| 105th Congress
1st Session | JOINT COMMITTEE PRINT | S. Prt.
105–10 |

COUNTRY REPORTS ON HUMAN RIGHTS PRACTICES FOR 1996

REPORT

SUBMITTED TO THE

COMMITTEE ON FOREIGN RELATIONS
U.S. SENATE

AND THE

COMMITTEE ON INTERNATIONAL RELATIONS
U.S. HOUSE OF REPRESENTATIVES

BY THE

DEPARTMENT OF STATE

IN ACCORDANCE WITH SECTIONS 116(d) AND 502B(b) OF THE FOREIGN ASSISTANCE ACT OF 1961, AS AMENDED

FEBRUARY 1997

Printed for the use of the Committees on Foreign Relations and International Relations of the U.S. Senate and House of Representatives respectively

U.S. GOVERNMENT PRINTING OFFICE
WASHINGTON : 1997

36–806 CC

For sale by the U.S. Government Printing Office
Superintendent of Documents, Mail Stop: SSOP, Washington, DC 20402-9328
ISBN 0-16-054190-5

COMMITTEE ON FOREIGN RELATIONS

JESSE HELMS, North Carolina, *Chairman*

RICHARD G. LUGAR, Indiana
PAUL COVERDELL, Georgia
CHUCK HAGEL, Nebraska
GORDON H. SMITH, Oregon
CRAIG THOMAS, Wyoming
ROD GRAMS, Minnesota
JOHN ASHCROFT, Missouri
BILL FRIST, Tennessee
SAM BROWNBACK, Kansas

JOSEPH R. BIDEN, Jr., Delaware
PAUL S. SARBANES, Maryland
CHRISTOPHER J. DODD, Connecticut
JOHN F. KERRY, Massachusetts
CHARLES S. ROBB, Virginia
RUSSELL D. FEINGOLD, Wisconsin
DIANNE FEINSTEIN, California
PAUL D. WELLSTONE, Minnesota

JAMES W. NANCE, *Staff Director*
EDWIN K. HALL, *Minority Staff Director*

COMMITTEE ON INTERNATIONAL RELATIONS

BENJAMIN A. GILMAN, New York, *Chairman*

WILLIAM GOODLING, Pennsylvania
JAMES A. LEACH, Iowa
HENRY J. HYDE, Illinois
DOUG BEREUTER, Nebraska
CHRISTOPHER SMITH, New Jersey
DAN BURTON, Indiana
ELTON GALLEGLY, California
ILEANA ROS-LEHTINEN, Florida
CASS BALLENGER, North Carolina
DANA ROHRABACHER, California
DONALD A. MANZULLO, Illinois
EDWARD R. ROYCE, California
PETER T. KING, New York
JAY KIM, California
STEVEN J. CHABOT, Ohio
MARSHALL "MARK" SANFORD, South Carolina
MATT SALMON, Arizona
AMO HOUGHTON, New York
TOM CAMPBELL, California
JON FOX, Pennsylvania
JOHN McHUGH, New York
LINDSEY GRAHAM, South Carolina
ROY BLUNT, Missouri
JERRY MORAN, Kansas

LEE HAMILTON, Indiana
SAM GEJDENSON, Connecticut
TOM LANTOS, California
HOWARD BERMAN, California
GARY ACKERMAN, New York
ENI F.H. FALEOMAVAEGA, American Samoa
MATTHEW G. MARTINEZ, California
DONALD M. PAYNE, New Jersey
ROBERT ANDREWS, New Jersey
ROBERT MENENDEZ, New Jersey
SHERROD BROWN, Ohio
CYNTHIA A. McKINNEY, Georgia
ALCEE L. HASTINGS, Florida
PAT DANNER, Missouri
EARL HILLIARD, Alabama
WALTER CAPPS, California
BRAD SHERMAN, California
ROBERT WEXLER, Florida
DENNIS KUCINICH, Ohio
STEVE ROTHMAN, New Jersey
VACANCY

RICHARD J. GARON, *Chief of Staff*
MICHAEL H. VAN DUSEN, *Democratic Chief of Staff*

CONTENTS

	Page
Foreword	VII
Letter of Transmittal	IX
Preface	XI
Overview	XIII

Africa:

Angola	1
Benin	8
Botswana	14
Burkina Faso	19
Burundi	24
Cameroon	32
Cape Verde	42
Central African Republic	45
Chad	51
Comoros	57
Congo	60
Cote d'Ivoire	66
Djibouti	73
Equatorial Guinea	79
Eritrea	85
Ethiopia	90
Gabon	98
Gambia, The	103
Ghana	109
Guinea	118
Guinea-Bissau	126
Kenya	130
Lesotho	143
Liberia	147
Madagascar	157
Malawi	162
Mali	168
Mauritania	173
Mauritius	183
Mozambique	187
Namibia	197
Niger	203
Nigeria	210
Rwanda	225
Sao Tome and Principe	230
Senegal	233
Seychelles	238
Sierra Leone	243
Somalia	249
South Africa	254
Sudan	264
Swaziland	274
Tanzania	281
Togo	290
Uganda	296
Zaire	307
Zambia	315
Zimbabwe	323

IV

	Page
LATIN AMERICA AND THE CARIBBEAN:	
Antigua and Barbuda	335
Argentina	338
Bahamas	344
Barbados	349
Belize	352
Bolivia	357
Brazil	364
Chile	380
Colombia	389
Costa Rica	407
Cuba	413
Dominica	425
Dominican Republic	428
Ecuador	434
El Salvador	442
Grenada	451
Guatemala	454
Guyana	468
Haiti	474
Honduras	481
Jamaica	490
Mexico	495
Nicaragua	512
Panama	521
Paraguay	532
Peru	540
St. Kitts and Nevis	553
Saint Lucia	555
Saint Vincent and the Grenadines	559
Suriname	562
Trinidad and Tobago	567
Uruguay	572
Venezuela	577
EAST ASIA AND THE PACIFIC:	
Australia	589
Brunei	593
Burma	598
Cambodia	607
China	616
Taiwan (China only)	643
Fiji	652
Indonesia	658
Japan	681
Kiribati	688
Korea, Democratic People's Republic of	690
Korea, Republic of	698
Laos	707
Malaysia	712
Marshall Islands	725
Micronesia, Federated States of	728
Mongolia	730
Nauru	735
New Zealand	738
Palau	741
Papua New Guinea	744
Philippines	752
Singapore	764
Solomon Islands	774
Thailand	778
Tonga	789
Tuvalu	792
Vanuatu	794
Vietnam	798
Western Samoa	807

Page

EUROPE AND CANADA:
Albania	813
Andorra	825
Armenia	828
Austria	836
Azerbaijan	840
Belarus	849
Belgium	859
Bosnia and Herzegovina	864
Bulgaria	876
Canada	887
Croatia	893
Cyprus	906
Czech Republic	913
Denmark	924
Estonia	927
Finland	934
France	937
Georgia	942
Germany	949
Greece	956
Hungary	968
Iceland	975
Ireland	977
Italy	983
Kazakstan	989
Kyrgyz Republic	1000
Latvia	1007
Liechtenstein	1015
Lithuania	1018
Luxembourg	1025
Former Yugoslav Republic of Macedonia	1028
Malta	1034
Moldova	1037
Monaco	1044
Netherlands, The	1047
Norway	1051
Poland	1054
Portugal (includes Macau)	1066
Romania	1075
Russia	1082
San Marino	1103
Serbia-Montenegro	1105
Slovak Republic	1114
Slovenia	1123
Spain	1126
Sweden	1135
Switzerland	1140
Tajikistan	1144
Turkey	1153
Turkmenistan	1173
Ukraine	1180
United Kingdom (includes Hong Kong)	1191
Uzbekistan	1211

NEAR EAST AND NORTH AFRICA:
Algeria	1221
Bahrain	1232
Egypt	1242
Iran	1256
Iraq	1265
Israel and the occupied territories	1278
Jordan	1307
Kuwait	1316
Lebanon	1325
Libya	1336
Morocco	1342
The Western Sahara	1353

NEAR EAST AND NORTH AFRICA—CONTINUED

	Page
Oman	1355
Qatar	1361
Saudi Arabia	1366
Syria	1375
Tunisia	1385
United Arab Emirates	1494
Yemen	1400

SOUTH ASIA:

Afghanistan	1407
Bangladesh	1417
Bhutan	1429
India	1435
Maldives	1451
Nepal	1456
Pakistan	1464
Sri Lanka	1483

APPENDIXES:

A. Notes on Preparation of the Reports	1497
B. Reporting on Worker Rights	1499
C. International Human Rights Conventions	1501
D. Explanation of Statistical Table	1505
E. FY 1995 U.S. Economic and Military Assistance—Actual Obligations	1506
F. 52d UNHRC Voting Record	1510

FOREWORD

The country reports on human rights practices were prepared by the Department of State in acco tions 116(d) and 502B(b) of the Foreign Assistance amended. They also fulfill the legislative requireme 505(c) of the Trade Act of 1974, as amended.

The reports cover the human rights practices of all are members of the United Nations and a few that are are printed to assist Members of Congress in the consid legislation, particularly foreign assistance legislation.

JESSE HELMS,
Chairman, Committee on Foreign Relati

BENJAMIN A. GILMAN,
Chairman, Committee on International Relations

LETTER OF TRANSMITTAL

DEPARTMENT OF STATE,
Washington, DC, January 29, 1997.

Hon. JESSE HELMS PELL,
Chairman, Committee on Foreign Relations.

DEAR MR. CHAIRMAN: On behalf of the Secretary of State, I am transmitting to you the Country Reports on Human Rights Practices for 1996, prepared in compliance with sections 116(d)(1) and 502B(b) of the Foreign Assistance Act of 1961, as amended, and section 505(c) of the Trade Act of 1974, as amended.

Sincerely,

BARBARA LARKIN,
Assistant Secretary, Legislative Affairs.

Enclosure:

PREFACE

1996 HUMAN RIGHTS REPORTS

Why The Reports Are Prepared

This report is submitted to the Congress by the Department of State in compliance with sections 116(d) and 502(b) of the Foreign Assistance Act of 1961 (FAA), as amended, and section 505(c) of the Trade Act of 1974, as amended. As stated in section 116(d)(1) of the FAA: "The Secretary of State shall transmit to the Speaker of the House of Representatives and the Committee on Foreign Relations of the Senate, by January 31 of each year, a full and complete report regarding the status of internationally recognized human rights, within the meaning of subsection (A) in countries that receive assistance under this part, and (B) in all other foreign countries which are members of the United Nations and which are not otherwise the subject of a human rights report under this Act." We have also included reports on several countries that do not fall into the categories established by these statutes and that are thus not covered by the congressional requirement.

The responsibility of the United States to speak out on behalf of international human rights standards was formalized in the early 1970's. In 1976 Congress enacted legislation creating a Coordinator of Human Rights in the U.S. Department of State, a position later upgraded to Assistant Secretary. In 1994 the Congress created a position of Senior Advisor for Women's Rights. Congress has also written into law formal requirements that U.S. foreign and trade policy take into account countries' human rights and worker rights performance and that country reports be submitted to the Congress on an annual basis. The first reports, in 1977, covered only countries receiving U.S. aid, numbering 82; this year 194 reports are submitted.

How The Reports Are Prepared

In August 1993, the Secretary of State moved to strengthen further the human rights efforts of our embassies. All sections in each embassy were asked to contribute information and to corroborate reports of human rights violations, and new efforts were made to link mission programming to the advancement of human rights and democracy. In 1994 the Bureau of Human Rights and Humanitarian Affairs was reorganized and renamed as the Bureau of Democracy, Human Rights, and Labor, reflecting both a broader sweep and a more focused approach to the interlocking issues of human rights, worker rights, and democracy. The 1996 human rights reports reflect a year of dedicated effort by hundreds of State

Department, Foreign Service, and other U.S. Government employees.

Our embassies, which prepared the initial drafts of the reports, gathered information throughout the year from a variety of sources across the political spectrum, including government officials, jurists, military sources, journalists, human rights monitors, academics, and labor activists. This information-gathering can be hazardous, and U.S. Foreign Service Officers regularly go to great lengths, under trying and sometimes dangerous conditions, to investigate reports of human rights abuse, monitor elections, and come to the aid of individuals at risk, such as political dissidents and human rights defenders whose rights are threatened by their governments.

After the embassies completed their drafts, the texts were sent to Washington for careful review by the Bureau of Democracy, Human Rights, and Labor, in cooperation with other State Department offices. As they worked to corroborate, analyze, and edit the reports, the Department officers drew on their own sources of information. These included reports provided by U.S. and other human rights groups, foreign government officials, representatives from the United Nations and other international and regional organizations and institutions, and experts from academia and the media. Officers also consulted with experts on worker rights issues, refugee issues, military and police matters, women's issues, and legal matters. The guiding principle was to ensure that all relevant information was assessed as objectively, thoroughly, and fairly as possible.

The reports in this volume will be used as a resource for shaping policy, conducting diplomacy, and making assistance, training, and other resource allocations. They will also serve as a basis for the U.S. Government's cooperation with private groups to promote the observance of internationally recognized human rights.

The Country Reports on Human Rights Practices cover internationally recognized individual, civil, political, and worker rights, as set forth in the Universal Declaration of Human Rights. These rights include freedom from torture or other cruel, inhuman, or degrading treatment or punishment; from prolonged detention without charges; from disappearance due to abduction or clandestine detention; and from other flagrant violations of the right to life, liberty, and the security of the person.

Universal human rights aim to incorporate respect for human dignity into the processes of government and law. All people have the inalienable right to change their government by peaceful means and to enjoy basic freedoms, such as freedom of expression, association, assembly, movement, and religion, without discrimination on the basis of race, religion, national origin, or sex. The right to join a free trade union is a necessary condition of a free society and economy. Thus the reports assess key internationally recognized worker rights, including the right of association; the right to organize and bargain collectively; prohibition of forced or compulsory labor; minimum age for employment of children; and acceptable work conditions.

OVERVIEW

THE GLOBAL STRUCTURE OF HUMAN RIGHTS

Half a century ago the building of a global structure of human rights protection was given special urgency by the unprecedented horrors of the Holocaust, of World War II, and of modern totalitarianism. So it was that the close of the war was followed by the Nuremberg Tribunals and the adoption in 1948 of the Universal Declaration of Human Rights. This effort has continued to the present day, and while it was given special impetus by the tragic events of our century, its foundations lie deep in the moral values of all humanity and the experience of oppressed people throughout history.

Throughout history, whenever fundamental human values have been assaulted by governments and their leaders, the result has come at horrific human and moral cost. That is what happened over the centuries, in every part of the world, including North America. And that is what happened in this century in the Armenian massacres, in the Nazi concentration camps, in the Soviet Gulag, in the Chinese Cultural Revolution, in the apartheid society of South Africa, in the killing fields of Cambodia, and more recently in the acts of genocide carried out in the former Yugoslavia, Rwanda, and Burundi. These and other massive human horrors, past and present, are a standing affront to civilization and all it stands for.

The idea of universal human rights and the measures taken to bring those ideas to life are the measure of these horrors and of the commitment of modern civilization not to repeat them. The evolving legal and political structure of human rights is a framework within which nations and governments seek to honor this commitment. It is, of course, a work in progress, and it is in many ways the most important work of governments and their citizens.

A broad consensus has been, and is, steadily emerging against such fundamental abuses of human beings as genocide, extrajudicial killings, torture, enslavement, sexual violence, the forced separation of families, the destruction of religion, and the suppression of thought and speech. Even those who engage in these practices rarely seek to justify their actions outright.

Contemporary disparagements of human rights take several forms. Some dismiss the very notion that there is an international consensus to support them, an argument belied by the deep striving for justice and dignity evidenced throughout history on every continent by people of goodwill. Others argue, for example, that there is no room for civil and political rights until economic development has been achieved, and even then, that such rights as free speech and association get in the way of economic well-being and social stability.

To the contrary, respect for human rights, free expression, the rule of law, and equal rights for all men and women serve to stabilize societies and the international community in the long term, and have a substantial and meaningful role to play in economic development in this burgeoning age of globalization and information technology. That was the position adopted by delegates to the World Conference on Human Rights in 1993, who unequivocally declared that: "While development facilitates the enjoyment of human rights, the lack of development may not be invoked to justify the abridgement of internationally-recognized human rights."

Indeed, it is now well established that the ultimate economic crisis—famine and mass starvation—is not occurring at the end of the 20th century in those countries whose rulers bear the consequences of their decisions, whose people participate in their own governance, and in which information freely circulates; that governments accountable to their citizens and to international law will be less prone to conflict and aggression; that the rule of law offers a solid ground for economic investment; and that civil society, fostered by freedom of association, supports the networks of social solidarity that are essential to successful, stable, long-term development.

While these truths are increasingly evident to vast numbers of people around the globe—indeed, the global movement for human rights is one of the most extraordinary political developments in modern history—they are still, sadly, far from being realized in many countries.

The greatest works of the human spirit take a long time to come into being, and they must be constantly nurtured lest they collapse, with horrific results. In particular, the evolving global network of laws and institutions protecting and promoting human rights has taken a long time, but its roots lie deep in the hopes, aspirations, and beliefs in human dignity of all cultures and societies.

CHALLENGES AND OPPORTUNITIES OF THE POST-COLD WAR WORLD

We have left the Cold War period in which human rights issues served as an ideological battleground. We have entered a period in which totalitarianism has been thoroughly discredited, and in which economies and societies around the world are afforded increased opportunities for integration and cooperation, due in large part to new technologies, as well as the passing of the Cold War, which divided much of the world into opposing blocs. Today, human rights concerns are increasingly incorporated into bilateral relations among countries, including with friends, and these efforts can be part of a genuine dialog among nations on the shape of the societies we hope to foster in the next century.

There are also greater opportunities for multilateral cooperation as the relationship between human rights, democracy, and development is becoming better understood, and we see greater strength and involvement of nongovernmental organizations (NGO's) in pressing for human rights and democracy in all parts of the world. The extraordinary activity and effectiveness of the NGO conference parallel to 1995's U.N. Conference on Women was a striking demonstration of this phenomenon.

Yet despite this promising situation, there is a yawning gap between the possibilities that these positive developments seem to present and the realities of a world in which there often seem to be more conflicts and human rights abuses than ever. Among the problems we are seeing are terrible ethnic and religious conflicts exploited by cynical leaders, refugee movements, and the persistence of authoritarianism in too many countries.

One way in which the international community is increasingly responding to this challenge is by fostering new institutions of justice, accountability, democracy, and civil society.

In particular, a series of new means and mechanisms of accountability have appeared in recent years in countries around the world, with institutions such as the National Truth Commissions of El Salvador, Haiti, and South Africa and National Human Rights Commissions in India, Indonesia, and Mexico. Meanwhile, regional bodies like the Organization of American States and the Organization for Security and Cooperation in Europe are deepening and broadening their human rights efforts and capabilities.

At the international level the most significant and promising of the institutions are the International Criminal Tribunals for the Former Yugoslavia and for Rwanda, which may herald a new era of international justice and pave the way for an International Criminal Court to bring to the bar of justice perpetrators of crimes against humanity throughout the world. The characterization of rape as a prosecutable war crime is another notable feature of the Tribunals' work. In addition, the Dayton Peace Agreement provides a case-in-point of how human rights and justice institutions can be synthesized with military intervention and other multilateral actions to effect a major effort of conflict resolution.

We are also witnessing the development of quasi-international human rights institutions. Nowhere is this more evident than in the former Yugoslavia, which witnessed the development in 1996 of both the Commission on Human Rights for Bosnia-Herzegovina, and the International Commission on Missing Persons in the Former Yugoslavia.

Created by states, managed by international human rights and humanitarian affairs experts, funded by the international community and yet having legal character under domestic law, these institutions represent creative attempts to forge new structures capable of protecting human rights and advancing humanitarian interests in the trying new circumstances of post-Cold War conflict.

AUTHORITARIAN REPRESSION

In 1996 patterns of repression and systemic human rights abuse continued in many countries, including some of the world's largest and most influential.

In China, where Marxist ideology has in recent years given way to economic pragmatism and increasingly robust ties of trade and commerce with the United States and many other countries, human rights abuses by a strong central Government persist in the face of legal reform efforts and economic and social change.

The Chinese Government in 1996 continued to commit widespread and well-documented human rights abuses, in violation of internationally accepted norms, stemming from the authorities' intolerance of dissent, fear of unrest, and the continuing absence of laws protecting basic freedoms. All public dissent against party and government was effectively silenced by intimidation, exile, or the imposition of prison terms, administrative detention, or house arrest. No dissidents were known to be active at year's end. Abuses included torture and mistreatment of prisoners, forced confessions, and arbitrary and lengthy incommunicado detention. Severe restrictions were also continued on freedom of speech, the press, assembly, association, religion, privacy (including coercive family planning), and worker rights. In minority areas such as Tibet and Xinjiang, controls on religion and other fundamental freedoms intensified. During 1996, Hong Kong's civil liberties and political institutions were threatened by restrictive measures taken by the Chinese Government in anticipation of Hong Kong's reversion to Chinese sovereignty in July of 1997.

In Nigeria the military council headed by General Sani Abacha, which seized power in 1993, remains in control, and its human rights performance remains dismal. Throughout the year General Abacha's Government regularly relied on arbitrary detention, arrests, and wide-scale harassment to silence its many critics. Security forces committed extrajudicial killings, tortured and beat suspects and detainees; prison conditions remained life threatening; and security officials continued routinely to harass human rights and democracy activists, labor leaders, environmentalists, and journalists. Nonparty local elections held in March were nullified by the Government, and numerous parliamentarians remain in jail. All these abuses occurred in a climate of infringements of freedom of speech, assembly, association, travel, and workers rights.

Cuba remains a totalitarian anachronism, where human rights deteriorated in 1996, and suppression of dissent worsened.

Despite formally ending Aung San Suu Kyi's house arrest, the military regime in Burma stepped up its "rolling repression" and systematic violation of human rights. North Korea remains an outpost of totalitarian rule.

After more than two decades in power, the Ba'thist regime exercises absolute dictatorial authority in Iraq. Elsewhere in the Middle East, repressive regimes in Iran, Syria, and Libya are responsible for the systematic denial of their citizens' basic human rights.

COUNTRIES IN TRANSITION

The extraordinary democratic revolution of the past decade is as yet unfinished. In many countries, democracy is still fragile, civil-military relations are not properly defined, elections are subject to manipulation, women cannot fully participate, and the institutions of justice and civil society that guarantee human rights over the long term have not yet fully emerged.

The picture in Russia is mixed. It continues to undergo profound transformations as its as yet unfinished democratic institutions and practices continue to evolve. July 1996 saw Russia's first-ever presidential election, and in December 1995 its second multiparty parliamentary elections. Human rights NGO's were generally free to operate. However, prison conditions—always harsh—have worsened, and lengthy pretrial detention continued. Violent hazing of military conscripts sparked new protests.

The major Russian media have functioned relatively unhindered and for the most part have reported freely on the Chechen conflict despite government pressure and heavy-handed treatment by Russian troops in the war zone. In addition, journalists throughout Russia covering controversial issues were subjected to pressure, physical violence, and even death, while the Government appeared unresponsive to requests for investigation of these cases. Legal reform has proceeded unevenly in the absence of the approval of key pieces of implementing legislation. The development of an independent judiciary continues but slowed considerably, and judges were often subject to manipulation by political authorities. Discrimination against minorities remains a problem, and discrimination against women in some sectors has intensified in recent years.

One genuine bright spot at year's end was the withdrawal of Russian forces from Chechnya, where conflict had claimed tens of thousands of lives.

Bosnia and Herzegovina enjoyed a year of comparative peace in 1996 as implementation of the 1995 Dayton Accords proceeded. The September elections for major offices were, despite their shortcomings, an important step in solidifying the foundations of peace and establishing representative institutions.

The largest challenge facing Bosnia has been to overcome the staggering effects of 3 years of warfare. In 1996 the international community sought to promote reconciliation. Yet political authorities continued, in varying degrees, to violate basic human rights. Members of the security forces mistreated citizens. Judicial institutions did not function effectively, freedom of movement was restricted, refugees were not able to return to their homes, freedom of the press and expression were curtailed, and ethnic discrimination was widespread. In the Serb entity and the Croat parts of the Federation, war criminals remained at large.

At year's end, the Serbian Government's blatant efforts to manipulate the results of the November 17 municipal elections had the effect of invigorating democratic forces, who were mounting the most serious challenge yet faced by the current regime.

Serious backsliding occurred in Belarus, where the President conducted a constitutional referendum generally regarded by the international community as illegitimate and subsequently replaced the Parliament with a rubber-stamp legislature while extending his own term. Progress toward democracy was set back by flawed elections in Armenia and fraudulent elections in Albania. Presidential power has grown in Kazakhstan and Kyrgystan to the point where the executive overshadows the legislature and the judiciary, while Uzbekistan—and to a greater extent Turkmenistan and Tajikistan—lag even further behind in the development of democracy and respect for human rights.

There was marked progress in Guatemala, where a peace accord between the Government and guerrillas ended a 36-year civil war. Some serious abuses did continue, although the Government demonstrated the political will to combat impunity, and courts have, in marked contrast to past years, convicted some members of the security services.

Haiti continued the democratic advances begun in 1994, although abuses and the poor condition of its judicial system remain issues of concern.

In the Middle East, the peace process suffered setbacks in 1996, which had negative effects on human rights in both the Occupied Territories and the areas administered by the Palestinian Authority. Terrorist acts had a deeply chilling effect on both diplomacy and human rights observance. The successful completion of elections for the Palestinian Council in March of 1996 marked a significant step in the development of Palestinian institutions; and there was some progress towards year's end in the easing of some aspects of Israel's closure of the Territories, in increased cooperation on the ground between Israeli and Palestinian authorities, and in the talks on Israeli redeployment within Hebron, which then reached a successful conclusion in January of 1997.

While Indonesia exhibits a surface adherence to democratic forms, its political system remains strongly authoritarian. The President, his associates, and the military still dominate the country and maintain an ideological program of social cohesion through the restriction of opposition, the repression of independent labor unions, the stifling of dissent, and other harsh measures. In the regions of Irian Jaya and East Timor the human rights climate is particularly harsh. Freedoms of assembly and association were curtailed in 1996 through arrests, surveillance, and other forms of intimidation. One positive development was the Government's tolerance of a National Human Rights Commission.

Some militaries continue to resist civilian, democratic oversight, as in Colombia, where entrenched conflict among security forces, guerrillas, paramilitaries, and narcotics traffickers has resulted in a climate of both abuse and impunity.

In some countries, such as Egypt and Turkey, campaigns against extremists have resulted in abuses, including torture.

RELIGION

A disturbing aspect of the post-Cold War world has been the persistence, and in some cases the intensification, of religious intolerance, religious persecution, and the exploitation of religious and ethnic differences for narrow and violent ends. In 1996 many religious groups around the world continued to face persecution and other difficulties in practicing their faiths and maintaining their cultural loyalties.

In China the Government intensified its policy of severely restricting and bringing under official control all religious groups, including Christians, Muslims, and Buddhists.

Christians are subject to difficulties ranging from interference to outright persecution in many countries, including Iraq, Pakistan, and the Sudan. In Cuba persecution continues, despite the easing of some of the harsher measures.

Non-Muslims are prohibited from public worship in Saudi Arabia, while elsewhere in the Middle East anti-Semitic materials regularly appear in government-controlled media. The Government of Iran continued its repressive practices against members of the

Baha'i faith. In Vietnam both Buddhists and Christians suffer from government restrictions.

Religious groups and figures are playing increasingly significant roles in the prevention and resolution of conflicts, in efforts at reconciliation among antagonistic groups, in fostering the peaceful evolution of civil society, and in respect for human rights.

These initiatives have taken a variety of forms, including peace activism, mediation, education for tolerance and nonviolence, and creating models of coexistence. In 1996 religious leaders and groups played an important peacemaking role in virtually every region, from Northern Ireland to Nicaragua to South Africa to Cambodia. Religious leaders such as the Pope, the Dalai Lama, Archbishop Tutu of South Africa, Bishop Belo of East Timor, and Maha Gosananda of Cambodia are engaged in efforts at mediation and the promotion of tolerance and human rights.

THE RIGHTS OF WOMEN

In the wake of the resoundingly successful U.N. Fourth World Conference on Women in Beijing in September of 1995, the year 1996 saw a tremendous increase in activity towards the protection and promotion of the human rights of women. Some governments have fulfilled obligations undertaken at the Conference and taken progressive actions to secure rights for women. Meanwhile, women's NGO's around the world have led the way, stepping up their activities, pressing governments for change, and providing new and creative services for women. The Conference's call to action and the resulting government and NGO activity is having a profound effect on democracy and economic development around the world.

Among the efforts underway are the development of legislation on family law in Namibia, on violence against women in Ecuador, and on women's political participation in the Philippines. Programs are being created for the economic and educational empowerment of women and for the prevention of sexual exploitation and trafficking of women and girls.

Alongside these gains, however, women all over the world continued in 1996 to encounter barriers of widespread political, economic, and social discrimination, often codified in law. Women are often strongly discouraged and prevented from participating in political life, are disproportionately poor, are denied the right to privacy, and face serious impediments to participating in economic life. In addition, laws meant to protect the human rights of women often go unenforced.

Discrimination reached new heights of severity in Afghanistan with the rise to power of the Taliban.

Violence against women, both in and outside the home, a particularly widespread and entrenched violation of women's rights, is either legally permitted or simply allowed to continue in many countries and is by no means restricted to the developing world. In a number of countries, the continued practice of female genital mutilation is a particularly egregious form of violence against women. Rape has been a particularly cruel tool of warfare in a number of conflicts. Despite the enormous strides of recent years, there is much that remains to be done.

THE RIGHTS OF CHILDREN

Children are perhaps the least represented members of society in the councils of government and among the most helpless victims of human rights abuse and other forms of political violence.

An estimated quarter of a million children, even as young as age 5, have been conscripted to serve as soldiers in dozens of armed conflicts around the world some with armed insurgencies, such as the Khmer Rouge, the Shining Path of Peru, and Palestinian groups in Lebanon, and some in regular armies, such as those of Cambodia, Uganda, Angola, and Sudan.

In Liberia, for example, children have been the greatest victims of the civil war, as education and nurture have been completely disrupted, while children have been recruited into the various warring factions.

But children suffer human rights abuse in contexts outside of conflict. Millions of children go uneducated and uncared for, and the so-called street children of the major cities find themselves caught in lives of crime and drug dependency and subject to harsh police measures. In a number of countries, incarcerated children suffer intolerable prison conditions.

The commercial sexual exploitation of children—through child prostitution, child pornography, and trafficking in children—is all too frequent in both developed and developing countries. The World Congress Against Commercial Sexual Exploitation of Children, held in Stockholm in August 1996, brought new attention to the problem and urged states and societies to take action against these abuses.

WORKER RIGHTS AND CHILD LABOR

Failure to respect basic worker rights as defined in several key International Labor Organization (ILO) Conventions continues to be a problem in many countries. These core worker rights include freedom of association, which is the foundation on which workers can form trade unions and defend their interests; the right to organize and bargain collectively; freedom from discrimination in employment; and freedom from child and forced labor.

Despite broad international recognition of these principles, free trade unions continue to be banned or suppressed in many countries; in many more, restrictions on freedom of association range from outright state control to legislation aimed at frustrating workers' legitimate efforts to organize. In 1996 the ILO criticized Nigeria, Indonesia, and Burma specifically, as well as a number of other countries for such practices. The ILO also repeated its call to Burma to cease its forced labor practices.

The relationships between worker rights and trade were the focus of discussion in a variety of international forums. The first ministerial meeting of the World Trade Organization held in Singapore in December adopted a declaration that renewed the WTO's "commitment to the observance of internationally recognized worker rights" and stated that "we believe that economic growth and development fostered by increased trade and further trade liberalization contribute to the promotion of those standards."

International focus on child labor intensified in 1996 in the ILO and other multilateral bodies. Consumers in developed countries have taken new notice of the issue, and this has had some effect on the acceptability of child labor in export-oriented countries. Nevertheless, the phenomenon continues, not only in developing countries but in some industrialized countries as well, with the overwhelming majority of child laborers in countries in Asia, Africa, and Latin America.

REFUGEES

Refugees are particularly vulnerable groups and at risk of human rights abuses. Although the human rights of refugees—especially women and children—are protected by international law, those rights are sometimes violated by the very governments to whom they have turned for protection.

These Country Reports for 1996 include specific information on the treatment of refugees and those who seek "first asylum." Although many nations treat these groups well, many other countries fail to provide meaningful protection to refugees and first asylum seekers.

CONCLUSION

In conclusion, let us remember on whose behalf we labor in the field of human rights and on whose behalf a global structure of protection is being built. This structure belongs to all of us, and it is being built for all of humanity. In building this structure the world is responding to the pain and need of men and women and children on all continents and to the historical conscience of mankind.

To those who dismiss those efforts as a form of cultural imperialism, let me offer in response the voices of indigenous NGO's working throughout the world to advance the cause of human rights. A powerful example is the presence of 110 NGO's from the Asia-Pacific region, which, meeting in Bangkok in 1993, sent the following message to the World Conference on Human Rights in Vienna:

> "We can learn from different cultures in a pluralistic perspective * * * to deepen respect for human rights. While we advocate cultural pluralism, those cultural practices which derogate from universally accepted human rights * * * must not be tolerated."

And let us recall the Declaration agreed to at Vienna in 1993 by all the nations of the world:

> "Human rights and fundamental freedoms are the birthright of all human beings; their protection and promotion is the first responsibility of governments."

It is true that human rights find their realization in a highly imperfect world. But that does not free us from responsibility to support respect for human rights in the processes of government and law and does not permit us to shirk this responsibility by invoking national sovereignty, or claims of social stability, economic development, or cultural difference.

As we near the dawn of a new century, the international community has an unprecedented opportunity to engage in respectful dialog on how best to promote human rights, freedom, and dignity. Every culture, tradition, and civilization brings its own genius to bear on this monumental effort, and that moral responsibility rests with every man and woman on this planet, calling us to a modern-day pursuit of an age-old quest for justice. In the words of the Talmudic sage Hillel: "If I am not for myself, who will be for me? If I am only for myself what am I? And if not now, when?"

JOHN SHATTUCK,
*Assistant Secretary of State for
Democracy, Human Rights, and Labor.*

AFRICA

ANGOLA

The Republic of Angola is in transition from a single party state to a multiparty democracy. The Popular Movement for the Liberation of Angola (MPLA) has ruled Angola since its independence from Portugal in 1975. The Constitution was revised in 1991 to provide for elections and for guarantees of basic human rights, but the Government does not generally respect its provisions in practice. In 1992 President Jose Eduardo dos Santos received a plurality of the votes in Angola's first elections, which United Nations' (U.N.) observers declared to be free and fair. Pending final resolution of the peace process, the President and the MPLA, backed by the security services, continue to dominate the Government. The judiciary is not independent of the President and the MPLA.

In November 1994, the Government signed the Lusaka Protocol peace accord with the National Union for the Total Independence of Angola (UNITA) in an effort to end 20 years of civil war. Under the auspices of the United Nations Angola Peacekeeping Mission (UNAVEM III) and with the help of three observer countries—the United States, Portugal, and Russia—the Government and UNITA continue to implement the Lusaka Protocol's provisions for a cease-fire, withdrawal of forces in contact, disarming and quartering of UNITA forces, integration of some UNITA soldiers into the Angolan armed forces, demobilization of remaining combatants, and creation of a Government of National Reconciliation. In May the National Assembly passed and President Dos Santos signed a blanket amnesty covering all crimes under military as well as civilian law against internal state security committed from May 31, 1991, to May 8, 1996. Passage of this law removed one of the last obstacles to UNITA's integration into Angola's armed forces.

The Ministry of the Interior is responsible for internal security. It exercises this function through the National Police and the paramilitary Rapid Intervention Police created in 1992 as an elite military force. The armed forces are responsible for external security. Prior to implementation of the Lusaka Protocol-mandated cease-fire, they were primarily engaged in fighting the civil war against UNITA. While civilian authorities generally maintain effective control of the security forces, there were frequent instances in which the security forces acted independently of government authority. Members of the security forces committed numerous, serious human rights abuses.

Angola's developing economy, in transition from a centrally directed to a market-based model, has significant potential to exploit extensive natural resource reserves and rich agricultural lands. Principal exports are petroleum and diamonds, which together with foreign aid are the country's leading sources of foreign exchange. Oil revenues for 1996 exceeded $4 billion and diamond revenues exceeded $850 million. Subsistence agriculture, the traditional livelihood for the majority of Angola's approximately 12 million citizens, was severely constrained by heavily mined fields and roads as well as by both government and UNITA restrictions on freedom of movement. In 1996 more than 3 million Angolans remained displaced or affected by the war, including 1.2 million who relied on emergency food aid supplied by the international donor community. Areas under government control suffered from hyperinflation, scarcity of consumer goods, massive unemployment and underemployment, and continuing pervasive corruption. While the Government took some measures to increase the availability and control prices of consumer staples, these initiatives did not remedy the root causes of economic instability and are not sustainable. Areas controlled by UNITA experienced scarcities of consumer goods along with massive unemployment and underemployment. Annual per capita gross national product is roughly $320, but much of the country's wealth remains concentrated in the hands of the small MPLA, military, and business elites. The average monthly salary of wage earners is equivalent to only about $10 ($50 to $100

(1)

in the Luanda area), which provides most of the population with a very low standard of living.

Although there was some improvement, the Government's human rights record continued to be poor, and it continued to commit numerous, serious abuses. Members of the security forces committed numerous extrajudicial killings, arbitrarily and secretly arrested and detained individuals, and routinely tortured and beat detainees. The Government did not take effective action to punish abusers. The Government continued to inhibit independent investigations of human rights abuses. Government leaders cited the 20-year civil war to justify allowing emergency considerations to override concerns over human rights abuses. Prison conditions were life threatening. The Government restricted freedom of expression, the press, assembly, and association. While some improvements were made, citizens' freedom of movement continues to be restricted. The judiciary is not independent from the President and the MPLA, and the judicial system does not assure fair trials. Although Angola is nominally a multiparty democracy, citizens have no effective means to change their government. Parliamentary elections due to be held in 1996 were postponed for between 2 and 4 years under the terms of the Lusaka Protocol; presidential elections are to be held when the United Nations determines that appropriate conditions exist. Discrimination and violence against women were widespread. Children and the disabled continued to suffer as a result of the civil war and poor economic conditions. The Government continued to dominate the labor movement, and there was no improvement in the poor worker rights situation.

UNITA human rights abuses in territories under its control included disappearances, arbitrary arrests and detentions, denial of fair public trial, forced conscription, and violations of humanitarian law, including attacks on civilian populations. UNITA also restricted freedom of speech, the press, assembly, association, and movement.

RESPECT FOR HUMAN RIGHTS

Section 1. Respect for the Integrity of the Person, Including Freedom From:

a. *Political and Other Extrajudicial Killing.*—Politically and economically motivated violence by state security forces and common criminal violence were often indistinguishable. A large number of violent crimes including robbery, vehicle hijackings, assault, kidnaping, rape, and murder were committed by members of the military and police forces both in and out of uniform. Although most criminal activity was committed by poorly and irregularly paid rogue elements of the security forces, there were credible reports that some of these attacks were carried out under orders from the Government. The Government did not take any effective action to punish abusers.

There were credible reports that the Rapid Intervention Police summarily executed people caught in the act of committing crimes. Frequent gun battles between members of the military and police, and fighting among soldiers, police, and bandits in streets, suburbs, and open air markets of major urban centers resulted in numerous civilian casualties.

There were credible reports that many prisoners died as a result of inadequate food and medical treatment (see Section 1.c.).

The 1995 killing of independent journalist Ricardo de Mello remains unsolved, as does the October murder of state-owned television journalist Antonio Casmiro in Cabinda (see Section 2.a.). Similarly the 1994 assassination of the Vice Governor of Malange province remains unsolved. The results of the investigation into the November 1993 death of opposition politician Carlos Simeao were never released. It is widely believed that these persons were killed for political reasons.

UNITA forces continued to kill civilians (see Section 1.g.). It was credibly alleged that dozens of prisoners died in UNITA custody (see Sections 1.c. and 1.d.).

In June private demining companies clearing oil production facilities in Soyo, Zaire province, uncovered a mass grave site. More than 100 bodies were found, and it is likely that many more will be uncovered as demining work progresses. Credible evidence indicates that these killings were committed by UNITA forces during their capture of the city in May 1993. UNAVEM observers have not yet concluded their investigation into this discovery. Given the over 500,000 war and war-related deaths attributed to Angola's 20-year civil war, it is likely that additional mass graves will be discovered.

b. *Disappearance.*—The Government and UNITA continued to accuse each other of abductions and disappearances of civilians. There are reportedly dozens of kidnapings, abductions, and disappearances per month.

There were no developments in the August 1994 disappearances of two individuals associated with Africare, Vincent Douma and Oliveira Lembe. The International Committee of the Red Cross (ICRC) and U.N. agencies continued searching for them throughout the year.

The ICRC reclassified 78 prisoners of UNITA as "disappeared." There were credible allegations that many of these persons died in UNITA custody.

   c. *Torture and Other Cruel, Inhuman, or Degrading Treatment or Punishment.*— There were credible firsthand reports that the police committed torture. Prison officials employed by the Interior Ministry routinely beat accused individuals in Comarca de Viana, a prison on the outskirts of Luanda, to extract information or confessions prior to trial. In many cases the police routinely beat and then released detainees rather than make an effort to prepare a formal court case. Government forces continued to rob and rape civilians (see Section 1.g.).

A Catholic priest who runs an orphanage in Twambo credibly reported that regional Ministry of Justice officials made threats against his life, reportedly because of his alleged sympathies with UNITA.

Prison conditions constituted a threat to the health and life of prisoners. The Government and the National Assembly Committee on Human Rights have acknowledged that conditions are inhuman. Cells are overcrowded and lack basic sanitary facilities. Many prisons, lacking financial support from the Government, were unable to supply prisoners with adequate food and health care. There were credible reports that many prisoners died of malnutrition and tuberculosis. Prison officials routinely beat detainees. Prisoners depended on families, friends, and international relief organizations for basic support.

The Government permitted prison visits by UNAVEM human rights monitors. UNITA forces continued to rob and rape civilians (see Section 1.g.).

   d. *Arbitrary Arrest, Detention, or Exile.*—Under the law a person caught in the act of committing a crime may be arrested and detained immediately. Otherwise, the law requires that an arrest warrant be signed by a judge or a provincial magistrate. Arrest warrants may also be signed by members of the judicial police and confirmed within 5 days by a magistrate. The Constitution provides for the right to a prompt judicial determination of the legality of the detention. Under the law the prosecution and defense have 90 days before trial to prepare a case, although this deadline may be extended by attorneys' general under extenuating circumstances. The Constitution also provides prisoners with the right to receive visits by family members. However, a scarcity of resources and the lack of qualified and motivated personnel in the judicial system limited the exercise of these rights.

In 1993 the Council of Ministers decided to transfer control of the judicial process and prison system from the Interior Ministry to the Justice Ministry. However, this transfer had not yet been made by year's end. Interior Ministry personnel continued to systematically, arbitrarily, and secretly arrest and detain persons for all categories of crime for indefinite periods of time, often without any apparent intent of bringing the detainees to trial.

The number of people detained by the Government and UNITA for political and security reasons is unknown.

The Lusaka Protocol provides for the release, under ICRC auspices, of persons detained for war-related reasons. As of September 10, the ICRC reported that 535 prisoners reported by the Government (369) and by UNITA (166) had been released. However, the ICRC has reclassified 78 prisoners originally reported to the ICRC by UNITA as "disappeared" because UNITA claimed that they were no longer in its possession. It was credibly alleged that most or all of these individuals died in UNITA custody.

The Government did not use forced exile.

   e. *Denial of Fair Public Trial.*—The Constitution provides for an independent judiciary, but in practice the court system lacked the means, experience, and training to be truly independent from the influence of the President and the ruling MPLA. The judicial system was largely destroyed during the civil war and during 1996 did not function in large areas of the country.

The court system comprises the Supreme Court at the appellate level, and municipal and provincial courts of original jurisdiction under the authority of the Supreme Court. The President has strong appointive powers, including appointment of Supreme Court judges, with no requirement for confirmation by the National Assembly. As of September, 12 of the 16 seats on the Supreme Court remained vacant. The Court serves as an appellate tribunal for questions of law and fact, but it does not have authority to interpret the Constitution. The Constitution reserves this role for a Constitutional Court, an entity that had not yet been constituted at year's end. The Constitution provides for the creation of an office of the "Provider of Justice," designated by the National Assembly for a 4-year term, to defend citizens rights and liberties. This office also had not yet been constituted at year's end.

Trials for political and security crimes are handled exclusively by the Supreme Court. There were no known political or security trials.

The Constitution provides defendants the presumption of innocence, the right to a defense and legal assistance, and the right of appeal. Amendments to the Code for Penal Process in 1991 provided for public trials, established a system of bail, and recognized the accused's right to counsel and to testify. However, the Government often did not respect these rights in practice. Municipal courts normally deal rapidly with routine civil and misdemeanor cases on a daily basis. Judges are normally respected laymen, not licensed lawyers. The judge and two laymen selected by the full court act as jury. Routine cases are normally dispatched by a court within 3 months. The verdict is pronounced the day following the conclusion of the trial in the presence of the defendant.

There are credible reports that the Government holds political prisoners; however, the number is unknown.

UNITA has established a military and a civilian court system in territories under its control and claims that its civil code is equivalent to the Portuguese Civil Code currently used by the Government. UNITA President Jonas Savimbi appoints judges personally, and UNITA trials are not open to the public. Juries consist of male elders chosen from the community. The accused reportedly has the right to a lawyer.

f. *Arbitrary Interference With Privacy, Family, Home, or Correspondence.*—The Government maintained a sophisticated security apparatus dedicated to surveillance, monitoring, and wire tapping of certain groups, including journalists, opposition party leaders, members and suspected sympathizers of UNITA, National Assembly deputies, and foreign diplomats. The law requires judicial warrants for searches of private homes. However, executive orders have been used to override normal legal provisions, as in the case of an executive order authorizing joint armed forces and police sweeps to seize weapons held by civilians in major urban areas in July and August. In August the Government began a 4-month operation, "Cancer II," that expelled over 4,000 Malian, Lebanese, Gabonese, and other foreign residents of Angola whose immigration status was deemed irregular. These prisoners were often held for more than 72 hours without appearance before a judge, and their deportations were carried out entirely within the executive branch without any judicial oversight or opportunity to challenge the legality of the decisions of police, customs, and immigration officers.

g. *Use of Excessive Force and Violations of Humanitarian Law in Internal Conflicts.*—Consolidation of the Lusaka Protocol peace process resulted in a significant decline in the widespread abuses of humanitarian standards committed by both government and UNITA forces during the previous 20 years. However, government and UNITA forces continued to subject hundreds of civilians to robbery, rape, or murder. "Bandits" (a term also applied to rogue elements of the armed forces) were also responsible for many attacks against civilian populations, with numerous confirmed incidents concentrated in the Quilenges, Huila province; and Chongoroi, Benguela province; areas. On May 22, armed bandits robbing a civilian truck in Quilenges fired on a passing UNAVEM vehicle. While no peacekeepers were hit, five civilians were killed and at least six injured.

Millions of mines, which were planted during the 20-year civil war to gain military advantage and to restrict the free circulation of people and goods, continued to kill and maim thousands of people. Many major roads were demined and reopened as a consequence of Government and UNITA commitments to allow the free circulation of people and goods throughout Angola. However, in many areas local authorities and military commanders of both parties continued to restrict free and safe passage of local populations, humanitarian organizations providing relief assistance, and United Nations observers. There were isolated incidents in the northeastern Lunda provinces and in Moxico where credible evidence indicates that demined roads were newly remined.

Section 2. *Respect for Civil Liberties, Including:*

a. *Freedom of Speech and Press.*—The Constitution provides for freedom of expression and of the press, and specifically provides that the press cannot be subject to political, ideological, or artistic censorship. However, the Government does not respect these rights in practice. Citizens, including deputies in the National Assembly, expect reprisals for public criticism of the Government or the MPLA, and the Government attempts to impede such criticism by monitoring and restricting access to political meetings. Journalists are intimidated into practicing self-censorship. The Government runs and tightly controls the only daily newspaper, the only television station, and the major radio station. It tightly restricts opposition leaders' access to these media. While two commercial radio stations and three private weekly and biweekly newspapers all practice self-censorship, several occasional newsletters are published that are openly critical of government officials and policy. The Government also allows UNAVEM to broadcast free of charge a series of "Roads of Peace" television and radio programs each week, although it has denied UNAVEM the right to establish its own radio station.

Media policy and censorship are controlled by a committee composed of the Minister of Social Communication, the press spokesman for the presidency, and the directors of the state-owned radio, television, and newspaper. The state-controlled national radio headquarters in Luanda cleared programs broadcast on national radio stations in provincial capitals.

Journalists admitted that they practice self-censorship and that repeated "errors in judgment" could result in dismissal and death threats. The January 1995 murder of Ricardo de Mello, editor of the independent newsletter Imparcial Fax, remains unsolved. It was a major blow to the development of a free press in Angola.

The Government was less restrictive with foreign news agencies such as the Voice of America, the British Broadcasting Corporation, and Cable News Network. Foreign journalists require authorization from the Minister of Interior in order to obtain access to government officials or travel within Angola. Both the Government and UNITA invited journalists to planned press events and to visit areas under their control.

UNITA runs a tightly controlled radio station whose broadcasts of often inflammatory material are heard throughout Angola. Lusaka Protocol provisions to convert this station into a nonpartisan private commercial station have not yet been completed. UNITA's newspaper, Terra Angolana, could not be found in government-controlled areas.

Academic life has been severely circumscribed by the civil war, but there is academic freedom, and academics do not practice self-censorship.

b. *Freedom of Peaceful Assembly and Association.*—The Constitution provides for the rights of association, assembly, and protest, but the Government does not respect these rights in practice. The Government strictly controls both assembly and association, the Rapid Intervention Police were mobilized twice in the capital during May to deter planned demonstrations. Legislation allows the Government to deny registration to private associations on security grounds, and the Government arbitrarily limits organized activities deemed inimical to its interests. The law also requires a minimum of 3-days' prior notice to authorities before public or private assemblies and makes participants liable for "offenses against the honor and consideration due to persons and to the organs of sovereignty" (see Section 2.c.).

In May Konrad Leibsher, a Catholic priest working with Luanda's poor, was arrested and tried for "crimes against the security of the state" for displaying placards decrying deteriorating economic conditions in Luanda. The government prosecutor argued that crowds drawn by the priest's placards violated the law on meeting and demonstrations, which requires prior government approval of gatherings which have the potential to endanger public order. The defense argument that freedom of speech guarantees are enshrined in the Constitution prevailed.

UNITA did not allow free assembly and association in areas under its control.

c. *Freedom of Religion.*—The Constitution provides for freedom of religion, including the separation of church and state, and the Government respects this right in practice. The authorities apparently did not enforce a 1995 government order prohibiting the practice of religion outside of approved locations.

During the May trial of Catholic priest Konrad Leibsher (see Section 2.b.), the government-controlled newspaper published a front page editorial accusing the priest of subversive activities, ordering the Church to stay out of social affairs, and insisting that sovereignty and order must be safeguarded. The Angolan Catholic Church issued a response supporting the priest, calling it the duty of every religious minister to confront issues of social justice.

d. *Freedom of Movement Within the Country, Foreign Travel, Emigration, and Repatriation.*—The Constitution provides for freedom of movement and residence within Angola and freedom of exit from and entry into the country, but the Government does not respect these rights in practice. As part of the peace process, both the Government and UNITA committed themselves to allow the free circulation of people and goods, but local authorities and military commanders continued to restrict movement in many areas. Nevertheless, many major roads were demined and opened to traffic, and part of Angola's 850,000 internally displaced persons and of the 325,000 refugees in neighboring countries began to return to their homes.

In a 4-month period beginning in August, the coordinated government operation Cancer II expelled more than 4,000 foreign residents whose immigration status was deemed irregular (see Section 1.f.).

Angola is a party to both the United Nations and Organization of African Unity conventions on refugees, and the Government cooperates with the U.N. High Commissioner for Refugees. The Government provides first asylum to refugees. An eligibility committee to evaluate asylum claims was established on paper in 1990, but was first staffed in 1995, and now meets regularly to evaluate asylum requests. There are approximately 9,600 Zairian refugees in Angola, at least 1,000 of whom have been officially granted refugee status. There were no reports of the forced expulsion of persons with valid claims to refugee status.

Section 3. Respect for Political Rights: The Right of Citizens to Change Their Government

The Constitution provides all adult citizens with the right to vote by secret ballot in direct, multiparty elections to choose the President of the Republic and deputies of the National Assembly. However, citizens have no effective means to change their government.

The President is elected by absolute majority. If no candidate obtains a majority of votes cast, there is a runoff between the two candidates with the highest number of votes. The National Assembly consists of 220 deputies, 130 elected on a national basis and 90 elected to represent the provinces. Ruling power is concentrated in the President who appoints the Prime Minister and other members of the Council of Ministers through which the President exercises executive power. The Council can enact decree-laws, decrees, and resolutions, thereby controlling most functions normally associated with the legislative branch.

The people exercised their new constitutional right to elect their government in September 1992 presidential and legislative elections. President dos Santos won 49.5 percent of the votes and should have faced UNITA leader Savimbi in a runoff election. UNITA and other parties accused the Government of massive electoral fraud, but U.N. observers declared the elections generally free and fair and called on UNITA to accept the results. The civil war resumed after UNITA rejected the election results, and the runoff in the presidential elections was postponed indefinitely. Subsequently, a small group within the MPLA has succeeded in maintaining a monopoly on governmental power. The U.N. is authorized by the Lusaka Protocol to declare when requisite conditions have been met to hold the second round of presidential elections. As part of the peace process, the Constitution was amended in 1996 to extend the mandate of the current Government and National Assembly past the November 1996 expiration of their terms to permit a smooth transition to a government of national reconciliation.

The National Assembly exercises little meaningful power independent of the ruling executive structure. Only 5 of 70 UNITA deputies elected to the National Assembly in the 1992 election occupied their seats, although the remainder are expected to do so when a government of national reconciliation and unity is formed. Several small parties are also represented in the National Assembly; however, few opposition deputies participated in National Assembly debate. One vocal opposition deputy was stripped of his parliamentary immunity by a vote of the MPLA majority to face charges of party registration fraud. Some MPLA deputies admitted that National Assembly debate was frequently superfluous, and the Assembly simply rubberstamped the presidency's initiatives.

There are no legal barriers to the participation of women in the political process. Only 3 of 19 cabinet ministries are headed by women, and 1 of the 12 Supreme Court judges is a woman. Women have been promoted to the rank of subcommissioner (major general equivalent) in the National Police.

Section 4. Governmental Attitude Regarding International and Nongovernmental Investigation of Alleged Violations of Human Rights

The Government impedes independent investigations of human rights abuses. Because of government suppression, the one functioning Angolan human rights monitoring group, the Angolan Human Rights Association, was moribund. The Human Rights Committee of the National Assembly remains weak and ineffective.

The UNAVEM Human Rights Monitoring Group (HRMG) held a number of national and regional human rights seminars with senior government and UNITA participation. UNAVEM's HRMG and military and civilian police observers were the only effective human rights monitors, but they did not make the conclusions of their investigations public. Additionally, the Government frequently interfered in UNAVEM's attempts to investigate complaints of human rights violations.

Amnesty International representatives were invited to participate in a June human rights seminar for police and prison officials. The Government granted the ICRC limited access to prisons in 1996. However, the Government denied the ICRC access to people allegedly being held as war-related prisoners (see Section 1.d.).

UNITA impedes independent investigations of human rights abuses in territory that it controls. It frequently interfered in UNAVEM's attempts to investigate complaints of human rights violations and denied the ICRC access to persons believed to be held prisoner (see Section 1.d.).

Section 5. Discrimination Based on Race, Sex, Religion, Disability, Language, or Social Status

Under the Constitution all citizens are equal before the law and enjoy the same rights and responsibilities regardless of color, race, ethnicity, sex, place of birth, religion, ideology, degree of education, or economic or social condition. The Government does not have the ability to effectively enforce these provisions.

Women.—Violence against women was widespread. Credible evidence indicated that a significant proportion of homicides were perpetrated against women, usually by their spouses. Due to dire economic circumstances, increasing numbers of women engaged in prostitution, and the clergy reported that marriages are breaking down at an alarming rate.

Despite constitutional protections, women suffered from discrimination. The law provides for equal pay for equal work, but in practice women are not compensated equally. Some women held senior positions in the military (primarily in the medical field) and civil service, but women were mostly relegated to low-level positions in state-run industries and in the small private sector. Adult women may open a bank account, accept employment, and own property without interference from their spouses. Women also have the right to inherit property. Upon the death of a male head of household, the widow automatically is entitled to 50 percent of any estate with the remainder divided equally among legitimate male and female children.

In much of the country women swelled the ranks of the disabled because they often set off land mines while foraging in the fields for food and firewood.

Children.—The Government gave only marginal attention to children's rights and welfare. Approximately 20 percent of children attend primary education classes. The Health Ministry worked with international donors to coordinate a successful child vaccination campaign against polio in September. Also in cooperation with international aid organizations, the Ministry of Social Integration has begun working to demobilize over 8,000 child soldiers in both government and UNITA armed forces. An increase in the number of street children in Luanda and other cities resulted from the breakdown of family structure caused by the resumption of the civil war in 1992 and the continuing deterioration of the economy. Child prostitution continued to be a pervasive sign of social decay in urban areas. Young girls often took jobs as domestic servants in private homes while young boys roamed the market places and streets. Living conditions in government youth hostels were so poor that the majority of homeless children preferred to sleep on city streets.

The government-sponsored National Institute for Children lacks the capacity to adequately assist efforts by international nongovernmental organizations to assist dispossessed youth. There are no active private children's rights advocacy groups. Medical authorities report that female genital mutilation (FGM), which is widely condemned by international health experts as damaging to both physical and psychological health, occurs rarely in remote areas of Moxico province, bordering Zaire and Zambia. Government health workers sporadically have campaigned against the practice.

People With Disabilities.—The number of physically disabled in Angola includes an estimated 70,000 people who required amputations due to mine explosions. While there is no institutional discrimination against people with disabilities, the Government is doing little to supplement current demobilization efforts to improve their physical, financial, or social distress. There is no legislation mandating accessibility for the disabled to public or private facilities, and, given the degradation of the nation's infrastructure, it is difficult for the disabled to find employment or participate in the educational system. There were a number of protests by disabled veterans seeking to improve their benefits and force government attention to their plight.

National/Racial/Ethnic Minorities.—Angola's population includes 1 to 2 percent of Khoisan and other linguistically distinct hunter-gatherer tribes scattered throughout the southern provinces of Namibe, Cunene, and Cuando Cubango. There is no evidence that they suffer from official discrimination or harassment, but they do not participate actively in the political or economic life of the country and have a marginal ability to influence government decisions concerning their interests.

The long civil conflict has deep ethnic and urban versus rural roots. Many of the small number of white and mixed race Angolans who occupy technical and governmental positions have strongly backed the MPLA. The Government accuses UNITA of exacerbating ethnic tensions by dwelling on the perceived colonial ties of these people.

Section 6. Worker Rights

a. *The Right of Association.*—The Constitution provides for the right to form and join trade unions, engage in union activity, and strike, but the Government does not respect these rights in practice. The Government dominated the National Union of Angolan Workers (UNTA), the labor organ of the ruling MPLA. A rival labor federation, the General Centrale of Independent and Free Labor Unions of Angola (CGSILA) was established in May. The law requires that labor unions be recognized by the Government. Restrictions on civil liberties effectively prevent any labor activity not approved by the Government.

The Constitution provides for the right to strike, and legislation passed in 1991 provides the legal framework for, and strictly regulates the exercise of, that right. The law prohibits lockouts and worker occupation of places of employment and provides protection for nonstriking workers. It prohibits strikes by military and police personnel, prison workers, and firemen. The law does not effectively prohibit employer retribution against strikers.

There were strikes against the Government by teachers, doctors, and nurses, among others. The Health and Education Ministries negotiated settlements but repeatedly failed to honor them because of lack of resources. On Labor Day, May 1, the Government deployed paramilitary police in all public spaces in Luanda to deter rumored labor demonstrations.

Unions have the right to affiliate internationally.

b. *The Right to Organize and Bargain Collectively.*—The Constitution provides for the right to organize, and the law provides for collective bargaining, but the Government does not respect these rights in practice. The Government dominates the economy through state-run enterprises. The Ministry of Public Administration, Employment, and Social Security sets wages and benefits on an annual basis. The Government failed to honor a February agreement between the teachers' union and the Education Ministry to provide teachers an indexed wage. In the small private sector, wages are based on multiples of the minimum wage set by the Government. Legislation prohibits discrimination against union members. Union members' complaints are adjudicated in the regular civil courts. Employers found guilty of antiunion discrimination are required to reinstate workers fired for union activities.

There are no export processing zones.

c. *Prohibition of Forced or Compulsory Labor.*—Current law authorizing forced labor for breaches of worker discipline and participation in strikes has been cited by the International Labor Organization as a violation of its Convention 105.

d. *Minimum Age for Employment of Children.*—The legal minimum age for employment is 14 years. The Inspector General of the Ministry of Public Administration, Employment, and Social Security is responsible for enforcing labor laws. This Ministry maintains employment centers where prospective employees register, and these centers screen out applicants under the age of 14. However, many younger children work on family farms, as domestic servants, and in the informal economy.

e. *Acceptable Conditions of Work.*—The minimum wage set by the Ministry of Public Administration, Employment and Social Security was set at roughly $20 per month (4 million kwanzas). However, the Government does not enforce this standard. Neither the minimum wage nor the average monthly salary, which is $10 ($50 to $100 in Luanda), is sufficient to provide a decent living for a worker and family. As a result, many wage earners depend on the thriving informal sector, subsistence farming, theft, corruption, or support from relatives abroad in order to survive.

A 1994 government decree established a 37-hour workweek. However, inadequate resources prevented the Ministry of Public Administration, Employment, and Social Security from enforcing this standard or from enforcing occupational health and safety standards. Workers cannot remove themselves from dangerous work situations without jeopardy to their continued employment.

BENIN

The Republic of Benin is a constitutional democracy headed by President Mathieu Kerekou, who was inaugurated on April 4 after elections generally viewed as free and fair. President Kerekou, who ruled Benin as a Socialist military dictator from 1972–1989, succeeded his democratically elected predecessor, and continued the civilian, democratic rule begun in the 1990–1991 constitutional process that ended his previous reign. There are 18 political parties represented in the unicameral, 83-member National Assembly; no party or political grouping commands a majority of seats. The Government respects the constitutional provision for an independent judiciary; however, the judiciary is inefficient and susceptible to corruption.

The civilian-controlled security forces consist of the armed forces, headed by a Minister Delegate for Defense Matters in the office of the President and the police force under the Interior Minister. The two Ministers also share authority over the gendarmerie, which exercises police functions in rural areas. The armed forces continued to play an apolitical role in government affairs despite concerns about morale within its ranks and its ethnic imbalance.

An extremely poor country with average yearly per capita income below $450, the economy is based largely on subsistence agriculture, cotton production, regional trade (including transshipment of goods to neighboring countries), and small-scale offshore oil production. The port of Cotonou serves as a major conduit for goods entering neighboring Nigeria legally and illegally. The new Administration continued, and in some cases stepped up, the austerity program begun by its predecessor; privatized state-owned enterprises; reduced fiscal expenditures; and deregulated trade. In spite of its bloated and inefficient bureaucracy, high debt servicing costs, and widespread unemployment, Benin's economic recovery continues under liberal economic policies instituted since the return to democracy. Inflation in 1996 was less than 3 percent with real growth estimated at between 5 and 6 percent.

The Government generally respected the human rights of its citizens. The major human rights problems continued to be the failure by police forces to curtail acts of vigilantism and mob justice; serious administrative delays in processing ordinary criminal cases with attendant denial of timely, fair trials; judicial corruption; harsh and unhealthy prison conditions; societal discrimination and violence against women and the abuse of children. The practice of female genital mutilation (FGM), is also a problem. The Constitutional Court demonstrated independence in a high profile challenge to the presidential elections and the prosecution of an army officer accused of threatening state security.

RESPECT FOR HUMAN RIGHTS

Section 1. Respect for the Integrity of the Person, Including Freedom From:

a. *Political and Other Extrajudicial Killing.*—There were no reports of political or other extrajudicial killings by government officials. However, a rising crime rate and a lack of police responsiveness led to more reports of mob justice. Vigilantism reportedly resulted in several cases of suspected criminals being killed or severely injured, particularly thieves caught in the act. Although a number of these incidents took place in urban areas and were publicized in the press, the Government apparently made no concerted attempt to investigate or prosecute anyone involved. Some press accounts suggested that the police deliberately ignored vigilante attacks.

b. *Disappearance.*—There were no reports of politically motivated disappearances.

c. *Torture and Other Cruel, Inhuman, or Degrading Treatment or Punishment.*— The Constitution prohibits such practices and there were no reports that officials employed them. The Government continued to make payments to victims of torture under the military regime which ruled from 1972 to 1989.

Prison conditions continue to be extremely harsh. Extensive overcrowding and lack of proper sanitation and medical facilities pose a risk to prisoners' health. The prison diet is seriously inadequate with malnutrition and disease common. Prisoners are allowed to meet with visitors.

d. *Arbitrary Arrest, Detention, or Exile.*—The Constitution prohibits arbitrary arrest, detention or exile, however, at times the authorities arbitrarily arrested and detained persons. The Constitution prohibits detention for more than 48 hours without a hearing by a magistrate whose order is required for continued detention. However, there were credible reports that authorities exceeded this 48-hour limit in many cases, sometimes by as long as a week, using the accepted practice of holding a person without specified time limit "at the disposition of" the public prosecutor's office before presenting the case to a magistrate. Approximately 75 percent of prisoners are pretrial detainees. Arbitrary arrest is not routine but does occur occasionally. In a highly publicized case, Colonel Maurice Kouandete was arrested for political reasons prior to the presidential election, allegedly for plotting against the security of the State. The Constitutional Court ruled that his detention was unconstitutional. He was not released, however, until President Kerekou took office on April 4.

On July 31, in his first address to the nation since taking office, President Kerekou announced that he would pardon certain categories of prisoners convicted between August 1, 1995, and June 15, 1996. All such prisoners were released by year's end.

The Constitution prohibits forced exile of citizens. Many citizens who went into exile prior to the establishment of democratic rule have returned.

e. *Denial of Fair Public Trial.*—The Constitution provides for an independent judiciary and the Government generally respects this provision in practice. However, the executive has important powers in regard to the judiciary.

The President appoints career magistrates as judges in civil courts, and the Constitution gives the Ministry of Justice administrative authority over judges, including the power to transfer them. Inadequate facilities, poorly-trained staff, and overcrowded dockets result in slow administration of justice. The low salaries of magistrates and clerks have a demoralizing effect on their commitment to efficient and timely justice and makes them susceptible to corruption.

The legal system is based on French civil law and local customary law. The Constitution provides for the right to a fair public trial. A defendant enjoys the presumption of innocence and has the right to be present at trial and to representation by an attorney, at public expense if necessary. In practice, the court provides indigent defendants with court-appointed counsel upon request. A defendant also has the right to confront witnesses and to have access to government-held evidence. Trials are open to the public, but in exceptional circumstances the President of the court may decide to restrict access to preserve public order or to protect the parties.

A civilian court system operates on the national and provincial levels. Military disciplinary councils deal with minor offense by military members, but have no jurisdiction over civilians. There is only one court of appeals. The Supreme Court is the court of last resort in all administrative and judicial matters. The Constitutional Court is charged with passing on the constitutionality of laws and disputes between the President and the National Assembly and with resolving disputes regarding presidential and National Assembly elections. Its rulings against both the executive and legislative branches indicated its independence from both these branches of Government. The Constitution also provides for a High Court of Justice to convene in the event of crimes committed by the President or government ministers against the State. Implementing legislation to create the High Court of Justice was passed in June. Although the legislation was passed, the Constitutional Court later found some of its provisions to be unconstitutional. As of year's end, the legislature had not passed revisions to bring the law into compliance with the Constitutional Court ruling.

At year's end there were no reports of political prisoners. During the year, one individual arrested in connection with a rocket attack on the site where the December 1995 international conference for the heads of French-speaking nations was held in special prison quarters, charged with "threatening national security," but tried under the Criminal Code. The individual was convicted and sentenced to 1 year in prison, but released on December 1 after paying a fine of $2,000 (1 million cfa).

f. *Arbitrary Interference With Privacy, Family, Home or Correspondence.*—The Constitution prohibits such practices and government authorities generally respect these prohibitions in practice. Police are required to obtain a judicial warrant before entering a private home, and usually observed this requirement in practice.

Section 2. *Respect for Civil Liberties, Including:*

a. *Freedom of Speech and Press.*—The Constitution provides for freedom of speech and of the press, and the Government respects these rights in practice. The Government entity with oversight responsibility for media operations is the High Authority for Audio-visual Media and Communications (HAAC), which requires broadcasters to submit weekly lists of planned programs and requires publishers to deposit copies of all publications with it. The requirement, however, is not observed by the media in practice.

There is a large and active privately owned press consisting of about a dozen newspapers. These publications criticize the Government freely and often, but their effect on public opinion is limited because of their urban concentration. The majority of Beninese are illiterate.

The Government continued to own and operate the media most influential in reaching the public. The only radio stations that transmit locally are Government owned: the Benin Office of Radio and Television (ORTB) transmits in FM, AM and short wave, in French and local languages. Radio France International (RFI) also transmits over a local FM band under an agreement with the Government. Five rural radio stations governed by local committees broadcast several hours a day exclusively in local languages. These stations receive support from ORTB. Radio is probably the most important information medium.

A similar arrangement is in place for television transmissions: ORTB broadcasts 5 hours per day on a signal that is easily received in urban areas. Approximately 80 percent of ORTB's television programming is in French. TV5, a commercial venture with investments by television broadcasting organizations in France, Canada, Belgium and Switzerland, broadcasts locally 24 hours a day entirely in French under an agreement with the Government. Although neither television station broadcasts partisan programs in support of or unduly critical of the Government, the vast majority of news programming centers on government officials' activities. By year's end, the National Assembly still had not approved guidelines for broadcasting, effectively blocking the demonopolization of electronic media.

The Government does not censor works by foreign journalists, authors, or artists. A special RFI correspondent covering the Presidential election was threatened with expulsion by the previous government because he transmitted reports of unofficial early election results that showed the government was losing. However, no action was taken against him.

HAAC regulations govern satellite reception equipment and movie and video clubs. There is little enforcement of these regulations.

In general, academic freedom is respected. University professors are permitted to lecture freely, conduct research, and publish their work.

b. *Freedom of Peaceful Assembly and Association.*—The Constitution provides for these rights, and the Government generally respects them in practice. The Government requires permits for use of public places for demonstrations and requires associations to register. It routinely grants both such permits and registrations. The Government did not take any actions against nonregistered organizations for failure or refusal to register. Security forces protected former President Soglo at a rally organized by the opposition coalition, following his return from a protracted stay abroad after the election. Soglo was allowed to use government-owned facilities for his homecoming speech and the rally was given prominent coverage on the government-owned radio and television stations.

c. *Freedom of Religion.*—The Constitution provides for freedom of religion, and the Government respects this right in practice.

d. *Freedom of Movement Within the Country, Foreign Travel, Emigration, and Repatriation.*—The Constitution provides for these rights, and the government generally respects them in practice. However, the presence of police, gendarmes, and illegal roadblocks impedes domestic movement. Although ostensibly meant to enforce automotive safety and customs regulations, many of these checkpoints serve as a means for officials to exact bribes from travelers. The Kerekou Government instituted measures to combat such petty corruption at roadblocks.

The Government's policy toward transhumance allows migratory Fulani herdsmen from other countries to enter freely; it does not enforce designated entry points. In recent years, friction between native farmers and itinerant foreign herders has sometimes led to violence.

The Government does not restrict international travel for political reasons, and those who travel abroad may return without hindrance.

Historically, the Government has cooperated closely with the United Nations High Commissioner for Refugees (UNHCR) and other humanitarian organizations in assisting refugees, including those in need of first asylum. The Government provided first asylum to up to 200,000 Togolese in the recent past. While most have returned to Togo, some 5,000 to 8,000 continue to receive first asylum. Several hundred Oganis from Nigeria were also provided first asylum in 1996. There were no reports of forced return of persons to a country where they feared persecution. There were no reports of forced expulsion of persons having a valid claim to refugee status.

As a result of political turmoil in neighboring Togo beginning in 1992, some 200,000 Togolese refugees were protected and assisted by the UNHCR. Since 1993 thousands of refugees have returned to Togo on their own. At the beginning of 1996, approximately 20,000 Togolese refugees remained in Benin. In mid-1996 UNHCR implemented its plan for organized voluntary repatriation of the Togolese. By year's end, all but about 5,000 to 8,000 had returned to Togo. Despite severe economic pressures limiting its ability to provide education for its own children, the Government allowed the Togolese to enroll their children in local schools and to participate in some economic activities. The country also hosts several hundred Nigerian refugees, primarily from the Ogoni ethnic group. Ogoni requests for asylum increased significantly when Ogoni leader Ken Saro-Wiwa was executed. Liberian, Rwandan, Burundian and Chadian refugees are among those also represented in smaller numbers.

Section 3. *Respect for Political Rights: The Right of Citizens to Change Their Government*

The Constitution provides citizens with the right peacefully to change their government. Citizens exercised this right in legislative elections in 1991 and 1995, and in presidential elections in 1991 and March, all considered free and fair. The Constitution provides for a 5-year term of office for the President (who is limited to two terms) and 4-year terms for National Assembly members (who may serve an unlimited number of terms). Seven candidates competed openly and vigorously during the March 3 presidential elections, with the two leaders contesting the runoff two weeks later. Although the losing incumbent challenged the final results, claiming fraudulent voting and other irregularities, those claims were rejected after consideration by the Constitutional Court.

Women participate actively in the political parties but are underrepresented in Government positions. There is now 1 woman in the 19-member Cabinet. The previous Government had four female cabinet members. There are 6 female deputies in the 83-member unicameral National Assembly. The President of the Constitutional Court is a woman; the HAAC and the Economic and Social Council have female members.

Section 4. Governmental Attitude Regarding International and Nongovernmental Investigations of Alleged Violations of Human Rights

A number of human rights groups—both domestic and international—operate without government restriction, investigating and publishing their findings on human rights cases. Government officials are generally cooperative and responsive to their views. Hundreds of electoral observers representing scores of international human rights groups traveled to Benin for the presidential elections. Nearly all of them reported that the Government had cooperated with them.

Section 5. Discrimination Based on Race, Sex, Religion, Disability, Language, or Social Status

The Constitution prohibits discrimination based on race, sex, and religion, but societal discrimination against women continues.

Women.—While no statistics are available, violence against women, including wife beating, occurs. The press sometimes reports incidents of abuse of women but judges and police are reluctant to intervene in domestic disputes, considering such disputes a family matter.

Although the Constitution provides for equality for women in the political, economic, and social spheres, women experience extensive societal discrimination, especially in rural areas, where they occupy a subordinate role and are responsible for much of the hard labor on subsistence farms. In urban areas, women dominate the trading sector in the open-air markets. By law, women have equal inheritance and property rights, but local custom in some areas prevents them from inheriting real property. Women do not enjoy the same educational opportunities as men, and female literacy is about 16 percent (compared with 32 percent for males).

There are active women's rights groups that have been effective in drafting a family code that would improve the status of women under the law.

Children.—The Ministry of Labor and Social Affairs is responsible for the protection of children's rights, primarily in the areas of education and health. In particular, the Government is trying to boost primary school enrollment, which is only about 66 percent. In some parts of the country, girls receive no formal education.

Some traditional practices inflict hardship and violence on children, including most prominently the custom of "vidomegon," whereby poor, often rural, families place a child, primarily girls, in the home of more wealthy families. In July a criminal court convicted and sent to prison the wife of a former Minister for beating to death a child in her employ under the vidomegon system. Other traditional practices include the killing of deformed babies, breach babies, and one of two newborn twins (all of whom are thought to be sorcerers in some rural areas). There is also a tradition in which a groom abducts and rapes his prospective child (under 14 years of age) bride. Criminal courts mete out stiff sentences to criminals convicted of crimes against children, but many such crimes never reach the courts.

The Government has been less successful in combating female genital mutilation (FGM), which is not illegal. FGM is widely condemned by international health experts as damaging to both physical and psychological health. FGM, or excision, is practiced on females ranging from infancy through 30 years of age. Studies vary widely and suggest that as few as 5 percent or as many as 50 percent of women are affected by this practice, mostly in the northern provinces. The actual incidence probably falls somewhere between these estimates. A prominent nongovernmental organization has made progress in raising awareness of the dangers of the practice; the Government has cooperated with its efforts. According to recent research, there is a strong profit motive in the continued practice of FGM by those who perform the operation, usually older women.

People With Disabilities.—Although the Constitution provides that the State look after the handicapped, the Government does not mandate accessibility for disabled persons. It operated a number of social centers for disabled persons to assist their social integration. Nonetheless, many are unable to find employment and must resort to begging to support themselves.

National/Racial/Ethnic Minorities.—There is a long history of regional rivalries. Although Southerners dominate the Government's senior ranks, Northerners dominate the military. The South has enjoyed more advanced economic development, a larger population, and has traditionally held favored status. In the 1996 elections, a Northerner was elected President.

Section 6. *Worker Rights*

a. *The Right of Association.*—The Constitution provides workers with the freedom to organize, join unions, meet, and strike, and the Government usually respects these rights in practice. The labor force of about 2 million is primarily engaged in subsistence agriculture and other primary sector activities, with less than 2 percent of the population engaged in the modern (wage) sector. Approximately 75 percent of the wage earners belong to labor unions. There are four union confederations, and unions are generally independent of Government and political parties. The Economic and Social Council, a constitutionally mandated body established in 1994, includes four union representatives. In August the Union of Workers of the Agency for Aviation Navigation (ASECNA) closed the country's only international airport for several days to protest government plans (initiated under the previous administration) to privatize airport operations. The strike was settled peacefully. In December ASECNA also struck in coordination with ASECNA workers in 14 other African countries. In February workers at the state-owned petroleum company, SONACOP, conducted a 72-hour strike to protest the company's privatization as proposed by the World Bank. The President agreed to renegotiate the terms of the privatization and the strike was settled peacefully.

There were no known instances of efforts by the Government to retaliate against union activity. Laws prohibit employer retaliation against strikers, and the Government enforces them effectively.

Unions may freely form or join federations or confederations and affiliate with international bodies.

b. *The Right to Organize and Bargain Collectively.*—The Labor Code provides for collective bargaining, and workers freely exercised these rights. Wages in the private sector are set in negotiations between unions and employers. A tripartite group, composed of unions, employers, and the Government, discussed and agreed to revisions in the Labor Code in 1995, but the new code had not been enacted into law by year's end The Government sets wages in the public sector by law and regulation.

The Labor Code prohibits employers from taking union membership or activity into account regarding hiring, work distribution, professional or vocational training, or dismissal. The Government levies substantial penalties against employers who refuse to rehire workers dismissed for lawful union activities.

There are no export processing zones.

c. *Prohibition of Forced or Compulsory Labor.*—The Labor Code prohibits forced or compulsory labor, and such labor is not practiced.

d. *Minimum Age for Employment of Children.*—The Labor Code prohibits the employment or apprenticeship of children under 14 years of age in any enterprise. However, the Ministry of Labor enforces the code in only a limited manner (and then only in the modern sector), due to the lack of inspectors. Children continue to work on rural family farms, on construction sites in urban areas, and as domestic servants. Children also commonly work as street vendors.

e. *Acceptable Conditions of Work.*—The Government administratively sets minimum wage scales for a number of occupations. The minimum wage is approximately $40 (cfa francs 20,300) per month, which is insufficient to cover the costs for food and housing of even a single worker living in an urban area. Many workers must supplement their wages by subsistence farming or informal sector trade. Most workers in the wage sector, however, earn more than the minimum wage.

The Labor Code establishes a workweek of from 40 to 46 hours, depending on the type of work, and provides for at least one 24-hour rest period per week. The authorities generally enforce legal limits on workweeks. The Labor Code establishes health and safety standards, but the Ministry of Labor does not enforce them effectively. The Labor Code does not provide workers with the right to remove themselves from dangerous work situations without jeopardy to continued employment. The Ministry of Labor has the authority to require employers to remedy dangerous work conditions but does not do so effectively.

BOTSWANA

Botswana is a longstanding, multiparty democracy. Constitutional power is shared between the President, Sir Ketumile Masire, and the 44-member popularly elected lower house of Parliament. The ruling Botswana Democratic Party (BDP) continued to dominate the National Assembly, holding 31 of 44 seats. The opposition Botswana National Front (BNF) holds the remaining 13 seats. In October 1994, the President was reelected in free and fair elections for a third 5-year term. The Government respects the constitutional provisions for an independent judiciary.

The civilian Government exercises effective control over the security forces. The military, the Botswana Defense Force (BDF), is responsible for external security. The Botswana National Police (BNP) are responsible for internal security. Members of the security forces occasionally committed human rights abuses.

The economy is market oriented with strong encouragement for private enterprise. Steady diamond revenues and effective economic and fiscal policies resulted in continuing growth, although the economy grew at a relatively modest annual rate of 4.5 percent following a downturn from 1991 to 1993. Per capita gross domestic product was approximately $3,000 in 1996. Over 50 percent of the population is employed in the informal sector, largely subsistence farming and animal husbandry. Rural poverty remains a serious problem, as does a widely skewed income distribution.

The Constitution provides for citizens' human rights, and the Government generally respects those rights in practice. Despite some continuing problems, Botswana's overall human rights record has been consistently positive since independence. There were credible reports that the police sometimes mistreated criminal suspects in order to coerce confessions. Women continued to face legal and societal discrimination, and violence against women is a continuing problem. Some Batswana, including groups not numbered among the eight "principal tribes" identified in the Constitution because they live in remote areas, still do not enjoy full access to social services and, in practice, are marginalized in the political process. In many instances the judicial system did not provide timely fair trials due to a serious backlog of cases. Trade unions continued to face some legal restrictions, and the Government did not always ensure that labor laws were observed in practice.

The Government continued to address human rights problems in 1996. Parliament ratified the Convention on the Elimination of All Forms of Discrimination Against Women (CEDAW) and adopted a national policy on women in July. However, the Government's plan announced in September 1995 to construct a separate detention facility for asylum seekers whose refugee claims have been rejected has been delayed pending resolution of a dispute between two government ministries over how improvements to the property will be made. The facility is now referred to by the Government as the Center for Illegal Immigrants. Until the Center is completed, refused asylum seekers continue to be detained in prison. Refugees and asylum seekers refused under Botswana's "first country of origin" policy are housed at Dukwe Refugee Camp.

RESPECT FOR HUMAN RIGHTS

Section 1. Respect for the Integrity of the Person, Including Freedom From:

a. *Political and Other Extrajudicial Killing.*—There were no reports of political killings. However, in February six members of the military intelligence unit of the BDF were implicated in the death of a man who died while under interrogation about stolen vehicles and computers. An alleged witness, who claimed that he had also been assaulted, charged that he saw the officers suffocate the deceased with a plastic bag.

In a case related to a violent student protest in early 1995, the 12-year sentence of a riot police officer convicted of murdering a man who apparently had no connection with the demonstrations was reduced at a February hearing.

b. *Disappearance.*—There were no reports of politically motivated disappearances.

c. *Torture and Other Cruel, Inhuman, or Degrading Treatment or Punishment.*— The Constitution explicitly forbids torture, inhuman, and degrading treatment or punishment. The authorities generally respect this prohibition in practice and, in some cases, have taken disciplinary or judicial action against persons responsible for abuses. However, instances of abuse do occur. While coerced confessions are inadmissible in court, evidence gathered through coercion or abuse may be used in prosecution. There were credible reports that police sometimes used intimidation techniques in order to obtain evidence or elicit confessions. In the past police sometimes suffocated criminal suspects with a plastic bag. There was one such allegation in 1996 (see Section 1.a.). In general, however, beatings and other forms of extreme physical abuse remained rare.In June the Government filed unlawful rioting and assault charges against several students who had been detained and released following violent student demonstrations in February 1995. Some of the students had alleged police assault when initially detained.

In January a district customary court sentenced nine young men to six strokes each on the buttocks for common nuisance. In October the House of Chiefs adopted a motion to request the Government to reinstate corporal punishment in the form of flogging across the back rather than the buttocks as is currently permitted. The House of Chiefs is an advisory body only.

Prison conditions meet minimum international standards, although overcrowding is a problem. Women in custody are placed in the charge of female officers. The Government permits visits by human rights monitors after a detailed inquiry procedure.

The Government neither forcibly repatriates nor deports failed asylum seekers, but it has incarcerated them alongside convicted felons. Asylum seekers refused under Botswana's "first country of origin" policy, who through mid-1995 were incarcerated, are now housed at Dukwe refugee camp, which is funded by the United Nations High Commissioner for Refugees (UNHCR) with support from the Government (see Section 2.d.). Asylum seekers who do not qualify as refugees are detained in prison. The Government's plan to build a dedicated facility for refused asylum seekers, announced in September 1995, has been delayed pending resolution of a dispute between two ministries over how improvements to the property are to be made. The facility, to be called the Center for Illegal Immigrants, will be administered jointly by the Department of Prisons and Rehabilitation with the Immigration Department, which will assist with processing asylum and immigration requests.

d. *Arbitrary Arrest, Detention, or Exile.*—Under the Constitution "every person in Botswana" is entitled to due process, the presumption of innocence, and freedom from arbitrary arrest. The authorities respected these guarantees in practice. Suspects must be informed of their legal rights upon arrest, including the right to remain silent, to be allowed to contact a person of their choice, and generally to be charged before a magistrate within 48 hours. A magistrate may order a suspect held for 14 days through a writ of detention, which may be renewed every 14 days. Most citizens charged with noncapital offenses are released on their own recognizance; some are released with minimal bail. Detention without bail is highly unusual, except in murder cases, where it is mandated. Detainees have the right to hire attorneys of their choice.

Poor police training and poor communications in rural villages make it difficult for detainees to obtain legal assistance, however, and authorities do not always follow judicial safeguards. The Government does not provide counsel for the indigent, except in capital cases, and there is no public defender service. Two nongovernmental organizations (NGO's)—the University of Botswana Legal Assistance Center and the Botswana Center for Human Rights—provide cost free legal services, but their capacity is limited. Constitutional protections are not applied to illegal immigrants, although the constitutionality of denying them due process has not been tested in court.

Following student demonstrations in February 1995 (see Section 1.c.), police detained and then released several hundred persons. In June the Government brought charges of unlawful rioting and assault against some of those who had been detained and released. This sparked renewed, although peaceful, student demonstrations. The Attorney General's Office has reviewed the charges and evidence and has decided to prosecute. Hearing dates had not been set by year's end.

The Government does not use exile for political purposes.

e. *Denial of Fair Public Trial.*—The Constitution provides for an independent judiciary, and the Government respects this provision in practice.The judiciary consists of both a civil court (including magistrates' courts, a High Court, and a Court of Appeal) and a customary (traditional) court system. The law provides for the right to a fair trial. The civil courts remained unable to provide for timely, fair trials in many cases, however, due to severe staffing shortages and an accumulated backlog of pending cases. The courts are making a major effort to clear this backlog, especially in murder cases.

Most trials in the regular courts are public, although trials under the National Security Act (NSA) may be held in secret. As a rule, courts appoint public defenders only for those charged with capital crimes (murder and treason). Those charged with noncapital crimes are often tried without legal representation if they cannot afford an attorney. As a result, many defendants may not be informed of their rights in pretrial or trial proceedings.

Implementation of the 1994 Anticorruption Act assuaged earlier concerns that it would weaken the defendant's constitutional presumption of innocence.

Most citizens encounter the legal system through the customary courts, under the authority of a traditional leader. These courts handle minor offenses involving land, marital, and property disputes. In customary courts the defendant does not have legal counsel and there are no precise rules of evidence. Tribal judges, appointed by the tribal leader or elected by the community, determine sentences, which may be appealed through the civil court system. The quality of decisions reached in the traditional courts varies considerably. In communities where chiefs and their decisions are respected, plaintiffs tend to take their cases to the customary court; otherwise, people seek justice from the civil courts.

There were no reports of political prisoners.

f. *Arbitrary Interference With Privacy, Family, Home, or Correspondence.*—The Constitution provides for the protection of privacy and the security of the person, and government authorities generally respect these rights.

Section 2. *Respect for Civil Liberties, Including:*

a. *Freedom of Speech and Press.*—The Constitution provides for freedom of expression, both individual and corporate, and the Government respects this right in practice. Botswana has a long tradition of vigorous, candid, and unimpeded public discourse.The independent press is small, but lively and frequently critical of the Government and the President. It reports without fear of closure or censorship. Concern has been expressed, however, that charges recently filed against a journalist may have an intimidating effect. In October the journalist was accused of violating a law that prohibits disclosure of the names of persons being investigated by the Directorate on Corruption and the Economic Crime Unit. However, a magistrate's court dismissed the charges on November 1. No further charges were brought either against the journalist or the reporter's two editors and the independent newspaper's coowners and publishers, who had been implicated at one point in the case.

The Government also subsidizes a free daily newspaper which depends heavily on the official Botswana Press Agency (BOPA) for its material. The broadcast media remain a government monopoly, with radio the most important medium of information in this highly dispersed society. Radio Botswana follows government policies and draws most of its stories from BOPA. Opposition leaders have access to the radio, but they complain—with some justification—that their air time is significantly limited. There are no privately owned radio or television stations, but there is a semilegal television station broadcasting to viewers in the capital city. Independent radio and television from neighboring South Africa are easily received.

On occasion the Government has taken steps, under loosely defined provisions of the NSA, to limit publication of national security information.

Academic freedom is not restricted.

b. *Freedom of Peaceful Assembly and Association.*—The Constitution provides for these rights, and the Government respects them in practice.

c. *Freedom of Religion.*—The Constitution provides for freedom of religion, and the Government respects this right in practice.

d. *Freedom of Movement Within the Country, Foreign Travel, Emigration, and Repatriation.*—There are no barriers to domestic and international travel or migration. Citizenship is not revoked for political reasons.The Government cooperates with the UNHCR and other humanitarian organizations in assisting refugees. Botswana has maintained a policy of considering resettlement requests only from refugees from contiguous countries. The Government has, however, permitted failed asylum seekers to remain in the country either at the Dukwe Refugee Camp or in jail. There were no confirmed reports of forced return of persons to a country where they feared persecution. Refugees and asylum seekers refused under Botswana's "first country of origin" policy are housed at Dukwe Refugee Camp until they are resettled or repatriated. New arrivals considered by the Government to be illegal immigrants are detained in prison until the Government's plan to construct a separate facility, announced in September 1995, has been completed. The plan, which is in the design stage, has been delayed pending resolution of a dispute between two ministries over how improvements to the property will be made.

Section 3. *Respect for Political Rights: The Right of Citizens to Change Their Government*

The Constitution provides citizens with the right to change their government peacefully, and citizens exercise this right in practice through periodic, free, and fair elections held on the basis of universal adult (21 years of age) suffrage. The Botswana Democratic Party continued to dominate Parliament following the October 1994 elections, ensuring the reelection of BDP leader Sir Ketumile Masire as President. The opposition Botswana National Front, the only opposition party to win seats, increased its representation from 3 to 13 seats.The House of Chiefs, an advisory upper chamber of Parliament with limited powers, is constitutionally restricted to the eight "principal tribes" of the Tswana nation. Consequently, other groups (e.g., the Basarwa "bushmen," Herero, Kalanga, Humbukush, Baloi, or Lozi) are not represented there. Given the limited authority of the House of Chiefs, the impact of excluding other groups of Botswana citizens is largely symbolic, but it is viewed as important in principle by some non-Setswana speakers. Members of the National Assembly are required to be able to speak English. This restriction has never been challenged in court.

In practice, women are underrepresented in the political process. Although women constitute just over 50 percent of the population, there are only 4 women among the 44 members of the National Assembly, and only 2 women in the Cabinet.

Section 4. *Governmental Attitude Regarding International and Nongovernmental Investigation of Alleged Violations of Human Rights*

Domestic and international human rights groups operate without government restriction, investigating and publishing their findings on human rights cases. Government officials are generally cooperative and responsive to such inquiries.

Section 5. *Discrimination Based on Race, Sex, Religion, Disability, Language, or Social Status*

The Constitution and Penal Code forbid discrimination on the basis of ethnicity, nationality, or creed, but do not address discrimination based on sex. These provisions are implemented in practice by the government authorities.

Women.—Violence against women, primarily beatings, remains a serious problem. Under customary law and in common rural practice men have the right to "chastise" their wives. Statistics are believed to underreport the levels of abuse against women. Police are rarely called to intervene in cases of domestic violence, and there were no court cases related to domestic violence in 1996. Spousal abuse is beginning to receive increased attention both from the media and from local human rights groups.

Women in Botswana do not have the same civil rights as men. However, one important step was the Government's accedence to the Convention on the Elimination of All Forms of Discrimination Against Women (CEDAW). In addition a national policy on women was adopted in July following consultations among the Government, NGO's and the private sector. The plan identifies six critical areas of concern, prioritized as follows: 1) women and poverty, 2) women and powersharing and decisionmaking, 3) education and training of women, 4) women and health, 5) the girl child, and 6) violence against women.

A number of other laws, many of which are attributed to traditional practices, restrict civil and economic opportunities for women. A woman married in "common property" is held to be a legal minor, requiring her husband's consent to buy or sell property, apply for credit, and enter into legally binding contracts. Women have, and are increasingly exercising, the right to marriage "out of common property," in which case they retain their full legal rights as adults. Polygyny is still legal under traditional law and with the consent of the first wife, but it is rarely practiced. In October the Government solicited bids for consultants to review existing laws alleged to discriminate against women.

Well trained urban women enjoy growing entry level access to the white collar job market, but the number of opportunities decreases sharply as they rise in seniority. Discrimination against women is most acute in rural areas where women work primarily in subsistence agriculture.

A number of women's organizations have emerged to promote the status of women. The Government has entered into a dialog with many of these groups. While some women's rights groups reportedly felt that the Government has been slow to respond concretely to their concerns, women's NGO's say that they are encouraged by the direction of change, and by the increasingly collaborative relationship with government authorities. Within the Ministry of Labor and Home Affairs, the Women's Affairs Unit, which is charged with handling women's issues, was upgraded to a division. Plans to make it a separate department had not yet been implemented.

Children.—The Government provides 7 years of education for children. The rights of children are addressed in the Constitution and the 1981 Children's Act. Under the act Botswana has a court system and social service apparatus designed solely for juveniles. There is no societal pattern of abuse against children.

People With Disabilities.—The Government does not discriminate on the basis of physical or mental disability, although employment opportunities for the disabled remain limited. The Government does not require accessibility to public buildings and public conveyances for people with disabilities, and the NGO community has only recently begun to address the needs of the disabled.

National/Racial/Ethnic Minorities.—The Tswana majority, of which the Constitution recognizes eight principal tribes, has a tradition of peacefully coexisting with "minor" tribes. Each of the eight principal tribes is represented in the advisory House of Chiefs, while the other groups are permitted only a subchief, who is not a member of the House. Other than the lack of schooling in their own language and representation in the House of Chiefs, Botswana's Bantu minorities and nonindigenous minorities, such as the white and Asian communities, are not subject to discrimination. However, the nomadic Basarwa remain marginalized; they have lost access to their traditional land and are vulnerable to exploitation. Their isolation, ignorance of civil rights, and lack of representation in local or national government have stymied their progress.

Section 6. Worker Rights

a. *The Right of Association.*—The Constitution provides for the right of association. In practice all workers, with the exception of government employees, are free to join or organize unions of their own choosing. Government workers may form associations that function as quasi-unions but without the right to negotiate wages. The industrial or wage economy is small, and unions are concentrated largely in the mineral and to a lesser extent in the railway and banking sectors. There is only one major confederation, the Botswana Federation of Trade Unions (BFTU), but there are no obstacles to the formation of other labor federations.

Unions are independent of the Government and are not closely allied with any political party or movement. Unions may employ administrative staff, but the law requires elected union officials to work full time in the industry the union represents. This severely limits union leaders' professionalism and effectiveness and has been criticized by the International Confederation of Free Trade Unions (ICFTU).

The law also severely restricts the right to strike. Legal strikes are theoretically possible after an exhaustive arbitration process, but in practice none of the country's strikes to date has been legal.

Unions may join international organizations, and the BFTU is affiliated with the ICFTU. The Minister of Labor must approve any affiliation with an outside labor movement, but unions may appeal to the courts if an application for affiliation is refused.

b. *The Right to Organize and Bargain Collectively.*—The Constitution provides for collective bargaining for unions that have enrolled 25 percent of a labor force. In reality only the mineworker unions have the organizational strength to engage in collective bargaining, and collective bargaining is virtually nonexistent in most other sectors.

Workers may not be fired for union-related activities. Dismissals may be appealed to labor officers or civil courts, but labor offices rarely do more than order 2-months' severance pay.

Botswana has only one export processing zone—in the town of Selebi-Phikwe—which is subject to the same labor laws as the rest of the country.

c. *Prohibition of Forced or Compulsory Labor.*—The Constitution specifically forbids forced or compulsory labor, and it is not practiced.

d. *Minimum Age for Employment of Children.*—Although education is not compulsory, the Government provides 7 years of free education to every child, and most children in Botswana take advantage of this opportunity. Only an immediate family member may employ a child 13-years-old or younger, and no juvenile under 15 years may be employed in any industry. Only persons over 16 years may be hired to perform night work, and no person under 16 years is allowed to perform hazardous labor, including in mining. District and municipal councils have child welfare divisions which are responsible for enforcing child labor laws. Because research on the issue of child labor is limited, it is difficult to state whether child labor laws are effectively enforced. Child labor is not perceived to be a significant problem in Botswana. The high level of primary and junior school attendance, coupled with the Government's policy of increasing the number of schools so as to accommodate more pupils for a greater number of years is a good indicator of dedication in principle and practice to deterring child labor.

e. *Acceptable Conditions of Work.*—The minimum monthly wage for full-time labor increased by $4.60 (16 Pula) in 1996 to $82 (286 Pula), which is less than 50 percent of what the Government calculates is necessary to meet the basic needs of a family of five. (Because of exchange rate changes, the dollar value of the minimum wage declined compared to 1995.) The Ministry of Labor is responsible for enforcing the minimum wage, and each of the country's districts has at least one labor inspector.

The Ministry of Labor began developing a small number of potential cases to take to the Industrial Court, but none had been brought before the Court by year's end.

Formal sector jobs almost always pay well above minimum wage levels. Informal sector employment, particularly in the agricultural and domestic service sectors where housing and food are included, frequently pay below the minimum wage. The Ministry of Labor recommends a monthly minimum wage of $92.60 (250 pula) for domestics, but this is not mandatory. Illegal immigrants, primarily Zambians and Zimbabweans, are easily exploited as they would be subject to deportation if they filed grievances against employers.

Botswana law permits a maximum 48-hour workweek, exclusive of overtime which is payable at time and a half for each additional hour. Most modern private and public sector jobs are on the 40-hour workweek.

Workers who complain about hazardous conditions cannot be fired. The Government's institutional ability to enforce its workplace safety legislation remains limited, however, by inadequate staffing and unclear jurisdictions between different ministries. Nevertheless, worker safety is generally provided for by employers, with the occasionally notable exception of the construction industry.

BURKINA FASO

President Blaise Compaore continued to dominate the Government of the Fourth Republic, assisted by members of his party, the Congress for Democracy and Progress (CDP). In spite of the existence of dozens of political parties, there is little viable opposition to the President and his Government, which includes one representative from a small self-described opposition party. The CDP controls the National Assembly with 86 of the 107 seats. Several opposition parties have token representation. In December 1995, the constitutionally mandated (though purely consultative) second chamber of the National Assembly was installed, completing the government structure envisaged in the 1991 Constitution. The Constitution provides for an independent judiciary; however, it is subject to executive influence.

The security apparatus consists of the armed forces, the paramilitary gendarmerie, controlled by the Ministry of Defense, and the police, controlled by the Ministry of Territorial Administration.

Over 80 percent of the population of 10 million engages in subsistence agriculture, which is highly vulnerable to rainfall variation. Frequent drought, limited communication and transportation infrastructure, in addition to a low literacy rate, are longstanding problems. The 50 percent devaluation of the cfa franc in 1994 added to the existing economic hardship of a structural adjustment program under way since 1991. That program seeks to limit government spending, especially on salaries and transfers, and open the economy to market forces, including privatization and reduction in the size of many inefficient state companies. Per capita income is about $150 per year, in postdevaluation terms.

There was continuing progress in the move towards greater democratization. Despite a functioning parliament structure and elected local governments, citizens are unable to exercise fully the right to change their government, and serious human rights abuses persisted. The extrajudicial killing of a villager by the local police and a general climate of impunity fostered by failure to prosecute previous abusers tarnished the Government's record. Prison officials continued to torture and mistreat detainees, and prison conditions remained harsh. A libel suit brought by the President against a political foe for particularly harsh public criticism left some members of the press apprehensive about a resurgence of self-censorship. The most egregious instances of violence against women remain those involving female genital mutilation, although women continue to campaign against this practice as well as against other forms of discrimination. Killings of criminal suspects by vigilante mobs remained a problem.

RESPECT FOR HUMAN RIGHTS

Section 1. Respect for the Integrity of the Person, Including Freedom From:

a. *Political and Other Extrajudicial Killing.*—In May members of the police stationed in the town of Reo shot and killed an unarmed villager during an operation to fine owners of unregistered vehicles. This incident, which still has not resulted in any punitive action by the Government against those responsible, marred an otherwise improving record regarding the security forces. The major problem with law enforcement is a general climate of impunity for human rights abusers fostered by the habitual failure of the Government's investigations to result in guilty findings or appropriate sanctions. Inquiries tend to drag until they are overshadowed by subsequent incidents, and then they are quietly shelved. Appeals by human rights organizations generally go unanswered. This failure to prosecute previous abuses remains a major hindrance to further human rights progress.

An official investigation into the May 1995 shooting to death of two unarmed high school demonstrators in Garango has yielded no results. The investigation into the July 1994 savage beating of two prisoners, who later died at the Maco prison in Ouagadougou, ended without calling for the punishment of those responsible. Nor were there any further developments regarding the July 1994 corruption scandal that led to the death in custody of two suspects under suspicious circumstances.

To date, the authorities have provided no explanation of the death of Doin Redan, who was found dead in 1994 a day after being detained by police. The Government continued to make no real effort to investigate the fate of a Ghanaian detainee, reportedly killed in 1993 while in police custody. Although international and local human rights groups pressured the official commission investigating the 1991 assassination of Clement Ouedraogo, a prominent opposition leader, to submit a report of preliminary findings to the Prime Minister, the report has not been made public. The case remains open, as do the cases of the 1989 "disappearance" of professor Guillaume Sessouma, detained for allegedly participating in a coup plot, and medical student Dabo Boukary in 1990, detained following student demonstrations. Credible reports indicated that security forces tortured and killed both.

Another disturbing trend was the persistence of vigilante killings by the public. There were numerous documented incidents of summary mob justice meted out to thieves caught by the citizenry, mostly in urban centers.

b. *Disappearance.*—There were no reports of politically motivated disappearances.

c. *Torture and Other Cruel, Inhuman, or Degrading Treatment or Punishment.*— While legally prohibited, torture and mistreatment of detainees, often to extract confessions, have been documented for a number of years. There are credible reports that officials at Maco prison continue to employ torture and degrading treatment, including beatings, cold showers, exposure to hot sun, and forcing persons to eat their own feces. The Government is not known to have taken any disciplinary action against those responsible, and the climate of impunity created by the Government's failure to prosecute abusers remains the largest obstacle to ending torture and other abuses.

Prison conditions are harsh, overcrowded, and can be life threatening. The federal prison in Bobo-Dioulasso, built in 1947, housed about 1,000 prisoners, although designed to hold less than half that number. The prison diet is poor, and inmates must often rely on supplemental food from relatives.

According to human rights monitors, prison visits are granted at the discretion of prison authorities. Permission is routinely granted, and advance permission is not required.

d. *Arbitrary Arrest, Detention, or Exile.*—The Constitution provides for the right to expeditious arraignment and access to legal counsel, and the law limits detention for investigative purposes without charge to a maximum of 72 hours, renewable for a single 48-hour period. In practice, however, police rarely observe these provisions. The average time of detention without charge is 1 week.

A few intellectuals, military officers, and former Government officials remain in self-imposed exile abroad following the October 1987 coup that brought Compaore to power, but most desiring to do so have repatriated themselves.

The Government does not use forced exile.

e. *Denial of Fair Public Trial.*—The Constitution provides for an independent judiciary; however, in practice it is subject to executive influence. The Constitution stipulates that the Head of State is also the President of the Superior Council of the Magistrature which nominates and removes some high-ranked magistrates and can examine the performance of individual magistrates.

The Constitution provides for the right to public trial, access to counsel, and has provisions for bail and appeal. While these rights are generally respected, the ability of citizens to obtain a fair trial remains circumscribed by ignorance of the law (80 percent of the population is illiterate) and by a continuing shortage of magistrates. A new penal code more relevant to modern requirements was adopted by Parliament and was expected to take effect in early 1997.

The Constitution provides that the Supreme Court is the highest court in the country. Beneath it are 2 courts of appeal and 10 provincial courts ("de grande instance"). There is also a High Court of Justice, with jurisdiction to try the President and senior government officials for treason and other serious crimes. The President has extensive appointment and other judicial powers. In 1995 the National Assembly passed legislation reforming the military court system, which had been susceptible to considerable executive manipulation, but there have been no further developments.

In 1995 the Government announced the creation of the Office of Ombudsman, called "Mediateur du Faso." Retired General Marc Garango was appointed to the position, which is responsible for mediating disputes between the State and its citizens. In addition to the formal judiciary, customary or traditional courts, presided over by village chiefs, handle many neighborhood- and village-level problems, such as divorce and inheritance disputes. These decisions are generally respected by the population, but citizens may also take a case to a formal court.

At year's end, there were no political prisoners in Burkina, according to local human rights organizations.

f. *Arbitrary Interference With Privacy, Family, Home, or Correspondence.*—The Constitution provides for these rights, and, in practice, the authorities generally do not interfere in the daily lives of ordinary citizens. In national security cases, however, a special law permits surveillance, searches, and monitoring of telephones and private correspondence without a warrant. By law and under normal circumstances, homes may be searched only with the authority of a warrant issued by the Minister of Justice. Except in certain cases, such as houses of prostitution and gambling dens, such warrants must be executed during "legal hours," defined as between 6 a.m. and 9 p.m.

Section 2. *Respect for Civil Liberties, Including:*

a. *Freedom of Speech and Press.*—The 1990 Information Code provides for freedom of speech and the press. In practice, these freedoms still remain circumscribed by a certain degree of self-censorship. The President and his Government remain sensitive to criticism. Provisions in the Code granting the Government strong legal powers to intimidate the press through a broad interpretation of defamation were removed in December 1993. As a result, journalists now charged with libel may defend themselves in court by presenting evidence in support of their allegations. Perhaps as a consequence, the independent press continued to exercise greater freedom of expression.

In February Bloc Socialiste Burkinabe (BSB) leader Nongma Ernest Ouedraogo was released after serving 5 months of a 6 month sentence for libel. In an August 1995 statement carried by a Ouagadougou daily, Ouedraogo alleged, among other things, that the President was corrupt and suggested that he fed human flesh to lions on his property. Ouedraogo was expeditiously tried under the law in a civil suit brought by President Compaore, at which he provided no evidence of his allegations. His appeal was turned down and he was fined a symbolic 1 franc and sentenced to 6 months in jail. The President's lawyer told the court that his client was not suing the paper over publication of the statement because he believes in freedom of the press. But the case reinforced a tendency toward self-censorship.

The independent press now includes four dailies, a dozen weekly newspapers, and a monthly news magazine. Although the official media, including the daily newspaper Sidwaya and the national radio, display progovernment bias, the presence of independent competition led government media to give more coverage to the political opposition. There are a half dozen thriving radio stations, one with eight branches, and one private television station.

Academic freedom is respected.

b. *Freedom of Peaceful Assembly and Association.*—The Constitution provides for freedom of assembly and association. Permits must, however, be obtained from municipal authorities for political marches. Applicants must indicate date, time, duration, and itinerary of the march or rally, and authorities may alter or deny requests on grounds of public safety. Denials or modifications may be appealed before the courts. Since early 1990, political parties and labor unions have usually been permitted to organize and hold meetings and rallies without seeking government permission. However, in March police broke up a student demonstration at Burkinabe University with tear gas, and in May security forces intimidated participants in a march by a labor union and forced them to change their route. The union had never received a response to its application for permission to march.

c. *Freedom of Religion.*—The Constitution provides for freedom of religion, and the Government respects this right in practice. Burkina Faso is a secular state. Islam, Christianity, and traditional religions operate freely without government interference. Neither social mobility nor access to modern sector jobs are linked to, or restricted by, religious affiliation.

d. *Freedom of Movement Within the Country, Foreign Travel, Emigration, and Repatriation.*—The Constitution provides for freedom of movement and authorities respect this right in practice. Gendarmes routinely stopped travelers within the country for identity and customs checks and the levying of road taxes at police and military checkpoints. There is no restriction on foreign travel for business or tourism.

Refugees are accepted freely in Burkina Faso. Due to civil unrest in neighboring countries, there are nearly 30,000 refugees and displaced persons, mostly Tuaregs from Mali and Niger. The Government cooperates with the Office of the United Nations High Commissioner for Refugees (UNHCR) and other humanitarian organizations in assisting refugees. The Government provides first asylum and provided it to over 20,000 refugees in 1996. The vast majority of those refugees were Tuaregs from Mali. There were no reports of forced return of persons to a country where they feared persecution. There were no reports of forced expulsion of those having a valid claim to refugee status.

Section 3. Respect for Political Rights: The Right of Citizens to Change Their Government

Citizens have the constitutional right to change their government through multiparty elections. In practice, however, they have been unable to exercise that right fully. Power remained in the hands of President Compaore and the CDP, most of whose members also played prominent roles in previous ruling parties. The Government includes a strong Presidency, a Prime Minister, a Council of Ministers presided over by the President, a two-chamber National Assembly, and the judiciary. The legislature is independent, but it remains susceptible to external influence from the executive branch.

The first municipal elections took place in 1995. The President's party secured over 1,100 of some 1,700 councillor seats being contested. On the whole, the balloting, which was monitored by representatives of several local human rights groups, proceeded freely and fairly. The Compaore Government faces legislative elections in 1997 and presidential elections in 1998.

In 1994 the Supreme Court ruled that an elected deputy in the National Assembly is not bound to the political party under which that person was elected and may change party affiliations as a representative in the legislature. This practice has been labeled "political nomadism" and is responsible for much of the factionalism in opposition parties.

There are no restrictions in law or practice on the participation of women or minority group members in politics. However, there are few women in positions of responsibility; 3 of the 23 ministers and 6 of the 107 National Assembly deputies are women.

Section 4. Governmental Attitude Regarding International and Nongovernmental Investigation of Alleged Violations of Human Rights

The Government's attitude toward local human rights groups has been mixed. It continued to tolerate the activities of the Burkinabe Movement for Human Rights (MBDHP), an independent group with representation in all 30 provinces. The Government is responsive to investigations by international nongovernmental organizations. However, the report of the special investigative committee into the 1995 killings in Garango has not been released, and the Government has not provided any information on the results of the inquiry.

Section 5. Discrimination Based on Race, Sex, Religion, Disability, Language, or Social Status

The Constitution prohibits discrimination on the basis of race, religion, or ethnic origin. Minority ethnic groups are, like the majority Mossi, represented in the inner circles of the Government, and government decisions do not favor one group over another.

Women.—Violence against women, especially wife beating, occurs occasionally. Cases of wife beating are usually handled through customary law and practice. The Government is attempting, using education through the media, to change attitudes toward women. The new penal code explicitly prohibits sexual harassment and female genital mutilation.

The Constitution provides for respect of human rights including those of women, but there is no specific constitutional protection for women, who face extensive discrimination. In general women continue to occupy a subordinate position and experience discrimination in such areas as education, jobs, property, and family rights. Overall, women represent 45 percent of the work force. In the modern sector, however, women make up one-fourth of the government work force, although usually in lower paying positions. Women still do much of the subsistence farming work.

Children.—The Constitution nominally protects children's rights. The Government has demonstrated its commitment to improving the condition of children by adopting a national policy to revitalize primary health care through the privatization of hospitals, which provided greater autonomy in hospital management. The Government has stated its commitment to improve access to primary education and has raised the literacy rate from 16 percent to 23 percent in recent years.

Females constitute approximately one-third of the total student population in the primary school system and are represented in the secondary and higher educational systems—although the percentage decreases dramatically beyond the primary level. Schools in rural areas have disproportionately fewer female students than schools in urban areas.

Female genital mutilation (FGM), which is widely condemned by international health experts as damaging to both physical and psychological health, is still widely practiced, especially in many rural areas, and is usually performed at an early age. The percentage of females who have undergone this procedure may be as high as 70 percent. The Government has made a strong commitment to eradicate FGM through educational efforts, and a national committee campaigns against the practice. The projected new Penal Code makes FGM a crime whose perpetrators are subject to 6 months' to 3 years' imprisonment and a significant fine. Nevertheless, FGM is still widely practiced. The Government has launched a sensitization campaign regarding the deleterious effects of this practice. Another form of mutilation, scarification of the faces of both boys and girls of certain ethnic groups, is gradually disappearing.

People With Disabilities.—While there is a modest program of government subsidies for workshops for the disabled, there is no Government mandate or legislation concerning accessibility for the disabled. There is no legislation to protect people with disabilities from discrimination. Programs to aid the disabled are limited, but human rights groups are not aware of any discrimination against the disabled.

Section 6. Worker Rights

a. *The Right of Association.*—Drafted in 1995, a new labor code remains before the National Assembly for review. Notwithstanding this pending legislation, workers, including civil servants, traditionally have enjoyed a legal right of association, which is recognized under the Constitution. There are 4 major labor confederations and 12 autonomous trade unions linked together by a National Confederal Committee. They represent a wide ideological spectrum, of which the largest and most vocal member espouses Socialist doctrine. Essential workers—police and fire workers—may not join unions.

The Constitution provides for the right to strike, and workers use strike actions to achieve labor goals. Employees of the largest commercial bank in the country went on strike for 2 days in September. In November health workers staged a 72-hour strike to demand better pay and working conditions.

Labor unions may affiliate freely with international trade unions.

b. *The Right to Organize and Bargain Collectively.*—Unions have the right to bargain for wages and other benefits, both directly with employers and with industry associations. These negotiations are governed by minimums on wages and other benefits contained in the Interprofessional Collective Convention and the Commercial Sector Collective Convention, which are established with government participation. If no agreement is reached, employees may exercise their right to strike. Either labor or management also may refer an impasse in negotiations to labor tribunals. Appeals may be pursued through the Court of Appeal to the Supreme Court, whose decision is binding on both parties. Collective bargaining is extensive in the modern wage sector but encompasses only a small percentage of workers.

The Labor Code prohibits antiunion discrimination. The Labor Ministry handles complaints about such discrimination, which the plaintiff may appeal to a Labor Tribunal. If the Tribunal sustains the appeal, the employer must reinstate the worker. Union officials believe that this system functions adequately.

There are no export processing zones.

c. *Prohibition of Forced or Compulsory Labor.*—The law prohibits forced labor, and it is not practiced.

d. *Minimum Age for Employment of Children.*—The Labor Code now in effect sets the minimum age for employment at 14 years, the average age for completion of basic primary school. However, the Ministry of Employment, Labor, and Social Security, which oversees labor standards, lacks the means to enforce this provision adequately, even in the small wage sector. Most children actually begin work at an earlier age on small, family subsistence farms, in the traditional apprenticeship system, and in the informal sector.

e. *Acceptable Conditions of Work.*—The Labor Code mandates a minimum monthly wage, a standard workweek of 40 hours with at least one 24-hour rest period, and establishes safety and health provisions. The current minimum monthly wage in the formal sector, about $48 (cfa 24,000), does not apply to subsistence agriculture, which employs about 85 percent of the population. The Government last set the minimum wage in 1995. It is not adequate for an urban worker to support a family. Wage earners usually supplement their income through reliance on the extended family and subsistence agriculture.

A system of government inspections under the Ministry of Labor and the Labor Tribunals is responsible for overseeing health and safety standards in the small industrial and commercial sectors, but these standards do not apply in the subsistence agricultural sector. Every company is required to have a work safety committee. If a workplace has been declared unsafe by the government labor inspection office for any reason, workers have the right to remove themselves from dangerous work without jeopardy to continued employment. In practice there are indications that this right is respected, but such declarations are relatively rare.

BURUNDI

Burundi's democratically elected president was overthrown in a military coup on July 25. Despite the coup, the National Assembly and political parties continue to operate, although under constraints. The present regime, under the self-proclaimed interim President, Major Pierre Buyoya, abrogated the 1992 Constitution and, during the so-called Transition Period, replaced the 1994 Convention of Government with a decree promulgated on September 13. Under this decree, the National Assembly does not have the power to remove the President of the Republic. The Prime Minister, appointed by the President, replaces the President in the event of the President's death or incapacity. Under the former constitution, the President of the National Assembly replaced the President.

Buyoya holds power in conjunction with the Tutsi-dominated military establishment. The judicial system remains under the control of the Tutsi minority, and most citizens consider it biased against Hutus. Violent conflict among Hutu and Tutsi armed militants and the army plunged the country into a civil war marked by ethnic violence, which included fighting between the army and armed rebel groups. The fighting resulted in the death, injury, and displacement of large numbers of civilians. Tens of thousands of people, both Hutu and Tutsi, have been massacred in ethnic violence since independence, especially in 1972, 1988, 1993, and since 1995. As the U.N. Commission of Inquiry in Burundi concluded in 1996, much, but not all, of the ethnic violence in Burundi since 1993 constituted genocide.

The security forces consist of the army and the gendarmerie under the Ministry of Defense, the judicial police under the Ministry of Justice, and the documentation police under the Ministry of the Interior. The army remains committed to protecting the interests of the Tutsi minority. The security forces committed numerous, serious, human rights abuses and also permitted Tutsi extremists to commit abuses.

Burundi is poor and densely populated, with over four-fifths of the population of 7 million engaged in subsistence agriculture. Per capita gross national product is estimated at less than $200 per year. The small modern sector, based largely on the export of coffee and tea, was damaged by an economic embargo imposed by neighboring countries July 31. The ongoing violence since October 1993 has caused severe disruptions and dislocations. Large numbers of internally displaced persons were unable to produce their own food crops and depended largely on international humanitarian assistance. Government efforts to privatize state-owned enterprises have come to a virtual halt.

The human rights situation continued to deteriorate. The security forces continued to commit numerous, serious human rights abuses, including extrajudicial killings. Military forces committed massacres of unarmed civilian Hutus and frequently permitted Tutsi extremists to engage in violence against Hutus. The Government was largely unable to prevent such abuses, and perpetrators generally went unpunished. Serious incidents of ethnically motivated extrajudicial killing and destruction of property occurred throughout the country. Armed troops and civilian militias killed both armed and unarmed ethnic rivals, including women, children, and the elderly. They also killed expatriates.

Government efforts to restore security were inadequate. Members of the armed forces and vigilante groups committed serious human rights violations with impunity. The continuing lack of accountability for killings and ethnic violence, and for those responsible for the 1993 coup attempt and the massacres that followed, contributed significantly to national insecurity. The dysfunctional justice system could not satisfactorily address these problems due to its own lack of independence, inefficiency, administrative disruption, and the partiality of Tutsi officials. The U.N. International Commission of Inquiry has issued a report about the events of October 1993, although no one involved has yet been brought to justice. Disappearances continued, and prison conditions remained life threatening. Arbitrary arrest and lengthy pretrial detention are problems. The court system suffers under a heavy backlog. The Government controls nearly all the media and banned public assembly. There are some restrictions on movement.

Legal and societal discrimination against women continues to be a serious problem; violence against women also occurs. Citizens do not have the right to change their government. Ethnic discrimination against Hutus is widespread. The Twa (Pygmy) minority remained almost completely marginalized.

Hutu rebel forces massacred both Hutu and Tutsi civilians, including women, children, the elderly, and expatriates, and the numbers killed increased, reflecting the increased scope of rebel activity during the past year.

RESPECT FOR HUMAN RIGHTS

Section 1. Respect for the Integrity of the Person, Including Freedom From:

a. *Political and Other Extrajudicial Killing.*—Amnesty International estimated that between October 1993 and December 1995 more than 100,000 people were killed in ethnic violence. The army was more responsible than any other group for these deaths. The United Nations Human Rights Rapporteur for Burundi estimated in June that 800 people per month were being killed; the majority of deaths continue to be attributed to government security forces. Organization for African Unity (OAU) military observers estimated that an average of 500 people per month were killed during the first 6 months of the year. Western nongovernmental organizations (NGO's) believe that about 10,000 people died in conflict during the year, although these sources acknowledge that their figures lack any degree of precision. In August the U.N. Center for Human Rights in Geneva issued a report that said that the Tutsi-led army killed 2,100 to 3,000 civilians in a series of incidents that took place between April and July. Between October and December, massacres of civilians by the military forces and the killing of innocent civilians by Hutu rebels occurred regularly. According to human rights monitors, there were more than 20 incidents in which civilians were killed, mainly by the army, but also by Hutu rebels. The number of civilians killed, estimated at 2,000 during the months of October through December, was the heaviest of the year. The U.N. International Commission of Inquiry concluded in 1996 that much but not all of the ethnic violence since the 1993 assassination of Burundi's president has constituted genocide.

A report released in February from the office of deposed President Sylvestre Ntibantunganya said that the army killed 44 civilians (9 men, 10 women, and 25 children) during an operation in late January at Kabarore in northern Burundi.

In March the Papal Nuncio reported that the municipal police killed a Hutu merchant from the Bujumbura central market along with five other Hutus near Bujumbura.

On April 26, the army—or possibly the Tutsi militia—reportedly killed 236 Hutu civilians, mostly women and children. An additional 42 people from Buhoro were treated for stab wounds at a nearby hospital. The army initially denied any involvement but said later that Hutu rebels had used civilians as "human shields" during the course of a military operation at Buhoro. Both U.N. human rights monitors and government investigators found 20 graves with an unknown number of corpses at Buhoro.

Government troops reportedly killed 14 civilians in Gitega province between April 20 and 27; Hutu rebels killed 5 civilians at a Catholic mission May 16.

U.N. human rights monitors investigated allegations of a possible massacre by government troops at Musigati in Bubanza province on May 6. The results of their investigation were inconclusive, although the U.N. investigators found 82 graves near Musigati.

In Gitega province, Western aid workers reported that six trucks carrying soldiers arrived at Kibimba Hill on June 13. According to the aid workers, the soldiers used machine guns and bayonets to kill between 70 and 100 Hutu civilians, including women and children.

Army troops reportedly killed about 40 Hutu civilians at a wedding ceremony on Mpfunda Hill in Kayanza province on July 13.

Government forces reportedly took revenge for Hutu extremist kills and killed about 60 Hutu civilians at Muzinda, 7 kilometers from Bujumbura, on July 23.

In late October, government radio reported that troops had killed 102 Hutu civilians in revenge for the killing of 26 Tutsis by Hutu rebels in Rutana province.

In October the military forces admitted that its troops had killed 40 civilians near Mutana October 14; an inquiry is under way. Credible sources also reported a massacre by military forces of between 100 and 400 recently returned refugees at a church in Murambi on October 22.

In November the U.N. Human Rights Observer Mission reported that soldiers killed between 200 and 400 Hutu refugees in a church in Murambi in Cibitoke province, supposedly in revenge for the killing of the governor of Citiboke hours earlier. A government inquiry was promised.

In early December, the military committed a series of killings in the southern portion of Kayanza province. According to U.N. Human Rights Observers, between 200 and 300 Hutus were killed as the army implemented a forced resettlement policy. In mid-December, military forces killed 70 civilians near Rumonge, and NGO's reported that an undetermined number of civilians were killed by troops in Makaba province December 13.

The three people accused of the 1995 killings of Italian religious workers in Bururi province have not been brought to justice. According to the public prosecutor, the Government is seeking the extradition of the three men accused of the killings from Rwanda and Uganda, where they are believed to have fled following their "escape from custody" in October 1995.

Criminal courts resumed operations this year after a lapse of more than 2 years. The courts tried 79 people for capital crimes, of whom 60 were found guilty and sentenced to death. The courts acquitted the other 19 defendants. Other cases are pending (see Section 1.e.).

During April and May, seven Hutu officials and one Tutsi military officer were killed by unknown assailants in Bujumbura. Two other prominent Hutus survived attempts to kill them. One National Assembly Deputy was killed and another wounded. No one has been brought to justice in connection with these murders and attempted murders. However, military forces claim that they arrested 25 suspects involved in these killings. Since 1993, 22 regular and alternate members of the National Assembly have been killed.

Numerous Hutu civilian administrators were also killed during the year.

On May 9, unknown gunmen fired automatic weapons and threw grenades into huts at a displaced persons' camp that housed about 6,000 Hutus in an outlying neighborhood of Bujumbura. Seven people were killed in the attack, and 32 others were wounded.

On June 4, unknown gunmen killed three expatriate employees of the International Committee of the Red Cross (ICRC) in Cibitoke province. A promised government investigation has produced no results.

In late February, Palipehutu rebels reportedly killed about 45 Hutu civilians in Cibitoke province, according to Hutu sources.

In late March, Hutu rebels near Songa in Bururi province killed about 110 Hutu and Tutsi civilians, according to OAU military observers. Houses were also burned. The Songa incident was the most severe of a series of rebel attacks in Bururi province during March and April.

On May 3, Hutu rebels attacked the King Khaled Hospital in Bujumbura, killing a guard and injuring three other people, including a baby girl. Rebels also attacked a hospital run by Medecins sans Frontieres-France in Makamba in early May.

Hutu rebels attacked a tea factory at Teza in Muramvya province on July 3. About 150 civilians, mainly Tutsis, were killed in the attack, according to local and expatriate sources.

A July 20 attack by Hutu rebels resulted in the deaths of a large number of Tutsi civilians at a displaced persons camp at Bugendana in Gitega province. A Western journalist counted 250 corpses at Bugendana, and government radio reported that 342 people had been killed in the massacre.

In September the Catholic archbishop of Gitega, a Tutsi, was killed in an ambush. It is not known who was responsible for his murder, but Church officials believe that Hutu rebels killed the archbishop.

Credible sources also reported that 87 civilians were killed in an attack by Hutu rebels in Cibitoke province December 18.

There is little reliable information about the interior since the July 25 coup. However, U.N. human rights monitors reported that an undetermined number of civilians were killed in Gitega province during fighting between rebel forces and government troops.

b. *Disappearance.*—Local human rights groups reported that abduction and disappearance were commonplace. Disappearances were the result of both ethnic and political rivalry. Reliable numerical estimates are not available, but the U.N. human rights monitoring mission is aware of three cases in Bujumbura and has received a report concerning the disappearance of 31 children in the interior. There was no further information on six Tutsis who disappeared in August and September 1994.

c. *Torture and Other Cruel, Inhuman, or Degrading Treatment or Punishment.*— The decree of September 13 and the suspended constitution prohibit these abuses, but they occur in practice.

Prison conditions were life threatening and characterized by severe overcrowding and inadequate hygiene, clothing, medical care, food, and water. Prisoners had to rely on family members to ensure an adequate diet, and officials acknowledged that digestive illness was a major problem among the prisoners. Women were held separately from men. U.N. human rights monitors reported that Tutsi prison guards permitted Tutsi prisoners to assault Hutu prisoners in Bujumbura's main prison.

U.N. human rights monitors and representatives of the ICRC were permitted to visit prisons.

d. *Arbitrary Arrest, Detention, or Exile.*—Arbitrary arrest and detention are problems. The law places no limit on the total length of pretrial detention. The police are obligated to obtain arrest warrants but have detained people for extended periods without announcing charges, certifying the cases, or forwarding them to the Ministry of Justice as required. Bail is permitted in some cases. Incommunicado detention reportedly exists, although the law prohibits it.

Presiding magistrates are authorized to issue arrest warrants. Regular police and gendarmes can make arrests without a warrant but must submit a written report to a magistrate within 48 hours of any arrest. A magistrate can order the suspect released or confirm the charges and continue detention, initially for 15 days, then subsequently for periods of 30 days, as necessary to prepare the case for trial. The Buyoya regime frequently and arbitrarily arrested foreign journalists (see Section 2.a.).

Despite the reestablishment of the criminal justice system, many of those arrested in conjunction with the events of 1993 remain in detention and have not faced trial. An attempt in April to bring foreign lawyers to the country to assist in the defense of those accused of crimes from 1993 failed.

The disruption of the political process and the general level of insecurity severely impeded the judicial process. Pretrial detainees constituted about 80 percent of the prison population of approximately 6,900 inmates.

The military Government has not used forced exile as a means of political control. However, many people remain in voluntary exile in Belgium, Kenya, Tanzania, and Zaire. Many senior officials continue to keep their families outside the country. A number of officials of the government of deposed President Sylvestre Ntibantunganya fled the country in August. The Buyoya regime has refused to allow Ntibantunganya and National Assembly President Leonce Ngendakuma permission to leave the country (see Section 2.d.).

e. *Denial of Fair Public Trial.*—The decree of September 13 provides for an independent judiciary, but in practice the judiciary is dominated by Tutsis.

When it operated normally, the judicial system was divided into civil and criminal courts with the Supreme Court at the apex. The military services have a separate judicial system.

Citizens do not have regular access to civilian and military court proceedings, although trials are ostensibly public. Defendants are presumed innocent and have the right to appeal. While defendants have a right to counsel and to defend themselves, few have legal representation in practice.

Most citizens assume that the courts still promote the interest of the dominant Tutsi minority, and members of the Hutu majority believe that the Tutsi-dominated judicial system is biased against them. Hutus accounted for only 13 of the country's 228 judges.

In February Tutsi extremists tried to use the judicial system to challenge the means by which former President Sylvestre Ntibantunganya had been chosen Chief of State. The Constitutional Court ruled against the extremists' legal challenge.

The criminal court system began to function again during the year. The vast majority of those arrested on criminal charges since October 1993 remained in custody awaiting trial. Criminal courts were reestablished in Bujumbura and in the provincial centers of Gitega and Ngozi. The criminal courts heard 79 cases relating to the 1993 massacres. According to the State Public Prosecutor, 60 of the cases resulted in convictions and in 19 cases the defendants were acquitted. All those found guilty received the death penalty. A further 400 cases are now ready to be heard before the courts. About 5,000 more cases were under investigation at year's end.

The civil court system functioned, although the lack of a well-trained and adequately supported judiciary constrained expeditious proceedings.

Besides the frequent lack of counsel for the accused, other major shortcomings in the legal system include the lack of adequate resources and trained personnel, and an outmoded legal code. Most citizens have lost confidence in the system to provide even the most basic protection. This circumstance has contributed to the growing level of vigilante violence.

There are no clearly identifiable political prisoners. However, police often bring charges of involvement in violent crimes or disturbance of the peace against detainees in connection with political issues.

f. *Arbitrary Interference With Privacy, Family, Home, or Correspondence.*—The decree of September 13 provides for the right to privacy, and the authorities generally respect the law requiring search warrants. Security forces are assumed to regularly monitor telephones.

g. *Use of Excessive Force and Violations of Humanitarian Law in Internal Conflicts.*—NGO's believe that about 10,000 persons died in conflict during the year (see Section 1.a.).

Continuing insecurity has limited international humanitarian relief operations in most areas outside of Bujumbura and brought them to a complete halt in Cibitoke and Bubanza provinces.

In May civilian relief supplies were stolen from a truck in Muyinga province.

The June 4 killing of three expatriate employees of the ICRC in Cibitoke province caused humanitarian workers to reevaluate their operations in some areas of the country. While operations continue in other areas, concerns about security remain.

Government forces have compelled Hutu peasants to leave their homes in Karuzi province and move into displaced persons' camps, according to international relief agency officials.

The army has also burned large numbers of civilian homes in the course of military operations in Gitega, Karuzi, Muramvya, Bubanza, Cibitoke, and Bujumbura rural provinces.

A series of killings in early December by military forces in the southern part of Kayanza province resulted in 200 to 300 civilian deaths, according to the U.N. High Commissioner for Refugees (UNHCR). These killings took place as the army was implementing a policy of forced resettlement of Hutus.

Hutu rebels killed Hutu civilians who refused to pay "taxes" to the rebels, according to sources in the interior.

Section 2. Respect for Civil Liberties, Including:

a. *Freedom of Speech and Press.*—There are no restrictions imposed on the press in the decree of September 13; however, the regime owns the only newspaper and the two major radio stations.

Newspapers, with the exception of the thrice-weekly government owned Le Renoveau, have ceased publication, generally for financial reasons. As a result, there is no opposition press. Newspaper readership remains limited. Numerous political tracts continue to circulate; however, these political pamphlets represent a variety of political viewpoints, often of an extremist nature.

Most people rely on the two government-owned radio stations for information. One station broadcast in Kirundi, the other in French, Swahili, and English. An independent radio station, Radio Umwizero, financed by the European Union, began broadcasting during the year but has no political content.

Since 1994 a clandestine radio station supporting Leonard Nyangoma's predominately Hutu insurgent group, the National Council for the Defense of Democracy, broadcasted intermittently and attacked the Government and the Tutsi establishment.

Foreign journalists were frequently questioned by the authorities. American, Belgian, British, Canadian, Danish, and French journalists were detained briefly by the gendarmerie.

No laws or regulations limit the academic freedom of professors at the university. Although no persons were persecuted for what they published or said, the university remains mostly a monoethnic institution. Hutu students are discouraged from returning by other students. The security forces entered the university campus to break up political meetings in October.

b. *Freedom of Peaceful Assembly and Association.*—The Government banned public political demonstrations. Prior to the July 25 coup, street demonstrations took place regularly in Bujumbura, often in contravention of the requirements then in force that demonstrations be authorized in advance.

The Government banned political parties immediately following the coup. Under the decree of September 13, they were again permitted to operate.

Political associations generally did not operate in the interior of the country.

c. *Freedom of Religion.*—There is no state religion, and the Government made no attempt to restrict freedom of worship by adherents of any religion. However, the Catholic archbishop of Gitega was murdered and other church officials have been wounded or killed in ambushes (see Section 1.a.). The Government has little ability to protect politically targeted clergy.

d. *Freedom of Movement Within the Country, Foreign Travel, Emigration, and Repatriation.*—The September 13 decree did not restrict citizens' travel, and in general, the Government made no attempt to restrict travel for political reasons either internally or abroad, although the right to travel of those under criminal investigation, including officials of the FRODEBU party, is limited. An additional exception was the refusal of the Buyoya regime to permit the departure from the country of President Sylvestre Ntibantunganya or National Assembly President Leonce Ngendakumana from the country.

In May the Government closed the border with Zaire. It has not been officially reopened. Despite the imposition of a postcoup economic embargo by neighboring countries, which included air travel, citizens continue to be able to leave by road.

Political parties and civilian militant groups at times prevented citizens from traveling to work and other locations.

Movement throughout the country has been restricted by security problems that the Government has not resolved. Increasing banditry and ethnic violence perpetrated by armed gangs and the military has rendered travel in the countryside perilous. In most of the country, Hutus rarely enter Tutsi areas; Tutsis rarely enter Hutu areas. Military security checkpoints throughout the country effectively restrict movement.

The UNHCR reported that about 180,000 Burundian refugees, most of them Hutu, remained in Zaire and Tanzania at year's end. Many had fled following the assassination of President Melchior Ndadaye in October 1993. Others fled as early as 1972. The UNHCR estimates that between 40,000 and 50,000 citizens left the country during the year. About 60,000 Burundian refugees returned in October and November following upheaval in eastern Zaire.

All but 223 of the 140,000 Rwandan refugees who were in Burundi at the beginning of the year were repatriated by July 25. Some of the repatriations may have been coerced, according to the UNHCR, especially those from Ntamba camp in January, and from the camps in Ngozi province in July. However, the majority of Rwandans returned to Rwanda voluntarily.

More than half the population of the provinces of Cibitoke, Bubanza, Bujumbura rural, and Karuzi were estimated to be internally displaced persons. At least 255,000 Burundians have been internally displaced, according to government estimates. Humanitarian agency officials believe that up to 400,000 Burundians may be internally displaced. The high level of insecurity continues to make it difficult to assess accurately the number of internally displaced people or to provide adequate humanitarian assistance for them.

The Government approved first asylum in recent years. This year, it hosted about 100,000 refugees from Rwanda. While the national government respected refuguee conventions, local authorities forced large numbers of Rwandans to return to that country during the year. Refugees returning to Burundi were killed by Burundian security forces this year (see Section 1.g.).

Refugees from other African countries, including Zaire and Somalia, have lived in the country for many years without encountering difficulties.

Section 3. Respect for Political Rights: The Right of Citizens to Change Their Government

The September 13 decree makes no provision regarding elections, and following the July coup citizens did not have the right to change their government.

Under the constitutional arrangements that were suspended by the coup, the now-deposed President should have remained in office until 1998, when legislative elections were also scheduled.

The decree of September 13 stipulates that the National Assembly consist of parliamentarians elected in 1993 who sat in the previous National Assembly. Under the decree, the interim President may appoint additional Parliamentarians, but he has not yet chosen to exercise this power. While the National Assembly has nominal budgetary oversight, the decree of September 13 allows the Council of Ministers to enact a budget if the National Assembly fails to do so, and it gives the interim President the authority to declare a state of emergency by decree and without reference to the National Assembly.

On September 13, Major Buyoya announced the restoration of the National Assembly and political parties with certain restrictions. In practice the National Assembly is not expected to meet regularly until its members determine under what authority it can act. Many of its members are unwilling to operate under the authority of Major Buyoya's decree of September 13, the regime's declared legal framework for the transitional period. Of the 81 members of the Assembly who were elected in 1993, 38 remain outside the country.

There are no legal restrictions on the participation of women or indigenous people in elections or politics. In practice, however, both women and ethnic Twa (Pygmies) who comprise about 1 percent of the population are underrepresented in government and in politics. Women currently hold 2 of the 22 Cabinet seats (no change from the number in the previous government) and 9 of the 81 seats in the National Assembly. There are no Twa in either the Cabinet or the National Assembly.

Section 4. Governmental Attitude Regarding International and Nongovernmental Investigation of Alleged Violations of Human Rights

Local human rights groups received varying degrees of cooperation from government ministries and local authorities. The human rights group Iteka continued to operate and publish a newsletter on the human rights situation. International human rights groups, including Amnesty International and Human Rights/Watch Africa visited the country. The United Nations deployed a five-member human rights observer mission in April. Its work was hampered, however, by insecurity in the countryside and by the Government's inability, and in some cases unwillingness, to protect human rights workers.

The 62-member OAU military observer mission was withdrawn by the OAU after the July 25 coup.

Local military authorities frequently refused access to areas of the interior to journalists, human rights workers, and international relief officials. Militant extremists, both Hutu and Tutsi, threatened the lives of people investigating human rights violations.

The U.N. International Commission of Inquiry worked in the country between October 1995 and May 1996, investigating the events surrounding the killing of President Melchior Ndadaye in October 1993 and the massacres that followed. The Commission produced a report that circulated in Bujumbura but was not officially released. The Government has asked for the establishment of an international tribunal to try those implicated in the events of 1993.

Section 5. Discrimination Based on Race, Sex, Religion, Disability, Language, or Social Status

The September 13 decree explicitly provides equal status and protection for all citizens, without distinction based on sex, origin, ethnicity, religion, or opinion. However, the Government failed to enforce effectively all these provisions. Hutus continue to perceive, correctly, that there is discrimination against them by the Tutsi-dominated Government.

Women.—Violence against women occurred, but there was no documentation of its extent. Wives have the right to bring physical abuse charges against their husbands; in practice, they rarely do so. Police do not normally intervene in domestic disputes, and the media do not report incidents of violence against women, including rape. There were no known court cases dealing with the abuse of women.

Women hold a secondary place in society and face both legal and societal discrimination. There continue to be explicitly discriminatory inheritance laws and discriminatory financial credit practices. Although women by law must receive the same pay as men for the same jobs, women are far less likely to hold any mid- or high-level positions. In rural areas, women traditionally perform hard farm work and have less opportunity for education than men.

Children.—The Government has taken no action to protect children's rights, nor has it addressed the growing problem of the increasing population of orphans that resulted from the continued violence since 1993. Children have not been spared by belligerents in the civil conflict; many of the victims of massacres have been children.

People With Disabilities.—The Government has not enacted legislation or otherwise mandated access to buildings or government services for people with disabilities. The rudimentary economy effectively excludes the physically disabled from many types of employment.

Indigenous People.—The Twa (Pygmy) minority remained almost completely marginalized—economically, socially, and politically. Most Twa continued to live in isolation, uneducated, and without access to government services, including health care. The Twa remain essentially outside of the political process.

National/Racial/Ethnic Minorities.—Burundi's fundamental problem continued to be ethnic conflict between the majority Hutus and the minority Tutsis. Tutsis have historically held power and still control the military and dominate educated society. The July 25 coup that deposed Hutu President Sylvestre Ntibantunganya replaced him with a Tutsi, Major Buyoya. Ethnic discrimination against Hutus, 85 percent of the population, affects every facet of society and institutions, including the military services and the judiciary.

There are few Hutus in attendance at the University of Burundi. A government effort in March to recruit Hutus into the army produced no positive results. The army remains overwhelmingly Tutsi.

Section 6. Worker Rights

a. *The Right of Association.*—The Labor Code nominally protects the rights of workers to form unions, although the army, gendarmerie, and expatriates working in the public sector are prohibited from union participation. Most union workers are urban civil servants.

The country's first national umbrella trade union, the Organization of Free Unions of Burundi (CSB), remains financially dependent on a system of checkoffs, as do local unions. The CSB represented labor in collective bargaining negotiations in cooperation with individual labor unions. Unions are Tutsi-dominated, reflecting Tutsi control of the formal sector of the economy. The unions have also been strong supporters of the Government.

The Labor Code permits the formation of additional unions or confederations outside the CSB. When settling disputes in which more than one labor union is represented, the law stipulates that the Minister of Labor will chose the union representing the greatest number of workers to participate in the negotiations.

The Labor Code provides workers with a restricted right to strike. There are several restrictions on the right to strike and to lock out employees: The action must be taken only after exhausting all other peaceful means of resolution; negotiations must continue during the action, mediated by a mutually agreeable party or by the Government; and, 6 days' notice must be given. The law prohibits retribution against workers participating in a legal strike, and this provision is upheld in practice.

In January activity in Bujumbura came largely to a standstill during a week-long general strike organized by extremist Tutsis.

Unions are able to affiliate with international organizations.

b. *The Right to Organize and Bargain Collectively.*—The Labor Code recognizes the right to collective bargaining, which had formerly been acknowledged only by ordinance. Since most workers in the formal sector are civil servants, government entities are involved in almost every phase of labor negotiations.

Public sector wages are set in fixed scales in individual contracts and are not affected by collective bargaining. In the private sector, wage scales also exist, but individual contract negotiation is possible.

The Labor Code gives the Labor Court jurisdiction over all labor dispute cases, including those involving public employees. Labor negotiations are still conducted largely under the supervision of the tripartite National Labor Council, the Government's highest consultative authority on labor issues. The Council represents government, labor, and management and is presided over and regulated by the Minister of Labor.

The Labor Code prohibits employers from firing or otherwise discriminating against a worker because of union affiliation or activity. This right is upheld in practice.

There are no export processing zones.

c. *Prohibition of Forced or Compulsory Labor.*—The law prohibits forced or compulsory labor, and it is not practiced.

d. *Minimum Age for Employment of Children.*—The Labor Code states that children under the age of 16 are not allowed to be employed by "an enterprise" even as apprentices, although it also states that they may undertake occasional work that does not damage their health or interfere with their schooling. In practice, in rural areas children under the age of 16 do heavy manual labor such as transporting bricks in daytime during the school year.

Children are legally prohibited from working at night, although many do so in the informal sector. Children are obliged by custom and economic necessity to help support their families by participating in activities related to subsistence agriculture, in family-based enterprises, and in the informal sector.

e. *Acceptable Conditions of Work.*—The formal minimum wage for unskilled workers is $0.46 (145 Burundi francs) per day in Bujumbura and Gitega and $0.38 (120 Burundi francs) per day in the rest of the country, with a graduated scale for greater skill levels. This amount does not allow a worker and family to maintain a decent standard of living, and most families rely on second incomes and subsistence agriculture to supplement their earnings. Employees working under a contract, particularly in urban areas, generally earn significantly more than the minimum wage. All employees in the public sector work under contract. The CSB estimates that 70 percent of employees working in the formal private sector are covered by a contract.

The Labor Code imposes a maximum 8-hour workday and a 45-hour workweek, except in cases where workers are involved in activities related to national security. Supplements must be paid for overtime work. The Labor Code establishes health and safety standards requiring an employer to provide a safe workplace and assigns enforcement responsibility to the Minister of Labor. However, the Ministry does not enforce the code effectively. Health and safety articles in the Labor Code do not directly address workers' rights to remove themselves from a dangerous work situation without fear of losing their jobs.

CAMEROON

Cameroon is a multiparty republic which continues to be dominated by President Paul Biya and a circle of advisers drawn largely from his own ethnic group and from his party, the Cameroon People's Democratic Movement (CPDM). The CPDM's power was last challenged in 1992 in relatively free National Assembly elections and highly flawed presidential elections in which Biya was elected to a 5-year term. The CPDM successfully dominates the National Assembly through its controlling share of a ruling coalition. In December 1995, the National Assembly passed amendments to the 1972 Constitution which were promulgated in January by President Biya. The amendments for the first time provide for presidential term limits and certain new legislative institutions, including an independent judiciary, which remains subject to political influence, a partially elected senate, and elected regional councils. However, the amendments have not yet been implemented and have done little to strengthen the independence of the judiciary or to moderate the President's power to dominate legislation, or rule by decree. In January the country held its first nationwide municipal elections.

Internal security responsibilities are shared by the national police, the National Intelligence Service (DGRE), the gendarmerie, the Ministry of Territorial Administration, military intelligence, the army, and to a lesser extent, the Presidential Security Service. The police and the gendarmerie have dominant roles in enforcing internal security laws. The security forces, including the military forces, remain under the effective control of the President, the civilian Minister of Defense, and the civilian head of police. The police and gendarmes continued to commit numerous human rights abuses.

Following nearly a decade of economic decline and widening financial imbalance, the 1994 cfa franc devaluation substantially restored external competitiveness. Economic growth recovered, averaging more than 3 percent annually over the last 3 years. The majority of the population is rural. The Government has begun implementing a program of structural reforms. Agriculture accounts for one-third of gross domestic product, while industry and the services sector account, for 26 and 33 percent, respectively. The petroleum sector has declined sharply as a share of public revenues. Principal exports include timber, coffee, cocoa, cotton, bananas, and rubber.

The Government's human rights record continued to be poor, although there was some improvement in certain areas. The Government continued to commit numerous serious human rights abuses. Citizens' ability to change their government remained limited. Security forces committed several extrajudicial killings and often beat and otherwise abused detainees and prisoners, generally with impunity. Conditions remained life threatening in almost all prisons. Security forces continued to arrest and detain citizens arbitrarily, often holding them for prolonged periods and, at times, incommunicado. The judiciary is corrupt, inefficient, and subject to political influence. Security forces conducted illegal searches, harassed citizens, infringed on their privacy, and monitored some opposition activists. A January law revoked formal press censorship and moved supervision of the press from the administrative authorities to the courts. However, the Government continued to impose some limits on press freedom. The authorities retain the power to seize publications deemed to put public order in jeopardy and used this power on at least two occasions. Although independent newspapers enjoyed considerable latitude to publish their views, journalists were subject to harassment, trial, and conviction under criminal libel laws. Authorities prosecuted and obtained convictions against several editors and journalists under these laws, and some received stiff fines and prison sentences. The Government sometimes restricted freedom of assembly and association. At times, security forces were used to inhibit political parties from holding public meetings. The Government restricts freedom of movement. Discrimination and violence against women remain serious problems.

Discrimination against ethnic minorities and Pygmies persists. The Government infringes on workers' rights, and slavery persists in an isolated northern region. Mob violence and intertribal disputes resulted in dozens of deaths. Nationwide multiparty municipal elections were relatively free and fair, although in some areas the Government restricted opposition candidate lists. After the election, the Government used legal but undemocratic means to ensure its control of municipal councils won by the opposition, provoking widespread protest and an attempt to conduct general strikes.

RESPECT FOR HUMAN RIGHTS

Section 1. *Respect for the Integrity of the Person, Including Freedom From:*

a. *Political and Other Extrajudicial Killing.*—There were no confirmed reports of political killings. However, the security forces continued to use excessive, lethal force and committed several extrajudicial killings.

In February an unarmed, unresisting taxi driver was shot and killed by a policeman near Bafut, Northwest province, in view of witnesses. The reasons for the shooting are unclear. The authorities took no action against the policeman, but an investigation into the case is underway.

On March 1, a pregnant woman was shot and killed by a soldier in the Limbe, Southwest province, market during a political demonstration by the Social Democratic Front (SDF) party. In the incident, the killer himself was immediately shot and killed by a fellow soldier. Security forces killed three other persons in an ensuing riot.

On March 15, Andre Tchieutcho, a suspected thief, was shot and killed inside the Mboppi gendarme headquarters.

On April 14, police outside Yaounde fired on a stolen vehicle, killing, in addition to the suspected perpetrators, two apparently innocent young men who had been given a ride by the alleged thieves.

On May 24, a Douala taxi driver, Joseph Desire Tuete Kuipo, was shot and killed by a policeman when he allegedly refused to pay a bribe at one of the ubiquitous and illegal police roadblocks. An outraged crowd attacked the policeman, seriously injuring him. At year's end, an investigation into the killing was underway. The police officer was suspended pending the results of the investigation.

In January Haman Daouda, a member of the National Union for Democracy and Progress (UNDP) party and a member of the National Assembly and members of his staff were assaulted while campaigning in the municipal elections in the territory of the Lamido (chief) of Mayo Rey, North province. The Lamido, an important supporter of the ruling CPDM party, reportedly directed his palace guard to injure or kill the parliamentarians. Haman Daouda died in February as a result of his injuries. UNDP demands for a government investigation were unsuccessful. A continuing series of intertribal land disputes in Northwest province resulted in several deaths and injuries.

In March residents of the villages of Babanki and Bambili, Northwest province, battled over the ownership of a section of land adjoining both villages. Seven persons died. This clash was but one of several that occurred during the year in Northwest province, resulting in an unknown number of deaths and injuries. In response, the Government sought to resolve the dispute with the assistance of traditional rulers. Several persons were arrested for their participation in the violence.

Mob violence directed at persons suspected of criminal activity or witchcraft resulted in a number of deaths and injuries.

b. *Disappearance.*—There were no reports of politically motivated disappearances. However, in June a prominent Bafoussam, West province, barrister and SDF activist, Joseph Lavoisier Tsapy, claimed that he had been seized by armed plainclothes policemen, blindfolded, and held for 4 days in an unknown location before being released unharmed. The period of his disappearance coincided with a planned SDF general strike in Bafoussam, for which Tsapy, President of the Town Council, was a leading organizer. While government authorities denied any involvement in Tsapy's disappearance, and the charges were never proved, many independent observers considered Tsapy's claim credible.

In September Nicolas Tejoumessie, editor of the newspaper Challenge Nouveau, was arbitrarily detained and beaten by four persons who claimed to be members of the secret police (see Section 1.c.).

c. *Torture and Other Cruel, Inhuman, or Degrading Treatment or Punishment.*—The Penal Code proscribes torture, renders inadmissible in court evidence obtained thereby, and prohibits public servants from using undue force against any person. In spite of this, there were credible reports that security forces inflicted beatings and other cruel and degrading treatment on prisoners and detainees. The beatings occurred not in prison facilities but in temporary detention areas in a police or gendarme facility.

Security forces subject prisoners and detainees to degrading mistreatment, including stripping, confinement in severely overcrowded cells, and denial of access to toilets or other sanitation facilities. Police and gendarmes often beat detainees to extract confessions and the names and whereabouts of alleged criminals. Sanctions against those responsible are rare.

Prison conditions are life threatening, especially outside major urban areas. Serious deficiencies in food, health care, and sanitation owing to the lack of resources occur in almost all prisons, including those run by traditional rulers in the north. Families are permitted to provide food and medicine. Beatings are common. Prisoners are reported to be chained at times in their cells and often denied adequate medical care. Juveniles and nonviolent prisoners are often incarcerated with violent adults. There are credible reports of sexual abuse of juvenile prisoners by adult inmates. Corruption among prison personnel is widespread. Some high profile prisoners are able to avoid some of the abuse that is routinely meted out to many common criminals. Some are held in elite wings of certain prisons where they enjoy relatively lenient treatment.

Following a March SDF demonstration in Limbe, security forces arrested 32 SDF members and held them under administrative detention in Buea Prison for more than 1 month pending investigation. There were credible reports that the prisoners suffered from excessive crowding and were denied adequate nutrition and medical care.

In the north, the Government permits traditional Lamibe (chiefs) to operate private prisons outside the government penitentiary system. Private prisons in the chiefdoms of Rey Bouba, Bibemi, and Tcheboa have the worst reputations. Members of the UNDP party alleged that their members have been detained in them and that some have died from mistreatment.

Because of the Government's refusal to guarantee the International Committee of the Red Cross (ICRC) access to all detention centers, official as well as unofficial, the ICRC has declined to visit any prisons since 1992, although both the Cameroonian Red Cross and the National Human Rights Commission make frequent visits.

In a May and June student strike at the University of Yaounde, a number of students were beaten both by police and by local thugs on university property, and as many as 30 were taken to prison and beaten there. Credible reports indicate that the troublemakers were encouraged by university authorities to help suppress the strike. Some of the students were held in prison for up to 40 days before being released pending court proceedings.

On September 8, Nicolas Tejoumessie, the editor of Challenge Nouveau, a prominent opposition newspaper, was seized at the doorway of his home in Douala by 4 men dressed in civilian clothing and taken to a location 30 kilometers outside the city, where he was severely beaten. His assailants allegedly claimed they were from the DGRE. During the beating, Tejoumessie's assailants reportedly interrogated him about his journalistic sources and warned him to cease his criticism of the Government. The identity of his assailants remains unknown.

d. *Arbitrary Arrest, Detention, or Exile.*—The Penal Code requires that detainees be brought promptly before a magistrate; however, security forces continued to arbitrarily arrest and detain citizens, although less frequently than in the past. Arbitrary, prolonged detention remained a serious problem as security forces often failed to bring detainees promptly before a magistrate and held them incommunicado.

Police may detain a person in custody in connection with a common crime for up to 24 hours, renewable 3 times, before bringing charges. However, the law only provides for the right to a judicial review of the legality of detention in the few majority Anglophone areas of the country. Elsewhere, the Francophone legal tradition applies, precluding judicial authorities from acting on a case until the administrative authority that ordered the detention turns the case over to the prosecutor. After a magistrate has issued a warrant to bring the case to trial, he may hold the detainee in "pretrial detention" indefinitely, pending court action. Furthermore, a 1990 law permits detention without charge for renewable periods of 15 days in order to combat banditry and maintain public order. Persons taken into detention are frequently denied access to both legal counsel and family members. The law permits release on bail only in the Anglophone provinces, where the legal system includes features of British common law. Even there, bail is granted infrequently.

In March, 32 SDF militants arrested following a demonstration in Limbe were arbitrarily detained for more than 1 month despite a court finding that there were no grounds for holding them (see Section 1.c.). Prison authorities cited the detention provisions of a 1990 law. The prisoners were finally released in mid-April without charges being filed. The Buea court, however, found the local government prefect in contempt and fined him for not respecting the court's earlier order to release the prisoners.

The courts punished some instances of arbitrary detention. A Yaounde court in March convicted six policemen (four of them in absentia) on charges of having arbitrarily arrested, beaten, and detained a deputy magistrate in October 1994. The court sentenced all the policemen to long prison terms and heavy fines.

In July a Bamenda, Northwest province, court ordered a police officer to pay a heavy fine to a woman whom he beat and wrongfully detained.

The Government does not practice political exile. Some opposition members who considered themselves threatened by the Government have voluntarily left the country and declared themselves to be in political exile.

e. *Denial of Fair Public Trial.*—Constitutional amendments ratified in January provide for an independent judiciary. However, the judiciary remains subject to political influence, and the Government took no concrete steps to implement the amendments. The courts did demonstrate a notable degree of independence in dealing with complaints in the aftermath of the January municipal elections.

The court system remains technically part of the executive branch, subordinate to the Ministry of Justice. The legal system is strongly influenced by the French legal system, although in the Anglophone provinces certain aspects of the Anglo-Saxon tradition apply. The court system includes the Supreme Court, a court of appeals in each of the 10 provinces, and courts of first instance in each of the country's 56 divisions. Some politically sensitive cases are never heard.

Traditional courts are important in rural areas. Their authority varies by region and ethnic group, but they are often the arbiters of property and domestic disputes and may serve a probate function as well. Most traditional courts permit appeal of their decisions to traditional authorities of higher rank.

Corruption and inefficiency in the courts remain serious problems. Justice is frequently denied or delayed. Powerful political or business interests appear to enjoy virtual immunity from prosecution, while critics of the Government are sometimes jailed under libel statutes considered by observers as unduly restrictive of press freedom. Prisoners may be detained indefinitely during pretrial proceedings.

Because appointed attorneys receive little compensation, the quality of legal representation for indigent persons is often poor. The bar association and some voluntary organizations, such as the Cameroonian Association of Female Jurists, offer free assistance in some cases. Trials are public.

In a highly charged case with political overtones that began in July 1994, 8 of 28 UNDP party militants were convicted in March and sentenced to lengthy prison terms for having participated in or abetted a riot to protest the visit to Maroua, Far North province, of a government official. One person was killed when rioters attacked the official's motorcade with stones. Court proceedings were characterized by repeated delays and irregularities that, at least in part, appear to have been politically motivated. Some of the defendants convicted were shown never to have been present at the demonstration but were sentenced on the presumption that they had encouraged the rioters. At year's end, the sentences were still under appeal. Credible observers disagree as to whether these convictions were based on political or criminal grounds.

f. *Arbitrary Interference With Privacy, Family, Home, or Correspondence.*—Both invasions of the home and tampering with correspondence are illegal in most circumstances, but there were a number of credible reports that police and gendarmes harassed citizens, conducted searches without warrants, and seized mail. Security forces frequently used roadblocks to extract bribes.

In April Conscience Africaine, a human rights organization, reported repeated tampering with its mail. The organization's headquarters was also burglarized; files as well as valuable equipment were taken. Police failed to conduct a serious investigation, in the view of Conscience Africaine.

In June the Governor of West province ordered gendarmes to seal off the house of barrister Joseph Lavoisier Tsapy for several days to prevent entry or egress. According to authorities, the measure was taken because Tsapy was engaged in encouraging violent civil disorder during an SDF-inspired general strike (see Section 1.b.). Authorities termed their action a legal measure intended to preserve public order.

Prior to the summit of the Organization of African Unity held in Yaounde in July, police conducted widespread preemptive searches in some neighborhoods for suspected criminals. These were aimed at providing security for the meeting. The searches included entry into private homes without warrants, an act permitted by the law. The law permits a police officer to enter a private home during daylight hours without a warrant if he is pursuing an inquiry and has reason to suspect that a crime has been committed. He must have a warrant to make such a search after dark. However, a police officer may enter a private home at any time in pursuit of a criminal observed committing a crime. An administrative authority may authorize police to conduct neighborhood sweeps in search of suspected criminals or stolen or illegal goods without individual warrants. Such sweeps are conducted frequently.

There were numerous credible reports that the Government kept some opposition activists and dissidents under surveillance.

Section 2. Respect for Civil Liberties, Including:

a. *Freedom of Speech and Press.*—The Constitution provides for freedom of expression and the press; however, the Government continued to impose some limits on these rights. In contrast with past years, the press enjoyed considerable liberty to publish due to the repeal of a law that had authorized press censorship by the Government. Nevertheless, the Government prosecuted nine editors and journalists on criminal libel charges, and courts imposed stiff fines and jail terms. In only one case did a journalist actually serve time in prison, however, and he was provisionally released after only 2 days. Some of these charges appeared to have been politically motivated. In addition, there were at least two instances in which the Government demanded that newspapers be seized under court orders, citing laws authorizing preservation of public order.

The Government publishes an official newspaper, the Cameroon Tribune, and operates all radio and television broadcasting. The law has provided since 1990 for the licensing of private radio and television stations, but the Government has not approved implementing regulations. Government reporters rarely criticize the ruling party or portray government programs in an unfavorable light, but sometimes do so implicitly. The government-controlled broadcast media provide broad coverage of CPDM functions, while giving relatively little attention to opposition events.

While 40 to 50 private newspapers are published sporadically, only about 10 were published on a regular basis during the year. These newspapers are often outspoken in their criticism of the President, the Government, corruption, and economic policies. Because of the high cost of a newspaper to an average citizen, as well as distribution problems, newspapers are not read widely outside the major cities.

Television and radio programming includes a weekly program that allows an opportunity for political parties represented in the National Assembly to present their views. In contrast with past years, the program faced no arbitrary suspensions although in September one UNDP program was censored. None of the country's non-parliamentary parties, including those that are known to have significant popular support, had access to the electronic media.

On February 27, Pius Njawe and Eyoum Ngangue, the publisher and editor, respectively, of Le Messager Popoli, were convicted in Douala of having libeled the President. The article in question was a satirical piece in which the President was referred to by an insulting name. Eyoum Ngangue was sentenced to 1 year in prison and a $600 fine; Pius Njawe was sentenced to 1 year in prison and a $200 fine. The two journalists appealed their sentences to an appeals court, which confirmed the sentences. Pius Njawe was subsequently arrested on October 29 and jailed in a Douala prison. Following widespread domestic and international criticism, he was released on November 15 on provisional liberty at the order of the Supreme Court, which agreed to review his request that the decision of the appeals court be invalidated. At year's end, Pius Njawe and Eyoum Ngangue remained at liberty and continued their journalistic activities.

In March two issues of the newspaper Dikalo were seized in Douala on orders of the governor of Littoral province on grounds that articles in the newspaper disturbed the public order. One of the offending articles charged that President Biya had placed government delegates as administrators of certain towns to counter the results of municipal elections in which opposition mayors were freely elected. A second article reported opposition party plans to stage a series of general strikes.

In April Pius Njawe and journalist Tietcheu Kameni were fined and sentenced to prison terms on charges of having libeled the Deputy Prime Minister in Charge of Territorial Administration. Their article accused the deputy Prime Minister of defrauding voters by interfering with the electoral registration process. While the two were found guilty of defamation of character, they were found not guilty of propagating false news. At year's end, the case was being reviewed on appeal, and neither Njawe or Kameni have yet served time in prison on these charges.

In May Vianney Ombey Ndzana, publisher of the newspaper Generation, was sentenced to a 5-month prison term and a heavy fine for having defamed the character of the director general of an important state-owned petroleum firm. An article in Ndzana's newspaper accused the Director General of financial improprieties. The court also suspended publication of his newspaper for 6 months. At year's end, both the prison term and the suspension remain under appeal, and neither had been implemented.

In June Njawe and journalist Paul Nyemb were ordered to pay a large sum to the former mayor of the town of Sangmelima on grounds that they had libeled him. At year's end, the court's decision remained under appeal.

In June Patrice Ndedi Penda, publisher of Galaxie, was sentenced to 2 years in prison and a large fine for having libeled the Minister of State in charge of agriculture. At year's end, Ndedi Penda had not been jailed, and his case remained under appeal.

In August Samuel Eleme, publisher of the newspaper La Detente and journalist Gaston Ekwalla were sentenced to 5 months' imprisonment and a heavy fine on charges that they libeled a CPDM (ruling party) member of the National Assembly. In addition, the newspaper was suspended from publication for 6 months. At year's end, the newspaper remained under suspension, but Eleme and Ekwalla had not been jailed. Their case remained under appeal.

On December 12, publisher William Mandio and reporter Daniel Atangana of the newspaper Le Front Independent were arrested by the presidential guard and held in the Center Province gendarmerie legion building in Yaounde. The motives for their arrest appeared to have been presidential guard's dissatisfaction with an article that the two had published that was critical of the unit. Mandio was released on December 15 and Atangana was released approximately 2 weeks later. At year's end, there were no charges pending against the two men.

In August Pierre Essama Essomba, the managing editor of the government Cameroon Tribune, was arrested and briefly detained on orders of the then-Minister of Justice on grounds that the editor had allowed a libelous letter about the Justice Minister to be published. Essama Essomba was released within hours of his arrest on orders of the Minister of State in charge of communication, who cited the editor's right to publish the letter.

Although there are no legal restrictions on academic freedom, state security informants operate on university campuses. Many professors believe that adherence to opposition political parties can have an adverse effect on their professional opportunities and advancement. Free political discussion at the University of Yaounde is dampened by the presence of armed security forces, as well as sometimes strident pro-opposition groups. Other universities and educational institutions appeared to be relatively free of the coercive presence of armed security forces or strident student groups. During a May-June strike at the University, university authorities used the police and vigilante gangs to suppress student activists. Several students were beaten and arrested during campus clashes (see Section 1.c.). Four alleged leaders of the strike have been banned from any Cameroonian universities and face trial on charges of assault. While the accused student leaders deny that they instigated violence, a number of university teachers and administrators claim that they were targets of death threats and intimidation by students.

b. *Freedom of Peaceful Assembly and Association.*—Freedom of assembly is provided for in the law, but the Government sometimes restricts this right in practice. The Penal Code prohibits public meetings, demonstrations, or processions without prior government approval.

In May the Governor of Southwest province issued an order banning all political activities within the province, including meetings and rallies. He took this step in response to efforts by the SDF and UNDP to organize general strikes to protest the Government's decision to impose government delegates on several municipalities won by the opposition in the January elections.

In March, Yaounde police used tear gas to break up a demonstration by aged retirees who had gathered in front of the National Social Security Office to demand payment of their back pensions. Several of the elderly victims were injured by the tear gas.

Freedom of association is provided for in the law, but the Government sometimes restricts this right in practice. Some 120 political parties operated legally together with a growing number of civic associations. In contrast with 1995, when many political parties faced government-imposed restrictions on their ability to assemble and operate, there were few such restrictions in 1996.

c. *Freedom of Religion.*—The Constitution provides for freedom of religion, and the Government generally does not restrict it in practice. Religious groups must be approved and registered with the Ministry of Territorial Administration in order to function legally.

d. *Freedom of Movement Within the Country, Foreign Travel, Emigration, and Repatriation.*—The law does not restrict freedom of movement within the country, but the Government does in fact impede domestic travel. Police frequently stop travelers to check identification documents, vehicle registrations, and tax receipts as security and immigration control measures. Police commonly demand illegal payments from citizens whom they stop at roadblocks or other points.

The Government occasionally uses its passport control powers against those whom it considers potential threats. Victorin Hameni Bieleu, the President of the Union of Cameroonian Democratic Forces (UFDC) party, had his passport withdrawn 5 years ago. He has since been unable to obtain a new one. Some student activists implicated in the May-June Yaounde clashes have also been unable to obtain passports.

In Bamenda, Northwest province, in May, antigovernment strikers prevented some citizens from traveling to work, using physical intimidation and smashing car windshields.

Cameroon has long served as a safe haven for displaced persons and refugees from nearby countries. Although the Government occasionally returns illegal immigrants, there were no reports of forced repatriation of recognized refugees. Some illegal immigrants have been subjected to harsh treatment, including imprisonment.

The Government cooperates with the office of the U.N. High Commissioner for Refugees (UNHCR) and other humanitarian organizations in assisting refugees. The Government provides first asylum to persons who arrive at the border without documentation and can show a valid claim to refugee status. There are currently 46,000 refugees in Cameroon for whom the country is a country of first asylum. The majority of these persons—nearly 42,000—are Chadian. The remainder are principally from Liberia, Sudan, Ethiopia, Rwanda, Burundi, and Zaire. There were 1,400 refugees who arrived in Cameroon as a country of first asylum in 1996. The Government accepts for resettlement refugees who are granted refugee status by the UNHCR. In 1996 Cameroon accepted approximately 30 Rwandan refugees from Tanzania for resettlement. There were no reports of forced expulsion of persons having a valid claim to refugee status during the year.

Section 3. Respect for Political Rights: The Right of Citizens to Change Their Government

Citizens have the Constitutional right to change their government, but dominance of the political process by the President and his party limit the ability of citizens to exercise this right. While the 1992 legislative elections were relatively free and fair, the 1992 presidential elections were highly criticized by international observers and widely viewed as fraudulent.

The January nationwide multiparty municipal elections were judged to be generally free and fair by domestic and international observers, including members of the diplomatic community. Opposition parties won victories in 104 of 336 elections contested. In most, but not all, locations, elections appeared to be conducted largely in accordance with the rules and to respect the will of the voters. Diplomatic observers watching the elections at booths around the country on voting day reported few signs of deliberate malfeasance on that particular day. Opposition parties, in particular, have complained that the vote in many places was skewed in favor of the Government by preelectoral manipulation of voter registration lists. These allegations have been very difficult to prove. Several parties complained that their lists of candidates in specific locations were arbitrarily and illegally rejected by government-controlled administrative authorities shortly before election day. Such claims form the basis of many of the challenges that were filed with the Supreme Court. The Court ruled itself incompetent to judge in many of these cases. Government authorities claim that they did not arbitrarily reject lists of opposition candidates. Rather, they say, the lists contained some error of format or procedure that rendered them inadmissible under the law.

While opposition parties scored major gains in the municipal elections in most urban areas and in the north and west, the center and south voted solidly for the President's CPDM party. Opposition parties charged that the Government illegitimately excluded them from contesting many localities, particularly in the center and south, in order to preserve the region as a CPDM stronghold. A total of 96 cases were filed with the Supreme Court. In the opinion of observers, the Supreme Court demonstrated a considerable degree of independence and respect for the law in its handling of these cases. By year's end, the Supreme Court had disposed of all 96 cases. Although the Court declared itself, on technical and legal grounds, unable to rule in a majority of the cases brought before it, in 18 cases it declared elections null and void. In annulling these elections, the Court demonstrated no bias for or against the ruling party. Contrary to the law, however, the Government has to date failed to organize new elections in those councils in which the elections were annulled, allowing councils with no legal authority to continue functioning.

A second aspect to the municipal election controversy involves the Government's appointment of delegates to head the administrations of several municipalities won by opposition parties. Under a 1993 decree the President has the authority to name a government delegate to head municipal councils in urban centers. Opposition parties viewed these appointments as a deliberate attempt by the Government to frustrate the will of the voters. To protest these appointments, the two major opposition parties, the SDF and the UNDP, sought to stage a series of rotating general strikes. These, however, failed to draw widespread support from the economically and politically dispirited population and were called off in June.

The Government's control over the country's administrative apparatus is broad and deep. The President appoints by decree the chief operating official (the government delegate) of Yaounde, Douala, Bamenda, and several other large cities. These delegates easily dominate the elected municipal councils, most of whose members belong to opposition parties. The governors of each of the provinces are also appointed directly by the President. Important lower level members of the provincial administrative structures, including the senior divisional officers, the divisional officers, and the district chiefs, are all career civil servants appointed by the Prime Minister. The governors and senior divisional officers wield considerable authority within the areas under their jurisdiction, including, significantly, the authority to ban political meetings that they deem likely to threaten public order. A majority of important government jobs are held by close confidants of the President, many of them drawn from his own ethnic group.

In December 1995, the National Assembly passed a set of government-introduced amendments to the 1972 Constitution, which established strongly centralized power. All debate was held behind closed doors. The amendments included term limits for the President, the creation of a partially elected (70 percent) and partially appointed (30 percent) Senate, and the creation of a set of regional councils with limited powers over local affairs. The amendments did not weaken presidential powers, and the independence of the judiciary remained questionable. The amendments were promulgated by the President in January, but have not yet been implemented.

There are no laws that specifically prohibit women or minorities from participating in government, in the political process, or in other areas of public life. Women are underrepresented in the President's Cabinet (2 of the 44 members), in the National Assembly (22 of the 180 members), and in the CPDM. Many of the key members of the Government are drawn from the President's own ethnic group; members of other ethnic groups and regions hold 32 seats in the Cabinet (compared with 12 held by members of the President's ethnic group), and 142 seats in the National Assembly (compared with 32 held by members of the President's ethnic group).

Section 4. Governmental Attitude Regarding International and Nongovernmental Investigation of Alleged Violations of Human Rights

Domestic and international human rights monitoring groups have considerable latitude to operate. A large number of independent human rights monitoring groups exist, although the activities of virtually all are limited by a shortage of funds and trained personnel. The Government did not generally prevent human rights monitors from operating, but on occasion harassed and obstructed them. The Government sometimes impedes the effectiveness of human rights NGO's by limiting access to prisoners and refusing to share information.

The most active human rights NGO's include the National League for Human Rights, the Organization for Human Rights and Freedoms, the Association of Women Against Violence, the Cameroonian Association of Female Jurists, the Cameroonian Association for Children's Rights, Conscience Africaine, the Movement for the Defense of Human Rights and Liberties, the Human Rights Defense Group, and the Human Rights Clinic and Education Center. A number of these groups issued press releases or reports detailing specific human rights violations. Many held seminars and workshops on various aspects of human rights.

The governmental National Commission on Human Rights and Freedoms, although hampered by a shortage of funds, conducted a number of investigations into human rights abuses and organized several human rights seminars aimed at judicial officials, security personnel, and other government officers. The Commission has never, however, published any results of its investigations. Its reports have been submitted to the Prime Minister and President but never released.

In February Cameroon hosted the first general conference of African National Human Rights Institutions in Yaounde. The conference, organized by the National Commission on Human Rights and Freedoms, sought to facilitate the exchange of information and strengthen cooperation among Africa's national human rights organizations and encourage states without human rights monitoring bodies to create them. In September the Government hosted a visit by the U.N. Nations Human Rights Commission. It requested that the Commission establish a regional human rights office in Yaounde. In mid-November, the Government cooperated with the

ICRC in holding a workshop attended by 23 African nations that addressed the relationship between international human rights and military operations. Military personnel participated in the workshop.

Section 5. Discrimination Based on Race, Sex, Religion, Disability, Language, or Social Status

The Constitution prohibits discrimination based on sex and mandates that "everyone has equal rights and obligations." It does not explicitly forbid discrimination based on race, language, religion, or social status. The Government does not effectively enforce these constitutional provisions.

Women.—Violence against women remains at high levels. Women's rights advocates report that the law does not impose effective penalties against persons who commit acts of domestic violence against women. Spouse abuse is not a legal ground for divorce. In cases of sexual assault, a victim's family or village often imposes direct, summary punishment upon the suspected perpetrator through means ranging from destruction of property to beating. While there are no reliable statistics on violence against women, the number of newspaper reports indicates that the frequency is high.

Despite constitutional provisions recognizing women's rights, women do not, in fact, enjoy the same rights and privileges as men. Polygyny is permitted by law and tradition, but polyandry is not. The extent to which a woman may inherit from her husband is normally governed by traditional law in the absence of a will, and customs vary from group to group. In many traditional societies, custom grants greater authority and benefits to male than to female heirs. In cases of divorce, the husband's wishes determine custody of children over the age of 6. While a man may be convicted of adultery only if the sexual act takes place in his home, a female may be convicted without respect to venue. In the northern provinces, some Lamibe reportedly prevent their numerous wives from ever leaving the palaces.

Children.—The Constitution provides for a child's right to education, and schooling is mandatory through the age of 14. Nevertheless, rising school fees and costs for books have forced many families to forego sending their children to school. Babies and small children are sometimes held in prison if their mothers are incarcerated. The degree of familial child abuse is not known but is one of several targeted issues of children's rights organizations.

Female genital mutilation (FGM), which has been condemned by international health experts as damaging to both physical and psychological health, is not widely practiced, but is practiced in some areas of Far North and Southwest provinces. It includes the most severe form of the abuse, infibulation, and is usually practiced on preadolescent girls. The Government does not recognize FGM as a problem and has not allocated resources to educate the public on the problem.

People With Disabilities.—A 1983 law and subsequent implementing legislation provide certain rights for persons with disabilities. These include access to public institutions, medical treatment, and education. The Government is obliged to bear part of a disabled person's educational expenses, to employ disabled persons where possible, and, as necessary, to provide them with public assistance. However, these rights are in fact rarely respected. There are few facilities for disabled persons and little public assistance of any kind. Lack of facilities and care for the mentally disabled is particularly acute. Society tends to treat the disabled as tainted, leaving churches or foreign NGO's responsible for providing assistance. The law does not mandate special access provisions for people with disabilities.

Indigenous People.—Cameroon's population of indigenous Baka Pygmies (a term which in fact encompasses several different ethnic groups) primarily resides in the forested areas of the south and southeast. While no legal discrimination exists, other groups often treat them as inferior and sometimes subject them to virtual slave labor.

National/Racial/Ethnic Minorities.—There are frequent and credible allegations of discrimination among Cameroon's more than 200 ethnic groups. President Biya's Beti ethnic group holds key positions in government, the security forces, and the military services. In other sectors, discrimination by other ethnic groups is common. Virtually all ethnic groups provide preferential treatment to fellow members where they are able to do so.

An important ethnic, political division falls along linguistic lines rooted in the colonial period. The Anglophone minority (20 percent) often charges that the Francophone majority does not share real power and that the Government provides fewer economic benefits to English-speaking regions.

Section 6. Worker Rights

a. *The Right of Association.*—A 1992 Labor Code allows workers to form and join trade unions of their choosing. The Labor Code permits groups of at least 20 workers to organize a union but also requires registration with the Ministry of Labor. In practice, independent unions have found it extremely difficult to obtain registration. Registered unions are invariably subject to government domination and interference.

Provisions of the Labor Code do not apply to civil servants, employees of the penitentiary system, or workers responsible for national security. In lieu of strikes, civil servants are required to negotiate grievances directly with the minister of the concerned department and with the Minister of Labor. Some sections of the Labor Code have never taken effect, as not all of the implementing decrees have been issued. No new implementing decrees were issued during the year.

There are two trade union confederations. In March 1995, the Government encouraged the creation of a new labor confederation, the Union of Free Trade Unions of Cameroon (USLC), with which it maintains close ties. Previously, the sole labor confederation had been the Confederation of Cameroonian Trade Unions (CCTU), formerly affiliated with the ruling CPDM party under the name Organization of Cameroonian Trade Unions. While both organizations appear to be dominated or at least thoroughly intimidated by the Government, the creation of the USLC was widely interpreted as an effort by the Government to create a rival trade union confederation more firmly under its control.

The Labor Code explicitly recognizes workers' right to strike but only after mandatory arbitration. Arbitration proceedings are not legally enforceable and can be overturned by the Government. The Labor Code provides for the protection of legal strikes and prohibits retribution against them.

There were several strikes during the year. In January workers from the disbanded Urban Transport Company demonstrated in front of the Prime Minister's office to demand social services and other assistance. Police broke up this peaceful demonstration.

In March employees of the national airline, Cameroon Airlines, staged a 1-day strike to protest staff retrenchment, nonpayment of retirement benefits, and plans to privatize the airline.

Throughout much of the year teachers in many parts of the country joined a rotating 2-days-per-week strike to protest nonpayment of back salaries and difficult working conditions.

In Bafoussam, West province, teachers' strikes severely disrupted the academic year. In some cases, striking teachers tried to prevent some of their colleagues from carrying out their duties. In an incident in Bafoussam, striking teachers tried to disrupt student examinations, leading to fights and 12 arrests. The arrested teachers were released after brief detentions.

The CCTU is a member of the Organization of African Trade Union Unity (OATUU) and the International Confederation of Free Trade Unions (ICFTU). The USLC filed applications for membership with these organizations in 1995. At year's end, the USLC was still awaiting a response to its bid to join the OATUU and ICFTU.

b. *The Right to Organize and Bargain Collectively.*—The Labor Code provides for collective bargaining between workers and management in work places, as well as between labor federations and business associations in each sector of the economy. Nevertheless, no sectoral collective bargaining negotiations had been undertaken by year's end.

In May some shop owners in West province and in Douala were reportedly punished by government authorities with fines and temporary closure for having heeded a call by SDF leaders to support a general strike.

The Labor Code prohibits antiunion discrimination, and employers guilty of such discrimination are subject to fines of up to $2,000. However, employers found guilty are not required to reinstate the workers against whom they discriminated. The Ministry of Labor reported no complaints of such discrimination during the year.

The International Labor Organization noted that the Government has failed since 1991 to recognize the National Union of Teachers of Higher Education.

There is an industrial free zone regime, but the Government did not grant approval to any firms to operate under it during the year. Free zone employers are exempt from some provisions of the Labor Code but must respect all internationally recognized worker rights.

c. *Prohibition of Forced or Compulsory Labor.*—Forced or compulsory labor is prohibited by the Labor Code. However, the authorities continued to allow prison inmates to be contracted out to private employers or used as communal labor for municipal public works.

There are credible reports that slavery continues to be practiced in the Lamidat of Rey Bouba, an isolated traditional kingdom in the North province.

d. *Minimum Age for Employment of Children.*—The Labor Code forbids the employment of children under the age of 14. However, Ministry of Labor inspectors responsible for enforcing the law lack resources for an effective inspection program. In rural areas, many children begin work at an early age on family farms. Often, rural youth, especially girls, are employed by relatives as domestic helpers, while many urban street vendors are under 14 years of age. There are no special provisions limiting working hours for children.

e. *Acceptable Conditions of Work.*—Under the Labor Code, the Ministry of Labor is responsible for setting a single minimum wage applicable nationwide in all sectors. The present wage is approximately $47 (23,500 cfa francs) per month. The minimum wage does not provide a decent standard of living for an average worker and family.

The Labor Code establishes a standard workweek of 40 hours in public and private nonagricultural firms, and 48 hours in agricultural and related activities. The Code makes compulsory at least 24 consecutive hours of weekly rest. The Government sets health and safety standards, and Ministry of Labor inspectors and occupational health doctors are responsible for monitoring these standards. However, they lack the resources for a comprehensive inspection program. There is no specific legislation permitting workers to remove themselves from dangerous work situations without jeopardy to continued employment.

CAPE VERDE

Cape Verde is a parliamentary democracy in which constitutional powers are shared between President Antonio Mascarenhas Monteiro, an independent, and Prime Minister Carlos Wahnon Veiga, and his party, the Movement for Democracy (MPD). The MPD dominates the National Assembly, in which three of the five official political parties are represented.

The Government controls the police, which have primary responsibility for maintenance of law and order. There were no reported human rights abuses committed by the police.

Cape Verde has a market-based economy but little industry and few exploitable natural resources. The country has a long history of economically driven emigration, primarily to Western Europe and the United States, and receipts from Cape Verdeans abroad remain an important source of income. Even in years of optimum rainfall, the country can produce food for only 25 percent of the population, resulting in heavy reliance on international food aid.

The Government generally respected the human rights of its citizens, and the law and judiciary provide effective means of dealing with instances of individual abuse. Domestic violence, discrimination against women and mistreatment of children continued to be serious problems. Although the Government supported legislation to ameliorate these problems, it failed to adopt, implement, and enforce policies designed to address the most critical challenges. There were instances of media self-censorship.

RESPECT FOR HUMAN RIGHTS

Section 1. Respect for the Integrity of the Person, Including Freedom From:

a. *Political and Other Extrajudicial Killing.*—There were no reports of political or other extrajudicial killings.

b. *Disappearance.*—There were no reports of politically motivated disappearances.

c. *Torture and Other Cruel, Inhuman, or Degrading Treatment or Punishment.*— The Constitution prohibits such practices, and there were no reports that officials employed them. Severe overcrowding of prisons is a problem. The Government permits both formal visits by human rights monitors to prisons and routine visits to individual prisoners.

d. *Arbitrary Arrest, Detention, or Exile.*—The law stipulates that authorities bring charges before a judge within 48 hours of arrest. Police may not make arrests without a court order unless a person is caught in the act of committing a felony. In exceptional cases, and with the concurrence of a court official, authorities may detain persons without charge for up to 5 days. These laws are observed in practice.

The Ministry of Justice has 40 days to prepare for trial in state security cases, and may detain persons until trial or for a period not to exceed 1 year. There is a functioning system of bail.

The Government does not use forced exile.

e. *Denial of Fair Public Trial.*—The Constitution provides for the right to a fair trial. A judiciary independent of the executive branch generally provides due process rights, but there are serious delays owing to understaffing.

The judicial system is composed of the Supreme Court and the regional courts. There are five Supreme Court judges, including one appointed by the President, one appointed by the National Assembly, and three appointed by the High Council of Magistrates. Judges are independent and may not belong to a political party.

Defendants are presumed to be innocent; have the right to public, nonjury trial; to counsel; to present witnesses; and to appeal verdicts. Free counsel is provided for the indigent. Regional courts adjudicate minor disputes on the local level in rural areas. The Ministry of Justice and Labor appoints local judges, who are usually prominent local citizens. Defendants may appeal regional court decisions to the Supreme Court.

The right to an expeditious trial is constrained by a seriously overburdened judicial system. A backlog of cases routinely leads to trial delays of 6 months.

There were no reports of political prisoners.

f. *Arbitrary Interference With Privacy, Family, Home, or Correspondence.*—The Constitution prohibits such practices, government authorities respect these prohibitions, and violations are subject to effective legal sanction.

Section 2. *Respect for Civil Liberties, Including:*

a. Freedom of Speech and Press.—The Constitution provides for freedom to express ideas by words, images, or any other means, and for freedom of the press without censorship. The Government generally respected these freedoms in practice. Nevertheless, there was increased criticism by independent political figures of the performance of the state-controlled television, radio, and print media for their failure to exercise vigorously their monitoring role in a multiparty system.

Journalists are independent of government control, and are not required to reveal their sources. However, self-censorship within government-controlled media, including the national television and radio networks as well as the state-owned newspaper Novo Jornal, influences media criticism of the Government.

Government authorization is not needed to establish newspapers, other printed publications, or electronic media. Independent media outlets experienced no direct pressure in their daily operations or business activities. The national radio station broadcasts live National Assembly sessions, and while independent media routinely criticize government policies and officials, state-controlled media have been criticized for failing to exercise their monitoring role vigorously in a democratic political system.

The Constitution provides for academic freedom, and the right is respected in practice.

b. *Freedom of Peaceful Assembly and Association.*—The Constitution provides for freedom of peaceful assembly and association without authorization and without harassment by the authorities. Throughout the year, labor organizations, opposition political parties, civic action groups, and numerous others exercised this right without government interference or objection.

c. *Freedom of Religion.*—The Constitution provides for the freedom of religion and the separation of church and state. It also prohibits the State from imposing religious beliefs and practices. The Government respects these rights in practice.

d. *Freedom of Movement Within the Country, Foreign Travel, Emigration, and Repatriation.*—The law provides citizens with the right to travel and establish residence without government restrictions. The Constitution provides for repatriation, and the Government respects this in practice.

The Constitution provides for the right of asylum by refugees, and no violations have been reported. According to credible media reports and the Human Rights Commission, Nigerian citizens suspected of involvement in criminal activity have encountered discrimination by immigration authorities and mistreatment by police.

The Government has not formulated specific policies regarding refugees or first asylum, and the issue of first asylum has never arisen.

Section 3. *Respect for Political Rights: The Right of Citizens to Change Their Government*

The citizens have the right to change their government and did so with legislative elections in December 1995, municipal elections in January, and presidential elections in February. The elections were judged free and fair by international observers.

The Constitution provides for separation of powers. Cabinet ministers are not required to be members of the National Assembly, but they are individually subject to confirmation by the President of the Republic. Collectively, they must retain the support of a parliamentary majority. The President may dismiss the Government with the approval of the Council of the Republic, which is composed of the president of the National Assembly, the Prime Minister, the president of the Supreme Court, the Attorney General, the president of the Regional Affairs Council, and four private members. Referendums may be held under specified circumstances but may not challenge individual political rights and liberties or the right of opposition parties to exist and function freely.

There are no restrictions in law or practice regarding the rights of women or members of minorities to vote or to participate in the political process. Women comprise 11 percent of the deputies elected to the National Assembly. There is one female cabinet minister.

Section 4. Governmental Attitude Regarding International and Nongovernmental Investigation of Alleged Violations of Human Rights

There is one private human rights groups in Cape Verde—the National Commission of the Rights of Man. No major human rights organizations conducted investigations during the year.

Section 5. Discrimination Based on Race, Sex, Religion, Disability, Language, or Social Status

The Constitution prohibits discrimination based on race, sex, religion, disability, language, or social status. However, the Government does not effectively enforce all its provisions, resulting in ongoing discrimination, particularly against women and children.

Women.—Domestic violence against women, including wife beating, remains common. Victims rarely report crimes such as rape and spousal abuse to the police. Women's organizations are seeking legislation to establish a special family court to address crimes of domestic violence and abuse.

Women continue to face discrimination in several ways. Despite constitutional prohibitions against sex discrimination and provisions for full equality, including equal pay for equal work, discrimination continues. Women experience difficulties in obtaining certain types of employment. Although they are often paid less than men, they are making modest inroads in the professions.

The Constitution prohibits discrimination against women in inheritance, family, and custody matters. However, largely because of illiteracy, most women are unaware of their rights. Women are often reluctant to seek redress of domestic disputes in the courts. The Organization of Cape Verdean Women alleges disparate treatment in inheritance matters despite laws calling for equal rights.

Children.—The Government has prepared studies of social policy priorities and legal rights for children and adolescents, and the Cape Verdean Institute for Children is being restructured in accordance with norms established in the Convention on the Rights of the Child. In education, the Government's priorities include extending mandatory education to 6 years for all children. In health, the Government seeks to reduce infant mortality and disease, combat drug and alcohol abuse, and discourage teenage pregnancy.

Child abuse and mistreatment are continuing problems, exacerbated by chronic poverty, large unplanned families, and traditional high levels of emigration of adult men. Mass media, including government-controlled media, continue to highlight children's problems, including sexual violence against children, juvenile prostitution, and drug abuse as well as health and education problems.

People With Disabilities.—The Government does not mandate access to public buildings or services for the disabled. Job discrimination against the physically disabled is prohibited. There are no official schools or trained teachers for the disabled, although several nongovernmental groups, including an association for the blind, are active.

Section 6. Worker Rights

a. *The Right of Association.*—The Constitution provides that workers are legally free to form and to join unions without government authorization or restriction. There are two umbrella union associations: The Council of Free Labor Unions, composed of 11 unions with about 14,000 members, and the National Union of Cape Verde Workers, formed by the former ruling party but operating independently, composed of 14 unions with about 16,000 members. The Government does not interfere with the activities of these organizations, but both suffer from a shortage of funds.

The Constitution provides union members with the right to strike, and the Government respects this right. By law, an employer must reinstate a worker fired unjustly.

Unions are free to affiliate internationally and have ties with African and international trade union organizations.

b. *The Right to Organize and Bargain Collectively.*—The Constitution provides for the right to organize and operate without hindrance and to sign collective work contracts. Workers and management in the small private sector, as well as in the public sector, reach agreement through collective bargaining. As the country's largest employer, the Government continues to play the dominant role by setting wages in the civil service. It does not fix wages for the private sector, but salary levels for civil servants provide the basis for wage negotiations in the private sector.

A 1991 legislative decree bans antiunion discrimination by employers, with fines for offenders. There were no reported cases of such discrimination.

There are no export processing zones.

c. *Prohibition of Forced or Compulsory Labor.*—Forced labor is forbidden by law and is not practiced.

d. *Minimum Age for Employment of Children.*—The legal minimum age for employment is 14 years. The law prohibits children under the age of 16 from working at night, more than 7 hours per day, or in establishments where toxic products are produced; but the Government rarely enforces the law. In practice the Ministry of Justice and Labor enforces minimum age laws with limited success, and then only in the urban, formal sectors of the economy.

e. *Acceptable Conditions of Work.*—There are no established minimum wage rates in the private sector. Large urban private employers link their minimum wages to those paid to civil servants which, for an entry level worker, is $120 (10,000 escudos) per month. The majority of jobs pay wages insufficient to provide a worker and family a decent standard of living; therefore, most workers also rely on second jobs, extended family help, and subsistence agriculture.

The maximum legal workweek for adults is 44 hours. While large employers generally respect these regulations, many domestic servants and rural workers work longer hours.

The Director General of Labor conducts periodic inspections to enforce proper labor practices and imposes fines on private enterprises which are not in conformity with the law. However, the Government does not systematically enforce labor laws, and much of the labor force does not enjoy their protection. There are few industries that employ heavy or dangerous equipment, and work-related accidents are rare.

There is no legal provision for workers to remove themselves from unsafe working conditions without jeopardy to continued employment.

CENTRAL AFRICAN REPUBLIC

The Central African Republic became a democracy in 1993 following free and fair elections in which Ange Felix Patasse, candidate of the Movement for the Liberation of the Central African People, was chosen President. Citizens also elected an 85-member National Assembly; no party holds a majority. In 1994 a Constitution providing for multiparty democracy was accepted in a national referendum. The judiciary is subject to executive interference.

The Government faced major crises during the year in the form of three mutinies by members of the armed forces. In April 200 soldiers protested their poor living conditions and the Government's failure to pay salary arrearages. The Government eventually paid the back salaries and restored order with the help of the French army. Following the mutiny, the President suspended political activity and public assembly, and restricted free movement out of the country. The political opposition demanded the resignation of the Government and new elections. In May approximately 500 soldiers again rebelled, ostensibly to protest the Government's transfer of control of the arsenal from the army to the Presidential Guard. More than 100 people were killed, many children were wounded, and soldiers detained the president of the National Assembly and other officials as hostages at Camp Kasai in the capital. French troops overwhelmed the rebels, who apparently had intended to overthrow the Government. After international diplomatic intervention and the efforts of civic leaders, the crisis was resolved in June with the formation of a Government of National Unity, a coalition arrangement that included members of major political parties. The agreement also included a protocol to increase the constitutional powers of the Prime Minister. Patasse appointed Jean-Paul Ngoupande to that post.

In mid-November the attempted arrest by the Government of former army officer Andre Saulet incited an ethnically based revolt by rebel government troops from the Yakoma ethnic group, supporters of former president Kolingba, a relative of Saulet.

The Yakoma, excluded from the current Government, comprised at least half the army. Some civilians, including several magistrates and private sector professionals, supported the rebellion goals of dismissal of President Patasse and the establishment of a new government. Four Organization of African Unity Francophone heads of state, from Chad, Mali, Burkina Faso, and Gabon, brokered an initial cease-fire. Negotiations for a lasting settlement continued into 1997 under the leadership of former Malian President, General Toumani Toure.

The military forces and the National Gendarmerie, under the Minister of Defense, share internal security responsibilities with the civilian police force, under the direction of the Minister of Public Security. Under President Patasse, the Presidential Security Guard was reduced in size and responsibility. Security forces committed serious human rights abuses.

The Central African Republic is a landlocked and sparsely populated country, most of whose inhabitants practice subsistence agriculture. Annual per capita gross domestic product is estimated at $357. Principal exports are coffee, cotton, timber, tobacco, and diamonds. The 1994 currency devaluation raised producers' prices, boosted rural income, and constrained consumption. The military and civil unrest during the year resulted in significant decreases in public revenues and higher unemployment.

The Government's human rights record remained the same, and serious human rights abuses continue in certain areas. There were credible reports of routine summary executions of suspected bandits by security forces. Police torture and beatings of detainees continued. The President granted amnesty to rebel forces, and the Government did not prosecute members of the armed forces who had committed abuses during the April and May mutinies. Some type of amnesty is expected for the November mutiny. Other human rights abuses included harsh prison conditions, abuse of prisoners, prolonged detention, limits on judicial independence and efficiency, restrictions on freedom of assembly and association, infringements on citizens' right to privacy, some limits on freedom of religion, restraints on press freedom to criticize the Government, a pattern of discrimination and violence against women, and discrimination against Pygmies.

Local human rights monitors expressed concern over the extended detention in excess of legal limits of ex-officials from the previous regime charged with corruption; some of these cases went to trial, but many remained pending. The new Constitutional Court named in January was sworn in during November.

RESPECT FOR HUMAN RIGHTS

Section 1. Respect for the Integrity of the Person, Including Freedom From:

a. *Political and Other Extrajudicial Killing.*—There were no known political killings (former Interior Minister Grelombe was killed by unknown persons during the November mutiny) but there were credible reports that the army and gendarmerie forces routinely conducted summary executions of suspected bandits in border regions. The Government did not prosecute members of the security forces for these killings or for other killings. Many prisoners died in custody at the Comissariat in connection with the repression of banditry, according to the Human Rights League.

Soldiers killed an estimated 200 persons during the army mutinies. President Patasse granted amnesty to the soldiers who had mutinied in April and May. As proposed by the mediation team, amnesty for the November rebellion was pending at year's end. The Government neither investigated nor prosecuted members of the armed forces for abuses committed during the mutinies.

b. *Disappearance.*—There were no reports of politically motivated disappearances.

c. *Torture and Other Cruel, Inhuman, or Degrading Treatment or Punishment.*—Although the Penal Code prohibits torture and specifies sanctions for those found guilty of physical abuse, the police continue to beat and otherwise abuse criminal suspects. There were reliable reports of abuse of prisoners. At one police station police tortured and abused all the individuals detained. Many deaths of prisoners due to official abuse were reported to the courts, but with no evident response taken. The Government has not punished those responsible. The August-September National Conference on Defense (Etats-Generaux) recommended the abolition of special secret police units due to their abusive treatment of detainees and their operation as a parallel and secret arm outside the normal enforcement structure.

Prison conditions are extremely harsh. Cells are overcrowded, and the basic necessities of life, including food, clothing, and medical care, are in short supply and routinely diverted by prison officials for their personal consumption. Prisoners are frequently forced to perform uncompensated labor at the residences of government officials. Male and female prisoners are confined separately in Bangui, but together elsewhere. Minors are routinely housed with adults and subjected to abuse. Following the May civil unrest, prisoners fled the infamous Ngaragba prison unhindered. Despite promises to construct a new facility, the Government has reopened the prison.

d. *Arbitrary Arrest, Detention, or Exile.*—The law stipulates that persons detained in cases other than those involving national security must be brought before a magistrate within 96 hours. In practice, the authorities often do not respect this deadline, in part due to inefficient judicial procedures. Judicial warrants are not required for arrest. By law, national security detainees, defined as "those held for crimes against the security of the State," may be held without charge for up to 2 months. Although previous governments used the national security provision of the law to arrest opponents for exercising internationally recognized human rights, the Patasse Government has not detained any persons for such actions.

Prolonged pretrial detention is a problem. Roughly one-half the male prison population are pretrial detainees. In September 1995, the criminal court began its first session in 2 years. On the docket were the cases of Kolingba regime (1981–93) officials charged with corruption who, in some cases, had been detained more than 18 months without trial. These cases remain pending, and some of the officials remain in custody. A parliamentary commission also investigating Kolingba-era corruption released its reports to the Ministry of Justice, but by year's end the Government had not published them.

The law does not permit the use of exile, and the Government did not employ it in practice. The Government has repeatedly stated that any person in exile for strictly political, rather than criminal, reasons may return without fear of persecution. At year's end, there were no known political self-exiles. Former Empress Catherine, wife of former Emperor Bokassa, briefly returned from exile.

e. *Denial of Fair Public Trial.*—The Constitution provides for an independent judiciary, but there are reliable reports of periodic executive interference.

The judiciary, which consists of regular and military courts, was reorganized in the 1994 Constitution. Legislation implementing this reorganization was passed at the beginning of the year.

In criminal cases, the accused are presumed innocent and have the right to legal counsel, to public trial, to be present at their trials, and to confront witnesses. The Government generally respects these safeguards in practice, but inefficient administration of the law, shortages of trained personnel and material resources hinder the process. The criminal court, for example, did not convene for 2 years for lack of money. Court proceedings are open to the public and frequently broadcast on national radio.

The August-September National Conference on Defense addressed many of the abuses in the military justice system and established long term recommendations for improvement.

There were no reports of political prisoners, although some observers note that anticorruption statutes at times appear to have been applied more rigorously to former officials of the previous regime than to current officials.

f. *Arbitrary Interference With Privacy, Family, Home, or Correspondence.*—The Government on rare occasions abused the law that prohibits invasion of the home without a warrant in civil and criminal cases. Police did, however, use Title IV of the Penal Code, governing certain political and security cases, which allows them to search private property without special authorization. The Government also monitored the telephones of some opposition figures and cut their telephone lines after the April mutiny.

Section 2. *Respect for Civil Liberties, Including:*

a. *Freedom of Speech and Press.*—The Constitution provides for freedom of the speech and the press. Although the Government generally allows the press to operate freely, it restricts press freedom to criticize the Government.

Citizens spoke freely and publicly about political developments, the President's handling of certain issues, and political parties. Opposition leaders, in particular, used press statements, manifestos, broadsides, and copies of open correspondence to the Government to circulate their views. Although not all this documentation was published in the government-controlled media, the Government made no apparent effort to censure, seize, or halt circulation of these materials elsewhere.

More than a dozen private newspapers were published over varying intervals, openly discussing a wide variety of views on political and social issues. The authorities did, however, restrict the ability of the press to criticize the Government. Government officials sued several journalists following accusations of corruption published by their newspapers. Many journalists regarded this as official harassment. In August 1995, the editor of former President Kolingba's Rassemblement Democratique Centrafricaine party newspaper was sentenced to 2 years in prison for defamation after publishing an article that accused President Patasse of conspiring to murder a labor leader. In January another journalist, a member of the opposition coalition CODEPO, was jailed for 1 month because he had accused the President of violating the Constitution in becoming president of his own political party. The court found that no justifiable complaint was lodged against him by President Patasse, and released him. In a separate case in September, a journalist from the independent newspaper Le Novateur was arrested by presidential guards, and jailed for 5 days without trial. He was subsequently reapprehended, tried, and sentenced to 5 months in prison for criticizing the slow due process of the judiciary system and for accusing a senior magistrate of incompetence.

The Government owns and controls one newspaper, which appears only sporadically, a more regular wire service news bulletin, and a radio and television station. Government reluctance to allow opposition access to the media was criticized by the opposition as a blatant effort to impede its activities. A private radio station, Africa No. 1, which is based in Libreville, Gabon, has been operating since 1995, and a church-affiliated station began operations the same year. The Government refused to allow the establishment of other private radio stations for fear that they would become voices for the opposition. The Government has not yet set up the High Council of Communication to regulate the management of private media and help enforce press ethics. The Government did not impede foreign journalists in their work.

The Government respects academic freedom. University faculty and students belonged to many political parties and expressed their views without fear of reprisal.

b. *Freedom of Peaceful Assembly and Association.*—The Constitution provides for the right of assembly, but the Government at times restricted this freedom. A 1992 decree requires organizers of demonstrations and public meetings to register with the Government 48 hours in advance and also prohibits political meetings in schools or churches. The Government forbade public assembly and demonstrations during the aftermath of the April military revolt; no such order was issued after the May or November crises. Police dispersed a November demonstration by civil servants over pay and working conditions, using tear gas and rubber bullets, injuring a number of protestors, and arresting 13 persons.

Associations are required to register with the Government to enjoy legal status. All political parties must register with the Ministry of Public Security in order to participate legally in politics. While the Government usually grants registration expeditiously, in one case in 1995 it revoked a party's registration after the Ministry of Justice mounted a legal challenge based on the party's religious nature.

There are more than 20 registered political parties and a variety of nonpolitical associations. The Government allowed them to hold congresses, elect officials, and publicly debate policy issues without interference.

c. *Freedom of Religion.*—The Constitution provides for freedom of religion, but includes fixed legal conditions and prohibits what the Government considers religious fundamentalism and intolerance. A 1994 constitutional provision prohibiting religious fundamentalism is widely understood to be aimed at Muslims. There is no state religion, and a variety of religious communities are active. Religious organizations and missionary groups are free to proselytize, worship, and construct places of worship. However, religious groups must register with the Government, and any group whose behavior the Government considers subversive remains subject to sanctions, although it imposed no sanctions on any group during the year.

d. *Freedom of Movement Within the Country, Foreign Travel, Emigration, and Repatriation.*—People are free to move within the country, but police and other officials harass travelers unwilling or unable to pay bribes at checkpoints along major intercity roads and at major intersections in Bangui. The Government effectively prevented former President Kolingba and members of his family and other dignitaries of the former regime from leaving Bangui. Some citizens, when attempting to leave the country, were informed by immigration authorities that their names were on unspecified official lists that forbade their departure. For example, in September Henri Pouziere, a well-known lawyer who lived in Libreville, Gabon and who recently defended a journalist, was refused permission to board an airplane for political reasons. After an investigation, he was authorized to leave the country. Another member of the opposition group Front Patriotique Pour Le Progres originally was forbidden to leave Bangui for Canada, his place of residence, because he was suspected of organizing a plot against the regime. Following pressure by the Human Rights League on the Ministers of Justice and Interior, he secretly fled the country.

The Government continued to work with the office of the United Nations High Commissioner for Refugees (UNHCR) in hosting Chadian and Sudanese refugees. Most refugees who were registered with the National Commission for Refugees remained in the country without difficulty. Many Chadians, however, have been accused of criminal activity. Applicants for asylum are generally well-treated and often accepted. Chadian applicants, however, have been viewed with suspicion and have appealed to the UNHCR for assistance.

Section 3. Respect for Political Rights: The Right of Citizens to Change Their Government

Citizens exercised their constitutional right to change their government by democratic means in the 1993 presidential and parliamentary elections. International observers deemed the elections free and fair. In 1995, for the first time in its history, the Parliament passed a vote of censure to change the Government.

The Constitution provides for multiple political parties and increased the powers and independence of the legislative and judicial branches at the expense of the executive branch. Local elections scheduled for 1994 never took place due to budget restrictions. In the interim, the Government appointed three successive mayors of Bangui, which engendered criticism from prodemocracy forces as reneging on a commitment. By-elections held in October 1995 to fill two vacant parliamentary seats were harshly criticized by the opposition for alleged irregularities.

Of the 85 Parliament members, three are women. One of the 20 Cabinet members is a woman. There are few Muslims in government. About 10 Muslims serve in the National Assembly.

Pygmies (Ba'aka), who represent from 1 to 2 percent of the national population, are not represented in the Government and have little political power or influence, although they voted in large numbers in the 1993 election.

Section 4. Governmental Attitude Regarding International and Nongovernmental Investigation of Alleged Violations of Human Rights

The Central African Human Rights League (LCDH) is a nongovernmental organization (NGO) with multiple goals, including publicizing human rights violations and pleading individual cases of human rights abuse before the courts. The LCDH distributed its pamphlets describing individuals' rights and judicial information to the prisons, police stations, courts, schools, and NGO's.

In the April and May mutinies the LCDH played an important role as mediator to help safeguard democratic institutions. In a letter to the President and government authorities, the LCDH criticized the Government's harassment of the press, excessive pretrial detentions in violation of the law, summary executions of suspected bandits, and the deaths of suspects while in police custody in Bangui. Several other NGO's, including the Movement for the Defense of Human Rights and Humanitarian Action and the Central African Red Cross, pursued human rights activities, including prison visits. The Government did not attempt to hinder any such activities.

There were no known requests by international human rights organizations for visits.

Section 5. Discrimination Based on Race, Sex, Religion, Disability, Language, or Social Status

The Constitution stipulates that all persons are equal before the law without regard to wealth, race, sex, or religion, but the Government does not effectively enforce these provisions, and significant discrimination exists.

Women.—Violence against women, including wife beating, occurs but it is impossible to quantify its extent as data are lacking, and victims seldom make reports. The courts try very few cases of spousal abuse, although litigants cite this abuse during divorce trials or in civil suits for damages. Some women reportedly tolerate abuse in order to retain a measure of financial security for themselves and their children. The Government did not address this issue during the year.

Despite the Constitution's provisions, in practice women are treated as inferior to men economically, socially, and politically. Women in rural areas, moreover, suffer more discrimination than women in urban areas. Sixty to 70 percent of urban females go to primary school, while only 10 to 20 percent of their rural counterparts do. Overall, at the primary level, females and males enjoy equal access to education, but the majority of young women drop out at the age of 14 or 15 due to social pressure to marry and bear children. Only 20 percent of the students at the University of Bangui are women. There are no accurate statistics on the percentage of female wage earners.

Polygyny is legal, although this practice faces growing resistance among educated women. There is no legal limit on the number of wives a man may take, but a prospective husband must indicate at the time of the marriage contract whether he intends to take further wives. In practice, many couples never formally marry because men cannot afford the traditional bride payment. Women who are educated and financially independent tend to seek monogamous marriages. Divorce is legal and may be initiated by either partner. The law does not discriminate against women in inheritance and property rights, but a welter of conflicting customary laws often prevails. A new family code drafted in 1995 by a conference sponsored by the Ministry of Social Affairs is designed to strengthen women's rights. The proposed family code still awaited National Assembly approval at year's end.

The Association of Central African Female Jurists' clinic advises women of their legal rights. It also published pamphlets in conjunction with the Ministry of Social Affairs on the dangers of female genital mutilation (FGM) and on food taboos.

Children.—Although there is no official discrimination against children, the Government spends little money on programs for children. There are few church and other NGO projects for youth. Most children are behind in their studies because of education strikes in the early 1990's. Education is compulsory beyond the age of 5, but parents are not prosecuted for truancy. Many Bangui street children survive by begging and stealing. Some are street vendors, part of the informal economy. Several charitable organizations strive to assist them.

Courts interpret the Penal Code as forbidding parental blows or injuries to children under age 15. The proposed family code is designed to strengthen children's rights. For example, illegitimate children would have the same rights as those born in wedlock.

An ordinance of February 22 formally abolished FGM, which is widely condemned by international health experts as damaging to both physical and psychological health. This traditional practice is found in certain rural areas, and to a lesser degree in Bangui, and is performed at an early age. Approximately 45 to 50 percent of females have undergone FGM. A campaign of awareness organized by the Ministry of Social Welfare and women's NGO's reduced the incidence of FGM in some rural areas. In 1996 the court registered one case of FGM that resulted in death.

People With Disabilities.—There is no codified or cultural discrimination against the disabled. There are several government-initiated programs designed to assist the disabled, including handicraft training for the blind and the distribution of wheelchairs and carts by the Ministry of Social Services. There is no legislated or mandated accessibility for the disabled.

Indigenous People.—Despite constitutional provisions, in practice some minorities are treated unequally. In general, the country's indigenous Pygmies have little ability to participate in decisions affecting their lands, culture, traditions, and the allocation of natural resources. In particular, indigenous forest-dwelling Pygmies are subject to social and economic discrimination and exploitation, which the Government has done little to correct. Pygmies often work for villagers at wages lower than those paid to members of other groups. The LCDH received reports and photos of a Pygmy child tortured by a villager who accused him of stealing at his farm. The villager had burned the child's hands. The court convicted him and sentenced him to prison.

Religious Minorities.—Muslims, particularly Mbororo (Peulh) herders, claim to have been singled out for harassment by the authorities, including shakedowns by police, due to popular resentment of their presumed affluence. Muslims play a preponderant role in the economy.

National/Racial/Ethnic Minorities.—There are about 90 ethnic groups, and in the past there was little ethnic balance at the higher levels of government. Under the Kolingba regime, members of the minority Yakoma ethnic group held a disproportionate number of senior positions in government, the armed forces, and state-owned firms. The Patasse Government has brought about a more representative ethnic balance in government. Even so, observers note that members of northern ethnic groups close to the President are a majority in Patasse's Cabinet and also receive favorable treatment in government appointments.

Section 6. Worker Rights

a. *The Right of Association.*—Under the Labor Code, all workers are free to form or join unions of their choosing without prior authorization. A relatively small part of the population has exercised rights of association, chiefly wage earners such as civil servants.

The current Labor Code does not refer to trade unions by name, a change from previous versions. The International Labor Organization (ILO) had requested this change to reflect the proliferation of new unions. There are now five recognized labor federations, including the Organization of Free Public Sector Unions and the Labor Union of Central African Workers (USTC). The USTC and its member unions continue to assert and maintain their official independence from the Government. The USTC never resolved its 1995 dispute with the Government concerning salary arrears.

Unions have the right to strike in both the public and private sectors. To be legal, strikes must be preceded by the union's presentation of demands, the employer's response to these demands, a conciliation meeting between labor and management, and a finding by an arbitration council that union and employer failed to reach agreement on valid demands. The union must also provide 8 days' notification in writing of planned strikes. The Labor Code states that if employers initiate a lockout that is not in accordance with the Code, then the employer is required to pay workers for all days of the lockout. Other than this, the Code does not provide for sanctions on employers for acting against strikers. It is not known to what extent this policy is actually followed. The May teachers' strike resulted in the detention of 14 union members for violation of the "Law of the Freedom to Work." The detainees were released after 1 day.

Labor federations are free to affiliate internationally. The USTC is affiliated with the International Confederation of Free Trade Unions.

b. *The Right to Organize and Bargain Collectively.*—In November police disbanded a demonstration by the Civil Service Trade Unions, who struck for better pay and working conditions. The police used tear gas and rubber bullets. They injured some demonstrators and arrested 13 persons.

The Labor Code accords trade unions full legal status, including the right to sue in court. It requires that union officials be employed full-time in the occupation as a wage earner, but they nonetheless conduct union business during working hours. The Code does not specifically provide that unions may bargain collectively. While collective bargaining has nonetheless taken place in some instances, the Government is usually involved in the process.

Wage scales are set by the Ministry of Labor and Civil Service and were in the process of revision at year's end. The nonpayment of salary arrears and higher consumer costs attributed to the 1994 devaluation continued to be the major complaints of the unions. The Government is undertaking reform in the civil service, including restructuring financial services.

The law expressly forbids discrimination against employees on the basis of union membership or union activity. The Labor Code does not state whether employers found guilty of antiunion discrimination are required to reinstate workers fired for union activities.

There are no export processing zones.

c. *Prohibition of Forced or Compulsory Labor.*—Forced labor is specifically prohibited by the Labor Code, and there were no reports of forced labor. Uncompensated prisoners are forced to work for government officials or magistrates.

d. *Minimum Age for Employment of Children.*—Employment of children under 14 years of age is forbidden by law, but the provision is only loosely enforced by the Ministry of Labor and Civil Service. In practice child labor is common in many sectors of the economy, especially in rural areas.

e. *Acceptable Conditions of Work.*—The Labor Code states that the Minister of Labor must set minimum wages by decree. Agricultural workers are guaranteed a minimum of $15 (cfa 7,800) per month, while office workers are guaranteed $36 (cfa 18,000). Minimum wages differ among the various sectors. The minimum wage assures a family the basic necessities but is barely adequate to maintain a decent standard of living. Most labor is performed outside the wage and social security system, especially by farmers in the large subsistence agriculture sector.

The law sets a standard workweek of 40 hours for government employees and most private sector employees. Household employees may work up to 55 hours per week. The law also requires that there be a minimum rest period of 48 hours.

There are also general laws on health and safety standards in the workplace, but the Ministry of Labor and Civil Service neither precisely defines nor actively enforces them, a matter about which the ILO has expressed concern to the Government for many years. The Labor Code states that a labor inspector may force an employer to correct unsafe or unhealthy work conditions, but it does not provide the right for workers to remove themselves from such conditions.

CHAD

Chad is governed by a transitional regime in which effective power is held by President Idriss Deby and his party, the Patriotic Salvation Movement (MPS). President Deby took power in a December 1990 coup and was confirmed as Chief of State by the Sovereign National Conference (CNS) of 1993. He won election against 14 other candidates in July under a Constitution adopted in a March 31 referendum and was inaugurated for a 5-year term on August 8. Elections for the Legislative

Assembly were scheduled for January 1997 to replace a provisional parliament, the Higher Transitional Council (CST), created by the CNS. The Government is headed by a prime minister appointed by the President. Prime Minister Djimasta Koibla has held office since March 1995. An ineffective and overburdened judicial system is subject to official interference.

The army, gendarmerie, police, and intelligence services are responsible for internal security. Officers of the ethnic group of President Deby dominate the Rapid Intervention Force, formerly known as the Republican Guard, and the National Security Agency (ANS), a counterintelligence organization that has acted as an internal political police force. The security forces were more subject to effective control by the Government. The security forces continued to commit human rights abuses.

The economy is based on subsistence agriculture, herding and fishing. Annual per capita income is an estimated $130 to $190. Chad has little industry; the chief export is cotton. The Government relies heavily on external financial and technical assistance.

The human rights situation improved in several respects during the year, although serious problems remain in certain areas. There were reports of continued abuses of human rights by both government and rebel forces. However, there were no reports of the massacres and terror campaigns that occurred in previous years. The security forces continued to abuse both suspects and detainees and use arbitrary arrest, detention, and illegal searches. However, after major reforms by the Minister of the Armies, reports of major violations by the security forces decreased significantly. The Government did not prosecute security personnel reportedly responsible in earlier years for murder, rape, torture, arbitrary arrest and detention, and illegal search and seizure. Prison conditions remained harsh. The presidential election was marred by widespread and credible reports of fraud, vote-rigging, and irregularities by local officials, although no major incidents of violence were reported. These actions were contrary to internationally accepted standards for free and fair elections. The irregularities apparently did not alter the overall outcome.

The Government at times also imposed illegal limits on freedom of assembly and association, particularly on opponents meeting to advocate a boycott of the second round of the presidential vote, and on occasion limited the freedom of movement of opposition presidential candidates. The judicial system remained ineffective and subject to government interference, unable to provide citizens with prompt trials. Detainees occasionally spend years in pretrial detention. The Government engages in telephone surveillance without judicial authority. Discrimination against women is common; violence against women is also believed to be common. There were infringements on worker rights, including reported instances of forced labor in agricultural communities and the military forces.

RESPECT FOR HUMAN RIGHTS

Section 1. Respect for the Integrity of the Person, Including Freedom From:
  a. *Political and Other Extrajudicial Killing.*—On August 16, Bichara Digui, a businessmen and former political prisoner with ties to both the political and armed opposition, was shot to death in what appeared to be a premeditated execution-style killing. There were reports that his opponents in the Government ordered his death; other reports claimed that he had received death threats from a fellow businessman who had lost a court case to him. The killing is under investigation by the police, but the motive for the shooting remained unclear at year's end. The Government made no effort to prosecute members of the security forces for killings committed in previous years. At least 20 extrajudicial killings of petty criminals by police occurred in November and December after adoption of a new law aimed at reducing street crime. The Government denied that it had ordered a shoot-to-kill policy aimed specifically at unarmed thieves but indicated that police would protect themselves when confronting armed criminals at crime scenes.

Two local human rights organizations reported, with credible supporting evidence, the public execution in Fianga on December 24 by security forces of nine criminal suspects, following a roundup of alleged thieves and highwaymen.
  b. *Disappearance.*—There were credible reports that several opposition party officials were abducted during the first round of the presidential campaign and later released.
  c. *Torture and Other Cruel, Inhuman, or Degrading Treatment or Punishment.*— The Constitution specifically prohibits torture and degrading or humiliating treatment; however, members of the security forces continued to commit some abuses. The Government took steps to halt acts of brutality by its security forces when President Deby appointed former Justice Minister Youssouf Togoimi Minister of the Armies in December 1995 in an effort to reform the military services. Deby and

Togoimi made significant efforts to end military corruption and abuse. Human rights advocacy groups reported only scattered abuses by the military in 1996, and credit Togoimi's reform actions. These abuses included harassment, illegal searches, and seizures of cattle, crops, and food. The Government took no effective measures to punish perpetrators of abuses from previous years.

On July 3 in Bebedjia in Eastern Logone province, security forces arrested former presidential candidate Ngarlejy Yorongar without a warrant, took him to the Bebedjia jail, and beat him (see Section 1.d.).

The army sometimes harassed residents of villages for their supposed collaboration with rebels, including unauthorized searches. Soldiers in army garrisons in certain towns often do not speak the local language, and this at times resulted in friction with the local population.

Prison conditions are harsh throughout the country, characterized by appalling overcrowding, poor sanitation, inadequate food, shelter, and medical facilities, and mixing of male and female prisoners. The Government took no effective action to improve these conditions. Prisoners are almost totally dependent on their families for food and clothing. All prisons are in need of major repairs, and escapes are frequent.

The Government permits some prison visits by human rights monitors such as the International Committee of the Red Cross.

d. *Arbitrary Arrest, Detention, or Exile.*—The Constitution and the Penal Code prohibit arbitrary arrest. Arrest warrants must usually be signed by a judicial official. However, the Government did not always respect these requirements.

Ngarlejy Yorongar, for example, was arrested in July without a warrant, by a local official. He was charged—only after being detained beyond the legal limit— with illegal campaigning for opposition candidate Wadal Abdelkader Kamougue and with arms trafficking with guerrilla forces. He was later transferred to N'Djamena where the Prosecutor General and the Justice Minister ruled that the charges were groundless and ordered him released.

The Government did not use exile as a political weapon.

e. *Denial of Fair Public Trial.*—The Constitution mandates an independent judiciary; however, the judiciary did not operate effectively, being underfunded, overburdened, and subject to official interference.

The national judicial system operates with courts located in provincial capitals. The N'Djamena Court of Appeals, the country's highest court, is supposed to conduct regular sessions in the provinces, but rarely does so. Applicable law can be confusing, as courts often tend to blend the formal French-derived legal code with traditional practices.

Official inaction and interference continued to plague the judiciary. Persons accused of crimes may have to endure up to several years of incarceration before being charged or tried, especially persons arrested for felonies in the provinces who often must await remand to the overcrowded and dangerous house of detention in N'Djamena. Salaries for justice officials are often low and in arrears. The Government has made reform of the judiciary a top priority.

The Military Code of Justice has not been enforced since the 1979–1980 Civil War, and courts-martial instituted early in the Deby Regime to try security personnel for crimes against civilians no longer operate. The remaining military magistrates now sit as civilian judges on the N'Djamena Court of Appeals.

People in rural areas usually do not have access to formal judicial institutions. In most civil cases they rely on traditional courts presided over by village chiefs, chefs de canton, or sultans. Decisions may be appealed to a formal court.

There are no reliable figures on political prisoners.

f. *Arbitrary Interference With Privacy, Family, Home, or Correspondence.*—The Constitution provides for the right to privacy of home, correspondence, and other communications, as well as freedom from arbitrary search. The Penal Code requires that authorities conduct searches of homes only during daylight hours and with a legal warrant. In practice, security forces ignored these provisions and conducted extrajudicial searches at any time.

The Government engages in wiretapping without judicial authority.

Section 2. *Respect for Civil Liberties, Including:*

a. *Freedom of Speech and Press.*—The Constitution and Transitional Charter provide for freedom of speech and the press, and the Government generally respected these rights. The official media, consisting of a national radio network, a press agency, and an N'Djamena television station, are subject to both official and informal censorship. The official media also tend to give priority to government officials and events while providing lesser coverage of the opposition. The Higher Council on Communications, an independent institution mandated by the CNS, acts as an arbiter whose main function is to promote free access to the media. It has no power of enforcement but successfully promulgated rules for equal access for official political statements broadcast during the constitutional referendum and the presidential election.

There are a number of limited-circulation independent newspapers published in the capital, some of which are vociferously critical of government policies and leaders. The Government did not censor these newspapers. It likewise did not interfere with the distribution of opposition tracts and press releases, but state radio officials sometimes refused to broadcast opposition political statements, even when the candidates had bought and paid for radio broadcast rights.

Academic freedom is respected.

b. *Freedom of Peaceful Assembly and Association.*—The Constitution provides for freedom of association and assembly, and the Government generally respected these rights in practice. Authorities routinely granted permits for political and nongovernmental organization (NGO) meetings and usually did not interfere with meetings or press conferences.

However, government forces were responsible for two serious abridgements of freedom of assembly. On June 28 and 29, forces directed by Secretary of State for Security Noudjalbaye Ngaryan prevented meetings of opposition political parties who were advocating a boycott of the second round of presidential elections. Police and gendarmes commanded by Secretary Noudjabaye also occupied the headquarters of the principal labor union in order to prevent a meeting called to discuss the boycott and revoked its legal charter for several weeks (see also Section 6.a.). Party and union officials reported that the security forces presented no court order authorizing them to prevent the meetings.

Opposition political parties also reported incidents of harassment by local officials during the election campaign. In one of the most violent incidents, a rally of presidential candidate Saleh Kebzabo in Kelo resulted in a riot allegedly instigated by the local officials. Several party members and officials were hospitalized as a results of injuries inflicted by the rioters, who also damaged or destroyed vehicles and equipment.

There are more than 60 registered political parties and several hundred NGO's. However, a confusion of laws governing NGO's enabled the Interior Ministry to threaten unions and human rights organizations with dissolution for alleged political activities during the election campaign (see Section 6.a.).

c. *Freedom of Religion.*—The Constitution states that the state is secular. It also provides for freedom of religion. All faiths worship without government constraint.

d. *Freedom of Movement Within the Country, Foreign Travel, Emigration, and Repatriation.*—The Constitution provides for these rights. However, several opposition presidential candidates reported that they were the object of government orders preventing them from traveling or leaving the country after the first round of presidential elections. In addition, Wadal Abdelkader Kamougue and Saleh Kebzabo, who finished second and third in the presidential vote, were both detained for several hours by security personnel at the N'Djamena airport at different times during the campaign and before being allowed to leave the country.

The Government does not require special permission for travel in most areas. However, armed bandits operate on many roads, exposing travelers to assault, robbery, and murder; many bandits have been identified as soldiers and deserters. Despite government efforts to clear the country's main routes of illegal roadblocks, elements of the security forces, guerrillas, and bandits continue to maintain them, extorting money from travelers.

Chadian refugees are free to repatriate, although several thousand remain in the Central African Republic, Niger, Nigeria, and Cameroon.

The Government cooperates with the U.N. High Commissioner for Refugees (UNHCR) and other humanitarian organizations assisting refugees. There were no reports of forced expulsion of those having a valid claim to refugee status. The country currently provides first asylum for refugees and has done so in past years. The Government has informally granted refugee and asylee status to persons and has allowed them to remain for resettlement.

The Government adheres to the 1951 U.N. Convention on Refugees and the 1967 protocol relating to their status. However, these accords were never ratified by Parliament and therefore do not carry force in local law. No official national structure has been created to deal with refugee affairs other than the repatriation committees, which focus solely on citizens returning from other countries. Since August 1993, however, the Government has registered refugees in N'djamena and sent their applications for refugee status to the UNHCR Central African Headquarters in Kinshasa, Zaire. If the application is accepted, then in principle the refugee will be enrolled in a 6-month care maintenance program, which includes a monthly subsistence allowance, medical care, and assistance in finding work. This program is funded by a local NGO.

Section 3. *Respect for Political Rights: The Right of Citizens to Change Their Government*

The March constitutional referendum and the July presidential election, both authorized by the Constitution, were the first national votes held in many years and the first under President Deby. The presidential election was marred by widespread and credible reports of fraud, vote-rigging, and irregularities by local officials, although no major incidents of violence were reported. These actions were contrary to internationally accepted standards for free and fair elections. The irregularities apparently did not alter the overall outcome.

The Constitution accords immunity to both the President and members of the National Assembly and includes no provision for recall. Local officials will continue to be appointed by the national Government until local elections in 1997.

Few women held senior leadership positions, although several served as Cabinet ministers; there were 4 women in the 52-member CST, which was disbanded late in the year.

Section 4. *Governmental Attitude Regarding International and Nongovernmental Investigation of Alleged Violations of Human Rights*

Human rights organizations operate with few overt restrictions, investigating and publishing their findings on human rights cases. Government officials are often accessible but generally unresponsive or hostile to the findings of these organizations.

Human rights NGO's gained recognition under the Deby regime and participate in key governmental institutions. They are courageous, if often partisan, in publicizing abuses through reports and press releases but only occasionally are able to intervene successfully with authorities. All are dominated by opponents of the Government, impairing their credibility. Two governmental bodies, the National Human Rights Commission and the Human Rights Committee of the CST, are also active.

The Government did not prohibit investigations by international human rights organizations. In April the United Nations Human Rights Commission considered a case against Chad under the confidential 1503 Procedure. The Commission voted to consider moving the case to the public process next year if there was no improvement in the human rights situation.

Section 5. *Discrimination Based on Race, Sex, Religion, Disability, Language, or Social Status*

The Constitution provides for equal rights for all citizens, regardless of origin, race, religion, political opinion, or social status. In practice, cultural traditions maintain women in a subordinate status, and the Government favors its ethnic supporters and allies.

Women.—While no statistics are available, domestic violence against women is believed to be common. By tradition, wives are subject to the authority of their husbands and have only limited legal recourse against abuse. Family or traditional authorities may act in such cases, but police rarely intervene.

Neither government nor advocacy groups have been able to redress discrimination against women. There are, however, a number of women's advocacy groups that are working to this end. Women do not have equal opportunities for education and training, making it difficult for them to compete for the few formal sector jobs. Property and inheritance laws do not discriminate against women, but traditional practice favors men. Exploitation of women is especially pervasive in rural areas, where women do most of the agricultural labor and are discouraged from formal schooling.

Children.—The Government has demonstrated little commitment to children's rights and welfare. It has not committed adequate funding to public education and medical care. Educational opportunities for girls are limited. About as many girls as boys are enrolled in primary school, but the percentage of girls enrolled in secondary school is extremely low, primarily because of early marriage. Although the law prohibits sex with a girl under the age of 14, even if married, this law is rarely enforced and families arrange marriages for girls as young as 11 or 12 years of age, sometimes forcibly, for the financial gain of a dowry. Many are then obligated to work long hours of physical labor for their husbands in fields or homes.

Female genital mutilation (FGM), which is widely condemned by international health experts as damaging to both physical and psychological health, is widespread and deeply rooted in tradition. Advocated by women as well as by men, the practice is strongest among ethnic groups in the east and south. It is usually performed prior to puberty as a rite of passage, an occasion many families use to profit from gifts from their communities. Opposition to its elimination is strong. Several female officials of the Health Ministry have unsuccessfully attempted to develop a public education program to change attitudes toward FGM. A number of women's groups are active in promoting change, but few are effective.

People With Disabilities.—There is no official discrimination against disabled persons. However, the Government operates few therapy, education, or employment programs for people with disabilities, and no laws mandate access to buildings for them.

National/Racial/Ethnic Minorities.—Ethnicity continues to influence government appointments and political alliances. There are approximately 200 ethnic groups from two general traditions: Arab and Saharana/Sahelian zone Muslims in the north, center and east, and Sudanian zone Christian or animist peoples in the south. Rivalries among these many groups have caused civil tensions and conflicts for decades.

Section 6. Worker Rights

a. *The Right of Association.*—The Constitution recognizes freedom of association and union membership as well as the right to strike. All employees, except members of the military, are free to join or form unions. Unions must receive authorization from the Government in order to operate legally. However, few workers belong to unions: most are subsistence cultivators or herders. The main labor organization is the Federation of Chadian Unions (UST), and its major constituent union is the Teachers' Union of Chad (SET). Neither has ties to the Government. A number of minor federations and unions, including the Free Confederation of Chadian Workers, also operate, some with ties to government officials.

The Government generally respected the right to organize and strike. However, armed police and gendarmes occupied UST offices for 2 days to prevent a meeting called to discuss a boycott of the second-round presidential vote. The Government revoked the union's charter on July 2 for alleged illegal political activity, but it reinstated it on July 31 following an international outcry, including a complaint filed with the International Labor Organization (ILO) by the International Confederation of Free Trade Unions, protesting suspension on that basis. The UST also had filed legal actions against the Government in the courts for similar attempts in 1993 and 1995 to suspend it and occupy its headquarters.

Isolated strikes over unpaid salaries by teachers and health workers occurred in several areas of the country, a marked improvement from previous years which were characterized by widespread strikes.

Unions may affiliate with international bodies.

b. *The Right to Organize and Bargain Collectively.*—The Constitution and the Labor Code contain only general provisions on the rights of labor and do not specifically protect collective bargaining. The Labor Code requires the Government to set minimum-wage standards and permits unions to bargain collectively, but it empowers the Government to intervene in the bargaining process under certain circumstances. The Government again failed to submit a draft labor code prepared in 1988 with ILO assistance for consideration by the CST.

The law does not specifically prohibit antiunion discrimination, and there is no formal mechanism for resolving such complaints. Three top union officials in Biltine Prefecture, Bakari Aoudou and Nadjingar Djimodundoudje of UST and Lokal Yokassi of SET were suspended from their jobs and expelled from the province at the behest of government officials in 1995, and have not been reinstated nor permitted to return.

There are no export processing zones.

c. *Prohibition of Forced or Compulsory Labor.*—The Constitution prohibits slavery and forced labor. However, the ILO maintained that several provisions of both pre- and post-independence legislation may permit forced labor under certain circumstances and has urged the government to take actions to repeal them. There is no evidence of the practice in the formal economy, but there have been reports of isolated instances among rural farming or herding communities and in military installations in the north. Human rights associations also indicate that the military routinely compels soldiers to perform forced labor at isolated outposts as punishment.

d. *Minimum Age for Employment of Children.*—The Labor Code stipulates that the minimum age for employment in the formal sector is 14 years. The Government does not enforce the law, but in practice children are rarely employed except in agriculture and herding. The Minister of the Armies stated publicly that the Government is attempting to muster out the approximately 600 underage soldiers currently serving in the armed forces.

e. *Acceptable Conditions of Work.*—The Labor Code requires the Government to set minimum wages. Although a 1994 Social Pact set the minimum wage at a range of $42 to $50 (cfa 21,000 to cfa 25,000)per month, most wages are insufficient to support a worker and family. Nearly all private sector and state-owned firms had applied the new standards by the end of 1995, but public sector wages remain below standard since the Government failed to submit legislation to implement them for its employees.

The Government record on salary payments improved significantly. Structural adjustment assistance from international institutions enabled it to pay most of its employees regularly and usually on time. Salary arrears to civil servants outside the capital, a problem in a country with few financial institutions, have been reduced to approximately 2 months from the previous 6 months. However, arrears to government employees from previous years remain unpaid. Moreover, some members of the military received only subsistence payments for most of the year. Many state employees must work second jobs, raise their own food crops, or rely on family for support.

The law limits most nonagricultural work to 48 hours per week, with overtime paid for supplementary hours, and agricultural work limited to 2,400 hours per year. All workers are entitled to 24 consecutive hours of rest per week, although in practice this is rarely enforced.

The Labor Code mandates occupational health and safety standards and inspectors with the authority to enforce them. These standards are rarely respected in practice, and the UST has alleged before the ILO that the labor inspection services are not allocated the funds necessary to perform their duties. In principle, workers can remove themselves from dangerous working conditions, but in practice they cannot without endangering their employment.

COMOROS

The Federal Islamic Republic of the Comoros comprises three islands and claims a fourth, Mayotte, which is still governed by France. The Comoros has a constitutional government but has been prone to coups since independence in 1975. The most recent came in September 1995, when foreign-led mercenaries and disaffected Comorian troops attempted to overthrow the elected government of President Said Mohamed Djohar. French military forces sent to the island 1 week later arrested the mercenaries, reinstalled the elected Prime Minister, and freed Djohar but removed him for "medical treatment" to the French Department of Reunion. Prime Minister Caabi El Yachroutou declared himself acting president, and pledged to hold new presidential elections. In January President Djohar returned to Comoros to assume ceremonial duties in accordance with an agreement brokered by the Organization for African Unity (OAU). In March Mohamed Taki Abdoulkarim was elected President. The elections were deemed to be free and fair by international observers. In April President Taki dissolved the National Assembly and postponed general elections beyond the 40 days within which the 1992 Constitution required they be held. President Taki appointed a committee to draft a new constitution which was approved in a referendum in October. Parliamentary elections were held in December.

The Comorian Defense Force (FCD) and the Gendarmerie are responsible for internal security. Both are under civilian control, but their loyalty is suspect as shown by the participation of several hundred soldiers in the 1995 coup. French officers serve as advisers to the FCD.

The economy of this extremely poor country is dominated by agriculture, but there is a shortage of arable land; soil erosion exacerbates this problem. Revenues from the main crops—vanilla, essence of ylang ylang, and cloves—continue to fall, while the population (about 500,000) is growing at an extremely high rate of about 3 percent. The per capita income is approximately $470. The Comoros is a part of the French franc monetary zone, but the 1994 devaluation of the franc did not improve the import-dependent economy, and it has had serious short-term consequences on government finances. The Comoros depends heavily on financial assistance from France and the European Union.

The human rights situation did not improve in 1996. Soldiers being held for allegedly participating in a 1992 coup attempt were released by the mercenaries in 1995 and later granted amnesty, but the Taki Government took steps to restrict freedom of speech and press. Prison conditions remain harsh but prisoners are rarely held overnight. Societal discrimination against women continued to be a serious problem.

RESPECT FOR HUMAN RIGHTS

Section 1. Respect for the Integrity of the Person, Including Freedom From:

a. *Political and Other Extrajudicial Killing.*—There were no reports of political or other extrajudicial killings.

As far as is known, there has been no official investigation into the deaths of two persons reportedly killed and secretly buried by the Gendarmerie on the eve of the legislative elections in December 1993 on the island of Anjouan.

b. *Disappearance.*—There were no reports of politically motivated disappearances.

c. *Torture and Other Cruel, Inhuman, or Degrading Treatment or Punishment.*—There were no substantiated reports of torture or other cruel, inhuman, or degrading treatment or punishment.

Prison conditions continued to be poor. A lack of proper sanitation, overcrowding, inadequate medical facilities, and poor diet are common problems. The Government has not taken action to remedy these problems. Because of these conditions, even prisoners found guilty of serious crimes are typically released in the evening to go home to sleep and are expected to return the next morning.

d. *Arbitrary Arrest, Detention, or Exile.*—The 1996 Constitution prohibits arbitrary arrest and imprisonment. It does not specify a time limit between arrest and appearance before a magistrate. The law does not specify how long prisoners held for security reasons may be detained without being charged.

The Government does not use forced exile as a means of political control.

e. *Denial of Fair Public Trial.*—The 1996 Constitution provides for an independent judiciary assured by the President. Trials are open to the public except for limited exceptions defined by law.

The High Council, made up of four members appointed by the President, three members elected by the Federal Assembly, and a member of each island council, also serves as the High Court of Justice and rules on cases of constitutional law.

The Constitution provides for equality before the law of all citizens. It does not mention right to counsel. There are very few lawyers in the country, making it difficult to obtain legal representation. The Government does not provide free legal counsel to the accused. The legal system incorporates Islamic law as well as French legal codes. Most disputes are settled by village elders or by a civilian court of first instance.

In September a man who allegedly murdered a pregnant woman in front of several witnesses was found guilty in a public, 2-day trial before a lay penal court. He had legal counsel. Prior to the conclusion of the man's trial and sentencing, President Taki stated publicly that the trial process was unnecessarily slow and called for harsher punishments for criminals. The man was publicly executed on September 16, and was the first person to be sentenced to death since the late 1970's.

There are no known political prisoners.

f. *Arbitrary Interference With Privacy, Family, Home, or Correspondence.*—There were no known cases of arbitrary interference with privacy or correspondence.

Section 2. Respect for Civil Liberties, Including:

a. *Freedom of Speech and Press.*—The Constitution does not provide for freedom of the press and the Government sought to restrict this freedom in January. The National Unity Government, which ruled between the restoration of civilian rule and the March presidential elections, arrested two journalists who criticized members of the Government for corruption. The journalists were released shortly thereafter. Several small, independent newspapers freely criticize the Government, but in June the Minister for Information convened journalists to remind them of their duty to support the country and the leadership. In July the Government shut down and confiscated the transmitter of the independent radio station, Tropic FM, accusing it of disseminating false news and inciting and provoking public disorder. Observers say that the Taki Government also has exerted more pressure on the semi-official weekly, Al-Watwan, whose editors are selected by the Minister for Information. Comorians discuss and criticize the Government and its leading personalities with more caution than in previous years.

The government-controlled radio station, Radio Comoros, is the only station in the country following the closure by the Government of Tropic FM. Comorians receive broadcasts from Mayotte Radio as well as from French television without interference, but these carry only limited news about Comoros developments. Satellite antennas are popular and amateur radio licenses are issued without hindrance. Foreign newspapers are available, as are books from abroad.

Although there is no university in the Comoros, secondary level teachers and students speak freely, and students occasionally engaged in meetings which criticized the Government.

b. *Freedom of Peaceful Assembly and Association.*—The 1996 Constitution does not provide for freedom of assembly and association, but the Government generally respects these rights in practice.

c. *Freedom of Religion.*—An overwhelming majority of the population is Sunni Muslim. The Constitution prohibits discrimination before the law based on religion or religious belief but establishes an ulamas council, which advises the President, Prime Minister, President of the Federal Assembly, the Council of Isles, and the island governors on whether bills, ordinances, decrees, and laws are in conformity with the principles of Islam. The Government permits non-Muslims to practice their faith, and Christian missionaries work in local hospitals and schools but are not allowed to proselytize.

In August President Taki announced a ban on alcohol and indecent apparel worn by women, citing a need to return to Islamic values.

d. *Freedom of Movement Within the Country, Foreign Travel, Emigration, and Repatriation.*—There are no restrictions on travel within the country or abroad, and exit visas are generally freely granted.

The Government has not formulated a policy regarding refugees, asylees, or first asylum.

Section 3. Respect for Political Rights: The Right of Citizens to Change Their Government

Citizens have the right, but it has not yet been fully demonstrated that they, in fact, have the ability to change their government peacefully through free and fair elections. The Constitution stipulates that sovereignty belongs to the people and is exercised by elected representatives or by referendum. Although the March presidential elections were characterized as free and fair by international observers, Djohar's removal from office by mercenaries and the subsequent stripping of his power by the National Unity Government was not a legal or democratic method of changing the government.

In October President Taki's proposed Constitution was approved in a national referendum. The new Constitution mandates that all political parties that did not win at least two seats per island in the December legislative elections are automatically dissolved unless they join other parties validly represented in the Federal Assembly. If only one party is represented in the assembly, the party or group obtaining the second largest number of votes is permitted to continue its activities.

Village chiefs and Muslim religious leaders tend to dominate local politics. Traditional social, religious, and economic institutions also importantly affect the country's political life.

Traditionally, Comorian society is male-dominated, making it very difficult for women to become involved in politics. Women have the right to vote and participate in the political process. There is one female minister. In National Assembly elections held in December, no women were elected.

Section 4. Governmental Attitude Regarding International and Nongovernmental Investigation of Alleged Violations of Human Rights

The Comoros Human Rights Association, established in 1990, continues to function, but many members are unwilling to criticize the Government vigorously for fear of losing their civil service positions. The Government cooperates with international human rights organizations, including the International Committee of the Red Cross.

Section 5. Discrimination Based on Race, Sex, Religion Disability, Language, or Social Status

The Constitution provides for the equality before the law without discrimination based on race, religion, or religious belief but is silent on sex, disability, language, and social status. The Government generally respects these provisions in practice, but discourages the practice of religions other than Islam.

Women.—Violence against women occurs, but medical authorities, the police, and women's groups believe that it is rare. In theory a woman could seek protection through the courts in the case of violence, but in reality the issue would most likely be addressed within the extended family or at the village level.

Men have the dominant role in Comorian society, and few women hold positions of responsibility in government or business. Societal discrimination against women is most apparent outside the major towns where women have onerous farming and child-rearing duties, with fewer opportunities for education and wage employment. In contrast change in the status of women is most evident in the major towns, where growing numbers of women are in the labor force and generally receive wages comparable to those of men engaged in similar work. While legal discrimination exists in some areas, in general inheritance and property rights do not disfavor women; for example, the house the father of the bride traditionally provides to the couple at the time of their marriage remains her property even in the case of divorce. In August President Taki announced a ban on indecent apparel worn by women (see Section 2.c.).

Children.—The Government, while committed to the protection of children's rights and welfare in theory, has an extremely limited ability to put this into practice. Population pressure and poverty force some families to place their children into the homes of others. These children, often as young as 7 years of age, typically work long hours as domestic servants in exchange for food and shelter. The few legal instruments which address the rights and welfare of children are not enforced because of a lack of inspectors.

Female genital mutilation, which is widely condemned by international health experts as damaging to both physical and psychological health, is not generally practiced, and child abuse appears to be rare.

People With Disabilities.—There is no evidence of widespread discrimination against the disabled in the provision of education or other services. No legislation is in force or pending concerning accessibility to public buildings or services for people with disabilities.

Section 6. Worker Rights

a. *The Right of Association.*—The Constitution does not provide for the right to unionize and strike, but these rights are practiced freely. Farming on small landholdings, subsistence fishing, and petty commerce make up the daily activity of most of the population. Hence, the wage labor force is small; less than 7,000 including government employees, and less than 2,000 excluding them. Teachers, civil servants, and dock workers are unionized. Unions are independent of the Government. Teachers and hospital workers go on strike intermittently, mostly because they do not get paid for months. There are no laws protecting strikers from retribution, but there were no known instances of retribution.

There are no restrictions on unions joining federations or affiliating with international bodies.

b. *The Right to Organize and Bargain Collectively.*—Unions have the right to bargain collectively, and strikes are legal. Wages are set by employers in the small private sector and by the Government, especially the Ministries of Finance and Labor, in the larger public sector. The Labor Code, which is only loosely enforced, does not set up a system for resolving labor disputes, and it does not prohibit antiunion discrimination by employers.

There are no export processing zones.

c. *Prohibition of Forced or Compulsory Labor.*—The Constitution does not mention forced or compulsory labor, but it is not practiced.

d. *Minimum Age for Employment of Children.*—The Labor Code defines 15 years of age as the minimum age for the employment of children. The Ministry of Labor has few resources to enforce this provision, but outside of domestic work child labor is not an issue due to the general lack of wage employment opportunities. Children generally help with the work of their families in the subsistence farming and fishing sectors.

e. *Acceptable Conditions of Work.*—The Government mandates minimum wage levels. The rates, which vary by occupation, have not been changed in over a decade and no longer reflect economic realities. The minimum wage for a laborer is about $11 (4,600 Comorian francs) per month. The Government periodically reminds employers to respect the Labor Code, which specifies 1 day off per week, plus 1 month of paid vacation per year, but does not set a standard workweek. There are no safety or health standards for the minuscule manufacturing sector.

CONGO

The Republic of the Congo continues its transition to democratic government. In 1992 Pascal Lissouba became its first democratically elected president after 24 years of one-party rule. Elections for the multiparty legislature followed in 1993. The Government continued to build upon the stable foundation provided by the Libreville Peace Accords, which ended a period of violent civil unrest in late 1992, 1993, and early 1994. The Government made some progress in establishing constitutionally mandated institutions, such as the Supreme Court; however it is still lagging in others. The Government continued to devolve power to regions and municipalities. The judiciary is independent although in some instances subject to government influence.

The national police and gendarmerie maintain internal security. The army and the border guard are responsible for external security but also have domestic responsibilities. While the civilian authorities generally maintain effective control of the security forces, some members of the security forces committed human rights abuses.

The economy depends heavily upon petroleum revenues and external capital. The Government made significant progress in economic liberalization and privatization. Per capita gross national product is $600.

The Government's human rights record was mixed, with improvements in some aspects but deterioration in other areas. Security forces continued to use severe beatings and abuse to extract confessions and as punishment, and to arbitrarily arrest and beat refugees in Brazzaville. Prison conditions remained life threatening. The Government arrested and beat four unionists who were sentenced to 4 months' imprisonment for "impeachment of the freedom to work" in a strike judged illegal. The Government passed a press law that intimidated many journalists and increased the frequency of self-censorship. The Government arrested two men for "attack against the state in peacetime"; the men were sentenced to 1 year in prison and exile from the capital. The judiciary is subject to political influence, and lengthy pretrial detention remains a problem. Societal discrimination and violence against women remained problems. Bantus continued to discriminate against and exploit Pygmies. Citizens sometimes resorted to vigilante justice, killing presumed thieves and "sorcerers." The partial disbandment and integration into the government security forces of private political militias early in the year reduced the incidence of citizen harassment, extortion, theft, and beatings carried out by these forces.

RESPECT FOR HUMAN RIGHTS

Section 1. Respect for the Integrity of the Person, Including Freedom From:

a. *Political and Other Extrajudicial Killing.*—There were no reports of political or other extrajudicial killings committed by the Government.

Civilians, however, continued to employ vigilante justice against presumed thieves and "sorcerers," sometimes beating them to death. Congo's leading human rights watch group, the Organization Congolaise des Droits de l'Homme (OCDH), reported 11 such killings. No judicial actions followed.

b. *Disappearance.*—There were no reports of politically motivated disappearances.

c. *Torture and Other Cruel, Inhuman, or Degrading Treatment or Punishment.*— The Constitution prohibits the use of torture and cruel, inhuman, or degrading treatment. In practice, however, some security force members routinely severely beat detainees both to extract "confessions" and as punishment. Security force members generally act with impunity.

Security forces beat four trade unionists prior to their trial (see Section 6.a.).

Prison conditions are dire and life-threatening. The death rate and the incidence of disease and malnutrition are considerably higher than among the general population. Buildings are dilapidated, security is lax, and food and medical care are inadequate. Most prisons, built during French colonial rule, were designed for short-term incarceration and low-inmate population. Although the maximum capacity of the Brazzaville prison is ostensibly 100, over 400 inmates were being held there in February. Prisoners often have to depend on their families to bring them food, as the Government does not provide meals. In the interior of the country, nonviolent inmates leave their cells during the day to forage for food in the surrounding towns. They return of their own accord in the evenings. With financial backing from the French Government, the Government's High Commissioner for Human Rights launched an initiative to improve prison conditions. The program managed to provide some mattresses, clothing, and limited medication. Much, however, remains to be done to bring the prisons up to international standards. Rape and sexual abuse of women and children by prison guards was not commonplace.

Political/security prisoners are held separately from the general prison population; however, their conditions do not differ significantly. Human rights groups reported difficulties in gaining access to prisons in the major urban centers of Brazzaville and Pointe-Noire. Access is facilitated, however, if an organization provides funds to ameliorate prison conditions.

d. *Arbitrary Arrest, Detention, or Exile.*—The Constitution prohibits arbitrary arrest, detention, or exile. The Code of Penal Procedure requires that an individual be apprehended openly and have a lawyer present during initial questioning. The code further stipulates that warrants be issued before arrests are made and that detainees be brought before a judge within 3 days and either charged or released within 4 months. In practice, the Government often violated these legal procedures and did not respect the constitutional mandates.

Detainees were promptly informed of the charges levied against them. However, many waited in prison for several months without being brought before a judge. Some detainees languish in jail for years because of lost files, oversights, and bureaucratic inertia. Except in a few cases with political overtones, lawyers and families had free access to detainees. Although the law provides for a system of bail, the average detainee lacks the financial means to meet bail. Over half of all persons in custody are pretrial detainees—70 percent at the central prison in Brazzaville. The Government often does not honor laws that provide for legal counsel for the indigent.

In May authorities arrested Colonel Bouissa Matoko at the airport after a search of his briefcase revealed "seditious" documents addressed to the former president, Denis Sassou Nguessou. Security forces conducted a raid on Matoko's home and found three guns and a small cache of grenades and ammunition. Colonel Matoko and the author of the "seditious" documents, Professor Gabriel Longombe, were convicted in September of "attack on the security of the state in peacetime." They were sentenced to 1 year in prison, followed by 1 year of probation and each was fined $2,000. The sentence further stipulates that while on probation, the two are exiled from Brazzaville.

In September the Government arrested Otto Mbongo for debts owed to the now bankrupt International Bank of Congo (BIDC). Mbongo was a key aide to former president Sassou Nguessou, and some allege that his arrest was politically motivated. The private media reported that Mbongo was arrested without a warrant, denied access to legal counsel, and refused family visitation. Mbongo is being held in an undisclosed location, separate from the general prison population. A trial date had not been set by year's end.

Three political detainees were being held as of year's end.

The Government does not use foreign exile.

e. *Denial of Fair Public Trial.*—The Constitution provides for an independent judiciary. Certain rulings, however, suggested that in some instances the courts were subject to political influence.

The judicial system consists of local courts, courts of appeal, and the Supreme Court.

In general, defendants are tried in a public court of law presided over by a state-appointed magistrate. The defense has access to, and the right to counter prosecution evidence and testimony. In formal courts, defendants are presumed innocent and have the right of appeal. The judiciary is overburdened with a caseload that far exceeds its capacity to ensure fair and timely public trials. Some cases never reach the court system, however. For example, it is common practice for citizens to beat thieves caught in the act, sometimes to death (see Section 1.a.). In rural areas, traditional courts continue to handle many local disputes, especially property and probate cases. Many domestic disputes are adjudicated under traditional law and within the extended family.

Colonel Bouissa and Professor Longombe (see Section 1.d.) were considered political prisoners by human rights observers.

f. *Arbitrary Interference With Privacy, Family, Home, or Correspondence.*—The Constitution provides for the privacy of homes as well as correspondence and telecommunications. Official searches of private properties and communications require a warrant, but in practice, warrants are not used in all instances. There is government surveillance of some telephone lines.

Section 2. *Respect for Civil Liberties, Including:*

a. *Freedom of Speech and Press.*—The Constitution provides for freedom of expression and calls for the establishment of an independent council to oversee private and electronic media and to safeguard speech and press freedoms. This council has not yet been established. In practice, individual freedom of expression is enjoyed, but press freedoms have been restricted. The Government retains monopoly power over radio and television.

In July Parliament passed a new press law that has been roundly criticized by local journalists and some international media experts as repressive and limiting press freedom. The law mandates that newspapers be deposited at several government offices before sale. The law also requires journalists, publishers, printers, and even vendors to register their place of residence with a court. Police authorities went to the homes of various journalists ostensibly to confirm their place of residence; however, some journalists reported feeling intimidated by these visits. Under the new law, journalists, publishers, printers, or vendors may be imprisoned for up to 5 years or fined up to $10,000 for a number of infractions including slander, inciting ethnic violence, and libel. The law allows the court to order the physical destruction of printing presses, if the court finds that the machinery was used to print an "inflammatory" article.

Workers employed by the Government in the state-owned radio and television enterprises often practice self-censorship. Although the new law has intimidated some of the private media, those with the political patronage of influential opposition members still criticize and disparage the Government.

In July journalists met with the Minister of Communication in an effort to moderate the new law. The Minister agreed to take their concerns under consideration, but no changes were made. In August the Government confiscated all journals not in compliance with the law. Journals reappeared for sale the following week, after having complied with the new regulations.

There were no known abridgements of academic freedom.

b. *Freedom of Peaceful Assembly and Association.*—The Constitution provides for freedom of assembly and association. In practice, any group wishing to hold a public assembly must inform the Minister of Interior, who reserves the right to forbid assemblies that threaten public order. The Minister of Interior, invoking this privilege, denied a request by a refugee organization to hold a meeting concerning problems being experienced with the government ministry charged with their protection (see Section 2.d.).

There are no restrictions on trade associations or professional bodies, and affiliation with international bodies is permitted.

c. *Freedom of Religion.*—The Constitution provides for freedom of religion, and the Government respects this right in practice.

d. *Freedom of Movement Within the Country, Foreign Travel, Emigration, and Repatriation.*—The Constitution provides for the right of all citizens to travel freely within Congo, and it specifically prohibits roadblocks and barriers. Nonetheless, military forces, political militias, and opportunists sometimes hindered free movement with barricades—generally demanding money. On occasion, motorists refusing to give money were detained for several hours. The National Conference Charter of Rights gives all citizens the right to travel abroad and return.

The approximately 3,000 refugees in Brazzaville continued to encounter serious human rights abuses. Security forces sometimes subjected Brazzaville-based refugees to arbitrary arrests, intimidation, and beatings, and the refugees also experienced bureaucratic ineptitude. Midyear the Government instituted a mandatory "sponsorship" policy, which requires refugee/asylum seekers to secure a pledge of financial support before it will process their claims. At year's end, the Brazzaville office of the United Nations High Commissioner for Refugees was working with the Government to reverse this requirement. There was one report of a forced expulsion, but this claim proved untrue.

In the Pointe-Noire area, the Congo hosts over 10,000 refugees, most of whom are from the Angolan enclave of Cabinda. There were no reports of human rights violations against this group. The Government provided first asylum to approximately 1,000 persons in 1996.

Section 3. *Respect for Political Rights: The Right of Citizens to Change Their Government*

The Constitution provides for popular election of the President and National Assembly. In a transition from one-party rule to democracy, the current President was elected in 1992. Legislative elections followed in 1993. A dispute over two legislative contests has not yet been resolved. The next presidential election is scheduled for 1997. In October successful, violence-free, indirect elections for one-third of the Senate's seats were carried out.

The Constitution divides power between the presidency and a government headed by a prime minister and formed with the approval of the National Assembly. The Constitution provides for 5-year terms of office for the President and National Assembly Deputies, all elected by universal suffrage, and 6-year terms for Senators, who are chosen by local councils. International monitors observed the last several rounds of legislative elections and found them to be free and fair.

The President sought to create a representative government by appointing members of each geographical region to the Cabinet.

There are no legal restrictions on representation by women or minority populations. However, women are underrepresented in government and politics. Women hold 4 of the 185 seats in the Senate and the National Assembly. Women occupy 3 of the 39 cabinet posts. Indigenous Pygmies are excluded from the political process (see Section 5).

Section 4. *Governmental Attitude Regarding International and Nongovernmental Investigation of Alleged Violations of Human Rights*

A wide variety of human rights groups operated with minimal government restriction, investigating and publishing their findings on human rights cases. Government officials were generally cooperative and responsive to their views, although prison visits by NGO's were sometimes restricted (see Section 1.c.). There were no visits by international human rights organizations.

Section 5. *Discrimination Based on Race, Sex, Religion, Disability, Language, or Social Status*

The Constitution specifically forbids such discrimination, but it persists in fact, particularly against women and Pygmies.

Women.—Domestic violence, including rape and beatings, is widespread but rarely reported. The problem is handled within the extended family and only in the most extreme instances is the matter brought to the police. Spousal abuse resulted in the death of eight women, according to a leading women's rights group. All of these cases are under judicial investigation.

There are no specific provisions under the law for spousal battery. Crises centers and hot lines are nonexistent. The problem of violence against women is largely ignored by the general population and the media.

The Constitution provides for the equality of all citizens, specifically prohibits discrimination based on sex, and specifically endorses the right of women to earn equal pay for equal work. In practice, however, women in the formal sector are underrepresented and encounter discriminatory promotion patterns. Most women work in the informal sector and thus have little or no access to credit. Women in rural areas are especially disadvantaged in terms of education and wage employment and are confined largely to family farm work, petty commerce, and childrearing responsibilities.

Marriage and family laws overtly discriminate against women. For example, adultery is illegal for women but not for men. Polygyny is legal; polyandry is not. While the Legal Code provides that 30 percent of an inheritance goes to the wife, in practice the wife generally loses all rights to the property. The "symbolic" nature of the brideprice set in the Family Code is often not respected, and men are forced to pay excessive amounts to the woman's family. As a result, the right to divorce is circumscribed for some women because they lack the financial means to reimburse the brideprice to the husband and his family. This problem is more prevalent in rural areas than in urban centers.

There are approximately 10 nongovernmental organizations that work on women's issues. Their effectiveness varies widely, however, and none is physically situated in rural areas. The Government's Ministry for the Integration of Women into Development is actively working with a number of nongovernmental organizations to educate women regarding their rights and to reform certain legal codes.

Children.—The Constitution states that the Government must protect children in accordance with international conventions. Child labor is illegal, and education is mandatory until age 16. In practice, limited state resources prevent public action toward achievement of these objectives, particularly in rural areas.

People With Disabilities.—The Constitution provides for "specific measures of protection in relation to their needs." In practice this means very little as the ministry charged with the welfare of the disabled has severe financial constraints. There is no overt discrimination against the disabled in employment and education. The Government has not implemented laws mandating access for people with disabilities.

Indigenous People.—The Constitution provides the same rights for Pygmies, an ethnic minority numbering in the tens of thousands, and living primarily in the northern forest regions, as it does for other citizens. In practice—in a society where Bantu Congolese predominate in every respect—Pygmies do not enjoy equal treatment. Pygmies are severely marginalized in the areas of employment, health, and education. They are often considered social inferiors, have no political voice, and are completely outside the political process. Many have never heard of the concept of voting and have no ability to influence government decisions affecting their interests.

Many Pygmies have a Bantu patron to whom they are obligated for perpetuity. Pygmies are inherited by their patron's eldest son upon his death. This arrangement has its roots in the ancestral tradition of pygmy slavery. In the informal sector, pygmy workers are generally underpaid for their labor relative to others, with compensation often being made in kind rather than wages, and they must gain permission from "their Bantu" before they can contract out their labor. Most Pygmies in the formal sector work for logging companies, and there are unconfirmed reports that Pygmies do not receive equal pay for equal work and are underrepresented in skilled labor and management positions.

There are credible reports that unless accompanied by a non-Pygmy, Pygmies are routinely denied medical treatment in the formal health sector; they are most often simply ignored or are asked to present documents that most Pygmies lack, such as national identification cards or national health cards. Credible sources also allege that Bantus are given first priority in national vaccination programs and that Pygmies are not vaccinated if there are not enough vaccination materials. In September a measles outbreak in Mbanza took the lives of 125 Pygmy children and 20 Bantu children, these figures are cited by one Western expert as proof that vaccination programs have historically prioritized Bantus over Pygmies. Investigation efforts by health officials reportedly focused exclusively on Bantu children.

Pygmy children who attend school are not always accorded equal treatment by their teachers and other educational authorities. Pygmy children are also routinely taunted by Bantu children, resulting in a difficult learning environment.

Section 6. Worker Rights

a. *The Right of Association.*—Both the Constitution and the Labor Code affirm the right to associate freely and allow no restriction on the formation of trade unions. Most workers in the formal (wage) sector are union members, and unions have made efforts to organize informal sectors such as agriculture and retail. The Constitution prohibits members of the security forces from forming unions or striking. There are six independent trade union organizations recognized by the State although not all are active.

Unions are free to strike but must file a letter of intent with the Ministry of Labor beforehand, thereby starting a process of arbitration. In theory, a strike may not take place until a process of nonbinding arbitration under the auspices of a regional labor inspector from the Labor Ministry has begun. The letter of intent must include the strike date, at which time the strike may legally begin even if arbitration is not complete. Employers have the right to fire workers if they give no advance notice of a strike.

In January negotiations broke down between the Government and the unions in four state-owned companies scheduled for privatization, and a strike was called. The Government ruled the strike to be illegal because the 3-day advance notice requirement was not observed. Workers not associated with the trade unions were requested to report to work. Armed members of the security forces reportedly went to the homes of known technicians (retired employees, etc.) and "encouraged" them to come to the assistance of the public service. The Government arrested four of the principal trade unionists and dismissed all workers who went on strike. Before going to trial, the four arrestees were beaten by security forces. Despite weak evidence, the four were convicted for "impeaching the freedom to work" and sentenced to 4 months in prison and fined. An international labor organization intervened on their behalf, raised bail money, and financed legal counsel. In March the four were granted a presidential pardon. The 120 dismissed striking workers were reinstated.

Unions are free to affiliate with international trade unions, and they maintain cooperative accords with other African, European, and American trade union organizations.

b. *The Right to Organize and Bargain Collectively.*—The Labor Code allows for collective bargaining and this provision is freely practiced. The Government sets industry-specific minimum wage scales, but unions are usually able to negotiate much higher wages for their members. Employers are prohibited from discriminating against employees who exercise their constitutional right to join a union. There were no reported firings for union activities.

There are no export processing zones.

c. *Prohibition on Forced or Compulsory Labor.*—The law prohibits forced or compulsory labor. There was, however, one instance when technicians were "encouraged" to come to the assistance of the public service (see Section 6.a.). There were also allegations that Pygmies experienced exploitation (see Section 5).

d. *Minimum Age for Employment of Children.*—The Constitution prohibits children under the age of 16 from working. The Ministry of Labor is responsible for enforcing child labor laws but concentrates its efforts only on the formal wage sector. Young children continued to work in the informal sector in cities, without government intervention.

e. *Acceptable Conditions of Work.*—The Government raised the minimum wage to $80 (CFAF 40,000) per month effective in March. This wage was not sufficient to provide a decent living for a worker and family. High urban prices and dependent extended families still obliged many workers to seek opportunities beyond their main employment or to practice subsistence agriculture.

The Constitution provides for reasonable pay, paid holidays, periodic paid vacation, and legal limits on allowable hours of work. The Labor Code stipulates that overtime must be paid for all work in excess of 40 hours per week and that regular days of leisure must be granted by employers. Although health and safety regulations require twice yearly visits by enforcement officers from the Ministry of Labor, in practice such inspections occur on a much less regular basis. There is no specific regulation granting workers the right to remove themselves from hazardous situations without jeopardy to continued employment, but unions are generally vigilant in calling attention to such situations.

COTE D'IVOIRE

From independence in 1960 until 1990, President Felix Houphouet-Boigny and his Democratic Party of Cote d'Ivoire (PDCI), then the only legal political party, governed the Republic of Cote d'Ivoire. The PDCI maintained this political dominance following multiparty presidential and legislative elections in 1990. Following Houphouet's death in 1993, National Assembly President Henri Konan Bedie became President by constitutional succession, and served out the remainder of Houphouet's term. Due to concerns about irregularities concerning the electoral code and voter registration, the major opposition parties boycotted the 1995 presidential election and tried to interfere with the voting process; however, President Bedie won 96 percent of the vote. The major political parties then reached an accord with Bedie, which allowed for full party participation in the 1995 legislative elections. The judiciary, although nominally independent, is subject to executive branch influence.

Security forces include the national police (Surete) and the Gendarmerie, a branch of the armed forces with responsibility for general law enforcement. The Gendarmerie is a national police force charged with maintenance of public order and territorial security. A new National Security Council, headed by the prior chief of the Gendarmerie, was formed in July to coordinate security policy, both internal and external. In August L'Etat Major de la Securite, a new structure focusing on internal security, and specifically on violent crime, earlier formed by the government began functioning. The Special Anti-Crime Police Brigade (SAVAC) continued its operations. Because of increased, violent incursions by armed Liberians, the Government designated Liberian border districts as part of a "military operational zone," where the armed forces are responsible for all security matters. The armed forces traditionally have accepted the primacy of civilian authority, although approximately 10 members of the military are in prison, accused of plotting a coup. Security forces including the SAVAC committed numerous human rights abuses.

The economy, largely market based but heavily dependent on the agricultural sector, performed poorly in recent years as high population growth coupled with economic decline resulted in a steady fall in living standards. Although the economy grew in 1995 and 1996 as major structural reforms continued, there has not yet been a significant reduction in poverty or improvement in social indicators such as mortality or literacy rates. Gross national product per capita in 1996 was about $730, and the economy expanded by about 7 percent. Principal exports are cocoa, coffee, and tropical timber; however, most of the rural population remains dependent on smallholder cash crop production. The country reached net self-sufficiency in oil and gas in 1995 with prospects for increased production.

The Government's human rights record improved in some areas, but serious human rights abuses continued. Members of the security forces committed extrajudicial killings, and the security forces beat and abused detainees and used force to disperse protestors. The Government also used arbitrary arrest and detention and failed to bring perpetrators of these abuses to justice. Prolonged detention is a problem, and prison conditions are harsh and life threatening. The judiciary does not ensure due process and is subject to executive branch influence, particularly in political cases. The Government limits citizens' right to change their government and restricts freedom of speech, the press, assembly, association, and movement. Three journalists imprisoned in December 1995 for criticizing the Government and Chief of State were pardoned on December 31. Discrimination and violence against women and female genital mutilation (FGM) remain problems. In September the Government announced a campaign to eliminate FGM.

RESPECT FOR HUMAN RIGHTS

Section 1. *Respect for the Integrity of the Person, Including Freedom From:*

a. *Political and Other Extrajudicial Killing.*—There were no reports of politically motivated killings by government forces. However, as violent civil crime continued at high levels, the security forces frequently resorted to lethal force and committed numerous extrajudicial killings. Credible media reports indicate that the Special Anticrime Police Brigade (SAVAC) continued its shoot-to-kill policy when pursuing criminal suspects. Corpses of alleged criminals killed by SAVAC or police personnel are regularly displayed on television and in the newspapers. According to press estimates, SAVAC and the regular police killed more than 20 persons. The Government did not prosecute SAVAC or police personnel for these killings.

In August police shot and killed a truck driver. The Minister of Security stated that the police implicated in the shooting had been questioned and justice was "following its course." By year's end, no arrests had been made.

Six detainees held since the "active boycott" of multiparty elections in October 1995 died in prison (see Section 1.c.).

The Government promised to investigate all killings that occurred in October 1995, during the "active boycott" of the election. These deaths included four protesters, eight demonstrators, and two security force members. However, by year's end the Government had taken no action.

b. *Disappearance.*—There were no reports of politically motivated disappearances.

c. *Torture and Other Cruel, Inhuman, or Degrading Treatment or Punishment.*—Despite legal protection for the rights of persons in custody, police sometimes beat detainees or prisoners as punishment, or to extract confessions, according to local human rights groups. There were no public reports of government officials being tried for these abuses.

A jurists' union official reported that police continue to beat suspects to obtain their confessions and that suspects are afraid to press charges against the police officers involved. Press photographs regularly show criminal detainees with swollen or bruised faces and bodies.

Police frequently use violence to restrain demonstrators. Riot police used tear gas and truncheons against unemployed demonstrators in January. Police used tear gas against transport workers demonstrating against the president of their union in August.

Prison conditions are harsh and life threatening. Problems include overcrowding, malnutrition, a high incidence of infectious disease, and lack of treatment facilities and medication, which are the conditions responsible for a high prisoner death rate throughout the prison community. Several journalists released last year reported that white-collar prisoners are accorded special treatment. According to press reports, six "active boycott" detainees died in prison, and one became paralyzed after an illness.

According to a Ivorian Human Rights League (LIDHO) report, conditions at the main prison of Abidjan are especially hazardous for women, with violent and nonviolent criminals, as well as minors, housed together. There are no health facilities for women, and reportedly a number of women have given birth at the prison without medical attention. There are credible reports of female prisoners being raped by prison guards.

Local human rights groups have difficulty gaining access to the prison. Officials denied LIDHO and other human rights groups access to the prison at various times this year.

d. *Arbitrary Arrest, Detention, or Exile.*—Under the Code of Penal Procedure, a public prosecutor may order the detention of a suspect for up to 48 hours without bringing charges. A magistrate may order detention up to 4 months but must also provide the Minister of Justice with a written justification for continued detention on a monthly basis. However, the law is often violated. Police have held persons for more than 48 hours without bringing charges. According to a representative of the jurists' union, this practice is common, and often magistrates are not able to verify that those not charged are released. Defendants are not guaranteed the right to a judicial determination of the legality of their detention. A judge may release pretrial detainees on provisional liberty if the judge believes that the suspect will not flee. However, according to LIDHO, many prisoners are detained for long periods, sometimes years, awaiting trial. While reliable statistics are lacking, pretrial detainees probably make up 10 percent of the prison population.

Information provided by one of the lawyers defending active boycott members suggests that approximately 100 are still being detained awaiting judicial action. An estimated 450 such persons were arrested; 19 were tried and released for lack of evidence; and 184 were released on provisional liberty awaiting trial. Of those tried and sentenced, 6 died in prison, 12 accepted a presidential pardon available to any nonviolent offender (after agreeing not to appeal their sentences), 6 were released on provisional liberty and have had their sentences overturned, 9 are serving their sentences, and 95 have completed their sentences. Figures on active boycott members published in the government-controlled newspaper are significantly lower. Three journalists, imprisoned for criticizing the President, had their final appeals denied, but were pardoned and released on December 31.

Although prohibited by law, police restrict access to some prisoners. Despite the frequency of arbitrary arrest, there is no accurate total of suspects held.

There are more than 10 military officers in detention, reportedly as the result of allegedly plotting a coup at the time of the October 1995 Presidential election.

The Government does not use forced exile.

e. *Denial of Fair Public Trial.*—According to the Constitution, the judiciary is independent of the executive branch in ordinary criminal cases. In practice, however, it follows the lead of the executive in national security or politically sensitive cases. There continue to be credible reports that those with ties to the opposition are treated more harshly by the judicial system than those with ties to the Government. Judges serve at the pleasure of the executive, and therefore reports of political pressure on the judiciary are credible.

The formal judicial system is headed by a Supreme Court and includes the court of appeals and lower courts.

In rural areas, traditional institutions often administer justice at the village level, handling domestic disputes and minor land questions in accordance with customary law. Dispute resolution is by extended debate, with no known instance of resort to physical punishment. The formal court system is increasingly superseding traditional mechanisms. In August a Grand Mediateur was appointed to settle disputes that cannot be settled at the traditional level. Although this mechanism is not yet active, it appears designed to bridge traditional and modern methods of dispute resolution.

Military courts do not try civilians. Although there are no appellate courts within the military court system, persons convicted by a military tribunal may petition the Supreme Court to set aside the tribunal's verdict and order a retrial.

The law provides for the right to public trial, although key evidence is sometimes given secretly. Those convicted have the right of appeal, and the Appellate Court, in a departure from the norm, overturned on appeal the convictions of several active boycott members. Several others had their sentences reduced.

Defendants accused of felonies or capital crimes have the right to legal counsel, and the judicial system provides for court-appointed attorneys for indigent defendants. In practice, many defendants cannot afford private counsel, and court-appointed attorneys are not readily available. According to one lawyer, even if a defendant has an attorney, he may not be notified of his trial date until the day before the trial, making it impossible for his lawyer to attend or provide a defense.

There were no reports of political prisoners in civilian jails at year's end. Regarded as political prisoners, the three journalists who were serving sentences throughout the year for criticizing the President lost their appeals, but were pardoned and released on December 31. For the last year, as many as 30 military officers and enlisted men have been held in detention, reportedly as the result of alleged coup plotting at the time of the presidential election in 1995. In November a military commission of inquiry met and seven of those held were dismissed from the army, six were returned to their units, and four were disciplined by being dismissed from the army for 16 months.

f. *Arbitrary Interference With Privacy, Family, Home, or Correspondence.*—The Code of Penal Procedure specifies that a police official or investigative magistrate may conduct searches of homes without a judicial warrant if there is reason to believe that there is evidence on the premises concerning a crime. The official must have the prosecutor's agreement to retain any evidence seized in the search and is required to have witnesses to the search, which may not take place between 9 p.m. and 4 a.m. In practice, police have sometimes used a general search warrant without a name or address. On occasion, police have entered homes of non-Ivorian Africans (or apprehended them at large), taken them to local police stations, and extorted small amounts of money for alleged minor offenses.

Security forces reportedly monitored some private telephone conversations, but the extent of the practice is unknown. There is no evidence that private written correspondence is monitored by authorities.

Section 2. Respect for Civil Liberties, Including:

a. *Freedom of Speech and Press.*—Although the Constitution provides for freedom of expression, and independent newspapers frequently criticize government policies, the Government imposes significant restrictions. The two government-owned daily newspapers offer little criticism of government policy, while government-owned radio and television offer none at all. Moreover, while independent and opposition newspapers (9 daily, several weekly), opposition leaders, and student groups voice their disapproval of governmental or presidential actions frequently and sometimes loudly, the Government does not tolerate what it considers insults or attacks on the honor of the country's highest officials. It is a crime, punishable by 3 months to 2 years in prison, to offend the President, the Prime Minister, foreign chiefs of state or government, or their diplomatic representatives, or to defame institutions of the State. Moreover, a 1991 press law created a Commission to enforce laws against publishing material "undermining the reputation of the nation or defaming institutions of the State." Journalists exercise considerable self-censorship, particularly in writing about the President.

In August the editor of the daily paper Le Populaire was arrested after publication of an article alleging an abuse of power by a public prosecutor. The article included a photo of an internal Gendarmerie document, and the editor was charged with possession of a controlled government document but subsequently released. Three opposition party journalists, convicted of insulting the President for the publication of an article attributing the poor performance of an Ivorian soccer team to his presence at an international match, stayed in prison throughout the year while exhausting their appeals. They were pardoned and released on December 31.

The Government owns both television channels and two major radio stations; only the primary government radio and television stations are broadcast nationwide. There are also four radio stations not controlled by the government (British Broadcasting Corporation, Radio France Internationale, Africa Number 1, and a private commercial station concentrating on entertainment). There is also a private television subscription service, Canal Horizon. While the independent stations have complete control over their editorial content, the Government continues to exercise considerable influence over official media program content, news coverage, and other matters, using these media to promote government policies. Much of the news programming is devoted to the activities of the President, the Government, the PDCI, and pro-Bedie groups.

Many prominent scholars are active in opposition politics and are not known to have suffered professionally, although some teachers and professors suggest that they have been transferred because of their political activities. According to press reports and student union statements, students continue to be used as informants at the University of Abidjan.

b. *Freedom of Peaceful Assembly and Association.*—The Constitution provides for freedom of assembly. In practice, however, that freedom is restricted when the Government perceives a danger to public order, as it did during the October 1995 elections, when it used lethal force to control antigovernment demonstrations, which it had banned by decree.

Groups that wish to hold demonstrations or rallies are required to submit a notice of their intent to do so to the Ministry of Security or Interior 48 hours before the proposed event. The Government sometimes denied the opposition permission to meet in public outdoor venues. Following opposition demonstrations in September 1995, the Government announced that "all marches and sit-ins would be banned for a 3-month period in all streets and public places." The decree was selectively applied; only opposition events were affected by the ban. Penalties for infraction ranged from no action to 12 months' imprisonment.

Police occasionally prohibit gatherings to prevent the expression of controversial views. An "anti-vandalism" law passed by the National Assembly in 1992 holds organizers of a march or demonstration responsible if any of the participants engage in violence. LIDHO and all major opposition parties condemned the law as unduly vague and as one that imposed collective punishment for the crimes of a few.

The Constitution states that people are free to organize associations, and the implementing law states that organizations must register, but does not require any authorization. Consequently, opposition parties assert that the Constitution permits private associations to form, and since the Constitution does not mention registration, requiring associations to register is unconstitutional. The Government rejects this interpretation and requires all organizations to register before commencing activities. There were no reports in the past 5 years of denial of registration.

The law prohibits the formation of political parties along ethnic or religious lines. In 1991 the Government banned the previously registered student union FESCI after a student was killed by other students. The ban was never rescinded, although FESCI was tolerated until May 1994 when the Government again insisted that the organization was banned, arresting several members of its executive bureau. FESCI remained banned but continues to contend that it was never legally banned and has been active in demonstrations, ceremonies, and political party conventions. There has never been a legal determination of its status.

In August the police burned a dormitory room and used tear gas to disperse a FESCI meeting. On December 11, when the body of a FESCI leader who died in self exile was returned to the country, the police harassed and beat a group of FESCI members at the airport. On December 12, the police broke up an informal memorial service organized by students and held on the university campus. On December 19, four FESCI leaders appeared at the office of the Minister of Security (reportedly at his invitation) but were arrested. On January 7, 1997 three of the four were convicted and sentenced to 2 years in prison under the "anti-vandalism" law and laws against disturbing the public order.

c. *Freedom of Religion.*—The Constitution provides for freedom of religion, and there are no known impediments to religious expression. There is no dominant religion, and no faith is officially favored. The Government permits the open practice of religion, and there are no restrictions on religious ceremonies or teaching. Nevertheless, some Muslims believe that their religious or ethnic affiliation makes them targets of discrimination by the Government with regard to high governmental positions and national identity documentation. Native Muslims are frequently subject to petty harassment as part of general pressure against Muslims from neighboring countries and, despite being a plurality of the population, are a definite minority at all levels of government.

d. *Freedom of Movement Within the Country, Foreign Travel, Emigration, and Repatriation.*—The law provides for these rights, and the Government respects them in practice. While the Government does not generally restrict internal travel, uniformed police regularly extort small amounts of money or goods for contrived or minor infractions by motorists or passengers on public conveyances. Citizens normally may travel abroad and emigrate freely and have the right of voluntary repatriation. There are no known cases of revocation of citizenship. However, the Government sometimes restricts foreign travel for political reasons.

Cote d'Ivoire is a signatory to the 1951 United Nations Convention on Refugees and its 1967 Protocol; it has signed but not ratified the Organization of African Unity convention governing the specific aspects of refugee problems in Africa. The right to first asylum is recognized by law and custom, and there are currently 305,000 Liberian refugees residing in Cote d'Ivoire. The Government cooperates with the United Nations High Commissioner for Refugees in health, education, and food distribution programs for refugees and agreed in principle to permit Liberians to cast absentee ballots should elections take place in their homeland in 1997.

In April serious factional fighting in Monrovia caused thousands of its residents to seek escape. On May 7, the Bulk Challenge, a Nigerian freighter carrying up to 3,500 passengers, arrived at San Pedro. Many passengers may have had a credible claim to asylum. U.N. and voluntary agencies expressed concern that the ship may have been unseaworthy, and that conditions aboard possibly posed a threat to life. The Government permitted most of the Liberian women and children to disembark temporarily. However, it did not authorize the UNHCR to screen the passengers for refugee status. Government officials cited a threat to national security, alleging that factional fighters were on board. The Government feared that more ships bearing asylum seekers would follow. After making repairs to the ship, the Government ordered the Bulk Challenge to reboard its passengers and sail for Ghana on May 9. Several deaths were reported before the ship reached Takoradi, Ghana, on May 13 where its passengers were granted asylum.

Section 3. *Respect for Political Rights: The Right of Citizens to Change Their Government*

Although the Constitution provides citizens with the right to change their government peacefully through democratic means, the Government limited this right in practice. The opposition complained that the Government used the 1994 electoral code to place formidable obstacles in the path of political rivals. The Rassemblement des Republicains held that Alassane Ouattara, a leading opposition rival to Bedie, had been unfairly excluded from entering the Presidential race due to the code's parentage, residency, and citizenship requirements. The opposition also complained of faulty voter registration procedures and of unfair restrictions on demonstrations after the Government issued a 3-month ban on marches and sit-ins in September 1995 in an attempt to guarantee public order (see Section 2.b.).

Under a multiparty system adopted in 1990, elections are held every 5 years by secret ballot. All citizens over 21 years of age can vote, and political parties are legally free to organize.

A presidential election was held in 1995. The major opposition parties boycotted the election due to the Electoral Code's candidacy requirements and voter registration irregularities. The Opposition defied the national laws regarding law and order and called for "active boycott" of the polls during the presidential election. They blocked polling places from access by voters and prevented delivery of election materials to the polls. Only the ruling PDCI and a single small opposition party, the PIT, fielded presidential candidates. President Bedie won 96 percent of the votes cast.

Afterward, the major political parties reached an accord that ensured full party participation in the 1995 legislative elections. These elections were, however, suspended in 3 of the 175 districts due to government concern over Bete-Baoule ethnic violence and voters displaced as a result of the active boycott. Election results from another three districts were declared invalid by the Constitutional Council. Elections in these six districts and two other open seats were held on December 29 and proceeded in an orderly, transparent manner. Of the eight legislative races, the PDCI won three and the FPI won five.

While there are no legal impediments to women assuming political leadership roles, only 14 of the 169 deputies elected to the National Assembly in November 1995 are women. Women hold 3 of the 17 leadership positions in the Assembly. There are 3 women in the 30-member presidential cabinet named in January, and 3 members of the Supreme Court are women. There are no impediments to the exercise of political rights by any of the over 60 ethnic groups.

Section 4. Governmental Attitude Regarding International and Nongovernmental Investigation of Alleged Violations of Human Rights

LIDHO, formed in 1987 and recognized by the Government in July 1990, has actively investigated alleged violations of human rights and issued press releases and reports, some critical of the Government. Other groups such as the International Movement of Democratic Women (MIFED) have held seminars and published press releases critical of government abuses of human rights. The Ministry of Family and Womens' Affairs and the Ministry of Communication have recently taken part in several NGO-sponsored campaigns to fight female genital mutilation (FGM) and violence against women.

Foreign government funding allowed Gerddes, a local NGO, to train the presidents of voting bureaus. Observatoire National des Elections (ONE), an umbrella group of local NGO's received official sanction and government cooperation for observing the December 29 elections.

The Government has cooperated with international inquiries into its human rights practices.

Section 5. Discrimination Based on Race, Sex, Religion, Disability, Language, or Social Status

Discrimination based on race, ethnicity, national origin, sex, or religion is prohibited by law, but in practice women occupy a subordinate role in society. In other respects, the Government enforces these provisions.

Women.—Representatives of women's organizations state that wife beating—while not widespread—does occur and often leads to divorce. Doctors state that they rarely see the victims of such violence. A severe social stigma is attached to domestic violence, and neighbors often intervene in quarrels to protect a woman who is the object of physical abuse. The courts and police view domestic violence as a family problem, unless serious bodily harm is inflicted or the victim lodges a complaint, in which case they may initiate criminal proceedings. The Ivorian Association for the Defense of Women (AIDF) and MIFED have protested the indifference of authorities to female victims of violence and called attention to domestic violence and FGM. The groups also reported that women who are the subject of rape or domestic violence are often ignored when they attempt to bring the violence to the attention of the police. The Government does not collect statistics on the rape or other physical abuse of women. The Government has no clear cut policy regarding spouse abuse beyond the strictures against violence in the Civil Code. In October the Minister of Communications opened an NGO-sponsored forum on violence against women and said that there would be more government action in this area.

In rural areas, ethnic custom dictates that women perform most menial tasks, although farm work by men is also common. Government policy encourages full participation by women in social and economic life, but there is considerable informal resistance among employers to hiring women, whom they consider less dependable by virtue of potential pregnancy. Women are underrepresented in some professions and in the managerial sector as a whole. Women in the formal sector, however, are paid on an equal scale with men.

Children.—The Ministries of Social Affairs and of Health and Social Protection seek to safeguard the welfare of children, and the Government has also encouraged the formation of NGO's such as the Abidjan Legal Center for the Defense of Children. In September the Government announced that it would hold parents legally and financially responsible for their abandoned children.

Primary education is compulsory but this requirement is not effectively enforced. Many children leave school after only a few years. There is a parental preference for educating boys, which is noticeable throughout the country but more pronounced in rural areas. According to an International Monetary Fund report, giving statistics for 1987–1992, stated that 81 percent of males and 58 percent of females attend primary schools. A 1996 United Nations Development Program report states that 1993 combined primary, secondary, and tertiary school enrollment was 31.1 percent of females and 47.5 percent of males. Sexual harassment of female students by male teachers is commonplace.

Female genital mutilation, which is widely condemned by international health experts as damaging to both physical and psychological health, is a serious problem. There is no legislation that specifically prohibits FGM, and it is considered illegal only as a violation of general laws prohibiting crimes against persons. It is practiced particularly among the rural population in the North and West. The procedure is usually performed on young girls or at puberty as part of a rite of passage; it is always done outside modern medical facilities. According to the World Health Organization, as many as 60 percent of women have undergone FGM.

A local NGO formed a committee in May to campaign against FGM. It opened with a series of seminars on FGM and violence against women. The NGO president enlisted President Bedie's support for the campaign and the Minister of Communications has lent personal support by attending and speaking at seminars. In September the Ministry of the Family and Women's Affairs announced a campaign against the practice. New laws prohibiting FGM reportedly are being prepared. However, traditional authorities continued to uphold the practice.

People With Disabilities.—There are no laws mandating accessibility for the disabled. Laws exist prohibiting the abandonment of the mentally or physically disabled, as well as enjoining acts of violence directed at them. Traditional practices, beliefs, and superstitions vary, but infanticide in cases of serious birth disabilities is less commonplace than in the past. Disabled adults are not the specific targets of abuse, but it is difficult for them to compete with able-bodied workers in the tight job market. The Government supports special schools, associations, and artisans' cooperatives for the disabled.

National/Racial/Ethnic Minorities.—Among both Ivorians and non-Ivorians, it is a widely-held perception that police routinely abuse and harass non-Ivorian Africans residing in Cote d'Ivoire (who represent one-third of the total population). This activity reflects the Ivorian conclusion that foreigners are responsible for high local crime rates and the concern over Ivorian national identity. Election law changes in 1995 limited candidates to those who could prove that both parents had been born in Cote d'Ivoire, and several recent, well-publicized cases have demonstrated that the concept of "Ivorianness" is being used to determine employability.

Members of the Bete ethnic group allege discrimination by the more powerful Baoule tribal group. The Baoules are the single largest tribal group in the country and have been politically dominant. According to the Bete, in 1970 members of the army (under Baoule command) killed 4,000 Bete in the Gagnoa region. Tensions between the groups escalated before the 1995 presidential elections, again in the Gagnoa region, and four people were killed during rioting (see Section 1.a.).

Section 6. Worker Rights

a. *The Right of Association.*—The law provides workers with the right to form unions. The government-sponsored labor confederation, the General Union of Workers of Cote d'Ivoire (UGTCI), dominated most union activity for decades. The UGTCI's hold on the labor movement loosened in 1991 when several formerly UGTCI-affiliated unions broke away and became independent. In 1992 11 formerly independent unions joined together to form the Federation of Autonomous Trade Unions of Cote d'Ivoire. Unions are free to join these and other groups. Registration of a new union requires 3 months under the law.

The right to strike is provided by the Constitution and by statute. The Labor Code requires a protracted series of negotiations and a 6-day notification period before a strike may take place, effectively making legal strikes difficult to organize. The UGTCI seldom calls strikes. Non-UGTCI unions have frequently called strikes. Transport workers in Youpougon struck in August after police shot and killed a driver, purportedly when he tried to run a traffic stop. The Minister of Security announced that the police had aimed for the vehicle's tires but missed.

Unions are free to join international bodies.

b. *The Right to Organize and Bargain Collectively.*—The Labor Code grants all citizens, except members of the police and military, the right to join unions and to

bargain collectively. Collective bargaining agreements are in effect in many major business enterprises and sectors of the civil service. In most cases in which wages are not established in direct negotiations between unions and employers, salaries are set by job categories by the Ministry of Employment and Civil Service. Labor inspectors have the responsibility to enforce a law that prohibits antiunion discrimination.
There are no export processing zones.

c. *Prohibition of Forced or Compulsory Labor.*—There were no reports of forced labor, which is prohibited by law. However, the International Labor Organization's Committee of Experts in its 1993 annual report questioned a decree that places certain categories of prisoners at the disposal of private enterprises for work assignments without their apparent consent. There has been no change in this decree.

d. *Minimum Age for Employment of Children.*—In most instances, the legal minimum working age is 16 years, and the Ministry of Employment and Civil Service enforces this provision effectively in the civil service and in large multinational companies. Labor law limits the hours of young workers, defined as those under the age of 18. However, children often work on family farms, and some children routinely act as vendors in the informal sector in cities. There are reliable reports of some use of child labor in informal sector mining and also of children working in "sweatshop" conditions in small workshops. Many children leave the formal school system at an early age; primary education is mandatory but far from universally enforced, particularly in rural areas.

e. *Acceptable Conditions of Work.*—The Government administratively determines monthly minimum wage rates, which were last adjusted following devaluation of the cfa franc in January 1994. A slightly higher minimum wage rate applies for construction workers. The Government enforces the minimum wage rates only for salaried workers employed by the Government or registered with the social security office. Minimum wages vary according to occupation, with the lowest set at approximately $71.49 (cfa 36,607) per month, which is insufficient to provide a decent standard of living for a worker and family. The majority of the labor force works in agriculture or in the informal sector where the minimum wage does not apply.

Through the Ministry of Employment and the Civil Service, the Government enforces a comprehensive Labor Code governing the terms and conditions of service for wage earners and salaried workers and providing for occupational safety and health standards. Those employed in the formal sector are reasonably protected against unjust compensation, excessive hours, and arbitrary discharge from employment. The standard legal workweek is 40 hours. The law requires overtime payment on a graduated scale for additional hours. The Labor Code provides for at least one 24-hour rest period per week.

Government labor inspectors can order employers to improve substandard conditions, and a labor court can levy fines if the employer fails to comply. In the large informal sector of the economy, however, involving both urban and rural workers, the Government's occupational health and safety regulations are enforced erratically at best. Workers in the formal sector have the right, under the Labor Code, to remove themselves from dangerous work without jeopardy to continued employment by utilizing the Ministry of Labor inspection system to document dangerous working conditions. However, workers in the informal sector cannot ordinarily remove themselves from such labor without losing their employment.

DJIBOUTI

Despite 1992 constitutional changes that permitted the creation of four political parties, President Hassan Gouled Aptidon and the People's Rally for Progress (RPP), in power since independence in 1977, continued to rule the country. Djibouti's two main ethnic groups are the politically predominant Issa (the tribe of the President, which is of Somali origin) and the Afar (who are also numerous in Ethiopia and Eritrea). The Afar comprise the largest single tribe in Djibouti but are outnumbered by the Issa and other Somali clans (Issak and Gadabursi) taken together. The judiciary is not independent of the executive.

In 1994, the Government and a faction of the Afar-led Front for the Restoration of Unity and Democracy (FRUD) signed a peace accord, ending 3 years of civil war. As part of the accord, the Government agreed to recognize the FRUD as a legitimate political party. The Government named two FRUD leaders to key cabinet posts in 1995, but no Afar has been named since then. The FRUD was legalized in March but a party congress had not been held by year's end. The other two officially recognized opposition parties, the Party for Democratic Renewal (PRD) and the National

Democratic Party (PND), do not hold parliamentary seats, in large part because the PND boycotted the 1992 legislative elections. As a result, the RPP won all 65 parliamentary seats. With the reelection of President Gouled in 1993, it now holds all significant government posts as well.

The 8,000-member National Police Force (FNP) has primary responsibility for internal security and border control and is overseen by the Ministry of Interior. The Ministry of Defense controls the army and the gendarmerie, and a small intelligence bureau reports directly to the President. Civilian authorities generally maintain effective control of the security forces, but there were instances in which the security forces acted independently of the Government's authority, and some members committed a number of human rights abuses.

Djibouti has little industry; services and commerce provide most of the national income, which is largely generated by the foreign expatriate community of 12,000, including 3,300 French soldiers, and the state-controlled maritime and commercial activities of the Port of Djibouti, the airport, and the Addis Ababa-Djibouti Railroad. Only a few mineral deposits exist in the country, and the arid soil is unproductive—only 10 percent is pasture and 1 percent is forested. People are free to pursue private business interests and to hold personal and real property. That part of the gross national product that benefits citizens (and thus excludes the expatriates) is estimated at about $250 per capita.

The Government's human rights record remained poor despite a limited multiparty political system. Members of the security forces committed several extrajudicial killings. There were credible reports that some members of the security forces beat detainees and denied proper medical treatment to some inmates. The Government continued to harass, intimidate, and imprison opponents. It continued to arrest and detain persons arbitrarily, holding them beyond the 48 hours permitted by law, and to infringe upon citizens' right to privacy. The judiciary is not independent of the executive. The Government permitted freedom of the press but cracked down heavily on union leaders and politicians critical of the President. Discrimination against women persists, and the practice of female genital mutilation continued to be nearly universal. Discrimination against ethnic minorities persists.

RESPECT FOR HUMAN RIGHTS

Section 1. Respect for the Integrity of the Person, Including Freedom From:

a. *Political and Other Extrajudicial Killing.*—Security forces were responsible for at least five extrajudicial killings. On January 9, while trying to break up a student demonstration over nonpayment of scholarships, the FNP in Ali Sabieh shot and killed 16-year-old Mohamed Idriss. Security forces killed two inmates at Djibouti's main Gabode prison during a February 3 riot over poor prison conditions (see Section 1.c.). On May 2, the FNP in Djibouti City shot and killed a bystander while breaking up a demonstration over the detention of the Government's former Treasurer. The Government has not punished the perpetrators of any of these killings.

In January there was a credible report that 26-year-old Mohamed Abdillahi Ismail died in his prison cell after not receiving treatment for tuberculosis. There were political undertones in the July 13 death in custody of Mohamoud Mohamed Ali; Ali was a potential witness in a criminal case against a former high-ranking politician, Moumin Bahdon Farah. The Government claimed that Ali died from tuberculosis. There was no police investigation and only a superficial autopsy. Another prisoner died from tuberculosis due to official negligence (see Section 1.e.).

There were no developments regarding the 1995 killings of Randa's religious leader, Ali Houmed Souleh, and an associate, Said Aramis. The Government continued to hold 11 soldiers accused of taking part in the killings.

b. *Disappearance.*—There were no reports of politically motivated disappearances. There were no developments in the 1995 abduction of four persons by armed men in the north, or the 1995 kidnaping of a traditional Afar chief at Alalli Dada by unknown persons.

c. *Torture and Other Cruel, Inhuman, or Degrading Treatment or Punishment.*—The Constitution states that no one shall be subjected to torture or to other inhumane, cruel, degrading, or humiliating punishments. Torture is punishable by 15 years in prison. However, there were credible reports that police and prison officials sometimes beat and otherwise physically abused prisoners and detainees. In January the PRD's newspaper reported that Djama Hersi Omar, a security guard allegedly involved in a theft case, was punched, kicked, hanged by his feet, and had his head dipped in ice water by members of the gendarmerie. The gendarmerie denied the accusations. In March the PND's newspaper reported that Djama Dabar Waberi was kicked and punched by security forces for his antigovernment views.

Prison conditions are harsh and characterized by severe overcrowding. Gabode prison, built for 300 persons, has more than twice that many inmates. Reportedly, prisoners must pay authorities to obtain food. The February 3 riot at Gabode prison was started by inmates who were unhappy about not being fed adequately. Security forces killed the inmates while suppressing the riot (see Section 1.a.). Several different groups of inmates went on hunger strikes during the year to protest poor nutrition and inadequate health care. Mohamed Abdillahi Ismail died of tuberculosis in his cell in January, according to the PND's newspaper. When the inmate's condition worsened, he was transferred to an isolated cell in the prison infirmary rather than transported to a local hospital. Reports also indicate that illegal aliens jailed for crimes sometimes have young children with them. There were, however, no reports of rape of female prisoners. The International Committee of the Red Cross (ICRC) staff no longer reside in the country. When present, they normally had access to all prisoners. An ICRC representative from Nairobi, Kenya visited the main prison in Djibouti during the year.

d. *Arbitrary Arrest, Detention, or Exile.*—The 1994 Penal Code stipulates that the State may not detain a person beyond 48 hours without an examining magistrate's formal charge. Detainees may be held another 48 hours with the prior approval of Djibouti's public prosecutor. Persons charged with political or national security offenses may be detained as long as an investigation is underway. Nevertheless, the police often disregarded these procedures, normally arresting persons without warrants and sometimes detaining persons for lengthy periods. The Penal Code provides for bail and expeditious trial. Incommunicado detention is used.

In May, in the midst of a strike by school teachers, security forces detained Mariam Hassan Ali, the Secretary General of the teachers union, and three union leaders for several hours without providing any explanation. In June the official newspaper reported that 18 inmates waited months to be released because of inaction by then-Justice Minister Moumin Bahdon Farah. Mohamed Mahamoud Ali, the potential witness in the theft case against Farah, was arbitrarily detained from June 20 until his death on July 13 (see Sections 1.a. and 1.c.). Amir Adaweh, the editor-in-chief of the PND's newspaper La Republique, spent several days in detention in July after being accused of organizing a protest in support of political prisoners. In August the Government sentenced five members of a splinter group within the ruling party, including three former ministers, to a 6-month prison term and fines of $1,200 for criticizing President Gouled (see Section 1.e.).

An Afar politician, Muhyadin Matdih Vedir, was allegedly arrested in August on political grounds at the request of the Ethiopian government. There were no developments in the cases of alleged terrorists Awalle Guelle Assone and Mohamed Hassan Farah, who were arrested in 1994 for the 1990 bombing of a cafe. The Government's investigation into their roles in the attack was ongoing at year's end. Mohamed Ali Areyte was arrested in 1995 as part of the same case. In April the French Government issued an international arrest warrant for PND president Aden Robleh Awaleh and his wife, Aicha Omar Dabar, for their part in the cafe bombing.

The Government does not use forced exile.

e. *Denial of Fair Public Trial.*—The Constitution provides for an independent judiciary, and magistrates are appointed for life terms. In practice, however, the judiciary is not independent of the executive. Constitutional provisions for a fair trial are generally respected in nonpolitical cases. There were reportedly political reasons for the May ouster of four of the five appellate court judges: Zakaria Abdillahi Ali, Emile David, Chantal Clement, and Nabiha Djama Sed. The Government also replaced Chief Prosecutor Ali Mohamed Afkada for political reasons.

In June 1995, the Government took steps to strengthen the rule of law by disbanding the special State Security Court, which in the past had handled cases of espionage, treason, and acts threatening the public order or "the interest of the republic" outside normal judicial channels. Another special court, the Superior Court of Justice, rules on cases of embezzlement of public funds and is theoretically empowered to try the President and government ministers. The Supreme Court is the only judicial body that can overrule decisions of the lower courts. A Constitutional Council rules on the constitutionality of laws, including those related to the protection of human rights and civil liberties. In August the Constitutional Council ruled that the Parliament's disciplinary committee wrongly denied the parliamentary immunity of three legislators. The Government ignored the Constitutional Council's ruling and launched a personal attack in the press on the Council's members.

The legal system is composed of legislation and executive decrees, French codified law adopted at independence, Shari'a (Islamic) law, and traditions of the native nomadic peoples. Crimes committed in urban centers are dealt with in accordance with French-inspired law and judicial practice in the regular courts. Civil actions may be brought in these courts or in the traditional courts. Shari'a law is restricted to civil and family matters.

The Constitution states that the accused is innocent until proven guilty, has the right to legal counsel, and the right to be examined by a doctor if imprisoned. Legal counsel is available to the indigent in criminal and civil matters. Court cases are heard in public before a presiding judge and two accompanying judges. The latter receive assistance from two persons—assessors—who are not members of the bench, but who possess a sufficient legal sophistication to comprehend court proceedings. The Government selects the assessors from the public at large, but credible reports indicate that political and ethnic affiliations may play a role in the appointment process.

There were five political prisoners: Moumin Bahdon Farah, the former Justice Minister; Ahmed Boulaleh Barreh, the former Defense Minister; Ali Mahamade Houmed, the former Industry Minister; Ismael Guedi Hared, the former presidential cabinet Director; and Abdillahi Guirreh, a former ruling party Annex President. Accused of inciting people to violence, using tribalism for political ends, and disseminating false information, the five were stripped of their party membership. After claiming in a published statement that President Gouled rules Djibouti by terror and force without regard to the Constitution, the five were sentenced to 6 months in jail, fined $1,200, and prohibited from running for elected office for a period of 5 years. The Constitution prohibits such condemnations of the President.

f. *Arbitrary Interference With Privacy, Family, Home, or Correspondence.*—The Constitution provides for the inviolability of the family, home, correspondence, and communications. The law also requires that the authorities obtain a warrant before conducting searches on private property. However, in practice, the Government does not always obtain warrants before conducting such searches, and it monitors the communications of some regime opponents (see Section 1.d.).

There was a credible report that members of the "political police" have kept attorney Aref Mohamed Aref under surveillance, threatened his life, and harassed his personal secretary. Aref often represents clients in high profile cases involving alleged human rights violations. The Centre for the Independence of Judges and Lawyers, which intervened on Aref's behalf, asked the Government to protect Aref and investigate the threats against him.

Section 2. Respect for Civil Liberties, Including:

a. *Freedom of Speech and Press.*—The Constitution provides for freedom of the press, and the Government generally respects this right in practice.

The Government owns the electronic media, the most important medium for reaching the public. It also owns the principal weekly newspaper, La Nation. The official media generally do not criticize the President or the Government. There are several opposition-run weekly and monthly publications which circulate freely and openly criticize the Government.

There are no specific laws or other criminal sanctions that threaten academic freedom. In general, teachers may speak and conduct research without restriction so long as they do not violate the laws on sedition.

b. *Freedom of Peaceful Assembly and Association.*—The right to free assembly is provided for in the Constitution, and the Government generally respected this right in practice. However, the Ministry of Interior requires permits for peaceful assembly and monitors opposition activities. Some opposition leaders effectively practiced self-censorship and, rather than provoke a government crackdown, refrained from organizing popular demonstrations.

The Constitution provides for four political parties. Nonpolitical associations must register with the Ministry of Interior in accordance with a preindependence law.

c. *Freedom of Religion.*—Islam is the state religion. Virtually the entire population is Sunni Muslim. The Government imposes no sanctions on those who choose to ignore Islamic teachings.

The foreign community supports Roman Catholic, French Protestant, Greek Orthodox, and Ethiopian Orthodox churches. Foreign clergy and missionaries may perform charitable works, but proselytizing, while not illegal, is discouraged.

d. *Freedom of Movement Within the Country, Foreign Travel, Emigration, and Repatriation.*—The Constitution allows freedom of movement. This right may be limited only by law.

In general citizens may travel or emigrate without restriction or interference. However, some Afar leaders have had their passports revoked or denied, and Muslim women planning to travel to certain Gulf countries may be prohibited from doing so unless accompanied by a spouse or an adult male.

Djibouti hosts almost 75,000 refugees and illegal immigrants, according to government sources. The U.N. High Commissioner for Refugees (UNHCR) acknowledges only the presence of some 21,000 refugees, largely from Somalia, resident in three main refugee camps. There are also 1,500 Ethiopian urban refugees registered with the UNHCR. Between 1994 and 1996, the UNHCR, in cooperation with the Government, organized repatriation to Ethiopia for 31,000 refugees and migrants from the city of Djibouti.

An estimated 10,000 to 18,000 Afars displaced by the civil war continue to live in Ethiopia, although not in refugee camps. The Government states that the Afars are welcome to return. However, Afar refugees perceive the northern region as unsafe. In addition, many of the Afars' homes and lands are occupied by Djiboutian soldiers and their families.

Section 3. Respect for Political Rights: The Right of Citizens to Change Their Government

Although the Constitution provides for the right of citizens to change their government, in practice citizens have not yet been allowed to exercise fully this right. The RPP has carefully controlled the implementation of the new four-party system, and, with the opposition largely refusing to participate, easily ensured total RPP control of the legislature in 1992 and President Gouled's reelection to a fourth term in 1993. Many Afars, particularly supporters of the FRUD, claim that the Constitution was crafted to ensure the President's domination of virtually all aspects of the Government, including the legislature and judiciary.

The Government signed a peace agreement with the FRUD in 1994, which set the stage for the inclusion of FRUD members in senior government posts. In June 1995, the Government named to a newly reshuffled Cabinet two FRUD faction leaders who signed the peace accord. No Afars have been named to the Cabinet since that time. The FRUD was registered as a political party this year but has not held a party congress. The Government recognizes only one of two FRUD factions. The two leaders who signed the peace accord are members of the recognized faction; the unrecognized faction includes members who refused to accept the terms of the accord.

Although legally entitled to participate in the political process, women are largely excluded from senior positions in government and in the political parties. There are no women in the Cabinet or in Parliament. The highest ranking woman in the country is Mrs. Khadija Abebe, President of the Court of Appeals. At least three other women serve as judges, and one is a director in the Ministry of Foreign Affairs.

Section 4. Governmental Attitude Regarding International and Nongovernmental Investigation of Alleged Violations of Human Rights

The Government has been hostile to the formation of local human rights groups. In 1993 the Government imprisoned Mohamed Houmed Souleh, the leader of the Association for the Defense of Human Rights and Liberties (ADDHL), after he criticized military abuses in the civil conflict. He was arrested and released several times thereafter. In 1996 Souleh and the ADDHL stopped publicly criticizing the Government, which continued to deny the ADDHL recognition. No other known human rights groups exist, and, except for the ICRC, no international human rights groups are known to have visited the country during the year (see Section 1.c.).

Section 5. Discrimination Based on Race, Sex, Religion, Disability, Language, or Social Status

While the Constitution prohibits discrimination on the basis of language, race, sex or religion, discrimination against women and ethnic minorities is widespread. In particular, the enforcement of laws to protect women and children is weak.

Women.—Violence against women exists but reported cases are few. The Government has been concerned about the problem of rape and included in the 1994 Penal Code, which entered into force in April 1995, stiff sentences for rapists, ranging up to 20 years in prison. However, there have as yet been no cases tried under the code. When violence against women occurs, it normally is dealt with within the family or clan structure rather than in the courts. The police rarely interfere in domestic violence cases, and the media report only the most extreme cases, such as murder.

Women legally possess full civil rights, but in practice, due to traditional societal discrimination in education and custom, they play a secondary role in public life and do not have the same employment opportunities as men. There are only a few women in the professions, and women are largely confined to wage employment in small trade, clerical, and secretarial fields. Customary law discriminates against women in such areas as inheritance, divorce, property ownership, and travel (see Section 2.d.). As the French-inspired legal code does not sanction such discrimination, educated women increasingly seek to defend their interests through the regular courts.

Children.—The Government devotes virtually no public resources to the advancement of children's rights and welfare. A few charitable organizations work with children.

According to an independent expert, as many as 98 percent of females 7 years or older have undergone female genital mutilation (FGM), which is widely condemned by international health experts as damaging to both physical and psychological health. In Djibouti FGM is generally performed on girls between the ages of 7 and 10. In 1988 the Djiboutian National Women's Union began an educational campaign against FGM, particularly infibulation, the most extensive and dangerous form of sexual mutilation practiced on women and girls. The campaign has had only marginal impact on the prevalence of this custom, which is pervasive in rural areas. Judicial reforms enacted in 1991 stipulate that anyone found guilty of genital mutilation of young girls may face a heavy fine and 5 years in prison. However, the Government has not convicted anyone under this statute or under the provisions of the Penal Code, which specifically prohibits FGM. The Government has not specifically addressed other forms of child abuse, which are often lightly punished. For example, when a child is raped or otherwise abused, the perpetrator is usually fined an amount sufficient to cover medical care for the injured child. The Government has yet to use provisions of the Penal Code to deal with domestic violence and child abuse more severely.

People With Disabilities.—The Government does not mandate accessibility to buildings or government services for people with disabilities. Although disabled persons have access to education and public health facilities, there is no specific legislation that addresses their needs, and there are no laws or regulations that prevent job discrimination against disabled people. The disabled have difficulty finding employment in an economy where approximately 60 percent of the able-bodied male adult population is underemployed or jobless.

National/Racial/Ethnic Minorities.—The Government continued to discriminate against citizens on the basis of ethnicity in terms of employment and job advancement. The Issa, the dominant Somali clan, control the ruling party, the civil and security services, and the military services. The President's subclan, the Mamassan, wields disproportionate power in affairs of state.

Section 6. Worker Rights

a. *The Right of Association.*—Under the Constitution, workers are free to join unions and to strike provided that they comply with legally prescribed requirements. In the small wage economy, about 70 percent of workers are union members, concentrated in individual private or state-owned enterprises. Previously, the Government exerted control over individual unions by making membership mandatory in the state-organized labor confederation, the General Union of Djiboutian Workers (UGTD). Since 1992 unions are free to join or form other confederations. While the UGTD is now nominally independent of the Government, it maintains close ties to the RPP. However, the Democratic Labor Union (UDT) has gained increasing union support despite government harassment.

The prescribed legal requirement for initiating a strike calls for the representatives of employees who plan to do so to contact the Interior Ministry 48 hours in advance. All strikes during the year were legal. In January secondary school teachers struck unsuccessfully over nonpayment of salaries and for better benefits. School teachers also struck unsuccessfully in April, May, June, and September over nonpayment of salaries and working conditions. Although the Labor Law prohibits employer retribution against strikers, the Government on one occasion arbitrarily arrested several hundred striking workers, including labor leaders. The Government also suspended, fired, or transferred scores of teachers active in the union to less desirable assignments in rural areas.

The Government replied to the International Labor Organization (ILO) concerning a complaint lodged by the International Confederation of Free Trade Unions (ICFTU) both in 1995 and in 1996. The Government stated that the unions were unwilling to negotiate and requested that the ILO furnish a consultant who could train trade unionists, draft a labor code, and review social legislation. The Government did not respond to the ICFTU's specific allegations. The ICFTU alleges that members of the Inter-Trade Union Association of Labor/General Union of Djibouti workers (UDT/UGTD) who struck on September 6, 1995, faced arbitrary arrest, threats, dismissals, or suspensions by the Government. Union headquarters were closed and sealed at that time. The workers were protesting the Government's refusal to enter into a dialogue with the trade unions over proposed legislation that would have had an adverse impact on their living standards. The ICFTU also lodged a complaint regarding the arrests of school teachers who struck in January. The Government said that it supports trade unions but added that police intervention was necessary to prevent social upheaval. In May security forces again seized the UGTD/UDT headquarters and froze their bank accounts.

Unions are free to maintain relations and exchanges with labor organizations abroad. The UDT has been a member of the ICFTU since 1994.

b. *The Right to Organize and Bargain Collectively.*—Although labor has the legal right to organize and bargain collectively, collective bargaining rarely occurs. Relations between employers and workers are informal and paternalistic. Wages are generally established unilaterally by employers on the basis of Ministry of Labor guidelines. When disputes about wages or health and safety issues arise, the Ministry of Labor encourages direct resolution by labor representatives and employers. Workers or employers may request formal administrative hearings before the Ministry of Labor's Inspection Service. The Service has been charged by critics with poor enforcement, due to its low priority and inadequate funding. The newly appointed Chief Labor Inspector promised in September to address these problems. The law prohibits antiunion discrimination, and employers guilty of such discrimination are legally required to reinstate workers fired for union activities. The Ministry generally enforces the law. In February the directors of the government-owned electric utility and telephone companies prohibited employees from attending a seminar on the role of unions in economic development sponsored by the UGTD, UDT, and the Conference Arabe pour les Accidents du Travail.

An export processing zone (EPZ) was established in December 1994. Firms in the EPZ are exempt from the Government's social security and medical insurance programs. Instead, they must provide either government or private accident insurance. The minimum wage in the EPZ is approximately $1 per hour. The regular workweek is 40 hours, while in the EPZ it is 45 hours. An employee having worked for the same firm in the EPZ for at least 1 year has the right to 15 days of annual leave compared to 30 days in the rest of the country (see also Section 6.e.).

c. *Prohibition of Forced or Compulsory Labor.*—The law prohibits forced or compulsory labor, and while this is generally observed, security forces reportedly sometimes compel illegal immigrants to work for them to avoid deportation.

d. *Minimum Age for Employment of Children.*—The minimum age for the employment of children is 14 years, and the law is generally respected. However, the shortage of labor inspectors reduces the likelihood of investigations being carried out, according to union sources. Children are generally not employed under hazardous conditions. Children may and do work in family-owned businesses, such as restaurants and small shops, at all hours. Many street beggars are young children whose parents have forced them to beg to help support the family.

e. *Acceptable Conditions of Work.*—Only a small minority of the population is engaged in wage employment. The Government administratively sets minimum wage rates according to occupational categories, and the Ministry of Labor is charged with enforcement. The monthly wage rate for unskilled labor, set in 1976, is approximately $90 (15,000 Djiboutian francs). However, some employers ask their employees to work up to 12 hours per day and pay them an additional wage. Some workers also receive housing and transportation allowances. Most employers pay more than the minimum wage, recognizing that it does not provide adequate compensation for a worker and family to maintain a decent standard of living.

By law the work week is 40 hours, often spread over 6 days. Workers are guaranteed daily and weekly rest periods and paid annual leave. The Ministry of Labor is responsible for enforcing occupational health and safety standards, wages, and work hours. Because enforcement is ineffective, workers sometimes face hazardous working conditions, particularly at the port. Workers rarely protest, as they fear replacement by others willing to accept the risks. There are no laws or regulations permitting workers to refuse to carry out dangerous work assignments without jeopardy to continued employment.

EQUATORIAL GUINEA

Equatorial Guinea is nominally a multiparty constitutional republic, but in reality power is exercised by President Teodoro Obiang Nguema through a small subclan of the majority Fang tribe, which has ruled since the country's independence in 1968. President Obiang was elected to a new 7-year term of office in February through elections marred by extensive fraud and intimidation. The President's Democratic Party of Equatorial Guinea (PDGE) controls the judiciary and the legislature, the latter also through fraudulent elections.

President Obiang exercises control over the police and security forces through the Minister of the Interior, who also serves as president of the national electoral board. The security forces committed numerous serious human rights abuses.

The majority of the population of approximately 400,000 lives by subsistence agriculture, supplemented by hunting and fishing. Barter is a major aspect of the economy in which the small monetary sector is based on exports of petroleum, cocoa, and increasing quantities of timber. Most foreign economic assistance has been suspended due to the lack of economic reform and the Government's repeated violations of human rights. Substantial new oil deposits were discovered in 1995, with exploitation beginning in 1996. The use and investment of oil revenues remains a closed process despite repeated calls from financial institutions and Equatoguinean citizens for financial openness. The country's economic potential continues to be undermined by fiscal mismanagement and a lack of transparency in public finance.

The Government's human rights record remained poor, and serious and systematic abuses continued, although there was some improvement in certain areas. Citizens do not have the right to change their government. Principal abuses by the security forces included: Physical abuse of prisoners; torture; beatings of detainees; arbitrary arrest and detention; extortion from prisoners; searches without warrants; and confiscation of property without due process. Officials took no action against security force members suspected of human rights violations. However, unlike the previous year, there were no reports of extrajudicial killing. Prison conditions remained life threatening. The judicial system does not ensure due process and is subject to executive influence. The Government severely restricts freedom of speech and the press. However, it permitted the establishment of two small, independent newspapers. The Government effectively limits the right of assembly. In the February presidential elections, the Government used arbitrary arrests, illegal detention, extensive roadblocks, beatings, and outright fraud to ensure President Obiang's hold on power. Discrimination and violence against women and foreigners remain serious problems. Discrimination against minorities persists.

RESPECT FOR HUMAN RIGHTS

Section 1. Respect for the Integrity of the Person, Including Freedom From:

a. *Political and Other Extrajudicial Killing.*—There were no reports of political or other extrajudicial killings.

b. *Disappearance.*—There were no reports of any unresolved disappearances. Reported disappearances usually involved detention for several days in secret locations without notification of family members or access to legal representation.

c. *Torture and Other Cruel, Inhuman, or Degrading Treatment or Punishment.*—These abuses are serious, frequent, and widespread. The police routinely beat detainees severely, and victims often require hospitalization after release. Access to prisoners is not generally permitted. The Government also uses the psychological effect of arrest, along with the fear of beating, to intimidate opposition party members. The security forces arrested prominent members of the opposition and beat and tortured them, the torture usually taking the form of beating of the soles of the feet.

Credible reports emerged that authorities arrested opposition politicians Victorino Bolekia, the mayor of Malabo, along with deputy mayor Santiago Obama and opposition figures Celestino Bacale and Julian Ehapo in February and badly beat them in detention. According to police, the prisoners—all of whom were elected in the municipal elections of 1995—were engaged in plotting a coup. However, credible sources report that rather than plotting, the four were attending French lessons at the French cultural center when the police raided the location. Mayor Bolekia was released within a few hours while the others remained incarcerated for 2 days. No official government action was taken against those responsible for the arrests and subsequent mistreatment of the prisoners in detention.

In March presidential candidate Amancio Gabriel Nze was reportedly arrested in Bata, chained to a wall, and beaten by Lt. Colonel Diosdado Nguema, police chief of Bata and reportedly a cousin of the President. Supporters arriving at the prison with food for Nze were allegedly also beaten.

In April Celestino Bacale was arrested again, this time for writing a memorandum calling attention to the Government's poor human rights record. He was secretly flown to Bata, on the African mainland, where he was allegedly tortured. In a rare show of independence, however, a magistrate reviewed Bacale's case and ordered his release.

While campaigning in Konibe, presidential candidate Secundino Oyono was reportedly fired upon by soldiers, later arrested, and tortured for 14 hours along with campaign worker Roque Maria Oyon. While there is no independent confirmation of the incident, it appears consistent with other accounts of arbitrary arrests and beatings. The Government has not prosecuted or punished any security officials for these abuses.

Prison conditions are primitive and life threatening. During a September roundup of foreigners for the purpose of extortion, authorities locked 29 detainees in a small cell for 1 week with only a bucket for a toilet. Several independent sources confirmed that prison guards beat a Togolese woman in her sixth month of pregnancy, causing a miscarriage. Rations are inadequate, and sanitary conditions practically nonexistent. Female prisoners are housed separately from men but are reportedly subjected to sexual abuse by guards.

Prison conditions are monitored by the International Committee for the Red Cross (ICRC), which makes recommendations to the Government. However, the ICRC recommendations are reportedly not released to the public. At the Government's insistence, they remain restricted to the ICRC, the Government, and the local Red Cross, which is charged with implementing the recommendations. There were credible reports that suggested changes, such as providing cells with cement floors and allowing prisoners access to clean water, had led to modest improvements in otherwise filthy conditions.

d. *Arbitrary Arrest, Detention or Exile.*—There are nominal but unenforced legal procedural safeguards regarding detention, the need for search warrants, and other protection of citizen's rights. These safeguards are systematically ignored by security forces.

Police routinely hold prisoners in incommunicado detention. The Government arrested political figures and detained them for indeterminate periods. Foreigners from neighboring countries are likewise subject to arbitrary mistreatment. On September 26 and 27, when security forces purportedly needed funds for the upcoming national day celebration on October 12, authorities took into custody hundreds of foreigners allegedly living without documentation. These included Nigerians, Ghanaians, Togolese, and Beninois. Many were taken from their beds and had their homes looted during raids. Bribes for release reportedly ranged from the equivalent of $10 to $100.

Even after paying bribes and being freed, some foreigners were reportedly arrested a second time and forced to pay again. Women seized during the raid were confined to a small cell without windows. One credible source described their detention chamber as "a sweat box" and said that their screaming could be heard all night. The guards verbally abused one person who attempted to bring food to jailed friends. A credible source reported that over 200 Nigerians were arrested and jailed. Many of these reportedly had their immigration papers in order, but were nevertheless jailed for the purpose of extortion. Authorities allegedly forced prisoners to pay rent on their cells for the time of incarceration. The authorities reportedly confiscated the documents and property of 35 Nigerians without due process, then loaded them onto a freighter, many clothed only in underwear, for forced repatriation to Nigeria.

On November 13, security agents arrested opposition figure Celestino Bacale for allegedly insulting the President in their presence. Reportedly, an intoxicated security agent accused Balale of plotting to kill President Obiang, and ordered Bacale's arrest, after Bacale refused to allow his briefcase to be searched. Authorities released him November 16, hours before a meeting between President Obiang and the Spanish President in Rome. The Government later ordered Bacale to present himself before a military court on the charge of insulting the President. Bacale went into hiding, with the Government reportedly broadcasting appeals to the public to apprehend him. He fled the country in December, with the charges pending against him.

There were no reports of long term political detainees. However, during the year, the Government arrested political leaders and detained them for indeterminate periods while they were interrogated, beaten, and tortured (see Section 1.c.).

The Government does not officially force its citizens into exile, but many persons who were able to travel abroad sought political asylum (see Section 2.d.).

e. *Denial of Fair Public Trial.*—The judiciary is not independent; judges serve at the pleasure of the President and are appointed, transferred, and dismissed for political reasons. Corruption is rampant.

The court system is composed of lower provincial courts, two appeals courts, and a Supreme Court. The President appoints members of the Supreme Court, who report to him. There are also traditional courts in the countryside, in which tribal elders adjudicate civil claims and minor criminal matters.

The Constitution and laws passed by the Chamber of Deputies provide for legal representation and the right to appeal. In practice, authorities often do not respect these provisions. Civil cases rarely come to public trial.

There were no reports of long term political prisoners. During the year, however, the Government arrested political leaders and detained them for indeterminate periods (see Section 1.d.).

f. *Arbitrary Interference With Privacy, Family, Home, or Correspondence.*—The Government does not enforce the law requiring judicial warrants for searches. Security forces regularly search homes and arrest occupants and generally do so without warrants.

The Government does not overtly force officials to join the PDGE. However, for lawyers, government employees, and others, party membership is necessary for employment and promotion. Even in the private sector, many citizens claim that party membership is necessary in order to be hired. The party banner is prominently displayed with the national flag in government offices, and many officials wear PDGE lapel pins.

There is surveillance of members of the opposition parties, resident diplomats, as well as accredited diplomats.

Section 2. *Respect for Civil Liberties, Including:*

a. *Freedom of Speech and the Press.*—The Constitution provides for freedom of speech and the press, but the Government severely restricts these rights in practice. Mild criticism of public institutions and government mismanagement is allowed. The Government, however, permits no criticism of the President or the security forces. All journalists must be registered with the Ministry of Information. According to trade sources, there are five or six independent reporters registered with the Ministry of Information. Between 30 and 40 reporters working for official party or government publications are also registered. Foreign reporters visiting Equatorial Guinea are required to be accompanied by guides from the Ministry of Information.

The Ministry of Information also allegedly requires publishers to submit copy for approval prior to publication. All local publications exercise self-censorship and are subject to prior restraint. However, the Government permitted the establishment of two small, independent newspapers, La Gaceta and El Sol. Some foreign publications are sold, though security forces reportedly peruse the contents of publications from Spain and confiscate literature critical of the Government. Outdated copies of Spanish and American newspapers are available to clients of prominent hotels. Shortwave broadcasts and government-controlled radio and television are available. Spanish broadcasts transmitted to Equatorial Guinea have been a source of friction between the two governments. Radio France International also transmits from Malabo.

Television broadcasts only a few hours each day. Cable is available, broadcasting the Cable News Network (CNN), Music TV (MTV), French news, movies, and cartoons. The Government withholds access to broadcasting by opposition parties, and rarely refers to the opposition in anything but a negative light when broadcasting the news.

There are no institutions of higher learning, although the Government is planning to open a university, with the foreign assistance, by combining teachers' training centers and other institutions.

b. *Freedom of Peaceful Assembly and Association.*—The right of assembly and association is provided for in the Constitution. However, government authorization must be obtained for meetings in private homes of more than 10 people for discussions that the regime considers political.

All parties must register with the Minister of Interior, and supply the names of members and a statement of purpose. Opposition parties must seek permits to hold meetings, including conferences and private meetings. Opposition members who have attempted to circumvent this regulation were beaten by security forces. Gatherings in public places, even small gatherings, are generally observed by security forces. The Government requires permits for public events, which it routinely grants but often quickly cancels, effectively undermining the right of assembly. Authorities granted, then canceled, permission for a meeting on the national day by opposition members who had planned to gather to discuss long-term strategies.

Credible sources state that citizens living in rural areas are hesitant to associate or even be seen with foreigners, fearing that doing so may lead to repercussions from government authorities.

c. *Freedom of Religion.*—The Government generally respects freedom of religion. There is no state religion, and the Government does not discriminate against any faith. However, a religious organization must first be formally recognized by the Ministry of Justice and Religion before its practice is allowed. Foreign missionaries reported a significant easing of restrictions on their activities during the year.

Nevertheless, the Government restricts the freedom of expression of the clergy. During the year, there were several incidents in which priests were arrested, beaten, and expelled from their parishes for allegedly preaching "political sermons." On February 13, Father Jose Carlos Esono was reportedly arrested in Bata and subjected to mistreatment by police who accused him of antigovernment activities. Reliable sources reported that a Nigerian priest was expelled in March for declining to celebrate mass for the President.

d. *Freedom of Movement Within the Country, Foreign Travel, Emigration, and Repatriation.*—In theory, freedom of movement and travel throughout the country are provided for in the law. However, local police routinely demand bribes from occupants of cars, taxis, and other vehicles traveling outside the capital. The Bubi ethnic group on the island of Bioko is unable to move about freely, according to credible sources, as the Government fears separatist sympathies among the Bubis. Roadblocks throughout the island reportedly prevent them from traveling between villages. Ethnic Fangs are also subject to extortion at random roadblocks.

During the 1996 Presidential elections, the Government systematically restricted the travel of opposition presidential candidates. According to credible reports, roadblocks on the island of Bioko and in continental Equatorial Guinea effectively kept opposition candidates away from their bases of popular support. Meetings were disrupted, and rallies canceled as a result. Election observers noted chains across major roads during the height of the political campaign.

Since the elections, the PDGE promulgated a directive to provincial bureaus to further restrict the free movement of opposition figures. The order entails confiscating property and documents of traveling members of the opposition, as well as searching them for "subversive documents." The directive has been described as "an order of permanent harassment."

Members of opposition parties frequently travel abroad but may face a hostile reception upon their return. For example, opposition figure Placido Mico was stopped and searched at the airport in October, following a visit to the United States. Authorities, led by the director general of national security, Antonio Mba (the President's brother), reportedly confiscated literature and souvenirs brought home from the trip. Nearly 90 percent of citizens who obtained visas for Spain in recent years reportedly never returned to Equatorial Guinea. Most sought political asylum.

There are both refugees and asylum seekers. According to a credible source, some 20 refugees from Liberia, Rwanda, Sudan, and Mauritania have sought political asylum. The Government generally grants these requests. Most refugees, however, do not declare themselves.

Section 3. Respect for Political Rights: The Right of Citizens to Change Their Government

The Constitution nominally provides citizens with the right to change their government peacefully, but in fact there have been no free, fair, and transparent presidential elections since independence in 1968. The President exercises complete power as Head of State, commander of the armed forces, and leader of the PDGE. Leadership positions with the Government are, in general, restricted to the President's subclan and closest supporters. While there is an elected Chamber of Deputies, it is not representative and is dominated by the Government. The Minister of the Interior also acts as president of the national electoral board.

The February presidential election, in which President Obiang claimed victory with 98 percent of the vote, was considered openly fraudulent by international observers. The President's early call for elections, ostensibly an effort to move toward democracy at the earliest opportunity, was perceived by many as a ploy to catch the opposition, as well as the nation's voters, off guard. The move met with repeated protests from the international community. It deprived opposition parties of sufficient time to organize their campaigns and meet with voters. Some opposition politicians who campaigned were beaten and jailed. Voting was done in the open and without secrecy, with opposition parties allegedly barred from access to polling areas. There were credible reports of widespread arrests and violence against opposition party members before the elections. Several countries refused to dispatch official observers. Accounts of observers who did attend included reports of beatings, roadblocks, stuffed ballot boxes, and open voting in the presence of security forces. Most opposition parties, claiming that it was futile to run amidst such blatant corruption, opted to boycott the elections.

Although there are no legal restrictions on the participation of women in politics, women remain seriously underrepresented. There are 2 women in the 42-member Cabinet, and 5 in the 80-member legislature.

Section 4. Governmental Attitude Regarding International and Nongovernmental Investigation of Alleged Violations of Human Rights

There are no effective local human rights nongovernmental organizations. One person who attempted to initiate a program with European Union funds to deal with human rights issues and the rehabilitation of torture victims was arrested and accused of running an illegal operation. According to credible reports, the person sought government approval and appealed to the Prime Minister for support, but the project failed and the individual left the country.

The United Nations Special Rapporteur for Human Rights visited once during the year and received government cooperation.

The United Nations Development Program's effort to encourage transparency in the 1995 municipal elections created friction with the Government. The Government requested the removal of the resident representative in 1995; he departed this year.

The Government established a parliamentary commission on human rights approximately 4 years ago. This organization, however, has rarely been heard from, and it has little credibility or influence.

Section 5. Discrimination Based on Race, Sex, Religion, Disability, Language, or Social Status

While the Constitution condemns all forms of discrimination, both governmental and social discrimination continue. These are reflected in traditional constraints on women's education and in the circumscribed opportunities for professional and occupational achievement of ethnic minorities. The Government deliberately limits potential opportunities for ethnic minorities.

Women.—Societal violence against women, particularly wife beating, is common. Public beating of wives is forbidden by government decree, but violence in the home is generally tolerated. The Government does not prosecute perpetrators of domestic violence.

Although the Constitution provides for equal rights, women are largely confined by custom to traditional roles, particularly in agriculture. Polygyny, which is widespread among the Fang, contributes to women's secondary status, as does limited educational opportunity; on average, women receive only one-fifth as much schooling as men.

There is no discrimination against women with regard to inheritance and family laws, but there is discrimination in traditional practice. For an estimated 90 percent of women, including virtually all ethnic groups except the Bubi, tradition dictates that if a marriage is dissolved, the wife must return the dowry given her family by the bridegroom at the time of marriage, while the husband automatically receives custody of their children.

Similarly, in the Fang, Ndowe, and Bisio cultures, primogeniture is practiced, and as women become members of their husband's families upon marriage, they are not usually accorded inheritance rights. According to the law women have the right to buy and sell property and goods, but in practice the male-dominated society permits few women access to sufficient funds to engage in more than petty trading or to purchase real property beyond a garden plot or modest home.

Children.—There are no legislated provisions for the welfare of children. The Government devotes little attention to children's rights or welfare and has no set policy in this area. Education is compulsory up to the age of 18, but the Government does not enforce the law.

People With Disabilities.—No constitutional or legal provisions exist for the physically disabled with respect to discrimination in employment or education. Nor is there legislation mandating accessibility to buildings or government services.

National/Racial/Ethnic Minorities.—There is no legal discrimination against ethnic or racial minorities, and the Government does not overtly limit participation by them, but the monopolization of political power by the President's Mongomo subclan of the Fang ethnic group persists.

In practice some members of minorities face discrimination because they are not members of the Fang ethnic group, or belong to a subclan other than the President's. Minorities do not face discrimination in inheritance, marriage, or family laws.

Several thousand citizens of Nigeria, Ghana, and Francophone Africa continue to reside in the country. Most are small traders and business people. There are numerous reports of their harassment by the police (see Section 1.d.)

Section 6. Worker Rights

a. *The Right of Association.*—Although the Constitution provides for the right to organize unions, the Government has not passed enabling legislation. A 1995 petition by service sector employees to form a union in the mainland capital of Bata has yet to be answered by the Government. In the small wage economy, no labor organization exists, although there are a few cooperatives with limited power. The law prohibits strikes. The Labor Code contains provisions to uphold worker rights, but the Government generally does not enforce them.

It is generally acknowledged that membership in the PDGE is a prerequisite for hiring and promotion in both public and private sectors. Membership in a rival political organization is considered grounds for dismissal from any position, public or private. Opposition politicians often claim to have been dismissed from their jobs after joining alternate political groups. Credible sources maintain that during the 1996 presidential elections several large private employers reportedly threatened to dismiss workers who did not vote for President Obiang. Now that the oil industry is a major employer, hiring is controlled by the Government, operating through an agency, APEGESA. Independent sources confirm that APEGESA screens applicants for positions and excludes those considered unfriendly or indifferent to the PDGE.

b. *The Right to Organize and Bargain Collectively.*—There is no legislation regarding these rights, or prohibiting antiunion discrimination. There is no evidence of collective bargaining by any group. Wages are set by the Government and employers, with little or no input from the workers. Employers must pay the minimum wages set by the Government, and most companies pay more than the government-established minimum.

c. *Prohibition of Forced or Compulsory Labor.*—The law forbids forced labor and slavery, and there is no evidence that such activity takes place. Convicted felons do, within the law, preform extensive labor outside prison without compensation.

d. *Minimum Age for Employment of Children.*—The legal minimum age for child employment is 18 years, but the Ministry of Labor does not enforce this law. The Government also does not enforce the law that stipulates mandatory education up to the age of 18. Underage youth perform both family farm work and street vending.

e. *Acceptable Conditions of Work.*—The law prescribes a standard 35-hour workweek and a 48-hour rest period which are observed in practice in the formal economy. The minimum monthly wage is approximately $53 (cfa 27,500). The minimum wage does not provide a decent standard of living for a worker and family. The Labor Code provides for comprehensive protection for workers from occupational hazard, but the Government does not enforce this in practice. Employees who protest unhealthy or dangerous working conditions risk the loss of their jobs.

ERITREA

Eritrea became an independent state in May 1993, following a U.N.-supervised referendum in which citizens voted overwhelmingly for independence from Ethiopia. The Eritrean People's Liberation Front (EPLF), which led the 30-year war for independence, has been in control of the country since it defeated Ethiopian army forces in 1991, and its leader, Isaias Afwerki, serves as the President. The EPLF, renamed the People's Front for Democracy and Justice (PFDJ), has outlined an ambitious program for transition to a democratically elected government by 1997. In April 1994, the National Assembly, partly appointed by the PFDJ leadership and partly elected, created a 50-member National Constitution Commission to draft a constitution by mid-1996. The Commission presented a draft to the public in September and debate continued through the end of the year. The draft constitution provides for democratic freedoms, including the rights of free assembly, free speech, and free association.

The Government made a sustained effort to reduce the armed forces, over 95,000 strong by the end of the war for independence, to its current 47,000 strength. The police are generally responsible for maintaining internal security, although the Government may call on the army, the reserves, and demobilized soldiers in times of internal disorder. The army is responsible for external and border security. Since 1993 the army has been forced to deal with the Eritrean Islamic Jihad (EIJ), a small, Sudan-based insurgent group that has mounted sporadic terrorist attacks in western Eritrea.

Eritrea underwent a transition from a centrally planned economy introduced by the former Ethiopian military dictatorship to a free-market economy introduced through the recent privatization of state-owned enterprises and liberalization of investment and trade. The economy is largely based on subsistence agriculture, with over 70 percent of the population of 3.6 million involved in farming and herding. The small industrial sector consists mainly of light industries with outmoded technologies. International economic assistance accounts for a significant portion of external revenues. The country is extremely poor, with an annual per capita income of less than $150.

The Government continued to enjoy strong public support and generally respected the rights of its citizens with the exception of Jehovah's Witnesses. Because of their refusal to vote or to participate in certain aspects of national service for religious reasons, the Government has imposed economic, employment, and travel restrictions on all Jehovah's Witnesses. A government proclamation issued in May requires that all private and nongovernmental organizations (NGO's) hire those who have completed their national service tour, demonstrating the Government's resolve to establish a national service program as a legal obligation of all citizens regardless of their religious beliefs. The Government has yet to permit prison visits, and an unknown number of persons suspected of association with the Ethiopian Mengistu regime, radical Islamic elements, or terrorists organizations remain in detention. The undeveloped judicial system limits the provision of speedy trials. There are no domestic human rights organizations. Despite the Government's efforts to support rights of women, they generally have a lower status than men, and female genital mutilation (FGM) remains widespread.

RESPECT FOR HUMAN RIGHTS

Section 1. Respect for the Integrity of the Person, Including Freedom From:
 a. *Political and Extrajudicial Killing.*—There were no reports of political or other extrajudicial killings.
 b. *Disappearance.*—There were no reports of politically motivated disappearances.
 c. *Torture and Other Cruel, Inhuman, or Degrading Treatment or Punishment.*—The Ethiopian Penal Code, as modified by the transitional Penal Code of Eritrea, prohibits torture, and there were no reports that the authorities employed it.

Prison conditions are Spartan but generally not inhuman. The Government does not permit prisoners to correspond with family and friends and restricts visitation privileges. There were no confirmed reports that prisoners were beaten or may have died due to lack of proper medical care. The Government does not permit independent monitoring of conditions in detention facilities.

 d. *Arbitrary Arrest, Detention, or Exile.*—The Penal Code stipulates that detainees may be held for a maximum of 30 days without being charged with a crime. In practice, the authorities sometimes hold persons suspected of crimes for much longer periods. In May 1995, on the second anniversary of independence, the Government pardoned and released 91 detainees who had been held for up to 4 years for collaboration with the Mengistu regime. An unknown number of additional suspected collaborators remain in detention without charge, despite a statement by President Isaias in September 1995 that their cases would be dealt with soon. An unspecified number of persons associated with radical Islamic elements or suspected terrorist organizations also remained in detention without charge. There were unconfirmed reports that the Government arbitrarily detained several Eritrean Liberation Front (ELF) members.

The Government does not use exile as a means of political control.
 e. *Denial of a Fair Public Trial.*—The judiciary is independent, and there were no known incidents of executive interference in the judicial process over the past year. The undeveloped judicial system, however, suffers from a lack of trained personnel, resources, and infrastructure that in practice limits the State's ability to grant accused persons a speedy trial. At independence Eritrea chose to retain the Ethiopian legal system based on the Napoleonic Code, until the new constitution is promulgated, which is expected in late 1997. Under this Code, simple crimes are brought to the lower court and are heard by a single judge. Serious crimes are tried publicly by a panel of three judges, and defendants have access to legal counsel, usually at their own expense. Although there is no formal public defender's office, the Government has successfully requested that attorneys work without fee to represent defendants accused of serious crimes who are unable to afford legal counsel. Defendants may appeal verdicts to the Appellate Court, which is composed of a president and five judges.

Since the population is largely rural, most citizens only have contact with the legal system through traditional courts. Village judges, appointed by a panel of government magistrates, provide justice in civil matters. Criminal cases are transferred to magistrates versed in criminal law. Many local issues, for example, property disputes and most petty crimes, are adjudicated by local elders according to custom or, in the case of Muslims, the Koran. These traditional courts cannot give sentences involving physical punishment.

Crimes committed by members of the military are handled by military courts.
There were no reports of political prisoners.

f. *Arbitrary Interference With Privacy, Family, Home, or Correspondence.*—Under the law, warrants are required before the Government can monitor mail, telephones, or other means of private communication. Warrants also are required in routine searches and seizures, except in cases where authorities believe individuals may attempt to escape or destroy evidence. There is no indication that the Government monitored private mail or telephone service.

The Government may ban any foreign publication from entering the country, and the press proclamation forbids the local reprinting of articles from banned publications.

Section 2. Respect for Civil Liberties, Including:

a. *Freedom of Speech and Press.*—The draft constitution, when enacted, will provide for freedom of speech and of the press, and citizens were generally free to express opinions in various forums. The Government controls all media, which include three newspapers, one radio station, and one television station. The Government continued to restrict the rights of the religious media to comment on politics or government policies. In theory nonreligious print media are free to criticize the Government. Nonetheless, criticism tends to be limited and fairly mild. Although there is no formal censorship body, it is likely that the media practice at least some self-censorship.

The Government's press proclamation allows for individuals to publish newspapers, although there are no privately owned newspapers or magazines published. It does not allow for private ownership of any broadcast media. The proclamation requires that all newspapers obtain a license from the Ministry of Information before publication and that all reporters register with the Ministry. The Government may also punish "whosoever insults, abuses, defames, or slanders the Government or one of the constituted legislative, executive, or judicial authorities," and forbids the publication of any matter that contravenes general morality.

Once the constitution is ratified, it will become the law of the land and all proclamations that conflict with it will be annulled. The constitutent assembly, once elected, is expected to ratify the new constitution by mid-1997.

Eritrea has one institution of higher education, the University of Asmara. All faculty members, including many from outside the country, are accorded full academic freedom.

b. *Freedom of Peaceful Assembly and Association.*—The Government requires a permit from the Ministry of Internal Affairs for a public meeting or demonstration. In general permits are granted freely for nonpolitical meetings or gatherings, and although no political demonstrations have occurred, there were no reports that permits for political demonstrations were denied. The draft constitution states that every citizen shall have the right to form organizations for political, social, economic, and cultural ends. However, the PFDJ has stated its opposition to the formation of religiously or ethnically based parties.

c. *Freedom of Religion.*—Although the draft constitution provides for freedom of religion, the Government has banned religious organizations from any involvement in politics. A July 1995 proclamation lists specific guidelines on the role of religion and religious affiliated NGO's in development and government, stating that development, politics, and public administration are the sole responsibility of the Government and people. As a result, religious organizations may fund, but not initiate or implement development projects. The proclamation also sets out rules governing relations between religious organizations and foreign sponsors.

The draft constitution provides for the "freedom to practice any religion and to manifest such practice." However, government persecution of the small community of Jehovah's Witnesses continued. In October 1994, the Government revoked the trading licenses of Jehovah's Witnesses and dismissed those who worked for the civil service. This government action resulted in economic difficulties for the Jehovah's Witnesses, especially former civil servants and businessmen.

The Witnesses' refusal on religious grounds to participate in national service or vote in a referendum applied to all. This spurred widespread criticism that the members were collectively shirking their civic duty. The harsh measures for refusal to participate in national service were applied only to the Jehovah's Witnesses. In addition to the Government's continued denial of passports, Jehovah's Witnesses are also denied identification cards, trading licenses, and government housing. However, they are not barred from meeting in private homes.

d. *Freedom of Movement Within the Country, Foreign Travel, Emigration, and Repatriation.*—The proposed constitution would provide fully for the rights of movement and emigration. In general citizens may live where they choose and travel freely internally. Some areas are restricted for security reasons. In particular, clashes between government forces and Eritrean Islamic Jihad members have led the

Government to restrict travel along much of the border with Sudan. Some areas remain heavily mined, a legacy of the war for independence, leading to additional travel restrictions.

Citizens are largely free to travel outside the country, although the Jehovah's Witnesses, former ruling party members, those who have not completed national service, and intending emigrants have been denied passports or exit visas and can only leave the country by traveling overland to Ethiopia. In general citizens are guaranteed the right to return. Instances in which citizens living abroad have run afoul of the law, contracted a serious contagious disease, or been declared ineligible for political asylum by other governments are considered on a case-by-case basis. The Government cooperates with the U.N. High Commissioner for Refugees (UNHCR) for the repartiation of Eritrean refugees from Sudan. A pilot refugee return program resulted in the successful repatriation of 25,000 refugees from Sudan in 1995. A further 100,000 of the estimated 150,000 to 300,000 Eritrean refugees remaining in Sudan have been unable to participate in a UNHCR-sponsored organized repatriation because of the failure of the Governments of Eritrea and Sudan to conclude an agreement on modalities of such a repatriation.

Section 3. *Respect for Political Rights: The Right of Citizens to Change Their Government*

Citizens do not currently enjoy this right, and credible reports suggest that authority within the Government is very narrowly held. The transitional government is dominated by the PFDJ.

The National Assembly in 1994 created a 50-member National Constitution Commission to draft a democratic constitution. The Commission completed a draft in July, and planned a series of public debates with presentation of a final draft to the National Assembly by year's end. The Constitution Commission also planned to finalish drafting election laws. Elections for the constituent assembly are scheduled to take place by late 1997 or early 1998. Ratification of the constitution is expected to take place soon thereafter with elections for a new National Assembly by late 1997 or early 1998.

In an effort to encourage broader participation by women in politics, the PFDJ named 3 women to the party's executive council and 12 women to the Central Committee. Women occupy seats on the Constitutional Commission and in the National Assembly and hold senior government positions, including the ministerial portfolios of justice and tourism. As part of a draft plan to establish regional legislatures, 30 percent of legislative seats would be reserved for women, who would also be able to compete for remaining seats.

Section 4. *Governmental Attitude Regarding International and Nongovernmental Investigation of Alleged Violations of Human Rights*

The Ministry of Foreign Affairs and the Ministry of Internal Affairs are jointly responsible for handling human rights inquiries. All NGO's also must register with the Eritrean Relief and Refugee Commission. There are no domestic human rights organizations in Eritrea. The Government reported no applications or registrations of human rights NGO's during the past year.

In 1995 the Government proclaimed that religious organizations, including religious-based NGO's, could not engage in development activities. The Government also removed religious-based indigenous NGO's completely from relief work in order to prevent the development of church-based organizations receiving money from abroad. All foreign NGO's are considered to be providing technical advice. If they are in Eritrea for more than 183 days, NGO's must pay an income tax of 38 percent of their salaries and allowances. This tax situation encourages the departure of NGO's and the loss of technical assistance.

Section 5. *Discrimination Based on Race, Sex, Religion, Disability, Language, or Social Status*

The Transitional Civil Code prohibits discrimination against women, children, and people with disabilities.

Women.—The Government has publicly taken a firm stand against domestic violence; health, police and judicial authorities say that no serious domestic violence problem exits.

The Government consistently advocated improving the status of women, many of whom played a significant role as fighters in the struggle for independence. In 1991 the provisional EPLF Government codified a broad range of rights for women, providing for equal educational opportunities, equal pay for equal work, and legal sanctions against domestic violence. In 1994 the Third Party Congress advocated more rights for women, including parity in the right to the use of land and other property. However, much of society remains traditional and patriarchal, and most women have an inferior status to men in their homes and communities. The law provides a framework for improving the status of women, but laws are unevenly implemented, because of both a lack of capacity in the legal system and ingrained cultural attitudes. In practice, males retain privileged access to education, employment, and control of economic resources, with disparities greater in rural areas than in cities.

Women aged 18 to 40 participate, by law, in the National Service Program.

Children.—The Ministry of Labor and Human Welfare is responsible for government policies concerning the rights and welfare of children. The Government recently reorganized and created under the Ministry of Social Affairs a department which includes the Children's Affairs Division. The Children's Affairs Division covers child care, counseling, and probation. Due to a shortage of schools and teachers, half the country's children are unable to attend school.

Female genital mutilation, which is widely considered by international health experts as damaging to both physical and psychological health, is practiced extensively on girls at an early age. The Government, through the Ministry of Health and the National Union of Eritrean Women, actively discourages this practice.

People With Disabilities.—The long war for independence left thousands of men and women physically disabled from injuries they received as guerrillas and as civilian victims. The Government spends a large share of its resources to support and train these war disabled, who are regarded as heroes, and does not discriminate against them in training, education, or employment. There are no laws mandating access for the disabled to public thoroughfares or public or private buildings.

Section 6. Worker Rights

a. *The Right of Association.*—There are no government restrictions regarding the formation of unions, including in the military, the police, and other essential services. Labor association is encouraged by the Government, which promulgated Proclamation 8 in 1991 providing workers with the legal right to form unions and to strike to protect their interests. The Government is presently rewriting the labor code, but it must wait until the new constitution is ratified. The National Confederation of Eritrean Workers, which was part of the EPLF during the war, has reorganized since independence and become independent of both the Government and the PFDJ. It represents over 20,000 workers from 129 unions. The largest union is the Textile, Leather, and Shoe Federation.

There were no strikes reported in 1996.

b. *The Right to Organize and Bargain Collectively.*—Eritrea is a member of the International Labor Organization (ILO) and worked closely with the organization in 1993 to prepare the draft labor code, which prohibits antiunion discrimination by employers and establishes a mechanism for resolving complaints of discrimination. The Government has indicated its intention to ratify several key ILO conventions on labor—freedom of association, the right to bargain, a labor administration system, and prohibitions against child labor—but still has not done so. The Ministry of Labor and Human Welfare indicated that ratification of the conventions may not occur until after the new constitution is promulgated. Wages are determined by the market.

There are no export processing zones.

c. *Prohibition of Forced or Compulsory Labor.*—There is no law or signed convention prohibiting compulsory labor. There were no known instances of forced labor. All citizens between 18 and 40 are required to participate in the national service program, which includes military training as well as civic action programs. High school students are also required to participate in a summer work program, for which they are paid.

d. *Minimum Age for Employment of Children.*—The legal minimum age for employment is 18 years, although apprentices may be hired at age 16. While the Ministry of Labor and Human Welfare is responsible for enforcement of laws pertaining to employment of children, there is no inspection system in place to monitor compliance. According to labor officials, 50 percent of children are not able to attend school due to a shortage of schools and teachers. Rural children who do not attend classes often work on their family farms, while urban children are often street vendors of cigarettes, newspapers, or chewing gum.

e. *Acceptable Conditions for Work.*—There are two systems regulating employment conditions: The civil service system, and the labor law system. There is no legally mandated minimum wage in the private sector. In the civil service sector wages vary from $40 to $473 (250–3000 birr per month), with factory workers (in Government-owned enterprises) earning the highest wages. The minimum wage does not provide the average worker and family a decent standard of living.

The standard workweek is 48 hours, but many people work fewer hours. There is no legal provision for a day of rest, but most workers are allowed 1 to 1 1a.2 days off per week. The Government has instituted occupational health and safety standards, but inspection and enforcement vary widely among factories. The draft labor law includes a number of provisions concerning women, including one that states that women during pregnancy shall not be assigned to jobs that could endanger their lives or the lives of their unborn children. Workers are permitted to remove themselves from dangerous work sites without retaliation.

ETHIOPIA

Ethiopia continued its transition from a unitary to a federal system of government. Prime Minister Meles Zenawi leads the Government of the Federal Democratic Republic of Ethiopia, which was elected in 1995 to replace a transitional government that was established following a long and brutal civil war. Most opposition groups boycotted the elections, and candidates affiliated with the dominant party within the transitional government, the Ethiopian Peoples' Revolutionary Democratic Front (EPRDF) won a landslide victory in national and regional contests. The EPRDF is in turn dominated by the Tigray Peoples' Liberation Front (TPLF). The judiciary is weak and overburdened, but showed increased signs of independence.

New federal regions, organized along ethnic lines, are increasingly autonomous, with greater local control over both fiscal and political issues. A history of highly centralized authority, great poverty, the recent civil conflict, and unfamiliarity with democratic culture all combine to complicate the implementation of federalism. The federal Government can not yet protect constitutional rights at the regional level, especially when local authorities are unwilling or unable to do so. Local administrative, police, and judicial systems remain weak in many regions.

Responsibility for internal security continued to shift from the military forces to the police in most regions. Throughout the year, military forces conducted low level operations against the Oromo Liberation Front (OLF) in parts of the Oromo regional state. The national police organization is subordinate to the Ministry of Justice. Some local officials and members of the security forces committed human rights abuses.

The economy is based on smallholder agriculture, with more than 85 percent of the population living in rural areas under very poor conditions. Per capita gross national product is estimated at $120 per year. Real economic growth in 1996 was 7 percent. Coffee accounts for about 60 percent of export revenues. The Government continued to implement an internationally supported economic reform program designed to liberalize the economy and bring state expenditures into balance with revenues.

The Government took a number of steps to improve its human rights practices, but serious problems remain. Security forces sometimes beat or mistreated detainees, and arbitrarily arrested and detained citizens. Prolonged pretrial detention is a problem. The judiciary lacks sufficient staff and funds, and consequently most citizens are denied the full protections provided for in the Constitution. The Government restricts freedom of the press and detained or imprisoned 14 journalists. At year's end, most were accused or convicted of inciting ethnic hatred or publishing false information in violation of the 1992 Press Law. The Government limits freedom of association and refused to register several nongovernmental organizations (NGO's), but otherwise did not prevent them from operating. Societal discrimination and violence against women and abuse of children remain problems; female genital mutilation is nearly universal. Societal discrimination against disabled persons is a problem.

The Government intensified measures to create a national, apolitical army by replacing thousands of demobilized Tigrayan soldiers with recruits from other ethnic groups. It implemented a training program in military justice and undertook programs to enhance the professional capacity and improve the performance of military personnel. It sought to strengthen the judiciary; additional civil and criminal judges were trained and assigned to regional courts, while efforts to eliminate judicial malfeasance resulted in the dismissal of many others. The Government sought to enhance transparency and accountability by publishing in state media several detailed reports of officials who were jailed or dismissed for abuse of authority, corruption, and violations of human rights. Governmental transparency, however, remains a problem. In October the Deputy Prime Minister and Minister of Defense was dismissed from all official posts for corruption.

The trial of the first group of defendants accused of war crimes under the brutal Marxist regime of Colonel Mengistu Haile Mariam (1974–1991), which began in December 1994, continued through the year. In December approximately 1,200 additional detainees were charged with war crimes.

RESPECT FOR HUMAN RIGHTS

Section 1. Respect for the Integrity of the Person, Including Freedom From:

a. *Political and Other Extrajudicial Killing.*—There were no confirmed reports of extrajudicial killings by government security forces. However, unconfirmed reports alleged that the Government was responsible for extrajudicial killings in parts of Oromiya regional state related to actions directed against the OLF.

In September a court convicted in absentia and sentenced to death three Egyptian Islamic militants for the attempted assassination of Egyptian President Hosni Mubarak in June 1995. Mubarak was unhurt, but two policemen were killed.

The Islamic extremist group Al'Ittihad Al'Islami claimed responsibility for three hotel bombings in which several people were killed, as well as for an attempt on the life of Minister of Transport and Communications Abdulmejid Hussein. The Minister was wounded and two bodyguards were killed. In November the Al'ittihad terrorist cells believed responsible for these actions were uncovered. The trial of those arrested continued at year's end.

The execution style killing in October of two foreigners in separate incidents in Dire Dawa is still under investigation. Banditry remained a serious problem in some parts of the country. Bandits, often heavily armed, killed civilians, police, and soldiers during robbery attempts. While government critics frequently ascribe political motives to bandit activity, most evidence suggests that these activities are primarily economically motivated.

b. *Disappearance.*—There were no confirmed reports, but numerous unconfirmed reports, of alleged disappearances.

c. *Torture and Other Cruel, Inhuman, or Degrading Treatment or Punishment.*— The Constitution prohibits the use of torture and mistreatment of prisoners. Nevertheless, there were numerous credible reports that security officials sometimes beat or mistreated detainees. Government media published occasional reports of officials who were jailed or dismissed for abuse of authority and violations of human rights.

Prison conditions are not generally life threatening and meet minimal international standards. Overcrowding, however, remains a serious problem. Prisoners are often allocated less than 2 square meters of sleeping space in a room that may contain up to 200 people. Prison food is adequate. Prisoners are typically permitted daily access to prison yards. Visitors are permitted, and many prisoners receive regular deliveries of food and other supplies from family members. Female prisoners are housed separately from men, and rape does not appear to be a problem.

There were credible reports that the army sometimes used military camps for the temporary detention and interrogation of OLF fighters and alleged supporters.

The Government permits independent monitoring of prison conditions, military camps, and police stations by the International Committee of the Red Cross (ICRC) and often by diplomatic missions. However, the ICRC does not have immediate access to government facilities and must either request permission or notify the government each time it wants to visit. Granting prison access is now the responsibility of regional governments. In most regions, permission to visit detention facilities is routinely granted.

There were several diplomatic visits to prominent detainees accused of war crimes who were held by the Special Prosecutor's Office (SPO), including Abera Yemaneab, Mamo Wolde, and Mekonnen Dori, who bore no signs of mistreatment by prison authorities.

d. *Arbitrary Arrest, Detention, or Exile.*—The Constitution and both the Criminal and Civil Codes prohibit arbitrary arrest and detention, but the Government does not always respect these rights in practice.

Under the Criminal Procedure Code, any person detained must be charged and informed of the charges within 48 hours and, in most cases, be offered release on bail. Those persons believed to have committed serious offenses may be detained for 15 days while police conduct an investigation, and for additional 15-day periods while the investigation continues. Some offenses, such as murder and treason, are not bailable. In practice, and especially in the regions, people are often detained without warrant, frequently not charged within 48 hours, and—if released on bail— never recalled to court. Nationwide, thousands of criminal suspects remained in detention without charge or trial at year's end. Most often these detentions resulted from the severe shortage and limited training of judges, prosecutors, and attorneys.

Federal and regional authorities arrested and detained hundreds of persons without charge or trial for activities allegedly in support of armed opposition groups. The vast majority of these took place in the Oromo regional state. In typical cases, security forces arrested and held these persons incommunicado for several days or weeks before eventually releasing them. Most detainees were accused of participating in armed actions by the OLF. Some 93 persons who were among a large group of OLF fighters detained in 1994 continued to be held.

In December the SPO filed charges against approximately 1,200 of the 2,000 persons jailed and accused of war crimes under the previous regime. Some of the defendants have been in pretrial detention for 5 years.

Exile is illegal and is not used.

e. *Denial of Fair Public Trial.*—The Constitution provides for an independent judiciary, and the federal courts showed increased signs of judicial independence.

Consistent with the 1994 Constitution, the Government continued to restructure the judiciary toward a decentralized federal system comprised of courts at the district and regional levels. In May the Government appointed 56 federal court justices. A judicial administrative commission was established to oversee the performance of the federal judiciary. The Federal High Court and Federal Supreme Court adjudicate cases involving federal law, transregional issues and national security and hear both original and appeal cases. The regional judiciary is increasingly autonomous. District (woreda), higher and supreme courts have been established, mirroring the structure of the federal judiciary. Regional supreme courts may be delegated authority by the federal courts to hear some federal cases. The Government may delegate some of the war crimes trials to supreme courts in the regions where the crimes were allegedly committed.

The military services have undertaken a sweeping overhaul of the military justice system. Foreign assistance is being used to train soldiers in topics which include judicial and nonjudicial punishment and the conduct of soldiers during military operations.

The Government's goal is a decentralized system that brings justice closer to the people; in practice, however, severe shortages of adequately trained personnel in many regions, as well as serious financial constraints, combine to keep the judiciary weak and overburdened and to deny most citizens the full protections provided for in the Constitution. Hundreds of individuals were detained, especially in the Oromo and Somali regions, without charge. Many were ultimately released without explanation or appearance before a judge. Such cases at times may reflect arbitrary actions on the part of heavy handed local officials, but also result from a shortage of trained and competent prosecutors and judges. The Government established regional offices of the Ministry of Justice to monitor local judicial developments, but the federal presence in the regions remains limited. Anecdotal evidence suggests that some local officials interpret decentralization to mean that they are no longer accountable to any higher authority, even within their own regions.

The Government is making concerted efforts to identify and train replacements for many lower court judges. Many judges were hastily appointed in 1991 and were subsequently dismissed for corruption, incompetence, or abuse of authority. The Government, aware of the severe lack of trained staff in the judicial system, began in 1995 to place greater emphasis on training new judges and prosecutors. Senior government officials charged with judicial oversight estimate that the creation of a truly independent and skilled judicial apparatus will take several decades. The Government has welcomed foreign financial and technical assistance.

Pending passage by regional legislatures of laws particular to their region, all judges are guided exclusively by the Federal procedural and substantive codes. Trials are public, and defendants have the right to a defense attorney. The Government established a public defender's office to provide legal counsel to indigent defendants, although its scope remains severely limited. The law does not allow the defense access to prosecutorial evidence before the trial.

The Constitution provides legal standing to some preexisting religious and customary courts and gives federal and regional legislatures the authority to recognize other courts. By law, both parties to a dispute must agree before a case may be heard by a customary or religious court. Shari'a (Islamic) courts hear religious and family cases involving Muslims. In addition, some traditional courts still function. Though not sanctioned by law, these courts resolve legal disputes for the majority of citizens who live in rural areas and who generally have little access to formal judicial systems.

The SPO was established in 1992 to create an historical record of the abuses during the Mengistu government and to bring to justice those criminally responsible for human rights violations. The trial of the first group of defendants charged with crimes against humanity during the former regime began in 1994 and continued intermittently through the year. Court appointed attorneys represent many of the defendants, following claims that they could not afford an adequate defense. Of the 73 defendants, the Government is trying 21 in absentia, including Colonel Mengistu Haile Mariam, the former dictator now in self-exile in Zimbabwe. In December approximately 1,200 additional detainees were charged with war crimes. Senior government officials expressed growing frustration with the slow pace of the work of the SPO. Local court observers believe that the remaining trials, once they begin, may last several years. Legal observers expect relatively few additional cases to be brought, with many defendants charged and tried collectively in each instance.

All Amhara People's Organization (AAPO) Chairman Professor Asrat Woldeyes and four other AAPO leaders were convicted in 1994 of planning armed action against the Government at a 1993 meeting. Asrat was also convicted of "incitement to war" in connection with a speech he made in 1992. He was sentenced to a total of 5 years' imprisonment. He still faces charges stemming from a May 1994 prison escape in Debre Berhan in which several guards were killed. Asrat is reportedly in good health.

Authorities arrested Dr. Taye Wolde Semayat, chairman of the Ethiopian Teacher's Association (ETA), in August upon his return from a trip abroad. Taye has been formally charged with leading an Amhara extremist organization that planned and carried out attacks against foreigners, including the attempted murder of a diplomat and a grenade attack on a diplomatic compound in Addis Ababa. The Government's case against Taye is not linked to his activities on behalf of the ETA. Taye's trial continued at year's end.

Opposition groups and the Ethiopian Human Rights Council allege that some of the persons detained by the SPO, as well as some other detainees, are held for political reasons. The Government denies that it holds political prisoners.

f. *Arbitrary Interference With Privacy, Family, Home, or Correspondence.*—The law requires judicial search warrants, but in practice they are seldom obtained outside Addis Ababa, as local governments vary in their understanding and practice of democratic norms. In Dire Dawa, for example, there were credible reports that some neighborhood officials searched residences without possessing warrants.

Section 2. Respect for Civil Liberties, Including:

a. *Freedom of Speech and Press.*—While the Constitution and the 1992 Press Law provide for the right to free speech and press, the Government often used legal mechanisms to restrict press rights in practice.

Journalists may fall victim to vague provisions of the Press Law concerning publishing false information or inciting ethnic hatred, and some journalists practice self-censorship. There were 14 journalists under government detention at year's end; most were accused or convicted of inciting ethnic hatred or publishing false information.

The editor of a private newspaper received a 6-month suspended sentence for not delivering two copies of the newspaper to the Ministry of Information, as specified by the Press Law, even though the breach had occurred a year earlier. In a similar case, the editor of a government magazine was fined about $80 for the same offense. According to a number of sources, the whereabouts of one independent editor have been unknown since March; a second allegedly missing editor later turned up in Germany.

At year's end, four journalists were serving sentences of from 6 months to 2 years. Four journalists were fined for their offenses, most for being unable to produce guarantors for bail. Ten journalists remained in detention without charge; six journalists were released after completing jail terms; and 13 others were free on bail. Bail for journalists is sometimes set at unreasonably high levels, often much more than their annual salaries.

The private press, which is often irresponsible, frequently reports that government forces or regional officials commit human rights abuses. Most private press accounts, however, are too imprecise to verify.

In general, the Government continued to deny access by private journalists to government press conferences, calling into question official affirmations of support for a responsible and dynamic free press. In December, however, for the first time, the Government invited several private newspapers to cover a major government press conference. One senior minister granted unprecedented interviews to several private newspapers. Critics note that the Press Law requires the Government to be accessible to those seeking information, but the Government more typically continued to ignore this provision. It usually denied access to information, even to government journalists. Both private and government journalists wrote extensively about problems of access to information. Most, but not all, government officials refuse to speak to the private press, even to confirm or deny an allegation.

Citizens are generally free to discuss publicly any topic they choose. A number of groups critical of the Government held press conferences and public meetings without apparent retribution.

Only about 1 percent of citizens regularly read any newspaper or magazine, and citizens outside Addis Ababa have extremely limited access to the print media. As a result of poor management, market forces, and government harassment, only about nine weekly newspapers appear regularly. Foreign journalists continued to operate freely and often wrote articles critical of government policies. They or their local affiliates were granted greater access to government officials than were local journalists.

Much of the private press continues to lack professionalism in its reporting. To address this problem, the Ministry of Information and Culture established the Ethiopian Mass Media Training Institute in April. In June the Government invited 10 private newspapers to participate in a 2-month training course, but only 2 attended.

Radio remains the most influential medium in reaching those who live in rural areas. The Press Law allows for private radio stations, but the only nongovernment radio license granted so far has been to Radio Fana, a station operated by the ruling EPRDF party. The Government operates the sole television station. It rescinded a previous ban on ownership of private satellite receiving dishes and dropped import restrictions on facsimile machines and modems. Internet access is unrestricted.

The official media, including broadcast, wire service, and print media, are legally autonomous and responsible for their own management and partial revenue generation, although they continue to receive government subsidies. Government reporters practice self-censorship but have, at times, questioned official policies. In April the Government created a Press and Information Department to act as official spokesman and to implement a new information policy which will guide contacts among government, the press, and the public. At year's end, the office was not yet fully functioning.

Academic freedom is respected. Students at Addis Ababa University, who have not been allowed to have a student council since 1993, were invited to elect representatives to a student committee following demonstrations in late 1995. In general, however, political activity is not encouraged on university campuses.

b. *Freedom of Peaceful Assembly and Association.*—The Constitution provides for the right of peaceful assembly, and the Government generally permitted groups to assemble during the year. Organizers of political meetings or demonstrations must notify the Government in advance and obtain a permit. Permits are required only for large meetings and are routinely granted. A number of large public demonstrations protesting various government actions took place in Addis Ababa. Protesters demonstrated against rent increases, an end to food subsidies, military pensions, the detention of Professor Asrat, government plans to commemorate the centennial of the victory at Adwa, and the policies of the Orthodox Patriarch. The Addis Ababa Municipal Government granted permits for each of these demonstrations, and there were no reports of violence.

The Constitution provides for freedom of association and the right to engage in unrestricted peaceful political activity. Government procedures for registration of NGO's were changed, and a number of policy issues regarding NGO's remain unclear. Primary responsibility for NGO registration now rests with the Ministry of Justice (MOJ), which has not yet issued written procedures. In 1995 the Government revoked the registration certificates of 47 domestic and international NGO's. It has refused to grant new registration to several of these NGO's despite their attempts to obtain it. The Ethiopian Human Rights Council, which the Government asserts is primarily a political organization, has applied for, but has not been granted, registration as an NGO.

The Government requires political parties to register with the National Election Board (NEB). Parties that do not participate in two consecutive national elections are subject to deregistration. There are about 60 organized political parties. Of these, eight are national parties, and the remainder operate only in specific regions. In July the NEB granted registration to the Council of Alternative Forces for Peace and Democracy in Ethiopia (CAFPDE) as a national party. CAFPDE has announced its intention to establish branch offices in several regions and has launched its own newspaper which is highly critical of government policies. The NEB also registered the opposition Oromo National Congress as a political party.

c. *Freedom of Religion.*—The Constitution provides for freedom of religion, including the right of conversion, and freedom of worship exists in practice.

d. *Freedom of Movement Within the Country, Foreign Travel, Emigration, and Repatriation.*—The Constitution provides for freedom of movement, including the right of domestic and foreign travel, emigration, and repatriation. Citizens may freely change their residence or workplace. Citizens and residents are required to obtain an exit visa before departing the country.

Exit visas are issued routinely, except to persons with pending court cases or unpaid debts.

All Ethiopian Jews (Falashas and Beta Israel) who wanted to emigrate to Israel are believed to have departed. The status of thousands of Feles Mora (Ethiopians who claim forced conversation to Christianity from Judaism during the past 100 years, but who have not been accepted as Jews by the Isranli Rabbinate) remains unresolved. Israel is handling Feles Nora applications on a case-by-case basis, and the two governments have agreed to grant about 110 visas per month for family reunification.

According to both the U.N. High Commissioner for Refugees (UNHCR) and foreign diplomats, the Government treats asylum seekers fairly and cooperates with the UNHCR and other humanitarian organizations in assisting refugees and returning citizens. It provided first asylum to more than 360,000 refugees this year; most are from Somalia and Sudan. There were no reports of forced expulsion on those having a valid claim to refugee status. Ethiopia is host to a total of approximately 400,000 refugees; most are from Somalia and Sudan.

Section 3. Respect for Political Rights: The Right of Citizens to Change Their Government

This right was exercised for the first time in Ethiopian history in 1995. However, most opposition groups chose to boycott the elections, despite a widespread finding that opposition participation was possible. Boycotting parties claimed that the Government impeded their ability to participate in the political process. Concerted efforts by Western governments to promote dialogue and political reconciliation between the Government and several key opposition groups leading up to the elections were not successful. Nevertheless, observers organized by Western donor governments, the Organization of African Unity, and a coalition of domestic NGO's judged the elections to be generally free and fair, although they cited numerous irregularities. The boycott was one factor leading to an overwhelming victory by candidates of the better funded and better organized EPRDF over candidates of the relatively weak and poorly organized opposition parties and independent candidates.

Political participation remains closed to a number of organizations that have not renounced violence and do not accept the Government as a legitimate authority. These groups include Medhin, the Coalition of Ethiopian Democratic Forces, the Ethiopian People's Revolutionary Party, the Oromo Liberation Front, and several smaller Somali groups.

Neither law nor practice restricts the participation of women or minorities in politics. While women's status and political participation are greater than ever, women are minimally represented in the Council of Ministers and among the leadership of all political organizations. Only 1 of the 15 members of the Council of Ministers is a woman; 2 other women hold ministerial rank, and a number of others hold senior positions. There are only 18 women among the 660 members of Parliament, and 4 of the 23 judges on the Federal High Court are women.

Section 4. Governmental Attitude Regarding International and Nongovernmental Investigation of Alleged Violations of Human Rights

Human rights organizations include the Ethiopian Human Rights and Peace Center, the Ethiopian Congress for Democracy, Action Professionals Association for the People, the Ethiopian Womens' Lawyers Association, and the Inter-Africa Group. These groups are primarily engaged in civic and human rights education, legal assistance and trial monitoring. The Ethiopian Human Rights Council, a self-proclaimed human rights monitoring organization, continues to operate without legal status as an NGO, since the Government considers it primarily a political organization.

The Government allows visits by the ICRC and international human rights groups and permits them to operate and travel freely, although prior approval is required from regional governments for prison visits. The ICRC conducts regular visits to detention centers throughout the country. While access has generally been excellent, access to some sites in the Oromo and Somali regions was a problem. The Government has encouraged human rights groups and foreign diplomats to observe the war crimes trials since court proceedings began in 1994. Delegations from Human Rights Watch/Africa, the Committee to Protect Journalists, Reporters sans Frontieres, and the Lawyers Committee for Human Rights all visited during the year. Representatives from these organizations held substantive discussions with a number of senior government officials, including Prime Minister Meles Zenawi. Officials of the Federal Security Authority have generally been responsive to requests for information from the diplomatic community.

Section 5. Discrimination Based on Race, Sex, Religion, Disability, Language, or Social Status

The Constitution states that all persons are equal before the law. The law provides that all persons should have equal and effective protection without discrimination on grounds of race, color, sex, language, religion, political or other opinion, national or social origin, wealth, birth, or other status. The Government, however, has not yet put fully into place mechanisms for effective enforcement of these protections.

Women.—The Constitution provides for the equality of women, but these provisions are often not applied in practice. Domestic violence, including wife beating and rape, are pervasive social problems. While women have recourse to the police and the courts, societal norms and limited infrastructure inhibit many women from seeking legal redress, especially in remote areas.

Although women played a prominent role (including service in combat) during the civil war and hold some senior government positions, in practice women do not enjoy equal status with men. The law considers men and women to be equal, but tradition and cultural factors place the husband as head of the household: in practice, men typically hold land tenure and property rights for all the family. Discrimination is most acute in the rural areas, where 85 percent of the population lives, and where women work more than 13 hours per day fulfilling household and farming responsibilities. In urban areas, women have fewer employment opportunities than men, and the jobs available do not provide equal pay for equal work. In 1993 the Government launched an initiative to promote the equality of women. As a result, statutes were changed, women's concerns were factored into the Government's development planning, and women's affairs desks were established in each of the ministries.

Children.—The Government has encouraged the efforts of domestic and international NGO's that focus on children's social, health, and legal issues. However, with daunting development challenges and severely limited resources, direct government support beyond efforts to provide improved health care and basic education remains limited.

Societal abuse against young girls continues to be a serious problem. Almost all girls undergo some form of female genital mutilation (FGM), which is widely condemned by international health experts as damaging to both physical and psychological health. Clitorectomies are typically performed 7 days after birth, and the excision of the labia and infibulation, the most extreme and dangerous form of FGM, can occur any time between the age of 8 and the onset of puberty. FGM is not specifically prohibited, although it is officially discouraged, and the Government has been very supportive of the National Committee on Traditional Practices in Ethiopia, which is dedicated to eradicating FGM. Nevertheless, early childhood marriage is common in rural areas, with girls as young as age 9 being party to arranged marriages. The maternal mortality rate is extremely high, due in part to food taboos for pregnant women, early marriage, and birth complications related to FGM, especially from infibulation.

Many thousands of street children live in Addis Ababa. These children beg, sometimes as part of a gang, or work in the informal sector in order to survive. Government and privately run orphanages are unable to handle the number of street children, and younger children are often abused by older children. There are credible reports that children are maimed or blinded by their "handlers" in order to raise their earnings from begging. Abandoned infants are often overlooked or neglected at hospitals and orphanages, and those children found to be HIV-positive are taken to an Addis Ababa orphanage where very limited medical care is available.

People With Disabilities.—The Constitution stipulates that the State shall allocate resources to provide rehabilitation and assistance to the physically and mentally disabled. Limited government resources restrict action in these areas. The Amhara Development Association operates a semigovernmental project to provide vocational training to disabled war veterans in Bahir Dar. A similar center has been established by the Tigray Development Association in Mehle. In 1994 the Government passed a law mandating equal rights for the disabled, but has not yet put into place mechanisms to enforce this law. Cultural attitudes toward the disabled are often negative. The Government does not have sufficient resources to mandate access to buildings or government services for persons with disabilities, and people with minor disabilities sometimes complain of job discrimination. An official at the government's rehabilitation agency estimated that, partly as a result of the long civil war, there are more than 5 million disabled persons in the population of about 56 million.

Religious Minorities.—Accurate information on the complex relationships among Ethiopia's religious groups is difficult to obtain, especially because religious differences are often related to ethnic distinctions. Religious tensions between Christians and Muslims, particularly in certain regions (most notably the Oromiya and Somali regions) persist, and anti-Christian sentiment is sometimes fueled by historical perceptions of Christians as elite. According to reports from NGO's, tension at the local level between and among Christians and Muslims has led to incidents of harassment, intimidation, and in some cases, violence.

National/Racial/Ethnic Minorities.—There are more than 80 ethnic groups. Although all these groups have had some influence on the political and cultural life of the country, Amharas and Tigrayans from the northern highlands have played a dominant role. Some ethnic groups such as Oromos, the largest single group, claim to have been subjugated during this period by Amharas and Tigrayans. In an attempt to address these concerns, the Government has established a federal system with political boundaries drawn along major ethnic lines. With federalism, for example, citizens of the Oromo region now have greater say over their own affairs and resources than at any time in the past century. Primary school students are increasingly being taught in their local languages, consistent with the new constitution. The military services have continued their efforts to recruit ethnic minorities at all levels. The demobilization of an additional 25,000 Tigrayan soldiers was completed, and these troops were replaced by recruits from other ethnic groups. All new recruits are screened as potential officer candidates, and those who qualify are offered officer training. As regional militia were disbanded, the Government integrated over 3,500 militia members into the national defense forces. The military services also welcomed back 7,000 soldiers who had served under the previous Marxist regime and who have important technical skills. These soldiers and former militia members are often permitted to retain their previous grade, up to the rank of colonel. Six of the military's nine general officers are non-Tigrayans.

Section 6. Worker Rights

a. *The Right of Association.*—Only a small percentage of the population is involved in wage labor employment, which is largely concentrated in urban areas. Approximately 85 percent of the work force lives in the countryside, engaged in subsistence farming.

The Constitution and the 1993 Labor Law provide most workers with the right to form and join unions and engage in collective bargaining, but only about 250,000 workers are unionized. Employees of the civil and security services (where most wage earners are found), judges, and prosecutors are not allowed to form unions. Workers who provide an "essential service" are not allowed to strike. Essential services include a large number of categories such as air transport, railways, bus service, police and fire services, post and telecommunications, banks, and pharmacies. There is no requirement that unions belong to the Confederation of Ethiopian Trade Unions (CETU), which was established in 1993. CETU includes nine federations organized by industrial and service sector rather than by region. In December 1994, the Government decertified CETU following a 30-day probationary period given to permit CETU to resolve serious internal management disputes. At year's end, CETU offices remained closed despite a court ruling that there were procedural violations in the Government's action to seal the CETU offices. The offices remained closed in part because the member trade unions have been unable to agree among themselves on a unified structure to govern CETU's assets and offices. By year's end, most CETU member federations were preparing to reorganize their organizations and were expected to receive government recognition of a new CETU. The Labor Law stipulates that a trade organization may not act in an overtly political manner.

The Labor Law explicitly gives workers the right to strike to protect their interests, but it also sets forth restrictive procedures that apply before a legal strike may take place. These apply equally to an employer's right to lock out workers. Strikes must be supported by a majority of the workers affected. The Labor Law prohibits retribution against strikers. Both sides must make efforts at conciliation, provide at least 10 days' notice to the Government, include the reasons for the action, and in cases already before a court or labor board, the party must provide at least a 30-day warning. If an agreement between unions and management cannot be reached, the Minister of Labor may refer the case to arbitration by a Labor Relations Board (LRB). The Government established LRB's at the national level and in some regions. The Minister of Labor and Social Affairs appoints each LRB chairman, and the four board members are composed of two each from trade unions and employer groups. Some efforts to enforce these regulations are made within the formal industrial sector.

Independent unions and those belonging to CETU are free to affiliate with, and participate in, international labor bodies.

b. *The Right to Organize and Bargain Collectively.*—Collective bargaining is protected under the Labor Law and under the Constitution, and it is practiced freely throughout the country. Collective bargaining agreements concluded between 1975 and the promulgation of the 1993 Labor Law are covered under the 1975 Labor Code and remain in force. Labor experts estimate that more than 90 percent of unionized workers are covered by collective bargaining agreements. Wages are negotiated at the plant level. The law prohibits antiunion discrimination by employers against union members and organizers. There are grievance procedures for hearings on allegations of discrimination brought by individuals or unions. Employers found guilty of antiunion discrimination are required to reinstate workers fired for union activities.

c. *Prohibition of Forced or Compulsory Labor.*—The Constitution proscribes slavery, which was officially abolished in 1942, and involuntary servitude. There are no reports of slavery. The Criminal Code specifically prohibits forced labor unless by court order as a punitive measure.

d. *Minimum Age for Employment of Children.*—Under the Labor Law, the minimum age for wage or salary employment is 14 years; children between the ages of 14 and 18 years are covered by special provisions. Children may not work more than 7 hours per day; work between the hours of 10 p.m. and 6 a.m.; work on public holidays or rest days; or perform overtime work. While some efforts to enforce these regulations are made within the formal industrial sector, large numbers of children of all ages grow and harvest crops outside most government regulatory control in the countryside, or work as street peddlers in the cities.

e. *Acceptable Conditions of Work.*—There is no minimum wage in the private sector. However, since 1985 a minimum wage has been set and paid to public sector employees, by far the largest group of wage earners. This public sector minimum wage is about $16 (105 Ethiopian birr) per month, which is insufficient to provide a decent standard of living for a worker and family. According to the Office of the Study of Wages and Other Remunerations, a family of five requires a monthly income of $61 (390 Ethiopian birr). Thus, even with two minimum wage earners, a family receives only about half the income needed for adequate subsistence.

The legal workweek, as stipulated in the Labor Law, is 48 hours, consisting of 6 days of 8 hours each, with a 24-hour rest period. However, in practice, most employees work a 40-hour workweek, 5 days of 8 hours each.

The Government, industry, and unions negotiate to set occupational health and safety standards. However, the Inspection Department of the Ministry of Labor and Social Affairs enforces these standards ineffectively, due to a lack of human and financial resources. Workers have the right to remove themselves from dangerous situations without jeopardy to continued employment.

GABON

A one-party state until 1990, Gabon held its first multiparty elections in 1991, with President Omar Bongo's party retaining a large majority in the National Assembly. President Bongo, in office since 1967, was reelected in 1993 in an election marred by serious irregularities. After several months of contention and civil unrest, political parties supporting the President and the principal opposition parties negotiated in October 1994 the "Paris Accords." These agreements included promises of reforms to amend electoral procedures, to include opposition leaders in government, and to assure greater respect for human rights. These were approved by a national referendum in July 1995. Opposition parties won disorganized municipal elections in the capital in October and November, while in December parties supporting the President won more than two-thirds of the seats in the National Assembly in elections that the opposition claimed were marred by massive fraud. The judiciary is independent but remains vulnerable to government manipulation.

The national police and the gendarmerie enforce the law and maintain public security. In conformity with the Paris Accords, the National Assembly reassigned authority over these security forces from the Ministry of Defense to the Ministry of the Interior and redesignated as the "Republican Guard," an elite, heavily armed corps that protects the President. In 1994 the Defense Minister used this corps for violent repression of public dissent, but more recently it has not acted with undue force. Security forces on occasion beat persons in custody.

The Government generally adheres to free market principles, particularly in the export sector, in which trade is dominated by petroleum, timber, and minerals. A majority of workers in the formal sector are employed by the Government or by large inefficient state-owned organizations. Per capita income is approximately $4,600 annually, and income distribution is badly skewed in favor of urban dwellers and a small economic elite. Immigrants from other African countries dominate the informal sector. The rural population is poor and receives few social services. Financial mismanagement and corruption have resulted in significant arrears in domestic and external debt. The Government continued to meet most of its structural adjustment performance goals.

The Government maintained a generally satisfactory human rights performance and made slow but measurable progress in instituting democratic electoral practices. Civil peace prevailed as the ruling Gabonese Democratic Party, members of the opposition coalition High Council of the Resistance, and other parties conducted negotiations, appealed to legal institutions, and used international mediation to resolve differences over interpretation and implementation of the Paris Accords. However, longstanding human rights abuses continued. The security forces beat and tortured prisoners and detainees, and prison conditions remained abysmal. Societal discrimination and violence against women, and exploitation of expatriate children as domestic and agricultural workers remained problems.

RESPECT FOR HUMAN RIGHTS

Section 1. Respect for the Integrity of the Person, Including Freedom From:

a. *Political and Other Extrajudicial Killing.*—There were no reports of political or other extrajudicial killing.

b. *Disappearance.*—There were no reports of politically motivated disappearances.

c. *Torture and Other Cruel, Inhuman, or Degrading Treatment or Punishment.*—The Constitution prohibits torture or cruel and inhuman punishment. However, security forces often beat or physically mistreat prisoners and detainees as punishment and to exact confessions.

Conditions in most prisons are abysmal and life threatening. Sanitation and ventilation are poor, and medical care is almost nonexistent. Prisons provide inadequate food for inmates. There were no known visits by human rights monitors to prisons during the year.

d. *Arbitrary Arrest, Detention, or Exile.*—The law provides for up to 48 hours of initial preventive detention, during which time police must charge a detainee before a judge. In practice, however, police rarely respect this provision. Bail may be set if there is to be a further investigation. Pretrial detainees have the right to free access to their attorneys. This right is respected in practice. Detainees have the right to an expeditious trial, as defined by the law. Pretrial detention is limited to 6 months for a misdemeanor and to 1 year for a felony charge. These periods may be extended up to 6 months longer by the examining magistrate. The Attorney General's office estimates that roughly 40 percent of persons in custody are pretrial detainees.

Exile is not used as a punishment nor as a means of political control, and there are no opposition leaders living in exile.

e. *Denial of Fair Public Trial.*—The Constitution provides for an independent judiciary. The judiciary is generally independent but remains vulnerable to government manipulation.

The Constitution provides for the right to a public trial and the right to legal counsel. These rights are generally respected in criminal cases. Nevertheless, procedural safeguards are lacking, particularly in state security trials. The law applies the concept of presumed guilt. A judge may thus deliver an immediate verdict at the initial hearing if sufficient evidence is presented by the State.

The judicial system includes the regular courts, a military tribunal, and a civilian State Security Court. The regular court system includes trial courts, appellate courts, and the Supreme Court. The Constitutional Court is a separate body charged with examining constitutional questions, including the certification of elections. There are no traditional or customary courts. In some areas, minor disputes may be taken to a local chief, but the Government does not recognize such decisions. The State Security Court, last convened in 1990, is constituted by the Government as required basis to consider matters of state security.

There were no reports of political prisoners.

f. *Arbitrary Interference With Privacy, Family, Home, or Correspondence.*—The Constitution provides for protection from surveillance, from searches without warrant, and from interference with private telecommunications or correspondence. As part of criminal investigations, police may request search warrants from judges, which they obtain easily, sometimes after the fact. The Government has used them in the past to gain access to the homes of opposition figures and their families. Government authorities also routinely monitor private telephone conversations, personal mail, and the movements of citizens.

Section 2. Respect for Civil Liberties, Including:

a. *Freedom of Speech and Press.*—The Constitution provides for freedom of speech and the press, and in practice, citizens speak freely and criticize leaders. Legislators in the National Assembly openly criticize government policies, ministers, and other officials.

The only daily newspaper is the government-owned L'Union, but there are more than a half-dozen weekly or periodical publications in newspaper format, representing independent views and those of various political parties. All—including L'Union—actively criticize the Government and political leaders of all parties. Most also criticize the President.

The National Communication Council (NCC), an appointed body, twice imposed restrictions on an opposition-owned radio station during election periods for broadcasting interviews and listener comments judged by the NCC to be dangerous to public order.

The Government controls national electronic media, which reach all areas of the country. Four private radio stations have been licensed and a fifth operates under a temporary permit. Journalists are subject to an extensive code of rights and responsibilities approved by the National Assembly in 1995.

The Government does not interfere with broadcasts of international radio stations Radio France 1, Africa No. 1, or the Voice of America. Foreign newspapers and magazines are widely available.

There are no restrictions on academic freedom, including research.

b. *Freedom of Peaceful Assembly and Association.*—Citizens and recognized organizations normally enjoy freedom of assembly and association which are provided for by the Constitution. Groups must obtain permits for public gatherings in advance, and the Government usually grants them.

c. *Freedom of Religion.*—The Constitution provides for religious freedom, and authorities do not engage in religious persecution or favoritism. There is no state religion. While the Government has not lifted its ban on Jehovah's Witnesses, neither has it enforced this ban.

d. *Freedom of Movement Within the Country, Foreign Travel, Emigration, and Repatriation.*—The Constitution provides for these rights. There are no legally mandated restrictions on internal movement. Police and gendarmes frequently stop travelers to check identity, residence, or registration documents, and members of the security forces regularly harass expatriate Africans working legally as merchants, service sector employees, and manual laborers. They extorted bribes and demanded services with the threat of confiscation of residence documents or imprisonment. Residence permits cost up to $1,000.

An unevenly enforced law requires married women to have their husbands' permission to travel abroad. An exit visa is no longer required for citizens to travel abroad. Aliens resident in the country must obtain a visa in order to leave and return.

The Government strictly controls the process of refugee adjudication. Coordination with the U.N. High Commissioner for Refugees (UNHCR) has improved in assisting refugees, and there were no credible reports that the Government had forcibly repatriated illegal aliens. There were about 350 refugees at year's end.

Section 3. Respect for Political Rights: The Right of Citizens to Change Their Government

The 1991 Constitution explicitly provides this right, but mismanagement and serious irregularities in both the 1990 legislative elections and the 1993 presidential election called into serious doubt the extent to which this right exists in practice.

In a July 1995 constitutional referendum, citizens approved by a 96 percent majority reforms previously agreed in the Paris Accords, including most significantly the establishment of an independent National Electoral Commission (NEC). The referendum was carried out under arrangements that assured that all political parties could monitor voting and vote counting.

National Assembly, Senate, and municipal elections scheduled for the Spring were postponed several times due to legislative inaction, government delays, and requests by the NEC for additional time. The NEC, created in May, institutionalized a process in which majority, opposition, and civil service representatives organized elections. Delays in registering voters and organizing elections were attributed by all sides to logistical rather than political obstacles.

Local elections scheduled for October 20 were poorly organized and were repeated on November 24 in the capital, Libreville. In each case, opposition parties won most of the municipal council seats in the capital. This result was reversed in the official results of legislative elections on December 15 and December 29, in which parties supporting the President took more than 80 of the 120 National Assembly seats, including 8 of the 10 seats representing the capital. Opposition parties claimed massive collaboration in fraud by the military and NEC magistrates in ensuring victory for parties supporting the President.

There are no restrictions on the participation of women and minorities in politics. There are 6 women among the 120 National Assembly representatives and 1 in the Cabinet. Women serve at all levels within the various ministries, the judiciary, and the opposition. Despite governmental protections, indigenous Pygmies rarely participate in the political process, and the Government has made only marginal efforts to include them (see Section 5).

Section 4. Governmental Attitude Regarding International and Nongovernmental Investigation of Alleged Violations of Human Rights

The Government officially allows the existence of independent human rights groups. There are two human rights groups, neither of which was active. There were no reports of harassment by officials.

There have been no active inquiries from foreign groups in recent years.

Section 5. Discrimination Based on Race, Sex, Religion, Disability, Language, or Social Status

The Constitution forbids discrimination based on national origin, race, gender, or opinion. The Government does not uniformly enforce these constitutional guarantees and tolerates a substantial degree of discrimination against women, especially in domestic affairs. It has also provided a lower level of health care and educational services to children of families of other African nationalities than it provided to citizens.

Women.—Violence against women is common and is especially prevalent in rural areas. While medical authorities have not specifically identified rape to be a chronic problem, religious workers and hospital staff report that evidence of physical beatings of women is common. Police rarely intervene in such cases, and women virtually never file complaints with civil authorities. Only limited medical and legal assistance is available.

The law provides that women have rights to equal access in education, business, and investment. Women own businesses and property, participate in politics, and work throughout the government and the private sector. Women nevertheless continue to face considerable societal and legal discrimination, especially in rural areas.

By law, couples must stipulate at the time of marriage whether they will adhere to a monogamous or a polygynous relationship. For monogamous married couples, a common property law provides for the equal distribution of assets after divorce. Wives who leave polygynous husbands suffer severe reductions in their property rights. In inheritance cases, the husband's family must issue a written authorization before his widow can inherit property. Common law marriage, which is socially accepted and widely practiced, affords a woman no property rights.

The law still requires that a woman obtain her husband's permission to travel abroad; however, this requirement is not consistently enforced. The 1995 National Assembly proposal allowing husbands to alter retroactively the legal status of their marriages from monogamous to polygynous was never formally introduced into the legislature.

Children.—The Government has used Gabon's oil revenue to build schools, to pay adequate teacher salaries, and to promote education, even in rural areas. Gabon has a relatively high infant mortality rate, and not all children have access to vaccination. Traditional beliefs and practices provide numerous safeguards for children, but children remain the responsibility of the extended family—including aunts, grandmothers, and older siblings. There is little evidence of physical abuse of children. Protection for children's rights is not codified in law.

There is concern about the problems facing the large community of children of African noncitizens. Almost all enjoy far less access to education and health care than do children of Gabonese, and are sometimes victims of child labor abuses (see Section 6.d.). While female genital mutilation is not practiced on Gabonese children, it does occur among the resident population of expatriate Africans.

People With Disabilities.—There are no laws prohibiting discrimination against persons with disabilities, nor providing for access to buildings or services.

Indigenous People.—Several thousand indigenous Pygmies live in northeastern Gabon. In principle they enjoy the same civil rights as other citizens. Pygmies are largely independent of formal authority, keeping their own traditions, independent communities, and local decisionmaking structures. Pygmies did not participate in government-instituted programs that integrated many small rural villages into larger ones along major roads. As a result, their access to government-funded health and sanitation facilities was limited. There are no specific government programs or policies to assist or hinder Pygmies.

National/Racial/Ethnic Minorities.—Persons from all major ethnic groups continued to occupy prominent positions in government, in the military services, and in the private sector. Credible reports suggest, however, that ethnic favoritism in hiring and promotion is pervasive. There was evidence, especially within the armed forces, that members of the President's ethnic group held a disproportionately large share both of senior positions and of jobs within the ranks.

Section 6. Worker Rights

a. *The Right of Association.*—The Constitution places no restrictions on the right of association and recognizes the right of citizens to form trade and labor unions. Virtually the entire formal private sector work force is unionized. Unions must register with the Government in order to be recognized officially. Public sector employees may unionize although their right to strike is limited if it could jeopardize public safety. Until 1990 there was only one recognized labor organization, the Gabonese Labor Confederation (COSYGA), to which all unionized workers contributed a mandatory percentage of their salaries. In 1992 the Government accepted the establishment of independent unions and abolished the mandatory contribution to COSYGA.

In November 1994, the National Assembly passed an extensively revised version of the Labor Code, which was published and implemented in early 1995. The Code provides extensive protection of worker rights.

Strikes are legal if they are held after an 8-day notice advising that outside arbitration has failed. The Labor Code prohibits direct government action against individual strikers who abide by the arbitration and notification provisions. It also provides that the Government cannot press charges against a group as a whole for criminal activities committed by individuals. Unions and confederations are free to affiliate with international labor bodies and participate in their activities. COSYGA is affiliated with the Organization of African Trade Union Unity, while the Gabonese Confederation of Free Unions (CGSL) is affiliated with the International Confederation of Free Trade Unions. Both COSYGA and CGSL have ties to numerous other international labor organizations.

b. *The Right to Organize and Bargain Collectively.*—The Labor Code provides for collective bargaining. Labor and management meet to negotiate differences, and the Ministry of Labor provides an observer. This observer does not take an active part in negotiations over pay scales, working conditions, or benefits. Agreements also apply to nonunion workers. While no laws specifically prohibit antiunion discrimination, the court may require employers found guilty by civil courts of having engaged in such discrimination to compensate employees.

There are no export processing zones.

c. *Prohibition of Forced or Compulsory Labor.*—The law prohibits forced labor, and there are no reports that it now exists.

d. *Minimum Age for the Employment of Children.*—Children below the age of 16 may not work without the express consent of the Ministries of Labor, Education, and Public Health. These ministries rigorously enforce this law with respect to Gabonese children, and there are few Gabonese under the age of 18 working in the modern wage sector. A significant number of children work in marketplaces or perform domestic duties. The U.N. Children's Fund (UNICEF) and other concerned organizations have reported that government officials often privately use foreign child labor, mainly as domestic or agricultural help. These children do not go to school, have only limited means of acquiring medical attention, and are often victims of exploitation by employers or foster families. Laws forbidding child labor theoretically extend protection to foreign children as well, but abuses often are not reported. There is no compulsory education law.

e. *Acceptable Conditions of Work.*—The Labor Code governs working conditions and benefits for all sectors and provides a broad range of protection to workers. The Code stipulates a 40-hour workweek with a minimum rest period of 48 consecutive hours. Employers must compensate workers for overtime work. All companies in the modern wage sector pay competitive wages and grant generous fringe benefits required by law, including maternity leave and 6 weeks of annual paid vacation.

Traditionally, representatives of labor, management, and the Government met annually to examine economic and labor conditions and to recommend a minimum wage rate within government guidelines to the President, who then issued an annual decree. This procedure was not followed in 1995 or in 1996, in part because the Government was pursuing a policy of wage austerity recommended by international financial institutions. The monthly minimum wage was kept at its 1994 level of about $125 (cfa 64,000). Wages do provide for a decent standard of living for a worker and family.

The Ministry of Health has established occupational health and safety standards but does not effectively enforce or regulate them. Application of labor standards varies greatly from company to company and between industries. The Government reportedly does not enforce labor code provisions in sectors where the bulk of the labor force is non-Gabonese. Foreigners, both documented and undocumented, may be obliged to work under substandard conditions; may be dismissed without notice or recourse; or may be physically mistreated, especially in the case of illegal aliens. Employers frequently require longer hours of work from noncitizen Africans and pay them less, often hiring on a short-term, casual basis in order to avoid paying taxes, social security contributions, and other benefits. In the formal sector, workers may remove themselves from dangerous work situations without fear of retribution.

THE GAMBIA

The Gambia is controlled by President Yahya A.J.J. Jammeh, the military leadership that joined him in a coup d'etat, and other members of the cabinet formed subsequently. Jammeh is the former chairman of the Armed Forces Provisional Ruling Council (AFPRC) that seized power in a coup d'etat in 1994, deposing the democratically elected government of Sir Dawda Jawara. Jammeh became President following controversial elections in September that observers considered neither free nor fair. Following his election, Jammeh dissolved the AFPRC and declared the Cabinet to be the sole ruling body until the National Assembly is elected in January 1997. President Jammeh and his party, the Alliance for Patriotic Reorientation and Construction (APRC), strongly backed by the armed forces, continue to dominate the Government and to repress most genuine opposition forces. The judiciary remained sensitive to government pressure.

The Gambian National Army (GNA) reports to the Minister of Defense (who is now the President). The police report to the Minister of Interior. The National Intelligence Agency (NIA), established in 1995 by government decree, reports directly to the Head of State but is otherwise autonomous. The AFPRC Government and some members of the security forces committed serious human rights abuses.

The Gambia's population of just over 1 million consists largely of subsistence farmers growing rice, millet, maize, and groundnuts (peanuts), the country's primary export crop. The private sector, led by reexporting, fisheries, horticulture, and tourism, contracted after the 1994 coup, but appears to be rebounding. Cuts in international economic assistance coupled with high population growth have worsened the economic decline.

The Government's poor human rights record continued as it committed widespread and repeated human rights abuses, but it improved somewhat during the year. Although the Government repealed a decree banning all political activities, in practice citizens still do not have an effective opportunity to change their government, although parliamentary opposition is becoming increasingly significant. Security forces beat and abused detainees. The AFPRC arrested and detained senior government officials and members of the press. It held detainees incommunicado and did not acknowledge their detentions; detained armed forces and police personnel without charge; banned political parties and specific individuals from political activity; curbed political activities, publications, and other communications; violently disrupted opposition campaign trips; and intimidated the press. The rights to travel and the right to transfer funds or assets for senior officials of the former Jawara government remained restricted in several cases. Prison conditions remained poor, and the courts remained subject to executive influence. AFPRC decrees abrogated due process and allowed the Government to search, seize, and detain without warrant or legal proceedings. The AFPRC ordered the arbitrary arrest, firing, and retirement of government officials and civil service employees loyal to the previous government. Discrimination against women persists. While health professionals have focused greater attention on the dangers of female genital mutilation (FGM), the practice is widespread and entrenched.

The AFPRC took some steps toward the formation of democratic institutions, but still retained control. A new Constitution defining most aspects of the Second Republic was approved in a national referendum in August and came into effect in January 1997 with the inauguration of the President. However, restrictive security decrees remain in effect. Given harsh press intimidation, the independent press has shown caution and practices self-censorship.

RESPECT FOR HUMAN RIGHTS

Section 1. Respect for the Integrity of the Person, Including Freedom From:

a. *Political and Other Extrajudicial Killing.*—There were no reports of political or other extrajudicial killings.

There were no developments in the 1995 deaths of Saidbou Haidara or Finance Minister Ousman Koro-Ceesay. The opposition used the lack of investigation in these cases to criticize the Government during the presidential campaign.

b. *Disappearance.*—There were no reports of politically motivated disappearances.

c. *Torture and Other Cruel, Inhuman, or Degrading Treatment or Punishment.*—The AFPRC did not suspend the previous Constitution's prohibition against torture and other cruel, inhuman, or degrading punishment and the new Constitution also forbids such practice. However, there were reports by detainees that agents of the State used torture or the threat of torture in interrogating them.

In January one of the detainees on trial for sedition testified that soldiers beat him in an attempt to obtain a confession from him. A woman on trial for sedition said that she was threatened with electric shock when she failed to answer questions regarding clandestine publications alleged to have been in her possession.

At the height of the September presidential election campaign, soldiers dragged 100 to 200 members of the opposition United Democratic Party (UDP) from their vehicles headed to Banjul. The soldiers ripped off the UDP members' party-labeled shirts, fired shots over their heads, confiscated their public address system, and burned UDP election materials. The opposition party members were forced to go to NIA headquarters where they were harassed and beaten, stripped of their clothing, and forced to run from the building. One senior member of the UDP leadership who refused to run was beaten with a rifle butt and suffered a broken hand.

Conditions at Mile 2 and Janjanbureh prisons remained poor. Mile 2 prison was reported to be austere, overcrowded, and lacking in medical facilities. Prisoners are locked in their cells for over 20 hours each day. Other reports indicate that the AFPRC assigned military guards to augment the corrections staff at the prison, and there were credible reports of malnourishment, illness, and beatings of military and security detainees. Women are housed separately.

Conditions in one local jail were reportedly unsanitary and overcrowded. Inmates slept on cement benches or the floor with no blankets. They were served two small meals a day, one consisting only of rice. There was one water tap in the cell area, but often no water.

The Government permitted no visits by international human rights groups. The African Center for Democracy and Human Rights Studies submitted numerous informal requests throughout the year to inspect prison conditions and the status of detainees, but its requests were repeatedly thwarted by the Government.

d. *Arbitrary Arrest, Detention, or Exile.*—The sections of the Constitution that protect against arbitrary arrest and detention were superseded by various decrees of the AFPRC. While there are provisions in the new Constitution that will provide protections, the restrictive security decrees that limited the previous Constitution remain in force. The AFPRC frequently and arbitrarily arrested military and police personnel, civil servants, parastatal staff, and media representatives. In 1995 the AFPRC declared by decree that the NIA would have the power to search, seize, detain, or arrest any individual or property without due process, and that the Minister of Interior could order a 90-day detention without charge and not subject to writ of habeas corpus. In January the AFPRC issued Decree 66, extending indefinitely the period the Minister of Interior may hold a person without charge. The new Constitution does not supersede these decrees, which remain in force.

The regime subjected prominent civilians in and out of government to lengthy surprise interrogations in uncomfortable circumstances, often lasting overnight, and detained some officials for extended periods.

Member of Parliament Lamin Waa Juwara was reported missing in March. Inquiries by family members were met with claims that the Government knew nothing about his detention or whereabouts. Senior government officials have privately acknowledged to a foreign diplomat that the Government is holding Juwara, but it has not publicly acknowledged his detention or charged him with any offense.

In January and in July, the Supreme Court rejected writ of habeas corpus applications for Housainou Njie and Momodou Cadi Cham, held in detention for political reasons since October 1995. The Court maintained that Decrees 57 and 66 give the Government the right to detain prisoners indefinitely. They were unconditionally released on November 4.

In January two visiting Senegalese journalists were seized and harassed by the NIA. They were later released only after repeatedly explaining their presence in the country.

A student and freelance reporter was arrested in February and detained for 7 days by the NIA, reportedly for submissions he made to the British Broadcasting Corporation Focus on Africa program.

The Government brought charges against all independent newspapers in March for failing to make annual returns (information regarding ownership of the paper and a signed bond). The newspapers said that the returns had been made, and the charges were subsequently dropped.

In April the NIA detained reporter S.B. Danso for 24 hours reportedly in reaction to a story he wrote about Mrs. Tuti Faal Jammeh, wife of the Head of State.

In June the NIA arrested and interrogated journalist Ansumana Badjie in connection with "negative reporting." He subsequently left the country fearing persecution.

In May journalists Alieu Badara Sowe and Bruce Asemota were arrested at their respective offices. They were held incommunicado for 16 days and then released. Both Badara and Sowe had written articles reporting fraud and dismissals in the national police department. While in detention, police demanded that they reveal their sources. Newspaper stories stated that Asemota was beaten.

Prior to the September 26 presidential election, opposition supporters were arrested and allegedly intimidated by the security and armed forces (see Section 1.c.). Following the election, there were several reports of opposition supporters being arrested and detained for allegedly making critical remarks about the government party.

In September the public relations officer for the opposition UDP disappeared following the party's launching ceremony. His mother said that men claiming to be NIA officers came to her residence looking for him. He appeared in Dakar a week later, claiming he had to flee his country because he was harassed and intimidated by the NIA.

The authorities generally did not permit families, independent observers, or other private citizens to visit military, police, or civilian detainees. Family members of detainees were subjected to intimidation and harassment by security forces, who made verbal threats and unannounced searches. In July two wives of detainees were followed home by NIA agents after meeting with a local human rights organization. Their houses were immediately searched and they were threatened with detention.

The AFPRC did not provide an accounting of detainees. Since the dissolution of the AFPRC, the President and the Cabinet govern. The decision regarding arrests and detentions lies with the executive branch. A journalist and a local nongovernmental organization named 29 military and police personnel whom they claimed have been arrested and detained since July 22, 1994. Of these 11 were released unconditionally on October 29. The reasons for these arrests and detentions are largely unknown. Along with military, police personnel, and civilians in long-term detention, the authorities detained an unknown number of additional people for shorter periods, ranging from hours to days. The majority of the 35 people arrested in October 1995, allegedly for attempting to organize a demonstration, were released by the end of 1996. The remainder reportedly have been charged with sedition. In August the AFPRC issued a decree banning a number of former political parties and their members from political activity for 30 years (see Section 3).

The Head of State pardoned 60 prisoners. In January four soldiers who had been detained since the 1994 military coup were granted amnesty. In February 20 prisoners, some who were political detainees from 1995, were pardoned. In July 13 political detainees were released. In October 11 security detainees were released, followed by 12 political detainees in November.

The government did not exile opponents. However, three senior officials of the former government, President Jawara, Vice President Sabally, and Secretary General Janha, remain outside the country under threat of arrest and detention if they return. Other officials who were outside the country at the time of the coup are at similar risk.

e. *Denial of Fair Public Trial.*—Although the Constitution provides for an independent judiciary, the courts are traditionally responsive to executive branch pressure.

The judicial system comprises a Judicial Committee of the Privy Council (based in London), the Supreme Court, the Court of Appeal, and the magistrate courts (one in each of the five divisions plus one in Banjul and one in Kanifing). The new Constitution provides for a reconfiguration of the courts in which a Supreme Court will replace the Privy Council as the ultimate court of appeal. Village chiefs preside over local courts at the village level. The AFPRC claimed that the judicial provisions of the Constitution remained in effect, but exempted its own decrees from court challenge and ignored due process with respect to arrest, detention, and trial.

The AFPRC appointed a number of commissions to investigate individuals and organizations suspected of corruption. These commissions have powers similar to a grand jury, including the authority to imprison and fine for contempt, and to imprison or demand bond from individuals considered likely to abscond. The commission findings recommended that the Government ban certain former politicians from running for political office for 5 to 20 years.

Despite these incidents, the judicial system remains structurally intact and recognizes customary Shari'a and general law. Customary law covers marriage and divorce for non-Muslims, inheritance, land tenure, tribal and clan leadership, and all other traditional and social relations. Shari'a law is observed primarily in Muslim marriage and divorce matters. Under Shari'a women receive half of what men receive in inheritance. General law, following the English model, applies to felonies, misdemeanors in urban areas, and the formal business sector. Trials are public, and defendants have the right to an attorney at their own cost.

Although total numbers are not available, most prisoners detained under the AFPRC's anticorruption campaign, or for security reasons, were political detainees. The bulk of those detained were released by year's end.

f. *Arbitrary Interference With Privacy, Family, Home, or Correspondence.*—Existing Constitutional safeguards against arbitrary search were abrogated as part of Decree 45. AFPRC priorities in security matters and corruption investigations override all Constitutional safeguards. Despite the new Constitution, Decree 45 remains in force.

Police seized private property and documents without due process and placed armed guards at homes and other properties suspected of having been acquired with embezzled or misappropriated funds. The AFPRC froze accounts of people under suspicion and prohibited by decree the transfer of their property. A number of instances remain unresolved. Observers assume that the Government monitors citizens engaged in activity that it deems objectionable. In the past, surveillance included monitoring of telephones and mail. The AFPRC also denied persons under house arrest access to international telephone service.

Opposition leader Ousainou Darboe fled his home and took refuge in the Senegalese embassy for 4 days following the presidential elections. The NIA posted agents outside Darboe's house, and Darboe claimed that the NIA made repeated death threats and harassed him. NIA agents were later withdrawn, and Darboe resumed his political activity.

Section 2. Respect for Civil Liberties, Including:

a. *Freedom of Speech and Press.*—The old and new Constitutions provide for freedom of speech and the press but in practice the AFPRC significantly restricted these freedoms. Until August political activities of all kinds, including possession and distribution of political literature or engaging in political discourse by any other means, was prohibited. Although Decree 89, promulgated in August, lifted some prohibitions on political activity, an atmosphere of fear remained regarding political action and relatively free exercise of political rights began only in December with the opening of the legislative electoral campaign.

The AFPRC attempted to require diplomats to secure government approval for all public statements.

The AFPRC used government decrees, summary arrest, interrogation, and detention to intimidate and silence journalists and newspapers that published articles that it deemed inaccurate or sensitive (see Section 1.d.). In March the AFPRC enacted Decrees 70 and 71, which required all newspapers to post a $10,000 bond or cease publication. While publishers posted the bonds within the allotted time frame, the Ministry of Justice rejected the bonds, claiming that the newspapers did not meet other conditions, not initially stipulated in the decree. As a result, nongovernmental newspapers ceased publication for 1 week until the Minister of Justice accepted the bonds. Fear of reprisals and government action forced all newspapers to exercise self-censorship. English, French, and other foreign newspapers and magazines are available. Although still independent, the nongovernment press grew cautious as the four major independent dailies practiced increasing self-censorship. Following the September presidential election, there was some lessening of restrictions on the press with greater visibility for opposition views and more criticism of government policies.

Although the AFPRC called for analysis and criticism of the way in which it governed, it frequently carried out reprisals against individuals who publicly criticized the Government. A government-sponsored television station, The Gambia's first, began broadcasting nationwide in September. During the presidential election campaign, the programming consisted mostly of government propaganda. The country also receives broadcasts from Senegal. Wealthy private consumers also use satellite systems.

Radio broadcasts from one government and two private stations normally did not reach listeners in the eastern part of the country until power was increased late in the year. Private radio stations simulcast news provided by Radio Gambia, the government station. Senegalese and international radio broadcasts attract wide audiences.

During the presidential elections, the government party dominated the public media. The Provisional Independent Electoral Commission reported that the Head of State had more than 1,400 minutes of air time, while the leading opposition candidate had only 60 minutes.

There is no university, but a university extension program completed its first academic year in August. There are no reports of any government restrictions on academic freedom.

b. *Freedom of Peaceful Assembly and Association.*—AFPRC decrees banned political organizations and political meetings of any kind throughout most of the year. While Decree 89 lifted the ban on political activities in August, the AFPRC's subsequent banning from politics of three major opposition political parties, all former presidents, vice presidents, and ministers, and other politicians; and its imposition of stiff penalties of life imprisonment or a $100,000 fine considerably restricted political activity and involvement.

c. *Freedom of Religion.*—The Constitution, which was partially suspended or modified after the AFPRC took power, and traditional laws provide for freedom of religion. Adherents of all faiths are free to worship without government restriction. The new Constitution provides for freedom of religion.

d. *Freedom of Movement Within the Country, Foreign Travel, Emigration, and Repatriation.*—The new Constitution provides for freedom of movement. Freedom of movement for ordinary citizens remained unimpeded, but the authorities prohibited those under investigation for corruption or security charges from leaving the country. Journalists and government officials have been required to produce travel clearances. Former ministers were not allowed to leave the country.

In June the Head of State instructed divisional commissioners not to issue passports to young people until after September, when the farming season ended.

The Government cooperates with the Office of the United Nations High Commissioner for Refugees (UNHCR) and other humanitarian organizations in assisting refugees. The Government provides first asylum and it did so for approximately 1,500 persons from Liberia and Sierra Leone in 1996, according to UNHCR. The Government works with the UNHCR in approving cases: the UNHCR identifies those that qualify for asylum or refugee status and the Government approves. There were no reports of persons forced to return to countries in which they feared persecution.

The Gambia continues to host approximately 2,000 Senegalese refugees from the Casamance region, and the AFPRC continued to work with the UNHCR, the Gambian Red Cross, and other organizations in dealing with refugees. Additionally, there are hundreds of refugees from Liberia and Sierra Leone. While there were no reports of forced expulsion of those having a valid claim to refugee status, in November the Government reevaluated the status of many of the refugees from Liberia and Sierra Leone, following an attack on a military barracks near the Senegalese border.

Section 3. Respect for Political Rights: The Right of Citizens to Change Their Government

Citizens do not have an effective right to change their government, although parliamentary opposition is becoming increasingly significant. The first decree issued by the AFPRC in 1994 suspended legislative and executive sections of the Constitution, including provisions for Parliament and elections. Although the Government repealed a decree banning all political activities, in practice citizens still do not have any effective means by which to change their government. Decree 89 allowed the resumption of political activities with serious limitations on specific organizations and individuals. The Decree banned all persons who held the offices of president, vice president, and minister since 1965 from involvement in politics for 30 years from the date of the AFPRC's coup d'etat. Banned under the same conditions were the People's Progressive Party, the National Convention Party, and the Gambia Peoples Party. The penalty for violation of the decree is a fine of $100,000 or possible life imprisonment. The Decree was widely interpreted as a tactic by the AFPRC to eliminate political opponents in the presidential elections.

Citizens attempted to exercise the right to change their government through a democratic process in presidential elections held in September. However, the few international observers that were present noted serious problems in the electoral process. Foreign governments condemned the election as not free and fair primarily because of restrictions imposed by the Government prior to the election.

The Constitution prohibits discrimination on the basis of sex, and there are no obstacles to the participation of women in government. Four of the 16 ministers in the AFPRC Executive Council (cabinet) were women. The AFPRC appointed more women to government positions than the previous government. The new Constitution will expand the voting rights of women at the local level.

Section 4. Governmental Attitude Regarding International and Nongovernmental Investigation of Alleged Violations of Human Rights

There are few organizations in The Gambia whose mandate permits human rights monitoring. The AFPRC promulgated Decree 81 requiring nongovernmental organizations (NGO's) to register with a National Advisory Council, to be appointed by the Government. This Council is to have the authority to deny, suspend, or cancel any NGO's right to operate, including international NGO's.

The AFPRC believes it inappropriate for international human rights observers to express concern for those whom the Government suspects of corruption or involvement in subversion, since the Government considers them criminals. There are two organizations whose primary mandate is the promotion of human rights—the International Society for Human Rights (ISHRA) and the African Center for Democracy and Human Rights Studies (ACDHRS). Both ISHRA and ACDHRS have conducted training in democratic rights and civic education. ACDHRS made numerous calls throughout the year for the Government to provide information on the judicial status of detainees, account for alleged disappearances and beatings at the hands of security forces, and release those held without charge. No visits of prisons were granted to international human rights organizations and inquiries as to the status of prisoners were often ignored or denied.

Section 5. Discrimination Based on Race, Sex, Religion, Disability, Language, or Social Status

The old and new Constitutions prohibit discrimination based on race, sex, religion, disability, language, or social status.

Women.—Domestic violence, including abuse, is occasionally reported, but its occurrence is not believed to be extensive. Police respond if cases are reported, and prosecute offenders if citizens file complaints. The media cover cases on trial.

Shari'a law is usually applied in divorce and inheritance. Marriages are usually arranged, and polygyny is practiced. Women normally receive a lower proportion of assets distributed through inheritance than do male relatives.

Employment in the formal sector is open to women at the same salary rates as men. No statutory discrimination exists in other kinds of employment, although women are generally employed in endeavors such as food vending or subsistence farming.

Women face extensive discrimination in education and employment but not at the hands of government. Families generally school male children before female children. Females constitute about one-third of primary school students and roughly one-fourth of high school students.

Children.—The Government does not mandate compulsory education and opportunities for secondary education are limited. The care and welfare of children in distress is considered primarily a family responsibility. Authorities intervene when cases of abuse or mistreatment are brought to their attention.

The practice of female genital mutilation (FGM), which is widely condemned by international health experts as damaging to both physical and psychological health, is widespread and entrenched. Reports place the number of women having undergone FGM anywhere from 60 to 90 percent. Seven of the 9 ethnic groups practice FGM at ages varying from shortly after birth until 18 years old. Although a newspaper article in August alleged female circumcision was a means to prevent AIDS, a subsequent article in the Government's newspaper said that "the Government backs the eradication of female circumcision". The Government, however, has not implemented legislation against FGM and, in the absence of legislation, the judiciary is not prepared to address the problem.

People With Disabilities.—There are no statutes or regulations requiring accessibility for the disabled. No legal discrimination against the physically disabled exists in employment, education, or other state services. Severely disabled individuals subsist primarily through private charity. Less severely disabled individuals are fully accepted in society and encounter no discrimination in employment for which they are physically capable.

Section 6. Worker Rights

a. *The Right of Association.*—Labor law remained unmodified by the AFPRC regime. The Labor Act of 1990 applies to all workers, except civil servants. The act specifies that workers are free to form associations, including trade unions, and provides for their registration with the Government. It specifically prohibits police officers and military personnel, as well as other civil service employees, from forming unions or striking. About 20 percent of the work force is employed in the modern wage sector, where unions are most active. Roughly 30,000 workers are union members, about 10 percent of the work force.

The Gambian Worker's Confederation and the Gambian Workers' Union are the two main independent and competing umbrella organizations. Both are recognized by the Government, but relations with the AFPRC were not tested.

The Labor Act authorizes strikes but requires that unions give the Commissioner of Labor 14 days' written notice before beginning an industrial action (28 days for essential services). It prohibits retribution against strikers who comply with the law regulating strikes. Upon application by an employer to the Supreme Court, the Court may prohibit industrial action that is ruled to be in pursuit of a political objective. The Court may also forbid action judged to be in breach of a collectively agreed procedure for settlement of industrial disputes. Because of these provisions and the weakness of unions, few strikes occur.

Unions may affiliate internationally, and there are no restrictions on union members' participation in international labor activities. The country applied in June 1995 to join the International Labor Organization. It has been accepted in principle, but must make modifications to its labor and employment laws.

b. *The Right to Organize and Bargain Collectively.*—The Labor Act of 1990 allows workers to organize and bargain collectively. Although trade unions are small and fragmented, collective bargaining takes place. Each recognized union has guidelines for its activities specified by the appropriate industrial council established and empowered by the Labor Act. Union members' wages exceed legal minimums and are determined by collective bargaining, arbitration, or agreements reached between unions and management after insuring that the agreements are in compliance with labor law. No denial of registration has been reported. The act also sets minimum contract standards for hiring, training, terms of employment, wages, and termination of employment. The act provides that contracts may not prohibit union membership. Employers may not fire or discriminate against members of registered unions engaged in legal union activities.

There are no export processing zones.

c. *Prohibition of Forced or Compulsory Labor.*—The Criminal Code prohibits compulsory labor, and it is not practiced.

d. *Minimum Age for Employment of Children.*—The statutory minimum age for employment is 18 years. There is no compulsory education, and because of limited secondary school openings, most children complete formal education by age 14 and then begin work. Employee labor cards, which include a person's age, are registered with the Labor Commissioner, but enforcement inspections rarely take place. Child labor protection does not extend to youth performing customary chores on family farms or engaged in petty trading.

e. *Acceptable Conditions of Work.*—Minimum wages and working hours are established by law through six joint Industrial Councils—Commerce, Artisans, Transport, Port Operations, Agriculture, and Fisheries.

Labor, management, and the Government are represented on these councils. The lowest minimum wage is about $1.35 (14 dalasis) per day for unskilled labor. This minimum wage is not adequate to sustain a suitable standard of living for a worker and family. Only 20 percent of the labor force, those in the formal economic sector, are covered by the minimum wage law. The majority of workers are privately or self-employed, often in agriculture. Most citizens do not live on a single worker's earnings but share resources within extended families.

The basic legal workweek is 48 hours within a period not to exceed 6 consecutive days. A 30-minute lunch break is mandated. In the private sector, the workweek includes 4 8-hour work days and 2 4-hour work days (Friday and Saturday). Government employees are entitled to 1 month's paid annual leave after 1 year of service. Private sector employees receive between 14 and 30 days of paid annual leave, depending on length of service.

The Labor Act specifies safety equipment that an employer must provide to employees working in designated occupations. The Factory Act authorizes the Ministry of Labor to regulate factory health and safety, accident prevention, and dangerous trades and to appoint inspectors to ensure compliance with safety standards. Enforcement is spotty owing to insufficient and inadequately trained staff. Workers may refuse to work in dangerous situations and may demand protective equipment and clothing for hazardous workplaces.

GHANA

Ghana continues its transition from a single-party, authoritarian system to a constitutional democracy. Flight Lieutenant (ret.) Jerry John Rawlings has ruled the country for 16 years. He became the first President of the Fourth Republic following controversial elections in 1992. This ended 11 years of authoritarian rule under Rawlings and his Provisional National Defense Council (PNDC), which had seized power from an elected government in 1981. The opposition fully contested the December 7 presidential and parliamentary elections, which were described as peaceful, free, and transparent by domestic and international observers. President Rawlings was reelected with 57 percent of the popular vote. Rawling's NDC party won 133 of the Parliament's 200 seats. The Constitution calls for a system of checks and balances, with an executive branch headed by the President, a unicameral Parliament, an independent judiciary, and several autonomous commissions, such as the Commission for Human Rights and Administrative Justice (CHRAJ). In reality this system of checks and balances is circumscribed by a Parliament monopolized by the President's party, a hesitant judicial service, and a system-wide lack of resources which hobbles the effectiveness of all three branches. The election of a significant number of opposition parliamentarians, however, may provide a more open process and debate in Parliament. The judiciary is subject to executive influence and lacks adequate resources.

Several security organizations report to various government departments. The police, under the jurisdiction of an 8-member Police Council, are responsible for maintaining law and order. An independent department, the Bureau of National Investigations (BNI) handles cases considered critical to state security and answers directly to the executive branch. Although the security apparatus is controlled by and responsive to the Government, monitoring, supervision, and education of the police in particular remain poor. Credible allegations continue of police involvement in human rights abuses, especially in areas remote from the capital.

The economy remains highly dependent on agriculture, with about 45 percent of gross domestic product derived from this sector. Gold, cocoa, and timber are the traditional sources of export earnings with gold growing in importance. The economy grew at a 4.5 percent rate in 1995, up from the 3.8 percent recorded in 1994. Increased gold production and a good cocoa harvest accounted for the slightly higher growth rate. However, inflation accelerated dramatically during 1995 and 1996 and at year-end registered 40 to 45 percent. The privatization of state-owned enterprises continues, but the pace of divestiture remains slow.

The Government's human rights record improved slightly, but problems remain in several areas. There were continued credible reports that members of the police beat prisoners and other citizens; arbitrarily arrested and detained persons; used excessive force, which resulted in a few instances of deaths in custody; and infringed on citizens' right to privacy. Newly organized municipal security forces, which fall outside the regular police service, injured a number of persons in using excessive force to control street vendors and public demonstrations. Prison conditions remained harsh despite modest reforms, and prolonged pretrial detentions remained a problem. Inadequate resources and a system vulnerable to political influence compromised the integrity of the overburdened judicial system. The Government failed to investigate the deaths of four demonstrators during a 1995 antigovernment protest.

The Government pressured the media. It resorted to an obscure 1960 law to prosecute several journalists, and there were a spate of criminal and civil libel suits that seemed to signal possible official harassment of the independent press. Nevertheless, the small but independent press, human rights monitoring groups, and opposition parties were again vigorous and out-spoken in criticizing various aspects of government policy. The CHRAJ, a government body, issued a critical report on the prison system and was successful in arbitrating individual human rights cases and in educating the public. Several new independent radio stations reflected the Government's public commitment to open airwaves.

The Government carefully controlled all aspects of the preelection procedures, but the participation of eight political parties and a large citizen turnout highlighted the gradually improving human rights situation.

Traditional practices still result in considerable discrimination and abuse of women and children, with violence against women a particular problem.

RESPECT FOR HUMAN RIGHTS

Section 1. Respect for the Integrity of the Person, Including Freedom From:

a. *Political and Other Extrajudicial Killing.*—There were no reports of political killings. However, on two separate occasions in attempting to control crowds, poorly trained Kumasi police killed two persons, reportedly as a result of stray bullets from warning shots. Police fired shots that accidentally killed a man after a December 1995 soccer match that ended in violence between the teams' supporters. In January another person was killed by a stray police bullet when police attempted to disperse demonstrating students who had erected road blocks. Police authorities announced that rubber bullets and water cannons had been ordered for crowd control.

There were two reports in the press of possible wrongful deaths of suspects in police custody. In January the official press reported that the authorities in the northern region had prosecuted two policemen for using excessive force in the death of a detainee, but that a court had subsequently acquitted the officers. In another case, at year's end the authorities had still not clarified or made arrests in the unexplained death of a man in a Central Region police cell in February, and the case remained open.

The Government continued to refuse to launch an inquiry into the deaths of four demonstrators during a protest of government tax policy in May 1995. There was credible evidence that the Minister of Youth and Sports had organized and armed the counter-demonstrators who were responsible for the killings. A police committee's report about the events surrounding the killings has never been publicly released. The police, however, claimed at a 1995 press conference that they were unable to identify any specific individuals responsible and that the matter was thus closed. The Minister of Youth and Sports has charged an independent newspaper with libel for reporting on the 1995 U.S. Government report on human rights practices in Ghana and his possible involvement in the killings.

In 1995 the police beat a Tetrem man in the Ashanti region who subsequently died. A police service inquiry determined that one of the two officers involved was primarily responsible for the suspect's death. Over 18 months later, the police officer's trial had not yet begun although the Attorney General has requested that the officer be charged with manslaughter. It is generally believed that severe beatings such as this occur throughout the country but go largely unreported.

Journalists were unsuccessful in their continued efforts to persuade the Government to investigate extrajudicial killings in the early years of PNDC rule, despite police professions in 1993 of willingness to investigate such killings.

b. *Disappearance.*—There were no reports of politically motivated disappearances.

c. *Torture and Other Cruel, Inhuman, or Degrading Treatment or Punishment.*—The Constitution states that the dignity of all persons shall be inviolable and that no one shall be subjected to torture or other cruel, inhuman, or degrading treatment or punishment, or any other condition that detracts from human dignity. Nonetheless, there were continued credible reports that members of the police beat prisoners and other citizens. Police used excessive force in attempting to control crowds, at times resulting in citizens' deaths (see Section 1.a.).

Security forces outside the control of the police service made a high-profile debut in 1996 and proved a threat to civil liberties. The Mayor's office in Accra dispatched a specially trained force, known as the City Crime Combating and Cleaning Unit, to eject forcefully unlicensed street vendors from city streets. The special force inflicted physical injuries on a number of vendors and destroyed much of their property. After withdrawing the forces for retraining, the Metropolitan Assembly decided in November to negotiate with the traders to resettle them in other less congested areas. In Tema a metropolitan security unit beat a taxi driver unconscious, and another unit, the so-called traffic task force, handed out unduly harsh penalties to and engaged in regular shake-downs of Kumasi taxi drivers. These actions sparked a demonstration by taxi drivers in August, and angry demonstrators burned vehicles and destroyed property, injuring 17 persons, some with gunshot wounds. Many reports indicated that most injuries were caused by metropolitan security forces. It was unclear if these injuries occurred before or after army troops were called in to restore order, or who caused the injuries.

Prisons are in most cases very poorly maintained, and conditions are extremely harsh. In March the CHRAJ published its long-anticipated report on prison conditions. It described prisons that are unsanitary, overcrowded, and poorly ventilated. Prisoners are malnourished (the daily food allowance per prisoner is about $0.35) and suffer from lack of medicines unless paid for by the inmates or provided by their families. The report concluded in part that prison conditions are "a flagrant violation of the individual's fundamental human rights." The CHRAJ's findings and recommendations generated much positive press coverage, but the only concrete action taken by the Government was a decree of amnesty for certain convicted prisoners and commuted sentences for others in order to relieve overcrowding in the prisons. Juvenile offenders were moved from prisons to schools for delinquent youths.

d. *Arbitrary Arrest, Detention, or Exile.*—The Constitution provides for protection against arbitrary arrest, detention, or exile and states that an individual detained shall be informed immediately, in a language the detained person understands, of the reasons for the detention, and of the right to a lawyer and to an interpreter, the latter at state expense. It also requires judicial warrants for arrest and provides for arraignment within 48 hours. In practice, however, many abuses occur, including detention without charge for longer than 48 hours and failure to obtain a warrant for arrest. The government press reported that the Inspector General of Police and the northern regional police commander were sued in January by a private businessman for unlawful arrest and detention.

The court has unlimited discretion to set bail, which can be excessive. It may refuse to release prisoners on bail and instead remand them without charge for an indefinite period, subject to weekly review by judicial authorities. It is common to remand a prisoner to investigative custody. The Constitution requires, however, that a detainee who has not been tried within a "reasonable" time shall be released either unconditionally or subject to conditions necessary to ensure that he appears at a later date for court proceedings.

Despite the provisions of the law, abuses occur. People are sometimes detained for trivial offenses or on unsubstantiated accusations. Approximately 30 percent of the prison population consists of pretrial detainees. In November the press reported the release of 5 suspects on bail who had been in prison from 5 to 10 years without trial. In December there were reports of remanded suspects languishing in prison without trial for up to 9 years. The suspects had petitioned the CHRAJ, which negotiated their release. The Commission was reported as saying at the time that it had other such instances under investigation.

The CHRAJ report on prison conditions recommended improvement in the administration of criminal justice, which currently denies many citizens their constitutional rights to be charged within 48 hours, to have bail posted within the same period, and to a speedy trial. The report concluded that the "penal system is unwittingly but inexorably punishing the innocent."

At the year's end, a Presidential Commission on the Police Service continued to hold public hearings in efforts to improve police effectiveness.

There were no known political arrests in 1996. However, an army captain, charged with plotting to overthrow the Government, was remanded into custody and awaited trial for treason.

The Government does not practice forced exile and encourages citizens with valuable skills who are living abroad to return, including dissidents. Some former government and discredited PNDC officials have returned and resumed careers and political activities.

e. *Denial of Fair Public Trial.*—The Constitution provides for an independent judiciary, but in practice the judiciary is subject to executive influence. The Constitution allows the Government to nominate up to 15 members of the Supreme Court; confirmation is the responsibility of a Parliament dominated by the President's party. Furthermore, the Chief Justice is empowered to impanel the justices of his choice to hear cases. These provisions along with a debilitating lack of resources have hindered the Court's role as a balance to the power of the executive branch. There were no official charges of judicial corruption but a recent survey revealed that 66 percent of the citizens believe that money influences the judicial system. Furthermore, the integrity of the legal system is compromised by a severe lack of financial, human, and material resources.

The Constitution establishes two basic levels of courts: superior and lower. The superior courts include the Supreme Court, the Appeals Court, the High Court, and regional tribunals. Parliament may establish lower courts or tribunals by decree. Legal safeguards are based on British legal procedures. Defendants are presumed innocent, trials are public, and defendants have a right to be present, to be represented by an attorney (at public expense if necessary), and to cross-examine witnesses. In practice the authorities generally respect these safeguards.

The CHRAJ's charter provides for it to investigate alleged violations of human rights and take action to remedy proven violations. It continues to hold workshops to educate the public, traditional leaders, the police, and the military on human rights issues. It mediates and settles cases brought to it by individuals with grievances against government agencies or private companies. In 1995 the CHRAJ received 6,173 petitions in its offices around the country and completed action on over 3,700 from 1995 and previous years. The majority of the complaints lodged with the commission were labor and workplace related, but cases involving human rights issues are increasing. In October the Commission concluded its lengthy corruption probe of high government officials. Its findings, damaging to the careers of three officials, were accepted as fair and reasonable.

The Chieftaincy Act of 1971 gives village and other traditional chiefs powers to mediate local matters, including authority to enforce customary tribal laws dealing with such matters as divorce, child custody, and property disputes. However, a number of laws passed during the PNDC era (1981–92) and the 1992 Constitution have steadily eroded the authority of traditional rulers and vested it in civil institutions, such as courts and district assemblies.

There were no reports of political prisoners. The last known political prisoner was Gershon Dompreh, who was released in January 1995.

f. *Arbitrary Interference With Privacy, Family, Home, or Correspondence.*—The Constitution provides that a person shall be free from interference within the privacy of his home, property, correspondence, or communication. This article has yet to be tested in court. In practice, although the law requires judicial search warrants, police do not always obtain them. Observers assume that the Government continues to engage in surveillance of citizens engaged in activities that it deems objectionable. In the past, this included monitoring of telephones and mail.

There have also been confirmed reports of interference in the affairs of private businessmen when they have been perceived as unsympathetic to the ruling NDC party. The Serious Fraud Office (SFO), created in 1994, has launched politically directed attacks on private business people perceived as unsympathetic to the regime. The SFO can freeze assets for up to a week without judicial review, a prerogative that it has not yet exercised. It has, however, attempted to seize passports of subjects of its investigations.

Section 2. Respect for Civil Liberties, Including:

a. *Freedom of Speech and Press.*—The Constitution provides for freedom of speech and the press, and opposition political parties and others have used these freedoms to criticize the Government. However, the Government dominates the print and electronic media and has continually pressured the government-run media for conformity. The Government controls the principal radio and sole television station and the two daily newspapers. The official media do not directly criticize government policies or President Rawlings although they report charges of corruption or mismanagement in government ministries and state-owned enterprises. The Government occasionally disciplines or dismisses journalists working in government-subsidized media for articles deemed unacceptable. The Government reportedly ended subsidies to the two state-owned publishing companies as a first step in partial divestiture.

Despite the Government's dominant position, the independent press continued to publish unimpeded, with newspapers and magazines critical of the Government, including personal attacks on the President, his wife, and his close advisers. However, independent newspapers and magazines tend to be small, with little circulation outside major cities.

While the Government has not overtly suppressed the independent print media, there were clear indications that the authorities were concerned and suspicious, particularly during an important election year. In November security forces detained a freelance journalist who, in his opinion column in an independent newspaper, alleged that the armed forces were prepared to rig or annul the results of the upcoming elections. The journalist was accused of "subversive activities leading to a treasonable offense," but was released on bail the day after having been taken into custody.

There was also a spate of libel charges against independent journalists and their editors during the year. These libel cases resulted largely in small fines and published apologies, but in general appeared to be officially inspired harassment of the independent press. However, two journalists and their editor face the more serious prospect of criminal prosecution and 10-year prison sentences under an obscure 1960 law, never before used, prohibiting defaming or slandering the "Ghanian State". The journalists and editor had essentially republished an article that originally appeared in a U.S.-based publication. They were first arrested in February, jailed, and then detained 10 days without bail before being released to prepare their case. By year's end, a decision had not yet been handed down. Prosecution under the criminal libel law became a more serious threat when the Supreme Court ruled in July that all citizens, rather than just those closely associated with the State, may avail themselves of the provisions of this law. Formerly criminal charges could only be sought when a false report was considered to have injured the credit or reputation of the State. Civil suits for libel are also allowed.

In July in another case, a contempt of court charge was leveled at a journalist reporting court proceedings in a case embarrassing to the President. The court sentenced the journalist to jail for 30 days, but more disturbing was the restraining ("gag") order the presiding judge imposed both on the case under consideration and reporting on the contempt charge. The independent press widely challenged the restraining order through noncompliance.

The Minister of Youth and Sports charged an independent newspaper with libel for its reporting on his possible involvement in the May 1995 deaths of four demonstrators (see Section 1.a.).

There were also accusations that the Government indirectly manipulates the independent press by refusing to do business with companies that advertise in opposition newspapers. However, advertising is steadily increasing in the independent newspapers. Foreign periodicals are sold in Accra and other major cities; they circulate freely and sometimes contain articles critical of the Government. Most Ghanaians obtain their news from the government-owned electronic media and the British Broadcasting Corporation radio service.

The Constitution states that individuals are free to own radio and television stations. While in the past the Government has been slow to grant licenses to independent broadcasters, six independent radio stations and a private television station began operations by year's end. While these stations are clearly independent, they cannot be characterized as outspoken critics of the Government.

There has been no restriction of academic freedom on university campuses, although the authorities clashed with demonstrating students on two occasions. In January a stray bullet fired by the Kumasi police killed a student protesting the lengthy closure of the universities (see Section 1.a.). The National Union of Ghanaian students, one of the more vocal critics of the Government, is allowed to organize and hold meetings. In June an appearance by President Rawlings at the Legon University campus ended in a brawl between demonstrating student union members and NDC supporters.

b. *Freedom of Peaceful Assembly and Association.*—The Constitution provides for freedom of peaceful assembly and association; it does not require permits for demonstrations. Parliament passed a public order law in late 1994 requiring that all organizers of "special events" or "processions" inform the police of their intentions so that the police can institute precautionary measures. The law also provides for curfews and arrest without warrants in specified instances. The authorities did not abuse the provisions of the law during the year.

In November five workers demonstrating in favor of union demands for improved working conditions were injured by bullets fired by the police. The proper authorities had been notified in advance, as required by law, that the demonstration would take place. The press secretary of the ruling NDC said that the party "regretted" the incident. The union chairman was quoted in the government press as saying that workers wanted a peaceful demonstration to remind management of union demands.

NGO's are required to register with the Registrar General's office, but this registration is routine. However, the possible threat of government interference in the form of mandatory NGO registration remains in a bill that has been languishing in a parliamentary committee for nearly 2 years. The council that would implement the law would consist primarily of government appointees and would have the authority to deny, suspend, or cancel an NGO's right to operate.

Political parties must be accredited by the Electoral Commission. The parties must show evidence of a "national character" such as official representation in all 10 of the country's regions. The Electoral Commission evaluates whether the party has shown evidence of a viable national support base before granting accreditation.

c. *Freedom of Religion.*—The Constitution provides for freedom of religion, and the Government respects this right in practice.

There is no state-favored religion and no apparent advantages or disadvantages attached to membership in any particular sect or religion. Foreign missionary groups have generally operated throughout the country with a minimum of formal restrictions.

During the year, there were a series of violent confrontations between religious groups, particularly among Islamic sects, but the issues involved were theological rather than political.

d. *Freedom of Movement Within the Country, Foreign Travel, Emigration, and Repatriation.*—The Constitution provides for these rights as an aspect of the provision for personal liberty.

Citizens and foreigners are free to move throughout the country without special permission. Police checkpoints exist countrywide to prevent smuggling, but most are left unmanned during daylight hours. Roadblocks and car searches are a normal part of nighttime travel in Accra.

Citizens are generally free to travel internationally and to emigrate or to be repatriated from other countries.

Ethnic tension and violence in the northern region diminished during the year. Army troops were deployed to the area and as a result Konkomba farmers were again able to travel to regional markets to sell produce (see Section 5).

The Government cooperates with the United Nations High Commissioner for Refugees (UNHCR) and other humanitarian organizations in assisting refugees. Ghana has a liberal policy of accepting refugees from other West African nations. The Government provides first asylum. It has provided first asylum in recent years to Togolese refugees, most of whom have returned to Togo as part of the UNHCR's organized voluntary repatriation program which was implemented in mid-year. It continues to provide first asylum to some 34,000 Togolese and approximately 18,000 Liberians who are still in Ghana. It provided first asylum to an additional 1,800 who arrived in 1996, most of whom arrived in April aboard the ship Bulk Challenge from Liberia, after other countries in the region refused to permit the passengers to disembark.

In June the Government did not authorize disembarkation of passengers from the Russian refugee ship, the Zolititsa, which had been searching for a port to disembark its 435 passengers, including many Liberians. There were no other reports of persons not being allowed to request asylum. There were no reports of forced return of persons to a country where they feared persecution. There were no forced expulsions of refugees with a valid claim to refugee status.

Section 3. Respect for Political Rights: The Right of Citizens to Change Their Government

The Constitution provides citizens with the right to change their government, and citizens exercised this right through a democratic process in presidential elections held in December.

In preparation for the elections, the Electoral Commission consulted closely with representatives of all registered political parties regarding election processes and laws. By October 1995, the Commission had registered over 9 million citizens. It was noteworthy that in five regions women registered in greater numbers than men; and in the Central Region women accounted for 54 percent of the total number registering. Over 6 million citizens returned to the 20,000 registration sites to ensure that their names were included on the registry.

As a result of these careful preparations, the elections proceeded smoothly, and observers judged them free and fair. The 77 percent turnout was significantly higher than the 52 percent in 1992, but the electorate was orderly. Hard work by the National Electoral Commission, political parties, and national and international NGO's contributed to the successful election. President Rawlings was reelected for a final 4-year term with 57 percent of the popular vote. The Great Alliance candidate, John Kufuor, received 40 percent. The NDC retained control of the 200-member Parliament with 133 seats, while opposition parties took 66 seats (1 seat was not contested due to a court injunction).

There are no obstacles to the participation of women in government. In 1996 there were 16 female parliamentarians and several ministers and Council of State members were women. In the December elections, 17 women were elected to the Parliament taking office in 1997.

Section 4. Governmental Attitude Regarding International and Nongovernmental Investigation of Alleged Violations of Human Rights

NGO's interested in human rights continued to grow in number and strength. These NGO's operate without government interference and, at year's end, without the need to register with the Government (see Section 2.b.). Prominent NGO's include the Red Cross, Amnesty International, the International Federation of Woman Lawyers (FIDA), and Women in Law and Development in Africa (WILDAF).

The Government cooperates with international humanitarian organizations including the International Committee of the Red Cross (ICRC).

Section 5. Discrimination Based on Race, Sex, Religion, Disability, Language, or Social Status

The Constitution prohibits discrimination on the basis of race, sex, religion, disability, language, or social status. The courts are specifically empowered to enforce these prohibitions, although enforcement by the authorities is generally inadequate, in part due to limited financial resources.

Women.—Violence against women, including rape and wife beating, remains a significant problem. These abuses usually go unreported and seldom come before the courts. The police tend not to intervene in domestic disputes. However, the media increasingly report cases of assault and rape. Women's groups have not yet raised the issue of domestic violence with the Government.

Women continue to experience societal discrimination. Women in urban centers and those with skills and training encounter little overt bias, but resistance to women in nontraditional roles persists. Few women enter college. Women, especially in rural areas, remain subject to burdensome labor conditions and traditional male dominance. Traditional practices and social norms often deny women their inheritances and property, a legally registered marriage (and with it, certain legal rights), and the maintenance and custody of children, all provided for by statute.

Women's rights groups are active in educational campaigns and in programs to provide vocational training, legal aid, and other support to women. The Government is also active in educational programs, and the President and First Lady are among the most outspoken advocates of women's rights. Although there has been no concrete policy change on the national level, the 1995 United Nations Conference on Women and the resulting platform for action generated widespread positive discussion about the status of women in Ghana.

Children.—Within the limits of its resources, the Government is committed to protecting the rights and welfare of children. There is little or no discrimination against females in education, but girls and women frequently drop out of school due to societal or economic pressures. Statistics show that from grades 1 to 6, 45 of every 100 pupils are girls; from grades 7 to 9, this number drops to 41. In the grades equivalent to high school (grades 10 to 12), the number of girls drops to 33 per 100 students, and drops even further to 25 per 100 students at the university level.

There are several traditional discriminatory practices that are injurious to female health and development. In particular, female genital mutilation (FGM), which is widely condemned by international health experts as damaging to both physical and psychological health, is a serious problem. According to one study, the percentage of women who have undergone this procedure may be as high as 30 percent, although most observers believe 15 percent to be more accurate. FGM is practiced mostly in Muslim communities in the far northeastern and northwestern parts of the country. As of 1994, FGM became a criminal act, and at least one practitioner and an accomplice were arrested during the year. Officials at all levels have been vocal in publicly speaking out against the practice of FGM, and a local NGO is making some inroads through its educational campaigns to encourage abandonment of FGM.

Trokosi, a traditional practice found among the Ewe ethnic group and primarily in the Volta region, is an especially severe abuse and a flagrant violation of children's and women's rights. It is a system in which a young girl, usually under the age of 10, is made a slave to a fetish shrine for offenses allegedly committed by a member of the girl's family. The belief is that if someone in that family has committed a crime, such as stealing, members of the family may begin to die in large numbers unless a young girl is given to the local fetish shrine to atone for the offense. The girl becomes the property of the fetish priest, must work on the priest's farm, and perform other labors for him. Because they are the sexual property of the priests, most trokosi slaves have children by him. Although the girls' families must provide for their needs, such as food, most are unable to do so. There are at least 4,500 girls and women bound to various shrines in the trokosi system, a figure that does not include the slaves' children. Even if released, generally without skills or hope of marriage, a trokosi woman has continued obligations to the shrine for the duration of her life. When the fetish slave dies, the family is expected to replace her with another young girl for the fetish shrine.

Although the Constitution outlaws slavery, Parliament has yet to pass a law explicitly prohibiting trokosi. The practice persists because of deeply entrenched traditional beliefs, and it is therefore unlikely that any legislative prohibition alone would eliminate the practice. Nevertheless, a local NGO has had some success in approaching village authorities and fetish priests and winning their confidence with the ultimate objective of securing the release of the trokosi slaves. There were 3 ceremonies where a total of over 120 trokosi women and girls were released through the efforts of this NGO, and the organization is working for additional releases.

Another traditional practice that violates the rights of children is forced childhood marriages. The prostitution of female children exists, despite its illegality.

People With Disabilities.—The Constitution specifically provides for the rights of people with disabilities, including protection against exploitation and discrimination. In practice, the disabled are not discriminated against in any systematic or overt manner. It also states that "as far as practicable, every place to which the public has access shall have appropriate facilities for disabled persons." In practice, however, this provision has yet to be implemented.

National/Racial/Ethnic Minorities.—Although the Government plays down the importance of ethnic differences, its opponents occasionally complain that it is dominated by the Ewe ethnic group from the eastern part of the country. The President and many of his close advisers are Ewe, but many ministers are of other ethnic origins.

To address the continuing tensions between the Konkomba and other ethnic groups in the north, the Government has created a permanent negotiating team comprised of religious leaders, NGO's, Council of State members, and other interested parties to help resolve the conflict. A series of highly publicized "peacemaking" ceremonies were held at which tribal leaders pledged to solve their differences through negotiations. The primary issue of contention among the northern ethnic groups is land.

There were numerous violent confrontations between and within ethnic groups related to chieftaincy issues, particularly those of succession. Beyond regular pleas by government officials for peace, there has been little effective intervention.

Section 6. Worker Rights

a. *The Right of Association.*—This right is restricted, as the Trades Union Ordinance confers broad powers on the Government to refuse to register a trade union. However, neither the PNDC nor the Government has interfered with the right of workers to associate in labor unions.

About 9 percent of workers belong to unions, a figure that has been declining slowly over the past several years. The Industrial Relations Act (IRA), initially written in 1958, and amended in 1965 and 1972, governs trade unions and their activities. The Trades Union Congress (TUC) is the only existing confederation, although it has no legal monopoly. In recent years it has been led by experienced union leaders who, aided by a revised union constitution and by-laws, continued to define an autonomous role for the TUC within the NDC regime. Since the 1992 elections, the TUC has taken a somewhat more confrontational stance vis-a-vis the Government and has criticized some of its economic policies. Civil servants have their own union, the Civil Servants Association, which operates outside of the TUC umbrella.

The law recognizes the right to strike. Under the IRA, the Government established a system of settling disputes, first through conciliation, then through arbitration. A union may call a legal strike if negotiations and mediation fail. However, because no union has ever gone through the complete process, there have been no legal strikes since independence. The IRA prohibits retribution against strikers, and this law is enforced. There has been no progress in implementing the Government's declared intention to establish labor tribunals to arbitrate industrial disputes certified as deadlocked.

Unions have the right to affiliate with international bodies. The TUC is affiliated with the Organization of African Trade Union Unity, headquartered in Accra, and is also a member of the International Confederation of Free Trade Unions.

b. *The Right to Organize and Bargain Collectively.*—The IRA provides a framework for collective bargaining and some protection against antiunion discrimination as well. Trade unions engage in collective bargaining for wages and benefits with both private and state-owned enterprises without government interference. The Government, labor, and employers negotiate together, however, through a tripartite commission to set minimum standards for wages and working conditions. The law requires employers found guilty of antiunion discrimination to reinstate workers fired for union activities. No union leaders have been detained in recent years for union or other activities.

Press reports in February claimed that management refused workers at the Volta garment factory in Teshie the right to unionize. This right, however, was ultimately respected, and in November the workers announced their decision to affiliate with the Industrial and Commercial Workers Union.

Legislation approving export processing zones (EPZ's) has been passed and a secretariat established, but at year's end there was no EPZ in operation. Existing labor law, however, will apply in any EPZ, including the right to organize.

c. *Prohibition of Forced or Compulsory Labor.*—The law prohibits forced labor, and it is not known to be practiced except in the trokosi system (see Section 5). The International Labor Organization (ILO) continues to urge the Government to revise various legal provisions that permit imprisonment with an obligation to perform labor for offenses that are not countenanced under ILO Convention 105.

d. *Minimum Age for Employment of Children.*—Labor legislation sets a minimum employment age of 15 and prohibits night work and certain types of hazardous labor for those under 18 years of age. In practice, child employment is widespread, and young children of school age often perform menial tasks during the day in the market or collect fares on local buses. An ILO survey conducted in three rural districts between 1992 and 1993 concluded that 11 percent of school age children were employed for wages and another 15 percent without remuneration. Observance of minimum age laws is eroded by local custom and economic circumstances that encourage children to work to help their families.

Officials only occasionally punish violators of regulations that prohibit heavy labor and night work for children. Inspectors from the Ministry of Labor and Social Welfare are responsible for enforcement of child labor regulations. They visit each work place annually and make spot checks whenever they receive allegations of violations.

e. *Acceptable Conditions of Work.*—In 1991 minimum standards for wages and working conditions were set by a tripartite commission composed of representatives of the Government, labor, and employers. The daily minimum wage, revised in 1996, combines wages with customary benefits, such as a transportation allowance. The daily minimum wage is $1.00 (1,700 cedis). This sum is insufficient for a single wage earner to support a family. Furthermore, there is widespread violation of the minimum wage law. In most cases households have multiple wage earners, and family members engage in some family farming and other family-based commercial activities.

The law sets the maximum workweek at 45 hours, with one break of at least 36 consecutive hours every 7 days. Through collective bargaining, however, the basic workweek for most unionized workers is 40 hours. In February, however, workers at the Spintex textile factory publicly charged that management was forcing them to work overtime without compensation under threat of layoffs. When workers formally requested that they be laid off, management refused the requests, which unleashed a worker protest that ended in the police using tear gas and firing warning shots. Workers have filed petitions with the CHRAJ, the Ministry of Employment and Social Welfare, and the Ministry of Labor. The status of the petitions was unknown at year's end.

Occupational safety and health regulations are in effect, and the Labor Department of the Ministry of Health and Social Welfare occasionally imposes sanctions on violators. Safety inspectors are few, however, and poorly trained. They take action if matters are called to their attention, but lack the resources to seek out violations. Workers have the right to withdraw themselves from dangerous work situations without jeopardy to continued employment, although they rarely exercise this right.

GUINEA

President Lansana Conte took office as Head of State of the Republic of Guinea in 1994, after multiparty elections in which the Government dominated the electoral process. Guinea held its first multiparty legislative elections in 1995, delivering more than 60 percent of Parliament's seats to President Conte's Party of Unity and Progress (PUP). The PUP is one seat short of the majority required to make constitutional amendments. Opposition leaders, some international observers, and segments of the citizenry voiced suspicion of PUP's considerable victories in both parliamentary and municipal elections. Although the PUP continues to dominate all three branches of government, opposition parties have on occasion persuaded PUP members of Parliament to vote with the opposition on specific legislative matters. The judiciary is subject to executive influence, particularly in politically sensitive cases.

Some 2,000 soldiers, protesting low salaries and meager benefits, mutinied February 2–3. The mutiny evolved into an attempted coup d'etat that nearly toppled the Government; it killed an estimated 30 to 50 people in Conakry, mostly civilians. President Conte fired his Minister of Defense on February 2, naming himself Minister, and appointed a Prime Minister and a new Government in July.

The gendarmerie and the national police share responsibility for internal security and sometimes play an oppressive role in the daily lives of citizens. The Red Berets—autonomous presidential guards—are accountable to almost no one except the President. Members of all the security forces, whom many citizens view as corrupt, ineffective, and even dangerous, frequently committed human rights abuses.

Eighty percent of Guinea's 7 million citizens engage in subsistence agriculture, and annual per capita gross domestic product is about $740. Major exports include bauxite, gold, diamonds, fruit, and coffee.

The Government continued to circumscribe human rights. Its tight control of the electoral process and lack of an independent electoral oversight mechanism call into serious doubt the ability of citizens to change the government. Major human rights abuses include: Extrajudicial killings by security forces; politically motivated disappearances related to the mutiny; police abuse of prisoners and detainees; use of torture by military personnel; inhuman prison conditions; instances of arbitrary arrest and detention; governmental failure to guarantee access by attorneys to clients in prison; the executive branch's influence over the judicial system and the electoral process; occasional instances of vigilante justice; infringement on citizens' privacy; restrictions on freedom of speech and the press; societal discrimination and violence against women; and prostitution and genital mutilation of young girls.

The Government dominated the electoral process. Leaders of the PUP called for the creation of an independent electoral commission. An independent press criticized the Government, but is subject to a broad range of restrictions, including arrest of reporters and suspension of publication. The Government owns and operates the electronic media, the major medium for reaching the vast majority of the public.

The Cabinet appointed in July announced measures to combat security force abuses (including the creation of a discipline council); several cabinet members publicly acknowledged shortcomings of the security apparatus and the need for substantial reform. The Ministry of Justice and the National Assembly attempted to educate the citizenry about the judicial process and individual rights.

RESPECT FOR HUMAN RIGHTS

Section 1. Respect for the Integrity of the Person, Including Freedom From:
  a. *Political and Other Extrajudicial Killing.*—There were no reports of targeted political killings, but there were several extrajudicial killings by security forces.

Soldiers involved in the February mutiny killed between 30 and 50 persons, mostly civilians who were victims of stray fire. The Government made numerous arrests and announced charges, but no trials have taken place. In March uniformed soldiers killed Colonel Seny Bangoura, Commander of the Alpha Yaya military camp in Conakry. The independent press reported several detentions in this case, but the Government did not announce any arrests or findings (see Section 1.c.).

The independent press reported that two detainees awaiting trial for murder and robbery in Telimele, Dian Oury Kante and Mahamed Diallo, died in custody in April. There was no investigation. Authorities confirmed that air force major Mamady Conde, detained in connection with the February mutiny, died in custody in Conakry in June. A prosecuting attorney said that Conde died from a diabetic attack. Conde's family called for an independent autopsy. The Government took no further action and announced no results.

Deaths in custody due to inhuman prison conditions and inadequate medical treatment are frequent (see Section 1.c.).

Liberian rebels killed dozens of Guineans and Liberian refugees during border incursions (see Section 2.d.).

There has been no investigation into the January 1995 deaths of 16 civilian prisoners while in police custody. There has been no action on the case of the policeman arrested for killing a youth following a rally in Conakry in June 1995 or the action against two police charged for killing a civilian in June in Kissidougou. Government authorities also blocked separate efforts by human rights groups and nongovernmental organizations to investigate political killings in the 1970's under then-president Sekou Toure and to protect victims' burial plots from urban encroachment.

Vigilante action by victims or other sometimes resulted in the beating to death of suspected criminals (see Section 1.e.).

  b. *Disappearance.*—In the months after the February mutiny, hundreds of soldiers and civilians disappeared during neighborhood sweeps conducted by unidentified members of security forces. After interrogations, dozens of soldiers were transferred to judicial authorities for legal proceedings related to the mutiny, and in August prosecutors released 63 detainees for lack of evidence. According to relatives, human rights groups, and the independent press, dozens—perhaps hundreds—of soldiers, civilians, and relatives of accused mutineers remained missing. The newspaper L'Independant reported that unidentified government authorities detained numerous relatives of alleged mutiny ringleader, Major Gbago Zoumanigui, missing since February and presumed to have fled the country. Most of Zoumanigui's family were released, but one relative, Baba Sarr, remained missing.

  c. *Torture and Other Cruel, Inhuman, or Degrading Treatment or Punishment.*— The Penal Code and the Constitution prohibit torture and cruel, inhuman, or degrading treatment. However, both civilian and military security forces often use beatings to extract confessions and employ other forms of brutality, including holding prisoners incommunicado without charges and under inhuman conditions. There were no reported judicial proceedings against officers suspected in these abuses.

Unidentified uniformed personnel used beatings, unsanitary conditions, and restrictions of food in secret prisons to obtain confessions from those suspected of involvement in the mutiny (see Section 1.d.).

Prison conditions are inhuman and life threatening. Family members and friends are responsible for feeding prisoners. Standards of sanitation remained poor, and there were several dozen deaths due to malnutrition and disease. Prisoners report threats and harassment by guards. There are credible reports from prisoners that female inmates are subject to harassment and sexual assault by guards.

The Guinean Organization for the Defense of Human and Citizen Rights (OGDH) determined that prisoners in at least one major prison, located in N'zerekore, suffered more from neglect and lack of resources than from mistreatment. According to the OGDH, the N'zerekore prison is a converted grain warehouse built in 1932 for 70 prisoners, but currently houses 120. There is no electricity or running water. The newly appointed Minister of Justice made televised visits to prisons in August and denounced the inhuman conditions. In June the Government authorized the creation of two nongovernmental organizations dedicated to ensuring prisoners' rights and prison conditions.

The Government occasionally permits prison visits by local human rights organizations.

d. *Arbitrary Arrest, Detention, or Exile.*—The Penal Code provides procedural safeguards for detainees. In practice, however, administrative controls over the police are ineffective, and security forces rarely follow the Penal Code; arbitrary arrest remained a persistent threat.

The Penal Code requires that detainees must be charged before a magistrate within 72 hours. Once charged, the accused may be held until the final outcome of the case, including a period of appeal. Release on bail is at the discretion of the magistrate who has jurisdiction. The Constitution proscribes incommunicado detention. The law provides for access by attorneys to their clients, but authorities frequently do not respect this provision.

From February through June, unidentified security forces detained hundreds of soldiers and civilians suspected of involvement in the February mutiny. Judicial authorities denied any responsibility for the arrests, yet took custody of dozens of detainees transferred by security forces. Bar Association attorneys, the independent press, and government sources described a parallel system of justice run by unidentified uniformed personnel who conducted midnight arrests, detained suspects, and used torture in secret prisons to obtain confessions before transferring detainees to prosecutors.

In August a government prosecutor released 63 detained soldiers for lack of evidence. The Government had charged a total of 43 soldiers with murder, looting, armed robbery, and abandonment of post in connection with the February mutiny and detained the rest without charges. The Government said that three unnamed soldiers remained in custody while human rights groups, the independent press, and government officials credibly reported that hundreds of soldiers and civilians were being detained illegally and without charges.

In September 1995, police in N'zerekore detained between 200 and 300 activists from the Rally of the Guinean People (RPG) party, following the killing of a police officer during an RPG demonstration that turned violent. According to credible reports, some of those detained were suspected in the killing; hundreds of others were detained for being RPG members or sympathizers. Most were subsequently released without charge, throughout much of the year 35 remained in detention without charges. The 35 were detained in military barracks, but human rights groups hesitated to demand that the detainees be turned over to judicial authorities for fear that they would suffer greater harm under the inhuman conditions of state-run prisons. In October 1996 most of the 35 were released with no further punishment than time served.

In December 1994, members of the presidential guard arrested, beat, and detained the U.S. Embassy React Team—composed of four Guinean employees—who were responding to a call by an American citizen for assistance. The team was detained for 12 days until the four were released without being charged with a crime. No action was taken against the members of the guard who were involved, and the Government has not returned the equipment that the guards seized.

The Government does not practice forced exile.

e. *Denial of Fair Public Trial.*—The Constitution provides for the judiciary's independence; however, the judiciary is susceptible to executive influence, particularly in politically sensitive cases. Magistrates are civil servants with no guarantee of tenure and are susceptible to influence by the executive branch. Judicial authorities often defer to central authorities in politically sensitive cases. Due to corruption and nepotism in the judiciary, relatives of influential members of the Government are virtually above the law. The Cabinet appointed in July stated that it will pursue those who violate the law but avoid punishment due to judicial corruption, including autonomous Red Berets. By year's end, no action had been taken.

The Judiciary includes courts of first instance, two Courts of Appeal, and the Supreme Court, the court of final appeal. There is also a State Security court, but it has not met since the trial of those allegedly involved in a 1985 coup attempt. Since 1988 civilian courts have rendered all judgments involving civilians under the Penal Code. A military tribunal prepares and adjudicates charges against accused military personnel, to whom the Penal Code does not apply. The armed services, however, made no use of a tribunal following the February mutiny and transferred dozens of detained soldiers to the judiciary (see Section 1.d.). The Government announced in September the creation of a Discipline Council for dealing with civil servants who abuse their positions as government employees.

The Penal Code provides for the presumption of innocence of accused persons, the independence of judges, the equality of citizens before the law, the right of the accused to counsel, and the right to appeal a judicial decision. Although in principle the Government is responsible for funding legal defense costs in serious criminal cases, in practice it rarely disburses these funds. The attorney for the defense frequently receives no payment. The Government provided counsel for dozens of soldiers charged in connection with the February mutiny and the quasi-independent Bar Association started a permanent legal defense fund.

Defense lawyers for soldiers detained in connection with the February mutiny complained that they had difficulty obtaining permission to meet with their clients, that prison guards eavesdropped on their conversations, denied family visits for the detainees, and that the Government cut their clients' salaries up to 60 percent to pay for prison meals.

In addition to corruption and nepotism, the administration of justice is plagued by numerous other problems, including shortages of magistrates (who generally are poorly trained) and lawyers, and the outdated and overly restrictive Penal Code.

A traditional system of justice exists at the village or urban neighborhood level. Litigants present their civil cases before a village chief, a neighborhood leader, or a council of wise men. The dividing line between the formal and informal justice systems is vague, and a case may be referred from the formal to the traditional system to ensure compliance by all parties. Similarly, if a case cannot be resolved to the satisfaction of all parties in the traditional system, it may be referred to the formal system for adjudication. The traditional system discriminates against women in that evidence given by women carries less weight.

Suspected criminals, notably thieves and rapists, are sometimes beaten to death by their victims or by others. Police authorities rarely intervene to rescue victims of vigilante justice.

The Government conducted a mid-year public awareness campaign on justice, using the government-controlled media to inform citizens of their rights. The campaign also included theatrical performances in French and in local languages to disseminate information on constitutional rights and judicial procedures.

The Government holds less than a dozen political prisoners. These prisoners are individuals incarcerated for allegedly politically motivated acts, such as protests, meetings and campaigns; but arrested and convicted under criminal laws such as those applying to creating disorder, inciting violence, and corruption. Some of these individuals consequently received disproportionately harsh punishment due to their political affiliation.

f. *Arbitrary Interference With Privacy, Family, Home, or Correspondence.*—The Constitution provides for the inviolability of the home, and judicial search warrants are required by law. However, police frequently ignore these procedures. Police and paramilitary police often ignore legal procedures in the pursuit of criminals and frequently detain private citizens at nighttime roadblocks in order to extort money. It is widely believed that security officials monitor mail and telephone calls.

Local businesses, especially expatriate companies, often complain of intimidation and harassment by public officials and authorities. Family members of alleged military mutineers reported harassment, arbitrary arrest, and searches.

Section 2. *Respect for Civil Liberties, Including:*

a. *Freedom of Speech and Press.*—The Constitution provides for freedom of expression, subject to certain limitations; however, despite government statements in support of free speech and a free press, the Government employs a broad range of restrictions that vitiate any real protection. The Government prohibits what it considers seditious talk or chants in public, has established defamation and slander as criminal offenses, and prohibits communications that personally insult the President, or incite violence, discrimination, or hatred, or that disturb the public peace.

The Government publishes the official newspaper, Horoya, and operates official television and radio (RTG). Reporters for the official press, who are government employees, practice self-censorship in order to protect their jobs. Several younger broadcast journalists reported critically about the Government and posed critical questions at official press conferences.

There is a vocal independent press which is critical of the President and the Government. For example, the weekly satirical newspaper Le Lynx publishes front page cartoons lampooning the Head of State and senior government officials. The government-controlled daily (Horoya) and two weekly newspapers (Le Lynx and L'Independant) publish regularly in Conakry and up to 10 other publications publish sporadically, although hampered by technical and financial difficulties. One newspaper, L'Espoir, is affiliated with the governing political party (PUP) and several other newspapers are affiliated with opposition parties. Other papers offer news and criticism of both the Government and the opposition.

The Government maintains control of the electronic media, and national radio serves as the most important means of reaching the public. French radio (RFI) is accessible on FM radio in Conakry and in September the Government authorized the FM transmission of Africa Number One, a private Gabonese radio station. Many Guineans listen regularly to foreign-origin shortwave radio and some Guineans have access to foreign television satellite broadcasts.

The Government has occasionally arrested journalists. In March the Government arrested the editor of Le Lynx, Souleymane Diallo, for publishing what authorities called falsification of an official document listing armed forces salaries. On March 28, a Conakry court declared Diallo innocent for lack of sufficient evidence; however, the Government prosecutor did not release him until April 2. Authorities arrested and convicted Diallo in 1995 for offending the Head of State after Le Lynx published a cartoon mocking one of President Conte's wives.

In May authorities arrested Le Citoyen's editor, Thierno Sadou, and in June its publisher, Siaka Kouyate, for publishing articles concerning the February mutiny and the theft of classified presidential documents. They were detained until August, when a Conakry judge convicted them for offending the Head of State and refusing to disclaim the article. They received a suspended sentence, a $500 fine and the judge suspended Le Citoyen from publishing for 2 months. Le Citoyen resumed publishing in September.

On July 2, the Government deported Serge Daniel, an RFI correspondent and citizen of Benin, for disseminating negative news. Among other items, Daniel had filed a report announcing that nearly $500,000 was missing from a Ministry of Health project funded by the U.N. Childrens Agency (UNICEF).

Political tracts occasionally circulate in Conakry and other urban areas. Some tracts support the Government while others specifically criticize senior officials. Foreign publications, some of which criticize the Government, are often available.

The Ministry of National Education and Scientific Research exercises limited control over academic freedom through its influence on faculty hiring and control over curriculum. In general teachers are not subject to classroom censorship.

b. *Freedom of Peaceful Assembly and Association.*—The law restricts freedom of assembly and the Government exercises its power to thwart unwanted political activity. The Penal Code bans any meeting that has an ethnic or racial character or any gathering "whose nature threatens national unity." Public gatherings are legal only if the Government receives notification 72 hours prior to the event.

The Government bans all street marches except for funerals. Pursuant to this statute, local authorities may cancel a demonstration or meeting if they believe that it will threaten public order. They may hold event organizers criminally liable if violence or destruction of property ensues.

Students at the University of Conakry went on strike in April and May demanding an increase in their scholarship payments. As a result of the strike, the students' demands were partially met. During this strike, police broke up a demonstration and arrested 22 students and a journalist from Le Lynx. Le Lynx reported that its journalist was beaten in custody but later released. The Government released 13 of the students for lack of evidence and convicted 9 for inciting violence and destruction of property. They were sentenced to 18 months' imprisonment (which was suspended) and fined $77 each. Freedom of association is protected by law, but there are cumbersome requirements to obtain government recognition. Political parties must provide information on their founding members and produce internal statutes and political platforms consistent with the Constitution before the Government recognizes them. There are approximately 46 legally recognized political parties; deputies of 9 different parties are represented in the National Assembly.

There were credible reports of harassment and oppression of the Rally of the Guinean People (RPG) party. In January the prefect of Kouroussa blocked two RPG National Assembly deputies from meeting in his district with party members. The RPG and human rights groups claimed that government authorities physically harassed Kouroussa citizens who did not vote for the government party, as well as RPG deputies traveling in Banankoro in August. The RPG and independent press reported that security forces harassed RPG leader Alpha Conde with tear gas and tanks at his Conakry residence.

c. *Freedom of Religion.*—The Constitution provides for freedom of religion and permits religious communities to govern themselves without state interference. The Government generally respects these rights in practice. Foreign missionaries and church-affiliated relief agencies operate freely. The Government and the quasi-governmental National Islamic League have spoken out against the proliferation of Shi 'ite fundamentalist sects, which they alleged were "generating confusion and deviation" within Guinean Islam, but have not restricted these groups.

d. *Freedom of Movement Within the Country, Foreign Travel, Emigration, and Repatriation.*—The Constitution provides citizens with the right to travel freely within the country and to change their place of residence and work. The Government requires all citizens to carry a national identification card, which they must present on demand at security checkpoints. Travelers face harassment by police and at military roadblocks, particularly late at night. It is common to pay bribes at these roadblocks.

The Government permits foreign travel, although it retains the authority to limit it for political reasons. The Government officially closed the borders during the December 1995 foreign ministers' meeting of the Organization of the Islamic Conference. In August commerce authorities restricted overland trade of some products in an effort to improve tax collection.

The Government cooperates fully with the United Nations High Commissioner for Refugees (UNHCR), the World Food Program, other humanitarian organizations, and donor countries to assist refugees. The Government provides first asylum in accordance with United Nations and Organization of African Unity conventions. In 1996 the Government provided first asylum for over 600,000 Liberian and Sierra Leonean refugees, including additional arrivals who fled renewed fighting in Liberia. There were no reports of forced return of persons to a country where they feared persecution.

The Government has provided school buildings, access to local medical facilities, and land for farming to assist those designated as refugees. However, relief organizations report that government authorities have demanded portions of donated fuel and food from delivery convoys.

While the Government has generally been hospitable toward refugees, there have been reports that local police and border patrol soldiers harassed refugees and demanded bribes or sexual favors for entry into Guinea. In reaction to violent Liberian rebel incursions in the Macenta forest region, which resulted in the death of dozens of Guinean and Liberian refugees, the Government increased its armed forces along the Liberian border in July and fought Liberian rebels.

There were no reports of forced repatriation.

Section 3. Respect for Political Rights: The Right of Citizens to Change Their Government

Although the 1990 Constitution provides for a popularly elected president and a multiparty parliament, the ability of citizens to exercise effectively this provision is restricted. The Government's tight control of the electoral process and lack of an independent electoral oversight mechanism call into serious doubt the ability of citizens to change the Government. The scheduled 1995 legislative elections in Kissidougou and Kaloum-Conakry did not take place. During the April session of the National Assembly, a majority of deputies rejected the then Minister of Interior's efforts to appoint, rather than elect, neighborhood councils; however, no elections were scheduled.

President Conte took office in 1994 after multiparty elections in December 1993 in which the Government dominated the electoral process. In 1995 the President's party, the Party of Unity and Progress, won 62 percent of the legislative seats (one seat short of the majority required to make constitutional amendments) and 56 percent of the municipal vacancies. The International Commission of Jurists reported seeing no seals on the legislative ballots, results envelopes left open, and various means of intimidation used at some polling places. The African-American Institute said that the National Electoral Commission—the supposed "moral guarantor of electoral fairnes'—had only a marginal role.

Opposition leaders deemed the entire process an "electoral masquerade" and "a comedy," and openly questioned the credibility and legitimacy of PUP's municipal and legislative landslide victories. Shortly after results were announced, nine opposition parties joined forces to form an umbrella organization, CODEM, dedicated "to act, organize, and combat together to make Guinea a land of liberty." These parties' deputies took their seats in the National Assembly and played an active role in budgetary and general sessions. Government radio and television provided live coverage of some legislative sessions.

Women are underrepresented in the Government. The President appointed a new Cabinet in July and reduced the number of women who hold positions in the 23-member Cabinet from 4 to 2. The women head the low profile ministries of Social Affairs and Youth, Sports, and Civic Education. There are only 9 female deputies in the 114-member National Assembly. There are few women at senior levels below minister and no women among senior military ranks. Women also play a minor role in the leadership of the major political parties.

The Cabinet and armed forces leadership include representatives of all major ethnic groups. However, a disproportionate number of senior military officers are Soussou, the President's ethnic group.

Section 4. Governmental Attitude Regarding International and Nongovernmental Investigation of Alleged Violations of Human Rights

Local nongovernmental organizations (NGO's) primarily interested in human rights issues include: The Guinean Organization for the Defense of Human Rights; the Guinean Human Rights Association; the Children of the Victims of Camp Boiro; S.O.S. Burial Grounds; the Association of Victims of Repression; Humanitarian Assistance for Prisons; Defense of Prisoners' Rights; Women Jurists for Human Rights; the Committee for the Defense of Civic Rights; and the Coordinating Committee on Traditional Practices Affecting Women's and Children's Health. Government officials are generally cooperative and responsive to their views; however, various officials have blocked private efforts to memorialize victims of the Sekou Toure regime.

Section 5. Discrimination Based on Race, Sex, Religion, Disability, Language, or Social Status

The Constitution states that all persons are equal before the law regardless of gender, race, ethnicity, language, beliefs, political opinions, philosophy, or creed, but the Government does not uniformly enforce these provisions.

Women.—Violence against women is common, although estimates differ as to the extent of the problem. Wife beating is a criminal offense and constitutes grounds for divorce under civil law; however, police rarely intervene in domestic disputes.

Although the Government has made regular statements in the media against sexual harassment, women working in the formal sector in urban areas complain of frequent sexual harassment. Refugees from Liberia and Sierra Leone report that some Guinean soldiers demand sex in exchange for entry into Guinea. There are credible reports from prisoners that female inmates are subject to harassment and sexual assault by guards. The social stigma attached to rape prevents most victims from reporting it. The Government has not vigorously pursued criminal investigations of alleged sexual crimes.

The Constitution provides for equal treatment of men and women, and the Ministry of Social Affairs and Women's Protection works to ensure such equality. Women face discrimination, however, particularly in rural areas, where opportunities for women are limited by custom and the demands of child-rearing and subsistence farming. Women are not denied access to land, credit, or businesses, but women receive less inheritance. Evidence given by women carries less weight than that given by men (see Section 1.c.). The Government has affirmed the principle of equal pay for equal work, but in practice, women receive less pay than men in most equally demanding jobs. According to a 1995 United Nations Development Program report, only 11 percent of females receive as much schooling as males and women constitute 38 percent of the labor force.

Children.—The Constitution provides that the Government has a particular obligation to protect and nurture the nation's youth, and the Government allocates a significant percentage of the budget to primary education. The President appoints a cabinet minister to defend women's and children's rights and a Minister of Youth.

Female genital mutilation (FGM), which is widely condemned by international health experts as damaging to both physical and psychological health, is practiced in all regions and among all religious and ethnic groups. FGM is performed on girls and women between the ages of 4 and 70. FGM is illegal under Article 265 of the Penal Code and senior officials have spoken out against the practice. According to an independent expert, between 70 and 90 percent of females have undergone this procedure. Infibulation, the most dangerous form of FGM, is practiced in the Forest region. Despite efforts by proponents of women's rights to call attention to the practice, and in spite of diseases resulting from crude and unsanitary surgical instruments and deaths resulting from the practice, the tradition continues, seriously affecting women's lives. The Government has made efforts to educate health workers on the dangers of this procedure and supports the efforts of the Committee on Traditional Practices Affecting Women and Children (CPTAFE), an NGO dedicated to eradicating FGM. An increasing number of men and women oppose the practice.

Prostitution exists in the informal economic sector and employs girls as young as 10. The Government takes prohibitive action if prostitution of minors is brought to its attention, but does not actively monitor child or adult prostitution.

People With Disabilities.—The Constitution provides that all persons are equal before the law. There are no special constitutional provisions for the disabled. The Government has not mandated accessibility for the disabled, and few disabled people work. Many disabled persons develop opportunities in the informal sector.

National/Racial/Ethnic Minorities.—While the Constitution and the Penal Code prohibit racial or ethnic discrimination, ethnic identification is strong. Mutual suspicion affects relations across ethnic lines, in and out of government. Promotions to senior government levels and the highest military ranks below the President include representatives of all three major ethnic groups.

Section 6. Worker Rights

a. *The Right of Association.*—The Constitution provides for the right of employees to form independent labor unions and prohibits discrimination based on union affiliation. Only an estimated 5 percent of the work force is unionized. Most union members are government employees, employees of the national utilities (electric, water, and telephone companies), or of foreign-controlled companies.

The Labor Code states that all workers, except military and paramilitary personnel, have the right to create and participate in organizations that defend and develop their individual and collective rights as workers. It requires elected worker representatives for any enterprise employing 25 or more salaried workers.

The National Confederation of Guinean Workers (CNTG) was the sole trade union before the Labor Code was enacted. Although there are now other trade unions and labor confederations, the CNTG remains the largest confederation.

The CNTG is indirectly funded by the State, although dissident members seek to increase the Confederation's freedom from government control. Independent unions and confederations have gained popularity, such as the Free Union of Teachers and Researchers of Guinea and the National Organization for Free Trade Unions of Guinea. Several disgruntled groups within the CNTG left the Confederation, citing corruption in its leadership. These groups joined with some independent unions to form the United Syndicates of Guinean Workers.

The Labor Code grants salaried workers, including public sector civilian employees, the right to strike 10 days after their representative union makes known its intention to strike. It prohibits strikes in sectors providing "essential services" (hospitals, radio and television, army, and police).

Unions may freely affiliate with international labor groups. The Government continues to designate CNTG to represent workers in the International Labor Organization conference.

Guinea's largest educators' union, SLECG, held a nonviolent strike in December 1995 to protest low salaries and poor benefits. The strike had wide participation in Conakry and several cities in the interior. High school students clashed with police and authorities arrested the union's Secretary General, Louis M'Bemba Soumah, and numerous union members. In January a Conakry court convicted seven union members for inciting violence and gave them 1-year suspended sentences.

b. *The Right to Organize and Bargain Collectively.*—Under the Labor Code, representative workers' unions or union groups may organize in the workplace and negotiate with employers or employer organizations. The law protects the right to bargain collectively concerning wages and salaries without government interference. Work rules and work hours established by the employer are developed in consultation with union delegates. The Code also prohibits antiunion discrimination. Union delegates represent individual and collective claims and grievances with management. Individual workers threatened with dismissal or other sanctions have the right to a hearing before management with a union representative present and, if necessary, to take the complaint to the Conakry Labor Court which convenes weekly to hear such cases. In the interior, civil courts hear labor cases.

There are no export processing zones.

c. *Prohibition of Forced or Compulsory Labor.*—The Labor Code specifically forbids forced or compulsory labor, and there is no evidence of its practice.

d. *Minimum Age for Employment of Children.*—According to the Labor Code, the minimum age for employment is 16 years. Apprentices, however, may start at 14 years. Workers and apprentices under the age of 18 are not permitted to work at night, nor for more than 12 consecutive hours, nor on Sundays. The Labor Code also stipulates that the Minister of Labor and Social Affairs must maintain a list of occupations in which women and youth under the age of 18 cannot be employed. In practice, enforcement by Ministry inspectors is limited to large firms in the modern sector of the economy. Children of all ages work on family farms, in small trades, and in the informal sector, such as street vending.

e. *Acceptable Conditions of Work.*—The Labor Code provides for the establishment by decree of a guaranteed minimum hourly wage, but the Government has not yet done so. There are also provisions in the code for overtime and night wages, which are fixed percentages of the regular wage. According to the Labor Code, regular work is not to exceed 10-hour days or 48-hour weeks, and there is to be a period of at least 24 consecutive hours of rest each week, usually Sunday. Every salaried worker has the legal right to an annual paid vacation, accumulated at the rate of at least 2.5 workdays per month of work. In practice, the authorities enforce these rules only in the relatively small modern urban sector.

The Labor Code contains provisions of a general nature regarding occupational safety and health, but the Government has not yet elaborated a set of practical workplace health and safety standards. Nor has it issued any of the ministerial orders laying out the specific requirements for certain occupations and for certain methods of work that are called for in the Labor Code. The Ministry of Labor and Social Affairs is responsible for enforcing labor standards, and its inspectors are empowered to suspend work immediately in situations hazardous to health. However, enforcement remained more a goal than a reality. Labor inspectors acknowledge that they cannot even cover Conakry, much less the entire country, with their small staff and meager budget.

Under the Labor Code, workers have the right to refuse to work under unsafe conditions without penalty.

GUINEA-BISSAU

Joao Bernardo Vieira was elected President in the Republic of Guinea-Bissau's first multiparty elections in 1994. Vieira has ruled the country since taking power in a 1980 coup. He is also the President of the African Party for the Independence of Guinea-Bissau and Cape Verde (PAIGC), which was the only legal political party from independence in 1974 until adoption of a multiparty constitution in 1991. The PAIGC holds 62 of the 100 seats in the National Assembly where 4 other parties are represented. The Constitution provides for an independent judiciary, but its functioning is hampered by a lack of resources and by corruption.

The police, under the direction of the Ministry of Internal Administration, have primary responsibility for the nation's internal security. The armed forces are responsible for external security and may be called upon to assist the police in internal emergencies. The police were responsible for human rights abuses.

The population of 1 million relies largely upon subsistence agriculture. Annual per capita gross domestic product is estimated at $840. The economy remained stable in 1996, but inflation continued at approximately 50 percent. The country is burdened by a heavy external debt and has inadequate tax revenues.

Political pluralism brought about greater transparency. However, the overall human rights situation did not improve during the year. Police continued to engage in arbitrary detention, physical mistreatment, and other forms of harassment. In addition, the police shot and killed one person and gravely injured another in the aftermath of a demonstration. The Government did not punish any members of the security forces for abuses. Prison conditions remain poor, and prolonged detention and a lack of due process continue. The Government restricts freedom of assembly. Journalists continue to practice self-censorship, and the Government infringes on citizens' right to privacy. Discrimination against women and children are problems.

RESPECT FOR HUMAN RIGHTS

Section 1. Respect for the Integrity of the Person, Including Freedom From:

a. *Political and Other Extrajudicial Killings.*—There was one known extrajudicial killing in 1996. In July the Minister of the Interior agreed to allow Spain to deport about 50 Africans of varying nationalities illegally resident in Spanish Morocco to Guinea-Bissau. The Spanish Government agreed to pay for the maintenance and repatriation of the deportees. On September 23, Guinean police shot and killed one of the deportees while he was sitting on a wall outside of the jail where they were being housed. This action was apparently in retaliation for a march earlier in the day that the deportees conducted in front of the Presidential palace to protest their conditions. In addition another deportee was shot and severely wounded. The Government has undertaken an investigation of this affair.

The 1992 death of Ussumane Quade, an army officer beaten to death while in police custody, remains unresolved. Human rights monitors continue to press for a thorough and impartial investigation of his death, ostensibly a suicide, but police have refused to cooperate.

b. *Disappearance.*—There were no reports of politically motivated disappearances.

c. *Torture and Other Cruel, Inhuman, or Degrading Treatment or Punishment.*— The Constitution prohibits cruel and inhuman punishment, and evidence obtained through torture or other coercion is invalid. However, the Government often ignores these provisions. Security and police authorities have historically employed abusive interrogation methods, usually in the form of severe beatings or deprivation. The Government rarely enforces provisions for punishment of abuses committed by security forces. Beatings and deprivation have continued to be used in prisons as a means of coercion. The head of the national police has initiated a program to educate police in the interior against using such methods.

Two policemen accused of rape in 1995 have yet to stand trial, and no trial date has been set. Human rights monitors report other incidents in which police accused of rape or mistreatment of prisoners have not been prosecuted.

The Prime Minister and his bodyguards slapped and pushed three citizens in three unrelated incidents. The attacks were not politically motivated, and no serious injuries occurred.

Prison conditions are poor, but generally not life threatening. The Human Rights League has offered to pay for prison improvements, but the Government has denied it access to prisoners.

d. *Arbitrary Arrest, Detention, or Exile.*—The legal system provides for procedural rights, such as the right to counsel, the right to release if no timely indictment is brought, and the right to a speedy trial. In practice, the judicial system generally fails to provide these rights.

Police detain suspects without judicial authority or warrants, occasionally through the devices of house arrest. The Government holds detainees without charge or trial for extended periods of time, sometimes incommunicado.

Human rights monitors estimate that pretrial detainees arrested without warrants and imprisoned without charge make up more than 90 percent of the prison population. The authorities do not routinely observe bail procedures.

The case of the deportees from Spain highlights this problem. They were initially housed in a jail in Bissau, although allowed to come and go as they pleased. Following the September 23 incidents, they were held without charges at a military prison outside of Bissau. Human rights groups and other interested parties were originally denied access to them. The deportees have since been released. The Nigerian, Guinean, and Spanish Governments repatriated the Nigerian refugees through Gambia. The remaining refugees are insisting on greater compensation in exchange for their agreement to leave the country.

The Government does not use forced exile.

e. *Denial of Fair Public Trial.*—The Constitution provides for an independent judiciary, but judges, who are poorly trained and paid, are sometimes subject to political pressures and corruption.

Trials involving state security are conducted by civilian courts. Military courts try only crimes under the Code of Military Justice committed by armed forces personnel. The Supreme Court is the final court of appeal for both civilian and military cases. The President has the authority to grant pardons and reduce sentences.

Despite its problems, the judicial system is sometimes capable of providing a fair trial, even in controversial cases. Several policeman accused of being accomplices to armed robbery in September 1995 were tried, convicted, and are now in prison.

Citizens who cannot afford an attorney have the right to a court-appointed lawyer. Traditional law still prevails in most rural areas, and urban dwellers often bring judicial disputes to traditional counselors to avoid the costs and bureaucratic impediments of the official system. Police often resolve disputes.

There were no reports of political prisoners.

f. *Arbitrary Interference With Privacy, Family, Home, or Correspondence.*—The Constitution provides for the inviolability of domicile, person, and correspondence, but the Government does not always respect these rights. The authorities examine international and domestic mail, the security forces seldom use judicial warrants, and the police sometimes force entry into private homes.

Section 2. Respect for Civil Liberties Including:
   a. *Freedom of Speech and Press.*—The Constitution provides for freedom of speech and the press, but journalists continue to practice self-censorship.
   In addition to the government-run newspaper, there is a daily newspaper and four weekly newspapers. However, the weekly newspapers have not published regularly due to financial constraints.
   There are currently five independent radio stations in Bissau in addition to the government-controlled station. Two of these are French and Portuguese radio stations, retransmitted in Bissau directly from Paris and Lisbon.
   In September and October, Radio Pindjiguiti, one of the private stations, alleged Government harassment due to its unfavorable coverage of the Government's handling of the African deportee situation and temporarily ceased news broadcasts. President Vieira intervened and guaranteed the safety of the station, allowing it to resume news broadcasts 48 hours later.
   Academic freedom is observed in schools and research institutions.
   b. *Freedom of Peaceful Assembly and Association.*—The Constitution provides for freedom of assembly and association, but the Government restricts the right in practice. Government approval is required for all assemblies and demonstrations. Requests are not always approved.
   In May the Government denied the Guinean Human Rights League permission to march peacefully in protest of Prime Minister Saturnino da Costa's management of the economy and three separate assaults by the Prime Minister and his bodyguards on citizens.
   In September the Government responded with excessive violence to an illegal protest in front of the Presidential palace by the African deportees from Spain. Police killed one deportee and injured another (see Section 1.a.).
   The Government does not prohibit or discourage actively the formation of associations, nor does it impose any restrictions on private associations.
   c. *Freedom of Religion.*—The Constitution provides for freedom of religion, and the Government respects this right in practice. While religious groups must be licensed by the Government, none has been refused. Various faiths, including Jehovah's Witnesses, continued missionary operations during the year.
   d. *Freedom of Movement Within the Country, Foreign Travel, Emigration, and Repatriation.*—The Government generally does not restrict movement within the country, foreign travel, or emigration. However, checkpoints and police harassment occur. Passports are issued by the Minister of Internal Administration. Citizens are guaranteed the right to return and are not subject to political revocation of their citizenship. There are no provisions for asylum.
   The Government provided first asylum to Senegalese refugees from the Casamance during that region's conflict. The number of Senegalese refugees has remained stable at 20,000 as tensions have eased in Senegal's Casamance region. The United Nations High Commissioner for Refugees (UNHCR) has set up a refugee camp in Jolomete well south of the Senegalese border. The Government requested this location in order to prevent refugees from being involved in the Casamance separatist movement, thereby eliminating conflicts between the Governments of Senegal and Guinea-Bissau. As of June, the Jolomete camp had about 550 refugees. There were no reports of forced return of Casamance refugees.
   In the case of other refugees, the Government has generally cooperated with the UNHCR. It granted first asylum to Liberian and Sierra Leonean refugees in 1996. There have been no reports of forced return of persons to a country where they feared persecution.

Section 3. Respect for Political Rights: The Right of Citizens to Change Their Government

   In 1994 voters were able to freely choose their government for the first time in the nation's history. The PAIGC retained power in elections judged to be free and fair by international observers, although they acknowledged some irregularities. The Minister of Territorial Administration scheduled local elections for December; however, these were postponed until the first quarter of 1997.
   Women are underrepresented in the political process. Eight of the 100 National Assembly deputies are women, and there is a women's caucus that cuts across party lines. Only 2 of 21 Cabinet ministers are women.

Section 4. Governmental Attitudes Regarding International and Nongovernmental Investigation of Alleged Violations of Human Rights

   The Government did not interfere with the Guinea-Bissau Human Rights League and international human rights groups, which continued to investigate human rights abuses objectively without government harassment. However, the League's planned conference on police and prison reform was canceled for the third consecutive year due to the Government's unwillingness to allow police to attend. The Government denied the Human Rights League access to some prisoners.

Section 5. Discrimination Based on Race, Sex, Religion, Disability, Language, or Social Status

The Constitution and law prohibit discrimination on the basis of sex, race, and religion. In practice, however, the Government does not effectively enforce these provisions.

Women.—Physical violence, including wife beating, is an accepted means of settling domestic disputes. Although police will intervene in domestic disputes if requested, the Government has not undertaken specific measures to counter social pressure against reporting domestic violence, rape, incest, and other mistreatment of women.

Discrimination against women persists although officially prohibited by law. Women are responsible for most work on subsistence farms and have limited access to education, especially in rural areas. Women do not have equal access to employment. Among certain ethnic groups, women can not own or manage land nor inherit property.

Children.—The Government allocates only limited resources for children's welfare and education.

Female genital mutilation (FGM), which is widely condemned by international health experts as damaging to both physical and psychological health, is widely practiced within certain ethnic groups, especially the Fulas and the Mandinkas. The practice is increasing as the population becomes more Muslim. The practice is also now being performed not only on adolescent girls, but also on babies as young as 4 months old. The Government has neither outlawed the practice nor taken effective action to combat it.

People With Disabilities.—There is no legislation mandating accessibility. The law does not specifically prohibit discrimination against people with disabilities, and the Government does not ensure equal access to employment and education. The State has made some efforts to assist disabled veterans through pension programs, but these programs do not adequately address veterans' health, housing, and food needs.

Section 6. Worker Rights

a. *The Right of Association.*—The Constitution provides all civilian workers with the freedom to form and join independent trade unions. However, the vast majority of the population works in subsistence agriculture. Most union members are government or parastatal employees; only a small percentage of workers are in the wage sector and are organized.

The Government registers all labor unions. There are 11 labor unions registered and operating. All unions are officially independent of the Government, but seven unions are affiliated with the National Trade Union Confederation (UNTG), which retains close informal ties with the PAIGC. The law does not favor UNTG-affiliated unions over others. The Constitution provides for the right to strike and protection from retribution against strike activities.

The only legal restriction on strike activity is the requirement for prior notice. Legal strikes were conducted by several unions, with no retribution against the strikers.

All unions are free to affiliate freely with national confederations and international labor organizations of their choice.

b. *The Right to Organize and Bargain Collectively.*—The Constitution does not provide or protect the right to bargain collectively, and there were no instances of genuine collective bargaining. Most wages are established in bilateral negotiations between workers and employers, taking into consideration the minimum salaries set annually by the Government's Council of Ministers.

The Government's provisions for the protection of workers against antiunion discrimination has very little effect due to low union membership. The Government has not taken further action, but no workers have alleged antiunion discrimination. The Government adopted no laws to establish penal sanctions against employers practicing such discrimination. The practice is not widespread.

There are no export processing zones.

c. *Prohibition of Forced and Compulsory Labor.*—Forced or compulsory labor is not permitted by law and is not known to exist. An individual accused of coercing labor in 1995 was found guilty and fined.

d. *Minimum Age for Employment of Children.*—The General Labor Act of 1986 established a minimum age of 14 years for general factory labor and 18 years for heavy or dangerous labor, including all labor in mines. These minimum age requirements are generally followed in the small-wage sector, but the Ministry of Civil Service and Labor does not enforce these requirements in other sectors. Children in cities often work in street trading, and those in rural communities do domestic and field work without pay. The Government does not attempt to discourage these traditional practices.

e. *Acceptable Conditions of Work.*—The Government's Council of Ministers annually establishes minimum wage rates for all categories of work but does not enforce them. The lowest monthly wage is less than $20 (600,000 pesos). This wage is inadequate to maintain a minimum standard of living, and workers must supplement their income through other work, reliance on the extended family, and subsistence agriculture. The maximum number of hours permitted in a normal workweek without further compensation is 45, but the Government does not enforce this provision.

The Ministry of Civil Service and Labor establishes legal health and safety standards for workers, with the cooperation of the unions, which are then adopted into law by the National Assembly. However, these standards are not enforced, and many persons work under conditions that endanger their health and safety.

Workers do not have a guaranteed right to remove themselves from unsafe working conditions without losing their jobs. Given high unemployment, a worker who left for such reasons would be readily replaced.

KENYA

After 9 years as a single-party state led by the Kenya Africa National Union (KANU), a 1991 constitutional amendment restored multiparty politics. However, President Daniel arap Moi and his KANU party continued to dominate the political system. In addition to his role as President, Moi also commands the military services, controls the security, university, civil service, judiciary, and provincial, district, and local governance systems. KANU controls a majority of the unicameral National Assembly's 200 seats. The judiciary is subject to executive branch influence.

The large internal security apparatus includes the Police Criminal Investigation Department (CID), the Paramilitary General Services Unit, the Directorate of Security and Intelligence (DSI), and the National Police. The CID and DSI investigate criminal activity and also monitor persons whom the State considers subversive. Members of the security forces committed serious human rights abuses, but fewer than in 1995.

The economy includes a well-developed private sector in trade, light manufacturing, and finance. The predominant agricultural sector provides food for local consumption, substantial exports of coffee, tea, cut flowers, and vegetables, and approximately 70 percent of total employment. Tourism remained the largest single foreign exchange earner. Tight monetary policies kept the annual inflation rate to a single digit. Annual per capita gross domestic product is $290.

The Government's human rights record showed some signs of improvement from its very poor level in 1995, but serious problems remain in many areas. Police committed numerous extrajudicial killings and tortured and beat detainees. The Government arrested and prosecuted some police officers responsible for abuses. Authorities continued to use arbitrary arrest and prolonged detention, although with reduced frequency. Prison conditions are life threatening, and authorities infringed on citizens' privacy rights. The judiciary is subject to executive branch influence, although several judges dismissed confessions obtained through coercion. Citizens' ability to change their government peacefully has not yet been fully demonstrated at the presidential level. The Government continued to harass and intimidate those opposed to the ruling party. The Government continued to detain critics of the ruling party, including opposition parliamentarians, journalists, politicians, clergy, members of civic organizations, and human rights activists. However, the number of parliamentarians arrested continued to decline. The Government continued to limit freedom of speech, assembly, and association, and block opposition leaders' access to their supporters and electronic media. Some journalists practice self-censorship. It also continued to deny registration to new political parties and to interfere with opposition party meetings, though fewer meetings were dispersed in 1996 than in 1995. The Government has not addressed the root causes of factional violence in the Rift Valley and elsewhere in Kenya. Discrimination against women and against and among ethnic groups, and violence against women and children remained serious problems. There were few incidents of ethnic violence; however, mob violence—at times resulting in death—remained a serious problem.

The Government established a standing committee on human rights in 1996 and made some effort to conduct a dialog with human rights organizations. It responded in print to a detailed critique by one human rights organization; allowed human rights organizations to witness autopsies of several people who had died in police custody; overturned the 1995 deregistration of Clarion, a human rights nongovernmental organization (NGO), and granted bail to members of Release Political Prisoners (RPP) detained for holding an "unlicensed" meeting. The standing committee presented its first report to President Moi on December 12, but details of the report were not made public.

RESPECT FOR HUMAN RIGHTS

Section 1. Respect for the Integrity of the Person, Including Freedom From:

a. *Political and Other Extrajudicial Killing.*—There was one killing with political undertones, the murder of Karimi Nduthu, Secretary General of RPP in March. Unknown assailants shot and killed Nduthu in his Nairobi home. There was no specific evidence tying the Government to the murder, but RPP activists reported that the assailants took nothing of commercial value.

Police frequently used lethal force in attempts to apprehend criminal suspects. According to government figures, police killed 74 "suspected robbers" between June 1995 and June 1996. The nongovernmental Kenyan Human Rights Commission (KHRC) reported that police killed 88 people in the first 9 months of the year, while a second organization reported 74 extrajudicial killings by security forces in the first 9 months of the year, including 12 by torture. According to the Attorney General's office, 12 police officers were charged with brutality and wrongful killing in 1996.

Human rights groups criticized some of these police shootings, claiming that the victims included innocent bystanders, and criticized the Government's failure to take appropriate action against the policemen responsible for the killings. The Government argued that some of the civilian victims in such cases were killed by criminals and that other killings were justifiable killings in pursuit of armed criminals in their drive to control rampant crime, a claim disputed by some human rights organizations. The Government prosecuted several police officers responsible for abuses, two of whom were convicted of murder.

Several persons died in police custody, reportedly as a result of torture. In March Peter Mukinyo Muhia died in police custody in Bombolulu. An autopsy showed the cause of death as internal bleeding and multiple bruises over his body inflicted while in police custody. In April Mwiniyi Khamas, a Mombasa security guard, died after 3 days in police custody; the post mortem report attributed her death to shock and severe bleeding. In May Joseph Kamau Kihara died in police custody in Makuyu, reportedly from torture during questioning about a car theft, and Noah Njuguna Ndung'u died in police custody in Kandara, apparently from beatings. The autopsy performed by a police pathologist and witnessed by a family doctor and human rights organizations found that Ndung'u died after being hit on the head and chest with a blunt object which caused severe internal bleeding. There were also wound marks on both buttocks, inflicted by a sharp object. The KHRC reported 17 deaths in police custody due to torture. Many prisoners died in custody due to life threatening prison conditions, including inadequate food and medical treatment (see Section 1.c.).

Police investigated some extrajudicial killings by security forces. According to the Attorney General's office, about 25 police officers faced charges of brutality and excessive force at the beginning of the year. A police officer was charged with the murder of musician Duncan Muiru Koronjo, who was beaten to death in Nairobi in March. However, there have been no effective police investigations into some of the more controversial cases of extrajudicial killing. These include the January murder in Nairobi of Joseph Kahungu Kamau in his shop, which eyewitnesses alleged was perpetrated by a plain clothes policeman; the February shooting death of Patrick Kariuki and four other men in Nairobi in what his family called a case of mistaken identity; and the March killing by police dogs of Peter Mukinyo Muhia while in police custody in Bombolulu. There was no investigation of the beating death of Nichodemus Mango'ri in Nakuru by Youth Wingers of the ruling KANU party, allegedly because he broke a hotel window. Opposition supporters claim that KANU youthwingers usually operate with tacit or explicit police approval. In June the High Court sentenced two administrative policemen to death for killing seven men in Nairobi in 1992. These were the first policemen known to be convicted of the use of excessive force. In June police reservist John Kangu was extradited from Singapore to face trial for the November 1994 deaths of a teacher and a church attendant whom he and another reservist mistook for thieves and killed. There has been no investigation of the November 1995 beating death in Murang'a of Jonathan Muni by three police officers, one of whom reportedly had a personal disagreement with

Muni. The trial of three constables implicated in the death of Charles Ireri, who died in police custody in 1994, began in January.

Police shot and killed three demonstrating students at Egerton and Kenyatta Universities on December 16 and 18. The Government announced a "thorough investigation" of the Kenyatta University shootings, but to date no report has been made public. No investigation into the Egerton slaying has been announced.

Mob violence remained a serious problem. The KHRC documented 30 cases between January and June in which suspected criminals were killed by angry crowds. These cases of "mob justice" included a father and son burned to death by mobs on suspicion of being wizards and two policemen killed in separate incidents when mistaken for thieves. The Government condemned the practice of mob justice and investigated such cases but has not arrested anyone for participation in the violence.

b. *Disappearance.*—There were no reports of politically motivated disappearances in 1996.

c. *Torture and Other Cruel, Inhuman, and Degrading Treatment or Punishment.*—The Constitution states that "No person shall be subject to torture or to inhuman or degrading punishment or other treatment."

There continued to be credible reports that police resorted to torture and brutality. The KHRC reported 90 cases of torture by police, including 17 deaths, in the first 9 months of 1996. The Attorney General's office reported that 12 police officers were charged with brutality and wrongful killing (see Section 1.a.).

According to KHRC, there were numerous cases of humiliation, intimidation, abuse and torture by police, typified by the cases below; in several instances, police use of torture resulted in death (see Section 1.a.). In March police arrested 13-year-old Phillip Eshialo in Kakamega and beat and tortured him for 10 days in connection with a bicycle theft involving his elder brother. Twenty people arrested in Kandara in May alleged that police whipped them, beat them with steel bars, pricked them in the buttocks with a sharp tool, and forced them to eat human waste. In January police detained and beat two Islamic leaders working with the Safina Party (see Sections 1.d. and 1.f.). In March police arrested and physically abused one journalist, then in May beat another (see Section 2.a.). In a particularly well-documented case, the KHRC published medical reports for the cases of Virginia Nyambura Wambui and Bernard Mirie Kariki, two of four people detained by Kiambu police in December 1995. The medical reports appeared to confirm the detainees' claims that they were whipped, kicked, beaten with sticks, and sexually abused, causing Wambui to suffer a miscarriage in her fifth month of pregnancy. All four were acquitted of robbery charges in July.

In the same report, the KHRC also published a personal statement by Josephine Nyawira Nengi describing the beatings and forced starvation that she experienced for 3 weeks while in detention following her May 1994 arrest on charges of robbery with violence. She was finally acquitted of all charges in March but detained again with 20 other members of RPP in July (see Section 1.d.). Police also reportedly abuse street children (see Section 5).

In the final weeks of 1996, there were a number of allegations of police torture. In November University of Nairobi (Kikuyu campus) student leader Solomon Muruli was reportedly detained by police for 5 days and tortured to obtain information on student unrest. The police commissioner responded to the public uproar by ordering an investigation into the allegations, but no report had been made by year's end. In December an unnamed woman was reportedly detained and tortured (beaten and sexually molested) by Kanu youthwingers; a number of similar incidents have been reported in Nakuru, with police making no effort to intervene or prevent. On December 9, a Kenyan military officer was reportedly detained and beaten by Nairobi police when he refused to make a holiday "contribution" after being stopped in his car.

Prison conditions are at times life threatening, due in part to a lack of resources, and in part to the Government's unwillingness to address deficiencies in the penal system. Prisoners are subjected to severe overcrowding, inadequate water, poor diet, substandard bedding, and deficient health care. In October 1995, Justice Emmanuel O'kubasu stated that prisons are "death chambers." The same month, Home Affairs Minister Francis Lotodo reported that 814 prisoners had died in jails in the first 9 months of 1995, due chiefly to dysentery and diarrhea. As of August 1994, Kenya's 78 prisons held a daily average of about 39,000 inmates, 12,000 of whom were awaiting trial. Prisons are severely overcrowded, averaging 30 percent above holding capacity. Some facilities, such as the Nairobi Remand Prison, are overcrowded by several hundred percent. Rape of both male and female inmates is a serious problem, as is the growing incidence of AIDS. Prisons do not have resident doctors, and only one prison had a doctor permanently assigned. A medical doctor at Kamiti prison reportedly threatened to bind Koigi Wa Wamere and his two associates—opposition activists convicted in 1995 on charges widely assumed to be politically motivated of trying to rob a police station of its armaments with a home-made weapon—and force the three prisoners to take antidepressants. In addition, the prison officer-in-charge refused to permit the special medical treatment and food ordered for them by the court.

Officially, there is separate confinement for men, women, and children. However, there are cases in which men and women have been put in the same cells, and youths (as young as early teenagers) are frequently kept in cells with adults in overcrowded prisons and remand centers. The Government does not permit independent monitoring of prison conditions.

d. *Arbitrary Arrest, Detention, or Exile.*—Despite constitutional protections, police continued to arbitrarily arrest and detain citizens. The Constitution provides that most persons arrested or detained shall be brought before a court "as soon as is reasonably practicable," which is statuatorily definable as within 14 days of arrest or from the start of detention. A 1988 constitutional amendment allows police to hold persons suspected of capital offenses, such as murder and treason, for 14 days before charging them in court. A 1993 amendment to the Penal Code excludes weekends and holidays from this 14-day period. In practice, however, suspects are often held for 2 to 3 weeks or longer before being brought to court.

Persons arrested and charged are usually allowed access to their families and attorney. Prisoners, however, may be visited by family members and attorneys only at the discretion of the State. For those who have been charged, it is often possible to be released on bail with a bond or guarantees of return.

The law does not stipulate the period within which the trial of a charged suspect must begin. The Government has acknowledged cases in which persons have been held in pretrial detention for several years, usually because of backlogs. There were credible reports of pretrial detention periods in excess of 5 years. Over 30 percent of prisoners are pretrial detainees.

The Preservation of Public Security Act (PPSA) allows the State to detain a person indefinitely without charge or trial upon a determination that it is necessary for the "preservation of public security." This provision includes "prevention and suppression of rebellion, mutiny, violence, intimidation, disorder and crime, unlawful attempts and conspiracies to overthrow the Government or the Constitution." The Chiefs' Authority Act, a legacy of the colonial period, empowers local officials called "chiefs" to arrest individuals and to restrict a person's movement without trial. No persons were detained under the PPSA or the Chief's Authority Act during the year.

The Task Force on the Reform of Penal Law and Procedures, created by the Attorney General in 1993, continued reviewing and proposing new statutes related to criminal investigation, arrest, detention, questioning, charge, and bail. The Task Force had still not submitted its final report by year's end.

The police continued to detain politicians, members of civic organizations, clergy, journalists, and other government critics, though in fewer numbers than 1995. The detainees were usually held for several hours before being released without charge. In some cases, detainees were held for longer periods, from several days to as long as several months.

Arrest of political and human rights activists by security forces decreased, compared with the previous year, but remained a serious problem. In January Mombasa police arrested two prominent Islamic leaders working with the Safina party. Police beat them while in custody and threatened them with charges of car theft; they released them 3 days later (see Sections 1.c. and 1.f.). In July Nairobi police arrested 21 members of the RPP, charging them with incitement and holding an illegal meeting, the first time in 12 months that the Government had brought charges of this nature. On August 6, however, the presiding magistrate granted bail to the detainees and set the hearing for November.

Security forces continued to harass, follow, inconvenience, and occasionally briefly detain opposition Members of Parliament (M.P.'s) and other government critics. However, the number of opposition M.P.'s arrested for sedition or incitement decreased. Nevertheless, in February, for example, security forces detained Ford-Asili M.P. George Nyanja for several hours. In July Nanyuki police arrested human rights attorney and opposition M.P. Paul Muite and several other members of Safina when they presented trophies to volleyball teams involved in a local competition. Police fired twice into the air to push back the crowd, which pelted police with stones as they took the detainees to the Nanyuki Police Station and held them for 2 hours.

The Government does not use exile as a means of political control. However, Sheik Khalid Balala, a former leader of the unregistered Islamic party of Kenya, has remained in a European country for more than 2 years because the Government has been unwilling to renew his passport.

e. *Denial of a Fair Public Trial.*—Although the Constitution provides for an independent judiciary, it is subject to executive branch influence in practice. The President has extensive powers over appointments, including that of the Chief Justice, the Attorney General, and Appeal and High Court Judges. The President can also dismiss judges and the Attorney General upon the recommendation of a special presidentially appointed tribunal. Judges do not have life tenure and serve on a contract basis.

The court system consists of a Court of Appeals, a High Court, and two levels of magistrates' courts, where most criminal and civil cases originate. Judges hear all cases; there is no jury system. Customary law is used as a guide in civil matters affecting persons of the same ethnic group so long as it does not conflict with statutory law. In 1989 High Court Justice Norbury Dugdale ruled that the "bill of rights" outlined in the Constitution was unenforceable; this decision reinforced the implicit power of the executive branch over the judiciary. The decision has not been overruled.

Civilians are tried publicly although some testimony may be held in secret. There is a presumption of innocence, and defendants have the right to attend their trial, to confront witnesses, and to present witnesses and evidence. Civilians can also appeal a verdict to the High Court and ultimately to the Court of Appeals. Military personnel are tried by military courts-martial, and verdicts may be appealed through military court channels. The Chief Justice appoints attorneys for military personnel on a case-by-case basis.

Defendants do not have the right to government-provided legal counsel, except in capital cases. For lesser charges, free legal aid is not usually available outside Nairobi. As a result, poor people without an attorney may be convicted for lack of an articulate defense. Although defendants generally have access to an attorney in advance of trial, defense lawyers do not always have access to government-held evidence, since the Government can plead the state security secrets clause as a basis for withholding evidence. The Government raised court fees for filing and hearing cases by several hundred percent in 1995. The daily rate for arguing a case before a judge, for example, rose from $10 to $50. The Law Society of Kenya and many attorneys strongly opposed the increase, saying that the new charges would deny the majority of citizens access to the courts.

The Constitution entitles the Attorney General to take over and discontinue proceedings in private prosecution cases. Attorney General Amos Wako has argued that citizens must first notify his office before initiating private prosecution. He has used this authority on a number of occasions to terminate cases against government officials, including a private suit by the Law Society of Kenya against Vice President Saitoti and others for allegedly embezzling funds from the treasury in the Goldenberg scandal.

There were several instances in which judges spoke out and sought to assert judicial independence. In May and August, a number of magistrates and judges called for greater judicial independence, complaining about the frequency of executive interference in court cases, and urged that the presidential power to appoint judges be transferred to Parliament. In several court cases, magistrates publicly rebuked the police for their brutal methods of interrogation and excluded confessions that were reportedly coerced. Judges have also urged that the Government publicly redress the inhuman conditions in prisons.

The Government does not currently hold political prisoners. In a well known human rights case, Koigi Wa Wamwere and his two associates were denied fair judicial process throughout most of the year. Their application for appeal of conviction was denied in July because the typing of the trial transcript had not been finished. On December 13, Koigi was granted bail on medical grounds, followed 1 month later by medical bail for his two associates. The three men remain at liberty while they pursue their appeal of conviction, but there are no indications as to when the trial manuscript typing will be finished.

f. *Arbitrary Interference With Privacy, Family, Home, or Correspondence.*—The Constitution permits searches without warrants in certain instances "to promote the public benefit." The Police Act clarifies that policemen may enter a home forcibly if the time required to obtain a search warrant would "prejudice" their investigations. Although security officers generally obtain search warrants, they occasionally conduct searches without warrants to apprehend suspected criminals or to seize property believed to be stolen. The courts have admitted evidence obtained without search warrants to support convictions.

There were instances during the year in which police conducted searches or seizures without warrants. One of the two Safina officers detained in Mombasa in January (see Sections 1.c. and 1.d.) was repeatedly beaten and threatened until he finally agreed to allow police to enter and search his home.

Security forces continued to employ various means of surveillance, including a network of informants to monitor the activities of opposition politicians and human rights advocates. Some opposition leaders report that the Government targets them with surveillance, telephone wiretaps, and interference with written correspondence.

Although citizens are free to choose their political affiliations, the Government discourages civil servants from membership in opposition parties.

Section 2. Respect for Civil Liberties, Including:

a. *Freedom of Speech and Press.*—Although the Constitution provides for freedom of speech and the press, the Government has interpreted broadly the existing colonial-era sedition and libel laws in order to limit free expression (see Section 1.d.). The Government has used these provisions to deny opposition parties the right to free speech. For example, security forces and local administration officials used these provisions as a pretext to disperse opposition rallies to prevent speakers from criticizing the Government. In June the President directed the police to disperse any meetings that maligned or abused government authorities. Despite these forms of obstruction, the press, civic organizations, and the opposition continued to present their views to the public.

The print media include three daily newspapers that report on national politics. The largest newspaper, The Nation, is independent and publishes articles critical of government policies. The second largest, The East African Standard, was sold in 1995 to an investment group with close ties to the Government. Despite the new management's pledge to maintain the newspaper's independent editorial policy, it has evolved into a tabloid that is less critical of the Government. The third daily newspaper, Kenya Times, reflects KANU party views. Weekly newspapers and magazines, many of which are openly critical of the Government, also have substantial audiences. On the whole, the print media remained outspoken and independent, despite continued government harassment.

According to members of the independent press, relations between the press and the Government have improved during the year. Even in cases in which government officials requested them to suppress damaging articles, the final decision was left to the editors. While the traditional taboos surrounding the President and his family remain in effect, political cartoons picturing President Moi, often in a negative light, have appeared. In January the Government withdrew a highly controversial proposed press law that would have significantly curtailed press freedoms. Nevertheless, newspaper and magazine editors continued to be subjected to varying degrees of government pressure to censor themselves, particularly regarding President Moi's family and corruption involving his advisers.

Overt harassment and occasional detention of journalists continued but at a reduced rate from the previous year. In January Kisumu police arrested East Africa Standard reporter Dennis Oluoch in connection with an article he had written, and Eldoret police arrested Nation correspondent Evans Kanini because of an article he had written about police corruption, charging him with being drunk and disorderly, a charge subsequently dismissed by the court. In March Eldoret police arrested Nation correspondent John Wanjala and reportedly physically abused him in custody because of his press reports critical of the police (see Section 1.c.). In May Kirinyaga police beat and confiscated the camera of East African Standard correspondent Munene Kamau; Kitui police arrested East African Standard correspondent James Owuor, and Nairobi police arrested Njehu Gatabaki, Ford-Asili M.P. from Githunguri and editor of Finance magazine, and detained him for 1 week. Gatabaki was already on trial for sedition for having alleged in Finance that President Moi had foreknowledge of the assassination of then-foreign minister Robert Ouko in 1990.

In June KANU youthwingers attacked East African Standard photographer Raphael Munge during a by-election campaign in Molo, stabbed him in the hand, stole his camera, and attacked East African Standard reporter Michael Giehua in Nakuru for damaging the party's reputation with his press reports. Police offered no protection in either case. Nakuru is notorious for its rampant and unrestrained KANU youthwingers and lack of police interference, verging on collusion. In September a group of Nairobi city councillors threatened to "fix" journalists who write about land scandals and other government irregularities. The offices of the independent weekly The People were bombed by persons unknown, and the newspaper received telephoned threats to desist from "writing those dirty things" about the Government.

The Government continued its ban on a number of books, including a Kiswahili play based on George Orwell's Animal Farm and a number of works by emigre author Ngugi Wa Thiong'o. In a speech on December 31, 1995, President Moi banned distribution of the book Family Life, published by the Girl Guides Association of America. He stated that it was immoral and promoted promiscuity and directed that it be removed from the shelves of the Kenyan Girl Guides and Boy Scouts.

In May the Minister of Education directed schools to teach the KANU party manifesto. After strong public protest, he modified this directive to include opposition party manifestos as well.

The Government and ruling party's tight control of the broadcast media has fostered unbalanced and unfair reporting. The Government maintains its monopoly control of the electronic broadcast media through tight control of broadcasting, particularly radio, the principal popular news medium. It controls the Kenya Broadcasting Corporation (KBC), which operates the country's premier radio, television, and cable television stations. KBC stations typically do not criticize the Government, give a large share of news time to government or ruling party functions, and neglect to give equal reporting to opposition activities. KANU supporters also own a second television station, Kenya Television Network, which airs news programs with more balanced political coverage. KANU supporters opened a third television network, Stellavision, in June and a new private F.M. radio station in September. The Minister of Information continued to delay action on numerous television and radio license applications, ostensibly waiting for the recommendations on media liberalization from the Attorney General's task force, which was charged with establishing operating rules for radio and television liberalization; it has made no recommendations after 3 years.

Representatives of the international media are generally free to operate. The Government complained that its hospitality to foreign correspondents indirectly worsens the national image because foreign journalists write so many negative articles about other countries which bear a Nairobi dateline.

b. *Freedom of Peaceful Assembly and Association.*—Freedom of Assembly is provided for in the Constitution but is seriously limited by the Government's use of the Public Order Act, which gives the authorities power to control public gatherings. This act prohibits meetings or processions of 10 or more persons without a license from the District Commissioner. In theory the law does not apply to persons meeting for social, cultural, charitable, recreational, religious, professional, commercial, or industrial purposes. In practice, meetings under almost all categories are subjected to the Public Order Act.

The Government continued to restrict the right of peaceful assembly by refusing to license, or by physically disrupting, opposition political meetings, despite President Moi's March 1 promise to opposition leaders that such gatherings would be permitted. The Government granted many meeting licenses, and the number of meetings dispersed was substantially fewer than in 1995. However, opposition parties reported that the Government blocked 26 public meetings of Ford-Kenya, Ford-Asili, Democratic Party, and Safina in the first 9 months of the year, compared with 72 for all of 1995. Government officials occasionally denied licenses to KANU as well, but almost always denied them to groups critical of the national party leadership.

According to press reports in January, the Nyeri district commissioner warned Safina party leaders to keep out of Nyeri, and Mombasa police stood by as ruling KANU party youthwingers blocked a Safina march to its new headquarters. In February Bondo police dispersed a meeting of women organized by the League of Kenya Women Voters. In March Nairobi police broke up an RPP meeting, Meru police blocked opposition leaders from addressing a by-election rally, and Kilifi police broke up an opposition meeting. In June Mombasa police arrested 24 opposition leaders for convening an "illegal" meeting (no license), KANU activists attacked Democratic Party supporters in Westlands (Nairobi), and police and armed KANU youthwingers blocked opposition leaders from entering Molo to campaign in the by-election there. In July police and opposition supporters clashed in Mwea when police armed with tear gas sought to disperse a licensed opposition rally. In August riot police in combat gear stopped a Democratic Party political seminar, and Nakuru police cordoned off a hotel to prevent invitees attending a women's seminar from entering. During one weekend in September, riot police disrupted three opposition meetings (in Kiambu, Meru, and Nyandarua) and a soccer contest in Nairobi, named in honor of a martyred student dissident.

In the last quarter of 1996, authorities disrupted a number of opposition and civil society meetings, sometimes forcefully. In a 1-week period in mid-October, Lokitau police broke up a civic education seminar on voting organized by the Catholic Diocese, Turkana police disrupted a civic education seminar sponsored by the Catholic Justice and Peace Commission, Gachako police dispersed a meeting to inaugurate a new Ford-Kenya office, and Kitui police disrupted a civic education meeting and detained and allegedly beat M.P. Charity Ngilu and two female journalists. In the ensuing uproar over the latter incident, the police commissioner suspended two police officers responsible for the incident, pending inquiry. In November, antiriot police halted a civic education workshop at the Saint Joseph Pastoral Centre in Machakos sponsored by the Catholic Justice and Peace Commission. In December police disrupted two Ford-Kenya (Odinga) meetings, and Kitui police halted a seminar on the "Values of Democracy" sponsored by the National Democratic Institute.

The Government restricts freedom of association by use of the Societies Act. The act states that every association must be registered or exempted from registration by the Registrar of Societies. Twelve political parties are currently registered under this statute: KANU, Ford-Kenya, Ford-Asili, Democratic Party, Social Democratic Party, Kenya Social Congress, Kenya National Congress, Party of Independent Candidates of Kenya, Kenya National Democratic Alliance, Labor Party Democracy, and National Development Party of Kenya. The Government has denied registration to 23 parties since 1992, while at year's end, 13 parties had applications pending.

Both the Public Order and the Societies Acts seriously restrict free political organization. They inhibit opposition party members from meeting with voters. The Government also continued to discourage civil servants from membership in opposition parties (see Section 1.f.). NGO's are registered by the Government's NGO Coordination Board under the NGO Act. In May the board formally revoked the ban on the Center for Law Research International (CLARION), a legal affairs NGO that was deregistered in 1995 because of its investigations of corruption.

c. *Freedom of Religion.*—The Constitution provides for freedom of religion, and the Government generally does not infringe upon religious activities, except to require registration by new churches.

Government officials virulently criticized the Catholic Church and the National Council of Churches of Kenya (NCCK) in August for their pastoral letters calling for constitutional reform and fair elections, accusing them of receiving assistance from unnamed foreigners. In September the Government accused the NCCK of subversive activities and planning to incite ethnic clashes in the Rift Valley.

d. *Freedom of Movement Within the Country, Foreign Travel, Emigration, and Repatriation.*—By law, citizens may travel freely within the country. However, the establishment of security zones in the 1992 elections and again following ethnic clashes in 1993, restricted the ability of many citizens to travel to those parts of the Rift Valley most affected by clashes. Although the security zones, such as in Molo and Burnt Forest, have not been officially lifted, access to the areas has been allowed in practice. Nonetheless, opposition party members have been stopped at police road blocks and prevented from visiting some of the areas.

The Government does not restrict emigration or foreign travel. The law requires a woman to obtain her husband's or father's permission prior to obtaining a passport (see section 5). Civil servants must obtain government permission for international travel, which was granted in all cases.

U.N. Development Program (UNDP) assistance to thousands of displaced ethnic clash victims came to a virtual standstill in January 1995. The Government tried to persuade the UNDP to restart this program, arguing that the different ethnic groups in the affected regions were once again living, working, and trading together. In fact, many of the rural people displaced by the clashes have still not returned to their homes and remain in refugee status in urban areas. In February the Government ordered 360 families displaced by ethnic violence in Burnt Forest to return to their farms or be evicted. Government officials insisted this was not forced relocation. Reportedly, no clash victims have returned to the Olenguruone area because of continued insecurity.

The Government provides first asylum and provided it to the approximately 168,000 UNHCR-registered refugees in 1996. The refugees are mostly Somali and Sudanese, living in camps, and an undetermined number living outside camps in cities and rural areas. Somalis account for about 75 percent of the total refugee population. Although 44,000 (mostly Somali) refugees repatriated in 1995, only a few thousand returned home in 1996, mainly due to poor security combined with crop failures in returnee areas. Most of those who chose to repatriate did so because they did not want to be relocated to camps on the northeast border of Somalia after one of the largest refugee camps near Mombasa was finally closed.

The law provides for the granting of asylum or refugee status in accordance with the standards of the 1951 U.N. Convention and its 1967 Protocol Relating to the Status of Refugees. Nevertheless, when over 400,000 refugees fleeing civil strife and drought arrived in Kenya from the neighboring countries of Somalia, Sudan, Ethiopia, and Uganda in 1991, the Government suspended indefinitely the process by which it ruled on applications for refugee or asylum. Since then, a handful of affluent individuals have effectively purchased de facto Convention status, but for practical purposes, an official asylum or refugee application process no longer exists. Consequently, resettlement is not an option in Kenya.

Incidents of rape of women and young girls in refugee camps continued to occur, though Kenyan police response has improved. Acts of violence, including carjackings and banditry, still occur with frequency in the camps and the Dadaab area, which sometimes led to the injury or death of some refugees and police.

Refugees living outside the camps are vulnerable to arrest, and those who purchase false identification documents and visa are even further at risk. Hundreds of refugees and illegal aliens have been arrested in police sweeps, supposedly targeting those involved in criminal activity in Nairobi. The UNHCR was allowed to facilitate the release of refugees who were ordered to camp, but other aliens were still being held at the end of 1996.

There were no reports of expulsions of those having a valid claim to refugee status. However, in late 1996, the Government moved forcefully to prevent a mass wave of persons fleeing drought conditions from crossing the Kenya/Somalia border. Once this flow of potential refugees was halted, the Government invited UNHCR and other humanitarian organizations to provide assistance in place to these individuals.

Section 3. Respect for Political Rights: The Right of Citizens to Change Their Government

The Constitution provides citizens with the right to change their government through free and fair multiparty elections, but their ability to do so has not yet been fully demonstrated at the presidential level. The 1992 presidential and parliamentary elections were marked by violence, intimidation, fraud, and other irregularities, but opposition candidates nevertheless won 63 percent of the vote, although split among several factions, thereby giving KANU a majority of seats in Parliament.

President Moi's election victory has allowed him and his KANU party to dominate the political process. At the local level, the President exercises sweeping power over the political structure. The President appoints both the powerful provincial and district commissioners and a multitude of district and village officials.

At the national level, the Constitution authorizes the President to dissolve the legislature and prohibits debate on issues under consideration by the courts. This law, in conjunction with the Speaker of the Assembly's ruling that the President's conduct is inappropriate for parliamentary debate, has limited the scope of deliberation on controversial political issues. M.P.'s are entitled to introduce legislation, but in practice it is the Attorney General who does so. As the head of KANU, which controls 124 of the Parliament's 200 seats, the President is also able to influence significantly the legislative agenda.

The Government continued to harass and intimidate the political opposition, although less frequently than in 1995. Its monopoly of the electronic media prevented opposition parties from reaching television and radio audiences (see Section 2.a.). The license provision of the Public Order Act kept opposition leaders from meeting their supporters, and the Government's use of colonial-era sedition laws restricted freedom of expression (see Sections 2.a. and 2.b.). The Electoral Commission, which oversees all elections, lacks statutory independence, since its members are appointed by the President. The opposition has also claimed that voter constituencies are apportioned in favor of KANU, which has resulted in a KANU parliamentary majority despite only receiving one-third of the popular vote. At the local level, officials have demonstrated partiality to the ruling party during parliamentary by-elections.

Five parliamentary by-elections were held in 1996 due to the deaths or disqualifications of sitting M.P.'s. The elections were generally free and fair, although journalists and diplomatic observers reported anomalies in voter registers and incidents of vote buying and continued use of government officials and vehicles, but not violence as in 1995. During the by-election in Hamisi, KANU youthwingers insured a KANU victory by keeping opposition supporters away from the polls. In the Siakago by-election, government employees and vehicles were blatantly used in support of KANU.

In latter months of 1996, the Government made a number of efforts which in effect, criminalized dissent. In September the Government charged several leading political and human rights activists with engineering a "guerrilla plot" to overthrow the Government or assassinate President Moi. That charge was not widely accepted, and the Government did not pursue it. Police who detained Nairobi University student Murali in November tried to force him (see Section 1.c.) to admit that student unrest at Nairobi University had been organized by the Safina Party. Government officials sought unsuccessfully to blame campus unrest at Egerton University near Nakuru on the opposition, specifically charging Safina. Government and police officials regularly accuse NGO's and churches involved in civic education of being "anti-Kenyan" and agents of unnamed foreign entities.

During his unprecedented March 1 meeting with leaders of the three main opposition parties, the President discussed ways to ensure fairness to all political factions. He agreed that the opposition should have greater access to the media and should receive licenses for meetings without hindrance. However, he did not follow through on these promises. Despite his promise to meet with opposition leaders in the future, no further meetings had been held by year's end.

Although there are no legal restrictions on the participation of women in politics, traditional attitudes circumscribe the role of women in politics. There was one female minister, the country's first, who was appointed by President Moi in 1995, and seven female M.P.'s in the Assembly. In August President Moi announced that women would henceforth be represented at local and provincial levels in KANU meetings. Within the opposition, women figure most significantly in the Democratic Party, in which 25 percent of the party's national office holders are women.

Members of all tribal and ethnic groups participate in the Government and political parties. However, since white Kenyan paleontologist Richard Leakey announced his involvement in the Safina party, President Moi has repeatedly cautioned against white Kenyans' participation in political activities. Numerous tribes—including Kisiis, Merus, Embus, Kambas, Kikuyus, Taitas, Kalenjins, Luhyas, Turkanas, Somalis, Maasai, Giriamas, and Luos—are represented in the President's Cabinet. However, the President reportedly relies on an inner circle of advisers, drawn mostly from his Kalenjin tribe.

Section 4. Governmental Attitude Regarding International and Nongovernmental Investigation of Alleged Violations of Human Rights

There are several well-organized and active human rights organizations. Two of these, the KHRC and RPP, not only produce regular reports on the human rights situation but also organize activities to publicize their causes. The Institute for Education in Democracy monitors parliamentary by-elections in cooperation with the Electoral Commission. Legal organizations, including the Public Law Institute, the Kenya Law Society, the International Commission of Jurists, and the International Federation of Women Lawyers, treat human rights issues as a priority.

Some opposition parties also maintain comprehensive files on human rights abuses, carefully tracking extrajudiciary violence and disruption of opposition political meetings. The Kenya Social Congress Party published a detailed study of human rights violations in one district in Nyanza province. The Citizens Coalition for Constitutional Change is an umbrella organization lobbying for constitutional reform. A large pool of attorneys represent the poor and human rights defendants without charge.

Human rights NGO's work actively to engage the Government on human rights issues and cases. In its Quarterly Repression Report, the KHRC frequently adds the parenthetical note that it was unsuccessful in obtaining information from government officials on a specific case.

While the Government often criticized domestic and international human rights NGO's, it also made some efforts to reach out and engage them. It allowed human rights organizations to witness autopsies of several persons who had died in police custody. It overturned the 1995 deregistration of the NGO Clarion (see Section 2.b.). The Kenya Electoral Commission facilitated the March visit of the U.S.-based International Foundation for Election Systems to analyze the electoral system. The same month, the Government published "Human Rights Situation in Kenya: The Way It Is" in order to rebut the KHRC's December 1995 Quarterly Repression Report. Despite allegations that the Government's pamphlet was meant to appease donor nations then meeting in Nairobi, the KHRC welcomed it as the beginning of a public dialog on human rights and reiterated that any errors in its own reports were due to the Government's failure to respond to the KHRC's numerous queries for case status reports.

In May the Government fulfilled its promise to create a Standing Committee on Human Rights. The 10-member committee was empowered to "investigate alleged violations of constitutional freedoms," including abuse of power by public officials. It was tasked with drafting recommendations on human rights problems and providing these to the government agencies under whose purview the problems fall. The committee announced that it was open to, and welcomed contact with, NGO's and would serve as the point of contact between them and the Government.

The Committee does not have sufficient funding to track human rights cases and investigate complaints. Moreover, its attention to mob violence, human rights education, and its lack of authority over government officials has led some observers to question its objectives and ability to affect the human rights situation. The Committee presented its first report to President Moi on November 27, but details of the report were not made public.

Section 5. Discrimination Based on Race, Sex, Religion, Disability, Language, or Social Status

The Constitution prohibits discrimination on the basis of a person's "race, tribe, place of origin or residence or other local connection, political opinions, color, or creed." However, authorities did not effectively enforce all these provisions.

Women.—Violence against women is a serious and widespread problem. The most recent police statistics published on the subject were released in 1994 and showed that in 1992 there were 454 cases of rape, 136 cases of attempted rape, 343 cases of indecent assault, 407 cases of defilement (e.g., child molestation), and 14 cases of incest. The statistics are probably underreported, however, since social mores deter women from going outside their families or ethnic groups to report sexual abuse. The Government has condemned violence against women, and the law carries penalties of up to life imprisonment for rape. Still, the rate of prosecution remains low because of cultural inhibitions against discussing sex, the fear of retribution, the disinclination of police to intervene in domestic disputes, and the unavailability of doctors who might otherwise provide the necessary evidence for conviction. Furthermore, traditional culture permits a man to discipline his wife by physical means and is ambivalent about the seriousness of spousal rape. This ambivalence was epitomized in the August statement by one magistrate that not all rape suspects deserved to be jailed because "some cases are not intentional," just a matter of men being "too impatient."

There were also numerous reported incidents of rape of refugee Somali women at the Dadaab camps; they were assaulted outside camp perimeters in the course of gathering firewood.

The Constitution does not specifically address discrimination based on gender, and women continue to face both legal and actual discrimination on several fronts. For example, a woman is legally required to obtain consent from her husband or father before obtaining a passport. In practice a woman must also have her husband's or father's approval to secure a bank loan. Also, women can legally work at night only in the export processing zones (EPZ's). Women have long dominated agricultural work in terms of numbers of laborers, and they have become more active in urban small business. Still, the average monthly income of women is about 37 percent lower than that of men. According to pension law, a widow loses her work pension upon remarriage, whereas a man does not. Not only do women have difficulty moving into nontraditional fields, they are also promoted more slowly than men and bear the brunt of job retrenchments.

Kenya's Law of Succession, which governs inheritance rights, provides for equal consideration of male and female children. In practice, most inheritance problems do not come before the courts. Women are often excluded from inheritance settlements or given smaller shares than male claimants. In addition, a widow cannot be the sole administrator of her husband's estate unless she has her children's consent.

Societal discrimination is most apparent in rural areas, where women account for 75 percent of the agricultural work force. Rural families are more reluctant to invest in educating girls than in educating boys, especially at the higher levels. The number of boys and girls in school is roughly equal at the primary and secondary levels, but men outnumber women almost 2 to 1 in higher education, and literate men significantly outnumber literate women.

The nation's best known women's rights and welfare organization, Maendeleo Ya Wanawake ("Development of Women" in Kiswahili) was established as a nonpolitical NGO during the colonial era, but now operates under the close supervision of the Government. A growing number of women's organizations are active in the field of women's rights, such as the National Commission on the Status of Women, the Education Center for Women in Democracy, and the Kenyan League of Women Voters.

Children.—The system of free education in the early years of Kenya's independence (1963) has given way to a "cost-sharing" education system in which students pay both tuition and other costs. These are a heavy burden on most families. While there is mandatory schooling for all up to grade 12, there is a very high drop out rate in part because of the heavy expenses to finance education. Moreover, the shortage of schools also obviates the legally required universal schooling. The health care system for school children, which once provided periodic medical checkups and free milk, now appears to be completely defunct.

Government-drafted legislation is under debate in Parliament to establish a National Council of Children's Services to supervise the planning and financing of child welfare activities. The bill would also revamp the juvenile court system. However, both KANU and opposition M.P.'s, as well as a number of local NGO's, have faulted the bill for portraying child offenders as criminals in need of discipline. Opponents of the bill also have noted that it does not address homelessness, female genital mutilation (FGM), forced labor, sexual abuse, and education. In November, a motion outlawing FGM was defeated in parliament just one week after that same body approved a motion to implement the provisions of the Beijing Women's Conference platform, one of which called for outlawing FGM.

Despite the Government's stated opposition, FGM, which is widely condemned by international health experts as damaging to both physical and psychological health, remains widespread, particularly among nomadic people. It is usually performed at an early age. Health officials estimate that roughly 50 percent of females nationwide have undergone this procedure. According to Maendeleo Ya Wanawake, that percentage is as high as 80 percent in some districts of the Eastern, Nyanza, and Rift Valley provinces.

Economic displacement and population growth continued to fuel the problem of homeless street children. The Child Welfare Society of Kenya estimated that the number of Nairobi's street children increased from 33,000 in 1990 to 44,000 in 1996, while the Government estimates their growth at 10 percent per year. According to the Attorney General's Task Force, these children are typically involved in theft, drug trafficking, assault, trespass, defilement, and property damage. There have been credible reports that police have treated street children inhumanely.

Child rape and molestation are rapidly growing human rights abuses. There were numerous and frequent press reports of rape of young girls. The rapists were typically older than the age of 40. Those convicted received prison sentences of between 5 and 20 years, plus several strokes of the cane. Child prostitution has emerged as a major problem in urban areas, often connected with the tourist trade. There were numerous press reports on the increase in child prostitution in Nairobi and Mombasa. A provincial government study in Nyanza province found that Kisumu city had 300 male and female child prostitutes 8 years of age and above and that the practice existed in small towns throughout the province.

People With Disabilities.—Government policies do not discriminate against people with disabilities with regard to employment, education, or state services. Disabled persons are frequently denied driving licenses, however. There is also no mandated provision of accessibility for the disabled to public buildings or transportation.

National/Racial/Ethnic Minorities.—According to the 1989 government census released in May 1994, the Kikuyu are the largest ethnic community, comprising 21 percent of the population. Luhya, Luo, Kamba, and Kalenjin (an amalgamation of nine small tribes) follow, each with more than 11 percent of the population.

Opposition politicians and local human rights groups report that the Government continued to discriminate against Rift Valley Kikuyus. They assert that provincial authorities have denied national identification cards to a substantial number of Kikuyu youths, even those born and raised there. Without identification cards these youths cannot marry, attend universities, obtain employment, or register to vote.

The Government has not been supportive—and was often critical—of private efforts to conciliate ethnic tensions in the Rift Valley. On several occasions, police blocked interparty reconciliation talks. The Government was critical of a series of meetings in August and September between Kikuyu and Kalenjin elders to foster reconciliation and facilitate resettlement of displaced people. Some government officials, for example, continued to aim harsh verbal barbs and threats at Kikuyus.

There continued to be tensions between Asian Kenyans (Kenyans of subcontinent descent) and black Kenyans; Asians are subject to official and societal discrimination. Black Kenyans generally resent Asians because of their affluence, their seeming reluctance to assimilate African culture and to employ black Kenyans in management positions, and the involvement of some, in league with influential black Kenyans, in corruption and theft of state funds. Politicians, both opposition and ruling party, from time to time sought to gain publicity by attacking Asian Kenyans, accusing them of usurping the natural inheritance of black Kenyans.

The Government has singled out the overwhelmingly Muslim ethnic Somalis as the only ethnic group required to carry an additional form of identification to prove that they are citizens. They must still produce upon demand their Kenyan identification card and a second identification card verifying "screening." Both cards are also required in order to apply for a passport. The continued presence of Somali refugees has exacerbated the problems faced by Kenyan Somalis.

Section 6. Worker Rights

a. *The Right of Association.*—Except for central government civil servants, including medical personnel and university academic staff, all workers are free to join unions of their choice. The law provides that as few as seven workers may establish a union, provided that the objectives of the union do not contravene the law, and that another union is not already representing the employees in question.

The Government may deregister a union, but the Registrar of Trade Unions must give the union 60 days to challenge the deregistration notice. An appeal of the Registrar's final decision may be brought before the High Court. President Moi deregistered the Kenya Civil Servants Union in 1980. Since 1989 the Central Organization of Trade Unions (COTU) has sought to reverse this decision.

There are at least 33 unions representing approximately 350,000 workers, less than 20 percent of the country's industrial work force. Except for the 150,000 teachers who belong to the Kenya National Union of Teachers, all other unions are affiliated with the one approved central organ—the COTU. The COTU leadership, however, generally does not pursue worker's rights vigorously, so that most union activity takes place at the shop steward level, which disadvantages the average worker in disputes with management.

The Government created COTU in 1965 as the successor to the Kenya Federation of Labor and the Kenya African Workers Congress. The 1965 decree establishing COTU gives the President the power to remove COTU's three senior leaders from office and grants nonvoting membership on the executive board to representatives of the Ministry of Labor and of KANU. A 1993 High Court decision nullified an attempt to install leaders more acceptable to the Government, but the plotters refused to vacate COTU headquarters. Following a 1994 Appellate Court order, however, the Registrar of Trade Unions agreed to recognize the old COTU leadership. Although the board is comprised of the leadership of affiliated unions, it is common for KANU to provide funding and other support for the election of senior union officials. In 1995 several trade union leaders from affiliated unions sought to bring about democratic reforms in the election and appointment of labor officials, independence from the Government, and establishment of links with any political party that supports worker rights. The reelection of the COTU leadership in July indicated that there would be no major changes in the near future.

The Trade Disputes Act permits workers to strike, provided that 21 days have elapsed following the submission of a written letter to the Minister of Labor. Members of the military services, police, prison guards, and members of the National Youth Service are precluded by law from striking. Other civil servants, like their private sector counterparts, can strike following the 21-day notice period (28 days if it is an essential service, such as water, health, education, or air traffic control). During this 21-day period, the Minister may either mediate the dispute, nominate an arbitrator, or refer the matter to the Industrial Court, a body of five judges appointed by the President, for binding arbitration. Once a dispute is referred to either mediation, fact-finding, or arbitration, any subsequent strike is illegal. However, the act gives the Minister of Labor broad discretionary power to determine the legality of any strike. In 1994 the Minister used this power to declare several strikes illegal, although the required notice had been given. The Minister did not declare any strikes illegal in 1995 or 1996; however, the Government's response to wildcat strikes is usually severe. This led worker rights groups to raise the problem with the International Labor Organization's (ILO's) Committee on Freedom of Association. Several unions, including municipal workers, bank employees, and some civil servants held brief strikes for back or increased wages.

Internationally, COTU is affiliated with both the organization of African Trade Union Unity and the International Confederation of Free Trade Unions. Many of its affiliates are linked to international trade secretariats.

b. *The Right to Organize and Bargain Collectively*.—While not having the force of law, the 1962 Industrial Relations Charter, executed by the Government, COTU, and the Federation of Kenya Employers, gives workers the right to engage in legitimate trade union organizational activities. Both the Trade Disputes Act and the Charter authorize collective bargaining between unions and employers. Wages and conditions of employment are established in negotiations between unions and management. In 1994 the Government relaxed wage policy guidelines to permit wage increases of up to 100 percent and renegotiation of collective agreements. Collective bargaining agreements must be registered with the Industrial Court in order to guarantee adherence to these guidelines.

The Trade Disputes Act makes it illegal for employers to intimidate workers. Employees wrongfully dismissed for union activities are generally awarded damages in the form of lost wages by the Industrial Court; reinstatement is not a common remedy. More often, aggrieved workers have found alternative employment in the lengthy period prior to the hearing of their cases.

Legislation authorizing the creation of Export Processing Zones (EPZ's) was passed in 1990. The EPZ Authority decided that local labor laws, including the right to organize and bargain collectively, would apply in the EPZ's, although it grants many exemptions in practice. For example, the Government waived aspects of the law that prevent women from working at night (see Section 6.e.). Labor and some government officials criticized health and safety conditions in the EPZ's.

c. *Prohibition of Forced or Compulsory Labor.*—The Constitution proscribes slavery, servitude, and forced labor. However, under the Chiefs' Authority Act, a local authority can require people to perform community services in an emergency, although this did not occur in 1996. The ILO Committee of Experts has found that these and other provisions of the law contravene ILO Conventions 29 and 105 concerning forced labor, but noted the Government's efforts to review the Chiefs' Authority Act.

d. *Minimum Age for Employment of Children.*—The Employment Act of 1976 makes the employment in industry of children under the age of 16 illegal. The act applies neither to the agricultural sector, where about 70 percent of the labor force is employed, nor to children serving as apprentices under the terms of the industrial training act. Ministry of Labor officers nominally enforce the minimum age statute, and the Government is making strong efforts to eliminate child labor, working closely with the ILO's International Program for the Elimination of Child Labor. Children often work as domestic servants in private homes, including those of relatives, in the informal sector, and in family businesses and commercial agriculture, although usually assisting parents rather than as employees in their own right. Given the high levels of adult unemployment and underemployment, the employment of children in the formal industrial wage sector in violation of the Employment Act rarely occurs.

e. *Acceptable Conditions of Work.*—The legal minimum wage for blue collar workers in the wage sector has 12 separate scales, varying by location, age, and skill level. The lowest minimum wages were $34 (1,700 shillings) per month in urban areas and $19.50 (955 shillings) in rural areas. The minimum wage is insufficient to meet the daily needs of a worker and family. A 2 percent wage increase in August had limited impact on worker income. Most workers relied on second jobs, subsistence farming, informal sector opportunities, or the extended family for additional support.

The Regulation of Wages and Conditions of Employment Act limits the normal workweek to 52 hours, although nighttime employees may be employed for up to 60 hours per week. Some categories of workers have a shorter workweek. As is the case with respect to minimum age limitations, the act specifically excludes agricultural workers from its purview. An employee in the nonagricultural sector is entitled to 1 rest day per week. There are also provisions for 1 month of annual leave and sick leave. The law also provides that the total hours worked (i.e., regular time plus overtime) in any 2-week period for night workers may not exceed 144 hours; the limit is 120 hours for other workers. Workers in some enterprises claimed that employers forced them to work extra hours without overtime pay. The Ministry of Labor is tasked with enforcing these regulations, and there are few reports of violations.

The Factories Act of 1951 sets forth detailed health and safety standards; it was amended in 1990 to include the agriculture, service, and government sectors. The 65 health and safety inspectors attached to the Ministry of Labor's Directorate of Occupational Health and Safety Services have the authority to inspect factories and work sites. As a result of the 1990 amendments, the Directorate's inspectors may now issue notices enjoining employers from practices or activities that involve a risk of serious personal injuries. Previously, only magistrates were vested with this authority. Such notices can be appealed to the Factories Appeals Court, a body of four members, one of whom must be a High Court judge. The number of factory inspections increased dramatically in 1993 and subsequently has continued at a high level. Workers are not forced by law to remain in hazardous conditions; however, many would be reluctant to remove themselves because of the high unemployment problem.

LESOTHO

Lesotho is a constitutional monarchy. Prime Minister Ntsu Mokhehle of the Basotholand Congress Party (BCP) is the Head of Government. Since winning free and fair elections in 1993, the BCP has controlled the Government and Parliament. Under the 1993 Constitution, the King has no executive authority. In 1994 King Letsie III unconstitutionally suspended Parliament and installed a Ruling Council. Local and international pressure led to a rapid return of constitutional government.

The security forces consist of the Lesotho Defense Force (LDF), the Lesotho Mounted Police (LMP), and the National Security Service (NSS). The Government adopted legislation to bring these services under more direct civilian control. The LDF now answers to the Prime Minister, through the Ministry of Defense. The NSS is directly accountable to the Prime Minister and the LMP reports to the Minister of Home Affairs. There were only isolated incidents of human rights abuses and disturbances.

A landlocked country surrounded by South Africa, Lesotho is almost entirely dependent on its sole neighbor for trade, finance, employment, and access to the outside world. A large proportion of the adult male work force is employed in mines in South Africa; miners' remittances account for slightly over one-third of gross national product (GNP). Real GNP grew an estimated 12 percent during 1996, with inflation predicted at less than 7 percent. Per capita GNP was approximately $790. State-owned organizations predominate in the agroindustrial and agribusiness sectors, but private sector activity dominates in manufacturing and construction. Under the traditional chieftainship structure, land is controlled by the chiefs and owned by the Kingdom, precluding private ownership of land.

The Government generally respected the human rights of its citizens; however, there continued to be problems in some areas. Discipline in the security services improved somewhat, but a few disturbances still occurred. Women's rights continued to be severely restricted, and domestic violence remained common. In September the police opened fire on striking construction workers, killing at least 4 and possibly as many as 15. In addition, the Government failed to prosecute anyone for extrajudicial killings and other abuses committed in previous years.

RESPECT FOR HUMAN RIGHTS

Section 1. *Respect for the Integrity of the Person, Including Freedom From:*

a. *Political and Other Extrajudicial Killing.*—There were no reports of political killings.

In September the police opened fire on striking construction workers, killing at least 4 and possibly as many as 15 persons. The authorities did not investigate or prosecute any security officials for the extrajudicial or summary killings committed during the political unrest of 1994. They also failed to investigate 1994 reports of police brutality, as well as pre-1994 reports of deaths in police custody of a number of unionists and criminal suspects.

b. *Disappearance.*—There were no reports of politically motivated disappearances.

c. *Torture and Other Cruel, Inhuman, or Degrading Treatment or Punishment.*—The Constitution expressly prohibits torture or inhuman or degrading punishment or other treatment, and there were no reports of its use. The Government did not investigate the numerous incidents that occurred in 1994 and previous years.

Prison facilities are overcrowded and in disrepair, but conditions do not threaten the health or lives of inmates. Conditions are not monitored independently.

d. *Arbitrary Arrest, Detention, or Exile.*—The Constitution prohibits arbitrary arrest and detention, and there were no known incidents of these abuses. However, the Government failed to investigate or prosecute anyone for the arbitrary arrests, detentions, and harassment of civilians which occurred during 1995 and previous years. Members of the NSS arbitrarily detained cabinet members and other senior government officials.

Pretrial detainees constitute a significant portion of total prison population, up to one-half in some locations. Because of backlogs, pretrial remand can last several years.

Persons detained or arrested in criminal cases and defendants in civil cases have the right to legal counsel. The 1981 Criminal Procedures and Evidence Act, as amended in 1984, makes provision for granting bail. Bail is granted regularly and generally fairly.

The Government has appealed the provisions of the Internal Security Act (ISA) of 1984 allowing for investigative detention.

The Government does not use forced exile.

e. *Denial of Fair Public Trial.*—The judiciary consists of the Court of Appeal (which meets semiannually), the High Court, magistrate's courts, and customary or traditional courts, which exist largely in rural areas to administer customary law. The High Court Chief Justice's decision in 1994 to swear in a provisional Ruling Council, in defiance of the Constitution, raised new questions about the independence of the judiciary. In particular, magistrates appear susceptible to governmental or chieftainship influence. Accused persons have and use the right to counsel and public trial. The authorities generally respect court decisions and rulings.

There is no trial by jury. Criminal trials are normally adjudicated by a single High Court judge who presides, with two assessors serving in an advisory capacity. In civil cases, judges normally hear cases alone. The High Court also provides procedural and substantive advice and guidance on matters of legal procedure to military tribunals; however, it does not participate in arriving at judgments. Military tribunals have jurisdiction only over military cases, and their decisions may not be appealed. Both law and custom severely limit the rights of women (see Section 5), but court treatment of women is not discriminatory.

There were no trials for political offenses. There were no reports of political prisoners.

f. *Arbitrary Interference With Privacy, Family, Home, or Correspondence.*—Although search warrants are usually required under normal circumstances, the ISA provides police with wide powers to stop and search persons and vehicles and to enter homes and other places for similar purposes without a warrant. The security services are believed to monitor routinely telephone conversations of Basotho and foreigners on national security grounds.

Section 2. Respect for Civil Liberties, Including:

a. *Freedom of Speech and Press.*—The Constitution provides for these rights, which are generally respected in practice. The independent newspapers, including one each controlled by the Roman Catholic and Lesotho evangelical churches, and two English-language weeklies, routinely criticize the Government. The official media, which consist of one radio station, a 1-hour daily newscast on a local television channel, and two weekly newspapers, faithfully reflect official positions.

The Government has withdrawn all of its advertising from a local newspaper linked to a dissident faction of the ruling BCP. Four government ministers have filed a civil lawsuit against the newspaper, seeking compensation for alleged defamation. In addition Parliament questioned its editors at some length, implicitly threatening another civil lawsuit.

The Government fully respects academic freedom. Although the Government owns and administers the country's only university-level institution of higher learning, academic staff represent the full political spectrum and are unhindered in expressing their views.

b. *Freedom of Peaceful Assembly and Association.*—Under a mid-1993 revision of the ISA, a public meeting, rally, or march no longer requires prior police permission, only advance notification. The police and local authorities generally respected these rights in 1996, unlike previous years. The Government did not investigate or prosecute any of the security personnel who killed and wounded several protestors at a peaceful 1994 progovernment demonstration.

In addition to the BCP and the Basotholand National Party (BNP), there are several smaller political parties. Political party meetings and rallies occurred regularly throughout Lesotho. There are no restrictions on political parties.

c. *Freedom of Religion.*—The Constitution provides for freedom of religion and the Government respects this right in practice.

d. *Freedom of Movement Within the Country, Foreign Travel, Emigration, and Repatriation.*—Citizens generally are able to move freely within the country and across national boundaries. The Government places no obstacles in the way of citizens who wish to emigrate.

In 1994 the Government allowed about 25 refugees to register with the U.N. High Commissioner for Refugees to study in Lesotho. They were expected to return to their countries of first asylum after completing their studies. Other than these students, Lesotho has no resident refugee population.

Section 3. Respect for Political Rights: The Right of Citizens to Change Their Government

In the first multiparty democratic elections in more than 20 years, the BCP swept into power in 1993 with complete control of the National Assembly. Despite the landslide electoral victory, the BCP Government was forced to contend with a number of challenges to its power in 1994. Those challenges culminated in August of that year when King Letsie III unconstitutionally suspended the Parliament and installed a Ruling Council. Many Basotho responded by demonstrating their support for the democratically elected BCP Government. Organized labor and others held two national "stayaways" to demonstrate support for the ousted Government, and there were numerous rallies at the National University. As a result of both local and international pressure, the King reversed himself, and the BCP regained control of the Government.

The 1994 Memorandum of Understanding between King Letsie III and Prime Minister Mokhehle, which was brokered by South Africa, Botswana, and Zimbabwe, called for reinstatement of the King's father, Moshoeshoe II, who had been deposed by the previous military government and exiled in 1990, as well as steps to broaden the political process. In early 1995, Moshoeshoe II was reinstated. However, King Letsie once again became king upon the death of his father in January 1996. The

1994 suspension of the Constitution by Letsie, although short-lived, highlighted the fragility of constitutional rule.

There are no legal impediments to women's participation in government or politics, but women remained underrepresented. There are 2 women in the 65-member Assembly and 7 women in the 33-member Senate. A woman serves as the Minister of Transportation and Communication.

Section 4. Governmental Attitude Regarding International and Nongovernmental Investigation of Alleged Violations of Human Rights

The Government did not hinder the activities of various nongovernmental human rights groups. These groups freely criticized both the Government and the short-lived Ruling Council.). The Government was cooperative during an Amnesty International visit in 1994.

Section 5. Discrimination Based on Race, Sex, Religion, Language, Disability, or Social Status

The Constitution prohibits discrimination based on race, color, sex, language, religion, political or other opinion, national or social origin, birth or other status, and the Government generally respected these prohibitions in practice.

Women.—Domestic violence, including wife beating, occurs frequently. Statistics are not available, but the problem is believed to be widespread. In Basotho tradition a wife may return to her "maiden home" if physically abused by her husband; in common law, wife beating is a criminal offense and defined as assault. Few domestic violence cases are brought to trial. Women's rights organizations, such as the local chapter of the International Federation of Women Lawyers, have taken a leading role in educating women regarding their rights under customary and common law, highlighting the importance of women fully participating in the democratic process.

Both law and custom severely limit the rights of women in such areas as property, inheritance, and contracts. Women have the legal and customary right to make a will and sue for divorce. However, under customary law, a married woman is considered a minor during the lifetime of her husband; she cannot enter into any legally binding contract, whether for employment, commerce, or education, without her husband's consent. A woman married under customary law has no standing in court and may not sue or be sued without her husband's permission. Senior government officials have publicly criticized customary practice which discriminates against women. The Government has committed to implement the plan of action from the Fourth International Conference on Women, held in Beijing in September 1995.

Children.—The Government has not addressed directly children's rights and welfare, although it has devoted substantial resources to primary and secondary education. There is no pattern of societal abuse against children, but many children work at a young age (see Section 6.d.).

People With Disabilities.—Discrimination against physically disabled persons in employment, education, or provision of other government services is unlawful. However, societal discrimination is common.

The Government has not legislated or mandated accessibility to public buildings for the disabled.

National/Racial/Ethnic Minorities.—Most citizens speak a common language and share common historical and cultural traditions. Small numbers of Asians (primarily ethnic Chinese and Indians) and South African whites are active in the country's commercial life. Economic and racial tension between the Chinese business community, specifically textile and garment industry employers, and the Basotho remained a problem.

Section 6. Worker Rights

a. The Right of Association.—Workers have the legal right to join or form unions without prior government authorization. A large percentage of the male labor force works in gold and coal mines in South Africa. The remainder are primarily engaged in traditional agriculture. There are small public and industrial sectors. A majority of Basotho mine workers are members of the South African National Union of Mineworkers (NUM). However, as a foreign organization, the NUM is not permitted to engage in union activities in Lesotho.

Under the 1993 Labor Code, prepared with the assistance of the International Labor Organization (ILO), all trade union federations require government registration. There are two trade union federations: The Lesotho Trade Union Congress and the Lesotho Federation of Democratic Unions. Unions are not tied to political parties. Overall, unionized workers represent only about 10 percent of the work force.

No legally sanctioned strike has occurred since independence in 1966. Legal protection for strikers against retribution has not always been enforced in cases of illegal strikes. Employers dismissed several hundred textile workers following wildcat strikes in 1994, and the Government maintained it could not oblige their employers to reinstate them. The Government was, however, successful in negotiating the reinstatement of employees following several illegal strikes in 1995 and 1996. Security forces violently suppressed some of the strikes in the textile, garment, and construction industries during 1994 and once during 1996.

There were no instances of governmental restrictions on international affiliations or contacts by unions or their members.

b. *The Right to Organize and Bargain Collectively.*—All legally recognized trade unions in principle enjoy the right to organize and bargain collectively, but in practice the authorities often restrict these rights. Although there was some bargaining between unions and employers to set wage and benefit rates, employers generally continued to set wage rates through unilateral action.

Lesotho has several industrial zones, in which mostly textile and apparel firms engage in manufacturing for export. All national labor laws apply in these industrial zones.

c. *Prohibition of Forced or Compulsory Labor.*—The 1987 Employment Act prohibits forced or compulsory labor, and there is no indication that such labor is practiced.

d. *Minimum Age for Employment of Children.*—The legal minimum age for employment in commercial or industrial enterprises is 14. In practice, however, children under 14 are often employed in the textile and garment sector and in family-owned businesses. As much as 15 percent of the textile work force of some 15,000 may be children between the ages of 12 and 15, according to a 1994 study by a foreign government. After visiting all 14 of Lesotho's nonartisan garment producers in 1994, the ILO, responding to a complaint by trade unions in the textile and clothing industry, was not able to confirm the unions' allegation of illegal child labor.

There are prohibitions against the employment of minors in commercial, industrial, or nonfamily enterprises involving hazardous or dangerous working conditions, but enforcement is very lax. The Ministry of Labor and Employment's Inspectorate is severely understaffed. Basotho youth under 18 years of age may not be recruited for employment outside of Lesotho. In traditional society, rigorous working conditions for the country's young "herdboys" are considered a prerequisite to manhood and a fundamental feature of Basotho culture beyond the reach of labor laws.

e. *Acceptable Conditions of Work.*—Wages are low. The monthly minimum wage for unskilled labor is $68 (320 maloti); for a heavy vehicle operator it is $131 (616 maloti). Minimum wages in lower skilled jobs are insufficient to ensure a decent standard of living for a worker and family. Most wage earners supplement their income through subsistence agriculture or remittances from relatives employed in South Africa. Many employers now pay more than minimum wages in an effort to attract and retain motivated employees.

The labor code spells out basic worker rights, including a maximum 45-hour workweek, a weekly rest period of at least 24 hours, 12 days of paid leave per year, and paid public holidays. The Code requires employers to provide adequate light, ventilation, and sanitary facilities for employees and to install and maintain machinery in a manner designed to minimize the risk of injury. In practice employers generally follow these regulations only within the wage economy in urban areas, and the Ministry of Labor and Employment enforces the regulations haphazardly. The Labor Code does not explicitly protect the right of workers to remove themselves from hazardous situations without prejudice to employment. However, labor code sections on safety in the workplace and dismissal imply that dismissal in such circumstances would be illegal.

LIBERIA

The Liberian civil war entered its seventh year with a continuation of death and destruction. In April and May, Monrovia was nearly destroyed by fighting in the capital. Up to 3,000 may have died and more than 2,000 foreign nationals were evacuated. Almost half the population of the capital of 850,000 inhabitants was displaced. The breakdown of law and order continued until West African peacekeepers (ECOMOG) regained control of the city in late May.

The fighting in Monrovia jeopardized the Abuja peace process that was launched in August 1995. A new peace accord—the fifteenth since the war began—was signed in Abuja, Nigeria, on August 17. It called for a cease-fire, disarmament, demobilization, reintegration, and the holding of national elections. The factions signing the new accord included: the National Patriotic Front of Liberia (NPFL); two ethnic wings—Krahn and Mandingo—of the United Liberation Movement for Democracy in

Liberia (ULIMO); and a coalition of anti-NPFL forces composed of the Liberian Peace Council (LPC), the Lofa Defense Force, and a breakaway-NPFL group called the Central Revolution Council (CRC). The second Abuja Accord contained provisions for sanctions—such as travel restrictions, exclusion from elections, and establishment of a war crimes tribunal—for factions not complying with the peace agreement.

Although the capital returned to relative quiet by late May, when ECOMOG reasserted its authority, the factions continued to wage war in the countryside beyond the scheduled cease-fire date of August 20. A new State Council chair, Ruth Sando Perry, assumed office on September 3, creating the third Liberian National Transitional Government (LNTG III). Given noncompliance with phase one of the peace process (implementation of a cease-fire and disengagement of fighters), phase two (disarmament and demobilization), which began November 22, faced formidable hurdles.

As an institution, the Armed Forces of Liberia (AFL) remained largely inactive. Many AFL Krahn soldiers, however, joined Krahn LPC troops in April and May to fight against the NPFL and ULIMO-Mandingo forces in Monrovia. There was a small corps of nonfactionalized AFL soldiers who remained neutral in the April-May events and stayed, unarmed, in the Barclay Training Center.

The Liberia National Police (LNP) and the National Security Agency (NSA), which report to the Ministry of Justice, together with the Special Security Services, which reports directly to the LNTG, also have responsibility for internal security, but they lacked the leadership, resources, and training to function effectively. The LNTG II appointment of a police director and top management team from one of the factions further reduced the effectiveness of the LNP. A special Rapid Response Unit (RRU), formed in 1995 to combat soaring violent crime in Monrovia, was infiltrated and corrupted by the NPFL. A new Minister of Justice appointed in September disbanded the RRU. However, she was dismissed in December and her successor announced he would reconstitute the RRU. Members of the RRU committed serious human rights abuses.

ECOMOG was the key military force supporting the LNTG III, as it was for all previous interim governments. At the end of 1996, ECOMOG claimed to have approximately 7,200 troops from 6 West African countries; over half were Nigerian. Regional governments, which had promised 2,700 additional troops for ECOMOG after the Abuja II Accord was signed, had not followed through on their commitments by the end of the year. In the absence of an effective central government, ECOMOG assumed many police powers in areas under its control. In contrast to previous years, there were no confirmed reports of ECOMOG committing human rights abuses.

The economy, ravaged by civil war, remained in severe disarray. No reliable information on the GDP is available. Prior to 1990, the economy was based primarily on iron ore, rubber, timber, diamond, and gold exports. Ninety-five percent unemployment, massive displacements of civilians throughout the country, and widespread destruction and looting devastated productive capacity, despite the country's rich natural resources and potential self-sufficiency in food. Meanwhile, the parallel black market economy thrived as the faction leaders and businessmen exploited and looted the wealth of the country. Using forced labor and stolen goods and fuel, they logged old growth timber, used environmentally unsound mining methods, and illegally tapped rubber trees in the areas under their control. The millions of dollars of profits from these enterprises were used to purchase more munitions, reinforcing the cycle of violence.

Factionally affiliated Government forces, factional forces, and agents were responsible for numerous human rights abuses. Some individual AFL members committed killings. RRU forces were responsible for killings, disappearances, and brutality. Factional members of the RRU actively participated in plundering and burning the capital in April and May, while threatening and, in some cases, murdering civilians. Ministry of Internal Affairs agents also used brutality against suspects. Conditions in government jails were life-threatening. Police arbitrarily arrested and detained persons, and at times infringed on citizens' privacy rights.

Because of the war, citizens have not been able to elect a representative government. The judicial system, already hampered by inefficiency and corruption, collapsed for 6 months following the outbreak of fighting in April. There were attempts by authorities to limit freedom of the press and freedom of association; journalists practiced self-censorship. Violence and discrimination against women are longstanding problems and have been widespread during the war. The war resulted in extensive abuse of children. The practice of female genital mutilation (FGM) persisted. Discrimination against minorities remains a problem. No progress was made in resolving outstanding incidents of past human rights abuses.

There were credible reports that some members of ECOMOG facilitated the delivery of—if they did not actually deliver—weapons and ammunition to the factions. Eyewitnesses also reported that some ECOMOG soldiers participated in the looting and destruction of Monrovia in April and May; this appeared to be limited to the Guinean contingent.

Although the 1985 Constitution, the Penal Code, and the Labor Code remain in effect, because of the civil war the rights provided for in these documents were largely not protected in practice.

The war has taken a horrendous toll on civilians. Of an estimated prewar population of 2.8 million, 200,000 died as a result of the civil conflict, 750,000 fled the country, and over 1.2 million are internally displaced. Approximately 1.5 million Liberians require humanitarian assistance to survive. The media, eyewitnesses, human rights groups, and international observers all reported flagrant disregard for human rights by the factional fighters. The factions committed summary executions, torture, individual and gang rapes, mutilations, and cannibalism. They burned people alive; looted and burned cities and villages; used excessive force; engaged in arbitrary detentions and impressment, particularly of children under the age of 18; severely restricted freedom of assembly, association, and movement; and employed forced labor.

Following the looting and destruction in Monrovia in April and May, which included facilities of the United Nations and humanitarian relief organizations, and left them without offices, vehicles, and resources; the few remaining NGO's had difficulty providing subsistence-level humanitarian relief, even within the Monrovia safehaven. The NGO's gradually rebuilt their staffs, even though fighters from various factions continued to hold up relief convoys, take relief workers hostage, and use civilians to attract humanitarian aid (see Section 1.g.).

RESPECT FOR HUMAN RIGHTS

Section 1. Respect for the Integrity of the Person, Including Freedom From:

a. *Political and Other Extrajudicial Killing.*—Political violence has been endemic to Liberia since the war began in 1989. Factional members of the RRU and AFL committed illegal killings. There were credible reports of extrajudicial killings by all factions during the April and May fighting in Monrovia and elsewhere throughout the year. NPFL-dominated RRU forces targeted and killed political opponents of NPFL head Charles Taylor in Monrovia. One outspoken NPFL critic was kidnaped in April by NPFL fighters and forced to view the headless bodies of people critical of Charles Taylor as a warning. On October 31, there was an assassination attempt by unidentified individuals against Charles Taylor at the executive mansion in Monrovia. Fighters—whether AFL, LPC or one of the ULIMO sub-factions—also targeted their enemies, fighters and civilians alike, removed their victims' body parts and ate them in front of civilians.

Although they publicly professed adherence to the rule of law, the leaders of the major warring factions condoned and in some instances seemingly appeared to encourage the murder and maiming of both civilians and combatants (see Section 1.g.). It was often impossible to determine whether these crimes were politically motivated or driven by tribal hatred (see Section 5). Among the many human rights atrocities in April, the Mandingo AFL Chief of Staff Mohammed Doumouyah was ritualistically tortured, mutilated, murdered, dismembered, and cannibalized by Krahn fighters in front of hostages at the AFL Barclay Training Center in Monrovia. There have been no arrests.

The majority of civilian deaths took place during factional raids on villages (see Section 1.g) in the countryside. ULIMO fighters executed civilians, and looted and burned their villages in Grand Cape Mount and Bomi counties. Even after the cease-fire of the Abuja II Accord went into effect in August, killings continued. Local human rights monitors reported that: On September 16, in Dia town 14 civilians were killed and the village—hometown of State Council chairwoman Ruth Perry—burned to the ground; on September 21, in Kango town, 16 civilians were murdered; on September 23, in Gunn town, 17 civilians were murdered; on September 28, in Sinje, another massacre took place (see Section 1.g) with more than 20 civilian victims; on December 7, in Zwanna Town (Royesville), 8 civilians were murdered; and on December 14 in Armadu Town, Bomi Highway, 4 people were killed. Fighting between the NPFL and LPC in the southeastern counties continued throughout the year, again resulting in many civilian deaths as villages repeatedly changed hands.

No progress was made in investigating the many killings from previous years, including the December 1994 massacre at DuPont Road. ECOMOG transferred the alleged perpetrators of the murder and cannibalization of a university student in August 1995 to civil authorities. The case has not yet been heard in court.

b. *Disappearance*.—There were no confirmed reports of disappearance perpetrated by the AFL, LNTG II or III regular police units or security forces, or by ECOMOG. However, there were credible reports of nighttime abductions and detention in secret jails by the NPFL-dominated RRU and other factions in Monrovia in April and May. The major factions were also responsible for many unexplained disappearances outside Monrovia (see Sections 1.g., 5, and 6.d.). Two Liberian nongovernmental organization workers in Zwedru disappeared on April 1 and are presumed dead. There are credible reports that NPFL fighters abducted civilians, including children, to use as combatants and for forced labor in illegal rubber tree tapping and timber operations. Both ULIMO factions used forced civilian labor to harvest alluvial gold and mine for diamonds.

The International Committee of the Red Cross (ICRC) runs a program allowing family members separated by the conflict to exchange Red Cross messages, mainly between people remaining in the country and relatives living abroad. Save the Children/UK reunited 140 children with their families during the year.

c. *Torture and Other Cruel, Inhuman, or Degrading Treatment or Punishment*.— The Constitution prohibits torture and other degrading treatment. There were no reports of torture by the LNTG II, or LNTG III police or security forces (with the exception of the RRU), or by ECOMOG. RRU forces were seen brutalizing civilians, burning houses, and looting during the April and May fighting in Monrovia. Men dressed in RRU trademark black clothes were involved in armed robberies and murders in the capital from June until September when they were disbanded.

Although the Supreme Court ruled that "trial by ordeal" or "sassywood"—commonly, the placement of a burning metal object on a suspect's body to induce confession in a criminal investigation—is unconstitutional, the Ministry of Internal Affairs continued to have licensed agents who subjected suspects to this practice A lawsuit brought in 1994 for injuries resulting from sassywood is still pending before the Supreme Court.

All major factions engaged in torture and other cruel, inhuman, and degrading treatment. Many victims exhumed in Monrovia after the April and May fighting had been "tarbeyed" before being killed—their arms tied tightly behind their backs at the elbow and wrist—an excruciating torture. Throughout the year, reports were received of rape, pillage, and the burning of villages in the western counties as the two ULIMO sub-factions fought for control. ULIMO-Mandingo fighters herded hundreds of displaced civilians into their Bomi county headquarters, Suehn, and held them hostage to attract relief food. When United Nations humanitarian workers were finally able to enter ULIMO-Krahn-controlled Tubmanburg in September, they found 20,000 starving civilians. Health care workers estimated the malnutrition rate at 83 percent; many people had died. Some civilians in Grand Cape Mount, when reached by the humanitarian community after 7 months, asked not to be given food because they feared that the fighters would kill them to get it (see Section 1.g.). LPC and NPFL fighters were accused of beating, torturing, and killing civilians, especially persons suspected of being sympathizers of the other faction, and burned their villages in the southeastern counties. Humanitarian relief workers were frequently detained and harassed by fighters, their personal property and vehicles confiscated, and food, intended for hungry civilians, stolen. Members of all factions practiced cannibalism (see Section 1.g.). The warring factions regularly committed violence against women, including individual and gang rapes.

Neither the LNTG II nor the LNTG III adequately addressed the life threatening conditions in government jails. There were incidents of starvation as the interim governments did not provide prisoners with adequate food or medical care. They did not pay guards for months. Cells were small, crowded, and filthy. Women, representing 5 percent of the central prison population, were held in separate cells, but there were no separate facilities for juvenile offenders. Ninety percent of the prisoners in the Monrovia central prison had been jailed for over 1 year without charge when the central prison was abandoned and the prisoners escaped during the fighting in early April. The central prison did not reopen until October 24 and very few of the escaped prisoners were recaptured.

The LNTG II and LNTG III granted human rights groups access to prisoners in Monrovia, and these groups frequently obtained needed medical treatment for prisoners. In a number of cases, the work of human rights groups and interested individuals resulted in the release of prisoners.

Reliable reports indicate that all warring factions operated secret jails both to enforce discipline in their own ranks and to intimidate or punish their enemies. The conditions in these clandestine jails were even worse than in government jails. Factions held prisoners in makeshift, substandard facilities and subjected them to various forms of inhuman treatment, both physical and psychological.

d. *Arbitrary Arrest, Detention, or Exile.*—The Constitution prohibits arbitrary arrest and provides for the rights of the accused, including warrants for arrests, and the right of detainees to be either charged or released within 48 hours. In practice some Liberian National Police officers in Monrovia and Buchanan often disregarded these rights and made arbitrary arrests. Many officers, whose average monthly salary was already less than $5.00, were not paid during the year and accepted bribes to arrest persons based on unsubstantiated allegations. As the police have no logistics or forensic investigative capabilities, they were unable to investigate crimes such as the August murder of Seh Vincent, a civilian representative in the Legislative Assembly.

In January the editors of a Monrovia newspaper were arbitrarily arrested and detained by the NPFL-appointed police director because of an article they published concerning the director (see Section 2.a.). On February 27, the NPFL-appointed Minister of Justice, acting without a warrant, arrested a journalist for an article he had written; the journalist was beaten but later released. On April 2, the NPFL detained a well-known religious leader and human rights activist on the fabricated charge of hindering law enforcement activities when he tried to mediate a dispute between faction leaders.

ECOMOG soldiers played the major role in policing the greater Monrovia and Buchanan areas. Many citizens continued to turn to ECOMOG rather than the unarmed, unpaid, and underequipped police force to arrest and detain alleged criminals. ECOMOG regularly turned detainees over to civilian authorities, as in the case of three men arrested for the October 17 murder, mutilation, and burning of two market women in Monrovia. There were no reports that ECOMOG officials coerced confessions from suspects.

Fighters outside of the ECOMOG safehavens of Monrovia and Buchanan did not honor due process safeguards and they arbitrarily detained numerous persons. Having almost unlimited power in practice to make warrantless arrests, they exercised that power often and capriciously, detaining persons, including international relief workers and missionaries, on spurious grounds or without charge for periods ranging from several hours to several weeks.

Approximately 750,000 citizens (over one-fourth of the prewar population), including former political leaders and human rights activists, fled the country because of the war.

The Government does not employ forced exile.

In April and May, over 2,000 foreign nationals, including United Nations agency and international humanitarian aid workers were evacuated when fighting broke out in Monrovia. In May approximately 5,000 civilians fled NPFL-LPC fighting in the southeast to seek refuge in Cote d'Ivoire. Approximately 2,000 civilians fled to Tabou, Cote d'Ivoire, when fighting began in September between the NPFL and LPC in Grand Gedeh county. Approximately 4,000 to 6,000 displaced Sierra Leoneans and 2,000 Liberians fled into Sierra Leone to avoid the fighting in the western counties in September. Many were forced back into Bo-Waterside in October and November due to fighting in Sierra Leone.

e. *Denial of Fair Public Trial.*—While the Constitution provides for an independent judiciary, the judiciary has always been subject to political, social, familial, and financial pressures. Corruption and lack of professionalism remained a recurrent problem. Because of the war, the judiciary did not function in most areas of the country.

Under the Constitution, defendants have due process rights conforming to internationally accepted norms of fair trial. Most of these rights, however, were ignored in practice. The NPFL-appointed Abuja II Minister of Justice rejected a court order releasing an NPFL defector, reasoning that the courts had no jurisdiction because this was an internal NPFL affair since the arrestee was an NPFL member.

The court structure is divided into four levels with the Supreme Court, whose members were appointed by the LNTG II, at its apex. All levels of the court system, including the Supreme Court in Monrovia, functioned erratically until fighting began in April. Subsequently the courts remained closed until September.

Customary law was also used both in Monrovia and the countryside. As in previous years, the Ministry of Internal Affairs subjected persons accused of occult practices and other crimes to "trial by ordeal," submitting defendants to physical pain to adjudicate guilt or innocence (see Section 1.c.).

In the areas controlled by the major factions, there was little pretense of due process; swift, arbitrary punishment was meted out by the faction leaders.

The Government does not hold political prisoners.

f. *Arbitrary Interference With Privacy, Family, Home, or Correspondence.*—While the Constitution provides for these rights, in wartime Liberia LNTG II and LNTG III authorities sometimes ignored them. The Constitution provides that police must obtain a warrant, or have a reasonable belief that a crime is in progress, or is about to be committed before entering a private dwelling. In practice some police forced entry without a warrant to carry out arrests and investigations.

The warring factions committed the most egregious abuses. Combatants looted the entire country with impunity. Widespread destruction in Monrovia in April and May included private homes, schools, hospitals and clinics, shops, churches, government buildings, and the offices of United Nations agencies and NGO's. Many buildings were burned. United Nations agencies and international NGO's were targeted by the factions and were looted of $30 million in equipment and vehicles in April.

g. *Use of Excessive Force and Violations of Humanitarian Law in Internal Conflicts.*—The major warring factions inflicted considerably more harm on noncombatants than on each other. They deliberately targeted, tortured, and murdered civilians, and regularly murdered women, children, and the elderly, indiscriminately ransacking villages and confiscating scant food supplies.

The massacre of more than 20 people, mostly women and children, at Sinje, Grand Cape Mount county, on September 28 illustrates the factions' disregard for humanitarian law. An exhumation of the bodies revealed that a baby girl's skull had been crushed. She was buried still strapped to her mother's back; her mother had been shot. Many more civilians were wounded, including an 8-month-old girl who had her foot cut off. Investigation has yet to determine which sub-faction of ULIMO—Krahn or Mandingo—was responsible. There were probably dozens of additional massacres in remote areas of conflict involving hundreds of victims which did not come to immediate public attention due to extensive political and social disruption throughout the year.

In June volunteer relief workers including the ICRC unearthed more than 520 corpses from shallow graves where they were temporarily buried during the factional fighting in the capital. Most of the victims died from bullet wounds, starvation, or disease.

There were credible reports that NPFL, ULIMO-Krahn, ULIMO-Mandingo, and LPC fighters committed acts of cannibalism (see Section 1.a.). In some instances, the fighters ate specific organs in the belief that it would make them stronger or invincible.

Relief organizations estimated that 1.2 million persons have been displaced since the war began. During this period, the factions have become experts at diverting humanitarian assistance. Most civilians are dependent on humanitarian aid for survival, but are often denied freedom to seek such assistance, as faction leaders and their followers forcibly detained them. These abducted civilians served as human shields for the fighters and were also used as forced labor (see Sections 1.b. and 6.c.). The factions often refused access by international and humanitarian relief agencies to distribute food until a medical and nutritional emergency existed, as was the case in Grand Cape Mount and Bomi counties when thousands of civilians were held hostage for over 7 months (see Section 1.c.). When assistance finally arrived for civilians, the armed groups frequently stole it. Fighters extorted humanitarian convoys at checkpoints, often insisting on providing "protection" for convoys, raiding upcountry warehouses, and taxing civilians in supplies after the delivery of food and medicines. Some civilians began asking that no food be delivered, as they did not want to be further brutalized by the factions. In October NPFL fighters looted 270 metric tons of food, then falsely accused two NGO workers of the theft. An NPFL spokesperson later declared that the food was intended for the civilians and, therefore, no crime was committed. The NPFL fighters were not disciplined. None of the warring factions returned the equipment or vehicles stolen during the fighting in April and May to the U.N. or to the relief organizations from which they had been stolen.

Section 2. *Respect for Civil Liberties, Including:*

a. *Freedom of Speech and Press.*—These freedoms are provided for in the Constitution and, with some significant limitations, were generally exercised in Monrovia. The former NPFL-appointed LNTG II Minister of Justice and the NPFL-appointed police director attempted to intimidate and restrict the press (see Section 1.d.). Citizens, including journalists, usually showed restraint and self-censorship in favor of the interim governments. Due to continued economic stagnation, all newspapers struggled to get their editions published. Following the April hostilities, the press was virtually moribund.

The restrictive Media Law, instituted during the Doe regime, remains in force and provides the Ministry of Information wide discretion in licensing and regulating journalists. A 1993 decree, which also remains in effect, set up guidelines for reporting on war-related issues.

Despite threats and harassment from the factions, the independent press continued to function until April/May. The independent press was among the first targets when fighting broke out in Monrovia. Only 1 of 13 independent newspapers escaped destruction, as it had changed its offices 2 weeks prior to the outbreak of fighting, but had not moved its trade sign. The independent press lost almost all of its equipment and supplies as did the two printing houses in Monrovia. No newspapers were printed for almost 4 months. Although by December six independent newspapers were publishing sporadically in Monrovia, they were financially weak. The other independent newspapers were still trying to reopen, but one, the Daily Observer, discouraged by the destruction and intimidation, remained closed until January 1997.

In addition to the independents, there was one pro-NPFL newspaper, The Patriot, and one pro-ULIMO-Mandingo newspaper, The National.

Although there once were three regional television stations in addition to one in Monrovia, television broadcasts ceased when the war started and have not resumed. Prior to the April and May destruction in Monrovia, there were six radio stations. With the exception of the NPFL-owned station, the others were looted or destroyed. In December only the government radio station, ELBC, the NPFL station, KISS-FM, and the independent Radio Monrovia were broadcasting regularly. In November the NPFL initiated a new short wave radio station from Totota.

Academic freedom was generally respected at the University of Liberia, however, it has been closed since April.

b. *Freedom of Peaceful Assembly and Association.*—The Constitution provides for the rights of peaceful assembly and association. The LNTG II and LNTG III generally permitted political parties and other groups to organize freely and hold public meetings in Monrovia. In February, however, both government officials and faction leaders vigorously opposed a civil society (including NGO's)-sponsored "stay at home day," the purpose of which was to express the popular demand for warring factions to disarm. In March the Women's Development Association of Liberia planned a public event on International Women's Day. The NPFL-appointed Minister of Justice publicly criticized the rally and denied the organizers permission to march in the capital. The organizers were granted permission by ECOMOG and the march was held as scheduled. For security purposes, however, ECOMOG continues to generally discourage large-scale parades or demonstrations.

The factions severely restricted freedom of assembly and association in areas they controlled.

c. *Freedom of Religion.*—The Constitution recognizes freedom of religion as a fundamental right, and Liberia has no established state religion. Although Islam is gaining adherents, as much as 40 percent of the population profess to be Christian. A significant portion of the population follows traditional animism or blends traditional religions with Christianity or Islam. Although the law prohibits religious discrimination, Islamic leaders complained that Muslims were discriminated against (see Section 5). There was no evidence of systematic violation of religious freedom by the warring factions.

d. *Freedom of Movement Within the Country, Foreign Travel, Emigration, and Repatriation.*—The Constitution provides for freedom of movement throughout the country as well as the right to leave or enter. To protect the 1 million people in Monrovia and Buchanan from rampant lawlessness and banditry, ECOMOG established a protective cordon around those cities and numerous checkpoints within the capital. In April and May, however, ECOMOG failed to protect Monrovia from factional fighting. It was not until May 27 that the Monrovia and Buchanan safehavens were reestablished. When ECOMOG could not guarantee safe passage upcountry, it restricted the movement of civilians and humanitarian aid workers at various times throughout the year.

Throughout the year, factional fighters prevented freedom of movement, restricting a range of activities from resettlement of displaced people to ordinary commerce and travel, throughout the areas they controlled. The warring factions also impeded the movement of relief workers and supplies, and extorted, humiliated, and harassed civilians throughout the country at checkpoints and makeshift barricades. Even after the seating of the LNTG III Council of State in September, there were reports that beatings of international humanitarian workers and thefts of foodstuffs and humanitarian vehicles by the warring factions continued. In November, on the eve of disarmament, aid workers reported that fighters in Tubmanburg threatened to hold them hostage if the aid workers did not distribute food as they desired (see Section 1.g.).

Since 1990 over 1.2 million citizens (of an estimated prewar population of 2.8 million) have been internally displaced. There are more than 750,000 Liberian refugees in neighboring West African countries. Some of the internally displaced returned to

Monrovia in January-March, but fled again when fighting resumed in April. Most subsequently returned, and there was no influx of displaced persons returning to Monrovia following the Ajuba II accord.

The Government provides first asylum. Although in 1995 there were approximately 120,000 Sierra Leonean refugees in Liberia, because of the fighting in western Liberia where most of the Sierra Leonean refugees lived, it is not known how many still remain.

The LNTG III cooperated with the Office of the United Nations High Commissioner for Refugees and other humanitarian organizations in attempting to assist refugees. However, inaccessibility to refugees due to fighting and security concerns severely limited the amount of relief assistance that could be provided. There were no reports of forced return of persons to a country where they feared persecution.

Section 3. Respect for Political Rights: The Right of Citizens to Change Their Government

Despite constitutional and statutory guarantees of free and fair elections, due to the civil war citizens could not exercise the right to change their government. A new interim government, the LNTG III, was installed on September 3, as a result of the signing of the Abuja II Accord on August 17. The Abuja II Accord calls for national elections in May 1997.

There are no restrictions on the participation of women in politics, however, they are underrepresented. Overall numbers of women in the LNTG II and LNTG III and the various political parties are small. With the advent of the LNTG III, a women chaired the Council of State, but there were no women as government ministers. A woman was appointed as chairman of the Elections Commission.

One vice councilman on the Council of State is a Muslim.

Section 4. Governmental Attitude Regarding International and Nongovernmental Investigation of Alleged Violations of Human Rights

The interim governments have generally permitted domestic and international groups to operate, but factional members of the Council of State have harassed, threatened, and beaten local human rights and humanitarian workers when they did not like their reports assessing responsibility for human rights violations.

The few domestic human rights organizations were underfunded, understaffed, and their personnel lacked adequate training. These groups were specifically targeted during the April and May fighting in Monrovia by factional fighters. Several influential human rights activists, who were the targets of RRU killers, left the country. Some have not returned. In December there were eight small human rights groups in the country; all struggled to rebuild looted offices and secure the funding needed to continue their work. The support structure for the consortium of human rights NGO's in Monrovia was destroyed during the April fighting and has not been reconstituted.

Prior to the fighting in Monrovia in April, some of the domestic human rights groups, as well as lawyers performing legal aid work, visited prisoners in government jails. None reported governmental interference with their activities. There were no domestic human rights organizations outside the cities of Monrovia and Buchanan due to insecurity associated with the warring factions' hostility to such organizations, but a few Monrovia-based human rights workers and members of the press sometimes were able, often at great risk to themselves, to visit the countryside to investigate reports of massacres and other human rights abuses.

Although the United Nations Observer Mission in Liberia (UNOMIL) has responsibility for monitoring human rights, for most of the year no one carried out this function. No UNOMIL reports on human rights were made public. The trained human rights observer assigned to UNOMIL in October 1995 resigned in November 1995, claiming lack of support for his work by the Special Representative of the Secretary General. He was replaced by another trained human rights observer in December 1996.

Section 5. Discrimination Based on Race, Sex, Religion, Disability, Language, or Social Status

The Constitution prohibits discrimination based on ethnic background, race, sex, creed, place of origin, or political opinion, but discrimination exists. There are no laws against gender-based discrimination, ethnic discrimination, or female genital mutilation (FGM).

Women.—In the massive violence inflicted on civilians during the conflict, women suffered the most (see Sections 1.c. and 1.g.). Rape was commonplace. Even prior to the war, domestic violence against women was extensive but never seriously addressed as an issue by the Government, the courts, the media, or women's groups. Since the war began, several women's organizations were established in Monrovia and Gbarnga to advance family welfare issues, to help promote political reconciliation, and to assist in rehabilitating former combatants as well as civilian victims of war. Several NGO's in Monrovia and Buchanan have developed programs for treating abused women and girls and increasing awareness of their human rights. Facilities and equipment were destroyed in the April fighting. At year's end, the NGO's were attempting to restart many of their programs.

The status of women varies by region, ethnic group, and religion. Before the outbreak of the civil war, women held one-fourth of the professional and technical occupations available in Monrovia. Some women currently hold skilled jobs in government, including in the judiciary. On the whole, however, the situation of women deteriorated dramatically with the onset of war, the closing of most schools, and the loss of their traditional role in production, allocation, and sale of food. In urban areas, women can inherit land and property. In rural areas, where traditional customs are stronger, a woman is normally considered the property of her husband and his clan and usually is not entitled to inherit from her husband.

Children.—Denied a normal childhood, Liberian youth have been seriously victimized by the civil war. The factions have abused children and have given no attention to their welfare; education and nurturing have been completely disrupted. Many who were disabled, orphaned, abandoned, or "lost" during a military attack on their homes or villages, accepted the protection and sustenance that joining a faction brought. The NPFL, LPC, and the two wings of ULIMO recruited and trained children as cooks, spies, errand runners, guards, patrols, and in many instances, combatants. Factions provided addictive drugs to children, thereby ensuring their compliance and continued participation in warfare. Many have been killed or wounded, have witnessed terrible atrocities, or themselves committed atrocities, becoming both victims and abusers in the conflict. There are no precise figures on the number of child soldiers, but some sources believe that 10 percent of the estimated 60,000 combatants are under 15 years of age; about 50 percent may be under 19. Many suffer from posttraumatic stress syndrome and have become addicted to drugs. Some NGO's and UNICEF initiated small retraining and rehabilitation programs for a limited number of former child fighters (see Section 6.d.), but these programs and facilities were destroyed during the April and May destruction of Monrovia.

Female genital mutilation (FGM) is widely condemned by international health experts as damaging to both physical and psychological health. FGM traditionally has been performed on young girls by northern, western, and central tribes, particularly in rural areas among traditional societies. Prior to the onset of civil war in 1989, approximately 50 percent of women in rural areas among northern, western, and central tribes between the ages of 8 and 18 underwent FGM. The war, however, has totally disrupted village life. Today probably less than 10 percent of females undergo FGM. In some instances, female health professionals in the tribes participated in the practice to the extent of providing hygienic conditions and postoperative care. The most extreme form of FGM, infibulation, is not practiced.

People With Disabilities.—The 7-year civil war has produced a large number of persons with permanent injuries in addition to persons disabled from other causes. There is no legal discrimination against the disabled, but in practice they do not enjoy equal access. There are no laws mandating accessibility to public buildings or services.

Religious Minorities.—The law prohibits religious discrimination. Some Muslims, however, who represent a growing share of the population, believe that Liberia's secular culture gives preference to Christianity in civic ceremonies and observances, and that discrimination spills over into areas of individual opportunity and employment. Although there are some Muslims in senior government positions, many Muslims believe that they are bypassed for highly sought-after government jobs.

National/Racial/Ethnic Minorities.—Although the Constitution bans ethnic discrimination, it also provides that only "persons who are negroes or of negro descent" may be citizens or own land, thus denying full rights to many persons who were born or lived most of their lives in Liberia. There has been no governmental initiative to repeal this racial test, but there are reports that non-Liberians have acquired Liberian passports. The 1975 economic "Liberianization" law prohibits foreign ownership of certain businesses, such as travel agencies, retail gasoline stations, and beer and soft-drink distributors.

The roots of the current civil conflict can be found to a large extent in the historical division between the Americo-Liberian minority who comprised 5 percent of the population and the 16 indigenous ethnic groups. Ethnic tensions were exacerbated during the Doe regime (1980–89) because of domination by his ethnic group, the Krahn. Throughout the civil war, the factions used an individual's language to identify ethnicity and often summarily executed those from groups considered hostile.

Section 6. Worker Rights

a. *The Right of Association.*—The Constitution states that workers, except military and police, have the right to associate in trade unions. The Constitution also states that unions are prohibited from partisan political activity. Government interference in union activities, especially elections and leadership conflicts, was commonplace both before and during the war.

Even though legal economic activity came almost to a complete halt during the on-going 7-year civil war, there were 32 functioning unions with the common objective of protecting the rights of their 60,000 members, who were largely unemployed. There is a proposal before the unions to merge into one body called the All Liberia Trade Union Unity Council which, if instituted, would encompass the Liberian Federation of Labor Unions. Despite this union activity, the actual power the unions exercised was extremely limited. The most vocal organization was the Liberian Seaman, Port and General Workers Union, which urged the government to pressure Liberian flag vessels to employ more Liberian workers.

The Constitution is silent on the right to strike, but labor laws protect this right. During the year, neither LNTG II nor LNTG III took discriminatory actions against organized labor. There were no noteworthy strikes during the year. Government officials were attempting to solve the problem of salary arrearages for all civil servants at year's end.

Liberia's status as a beneficiary of trade preferences under the United States' generalized system of preferences (GSP) program was suspended in 1990 as a result of the Doe government's failure to take steps to provide internationally recognized worker rights.

Labor unions have traditionally affiliated with international labor groups, such as the International Confederation of Free Trade Unions.

b. *The Right to Organize and Bargain Collectively.*—With the important exception of civil servants, workers (including employees of public corporations and autonomous agencies) have the right to organize and bargain collectively. In the past, agreements were negotiated freely between workers and their employers without government interference. In 1996 these rights were largely moot because of the lack of economic enterprise, especially in Monrovia, where only a few businesses resumed operations, usually with greatly reduced staffing, after the April and May fighting.

There are no export processing zones. All were destroyed when the war started.

c. *Prohibition of Forced or Compulsory Labor.*—The Constitution prohibits forced labor, but even before the civil war this prohibition was widely ignored in rural areas where farmers were pressured into providing free labor on "community projects" which often benefited only local leaders. During the year the warring factions continued to use forced labor for all purposes, including the exploitation and theft of national resources. Displaced persons reported that the LPC and the NPFL forced civilians to labor in the illegal timber cutting business throughout the southeast.

d. *Minimum Age for Employment of Children.*—Even before the civil war, enforcement of the law prohibiting employment of children under age 16 during school hours in the wage sector was lax. Small children continued to assist their parents as vendors in local markets and on family subsistence farms. This practice persists, particularly in those areas affected by the war, where there are no schools. All factions recruited young children as soldiers. Many of these children remained under arms (see Section 5). Based on extensive interviews, one NGO reported that only the LPC abducted children and forced them to serve in the war.

e. *Acceptable Conditions of Work.*—The Labor Law provides for a minimum wage, paid leave, severance benefits, and safety standards, but with the war, the enforcement mechanisms collapsed. In the war-ravaged economy, citizens were forced to accept any work they could find, regardless of wage. A legal minimum wage of approximately $0.90 per day for agricultural workers and 3 or 4 times that amount for industrial workers remains in force, but because of the war, it was not enforced.

The Labor Code provides for a 48-hour, 6-day regular workweek with a 30-minute rest period per 5 hours of work. The 6-day workweek may extend to 56 hours for service occupations and to 72 hours for miners, with overtime pay beyond 48 hours. Prior to 1990 there also were government-established health and safety standards, enforced in theory by the Ministry of Labor. Because of the war these regulations were not in fact enforced. Even under the Labor Code, workers did not have a specific right to remove themselves from dangerous work situations.

MADAGASCAR

Madagascar completed its transition from 16 years of authoritarian Socialist rule with the free and fair election of Albert Zafy as President in 1993. Under the 1992 Constitution, power is divided between the President, the Prime Minister, and his Government and a bicameral legislature (Senate and National Assembly). A number of institutions provided for in the Constitution, including the Senate, an independent judiciary, and new courts that require Senate appointments, had not been established by year's end. Communal elections, the first step toward the creation of the Senate, were held in November 1995. Departmental and regional elections, which must also precede a Senate election, were postponed in July due to impeachment proceedings against President Zafy. His impeachment became effective in September, with Prime Minister Norbert Ratsirahonana becoming acting Head of State while retaining his post as Prime Minister. In December former president Didier Ratsiraka defeated Zafy in a runoff presidential election.

The Ministry of National Police is responsible for law and order in urban areas. The Ministry of Armed Forces comprises the National Army, including army troops, air force, navy, and the gendarmerie. The gendarmerie has primary responsibility for security except in major cities, and is assisted in some areas by regular army units in operations against bandit gangs and cattle thieves. In August the Minister of Armed Forces issued a statement reiterating the armed forces' commitment to abide by the law as the impeachment struggle came to dominate national politics. The armed forces assiduously observed this order. Military force strength gradually declined to about 20,000 troops. There are also village-level law enforcement groups, or vigilance committees, known as dina. There were occasional reports that police and gendarmes committed human rights abuses, as did the dina.

Madagascar is a very poor country. The economy relies heavily on agriculture; production of coffee and vanilla fell, but shrimp exports rose, and rice, the major staple, remained at near-sufficiency. Manufacturing in export processing facilities increased modestly. Smuggling of vanilla, gold, precious stones, and cattle continued to be major concerns. Overall economic performance stabilized, but three-fourths of the population of 14 million still live in poverty. Foreign assistance remains a major source of national income. Living standards are low, with per capita gross domestic product estimated at $250. Inflation was 49 percent in 1995, but fell rapidly in 1996. Unemployment, especially among youth, remained high. The Government plans to implement a program of economic reform and structural adjustment to foster a market economy.

The human rights situation did not change significantly from 1995. There was little political violence, despite strikes, demonstrations, and heated political debate between the President and his opponents in the National Assembly. There were occasional reports of police brutality against criminal suspects and detainees, as well as instances of arbitrary arrest and detention. Prison conditions remained harsh and life threatening, and in some prisons women may experience physical abuse, including rape. The authorities took no action to relieve the overburdened judiciary. As a result, suspects were held in lengthy pretrial detention that often exceeded the maximum sentence for the alleged offense. Dina were responsible for summary justice in rural areas where the Government's presence was weak. Women continued to face societal discrimination.

RESPECT FOR HUMAN RIGHTS

Section 1. Respect for the Integrity of the Person, Including Freedom From:

a. *Political and Other Extrajudicial Killing.*—There were no reports of political killings by government forces. However, harsh prison conditions and the authorities' failure to provide adequate food and medical treatment resulted in an unknown number of deaths in custody (see Section 1.c.). Village dina continued to mete out summary justice, including executions, to combat rising rural banditry. The Malagasy Young Lawyers Association reported more than a dozen executions following dina trials, usually for cattle theft. Mobs took violent action against suspected thieves in some areas, particularly major cities, resulting in injury or death.

There were no developments in several pre-1996 incidents: The 1994 beating death of radio journalist Victor Randrianirina, who had allegedly reported on sapphire smuggling; several 1991–93 incidents in which security forces killed or injured unarmed civilians; the deaths of more than 30 demonstrators who were killed by then-President Ratsiraka's presidential guard at Iavoloha palace on August 10, 1991; or a March 31, 1992, incident in which soldiers killed 6 pro-Ratsiraka supporters at the National Forum (Constitutional Convention).

b. *Disappearance.*—There were no reports of politically motivated disappearances.

c. *Torture and Other Cruel, Inhuman, or Degrading Treatment or Punishment.*—The Constitution specifically provides for the inviolability of the person. However, there were occasional reports that police or other security forces mistreated prisoners or detainees. There were rare instances of dina trials in which torture was used to elicit confessions.

Prison conditions are harsh and life threatening. Prisoners' diets are inadequate, and family members must augment daily rations. Prisoners without relatives nearby sometimes go for days without food. Prison cells average less than 1 square meter of space per inmate. The authorities do not provide adequate medical care. The prison population of 20,000 suffers a range of medical problems that are rarely treated, including malnutrition, infections, malaria, and tuberculosis. These conditions have caused an unknown number of deaths.

Women in prisons suffer abuses, as do the children who are sometimes confined with them. Gender segregation is not absolute, and some rapes were reported.

The Government permits prison visits by the International Committee of the Red Cross, religious and nongovernmental organizations (NGO's), and a Malagasy legal association investigating excessive pretrial detention.

d. *Arbitrary Arrest, Detention, or Exile.*—The Constitution provides for due process for accused persons, but in practice the authorities do not always observe legal safeguards against arbitrary arrest and detention. In particular, excessive investigative detention of suspects results in denial of due process.

According to law, a criminal suspect must be charged, bound over, or released within 3 days of arrest. An arrest warrant may be obtained but is not always required. According to the Penal Code, defendants in ordinary criminal cases have the right to be informed of the charges against them, must be charged formally within the specified time permitted, and must be allowed access to an attorney. Court-appointed counsel is provided for indigent persons accused of crimes that carry a minimum 5-year jail sentence. An attorney or the accused may request bail immediately after arrest, after being formally charged, or during the appeal process, but it is rarely granted in the case of violent crimes.

More than 70 percent of the estimated 20,000 persons in custody were in pretrial detention. Despite existing legal safeguards, investigative detention often exceeds 1 year, and 3 or 4 years of detention are common, even for crimes for which the maximum penalty may be 2 years or less. The accused may wait years in prison only to be ultimately exonerated in court. A Catholic NGO, Aumonerie Catholique, in partnership with the Young Lawyers' Association, pursued case reviews of a number of detainees.

Although the law allows detainees to sue the Government for damages in cases of unlawful detention, no such suits were reported. By law, persons accused of subversive activity may be detained incommunicado for 15 days and are subject to indefinite detention if considered necessary by the Government; however, this law was not invoked during the year.

The Government does not use forced exile.

e. *Denial of Fair Public Trial.*—The Constitution provides for an independent judiciary; however, implementing legislation has not been passed. The establishment of a number of courts also provided for in the Constitution awaits the long-delayed inauguration of the Senate.

The judiciary has three levels of jurisdiction: local courts for civil and criminal cases carrying limited fines and sentences; the Court of Appeals, which includes a criminal court for cases carrying sentences of 5 years or more; and the Supreme Court. The judiciary also includes courts designed to handle specific kinds of cases such as cattle theft. The High Constitutional Court is an autonomous court that undertakes technical reviews of laws, decrees, and ordinances, and certifies election results.

While awaiting reform, the judiciary remained under the Ministry of Justice. Lack of internal controls and relatively low salaries for magistrates encourage corruption. With judicial reform stagnated, the pace of court proceedings has slowed and created a huge backlog, contributing to the problem of excessive investigative detention.

Trials are public, and defendants have the right to an attorney, to be present at the trial, to confront witnesses, and to present evidence. Defendants enjoy a presumption of innocence under the Penal Code.

The right of traditional village institutions to protect property and public order is codified in the Constitution as well as earlier laws. Dina adjudicate or arbitrate civil disputes within and between villages. Dina are also established in some urban areas. In practice dina increasingly deal with criminal cases because of increasing crime, the physical isolation of many rural areas, and the ineffectiveness of the police and the judiciary outside major centers. Dina punishments were at times severe and in some cases included capital punishment. In late 1995, the Government began to combat crime and insecurity in isolated rural regions by augmenting the gendarmerie—traditionally responsible for law and order in rural areas—with army units.

In November 1994, the National Assembly formally recognized the role of dina in reducing crime when it passed legislation that gave dina verdicts the same weight as judgments by lower courts. This legislation also increased fines and the severity of prison sentences for those refusing to abide by dina decisions. However, the 1994 law remained under review by the High Constitutional Court and did not become effective. Decisions by dina are not subject to codified safeguards for the accused, but in some instances may be challenged at the appeals court level. Some cases have also been referred to the Office of the Mediator (ombudsman), which investigates and may seek redress from formal judicial authorities.

Military courts are integrated into the civil judicial system, and differ only in the kinds of cases tried and in the inclusion of military officers on jury panels. Such courts have jurisdiction over some cases involving national security, including acts allegedly threatening the nation and its political leaders; invasion by foreign forces; and rioting that could lead to the overthrow of the Government. Defendants in military cases, as in civil law, enjoy an appeals process that reexamines points of law rather than the facts of the case. A civilian magistrate, usually joined on the bench by a panel of military officers, presides over military trials.

There were no reports of political prisoners.

f. *Arbitrary Interference With Privacy, Family, Home, or Correspondence.*—The Constitution prohibits such practices, government authorities generally respect these prohibitions, and violations are subject to effective legal sanction.

Section 2. *Respect for Civil Liberties, Including:*

a. *Freedom of Speech and Press.*—The Constitution provides for freedom of the speech and of the press, and the Government respects these rights in practice. The press is independent, and the judiciary functions effectively in this area.

Academic freedom is respected.

b. *Freedom of Peaceful Assembly and Association.*—The Constitution provides for these rights, and the Government respects them in practice.

c. *Freedom of Religion.*—The Constitution provides for freedom of religion, and the Government respects this right in practice.

d. *Freedom of Movement Within the Country, Foreign Travel, Emigration, and Repatriation.*—The Constitution provides for these rights, and the Government respects them in practice. However, fear of crime effectively restricts travel to some places, especially at night. Malagasy and foreign residents require exit visas, but these are almost never refused unless the person is involved in legal proceedings.

The Government generally cooperates closely with the United Nations High Commissioner for Refugees in processing the small number of refugees or asylum seekers. However, the Government has failed to resolve the status of approximately 127 Ethiopian asylum seekers who have been in Madagascar for several years. A group of approximately 40 Ethiopians staged a hunger strike from September 30 to October 6 to protest the Government's failure to recognize them as refugees. There were no reports of forced expulsion of those with recognized or pending claims to refugee status. The issue of the provision of first asylum has never arisen.

Section 3. *Respect for Political Rights: The Right of Citizens to Change Their Government*

Citizens have the right to change their government through direct universal suffrage and secret ballot. Albert Zafy was elected to a 5-year term as President in 1992 in the first election under the current constitution. In 1993 138 members of the National Assembly were elected for 4-year terms. Local government mayors and councils were elected in 1995. A referendum to amend the Constitution was also held in 1995. These by-elections were generally free and fair.

Under the Constitution, the President has primary responsibility for national defense and foreign policy, while the Prime Minister is head of government and responsible for domestic policy. The President selects the Prime Minister under provisions of a 1995 referendum that amended the Constitution. The Prime Minister is appointed when a new National Assembly is elected every 4 years, or upon a vacancy. The Constitution gives the President, acting in conjunction with the Council of Ministers, the right to dissolve the National Assembly if there have been two governmental crises in the previous 18 months. The High Constitutional Court must rule that such crises have occurred. The Prime Minister is required to submit his resignation, as must the Cabinet, if a motion of censure is passed by a two-thirds majority of the National Assembly.

Relations between the President and the National Assembly progressively deteriorated following the 1995 referendum in which the President acquired the right to name the Prime Minister. The President's insistence on the right to select political allies for several crucial ministries in the successor government of Prime Minister Ratsirahonana ultimately led to a motion of impeachment against him in July. In September the High Constitutional Court validated the National Assembly's vote.

The Senate had not yet been created by year's end. Two-thirds of the Senate's members are to be selected by local, department, and regional government officials, while one-third of the members are to be appointed by the President. Although local government elections were held in November 1995, the departmental and regional elections scheduled for 1996 were postponed.

There are no legal impediments to women's participation in government or politics, but in practice they are underrepresented in both areas. Only one ministerial post has been held by a woman in any one of the successive governments since 1992, and women hold only 6 percent of National Assembly seats. However, nearly half of the magistrates are women.

Section 4. Governmental Attitude Regarding International and Nongovernmental Investigation of Alleged Violations of Human Rights

A number of human rights groups operate without government restriction, investigating and publishing their findings on human rights cases. Government officials are usually cooperative and responsive to their views. The Constitution provides for an independent office to promote and protect human rights. In 1994 the National Assembly assigned that role to the Office of the Mediator (ombudsman), which relies on moral suasion to correct abuses. The Office publishes annual reports on its activities, and produced and distributed a series of brochures to educate citizens on their rights and responsibilities, outline the rights of women and children, and bring public attention to the potential for human rights violations by dina.

The Government is open to visits by international human rights groups and to domestic and international election observers, although no foreign groups applied to observe any elections.

Section 5. Discrimination Based on Race, Sex, Religion, Disability, Language, or Social Status

The Constitution prohibits all forms of discrimination and outlaws groups that advocate ethnic or religious segregation. However, there are no government institutions that enforce these antidiscrimination provisions.

Women.—Violence against women is not widespread. Police and legal authorities intervene when physical abuse is reported. There is no law dealing specifically with violence against women except rape. Spouses can be tried for nonrape abuses, generally under civil law.

There is societal discrimination against women. Such discrimination is less salient in urban areas where many women manage or own businesses or fill management positions in state industries.

Under a 1990 law, wives have an equal voice in selecting the location of a married couple's residence, and they generally receive an equitable share of common property on divorce. Widows with children inherit half of joint marital property. A tradition known as "the customary third" is still observed in some areas. Under this custom, the wife has a right to only one-third of a couple's joint holdings. However, a widow receives a pension, while a widower does not.

Children.—While official expenditures on children's welfare are low, the Government has maintained spending levels of the ministries of Health and Education despite increasing fiscal austerity. However, these levels are not sufficient to maintain public services under current economic conditions. The Government provides education through the secondary or vocational level, and it is compulsory through the age of 14. In practice, however, attendance at primary schools is estimated to be about 70 percent.

There is no societal pattern of abuse of children.

People With Disabilities.—There is no systematic discrimination against disabled persons in employment, education, or in the provision of other state services. There is no law mandating access to buildings for people with disabilities. One NGO, Fondation Ikoriatsoa, has begun work on a draft law to define the rights of the disabled.

National/Racial/Ethnic Minorities.—The Malagasy, who are of mixed Malayo-Polynesian, African, and Arab heritage, include 18 distinct groups differing in regional and ancestral affiliation. Although there are some linguistic differences, nearly all speak a dialect of the Malagasy language. None of these groups constitutes a majority of the population.

A long history of military conquest and political consolidation raised the political and economic status of highland ethnic groups of Asian origin above that of coastal groups of more African ancestry. Centralized administration and economic planning since independence reinforced the concentration of economic and political power in the central highlands, where the capital is situated. These policies fed enduring tension between coastal and highland peoples. Ethnic, caste, and regional solidarity are often factors in hiring practices.

An Indo-Pakistani community has resided in Madagascar since the early part of the century. This community, traditionally focused on commerce, now numbers about 20,000. Few of these individuals have made successful claims to Malagasy nationality, which is customarily acquired through a native-born Malagasy mother. Indo-Pakistanis are widely mistrusted. In past years, their shops have been looted and ransacked during civil disturbances.

Section 6. Worker Rights

a. *The Right of Association.*—The Constitution and the 1995 Labor Code provide workers in the public and private sectors with the legal right to establish and join labor unions of their choosing without prior authorization. However, essential service workers, including police and military, may not form unions. Unions are required to register with the Government, and registration is routinely granted. About 80 percent of the labor force of 5 million is engaged in agrarian production. Union members account for only about 5 percent of the total labor force.

There are a number of trade union federations, many affiliated with political parties. Neither public nor private sector unions have played a major political or economic role in recent years. The Government exercises very limited control over organized labor.

The Labor Code and the Constitution include the right to strike, including in export processing ("free trade") zones (EPZ's). Workers in essential services have a recognized but restricted right to strike, although in practice short strikes took place without reprisal. The code requires workers to exhaust conciliation, mediation, and arbitration procedures before striking, but has not in practice been a significant deterrent to legal strikes.

Strikes took place in virtually every major city as workers added their voice to the political struggle between the President and the National Assembly and protested declining incomes and poor economic conditions. Government workers and university students also called strikes to protest austerity measures.

The ILO noted a number of instances in which the Government has failed to bring law and regulation into conformity with existing conventions or otherwise submit texts for ILO review, including those addressing forced labor, freedom of association, guarding of machinery, hygiene in commerce and offices, and weight limits. In most instances, these failures indicate legislative inertia rather than abuses.

Unions freely join and participate in international bodies and may form federations or confederations.

b. *The Right to Organize and Bargain Collectively.*—Both the Labor Code and the Constitution provide for the right to bargain collectively. The code states that collective bargaining may be undertaken between management and labor on the initiative of either party. Collective bargaining agreements are rare. The Government is often involved in the bargaining process, in part because of the large percentage of public employees who are union members.

The Labor Code prohibits discrimination by employers against labor organizers, union members, and unions. In the event of antiunion activity, unions or their members may file a case against the employer in civil court. Labor laws apply uniformly throughout the country, including in the EPZ's. However, the Government's enforcement of labor laws and regulations is hampered by lack of staff and financial resources. The 27 Ministry of Labor inspectors visit industrial work sites with some regularity but most often those located near the capital.

There are several EPZ's which are, in practice, firms operating under special import and export rules. Such firms are required to follow all pertinent labor law and regulation, including minimum wage laws.

c. *Prohibition of Forced or Compulsory Labor.*—The Labor Code explicitly prohibits forced labor Code, and it is not practiced.

d. *Minimum Age for Employment of Children.*—The Labor Code defines a child as any person under the age of 18 years. The legal minimum age of employment is 14 years, and work by individuals under the age of 18 is prohibited at sites where there is apparent and imminent danger. The Government enforces child labor laws in the small formal economic sector through inspectors of the Ministry of Civil Service, Labor, and Social Redressment. In the large agricultural sector, many young children work with parents on family farms at much younger ages. In urban areas, many children work as petty traders and beggars.

Education is compulsory to the age of 14. In practice, however, only about 70 percent of children attend primary school.

e. *Acceptable Conditions of Work.*—The Labor Code and implementing legislation prescribe working conditions and wages, which are enforced by the Ministry of Civil Service, Labor, and Social Redressment. The law makes separate provisions for agricultural and nonagricultural labor.

The minimum wage is set by the Government. Other wages are set by employers with individual employees, sometimes below the standard minimum wage. When there is a failure to reach agreement, the Ministry of Labor convenes a Committee of Employment Inspectors to resolve the matter. If this process fails, the Committee refers the matter to the chairman of the Court of Appeals for final arbitration. No such cases reached the Court of Appeals during the year. The minimum wage is $30.50 (fmg 121.605) per month. This wage does not provide a decent living for a worker and family and must be supplemented by subsistence agriculture, petty trade, support from relatives, or employment of other family members. Minimum wage rates are not always respected, since high unemployment and widespread poverty lead workers to accept wages at lower levels.

The standard legal workweek in nonagricultural and service industries is 40 hours, and 42½ hours in agriculture. At least one 24-hour rest period each workweek is mandated. The Labor Code sets rules and standards for worker safety and work site sanitation. Ministry of Civil Service, Labor and Social Redressment officials monitor labor conditions. However, they are usually able to cover only the capital region effectively. If violators do not remedy cited violations within the time allowed, they may be legally sanctioned or assessed administrative penalties. In some sectors, safety equipment is not used due to the expense of protective clothing and other safety devices. There have been no published reports of occupational health hazards or accident trends. There is no explicit right for workers to leave dangerous workplaces without jeopardizing their employment.

MALAWI

The Republic of Malawi held its first democratic, multiparty elections since independence in May 1994. President Bakili Muluzi principally relies on the ruling United Democratic Front (UDF), which holds 82 of the 177 seats in the National Assembly. The opposition Malawi Congress Party (MCP), formerly the sole legal party, holds 52 seats. The Alliance for Democracy (AFORD) split over the UDF–AFORD coalition and the continued presence of AFORD Members of Parliament (MP) in the Cabinet, reducing AFORD's number of MP's to 27. Six former AFORD MPs and one former MCP MP sit as independents. Both the MCP and AFORD opposition alleged government corruption; AFORD also protested Muluzi's appointment of AFORD members as ministers without consulting with the party leadership. In July the MCP and AFORD withdrew from the National Assembly, arguably depriving that body of its quorum. The parties referred the political impasse to the judiciary for resolution. The judiciary has demonstrated independence in several high profile political cases, although there are frequent, but unproven, allegations that its decisions result from political bias or bribery.

The National Police, headed by the Inspector General of Police under the Ministry of Home Affairs, is responsible for internal security. Although the army is apolitical, the police occasionally called on the army for support. While violence and common crime have become frequent, there was no indication of organized activity in Malawi or abroad by remnants of the Malawi Young Pioneers (MYP), formerly the MCP's paramilitary wing. Despite notable improvements, there continued to be credible allegations of human rights abuses by the police.

Small, densely populated, and landlocked, Malawi's economy is predominantly agricultural. Over 85 percent of the population derives its income from agriculture. Tobacco remains the primary foreign exchange earner; other cash crops include tea, coffee, and sugar. Foreign aid remains a critical source of income. The Government continued to extend market pricing in the agricultural sector and began privatizing the ownership of public enterprises. The high inflation that has plagued Malawi for several years abated toward the end of 1996, following the country's first good rainy season in several years. The economy was expected to grow by 11 percent in real terms. Per capita income is below $200. Wealth remains concentrated in the hands of a small elite, many of whom remain aloof from national politics.

The Government generally respected the human rights of its citizens, but serious problems remained. The police continued to abuse detainees and to use excessive force in handling criminal suspects. There were instances of deaths of detainees while in, or shortly after release from, police custody. In implementing reforms the Inspector General of Police stressed public accountability and transparency. Prison conditions remained poor. Lengthy pretrial detention, the inefficient and understaffed judicial system, and limited resources called into question the ability of defendants to receive a timely and, in some cases, a fair trial. High levels of crime prompted angry mobs to summarily execute alleged criminals.

The Government remained in control of the broadcast content of the nation's radio stations. It delayed consideration of proposed legislation on the reform of the Malawi Broadcasting Corporation and did not issue any new broadcasting licenses. By contrast the print media continued to report freely. The Human Rights Commission mandated by the Constitution to explore human rights violations was established but made very little progress. Women continued to experience severe societal discrimination, and violence against women and children remained a problem. The Government has taken steps to assist disadvantaged women in its economic development programs.

RESPECT FOR HUMAN RIGHTS

Section 1. Respect for the Integrity of the Person, Including Freedom From:

a. *Political and Other Extrajudicial Killings.*—There were incidents of deaths of detainees while in, or shortly after release from, police custody. Most serious were the March 5 deaths from suffocation in severely overcrowded cells of 17 prisoners. The Government and police responded to this incident of police negligence by promptly laying out the facts of the incident. Although the police normally do not issue statements on deaths in custody, the Inspector General released on March 7 a statement to the press describing this incident and announcing an inquiry. A presidential inquiry as well as a joint Inspectorate of Prisons/Human Rights Commission inquiry were subsequently announced on March 7 and 8. (Of the three, only the Inspectorate/Human Rights Commission inquiry eventually delivered its report. The report acknowledged the full cooperation and helpful assistance of the Inspector General, who made witnesses and records available.) The station officer and officer in charge were indicted, and the prison officials on duty were suspended on March 8. During the course of the inquiry, the Inspector General of Police informed the Inspectorate/Human Rights Commission that an internal inspectorate had been established to address these and other issues. During a September followup visit, the Inspectorate of Prisons noted that many of the recommended improvements to the facility had been carried out and that prison recordkeeping was much improved.

The inquest into the April 1995 shooting of former Army Commander Manken Chigawa revealed not only sketchy police investigation into his death, but serious inconsistencies between police and witness accounts of the deaths while in police custody of his two alleged killers. These accounts and the apparent attempts by some police subordinates to hide deaths or incidents of mistreatment prompted the Inspector General to establish the internal inspectorate to address issues of police misconduct.

Frustrated by inadequate law enforcement and rising crime, angry mobs sometimes resorted to vigilante justice in beating, stoning, or burning suspected criminals to death. The Government made no discernible effort to punish individuals who carried out these abuses.

b. *Disappearance.*—There were no reports of politically motivated disappearances.

c. *Torture and Other Cruel, Inhuman, or Degrading Treatment or Punishment.*—The Constitution prohibits torture and other cruel, inhuman, or degrading treatment. Although that provision is generally respected, the Inspectorate of Prisons, an investigative body mandated by the Constitution, confirmed that the police continued to physically abuse detainees. However, the incidence of abuse has dropped. While higher ranking officials demonstrated familiarity with new standards for the humane treatment of prisoners, their subordinates commonly employed unacceptable techniques. According to an October Inspectorate of Prisons report, unacceptable techniques included beatings, whippings, dog attacks, knifings, and the intentional deprivation of food, water, toilet facilities, and medical care to force confessions. These abuses are sometimes hidden by keeping a prisoner in police custody until wounds heal before turning the prisoner over to the prison system for remand. The mistreatment is partly due to the mistaken belief of many police officers that the law requires them to present a case (not just charges) to the court within 48 hours of arrest. The Government also sought community involvement in its comprehensive reform of the police.

Prison conditions remained poor. Overcrowding, inadequate nutrition, and substandard sanitation and health facilities remained serious problems. While not kept in separate facilities, women are segregated within the prison compound and tended by female guards. The Inspectorate of Prisons and local organizations monitor police behavior and prison conditions without government interference.

d. *Arbitrary Arrest, Detention, or Exile.*—The law permits the accused to challenge the legality of detention, to have access to legal counsel, and to be released or informed of charges by a court of law within 48 hours. In an effort to comply with the 48-hour rule, police occasionally resorted to beatings in order to extract information necessary to their case. In cases where the court determines that a defendant cannot afford to supply his own counsel, legal services are supposed to be provided by the Government. With few persons able to afford legal counsel, the country's four public defenders were not sufficient to meet the needs of indigent detainees. Bail is frequently granted to reduce prison overcrowding. Its use often bears only a tenuous relation to the merits of an individual's situation. September statistics indicate that approximately 35 percent of the 4,887 prison inmates are detainees awaiting trial.

On August 29, William Phakamisa and two others were arrested for allegedly conspiring to kill key government and UDF officials. Police officials subsequently told his family that Phakamisa had been released from custody when in fact he was being held incommunicado at police facilities. Phakamisa claimed that the detention was intended to extract his cooperation in implicating opposition leaders in a plot.

Exile is not used as a means of political control. However, against the directive of its own High Court, the Government acquiesced in the exile to Malawi of Zambian political dissidents.

e. *Denial of Fair Public Trial.*—The Constitution provides for an independent judiciary, and the Government respects this provision in practice. The judiciary demonstrated a high degree of independence from elected officials in several high profile political cases. Allegations that individual judges were corrupt or politically biased were common but unproven.

The Constitution provides for a High Court, a Supreme Court of Appeal, and subordinate magistrate courts. The Chief Justice is appointed by the President and confirmed by the National Assembly. Other justices are appointed by the President following a recommendation by the Judicial Service Commission. All justices are appointed until the age of 65 and may be removed only for reasons of incompetence or misbehavior, as determined by a majority in Parliament and the President.

By law defendants have the right to a public trial but not to a trial by jury. In dealing with murder cases, the High Court nevertheless used juries of seven persons from the defendant's home district. Defendants are also entitled to an attorney, the right to adduce and challenge evidence and witnesses, and the right of appeal. However, the judiciary's budgetary and administrative problems effectively denied expeditious trials for many defendants. No murder trials by jury have been conducted before the High Court since December 1995. Nevertheless, prisoner deaths and the release of those held on the basis of weak evidence decreased the backlog of homicide cases.

The judicial system is also handicapped by serious weaknesses, including poor record keeping, shortage of trained personnel, and a heavy caseload. Traditional court judges, absorbed into the magistrate court system, received training to acquaint them with court procedure and the body of law they are now expected to administer.

Many of the country's old repressive laws were superseded by the new Constitution. The High Court overturned old laws that were in conflict with the Constitution. In consultation with nongovernmental organizations (NGO's) and parliamentarians, the Law Commissioner undertook to clarify ambiguities in the Constitution and to bring legislation on women into compliance with new constitutional standards.

Juvenile offenders have special rights under the Constitution, including the right to be separated in custody from adults, to be treated in a manner that accounts for age and the possibility for rehabilitation, and to be exempted from the punishment of life imprisonment without the possibility of release.

There were no reports of political prisoners.

f. *Arbitrary Interference With Privacy, Family, Home, or Correspondence.*—Government authorities generally respected the constitutional right to privacy regarding person, family, home, and private communications. However, army and police forces, in carrying out sweeps for illegal weapons, did not obtain search warrants as required by law. Postal authorities have apparently ceased their past practice of opening and inspecting private correspondence.

Section 2. Respect for Civil Liberties, Including:

a. *Freedom of Speech and Press.*—The new Constitution superseded old laws restricting the press and now provides for freedoms of speech and press. The Government generally respected these rights in practice. The Government also generally tolerated the broad spectrum of political and ideological opinion presented in the country's two dozen newspapers. However, media representatives complained about government secrecy and periodic verbal threats against members of the press by government officials. In May the Government launched its own official weekly newspaper.

Malawi has two radio stations. A small private station broadcasts only religious programming and is not permitted to broadcast news. State-owned Malawi Broadcasting Corporation (MBC), however, is the most important medium for reaching the public. MBC programming was dominated by reporting on the activities of senior government figures and official government positions. Parties and groups opposed to the Government largely were denied access to the broadcast media. MBC reporters were disciplined or fired for their reporting on opposition parties. News stories were pulled in midbroadcast and press conferences heavily edited to avoid politically sensitive material. MBC refused to air paid public announcements of labor union events. The Government effectively blocked consideration of legislation to make MBC a more independent public broadcasting entity and continued to deny applications to establish new private radio stations.

There were no restrictions on academic freedom.

b. *Freedom of Peaceful Assembly and Association.*—The Constitution provides for freedom of assembly and association, and the Government respects these rights in practice. Authorities routinely granted official permits, which are required by law for large meetings. The Government requires organizations, including political parties, to register with the Registrar General in the Ministry of Justice. Despite frequent lengthy delays, there were no reports of groups being denied registration.

c. *Freedom of Religion.*—The Constitution provides for freedom of religion, and the Government respects this right in practice. Religious groups must register with the Government.

d. *Freedom of Movement Within the Country, Foreign Travel, Emigration, and Repatriation.*—Citizens have freedom of movement and residence within the country, and the right to leave and return. The National Assembly took the final steps to lift the remaining restrictions on where Asians, whether citizens or not, could reside and work. To date there has been little movement by Asians and other expatriates from cities and towns to rural areas.

The Government cooperated with the Office of the United Nations High Commissioner for Refugees (UNHCR) in managing the refugee community. According to the UNHCR, Malawi now hosts approximately 1,500 refugees. There were 200 new cases in December alone, primarily due the crisis in the Great Lakes region of Africa. This influx had not diminished by year's end. Approximately 1 million refugees from Mozambique left Malawi in 1995. Although the Government grants refugee status, it does not accept refugees for resettlement and does not permit them to work or study. There were no reports of forced return of persons to a country where they feared persecution. Approximately 1,500 refugees, primarily from Somalia and the Great Lakes region, are housed at Malawi's Refugee Center. Asylum applicants are granted hearings to make their case for refugee status. Although there were no reports of bona fide refugees seeking first asylum being turned away, NGO sources have expressed concern that some of those found not to be bona fide refugees—primarily Zaireans—were rejected because of poor quality translation or ambiguous questions that trapped or misled otherwise qualified refugees. The Government is increasingly wary of those who travel long distances to seek asylum in Malawi. Foreign Minister George Ntafu, responding to reports of a Great Lakes refugee trek to Malawi, declared in December that the refugees would not be permitted into the country. In that month, nine Rwandan refugees were intercepted and returned to Tanzania after illegally crossing into Malawi, but hundreds more have succeeded in making their way into the refugee camp.

Section 3. Respect for Political Rights: The Right of Citizens to Change Their Government

Citizens are generally able to exercise this constitutional right. Malawi has universal suffrage for citizens 18 years of age and older. There were allegations of vote buying, intimidation, and the misuse of government assets during by-elections, which were common practices under the Banda regime. In one case where voters were permitted to cast ballots despite allegedly selling or losing their registration cards, the Electoral Commission determined that the violation did not affect the outcome of the election and declined to strike down the election result.

President Muluzi, Vice President Justin Malewezi, and a 25-member Cabinet exercise executive authority. The Second Vice Presidency remains vacant following the resignation of Chakufwa Chihana and the collapse of the UDF–AFORD coalition. While the executive and the legislature were elected in free, democratic elections, the executive in fact exerted considerable influence over the legislature. Local elections have been postponed due to a lack of funds, effectively preventing the citizenry from selecting new local leadership. However, in November the Minister of Local Affairs reaffirmed the Government's commitment to the ongoing reorganization of local government structures. Although the Government does not prevent the operation of opposition political parties, the parties have alleged that the Government utilizes bribery and other inducements to encourage opposition party divisions and defections of key personnel to the UDF.

There are no laws that restrict the participation of women or minorities in the political process. In practice, however, there are very few women in prominent government positions. Only two ministers and two deputy ministers are women, and there are nine women in the National Assembly. Despite the small number of female parliamentarians, the parliamentary women's caucus has worked effectively with the Law Reform Commissioner on draft legislation to bring the law into compliance with constitutional guarantees protecting women.

Section 4. Governmental Attitude Regarding International and Nongovernmental Investigation of Alleged Violations of Human Rights

A wide variety of local and international human rights groups operated without government restriction, training civic educators, advocating changes to existing laws and cultural practices, and investigating and publishing their findings on human rights cases. Government officials are generally cooperative and responsive to their views.

The Ombudsman, mandated by the Constitution to investigate and take legal action against government officials responsible for human rights violations and other abuses, began functioning. However, the Ombudsman's freedom of action was circumscribed by legislation that requires a warrant and a 3-day waiting period to gain access to certain government records. The Constitution also provides for a National Compensation Tribunal (NCT) to entertain claims of criminal and civil liability against the former government. As of September the NCT had awarded nearly $200,000 to 200 claimants. Other large sums were disbursed to settle non-NCT lawsuits against the Government for similar human rights violations. However, the prominence of many of both the NCT and non-NCT recipients raised concerns of favoritism. With two members named, the constitutionally mandated Human Rights Commission, also entrusted with monitoring and protecting against violations of constitutional rights, had barely begun to function by year's end and awaits further legislation on membership and procedures.

Section 5. Discrimination Based on Race, Sex, Religion, Disability, Language, or Social Status

The Constitution specifically provides for equal rights for women; forbids discrimination based on language, culture, or religion; and generally provides every citizen the right to equality and recognition before the law. In practice the capacity of government institutions to assure equal rights for all citizens is limited.

Women.—Spousal abuse, especially wife beating, is common. Malawian society has begun to take problems of violence against women more seriously. The press published more frequent accounts of rape and abuse, and the judiciary imposed heavier penalties on those convicted of rape. However, domestic violence is not discussed openly by women, reportedly even among themselves, and there are no confidential shelters or facilities for treatment of women who suffer physical or sexual abuse. Police do not normally intervene in domestic disputes.

Under the new Constitution, women have the right to full and equal protection by law and may not be discriminated against on the basis of their sex or marital status. In practice, however, discrimination against women is pervasive, and women do not have opportunities equal to those available to men. Women, especially in rural areas, historically have been unable to complete even a primary education and are therefore at a serious disadvantage in the job market. Women often do not have equal access to legal and financial assistance, and wives are often victims of discriminatory inheritance practices in which the majority of the estate is taken unlawfully by the deceased husband's family. Women are usually at a disadvantage in marriage, family, and property rights but have begun to speak out against abuse and discrimination. The Law Reform Commissioner took steps to bring legislation on women into compliance with new constitutional standards (see Section 1.e.).

The Government addresses women's concerns through the Ministry of Women and Children Affairs and Community Development. The National Commission on Women in Development (NCWID) coordinates Government and NGO activities. After the President remarked that he wished to appoint more women but did not know of suitable candidates, the NGO Women's Voice prepared a book for him containing resumes of 250 prominent women. The book subsequently served as a source for recent appointments to boards of parastatal (state-owned) organizations.

Children.—The Constitution provides for equal treatment for children under the law, and the Government greatly increased spending on children's health and welfare. The Government has established free primary education for all children, although education is not compulsory. A few charitable organizations attempted to reduce the number of child beggars in urban areas and find alternative care for them. The problem of street children worsened as the number of orphans whose parents died from HIV/AIDS increased.

There are societal patterns of abuse of children. A few small ethnic groups practice female genital mutilation (FGM), which is widely condemned by international health experts as damaging to both physical and psychological health. The media have also begun to report on the sexual abuse of children, especially in relation to traditional practices of initiation. While still shrouded in secrecy, emerging data on rites to initiate girls into their future adult roles suggest that abusive practices are widespread and more damaging than previously believed. Also, the common belief that sex with children reduces the risk of AIDS contributes to the sexual abuse of minors.

People With Disabilities.—The Government has not mandated accessibility to buildings and services for the disabled, but one of the national goals listed in the new Constitution is to support the disabled through greater access to public places, fair opportunities in employment, and full participation in all spheres of society. Special schools and training centers, which assist individuals with disabilities, and several self-supporting businesses run by and for the disabled have existed for some time.

National/Racial/Ethnic Minorities.—Malawians of African heritage are members of indigenous tribes and are not discriminated against by government or society. Although former restrictions on where Asians could live and work are now unconstitutional, only a few Asians tested the new policy (see Section 2.d.).

The Government considered various proposals on temporary employment permits for expatriates but has yet to clarify its policy and procedures. The Government's decision not to automatically renew the permits caused concern and sometimes hardship to businessmen, teachers, health workers, and missionaries. Business residence permits are readily granted to new investors.

Section 6. Worker Rights

a. *The Right of Association.*—Although signed into law in June, the Labour Relations Act of 1996 did not enter into force. Thus, labor issues continue to be covered by the old legislation. Workers have the legal right to form and join trade unions, but unions must register with the Ministry of Labour and Manpower Development (MOLMD). Unionization is on the rise, but resistance on the part of many employers remained. Army personnel and police may not belong to trade unions, but other civil servants are allowed to form unions. There were 13 registered trade unions. Given the low percent of the work force in the formal sector (about 12 percent), plus the lack of awareness of worker rights and union benefits, only a minuscule percent of the work force are union members. Statistics on the numbers of union members are not available. Unions are independent of the Government, parties, and other political forces. Although there are no restrictions on the number of union federations, Malawi has only one, the Malawi Congress of Trade Unions (MCTU). All unions are affiliated with it. According to the MOLMD, there are no unusually difficult registration procedures that would prevent a trade union from registering.

Members of registered unions in "essential services" have the right to strike after having carried out prescribed procedures. Essential services are nowhere specified; they are determined by the Minister of Labour. The Trade Union Act requires that labor disputes in essential services be reported in writing to the Minister of Labour, who then attempts to negotiate a settlement. He may refer the case to a tribunal within 28 days of receiving the dispute report if it is not possible to reconcile the parties. The law implies that if a trade dispute has gone through this process, and if it has not been resolved or referred to a tribunal, workers in essential services may strike. There were a handful of strikes, with no clear agreement on which strikes were legal. As the Trade Union Act requires that unions must approve strikes by secret ballot, all the strikes may have been illegal.

The laws do not specifically prohibit retaliation against strikers. There is no prohibition on actions against unions that are not legally registered. Arbitration rulings are legally enforceable.

Unions may form or join federations and affiliate with international organizations with government permission.

b. *The Right to Organize and Bargain Collectively.*—Unions have the right to organize. The right to bargain collectively, although practiced, is only implied and not expressly protected by law.

The Ministry of Labour sets minimum wage rates based on recommendations of the Tripartite Wages Advisory Board.

The law prohibits antiunion discrimination by employers, but there are no effective mechanisms for resolving complaints, and there is no legal requirement that employers reinstate workers dismissed because of union activities.

In August 1995, Parliament approved legislation to establish six export processing zones (EPZ's); four were operational by year's end. The full range of labor legislation applies to the EPZ's.

c. *Prohibition of Forced or Compulsory Labor.*—The new Constitution prohibits forced labor, and such labor is not employed.

d. *Minimum Age for Employment of Children.*—The Constitution defines children as those under the age of 16 years and prohibits the employment of children in work that is hazardous, harmful, industrial, or interferes with their education. However, while primary education is now free and universal, it is not compulsory. Enforcement by police and labor inspectors in the MOLMD is not effective because of budgetary constraints. There is significant child labor on tobacco and tea estates, subsistence farms, and in domestic service. There is no special legal restriction on children's daytime work hours.

e. *Acceptable Conditions of Work.*—There are two legislated minimum wage rates, but the administratively set minimum wages are insufficient to support a worker and family. Wage earners tend to supplement their incomes through farming activities carried out through the extended family network. The urban minimum wage is roughly $0.78 (MK11.85) per day, including $0.08 for rent; in all other areas it is roughly $0.56 (MK8.50) per day, including $0.07 for rent. The MOLMD is unable to effectively to enforce the minimum wage. The prescribed minimum wages are largely irrelevant for the great majority of citizens who earn their livelihood outside the formal wage sector.

The maximum legal workweek is 48 hours, with a mandatory weekly 24-hour rest period. The laws require payment for overtime work and prohibit excessive compulsory overtime. However, labor inspections are more the exception than the rule, and the statutory restrictions are frequently violated.

The Workers' Compensation Act includes extensive occupational health and safety standards. Enforcement of these standards by the MOLMD is erratic, and workers—particularly in industrial jobs—often work without basic safety clothing and equipment. MOLMD officials say that workers have the right to remove themselves from dangerous work situations without jeopardy to continued employment. However, given the low level of education of most workers and the high level of unemployment, they are unlikely to exercise this right. Workers dismissed for filing complaints about workplace conditions can theoretically file a complaint with the nearest labor office or sue the employer for wrongful dismissal.

MALI

Mali is a constitutional democracy. The Government is headed by Prime Minister Ibrahim Boubacar Keita. In the country's first democratic elections in 1992, which were judged to be free and fair by international observers, citizens ratified a new constitution, elected the National Assembly, and chose President Alpha Oumar Konare as Head of State. These elections completed a 14-month transition following the 1991 overthrow of the Moussa Traore regime. The peace agreement reached with Tuareg and Maur rebel groups in 1995 remained in force. At a ceremony in March, the Government officially celebrated the end of the rebellion, and the majority of rebel movements formally dissolved themselves.

Security forces are composed of the army, air force, Gendarmerie, the National Guard, and the police. The army and air force are under the control of the civilian Minister of Defense, as are the Gendarmerie and the National Guard. The police are under the Ministry of Territorial Administration. The police and gendarmes share responsibility for internal security.

Mali is a very poor country. Its economy is based primarily on farming and animal husbandry, making it highly dependent on adequate rainfall for its economic well-being. The Government continues to make progress in implementing reforms aimed at modernizing the economy. Nevertheless, Mali continues to be beset by economic problems, including a poor infrastructure, the lack of an industrial sector, and heavy dependence on foreign assistance. Social ills, including a literacy rate of only 23 percent and a high population growth rate, also contribute to Mali's poverty.

The Government generally respected constitutional provisions for freedom of speech, press, assembly, association, and religion. However, prison conditions are poor, and the judicial system's large case backlog results in long periods of pretrial detention. The executive branch retains influence over the judiciary. Social and cultural factors continued to sharply limit economic and educational opportunities for most women. Societal violence against women and children, including spousal abuse and female genital mutilation, is widespread.

RESPECT FOR HUMAN RIGHTS

Section 1. Respect for the Integrity of the Person, Including Freedom From:

a. *Political and Other Extrajudicial Killing.*—There were no reports of political or other extrajudicial killings.

There were no developments in the October 1994 deaths of the Swiss Cooperation Mission director and his two Malian colleagues, who were killed by an army patrol in Niafunke. A Government mission of inquiry into their deaths determined in December 1994 that the patrol's actions were unwarranted and unjustified. However, to date, the Government has neither identified publicly the responsible parties, nor made attempts to expedite the case, which remains on file at the regional court in Mopti.

b. *Disappearance.*—There were no reports of politically motivated disappearances.

c. *Torture and Other Cruel, Inhuman, or Degrading Treatment or Punishment.*—The Constitution prohibits such practices, and there were no reports that officials employed them.

Prison conditions continue to be characterized by overcrowding, inadequate medical facilities, and limited food supplies. They remain below minimum international standards. Several organizations, including the Malian Association of Human Rights, and the Malian Association of Women Jurists, visited prisoners in 1996 and are working with women and juvenile prisoners to improve their conditions. The International Committee of the Red Cross (ICRC) continued to visit detainees held in connection with the tensions in the north, as well as the leading members of the former government. In Bamako juvenile offenders are usually held in the same prison as adult offenders but are kept in separate cells. Women are housed in the same prison facility as men but live in a separate compound. In regional prisons outside the capital, men and women are housed in the same building but in separate cells. In these facilities, children share cells with adult prisoners of the same sex.

d. *Arbitrary Arrest, Detention, or Exile.*—The Constitution provides that suspects must be charged or released within 48 hours and are entitled to counsel. In practice, however, detainees are not always charged within the 48-hour period. Moreover, administrative backlogs and insufficient lawyers, judges, and courts often cause lengthy delays in bringing people to trial. In extreme cases, individuals have remained several years in prison before coming to trial. Judicial warrants are required for arrest. Local lawyers have estimated that about half of prison inmates are pretrial detainees. Bail does not exist. On occasion the authorities release defendants on their own recognizance.

The Government does not practice forced exile.

e. *Denial of Fair Public Trial.*—The Constitution provides for an independent judiciary, but the executive branch continues to exert considerable influence over the judicial system. The Ministry of Justice appoints judges and supervises both law enforcement and judicial functions, and the President heads the Superior Judicial Council, which oversees judicial activity.

The Supreme Court has both judicial and administrative powers. The Constitution established a separate Constitutional Court which oversees issues of constitutionality and acts as an election arbiter. The Constitution also provides for the convening of a High Court of Justice with the power to try senior government officials in cases of treason.

Except in the case of minors, trials are public, and defendants have the right to be present and have an attorney of their choice. Defendants are presumed innocent and have the right to confront witnesses and to appeal decisions to the Supreme Court. Court-appointed attorneys are provided for the indigent without charge. The majority of disputes in rural areas are decided by the village chief in consultation with the elders. If these decisions are challenged in court, only those found to have legal merit are upheld.

Women and minorities are not discriminated against in courts, but traditional practice discriminates against women in inheritance matters.

There were no reports of political prisoners.

f. *Arbitrary Interference With Privacy, Family, Home, or Correspondence.*—The Constitution provides for the inviolability of the home, and the Government respects this right in practice. Police searches are infrequent and require judicial warrants. Security forces do, however, maintain physical and technical surveillance of individuals and groups believed to be threats to internal security, including surveillance of telephone and written correspondence of individuals deemed to be a threat to national security.

Section 2. *Respect for Civil Liberties, Including:*

a. *Freedom of Speech and Press.*—The Constitution provides for freedom of speech and the press, and the Government respects these rights in practice. There are approximately 40 independent newspapers and journals, in French, Arabic, and local languages. There are three daily newspapers: two are independent; one is government controlled.

The Government controls one television station and one of many radio stations, but all operate on a semi-independent basis and present a wide range of views, including those critical of the Government, the President, the Prime Minister, and other politicians.

Fifteen independent radio stations exist in Bamako, and there are approximately 40 additional stations throughout the country. Two private television companies rebroadcast French, British, South African, and American television programs, including news bulletins. The Government made little progress toward private television licensing during the year.

Laws passed in 1993 regulate the press and provide for substantial penalties, including imprisonment, for slander and for public injury to the Head of State, other officials, and foreign diplomats; these laws leave injury undefined and subject to judicial interpretation.

Academic freedom is respected.

b. *Freedom of Peaceful Assembly and Association.*—The Constitution provides for these rights, and the Government respects them in practice. The Government does not interfere with political meetings, which take place openly.

c. *Freedom of Religion.*—The Constitution provides for freedom of religion and declares Mali to be a secular state. The Government does not discriminate on religious grounds, and citizens are free to practice their faiths. Although legal restrictions on the Baha'i faith still exist, the Government does not enforce them, and Baha'i worship freely. The Minister of Territorial Administration can prohibit religious publications that he concludes defame another religion, but there were no known instances of publications being prohibited.

d. *Freedom of Movement Within the Country, Foreign Travel, Emigration, and Repatriation.*—The Constitution provides for these rights, and the Government generally respects them in practice. The Government generally does not restrict internal movement, and does not restrict international travel. However, police routinely stop and check both citizens and foreigners to restrict the movement of contraband and to verify vehicle registrations. Some police and gendarmes use the occasion to extort bribes.

The Government cooperates with the Office of the United Nations High Commissioner for Refugees (UNHCR) and other humanitarian organizations in assisting refugees. Although Mali has no legislation regarding refugee asylum and resettlement, the Government, in practice, provides first asylum for refugees. Those granted refugee status by the UNHCR are permitted to remain, albeit in a legal vacuum due to the absence of resettlement legislation. There were no reports of forced return of persons to a country where they feared persecution.

Of the estimated 120,000 Taureg and Maur Malian refugees who fled to neighboring countries during the 1990–95 Taureg-Maur rebellion, approximately 87,000 remain in neighboring countries. In July the UNHCR appealed to the international community to fund its program for repatriating the remaining Malian refugees. With the consolidation of peace in northern Mali, both UNHCR-assisted and spontaneous refugee repatriations continued throughout the year. The Government asserts that there are approximately 16,700 Mauritanian Peuhl refugees residing in Mali. Some expatriates who work in the development and refugee fields believe that the figure is lower.

Section 3. Respect for Political Rights: The Right of Citizens to Change Their Government

Citizens have the right to change their government and did so for the first time in 1992, voting by secret ballot in elections that were generally free, fair, and broad based, despite some irregularities. Twenty-one political parties participated in the elections, and 11 are represented in the National Assembly. The President's party, the Association for Democracy in Mali, holds the majority of the seats in the Assembly.

Under the Constitution, the President is Chief of State and Commander-in-Chief of the armed forces and is elected for a term of 5 years with a limit of two terms. The President appoints the Prime Minister.

There are no restrictions on voting, legal or otherwise, for women or minorities. However, women are underrepresented in politics. Only 3 women hold seats in the 116-member National Assembly, and 2 cabinet ministers are women. A third woman, the Secretary for the Promotion of Women, holds ministerial rank. Nomadic peoples, including Fulani and Taureg, are represented in both the Cabinet and National Assembly. The President of the Assembly is Fulani.

Section 4. Governmental Attitude Regarding International and Nongovernmental Investigation of Alleged Violations of Human Rights

Independent human rights organizations—including the Malian Association for Human Rights (AMDH), a smaller Malian League of Human Rights, and a local chapter of Amnesty International—operate openly and without interference from the Government. Since 1994 the Government has held an annual democratic forum in December to which it invited citizens to voice discontent and grievances against the Government publicly in the presence of international human rights observers. The events are well attended by local citizens from all walks of life who speak freely. International media and human rights observers were present at the forum. The ICRC has an office in Bamako and has strengthened its presence in the north by opening offices in Timbuktu and Gao.

Section 5. Discrimination Based on Race, Sex, Religion, Disability, Language, or Social Status

The Constitution prohibits discrimination based on social origin, color, language, sex, or race, and the Government respects these provisions in practice. However, social and cultural factors give men a dominant role.

Women.—Although the Constitution prohibits discrimination based on sex and provides for the basic rights of all persons, violence against women, including wife beating, is tolerated and common.

Women's access to jobs in the professions and government is limited, as are their economic and educational opportunities. For example, a 1995–96 national demographic and health survey found that 81 percent of women between the ages of 15 and 49 received no education (compared with 69.3 percent of men). Women comprise 15 percent of the labor force. The Government, the major employer, pays women the same as men for similar work. Women often live under harsh conditions, especially in the rural areas, where they perform hard farm work and do most of the childrearing. Despite legislation giving women equal rights regarding property, traditional practice and ignorance of the law prevent women from taking full advantage of this reform. In March the Government launched a 4-year national plan of action for the promotion of women. The plan, financed by national, regional, and local community budgets, seeks to reduce inequalities between men and women in six target areas, including education, health, and legal rights.

There are numerous active women's groups that promote the rights of women and children, and the female head of the Commission for the Promotion of Women enjoys the rank of minister. Women have very limited access to legal services. They are particularly vulnerable in cases of divorce, child custody, and inheritance rights, as well as in the general protection of civil rights.

Children.—Only one in five children receives basic education. There is no constitutional or legal provision to protect the interests and rights of children, and no juvenile court system. However, the Malian Social Services Department investigates and intervenes in cases of reported child abuse or neglect.

Female genital mutilation (FGM), which is widely condemned by international health experts as damaging to both physical and psychological health, is still common, especially in rural areas, and is performed on girls at an early age. According to the 1995–96 national demographic and health survey, at least 93.7 percent of women have undergone this mutilation. The Government has not proposed legislation prohibiting FGM. However, it supports educational efforts to eliminate the practice through seminars and conferences and provides media access to proponents of its elimination.

People With Disabilities.—There is no specific legislation protecting the rights of the physically or mentally disabled, nor mandating accessibility. The Government does not discriminate against the physically disabled in regard to employment, education, and other state services. Given the high unemployment rate, however, the physically disabled are often unable to find work.

Section 6. Worker Rights

a. *The Right of Association.*—The Constitution and the Labor Code specifically provide for the freedom of workers to form or join unions and protect freedom of association. Only the military, the Gendarmerie, and the National Guard are excluded from forming unions. Virtually all salaried employees are organized. Workers have established independent unions for teachers, magistrates, health workers, and senior civil servants, and most are affiliated with the National Union of Malian workers (UNTM) confederation. The UNTM has maintained its autonomy from the Government.

The Constitution provides for the right to strike, although there are restrictions in some areas. For example, civil servants and workers in state-owned enterprises must give 2 weeks' notice of a planned strike and must enter into negotiations with the employer and a third party, usually the Ministry of Labor. The Labor Code prohibits retribution against strikers, and the Government respects this requirement in practice. Workers at the privately owned Syama gold mine in Sikasso region went on strike in January and March to demand a pay increase and a reduction in working hours. In June, 6 of the 12 UNTM unions staged a legal 2-day walkout to support demands for increased wages.

Unions are free to associate with and participate in international bodies.

b. *The Right to Organize and Bargain Collectively.*—The growth of independent unions has led to more direct bargaining between these unions and their employers. Wages and salaries, however, for those workers belonging to the UNTM unions are set by tripartite negotiations between the Ministry of Labor, labor unions, and representatives of the federation of employers of the sector to which the wages apply. These negotiations usually set the pattern for unions outside the UNTM. The Ministry of Labor acts as a mediator in labor disputes.

Neither the Constitution nor the Labor Code addresses the question of antiunion discrimination, but there have been no reports or complaints of antiunion behavior or activities. If the parties cannot come to agreement, the dispute goes to the Labor Court for decision.

There are no export processing zones.

c. *Prohibition of Forced or Compulsory Labor.*—The Constitution prohibits forced or compulsory labor. Slavery persists, however, throughout the North. Expatriate health, development, and refugee workers report that traditional enslavement of members of the Bellah ethnic group by Taureg factions remains widespread throughout the North. Rumors persist of slavery in the remote salt mining communities of Taoudeni north of Timbuktu. These rumors are difficult to verify, and other reports indicate that the members of the Bellah ethnic group who work the mines now receive wages, however meager.

d. *Minimum Age for Employment of Children.*—The minimum legal age for employment is 14 years, but children may work with parental permission as apprentices at the age of 12. This regulation is often ignored in practice. Moreover, it has no effect on the vast number of children who work in rural areas, helping with family farms and herds, and in the informal sector, e.g., street vending. These children are not protected by laws against unjust compensation, excessive hours, or capricious discharge. The Labor Inspection Service of the Ministry of Labor is responsible for, and reasonably effective in, enforcement of child labor laws, but only in the modern sector.

e. *Acceptable Conditions of Work.*—The Labor Code specifies conditions of employment, including hours, wages, and social security, but in practice many employers either ignore or do not comply completely with the regulations. The national minimum wage rate, set in October 1994, is approximately $40 (cfa 21,000) per month. Workers must be paid overtime for additional hours. The minimum wage is supplemented by a required package of benefits, including social security and health care. While this total package could provide a minimum standard of living for one person, in practice most wage earners support large extended families and must supplement their income by some subsistence farming or work in the informal sector.

The normal legal workweek is 40 hours, with a requirement for at least one 24-hour rest period. The Social Security Code provides a broad range of legal protection against hazards in the workplace, and workers' groups have brought pressure on employers to respect parts of the regulations, particularly those affecting personal hygiene. With unemployment high, however, workers are often reluctant to report violations of occupational safety regulations. The Labor Inspection Service of the Ministry of Labor oversees these standards but limits enforcement to the modern, formal sector. Workers have the right to remove themselves from dangerous work situations and request an investigation by the Social Security Department, which is responsible for recommending remedial action where deemed necessary.

MAURITANIA

Mauritania is an Islamic republic. The 1991 Constitution provides for a civilian government composed of a dominant executive branch, a Senate and National Assembly, and an independent judiciary. President Maaouya Ould Sid'Ahmed Taya has governed since 1984, first as head of a military junta, and since the 1992 election as head of a civilian government. President Taya won 62 percent of the vote in the four-way presidential contest, which was widely regarded as fraudulent. Most opposition parties boycotted subsequent parliamentary elections. Opposition parties participated in Senate elections in 1994 and 1996 but gained only one seat. In the country's first multiparty legislative elections held in October, only 1 opposition and 6 independent candidates were elected to the 79-member National Assembly. The outcome of the election was marred by fraud on all sides and pervasive government intervention, representing a backward step in the country's efforts to establish a pluralist democracy.

The Government maintains order with regular armed forces, the National Guard, the Gendarmerie (a specialized corps of paramilitary police), and the police. The Ministry of Defense directs the armed forces and Gendarmerie; the Ministry of Interior directs the National Guard and police. The armed forces are responsible for national defense. The National Guard performs police functions throughout the country in areas in which city police are not present. The Gendarmerie is a paramilitary group responsible for maintenance of civil order in and outside metropolitan areas. Security forces are under the full control of the Government and responsible to it. Some members of the security forces committed human rights abuses.

Mauritania, with a population of 2.28 million, has a generally market-oriented economy based on subsistence farming, herding, and a small commercial sector. Drought, desertification, insect infestation, rapid urbanization, extensive unemployment, pervasive poverty, and a burdensome foreign debt handicap the economy. Inadequate recent rainfall has also contributed to urbanization, further straining government finances. Annual per capita national income has declined in recent years and is estimated at $480 (1995 figure). Mauritania receives foreign assistance from various bilateral and multilateral sources.

The Government's human rights record was poor, and problems remain in certain areas. Democratic institutions are still rudimentary, and the Government circumscribes citizens right to change their government. Police often used brutal methods, including excessive force and torture, as well as arbitrary arrest, illegal searches, and incommunicado prearraignment detention. Pretrial detention is often very lengthy. The Government has failed to bring to justice officials who commit abuses. Prison conditions are harsh and unhealthy. Although the Government has instituted some judicial reforms, the executive continues to exercise significant pressure on the judiciary, and in practice the right to a fair trial frequently is restricted. The Government broadened the scope for opposition activity and improved its access to government-owned media, but continued to seize and suspend publications, and limit freedom of religion. Societal discrimination against women continues and female genital mutilation remains a serious concern. Ethnic tensions are gradually easing, but many members of the Halpulaar, Soninke, and Wolof ethnic groups are underrepresented and feel excluded from effective political representation.

The Government took further steps to resolve a serious abuse from the 1989-91 period, in which approximately 70,000 Mauritanians were expelled or fled, by facilitating cooperation between the Mauritanian Red Crescent Association and the United Nations High Commissioner for Refugees, to assist returnees from the refugee camps in Senegal. The UNHCR estimates that 30,000-35,000 have returned; 10,000-15,000 during the year. The Government has yet to address fully another major abuse from the 1989-91 period, when 503 members of the military were killed, tortured, and maimed, almost entirely from the Halpulaar ethnic group. In 1993 the Parliament passed an amnesty bill to preclude legal pursuit of those responsible. The Government has given pensions to the widows of some of those killed and in 1996 extended that benefit to some of those who survived the purge. However, the Government has not acknowledged responsibility or wrongdoing nor has it provided honorable discharge papers to survivors or other compensation to families of those killed to enable their reintegration into society.

Slavery, in the form of unofficial forced or involuntary servitude, exists. Many persons continue to live in conditions of unofficial paid or unpaid servitude and many persons still consider themselves to be slaves.

RESPECT FOR HUMAN RIGHTS

Section 1. Respect for the Integrity of the Person, Including Freedom From:

a. *Political and Other Extrajudicial Killing.*—There were no reports of political killings, but one person is known to have died while in police custody. A Burkinabe arrested in Nouadhibou in June died in police custody; police stated that the cause of death was suicide, although credible observers believe that police mistreatment was the cause of death.

Extrajudicial killings from past years, primarily of Afro-Mauritanians (members of one of the three sub-Saharan ethnic groups, Halpulaar, Soninke, or Wolof), remained unresolved. The principal example of such killing involves the 1990–91 deaths while in military custody of 503 largely Halpulaar and Soninke military personnel and civilians detained in the investigation of an alleged coup attempt. The military has not released the results of its 1991 internal investigation, and in 1993 the National Assembly passed an amnesty law that prevents any charges from being brought against members of the armed forces, security forces, or other citizens involved in the abuses committed between January 1990 and April 1992. In July 1993, the Government began to provide pension benefits to some of the widows and families of those killed, and in 1996 the Government recognized the prior Government service of some of the civilian survivors and began to pay them pensions. However, the Government has not given military survivors the discharge papers that are necessary for alternative employment.

The Government's failure to bring to justice officials who commit abuses and fail to observe legal procedures has contributed to widespread popular dissatisfaction with the judicial system and the belief that security officials are a force apart from government authority and not subject to legal restraints.

b. *Disappearance.*—There were no reports of politically motivated disappearances.

c. *Torture and Other Cruel, Inhuman, or Degrading Treatment or Punishment.*—The law prohibits torture and other forms of cruel or inhuman punishment, but the police continue on occasion to beat criminal suspects while in custody. Police in some instances used excessive force to break up peaceful demonstrations or disperse crowds. There were credible reports that some of those arrested in June in a crackdown on local drug traffickers were tortured by police during pretrial detention. Methods of torture include beatings, around the clock questioning, and, in one instance, a detainee was subjected to the "jaguar" (in which an individual's hands and feet are bound, the individual is suspended from a pole from his hands and feet, and he is beaten). Authorities have not tried or punished persons suspected of committing such abuses.

Prison conditions are harsh and do not meet minimum international standards. There is severe overcrowding, unsanitary conditions, and inadequate food and medical treatment. The independent press and human rights activists regularly report the deaths of prison inmates; authorities cite natural causes, although witnesses claimed to have evidence of mistreatment. There was also a report of a detainee's death (see Section 1.a.). The central prison in Nouakchott, which was built for a prison population of 200 men, now houses more than 700. Observers report better conditions at the women's prison and children's detention center in Nouakchott. A French nongovernmental organization (NGO), Pharmaciens sans Frontieres, which was asked in 1994 by the Government to coordinate international assistance for a large-scale project to improve overall prison conditions, completed its plans in 1995 and is soliciting international assistance. In conjunction with its recommendations, the Government is enlarging the central prison in Nouakchott, and is building a new prison in Akjoujt.

The Government permits visits by human rights monitors.

d. *Arbitrary Arrest, Detention, or Exile.*—The Constitution provides for due process and the presumption of innocence until proven guilty by an established tribunal. It stipulates that authorities cannot arrest, detain, prosecute, or punish anyone except as provided for under the law. Actual application of these safeguards continued to vary widely from case to case.

The law requires that courts review the legality of a person's detention within 48 hours of arrest. The police may extend the period for another 48 hours, and a prosecutor or court may detain persons for up to 30 days in national security cases. Only after the prosecutor submits charges does a suspect have the right to contact an attorney.

During the June crackdown against drug traffickers, authorities held suspects in prearraignment detention in excess of the legally established limit, but did grant detainees access to counsel and family. There were credible reports that police detained other persons incommunicado and without access to counsel for extended periods prior to arraignment, although human rights activists report that police are showing greater respect for legally mandated procedures. Pretrial detention after arraignment is extensive, and approximately 50 percent of the prison population has not been tried.

Some indicted prisoners are released before trial without explanation; familial, tribal, or political connections may explain some of these cases. There is a provision for granting bail, but it is rarely used.

Occasional reports of arbitrary arrests and intimidation committed by security forces continued, particularly among returned refugees in communities along the Senegal River, but the extent of abuses declined, as the Government, in conjunction with the UNHCR and Mauritanian Red Crescent Society, made efforts to resettle returnees (see Section 2.d.).

The Government does not employ forced exile.

e. *Denial of Fair Public Trial.*—Although the Constitution provides for the independence of the judiciary, in practice the executive branch exercises significant pressure on the judiciary through its ability to appoint and influence judges. In addition, the judicial system's fairness is limited by poorly educated and poorly trained judges who are susceptible to social, financial, tribal, and personal pressures.

The judicial system includes lower, middle, and upper level courts, each with specific jurisdictions. A dual system of courts, one based on modern law and one based on Shari'a, has been replaced by a single system as the country moves to a modernized legal system that is in conformity with the principles of Shari'a. Departmental, regional, and labor tribunals are the principal instances at the lower level. The 53 departmental tribunals, composed of a president and magistrates with traditional Islamic legal training, hear civil cases involving sums less than $72 (10,000 UM) and family issues (e.g., domestic, divorce, and inheritance cases). Thirteen regional tribunals accept appeals in commercial and civil matters from the departmental tribunals and hear misdemeanors. Three labor tribunals, composed of a president and two assessors (one who represents labor and one who represents employers), serve as final arbiters for labor disputes. At the middle level, three courts of appeal, each with two chambers (a civil and commercial chamber, and a mixed chamber) hear appeals from the regional courts and have original jurisdiction for felonies. Nominally independent, the Supreme Court is headed by a magistrate appointed to a 5-year term by the President. The Supreme Court reviews decisions and rulings made by the courts of appeal to determine their compliance with the law and procedure. Constitutional review is the purview of a six-member Constitutional Council, composed of three members named by the President, two by the National Assembly President, and one by the Senate President. Annual review of judicial decisions is undertaken by the Supreme Council of the Magistrature, over which the President presides; the President and Senior Vice President of the Supreme Court, the Minister of Justice, three magistrates, and representatives from the Senate and National Assembly are members of this Council. The annual review is intended to determine whether courts applied the law correctly and followed proper procedures.

All defendants, regardless of the court or their ability to pay, have the legal right to representation by counsel during the proceedings, which are open to the public. If defendants lack the ability to pay for counsel, the court appoints an attorney, from a list prepared by the national order of lawyers, who provides defense free of charge. The law provides that defendants may confront witnesses, present evidence, and appeal their sentences, and these rights are generally observed in practice.

Because Shari'a provides the legal principles upon which the law and legal procedure are based, courts do not in all cases treat women as equals of men, for example, the testimony of two women is necessary to equal that of one man. In addition, in awarding an indemnity to the family of a woman who has been killed, the courts grant only half the amount they would award for a man's death. There are no female magistrates. However, for commercial and other modern issues not specifically addressed by Shari'a, the law and courts treat women and men equally.

In January the Government, with international assistance, began a far-reaching effort to improve judicial performance and independence. A training program to improve the skills of magistrates was begun, and in May the Government increased the salaries of magistrates and police officials in an attempt to combat corruption and improve independence.

In January, in an important display of judicial independence, the December 1995 convictions of Baathists for membership in an illegal political organization were overturned by the appellate judge, whose decision was based largely on his finding that security forces and the prosecution had failed to follow legally required procedures for interrogation and finding evidence.

There were no reports of political prisoners.

f. *Arbitrary Interference With Privacy, Family, Home, or Correspondence.*—The law requires judicial warrants in order to execute home searches, but the authorities often ignore this requirement. During the detention of drug traffickers, authorities conducted searches of their residences without warrants and also failed to submit the required reports on the results of these searches to the prosecutor.

Government surveillance of dissidents and the political opposition is believed to continue, although the extent to which the Government used informants is unknown.

Section 2. *Respect for Civil Liberties, Including:*

a. *Freedom of Speech and Press.*—The Constitution provides for freedom of speech and the press, but the Government continues to restrict these rights through prepublication press censorship by the Interior Ministry. NGO's and the privately owned press openly criticized the Government and its leaders. Antigovernment tracts, newsletters, and petitions circulate widely in Nouakchott and other towns.

All newspapers and political parties must register with the Ministry of the Interior. Although the Government did not refuse to register any journal, it suspended for 3 months the right to publish of two independent weeklies, Mauritanie Nouvelles in April and Le Calame in October, in both their French and Arabic editions. Some 37 independent, privately owned newspapers were published during the year, many on an irregular basis. For the most part, these journals are weeklies, published in Arabic or French, and reach limited audiences. Mauritanie Nouvelles experimented for several months with daily publication, but for financial reasons reverted to weekly publication. Several journals increased the frequency of their publication prior to the National Assembly elections. Readership of the independent press increased, in particular during the electoral period. Independent journals reported openly and critically on the opposition and government alike, and published party declarations and tracts without government censure or restraint.

The Ministry of the Interior reviews all newspaper copy prior to publication. The Press Law provides that the Minister of the Interior can stop publication of material discrediting Islam or threatening national security. Although the Ministry did not excise material from journals or otherwise censor individual articles, the authorities seized 23 individual issues of various journals; by comparison, in 1995 14 individual issues were seized. The Government provided no specific reason for the seizures.

The electronic media (radio and television) and two daily newspapers, Horizon and Chaab, are government owned and operated. Radio is the most important medium in reaching the public, and the official media strongly support government policies. The law requires both radio and television to provide equal broadcast time to all political parties during electoral campaigns, which they did during the Senate and National Assembly elections. Although government-owned Horizon and Chaab offered to publish free of charge a limited number of communiques by political parties, they refused during the electoral campaign to publish some opposition party declarations because they viewed them as inflammatory. Opposition parties' access to radio broadcast facilities is sharply limited at other times. However, in a significant departure from past practice, government-owned media provided limited but factual coverage of the activities of opposition political parties prior to the National Assembly elections. The Government granted permission to a French radio network to transmit locally, but denied private applications to establish radio stations.

The one university is government funded and operated. Academic freedom is generally respected, and there were no cases in which the Government prevented research or publication, or censored lectures.

b. *Freedom of Peaceful Assembly and Association.*—The Constitution provides for freedom of assembly and association, and for the most part the Government respects these rights, although there were occasions when it restricted public gatherings. The law requires that all recognized political parties and NGO's apply to the local prefect for permission for large meetings or assemblies. Permission is generally freely granted, and although there were no known instances in which a prefect denied permission for gatherings of opposition political parties, authorities impeded access to some meetings. Although the two recognized labor confederations held Labor Day rallies, authorities in Nouakchott denied permission to the Free Confederation of Mauritanian Workers (CLTM) to march, on the grounds that it was not recognized by the Government (see Section 6.a.).

The number of political parties, labor unions, and NGO's continued to increase. Some 21 political parties and a wide array of NGO's, many of them highly critical of the Government, met openly, issued public statements, and chose their own leadership. The Government in January issued new regulations to facilitate the establishment of NGO's engaged in economic and social development, environmental protection, and humanitarian assistance. These streamlined procedures facilitated the recognition of several existing NGO's and led to the establishment and recognition of a large number of new NGO's. The Government has not yet granted some NGO's official standing but allowed them to operate. Among these is the Mauritanian Association for Human Rights; the Government claims that it appeals to specific ethnic groups, namely the Afro-Mauritanian community, and is a potentially divisive force. The Government also has not recognized two antislavery NGO's, the independent "SOS–Esclaves" and the progovernment "National Committee for the Eradication of the Vestiges of Slavery in Mauritania." However, the Government allows these associations to function, issue reports and statements, and, in the case of SOS–Esclaves, assist individuals in their dealings with the Government to resolve problems.

c. *Freedom of Religion.*—The 1991 Constitution established Mauritania as an Islamic republic and decrees that Islam is the religion of its people and the State. All but a small number of Mauritanians are Sunni Muslims and are prohibited by their religion from converting to another religion. The Government prohibits proselytizing by non-Muslims. Christian churches have been established in Nouakchott, Atar, Zouerate, Nouadhibou, and Rosso. The expatriate community of Christians and the few Mauritanian citizens who are considered Christians from birth practice their religion openly and freely in these churches. Mauritanian Muslims freely attend Christian weddings and funerals when invited and on occasion have performed the formal witness role at Catholic weddings. The possession of Bibles and other Christian religious materials in private homes is not illegal, although there are confirmed cases in which authorities have detained and harassed individuals who have shared such materials with others.

d. *Freedom of Movement Within the Country, Foreign Travel, Emigration, and Repatriation.*—The Constitution provides for freedom of movement and residence within all parts of the territory, and guarantees the freedom to enter and leave. Historically there were few restrictions on travel in Mauritania's nomadic society. With urbanization and automobile travel, the Government set up regular road checkpoints where the Gendarmerie checks papers of travelers. The Government imposed no nighttime curfews. There were no reported cases of persons being denied passports for political reasons.

The Government cooperates with the Office of the United Nations High Commissioner for Refugees (UNHCR) and other humanitarian organizations in assisting refugees. The UNHCR operates a camp for Malians in eastern Mauritania. Refugees from other countries reside in the country as well. The Government has provided first asylum to Malians and others in the recent past. While many Malians have returned to their country, some 25,000 continue to receive first asylum.

Of the approximately 70,000 Afro-Mauritanians who were expelled by Mauritania or fled to Senegal during the 1989–91 crisis, the UNHCR estimates that 30,000 to 35,000 have returned; 10,000 to 15,000 of these in 1996. An estimated 50,000 to 55,000 refugees remain in refugee settlements in Senegal, including 15,000 children born there since 1989. Many of the 15,000 Mauritanian Halpulaar who took refuge in Mali during the crisis have integrated into the population and 5,000 are estimated to have returned to Mauritania. The UNHCR discontinued at the end of 1994 the limited assistance it had been providing to them. According to the UNHCR, the return of refugees is accelerating and the Government is making satisfactory efforts to assist those who return from Senegal. In June the UNHCR and the Ministry of Interior signed an agreement under which the UNHCR will provide assistance for government efforts to issue identity and other documents to returnees in the riverine area. Authorities actively identified projects that were undertaken by the UNHCR, the Mauritanian Red Crescent Society (CRM), and NGO's under the UNHCR-financed "special plan for rapid insertion" to assist returnees. The Government began to issue identification cards to some, and returned land, houses, and even personal property when it could be located and identified. Many whole villages and almost all Peulh (nomadic herders of the Halpulaar ethnic group) have returned.

Section 3. Respect for Political Rights: The Right of Citizens to Change Their Government

The Constitution provides citizens with the right to change their government, but the Government circumscribes it in practice. The 1992 multiparty election of a civilian president ended 14 years of military rule, but both the opposition and international observers concluded that the elections were fraudulent. The military continued to provide strong support to the regime. Although all ministerial-level positions were filled by civilians, some members of the former Military Council, in addition to President Taya, remained in positions of power within the executive branch, the National Assembly, the armed forces, and government-owned enterprises.

In the country's first multiparty legislative elections held in October, only 1 opposition and 6 independent candidates were elected to the 79-member National Assembly. The outcome of the elections was marred by fraud on all sides, pervasive intervention by government and election officials, and use of government resources to support candidates from the ruling PRDS party. Although the Government made procedural improvements that resulted in orderly voting, the elections represent a backward step in the country's efforts to establish a pluralist democracy.

Women have the right to vote, and are active in election campaigns, although few are in positions of political leadership. There are seven women in senior government positions, including one Cabinet member, one mayor, and several in the office of the Presidency. There are three female members of the National Assembly (including one Haratine and one Soninke from the Forgeron caste), but no female members in the Senate. Halpulaars, Soninkes, and Wolofs are underrepresented in senior Government positions. Of the Government's 23 ministerial posts, 1 incumbent is Haratine, 3 Halpulaar, 1 Soninke, and 1 Wolof; the remainder are of either White Moor or of mixed White Moor/Haratine ethnicity (see Section 5).

Section 4. *Governmental Attitude Regarding International and Nongovernmental Investigation of Alleged Violations of Human Rights*

There are an increasing number of human rights organizations. The oldest is the Mauritanian League for Human Rights, an independent but government-recognized body. A second and still unrecognized organization, the Mauritanian Human Rights Association (AMDH), while not affiliated with the opposition, has many opposition members. It has been more critical of the Government than the League, particularly on the unresolved abuses of the 1989–91 period.

Various other organizations address human rights issues. The pan-African organization Gerddes-Africa, or International Study and Research Group on Democracy and Economic and Social Development in Africa, established a branch in Mauritania in 1994. Two other groups, SOS–Esclaves and the National Committee for the Struggle Against the Vestiges of Slavery in Mauritania, focus their efforts on overcoming the country's vestiges of slavery (see Section 6.c.). SOS–Esclaves was particularly active in drawing public attention to this issue, issuing in March a report detailing its activities and a petition appealing to national and international audiences to support measures to eradicate slavery. SOS–Esclaves also intervened effectively with government authorities to push resolution of some of the cases, in particular child custody cases, brought to the organization by former slaves.

The Committee of Solidarity with the Victims of Repression in Mauritania is concerned with the plight of the 1989 expellees. The Consultative Group for the Return of the Refugees was founded to promote the return of the remaining Mauritanian refugees in Senegal. The Collective of Workers Victims of the 1989 Events seeks redress for government employees who lost their jobs in the events of 1989. The Committee of the Widows and the Collective of Survivors focus on the sufferings of the victims of the 1990–91 military purge and their families. The Collective of Survivors of Political Detention and Torture (CRAPOCIT) was established this year to seek redress for abuses committed during the 1986–87 period. These, and other groups of individuals with common concerns, function openly and actively, but their efforts are somewhat circumscribed because they are not officially recognized (see Section 2.b.).

Representatives from a variety of European, African, American, and Arab human rights organizations visited Mauritania. The International Federation of Human Rights dispatched a legal expert to observe the trial of Baathists at the behest of the AMDH. The African Commission on Human and Peoples Rights, which visited for 10 days in June, met with government officials and activists and subsequently presented its report to President Taya. The Senegalese human rights group RADO visited, as did the Arab Institute for Human Rights (Tunis), the Union of Arab Jurists, and the Arab League for Human Rights. Representatives of the American NGO, Africare, visited in August. Local human rights activists report that these groups were allowed free access and that there were no reports of harassment or reprisal against Mauritanian interlocutors during or following the visits.

Section 5. Discrimination Based on Race, Sex, Religion, Disability, Language, or Social Status

The Constitution provides for equality before the law for all citizens, regardless of race, national origin, sex, or social status, and prohibits racially or ethnically based propaganda. In practice, the Government often favors individuals on the basis of ethnic and tribal affiliation, social status, and political ties. Discrimination against women, strongly rooted in traditional society, is endemic, although the situation is improving.

Women.—Human rights monitors and women lawyers report that physical mistreatment of women by their husbands is limited. The police and judiciary occasionally intervene in domestic abuses, but women in traditional society usually do not seek legal redress, relying instead upon family and ethnic group members to resolve domestic disputes. The incidence of rape is low. It occurs, but newspaper accounts of attacks are rare.

Traditional forms of mistreatment of women continue, mostly in isolated rural communities, but these practices appear to be on the decline. Such mistreatment consists of forced feeding of adolescent girls (gavage) and female genital mutilation.

Women have legal rights to property and child custody, and, among the more modern and urbanized population, these rights are recognized. In accordance with Shari'a, marriage and divorce do not require the woman's consent, polygyny is allowed, and a woman does not have the right to refuse her husband's wish to marry additional wives. In practice, polygyny is very rare among Moors although common among Afro-Mauritanians. Arranged marriages are also increasingly rare, particularly among the Moor population. Women frequently initiate the termination of a marriage, which most often is done by husband or wife by repudiation rather than divorce. It is also common in Moor society for a woman to obtain, at the time of marriage, a contractual agreement that stipulates that her husband must agree to end their marriage if he chooses an additional wife. The rate of divorce among Moors is estimated to be 37 percent and the remarriage rate after divorce 72.5 percent.

Women still face some legal discrimination. For example, the testimony of two women is necessary to equal that of one man, and the value placed on women's lives in court-awarded indemnities is only half the amount awarded for a man's death (see Section 1.e.). Women do not face legal discrimination, however, in other areas not specifically addressed by Shari'a.

There are no legal restrictions on the education of girls and women. Some 75 percent of school age girls attended school in 1995, up from 44.8 percent in 1990 (compared with 85.9 percent for boys, up from 58.3 percent). Increasing numbers of women attend the university, women made up 14.9 percent of the university's 1992–93 enrollment.

The Government seeks to open new employment opportunities for women in areas that are traditionally filled by men, such as health care, communications, police, and customs services.

The law provides that men and women receive equal pay for equal work. While not universally applied in practice, the two largest employers, the civil service and state mining company, respect this law. In the modern wage sector, women also receive generous family benefits, including 3 months of maternity leave.

Children.—The Government does not require attendance at school and a lack of financial resources limits available educational opportunities. However, almost all children, regardless of sex or ethnic group, attend Koranic school from the ages of five to seven and gain at least rudimentary skills in reading and writing Arabic in addition to memorizing Koranic verses.

The law makes special provisions for the protection of children's welfare, and the Government has programs to care for abandoned children. These programs are, however, hampered by inadequate funding. The Government relies on foreign donors in such areas as child immunization. Moreover, it does not enforce existing child labor laws, and children perform a significant amount of labor in support of family activities. There are isolated but credible press reports of parents agreeing, in exchange for money, to send their young children to work in foreign countries. The most common cases are of boys aged 8 to 10 years sent to work as "jockeys" or herders in the United Arab Emirates or Qatar (see Section 6.d.).

Female genital mutilation (FGM) is widely condemned by international health experts as damaging to both physical and psychological health. It is performed most often on young girls, often on the seventh day after birth and almost always before the age of 6 months, and it is practiced among all ethnic groups except the Wolof. Reportedly, 95 percent of Soninke and Halpulaar women undergo FGM, as do 30 percent of Moor women. Local experts agree that the least severe form of excision is practiced, and not infibulation, the most severe form of FGM. Evidence indicates that the practice of FGM is decreasing in the modern urban sector. The Government does not attempt to interfere with these practices, but does not allow them in hospitals. It is the clear public policy of the Government, through the Secretariat of Women's Affairs, that the practice should be stopped. Public health workers and NGO's educate women to the dangers of FGM and to the fact that FGM is not a requirement of Islam. A recent, officially produced Guide to the Rights of Women in Mauritania (with religious endorsement) stresses that Islam does not require FGM and that if medical experts warn against it for medical reasons, it should not be done.

People With Disabilities.—The law does not specifically provide for people with disabilities, and the Government does not mandate preference in employment or education or public accessibility for disabled persons. It does, however, provide some rehabilitation and other assistance for the disabled.

National/Racial/Ethnic Minorities.—Ethnic and cultural tension and discrimination arise from the geographic and cultural line between traditionally nomadic Arabic-speaking (Hassaniya) Moor herders and Afro-Mauritanian sedentary cultivators of the Halpulaar, Soninke, and Wolof ethnic groups in the south. Although culturally homogeneous, the Moors are divided among numerous ethno-linguistic clan groups and are racially distinguished as White Moors and Black Moors. The majority of what are known as Black Moors are Haratine, literally "one who has been freed," although some Black Moor families were never enslaved. The Halpulaar (the largest Afro-Mauritanian group), the Wolof, and the Soninke ethnic groups are concentrated in the south. "White" Moors, large numbers of whom are dark-skinned after centuries of intermarriage with members of Sub-Saharan African groups, dominate positions in government, business, and the clergy. The Halpulaar, Soninke, and Wolof ethnic groups are underrepresented in the military and security sectors.

Ethnic tensions surfaced dramatically in the mass expulsions of Afro-Mauritanians in 1989–90 and the purge of Afro-Mauritanians from the military in 1991. Few regained their positions.

The Constitution designates Arabic along with Pulaar, Soninke, and Wolof as Mauritania's national languages. Successive governments—both civil and military—have pursued various policies of "Arabization" in the schools and in the workplace. Non-Arabic-speaking ethnic groups have protested this policy, as have Arabic-speaking groups that want their children to obtain a bilingual Arabic-French education. As a consequence, the availability of bilingual Arabic-French programs is increasing. Elementary school classes are also available in the other national languages in some localities.

Overt tensions between ethnic groups have lessened since the explosive ethnic violence of 1989–91, when the Government conducted extrajudicial expulsions and purges of the security forces clearly based on ethnicity. Nevertheless, some hostility and bitterness persist between ethnic groups although political coalitions among the groups are increasingly important.

Section 6. Worker Rights

a. The Right of Association.—The Constitution provides for freedom of association and the right of citizens to join any political or labor organization. All workers except members of the military and police are free to associate in and establish unions at the local and national levels.

Prior to the 1993 amendment of the Labor Code, which repealed provisions restricting trade union pluralism, the government-controlled labor central, the Union of Mauritanian Workers (UTM), was the only labor confederation allowed by law. Since 1993 two new labor confederations have formed and the UTM, which many workers still view as closely allied with the Government and the PRDS, has lost ground to these organizations. The Government recognized a new confederation in 1994, the General Confederation of Mauritanian Workers (CGTM). The CGTM is not affiliated with any political party, although most of its members favor the opposition; it continued to gain considerably in strength during the year, in part because of the UTM's internal discord. The Government, which previously subsidized only the UTM, began in the spring to provide funds also to the CGTM, proportional to its membership. Both confederations provided representatives to the country's three labor tribunals, and the CGTM was included in most government deliberative or consultative bodies in which the UTM alone has participated in the past. A third labor confederation, the Free Confederation of Mauritanian Workers (CLTM), formed in 1995, has not been recognized by the Government but is nevertheless allowed to function. Several independent trade unions, in particular three for teachers at the elementary, secondary, and university levels, were also active.

The bulk of the labor force is in the informal sector, with most workers engaged in subsistence agriculture and animal husbandry; only 25 percent are employed in the wage sector. However, nearly 90 percent of the industrial and commercial workers are organized. The law provides workers with the right to strike, and there were several strikes and partial work stoppages. Most strikes were settled quickly due to limited worker and union resources. Moreover, the law provides for tripartite arbitration committees composed of union, business, and government representatives. Once all parties agree to arbitration, the committee may impose binding arbitration that automatically terminates any strike.

International trade union activity increased. The Government included both CGTM and UTM representatives in its delegation to the International Labor Organization in June, and the ILO conducted an extensive series of training workshops in which both confederations participated. The CGTM and UTM have applied for membership in the ICFTU, the UTM participated in regional labor organizations, and the CGTM was accepted as a member of the Organization of African Trade Union Unity (OATUU).

The Government did not petition the United States for reconsideration of Generalized System of Preferences (GSP) trade privileges. The United States revoked GSP benefits in July 1993 for failure to respect freedom of association or to take steps to eliminate forced labor, including vestiges of slavery (see Section 6.c.).

b. *The Right to Organize and Bargain Collectively.*—The law provides that unions may freely organize workers without government or employer interference. General or sectoral agreements on wages, working conditions, and social and medical benefits are negotiated in tripartite discussions and formalized by government decree. Wages and other benefits can also be negotiated bilaterally between employer and union and the results of such negotiations are filed with the Directorate of Labor.

Laws provide workers with protection against antiunion discrimination and employees or employers may bring labor disputes to three-person labor tribunals administered jointly by the Ministries of Justice and Labor with the participation of union and employer representatives.

There are no export processing zones.

c. *Prohibition of Forced or Compulsory Labor.*—Mauritanians continue to suffer the effects of generations of the practice of slavery in Moor society, and of caste distinctions that include slaves in country's Afro-Mauritanian ethnic communities. Slavery was officially abolished three times in Mauritania, most recently by the post-independence government in 1980. Nevertheless, there are many individuals who continue to live in conditions of paid or unpaid servitude, and many persons still consider themselves to be slaves.

Slavery in the form of officially sanctioned forced or involuntary servitude, is extremely rare, and a system of slavery in which government and society join to force individuals to serve masters no longer exists. Adult males can no longer be obliged by law to remain with their masters nor can they be returned if they leave. Adult females with children, however, may have greater difficulties and may be compelled by pressures other than physical force to remain in a condition of servitude. For example, in some cases masters refuse to allow children to accompany their mothers; in other cases the greater economic responsibility of a family may be the principal impediment to seeking a new life. Children's legal status is more tenuous than that of adults.

There are occasional confirmed cases of "transfers" of individuals—often children—from one employer or master to another, usually of the same family. Reports of sales are rare, cannot be confirmed, and are confined to past years.

The Government's record in cases in which an individual's civil rights are affected because of his or her status as a former slave is extremely weak. Punishment is extremely rare for individuals who in such cases break laws (e.g., those that prohibit detention of an individual against his or her will by another individual, or kidnaping) and there were no known instances this year in which the Government punished individuals for such infractions. Nevertheless, when complaints are filed with the Government to remedy such cases, it generally intervenes in accordance with the law, although sometimes only after considerable prodding and passage of time. When called upon to assist or adjudicate, administrative officials or courts on occasion rule in favor of former masters (e.g., in child custody cases in which a former master claims parentage, or in inheritance cases) if it finds this justified because of the facts of the case. A mother appealed the February ruling by a magistrate in Brakna giving custody of her two children to a former master who claimed to be their father. The appeals court had not ruled on the case by year's end. According to the Minister of Justice, the appeals court is still establishing the facts in the case, in particular, whether the former master was married to the mother. Determination could be problematic in a country where there is polygyny, "secret" marriages, no written records, and divorce by repudiation. The court is willing to pursue the concept of genetic testing to determine paternity.

Countless numbers of citizens, whether Moor or Afro-Mauritanian, continue to call themselves "slave" even though they are legally free to live and work where they choose. This is exacerbated by the government's extremely weak record of enforcing the ban on slavery. However, many still live with masters or former masters. Extremely difficult economic conditions provide few economic alternatives for many and leave some former slaves open to exploitation by former masters. Significant numbers, especially in the cities, work for former masters for a pittance or in exchange for room and board, clothing, and medical benefits. Invisible but crippling psychological bonds make it difficult for many individuals who have generations of forbearers who were slaves to think of themselves as free from former masters. Because of religious instruction in the past, some individuals continue to link themselves to former masters and fear religious sanction if that bond is broken by anyone else.

"Slave" as a caste designation is common to all ethnic groups—sub-Saharan Afro-Mauritanian groups as well as Moor. The legacy of these caste distinctions continues to affect the status and opportunities available to members of these non-Moor communities. In some groups, for example, individuals of a higher caste who seek to marry someone of a lower caste may be barred by the community and in Soninkie communities members of the slave caste cannot be buried in the same cemetery as other castes.

Three NGO's, SOS-Esclaves, the National Committee for the Struggle Against the Vestiges of Slavery in Mauritania, and the Initiative for the Support of the Activities of the President, had as their focus issues related to the history of Slavery in Mauritania. Of these, SOS-Esclaves was particularly active in bringing to public attention cases in which it found the rights of former slaves to have been abridged, and in assisting former slaves in their difficulties with former masters. Other human rights and civic action NGO's also follow this issue closely. The independent press which includes journals that are published by Haratines and Afro-Mauritanians who emphasize issues of importance to these ethnic groups, is also quick to report any incident that comes to its attention in which the rights of former slaves have not been respected.

Inheritance disputes between Haratines and the descendants of their former masters arose several times and were adjudicated in court. While most such disputes are decided in accordance with the law and rule that the descendants of the former slaves should inherit their property, the independent press reported one case in which a magistrate (Qadi) in Nema in 1994 ruled in favor of the former master; the implementation of this ruling was blocked in 1995 while the former slave's descendants appealed. The case was decided against the children by the Supreme Court in 1995. The Minister of Justice has ordered the courts to consult with each other and review their decisions. He said that contrary to allegations, although the case is between Haratines and White Moors, it does not involve the descendants of slaves and the descendants of masters. Rather, it is a land tenure dispute, which is "very common" in Mauritania, and one that in which the disputants had no past relationship of master and slave.

Inheritance disputes between Haratines and the descendants of their former masters are now adjudicated in court. A 1994 land inheritance case which ruled against Haratines who wanted title to a master's property is under review. The results of this review remain outstanding.

In a 1995 case, the Supreme Council of the Magistrature removed a magistrate from the bench because he ruled, contrary to the law, that a former master, rather than the former slave's descendants, should inherit the possessions of an ex-slave. On December 28, the Supreme Council of the Magistrature removed the magistrate in Kankossa from the bench because he refused to accept the provisions of the 1980 law abolishing slavery. The removal of this magistrate reinforces to other judges that the provisions of the 1980 law apply.

d. *Minimum Age for Employment of Children.*—Education is not compulsory, and for financial and other reasons, 20 percent of school-age children do not regularly attend government schools. Labor law specifies that no child under the age of 13 years may be employed in the agricultural sector without the permission of the Minister of Labor, nor under the age of 15 years in the nonagricultural sector. The law provides that employed children of age 14 to 16 years should receive 70 percent of the minimum wage, and those from age 17 to 18 years should receive 90 percent of the minimum wage. The Labor Ministry's few inspectors provide only limited enforcement of child labor laws (see Section 5).

Young children in the countryside commonly pursue herding, cultivation, fishing, and other significant labor in support of their families' activities. In keeping with longstanding tradition, many children serve apprenticeships in small industries and in the informal sector.

   e. *Acceptable Conditions of Work.*—The minimum wage for adults is approximately $67 (8,300 ouguiya) per month and has not been raised since October 1992. It is difficult for the average family to meet its minimum needs and maintain a decent standard of living at this salary. The standard, legal, nonagricultural workweek may not exceed either 40 hours or 6 days without overtime compensation, which is paid at rates that are graduated according to the number of supplemental hours worked. The Labor Directorate of the Ministry of Labor is responsible for enforcement of the labor laws, but in practice inadequate funding limits the effectiveness of the Directorate's enforcement.

   The Ministry of Labor is also responsible for enforcing safety standards but does so inconsistently, due to inadequate funding. In principle workers can remove themselves from hazardous conditions without risking loss of employment; in practice, they cannot.

MAURITIUS

Mauritius is a parliamentary democracy governed by a Prime Minister, a Council of Ministers, and a National Assembly. The Head of State is the President, who is nominated by the Prime Minister and confirmed by the Assembly, and whose powers are largely ceremonial. Fair and orderly national and local elections, supervised by an independent commission, take place at regular intervals, most recently in 1995. The judiciary is independent, there are numerous political parties, both large and small, and partisan politics are open and robust.

A paramilitary Special Mobile Force and Special Supporting Units under civilian control are responsible for internal security. These forces, under the command of the Commissioner of Police, are backed by a general duty police force. They are largely apolitical and generally well-trained, but the police committed some human rights abuses.

The economy is based on labor-intensive, export-oriented manufacturing (mainly textiles), as well as sugar and tourism. About 85 percent of arable land is planted with sugar cane. There is a generally high standard of living; annual per capita income is approximately $3,195. The country weathered well the global economic slowdown of the early 1990's and is now attempting to diversify its economy by promoting investment in new sectors, such as electronics, and developing the country as a regional financial center.

The Government's human rights record improved, but problem areas remained. There continued to be occasional reports that police abused suspects and detainees. The Government continued to use the National Intelligence Unit to monitor opposition party activities. On at least two occasions the police denied demonstration permits, which are normally routinely granted. Violence against women and child labor appeared to be on the rise, despite government efforts to address these problems.

RESPECT FOR HUMAN RIGHTS

Section 1. Respect for the Integrity of the Person, Including Freedom From:

   a. *Political and Extrajudicial Killing.*—There were no reports of political killings. The investigation into the 1994 case of a suspect in police custody who burned to death in his cell is complete but the district magistrate has not communicated his findings to the Director of Public Prosecutions.

   In December a suspect held in a police holding cell for 3 nights died of multiple blows. The Commissioner of Police called for an investigation, but observers complained that the police should not be responsible for investigating themselves in such matters.

   b. *Disappearance.*—There were no reports of politically motivated disappearances.

   c. *Torture and Other Cruel, Inhuman, or Degrading Treatment or Punishment.*— The law prohibits torture and inhuman punishment, but there were several unofficial reports of police brutality, involving mistreatment of individuals on the street as well as of suspects in custody. One prisoner died in custody as result of multiple blows. (See Section 1.a.).

   Because of the Police Commissioner's crackdown on crime, prisons have become overcrowded and prison sanitation inadequate.

   d. *Arbitrary Arrest, Detention, or Exile.*—The Constitution prohibits arbitrary arrest, detention, or exile and the Government generally observes these prohibitions. A 1994 constitutional amendment allows the police to hold a person arrested or detained for a drug offense without bail until a final determination has been made in the case. Parliament has not enacted implementing legislation or otherwise specified which drug offenses will be covered by this amendment (see Section 1.e.).

The Government does not use exile as a means of political control.

e. *Denial of Fair Public Trial.*—The Constitution provides for an independent judiciary, and the Government generally respects this provision in practice. Some critics believed that the executive interfered with the judiciary. Legal experts noted concern about overt manipulation of the judiciary as well as political influence over the Commissioner of Police, the Director of Public Prosecutions, and the Anticorruption Tribunal.

The judicial system consists of the Supreme Court, which has appellate powers, and a series of lower courts. Final appeal may be made to the Judicial Committee in the United Kingdom (the Privy Council). There are no political or military courts. The judiciary provides citizens with a fair judicial process.

Defendants have the right to private or court-appointed counsel. The 1995 draft dangerous drugs act, which would permit law enforcement authorities to hold suspected drug traffickers for up to 36 hours without access to bail or legal counsel, is being examined by a select committee before it is considered by the National Assembly. The constitutionality of the law may be questioned.

There were no reports of political prisoners.

f. *Arbitrary Interference With Privacy, Family, Home, or Correspondence.*—The sanctity of the home is provided for in law and generally respected in practice. Search of personal property or premises is allowed only under clearly specified conditions by court order or by police action to stop a crime in progress. The Government's intelligence apparatus continued to carry out illegal surveillance of local opposition leaders and other major figures.

Section 2. Respect for Civil Liberties, Including:

a. *Freedom of Speech and Press.*—The Constitution provides for freedom of speech and of the press, and the Government generally respects these rights in practice. Debate in the National Assembly is lively and open. There were occasional complaints of government influence in editorial policies, but more than a dozen privately owned daily, weekly, and monthly newspapers presented varying political viewpoints, and they expressed partisan views freely. The Government has the ability to counter press criticism by using strict libel laws; however, the Government did not use these laws to inhibit the press in 1996. Libel suits between private parties are common.

The Government monopoly in broadcasting continued, after the Ramgoolam Government took office in December 1995 and postponed introduction of legislation to liberalize the radio and television industries, saying that it needed to review the 1995 report that the previous Government had commissioned. Television and radio news reporting maintained a progovernment slant which drew sharp criticism from newspaper editors. Under a new management team, Mauritius Broadcasting Corporation began to allow opposition figures slightly more air time. "Sky News" from the United Kingdom and "Canal Plus" from France are available to the public on a subscription basis.

The Government generally respects academic freedom but has occasionally censored books, usually citing national security reasons.

b. *Freedom of Peaceful Assembly and Association.*—The Constitution provides for these rights, and the Government generally respects them in practice. Police permission is required for demonstrations and mass meetings; such permission is rarely refused and groups have the right to challenge denials. The Commissioner of Police denied at least two permits for demonstrations. One denial was based on a parliamentary act disallowing public gatherings on days during which the Parliament is sitting, although exceptions to the act had been made in the past. The permit denial was not delivered at least 48 hours prior to the planned demonstration, as is customary, and police arrested 11 labor leaders who attended. Their cases were pending.

c. *Freedom of Religion.*—The Constitution provides for freedom of religion, and the Government respects this right in practice.

d. *Freedom of Movement Within the Country, Foreign Travel, Emigration, and Repatriation.*—The Constitution provides for these rights, and the Government respects them in practice.

There are no refugees, and the Government deals with asylum requests on a case by case basis. The issue of the provision of first asylum has never arisen. There were no reports of forced return of persons to a country where they feared persecution.

Section 3. Respect for Political Rights: The Right of Citizens to Change Their Government

The Constitution provides citizens with the right peacefully to change their government, and citizens exercise this right in practice. Free and fair elections based on universal suffrage were held in December 1995. The opposition coalition won all elected seats in the National Assembly, and Labor Party leader Navinchandra Ramgoolam was sworn in as Prime Minister, replacing Anerood Jugnauth, who had led the Government since 1982.

The remote and isolated islands of Agalega and St. Brandon are an exception to universal suffrage. Their nearly 500 citizens are not registered as voters and have no representation in Parliament.

In the National Assembly, up to eight members are appointed through a "best loser" system to ensure that all ethnic groups are represented. Political parties often match the ethnicity of their candidates to the ethnic composition of particular electoral districts.

Six of the 66 members of the Assembly are women.

Section 4. Governmental Attitude Regarding International and Nongovernmental Investigation of Alleged Violations of Human Rights

A variety of human rights groups operate without government restriction, investigating and publishing their findings on human rights cases. Government officials are cooperative and responsive to their views.

In October Mauritius hosted the 20th Ordinary Session of the African Commission on Human and Peoples' Rights. Mauritian NGO's actively participated in the NGO workshop that preceded the event. Issues such as the Dangerous Drug Act and stringent immigration policies were debated openly.

Section 5. Discrimination Based on Race, Sex, Religion, Disability, Language, or Social Status

The Constitution specifically prohibits discrimination on the basis of race, caste, place of origin, political opinion, color, creed, or sex. The Government generally respects these provisions.

Women.—Violence against women, particularly spousal abuse, is widespread and increasing, according to the Ministry of Women's Rights and Family Welfare, attorneys, and NGO's. In 1995 the number of reported cases of domestic violence against women rose to 966 compared with 425 in 1994. In the first half of 1996, 1,062 cases were reported to Children and Women Protection unit. The Government is working to increase awareness of the problem and to provide relief for victims by providing counseling and temporary shelter. It is also promulgating a law that would specifically address domestic violence. There are no special legal provisions concerning family violence. Police are generally reluctant to become involved in cases of spousal abuse.

Women have traditionally occupied a subordinate role in society, and societal discrimination continues. Nearly half of Mauritian women work outside the home.

Children.—The Government placed strong emphasis on the health and welfare of children, and displayed a commitment to expand educational opportunities for children. Reported incidents of child abuse are infrequent and isolated, although private voluntary organizations claim that the problem is more widespread than publicly acknowledged. At present, most government programs are administered by the state-funded National Children's Council, which provides counseling and investigates reports of child abuse as well as remedial action to protect affected children.

People With Disabilities.—There is no discrimination against disabled persons in employment, education, or in the provision of other state services. The law requires organizations which employ more than 10 people to set aside at least 3 percent of their positions for people with disabilities. The law does not, however, require that work sites be accessible to the disabled, making it difficult for people with disabilities to fill many jobs. There is no law mandating access to public buildings or facilities.

National/Racial/Ethnic Minorities.—Tensions between the Hindu majority and Creole and Muslim minorities persist. A 1995 law that would have favored Hindu children in educational opportunities brought racial tension to the forefront during the December 1995 electoral campaign. The law was struck down by the Supreme Court and the tension eased, but bitterness remains, and the Creole and Muslim minorities attempted to keep public attention focused on alleged societal injustices against them. In March a soccer match erupted into a riot when spectators realized that Mauritian Muslims were cheering for an Egyptian team instead of the Mauritian team. Creole political groups claimed that cases of brutality by the predominantly Hindu police force are perpetrated almost exclusively against Creoles.

There were numerous credible reports of the predominantly Hindu police force mistreating the predominantly Creole population of Rodrigues.

Section 6. Worker Rights

a. *The Right of Association.*—The Constitution explicitly protects the right of workers to associate in trade unions, and there is an active trade union movement. More than 300 unions represent over 100,000 workers, more than 20 percent of the total work force. With the exception of members of the "disciplined force" (i.e., the police and the Special Mobile Force) and persons in state services who are not public officers (e.g., contractors), workers are free to form and join unions and to organize in all sectors including in the export processing zone (EPZ). In the EPZ, however, only 10 percent of the work force is unionized, and employers continued to intimidate prospective union members. Labor unions are independent from the Government. Unions press wage demands, establish ties to domestic political parties, and address political issues. Unions are free to establish federations.

Under the Industrial Relations Act (IRA), unions have the legal right to strike. In practice, however, the IRA requires a prestrike 21-day cooling-off period, followed by binding arbitration, which has the effect of making most strikes illegal. Moreover, the IRA states that worker participation in an unlawful strike is sufficient grounds for dismissal, but workers may seek remedy in the industrial court if they believe that their dismissal is unjustified. According to Ministry of Labor statistics, there were five work stoppages.

Statutory minimum wage levels in the export processing zone (EPZ) are somewhat lower than elsewhere, but due to the country's labor shortage, actual wage levels are nearly double the minimum wage. Under the law, unions may and do establish ties with international labor bodies.

b. *The Right to Organize and Bargain Collectively.*—The law protects the right of employees to bargain collectively with their employers. However, the collective bargaining process is weakened by excessive government intervention in the form of wage-setting in the state sector, which is generally used as the basis for private-sector pay. Wages are set by the National Remuneration Board, whose chairman is appointed by the Minister of Labor. About 12 percent of the labor force works for national or local government. The IRA prohibits antiunion discrimination. There is an arbitration tribunal which handles any such complaints.

The EPZ employs about 90,000 people. While there are some EPZ-specific labor laws, such as provisions allowing EPZ employers to require up to 10 hours per week of paid overtime from their employees, workers in this sector enjoy the same basic protections as non-EPZ workers.

c. *Prohibition of Forced or Compulsory Labor.*—Forced or compulsory labor is prohibited by law, and not practiced in fact.

d. *Minimum Age for Employment of Children.*—The legal minimum age for employment of children is 15 years. The Ministry of Labor is responsible for enforcement and conducts frequent inspections. A threefold increase in the number of underage workers found by government inspectors in latter half of 1995 over the same period in 1994 led to increased government inspections. Inspectors issued warnings to the culpable employers. The Government estimated that children make up 0.7 percent of the work force. Child labor in homes, on farms, and in shops is common in Rodrigues, which remained difficult to monitor.

e. *Acceptable Conditions of Work.*—The Government administratively establishes minimum wages, which vary according to the sector of employment, and it mandates minimum wage increases each year based on inflation. The minimum wage for an unskilled worker in the EPZ is about $11.55 (231.28 rupees) per week effective July 1, while the lowest weekly wage for a non-EPZ worker is about $12.50 (250.05 rupees). While this is significantly below the level needed to provide an acceptable standard of living, the actual market wage for most workers is much higher due to the present labor shortage.

The standard legal workweek in the industrial sector is 45 hours. In the EPZ an employee may be required to work an additional 10 hours per week, although at a higher hourly wage.

The Government responded to a 1995 complaint to the International Labor Organization regarding the wages and living conditions of foreign workers by increasing the number of inspections carried out by the Foreign Labor Inspection Squad. Observers complain that the inspectors are easily bribed and are the only people allowed access to foreign workers who are not being otherwise protected by the labor laws.

The Government sets health and safety standards, and Ministry of Labor officials inspect working conditions and ensure compliance with the 1988 Occupational Safety, Health, and Welfare Act. The small number of inspectors limits the Government's enforcement ability, but the number of occupational accidents has been cut nearly in half since the act's passage. Workers have the right to remove themselves from dangerous situations without jeopardy to continued employment.

MOZAMBIQUE

Mozambique has a constitutional government headed by President Joaquim Chissano who was elected in the country's first multiparty elections in October 1994. President Chissano and the leadership of his party, the Front for the Liberation of Mozambique (FRELIMO), which has ruled the country since independence in 1975, control policymaking and implementation. The National Assembly, the only multiparty institution beside the defense force, provided useful debate on national policy issues. However, the Assembly's FRELIMO majority did not exert significant authority or independence from the executive with regard to policymaking. The judiciary began to openly discuss its weaknesses, but it remained unable to implement constitutional provisions safeguarding individual human rights or to provide an effective check on the power of the executive branch. Although the foundations of democracy remained fragile, Mozambique's political transition continued to be largely successful, and reintegration of areas controlled by the Mozambican National Resistance (RENAMO) during the war continued, with tensions limited to only a few districts.

The integration of the FRELIMO and RENAMO defense forces continued, although a lack of resources and political will has hampered the development of a nonpartisan professional military. There are several forces responsible for internal security under the Minister of Interior, the Criminal Investigation Police (PIC), the Mozambican National Police (PRM), and the Rapid Reaction Police (PIR). The State Information and Security Service (SISE) reports directly to the President. These ill-trained and ill-disciplined units continued to be the focus of much controversy. Members of the security forces committed numerous human rights abuses.

Approximately 80 percent of the population is employed in agriculture, mostly on a subsistence level. Major exports are shrimp, sugar, cotton, and cashew nuts. The transition to a market economy in the small formal economy accelerated during the latter half of the year with increasing privatization of state-owned enterprises and progress in financial sector reform. Starting from an extremely low base, the gross domestic product grew 3 percent in 1995 and was forecast to grow at a significantly higher rate in 1996. Inflation fell significantly with an estimated annual inflation rate of approximately 21 percent, below the International Monetary Fund target for the year. Although the general economic outlook improved with good rains and a good harvest, the economy and the Government's budget remained heavily dependent on foreign aid; the economy experienced a $613 million trade deficit in 1995. Extensive corruption at all levels of the Government continues to be a problem. The annual per capita income of around $90 remains very low, and unemployment is high.

While the status of political and civil liberties improved, the Government's overall human rights record continued to be marred by a pattern of abusive behavior by the security forces and an ineffective judicial system which is only nominally independent from the FRELIMO-controlled executive. Poorly trained and undisciplined police forces and local officials continued to commit human rights abuses, including extrajudicial killings, excessive use of force, and arbitrary detention. Security forces and police routinely beat, tortured, or otherwise abused detainees, including street children. Extremely poor prison conditions resulted in the deaths of dozens of inmates. Arbitrary arrests and lengthy detentions without fair and expeditious trials remained problems. The Government continued to restrict press freedom; the media remained largely owned by the Government and state enterprises and manipulated by factions within the ruling party, but there was greater criticism of government policies. Also, with increased press and NGO scrutiny, more abuses by security forces came to light than in previous years, and in some instances the Government investigated and punished those responsible. However, in view of the common perception that the police force is unreliable and corrupt, many citizens resorted to mob justice. Late in the year, the President dismissed the unpopular Minister of Interior, and the Government promised long-needed reforms of the police forces. Societal discrimination and violence against women, and violence against children remain problems.

RESPECT FOR HUMAN RIGHTS

Section 1. Respect for the Integrity of the Person, Including Freedom From:

a. *Political and Other Extrajudicial Killing.*—There were no known cases of political killings, but there were reports of extrajudicial killings. RENAMO officials charged that security forces had killed several of its members. In May the General Secretary of RENAMO, Francisco Marcelino, accused police of intimidating, persecuting, detaining, and executing RENAMO followers in Manica, Sofala, Nampula, and Tete provinces. The Government did not investigate these charges, but there were no independent verifications of the alleged killings.

According to the Mozambican League of Human Rights (LDH), in June police were responsible for the death in police custody of an accused car thief, Frenque Tchembene, and the disappearance of another suspect, Abdul Mota (see Section 1.b.). According to Frenque's wife, who was present during his interrogation, Frenque was beaten with iron bars and AK–47 rifles, submerged in dirty water, and struck in the genital area. His medical report indicated that he died later the same week from these police-inflicted injuries. After protest by the LDH, the authorities arrested a sergeant and charged him and four other officers with murder.

A press report stated that police killed three people—two by gunshot and the third by beating—early in the year in Central Zambezia province. The police involved were briefly detained then released. In March the independent press reported that a police officer in Machava, a Maputo suburb, tortured a man to death after a complaint that the man was harassing a neighbor.

Extremely poor prison conditions led to the deaths of many persons in custody (see Section 1.c.).

There were no known disciplinary actions taken in the 1995 killing of Fern Macongue Sitoe. The police shot Sitoe in the course of attempting to settle a local dispute.

Mob and vigilante killings continued to be common. For example in March a group of residents in Manjacaze lynched two suspected armed robbers. While the authorities rarely prosecuted mob participants, in June police in Matola prevented a mob from burning to death four thieves. There were numerous but unverified reports during the year that regulos (traditional chiefs) and curandeiros (traditional healers) had imposed and carried out death sentences against persons accused of witchcraft.

b. *Disappearance.*—There were no reports of politically motivated disappearances.

In May Abdul Mota, a suspected car thief, disappeared after an argument with an officer of the paramilitary "lightning brigade" that patrols the Maputo-Ressano Garcia highway. Mota disappeared after last being seen with a senior officer of the brigade. The authorities failed to conduct a thorough investigation, and no report on the incident had been issued by year's end. Mota remained missing at year's end.

The fate of thousands of Mozambicans who disappeared during the civil war still remains unresolved. However, a FRELIMO National Assembly deputy reported publicly for the first time that the FRELIMO leadership had had one such person— Lazaro Nkavandame, one of FRELIMO's founders—executed by firing squad for treason, as were others during the conflict.

In March another FRELIMO National Assembly deputy alleged that RENAMO continues to hold kidnaped children in Niassa province.

c. *Torture and Other Cruel, Inhuman, or Degrading Treatment or Punishment.*— The 1990 Constitution expressly prohibits torture and cruel or inhuman treatment, but the Mozambican police forces continued to commit serious abuses. The police often used excessive force, and there were continuing reports that police routinely beat and whipped detainees. In February one senior PRM officer stated publicly that in order to restore public order police have to beat people.

Corruption in the police forces extends throughout the ranks, and the PRM used violence and detention to intimidate people from reporting abuses. In July the Director of the Criminal Investigation Police (PIC), Domingos Maita, publicly stated that the police forces are infiltrated by crime syndicates. A press report in September from Gaza province's capital Xai Xai indicated that the local police regularly extorted money from street vendors (predominately widowed and divorced women), beat the women, and confiscated their produce. Police also beat street children (see Section 5).

The vast majority of these cases were never investigated, but one case received nationwide publicity due to the LDH's investigation. The LDH accused the PRM of deliberately torturing nine workers on the Mozambican National Airline (LAM) at the end of 1995. The report stated that the police officers tortured the workers with saws, hammers, and by sticking guns up the workers' nostrils or in their ears, leaving some of the workers with hearing impairments. Although the LDH sent letters to various authorities, including the Prime Minister and the Minister of the Interior, by the end of 1996 no investigation into the alleged torture had taken place.

Credible reports indicated that the paramilitary "lightning brigade" guarding the Ressano Garcia-Maputo road continued to beat and torture suspected car thieves, keeping them shackled for days without due process.

A RENAMO provincial official, Tome Fernandes, accused the police in May of intimidating citizens of the RENAMO constituency in Cabo Delgado province. Although RENAMO presented Prime Minister Pascoal Mocumbi with a series of such allegations, it does not appear that any investigation has taken place. A civil court in March settled the 1994 case of torture of a bank official by "PROTEG" private security forces involving the use of electric shocks. The court ordered the Commercial Bank of Mozambique to reemploy the official and pay him 17 months' back wages. However, the criminal case concerning the torture allegations had not been heard by year's end.

RENAMO officials continued to allege that on numerous occasions police harassed, detained, and beat its members (see Sections 1.a. and 3).

On occasion the Government took action to counter the abuses arising from police corruption and excessive use of force. In June the Maputo provincial police commander, Raimundo Macie, stated that in 1995 the Maputo command disciplined 66 policemen and expelled 19 from the force for collaborating with criminals. In August two police officers were found guilty of sexually violating two minors, 12 and 14 years of age. There were isolated instances of disciplinary actions in other parts of the country. In November President Chissano relieved the unpopular Interior Minister and his deputy, and the new Minister took steps to discipline or expel dozens of police officers as well to begin a program of reform inside the police force.

Prison conditions throughout the country are extremely poor and continued to deteriorate; they posed a severe threat to inmates' life and health. Medical and food supplies are usually insufficient, with little medical care available, and some prisoners being fed only once a day or less. It is estimated that some prisons hold up to four times their intended prisoner capacity. Throughout the year Justice Minister Jose Abudo reported on the serious conditions in the prisons. He made highly publicized visits to prisons, reporting that severe overcrowding, food shortages, and disease, including scabies, malaria, tuberculosis, and anemia, had led to the deaths of prisoners. He also found that management irregularities in many of the country's prisons, including embezzlement of prison funds, had exacerbated prison conditions. In June Abudo stated that the Justice Ministry was unable to fund three meals a day for prisoners and that, in general, prisoners throughout the country received barely one daily meal, often of extremely poor quality.

There were many reports of deaths in overcrowded prisons. For example, in June prison director Pedro Nharrugula said that at least five prisoners had died of diarrheal diseases during the previous 10 months in the main prison in Quelimane, the capital of Central Zambezia province. He said that the Quelimane prison, built to accommodate 90 inmates, currently held 406. Other reports indicated that at least 25 prisoners had died in Manica provincial prison by the end of March. The Manica prison, built to hold 300, contained more than 900 persons. The Beira central prison director, Luis Alberto Sucane, admitted that overcrowding and poor sanitary conditions had caused numerous deaths in the Beira prison, which, despite a capacity of 200, contained 800 prisoners.

Interior Minister Manuel Antonio declared in January that if prisoners die of hunger, they only have themselves to blame. His comments evoked severe national criticism. Calls by a variety of national figures for his resignation went unheeded by the Government. However, in order to combat these poor prison conditions, in February the Ministry of Justice began an initiative whereby prisoners in Sofala, Central Zambezia, and Manica provinces were given their own plots of land to cultivate for food, and in Quelimane prisoners were contracted out as laborers to local businesses.

Although the majority of cases of abuse in prison are due to overcrowding and lack of food and medical attention, prisoners continued to regularly report police beatings, rapes, and demands for money in exchange for freedom. In an April letter by a group of inmates to a national newspaper, the prisoners charged that police officers beat and tortured them, sexually abused prisoners and their wives, and demanded money for food and sometimes freedom. Many pretrial detainees are minors who are incarcerated with adult inmates. As a result, child molestation and other violence against children are rampant in the country's prisons. Military and civilian prisoners are held in the same prisons.

International human rights groups are given access to prisoners.

d. *Arbitrary Arrest, Detention, or Exile.*—The Constitution provides that the duration of preventive imprisonment be set by law; however the police continue to arbitrarily arrest and detain citizens. Under Law 2/93, the maximum preventive imprisonment is 48 hours. Within that time period, a detainee has the right to have his case reviewed by judicial authorities, after which he can be detained up to another 60 days while his case is investigated by the PIC. However, persons accused of the most serious crimes, i.e., security offenses or these requiring a sentence of more than 8 years, may be detained up to 84 days without being formally charged. With court approval such detainees may be held for two additional periods of 84 days while the police complete their investigation. In practice, however, the authorities often ignore these rules, as well as a detainee's constitutional right to counsel and to contact relatives or friends. Although Law 19/91 provides definitions of crimes against the State, such as treason, terrorism, and sabotage, the Government retains the discretion to determine which crimes constitute security offenses.

Most citizens are unaware of their rights, particularly those granted under the 1990 Constitution and Law 2/93, and detainees can spend many months, even years, in pretrial status. In August the President of the Supreme Court, Mario Mangaze, publicly admitted that detainees' rights under Law 2/93 regarding preventive imprisonment were being abused due to a severe shortage of qualified judicial authorities to review cases. The bail system remains poorly defined, and prisoners, their families, and NGO's complained that police and prison officials often take bribes to release those who can afford to pay. The law provides that if the prescribed period for investigation has been completed and no charges have been brought, the detainee must be released. In practice, however, this law is often ignored, in part because of the severe lack of administrative personnel, trained judges, and sufficient lawyers to monitor the judicial system (see Section 1.e.).

A large backlog of prisoners continue to await trial. Official data for 1995 indicated that there were 2,572 persons in prison and that over half (1,451) were still awaiting trial. In July the Minister of Justice reported that of Pemba prison's 321 inmates, 61 awaited trial and 170 had not even been charged. In Beira central prison 322 of the 743 inmates reportedly had already been in pretrial detention for periods longer than the potential jail terms applicable for their alleged crimes, and 278 of the 639 prisoners in Manica central prison were in similar status. In Guelimane provincial prison 245 of the 406 prisoners were awaiting judicial hearing, many for over 6 months.

The Constitution expressly prohibits exile, and the Government does not use exile as a form of political control.

e. *Denial of Fair Public Trial.*—The Constitution formally established an independent judiciary and specifically states that the decisions of the courts take precedence over all other authorities and individuals and must be obeyed. Nevertheless, the executive, and by extension the FRELIMO party, dominates the judiciary. Judges largely owe their positions to the ruling FRELIMO party, which continues to exercise significant influence on all aspects of public life through the executive and party organs.

The President appoints the President and Vice President of the most important tribunal, the Supreme Court. These selections are then sent to the National Assembly for approval. Although the Supreme Council of Judicial Magistrates assembles a list of qualified persons for the remaining Supreme Court positions, the President selects the justices off the list. No National Assembly approval is needed for these choices. In May the FRELIMO-dominated National Assembly succeeded in electing its list of four candidates to the Supreme Council. The President also appoints the Attorney General. The National Assembly has yet to assert it prerogatives in the judicial area.

There are two complementary formal justice systems: The civil/criminal which includes customary courts; and the military. A 1991 law empowered the Supreme Court to administer the civil/criminal; it also hears appeals, including military cases, although the Ministry of Defense administers the military courts. Below the Supreme Court there are provincial and district courts. There are also special courts that exercise limited subject-matter jurisdiction, e.g., administrative courts, customs courts, fiscal courts, maritime courts, and labor courts. As with the provincial and district courts, these specialized courts are ineffective because they suffer from a lack of qualified professionals. Civilians are not under the jurisdiction of, or tried in, the military courts. Local customary courts handle matters such as estate and divorce cases.

Persons accused of crimes against the State are tried in regular civilian courts under standard criminal judicial procedures. The Supreme Court has original jurisdiction over members of the National Assembly and anyone else who is immune from trial in the lower courts. A judge may order a trial closed because of national security interests or to protect the privacy of the plaintiff in cases concerning rape.

In regular courts, all accused persons are in theory presumed innocent and have the right to legal counsel and the right of appeal, but the authorities do not always respect these rights, and in fact the great majority of the population is either unaware of these rights or does not possess the means to obtain any form of legal counsel. There is a serious shortage of qualified judicial personnel. In April Supreme Court President Mangaze reported that at the provincial level, only one licensed judge exists in Cabo Delgado, Gaza, and Zambezia provinces, respectively. He reported that at the district level there are districts with no courts or judges at all. In August Supreme Court President Mangaze further admitted that the grave problems of a lack of human and financial resources and problems with outdated legislation have impeded the judiciary's effectiveness. Exacerbating the problem is the lack of licensed attorneys, with less than 200 in the country and the vast majority centered in Maputo. In an effort to replace the public organization previously responsible for providing counsel for indigent defendants, some NGO's, such as the Mozambican League of Human Rights and the Association of Mozambican Women in Judicial Careers, offer limited legal counsel at no or little cost.

The President of the Supreme Court has also acknowledged that the judicial system in plagued by bribery and extortion. In June a judge in Gaza province was accused of confiscating private goods, including cars of local citizens.

In November the presiding judge of the Manica provincial court was accused of murdering his domestic servant. The victim's widow filed a case against the judge with the provincial attorney who forwarded it to the relevant authorities in Maputo. As a result of these charges, the Deputy President of the Supreme Court traveled to the provincial capital of Chiomoio to conduct an investigation. By year's end, there had not been any disciplinary action taken.

The Government, with international assistance, has developed a comprehensive plan for improving the professional level and efficiency of the judiciary. In an effort to combat the lack of human resources, in mid-September a Center for Judicial Formation (with European funding) opened, which will train nonlicensed persons for the role of district magistrates.

Efforts to reintegrate RENAMO-controlled zones into central administrative structures continued, but RENAMO still exercises informal control over a number of areas through a rudimentary form of civil administration and traditional courts, with extensive use of traditional authorities as judges. In September the RENAMO National Assembly deputy for Inhambane, Fernando Pries, acknowledged the existence of a RENAMO administrative structure in the district of Chipandzane. A traditional chief in the district of Rovuro was accused of trying to collect taxes, and another in Inharrime district forced residents to build huts and latrines.

There were no reports of political prisoners.

f. *Arbitrary Interference With Privacy, Family, Home, or Correspondence.*—The 1990 Constitution provides for the right of privacy and expressly forbids the use of surveillance techniques. By law police need a warrant to enter homes and businesses. Although there are fewer reports of such activity, incidents of illegal telephone wiretapping by government intelligence agencies allegedly still occur. Security forces keep watch on RENAMO members and supporters and other members of the opposition.

Section 2. Respect for Civil Liberties, Including:

a. *Freedom of Speech and Press.*—The Constitution, the 1991 Press Law, and the 1992 Rome Peace Accords provide for freedom of expression and the press but with restrictions in cases involving national defense considerations. Although there was some progress toward greater transparency and criticism in reporting on government policies and more independent editorial content, the Government continued to restrict press freedom. While criticism of the President is not legally prohibited, the 1991 Press Law holds that, in cases of defamation against the President, truth is not a sufficient defense against libel. Although this law has not been tested in court, it resulted in considerable self-censorship, and there is almost no direct criticism of the President.

The Government dominates the media, which reflect a bias toward state interests. The Government and state enterprises own the greater part of the country's media, including Mozambique's two daily newspapers, the only Sunday newspaper, the only weekly news magazine, and the national radio and television stations. Radio Mozambique is the public's most important source of information and receives the largest single subsidy from the state budget of any public company. The Government also has its own wire service, the Mozambican News Agency.

The government-controlled media continued to orchestrate disinformation campaigns regarding RENAMO activities. For example, the government-controlled press repeatedly claimed that members of an obscure Zimbabwean dissident group, allegedly operating along the two country's borders, had ties to RENAMO and that RENAMO was keeping armed men in hiding. No credible evidence was ever produced for these allegations, and the claims died out in the latter half of the year. More generally, the press tended deliberately to portray RENAMO in a bad light although this too was less evident as the year wore on.

The development of the small independent media continued over the past year. In addition to the two weekly newspapers, Demos and Salvana, and two facsimile daily news sheets, Medifax, and Imparcial, two monthly newspapers appeared; Renascer oriented to general news, and Gaseta Mercantil covering economic issues. There were attempts at other news sheets, and independent newspapers with mimeographed formats appeared in two provinces. The second television station and a few limited range radio stations also continued to operate.

The small independent press carried opposition viewpoints and generally enjoyed far greater credibility, but its influence (and that of the official press as well) is limited largely to Maputo and the provincial capitals because of the logistical difficulty of distribution of any publication in rural areas. Only a small minority of the population receives news through either television or the print media.

Journalists who criticized government officials or policy were at times subjected to threats and intimidation. For example, in April, in violation of the 1991 Press Law, police in Nacala detained, harassed, and destroyed the film of two journalists of the independent newspaper Savanna who had photographed local traffic police.

Government domination of newspaper printing presses led to allegations of official harassment of the independent press, but there was no evidence this affected publication or content of the independent publications.

Abolition of the Ministry of Information in late 1994 did not notably result in greater independence of the media, and a new information office under the Prime Minister continues to at least informally monitor press content. A Mozambican chapter of the Media Institute of Southern Africa, whose goal is the creation and development of a free and pluralistic press in southern Africa, was founded in July.

There are no formal restrictions on academic freedom. In practice, however, teachers routinely adhere to self-censorship since their employment depends on the State. During a June strike of students (demanding an increase in living allowances) at the University of Eduardo Mondlane, the university rector made credible allegations of political interference in the functions of the university.

b. *Freedom of Peaceful Assembly and Association.*—The Constitution provides for freedom of assembly and association. Throughout the year political parties and other groups freely held congresses, press conferences, workshops, and other public gatherings. No groups were known to have been denied permission to hold public marches. For example, RENAMO's Maputo city branch organized celebrations of the fourth anniversary of the signing of the Rome Peace Accords in October and held other meetings throughout the country. NGO's and church organizations were also active in hosting conferences and rallies, and faced no governmental obstacles or harassment. The Mozambican Christian Council continued its project of collecting arms throughout the country without interference.

Legislation promulgated in 1991 ensures the process of registration of political parties. Currently there are over 15 registered, active political parties. Under 1992 legislation a political party must demonstrate that it has no racial, ethnic, or religious exclusiveness and secure at least 2,000 signatures of citizens in order to be recognized legally.

Other groups and associations continued to organize themselves or become more active, including Foro Mulher, an umbrella women's NGO group, which hosted a conference on women's rights (see Section 5). The Government requires nonpolitical groups, except religious organizations, to register, but it rarely rejects applications from new associations.

c. *Freedom of Religion.*—The Constitution provides that all citizens have the freedom to practice or not to practice a religion and gives religious denominations the right to pursue their religious aims freely. The Government respects these rights in practice. The Government does not require religious organizations or missionaries to register, and foreign missionaries are routinely granted visas. The Constitution also gives religious groups the right to own and acquire assets, and these institutions are allowed by law to operate schools. Small Christian evangelical groups continued to form throughout the year, and an Islamic group provided funds for the construction of schools in Niassa, Nampula, and Maputo provinces.

Relations between the Government and the religious organizations, tense in the early years after independence, began to improve in 1992 and have improved further as the Government sought political support from these organizations in the multiparty system. Muslim deputies introduced an Islamic holiday proposal in the National Assembly's fourth session (February–May), but President Chissano requested that the Supreme Court make a ruling on its constitutionality. A variety of national figures, including the Catholic Church's Archbishop of Beira, charged that the proposal conflicts with the Constitution, which declares that Mozambique is a secular state. The Supreme Court in December ruled that the Islamic Holidays Law was unconstitutional since it conflicted with constitutional provisions guaranteeing the secular nature of the Mozambican State.

d. *Freedom of Movement Within the Country, Foreign Travel, Emigration, and Repatriation.*—The Constitution provides for freedom of travel within the country and abroad. The Government no longer requires citizens to obtain permits from local authorities in order to travel within the country. The Government continues to enforce a law fining foreigners who overstay their visas; increasing the amount to $350 per day.

Throughout the year, security force roadblocks and patrols affected freedom of movement. Police harassment throughout the country's road network increased over the past year, with many incidents of officers demanding bribes on trumped-up charges. Confiscating people's possessions under flimsy pretexts has become a common police practice.

Although several riots throughout the country by unemployed demobilized soldiers occurred in midyear, the disturbances were small in scale and largely confined to urban areas. In the countryside, where most of the demobilized soldiers reside, former soldiers appeared to be reintegrating peacefully with no threats to freedom of movement.

In July the United Nations High Commissioner for Refugees (UNHCR) officially ended its repatriation and reintegration program for Mozambican refugees. In the 30-month period following the signing of the October 1992 Rome Peace Accord, approximately 1.7 million Mozambican refugees returned to the country from six countries of asylum. During the same time period, most of the country's 3.6 million internally displaced persons moved back to their homes.

In recent years, Mozambique has been primarily a refugee generating country. Historically, however, Mozambique has provided asylum to large numbers of refugees from neighboring countries. The Government cooperates with the UNHCR and other humanitarian organizations in assisting refugees, including providing first asylum. At year's end, there was a small caseload of 48 refugees who have been granted asylum in Mozambique, primarily from other African countries (Rwanda, Burundi, Zaire, and Somalia). Of these 48 persons, 28 individuals were granted asylum in 1996. The UNHCR also manages a moderate caseload of individuals who have been refused refugee status but are in the process of appealing this decision and of those who are still in the application process. There were no reports of forced return of persons to a country where they feared persecution.

Section 3. Respect for Political Rights: The Right of Citizens to Change Their Government

The Constitution provides that citizens have the right to elect their representatives by universal, direct, secret, and periodic elections. In October 1994 citizens freely exercised for the first time their right to vote in multiparty elections, which U.N. and other international observers declared to be free and fair. President Chissano was elected, with the ruling FRELIMO party winning 129 of the 250 National Assembly seats. RENAMO surprised many observers with its strong showing in the elections, winning majorities in the country's five most populous provinces. Although the opposition parties are in a minority status in the Assembly and lacked previous legislative experience, the two 1996 parliamentary sessions were marked by an improvement in both the overall quality of debate as well as the effectiveness of individual deputies from all parties.

Although debate and the airing of issues of national concern increased in the National Assembly during the year, the Assembly with its FRELIMO majority did not provide any significant check on the power of the executive branch. The executive continued to gain parliamentary approval on even the most controversial issues, such as the composition of the newly created National Defense Council.

The President and the FRELIMO leadership continued to control policymaking and implementation, and all cabinet positions and provincial governorships went to FRELIMO party members, even in provinces where RENAMO had won overwhelming majorities in the 1994 elections. The Government's strategy appeared increasingly to be to use its patronage and power to build support in areas that supported RENAMO during the 1994 elections. RENAMO parliamentarians complained of a lack of support from provincial and district officials during visits to their constituencies. Working relationships between the parties at the national and local level appeared to improve, however, as the year wore on.

Although FRELIMO administrators in some areas continued to accuse RENAMO officials of running parallel governmental structures and harassing central government appointed officials, by year's end these allegations diminished as the Government began to operate more freely in RENAMO-dominated areas.

Momentum behind local elections grew throughout the latter part of 1996 culminating in the National Assembly's approval of the Municipalities Law in December. Local elections were expected to take place in late 1997 in several dozen localities covering a significant proportion of the population. RENAMO officials, who had previously resisted the concept of gradualism in local elections, by year's end had accepted this phased approach to the polls.

While there are no legal restrictions hindering women's involvement in government, cultural factors have inhibited their political advancement. Nonetheless, 62 of the 250 (28 percent) National Assembly deputies are women, even though these female deputies are not believed to play a significant role in either the Parliament's or the individual parties' decisionmaking processes. One women serves as a minister and five as vice ministers.

Section 4. Governmental Attitude Regarding International and Nongovernmental Investigation of Alleged Violations of Human Rights

There are no legal obstacles to the formation of local human rights groups. The Mozambican League of Human Rights has focused efforts on educating the public regarding its rights. It uncovered many of the grave abuses within the prison system. The Government has permitted the League access to Maputo and Nampula prisons under the jurisdiction of the Ministry of Justice. The League has also publicly criticized widespread abusive behavior by the police and the Minister of Interior himself. In May a new group, the Mozambican Human Rights Association, was formed with a primary mission of human rights education. In late December, a third group, Human Rights and Discovery, was formed with stated aims of promoting, protecting, and developing human rights.

The Government has been receptive to visits by international human rights monitoring groups, including the International Committee of the Red Cross and the International Commission of Jurists.

Section 5. Discrimination Based on Race, Sex, Religion, Disability, Language, or Social Status

The Constitution forbids discrimination based on race, sex, religion, or disability, but the Government does not ensure in practice that such discrimination does not occur.

Women.—Although official statistics are not kept, according to health officials, women's groups, and other sources violence against women—particularly wife beating and rape—is widespread, especially in rural areas. Many women believe that their spouses have the right to beat them, and cultural pressures make it highly unlikely for most women to press for legal action against abusive spouses. While rape can theoretically be prosecuted in the courts, no civil laws exist whereby domestic violence is specifically considered a crime. The police do not normally intervene in domestic disputes, and cases are rarely brought before the courts. When victims of physical abuse are brought to the hospital, such cases are rarely registered as caused by domestic violence.

Nevertheless, an increasing number of women's groups have been calling for a revision in the Penal Code to include provisions for prosecuting such violence, documenting cases of domestic violence, and encouraging victims of domestic and sexual violence to press charges. In July the President described domestic violence against women as a violation of human rights and an obstacle to social harmony. The President stated that the Government is committed to fighting against domestic violence and called for the establishment of hostels for the victims of domestic violence. A group of NGO's active in the women's rights area established the Kulaya Center for Victims of Domestic Violence in midyear. The Center, which operates out of the Maputo central hospital, currently has approximately 15 beds and relies on foreign funding.

Despite constitutional protections providing for the equality of men and women under law in all aspects of political, economic, social, and cultural life, civil and commercial legal codes that predate independence frequently contradict each other and the Constitution. Under the Law of the Family (through both court interpretation and precedent), the husband (or father) is the head of the household, and women (both wives and daughters), must ensure male approval of any and all undertakings that women assume. For example, in order to start a business, a woman must first have the written approval of her husband or father (or closest male relative). Without this approval, a woman is unable to lease a building, obtain a loan, or contract for goods and services. The legal domicile of a married woman is her husband's house, and she may only work outside the home with the express consent of her husband.

Family law also dictates that a couple's possessions belong to the husband, and he has full authority to decide on the disposition of these goods. Upon the death of a husband, a widow is only fourth in line (after sons, fathers, and brothers) for inheritance of the household goods. Although the law states that the widow is entitled to half of the goods acquired during the marriage, in practice women rarely know of or insist upon this right.

Several women's groups have argued that the Constitution discriminates against women because it only grants Mozambican citizenship to the foreign wife of a Mozambican male, but not to the foreign-born spouse of a Mozambican woman.

Customary law or traditional law offers women even fewer protections than family law. Unless a marriage is registered, a woman has no recourse to the judicial branch for enforcement of the few rights provided to women by the civil codes. Although women are the primary cultivator of family land in rural areas, under customary law they have no rights to the disposition of the land. Generally, land tenure is passed on through male relatives, not female ones.

Women also experience economic discrimination in practice and sexual harassment in the workplace. The Organization of Mozambican Workers (OTM) reported in March that women are the principal victims of retrenchments due to economic restructuring and are often fired under the pretext of low productivity. Women are rarely given the same opportunities for technical training as men. According to the Secretary General of the National Union of Agricultural and Forestry Workers, female workers were fired from their jobs for not allowing sexual advances. In April another trade union, the National Union of Road Transport and Technical Assistance Workers, alleged that women experience sexual assault, are overworked, and work in conditions lacking basic sanitation and bodily protection. In March the Chemical Workers' Union accused company managers of sexually harassing female workers. In May the Mozambican Association of Demobilized Soldiers noted that demobilized female soldiers from both government and RENAMO forces were still facing discrimination in the reintegration process. The demobilized female soldiers claimed, for example, that the majority of microenterprise projects benefited demobilized males.

Women have less access than men to educational institutions above the primary level. Although roughly equal proportions of male and female children enter primary school, by secondary school males greatly outnumber females. Discrimination against women is most apparent in rural areas where over 80 percent of the population live, and where women are engaged mainly in subsistence farming and child rearing, with little opportunity for schooling or access to health care.

Foro Mulher, an umbrella for women's NGO groups, has approximately 21 registered members. These women's NGO's have become increasingly active over the last year in their efforts to highlight a variety of women's issues, including domestic violence, legal inequities, and economic empowerment. Funded through a host of different means, some of these NGO's provide basic legal advice for women, others conduct training seminars, and still others lobby for changes in governmental legislation. Although these groups have organized successful programs, their effectiveness is often limited because the programs are concentrated in Maputo or other urban areas while the vast majority of women live in the rural zones.

Children.—The Government has not made children's rights and welfare a priority but is making some efforts to deal with a corrupt and overcrowded educational system. It is widely reported that school children (or their parents) must bribe teachers for passing grades. Reportedly about 60 percent of the country's children now attend school.

The Government has also made little attempt to alleviate the plight of the increasing numbers of urban street children, many of whom were orphaned by the war. In March Minister of Health, Dr. Aurelio Zilhao reported that 300,000 children, traumatized by the war, orphaned, and abandoned, require social reintegration. Street children are beaten by police and are often victims of sexual abuse. In January a press article reported that police in Maputo imprisoned a 15-year-old child for 9 days with no recourse to justice for allegedly stealing a tape cassette. The same minor was then allegedly given 12 lashes by the police before being released. In February a parliamentary deputy discovered five street children detained in a Montepuez, Cabo Delgado prison.

People With Disabilities.—Although the Constitution expressly states that "disabled citizens shall enjoy fully the rights enshrined in the Constitution," the Government provided few resources to make this a reality. It has relied on NGO's to assist the disabled. Founded in 1991, the Association of Mozambican Disabled

(ADEMO) addresses the social and economic needs of the disabled. Since then, smaller NGO's have formed, such as the Association of Handicapped Military and Paramilitary Mozambicans (ADEMINO), which represents disabled demobilized soldiers, and the Association of Blind and Visually Impaired Mozambicans. Although poorly funded, these groups provide training, raise public awareness of the need to integrate the disabled into society, and lobby the Ministry of Labor to initiate legislation to support the working rights of the disabled. In May ADEMIMO charged that the Government had not yet authorized medical pensions for disabled soldiers. Also in May the press reported that more than 9,000 disabled former military personnel in Sofala province were living in dire conditions due to the Ministry of Planning and Finance's refusal to institute disability pensions.

The only provisions that the Government has enacted for accessibility to buildings and transportation for the disabled were in the electoral law governing the country's first multiparty elections, which addressed the needs of disabled voters in the polling booths. No special access facilities exist.

National/Racial/Ethnic Minorities.—There was no systematic persecution or discrimination on the basis of race or ethnicity, although the FRELIMO Government has traditionally included at all levels a disproportionate number of southerners, mostly from the Shangaan ethnic group. However, the Government took some steps to address this imbalance by appointing provincial governors native to their respective provinces. The Government also included more nonsoutherners in the FRELIMO parliamentary delegation.

RENAMO leadership is predominately from the Shona ethnic group. There is no indication that the conflict between the Government and RENAMO was primarily motivated by ethnicity, although ethnic and regional factors may have played some role and explain some of the civil war violence.

Section 6. Worker Rights

a. *The Right of Association.*—The Constitution specifies that all workers are free to join or refrain from joining a trade union. The 1991 Labor Law further protects workers' right to organize and to engage in union activity at their place of employment. The legislation gave existing unions the right to register independently from the Organization of Mozambican Workers (OTM).

Until 1992 the only trade union federation in Mozambique was the OTM, which was affiliated with the FRELIMO party, and from its inception FRELIMO dominated the union. Its leadership was dictated by FRELIMO. With the passage of the 1991 legislation, three unions broke away from OTM in 1992, and by 1994 had formed their own central union, the Free and Independent Union of Mozambique (SLIM). SLIM maintains a working relationship with the OTM. The OTM claims almost 67 percent worker affiliation within its constituent unions, and SLIM claims 60 percent worker affiliation.

At its third National Congress in May 1994, the OTM declared itself free of commitments to any political party, company, or religious group, and ruled that its members affiliated with any political party would not be eligible to hold elected offices. However, independent unions continue to charge that the OTM lacks sufficient independence from the Government.

The Constitution explicitly provides for the right to strike, with the exception of government employees, police, military personnel, and employees engaged in other essential services (which include sanitation, firefighting, air traffic control, health care, water, electricity, fuel, post office, and telecommunications). Throughout the year there were sporadic strikes at a variety of companies throughout the country, where workers' demands usually centered around the issues of salaries in arrears or increases in wage levels. In August workers of a fishing company in Nampula province went on strike, demanding an increase in their minimum wage of $19 per month (the national minimum wage is $22.50 per month).

The 1991 Labor Law forbids retribution against strikers, the hiring of substitute workers, and lockouts by employers. There were no known instances of employer retribution against striking workers. Specific labor disputes are generally arbitrated through ad hoc workers' commissions, formally recognized by the Government. In May an ad hoc workers' commission at one company met with the employer to discuss striking workers' allegations that officials of the company verbally and physically abused workers.

The Constitution and labor legislation give unions the right to join and participate in international bodies. The OTM is a member of the Organization of African Trade Union Unity and the Southern African Trade Union Coordinating Council.

b. *The Right to Organize and Bargain Collectively.*—The Labor Law protects the right of workers to organize and to engage in collective bargaining. The Government has become less involved in the bargaining process despite the large number of state-owned enterprises. In late 1991 the Government decreed that it would no longer set all salary levels and left negotiations for wage increases in the hands of existing unions. The Social Pact Committee, which involves the Government, the OTM, the SLIM, the teachers' and journalists' unions, and employers' associations is important in resolving labor-management issues. This Committee negotiated a revision of the minimum wage in May. In April the Minister of Labor agreed to submit any proposed change to the Labor Law to the committee for review.

The Labor Law expressly prohibits discrimination against organized labor, although antiunion discrimination has not been as issue because, until recently, unions were government-controlled organizations.

While Mozambique has enacted legislation for the establishment of export processing zones, no zones have been created.

  c. *Prohibition of Forced or Compulsory Labor.*—Forced or compulsory labor is prohibited by law, and there have been no reports of such labor practices.

  d. *Minimum Age for Employment of Children.*—Child labor is regulated by the Ministry of Labor. In the wage economy, the minimum working age is 16 years. Because of high adult unemployment, estimated at around 50 percent, few children are employed in regular wage positions. However, children of younger ages commonly work on family farms or in the urban informal sector, where they perform such tasks as guarding cars, collecting scrap metal, or selling trinkets and food in the streets.

  e. *Acceptable Conditions of Work.*—The Government sets minimum wage rates administratively. The minimum wage rate enacted in May was approximately $22.50 (271,126 meticais) per month. It is estimated that a salary of about $62.00 (700,000 meticais) per month is needed in order to provide a decent standard of living for a worker and family. As the minimum wage is not considered sufficient to sustain an average urban worker and family, many workers must turn to a second job, if available, as well as work garden plots to survive.

The Ministry of Labor is responsible for enforcing the minimum rates in the private sector, and the Ministry of Finance is responsible in the public sector. Violations of minimum wage rates are usually investigated only after workers register a complaint. It is customary for workers to receive additional benefits such as transportation and food.

The standard legal workweek is 44 hours, with a weekly 24-hour rest period stipulated. In the small modern sector, the Government has enacted health and environmental laws to protect workers. However, the Ministry of Labor enforces these laws ineffectively, and the Government has only occasionally closed firms for noncompliance. A report issued in July indicated that violations of health and safety norms and regulations in 1995 caused 524 accidents in the building, timber, and mining sectors alone. Workers have the right to remove themselves from work situations that endanger their health or safety without jeopardy to their continued employment.

NAMIBIA

Namibia is a multiparty, multiracial democracy with an independent judiciary. President Sam Nujoma, leader of the South West Africa People's Organization (SWAPO), won Namibia's first free elections in November 1989. President Nujoma and the SWAPO party received just over 70 percent of the vote in the December 1994 Presidential and National Assembly elections, which, despite some irregularities, were generally regarded as free and fair.

The police, supervised by the Ministry of Home Affairs, and the Namibian Defense Force (NDF), supervised by the Ministry of Defense, share responsibility for internal security. The civilian authorities maintain effective control of the security forces, although individual members of the police forces occasionally committed human rights abuses.

Namibia's modern market sector produces most of its wealth while a traditional subsistence agricultural sector (mainly in the north) supports most of its labor force. The principal exports are diamonds and other minerals, cattle, and fish. Mining, ranching, and fishing—the mainstays of the market sector—are still largely controlled by white Namibians and foreign interests. Government policy, however, is to "Namibianize" the increasingly important fishing sector, so that more indigenous entrepreneurs are able to participate, and to provide opportunities for black Namibians in the potentially lucrative and labor-intensive tourism industry. The gross domestic product is $1,663 per capita. However, there remains a wide disparity between income levels of blacks and whites.

The Government generally respected the human rights of its citizens; although problems remained in several areas. There continued to be credible reports that police abused criminal suspects. Despite the release of the "Heroes Book," SWAPO continued to fail to provide a complete accounting for missing detainees held during the preindependence period. Prison conditions remain harsh, but the Government took several steps during the year to improve them and to increase the emphasis on rehabilitation. A large court backlog leads to lengthy delays of trials.

The Married Persons Equality Act, signed into law in May, eliminated discriminatory practices against women in civil marriages. Women married under customary law, however, continued to experience serious legal and cultural discrimination. Although violence against women and children, including rape and child abuse, continues to be a serious problem, the issue received increased attention from government officials and human rights activists. In September the President elevated the head of the Department of Women's Affairs to cabinet-level rank. Inherited problems of racial and ethnic discrimination and glaring disparities—especially in education, health, employment, and working conditions—continued, despite sustained efforts by the Government to reduce them. Societal discrimination against indigenous peoples persists.

RESPECT FOR HUMAN RIGHTS

Section 1. Respect for the Integrity of the Person, Including Freedom From:
  a. *Political and Other Extrajudicial Killing.*—There were no reports of political or other extrajudicial killings. There were no developments concerning the reported shooting of civilians in border areas in 1995 and no reports of such instances in 1996.

According to press reports, the Namibian and South African Governments held discussions regarding the extradition from South Africa of those implicated in the murder of SWAPO activist Anton Lubowski. In 1994 the Namibian High Court determined that Lubowski had been killed at the behest of the former South African Civil Cooperation Bureau (CCB). While the Attorney General later ruled that there was insufficient evidence to prosecute the assassins, the Prosecutor General decided to reopen the 1989 inquest in 1995.

  b. *Disappearance.*—There were no reports of politically motivated disappearances.
Human rights organizations, political parties, and the public continued to call for a full accounting of unexplained disappearances of persons detained by SWAPO prior to independence. In August President Nujoma released the long-promised, official SWAPO memorial book, known as the Heroes Book, which lists the names of nearly 8,000 people who died during the liberation struggle. Local human rights organizations harshly criticized the book, characterizing it as an unconvincing coverup and declaring that the listing is fraught with inaccuracies and omissions regarding those who died or disappeared in SWAPO detention camps. SWAPO was viewed widely as having failed, once again, to deal forthrightly with the missing detainee issue. While some of the Government's critics would be satisfied with an official apology for SWAPO abuses against these detainees, others are pressing for full accountability through a truth commission, prosecutions, and convictions.

  c. *Torture and Other Cruel, Inhuman, or Degrading Treatment or Punishment.*—
The Constitution provides that "no persons shall be subject to torture or to cruel, inhuman, or degrading treatment or punishment." There were credible reports, however, that members of the police beat or otherwise abused civilians, either during arrest or in police station houses. According to human rights organizations, the overall number of such instances appears to be decreasing, although the problem remains particularly acute in northern areas. In November a policeman accused of abusing a criminal suspect was charged with attempted murder, assault, and kidnaping. The police launched internal investigations of alleged abuse of prisoners but there were no public reports that abusers were punished.

Prison conditions are harsh, but do not pose a serious threat to life or health. Human rights organizations continued to complain about prison overcrowding. In March 1995 the Government created a Ministry of Prisons and Correctional Services, charged with administering the country's prisons and jails. The Ministry emphasizes correctional and rehabilitation functions, including vocational training, and has made some concrete progress. For example in 1996 the Government opened two new rehabilitation facilities where inmates are taught skills for use upon their release. The Government also expanded its model program to separate youthful offenders from adult criminals, although in many remote and rural areas juveniles continue to be held with adults.

The Government continued to grant nongovernmental organizations (NGO's) and diplomatic officials regular access to prisons and prisoners.

d. *Arbitrary Arrest, Detention, or Exile.*—The Constitution forbids arbitrary arrest or detention, and the Government generally respected these provisions in practice. According to the Constitution, persons who are arrested must be informed of the reason for their arrest and must be brought before a magistrate within 48 hours of their detention. The accused are entitled to defense by legal counsel of their choice, and those who cannot afford a lawyer are entitled to state-provided counsel. In practice, however, many accused persons in remote and rural areas are not legally represented, primarily due to resource constraints. A trial must take place within "a reasonable time," or the accused must be released. Human rights organizations criticized the length of time that pretrial detainees were held, which stretched up to 1 year in many cases while investigations were pending.

Some traditional leaders reportedly continued to detain and imprison persons accused of minor offenses without recourse to police or judicial review. The Government continued training traditional leaders on the legal limits of their authority.

The Government does not use forced exile.

e. *Denial of Fair Public Trial.*—The Constitution provides for an independent judiciary, and the Government respects this provision in practice.

The formal court system has three levels: 30 magistrates' courts, the High Court, and the Supreme Court. The latter also serves as the court of appeals and as a constitutional review court.

Most rural Namibians first encounter the legal system through the traditional courts, which deal with minor criminal offenses, such as petty theft and infractions of local customs, among members of the same ethnic group. A special commission, created to make recommendations on the prospective jurisdiction of traditional courts, concluded that traditional cultural practices and structures should be maintained, provided that they were consistent with constitutional protections and existing laws. The Traditional Authorities Act delineates which offenses may be dealt with under the traditional system.

The constitutional right to a fair trial, with a presumption of innocence until proven guilty, is generally afforded by the judiciary. However, long delays in hearing cases in the regular courts and problems associated with the traditional system limit this right in practice.

The lack of qualified magistrates, other court officials, and private attorneys has resulted in a serious backlog of criminal cases, which often translated into long delays—sometimes 6 months or more—between arrest and trial. To address these problems, the Government, together with the University of Namibia, provided inservice legal training to magistrates and other court officials at the University's training center.

There were no reports of political prisoners.

f. *Arbitrary Interference With Privacy, Family, Home, or Correspondence.*—The Constitution provides all citizens with the right to privacy and requires arresting officers to secure a judicial warrant for certain listed offenses before conducting a search. Government authorities respected these rights in practice, and violations are subject to legal sanction.

Section 2. Respect for Civil Liberties, Including:

a. *Freedom of Speech and Press.*—The Constitution provides for freedom of speech and of the press, and the Government generally respected these rights.

The government-owned Namibian Broadcasting Corporation (NBC) operates most radio and television services. Although the NBC provides significant coverage of the opposition, there were growing complaints that the NBC, in particular the television service, became even less balanced in its coverage of sensitive issues than in 1995 and did not cover certain issues at all. This was especially evident relating to coverage of the missing detainees question where private organizations involved in the issue have been critical of the lack of coverage of press conferences dealing with the question. In April the Journalists' Association of Namibia adopted a resolution condemning the Government for attempting to suppress public debate on the detainee issue. NBC radio has a much wider audience than the television service and is acknowledged to be somewhat more balanced in its reporting.

There are three private radio stations and a private cable television service which broadcasts Cable News Network and South African news and entertainment programs. A variety of privately owned newspapers operate without government restriction. While there is evidence of self-censorship in state-owned media, reporters for independent newspapers criticize the Government openly and do not engage in evident self-censorship.

In April the National Assembly passed the Powers, Privileges, and Immunities of Parliament Act which included a clause making publication of leaked documents or false information about parliamentary matters a criminal offense. However, when the Media Institute of Southern Africa, other civil liberties groups, and foreign diplomats criticized this attempt at limiting press freedom, the Government and the National Council amended the bill to exclude this provision.

The Government respects academic freedom.

b. *Freedom of Peaceful Assembly and Association.*—The Constitution provides for freedom of assembly and association, and the Government respects these rights in practice. Various organizations, including political parties and religious groups, held large meetings and public gatherings without interference.

c. *Freedom of Religion.*—The Constitution provides for freedom of religion, and the Government respects this right in practice.

d. *Freedom of Movement Within the Country, Foreign Travel, Emigration, and Repatriation.*—The Constitution provides for these rights, and the Government respects them in practice.

The Government cooperates with the United Nations High Commissioner for Refugees (UNHCR), and UNHCR officials have observed a marked improvement in the Government's refugee policy. However, in a number of cases the status of the asylum applicants had not yet been decided. In an attempt to deal with this backlog, the UNHCR recently appointed a nongovernmental legal organization to screen cases. There were no reports of forced expulsion of those having a valid claim to refugee status. Human rights organizations, however, reported cases where authorities initially denied detained illegal immigrants the right to apply for refugee status until human rights organizations or attorneys intervened.

Namibia is a first asylum country and continues to permit asylum seekers to enter the country. It does not turn back asylum seekers. There are presently 2,020 refugees and asylum seekers at the Osire refugee camp, 90 percent of whom are from Angola. The rest are from Zaire, Rwanda, Burundi, Tanzania, and other African countries. Asylum seekers are interviewed by host country officials and those granted refugee status are permitted to work and attend school or the University of Namibia. Schools have been established for refugees and asylum seekers at Osire camp. Its residents are permitted to leave the camp, which is not fenced.

Section 3. Respect for Political Rights: The Right of Citizens to Change Their Government

Citizens exercised this constitutional right for the second time in December 1994 in what were generally agreed—despite some irregularities—to be free and fair presidential and parliamentary elections. The Government printed and distributed useful and informative voter guides with lists of government and opposition candidates and requested international election observers. There were televised debates, and the opposition parties were able to campaign freely.

The Constitution establishes a bicameral parliament and provides for general elections every 5 years and regional elections every 6 years. Incumbent President Nujoma was reelected to a second 5-year term of office during the country's first postindependence elections for the National Assembly and Presidency in December 1994. The ruling SWAPO party won 53 of the 72 elected National Assembly seats, the Democratic Turnhalle Alliance (DTA, the major opposition party) secured 15 seats, and three smaller parties obtained a total of 4 seats.

The DTA unsuccessfully challenged the results of the election, based on discrepancies in four constituencies in the north where votes cast exceeded the number of registered voters. In March 1995, the High Court rejected the DTA's challenge; this decision was upheld by the Supreme Court in midyear.

Women are increasingly involved in the political process but remain seriously underrepresented. There are 3 female ministers and 3 female deputy ministers out of a total of 22 ministerial and 22 deputy ministerial positions. In addition two women hold cabinet-level positions, Director of the National Planning Commission and Ombudsman. Women hold 16 of 98 parliamentary seats. In June female legislators formed a Women's Caucus in Parliament to review legislation for gender sensitivity. Historic economic and educational disadvantages have served to limit the participation of the indigenous San ethnic group in politics.

Section 4. Governmental Attitude Regarding International and Nongovernmental Investigation of Alleged Violations of Human Rights

Local nongovernmental organizations, such as the National Society for Human Rights (NSHR) and the Legal Assistance Center, operated freely, criticizing the Government's handling of the SWAPO detainee issue, misconduct by members of the police, and discrimination against women and indigenous ethnic groups. In addition other human rights organizations such as the Namibia Institute for Democracy, the Human Rights Documentation Center, the Center for Applied Social Sciences, and the Media Institute of Southern Africa worked openly on a variety of human rights issues affecting women, ethnic minorities, and other groups.

Representatives of international human rights organizations traveled to Namibia and discussed human rights issues with governmental and nongovernmental representatives.

Section 5. *Discrimination Based on Race, Sex, Religion, Disability, Language, or Social Status*

The Constitution prohibits discrimination based on race, creed, gender, or religion, and specifically prohibits "the practice and ideology of apartheid." However, the Government has not taken effective action against discrimination faced by women and the disabled.

Women.—Violence against women, including beating and rape, is widespread. Because of traditional attitudes regarding the subordination of women, many incidents of abuse are never reported to the authorities. In those few grave abuse cases where legal action has been initiated, however, the courts often sentenced male offenders, including spouses, to long terms of imprisonment. An historical problem of low bail, which has allowed some males to repeat their offenses, appears to be lessening. The courts sentenced convicted rapists to prison terms averaging 6 to 9 years. In April the Namibian Women's Organization praised the decision by the High Court to sentence a convicted rapist to life imprisonment. The man had sexually assaulted a woman in front of her children in 1995. This was the first time a convicted rapist was given a life sentence. Centers for abused women and children in Oshakati, Windhoek, Keetmanshoop, and Rehoboth are staffed with specially trained female police officers to assist victims of sexual assaults.

Despite constitutional protections and new legislation, women face persistent discrimination arising out of deep-rooted traditions of all ethnic groups and customary law. The Government, prodded by active women's rights organizations, has begun to address some forms of discrimination. In September the President elevated the head of the Department of Women's Affairs to cabinet-level rank. In addition the Married Persons Equality Act, promulgated in May, provides women in civil marriages who are married under community property laws with status equal to that of their husbands. Married women are now permitted to open bank accounts, sign contracts, and serve on the boards of companies without having to obtain their husbands' permission. This new legislation, however, does not apply to customary (traditional) marriages, where women continue to face legal and cultural discrimination. Traditional practices also continue to permit family members to confiscate the property of deceased men from their widows and children.

Children.—Children's rights, including those of protection from economic exploitation and from work that is hazardous or harmful to their health, education, mental, spiritual, moral, or social development, are enumerated in the Constitution. In practice the Government has been able to commit only limited resources to the protection of children's welfare. The Government devotes 31 percent of the national budget to education. The Government, with the assistance of international organizations, launched a national polio eradication campaign as part of its ongoing immunization program. A seminar for parliamentarians, organized under U.N. auspices, was held on the Convention on the Rights of the Child. A juvenile justice diversion program was expanded to separate juvenile offenders from adults in the criminal justice system.

Child abuse is a serious and increasingly acknowledged problem. The authorities vigorously prosecuted cases involving crimes against children, particularly rape and incest, and encouraged discussion and the issuance of printed materials in schools. In September a child rapist was given a 20-year sentence for sexually abusing a 10-year-old girl. The centers for abused women and children also worked to reduce the trauma suffered by abused children and provided training to police officials on handling this problem.

People With Disabilities.—While discrimination on the basis of disability is not addressed in the Constitution, the Labor Act of 1992 prohibits discrimination against disabled persons in employment.

The Government does not legally require special access to public buildings for the disabled. Some municipal governments, however, have installed ramps and special curbing at street crossings for the disabled.

Indigenous People.—The San people, the country's earliest known inhabitants, historically have been exploited by other ethnic groups. The Government has taken a number of measures to end this societal discrimination against the San, including seeking their advice about proposed legislation on communally held lands and increasing their access to primary education. Similarly, the Government has sought the views of the Himba people in northwest Namibia in connection with feasibility studies for the construction of a major hydroelectric dam in the heart of their traditional territory. By law all indigenous groups are able to participate equally in decisions affecting their lands, cultures, traditions, and allocations of natural resources. Nevertheless, the San and other indigenous Namibians have been unable to exercise fully these rights as a result of historically minimal access to education and economic opportunities under colonial rule, coupled with their relative isolation in remote areas of the country.

The Traditional Authorities Act, which came into effect in December 1995, defines the role, duties, and powers of traditional leaders. The act provides that customary law that is inconsistent with provisions of the Constitution is invalid and delineates which types of crimes may be dealt with in traditional courts. The act assigns to traditional leaders the role of guardians of culture and tradition, and also mandates that traditional leaders elected to Parliament must choose between their traditional and elected offices before the end of 1996. Some traditional leaders and human rights organizations have maintained that this provision is unconstitutional, and a court challenge is being pursued.

National/Racial/Ethnic Minorities.—The Constitution prohibits discrimination based on race and other factors and specifically prohibits "the practice and ideology of apartheid." Nevertheless, as a result of more than 70 years of South African administration, societal, racial, and ethnic discrimination persists, and some apartheid-based statutes have not yet been repealed or replaced by the Parliament. Many nonwhites continued to complain that the Government was not moving quickly enough in education, health, housing, employment, and access to land.

Also some opposition parties, including members of the Herero and Nama ethnic groups, complained that the SWAPO-led Government provided more development assistance to the numerically dominant Ovambo ethnic group of far northern Namibia than to other groups or regions of the country. In June 1995, the High Court denied the application by the "Basters" community for the Government to return its traditional land in the Rehoboth area, ruling that the community's "traditional lands" reverted to the central Government upon independence. The Supreme Court agreed with the High Court's judgment and dismissed the Basters final appeal in May.

Section 6. Worker Rights

a. *The Right of Association.*—The Constitution provides for freedom of association, including freedom to form and join trade unions. The 1992 Labor Act extended that right to public servants, farm workers, and domestic employees. Trade unions have no difficulty registering, and there are no government restrictions on who may serve as a union official. No union has been dissolved by government action. During the year, the Namibian public service held vigorously contested union elections.

Unions are independent of Government and may form federations. The two principal trade union umbrella organizations are the National Union of Namibian Workers (NUNW), and the Namibia People's Social Movement (NPSM). The larger NUNW continues to maintain its strong affiliation with the ruling SWAPO party. Roughly half of the wage sector is organized to some degree, although less than 20 percent of full-time wage earners are organized.

Except for workers providing essential services (e.g., jobs related to public health and safety) and workers in the nascent export processing zones (EPZ's), workers enjoy the right to strike once conciliation procedures have been exhausted. Under the Labor Act, strike action can only be used in disputes involving specific worker interests, such as pay raises. Disputes over worker rights, including dismissals, must be referred to a labor court (which is convened when needed in the existing magisterial districts) for arbitration. The Labor Act protects legally striking workers from unfair dismissal.

Unemployment, which is nearly 40 percent, remained a significant problem in Namibia, affecting largely the black majority. Apartheid-era attitudes among some employers contributed to a divisive, 10-week strike at a major mining firm. While the atmosphere at the three mine sites was tense and occasionally violent, the confrontation was eventually defused by high-level government intervention.

Trade unions are free to exchange visits with foreign trade unions and to affiliate with international trade union organizations. Unions have exercised this right without interference. The American Federation of Labor-Congress of Industrial Organizations, through its African-American Labor Center representative in South Africa, provided technical assistance to the NUNW during regular visits to Namibia.

b. *The Right to Organize and Bargain Collectively.*—The 1992 Labor Act provides employees with the right to bargain individually or collectively. Collective bargaining is not widely practiced outside the mining and construction industries; wages are usually set by employers. As unions become more active, however, informal collective bargaining is becoming more common.

The Labor Act provides a process for employer recognition of trade unions and protection for members and organizers. The law also empowers the labor court to remedy unfair labor practices and explicitly forbids unfair dismissals, which may be appealed to the labor court.

The Labor Act applies to the prospective EPZ in Walvis Bay. A compromise on this point was reached by the Government and NUNW representatives in August 1995. However, trade unionists continued to challenge the constitutionality of the compromise because it precludes strikes and lockouts. Under the compromise, labor-related issues in the EPZ would be referred to a special EPZ Dispute Settlement Panel, composed of employers and workers, for expeditious resolution. As business activity in the Walvis Bay EPZ had just begun to get under way by year's end, the effectiveness of this compromise in securing the rights of workers in the EPZ could not yet be determined.

c. *Prohibition of Forced or Compulsory Labor.*—Forced labor is prohibited by law. Although there were no formal complaints filed with the Ministry of Labor, there were ongoing reports in the media that farm workers often receive inadequate compensation for their labor and are subject to strict control by farm owners. Ministry of Labor inspectors sometimes encountered problems in gaining access to the country's large, privately owned commercial farms in order to document possible Labor Code violations.

d. *Minimum Age for Employment of Children.*—Under the 1992 Labor Act, the minimum age for employment is 14 years, with higher age requirements for certain sectors such as mining, construction, and night work. Ministry of Labor inspectors generally enforce minimum age regulations, but children below the age of 14 often work on family and commercial farms, and in the informal sector. A report on the status of children estimates that 13,800 children under 15 years of age are already in the labor force. Of these, 41 percent are working as unpaid laborers on family and commercial farms. Boys in rural areas traditionally start herding livestock at age 7. According to 1991 figures, approximately 2 percent of farm workers are children (mainly from the San ethnic group). There were also reports that Angolan and Zambian children, who are not protected by the Labor Act, worked on communal and cattle farms in border areas.

e. *Acceptable Conditions of Work.*—There is no statutory minimum wage law. In Windhoek's nonwhite townships, many workers and their families have difficulty maintaining a minimally decent standard of living. White citizens earn significantly more on average than do black citizens, in large part because whites own most of the country's productive resources and have had access to education that enables them to take advantage of the skilled labor shortage.

After independence the standard legal workweek was reduced from 46 to 45 hours, and includes at least one 24-hour rest period per week. An employer may require no more than 10 hours per week of overtime. The law mandates 24 consecutive days of annual leave, at least 30 workdays of sick leave per year, and 3 months of unpaid maternity leave. In practice, however, these provisions are not yet rigorously observed or enforced by the Ministry of Labor. During 1996 two important NGO studies—one of farm workers and the other of domestic employees—highlighted the dismal conditions which some employees encounter while working in these occupations.

The Government mandates occupational health and safety standards. The Labor Act empowers the President to enforce them through inspections and criminal penalties. The law requires employers to ensure the health, safety, and welfare of their employees. It provides employees with the right to remove themselves from dangerous work situations.

NIGER

Niger began the year as a multiparty parliamentary democracy, but on January 27 a group of army officers led by then Colonel Ibrahim Mainassara Bare overthrew the elected government. The leaders of the coup d'etat quickly established a Military Council of National Salvation (CSN) and a subordinate interim cabinet. The CSN suspended the 1992 Constitution, dissolved the National Assembly, implemented a state of emergency, and temporarily prohibited political activity. Top civilian government leaders were put under house arrest. The Government subsequently organized a Constitutional Conference, held a referendum on the new Constitution, and conducted a seriously flawed presidential election, which was won by Bare, the coup leader. November legislative elections were boycotted by the opposition. Progovernment parties and sympathizers claimed all 80 National Assembly seats.

Security forces consist of the army, the Republican Guard, the gendarmerie (paramilitary police), and the national police. The police and the gendarmerie traditionally have primary responsibility for internal security. However, since the coup the army has had a much more prominent role. The January coup was led by army officers with some support from the gendarmerie. Since the coup, members of all security forces have committed human rights abuses.

The economy is based mainly on traditional subsistence farming, herding, small trading, and informal markets. Less than 15 percent of the labor force is in the modern sector. Uranium is the most important export. Per capita income is less than $260. Persistent drought, deforestation and soil degradation, low literacy, a flat uranium market, high import prices, and burdensome debt further weakened the already troubled economy. Niger is heavily dependent on foreign assistance, and one of the aftermaths of the coup was a sharp fall in foreign aid.

The Government's human rights record worsened in 1996 as the Government committed numerous abuses. The fraudulent presidential election effectively disenfranchised Nigeriens, preventing them from exercising their right to change their government. Security forces beat political opponents and violated laws governing searches, treatment of prisoners, and length of detention. Prison conditions remained poor. The overloaded judicial system and delays in trials resulted in long periods of pretrial confinement. The Government intimidated the private press and radio, arresting and mistreating journalists and publishers, and temporarily closing two private radio stations. Civic and political organizations were banned from holding gatherings or demonstrations for much of the year, under a declared state of emergency and other bans. Societal discrimination and domestic violence against women continued to be serious problems. Female genital mutilation persists.

RESPECT FOR HUMAN RIGHTS

Section 1. Respect for the Integrity of the Person, Including Freedom From:

a. *Political and Other Extrajudicial Killing.*—There were no reports of political or other extrajudicial killings by government officials.

Violence in the North has been minimal since the signing of the April 1995 peace pact between Tuareg separatists and the Government. A similar agreement in April between the Government and the Arab/Toubou/Kanouri Front (CRA) based in eastern Niger, which seeks independence for its region, also lessened sporadic violence in that area. After an attack in February on Dirkou and its small military base by a CRA subgroup, the Government reported CRA casualties of 12 dead and 8 wounded. Skirmishes with the same group in the Lake Chad area in January and February produced a similar number of deaths with casualties on both sides. The group also killed and wounded several civilian road workers in an attack in June in the same area. The Government has not yet met its peace accord commitment to disarm Arab militias and has produced no report of a promised investigation into the 1995 killing of a Tuareg rebel leader, reportedly by Arab militia.

b. *Disappearance.*—There were no reports of politically motivated disappearances.

c. *Torture and Other Cruel, Inhuman, or Degrading Treatment or Punishment.*—Although the Constitution prohibits such practices, there were reports that police or military personnel beat or otherwise abused several political leaders and their supporters. Mamane Abou, editor of the weekly newspaper, Le Republicain, and president of the private press association, was detained briefly by police on July 21, who shaved his head bald to humiliate him (see Section 2.a.).

Prisons are underfunded and understaffed. They are overcrowded and diet, health, and sanitary conditions for prisoners are very poor. For example, the Agadez prison's health budget for 182 prisoners was $825 a year.

Prisoners are segregated by sex. Family visits are allowed, and prisoners can receive supplemental food and other necessities from their families. There are no reports of unduly harsh treatment, beyond the very poor conditions of detention noted above, but petty corruption among prison staff is also reported rampant.

Human rights monitors visit the prisons.

d. *Arbitrary Arrest, Detention, or Exile.*—Although the Constitution prohibits arbitrary detention, and laws officially prohibit detention without charge in excess of 48 hours, police violate these provisions in practice. If police fail to gather sufficient evidence within the detention period, the prosecutor gives the case to another officer, and a new 48-hour detention period begins.

Authorities detained numerous political party leaders, generally for brief periods, and sometimes roughly treated them, as part of an effort to intimidate the opposition. Authorities placed the four political party candidates who contested the July

7 to 8 presidential elections under house arrest after the elections and held them until July 22. One candidate, Nigerien Party for Democracy and Socialism (PNDS) head Mahamadou Issoufou, was put under house arrest again by authorities from July 27 to August 12, and two other party leaders were detained for 3 days, after party members staged a protest on July 27 against the election fraud. In February authorities arrested eight members of former President Ousmane's party, reportedly to prevent them from helping him seek asylum in a Western embassy. They were released within a few days; no charges were filed. Two PNDS party leaders were detained by soldiers for 5 days in early May without explanation; one was beaten. The Government arrested several dozen protesters at the time of the July elections but released them by July 22. At least one, possibly more, were beaten while in custody.

The judicial system is seriously overloaded. There are no statutory limits on pretrial confinement of indicted persons; detention frequently lasts months or years. As many as 80 percent of prisoners in Niamey are awaiting trial.

The law provides for a right to counsel, although there is only one defense attorney known to have a private practice outside the capital. A defendant has the right to a lawyer immediately upon detention. The State provides a defense attorney for indigents.

Bail is available for crimes carrying a penalty of less than 10 years' imprisonment. Widespread ignorance of the law and lack of financial means prevent full exercise of these rights.

In August President Bare pardoned most prisoners with less than 2 years yet to serve and substantially reduced the sentences of most others. All juveniles, nursing and pregnant women, elderly prisoners, and those with certain illnesses were released regardless of the time remaining on their sentences.

The Constitution prohibits exile, and there were no reports of its use.

e. *Denial of Fair Public Trial.*—The Constitution provides for an independent judiciary. Although the Supreme Court has on occasion asserted its independence, human rights groups assert that family and business ties influence the lower courts and undermine their integrity. Judges sometimes fear reassignment or having their financial benefits reduced if they render a decision unfavorable to the Government, though such coercive tactics are reportedly less frequently used.

Defendants and prosecutors may appeal a verdict, first to the Court of Appeals, then to the Supreme Court. The Court of Appeals reviews questions of fact and law, while the Supreme Court reviews only the application of law and constitutional questions.

A traditional chief or a customary court try cases involving divorce or inheritance. Customary courts, located only in large towns and cities, are headed by a legal practitioner with basic legal education who is advised by an assessor knowledgeable in the society's traditions. The judicial actions of chiefs and customary courts are not regulated by code, and defendants may appeal a verdict to the formal court system. Women do not have equal legal status with men and do not enjoy the same access to legal redress (see Section 5).

The law provides that the Government constitute a State Security Court to try high crimes against the State in secret, but due process provisions still apply. Civil and criminal trials are public except in security-related cases. Defendants have the right to counsel, to be present at trial, to confront witnesses, to examine the evidence against them, and to appeal verdicts. The Constitution affirms the presumption of innocence.

The law provides for counsel at public expense for minors and indigent defendants charged with crimes carrying a sentence of 10 years or more. Although lawyers comply with government requests to provide counsel, they are generally not remunerated by the Government.

There were no reports of political prisoners.

f. *Arbitrary Interference With Privacy, Family, Home, or Correspondence.*—The law requires that police have a search warrant, normally issued by a judge. Police may search without warrants when they have strong suspicion that a house shelters criminals or stolen property. The police routinely violated required procedures when invading the homes and interfering in the affairs of political party leaders and journalists after the July presidential elections. These actions confirm human rights organizations' reports that police often conduct routine searches without warrants.

Section 2. *Respect for Civil Liberties, Including:*

a. *Freedom of Speech and Press.*—Like its predecessor, the 1996 Constitution, approved by referendum in May, provides for freedom of speech and the press. Nevertheless the current Government, following the January coup and through the fraudulent July presidential elections, took actions to limit press freedom and stifle political discussion, through intimidation, harassment, and detention. The editor of Le Soleil newspaper was kidnaped and beaten by unknown persons, presumed to be government agents. The Government detained the editor of The Alternative newspaper in April, after he published an article critical of the Bare regime. On May 3, an edition of the (antimilitary) Tribune du Pueple containing an editorial critical of the Government was seized at the printers. On May 5, the Government detained and imprisoned without charges the editor of Tribune du Pueple.

On July 7, during presidential voting and after independent radio station R and M aired comments by a party candidate critical of the regime, police temporarily shut down the station and arrested the editor in chief. On July 8, military authorities closed independent radio station Anfani, which had also carried remarks the previous day by a political leader opposing Bare. The station was not allowed to resume broadcasting until early August. Mamane Abou, editor of the weekly newspaper, Le Republicain, and president of the private press association, was detained briefly by police on July 21, who shaved his head bald to humiliate him. Police also arrested Amadou Hamidou, publisher of Tribune du Pueple, in July. British Broadcasting Corporation correspondent Abdoulaye Seyni was briefly detained by the Government and released in early August. All arrested persons listed above were released after brief detention.

Despite these governmental efforts to control media content, the local independent press remained relatively assertive in protesting the July electoral fraud and other government actions. No newspaper was forced to shut down. Foreign journals circulated and reported freely.

Government harassment of the private media continued during the legislative elections with the private radio station Anfani being most repeatedly targeted. Station managers decided to suspend all news programming for the weekend of the election because of concerns that government officials would arbitrarily detain both staff and management.

The most important public medium is the government-operated, multilingual national radio service. It provided only minimal air time for opposition political activities. The Government publishes the French-language daily, Le Sahel, and its weekend French edition. There are about 12 private French and Hausa language weeklies or monthlies, some published by political parties.

Academic freedom is respected.

b. *Freedom of Peaceful Assembly and Association.*—The Constitution provides for freedom of assembly and association. Nevertheless, the Government retains the authority to prohibit gatherings either under tense social conditions or if advance notice (48 hours) is not provided. A decree prohibiting political party activity remained in effect from January until May 20. In addition, the Government declared a state of emergency after the coup, under which it selectively banned public assemblies or gatherings until lifting it on May 23. Authorities used a ban on public demonstrations issued after the July elections to mute public protest of the results. On July 10 and 11, police dispersed opposition supporters, who defied the ban in large numbers in Niamey and Zinder respectively, with tear gas and baton charges, assisted by armed forces personnel.

Opposition parties which boycotted the legislative elections were not permitted to hold meetings or demonstrations during the campaign period. Government spokesmen claimed that only parties contesting elections had such a right although the Constitution makes no such distinction.

Under the Constitution, Nigeriens may form political parties of any kind, except those that are based on ethnicity, religion, or region, and the Government respects this right in practice.

c. *Freedom of Religion.*—The Government respects freedom of religion. Most Nigeriens practice Islam. Christians (including Jehovah's Witnesses) and Baha'i practice freely. Foreign missionaries work freely, but their organization must be registered as a Nigerien association.

d. *Freedom of Movement Within the Country, Foreign Travel, Emigration, and Repatriation.*—The law provides for freedom of movement. Neither emigration nor repatriation is restricted. The coup-installed Government closed the country's airports and land borders immediately following the coup but reopened them several days later.

Among the Hausa and Fulani peoples in eastern Niger, some women are cloistered and may leave their homes only if escorted by a male and usually only after dark. Security forces at checkpoints monitor travel of persons and the circulation of goods, particularly near major population centers and sometimes demand extra payments. Attacks by bandits on major routes to the North have declined considerably, although people often travel in convoy with military escort for security.

The Government cooperates with the Office of the United Nations High Commissioner for Refugees (UNHCR) and other humanitarian organizations in assisting refugees.

The Government has provided first asylum in the recent past to several thousand Chadian refugees. Thousands of Malian refugees have resided in recent years in western Niger. The issue of first asylum is not known to have arisen in any new cases in 1996. There are 1,500 Chadian refugees in eastern Niger. In addition, 20,000 to 25,000 Tuareg refugees from Mali reside in Niger. A tripartite agreement was negotiated by Mali, Niger, and the UNHCR for the repatriation of Malian refugees beginning in early 1997. Many refugees have begun to return voluntarily to Mali with assistance from the Governments of Niger and Mali, the International Committee of the Red Cross, and the UNHCR.

There were no reports of forced repatriation of refugees. There were no reports of forced return of persons to a country where they feared persecution.

Section 3. Respect for Political Rights: The Right of Citizens to Change Their Government

President Bare, through the Military Council of National Salvation and his Council of Ministers, rules by decree. The January coup d'etat led by then Colonel Bare overthrew the democratically elected government. In the days following the coup, Bare and the coup leadership dissolved the National Assembly; banned political party activity; suspended the 1992 constitution; and declared a state of emergency. Bare scheduled presidential elections for July and legislative elections for a new National Assembly for September, later postponed until November.

In a May 10 referendum with a low turn-out, voters approved a new Constitution that reiterates rights granted under the 1992 document. Citizens 18 years of age and over can vote, and balloting is by secret ballot. The Constitution provides for a political system with checks and balances, an ethnically representative 83-seat National Assembly, and an independent judiciary. The most prominent constitutional changes are the provisions for a stronger presidency, which make the Prime Minister more clearly subordinate to the President.

The military government organized presidential elections on July 7 and 8, in which General Bare (promoted from colonel in May), the leader of the coup, ran against four political party candidates. However, midway through the voting, the regime dismissed the independent electoral commission, took control of ballot boxes, and prevented political party representatives and neutral observers from monitoring the vote tabulation. Bare claimed 52 percent of the votes, a result widely viewed as fraudulent by both local and international observers. An association of nongovernmental organizations (NGO's), the Collectif, issued in mid-July a very critical report on the Government's organization of the presidential elections, including the vote-counting phase. The report cited numerous violations of the electoral code and concluded that the elections were not transparent and therefore not credible. General Bare was sworn into office on August 7.

Circumstances were similar for the legislative elections, postponed until November 23 from their original September date. The Government and opposition attempted to negotiate terms for full and free political participation, with the opposition seeking to annul the presidential election and further postpone legislative elections. During this period of negotiation, the Government arrested Bello Tiousso Garba, the leader of a small opposition party, after he criticized the Government in an interview on a local radio station. Although Garba was released within 24 hours, the Minister of the Interior subsequently prohibited the party from all activities for 3 months. Ultimately the sides could not reach agreement, and when the Government moved forward with the elections as scheduled, the opposition called for a boycott. The elections were characterized by a modest turnout with the Government claiming 36 percent participation, but foreign observers indicated a more accurate figure was 25 percent.

Women traditionally play a subordinate role in politics. The societal practice of husbands' voting their wives' proxy ballots effectively disenfranchises many women. This practice was widely used in recent presidential and National Assembly elections.

In the now-dissolved National Assembly, 3 of the 83 members were women. In the Assembly elected in November only 1 of the 80 elected members is female. The last Government appointed 5 women to ministerial positions; the present Government has appointed 4 women. Many women were active in the brief summer electoral campaign, focusing on getting out the female vote, voter registration, and organizing campaigns.

Section 4. Governmental Attitude Regarding International and Nongovernmental Investigation of Alleged Violations of Human Rights

Several independent human rights groups and associations operate without explicit governmental hindrance, although a certain atmosphere of intimidation has prevailed since the coup. Dominant among the associations are the Nigerien Association for the Defense of Human Rights (ANDDH); Democracy, Liberty, and Development (DLD); the National League for Defense of Human Rights; Adalci; the Network for the Integration and Diffusion of Rights in the Rural Milieu (known as "Ridd-Fitla"); and the Association of Women Jurists of Niger. There are several other women's rights groups. The International Committee of the Red Cross is active in Niger.

An association of local NGO's representing all political views created an umbrella association, the "Collectif", to promote human rights and democracy. (see Section 3)

Section 5. Discrimination Based on Race, Sex, Religion, Disability, Language, or Social Status

The Constitution prohibits discrimination based on sex, social origin, race, ethnicity, or religion. In practice, however, there is discrimination against women, children, ethnic minorities, and disabled persons, including limited economic and political opportunities.

Women.—Domestic violence against women is widespread, although firm statistics are lacking. Wife beating is reportedly common, even in upper social strata. Families often intervene to prevent the worst abuses, and women may (and do) divorce because of physical abuse. While women have the right to seek redress in the customary or modern courts, few do so from ignorance of the legal system, fear of social stigma, and fear of repudiation. Women's rights organizations report that prostitution is often the only economic alternative for a woman who wants to leave her husband.

Despite the Constitution's provisions for women's rights, the deep-seated traditional belief in the submission of women to men results in discrimination in the political process (see Section 3), in education, employment, and property rights. Discrimination is worse in rural areas, where women do much of the subsistence farming as well as childrearing. Despite being 47 percent of the work force, women have made only modest inroads in civil service and professional employment and remain underrepresented in these areas.

Women's inferior legal status is evident since, for example, a male head of household has certain legal rights; but divorced or widowed women, even with children, are not considered to be the heads of their households. In 1995 the Government considered a draft family code modeled on codes in other African Muslim countries intended to eliminate gender bias in inheritance rights, land tenure, and child custody, as well as end the practice of repudiation, which permits a husband to obtain an immediate divorce with no further responsibility for his wife or children. In June 1995, when Islamic associations condemned the draft code, the Government suspended discussions and has taken no further action. Islamic militants reportedly threatened women who supported the code with physical harm.

Children.—Although the Constitution provides that the State promote children's welfare, financial resources are extremely limited. Only about 25 percent of children of primary school age attend school, and about 60 percent of those finishing primary school are boys. The majority of young girls are kept at home to work and rarely attend school for more than a few years, resulting in a female literacy rate of 7 percent versus 18 percent for males. Tradition among some ethnic groups allows young girls from rural families to enter marriage agreements on the basis of which girls are sent at the age of 10 or 12 to join their husband's family under the tutelage of their mother-in-law. There are credible reports of underage girls being drawn into prostitution, sometimes with the complicity of their families.

According to international experts, female genital mutilation (FGM), which is widely condemned by international health experts as damaging to both physical and psychological health, is practiced by several ethnic groups in the western and the far eastern areas of the country. Clitoridectomy is the most common form of FGM.

People With Disabilities.—The Constitution mandates that the State provide for people with disabilities. However, the Government has yet to implement regulations that call for accessibility and education for those with special needs.

National/Racial/Ethnic Minorities.—Ethnic minorities—Tuareg, Fulani, Toubou, Kanouri, and Arab—continue to assert that the far more numerous Hausa and Djerma ethnic groups discriminate against them. The Hausa and Djerma dominate government and business. The Government has supported greater minority representation in the National Assembly and increased education and health care. It supports in principle the April 1995 peace accord calling for special development efforts in the north where the Tuareg population is dominant. However, nomadic peoples, such as Tuaregs and many Fulani, continue to have less access to government services.

Section 6. Worker Rights

a. *The Right of Association.*—The Constitution provides formal recognition of workers' longstanding right to establish and join trade unions. However, more than 95 percent of Niger's work force is employed in the nonunionized subsistence agricultural and small trading sectors.

The National Union of Nigerien Workers (USTN), a federation made up of 42 unions, represents the majority of salary earners; most are government employees, such as civil servants, teachers, and employees in state-owned corporations. The USTN and the affiliated National Union of Nigerien Teachers (SNEN) profess political autonomy but, like most unions, have informal ties to political parties. There is also an independent magistrate's union.

However, in February the Government suspended the two national police unions, with the purported aim of restoring order within the police service. It also suspended the customs, and water and forest workers' unions in April, because of their "paramilitary nature."

The Constitution provides for the right to strike, except for security forces and police. In March 1994, the National Assembly passed a new strike law specifying that labor must give notice and begin negotiations before work is stopped; that public workers must maintain a minimum level of service during a strike; that the Government can requisition workers to guarantee minimum service; and that striking public sector workers will not be paid for the time they are on strike. The latter condition already prevailed in the private sector.

During the year, labor challenged the Government on the budget and a new law regulating strikes. The USTN staged several short strikes, most over pay demands. Civil servants struck for 2 days over salary arrears in January, and uranium and coal mine workers struck for several days in February and March over expanded pay and benefits. Television journalists and announcers struck briefly in March over allowances. In June USTN orchestrated a 48-hour general strike to protest salary arrears that it claimed were due to civil service and parastatal workers. These strikes largely failed to achieve their objectives but demonstrated that the right to strike, within accepted procedures, would be honored. Following the tainted July presidential elections, USTN called a poorly heeded strike to protest the dissolution of the independent electoral commission midway through the voting and vote counting. However, the Government announced that the strike was illegal, because its goal was not to advance workers' "material and moral" interests but was only to make a "political demand" outside the unions' competence.

The USTN is a member of the Organization of African Trade Union Unity and abides by that organization's policy of having no formal affiliations outside the African continent. However, it enjoys assistance from some international unions, and individual unions such as the teacher's union are affiliated with international trade secretariats.

b. *The Right to Organize and Bargain Collectively.*—In addition to the Constitution and the Labor Code, there is a basic framework agreement, negotiated by the USTN's predecessor, employers, and the Government, which defines all classes and categories of work, establishes basic conditions of work, and defines union activities. In private and state-owned enterprises, unions widely use their right to bargain collectively with management without government interference for wages over and above the statutory minimum as well as for more favorable work conditions. Collective bargaining also exists in the public sector. However, since most organized workers, including teachers, are government employees, the Government is actually involved in most bargaining agreements. The USTN represents civil servants in bargaining with the Government, and labor/management agreements apply uniformly to all employees.

The Labor Code is based on International Labor Organization principles; it protects the right to organize and prohibits antiunion discrimination by employers. Labor unions reported no such discrimination.

There are no export processing zones.

c. *Prohibition of Forced or Compulsory Labor.*—The Labor Code prohibits forced or compulsory labor, except for legally convicted prisoners. There were no reports of violations.

d. *Minimum Age for Employment of Children.*—Child labor in nonindustrial enterprises is permitted by law under certain conditions. Children under the age of 14 must obtain special authorization to work, and those 14 to 18 years of age are subject to limitation on hours (a maximum of 4.5 hours per day) and types of employment (no industrial work) so that schooling may continue. Minimum compulsory education is 6 years, but far fewer than half of school-age children complete 6 years of education.

The law requires employers to ensure minimum sanitary working conditions for children. Law and practice prohibit child labor in industrial work. Ministry of Labor inspectors enforce child labor laws. Child labor is practically nonexistent in the formal (wage) sector, although children work in the unregulated agricultural, commercial, and artisan sectors. Rural children (the majority) regularly work with their families from a very early age—helping in the fields, getting firewood and water, and other similar tasks. There is no official regulation of this labor.

e. *Acceptable Conditions of Work*.—The Labor Code establishes a minimum wage for salaried workers of each class and category within the formal sector. The lowest minimum is approximately $38 (cfa 20,500) per month. Additional salary is granted for each family member and for such working conditions as night shifts and required travel. Minimum wages are not sufficient to provide a decent living for workers and their families. Most households have multiple earners (largely informal commerce) and rely on the extended family for support.

The legal workweek is 40 hours with a minimum of one 24-hour rest period. However, for certain occupations the Ministry of Labor authorizes longer workweeks—up to 72 hours. There were no reports of violations.

The Labor Code also establishes occupational safety and health standards; Ministry of Labor inspectors enforce these standards. Due to staff shortages, however, inspectors focus on safety violations only in the most dangerous industries: mining, building, and manufacturing. Although generally satisfied with the safety equipment provided by employers, citing in particular adequate protection from radiation in the uranium mines, unions say workers should be better informed of the risks posed by their jobs. Workers have the right to remove themselves from hazardous conditions without fear of losing their jobs.

NIGERIA

General Sani Abacha, who seized power in a palace coup in November 1993, remained Head of State throughout 1996. Under Abacha, the main decisionmaking organ is the exclusively military Provisional Ruling Council (PRC), which rules by decree. The PRC oversees the 32-member Federal Executive Council composed of military officers and civilians. Pending the promulgation of the Constitution written by the Constitutional Conference in 1995 and subsequently approved by the Head of State, the Government observes some provisions of the 1979 and 1989 Constitutions. The decree suspending the 1979 Constitution was not repealed and the 1989 Constitutions has not been implemented. In 1995 Abacha announced a transition timetable which purports to return the country to democratically elected civilian government by October 1, 1998.

The Government continued to enforce its arbitrary authority through the Federal Security System (the military, the state security service, and the national police) and through decrees blocking action by the opposition in the courts. All branches of the security forces committed serious human rights abuses.

Most of the 100 million population is rural, engaging in small-scale agriculture. Nigeria depends on oil exports for over 90 percent of its foreign exchange earnings. The economy was estimated to have grown at a higher rate than the 2.2 percent of 1995 and the 1.0 percent of 1994, but at little or no margin above the population growth rate so that gross domestic product per capita did not change appreciably. Even that growth is deceptive, however, since much of it came from the petroleum sector with limited effect on the rest of the economy. The general level of economic activity continues to be depressed with factory capacity utilization remaining in the 30 percent range and many major companies reporting lower profits and expanding inventories. Endemic corruption further hindered the functioning of the economy. The Government has instituted liberalizing economic reforms through its "guided deregulation" program, e.g., investment and foreign exchange rules; but its controls over the economy remain extensive, including government-mandated, below-market fuel prices. There is a continued lack of transparency in government transactions.

The human rights record remained dismal. Throughout the year, General Abacha's Government relied regularly on arbitrary detention and harassment to silence its many critics. The winner of the annulled 1993 presidential election, Chief Moshood K.O. Abiola, remained in detention on charges of treason, and in June unidentified persons murdered Abiola's senior wife under mysterious circumstances. The Government's investigation to date has been perfunctory. Security forces committed extrajudicial killings and used excessive force to quell antigovernment protests as well as to combat a growing wave of violent crime, killing and wounding a number of persons, including innocent civilians. Police tortured and beat suspects and detainees, and prison conditions remained life threatening; many prisoners died in custody. Security services continued routine harassment of human rights and prodemocracy groups, including labor leaders, journalists, and student activists. The Government also infringed on citizens' right to privacy.

Citizens do not have the right to change their government by peaceful means. Despite the announced timetable for transitions from military to multiparty rule, there was little meaningful progress toward democracy. In the March 16 nonparty local elections, the Government disqualified many candidates and promulgated a decree allowing replacement without cause of elected officials by government-selected administrators, effectively nulifying the results. Local government elections on a party basis, originally scheduled for the fourth quarter of 1996, were postponed until 1997. The Government's reliance on tribunals, which operate outside the constitutional court system, and harsh decrees prohibiting judicial review seriously undermine the integrity of the judicial process and often result in legal proceedings that deny defendants due process, as in the 1995 cases of Ken Saro-Wiwa and eight others (who were executed) and former Head of State Olusegun Obasanjo (who was convicted by a secret military tribunal). Obasanjo, his erstwhile deputy and outspoken National Constitutional Conference delegate Shehu Musa Yar'Adua, and more than 20 others, remained in prison for their roles in an alleged March 1995 coup plot. The Government's frequent refusal to respect court rulings also undercuts the independence and integrity of the judicial process.

Other human rights problems included infringements on freedom of speech, press, assembly, association, travel, and workers rights, and violence and discrimination against women. There were many reports of sexual abuse of female prisoners. The regime established a National Human Rights Commission (NHRC) in June, but it was never taken seriously by nongovernmental human rights groups and by year's end had no discernible effect on the human rights climate.

RESPECT FOR HUMAN RIGHTS

Section 1. Respect for the Integrity of the Person, Including Freedom From:

a. *Political and Other Extrajudicial Killing.*—As in previous years, police and security services commonly committed extrajudicial killings and used excessive force to quell antigovernment and prodemocracy protests. Credible, though unconfirmed, reports by Nigerian human rights groups indicate numerous deaths of suspects in police custody. These reports are consistent with other credible reports of police abuse, including the use of torture to extract criminal confessions. The Government seldom holds police and security forces accountable for their use of excessive, deadly force or for the death of individuals in custody. The Government's actions have fostered a climate of impunity in which these abuses flourish. Increasing and widespread violent crime prompted police to employ roadblocks and checkpoints where extortion, violence, and lethal force are common.

In one widely reported incident, Lukman Ololade, an independent bus driver, was shot by police in early February as he and other drivers attempted to push his disabled minibus to the side of the road. According to transport workers present at the time, police officers stopped by the bus and an argument ensued between the officers and transport workers. In the course of the argument, a policeman opened fire, fatally wounding Ololade. The Committee for the Defense of Human Rights, a Nigerian nongovernmental organization (NGO), highlighted in its September newsletter the deaths of a bus driver and passenger shot by a security officer as the bus passed a roadside checkpoint. Accounts of security officers shooting at transport workers and individual drivers who refuse to pay bribes at checkpoints or appear "suspicious" were common.

There were several reports that the Lagos State Environmental Task Force (see Section 1.c.) members also killed citizens who failed to stop at checkpoints or comply with task force orders.

Credible reports of mobile anticrime police shooting people suspected of armed robbery continued throughout the year. On October 24, four armed suspects in a carjacking near a foreign embassy in Lagos were shot and killed by police officers. Two of the suspects were fatally wounded while attempting to flee; eyewitnesses reported that the other two suspects were injured and disabled by police during the chase and subsequently shot dead 50 feet from the gate of an embassy. Reliable sources reported that police officers involved acted under standing instructions to shoot to kill.

In September 39 people were reported dead in the northern cities of Kaduna and Zaria after police attempted to break up demonstrations protesting the detention of Muslim cleric and religious leader Sheikh Ibrahim Al-Zakzaky. The Civil Liberties Organization (CLO) reported that the protesters were unarmed and the demonstrations peaceful until police fired tear gas into the crowd, creating confusion. During the resulting melee, police opened fire, killing and wounding both protestors and police officers.

The harsh interrogation methods reportedly practiced by some security officers resulted in the deaths while in custody of several people. Joseph Kporok, a 30-year-old Movement for the Survival of the Ogoni People (MOSOP) activist, was arrested after a dispute with his mother-in-law over land. Once in custody at the Rivers state internal security task force headquarters, Kporok was interrogated about his Mosop affiliation and beaten. He was then transferred to state police headquarters in Port Harcourt where he died on October 22. In July, 26-year-old Kenneth Nwokoye was beaten to death by uniformed officers who arrested him after raiding and searching his house. The officers did not present a search or arrest warrant.

Paralleling the year's noticeable increase in violent crime was the mysterious and brutal murder in June of Kudirat Abiola, the senior wife of M.K.O. Abiola, who was shot in her car multiple times by unknown persons. The Government conducted a perfunctory investigation of the murder that included the detention of leading National Democratic Coalition (NADECO) activists and Abiola family members. All have been released. There have been no further arrests.

In November Suliat Adedeji, an outspoken politician and successful businesswoman, was beaten and shot by armed men who invaded her home in Ibadan. Despite brutal demands for "ransom," nothing was taken from the Adedeji home. Alex Ibru, publisher of The Guardian, one of the country's leading independent daily newspapers, was shot and permanently injured in February by gunmen.

b. *Disappearance.*—There were no confirmed reports of politically motivated disappearances. However, government detention practices have the effect of causing many persons to be "missing" for extended periods (see Section 1.d.).

c. *Torture and Other Cruel, Inhuman, or Degrading Treatment or Punishment.*—The 1979 Constitution (suspended) and the 1989 Constitution (never implemented) prohibit torture and mistreatment of prisoners and provide criminal sanctions for such excesses. The Evidence Act of 1960 prohibits the introduction of evidence obtained through torture. Nevertheless, detainees frequently die while in custody (see Section 1.a.), and there were credible reports that police seeking to extract confessions regularly tortured and beat suspects and that interrogators beat and nearly tortured to death convicted "coup plotters". The authorities reportedly tortured convicted coup plotter and TSM magazine editor in chief Chris Anyanwu while in detention, and they beat Bunmi Aborishade, editor of the defunct June 12 weekly, when he was arrested in April. Detainees are regularly kept incommunicado for long periods of time (see Section 1.d.).

There were numerous credible reports of torture in Ogoniland perpetrated by the Rivers State Internal Security Task Force. The abuses reportedly increased just before the April visit of the United Nations fact-finding team dispatched to examine human rights and the transition process. Abuses continued at the higher level throughout the remainder of the year. In March there were credible reports that task force members beat and detained Ogonis who refused to leave their homes as instructed or otherwise attempted to foil alleged government plans to replace residents with government agents in preparation for the U.N. team's visit. The most egregious example was the case of Nsaa Korsi, an elderly widow, who refused the soldiers' demands to leave her house. They dragged her out, flogged her, and walked on her back while wearing boots. She reportedly suffered brain and spinal damage to the extent that she can no longer walk or speak coherently.

Early in the Abacha regime, Lagos state administrator, Colonel Olagunsoye Oyinlola, formed the Lagos State Environmental Task Force as part of its "war on indiscipline and corruption." Under Colonel Oyinlola's direct supervision, the task force used brutal force on individuals in its attempts to rid Lagos of illegal street traders and copious accumulated garbage. task force soldiers routinely beat and arrested anyone they perceived as "undisciplined," usually unarmed market women and traders, but also including jaywalkers, errant drivers, children, and young street hawkers. For the most part, the Government neither acknowledged nor denied that these abuses occurred and left their perpetrators unpunished. However, new Lagos state administrator Colonel M.B. Marwa has acknowledged that there have been abuses and said he would try to curb them.

There also were reliable reports of caning used as a form of punishment for minor infractions or public disturbances.

Prison conditions remain life threatening. Lack of potable water, inadequate sewage facilities, and shortage of medical supplies result in deplorable sanitary conditions. Disease runs rampant in the cramped, poorly ventilated facilities. Prison inmates are seldom allowed outside their cells for recreation, and many inmates must provide their own food. In such cases, only those with money or whose relatives bring food regularly have something to eat. Poor inmates rely on handouts from others to survive. Prison officials and police often deny inmates food and medical treatment as a form of punishment or to extort money from them. Many prisoners are routinely denied adequate medication and medical care. Severe overcrowding worsens the problem. For example, Ikoyi Prison in Lagos, built to house about 800 inmates, holds over 2,000. The convicted "coup plotters" and other detainees have been dispersed to various prisons around the country since October 1995, hindering access to their families and food.

Reports of sexual abuse of female prisoners are common. The Government derives considerable savings from the practice of leaving children born in prison with their jailed mothers rather than placing them in foster homes.

d. *Arbitrary Arrest, Detention, or Exile.*—The regime repeatedly engaged in arbitrary arrest and detention. Police are empowered to make arrests without warrants if they believe that there is a reasonable suspicion that a person committed an offense; they often abuse this power. The law requires that the arresting officer inform the accused of charges at the time of arrest and take that person to a station for processing within a reasonable time. By law, police must provide suspects with the opportunity to engage counsel and to post bail. However, police generally do not adhere to these safeguards and often hold suspects incommunicado under harsh conditions for extended periods without charge. Over 100 supporters of Shi'ite religious leader Sheikh Ibrahim Al-Zakzaky (see Section 1.a.) were arrested during and after public protests over his detention in the northern part of the country. The detained supporters were scheduled to appear in court in late December, but officials said "security concerns" precluded their appearance in public. By year's end no action had been taken to prosecute or release the detainees. Accurate numbers of detainees were unavailable, but official sources put the number at "over 100 but probably less than 200."

Police also commonly place relatives and friends of wanted suspects in detention without criminal charge to induce suspects to surrender to arrest (see Section 1.f.). Police detained a 13-year-old boy with British citizenship in April and held him for a month when Directorate of Military Intelligence officials were seeking to arrest the boy's Nigerian relative. He was eventually released following intervention by a foreign government.

The State Security (Detention of Persons) Decree of 1984 (Decree Two) allows the Government to detain without charge persons suspected of acts prejudicial to state security or harmful to the economic well-being of the country. When invoked, the decree suspends the detainee's civil liberties and precludes judicial review. Many citizens consider Decree Two the main threat to their basic freedoms because the judicial ouster clause encourages arbitrary detention and fails to define what constitutes acts under the decree's purview. Decree 11 of 1994 authorizes the PRC Vice Chairman or the Commissioner of Police to detain persons for up to 3 months.

In June the Government announced the repeal of Decree 14 of 1994, which had effectively suspended the right of habeas corpus by forbidding courts to hear cases demanding the Government produce in court those detained under Decree Two of 1984. The Government also announced a decree amending the Civil Disturbances (Special Tribunal) Decree of 1987 to remove members of the armed forces from the membership of the tribunal and allow for a right of appeal by a convicted person to the Special Appeal Tribunal (see Section 1.e.). At year's end, the full details of the new decrees were not known as the texts had not yet been released. However, despite the new decrees, the Government still retains full authority under Decree Two and Decree 12 of 1994 to detain citizens and dispense with habeas corpus challenges.

The Government routinely arrested and detained without charge leading human rights and prodemocracy activists, including prominent attorney Gani Fawehinmi in January, and in February human rights activist lawyer Femi Falana and prodemocracy activist and organizational secretary of Fawehinmi's National Conscience Party Femi Aborisade. Immediately prior to a November visit by representatives of the Commonwealth Ministerial Action Group to review the human rights situation, the Government released Fawehinmi, Falana, and Aborisade.

In June following the murder of Kudirat Abiola (see Section 1.a.), senior wife of M.K.O. Abiola, the authorities detained seven Abiola family members and four prominent members of the opposition group NADECO in connection with Mrs. Abiola's murder. All seven family members were released in July. One of the

NADECO members, octogenarian Solanke Onasanya, was released after 3 weeks to seek medical attention. The three remaining NADECO members, Abraham Adesanya, age 74, Ayo Adebayo, age 68, and Ganiu Dawodu, age 63, remained in detention without charge for several months.

The Government released several prominent detainees in June just before the Commonwealth Ministerial Action Group was set to meet in London to consider issues including additional sanctions. The authorities held Tunji Abayomi, chairman of the Founder's Council of Human Rights Africa and Obasanjo's lawyer, originally detained in July 1995, until June; Fred Eno, an aide to M.K.O. Abiola, from August 1994 to June; and Abdul Oroh, executive director of the CLO from July 1995 to June. Ayo Opadokun, General Secretary of NADECO, who had been detained since October 1994, was released June 25, only to be rearrested the following day and held in detention without charge until November 2. Expectations that the releases might presage real human rights improvements were not fulfilled, as the Government continued its policies of arbitrary arrest and detention, including the December arrest and detention of prodemocracy activist Dr. Fred Fasehun and former presidential candidate and NADECO supporter Olabiyi Durojaiye. Both remained in detention at year's end.

Several leading labor and prodemocracy activists who were arrested in 1993 remained in detention, including M.K.O. Abiola and Frank Kokori, General Secretary of the National Union of Petroleum and Natural Gas Workers (NUPENG). In January security forces arrested Milton Dabibi, who was General Secretary of the Petroleum and Natural Gas Senior Staff Association (PENGASSAN) before the Government dissolved the executive structure of the union and installed a sole administrator. At year's end, Dabibi remained in detention (see Section 6.a.).

The Government routinely detained human rights monitors, journalists, and political opponents for making or publishing critical statements (see Sections 2.a., 2.b., and 4). Government security forces also frequently harassed, arrested, and detained journalists for a variety of reasons, including the alleged spreading of false information and stories that exposed the actions of government officials.

Often the authorities did not charge detainees but held them for brief periods and questioned them about their activities and statements. In September security agents briefly detained and beat a Nigerian employee of the information service of a foreign embassy in Abuja after she refused to answer questions concerning the nature of her work.

The total prison population is estimated at 70,000. A precise figure for the number of persons detained without charge is unavailable. However, the Constitutional Rights Project, which recently completed a study on the failure of prosecution of criminal suspects, estimates that 40,000 prisoners, nearly 60 percent of the total prison population, are still awaiting trial. Official government figures put the number of prisoners awaiting trial at almost the same level, 35,575. Some have been detained as long as 12 years without trial.

There are no reliable figures for the number of political detainees, but local human rights groups' estimates range between 100 and 200 (see also Section 1.e.). At year's end, M.K.O. Abiola remained in prison despite a November 1994 ruling by the Kaduna Federal High Court of Appeals granting him bail on the condition that he "not disturb the peace." In May 1995, eight Supreme Court justices, including Chief Justice Mohammed Bello, withdrew from hearing the case because of a libel suit they had pending against Abiola's Concord Press, effectively suspending hearings on Abiola's appeal until new justices were named to the Court. Abiola's trial on treason charges remained suspended indefinitely on orders from the regime.

There were no known instances of forced exile as a means of political control, although several NADECO members, including former Senator Bola Tinabu, retired Air Commodore Dan Suleiman, Nobel laureate Wole Soyinka, and elder statesman and senior NADECO figure Anthony Enahoro live in self-imposed exile. Other activists such as Owens Wiwa, brother of executed minority rights activist Ken Saro-Wiwa, and his wife Diana joined them. An unknown number of Ogoni reportedly fled to neighboring countries, North America, or Europe in search of asylum.

e. *Denial of Fair Public Trial.*—The Government has taken several steps to undercut the independence and integrity of the judiciary. To suppress opposition to its rule, the regime first bypassed the regular courts in favor of "tribunals" and then declared itself above the law by prohibiting court review of any government action. Tribunal sentences are generally severe. The Government's reliance on tribunals, which operate outside the constitutional court system, seriously undermine the integrity of the judicial process and often result in legal proceedings that deny defendants due process, as the case of Ken Saro-Wiwa and his eight codefendants. The Government's frequent refusal to respect court rulings also undermines the integrity of the judicial process.

The regular court system is composed of both federal and state trial courts, state appeals courts, the federal Court of Appeal, and the federal Supreme Court. Under the 1979 Constitution, courts of the first instance include magistrate or district courts, customary or area courts, Shari'a (Islamic) courts, and for some specified cases, the state high courts. The nature of the case usually determines which court has jurisdiction. In principle customary and Shari'a courts have jurisdiction only if both plaintiff and defendant agree. In practice, however, fear of legal cost, delay, and distance to alternative courts encourage many litigants to choose these courts.

Decree One of 1984, the basic Constitution (modification and suspension) decree, the first decree promulgated by the military officers who overthrew the civilian regime of President Shehu Usman Aliyu Shagari in 1983, left the institutional framework of the judiciary relatively intact. However, it established a parallel system of military tribunals with sole jurisdiction over certain offenses, such as coup plotting, corruption, armed robbery, and illegal sale of petroleum. A 1991 decree amended Decree One by providing that only sitting or retired civilian judges may preside over tribunals hearing nonmilitary cases. Decree 12 states that "no act of the federal military Government may henceforth be questioned in a court of law" and "divests all courts of jurisdiction in all matters concerning the authority of the federal Government."

Criminal justice procedures call for trial within 3 months of arraignment for most categories of crimes. Inefficient administrative procedures, petty extortion, bureaucratic inertia, poor communication between police and prison officials, and inadequate transportation continue to result in considerable delays, often stretching to several years in bringing suspects to trial.

Trials in the regular court system are public and generally respect constitutionally protected individual rights, including a presumption of innocence, the right to be present, to confront witnesses, to present evidence, and to be represented by legal counsel. However, there is a widespread perception that judges are easily bribed or "settled," and that litigants cannot rely on the courts to render impartial judgment.

There are no legal provisions barring women or other groups from testifying in civil court or giving their testimony less weight. The testimony of women is, however, accorded less weight in Shari'a courts.

In most cases before the tribunals, the accused have the right to legal counsel, bail, and appeal, although some tribunals substitute a presumption of guilt for the presumption of innocence, and conviction rates in the tribunals reportedly exceed conviction rates in the regular courts.

In practice tribunal proceedings often deny defendants due process as in the trial before the Ogoni Civil Disturbances Special Tribunal of Ken Saro-Wiwa and others for their alleged roles in the killings of four prominent Ogoni politicians in May 1994. On October 31, 1995, the Tribunal announced guilty verdicts and death sentences for Saro-Wiwa and eight other activists. The PRC "confirmed" this decision on November 8, 1995, and quickly executed all nine on November 10, 1995. In that case, the Government refused to comply with a tribunal order to produce a videotape recorded on May 22, 1994, with Rivers' state administrator Lt. Colonel Dauda Komo who proclaimed in advance that Saro-Wiwa was "guilty of murder." This led the 18-member defense team, led by Gani Fawehinmi, to withdraw in protest.

In June in response to the report of the U.N. fact-finding team sent to investigate human rights and the transition process, the Government announced two decrees, one repealing Decree 14 of 1994 which had effectively suspended the right of habeas corpus (see Section 1.d.) and the other amending the Civil Disturbances (Special Tribunal) Decree of 1987 to remove members of the armed forces from the membership of the tribunal and allow for a right of appeal to the Special Appeal Tribunal. While the texts had not yet been released by year's end, the Government quickly clarified that appeals to the Special Appeals Tribunal would not be allowed for military personnel convicted of coup plotting. It remained silent regarding appeals for civilians convicted of coup plotting, but all indications are that the new decree was never meant to apply to them.

Additional Ogoni defendants were arrested in 1994, one of whom died while in custody. Known as the Ogoni 19, these individuals were arraigned in July in connection with the murder of the 4 Ogoni politicians. The new decree amending the Civil Disturbances (Special Tribunal) Decree of 1987 would seem to preclude the possibility of the Ogoni 19 being tried by a Special Tribunal. At year's end, no significant progress had been made in the case.

A motion demanding the immediate release of the detainees filed by the law offices led by Azibaola Robert was thrown out by the High Court on a technicality. Moreover, government agents subjected the Ogonis' lawyers to harassment and intimidation. In addition to surveillance, government agents arrested the lawyers following a court appearance in July when the agents tried to force a photographer, who had been brought to court to take pictures of the accused, to surrender his camera. The ensuing scuffle caused the magistrate, who had granted permission for the photographs with no objection from the prosecution, to seize the camera pending a decision on the matter. The agents reported back to their superiors, who immediately dispatched agents to arrest the lawyers and the photographer. The photographer escaped detention because he was not in the room at the time, but the agents seized his camera from the magistrate. The Government is pursuing prosecution of the lawyers on charges of obstructing the arrest of the photographer, an employee of The Vanguard newspaper. At year's end, the lawyers were no longer in custody, but subjected to continued harassment.

The number of political prisoners (as distinct from political detainees) held by the Government is also unknown (see Section 1.d.). Thirty-five individuals convicted in 1995 by a secret military tribunal of coup plotting and related charges remained in prison. These included former Head of State Olusegun Obasanjo; his erstwhile deputy and National Constitutional Conference delegate Shehu Musa Yar'Adua; editor in chief of The Sunday Magazine Chris Anyanwu; Tell magazine assistant editor George Mbah; The News magazine editor Kunle Ajibade; Weekend Classique editor Ben Charles Obi; and chairman of the prominent human rights organization Campaign for Democracy (CD) Beko Ransome-Kuti. They continued to serve reduced sentences which still ran as long as 25 years.

The only exceptions were six individuals convicted in the alleged coup plot who were released in March at the completion of their commuted sentences, although their families had to file petitions in court to obtain their release. Queenette Allogoa, also sentenced to 6 months, remained in prison despite having finished her sentence. The Government offered no explanation for her continued detention.

f. *Arbitrary Interference With Privacy, Family, Home, or Correspondence.*—Provisions of the 1979 and 1989 Constitutions provide for the rights to privacy in the home, in correspondence, and in oral electronic communications. However, the military Government regularly interfered in the lives of citizens, and if the authorities desired to use a warrant in a particular search case, they often secured it from a military tribunal rather than a regular court. Human rights and prodemocracy leaders reported that security agents regularly followed them and cut off or monitored their organizations' telephones. Police routinely detain relatives and friends of suspects without charge to induce suspects to surrender (see Section 1.d.). Credible sources report an increase in harassment and intimidation of citizens by police and military units in Ogoniland following the late March to early April visit of the United Nations fact-finding team sent to investigate human rights and the transition program. Abuses perpetrated in Ogoniland included arbitrary detention without charge and random search of houses and cars without warrants or probable cause.

The November 10 first anniversary of the hanging of the Ogoni 9 passed largely without incident. As has been done in the past, the Government prevented the holding of even peaceful public demonstrations of mourning, including the wearing of black clothing. Fear of government reprisals kept most people indoors and a strict curfew enforced by security officials stopped many planned memorial services and all public displays of mourning.

Section 2. Respect for Civil Liberties, Including:

a. *Freedom of Speech and Press.*—Constitutional provisions providing for freedom of speech and the press are not enforceable because of continued suspension of constitutional rights. The Abacha regime often publicly declared its support for these freedoms, but it nevertheless sought to limit or confine public political dialog. The regime also increased its systematic intimidation of the press through legal and extralegal means throughout the year.

Although there is a large and vibrant indigenous independent press which is frequently critical of the Government, the Government also owns or controls many newspapers. All newspapers and magazines are required to register with the Government under the Newspaper Registration Board Decree 43 of 1993, and the Minister of Culture and Information declared in December that beginning in 1997 any publication not registered with the board will be prosecuted. The fee for registration is high. The Abacha regime has, at various times, shut down independent newspapers for various offenses. Journalists continue to be subject to close scrutiny and routine harassment by security forces.

The Government granted broadcasting rights to private radio stations in 1994, but it keeps a careful watch over radio broadcasts, the most important means of reaching the public. In May the National Broadcasting Commission banned Ray Power, a private Lagos radio station, from transmitting British Broadcasting Corporation (BBC) programs, ostensibly under Decree 38, which states that transmissions must have equity and reciprocity. Since BBC does not broadcast Nigerian programs, Ray Power could not broadcast BBC programs. Television, both Nigerian and otherwise, is widely available. Access is limited more by substandard cable installation, electrical power surges and outages, and technical broadcasting difficulties than by government intervention. However, government-controlled broadcast media still dominate the country, and even private broadcasters do not transmit stories that criticize the Government.

Throughout the year, government security agents frequently harassed, arrested, and detained journalists. Four journalists convicted of involvement in an alleged 1995 coup plot remained in prison (see Section 1.e.). The Government detained without charge Nosa Igiebor, editor in chief of Tell magazine, from December 1995 to June. In March the Government briefly detained Emeka Omeihe, editor of the newspaper Daily Champion, and three top editorial staff of The Guardian newspaper over reports in their newspapers that the Directorate of Military Intelligence (DMI) had ruled out sabotage in the presidential plane crash in January that killed Ibrahim Abacha, the Head of State's son. Others detained for shorter or longer periods, usually without charge, included in April Bunmi Aborishade, editor of the defunct weekly June 12; in May George Onah, defense correspondent of The Vanguard newspaper, who remained in custody at year's end; in May Tunji Adegboyega, editor of The Punch newspaper, for a front-page story relating to the arson attack on the home of one of the prominent NADECO members in self-exile; also in May, Kate Odigie-Oyegun, the general manager of the newspaper company that publishes The Observer over a story that speculated about changes in the military following largescale military promotions to the rank of general; in August Alphonsus Agborh, The Punch newspaper's Port Harcourt correspondent, for a story concerning imported arms; and in September Ola Awoniyi, Abuja bureau chief for The Nigerian Tribune after reporting allegations of espionage and corruption in the Air Force.

Virtually all senior editors of the weeklies Tell, Dateline, The News, and Tempo, and the daily A.M. News are subject to surveillance and harassment by security agents. They have been driven underground by constant fear of arrest and now operate clandestinely from numerous scattered locations throughout Lagos. Security forces routinely seized entire runs of Tell magazine when cover stories offended the Government. Agents harassed and intimidated vendors and printers to the point that in some parts of the country Tell is no longer available. The seizures and intimidation caused great financial distress for Tell and were partially responsible for the weekly's decision to discontinue publication of its sister magazine Dateline.

The Government also denied entry to and threatened to deport foreign journalists. Christian Science Monitor and Financial Times correspondent Paul Adams was arrested in January and detained incommunicado for several days. He was released on bail in mid-January, but his trial on trumped-up charges of possession of "seditious" materials dragged on until he was finally acquitted in April. In February a U.S. citizen working as a BBC correspondent was detained and held incommunicado for a day. The Government gave no reason for her arrest and never charged her with any crime. However, it was clear that the Government was not pleased by her aggressive research into reports of a possible coup attempt. Numerous other journalists had to cancel trips because they were unable to obtain visas. In addition to harassing individual journalists, the Government attacked the foreign press by blocking the distribution of international editions of foreign publications such as Newsweek that carried stories unfavorable to the regime.

The military Government used a number of other means to intimidate the press. These included a decree banning government offices from advertising in nongovernment media, periodic directives to government offices forbidding the purchase of certain publications, personal attacks by government-controlled media against journalists and others who challenged government policies, and threats of harassment of potential advertisers and investors in antigovernment publications. The Information Minister has repeatedly made intimidating speeches against the prodemocracy press. There are credible reports that he sent a letter to the advertising practitioners association cautioning members to avoid advertising in such prodemocracy publications as AM News, PM News, TSM, and Tell, or risk losing government patronage. In December he announced that the Ministry would establish "press courts" to try journalists who write "false" reports. Other common means of harassment include the disruption of public performances, conferences, book promotions, and other forums that security forces believe prodemocracy groups use to spread their message.

In February security forces canceled the performance of a play written by self-exiled Nobel prize winner Wole Soyinka. In March they prevented NADECO members from meeting with a United Nations team sent to Nigeria to examine human rights and the transition to democracy; broke up a conference in Jos sponsored by a foreign embassy information service entitled "Dilemmas of Democracy," briefly arresting two of the organizers and dispersing the participants; shut down the CLO-sponsored launch of the book "The Church and Human Rights: A Human Rights Education Manual for Churches;" and canceled the American Studies Association of Nigeria (ASAN) fifth annual conference in Kaduna. In April security forces canceled the introduction of a book at the government-affiliated Nigerian Institute of International Affairs by a former governor with strong ties to NADECO. In May armed policemen forcibly canceled a Nigerian Union of Journalists lecture and meeting with 100 journalists marking the first anniversary of the arrest and detention of four colleagues sentenced to 15 years' imprisonment for coup plotting (see Section 1.e.).

Academic freedom is generally respected, although security forces routinely monitor and on occasion break up conferences they perceive as forums for prodemocracy groups (see Section 2.b.). The Government tape records faculty conversations. The Government in May banned all activities on a national level by the National Association of Nigerian Students (NANS). The Government also banned university staff unions (see Section 6.a.). Nigerian embassies often refuse to issue visas to visiting lecturers and musicians. This policy has precluded discussions between foreign and Nigerian academicians on topics of mutual interest.

Some student groups believe university authorities follow government directives to suspend or expel activist students. On August 26 in Bauchi, the authorities detained for a day four professors belonging to the striking Academic Staff Union of Universities (ASUU) (see Section 6.a.).

b. *Freedom of Peaceful Assembly and Association.*—The two Constitutions provide citizens with the right to assemble freely and associate with other persons in political parties, trade unions, or other special interest associations. However, the Government proscribed all political activity 1 day after coming to power in 1993. The Government arbitrarily canceled or prevented a number of public meetings during the year, including cultural events, academic conferences, book promotions, and human rights meetings (see also Section 2.a.).

While permits are not normally required for public meetings indoors, and permit requirements for outdoor public functions are often ignored by both government authorities and those assembling, the Abacha Government retained legal provisions adopted by the Babangida government, banning gatherings whose political, ethnic, or religious content it believed might lead to unrest. Security forces used permit requirements as one of the justifications for their regular practice of disrupting prodemocracy conferences, book introductions, and seminars. Open-air religious services away from places of worship remained prohibited in most states due to religious tensions in various parts of the country (see also Section 2.c.).

In August 1994, General Abacha announced that "individuals or groups may henceforth canvass political ideas, but they cannot form political parties for now." In June 1995, Abacha announced a partial lifting of the ban on political activity, but it was not until June that a reconstituted National Electoral Commission of Nigeria (NECON) finally announced cumbersome and impractical requirements for registering political parties. NECON gave the parties an unrealistic 6-week period in which to satisfy such requirements as registering 40,000 members in each of the 30 states and 15,000 in the federal capital territory of Abuja, as well as issuing photo identification cards to each of them. Despite the practical impossibility of satisfying NECON's requirements, 23 parties purchased registration forms from NECON for approximately $6,000; 18 of them submitted the forms and supporting documentation by the July 25 deadline. In response to widespread protests over the party registration process, NECON announced a new exercise allowing the 18 groups to apply for mergers. The merger requests had to be accompanied by another burdensome set of documentation, including a party resolution agreeing to the merger; the new name, constitution, acronym, symbol, and manifesto of the party; addresses of the national, state, and local government area and council level chapters of the party; and the names of proposed executive staff at all levels of the organization. By September NECON announced the registration of five parties and ordered dissolved all unregistered political parties, effectively preventing the participation of other political parties, which included the majority of established politicians and potential opposition leaders.

Although Abacha announced the lifting of all restrictions on political activities in his October 1, 1995, Independence Day address, he did not issue the enabling decree until February. The Government continued to repress the political activities of opposition groups. In February the Government announced three new decrees lifting the restrictions on political activity, laying out the transition timetable, and empowering the transition bodies. When the texts of the decrees were released in March, however, it became clear that the regime had negated its decree lifting restrictions on political activity by including language that established vague new categories of crimes for impeding the transition to democracy and imposed a penalty of 5 years in prison for those found guilty of such crimes. This action effectively allowed the regime to remove its opponents from the political scene until after the completion of the transition timetable (see Section 3).

Religious, professional, and other organizations need not register with the Government and are generally permitted to associate freely with other national and foreign bodies. The PRC retained its ban on several political organizations that it contended were founded primarily along ethnic, tribal, religious, or other parochial lines for the purpose of sponsoring various political candidates.

c. *Freedom of Religion.*—The Government generally respects freedom of belief, practice, and religious education provided for by the suspended 1979 and 1989 Constitutions. Both Constitutions also prohibit state and local governments from adopting a state religion. The Government instituted a ban in 1987 (which is still in effect) on religious organizations on campuses of primary schools, although individual students retain the right to practice their religion in recognized places of worship.

In Kwara state in March, state authorities ordered the closure of Christian schools that refused to include Islamic studies in their curriculum. Reportedly, the Christian community in Kwara state was refusing to teach Islamic studies in Christian schools because Islamic schools are not being required to teach Christian studies. After the transfer of the state military administrator, the situation was resolved and the Christian schools reopened. No further incidents have been reported.

Distribution of religious publications is generally unrestricted. There is a lightly enforced ban on published religious advertisements, and religious programming on television and radio remains closely controlled by the Government. Both Christian and Muslim organizations allege that the Ministry of Foreign Affairs and the Immigration Department continue to restrict the entry into the country of certain religious practitioners, particularly persons suspected of proselytizing. While it has not outlawed the practice, the Government discourages proselytizing in the belief that it stirs up religious tensions, particularly in the predominantly Islamic north. The Government also bans open-air religious services away from places of worship (see Section 2.b.).

In September the authorities arrested Shia activist Ibrahim al-Zakzaky (see Section 1.d.) and charged him with an alleged attempt to set up a clandestine radio station.

d. *Freedom of Movement Within the Country, Foreign Travel, Emigration, and Repatriation.*—The two Constitutions entitle citizens to move freely throughout the country and reside where they wish. However, increasing violent crime in many parts of the country prompted police to set up roadblocks and checkpoints, where officers commonly engaged in extortion, violence, and excessive use of force.

The Constitutions also prohibit expulsion or the denial of exit or entry to any citizen. In practice, however, women must often obtain permission from a male family member before being granted a passport, and the Government, like its predecessors, occasionally prevented travel for political reasons. Throughout the year, the Government routinely seized the passports of its critics, including those of Movement for the Survival of Ogoni People (MOSOP) Vice President Ledum Mitee, CLO President Ayo Obe, Nigerian Association of University Women President and African-American Institute program representative Clara Osinulu, lawyer Priscilla Kuye, United Nations hunger award recipient Chief Bisi Ogunleye, and human rights activist, lawyer, and CLO cofounder Olisa Agbakoba.

Journalists reported harassment at the nation's airports by security officials throughout the year, including having to fill out a special entry and exit form detailing their movements abroad, reasons for making their trip, and names of friends and associates overseas. Security officials harassed or temporarily confiscated the passports of journalists who refused to complete the form. The Government assigned security personnel to Murtala Mohammed International Airport (MMIA) to screen departing passengers to apprehend prodemocracy supporters. Government security agents questioned extensively citizens who had been issued United States visas. If the agents were not satisfied with the responses, they had orders to seize passports and turn the citizens over to military intelligence and state security service personnel for additional questioning.

The Government cooperates with the Lagos Office of the United Nations High Commissioner for Refugees (UNHCR) and other humanitarian agencies in assisting refugees through the National Commission for Refugees and the Federal Commissioner. Regulations governing the granting of refugee status, asylum, and resettlement are outlined in Decree 52 of 1989 which incorporates many aspects of the 1951 U.N. Convention. Refugee and resettlement applications are reviewed by the Eligibility Committee established under Decree 52. A representative from the UNHCR participates in the Eligibility Committee.

There are an estimated 5,000 Liberian, 1,400 Chadian, 1,500 Cameroonian, 140 Ghanaian, and an undetermined number of Togolese, Somalian, Sudanese, and Ethiopian refugees. The issue of the provision of first asylum did not arise in 1996 and has not arisen since the establishment of the National Commission for Refugees under Decree 52. There were no reports that refugees were expelled.

Section 3. Respect for Political Rights: The Right of Citizens to Change Their Government

Citizens could not exercise this right in 1996, and there was little indication that General Abacha's military regime was willing to permit them to do so on any basis other than a process tightly controlled by the regime. Throughout the year, the regime committed numerous, repeated, and egregious human rights abuses in its effort to prevent citizens from opposing it by peaceful political means.

After coming to power, the Provisional Ruling Council headed by General Abacha promised to return to civilian, democratic rule but did not provide a timetable until Abacha's 1995 Independence Day address. Then Abacha announced a transition timetable, leading to inauguration of a civilian president on October 1, 1998. The transition process provides for a series of local, state and federal elections over a period of 3 years.

By year's end, there was little meaningful progress towards democracy despite Abacha's 3-year transition program. The first substantial deviation from the transition timetable occurred in June when the Government missed the deadline for creation of new states and local governments. The timetable showed further signs of slippage when the Government extended to mid-September the cumbersome and impractical party registration process scheduled for completion at the end of August (see Section 2.b.). The government body set up to screen political parties seeking registration had the authority to disqualify parties. The process was not subject to public scrutiny or review. In September NECON announced the registration of five parties and ordered dissolved all unregistered political parties, effectively preventing the participation of other political parties, which included the majority of established politicians and potential opposition leaders, in the electoral process. The reviewing body also retains the option to revoke registration at any time, leaving a loophole for later disqualification of any parties that annoy the regime. Individual members of unregistered parties are theoretically permitted to join the officially registered parties, but whether they will be permitted to run for office remains to be seen (see Section 2.b.). Local government elections on a party basis, originally scheduled for December, were postponed until March 1997.

In August Abacha removed all state administrators from their posts, redeploying three of them to new states, and returning the rest to their respective branches of the armed forces. Ten of the former administrators are reportedly being subjected to a government probe of their actions in office. At year's end, none of the administrators had been formally charged or tried.

Politics remained dominated by men. However, there are no legal impediments to political participation or voting by women or members of any minority group. There are three women in the Federal Executive Council and female judges and magistrates at all levels of the judiciary.

Section 4. Governmental Attitude Regarding International and Nongovernmental Investigation of Alleged Violations of Human Rights

The Government permitted local human rights groups to operate but often interfered with their activities, detaining their members and preventing them from criticizing the Government's human rights record (see Sections 1.d. and 2.a.). High-level government officials regularly denounced the activities of Nigeria's human rights community, often accusing its members and the independent press of participating in foreign-inspired plots to destabilize the country.

Notwithstanding the Government's hostile attitude, national and international human rights groups engaged in a vocal and public campaign for the promotion of human rights. Among the most active organizations are: The CLO, the Committee for the Defense of Human Rights, the Constitutional Rights Project, the National Association of Democratic Lawyers, Human Rights Africa, and the Legal Research and Resource Development Center. A number of prominent authors, artists, educators, and jurists, in addition to professional and labor organizations spoke out frequently on human rights issues as well. Amnesty International (AI) is active, and the International Committee of the Red Cross has a regional office in Lagos.

The regime established a National Human Rights Commission in June, but the commission lacked credibility as an independent monitoring body. By year's end the commission had only limited funding, no permanent office space, no working telephones and no clear mandate to do anything other than convene meetings. Nongovernmental human rights groups did not view the commission as a serious entity, and members of the commission purported to represent leading NGO's were unknown to the groups they allegedly represented. The commission held two meetings and sponsored a public lecture on World Human Rights Day but had no discernible effect on the overall human rights situation.

The Government impeded foreign human rights monitoring groups and individuals from visiting the country by delaying or refusing visas and attempting to manipulate their schedules. The most notable example was the United Nations factfinding team dispatched in late March to examine human rights and the transition process. The Government first proposed a program almost entirely lacking in exposure to nongovernment groups or individuals, then attempted to prevent opposition groups from meeting with the team by arresting or intimidating those who sought meetings. There were credible reports that the Government stepped up repression in politically sensitive Ogoniland and surrounding areas of Rivers state just before the U.N. team's visit and kept the new higher levels of abuse in place after its April departure. In November the Government detained three AI officials, including visiting AI development field organizer for west and central Africa, for carrying "seditious literature" which included the text of a speech by AI Secretary General Pierre Sane. The three were held until 10:00 p.m. and then released but told to report in the following day. They were required to report to officials each day for 4 days. Other organizations have also reported similar restrictions.

Section 5. Discrimination Based on Race, Sex, Religion, Language, Social Status, or Disability

Both the 1979 and 1989 Constitutions provide citizens with the right to freedom from discrimination based on "community, place of origin, ethnic group, sex, religion, or political opinion." However, customary and religious discrimination against women persists, while tension between the Government and disaffected minority groups persisted.

Women.—Reports of spousal abuse are common, especially wife beating in polygynous families. Police do not normally intervene in domestic disputes, which are seldom discussed publicly. In more traditional areas, it is questionable whether the courts and police intervene to protect women who formally accuse their husbands if the level of alleged abuse does not exceed customary norms in the area. Purdah, the Islamic practice of keeping girls and women in seclusion from men outside the family, is prevalent in parts of the far north. Women also bear the brunt of attacks for social and religious reasons, particularly for "immodest" or "inappropriate" behavior.

Women experience considerable discrimination as well as physical abuse. There are no laws barring women from particular fields of employment, but women often experience discrimination because the Government tolerates customary and religious practices that adversely affect them. Approximately 35 percent of women are active in the labor force. While the number of women employed in the business sector increases every year, women do not receive equal pay for equal work and often find it extremely difficult to acquire commercial credit or obtain tax deductions or rebates as heads of households.

While some women have made considerable individual progress, both in the academic and business world, most are underprivileged. Although women are not legally barred from owning land, under some customary land tenure systems only men can own land, and women gain access to land through marriage or family. In addition, many customary practices do not recognize a woman's right to inherit her husband's property, and many widows are rendered destitute when their in-laws take virtually all of the deceased husband's property. In other areas, a widow is considered part of the property, and she too may be "inherited" by the husband's eldest male relative. Polygyny is widely practiced among all ethnic groups in both Christian and Islamic communities. Women often must provide permission from a male family member to obtain a passport (see Section 2.d.).

Children.—The Government remains only sporadically committed to children's rights and welfare. Public schools continue to deteriorate, and limited facilities precluded access to education for some children. While the Government increased spending on children's health in recent years, it seldom enforced even the inadequate laws designed to protect the rights of children. Although the law stipulates that "no child shall be ordered to be imprisoned," juvenile offenders are routinely denied bail and incarcerated along with hardened criminals.

There are a range of problems involving children. The Government only occasionally condemns child abuse and neglect and makes little effort to stop customary practices, such as the sale of children into marriage. There are credible reports that poor families often sell their daughters into marriage as a means of supplementing their incomes. There are also reports that many young girls are forced into marriage as soon as they reach puberty, regardless of age, to prevent "indecency" associated with premarital sex.

The Government publicly opposes female genital mutilation (FGM), which is widely condemned by international health experts as damaging to both physical and psychological health. However, the Government has taken no action to abolish the procedure, and many ethnic groups subject young females to it. Nigerian experts estimate that as many as 50 percent of women, primarily in the Christian south but less in the north, may have undergone FGM, which varies from simple removal of the clitoral hood or labia minora to excision of the clitoris and the most dangerous form, infibulation. A U.N. report states that 60 percent of the population, 32.7 million women, have been subjected to some form of FGM.

The age at which females are subjected to FGM varies from the first week of life to after a woman delivers her first child. The Ministry of Health and NGO's sponsor public awareness and education projects to inform communities of the health hazards of FGM. The press openly condemned the practice on a number of occasions.

People With Disabilities.—While the Government called for private businesses to institute policies ensuring fair treatment for the 2 percent of the work force that it claims is disabled, it has not enacted any laws fostering greater accessibility to buildings and public transportation, nor has it formulated any policy that specifically ensures the right of the disabled to work.

Religious Minorities.—The law prohibits religious discrimination. Nonetheless, it is commonly reported that government officials often discriminate against persons practicing a religion different from their own. Religious tensions often lead to violence. There were regular clashes in the fall between the Muslim Brothers, a Shiite group, and Sunni Muslims in Zaria in Kaduna state. Shiites reportedly stormed Sunni mosques in an attempt to install their own imams as preachers. More than 20 protestors and security personnel were killed in religion-related violence that began in mid-September when the Government arrested a leader of the Shi'ite Muslim Brotherhood, Sheikh Ibrahim Al-Zakzaky (see Sections 1.d. and 2.c.). Zakzaky remains in detention and has not been charged with an offense.

National/Racial/Ethnic Minorities.—The Government has promulgated no official policy concerning discrimination against any of the 250 ethnic groups, and laws do not favor one group over another. However, there is a long history of tension among the diverse ethnic groups. Clashes continued between rival ethnic groups in Delta, Rivers, Benue, Cross River, Kaduna, Plateau, and Taraba states, often resulting in casualties. Tradition continues to impose considerable pressure on individual government officials to favor their own ethnic group, and ethnic favoritism persists. During nonpartisan local government elections in March, nonindigenous residents of certain states, notably Kaduna, were barred from exercising their right to vote.

The Ogoni, an ethnic group indigenous to Rivers state in eastern Nigeria (one of the oil-producing regions), maintain that the Government continues to engage in a systematic campaign to deprive them of their land and its wealth. Members of the Ogoni group claim that the Government seizes Ogoni property without fair compensation, ignores the environmental impact of oil production on Ogoni land, and fails to provide adequate public services, such as water and electricity. The confrontation between the Government and the Ogoni remains violent. MOSOP, which campaigns for Ogoni autonomy, often describes government policy towards the Ogoni as genocide. Ogoni concerns about environmental degradation and the quality of social services have merit. The Ogoni 19, accused of murdering 4 Ogoni politicians in July 1994, remained in detention at year's end (see Section 1.e.).

Other ethnic minorities, particularly in Delta, Rivers, and Akwa Ibom states, have echoed Ogoni claims of environmental degradation and government indifference to their development. Groups such as the Ijaw, Itsekiri, and Urhobo have grown increasingly vocal in expressing their unhappiness, while the prevalence of ethnic conflict and confrontation with government forces increased in these areas.

Section 6. Worker Rights

a. *The Right of Association.*—The Government continued its pattern of interference in the affairs of organized labor through the issuance of decrees that restricted unions in the selection of leaders, directed various unions to merge, and proscribed certain unions entirely. The Government also employed a variety of tactics to divide and intimidate labor. Although basic labor legislation dating to 1974 remains in place, decrees enacted in 1994 that dissolved elected national executive councils of the Nigeria Labor Congress (NLC) and two key oil sector unions and placed them under the authority of government-appointed sole administrators have marginalized the labor movement. The Government's exercise of absolute power over the affairs of the NLC, the National Union of Petroleum and Natural Gas

Workers (NUPENG), and the Petroleum and Natural Gas Senior Staff Association (PENGASSAN) continued, in blatant disregard of International Labor Organization (ILO) conventions that it has signed and ratified.

Workers, except members of the armed forces and employees designated essential by the Government, may join trade unions. Essential employees include fire fighters, police, employees of the central bank, the security printers (printers of currency, passports, and government forms), and customs and excise staff. In May 1993, the Government promulgated the Teaching Essential Services Decree, declaring education an essential service. The Decree did not, however, proscribe education sector unions.

Approximately 70 percent of the work force is employed in agriculture. Agricultural workers, except for small numbers in the food processing sector, are not unionized. Most of the informal sector and practically all small industries and businesses remain nonunionized. Approximately 11.5 percent of the total work force belong to unions. Nonagricultural enterprises that employ more than 50 employees are obliged by law to recognize trade unions and to pay or deduct a dues checkoff for employees who are members. Organized labor has accused some employers of deliberately organizing their industries into multiple units employing less than 50 workers to avoid unionization. The Government has threatened in the past to withdraw the dues checkoff provision and make the payment of union dues completely voluntary if unions pursue strikes, as in the cases of the 1993 general strike, and the 1994 petroleum strike.

In contravention of the ILO Convention on Freedom of Association, the Government has decreed that the NLC is the single central labor body. Although state executive councils of the NLC continue to function, government interference makes it difficult for the NLC to represent workers effectively. The NLC claims to represent 3 million workers of a total work force of 30 million. This figure is difficult to verify and may have dropped in light of continued depression in the manufacturing sector and significant public sector reductions in force. The Government continued to resist attempts by higher graded workers and middle management to form and register an independent labor central. However, the Senior Staff Consultative Association of Nigeria (SESCAN) continues to serve as an unregistered labor central for the senior staff associations.

The Government used threats of arrest and short-term and long-term detention without charge to intimidate labor activists throughout the year. NUPENG President Wariebe Agamene and two other labor leaders were released from detention over the 1996 New Year holiday, but the Government continued to hold without charge NUPENG General Secretary Frank Kokori, detained since August 1994 and former PENGASSAN General Secretary and current Secretary General of SESCAN, Milton Dabibi, detained since January. In March a special assistant to the Minister of Labor and Productivity quit his employment claiming that the Minister was planning to arrest and probe union leaders for alleged financial wrongdoing. In May protesters who claimed to support government positions on controversial labor issues disrupted a meeting of union activists in Ogun state. The following day, the authorities arrested Adams Oshiomhole, General Secretary of the Textile Workers Union, and held him 26 hours for questioning. A similar meeting held at the University of Lagos in September was disrupted by violence from progovernment supporters.

The Government demonstrated its indifference to the ILO Convention on Freedom of Association when it issued Decree Four, Trade Union (amendment) Decree. Dated January 5, but only released in late February, the decree reduced the number of industrial trade unions from 41 to 29 through directed mergers, barred general secretaries from seeking elective positions in the NLC or in the unions that employed them, directed employers to act as dues collecting agents of the NLC, and included an ouster clause to bar judicial challenges to the decree. While the merger exercise was accomplished without much rancor, the Minister of Labor was publicly accused of attempting to manipulate several elections of new union executive councils, and union activists, led by the general secretaries of key unions, rallied on several occasions to condemn government interference in trade union activities. Eventually, in June a delegation of union activists presented labor views directly to the Head of State, but at year's end the decree has not been amended or withdrawn.

Despite promises made by government spokesmen at the ILO Conference in June 1995 that elected executive councils would replace sole administrators at the NLC, NUPENG, and PENGASSAN, the Government took no credible steps to hold such elections. The unwillingness of the Government to allow elections to proceed at the two oil workers unions was clear evidence of the Government's overall lack of sincerity on the issue. At the 1996 Conference, the Government disingenuously blamed workers for obstructing elections and promised again that sole administrators would be removed from the three bodies. The promise remained unfulfilled at year's end.

The Government further violated the freedom of association of workers when it proscribed three campus unions on August 21. It dissolved the Academic Staff Union of Universities (ASUU), which had been on a nationwide strike since April, plus two nonstriking unions—the Nonacademic Staff Union (NASU) and the Senior Staff Association of Nigerian Universities (SSANU)—and seized their assets. In the aftermath of the proscription order, the Government ordered all academics who wanted to keep their positions to return to work. After 6 months, the strikers returned to work.

For the third year in succession, the ILO faulted Nigeria for its disregard of worker rights and its violation of Convention 87. In 1995 a "special paragraph" took the Government to task for denying trade unions the right to elect their leaders freely and supplemented a 1994 finding of the ILO Committee on Freedom of Association that the Government's interference in the administration of labor unions and its restriction of worker rights directly contravened ratified conventions. The Committee had recommended that the Government remove appointed administrators from labor bodies, restore suspended union executives, allow them access to the premises of union headquarters, and restore dues checkoff where suspended. By year's end, none of these demands had been met. Once again the Committee on the Application of Conventions and Recommendations adopted a "special paragraph". The Government took advantage of a predetermined rotation among African states to take a seat on the ILO governing body, but withdrew a bid for chairmanship of the Technical Cooperation Committee after repeated criticism of its continued contempt for ILO recommendations.

The right to strike is recognized by law except for those performing essential services. However, workers are required to give 21 days' notice prior to commencing a strike. Strikes in the public sector occurred in many of the 30 states, typically when underfunded state and local governments failed to fulfill previously negotiated contract provisions relating to salaries and allowances. The National Association of Resident Doctors struck several times over wage-related concerns.

There are no laws prohibiting retribution against strikers and strike leaders, but strikers who believe that they experience unfair retribution may submit their cases to the Industrial Arbitration Panel whose decisions are binding on all parties.

In August 1991, under Decree 32, the Government revoked past policy and permitted international labor affiliation with non-African international labor organizations. Negotiations commenced with the International Confederation of Free Trade Unions (ICFTU) for formal affiliation, but the removal of the NLC executive and the protracted political confrontation precluded further progress on these applications. Following a December 1995 ICFTU resolution critical of the Government's labor policies and actions, the Government refused to permit the ICFTU to send a delegation, although a representative of an ICFTU-affiliated African labor organization was allowed to visit for several days in May.

b. *The Right to Organize and Bargain Collectively.*—The labor laws provide for both the right to organize and the right to bargain collectively between management and trade unions. Collective bargaining is, in fact, common in many sectors of the economy. Laws further protect workers against retaliation by employers for labor activity through an independent arm of the judiciary, the Nigerian Industrial Court (NIC), which handles complaints of antiunion discrimination. Before cases can be brought to the NIC, parties are required to seek mediation and conciliation through the Ministry of Labor. Unresolved disputes may subsequently be taken to the Industrial Arbitration Panel and the NIC. Union officials have, however, questioned the independence of the NIC in light of its refusal to resolve various disputes stemming from the Government's failure to fulfill contract provisions for public employees.

There have been no significant reforms in labor practice since January 1991, when the Government abolished the uniform wage structure for all government entities. This move allowed each tier of government—federal, state, local, and state enterprises—freedom to negotiate its own level of wages, benefits, and conditions of employment. As a result, negotiations previously conducted on a nationwide basis under the direct supervision of the Labor Ministry are now conducted on a local, often plant-wide, basis with less government involvement.

One export processing zone remains in development in Calabar, Cross River state. Workers in such zones are subject to national labor laws.

c. *Prohibition of Forced or Compulsory Labor.*—The 1974 Labor Decree and the 1979 and 1989 Constitutions prohibit forced or compulsory labor. There are no reports of forced or compulsory labor. However, the ILO has noted that with no constitution in force, the Government may be unable to enforce the ILO Convention against forced labor.

d. *Minimum Age for Employment of Children.*—The 1974 Labor Decree prohibits employment of children under 18 years of age in commerce and industry and restricts other child labor to home-based agricultural or domestic work. The law further stipulates that children may not be employed in agricultural or domestic work for more than 8 hours per day. The decree allows the apprenticeship of youths at age 13 under specific conditions.

Primary education is compulsory, although this is rarely enforced, and recent studies show declining enrollment due mainly to the continuing deterioration of public schools. This lack of sufficient primary school infrastructure has ended some families' access to education, forcing them to place their children in the labor market. The ILO and the United Nations Children's Fund, in consultation with the NLC, have concluded that child labor, while not yet endemic, is increasing and could become a serious problem.

e. *Acceptable Conditions of Work.*—The 1974 Labor Decree sets a minimum wage, which is reviewed on an ad hoc basis. The last review in 1991 was undertaken by a tripartite group consisting of representatives of the NLC, the Nigeria Employers' Consultative Association, and the Ministry of Labor. With the considerable decline in the naira, the group raised the minimum wage from $2.90 (250 naira) to $5.00 (450 naira) per month, a level which does not provide a decent living for a worker and family.

The 1974 Labor Decree also established a 40-hour workweek, prescribed 2 to 4 weeks of annual leave, and stipulated that workers must be paid extra for hours worked over the legal limit. The decree also stated that workers who work on Sundays and statutory public holidays must be paid a full day's pay in addition to their normal wages. There is no law prohibiting excessive compulsory overtime.

The Labor Decree contains general health and safety provisions, some aimed specifically at young or female workers. While it requires that the factory inspectorate of the Ministry of Labor and Employment inspect factories for compliance with health and safety standards, this agency neglects safety oversight of construction sites and other nonfactory work. The decree also requires employers to compensate injured workers and dependent survivors of those killed in industrial accidents. The Labor Decree does not provide workers with the right to remove themselves from dangerous work situations without loss of employment. The Labor Ministry, which is charged with enforcement of these laws, has experienced large staff turnover and has been largely ineffective in identifying violations. The Government has failed to act on various ILO recommendations since 1991 to update its moribund inspection and accident reporting program.

RWANDA

The largely Tutsi Rwandan Patriotic Front (RPF), which took power following the civil war and genocide of 1994, is the principal political force in the Government of National Unity. President Pasteur Bizimungu, an ethnic Hutu, and Vice President and Minister of Defense Paul Kagame, an ethnic Tutsi, both belong to the RPF. The mainly Hutu Republican Democratic Movement (MDR) retains the office of Prime Minister. Prime Minister Pierre Rwigema runs the Government on a daily basis and is responsible for relations with the National Assembly. The judicial system is functioning on a limited basis.

The Minister of Defense is responsible for internal security and military defense; the Minister of Interior is responsible for civilian security matters. The security apparatus consists of the Rwandan Patriotic Army (RPA) and the gendarmerie, largely made up of RPA soldiers. Civilian police with limited arrest powers work in some rural communes. They report to the bourgemestre, or local mayor. The RPA and gendarmerie committed numerous serious human rights abuses prior to the mass repatriation of refugees.

The economic situation remains difficult. The interethnic violence from 1990 onward and especially the massive genocide of 1994 resulted in the neglect and widespread destruction of much of the country's economic infrastructure, including utilities, roads, and hospitals. Most citizens are subsistence farmers, and food production even before the war had barely kept pace with population growth. Small-scale commercial activities are on the increase, but the industrial base remains neglected.

The Government continued to be responsible for numerous serious human rights abuses, although the country took a major step toward national reconciliation with the voluntary return of hundreds of thousands of refugees in November. Citizens do not have the right to change their government. The RPA killed hundreds of people; some killings were for political reasons, some were acts of revenge. Still other victims were innocent civilians, including hundreds of civilians killed in security sweeps in the countryside. The number of such abuses dropped after the mass repatriation, and related military setbacks for Hutu rebels late in the year. Prison conditions are harsh. Authorities hold more than 80,000 prisoners in overcrowded jails; most are accused of participating in the genocide. In November the Government announced that it would begin releasing prisoners whose arrest files do not meet strict standards concerning potential guilt. Due process rights guaranteed by the Constitution are not assured. The Government arrested genocide suspects at the rate of about 800 every week during the first 6 months of the year; the rate dropped sharply thereafter. Nearly all such arrests appear arbitrary and are often based on oral complaints and unsubstantiated accusations. In late December, the Government began to hold the first trials of suspects accused in the killing of some half-million people in 1994.

In November and December, more than 1.1 million Rwandan refugees returned from Tanzania, and from Zaire in the wake of a rebellion in North and South Kivu. The Government welcomed the refugees and assisted them in returning to their home communes. Among the returnees were thousands of people suspected of complicity in the genocide of 1994; however, the Government immediately suspended arrests of suspected war criminals, except in notorious cases.

The authorities harassed and threatened journalists, and freedom of assembly, movement and political activity are restricted. Discrimination and violence against women, and discrimination against indigenous people are problems.

During the genocide and war of April to July 1994 approximately two-thirds of the population was uprooted. More than 1.7 million people fled to bordering countries; another 2 million were internally displaced. The internally displaced returned to their homes by year's end.

Hutu insurgents committed many serious human rights abuses, including killings of unarmed civilians.

RESPECT FOR HUMAN RIGHTS

Section 1. Respect for the Integrity of the Person, Including Freedom From:

a. *Political and Other Extrajudicial Killing.*—The RPA committed hundreds of killings for political reasons, in revenge for earlier violence, and in security sweeps (see Section 1.g.). The RPA killed many civilians during these operations. Many of these killings were in response to rebel infiltrations from Zaire.

Genocide survivors and Hutu politicians at the local level have been the targets of infiltrators. On June 18, unknown persons presumed to be infiltratiors killed 15 genocide survivors and 1 RPA trooper in an attack on a makeshift settlement in Kibuye prefecture. These killings were apparently part of an effort to silence witnesses to the genocide of 1994.

On March 30, ex-FAR infiltrators killed Andre Ndayobotse, counselor of Nyamubembe sector in Nyakabuye prefecture, Cyangugu. On May 10, infiltrators in Cyangugu killed Anne Marie Mukandori, the bourgemestre of Karengera Commune. The commune of Bugarama was the scene of several murders of local officials and their families by infiltrators, deaths due to land mines, and an armed attack by ex-FAR soldiers on the municipal offices and jail. These killings took place during March and April.

b. *Disappearance.*—There were a few reports of disappearances, particularly in connection with RPA cordon and search operations. Human rights observers report, however, that due to the tense security situation and the mobility of returnees, it was often difficult or impossible to characterize definitively whether the disappearance of "missing" persons was involuntary or the result of force. In addition, there were a growing number of incommunicado detentions by agents of the State, which resulted in the effective disappearance of many persons.

One particularly blatant and well-documented disappearance occurred on July 11, when unknown individuals seized the Bourgemestre of Nyabikenke Commune in Gitarama prefecture, and forced him, with his motorcycle, into an RPA truck. He has not been seen since and is presumed dead. Police made no arrests.

c. *Torture and Other Cruel, Inhuman, or Degrading Treatment or Punishment.*—Torture is contrary to the Fundamental Law, and there were no reports of systematic torture. Various observers have accused local authorities of using excessive force in arrests and interrogation, but there have been no documented cases.

Prison conditions are harsh. Overcrowding and sanitation are serious problems. There are approximately 80,000 persons held in some 250 prisons and jails having a much smaller design capacity.

The International Committee of the Red Cross (ICRC), human rights organizations, diplomats, and journalists have regular access to the prisons. The ICRC feeds detainees in the 14 main prisons and also provides additional expertise and logistical and material support to improve conditions for detainees. New detention centers are being built.

d. *Arbitrary Arrest, Detention, and Exile.*—The justice system began functioning on a limited basis at midyear, hearing nongenocide criminal and civil cases. Under these circumstances in which the Government has little capacity to ensure due process, almost all arrests appeared to arbitrary.

The Government arrested genocide suspects at the rate of 800 per week in the first 6 months of the year; thereafter the rate dropped to 400. Arrests are often based on oral complaints and, it is believed, at times on false accusations.

Exile is not practiced.

e. *Denial of Fair Public Trial.*—The judicial system again began functioning late at midyear. Never a model of free and fair justice, the system collapsed during the war and genocide of 1994. The Government, with the help of the international community, is attempting to rebuild the judiciary and appoint lower court officials.

The law provides for public trials with the right to a defense. There were only a few trials of criminal suspects and a few genocide trials. Despite the lengthy incarceration of about 80,000 genocide suspects, genocide trials only began at the end of December.

In August the Parliament passed a new genocide law, designed to elicit confessions in exchange for reduced sentences for the vast majority of those involved in the genocide. Trials are envisioned for only the most highly placed organizers of the massacres and those who participated with special zeal.

There were no reports of political prisoners.

f. *Arbitrary Interference With Privacy, Family, Home, or Correspondence.*—The Fundamental Law prohibits such practices. Authorities generally respect these prohibitions and prosecute violations.

g. *Use of Excessive Force and Violations of Humanitarian Law in Internal Conflicts.*—The insurgency along the western border led to many instances of the use of excessive force. A typical pattern was for infiltrators from Zaire to kill a local official or attack municipal offices; in many instances, the RPA reaction included the killings of innocent civilians. In April the RPA and insurgents killed more than 30 local residents in Rutsiro commune in Kibuye prefecture in an armed clash between the two groups. The RPA and insurgents killed between 40 and 50 persons during an armed clash at the detention center in Satinsyi commune, Ginsenyi prefecture. Of some 170 killed in 45 aggravated incidents in April, 124 are thought to have been killed by agents of the State, and 15 by infiltrators.

Between July 5 and 13, the RPA killed more than 100 people during military operations in Gisenyi and Ruhengeri prefectures. Some of those killed were members of the defeated former army and Interahamwe militias, but many were reported to be unarmed civilians.

In June, July, and August the army conducted a series of cordon and search operations in the countryside in an effort to flush out infiltrators. During these operations, the military killed several hundred civilians. Infiltrators also killed many persons, including Tutsi survivors of the genocide and local Hutu officials.

In July some 365 people were killed in 93 separate incidents. 220 deaths were in Gisenyi prefecture, the site of the most intensive infiltrations. An estimated 226 of the killings were attributed, according to human rights observers, to agents of the State, including the RPA; 45 were attributed to infiltators. In August about 110 people were killed by agents of the state.

Members of the former Hutu extremist government and the former army (ex-FAR), based just across the border in Zaire, threatened to renew the civil war; cross-border incidents continued to exacerbate the troubled security situation until the ex-FAR's military setbacks by Zairian rebels in November and the massive return of refugees.

Section 2. *Respect for Civil Liberties, Including:*

a. *Freedom of Speech and Press.*—The Fundamental Law provides for freedom of the press; however, the Government at times harassed and intimidated the media.

Government agents harassed journalists whose reporting was contrary to official views. In August the authorities temporarily closed the Intego, a Kigali weekly newspaper after its publisher and two journalists were detained arbitrarily by members of the security forces. The publisher was detained without charge for 1 week and was treated harshly. The Government did not officially close or sanction the newspaper, but the publisher thought it prudent to suspend operations, prior to reopening in November.

There are several privately owned newspapers, the government-owned Radio Rwanda, and the U.N.-operated Radio Unamir.

The University has reopened, and academic freedom is respected.

b. *Freedom of Peaceful Assembly and Association.*—The Fundamental Law provides for freedom of peaceful assembly, but authorities may legally require advance notice for outdoor rallies, demonstrations, and meetings. Political activity below the executive committee level of political parties was suspended by agreement of the parties. The National Revolutionary Movement for Democracy and Development (MRND), and the Coalition for Defense of the Republic (CDR), both implicated in planning and executing the 1994 genocide, have been banned by law.

c. *Freedom of Religion.*—The 1991 Constitution provides for freedom of religion, and the Government respects this right in practice.

d. *Freedom of Movement Within the Country, Foreign Travel, Emigration, and Repatriation.*—The Constitution provides for these rights, and the Government generally respects them in practice. However, the Government canceled all tourist passports effective September 30. This action gave the Ministry of the Interior more control over the movements of Rwandans outside the country.

Up to 300,000 Rwandans who fled in July 1994 remain outside the country. Repatriation of 600,000 from Zaire took place in November and December. More than 50,000 refugees repatriated from Burundi in July and August. In December, 480,000 additional refugees returned from Tanzania on the basis of decisions made by the government of that nation. The Government, aided by international humanitarian organizations, received and processed these refugees and facilitated their return to their homes, largely without incident.

Section 3. Respect for Political Rights: The Right of Citizens to Change Their Government

Citizens do not have the right to change their government through democratic means. The 1992 powersharing agreement crafted in the Arusha negotiations and ratified by the 1993 peace accord was not fully implemented prior to then-President Habyarimana's death in April 1994, but it remains the basis of planning. Despite the events of 1994, the RPF brought representatives of four other opposition parties into the Government after the RPF military victory, but none of these officials were elected. An appointed multiparty National Assembly is now functioning, with nine political parties represented, including the RPF.

The national constitution known as the Fundamental Law is comprised of four 1exts: the Constitution of 1991; the Arusha Accords of 1993; the RPF Declaration of August 1994; and the Interparty Accords of 1994. These texts apply in a complicated legal precedence based loosely on their dates of execution.

There are no legal restrictions on the participation of women in political life, but women remain poorly represented in politics and government, including both the Cabinet and the National Assembly. The Batwa ethnic group is also underrepresented.

Section 4. Governmental Attitude Regarding International and Nongovernmental Investigation of Alleged Violations of Human Rights

A wide variety of local and international human rights groups operate without government restriction, investigating and publishing their findings on human rights violations. They include the U.N. High Commissioner for Human Rights, which operates a field office with branches throughout the country, and nongovernmental organizations (NGO's) including Journalists Sans Frontieres. Government officials are generally cooperative and responsive to their views. The ICRC is also active.

The International War Crimes Tribunal, which is to hold trials of genocide suspects in Arusha, Tanzania, began and subsequently postponed trials in 1996. The Government has criticized the tribunal for its slow start.

Section 5. Discrimination Based on Race, Sex, Religion, Disability, Language, or Social Status

The Constitution provides that all citizens are equal before the law, without discrimination on the basis of race, color, origin, ethnicity, clan, sex, opinion, religion, or social standing. The Government provides only limited enforcement of these provisions, however.

Women.—Violence against women continues. Wife beating and domestic violence are normally handled within the context of the extended family and rarely come before the courts. Despite constitutional provisions, women continue to face serious discrimination. They traditionally perform most of the subsistence farming and have a limited wage-earning role in the modern sector. They have only limited opportunities for education, employment, and promotion. The Family Code of 1992 has generally improved the legal position of women in matters relating to marriage, divorce, and child custody, but still does not meet the constitutional commitment to gender equality. For example, it formally designates men as heads of households. Also, the absence of succession laws limits a woman's right to property, thus jeopardizing her status and ability to provide for her family should she survive her husband. This omission is particularly onerous in the post-genocide period, since widows are very numerous and surviving male relatives who would normally inherit and provide for them are relatively few.

Children.—The Government is attempting to provide an education and to guarantee health care to every child. More than 50,000 children separated from their parents during the genocide and national upheaval remain in the care of strangers or international organizations. Although the Penal Code prohibits the imprisonment of children with adults, the Government reports that hundreds of children are in fact incarcerated with adults throughout the prison system. A detention center for children funded by the U.N. Children's Fund opened in October 1995; it houses about 150 boys.

People with Disabilities.—Although there are no laws restricting people with disabilities from employment, education, or other state services, in practice few disabled persons have access to education or employment. There are no laws or provisions that mandate access to public facilities.

Indigenous People.—Less than 1 percent of the population comes from the Batwa ethnic group. These indigenous people, survivors of the Pygmy (Twa) tribes of the mountainous forest areas bordering Zaire, exist on the margins of society and continue to be treated as inferior citizens by both Hutus and Tutsis. The Batwa have been unable to protect their interests, which center on access to land and housing. Few Batwa have gained access to the educational system, resulting in minimal representation in government institutions. There is no reliable information on specific human rights abuses perpetrated against the Batwa population during the 1994 upheaval. A group of several hundred Batwa refugees was discovered in 1994 living in a forested area outside Goma, Zaire, its members deeply traumatized by the events they had witnessed. They did not confirm, however, whether they or other Batwa had been victims of massacres by either side.

National/Ethnic/Racial Minorities.—Before April 1994, an estimated 85 percent of citizens were Hutu, 14 percent were Tutsi, and 1 percent Batwa. The subsequent mass killings and migrations affected the ethnic composition of the population, but the extent of the changes is unknown.

The Government has called for ethnic reconciliation and committed itself to abolishing policies of the former government that had created and deepened ethnic cleavages. It promised to eliminate references to ethnic origin from the national identity card, a provision of the 1993 Peace Accord. The Government has not statutorily addressed the issue of ethnic quotas in education, training, and government employment. It has partially integrated more than 2,000 former government soldiers into RPF forces, although not by the formula prescribed by the 1993 Arusha Accord. Tutsi clergy and businessman, who were well represented in these sectors of society, were killed in great numbers in the genocide. Following the 1994 victory by the RPF, Tutsis returning from exile took over many of the business and professional positions formerly held by Hutus and Tutsis.

Section 6. Worker Rights

a. *The Right of Association.*—In practice Rwanda does not have a fully functioning labor movement, given the massive disruptions caused by the 1994 genocide. However, unions are slowly regrouping and asserting themselves. Although preconflict labor law technically remains in effect, the Government is unable to implement its provisions.

The Constitution provides for the right of citizens to create professional associations and labor unions. Union membership is voluntary and open to all salaried workers, including public sector employees. There are no restrictions on the right of association, but all unions must register with the Ministry of Justice for official recognition. There are no known cases in which the Government has denied such recognition. Unions are prohibited by law from having political affiliations, but in practice this is not always respected.

Organized labor represents only a small part of the work force. More than 90 percent are engaged in small-scale subsistence farming. About 7 percent work in the modern (wage) sector, including both public and private industrial production, and about 75 percent of those active in the modern sector are members of labor unions.

Before 1991 the Central Union of Rwandan Workers (CESTRAR) was the only authorized trade union organization. With the political reforms introduced in the Constitution, CESTRAR officially became independent of the Government and the MRND.

The Constitution provides for the right to strike, except for public service workers. A union's executive committee must approve a strike, and a union must first try to resolve its differences with management according to steps prescribed by the Ministry of Labor and Social Affairs. The Government never enforced laws prohibiting retribution against strikers.

Labor organizations may affiliate with international labor bodies. CESTRAR is affiliated with the Organization of African Trade Union Unity and the International Confederation of Free Trade Unions.

b. *The Right to Organize and Bargain Collectively.*—The Constitution provides for collective bargaining, although only CESTRAR had an established collective bargaining agreement with the Government. In practice, since most union members are in the public sector, the Government is intimately involved in the process (see Section 6.e.).

The law prohibits antiunion discrimination, and it has not occurred in practice. There are no formal mechanisms to resolve complaints involving discrimination against unions.

There are no export processing zones.

c. *Prohibition of Forced or Compulsory Labor.*—The law prohibits forced labor, and there are no reports that it occurs in practice.

d. *Minimum Age for Employment of Children.*—Except in subsistence agriculture, the law prohibits children under the age of 18 from working without their parents' or guardians' authorization, and they generally may not work at night. The minimum age for full employment is 18 years and for apprenticeships 14 years, providing that the child has completed primary school. The Ministry of Labor has not enforced child labor laws effectively.

e. *Acceptable Conditions of Work.*—The Ministry of Labor sets minimum wages in the small modern sector. The minimum wage is $1.08 (310 Rwandan francs) for an 8-hour workday. The Government, the main employer, effectively sets most other wage rates as well. The minimum wage was inadequate to provide a decent standard of living for an urban family. Often families supplement their incomes by work in small business or subsistence agriculture. In practice, however, workers will work for less than the minimum wage.

Officially, government offices have a 40-hour workweek. Negotiations in 1993 between the unions, Government, and management were held to reduce the workweek from 45 to 40 hours in the private sector as well, but by year's end, no such reduction had occurred. Hours of work and occupational health and safety standards in the modern wage sector are controlled by law, but labor inspectors from the Ministry of Labor enforce them only loosely. Workers do not have the right to remove themselves from dangerous work situations without jeopardizing their jobs.

SAO TOME AND PRINCIPE

The Democratic Republic of Sao Tome and Principe is a multiparty democracy. The Government is composed of an executive branch, a unicameral legislature (the National Assembly), and an independent judiciary. The President appoints the Prime Minister, who in turn appoints the ministers of the Government. Miguel Trovoada, an independent, was re-elected President in 1996 for a second 5-year term. The Movement for the Liberation of Sao Tome and Principe (MLSTP), which had ruled prior to 1990 as the sole legal party, won a plurality in free and fair parliamentary elections in 1994 and holds 5 of 9 seats in the current Government. Presidential elections held in June and July were deemed generally free and fair by international observers and the results were ratified in late August, despite allegations of an unconstitutional modification of voter lists between the first and second rounds.

The Minister of National Defense, Security, and Internal Order supervises the military, many of whose members are part-time farmers or fishermen, and the police. A week-long military mutiny in August 1995 was ended by an agreement mediated by the Foreign Minister of Angola, forestalling a threatened overthrow of the Government. The National Assembly passed an amnesty for the mutineers which was proclaimed by the President. The Government and international donors have dedicated resources to improving soldiers' living conditions.

The economy is based on the export of a single product, cocoa, produced in an archaic state-run system of plantations called "empresas." The Government has privatized some of the state-held land but has had limited success in privatizing state-owned enterprises. The Government is following structural adjustment guidelines, but the economy continues to face serious difficulties. The annual inflation rate is 35 percent, unemployment is 27 percent, total external debt is six times gross domestic product, and the country is highly dependent on foreign aid. Per capita income is less than $250 per year.

The Government continued to respect the rights of its citizens. The principal human rights problems continued to be an inefficient judicial system, harsh prison conditions, discrimination and violence against women, and outdated plantation labor practices that limit worker rights.

RESPECT FOR HUMAN RIGHTS

Section 1. Respect for the Integrity of the Person, Including Freedom From:

a. *Political and Other Extrajudicial Killing.*—There were no reports of political or other extrajudicial killings.

b. *Disappearance.*—There were no reports of politically motivated disappearances.

c. *Torture and Other Cruel, Inhuman, or Degrading Treatment or Punishment.*— The Constitution prohibits torture or cruel and inhuman punishment. There were no reports of violations such as beatings or other cruel treatment during arrests or interrogations.

Prison conditions are harsh but not life threatening. While there is no indication that human rights monitors have requested permission to make prison visits, it is believed the Government would permit such visits if requested.

d. *Arbitrary Arrest, Detention, or Exile.*—The Constitution prohibits arbitrary arrest, detention, or exile, and the Government observes these prohibitions.

Exile is not used as a punishment, and all those exiled under the one-party regime of 1975–1990 are free to return.

e. *Denial of Fair Public Trial.*—The Constitution provides for an independent judiciary, and the judiciary has returned verdicts against both the President and the Government. The legal system is based on Portuguese law and customary law, with the Supreme Court at the apex. The Government has important powers relating to the judiciary, including setting salaries for judges and all ministerial employees in accordance with standard government salary guidelines. Government salaries are extremely low, and the authorities are concerned that judges may be tempted to accept bribes. The authorities maintain that they continue to respect the independence of the judiciary.

The Constitution provides for the right to fair public trial, the right of appeal, and the right to legal representation. In practice, however, the judicial infrastructure suffers from severe budgetary constraints, inadequate facilities, and a shortage of trained judges and lawyers, causing long delays in bringing cases to court and greatly hindering investigations in criminal cases.

There were no reports of political prisoners.

f. *Arbitrary Interference With Privacy, Family, Home, or Correspondence.*—The Constitution provides for the integrity of the person and the right to privacy of home, correspondence, and private communication. The Government does not engage in intrusive practices, such as surveillance of people or the monitoring of communications. The judicial police are responsible for criminal investigations and must obtain authorization from the Ministry of Justice to conduct searches.

Section 2. Respect for Civil Liberties, Including:

a. *Freedom of Speech and Press.*—The Constitution provides for freedom of expression and freedom of the press, and the Government generally respects these rights in practice. One government-run and four independent newspapers have published in the past; none appeared regularly in 1996 due to financial constraints and the lack of printing facilities.

Television and radio are state-operated. While there are no independent local stations, there are no laws forbidding them. The Voice of America, Radio International Portugal, and Radio France International are rebroadcast locally. The law grants all opposition parties access to the state-run media, including a minimum of 3 minutes per month on television.

All parties freely distribute newsletters and press releases giving their views and criticizing the Government, the President, and one another. There were no reports of government censorship or threats of censorship from any group, nor any reports of efforts by national security forces to suppress criticism.

b. *Freedom of Peaceful Assembly and Association.*—The Constitution provides for these rights, and the Government respects them in practice. Political rallies during the election campaign were numerous and unhindered. The Government requires that requests for authorization of large-scale events be filed 48 hours in advance and usually grants the appropriate permits.

c. *Freedom of Religion.*—The Constitution provides for religious freedom, and the Government respects this right in practice. There are no restrictions on the activities of foreign clergy.

d. *Freedom of Movement Within the Country, Foreign Travel, Emigration, and Repatriation.*—Under the Constitution and in practice, citizens have the right to move freely within the country, to travel abroad, and to emigrate and return. Authorities have traditionally welcomed those seeking refuge or asylum. The issue of provision of first asylum did not arise during the year.

Section 3. *Respect for Political Rights: The Right of Citizens to Change Their Government*

Citizens exercised this right for the first time in free and fair presidential and legislative elections in 1991 and again in the legislative elections of October 1994. These elections resulted in the peaceful transfer of power between political party coalitions. More than 80 percent of those eligible to vote cast their ballots in the 1996 presidential elections. International observers judged the contest to be free and fair. The National Electoral Commission acknowledged minor discrepancies in the registration process and in voter rolls while asserting that these were insufficient to call the results into question. After some controversy, the Supreme Court ratified the results. Each of the three principal political parties has significant representation in the unicameral National Assembly. Elections are by secret ballot on the basis of universal suffrage for citizens 18 years of age or older.

The Constitution provides for the election of the President, who as Head of State names the Prime Minister. The Prime Minister appoints members of the Government.

There are no restrictions in law or in practice on the participation of women in politics. However, women are underrepresented in the legislature. They currently hold 3 of 55 seats in the National Assembly. One woman was a presidential candidate in the 1996 elections and received 16 percent of the first-round vote.

Section 4. *Governmental Attitude Regarding International and Nongovernmental Investigation of Alleged Violations of Human Rights*

A small number of local human rights groups have formed since 1991 and operate without restriction or governmental interference. There were no known requests by international human rights groups to visit the country.

Section 5. *Discrimination Based on Race, Sex, Religion, Disability, Language, or Social Status*

The Constitution provides for the equality of all citizens regardless of sex, race, racial origin, political tendency, creed, or philosophic conviction. However, the Government has not sought actively to enforce these provisions.

Women.—While the extent of the problem is unknown, violence against women occurs, and medical professionals and officials report firsthand experience in dealing with violence, including rape. They also report that although women have the right to legal recourse—including against spouses—many are reluctant to bring a complaint or are ignorant of their rights under the law. Traditional beliefs and practices also inhibit women from taking domestic disputes outside the family.

While the Constitution stipulates that women and men have equal political, economic, and social rights, and while many women do have access to opportunities in education, business, and government, in practice women still encounter significant societal discrimination. Traditional beliefs concerning the division of labor between men and women leave women with much of the hard work in agriculture, with most child-rearing responsibilities, and with less access to education and to the professions. Female literacy is approximately 62 percent (compared with male literacy of 85 percent).

Children.—A number of government and donor-funded programs have been established to improve conditions for children. There has been improvement in maternity and infant care, in nutrition, and in access to basic health services, especially in urban areas. Mistreatment of children is not widespread. There remain few social protections for orphans and abandoned children.

People With Disabilities.—The law does not mandate arrangements to provide access to buildings, transportation, or services for persons with disabilities.

Section 6. *Worker Rights*

a. *The Right of Association.*—The Constitution provides for freedom of association and the right to strike. Few unions exist in the very small modern wage sector. One confederation, the Independent Union Federation, has been attempting to organize workers on the large state-owned plantations, but it has met with only limited success. Independent cooperatives, on the other hand, have taken advantage of the government land distribution program to attract workers and in many cases significantly to improve production and incomes. Public sector employees still comprise the great majority of wage earners. Government employees and other essential workers are allowed to strike and did so repeatedly. There are no laws or regulations prohibiting employers from retaliating against strikers.

There are no restrictions barring trade unions from joining federations or affiliating with international bodies.

b. *The Right to Organize and Bargain Collectively.*—The Constitution provides that workers may organize and bargain collectively. However, due to its role as the principal employer in the wage sector, the Government remains the key interlocutor for labor on all matters, including wages. There are no laws prohibiting antiunion discrimination.

There are no export processing zones.

c. *Prohibition of Forced or Compulsory Labor.*—The law prohibits forced or compulsory labor, and such labor is not practiced.

d. *Minimum Age for Employment of Children.*—Employers in the modern wage sector generally respect the legally mandated minimum employment age of 18 years. The Ministry of Justice and Labor is responsible for enforcing this law. In subsistence agriculture, on plantations, and in informal commerce, children do work, sometimes from an early age.

e. *Acceptable Conditions of Work.*—Working conditions on many of the state-owned plantations—the biggest wage employment sector—border on the medieval. There is no legally mandated minimum wage. The average salary for plantation workers does not permit a decent standard of living, and its real value is constantly eroded by high rates of inflation. In principle, workers are provided free (but inadequate) housing, rudimentary education, and health care, as well as the privilege of reduced prices and credit at the "company store." These arrangements are intended to subsidize food and clothing. Corruption is an everyday fact, however, and international lending institutions have criticized the Government for ineffective administration of these subsidies. Workers are often forced to pay higher prices on the parallel market to obtain the goods theoretically provided at a discount as part of their compensation.

The legal workweek is 40 hours with 48 consecutive hours mandated for a rest period, a norm respected in the modern wage sector. The Social Security Law of 1979 prescribes basic occupational health and safety standards. Inspectors from the Ministry of Justice and Labor are responsible for enforcement of these standards, but their efforts are ineffective. Employees have the right under the law to leave unsafe working conditions.

SENEGAL

Senegal is a republic with an elected president, Abdou Diouf, who has been in office since 1981, and a unicameral legislature dominated by the President's Socialist Party (PS) since independence from France in 1960. During the year, the Government decentralized its regional and local administrations. The stability brought about by the entry of the principal opposition party into government in 1995 continued, with the smaller parties choosing to remain in government while contesting the elections. The judiciary is independent although subject to governmental influence and pressure.

The armed forces are professional and generally disciplined. They traditionally remain aloof from politics and are firmly under civilian control. The paramilitary gendarmerie and the police are less professional and less disciplined. Some members of the gendarmerie and the police continued to commit serious human rights abuses.

Senegal is predominantly agricultural with more than 70 percent of the labor force engaged in farming, largely peanut production. Since the devaluation of the cfa franc in 1994, the Government implemented a series of economic policy reforms to enhance competitiveness, and is phasing out most qualitative restrictions on imports, dismantling monopolies, liberalizing the labor market, and privatizing several important state-owned industries. Supported by the international donor community, Senegal remains dependent on foreign assistance as an important part of its national budget.

The Government generally respected the human rights of its citizens, however, there were serious problems in some areas, particularly torture by police of suspects during questioning, arbitrary arrest, and lengthy pretrial detention. The Government tried or punished few military, gendarmes, or police for previous human rights abuses, particularly for those in the Casamance. The Socialist Party's domination of political life, including irregularities and fraud in the 1996 regional and local elections, calls into question the extent to which citizens can meaningfully exercise their right to change the government. Poor prison conditions, a judiciary subject to government influence and pressure, domestic violence and discrimination against women, and some abuse of children are also problems.

Although there were credible reports of infrequent human rights abuses perpetrated by Casamance rebels, a cease-fire during the year effectively restored the security and safety of the Casamance.

RESPECT FOR HUMAN RIGHTS

Section 1. Respect for the Integrity of the Person, Including Freedom From:

a. *Political and Other Extrajudicial Killing.*—There were no confirmed reports of political or extrajudicial killings by government officials.

b. *Disappearance.*—There were no reports of politically motivated disappearances.

c. *Torture and Other Cruel, Inhuman, or Degrading Treatment or Punishment.*—There are credible reports that police and gendarmes often beat suspects during questioning and pretrial detention, in spite of constitutional prohibitions against such treatment. Torture perpetrated by police, usually beatings, remains an embarrassing public issue for the Government, and is regularly reported in the press. In April two police officers were arrested for torturing a suspect by spraying paint thinner on his buttocks and igniting it. At year's end, the accused officers were on bail pending trial. The Government proposed and Parliament is reviewing a law designed to strengthen legal provisions forbidding torture.

Prison conditions are poor. Prisons remain overcrowded, and food and health care are inadequate. However, there have been no reported deaths in prison due to these conditions.

During the year, a cease-fire was in effect between the Government and the Movement of Democratic Forces in the Casamance (MFDC). The very few incidents which seemed to involve the MFDC were directed against civilians. Although precise data are lacking, the cease-fire has apparently reduced the numbers of persons displaced in the Casamance.

The Government permits visits by government, nongovernmental, and international human rights monitors.

d. *Arbitrary Arrest, Detention, or Exile.*—The Constitution prohibits arbitrary arrest and detention, however, authorities at times violate these constitutional prohibitions.

The law specifies that warrants, issued by judges, are required for arrests. However, laws also grant the police broad powers to detain prisoners for lengthy periods of time. Police may legally hold without charge a person suspected of a crime for 48 hours after arrest and for up to 72 hours if ordered by a public prosecutor. This period may be doubled in the case of crimes against the security of the state. The prosecutor decides whether to forward the case to an investigating judge who may open an investigation. At this point, the suspects are preliminarily charged and may be held or released on their own recognizance. There is a system of bail, but it is rarely used. During temporary detention the accused has no access to family or an attorney but has the right to demand a medical exam. Once charged, a prisoner is permitted visits by both family and legal advisors. The accused may be held in custody for 6 months, and the investigating magistrate can certify that an additional 6 month extension is required. Such extensions may be reviewed by a court on appeal from the accused's attorney.

Police are rarely prosecuted for violations of arrest and detention procedures, and the authorities may detain a prisoner for long periods of time while they investigate and build a case against a suspect. The authorities may and routinely do hold prisoners in custody unless and until a court demands their release. Despite the 6-month limitations on detention, the time between the charging phase and trial averages 2 years. In a particularly egregious case, in October three defendants were acquitted by a court after 5 to 7 years of detention.

In January the Government released from house arrest MFDC leader Abbe Diamacoune Senghor and four military/political advisors who had been extradited from Guinea-Bissau in 1994. The individuals had been charged but not convicted of compromising the security of the state.

Approximately 120 suspected MFDC members remained in political detention at year's end. Throughout the year, the Government released small groups of MFDC members to suggest good faith in negotiations.

The Constitution prohibits exile and it is not used.

e. *Denial of Fair Public Trial.*—The Constitution provides for a judiciary independent of the executive, the legislature, and the armed forces. However, magistrates are vulnerable to outside pressures due to low pay, poor working conditions, and family and political ties. Also, the Minister of Justice and subordinate authorities have extensive authority to influence judicial procedures, e.g., in keeping the accused in pretrial detention. Political and governmental pressure reportedly came to bear on the court when it fined Sud Communication, a privately owned media group, an unprecedented $1 million and sentenced five of its journalists to jail for defamation. Sud Communication and the journalists are appealing the decisions.

The legal system is based on French civil law and is composed of ordinary courts and a number of higher and special courts, including the three created in May 1992 to replace the Supreme Court: The Council of State for Administrative Questions, the Constitutional Council, and a Court of Appeal. These Courts remain understaffed, and many of the special courts, including the Unlawful Enrichment Court and special courts to try government officials for treason and malfeasance, are dormant. Muslims have the right to choose customary law or civil law for certain civil cases, such as those concerning inheritance and divorce. However, customary law decisions are rendered by civil court judges. There is a separate system of military courts for members of the armed forces and the gendarmerie. The right of appeal exists in all courts except military courts and the special "illegal enrichment" court. Military courts may not try civilians.

In principle the accused is innocent until proven guilty, and when brought to trial it is the State's burden to prove that the accused is guilty of the charges. Trials are public, and defendants have the right to be present in court, to confront witnesses, to present evidence, and to have an attorney. In practice, however, some defendants are denied legal assistance at public expense due to lack of funding. Evidentiary hearings may be closed to the public and the press. A panel of judges presides over ordinary courts for both civil and criminal cases; in criminal cases citizens also serve on the panel.

There were no reports of political prisoners.

f. *Arbitrary Interference With Privacy, Family, Home, or Correspondence.*—The Constitution prohibits arbitrary invasion of the home, and there was little government interference in the private lives of citizens, particularly in rural areas. The law requires search warrants, and only judges may issue them. During high-profile or politically charged investigations, police often proceed without the required search warrants.

Section 2. Respect for Civil Liberties, Including:

a. *Freedom of Speech and Press.*—The Constitution provides for freedom of speech and press, and the Government generally respects these rights in practice. Laws prohibit the press from the expression of views that "discredit" the State, incite the population to disorder, or disseminate "false news." However, the Government did not prosecute any groups or persons under these statutes during the year.

A broad spectrum of thought and opinion is available to the public through magazines and newspapers, including foreign publications, and numerous independent radio stations. Political and economic views expressed in the independent press are often critical of the Government and its programs. While publishers are required to register prior to starting publication, the Government routinely approves such registrations. A government monopoly controls local television, an important source of news. French-owned pay television is available but offers no local news.

Academic freedom is respected.

b. *Freedom of Peaceful Assembly and Association.*—The Constitution provides for these rights, and the Government generally respects them in practice. The Government requires prior authorization for public demonstrations, which it usually grants. After permitting large gatherings earlier in the year, the Government lifted its formal ban on the Moustarchidine movement in the fall.

Citizens wishing to form associations must register with the Ministry of Interior. Business-related associations register with the Ministry of Commerce. By law and in practice, the Ministry of Interior must register such groups so long as the objectives of the association are clearly stated and they do not violate the law.

c. *Freedom of Religion.*—The Constitution provides for freedom of religion, and the Government respects this right in practice.

d. *Freedom of Movement Within the Country, Foreign Travel, Emigration, and Repatriation.*—The Constitution provides for these rights, and the Government generally respects them in practice. Certain public employees must obtain government approval before departing Senegal.

The Government cooperates with the Office of the United Nations High Commissioner for Refugees (UNHCR) and other humanitarian organizations in assisting refugees. More than 60,000 Mauritanian refugees resident in Senegal since 1989 as the country of first asylum, and members of other refugee groups, may move freely throughout the country. In 1996 Senegal offered first asylum to many residents of Liberia who were forced to flee the fighting in that country. All either returned to

Liberia or settled in other countries by the end of the year. There were no reports of forced return of persons to a country where they feared persecution.

Section 3. Respect for Political Rights: The Right of Citizens to Change Their Government

Citizens have the constitutional right to change their government through periodic multiparty elections. However, the Socialist Party's domination of political life—it has held power since independence—and irregularities and fraud in the regional and local elections have called into question the extent to which citizens can meaningfully exercise this right.

The PS holds a 73 percent majority in Parliament with 88 parliamentary seats, 2 more than in 1995 due to opposition member defections. The opposition holds 32 seats. There are 25 legal opposition parties. Five members of the leading opposition party, the Senegalese Democratic Party (PDS), and 4 independent and/or minor opposition members are in President Diouf's 33-member cabinet.

Despite its preeminent position, the PS continued to suffer extensive factional infighting during the first part of the year, which in some cases resulted in serious injuries. This internal PS conflict was responsible, at least in part, for the Government's decision to cancel the November 1995 municipal elections and reschedule them to coincide with the November 1996 rural elections. There were credible allegations that the Government engaged in gerrymandering, illegal fundraising, voter list manipulations, and other irregularities in its manipulation of the electoral process prior to the November elections.

The regional and local elections held on November 24 and 27 were marked by allegations of fraud and many serious procedural and other irregularities. Many polling places in the capital opened late or not at all. There were reports of similar problems elsewhere, but apparently not on the same scale as in Dakar. One million extra blank voter's identification cards were printed, an amount far exceeding the legal limit. Although 500,000 of the extra cards were publicly burned, allegations remained that 300,000 blank cards were not accounted for. Almost all opposition politicians and civic leaders renewed their calls for the creation of an independent national electoral commission to administer elections. In spite of strong sentiment supporting such a measure, the Government refused to create an independent electoral commission.

Women are underrepresented in the political process. While there are no legal impediments to their participation in government and politics, cultural and educational factors hamper them. Only 3 of the 33 ministers who comprise the President's Cabinet are women, and there are only 2 in the 19-member Economic and Social Council, the Government's quasi-policymaking body. Women won two mayoralty elections and one rural commune in the November local elections. There are no women heading political parties, and only 14 female Deputies in the 120-member National Assembly. Women's lower representation reflects not only disparity in education (see Section 5), but also cultural pressures. Political parties often rank women low on party lists, making it difficult for them to be elected to the National Assembly or be appointed ministers.

Section 4. Governmental Attitude Regarding International and Nongovernmental Investigation of Alleged Violations of Human Rights

A wide variety of human rights groups operate without government restriction, investigating and publishing their findings on human rights cases. Government officials are generally cooperative and receptive to their views.

Section 5. Discrimination Based on Race, Sex, Religion, Disability, Language, or Social Status

The Constitution states that "men and women shall be equal in law" and prohibits discrimination based on race, religion, sex, class, or language. However, de facto discrimination against women is pervasive, and the Government frequently does not enforce antidiscrimination laws.

Women.—There are credible reports that violence against women, usually wife beating, is common, particularly in rural areas. The Government and cooperative newspapers led a yearlong media campaign against spouse abuse. Police do not usually intervene in domestic disputes, and most people are reluctant to go outside the family for redress. The law and society view rape as a very serious crime, and the law stipulates that persons convicted of rape may be imprisoned up to 10 years, more if the victim is a minor. Rape trials often result in convictions. In the past, vigilante action was often meted out to the accused before the police were able to arrest rape or family violence suspects.

Despite constitutional protections, women face extensive societal discrimination, especially in rural areas where Islamic and Senegalese customs, including polygyny and Islamic rules of inheritance, are strongest, and women are generally confined to traditional roles. In the countryside, women perform much of the subsistence farming and childrearing and have limited educational opportunities. Although the Government has committed itself to equalizing male/female primary school enrollment, there is still much social and official discrimination against women in educational opportunities. Only 19 percent of females over 15 years of age are literate, while the rate for males over age 15 is 30 percent.

According to the U.N. only 20 percent of women are engaged in paid employment. Traditional practices, moreover, make it difficult for women to obtain bank credit. Women usually marry young (the majority by age 16 in rural areas), and average 6 live births (down from 7 in 1995). About half of all women live in polygynous unions.

In urban areas women encounter somewhat less discrimination and are active in government, political life, the legal profession, and business. About 14 percent of lawyers are women. Urban women are more likely to take advantage of the Government's efforts to increase respect for women's legal rights to divorce, alimony, and child support, and to seek education and employment. In general, urban women receive equal pay for equal work.

Children.—The Ministry of Women, Children, and the Family, established in 1990, is responsible for promoting children's welfare. Numerous organizations assist the Ministry in support of children's rights, including the Ministry of Health which maintained a nationwide effort focusing on child survival. Organized street begging by children who are Koranic students results in a significant interruption of their education. The Government continues to increase the number of classrooms and encourage more children, particularly females, to enter and stay in school.

There are no laws or regulations concerning female genital mutilation (FGM), which is widely condemned by international health experts as damaging to both physical and psychological health. However, the Ministry of Women, Children, and the Family sponsors programs to educate women to the dangers of FGM. FGM is not practiced by Senegal's largest ethnic group, the Wolofs (representing 43 percent of the population), but it is performed on girls belonging to some other ethnic groups. Infibulation, the most extreme and dangerous form of FGM, is practiced by members of the Toucouleur and Peulh ethnic groups, particularly those in rural areas. Unsubstantiated recent studies estimate that between 5 and 20 percent of females undergo the procedure.

People With Disabilities.—There is no official discrimination against disabled persons. There are no laws that mandate accessibility for the disabled, and in practice most persons with disabilities are generally unable to participate in many occupations due to physical barriers and a lack of equipment and training opportunities that would make such participation possible.

Religious Minorities.—Approximately 92 percent of the population are Muslim. There are small Christian (2 percent) and indigenous (6 percent) religious communities. Officially, adherence to a particular religion confers no advantage or disadvantage in civil, political, economic, military, or other matters. In practice, however, membership in an Islamic subgroup may afford certain political and economic protections and advantages.

Section 6. Worker Rights

a. *The Right of Association.*—The Constitution and the Labor Code provide all workers with the right of association, and they are free to form or join unions. A minimum of seven persons, each having worked in the trade for at least 1 year, may form a trade union by submitting a list of members and a charter to the Ministry of Interior. While the Ministry does not always grant initial recognition to a union, once it gives recognition, the Ministry virtually never withdraws it. It may, however, disband a union if its activities deviate from its charter. The Labor Code does not apply to the informal and agricultural sectors where most people work.

Although they represent a small percentage of the working population, unions wield significant political influence because of their ability to disrupt vital sectors of the economy. The small industrial component of the total work force of 4 million is almost totally unionized. The only union in the agrarian sector is one representing workers at a privately owned sugar company. Some farmers are organized into the National Farming Association, an advocacy organization.

The National Confederation of Senegalese Workers (CNTS), the largest union organization, has close ties to the ruling Socialist Party, and union members hold a considerable number of government positions. One is a PS minister, and four others hold PS seats in Parliament. While ostensibly an independent organization, the umbrella CNTS consistently supports government policies.

The rival to the CNTS is the National Union of Autonomous Labor Unions of Senegal (UNSAS). UNSAS is a federation of strategically important unions such as those of electricians, telecommunication workers, teachers, water technicians, and hospital, railroad, and sugar workers.

The Constitution and the Labor Code provide for the right to strike, but with restrictions. Unions representing members of the civil service must notify the Government of their intent to strike no less than 1 month in advance, and private sector unions must make a similar notification 3 days in advance. The Government or the employer can use the time to seek a settlement to the dispute but cannot stop the strike. There were numerous legal—but no illegal—strikes in 1996. Regulations prohibit employers from retaliating against legal strikers, and these regulations are enforced through the Labor Court.

The Labor Code permits unions to affiliate with international bodies. The CNTS is active in regional and international labor organizations and is the dominant Senegalese member of the Organization of African Trade Union Unity.

b. *The Right to Organize and Bargain Collectively.*—The law provides unions with the right to organize and to bargain collectively, and these rights are protected in practice. There are also legal prohibitions governing discrimination by employers against union members and organizers. Employers found guilty of antiunion discrimination are required to reinstate workers. There were no known instances in which workers were prevented from exercising the right to organize and bargain collectively. The Ministry of Labor can intervene in disputes between labor and management if requested, and it plays a mediation role in the private and state enterprise sectors.

Labor laws apply to all industrial firms including those in the Dakar Industrial Free Trade Zone.

c. *Prohibition of Forced or Compulsory Labor.*—There were no reports of forced labor, which is prohibited by law.

d. *Minimum Age for Employment of Children.*—The minimum age for employment is 16 years for apprenticeships and 18 for all other types of work. Inspectors from the Ministry of Labor closely monitor and enforce these restrictions within the small formal wage sector, which includes state-owned corporations, large private enterprises, and cooperatives.

However, children under the age of 16 frequently work in the much larger traditional or informal sectors, such as family farms in rural areas or in small businesses, where the Government does not enforce minimum age and other workplace regulations.

e. *Acceptable Conditions of Work.*—Legislation mandating a monthly minimum wage has been in force since the country's independence in 1960. The Ministries of Labor and Finance determine wage rates after negotiating with the unions and management councils. The minimum wage of less than $.40 (202 cfa francs) per hour, last negotiated in 1989, is not adequate to support a worker and a family.

Within the formal sector, the law mandates: a standard workweek of 40 to 48 hours for most occupations, with at least one 24-hour rest period and 1 month per year of annual leave; enrollment in government systems for social security and retirement; safety standards; and a variety of other measures. These regulations are incorporated into the Labor Code and are supervised by inspectors from the Ministry of Labor. However, the authorities' enforcement is uneven, especially outside the formal sector. There is no explicit legal protection for workers who file complaints about unsafe conditions. While there are legal regulations concerning workplace safety, government officials do not often enforce them.

In theory workers have the right to remove themselves from unsafe working conditions, but in practice the right is seldom exercised in circumstances of high unemployment and a slow legal system.

SEYCHELLES

President France Albert Rene and his Seychelles People's Progressive Front (SPPF) have governed since a 1977 military coup. In the 1990's the SPPF guided the return to a multiparty political system, which culminated in July 1993 in the country's first free and fair presidential and parliamentary elections since 1977. President Rene was continued in power, and the SPPF won 27 of the 33 National Assembly seats, 21 by direct election and 6 by proportional representation. Despite the elections, the President and the SPPF continued to dominate the country through a pervasive system of political patronage and control over government jobs, contracts, and resources.

The Constitution was amended in 1995 to allow for the appointment of a vice president. The President has complete control over the security apparatus, which includes a national guard force, the army, and the police. There is also an armed paramilitary Police Mobile Unit. There were several credible reports that the security forces abused persons in custody.

In recent years, the Government continued in an unsystematic way its program to privatize the economy, imposed cuts in domestic spending, reintroduced import licensing to improve the country's foreign exchange position, and passed laws with tax cuts and abatements to encourage and attract foreign investment. In addition, the Government tried to reduce the high dependence on tourism—approximately 70 percent of hard currency earnings—by promoting the development of fishing and light manufacturing. Despite these efforts, the public and quasi-public sectors continued to drive the economy. The Government, through the Seychelles Marketing Board, other state organizations, and the use of banking regulations, continued to dominate most aspects of the economy.

The human rights situation continued to improve, and the Government generally respected the rights of its citizens. However, despite parliamentary formalities, the President continued to wield power virtually unchecked. Security forces used excessive force in a few instances, although police brutality was not widespread. The authorities investigated complaints of police abuse. Violence against women and child abuse remained problems.

RESPECT FOR HUMAN RIGHTS

Section 1. Respect for the Integrity of the Person, Including Freedom From:

a. *Political and Other Extrajudicial Killing.*—There were no reports of politically motivated or other extrajudicial killings.

b. *Disappearance.*—There were no reports of disappearances.

c. *Torture and Other Cruel, Inhuman, or Degrading Treatment or Punishment.*—The Constitution expressly forbids torture, but there have been instances of excessive use of force by police. The authorities have investigated and punished offenders in the past.

Conditions at Long Island prison are Spartan. Family members are allowed monthly visits, and prisoners have access to reading but not writing materials. There is no regular system of independent monitoring of prisons.

d. *Arbitrary Arrest, Detention, or Exile.*—The Constitution provides that persons arrested must be brought before a magistrate within 24 hours. This provision is applied in practice to the extent possible (with allowances for boat travel from distant islands). In October the National Assembly amended this to allow, with a court order, 4 days' detention without a formal charge. With a judge's approval this period can be extended to 7 days. Detainees have access to legal counsel, and free counsel is provided for the indigent. The law provides for judicial review of the legality of detention, and bail is available for most offenses.

Several persons have brought civil cases against the police for unlawful arrest or entry, with limited success.

There were no cases of forced exile. Following the 1977 coup, a number of persons went into voluntary exile, and others were released from prison with the proviso that they immediately leave the country. A number of these former exiles who returned were able to reacquire their property, but the large majority have not. There were some instances in which the Government rejected valid compensation claims for confiscated properties of returning exiles, apparently for political reasons.

e. *Denial of Fair Public Trial.*—The Constitution provides for an independent judiciary, but there are questions about its independence. The judicial system includes magistrates' courts, the Supreme Court, the Constitutional Court, and the Court of Appeal. Criminal cases are heard by a magistrates' court or the Supreme Court, depending on the gravity of the offense. A jury is used in cases involving murder or treason. Trials are public, and the accused is considered innocent until proven guilty. Defendants have the right to counsel, to be present at their trial, to confront witnesses, and to appeal. However, there are few well-trained lawyers. The Constitutional Court convenes weekly or as necessary to consider constitutional issues only. The Court of Appeal convenes twice a year to consider appeals from the Supreme Court and Constitutional Court only.

Defendants generally have the right to a fair trial. All judges are appointed for 5 years, and can be re-appointed by the Constitutional Appointment Committee. All were hired from other British Commonwealth countries, and none is Seychellois. Some observers criticized expatriate judges for a perceived lack of sensitivity on issues such as domestic violence. Legal organs of the Government, such as the Attorney General's office and the Ombudsman, are reluctant to pursue charges of wrongdoing or abuse of power against senior officials.

There were no reports of political prisoners.

f. *Arbitrary Interference With Privacy, Family, Home, or Correspondence.*—The Constitution provides for the right to privacy and freedom from arbitrary searches. The law requires a warrant for police searches, and the authorities generally respected this requirement in practice. The law requires that all wiretaps be justified on the grounds of preventing a serious crime and be approved by a judge. The Government maintains telephone taps on some political figures.

Section 2. Respect for Civil Liberties, Including:

a. *Freedom of Speech and Press.*—The Constitution provides for freedom of speech and the press, but it also provides for restrictions on speech "for protecting the reputation, rights, and freedoms of private lives of persons" and "in the interest of defense, public safety, public order, public morality, or public health." Both freedom of speech and the press are thus constrained by the ease with which civil lawsuits can be filed to penalize journalists for alleged libel. In most instances, citizens speak freely, including in Parliament.

The Government has a near-monopoly on the media, owning the only television and radio stations, the most important means for reaching the public, and The Nation, the only daily newspaper. The official media adhere closely to the Government's position on policy issues and give the opposition and news adverse to the Government only limited coverage.

While both of the opposition parties publish an assortment of newsletters and magazines, only one significant opposition newspaper, the weekly Regar, is currently in circulation. Government figures have sued Regar for libel six times in the past 3 years, including once in 1996.

A second weekly, The Independent, ceased publication in 1995 because of dwindling circulation and the financial effect of losing a libel suit brought by a government official. Independent publications are also potentially vulnerable to government pressure now that the only printing press has been sold to an SPPF National Assemblyman. In general, government harassment of opposition publications is diminishing.

Academic freedom is limited since, for example, one cannot reach senior positions in the academic bureaucracy without demonstrating at least nominal loyalty to the SPPF. There are no universities; secondary school teachers are largely apolitical. The Government controls access to the Polytechnic, the most prestigious learning institution, and public school graduates wishing admission are given preference based on their participation in the National Youth Service (NYS), a year-long program that now emphasizes educational instruction, although in the past it has stressed paramilitary training and SPPF ideology.

b. *Freedom of Peaceful Assembly and Association.*—The Constitution provides for these freedoms, and in practice the Government generally permitted peaceful assembly and association without interruption or interference. In addition to the SPPF, there are two other political parties. In 1996 the Government once denied permission to the United Opposition Party to hold a public demonstration the day of the President's State of the Nation address. Opposition parties cited several cases in which supporters lost government jobs solely because of their political beliefs. Political criteria also weigh in government decisions regarding licenses and loans.

c. *Freedom of Religion.*—The Constitution provides for freedom of religion, and the Government respects this right in practice.

d. *Freedom of Movement Within the Country, Foreign Travel, Emigration, and Repatriation.*—The Constitution provides for freedom of movement, and there was no known abridgement of domestic or international travel. Although it was not used, the 1991 Passport Act allows the Government to deny passports to any citizen if the Minister of Defense finds that such denial is "in the national interest." There were no known requests for asylum and no refugees in the Seychelles.

Section 3. Respect for Political Rights: The Right of Citizens to Change Their Government

Citizens freely exercised the right to change their government in the July 1993 National Assembly and presidential elections, which were judged by international and national observers to have been free and fair. However, President Rene and the SPPF dominated the electoral process and continued to rule—as they have since 1977. The elections served to provide a voice to other parties.

The President's SPPF party has utilized its political resources and those of the Government to develop a nationwide organization that extends to the village level.

The opposition parties have been unable to match the SPPF's organization and patronage, in part because of financial limitations.

The main opposition party, the Democratic Party, is led by Sir James Mancham, the country's first elected president, who was forced into a 15-year exile in 1977. Mancham was reelected president of the Democratic Party by acclamation at a controversial party convention in March. Critics of Mancham alleged that his ties to the ruling SPPF were too close and that he discouraged his own party members from criticizing the Government.

There are no legal restrictions on the participation of women or members of minority groups in politics. Women hold 3 ministerial positions in the 11-person Cabinet and 8 seats in the 33-member National Assembly. The white minority of Seychelles continues to dominate governmental institutions, but some Creoles (African Seychellois) have risen to senior positions of responsibility, particularly in the military forces. Of the six members of the Defense Forces Council, four are Creole.

Section 4. Governmental Attitude Regarding International and Nongovernmental Investigation of Alleged Violations of Human Rights

There are no private groups devoted exclusively to investigating human rights practices. However, both the churches and some nongovernmental organizations (NGO's) have been strong voices for human rights and democratization, and the Government has not interfered with their activities. There were no known requests by international human rights groups to visit the Seychelles.

Section 5. Discrimination Based on Race, Sex, Religion, Disability, Language, or Social Status

The Constitution affirms the right to be free from all types of discrimination, but it does not specifically prohibit discrimination based on these factors. In practice, there is no overt discrimination in housing, employment, education, or other social services based on race, sex, ethnic, national, or religious identification.

Women.—Violence against women, particularly wife beating, remains a problem. Police seldom intervene in domestic disputes, unless the dispute involves a weapon or major assault. The few cases that reach a prosecutor are often dismissed, or if a case reaches court, the perpetrator is usually given only a light sentence. There is growing societal concern about domestic violence and increased recognition of the need to address it.

This society is largely matriarchal, and women have the same legal, political, economic, and social rights as men. There is no officially sanctioned discrimination in education or employment, and women are well represented in politics and business.

Children.—Children have legal protection from labor and physical abuse and are required to attend school. Free public education is available. In June 1995, the Government created an institutional framework for aiding children.

Sexual abuse of young girls, usually in low-income families, is a serious problem. While complete statistics are not available, Ministry of Health data and press reports indicate that there are a significant number of rapes committed against girls under the age of 15. Very few child-abuse cases are actually prosecuted in court. The strongest public advocate for young victims is a semiautonomous agency, the National Council for Children, not the Government. There is criticism that the police fail to investigate charges of child abuse with vigor.

People With Disabilities.—The Government does not discriminate against people with disabilities in housing, jobs, or education. However, there is no legislation providing for access to public buildings, transportation, or government services. The Government has promised the International Labor Organization (ILO) that it would implement a law providing for more jobs for disabled workers.

National/Racial/Ethnic Minorities.—There is a longstanding education gap between Creoles and Seychellois of white or Asian origin, which has been a factor in the continuing political and economic domination of the country by whites and Asians. Despite a significant Creole majority, the President, the Industry Minister, the Foreign Minister, most principal secretaries, and almost the entire merchant and financial class are white or Asian. The Government is attempting to reduce this gap through universal access to public education, but the formalization and teaching of Creole has increased the difficulty that Creole students experience in learning English and French at a competitive level. Further, the political domination by whites seems unyielding since the elected leadership of the majority party and of one of the two main opposition parties is white.

Section 6. Worker Rights

a. *The Right of Association.*—Under the 1993 Industrial Relations Act (IRA), workers have the right to form and join unions of their own choosing. Police, military, prison, and fire-fighting personnel may not unionize. Under the act, the former government-controlled union, the National Workers Union, lost its monopoly position.

There are currently four registered unions: two dominated by the SPPF and two independents. An attempt to organize an independent union incorporating employees from both governmental ministries and government-owned entities was thwarted by government legal action.

Unions can freely affiliate with international bodies.

b. *The Right to Organize and Bargain Collectively.*—The IRA provides workers with the right to engage in collective bargaining. However, in practice free collective bargaining does not normally take place. The Government has the right to review and approve all collective bargaining agreements in the public and private sectors. There is little flexibility in the setting of wages. In the public sector, which employs about 60 percent of the labor force, the Government sets mandatory wage scales for employees. Wages in the private sector are generally set by the employer in individual agreements with the employee, but in the few larger businesses, wage scales are subject to the Government's right of review and approval. Private employers historically have paid higher wages than the Government in order to attract qualified workers. However, economic problems this year have led to downward pressures on wages.

The law prohibits antiunion discrimination by employers against union members. Independent unions allege that their members in the public sector have encountered discrimination on the job because of their affiliation with non-SPPF unions.

The Employment Acts of 1987 and 1995 constitute the basic labor law. They authorize the Ministry of Employment and Social Affairs to establish and enforce employment terms, conditions, and benefits. Workers have frequently obtained recourse against their employers through the Ministry.

There are no export processing zones, but the Government is actively attempting to create one.

c. *Prohibition of Forced or Compulsory Labor.*—The law prohibits forced or compulsory labor, and it does not exist.

d. *Minimum Age for Employment of Children.*—The minimum age for employment is 15 years, and children are encouraged to attend school until the tenth grade or the age of 17, whichever occurs first. The Government strongly encourages children to fulfill 1 year of NYS before entering the work force at the age of 16 or the Polytechnic School for Vocational Training, and it discourages public or private sector employment of workers under the age of 16. The Government sponsors apprenticeships and short-term (up to 6 months) work programs for those who leave school and do not participate in the NYS. Children in these programs receive a training stipend which is below the minimum wage. The Government enforces child labor laws through inspections by the Ministry of Employment and Social Affairs.

e. *Acceptable Conditions of Work.*—Seychelles has a complicated minimum wage scale, which is administratively regulated by the Government; it covers the public and state-owned sectors and differentiates among various job classifications. The Ministry of Employment and Social Affairs enforces minimum wage regulations. The official minimum wage is about $320 (1,600 Seychelles rupees) per month. Trade unions contend that government entities pay some workers at less than the legal minimum. Even with the free public services that are available, primarily health and education, independent labor unions dispute that a single salary at the low end of the pay scale provides a worker and family with even a Spartan standard of living.

Many families deal with the high cost of living by earning two or more incomes, although the number of households with two persons employed has reportedly dropped to 30 percent. In recent years there has been a growing trend in government policy to import foreign workers, primarily from India and elsewhere in Asia, to work in the construction and commercial fishing sectors. Although it is difficult to determine the living and working conditions of these workers, there is strong evidence that the labor laws are routinely flouted by their employers, with the Government's knowledge. These workers are paid lower wages and forced to work longer hours than Seychellois, sometimes with the express consent of the Government.

The legal maximum workweek varies from 45 to 52 hours, depending on the economic sector, while government employees work shorter hours. Each full-time worker is entitled to a half-hour break per day and a minimum of 21 days of paid annual leave. Workers are permitted to work overtime up to 60 additional hours per month. The Government generally enforces these ceilings. Foreign workers do not enjoy the same legal protections.

The Government issued comprehensive revised occupational health and safety regulations in October 1991. The Ministry of Employment and Social Affairs has formal responsibility for enforcing these regulations; however, the Ministry of Health seeks a role in this area. An ILO team which visited in early 1995 found serious deficiencies in the management and effectiveness of government monitoring and enforcement efforts. Occupational injuries are most common in the construction, marine, and port industries. A worker who removes himself from a potentially dangerous situation on the job is considered to have resigned. Safety and health inspectors rarely visit job sites. In 1994 there were four deaths and 162 on-the-job injuries officially reported. In 1995 there were two deaths and 57 on-the-job injuries. The Ministry did not release statistics for this year.

SIERRA LEONE

The country is governed by the 1991 Constitution; provisions suspended by the National Provisional Ruling Council (NPRC) have been reinstituted. In an internal NPRC power struggle, General Julius Maada Bio ousted NPRC chairman (Captain) Valentine Strasser in January 1996. After 4 years of military government, which followed 25 years of one party rule, the Republic of Sierra Leone returned to civilian government after elections in March. With 70 percent of the electorate participating, Alhaji Ahmad Tejan Kabbah was elected President in the first free and fair elections since 1967 and took office in March in a peaceful transfer of power from the NPRC. The judiciary is no longer subject to the intervention of special commissions of inquiry that were established by the NPRC to circumvent the judicial system.

On November 30, President Kabbah signed a peace accord with the Revolutionary United Front (RUF) which had been attempting to overthrow successive governments since March 1991. Joint Government and RUF committees will oversee disarmament and demobilization of RUF and government forces.

The Sierra Leone Military Force (RSLMF) is responsible for external defense. During the civil war, the RSLMF and the police force provided internal security. The RSLMF was supported by Nigerian and Guinean military contingents and by Executive Outcomes, a private South African mercenary firm. The April cease-fire was broken by both sides, but ultimately the RSLMF and civil defense militias (Kamajohs) applied sufficient military pressure on the RUF to lead to successful peace negotiations. The Kamajohs were not under full governmental control. Clashes between the RSLMF and the Kamajohs occurred. Government security forces committed numerous serious human rights abuses.

Sierra Leone is a very poor country with alarming health statistics. The average life expectancy for a women is 47 years and 42 years for a man. One child out of four dies before age 5. Before the war, more than 70 percent of the 4.5 million citizens were involved in some aspect of agriculture, mainly subsistence farming. Although the country is rich in minerals, including rutile (titanium dioxide), diamonds, gold, and bauxite, official receipts from legal exports of gold and diamonds have decreased over recent years. Significant portions of the gold and diamonds are smuggled abroad. Government revenues from the mineral sector were far below preconflict levels.

Although the Government's human rights record has improved, serious problems remain. The security forces were responsible for extrajudicial killings, beatings, arbitrary arrest and detention, and illegal searches. There were reports that police abused suspects during arrest and interrogation. Prison conditions remain life threatening, and lengthy delays in trials, prolonged pretrial detentions, and violations of due process remain problems. Over half of the 640 persons detained at the Pademba Road prison are awaiting trial. Most abuses, including extrajudicial killings by RSLMF units, were committed chiefly in the area of armed conflict. The Government has harassed, arrested, and detained journalists. Discrimination and violence against women remain widespread, as does violence against children.

RUF rebels were responsible for numerous serious human rights abuses, including extrajudicial killings, torture, rape, and mutilation of civilians.

RESPECT FOR HUMAN RIGHTS

Section 1. Respect for the Integrity of the Person, Including Freedom From:

a. *Political and Other Extrajudicial Killing.*—Both government forces and RUF rebels engaged in these abuses. A cease-fire was in effect, but there were violations by renegade RSLMF soldiers and RUF forces.

Armed forces personnel were reportedly involved in political and extrajudicial killings. Renegade soldiers killed civilians while engaged in looting, robbery, and extortion (see Section 1.g.). The military court-martialed three soldiers for murder, but none was sentenced to death.

There were several attempted political killings. On February 26, the night of the presidential elections, unknown persons attempted to kill Paul Kamara, the former editor of For Di People newspaper, and a critic of the NPRC. Kamara accepted an appointment on January 19 as NPRC Minister for Lands, Housing, and the Environment. Assailants dressed in military fatigues used military weapons in the attack in which Kamara was shot five times in the leg at close range. NPRC delays in seeking appropriate medical treatment hindered his recovery. The Government made no arrests.

On February 18, prior to the February election, an attempt was made to kill Dr. James Jonah, the head of the Interim National Election Commission, when a hand grenade was thrown into his residential compound. The Government made no arrests.

Three policemen were charged with manslaughter for allegedly beating a suspect to death on July 4 at the central police station.

Eight prisoners died in custody due to lack of food and inadequate medical treatment (see Section 1.c.).

RUF forces killed civilians while engaged in looting, robbery, and extortion (see Section 1.g.).

b. *Disappearance.*—Since the civilian Government assumed power, there have been no reports of disappearances of captured persons who were suspected to be rebels.

c. *Torture and Other Cruel, Inhuman, or Degrading Treatment or Punishment.*—Although the Constitution prohibits torture, the police and armed forces personnel beat suspects during arrest and interrogation. Armed forces personnel engaged in combat operations sometimes physically abused or killed civilians (see Section 1.g.). The Government made some effort to investigate the incidents and punish those involved.

On February 12, soldiers assaulted presidential candidate Thaimu Bangura in Freetown, preventing him from attending the National Consultative Conference. Soldiers dragged Bangura from his car beat him, and stole his car. The NPRC found and returned his car, but was unable to find Bangura's assailants.

Prior to elections, both government soldiers and rebel forces terrorized many villages, cutting off fingers, hands, arms, ears, or lips with machetes. Some had slogans denouncing the elections cut into their backs and chests. While the RUF conducted many attacks in the northern province, responsibility in the southern province was harder to determine. Several victims in villages in Kakunya Chiefdom (Moyamba District) and Lubu Chiefdom (Bo District) from 19-22 February had their hands amputated. Others had "No Elections" cut into their backs or RUF cut into their foreheads. Fingers, upper lips, and ears were amputated. On February 22, one man from Sumbuy, Lubu Chiefdom had "RUF" and "No Elections" cut into his forehead and back. His upper lip and right ear were cut off.

Prison conditions at times remain life threatening. The civilian Government worked to improve conditions. While still overcrowded with 5 occupants in a cell built for 1 inmate, the civilian Government reduced numbers of prisoners in the Pademba Road prison by nearly one-half (1,200 to 640). Diet and medical care in the prison was often inadequate. Eight of 70 suspected rebels detained by the NPRC Government in 1995 died of malnutrition and lack of medical supervision. While the new Government provides better supervision of food and medical services for inmates, these programs lack the required monitoring. Detainees sleep on mattresses on the floor, and toilet facilities are rudimentary. Over half of the 640 prisoners are awaiting trial. Male and female inmates are imprisoned separately but together with juveniles. Homosexual rape is common.

A nongovernmental group, Prison Watch, has been organized to focus attention on prison conditions. The Government continued to grant the International Committee of the Red Cross (ICRC) access to prisoners, including alleged rebels.

d. *Arbitrary Arrest, Detention, or Exile.*—In practice, the Government does not provide adequate safeguards against arbitrary or unjust detentions, nor for their formal review. By law, after an initial 24 hour detention, detainees must have access to legal counsel, families, and medical care, but detainees are seldom provided with these services unless they can afford legal counsel to demand compliance. The Government repealed NPRC decrees under which high-ranking police and military officials could arrest without warrant and detain indefinitely any person suspected of posing a threat to public safety. In practice, soldiers arrest or detain civilians without charge. Arrested foreigners are often released but may not depart the country.

The Government provides legal representation for the indigent only in cases of capital offenses. Lack of counsel in other cases frequently leads to wrongful conviction. Many indigent detainees are unaware of their rights and assume, sometimes correctly, that law enforcement or judicial authorities will be paid by the accuser to rule against them. The Society for the Protection of Human Rights provides free legal counsel to some indigent detainees, and some local nongovernmental organizations (NGO's) provide counsel and advice to women concerning their rights.

During military operations, a number of rebels were captured by army forces. They were held at brigade headquarters in provincial capitals and at the defense headquarters in Freetown. After initial interrogation, the RUF combatants were released to family members who signed a guarantee to the military that the family was responsible to return the RUF combatant to the military if further discussions were needed. Under the peace accord, RUF combatants will be pardoned from incidents connected with the war. The four high ranking RUF officials arrested by Guinean authorities in 1995 were initially held at army headquarters but at year's end were in custody at the police Criminal Investigation Division (CID) headquarters and expected to be released soon as part of the Government's compliance with the peace accord.

In April the authorities released the last three political detainees held by the Government.

The Government does not use exile to circumvent the judicial system. However, senior NPRC officials were offered short-term educational programs abroad by international organizations to entice them to leave the political scene following the change of government. There are no restrictions on their return.

e. *Denial of Fair Public Trial.*—There are constitutional provisions for an independent judiciary. No special commissions of inquiry operate under the new civilian government. A board headed by a justice on loan from the Commonwealth is reviewing actions taken by the previous special commissions of inquiry to determine whether actions by the special commissions were injurious to citizens.

There are three judicial systems: Regular courts; local or traditional courts; and courts-martial. The regular court system is based on the British model and consists of a Supreme Court, an intermediate Court of Appeals, a High Court of Magistrates, and Magistrates Courts. There are criminal and civil courts. Decisions by lower courts may be appealed in the high courts. Under previous governments, there have been delays of up to 5 years in bringing some cases to trial. The new Government is attempting to improve working conditions and facilities for the judiciary to improve its performance, but the backlog of cases is of major concern.

Judges in the regular court system may serve until they reach the mandatory retirement age of 65, unless their appointment is revoked. There were no known instances of judges being fired or transferred for political reasons. Elected indigenous leaders preside over the local courts and administer tribal law in civil cases. Local courts are often the only legal institution in rural areas, however, local courts in the eastern and southern provinces are still not functioning due to the unsettled conditions in these areas.

The courts-martial system, based on British military codes and common law, provides for adjudication of minor offenses by the military unit commander. Soldiers accused of more serious offenses are transferred from field units to Headquarters for trial. Although exact statistics are unavailable, the courts-martial system has convicted military personnel for murder, robbery, and other offenses. This year no military personnel were sentenced to death for capital offenses and no executions were conducted. The senior officer sentenced to death under the NPRC government in 1995 was released by the current Government.

The right to minimum due process is not always respected. Authorities sometimes beat detainees or otherwise punish them prior to incarceration or a court hearing. There were no allegations of mutilation of detainees by law enforcement officials this year (see Section 1.c.). In addition the regular court system accepts and sanctions provisions of tribal, traditional, and Islamic law that discriminate against women and minorities.

f. *Arbitrary Interference With Privacy, Family, Home, or Correspondence.*—The Government has repealed the NPRC decrees that provided broad authority to monitor actions or conversations within homes, to prevent a person from acting in a manner deemed prejudicial to public safety, to impose restriction on employment or business, to control association or communication with other persons, and to interfere with correspondence. However, in practice, there were numerous occasions of abusive treatment of citizens by soldiers and police, both within and outside the war zones. These abuses included forced entry into homes, robberies, and assaults. A number of soldiers accused of looting were court-martialed.

g. *Use of Excessive Force and Violations of Humanitarian Law in Internal Conflicts.*—The internal conflict involves multiple ethnic groups and has resulted in an estimated 15,000 deaths since 1991. Also, an estimated 1.7 million Sierra Leoneans have been displaced internally or are living as refugees in neighboring countries because of the war. Guinean and Nigerian troops continued to assist the Sierra Leonean military.

There were many serious violations of humanitarian law in the internal conflict throughout the war zone, including summary executions of prisoners and noncombatants, and torture, rape, mutilation, and killing of civilians.

On March 14, the NPRC with the assistance of the Government of Cote D'Ivoire negotiated an unconditional cease-fire with the RUF. The ICRC acted as a facilitator in its role of neutral intermediary. The new civilian Government continued talks with the RUF, and on April 22, the sides agreed to extend the cease-fire and appointed groups to draft peace and disarmament accords. On May 28, the RUF suspended talks and said it would not disarm until Executive Outcomes, a private mercenary organization employed by the government, left Sierra Leone. The cease-fire generally continued to hold, although there were serious security incidents. The Government and the RUF signed a peace accord on November 30.

Despite the cease-fire, government security forces and RUF rebels continued to loot villages and ambush truck convoys. RUF forces abducted villagers and vehicle passengers and forced them to carry looted goods to RUF bases. Civilians were maimed, tortured, and murdered in these incidents. On August 29, between Gbaima and Mafombo on the Bo-Taiama highway, a car carrying seven passengers was ambushed, reportedly by RUF combatants. Six persons were shot, and two died. In some cases, the perpetrators could not be identified; however, it is generally believed that undisciplined armed forces personnel, the RUF forces, and thieves committed attacks on civilians. The towns of Kamakwie, Kamallu, and Pendembu in Kambia and Bombail districts in the northern province were attacked. Many abductees were taken to a RUF camp in the Malal hills. The village of Kpatobu, Lubu Chiefdom, was attacked by an armed group in both military uniforms and civilian clothes, armed with sticks, machetes, guns, and rocket propelled grenades. The attackers killed two villagers and mutilated at least four others.

There appears to have been little ethnically motivated violence in the hostilities.

Section 2. Respect for Civil Liberties, Including:

a. *Freedom of Speech and Press.*—The 1991 Constitution provides for freedom of speech and press. However, in practice, authorities arrested, beat, harassed, and detained journalists, and temporarily banned two newspapers for publishing unflattering articles about the Government. There are 28 newspapers covering a wide political spectrum. Many feature sensational, undocumented headlines and articles.

In April police arrested the editor of the Concord Times for a story critical of government spending. Released after 10 hours, the editor was later charged with seditious libel; the charges were dropped after the editor admitted inaccuracy in the story. In May police harassed and beat a reporter for Afro Times investigating a story at CID headquarters. In July police arrested the editor of The Point for a story concerning corruption and detained him for 10 hours. In August police detained the editor of Expo Times for 8 hours, and searched his office, for a story concerning the internal conflict between the RUF and government forces.

The capital has four radio stations: one is controlled by the Government; one is privately owned; and two are operated by Christian missionaries and broadcast religious programming and foreign news. A privately owned station operates in the provincial capital of Bo. The Government owns and operates the only television station, which is seen only in the capital.

The Government respects academic freedom. There were no reports of detention of educators or threats to them for their teaching activities.

b. *Freedom of Peaceful Assembly and Association.*—The 1991 Constitution provides for freedom of assembly as well as the right to form political, economic, social, and professional organizations. The Government has placed no restrictions on any of these provisions in practice.

In September the NPRC decree banning 57 individuals from political activity for 10 years was repealed.

c. *Freedom of Religion.*—The Constitution provides for freedom of religion, and the Government respects this right in practice.

d. *Freedom of Movement Within the Country, Foreign Travel, Emigration, and Repatriation.*—There are no official restrictions on travel within the country, but numerous military checkpoints make travel difficult. As security increased in the countryside, more travel by road occurred between major cities. However, at various times, vehicles were ambushed or hijacked by armed forces and RUF personnel. A police clearance is required for citizens traveling outside the country.

There are no restrictions on emigration or repatriation. Approximately 1.7 million citizens are displaced within the country. An estimated 350,000 Sierra Leoneans are refugees in Guinea and Liberia.

The Government cooperates with the Office of the United Nations Commissioner for Refugees (UNHCR) and other humanitarian organizations in assisting refugees. The Government has provided first asylum to Liberians during the 1990's. It continues to provide first asylum to some 12,000 Liberians and provided it to an additional 1,176 persons in 1996.Although in May the Government provided food and water to the Victory Reefer, a ship carrying some 100 Liberian refugees which had been searching for a port to disembark its passengers, it did not authorize disembarkation. With the exception of the Victory Reefer, there were no reports of forced return of persons to a country in which they feared persecution. There is no formal process for granting political asylum.

Section 3. Respect for Political Rights: The Right of Citizens to Change Their Government

With the 1991 Constitution restored, citizens have the right to change their government. As a result of great international and domestic pressure, the NPRC allowed presidential elections in February and March.

Women were substantially involved in ensuring that elections took place, but they are underrepresented in government. In the new Government, women head 2 of 21 ministries. The recently appointed foreign minister is a woman. Freetown and Bo, the largest cities in the country, have appointed female mayors. A few senior civil service, police, and judicial positions are held by women.

Section 4. Governmental Attitude Regarding International and Nongovernmental Investigation of Alleged Violations of Human Rights

Active human rights groups include the National League for Human Rights and the Network Movement for Justice. There is a local chapter of Amnesty International in Freetown and human rights groups operate without restriction. Several organizations are providing human rights training.

The Government allows the ICRC to visit prisoners and suspected rebels in the Pademba Road Prison and various military barracks. Amnesty International also continues to visit the prison.

Section 5. Discrimination Based on Race, Sex, Religion, Disability, Language, or Social Status

The Constitution prohibits discrimination against women and provides for protection against discrimination on the basis of race and ethnicity, except for the prohibition against citizenship for persons with a non-African father. This provision effectively blocks citizenship and political participation of the Lebanese community, persons of Afro-Lebanese descent, and other persons with non-African fathers.

Women.—Violence against women, especially wife beating, is common. Police are unlikely to intervene in domestic disputes except in cases of severe injury or death. Few cases of such violence go to court. Sierra Leone does not recognize domestic violence against women as a societal problem, and the new Government has not given it high-level attention.

Rape remains a recognized societal problem. It is punishable by up to 14 years' imprisonment. The Government enforces this law.

The Constitution provides for equal rights for women, but in practice women face both legal and societal discrimination. Their rights and status under traditional law vary significantly, depending upon the ethnic group. The Temne and Limba tribes of the north afford greater rights to women to inherit property than does the Mende tribe, which gives preference to male heirs and unmarried daughters. However, in the Temne tribe, women cannot become paramount chiefs. In the south there are a number of female paramount chiefs.

Women do not have equal access to education, economic opportunities, health facilities, or social freedoms. In rural areas, women perform much of the subsistence farming, all of the child rearing, and have little opportunity for education. The average educational level for women is markedly below that of men; only 6 percent are literate. At the university level, men predominate. A local NGO, Women Organized for a Morally Enlightened Nation, seeks to educate women throughout the country on their civic and civil rights and responsibilities.

Children.—The Government is committed to improving childrens' education and health. The Government's Ministry of Gender and Children's Affairs seeks to work with all ministries to ensure children's concerns are addressed.

With a peace agreement, the Government's demobilization program for both rebel and military forces will address the issue of "boy soldiers". Many underage boys were allowed to join military operations early in the war. Rebel forces routinely conscripted young men and women into their ranks when they attacked rural villages. The new Government continued work with NGO's to address the integration of "boy soldiers" back into society.

Although statistics are not yet available for the year, infant and child mortality is very high. Statistics are expected to be similar to 1995 with one child in four dying before the age of 5 and one-third of children under the age of 5 being underweight.

Instances of ritual murders of boys and girls, as well as adults, associated with animist religious groups in the provinces, continued. Four women have been convicted of manslaughter and are serving prison sentences for their participation.

Female genital mutilation (FGM), which is widely condemned by international health experts as damaging to both physical and psychological health, is widely practiced on young women and girls, especially in traditional ethnic groups and among the less-educated. While one independent expert estimates the percentage of females who have undergone this procedure may be as high as 90 percent, local groups believe that this figure is overstated. Membership in female secret societies that practice FGM in their initiation rites has been declining.

There has been an active press campaign by secret societies that attempts to counter the well-publicized international condemnation of FGM. On August 17, a 28-year-old woman was abducted by the Secret Bundo Society in Freetown and was subjected to FGM. The woman is bringing criminal charges against the Society and has retained a lawyer, but at the end of the year the case had not gone to trial.

People With Disabilities.—Questions of public facility access and discrimination against the disabled have not become public policy issues. The Department of Education has an official whose function is to further mainstream education of students with learning disabilities.

No laws mandate accessibility to buildings or provide for other assistance for the disabled. While there does not appear to be outright discrimination against the disabled in housing or education, with the high rate of unemployment, few disabled persons work in offices or factories.

National/Racial/Ethnic Minorities.—Ethnic loyalty remains an important factor in government, the military, and business. Complaints of corruption and ethnic discrimination in government appointments, contracts, military commissions, and promotions are common.

Residents of non-African descent face institutionalized political restrictions. The Constitution restricts citizenship to persons of Negro-African descent following a patrilineal pattern. This constitutional restriction effectively denies citizenship to many long-time residents, notably the Lebanese community.

Section 6. Worker Rights

a. *The Right of Association.*—The Constitution provides for the right of association. All workers, including civil servants, have the right to join trade unions of their choice. Unions are independent of the Government. All labor unions have by custom joined the Sierra Leone Labor Congress (SLLC), but membership is voluntary. There is no legal prohibition against SLLC leadership holding political office, and leaders have held both elected and appointed government positions.

Under the Trade Union Act, any five persons may form a trade union by applying to the Registrar of Trade Unions, who has statutory powers under the act to approve the creation of trade unions. The Registrar may reject applications for several reasons, including an insufficient number of members, proposed representation in an industry already serviced by an existing union, or incomplete documentation. If the Registrar rejects an application, his decision may be appealed in the ordinary courts, but applicants seldom take such action. Approximately 60 percent of workers in urban areas, including government employees, are unionized, but unions have had little success in organizing workers in the agricultural and mining sectors.

Unions have the right to strike without exception, but the Government may require 21 days' notice. The new Government repealed the NPRC decree that prohibited disruption of public tranquility or disruption of supplies, which could be used to prevent a prolonged strike. Although union members may be fired for participating in even a lawful strike, no such incidents were reported.

Unions are free to form federations and confederations and to affiliate internationally. The SLLC is a member of the International Confederation of Free Trade Unions, and there are no restrictions on international travel or contacts of trade unionists.

b. *The Right to Organize and Bargain Collectively.*—The legal framework for collective bargaining is the Regulation of Wages and Industrial Relations Act. Collective bargaining must take place in trade group negotiating councils, each of which has an equal number of employer and worker representatives. Most enterprises are covered by collective bargaining agreements on wages and working conditions. The SLLC provides assistance to unions in preparation for negotiations. In case of a deadlock, the Government may intervene. It has not, however, used decrees to prevent strikes.

No law prohibits retribution against strikers. Should an employee be fired for union activities, the individual may file a complaint with a labor tribunal and seek reinstatement. Complaints of discrimination against unions are made to an arbitration tribunal. Individual trade unions investigate alleged violations of work conditions to try to ensure that employers take the necessary steps to correct abuses.

Labor laws apply to enterprises located in export processing zones.

c. *Prohibition of Forced or Compulsory Labor.*—Under the Chiefdom's Council Act, compulsory labor may be imposed by individual chiefs, requiring members of their villages to contribute to the improvement of common areas. This practice exists only in rural areas. There is no penalty for noncompliance.

The Government does not require compulsory labor. However, an NPRC decree retained by the current Government requires that homeowners, businessmen, and vendors clean and maintain their premises. Failure to comply is punishable by fine or imprisonment. The last Saturday of each month is declared a National Cleaning Day, and there have been reports under the new Government of security forces publicly humiliating citizens to ensure compliance.

d. *Minimum Age for Employment of Children.*—The minimum age for employment is officially 18 years, but in practice there is no enforcement because there is no government entity specifically charged with this task. Children routinely assist in family businesses, especially those of vendors and petty traders. In rural areas, children work seasonally on family subsistence farms.

Because the adult unemployment rate is high (an estimated 70 percent in some areas), few children are involved in the industrial sector. There have been reports that young children have been hired by foreign employers to work as domestics overseas at extremely low wages and in poor conditions. The Department of Foreign Affairs and International Cooperation is responsible for reviewing overseas work applications to see that no one under the age of 14 is employed for this purpose and to enforce certain wage standards.

e. *Acceptable Conditions of Work.*—There is no minimum wage. Purchasing power continued to decline, and most workers have to pool incomes with their extended families and engage in subsistence food production to maintain a minimum standard of living. The Government's suggested standard workweek is 38 hours, but most workweeks exceed 38 hours. The Government sets health and safety standards, but the standards are outmoded and often not enforced. The Health and Safety Division of the Department of Labor has inspection and enforcement responsibility, but inadequate funding and transportation limit its effectiveness.

Health and safety regulations are included in collective bargaining agreements, but there is no evidence of systematic enforcement of those health and safety standards. Trade unions provide the only protection for workers who file complaints about working conditions. Initially, a union makes a formal complaint about a hazardous work condition. If this is rejected, the union may issue a 21-day strike notice. If workers remove themselves from dangerous work situations without making a formal complaint, they risk being fired.

SOMALIA

Somalia has been without a recognized central government since its last president, dictator Mohamed Siad Barre, fled the country in 1991. Subsequent fighting among rival faction leaders resulted in the killing, dislocation, and starvation of thousands of Somalis and led the United Nations to intervene militarily in 1992.

With the exception of the capital city of Mogadishu and the region outside the provincial city of Baidoa, little serious interclan fighting occurred in 1996. Sporadic fighting continued in parts of the northwest. Although the death of self-proclaimed President Mohammed Farah Aideed in late July prompted his successor and the leaders of rival factions to declare a cease-fire in Mogadishu, this encouraging development was not implemented and failed to speed progress toward national reconciliation. Nonetheless, various intermediaries acting on behalf of the Organization for African Unity and the Arab League persevered in efforts to reconcile the competing factions.

Following "President" Aideed's death, members of his faction selected his son Hussein Farah Aideed as president of the putative national government formed by Aideed in 1995. In the northwest, the breakaway "Republic of Somaliland" continued to proclaim its independence. Neither "government," however, received international recognition. After the withdrawal of the last U.N. Nations peacekeepers in

1995, the persistent absence of a central government prompted citizens in most regions to continue the process of establishing rudimentary local administrations. Most are based on the authority of the predominant clan and faction in the area. These continued to function with varying degrees of effectiveness. Local authority remained contested, however, in the Kismayo area, parts of the northwest, in Gedo and in Mogadishu. In most regions, the judicial system relies on some combination of traditional and customary justice, Islamic (Shari'a) law, and the pre-1991 penal code.

While Somalia remains desperately poor, the economy continued to improve, especially in comparison with its state during the mass starvation in 1992. However, limited rainfall and continued closure of seaports hindered progress. Relative peace in much of the country, coupled with an increasing level of commercial activity, contributed to this recovery. Annual gross domestic product per capita is estimated at $600. Livestock and fruit exports continued to expand, although the latter were disrupted by the closure of Mogadishu seaport throughout the year. Factional differences also impeded banana exports through the port of Merca. The country remains chronically deficit in food, however, and some of the most fertile agricultural regions suffered from drought or serious flooding. Lack of employment opportunities caused pockets of malnutrition in Mogadishu and some other communities.

Human rights abuses continued. Many civilian citizens were killed in factional fighting, especially in Mogadishu among the Hussein Aideed, Osman Atto, Ali Madhi, and Musa Sude factions. However, due to the decrease in interclan fighting, there were fewer reported abuses than in previous years. Other key problems remained the lack of political rights in the absence of a central authority, the reliance of some communities on harsh Shari'a punishments, including amputations and stoning, societal discrimination against women, and the mistreatment of women and children, including the nearly universal practice of female genital mutilation (FGM). There is no effective system for the protection of worker rights.

RESPECT FOR HUMAN RIGHTS

Section 1. Respect for the Integrity of the Person, Including Freedom From:

a. *Political or Other Extrajudicial Killing.*—Political violence and banditry have been endemic since the 1991 revolt against Siad Barre. Tens of thousands of citizens, mostly noncombatants, have since died in interfactional and interclan fighting (see Section 1.g.).

Although many civilians died as a result of interfactional and interclan fighting during the year, politically motivated extrajudicial murder was less common. Early in January, an anti-Aideed group claimed that pro-Aideed fighters had massacred 18 people in Baidoa. There was no independent confirmation of the report. On March 9, unknown gunmen killed South Mogadishu peace activist Alman Ali Ahmed, apparently for political reasons. In August two Ethiopian businessmen were killed in Galcayo, reportedly in retaliation for the Ethiopian military incursion that took place on August 9–11. In September a businessman allied with opponents of the Aideed Government was shot and killed by pro-Aideed militia.

b. *Disappearance.*—There were no known reports of unresolved politically motivated disappearances, although cases might easily have been concealed among the thousands of returnees, displaced, and war dead. Kidnaping remained a problem, particularly for relief workers and critics of the faction leaders (see Section 1.d.).

c. *Torture and Other Cruel, Inhuman, or Degrading Treatment or Punishment.*— There were no reports of the use of torture by warring militiamen against each other or against civilians.

In Sorth Mogadishu, parts of South Mogadishu, the middle Shabelle, and parts of the Gedo and Hiran regions, Shari'a courts regularly sentence convicted thieves to public lashings, stonings, and less frequently, to the amputation of their hands (see Section i.e.).

Prison conditions varied by region. Conditions at the South Mogadishu Prison, controlled by the Aideed forces, improved markedly after the start in 1995 of visits by international organizations, while conditions at the North Mogadishu Prison controlled by the Shari'a court system deteriorated to the point that prisoners staged a hunger strike starting in early September. The head of the court system promised improvements, but this announcement did not satisfy the prisoners, who continued fasting for several weeks. Conditions elsewhere reportedly were less severe, according to international relief agencies. In many areas, prisoners receive food from family members or relief agencies. The International Committee of the Red Cross (ICRC) delegates were permitted to visit prisons in some parts of the country, as were Western diplomats.

d. *Arbitrary Arrest, Detention, or Exile.*—In the absence of constitutional or other legal protections, Somali factions and armed bandits continued to engage in arbitrary detention, including the kidnaping of international relief workers. In January the Shari'a court arrested 18 s3pporters of General Aideed in north Mogadishu after they announced the formation of a political organization in support of his claimed government. Some of those arrested also had accepted positions in the Aideed regime. The courts later released the group. On May 3, General Aideed's forces arrested an Islamic court judge as a result of a political dispute.

As in past years, kidnapers continued to target foreigners. Among the most notable incidents were: the March 21 abduction of five U.N. staff members from Bale Dogle airfield; the kidnaping 2 days later in Bosasso of an American relief agency employee; and the seizure of three aid workers in the northwest in mid-May. U.S. citizen Daniel Suther was kidnaped at gunpoint in north Mogadishu on September 17. With assistance from a U.N. security officer and local elders, Suther was released on September 18. In each instance, the victims managed to gain their release, generally within days. One incident took far longer to resolve, the May 25 "arrest" of an Australian pilot by forces loyal to General Aideed. Accused of illegally entering Somali air space, the pilot remained in custody until October. Four Russian pilots detained in the northwest in mid-July regained their freedom after payment of a $45,000 "fine."

e. *Denial of Fair Public Trial.*—There is no national judicial system. The judiciary in most regions relies on some combination of traditional and customary justice, Islamic (Shari'a) law, and the pre-1991 penal code. Islamic (Shari'a) courts continued to operate in several regions of the country, partially filling the vacuum created by the absence of normal government authority. Shari'a courts traditionally ruled in cases of civil and family law, but their jurisdiction was extended to criminal proceedings in some regions beginning in 1994. In Bosasso and Afmedow, for example, authorities turn criminals over to the families of their victims, who exact blood compensation in keeping with Somali tradition. In the northwest, the so-called Republic of Somaliland continues to use the pre-1991 Somali penal code, pending adoption of a new constitution and related laws. In Bardera courts apply a combination of Islamic Shari'a law and the pre-1991 penal code. In North Mogadishu, a segment of South Mogadishu, the Middle Shabelle, and parts of the Gedo and Hiran regions, court decisions are based solely on Shari'a law.

The right to representation by an attorney and the right to appeal do not exist in those areas applying traditional and customary judicial practices or Shari'a law. These rights are more often respected in regions that continue to apply the pre-1991 penal code.

There were no reports that political prisoners were being held by the various factions.

f. *Arbitrary Interference With Privacy, Family, Home, or Correspondence.*—Looting and forced entry into private property continued but at levels reduced from previous years, when large numbers of invading militiamen occupied many urban properties. In January rival factions set fire to the homes of Aideed supporters in central Somalia. In Gedo region, representatives of the local administration seized 163 metric tons of food, office equipment, and other supplies after relief agencies refused to comply with payment demands. In April General Aideed's militia forcibly removed 220 patients, then seized control of Martini Hospital in Mogadishu. The facility subsequently became a military encampment. Also in April, local militia looted a relief agency's offices in Jowhar, prompting the agency to suspend operations.

Most properties that were forcibly occupied during militia campaigns in 1992–93, notably in Mogadishu and the lower Shabelle, remained in the control of persons other than their owners.

g. *Use of Excessive Force and Violations of Humanitarian Law in Internal Conflicts.*—Warring factions continued to commit violations of humanitarian law, including the killing of civilian noncombatants. Beginning in early January, sporadic fighting in the Mogadishu area between pro- and anti-Aideed militia led to scores of civilian dead and hundreds wounded. Numerous combatants also lost their lives. Both sides shelled targets located in densely populated neighborhoods and, on several occasions, combatants used hospitals for military positions. Among the most egregious incidents were the shelling in early April of a Mogadishu internally displaced persons' camp, which resulted in at least 16 deaths, and a July incident in which warring factions shelled a soccer stadium. At least three noncombatants were killed. Fourteen civilians were killed when a mortar shell landed on a private house in Mogadishu, also in July. In April Aideed militiamen killed a number of worshipers at a mosque in Mogadishu. Occasional fighting in and around Baidoa in Bay region also claimed a number of noncombatant lives as local militia battled General Aideed's fighters for control of the area. The year ended with the most fierce fighting in Mogadishu since the death of General Aideed. Factional fighting in Mogadishu from December 15 to 19 resulted in 132 known deaths. Another 1,500 persons, according to the ICRC, were hospitalized.

Ethiopian troops entered the Gedo region on August 8 and 9, displacing several hundred thousand civilian citizens, most of whom returned by mid-September. An estimated 300 persons, including combatants, died as a result of the fighting between Ethiopian troops and members of the Islamic fundamentalist group Al-Ittihad Al'Islami. Ethiopian officials believed that members of Al-Ittihad Al'Islami were responsible for a number of terrorist acts inside Ethiopia, including the bombing of several hotels. On December 21, Ethiopian forces reportedly repulsed an attack by Somali-based Al-Ittihad extremists in the Somali border town of Dolo. The Ethiopian government believes that Al-Ittihad Al'Islami forces were assisted by forces loyal to Hussein Aideed's Somali National Alliance. Ethiopian officials claim that 100 attackers were killed with 12 Ethiopian casualties, but these figures could not be confirmed.

Section 2. Respect for Civil Liberties, Including:

a. *Freedom of Speech and Press.*—Most citizens obtain news from foreign news broadcasts, notably the British Broadcasting Corporation, which transmits a daily Somali language program. The major faction leaders in Mogadishu, as well as the authorities of the Republic of Somaliland, operate small radio stations. The print media consist largely of short, photocopied dailies, published in the larger cities and often linked to one of the factions. Several of these newspapers are nominally independent and are critical of the faction leaders.

In January the head of the North Mogadishu Shari'a courts ordered the arrest of comedians and other actors at public entertainment sanctioned by the area's dominant political leader. Journalists came under threat as well, including an incident in early September when pro-Aideed gunmen briefly besieged several foreign correspondents who were in the city to interview political leaders.

b. *Freedom of Peaceful Assembly and Association.*—Many clans and factions held meetings during the year without incident, albeit usually under tight security. Although citizens are free to assemble in public, the lack of security effectively limits this right in many parts of the country. Few public rallies took place during the year without the sponsorship one of the armed groups.

Some professional groups and local nongovernmental organizations (NGO's) operate as security conditions permit.

c. *Freedom of Religion.*—Somalis are overwhelmingly Sunni Muslim. Local tradition and past law make it a crime to proselytize adherents for any religion except Islam. Some local administrations have made Islam the official religion in their regions, in addition to establishing a judicial system based on Shari'a law (see Section 1.e.). Non-Sunni Muslims are often viewed with suspicion by the Sunni majority. There is strong social pressure to respect Islamic traditions, especially in fundamentalist enclaves such as Luuq, in the Gedo region. There is a small, low-profile, Christian community. So long as they refrain from proselytizing, Christian-based international relief organizations generally operate without interference.

In late April, militia loyal to General Aideed attacked worshipers at the Jumma Mosque in Mogadishu, killing a number of persons and robbing others; their motive remains unclear.

d. *Freedom of Movement Within the Country, Foreign Travel, Emigration, and Repatriation.*—Freedom of movement continued to be restricted in most parts of the country. Checkpoints manned by militiamen loyal to one clan or faction inhibited passage by members of other groups. In the absence of a recognized national government, most citizens lack documents needed for international travel. As security conditions improved in many parts of the country, refugees and internally displaced persons continued to return to their homes. Despite sporadic harassment, including the theft of U.N. High Commissioner for Refugees (UNHCR) food assistance packages by militiamen, repatriation generally took place without incident.

The number of Somali refugees in Kenya dropped to approximately 125,000 by year's end, down from more than 400,000 at the height of the humanitarian crisis in 1992. In Ethiopia, however, the number of Somali refugees remained steady at approximately 275,000. There are 21,000 Somali refugees in Djibouti. As Somalia has no functioning government, there is no policy of first asylum, although in 1996 approximately 560 Ethiopian refugees remained in northwestern Somalia near Hargeisa. The central authorities in northwest Somalia have cooperated with the UNHCR and other humanitarian organizations in assisting refugees, although agreement on the return of refugees to the coastal areas of the Awdal region has still not been reached. There were no reports of forced expulsion of those having a valid claim to refugee status.

Section 3. Respect for Political Rights: The Right of Citizens to Change Their Government

Citizens did not have this right as there is no government. There was no widely supported, effective national government recognized domestically or internationally. In most regions, however, local clan leaders in fact function as rulers. Although many such groups derive their authority from the traditional deference given clan elders, most face opposition of varying strength from political factions and radical Islamic groups. In the northwest, the so-called Republic of Somaliland was endorsed by clan elders in 1991 and 1993 and has since created functional administrative institutions, albeit in only a small portion of the territory it claims to rule. In Kismayo the dominant faction leader seized the town in 1993, but is dependent on elders from several subclans in order to govern the community. Following the death of General Aideed, his supporters selected his son Hussein to succeed him as president of his claimed central government, which effectively exercises its authority in parts of South Mogadishu, Bay Region, and the lower Shabelle. Ali Mahdi and his Abgal subclan supporters, in cooperation with leaders of the Islamic Shari'a courts, function as the governing authorities in North Mogadishu and the middle Shabelle.

Although several women are important behind-the-scenes figures in the various factions, women as a group remain outside the political process. No women hold prominent public positions and few participated in regional reconciliation efforts.

Section 4. Governmental Attitude Regarding International and Nongovernmental Investigation of Alleged Violations of Human Rights

There were no local human rights organizations active during the year. The ICRC visited prisons in some parts of the country. The U.N. Nations Special Rapporteur on Human Rights visited the country from February 25 to March 10, and prepared a report for the Secretary General; it is to be released in 1997. International humanitarian NGO's and U.N. agencies continued to operate, but the poor security situation limited their activities in some areas.

Section 5. Discrimination Based on Race, Sex, Religion, Disability, Language, or Social Status

Societal discrimination against women and widespread abuse of children continued to be serious problems.

Women.—Women suffered disproportionately heavily in the civil war and strife that has followed. During the past year, however, there were no reports of systematic attacks on women in connection with the continuing civil strife.

Women are systematically subordinated in the overwhelmingly patriarchal culture. Polygyny is lawful; polyandry is not. Under laws issued by the former government, female children can inherit property, but only half the amount to which their brothers are entitled. Similarly, according to the tradition of blood compensation, those found guilty of the death of a woman must pay only half as much (50 camels) to the aggrieved family as they would if the victim were a man (100 camels).

Children.—Children remain among the chief victims of the continuing violence. Boys as young as 14 or 15 years of age have participated in militia attacks, and many are members of the marauding gangs known as "Morian."

Female genital mutilation, which is widely condemned by international experts as damaging to physical and mental health, is widely practiced. An independent expert in the field estimates that 98 percent of females have been subjected to it.

People With Disabilities.—There were no laws mandating accessibility to public buildings, transportation, or government services for the disabled before the collapse of the state. No functioning government is yet in place that could address these issues.

National/Racial/Ethnic Minorities.—More than 80 percent of the people share a common ethnic heritage, religion, and nomadic culture. The largest minority group consists of "Bantu" Somalis, who are descended from slaves brought to the country about 300 years ago. In virtually all areas, the dominant clan excludes members of groups other than itself from effective participation in governing institutions and subjects them to discrimination in employment, judicial proceedings, and access to public services. Members of minority groups are subjected to harassment, intimidation, and abuse by armed gunmen of all affiliations.

Section 6. Worker Rights

a. *The Right of Association.*—The 1990 constitution provided workers with the right to form unions, but the civil war and factional fighting negated this provision and shattered the single labor confederation, the then government-controlled General Federation of Somali Trade Unions. Given the extent of Somalia's political and economic breakdown and the lack of legal enforcement mechanisms, trade unions could not function freely in the country.

b. *The Right to Organize and Bargain Collectively.*—Wages and work requirements in traditional Somali culture are largely established by bartering, based on supply, demand, and the influence of the clan from which the worker originates. As during past years, labor disputes sometimes led to the use of force or kidnaping (see also Section 1.d.).

There are no export processing zones.

c. *Prohibition of Forced or Compulsory Labor.*—Local partners of multinational fruit export firms reportedly used forced labor in some areas of the lower Shabelle.

d. *Minimum Age for Employment of Children.*—Formal employment of children was rare, but youths are commonly employed in herding, agriculture, and household labor from an early age.

e. *Acceptable Conditions of Work.*—There was no organized effort by any of the factions or putative regional administrations to monitor acceptable conditions of work.

SOUTH AFRICA

South Africa's governing institutions and society continued to consolidate the democratic transformation initiated by the historic 1994 national elections. Areas where local elections had been postponed in late 1995 held peaceful polls to select local councilors in mid-1996. The Government of National Unity, comprising ministers from the African National Congress (ANC), the National Party (NP), and the Inkatha Freedom Party (IFP) functioned successfully through the first half of the year, with the NP voluntarily deciding to withdraw from both national and provincial executive branches on June 30. With the withdrawal of the NP, the Parliament took on an even more central role in the national debate. In addition to the 3 major parties, the 400-member National Assembly includes the Democratic Party (DP), the Freedom Front (FF), the Pan Africanist Congress (PAC), and the African Christian Democratic Party (ACDP). The Government continues to operate under an Interim Constitution. However, following year-long negotiations in the Constitutional Assembly (the National Assembly and Senate sitting jointly), the Constitutional Court certified a revised draft Constitution as complying with the Interim Constitution's required 34 principles. President Mandela signed the new Constitution into law on December 10 and it is scheduled to come into effect in February 1997. The judiciary, including the Constitutional Court, is independent.

The South African Police Service (SAPS) has primary responsibility for internal security, although the Government continues to call on the South African National Defense Force (SANDF) to provide support for the SAPS in internal security situations. The Deputy Defense Minister stated in August that at least 8,000 SANDF troops are deployed daily in support of the SAPS countrywide. The SAPS is undergoing a major restructuring and transformation from a primarily public order security force largely dedicated to enforcing apartheid laws to a more accountable, community service oriented police force. The SANDF and the newly created SAPS border control and policing unit share responsibility for external security. The civilian authorities maintain effective control of the security forces. However, some members of these forces committed human rights abuses.

South Africa has a diversified and productive economy with strong agricultural, mining, and industrial sectors. In 1995 the manufacturing sector accounted for 24.3 percent of the gross domestic product valued at $105.4 billion. The inequality of opportunity and the skewed government spending of the apartheid era have resulted in widespread illiteracy, high unemployment, a lack of adequate health care, and other socioeconomic ills among the black majority population. Official unemployment rates for the formal sector fluctuate between 32 and 40 percent. Over 60 percent of the black population is either unemployed, underemployed, or working in the informal sector. Although the Government is working hard to redress the gross inequities of the economy through the promotion of small, medium, and microenterprises and by attracting large levels of foreign direct investment, the socioeconomic legacy of apartheid is expected to remain a problem for many years.

The Government generally respects the human rights of its citizens, and the laws and newly independent judiciary provide an effective means of dealing with instances of individual abuses. Some members of the security forces committed human rights abuses, including use of excessive force during arrest, torture, and other physical abuse. Deaths in police custody remain a problem. The Government has taken action to investigate and punish some of those involved. The judiciary is overburdened, and lengthy delays in trials are a problem. Discrimination against women and the disabled continued. Violence against women and children remains a serious problem. Although there were still hundreds of political and extrajudicial killings, political violence continued to decrease, both in KwaZulu/Natal and countrywide.

The Truth and Reconciliation Commission (TRC), created to investigate apartheid-era human rights abuses, compensate victims, and grant amnesty for full disclosure of politically motivated crimes, began intensive rounds of hearings in April, which continued through the end of the year. Parliament continued to revise or repeal discriminatory legislation, and it passed an Interim Protection of Informal Land Rights Act. A new labor relations regime was adopted that improves the climate for worker rights.

RESPECT FOR HUMAN RIGHTS

Section 1. Respect for the Integrity of the Person, Including Freedom From:

a. *Political and Other Extrajudicial Killing.*—Deaths in police custody remain a problem. There were at least 32 deaths in custody during the year, although final statistics were not available. A number of cases of deaths in police custody are under investigation by the authorities. Deaths due to use of excessive force during apprehensions are a serious problem.

The number of political and extrajudicial killings continued to decrease in 1996, following the general trend after the April 1994 national elections. The Human Rights Commission (HRC) reported that political violence resulted in 970 deaths in the first 11 months of 1996, compared with 1,296 for the same period in 1995. The South African Institute for Race Relations (SAIRR) reported 683 politically motivated killings in the first 11 months of 1996, compared with 1,044 for the same period in 1995.

Beginning shortly before the peaceful community elections in KwaZulu/Natal in June, IFP and ANC leaders and grassroots supporters intensified their efforts to promote the fledgling provincial peace process. Reputed warlords from both parties held joint rallies in the Natal midlands to promote tolerance, and a joint IFP–ANC provincial commission is working on guidelines for free political campaigning. The increased emphasis on peace is reflected in the continued fall in the number of politically motivated killings in KwaZulu/Natal. The HRC reports that politically motivated killings in the province fell to an average of 41 per month through August, compared with an average of 67 per month in 1995. One of the most egregious examples of political violence was the murder of Zulu Princess Nonhlanhla in April, in an attack on a royal palace in which Zulu Queen Buhle and Princess Sibusile Zulu were badly injured. The police have made arrests in the case. On March 22, 11 bodies were found in KwaZulu/Natal's south midlands and an additional 6 people were killed in another incident.

Vigilante action and mob justice were problems. People Against Gangsterism and Drugs (PAGAD), a community-based organization calling for stronger action by the Government and police against crime and drugs, engaged in acts of intimidation and violence against suspected drug dealers and gang leaders. In one incident in Cape Town in August, an angry PAGAD crowd shot and burned to death alleged drug dealer and gang leader Rashaad Staggie in the presence of police. The Government condemned the action and subsequent PAGAD violence, and it has taken steps to arrest some of those who participated in the violence. Several PAGAD leaders were subsequently taken into custody for violating their bail conditions during ongoing judicial investigations.

Three people were arrested for the 1987 murder of Zazi Kuzways. In Johannesburg eight persons standing in a line of job seekers outside a plant were shot and killed by unknown assailants.

There were a number of killings due to factional fights between either political or ethnic groups, many of them in and around mining operations. For example in September, 21 miners were killed at a mine as a result of factional fighting between Xhosa and Sotho. Over 30 squatters were killed in factional clashes near a platinum mine in Northwest province.

There were occasional reports of killings linked to the continued practice of witchcraft in some rural areas. In the Northern province, where traditional beliefs regarding witchcraft remain strong, officials reported dozens of killings of people suspected of witchcraft. The Government has instituted educational programs to prevent such actions.

The TRC's investigative unit is looking into a number of cases of alleged political or extrajudicial killings committed in previous years that have been brought to its attention through TRC hearings. Also, special police investigative teams continue to make arrests in the cases of the 1995 Christmas season massacres.

In March the Rand Supreme Court found nine members of the Afrikaner Weerstandsbeweging (AWB) guilty of murder charges in connection with the April 1994 preelection bombing campaign. Another 13 AWB members were convicted of lesser charges (possessing arms and explosives), and 4 were acquitted.

A resurgence of violence attributed to extreme right Afrikaner nationalist groups occurred late in the year. A previously unknown group calling itself the "Boere Attack Troops" claimed responsibility for a Christmas Eve bombing in the Western Cape town of Worcester that resulted in four deaths.

In August retired SAP Colonel Eugene de Kock, who commanded a police unit allegedly used for "third force" activities, was found guilty on 89 charges, including 6 murder charges, and sentenced in October to 2 life sentences plus an additional 212 years' imprisonment. De Kock is in the process of applying for amnesty from the TRC.

On October 11, a court acquitted former Defense Minister Magnus Malan of murder and conspiracy charges. Fourteen other defendants were acquitted, including 6 Zulu policemen acquitted a day earlier. The State had charged General Malan and the others with involvement in the January 1987 murder of 13 people at Kwamakhuta, near Durban.

No charges have been filed to date in the case of the 1994 assassination of former Dutch Reformed Church moderator Johan Heyns; this situation is unlikely to change. Five men were arrested in the 1981 murder of Griffiths Mxenge. Their trial was postponed until April 1997, pending amnesty hearings involving at least three of the accused.

b. Disappearance.—There were no new reports of politically motivated disappearances caused by government authorities or agents. Starting in April the TRC heard public testimony regarding numerous politically motivated disappearances between 1960 and 1993. Investigations into a number of these disappearances were subsequently begun by the TRC's investigative unit, as well as by the relevant provincial attorney general in some cases.

c. Torture and Other Cruel, Inhuman, or Degrading Treatment or Punishment.—The Interim Constitution stipulates that "no person shall be subject to torture of any kind, whether physical, mental, or emotional, nor shall any person be subject to cruel, inhuman, or degrading treatment or punishment." Some members of the police used excessive force and tortured and otherwise abused suspects and detainees. However, broad efforts to reform police practices have substantially reduced such activities.

Monitoring organizations continued to make credible reports of police abuse of detainees while in custody, including beatings, suffocation with rubber tubing, electric shock, and rape. In August an attorney was appointed Executive Director of the Independent Complaints Directorate (ICD). The ICD is a civilian channel for complaints operating separately from the SAPS. It investigates allegations of misconduct and corruption by members of the police. Also, several human rights education programs for the SAPS were conducted by nongovernmental organizations (NGO's).

The SAPS has continued to undergo sweeping, positive changes, including the institution of reforms designed to create partnerships between local police forces and the communities they serve. Resignations and retirements of senior police officials have permitted the infusion of new personnel at senior levels, from both inside and outside the SAPS, and these appointments have also served to further affirmative action within the SAPS.

Prison conditions meet minimum international standards, and the Government permits independent monitoring of prison conditions, including visits by human rights organizations.

d. Arbitrary Arrest, Detention, or Exile.—The Interim Constitution expressly prohibits detention without trial. It also provides that every detained person has a number of other rights, including the right to be informed promptly of the reasons for detention; to be charged within 48 hours of arrest; to be detained in conditions of human dignity; to consult with legal counsel at every stage of the legal process; to communicate with relatives, medical practitioners, and religious counselors; and to be released with or without bail, unless the interests of justice require otherwise.

Courts and police generally acted in good faith to respect these rights, although there was a growing problem with bringing detained persons to trial in a prompt fashion. According to the HRC, prisoners wait on average for 6 months to be tried, although in extreme cases this can extend up to 2 years. This problem is due in large measure to the overburdened judiciary, which has more cases than it can handle efficiently, and insufficient staff and resources.

There were no reports of forced exile.

e. *Denial of Fair Public Trial.*—The Interim Constitution provides for an independent and impartial judiciary subject only to the Constitution and the law, and the Government respects this provision in practice. The independence and impartiality of the judiciary were underscored by the Constitutional Court's September 6 decision to decline to certify the new draft constitution (see Section 3).

While the precise relationship between the Constitutional Court and the Appellate Division of the Supreme Court (which was formerly the country's supreme judicial body) remains unclear, the Interim Constitution makes the former the highest court for interpreting constitutional issues; the latter remains supreme in all others.

Judges try criminal cases. The jury system was abolished in 1969. Serious offenses are tried in the Supreme Court, while magistrates hear lesser offenses. The presiding judge or magistrate determines guilt or innocence.

The Interim Constitution's section on fundamental rights provides for due process, including the right to a fair, public trial within a reasonable time of being charged and the right to appeal to a higher court. It also gives detained persons a right to state-funded legal counsel when "substantial injustice would otherwise result."

The Government and legal bodies have acted to redress historic racial and gender imbalances in the judiciary and the bar. The ranks of judges, magistrates, senior counsels, and attorneys are now more reflective of society, although still far short of a representative composition.

By year's end approximately 4,000 written applications for amnesty had been received by the TRC, of which about half were from those already incarcerated for crimes which they claim were committed for political reasons. On August 29, the TRC granted its first amnesty to two men convicted of killing Glad Mokgatle, an ally of Bophuthatswana strongman Lucas Mangope, ruling that their actions fit the required definition of a political crime. The two were released on August 30.

f. *Arbitrary Interference With Privacy, Family, Home, or Correspondence.*—The Interim Constitution prohibits such practices, government authorities generally respect these prohibitions, and violations are subject to effective legal sanction.

A Constitutional Land Court was established to adjudicate, among other matters, claims of persons dispossessed and removed from land during the apartheid era. Several thousand land claims have already been lodged with the Commission on Restitution of Land Rights, which has been set up to process, investigate, and attempt to settle claims. The Commission's decisions are to be referred to the Court for approval, and complex claims are to be heard and decided by the Court. The Court has the power to order the State to compensate victims or to expropriate their former land. The revised deadline for lodging claims is April 1998, and the Court must complete its work within 5 years.

Section 2. Respect for Civil Liberties, Including:

a. *Freedom of Speech and Press.*—The Constitution provides for freedom of speech and of the press, and the Government respects these rights in practice. These rights can, however, be limited by general law under some circumstances. Coverage of news and expression of opinion is vigorous and unfettered. Self-censorship is not a serious problem. While most major broadcast media are still state-owned, their editorial independence appears genuine and the Government is taking steps to end its broadcast monopoly. The South African Broadcasting Corporation (SABC) controls all broadcast television and most radio. Once seen as the Government's voice, the SABC is in the midst of an historic reorganization and change of direction. SABC news programming offered balanced coverage of the Government and the leading opposition parties, although the smaller opposition parties regularly complained of insufficient coverage of their activities.

The work of the Independent Broadcast Authority (IBA) is contributing to major changes in the electronic media. The IBA granted 81 licenses for community radio broadcasters and approximately 60 of these small, not-for-profit stations were broadcasting in 1996. The IBA also held hearings on issuance of eight commercial licenses and the sale of six SABC radio stations to private investors. Although some parties (notably potential commercial broadcasters) have complained about the slow progress, the IBA's work has begun to bring real competition to the country's airwaves for the first time.

Several laws remained in effect that permit the Government to restrict the publication of information about the police, the national defense forces, prisons, and mental institutions. While these laws were not often employed, they remained a genuine threat to freedom of the press. In August the Attorney General of the Western Cape province invoked the Criminal Procedure Act in an effort to compel journalists to turn over all written and graphic material related to an episode of gang violence. Editors were threatened with subpoenas but refused to turn over any materials. Through reporting and editorials, journalists publicized the threat and argued that the media could not become agents of the police. The Attorney General backed down, but the incident demonstrated the media's vulnerability to such laws.

Similar events in Cape Town also brought threats to the media from members of the community action organization PAGAD (see Section 1.a.). Journalists who covered the mob murder of a reputed drug dealer by PAGAD members were threatened with death if they made their notes or graphic materials available to the police.

In October the newly formed South African Editors' Forum criticized President Mandela for an attack on black journalists. Mandela had complained that black journalists were unfairly criticizing the Government in order to please white press owners.

The South African Board of Censors reviews and passes judgment on written and graphic materials published in or imported into the country. The Board of Censors has the power to edit or ban books, magazines, movies, and videos. It regularly exercises that power.

There are no official restrictions on academic freedom.

b. *Freedom of Peaceful Assembly and Association.*—The Interim Constitution provides for freedom of assembly and of association, and the Government respects these rights in practice. Political parties and organizations operate freely.

c. *Freedom of Religion.*—The Interim Constitution provides for freedom of religion, and the Government respects this right in practice.

d. *Freedom of Movement Within the Country, Foreign Travel, Emigration, and Repatriation.*—The Interim Constitution provides for these rights, and the Government respects them in practice.

In January the Government formally acceded to the 1951 United Nations Convention Relating to the Status of Refugees and its 1967 Protocol. In July South Africa signed a memorandum of understanding with the U.N. High Commissioner for Refugees (UNHCR) on standardization of regional refugee policies, which is designed to shift more responsibility for handling refugee flows onto first asylum countries in the region.

The Government cooperates with the UNHCR and other humanitarian organizations in assisting refugees. The Government provides first asylum, granting applicants the right to work and study. Over 16,000 asylum seekers were registered by the Government in 1996. In May the Government and the UNHCR completed the Mozambican repatriation program. About 70 percent of the tens of thousands of illegal immigrants deported during the year came from Mozambique. Despite numerous procedural safeguards, energetic efforts to combat a mounting illegal immigration problem sometimes resulted in wrongful deportations.

Parliament passed an amnesty bill in June permitting certain illegal aliens who have lived in South Africa for 5 years or more to become legal residents. Despite predictions that up to a million of the estimated 5 million illegal aliens in the country would apply for the amnesty, by year's end only about 10,000 had taken advantage of the measure.

Section 3. Respect for Political Rights: The Right of Citizens to Change Their Government

Citizens exercised the right to change their government in 1994 elections that international observers deemed to be substantially free and fair. The country continued to be governed pursuant to an Interim Constitution that provides for a bicameral parliament, an executive state president, and an independent judiciary, including a constitutional court. The Parliament comprises the National Assembly (400 members elected by proportional lists) and the Senate (90 members, 10 from each province, elected by the provincial parliaments). The two houses are generally coequal. Seven parties are represented in the Assembly, with the African National Congress, the National Party, and the Inkatha Freedom Party holding the majority of the seats (252, 82, and 43 respectively). All citizens over 18 years of age are permitted to vote in elections.

Until the National Party withdrew from the Government on June 30, these three parties shared executive power in a Government of National Unity (GNU) under the Interim Constitution. The Interim Constitution provides for an executive deputy president from any party garnering more than 20 percent of the total vote. Thus, in addition to President Nelson Mandela, who is the Executive Head of State, South Africa had two Executive Deputy Presidents, Thabo Mbeki from the ANC and F. W. de Klerk (the former State President) from the NP. This arrangement was altered on June 30, when the National Party voluntarily withdrew from the GNU, de Klerk relinquished his deputy presidency, and only the ANC and the IFP were left in the executive branch. Mbeki became the sole Executive Deputy President. The ANC filled 24 of the 27 cabinet positions.

According to the Interim Constitution, the Constitutional Assembly (CA) was required to draft and approve a permanent constitution by May 9. The draft was required to comply with 34 constitutional principles spelled out in the Interim Constitution. On May 8, the CA (minus the IFP, which walked out of constitutional negotiations in February 1995) approved a document, which was referred to the Constitutional Court. Hearings were held in July, and on September 6 the court referred the document back to the CA, citing seven provisions and one whole chapter that did not comply with the principles. Following intensive negotiations in September and October, the CA submitted a revised draft, which was certified by the Constitutional Court on December 2. President Mandela signed the new Constitution into law on December 10.

In addition to certification of the new Constitution, the Constitutional Court also has the responsibility to interpret, defend, and enforce the Constitution. The Court has the power to overturn any law or executive act that it deems unconstitutional. The Interim Constitution also provides that the Court protect over 25 fundamental rights of citizens, pending entry into force of the new Constitution.

Local councils elected in November 1995 were in place in seven of South Africa's nine provinces (and in some areas of the Western Cape) throughout 1996. Disputes that had delayed local polls in parts of the Western Cape and KwaZulu/Natal were successfully resolved, and peaceful elections were held in those provinces on May 29 and June 26 respectively.

There are no legal impediments to women's participation in government and politics. Over one-fourth of the National Assembly members are women, women won 20 percent of the Senate seats in the 1994 elections, women chair approximately one-quarter of the 60 National Assembly committees, and women fill both the Speaker and Deputy Speaker positions in the National Assembly. In the Cabinet, female representation increased somewhat in 1996. Women hold 4 of 27 ministerial positions, as well as 8 deputy ministerial slots.

Section 4. Governmental Attitude Regarding International and Nongovernmental Investigation of Alleged Violations of Human Rights

A number of human rights groups operate without government restriction, investigating and publishing their findings on human rights cases. Government officials are generally cooperative and responsive to their views. Many organizations now participate in governmental bodies seeking to gather public input and to fashion policies related to human rights.

During 1996 the Truth and Reconciliation Commission was constituted and began its work. Under the 1995 enabling legislation, the TRC is empowered: To look into apartheid-era gross human rights abuses committed between 1960 and 1993; to grant amnesty to perpetrators of a broad range of politically motivated crimes; and to recommend compensation for victims of human rights abuses. The TRC began public hearings into human rights abuses in April, and held its first amnesty hearings in May. By year's end, thousands of statements from victims of human rights abuses had been received by the TRC, and hearings held throughout the country. Approximately 4,000 amnesty applications had also been submitted.

President Mandela announced on December 13 that the deadline for submitting amnesty applications to the TRC would be extended from December 14, 1996 to May 10, 1997. Mandela also said that he would request that the National Assembly extend the amnesty period cutoff date from December 6, 1993 to May 10, 1994 (the date on which Mandela was inaugurated as South Africa's first democratically elected president). The TRC had strongly urged Mandela to extend both deadlines, arguing that the extensions would encourage additional perpetrators to apply for amnesty.

In their institutional testimony before the TRC, both former government and liberation movement representatives conceded that human rights abuses had been committed by individuals acting on their own, but denied that abuses had been authorized at the highest levels. Investigations into these statements continued at year's end.

TRC officials emphasized throughout the year that the Commission's mandate is to investigate human rights abuses committed by all parties, and that all parties are bound by the legislation's amnesty provisions. Comments by some ANC officials that appeared to suggest that the ANC was exempting its members from the amnesty process prompted concern that the Commission's independence was being undermined. However, senior ANC officials assured TRC Chairman Desmond Tutu in a meeting late in the year that the party respected the Commission's authority and was encouraging its members to apply for amnesty where appropriate.

By year's end, a number of former government officials, including one former minister and a top-level police official, had indicated that they would apply for amnesty.

Hearings had been held involving nearly 50 applicants, including 5 former senior security policemen who presented evidence to the Commission on approximately 40 cases of disappearance, bombings, and murder. Former security force Colonel Dirk Coetzee, one of the first apartheid government "defectors" to expose security force human rights violations, also testified before the Amnesty Committee; two others accused with him in the murder of Griffiths Mxenge have submitted amnesty applications.

On August 29, the TRC granted its first amnesty to two men convicted of killing Glad Mokgatle, an ally of Bophuthatswana strongman Lucas Mangope, ruling that their actions fit the required definition of a political crime. The two were released on August 30. In December the TRC granted amnesty to former policeman Brian Mitchell, who was serving a 30-year sentence for his part in the 1988 murder of 11 people, known as the Trust Feed massacre. Amnesty was granted in half the nearly two dozen cases adjudicated by year's end.

The government-created Human Rights Commission is tasked with promoting the observance of fundamental human rights at all levels of government and throughout the general population. The HRC also has the power to conduct investigations, issue subpoenas, and hear testimony under oath. While commissioners were named in late 1995, the Commission's powers were not formally determined until May 17. Operations have been hampered by red tape, budgetary concerns, the absence of civil liberties legislation, and uncertainty over the entry into force of the new Constitution, which will, among other provisions, expand bill of rights provisions to cover actions between private individuals.

The Office of Public Protector, which was also mandated under the Interim Constitution, functioned throughout the year. Its role is to investigate abuse and mismanagement by the Government. In its highest profile case, the Public Protector examined the handling of the contract and funding for the AIDS-awareness play "Sarafina II" by officials of the Department of Health. The Government indicated that it would accept the recommendations of the inquiry, some of which were critical of government action.

Section 5. Discrimination Based on Race, Sex, Religion, Disability, Language, or Social Status

The Interim Constitution prohibits discrimination on grounds of race, gender, ethnic or social origin, color, sexual orientation, age, disability, religion, conscience, belief, culture, language, sex, pregnancy, marital status, or birth. Legal recourse is available to those who believe they have been discriminated against.

Women.—There is a high rate of violence against women. Newspapers report that every 6 days a woman is killed by her husband or boyfriend. According to a study conducted by the NGO, People Opposing Women Abuse, the figures for reported rape have risen consistently each year, from 32,000 cases in 1994 to nearly 37,000 in 1995 (the last year for which figures are available). Unofficial estimates by the National Institute for Crime Prevention and Rehabilitation of Offenders suggest that only 1 rape in 20 is reported to police.

The Prevention of Family Violence Act of 1993 defines marital rape as a criminal offense and provides a simpler, cheaper, and more effective procedure for women to obtain injunctions against their abusive husbands and partners. However, to date only a handful of women have pressed complaints under the law, despite government and NGO efforts to increase public awareness of it.

Given the high incidence of violence against women, the Government pledged to establish more centers for battered women. However, by year's end few such centers had been opened and women's advocacy groups were calling on the Government to speed implementation of its pledge. The SAPS created new police units dealing specifically with domestic violence, child protection, and sexual violence, which are intended in part to increase victims' confidence in the police, resulting in more victims coming forward to report such crimes. In October the TRC conducted a special hearing on abuses suffered by women before an all-female commission.

In March the Government established an Office on the Status of Women, located in the Deputy President's Office. The Office is intended to coordinate gender desks in each department, which will be charged with reviewing department policy and developing strategies to ensure integration of gender concerns in policy and planning, and to undertake investigations of reported gender discrimination.

The Commission on Gender Equality Bill was passed by Parliament in June. The act established a government body to promote gender equality and to advise and make recommendations to Parliament on any legislation affecting women. In November the National Assembly approved the list of appointees (which included 10 women and 2 men) to the country's first gender commission.

Discrimination against women remains a serious problem despite legal and constitutional advances and government attention to this issue. For example under some traditional laws, women are prevented from owning land and inheriting property. The new Interim Protection of Informal Land Rights Act protects persons who have insecure and informal rights and interests in land; many women are in this category. Some steps were taken to achieve greater economic advancement for women such as establishing an investment fund. The Affirmative Action Monitor, published by the consulting group FSA-Contact, reported that there was a 25 percent increase in the number of female professionals in the organizations surveyed.

In January the Government ratified the U. N. Convention on the Elimination of All Forms of Discrimination Against Women.

The Women's National Coalition (formed in 1994) includes more than 90 women's groups from labor, political parties, religious groups, trade unions, cultural and social interest groups, and business and professional bodies. Government participants in the U. N. Fourth World Conference on Women in Beijing developed a national plan of action and induced government departments to make concrete commitments to address gender issues. During parliamentary deliberations on the 1996 budget, many officials provided information assessing gender-specific implications of their budgets, as well as their departments' efforts to promote women.

The new Constitution includes an equality clause that prohibits discrimination on the grounds of gender, sex, pregnancy, marital status, or sexual orientation. The Government used the Platform of Action from the Beijing Conference as a reference guide in the drafting of this and other provisions of the law.

Polygyny continues to be practiced in several ethnic groups. However, generally only one marriage is registered under civil law; subsequent marriages are conducted under traditional rites. Bride price ("lobola") is also a traditional practice of some ethnic groups.

Children.—The Interim Constitution stipulates that children have the right "to security, education, basic nutrition, and basic health and social services." The Government remains firm in its commitment to provide these services, and has made some progress toward developing the mechanisms for delivering necessary services. However, the demand for such services far outstrips the resources currently available.

The Schools Bill passed by Parliament aims to achieve greater educational opportunities for black children. It introduces compulsory education from ages 7 to 15, a single syllabus, and more equitable funding. The Government plans to redeploy teachers from predominantly white to predominantly black schools in order to equalize student/teacher ratios, and to redistribute funding from relatively rich to relatively poor school districts. Student populations on university campuses are becoming more representative of the country's racial profile, with previously all-white universities reaching out to recruit students from black and colored townships.

Social programs known as "Presidential Initiatives," which were included in the former Reconstruction and Development Program, continue to receive government support. These initiatives offer free health care to pregnant women and to children under 6 years of age, and provide nutritious meals for primary school children.

Violence against children remains widespread. A report conducted by the Human Sciences Research Council and the Child Protection Unit concludes that crimes committed against children are currently rising at an annual rate of 29 percent. Reported cases have increased 65 percent between 1993 and 1995. The increase in reported cases can be attributed to the creation of special units to deal with these crimes, growing emphasis on children's rights, and increased attention to the problem by the public and the media. However, a lack of coordinated and comprehensive strategies to deal with such crimes continues to impede the delivery of needed services to young victims.

Child prostitution is on the rise, primarily in Cape Town, but in Durban and Johannesburg as well. An increase in the number of children living on the streets has contributed to the growing number of child prostitutes. The child sex industry has become increasingly organized, with children either being forced into prostitution or exploited by their parents to earn money for the family.

Female genital mutilation, which is widely condemned by international health experts as damaging to both physical and psychological health, is traditionally practiced in some remote areas of South Africa, although the practice is not thought to be widespread. Traditional circumcision of teenage boys results in the hospitalization, mutilation, or even death of several youths each year.

In March amendments to prison legislation were passed permitting the detention of 14- to 18-year old juveniles who were awaiting trial for serious crimes such as rape and murder. In August Correctional Services Minister Sipo Mzimela initiated a national debate on the incarceration of juveniles by claiming that 62 percent of the 398 juveniles awaiting trial in top security jails—some as young as 12 years old—should not be there because they were being tried on relatively minor charges.

People With Disabilities.—The Interim Constitution and Bill of Fundamental Rights prohibit discrimination on the basis of disability. Society continues to promote an increasingly modern concept of people with disabilities as a minority whose civil rights must be protected. The Government attempts to ensure that all government-funded projects take account of the needs of its disabled citizens.

However, in practice government and private sector discrimination in employment still exists, given the wide discretion allowed managers in hiring practices. According to the Affirmative Action Monitor, fewer than two-thirds of South African companies target the disabled as part of their affirmative action programs. The law mandates access to buildings for people with disabilities, but such regulations have rarely been enforced and until recently, public awareness of them was virtually nonexistent. The National Environmental Accessibility Program, an NGO comprising disabled consumers as well as service providers, has established a presence in all nine provinces in order to lobby for compliance with the regulations and to sue offending property owners when necessary.

Indigenous People.—The Interim Constitution provides for the recognition of "the institution, status, and role of traditional leadership," and requires the courts to "apply customary law when that law is applicable, subject to the Constitution and any legislation that specifically deals with customary law."

The Interim Constitution further permits legislation for the establishment of provincial houses of traditional leaders and a national council of traditional leaders, both of which would deal with matters relating to traditional leadership, the role of traditional leaders, indigenous and customary law, and the customs of communities observing a system of customary law.

National/Racial/Ethnic Minorities.—The Interim Constitution and Bill of Fundamental Rights prohibit discrimination on the basis of race, ethnic or social origin, and culture. The Government has begun reorganizing and redesigning the educational, housing, and health care systems to benefit all racial and ethnic groups in society more equally. The public and private sectors continue to pursue affirmative action programs, which are permitted under terms of the Interim Constitution. The Government has instituted an effective affirmative action program, and has strongly encouraged private firms to do so. According to a Department of Labor survey, 82 percent of private sector firms have instituted affirmative action programs.

The new Interim Protection of Informal Land Rights Act, which protects people with insecure and informal rights and interests in land, supplements the many 1994 land and housing acts which were passed to redress former discriminatory practices and to promote equality in access to land and housing resources.

According to Affirmative Action Monitor, affirmative action policies have had little impact on the top echelons in business. The number of white senior and middle managers has been reduced by less than 2 percent. The number of black senior and middle managers has increased by less than 1 percent. The number of companies with affirmative action programs decreased over the last year, declining from 94 percent in 1995 to 82 percent in 1996. Based on the consultants' survey, one-third of the organizations with no current programs did not intend to implement one. Twelve percent of the companies surveyed said that they had experienced a drop in standards or deterioration in quality of work due to affirmative action. However, the country's black majority increasingly is making inroads into the previously all-white entrepreneurial sector through pooled investments and acquisitions.

Section 6. Worker Rights

a. *The Right of Association.*—Freedom of association and the right to strike are provided by the Interim Constitution and given statutory effect in the Labor Relations Act (LRA), which entered into force on November 11. All workers in the private sector are entitled to join a union. Most workers in the public sector, with the exception of members of the National Defense Force, the National Intelligence Agency, and the South African Secret Service, are also entitled to join a union. No employee can be fired or prejudiced because of membership in or advocacy of a trade union. There are 227 registered trade unions and about 40 unregistered trade unions, with a total approximate membership of 3.2 million, or about 42 percent of the employed, economically active population.

The largest trade union federation, the Congress of South African Trade Unions (COSATU) is formally aligned with the ANC and the South African Communist Party. Over 60 former COSATU members serve in national and provincial legislatures and administrations, and scores more entered local government following the November 1995 local elections. The much smaller National Council of Trade Unions, while officially independent of any political grouping, has close ties to the Pan

Africanist Congress and the Azanian Peoples Organization. A third major federation, the Federation of South African Labor, comprises primarily white-collar professional employees. A federation of public service employees called the Federation of Organizations Representing Civil Employees was created in early 1996 but has not yet been formally registered.

The LRA has established a simple procedure for a protected strike. All that is required is that the dispute be referred for conciliation. If conciliation fails to resolve the dispute, then a trade union is entitled to engage in a legal strike. Such a strike is not liable to criminal or civil action. The LRA allows employers to hire replacement labor for striking employees, but only after giving 7 days' notice to the striking trade union.

The LRA applies to public sector as well as private sector workers. Therefore, public sector employees are also guaranteed the right to strike, with the exception of essential services and the three components of the security services mentioned above. While this right was first asserted in the Public Sector Labor Relations Act of 1993, the LRA simplifies and rationalizes collective bargaining in the public sector and the resort to industrial action. Moreover, through the LRA, Parliament has granted employers the right to lock out workers if certain conditions are met. However, a controversial attempt to establish this right in the Constitution was rejected by the Constitutional Court in September.

The Government does not restrict union affiliation with regional or international labor organizations.

The International Labor Organization readmitted South Africa in 1994; the country had withdrawn from the Organization in 1964.

b. *The Right to Organize and Bargain Collectively.*—The law defines and protects the rights to organize and to bargain collectively. The Government does not interfere with union organizing and generally has not interfered in the collective bargaining process. The new LRA statutorily entrenches "organizational rights," such as trade union access to work sites, deductions for trade union subscriptions, and leave for trade union officials, which strengthen the ability of trade unions to organize workers.

Union participation as an equal partner with business and government in the tripartite National Economic Development and Labor Council, a tripartite negotiating forum, ensures a direct voice for labor in the formulation of economic, social, and labor policy.

The new LRA creates workplace forums that are intended to promote better shop floor communication between management and labor over issues of work organization and production. The forums, to receive statutory protection, can only be initiated by trade unions in businesses with more than 100 employees. However, the law is designed to build wide support within the trade union movement and business for new workplace relationships.

To further reduce the adversarial nature of labor relations, the LRA also creates a Commission for Conciliation, Mediation, and Arbitration (CCMA), which is intended to play an aggressive, interventionist role to resolve disputes before they become full-fledged strikes or lockouts. In the event the CCMA is unable to resolve a dispute, it may be referred to the Labor Court. However, the intent of the bill is to reduce judicial intervention into labor relations, relying on the parties to resolve the dispute whenever possible.

There are no export processing zones.

c. *Prohibition of Forced or Compulsory Labor.*—Forced labor is prohibited by the Interim Constitution, and the law is effectively enforced.

d. *Minimum Age for Employment of Children.*—Employment of minors under age 15 is prohibited by law. However, the law gives discretionary powers to the Minister of Welfare to exempt certain types of work to allow individual employers or groups of employers to hire children under certain conditions. This is common practice in the agricultural sector. Use of child labor in the informal economy is also common. The Ministries of Labor and Justice do not effectively enforce child labor laws, acting largely in response to complaints made against specific employers.

e. *Acceptable Conditions of Work.*—There is no legally mandated national minimum wage. Instead, the LRA provides a mechanism for negotiations between labor and management to set minimum wage standards, industry by industry. Currently, 100 industries covering most manufacturing workers come under the provisions of the act. In those sectors of the economy not sufficiently organized to engage in the collective bargaining processes which establish minimum wages, the Wage Act gives the Minister of Labor the authority to set minimum wages and conditions. The Wage Act, however, does not apply to farm or domestic workers.

Occupational health and safety issues are a top priority of trade unions, especially in the mining and heavy manufacturing industries. Although attention to these issues has increased dramatically, including passage in 1993 of the Occupational Health and Safety Act, industrial and mining processes are dangerous and sometimes deadly. Government attempts to reduce mining fatalities culminated in June in the Mine Health and Safety Act. The act had its genesis in a report issued last year by a commission of inquiry convened to look into health and safety issues at South African mines. The new act establishes the right of an employee to remove himself from a work place he deems a danger to his health and safety. Moreover, it establishes a tripartite Mine Health and Safety Council, and an Inspectorate of Mine Health and Safety tasked with enforcing the act and monitoring compliance with its provisions. The act specifically makes it an offense for a company to discriminate against an employee who asserts a right (e.g., to leave a hazardous work site) granted by the act, and requires mine owners to file annual reports that provide statistics on health and safety incidents for each mine being worked.

SUDAN

The 1989 military coup that overthrew Sudan's democratically elected government brought to power Lt. General Omar Hassan Al-Bashir and his National Salvation Revolution Command Council (RCC). Bashir and the RCC suspended the 1985 constitution, abrogated press freedom, and disbanded all political parties and trade unions. In 1993 the RCC dissolved itself and appointed Bashir President. In March Bashir won highly structured national elections as President, while an elected National Assembly replaced the transitional national assembly. The opposition boycotted the electoral process. Despite promulgation of new national institutions and an interim constitution through constitutional decrees, the new Government has continued to restrict most civil liberties. Since 1989 real power has rested with the National Islamic Front (NIF), founded by Dr. Hassan Al-Turabi. He became Speaker of the 1996 National Assembly. NIF members and supporters continue to hold key positions in the Government; security forces; judiciary; academia; and the media. The newly created supreme political institution, the National Convention, which sets national policy guidelines, is also under NIF control. The judiciary is subject to government influence.

The civil war, which has resulted in the death of more than 1.5 million Sudanese, continued into its 13th year. The principal insurgent factions are the Sudanese People's Liberation Movement (SPLM) and the South Sudan Independence Movement (SSIM). Neither side has the apparent ability to win the war militarily. Informal peace efforts included one meeting in May following the U.N. Educational and Science agency's (UNESCO's) 1995 "Culture of Peace" effort to initiate a dialog between the Government and insurgent leaders. These meetings did not, however, constitute peace negotiations.

Government efforts led one insurgent faction leader, Riak Machar of the SSIM and a number of less significant figures, to sign a "political charter" on April 10. However, the SPLM, the major insurgent movement, has regarded the document with suspicion. Regional nations of the renamed Intergovernmental Authority on Development (IGAD) played no role in the peace process in the wake of the 1995 government rejection of the IGAD declaration of principles.

In addition to the regular police and the Sudan People's Armed Forces (SPAF), the Government maintains an external security organ, an internal security organ, a militia known as the Popular Defense Forces (PDF), and a parallel police force, the Popular Police, whose mission includes enforcing proper social behavior, including restrictions on alcohol and "immodest dress." Members of the security forces committed numerous human rights abuses.

Civil war, economic mismanagement, over 3 million internally displaced persons in a country of 27.5 million, and a refugee influx from neighboring countries have devastated Sudan's mostly agricultural economy. Exports of gum arabic, livestock, and meat accounted for more than 50 percent of export earnings. Reforms aimed at privatizing state-run firms and stimulating private investment failed to revive a moribund economy saddled with massive military expenditures and a huge foreign debt of approximately $16 billion. Per capita national income is estimated at $900 per year.

The human rights situation remained extremely poor, as both the Government and insurgents committed serious human rights abuses. Government forces were responsible for extrajudicial killings, disappearances, forced labor, slavery, and forced conscription of children. Government security forces regularly harassed, arbitrarily arrested and detained, tortured, and beat opponents or suspected opponents of the Government with impunity. Prison conditions are harsh, and the judiciary is largely subservient to the Government. The authorities do not ensure due process, and the military forces summarily tried and punished citizens.

The Government continued to restrict freedom of assembly, association, religion, privacy, and movement. Citizens do not have the ability to change their government peacefully. In the context of the Islamization and Arabization drive, pressure—including forced Islamization—on non-Muslims remained strong. Fears of Arabization and Islamization and the imposition of Shari'a (Islamic Law) fueled support for the southern insurgency. Discrimination and violence against women and abuse of children continued. Discrimination against religious and ethnic minorities persisted, as did government restrictions on worker rights. Child labor is a problem.

On a positive note, the Government resumed cooperation with international human rights monitors. The U.N., including the Special Rapporteur on Sudan and the Rapporteur on Religious Intolerance visited areas under the Government's control. The Government also invited the Rapporteur on Freedom of Expression to visit.

Cooperation with U.N.-sponsored relief operations was mixed. Government forces periodically obstructed the flow of humanitarian assistance. Problems with relief flights in the south centered on the Government's denial of more than a dozen destinations to both the U.N. Operation Lifeline Sudan and the International Committee of the Red Cross (ICRC). In December U.S. Congressman Bill Richardson helped conclude an agreement between the ICRC and an insurgent leader allied with the Government, Kerubino Kwanyin Bol, which freed three ICRC hostages Kerubino had captured from an ICRC flight. The agreement gave Kerubino some relief supplies in return for the release of three expatriate ICRC staff members. The other five hostages, SPLA soldiers (from the SPLM's military wing) being returned under accepted ground rules to their place of origin by the ICRC after treatment for wounds at an ICRC hospital, were given the choice of returning to Khartoum with the other released hostages, returning to territory held by SPLA by walking, or staying under Kerubino's control. They chose the latter, but their current whereabouts are unknown. In July authorities restored permission for relief flights by C-130 aircraft with large cargo capacity.

Insurgent groups continued to commit numerous, serious human rights abuses. The SPLM continued to violate citizens' rights, despite its claim to be implementing a 1994 decision to assert civil authority in areas that it controls, and in many cases, has controlled for many years. The SPLM was responsible for extrajudicial killings, kidnapings, arbitrary detention, and forced conscription, and occasional arrest of foreign relief workers without charge. The SPLM failed to follow through on its promise to investigate a 1995 massacre. The ICRC publicly noted that the SPLM taught courses to officers of the SPLA at the request of that organization. The ICRC also noted that the SPLA has begun to observe some basic laws of war: It takes prisoners on the battlefield and permits ICRC visits to them. However, the SPLA did not allow the ICRC to visit rebels accused by the insurgent group of "treason" or other crimes. The Government still does not apply the laws of war to the southern insurgency and takes no prisoners.

RESPECT FOR HUMAN RIGHTS

Section 1. Respect for the Integrity of the Person, Including Freedom From:

a. *Political and Other Extrajudicial Killing.*—No substantiated reports of political or other extrajudicial killings came from insurgent zones, possibly due to the limited access to such zones by outside observers. In their attacks on insurgent forces, government troops also killed civilians (see Section 1.g.). Police also used excessive force against demonstrators. According to conflicting reports, police killed six or seven demonstrators in an incident in Omduran (see Section 2.b.).

Insurgent forces are believed to have committed political and other extrajudicial killings, with details generally unavailable. Rebels also killed civilians during their attacks on government forces (see Section 1.g.).

b. *Disappearance.*—There were continued allegations that the Government was responsible for the arrest and subsequent disappearance of those suspected of supporting rebels in government-controlled zones of the south and the Nuba Mountains. The Government established a Committee to Investigate Slavery and Disappearances in the Nuba Mountains in response to a resolution passed by the 1995 U.N. General Assembly. The Committee reportedly interviewed or obtained reliable information on the whereabouts of all but about 3 dozen of the more than 200 persons whose cases of disappearance the U.N. had cited.

Scores of persons arrested by government forces in Juba in 1992, including two Sudanese employees of the U.S. Agency for International Development, Domonic Morris and Chaplain Lako, remained unaccounted for; most are believed dead. In spite of reliable reports that a few of those arrested in Juba in 1992 are held in a Khartoum prison, the Government denied any knowledge of their whereabouts.

c. *Torture and Other Cruel, Inhuman, or Degrading Treatment or Punishment.*— The Government's official and unofficial security forces continued to torture and beat suspected opponents. From December 1995 through January 1996, authorities in Juba beat and tortured a young man of the Toposa ethnic group to extract a confession that he had organized antigovernment cells. They detained and demanded a confession from a Roman Catholic priest of the same ethnic group, threatening to kill the youth and others unless the priest confessed to antigovernment activities, which he did.

Reports continued to decline of use of, and torture in, "ghost houses," places where security forces detained government opponents incommunicado under harsh conditions for an indeterminate time with no supervision by the courts or other independent authorities with power to release the detainees. Their use has likely declined due to the increased control of the NIF regime, which decreased the need to intimidate opposition groups. The west wing of Khartoum's main Kober prison remains under the supervision of the security services. It was removed from prison services' control in 1995. While other prison wardens are accountable to courts of law for abuses they perpetrate, security forces are not. Despite the widespread use of torture, the Government has never publicly disciplined any security official for employing it.

The 1991 Criminal Act, based on an interpretation of Shari'a law, prescribes specific "hudud" punishments, including amputation, stoning, and lashing for some offenses. The courts continued their informal suspension of the amputation and stoning penalties and did not impose sentences involving them during the year. The courts routinely meted out lashings, most often to persons convicted of brewing or consuming alcohol. Two U.S. citizens of ethnic Sudanese origin were lashed in early 1996.

Conditions in government prisons remain harsh, but not life threatening. Built before Sudan's 1956 independence, most prisons are poorly maintained, and many lack basic facilities such as toilets or showers. Health care is primitive and food inadequate. Minors are often held with adults. Female prisoners are housed separately from men; rape in prison is reportedly rare. Prison officials arbitrarily denied family visits. While there are currently no independent Sudanese human rights organizations, international human rights officials have visited prisons in the past.

There are credible reports of beatings and other punishment of prisoners, often by SPLA and SSIA rebels, but the only verifications have been reports by ICRC and others who have been to SPLM prisoner of war camps. The SPLM allows the ICRC to visit battlefield prisoners, except those accused of treason or other crimes. The SSIM permits no such visits.

d. *Arbitrary Arrest, Detention, or Exile.*—Legal provisions under the 1992 and 1995 National Security Acts and Criminal Code effectively set a fairly simple process to detain anyone for 3 months, with presidential determination, backed by a magistrate, available to detain for an additional 3 months. In July the authorities moved to charge and court martial a number of persons accused following a March coup attempt. Allegations continue that some individuals are detained indefinitely.

The law allows for bail, except for those accused of crimes punishable by death or life imprisonment. In theory, the Government provides legal counsel for indigent persons in such cases. However, reports continue that defendants do not always receive this right, and that counsel in some cases may only advise the defendant and may not address the court.

Authorities continued to detain political opponents of the Government during the year. In the wake of antigovernment demonstrations, especially by students, authorities arrested many individuals. A number of medical personnel were detained following protests and a confrontation with public order personnel at Khartoum hospital. A notable incident of harassment was the arrest and brief detention of former vice president Abel Alier, who refused to be turned away from attending a gathering at former prime minister Sadiq Al-Mahdi's residence. Mr. Alier later publicly described degrading treatment that he received from security forces.

In August a military officer of the SPLA in charge at Akot detained six missionaries without charge for 12 days, contravening the SPLM's April resolution that "no person shall be held in incommunicado detention without charge or trial." During the detention, the SPLM military officers refused to accede to the demand of the SPLM civil authority "commissioner" for that county, who demanded the missionaries' release, calling into serious question the powers of that civil authority. The six were released only when the more powerful SPLA authorities intervened. By year's end, an investigation had been organized by the SPLM and the new Sudan Council for Churches, but no action had been taken against the perpetrators.

e. *Denial of Fair Public Trial.*—The judiciary is not independent and is largely subservient to the Government. The Chief Justice of the Supreme Court, formerly elected by sitting judges, is now appointed. As the senior judge in the judicial service, he also controls the judiciary.

The judicial system includes four types of courts: Regular courts, both criminal and civil; special mixed security courts; military courts; and tribal courts in rural areas to resolve disputes over land and water rights and family matters.

The 1991 Criminal Act governs criminal cases, whereas the 1983 Civil Transactions Act still applies to most civil cases. Military trials, which are sometimes secret and brief, do not provide procedural safeguards, have sometimes taken place with no advocate nor counsel permitted, and no effective appeal from a death sentence. Other than for clemency, witnesses may be permitted.

Trials in regular courts nominally meet international standards of legal protections. For example, the accused normally have the right to counsel, and the courts are required to provide free legal counsel for indigent defendants accused of crimes punishable by death or life imprisonment. In practice, however, these legal protections are unevenly applied.

In 1989 the Special Courts Act created special three-person security courts to deal with a wide range of offenses, including violations of constitutional decrees, emergency regulations, some sections of the penal code, as well as drug and currency offenses. Special courts, on which both military and civilian judges sit, handle most security related cases.

Attorneys may advise defendants as "friends of the court" but normally may not address the court. Lawyers complain that they are sometimes granted access to court documents too late to prepare an effective defense. Sentences are usually severe and implemented at once. Death sentences, however, are referred to the Chief Justice and the Head of State. Defendants may file appellate briefs with the Chief Justice.

The RCC dissolved the respected Sudanese Bar Association in 1989 and reinstated it with an NIF-controlled leadership. Lawyers who wish to practice in Sudan must maintain membership in the Bar Association. Human rights monitors report that the Government continued to harass, detain, and torture members of the legal profession whom it viewed as political opponents.

The Government officially exempts the 10 southern states, whose population is mostly non-Muslim, from parts of the Criminal Act. However, the Act permits the possible future application of Shari'a law in the south, if the state assemblies so decide. There were no reports that hudud punishments, other than lashings, were carried out by the courts in government-controlled areas of the south. Fear of the imposition of Shari'a law remained a key issue in the rebellion.

Parts of the south and the Nuba Mountains fell outside effective judicial procedures and other governmental functions. According to credible reports, government units summarily tried and punished those accused of crimes, especially for offenses against civil order.

In July the Government brought to military court 31 persons alleged to have plotted a coup in March. The Commander-in-Chief, President Bashir, asked that the Attorney General approve, under the relevant provision of law, that 10 of the civilians accused be tried in the military court. The Attorney General so approved. The trial continued at year's end.

Magistrates in SPLM-held areas follow a penal code roughly based on the 1925 Sudan code. In rural areas outside effective SPLM control, tribal chiefs apply customary laws. The SPLM proclaimed a civilian structure to eliminate the secret and essentially political trials conducted by military commanders in previous years, but at year's end there was no evidence to indicate that any such civilian trials had been held.

The Government maintains that it holds no political prisoners, although credible reports persist that the Government holds several political detainees (see Section 1.d.).

f. *Arbitrary Interference With Privacy, Family, Home, or Correspondence.*—The Government routinely interferes with its citizens' privacy. Security forces frequently conducted night searches without warrants. They targeted persons suspected of political crimes or, in northern Sudan, of distilling or consuming illegal alcoholic beverages. The Government razed the homes of thousands of squatters (see Section 2.d.).

A wide network of government informants conducted pervasive surveillance in schools, universities, markets, workplaces, and neighborhoods. The Government disbanded political parties and prevented citizens from forming new political groups. The Government continued to summarily dismiss military personnel and other government employees whose loyalty was suspect. The government committee set up in August 1995 to review cases of persons summarily dismissed since the 1989 coup continued to function. In May the government press reported that 124 government employees laid off after the coup had been reinstated and, on the recommendation of the committee, the President improved the pension status of 582 others. This action followed the reinstatement of 63 government employees in February.

Security personnel routinely opened and read mail and monitored telephones. The Government continued to restrict ownership of satellite dishes by private citizens by enforcement of its licensing requirement.

A Muslim man may marry a non-Muslim, but a Muslim woman cannot marry a non-Muslim, unless he converts to Islam. However, this prohibition is not universally observed, particularly in the south and among Nubians. Non-Muslims may only adopt non-Muslim children; no such restrictions apply to Muslims.

Various government bodies have decreed on different occasions that women must dress according to modest Islamic standards (see Section 5.).

A wide variety of Arabic and English publications are available, but they are subject to censorship.

Government-instituted neighborhood "popular committees"—ostensibly a mechanism for political mobilization—served as a means for monitoring households' activities. These committees caused many citizens to be wary of neighbors who could report them for "suspicious" activities, including "excessive" contact with foreigners. The committees also furnished or withheld documents essential for obtaining an exit visa. In high schools, students were sometimes pressured to join pro-regime youth groups.

Both the Government and rebel factions continued to forcibly conscript citizens (see Section 6.c.).

The insurgent SPLM is not known to interfere with privacy, family, home or correspondence in areas it controls, although correspondence is difficult in war zones.

g. *Use of Excessive Force and Violations of Humanitarian Law in Internal Conflicts.*—Since the civil war resumed in 1983, more than 1.5 million people have been killed as a result of fighting between the Government and insurgents in the south. The civil war continued unabated, and all sides involved in the fighting were responsible for abuses in violation of humanitarian norms. At year's end, the Government controlled virtually all the northern two-thirds of the country and some areas of the southern third. Insurgents operating under the National Democratic Alliance began small scale activities along the Ethiopian and Eritrean border areas in January. Government aircraft and helicopter gun ships bombed or attacked civilian areas at Kotobi, Tambura, and Maridi, and other places in the south.

Government forces routinely killed rebel soldiers captured on the battlefield. Only a small group of prisoners captured before the 1989 coup are reported being held as prisoners of war in government-controlled areas. These persons are held in Juba and have been visited by the ICRC.

The Government did not detain nongovernmental organization (NGO) workers in areas captured by its forces; however, government restrictions in practice limited or denied travel by relief NGO's to many areas long controlled by insurgents.

Rape of women is committed by both parties to the conflict in the south.

Both sides routinely displaced and often killed civilians or destroyed clinics and dwellings intentionally during their offensive operations. Insurgent forces along the Eritrean border laid land mines which caused casualties to civilian travelers as well as to military forces.

Northern Muslim opposition groups under the 1995 "National Democratic Alliance" (NDA) umbrella structure, which includes the SPLA, took military action against the Government. The NDA claimed to have attacked government garrisons and strategic points near the Ethiopian and Eritrean borders. They also indiscriminately laid land mines on roads and paths, which killed and maimed both soldiers and civilians.

The SPLM has taken a number of prisoners over the years, many during its offensive from October to December 1995. The ICRC has publicly confirmed that it regularly visits more than 300 such detainees, but was refused permission to visit SPLA criminal and civil prisoners. The SPLM has returned some prisoners of war to the Government under parole.

Rhetoric and meetings to advance a dialog for peace continued during the year. In May meetings under UNESCO's "Culture of Peace" effort took place in the Netherlands, following the initial meeting of September 1995. Government and rebel representatives participated.

An unrelated government effort with splinter SSIM leader Riak Machar resulted in the signature of a "political charter" in April, which gained a few more signatures of figures previously associated with Riak's faction or dissidents from the SPLM.

The SPLM and NDA did not sign and remain suspicious that the political charter is a trick by the Government to forestall negotiations.

Section 2. *Respect for Civil Liberties, Including:*

a. *Freedom of Speech and Press.*—The Government severely curtails freedom of speech and press. Government intimidation and surveillance, fostered in part by an informer network, continued to inhibit open, public discussion of political issues. Radio, television, and much of the print media are controlled directly by the Government and are required to reflect government and NIF policies. However, some lively discussions of domestic and foreign policy do take place in the press. All journalists, even in the privately owned Arabic daily press, practice self-censorship. Sudan Television has a permanent military censor to ensure that the news reflects official views.

Of the four privately-owned daily newspapers operating in October, Akhbar Al-Youm followed a careful line and did not encounter any problems. The Government closed Al-Rai Al-Akher in July for publishing articles "harming the National security and social stability," and tried to cancel the publishing license of Dar Al-Ahlia publishing house as well. The owners sued the authorities over the issue. No judgment has yet been rendered. A new Press Law came into effect in November. Under its provisions, actions such as those taken by Al-Rai Al-Akher are not possible. Three new daily newspapers regarded as pro-NIF were launched.

The Government often charged that the international, and particularly the Western, media have an anti-Sudan and anti-Islam bias. Government press policy eased during the year, and the Government granted a number of foreign journalists visas to report on the March elections. Rebel movements have provided relatively few opportunities for journalists to report on their activities.

In spite of the restrictions on ownership of satellite dishes, citizens do have access to foreign electronic media. Foreign radio signals are not jammed. In addition to its own domestic and satellite television services, Sudan Television offers a pay cable network of six channels, which directly rebroadcasts uncensored Cable News Network (CNN), the London-based, Saudi-owned, Middle East Broadcasting Corporation (MBC), Dubai TV, and Kuwait TV.

Academic debate includes a vigorous campus polemic with pro-NIF and antigovernment sentiments prominently displayed and heard. NIF students have tried to influence the outcome of student government elections, and burned the offices of the head of a private university who had approved student elections which brought a pro-NDA slate to power. The Minister of Higher Education temporarily closed the University due to subsequent death threats against the university official. The government security forces continued to arrest and detain academic staff linked with opposition parties. The Government continued to use political criteria whenever possible in appointing new faculty members.

b. *Freedom of Peaceful Assembly and Association.*—The authorities severely restricted these freedoms, permitting only Government-authorized gatherings. The declaration of the state of emergency and of martial law on June 30, 1989, effectively eliminated the right of assembly. Demonstrations occurred repeatedly throughout the year, organized by students, by other residents of Omduran unhappy at lack of water, and by those especially disaffected by skyrocketing prices. Police brutally suppressed all these demonstrations, arresting scores of protestors, and killing others. For example, in September demonstrators clashed with police in protests triggered by new government regulations on the weight of bread loaves. That prompted bakeries to shut down. In September police killed between 6 and 11 demonstrators and injured several others. Scores of protestors were arrested in the September riots. A government newspaper reported that 35 persons were sentenced to receive up to 20 lashes.

The Government dissolved all political parties in 1989, and prohibits citizens from forming new political groups or other associations. In 1989 the Government dissolved the Bar Association and reinstated it under NIF leadership with highly controlled elections. All lawyers who wish to practice in Sudan must maintain membership in the organization (see Section 1.e.).

c. *Freedom of Religion.*—Although the Government has stated that all religions should be respected and that freedom of worship is ensured, in practice the Government treats Islam as the state religion and has declared that Islam must inspire the country's laws, institutions, and policies. The October 1994 Societies Registration Act replaced the controversial Missionary Societies Act of 1962. It theoretically allows churches to engage in a wider range of activities than did the Missionary Act, but churches are subject to the restrictions placed on nonreligious corporations. The Government permits non-Muslims to partcipate in services in existing and otherwise authorized places of worship. The Government continued to deny permission to build churches. In December the Papal Nuncio detailed the continuing government policy to deny permits to build churches; since independence, only one Roman Catholic church has been built. Some makeshift structures have been permitted. While non-Muslims may convert to Islam, the 1991 Criminal Act makes apostasy (which includes conversion to another religion) by Muslims punishable by death.

Authorities continued to restrict the activities of non-Muslims, and there continued to be reports of harassment and arrest for religious beliefs and activities. There were reports that three Muslim Nubian women and a Christian clergyman were arrested after the clergyman converted the women to Christianity. The women were later released without charge.

Muslims may proselytize freely, but non-Muslims are forbidden to proselytize. Foreign missionaries and religiously oriented organizations continued to be harassed by authorities, and their requests for work permits and residence visas are delayed.

Children, regardless of presumed religious origin, who have been abandoned or whose parentage is unknown, are considered Muslims and can only be adopted by Muslims. Non-Muslims may adopt other non-Muslim children. No equivalent restriction is placed on adoption by Muslims. Foundlings or other abandoned children are considered by the State to be Sudanese citizens and Muslims and therefore can only be adopted by Muslims. In accordance with Islamic law, Muslim adoptees do not take the name of their adoptive parents and are not automatic heirs to their property.

Popular Defense Force (PDF) trainees, including non-Muslims, are indoctrinated in the Islamic faith. In prisons, Government-supported Islamic NGO's offer inducements to, and pressure on, non-Muslim inmates to convert. Islamic NGO's in war zones are reliably reported to withhold food and other services from the needy unless they convert to Islam. Children, including non-Muslim children, in camps for vagrant minors are required to study the Koran (see Section 5).

In rebel-controlled areas, Christians, Muslims, and followers of traditional African beliefs generally worship freely.

d. *Freedom of Movement Within the Country, Foreign Travel, Emigration, and Repatriation.*—The Government restricted freedom of movement by denying exit visas to some categories of persons, including policemen and doctors. The Government also kept lists of political figures and other citizens not permitted to travel abroad. Because of tensions with Egypt, the authorities denied many requests for travel to that country.

Women may not travel abroad without the permission of their husbands or male guardians. Some former political detainees were forbidden to travel outside Khartoum. Movement was generally free for other citizens outside the war zones, but those who failed to produce an identity card at checkpoints risked arrest. Foreigners needed permits, which were difficult to obtain and often refused, for domestic travel outside of Khartoum. Foreign diplomats, however, could travel to many locations under government escort. Foreigners had to register with the police on entering the country, seek permission to move from one location to another, and reregister at each new location within 3 days of arrival. Foreign NGO staff sometimes had problems obtaining entry visas or work or travel permits once they had entered the country.

Insurgent movements also required that foreign NGO personnel obtain permission before traveling to areas that they control, although such permission was granted regularly.

Tens of thousands of persons, largely southerners and westerners displaced by famine and civil war, continued to live in squatter slums in the Khartoum area. Throughout 1996 the Government razed thousands of squatter dwellings in this area; inhabitants knew that their homes were slated for destruction, but not when it would occur. Bulldozers would typically arrive unannounced in a neighborhood and carry out the razing the same day. Although the Government promised to sell the inhabitants a plot of land for approximately $145, tens of thousands were made homeless temporarily. Usually, the inhabitants established temporary shelters on the site of their razed dwellings until they could gain title to a plot of land. Muslims who did not have sufficient money to purchase the land and construct a dwelling could obtain assistance from Islamic charities; others could not.

The Government cooperated with the U.N. High Commissioner for Refugees (UNHCR) and other humanitarian assistance organizations and accorded refugees relatively good treatment. It provided first asylum, although no figures are available for 1996. In April a UNHCR census revealed a total refugee population of 139,874, of whom an estimated 124,000 were Eritreans, in camp for many years. In December the Government, together with the government of Eritrea, agreed to begin discussion of repatriation of Eritrean refugees in a technical committee which would include the UNHCR. Approximately 28,000 Ethiopians repatriated early in the year, leaving about 15,000 in camps. Many refugees, including an estimated 26,000 Eritreans, live in villages and towns in Sudan. There were no reports of forcible repatriation of refugees, regardless of their status. Some reports cited mistreatment of refugees, including beatings and arbitrary arrests. Refugees could not become resident aliens or citizens, regardless of their length of stay. The Government allowed a large number of refugees to work. An estimated 600,000 Sudanese refugees, including 230,000 in camps, remained in Uganda, as a result of fighting between the Government and insurgents. Refugees flowed from Sudan to Ethiopia, Eritrea, and Kenya.

Section 3. Respect for Political Rights: The Right of Citizens to Change Their Government

Citizens had no genuine opportunity to change their government peacefully through the March elections. The elections were structured in a way that ensured that the NIF would retain control of the government and that its vision of national institutions, including ultimately a new constitution, would prevail.

In June, 10 leading political figures sent a memorandum to President Bashir, addressing him merely as "Commander-in-Chief," which criticized the NIF and cited various NDA documents and resolutions. They urged that the "ruling authority" resign in favor of an interim administration. International human rights organizations reported that a number of political opponents of the Government (none signatory to the memorandum) were detained following release of the memorandum.

In 1989 the RCC abolished all political parties and temporarily detained the major party leaders. In 1990 the RCC rejected both multiparty and one party systems, establishing 2 years later an entirely Government-appointed Transitional National Assembly, based on a Libyan-style political structure with ascending levels of nonpartisan assemblies. The essentially powerless appointed legislature was replaced following the March elections by an elected National Assembly, in which 125 of its 400 members were appointed from the National Convention. Opposition parties boycotted the election.

The federal system of government was instituted in August 1995, and is slowly developing a structure of 26 states, which the Government sees as a possible inducement to the insurgents for accommodation through a principle of regional autonomy.

Women are underrepresented in government and politics. There is one woman in the Cabinet, the Minister of Health. Women have the right to vote, and seats in the National Assembly are set aside for representatives of women's organizations and for female student representatives. There are 25 women in the National Assembly.

Section 4. Governmental Attitude Regarding International and Nongovernmental Investigation of Alleged Violations of Human Rights

The Government began to implement international conventions and basic human rights practices. Previously it had vigorously sought to suppress domestic criticism on human rights issues. During the year, it resolved serious differences with U.N. Special Rapporteur Gaspar Biro, who visited in July. The Government also received the Rapporteur of the Committee on Religious Intolerance and invited the Rapporteur of the Committee on Freedom of Expression.

Sudan's Human Rights Advisory Council, a government body whose rapporteur is the Solicitor General for Public Law, has taken an increasing role in addressing human rights issues within the Government. There are no human rights NGO's; however, individual human rights activists operate in anonymity.

Section 5. Discrimination Based on Race, Sex, Religion, Disability, Language, or Social Status

A governmental decree prohibits discrimination based on religion or sex. Redress is provided through the administrative courts or the Labor Office. The 1992 General Education Act stipulates equal opportunity in education for the disabled. Mechanisms for social redress, especially with respect to violence against women and children, are particularly weak.

Women.—Violence against women continues to be a problem, although accurate statistics on violence against women do not exist. Many women are reluctant to file formal complaints against such abuse, although domestic violence is a legal ground for divorce. The police do not normally intervene in domestic disputes. Displaced women from the south were particularly vulnerable to harassment, rape, and sexual abuse. The Government did not address the problem of violence against women, nor was it discussed publicly.

Some aspects of the law and many traditional practices discriminate against women. Gender segregation is common in social settings. In keeping with Islamic law, a Muslim woman has the right to hold and dispose of her own property without interference. Women are ensured inheritance from their parents. However, a daughter inherits half the share of a son, and a widow inherits a smaller percent. It is much easier for men to initiate legal divorce proceedings than for women. These rules apply only to Muslims and not to those of other faiths, for whom religious or tribal law apply. Although a Muslim man may marry a non-Muslim, a Muslim woman cannot marry a non-Muslim unless he converts to Islam. Women cannot travel abroad without the permission of their husbands or male guardians (see Section 2.d.).

A number of government directives require that women in public places and government offices, and female students and teachers conform to what it deemed an Islamic dress code. This, at the least, entailed wearing a head covering. However, enforcement of the dress code regulations was uneven.

Credible but unconfirmed reports continued that women held in special camps in the south were sold to northerners to work as domestic servants (see Section 6.c.).

Children.—A considerable number of children suffered serious abuse, including enslavement and forced conscription in the war zones. There continued to be credible but unconfirmed reports of the existence of special camps in the south in which people from the north or from abroad came to purchase women and children for work as domestic servants (see Section 6.c.).

The Government forcibly conscripted young men and boys into the military forces, as did the insurgents. In the late 1980's, the SPLM forcibly recruited an estimated 17,000 boys between the ages of 12 and 15 years for military duty; it trained them in camps that it operated in Ethiopia. These recruits were kept separated from other SPLM forces until the SPLM was expelled from Ethiopia in 1991; thereafter, approximately 10,000 traveled with the SPLM forces until they either reached the Kenyan refugee camp at Kakuma, settled in other areas controlled by the SPLM, or were absorbed into regular SPLM military units. In September the SPLM and U.N. children's agency, UNICEF, repatriated more than 160 boys to their parents, perhaps the last group that has not since come of legal military age.

The Government has operated camps for vagrant children. Police periodically sweep the streets of Khartoum and other major cities, taking children whom police personnel deem homeless to these camps where they are detained for indefinite periods. Until recently, these children were not allowed to leave the camps and are subjected to strict discipline and physical and military training. Health care and schooling at the camps are generally poor; basic living conditions are often primitive. All the children, including non-Muslims, must study the Koran, and there is pressure on non-Muslims to convert to Islam. Teenagers in the camps are often conscripted into the PDF.

Female genital mutilation (FGM), which is widely condemned by international health experts as damaging to both physical and psychological health, is widespread, especially in the north. It is estimated that as many as 90 percent or more of females in the north have been subjected to FGM, with consequences that sometimes have included severe urinary problems, infections, and even death. Infibulation, the severest type of FGM, is the most common and is usually performed on girls between ages 4 and 7. It is often performed by traditional practitioners in improvised, unsanitary conditions, causing severe pain and trauma to the child. No form of FGM is illegal under the Criminal Code. However, the health law forbids doctors and midwives from practicing its severest form, Pharaonic circumcision or infibulation. Women displaced from the south to the north reportedly are increasingly imposing FGM upon their daughters, even if they themselves have not been subjected to it. The Government has neither arrested nor prosecuted any persons for violating the health law against FGM.

Two NGO's with funding from the U.N. and a government agency are actively involved in eradication of FGM, which they describe as a "harmful practice." A small but growing number of urban, educated families are completely abandoning the practice. A larger number of families, in a compromise with tradition, have adopted the least severe form of FGM as an alternative to infibulation.

People With Disabilities.—The Government does not discriminate against disabled persons but has not enacted any special legislation or taken other steps, such as mandating accessibility to public buildings and transportation for the disabled. The 1992 General Education Act requires equal educational opportunities for the disabled.

Religious Minorities.—Although the law recognizes Sudan as a multireligious country, in practice, the Government treats Islam, the religion of the majority, as the state religion. Muslims predominate in the north, but are in the minority in the south where most people practice Christianity or traditional African religions. One to two million displaced southerners who practice Christianity or traditional African religions and about 500,000 Coptic Christians live in the north.

In Government-controlled areas of the south, there continued to be credible evidence of a policy of Islamization of public institutions. Some non-Muslims lost their jobs in the civil service, the judiciary, and other professions. Few non-Muslim university graduates found government jobs. Some non-Muslim businessmen complained of petty harassment and discrimination in the awarding of government contracts and trade licenses. There were also reports that Muslims receive preferential treatment for the limited services provided by the Government, including access to medical care.

National/Racial/Ethnic Minorities.—Sudan's population of 27.5 million is a multiethnic mix of over 500 Arab and African tribes with scores of languages and dialects. The Arab, Muslim culture in the north and central areas and the non-Muslim, African culture in the south are the two dominant cultures. Northern Muslims, who form a majority of about 16 million, have traditionally dominated the government. The southern ethnic groups fighting the civil war (largely followers of traditional African religions or Christians) seek independence, or some form of regional self-determination, from the north.

The Muslim majority and NIF-dominated Government continued to discriminate against ethnic minorities in almost every aspect of society. Citizens in Arabic-speaking areas who do not speak Arabic experienced discrimination in education, employment, and other areas. The use of Arabic as the medium of instruction in higher education discriminated against non-Arabs. For university admission, students completing high school are required to pass examinations in four subjects: English; Mathematics; Arabic; and Religious Studies. Even at the university level, examinations in all subjects except English were in Arabic, placing non-native speakers of Arabic at a disadvantage.

Section 6. Worker Rights

a. *The Right of Association.*—Although there was a strong labor union movement during the government of Sadiq Al-Mahdi, the RCC abolished the precoup labor unions, closed union offices, froze union assets, forbade strikes, and prescribed severe punishments, including the death penalty, for violations of RCC labor decrees. The Government dismissed many labor leaders from their jobs or detained them, although most of those arrested were later freed.

The Sudan Workers Trade Unions Federation is the leading blue-collar labor organization with about 800,000 members. In 1992 local union elections were held, after a delay to permit the government-controlled steering committees to arrange the outcomes. The elections resulted in government-approved slates of candidates voted into office by prearranged acclamation.

The U.S. Government in 1991 suspended Sudan's eligibility for trade benefits under the generalized system of preferences because of its violations of worker rights.

Unions remained free to form federations and affiliate with international bodies, such as the African Workers' Union and the Arab Workers' Union.

b. *The Right to Organize and Bargain Collectively.*—A 1989 RCC constitutional decree temporarily suspended the right to organize and bargain collectively. Although these rights were restored to labor organizing committees in September, government control of the steering committees meant in practice that the Government dominates the process of setting wages and working conditions. The continued absence of labor legislation allowing for union meetings, filing of grievances, and other union activity greatly reduced the value of these formal rights. Although local union officials raised some grievances with employers, few carried them to the Government. Wages are set by a tripartite committee comprising representatives of the Government, labor unions, and business. Specialized labor courts adjudicate standard labor disputes.

In 1993 the Government created two export processing zones (EPZ's); it later established a third at Khartoum International Airport. At year's end, only the EPZ at Khartoum International Airport was open. The labor laws do not apply in EPZ's.

c. *Prohibition of Forced or Compulsory Labor.*—Although the law prohibits forced or compulsory labor, slavery persists. According to the report by the U.N. Special Rapporteur, reports and information from a variety of sources after February 1994 indicate that the number of cases of slavery, servitude, slave trade, and forced labor have increased alarmingly. The taking of slaves, particularly in war zones and their export to parts of central and northern Sudan continued. There also continued to be credible, but unconfirmed, reports that women and children were sold and sent to the north or abroad to work as domestic servants, agricultural laborers, and sometimes concubines. The Government has not taken any action to halt these practices. In May two reporters from The Baltimore Sun, a U.S. newspaper, bought two children in an alleged slave market; the children were returned to their parents by the reporters. Others, such as representatives of Christian Solidarity International, have also confirmed the practice of slavery by arranging the purchase of children. The average price per child is reportedly about $300 worth of cattle; the price is $500 if the purchaser is a Westerner.

Reliable reports indicate the direct and general involvement of the SPAF, the PDF, and armed militias, backed by the Government, in the abduction and deportation of civilians from the conflict zones to the north. These practices all have a pronounced racial aspect, as the victims are exclusively black southerners and people belonging to the indigenous tribes of the Nuba mountains.

In some instances, local authorities took action to stop slavery; in other cases the authorities did nothing to stop the practice. In response to a resolution of the 1995 U.N. General Assembly, the Government in May established a committee to investigate charges of slavery. This committee submitted a report to the Government, which was communicated to the U.N. General Assembly.

Both the Government and rebel factions continued to use force to conscript men of military age into the fighting forces. For example, in February a group of national service trainees were unexpectedly taken to Khartoum and flown to Juba, where they were expected to serve in combat. Conscripts face significant hardship and abuse in military service. The rebel factions continued to force southern men to work as laborers or porters.

d. *Minimum Age for Employment of Children.*—The legal minimum age for workers is 16 years, but the law is loosely enforced by inspectors from the Ministry of Labor and in the official or wage economy. Children as young as 11 or 12 years of age worked in a number of factories, particularly outside the capital, including the edible oil factories at Um Ruwaba. In addition, severe poverty has produced widespread child labor in the informal, unregulated economy. In rural areas, children traditionally assist their families with agricultural work from a very young age.

e. *Acceptable Conditions of Work.*—The legislated minimum wage is enforced by the Ministry of Labor, which maintains field offices in most major cities. Employers generally respect the minimum wage. Workers who are denied the minimum wage may file a grievance with the local Ministry of Labor field office, which is then required to investigate and take appropriate action if there has been a violation of the law. At year's end, a new minimum wage of approximately $10 (15,000 Sudanese pounds) per month had been approved but not implemented. This wage is insufficient to provide a decent standard living for an average worker and family. The workweek is limited by law to six 8-hour days, with a day of rest on Friday. Although the laws prescribe health and safety standards, working conditions were generally poor, and enforcement by the Ministry of Labor minimal. The law does not address the right of workers to remove themselves from dangerous work situations without loss of employment.

SWAZILAND

Swaziland is governed as a modified traditional monarchy with executive, legislative, and (with some limitations) judicial powers ultimately vested in the King (presently Mswati III). The King rules according to unwritten Swazi law and custom, in conjunction with an elected parliament and an accompanying structure of published laws, implementing agencies, and an independent judiciary. Despite the 1993 parliamentary elections, the election of regional and local councils in 1994, and municipal elections in 1995, political power continues to rest largely with the King and his circle of traditional advisers. The 1968 Constitution was suspended by the present King's father in 1973; however, there were demands that the suspension be lifted. Based upon the 1973 suspension, the King has the authority to issue decrees that carry the force of law (although he did not exercise this authority in 1996). In April the King formally announced a constitutional initiative, involving a review of the suspended 1968 Constitution and the establishment of a constitutional commission to draft a new constitution. Members of the Constitutional Review Commission were announced in late July, and it met in September. The Commission has 2 years to complete its report.

Both the Umbutfo Swaziland Defense Force and the Royal Swaziland Police operate under civilian control and are responsible for external and internal security. The police harassed and arrested political activists from prohibited political organizations. Some members of the police use excessive force and abuse in the interrogation of criminal suspects.

Swaziland has a free market economy, with relatively little government intervention. The majority of Swazis are engaged in subsistence agriculture, although a relatively diversified industrial sector now accounts for the largest component of the formal economy. The economy relies heavily on the export sector, especially the soft drink concentrate, sugar, and wood pulp industries, which are composed primarily of large firms with predominantly foreign ownership. A governmental organization maintains large investments in all major sectors of the economy, including industry, agriculture, and services.

There was little change in the overall human rights situation. Despite the constitutional initiative, citizens are still not able to change their Government. The Government restricted freedom of speech and assembly and continued prohibitions on political activity. The media practiced self-censorship. A journalist from the government newspaper, members of political groupings, and labor union leaders were detained or arrested. Some members of the police continued to use physical abuse and excessive force, especially during the interrogation of suspects, and the authorities rarely punished those who committed such acts. The Government's use of a nonbailable offense provision, strengthened by act of Parliament in 1994, continued to cause overcrowding in detention facilities. Prison conditions are poor. The Government adopted revised industrial relations legislation, containing draconian penalties for various violations of the law, which both unions and organized business rejected. Legal and cultural discrimination and violence against women, as well as abuse of children, remained problems.

RESPECT FOR HUMAN RIGHTS

Section 1. Respect for the Integrity of the Person, Including Freedom From:

a. *Political and Other Extrajudicial Killing.*—At the height of the January mass labor action, police shot and killed a female protestor in Manzini.

b. *Disappearance.*—There were no reports of politically motivated disappearances.

c. *Torture and Other Cruel, Inhuman, or Degrading Treatment or Punishment.*—There were credible reports by criminal defendants of the use of torture during interrogation. A number of defendants accused police of employing the "tube" style of interrogation, in which police suffocate suspects through use of a rubber tube around the face and mouth. Police routinely beat criminal suspects in the course of interrogations. The Government failed to prosecute or otherwise discipline police officers for such abuses. Courts did, however, throw out confessions induced through such physical abuse.

In January police used excessive force in breaking up a protest by street vendors, injuring scores of people (see Section 2.b.). In the same month police and army units assaulted students attempting to hold a meeting (see Section 2.b.). In October police detained over 20 students protesting in Big Bend, beat them, and threatened them with prosecution and the loss of scholarships.

Prison conditions are poor. Food is generally adequate, although sometimes family members must bring food to supplement the sparse prison diet. Medical care is inadequate. Use of the nonbail provision led to continued overcrowding in government remand centers, where suspects are held during pretrial detention (see Section 1.d.). Women and juveniles are held in separate prison facilities. The Government permits prison visits by human rights monitors.

d. *Arbitrary Arrest, Detention, or Exile.*—The law requires warrants for arrests in most circumstances, except when police observe a crime being committed or have reason to believe that a suspect will flee. Detainees may consult with a lawyer of their choice and must be charged with violation of a statute within a reasonable time, usually 48 hours, or, in remote areas, as soon as the judicial officer appears. The authorities generally respect these rights in practice.

The Government continued to limit provisions for bail for crimes appearing in the Nonbailable Offenses Order, effective August 24, 1993. The Minister of Justice may amend the list, which currently has 10 offenses, by his own executive act. An 11th offense, involving narcotics, is reportedly in the preparation stage, because of growing concern regarding drug use and drug dealers. The mere charge of the underlying offense, without any evidentiary showing that the suspect is involved, is sufficient to employ the nonbail provision.

Overcrowding, poor diet, and delays in bringing cases to court led to a brief hunger strike by criminal detainees in February protesting their continuing detention without trial.

In January police detained a journalist for the government newspaper for photographing police assaulting street vendors (see Section 2.a.).

In January the Government arrested and held incommunicado three labor leaders during the nationwide mass stay away conducted by the Swaziland Federation of Trade Unions (see Section 6.a.). The unionists were charged with inciting public violence under the Public Order Act, a nonbailable offense (see Section 6.a.). The leaders were released after 3 days' detention; all charges were dropped. In March the Government charged the three men with various offenses under the Industrial Relations Act for alleged illegal acts stemming from the same mass stay away. The case was subsequently postponed indefinitely by the High Court.

The Government does not use forced exile. There are no formal barriers to prevent the return of dissidents.

e. *Denial of Fair Public Trial.*—The judiciary is independent; however the King has certain judicial powers. Judicial powers are vested in a dual system, one independent and based on Western law, the other based on a system of national courts that follows unwritten traditional law and custom. In treason and sedition cases, the King can circumvent the regular judiciary by appointing a special tribunal, which may adopt rules and procedures different from those applied in the High Court. However, this power was last used in 1987.

The modern judiciary consists of the Court of Appeals, (composed entirely of expatriate, usually South African, judges), the High Court, and magistrates' courts, all of which are independent of executive and military control and free from intimidation from outside forces. The expatriate judges, often distinguished members of their respective bars, serve on the basis of 2-year, renewable contracts. Local judges serve indefinitely on good behavior. In magistrates' courts, the defendant is entitled to counsel at his or her own expense. Court-appointed counsel is provided in capital cases or when difficult points of law are at issue. There are well-defined appeal procedures up to the Court of Appeals, the highest judicial body.

Most Swazis who encounter the legal system do so through the traditional courts. The authorities may bring ethnic Swazis to these courts for relatively minor offenses and violations of traditional law and custom. In traditional courts, defendants are not permitted formal legal counsel but may speak on their own behalf and be assisted by informal advisers. Sentences are subject to review by traditional authorities and to appeal to the High Court and the Court of Appeals. By law the public prosecutor has the authority to determine which court should hear a case, but in practice the police usually make the determination. Accused persons have the right to transfer their cases from the traditional courts. Delays in trials are common.

The court has delayed the trial of 49 members of the People's United Democracy Movement (PUDEMO) and its sister organization, the Swaziland Youth Congress (SWAYOCO), for nearly 2 years. They were arrested by police in late December 1994 when the two groups staged a public rally in Siteki. The 49 have been charged by the Government with holding a political meeting without a permit, possession of political pamphlets, and disturbing traffic. While the case remains pending, the defendants are free on bail but must report to the courtroom on a regular basis.

There were no reports of political prisoners.

f. *Arbitrary Interference With Privacy, Family, Home, or Correspondence.*—The law requires a warrant from a magistrate before police may search homes or other premises, and police generally respect this requirement in practice. However, police officers with the rank of subinspector or higher have the right to search without a warrant if they believe evidence might be lost through delay in obtaining a warrant. While searches without warrants occur occasionally, the issue of legality of evidence rarely arises in court.

Section 2. Respect for Civil Liberties, Including:

a. *Freedom of Speech and Press.*—Freedom of speech, especially on political matters, remains limited, including in the Parliament. The media, both government-controlled and private, practice self-censorship in regard to the immediate royal family and national security policy. In January police detained a photographer for the government newspaper for taking photographs of police assaulting street vendors during a protest in Manzini. The photographer was released the same day. In June the Minister of Broadcasting interrupted the evening news broadcast of the government television station and radio station and prevented the reading of news items concerning the ongoing labor turmoil in the country. The Government continued to refuse to grant the expatriate owner and publisher of the independent newspaper a renewal of his work permit, now pending for over 2 years. After publishing a report critical of the alleged financial dealings of the King, a senior editor of the independent newspaper was forced under pressure and alleged threats of arrest to issue a public apology.

Both government-owned and independent newspapers continued to treat a wide variety of sensitive topics and to criticize government corruption, inefficiency, and waste. The government-owned television and radio stations—the most influential media in reaching the public—generally followed official policy positions. Private companies and church groups own several newsletters, magazines, and one radio station that broadcasts throughout the region, but these avoid political controversy.

The practice of self-censorship and the prohibition of political gatherings limit academic freedom.

b. *Freedom of Peaceful Assembly and Association.*—King Sobhuza's 1973 decree prohibits political parties, as well as meetings of a political nature, processions, or demonstrations in any public place without the consent of the Commissioner of Police. The authorities did not generally grant permission to hold meetings but did not rigidly enforce the 1973 decree. Political organizations, including PUDEMO and SWAYOCO, often met without the required permission without repercussions. However, the threat of police intervention is pervasive, and on several occasions police harassed political and labor groups taking part in political activities, such as peaceful meetings, rallies, and demonstrations. Police in January broke up a protest march by street vendors in Manzini with baton charges, firing tear gas and live ammunition. Scores of people were injured, including two shot by police.

Also in January police and army units assaulted students with batons at the University of Swaziland when students attempted to hold a meeting concerning the ongoing nationwide strike by trade unions. A number of students were injured by police. In April a SWAYOCO activist was convicted of subversive activities and public violence for hauling down the Swazi flag during the nationwide union strike in January. The activist received a suspended sentence. In June police broke up another student meeting at a public park in Manzini, where the students were attempting to rally in favor of striking teachers. In September and October police and military personnel prevented a public meeting called by PUDEMO and the Swazi Democratic Alliance to discuss matters regarding the Constitutional Review Commission.

A revised Industrial Relations Act severely restricts the ability of trade union organizations to participate in the social and political affairs of the nation. The Act prohibits unions from striking or agitating over such issues (see Section 6.a.).

There was no progress in the case of the 49 members of PUDEMO and SWAYOCO who were arrested for staging a public rally in December 1994 (see Section 1.e.).

Several traditional forums exist for the expression of opinion, including community meetings, national councils, and direct dialog with village chiefs, but they often depend on the sufferance of leaders and are not effective channels for expressing real political dissent.

c. *Freedom of Religion.*—Followers of all religious faiths are free to worship without government interference or restriction.

d. *Freedom of Movement Within the Country, Foreign Travel, Emigration, and Repatriation.*—Swazis may travel and work freely within the country. However, under traditional law a married woman requires her husband's permission to apply for a passport for travel abroad, and unmarried women require the permission of a close male relative. A Citizenship Law passed in 1992 removed several ambiguities relating to Swazi citizenship and nominally enabled nonethnic Swazis to obtain passports and citizenship documents. Bureaucratic delays, however, plagued individuals seeking these documents during the year, in part due to the common perception that mixed race and white Swazis are not real Swazis. Mixed race citizens in particular are sometimes subject to unfair and discriminatory treatment.

The Government treats several thousand ethnic Swazis from the former homeland of KwaZulu in South Africa as virtually indistinguishable from local Swazis and routinely grants them travel and citizenship documents.

Swaziland's treatment of refugees is considered excellent by the United Nations High Commissioner for Refugees (UNHCR) as well as the various nongovernmental organizations (NGO's) involved in the care of these groups. The UNHCR officially registered several hundred refugees in Swaziland, the majority coming from east and central Africa. The issue of provision of first asylum has not arisen in recent years.

Section 3. Respect for Political Rights: The Right of Citizens to Change Their Government

Citizens are not able to exercise this right. The King retains ultimate executive and legislative authority, and political parties are prohibited. Passage of legislation by Parliament requires the King's assent to become law, which he is not obliged to give. When Parliament is not in session, the King may legislate by decree under his residual emergency powers. The King chooses the Prime Minister and, in consultation with the Prime Minister, the Cabinet, as well as many senior civil servants, and heads of government offices.

Pressure has been building to modernize the political system. In July the King chose the members of a Constitutional Review Commission, to examine the suspended 1968 Constitution, and begin work on a new document. However, the exact duties of the Commission remained unclear. The Commission has 2 years to complete its work.

Women have full legal rights to participate in the political process. There are 2 women in the 65-member House of Assembly, and 6 women hold seats in the 30-member Senate. There are no women in the Cabinet. Three women serve as principal secretaries, the most senior civil service rank in the ministries. There are women on the 30-person Constitutional Review Commission.

Section 4. Governmental Attitude Regarding International and Nongovernmental Investigation of Alleged Violations of Human Rights

The Government permits domestic human rights groups to operate. In 1996 two local human rights groups spoke out on human rights issues and served as mediators in land and labor disputes. The groups criticized the Government on a number of occasions, including the Government's handling of labor disputes, detention of labor leaders, and the lack of accountability and transparency in government circles. There were no visits by international human rights organizations.

Section 5. Discrimination Based on Race, Sex, Religion, Disability, Language, or Social Status

The 1968 Constitution remains suspended. However, the Employment Act of 1980 forbids employers to discriminate on the basis of race, religion, sex, or political affiliation. Under the act employees may bring suit against employers for discrimination, and there are also provisions for criminal prosecutions. However, there is no record of any suits or prosecutions. Reportedly, the act has been used on occasion to bring moral suasion to bear against employers. Mixed race citizens sometimes experience discrimination.

Women.—Violence against women, particularly wife beating, is frequent, despite traditional strictures against this practice. Women have the right to charge their husbands with assault under both the traditional and modern legal systems and frequently do so, usually in extreme cases when intervention by extended family members fails to end such violence. The traditional courts, however, can be unsympathetic to "unruly" or "disobedient" women and are less likely than the modern courts to convict men for wife beating. Rape is also a common crime and is regarded by many men as a minor offense. Even in the modern courts, sentences frequently amount to no more than several months in jail, a fine, or both. The Legal Code addresses legal protection from sexual harassment, but its provisions are vague and largely ineffective.

Several NGO's provide support to groups affected by discrimination or abuse, including the Swaziland Action Group Against Abuse, which has relations with other civic organizations as well as the Government. They provide forums to discuss spousal and child abuse and to educate the public on the rights of abuse victims.

Women have traditionally occupied a subordinate role in society, and the dualistic nature of the legal system complicates the issue of women's rights. As traditional marriage is governed by uncodified law and custom, women's rights are often unclear and change according to where and by whom they are interpreted. In both traditional and civil marriages, wives are legally treated as minors, although those who marry under civil law may be accorded the legal status of adults, if stipulated in a signed prenuptial agreement.

Changing socioeconomic conditions, urbanization, and the increasing prominence of female leaders in government and civic organizations are breaking down barriers to equality. Wives now routinely and successfully execute contracts and enter into a variety of transactions in their own names. Nevertheless, despite the 1980 Employment Act requiring equal pay for equal work, men's average wage rates by skill category usually exceed those of women. Moreover, a woman generally requires her husband's permission to borrow money, open a bank account, leave the country, gain access to land, or, in some cases, take a job. Unmarried women require a male relative's permission to obtain a passport (see Section 2.d.).

Traditional marriages consider children to belong to the father and to his family if the couple divorces. Children born out of wedlock are viewed as belonging to the mother. In traditional marriages, a man may take more than one wife. A man who marries a woman under civil law legally may not have more than one wife, although in practice this restriction is sometimes ignored. Under the Citizenship Act of 1992, a Swazi woman does not automatically pass citizenship to her children.

Couples often marry in both civil and traditional ceremonies, creating problems in determining which set of rules applies to the marriage and to subsequent questions of child custody and inheritance in the event of divorce or death.

The Government has committed itself to various women's initiatives in the wake of the 1995 Beijing Conference on Women, and the Ministry of Home Affairs coordinates women's issues.

Children.—The Government is concerned with the rights and welfare of children, and a number of laws directly address children's issues. The Adoption of Children Act of 1952 includes a number of provisions for protecting children under consideration for adoption, and the Maintenance Act of 1970 includes various provisions regarding the enforcement of maintenance decrees for the benefit of women and children. A government task force continued to educate the public on children's issues.

Child abuse is a problem in Swaziland. Children convicted of crimes sometimes are caned as punishment. In May two 10-year-olds were caned for housebreaking. Fueled by demographic and social pressure, there are growing numbers of street children in Mbabane and Manzini.

People With Disabilities.—The Government, through the Ministry of Home Affairs, has called for equal treatment of the disabled but has not initiated legislation to prohibit discrimination against the disabled. For example, there are no laws mandating accessibility for the disabled to buildings, transportation, or government services.

Section 6. Worker Rights

a. *The Right of Association.*—The new Industrial Relations Act (IRA), a revision of the 1980 act, affirms the right of trade unions to organize and associate freely in the context of traditional trade union concerns. However, it imposes harsh criminal penalties for union activity in favor of social or political issues outside core union concerns. Although the Act permits workers in all sectors of the economy, including the public sector, to join unions, their ability to express themselves is severely restricted. Unions can operate independently of government or political control, provided that they act as economic, other than political, organizations. The main trade union federation is the Swaziland Federation of Trade Unions (SFTU). The Swaziland Federation of Labor, a breakaway federation formed from the SFTU in 1993, gained formal Government recognition in 1994.

Unions are free to draw up their own constitutions within the framework of the IRA. The act specifies a number of provisions that must be addressed in a constitution, including the election of officers by secret ballot. The Labor Commissioner must approve the union constitution, and he can strike out or amend provisions that violate the law. The Government may dissolve unions that fail to maintain proper registration with the Labor Commissioner without recourse to judicial review, but it has never exercised this authority. The law prohibits strikes in "essential" services, which cover electricity, water, firefighting, health, sanitary, telephone, telegraph, and broadcast, as well as many civil service positions. The teaching profession was removed from the list of essential services.

The IRA details the steps to be followed when disputes arise, including what determines a legal or illegal strike. The act empowers the Government to mediate employment disputes and grievances and to enjoin a union from striking. When disputes arise, the Government often intervenes to try to reduce the chances of a strike, which may not be legally called until all avenues of negotiation have been exhausted and a secret ballot of union members has been conducted.

The act forbids labor federations or their officers to engage in any act that "causes or incites" the slowdown or cessation of work or economic activity, or to act in any way that might be construed as a "restraint of trade." The maximum penalty for violation of these provisions is 5 years' imprisonment. The Act also provides that any labor federation that devotes more of its funds and officers' time to issues of "public policy or public administration" than to union activities may be suspended or closed down. In September the Prime Minister noted his Government's readiness to consider amending the IRA; however the Government had taken no steps to do so by year's end. In October a panel of legal experts advised that the IRA was improperly adopted, raising questions regarding its legal validity. The matter was under court review at year's end.

There were a number of strikes, usually over wages and benefits, or dismissal of fellow workers. In January the SFTU conducted a mass stay away related to 27 demands presented to the Government in 1994 and to calls for fundamental political change. These demands and calls addressed a wide range of issues, including recognition of affirmative action, a national uniform minimum wage, an end to discrimination against women, the provision of better housing for workers, inclusion of worker representatives in constitutional discussions, and the lifting of the 1973 decree that suspended the Constitution and outlawed political parties. The stay away, which shut down the economy and large parts of the Government, ended after 8 days upon a command from the King that workers return to their workplaces or face the use of force. At the height of the stay away, police shot and killed a woman demonstrator in Manzini; arrested three top SFTU leaders, charged them with violations of the Public Order Act, and held them incommunicado for several days. The Government then released the leaders and dropped all charges. In March the Government reopened the case against the three leaders, this time alleging violation of the IRA. After a single hearing on the charges, the High Court indefinitely postponed the case. In July one of the three leaders, charged with fraud in connection with his former employment by a parastatal government insurance corporation, was acquitted. (These charges were filed in the aftermath of the January stay away). Also in July the Government filed an approximately $1 million claim against the SFTU for losses incurred during the January stay away.

In June the Swaziland National Association of Teachers (SNAT), and the Swaziland National Association of Civil Servants (SNACS) went on nationwide strikes for higher wages. In July both organizations suspended their strikes, after the King agreed to investigate their wage demands.

The International Labor Organization (ILO) Committee of Experts (COE) has noted discrepancies between the IRA and ILO Convention 87 on Freedom of Association and ILO Convention 98 on the Right to Organize and Bargain Collectively, both of which Swaziland ratified in 1978. The COE concerns include the powers accorded government officials to control union activity and the strictures on the ability of workers to form unions and associate with other unions at home and abroad. The Government tolerates the unions' international affiliations but does not recognize them.

b. *The Right to Organize and Bargain Collectively.*—The IRA provides for the right to organize and bargain collectively and outlaws antiunion discrimination. Collective bargaining is widespread; approximately 80 percent of the formal private sector is unionized. The Industrial Court may refuse to register collective bargaining agreements in the event of nonobservance of any requirement of the IRA. The law obliges employers to recognize a union when it achieves over 50 percent membership among employees. Disputes are referred to the Labor Commissioner and the Industrial Court, if necessary. Employers must allow representatives of legally recognized unions to conduct union activities on company time. Although many employers resist recognition and force the issue to the Industrial Court, the Court has generally ruled in favor of the unions on recognition.

In the case of unfair dismissal, the Court may order reinstatement and may award compensation of up to 24 months' salary. Union leaders made credible charges that management in various industries summarily dismissed workers for union activity. The Government sometimes instigates such dismissals.

There are no export processing zones.

c. *Prohibition of Forced or Compulsory Labor.*—The law prohibits forced labor, and it is not known to exist.

d. *Minimum Age for Employment of Children.*—The Employment Act of 1980 prohibits the hiring of a child below the age of 15 years in an industrial undertaking, except in cases where only family members are employed in the firm, or in technical schools where children are working under the supervision of a teacher or other authorized person. Legislation limits the number of night hours that can be worked on schooldays and limits children's work hours overall to 6 per day or 33 per week. Employment of children in the formal sector is not customary.

However, children below the minimum age are frequently employed in the agricultural sector, particularly in the eastern cotton-growing region. Children are also employed as domestic workers, and as herd boys in rural areas. The Ministry of Labor is responsible for enforcement of child labor regulations, but its effectiveness is limited by personnel shortages.

e. *Acceptable Conditions of Work.*—Swaziland has a legally mandated sliding scale of minimum wages depending on the type of work. These minimum wages generally provide a worker and family with an adequate standard of living within the context of Swazi society. The minimum monthly wage for a domestic worker is approximately $40 (180 emalangeni), for an unskilled worker $65 (280 emalangeni), and for a skilled worker $100 (450 emalangeni).

Labor, management, and government representatives have negotiated a maximum 48-hour workweek in the industrial sector, except for security guards, who work up to six 12-hour shifts per week. The Employment Act and the Wages Act entitle all workers to 1 day of rest per week. Most workers receive a minimum of 12 days annual leave. The Labor Commissioner enforces standards in the formal sector.

Extensive legislation protects worker health and safety. The Government sets safety standards for industrial operations and encourages private companies to develop accident prevention programs. Recent growth in industrial production has necessitated more government action on safety issues. However, the Labor Commissioner's Office has conducted few safety inspections in recent years because of staffing deficiencies. Workers have no formal statutory rights to remove themselves from dangerous work places without jeopardizing their jobs; nor do any collective bargaining agreements address the matter.

TANZANIA

The United Republic of Tanzania amended its Constitution in 1992 to become a multiparty state, and, in late 1995, conducted its first multiparty general elections for president and parliament in more than 30 years. The ruling party, Chama Cha Mapinduzi (CCM), continued to control the Union Government, winning 186 of the 232 elective seats in Parliament. The CCM presidential candidate, Benjamin Mkapa, won a four-way race with 61.8 percent of the vote. The islands of Zanzibar are integrated into the United Republic's governmental and party structure; however the Zanzibar Government, which has its own president and parliament, exercises considerable autonomy. Elections for the president and parliament of Zanzibar were also held in 1995. International observers noted serious discrepancies during the vote-counting process, calling into question the reelection of CCM incumbent Dr. Salmin Amour Juma as Zanzibar's President. In the period since that election, opposition parties called for new elections, prompting reprisals by the authorities, and, in response, most donors halted aid to Zanzibar.

The police have primary responsibility for maintaining law and order. They had formerly been supported by citizens' anticrime groups and patrols known as "Sungusungu," but these generally became inactive after the elections. The police regularly committed human rights abuses.

Agriculture provides 85 percent of employment. Cotton, coffee, sisal, tea, gemstones, and tourism account for most export earnings. The industrial sector is small. Economic reforms undertaken since 1986, including liberalization of agricultural policy, the privatization of state-owned enterprises, rescheduling of foreign debt payments, and the freeing of the currency exchange rate, have helped stimulate economic growth, as has the decline in the rate of inflation. However, poor government fiscal management and corruption limit economic progress.

The Government's human rights record did not improve and problems persisted. Although the 1995 multiparty elections represented an important development, citizens' right to change their government in Zanzibar is severely circumscribed. Although new opposition parties were competitive in many 1995 races and won in some constituencies, police often harassed and intimidated members and supporters of the political opposition. Other human rights problems included police beatings and mistreatment of suspects which sometimes resulted in death. Soldiers attacked civilians, and police in Zanzibar used torture, including beatings and floggings. Prison conditions remained harsh and life threatening. Arbitrary arrest and prolonged detention continued, and the inefficient and corrupt judicial system did not provide expeditious and fair trials for many citizens and foreigners. There were limitations on freedom of the press, association, assembly, and worker rights, and infringements on citizens' privacy. The Government obstructed formation of local human rights groups. Mob justice remained severe and widespread. Discrimination and violence against women remained serious problems. Some abuse of children and child labor continued. Following a change in 1995 in its longstanding policy of offering asylum, the Government formally closed its borders to new asylum seekers from Rwanda and Burundi and refused entry to or forcibly repatriated several hundred. In December several hundred thousand asylum seekers left Tanzania to return to Rwanda.

RESPECT FOR HUMAN RIGHTS

Section 1. Respect for the Integrity of the Person, Including Freedom From:

a. *Political and Other Extrajudicial Killing.*—There were no reports of political killings. Credible observers estimate that as many as 10 prisoners die each year in part as a result of inadequate nutrition, health care, and sanitation, but the majority of these die as a result of police beatings of persons in detention (see Section 1.c.). In one instance, Dar es Salaam police have not explained the March death of a young man who died in their custody.

There were no developments in the 1993 police killing of a member of the opposition party Civic United Front (CUF) on the island of Pemba. After a lengthy investigation, the policeman who fired the shots was charged with murder without intent and remains free on bail. CUF leaders complained that the President and Attorney

General of Zanzibar blocked the prosecution of the police officer. Nearly 4 years after the event, the trial was still pending.

Instances of mob justice against suspected criminals continued to claim dozens of lives. The media reported numerous incidents in which mobs kill suspected thieves who have been stoned, lynched, beaten to death, or doused with gasoline and set on fire. Such events are so commonplace that they are often bunched together with reporting on car accidents and other mishaps. Many instances are never reported. In September a mob attacked a suspected thief in front of the home of a diplomat; security guards at the residence rescued the seriously injured suspect who was taken by security patrol to police custody. The widespread belief in witchcraft has led, in some instances, to killing of alleged witches by their "victims," aggrieved relatives, or mobs. A deputy minister estimated that one hundred mostly older women in the Mwanza and Shinyanga regions are killed every year by those who believe them to be witches. Government officials have condemned these practices, but in only one known instance, in Kwimba, were authorities able to identify and arrest individuals for engaging in mob violence. No preventive measures have been taken.

b. *Disappearance.*—There were no reports of politically motivated disappearances.

c. *Torture and Other Cruel, Inhuman, or Degrading Treatment or Punishment.*—The Constitution prohibits the use of torture and inhuman or degrading treatment, but the police regularly threaten, mistreat, and occasionally beat suspected criminals during and after their apprehension and interrogation. Although government officials usually condemn these practices, the Government seldom prosecutes officials for such abuses. The People's Militia Laws, as amended by Parliament in 1989, bestow quasi-legal status on the traditional Sungusungu neighborhood and village anticrime groups. In the past, these groups were criticized for using excessive force with criminal suspects, but they became largely moribund following the installation of the new government.

There have been repeated reports from credible sources of torture, including beatings and floggings by police, in Zanzibar, notably on Pemba island. The Zanzibar and Union Governments have both denied these charges.

On May 30, eight soldiers attacked residents of Songea, allegedly to retaliate for the theft of a soldier's bicycle. In June another group of soldiers attacked Mererani village near Arusha, looting and setting homes ablaze, reportedly in revenge for the stabbing of a soldier several days earlier. Some of the troops interfered with villagers' efforts to protect their property and defend themselves. A government commission of inquiry was established, but it has not reached any conclusions. Similar incidents involving soldiers, such as an attack on residents of Boko-Kunduchi in late 1995, have also been reported.

Prison conditions remained harsh and life threatening. Government officials acknowledged that prisons are overcrowded and living conditions poor. Prisons are authorized to hold 21,000 prisoners, but their population was estimated at 47,000. The Government is expanding prisons to accommodate the increased population, and some prisoners are paroled or receive suspended sentences as a means of relieving congestion. One person released from Ukonga prison told of guards beating and abusing prisoners, particularly during monthly searches during which time all prisoners were assembled and required to strip. Serious diseases, such as dysentery, malaria, and cholera, are common and result in deaths. Medical treatment is limited, and friends and family of prisoners generally need to provide medication or the funds with which to purchase them. In February a prisoner held in pretrial detention in Mbeya died of diarrhea as he was entering court. Convicted prisoners are not allowed to receive food from the outside and are often moved to different prisons without notification to their families. Pretrial detainees are held together with those serving sentences but are allowed to receive food from the outside.

There is no outside monitoring of prison conditions.

d. *Arbitrary Arrest, Detention or Exile.*—The Criminal Procedure Code, amended in 1985, requires that a person arrested for a crime, other than a national security charge under the Preventive Detention Act, be charged before a magistrate within 24 hours. However, in practice, the police often fail to do so. An opposition member of the Pemba House of Representatives was detained by the police for more than 3 weeks from late February to mid-March without charge. The 1985 amendments also restricted the right to bail and imposed strict conditions on freedom of movement and association when bail is granted. Because of backlogs, an average case still takes 2 to 3 years or longer to come to trial. Thirty-five people charged with causing disturbances during the 1995 election campaign remained in police custody for more than 9 months. The code provides for a right to defense counsel. The Chief Justice assigns lawyers to indigent defendants charged with serious crimes such as murder, manslaughter, and armed robbery. There are only a few hundred practicing lawyers in Tanzania, and most indigent defendants charged with lesser crimes do not have legal counsel.

Under the Preventive Detention Act, the President may order the arrest and indefinite detention without bail of any person considered dangerous to the public order or national security. This act was also amended in 1985 to require the Government to release detainees within 15 days of detention or inform them of the reason for their detention. The detainee was also allowed to challenge the grounds for detention at 90-day intervals. Despite a landmark ruling by the Court of Appeal in 1991 that the Preventive Detention Act could not be used to deny bail to persons not considered dangerous to society, the Government has still not introduced corrective legislation. The Preventive Detention Act was not used in 1996. While the Law Reform Commission recommended that the act be repealed, the President said that repeal is unnecessary if the law is not being used. The Government has additional broad detention powers under the Regions and Regional Commissioners Act and the Area Commissioners Act of 1962. These acts permit regional and district commissioners to arrest and detain for 48 hours persons who may "disturb public tranquility."

Police continued to make arbitrary arrests, although less frequently than in the past. For example, the police occasionally arrest relatives of criminal suspects and hold them in custody without charge for as long as several years in efforts to force the suspects to surrender. Such relatives who manage to get their cases before a judge are usually set free, only to be immediately rearrested when they leave the courtroom. The Government has not taken any legal action to correct these abuses.

Since the 1995 election, police in Zanzibar, particularly on Pemba, have regularly detained, arrested, and harassed CUF members, and suspected supporters. Despite orders from the Union Government's Inspector General of Police, officers in Zanzibar continued these activities.

e. *Denial of Fair Public Trial.*—The Constitution provides for an independent judiciary, and in practice, the judiciary has been increasingly willing to demonstrate its independence of the Government. In the past, senior police or government officials pressured and sometimes reassigned judges who made unpopular rulings. No such incidents occurred in 1996. Independent observers, however, continue to view the judiciary as corrupt and inefficient, and question a defendant's ability to obtain an expeditious and fair trial.

The legal system is based on the British model, with modifications to accommodate customary and Islamic law in civil cases. Military courts do not try civilians, and there are no security courts. Defendants in civil and military courts may appeal decisions to the High Court and Court of Appeal.

Zanzibar's court system generally parallels the mainland's legal system but retains Islamic courts to handle Muslim family cases such as divorce, child custody, and inheritance. Cases concerning Zanzibar constitutional issues are heard only in Zanzibar's courts. All other cases may be appealed to the Court of Appeal of the United Republic of Tanzania.

The majority of individuals held in the two major prisons in Dar es Salaam are awaiting trial. In many instances, bribes determine whether bail is granted or even whether a case is judged as a civil or criminal matter. The Government initiated efforts as early as 1991 to highlight judicial corruption and increased its oversight in 1996, but scant progress has been made.

Criminal trials are open to the public and to the press; courts must give reasons on the record for holding secret proceedings. Criminal defendants have the right of appeal.

There were no reports of political prisoners.

f. *Arbitrary Interference With Privacy, Family, Home or Correspondence.*—The State continued to interfere with these rights, which are generally provided for in the Constitution. The CCM has historically penetrated all levels of society through local cells, varying in size from single family homes to large apartment buildings and containing from 10 to 200 persons. Unpaid party officials serve as 10-cell leaders with authority to resolve problems at the grassroots level and to report to authorities any suspicious behavior, event, or noncompliance with compulsory night patrol service in the neighborhood. In 1993 elections were held for new grassroots leaders to replace the CCM 10-cell leaders in nonparty business. Few voters participated in these elections, which were boycotted by the opposition and the 10-cell leaders retain nearly all of their power and influence.

CCM membership is voluntary and is estimated at 2 to 3 million card holders. While in the past, CCM membership had been necessary for advancement in political and other areas, the importance of such membership is waning.

The Criminal Procedures Act of 1985 authorizes police officials and official civilian anticrime units to issue search warrants; however, the act also authorizes searches of persons and premises without a warrant if necessary to prevent the loss or destruction of evidence connected with an offense or if circumstances are serious and urgent. In practice warrants are rarely requested, and police and other security services search private homes and business establishments at will. The security services reportedly monitor telephones and correspondence of some citizens and selected foreign residents.

The police occasionally arrest relatives of criminal suspects and detain them without charge in an effort to force suspects to surrender (see Section 1.d.).

National employment directives stipulating the nature of employment and location of residence give authorities the right to transfer citizens to another area to ensure productive employment (see Section 2.d.).

Compulsory participation in Sungusungu anticrime groups ended after the November elections. The Sungusungu now exist essentially in name only.

Section 2. Respect for Civil Liberties, Including:

a. *Freedom of Speech and Press.*—The Constitution provides for freedom of speech and the press, however, the Government pressures journalists to practice self-censorship. Opposition political party members and others openly criticize the Government and ruling party in public forums.

Private radio and television stations broadcast in Dar es Salaam and in a few other urban areas. On Zanzibar radio and television are controlled by the Government which also practices a restrictive policy with regard to print media. Private mainland newspapers are widely available, and many residents of Zanzibar can receive mainland television.

The press in Tanzania is, on the whole, lively and outspoken, and even the government-owned newspaper occasionally reports events that portray the Government in an unflattering light. There are 9 daily newspapers and 15 other newspapers in English and Kiswahili, along with another dozen periodicals, some of which are owned or influenced by political parties, both CCM and opposition. During 1996 the rising cost of newsprint resulted in the closure of 15 newspapers. There is no official censorship, but throughout the year the Government continued to pressure newspapers to kill or ameliorate unfavorable stories. In fear of government reprisals the media continued to practice self-censorship.

On January 25, the Government of Zanzibar banned from the islands the circulation of the privately owned Kiswahili daily Majira on the grounds that it was carrying antigovernment articles. Also in January, the local government barred a Zanzibari journalist from further reporting, charging that he had written articles "aimed at disrupting the peace and national unity in Zanzibar." The Kiswahili tabloid Heko was banned nationally in July; the ban was lifted in early October after the managing editor issued a letter of apology to the Government.

In an October incident, police roughed up and arrested two photographers attempting to take pictures of the roundup of illegal street vendors in Dar es Salaam; the photographers were not charged and were subsequently released. Also in October, subsequent to a high-profile by-election won by the opposition, police stifled media coverage of the new Member of Parliament. Television cameramen attempting to record his swearing in were detained and not released until after the end of the ceremony. Perhaps in response to these incidents, the following month the Dar Es Salaam police commissioner warned his officers not to harass working journalists (see Section 2.b.).

The Union Government sought to maintain some control over the private media with the establishment of a code of conduct for journalists and a Media Council. Led by the Tanzanian chapter of the Media Council for Southern Africa and the Association of Journalists and Media Workers, journalists forced the Government to agree to a voluntary code of ethics and the establishment of a media council intended to preserve and expand media freedom. The council came into existence with government approval on February 14, but has proven ineffectual.

Academic freedom exists in theory and largely in practice, particularly at the university level. Academics have been increasingly outspoken in their criticism of the Government and calls for reform.

b. *Freedom of Peaceful Assembly and Association.*—The Constitution provides for the freedom of peaceful assembly and association, and, except in Zanzibar, citizens generally enjoyed the right to discuss freely political alternatives. However, the Constitution and other laws and regulations limit these rights and stipulate that citizens cannot run for public office unless they are members of a registered political party.

Political parties must give police 48 hours' advance notice of rallies. Police have the authority to deny permission for political rallies on public safety or security grounds, or if the permit seeker belongs to an unregistered organization or political party. Persons are arrested for assembling without the appropriate permit. Opposition parties, other than in Zanzibar, are able to hold rallies. Local government officials there prohibited the assembly of CUF supporters and use of CUF slogans from the October 1995 election until August. During that 10-month period, Zanzibar officials refused CUF applications for permits, citing a threat to public order. Police dispersed meetings attended by persons thought to be opposed to the Zanzibar Government.

On the mainland, a by-election in the Dar es Salaam district of Temeke was marked by scattered violent incidents against individuals and property, though there was tight security at polling places. The opposition candidate won the election. When the opposition sought to hold a victory procession, however, the Inspector General of Police sent a letter to the opposition party's secretary general directing that no march be held under threat of arrest (see Section 2.a.), and the march was canceled.

In May students demonstrating outside the Ministry of Higher Education were attacked by riot police. The police used tear gas and nightsticks and 30 people were injured, 4 seriously. The police arrested 74 people.

The Registrar of Political Parties has sole authority to approve or deny the registration of any political party and is responsible for enforcing strict regulations on registered or provisionally registered parties. The electoral law prohibits independent candidates; requires any Member of Parliament to resign if they join another party; requires all political parties to support the union with Zanzibar; and forbids parties based on ethnic, regional, or religious affiliation. Parties granted provisional registration may hold public meetings and recruit members. They have 6 months to submit lists of at least 200 members in 10 of the country's 25 regions, including two regions in Zanzibar, in order to secure full registration and to be eligible to field candidates for election. Nonregistered parties are prohibited from holding meetings, recruiting members, or fielding candidates.

The most prominent unregistered party was Reverend Christopher Mtikila's Democratic Party, which advocates the dissolution of the union and the expulsion of minorities from the mainland. Despite his political party's lack of government recognition, Mtikila, was able to publicize his views through his legally registered church and through ongoing lawsuits against the Government.

In November the Registrar of Political Parties told a workshop on the Constitution that conditions for registration under the Political Parties Act of 1992 were too "harsh" and suggested that changes be made to permit other parties to compete in elections.

Under the Societies Ordinance, the Ministry of Home Affairs must approve any new association. Several nongovernmental organizations (NGO's) were formed in the last few years to address the concerns of families, the disabled, women, and children. In September the Ministry of Home Affairs suspended the registration of the National Women's Council, allegedly because it engaged in political activity. The Government has called on the organization to rewrite its constitution to prevent it from involvement in such activity. The Deputy Minister said that if the council's constitution were not revised and such activity halted, it would be stricken from the official registry.

A number of professional, business, legal, and medical associations exist. Representatives of the business community and President Mkapa held three meetings, the most recent of which included the Cabinet and lasted 5 hours, seeking radical changes in the tax and investment codes. The Government, for more than 2 years, has withheld registration from an NGO called Defenders of Human Rights in Tanzania (see Section 4). Opposition leaders complain that the Zanzibar Government is even more restrictive in registering societies than the Union Government.

c. *Freedom of Religion.*—The Constitution provides for freedom of religion, and the Government generally respects this right in practice. Missionaries are allowed to enter the country freely to proselytize, and citizens are allowed to go abroad for pilgrimages and other religious practices.

d. *Freedom of Movement Within the Country, Foreign Travel, Immigration, and Repatriation.*—The Government imposes some limits on these rights. Short-term domestic travel is not restricted, but citizens must follow national employment directives stipulating the nature of employment and location of the residence. The Human Resources Deployment Act of 1983 requires local governments to ensure that every resident within their area of jurisdiction engages in productive and lawful employment. Those not employed are subject to transfer to another area where employment is available. These laws are also used by police as a means of soliciting bribes and intimidating urban residents. The Dar es Salaam City Council rounds up beggars for return to their home areas, but many return to the capital.

Passports for foreign travel can be difficult to obtain, mostly due to bureaucratic inefficiency, and authorities subject those planning to travel or emigrate to close scrutiny. Citizens who leave the country without permission are subject to prosecution upon their return.

Mainlanders are required to show identification to travel to Zanzibar, and are not allowed to work or own land on the islands.

Tanzania traditionally maintained a generous open border policy with regard to asylum seekers from neighboring countries. However, in early 1995, following the influx of over a half million Rwandan asylum seekers, the Government closed its borders with Rwanda and Burundi. In practice asylum seekers continue to enter the country. During the year, the authorities used laws, such as those on poaching, trespassing and illegal migration, to force several hundred persons previously admitted to return to both Rwanda and Burundi. In December, following the repatriation of Rwandans from eastern Zaire, the Government, in cooperation with the United Nations High Commissioner for Refugees, made a controversial decision that conditions in their homeland were such that Rwandans should leave Tanzania and return to Rwanda. Faced with the government decision, and the presence of Tanzanian troops, by year's end virtually all of the asylum seekers had departed the country. A relatively small number who feared for their safety were permitted to remain in Tanzania temporarily. Some humanitarian refugee organizations had limited access to the process.

Tanzania continued to offer first asylum to about 300,000 other refugees, principally from Burundi and Zaire.

Section 3. Respect for Political Rights: The Right of Citizens to Change Their Government

A multiparty political system was officially introduced in 1992. Three years later, for the first time in more than 30 years, citizens exercised their right to change their government through national elections for president and parliament. The CCM, with huge advantages over opposition parties in membership and access to resources including its own daily Kiswahili-language newspaper, retained the presidency and 186 of 232 elective seats in Parliament. The Government employed tactics to restrict or delay activities of opposition parties, which nonetheless made credible challenges in many districts and for president.

Because of widespread problems with the distribution of ballots on election day, the Government nullified the results and conducted new elections in seven Dar es Salaam constituencies. Some opposition parties demanded that the election be rerun nationwide and boycotted the new elections in Dar es Salaam.

The Constitution of Zanzibar allows citizens the right to change their government peacefully; however, this right has been severely circumscribed. The 1995 presidential election in Zanzibar was seriously flawed. Government-owned broadcast media in Zanzibar were biased in favor of CCM incumbent President Salim Amour Juma. The government party intimidated and harassed the opposition and did not permit opposition rallies until 2 months prior to the election. Further, registration was limited to persons who had maintained the same residence for 5 years, which disenfranchised many voters. CUF party members also were detained by police when they attempted to campaign in rural areas.

Election observers in Zanzibar were denied access to the tabulation of votes from polling stations. After 4 days, the Zanzibar Electoral Commission (ZEC) appointed by the Amour government, announced that Amour had won by 0.5 percent of the vote. Figures tabulated by the CUF showed a similarly close victory for its candidate. After efforts by the international community to reconcile discrepancies in the vote counting, observers concluded that the official results may have been inaccurate. Critics questioned the probity of the ZEC chairman who defended the election and its outcome when soon thereafter he purchased an expensive home. The Zanzibar and Union Governments both rejected calls to overturn the result and conduct a new election. In April Zanzibar police raided the home of the CUF's presidential candidate, citing "the duty of police to maintain law and security."

In the year since the election, government security forces and CCM gangs harassed and intimidated CUF members on both of the two main Zanzibar islands, Pemba and Ugunja. Because CUF won all 20 seats on Pemba, Pembans living on Ugunja were regarded as CUF supporters and as a result were harassed. CUF members accused police of detaining dozens of its members, including several local leaders. Many CUF supporters have deserted Ugunja for Pemba or the mainland. Safety is not ensured in Pemba, where security forces dispersed gatherings, intimidated and roughed up individuals, and expelled two tourists in September for their contact with CUF members. Most international donors have suspended direct assistance to Zanzibar in response to activities of the authorities.

There are no restrictions in law on the participation of women in politics and government. In practice, however, few women are politically active. Eight of 232 elected members of the Union Parliament are women. In addition, 37 women from both the CCM and opposition parties were appointed to Parliament to seats reserved for women. Three of the cabinet's 23 ministers are women.

Section 4. Governmental Attitude Regarding International and Nongovernmental Investigation of Alleged Violations of Human Rights

The Government has obstructed the formation of local human rights groups. Persons seeking to register human rights NGO's such as the Defenders of Human Rights in Tanzania and the Tanzania Human Rights Education Society, complained that the Ministry of Home Affairs continued to delay action on their applications (see Section 2.b.). This hampered their access and efforts to monitor violations of human rights. The Government refused to register the African Human Rights and Justice Protection Network on the grounds that it was politically oriented.

Government officials have said that international human rights groups are welcome to visit Tanzania.

Section 5. Discrimination Based on Race, Sex, Religion, Disability, Language, or Social Status

The Constitution prohibits discrimination based on nationality, tribe, origin, political affiliation, color, religion, or lifestyle. Discrimination based on sex, age, or disability is not specifically prohibited by law but is publicly discouraged in official statements.

Women.—Violence against women remained widespread. Legal remedies exist but in practice are difficult to obtain. Traditional customs subordinating women remain strong in both urban and rural areas, and often local magistrates upheld such practices. Women may be punished for not bearing children. It is accepted for a husband to treat his wife as he wishes, and wife beating can occur at all levels of society. Cultural, family, and social pressure prevent many women from reporting abuses to authorities. Government officials frequently make public statements decrying such abuses, but rarely take action against perpetrators.

Although the Government advocates equal rights for women in the workplace, it does not ensure these rights in practice. In the public sector, which employs 80 percent of the salaried labor force, certain statutes restrict women's access to some jobs or hours of employment. While progress on women's rights has been more noticeable in urban areas, strong traditional norms still divide labor along gender lines and place women in a subordinate position. Discrimination against women is most acute in the countryside, where women are relegated to farming and raising children with almost no opportunity for wage employment. Custom and tradition often hinder women from owning property such as land, and these may override other laws that provide for equal treatment. Women seeking higher education may be harassed by male colleagues; the authorities have largely ignored the practice.

The overall situation for women is even less favorable in heavily Muslim Zanzibar. Women there, and in many parts of the mainland, face discriminatory restrictions on inheritance and ownership of property because of concessions by the Government and courts to customary and Islamic law. While provisions of the Marriage Act provide certain inheritance and property rights for women, the decision to apply customary, Islamic, or statutory law depends on the lifestyle and stated intentions of the male head of household. The courts have thus upheld discriminatory inheritance claims, primarily in rural areas. Under Zanzibari law, unmarried women under the age of 21 who become pregnant are subject to 2 years' imprisonment.

Several NGO's provide counseling and education programs on women's rights issues, particularly sexual harassment and molestation.

Children.—Government funding of programs for children's welfare remained minuscule. The Government made some constructive efforts to address children's welfare, including working closely with NGO's to assess the well-being of orphans and neglected children.

The law provides for 7 years of compulsory schooling. In the past, girls who became pregnant were expelled from school. During 1996 procedures were put into effect to permit such girls to continue their education following their maternity absence.

Female genital mutilation (FGM) is widely condemned by international health experts as damaging to both physical and psychological health. Although the Government officially discourages FGM, it is still performed at an early age by approximately 20 of the country's 130 main ethnic groups, affecting perhaps 10 percent of the population. In some groups, FGM is compulsory, and, in others, a woman who has not undergone the ritual might not be able to marry. Government officials have called for changes in customs that adversely affect women, but no legislation has been introduced that would specifically restrict the practice of FGM. Some local government officials have begun to combat the practice, and in 1996 five persons were convicted and imprisoned for assault for mutilating young girls between the ages of 1 and 3 years. Seminars sponsored by various governmental and nongovernmental organizations are regularly held in an attempt to educate the public on the dangers of these and other traditional practices. Health authorities believe the practice is declining, but other sources maintain that it is on the rise, especially in central Tanzania.

People With Disabilities.—The Government does not mandate access to public buildings, transportation, or government services for people with disabilities. Although there is no official discrimination against the disabled, in practice the physically disabled are effectively restricted in their access to education, employment, and provision of other state services due to physical barriers. The Government provides only limited funding to special facilities and programs.

Religious Minorities.—The Muslim community claims to be disadvantaged in terms of its representation in the civil service and government and in state-owned business, in part because both colonial and past, post-independence administrations refused to recognize the credentials of traditional Muslim schools. As a result, there is widespread Muslim resentment of the perceived advantages enjoyed by Christians. Christians, in turn, have been critical of what they perceive as undue favoritism accorded to Muslims in appointments, jobs, and scholarships by former President Mwinyi, a Muslim. Some leaders in both camps appear to be playing up religious tensions. In fact there does not at present appear to be any serious problem of discrimination due to religion in access to employment or educational opportunities.

National/Racial/Ethnic Minorities.—In the past, the Government discriminated against the Barabaig and other nomadic people in northern Tanzania. These ethnic groups continued to complain of government discrimination based on government efforts to make them adopt a more modern lifestyle and to restrict their access to land that was turned into large government wheat farms.

The Asian community has declined by 50 percent, over the years, to about 50,000, a result of considerable antipathy by many African Tanzanians. There are, however, no laws or official policies which discriminate against them. As the Government places greater emphasis on market-oriented policies and privatization, public concern regarding the Asian community's economic role has increased. This has led to demands for policies of "indigenization" to ensure that privatization does not increase the Asian community's economic predominance at the expense of the country's African population.

Section 6. Worker Rights

a. *The Right of Association.*—Both the Constitution and the 1955 Trade Union Ordinance refer to the right of association of workers. Nevertheless, workers do not have the right to form or join organizations of their own choice. The Organization of Tanzania Trade Unions Act of 1991 addresses all labor union issues. The act created the Organization of Tanzania Trade Unions (OTTU) which is the only trade union organization in Tanzania. Renamed the Tanzania Federation of Trade Unions (TFTU), subject to parliamentary approval of its new constitution, OTTU/TFTU is comprised of 11 independent trade unions. The individual unions are given the right to leave the TFTU and to collect their own dues, 5 percent of which must be contributed to the federation. More than a year after the labor reorganization, only 1 of the 11 new independent unions, the Tanzanian Teachers Union, is fully registered.

OTTU/TFTU represents 60 percent of workers in industry and government, but it has little influence on labor policy. Overall, roughly 25 percent of Tanzania's 2 million wage earners are organized. All workers, including those classified as "essential" service workers, are permitted to join unions, but essential workers are not permitted to strike.

There are no laws prohibiting retribution against legal strikers. Workers have the legal right to strike only after complicated and protracted mediation and conciliation procedures leading ultimately to the Industrial Court, which receives direction from the Minister of Labor and Youth Development. If the OTTU/TFTU is not satisfied with the decision of the Industrial Court, it can then conduct a legal strike. These procedures can prolong a dispute by months without resolving it. Pending a resolution, frustrated workers have staged impromptu, illegal, wildcat strikes and walkouts.

The TFTU expanded beyond its forerunner's membership in regional and pan-African trade union organizations by joining the International Confederation of Free Trade Unions.

b. *The Right to Organize and Bargain Collectively.*—Collective bargaining is protected by law but limited to the private sector. Wages for employees of the Government and state-owned organizations, which account for the bulk of the salaried labor force, are administratively set by the Government.

Although the OTTU/TFTU negotiates on behalf of most private sector employees with the Association of Tanzanian Employers, collective agreements must be submitted to the Industrial Court for approval. The International Labor Organization (ILO) has observed that these provisions are not in conformity with ILO Convention 98 on Collective Bargaining and the Right to Organize. Tanzania's Security of Employment Act of 1964 prohibits discriminatory activities by an employer against union members. Employers found guilty of antiunion activities are legally required to reinstate workers.

There are no export processing zones (EPZ's) on the mainland, but there are three in Zanzibar. Work conditions are comparable to those in other work places. Labor law protections apply to EPZ workers.

c. *Prohibition of Forced or Compulsory Labor.*—The Constitution prohibits forced labor, though the ILO observed that provisions of various laws are incompatible with ILO Conventions 29 and 105 on forced labor. Specifically, the Human Resources Deployment Act of 1983 requires every local government authority to ensure that able-bodied persons over 15 years of age not in school engage in productive or other lawful employment. In some rural areas, villagers are obligated to work in the village communal gardens or on small construction projects such as repairing roads.

d. *Minimum Age for Employment of Children.*—Children under 12 years of age are prohibited by law from working in the formal wage sector in both urban and rural areas. However, this provision does not apply to children working on family farms or herding domestic livestock. Children between the ages of 12 and 15 may be employed on a daily wage and on a day-to-day basis, but they must have parental permission and return to the residence of their guardian at night.

The minimum age for entry into work of a contractual nature in approved occupations is set at 15 years. The law prohibits a young person from employment in any occupation that is injurious to health and that is dangerous or otherwise unsuitable. Young persons between the ages of 12 and 15 may be employed in industrial work but only between the hours of 6 a.m. and 6 p.m., with some exceptions allowed. The Ministry of Labor and Youth Development is responsible for enforcement, but the number of inspectors is inadequate to police conditions. The effectiveness of government enforcement has reportedly declined with increased privatization. Approximately 3,000 to 5,000 children engage in seasonal employment on sisal, tea, tobacco, and coffee plantations. Children working on plantations generally receive lower wages than their older counterparts, although they may be in comparable jobs. Work on sisal plantations is particularly hazardous and detrimental to children. On one sisal plantation, children made up 30 percent of the work force; only half of the children had completed primary school. They had a high incidence of skin and respiratory problems, were not provided protective clothing, and lacked adequate nourishment and lodging. Another 1,500 to 3,000 children work in unregulated gemstone mines. In the informal sector, children assist their parents in unregulated piecework manufacturing.

e. *Acceptable Conditions of Work.*—There is a legal minimum wage for employment in the formal sector. The TFTU often negotiates higher minimum wages with individual employers, depending on the financial status of the business. The legal minimum wage is $30 (17,500 Tanzanian shillings) per month. Even when supplemented with various benefits such as housing, transport allowances, and food subsidies, the minimum rate may not always be sufficient to provide an adequate living for a worker and family, and workers often must depend on the extended family, or a second or third job. Despite the minimum wage, many workers, especially in the informal sector, are paid less.

There is no standard legal workweek. However, a 5-day, 40-hour workweek is in effect for government workers. Most private employers retain a 6-day, 44- to 48-hour workweek. In general women may not be employed between 10 p.m. and 6 a.m. Several laws regulate safety in the workplace. An occupational health and safety factory inspection system, set up with the assistance of the ILO, is managed by the Ministry of Labor and Social Welfare and Youth Development. Its effectiveness, however, is limited.

OTTU/TFTU officials have claimed that enforcement of labor standards is effective in the formal sector, but no verification studies have been performed. Workers may take an employer to court through their TFTU branch if their working conditions do not comply with the Ministry of Labor's health and environmental standards. Workers making such complaints have not lost their jobs as a result. However, workers do not have the have the right to remove themselves from dangerous situations without jeopardizing their employment. Enforcement of labor standards is nonexistent in the informal sector.

TOGO

President General Gnassingbe Eyadema and his Assembly of the Togolese People (RPT) party, strongly backed by the military, continue to dominate the exercise of political power. During the year, the RPT party was able to persuade three opposition Assembly deputies to vote with it, thus gaining an effective majority in the legislature. The RPT then manipulated the rules governing the electoral process, and thus further consolidated its majority in the legislature through by-elections held in August. Despite an effort to create a government of national unity, the opposition's refusal to participate resulted in a new government formed in the wake of the by-elections with an overwhelming majority of RPT ministers. The Eyadema Government, which also exerts control over the judiciary, made little progress in its professed intention to move from an authoritarian legacy to democracy.

The security forces consist primarily of the army (including the elite Presidential Guard), navy, air force, the Surete Nationale (including the national police), and the Gendarmerie. Approximately 90 percent of the army's officers and 70 percent of its soldiers come from the President's northern (Kabye) ethnic group. The Minister of the Interior, an army colonel, is in charge of the national police and the Defense Minister has nominal authority over the other security forces. In practice there is little differentiation between civilian and military authorities. Security forces remain overwhelmingly loyal to their chief, President Eyadema, subject to his direct control, and carry out his orders. Some members of the security forces committed serious human rights abuses.

About 80 percent of the country's estimated 4.25 million people are engaged in subsistence agriculture, but there is also an active commercial sector. The main exports are phosphates, cotton, and cocoa, which along with revenue from Lome's port, are the leading source of foreign exchange. Annual per capita gross domestic product is around $300. The country is slowly moving toward structural adjustment under programs of international financial institutions and has resumed moderate growth.

The Government's human rights record continued to be poor. The Government restricted citizens' right to change their government. Security forces were responsible for extrajudicial killings, beatings, arbitrary detentions, and interference with citizens' movement and privacy rights. The Government did not, in general, investigate or effectively punish those who committed such abuses. Prolonged pretrial detention was commonplace, and prison conditions remained very harsh. The Government continued to influence the judiciary, defendants' rights to fair and expeditious trials are not ensured, and some detainees wait years to be judged. There were instances of infringement of freedom of speech and the press by security forces and the Government, including investigative detention to harass journalists and political opponents, and suspension of newspaper publication. Societal discrimination and violence against women, as well as abuse of children, continued.

RESPECT FOR HUMAN RIGHTS

Section 1. Respect for the Integrity of the Person Including Freedom From:

a. *Political and Other Extrajudicial Killing.*—A heavy security presence combined with habitual impunity enjoyed by members of the security forces has created a climate in which excessive force can be used without legal consequences. The security forces were responsible for at least three extrajudicial killings.

Captain Philippe Azote of the Togolese Armed Forces was shot in the back and killed at a security checkpoint in Lome by security forces on January 7. As was his longstanding practice, Azote was jogging when stopped and questioned. The Government claimed that Captain Azote was mistaken for a terrorist since he was armed. Azote had been dismissed from the military earlier in his career for suspicion of taking part in the killing of General Amegee, and sources close to the military claim Azote's death was revenge by a military faction which supported Amegee. The soldier who shot Azote was originally commended for his antiterrorism work; after Azote was identified, the soldier was arrested. There has been no trial.

Security forces killed Thomas Rupprecht, a German embassy employee with diplomatic status, at a security checkpoint in Lome on March 27. An investigation report indicates that Rupprecht was shot numerous times while attempting to drive away after arguing about a demand to be searched. Two soldiers were arrested, and the

Government has given compensation to the family, but there has not been a trial for the accused perpetrators.

A Togolese soldier at a security checkpoint shot and killed Anthony Dogbo, a Ghanaian taxi driver, on the outskirts of Lome on April 11. Despite several requests from the Ghanian Embassy to compensate the deceased's family or to punish the perpetrator, the Government has not responded, and there has been no known investigation.

In addition to these confirmed incidents, opponents of the Government alleged other killings linked to security forces. Unidentified persons in military uniform were responsible for the murder of Rose Lebene Woenagno on January 26. State Inspector Amouzou Efoe Paul Adjakly, whose responsibilities gave him access to sensitive government accounting files, was killed on February 17 by unknown persons. Adjakly was found by a road outside Lome with injuries to his head; his motorcycle revealed no signs of an accident, and his briefcase lay untouched next to him. On April 29, a group of unidentified persons carrying machine guns tortured and killed retired mason Komlavi Yebesse. Media coverage of the Yebesse incident, insinuating security force involvement, led to the suspension of an opposition newspaper (see Section 2.a.).

On October 14, three soldiers manning an armed security checkpoint in Lome near the Ghana border were killed by gunfire. The attack was credibly alleged to be carried out by opposition elements and a previously unknown group, the Interior Committee for Democracy and Salvation, claimed responsibility.

Numerous prisoners died due to lack of medical facilities and widespread disease in prisons (see Section 1.c.).

There were no developments in the 1995 murder in Ghana of opposition leader Lt Vincent Tokofai, the 1994 killing of Gaston Edeh, or the 1992 killings of Marc Atidepe and Tavio Amorin.

b. *Disappearance.*—There were no reports of politically motivated disappearances.

There were, however, no developments in the 1994 disappearance of David Bruce, or in the disappearance of Afougnilede Essiba, Adanou Igbe, Kobono Kowouvi, and another companion, all four of whom were arrested by soldiers at an armed security checkpoint in Adetikope in 1994. In 1994 the Government began an investigation of the Bruce disappearance but has not reported any results.

c. *Torture and Other Cruel, Inhuman, or Degrading Treatment or Punishment.*— The law prohibits these practices, but security forces often beat detainees immediately after arresting them. Some suspects have credibly claimed to have been tortured, including beatings and lack of access to food and medical attention. The Government did not investigate, prosecute, or punish any officials for these abuses.

Prison conditions remained very harsh, with serious overcrowding and inadequate sanitation and food. Medical facilities are practically nonexistent, and widespread disease in prisons led to an estimated 15 deaths of incarcerated individuals. Prison guards in the overcrowded Civil Prison of Lome charge prisoners a small fee to shower, use the toilet, or have a place to sleep. Children are often incarcerated with convicted adults. Women are housed separately. International and local private organizations have access to prisons for monitoring purposes.

d. *Arbitrary Arrest, Detention, or Exile.*—The law allows authorities to hold arrested persons incommunicado without charge for 48 hours, with an additional 48-hour extension in cases deemed serious or complex. In practice, detainees can be and often are detained without bail for lengthy periods with or without the approval of a judge. Family members and attorneys officially have access to a detainee after the initial 48- or 96-hour detention period, but authorities often delay, and sometimes deny, access.

Judges or senior police officials issue warrants. Although detainees have the right to be informed of the charges against them, police sometimes ignore this right. The law stipulates that a special judge conduct a pretrial investigation to examine the adequacy of evidence and decide on bail. However, a shortage of judges and other qualified personnel plus official indifference have resulted in lengthy pretrial detentions—in some cases several years—and confinement of prisoners beyond their sentences. An estimated 50 percent of the prison population were pretrial detainees. Increasingly, the Government used brief investigative detentions of less than 48 hours to harass and intimidate opponents and journalists for alleged defamation of Government officials (see Section 2.a.). The Government often resorts to false charges of common crimes to detain and intimidate opponents.

There were instances of arbitrary arrests and detention. Nicoue Broohm, Counselor for Social Affairs and Human Rights for Prime Minister Kodjo and member of Kodjo's Democratic Union of Togo Party (UTD), was arrested by gendarmes in June and detained for 3 days for allegedly helping a student with a study of the President's chances of winning a referendum on the Constitution. Kokouvi Adakou, a UTD Vice President, was arrested by gendarmes and questioned a week before legislative by-elections in Notse. Adakou was released the same day. David Oladokoun, a UTD leader in Atakpame, was arrested by gendarmes in May and detained for 3 days for expressing his opinion on the 1998 presidential elections. He was released and arrested again within 24 hours, but again released 2 days later. Alfred Adomayakpo, former chief of security for Kodjo and former Director of National Security, was arrested by gendarmes on July 10 for allegedly editing tracts calling for armed revolt. Denied access to a lawyer for 10 days, he was not released until September 23. The Gendarmarie arrested Minister of Rural Development and Tourism, Yao Doh-Feli, also of the UTD, on August 13, and released him 2 hours later.

Commander of the Gendarmarie Pitalouani Laokpessi claimed that security forces were looking for another person of the same last name.

The Constitution prohibits exile, and the Government respects this prohibition.

e. *Denial of Fair Public Trial.*—Although the Constitution provides for an independent judiciary, in practice the executive branch continued to influence the judiciary.

The Supreme Court stands at the apex of the court system. The civil judiciary system includes the Sessions (Court of Assizes) and Appeals Courts. A military tribunal exists for crimes committed by security forces, but its proceedings are closed. Traditional law discriminates against women, particularly in the area of inheritance.

The court system remained overburdened and understaffed (see Section 1.d.). Magistrates, like most government employees, are not always paid on time. The judicial system employs both African traditional law and the Napoleonic Code in trying criminal and civil cases. Trials are open to the public, and judicial procedures are generally respected. Defendants have the right to counsel and to appeal. The Bar Association provides attorneys for the indigent. Defendants may confront witnesses, present evidence, and enjoy a presumption of innocence. In rural areas, the village chief or council of elders may try minor criminal and civil cases. Those who reject the traditional ruling may take their cases to the regular court system, which is the starting point for cases in urban areas.

The Government released political prisoners in late 1994 and early 1995 under the December 1994 general amnesty. The amnesty law, however, was not consistently applied. Dodji Agbaglo, Alex Kpayedo, Paul Hooper, Pierre Hooper, and Edmond Atto, members of the radical youth opposition group M05 arrested in 1994 for an alleged plot to blow up an electrical station at the state-owned Togolese Office of Phosphates, were sentenced on July 3 to between 5 and 7 years in prison. Despite the apparent political motivation of the crime, the State Prosecutor exercised his discretion and refused to apply the December 1994 general amnesty law to this case. Other members of M05 were released under the General Amnesty.

f. *Arbitrary Interference With Privacy, Family, Home, or Correspondence.*—In criminal cases, a judge or senior police official may authorize searches of private residences. In political and national security cases, the security forces need no prior authorization. Police conducted searches without warrants, searching for dissidents' arms caches as well as for criminals, often under the guise of searching for identity cards. Armed security checkpoints exist throughout the country, and security forces arbitrarily interfere with privacy by searching vehicles, baggage, and individuals in the name of security. The Government monitors telephones and correspondence and maintains the police and Gendarmerie as domestic intelligence services.

Section 2. Respect for Civil Liberties, Including:

a. *Freedom of Speech and Press.*—The Constitution provides for freedom of speech and the press, and the Government generally respects these rights in practice although on occasion it intimidated journalists through threats, detention, and persecution.

There is a lively press consisting of approximately 10 independent newspapers, some of which are often extremely critical of President Eyadema. There are four independent radio stations, and two private television companies retransmitting international satellite stations, but none of the independent broadcasters provides any reporting of local or national events. The official media consist of one radio station, one television station, and one daily newspaper. Although they were generally slanted in favor of President Eyadema and the Government, they allowed the opposition limited access.

There were instances of detention and censorship. Moreover, intimidation of the press leads to self-censorship. Moudassirou Katakpaou Toure, director of the opposition newspaper, The Letter of Tchaoudjo, was sentenced on January 17 without being present at the trial or sentencing to 5 years in prison and a $10,000 fine for "defamation of the Chief of State." The Letter of Tchaoudjo was suspended indefinitely. On June 19, the opposition newspaper, The Tribune of Democrats, was fined $6,000, suspended for 6 months, and its director of publication, Eric Lawson, was sentenced without being present at the trial or sentencing to 5 years in prison for "inciting hate and spreading false news" regarding a series of articles blaming a murder on an unidentified commando squad of persons in uniform. The Government never exercised its right of reply nor called on the paper to print a retraction, and the trial was held in secret without informing The Tribune or Lawson of the charges against them. In September the opposition newspaper, The Crocodile, claimed uniformed security forces harassed its vendors in northern Togo and, through intimidation, prevented the distribution of independent newspapers.

In November journalists from three opposition newspapers: Le Combat du Peuple; Le Crocodile; and Forum Hebo, were detained and questioned for periods up to 48 hours, ostensibly for articles accusing a gendarme of killing his wife. However, Lucien Messan, Director of Publication for Le Combat du Peuple, was questioned concerning his intentions for printing an article accusing security forces personnel of participating in a stolen car ring. Messan's interrogators included Gendarmerie commander Laokpessi, who was among those implicated in the article.

At the University of Benin, Togo's sole university, academic freedom is constrained by concern among professors about potential harassment by the Government or antiopposition militants and the lack of a faculty-elected rector. Opposition student groups are intimidated by an informer system that has led in the past to government persecution. The only recognized student group is pro-Eyadema.

b. *Freedom of Peaceful Assembly and Association.*—Under the Constitution, citizens are free to organize in associations and political parties, and in practice political parties are able to hold congresses, elect officers, register, and meet. However, fear of informants and harsh reaction from the Government has reduced public demonstrations. In August a preelection rally by Prime Minister Kodjo in Mango was forced to be relocated, then canceled, when RPT activists, some with machetes, disrupted the event. On November 16 and 17, a delegation of CAR leaders was harassed when roadblocks were set up outside towns in Amou prefecture where they were to hold political rallies. While the rallies ultimately took place, the delegation had to transit numerous barricades, and at one point members of the delegation were assaulted by an RPT supporter. There are many active nongovernmental organizations.

c. *Freedom of Religion.*—The Constitution provides for freedom of religion, and the Government generally respects this right in practice.

d. *Freedom of Movement Within the Country, Foreign Travel, Emigration, and Repatriation.*—The Constitution provides for these rights, however, armed security checkpoints and arbitrary searches of vehicles and individuals are commonplace. The lack of discipline of the soldiers manning the roadblocks and their actions, such as firing at vehicles and frequently demanding bribes before allowing citizens to pass, impede free movement within the country.

The Government generally cooperates with the Office of the United Nations High Commissioner for Refugees (UNHCR) and other humanitarian organizations in assisting refugees. While there is no legislated body to determine asylum or refugee status, the Government routinely accepts the decision of the UNHCR office resident in Lome. The Government provides first asylum (and provided it to approximately 400 persons in 1996). Although in June the Government provided medical supplies, foodstuffs, and water to a Liberian refugee ship, the Zolotitsa, which had been searching the coast for a port to disembark its 435 passengers, it did not authorize disembarkation. With the exception of the Zolotitsa incident, there were no reports of forced return of persons to a country where they feared persecution.

The August 1995 agreement with UNHCR for the repatriation of an estimated 45,000 Togolese refugees living in Benin and 75,000 to 80,000 living in Ghana neared completion by year's end. The UNHCR estimates there will be 25,000 refugees remaining at year's end. They have extended the repatriation program to April 1997, at which time they estimate 15,000 refugees will remain expatriated. The Government also accommodates roughly 8,500 refugees, mainly Ghanaians.

Section 3. Respect for Political Rights: The Right of Citizens to Change Their Government

The Constitution provides for the right of citizens peacefully to change their government. In recent elections, however, this right was only partly respected. In August by-elections, President Eyadema and his RPT party manipulated the rules governing the electoral process and thus further consolidated their majority in the legislature. There were reports of security forces visiting towns weeks in advance of the election and warning their populations of violence if opposition candidates were elected. An RPT parliamentarian threatened at a public meeting in Mango that opposition candidates would be killed if they won.

Institutions created to ensure transparency in electoral procedures and to adjudicate election disputes, such as the National Electoral Commission and the Constitutional Court, are either controlled by the President or still not in place. International observers found the 1993 presidential election to be seriously flawed. Eyadema maintains a highly centralized government, including influencing important nominations of ministers, prefects, mayors, and traditional chiefs. The Government does not openly restrict the functioning of political opponents, but the President uses the strength of the military and his government allies to intimidate and harass citizens and opposition groups. Eyadema also continues to influence the judiciary.

The Constitution provides for universal suffrage and a secret ballot, and these provisions are respected in practice.

There are no legal restrictions on the participation of women or members of ethnic minorities in politics or government. Although many women are members of political parties, there was only one female minister in government and one female deputy in the National Assembly.

Section 4. Governmental Attitude Regarding International and Nongovernmental Investigation of Alleged Violations of Human Rights

There are several local private human rights groups, including the Togolese Human Rights League and the Center of Observation and Promotion of the Rule of Law. In general the Government allows groups access to investigate alleged violations of human rights. However, the Government usually does not follow up on investigations of abuses. Years of government threats and intimidation of human rights leaders, combined with a lack of results from human rights initiatives, have led some human rights monitors to end their public activities.

The Government includes a Ministry of Justice and Human Rights. The National Assembly voted in November to enact a ministerial decree to reorganize the government-sponsored and government-funded National Human Rights Commission (CNDH). The opposition, which boycotted the assembly vote, criticized the new law for allowing the President to control the composition, and ultimately the actions, of the CNDH. In practice neither the Ministry of Justice and Human Rights nor the CNDH operate independently from the President. The International Committee of the Red Cross has a permanent representative in Togo.

Section 5. Discrimination Based on Race, Sex, Religion, Disability, Language, or Social Status

The Constitution prohibits discrimination on the basis of ethnic group, regional or family origin, sex, religion, social or economic status, or personal political or other convictions. However, the Government does not provide effective redress for discrimination complaints, and discrimination based on both ethnic group and sex is common.

Women.—Violence against women continues. Although mechanisms exist within both the traditional extended family and formal judicial structures for redress, the police rarely intervene in traditional or domestic violence cases. Wife beating affects an estimated 10 percent of married women and continues with impunity. Local houses of prostitution exist, and some trafficking in Togolese women for the purposes of prostitution or for exploiting women as domestic servants occurs with no visible effort by the Government to curtail these abuses. There is a Ministry of Feminine Promotion and Social Protection, which, along with independent women's groups and related nongovernmental organizations, have active campaigns to inform women of their rights.

Despite a constitutional declaration of equality under the law, women continue to experience discrimination, especially in education, pension benefits, inheritance, and as a consequence of traditional law. A husband may legally oppose his wife's right to work and control her earnings, and he may also decide where his family will live. Employers are often reluctant to hire women, especially for higher-level positions. Far fewer women than men attend university, and fewer women graduate from secondary school. Families traditionally give boys priority over girls when deciding who shall attend school. In urban areas, women and girls dominate local market activities and commerce with neighboring countries. However, harsh economic conditions in rural areas, where most of the population lives, leave women with little time for activities other than taxing domestic and agricultural field work. Under traditional law, which applies to the vast majority of women, a wife has no rights of survivorship in the event of divorce, separation, or the death of her husband.

Children.—Although the Constitution and family code laws provide for the protection of children's rights, in practice government programs often suffer from a lack of money, materials, and enforcement. The Government provides free education in state schools, and there are social programs to provide free health care for poor children. Orphans and other needy children receive some aid from extended families or private organizations but less from the State. There are few juvenile courts, and children are often jailed with adults. There are credible reports of trafficking in children for the purpose of forced labor (see Section 6.c.).

Female genital mutilation (FGM), which is widely condemned by international health experts as damaging to both physical and psychological health, remains a current, although diminishing, practice in Togo. Approximately 12 percent of Togolese girls and women have undergone FGM. Although many of the largest ethnic groups in Togo do not practice FGM, the practicing groups have rates ranging from 40 to 98 percent. In theory women and girls are protected by the Constitution from FGM, and the Government claims that it would protect any woman bringing a claim of FGM to its attention. However, in practice, the prohibition is not enforced, and traditional customs often supersede the legal system in various ethnic groups.

People With Disabilities.—The Government does not mandate accessibility to public or private facilities for people with disabilities. Although the Constitution nominally obliges the Government to aid disabled persons and shelter them from social injustice, the Government provides only limited assistance in practice. While there is no overt state discrimination against disabled persons and while some hold responsible government positions, the disabled have no meaningful recourse against private sector discrimination, which compels many to beg.

National/Racial/Ethnic Minorities.—Members of northern ethnic groups dominate the security forces, while southerners dominate most commerce and the professions. With a few exceptions, southerners and northerners are also divided along political lines. Civil unrest in recent years and inadequate or prejudicial law enforcement exacerbated ethnic rivalries dating from precolonial times. With the rise in north-south tensions, majority ethnic group members in those regions have harassed and attacked their neighbors belonging to minority groups, forcing them back to their home regions. In recent years, many Togolese, predominantly southerners, fled to neighboring Benin and Ghana, and members of northern ethnic groups were internally displaced.

Section 6. Worker Rights

a. *The Right of Association.*—The Constitution provides most workers with the right to join unions and the right to strike. Security forces, including firemen and policemen, do not have these rights; government health care workers may join unions but may not strike. The work force in the formal (wage) sector is small, involving about 20 percent of the work force, of whom 60 to 70 percent are union members or supporters.

The Constitution also prohibits discrimination against workers for reasons of sex, origin, beliefs, or opinions. There is no specific law prohibiting retribution against strikers.

There are several major trade union federations. These include the National Confederation of Togolese Workers (CNTT), closely associated with the Government; the Labor Federation of Togolese Workers (CSTT); the National Union of Independent Syndicates (UNSIT); and the Union of Free Trade Unions.

Federations and unions are free to associate with international labor groups. The CNTT and the UNSIT are affiliates of the International Confederation of Free Trade Unions.

b. *The Right to Organize and Bargain Collectively.*—The Labor Code nominally provides workers with the right to organize and bargain collectively. All formal sector employees are covered by a collective bargaining agreement. However, true collective bargaining is limited by the Government's role in producing a single tripartite bargaining agreement signed by the unions, management, and the Government. This agreement sets wage standards for all formal sector employees. Individual groups in the formal sector can attempt through collective bargaining to negotiate a more favorable package, and some do, but this approach is not common.

The Labor Code prohibits antiunion discrimination. The Ministry of Labor is charged with resolving labor-related complaints but does not always do so effectively.

A 1989 law allows the establishment of export processing zones (EPZ's). Many companies have EPZ status, and about 20 are currently operating. The EPZ law provides exemptions from some provisions of the Labor Code, notably the regulations on hiring and firing. Employees of EPZ firms do not enjoy the same protection against antiunion discrimination as do other workers.

c. *Prohibition of Forced or Compulsory Labor.*—The law does not specifically address this question, and children are sometimes engaged in forced labor, primarily as domestic servants. Credible sources have confirmed the international trafficking of children, most often to other West and Central African countries, but also to the Middle East and Asia. In rural areas, parents sometimes force young children into domestic work in other households in exchange for cash. The Government has done nothing to stop this practice.

d. *Minimum Age for Employment of Children.*—The Labor Code prohibits the employment of children under the age of 14 in any enterprise. Some types of industrial and technical employment require a minimum age of 18. Inspectors from the Ministry of Labor enforce these age requirements but only in the formal sector in urban areas. In both urban and rural areas, particularly in farming and petty trading, very young children traditionally assist in their families' work. Under the Constitution, school is mandatory for both sexes until the age of 15, but this requirement is not strictly enforced.

e. *Acceptable Conditions of Work.*—The Government sets minimum wages for different categories, ranging from unskilled labor through professional positions. Less than the official minimum wage is often paid in practice, mostly to less-skilled workers. Official monthly minimum wages, including the 5 percent nationwide increase implemented in July, range from approximately $30 to $46 monthly (cfa 14,700 to cfa 23,100). The July increase represents the first since 1987, despite the 50 percent devaluation of the cfa in 1994. Many workers cannot maintain a decent standard of living at the lower official minimum wages, and many must supplement their incomes through second jobs or subsistence farming. The Ministry of Labor is ostensibly responsible for enforcement of the minimum wage system but does not enforce the law in practice. The Labor Code, which regulates labor practices, requires equal pay for equal work, regardless of sex. However, this provision is generally observed only in the formal sector.

Working hours of all employees in any enterprise, except for agricultural enterprises, normally must not exceed 40 hours per week; at least one 24-hour rest period per week is compulsory, and workers must receive 30 days of paid leave each year. The law requires overtime compensation, and there are restrictions on excessive overtime work. The Ministry of Labor's enforcement is weak, however, and employers often ignore these provisions.

A technical consulting committee in the Ministry of Labor sets workplace health and safety standards. It may levy penalties on employers who do not meet the standards, and employees ostensibly have the right to complain to labor inspectors of unhealthy or unsafe conditions without penalty. In practice, the Ministry's enforcement of the various provisions of the Labor Code is limited. Large enterprises must legally provide medical services for their employees and usually attempt to respect occupational health and safety rules, but smaller firms often do not.

UGANDA

During the first 6 months of the year, President Yoweri Museveni continued to rule through the National Resistance Movement (NRM), as he had since 1986. The President dominated the Government, the NRM, and the transition process to constitutional government. The October 1995 Constitution provided for a 276-member unicameral Parliament and an autonomous, independently elected President. The Constitution formally extended Uganda's one-party "movement" form of government for 5 years and severely restricted political party activities, with a national referendum on the role of multiple political parties scheduled for the year 2000. In June and July, separate generally peaceful and orderly presidential and parliamentary elections were held; Museveni was elected President by a wide margin, and NRM supporters won an overwhelming majority of seats in the new Parliament. However, provisions of the election laws heavily favored the NRM, and restrictions on political party activities, NRM use of state institutions, inaccuracy in the voters register, and a proliferation of fraudulent voter cards led to a flawed election process. Technical aspects of the election were generally carried out in a transparent manner. The judiciary is generally independent, but weak; the President has extensive legal and extralegal powers.

The Uganda People's Defense Force (UPDF) is the key security force. The new Constitution maintains civilian control of the UPDF, with the President designated as commander-in-chief. The UPDF's demobilization program, which concluded in 1995, was partially reversed due to increasing instability in the north, and some soldiers were reactivated to combat the rebels. Efforts against northern insurgents were placed under the command of President Museveni's brother, Major General Salim Saleh. UPDF soldiers and members of local defense units (LDU's) assist the police in rural areas, although the LDU's continued to operate without a legal mandate. The Internal Security Organization (ISO) remained under the direct authority of the President. Although primarily an intelligence gathering body, ISO operatives occasionally detained civilians. The ISO's record showed improvement over previous years, although the UPDF, police, and LDU'S committed human rights abuses.

Primarily based on agriculture, the economy grew 8.5 percent during the fiscal year that ended June 30. Coffee remained the chief export crop and foreign exchange earner. In addition, the value of cotton exports jumped by 50 percent, while production of sugar, milk, poultry, and fisheries saw more modest increase. As the privatization of state-owned companies continued, companies ranging from soft drinks to cement received large infusions of private-sector capital. To fight rural poverty (annual gross domestic product was estimated at $220 per capita), the Government continued its infrastructure modernization programs and relied heavily on foreign aid to support its development program. Foreign assistance accounted for approximately 51 percent of government spending.

The Government's human rights record improved somewhat, but numerous, serious problems remain. Citizens have the right to change their government, but NRM domination of the flawed election process limited this right. Security forces used excessive force, at times resulting in death. Government forces committed or failed to prevent some extrajudicial killings of suspected rebels and civilians. Police, UPDF, and LDU forces regularly beat and sometimes tortured suspects, often to force confessions. Despite measures to improve the discipline and training of security forces, and despite the punishment of some security force officials guilty of abuses, security force abuses remained a problem throughout the country.

Prison conditions remained harsh. Prolonged pretrial detention remained a problem. Poor judicial administration, lack of resources, a large case backlog, and lengthy trial delays circumscribed due process and the right to a fair trial. The UPDF at times infringed on citizens' privacy rights. The Government at times restricted freedom of the press. Although independent newspapers generally published freely, the Government dominated the media, limited freedom of speech during the election campaigns, occasionally used outdated sedition laws, and imprisoned some members of the media. This led some journalists to practice self-censorship. In July the UPDF began censoring press reports about the northern insurgencies. The Government has required many students to take NRM political education courses; however, this program was suspended for much of the year. The new Constitution extended previously existing restrictions on political activity for an additional 5 years, effectively limiting freedom of assembly and association. Discrimination against women, domestic violence, and the rape of women and children remained serious problems. Child labor is widespread.

Insurgent forces committed numerous serious abuses. The Lord's Resistance Army (LRA), led by Joseph Kony, continued to kill, torture, maim, rape, and abduct large numbers of civilians. The West Nile Bank Front (WNBF) also committed killings.

RESPECT FOR HUMAN RIGHTS

Section 1. Respect for the Integrity of the Person, Including Freedom From:

a. *Political and Other Extrajudicial Killing.*—There were no reports of politically motivated killings by government forces. However, in the course of official operations, police, UPDF, and LDU personnel sometimes used excessive force, resulting in deaths. In one incident, an LDU guard killed an unarmed civilian to protect an accused thief from a mob. In another incident, an LDU guard killed 11 persons by rolling a grenade into a dance hall after he saw another man with his girlfriend. The guard and a dozen of his LDU companions were arrested following the incident. In Mbale district, the army began disarming the LDU's to counter such offenses. In the northern town of Gulu in August, UPDF personnel stood aside while a mob beat to death four prisoners believed to be members of the LRA. In another incident in April, UPDF soldiers reportedly killed an unarmed LDU guard in the Gulu area while he was in the process of surrendering to arrest. In June two persons residing in the Gulu town barracks were shot to death under suspicious circumstances. In November a police officer in Kampala opened fire on a crowd that was restraining police from stripping naked a suspected thief (a common mode of informal justice); one person was killed and four seriously wounded. No government action in response to these incidents was reported. Poor conditions and lack of adequate medical treatment caused many deaths in prisons (see Section 1.c.).

At year's end, the case of the policeman arrested in June 1995 for killing a striker at the Lugazi Sugar Corporation was still pending. Vigilante justice was a problem (see Section 1.c.).

The LRA was responsible for the killing of numerous civilians (see Section 1.g.).

b. *Disappearance.*—There were no reports of politically motivated disappearances at the hands of government forces.

On August 4, the LRA abducted Alfred Ocen Lalur, the chief administrative officer of Lira. His whereabouts remain unknown (see also Section 1.g.). In addition, the LRA abducted dozens of school-age children, reportedly for indoctrination in Sudan as LRA guerrillas, for sale as slaves, or for sexual purposes. While some of those abducted later escaped or were recaptured, the whereabouts of many children remained unresolved at year's end.

c. *Torture and Other Cruel, Inhuman, or Degrading Treatment or Punishment.*— The Constitution prohibits "any form of torture, cruel, inhuman, or degrading punishment." Police and UPDF commonly beat and sometimes tortured suspected criminals, often to force confessions. In one instance, three police officers were disarmed and beaten by a group of disgruntled citizens. Reinforcements returned shortly thereafter to arrest 70 perpetrators, who were in turn beaten by the police.

LDU's, which frequently lack training, are guilty more often than police of mistreatment of prisoners and detainees. Although they have no authority to make arrests, LDU's continued to do so in rural areas. The Government investigated some cases of abuse, trying and punishing some offenders. One LDU guard was arrested in January after he allegedly shot a person in his custody.

There were scattered instances in which mobs attacked suspected thieves and other offenders caught in the commission of crimes. These mobs engaged in stoning, beatings, and other forms of mistreatment, such as tying the suspect's wrists and ankles together behind his back, or forcing accused criminals to hop painfully on the sides of their ankles. The authorities rarely prosecuted persons engaged in mob justice. On occasion mob violence resulted in death.

Prison conditions remained harsh. There are two civilian prison systems: One State-funded and run by the Ministry of Internal Affairs, and a second run at the local administration level, under the auspices of the Ministry of Local Government. Conditions are particularly harsh in the 133 local prisons, which received no central government funding. Additionally, although the law states that civilians are never to be held in military barracks, civilians continued to be detained in barracks for years, often without trial. Both civilian and military prisons have high mortality rates from overcrowding, diseases spread by unsanitary conditions, malnutrition, and AIDS, a disease that is widespread among the general population. No accurate estimates are available on the number of deaths due to poor conditions and lack of medical care. According to reports by nongovernmental organizations (NGO's), however, at least three persons died in early 1996 at Kangulumira prison in eastern Uganda from a combination of poor food, hard labor, and beatings. The predominant cause of death among prisoners, however, was AIDS. In the local prisons, the uniforms and bedding stipulated by law are rarely provided, although there is evidence that wardens do attempt to obtain these items. In large part, harsh conditions result from inadequate funding. The centrally funded prisons are sufficiently organized to grow maize, millet, cassava, beans, eggplant, carrots, and other crops. Prison conditions come closest to international norms in Kampala, where prisons provide medical care, running water, and sanitation. On the other hand, these centrally funded prisons are the most overcrowded. Luzira upper (maximum security) prison regularly holds twice its maximum planned capacity. In June the chief magistrate ordered all judges to visit a prison, so that they would understand the reality of prison life before passing sentences. Human rights groups, especially the Uganda Law Reform Commission, continued to lobby for expanded noncustodial sentencing. Although the law provides for access to prisoners by families, ignorance of this right, and fear of prison authorities, often limit family visits.

At the local level, due to a lack of space, juveniles are often kept in prison with adults. The central prison system maintains one juvenile prison and two lower security reformatory halls. School facilities and health clinics in all three institutions are defunct; prisoners as young as age 12 perform manual labor from dawn until dusk. Women have segregated wings in the prisons, with female staff. According to human rights advocates, rape is not generally a problem. The central prison system has launched a 3-year program to improve prison buildings, water and sanitation systems, food, and uniforms. Most of these items are made within the prison system itself.

In September the Government co-hosted an international conference on prison conditions throughout Africa. The conference produced a declaration on amelioration of prison conditions that is being used by the Government as a guide for its program of prison improvement. As part of this effort, the Government is revising the Prisons Act, which provides the legal basis for prison management. In addition, the Government initiated a plan to integrate local prisons with the central prison system.

Media access to prisons remained limited, but the Government permitted full access to prisons by the International Committee of the Red Cross (ICRC) and local NGO's, principally the Foundation for Human Rights Initiative (FHRI) and the Uganda Prisoners' Aid Foundation (UPAF). Prison authorities require advance notification of visits, a process that is often subject to administrative delays.

d. *Arbitrary Arrest, Detention, or Exile.*—According to the 1995 Constitution, a suspect must be charged within 48 hours of arrest and be brought to trial or released on bail within 120 days (360 days for a capital offense). In practice, however, the authorities enforced neither requirement. Other laws, such as the Public Order and Security Act of 1967 (the Detention Order), provide for unlimited detention without charge, but these laws have never been formally invoked by the NRM Government. Legal and human rights groups sharply criticized the excessive length of detention without trial—in many cases amounting to several years—for alleged offenses under other laws.

Pretrial detainees comprise nearly three-fourths of the prison population. At year's end, there were 11,527 prisoners in the central prison system, of whom 4,126 had been convicted and 7,401 were in pretrial detention (remand). Congestion and delay in the legal system have produced similar figures for several years. At the local level, the situation is far worse. Most of the approximately 4,000 local prisoners have not yet had a fair trial. Civilians detained in military barracks are almost invariably deprived of a fair, civilian trial. The actual numbers of such detainees are unknown, but there are believed to be fewer than in local prisons. Across all types of prisons, the average time in pretrial detention is from 2 to 3 years.

Some incidents of apparently politically motivated arrests were reported, although the number of political detainees is believed to be small. In one case, some 18 Muslim men were reportedly detained in the Kampala area in February by military intelligence officers and confined in a military barracks without charge.

Arbitrary arrest is rare. However, in May a prominent member of the political opposition and a journalist were arrested during the presidential campaign and charged with sedition (see Section 2.a.).

The Government did not use exile as a means of political control. A presidential amnesty for former LRA/WNBF rebels remains in effect, although those who return risk capture by mobs or the UPDF, either of which may subject them to violent retribution.

e. *Denial of Fair Public Trial.*—The Constitution provides for an independent judiciary. However, while the judiciary is generally independent, the President has extensive legal and extralegal powers that may influence the exercise of this independence. He nominates, for the approval of Parliament, members of the Judicial Service Commission, which makes recommendations on High Court and Supreme Court appointments. The President's influence has also been felt in the Industrial Court (IC) (see Section 6.a.). The highest court is the Supreme Court, followed by (in descending order) the Court of Appeal/Constitutional Court, the High Court, the chief magistrate's court, local council (LC) 3 (subcounty), LC 2 (parish), and LC 1 (village). A minimum of six justices may sit on the Supreme Court and the Court of Appeal/Constitutional Court. Although once considered a useful innovation, the LC courts are now often thought to be sources of injustice due to such factors as bribery and male dominance in rural areas. In addition, there are a few specialized courts to deal with industrial or other matters. The IC for arbitration of labor disputes is structurally parallel to the chief magistrate's court.

At the lower end of the judicial system, the local village councils 1) have the authority to settle civil disputes, including land ownership and payment of debts. These courts, often the only ones available to villagers, frequently exceed their authority by hearing criminal cases, including murder and rape. LC decisions may be appealed to magistrate's courts, but often there are no records made of the case at the village level, and many defendants are not aware of their right to appeal. The civilian judicial system contains procedural safeguards, including the granting of bail and appeals to higher courts.

The right to a fair trial has been circumscribed for many years by an inadequate system of judicial administration and resources, resulting in a serious backlog of cases. Criminal cases may take 2 years or more to reach the courts. Although the case backlog remains huge, some courts began to adhere to the constitutionally prescribed limits on pretrial detention. The Buganda Road Court continued to dismiss cases after 6 months if prosecutors could not produce sufficient evidence to commence a trial. The Mbale court dismissed four persons accused of plotting to assassinate the Speaker of Parliament because their pretrial detention exceeded the legal limit by a day. Chief magistrate Lawrence Gidudu ordered all chief magistrates and magistrates grade 1 to cease granting adjournments if the prosecution does not present convincing reasons for the delay. In August a Kampala court ordered the release of a Kenyan, arrested for illegally entering the country, who had been detained in Lubiri barracks for 4 months.

Many defendants cannot afford legal representation. The Constitution requires that the Government provide an attorney for indigent defendants accused of capital offenses, but there is rarely enough money to retain adequate counsel. The Uganda Law Society (ULS) operates legal aid clinics in four regional offices. It assists military defendants as well as civilians. The Uganda Association of Women Lawyers (FIDA) and the FHRI also practice public-interest law from offices in Kampala.

The military court system does not assure the right to a fair trial. Although the accused has the right to legal counsel, military defense attorneys are often untrained and may be assigned by the military command, which also appoints the prosecutor and the adjudicating officer. The sentence passed by a military court, which may invoke the death penalty, may be appealed to the high command, but not to the High or Supreme Courts. The ULS in 1995 petitioned the Government to address the lack of an appeals process in the military courts but as of the year's end it had received no response, and the issue appeared to be in abeyance. The Government continued to arrest and charge persons for treason. In the past, numerous human rights abuses were committed in connection with treason cases, including political detentions, detentions without charge, and mistreatment of prisoners. Such abuses reportedly occurred at times in 1996, such as the confinement for 2 weeks in a military barracks of some 25 persons detained on suspicion of treason in southwestern Uganda in September. During the year, the Government charged at least 84 people with treason and related crimes, in addition to at least 100 pending cases in various stages of the legal process. Most were cases in which persons were accused of attempting to overthrow the Government. At least 63 people arrested in 1995 on treason charges for attempting to establish a rebel training camp in Buseruka remain in custody, and their case has moved to the high court. Six suspected LRA rebels remain in custody, and their case has gone to the high court as well, as have the cases of businessman Joseph Lusse and two UPDF soldiers arrested for treason in July 1995. Francis Kilama, charged with treason in July 1995, remains in pretrial detention pending police investigation. In November retired UPDF soldier Eddy Waswa, who had been charged with treason in October, died in Luzira prison, reportedly of natural causes. Several persons previously charged with treason, including businessman Salim Okulla, were released after dismissal of the charges, in some instances for procedural reasons.

The number of political prisoners is unknown. The case of Bright Gabula Africa, whose death sentence for treason was upheld by the Supreme Court in May 1995, remains pending. According to the authorities, no executions for treason occurred during the year.

f. *Arbitrary Interference With Privacy, Family, Home, or Correspondence.*—The Constitution provides for the protection of privacy, which the Government generally observes. The law requires that police have search warrants before entering private homes or offices, and the police generally observed this law in practice, although in its effort to combat the rebel movement in the north, the UPDF on occasion invaded private homes without warrants. UPDF forces in the north also allegedly beat civilians and confiscated civilian property, such as cattle. The police sometimes searched vehicles without prior warrants. Prison officials routinely censor the mail of prisoners.

g. *Use of Excessive Force and Violations of Humanitarian Law in Internal Conflicts.*—Reports of violations of humanitarian law increased over previous years. In August the UPDF herded 10,000 unarmed residents of the Gulu area into a stadium and interrogated them to identify rebel collaborators. They dubbed the exercise "Operation Panda Gari" (Kiswahili for "get in the truck"). All but 18 were released within days.

In the north, forces of the LRA led by Joseph Kony regularly attacked civilian and military targets including Sudanese refugee camps, causing widespread death and destruction of homes and property. The LRA continued to kill, maim, rape, and abduct large numbers of civilians. Newspapers reported that Kony offered bounties for the killing of prominent Ugandan military personnel, including the Minister of State for Defense. In one incident, approximately 20 civilians were killed near Gulu at the end of July. Their mutilated bodies were displayed along the main road. LRA soldiers reportedly committed this atrocity to intimidate local citizens. Such extrajudicial killings occurred frequently. The LRA massacred 108 unarmed civilian Sudanese refugees in an attack on the Achol-Pii refugee camp in July. Rebel forces terrorized civilians with tactics that included cutting off noses and ears and breaking legs with hammers. The LRA regularly abducted children of both sexes for impressment into its own ranks. The young abductees were taken to clandestine bases, where they were virtually enslaved as concubines, guards, and soldiers. LRA forces also engaged in the destruction of property, often setting ambushes for military and civilian vehicles. In the north, civilians were routinely abducted by the LRA. The New Vision newspaper reported that the LRA had abducted more than 1,200 people by the end of August, roughly half of whom were later freed. LRA rebels also planted land mines on roads in Gulu and Kitgum district throughout the year. Land mines on the few roads to the border hinder the transport of food to more than 200,000 Sudanese refugees in camps near the border.

In the northwestern region bordering Sudan and Zaire, the WNBF similarly laid land mines on major roads used for relief shipments to refugee camps as well as for local commerce. In September WNBF forces also reportedly attacked trucks transporting refugees, killing 14 persons.

Another rebel group, the Allied Democratic Forces (ADF) invaded the Kasese region from Zaire in November. Before being driven out by the UPDF, the ADF abducted hundreds of civilians from the locality. A number of abductees, including at least seven government officials, were subsequently murdered.

Section 2. Respect for Civil Liberties, Including:

a. *Freedom of Speech and Press.*—The Constitution provides for freedom of speech and the press, but the Government at times restricted these rights in practice. The media were dominated by the New Vision, a Government-funded daily newspaper with a circulation of 40,000 (with up to 10 readers sharing each copy) and a Government-controlled radio station, Radio Uganda. These news sources were of a fairly high quality and often included reporting critical of the Government. The Government's occasional use of outdated sedition laws and imprisonment of some members of the media led some journalists to practice self-censorship. During the election campaigns, the New Vision exhibited a clear pro-NRM editorial bias, and gave more prominent coverage to NRM supporters running for office.

However, the availability of rival nongovernment publications increased. The independent Monitor newspaper equaled the New Vision by increasing its circulation to 40,000; another independent, The Crusader, which began publication in December 1995, quickly expanded its circulation and credibility. The East African, a Nairobi-based weekly publication that covers Uganda extensively, expanded its circulation without government hindrance.

The editor of the most outspoken biweekly, Teddy Seezi Cheeye of the Uganda Confidential, was convicted for defamation of Chief Justice Wambuzi and "the publication of false news." He continued to face various civil suits for defamation as a result of his emphasis on highly personalized and derogatory news and comments; the loss of these suits could result in imprisonment.

The Government controls one television station and the radio station with the largest audience. There are three local television stations, three local radio stations, and five stations available by satellite. Uncensored Internet access became widely available through three commercial service providers in major cities, although its price was prohibitive for all but the most affluent noninstitutional users.

Freedom of speech did not fare well in the context of the transition to constitutional government, including the presidential and parliamentary elections. Guidelines imposed by the Ministry of Internal Affairs prevented members of the former constituent assembly from addressing groups outside their constituencies. Electoral rules prohibited "campaigning" by presidential challengers until the official start of the campaign 39 days before the election. However, in their official capacity, President Museveni and senior members of the Government were free to travel throughout the country for months prior to the election. Rallies in support of all three presidential candidates suffered varying levels of harassment from thugs, in some cases resulting in physical injuries. It appeared, however, that such incidents were particularly directed at President Museveni's opponents.

Yusef Nsubuga Nsambu, a leader of the Conservative party and a supporter of presidential challenger Dr. Paul Ssemogerere, was arrested in May and charged with sedition for his unflattering descriptions of President Museveni. He was released unharmed 2 days later.

The press and media law, passed in June, requires that journalists be licensed and meet certain standards, including holding a university degree. The law provides for a Media Council to monitor and discipline journalists. The law also gives the Government power to suspend newspapers and to deny access to state information. Although the Media Council was established, government officials were not vigorously enforcing the law, both for practical and political reasons. In October a producer at an independent radio station was briefly detained for broadcasting a program in which guests criticized the government's new value-added tax (VAT). About 11 others, including a Member of Parliament, were also briefly detained on suspicion of inciting a week-long protest by business owners against the VAT.

A considerable degree of academic freedom exists at the two public and five private universities, with no government interference in teaching, research, or publication. Students have sponsored wide-ranging political debates in open forums on campus, including an interdisciplinary conference on human rights at Makerere University.

In the past, the Government has required many students and government officials to take NRM political education and military science courses known as "Chaka Mchaka." These courses have been criticized as indoctrination in NRM political philosophy, including the view that political parties were responsible for the country's civil conflicts before 1986. There were reports that the techniques used in some of the courses included intimidation, physical and mental abuse, and sexual harassment. Although this program was largely in abeyance in 1996, legislation providing funding for the Government's "mass mobilization" program was criticized as indirectly supporting the NRM and could result in the program's revival.

b. *Freedom of Peaceful Assembly and Association.*—The Constitution provides for freedom of assembly, but the Government restricts this right in practice. The Constitution bans political parties both from holding national conventions and opening branch offices outside the capital for 5 years.

During the parliamentary election, the Government denied permits for public gatherings and rallies by opposition politicians. In Mbale, LDU's fired into the air during a campaign meeting held by the main presidential challenger, Paul Ssemogerere. The police issued administrative permits for public gatherings, but retained the right to deny permits in the interest of public safety. The police prevented or dispersed at least 13 rallies, seminars, and other public events organized by opposition leaders, including Ssemogerere, Uganda People's Congress Acting Secretary General Cecilia Ogwal, the National Freedom Party, and profederalist activists.

The Constitution provides for freedom of association, but the Government restricts this right in practice. NGO's are required to register with the Nongovernmental Organizations Board, which includes representation from the Ministry of Internal Affairs as well as other ministries. The Government generally approves NGO registration, although there have been instances in which NGO's considered to be opposed to the Government politically have encountered serious difficulties in obtaining registration.

c. *Freedom of Religion.*—The Constitution protects freedom of religion, and the Government respects this right in practice. There is no state religion. Prisoners are given the opportunity to pray on the day appropriate to their faith. Muslim prisoners are usually released from work duties during the month of Ramadan.

d. *Freedom of Movement Within the Country, Foreign Travel, Emigration, and Repatriation.*—The Constitution provides for these rights, and the Government respected them in practice. A married woman needs to obtain her husband's signature on her passport application if children are travelling on the same passport.

The Government has a policy of providing first asylum for refugees and has repeatedly provided such asylum in recent years to citizens of each of its neighboring countries. In 1996 first asylum was granted to nearly 16,000 Zairian asylum seekers. Approximately 2,000 Rwandan refugees, who have had refugee status in Tanzania since 1994, entered Uganda in December to avoid repatriation to Rwanda and were allowed to remain, although at the year's end they had not been granted refugee status.

The Government cooperated with the U.N. High Commissioner for Refugees and other humanitarian organizations in assisting refugees. There were no reports of forced expulsion of those having a valid claim to refugee status. The Government provides first asylum, and in 1996 provided first asylum to more than 240,000 refugees, the majority from Sudan, the remainder from Rwanda and Zaire. The Government pursues an active program for permanent resettlement of those refugees who believe that they can return to their country of origin.

There were several incidents late in the year in which the Government was unable to provide protection to the Sudanese refugee camps in the north of the country when these camps were attacked by rebel forces (see Section 1.g.).

Section 3. Respect for Political Rights: The Right of Citizens to Change Their Government

Citizens have the right to change their government, but NRM domination of the flawed election process limited the effective exercise of this right. In May President Museveni was elected with approximately 76 percent of the vote. In June parliamentary elections were held in which supporters of the NRM won an overwhelming majority of parliamentary seats. Both elections were conducted in a peaceful and orderly manner throughout most of the country. The interim electoral commission generally succeeded in carrying out technical aspects of the election in a transparent manner. However, constitutional restrictions on political parties and provisions of the parliamentary and presidential election laws heavily favored the NRM. Voter registers were often inaccurate and not always available for public scrutiny, which facilitated a proliferation of fraudulent voters' cards. In some cases, local government officials acted in support of particular candidates for office. The interim electoral commission undertook nationwide voter education and civic education programs. Although in some rural villages, NRM loyalists altered the instruction programs to direct voters toward candidates supporting the NRM, the majority of these education efforts were well-conceived and productive. Universal suffrage is accorded to adults 18 years of age and older. Contrary to the Constitution, this right was denied to prisoners.

Although women are underrepresented in government and politics, women play a prominent role in national politics. The vice president and the deputy speaker of Parliament are women. In addition, each of the nation's 39 districts elected 1 woman to Parliament to fill a seat reserved for women by provisions of the Constitution. Six other women won openly contested seats in the 276-member Parliament.

Section 4. Governmental Attitude Regarding International and Nongovernmental Investigation of Alleged Violations of Human Rights

Numerous human rights groups operate in Uganda. Among them are: The FHRI; the Uganda chapter of FIDA; the UPAF, which monitors prison conditions; the National Organization for Civic Education and Elections Monitoring, which deals with concerns related to civil society and political rights; and the National Women's Organization of Uganda. These groups operate without government restriction, investigating and publishing their findings on human rights cases. HURINET, the human rights network, an umbrella organization for nine human rights organizations active in the country, began publishing a quarterly human rights newsletter in January. Amnesty International began talks with the Government about opening a branch office in Kampala in 1997.

The Constitution established a Human Rights Commission as a permanent independent body with judicial powers. Members of the Commission were named in 1996, but by year's end had issued no rulings. Government officials were generally cooperative and responsive to NGO views. They frequently attended conferences and seminars hosted by NGO's on social issues. The Government allowed access by international human rights NGO's, the U.N. High Commissioner for Refugees, and the ICRC. Scattered reports were received during the presidential election campaign that there was harassment of workers associated with some NGO's thought to be opposed to President Museveni.

Section 5. Discrimination Based on Race, Sex, Religion, Disability, Language, or Social Status

The Constitution prohibits discrimination based on these factors, but the Government does not effectively enforce the law in matters of local or culturally accepted discrimination against women, children, people with disabilities, or certain ethnic groups. In Parliament there are special seats designated for women, the disabled, and members of the UPDF. Nothing precludes members of these groups from running for ordinary seats. Race was not a significant factor in national politics. The escalating tension in the north, and particularly the unconstitutional "Operation Panda Gari," led to violations of the rights of many Acholi, the ethnic group which comprises a significant part of the northern population.

Women.—Violence against women, including rape, remained common. There were no laws passed to protect battered women apart from a general law on assault. However, legislation was passed to establish a Family and Children's Court; a task force was established to implement it. Public opinion and law enforcement officials continued to view wife beating as a man's prerogative and rarely intervened in cases of domestic violence. Cases were reported in which husbands beat their wives for failure to vote according to her husband's wishes. Women remained more likely to sue for divorce than to raise assault charges against their husbands while still married. These issues received growing public attention, and female judges, NGO's, and other interested parties hosted an international conference on domestic violence, marriage, and property rights in August.

Traditional and widespread discrimination against women continued, especially in rural areas, despite constitutional provisions to the contrary. Many customary laws discriminate against women in the areas of adoption, marriage, divorce, and devolution of property on death. In most areas in the country, women may not own or inherit property, nor may they have custody of their children under local customary law. Divorce law sets stricter evidentiary standards for women to prove adultery. Women do most of the agricultural work but own only 7 percent of the land. Since the implementation of the new Constitution, foreign-born husbands of Ugandan women could become citizens. The previous law had allowed only men to sponsor their foreign spouses for citizenship. There are limits on a married woman's ability to travel abroad with her children (see Section 2.d.).

There are active women's rights groups, including FIDA, Action for Development, the National Association of Women Judges of Uganda, and the National Women's Organization of Uganda, which promote greater awareness of the rights of women and children. FIDA is conducting a 3-year project to reform outdated and discriminatory laws.

Children.—Although it has devoted only limited funds to children's welfare, the Government demonstrated a commitment to improving children's welfare with the passage of a children's bill to consolidate laws relating to children and provide for their care and protection. The bill stipulated various children's rights and parents' responsibilities, including the requirement that "no child shall be employed or engaged in any activity that may be harmful to his or her health, education, mental, physical or moral development." Nevertheless, the large size of the youth population makes it difficult for the Government to enforce prohibitions on child labor (see Section 6.d.). Half the population is under age 18. Current estimates based on 1991 figures (the most recent ones available) suggest that the number of orphaned children was approximately 1.3 million in 1996 (children missing either parent are considered orphans). The high number of orphans can be attributed to previous civil wars, internal displacement of persons, and AIDS.

There was no system of compulsory education as the Government does not have the resources to provide universal schooling. Parents are required to pay for school fees, books, and uniforms. During the elections, the President announced a policy of providing free education through seventh grade for a maximum of four children per family. In December legislation to implement this program was introduced; it was still pending at year's end. This proposed policy caused some consternation for the large, often polygynous Ugandan families. Girls and boys theoretically have equal access to education, and lower grades are about evenly divided by sex, but some observers believe that this new government provision may further support the trend of parents to favor education for boys. Parents' inability to afford schooling correlates highly with child labor (see Section 6.d.).

Child abuse remained a serious problem, particularly the rape of young girls (known locally as "defilement"). Only a small fraction of these cases are reported, especially when the perpetrator is a family member, neighbor, or teacher, as is often the case. Few accusations reach the courts. Neither conviction nor punishment was common. Cases were reported frequently in newspapers, but a payment to the girl's parents often ended the matter. There are increasing numbers of cases being prosecuted, such as that of a headmaster in Bushenyi who had raped one of his 12-year-old students and received a 13-year jail term.

Corporal punishment persisted in many schools. In March a teacher in Mpigi reportedly beat an 8-year-old child to death; he was arrested, and at year's end he was free on bail. In August a headmaster in Bulegna reportedly beat a 17-year-old girl to death. He was arrested and charged in October with committing an act intended to cause grievous harm. He denied the charge, and at year's end he was free on bail of about $500.

Female genital mutilation (FGM), which is widely condemned by international health experts as damaging to both physical and psychological health, is practiced only by the Sabyni tribe in the Sebei locality in eastern Uganda whose members number fewer than 10,000. There is no law against the practice, but government and women's groups working with the U.N. Fund for Population Activities have a program to combat the practice through education. In October officials of eastern Uganda's Kapchorwa district (Sebei) discontinued collecting fees from parents of young girls who undergo FGM; circumcision fees for boys remained. The step was taken in part in response to protests by female health workers, who claimed that use of FGM as a source of revenue discouraged officials from helping to end the practice.

People With Disabilities.—The law does not mandate government services or facilities such as accessibility of buildings for the disabled. Most buildings are one-story, but in the larger towns with multistory buildings, there are often no elevators and, even where they do exist, they are rarely reliable. Widespread discrimination by society and employers limits job and educational opportunities for those with physical disabilities. A small office for the disabled within the Ministry of Local

Government lacks sufficient funding. Special elections to fill five parliamentary seats allotted to disabled persons were hotly contested, and the media gave extensive coverage to the issues raised by the candidates. Since being elected, the disabled members have been active in emphasizing issues of concern to people with disabilities.

Section 6. Worker Rights

  a. *The Right of Association.*—The Constitution provides for the right of every person to join associations or trade unions. In practice, the Government respects the right to form unions, and since 1993 this right has been extended to civil servants. However, many "essential" government employees are not permitted to form unions; these include the police, army, permanent secretaries in the ministries, heads of departments and state-owned enterprises, school principals, and other management level officials.

  The National Organization of Trade Unions (NOTU), the largest labor federation, includes 17 unions and is independent of the Government and political parties. Its membership was expanded by the recent addition of medical workers, including doctors, and the civil service union. Nevertheless, NOTU's influence on the overall economy remains marginal, since about 90 percent of the work force consists of peasant farmers. Even in areas where cash crops are significant, unionization remained virtually nonexistent. According to the 1988–89 census, about 20 percent of an estimated 400,000 workers in the industrial or modern wage sector of the economy were unionized.

  The Constitution confirms the right to strike, but government policy requires that labor and management make "every effort" to reconcile labor disputes before resorting to strike action. This directive presents unions with a complicated set of restrictions. If reconciliation does not seem possible, labor must submit its grievances and notice to strike to the Minister of Labor, who usually delegates the dispute to the Industrial Court (IC). The IC, however, has issued no prolabor rulings since President Museveni expressed his displeasure with its hostility toward the business community in 1995. In the absence of verdicts from the IC, the Minister of Labor generally did not permit strikes, on the basis that "every effort" had not been exhausted. Frustrated laborers often went on strike anyway, protesting credibly that they were not paid a living wage. Housing conditions and pay complaints led to a violent strike in October at the Kakira sugar plantation, resulting in 74 arrests.

  There were 12 major strikes by both union and nonunion labor, including bankers, teachers, doctors, health care workers, and sugar cane and tea factory workers. Unionized bank employees settled their longstanding dispute with bank owners, but their success prompted the nonunion Uganda Commercial Bank (UCB) workers to follow suit. UCB workers complained that the settlement created anomalies in the pay scales. The Government respected the rights of striking workers once they walked out. One exception occurred during the Kasaku tea estates strike, where workers in a confrontation with management allegedly set fire to the tea fields, permanently destroying 2,500 tea bushes. In spite of a complete lack of evidence, police arrested those persons identified by management as troublemakers. The arrested workers remained in jail for weeks without bail. The case of the police officer arrested in 1995 for killing a striker at the Lugazi Sugar Corporation was still pending at year's end. In the case of three union leaders of the Ugandan Medical Workers Association arrested in 1995, the case was delayed several times at the prosecution's request and was still pending at year's end. The magistrate threatened to dismiss the charges unless the prosecution produced its witnesses.

  Labor unions freely exercised the right to affiliate with and participate in regional and international labor organizations.

  b. *The Right to Organize and Bargain Collectively.*—The law provides for the right to organize and bargain collectively, but true collective bargaining takes place only in the small private sector of the modern economy. In the modern sector, the Government is by far the largest employer (civil service and state-owned enterprises) and it dominates the bargaining process. The Government has, however, adopted a tripartite (government-employers-labor) cooperative approach to setting wages and resolving labor issues. Both the Government and employers may refer disputes to the Industrial Court. The law does not prohibit antiunion discrimination by employers, but apart from a tea plantation arson case (see Section 6.a.), there were no reported incidents of government harassment of union officials.

  There are no export processing zones.

  c. *Prohibition of Forced or Compulsory Labor.*—The Constitution prohibits compulsory labor. However, there is strong evidence that prison officials hired out prisoners to work on private farms and construction sites. Throughout the country, prison officials routinely augmented their meager pay with crops grown by prisoners on the prison grounds. Male prisoners performed arduous physical labor while female prisoners produced marketable handicrafts such as woven basketry. None received compensation, although the law demands that pretrial detainees must receive back pay for all work that they have performed, once they are released. The Government has not reported on the International Labor Organization (ILO) Convention on Forced Labor, for which it was cited by the ILO in 1995. The Government was again cited in 1996 by the ILO for failure to report. According to the Government, the 1995 report has been completed and is awaiting submission to the ILO.

d. *Minimum Age for Employment of Children.*—Employers are prohibited by law from hiring workers below the age of 18, but child labor is widespread. The Ministry of Social Services is charged with enforcing the law on child labor, but it has few resources to do so. Part of the problem is demographic, as half the population is under 18 years of age. School fees make it impossible for many parents—particularly poor farmers, the majority of the population—to give their children an education. As a result, there is an incentive to leave school and go into agricultural or domestic work in order to help meet expenses or perform the work of absent or infirm parents, a common situation throughout the country. About 55 percent of school-age children are in school.

Most working children are employed in the informal sector, often on the subsistence farms of extended family members or as domestic servants. In urban areas, children peddle small items on the streets, become involved in the sex trade, or beg for money. Some of the largest sectors also employ child labor. The vast tea plantations pay by the weight of tea leaves harvested; although most tea harvesting is done by adults, some children are also employed.

Smuggling, one of the nation's larger informal industries, illegally employs large numbers of child laborers at the Kenyan and Tanzanian borders. Children walk back and forth across the unguarded borders transporting small amounts of coffee, fuel, sugar, or other commodities.

e. *Acceptable Conditions of Work.*—The Government does not set a minimum wage. Wages continued to be determined through negotiation between individuals and their employers, unions and proprietors, or through negotiation within the boards of directors at state-owned industries. Salaries are usually augmented by other incentives such as housing and transport allowances, which often equal base wages. The Ministry of Labor's salary scale for civil servants starts with unskilled labor at $50 (51,133 shillings) per month, up to supervisors at $400 (414,738 shillings) per month, plus modest increases for years served. All include provisions for paid overtime. The higher end of this scale would provide minimal support for a worker and family, but most civil servants have great difficulty earning enough money to pay their children's school fees. Many civil servants and their dependents work in second jobs, grow their own food, or seek other ways to feed themselves.

In industries that employ workers on an hourly basis, the normal workweek was 40 hours. Although there was no legal maximum workweek, a time-and-a-half rate was paid for each additional hour worked. Many industries pay workers by piecework, which avoids overtime and circumvents the prohibition on child labor.

The condition of employee housing on the tea and sugar plantations, at the major state-owned corporations, and within military and police barracks was substandard. Such conditions contributed to one strike in October (see Section 6.a.). Sanitation and water facilities are often lacking.

In downtown Kampala, buildings are routinely expanded upward by the addition of several cement floors. Some structures have tripled in height above the original foundations, leading local engineers to express reservations about the structural integrity of these workplaces. Factories are generally sound, but machinery almost always lacks safeguards. The Federation of Uganda Employers held a training convention in May to address the enhancement of the currently inadequate occupational health and safety practices and training.

Vestiges of occupational health and safety legislation are contained in the outdated Factories Act of 1954, the Employment Decree of 1975, and the Workmen's Compensation Act of 1964. None of these acts addresses present-day working hazards. The acts do not protect workers who refuse to perform dangerous work from being fired, although strong unions in certain dangerous industries do protect such workers. The Ministry of Labor's Department of Occupational Health is responsible for enforcement of the limited occupational safety regulations, but in practice inspections are rare, due primarily to the lack of inspectors' vehicles. Under the outdated legislation, the maximum award payable in workers' compensation to a disabled employee, or to the estate of employees killed on the job, is $38.

ZAIRE

After 31 years of authoritarian rule, President Mobutu Sese Seko is generally considered to remain in control of the Government, although his poor health and prolonged absence from the country signaled a significant decline in his authority. A Sovereign National Conference (CNS) in 1992 formulated a new constitution and enacted legislation establishing a transitional government, directly challenging Mobutu.

Following a turbulent contest for political leadership in the ensuing 2 years between the governments of Etienne Tshisekedi and Faustin Birindwa, Mobutu allies and opposition leaders in 1994 passed a Transitional Act, creating a transition constitution and a Combined Transitional Parliament, the High Council of the Republic-Transitional Parliament (HCR–PT). In 1994 the HCR–PT elected Leon Kengo Wa Dondo as Prime Minister. A lawsuit contesting the legality of the election was set aside in September, but continuing political challenges and the protracted transition have left the Kengo Government with little effective authority. In 1995 the HCR–PT extended the transition period and scheduled new elections for mid-1997.

The HCR–PT officially installed a National Election Commission (NEC) in April, which established an electoral calendar providing for a constitutional referendum and national elections in 1997. The HCR–PT approved the draft constitution in October for approval by popular referendum.

President Mobutu's authority rests on his control of key security forces, which include the Civil Guard, a police force with paramilitary and antiterrorist capabilities, and the 7,000-member Special Presidential Division (DSP). Both remain under the command of Mobutu loyalist generals. There exist, in addition, the regular armed forces and a gendarmerie. The security forces suffer from major discipline problems due to irregular pay and a lack of trained commissioned and noncommissioned officers. Members of all the security forces committed numerous and serious human rights abuses.

Most sectors of the economy have been contracting since the late 1970's, and in the 1990's the decline accelerated. Production and incomes have fallen steadily, as the modern sector has virtually collapsed. Physical infrastructure has suffered serious damage, financial institutions have collapsed, and human capital has significantly eroded. Annual per capita national income is estimated at $115. Subsistence activities, a growing informal sector, corruption, and widespread barter characterize much of the economy. The insolvent public sector cannot provide even basic public services, and foreign economic assistance is limited, pending the 1997 elections.

Amid a general atmosphere of economic and personal insecurity, the Government continued to tolerate and commit serious human rights abuses. Security forces continued to commit numerous human rights abuses, including extrajudicial killings, torture, looting, and arbitrary detention. In general, the authorities did not punish the perpetrators, and the problem of impunity remained.

Most prison conditions remain life threatening. Large scale military pillaging largely stopped in 8 of the 11 regions when the Government met most military payrolls. Extensive pillaging occurred, however, in North and South Kivu and Haut Zaire as the Zairian Armed Forces (FAZ) fled advancing rebels.

Citizens were not able to vote to change their government in multiparty elections. Prolonged pretrial and extrajudicial detention is a problem. The judicial system was not independent and was plagued by corruption, lack of due process, lack of resources, and many other problems. It remained largely ineffective as a deterrent or corrective force to human rights abuses. Security forces continued to violate citizens' rights to privacy. Although freedom of expression continued to increase, and was particularly evident in the proliferation of independent newspapers, authorities sought to limit freedom of speech and the press. Military and civilian security forces detained or arrested journalists, editors, and newspaper vendors. The authorities permitted some political demonstrations to proceed unhindered, but at other times the police or Civil Guard intervened, using intimidation, violence and arrests. The Government and security forces restricted freedom of movement. Discrimination against women, ethnic minorities, and Pygmies occurred. Violence against women is seldom punished.

Severe, lethal ethnic conflict in eastern Zaire resulted in many deaths. The continued refugee presence resulting from the 1994 influx from Rwanda exacerbated existing tensions and contributed to a revolt by Banyamulenge ethnic Tutsis and other groups, which many observers conclude was supported by Rwanda and Uganda.

RESPECT FOR HUMAN RIGHTS

Section 1. Respect for the Integrity of the Person, Including Freedom From:

   a. *Political and Other Extrajudicial Killing.*—Security forces, including police, are alleged to have committed over 100 killings during the year although precise estimates are unavailable. Given the administrative and security breakdown throughout the country and the often anecdotal nature of the accounts of these killings, it was often difficult to determine whether these killings were committed for political, monetary, personal, or law enforcement reasons. The Zairian Association for the Defense of Human Rights (AZADHO), a respected human rights group based in Kinshasa, reported 102 cases of extrajudicial killing for the year. Reports often linked security forces to killings and random acts of robbery or extortion. For example, the local press in Kinshasa in August reported that a soldier shot and killed a merchant in the central market because she refused to pay for protection; the soldier was not arrested or charged with a crime. Only rarely have there been reports that civil or military authorities made inquiries into such incidents. In the east, interethnic conflicts led to many deaths (see Section 1.g.).

   Persons incarcerated in the country's prisons are reportedly beaten by prison officials, while other prisoners die of illness or starvation (see Section 1.c.).

   In July 1995, in a particularly egregious example of extrajudicial killing, civil guards used lethal force to put down an unauthorized demonstration in Kinshasa by the Unified Lumumbist Party (PALU), led by Antoine Gizenga. Human rights monitors stated that there were 14 deaths, including a soldier; 54 others were seriously wounded. The Government claimed, however, that there were four deaths plus one soldier killed by the protesters. Gizenga was detained for several days and released on bail. He reportedly was charged with organizing an unauthorized demonstration and possessing an M-16 assault rifle which authorities claimed was found in his house. Military forces attacked Gizenga's home and raped and killed a member of his family immediately after the 1995 incident. The military services launched official inquiries into the incident in August 1995 but failed to make public any results. The charges were dropped on February 29.

   In several cases, notably in the interior, citizens responded to military aggression in kind, sometimes killing soldiers. On February 15, for example, Goma residents killed a soldier whom they believed had earlier murdered a civilian. In Kinshasa in July, a group of citizens destroyed a courthouse after a gendarme working there shot and killed a taxi driver for refusing him free transportation. There are no reports that the gendarme was ever tried or sentenced for the crime. There were extrajudicial killings of Zairian officials by Banyamulenge rebels and their allies in the Kivus in November (see Section 1.g.).

   b. *Disappearance.*—There were several reported cases of disappearances, although the number appears to be down from previous years. As in the past, some of these disappearances may have been criminal, rather than political, in nature. Security forces regularly hold alleged suspects in secret detention for varying periods of time before acknowledging that they are actually in custody. The most frequent accounts describe unidentified assailants who abduct, threaten, and often beat their victims before releasing them. Journalists and opposition party members claim that they are targets for such actions. Patrick Shotsha On'oto, a youth leader who had been periodically harassed by uniformed personnel since participating in the 1992 Christian Students' March, disappeared in April 1995 after giving a lecture on the role young people should play in elections. His whereabouts remain unknown. In Kisangani a human rights nongovernmental organization (NGO), Friends of Nelson Mandela, reported the disappearance of Damadu Mbula, exact date unknown. Mbula has not been located. Mbula Kwete, a journalist based in Kinshasa, disappeared in September. According to a local newspaper, Kwete had been sought by the authorities for some time due to his political beliefs.

   c. *Torture and Other Cruel, Inhuman, or Degrading Treatment or Punishment.*—Although the law forbids torture, security forces and prison officials routinely disregard this prohibition, often beating prisoners in the process of arresting or interrogating them. In March in Bunia, in the region of Haut Zaire, according to the National League for Free and Fair Elections (LINELIT), a local NGO, two members of the Union for Democracy and Social Progress (UDPS) were arrested and tortured by members of the Civil Guard because of their political activities. AZADHO reported in August that two members of the government tax collectors' union were arrested and tortured for requesting an audit of the Director General of Taxation. AZADHO reported torture marks on the bodies of the two unionists. An American citizen was arrested in May and again in August. Akerele's mother, a Zairian, is a declared candidate for President. On both occasions, police beat Akerele; the second time police shaved his head and inscribed the letters "p.m." He was never charged with any crime. Several other released prisoners claim to have been struck, kicked, whipped, and suspended upside down for long periods of time. The authorities, including the judiciary, rarely investigate claims of torture, despite their prevalence. Members of all the security forces routinely prey on civilians, generally without official rebuke. They continued to commit many criminal infractions, including robbery, extortion, and looting.

Conditions in most of the 220 known prisons and places of detention remain life threatening. There are no precise numbers of prisoners; however, AZADHO reports that there are 1,067 prisoners in the Makala and Ndolo prisons in Kinshasa. The Government does not acknowledge any responsibility to furnish prisoners food or medical supplies. Prison facilities are grossly inadequate; living conditions are harsh and unsanitary, and prisoners are poorly treated. The system has severe shortages of funds, medical facilities, food, and trained personnel. Overcrowding and corruption are widespread. Reports of prisoners being tortured, beaten to death, deprived of food and water, or dying of starvation are common. Prisoners are wholly dependent on personal resources of family or friends for their survival. Inmates at Makala Central Prison in Kinshasa sleep on the floor without bedding and have no access to sanitation, potable water, or adequate health care. Even in Makala's best-equipped ward, over 100 white collar criminals share one latrine. Tuberculosis, red diarrhea, and other infectious diseases are rampant. Although authorities have not targeted women for abuse, rapes occur. Of the 50 women in Makala Prison in August, 5 were accompanied by children under the age of 5 years. Political prisoners are held in a separate ward and are allowed little, if any, direct contact with visitors. On December 27, 1995, the Minister of Justice issued an order prohibiting the use of 25 of the 73 detention centers in the region of Kinshasa following a Judicial Commission's report that these facilities were in "an advanced state of unhealthiness incompatible with human dignity." Makala Central Prison was not listed among the 25 prisons prohibited from use. In August, 20 of these prisons were reportedly still being used.

The International Committee of the Red Cross (ICRC), religious organizations, and local human rights organizations report that they have regular access to prisons nationwide. In some cases, however, the unpublicized creation of unofficial detention sites by the civil and military authorities circumvents their access to all prisoners and detainees.

d. *Arbitrary Arrest, Detention, or Exile.*—Despite legal provisions governing arrest and detention procedures, the security forces were responsible for numerous cases of arbitrary arrest and detention.

Under the law, serious offenses (those punishable by more than 6 months' imprisonment) do not require a warrant for a suspect's arrest. Only a law enforcement officer with "judicial police officer" status is empowered to authorize arrest. This status is also vested in senior officers of the security services. The law instructs security forces to bring detainees to the police within 24 hours. The law also provides that detainees must be charged within 24 hours and be brought within 48 hours before a magistrate, who may authorize provisional detention for varying renewable periods.

In practice, these provisions are rarely followed. Gendarmes and civil guards commonly detain civilians without any legal authority. The security forces—especially those carrying out the orders of any official who can claim authority—use arbitrary arrest to intimidate outspoken opponents and journalists. Charges are rarely filed, and the political motivation for such detentions are often obscure. When the authorities do press charges, the claims that they file are sometimes contrived or recitations of archaic colonial regulations.

Estimates of political detainees are unreliable due to detention in clandestine locations and military facilities. The practice of detaining people for their political views declined from past years.

Political detainees are typically held incommunicado, sometimes in unofficial detention sites, with irregular or no access to legal counsel. Newspaper journalist Sumalili Kilue, arrested and released in February by the military forces, was never charged with a crime.

On May 3, the authorities in North Kivu released Malira Kabuya, Byamungu Kahima, Ndasimwa Malira, and Bonane (Hunde ethnic group). They were never charged, and there was no action on the part of the authorities to investigate their severe mistreatment by the police.

Authorities detained five individuals on different occasions in incidents related to the outbreak of hostility in the Kivus. Political opposition members Willy Mishiki and Joseph Olenga Nkoy were detained for, respectively, inciting student demonstrations and for criticizing the Government's handling of the Kivu crisis. Both were released on December 13.

Three members of the local NGO La Voix des Sans Voix, including the organization's president Floribert Cheyeba, were detained for having inquired about the welfare of prisoners of war; authorities released the three on November 2.

Corrupt local officials routinely use detention as a means of extortion, arresting people on fabricated charges, releasing them only after payment of a "fine."

Of the 1,067 detainees accounted for in Makala and Ndolo Prisons in August, more than 75 percent had yet to come before a judge, although many had spent as long as 2 years in prison.

The Transitional Act specifically forbids exile, and there were no known cases.

e. *Denial of Fair Public Trial.*—Despite provisions for independence in the Transitional Act, the judiciary is not independent of the executive branch, and the latter can and does manipulate it.

Civil and criminal codes are based on Belgian and customary law. The legal system includes lower courts, appellate courts, the Supreme Court, and the Court of State Security. There is a separate system of military tribunals with an appeals structure that parallels that of civilian courts. Decisions from the military tribunals may be appealed to the Supreme Court. Charges of misconduct against senior government officials must be filed directly with the Supreme Court.

The Transitional Act provides for the right to a speedy public trial, the presumption of innocence, and legal counsel at all stages of proceedings. Defendants have the right to appeal in all cases except those involving national security, armed robbery, and smuggling, all of which are adjudicated by the court of state security. The law provides for court-appointed counsel at state expense in capital cases, in all proceedings before the Supreme Court, and in other cases when requested by the court. In practice, the authorities ignore these protections.

Adherence to established legal procedures varies considerably, and fair public trial is rare. Corruption is pervasive, particularly among magistrates, who are very poorly and intermittently paid and are poorly trained. The judicial system is further hobbled by major shortages of personnel, supplies, and infrastructure. Defendants never meet their counsel or do so only after months of detention and interrogation. Cases are heard only when the defendant or plaintiffs pay all court costs, including salaries, a situation that routinely results in corruption.

Judicial officials assigned to remote areas in the country in some cases either refused to assume their posts or fled from them in ethnic purification campaigns, particularly in Maniema and Shaba. As a result, local authorities usurped judicial proceedings in some parts of the country.

There are no reliable statistics on the number of political prisoners, but the trend of incarcerating people for their political views was down from past years. There were no reported cases of individuals formally accused, tried, and imprisoned for political beliefs.

f. *Arbitrary Interference With Privacy, Family, Home, or Correspondence.*—Security forces routinely ignore the Transitional Act provisions for the inviolability of the home and of private correspondence. They ignore the requirement for a search warrant, entering and searching homes at will. In January, for example, four civil guards entered the home of Denis Wathum without a warrant, detained him at a military precinct, and asked for money. He was later released.

The threat of rape, sometimes perpetrated by uniformed persons, restricts the freedom of movement at night for women in many neighborhoods. Groups of citizens have implemented neighborhood watch programs, but women in many parts of Kinshasa do not leave their homes at night.

Elements of the DSP and Civil Guard have reportedly been used to intimidate private businesses for the commercial gain of individuals. For example, the DSP in 1995 intervened in a private commercial dispute between a foreign-owned company and a local competitor owned by one of Mobutu's closest associates, and in September a house owned by the central bank was seized. Members of the armed forces are employed as security guards and enforcers. The Kengo Government strongly supports the contractual rights of foreign investors and has sought, albeit unsuccessfully in most cases, to curtail arbitrary interference by elements of the military forces. Uniformed personnel routinely interfere with daily business activities, especially those of the informal economy. Currency vendors are particularly at risk and remain subject to repeated robberies by uniformed assailants. In February and in November soldiers robbed several currency vendors in downtown Kinshasa's Wall Street district. They were never charged or brought to trial.

Citizens are free to join or refrain from participating in any political party. However, opposition party members complain that they are followed or harassed by troops loyal to the President. In July Christian Badibangi, a member of the radical opposition, was shot and wounded by unknown persons in his home. No one has been charged. Citizens widely assume that the Government monitors mail and telephone communications. The Government does not restrict access to foreign publications.

g. *Use of Excessive Force and Violations of Humanitarian Law in Internal Conflicts.*—The July 1994 influx and protracted presence of refugees and former Rwandan soldiers aggravated longstanding conflicts between Zairian groups, and violent ethnic clashes, described as ethnic cleansing, took place in North Kivu in several subregions north of Goma in February. Also, ambiguities in Banyarwanda (peoples of Rwandan origin) legal status, caused by conflicting laws that bestow and then revoke citizenship, further inflamed tensions, especially with the prospect of multiparty elections. In the Masisi region of North Kivu almost all ethnic Tutsi citizens were forced out of the country due to fear of ethnic violence and are now refugees in Rwanda. Hutus were the dominant ethnic group in the Masisi region until October. These violent ethnic clashes in eastern Zaire included widespread human rights abuses, despite the deployment of additional Zairian troops to the region in February and March. These tribal conflicts encouraged ethnic groups in the region to engage in violent attacks against other tribes. Violence, or the threat of violence was carried out by Hutu, Hunde, Nande, and other Zairian ethnic groups, some of which formed bands of youth to terrorize the ethnic minority Tutsi. From February to October, more than 1,000 people were reported killed in the Masisi region as a result of fighting between the Banyarwanda and indigenous ethnic groups.

In October a rebellion nominally led by the ethnic Tutsis in South Kivu resulted in open warfare and the expulsion of Hutu refugees from the immediate area of the refugee camps in North and South Kivu, and loss of life of all sides (see Section 2.d.). The rebellion expanded in November and December, and many observers concluded that the rebellion was supported by Rwanda and Uganda. Rebels have been accused of massacring segments of the refugee population, of summarily executing business people who did not comply with rebel directives, and of killing political leaders closely associated with the Government. Tutsi led rebels reportedly massacred 500 men at a camp for Rwandan refugees and Zairian displaced persons south of Bukavu in November. A Bukavu Catholic bishop was executed, allegedly by the FAZ for a public statement supporting Banyamulenge rights. The Catholic archbishop of Bukavu was murdered, apparently by the rebels.

In contrast, there were no reports of violence against Kasaians living in Shaba since the expulsion of 1992. The last groups of displaced Kasaians forced to flee Shaba were resettled in July 1995.

Section 2. Respect for Civil Liberties, Including:

a. *Freedom of Speech and Press.*—The Transitional Act provides for freedom of expression as a fundamental civil right. However, while the press and the public can exercise freedom of expression much more openly than before the transition began in April 1990, in practice the Government—notably those elements loyal to the President—continues to restrict freedom of speech and the press to a considerable extent.

Newspaper publishers are required to deposit copies of each issue with the Ministry of Information prior to publication. The Government continued arbitrarily to intimidate, harass, and detain journalists and other media officials for publishing controversial articles. On September 17, Ladi Luya, the editor of Le Palmares, a pro-opposition newspaper, was arrested for publishing an article speculating on the President's health. He was released on September 28. In March the Minister of Information suspended the publishing of two newspapers because of an article entitled, "The Financial and Budget Mismanagement of the Zairian Armed Forces." Their publisher, Bonsanje Yema, was held briefly in detention but is now free. Though the two newspapers are still banned, Bonsanje is publishing a newspaper under a different title. In August the Governor of Haut Zaire banned the NGO LINELIT from having access to the government owned radio and television stations. They are still banned. Several church radio stations in Kisangani and Bunia (Haut Zaire) have been banned from broadcasting any nonreligious programs. In some cases, government and military authorities have targeted media reporters and officials for extortion purposes.

The principal means of communication with the public are radio and television, both of which remain under presidential control. Although there is no specific policy prohibiting opposition access to radio and television, opposition parties complain that they are unable to gain access to such media.

In December 1995, the Parliament passed a new press law after consultations with media representatives, but the President refused to sign it and sent the legislation back to Parliament for reconsideration. However, on June 22, President Mobutu signed the law into effect. While the law deals mainly with media administrative issues, it also codifies the law in libel cases and requires journalists to reveal sources "when required by the law."

In principle, academic freedom is provided for in the Transitional Act. However, in the past when teachers and academic staff have organized to protest their salaries and working conditions, they were met with repression.

b. *Freedom of Peaceful Assembly and Association.*—The Transitional Act upholds the right to assemble and associate. The full exercise of the right of assembly is subordinate to the maintenance of "public order." The Government requires all organizers to apply for permits, which are granted or rejected at its discretion. In some cases, the Government uses this power to discriminate against political opponents, and has revived a 1959 colonial ordinance to justify banning public meetings. The Government allowed several groups, including the radical opposition, to hold several large gatherings, the last one on July 26, during which security forces exercised restraint. Nevertheless, in other instances security forces repressed unauthorized political and other demonstrations, sometimes violently (see Section 1.a.). On July 19, several UDPS members of the opposition who tried to hold a banned march were arrested and tortured. Dieudonne Nyengele was detained for almost a month but was released on August 16. NGO's in Bunia reported that opposition political parties' rallies were usually banned by regional authorities. (Bunia was in rebel hands at year's end.)

The Government requires that NGO's and political parties register with the Minister of Justice, but there have been no reported cases in which an organization has been refused registration.

c. *Freedom of Religion.*—The Transitional Act provides for freedom of religion, and the Government respects this provision in practice, with the reservation that the expression of this right neither disturb public order nor contradict commonly held morals. There is no legally established or favored church or religion.

A 1971 law regulating religious organizations grants civil servants the power to establish and dissolve religious groups. Although this law restricts the process for official recognition, officially recognized religions are free to establish places of worship and to train clergy. Many recognized churches have external ties, and foreign nationals are allowed to proselytize. The Government generally does not interfere with foreign missionaries. Many missionaries, however, report that local security forces and government authorities often demand money for alleged taxes and that they are never given receipts for the sums paid. There has been no known persecution of Jehovah's Witnesses or any other groups for practicing their faith in recent years. The Jehovah's Witnesses, formally unbanned in 1993, were permitted to construct a headquarters in Kinshasa.

d. *Freedom of Movement Within the Country, Foreign Travel, Emigration, and Repatriation.*—The Transitional Act allows for freedom of movement, but the Government, and in particular the security forces acting independently, often restrict this freedom. All citizens, refugees, and permanent residents are nominally required to carry identity cards. However, the Government has not officially issued identity cards since 1987 when it invalidated the old ones, then banned the new ones. Consequently, some citizens carry both cards, while other citizens have none. Security forces erect checkpoints at airports, ferry ports, and roadblocks, usually to extort money from travelers. Passports and exit permits are available in principle to all citizens but often at exorbitant cost from corrupt officials. Women must have the permission of their husbands to apply for a passport (see Section 5).

The Government provides first asylum. Zaire housed nearly 1 million Rwandan Hutu refugees, mostly 1994 first asylum cases, along its densely populated eastern border until a revolt, led by Banyamulenge ethnic Tutsis and other groups, led to the November repatriation of the majority of the refugees.

The Government cooperated with the U.N. High Commissioner for Refugees (UNHCR) who estimated that there were also approximately 150,000 Burundi Hutu refugees located in the area. Extreme regional insecurity and open warfare between ethnic Tutsis, Hutu extremists, and Zairian security forces, prompted the United Nations and donor nations to request a military operation in the region of the Kivus in November. Plans for such an operation were suspended after the majority of the refugees in the Kivu camps returned to Rwanda.

The 1,500 members of the Zairian camp security contingent troops (CZSC) from the Special Presidential Division generally performed their duties well in the camps throughout the year. However, cross-border violence rendered the overall refugee security situation unstable, and refugees were subject to extortion, robbery, and sexual abuse. The UNHCR reported that rapes in and outside the refugee camps were on the rise since January. There were reported abuses by the former Rwandan military forces located in the camps, by civilian refugees, and by local Zairians. The Kengo Government removed some intimidators from the refugee camps throughout the year. Most of the Rwanda Hutu hardliners, however, remained and moved deeper into Zairian territory following the massive return of refugees to Rwanda in November.

Zaire is a signatory to the 1951 U.N. Convention and its 1967 Protocol related to the treatment of refugees.

Section 3. Respect for Political Rights: The Right of Citizens to Change Their Government

The Transitional Act mandates the right of citizens to change their government, but citizens have not been able to exercise this right by voting in multiparty elections. President Mobutu, who in 1990 promised democratic reform, continued to impede democratic progress through his control over key parts of the state apparatus, especially the military forces, and by distracting factions of the political opposition, often with spurious promises. In the process, the President exacerbated party maneuvering and political posturing in the HCR–PT and reinforced Tshisekedi's and the radical opposition's intransigence in Parliament. Despite these impediments, the Parliament passed implementing legislation establishing a National Electoral Commission (NEC) to conduct a nationwide census, register voters, publish a list of candidates, and supervise eventual elections. On January 1, the HCR–PT broke the deadlock over the question of the NEC's membership. In October the HCR–PT completed its deliberations on the draft constitution and implementing legislation for the referendum. President Mobutu promulgated the draft constitution in late December.

There are no official restrictions on the participation of women or minorities in politics. However, in practice, there are few women or Muslims in senior positions in the Government or in political parties. In the new cabinet established December 24, there is one female minister. A U.N. Children's Fund (UNICEF) study on women reported that there were 38 women in the HCR–PT of a total membership of 739.

Section 4. Governmental Attitude Regarding International and Nongovernmental Investigation of Alleged Violations of Human Rights

While the Government rarely responds to human rights accusations, it permits a number of effective human rights organizations to operate, including AZADHO, LINELIT, and the Voice of the Voiceless. These organizations investigate and publish their findings on human rights cases, largely without government restriction. The Government acknowledged AZADHO's 1995 report of human rights abuses, although it disagreed with the group's figures.

The security forces continued occasionally to harass and intimidate human rights monitors, although there were fewer NGO reports of this activity than in 1995. The Government permitted international organizations to visit and discuss abuses; the ICRC was allowed to visit prisons on a regular basis.

In December the U.N. Human Rights Commission established a two-person field office in Kinshasa, with a mandate to assess human rights conditions.

Section 5. Discrimination Based on Race, Sex, Religion, Disability, Language, or Social Status

The Transitional Act forbids discrimination based on ethnicity, sex, or religious affiliation, but the Government made little headway in advancing these provisions. Societal discrimination remained an obstacle to the advancement of certain groups, particularly women, Muslims, and the Pygmy (Batwa) ethnic group.

Women.—Domestic violence against women, including rape, is believed to be common, but there are no known government or NGO statistics on the extent of this violence. Rape is a crime in Zaire, but the press rarely printed articles about specific incidents of violence against women or children. When the press reports a rape, it is generally as a consequence of some other crime, but rarely because of the act of rape itself. AZADHO listed only three reported rapes in 1996. The police rarely intervene in domestic disputes, and local NGO's dealing with women's issues stated that they were unaware of any Kinshasa court cases this year involving rape or spousal abuse.

Despite constitutional provisions, women are relegated to a secondary role in society. They comprise the majority of primary agricultural laborers, and small-scale traders and are almost exclusively responsible for childrearing. In the nontraditional sector, women commonly receive less pay for comparable work. Only rarely do they occupy positions of authority or high responsibility. A UNICEF study on women in Zaire reported that only 85 of the country's approximately 600 lawyers are women. Women also tend to receive less education than men. The UNICEF study reported that, as of 1995, 14 percent of children between the ages of 10 and 14 had never been to school. Ranked by sex for this age group, 17.8 percent of girls had never attended school, compared with 10 percent for boys.

Women are required by law to obtain their spouse's permission before engaging in routine legal transactions, such as selling or renting real estate, opening a bank account, accepting employment, or applying for a passport (see Section 2.d.). A 1987 revision of the Family Code permits a widow to inherit her husband's property, to control her own property, and to receive a property settlement in the event of divorce. In practice, sometimes consistent with customary law, women are denied these rights. Widows are commonly stripped of all possessions—as well as their dependent children—by the deceased husband's family. Human rights groups and church organizations are working to combat this custom, but there is generally no government intervention or legal recourse. Women also are denied custody of their children in divorce cases, but they retain the right to visit them. Polygyny is practiced although it is illegal. Children of polygynous unions are legally recognized, but only the first wife is legally recognized as a spouse.

Children.—Government spending on children's programs is nearly nonexistent. Most schools, for example, only function in areas where parents have formed cooperatives to pay teachers' salaries.

There are no documented cases in which security forces or others target children for specific abuse, although children suffer from the same conditions of generalized social disorder and widespread disregard for human rights that affect society as a whole. These conditions sometimes render parents unable to meet their children's basic human needs.

Female genital mutilation, which is widely condemned by international health experts as damaging to both physical and psychological health, is not widespread, but it is practiced on young girls among isolated groups in the north.

People With Disabilities.—The law does not mandate accessibility to buildings or government services for the disabled. There are some special schools, many with missionary staff, that use private funds and limited public support to provide education and vocational training to blind and physically disabled students.

Indigenous People.—Societal discrimination continued against the Pygmy (Batwa) population of less than 10,000. Although citizens, Pygmies living in remote areas took no part in the political process.

National/Racial/Ethnic Minorities.—The last official census was taken in 1984. It is estimated that the population is now 45 to 50 million, and comprises more than 200 separate ethnic groups. Four indigenous languages have national status. French is the language of government, commerce, and education. Members of President Mobutu's Ngbandi ethnic group are disproportionately represented at the highest levels of the military and intelligence services. Violent clashes between Banyamulenge ethnic Tutsis and other ethnic groups and government security forces in the North and South Kivu regions led to open warfare, ethnic cleansing, and loss of life (see Section 2.d.). Rwandan and ethnic Tutsis elsewhere in Zaire, notably in major urban centers like Kinshasa, Lubumbashi, and Kisangani, were targeted for harassment, systematic theft at their homes and businesses, and physical abuse following the outbreak of hostilities in the Kivus. Hundreds were forced to flee the country.

Section 6. Worker Rights

a. *The Right of Association.*—The Transitional Act and other legislation permit all workers except magistrates and military personnel to form and join trade unions.

Before 1990 the law required all trade unions to affiliate with the National Union of Zairian Workers (UNTZA), the sole recognized labor confederation and which also formed part of Mobutu's Popular Movement of the Revolution (MPR) party. When political pluralism was permitted in April 1990, UNTZA disaffiliated itself from the MPR and reorganized under new leadership chosen through elections deemed fair by outside observers. Although UNTZA remains the largest labor federation, almost 100 other independent unions are now registered with the Labor Ministry and two other large federations are active. Some of these are affiliated with political parties or associated with a single industry or geographic area.

The law recognizes the right to strike; however, legal strikes rarely occur since the law requires prior resort to lengthy mandatory arbitration and appeal procedures. Labor unions have not been able to defend effectively the rights of workers in the deteriorating economic environment. In July and August, several government employees were arrested and released several times for being members of the Solidarity trade union. Illegal general, sector, and other strikes, often called by political parties and not necessarily organized by unions, occur despite their illegality. The law prohibits employers or the Government from retaliating against strikers, but it is rarely enforced.

In November 1995, the International Labor Organization Committee on Freedom of Association (CFA) cited Zaire for serious violations of the principles of freedom of association on the basis of complaints arising from events between mid-1993 and March 1995. The CFA expressed "deep concern" about "arrests, detentions, and torture of trade unionists, acts of repression against demonstrators, the hampering of trade union activities, and acts of antiunion discrimination, including the dismissal of officials, prohibition of union meetings in the health services, refusal to register trade unions, creation of trade unions by the authorities, and the Government's refusal to negotiate with representative trade unions." The CFA regretted the Government's failure to respond to these allegations and called on it to make restitution where possible and to desist from such actions in the future. Trade unions report that in 1996 the Government did not officially stop this type of harassment.

Unions may affiliate with international bodies. The UNTZA participates in the Organization of African Trade Union Unity, and the Central Union of Zaire is affiliated with the World Confederation of labor.

b. *The Right to Organize and Bargain Collectively.*—The law provides for the right to bargain collectively, and an agreement between the UNTZA and the employers association provided for wages and prices to be jointly negotiated each year under minimal government supervision. This system, which functioned until 1991, broke down as a result of the rapid depreciation of the currency. While collective bargaining still exists in theory, continuing hyperinflation has encouraged a return to pay rates individually arranged between employers and employees.

The collapse of the formal economy has also resulted in a decline in the influence of unions, a tendency to ignore existing labor regulations, and a buyer's market for labor. The Labor Code prohibits antiunion discrimination, although this regulation is not strongly enforced by the Ministry of Labor. The law also requires employers to reinstate workers fired for union activities. In the public sector, the Government sets wages by decree; public sector unions act only in an informal advisory capacity.

There are no export processing zones.

c. *Prohibition of Forced or Compulsory Labor.*—The law prohibits forced labor, and such labor is not practiced.

d. *Minimum Age for Employment of Children.*—The legal minimum age for employment is 18 years. Employers may legally hire minors between the ages of 14 and 18 with the consent of a parent or guardian, but those under 16 may work a maximum of 4 hours per day; those between the ages of 16 and 18 may work up to 8 hours. Employment of children of all ages is common in the informal sector and in subsistence agriculture. Neither the Ministry of Labor, which is responsible for enforcement, nor the labor unions make an effort to enforce child labor laws. Larger enterprises do not commonly exploit child labor.

e. *Acceptable Conditions of Work.*—Most citizens are engaged in subsistence agriculture or commerce outside the formal wage sector. The minimum wage, last adjusted by government decree in 1990, is irrelevant due to rapid inflation. Most workers rely on the extended family and informal economic activity to survive. The maximum legal workweek (excluding voluntary overtime) is 48 hours. One 24-hour rest period is required every 7 days.

The Labor Code specifies health and safety standards, and, while the Ministry of Labor is officially charged with enforcing these standards, its efforts to do so remained insufficient. There are no provisions in the Labor Code permitting workers to remove themselves from dangerous work situations without penalty.

ZAMBIA

Zambia is a republic governed by a president, a unicameral national assembly, and a constitutionally independent judiciary. After two decades of one-party rule, free and fair multiparty elections in 1991 resulted in the victory of the Movement for Multiparty Democracy (MMD) and the election of President Frederick J. T. Chiluba, a former trade unionist. In the November 18 elections, President Chiluba was reelected and his party gained 131 of 150 seats in the National Assembly. There were 5 presidential and over 600 parliamentary candidates from 11 parties. Elections took place peacefully. Following the ballot, several opposition parties and nongovernmental organizations (NGO's) declared the electoral process neither free nor fair, in part due to constitutional amendments enacted in May that disqualified former President Kenneth Kaunda, the main opposition leader, from seeking the Presidency. Kaunda's United National Independence Party (UNIP) had boycotted the parliamentary polls, alleging that the results were fixed beforehand. Although reputable reports indicated some voting irregularities, no evidence of substantial or widespread vote rigging or vote-counting fraud has been presented.

The police, divided into regular and paramilitary units operating under the Ministry of Home Affairs, have primary responsibility for maintaining law and order. The Zambia Intelligence Security Service, under the Office of the President, is responsible for intelligence and internal security. Despite reform efforts begun in 1994, including human rights training and punishment of some offenders, the police force lacks sufficient professionalism and discipline. Police continued to commit numerous, and at times serious, human rights abuses.

Throughout the year the Chiluba Government continued its free market economic reform program. New taxes slowed economic growth and allegations of high-level government corruption continued. Rains during the 1995–96 growing season produced a good harvest of maize, the staple food, improving the food security of most Zambians. The key copper industry, scheduled for privatization in 1997, suffered from a gradual weakening of world prices and a fall in production. The resulting lost income contributed to a fall in the value of the kwacha. Successful privatization in other industries and the development of nontraditional agricultural exports created some new jobs.

The Government took steps to address some human rights problems, but serious abuses continued in several areas. The police were responsible for extrajudicial killings as well as beatings of criminal suspects and detainees. Prison conditions are harsh and deteriorated further, posing an increased threat to the health and lives of inmates. Arbitrary arrests, prolonged detention, and long trial delays remain problems. Police authorities continued efforts to address police brutality, adopting community based policing methods, introducing human rights training into the curriculum of the police training college, and instituting a program of human rights seminars for midlevel and senior officers.

The Government unsuccessfully sought to reduce the independence of the judiciary, persisted in attempts to limit freedom of the press, and restricted citizens' right of peaceful assembly. The Government announced its intention not to privatize government-owned mass media, contrary to its 1991 promises. The Government rejected most elements of a draft constitution prepared in 1995 by a presidentially appointed review commission, choosing instead to pass amendments to the 1991 Constitution. The principal purpose of the amendments was to disqualify Kaunda, the main opposition leader (and many other citizens), from contesting the Presidency by making only second-generation Zambians eligible. These amendments restricted the right of citizens to change their government. Women continued to experience discrimination in both law and fact. Wife beating, rape, and denial of widows' inheritance rights remained widespread.

RESPECT FOR HUMAN RIGHTS

Section 1. Respect for the Integrity of the Person, Including Freedom From:

a. *Political and Other Extrajudicial Killing.*—There were no reports of political killings during the year, but police continued to use excessive force that resulted in extrajudicial killings. Press accounts reported that police killed 12 people during the year. Most were killed while reportedly trying to escape capture. One of the 12 was an innocent woman killed by police gunfire during a gun battle with suspects in September. Police acknowledged their mistake and promised to compensate the victim's family. According to the police spokesmen, one suspect died in jail when officers failed to provide necessary medical attention.

On December 28, a woman died in police custody in Kasempa. Townspeople, alleging that police officers had beaten her to death, attacked government offices in Kasempa in an attempt to avenge her death.

Throughout the year, government officials, nongovernmental organizations, and the press closely scrutinized police involvement in human rights abuses, criminal activity, and corruption. Francis Ndhlovu, Inspector General of Police, continued to exercise his mandate to reform the force. Ndhlovu has instituted a variety of measures designed to restore discipline, professionalism, and respect for human rights, including police training in respect for human rights. Ndhlovu's efforts suffered a setback in May when a State House official ordered police to attack a peaceful march by students, overruling the police commander on the scene. In September Ndhlovu testified that he had placed illegal wiretaps on a telephone at The Post newspaper office. By year's end, the Government had not taken disciplinary action against him.

The police undertook investigations of instances of police use of excessive force, disciplining officers who committed human rights abuses. The police adopted community based policing methods. Middle-ranking and senior police officers were enrolled in human rights training seminars at the Police Academy. According to statistics made available by the police command, at least eight police officers were the subjects of internal investigations or prosecutions. Further, according to official statistics, the authorities arrested at least 12 police officers on such criminal charges as robbery and possession of illegal narcotics.

The government-appointed Human Rights Commission, chaired by prominent attorney Bruce Munyama, aggressively examined police human rights abuses in public hearings held throughout 1995. In September 1995, the Commission submitted its final report to the President, including recommendations to improve the human rights performance of the police. The report was released by the Government in October when the Parliament also passed legislation creating an autonomous human rights commission.

Many prisoners died as a result of harsh prison conditions (see Section 1.c.).

In June a bomb exploded at the Lusaka airport, killing one police officer who reportedly arrived at the scene to investigate reports of the bomb's presence. In December 1995, army recruits near Kapiri Mposhi went on a rampage in retaliation for the death of a comrade at the hands of local villagers. They destroyed 10 small villages and killed two villagers. Neither the police nor the Ministry of Defense had brought charges against the recruits by year's end.

b. *Disappearance.*—On December 30, The Post newspaper reported the disappearance and detention of Chronicle reporter George Jambwe who had entered the Army Headquarters (Arakan Barracks) in an effort to interview the army commander. He was released to police custody after 3 days and charged with criminal trespass.

c. *Torture and Other Cruel, Inhuman, or Degrading Treatment or Punishment.*—Although the 1991 Constitution prohibits torture, police regularly used excessive force when apprehending, interrogating, and detaining criminal suspects or illegal aliens. In most such instances, detaining officers beat suspects. In March police at the Chawama station severely beat a suspect, denied him necessary medical attention, and then released him without filing charges. In May police crushed the testicle of a detainee. No officers have been disciplined or arrested for these acts. By year's end, the Government had not disciplined or prosecuted any of the individuals allegedly involved in the torture of persons detained in connection with the 1993 state of emergency.

On October 18, police clashed with supporters of a local politician in Kabwe. Television coverage that evening showed police kicking and beating many of those who had been detained and handcuffed. Police action followed President Chiluba's instructions to MMD Secretary General Michael Sata, heard on the public address system at the MMD rally in Kabwe, to "sort them, Michael, sort them out."

Prison conditions are harsh. Deteriorating prison conditions posed an increased threat to prisoners' lives. According to official statistics, prisons designed to hold 6,000 prisoners held over 12,000. This severe overcrowding, combined with poor sanitation, inadequate medical facilities, meager food supplies, and lack of potable water resulted in serious outbreaks of dysentery, tuberculosis, and other diseases at various prisons throughout the year. In a report submitted to Parliament, the Director of Prisons said 975 prisoners had died in prison between January 1991 and December 1995. Of these 203 died of AIDS-related illnesses, the rest from harsh conditions or other illnesses. Prisoners continued to die at about the same rate in 1996.

The Government permits prison visits by both domestic and international human rights monitors.

d. *Arbitrary Arrest, Detention, or Exile.*—Criminal suspects are often arrested on the basis of flimsy evidence or an uncorroborated accusation. In these and other criminal cases, the law requires that a detainee be charged and brought before a magistrate within 24 hours. Attorneys and family members are allowed pretrial access to detainees. In practice the authorities hold most detainees for more than 1 month from the time of arrest to first appearance before a magistrate. In many cases an additional period of 6 months elapses before the magistrate commits the defendant to a high court for trial. Following committal, preparation of the magistrate court record for transmittal to a high court takes months—in some cases as long as a year. Once a case reaches a high court for trial, court proceedings last an average of 6 months.

Approximately 2,000 of the 12,000 jailed prisoners are awaiting trial on criminal charges. In some cases defendants have been awaiting trial for 10 years. These long delays are the result of inadequate resources, inefficiency, lack of trained personnel, and broad rules of procedure that give wide latitude to prosecutors and defense attorneys to request adjournments. In 1996 the High Court Commissioner began releasing detainees if the police failed to bring the case to trial.

Although there is a functioning bail system, overcrowded prisons reflect the large number of detainees accused of serious offenses for which bail is not granted. These include treason, murder, aggravated robbery, and violations of the narcotics laws. Also, poor or indigent detainees rarely have the financial means to post bail. The government legal aid office is responsible for providing legal representation to poor or indigent detainees and defendants in criminal or civil cases. In practice few receive assistance. In 1996 the office had 14 attorneys to cover the entire country and a budget of $110,000.

Police stations frequently become "debt collection centers," where police officers, acting upon an unofficial complaint, will detain a debtor without charge indefinitely until he or she pays the complainant. The police receive a percentage of the paymentin return. This situation is commonplace. The authorities held approximately 500 foreigners, principally from neighboring countries, as illegal aliens until they could deport them. At times these detentions last months or years (see Sections 1.f. and 2.d.).

The Speaker of the National Assembly ordered the indefinite incarceration of Post newspaper writers Fred Mmembe, Bright Mwape, and Lucy Sichone for contempt of the House. A high court later quashed the sentences, ruling that the Speaker had no authority over private citizens, but only after Mmembe and Mwape had spent several weeks in prison.

The Government arrested eight United National Independence Party (UNIP) leaders on charges of treason (a nonbailable offense). The prosecution delayed arraignment and sought to delay the opening of the trial. After several weeks, however, the High Court insisted that the government prosecutor pursue the case. Two suspects were later released due to failure to prosecute. The other six were acquitted after a 6 week trial. The health of all eight suffered while they were imprisoned. Many attorneys considered the charges purely political. Although technically the Government arrested them for their alleged involvement in bombings, their status in the opposition and the Government's failure to produce any convincing evidence raised the suspicion that they were really political detainees.

In an effort to intimidate students and discourage them from publicly criticizing the Government, the police arrested Emmanuel Tembo, president of the University of Zambia's students' union in July, questioned him about campus demonstrations against the Government's constitutional amendments, and released him on the following day.

The Government has not used exile for political purposes, but it has used deportation or the threat of deportation for such purposes. The case of John Chinula, a member of the Central Committee of UNIP (the former ruling party), whom the Government had deported in 1994, continued to attract the attention of human rights advocates. They protested his deportation, asserting that Chinula had been born in Zambia and that the deportation was a denial of due process. However, those advocating his case were quieted by a Lusaka High Court decision denying habeas corpus to Chinula in September 1995, in which the Court stated that he was, in fact, a citizen of Malawi. In December Malawi's Supreme Court ordered Chinula returned to Zambia. Zambian immigration officials and the Minister of Home Affairs announced that Chinula would be arrested and deported if he entered Zambia. His whereabouts were unknown at year's end. Chinula's longstanding ties to Zambia and his prominence as a politician continue to raise questions about the Government's motives in deporting him.

e. *Denial of Fair Public Trial.*—The Constitution provides for an independent judiciary. Although the Government has generally respected the independence of the judiciary, it tried unsuccessfully to limit its independence during the year. The President nominates and the National Assembly confirms the Chief Justice and the other eight members of the Supreme Court. The Court has appellate jurisdiction for all legal and constitutional disputes. Several high courts have authority to hear criminal and civil cases and appeals from lower courts. Magistrate courts have original jurisdiction in some criminal and civil cases, while local, or customary, courts handle most civil cases at the local level.

In April the Government introduced constitutional amendments that would have virtually eliminated the independence of the high courts and the Supreme Court. The amendments would have granted the President the power to dismiss judges, subject only to concurrence by the National Assembly. The President alone would have been able to decide what constituted grounds for dismissal. Following strong public protest, the Government withdrew the amendments in May.

Local courts employ the principles of customary law, which vary widely throughout the country. Lawyers are barred from participating, and there are few formal rules of procedure. Presiding judges, who are usually prominent local citizens, have great power to invoke customary law in rendering judgments regarding marriages, divorces, inheritances, other civil proceedings, and minor criminal matters. Judgments are often not in accordance with the Penal Code; for example, they tend to discriminate against women in matters of inheritance (see Section 5).

Trials in magistrate courts are public, and defendants have the opportunity to confront accusers and present witnesses. Many defendants, however, are too poor to retain a lawyer, and the poor state of the Government's Legal Aid Department means that many citizens entitled to legal aid find that it is unavailable.

There were no reports of political prisoners.

f. *Arbitrary Interference With Privacy, Family, Home, or Correspondence.*—The Constitution provides for respect for privacy and the inviolability of the home, and the authorities generally respected these rights in practice.

Except during a state of emergency, the law requires a warrant before police may enter a home; however, police routinely ignored this requirement. The Constitution grants the Drug Enforcement Commission and the Zambian Intelligence Security Service authority to wiretap telephones. In September the Inspector General of Police admitted in open court that he had ordered illegal wiretaps on a telephone at the offices of The Post, an independent daily newspaper.

Roundups of suspected illegal aliens in the home or workplace continued. According to the government Commissioner for Refugees, immigration officials are empowered under the law to conduct these roundups without a warrant (see Section 2.d.).

Section 2. Respect for Civil Liberties, Including:

a. *Freedom of Speech and Press.*—While the Constitution provides for freedom of expression and of the press, the Penal Code lists various prohibited activities that may be interpreted to restrict these freedoms. In February the Government banned issue 401 of The Post for allegedly revealing "state secrets" (these were transcripts of cabinet discussions of MMD election campaign strategy). It later ordered ZAMNET, the Zambian Internet provider, to delete the issue from The Post's home page. The Government invoked restrictive laws—for example, prohibiting defamation of the President—in other selected cases. A magistrate in the copperbelt town of Kitwe sentenced William Banda to 3 years' imprisonment for publicly insulting President Chiluba during his visit to a housing project. Banda was immediately taken into custody by a local official of the ruling MMD party. The Government or its appointed officials filed numerous libel and defamation suits against The Post in response to a series of headlines and stories focusing on issues of corruption and controversial government policies. At year's end over 90 of these cases remained to be adjudicated.

The law includes provisions for investigative tribunals to call as witnesses journalists and media managers who print allegations of parliamentary misconduct. Failure to cooperate with the tribunal may result in charges of contempt punishable by up to 6 months in jail. This is seen by the media as a clear infringement on press freedom and a means for parliamentarians to bypass the clogged court system in dealing with libel suits against the media. The Press Association of Zambia has its own media ethics code and voluntary industry ethics board. The indefinite incarceration of three Post writers (see Section 1.e.) on orders of the Speaker of the House infringed upon freedom of expression.

A number of independent newspapers actively question government actions and policies. They circulate without government interference. Throughout the year the leading independent daily, The Post, had a home page on the World Wide Web that attracted over 15,000 readers per month. The State House and the government-controlled Times of Zambia established home pages in April.

The Government owns the two most widely circulated newspapers, as well as the sole television station, ZNBC. In addition to the government-controlled radio station, two church-related stations and one private commercial station operate in Zambia. MNET, a South African company, provides a subscriber television service. It carries British Broadcasting Corporation (BBC) world news but provides no local news coverage. The Government exercises considerable influence over the government-owned media, which have followed the government line on important issues to an increasing degree. The government-sponsored radio stations carry some BBC and German World Service news programs. In August the Government announced its intention not to privatize government-owned mass media, contrary to its 1991 promises.

Although the Government attempted to influence the politics of university students (see Section 1.d.), it took no action restraining academic freedom during the year. Following a rock-throwing incident involving university students, the Faculty Senate at the University of Zambia closed the campus 1 week before the November 18 general election. Although the Senate insisted that it acted independently, university and police actions before the incident indicate the Senate succumbed to government influence.

b. *Freedom of Peaceful Assembly and Association.*—The Constitution provides for freedom of peaceful assembly and association, but the Government restricted these rights in practice. On January 10, the Supreme Court ruled unconstitutional key provisions of the 1955 Public Order Act, which had been used to restrict the right of peaceful assembly. Subsequently, the National Assembly passed legislation requiring 14 days prior notification to the police in order to hold a public meeting. President Chiluba reduced this to 7 days in September. In practice the police did not interfere with peaceful rallies whose leaders had followed the prior notification rule.

All organizations must apply formally for registration to the Registrar of Societies. In most cases the authorities routinely approved these applications. During the year there were 36 political parties in operation and dozens of NGO's.

Following the November elections, several NGO's declared that the elections were neither free nor fair. The Government accused them of colluding with foreign powers and of engaging in unpatriotic activity. Subsequently police briefly detained the directors of two of these groups, Alfred Zulu of the Zambian Independent Monitoring Team and Ngande Mwanajiti of the Clean Campaign Committee. Police also searched the offices, confiscated materials, and froze the bank accounts of the two organizations. At year's end, police charged Alfred Zulu with illegal reception of foreign funds. The assets of both organizations remained under court control.

c. *Freedom of Religion.*—A 1996 amendment to the Constitution declares Zambia a Christian nation while providing for freedom of religion. The Government respects the rights of all faiths to worship freely in practice.

d. *Freedom of Movement Within the Country, Foreign Travel, Emigration, and Repatriation.*—The Constitution provides citizens with the right to move freely throughout Zambia, to reside in any part of the country, and to depart and return to the country without restriction. The authorities generally respected these rights, but police roadblocks to control criminal activity continued, and police sometimes extorted money and goods from motorists.

The United Nations High Commissioner for Refugees (UNHCR) estimated that there were approximately 120,000 refugees, mainly Angolans, in Zambia in 1996. Approximately 500 refugees from Africa's great lakes region were present in Zambia at year's end. The Government cooperates fully with UNHCR. As in the past, the Government continues to provide first asylum to refugees from several countries and allows refugees to resettle in Zambia. There were no reports of forced return of persons to a country where they feared persecution or a pattern of abuse.

A steady trickle of Zairians continued to cross into Zambia during the year. In response to alleged criminal activities of many Zairians in the border region, the Government rounded up, arrested, and deported many Zairians and other illegal aliens throughout the year. The authorities held approximately 500 foreigners, principally from neighboring countries, as illegal aliens pending their deportation. On occasion such detentions last for months or years (see Sections 1.d. and 1.f.). The deportation of illegal aliens is lawful, but Zairians and others who had been accorded refugee status by the UNHCR were sometimes picked up and held for varying lengths of time before being released. In several cases the Government deported refugees who were registered with the UNHCR. The Government detained 12 Rwandans accused of war crimes. The Government cooperated fully with U.N. and International Criminal Tribunal for Rwanda (ICTR) officials. The courts ordered four of the suspects transported to Arusha, Tanzania for trial by the ICTR and released eight others for lack of evidence.

Section 3. Respect for Political Rights: The Right of Citizens to Change Their Government

Citizens exercised the right to change their Government in multiparty elections in November. Constitutional amendments barring first-generation Zambians from contesting the Presidency and preventing traditional chiefs from running for political office restricted the right of citizens to change their Government. The former provision barred the most popular opposition candidate, former President and UNIP leader Kenneth Kaunda, from running for President; the latter provision barred UNIP's number two, Senior Chief Inyambo Yeta.

Under the 1991 Constitution, as amended, the President wields broad authority. Although the National Assembly ratifies major appointments and has other powers, in practice it continued to provide only a limited check on executive authority.

Although the principal opposition party, UNIP, boycotted the parliamentary balloting, a total of 11 parties contested 150 parliamentary seats. Five candidates contested the Presidency. Just under 50 percent of eligible voters registered. Of these, approximately 60 percent cast ballots. While the MMD's use of government resources (civil servants as campaign workers, use of government vehicles, and the state-owned media) apparently did not change the overall outcome, it called into question the fairness of the process. The Government's failure to implement a transparent registration project raised doubts about the Government's willingness to have an open electoral process.

The number of women in politics and government is increasing, but their numbers remain small. There are 13 women in the 158-member National Assembly. Women serve as cabinet ministers, deputy ministers, and ministerial permanent secretaries. Chiluba's post-election Cabinet has two female ministers and one minister of Asian (Indian) descent.

Section 4. Governmental Attitude Regarding International and Nongovernmental Investigation of Alleged Violations of Human Rights

A number of human rights and civic organizations generally operated without government hindrance. These include the Law Association of Zambia, the Foundation for Democratic Process, and the Zambia Civic Education Association. Other groups were active in promoting women's civil and political rights. The Government announced that it would establish an autonomous human rights commission before year's end and continued to be receptive to criticism from human rights and civic organizations. On occasion, however, government officials accused human rights monitors of abetting crime and thwarting the work of the police through their focus on the victims of police brutality, which the Government apparently interpreted as an effort to discredit the authorities. The Government was receptive to inquiries and visits by international human rights organizations.

Section 5. Discrimination Based on Race, Sex, Religion, Disability, Language, or Social Status

The Constitution prohibits discrimination based on race, tribe, sex, place of origin, marital status, political opinion, color, or creed. Constitutional amendments barring native born Zambians of partial or full foreign ancestry from the Presidency were unsuccessfully challenged in court.

Women.—Violence against women remained a serious problem. Wife beating and rape were commonplace. According to official statistics, over 3,000 rape cases were reported to the police between 1991 and 1996. Of these, approximately 30 percent resulted in conviction and 5 percent acquittal. The remainder were either dismissed or remain unresolved. Defendants convicted of rape normally were sentenced to prison at hard labor. Since many rapes are not reported to the police, the actual number is considered much higher. Domestic assault is a criminal offense, but in practice police are often reluctant to pursue reports of wife beating, preferring to broker a reconciliation. The Government and NGO's expressed increasing concern about violence against women, and the media devoted considerable publicity to it during the year.

The Constitution and other laws entitle women to full equality with men in most areas. In practice, however, women are severely disadvantaged compared to men in formal employment and education. Married women who are employed often suffer from discriminatory conditions of service. For example, allowances for housing and children and tax rebates to which they as employees are entitled often accrue to their husbands. Similarly, women have little independent access to credit facilities; in most cases, they remain dependent on husbands, who are required to sign for loans. As a result, few women own their own homes.

Customary law and practice also place women in subordinate status with respect to property, inheritance, and marriage, despite various constitutional and legislative provisions. Under traditional customs prevalent in most ethnic groups, all rights to inherit property rest with the deceased man's family. The 1989 Intestate Succession Act is designed to guarantee women a share of the joint estate. Under the act, the children of a deceased man share 50 percent equally among themselves; the widow receives 20 percent; the parents 20 percent; and relatives 10 percent. A 1996 "reform" of the act places the widow's share as 20 percent to be divided equally among the women who have a claim. Formerly one was considered a widow only if there was a registered church wedding or weddings. (Polygamy was and is permitted if the first wife agrees to it at the time of the first wedding.) Now the widow or widows must share the inheritance with any other women who can prove a marital relation (not a registered or recorded marriage) with the deceased man, thus granting inheritance rights to mistresses or concubines.

In practice "property grabbing" by the relatives of the deceased man continues to be rampant, particularly when local customary courts have jurisdiction. These courts often use a different law, the Local Courts Act, to distribute inheritances without reference to the percentages mandated in the Succession Act. As a result, many widows receive little or nothing from the estate. Fines mandated by the Succession Act for property grabbing are extraordinarily low.

Children.—The Government seeks to improve the welfare of children, but scarce resources and ineffective implementation of social programs adversely affected the welfare of children and adults alike. Due to harsh economic conditions, both rural and urban children often must work in the informal sector to help families make ends meet (see Section 6.d.). There was no societal pattern of discrimination or abuse against children.

People With Disabilities.—Persons with disabilities face significant societal discrimination in employment and education. The Government continued to take steps to ameliorate their hardships, including establishing a national trust fund to provide loans to the disabled to help them start businesses, but its efforts are limited by scarce resources. The Government has not legislated or otherwise mandated accessibility to public buildings and services for the disabled.

Section 6. Worker Rights

a. *The Right of Association.*—The Constitution provides for the right of citizens to form trade unions, and approximately 60 percent of the 300,000 formal sector workers are unionized. Fourteen of the country's 19 large national unions, organized by industry or profession, are affiliated with the Zambia Congress of Trade Unions (ZCTU). The ZCTU is democratically operated and, like its constituent unions, is independent of any political party and the Government. By a majority vote of its members, a union may decide on affiliation with the ZCTU or with trade unions or organizations outside Zambia. The Mine Workers Union of Zambia and four other ZCTU constituent unions broke away from ZCTU and have established a rival umbrella organization.

The ZCTU is a member of the International Confederation of Free Trade Unions. Labor leaders travel without restriction to international conferences and to visit counterparts abroad.

The 1993 Industrial and Labor Relations Act (ILRA) reestablished the "one industry, one union" principle. In December the Government ratified articles 97 and 98 of the International Labor Organization Convention allowing the establishment of more than one labor confederation. The Bankers Union of Zambia, a new union, was duly registered with the Government in 1993 but has been unable to operate because the employers recognize the existing Zambia Union of Financial and Allied Workers. In November 1993 the Ndola High Court ordered the Government to register the Secondary School Teachers Union of Zambia. The Government continues to argue that the Zambia National Union of Teachers represents secondary school teachers and has administratively delayed recognition of the new secondary teachers union.

All workers have the right to strike, except those engaged in essential services, the Zambia Defense Force, the judiciary, the police, the prison service, and the Intelligence Security Service. The ILRA defines essential services as power, medical, water, sewage treatment, firefighting, and certain mining occupations as essential to safety. It permits strikes only after all other legal recourse has been exhausted, and in practice virtually all work stoppages during the year were illegal. The ILRA prohibits employers from retribution against employees engaged in legal trade union activities. Workers engaged in illegal strikes do not enjoy this protection.

b. *The Right to Organize and Bargain Collectively.*—The ILRA provides for the right to organize and bargain collectively. Employers and unions in each industry negotiate collective bargaining agreements through joint councils in which there is no government involvement. In practice the industry joint councils function effectively as collective bargaining units. Civil servants and teachers, as public officials, negotiate directly with the Government. Collective bargaining disputes are first referred to a conciliator or a board of conciliation. If conciliation fails to resolve the dispute, the parties may refer the case to the Industrial Relations Court or, in the case of employees, vote to strike. In practice legal strikes under the ILRA are rare, totalling two during the year. The ILRA prohibits antiunion discrimination by employers against union members and organizers. An employee who believes he or she has been penalized for union activities may, after exhausting any existing administrative channels for relief, file a complaint with the Industrial Relations Court. This Court has the power to order appropriate redress for the aggrieved worker. The complainant may appeal a judgment of the Industrial Relations Court to the Supreme Court. In practice the Court often orders employers to reinstate workers found to have been the victims of discrimination.

There are no export processing zones.

c. *Prohibition of Forced or Compulsory Labor.*—The Constitution prohibits slavery and involuntary servitude, but it authorizes citizens to be called upon to perform labor in specific instances, for example, during national emergencies or disasters. Moreover, a citizen can be required to perform labor that is associated with traditional civic or communal obligations, as when all members of a village are called upon to assist in preparing for a visit by a traditional leader or other dignitary.

d. *Minimum Age for Employment of Children.*—The minimum legal age for employment of children is 16 years. The Labor Commissioner effectively enforces this law in the industrial sector in which, because of the high demand for employment by adults, there are no jobs available for children. The law is not enforced, however, for those who work in the subsistence agricultural, domestic service, and informal sectors, where persons under age 16 are often employed. In urban areas children commonly engage in street vending.

e. *Acceptable Conditions of Work.*—The minimum wage for nonunionized workers is set at $0.06 (70.30 kwacha) per hour. Assuming a 48 hour workweek—the legal maximum for nonunionized workers—a worker earning the minimum wage would receive about $11.30 (14,600 kwacha) per month. The minimum wage covers nonunionized workers in categories such as general workers, cleaners, office orderlies, and watchmen. The minimum wage is insufficient to provide an adequate standard of living for a worker and family, and most minimum wage earners must supplement their incomes through second jobs, subsistence farming, or reliance on the extended family.

With respect to unionized workers, each industry sets its own wage scales and maximum workweek limits through collective bargaining. In practice almost all unionized workers receive salaries considerably higher than the nonunion minimum wage. The minimum workweek for full-time employment is 40 hours and is, in practice, the normal workweek. The law requires 2 days of annual leave per month of service.

The law also regulates minimum health and safety standards in industry. The Department of Mines is responsible for enforcement. Factory safety is handled by the Inspector of Factories under the Minister of Labor, but staffing problems chronically limit enforcement effectiveness. There are no legislative provisions to protect a worker who refuses to work on safety grounds.

ZIMBABWE

President Robert Mugabe and his Zimbabwe African National Union-Patriotic Front (ZANU–PF) have dominated the legislative and executive branches of Zimbabwe's Government since independence in 1980. The Constitution allows for multiple parties; in addition to ZANU–PF, there are a large number of smaller parties. However, they are poorly organized and led, poorly financed, and subject to periodic intimidation by the ruling party and government security forces. The judiciary is independent, but the Government occasionally refuses to abide by court decisions.

The Zimbabwe Republic Police (ZRP) are responsible for maintaining law and order. The Zimbabwe National Army and Air Force are responsible for external security. The Central Intelligence Organization (CIO) under the Ministry of State Security is responsible for internal and external security but no longer has powers of arrest.

Zimbabwe's economy is agriculturally based, with strong mining and tourism sectors and a diversified manufacturing base. It is increasingly market based under the 1991–95 structural adjustment program. Primary exports are tobacco, cotton, oil seeds, livestock, gold, and nickel. Over 60 percent of the population engages in subsistence agriculture. The formal sector unemployment rate remains above 45 percent. Indigenization (black economic empowerment) is a government priority to redress economic disparities between the majority black population and a small white elite. The estimated 1996 annual per capita gross domestic product of $588 is expected to rise as the economy continues its recovery from drought.

The Government generally respected the human rights of its citizens; however, there were significant problems in some areas, including incidents of police brutality, harsh prison conditions, the Government's refusal to abide by several court rulings, CIO intimidation of opposition party candidates and their supporters, restrictions on academic freedom, infringements on citizens' privacy, and the banning of the Gays and Lesbians of Zimbabwe's stand at the Harare International Book Fair (which was overturned by the courts).

Members of the security forces committed human rights abuses. Despite cases of police brutality, human rights organizations report a marked improvement in overall police treatment of suspects and members of the public.

Although the legislative and campaign climate remained tilted in favor of the ruling party and the March presidential elections were marred by opposition candidates' last minute attempts to withdraw, impartial election monitors found the elections generally free and fair. As a result of the Government's improper handling of nominations, the High Court nullified the results of the October 1995 Harare and Bulawayo mayoral elections. Cases challenging the validity of the Chitungwiza, Gweru, and rerun Harare mayoral elections were still pending at year's end. Although the small independent press was increasingly open and critical of the Government, the electronic media—the major source of information for most Zimbabweans—remained government-controlled, and strict antidefamation laws led to self-censorship. The Zimbabwe Broadcast Corporation issued an order banning coverage of several businessmen and opposition politicians. Domestic violence against women remained widespread, and traditional, often illegal, discrimination against women and the disabled continued.

RESPECT FOR HUMAN RIGHTS

Section 1. Respect for the Integrity of the Person, Including Freedom From:

a. *Political and Other Extrajudicial Killing.*—There were no reports of political killings by government security forces. However, police killed three people in shooting incidents during the year. All occurred in the line of duty, and there were no suspicious circumstances.

Harsh prison conditions contributed to the average of 25 deaths per month of prisoners in custody (see Section 1.c.).

The Legal Resource Foundation and the Catholic Commission for Justice and Peace (CCJP) interviewed thousands of victims or relatives of victims of atrocities committed during the 1982-87 Matabeleland crisis and are scheduled to present their findings to the President in early 1998. No action has been taken on the 1993 Simplicius Chihambakwe Commission investigation of the Matabeleland crisis. Despite calls by the CCJP for an investigation, the Government took no further action on the bodies discovered at Antelope Mine in Kezi in 1992; the bodies have not been identified or properly buried. The trial of the police officer charged with murder after allegedly shooting another officer, who had ordered him not to urinate in public, began in September. There were no developments in the cases concerning the 1992 death in custody of 15-year-old Happy Dhlakama, the 1991 death of Lieutenant Shepard Chisango, or the 1988 death of Captain Edwin Nyela.

b. *Disappearance.*—There were no reports of politically motivated disappearances. There were no developments in the 1990 disappearance of Rashiwe Guzha.

c. *Torture and Other Cruel, Inhuman, or Degrading Treatment or Punishment.*—The Constitution prohibits torture, and cruel and inhuman treatment. There were no credible reports of torture. The ZRP service charter and improved training have resulted in markedly better treatment of suspects and the public. However, there are still reports of occasional police brutality. For example in November police fired tear gas at a group of striking nurses trying to peaceably enter a magistrate's court to attend the hearing of fellow strikers. Also in November, police beat students fleeing demonstrations at the University of Zimbabwe. Police occasionally beat suspects as they are arrested.

The Government has not actively pursued past allegations of torture, nor prosecuted CIO or ZRP officers for such abuses. The CIO continued to refuse to pay court-ordered damages to a 1990 torture victim.

Prison conditions remained harsh and have improved little since the CCJP issued its 1993 report describing extreme overcrowding, shortages of clothing, and poor sanitary conditions. In August, 4,000 prisoners were released under a presidential amnesty, helping to ease serious overcrowding. Overcrowding and poor sanitation aggravated outbreaks of cholera, diarrhea, and AIDS-related illnesses. An average of 25 prisoners a month died in custody, 18 from AIDS-related illnesses. Zimbabwe has established a successful community service sentencing program to try to alleviate prison overcrowding. The Legal Resource Foundation, in cooperation with the prison service, established a human rights training program for prison officials. Officials who mistreat prisoners are routinely punished.

The Government permits international human rights monitors to visit prisons.

d. *Arbitrary Arrest, Detention, or Exile.*—The Constitution prohibits arbitrary arrest, detention, or exile, and the Government observes these prohibitions. The law requires that police inform an arrested person of the charges against him before he is taken into custody. Warrants of arrest issued by the courts are required except in cases of serious crimes or where there is the risk of evidence disappearing. The Ministry of Home Affairs pays an average of $150,000 (Z$1.5 million) each year in damages in wrongful arrest cases. In September the Minister issued a strongly worded statement warning police to observe proper procedures.

Although a preliminary hearing before a magistrate is required within 48 hours (or 96 hours over a weekend), the law is often disregarded if a person does not have legal representation. A 1992 amendment to the Criminal Procedures and Evidence Act substantially reduced the power of magistrates to grant bail without the consent of the Attorney General or his agents. In practice, however, a circular issued by the Attorney General giving a general authority to grant bail has lessened the negative impact of the rule. High Court judges grant bail independently.

The Government still enjoys a wide range of legal powers under the Official Secrets Act and the Law and Order Maintenance Act (LOMA). Originally promulgated 30 years ago and widely used in the past to prosecute political opponents of the Government, the LOMA gives extensive powers to the police, the Minister of Home Affairs, and the President to address political and security crimes that are not clearly defined. The Government invoked the LOMA during the civil service strike in September when it briefly arrested two leaders of the Public Service Association. In November two leaders of the junior doctors strike and the head of the Zimbabwe Teachers' Union were arrested under the LOMA. The Supreme Court has agreed to hear a constitutional challenge to the LOMA as part of their defense. A supporter of the independent Member of Parliament (M.P.) was fined under the LOMA for removing his vehicle, which had been driven by an unlicensed driver, from police impoundment during the Harare South by-election campaign. William Namakonya and Simba Mhlanga received 12- and 15-year sentences respectively under the LOMA for conspiring to assassinate President Mugabe. Opposition leader and M.P. Ndabadingi Sithole is still on bail pending trial on the same charge. In November the Supreme Court agreed to hear a constitutional challenge to the LOMA's provisions that the accused must prove their innocence as part of Sithole's defense.

Pretrial detainees, who make up 21 per cent of the overall prison population, spent an average of 6 months in prison before their trials because of a critical shortage of magistrates and court interpreters. In an extreme case, Daniel Machabe was released in 1994 after spending more than 7 years in remand without trial.

The Government does not use exile as a means of political control.

e. *Denial of Fair Public Trial.*—The Constitution provides for an independent judiciary, and the judiciary has a well-deserved reputation for independence. However, on occasion the Government refuses to abide by its decisions. Judges are appointed for life and can be removed from the bench only for gross misconduct. They are not discharged or transferred for political reasons. Magistrates, who are part of the civil service rather than the judiciary, hear the vast majority of cases and are sometimes subject to political pressure. Military courts deal with disciplinary or court martial proceedings. Police courts, which can sentence a police officer to confinement to camp or demotion, handle disciplinary and misconduct cases. Trials in both these latter courts meet internationally accepted standards for fair trials; defendants in these courts have the right to appeal to the Supreme Court. All levels of the judiciary often make rulings unpopular with the Government.

The Customary Law and Local Courts Act of 1990 created a unitary court system, consisting of headmens' courts, chiefs' courts, magistrates' courts, the High Court, and the Supreme Court. With this restructuring, civil and customary law cases may be heard at all levels of the judiciary, including the Supreme Court. In July the police criticized the customary courts for ruling on rape cases, over which they have no jurisdiction.

The Constitution provides for the right to a fair trial, and the judiciary rigorously enforces this right. Every defendant has the right to a lawyer of his choosing. However, well over 90 percent of defendants in magistrates' courts go unrepresented. In criminal cases, an indigent defendant may apply to have the Government provide an attorney, but this is rarely done and rarely granted. However, in capital cases the Government provides an attorney for all defendants unable to afford one. Litigants in civil cases can request legal assistance from the Legal Resources Foundation or the Citizens Advice Bureau. All litigants are represented in the High Court. The Supreme Court has instructed magistrates to ensure that unrepresented defendants fully understand their rights and to weigh any mitigating circumstances in criminal cases, whether or not the accused presents them as part of his defense.

The right to appeal exists in all cases and is automatic in cases in which the death penalty is imposed. Trials are open to the public except in certain security cases. Defendants enjoy a presumption of innocence and the right to present witnesses and question witnesses against them. Defendants and their attorneys generally have access to government-held evidence relevant to their cases. The legal system does not discriminate against women or minorities.

The Government generally abided by court decisions even when it was strongly opposed to the rulings. However, in January the Immigration Department deported a Nigerian national despite a High Court stay of the deportation order. In addition the Government routinely delayed payment of court costs or judgments awarded against it. For example, the CIO continued its refusal to pay damages awarded by the High Court to a former opposition party official whom CIO agents had tortured in 1990. The Attorney General's office was unable to ensure CIO compliance with the judgment.

Legal and human rights activists continued to criticize the Government's efforts to adopt constitutional amendments in order to overturn Supreme Court rulings. For example, Amendment 11 (1992) changed the Constitution to allow corporal punishment of minors after the Supreme Court ruled that caning of minors constituted cruel and inhuman punishment. Amendment 14 (1996), which denies both men and women the right to confer automatic residency on their foreign spouses, was passed in response to a 1994 Supreme Court ruling declaring that women should have the same rights as men to confer residency and citizenship on their spouses (see Section 2.d.).

There were no reports of political prisoners.

f. *Arbitrary Interference With Privacy, Family, Home, or Correspondence.*—The Constitution prohibits arbitrary interference with privacy, family, home, or correspondence. Human rights groups are concerned that Amendment 14 erodes these constitutional rights by repealing Section 11 of the Constitution which specifies protection for the right to the privacy of one's home and from the compulsory acquisition of property without compensation. Although government authorities generally respect citizens' right to privacy and violations are subject to legal sanction, it is widely known that the Government sometimes monitors private correspondence and telephones, particularly international communications.

The need for land reform in Zimbabwe is almost universally accepted; however, problems have arisen with implementation of the 1992 Land Acquisition Act. Farmers whose lands have been designated for acquisition may only appeal the amount of compensation in administrative courts, not the initial decision to acquire their farms. In the past this act was implemented largely along racial lines; the Government stated that black-owned commercial farms would not be subject to designation. In a few cases, land was designated for acquisition to achieve political goals. Opposition party leader M.P. Ndabadingi Sithole continued to fight the Government over its 1993 acquisition of his farm.

Section 2. Respect for Civil Liberties, Including:

a. *Freedom of Speech and Press.*—The Constitution provides for freedom of expression but allows for legislation to limit this freedom in the "interest of defense, public safety, public order, state economic interests, public morality, and public health." Although the independent press is increasingly open and critical of the Government, there is a high degree of self-censorship in both the government-controlled and independent press. Self-censorship is aggravated by antidefamation laws that make no distinction between public and private persons. For example in December the former head of the army was awarded substantial damages in a defamation suit because an independent monthly had pondered how his "goings on" would be reported. In addition an extremely broad Official Secrets Act makes it a crime to divulge "any information acquired in the course of official duties."

The major print media (seven English language newspapers and one vernacular broadsheet) belong to the Mass Media Trust, a holding company heavily influenced by the Government and ruling party. The Ministry of Information controls the Zimbabwe Inter-Africa News Agency wire service. The Government influences mainstream media through indirect ownership, editorial appointments, directives to editors, and removal of wayward editors. The small independent press consists primarily of two economic weeklies and three monthly magazines. They carefully monitor government policies and open their pages to opposition critics. Other minor independent publications exist with fewer than 3,000 subscribers.

Radio and television are entirely government owned and controlled. Journalists report that ZANU–PF Secretary for Information Nathan Shamuyarira is often involved in determining what news is broadcast. Despite a Supreme Court ruling that the Government's monopoly on telecommunications was unconstitutional because it interfered with the constitutional right to freedom of expression, the Government has repeatedly refused to license independent radio and television stations. The Zimbabwe Broadcasting Corporation (ZBC), which still enjoys a monopoly under the Broadcast Act, issued an order banning coverage of several prominent businessmen and opposition politicians. In addition all of the government-controlled media refused to report the statements of the Public Service Association during the civil service strike in August. The ZBC gave all candidates 30 minutes of free broadcast time during the Presidential campaign.

Books and films are subject to review by the Zimbabwe Board of Censors. In February the police briefly seized the negative of a film, still in production, on the liberation struggle which the National War Veteran's Association claimed was offensive. However, the Southern African Film Festival was held in Harare in September without interference from the Board of Censors.

In July the government spokesman announced that the Gays and Lesbians of Zimbabwe (GALZ) exhibit on AIDS counseling and prevention at the Harare International Book Fair had been banned. The Board of Censors subsequently issued an official banning order, but the High Court overturned the order on the grounds that the Board of Censors could not ban materials it had not screened.

The University of Zimbabwe (UZ) Amendment Act and the National Council for Higher Education Act curtail academic freedom by restricting the independence of universities, making them subject to government influence, and extending the disciplinary powers of the university authorities against staff and students. Th UZ suspended or expelled 20 students under the act after students wrecked the university cafeteria protesting poor food. A large number of Harare Polytechnic and UZ students were suspended in July for participating in unruly demonstrations demanding increased allowances.

b. *Freedom of Peaceful Assembly and Association.*—The Constitution provides for the right of assembly and association for political and nonpolitical organizations, including a broad spectrum of economic, social, professional, and recreational activities. Permits are no longer required for meetings or demonstrations. A draft public order act, the purported successor to the Law and Order Maintenance Act, has been circulated for comment to human rights groups. The law would make organizers of demonstrations civilly liable if the demonstrations turn violent.

The formation of unions and political parties is not restricted. Organizations are generally free of governmental interference as long as their activities are viewed as nonpolitical. However, under the Private Voluntary Organizations Act of 1995, the Minister of Social Welfare, Labor, and Public Service is empowered to suspend the executive body or "any member of the executive committee of an organization and to appoint persons to manage the affairs of the organization for a specified time." A case challenging the Minister's November 1995 removal of the board of a women's nongovernmental organization (NGO) is pending in the Supreme Court. The National Association of NGO's (NANGO) is negotiating with the Government for revision of the act. As a result of the act, several newly established NGO's decided to establish their organizations as "associations" connected with established NGO's so that their executive bodies would not be subject to government interference.

c. *Freedom of Religion.*—The Constitution provides for freedom of religion, and the Government respects this right in practice.

d. *Freedom of Movement Within the Country, Foreign Travel, Emigration, and Repatriation.*—The Constitution provides for these rights, and the Government generally respects them in practice.

The new Zimbabwean Citizenship and Immigration bill, presented to Parliament in mid-1994 but not yet law, tightens prohibitions against dual citizenship. Human rights groups are concerned that these provisions will most affect white Zimbabweans, many of whom hold dual citizenship, and will interfere with citizens' right of return.

In response to a 1994 Supreme Court ruling that Zimbabwe's practice of allowing men, but not women, to confer residency rights on their foreign born spouses was discriminatory, the Government proposed a constitutional amendment establishing the practice in the Constitution. After an outcry from civic, particularly women's, organizations, the Government withdrew the amendment and proposed a revised bill that allows neither men nor women to confer citizenship on their foreign born spouses automatically. Parliament passed the amendment in October.

The Government cooperates with the Office of the United Nations High Commissioner for Refugees and other humanitarian organizations in assisting refugees. Zimbabwe provides first asylum. Forty persons were granted first asylum and 36 denied it in 1996. There were no reports of forced expulsion of those having a valid claim to refugee status nor of forced return of persons to countries where they feared persecution. There were approximately 350 refugees from a variety of African nations.

Section 3. Respect for Political Rights: The Right of Citizens to Change Their Government

Citizens have the legal right to change their government democratically, however, the political process continued to be tilted through various means in favor of the ruling party. President Mugabe and his ZANU–PF Party remained the dominant political force within the country. In the 1995 general elections, ZANU–PF captured

117 of the 120 elected seats. The 10 chiefs who sit as M.P.s are elected by their peers. The President also appoints 8 provincial governors, who sit as M.P.s, and 12 nonconstituency M.P.s. The net result of several constitutional amendments has been to consolidate the power of the executive branch and to limit M.P.s' independence. There is no effective parliamentary opposition, and the legislature remained subordinate to the executive branch. However, in 1996 Parliament had greater influence on the content of proposed legislation in ruling party caucus debate and during the committee phase than in previous years.

There are many small opposition parties. However, their growth is inhibited by a variety of factors, including the Political Parties Finance Act (PPFA) and the government monopoly on the electronic media. The PPFA provides government funding only to those parties that have more than 15 parliamentary seats, effectively giving all public funding to the ruling party. An opposition party's constitutional challenge of the Electoral Act is still pending before the Supreme Court. There were credible reports of continued CIO harassment of opposition and independent candidates and their supporters. In addition to these serious institutional problems, however, the opposition parties' poor leadership, infighting, and lack of coherent platforms played an important role in their poor electoral showing.

The week before the March presidential elections both opposition candidates attempted to withdraw, claiming that until the PPFA, the Electoral Act, and the Broadcast Act were substantially revised, they would be unable to surmount the hurdles placed before them by the electoral system. However, the Registrar General ordered that the elections be held with their names on the ballots because they did not withdraw within the period required by the Electoral Act.

Voting in the presidential elections was peaceful and generally free and fair. The turnout was very low (30.4 percent). The relatively high ratio of spoiled ballots (over 4 percent) was thought to indicate a need for more thorough voter education, particularly in rural areas. Human rights organizations praised the conduct of the ZRP during the elections. There were no reports of bias or intimidation by election officials. The Electoral Supervisory Commission (ESC) deployed hundreds of NGO election monitors nationwide, but at year's end the ESC had not presented its report on the Presidential election to the Minister of Justice.

In March the High Court nullified the results of the October 1995 Bulawayo and Harare mayoral elections because the returning officers (supervising election officials) had conducted nominations improperly. An opposition party is appealing the High Court's ruling that the Gweru mayoral elections were handled properly, alleging that the President abused the Presidential Powers Act in calling for mayoral elections before Parliament passed a new Urban Councils Act establishing the post of executive mayor.

New Bulawayo and Harare elections were held in August and September. The campaign in Harare was marked by lopsided media coverage and CIO and ZANU-PF official harassment of opposition party supporters. There were isolated incidents of violence by supporters of both candidates. Before the election, the independent candidate successfully sued to have the Town Clerk, who was a candidate in the 1995 ruling party parliamentary primaries, removed as returning officer. His suit to have the new election results nullified, on the grounds that the voters' roll was not in order and that vote counting was handled improperly, was still pending in the High Court at year's end. NGO election observers described the vote counting as "chaotic" and noted that the agents of the independent candidate were not present when counting began. Also in September the independent candidate for Mayor of Chitungwiza (a newly designated municipality) filed a High Court suit to have the election results nullified because gross irregularities in the voters' roll resulted in persons not on the roll being allowed to vote fraudulently and persons on the roll being refused the right to vote. There were 20 affidavits attached to his suit detailing abuses ranging from violence and intimidation by supporters of the ruling party, to vote buying, to voters being told they were "too old to vote."

There are institutional problems with the management and supervision of elections. Although the Ministry of Justice technically administers the Electoral Act, the Registrar General's Office falls under the Ministry of Home Affairs. With a meager budget and a tiny staff seconded from the Ministry of Justice, the Electoral Supervisory Commission lacks the institutional capacity to oversee all of the country's polling stations. Nor do commissioners have the executive authority to order that an irregularity be corrected. Despite an attempt to computerize the voters' roll, it contains a very large number of redundancies or errors, including misspellings, multiple entries, and names of the deceased. In the March presidential elections, thousands of voters were turned away because their names were missing from or improperly listed on the roll. An opposition party's challenge of the results of the July

1995 parliamentary by-election in Gweru on the grounds that registration irregularities affected the outcome was still before the High Court at year's end.

Women participate in politics without legal restriction. However, according to local women's groups, husbands—particularly in rural areas—commonly force their wives to vote for the husband's preferred candidates.

There are 20 women in the 150-member Parliament, including the Deputy Speaker. There are three female cabinet ministers and three deputy ministers. All major ethnic groups are represented in Parliament and in the Government.

Section 4. Governmental Attitude Regarding International and Nongovernmental Investigation of Alleged Violations of Human Rights

Although the Government permits local civic and human rights groups to operate, it monitors their activities closely, in particular those of the Catholic Commission for Justice and Peace and ZIMRIGHTS. Other groups that promote human rights include the Legal Resource Foundation, the Southern African Federation of the Disabled, Zimbabwe Lawyers for Human Rights, the Child and Law Project, the Zimbabwe Women Lawyer's Association, and the Southern African Human Rights Research and Documentation Trust. The Foundation for Democracy in Zimbabwe (FODEZI) was established in July as a watchdog organization to support independent candidates. Amnesty International, Transparency International, and the International Committee of the Red Cross operate in Zimbabwe. The Government does not discourage representatives from international human rights groups from visiting Zimbabwe.

Section 5. Discrimination Based on Race, Sex, Religion, Disability, Language, or Social Status

The Constitution provides that "every person in Zimbabwe" is entitled to fundamental rights whatever his race, tribe, place of origin, political opinions, color, creed, or sex.

Women.—Domestic violence against women, especially wife beating, is common and crosses all racial and economic lines. Women's groups have noted that every police station in Zimbabwe has handled at least one case of a woman killed by her husband. According to Women in Law and Development in Africa (WILDAF), domestic violence accounts for more than 60 percent of murder cases in the Harare High Court. In 1992 (the last year for which official statistics are available), 4,437 official complaints of wife beating were filed. Human rights groups have noted that increased training has improved police community relations officers' handling of these cases. There were 3,148 cases of rape reported in 1995 (the majority involving girls under the age of 14), resulting in 727 convictions. There were 1,400 cases of rape in the first half of 1996. Women's groups and the police believe the actual number is much higher, but the majority of cases go unreported because of the social stigma of rape. When cases come to court, the courts generally impose stiff sentences for rape and wife beating. However, a "binding over" order (an order to appear in court to respond to an accusation of violent behavior) is issued based only on actual physical abuse and not on threats of violence. In addition the courts do not have the power to oust an abusive spouse from a matrimonial home.

Since independence the Government has enacted major laws aimed at enhancing women's rights and countering certain traditional practices that discriminate against women. However, women remain disadvantaged in Zimbabwean society. Illiteracy, economic dependency, and prevailing social norms prevent rural women in particular from combating societal discrimination. Despite legal prohibitions, women are still vulnerable to entrenched customary practices, including "kuzvarira," the practice of pledging a young women to marriage with a partner not of her choosing; "nhaka," the custom of forcing a widow to marry her late husband's brother; and the customary practice of offering a young girl as compensatory payment in interfamily disputes.

Although two women preside as chiefs in Mashonaland, a dispute has erupted over the ascension of a female chief, sanctioned by the President, in Matabeleland South. Provincial Governor Welshman Mabhena declared that "under Ndebele custom a woman can never preside over a man. It is a mockery of our culture."

The Legal Age of Majority Act and the Matrimonial Causes Act recognize women's right to own property independently of their husbands or fathers. However, while unmarried women may own property in their own names, women married under customary law are not allowed to own property jointly with their husbands. Inheritance laws remain unfavorable to widows. The Government took no legislative action on a draft inheritance law that would address the issue of unfair and unequal distribution of inherited assets. Divorce and maintenance laws are favorable toward women, but women generally lack awareness of their rights under the law.

Although labor legislation prohibits discrimination in employment on the basis of gender, women are concentrated in the lower echelons of the work force and commonly face sexual harassment in the workplace.

Several active women's rights groups in Zimbabwe, including WILDAF, the Musasa Project, the Zimbabwe Women Lawyers' Association, and the Women's Action Group, concentrate on improving women's knowledge of their legal rights, increasing women's economic power, and combating domestic violence. There is no government office specifically responsible for women's affairs.

Children.—The Government continued to demonstrate its strong commitment to children's rights and welfare through a system of primary health care and education overseen by the Ministry of Health and Child Welfare. The Children's Protection and Adoption Act, the Guardianship of Minors Act, and the Deceased Person's Maintenance Act all protect the legal rights of minor children. While there is no compulsory education, Zimbabwe has made considerable progress in providing education for girls, and overall primary school attendance has increased by more than 400 percent since independence. About 93 percent of children reach grade 5. With the reintroduction of school fees in urban schools and rural secondary schools, however, enrollment has declined. If a family is unable to pay tuition costs, it is most often female children who leave school. There are an estimated 12,000 homeless "street kids" in Zimbabwe, many of them the children of former Mozambican refugees or AIDS orphans. Child abuse—including incest (long taboo in Zimbabwean society), infanticide, child abandonment, and rape is increasing but still is not widespread.

The Ministry of Justice's Vulnerable Witnesses Committee established two pilot projects to improve the judicial system's handling of child victims of rape and sexual abuse. The criminal justice system has special provisions for dealing with juvenile offenders.

Female genital mutilation (FGM), which is widely condemned by international health experts as damaging to both physical and psychological health, is rarely performed in Zimbabwe. However, according to press reports, the initiation rites practiced by the small Remba ethnic group in Midlands Province include infibulation, the most extreme form of FGM.

People With Disabilities.—President Mugabe appointed a disability activist to Parliament in 1995 to represent the needs of the disabled. The Disabled Persons Act of 1992 specifically prohibits discrimination against people with disabilities in employment, admission to public places, or provision of services and is viewed by advocates of the disabled as model legislation. In practice, however, the lack of resources for training and education severely hampers the ability of disabled people to compete for scarce jobs. Although the act stipulates that government buildings should be accessible to disabled persons, for budgetary reasons this is rarely implemented. Disabled people face particularly harsh customary discrimination. According to traditional belief, people with disabilities are considered bewitched, and reports of disabled children being hidden when visitors arrive are common.

National/Racial/Ethnic Minorities.—The Shona ethnic group makes up 77 percent of the population, Ndebele 14 percent, Kalanga 5 percent, whites 1 percent, and other ethnic groups 3 percent. Government services are provided on a nondiscriminatory basis, and the Government has sought to expand and improve the previously "whites only" infrastructure in urban areas to provide health and social services to all citizens. Nevertheless, in social terms Zimbabwe remains a racially stratified country. While schools and churches are all integrated, social interaction among racial groups is still limited. Although intertribal relations are generally very good, the disproportionate number of Shona speaking teachers and headmasters in Matabeleland schools remained a sensitive issue.

Section 6. Worker Rights

a. *The Right of Association.*—The Labor Relations Act (LRA) provides private sector workers with freedom of association and the right to elect their own representatives, publish newsletters, and set programs and policies that reflect the political and economic interests of labor. Workers are free to form or join unions without prior authorization. The LRA allows for the existence of multiple unions per industry, provided that each is registered with the Ministry of Public Service, Labor, and Social Welfare (MPSLSW). While the Government may deregister individual unions, the High Court has ruled that the LRA does not give the Minister the power to suspend or deregister the national umbrella labor confederation, the Zimbabwe Congress of Trade Unions (ZCTU).

Approximately 30 percent of the formal sector work force belongs to the 33 unions that form the ZCTU. ZCTU officers are elected by delegates of affiliated trade unions at congresses held every 5 years. While the Government encouraged the ZCTU's formation, anticipating that it would form the labor arm of ZANU–PF, it no longer directly influences ZCTU actions. The Government and the ZCTU often clash on economic policy, particularly the Economic Structural Adjustment Program (ESAP). The Government usually does not consult either the ZCTU or employers before implementing policy decisions affecting the workplace. This lack of consultation often results in reactions that disrupt labor relations, thereby promoting uncertainty and even strikes. At its 1995 Congress, the ZCTU called for the formation of a standing committee consisting of labor, government, and industry representatives that would comment on all government policy decisions affecting labor. The LRA allows for the formation of multiple national federations. A second umbrella labor organization, the Zimbabwe Federation of Trade Unions (ZFTU), was launched in October with the stated purpose of providing an alternative of the ZCTU. The new organization states that its goal is to work in collaboration with the Government and is openly critical of the ZCTU. The ZFTU's origin, leadership, and membership remained unclear at year's end. Although key personnel have not been publicly identified, most observers believe that they are principally former senior ZCTU leaders, some of whom were involuntarily separated from that organization. No ZFTU activity has been observed other than the fact of its formation.

Public servants and their associations, the Public Service Association (PSA), the Zimbabwe Teachers Association (ZIMTA), and the Zimbabwe Nurses Association (ZINA), are not covered by the provisions of the LRA. Instead, their conditions of employment are provided for under the Constitution. Although civil servants are constitutionally barred from forming unions, in 1995 ZIMTA stated its intention to join the ZCTU and the PSA joined in August. All public servants are deemed essential and are prohibited from striking. Nonetheless, in late August at least 20,000 civil servants went on nationwide strike with many more unable or unwilling to report to work. The Government declared the strike illegal, briefly arrested PSA leaders, and announced the dismissal of striking workers. After a 20-day strike, the Government rescinded the dismissal order and agreed to implement previously promised pay raises. The Government also agreed to enter negotiations on other worker demands such as unifying the public and private sectors under one LRA. In late October, over 2,000 government nurses and 300 government doctors from Zimbabwe's principal hospitals resumed their portion of the civil servant strike, citing as justification lack of Government good faith in the negotiations. The Government declared the strike illegal, dismissed the striking workers, arrested several of their representatives, and banned demonstrations, use of protest placards, and public gatherings related to the strike. In November the ZCTU called a national 2-day work stoppage after riot police broke up a peaceful demonstration using truncheons and tear gas. The police briefly detained the ZCTU's Secretary General during the demonstration. The call for a work stoppage went unheeded. By early December, most nurses and doctors had returned to work, but the Government refused to reinstate two doctors and several nurses who were in the forefront of the strike.

The Labor Relations Amendment Act (LRAA) of 1992 specifies that workers may establish independent worker committees, which exist side by side with unions, in each plant. Worker committees must also be registered with the MPSLSW, which is free to refuse registration. Trade union officials believe that the formation of worker committees was an attempt to dilute union authority. However, the ineffectiveness of worker committees demonstrated the need for the experienced worker representation of the established trade unions.

The International Conference of Free Trade Unions (ICFTU) has criticized Zimbabwean labor legislation for giving "wide scope to the authorities to declare that a given enterprise or industry constitutes an essential service, and then impose a ban (on strikes) on it." The authority to reclassify a previously nonessential service as essential was not used in 1996. Workers in sectors deemed "nonessential" have the right to strike provided the union advises the Government 2 weeks in advance of its intention to do so. If the MPSLSW finds that administrative requirements were not met for a strike, it can issue a disposal order that gives the employer the right to dismiss striking workers. There were no reports that this occurred in 1996. There were 30 cases of collective job actions during the first 5 months of 1996.

The ZCTU and its officials are free to associate with international labor organizations and do so actively. The ZCTU is affiliated with the ICFTU and the Southern African Trade Union Coordinating Council. The African American Labor Center (AALC) maintains a regional office based in Harare.

b. *The Right to Organize and Bargain Collectively.*—The LRA provides workers with the right to organize. As originally enacted, this act was silent on the right to bargain collectively. However, the 1992 LRAA permits unions to bargain collectively over wages. Worker committees, which are by law not organizationally part of the unions or the ZCTU, are empowered to negotiate with the management of a particular plant on the conditions of labor and codes of conduct in the workplace, except for wages.

Collective bargaining wage negotiations take place on an industrywide basis between the relevant union and employer organizations sitting on joint employment boards or councils. These bodies submit their agreements to the Registrar in the MPSLSW for approval. The Government retains the power to veto agreements that it believes would harm the economy. However, it did not directly involve itself in labor negotiations unless requested to do so by one of the two parties. When no trade union represents a specific sector, representatives of the organized workers, i.e., the professional associations, meet with the employer associations, under the mediation of labor officers from the MPSLSW. Public sector wages are determined by the Salary Service Department of the MPSLSW, subject to the approval of an independent Public Service Commission (PSC). Each year PSC officials meet with PSA representatives to review wages and benefits. These reviews result in a recommendation that is forwarded to the MPSLSW. The Minister is not required by law to accept the recommendation.

Employees designated as being in managerial positions are excluded from union membership and thus from the collective bargaining process. The presence of the ZCTU or specific national unions in individual shop floor or worker committee negotiations is not mandated.

The LRA prohibits antiunion discrimination by employers against union members. Complaints of such discrimination are referred to labor relations officers and may subsequently be adjudicated by the Labor Relations Tribunal (LRT). Such complaints are handled under the mechanism for resolving cases involving "unfair labor practices." The determining authority may direct that workers fired due to antiunion discrimination should be reinstated, although this has yet to be utilized in practice.

The LRAA streamlined the procedure for adjudicating disputes by strengthening the LRT. Now, labor relations officers hear a dispute; their decision may be appealed to regional labor relations officers, after which the LRT may hear the case. Ultimately, it may be appealed to the Supreme Court. In 1993 the Government filled long vacant positions on the LRT, but at year's end the LRT boards were still not fully staffed. The LRT has a backlog of over 2,000 cases, some of which have been awaiting a hearing for more than 7 years.

The Export Processing Zones Act states the LRA shall not apply to workers in export processing zones (EPZ's). Although President Mugabe publicly agreed in 1994 that the act should be revised to make the LRA applicable in the EPZ's, the Government has taken no action to amend the act. Applications for companies to be established in the newly created EPZ's are currently being processed.

c. *Prohibition of Forced or Compulsory Labor.*—Compulsory labor is prohibited by law, and there were no reports that it was practiced.

d. *Minimum Age of Employment of Children.*—The law affords little protection to working children. There is no specific legal prohibition of child labor; the LRA only states that contracts of employment shall not be enforceable against any person under the age of 16. Although schooling is not compulsory, over 90 percent of children attend school through grade 5 (see Section 5).

The presence of child labor in industry is marginal since a ready supply of adult labor at relatively low wages gives firms little incentive to employ children. Children are most often employed as casual farm workers, domestics, or in the informal sector; only a tiny percentage of children work full-time. Among the peasant farmers, financial necessity often dictates the use of child labor during the harvest season and for tending livestock. There were anecdotal reports of an increase in the number of children working full-time in the informal sector and small-scale alluvial gold panning. The Government formed a task force in late 1993 to define child labor, determine problem areas, and suggest legislation to alleviate these problems. The task force referred its recommendations to the Attorney General's office which to date has taken no action.

e. *Acceptable Conditions of Work.*—The maximum legal workweek is 54 hours, and the law prescribes a minimum of one 24-hour rest period per week. Working conditions are regulated by the Government on a specific industries basis. The Constitution empowers the PSC to set conditions of employment in the public sector. Government regulations for each of the 22 industrial sectors continue to specify minimum wages, hours, holidays, and required safety measures. In recent years, in an effort to opt out of the wage bargaining system, the Government mandated wage parameters and specified minimum wage increases only for domestics and gardeners. Due to an ineffective monitoring system, many such workers are remunerated below the minimum wage.

The minimum monthly wage for domestics and gardeners of approximately $31 (Z$308.49 and Z$304.83 respectively) is the de facto minimum wage. In most instances the employer must provide housing and food to workers or allowances for such. On commercial farms, the employer may provide schooling for workers' children. The minimum wage is not sufficient to sustain a decent standard of living for a worker and family. Workers in sectors covered under collective bargaining agreements received wage increases averaging a few points below the 25 percent inflation rate. Minimum monthly wage rates ranged from $29 (Z$290) in the agricultural sector to approximately $73 to $82 (Z$731 to Z$817) in the various manufacturing sectors. In theory labor relations officers from the MPSLSW are assigned to monitor developments in each plant to assure that government minimum wage policy and occupational health and safety regulations are observed. In practice these offices are understaffed, cannot afford to routinely inspect workplaces, and must rely on voluntary compliance and reporting by employers.

Safety in the workplace is a continuing problem. The most recent figures show that there were 252 deaths in 19,861 reported occupational injuries during 1995, numbers consistent with those for preceding years. Many of the basic legal protections do not apply to the vast majority of farm, mine, and domestic workers. Unions charge that there are no general standards for the work environment, such as threshold limits for manually lifted weights or conditions for pregnant workers. Health and safety standards are determined only on an industry-specific basis. The Government intervenes on a selected basis (and often seemingly in response to the most recent accident) and sets standards by regulation in some industries. In theory workers have a legal right to remove themselves from dangerous work situations without jeopardy to continued employment; in practice they risk the loss of their livelihood.

LATIN AND THE CARIBBEAN

ANTIGUA AND BARBUDA

Antigua and Barbuda is a multiparty, parliamentary democracy and a member of the Commonwealth of Nations. A Prime Minister, a cabinet and a bicameral legislative assembly compose the Government. A Governor General, appointed by the British monarch, is the titular head of state, with largely ceremonial powers. Prime Minister Lester B. Bird's Antigua Labor Party (ALP) has controlled the Government and Parliament since 1976. During the last elections in March 1994, the ALP retained power by capturing 10 of 17 parliamentary seats, down from the 15 it held under the administration of V.C. Bird Sr., the current Prime Minister's father. The Governor General appoints the 15 senators, 11 with the advice of the Prime Minister and 4 with the advice of the opposition leader.

Security forces consist of a police force and the small Antigua and Barbuda Defence Force. The police are organized, trained, and supervised according to British law enforcement practices and have a reputation for respecting individual rights in the performance of their duties.

Antigua and Barbuda has a mixed economy with a strong private sector. Tourism is the most important source of foreign exchange earnings. The country is burdened by a large and growing external debt which remains a serious economic problem.

Although the Government generally respected constitutional provisions for political and civil rights, opposition parties complained that they received no coverage or opportunity to express their views on the government-controlled electronic media. Societal discrimination and violence against women also continued to be problems.

RESPECT FOR HUMAN RIGHTS

Section 1. Respect for the Integrity of the Person, Including Freedom from:

a. *Political and Other Extrajudicial Killing.*—There were no reports of political or other extrajudicial killings.

b. *Disappearance.*—There were no reports of politically motivated disappearances.

c. *Torture and Other Cruel, Inhuman, or Degrading Treatment or Punishment.*—The Constitution prohibits such practices, and the authorities generally respected these prohibitions.

Conditions at the lone, 18th-century-vintage prison are primitive and repairs are still being carried out a year after hurricane Luis hit Antigua. While the prison is not overcrowded, death row prisoners get exercise only three times a week, and all prisoners receive only one meal a day, consisting mostly of cornmeal mush and a small piece of fish or chicken. Prisoners are permitted to supplement their diet if their relatives are able to bring food to the prison.

d. *Arbitrary Arrest, Detention, or Exile.*—The Constitution prohibits arbitrary arrest and detention, and the Government respects these provisions in practice. Criminal defendants have the right to a judicial determination of the legality of their detention. The police must bring detainees before a court within 48 hours of arrest or detention. Opposition leaders claim the Government has developed a pattern of arresting suspects on Fridays and holding them until Tuesdays in order to prolong the incarceration. Most of these cases involve youths suspected of narcotics violations.

There were no reports of involuntary exile.

e. *Denial of Fair Public Trial.*—The judicial system is part of the Eastern Caribbean legal system and reflects historical ties to the United Kingdom. The Privy Council in London is designated by the Constitution as the final court of appeal, which is invariably employed in the case of death sentences. There are no military or political courts. The Constitution provides that criminal defendants receive a fair, open, and public trial. In capital cases only, the Government provides legal assistance at public expense to persons without the means to retain a private attorney.

Courts can reach verdicts quickly, with some cases coming to conclusion in a matter of days.

There were no reports of political prisoners.

f. *Arbitrary Interference with Privacy, Family, Home, or Correspondence.*—The Constitution prohibits such practices. Government authorities generally respect these prohibitions, and violations are subject to effective legal sanction.

Section 2. Respect for Civil Liberties, Including:

a. *Freedom of Speech and Press.*—The Constitution provides for freedom of speech, the press, and other forms of communication. The authorities generally respect these provisions in practice. However, the Government dominates the electronic media—the only daily source of news—and effectively denies equal coverage to opposition parties. The Government owns one of the two general interest radio stations and the single television station. A religious station broadcasts without impediment. One of the Prime Minister's brothers owns the second radio station, and another brother is the principal owner of the sole cable television company. The government-controlled media report regularly on the Government's and the ruling party's activities but the opposition party has alleged that it is provided neither coverage in the electronic media, nor access.

The sole daily newspaper criticizes the Government on a variety of issues. When the newspaper tried to start a radio station, police shut down the station claiming that it did not have a license to operate. The owners sued the State for illegal search and seizure and claimed that their constitutional right to broadcast had been violated.

Political opposition parties and private sector organizations such as the Chamber of Commerce publish several weekly newspapers which offer a variety of opinions without government interference.

The Government does not restrict academic freedom.

b. *Freedom of Peaceful Assembly and Association.*—The Constitution provides for the right of peaceful assembly. The police normally issue the required permits for public meetings, but sometimes deny them in order to avert violent confrontations. While the authorities placed some restrictions on demonstrations in the past, the opposition held numerous rallies, public meetings, and a large march with no interference.

c. *Freedom of Religion.*—The Constitution provides for freedom of religion, and the Government respects this right in practice.

d. *Freedom of Movement Within the Country, Foreign Travel, Emigration, and Repatriation.*—The law provides for these rights, and the Government respects them in practice.

There were no reports of forced expulsion of anyone having a valid claim to refugee status. The issue of provision of first asylum did not arise. However, government practice on refugee and asylum cases remains undefined.

Section 3. Respect for Political Rights: The Right of Citizens to Change Their Government

The Constitution provides for a multiparty political system accommodating a wide spectrum of political viewpoints. All citizens 18 years of age and older may register and vote by secret ballot. The Constitution requires general elections at least every 5 years. The law obligates the Government to hold voter registration during a fixed period (of only 5 days) each year, and parties conduct their own registration drives free of government interference.

Except for a period in opposition from 1971 to 1976, the ALP has held power continuously since 1951. The opposition has charged that the ALP's longstanding monopoly on patronage and its influence over access to economic opportunities make it extremely difficult for opposition parties to attract membership and financial support. In 1992 public concern over corruption in government spawned the merger of three opposition political parties into the United Progressive Party (UPP). The UPP succeeded in increasing its representation to seven seats from five during the 1994 election. Opposition and press regularly charge members of the Government with corrupt practices.

No women have been elected or currently serve in the House of Representatives. Two women are senators, which are appointed positions. Eight of the 14 ministry Permanent Secretaries (the top civil servant position in ministries) are women.

Section 4. Governmental Attitude Regarding International and Nongovernmental Investigation of Alleged Violations of Human Rights

While there are no governmental restrictions, no local human rights groups have been formed. There were no requests for human rights investigations or inquiries from individuals or international human rights groups during the year.

Section 5. Discrimination Based on Race, Sex, Religion, Disability, Language, or Social Status

The law prohibits discrimination based on race, sex, creed, language, or social status, and the Government generally observed its provisions.

Women.—Violence against women is a recognized social problem. It is treated as a matter of public conscience, and there are nongovernmental social welfare groups focused on the problem. Women in many cases are reluctant to testify against their abusers. Police generally refrain from intervening in cases of domestic violence, and some women have charged credibly that the courts are lenient in such cases.

While the role of women in society is not legally restricted, economic conditions tend to limit women to home and family, particularly in rural areas, although some women work as domestics, in agriculture, or in the large tourism sector. The Government promised in previous years to provide better programs and educational opportunities for both sexes as well as family planning services, but failed to implement any new programs during the year. The Directorate of Women's Affairs exists to help women advance in government and the professions, but progress was slow.

Children.—Child abuse remains a hidden problem. While the Government repeatedly expressed its commitment to children's rights, it made no significant efforts to protect those rights in practice, and abuse tends to go unpunished.

People With Disabilities.—There are no specific laws mandating accessibility for the disabled, but there are constitutional provisions that prohibit discrimination against the physically disabled in employment and education. There is no evidence of widespread discrimination against physically disabled individuals, although the Government does not visibly enforce the constitutional antidiscrimination provisions.

Section 6. Worker Rights

a. *The Right of Association.*—Workers have the right to associate freely and to form labor unions, and the authorities generally respect these rights in practice. Although fewer than 50 percent of workers belong to unions, the important hotel industry is heavily unionized. Antigua and Barbuda has two major trade unions: the Antigua Trades and Labour Union (ATLU) and the Antigua Workers' Union (AWU). The ATLU is associated with the ruling ALP, while the larger and more active AWU is rather loosely allied with the opposition.

The Labor Code recognizes the right to strike, but the Court of Industrial Relations may limit this right in a given dispute. Once either party to a dispute requests the court to mediate, there can be no strike. Because of the delays associated with this process, unions often resolve labor disputes before a strike is called.

Unions are free to affiliate with international labor organizations and do so in practice.

b. *The Right to Organize and Bargain Collectively.*—Labor organizations are free to organize and bargain collectively. The law prohibits antiunion discrimination, and there were no reports that it occurred. Employers found guilty of antiunion discrimination are not required to rehire employees fired for union activities, but must pay full severance pay and full wages lost by the employee from the time of firing until the determination of employer fault. There are no areas of the country where union organization or collective bargaining is discouraged or impeded.

There are no export processing zones.

c. *Prohibition of Forced or Compulsory Labor.*—The Constitution forbids slavery and forced labor, and they do not exist in practice.

d. *Minimum Age for Employment of Children.*—The law stipulates a minimum working age of 13, which is respected in practice. The Ministry of Labour, which is required by law to conduct periodic inspections of workplaces, has responsibility for enforcement. There have been no reports of minimum age employment violations. The political strength of the two major unions and the powerful influence of the Government on the private sector combine to make the Ministry of Labour very effective in enforcement in this area.

e. *Acceptable Conditions of Work.*—The law established minimum wages for various work categories in 1981. The lowest minimum wage, for domestic workers, is $0.46 (EC$1.25) per hour; the highest minimum wage, for skilled labor, is $1.30 (EC$3.50) per hour. Most minimum wages would not provide a decent standard of living for workers and their families, but in practice the great majority of workers earn substantially more than the minimum wage.

The law permits a maximum 48-hour, 6-day workweek, but in practice the standard workweek is 40 hours in 5 days. The law provides workers a minimum of 12 days of annual leave and up to 13 weeks of maternity leave.

There are no occupational health and safety laws or regulations; thus there is no provision for a worker to leave a dangerous workplace situation without jeopardy to continued employment.

ARGENTINA

Argentina is a federal constitutional democracy with an executive branch headed by an elected president, a bicameral legislature, and a separate judiciary. In 1995 voters reelected President Carlos Saul Menem to a second term that runs until 1999. His Justicialist party won a majority of seats in both houses of Congress.

The President is the constitutional commander in chief, and a civilian Defense Minister oversees the armed forces. The responsibility for maintaining law and order is shared by several law enforcement agencies. The Federal Police report to the Interior Minister, as do the Border Police and Coast Guard. Provincial police are subordinate to the respective provincial governors. Provincial policemen continued to commit human rights abuses.

Argentina has a mixed agricultural, industrial, and service economy. An economic reform and structural adjustment program, begun in 1989, led to 3 years of high growth with sharply reduced inflation, and spurred competitiveness. As a result of privatization, private sector adjustment, and a lingering recession, however, the national unemployment rate remained high at 17.2 percent. The high cost of living affected those on low fixed incomes the most, although the entire country benefited from the end of hyperinflation.

The Government generally respected the human rights of its citizens; however, there were problems in some areas. There continue to be instances of extrajudicial killings and physical mistreatment of detainees by local police, who also arbitrarily arrest and detain citizens. However, provincial authorities investigated, tried, and convicted a number of police officials for such abuses. Prison conditions are poor. The judicial system is subject to political influence at times and to inordinate delays, resulting in lengthy pretrial detention. Discrimination and violence against women are also problems. Revelations of extrajudicial killings by former military officers who served under the 1976–83 military government sparked a national debate over a full accounting of those who disappeared during that period. The Government and the armed forces said, however, that they have no information about those who disappeared beyond that released in 1984 by the National Commission on Disappeared Persons and collected since then by the Interior Ministry's Subsecretariat for Human and Social Rights.

RESPECT FOR HUMAN RIGHTS

Section 1. Respect for the Integrity of the Person, Including Freedom From:

a. *Political and Other Extrajudicial Killing.*—There were no reports of politically motivated extrajudicial killings.

Provincial police, however, were believed responsible for a number of other extrajudicial killings and were sometimes accused of being "trigger happy." Provincial governments have investigated and in some instances detained and tried the officers involved. For example, in February the authorities placed a Buenos Aires provincial policeman in preventive custody for the killing of Ramon Roldan, shot while seated in the back of a car that was rushing his daughter to a hospital. In March four police officers in the same province were arrested, and their supervisors relieved of duty, in connection with the killing of a 16-year-old boy, Cristian Campos, and the burning of his remains. In June the authorities arrested a policeman in the province of Cordoba in connection with the shooting death of 19-year-old Ariel Lastra.

In March the governor of the province of Tucuman dismissed the chief of the provincial police after the latter was quoted as saying he would like to "put a few bullets" into thieves in the province. In September the chief of police of the province of Buenos Aires was also replaced.

Two gunmen attempted to kill a former police doctor, Jorge Antonio Berges, who had been convicted in December 1986 of aiding in the torture of prisoners and of delivering the babies of illegally detained women in the 1970's and facilitating their fraudulent adoptions. A domestic criminal group, the People's Revolutionary Organization, claimed responsibility for the attack and said it tried to kill Berges in the name of all those who had suffered at the hands of the "torturers" of the military dictatorship.

In January a court sentenced an army officer and two noncommissioned officers to up to 15 years in prison for the 1994 murder of Omar Carrasco, a young army recruit who was beaten to death during a hazing incident in Neuquen. In August the authorities indicted two army officers in an investigation of alleged attempts to cover up the crime. In May a court sentenced three officers in the province of Jujuy to prison terms of 16 years for the kidnap and murder in 1994 of a young engineer, Diego Rodriguez Laguens.

The authorities arrested 15 members of the Buenos Aires provincial police, including 3 high-ranking officers and a former officer, in connection with the 1994 bombing of the AMIA Jewish cultural center in Buenos Aires. In August they charged the 4 officers with homicide on the grounds that they allegedly supplied the van that was filled with explosives; the bomb killed 87 people and injured 250 others. At year's end, the 4 remained in jail; all 15 will be tried.

b. *Disappearance.*—There were no reports of politically motivated disappearances.

In May a judge in La Plata ordered the arrest of two police officers accused of torturing to death a 23-year-old student, Miguel Bru, who disappeared in 1993. In June the province of Mendoza appointed two commissions to investigate the disappearances of three men (Adolfo Garrido, Raul Baigorria, and Cristian Guardatti) in two separate incidents in 1990 and 1992, and to determine appropriate levels of compensation for their families. According to witnesses, the three were in the custody of provincial police when they were last seen. The families had filed suit in the Inter-American Court of Human Rights, and in January the President instructed the Foreign Ministry to enter into discussions with them in order to arrive at a settlement. According to the Inter-American Commission on Human Rights (IACHR), an ad hoc investigative commission established an arbitration award to be paid to the victims and issued a report on August 16. The IACHR stated in October, however, that the recommendations of the ad hoc committee had not been carried out and that no settlement had been reached and called on the Government to publish and distribute the ad hoc committee's report.

Revelations concerning disappearances under the 1976–83 military regime continued to claim public attention, and a federal court promised anonymity to anyone who would come forward with new information. The court reactivated the cases of two French nuns and a Swedish student who disappeared at different times during the period of military rule, in an attempt to determine their fate. The navy officer convicted in absentia in France for the disappearance of the nuns, and wanted in Sweden for the disappearance of the Swede, took early retirement.

In September a federal judge in Spain opened a criminal investigation into the torture, disappearance, and killing of 266 Spanish citizens in Argentina during the military regime. He charged 97 former and active military and police officers in the case and seeks to interrogate them in Spain or Argentina. They reportedly include members of military juntas, commanders of clandestine jails, and doctors who attended torture sessions. A parallel investigation focuses on the alleged abduction of 54 children of Spanish citizens who remain missing.

Most reliable estimates place the number of those who disappeared between 10,000 and 15,000. In 1984 the National Commission on Disappeared Persons issued a report that lists 8,961 names based on public testimony from friends, relatives, and other witnesses. Since then, the Ministry of the Interior's Subsecretariat for Human and Social Rights has added approximately 2,500 new names, also based on voluntary reporting.

The Grandmothers of the Plaza de Mayo, a human rights group, continued efforts to reunite the children of couples who disappeared under the military regime with their biological next-of-kin. The group is working with the National Commission on the Right to Identity, an agency of the Subsecretariat for Human and Social Rights.

c. *Torture and Other Cruel, Inhuman, or Degrading Treatment or Punishment.*— The Constitution prohibits torture, and the Criminal Code provides penalties for torture that are similar to those for homicide. Nevertheless, police brutality remains a serious problem. In February a court sentenced a policeman in Mar del Plata to 9 years in prison for torturing a 15-year-old boy who had been arrested on suspicion of raping a child. In April the authorities arrested two policemen in Posadas on suspicion of raping a 13-year-old girl in a police station where they had taken her in what they said was a crackdown on prostitution. In April two policemen in Cordoba were detained on suspicion of raping a young woman who had come to a local jail to visit a prisoner.

In February the government of Buenos Aires province announced the suspension, pending further investigation, of 11 police officers, including 1 inspector and 2 deputy inspectors, for their role in violently repressing a student demonstration at the La Plata police headquarters. This and other incidents of hasty use of force by the provincial police impelled President Menem to meet with his senior security officials and the police chiefs of all the provinces in order to analyze the problem. They adopted an action plan calling for more human rights training for police officers, more careful recruiting, and closer community liaison, among other measures.

On September 13, the Government agreed to an out-of-court settlement with Jose Siderman, who had sued it in a U.S. court for torture and other abuses that he suffered at the hands of the l976–83 military regime, as well as abuses committed by later governments.

Prison conditions are poor in a number of overcrowded jails where the facilities are old and dilapidated. Severe overcrowding apparently contributed to a riot in March in the Villa Floresta prison near Bahia Blanca, the second riot there in 3 months. In March inmates at the Sierra Chica maximum security penitentiary in Buenos Aires province mutinied after a botched escape attempt. In the ensuing battles between rival gangs, one inmate was killed, seven died in a fire touched off by the riot, and other prisoners were reported missing. In addition, the rioters took hostages, including a judge who arrived to negotiate an end to the uprising.

In April there was a wave of prison riots in the province of Buenos Aires and elsewhere in the nation. A total of 17 prisons were affected, throughout the country, with an estimated 5,600 prisoners in active revolt. An additional 6,000 prisoners participated in hunger strikes or signed petitions, out of a national prison population of 27,000. The prisoners complained about overcrowding in the jails, the slow pace of resolving their cases, excessive bail amounts, and incongruous criminal penalties (e.g., the sentence for auto theft is 9 years longer than that for manslaughter). In the Buenos Aires provincial penitentiary system, courts have yet to try and convict 70 percent of the prisoners. The prisoners sought compliance with a 1994 law that gives unsentenced prisoners 2 days' credit toward their final sentence for every day served prior to sentencing, after a period of 2 years.

To help relieve prison overcrowding in the province of Buenos Aires, the Government solicited bids for the construction of two new prisons designed to be more secure and to offer better living conditions for inmates. The Government is also exploring the possibility of contracting some prison services to private firms in order to upgrade conditions.

The Government permits prison visits by independent human rights monitors.

d. *Arbitrary Arrest, Detention, or Exile.*—The Penal Code places limits on the arrest and investigatory power of the police and the judiciary, but provincial police often ignored these restrictions. Human rights groups find it difficult to document such incidents, because victims are reluctant to file complaints.

Police detain teenagers and young adults, sometimes overnight, sometimes for an entire weekend, without formal charges. They do not always provide such detainees with the opportunity to call their families or an attorney. These detainees are released only upon a complaint from relatives or legal counsel.

The law provides for the right to bail, and it is utilized in practice. Nonetheless, the law allows pretrial detention for up to 2 years, and the slow pace of criminal trials often results in lengthy pretrial detention periods.

The law does not permit involuntary exile, and it is not practiced.

e. *Denial of a Fair Public Trial.*—The Constitution provides for an independent judiciary. While it is nominally independent and impartial, its processes are inefficient, complicated, and, at times, subject to political influence.

The judicial system is divided into federal and provincial courts, each headed by a Supreme Court with chambers of appeal and section courts below it. The system is hampered by inordinate delays, procedural logjams, changes of judges, and incompetence. Allegations of corruption are widely reported, especially in civil cases.

Trials are public and defendants have the right to legal counsel and defense witnesses. A panel of judges decides guilt or innocence. In 1992 some federal and provincial courts began deciding cases using oral trials instead of the practice of written submissions. Oral trials are less time consuming, and they have helped reduce the number of prison inmates awaiting trial. Nevertheless, lawyers and judges are still struggling to adjust to the new procedures, and substantial elements of the old system remain. For example, before the oral part of a trial begins, judges receive written documentation regarding the case which, according to prominent legal experts, can bias a judge before oral testimony is heard.

Constitutional reforms in 1994 provided for a blue-ribbon judicial council that would have responsibility for federal court administration and the selection and removal of judges. However, due to disagreement over the composition of the council, Congress has not yet passed the necessary enabling legislation.

International human rights groups have claimed that Juan Antonio Puigjane, a Capuchin monk sentenced to prison with 19 others in a 1989 attack on an army barracks, is jailed for political reasons. Argentine officials maintain, however, that Puigjane was properly tried and convicted for involvement in a violent rebellion against a democratically elected government. There were no other reports of political prisoners.

f. *Arbitrary Interference with Privacy, Family, Home or Correspondence.*—The Constitution prohibits such practices, and government authorities generally respect these prohibitions. Violations are subject to legal sanction, although in practice, local police have the right to stop and search individuals without probable cause.

Section 2. Respect for Civil Liberties, Including:

a. *Freedom of Speech and Press.*—The Constitution provides for freedom of speech and the press, and the Government respects these rights in practice. An independent press and a functioning democratic political system combine to ensure freedom of speech and of the press, including academic freedom.

There were several reported attacks on journalists. In February gunshots were fired at the office of a news photographer in Cordoba who had taken graphic photos of a prison riot. In August two journalists in the province of San Juan complained to the Association of Argentine News Organizations (ADEPA) that their homes had been deliberately set on fire. The perpetrators of the attacks were unknown. In June ADEPA released a statement criticizing proposed laws it said would threaten freedom of the press, including a bill to increase fines for publishing information about offenses by minors and a draft anticorruption law that included penalties for publishing financial disclosure statements concerning inheritances. The Government described the accusation as "profoundly unfair" and called on ADEPA to acknowledge the extent of press freedom that existed; ADEPA said that it would continue to warn against such proposals.

In March the judges hearing a controversial murder case in Catamarca province announced a suspension of radio and television coverage of the trial, thereby provoking sharp public reaction and rallies throughout the country. Although fascination with the soap opera-like courtroom drama is partly responsible for the outcry, many also believed that the judges decided to ban media access as part of a deal to get the defendant, the son of an influential politician, an acquittal. Less than 48 hours later, the Catamarca Supreme Court ordered the trial to resume media coverage, but the judges hearing the case subsequently resigned, charging political interference in the process.

b. *Freedom of Peaceful Assembly and Association.*—The Constitution and laws provide for these rights, and the Government respects them in practice.

c. *Freedom of Religion.*—The Constitution provides for freedom of religion, and the Government respects this right in practice.

d. *Freedom of Movement Within the Country, Foreign Travel, Emigration, and Repatriation.*—The Constitution and law provide for these rights, and the Government respects them in practice.

The Government recognizes as refugees those persons who meet the criteria of the 1951 United Nations Convention on Refugees and its 1967 Protocol. The refugee eligibility committee, composed of representatives of the Ministries of Justice, Foreign Affairs, and the Interior is responsible for determining a refugee's status. A representative of the U.N. High Commissioner for Refugees may participate in committee hearings, but may not vote. The Government has granted refugee status to numerous persons and accepted them for resettlement. The issue of the provision of first asylum, however, has rarely arisen. There were no reports of the forced return of persons to a country where they feared persecution.

Section 3. Respect for PoliticalRights: The Right of Citizens to Change their Government

Since its return to democratic government in 1983, Argentina has held periodic free and fair elections to choose federal, provincial, and municipal office holders. Universal adult suffrage is obligatory in national elections. Political parties of varying ideologies operate freely and openly. The revised Constitution provides that all adult citizens shall enjoy full participation in the political process, and they do so in practice.

The Constitution stipulates that the internal regulations of political parties and party nominations for elections be subject to affirmative action requirements to assure that women are represented in elective office. A 1993 decree implementing a 1991 law required that a minimum of 30 percent of all political party lists of candidates be female. As a result, the presence of women in the Congress is increasing. There are 72 women in the 257-seat Chamber of Deputies and 4 of 50 Senators are women. Women are also assuming positions of greater authority in provincial and local governments.

Section 4. Governmental Attitude Regarding International and Nongovernmental Investigation of Alleged Violations of Human Rights

A wide variety of human rights groups operate without government restriction, investigating and publishing their findings on human rights cases. Government officials are generally cooperative and responsive to their views.

Section 5. Discrimination Based on Race, Sex, Religion, Disability, Language or Social Status

The Constitution and federal law provide for equality for all citizens. The 1988 Antidiscrimination Law establishes a series of penalties from 1 month to 3 years' imprisonment for anyone who arbitrarily restricts, obstructs, or restrains a person based on "race, religion, nationality, ideology, political opinion, sex, economic position, social class, or physical characteristics." There is no evidence of any systematic effort to abridge these rights by the Government or by private groups.

Women.—Violence and sexual harassment against women are problems. Insensitivity among police and judges sometimes discourages women from reporting assaults, especially domestic violence. The National Women's Council has been working with law enforcement authorities to include in their police training curriculum material on handling cases of violence against women. Many public and private institutions offer prevention programs and provide support and treatment for women who have been abused.

Women still encounter economic discrimination and occupy a disproportionate number of lower paying jobs. Often they are paid less than men for equal work, even though this is explicitly prohibited by law. Female labor leaders pressed their male counterparts for affirmative action programs within the trade union movement to counteract this. Women are also found disproportionately in the informal sector, where they are effectively denied work-related economic and social benefits enjoyed by those in the formal sector.

The National Women's Council, created in 1992 in response to recommendations in the United Nations Convention on the elimination of all forms of discrimination against women, carried out programs to promote equal opportunity for women in education and employment, encourage the participation of women in politics, and support women's rights programs at the provincial level. Provisions in the revised Constitution have greatly increased women's participation in politics.

Children.—The 1994 Constitution incorporates the U.N. Convention on the Rights of the Child. The Ministry of Interior's Subsecretariat for Human and Social Rights works with the United Nations Children's Fund and other international agencies to promote children's rights and well-being.

Historically, Argentina has had numerous programs to provide public education, health protection, and recreational services for all children, regardless of class or economic status. According to some nongovernmental organization (NGO) and church sources, however, child abuse and prostitution are on the rise, and the National Council on Children and the Family believes that those affected tend to be younger than previously. The Council, which the Government established in 1990, works actively with federal and local agencies to improve child protection programs. The federal capital, most of the 24 provinces, and the Federal Government have passed child protection laws.

People With Disabilities.—A 1994 law aimed at eliminating physical barriers to disabled persons regulates standards regarding access to public buildings, parks, plazas, stairs, and pedestrian areas. An increasing number of street curbs in Buenos Aires have been modified to accommodate wheel chairs, but few buildings and public areas in the capital or other cities offer easy access to persons with disabilities.

In June Congress passed a law creating a federal disabilities council composed of national, provincial, and NGO representatives and chaired by the President of the National Advisory Commission for the Integration of Disabled Persons, who has the rank of state secretary within the Federal Government. Federal law also prohibits discrimination against the disabled in employment. Since establishment of the National Program Against Discrimination in 1994, the largest single group bringing complaints has been disabled persons.

Indigenous People.—The revised Constitution provides the right of minorities to be represented in government and incorporates international agreements intended to promote their economic, social, and cultural rights. Estimates of the size of the indigenous population vary from 60,000 to 150,000, but the National Statistical Institute put the figure at below 100,000 as of 1992. Most live in the northern and northwestern provinces and in the far south. Their standard of living is considerably below the average, and they have higher rates of illiteracy, chronic diseases, and unemployment. Indigenous groups are sometimes involved in disputes over tribal lands, which tend to be prolonged due to an inefficient court system unable to expedite conflicting land title claims.

The Kolla Indians made some progress in their efforts to obtain title to ancestral lands, following a protest and the blocking of roads in July. The Mapuche Indians in Patagonia organized protests for similar reasons.

Religious Minorities.—The large Jewish community alleges that anti-Semitism exists in the military and security services and that this may have affected the Government's investigation of the 1992 bombing of the Israeli embassy and the 1994 bombing of AMIA, a Jewish cultural center. The Government denies these allegations and cites the immense complexity of investigating terrorist cases as the principal reason for the lack of definitive results to date. There were concrete, if modest, advances in the AMIA investigation, including the arrest of several senior provincial police officers alleged to have procured a van used as a carbomb in the attack (see Section 1.a.). In November the Government announced an increase in the reward it had offered since 1994 for information or evidence to "clarify the acts of international terrorism" against the Israeli embassy and the AMIA center from $2 million to $3 million.

The Government's desire to accommodate the sensitivities of the Jewish community was evident in July, when Justice Minister Rodolfo Barra, already a controversial figure for other reasons, resigned abruptly, in the face of growing evidence that he had been a member of a pro-Nazi youth movement. (Barra later became a legal adviser to the Senate.) When an Italian court acquitted Nazi officer Erich Priebke, who had resided in Argentina until his extradition for trial in Rome, the Government immediately announced that Priebke would not be allowed to reenter the country.

In October vandals desecrated the predominantly Jewish La Tablada cemetery outside Buenos Aires, in the third incident of its kind during the year. The vandals smashed or defaced scores of tombstones and mausoleums, painting swastikas on many tombstones. The Government was quick to condemn the act, and the authorities arrested four suspects in the case and charged them with desecrating 60 tombs.

Section 6. Worker Rights

a. *The Right of Association.*—With the exception of military personnel, all workers are free to form unions. Estimates regarding union membership vary widely. Most union leaders believe it to be about 40 percent of the work force; government figures indicate union membership at 30 percent. Trade unions are independent of the Government or political parties, although most union leaders are affiliated with President Menem's Justicialist party. Unions belong to either the General Confederation of Labor (CGT), the largest union federation; the Movement of Argentine Workers, a dissident group within the CGT; or the independent Congress of Argentine Workers. Unions have the right to strike, and members who participate in strikes are protected by law. The CGT staged general work stoppages in August, September, and December to protest the Government's labor and social policies. During the September stoppage, about 70,000 workers staged a peaceful protest outside Government House in Buenos Aires.

Unions are members of international labor associations and secretariats and participate actively in their programs.

b. *The Right to Organize and Bargain Collectively.*—The law prohibits antiunion practices, and the Government enforces this prohibition. The trend towards bargaining on a company level, rather than negotiating on a sectoral basis, continued, but the adjustment has not been an easy one for either side. Both the Federal Government and a few highly industrialized provinces are working to create mediation services to promote more effective dispute resolution.

Export processing zones, known as "zonas francas," exist or are planned in several provinces. The same labor laws apply in these zones as in all other parts of the country.

c. *Prohibition of Forced or Compulsory Labor.*—The Constitution prohibits forced labor, and there were no reports that it was practiced.

d. *Minimum Age for Employment of Children.*—The law prohibits employment of children under 14 years of age, except in rare cases where the Ministry of Education may authorize a child to work as part of a family unit. A small number of children work with their parents harvesting fruits and vegetables. Minors aged 14 to 18 may work in a limited number of job categories but not more than 6 hours a day or 35 hours a week. The law is effectively enforced except in some isolated rural areas where government enforcement capabilities are stretched thin. A report by the International Labor Organization indicated that 140,000 children under 14 years of age (4 percent of the population aged 10 to 14) work.

e. *Acceptable Conditions of Work.*—The national monthly minimum wage is $200 (200 pesos), which is not sufficient to sustain an average family of four.

Federal labor law sets standards in the areas of health, safety, and hours. The maximum workday is 8 hours and workweek 48 hours. As part of its economic restructuring program, the Government enacted into law reforms aimed at giving small and medium enterprises greater flexibility in the management of their personnel. The Government is also proposing to modernize the system of workers' compensation.

Occupational health and safety standards are well developed, but federal and provincial governments lack sufficient resources to enforce them fully. In spite of union vigilance, the most egregious cases of inhumane working conditions involve illegal immigrants, who have little opportunity or knowledge to seek legal redress.

Workers have the right to remove themselves from dangerous or unhealthful work situations, after having gone through a claim procedure, without jeopardy to continued employment. Nevertheless, workers who leave the workplace before it has been proven unsafe run the risk of being fired; in such cases, the worker has the right to judicial appeal, but this process can be very lengthy.

BAHAMAS

The Commonwealth of the Bahamas is a constitutional, parliamentary democracy and a member of the Commonwealth of Nations. Queen Elizabeth II, the nominal head of state, is represented by an appointed Governor General. Prime Minister Hubert A. Ingraham's Free National Movement (FNM) has controlled the Government and Parliament since August 1992. The judiciary is independent.

The police and the small Bahamas Defence Force answer to civilian authority and generally respect laws protecting human rights. However, there continue to be reports that police occasionally abuse detainees.

The economy depends primarily on tourism, which accounts for over two-thirds of the gross domestic product. Financial services, particularly offshore banking and trust management, are also a major source of revenue. While some citizens enjoy relatively high average income levels, there is considerable underemployment and poverty. The official unemployment rate is over 13 percent, but unofficial estimates range up to twice that figure.

Citizens enjoy a wide range of democratic freedoms and human rights. The principal human rights problems include reports of occasional police abuse of detainees, continuing harsh conditions at the only prison, delays in trials, violence and discrimination against women, and violence against children.

RESPECT FOR HUMAN RIGHTS

Section 1. Respect for the Integrity of the Person, Including Freedom From:

a. *Political and Other Extrajudicial Killing.*—There were no reports of politically motivated killings.

In September a bank robber was shot and killed during an exchange of fire. Police officials denied responsibility for the shooting, and some evidence reportedly supports their contention. Investigations were not complete by year's end. In another case, a court acquitted the two police officers dismissed from the force and charged with murder in the 1995 death of a third officer.

b. *Disappearance.*—There were no reports of politically motivated disappearances.

c. *Torture and Other Cruel, Inhuman, or Degrading Treatment or Punishment.*—The Constitution prohibits torture and other cruel and degrading treatment or punishment, but corporal punishment—abolished in 1984—was reinstated in 1991.

In February police officers shot a citizen after a high-speed chase in Nassau. The victim was driving a car similar to one from which shots had been fired at police officers. The Government almost immediately offered a public apology to the victim and his family and made financial arrangements for his medical treatment and other compensation. The police claim that the use of deadly force was justified under the circumstances and did not discipline the officers involved.

Human rights monitors and members of the general public continued to express concern over instances of police abuse against criminal suspects. Many of the charges of abuse involved beatings in order to extract confessions. Police officials denied that there have been violations of defendants' rights. According to the officials, a defendant's rights are protected by the trial judge, who determines the admissibility of a defendant's statement as evidence at trial. The Police Complaints and Discipline Unit, which reports directly to senior police officials, is responsible for investigating allegations of police brutality.

Conditions at Fox Hill, the only prison, continue to improve, but remain harsh and overcrowded. The men's prison, originally built in 1953 to house about 600 inmates, holds over 1,200 prisoners. The women's prison population is around 30, considerably less than full capacity. Male prisoners are crowded into poorly ventilated cells that generally lack running water and adequate sanitation facilities. There are no separate facilities for inmates being held on remand, although some are eventually segregated in a medium security wing after being processed through maximum security. Prison officials estimate that about 13 percent of the incoming prisoner population is infected with the HIV virus. Most prisoners lack beds, many sleep on concrete floors, and most are locked in their cells 23 hours per day. Facilities for women are less severe and do have running water. Organizations providing aid, counseling services, and religious instruction have regular access to inmates.

The Government provided funds to enable prison officials to make improvements in prison facilities and to continue prisoner rehabilitation programs. Modern training facilities include new computers and personnel to train the officers and staff. The prison has installed a computer system for its records, with plans for future links with the courts as well as law enforcement entities. A new entrance facility and visitor center was completed, with equipment to screen visitors for contraband. As prisoners are moved into two planned new facilities, much-needed renovation is set for the maximum security unit.

Local and international human rights groups were able to visit the prison during the year.

d. *Arbitrary Arrest, Detention, or Exile.*—The Constitution prohibits arbitrary arrest and detention. The authorities conduct arrests openly and, when required, obtain judicially issued warrants. Serious cases, including those of suspected narcotics or firearms offenses, do not require warrants where probable cause exists. Arrested persons appear before a magistrate within 48 hours (or by the next business day for cases arising on weekends and holidays) to hear the charges against them. They may hire an attorney of their choice. The Government does not provide legal representation except to destitute suspects charged with capital crimes. Police sometimes deviate from prescribed procedures, however, and act arbitrarily. The Government respects the right to a judicial determination of the legality of arrests.

Judges tend not to grant bail to foreign suspects, particularly on more serious offenses, since the authorities consider foreign offenders likely to flee if released on bail. Judges sometimes authorize cash bail for foreigners arrested on minor charges, but in practice, foreign suspects generally prefer to plead guilty and pay a fine rather than pursue their right to defend themselves, given possible delays in court cases and harsh conditions in the prison. There were complaints of excessive pretrial detention. In December Parliament amended the Bail Act to prohibit bail for repeat offenders and those accused of certain violent crimes.

The authorities detain illegal migrants, primarily Haitians and Cubans, at the Carmichael Road Detention Center until arrangements can be made for them to leave the country. Illegal migrants convicted of crimes other than immigration violations are held at the prison and remain there for weeks or months, pending deportation after serving their sentences, unless they can arrange private means for their repatriation. Security concerns again forced the authorities to transfer groups of Cuban detainees temporarily from the detention center to the prison. These detainees have all since been released or deported.

Exile is illegal and is not practiced.

e. *Denial of Fair Public Trial.*—The justice system derives from English common law. The judiciary, appointed by the Governor General on the advice, in most cases, of the Judicial and Legal Services Commission, has always been independent. Magistrate's courts are the lowest level courts and only handle crimes with a maximum sentence of 5 years. Trial by jury is only available in the Supreme Court, which is the trial court that handles most major cases. Its decisions may be appealed to the the Court of Appeal, with the Privy Council in London being the final court of appeal.

Trials are fair and public; defendants enjoy the presumption of innocence and the right to appeal. The judicial system is plagued by a large backlog of cases. This situation improved somewhat over the year because of the efforts of the Government to introduce a case management system. The training of court reporters, completed in 1996, also helped to speed up trials. Despite these measures to improve efficiency in the courts, complaints persist of excessive pretrial detention and delayed justice for victims.

There were no reports of political prisoners.

f. *Arbitrary Interference with Privacy, Family, Home, or Correspondence.*—The Constitution prohibits arbitrary entry, search, or seizure, and the Government generally respects these prohibitions in practice. The law usually requires a court order for entry into or search of a private residence, but a police inspector or more senior police official may authorize a search without a court order where probable cause of a weapons violation exists. Such an official may also authorize the search of a person (which extends to the vehicle in which the person is traveling) without a court order, should probable cause exist for drug possession.

Section 2. Respect for Civil Liberties, Including:

a. *Freedom of Speech and Press.*—The Government respects the constitutional provision for the right of free expression, and the political opposition criticizes the Government freely and frequently. Three daily and several weekly newspapers, all privately owned, express a variety of views on issues of public interest, including varying degrees of criticism of the Government and its policies. Foreign newspapers and magazines are readily available.

There is a government-run radio station and three privately owned radio broadcasters. The country's sole television station, the state-owned Broadcasting Corporation of the Bahamas, presents a variety of views, although opposition politicians claim with some justification that their views do not receive as extensive coverage as those of the Government.

The Government does not restrict academic freedom.

b. *Freedom of Peaceful Assembly and Association.*—The Constitution provides for the rights to free assembly and association, and the authorities respect these rights in practice. The law permits private associations, but groups must obtain permits to hold public demonstrations. The authorities grant such permits almost without exception.

c. *Freedom of Religion.*—The Constitution provides for freedom of religion, and the Government respects this right in practice.

d. *Freedom of Movement Within the Country, Foreign Travel, Emigration, and Repatriation.*—The Constitution provides for these rights, and the Government respects them in practice.

The Government cooperates with the U.N. High Commissioner for Refugees (UNHCR) and other humanitarian organizations in assisting refugees. The Government provided first asylum to 47 persons (46 Cuban nationals and 1 Liberian) in 1996, based on recommendations by the UNHCR. There were no reports of forced return of persons to a country where they feared persecution.

Although the repatriation agreement between the Bahamas and Haiti expired at the end of 1995, the Government continued to repatriate illegal Haitian immigrants based on the terms of the agreement. The Bahamas signed a repatriation agreement with the Government of Cuba in January, and since then the authorities successfully repatriated illegal Cuban immigrants.

Section 3. Respect for Political Rights: The Right of Citizens to Change their Government

The Constitution provides citizens with the right to change their government peacefully, and citizens exercise this right in practice through periodic, free, and fair elections held on the basis of universal suffrage.

The Bahamas is a constitutional, parliamentary democracy with two major political parties and general elections at least every 5 years. An elected Prime Minister and Parliament govern. The political process is open to all elements of society, and citizens 18 years of age and older are eligible to register and vote; voting is by secret ballot. Parliamentary elections are scheduled to be held in 1997. In the 1992 elections, slightly more than 92 percent of registered voters cast valid ballots. The two principal political parties are the ruling Free National Movement and the opposition Progressive Liberal Party (PLP). The PLP led the country for 6 years of internal self-government from 1967 to 1973, and held power from independence in 1973 until 1992.

The FNM holds 32 of 49 seats in the House of Assembly, and the PLP holds 17. Both the ruling party and the opposition name members to the upper house—the Senate—in compliance with constitutional guidelines. Although it does pass legislation, the Senate is primarily a deliberative body that serves as a public forum to discuss national problems and policies to address them.

The Parliament has four elected female members, including the deputy speaker of the House, and three appointed female Senators, including the government leader in the Senate. A woman serves as Minister of Foreign Affairs and Attorney General.

Section 4. Governmental Attitude Regarding International and Nongovernmental Investigation of Alleged Violations of Human Rights

Individual human rights monitors and several local human rights groups, as well as representatives of international human rights organizations, operate freely, expressing their opinions and reporting their findings on alleged human rights violations without government restriction. The Government allows them broad access to institutions and individuals.

Section 5. Discrimination Based on Race, Sex, Religion, Disability, Language, or Social Status

The Government generally respects in practice the constitutional provisions for individual rights and freedoms regardless of race, place of origin, political opinion, creed, or sex. However, both the Constitution and the law discriminate against women in several respects.

Women.—Domestic violence against women continued to be a serious problem, with many women seeking shelter at the private, but government-supported, crisis center in Nassau. The Government has established a nationwide toll-free hot line, with two trained volunteers on each of the inhabited islands on call to respond in the event of a crisis. The crisis center, with help from the Government, instituted a public awareness campaign to highlight the problems of abuse and domestic violence. The Domestic Court, which deals exclusively with family issues such as spousal abuse, maintenance payments, and legal separation, continued to receive a high volume of cases. The court can and does impose various legal constraints to protect women from abusive spouses or companions.

The Constitution discriminates against women by not providing them with the same right as men to transmit citizenship to their foreign-born spouses. Additionally, the law makes it easier for men with foreign spouses to confer citizenship on their children than for women with foreign spouses. Some inheritance laws also favor men over women. For example, when a person dies without a will, the estate passes to the oldest legitimate son, or in cases where there is no son, the closest legitimate male relative. Prominent women of all political persuasions continue to push for an amendment to the Constitution and related laws to redress this situation.

Women participate fully in society and are well represented in the business and professional sectors, as well as in the judiciary and the Government. The Minister of Foreign Affairs and Attorney General, Janet Bostwick, also directs the Bahamian Bureau of Women's Affairs, which is within the Ministry of Foreign Affairs.

Children.—The Government places priority on maintaining adequate expenditures for child welfare and education. However, child abuse and neglect remain serious problems. The law requires that anyone having contact with a child they believe to be sexually abused must report their suspicion to the police. The same reporting requirement does not apply to cases of physical abuse, which nonetheless are high. The police refer reported cases of sexual and physical abuse to the Department of Social Services, which investigates them and can bring criminal charges against perpetrators. The Department may remove children from abusive situations if the court deems it necessary.

People With Disabilities.—Although the 1973 National Building Code mandates certain accommodations for the physically disabled in new public buildings, the authorities rarely enforce this part of the code. The code fails to mandate accommodation in new private buildings, however, which often lack accessibility as well.

The Disability Affairs Unit of the Ministry of Social Development and National Insurance works with the Bahamas Council for Disability, an umbrella organization for groups offering services for the disabled, to provide a coordinated public and private sector approach to the needs of the disabled. A mix of government and private residential and nonresidential institutions provides a range of educational, training, and counseling services for both physically and mentally disabled adults and children. In January the Government opened a new training center, with emphasis on computer training, within a private residential institution. Graduates of the center were working within government and the private sector by the end of the year. The Ministry's national policy statement, presented to the Government in January, is still under consideration.

National/Racial/Ethnic Minorities.—An estimated 30,000 Haitians reside in the Bahamas legally and productively, but social, economic and political sensitivities remain. Members of the Haitian community reported that some police and immigration officials have taken Haitians off the streets into custody before allowing them a chance to produce their residency permits. Haitians also complained that officials sometimes came to their residences late at night, a violation of the terms of the expired Bahamas-Haiti repatriation agreement. These alleged violations are difficult to confirm, but some similar past complaints resulted in procedural changes by the authorities.

Section 6. Worker Rights

a. *The Right of Association.*—The Constitution provides that labor unions have the right of free assembly and association. Private sector and most public sector workers may form or join unions without prior approval. Members of the police force, defense force, fire brigade, and prison guards may not organize or join unions. Workers exercise the right of association extensively, with almost one-quarter of the work force (and one-half the workers in the important hotel industry) belonging to unions.

The country's two major umbrella labor organizations, the National Workers Council of Trade Unions and Associations and the Trade Union Congress (TUC), and individual labor unions all function independent of government or political party control. A third umbrella organization, the National Congress of Trade Unions, continued to grow, adding the third largest union, the Bahamas Union of Teachers, to its membership.

The Industrial Relations Act requires that, before a strike begins, a simple majority of a union's membership must vote in favor of a motion to strike. The Department of Labor must supervise the vote. Unions have instituted slowdowns or stoppages at the Bahamas Electricity Corporation, the Water and Sewerage Corporation, the Ministry of Public Works, Bahamasair, and a popular restaurant in Nassau. In order to resolve trade disputes more quickly, the Industrial Relations Act was amended in July to establish the industrial tribunal. According to the act, trade dispute matters are first filed with the Ministry of Labor and then if not resolved, turned over to the tribunal. The tribunal will follow normal court procedures for the admission of evidence, direct examination, and cross examination. The tribunal's decision is final and is only appealable in court on a strict question of law.

All labor unions have the right to maintain affiliations with international trade union organizations.

b. *The Right to Organize and Bargain Collectively.*—Workers freely exercise their right to organize and participate in collective bargaining, which the law protects. Unions and employers negotiate wage rates without government interference.

The Constitution and the Industrial Relations Act prohibit antiunion discrimination by employers. The act requires employers to recognize trade unions, and it requires the reinstatement of workers fired for union activities. Employers may dismiss workers in accordance with applicable contracts, which generally require some severance pay. The Government enforces labor laws and regulations uniformly throughout the country. City Markets, one of the largest grocery chains, filed a lawsuit in September to void the certification of the Commercial Stores, Supermarkets, and Warehouse Workers' Union as the bargaining agent for its workers.

There are two small free trade zones. Labor law and practice in these zones do not differ from those in the rest of the country.

c. *Prohibition of Forced or Compulsory Labor.*—The Constitution prohibits forced or compulsory labor, and such labor does not exist in practice.

d. *Minimum Age for Employment of Children.*—The law prohibits the employment of children under the age of 14 for industrial work, work during school hours, or work at night. There is no legal minimum age for employment in other sectors, and some children work part time in light industry and service jobs.

e. *Acceptable Conditions of Work.*—The Fair Labor Standards Act limits the regular workweek to 48 hours and provides for one 24-hour rest period. The act requires overtime payment (time and a half) for hours beyond the standard. The act permits the creation of a Wages Council to recommend the setting of a minimum wage, but the Government has never established such a council or a general minimum wage. However, in September the Government established a specific minimum wage for all hourly and temporary workers throughout the public sector.

The Ministry of Labor, responsible for enforcing labor laws, has a team of inspectors who conduct on-site visits to enforce occupational health and safety standards and investigate employee concerns and complaints, but inspections occur only infrequently. The Ministry normally announces inspection visits in advance, and employers generally cooperate with inspectors to implement safety standards.

The national insurance program compensates workers for work-related injuries. The Fair Labor Standards Act requires employers to find suitable alternative employment for employees injured on the job but still able to work. The law does not provide a right for workers to absent themselves from dangerous work situations without jeopardy to continued employment.

BARBADOS

Barbados, a member of the Commonwealth of Nations, is a constitutional democracy with a multiparty, parliamentary form of government. The Queen is Head of State and is represented by an appointed Governor General. Prime Minister Owen Arthur is the Head of Government and governs with an appointed Cabinet.

The Royal Barbados Police Force is charged with maintaining public order. The small volunteer Barbados Defence Force (BDF), responsible for national security, can be employed to maintain public order in times of crisis, emergency, or other specific need. The BDF has assisted the police since 1993 by patrolling certain tourist areas in response to an increase of crime. On the whole, the police respected constitutional and legal provisions protecting human rights, but there continued to be infrequent reports of incidents of use of excessive force by police.

The economy is based on tourism, services, light manufacturing, and agriculture, which makes it vulnerable to external economic developments. Per capita gross domestic product exceeds $6,000 per year. Barbados has experienced a moderate recovery after a recession in the early 1990's. In 1996 the economy was expected to grow at over 4 percent, based primarily on increases in tourism.

Citizens enjoy a wide range of rights and freedoms, and the Government respects constitutional provisions regarding human rights. Principal human rights problems continued to be societal violence against women and children and occasional instances of excessive use of force by police.

RESPECT FOR HUMAN RIGHTS

Section 1. Respect for the Integrity of the Person, Including Freedom From:

a. *Political and Other Extrajudicial Killing.*—There were no reports of political or other extrajudicial killings.

b. *Disappearance.*—There were no reports of politically motivated disappearances.

c. *Torture and Other Cruel, Inhuman, or Degrading Treatment or Punishment.*—The Constitution specifically prohibits torture and cruel, inhuman, or degrading treatment or punishment. However, the Caribbean Human Rights Network and the local press reported numerous allegations of coerced confessions. There continued to be credible reports that law enforcement officials sometimes used force during detention to extract confessions from detainees.

Police procedures provide that the police may question suspects and other persons they hold only at a police station, except when expressly permitted by a senior divisional officer. An officer must visit detainees at least once every 3 hours to inquire about the detainees' condition. After 24 hours, the detaining authority must submit a written report to the deputy commissioner. The authorities must approve and record all movements of detainees between stations. The Caribbean Human Rights Network is satisfied that the authorities generally adhere to these basic principles, although officials occasionally used excessive force.

Barbados is in the forefront of an initiative to standardize police procedures throughout the English-speaking Caribbean region. The authorities issued firearms to special units and some foot patrols in high-crime areas in response to the 1993 shooting death of a policeman and a rise in gun-and drug-related crime. Aside from this development, the police force is still mainly unarmed, in keeping with its British traditions.

The only prison is overcrowded, with over 800 inmates in a structure built for 350 inmates, and has very antiquated equipment. The Caribbean Human Rights Network has publicly urged the establishment of a detention and rehabilitation center for students and first offenders. The Government reported that it investigated the 1995 allegation of a gang rape of a young prisoner by other inmates and determined it to be without foundation.

The Government allows private groups to visit prisons to ascertain conditions.

d. *Arbitrary Arrest, Detention, or Exile.*—The Constitution prohibits arbitrary arrest and imprisonment and requires detainees to be brought before a court of law within 72 hours of arrest. The Government generally respects these provisions in practice. Criminal defendants have the right to counsel, and attorneys have ready access to their clients. The authorities do not use exile as a punishment or means of political control.

e. *Denial of Fair Public Trial.*—The judiciary acts independently and is free of intervention by other branches of government. The Constitution provides that persons charged with criminal offenses be given a fair public hearing within a reasonable time by an independent and impartial court, and the Government respects this right in practice. The judicial system provides for the right of due process at each level. The law presumes defendants innocent until proven guilty. The Government provides free legal aid to the indigent with the exception of a 1,000 pounds sterling cap on expenses incurred for appeals by death row prisoners to the Privy Council in London. Two inmates are suing the Government on the grounds that this limitation deprives them of their right to due process.

There were no reports of political prisoners.

f. *Arbitrary Interference with Privacy, Family, Home, or Correspondence.*—The Constitution prohibits arbitrary entry, search, or seizure, and the law requires warrants to be issued before privately owned property may be entered and searched.

The Government does not routinely interfere in the private lives of its citizens. Nonetheless, there continued to be credible reports that, in response to increased drug-related crime, the police resorted to searches of homes in certain neighborhoods, sometimes without warrants. The Government does not censor mail. However, the Government restricts the receipt of foreign publications deemed to be pornographic. Other foreign publications of a non-prurient nature are allowed without restriction.

Section 2. Respect for Civil Liberties, Including:

a. *Freedom of Speech and Press.*—The Constitution provides for freedom of speech and the press, and the authorities respect these rights in practice. There are two independent daily newspapers, both of which present opposition political views. The Government regularly comes under attack in the newspapers and on daily call-in radio programs. There are five radio stations, two of which are owned by the Government. The Caribbean Broadcasting Corporation (CBC) television service (the only television source, excluding direct satellite reception) is government owned. Though CBC is a state enterprise, it regularly reported views opposing government policies. Although critics allege that the Government sometimes uses its influence to discourage media reporting on sensitive issues, the press remained vigorously critical of the Government on a broad span of issues. The Government prohibits the production of pornographic materials.

The Government does not restrict academic freedom.

b. *Freedom of Peaceful Assembly and Association.*—The Government observes the constitutional provisions for peaceful assembly and private association in practice. Political parties, trade unions, and private organizations function and hold meetings and rallies without hindrance.

c. *Freedom of Religion.*—The Constitution provides for freedom of religion, and the Government respects this right in practice.

d. *Freedom of Movement Within the Country, Foreign Travel, Emigration, and Repatriation.*—Citizens and legal residents move freely within Barbados and leave and enter the country without restriction.

The Government has not formulated a policy regarding refugees, asylees, or first asylum. The issue of the provision of first asylum did not arise. There were no reports of forced expulsion of anyone having a valid claim to refugee status. However, government practice remains undefined.

Section 3. Respect for Political Rights: The Right of Citizens to Change Their Government

Citizens have this right in law and exercise it in practice. Political parties freely compete in fair elections by secret ballot at least every 5 years. In the most recent election in September 1994, the Barbados Labour Party won a decisive victory, gaining a 19-to-8 majority over the Democratic Labour Party. The New Democratic Party won one seat, its first ever in Parliament. There are no impediments to participation in the political process, and all citizens over age 18 may vote. The Prime Minister exercises executive power along with the Cabinet of Ministers he appoints, balanced by the bicameral Parliament and the judicial system.

Women are well represented at all levels of government and politics. After the September 1994 elections, Prime Minister Arthur appointed women to several cabinet-level portfolios. The Deputy Prime Minister is a woman (she also serves concurrently as Foreign Minister), and the Ministries of Health and Education are also headed by women.

Section 4. Governmental Attitude Regarding International and Nongovernmental Investigation of Alleged Violations of Human Rights

Local groups involved with human rights operate freely and without Government hindrance. The Caribbean Human Rights Network, a Caribbean-wide human rights organization which has its headquarters and a small staff in Barbados, investigates and reports on allegations of human rights violations throughout the region.

Section 5. Discrimination Based on Race, Sex, Religion, Disability, Language, or Social Status

The Constitution provides for equal treatment under the law, regardless of race, religion, or sex. The Government respects these rights in practice.

Women.—Women actively participate in all aspects of national life and are well-represented at all levels of both the public and private sectors. They form a large percentage of heads of household and are not discriminated against in public housing or other social welfare programs. However, violence against women and children continued to be a significant social problem. Women's rights groups reported that the known incidence of sexual assaults, domestic violence, incest, and rape increased, despite the fact that there is still some reluctance on the part of victims to report such incidents. There are public and private counseling services for domestic violence, rape, suicide, and child abuse.

The 1992 Domestic Violence Law specifies the appropriate police response to domestic violence, intended to protect all members of the family, including men and children. It applies equally to marriages and to common law relationships. Criminal penalties for violent crimes are the same, regardless of the sex of the offender or the victim. The courts heard a number of cases of domestic violence against women involving assault or wounding. Victims may request restraining orders, which the courts often issue. The courts can sentence an offender to jail for breaching such an order. Human rights monitors continued to criticize the inconsistency in sentencing for rape, incest, and statutory rape, which is often left to the discretion of the judge. They noted that the lack of sentencing guidelines resulted in longer sentences for persons convicted of petty theft than for incest; and lesser sentences for incest than for rape or sexual assault of nonfamily members.

Children.—The Government is committed to children's human rights and welfare, although violence against children remains a serious problem. The Child Care Board is the key agency responsible for monitoring and responding to the critical welfare needs, interests, and rights of children.

People With Disabilities.—The law does not prohibit discrimination against the physically disabled in employment, education, or the provision of other state services. The Labour Department, which is responsible for finding jobs for the disabled, unsuccessfully advocated the introduction of such legislation in the 1980's. Similarly, there is no legislation mandating provision of accessibility to public thoroughfares or public or private buildings. Interest groups have lobbied for this type of legislation from time to time, but without success.

Section 6. Worker Rights

a. *The Right of Association.*—Workers freely exercise their right to form and belong to trade unions and to strike. There are two major unions and several smaller ones, representing various sectors of labor. The public service union, the National Union of Public Workers, is independent of any political party or the Government. The largest union, the Barbados Workers' Union (BWU), was historically closely associated with the Barbados Labour Party prior to 1954. After 1954, officers of the BWU became personally associated with the Democratic Labour Party.

The law accords full protection to trade unionists' personal and property rights. Another law prohibits strikes against public utilities. All private and public sector employees are permitted to strike, but essential workers may strike only under certain circumstances and after following prescribed procedures. There were no major strikes or long-term work stoppages, except for a strike in July by junior doctors at the main hospital that disrupted clinical services for 1 week.

Trade unions are free to form federations and are in fact affiliated with a variety of regional and international labor organizations. The Caribbean Congress of Labor has its headquarters in Barbados. A new Congress of Trade Unions and Staff Associations was inaugurated in August 1995. Most unions belong to this organization.

b. *The Right to Organize and Bargain Collectively.*—The law provides for the right to organize and bargain collectively, and authorities respected it in practice. Recent losses of jobs in the economy resulted in a reduction in union membership to about 20 percent of the working population. Normally, wages and working conditions are negotiated through the collective bargaining process, but a tripartite prices and incomes policy accord signed in the summer of 1993 established a 2-year wage freeze. The revised (second) protocol makes provision for negotiated increases in basic wages and increases based on productivity. The new accord covers 1995–1997, and was noted by Parliament on January 16.

Employers have no legal obligation to recognize unions under the Trade Union Act of 1964, but most do so when a majority of their employees signify a desire to be represented by a registered union. While there is no specific law prohibiting antiunion discrimination, the courts provide a method of redress for employees alleging unfair dismissal. The courts commonly award monetary compensation but rarely order reemployment.

There are no manufacturing or special areas where collective bargaining rights are legally or administratively impaired. There are no export processing zones.

c. *Prohibition of Forced or Compulsory Labor.*—The Constitution prohibits forced or compulsory labor, and there were no reports of its use.

d. *Minimum Age for Employment of Children.*—The legal minimum working age of 16 is generally observed. Compulsory primary and secondary education policies, which require school attendance until age 16, reinforce minimum age requirements. The Labour Department has a small cadre of labor inspectors who conduct spot investigations of enterprises and check records to verify compliance with the law. These inspectors may take legal action against an employer who is found to have underage workers.

e. *Acceptable Conditions of Work.*—The law sets and the authorities establish minimum wages for specified categories of workers. Only two categories of workers have a formally regulated minimum wage—household domestics and shop assistants (entry level commercial workers). Household domestics receive a minimum wage of about $32.50 (bds $65.00) per week, although in actual labor market conditions, the prevailing wage is almost double that amount. There are two age-related minimum wage categories for shop assistants. The adult minimum wage for shop assistants is $1.87 (bds $3.75) per hour; the juvenile minimum wage for shop assistants is $1.62 (bds $3.25) per hour. There is a minimum wage in place for workers (for example, sugar plantation workers) but the wage actually paid is a negotiated rate much higher than the legislated rate. This is a matter of practice but not of law.

The minimum wage for shop assistants is marginally sufficient to meet minimum living standards; most employees earn more. In 1992 an International Labor Organization (ILO) Committee of Experts (COE) cited Barbados for not adhering to the ILO convention on equal remuneration in its wage differentials in the sugar industry. The COE admonished the Government to ensure the application of the principle of equal remuneration for work of equal value to male and female workers in the sugar industry or to provide further information on job descriptions which might justify such wage distinction. This case was not resolved by year's end.

The standard legal workweek is 40 hours in 5 days, and the law requires overtime payment for hours worked in excess. Barbados accepts ILO conventions, standards, and other sectoral conventions regarding maximum hours of work. However, there is no general legislation that covers all occupations. Employers must provide workers a minimum of 3 weeks' annual leave. Unemployment benefits and national insurance (social security) cover all workers. A comprehensive, government-sponsored health program offers subsidized treatment and medication.

The Factories Act of 1983 sets out the officially recognized occupational safety and health standards. The Labour Department enforces health and safety standards and follows up to ensure that problems cited are corrected by management. The Factories Act requires that in certain sectors firms employing more than 50 workers set up a safety committee. This committee can challenge the decisions of management concerning the occupational safety and health environment. Trade unions have called on the Government to increase the number of factory inspectors in order to enforce existing and proposed safety and health legislation more effectively, and to follow up to ensure that problems cited are corrected by management. Government-operated corporations in particular were accused of doing a "poor job" in health and safety. The Government has promised to undertake inspections of government-operated corporations and manufacturing plants as a priority. Workers have a limited right to remove themselves from dangerous or hazardous job situations without jeopardizing their continued employment.

BELIZE

Belize is a parliamentary democracy with a constitution enacted in 1981 upon independence from the United Kingdom. The Prime Minister, a cabinet of ministers, and a legislative assembly govern the country. The Governor General represents Queen Elizabeth II in the largely ceremonial role of head of state. Both local and national elections are scheduled on a constitutionally prescribed basis. The Constitution provides for an independent judiciary.

The Police Department has primary responsibility for law enforcement and maintenance of order. The Belize Defense Force (BDF) is responsible for external security, but when deemed appropriate by civilian authorities may be tasked to assist the police department. Both the police and the BDF report to the Minister of National Security and are responsible to and controlled by civilian authorities. There were occasional reports of abuse by the police.

The economy is primarily agricultural, although tourism has become the principal source of foreign exchange earnings. The agricultural sector is heavily dependent on preferential access to export markets for sugar and for bananas. The Government favors free enterprise and generally encourages investment, although domestic investors are given preferential treatment over foreign investors in a number of key economic sectors. Preliminary estimates put 1996 gross domestic product growth at 4.5 percent in real terms. Annual per capita income was about $2,359.

The Constitution provides for, and citizens enjoy in practice, a wide range of fundamental rights and freedoms. Principal human rights abuses include occasional use of excessive force by the police when making arrests, lengthy pretrial detention, political influence on the judiciary, discrimination and domestic violence against women, and employer mistreatment of immigrant workers in the banana industry.

RESPECT FOR HUMAN RIGHTS

Section 1. Respect for the Integrity of the Person, Including Freedom From:

a. *Political and Other Extrajudicial Killing.*—There were no reports of political or other extrajudicial killings.

b. *Disappearance.*—There were no reports of politically motivated disappearances.

c. *Torture and Other Cruel, Inhuman, or Degrading Treatment or Punishment.*—The Constitution forbids torture or other inhuman punishment. There were several credible reports of mistreatment and abuse by the police. In at least two cases, police authorities took internal disciplinary measures against officers accused of abuse, although the authorities did not lodge criminal charges. The Police Department, the Police Complaints Board, and on occasion special independent commissions appointed by the Prime Minister investigate allegations of official abuse.

The Hattieville prison opened in 1993 and replaced the notoriously decrepit Belize City prison. Although designed to house 500 inmates, it actually held 960, or about 5 prisoners per 10-by-12-foot cell. There are rare reports of human rights abuses at the prison, in the form of physical brutality by prison wardens. The press also carried credible reports that prisoners were used as a labor force to build homes for family members of the minister with oversight responsibility for the prison.

The Government permits prison visits by independent human rights monitors.

d. *Arbitrary Arrest, Detention, or Exile.*—The Constitution prohibits arbitrary arrest or detention, and the Government generally observes these prohibitions. The law requires the police to inform a detainee of the cause of detention within 48 hours of arrest and to bring the person before a court within 72 hours. In practice, the authorities normally inform detainees immediately of the charges against them. Bail is granted in all but the most serious cases. In cases involving narcotics, the police cannot grant bail, but a Magistrate's court may do so after a full hearing. Many detainees cannot afford bail, however, and backlogs in the judicial system often cause considerable delays and postponements of hearings, resulting in an overcrowded prison and prolonged incarceration before trial.

The Constitution forbids exile, and it does not occur.

e. *Denial of Fair Public Trial.*—The Constitution provides for an independent judiciary, and the Government generally respects this provision in practice. The judiciary consists of the magistrate's courts, the Supreme Court, and the Court of Appeal.

Notwithstanding constitutional provisions, the fact that prominent government leaders continue to practice law while in office brought the judiciary's independence into question. The Chief Justice of the Supreme Court publicly stated that judges should not interpret laws in such a way as to frustrate the intention of the legislature, saying that this practice is an abuse of the power of the courts. The appearance of judicial independence from the executive branch is also compromised because judges and the director of public prosecutions must negotiate renewal of their employment contracts with the Government and thus may be vulnerable to political interference.

An inordinate number of significant narcotics-related cases are taking years to resolve. In these cases, defendants are released on minimal bail payments, and the defense lawyers and their firms are closely connected to sitting ministers of government, including the Attorney General.

Persons accused of civil or criminal offenses have constitutional rights to presumption of innocence, protection against self-incrimination, defense by counsel, a public trial, and appeal. Trial by jury is mandatory in capital cases. The Supreme Court and magistrate courts suffer backlogs aggravated by the inability to maintain a full complement of judges.

Those convicted by either a magistrate's court or the Supreme Court may appeal to the Court of Appeal. In some cases, including those resulting in a capital sentence, the convicted party may make a final appeal to the Privy Council in the United Kingdom. The Privy Council has agreed to hear several such appeals in 1996; this delayed carrying out the capital sentences.

There were no reports of political prisoners.

f. *Arbitrary Interference with Privacy, Family, Home, or Correspondence.*—The Constitution prohibits such practices, government authorities generally respect these prohibitions, and violations are subject to legal sanctions. However, there were several cases in which the Government has expropriated private land. The law requires that the Government assess and pay compensation in these instances, but these cases take many years to settle.

Section 2. *Respect for Civil Liberties, Including:*

a. *Freedom of Speech and Press.*—The Constitution provides for freedom of speech and of the press, but also permits the authorities to make "reasonable provisions" in the interests of defense, public safety, public order, public morality, or public health. These provisions include forbidding any citizen to question the validity of the financial disclosure statements submitted by public officials. Anyone who questions these statements orally or in writing outside of a rigidly prescribed procedure is subject to a fine of up to $5,000 or imprisonment of up to 3 years, or both.

A wide range of viewpoints is publicly presented without government interference in six privately owned weekly newspapers (there is no daily press), half of which are directly subsidized by major political parties. All newspapers are subject to the constraints of libel laws.

Since the first privately owned commercial radio station began broadcasting in 1990, other stations have been established, broadening the audience's choices. Popular radio call-in programs are lively and feature open criticism of and comments on government and political matters. Through financial subsidies, the Government continues to exert substantial editorial influence over the nominally autonomous Broadcasting Corporation of Belize (BCB) and its two radio stations; BCB once held a monopoly on radio in the country. The Government utilizes BCB studios and facilities to produce partisan advertisements and party propaganda.

There are eight privately owned television broadcasting stations, including several cable networks in Belize City and the major towns. The Government's Belize Information Service and two independent television stations produce local news and feature programs. The Belize Broadcasting Authority (BBA) regulates broadcasting and asserts its right to preview certain broadcasts, such as those with political content, and to delete any defamatory or personally libelous material from political broadcasts. As far as is known, the BBA did not exercise this authority during 1996 although there appeared to be ample opportunity to do so during the aggressive and negative media campaigns each party waged during local elections held earlier in the year.

The Belize Press Association, formed in 1995 to seek common ground among the disparate members of the press, continued this effort in the face of strong internal partisan debate. One of the association's main goals is to obtain increased access to government information, utilizing the country's Freedom of Information Act. In September the Prime Minister challenged the media to exercise this right, noting that only one case had been filed in the 3 years since the law had been passed. Frustrating the media's attempts to use the Freedom of Information Act are statements by the Supreme Court warning journalists that questioning the integrity of the court or its members could result in criminal contempt of court charges.

The law provides for academic freedom, and the Government respects it in practice.

b. *Freedom of Peaceful Assembly and Association.*—The Constitution provides for freedom of assembly and the authorities honor it in practice. Political parties and other groups with political objectives freely hold rallies and mass meetings. The organizers of public meetings must obtain a permit 36 hours in advance of the meetings; such permits are not denied for political reasons and are routinely granted in practice.

The Constitution permits citizens to form and join associations of their choice, both political and nonpolitical.

c. *Freedom of Religion.*—The Constitution provides for freedom of religion, and the Government respects this right in practice.

d. *Freedom of Movement Within the Country, Foreign Travel, Emigration, and Repatriation.*—The Constitution provides for these rights, and the Government respects them in practice.

The Government generally cooperates with the United Nations High Commissioner for Refugees (UNHCR) and other humanitarian organizations in assisting refugees. The UNHCR provides the majority of funding for refugee programs in the country, including the salaries of most of the employees in the Government's Department of Refugees. A government committee to review applications for asylum meets weekly and includes a UNHCR representative as a member. The Government turned down approximately 500 requests for asylum in 1996. The Government honors the principle of first asylum, and most recently provided it to four persons in 1995.

In the wake of the civil conflicts in Central America during the 1980's, over 40,000 mostly Hispanic immigrants came to Belize, many of them entering illegally and living in the country without documentation. The Government has granted asylum and allowed local resettlement of about 8,000 refugees. Despite the signing of the Peace Treaty ending Guatemala's civil war, the Government does not plan to send Guatemalan refugees back until it deems the situation in that country to be conducive to such return.

Section 3. Respect for Political Rights: The Right of Citizens to Change Their Government

Belize is a democracy governed by a Legislative Assembly, with executive direction from a cabinet of ministers headed by Prime Minister Manuel Esquivel. The law requires national elections at least every 5 years.

All elections are by secret ballot, and suffrage is universal for citizens 18 years and older. National political parties include the People's United Party (PUP), the United Democratic Party (UDP), the National Alliance for Belizean Rights (NABR), and the People's Democratic Party (PDP). The nation's ethnic diversity is reflected in each party's membership. The Government changed hands (for the third time since independence in 1981) in 1993 when a coalition of the UDP and the NABR won 16 of 29 seats in the House of Representatives.

No laws impede participation of women in politics; their scarcity in electoral politics can be attributed to tradition and socioeconomic factors. Women hold a number of appointive offices, including three of nine Senate seats. One member of the 29-seat House of Representatives is a woman, but women in elective office are the exception. None hold senior positions higher than membership on the executive committees of the political parties.

Section 4. Governmental Attitude Regarding International and Nongovernmental Investigation of Alleged Violations of Human Rights

A number of human rights groups operate without government restriction, investigating and publishing their findings on human rights cases. Government officials are generally cooperative and responsive to their activities. The Human Rights Commission of Belize (HCRB), a nongovernmental organization (NGO) affiliated with regional human rights organizations and partly funded by the UNHCR, operates free of government restriction on a wide range of issues, including refugee and agricultural workers' rights, cases of alleged police abuse, and cases of alleged illegal deportations of Central American nationals. The HCRB publicizes, and urges police and other government bodies to act upon complaints it receives. However, the HCRB appears to have been largely inactive in 1996, reportedly due to financial difficulties.

Local and international human rights groups operate freely, and the Government cooperates with independent investigations of human rights conditions. However, when native Belizean Maya organizations voiced concern over what they considered an environmentally questionable and socially disruptive highway improvement project in the Toledo district, the Government dismissed their arguments and reportedly accused the leaders of being foreign immigrants.

Section 5. Discrimination Based upon Race, Sex, Religion, Disability, Language, or Social Status

Belize is a multiracial, multiethnic country, and the Government actively promotes tolerance and cross-cultural understanding. Discrimination on ethnic or religious grounds is illegal and not common, although ethnic tension, particularly resentment of recently arrived Central American and Asian immigrants, continued to be a problem. The Government continues to reserve certain professions for Belizean nationals, granting permits and licenses to non-Belizeans only in specific cases. These occupations include fishing, souvenir manufacturing, sightseeing tours, accounting, insurance, real estate, and legal services.

Women.—Domestic violence against women is a chronic problem. Women Against Violence, an NGO with branches throughout the country, runs a shelter for battered women and a hot line for rape victims.

Despite constitutional provisions for equality, women face social and economic prejudices. For example, women find it more difficult than men to obtain business and agricultural financing and other resources. Most employed women are concentrated in female-dominated occupations with traditionally low status and wages. A women's bureau in the Ministry of Labor and Social Services is charged with developing programs to improve the status of women. A number of officially registered women's groups work closely with various government ministries in promoting social awareness programs. Women have access to education and are active in all spheres of national life, but relatively few are found in top managerial positions. While the law mandates that women receive equal pay for equal work, female wage earners often earn less than men in similar jobs. There are no legal impediments to women owning or managing land or other real property.

Children.—Education is compulsory for children ages 5 to 14. There is a family services division in the Ministry of Human Resources devoted primarily to children's issues. The division coordinates programs for children who are victims of domestic violence, advocates remedies in specific cases before the family court, conducts public education campaigns, and works with NGO's and the United Nations Children's Fund to promote children's welfare. There is also a national committee for families and children, chaired by the Minister of Human Resources. There is no societal pattern of abuse of children.

People With Disabilities.—The law does not mandate specifically the provision of accessibility for disabled persons nor prohibit job discrimination against them. The Government's Disability Services Unit, as well as a number of NGO's such as the Belize Association of and for Persons with Disabilities and the Belize Center for the Visually Impaired provide assistance to physically disabled persons. Disabled children have access to government special education facilities.

Section 6. Worker Rights

a. *The Right of Association.*—By statute and in practice, workers are free to establish and join trade unions. Eleven independent unions, with approximately 11 percent of the labor force, represent a cross-section of white-collar, blue-collar, and professional workers, including most civil service employees. Several of these unions, however, were inactive. The Ministry of Labor recognizes unions after they file with the office of registry. The law empowers members to draft the by-laws and constitutions of their unions, and they are free to elect officers from among the membership at large. Unions that choose not to hold elections may act as representatives for their membership, but the national Trade Union Congress permits only unions that hold free and annual elections of officers to join its ranks. Both law and precedent effectively protect unions against dissolution or suspension by administrative authority.

The law permits unions to strike, but unions representing essential services may strike only after giving 21 days' notice to the ministry concerned.

Although no unions are officially affiliated with political parties, several are sympathetic to one or the other of the two main parties (the UDP and the PUP). Unions freely exercise the right to form federations and confederations and affiliate with international organizations.

b. *The Right to Organize and Bargain Collectively.*—The law provides for collective bargaining and unions freely practice it throughout the country. Employers and unions set wages in free negotiations, or, more commonly, employers simply establish them. The Labor Commissioner acts as a conciliator in deadlocked collective bargaining negotiations between labor and management, offering nonbinding counsel to both sides. Historically, the Commissioner's guidance has been voluntarily accepted. However, should either union or management choose not to accept the Commissioner's decision, both are entitled to a legal hearing of the case, provided that it is linked to some provision of civil or criminal law.

The Constitution prohibits antiunion discrimination both before and after a union is registered. Unions may freely organize, but the law does not require employers to recognize a union as a bargaining agent. Some employers have been known to block union organization by terminating the employment of key union sympathizers, usually on grounds purportedly unrelated to union activities. Effective redress is extremely difficult in such situations. Technically, a worker may file a complaint with the Labor Department, but in practice it was virtually impossible to prove that a termination was due to union activity. The United Banners Banana Workers Union is seeking to organize the mainly foreign laborers in the banana industry and in the process is testing the Government's commitment to a number of these legal provisions. The Government has refused to recognize the union until the union submits its membership list for inspection. The union's members have expressed concern over possible government reprisals.

The Labor Code applies in the country's two export processing zones (EPZ's). There are no unions in the EPZ's, however, reflecting the general weakness of organized labor in the country.

c. *Prohibition of Forced or Compulsory Labor.*—The Constitution forbids forced labor, and it is not generally known to occur. However, prisoners were reportedly used to build homes for relatives of senior officials (see Section 1.c.).

d. *Minimum Age for Employment of Children.*—The minimum age for employment is 14 years, or 17 years for employment near hazardous machinery. Inspectors from the Ministries of Labor and Education enforce this regulation, although in recent years school truancy officers, who have historically borne the brunt of the enforcement burden, have been less active. The law requires children between the ages of 5 and 14 to attend school, but there are many truants and dropouts.

e. *Acceptable Conditions of Work.*—The minimum wage is $1.12 (BZ$2.25), except in export industries where it is $1.00 (BZ$2.00) per hour. For domestic workers and shop assistants in stores where liquor is not consumed, the rate is $0.87 (BZ$1.75) per hour. The minimum wage law does not cover workers paid on a piecework basis. The Ministry of Labor is charged with enforcing the legal minimum wage, which is generally respected in practice. The minimum wage as a sole source of income is inadequate to provide a decent standard of living for a worker and family. Most salaried workers receive more than the minimum wage.

The law sets the normal workweek at no more than 6 days or 45 hours. It requires payment for overtime work and an annual paid vacation of 2 weeks. A patchwork of health and safety regulations covers numerous industries, and the Ministries of Labor and Public Health enforce these regulations to varying degrees. Enforcement is not universal, and the ministries commit their limited inspection and investigative resources principally to urban and more accessible rural areas where labor, health, and safety complaints have been registered. Workers have the legal right to remove themselves from a dangerous workplace situation without jeopardy to continued employment.

The exploitation of undocumented Hispanic workers, particularly young service workers and workers in the banana industry, continues to be a major issue for the Government, the HCRB, and other concerned citizens. Undocumented immigrants working in the Stann Creek area banana industry have cited for years poor working and living conditions and routine nonpayment of wages. However, little progress has been made in resolving or preventing these systemic problems.

BOLIVIA

A constitutional, multiparty democracy with an elected president and bicameral legislature, Bolivia has separate executive, legislative, and judicial branches with an attorney general independent of all three. The judiciary, while independent, is corrupt and inefficient. The executive and legislative branches share these defects to some extent. Constitutional amendments to reform the political and judicial systems that were approved in August 1994 were partially implemented by the end of 1996.

The National Police have primary responsibility for internal security, although the army, navy, and air force can be called upon for help in critical situations. A special antinarcotics force (FELCN), including the Mobile Rural Patrol Unit (UMOPAR), is dedicated to antinarcotics enforcement. Civilian authorities maintain effective control of the security forces, but some members of these forces committed human rights abuses.

Although rich in minerals and hydrocarbons, Bolivia has an annual per capita gross domestic product of about $1,000. Principal exports are minerals, natural gas, and other raw materials; traditional agriculture dominates the domestic economy. Poverty is endemic. Many citizens lack such basic services as water, electricity, sewers, and primary health care. The centralized economy has long depended heavily on foreign aid. To promote development and a transition to a market economy, the Government is carrying out a program of privatization, deficit reduction, to strengthen the banking system, and encourage increased exports and foreign investment.

The Government generally respected the human rights of its citizens; however, legal and institutional deficiencies prevented their full protection. The Government continued its initiatives to improve this situation, but implementation was slow. The most pervasive human rights abuse continued to be prolonged incarceration of detainees due to antiquated procedures, inefficiency, and corruption in the judicial system.There were credible reports of abuses by police, including excessive force, petty theft, extortion, and improper arrests. Prison guards beat prisoners. Human rights groups criticized the FELCN and the UMOPAR for abuses, particularly against coca growers and peasants in the Chapare region. Although the authorities disciplined or brought charges against 40 members of these units, in general police remained reluctant to prosecute their own colleagues for offenses. Investigations of alleged official abuses were slow. Other problems include harsh prison conditions, violence and discrimination against women, discrimination against and abuse of indigenous people, abuse of children, and inhuman working conditions in the mining industry. Controversy continued as to whether certain actions, such as temporary detentions taken to implement a state of siege in April 1995, were unconstitutional and violated human rights.

RESPECT FOR HUMAN RIGHTS

Section 1. Respect for the Integrity of the Person, Including Freedom From:

a. *Political and Other Extrajudicial Killing.*—There were no reports of politically motivated killings. However, there were two instances in which security forces killed protesters while trying to control demonstrations.

Two deaths resulted from confrontations between demonstrators and security authorities in connection with teachers' union protests. On March 25 a police antiriot shotgun pellet evidently killed Rosendo Chino Olori, a market porter, in central La Paz. Chino was an innocent passerby caught up in a battle between teachers' union demonstrators armed with slings and dynamite, and police using tear gas and rubber shotgun pellets. Demonstrators at first prevented police from reaching Chino's body, claiming that he was a murdered fellow teacher. They roughed up a television camera crew at the scene. Police initially asserted that Chino died because the teachers did not allow him to receive medical assistance. However, a televised autopsy confirmed what closeup news photos of the corpse had suggested, i.e., that Chino's chest wound was massive and that no treatment could have saved him. A pathologist displayed on camera what appeared to be a large plastic pellet he removed from Chino's body and stated that it had been fired at close range causing nearly instantaneous death. The authorities did not deny that a police weapon killed Chino, although they said they had not authorized government forces to fire. The Government closed its investigation after failing to determine which policeman fired the shot.

Wilber Ferreira Cespedes, age 15, was killed in Cobija, Pando department, on May 23. The death occurred when demonstrators stoned the department administrative offices where officials were signing an agreement to end a 2-month teachers strike. A shotgun projectile fired by a police official guarding the building struck Ferreira. One pathologist identified it as a lead pellet, and another as a rubber pellet. An investigation was still in progress at year's end.

The final results of these investigations, and of the investigations into the five law enforcement-related deaths in the Chapare in 1995, have not been released. No action is known to have been taken against any official involved. The police officer accused in 1994 of murdering coca worker Felipe Perez Ortiz, who escaped from custody in September of that year, has not been recaptured. The investigation continued in the case of five police officials arrested at the end of 1994 and charged with culpable negligence in the death of a prisoner, and the five officers remained free pending its completion. The Government's failure to complete effective investigations and publish the findings within a reasonable time amounts to impunity despite contrary government policies.

b. *Disappearance.*—There were no reports of politically motivated disappearances.

c. *Torture and Other Cruel, Inhuman, or Degrading Treatment or Punishment.*—The Government honors the constitutional prohibition against torture. However, there were reports that police used undue force in detaining farm workers during antinarcotics operations. Although many such allegations clearly were politically motivated exaggerations, the similarity and volume of such claims suggest that they had some basis in truth. However, no security personnel were charged or tried. In July the National Police announced activation of a special Police Control Corps to monitor police behavior and to discipline officials who commit abuses. Beginning with an 18-member unit in La Paz, the Government plans to extend the corps throughout the country.

The authorities disciplined or held for prosecution 40 members of the FELCN and the UMOPAR for offenses including corruption, extortion, and attempted rape. The three policemen accused of raping a juvenile prisoner in 1995 were discharged and in jail awaiting trial at year's end. In general, however, the police were reluctant to prosecute their own colleagues for offenses. Congress has yet to take action on the 1995 report of its Human Rights Committee resurrecting allegations that police officials had in past years tortured captured terrorists and recommending that criminal proceedings be opened against a number of named officers.

There were credible reports that guards beat some prisoners for attempting to escape from custody. The authorities suspended some prison personnel pending investigation.

Prison conditions are harsh. Prisons are overcrowded, and conditions can be life threatening for inmates without money. Ability to pay can determine cell size, visiting privileges, day-pass eligibility, and place or even length of confinement. Cell prices range from $20 to $5,000, paid to prior occupants or to prisoners who control cell blocks. In the poorest parts of La Paz' San Pedro prison, for example, inmates occupy tiny cells (3 by 4 by 6 feet) with no ventilation, lighting, or beds. Crowding in some "low-rent" sections obliges inmates to sleep sitting up. Children up to 6 years old may live with an incarcerated parent; an estimated 400 children do so. The authorities worked to get such children out of prisons, but many have nowhere else to go. The standard prison diet, according to a 1995 study, can cause anemia. Drugs and alcohol are readily available for those who can pay. There is no adequate health care within the prisons, and it is very difficult for prisoners to get permission for medical treatment outside. Affluent prisoners, however, can obtain transfers to preferred prisons or even to outside private institutional care for "medical" reasons.

Convicted juvenile prisoners are not segregated from adult prisoners in jails. Rehabilitation programs for juveniles or other prisoners are scarce to nonexistent. The Government has acknowledged these problems but does not have sufficient resources to correct them quickly.

The Government permits prison visits by human rights monitors and news media representatives.

The incidence of violence was far lower in the Chapare coca growing region than in 1995, as more growers agreed to have their crops eradicated in exchange for compensation. However, there were credible reports that coca growers unions used physical coercion and intimidation to prevent farm workers from cooperating with the Government in coca eradication. Indigenous groups complained that armed coca growers invade their lands by force and coerce or bribe their members to cultivate illegal coca.

Indigenous communities in areas with little or no central government presence impose corporal punishment such as whipping on members who violate traditional laws or rules, although such punishment is forbidden by the Constitution.

d. *Arbitrary Arrest, Detention, or Exile.*—Arrests are carried out openly. The law requires a valid warrant, which a court must confirm within 48 hours. However, there were credible reports that these legal safeguards were violated in some cases.

Denial of justice through prolonged detention remains the most pervasive human rights problem. Judicial corruption, a shortage of public defenders, inadequate case-tracking mechanisms, and complex criminal justice procedures keep persons incarcerated for months, or even years, before trial. A survey in September of the largest prison, San Pedro, revealed that about 80 percent of the inmates still were awaiting either trial or sentence. The Constitution provides for judicial determination of the legality of detention. Prisoners are released if a judge rules detention illegal, but the process can take months. Prisoners may see a lawyer, but approximately 70 percent cannot afford legal counsel, and public defenders are overburdened. Bail exists, except in some drug cases, and is generally granted.

The Government continues to address the problem of delay of justice by implementing the 1994 constitutional reforms to streamline the judicial system and taking measures to correct other deficiencies as they come to light. The Personal Recognizance Law promulgated in February permits pretrial release on personal recognizance for those unable to post bond, and provisional liberty for those declared innocent but awaiting review or appeal, or those already imprisoned longer than the maximum sentence for their alleged offense. The new law also shortens the permissible time for various stages of the penal process, including preventive detention. The authorities freed more than 1,000 prisoners provisionally or permanently under this law in its first 7 months. When it became known that hundreds of cases were suffering long delays because the defendants could not pay postage costs to transfer their files between judicial offices, a Supreme Decree eliminated that obligation.

The Public Defender program, still being expanded with a current total of 16 offices nationwide, has in its first 3 years of existence freed nearly 18,000 persons who probably would have remained imprisoned for lack of legal defense. From its establishment in October 1994 until September 1996, the Public Defender's office in the coca-growing Chapare region—where most allegations of official abuse arise—represented persons in 2,141 cases, obtaining liberty for the defendants in 1,502 of them. The office is taking an active approach by distributing concise information about human rights to the populace and seeking to be involved in arrest cases at the earliest possible juncture to ensure that human rights and due process are honored. A new program of mobile public defenders who can reach out to the more remote parts of the area has proven effective, and is being extended to other isolated regions of the country.

Children from 11 to 16 years of age can be detained indefinitely in children's centers for known or suspected offenses, or for their protection, simply on the orders of a social worker. There is no judicial review.

The Government does not use forced exile as a punishment.

e. *Denial of Fair Public Trial.*—The judiciary is independent, but corruption and intimidation in the judicial system remain major problems. Poor pay and working conditions help make judges and prosecutors susceptible to bribes. Five Supreme Court ministers face investigations and possible corruption charges. Several lower court judges, as well as some prosecutors, were the subjects of similar allegations during the year, resulting in some firings and pending legal actions.

The judicial system has four levels: Investigative, trial, and superior courts, with the Supreme Court at the apex. In mid-1995, the Congress approved five new justices to complete the Supreme Court bench, ending a period of 18 months in which the court was not fully staffed or fully functional. The justices admit, however, that it is still difficult to assemble the quorum needed for decisions, and rulings are unduly delayed.

Police present the case of an arrested person to a prosecutor. If the prosecutor decides to prosecute, the case is then submitted to an investigative court which decides whether there is sufficient evidence to issue an indictment; if so, the case goes to a trial court. The trial court's decision may be appealed to superior court and, eventually, to the Supreme Court. Bail is usually available. Cases of persons arrested under the counternarcotics law go directly from a special prosecutor to the trial court. There is no bail in narcotics cases. The trial court's decision must be reviewed by the district superior court, which may confirm, lower, raise, or annul the sentence, or impose a sentence where there was none before. Both the district prosecutor and the defense attorney may make recommendations and comments at this stage. Superior court decisions in narcotics cases must be reviewed by the Supreme Court whose decision is final. Under the Personal Recognizance Law, persons who are absolved or found innocent in either of the two first instances may then be granted provisional liberty while they await the mandatory higher reviews.

The authorities generally respect the constitutional guarantee of the right to a fair public trial. However, the maximum time periods permitted by law for different stages of the judicial process frequently are exceeded. Defendants have the right to an attorney, to confront witnesses, to present evidence, and to appeal judicial decisions. The authorities generally honor these rights. Although the law provides for a defense attorney at public expense if needed, one is not always promptly available. The highly formal and corrupt judicial system makes it difficult for poor, illiterate persons to have effective access to courts and legal redress.

There were no reports of political prisoners.

f. *Arbitrary Interference with Privacy, Family, Home, or Correspondence.*—The Constitution provides for the sanctity of the home and the privacy of citizens, and government authorities generally respect these provisions. There were credible allegations of UMOPAR abuses involving illegal searches and thefts of property from homes. However, residents in the coca growing areas generally are reluctant to file and pursue formal complaints. In August 1995, the Government and coca growers' union representatives agreed to form a mixed commission with offices throughout the Chapare coca-growing region, where most offenses allegedly occur. These offices would accept and pursue complaints of human rights abuses committed by anyone, including police, narcotics traffickers, or coca growers. The first such office began to function in Chimore in December 1995 and has been active in investigating some complaints.

Section 2. Respect for Civil Liberties, Including:

a. *Freedom of Speech and Press.*—The Constitution provides for the fundamental right to express ideas and opinions freely by any means of dissemination. There are, however, some limitations on freedom of speech. The Penal Code provides that persons found guilty of insulting, defaming, or slandering public officials for carrying out their duties may be jailed from 1 month to 2 years. If the insults are directed against the President, Vice President, or a Minister, the sentence may be increased by one-half. Although this law was rarely enforced, in March the authorities jailed former attorney general Manuel Morales Davila for accusing the President of treason. At year's end, Morales Davila was at liberty pending trial.

State-owned and private radio and television stations operated freely. Newspapers are privately owned; most adopt antigovernment positions.

The Government respects academic freedom, and the law grants public universities autonomous status. Some Marxist groups of teachers and students sought to deny academic freedom and to impose their political agenda on the education process. Radical, Trotskyite elements of the La Paz teachers' union symbolically burned books to be used in the Government's education reform plan, which removes the teachers' control of the curriculum and subjects them to quality review by parents and civic authorities.

b. *Freedom of Peaceful Assembly and Association.*—The law provides for the rights of peaceful assembly and association, and the authorities respect them in practice.

The Government routinely grants permits for marches and rallies and, as a rule, the authorities try to avoid confronting demonstrators. However, police clashed with union and other demonstrators on many occasions. Labor, political, and student groups carried out many demonstrations and rallies in La Paz and other cities throughout the year, particularly during the first quarter. The authorities intervened only when they became dangerously violent or interfered substantially with normal civic activity.

c. *Freedom of Religion.*—Roman Catholicism predominates, and the Constitution recognizes it as the official religion. However, citizens may practice the religion of their choice. About 400 religious groups, mostly Protestant, are active. Missionary groups must register with the Foreign Ministry as nongovernmental organizations (NGO's); there was no indication that they were treated differently from other NGO's. The Ministry did not disallow any registrations by missionary groups.

d. *Freedom of Movement Within the Country, Foreign Travel, Emigration, and Repatriation.*—There are no restrictions on travel. The law permits emigration and provides for the right to return. The Government does not revoke citizenship for political reasons.

The Government cooperates with the United Nations High Commissioner for Refugees and other humanitarian organizations in assisting refugees. Some refugees were accepted for resettlement. The issue of the provision of first asylum did not arise. Early in 1996, the authorities returned some Peruvians deemed to be improperly in the country in the wake of the 1995 kidnaping of industrialist Samuel Doria Medina by the Tupac Amaru terrorist group, but there were no reports that they were subsequently persecuted in Peru.

Section 3. Respect for Political Rights: The Right of Citizens to Change Their Government

The Constitution provides citizens with the right to change their government peacefully, and citizens exercise this right in practice through periodic, free, and fair elections held on the basis of universal suffrage. Political parties ranging from far left to moderate right function openly. Implementing regulations for the 1994 constitutional revisions provide for more than half of the congressional deputies to be elected individually and directly, rather than from party lists.

No legal impediments exist to women or indigenous people voting, holding political office, or rising to political leadership. Nevertheless, the number of women and indigenous people who have prominent positions in politics remains small. Most of the political parties have said that they will accede to demands from women that they be allocated a fair share of the candidacies in the 1997 national elections. There are 13 women in the 130-seat Chamber of Deputies, but none in the Senate or the Cabinet. The Vice President, Victor Hugo Cardenas, is an Aymara.

Section 4. Governmental Attitude Regarding International and Nongovernmental Investigation of Alleged Violations of Human Rights

A number of human rights groups operate without government restriction, investigating and publishing their findings on human rights cases. Government officials are generally cooperative and responsive to their views. However, they criticize human rights advocates for paying attention exclusively to the negative aspects of the Government's performance. The Human Rights Committee of the Congress is very active and frequently criticizes the Government publicly.

Section 5. Discrimination Based on Race, Sex, Religion, Disability, Language, or Social Status

The Constitution prohibits discrimination based upon race, sex, language, religion, political or other opinion, origin, or economic or social condition. Nonetheless, there was significant discrimination against women, indigenous people, and the small black minority.

Women.—Violence against women is pervasive. A study by the National Institute of Statistics covering the July 1992-June 1993 period found that 40 percent of all reported violent attacks in La Paz department were perpetrated against women. Ninety-five percent of the attackers were male; in 71 percent of the cases the attacker was closely related to the victim. Of these domestic violence complaints, 52 percent involved physical mistreatment and 48 percent involved psychological abuse. A total of 11,069 complaints of violence against women were registered in La Paz during this period. The Government estimates that there are about 100,000 incidents of violence against women annually nationwide and that as many as 95 percent of them go unpunished. The Congressional Committee on Women stated that an average of 3.5 cases of rape or statutory rape were reported each day for the first half of 1995 and estimated that twice that many cases were not reported.

The Government continued to implement a program to protect women. In December 1995, the Government promulgated the Law on Domestic Violence, which makes rape a public crime and broadens the definition of family member abuse. Public agencies state that reported incidents of abuse have increased markedly as a result of the new law, as citizens become more aware of the problem and of the availability of help.

Comprehensive legal services offices continued to be established to help and support women. There were 26 such offices operating throughout the country by early 1996. Family protection police units, staffed by specially trained officers including women, were also expanded with a target of 10 by mid-year. Other elements of the program include revisions to school curriculums and educating health care providers about the appropriate manner of dealing with female patients.

A new medical security program inaugurated in July guarantees free medical care to women of reproductive age and to children under the age of 5, based on economic need.

The Penal Code does not define sexual harassment as a crime; the authorities must try persons accused of harassment under other penal provisions. There are no statistics on the incidence of sexual harassment, but the problem is generally acknowledged to exist widely in the male-oriented society.

Women generally do not enjoy a social status equal to that of men. Many women do not know their legal rights; traditional prejudices and social conditions remain obstacles to advancement. Women generally earn less than men for equal work. Young girls often leave school to work at home or on the economy. Although not effectively enforced, the national labor law is overprotective in some aspects, limiting women to a workday 1 hour shorter than that of men and prohibiting them from working at night.

Children.—The Government is aware of the precarious situation of children and the need to provide legal and institutional infrastructure for their protection. However, the Government has not given the situation sufficient political priority to ensure that it will be corrected quickly and effectively.

Statistics from the Ministry of Planning's Education Reform Team show that in rural areas, only 0.7 percent of girls and 1.4 percent of boys finish high school; in urban areas, 26 percent of girls and 31 percent of boys do so. The 1994 Education Reform Act sought to improve the situation of children; even optimistic observers, however, noted that it will take years for it to have an impact.

The National Institute of Statistics calculated in 1995 that 47 percent of children in La Paz were chronically undernourished, and that 10 percent of the children migrating from rural areas showed evidence of acute malnutrition.

Many children, particularly from rural areas, lack the birth certificates and identity documents they need to secure social benefits and protection. There were credible allegations that as many as 200 juveniles, for instance, were incarcerated as adults in the San Pedro jail for lack of reliable civil documents proving their ages. The Minor's Code promulgated in 1992 has proven inadequate.

According to a 1995 report by the director of the National Institute of Child Development, 96,000 children have mental disabilities, 37,000 have physical disabilities, 4,000 have hearing impairments, and 2,500 have visual impairments. Because of scarce resources, only about 400 of these children were treated in government facilities.

Government surveys suggest that about 1 million children (or about 1 child in 3) suffer physical or psychological abuse—13 percent of them at school, where corporal punishment and verbal abuse are common, and 87 percent at home. About 20 percent of all children suffer abuse severe enough to result in bruises, scars, or burns. Although laws provide safeguards against children working, they are not effectively enforced, and about 216,000 children work, usually to help provide for family subsistence, in uncontrolled and sometimes unhealthy conditions (see Section 6.d.).

The old practice of "criadito" service still persists in some parts of the country. Criaditos are indigenous children of both sexes, usually 10 to 12 years old, whom their parents indenture to middle- and upper-class families to perform household work in exchange for education, clothing, room, and board. There are no controls over the benefits to, or treatment of, such children, who may become virtual slaves for the years of their indenture.

People With Disabilities.—In December 1995, the Congress passed a law on disabilities drafted by the Senate Commission on Social Development and interested NGO's. The law provides for equal employment and social rights for the disabled, provides incentives to employers, and requires national and local governmental agencies to strengthen or create units charged with responsibility for the disabled. It also establishes the right of access to public and private facilities "without architectural impediment" for people with disabilities. The new electoral law made arrangements for blind voters. In general, however, there are no special services or infrastructure to accommodate people with disabilities. A lack of adequate resources impedes full implementation of the new law. Social attitudes keep many disabled persons at home from an early age, limiting their integration into society.

Indigenous People.—Discrimination against, and abuses of, indigenous people continued. The indigenous majority generally remains at the low end of the socioeconomic scale, facing severe disadvantages in health, life expectancy, education, income, literacy, and employment. Lack of education, inefficient farming and mining methods, indigenous cultural practices, inability to speak Spanish, and societal biases keep the indigenous people poor. They continued to be exploited in the workplace. Some rural indigenous workers are kept in a state of virtual slavery by employers who charge them more for room and board than they earn. Although the October Agrarian Reform Law extended the protection of the national labor law to all paid agricultural workers, including indigenous workers, the problem persists for lack of effective enforcement.

The Agrarian Reform Law also provides for indigenous communities to have legal title to their communal lands and for individual farmers to have title to the land they work. The Government and indigenous leaders jointly developed provisions of this law; the authorities presented the first communal titles to seven indigenous groups in December.

Indigenous people complain that their territories are not legally defined and protected, and that their resources are exploited by outsiders. Specific offenders allegedly are coca growers and timber pirates. Indigenous groups have taken advantage of the Popular Participation Law to form municipalities that offer them greater opportunities for self-determination.

Section 6. Worker Rights

a. *The Right of Association.*—Workers may form and join organizations of their choosing. The Labor Code requires prior government authorization to establish a union, permits only one union per enterprise, and allows the Government to dissolve unions; however, the Government has not enforced these provisions in recent years. While the code denies civil servants the right to organize and bans strikes in public services, including banks and public markets, nearly all civilian government workers are unionized. Workers are not penalized for union activities. In theory, the Bolivian Labor Federation (COB) represents virtually the entire work force; however, only about one-half of workers in the formal economy actually belong to labor unions. Some members of the informal economy also participate in labor or trade organizations.

Workers in the private sector frequently exercise the right to strike. Solidarity strikes are illegal, but the Government has not prosecuted those responsible nor imposed penalties. Significant strikes centered around annual negotiations over salaries and benefits for public employees. However, their real targets were the Government's economic and social reform programs. Most strikes were conducted and led by the militant Trotskyite element of the Urban Teachers Union. Other disturbances occurred in the Chapare region where the coca growers' unions opposed government eradication efforts. Normal activity in major cities was sometimes paralyzed by rioting unionists in the first quarter of the year.

Unions are not free from influence by political parties. The COB itself is a political organization directed by Marxist ideologues. Its stated aim is to overthrow the Government's neoliberal economic program, and it gives little attention to serious collective bargaining. Most parties have labor committees that attempt to influence union activity and also have party activists inside the unions.

The law allows unions to join international labor organizations. The COB became an affiliate of the Communist, formerly Soviet-dominated, World Federation of Trade Unions in 1988.

b. *The Right to Organize and Bargain Collectively.*—Workers may organize and bargain collectively. In practice, collective bargaining, defined as voluntary direct negotiations between unions and employers without participation of the Government, is limited. Consultations between government representatives and labor leaders are common, but there are no collective bargaining agreements as defined above. In state industries, the union issues a list of demands and the Government concedes some points. Private employers often use public sector settlements as guidelines for their own adjustments, and some private employers exceed the government settlements. The Government, conscious of International Monetary Fund guidelines, rarely grants wage increases exceeding inflation.

The law prohibits discrimination against union members and organizers. Complaints go to the National Labor Court, which can take a year or more to rule. The court has ruled in favor of discharged workers in some cases and successfully required their reinstatement. However, union leaders say problems are often moot by the time the court rules.

Labor law and practice in the seven special duty-free zones arethe same as in the rest of the country.

c. *Prohibition of Forced or Compulsory Labor.*—The law prohibits forced or compulsory labor. However, the practices of child apprenticeship and agricultural servitude by indigenous workers (see Section 5) constitute violations, as do some individual cases of household workers effectively imprisoned by their employers.

d. *Minimum Age for Employment of Children.*—The law prohibits employment of persons under 18 years of age in dangerous, unhealthy, or immoral work. The Labor Code is ambiguous on conditions of employment for minors from 14 to 17 years of age, and permits apprenticeship for those 12 to 14 years old. This practice has been criticized by the International Labor Organization.

Responsibility for enforcing child labor provisions resides in the Labor Ministry, but it generally does not enforce provisions about employment of children. Although the law requires all children to complete at least 5 years of primary school, the requirement is poorly enforced, particularly in rural areas. Urban children sell goods, shine shoes, and assist transport operators. Rural children often work with parents from an early age. Children are not generally employed in factories or formal businesses but, when employed, often work the same hours as adults.

e. *Acceptable Conditions of Work.*—In conformity with the law, the minimum wage is subject to annual renegotiation and was adjusted in April to approximately $43.30 (223 Bolivianos) per month plus bonuses and fringe benefits. The minimum wage does not provide a decent standard of living for a worker and family, and most workers earn more. Although the minimum wage falls below prevailing wages in most jobs, certain fringe benefits are pegged to it. The minimum wage does not cover about 20 percent of urban workers—vendors and shoe polishers, for example—nor does it cover farmers, some 30 percent of the working population.

Only half the urban labor force enjoys an 8-hour workday and a workweek of 5 or 5½ days, because the maximum workweek of 44 hours is not enforced. The Labor Ministry's Bureau of Occupational Safety has responsibility for protection of workers' health and safety, but relevant standards are poorly enforced. Working conditions in the mining sector are particularly bad. Although the State Mining Corporation has an office responsible for safety, many mines, often old and using antiquated equipment, are dangerous and unhealthy. In some mines operated as cooperatives, miners earn less than $3 per 12-hour day. They work without helmets, boots, or respirators in mines where toxic gases abound; they buy their own supplies, including dynamite, have no scheduled rest periods, and must survive underground from 24 to 72 hours continuously with little water and food. There are no special provisions in law defining when workers may remove themselves from dangerous situations. Unless the work contract covers this area, any worker who refuses to work based on the individual's judgment of excessively dangerous conditions may face dismissal.

BRAZIL

Brazil is a constitutional federal republic composed of 26 states and the federal district. In 1994 voters elected a new president, two-thirds of the senate, and 513 federal deputies. It was the second time since the end of military rule in 1985 that citizens freely chose their president and elected the legislative bodies in accordance with the 1988 Constitution. Fernando Henrique Cardoso became President on January 1, 1995, and is serving a 4-year term, reduced from 5 years by a 1994 constitutional amendment.

Police forces fall primarily under the control of the states. State police are divided into two forces: The civil police, who have an investigative role, and the uniformed police, known locally as the "Military Police," who are responsible for maintaining public order. Although controlled by the individual state governments, the Constitution provides that the uniformed police can be called into active military service in the event of an emergency, and they maintain some residual military privileges, including a separate judicial system. The federal police force is very small and plays little role in maintaining internal security. State police officers are charged with many serious human rights abuses.

Brazil has a market-based economy, although the Government has traditionally played a dominant role in shaping economic development. The Government is encouraging greater private sector participation in the economy through privatization of state enterprises, deregulation, and removal of impediments to competition. Industrial production, including mining operations, and a large and diversified capital goods sector, accounts for approximately 34 percent of gross domestic product (GDP); agriculture contributes about 13 percent. Brazil exports both manufactured and primary goods. Among the principal exports are coffee, soybeans, textiles, leather, metallurgical products, and transportation equipment. GDP was $563 billion in 1995, and the economy grew at a rate of 4.1 percent. The large gap in income distribution narrowed slightly in 1995. The poorest tenth of the population earned 1 percent of national income, compared with 0.7 percent in 1993, while the richest tenth earned 47.1 percent, down from 49 percent in 1993.

The most serious human rights abuses continued to be extrajudicial killings and torture. State police killed 19 landless workers in southern Para in April; they summarily executed at least 10 of the victims. In urban areas, the police are frequently implicated in killings and abuse of prisoners, but special courts for the uniformed police are, in many cases, overloaded, rarely investigate effectively or bring fellow officers to trial, and seldom convict abusers. This separate system of special state police courts contributes to a climate of impunity for police elements involved in extrajudicial killings or abuse of prisoners and is thought to be the single largest obstacle to eliminating such abuses by police. It is too early to tell what may be the effect upon impunity of the new legislation giving civil courts jurisdiction over crimes of intentional homicide committed by uniformed police officers.

The poor bear the brunt of most violence, whether committed by the police or by criminals. Prison conditions range from poor to harsh. The judiciary has a large case backlog and is often unable to ensure the right to a fair trial. Justice is slow and often unreliable, especially in rural areas where powerful landowners use violence to settle land disputes and influence the local judiciary. Violence against homosexuals and women and discrimination against women and minorities are problems. Child prostitution is also a problem. Despite constitutional provisions safeguarding their rights, indigenous people continue to be victimized by outsiders who encroach on Indian lands and to be neglected by governmental authorities. The authorities do not adequately enforce laws against forced labor, and the sugar and charcoal industries exploit children. A free press and active human rights organizations expose abuses and demand action to stop them.

The Government introduced an action plan to address human rights abuses, but many human rights groups expressed concern about congressional opposition to some elements of the plan and about what specific means would be used to accomplish its goals. President Cardoso created an interministerial group in late 1995 to fight what he publicly acknowledged as Brazil's serious problem with racism and discrimination. In addition, the Government has increased significantly the number of roving inspectors charged with clamping down on forced labor, and it launched a national effort, in partnership with state governors and local organizations, aimed at eradicating child labor. The government tourist agency embarked on a nationwide campaign against sex tourism and the attendant problem of child prostitution. However, the increased commitment by politicians at the national level still has not had a significant impact in many of the states where human rights violations are most common.

RESPECT FOR HUMAN RIGHTS

Section 1. Respect for the Integrity of the Person, Including Freedom From:

a. *Political and Other Extrajudicial Killing.*—Extrajudicial killings continued to be a serious problem throughout the country. In urban areas, a high crime rate, a failure to apprehend most criminals, and an inept criminal justice system all contribute to public acquiescence in police brutality and killings of criminal suspects.

According to the newly created Sao Paulo police ombudsman office, police killed 119 citizens in the first 6 months of 1996, a figure that does not include persons who are wounded and die later in a hospital. The figure reflects both the city's high level of violent crime and excessive use of force by the police. Many Sao Paulo-based human rights groups claim that the uniformed police, who openly doubt the judiciary's ability to convict those they apprehend, often decide to summarily execute suspected criminals rather than apprehend them.

In May the authorities arrested a Sao Paulo police officer, Jose Rogerio de Araujo Felismino, and his brother and charged them with the murder of a prominent AIDS activist; they were awaiting trial at year's end. In a separate case, Sao Paulo police badly beat 36-year-old Jaerte Antonio at his home, where a drunk Antonio had threatened his mother with violence. They took Antonio to a hospital, where he died soon afterward. The police Inspector General is investigating Antonio's death but had charged no one by the end of the year. In February police shot a man in the coastal town of Peruibe, Sao Paulo, twice after his arrest on drug possession charges. According to the man's family, the police shot him while in custody, later tortured him, then took him to a hospital, where he died 3 days later from his injuries. An internal police investigation was still in progress at the end of the year.

By mid-December, there had been 155 victims in 47 instances of "mass murder" in Sao Paulo. Although suspects had been identified in only 10 of these execution-style killings, most appeared to be perpetrated by criminal gangs and drug traffickers. Human rights monitors and public prosecutors believe that police are responsible for some of the unresolved cases, which often result from police involvement in drug deals gone awry or from retaliation for witnesses' cooperation with prosecutors or investigators. These monitors point as evidence to the wave of arrests of low-ranking police officers, and some senior officers, in the first half of the year for involvement in a variety of criminal activities. For example, the authorities arrested 4 military police officers, all members of the elite "Rota" strike force, and charged them with the murders of 25 people in 6 separate massacres, and with 3 bank robberies. The leader of the four, Hellmans Hoffman de Oliveira, was known as "Robocop" because he illegally carried a .45 caliber revolver. The gang members are under detention pending trial in a civil court.

Sao Paulo Governor Mario Covas continued to push for reforms intended to curb abuses by the state police. He appointed human rights activists as his attorney general and secretaries of public security, justice, and state prisons; he also created Sao Paulo's first civilian police ombudsman. The ombudsman has been effective in calling attention to police abuses and bringing to trial criminal elements within the police. From November 1995 through June—principally due to the ombudsman's efforts—Sao Paulo police opened more than 100 internal criminal investigations; prior to 1996, the annual number of internal investigations had never exceeded 40. Private citizens seemed to take full advantage of the opportunity to lodge complaints, as the ombudsman's office received an average of 90 calls a week on its toll-free telephone number. The ombudsman convinced the police to increase community patrols in peripheral neighborhoods, where violence is common, while the state public security secretary added courses on human rights and discrimination to the civil police training curriculum. In addition, since September 1995, Sao Paulo police officers who kill citizens are removed from their jobs and obliged to participate in a program in which they receive psychological counseling as well as classes on community policing, abuse of power, and the Penal Code. According to the weekly magazine Veja, the number of people killed by Sao Paulo police dropped from an average of 33 per month when the program was instituted to 18 per month by the end of March.

Acts of intimidation often hindered investigations, including death threats against witnesses, prosecutors, judges, and human rights monitors. In May Valdemir Lima de Oliveira, a witness against three policemen accused of corruption, was murdered as he was leaving a Sao Paulo police station after giving a deposition. The civil police chief in Franco da Rocha, and members of his staff, have received death threats since beginning their investigation of the clandestine dumping site for the victims of death squads; one investigator resigned as a result.

At least 596 minors in Rio de Janeiro were victims of homicide in 1995, according to the Rio-based Advanced Institute for Religious Studies. Execution-style killing of street children continued in 1996, but comprehensive statistics were not available. On April 23, two unidentified street youths were shot at point-blank range in the head and neck in Rio de Janeiro's affluent Laranjeiras neighborhood. The use of unprofessional autopsy procedures and inexplicable delays in the investigation led human rights groups to suspect that the murders were the work of police officers. No suspects have been identified.

In early March, three street children—Gilmar Ferreira de Franca, 14, Jamil Martins Murilo, 15, and Junior Santos Marques Lelo, 17—were found dead in the Taquaril neighborhood of Belo Horizonte. Their hands were tied, and they had been shot in theback. A group calling itself "Reaction" claimed responsibility,writing in a note that the minors had been killed to protest the low salaries paid to civil police. According to human rights groups in Belo Horizonte, there is significant evidence that Reaction is composed of active duty and former police officers. A police investigator charged one police officer in the slaying and said that several others are under investigation.

The number of citizens killed in conflicts with Rio police rose significantly. According to the daily newspaper Jornal do Brasil, prior to June 1995, an average of 3.2 persons per month were killed by police, while that figure rose to 20.5 per month in the first 6 months of 1996. Human rights groups blame financial awards and promotions for police "bravery," instituted in November 1995 by Nilton Cerqueira, the Rio state secretary for public security, for encouraging police to use excessive force. When the Brazil-based representative of Human Rights Watch/Americas privately urged Cerqueira to announce that he would give the awards only to police officers who brought in suspects alive, Cerqueira reportedly replied that the important point was that criminals should be stopped, dead or alive.

In June the President of the Federal Chamber of Deputies human rights committee visited Manaus, the capital of Amazonas state, to urge state officials to investigate the activities of a death squad known as "the firm." According to the state bar association, local human rights organizations, and a state prosecutor, current and former police officers comprise this group, which is involved in summary executions, illegal arrest, torture, and drug trafficking. The death squad is suspected, among other crimes, of executing 20 people and torturing 8 adolescents in the first 6 months of 1996.

A deputy prosecutor general in Brasilia recommended that the President order federal intervention in the western state of Acre to prevent the systematic violation of human rights there. Federal prosecutors in Acre reported that there had been a "dizzying increase in urban violence" during the previous 2 years, due almost exclusively to widespread human rights violations committed by the state's uniformed police. The situation worsened dramatically on June 30, when convicted drug trafficker Jorge Hugo shot and killed Itamar Pascoal, a police officer and brother of a state deputy (and retired policeman) Hidelbrando Pascoal. Hugo went into hiding, while the police, under the personal command of Hidelbrando Pascoal (according to the prosecutors' report), went on a rampage of kidnaping, torture, and murder. The federal prosecutors' report quoted Hidelbrando Pascoal as saying he would kill Hugo and anyone who had helped him to escape. The state governor was unwilling or unable to exercise any control over the military police.

The Permanent Forum Against Violence, a human rights organization in the northeastern state of Alagoas, condemned what it called an "uncontrollable rise in criminality and brutal disrespect for human rights" in the state and involvement by elements of the public security apparatus. The Forum reported that 192 murders were committed in the state in the first 3 months of 1996, a 21 percent increase over the same period in 1995. Suspects were identified in only 47 cases, 25 percent of whom were military or civil policemen.

The state police killing of 19 landless workers on April 17 in El Dorado de Carajas, in the northern state of Para, illustrates the tensions created by land invasions and the excessive violence often used by policemen in dealing with squatters. Several hundred landless workers blocked a highway to focus attention on the group's demand to be resettled, and to have state officials provide food and buses to take the marchers to Belem, the state capital. The state authorities sent 157 policemen to clear the highway. After erecting barricades on either side of the protestors, the police launched canisters of tear gas into the crowd and fired machine guns into the air to disperse it. It is unclear who began firing first—each side accused the other—but the police opened fire with machine guns from both sides of the crowd. Autopsy reports subsequently revealed that 10 of the victims had been summarily executed; 3 had been shot at point-blank range, and 7 had been killed with knives or sickles. The authorities charged all 157 policemen involved in the massacre with intentional homicide and will try them in a civil court.

Human rights groups cite the high level of crime and the failings of the judicial system as contributing factors to public tolerance of vigilante lynchings of suspected criminals. According to the daily newspaper Correio Braziliense, citizens lynched 22 people in the northeastern state of Bahia, usually the leader among states in this category, through mid-December. In an incident on September 3, 15 bus passengers in the city of Salvador beat to death a man who had tried to rob 2 couples riding on the bus.

In rural areas, new conflicts between rural landowners and the landless intensified in 1996, in part due to land invasions organized by the rural Landless Workers' Movement (MST) to pressure the federal Government to speed up settlement of landless families. The MST illegally occupied hundreds of plots of land identified as unproductive, blocked highways, and occupied government buildings, raising tensions and increasing confrontations with landowners, their gunmen, and, in many cases, policemen. Forty-five people died in land disputes in the first 8 months of 1996. Such killings usually go unpunished, because the landowners thought to be responsible for many of them often control the police in isolated areas, and intimidate local judges and lawyers with violence and threats of violence.

After significant pressure from human rights groups, the governor of the northeastern state of Rio Grande do Norte suspended his assistant secretary for public security, Maurilio Pinto de Medeiros, pending clarification of his involvement in serious human rights abuses. The most serious allegation against Medeiros is that he is suspected of heading a death squad composed of uniformed and investigative policemen, according to a report by a special commission of prosecutors formed in May 1995 to investigate the many allegations against Medeiros. As a result of the commission's investigation, the authorities filed a number of criminal complaints against Medeiros in a local court, but no trial date has been set. Francisco Gilson Nogueira, a prominent local human rights attorney and public critic of Medeiros, was fatally shot on October 20. The federal police are investigating the case but had not arrested any suspects at year's end.

The authorities charged the commander and 19 other police officers involved in the August 1995 massacre of 9 squatters in Corumbiara, Rondonia, with intentional homicide, meaning the accused will be tried in regular courts rather than a special police tribunal. They also charged four squatter leaders with intentional homicide for the deaths of two policemen, as well as for the deaths of the nine squatters. The authorities justified the latter charges by declaring that the leaders were responsible for the land invasion that sparked the confrontation. The medical examiner reported that most of the squatters killed had been shot in the back at short range and that many of the bullets had traveled from the top of the body downward, indicating that the victims had been killed from behind while kneeling.

In April a court convicted Rio de Janeiro police officer Marcos Vinicius Emmanuel for his involvement in the 1993 massacre of eight street children in downtown Candelaria square after he confessed to the crime, and sentenced him to 309 years in prison (reduced to 89 years on appeal). The courts convicted another policeman, Nelson Cunha, on similar charges in November and sentenced him to 261 years in prison. Cunha has the right to a retrial, but no date has been set. The trial of a third policeman, Marcos Aurelio Alcantara, who also confessed his involvement in the Candelaria killings, is set for May 1997. Candelaria survivor and key witness Wagner dos Santos identified policeman Carlos Jorge Liaffa Coelho as one of those who shot him. Although the authorities briefly detained Liaffa after they found a gun reportedly used in the massacre in his father's home, they subsequently released him for lack of evidence. A jury acquitted three of the original suspects in the case on December 10, at the request of both the prosecution and the defense, even though Dos Santos had consistently maintained that one of them was involved in the killings.

The investigation of police gang members accused of murdering 21 Vigario Geral residents in 1993 continues to progress slowly.

In March the Sao Paulo civil police's Department of Homicides and Personal Protection (DHPP) took over the investigation from the local police in the case of Franco da Rocha, one of Sao Paulo state's poorest communities, and location of a clandestine dumping site for the victims of death squads. Since 1993 at least 212 bodies have been found there, 50 victims killed with bullets to the head, while the arms and heads of some of the bodies had been removed in an apparent attempt to conceal the victims' identities. Investigators succeeded in identifying most of the victims, and linking them to previously unexplained disappearances. By year's end, the DHPP had not arrested or charged any suspects, but both human rights groups and Franco da Rocha police agreed that a thorough investigation was being conducted.

Progress in the investigation of the 121 Sao Paulo police accused of the 1992 Carandiru prison massacre was effectively stalled by disagreement over which court had jurisdiction—the special police courts or a civil court. The legislation signed in August by President Cardoso transferring all trials of uniformed police charged with intentional homicide to regular courts is likely to apply to the defendants in the Carandiru case. The Inter-American Commission on Human Rights (IACHR) began censure proceedings against the Government in October for its failure to punish those responsible for the Carandiru killings. However, the expected transfer of the case to ordinary courts, and the human rights reforms being implemented by the state government, led the IACHR to suspend consideration of censure.

In a high profile Sao Paulo case—the "42nd Delegacia"—uniformed and civil police were accused of the 1989 murder of 18 prisoners asphyxiated when police crammed 51 prisoners into a tiny, unventilated cell as punishment. Although the civil police defendants have been tried and sentenced in civil court, the 7-year-old case against the uniformed police officers continues to languish in the special police tribunal. In March the IACHR censured the Government for the lack of progress in bringing to justice those responsible for the 42nd Delegacia massacre.

In the Chico Mendes murder case, almost 3½ years after his convicted killers escaped through the front door of a penitentiary in the western state of Acre, where they had been serving a 19-year sentence for the 1988 murder of the renowned rubber tapper and rural union leader, federal police agents recaptured Darly Alves da Silva in southern Para on June 30 and his son Darci on November 25. Both men were returned to prison.

The case of the 1985 murder of Joao Canuto, the first president of the rural workers union in Rio Maria, Para, has been in the state prosecutor's office awaiting a trial date since August 1993, 8 years after the beginning of the investigation. No one has been charged in the case.

b. *Disappearance.*—There were no reports of politically motivated abductions. However, human rights groups often blamed the police or vigilante groups for the disappearance of street children or persons believed to be criminals.

On January 10, an eyewitness in a rape case against a Sao Paulo police officer disappeared. Shortly after she and the victim reported the December 1995 rape, the witness began receiving threats. By midyear the rape investigation was in progress, and both the civil police and police ombudsman were investigating the disappearance.

In 1995 Congress passed legislation recognizing and assuming government responsibility for the deaths of 136 political activists who "disappeared" during the military regime while in the custody of public officials, and obligating the Government to pay indemnities of between $100,000 and $150,000 to each of the families. The law created a commission to determine the amount of each indemnity and to evaluate additional requests from families who believed that they might qualify as well. By mid-December, the commission had approved 108 additional indemnity requests and rejected 43, with 84 cases still pending.

c. *Torture and Other Cruel, Inhuman, or Degrading Treatment or Punishment.*—The Constitution prohibits torture and contains severe legal penalties for torture or acquiescence in it. The Penal Code fails to define torture, however, and there are frequent credible reports that police beat and torture criminal suspects to extract information, confessions, or money. Such torture can result in death (see Section 1.a.) The Government estimated in its 1994 report on the internal human rights situation that fewer than 10 percent of cases of mistreatment by police are reported. Victims are generally poor, uneducated about their rights, and—most of all—afraid to come forward for fear of reprisals.

Fabio Luciano dos Reis, age 20, and Emerson Moreira da Silva, age 21, accused Sao Paulo policemen of beating them in March. Reis further alleged that police had held him down and "scalped" him; he was later treated at a Sao Paulo hospital for knife wounds to the skin covering the cranium. Three officers were charged with the crime. In a case that received widespread media attention, the authorities charged 11 Sao Paulo policemen with causing bodily injury and abuse of authority in the alleged torture of a couple in October 1995. The police officers raided the house of Messias Francisco de Souza, age 63, and his wife, Dirce Maria Anacleto, age 52, in the mistaken belief that the couple had been involved in the recent murder of a policeman. They subjected De Souza and Anacleto to kicks, electric shocks, and beatings with pistols, sticks, and fists. At year's end, the 11 policemen were awaiting trial, and the authorities were protecting the couple, who complained of receiving threats.

Mario Cesar Machado Monteiro, a military court judge in Rio de Janeiro, acquitted two army captains accused of torturing an army corporal who had deserted during "Operation Rio," the 1995 joint army-police operation against crime and drug trafficking in Rio, despite evidence suggesting that the captains had used smothering and other forms of torture on the corporal. The judge, however, justified his decision by ruling that "the necessary rigor was used to intimidate the corporal into admitting his involvement in drug trafficking." Human rights groups widely criticized the ruling.

Prison conditions range from poor to harsh. According to the Government's 1995 penitentiary census, the overcrowded prisons held 129,169 inmates in space designed for 59,954. There are often six to eight prisoners in a cell meant for three; some prisoners force others to pay for the use of a bed. Due to the severe overcrowding in prisons, police stations are often used as prisons, where sentenced criminals share cells with detainees.

Sao Paulo's prison system in particular suffers from chronic overcrowding, corrupt and abusive local prison management, and prisoner access to weapons and drugs. The police precincts and state's 43 penitentiaries—the majority of them dilapidated and dirty—house 68,500 prisoners in facilities designed to hold less than 32,000. Discipline is difficult to maintain under such conditions, and prison officials often resort to inhuman treatment to maintain order. A report issued in April by the Sao

Paulo state assembly revealed extremely harsh prison conditions, including rat- and mosquito-infested cells, lack of sanitary facilities, and kitchens that served raw or spoiled food. Scabies and tuberculosis, diseases not common in the general population, are endemic in Sao Paulo prisons. The report indicated that denial of first aid and other medical care is sometimes used as a form of punishment.

In the second half of the year, the severe overcrowding in Sao Paul prisons led to an increase in the number of prisoner revolts and the violence associated with them. An October riot at Carandiru prison left four prisoners and one guard dead, while in November, police killed four prisoners when they quelled an uprising at a prison in Praia Grande. A total of 1,442 prisoners escaped from Sao Paulo's prisons through the end of June. A surge in crime rates among minors has overwhelmed juvenile detention facilities, where conditions are no better than in regular prisons.

The Government permits prison visits by independent human rights monitors.

d. *Arbitrary Arrest, Detention, or Exile.*—The Constitution limits arrests to those caught in the act of committing a crime or those arrested by order of a judicial authority. The authorities usually respect the constitutional provision for a judicial determination of the legality of detention, although some convicted inmates are held beyond their sentences due to poor record keeping. The law permits provisional detention for up to 5 days under specified conditions during a police investigation, but a judge may extend this period. According to groups that work with street children, however, the police sometimes detain street youths illegally without a judicial order or hold them incommunicado.

The Constitution prohibits forced exile, and it is not practiced.

e. *Denial of Fair Public Trial.*—The judiciary is an independent branch of government, but in many instances it is unable to ensure the right to fair trial.

The judicial system, with the federal Supreme Court at its apex, includes courts of first instance and appeals courts. States organize their own judicial systems but must adhere to the basic principles in the federal Constitution. There is also a system of specialized courts dealing with police, labor, elections, juveniles, and family matters.

Special police courts have jurisdiction over state uniformed police; the record of these courts shows that punishment is the exception rather than the rule. A human rights group in the northeast, studying police crimes against civilians tried in police courts from 1970 to 1991, found that only 8 percent of the cases resulted in convictions. In Sao Paulo, another study found that only 5 percent of cases resulted in convictions. The courts (which are separate from the courts-martial of the armed forces, except for the final appeals court) are composed of four ranking state uniformed police officials and one civilian judge. With too few judges for the caseload there are backlogs, and human rights groups note a lack of zeal among police charged with investigating fellow officers.

In August the President signed legislation giving ordinary courts jurisdiction over cases in which uniformed police officers are accused of intentional homicide against civilians. Human rights groups are dubious about the new law's likely impact on impunity, since it is the internal police investigation that determines whether the homicide was intentional or not, and the police tribunal that decides whether to forward a case to civil court for trial.

Defendants are entitled to counsel and must be made fully aware of the charges against them. According to the Ministry of Justice, approximately 85 percent of prisoners cannot afford an attorney. In cases in which a defendant cannot afford an attorney, the court must provide one at public expense; courts are supposed to appoint private attorneys to represent poor defendants when public defenders are unavailable, but often no effective defense is provided. Juries try only cases of willful crimes against life; judges try all others.

The right to a fair public trial as provided by law is generally respected in practice, although in rural areas the judiciary is generally less capable and more subject to the influence of local landowners, particularly in cases related to indigenous people and rural union activists. Similarly, local police are often less zealous in investigating, prosecutors are reluctant to initiate proceedings, and judges find reasons to delay when cases involve gunmen contracted by landowners to eliminate squatters or rural union activists.

The need for judicial reform is widely recognized because the current system is inefficient, with backlogs of cases and shortages of judges. Lawyers often drag out cases as long as possible in the hope that an appeals court might render a favorable opinion and because they are paid according to the amount of time they spend on a case. According to the Institute of Economic, Social, and Political Studies of Sao Paulo, however, 90 percent of appeals court decisions confirm decisions made in lower courts. Low pay, combined with exacting competitive examinations that in some years eliminate 90 percent of the applicants, make it difficult to fill vacancies on the bench. The system requires that a trial be held within a certain period of time from the date of the crime (similar to a statute of limitations). However, due to the backlog of cases, old cases are frequently dismissed. According to a former judge, this encourages corrupt judges purposely to delay certain cases, so that they can be dismissed.

A federal law approved in September 1995 created small claims courts to handle, and resolve quickly, less serious criminal and civil cases. In Sao Paulo, the new courts resolved 80 percent of their cases within 60 days, and cleared from the state docket some 45,000 backlogged cases.

There were no reports of political prisoners.

f. *Arbitrary Interference with Privacy, Family, Home, or Correspondence.*—The Constitution provides for freedom from arbitrary intrusion into the home, although wiretaps authorized by judicial authority are permitted. There were no reports of illegal entry for political reasons, but illegal entry into homes without a warrant occurs in searches for criminal suspects. The inviolability of private correspondence is respected. The law regulating the conditions under which wiretaps may be used appears to strike a fair balance between giving the police an effective law enforcement tool and protecting the civil liberties of citizens. Several test cases are required, however, to determine whether that balance is maintained in practice.

Section 2. *Respect for Civil Liberties, Including:*

a. *Freedom of Speech and Press.*—The 1988 Constitution abolished all forms of censorship and provides for freedom of speech and a free press. The authorities respect these rights in practice. Newspapers and magazines, which are privately owned, vigorously report and comment on government performance. Both the press and broadcast media routinely discuss controversial social and political issues and engage in investigative reporting.

Most radio and television stations are privately owned; but the Government has licensing authority, and politicians frequently obtain the licenses. Many television and radio stations are owned by current or former congressmen, some of whom are or were members of the committee overseeing communications. It is difficult to determine how many media outlets are indirectly controlled by politicians since concessions are often registered in the names of family members or friends linked to them. In addition, concessions are regularly transferred to other names, with little oversight by the Government.

The penalty for libel under the 1967 press law—a prison term—is considered extreme by judges. Press criticism has described it as an archaic and authoritarian law inherited from the military regime. Congress has considered, but has not yet eliminated, the press law's provisions for prison terms.

There were reports of harassment against journalists. According to the Inter-American Press Association, radio commentator Carlos Alberto Salvador received death threats from the mayor of Boa Viagem, in the northeastern state of Ceara, after denouncing a number of irregularities in the mayor's administration. Salvador filed a criminal complaint with the state secretary of public security in January. On January 24, a police officer, Major Adalberto Carvalho de Souza, tried to prevent the Recife-based newspaper, Jornal do Comercio, from reporting the arrest of a sergeant from his battalion, who was accused of stealing 10 cases of beer from a supermarket. Late on the night of February 19, two shots were fired through the windows of the central office of the national daily newspaper Jornal do Brasil, based in Rio de Janeiro. Only six journalists were in the building at the time, and none was injured. The police are investigating but have identified no suspects. On May 15, reporters Warner Filho and Tina Coelho, of the Brasilia daily Correio Braziliense, were covering police carrying out an eviction order of squatters in Cristalina, Goias. When the reporters tried to photograph police destroying six temporary shelters erected by the squatters, the police handcuffed and beat them and arrested them for obstruction of justice and disrespect for authority.

Foreign publications are widely distributed in Brazil; prior review of films, plays, and radio and television programming is practiced only to determine a suitable viewing age.

Academic freedom is respected.

b. *Freedom of Peaceful Assembly and Association.*—The Constitution provides for the right to assemble peacefully, and the Government respects this right in practice. Permits are not required for outdoor political or labor meetings, and such meetings occur frequently.

The Constitution also provides for the right of freedom of association, and the Government respects this right in practice.

c. *Freedom of Religion.*—The Constitution provides for freedom of religion, and the Government respects this right in practice. There is no favored or state religion. All aiths are free to establish places of worship, train clergy, and proselytize, although the Government controls entry into Indian lands.

d. *Freedom of Movement Within the Country, Foreign Travel, Emigration, and Repatriation.*—There are no restrictions on movement within Brazil, except for the protected Indian areas, nor are there any restrictions on emigration or return. A parent, however, is not allowed to leave the country with children without the permission of the other parent.

The Government cooperates with the office of the United Nations High Commissioner for Refugees (UNHCR) in assisting refugees. The Government does not provide first asylum; rather, those physically present in the country whom the UNHCR determines to be refugees are accepted for resettlement. In 1996, 375 people applied for refugee status. The Government approved 115 applications, denied 167, and decisions were pending on the others at year's end. There were no reports of forced repatriation of persons to countries in which they feared persecution.

Section 3. Respect for Political Rights: The Right of Citizens to Change their Government

The Constitution provides for the right of citizens to change their government through free elections, and citizens most recently exercised this right in 1994, filling executive and legislative offices throughout the country. Voting is secret and mandatory for all literate Brazilian citizens age 18 to 70, except military conscripts who may not vote. It is voluntary for minors age 16 to 18, for the illiterate, and for those age 70 and over.

Women have full political rights under the Constitution and are becoming active in politics and government. However, they comprise only 6.5 percent of the national Congress; 34 women serve in the Chamber of Deputies (out of 513 seats), and 6 serve in the Senate (out of 81 members). In the 1994 elections, voters elected one female governor. To boost the participation of women in government, Congress passed legislation requiring that 20 percent of each party's candidates in the 1996 municipal elections be women. In November voters in Sao Paulo elected the city's first black mayor. The 1988 Constitution gave Indians the franchise, but their ability to protect their own interests is severely limited (see Section 5).

Section 4. Governmental Attitude Regarding International and Nongovernmental Investigation of Alleged Violations of Human Rights

Nongovernmental organizations (NGO's) actively investigate allegations of human rights violations and often initiate legal proceedings. Government officials are generally cooperative with them. Several international NGO's either maintain offices in Brazil or visit periodically. In a 10-day visit to Brazil in August, the executive director of Human Rights Watch/Americasidentified a number of areas of concern but found the federal officials open in discussing human rights problems. Government offices such as the Ministry of Justice's secretaries for citizenship and human rights and the federal prosecutor's office respond readily to inquiries about human rights cases and launch their own investigations.

Both the federal and some state governments formed partnerships with NGO's in a number of significant initiatives. For example, the Ministry of Justice asked the University of Sao Paulo-based Nucleus for the Study of Violence to draft the national human rights action plan. In addition, in a series of seminars around the country, the Government solicited the input of a broad range of human rights groups for the final version of the plan, announced by President Cardoso in May. The northeastern state of Pernambuco created a witness protection program, the first in Brazil, to protect witnesses or victims of violent crimes. Development and administration of the nascent program was the result of a unique partnership between the state government and GAJOP, a human rights NGO.

Section 5. Discrimination Based on Race, Sex, Religion, Disability, Language, or Social Status

Discrimination on the basis of sex, race, religion, and nationality is unconstitutional, yet women, blacks, and indigenous people continued to experience discrimination. The International Labor Organization (ILO) notes that important differences in wages continue to exist to the detriment of women and blacks, particularly in rural areas.

There continued to be reports of violence against homosexuals, although it was not always clear that the victims' sexual orientation was the reason. The Grupo Gay da Bahia, Brazil's best known homosexual rights organization, reported that 65 homosexuals were killed in the first 7 months of 1996, but the group's report did not specify whether all the victims were specifically targeted because they were homosexual or were killed for other motives. Ten homosexuals were murdered, and 3 disappeared, in Brasilia in the first 7 months of 1996. Most were apparently the victims of male prostitutes, some of whom reportedly were low-ranking soldiers trying to earn extra money.

There were several attacks by neo-Nazi skinhead groups in cities in southern Brazil. In March neo-Nazi skinheads murdered Carlos Adilson de Siqueira, a 23-year-old gay black man, in the southern city of Curitiba. The confessed killer, a 17-year-old office boy, was a member of "Carecas do Brasil," a skinhead gang composed of adolescents from well-off families. The group denied that it targets blacks but admitted to persecuting homosexuals and drug addicts. According to the Curitiba police, at least three neo-Nazi groups, totalling about 30 members, were active in Curitiba. In June a gang of some 30 neo-Nazis stormed into two gay bars in Sao Paulo, assaulted many customers, and killed a gay artist, Nilton Verdini Silva. No one has been charged for Silva's murder.

Women.—There is a high incidence of physical abuse of women. Most major cities and towns have established special police offices to deal with crimes against women, including 124 cities in Sao Paulo state, 54 in Minas Gerais, and 5 in the state of Rio de Janeiro. The special police office in Brasilia has seen a steady increase in reports of crimes against women during the last 6 years, from 1,003 in 1992 to 3,818 in 1995, and 2,404 in the first 7 months of 1996. Police and social workers attribute the increase in reported complaints not to a rising level of violence against women, but to greater awareness by women of their rights and less willingness to tolerate abuse than in the past. The Brasilia office produced and distributed widely a pamphlet containing tips for women on how to avoid being raped, which played an integral role in making women throughout the Federal District aware of the special office's services. The office for protection of human rights in the Belo Horizonte mayor's office noted a "frightening escalation of violence against women" in that city. In the first 5 months of 1996, 90 rapes, 68 murders of women, and 1,237 cases of bodily harm were reported to Belo Horizonte police stations.

In rural areas, abused women have little recourse since there are no specialized police offices available to them. Men who commit crimes against women, including sexual assault and murder, are unlikely to be brought to trial. Although the Supreme Court in 1991 struck down the archaic concept of "defense of honor" as a justification for wife murder, courts are still reluctant to prosecute and convict men who attack their wives. In April the Supreme Court voted to absolve a man convicted by a lower court of rape for having sexual intercourse with a 12-year-old girl. Even though the age of consent is 14, the court stated in its ruling that the man had not committed a crime because the girl had given her permission. One federal deputy praised the "courage" of the court's decision and introduced a bill to lower the age of consent from 14 to 12.

The Constitution prohibits discrimination based on sex in employment or pay and provides for 120 days of paid maternity leave. However, the provision against wage discrimination is rarely enforced. According to the most recent official statistics, women earn, on average, 54 percent of the salaries earned by men. A recent study by a sociologist showed that women who started working in positions in which they earned twice the minimum wage advanced in pay after 10 years to a wage of seven times the minimum wage. Men starting in the same positions earned 2.6 times the minimum wage and advanced to a wage of 10.9 times the minimum wage after 10 years. A Ministry of Labor survey revealed that the average starting salary for high school-educated women in Sao Paulo hired between January and May was about $850, fully one-third less than the $1,300 average starting salary for high school-educated men during the same period.

In Sao Paulo in early September, several thousand students took the entrance exam to become judges. According to the daily newspaper Folha de Sao Paulo, women wearing pants were not allowed to take the exam, as test administrators told them that they were not dressed in accordance with the "tradition of the judiciary."

In response to the maternity leave law, some employers seek sterilization certificates from female job applicants or try to avoid hiring women of childbearing age. Hoping to clamp down on such practices, President Cardoso signed a law in April 1995 prohibiting employers from requiring applicants or employees to take pregnancy tests or present sterilization certificates. Employers who violate the law are subject to a jail term ranging from 1 to 2 years, while the company must pay a fine equal to 10 times the salary of its highest paid employee.

Children.—Despite progressive laws to protect children and a growing awareness of their plight through media and NGO campaigns, millions of children continue to fail to get an education, must work to survive, and suffer from the poverty afflicting their families. In a positive development, a report issued by the Brazilian Institute for Geography and Statistics (IBGE) stated that the number of children between the ages of 10 and 14 who were employed decreased by 163,000 from 1993 to 1995.

However, more than 3 million children in the same age range continue to work, many of them together with their parents, under conditions approximating forced labor or debt bondage (see Section 6.d.). Many other children beg on the streets of cities.

There are no reliable figures on the number of street children, some of whom are homeless, but the majority of whom return home at night. In Rio de Janeiro, an organization aiding street children estimated recently that 30,000 frequent the streets by day but probably less than 1,000 sleep there. NGO's have made enough shelters available for homeless children, but some children prefer the freedom and drugs that street life offers. In Sao Paulo, NGO's aiding street children estimated that some 12,000 children roam the streets by day and that from 3,000 to 5,000 of them live permanently on the streets. The NGO's report that extreme poverty at home or sexual abuse by fathers and stepfathers are the principal reasons so many children choose to live on the streets. An IBGE study reported that 47 percent of Sao Paulo children come from families that earn less than $200 per month.

Because street children have a high rate of drug use and have been involved in assaults and robberies, a significant portion of the public supports harsh police measures against them, viewing the issue as one of crime and security, not human rights. Of the 562 reported homicides in the northeastern state of Pernambuco in the first 8 months of 1995, 10 percent of the victims were under 18 years of age. A local human rights group suspects that many of these minors are killed by off-duty policemen and private security guards hired by area businessmen to rid their areas of street children. Rio de Janeiro's Advanced Institute for Religious Studies reported that 596 minors were murdered in Rio in 1995, a significant increase from the 513 killed the previous year. Federal, state, and local governments devote insufficient resources to street children. NGO's sponsor relief efforts, but demand far outstrips available resources.

In January Embratur, the national tourist agency, embarked on a national campaign against sex tourism and child prostitution, a significant problem throughout Brazil, but particularly prevalent in the major tourist cities in the northeast. The agency banned the use of images of scantily clad women in its promotional materials, and launched a nationwide program, in conjunction with private travel agencies and NGO's, to warn hotel guests of the prohibition on sex with minors by placing posters inside their rooms. Through a series of workshops, Embratur also attempted to educate travel agents and state tourism agencies about existing legislation on child prostitution. The government of the Federal District launched a comprehensive program, "Brasilia Crianca," aimed at combating the sexual exploitation of children. The program involves a broad range of concrete actions, including creating a 24-hour number for reporting cases of sexual abuse; creating a special police office to investigate sexual crimes against children; requiring schools to discuss violence against children; requiring the formation of teams within each clinic and hospital trained to treat child victims of violence or sexual abuse; and developing formal education classes and professional training for adolescents from low-income families who have had little education.

People With Disabilities.—The 1988 Constitution contains several provisions for the disabled, stipulating a minimum wage, educational opportunities, and access to public buildings and public transportation. Groups that work with the disabled, however, report that state governments completely failed to meet the legally mandated targets for educational opportunities and work placement.

There was little progress in the elimination of architectural barriers to the disabled. However, the Federal District government made some efforts to eliminate architectural barriers by building access ramps and enlarging restrooms at Brasilia's central bus station, the zoo, the city park, and the southern commercial area. In addition, the city opened bidding for the acquisition of five access lifts to be installed in buses by year's end. Federal District legislation requires public buses to reserve four seats for the disabled, but other riders normally do not respect the rule, and drivers rarely enforce it. The Federal District government offered 22 professional training courses to 750 disabled people, and was negotiating with private companies to find positions for course graduates. Through the end of August, 12 people with disabilities had begun working for the city after receiving training.

Indigenous People.—Brazil's approximately 320,000 Indians, who speak 170 different languages, have a constitutional right to their traditional lands. Indigenous rights groups, however, expressed concern that in practice the authorities allow most indigenous people only limited participation in decisions affecting their lands, cultures, traditions, and the allocation of natural resources. The 1988 Constitution charged the federal Government with demarcating 519 indigenous areas within 5 years, but the authorities have yet to complete more than half the demarcations and entitling decrees. In January the Government issued decree 1775, altering the demarcation process to permit challenges to proposed demarcations from nonindigenous interested parties, despite the fact that the Constitution allows the federal Government to expropriate land with just compensation.

A total of 419 separate challenges, covering 34 Indian areas, were filed. FUNAI, the National Indian Foundation, rejected all of the claims, and forwarded them to Justice Minister Nelson Jobim, who made the final decision. Jobim rejected all but 33 challenges, covering 8 different areas. He returned these to Funai asking for clarification of what he called technical errors in the anthropological reports, the basis for each demarcation.

The concerns of Indian rights groups and the federal prosecutor's office that the change in the demarcation process would reopen land claims in previously demarcated Indian reserves, and encourage land invasions by non-Indians hoping to stake new claims, resulting in increased violence, seem to be well-founded. According to COIAB, an umbrella group of indigenous rights organizations in the Amazon region, lumberjacks, fishermen, agricultural workers, and miners intensified invasions of at least 18 indigenous lands in Amazonas, Para, Parana, Rondonia and Roraima within 2 weeks after the new demarcation decree took effect. Lumberjacks invaded the Mamia reservation in Amazonas, home to 150 Munduruku Indians, where they cut down dozens of trees, and beat an Indian resident. Some 100 miners invaded the Munduruku reservation of Jacareacanga in southern Para, raising tensions with the Indians, who threatened to attack the miners if they were not removed.

The challenge to the Raposa-Serra do Sol reserve in Roraima, inhabited by some 12,000 Macuxi, Wapixana, Ingariko, and Taurepang Indians, was among the 8 that Justice Minister Jobim did not reject. The area was identified as traditional Indian land by Funai anthropologists in 1993, but the demarcation order awaited the Justice Minister's approval for 3 years. The area has been torn by constant conflict between Indians and nonindigenous occupants. Jobim had asked for further information on Raposa-Serra do Sol, citing the existence of a recently created municipality near the boundaries of the area. On December 20, Jobim ordered a reduction in the boundaries of the reservation and determined that several settlements by non-Indians would be allowed to remain within the area.

The Constitution provides Indians with the exclusive use of the soil, waters, and minerals found in their lands, subject to congressional authorization. The regulations necessary for economic exploitation, however, are still pending before the Congress as part of the bill known as the statute of indigenous societies. Illegal mining, logging, and ranching are a constant problem on Indian lands, as a majority of these lands have been occupied by non-Indians.

Several thousand gold miners invaded the Yanomami reserve in the state of Roraima, after the Government, citing a lack of resources, suspended its efforts to expel miners from the area. The influx of miners caused a surge in the number of Indians dying from malaria. At least 36 Yanomami died from malaria, and 136 from other diseases, including pneumonia and tuberculosis, in part due to the federal Government's failure to provide adequate medical care for indigenous people. The Catholic Church-affiliated Indigenist Missionary Council (CIMI) was alarmed at the lack of access to health care of the Deni Indians, who live in groups of some 60 Indians each along the Xerua river in the Amazon region. According to CIMI, a measles epidemic in 1991 killed 60 of 500 Deni Indians, and approximately 25 percent of the Deni population has died since then of preventable diseases such as tuberculosis and malaria. Since the Deni live in extremely isolated areas, sick Indians must travel 10 days by boat to get to the nearest Funai health clinic in Manaus. According to a report by the Manaus-based Institute of Tropical Medicine, the average life expectancy of Brazilian Indians dropped from 48.2 years in 1993 to 42.6 years in 1995.

The 1993 case against the Brazilian gold miners who were accused of killing 16 Yanomami on the Venezuelan side of the border remains mired in legal problems. None of the accused miners is in custody. Yanomami witnesses failed to recognize two of the accused, and other witnesses have disappeared. Indigenous rights groups expressed concern that the process was completely paralyzed and that those responsible for the massacre may never be brought to justice.

CIMI reported that more than 7,000 Indians were trapped into forced labor (see Section 6.c.). The majority were Guarani Indians in the state of Mato Grosso do Sul, where a high rate of suicide (11 among the Guarani through July) was reported.

National/Racial/Ethnic Minorities.—Although racial discrimination has been illegal since 1951, darker skinned citizens say they frequently encounter discrimination. Most blacks are found among the poorer sectors of society. Even though nearly half of the population has some African ancestry, very few senior officials in government, the armed forces, or the private sector are black. Black consciousness organizations challenge the view that Brazil is a racial democracy with equality for all regardless of skin color. They assert that racial discrimination becomes most evident when blacks seek employment, housing, or educational opportunities.

According to government statistics, the monthly per capita income for white males is 6.3 times the minimum wage; for white women, 3.6 times the minimum wage; for black men, 2.9; and for black women, 1.7.

A 1995 survey conducted by a prominent polling service provided insight into the perceptions of different segments of the population about the problem of racism. The survey showed that 89 percent of the population believes that whites are prejudiced against blacks. Ten percent of nonblacks admitted that they were prejudiced against blacks, and, according to the pollsters, 87 percent of whites displayed signs of racism in their answers to at least 1 of 12 questions asked in the poll. A 1996 survey (by a different polling group) of people in 11 state capitals revealed that 83 percent of those interviewed believe that blacks suffer from discrimination. In Sao Paulo 58.9 percent of respondents and in Belo Horizonte 68.1 percent of respondents believed that measures should be taken to discourage natives of the northeast, many of whom are black, from migrating to those cities.

Blacks are often the victims of violence at a level disproportionate to their percentage in the population. For instance, a well-respected human rights NGO active in the northeast, the Luiz Freire Cultural Center, reported that, of the 1,378 murder victims in Recife in 1994, 87 percent were black. The weekly newsmagazine, Isto E, reported that, on June 17, Luciano Soares Ribeiro, a black data entry operator, was riding his bicycle in the town of Canoas, near Porto Alegre, the capital of Rio Grande do Sul, when he was hit by a white man driving a car. The driver, Rogerio Ferreira Pansera, later told the police that he had not stopped to help Ribeiro because he assumed that Ribeiro was a bike thief. Two passers-by took Ribeiro to a nearby hospital. When his mother arrived 4 hours later, she learned that the neurologist, Antonio Carlos Marrone, had refused to treat her son because he assumed that he was a common criminal and would not be able to pay his medical bill. Ribeiro died 2 days later from cranial trauma.

Racism as a crime is difficult to prove, although both Sao Paulo and Rio de Janeiro have designated special police units to investigate it. In a positive development, however, the daily newspaper, Folha de Sao Paulo, reported that, in January, a Rio de Janeiro court ordered Pires security services to pay an indemnity of $1 million for moral damages to the family of a black bookseller, Valdemir Damiao da Purificacao. In February 1995, a security guard shot and killed Purificacao as he entered a Bank of Brazil office in the Tijuca district of Rio de Janeiro where he went regularly to sell books. In his statement to police afterward, the security guard said he thought Purificacao was a thief, "because he was black and was carrying a large vinyl bag."

In a case that generated considerable media attention, a well-known entertainer named "Tiririca" released a record called "look at her hair," whose lyrics many criticized as racist. The lyrics describe his wife, who is black, as a "stinking beast whose odor is worse than a skunk." Tiririca himself is the son of an Afro-Brazilian mother and is considered a mixed-race mulatto by Brazilian standards. The Ministry of Justice filed racism charges against Tiririca in Rio de Janeiro, where the judge ordered Sony records to withdraw all copies of the compact disc and cassettes. Subsequently, a federal prosecutor told Sony's president that producing or making the song public would be considered a criminal act, and recommended that he withdraw all copies from the national market. He told Sony that it would be allowed to re-release it only after the song is removed.

A much higher percentage of blacks are convicted by Brazilian courts than whites, according to professor Sergio Adorno, of the University of Sao Paulo's Nucleus for the Study of Violence. Adorno analyzed 500 criminal cases judged in Sao Paulo courts in 1990 and found that 60 percent of whites able to afford their own lawyers were acquitted, while only 27 percent of blacks who hired lawyers were found not guilty.

President Cardoso created in November 1995 an interministerial working group to fight what he acknowledged as Brazil's serious problem with racism and discrimination. The group was charged with proposing public policies to increase the participation and access of Afro-Brazilians in society. The President's public acknowledgment that racism and discrimination existed in Brazil was unprecedented for Brazilian presidents, who have maintained in the past that people were discriminated against because they were poor, not because of their skin color. The interministerial group's subgroup on health launched a national campaign to educate health workers and others about sickle cell anemia, and began requiring that race be indicated on all birth and death certificates, intending to use the information gathered to build a comprehensive database of statistics on race. Another subgroup is studying the possibility of implementing affirmative action programs in three principal areas:

Education, the labor market, and government-sponsored radio and television advertising.

Section 6. Worker Rights

a. The Right of Association.—The Labor Code provides for union representation of all workers (except for military, police, and firemen) but imposes a hierarchical, unitary system, funded by a mandatory "union tax" on workers and employers. Under a restriction known as "unicidade" (one per city), the code prohibits multiple unions of the same professional category in a given geographical area. The 1988 Constitution freed workers to organize new unions out of old ones without prior authorization by the Government but retained other provisions of the old labor code. Elements of the labor movement and the International Confederation of Free Trade Unions (ICFTU) criticize the retention of unicidade and the union tax.

In practice, unicidade has proven less restrictive in recent years, as more liberal interpretations of its restrictions permitted new unions to form and—in many cases—to compete with unions and federations that had already enjoyed official recognition. The sole bureaucratic requirement for new unions is to register with the Ministry of Labor which, by judicial decision, is bound to receive and record their registration. The primary source of continuing restriction is the system of labor courts, which retain the right to review the registration of new unions and to adjudicate conflicts over their formation. The power of the labor courts to define jurisdictions came to the fore again during 1996 when the Sole Workers Central (CUT—the largest and most activist of the three labor confederations) ABC metalworkers' federation was riven by a group of dissidents who attempted to establish their own local union in one of the suburban Sao Paulo municipalities that the federation comprises. Although a majority of federation members clearly appeared to favor the unified structure, the dissidents sought redress by filing suit with the labor court.

Otherwise, unions are independent of the Government and of political parties. Approximately 20 to 30 percent of the work force is organized, with well over half of this number affiliated with an independent labor central. Intimidation of rural labor union organizers by landowners and their agents continues to be a problem (see Section 1.a.).

The Constitution provides workers with the right to strike, including civil servants (except again, for military, police, and firemen). Enabling legislation passed in 1989 stipulates that essential services must remain in operation during a strike and that workers must notify employers at least 48 hours before beginning a walkout. The Constitution prohibits government interference in labor unions but provides that "abuse" of the right to strike (such as not maintaining essential services or failure to end a strike after a labor court decision) is punishable by law.

The Constitution specifies the right of public employees to strike, subject to conditions enacted by the Congress. Since the Congress has yet to pass the complementary legislation, labor law attorneys continue to debate the limits on the right to strike of public employees. In practice, the Government has not interfered with their right to strike, though a month-long strike by Petrobras (the public oil monopoly) employees in May 1995, which greatly inconvenienced the public, was judged abusive by the Supreme Labor Court, and led many—including some labor leaders—to call for limits on public employees' right to strike.

CUT, the parent central to the petroleum workers, submitted a complaint to the International Labor Organization (ILO) Committee on Freedom of Association in May 1995 arguing that the firing of 59 union members for their involvement in the strike violated their right to strike. In November 1995, the ILO body found that the nature of the labor court's procedures, which allow either party to submit a dispute for what amounts to binding arbitration, "may effectively undermine the right of workers to strike and does not promote effective collective bargaining." The ILO suggested that the legislation be amended to permit submission of disputes to judicial authorities only with the permission of both parties or in case of the interruption of essential services. The ILO also suggested that the 59 workers be rehired.

Train and municipal transit workers, autoworkers, metalworkers, university professors, electrical generating authority employees, and dockworkers all went on strike. In addition, the three trade union confederations called a 1-day general strike in June, in which nearly all organized sectors of the economy participated to some degree. Formerly, the courts ruled almost automatically that strikes were abusive; in recent years, however, the courts have applied the law with more discretion. The 1989 strike law prohibits dismissals or the hiring of substitute workers during a strike, with certain exceptions, provided the strike is not ruled abusive.

Although the law makes no provision for a central labor organization, three major groups have emerged: The Sole Workers Central, the General Workers Confederation, and Forca Sindical. The centrals do not have legal standing to represent professional categories of workers, but all three centrals can effectively acquire such standing by affiliating with existing statewide federations or nationwide confederations or by forming new federations and confederations.

Unions and centrals freely affiliate with international trade union organizations. All three major confederations are affiliated with the ICFTU.

b. *The Right to Organize and Bargain Collectively.*—The Constitution provides for the right to organize. With government assistance, businesses and unions are working to expand and improve mechanisms of collective bargaining. The scope of issues legally susceptible to collective bargaining is narrow, however, and the labor court system exercises normative powers with regard to the settlement of labor disputes, thus discouraging direct negotiation. The Cardoso Government made expansion of collective bargaining one of its major objectives in the labor sector. In mid-1995, the Government promulgated a provisional measure that ended the indexing of wages to inflation, reduced the role of labor courts in wage negotiations, allowed for mediation if the parties involved requested it, and provided greater latitude for collective bargaining. Unions welcomed these changes, since previously labor courts and the Labor Ministry had mediation responsibility in the preliminary stages of dispute settlement. In many cases, free negotiations set wages; labor court decisions set them in others. Under the terms of the provisional measure, parties may now freely choose mediation. The ILO notes that important differences in wages continue to exist to the detriment of women and blacks, particularly in the rural sectors (see Section 5).

The Constitution incorporates a provision from the Labor Code that prohibits the dismissal of employees who are candidates for or holders of union leadership positions. Nonetheless, dismissals take place, with those dismissed required to resort to a usually lengthy court process for relief. In general, the authorities do not effectively enforce laws protecting union members from discrimination. Union officials estimate that only 5 percent of such cases reaching the labor court system are resolved within days through a preliminary judicial order. The other 95 percent generally take 5 to 10 years (and sometimes more) to resolve.

Labor law applies equally in the free trade zones. However, unions in the Manaus Free Trade Zone, like rural unions and many unions in smaller cities, are relatively weaker vis-a-vis industry compared with unions in the major industrial centers.

c. *Prohibition of Forced or Compulsory Labor.*—Although the Constitution prohibits forced labor, there were credible reports of forced labor in many parts of Brazil. In 1996 the Catholic Church-affiliated Pastoral Land Commission (CPT) reported 21 cases of forced labor, involving a total of 26,047 workers in 8 states. The number of workers involved represents a small increase over the 25,193 reported the previous year and a large increase over the 19,940 reported in 1994. Forced labor is common on farms producing charcoal for use in the iron foundries and steel industries and in the sugar industry (see also Section 6.d.).

Local police admitted that overseers or owners of many farms withhold pay from migrant laborers and use force to retain and intimidate them, but such violations fall within the jurisdiction of the Federal Ministry of Labor. The Ministry of Labor increased the number of roving inspectors from 2,300 in 1995 to some 3,000 in 1996, but admits that its enforcement mechanisms are still inadequate. Labor organizations allege that in mining and the rural economy thousands of workers, including minors, are hired on the basis of false promises, subjected to debt bondage and forced prostitution, with violence used to retain or punish workers who attempt to escape. The people responsible for exploiting forced labor usually go unpunished because freed workers are often afraid to testify against those who recruited and oversaw them, and because the authorities have found it difficult to identify and locate the owners of farms or businesses that exploit forced labor.

The CPT reported that local authorities varied in their responses to allegations that forced labor existed in their jurisdictions. The governor of Minas Gerais denied that forced labor existed in his state even though, according to the CPT, inspections found some 8,000 people who were being forced to work on charcoal farms without payment and under subhuman conditions. In the western state of Acre, however, the state prosecutor general for labor appointed two special prosecutors to investigate allegations of forced labor there.

In mid-1995 the largest trade union confederation, CUT, initiated a 24-hour hot line with a toll-free number for reporting instances of forced labor. CUT president Vicente Paulo da Silva inaugurated the campaign by personally inspecting charcoal refineries in the state of Mato Grosso do Sul. Shortly after the CUT initiative, President Cardoso announced the formation of a task force to combat forced labor. Cardoso said that the Government would no longer provide loans, subsidies, or rollover of outstanding debt to farms or companies found to employ forced labor and that they would be ineligible to bid on public contracts. One important practice instituted by the task force was the use of federal law enforcement officers from other states for inspections, so that enterprises using forced labor cannot rely on friendly local authorities to avoid detection and punishment. The CPT noted that the effectiveness of surprise inspections was often hampered by the inability of inspection teams to arrive in an area without advance warning and by often spotty collaboration from the federal police. The Minister of Labor issued a decree in late 1995 providing that farms caught a second time using forced labor would be seized, and used to settle landless families as part of the federal Government's agrarian reform program.

d. *Minimum Age for Employment of Children.*—The minimum working age under the Constitution is 14 years, except for apprentices. Judges can authorize employment for children under 14 years of age when they feel it appropriate. However, in October the Cardoso administration introduced a proposed constitutional amendment that would prohibit all child labor under the age of 14. The authorities rarely enforce legal restrictions intended to protect working minors under the age of 18, however, and the problem is widespread. The law requires permission of the parents or guardians for minors to work, and they must attend school through the primary grades. The law bars all minors from night work, work that constitutes a physical strain, and employment in unhealthful, dangerous, or morally harmful conditions. The Ministry of Labor is responsible for enforcement of child labor laws, but it has too few inspectors to do so effectively. The widely held view that it is better for minors to work than to be involved in street crime also hampers enforcement efforts.

Despite legal restrictions, however, official figures state that more than 3 million 10- to 14-year-old children (or 4.6 percent of the work force) were employed. Many children work alongside their parents in cane fields, cutting hemp, or feeding wood into charcoal ovens; accidents, unhealthy working conditions, and squalor are common in these workplaces. According to a comprehensive 1995 report in the weekly magazine Veja on the problem of child labor, it is common to find children in the interior of Bahia who have lost fingers and forearms feeding sisal into grinding machines. Carlos Silva de Jesus, age 14, for instance, has been blind since the age of 8 when, while working in a sisal field in Retirolandia, Bahia, he stabbed his left eye with a sisal leaf and shortly afterward punctured his right eye with a knife because he could not see very well.

In a public ceremony in the Presidential Palace on September 6, President Cardoso, accompanied by eight state governors and much of his cabinet, signed three protocols with state governors and NGO's expressing the commitment of the signatories to eradicate child labor in Brazil. In remarks at the signing ceremony, Cardoso said that child labor was "unacceptable" because it involved the degradation of human beings, which reflected badly on all Brazilians. Cardoso acknowledged that child labor has long existed in Brazil, but he insisted that the situation was different now because the federal Government, in cooperation with state governments, businesses, and NGO's, was taking concrete steps to combat it.

Cottage industry subcontractors for independent shoe manufacturers in Franca (Sao Paulo) have, in the past, employed thousands of children under the age of 14, in violation of the law. Public prosecutors, however, brought several suits in late 1994 and 1995 against Franca manufacturers for illegally subcontracting work that led to the exploitation of child labor. The labor court fined the manufacturers and ordered the practice stopped. Subsequently, the Franca shoe manufacturers' association signed an agreement with ABRINQ (the Brazilian toy manufacturers' foundation for children's rights) agreeing to end the use of child labor by its subcontractors.

According to a recent 2-year study carried out by an NGO based in Pernambuco, the Centro Josue de Castro, the use of child labor is common on sugar cane plantations. The study estimated that 54,000 minors work on sugar cane plantations in Pernambuco, and 40,000 in Sao Paulo. In 40 percent of the families the researchers interviewed, children contributed 30 to 50 percent of the family income. In the sugar cane industry in Pernambuco, 25 percent of the workers are younger than 18 years, 90 percent of whom began working on the plantations between the ages of 7 and 13. CUT, the nationwide labor confederation, reported that child labor is common among orange pickers in Sao Paulo. The CPT received reports of child labor in the charcoal production industry in Minas Gerais, Mato Grosso, Mato Grosso do Sul, and Para; on sisal plantations in Bahia and Paraiba; on cotton plantations in Parana; and in the area of reforestation, where children are used principally to put toxic chemicals on trees and anthills, in Minas Gerais, Bahia, and Espirito Santo.

ABRINQ has been active in trying to remedy many of these abuses. It convinced the state's sugar producers and Abecitrus, the association of state citrus exporters, to sign accords agreeing to remove child labor from their operations. At ABRINQ's encouragement, Volkswagen, General Motors, and other auto manufacturers are investigating the role of child labor in operations related to their plants (children are involved in producing charcoal, which is used to produce the cast iron and steel used in cars).

In its efforts to convince state governments to crack down on child labor, ABRINQ has emphasized the need to provide educational opportunities for the children involved. The state government of Mato Grosso do Sul, in conjunction with the federal Government, implemented a pilot project intended to take children from charcoal farms and place them in classrooms. The parents are paid a salary slightly higher than the child's monthly earnings on the charcoal farm so long as the child remains in school. If the program is successful, the state government plans to expand it from the initial group of 1,000 children.

e. *Acceptable Conditions of Work.*—Prior to July 1994, the Government adjusted the national minimum wage every month. Upon introduction of the economic stabilization plan in 1995, it set the minimum wage at $83 (70 reais) per month. In May 1995, President Cardoso raised the minimum wage to $111 dollars (100 reais) per month, and, in May 1996, raised it again to $115 (112 reais). The minimum wage is not sufficient to provide a decent standard of living for a worker and family. The Interunion Department for Socioeconomic Studies and Statistics estimated that the minimum wage is slightly more than one-fourth that necessary to support a family of four (the standard set by the 1988 Constitution). The most recent national survey (for 1990) showed that 35 percent of economically active individuals, including minors from 10 to 14 years of age, earned no more than the minimum wage. Many workers, particularly outside the regulated economy and in the northeast, reportedly earned less than the minimum wage.

The 1988 Constitution limits the workweek to 44 hours and specifies a weekly rest period of 24 consecutive hours, preferably on Sundays. The Constitution expanded pay and fringe benefits and established new protections for agricultural and domestic workers, although not all of these provisions are enforced.

Unsafe working conditions are prevalent throughout the country. Incomplete figures from the Ministry of Social Welfare on workplace accidents and fatalities in 1995 showed 424,137 reported accidents, of which 3,967 were fatal and 15,156 caused permanent disabilities. Fundacentro, part of the Ministry of Labor, sets occupational health and safety standards. However, the Ministry has insufficient resources for adequate inspection and enforcement of these standards. There were also credible allegations of corruption within the enforcement system. If a worker has a problem in the workplace and has trouble getting relief directly from his employer, he or his union can file a claim with the regional labor court, although in practice this is frequently a cumbersome, protracted process.

The law requires employers to establish internal commissions for accident prevention in workplaces. The law protects employee members of these commissions from being fired for their activities. Such firings, however, do occur, and legal recourse usually requires years for resolution. While an individual worker does not have the legal right to remove himself from workplaces with hazardous conditions, workers may express such concerns to the internal commission, which would conduct an immediate investigation.

CHILE

Chile is a multiparty democracy with a constitution that provides for a strong executive, a bicameral legislature, and an independent judiciary. Approved by referendum in 1980, the Constitution was written under the former military government and establishes institutional limits on popular rule. President Eduardo Frei, a Christian Democrat, began his 6-year term in 1994. The National Congress comprises 120 deputies and 46 senators. The government coalition of six parties holds a majority in the lower house. An opposition coalition, together with several independent and eight appointed senators, controls the upper chamber. Appointees of the former president, General Augusto Pinochet, continue to influence the constitutionally independent judicial branch. However, turnover in the courts has led to a significant diminution of that influence.

The armed forces are constitutionally subordinate to the President through an appointed Minister of Defense but enjoy a large degree of legal autonomy. Most notably, the President must have the concurrence of the National Security Council to remove service chiefs. The Carabineros (the uniformed national police) have primary responsibility for public order and safety and border security. The civilian Investigations Police are responsible for criminal investigations and immigration control. Both organizations—although formally under the jurisdiction of the Ministry of Defense, which determines their budget—are under operational control of the Ministry of Interior. Some alleged perpetrators of human rights abuses during the military regime remain on active duty in the army. The security forces committed a number of human rights abuses.

The export-led, free market economy experienced its 13th consecutive year of expansion. The most important export was copper; forestry products, fresh fruit, fish meal, and manufactured goods were also significant sources of foreign exchange. Gross domestic product grew at 8.5 percent, unemployment remained steady at around 5.5 percent, and inflation increased slightly to 8.2 percent. Since 1987 the percentage of the population living below the poverty line has decreased from 45 to 25 percent at the end of 1996. Annual per capita income rose above $4,700 in 1995.

The Government generally respected its citizens' human rights. However, there continued to be some problem areas. The most serious cases involved allegations of torture, brutality, and police use of excessive force. There continue to be reports of physical abuse in jails and prisons. Discrimination and violence against women, and violence against children are problems. Many indigenous people remain marginalized.

Almost all other human rights concerns are related to abuses that occurred during the former military government, primarily between 1973 and 1978. Efforts to bring abusers to justice in cases dating back to the early years of the military government are limited by the conflicting demands for justice and for national reconciliation. Military authorities continue to resist disclosing abuses from the past. In particular, the courts continue to struggle with the application of the 1978 Amnesty Law to cases that occurred during the first 5 years of military rule. Over the past 2 years, the Government and the opposition debated various proposals that would effectively close all cases covered by the Amnesty Law that are still under judicial investigation. These efforts, however, have largely stalled, and the judicial system continues to investigate and close pending human rights cases.

RESPECT FOR HUMAN RIGHTS

Section 1. Respect for the Integrity of the Person, Including Freedom From:
    a. *Political and Other Extrajudicial Killing.*—There were no reports of political killings.

The Committee for the Defense of People's Rights (CODEPU) reported that at least three individuals died as a result of the use of excessive force by the police, including one innocent bystander who died when caught in a crossfire between criminals and the police. In addition, army personnel shot and killed another individual who was trespassing on army property. These deaths received wide media coverage, and the cases are under investigation by the courts.

The courts made several landmark decisions during the year on cases that occurred under the military regime. In June the Supreme Court invoked the Amnesty Law to end all action in the 1976 murder of Carmelo Soria, a Spanish citizen employed by the United Nations. As a result, the authorities dismissed charges against two ex-agents of the National Intelligence Center (CNI) who were indicted in June 1995 as author and accomplice in this crime; any further official investigation was terminated. This decision provoked concern and condemnation from a broad spectrum, including the embassies of the European Union states, Chilean members of congress, and political parties. In September a group of parliamentarians belonging to the government coalition, charging denial of justice, introduced an impeachment motion against four Supreme Court justices, including Eliodoro Ortiz, the investigating judge who decided that the Amnesty Law applied. Some observers criticized the legislators' effort, however, as an attempt to intimidate the judiciary.

In another high-profile case, retired General Manuel Contreras and Brigadier Pedro Espinoza continue to serve their 7- and 6-year prison terms, respectively, as the intellectual authors of the 1976 murder in Washington, D.C. of former Chilean Foreign Minister Orlando Letelier and his U.S. citizen assistant, Ronni Moffit. Both filed petitions for pardon but neither has been approved. However, the authorities granted Contreras credit for the 50 days he served while under house arrest pending resolution of the U.S. Government's extradition request in 1978. In addition, Italian courts convicted Contreras and Raul Iturriaga, another former DINA (National Intelligence Directorate) officer, in absentia for the attempted murder of former Chilean Vice President Bernardo Leighton and his wife Anita Fresno, and sentenced each man to 18 years in prison. The Italians have requested neither their extradition nor that they serve their sentences in Chile.

The January arrest in Argentina of former Chilean intelligence agent Enrique Arancibia Clavel once again drew attention to the 1974 assassination in Buenos Aires of former Chilean army chief Carlos Prats. Prats was the army commander under President Salvador Allende and was succeeded by General Pinochet in August

1973. He left Chile for Argentina several days after the coup against Allende. The case was reopened in 1992 as a result of a petition filed by the Prats family containing new evidence. The Government has agreed to be a coplaintiff in the Argentine trial of Arancibia.

In the case involving the 1982 murder of Tucapel Jimenez, the third chamber of the court of appeals unanimously denied bail to retired army Major Carlos Herrera on the grounds that he is a danger to society. Herrera, previously convicted of unnecessary violence which resulted in the 1984 death of political activist Mario Fernandez, began serving his 10-year sentence in Punta Peuco prison in January.

After more than 9 years, a military judge dismissed the case of the June 1987 deaths from "Operation Albania," in which CNI agents killed 12 people connected to the Manuel Rodriguez Patriotic Front (FPMR). This was in spite of a unanimous ruling in 1995 by the military tribunal—a higher court—that the deaths were homicides and that the cases should go to trial. At the time, the authorities claimed that all 12 died in shoot-outs with security officers, and therefore no crime was committed. The authorities implicated 28 former officers and enlisted men in this case. The decision to close the case has been appealed to the Supreme Court.

On April 10, Supreme Court Justice Alfredo Pfeiffer reopened the investigation of the April 1991 assassination of Democratic Independent Union (UDI) founder and Senator Jaime Guzman, due to controversial public statements made by Jorge Barraza, the police detective in charge of the 1991–93 investigation. According to Barraza, the assassination's intellectual author was FPMR leader Juan Gutierrez Frischman, also known as "El Chele," who also happened to be married at the time to Cuban armed forces chief Raul Castro's daughter. Barraza charged that his superiors in the Interior Ministry removed him from the case in 1993 because they feared that his investigation would reveal crimes committed by confidential informants. As a result of the initial investigation, the courts found two members of the FPMR guilty and gave them life sentences. The courts found three other FPMR members guilty in absentia but the authorities never apprehended them. Gutierrez was not listed then as a conspirator. Barraza claims that when he presented a secret document to his Interior Ministry superiors in August 1993 detailing Gutierrez's role, he was transferred, and his investigative unit disbanded.

Pfeiffer resigned in June, claiming death threats and political pressure to drop the case, and Raquel Camposano was appointed in his place. On December 18, as a result of her investigation, Camposano issued an arrest warrant for Investigations Police director Nelson Mery, charging him with obstruction of justice for withholding from judicial authorities a key surveillance videotape of the terrorist cell involved in the Guzman assassination. Separately, the judge also issued indictments against former Deputy Director of Public Security Marcelo Schilling, his assistant, and several subordinates for having illegally obtained information from leftwing terrorists in exchange for immunity from prosecution. President Frei declined to accept resignations from Mery and Schilling; an appeals court subsequently dismissed the cases, and the Supreme Court upheld the dismissal.

b. *Disappearance.*—There were no reports of politically motivated disappearances.

The major human rights controversy involved past disappearances and efforts by all political forces and the Government to reinterpret the 1978 amnesty in such a way as to achieve both justice and national reconciliation. As interpreted under the so-called Aylwin Doctrine (named after former president Patricio Aylwin), the courts should not close a case involving a disappearance (those who disappeared are considered to have been "kidnaped") until either the bodies are found or credible evidence is provided to indicate that an individual is dead. This could affect up to 542 cases, which cover about 1,100 persons still classified as "detained or missing" from the early years of the military regime. The application of the Aylwin Doctrine, however, has been uneven, as some courts continued the previous practice of applying the 1978 amnesty to disappearances without conducting an investigation to identify the perpetrators. The court closed 16 cases during the first half of the year through application of the amnesty; 170 cases are active; and an additional 356 cases are temporarily closed but subject to being reopened.

The Government attempted to alter implementation of the amnesty through a proposal negotiated by Minister of the Interior Carlos Figueroa and opposition leader Miguel Otero. The bill they introduced proposed to keep secret the identity of key witnesses, including those implicated in the crimes, in exchange for whatever confidential information they might provide on the fate of those who disappeared. This information, which would never be available to the public, would serve as the basis for the permanent closure of the case. However, the proposal was criticized by both the right and the left and never came to a vote.

The Social Aid Foundation of Christian Churches (FASIC) brought four disappearance cases that had been closed in 1995 with the fate of the victims still unknown to the attention of the Inter-American Commission on Human Rights (IACHR). While the commission has made rulings on these cases, they have yet to be published. The FASIC also appealed an additional 14 cases to the IACHR.

Some progress has been made in locating a number of those who disappeared. The remains of three bodies were discovered in early December 1995 on the grounds of a military camp situated 25 miles north of Santiago. The authorities identified two of them as Manuel Weibel Navarrete and Ignacio Orlando Gonzalez Espinoza, both former members of the Chilean Communist Party. There are suspicions that a large number of bodies were buried in military precincts, but the military authorities refuse access to these areas, thus preventing the possible closure of a number of these cases.

c. *Torture and Other Cruel, Inhuman, or Degrading Treatment or Punishment.*—The Constitution forbids "the use of illegal pressure" on detainees, but CODEPU has received reports of instances of mistreatment and abuse by some Carabinero and Investigations Police units. CODEPU lawyers visit detainees during their interrogation (see Section 1.d.) and represent many suspected terrorists in court. CODEPU alleged that there were some cases of use of excessive force against detainees during the year. It found a significant improvement in the record of the plainclothes Investigations Police, while complaints against the uniformed Carabineros increased in number. The Minister of Interior normally asks the courts to conduct independent investigations of credible complaints of police abuse, but such investigations rarely result in arrests, due in part to the reluctance of judges to pursue the issue vigorously. The courts convicted and sentenced only four police officials for committing acts of violence against detainees. However, as indicated in the CODEPU report, police authorities often impose administrative sanctions on abusive officers without waiting for a judicial ruling.

According to a report by the United Nations Commission on Human Rights, while considerable progress has been made since the return to civilian rule in 1990, acts of torture still continue. A study by Diego Portales University indicated that 71 percent of detainees interrogated had suffered some form of ill treatment. The United Nations report concluded that although abuses are not systemic, the Government has taken insufficient action to ensure that the activities of the Carabineros are in accord with the law. It recommends that the Carabineros be entirely subordinated to the Ministry of Interior.

Prisons are overcrowded and antiquated, but the conditions are not life threatening. Food meets minimal nutritional needs, and prisoners may supplement the diet by buying food. Those with sufficient funds can often rent space in a better wing of the prison. Prison guards have been accused of using excessive force to stop attempted prison breaks. Although most reports state that the guards generally behave responsibly and do not mistreat prisoners, several prisoners have complained of beatings. There are about 300 minors in adult prisons (see Section 5).

The maximum security prison houses 79 prisoners, most of them charged with or convicted of terrorism. Prisoners continue to complain that strict security measures, prohibition of visitors, hidden cameras, and the extremely rigid regulations violate their rights. Recently, the president of the Santiago Court of Appeals confirmed the existence of listening devices in prison cells. In a reply to this report, the Minister of Justice confirmed that microphones were present but said that they were never used.

In June 1995, a new prison at Punta Peuco, 25 miles north of Santiago, was completed. This prison was constructed specifically for government and military officers sentenced to jail. As of August, it had 15 inmates including Brigadier Pedro Espinoza and retired General Manuel Contreras.

The Government permits prison visits by independent human rights monitors.

d. *Arbitrary Arrest, Detention, or Exile.*—The Constitution allows civilian and military courts to order detention for up to 5 days without arraignment and to extend the detention of suspected terrorists for up to 10 days. The law affords detainees 30 minutes of immediate and daily access to a lawyer (in the presence of a prison guard) and to a doctor to verify their physical condition. The law does not permit a judge to deny such access; police authorities generally observed these requirements.

As of September, 9 percent of the general prison population were under investigation but not charged with a crime, 50 percent were charged with an offense and were awaiting trial or sentencing, and 41 percent were serving sentences.

The police have the authority to make arrests based on suspicion, particularly of youth in high crime areas late at night. In practice, the detainees are not promptly advised of charges against them, nor are they granted a speedy hearing before a judge. The Constitution provides for the right to legal counsel, but this is a reality only for those who can afford to pay. The poor, who account for the majority of cases, may be represented by law students doing practical training (who are often overworked) or, on occasion, by a court appointed lawyer. Arrest procedures do not require police to allow detainees to telephone relatives or a lawyer. The Constitution allows judges to set bail.

Law enforcement authorities often failed to inform foreign embassies when their nationals were arrested.

There were no cases of forced exile.

e. *Denial of Fair Public Trial.*—The Constitution calls for a judicial system independent of the other branches of government.

Cases decided in the lower courts can be referred to the appeals courts, and ultimately to the Supreme Court. Although the judiciary, and particularly the Supreme Court, has been dominated by appointees of the former military regime, the passage of time is changing this legacy. Criminal court judges are appointed for life, and appointments to the Supreme Court and the appeals courts are made by the President from lists prepared by the Supreme Court. Of the 16 justices on the Supreme Court, 7 have been appointed since the end of the military regime. The Supreme Court continues to work with the other branches of government on broad judicial reform.

The jurisdiction of military tribunals is limited to cases involving military officers. If formal charges are filed in civilian courts against a military officer, including Carabineros, the military prosecutor asks, and the Supreme Court normally grants, jurisdiction to the military. This is of particular consequence in the human rights cases dating from 1973 to 1978, the period covered by the 1978 Amnesty Law. In addition, military courts have the authority to charge and try civilians for defamation of military personnel and for sedition, but their rulings can be appealed to the civilian Supreme Court.

Based on the Napoleonic Code, the judicial system does not provide for trial by jury, nor does it assume innocence until proven otherwise. Criminal proceedings are inquisitorial rather than adversarial. The Constitution provides for the right to legal counsel, but the poor do not always get effective legal representation (see Section 1.d.).

CODEPU reports that there are four political prisoners; however, these individuals were convicted of crimes related to terrorist acts.

f. *Arbitrary Interference with Privacy, Family, Home, or Correspondence.*—The Constitution prohibits such practices, government authorities generally respect these prohibitions, and violations are subject to effective legal sanctions. The 1995 Privacy Law bars obtaining information by undisclosed taping, telephone intercepts, and other surreptitious means, as well as its dissemination.

Section 2. Respect for Civil Liberties, Including:

a. *Freedom of Speech and Press.*—The Constitution provides for freedom of speech and the press, and the authorities generally respected these rights in practice.

The press maintains its independence, criticizes the Government, and covers issues sensitive to the military, including human rights. The Privacy Law also applies to the media, which are not exempt from its provisions.

The print and electronic media are largely independent of government control. The State is majority owner of La Nacion newspaper, but the newspaper is editorially independent. However, La Nacion's editorial policy rarely, if ever, disagrees with government policy. The Television Nacional network is state owned but not under direct government control. It receives no government subsidy and is self-financing through commercial advertising. It is editorially independent and is governed by a board of directors which, although politically appointed, encourages the expression of varied opinions over the network.

Military courts have the authority to charge and try civilians for defamation of military personnel and for sedition, but their rulings can be appealed to the civilian Supreme Court.

A draft press law, building on one proposed by the Aylwin government in 1993, would transfer cases involving freedom of speech (including charges of defamation and sedition) for nonmilitary personnel from military to civilian courts. As the bill moved from the House to the Senate, it remained the subject of considerable controversy, with the press arguing that some of its provisions might undermine aspects of freedom of expression. The bill was still under consideration in the Senate at year's end.

It is a criminal offense to besmirch the honor of state institutions and symbols, such as the Congress, the military services, the flag, and the President. In December 1995, the courts convicted a former cabinet minister in Pinochet's government of defaming state institutions after he charged that unnamed members of congress used drugs and jailed him until he agreed to accept a suspended sentence and a nominal fine. The Santiago court of appeals overturned the verdict in January, but the Supreme Court reinstated it in May.

On October 29, the Investigations Police arrested Gladys Marin, Secretary General of the Communist Party, and jailed her on charges of having slandered army commander-in-chief Augusto Pinochet. The army brought charges against Marin under the National Security Law for public statements she made on September 11 characterizing Pinochet as a psychopath and accusing him and the army of human rights violations. The army subsequently dropped the charges, and Marin was released on October 21. Prior to the charges being dropped, however, both the court of appeals and the first chamber of the Supreme Court upheld the warrant for Marin's arrest.

In June a Santiago court ordered the arrest of Eduardo Meneses, leader of the rap group Panteras Negras. In January 1995, police officers, with the support of the Council for the Defense of the State, had filed a suit against Meneses under the military penal code for insulting the police, citing the lyrics of his song "War in the Streets." The song was included in a December 1995 concert at which members of the police had been present.

In the only case involving film censorship to reach the courts during the year, the Film Classification Board on November 11 voted to reclassify the banned 1988 film "The Last Temptation of Christ" as suitable for theater showings for those over the age of 18. However, on November 14, the court of appeals accepted a motion by the conservative group "Chile's Future" ("El Porvenir de Chile") to prohibit the film's showing pending further judicial review. The controversy was front page news; the conservative group argued that the board's reclassification was illegal and that the film is an attack against the honor of the Catholic Church, Christ, and Christians. Party for Democracy Deputy Victor Barrueto and other opponents of film censorship have proposed amending the Constitution to prohibit film censorship and to restrict the board's power to that of simply rating films.

Francisco Martorell, the author of the book "Diplomatic Impunity," returned from self-imposed exile in Argentina to present himself for sentencing for slander against prominent figures in a case that dates back to 1993. Martorell's book alleged sexual promiscuity and other misconduct by a number of prominent figures in society and politics while recounting the exploits of the Argentine Ambassador to Chile in 1989–91. The prison sentence was suspended, but Martorell was fined about $25,000 (10 million pesos). His book is still banned.

The courts rarely issued orders prohibiting media coverage of cases in progress, although one prominent instance drew wide protests. When the courts renewed investigation into the 1990 assassination of Senator Jaime Guzman, a gag order was imposed, then lifted 2 months later. The law does not set any limits on a judge's power to impose such prohibitions nor does it require the reasons for the ban to be cited. In reaction to the presence of the media when the Investigations Police arrested a Carabinero, the court of appeals reaffirmed provisions of the Code of Penal Procedure that prohibit police from publicly disclosing the findings of their investigations.

The Government does not restrict academic freedom.

b. *Freedom of Peaceful Assembly and Association.*—The Constitution provides for these rights, and the Government respects them in practice.

c. *Freedom of Religion.*—The Constitution provides for freedom of religion, and the Government respects this right in practice. All denominations practice their faiths without restriction. Although church and State are officially separate, the Roman Catholic Church receives official preferential treatment. A 1995 municipal ordinance made it illegal to cause disturbances in the streets, which has been interpreted by some evangelical groups as an attempt to prevent them from proselytizing and preaching in public.

The small Jewish population is free to practice its religion but faces some discrimination in public life. In October a cabinet minister and a subcabinet member were reported to have made anti-Semitic comments in government meetings. Subsequently a Jewish vice minister resigned his post. Knowledgeable sources believed this was partly the result of internal policy differences and partly because of the Government's failure even to acknowledge that the remarks had been made.

d. *Freedom of Movement Within the Country, Foreign Travel, Emigration, and Repatriation.*—The Constitution provides for these rights, and the Government generally respects them in practice. For minor children to leave the country, either alone or with only one of their parents, they must have notarized permission from both parents.

The Government cooperates with the United Nations High Commissioner for Refugees and other humanitarian organizations in assisting refugees. The issue of the provision of first asylum has never arisen. There were no reports of forced return of persons to a country where they feared persecution.

Section 3. Respect for Political Rights: The Right of Citizens to Change Their Government

Chile is a constitutional democracy, and citizens have the right to change their government through periodic elections. There is universal suffrage for citizens 18 years of age and over. The Government still operates under some political restraints that were imposed by the previous regime. Under the 1980 Constitution, various national institutions—including the President, the Supreme Court, and the armed forces-dominated National Security Council—appointed an additional nine senators (beyond those elected) to 8-year terms prior to the transition to democracy. These senators, whose terms expire in 1997, were appointed by then-president Pinochet, and they join with the opposition on most matters. The legislative branch, with the exception of the institutional senators, is freely elected and independent from the executive branch.

The former military government wrote the 1980 Constitution and amended it slightly in 1989 after losing a referendum on whether General Pinochet should stay in office as president. It provides for a strong presidency and a legislative branch with limited powers. In addition, the Constitution includes provisions designed to protect the interests of the military and the rightwing political opposition.

These provisions, according to their defenders and even some critics, assured stability in the political process during the transition. Some of these provisions are characterized by critics as "authoritarian enclaves" left over from the previous regime; while advocates describe them as integral to the system of checks and balances. They include limitations on the President's right to remove military service chiefs, including chief of the army (the position General Pinochet can hold until 1998); an electoral system that gives the second place party (or coalition) in each district disproportionate representation in Congress; and the provision for nonelected institutional senators.

Women have had the right to vote in municipal elections since 1934 and in national elections since 1949, and they are active in political life at the grassroots level. Women make up a majority of registered voters and of those who actually cast ballots, but there are few women in leadership positions. There are 9 women among the 120 deputies, 3 women in the 46-seat Senate (including one of the designated senators), and 3 of 21 cabinet ministers are women. The level of female participation is not increasing. The percentage of female candidates in the 1996 municipal elections increased only slightly from 1994—to 17.7 percent from 16.7 percent.

The over 1 million indigenous people have the legal right to participate freely in the political process, although relatively few are politically active. While their participation has increased since the 1990 democratic transition, there is only one member of Congress of indigenous descent. In 1994 the Government created the National Corporation for Indigenous Development and placed it under the Planning Ministry; in 1995, indigenous people elected their representatives to this body.

Section 4. Governmental Attitude Regarding International and Nongovernmental Investigation of Alleged Violations of Human Rights

The Chilean Human Rights Commission, a nongovernmental organization (NGO), is affiliated with the International League of Human Rights and continues to gather evidence of police abuses. The CODEPU provides legal counsel to those accused of politically related crimes and to victims of human rights abuses. NGO's say that the Government has cooperated with their efforts to investigate accusations of continued human rights violations. Many international NGO's also continue to follow closely human rights issues.

The National Commission on Truth and Reconciliation (Rettig Commission) issued a report in 1991 that helped many Chileans come to terms with human rights abuses under the military government. The successor to the commission, the National Corporation for Compensation and Reconciliation, continues to investigate cases. Its mandate was extended until the end of 1996 to allow it to complete investigations of the last cases on which it has information. In August it delivered its final report, which confirmed 899 cases in addition to those documented by the Rettig Commission, bringing the total number of victims of killings and disappearance cases to 3,197. The corporation also provides compensation to family members of human rights victims.

Section 5. Discrimination Based on Race, Sex, Religion, Disability, Language, or Social Status

The Constitution provides for equality before the law, but it does not specifically ban discrimination based on race, sex, religion, or social status.

Women.—The public is only beginning to appreciate the extent of abuses such as wife beating. The National Women's Service (SERNAM), created in 1991 to combat discrimination against women, found in a 1992 study that 26.2 percent of women it surveyed said that they had been subjected to some form of physical violence by their husband or partner while another 33.5 percent reported some form of psychological abuse. However, only 16 percent reported such violence to the police. SERNAM is now conducting courses on the legal, medical, and psychological aspects of domestic violence for Carabineros, who are usually the first public officials to intervene in such incidents. These courses have been expanded to include judicial and municipal authorities.

The courts may order counseling for those involved in intrafamily violence. As of July 12, there were 8,147 court cases involving intrafamily violence in Santiago. The Carabineros also reported that its family affairs unit received more than 463 complaints of rape or sexual abuse during the first 8 months of the year.

Legal distinctions between the sexes still exist, despite a 1989 decision to give human rights treaties to which Chile is a party precedence over local laws. The law permits legal separation, but not divorce, so those who wish to remarry must seek annulments. Since annulment implies that a marriage never existed under the law, former spouses are left with little recourse for financial support. Although a recent law created conjugal property as an option in a marriage, some women saw this as a step backward, since the law on separate property (which still exists) gives women the right to one-half their husbands' assets but gives husbands no rights to theirs.

Another SERNAM study found that the average earnings of female heads of household are only 71 percent of those of male heads of household. Women with no schooling received a salary that was 87 percent of that of their male counterparts without schooling, while female heads of household with university training earned only 57 percent as much as their male contemporaries. SERNAM has a pilot program providing occupational training and child care in an effort to alleviate this disparity.

Children.—The Government provides free education through high school (compulsory up to the eighth grade). A survey by the National Minors Service indicated that sexual abuse of minors occurs but that few cases were reported. A United Nations Children's Fund (UNICEF) report shows that 34 percent of children under 12 years of age experience serious physical violence, although only 3.2 percent of the victims of intrafamily violence reported to the Carabineros family affairs unit were below the age of 18. The 1994 Law on Intrafamily Violence was designed in part to deal with this problem. UNICEF estimates that over 100,000 children are in the work force (see Section 6.d.).

Congress enacted a law that segregates juvenile offenders from adult prisoners. Although juvenile offenders (i.e., those under the age of 18) had long received special treatment in the courts, some of them had been incarcerated with adults. The Government has reduced the number of minors in adult prisons from 6,630 in 1992 to around 300 in 1996.

People With Disabilities.—Congress passed a law in 1994 to promote the integration of people with disabilities into society, and the National Fund for the Handicapped (FONDIS) has a $1.5 million budget. The 1992 census found that 288,000 citizens said that they had some form of disability, but FONDIS estimates that the actual number is closer to 1 million. The disabled still suffer some forms of legal discrimination; for example, blind people cannot become teachers or tutors. Although the law requires that new public buildings provide access for the disabled, the public transportation system does not make provision for wheelchair access, and a new subway line under construction provides no facilitated access for the disabled.

Indigenous People.—The Mapuches from the south comprise over 90 percent of the indigenous population, but there are small Aimara, Atacameno, Huilliche, Rapa Nui, and Kawaskhar populations in other parts of the country. A committee composed of representatives of indigenous groups participated in drafting the 1993 law that recognizes the ethnic diversity of the indigenous population and gives indigenous people a voice in decisions affecting their lands, cultures, and traditions. It provides for eventual bilingual education in schools with indigenous populations, and it replaced a statute that emphasized assimilation of indigenous people. However, out of the population that identifies itself as indigenous (nearly 1 million, according to the 1992 census), about half remain separated from the rest of society, largely because of historical, cultural, educational, and geographical factors. In fact, the ability of indigenous people to participate in decisions affecting their lands, cultures, traditions, and the allocation of natural resources is marginal.

National/Racial/Ethnic Minorities.—Chile assimilated a major European (mainly German) migration in the last century and a major Middle Eastern and Croatian migration in the early part of this century. Smaller racial and ethnic minority groups (Indians, Chileans of Asian descent, and African-Chileans) experience some societal intolerance.

Section 6. Worker Rights

a. *The Right of Association.*—Workers have a right to form unions without prior authorization and to join existing unions; 13 percent of the work force is organized. A 1995 law provides government employee associations with the same rights as trade unions, and implementing regulations have been adopted. Only the police and military are not allowed to form unions.

The 1992 Labor Code permits nationwide labor centrals, and the Unified Workers Central (CUT), the largest and most representative of them, legalized its status in April 1992. Unions are independent of the Government, but union leaders are usually elected from lists based on party affiliation and often receive direction from parties' headquarters.

Reforms to the Labor Code in 1990 removed many restrictions on the right to strike, although some remain. Employers may no longer fire striking workers without paying severance benefits. Employers must show cause to fire workers, but layoffs are permissible. Union leaders claim that some employers invoke this clause to fire employees who are attempting to form unions or who are active in collective bargaining. There is no specific information from union sources on particular cases where layoffs were used by employers to dismiss workers for prounion activities. Moreover, such acts and antiunion discrimination in general are illegal.

The CUT and many other labor confederations and federations maintain ties to international labor organizations.

b. *The Right to Organize and Bargain Collectively.*—Although the climate for collective bargaining has improved since the return to democratic government in 1990, most workers continue to negotiate individual contracts. Employers say that this is due to the worker's preference, distrust of union leaders, and to loyalty to their companies. Union leaders counter that the Labor Code—which among other things does not allow closed shops—prevents them from successfully organizing in many sectors. Employers may also include a clause in individual employment contracts that some classes of employees are not allowed to participate in collective bargaining, although this applies only to supervisory personnel. Employees may object to the inclusion of such clauses in their contracts and may appeal to the Ministry of Labor for their excision.

The Ministry is able to arbitrate about one-half of the complaints that it receives. Workers are free to take unarbitrated cases before the courts and, if they succeed in proving that they were fired unjustly, the employer must pay the discharged employees twice their normal severance payment. There are no statistics available concerning the disposition of complaints of antiunion behavior. There are allegations that employers fire workers for prounion activity and attempt to avoid a complaint by immediately paying them twice the normal severance pay.

Temporary workers—defined in the Labor Code as those in agriculture and construction, as well as port workers and entertainers—may now form unions, but their right to collective bargaining remains dependent on employers agreeing to negotiate with unions of temporary workers. The Labor Code provides sanctions for unfair bargaining practices, which protect workers from dismissal during the bargaining process, but labor leaders claim that companies invoke the needs of the company clause to fire workers after a union has signed a new contract, particularly when negotiations result in a prolonged strike.

The same labor laws apply in the duty free zones.

c. *Prohibition of Forced or Compulsory Labor.*—The Constitution and the Labor Code prohibit forced or compulsory labor, and there is no indication that it is practiced.

d. *Minimum Age for Employment of Children.*—The law allows children between the ages of 15 and 18 to work with the express permission of their parents or guardians. Children 14 years of age may also work legally with such permission, but in addition they must have completed their elementary education, and the work involved may not be physically strenuous or unhealthy. Additional provisions in the law protect workers under 18 years by restricting the types of work open to them (for example, they may not work in nightclubs) and by establishing special conditions of work (they may not work more than 8 hours in 1 day). Labor inspectors enforce these regulations and compliance is good in the formal economy. Many children are employed in the informal economy, however, which is difficult to regulate. UNICEF estimates that approximately 107,000 children between 12 and 19 years of age were in the work force. The majority of these were males from single parent households headed by women; these children worked more than 40 hours per week and did not attend school.

e. *Acceptable Conditions of Work.*—The law sets minimum wages, hours of work, and occupational safety and health standards. The legal workweek is 48 hours which can be worked in either 5 or 6 days. The maximum workday length is 10 hours, but positions such as caretakers and domestic servants are exempted. All workers enjoy at least one 24-hour rest period during the workweek, except for workers at high altitudes who voluntarily exchange a workfree day each week for a number of consecutive workfree days every 2 weeks.

A tripartite committee comprising government, employer, and labor representatives normally suggests a minimum wage based on projected future inflation and increases in productivity. On May 14, the Senate approved the Government's proposal with little dissent, setting the minimum monthly wage at about $160 (65,500 pesos), which took effect on June 1. The minimum wage is adjusted annually. This wage is designed to serve as the starting wage for an unskilled single worker entering the labor force and does not provide a family with an acceptable standard of living. Only 11 percent of salaried workers earn the minimum wage.

Occupational health and safety is protected under the law and administered by the Ministry of Health. Ministry of Labor inspectors enforce laws covering working conditions. The Government has increased resources for inspections and targeted industries guilty of the worst abuses. As a result, enforcement is improving, and voluntary compliance is fairly good. Insurance mutual funds provide workmen's compensation and occupational safety training for the private and public sectors. They reported a 24-percent decline in occupational injuries over the past 5 years, although 11 percent of the work force still submitted claims. Workers who remove themselves from situations that endanger their health and safety have their employment protected, provided that they ask a workers' delegate to bring the problem to the attention of labor inspectors. A new law entered force on December 15 that increases the number of annual occupational health and safety inspections and provides that they will be carried out by an expanded labor inspection service in the Ministry of Labor.

COLOMBIA

Colombia is a constitutional, multiparty democracy in which the Liberal and Conservative parties have long dominated politics. President Ernesto Samper avoided possible removal from office on June 13 when the House of Representatives voted that there was insufficient evidence to impeach him on charges that he knowingly accepted contributions from narcotics traffickers during his 1994 campaign. The ongoing crisis diminished the President's moral authority to govern, but he vowed to complete his term of office through August 1998. The judiciary is largely independent.

Widespread internal armed conflict and rampant killings continued to overwhelm society. An estimated 10–15,000 full-time guerrillas organized in over 100 groups represented a growing challenge to government security forces—and exercised a degree of permanent influence in more than half of the country's municipalities. The major guerrilla groups showed no serious interest in peace talks. Some guerrilla groups continued to collaborate with narcotic traffickers, especially in rural regions in the eastern part of the country. Paramilitary forces played a major role in the internal conflict.

The Ministry of Defense is responsible for internal security and oversees both the armed forces and the national police. The Department of Administrative Security (DAS), with broad intelligence gathering, law enforcement, and investigative authority, reports directly to the President. The armed forces and the police committed numerous, serious human rights abuses.

Colombia has a mixed private and public sector economy. The Government continued an economic liberalization program and the privatization of selected public industries, although at a slower pace than in 1995. Crude petroleum rivaled coffee as the principal export; two new fields of as yet unverified size are expected to increase petroleum's importance to the economy. Narcotics traffickers controlled vast numbers of enterprises, and drug-related corruption exerted enormous influence throughout society and political life.

The Government took some steps to reduce human rights violations, but its overall human rights record remained poor. Although extrajudicial killings by the security force declined somewhat, the armed forces and the police continued to be responsible for serious abuses including, according to credible reports, instances of death squad activity within the army. Such killings specifically attributed by credible nongovernmental organizations (NGO's) to government security forces declined by approximately 11 percent in the first 9 months of the year, compared with the same period in 1995. With notable exceptions, the security forces generally exercised restraint in dealing with protesters. However, soldiers reportedly killed several militant coca farmers and field workers ("cocaleros") and injured hundreds who—supported in part by guerrillas and narcotics traffickers—were seeking to impede antinarcotics programs in the south in August; guerrillas also were responsible for some of the deaths. Security forces were responsible for dozens of disappearances. Police and soldiers continued to torture and beat detainees. Prison conditions are generally harsh. Arbitrary arrest and detention, as well as prolonged pretrial detention, are problems. The judiciary is severely overburdened, and has a huge case backlog estimated at over 1 million cases. The use of "faceless" prosecutors, judges, and witnesses, under cover of anonymity for security reasons, continued.

The independent Prosecutor General's office achieved a record number of human rights indictments and arrests, including that of a retired three-star general. However, in many instances including that of the general, the Prosecutor General's office was subsequently compelled to transfer the cases to the military justice system, which has established an almost unbroken record of impunity. The Government allows the military to exercise primary jurisdiction over military personnel accused of abuses; the most prevalent form of sanction is informal dismissal from the service without benefit of court-martial. Moreover, the Government's early, high priority on human rights became a casualty of the crisis over contributions by drug traffickers to the President's election campaign.

Rampant impunity is at the core of the country's human rights violations. According to government reports, in from 97 to 99.5 percent of all crimes, the lawbreakers are never brought to justice. Victims never even report an estimated 74 percent of all crimes to the authorities. The Prosecutor General's office, however, increased efforts to prosecute high-profile human rights cases involving grave violations such as massacres and forced disappearances committed by government forces, paramilitary groups, and guerrillas. While the National Human Rights Ombudsman confirmed that documented cases of security force abuse had declined, he cautioned that the situation remained critical. At the Government's request, the United Nations High Commissioner for Human Rights agreed to open a field office in early 1997.

The Samper administration has not taken action to curb increased abuses committed by paramilitary groups, verging on a policy of tacit acquiescence. Even in areas where they had heavy influence, the armed forces seldom restrained paramilitary activity and abuses.

For 36 of the past 44 years, including much of 1996, the Government has operated under declared states of emergency that enabled the executive to rule by decree in broad areas of the country. The decrees frequently limited due process rights and freedom of movement. The Government created special "public order zones" to permit military commanders in areas of high conflict to direct all government security efforts—including, with authorization by the elected governor or president, imposing curfews, check-points, and requiring safe conduct passes. A Samper administration reform proposal to expand presidential emergency decree powers and remove declarations of states of emergency from oversight by the Constitutional Court moved forward in Congress, and debate on the proposal was scheduled to resume in 1997. The presence of paramilitary, guerrilla, and narcotics trafficking organizations, and the armed confrontations among them, as well as with the armed forces, has displaced 750,000 persons; this total increased by 25 percent compared with 1995.

The Government increased pressure on the media to influence reporting, and in December, the President signed a bill that is expected to lead to intrusive, partisan censorship of television newscasts. Violence against women and children is a serious problem. Unofficial but extensive discrimination against women, minorities, and the indigenous continued. Child labor is a widespread problem. Vigilante groups that engaged in "social cleansing"—the killing of street children, prostitutes, homosexuals, and others deemed socially undesirable—continued to be a serious problem.

Guerrilla forces continued to be responsible for numerous killings and disappearances, as well as 30 to 50 percent of all kidnapings. The Revolutionary Armed Forces of Colombia (FARC) guerrilla group showed no interest in releasing three American missionaries whom the FARC kidnaped on January 31, 1993. According to credible NGO sources, during the first 9 months of the year, members of paramilitary groups committed 59 percent of politically motivated extrajudicial killings; guerrillas were responsible for 33 percent; and government forces for 8 percent of them.

RESPECT FOR HUMAN RIGHTS

Section 1. Respect for the Integrity of the Person, Including Freedom From:
   a. *Political and Other Extrajudicial Killing.*—Political and extrajudicial killing continued to be a serious problem. Members of the security forces continued to commit extrajudicial killings, at a somewhat reduced rate. According to the Bogota-based NGO Intercongregational Justice and Peace Commission and the Center for Investigation and Popular Education (CINEP), the security forces were responsible for about 8 percent of political murders in which the perpetrators could be identified. This represented a decline from the 16 percent reported for the same period in 1995. However, this marked a small drop in absolute numbers, from 55 to 49, due to generally escalated violence throughout the country. A study by the Colombian Commission of Jurists (CCJ) also indicated a downward trend in security force abuses. CCJ reported that in 1995, agents of the State committed 16 percent of political killings, forced disappearances, and social cleansing operations in which perpetrators could be generically identified, compared with 54 percent in 1993. Preliminary figures for 1996 indicate a continuation of this trend, with 18 percent of abuses attributed to the security forces.

According to its 1996 report, the independent, state-sponsored Defensoria del Pueblo (National Human Rights Ombudsman) received 219 complaints in 1995 against the army alleging murder, forced disappearances, and threats. The same report cited 169 complaints against the police for murder, disappearances, and threats. The Ombudsman's figures for 1996 are not yet available, but he praised the police for substantially improving their human rights record. The Attorney General's office reported that of the 3,000 complaints against public officials received between June 1995 and October 1996 (some of which occurred before that reporting period), it opened proceedings in 1,338 cases, including 28 massacres and 202 homicides. Some of the other cases did not involve public officials and were passed on to other government investigative bodies. Government officials give credence to reports of isolated death squad activity by at least one army unit, the 20th Intelligence Brigade.

Although security forces generally exercised restraint in dealing with protesters, soldiers reportedly killed several militant coca farmers and field workers and injured hundreds in August (see Section 2.b.).

While security force killings declined slightly, killings by paramilitary forces increased, and killings by guerrillas and narcotics traffickers also continued to be a serious problem. According to the Institute of Legal Medicine, there were 25,274 murders in 1995, down from 26,764 in 1994. The Institute reported an average of 77.4 violent deaths per 100,000 inhabitants. The National Police reported that 12,824 citizens were victims of homicide during the first 6 months of 1996, down from 13,001 during the last 6 months of 1995.

The police and the judiciary have insufficient resources to investigate most killings adequately. In June the Superior Council of the Judiciary reported that 74 percent of all crimes go unreported, and between 97 and 98 percent of all crimes go unpunished. The government commission on public spending placed the impunity rate for all crimes at 99.5 percent. Although data were lacking in a majority of murder cases, the CCJ study estimated that the killers targeted 4 out of every 10 murder victims for their involvement with political, labor, or social causes.

The CCJ study also indicated that as the number of political killings and forced disappearances carried out by members of the armed forces and police decreased since 1993, those committed by paramilitary organizations increased. In cases of political killings, forced disappearances, and social cleansing during 1995 in which perpetrators could be generically identified, the CCJ concluded that paramilitary members committed 46 percent of those offenses, compared with 18 percent in 1993; and that guerrilla organizations committed 38 percent of those offenses, compared with 28 percent in 1993. Preliminary figures for 1996 indicate a continuation of this trend, with 48 percent attributed to paramilitary organizations and 38 percent to guerrilla organizations, from October 1995 through March. The CCJ claimed the impunity rate for politically motivated crimes is virtually 100 percent.

Another source came to a similar finding. Combined data collected by the Justice and Peace Commission and CINEP showed evidence sufficient to establish a probable perpetrator in 582 extrajudicial killings (including unresolved forced disappearances) known or presumed to be politically motivated during the first 9 months of 1996, compared with 342 political murders during the first 9 months of 1995. Of the perpetrators generically identified in 1996, 6 percent were military, 2 percent were police, 59 percent were members of paramilitary groups, and 33 percent were guerrillas. In absolute numbers, extrajudicial killings attributed to the military and police dropped slightly (55 to 49), representing 8 percent of such killings compared to 16 percent in 1995, even though the overall level of violence escalated. Comparing January through September for 1995 and 1996 respectively, paramilitary killings (334 in 1996; 164 in 1995) increased from 48 percent to 59 percent of the total, while guerrilla killings (189 in 1996; 123 in 1995) accounted for 33 percent of the total, down slightly from 36 percent in 1995. Thus both paramilitary and guerrilla killings increased significantly in absolute numbers during the months of January through September. The CINEP, the Justice and Peace Commission, and the CCJ caution, however, that these relative comparisons could change significantly if all the perpetrators could be identified. They agree that the statistics represent rough approximations which at best point to general trends.

Human rights monitors reported continued incidents of social cleansing—including attacks and killings—directed against individuals deemed socially undesirable such as drug addicts, prostitutes, transvestites, beggars, and street children. The Justice and Peace Commission reported 60 cases of social cleansing during the months of January through June; it attributed 22 of those cases to members of paramilitary or private justice groups. In the remaining cases, a likely perpetrator could not be identified. (During the same time period in 1995, Justice and Peace reported 71 cases of social cleansing, and attributed 15 to the police, 6 to paramilitaries, and 12 to the guerrillas.) The Attorney General reported one case under investigation that may have involved a state security agent. The regional prosecutor in Medellin had a former policeman under investigation for participation in a social cleansing group and other crimes.

Killings by paramilitary groups increased significantly, often with the alleged complicity of individual soldiers or of entire military units and with the knowledge and tacit approval of senior military officials. The groups targeted teachers, labor leaders, community activists, mayors of towns and villages, town council members, and, above all, peasants. Many of these victims included members of indigenous communities. The Ombudsman reported that despite a 60 percent increase in various forms of paramilitary activity since 1992, the military failed to give priority to confronting those illicit groups. Whether organized as drug traffickers' private armies or landowners' private defense groups in response to kidnaping threats and extortion demands, these illegal groups reportedly killed suspected guerrilla members and supporters on sight as normal operating procedure.

Allegations of cooperation by members of the armed forces with paramilitary groups, including tacit support and direct collaboration by members of the armed forces, in particular the army, continued to generate controversy. The army commander categorically denied the charge that such cooperation existed, but informed observers reported that tacit arrangements between local military commanders and paramilitary groups did occur in some regions. Both government human rights advocates and academics reported that paramilitary groups freely operated in some areas that were under military control. As paramilitary violence surged in November and December, the Government offered a reward of over $1 million (1 billion pesos) for the capture of paramilitary leader Carlos Castano. Belatedly, the army sent special troops to Sucre department, one of the regions most affected by paramilitary attacks. Concrete results of the Government's efforts by year's end could not be measured.

The Ombudsman and the Prosecutor General's office agreed that some cases show that some members of the armed forces have collaborated with paramilitary groups. The prosecutor ordered the arrest of an army captain and a paramilitary leader implicated in the April massacre of 15 persons in the town of Segovia. It also ordered the arrest of retired three-star army General Farouk Yanine, who voluntarily returned to Colombia to face charges of having supported paramilitary groups in the mid to late 1980's. He is accused of implementing a strategy to have paramilitary groups carry out counterguerrilla activities the army was prohibiting from doing, and with having had knowledge of the 1987 massacre by paramilitaries of 19 civilians suspected of aiding guerrillas. In November the Superior Council of the Judiciary transferred the case to the military justice system. While acquiescing to the Council's ruling, the civilian Prosecutor General demurred that formation of a paramilitary group did not constitute an act of service. General Yanine remained under detention but as yet unindicted while the investigation continued as of year's end.

Although most paramilitary killings remain unsolved, in June the regional prosecutor in Bogota indicted 185 members of paramilitary groups active in the Magdalena Medio region since 1991. The Prosecutor General's human rights unit conducted a broad investigation into the paramilitary groups active in this region since the 1980's. The investigation included extensive testimony of an imprisoned paramilitary member (and former guerrilla) implicated in at least 200 crimes and the deaths of as many as 700 people. In addition to General Yanine, the prosecutor arrested an army colonel and a sergeant and issued a warrant for an army major.

In the case of all four suspects, the Superior Council of the Judiciary transferred jurisdiction to the military justice system. However, paramilitary leaders such as known drug traffickers Fidel and Carlos Castano and emerald magnate Victor Carranza remained beyond the reach of justice.

The Ombudsman attributed the majority of massacres committed in Uraba, Cesar, Cordoba, Magdalena Medio, and the eastern plains to paramilitary groups. Of the 1,379 political murders and 323 disappearances registered by the Permanent Committee for the Defense of Human Rights from January through August, the committee likewise attributed a majority to paramilitary groups and paid killers. The committee cautioned that these totals could rise by 30 to 40 percent if statistics gathered by other NGO's were taken into account.

The leftist coalition party known as the Patriotic Union (UP) continued to be the target of political killing. It has lost approximately 3,500 members in what the UP perceived as a campaign of targeted killings waged against its leadership over the last 11 years. There were 600 reported murders of UP members in Meta department alone since the campaign began, including the head of the Meta Committee for Human Rights, Josue Giraldo, who was killed in October. The Inter-American Commission on Human Rights (IACHR) adopted a resolution requesting the Government to prosecute anyone targeting human rights advocates for murder and to provide protection for Giraldo's family. In May, Aida Abella, national head of the UP and Bogota city council member, was nearly killed in an attack by unknown persons.

The UP brought a complaint before the IACHR that charges the Government with "action or omission" in what the UP terms "political genocide" against the UP and the Communist Party. In its October submission to the IACHR, the human rights organization Fundacion Reiniciar reported that, between January 1 and September 20, UP activists were killed at the rate of one every other day. Many murdered UP members held or had previously held elected office: 1 regional deputy, 13 municipal council members, 2 former mayors, and 3 former council members. UP leader Hernan Motta is the party's member of the Senate, replacing UP leader Manuel Vargas Cepeda who was killed in 1994. An investigation of two army colonels and two army sergeants implicated in his murder was still underway at year's end. A court sentenced the murderers of UP leader Jaime Pardo Leal to prison nearly 10 years after his killing.

In Cesar department, paramilitary enforcers violently displaced peasants from land on the Hacienda Bellacruz in a land dispute in which the national Government had ruled in favor of the peasants. On September 28, paramilitary members killed Eliseo Narvaez, one of the peasant leaders and negotiators, and his brother Eder, bringing to 15 the number of small farmers killed in this dispute since January, according to a report by the National Association of Peasants for Unity and Reconstruction. NGO's cite this case as an example of the central Government's inability or lack of will to enforce the law in the face of deadly paramilitary force.

Overall, paramilitary killings escalated not only in all of the areas which in 1995 suffered the greatest concentration of violence, such as Meta, Uraba, Cordoba and Cesar, but in other regions as well, including Sucre, parts of Antioquia beyond Uraba, Magdalena Medio, and Putumayo. This increase reflects the intensified competition between paramilitary and guerrilla organizations for control across a broad sweep of territory (see Section 1.g.). The victims of paramilitary killings, however, were overwhelmingly unarmed, noncombatant civilians whose summary murders the paramilitary forces rationalized as punishment for possible ties to the guerrillas.

In January unknown assailants shot and killed Marta Elena Sanchez, director of Palmira prison outside Cali. Other unknown assailants killed Miraflores mayor Mauro Restrepo Oliveros that month. In June FARC guerrillas allegedly were responsible for killing the governor of Caqueta department, Jesus Angel Gonzalez.

There was some progress in the case of the 1995 murder of American missionaries Timothy Van Dyke and Steven Walsh. The authorities identified the FARC commanders responsible for these killings and issued warrants for their arrest; however, they were not in custody at year's end (see Section 1.e.).

b. *Disappearance.*—Colombia continued to suffer from extremely high overall rates of disappearance and kidnaping. In July the private foundation Pais Libre and the directorate for the Government's special antikidnaping task forces reported 557 kidnapings during the first half of the year. They estimated that this represented only one-half the actual total because many families of kidnaping victims chose not to report kidnapings in order to conceal ransom negotiations. A U.S. security consulting firm estimated an annual total of 3,500 kidnapings.

The law codifies kidnaping for extortion and "simple kidnaping" as crimes. Efforts to identify the act of forced disappearance as a crime have not been successful, however, in part because the military justice system may treat forced disappearances as acts performed in the line of duty. By October the Attorney General for Human

Rights reported 40 forced disappearances attributed to members of the armed forces, police, and the DAS. NGO's reported several cases of forced disappearances allegedly committed by government forces during the coca cultivators' protests of July and August.

Guerrillas were responsible for between 30 and 50 percent of all kidnapings. They continued to deny, implausibly, that their practice of kidnaping constitutes common criminal extortion. Arrests or prosecutions in any of these cases were rare. Foreigners were attractive targets for kidnaping by both the FARC and the ELN, which generally demanded exorbitant ransom payments for their release.

In April members of an ELN splinter group known as JEGA (Jorge Eliecer Gaitan Alianza) kidnaped Juan Carlos Gaviria, brother of former Colombian president and current OAS Secretary General Cesar Gaviria. JEGA issued a number of incoherent demands for political concessions during the 2 ensuing months, but in June his captors released Gaviria in return for safe conduct to Cuba. This case generated considerable controversy because it represented a departure from government policy not to grant concessions to kidnapers.

In July the paramilitary group headed by Fidel and Carlos Castano began a retaliation campaign of kidnapings, targeting relatives of FARC and ELN leaders. In October the Costa Rican Government granted refuge to 20 threatened guerrilla family members at the petition of the U.N. High Commissioner for Refugees and the Red Cross. Interior Minister Horacio Serpa played a key role in convincing the Costa Rican Government to accept the guerrillas' relatives. As in the Gaviria case, Serpa's intervention marked a departure from the Government's handling of other kidnapings.

FARC guerrillas kidnaped American missionaries David Mankins, Mark Rich, and Rick Tenenoff near the border with Panama on January 31, 1993. Mankins, Rich, and Tenenoff along with their wives and families were members of the New Tribes Mission (NTM) at the time of their kidnaping. For more than 2 years, the FARC has failed to discuss the release of the three missionaries, despite numerous efforts by NTM representatives to contact the FARC.

The Prosecutor General's human rights unit continued its investigation of the 1987 forced disappearance, torture, and murder of Nydia Erika Bautista, a member of the April 19th Movement, or M-19. However, in December the Superior Council of the Judiciary transferred this case to the military justice system. In October the Administrative Tribunal of Cundinamarca ruled that the Government was responsible for the 1990 disappearance of human rights activist Alirio de Jesus Pedraza and ordered that his family receive financial indemnification.

c. *Torture and Other Cruel, Inhuman, or Degrading Treatment or Punishment.*—The law prohibits torture, but reports of incidents of police and military beatings and torture of detainees continued. There was no appreciable decrease in cases of torture committed by individuals from various government security agencies. The Attorney General for Human Rights reported investigating 462 cases of torture committed by the police, DAS, army, prison officials, and other agents of the State during the period from June 1995 to October 1996. These abuses often occurred in connection with illegal detentions in the context of counterinsurgency or counternarcotics operations. In August soldiers beat a cameraman because he had filmed them beating an unarmed civilian during a protest by coca growers and harvesters (see Section 2.a.). Paramilitary groups operating in rural areas were also reportedly responsible for many instances of torture, which, however, cannot be documented. In cases of extrajudicial killings, the authorities rarely sent bodies that bore the traces of physical torture for extensive forensic investigation.

Prison conditions are generally harsh, especially for those prisoners without significant outside support. Overcrowding and dangerous sanitary and health conditions remained a serious problem. Local or regional commanders do not always prepare mandatory detention registers or follow notification procedures, and as a result, accurate detainee counts do not exist.

The International Committee of the Red Cross (ICRC) continued to have access to most prisons and police and military detention centers.

d. *Arbitrary Arrest, Detention, or Exile.*—The Constitution includes several provisions designed to prevent illegal detention; however, the authorities continued to arrest and detain citizens arbitrarily.

Suspects must be brought before a judge within 36 hours of their arrest, and they have a right to petition for habeas corpus from any judge. The judge must act upon that petition within 36 hours of its application. Despite these legal protections, instances of arbitrary detention continued, and a significant percentage of the prison population remained in an undetermined pretrial status. Justice and Peace received 598 reports of arbitrary detentions during the first 6 months of the year, a number far higher than the Ombudsman's full-year count of 374 illegal or arbitrary arrests in 1995. Although the Ombudsman's 1996 figures were not yet available, a similar discrepancy with the NGO's was likely because of different reporting criteria.

The state of emergency permits preventive detention with or without prior judicial authorization but requires the authorities to bring detainees before a judicial officer within 36 hours of arrest. Although the authorities were able to increase the number of arrests, in many cases they failed to bring the detainees before the judicial authorities within the required time. Citizens were thus often held without formal justification before eventually being released. The Government failed to anticipate the impact which its declarations of states of emergency would have on an overburdened judicial system that could not address the needs of citizens even under normal circumstances.

Exile is not practiced.

e. *Denial of Fair Public Trial.*—The judicial system, reorganized under the 1991 Constitution, is largely independent of the executive and legislative branches, both in theory and practice.

The judiciary includes the Constitutional Court, Supreme Court of Justice, the Council of State, the Higher Judiciary Council, tribunals, and courts. The 1991 Constitution modified the structure of the judicial branch by creating the Office of the Prosecutor General as an independent prosecutorial body.

The judiciary has long been subject to threats and intimidation when dealing with cases against members of paramilitary, guerrilla, and narcotics organizations. Although violent attacks against prosecutors and judges dropped with the decline in drug-related terrorism in the late 1980's (and as extradition of Colombian citizens was halted in 1991), prosecutors, judges, and defense attorneys are still subject to threats and acts of violence. In August alleged ELN guerrillas abducted and killed Pedro Alfonso Marquez, director of the prosecutor's office of investigations in La Guajira department. In February a member of the Attorney General's office designated to investigate corruption among government intelligence services was killed with her husband in what appeared to be a contract murder, although no direct link to her work could be established. A civil municipal judge was killed in Cali in August. Other victims included prosecuting attorneys, investigators working on their cases, as well as other employees of courts and prosecutors' offices. Justice and Peace received reports of seven attorneys murdered for political reasons during the first 6 months of the year.

The Constitution specifically provides for the right to due process. The accused has the right to representation by counsel, although representation for the indigenous and the indigent historically has been inadequate. The Government continued to labor under staffing and funding shortages in an effort to develop a credible public defender system. As in past years, the judiciary remained overburdened and often in a state of chaos, staggering under a backlog estimated at over 1 million cases.

The system of justice incorporates regional or public order jurisdictions to prosecute cases involving the crimes of narcotics trafficking, terrorism, kidnaping, subversion, and extortion. In these courts, faceless prosecutors, judges, witnesses, and attorneys act under cover of anonymity for security reasons. The Government intends to end the system of regional jurisdictions in 1999. Human rights groups continued to charge that this system violates basic legal norms and procedural rights, and the Prosecutor General agreed that these cases needed stricter controls and limits. While a late 1993 reform of the Criminal Procedures Code addressed certain procedural shortcomings within the system, problems remained. It was still difficult for defense attorneys to impeach or cross-examine anonymous witnesses, and often they did not have unimpeded access to the State's evidence. As a result of such concerns, judges may no longer base a conviction solely on the testimony of an anonymous witness. Prosecutors, judges, and witnesses generally maintained, however, that the protection of anonymity that is provided by a faceless system is essential to the successful investigation and prosecution of human rights cases in a country where violence is endemic and acts of revenge against those prosecuting violent crime may be expected.

Human rights groups also criticized the Government's policy of allowing major narcotics traffickers to surrender voluntarily and negotiate their sentences. These critics charged that lower-income defendants were at a disadvantage under the system, while powerful criminals received deferential treatment. They also charged that the system, lacking resources, could not effectively prosecute the major guerrilla leaders and was left to handle only low-level criminals suspected of subversive activity. Prosecutors reported, moreover, that potential witnesses in major cases often lacked faith in the Government's ability to protect their anonymity and were unwilling to testify.

The Attorney General's office is part of the Public Ministry. It investigates misconduct by public officials and orders administrative sanctions as applicable. The Attorney General for Human Rights investigates some allegations of human rights abuses by members of the state security apparatus, drawing upon a network of government human rights ombudsmen covering over 1,000 municipalities. The office of the human rights Ombudsman has the constitutional duty to ensure the promotion and exercise of human rights, but it is severely underfunded. In addition to providing public defense attorneys in criminal cases, the Ombudsman's offices throughout the country provide a legal channel for thousands of complaints and allegations of human rights violations. The new Ombudsman, who took office on August 30, reported that his office needed a minimum of 2,000 public defenders to fulfill its constitutional duty. By year's end, however, there were only 500 public defenders. Moreover, the budget the Finance Ministry presented to Congress fell significantly short of the Ombudsman's basic requirements to cover staffing and technical infrastructure.

The Prosecutor General's specially designated human rights unit achieved major results in 1996. Under the direction of a coordinating prosecutor and supported by a team of investigators, this group of 25 faceless prosecutors addressed approximately 100 cases involving massacres, extrajudicial killings, kidnapings, and forced disappearances. They issued numerous arrest warrants against members of the armed forces, paramilitary groups, guerrilla organizations, and drug trafficking organizations and had successfully arrested some of those suspects by year's end (see Section 1.a.). For the first time, the authorities ordered the arrest of a retired three-star general, Farouk Yanine, alleged to have supported paramilitary activity in Magdalena Medio region. The unit also ordered the arrest of an army colonel on similar charges. In addition, the unit identified and issued arrest warrants for the FARC commanders responsible for the June 1995 murders of FARC-abducted American missionaries Timothy Van Dyke and Steve Welsh. In another major case, the authorities arrested an army major and a paramilitary leader on charges of complicity in the April massacre of 15 civilians in the city of Segovia, Antioquia department. Although top military leaders hailed the cases brought against guerrilla leaders, they strongly objected, and in some cases tried to obstruct, prosecution of cases against members of the armed forces and of paramilitary organizations. Decisions by the Superior Council of the Judiciary in November and December to transfer certain key cases to military courts suggested a reversal of its position on military versus civilian jurisdiction earlier in the year and aroused concern that additional cases involving allegations of military collaboration with paramilitary organizations would likewise be passed on to the military courts.

Faceless prosecutors handle most cases involving criminal violations of human rights, with caseloads that commonly exceed 100. In March a faceless judge sentenced four persons to a total of 114 years and 5 months for the 1994 massacre of 20 members of the indigenous Guataba community in Caloto, Cauca department.

The Government states that it does not hold political prisoners. However, the ICRC reported that it monitored approximately 2,000 cases of citizens imprisoned under accusations of rebellion or aiding and abetting the insurgency, which are punishable under law. Critics charge that prisoners held under suspicion of collaboration with guerrillas are detained for political reasons. Many of these prisoners were noncombatants who in some cases were held for months during preliminary proceedings before their cases could be dismissed.

f. *Arbitrary Interference with Privacy, Family, Home, or Correspondence.*—The law generally requires a judicial order for authorities to enter a private home, except in cases of hot pursuit. In remote regions, the military forces have civilian prosecutorial units attached to them. Some human rights groups charged that these attached units were unconstitutional, and Congress has so far refused to grant them permanent status. To address this problem, the Ministry of Defense continued training in legal search procedures that comply with constitutional and human rights.

A judicial order is likewise required to authorize telephone monitoring and the interception of mail. This protection extends to prisoners held in jails. However, various state authorities monitor telephones without obtaining authorization.

g. *Use of Excessive Force and Violations of Humanitarian Law in Internal ConflictsThe internal armed conflict and narcotics trafficking are the central causes of violations of human rights and humanitarian law. Guerrilla and paramilitary groups, in particular, but also government security forces violated international humanitarian law in Colombia's internal conflict. The ICRC reported that the Government, including military authorities, followed an open door policy toward the ICRC and incorporated Red Cross curriculums on international humanitarian law in standard military training. A persistent, if unofficial, emphasis by the army on body count as a means of assessing field performance is a main contributing cause of vio-*

lations of international humanitarian law. With rare exceptions, according to military sources, local commanders typically preferred to discharge soldiers accused of raping civilian women and other serious human rights violations, rather than to initiate court martial proceedings.

A consortium of NGO's in eastern Antioquia reported an operation conducted on January 29 by 40 soldiers of a battalion stationed at Rionegro together with a number of civilians, who surrounded the San Vicente home of the Diaz Alzate. The attackers fired indiscriminately and threw two grenades at the house in which two elderly members of the family, two adults, and one child were present. The head of the household was wounded and taken to the military base where he was held for 24 hours before the family was informed of his whereabouts. Also in January, witnesses reported receiving threats from paramilitary groups in the city of Ocana that they should attend a meeting of business people, allegedly guarded by soldiers, at which members of paramilitary groups subjected the attendees to death threats and extortion if they did not cooperate with the military forces in the region.

In Sucre, during the first 113 days of the year, paramilitary or self-defense groups killed 137 persons. This escalation of violence effectively forced 800 families to abandon their land. The victims were typically campesinos, teachers, civic leaders, and other noncombatants suspected of sympathizing with guerrillas. The violence continued throughout the year, with a marked upsurge beginning in late November. The paramilitary massacre of 17 peasants during a 1-day campaign was just one of a number of paramilitary attacks in Sucre. The CINEP reported that Putumayo department had surpassed Uraba with Colombia's highest violent death rate, 425 per 100,000 persons, in 1995. Firearms were used in 95 percent of these killings. That violence escalated in the first months of 1996, according to the CINEP and the Putumayo Departmental Committee for Human Rights. Both attributed the violence to drug traffickers, guerrillas, and paramilitary groups. A paramilitary group massacred 15 people in Segovia, Antioquia, in April. In May the prosecutor arrested an army captain and a paramilitary organization member in connection with the massacre. Parts of Antioquia also saw an escalation of paramilitary violence during November and December. The year ended with a massacre on December 31 by paramilitaries of as many as 11 civilians, including 2 indigenous leaders of the Nendo community in Dabeiba, Antioquia.

On February 15, Protocol II of the Geneva Convention entered into force. The Constitutional Court had earlier ruled that the law ratifying the protocol would be equally applicable to government and guerrilla forces. Despite some pronouncements of support, guerrilla organizations continued to pursue a strategy that included kidnaping, targeting of civilian populations and installations, deployment of land mines, and recruitment of minors.

The loosely organized guerrilla groups of the Simon Bolivar Coordinating Body, which include primarily the FARC and ELN, commanded an estimated 10,000 to 15,000 full-time guerrillas organized in over 100 "fronts." These groups exercised a degree of permanent influence in over half of Colombia's local municipalities. They committed a host of violations, including killings, kidnapings, deployment of antipersonnel land mines, oil pipeline bombings, and other acts of sabotage.

According to estimates by CINEP and Justice and Peace, guerrillas were responsible for killing at least 189 civilians between January and September. In the continuing struggle for control of the narcotics and arms trafficking corridor of Uraba, guerrilla retaliation for paramilitary attacks regularly victimized innocent civilians, although some direct clashes with paramilitary units did occur. To justify summary executions of civilians, guerrillas typically charged that their victims were either informants for the army or related in some other way to the State, or that they simply refused to support the guerrillas' operations.

The FARC continued its campaign of assassination against the Hope, Peace, and Freedom Movement, whose members had left the EPL in the early 1990's and had since become active in the National Syndicate of Agro-Industry Workers in Uraba. FARC guerrillas killed 2 children near Miraflores, Guaviare, when they detonated 1 of 50 land mines that their forces had deployed in the area. The FARC's September attack on unarmed policemen playing sports in the town of Uramita, Antioquia, was typical. In addition to one policeman and one adult civilian, the FARC killed a 3-year-old child during the attack. In another incident the FARC killed four policemen transporting prisoners in Antioquia. They then released the prisoners, including three murderers and one narcotics trafficker. In August and September, FARC forces killed over 100 people, at one point paralyzing traffic in half the country's departments by threatening to burn vehicles on the highway.

The National Liberation Army (ELN) also targeted civilians. In one incident in May, ELN guerrillas intercepted a bus and shot four of its passengers. There are confirmed reports of continued instances of ELN and FARC death threats against the girlfriends, fiancees, and wives of policemen and soldiers. According to press reports, in November an ELN front active in southern Antioquia summarily executed 11 of its own members.

In May a FARC guerrilla attack killed at least 16 persons, including 2 children, in the fishing town of Turbo, Uraba. The guerrillas burned numerous houses; 20 persons were victims of forced disappearance. In September members of the fifth FARC front summarily executed four rural community leaders near Apartado, Uraba. In February the ELN attacked and nearly killed the 17-year-old girlfriend of a policeman.

On March 13, FARC guerrillas attacked a police station in Chalan, Sucre, killing 11 police members. The police accused townspeople of advance knowledge of the attack, and eventually withdrew from the town center. Paramilitaries moved in shortly thereafter. On April 15, a guerrilla ambush killed 31 soldiers on patrol, and Jose Maya Garcia, chair of the Chamber of Representatives' peace commission, was kidnaped. These assaults prompted President Samper to create special public order zones by decree 2 days later.

On August 30, FARC and ELN guerrillas coordinated forces to launch a major offensive, with 28 attacks in 11 departments during a 48-hour period. The most notable attack was the FARC assault on an army outpost in Las Delicias, Putumayo department. The guerrillas killed 29 soldiers and took another 60 hostage. At year's end, the soldiers remained in FARC custody, with negotiations for their release at an impasse. Guerrilla violence continued at an escalated level throughout September and October, with roadblocks and sporadic killings throughout the country.

Initial reports implicated guerrillas in the social cleansing homicide of two other individuals in Valle del Cauca department in February. Guerrilla organizations continued to recruit minors between the ages of 12 and 15; some press accounts reported cases of children under the age of 12 among guerrilla ranks. Once recruited, the child guerrillas are virtual prisoners of their commanders and subject to various forms of widespread abuse. Sexual abuse of young girls is a particular problem.

In general, the guerrilla leadership continued to exploit the issue of human rights violations for propaganda purposes but took no measurable steps to abide by international standards. In March the Dutch NGO Pax Christi sharply criticized the FARC leadership for their human rights practices. The FARC demonstrated this lack of good faith by drawing out negotiations for the release of the soldiers captured during the attack on Las Delicias and reneging on their promise to release the soldiers to the ICRC. The president of the Catholic Conference of Bishops criticized the FARC leadership for prolonging the captive soldiers' ordeal and made a direct televised appeal for their immediate release, to no avail.

A CINEP report on violence in Putumayo department also cited guerrilla violations of international humanitarian law. Other accounts of guerrilla abuse included reports that the bodies of 20 soldiers killed at La Carpa in Guaviare department in September showed signs of mutilation by dogs. The FARC force had overwhelmed a small army unit called in to aid a small community that had been harassed and intimidated by the guerrillas.

In 1994 the Government initiated a program to organize and register legal civilian rural defense cooperatives, known collectively as Convivir, which were to provide counterinsurgency intelligence to local military commanders. These groups numbered approximately 200 by June, primarily in central and northern Colombia, according to the CINEP. Although the authorities originally intended these groups to be unarmed, by mid-1996 they had authorized a number of them to carry arms. By year's end, government officials had received the first citizen complaints that some of these groups had exceeded their authority and were acting as vigilantes.

Although the governor of Antioquia expressed the belief that the Convivir groups could be controlled, some mayors and other local officials in Antioquia disagreed. The Ombudsman's 1996 report to Congress reiterated his office's opposition to the Convivir program. Citing the Government's inability to control such groups in past administrations, the Ombudsman expressed concern that the Convivir cooperatives, too, would lack accountability. Other government human rights monitors expressed similar concerns.

Drug traffickers, guerrillas, and common criminals continued to target soldiers and police on a daily basis. A FARC ambush that killed 31 soldiers in April was typical of the guerrilla strategy of attacking small and vulnerable units. Guerrillas intensified this strategy during the September offensive which began with the attack on Las Delicias.

Section 2. Respect for Civil Liberties, Including:

a. *Freedom of Speech and Press.*—The authorities generally respected these constitutionally protected rights, but were quick to apply subtle (and not so subtle) pressure on the media when their core interests were threatened. Most media resisted such pressure, but the less powerful media organizations submitted to it. Other signs of government efforts to influence the media included occasional calls on patriotic grounds to limit negative reporting that might hurt the country's image in the world. On January 30, a member of the National Television Commission ordered the state-controlled television network to cut off the live broadcast of congressional debate that followed the President's address to a special session of Congress. The Government thus cut off a Senator in the midst of her denunciation of the President, based on her first-hand knowledge, for having solicited contributions from drug traffickers for his presidential campaign.

The National Television Commission threatened to review the license of the television newscast "24 HOURS" unless the news director appeared before the commission and justified an interview with a foreign ambassador that was critical of the President. The threat was an obvious effort by Samper administration allies on the commission to intimidate newscasts into softening their stances toward the Government.

In December the National Television Commission singled out "TV HOY," a national television news network, by threatening to impose a fine and a 2-day broadcast suspension for an inaccurate report. The network retracted the broadcast report, but at year's end, the issue of the fine and the suspension remained unresolved. Critics charged that the Commission was selectively applying standards of accuracy, its primary criterion apparently being whether a report reflected positively on President Samper's image.

Congressional allies of the Samper administration introduced legislation that would suspend the licenses of 12 television newscasts, valid under existing law until December 31, 2003. Ignoring concerns expressed by the Inter-American Press Association (IAPA), Congress passed and in late December, President Samper signed into law fundamental changes in treatment of television newscasts that are expected to have a chilling effect on freedom of the press. The new law revoked previous hands-off licensing procedures and made license holders of television newscasts on the three government channels subject to review—and possible revocation and mandatory exclusion from television newscasting for 5 years—every 6 months. This law also opens the door to the creation of two new private television channels that will fall under the ownership of economic conglomerates that have historically enjoyed a privileged relationship with whatever government is in power. While court challenges are expected, the new law is an obvious effort by the Samper administration to eliminate troubling television news coverage of a scandal-ridden administration and to reward its powerful backers for remaining loyal. Television news, previously relatively free, albeit prone to sensationalism and low journalistic standards, is now subject as never before to intrusive government censorship.

The privately owned print media published a wide spectrum of political viewpoints and often voiced harsh antigovernment opinions without administrative reprisals. The Government imposed some restrictions on electronic media coverage of incidents of public disorder and of drug terrorist activity and reserved the right to prohibit coverage of certain news events that could affect state security. During the protest of coca growers and harvesters in Caqueta department in August, army soldiers injured two television cameramen. The soldiers severely beat one cameramen because he had filmed them beating an unarmed civilian.

Under a state of emergency the Government may regulate the media only to the extent of controlling information that may endanger lives or directly induce public disturbances. The Government may use television and radio stations as it deems appropriate but may not prohibit reports of human rights violations. The Government may not establish an official censorship board, but accredited media associations are to act as a self-regulatory tribunal.

All citizens have the right to seek a judicial injunction or motion (tutela) in cases involving violations of basic constitutional rights. This provides all persons and organizations, including the media, with a mechanism to denounce both private and government violations of basic constitutional rights.

In October unknown assailants murdered journalist Norvey Diaz in Cundinamarca department. For over 5 years, Diaz had investigated and reported the existence of social cleansing groups, which he claimed had links to the police in the city of Girardot. He had received death threats throughout the year. The Ombudsman reported in 1995 that 107 journalists had been murdered since 1980—often victims of paramilitary organizations, guerrilla groups, and narcotics traffickers.

Both Colombian and international journalists typically work in an atmosphere of threat. In January Mexican journalist Jorge Ramos of the Univision News Network curtailed his stay because of death threats he received after an interview with former Defense Minister Fernando Botero. During that interview, Botero accused President Samper of being behind the strategy to solicit campaign donations from drug traffickers. In February DAS agents detained a journalist who was collaborating with Botero on a forthcoming book. They questioned her at the Bogota airport and reportedly photocopied her notes before permitting her departure. Another Univision journalist, Colombian Raul Benoit, was the target of a murder attempt in March in connection with his work.

The Government generally respected academic freedom, and there exists a wide spectrum of political activity throughout the country's universities. Paramilitary groups and guerrillas, however, often targeted teachers at the elementary and secondary levels in areas of conflict. They also threatened university-level academics doing studies on internal conflict and human rights.

b. *Freedom of Peaceful Assembly and Association.*—The Constitution provides for freedom of peaceful assembly and association, and the Government respects these rights in practice. The authorities do not normally interfere with public meetings and demonstrations and usually grant the required permission except when they determine that there is imminent danger to public order. In Bogota, however, officials who routinely issue demonstration permits indicated they were under pressure to discriminate against some of the civic action groups that organized to criticize the President. Any organization is free to associate with international groups in its field.

NGO's criticized the Government's response to protest demonstrations involving an estimated 80,000 to 150,000 "cocaleros" (coca cultivators and field workers, supported in part by guerrillas and narcotics traffickers) who mobilized in July, August, and early September to impede the Government's counternarcotics operations in coca-growing regions. In the resulting confrontations, government forces generally abided by standing orders not to employ deadly force. However, soldiers did kill some protesters, and some abuses were alleged. Investigators sent to the region by a consortium of NGO's attributed 13 killings to the army, 1 to the police, and 4 to guerrillas. They cautioned, however, that the death toll may have been higher. An estimated 200 demonstrators were injured; soldiers and police also sustained injuries. The NGO delegation reported other types of abuse, including incidents of excessive use of force, forced disappearances, arbitrary arrests, destruction of private property, and eradication of legitimate crops. The NGO's also reported that the murder of two soldiers may have been related to the protest.

c. *Freedom of Religion.*—The Constitution provides for complete religious freedom, and the Government respects this right in practice. There is little religious discrimination. Roman Catholic religious instruction is no longer mandatory in state schools, and a Constitutional Court decision in 1994 found unconstitutional any official government reference to religious characterizations of the country. The Government permits proselytizing among the indigenous population, provided that it is welcome and does not induce members of indigenous communities to adopt changes that endanger their survival on traditional lands. The law on the freedom of cults provides a mechanism for religions to obtain the status of recognized legal entities.

d. *Freedom of Movement Within the Country, Foreign Travel, Emigration, and Repatriation.*—The Constitution provides citizens with the right to travel domestically and abroad. Outsiders wishing to enter Indian tribes' reserves must be invited. In areas where military operations against guerrillas are underway, police or military officials occasionally required civilians to obtain safe-conduct passes; guerrillas reportedly used similar means to restrict travel in areas under their control. Guerrilla incursions, military counterinsurgency operations, guerrilla and paramilitary conscription, and land seizures by narcotics traffickers often forced peasants to flee their homes and farms. In October the office of the President's adviser for human rights reported that 750,000 out of a total population of 35 million are displaced persons. This marks a significant increase since 1995, when the Colombian Conference of Bishops reported 600,000 displaced persons. The President's adviser attributed the mass displacement to the presence of paramilitary, guerrilla, and narcotics trafficking organizations in many regions and the armed confrontations among them, as well as with the armed forces. The report cited factors such as threats, murder attempts, selective killings, massacres, torture, and aerial combat operations provoked by participants in the armed conflict. The adviser's office further estimated that 195 persons per day must leave their homes because of the violence.

According to the System of Information on Households Displaced by Violence (SISDES), the army was responsible for 16 percent of the displacement, paramilitary organizations for 32 percent, and guerrilla organizations for 26 percent. SISDES attributed the remaining 26 percent to the influence of the police, urban militias, and drug traffickers. The Uraba region of Antioquia and Choco departments suffered the greatest displacement. The Ombudsman reported that 300,000 persons fled Uraba for other regions during the last 10 years.

A case that aroused considerable controversy was that of 106 families violently displaced by members of paramilitary groups from land in Cesar department that the Colombian ambassador to the European Union claims to be his property. Many of these families sought shelter with the Ombudsman in Bogota, where they remained at year's end for lack of other refuge. On November 5, the ambassador resigned, following an October 24 resolution by the European Parliament criticizing the Government for gross human rights violations and calling for the ambassador to step down. Displaced persons continued to face a crucial dilemma: They could not stay in conflict zones because of legitimate fears for their safety, but they also were rejected and perceived as an economic burden by the regions and cities that were their most common destinations.

Colombia has had a tradition of providing political asylum since the 1920's. During the 1970's, Colombia granted asylum to Argentine, Chilean, Uruguayan, and Paraguayan citizens seeking refuge from dictatorial regimes in their own countries.

The Government cooperates with the office of the United Nations High Commissioner for Refugees and other humanitarian organizations in assisting refugees. The Government reserves the right to determine eligibility for asylum, based upon its own assessment of the political nature of the persecution an applicant may have suffered. The issue of the provision of first asylum did not arise. There were no reports of the forced return of persons to a country where they feared persecution.

Section 3. Respect for Political Rights: The Right of Citizens to Change Their Government

Citizens exercise this right in regular, secret ballot elections that have historically been considered fair and open. However, critics question if they are indeed fair, pointing out that vote buying is a regular feature of elections in some regions, and that President Samper's 1994 election campaign solicited and received contributions from drug traffickers. Presidential elections are held every 4 years. The Liberal and Conservative parties have long monopolized the formal political process with one or the other customarily winning the presidency. The President serves only one term and may not be reelected. All citizens are enfranchised at the age of 18. Public employees are not permitted to participate in campaigns but, with the exception of the military, may vote. Officially, all political parties operate freely without government interference. Those that fail to garner 50,000 votes in a general election may lose the right to present candidates and may not receive funds from the Government. However, they may reincorporate at any time by presenting 50,000 signatures to the National Electoral Board.

The 1991 Constitution created the office of vice president, replacing an arguably less significant "presidential designate," elected by Congress. In 1994 the country held a national presidential election as well as congressional, gubernatorial, and mayoral elections. For the first time, the country also elected a Vice President, Humberto de la Calle, who ran on the Liberal Party ticket with presidential candidate Ernesto Samper. (Carlos Lemos Simmonds replaced De la Calle, who resigned in September.) Liberal Party representatives made a strong showing in the congressional elections, providing a Liberal majority in both houses. However, bipartisan coalitions were still often necessary for the Liberals to enact legislation. A group of Conservative Party supporters was key in the 111-to-44 vote not to impeach Samper on charges of knowingly receiving campaign contributions from drug traffickers.

The high level of violence has a profound effect on the political process: Reiniciar's report to the IACHR listed freely elected officials forced to leave Colombia because of death threats. In addition to the murdered UP officials (see Section 1.a.), the office of the High Commissioner for Peace reported that 1,143 civic and political leaders of other parties were killed between 1990 and 1995.

There are no legal restrictions, and few practical ones, on the participation of women or minorities in the political process. Seven female senators and 19 female representatives served among the 267 members of Congress, including the first vice president of the House of Representatives. The Ministers of Foreign Affairs, Agriculture, Education, and Health were women, as were the President's advisers for juridical affairs, for Bogota, for Medellin, and for public administration affairs.

The Constitution reserves 2 seats in the 102-seat Senate for representatives of the indigenous population, and a 1993 law set aside 2 seats in the 165-seat House of Representatives for citizens of African heritage. In September, however, the Constitutional Court declared the latter law unconstitutional. The Court tasked the two African-Colombian representatives to redraft the law during the remaining 2 years of their terms in order to establish the permanent seats in a manner consistent with provisions of the 1991 Constitution.

Section 4. Governmental Attitude Regarding International and Nongovernmental Investigation of Alleged Violations of Human Rights

A large nongovernmental human rights community is active. It includes the Center for Investigations and Popular Research, the Colombian Commission of Jurists, the Intercongregational Commission for Justice and Peace, the Permanent Committee for the Defense of Human Rights, the Catholic Bishops Conference, the Latin American Institute for Alternative Legal Services, the Association of Families of Detained and Disappeared Persons, and Peace Brigades International.

NGO's investigated and reported on human rights abuses committed by government forces, the paramilitaries, and guerrillas. They expressed serious concern at what they viewed to be the increasing militarization of Colombia as the internal armed conflict escalated, and with it, a loss of interest in seeking peace through negotiation. NGO's almost unanimously criticized the deterioration of the Samper administration's human rights policies, particularly his reliance on declared states of emergency and establishment of special order zones—which they characterized as allowing the military to displace civil authority, and imposing abusive restrictions on citizens. NGO's were highly critical of the Government's handling of the protest of the cocaleros, whom they believed unfairly bore the brunt of the Government's antidrug policy.

The Government in November took a significant step to expand human rights monitoring by signing an agreement with the United Nations High Commissioner on Human Rights to establish a field office in Bogota. This seven-person office, scheduled to open in February 1997, is to monitor, analyze, and report on human rights abuses throughout the country. It is expected to serve as an experiment and model for other countries under U.N. scrutiny for their high incidence of human rights violations.

The Government has an extensive human rights apparatus, which includes the office of the President's Adviser for Human Rights, the Ombudsman and its regional representatives, the Attorney General's office for human rights and regional representatives, and a special unit within the Prosecutor General's office. The Ministry of Defense has had a Secretariat for Human Rights since 1994, with a system of 208 human rights offices, down to the battalion level, distributed through all branches of the armed services, including the police. By year's end, the Interior Ministry had selected a candidate to head its new human rights office, which is to expand existing programs within the Ministry. The Red Cross and presidential adviser collaborated with the armed services to expand training in human rights and international humanitarian law.

In general, a state of estrangement continued between the Samper administration and the NGO's, which found no reason to return to the Joint Commission on Human Rights which they left in 1995. Prominent military officials voiced feelings of frustration and outright hostility toward the NGO community. After much debate, a majority of NGO's agreed that the establishment of a field office of the U.N. Commissioner for Human Rights was a workable alternative to a Special Rapporteur. This agreement implied recognition for the efforts of the Government's civilian human rights officials who proposed the office despite fierce opposition from high-ranking military officials. Nevertheless, the corps of government human rights advisers and monitors was often unsuccessful in getting its recommendations adopted on government policy issues.

Although the Government generally did not interfere with the work of human rights NGO's, staff members and volunteers often faced threats and intimidation by individual members of the police and armed forces, paramilitary groups, or guerrillas. Since October human rights lawyer Pedro Julio Macheca Avila has been under surveillance by unidentified individuals who also attempted to locate members of his family. The motivation for this pattern of harassment may be Macheca Avila's legal representation of controversial figures, among whom are acknowledged members of the ELN guerrilla group. Macheca Avila's representation of peasant families threatened by paramilitaries in Cesar department may also be the cause of the harassment.

Peace Brigades International expressed concern that an investigation of the organization in June by the SIJIN (local police investigators), possibly working with the army, may have been part of an effort to intimidate and discredit the organization. Many prominent human rights monitors worked under constant fear for their physical safety. The executive director of the Permanent Committee for the Protection of Human Rights left the country in May after narrowly escaping an attempt on his life by armed assailants.

The outgoing Ombudsman expressed serious concern over the Samper administration's declining commitment to human rights programs initiated during the President's first year in office. This decline began in mid-1995 with the onset of the political crisis related to formal testimony indicating that President Samper knew of and welcomed donations from drug traffickers to his 1994 presidential campaign. Many government and NGO human rights monitors expressed concern that Samper's failure to promote reform of the military justice system, coupled with hard-line Senators' "counterreform" proposals, indicated a growing willingness by both the executive and legislative branches to cede to the military some of the already limited checks that the Attorney General and Prosecutor General exercise under the 1991 Constitution. Such counterreforms are scheduled for congressional debate in 1997.

Section 5. Discrimination Based on Race, Sex, Religion, Disability, Language, or Social Status

The Constitution specifically prohibits discrimination based on race, sex, religion, disability, language, or social status. In practice, however, many of these provisions are not enforced.

NGO's report that homosexuals are occasional victims of violence and the vigilante killings known as social cleansing.

Women.—Rape and other acts of violence against women are pervasive in society, and like other crimes, are seldom prosecuted successfully. Spousal abuse in itself is not considered a crime. The quasi-governmental Institute for Family Welfare (ICBF) and the Presidential adviser's Office for Youth, Women, and Family Affairs continued to report high levels of spouse and partner abuse throughout the country. The ICBF conducted programs and provided refuge and counseling for victims of spouse abuse, but the level and amount of these services were dwarfed by the magnitude of the problem.

The law provides relatively mild sentences, ranging from 6 months to 8 years, for crimes of sexual abuse and allows for significant sentence reductions based on the conduct of the convicted perpetrator. In cases of sexual abuse, police may not legally detain the perpetrators unless the abuse was committed in conjunction with other crimes. In most cases, the assailant is released because the law permits the probationary release of criminals convicted of crimes carrying minimum sentences of less than 2 years. In July President Samper signed Law 294 on family violence, which identifies as crimes violent acts committed within families, including spousal rape. It also provides legal recourse for victims of family violence, immediate protection from physical or psychological abuse, and judicial authority to remove the abuser from the household. The law also allows a judge to oblige an abuser to seek therapy or reeducation. For acts of spousal sexual violence, the law mandates sentences of 6 months to 2 years. It denies probation or bail to offenders who disobey court restraining orders. At year's end, it was too soon to measure the effect the new law may have.

The Constitution prohibits any form of discrimination against women and specifically requires the authorities to "guarantee adequate and effective participation by women at decisionmaking levels of public administration." Even prior to implementation of the 1991 Constitution, the law had provided women with extensive civil rights. Despite these constitutional provisions, however, discrimination against women persists. According to figures published by the United Nations, women's earnings for formal sector, nonagricultural work correspond to approximately 85 percent of men's earnings for comparable work, and women must demonstrate higher qualifications than men when applying for jobs. Moreover, women constitute a disproportionately high percentage of the subsistence labor work force, especially in rural areas. Women's groups such as Promujer and the Association of Twenty-First Century Women reported that the social and economic problems of single mothers remained great throughout the year, despite government efforts to provide them with training in parenting skills.

Children.—The Government provide public education, which is compulsory for children 6 through 14 years of age. Nevertheless, an estimated 25 percent of children in this age group do not attend school, due to lax enforcement of truancy laws and inadequate classroom space.

Despite significant constitutional and legislative commitments to the protection of the rights of children, these were only minimally implemented. The Constitution imposes the obligation on family, society, and the State to assist and protect children, to foster their development, and to assure the full exercise of these rights. A special Children's Code sets forth many of these rights and establishes services and programs designed to enforce the protection of minors. Children's advocates reported the need to educate citizens with regard to the code as well as the new Law on Family Violence, which was drafted particularly to increase legal protection for women and children. The ICBF oversees all government child protection and welfare programs and funds nongovernmental and church programs for children.

Child prostitution was commonplace in the five major cities. In Medellin the city initiated in August a program called "Street Dwellers" as an outreach program to assist child prostitutes ranging in age from 8 to 18 years. Street children continued to be the targets of social cleansing gangs. In conflict zones, children were also often caught in the crossfire between the security forces, paramilitary groups, and guerrilla organizations. Deadly land mines known as "leg breakers" laid by guerrillas killed or mutilated many children in these areas. Guerrilla groups continued to recruit minors, and there were increased reports that they sexually abused teenage female recruits. According to figures published by the army, approximately 2,000 children participated in some fashion in the guerrilla combat. An estimated 48 percent of all persons displaced by violence are children. According to statistics compiled by the President's antikidnaping czar and the Pais Libre foundation, children surpassed businessmen and ranchers as prime kidnaping targets during the first months of the year.

People With Disabilities.—The Constitution enumerates the fundamental social, economic, and cultural rights of the physically disabled, but serious practical impediments exist to prevent disabled persons' full participation in society. There is no legislation that specifically mandates access for people with disabilities. According to the Constitutional Court, physically disabled individuals must have access to receive assistance at voting stations. Also according to a Constitutional Court ruling, the social security fund for public employees cannot refuse to provide services for the disabled children of its members, regardless of the cost involved.

Indigenous People.—There are approximately 82 distinct ethnic groups among the 800,000 indigenous inhabitants. The Constitution gives special recognition to the fundamental rights of indigenous people. It provides for a special criminal and civil jurisdiction, based upon traditional community laws, within Indian territories. The Ministry of Interior, through the Office of Indigenous Affairs, is responsible for protecting the territorial, cultural, and self-determination rights of Indians. Ministry representatives are located in all regions of the country with indigenous populations and work with other governmental human and civil rights organizations to promote Indian interests and investigate violations of indigenous rights. Nonetheless, members of indigenous groups suffer discrimination in the sense that they have traditionally been relegated to the margins of society. Few opportunities exist for those who might wish to participate more fully in modern life.

Traditional Indian authority boards operate some 334 designated Indian reserves; the boards handle national or local funds and are subject to fiscal oversight by the national Comptroller General. These boards administer their territories as municipal entities, with officials elected or otherwise chosen according to Indian tradition. Indigenous communities are free to educate their children in traditional dialects and in the observance of cultural and religious customs. Indigenous men are not subject to the national military draft.

In June members of the Wayuu community occupied the headquarters of the Government's Office of Indigenous Affairs to protest what the wayuu considered the Government's condescending treatment of the community. The protesters subsequently moved their protest to the offices of the Colombian Conference of Bishops. The protest ended after 36 days, when the Government issued two decrees creating a human rights commission for indigenous communities and a permanent board for coordination with the indigenous communities.

Indigenous communities suffer disproportionately from the internal armed conflict. In September 4,000 members of indigenous communities gathered in Popayan, the capital of Cauca department to protest the presence of government forces paramilitaries, and guerrilla in their territories and to meet with government authorities to initiate a dialog on better health and education services, environmental protection, and agricultural development.

A contract that Ecopetrol, the national oil company, awarded to Occidental Petroleum caused a direct conflict with the W'wa indigenous community. Despite a provision of the 1991 Constitution obliging the Government to consult indigenous populations before allowing any development or change on indigenous territory, the contract called for Occidental Petroleum to conduct a geological survey for petroleum sources. In response to a formal request by the Ombudsman, a Bogota tribunal issued an injunction ordering the Government to respect the w'wa community's rights in this matter. The Supreme Court subsequently granted an appeal filed by Ecopetrol and Occidental. That decision in turn threw the case to the Constitutional Court for a final ruling which was still pending at year's end.

Despite official government policy to protect indigenous populations, members of indigenous communities were frequently the victims of violence throughout the year. By August 12 members of the Senu community of the San Andres de Sotavento indigenous reserve, including the community's mayor, had been killed. In zones where the guerrillas were active, such as the Sierra Nevada and Valle de Cauca, the security forces often suspected the indigenous population of complicity with narcotics traffickers and guerrillas. However, most of the incidents in which people attacked or threatened Indians stemmed from land ownership disputes concerning the designated Indian reserves. The National Land Reform Institute estimated that some 40 indigenous communities had lost legal title to land that they claimed as their own and that roughly 100 other groups had title claims that were not recognized or reconciled.

National/Racial/Ethnic Minorities.—Approximately 2 million citizens of African heritage live primarily in the Pacific departments of Choco, Valle del Cauca, and Narino, and along the Caribbean coast. They represent roughly 4 percent of the total population, although representatives of the African-Colombian community believe their population is much larger. Blacks are entitled to all constitutional rights and protections but have traditionally suffered from economic discrimination.

Despite the passage of the African-Colombian Law in 1993, little concrete progress was made in expanding public services and private investment in the Choco or other predominantly black regions. In September the Government established a special fund to provide scholarships and credits to expand African-Colombians' access to higher education. Allegations of discrimination and hazing by the military against African-Colombians continued. The navy makes little effort to recruit African-Colombians, despite their traditional ties to the sea and maritime commerce. Like other communities on the margins of society, Afro-Colombians suffered disproportionately from political violence, particularly in the struggle between paramilitary and guerrilla forces for control of Uraba. Unemployment among African-Colombians is as high as 76 percent in some communities.

Section 6. Worker Rights

a. *The Right of Association.*—The law recognizes the rights of workers to organize unions and strike. The Labor Code provides for automatic recognition of unions that obtain at least 25 signatures from the potential members and comply with a simple registration process at the Labor Ministry. The law penalizes interference with freedom of association. It allows unions to determine freely internal rules, elect officials, and manage activities, and forbids the dissolution of trade unions by administrative fiat. According to Labor Ministry estimates, approximately 7 percent of the work force is organized in 2,235 unions.

The 1991 Constitution provides for the right to strike by nonessential public employees and authorizes Congress to pass enabling legislation that would define "essential," but legislation that prohibits public employees from striking is still in force. Before staging a legal strike, unions must negotiate directly with management and—if no agreement results—accept mediation. By law, public employees must accept binding arbitration if mediation fails; in practice, public service unions decide by membership vote whether or not to seek arbitration.

In 1993 the International Labor Organization (ILO) criticized 10 provisions of the law, including: The supervision of the internal management and meetings of unions by government officials; the presence of officials at assemblies convened to vote on a strike call; the legality of firing union organizers from jobs in their trades once 6 months have passed following a strike or dispute; the requirement that contenders for trade union office must belong to the occupation their union represents; the prohibition of strikes in a wide range of public services that are not necessarily essential; various restrictions on the right to strike; the power of the Minister of Labor and the President to intervene in disputes through compulsory arbitration when a strike is declared illegal; and the power to dismiss trade union officers involved in an unlawful strike.

On October 14 truck drivers staged a major strike that paralyzed cargo transport in many regions of the country. The Minister of Transportation declared the strike illegal and ordered the truckers back to work. When they refused, the Government declared that it would consider taking legal action against 105 trucking companies, arrested 60 drivers, and investigated 216 cargo vehicle owners. The strike ended after 11 days, when government and trucking representatives reached an accord raising the allowable cost of cargo transport.

A collective work convention signed in 1995 between Ecopetrol and the Union of Syndicated Labor (USO) remained in effect. That accord was the result of the Government's restructuring, rather than privatizing, Ecopetrol to avoid massive layoffs. The USO leadership remained in open conflict with the Government on many issues. USO leaders reported further that its members continued to receive death threats from presumed paramilitary groups active in the oil-producing Magdalena Medio region.

Labor leaders throughout the country continued to be the target of attacks by the military, police, paramilitary groups, guerrillas, narcotics traffickers, and their own union rivals. In April the Latin American Central of Workers reported that at least 2,000 Colombian union members and leaders had been killed since 1991. According to figures published by Justice and Peace, during the first 6 months of 1996, 14 labor activists were murdered in connection with their labor activities. The report listed 2 presumed murdered because of their labor activities, 2 forcible disappearances, and 12 illegal detentions. In the banana-producing region of Uraba, organized workers historically belonged to the extreme left wing of the labor movement but refused to cooperate with the FARC. Paramilitary and guerrilla organizations carried out a rash of massacres in Uraba throughout the year. Approximately half the victims of the FARC massacres were former EPL members, targeted for their participation in or sympathy with the National Syndicate of Agro-Industry Workers, a labor union closely associated with the Hope, Peace, and Freedom Movement of demobilized EPL guerrillas.

The list of killings, intimidations, and arbitrary arrests of labor union leaders included the murder of Norte de Santander Workers Union president Elba Hernandez de Aguilera in August and the forced disappearance and murder of Unified Workers' Central member Hector Posada, found in a mass grave in March in Uraba. The Justice and Peace data bank reported 61 threats against other labor leaders were reported from January through June.

Unions are free to join international confederations without government restrictions.

b. *The Right to Organize and Bargain Collectively.*—The Constitution protects the right of workers to organize and engage in collective bargaining. Workers in larger firms and public services have been most successful in organizing, but these unionized workers represent only a small portion of the economically active population. High unemployment (about 12 percent), traditional antiunion attitudes, and weak union organization and leadership limit workers' bargaining power in all sectors.

The law forbids antiunion discrimination and the obstruction of free association. Government labor inspectors theoretically enforce these provisions, but because of the small number of inspectors and workers' fears of losing their jobs, the inspection apparatus is weak. The Labor Code calls for fines to be levied for restricting freedom of association and prohibits the use of strike breakers.

Collective pacts—agreements between individual workers and their employers—are not subject to collective bargaining and are typically used by employers to obstruct labor organization. Although employers must registered collective pacts with the Ministry of Labor, the Ministry does not exercise any oversight or control over them.

The Labor Code also eliminates mandatory mediation in private labor-management disputes and extends the grace period before the Government can intervene in a conflict. Federations and confederations may assist affiliate unions in collective bargaining.

Labor law applies to the country's seven free trade zones (FTZ's), but its standards are difficult to enforce. Public employee unions have won collective bargaining agreements in the FTZ's of Barranquilla, Buenaventura, Cartagena, and Santa Marta, but the garment manufacturing enterprises in Medellin and Risaralda, which have the largest number of employees, are not organized. National labor leaders claim that in these FTZ's the provisions of the Labor Code dealing with wages, hours, health, and safety are not honored.

c. *Prohibition of Forced or Compulsory Labor.*—The Constitution forbids slavery and any form of forced or compulsory labor, and this prohibition is respected in practice.

d. *Minimum Age for Employment of Children.*—The Constitution bans the employment of children under the age of 14 in most jobs, and the Labor Code prohibits the granting of work permits to youths under the age of 18. This provision is respected in larger enterprises and in major cities. Nevertheless, the extensive informal economy remains effectively outside government control. Some 800,000 children between the ages of 12 and 17 work, according to Labor Ministry studies. These children work—often under substandard conditions—in agriculture or in the informal sector, as street vendors, in leather tanning, and in small family-operated mines. Working children are exposed to the same risks that affect adult workers, including exposure to toxic substances and accidental injuries, all of which contribute to impaired physical development. The ICBF continued its outreach campaign to inform child laborers of their rights and where to turn for help. No figures were available to measure the impact of this effort.

e. *Acceptable Conditions of Work.*—The Government sets a uniform minimum wage for workers every January to serve as a benchmark for wage bargaining. The minimum wage was approximately $140 (col$ 140,000) per month. The minimum wage does not provide a decent standard of living for a worker and family. Because the minimum wage is based on the Government's target inflation rate, the minimum wage has not kept up with inflation in recent years. By government estimates, the price of the family shopping basket is 2.4 times the minimum wage. However, 60 percent of all workers earn no more than, and often much less than, twice the minimum wage.

The law provides for a standard workday of 8 hours and a 48-hour workweek, but it does not specifically require a weekly rest period of at least 24 hours, a failing criticized by the ILO. Legislation provides comprehensive protection for workers' occupational safety and health, but these standards are difficult to enforce, in part due to the small number of Labor Ministry inspectors. In addition, unorganized workers in the informal sector fear that they will lose their jobs if they exercise their right to denounce abuses, particularly in the agricultural sector. According to the Labor Code, workers have the right to withdraw from a hazardous work situation without jeopardizing continued employment. In general, a lack of public safety awareness, inadequate attention by unions, and lax enforcement by the Labor Ministry result in an alarmingly high level of industrial accidents and unhealthy working conditions. Over 80 percent of industries lack industrial security plans. The Social Security Institute reported 115,000 work-related accidents for 1995, 17,000 of which resulted in deaths. Informed observers reported that the level of work-related accidents was expected to remain at comparably high levels in 1996.

COSTA RICA

Costa Rica is a longstanding, stable, constitutional democracy with a unicameral Legislative Assembly directly elected in free multiparty elections every 4 years. Jose Maria Figueres of the National Liberation Party won the presidency in the February 1994 elections, in which approximately 80 percent of eligible voters cast ballots. The Government respects constitutional provisions for an independent judiciary.

The 1949 Constitution abolished the military forces. The Ministry of Public Security—which includes the Border Guard, the Rural Guard, and the antidrug police—and the Ministry of the Presidency share responsibility for law enforcement and national security. The Judicial Police, under the Supreme Court, conduct investigations, while the San Jose Metropolitan Police and the Transit Police within the Ministry of Public Works and Transportation also have limited police powers. Public security forces generally observe procedural safeguards established by law and the Constitution.

The market-based economy is based primarily on agriculture, light industry, and tourism. The pace of economic growth slowed from a 2.5 percent increase in 1995 to a projected rise of 1 to 1.5 percent in 1996. The Government also faced a growing fiscal deficit in 1995 equivalent to 3.8 percent of gross domestic product (GDP). Despite several tax increases in 1995, the projected public sector deficit for 1996 was equivalent to 3 percent of GDP. The Constitution protects the right to own private property; however, domestic and foreign property owners encounter difficulty gaining adequate, timely compensation for lands expropriated for national parks and those set aside for indigenous people or invaded by squatters.

Citizens enjoy a wide range of individual rights and freedoms. The Government fully respects the human rights of its citizens, and the law and judiciary provide effective means of dealing with instances of abuse of individual rights. Nonetheless, the judicial system moves very slowly in processing criminal cases, resulting in lengthy pretrial detention for some suspects. There were two reported instances of physical abuse by police. The Government has identified domestic violence as a serious problem and sponsored a public awareness program to deter such abuse. Abuse of children also remains a problem. Traditional patterns of unequal opportunity for women and racial minorities remain, in spite of continuing government and media efforts to advocate change.

RESPECT FOR HUMAN RIGHTS

Section 1. Respect for the Integrity of the Person, Including Freedom From:

a. *Political and Other Extrajudicial Killing.*—There were no reports of political or other extrajudicial killings.

Although labor demonstrations in August in the port of Limon were peaceful, the police used tear gas to disperse a rock-throwing crowd that had barricaded a road near Limon. The use of tear gas resulted in injuries and the death of an asthmatic woman asphyxiated in a nearby house.

The 1992 "Cobra Command" case was finally resolved. A court convicted 3 former members of the Cobra Command—a now-defunct antinarcotics unit of the Rural Guard—for the 1992 murder of 2 suspected drug traffickers, the rape of 2 indigenous women, and the illegal detention and harassment of 11 indigenous people. These crimes occurred during an unsuccessful search for marijuana plantations in the Talamanca region. The court cleared eight former members of the unit of all criminal charges; the authorities could not locate one former member. The court sentenced two of the three guilty Cobra Command members to terms of 42 years and 32 years, for rape, murder, and illegal detention. The third was sentenced to 5 years for rape.

At the end of the year, the three policemen accused in the 1994 Ciro Monge case and the seven accused in the 1993 Malcom case remained free on bail and awaiting trial. The authorities scheduled the trial in the Ciro Monge case for September 1997 but had not set a date for the other trial.

b. *Disappearance.*—There were no reports of politically motivated disappearances.

c. *Torture and Other Cruel, Inhuman, or Degrading Treatment or Punishment.*—The Constitution prohibits cruel or degrading treatment and holds invalid any statement obtained through violence. The authorities generally abide by these prohibitions. An effective mechanism for lodging and recording complaints of police misconduct exists. In 1995, the most recent year for which statistics are available, 1,262 cases of police abuse of authority or misconduct were reported. The Ombudsman's office investigates complaints and, where appropriate, initiates suits against officials. In August the authorities charged three police officers with false arrest as a result of a January 1994 complaint brought by the Ombudsman himself. According to the complaint, the officers arrested the Ombudsman after he had questioned the conduct of one of the officers at the scene of a traffic accident. The courts sentenced the three officers to 3 years in prison for false arrest, but suspended the sentences and put them on 5 years' probation and imposed a 6-month prohibition from public or private security employment.

In January a man accused three Rural Guard members of intimidating a woman and threatening to shoot him when he tried to help her. At year's end, the authorities were investigating the case and had suspended the three policemen. In March a Nicaraguan complained to authorities that three policemen had beaten and illegally detained him earlier that month. In this case the authorities also suspended the accused policemen and were investigating the case.

A large percentage of police personnel owe their appointments to political patronage. The Figueres administration continued implementation of the 1994 Police Code designed to professionalize and depoliticize the police force. The Government's long-term plan is to establish permanent, professional cadres, eventually resulting in a nonpolitically appointed career force. The basic course for new police recruits includes training using a human rights manual developed by the Ministry of Public Security.

Prisoners generally receive humane treatment. While guards rarely abuse prisoners physically, there are credible reports that prisoners are sometimes subjected to other forms of abuse such as extortion. The Prison Rights Ombudsman investigates complaints and refers serious cases of abuse to the Public Prosecutor. Penitentiary overcrowding is a growing problem, with the prison population about 83 percent above planned capacity. Illegal narcotics are readily available in the prisons, and drug use is common. In March the Supreme Court's Constitutional Chamber issued an order to the San Sebastian prison in San Jose—at 123 percent over capacity the third most crowded prison in the country—giving the institution 1 year to achieve minimally acceptable conditions for the prisoners.

The Government permits prison visits by independent human rights monitors.

d. *Arbitrary Arrest, Detention, or Exile.*—The Constitution and law prohibit arbitrary arrest, detention, or exile, and the Government generally respects these prohibitions.

The law requires issuance of judicial warrants before making arrests. The Constitution entitles a detainee to a judicial determination of the legality of the detention during arraignment before a court officer within 24 hours of arrest. The authorities generally respect these rights.

The law provides for the right to release on bail, and the authorities observe it in practice. Generally, the authorities do not hold detainees incommunicado. With judicial authorization, the authorities may hold suspects for 48 hours after arrest or, under special circumstances, for up to 10 days.

The Constitution bars exile as punishment.

e. *Denial of Fair Public Trial.*—The Constitution and law provide for an independent judiciary, and the Government respects this provision in practice. The Constitution provides for the right to a fair trial, and an independent judiciary vigorously enforces this right.

The Supreme Court supervises the work of the lower courts, known as tribunals. The Legislative Assembly elects the 22 Supreme Court Magistrates to 8-year terms, subject to automatic renewal unless the Assembly decides otherwise by a two-thirds majority. Accused persons may select attorneys to represent them, and the law provides for access to counsel at state expense for the indigent.

Persons accused of serious offenses and held without bail, however, sometimes remain in pretrial custody for long periods. Lengthy legal procedures, numerous appeals, and large numbers of detainees cause delays and case backlogs. There were 1,281 accused persons, representing 28 percent of the prison population, jailed awaiting trial as of September.

There were no reports of political prisoners.

f. *Arbitrary Interference with Privacy, Family, Home, or Correspondence.*—The Constitution prohibits such practices. Government authorities generally respect these prohibitions, and violations are subject to effective legal sanction. The law requires judicial warrants to search private homes. Judges may approve use of wiretaps in limited circumstances, primarily to combat narcotics trafficking.

Section 2. *Respect for Civil Liberties, Including:*

a. *Freedom of Speech and Press.*—The Constitution provides for freedom of speech and the press, and the Government respects these rights in practice. An independent press, a generally effective judiciary, and a functioning democratic political system combine to ensure freedom of speech and of the press, including academic freedom.

There are 9 major privately owned newspapers, several periodicals, 6 privately owned television stations, and over 70 privately owned radio stations, all of which pursue independent editorial policies. While the media generally criticize the Government freely, there were unconfirmed allegations that the Government withheld advertising from some publications in order to influence or limit reporting. The Assembly passed a "right of response" law that provides persons criticized in the media an opportunity to reply with equal attention and at equal length. Critics charge that this law could have a chilling effect on press criticism of elected officials.

The Office of Control of Public Spectacles rates films and has the authority to restrict or prohibit their showing; it has similar powers over television programs and stage plays. Nonetheless, foreign and particularly American films spanning the U.S. rating system are offered to the public. A tribunal reviews appeals of the office's actions. In January the Supreme Court's Constitutional Chamber ruled unconstitutional a 1989 decision by the office to prohibit public showing of the film "The Last Temptation of Christ." This film, and the graphic depiction of violence and sex in popular television and movies, have generated heated debate. In May over 70 prominent citizens, decrying "violence, hate, and pornography" in the mass media, signed a public letter to the President urging him to enforce Article 28 of the Constitution, which authorizes the prohibition of acts which "are harmful to morality or public order."

b. *Freedom of Peaceful Assembly and Association.*—The Constitution provides for these rights, and the Government respects them in practice.

c. *Freedom of Religion.*—The Constitution provides for freedom of religion, and the Government respects this right in practice. While the Constitution establishes Roman Catholicism as the state religion, people of all denominations freely practice their religion without government interference. Foreign missionaries and clergy of all denominations work and proselytize freely.

d. *Freedom of Movement Within the Country, Foreign Travel, Emigration, and Repatriation.*—The Constitution provides for these rights, and the Government respects them in practice. There are no restrictions on travel within the country, on emigration, or the right of return.

There is a long tradition of providing refuge to people from other Latin American countries. In a controversial decision, the Government in March granted political asylum to former vice president of Ecuador Alberto Dahik. In October 1995 while still vice president, Dahik fled from Ecuador to Costa Rica to avoid arrest on charges of misuse of public funds. Dahik claimed the charges were fabricated by his political enemies. In June the Government allowed Venezuelan citizen Luis Escobar Ugaz to enter the country to apply for political asylum. Ugaz, a member of the Bolivarian Revolutionary Movement, had sought refuge in the Costa Rican embassy in Caracas, claiming persons with connections to the Venezuelan police had kidnaped and tortured him. By year's end, the Government had not yet reached a decision in Ugaz' case.

The Government cooperates with the office of the U.N. High Commissioner for Refugees and other humanitarian organizations in assisting refugees. The Government makes a distinction between political asylum and refugee status; the issue of the provision of first asylum did not arise. The Constitution specifically prohibits repatriation of anyone subject to potential persecution, and there were no reports of forced expulsion of persons to a country where they feared persecution. The authorities regularly repatriated undocumented Nicaraguans, most of whom entered the country primarily for economic reasons. In August nine Nicaraguans accused border police officials in Los Chiles of using undue force when repatriating them. The Government is investigating the allegations.

Section 3. Respect for Political Rights: The Right of Citizens to Change Their Government

The Constitution provides citizens with the right to change their government peacefully, and citizens exercise this right in practice through free and fair elections held on the basis of universal suffrage and by secret ballot every 4 years. The independent Supreme Electoral Tribunal ensures the integrity of elections, and the authorities and citizens respect election results. The Constitution bars the President from seeking reelection, and Assembly members may seek reelection only after at least one term out of office. In the 1994 elections, President Figueres' National Liberation Party gained a plurality in the Legislative Assembly, winning 28 of 57 seats. The Social Christian Unity Party won 25 seats, the Democratic Force won 2 seats, and 2 provincial parties each garnered 1 seat. After an intraparty dispute, one of the Democratic Force legislators formed a new party in February. As a result, the Democratic Force now has one seat, and the new party—the New Democratic Party—has one seat.

Women encounter no legal impediments to their participation in politics. While they are underrepresented in leadership positions of the Government and political parties, this situation has begun to change. A woman serves concurrently as Vice President and as a cabinet minister; another woman is Minister of Public Security. In addition, six vice ministers, nine Legislative Assembly members, and five directors of autonomous institutions are women. In June the opposition Social Christian Unity Party reformed its statutes to mandate that a minimum of 40 percent of posts in party councils be occupied by women. Lorena Vasquez became the party's first female Secretary General. The ruling National Liberation Party is also considering statutory reforms to increase female participation in party decisionmaking.

Indigenous people may participate freely in politics and government. In practice, they have not played significant roles in these areas, except on issues directly affecting their welfare, largely because of their relatively small numbers and physical isolation. Costa Rica's 30,000 blacks, largely resident on the Caribbean coast, enjoy full rights of citizenship, including the protection of laws against racial discrimination. The Legislative Assembly includes one black member; one vice minister is black.

Section 4. Governmental Attitude Regarding International and Nongovernmental Investigation of Alleged Violations of Human Rights

Various human rights groups operate without government restriction, investigating and publishing their findings on human rights cases. Government officials are cooperative and responsive to their views. The Costa Rican Commission for Human Rights, the Commission for the Defense of Human Rights in Central America, and the Family and Friends of Political Prisoners of Costa Rica, monitor and report on human rights.

Several international organizations concerned with human rights, including the Inter-American Institute for Human Rights and the Inter-American Court of Human Rights, are located in San Jose.

Section 5. Discrimination Based on Race, Sex, Religion, Disability, Language, or Social Status

The Constitution pronounces all persons equal before the law, and the Government generally respects these provisions.

Women.—The Government has identified domestic violence against women and children as a serious societal problem. The authorities have incorporated training on handling domestic violence cases in the basic training course for new police personnel. In April the Legislative Assembly passed the Law Against Domestic Violence, which classifies certain acts of domestic violence as crimes and mandates their prosecution. Previously, courts had sometimes treated such acts as mere infringements of the law and not serious enough to merit prosecution. The law requires public hospitals to report cases of female victims of domestic violence. Television coverage of this issue has increased in news reporting, public service announcements, and feature programs.

Women constitute 49.5 percent of the population. The 1990 Law for the Promotion of the Social Equality of Women not only prohibits discrimination against women but obligates the Government to promote political, economic, social, and cultural equality. In March the Government's National Center for the Development of Women and the Family presented its 3-year National Plan for Equality of Opportunity between Women and Men. The plan is based in great measure on the Platform for Action adopted at the Fourth World Conference on Women in Beijing.

According to the 1993 census, 30 percent of working-age women earn wages outside the home, compared with 79 percent of working-age men. One-fifth of all families depend primarily on the earnings of women. Most women work in the services sector, with others working in industry and agriculture. While laws require that women and men receive equal pay for equal work, average salaries for women remain somewhat below those of male counterparts. According to the 1995 report on human development prepared by the United Nations Development Program, women receive about 83 percent of the salary of men for equal work. The average life expectancy for women increased by 12 years since the early 1970's to 77 years, higher than the 72-year average for men.

Children.—The Government is committed to children's rights and welfare through well-funded systems of public education and medical care. The Government spends more than 4 percent of GDP on education and over 5 percent on medical care. Accordingly, the country has a high rate of literacy (94 percent) and a low rate of infant mortality (13.4 persons per 1,000). The law requires 6 years of primary and 3 years of secondary education for all children. There is no difference in the treatment of girls and boys in education or in health care services. The autonomous National Institute for Children (PANI) oversees implementation of the Government's programs for children. The Catholic Church is building a home both for teenage mothers and for children with AIDS, which the Church will operate with help from the PANI.

In recent years, the PANI has increased public awareness of crimes against children. In the first 6 months of 1995, the most recent year for which statistics are available, the Institute intervened in 3,800 cases of abandonment, 1,158 cases of physical abuse, 1,318 cases of sexual abuse, and 116 cases of psychological abuse of children. Abuses appear to be more prevalent among impoverished, less-educated families. Traditional attitudes and the inclination to treat such crimes as misdemeanors sometimes hamper legal proceedings against those who commit crimes against children.

In February the PANI announced a comprehensive plan to improve the conditions of the poorest children. According to Institute estimates, 17 percent of children between the ages of 5 and 17 are involved in income-producing activities, and 25,000 childrenwork rather than attend school. The Government, police sources,and representatives of the United Nations Children Fund acknowledge that child prostitution is a growing problem but say the exact magnitude of the problem is as yet undetermined. Official sources assert that unofficial studies which estimate that from 2,000 to 3,000 children are involved in prostitution in San Jose are "not scientifically verified."

People With Disabilities.—In May the Law of Equal Opportunity for Persons with Disabilities went into effect. It prohibits discrimination, provides for health care services, and mandates provision of access to buildings for persons with disabilities. A number of public and private institutions have made individual efforts to improve access.

Indigenous People.—The population of about 3.3 million includes nearly 29,000 indigenous people among 8 ethnic groups. Most live in traditional communities on 22 reserves which, because of their remote location, often lack access to schools, health care, electricity, and potable water. The Government, through the National Indigenous Commission, completed distribution of identification cards to facilitate access to public medical facilities. The Government also built a medical clinic and several community health centers in indigenous areas. The Ombudsman has established an office to investigate violations of the rights of indigenous people.

Section 6. Worker Rights

a. *The Right of Association.*—The law specifies the right of workers to join unions of their choosing without prior authorization, although barriers exist in practice. About 15 percent of the work force is unionized, almost entirely in the public sector. Unions operate independently of government control.

Some trade union leaders contend that "solidarity" associations, in which employers provide access to credit unions and savings plans in return for agreement to avoid strikes and other types of confrontation, infringe upon the right of association. After the International Labor Organization (ILO) Committee on Freedom of Association ruled that solidarity associations and their involvement in trade union activities violated freedom of association, the Government amended the Labor Code in 1993. The following year, the ILO Committee of Experts (COE) ruled that these and other planned changes fostered greater freedom of association. In 1995 the COE encouraged the Government to approve legislation to allow unions to administer compensation funds for dismissed workers and to repeal labor code provisions restricting the right to strike in certain nonessential public, agricultural, and forestry sectors. This recommendation remained under government consideration at year's end.

There are no restrictions on the right of private sector workers to strike, but very few workers in this sector belong to unions. Accordingly, private sector strikes rarely occur. The Constitution and Labor Code restrict the right of public sector workers to strike. In August stevedores and other workers from Limon province staged several work stoppages and protests to protest lowered wages, lack of work, and insufficient infrastructure. In September the Government signed an agreement with the activist group "Struggling Limon" to address the needs of this area, site of the country's principal port.

Unions may form federations and confederations and affiliate internationally.

b. *The Right to Organize and Bargain Collectively.*—The Constitution protects the right to organize. Specific provisions of the 1993 labor code reforms provide protection from dismissal for union organizers and members during union formation. The revised provisions require employers found guilty of discrimination to reinstate workers fired for union activities.

Public sector workers cannot engage in collective bargaining because the Public Administration Act of 1978 makes labor law inapplicable in relations between the Government and its employees. Private sector unions have the legal right to engage in collective bargaining.

All labor regulations apply fully to the country's nine export processing zones (EPZ's). The Labor Ministry oversees labor regulations within the EPZ's, but acknowledged that it has only 1 inspector for every 30,000 workers.

c. *Prohibition of Forced or Compulsory Labor.*—The Constitution prohibits forced or compulsory labor, and there were no known instances of such practices.

d. *Minimum Age for Employment of Children.*—The Constitution provides special employment protection for women and children and establishes the minimum working age at 12 years, with special regulations in force for workers under the age of 15. Children between 15 and 18 years of age can work a maximum of 7 hours daily and 42 hours weekly, while children between the ages of 12 and 15 can work a maximum of 5 hours daily and 30 hours weekly. The PANI, in cooperation with the Labor Ministry, effectively enforces these regulations in the formal sector. After two adolescents died from chemical poisoning while working on banana plantations in 1993, the authorities prohibited employment of youths under the age of 18 in the banana industry. Nonetheless, child labor remains an integral part of the large informal economy. According to a PANI survey, about 152,000 children worked during 1995, of whom nearly 93,000 had prior PANI approval.

e. *Acceptable Conditions of Work.*—The Constitution provides for a minimum wage. A National Wage Council, composed of three members each from government, business, and labor, sets minimum wage and salary levels for all sectors. Monthly minimum wages, last adjusted in July for the private sector, range from $122 (25,636 colones) for domestic servants to $591 (124,255 colones) for certain professionals. Public sector negotiations, based on private sector minimum wages, normally follow the settlement of private sector negotiations. The Ministry of Labor effectively enforces minimum wages in the San Jose area, but less effectively in rural areas. Workers with families at the lower end of the wage scale, as well as those in the middle class, encounter difficulty in keeping up with the rising cost of living.

The Constitution sets workday hours, overtime remuneration, days of rest, and annual vacation rights. Although often circumvented in practice, it also requires compensation for discharge without due cause. Generally, workers may work a maximum of 8 hours during the day and 6 at night, up to weekly totals of 48 and 36 hours, respectively. Nonagricultural workers receive an overtime premium of 50 percent of regular wages for work in excess of the daily work shift. Agricultural workers do not receive overtime, however, if they voluntarily work beyond their normal hours. Little evidence exists that employers coerce employees to perform such overtime.

For several years, the ILO COE asked the Government to enact provisions regarding accident prevention for seafarers, as required by ILO Convention 134 on the "Prevention of Accidents (Seafarers)." The COE had not yet received the requested regulations at year's end.

A 1967 law on health and safety in the workplace requires industrial, agricultural, and commercial firms with 10 or more workers to establish a joint management-labor committee on workplace conditions and allows the Government to inspect workplaces and to fine employers for violations. Most firms subject to the law establish such committees but either do not use the committees or neglect to turn them into effective instruments for improving workplace conditions. While workers have the right to leave work if conditions become dangerous, workers who do so may find their jobs in jeopardy unless they file written complaints with the Labor Ministry. Due partly to budgetary constraints, the Ministry has not fielded enough labor inspectors to ensure consistent maintenance of minimum conditions of safety and sanitation, especially outside San Jose.

CUBA

Cuba is a totalitarian state controlled by President Fidel Castro, who is Chief of State, Head of Government, First Secretary of the Communist Party, and Commander in Chief of the armed forces. President Castro exercises control over all aspects of Cuban life through the Communist Party and its affiliated mass organizations, the government bureaucracy, and the state security apparatus. The party is the only legal political entity, and President Castro personally chooses the membership of the select group that heads the party. The party controls all government positions, including judicial offices.

The Ministry of Interior is the principal organ of state security and totalitarian control. The Revolutionary Armed Forces (FAR), led by President Castro's brother Raul, exercises control over this Ministry. In addition to regulating migration and controlling the Border Guard and the police forces, the Interior Ministry investigates and actively suppresses organized opposition and dissent. It maintains a pervasive system of vigilance through undercover agents, informers, the Rapid Response Brigades, and the Committees for the Defense of the Revolution (CDR's). While the Government traditionally used the CDR's to mobilize citizens against dissenters, impose ideological conformity, and root out "counterrevolutionary" behavior, severe economic problems have reduced the willingness of citizens to participate in the CDR's and thereby lessened their effectiveness. Other mass organizations also inject government and Communist Party control into every citizen's daily activities at home, work, and school. There were instances in which members of the security forces committed human rights abuses.

The Government continued to control all significant means of production and remained the predominant employer, despite permitting some carefully controlled foreign investment and legalization of some minor categories of self-employment. Although the Government forecast a 5 percent economic growth rate for 1996, the economy remained in a slump due to the inefficiencies of the centrally controlled economic system, the collapse of Cuba's trade relations with the former Soviet bloc, and the end of the $4 to $5 billion in annual Soviet subsidies. Despite some economic recovery, gross domestic product is still only about two-thirds the 1989 level, and total foreign trade about one-fourth the 1989 level. For the sixth straight year, the Government continued its austerity measures known euphemistically as the "special period in peacetime." Agricultural markets, legalized in 1994, gave consumers wider access to meat and produce, although at prices beyond the routine reach of most Cubans living on peso-only incomes. The system of "tourist apartheid" continued, in which foreign visitors receive preference over citizens for food, consumer products, and government services, as well as access to hotels and resorts from which Cuban citizens remain barred.

The Government's human rights record worsened in 1996 with the large-scale crackdown against the prodemocracy umbrella group "Concilio Cubano," the shootdown of two U.S. civilian airplanes in international airspace, increased reports of deaths due to the excessive use of force by police, further restrictions on the distribution of foreign publications, increased use of exile and internal exile to control the activities of independent journalists and human rights advocates, antagonism to any foreign diplomatic criticism of human rights practices, restrictions on foreign contacts with human rights activists, the denial of visas to prominent U.S. journalists, and the expulsions of visiting foreign journalists. The authorities continued routinely to harass, threaten, arbitrarily arrest, detain, imprison, defame, and physically attack human rights advocates and members of independent professional associations, including journalists, economists, and lawyers, often with the goal of encouraging them to leave Cuba. Members of the security forces and prison officials continued to beat and otherwise abuse detainees and prisoners. The Government continued to restrict sharply basic political and civil rights, including: The right of citizens to change their government; the freedoms of speech, press, assembly, association, religion, and movement; the right to privacy; and various worker rights. The judiciary is completely subordinate to the Government and to the Communist Party. The Government denied human rights advocates due process and subjected them to unfair trials. Political prisoners were offered the choice of exile or continued imprisonment. Prison conditions remained harsh.

In April the United Nations Human Rights Commission (UNHRC) once again passed a resolution endorsing the report of the UNHRC Special Rapporteur, which detailed Cuba's violations of human rights. The Government continued to refuse the Special Rapporteur permission to visit Cuba.

RESPECT FOR HUMAN RIGHTS

Section 1. Respect for the Integrity of the Person, Including Freedom From:

a. *Political and Other Extrajudicial Killing.*—Reports increased of deaths due to the excessive use of force by police. Policeman Jose Angel Merino Fragoza of the Sixth Precinct of Marianao in Havana reportedly shot and killed 30-year-old Renzo Falbello Gallego on the night of September 14 for not stopping when Merino called out, "Halt, Jose." Falbello apparently did not believe that the policeman was addressing him. The Government tried Merino for manslaughter and a court and sentenced him to 7 years in prison on December 20.

On May 24, a policeman shot and killed 28-year-old Ivan Agramonte Arencibia in Havana. Agramonte, who was reportedly carrying contraband pizza dough on the back of his bicycle, had fled a policeman's order to halt. Policemen Yosvani Maturell Fernandez and Omar Castro pursued Agramonte, knocking him off his bicycle and then beating him. While Agramonte lay semi-conscious on the ground, Maturell took out his pistol and shot him in the head. He died shortly thereafter at a nearby hospital. On September 6, the Government tried Maturell for manslaughter and sought a prison sentence of 14 years. The court had not issued its verdict at year's end. The authorities detained Omar Castro for 5 days and then released him.

On March 9, policeman Francisco Valdes shot and killed 26-year-old Osmany Campos Valle on his family's small ranch in Guane, in the province of Pinar del Rio; Valdes had just returned from a party at which alcoholic beverages had been served. On seeing some movement on the ranch, Valdes had asked the person's identity and, although Campos reportedly repeated his nickname several times, Valdes shot him. The authorities tried Valdes on May 22 in a Ministry of Interior courtroom for "special cases." The prosecution sought a 12-year prison sentence and monthly support payments of about $1.50 (30 pesos at the prevailing legal exchange rate) for each of Campos' two young children. On appeal, the court sentenced Valdes to 8 years' imprisonment.

Late in the evening of December 16, 1995, a policeman in Camaguey shot at Yoel Leyva and Pedro Roque, whom he had ordered to halt. The 18-year-old Leyva died the following day. The youths reportedly had told the policeman that they could not stop because the bicycle they were riding had no brakes. At the wake, Carlos Diaz Barranco, First Secretary of the Communist Party of Camaguey, pledged to bring the policeman to justice. The policeman was tried on December 16, 1995 and released in February.

On April 18, the Government tried the prison officials and inmates alleged to have been involved in the September 12, 1995 death in police custody of Estanislao Gonzalez Quintana. While the court determined that Gonzalez' death was the result of alcoholism-related heart problems, not the beating he received at the hands of the defendants, the prosecution nevertheless sought prison sentences of 10 years for the prison guard, 12 years for one of the inmates, and from 1 to 4 years on the charge of dereliction of duties for other prison officials. Gonzalez' widow denied that Gonzalez had suffered from heart problems or alcoholism. The court sentenced the prison guard and the inmate to 2 years' imprisonment and the other prison officials to 8 months' house arrest. The widow appealed the sentences, and appeals trials were pending as of November.

On February 24, the Cuban Air Force shot down two unarmed civilian aircraft from the United States, killing all four people aboard. The report issued by the International Civil Aviation Organization (ICAO) found that the shootdown occurred in international airspace and without warning. The ICAO Council "reaffirmed its condemnation of the use of weapons against civil aircraft in flight as being incompatible with elementary considerations of humanity and the rules of customary international law." The U.N. Security Council endorsed the report and the ICAO Council resolution and "noted that the unlawful shooting down by the Cuban Air Force of two civil aircraft on 24 February 1996 violated the principle that states must refrain from the use of weapons against civil aircraft in flight and that, when intercepting civil aircraft, the lives of persons on board and the safety of the aircraft must not be endangered." The UNHRC expressed its "dismay [over] the loss of human life and disregard for human rights norms shown by the Government of Cuba."

On October 16, the Inter-American Commission on Human Rights (IACHR) issued its final report on the Government's July 13, 1994 sinking of the "13th of March" tugboat in which 41 individuals died. The Government did not respond to the IACHR's preliminary report issued on May 3. The IACHR concluded that the Government violated Article I of the American Declaration on the Rights and Duties of Man, which guarantees the rights to life and the integrity of the person, and Articles VIII and XVIII, which guarantee the rights of transit and justice, respectively. The report found the Government legally obligated to indemnify the survivors and the relatives of the victims for the damages caused.b. DisappearanceThere were no reports of politically motivated disappearances.

c. *Torture and Other Cruel, Inhuman, or Degrading Treatment or Punishment.*—The Constitution prohibits abusive treatment of detainees and prisoners, but there were instances in which members of the security forces and prison officials beat and otherwise abused human rights advocates, detainees, and prisoners. At the police station in Nueva Gerona, on the Isle of Youth, policeman Gerardo Acedia Frometa reportedly subjected detainee Octavio Rodriguez Gonzalez to electric shocks during an interrogation in June. Rodriguez allegedly was taken to an extremely cold interrogation room and seated on, and handcuffed to, a metal chair which was bolted to the floor. The policeman then reportedly applied electric shocks to the chair.

Individuals linked to state security forces subjected human rights advocates to physical aggression. Four men attacked Diosdado Gutierrez Hernandez, a member of the Human Rights Party of Cuba, on the street the night of April 20 in Pinar del Rio and whispered "take your human rights" while punching him in the stomach. They did not rob him.

In May the Cuban Psychiatric Society (CPS) withdrew its 1993 invitation to the American Psychiatric Association's (APA) Committee on International Abuse of Psychiatry and Psychiatrists which had planned to visit Cuba to investigate charges that the Government was repressing political dissidents through abusive psychiatric interventions. The CPS reportedly found APA's conditions that a Cuban-American psychiatrist be included on the delegation and that interviews with dissident psychiatrists be permitted to be "colored by political interests."

Prison conditions continued to be harsh. The Government claims that prisoners have guaranteed rights, such as family visitation, adequate nutrition, pay for work, the right to request parole, and the right to petition the prison director. However, police and prison officials often denied these rights and used beatings, neglect, isolation, denial of medical attention, and other abuse against detainees and prisoners, including those convicted of political crimes or those who persisted in expressing their views. There are separate prison facilities for women and for minors.

The IACHR reported that prison authorities subjected prisoners who protested the conditions or treatment to reprisals such as beatings, transfer to punishment cells, transfer to prisons far from their families, suspension of family visits, or denial of medical treatment.

A member of the France-Liberte delegation that interviewed political prisoners in May 1995 stated that lengthy and often incommunicado pretrial detention constitutes a form of psychological torture. State security officials also subjected dissidents to systematic psychological intimidation, including sleep deprivation, imprisonment in cells with common criminals, aggressive homosexuals, or state security agents, and threats of physical violence, in an attempt to coerce them to sign incriminating documents or to collaborate. Human rights advocate Alberto Perera Martinez, detained as part of the Government's crackdown against the Concilio Cubano (see Section 1.d.), reported that prison guards deprived him of sleep for 17 consecutive days, woke him at regular intervals throughout the night for questioning, and kept him in a cell with 24-hour-a-day illumination in order to pressure him to sign false statements. During the crackdown, the authorities held human rights advocate Eugenio Rodriguez Chaple, a diminutive man in poor health, in the same cell as a boxer who was detained on criminal charges.

At the Kilo 8 prison in Camaguey, Jesus Chamber Ramirez, who sentenced to 10 years' imprisonment for enemy propaganda and disrespect against government authority, was regularly denied family visits because of his insistence on treatment as a political rather than a common prisoner. Prison authorities often placed political prisoners in cells with common and sometimes violent criminals and required that they comply with the rules for common criminals.

The rights to adequate nutrition and medical attention were also regularly violated. The IACHR described the nutritional and hygienic situation in the prisons, together with the deficiencies in medical care, as "alarming." Both the IACHR and the U.N. Special Rapporteur, as well as other human rights monitoring organizations, reported widespread incidence in prisons of tuberculosis, scabies, hepatitis, parasitic infections, and malnutrition. In the Guamajal prison in Villa Clara, several tuberculosis-infected prisoners staged a hunger strike in mid-July to protest the lack of appropriate medical care. On February 9, a guard at the same prison hit a hungry prisoner, Eleodoro Sanches, on the head with a metal spoon, causing a gash that required two stitches, for eating a stolen plate of boiled bananas in the kitchen where he worked.

The authorities regularly denied prisoners other purportedly guaranteed rights, such as the right of correspondence. At the Guamajal prison on January 15, political prisoners gave their personal correspondence to a prison official to send to their relatives. Those letters were found later that day torn and discarded in a wastepaper basket.

Three prison guards severely beat Ramon Varela Sanchez, Vice President of the Marti Civic League, on his head, back, and chest on May 3 after he intervened on behalf of another prisoner who was denied medical attention for an abscessed molar. Due to the severity of his injuries, the authorities transferred Varela to a prison hospital where he remained for 6 days. Varela's lawyer presented a formal complaint to the Ministry of Interior official responsible for prisons, but no action was taken against the prison guards. Varela, who had been held without charges since July 30, 1995, was finally tried on September 25. The Government alleged that Varela was the intellectual author of an arson attack on a train station in the Calabazar municipality of Havana and sought 5 years' imprisonment. During the trial, however, the authorities changed the charge, and the court sentenced him to 2 years' imprisonment for inciting to commit delinquent acts.

Prison officials also confiscated medications and food brought by family members for political prisoners. In March a prison official at the Kilo 8 prison seized the medications and food brought by relatives for political prisoners Eduardo Gomez Sanchez, Jorge Luis Garcia Perez, Alejandro Mustafa Reyes, and Luis Gustavo Dominguez Gutierrez. They were threatened with beatings if they complained.

In March the prison warden at Kilo 8 denied pastoral visits and confiscated religious books, including the Bible, from political prisoner Jorge Luis Garcia Perez. Garcia, who staged several hunger strikes in protest, is a member of the group of political prisoners at Kilo 8 who publicly denounce human rights violations occurring in the prison.

Prison officials at Kilo 8 mounted a campaign to find and seize any reports of human rights violations within the prison. In a meeting with a group of prisoners in mid-April, a prison official promised that those who passed notes from counterrevolutionary prisoners to visiting relatives would be expelled from their prison jobs, while those who turned them in to the authorities would receive conjugal visits and other benefits.

The Government does not permit independent monitoring of prison conditions by international or national human rights monitoring groups.

d. *Arbitrary Arrest, Detention, or Exile.*—The Law of Penal Procedures requires police to file formal charges and either release a detainee or bring the case before a prosecutor within 96 hours of arrest. It also requires the authorities to provide suspects with access to a lawyer within 10 days of arrest. However, the Constitution states that all legally recognized civil liberties can be denied anyone actively opposing the "decision of the Cuban people to build socialism." The authorities routinely invoke this sweeping authority to deny due process requirements to those detained on purported state security grounds.

The authorities routinely engage in arbitrary arrest and detention of human rights advocates, subjecting them to interrogations, threats, and degrading treatment and conditions for hours or days at a time. The police detained Ronald Faxas Maceo on January 31 in Old Havana for distributing copies of the Spanish-language version of the Miami Herald and the magazine Dissident. They held him overnight, fined him about $5 (100 pesos) for disrespect, and warned that he could be imprisoned for 4 to 5 years for spreading enemy propaganda. On July 22, police detained Marvin Hernandez and Benito Fojaco and held them for 4 days in Cienfuegos for meeting with a foreign diplomat. The authorities detained human rights advocate Osmel Lugo Gutierrez on May 22, held him for a month at the state security headquarters in Havana, and then transferred him to the 1580 prison pending trial on charges of disrespect and inciting to commit a delinquent act. The secretary of his human rights organization, Grisel Galera Gomez, faced similar charges but was released on bail. The charges reportedly stemmed from their organization's petition drive and other efforts to protest the forcible eviction of squatters in a shantytown in the San Miguel del Padron municipality of Havana. As of November, no trial date had been set.

On January 6, state security agents arrested John Sweeney, a visiting researcher with the Heritage Foundation, and interrogated him for 4 hours about the purpose of his visit and his contacts in Cuba. They reportedly said that they had "accompanied" him since his arrival in Cuba.

Amnesty International noted that the Government had changed its tactics in dealing with human rights advocates, and "rather than arresting them and bringing them to trial, the tendency was to repeatedly detain them for short periods and threaten them with imprisonment unless they gave up their activities or left the country." The Government applied this tactic to dozens of members of Concilio Cubano, a prodemocracy umbrella group composed of over 130 human rights, political opposition, and independent professional organizations, which was founded in October 1995. The harassment intensified in the weeks surrounding Concilio Cubano's planned February 24 meeting to discuss Cuba's future. State security agents visited, harassed, threatened, or briefly detained over 200 individuals, including 4 of the 5 members of the Concilio Cubano secretariat (see Section 1.e.). The UNHRC "deplored" the detention and harassment of Concilio Cubano members.

The authorities detained Concilio Cubano activists Eugenio Rodriguez Chaple, Rafael Solano, Alberto Perera Martinez, Nestor Rodriguez Lobaina, Heriberto Leyva, and Radames Garcia de la Vega for 6 to 8 weeks, much of the time incommunicado. They subjected them to physical threats, several interrogations daily, imprisonment in cells with aggressive common criminals, sleep deprivation, confiscation of food, vitamins, and medications brought by relatives, and strictly supervised and limited family visits. When released, all were told that they would be brought to trial and given lengthy prison terms if they did not leave the country.

The Penal Code also includes the concept of "dangerousness," defined as the "special proclivity of a person to commit crimes, demonstrated by his conduct in manifest contradiction of socialist norms." If the police decide that a person exhibits signs of dangerousness, they may bring the offender before a court or subject him to "therapy" or "political reeducation." Government authorities regularly threaten prosecution under this article. Both the UNHRC and the IACHR condemned this concept for its subjectivity, the summary nature of the judicial proceedings employed, the lack of legal safeguards, and the political considerations behind its application. According to the IACHR, "the special inclination to commit crimes referred to in the Cuban Criminal Code amounts to a subjective criterion used by the Government to justify violations of the rights to individual freedom and due process of persons whose sole crime has been an inclination to hold a view different from the official view."

On May 7, a court tried human rights advocate Ernesto de la O Ramos in San Juan y Martinez in the province of Pinar del Rio and sentenced him to 2 years' imprisonment on the charge of dangerousness for belonging to a dissident organization and disseminating news about Cuba on foreign radio stations. As of November, De la O Ramos also faced trial on a separate charge of disseminating enemy propaganda.

The Government also used exile as a tool for controlling and eliminating the internal opposition. The Government regularly offered exile as the condition for release to political prisoners. In January the Government released political prisoners Luis Grave de Peralta Morell, Carmen Julia Arias Iglesias, and Eduardo Ramon Prida Gorgoy at the request of visiting U.S. Congressman Bill Richardson. They were taken from prison directly to the airport for departure.

In contrast to its general practice of offering exile only after imprisonment, the Government increasingly threatened to charge, try, and imprison human rights advocates and independent journalists if they did not leave the country. Human rights advocates Mercedes Parada Antunez, Eugenio Rodriguez Chaple, Alberto Perera Martinez, Luis Felipe Lores Nadal, Lucila Irene Almira, and Miguel Angel Aldana, and independent journalists Rafael Solano, Roxana Valdivia Castilla, and Olance Nogueras Rofe, were among those threatened. Amnesty International expressed "particular concern" about this practice, which "effectively prevents those concerned from being able to act in public life in their own country."

The Government also increasingly began to employ internal exile as a means to restrict the activities of independent journalists and human rights advocates. The authorities prohibited independent journalists Olance Nogueras Rofe and Roxana Valdivia Castilla from traveling to Havana from their hometowns of Cienfuegos and Ciego de Avila, respectively, unless the travel was for the purpose of making arrangements to leave the country.

One June 6, police arrested university reform advocates Nestor Rodriguez Lobaina and Radames Garcia de la Vega, who had remained in Havana following their release from detention in April despite orders to return to their homes in the eastern provinces. A court tried them on June 12 for resisting authority and disobedience and sentenced them to 6 months and 1 year, respectively, of restricted movement in their hometowns, 5 years of internal exile in their home provinces, and to report periodically to the local police. According to Amnesty International, "the sentence is believed to have been imposed to prevent them from returning to the capital to carry on with their activities." Rodriguez and Garcia remained in Havana pending the results of their appeal and the police arrested them again on June 25 for breach of sentence. The following day, when taken to the courthouse, Rodriguez reportedly appeared with facial bruises and accused a civilian-clad security agent of having beaten him. While handcuffed, he was attacked and again beaten by the agent. The authorities forcibly sent Rodriguez and Garcia to the provinces of Guantanamo and Santiago, respectively, on July 1. The authorities also confiscated their identity documents, which Cuban citizens are required to carry at all times, as a means of enforcing the restriction on their movement. In mid-July, state security agents threatened Rodriguez and Garcia with imprisonment if they continued their political activities.

e. *Denial of Fair Public Trial.*—Although the Constitution provides for independent courts, it explicitly subordinates them to the National Assembly (ANPP) and the Council of State, which is headed by Fidel Castro. The ANPP and its lower level counterparts elect all judges. The subordination of the courts to the Communist Party further compromises the judiciary's independence.

Civil courts exist at municipal, provincial, and Supreme Court levels. Panels composed of a mix of professionally certified and lay judges preside over them. Military tribunals assume jurisdiction for certain counterrevolutionary cases. Cuban law and trial practices do not meet international standards for fair public trials. Almost all cases are tried in less than a day.

There are no jury trials. While most trials are public, trials are closed when state security is allegedly involved. Prosecutors may introduce testimony from a CDR member as to the revolutionary background of a defendant, which may contribute to either a longer or shorter sentence. The law recognizes the right of appeal in municipal courts but limits it in provincial courts to cases such as those involving maximum prison terms or the death penalty. The law requires that an appeal be filed within 5 days of the verdict.

Criteria for presenting evidence, especially in cases of human rights advocates, are arbitrary and discriminatory. Often the sole evidence provided, particularly in political cases, is the defendant's confession, usually obtained under duress and without the legal advice or knowledge of a defense lawyer. The authorities regularly deny defendants access to their lawyers until the day of the trial. Several dissidents who have served prison terms report that they were tried and sentenced without counsel and were not allowed to speak on their own behalf. Amnesty International stated that "trials in all cases fall far short of international standards for a fair trial."

The law provides the accused the right to an attorney, but the control that the Government exerts over the livelihood of members of the state-controlled lawyers' collectives—especially when they defend persons accused of state security crimes—compromises their ability to represent clients. Attorneys have reported reluctance to defend those charged in political cases out of fear of jeopardizing their own careers.

The Government summarily tried and imprisoned four members of the Concilio Cubano (see Section 1.d.). The police arrested Concilio Cubano founder Leonel Morejon Almagro on February 15. A court sentenced him on February 23 to 6 months' imprisonment for resisting authorities; on appeal, it sentenced him to an additional 9 months' imprisonment for disobedience. The court also fined his defense attorney, Jose Angel Izquierdo Gonzalez, for characterizing the trial as a "sham." In August the authorities transferred Morejon from Vallegrande prison on the outskirts of Havana to Ariza prison in Cienfuegos, on the southern coast of Cuba, for refusing to accept the prison's reeducation system.

The police also arrested Concilio Cubano secretariat member Lazaro Gonzalez Valdes on February 15, and a court sentenced him on February 22 to 14 months' imprisonment for disobedience and disrespect. Izquierdo, who also represented Gonzalez, was only informed of the charges a few hours before the trial and was only able to speak to his client a few minutes beforehand. People believed to be members of the Government's Rapid Response Brigade, armed with iron bars and sticks, reportedly surrounded the courthouse during the trial.

The police arrested Juan Francisco Monzon Oviedo, an alternate member of the coordinating body of Concilio Cubano, on March 18, and a court sentenced him on March 21 to 6 months' imprisonment for illegal association. His attorney did not appear for the trial. The authorities detained human rights advocate Roberto Lopez Montanez on February 23, and held him until a court tried and sentenced him on July 16 to 15 months' imprisonment for disrespect and falsification of documents. Despite serious health problems, the Government refused to release Lopez on bail pending trial.

According to Amnesty International, some 600 persons were imprisoned for various political crimes. Other human rights monitoring groups estimate that between 1,000 and 1,500 individuals—not including those held for dangerousness—were imprisoned on such charges as disseminating enemy propaganda, illicit association, contempt for authorities (usually for criticizing Fidel Castro), clandestine printing, or the broad charge of rebellion, often brought against advocates of peaceful democratic change. In a television interview in October 1995, President Castro acknowledged and attempted to justify the existence of political prisoners in Cuba by stating that this was a normal practice in many other countries.

f. *Arbitrary Interference with Privacy, Family, Home, or Correspondence.*—Although the Constitution provides for the inviolability of one's home and correspondence, official surveillance of private and family affairs by government-controlled mass organizations, such as the CDR's, remains one of the most pervasive and repressive features of Cuban life. The State has assumed the right to interfere in the lives of citizens, even those who do not actively oppose the Government and its practices. The Communist Party controls the mass organizations that permeate society. Their ostensible purpose is to "improve" the citizenry, but in fact their goal is to discover and discourage nonconformity. Citizen participation in these mass organizations has declined; the economic crisis has both reduced the Government's ability to provide material incentives for their participation and forced many people to engage in black market activities, which the mass organizations are supposed to report to the authorities.

The authorities utilize a wide range of social controls. The Interior Ministry employs an intricate system of informants and block committees (the CDR's) to monitor and control public opinion. While to a lesser extent than in the past, CDR's continue to report on suspicious activity, including conspicuous consumption; unauthorized meetings, including those with foreigners; and defiant attitudes toward the Government and the revolution.

State security often reads international correspondence and monitors overseas telephone calls and conversations with foreigners. The Government controls all access to the Internet, and all electronic mail messages are subject to censorship. Citizens do not have the right to receive publications from abroad, although newstands in foreigners-only hotels and outside certain hard currency stores do sell foreign newspapers and magazines. The Government continued to jam U.S.-operated Radio Marti and Television Marti; Radio Marti broadcasts frequently overcame the jamming attempts. Security agents subject dissidents, foreign diplomats, and journalists to harassment and surveillance.

The authorities regularly search people and their homes, without probable cause, to intimidate and harass them. During the Government's crackdown on Concilio Cubano, state security agents searched the homes of dozens of human rights advocates and independent journalists, seizing typewriters, personal and organizational documents, books, and foreign newspapers. On April 26, state security agents searched the office of the Independent Press Bureau of Cuba and seized files, correspondence, magazines, two typewriters, a computer, a printer, and office supplies.

The authorities regularly detained human rights advocates after they visited the U.S. Interests Section, confiscated their written reports of human rights abuses, and seized copies of U.S. newspapers and other informational material.

Section 2. Respect for Civil Liberties, Including:

a. *Freedom of Speech and Press.*—The Government does not allow criticism of the revolution or its leaders. Laws against antigovernment propaganda, graffiti, and insults against officials carry penalties of from 3 months to 1 year in prison. If President Castro or members of the National Assembly or Council of State are the object of criticism, the sentence is extended to 3 years. Local CDR's inhibit freedom of speech by monitoring and reporting dissent or criticism. Police and state security officials regularly harassed, threatened, beat, and otherwise abused human rights advocates in public and private as a means of intimidation and control.

The Constitution states that electronic and print media are state property and "cannot become in any case private property." The Communist Party controls all media as a means to indoctrinate the public. All media must operate under party guidelines and reflect government views. In late June, the Cuban Institute of Radio and Television demoted translator Pedro Hernandez Diaz for refusing to "soften" the subtitled translation of the last two lines of the "Star Spangled Banner" in a movie to be shown on Cuban television.

At year's end, the authorities fired the director and three writers and editors of the Havana Tribune, a weekly published by Havana province's Communist Party, for two pieces that appeared on December 22. One was an article that appeared to attack the pet project of two influential officials and the other an editorial subject to interpretation as a subtle criticism of the regime. These firings highlighted the ideological rigidity within which the official media must operate, and are expected to cause reporters and editors to follow the official line even more stridently in the future.

The Government usually did not jam foreign radio broadcasts; however, it continued to jam U.S.-operated Radio Marti and Television Marti (see Section 1.f.)

The Committee to Protect Journalists (CPJ) listed Cuba as one of the 10 worst "enemies of the press" because of the Government's prohibition against any independent publications or broadcasters. The Government subjects independent journalists to internal travel bans, periodic overnight detentions, the harassment of friends and relatives, seizures of written manuals and computer and facsimile equipment, and repeated threats of prolonged imprisonment. The CPJ publicly complained about the denial of essential telecommunications services to independent journalists. The Inter-American Press Association awarded its 1996 Grand Prize for Press Freedom to the Independent Press Bureau of Cuba, the Association of Independent Journalists of Cuba, Havana Press, CubaPress, and La Patria—all independent press agencies—for their work in the face of constant government harassment and threats.

Several visiting foreign journalists who met with independent journalists were harassed or expelled from the country. On June 12, four men seized Rodrigo Alonso, a Chilean national in Cuba to prepare a program on the life of Che Guevara, as he left his hotel. They forced him into a car, drove him around Havana for about 4 hours, and questioned him aggressively about his activities in Cuba. The authorities expelled Susan Bilello, a representative of the CPJ, and Jacques Perrot, a representative of the French-based "Reporters Sans Frontieres," from Cuba on June 20 and July 12, respectively.

The Government rigorously monitored other forms of expression and often arrested people for the crimes of enemy propaganda and clandestine printing. Enemy propaganda was considered to include materials ranging from the Universal Declaration of Human Rights, to reports of human rights violations, to mainstream foreign newspapers and magazines. In September state security agents searched the library of the Grand Masonic Lodge, seized "illegal" newspapers and magazines, and then met with the Masonic leadership. On September 15, before representatives of over 200 lodges, Grand Mason Eriberto Saborit Verdecia announced that Gustavo Pardo had been fired from his position as library director and expelled from the Masonic Lodge. He presented five cartons of books, which he suggested be burned.

The Government prohibits all diplomatic missions in Havana from printing or distributing publications, particularly newspapers or newspaper clippings, unless those publications deal exclusively with conditions in the mission's home country and receive prior government approval. The Government reacted negatively against foreign diplomats who focused on human rights problems in Cuba. It withdrew official approval for a new foreign ambassador because of his public comments that his door would be open to dissidents, and refused to renew the visa of another diplomat who maintained contacts with human rights activists, requiring that she leave the country for allegedly engaging in "activities incompatible with her diplomatic status." Foreign Ministry officials accused the diplomat of distributing antigovernment literature to dissident groups, citing such volumes as George Orwell's novel "Animal Farm" and biographies of Cuban independence heroes Jose Marti and Antonio Maceo.

On December 24, the ANPP rubber-stamped a new law proscribing citizens from seeking or providing any information to any representative of the U.S. Government that might be used directly or indirectly in the application of U.S. legislation. This includes accepting or distributing any publications, documents, or other material from any origin which the authorities might interpret as facilitating implementation of such legislation.

The Government circumscribes artistic, literary, and academic freedoms. In a March 23 speech to the Fifth Plenary Session of the Communist Party, Party Second Secretary Raul Castro chastised intellectuals, Communist Party members, artists, and the media for ideological laxity. The Communist Party shortly thereafter replaced the director of the Center for the Study of the Americas, a think tank that

Raul Castro had specifically criticized for having succumbed to foreign ideas and lifestyles. The authorities fired Jorge Luis Acanda, chairman of the Marxist Studies Department at the University of Havana, on April 19 after foreign news reports quoted him describing declining student enrollment in Marxist studies courses. They discharged University of Havana professors Miriam Gras and Gloria Leon without right of retirement in early September. The Communist Party had previously expelled the two professors. The party and the university reportedly objected to the regular professional contacts that Gras, a professor of political science, and Leon, a professor of American studies, maintained with foreign diplomats and visiting academics.

The educational system teaches that the State's interests have precedence over all other commitments. The Ministry of Education requires teachers to evaluate students' ideological character and note it in the records that students carry throughout their schooling, and which affect their future educational and career prospects. In many cases, the Government demands that teaching materials for courses such as mathematics or literature have an ideological content.

b. *Freedom of Peaceful Assembly and Association.*—Although the Constitution grants limited rights of assembly and association, these rights are subject to the requirement that they may not be "exercised against * * * the existence and objectives of the Socialist State." The law punishes any unauthorized assembly, including for private religious services, of more than three persons, even in a private home, by up to 3 months in prison and a fine. The authorities selectively enforce this prohibition and often use it as a legal pretext to harass and imprison human rights advocates. The authorities have never approved a public meeting of a human rights group. The Government did not formally respond to the December 22, 1995 written request to the Council of State from the Concilio Cubano for authorization to hold a meeting on February 24–27 to discuss Cuba's future. State security officials informed human rights leader Gustavo Arcos Bergnes verbally on February 16, the day after the crackdown began, that the Government would not permit such a meeting.

The Penal Code specifically outlaws "illegal or unrecognized groups." The Ministry of Justice, in consultation with the Interior Ministry, decides whether to give organizations legal recognition.

Along with recognized churches, the Roman Catholic humanitarian organization CARITAS, small human rights groups, and several nascent fraternal or professional organizations are the only associations outside the control of the State, the party, and mass organizations. The authorities continue to ignore these groups' applications for legal recognition, thereby subjecting members to potential charges of illegal association.

All other legally recognized nongovernmental groups are affiliated with or controlled by the Government. Referring to the research institutes that he had criticized in his March 23 speech, Raul Castro stated in April that "the party has the right to question and analyze whether a [research] center that depends on it for material and human resources is doing what it is supposed to do and, if not, to correct things." Several of these research institutes applied for and received consultative status as nongovernmental organizations with the U.N. Economic and Social Council (ECOSOC). Under ECOSOC rules, government support may be acceptable for a nongovernmental organization but should at no time "interfere with the free expression of views of the organization."

c. *Freedom of Religion.*—In recent years, the Government has eased the harsher aspects of its repression of religious freedom. In 1991 it allowed religious adherents to join the Communist Party. In 1992 it amended the Constitution to prohibit religious discrimination and removed references to "scientific materialism," i.e., atheism, as the basis for the Cuban State. Nevertheless, the State prohibits members of the armed forces from allowing anyone in their household to observe religious practices, except elderly relatives if their religious beliefs do not influence other family members and are not "damaging to the revolution."

Despite continued prohibitions on access to the media and establishment of religious schools, and restrictions on the number of foreign priests and nuns, the Roman Catholic Church has observed that it has relatively more latitude in which to carry out its pastoral mission. Church attendance in all denominations has grown in recent years.

However, religious persecution continues. In December 1995, the Government issued a resolution preventing any Cuban or joint enterprise from selling computers, fax machines, photocopiers, or other equipment to any church. A December 1, 1995 decree signed by Politburo member Jose Ramon Machado Ventura prohibited Christmas trees and decorations in public buildings, except those related to the tourist or foreign commercial sector, and completely prohibited Nativity scenes. (Official recognition of all religious holidays ended in 1961.) In February the Union of Communist Youth (UJC) affiliate within the lawyers' collective in the town of Palma Soriano expelled attorney Cesar Antonio Martinez Melero from his longstanding membership because of his active involvement in the Roman Catholic Church. In April a disciplinary board of the Julio Mella Polytechnic Institute suspended Raul Leyva Amaran's student stipend for 6 months for refusing on religious grounds to participate in a February 27 rally in support of the Government's shootdown of two civilian U.S. aircraft. Leyva had said that as a Catholic, he "did not support the violent death of anyone and for reasons of conscience [he] could not go to the rally."

The Government continued its 1961 prohibition on nearly all religious processions outside churches and denied churches access to the mass media.

The Government requires churches and other religious groups to register with the provincial registry of associations to obtain official recognition. The Government prohibits, with occasional exceptions, the construction of new churches, forcing many growing congregations to violate the law and meet in people's homes. Government harassment of private houses of worship continued, with evangelical denominations reporting evictions from, and bulldozing of, houses used for these purposes. In the province of Las Tunas, neighbors of one private house of worship tried to provoke fights with parishioners, blared music during religious services, and tried to pour boiling water through the windows during a religious service. In the western mining town of Moa, a group of evangelical leaders submitted a written appeal to the local Communist Party to stop the harassment of church members and the demolition of private houses of worship and to lift the prohibition on the construction, expansion, or remodeling of churches. The authorities warned religious leaders in Havana that they would impose fines from $550 to $2,800 (10,000–50,000 pesos), imprison leaders and withdraw official recognition from the religious denomination itself unless the private houses of worship were closed.

The Government, however, relaxed restrictions on members of the Jehovah's Witnesses, whom it had considered "active religious enemies of the revolution" for their refusal to accept obligatory military service or participate in state organizations. The Government authorized small assemblies of Jehovah's Witnesses, the opening of a Havana central office, and the publishing of the Jehovah's Witnesses' Watchtower magazine and other religious tracts.

State security officials regularly harassed human rights advocates prior to religious services commemorating special feast days or before significant national days. A crowd of thugs, armed with wooden clubs hidden inside rolled-up newspapers, surrounded the Sacred Heart Church in central Havana before a mass on July 13, the second anniversary of the Cuban Coast Guard's sinking of the "13th of March" tugboat in which 41 people died.

d. *Freedom of Movement Within the Country, Foreign Travel, Emigration, and Repatriation.*—The Government generally does not impose legal restrictions on domestic travel, except for persons found to be HIV-positive, whom it initially restricts to sanitoriums for treatment and therapy before conditionally releasing them to the community. However, state security officials forbade some human rights advocates and independent journalists from traveling outside their home provinces and has begun to sentence others to internal exile (see Section 1.d.).

The Government imposes some restrictions on both emigration and temporary foreign travel. It allows the majority of persons who qualify for immigrant or refugee status in other countries to leave Cuba. In certain cases, however, the authorities delay or deny exit permits, usually without explanation. Some of the denials involve professionals who have tried to emigrate and whom the Government subsequently banned from working in their occupational field. The Government refused permission to others because it considers their cases sensitive for political or state security reasons. The Government also routinely denies exit permits to young men approaching the age of military service until their 27th birthday, even when it has authorized the rest of the family to leave. However, most of those cases approved for migration to the United States under the September 9, 1994 U.S.-Cuban migration agreement eventually receive exemption from obligatory service and exit permits.

Migrants who travel to the United States must pay fees of $600 per adult, $400 per child, plus airfare. Such fees—which must be paid in dollars—are equivalent to 2½ years of a professional person's salary. In April a ministerial decree reduced the fee by half for 1,000 individuals, but by year's end, 238 of these individuals still could not pay even this reduced amount. The International Organization for Migration is considering options to handle the fees for those refugees.

The Government denied temporary exit permits to several human rights advocates, including Osvaldo Paya Sardinas, Vladimiro Roca Antunez, and Rene Gomez Manzano.

The Penal Code provides for imprisonment from 1 to 3 years or a fine of $15 to $50 (300 to 1,000 pesos) for unauthorized departures by boat or raft. The office of the U.N. High Commissioner for Refugees (UNHCR) has stated that it regards any sentence for illegal exit of over 1 year as harsh and excessive. Under the terms of the May 2, 1995 U.S.-Cuba migration accord, the Government agreed not to prosecute or retaliate against rafters returned to Cuba from international or U.S. waters.

In August 1994, the Government eased restrictions on visits by, and repatriation of, Cuban emigrants. Cubans who establish residency abroad and who are in possession of government-issued "permits to reside abroad" may travel to Cuba without visas. The Government reduced the age of people eligible to travel abroad from 20 to 18 years and extended the period for temporary stay abroad from 6 to 11 months. In November 1995, the Government announced that emigrants who are considered not to have engaged in "hostile actions" against the Government and who are not subject to criminal proceedings in their country of residence may apply at Cuban consulates for renewable, 2-year multiple-entry travel authorizations.

The Constitution provides for the granting of asylum to individuals persecuted "for their ideals or struggles for democratic rights against imperialism, fascism, colonialism, and neocolonialism; against discrimination and racism; for national liberations; for the rights of workers, peasants, and students; for their progressive political, scientific, artistic, and literary activities, for socialism and peace." The Government honors the principle of first asylum and provided it to a small number of persons in 1996. According to the UNHCR, five foreign nationals sought asylum or refugee status from the Government in 1996. There were no reports of the force return of persons to countries where they feared persecution.

Section 3. Respect for Political Rights: The Right of Citizens to Change Their Government

Citizens have no legal right to change their government or to advocate change. The Constitution proscribes any political organization other than the Communist Party. A small group of leaders select members of its highest government bodies—the Politburo and the Central Committee.

The authorities tightly control all elections. The Government has ignored calls for democratic reform. The European Union suspended negotiations toward a cooperation agreement in February because of lack of progress toward political or economic reform and in December adopted a common position binding on all member states. It directly links improvement of European Union relations with Cuba to progress toward a democratic transition and an improvement in the human rights situation. The Government rejects any change judged incompatible with the revolution. The Government has systematically retaliated against those who have peacefully sought political change.

Although not a formal requirement, Communist Party membership is in fact a prerequisite for high-level official positions and professional advancement.

Government leadership positions continued to be dominated by men. There are very few women or minorities in policymaking positions in the Government or the party. There are three women on the Politburo. Two of the 14 provincial party secretaries are women, the first chosen in 1993. The head of the Union of Communist Youth is a woman. Although blacks and mulattos make up over half the population, they hold only 2 seats in the 26-member Politburo.

Section 4. Governmental Attitude Regarding International and Nongovernmental Investigation of Alleged Violations of Human Rights

The Government does not recognize any domestic human rights groups, or permit them to function legally. The Government subjects domestic human rights advocates to intense intimidation, harassment, and repression. In violation of its own statutes, the Government refuses to consider applications for legal recognition submitted by human rights monitoring groups.

The Government has steadfastly rejected international human rights monitoring. In 1992 Cuba's U.N. representative stated that Cuba would not recognize the UNHRC mandate on Cuba and would not cooperate with the Special Rapporteur, despite being a UNHRC member. This policy remains unchanged. The Government consistently refused even to acknowledge requests by the Special Rapporteur to visit Cuba.

Section 5. Discrimination Based on Race, Sex, Religion, Disability, Language, or Social Status

Cuba is a multiracial society with a black and mixed race majority. The Constitution forbids discrimination based on race, sex, or national origin, although evidence suggests that racial and sexual discrimination occur often.

Women.—Violent crime is rarely reported in the press, and there are no publicly available data regarding the incidence of domestic violence. The law establishes strict penalties for rape, and the Government appears to enforce the law. Prostitution has increased greatly in the last few years; press reports indicate that tourists from various countries visit specifically to patronize inexpensive prostitutes. During its 1995 annual meeting, the official Federation of Cuban Women criticized government-sponsored advertising that promoted sex-related tourism.

The Family Code states that women and men have equal rights and responsibilities regarding marriage, divorce, raising children, maintaining the home, and pursuing a career. Women are subject to the same restrictions on property ownership as men. The Maternity Law provides 18 weeks of maternity leave and grants working women preferential access to goods and services. About 40 percent of all women work, and they are well represented in the professions.

Children.—The Constitution states that the Government will protect "family, maternity, and matrimony." It also states that children, legitimate or not, have the same rights under the law and notes the duties of parents to protect them. Education is free and is grounded in Marxist ideology. State organizations and schools are charged with the "integral formation of children and youth." The national health care system covers all citizens. There is no societal pattern of abuse of children.

People with Disabilities.—The law prohibits discrimination based on disability, and there have been few complaints of such discrimination. There are no laws that mandate accessibility to buildings for people with disabilities.

National/Racial/Ethnic Minorities.—Many blacks have benefitted from the social changes of the revolution. Nevertheless, there have been numerous reports of disproportionate police harassment of black youths.

Section 6. Worker Rights

a. *The Right of Association.*—The Constitution gives priority to state or collective needs over individual choices regarding free association or provision of employment. The "demands of the economy and society" take precedence over an individual worker's preferences. The law prohibits strikes; none are known to have occurred. Established labor organizations have a mobilization function and do not act as trade unions or promote or protect worker rights, including the right to strike. Such organizations are under the control of the State and the Party.

The Communist Party selects the leaders of the sole legal confederation, the Confederation of Cuban Workers, whose principal responsibility is to ensure that government production goals are met. Despite disclaimers in international forums, the Government explicitly prohibits independent unions and none exist. There has been no change since the 1992 International Labor Organization (ILO) finding that independent unions "do not appear to exist" and its ruling that Cuba violated ILO norms on freedom of association and the right to organize. Those who attempt to engage in union activities face government persecution.

Workers can lose their jobs for their political beliefs, including their refusal to join the official union. The authorities dismissed Blanca Nieves Cruz Rivero, a secretary for 13 years with the Ministry of Justice in the province of Pinar del Rio, from her job on April 16. According to her dismissal letter, Nieves violated her work contract by "refusing to participate in the mass organizations and to be affiliated with the public administration union; and for having contact with people who do not share the philosophy of the revolution and for opposing it in an open manner as an activist of so-called human rights groups; and for having realized activities such as speaking on enemy radio stations that transmit from abroad messages of a counterrevolutionary content." Nieves had written an open letter to Raul Castro on April 2 criticizing his speech to the Fifth Communist Party Congress and had been interviewed on Radio Marti.

b. *The Right to Organize and Bargain Collectively.*—Collective bargaining does not exist. The State Committee for Work and Social Security sets wages and salaries for the state sector. Since all legal unions are government entities, antiunion discrimination by definition does not exist.

In 1993 the Government removed some of the restrictions on self-employment imposed in 1968 and allowed people to apply for licenses to work in over 125 different occupations, expanded to over 160 in 1994. Besides adding another 20 occupational categories, in 1995 the Government removed its previous ban on self-employment licenses for university graduates. However, university graduates cannot get self-employment licenses to work in their professional field and must remain employed in their state job to qualify for a self-employment license.

There are no functioning export processing zones in Cuba, although the 1995 Foreign Investment Law (Law 77), authorizes the establishment of free trade zones and industrial parks. Law 77 continued to deny workers the right to contract directly with foreign companies investing in Cuba. The Government requires foreign investors to contract workers through state employment agencies, which are paid in foreign currency and, in turn, pay their workers in pesos. Workers subcontracted by state employment agencies must meet certain political qualifications. According to Marcos Portal, Minister of Basic Industry, the state employment agencies consult with the party, the Confederation of Cuban Workers, and the Union of Communist Youth to ensure that the workers chosen deserve to work in a joint enterprise.

c. *Prohibition of Forced or Compulsory Labor.*—Neither the Constitution nor the Labor Code prohibit forced labor. The Government maintains correctional centers where it sends people for crimes such as dangerousness. They are forced to work on farms or building sites, usually with no pay and inadequate food. The authorities often imprison internees who do not cooperate. The Government employs special groups of workers, known as "microbrigades," on loan from other jobs, on special building projects. These microbrigades have increased importance in the Government's efforts to complete tourist and other priority projects. Workers who refuse to volunteer for these jobs often risk discrimination or job loss. Microbrigade workers, however, reportedly receive priority consideration for apartments. The military channels some conscripts to the Youth Labor Army, where they serve their 2-year military service requirement working on farms that supply both the armed forces and the civilian population.

d. *Minimum Age for Employment of Children.*—The legal minimum working age is 17 years. The Labor Code permits employment of 15- and 16-year-olds to obtain training or fill labor shortages. All students over age 11 are expected to devote 30 to 45 days of their summer vacation to farm work, laboring up to 8 hours per day. The Ministry of Agriculture uses "voluntary labor" by Student Work Brigades extensively in the farming sector. The law requires school attendance until the ninth grade, and this law is generally respected.

e. *Acceptable Conditions of Work.*—The minimum wage varies by occupation and is set by the Bureau of Labor and Social Security. The minimum monthly wage for a maid, for example, is $8.25 (165 pesos); for a bilingual office clerk, $9.50 (190 pesos); and for a gardener $10.75 (215 pesos). The Government supplements the minimum wage with free medical care, education, and subsidized housing and food. Even with these subsidies, however, a worker must earn far more than the average monthly wage to support a family. The Government rations most basic necessities such as food, medicine, clothing, and cooking gas, which are in very short supply, if available at all.

The standard work week is 44 hours, with shorter workdays in hazardous occupations, such as mining. The Government also reduced the workday in some governmental offices and state enterprises to save energy. Workplace environmental and safety controls are usually inadequate, and the Government lacks effective enforcement mechanisms. The Labor Code establishes that a worker who considers his life in danger because of hazardous conditions has the right not to work in his position or not to engage in specific activities until such risks are eliminated. According to the Labor Code, the worker remains obligated to work temporarily in whatever other position may be assigned him at a salary prescribed by law. Industrial accidents apparently are frequent, but the Government suppresses such reports.

DOMINICA

Dominica is a multiparty, parliamentary democracy and a member of the Commonwealth of Nations. A Prime Minister, a Cabinet and a unicameral Legislative Assembly compose the Government. A President, nominated by the Prime Minister in consultation with the leader of the opposition party, elected for a 5-year term by the Parliament, is head of state. The United Workers Party (UWP), led by Prime Minister Edison James, won 11 of 21 seats in Parliament in free and fair elections in June 1995. The UWP gained an additional seat in 1996 when the party won a by-election for a seat vacated by a member of the opposition. The Constitution calls for elections at least every 5 years.

The Dominica Police is the only security force. It is controlled by and responsive to the democratically elected Government.

Dominica's primarily agrarian economy depends on earnings from banana exports. The Government is attempting to develop the tourist industry, to diversify agricultural production, and to promote exports of raw fruits, vegetables, and coconut products, both within and outside the region. Per capita gross domestic product was about $2,400 in 1994.

Human rights are generally well respected. The principal human rights problems continued to be societal violence against women and children, and occasional instances of use of excessive force by police.

RESPECT FOR HUMAN RIGHTS

Section 1. Respect for the Integrity of the Person, Including Freedom From:

   a. *Political and Other Extrajudicial Killing.*—There were no reports of political or other extrajudicial killings.

   b. *Disappearance.*—There were no reports of politically motivated disappearances.

   c. *Torture and Other Cruel, Inhuman, or Degrading Treatment or Punishment.*—The Constitution prohibits such practices. There were, however, two reports of police brutality during the year. The police allegedly beat a young man in Grand Bay, but the Government has not charged anyone in the incident. In another case, police allegedly beat up a suspected drug dealer. The director of public prosecutions decided not to file charges in that case.

   Overcrowding and unsanitary conditions continue to be problems in Dominica's only prison facility. The prison provides work therapy, sports programs, educational opportunities, and counseling for inmates.

   d. *Arbitrary Arrest, Detention, or Exile.*—The law requires that police charge persons with a crime within 24 hours after arrest or detention or release them from custody. This is generally honored in practice, although often those arrested on Fridays remain the weekend in jail and are not charged until the following Monday. The other exception to usual practice is if the detainee cannot afford legal counsel.

   The Government does not use forced exile.

   e. *Denial of Fair Public Trial.*—The law provides for public trial before an independent, impartial court. Criminal defendants are presumed innocent until proven guilty, are allowed legal counsel, and have the right to appeal. Courts provide free legal counsel to the indigent only in capital cases.

   There were no reports of political prisoners.

   f. *Arbitrary Interference with Privacy, Family, Home, or Correspondence.*—The Constitution prohibits such practices. Government authorities generally respect these prohibitions, and violations are subject to effective legal sanction.

Section 2. Respect for Civil Liberties, Including:

   a. *Freedom of Speech and Press.*—The Constitution provides for the right of free expression, and the Government respects this in practice. The political opposition openly criticizes the Government. Dominica's main radio station is state owned and has a government-appointed board. There is also an independent radio station owned by the Catholic Church.

   The print media consist of three private newspapers. Dominicansenjoy good access to independent news sources through cable television and radio reception from neighboring islands. The print media consist of two private newspapers and political party journals; all publish without censorship or government interference.

   The Government does not restrict academic freedom.

   b. *Freedom of Peaceful Assembly and Association.*—The Constitution provides for these rights, and with one exception in 1996, the Government has respected them in practice. In August Prime Minister James banned political meetings in the Mahaut constituency when the ruling United Workers Party and the opposition Dominica Freedom Party failed to reach agreement on the use of a school and school grounds for a political rally. Both parties had scheduled a rally at the same time and place. Saying that there was a possibility of a breakdown in law and order, Prime Minister James banned all political meetings in the constituency for one weekend. The opposition Dominica Labour Party called the ban undemocratic. All parties, however, respected the order and no incidents were reported.

   c. *Freedom of Religion.*—The Constitution provides for freedom of religion, and the Government respects this right in practice.

   d. *Freedom of Movement Within the Country, Foreign Travel, Emigration, and Repatriation.*—The law provides for these rights, and the authorities respect them in practice. The Government may revoke passports if subversion is suspected but has not done so in recent times.

   The Government has not formulated a policy regarding refugees, asylees, or first asylum. The issue of the provision of first asylum did not arise. There were no reports of forced expulsion of anyone having a valid claim to refugee status; however, government practice remains undefined.

Section 3. Respect for Political Rights: The Right of Citizens to Change Their Government

The Constitution provides citizens with the right to change their government peacefully, and citizens exercise this right in practice through periodic, free, and fair elections held on the basis of universal suffrage.

In the last national elections in June 1995, the United Workers Party defeated the incumbent Dominica Freedom Party, taking 11 of 21 seats in Parliament. In a by-election in August, the UWP gained an additional seat when it won a seat vacated by a member of the Dominica Freedom Party, giving the UWP a total of 12 seats. The Dominica Freedom Party currently holds four seats, and the Dominica Labour Party holds five seats.

There are no impediments in law or in fact to the participation of women in leadership roles in government or political parties. Voters elected two women to Parliament in the June 1995 elections. Indigenous Carib Indians participate in national political life and enjoy the same civil rights accorded other Dominican nationals.

Section 4. Governmental Attitude Regarding International and Nongovernmental Investigation of Alleged Violations of Human Rights

There are no government restrictions on the formation of local human rights organizations, although no such groups exist. Several advocacy groups, such as the Association of Disabled People and a women's and children's self-help organization, operate freely and without government interference. There were no requests for investigations of human rights abuses from international or regional human rights groups.

Section 5. Discrimination Based on Race, Sex, Religion, Disability, Language, or Social Status

The Constitution includes provisions against racial, sexual, and religious discrimination, which the authorities respect in practice.

Women.—Beyond the general protection of the Constitution, women do not benefit from any specific civil rights legislation. There is little open discrimination against women, yet sexual harassment and domestic violence cases are common, and there is no family court to deal specifically with domestic violence issues. Women can bring charges against husbands for battery, and both the police and the courts prosecute cases of rape and sexual assault, but there are no specific spousal abuse laws. The Welfare Department assists victims of abuse by finding temporary shelter, providing counseling to both parties, or recommending police action. The Welfare Department reports all cases of abuse to the police. The courts may issue protective orders, but the police do not consistently enforce them.

Property ownership continues to be deeded to "heads of households," who are usually males. When the husband head of household dies without a will, the wife cannot inherit the property or sell it, although she can live in it and pass it to her children. In the civil service, the law establishes fixed pay rates for specific jobs, whatever the gender of the incumbent. There is no law requiring equal pay for equal work for private sector workers.

Children.—Various laws enumerate children's rights, but their enforcement is hampered by lack of staffing in government agencies. Reported cases of child abuse have more than doubled since 1993, when 253 were recorded; the Government has not responded with any increase in the number of social workers assigned to handle such cases. The Social Welfare Office, which has only six staff members to deal with all welfare problems, handles complaints of child abuse.

Although the maximum sentence for sexual molestation (rape, incest) is life imprisonment, the normal sentence given is 15 years except in the case of murder. The age of consent to sexual relations is 16 years.

People With Disabilities.—Beyond the general protection of the Constitution, there is no specific legislation dealing with the disabled. There is no requirement mandating access for those with disabilities.

Indigenous People.—There is a significant Carib Indian population, estimated at 3,000, of a total population of 72,000. Most live on a 3,700-acre reservation created in 1903. School, water, and health facilities available on the Carib reservation are rudimentary but similar to those available to other rural Dominicans.

Section 6. Worker Rights

a. *The Right of Association.*—All workers have the legal right to organize, to choose their representatives, and to strike, but unions represent less than 10 percent of the work force. All unions are independent of the Government. While there are no direct ties, members of certain political parties dominate some unions There is no restriction on forming labor federations, and unions are affiliated with various international labor bodies.

b. *The Right to Organize and Bargain Collectively.*—Unions have legally defined rights to organize workers and to bargain with employers. Collective bargaining is widespread in the nonagricultural sectors of the economy, including the government service, and there is also recourse to mediation and arbitration by the Government. The law prohibits antiunion discrimination by employers, and judicial and police authorities enforce union rights. In addition, employers must reinstate workers fired for union activities. It is legally compulsory for employers to recognize unions as bargaining agents once both parties have followed appropriate procedures. Department of Labour inspectors under the supervision of the Labour Commissioner enforce labor legislation, but the small Labour Inspection Office lacks qualified personnel to carry out its duties.

Labor regulations and practices governing Dominica's industrial areas and export firms do not differ from those prevailing in the rest of the economy.

c. *Prohibition of Forced or Compulsory Labor.*—The law prohibits forced or compulsory labor, and such labor is not known to exist.

d. *Minimum Age for Employment of Children.*—The minimum legal age for employment is 15 years. Employers generally observe this law without government enforcement.

e. *Acceptable Conditions of Work.*—The law sets minimum wages for various categories of workers. These were last revised in November 1989. The minimum wage rate for most categories of workers is $0.56 (EC$1.50) per hour, but for domestic servants it is $0.37 (EC$1.00) per hour if meals are included, and $0.46 (EC$1.25) per hour if meals are not included. The minimum wage is not sufficient to provide a decent standard of living for a worker and family. However, most workers (including domestics) earn more than the legislated minimum wage.

The standard legal workweek is 40 hours in 5 days. The law provides for a minimum of 2 weeks' paid vacation per year. The Employment Safety Act provides occupational health and safety regulation. Local nongovernmental organizations and one major union consider it to be consistent with international standards. The Advisory Committee on Safety and Health is an established body but has never met. The rarely used enforcement mechanism consists of inspections by the Department of Labour, which can and does prescribe specific compliance measures, impose fines, and prosecute offenders. Workers have the right to remove themselves from unsafe work environments without jeopardy to continued employment.

DOMINICAN REPUBLIC

The Constitution provides for a popularly elected President and a bicameral Congress. In practice, the distribution of power has favored the executive branch. Following a free and fair presidential election in which political parties across the ideological spectrum participated, Leonel Fernandez of the Dominican Liberation Party assumed the presidency August 16. He replaced Joaquin Balaguer, who served as president for 22 of the past 30 years. The Government began an overhaul of the nominally independent judiciary, which was highly politicized in the past.

The security forces are the National Police (PN), the National Department of Investigations (DNI), the National Drug Control Directorate (DNCD), and the military (army, air force, and navy). The PN is under the Secretary of the Interior and Police; the military is under the Secretary of the Armed Forces; and the DNI and DNCD, which have personnel from both the police and the military, report directly to the President. The security forces are generally responsive to civilian executive branch authority. However, some members of the security forces continued to commit human rights abuses, sometimes with the tacit acquiescence of the civil authorities.

The economy, once heavily dependent on sugar and other agricultural exports, has diversified; tourism and Free Trade Zones (FTZ's) are now major sources of income and employment. Remittances from abroad provide an estimated 10 percent of gross domestic product, which is about $1,572 per capita. State-owned firms such as the State Sugar Council (CEA), the Corporation for State Enterprises, and the Dominican Electricity Corporation have impeded economic growth because of financial and administrative ineptitude.

Principal human rights problems include continuing instances of extrajudicial killings by police, arbitrary detention and beatings of suspects, security services' refusal to obey judicial orders, interference with the judiciary, judicial corruption, maladministration of the courts, poor prison conditions, detention of suspects' relatives, abuses of Haitian migrants, compulsory labor, and impediments to free association. Workers in the state-owned sugar plantations and mills continued to work under deplorable conditions. Discrimination, violence against women, and prostitution are also serious problems.

RESPECT FOR HUMAN RIGHTS

Section 1. Respect for the Integrity of the Person, Including Freedom From:

a. *Political and Other Extrajudicial Killings*There were no reports of political killings, but there were 85 reports of extrajudicial killings by the security forces. These were usually committed by police pursuing suspects. In February an army patrol killed a child and wounded four others in the city of Santiago when it fired upon a vehicle which did not obey orders to stop. The officials were dismissed. In another incident, a pregnant 19-year-old woman died in police custody, allegedly from beating during interrogation. In another incident, according to the press and human rights activists, a police officer entered a private home and shot a 17-year-old while he slept with his infant child. Although police dispute the killer was actually a police officer, human rights activists report the alleged killer has since been promoted.

Military courts try military personnel charged with extrajudicial killings. Police tribunals have on occasion tried, convicted, and sentenced personnel charged with extrajudicial killings. According to press reports, police referred two cases of extrajudicial killings to civilian criminal courts in 1996.

b. *Disappearance.*—There were no reports of politically motivated disappearances.

The case of Narciso Gonzalez, a university professor and critic of the Balaguer government, who disappeared in May 1994, continued to languish in the court system. The case came before the Inter-American Commission on Human Rights (IACHR) in October. The Fernandez Government then reopened the case. The police gave the Attorney General a detailed report of their findings, and the investigating judge interviewed dozens of people. Although there have been no indictments, the authorities appeared to be pursuing the case seriously and submitted a response to the IACHR in November.

c. *Torture and Other Cruel, Inhuman, or Degrading Treatment or Punishment.*—Torture and other forms of physical abuse are illegal, but instances of security service personnel physically abusing detainees continued. Lack of supervision, training, and accountability throughout the law enforcement and corrections systems exacerbate the problem of physical abuse. Human rights groups and the press reported numerous incidents of physical abuse of detainees while in custody. Such incidents included the reported beating of four accused car thieves while they were suspended by their wrists for several hours. In December the Attorney General publicly accused the DNCD of practicing torture and called upon its director to stop the practice. The authorities usually order little or no punishment for perpetrators of such abuse. Although punishment may range up to 5 years' incarceration for serious cases of abuse, as a rule judges have sentenced convicted officials to sentences ranging from a 1-month suspension to 6 months' incarceration.

Prison conditions are poor. Prisons are grossly overcrowded, and health and sanitary conditions are substandard. Conditions at the largest prison, La Victoria, pose a serious threat to life and health. Suspects awaiting trial are kept with convicts serving their sentences. The Government estimated that in September there were 500 prisoners awaiting trial at La Victoria who have been jailed longer than the maximum sentence for their crime.

Juveniles are at times held with adult offenders. The Attorney General in September estimated that as many as 300 minors were in custody in La Victoria prison. Some prison personnel reportedly engage in extortion and other corrupt activities, and most prisoners find it necessary to rely on relatives or their own finances to be fed adequately. Medical care suffers from a lack of supplies and available physicians.

Shortly after the new Government took office, inmates rioted in several prisons, including three times at La Victoria. The Government responded with an overhaul of the penal system in conjunction with its program of judicial reform. The authorities took a census of all the prisons, and the Attorney General's office began a case-by-case review of all prisoners. The authorities segregated minors, the infirm, and the mentally ill from other prisoners. They began a renovation program, starting at La Victoria, and sent medical teams to visit the prisons. Prisoners are now allowed access to telephones and recreation programs are under consideration.

The Government permits prison visits by independent human rights monitors.

d. *Arbitrary Arrest, Detention, or Exile.*—The Constitution stipulates that authorities may detain suspects for a maximum of 48 hours before arraignment, after which they must charge or release them. However, in special circumstances, suspects may be detained for longer periods with the approval of the prosecutor's office. Security forces continued to violate constitutional provisions by detaining suspects for "investigation" or "interrogation" beyond the prescribed 48-hour limit. Security forces traditionally detain all suspects and witnesses in a crime and use the investigative process to determine which ones are innocent and merit release and which ones they should continue to hold. Under the new Government, police commanders must report the previous day's arrests to the local prosecutor to preclude abuse of the 48-hour limit.

The DNCD and National Police continued to engage in indiscriminate roundups of people in poorer neighborhoods. The security forces also continued to detain relatives and friends of suspected criminals with the aim of forcing the surrender of suspects. Civil authorities have not acted to curb these abuses.

While the law does not prohibit exile, there are no known cases of citizens in forced exile. Before the June 30 presidential election, a former prosecutor, who while abroad charged that senior Dominican officials were involved in corruption and drug trafficking, was not allowed to return. The IACHR heard the case but has not released any findings. After the election, she entered the country without incident.

e. *Denial of Fair Public Trial.*—Although the Constitution stipulates an independent judiciary, in practice, interference from other public and private entities, including the executive branch, substantially undermines judicial independence.

The judicial system was in flux during the second half of the year. In August the National Judicial Council (CNM) was finally named after being mandated by the 1994 constitutional reforms. The seven-member CNM includes the President and legislators from both houses of Congress, the president of the Supreme Court, and a second supreme court justice. Beginning in September, the council held its first meetings, which dealt with procedural matters. Historically the Senate chose all judges, but the constitutional reforms ended the Senate's exclusive role in appointing judges and provide for a professional career service for judges, including lifelong appointments. The CNM is to appoint justices of the Supreme Court, and they will name judges to the lower courts. At year's end, the CNM had not named the justices for the new Supreme Court. The autonomy of the judiciary remains in question.

The Constitution provides for public trial. The courts normally appoint lawyers at public expense for indigent defendants in felony cases but rarely in criminal misdemeanor cases. The judicial system is plagued by chronic delays. Many suspects suffer long pretrial detention; nearly 86 percent of the prison population is awaiting trial. There are also perennial accusations of corruption. The judicial system provides for bail. However, cases in which bail is posted rarely come to trial, circumventing the intended purpose of bail.

Military or police courts have jurisdiction over members of the security forces, but a military or police board frequently remands cases involving capital crimes (murder, rape, etc.) to civilian courts for review after dishonorable discharge.

There were no reports of political prisoners.

f. *Arbitrary Interference with Privacy, Family, Home, or Correspondence.*—Generally, the Government does not arbitrarily use wiretapping or other surreptitious methods to interfere with the private lives of persons or families and observes constitutional provisions against invasion of the home. The authorities may only search a residence in the presence of a prosecutor or an assistant prosecutor, or in cases of "hot pursuit," or where there is reason to believe that a crime is in progress.

The security forces continued to detain relatives and friends of suspects to try to compel suspects to surrender (see Section 1.d.).

Section 2. Respect for Civil Liberties, Including:

a. *Freedom of Speech and Press.*—The law provides for these freedoms, and the Government usually respects them in practice. During the presidential campaign, a court tried a journalist, Juan Bolivar Diaz, in absentia and sentenced him to 6 months' imprisonment for libel for a book that set forth the case for fraud in the 1994 elections. The incident provoked vigorous public protest; Diaz appealed the sentence and remained free at year's end.

Citizens of all political persuasions exercise freedom of speech. The numerous privately owned radio and television stations broadcast all political points of view. A 1971 law prohibits foreign-language broadcasts.

The Government controls one television station but no major newspapers. Newspapers freely reflect independent and opposition points of view. Although journalists operate in a relatively tolerant environment, some self-censorship exists for fear of retaliation, ranging from loss of influence to loss of employment.

Public and private universities enjoy broad academic freedom. The main public university, the Autonomous University of Santo Domingo, with approximately 35,000 students, has no restrictions on enrollment and maintains a policy of nonintervention (other than curriculum development) in classroom affairs. The Government exerts no control over private universities, except for the preservation of standards, and teachers are free to espouse their own theories without government oversight.

b. *Freedom of Peaceful Assembly and Association.*—The Constitution provides for these freedoms, which the Government commonly respects in practice. Outdoor public marches and meetings require permits, which the Government usually grants. Political parties freely affiliate with their foreign counterpart organizations. Professional organizations of lawyers, doctors, teachers, and others function freely and can maintain relations with counterpart international bodies of diverse political philosophies.

c. *Freedom of Religion.*—The Constitution prohibits discrimination on religious grounds, and the Government does not interfere with the practice of religion.

d. *Freedom of Movement Within the Country, Foreign Travel, Emigration, and Repatriation.*—Citizens face no unusual legal restrictions on travel within or outside the country.

Haitians continue to come to the Dominican Republic, some legally but most undocumented, in search of economic opportunity. Throughout the year, security forces, particularly the army, repatriated undocumented Haitian nationals believed to be in the country illegally. The expulsions occurred in various regions of the country. Thousands were expelled immediately prior to the May 16 presidential election, but there was no noticeable upsurge in expulsions prior to the June 30 runoff election or since. According to international and Dominican human rights groups and the United Nations High Commissioner for Refugees (UNHCR), during the first few months of the year, Haitian deportees were humiliated by having their heads shaved and painted and being left without their belongings far from where they live in the country. The UNHCR reported that there were 607 Haitian refugees.

According to a 1984 law, an applicant for refugee status must be referred to the National Committee for Refugees by the National Office of Refugee Affairs, which has not been established. Instead, the Department of Immigration issues documentation to UNHCR-certified refugees. While these documents are accepted by the police and immigration officials, the process by which they are issued does not comply with the law.

The Government cooperates with the UNHCR and other humanitarian organizations in assisting refugees. The Government provides first asylum and resettlement. The Government provided documentation in 14 asylum cases in 1996; there were no resettlements. There were no reports of the forced return of persons to a country where they feared persecution.

Section 3. Respect for Political Rights: The Right of Citizens to Change Their Government

The Dominican Republic is a constitutional democracy. The President, all 150 members of the Senate and Chamber of Deputies, and the mayors and city council members of more than 100 municipalities are freely elected every 4 years by secret ballot and universal adult suffrage. Active duty police and military personnel may not vote. The President appoints the governors of the 29 provinces. Opposition groups of the left, right, and center operate openly.

Presidential elections were held on May 16 with a runoff election between the two top contenders on June 30. A new system of voting was used to reduce opportunities for fraud. There were accusations from all sides of attempted fraud and other irregularities, including vote suppression through buying or confiscating voter identification cards. In spite of these accusations, international and Dominican observers praised the process as the cleanest elections in the country's history; the losing candidates accepted the results; and power was transferred peacefully and smoothly.

The nation has a functioning multiparty system. In practice the President can dominate public policy formulation and implementation. He can exercise his authority through the use of the veto, discretion to act by decree, and influence as the leader of his party. Traditionally, the President has predominant power in the Government, effectively making many important decisions by decree.

Congress had limited power under the previous government. The two main opposition parties and their allies combined hold 88 and 96 percent of the lower and upper houses, respectively, leaving President Fernandez's party with scant congressional presence. The Congress also provides an open forum for the free exchange of views and debate.

Women and minorities confront no serious legal impediments to political participation. Women hold 14 seats in the 120-member House of Deputies and 1 seat in the 30-member Senate. Women continue to have representation in appointed positions, albeit limited. One of the 15 Cabinet secretaries is a woman, and women hold 3 of 29 provincial governorships.

Section 4. Governmental Attitude Regarding International and Nongovernmental Investigations of Alleged Violations of Human Rights

Nongovernmental human rights organizations operate freely without governmental interference. In addition to the Dominican Human Rights Committee, several other Haitian, church, and labor groups exist.

Section 5. Discrimination Based on Race, Sex, Religion, Disability, Language, or Social Status

The law prohibits discrimination based on race and sex. Such discrimination exists in society, but the Government has not acknowledged its existence or made efforts to combat it.

Women.—Domestic violence and sexual harassment are widespread. There are no laws protecting citizens from abuse by their spouses, and victims rarely report such abuse.

The Government does not vigorously enforce prostitution laws. Sex tourism is a growing industry, particularly in the north coast resort city of Sosua. The Government has no program in the area to educate prostitutes about the dangers of sexually transmitted diseases. Dominican women are also victims of rings that smuggle third-world women to Europe to work as prostitutes in conditions rife with exploitation and mistreatment. Corruption and a reluctance to restrict emigration hinder enforcement of the law.

Divorce is easily obtainable by either spouse, and women can hold property in their own names apart from their husbands. Traditionally, women have not shared equal social and economic status or opportunity with men, and men hold the overwhelming majority of leadership positions in all sectors. In many instances women are paid less than men in jobs of equal content and equal skill level. Some employers in industry reportedly give pregnancy tests to women before hiring them, as part of a medical examination. Some employers have stated, and workers confirm, that pregnant women are not hired.

Children.—The former government did not support its professed commitment to child welfare with financial and human resources. Despite the existence of government institutions dedicated to child welfare, private social and religious organizations carry the principal burden. The private institutions receive no government financing. In September at a gathering of children celebrating National Children's Rights Day, President Fernandez promised the Government's full support to the entities charged with implementing the 1994 Minor's Code. The law requires only 6 years of formal education.

The most serious abuse involving children is the failure of the judicial system to protect the status of minors in criminal cases. The authorities sometimes treated minors as adults and incarcerated them in prison rather than juvenile detention centers. Courts for minors, mandated by the code, have not been established.

The unimplemented Minor's Code contains provisions against child abuse, including physical and emotional mistreatment, sexual exploitation, and child labor. It also provides for removal of a mistreated or delinquent child to a protective environment. However, according to local monitors, instances of child abuse were underreported because of traditional beliefs that family problems should be dealt with inside the family. Some in the tourist industry have provided or facilitated sexual exploitation of children. Tours are marketed overseas with the understanding that boys and girls can be found for sex partners.

People With Disabilities.—Disabled persons encounter discrimination in employment and provision of other services. Although the law contains provisions for physical access for the disabled to all new public and private buildings, the authorities have not uniformly enforced this law.

National/Racial/Ethnic Minorities.—Dominicans are strongly prejudiced against Haitians, many of whom are illegal immigrants and constitute a significant percentage of the unskilled manual labor force. The Government has not acknowledged the existence of this discrimination nor made any efforts to combat it. Darker-skinned Dominicans also face informal barriers to social and economic advancement.

Credible sources charge that the Government at times refuses to recognize individuals of Haitian ancestry born in the country as Dominican citizens. Lack of documentation also sometimes hinders the ability of children of Haitian descent to attend school where there is one available; some parents fail to seek documentation for fear of being deported.

Section 6. Worker Rights

a. *The Right of Association.*—The Constitution provides for the freedom to organize labor unions and also for the right of workers to strike (and for private sector employers to lock out workers). All workers, except the military and police, are free to organize, and workers in all sectors exercise this right.

Requirements for calling a strike include the support of an absolute majority of the workers of the company, a prior attempt to resolve the conflict through arbitration, written notification to the labor secretariat, and a 10-day waiting period following notification before proceeding with a strike. The Government respects association rights and places no obstacles to union registration, affiliation, or the ability to engage in legal strikes.

The Labor Code specifies in detail the steps legally required to establish a union, federation, and confederation. The code calls for automatic recognition of a union if the Government has not acted on its application within a specific time. In practice, the Government has readily facilitated recognition of labor organizations. Organized labor represents little more than 10 percent of the work force and is divided among three major confederations, four minor confederations, and a number of independent unions. Unions are independent of the Government and political parties.

There were two instances of union members being fired without cause. The unions have brought these cases to court, and the cases were still under consideration at year's end. Widespread discreet intimidation of union activity was reported. For example, union members in free trade zones (FTZ's) report that they hesitate to discuss union activity at work, even during break time, for fear of losing their jobs.

Labor unions can and do freely affiliate regionally and internationally.

b. *The Right to Organize and Bargain Collectively.*—Collective bargaining is lawful and may take place in firms in which a union has gained the support of an absolute majority of the workers. Only a minority of companies has collective bargaining pacts. The Labor Code stipulates that workers cannot be dismissed because of their trade union membership or activities.

The Labor Code establishes a system of labor courts for dealing with disputes, but their effectiveness is limited by lack of resources and political judges. Some labor courts enjoy reputations for honesty, depending on the presiding judge. Labor courts exist in five jurisdictions, but the problems that the courts were established to address still prevail in the rest of the country.

The Labor Code applies in the 32 established FTZ's, which employ approximately 170,000 workers, mostly women. Workplace regulations and their enforcement in the FTZ's do not differ from those in the country at large, although working conditions are sometimes better. Some FTZ companies have a history of discharging workers who attempt to organize unions. Although there are approximately 70 unions in the FTZ's, many exist only on paper. The majority are affiliated with the National Federation of Free Trade Zone Workers.

The State Sugar Council (CEA) employs workers from more than 100 unions. Dominican workers predominate in most of the unions, although two unions are Haitian-dominated. The CEA has long maintained a negative attitude toward additional organizing efforts.

c. *Prohibition of Forced or Compulsory Labor.*—The law prohibits forced or compulsory labor.

There were numerous credible reports of forced or coerced overtime in factories. Employers, particularly in the FTZ's, sometime locked the exit doors of factories at the normal closing time so that workers could not leave. There have been reports of workers being fired for refusing to work overtime, and both employers and workers state that newly hired workers are not informed that overtime is optional.

Haitian sugar cane workers continued to encounter restrictions on their freedom of movement. These include armed guards on the plantations who try to find departing workers before they leave company lands. While pay is still low and living conditions harsh, experts from NGO's and unionists agree that working and living conditions among Haitian cane workers have improved in the past 5 years.

d. *Minimum Age for Employment of Children.*—The Labor Code prohibits employment of children under 14 years of age and places restrictions on the employment of children under the age of 16. These restrictions include a limitation of no more than 6 hours of daily work, no employment in dangerous occupations or establishments serving alcohol, and limitations on nighttime work. The law requires 6 years of formal education.

The high level of unemployment and lack of a social safety net create pressures on families to allow children to earn supplemental income. Tens of thousands of children work selling newspapers, shining shoes, or cleaning cars, often during school hours. The Government has proposed a fine for the parents of truant children.

There were no reports of child labor among cane cutters.

e. *Acceptable Conditions of Work.*—The Constitution provides the Government with legal authority to set minimum wage levels and the Labor Code assigns this task to a National Salary Committee. Congress may also enact minimum wage legislation. The minimum wage is approximately $75 (1,014 pesos) per month. This covers only a fraction of the living costs of a family in Santo Domingo, but many workers receive only the minimum wage. For example, 60 percent of government employees earn only the minimum wage.

The Labor Code establishes a standard work period of 8 hours per day and 44 hours per week. The code also stipulates that all workers are entitled to 36 hours of uninterrupted rest each week. In practice, a typical workweek is Monday through Friday plus a half a day on Saturday, but longer hours are not unusual. The code grants workers a 35 percent differential for work over 44 hours up to 68 hours per week and double time for any hours above 68 hours per week.

The Dominican Social Security Institute (IDSS) sets workplace safety and health conditions. The existing social security system does not apply to all workers and is underfunded. Both the IDSS and the Labor Secretariat have small corps of inspectors charged with enforcing standards. Inspector positions are customarily filled through political patronage. In practice, workers cannot remove themselves from hazardous workplace situations without jeopardy to continued employment.

Conditions for agricultural workers are in general much worse, especially in the sugar industry. On many sugar plantations, cane cutters are paid by the weight of cane cut rather than hours worked. Many cane cutters earn approximately $3.70 (50 pesos) per day. Many worker villages have high rates of disease and lack schools, medical facilities, running water, and sewage systems.

ECUADOR

Ecuador is a constitutional republic with a president and an 82-member unicameral legislature chosen in free elections. President Abdala Bucaram's governing coalition controls only 30 seats in the Congress. Congress has sweeping powers to question and censure cabinet ministers; such censure results in automatic dismissal of the minister in question. This is often used as a political tool by opposition political parties. Members of the Supreme Court preside over a judiciary that is constitutionally independent but in practice is susceptible to outside pressure.

The military enjoys substantial autonomy, reinforced by guaranteed revenues from the nation's oil exports, as well as from civil aviation, shipping, and other commercial sectors. The military has maintained a low profile in domestic politics since the return to constitutional rule in 1979. The National Police, responsible for domestic law enforcement and maintenance of internal order, falls under the civilian Ministry of Government and Police. There continued to be credible allegations of human rights abuses by the police and, in some isolated cases, members of the military.

The economy is based on private enterprise, although there continued to be heavy government involvement in key sectors such as petroleum, utilities, and aviation. The gross domestic product of $1,559 per capita provides most of the population with a low standard of living. The inflation rate for the year was 26 percent. The principal exports are oil, bananas, and shrimp, which are the country's leading sources of foreign exchange. Manufacturing for regional export markets is of growing importance. Most citizens are employed in the urban informal sector or as rural agricultural workers; rural poverty is extensive, and underemployment is high.

The most fundamental human rights abuse stems from shortcomings in the politicized and inefficient legal and judicial system. People are subject to arbitrary arrest; once incarcerated, they may wait years before coming to trial unless they resort to paying bribes. Other human rights abuses included isolated instances of extrajudicial killings; torture and other mistreatment of prisoners and detainees by the police; poor prison conditions; government failure to prosecute and punish human rights abusers; and violence and pervasive discrimination against women, Afro-Ecuadorians, and indigenous people. In August the Supreme Court resolved a controversial human rights case involving those accused of a 1993 ambush of a joint military and police riverine unit, by absolving the seven peasants of murder charges on the grounds that their confessions were obtained through torture. In September the President established a Truth and Justice Commission to investigate human rights abuses since the 1979 restoration of democracy.

RESPECT FOR HUMAN RIGHTS

Section 1. Respect for the Integrity of the Person, Including Freedom From:

a. *Political and Other Extrajudicial Killing.*—There were no reports of politically motivated killings. There continued to be credible reports of police involvement in extrajudicial killings, although the number of such reports declined significantly. The police often acted with impunity in such cases, because disciplinary action is the responsibility of the police itself. Although special police courts usually try cases involving police officers as defendants, the Government in some cases revoked this right and tried officers in civil courts.

The Ecumenical Committee for Human Rights (CEDHU) reported a total of nine extrajudicial killings. Six of these involved individuals killed by the police in the course of pursuing criminals, one involved a drunk policeman killing a citizen, and two were apparently the result of personal fights between victims and off-duty policemen.

In February policemen in the Amazonian town of Sucumbios chased a young black man named Jose Landazuri into a swamp, following reports that he had been involved in a robbery. Bystanders heard Landazuri shout "Don't shoot me," followed by the sound of gunfire. The police left the swamp without Landazuri. The family later found the body of Landazuri in the swamp with a bullet through his forehead. A police investigation concluded that he had been shot while resisting arrest.

On September 17, police shot and killed an alleged criminal, 16-year-old Miguel Manrique, during a drug raid on his house in the La Toja neighborhood of Quito. The police broke into Manrique's house without a warrant and said they shot him in a scuffle. The family claims that the youth was sleeping when the police broke in, and that the police shot him in the face at close range while he was wiping the sleep out of his eyes. On October 2, after a public outcry a criminal court ordered the arrest of police sergeant Ulvio Munoz in connection with Manrique's murder.

There were also instances in which citizens took the law into their own hands, leading to mob violence that resulted in deaths (see Section 1.e.). Faced with a growing number of such cases and complaints from human rights groups that the police were tolerant of vigilante justice, late in the year the police began to crack down on the practice. There were a number of news reports of police saving criminals from lynchings. For example, on September 30, policemen in the poor neighborhood of Santa Elena, Machala, rescued a thief who had been tied to a post by a crowd, beaten, and doused with gasoline. As members of the crowd looked for a match, the police cut him loose and took him to a hospital.

There were no reports of individuals killed by the military. A provincial court is investigating the apparent death of one Peruvian at the hands of local authorities in 1995 (see Section 1.b.).

In August a former policeman published a book and gave a series of interviews in which he claimed that police special units had participated in the execution of suspected leftist guerrillas during the 1980's. His revelations were questioned by some, but prompted Congress to create an investigating committee in September. Among other information, the former policeman provided the location of two alleged clandestine graveyards where he claimed the police buried the bodies of prisoners killed during interrogations in 1984–88. The Government promised a full investigation. Initial surveys of the sites by members of the press failed to indicate the presence of buried bodies.

Attorney General Leonidas Plaza told reporters on October 2 that the Inter-American Court of Human Rights had no jurisdiction in the case of Consuelo Benavides, a school teacher whom the army killed in 1985 because of alleged subversive activities. Plaza said that the courts had already tried the case and found several members of the military guilty. He noted that Congress authorized an indemnity to the Benavides family but said the country does not have $10 million the family seeks. President Bucaram told the press earlier that the Benavides family has a just claim, but that the Government has no money to pay it. He said that the Benavides family should seek compensation from then-President Febres Cordero, as the Bucaram Government had not committed the crime. The Benavides case is the first Ecuadorian case before the Inter-American Court. Human rights groups note that while the Government did eventually prosecute some of the military personnel involved in this murder, several of the most high-ranking suspects "escaped" from military confinement, and the statute of limitations spared others due to slow progress of the case in court.

b. *Disappearance.*—There were no reports of politically motivated disappearances.

In the wake of border hostilities with Peru in 1995, the Government of Peru claimed that 15 of its citizens had disappeared at the hands of Ecuadorian authorities. The Provincial Court in Loja province is investigating the apparent death of one Peruvian at the hands of local authorities, and another Peruvian detained in a military hospital in Quito has not been accounted for. However, there is no evidence that the 13 other Peruvian nationals were ever in Ecuador.

In September President Bucaram established a Truth and Justice Commission to investigate human rights abuses since the 1979 restoration of democracy. The Commission, made up of representatives of human rights organizations, the Church, and the Government, will have no judicial powers but is to report on unresolved human rights cases. In its first week, the Commission received 211 allegations of disappearances, although only 14 persons were alleged to have disappeared due to actions by agents of the State.

c. *Torture and Other Cruel, Inhuman, or Degrading Treatment or Punishment.*—Although the law prohibits torture and similar forms of intimidation and punishment, police continued to physically mistreat suspects and prisoners, usually with impunity. The CEDHU regularly published detailed reports on suspects who charged the police with torture. In these reports the CEDHU frequently named police officials alleged to be responsible and often included photographs of the victims with their wounds. In most cases, the police appeared to have abused such persons during investigations of ordinary street crime. According to the CEDHU and other human rights organizations, the victims reported that the police beat them, burned them with cigarettes, applied electric shocks or threatened them psychologically. In Guayaquil a television camera crew videotaped a police officer stomping on the head and kicking the face of a robbery suspect who had already been handcuffed and was lying on the ground.

Defense Ministry officials continued to deny mistreatment by the military of four Colombians whom they detained in August-September 1995 and who, according to the police, had suffered numerous contusions by the time the military handed them over to police custody. The Defense Ministry claimed that the contusions resulted from the detainees throwing themselves against the walls and floor during interrogation.

The Supreme Court rendered a landmark decision in August rejecting the admissibility of confessions obtained through torture. It overturned the conviction of 7 peasants accused of participating in the December 1993 ambush of a joint military and police riverine patrol along the Putumayo River in which 11 soldiers and police officers died. A lower court, which had found the defendants guilty of murder, acknowledged that the only evidence against the defendants consisted of their own confessions and noted in the court record that these confessions had been obtained through torture. The police investigation further substantiated that the defendants had been physically abused while in military custody. The "Putumayo seven" were released from prison in September, following 2½ years of detention. Human rights groups point to the Supreme Court decision as a factor that may encourage the police to cease the use of torture to extract confessions and turn to legitimate, if more resource-intensive, methods of investigating common crime.

The law permits police or military courts to try police officers and military defendants in closed sessions, in accordance with the respective military and police court martial manuals. Only the Supreme Court may try cases involving flag-rank officers. The police court in particular does not announce verdicts or punishments, if any, creating the strong impression that the police are immune from prosecution.

Conditions in detention centers generally continued to be poor. Prisons in the tropical coastal areas tend to be worse than those in the temperate highlands. Overcrowding is a chronic problem, although conditions are notably better in the women's prison in Quito than in other facilities. A midyear census of the prison system found that 9,369 male prisoners were crowded into prisons designed to hold 5,049. There are no separate facilities for hard-core or dangerous criminals, nor are there effective rehabilitation programs.

The Government permits prison visits by independent human rights monitors.

d. *Arbitrary Arrest, Detention, or Exile.*—The Constitution and the Penal Code provide that no one may be deprived of liberty without a written order from a governmental authority, but the authorities often violated these legal protections against arbitrary arrest or detention. By law, the authorities must issue specific written orders within 24 hours of detention—even in cases in which a suspect is caught in the act of committing a crime—and must charge the suspect with a specific criminal offense within 48 hours of arrest. All detained persons may have the legality of their detention reviewed within 48 hours of their arrest. This review is supposed to be conducted by the senior elected official (usually the mayor) of the locality in which the suspect is held. Regardless of the legality of a detention, a prisoner may only be released by court order. In some cases, detainees who are unaware of this, or who do not have the funds to hire a lawyer, may remain in prison for an extended period before being released. Bail is not generally available. Families of detainees sometimes intervene in an attempt to secure the prisoners' freedom through illegal means.

In its first months after taking office in August, the Bucaram Government ordered the arrest of suspected corrupt civil servants, as well as some business executives, without proper evidence. Although the authorities released them within a few days in most cases, this practice led to numerous complaints of arbitrary arrest.

Human rights organizations reported occasional cases of incommunicado detention, although the law prohibits this practice. Despite provisions of the Penal Code, the police often detained suspects without the required written order. Even when an order was obtained, those charged with determining the validity of detention often allowed frivolous charges to be brought, either because they were overworked or because the accuser bribed them. In many instances, the system was used as a means of harassment in civil cases in which one party sought to have the other arrested on criminal charges. The authorities frequently detained suspects longer than 24 hours before court orders were signed and often failed to bring charges against suspects within 48 hours of arrest. Preventive detention up to and including trial is legal under certain circumstances.

The Government does not use exile as a method of political control.

e. *Denial of Fair Public Trial.*—The Constitution provides for an independent judiciary. In practice, however, the judiciary is susceptible to outside pressure.

The regular court system tries most nonmilitary defendants, although some indigenous groups try members independently for violations of tribal rules. Despite efforts begun in 1992 to depoliticize and modernize the court system, the judiciary continues to operate slowly and inconsistently. Judges reportedly rendered decisions more quickly or more slowly depending on political pressure or the payment of bribes. However, the norm is for lengthy periods before cases come to the courts.

The failure of the justice system led to a growing number of cases of communities taking the law into their own hands (see Section 1.a.). Through the first week of December, there were 23 reports of fatal lynchings and burnings of alleged criminals by enraged citizens. These occurred particularly in indigenous communities and poor neighborhoods of the major cities where there is little police presence. One of the most dramatic cases occurred in July in the town of Mana, Cotopaxi province, when an angry crowd stopped a police vehicle transporting a group of five car thieves and, after wresting them from police custody, beat them to death and burned their bodies. The group reportedly had killed an individual in the course of stealing his car only days earlier, and the family of the victim and other townspeople ambushed the police escort to exact their own justice.

The law provides for internationally accepted due process rights for criminal defendants, but the authorities often did not observe these rights in practice. By law, the accused is presumed innocent until proven guilty, and defendants have the right to a public trial, defense attorneys, and appeal. They may present evidence, refuse to testify against themselves, and may confront and cross-examine witnesses. Although a public defender system exists, in practice there are relatively few attorneys available to defend the large number of indigent suspects.

The legislature amended the Constitution in 1995 to stipulate that no testimony taken from a prisoner may be used as evidence in court unless the individual's lawyer was present at the taking of testimony. Implementing legislation, however, remains to be passed.

Trial is supposed to begin within 15 to 60 days of the initial arrest, but in practice, initiation of the trial phase can take years. Less than 40 percent of all prisoners have been to trial. Indigenous people and other minorities are disproportionately affected by these delays as they are more likely to be poor and unable to buy their way out of pretrial detention. However, there was no evidence of a systematic effort to discriminate against women or minorities.

A foreign assistance program begun in 1994 has enabled the courts to computerize the National Register of Prisoners. Use of this system made it possible for the courts to track prisoners' status more easily. Since its inception, the courts released over 800 prisoners, who had either completed their sentences or who had never been tried but had served the maximum sentence for the alleged crime.

There were no reports of political prisoners.

f. *Arbitrary Interference with Privacy, Family, Home, or Correspondence.*—The law prohibits such practices, government authorities generally respect these prohibitions, and violations are subject to effective legal sanctions.

Section 2. *Respect for Civil Liberties, Including:*

a. *Freedom of Speech and Press.*—The Constitution provides for freedom of speech, and the authorities generally respected this provision in practice, but with some notable exceptions. A case remains before the Supreme Court in which an independent congressman, Fernando Larrea, was charged with treason for remarks he made on a provincial radio station in 1995 in which he ridiculed the president of the Supreme Court and the commander of the army. (He spoke derisively of the role the army commander had played in the border hostilities with Peru.) While not releasing the tape or transcript of Larrea's intemperate remarks, the military proceeded to charge Larrea with treason under the National Emergency Decree then in force and initiated proceedings against him in a military court. The Supreme Court has yet to determine if the military court has jurisdiction.

All of the major media organs—television, newspapers, and radio—are in local, private hands except for two government-owned radio stations. The law limits foreign investment in broadcast media. Using a law (promulgated by the last military regime) that requires the media to give the Government free space or air time, the Government can and does require television and radio to broadcast government-produced programs featuring the President and other top administration officials.

Ecuador has a free and vigorous press. Ownership of the media is broad based, and editorials represent a wide range of political views and often criticize the Government. However, some degree of self-censorship in the print media occurs, particularly with respect to politically sensitive issues or stories about the military and its related industries.

The Government does not interfere in issues involving academic freedom.

b. *Freedom of Peaceful Assembly and Association.*—The Constitution provides for the rights of free assembly and association for peaceful purposes, and the Government generally respected these rights in practice. Public rallies require prior government permits, which are generally granted, although exceptions occur. Numerous labor and student demonstrations took place without incident in the capital and the outlying regions. In general the security forces intervened in demonstrations only when there was violence against bystanders or property. During a strike in March by bus drivers in Quito, the authorities called in the military to clear blocked roads after 5 days of inaction by the police. The military injured several striking drivers in the course of the operation.

c. *Freedom of Religion.*—The Constitution provides for freedom of religion, and the Government respects this right in practice. Numerous foreign religious orders and missionary groups are active.

d. *Freedom of Movement Within the Country, Foreign Travel, Emigration, and Repatriation.*—The Constitution provides for these rights, and the Government respects them in practice. The Government cooperates with the United Nations High Commissioner for Refugees and other humanitarian organizations in assisting refugees. The issue of provision of first asylum did not arise. There were no reports of forced return of persons to a country where they feared persecution.

Section 3. Respect for Political Rights: The Right of Citizens to Change Their Government

The Constitution provides citizens with the right to change their government peacefully, and citizens exercise this right in practice through periodic, free, and fair elections held on the basis of universal suffrage. Since the return to civilian rule in 1979, citizens have actively exercised their right to change their national and local governments. There were 18 political parties spanning the ideological spectrum that participated in the 1996 national elections, 11 of which won representation in Congress. These elections resulted in the peaceful transfer of power from a center-right government to a populist government, as well as a realignment of power within the legislature.

Voting is mandatory for literate citizens over 18 years of age and voluntary for illiterate citizens. The law does not permit active duty members of the military to vote. The Constitution bars members of the clergy and active duty military personnel from election to Congress, the presidency, or vice presidency.

Traditional elites tend to be self-perpetuating. Consequently, very few women, Afro-Ecuadorians, and indigenous people are found in high positions in government, although no specific laws or policies prevent women or minorities from attaining leadership positions. Women hold 4 of 82 seats in Congress. In July voters elected Rosalia Arteaga as the first female Vice President in the country's history.

There are no Afro-Ecuadorians in Congress or in any senior level government jobs. Afro-Ecuadorian political leaders in Esmeraldas province (whose population is largely Afro-Ecuadorian) attribute this in part to the lack of identification of the Afro-Ecuadorian population with their own politicians.

The indigenous movement, which long shunned traditional politics, formed an electoral movement called Pachakutik (which means "cataclysmic change" in Quichua) and ran candidates for national, provincial, and local office in the elections. Pachakutik succeeded in electing eight members of congress (one national deputy and seven provincial deputies) and mayors of several cities, including Cuenca—the third largest city. Although Pachakutik only received about 8 percent of the vote nationwide, its representation in Congress and at the provincial and municipal level assures the indigenous community a greater voice in government. Pachakutik's success also forced traditional political parties to focus attention on issues of importance to the indigenous population—long neglected by the political process.

Section 4. Governmental Attitude Regarding International and Nongovernmental Investigation of Alleged Violations of Human Rights

A number of human rights groups, both domestic and international, operate without restriction, investigating and publishing their findings on human rights cases. Domestic human rights groups, such as the CEDHU and the Regional Latin American Human Rights Association (ALDHU), were outspoken in their criticism of the Government's record on specific cases. Nevertheless, the Government contracted with the ALDHU to provide human rights training to the military and the police.

Section 5. Discrimination Based on Race, Sex, Religion, Disability, Language, or Social Status

The Constitution prohibits discrimination based on race, religion, sex, or social status. However, women, Afro-Ecuadorians, and indigenous people face significant discrimination.

Women.—Although the law prohibits violence against women, including within marriage, it is a widespread practice. Many rapes go unreported because of the victims' reluctance to confront the perpetrators. Women may only file complaints against a rapist or an abusive spouse or companion if they produce a witness. While some communities have established their own centers for counseling and legal support of abused women, the Government only began to address this question seriously with the formation of the "Comisaria de la Mujer," or Women's Bureau, in 1994. Although this office can accept complaints about abuse of women, it has no authority to act on them.

A 1995 Law Against Violence Affecting Women and Children, drafted by a coalition of women's organizations, criminalizes spousal abuse for the first time, including physical, sexual, and psychological abuse. It also creates family courts and reforms the Penal Code to give courts the power to separate an abusive spouse from the home. Congress approved the law in record time.

Discrimination against women is pervasive in society, particularly with respect to educational and economic opportunities for those in the lower economic strata. The increasingly active women's movement blames culture and tradition for inhibiting achievement of full equality for women. There are fewer women in the professions and skilled trades than men, and pay discrimination against women is common.

Women's groups accused the Bucaram administration of ignoring the cause of reducing violence against women because of the President's steadfast support for his Minister of Energy, who made denigrating public statements about women and who has been accused of physically assaulting women.

Children.—The Government is committed in principle to the welfare of children but has not taken effective steps to promote it. The Government rarely enforces the constitutional requirement of education through the age of 14.

There is no societal pattern of abuse against children. Government resources to assist children have traditionally been limited, although it instituted a program to care for the children of the working poor called "Operation Child Rescue." Several private organizations are very active in programs to assist street children, and the U.N. Children's Fund also runs a program in conjunction with the Central Bank. Especially in urban areas, the children of the poor often experience severe hardships. It is common to see children as young as 5 or 6 years of age selling newspapers or candy on the street to support themselves or to augment the family income. Also, there are instances of prostitution by girls under 18 years of age in urban areas. In rural areas, young children often must leave school at an early age to help out on the family's plot of land.

People With Disabilities.—There is no official discrimination against disabled persons in employment, education, or the provision of other state services. However, there are no laws to guarantee disabled people access to public buildings or services, nor are they provided any other special government assistance.

Indigenous People.—While at least 85 percent of all citizens claim some indigenous heritage, culturally indigenous people make up about 15 to 20 percent of the total population. The vast majority of these people live in rural areas, and most live in varying degrees of poverty. Land is scarce in the more heavily populated highland areas where high infant mortality, malnutrition, and epidemic disease are also common. In addition, electricity and potable water are often unavailable. Although the rural education system is seriously deficient, many indigenous groups participated actively with the Ministry of Education in the development of the bilingual education program used in rural public schools.

Indigenous people enjoy the same civil and political rights as other citizens and also have several special privileges designed to allow them to manage their own affairs within their own communities. This is particularly true in the Amazon area where indigenous groups have claim to specific tracts of land. These groups also have begun to play an active role in decisionmaking with respect to the use of their lands for oil exploration and production, by lobbying the Government and enlisting the help of foreign nongovernmental organizations. Environmental groups and indigenous organizations continued to blame oil companies for causing major environmental damage and to criticize their damage control efforts as insufficient.

Despite their increasing political influence (see Section 3) and the efforts of grassroots community groups, which were increasingly successful in pressuring the central Government to assist them, Indians continue to suffer discrimination at many levels of society. In an August beauty pageant in the predominantly Indian town of Otavalo, young women of indigenous background were denied participation in the contest based on their Indian heritage. Even after this blatant discrimination received national attention in the press and had provoked an appeal by President Bucaram, organizers of the event refused to admit contestants of Indian background.

National/Racial/Ethnic Minorities.—The population of the rural, northern coastal area includes large numbers of Afro-Ecuadorian citizens. They suffer widespread poverty and pervasive discrimination, particularly with regard to educational and economic opportunity. There were no special government efforts to address these problems.

There are five major Afro-Ecuadorian organizations active in the country, and these organizations estimate that Afro-Ecuadorians account for 700,000 people, or about 6 percent of the total population. While the presence of Afro-Ecuadorians has grown in the fields of sports and culture (the country's most prominent soccer stars and 1996 Miss Ecuador were Afro-Ecuadorian), educational opportunities continue to be limited. A recent census listed only 359 Afro-Ecuadorian lawyers, engineers, doctors, and economists.

The press has focussed on lingering racism among all strata of society. Afro-Ecuadorian organizations note that despite the absence of official discrimination, societal discrimination continues to affect them. For example, they assert that the police stop Afro-Ecuadorians for document checks with greater frequency than other citizens.

Section 6. Worker Rights

a. *The Right of Association.*—The Constitution and Labor Code provide most workers with the right to form trade unions. Members of the police and the military, and public sector employees in nonrevenue producing entities are not free to form trade unions. The 1991 Labor Code reforms raised the number of workers required for an establishment to be unionized from 15 to 30, which the International Labor Organization's Committee on Freedom of Association considered too stringent a limitation at the plant workers' council level.

While employees of stated-owned organizations enjoy rights similar to those in the private sector, the law technically prevents the majority of public sector employees from joining unions or exercising collective bargaining rights. Nevertheless, most public employees maintain membership in some labor organization, and there are frequent "illegal" strikes. Despite official threats, the Government rarely takes action against striking public workers. Although the five umbrella organizations are politically independent, the two largest single labor unions, the Teachers' Union and the Union of Social Security Workers, are allied with the Movimiento Politico Democratico, the far-left socialist party.

Approximately 12 percent of the work force is organized. There are four large labor centrals or confederations, three of which maintain international affiliation. None of the main labor centrals is firmly connected to any one political party, and there are no ties between the Government and any labor union.

There are few restrictions on the right of workers to strike, although a 20-day cooling-off period is required before a strike is declared. The Labor Code revisions limit solidarity strikes or boycotts to 3 days, provided that they are approved by the Labor Ministry. In a legal strike, workers may take possession of the factory or workplace, thus ending production at the site, and receive police protection during the takeover. The employer must pay all salaries and benefits during a legal strike; the Labor Code protects strikers and their leaders from retaliation. The only significant strikes were by public sector employees such as teachers and medical workers. None of the strikes resulted in violence.

b. *The Right to Organize and Bargain Collectively.*—The labor market is highly segmented, with a minority of workers in skilled, usually unionized, positions in state-run enterprises or in medium to large industries. Most of the economically active population is employed in the agricultural sector or the urban informal sector; the vast majority of these workers are not organized. The Labor Code requires that all private employers with 30 or more workers belonging to a union must negotiate collectively when the union so requests. Although approximately 12 percent of the work force is organized, collective bargaining agreements cover only one-quarter of these workers.

The Labor Code streamlined the bargaining process in state enterprises by requiring workers to be represented by one labor union only. It prohibits discrimination against unions and requires that employers provide space for union activities upon the union's request. The law does not permit employers to dismiss a worker without the express permission of the Ministry of Labor, rulings that are not subject to judicial review. If the Ministry of Labor rules that a dismissal is unjustified, it can require the employer to pay large indemnities or separation payments to the worker, although the reforms set a cap on such payments. The Labor Code provides for resolution of labor conflicts through an arbitration and conciliation board comprising one representative of the Ministry of Labor, two from the union, and two representatives of management.

The Maquila (in bond) Law passed in 1990 permits the hiring of temporary workers for the maquila industries only. While there is no express prohibition on association rights in the Maquila Law, in practice it is difficult to organize temporary employees on short-term contracts. Since temporary workers are not recognized by the Labor Code, they do not enjoy the same level of protection offered to other workers. The maquila system allows a company and its property to become an export processing zone wherever it is located. Many such "zones" have thus been established; most are dedicated to textiles and fish processing.

c. *Prohibition of Forced or Compulsory Labor.*—The Constitution and the Labor Code prohibit compulsory labor, and there were no reports of it.

d. *Minimum Age for Employment of Children.*—The Constitution establishes that children must attend school until the equivalent of 14 years of age. However, because of the lack of schools in many rural communities and the need for children to work, this provision is rarely enforced. The law prohibits persons less than 14 years old from working, except in special circumstances such as apprenticeships. It requires those between the ages of 14 and 18 years to have the permission of their parent or guardian to work. The law prohibits children between the ages of 15 and 18 years from working more than 7 hours per day or 35 hours per week, and it restricts children below the age of 15 years to a maximum of 6 hours per day and 30 hours per week. In practice, the Ministry of Labor fails to enforce child labor laws. In rural areas many children attend school only sporadically after about 10 years of age in order to contribute to household income as farm laborers. In the city many children under 14 years of age work in family-owned "businesses" in the informal sector, shining shoes, collecting and recycling garbage, or as street peddlers.

e. *Acceptable Conditions of Work.*—The Ministry of Labor has the principal role in enforcing labor laws and carries this out through a corps of labor inspectors who are active in all 21 provinces. The Labor Code provides for a 40-hour workweek, a 15-day annual vacation, a minimum wage, and other employer-provided benefits, such as uniforms and training opportunities.

The Ministry of Labor sets the minimum wage every 6 months in consultation with the Commission on Salaries, but Congress may also adjust it. The statutory minimum wage is not adequate to provide a decent standard of living for a worker and family. As of September, the minimum wage plus mandated bonuses provided a gross monthly compensation of approximately $160 (S/513,583). Most organized workers in state industries and formal sector private enterprises earned substantially more than the minimum wage and also received significant other benefits through collective bargaining agreements. The majority of workers, however, work in the large informal and rural sector without recourse to the minimum wage or legally mandated benefits.

The Labor Code also provides general protection for workers' health and safety on the job. A worker may not leave the workplace of his own volition, even if there is a hazardous situation. The worker is allowed to request that an inspector from the Ministry of Labor come to the workplace and confirm the hazard; that inspector may then close down the workplace.

The Government enforces health and safety standards and regulations through the Social Security Institute. In the formal sector, occupational health and safety is not a major problem. However, there are no specific regulations governing health and safety standards in the agricultural sector and, in practice, there is no enforcement of safety rules in the small mines that make up the vast majority of the mining sector.

EL SALVADOR

El Salvador is a constitutional, multiparty democracy with an executive branch headed by a president, a unicameral legislative assembly, and a separate, politically appointed, independent judiciary. Armando Calderon Sol of the Nationalist Republican Alliance Party (ARENA) was inaugurated President for a 5-year term in June 1994. In the Legislative Assembly, the ARENA party holds a plurality. Seven other parties also hold seats, including the ex-guerrilla organization Farabundo Marti Front for National Liberation (FMLN), and its offshoot, the Democratic Party.

Since the Peace Accords ended the 12-year civil war in 1992, the Government has reduced the armed forces (including civilian employees) by over 70 percent, created a new Civilian National Police (PNC); redefined the role of the military; integrated the former guerrillas into political life; and completed a land transfer program. The military continues to provide protection for PNC patrols in rural areas, a measure begun in 1995 in response to action by well-armed criminal bands. Members of the PNC were charged with having committed human rights abuses.

El Salvador has a mixed economy largely based upon agriculture and light manufacturing. The Government is committed to privatization and free market reforms. People are free to pursue economic interests, and private property is respected. The rate of real economic growth continued to be strong, and per capita gross domestic product was about $1,710. About 40 percent of the population lives below the poverty level.

The Government's human rights record improved somewhat. There were two cases in which police agents face charges of extrajudicial killings. Occasional use of excessive force by the police, denial of due process, lengthy pretrial detention, and long delays in trials were also problems. Prison conditions remain poor, although overcrowding was reduced somewhat. The judiciary is inefficient and subject to corruption. The Supreme Court did not move quickly enough to discipline or dismiss incompetent judges. The resulting widespread impunity continues to be a problem. Politically motivated assassinations appear to have ended, although a number of cases from past years remain unsolved. Some public figures reported death threats, but none was substantiated. Discrimination against women, the disabled, and indigenous people, violence against women, and abuse of children are also problems. The level of criminal violence, particularly murder, assaults, kidnaping, and robberies, remained high. In March growing public demand for firm action against crime led to the passage of an Emergency Law against Common and Organized Crime, which won the support of all political parties represented in the Legislative Assembly, except the FMLN. Shortly after the law's passage, the Government's Human Rights Ombudsman and other critics filed several constitutional challenges against it; at year's end, the Supreme Court had not ruled on the law's constitutionality. On December 4, the Legislature approved a new Criminal Procedures Code, as called for by the Peace Accords.

In April the United Nations General Assembly (UNGA) reduced the U.N. Mission to El Salvador to a small office of verification, reflecting continued progress in implementation of the Peace Accords. The UNGA further scaled back the U.N. presence in December and eliminated the position of Special Representative of the Secretary General. The Human Rights Ombudsman, whose office was created by the Peace Accords, continued to speak out on issues such as harsh prison conditions and the emergency law, but the investigative capacity of her agency, the Office of the Counsel for the Defense of Human Rights (PDDH), remained limited. Nonetheless, polls indicate that the PDDH retains a high level of public trust.

RESPECT FOR HUMAN RIGHTS

Section 1. Respect for the Integrity of the Person, Including Freedom From:

a. *Political and Other Extrajudicial Killings.*—There were no confirmed cases of political killings. However, there were two cases in which the authorities charged PNC officers with extrajudicial killing. Six PNC agents and two PNC drivers face charges of killing four persons (including a minor) during a brawl in San Pedro Masahuat in March. After a justice of the peace ordered the arrest of the agents, a trial judge released two of them on the grounds that there was insufficient evidence. A higher court ordered the two back into confinement, but one fled in the meantime. Officials of the Attorney General's office alleged that PNC agents in San Pedro Masahuat attempted to intimidate witnesses and interfere with the proceedings in an effort to protect their colleagues. The justice of the peace has received police protection at the request of the Supreme Court.

In October a PNC agent shot and killed Francisco Manzanares in what the police said was investigation of an extortion case. Although not active in politics at the time of his death, Manzanares' past as an FMLN combatant and party member raised the issue of political killing. The authorities charged PNC agent Guillermo Linares with wrongful death and detained three other PNC agents for having removed the body from the crime scene when they took Manzanares to a hospital. The incident was under active investigation at year's end; preliminary evidence indicated improper police procedures rather than a deliberate killing.

In September unidentified assailants shot and killed Siegfried Guth Zapata, the nephew of ARENA's then president, in San Salvador. The motive is unknown; the case remained under investigation at year's end.

Politically motivated threats were made during the year, but the existence of organized groups was never proven. Since May a previously unknown group calling itself the "Roberto D'Aubisson Nationalist Force" (FURODA) had made politically motivated threats against 15 prominent citizens, including the Human Rights Ombudsman and other government officials. The existence of this and other groups was never proven, and although threats continued in some cases, none were carried out. In November Ombudsman Dr. Marina de Aviles publicized the FURODA threats against her and her staff but vowed to continue her work. Government and ARENA party officials condemned the threats, and the PNC director said the police were working directly with the Ombudsman to provide collaboration and security.

Tomas Coronado Valles, the PNC officer who killed a protester with a rubber bullet in November 1995, remained under a charge of manslaughter. The Ministry of Public Security and the PDDH completed work on the details of an agreement, signed after the November 1995 incident, to govern coordination in situations such as violent public demonstrations.

The authorities detained, but later released, PNC agents in connection with the controversial 1995 death of medical student Adriano Vilanova. A December PDDH report concluded that a government autopsy that exculpated the police was botched and that Vilanova was beaten to death, not struck by a car or impaired by drugs or alcohol as the authorities had claimed. The PDDH report suggested that PNC members were guilty of extrajudicial killing and that a judge had impeded investigation of the case, but it did not contain any new evidence to support these allegations. The President, the Attorney General, and the Supreme Court president announced that the Government would do everything in its power to identify and punish the perpetrators. The case remained open at year's end.

Prosecutions continued in the case of the so-called Sombra Negra (Black Shadow) vigilante group, which surfaced in San Miguel in 1994 and allegedly killed 20 people whom it claimed were criminals. However, a court released several suspects from pretrial confinement when it determined that there was insufficient evidence against them. Nine suspects who were alleged members of the group still faced charges at year's end, including at least two of the four PNC members arrested in July 1995.

There was little progress in cases from past years in which political motivation was a possibility, with the exception of the investigation of the 1993 murder of FMLN leader Darol Francisco Velis Castellanos. In that case, the authorities extradited a former PNC detective, Carlos Romero Alfaro, from the United States in March. Following his extradition, they arrested another former agent in connection with the murder and investigated two others. The case remained active at year's end.

b. *Disappearance.*—There were no confirmed reports of politically motivated disappearances.

Vague and unsubstantiated rumors of political motivation surrounded the kidnaping of Andres Suster, the 15-year-old son of a close associate of former President Alfredo Cristiani. Suster was kidnaped in September 1995 and released in September. While political motivations cannot be ruled out, available evidence suggests that this was a criminal act for personal gain.

c. *Torture and Other Cruel, Inhuman, or Degrading Treatment or Punishment.*— The Constitution prohibits such practices, but complaints against the PNC for excessive use of force and denial of due process continued. Some of these complaints were investigated and found to be warranted, but most were not thoroughly explored due to institutional weaknesses of the PDDH and the PNC Inspector General's office.

The PNC continued to be the subject of more complaints of human rights violations than any other government institution. This reflects their license to use force and carry out arrests, as well as their inexperience (the 1992 Peace Accords created the PNC as a replacement for the old, discredited security forces; the first PNC deployment occurred in March 1993). The majority of the complaints against the PNC continued to be for denial of due process. The authorities have investigated and disciplined some PNC agents for misconduct, including human rights violations, and jailed a few for criminal activity.

The PNC Inspector General briefly threatened to resign in June, claiming that the Deputy Director of the PNC and the Public Security Ministry were undermining his ability to do his job. He withdrew his resignation after receiving public reassurances of the importance of his office.

Despite the volume of human rights complaints, public opinion polls gave the PNC relatively high marks amidst general dissatisfaction with government institutions as a whole. In an August poll conducted by the Institute of Public Opinion of the Central American University, the PNC came in second place in a ranking of those institutions that best defended human rights. A plurality of respondents, however, stated no institutions effectively defended human rights or that they had no opinion. Two other separate polls by the Salvadoran Investigation Center for Public Opinion of the University of Technology also gave relatively high marks to the PNC.

In the only terrorism-related arrests, the authorities detained four university students in June in connection with a car bombing in April and an explosion at an insurance company in May. No one was injured in either incident, and the motives remain unclear. The four students allegedly belong to a leftwing terrorist group; one of the four was released for lack of evidence.

Prison conditions remained poor, but the Government opened a new 2,000-inmate prison in September. This reduced severe overcrowding, although there were still 3,000 excess prisoners. The prisons are filled with violent inmates, and guards exercise little control. Killings among prisoners are common. The Human Rights Ombudsman said in June that prison conditions constituted a systematic violation of human rights. She blamed judges for using pretrial detention too freely and trying cases too slowly. The Ombudsman recommended approval of pending criminal codes, the use of pretrial detention only as a last resort, acceleration of judicial procedures, seeking alternatives to imprisonment, and developing a policy on crime and prisons.

Prison problems attracted public attention when protesting prisoners organized a "lottery of death" in which they randomly selected inmates for execution. No executions were carried out, but other prisoners began hunger strikes, some with their mouths crudely sewn shut, to gain attention for their demands for better conditions, provisions for bail, speedy trials, and early release programs. The Government responded by asking the courts to speed up trials (the Supreme Court began a nationwide review of pending cases) and promising to relocate prisoners, measures which seemed to relax tensions.

The Government permits prison visits by independent human rights monitors, NGO's, and the media.

d. *Arbitrary Arrest, Detention, or Exile.*—The Constitution prohibits arbitrary arrest and detention, and the number of complaints of arbitrary arrest and detention continued to decline. Complaints that PNC officers violated due process rights of detainees also continued, but few of these complaints were fully investigated. The courts generally enforced a ruling that interrogation without the presence of a public defender amounts to coercion, and that any evidence so obtained is inadmissible. As a result, police authorities generally delayed questioning until a public defender arrived. However, since low salaries and insufficient supervision limit the number of cases that public defenders handle, they are not always available when needed.

By law, the police may hold a person for 72 hours before delivering the suspect to court, after which time the judge may order detention for an additional 72 hours to determine if an investigation is warranted. Because of a lack of holding cells, such detainees are often sent to the prisons where they may be mixed with violent criminals. The law allows 120 days to investigate serious crimes and 45 days for lesser offenses before a judge must bring the accused to trial or dismiss the case. The Emergency Law Against Common and Organized Crime, passed in March and effective for 2 years, shortened these periods, but in practice the authorities rarely observed the time limits. The Assembly also considered a second measure in response to the crime wave, a sweeping vagrancy law that would have allowed the police to make arrests for a variety of only vaguely defined activities not heretofore criminal. However, the Assembly dropped this proposal after it was sharply criticized by human rights advocates.

Although the law permits the release of detainees pending trial for crimes for which the maximum penalty does not exceed 3 years, many crimes (homicide, manslaughter, rape, and crimes against property) carry penalties in excess of 3 years, thereby precluding release pending trial. Because it may take several years for a case to come to trial, some prisoners have been incarcerated longer than the maximum legal sentence for their crimes. Any detainee may request a review (habeas corpus) by the Supreme Court, but the Court denies the overwhelming majority of such requests. Nearly 80 percent of all inmates are awaiting trial or sentencing.

The Constitution prohibits compulsory exile, and it is not practiced.

e. *Denial of Fair Public Trial.*—The Constitution provides for an independent judiciary, and the Government respects this provision in practice.

The court structure has four levels: Justices of the peace, trial courts, appellate courts, and the Supreme Court. Judges, not juries, rule in many cases. A jury verdict cannot be overruled by a judge nor appealed by the defendant; however, defendants may appeal the sentence to the Supreme Court.

Legislation passed in 1995 provided for oral trials and new rights for the parties, and it also established two new court systems for family and juvenile offenders. Both systems stress conciliation as an alternative to adjudication. The Juvenile Legal Code that went into effect in March 1995 included greater provisions for due process, raised the age of majority from 16 to 18 years, limited sentences to a maximum of 7 years, and introduced alternatives to incarceration. However, the Emergency Law Against Common and Organized Crime lowered the age of minors to 14 years and made imprisonment the remedy of choice. The new Juvenile Code continues to suffer from the weaknesses of the institutions involved in its execution.

Under the Constitution, defendants have the right to a presumption of innocence, protection from self-incrimination, legal counsel, freedom from coercion, and compensation for damages due to judicial error. They also have the right to be present in court and to confront witnesses. While still far from satisfactory, compliance with these provisions has improved, in large part due to judicial training programs and to evaluations of judges conducted by the National Council of the Judiciary (an independent body provided for in the Constitution to nominate, train, and evaluate judges) and the Supreme Court. Although legal counsel is supposed to be available at government expense for the indigent, there continued to be far too few public defenders to make this a reality.

On December 4, the Legislative Assembly approved a new Criminal Procedures Code, as called for by the Peace Accords. The new code replaces a criminal system based on civil law with one in which oral argument is the norm. The legislature is expected to take up other legal reforms mandated by the Peace Accords, including a new criminal code and a sentencing law, in early 1997.

Problems of corruption and incompetence in the judicial system remain. The Supreme Court, which has the authority to discipline judges, has moved slowly. Judicial salaries are now high enough to attract qualified judges, but are still inadequate for prosecutors or public defenders. Training programs are insufficient to compensate for inadequate university training, low pay, and poor supervision. While new laws represent a marked improvement, they also add to the confusion. Impunity, especially of the politically, economically, or institutionally well-connected, continued to be a problem. The deficiencies of the judicial system contribute to this impunity as well as to the increase in crime.

There were no reports of political prisoners.

f. *Arbitrary Interference with Privacy, Family, Home, or Correspondence.*—According to the Constitution, the police must have the resident's consent, a warrant, or a reasonable belief that a crime is being or is about to be committed, before entering a private dwelling. Government authorities generally respected these rights. Wiretapping of telephone communications by the Government, private persons, and political parties is illegal but occurs.

Section 2. Respect for Civil Liberties, Including:

a. *Freedom of Speech and Press.*—The Constitution provides for freedom of the press, and the Government respects this right in practice.

There are 4 daily newspapers, 10 television stations, approximately 100 licensed radio stations, and 2 major cable television systems. Print and broadcast journalists regularly criticize the Government and report opposition views. According to most major media associations, in general the Government did not use direct or indirect means to control the media.

In 1995 the Government's National Telecommunications Association (ANTEL) closed 11 low-power, unlicensed radio stations operating in small rural communities. These so-called community radio stations alleged an attempt to restrict free speech, while ANTEL claimed that the stations' signals interfered with licensed users, a charge the community radio stations denied. In January the Supreme Court ruled that the Government had improperly confiscated the community radio equipment, ordered its return, and overturned a fine levied by ANTEL. However, the Court said that the stations must get permits before broadcasting. In practice, it takes years to get licenses, and the spectrum is already over subscribed. ANTEL has offered the community stations various alternatives, all of which have been rejected. Of the 11 stations, 10 have resumed unlicensed broadcasting. The community radio stations tried unsuccessfully to persuade the Legislative Assembly to grant them special regulatory status under the new telecommunications law passed in September.

In July the police arrested Francisco Elias Valencia, editor of a newspaper usually identified with the left, on libel charges after his newspaper accused a PNC official of corruption. Valencia was quickly released under bond, but journalists from across the political spectrum condemned his arrest as an attack on freedom of the press. The incident appeared to be unique (in part a result of the country's unusually strict libel laws) and not part of a larger effort to intimidate the press.

Some media outlets accused the Government of favoritism in the apportionment of its advertising, but they did not produce any firm evidence to substantiate their complaints. In June some media figures received threats purportedly from a previously unknown clandestine group, but the threats were never carried out.

The Constitution provides for academic freedom, and the Government respects this right in practice.

b. *Freedom of Peaceful Assembly and Association.*—The Constitution provides for peaceful assembly and association for any lawful purpose, and the Government respects these rights in practice. There is no requirement for permits to hold public meetings, and public demonstrations are common. Incidents of alleged police brutality in breaking up demonstrations in 1995 were not repeated.

In November the Assembly passed a law giving the Ministry of Interior the authority to regulate, supervise, and financially oversee both domestic and international nongovernmental organizations (NGO's) and religious groups working in the country. The law exempts organizations such as unions, cooperatives, and the Catholic Church, and the Interior Minister stated it will not affect other churches. International NGO's had lobbied for regulation of their organizations to remain with the Foreign Ministry. Smaller and domestic NGO's and the FMLN opposed the law, arguing that it abridges freedom of association. The NGO community and others expressed concern that the Interior Ministry will politicize registration and regulatory oversight decisions.

c. *Freedom of Religion.*—The Constitution provides for freedom of religion, and the Government respects this right in practice.

d. *Freedom of Movement Within the Country, Foreign Travel, Emigration, and Repatriation.*—The Constitution provides for these rights, and the Government respects them in practice.

The Government cooperates with the office of the United Nations High Commissioner for Refugees and other humanitarian organizations in assisting refugees. The issue of the provision of first asylum did not arise in 1996 and has not arisen in recent years. There were no reports of forced return of persons to a country where they feared persecution.

Section 3. Respect for Political Rights: The Right of Citizens to Change Their Government

Citizens exercise the right to change their government peacefully through regularly scheduled elections. The President and Vice President are elected every 5 years; legislative and municipal elections are held every 3 years. The Constitution bars the President from election to consecutive terms. Voting is by secret ballot, and there is universal suffrage.

In November the Assembly approved a package of reforms to the Electoral Code that make it more difficult for political parties to form and maintain official status. In addition, the reforms provide government funding only to parties that meet the minimum requirements for official status or that have at least one member serving in the Legislative Assembly. (There were eight political parties with a least one Assembly deputy and four parties without a deputy and with membership insufficent to qualify for government funding.) The Assembly also voted to dismiss one of the members of the Supreme Electoral Tribunal. The Assembly's moves were criticized for creating the perception of manipulation of the electoral process or the electoral authorities during the sensitive period prior to the March 1997 national legislative and municipal elections.

Although women represent 50.6 percent of the registered voters, the number of women active in politics is relatively small. In the 1994 elections, voters elected 9 women to the 84-member Legislative Assembly, a slight increase from the number in the previous Assembly. The president and 1 of the 4 vice presidents of the Assembly are women, as are 2 of the 15 Supreme Court justices. One cabinet minister is a woman, as are 31 of the country's 262 mayors. A woman serves as the Government's highly visible Human Rights Ombudsman.

Section 4. Governmental Attitude Regarding International and Nongovernmental Investigation of Alleged Violations of Human Rights

The Government demonstrated a willingness to discuss human rights issues and problems with international, local, and nongovernmental organizations. Numerous local NGO's operate freely as do various international human rights groups, including migration and other humanitarian and technical assistance groups. However, several NGO's registered their concern that the Ministry of Interior could use its new regulatory powers under the NGO registration law passed in November to restrict NGO activity (see Section 2.b.).

The Peace Accords specifically provided for creation of the PDDH, which was formally established by a constitutional amendment that defined its role. The PDDH's investigative capacity remains limited, however, and the Assembly voted to reduce its budget by 10 percent in December, as part of government-wide reductions. Nonetheless, the Ombudsman continued to speak out on issues such as prison conditions and the emergency law, and polls indicate that the PDDH retains a high level of public trust.

In April the U.N. General Assembly reduced the U.N. Mission to El Salvador to a small office of verification called ONUV, reflecting continued progress in implementation of the Peace Accords. The UNGA further scaled back the U.N. presence in December and eliminated the position of Special Representative of the Secretary General. The U.N. Development Program office assists the police, the judiciary, and the PDDH.

Section 5. Discrimination Based on Race, Sex, Religion, Disability, Language, or Social Status

The Constitution states that all people are equal before the law and prohibits discrimination based on nationality, race, sex, or religion. In practice, discrimination against women and the disabled occurs in salaries, in hiring, and in access to credit and education.

Women.—Violence against women, including domestic violence, is widespread and a serious problem. Government institutions such as the PDDH, the Attorney General's office, the Supreme Court, and the PNC coordinate efforts to combat family violence, and the National Secretariat for the Family maintains a hot line for victims to report domestic abuse. From March 1995 to March 1996, there were 10,032 reported cases of domestic violence against women, according to the Institute for Women. The Institute of Legal Medicine, using different criteria, reported 441 cases from January to October. The Center for Women, a leading women's group, reported that out of the 571 women who requested legal advice on problems such as housing, alimony, sexual abuse, and child custody in the first 6 months of 1995, 451 said they had been mistreated by their spouse. The Attorney General's office received on average 10 cases a day of family violence, women being the main victims.

The authorities believe that cases of domestic violence and rape are underreported because of economic and societal pressures and the belief that cases are unlikely to be resolved. The PDDH says that in previous years hundreds of domestic abuse victims who underwent psychotherapy refused to report their cases formally. One benefit of the controversial Emergency Law Against Common and Organized Crime enacted in March was that it did away with a provision of the Penal Code that allowed a rapist to escape criminal liability by obtaining pardon from or by marrying the victim, a provision that invited intimidation of the victim. Reports of sexual abuse of women continued to rise. From January to October, the Institute for Legal Medicine received 367 reports of sexual abuse of women, compared with 375 reports for all of 1995. A main concern for women is that due to the lack of corroborating witnesses, only 10 percent of rape cases result in convictions.

The Constitution grants women the same legal rights as men, but they suffer discrimination in practice. A new Family Legal Code went into effect in October 1994, which amended some laws that discriminated against women, most notably the large number living in common law marriages. The new law also established courts to resolve family disputes. Several NGO's are engaged in promoting women's rights and have conducted several rights awareness campaigns in the media.

Women suffer from economic discrimination and in practice do not have equal access to credit and land ownership. Women are often paid less than men, and over 25 percent of working women earn less than the minimum wage. Of the economically active female population, 65 percent work in the informal economy. Training for women is generally confined to low-wage occupational areas where women already hold most positions, such as teaching, nursing, home industries, or small businesses.

Children.—Government concern for children's rights and welfare is reflected more in its efforts to reduce poverty and promote family stability through economic growth than in direct expenditure on children. The law requires education through the ninth grade, but this is only feasible in the country's larger urban centers. The Salvadoran Institute for the Protection of Children (ISPM), an autonomous entity, is responsible for protecting and promoting children's rights. The Emergency Law Against Common and Organized Crime negated many provisions of the 1995 Juvenile Code by lowering the age of majority for juvenile offenders to 14 years.

The Government works closely through state institutions and with the United Nations Children's Fund to promote protection and general awareness of children's rights. However, children continued to fall victim to physical and sexual abuse, abandonment, exploitation, and neglect. ISPM has an estimated 5,000 children in its shelters, some abandoned and others victims of mistreatment. ISPM received around 2,000 complaints of abuse during the year. Estimates of the numbers of children living on the streets of San Salvador run as high as 2,000. Many appear to be involved in substance abuse (glue and paint sniffing), and there are allegations that they suffer from police brutality. The PNC denies these charges; the PDDH has provided human rights training to those police units that have the most contact with juveniles. The PDDH has also called for the creation of drug treatment centers for minors.

The Institute of Legal Medicine recorded an increase in reports of sexual abuse of children under 14 years of age, with 315 reports in the first 9 months of 1996, compared with 313 for all of 1995. The Attorney General's office also registered an increase in offenses against children, nearly one half of which were sexual abuse cases. According to the PDDH, over 85 percent of all abuse occurs in schools and at home, with only a small percentage being reported. Out of the 1,857 children attended at San Salvador's largest children's hospital between 1989 and 1993, nearly one quarter were treated for sexual abuse carried out by family members or friends of the family.

The PDDH estimates there are some 270,000 minors working, mostly as street vendors. Most of these are believed to come from single-parent families. Besides losing their opportunity for an education, these children often fall victim to sexual abuse and are exploited as prostitutes.

Infant malnutrition is also a problem. Ministry of Health figures indicated that 50 percent of infants under the age of 5 are undernourished. The Government has a National Plan for Infants designed to increase access to potable water, iodized salt, vitamins, and to encourage breast feeding, but all of these remain problem areas, especially among the rural poor.

People With Disabilities.—Except for the war wounded, who have secured both government and international funding for rehabilitation and retraining programs, the Government has no program to combat discrimination against the disabled. There are no laws mandating provision of access to public or private buildings for people with disabilities. The Government has not enforced a decree passed in 1984 stating that 1 of every 500 employees must be a person with disabilities. Access to basic education is limited due to lack of facilities and appropriate transportation. There is no provision of state services for the physically disabled. Only a few of the Government's community-based health promoters have been trained to treat the disabled, and they rarely provide such service, tending rather to focus on life-threatening conditions and preventive care for mothers and children. It is estimated that between 7 and 10 percent of the population is afflicted by some form of disability.

There are few organizations dedicated to protecting and promoting the rights of people with disabilities. Foreign funds for badly needed rehabilitation services channeled through the Telethon Foundation Pro-Rehabilitation, a local private voluntary organization, help address numerous rehabilitation issues and provide alternatives for the education and rehabilitation of the disabled population. A semiautonomous institute, the Salvadoran Rehabilitation Institute for the Disabled (ISRI), also provides assistance to the disabled. ISRI offers medical treatment and counseling, special education programs, and professional training courses. Founded in 1957, ISRI has 10 centers throughout the country and receives assistance from the Government and national and international private and nongovernmental organizations.

There was continued unrest in a home for the blind. Members of the Association of the Blind of El Salvador (ASCES) denounced the school's director alleging corruption and demanded his dismissal. They also complained that ISRI had failed to give them a voice in naming the school's director. Instead of the hunger strikes used in 1995, ASCES staged a takeover of the school in January. However, the National Association of Blind Salvadorans and the Independent Association of Blind Progressives denounced the takeover as too radical a move. The PDDH moved students at the school to another location, and the takeover continued until March when, without modifying their demands, ASCES members left the school in what they called a gesture of good faith. Negotiations between ASCES and ISRI continue with the PDDH mediating.

Indigenous People.—El Salvador is an ethnically homogeneous country, although a very small segment of the population claims to have descended solely from indigenous people. In 1932 government forces killed approximately 30,000 mostly indigenous people following an uprising. In the face of such repression, most remaining indigenous people adopted local customs and successfully assimilated into the general population. There remain a few very small communities of indigenous people who still wear traditional dress and maintain traditional customs without repression or interference. The Constitution makes no specific provisions for the rights of indigenous people.

The indigenous population is believed to be the poorest group in the country. In a 1994 study, the Human Rights Ombudsman found that 90 percent of indigenous people lived in conditions of extreme poverty, with average monthly incomes one-half the legal minimum wage. Employment opportunities in rural areas are few; domestic violence is a problem. Indigenous people reportedly earn less than other agricultural laborers, and indigenous women in particular have little access to educational and work opportunities since they head most of the households. Access to land is a growing problem confronting indigenous people. Few possess titles to land, and access to bank loans and other forms of credit is extremely limited.

The leader of what is probably the largest indigenous association, the National Association of Indigenous Salvadorans (ANIS), remains involved in a long-running land dispute with a neighboring cooperative. The controversy has resulted in a law suit and may have been the motive for death threats received by ANIS leaders. ANIS sponsored the first meeting of the indigenous population in August 1995. Leaders at the event called for respect for indigenous rights, as well as for constitutional recognition of their existence.

Section 6. Worker Rights

a. The Right of Association.—The Constitution prohibits the Government from using nationality, race, sex, creed, or political philosophy as a means to prevent workers or employers from organizing themselves into unions or associations. Numerous and sometimes conflicting laws governing labor relations impede full realization of the freedom of association, although Labor Code amendments developed by the International Labor Organization (ILO) and approved in 1994 brought about some improvements. The Labor Code prohibits partisan political activity by unions, but they routinely ignore this prohibition.

In the 1992 Peace Accords, the Government committed itself to seek consensus on revised labor legislation through the Socioeconomic Forum with equal representation from labor (including groups aligned with the FMLN), the Government, and the private sector. The Assembly passed legislation in 1994 streamlining the process required to form a union, extending union rights to agricultural, independent, and small-business workers, and extending the right to strike to union federations. The legislation also established a tripartite National Labor Council to replace the Socioeconomic Forum.

There are approximately 150 active unions, public employee associations, and peasant organizations, which represent over 300,000 Salvadorans, approximately 20 percent of the total work force. Only private sector workers have the right to form unions and strike; employees of nine autonomous public agencies may form unions but not strike. Nevertheless, many workers including those in the public sector form employee associations that frequently carried out strikes that, while technically illegal, were treated as legitimate.

Negotiations between public employee associations and the Government generally settle public sector strikes, although the Labor Code provides for mandatory arbitration of public sector disputes. Government downsizing and privatization efforts left public workers disgruntled and public workers' unions claimed that the Government failed to bargain in good faith.

The law prohibits antiunion actions before a union is legally registered. However, under the previous labor code, there were credible charges that the Government impeded union registration through exacting reviews of union documentation and strict interpretation of the Constitution, Labor Code, and union statutes. ILO-drafted changes have streamlined the process and it is now difficult for management to use bureaucratic inertia to impede the formation of a union.

The Labor Code forbids foreigners from holding leadership positions in unions, but unions freely affiliate with international labor organizations.

b. *The Right to Organize and Bargain Collectively.*—The Constitution and the Labor Code provide for collective bargaining rights, but only to employees in the private sector and in autonomous government agencies, such as utilities and the port authority. However, both private sector unions (by law) and public sector employee associations (in practice) use collective bargaining extensively.

The Ministry of Labor oversees implementation of collective bargaining agreements and acts as conciliator in labor disputes in the private sector and autonomous government institutions. In practice, ministers and the heads of autonomous government institutions often negotiate with labor organizations directly, relying on the Labor Ministry only for such functions as officially certifying unions. The Ministry often seeks to conciliate labor disputes through informal channels rather than attempting to enforce regulations strictly, leading to charges that the Ministry is biased against labor. Corruption continues to be a serious problem affecting labor inspectors and courts.

The Constitution prohibits discrimination against unions. It provides that union officials at the time of their election, throughout their term, and for 1 year following their term shall not be fired, suspended for disciplinary reasons, removed, or demoted except for legal cause. Employers generally observed this provision in practice, but in the past they have in some cases fired those attempting to form unions before receiving their union credentials. The law requires employers to rehire employees fired for any type of union activity, although the authorities sometimes fail to enforce this requirement. In many cases, employers convince fired employees to take a cash payment in lieu of returning to work.

There are nine Export Processing Zones (EPZ's). Labor regulations in these zones are identical to those throughout the country. Companies operating in the EPZ's, while providing higher salaries and benefits than companies outside the EPZ's, strongly discourage organizing. In past years there were credible reports of some foreign-owned factories dismissing union organizers. In addition, unions accused some companies of physically abusing their workers. While labor inspectors and courts were ineffective in the face of such complaints, the Government formed interagency committees (consisting of representatives of the Labor Ministry, Economic Ministry, and the PDDH) to investigate alleged violations.

In January the Legislative Assembly passed laws reforming the Labor Ministry and giving the Government the power to take away free zone privileges from companies breaking labor regulations. The new Labor Minister began reorganizing his Ministry, aided by an April law modernizing the Ministry and increasing the number of labor inspectors. The Labor Ministry also opened field offices in two EPZ's. In August the Government established a tripartite (government, business, and labor) commission to help resolve conflicts in free trade zones and bonded companies. In addition, factory operators and owners continue efforts at setting up an industrywide operating code defining internationally recognized labor standards, as well as a mechanism to monitor its enforcement.

c. *Prohibition of Forced or Compulsory Labor.*—The Constitution prohibits forced or compulsory labor, except in the case of calamity and other instances specified by law. This provision is followed in practice.

d. *Minimum Age for Employment of Children.*—The Constitution prohibits the employment of children under the age of 14. It provides for exceptions only where such employment is absolutely indispensable to the sustenance of the minor and his family. This is most often the case with children of peasant families who traditionally work during planting and harvesting seasons. Children also frequently work as street vendors and general laborers in small businesses, especially in the informal sector. Parents of children in circumstances such as these often do not allow their children to complete schooling through the ninth grade as the law requires, since the labor the children perform is considered vital to the family. Child labor is not usually found in the industrial sector. (One well-publicized 1995 case of child labor involved a minor who used forged identity papers to pass as an adult.) The Ministry of Labor is responsible for enforcing child labor laws.

e. *Acceptable Conditions of Work.*—The minimum wage for commercial, industrial, service, and agroindustrial employees is $4.40 (38.50 colones) per day for industrial and service workers, and $3.30 (28.60 colones) per day, including a food allowance, for agroindustrial employees. Full-time employees who are paid the minimum wage receive pay for 30 days a month. However, the minimum wage with benefits is not sufficient to provide a decent standard of living for a worker and family. Minimum wages did not keep up with the Ministry of Economy's estimate of the increase in the cost of living. The Labor Ministry is responsible for enforcing minimum wage laws and does so effectively in the formal sector.

The law limits the workday to 6 hours for youths between 14 and 18 years of age and 8 hours for adults, and it mandates premium pay for longer hours. The Labor

Code sets a maximum normal workweek of 36 hours for youths and 44 hours for adults. It requires for all workers bonus pay for overtime and limits the workweek to no more than 6 days.

The Constitution and the Labor Code require employers, including the Government, to take steps to ensure that employees are not placed at risk in their workplaces and prohibit the employment of persons under 18 years of age and all women in occupations considered hazardous. Nevertheless, health and safety regulations are outdated, and enforcement is inadequate. Workers can remove themselves from dangerous work situations without jeopardizing their employment only in situations where they can present a medical certificate issued by a doctor or the Social Security Institute indicating that their health is at risk while using certain equipment or substances. The Ministry of Labor attempts to enforce the applicable regulations and conducts investigations which sometimes lead to fines or other findings favoring workers. The Ministry has very limited powers and only limited resources to enforce compliance.

GRENADA

Grenada is a parliamentary democracy, with a Governor General as titular Head of State. In June 1995 parliamentary elections, Prime Minister Dr. Keith Mitchell's New National Party (NNP) won 8 of 15 seats and formed a majority government. The elections were openly and fairly contested, and were free of violence. Since the elections, 2 members of the opposition joined the Government to give it 10 seats in Parliament.

The 750-member Royal Grenada Police Force is responsible for maintaining law and order. It is controlled by and responsive to civilian authorities.

Grenada has a free market economy based upon agriculture and tourism. The real economic growth rate was 2.6 percent for 1995, and the government-estimated annual growth for 1996 was 3 percent.

Citizens enjoy a wide range of civil and political rights. Human rights problems included allegations of police brutality in the course of criminal investigations, but there were no documented cases. The Commissioner of Police has spoken out strongly against police use of unlawful force. Violence against women is common.

RESPECT FOR HUMAN RIGHTS

Section 1. Respect for the Integrity of the Person, Including Freedom From:

a. *Political and Other Extrajudicial Killing.*—There were no reports of political or other extrajudicial killings.

b. *Disappearance.*—There were no reports of politically motivated disappearances.

c. *Torture and Other Cruel, Inhuman, or Degrading Treatment or Punishment.*— The Constitution prohibits such practices, and there were no reported incidents of torture. Flogging, a legal form of punishment, is rare but has been used recently in sex crime and theft cases.

The press occasionally reported claims of police brutality, some of which arose following the complainants' alleged attempts to resist arrest. Allegations of police brutality are investigated internally by the police, with no disciplinary actions reported for 1996. No one brought a case of police brutality before the courts during the year. The Police Commissioner can discipline officers in valid cases of brutality with penalties that may include dismissal from the force. The Police Commissioner has spoken out strongly against police use of unlawful force.

Prison conditions meet minimum international standards, and the Government permits visits by human rights monitors.

d. *Arbitrary Arrest, Detention, or Exile.*—The law provides the police with the right to detain persons on suspicion without a warrant, but they must bring formal charges within 48 hours. The police adhered to this time limit in practice. If the police do not charge a detainee within 48 hours, they must release the person.

The law provides for a judicial determination of the legality of detention within 15 days after arrest on a criminal charge. The police must formally arraign or release a detained person within 60 days, and the authorities generally followed these procedures. There is a functioning system of bail, although persons charged with capital offenses are not eligible. Persons charged with treason may be accorded bail only upon recommendation of the Governor General.

Exile is not practiced.

e. *Denial of Fair Public Trial.*—The judiciary, a part of the Eastern Caribbean legal system, is highly regarded and independent. Final appeal may be made to the

Privy Council in the United Kingdom. There are no military or political courts. Those arrested on criminal charges are brought before the independent judiciary. Following a determination by a judicial hearing that there is sufficient evidence to substantiate a criminal charge, the judge remands the defendant for trial.

The law provides for the right to a fair public trial, and the authorities observe it in practice. There is a presumption of innocence, and the law protects persons against self-incrimination and requires the police to explain a person's rights upon arrest. The accused has the right to remain silent and to seek the advice of legal counsel. A defense lawyer has the right to be present during interrogation and may advise the accused how to respond or not to respond to questions. The accused has the right to confront his accuser.

The court appoints attorneys for indigents only in cases of murder or other capital crimes. In other criminal cases that reach the appellate stage, the court will similarly appoint a lawyer to represent the accused if he was not previously represented or reappoint the defendant's earlier counsel if the appellant can no longer afford the lawyer's services. Due to the backlog of cases caused by a shortage of judges and facilities, up to 6 months can pass before those charged with serious offenses face trial in the high court. With the exception of murder and foreign-born drug suspects, the courts grant most defendants bail while awaiting trial.

There were no reports of political prisoners.

f. *Arbitrary Interference with Privacy, Family, Home, or Correspondence.*—The Constitution provides for protection from these abuses, and there were no reports of such actions. The law generally requires judicially issued warrants for searching homes, except in cases of hot pursuit. The Firearms Act of 1968 and the Drug Abuse Prevention Act Number 7 of 1992 contain other exceptions that give the police and security units legal authority to search persons and property without warrants in certain circumstances. In practice, police obtain warrants in the majority of cases before conducting any search.

Section 2. Respect for Civil Liberties, Including:

a. *Freedom of Speech and Press.*—The Constitution provides for freedom of speech and the press, and the Government does not restrict these rights. There are four weekly newspapers and several newspapers which publish irregularly. One of the weeklies is affiliated with an opposition political party, but the three most widely circulated newspapers are independent and often critical of the Government. The newspapers frequently carry press releases by the opposition parties, one of which regularly provides a weekly column expressing the opposition party's views.

Grenada has four radio stations. The main station is part of the Grenadian Broadcasting Corporation (GBC), a statutory body not under direct government control. Grenada's main television station is also part of the GBC. A privately owned television station began broadcasting in 1992, when a cable company began operating in the capital area with plans to expand eventually throughout the country. Throughout 1996 the television news often carried reports on opposition activities, including coverage of the political rallies of the various political parties and candidates, public forums featuring political leaders of each of the major parties, and other public service broadcasts. The Government granted several new licenses for radio stations during the year.

The Government does not restrict academic freedom.

b. *Freedom of Peaceful Assembly and Association.*—The Constitution provides for the right to assemble for any peaceful purpose. Supporters of political parties meet frequently and hold public rallies; the authorities require permits for the use of a public address system but not for public meetings themselves.

c. *Freedom of Religion.*—The Constitution provides for freedom of religion, and the Government respects this right in practice.

d. *Freedom of Movement Within the Country, Foreign Travel, Emigration, and Repatriation.*—The Constitution provides for freedom of movement within the country, and all citizens have the right to enter and leave the country, except in special circumstances as outlined in and limited by the 1986 Act to Restrict the Freedom of Movement of Certain Persons. This law allows the Minister for National Security to restrict travel out of Grenada by any person whose aims, tendencies, or objectives include the overthrow of the democratic and parliamentary system of government; it has not been invoked in the past few years. Anyone so restricted may appeal after 3 months to an independent and impartial tribunal. The Chief Justice appoints an accredited lawyer to preside over such a tribunal.

No formal government policy toward refugee or asylum requests exists. The issue of provision of first asylum did not arise. There were no reports of forced expulsion of anyone having a valid claim to refugee status; however, government practice remains undefined.

Section 3. Respect for Political Rights: The Right of Citizens to Change Their Government

The Constitution provides citizens with the right to change their government peacefully, and citizens exercise this right in practice through periodic, free, and fair elections held on the basis of universal suffrage. The next parliamentary elections must be held by October 2000.

There are no restrictions in law or practice on participation by women in government and politics. Three of the 15 elected members of Parliament are women, as well as 1 of the 13 appointed Senators (who also serves as Deputy President of the Senate). Women account for 8 of the 12 permanent secretaries, the highest civil service position in each ministry; in addition, a woman is the Cabinet Secretary, the highest civil service position in the Government.

Section 4. Governmental Attitude Regarding International and Nongovernmental Investigation of Alleged Violations of Human Rights

Local human rights groups operate without government restriction, and the Government cooperates with visits from international human rights organizations.

Section 5. Discrimination Based on Race, Sex, Religion, Disability, Language, or Social Status

The Constitution prohibits discrimination based upon race, place of origin, political opinions, color, creed, or sex, and the Government generally adheres to these provisions.

Women.—Knowledgeable women's rights monitors report that violence against women is common and that most cases of spousal abuse go unreported. The police confirm that most cases of alleged abuse are not reported and others are settled out of court. Grenadian law stipulates a sentence of 15 years' imprisonment for a conviction of rape. Sentences for assault against a spouse vary according to the severity of the incident. There is no evidence of official discrimination in health care, employment, or education. Women frequently earn less than men performing the same work; such wage differences are less marked for the more highly paid jobs.

Children.—The Social Welfare Division within the Ministry of Labour provides probationary and rehabilitative services to youths, day care services and social work programs to families, assistance to families wishing to adopt or foster children, and financial assistance to the three children's homes in Grenada run by private organizations.

The Government reported 40 cases of child abuse during the year. The law provides for harsh penalties against those convicted of child abuse and disallows the victim's alleged "consent" as a defense in cases of incest.

People With Disabilities.—The law does not protect job seekers with disabilities from discrimination in employment, nor does it mandate provision of accessibility for public buildings or services. The National Council for the Disabled, which receives a small amount of financial assistance from the Government, was instrumental in placing visually impaired students into community schools, which were previously reluctant to accept them in some cases. The Council also approached architects to assist in construction of ramps at various hotels and public buildings, and ramps have already been installed at some hotels.

Section 6. Worker Rights

a. *The Right of Association.*—All workers are free to organize independent labor unions. Labor Ministry officials estimate that the percentage of the work force that is unionized is between 20 and 25 percent. Union leaders play a significant role in the political process, and one labor leader serves in the Senate on behalf of the Grenada Trades Union Council (GTUC).

Workers in the private and public sectors are free to strike, once legal and procedural requirements are met. There were several incidents of industrial action, including strikes, but all were short-lived and settled with the intervention of the Ministry of Labor or the Prime Minister. All unions are technically free of government control, and none receive government financial support. However, all the major unions belong to one umbrella labor federation, the GTUC, which is subsidized by the Government. The GTUC holds annual conventions and determines some policies for member unions. The GTUC and its unions freely affiliate with regional and international trade union groups.

b. *The Right to Organize and Bargain Collectively.*—Workers are free to organize and to participate in collective bargaining. Legislation requires employers to recognize a union that represents the majority of workers in a particular business. The law prohibits discrimination by employers against union members and organizers. If a complaint of discrimination arises, mechanisms exist to resolve it. After all avenues for resolving a complaint have been exhausted between union representatives and employers, both sides may agree to ask for the assistance of the Labor Commissioner. If the Labor Commissioner is unable to find a resolution to the impasse, the Minister of Labor intervenes and, if unable to reach an agreement, may appoint an arbitration tribunal if both parties agree to abide by its ruling. The law requires employers found guilty of antiunion discrimination to rehire dismissed employees, but in most cases the employee accepts the option of compensation. There were no cases of antiunion discrimination reported to the Ministry in 1996.

Unions may organize and bargain anywhere in the country, including, in theory, export processing zones (EPZ's), which are not exempted from Grenada's labor legislation.

c. *Prohibition of Forced or Compulsory Labor.*—The Constitution specifically prohibits forced labor, and there were no reports of it.

d. *Minimum Age for Employment of Children.*—Child labor is illegal and does not occur. The statutory minimum age for employment of children is 18 years. Inspectors from the Ministry of Labor enforce this provision in the formal sector by periodic checks. Enforcement efforts in the informal sector are lax.

e. *Acceptable Conditions of Work.*—Legislation sets minimum daily wage rates for the agricultural, industrial, and commercial sectors. Most recently revised in 1994, minimum wages for farm laborers are $5.73 (EC$15.48) per day for men and $5.33 (EC$14.40) for women. Most workers, including nonunionized ones, receive other benefits from their employers through the collective bargaining agreements reached with that firm's unionized workers. Even when these benefits are added to wages from a full-time minimum wage job, it is insufficient to provide a decent standard of living.

The law does not prescribe a set number of hours as the standard workweek, except for the public sector which is expected to work a 40-hour week Monday through Friday. The normal workweek in all sectors seldom exceeds 40 hours, although in the commercial sector this includes Saturday morning work.

The Government sets health and safety standards, but they are minimal, and the authorities do not effectively enforce them. Workers can remove themselves from dangerous workplace situations without jeopardy to continued employment.

GUATEMALA

The 1985 Constitution provides for election by universal suffrage of a one-term president and a unicameral congress. It also mandates an independent judiciary and a Human Rights Ombudsman (PDH), who is elected by and reports to the Congress. Elections for president, vice president, congress, and municipal offices held on November 12, 1995, resulted in the National Advancement Party (PAN) winning 42 of the 80 congressional seats; however, no presidential candidate received an absolute majority of the votes. Alvaro Arzu Irigoyen of the PAN won the runoff presidential election and took office January 14. Reflecting a greater opening for political activity, 24 parties, including a broad front coalition composed of civic, human rights, and labor leaders, campaigned in the free and fair elections.

Peace talks between the Government and the leftist insurgent Guatemalan National Revolutionary Unity (URNG) resulted in a negotiated end to the 36-year-long civil war, with a final peace accord signed on December 29. Guerrilla groups unilaterally ceased offensive action in March, and government forces immediately responded by halting counterinsurgency patrols. In May the URNG announced that it would cease collection of "war taxes" following signature of an accord dealing with socioeconomic and agrarian issues. Even before the final peace agreement, the Government began demobilizing the rural civil self-defense groups called Civilian Defense Patrols (PAC's), a process largely completed in November. The peace accords call for restructuring and downsizing the military, abolishing all PAC's, and strengthening the civil government, including increased spending on education and health. The army's budget and authorized strength of 43,000 men are to be reduced by one-third by 1999, and the Government is to propose a constitutional amendment to permit a civilian Minister of Defense. The agreements also call for the creation of a new police force with increased training and for the army to be removed from all internal security functions. A broad range of civic groups, including prominent human rights groups, endorsed the final accords.

The U.N. Human Rights Verification Mission (MINUGUA), established by a 1994 Government-URNG accord on human rights, maintains a large staff with regional offices to monitor compliance with the human rights accord. It is expected to assume expanded responsibilities in the wake of the final peace agreement. A military observer component will be added to MINUGUA for a short time to monitor demobilization. MINUGUA has served as an important deterrent to human rights abuses.

The Minister of Government oversees the National Police and the Treasury Police, which shared responsibility for internal security with the army. There are no members of the military in the police command structure. More than 200,000 men served in the PAC's at the beginning of the year, and some PAC's still conducted counterinsurgency patrols then. An estimated 137,000 men participated in Peace and Development Committees (PDC's) at the beginning of the year. While PDC's are voluntary associations that have no official links to either the military or the PAC's, they are often composed of former PAC members. By the end of the year, the PAC's had been disbanded, over 215,000 PAC members demobilized, with over 10,000 weapons surrendered. Although the Constitution requires that service be voluntary, the PDH's office, the Catholic Archbishop's Human Rights Office (ODHAG), and MINUGUA reported that in some regions certain PAC's were still compelling members to join or remain in the patrols in the first half of the year. Security forces, especially PAC's and members of the police, committed numerous serious human rights violations.

The agricultural-based, private sector-oriented economy grew by approximately 3.1 percent in real terms. Coffee, sugar, and bananas are the leading exports, with more than half the work force engaged in agricultural labor. Inflation was 11 percent.There is a marked disparity in income distribution, and poverty is pervasive, particularly in the large indigenous community. According to U.N. statistics, approximately 80 percent of Guatemalans live in poverty, with 59 percent in extreme poverty. Per capita gross national product was approximately $1,400.

There was marked improvement in the overall human rights situation, as demonstrated by a decrease in the number of serious violations, but problems remain in several areas. The improvement was the result of the March cessation of hostilities, the December final peace accord, the Government's initial reforms of the security services, including disbanding the PAC's, as well as increased political will to combat impunity. These favorable military and political developments resulted in a greatly reduced number of conflict-related violations. Nonetheless, the PAC's, former civilian military commissioners, members of the army, and the police committed serious human rights violations, including extrajudicial killings, physical abuse, arbitrary arrest and detention, and death threats. The security forces generally enjoyed impunity from the law. However, in contrast to past years, the Government prosecuted and civilian courts convicted members of several PAC's and some police officers, and the authorities indicted several members of the military for human rights abuses. In December Congress passed a controversial national reconciliation law to implement the peace accord's provisions on reintegrating the URNG into civilian life. The law provides exemption from prosecution for specific war-related acts; MINUGUA stated that it was consistent with international standards.

Even before the final agreements, the Arzu Government took important steps to begin to reduce the extensive institutional and legal autonomy of the army and police in military and security matters. In January the President restructured the military command, reducing the number of general officers from 23 to 8 and retiring or leaving without assignment numerous officers alleged to be involved in corruption or other abuses. In September the President dismissed two other generals, including the Deputy Defense Minister, on corruption charges. Earlier, in June the Congress enacted a law removing from military jurisdiction cases involving members of the military involved in common crimes; as a result 347 cases were transferred from military to civilian courts. In January the Government also dismissed over 100 police officers for corruption and other crimes, many of whom were also the subject of criminal investigations at year's end. In addition, it dismissed 25 members of the Treasury Police for similar reasons in the first half of the year.

Nonetheless, government policy changes and a more aggressive stance by the Minister of Government and the Director of the National Police, while having important positive effects and demonstrating increased political will, have not yet been sufficient to eliminate completely the impunity commonly enjoyed by government security forces and others. A climate of lawlessness persisted throughout the year, and violent acts were committed against all sectors of society, in particular striking such groups as media representatives and human rights monitors. With judges and other law enforcement officials subject to intimidation, corruption, and inadequate resources, the judicial system was often unable to ensure fair trials. Both legal and societal discrimination and violence against women persisted. Societal abuse of children and discrimination against indigenous people continued as well. Guerrillas, as well as leftwing and rightwing extremist groups, committed major human rights violations. Guerrilla abuses included death threats, kidnaping for profit, the use of mines and explosives in civilian areas, and forced recruitment of minors.

RESPECT FOR HUMAN RIGHTS

Section 1. Respect for the Integrity of the Person, Including Freedom From:
   a. *Political and Other Extrajudicial Killing.*—Politically motivated killings continued with disturbing frequency, albeit at lower levels than in recent years. PAC members, police and military personnel, and rightwing extremist groups were all responsible for political and extrajudicial killings. Because of the scarcity of law enforcement resources and a weak and ineffective judicial system, the Government did not successfully investigate many killings or other crimes fully or detain and prosecute perpetrators. The Government's inability to identify, prosecute, or punish those responsible for such offenses remains an impediment to human rights progress.

The PDH's office, which generally compiles data based on personal interviews with victims and their families, listed 173 cases of possible extrajudicial killings in 1996, compared with 216 in 1995. Using media reports and interviews with victims and their relatives, the ODHAG reported 120 extrajudicial killings, compared with 215 in 1995 and 287 in 1994. For its part, MINUGUA listed 69 complaints of extrajudicial killings for the period between January 1 and June 30, but it was able to confirm only 6. None of these human rights offices broke down the figures according to the organization believed responsible, but government security forces, former military commissioners, and current and former PAC members committed such offenses.

The ODHAG and MINUGUA also accused some members of the army and the National Police of directing an extrajudicial "social cleansing" campaign in which they or their agents kill minors and adults believed to have committed common crimes.

PAC members continued to commit human rights abuses, including extrajudicial killings, extorting money from those who did not want to participate (see Section 1.f.), and general criminal activity including burglary and assault. Former PAC members and former military commissioners, who often form an important part of the local power structure in the absence of day-to-day central government authority in outlying areas, are feared in many rural communities. (Military commissioners, formally decommissioned September 15, 1995, were generally local civilian leaders who represented the army, serving as intermediaries with PAC members.) Despite the peace accords and the Government's success in disarming and disbanding the PAC's, there exists a widespread perception that the PAC's and former PAC members enjoy army backing and immunity from prosecution. The ODHAG and the Runujel Junam Council of Ethnic Communities (CERJ, an indigenous human rights organization), reported that the executive branch failed to carry out arrest warrants against a number of military commissioners and PAC members for their involvement in human rights crimes. PAC members and military commissioners are rarely convicted for their crimes. Nonetheless, in an improvement over past years, the courts convicted and sentenced 4 PAC members during the year, with 15 still pending trial. In several of these cases, CERJ acted as a joint complainant (see Section 1.e.).

Since the 1994 killings at the La Exacta farm, the Ministry of Government has modified its procedures and has promoted improved discipline and greater restraint in the use of force in property eviction tactics employed by the authorities. They carried out at least 20 evictions without incident during the year. Nonetheless, on April 17, the commander of the Police Rapid Reaction Force, Ernesto Soto, and Roberto Velasquez, a peasant participating in the occupation of El Tablero farm, were killed when peasants clashed with police attempting to dislodge them. It is unclear who instigated the confrontation; MINUGUA, the PDH, and the ODHAG each issued conflicting statements.

There was no significant progress in the case of the 1993 murder of newspaper publisher and former presidential candidate Jorge Carpio. In November the prosecuting attorney announced he was quitting and going into voluntary exile because of continued threats and harassment. At year's end, the case continued under a different attorney.

On January 6, assailants killed CERJ member Miguel Us Mejia and his wife Lucia Tiu Tum, a member of the Guatemalan Conference of Widows (CONAVIGUA), who were returning from a wedding in a remote village in Quiche department. The killer stabbed Us Mejia more than 20 times and shot Tiu Tum twice. The authorities have not arrested anyone for the crime; the violence of the attack and the absence of robbery suggest political motives. Human rights groups accused local PAC members of committing the murders.

On January 23, Miguel Mijanos, a member of a military patrol, shot and killed Narciso Alcor along the Central American highway in Chimaltenango. Alcor had approached the patrol late at night and apparently disregarded several orders to halt. Mijanos fired shots in the air, at which point Alcor fled. Mijanos then shot Alcor twice in the back. Mijanos was detained and under investigation for extrajudicial execution at year's end. There was no indication of a political motive.

On September 20, a Treasury Police agent, Armando Ramirez, killed 16-year-old Ronald Raul Ramos Hernandez. According to Casa Alianza, an organization dedicated to assisting street children, Ramirez—apparently under the influence of alcohol—approached and demanded money from Ramos and other street children sleeping under a bridge in Tecun Uman on the Mexican border. The agent then beat Ramos and shot him once in the head. The authorities issued a warrant to arrest Ramos, but he apparently fled the country. Casa Alianza charged that the refusal of local officials to investigate the case and detain Ramirez facilitated his escape.

Popular frustration with the inability of the authorities to combat crime resulted in a series of lynchings and mob attacks throughout the year. Mobs killed at least 31 people who were suspected of crimes ranging from murder to petty theft and injured many other suspected criminals. There were allegations that some of these mobs had been incited for political purposes, but the majority of incidents appeared to be spontaneous. Efforts by volunteer firemen and police, sometimes assisted by the military, to aid the victims were often unsuccessful. With few exceptions, the Government made no effort to arrest or prosecute the perpetrators of these attacks.

Congress passed a National Reconciliation Law in December to implement the provisions of the peace accord on reintegration of the URNG into political life. The law provides amnesty for political crimes directly related to the war. However, it states that those who committed serious human rights violations—torture, forced disappearance, genocide, illegal treatment of prisoners, and those crimes not subject to a statute of limitations or to amnesty by domestic law or international treaty—do not receive relief from criminal responsibility. The law provides for a special review by the Appeals Court, on a case-by-case basis, for common crimes committed in connection with war-related acts to determine if any exemption from prosecution applies. Human rights activists criticized the law as too lenient, but MINUGUA stated that it was consistent with international standards.

There were developments in some high-profile cases from previous years:

The ODHAG and MINUGUA issued separate reports concluding that the October 1995 killing of 11 returned refugees at the Xaman Ranch in Alta Verapaz by an army patrol was not premeditated or ordered by the military command. In February an appellate judge ordered the criminal case against the soldiers involved transferred to civilian jurisdiction. In June the civilian judge granted bail for 8 of the 26 soldiers in the case, including the commanding officer, Lieutenant Lacan Chaclan. The prosecution appealed this decision, and, based upon irregularities in the way this and other decisions were made, the authorities subsequently suspended the judge and returned the eight to jail. The case continued under a different civilian judge at year's end.

Victor Roman, the alleged perpetrator of the 1995 murder of evangelical pastor Manuel Saquic and the 1994 murder of pastor Pascual Serech, remained at large at year's end, despite an arrest warrant and the offer of a $3,300 (20,000 quetzales) reward. In September the Public Ministry filed charges against two other persons allegedly involved in the Serech murder, including Serech's wife, and filed charges in absentia against Roman. Members of the presbytery to which both Saquic and Serech belonged received numerous death threats during the year, presumably related to their continued demands for the apprehension of Roman and their testimony before the Inter-American Commission on Human Rights (IACHR). In June the IACHR issued a resolution faulting the Government for a lax investigation and ordered protection of the witnesses involved and monthly reports from the Government on the progress of the case.

Partly in response to the Commission's findings, the Government established regular meetings between civilian and military authorities responsible for the case and members of the presbytery. In August the presbytery withdrew from the meetings citing a lack of progress in the investigation and a lack of cooperation from the military. A search of local military facilities where Roman allegedly had been sighted failed to uncover Roman or further leads.

In the April 1994 killing of Constitutional Court President Epaminondas Gonzalez Dubon, an appeals court overturned the verdict of two of the six persons convicted; they were released in March. The Constitutional Court later reversed this decision after an appeal by the Public Ministry. One of the accused had been arrested on unrelated charges but subsequently escaped in August and remained at large at year's end. The other was recaptured in September. Meanwhile, the authorities indicted Antonio Trabanino Vargas, already in prison on other charges, for involvement in the killing. Judicial proceedings against Trabanino continued at year's end. Although the Public Ministry ruled out any motive other than robbery, there was widespread speculation that Gonzalez Dubon was killed because he had decided to uphold the constitutionality of an extradition order to the United States for former Lieutenant Colonel Carlos Ochoa Ruiz on drug-related charges.

A videotape of a November 1994 demonstration by university students showed policemen severely beating student Mario Lopez Sanchez after he was injured and incapable of resistance. Lopez later died from his injuries. Judicial proceedings continued at year's end. An appellate court reinstated a previously dismissed wrongful death lawsuit for $1.6 million (10 million quetzales) against the Government filed by the family. MINUGUA reports that, since Lopez' death, there have been incidents of torture, kidnaping, and intimidation directed against witnesses and others involved in the prosecution of the case.

The authorities arrested seven police officers in connection with the August 1994 killing of three workers at the La Exacta farm. The seven were still awaiting trial at year's end. According to MINUGUA, however, Public Ministry officials have neglected to carry out some basic investigative inquiries into this incident.

There were major developments in the case against three former army officers accused of ordering the 1990 murder of anthropologist Myrna Mack. An October Supreme Court decision to proceed with the case under the former penal procedures code rendered inadmissible all evidence previously gathered by the Public Ministry and cocomplainant Helen Mack, effectively ending the prosecution. The Public Ministry and Mack appealed the ruling to the Constitutional Court. The convicted material author of the crime, Jose Noel Beteta, is in prison serving a 30-year sentence. There was no progress in the presumably related case of detective Jose Luis Merida Escobar, killed in 1991 while investigating Myrna Mack's death.

The 1988 "white van case," in which members of the Treasury Police allegedly abducted, tortured, and murdered victims using a white van, remained open at year's end. In June the Public Ministry announced that unknown individuals had broken into its offices and searched the prosecution's file on the case.

On April 11, a court acquitted members of a PAC in Colotenango —which was disbanded on August 9—due to lack of evidence in the August 1993 murder of Juan Chanay Pablo, an anti-PAC demonstrator. The Public Ministry is appealing the decision. Family members also brought the case to the IACHR. For the first time in any such case, the Government is seeking to negotiate a settlement with the plaintiffs.

There was no progress in resolving numerous other past extrajudicial killings: The 1985 killings of Nicholas Blake and Griffith Davis; the 1989 disappearances and murders of university students; the 1990 Hector Oqueli Colindres and Gilda Flores killings; the 1990 disappearance of Maria Tiu Tojin and her daughter; the 1991 disappearance of Diego Domingo Martin; the 1992 kidnaping, torture, and murder of Huehuetenango peasant Lucas Perez Tadeo; the 1993 shooting of street children Henry Yubani Alvarez and Francisco Tziac; and the 1993 shooting of student protester Abner Abdiel Hernandez Orellana.

b. *Disappearance.*—In contrast to past years, there were no credible reports of disappearances attributed to official forces.

The PDH's office received 47 complaints of forced disappearance, compared with 77 for 1995. While motives in the incidents reported by the PDH are difficult to determine, the victims were not, in general, politically active. Using a more restrictive definition than the PDH, the ODHAG reported no forced disappearances during the year.

Disappearances in high-profile cases from recent years remained unresolved at year's end. Arnoldo Xi, a community leader in Tixila, Purulha, Baja Verapaz and a member of CONIC (an indigenous human rights organization dedicated to saving Mayan culture), reportedly wounded by gunfire and abducted by armed men on March 23, 1995, remained missing. The whereabouts were unknown of Salvador de la Rosa, a member of a military patrol who disappeared in March 1995, and of Lorenzo Quiej Pu, a member of CONDEG (an organization dedicated to helping Guatemalans internally displaced due to the armed conflict), who disappeared in January 1994. The disappearances of San Marcos PAC members Margarito Lopez and Obdulio Zapeta, army enlisted man Diego Chel Matom, and farmers Ramona Munoz and Maritza Gil, who were allegedly kidnaped in 1993 by guerrillas, also remained unresolved at year's end.

c. *Torture and Other Cruel, Inhuman, or Degrading Treatment or Punishment.*— The Constitution provides for the integrity and security of the person and prohibits the physical or psychological torture of prisoners. There were credible reports of mistreatment by members of the security forces, including sexual abuse of minors and adults and use of excessive force at the time of arrest. Additional reports indicated that, especially in rural areas, the army, civil defense patrols, former military commissioners, and police all at times used excessive force against the civilian population.

Many bodies were found in various parts of the country bearing signs of severe disfigurement or mutilation. It was difficult to determine those responsible, in part because the authorities do not have the capacity to undertake serious investigations. The PDH's office listed 12 potential cases of torture, compared with 9 in 1995. The ODHAG listed 4 cases of torture, compared with 5 cases in 1995 and 17 cases in 1994. Some of these incidents were believed to be politically motivated, such as the case of radio reporter Vinicio Pacheco (see Section 2.a.) Evidence of torture and severe mistreatment are also prevalent in murders arising from nonpolitical disputes, particularly those related to narcotics trafficking.

Casa Alianza reported various instances in which the National Police abused street children. It also reported that the criminal case against the five policemen charged in the March 1994 baton beating of Luis Antonio Roldan Izeppi remained pending because two policemen have not testified. One of the five has since left the force. Also according to Casa Alianza, private security guards routinely abuse street children. The courts convicted five people, including two police officers and one military officer, of abusing street children. Guerrilla forces also occasionally abused the civilian population, especially in rural areas.

There were no new developments in the investigation of abuses suffered by U.S. citizen Sister Dianna Ortiz in November 1989.

Prison conditions are harsh but not life threatening. The Government reports that prison capacity is 7,100 persons. However, prisoners frequently complain of overcrowding, even though there were less than 5,700 inmates at year's end. Prisoners also complain of inadequate food, and fights among inmates led to the deaths of several prisoners. Corruption—especially drug-related—is widespread, and the authorities replaced the director of prisons in November due to allegations of corruption. Women prisoners are held in facilities separate from men, and minor children are held in separate detention facilities.

The Government permits access to prisons by family members as well as independent international monitors.

d. *Arbitrary Arrest, Detention, or Exile.*—Despite legal safeguards, there were frequent credible reports of arbitrary arrest, incommunicado detention, and failure to adhere to prescribed time limits in legal proceedings by the security forces. The Constitution requires that a court-issued arrest warrant be presented to a suspect prior to arrest unless he is caught in the act of committing a crime. Police may not detain a suspect for over 6 hours without bringing the case before a judge. The law also provides for bail and access to lawyers.

There are no reliable data on the number of arbitrary detentions, although most accounts agree that the security forces routinely ignore writs of habeas corpus in cases of illegal detention. There were 5,400 men and 277 women in prison at year's end. Reliable estimates suggest that about 70 percent have been sentenced, and 30 percent are awaiting sentences. Prisoners are often detained past their legal trial or release dates. The ODHAG has charged that prisoners are sometimes not released in a timely fashion after completing their sentences due to the failure of judges to issue the necessary court order.

There were numerous reports that policemen illegally detained street children; the authorities rarely took action in any of these incidents.

The Constitution prohibits exile, and it is not officially practiced. There are instances of threatened individuals fleeing the country out of fear for their lives.

e. *Denial of Fair Public Trial.*—The Constitution provides for an independent judiciary. However independent in fact, in practice the judicial system often fails to provide fair trials. International organizations, including MINUGUA, continued to note the Government's failure to investigate, prosecute, and punish many suspects, especially in cases involving members of the military and public security forces.

The judiciary is composed of a Constitutional Court, a Supreme Court, appellate courts, lower courts, and courts of special jurisdiction (e.g., labor courts). The Constitution provides that the Congress elect Supreme Court and appellate court magistrates from lists prepared by panels comprised of active magistrates, the Bar Association, and law school deans.

The new Criminal Procedures Code, which came into effect in mid-1994, fundamentally alters the administration of criminal justice by strengthening the prosecutorial function, establishing a public defender program, and instituting oral adversarial proceedings at the trial phase. Its key precepts include the accused's presumption of innocence, the right to be present at trial, the right to counsel, and the possibility of release on bail. Trials are public. The new code also provides for language interpretation for those who require it (see Section 5).

Because of the difficulty in implementing the new code, however, the commitment to transform a dysfunctional judicial system into an effective one is being seriously tested. Despite evidence of increased political will and some concrete advances, the legal obligation of the State (through its Public Ministry) to investigate crimes, prosecute offenders, and administer punishment has been severely hampered by inadequate training and equipment, as well as insufficient numbers of investigators. The courts' response to human rights violations, as well as to general criminal activity, has been very slow. The authorities often avoid conducting investigations that might lead them into conflict with powerful forces. There is apparently no set procedure within the Public Ministry to govern criminal investigations and thus to ensure a viable response to criminal activity. In an effort to improve coordination and set an example for other investigative units, a specially trained investigative task force began operating in May. The task force is made up of members of the Public Ministry and Ministry of Government and is assigned to high priority cases. By year's end, the task force had made arrests in a number of kidnaping and murder cases.

Coordination between the Public Ministry and the National Police with regard to investigations is inadequate. Security forces personnel are reluctant to investigate cases potentially involving colleagues. Police are poorly paid, relatively few in number, and lack adequate resources and training. Judges and prosecutors are susceptible to intimidation and corruption and suffer from low pay, poor working conditions, and low morale. Such factors, combined with the small number of prosecutors and the interference of the Supreme Court with the lower courts, demonstrate that the Government's efforts to date have been insufficient to combat the existing pervasive atmosphere of impunity.

There are, however, signs that the reforms are taking root. There were over 600 oral trials held under the new procedures; of which approximately 100 resulted in acquittals. In contrast with the past, during the year the authorities tried and convicted some police officials and current and former members of PAC's and arrested several members of the military, including high-ranking officers, who awaited trial at year's end (see Section 1.a.). The Public Ministry was successful in prosecuting a number of other high-profile cases of common crime as well, including the 1994 murder of Karin Fleischmann, for which a court sentenced Ricardo Ortega del Cid to 30 years in prison. In an effort to improve the functioning of the court system in rural areas, the judicial system added 19 judges and 5 justices of the peace in August and announced plans to expand the court system in rural areas.

Members of the judiciary, as well as prosecutors, continued to receive threats, either in an attempt to influence current decisions or as reprisals for past decisions. According to the Secretary General of the Supreme Court, early in the year, 40 judges had reported receiving threats related to their cases. Public prosecutors, private plaintiffs, and officials from MINUGUA, the ODHAG, and the PDH's office also received threats.

Corruption continues to impede the proper functioning of the police force, and there are credible allegations of some police involvement in narcotics trafficking. In numerous criminal cases, police were unwilling to execute arrest warrants. In January the Arzu administration began an effort to combat corruption in the security forces by dismissing over 100 National Police and 25 Treasury Police officers. By the middle of the year, more than 100 of these officers were facing judicial proceedings. In a further effort to professionalize the police force, the Ministry of Government initiated a mandatory 6-month training course for all newly hired police officers. In the past, many officers received no formal training. The new training program includes instruction on human rights given by the PDH and Casa Alianza and was developed with assistance from MINUGUA and other international organizations. The first officers graduated from the new course in mid-summer. Plans incorporated into the final peace agreement include the unification of the civilian security forces into a single police force, a professional training and development program, and a significant increase in the number of officers. All new officers are to pass the 6-month training course.

There were no reports of political prisoners.

f. *Arbitrary Interference with Privacy, Family, Home, or Correspondence.*—The Constitution provides for the inviolability of home, correspondence, and private documents, but the authorities at times disregard these provisions. Elements of the security forces reportedly continue to monitor private communications. As recently as 1995, Ministry of Defense officials admitted that the military monitors communications "when necessary." In January the daily newspaper Siglo Veintiuno charged that the Presidential Military Staff had tapped its fax machine. Many human rights workers alleged surveillance of their movements and activities.

MINUGUA reports that the military has honored the June 1994 presidential order to suspend all conscription, including forced recruitment. However, while the Constitution requires that PAC service be voluntary, in some regions, army officers and PAC leaders pressured men to become and remain members or extorted a fee from individuals in exchange for permission to resign. There are credible reports that individuals refusing to serve in PAC's suffered threats and other abuses. The Government's action to disband the PAC's was a major step toward ending these abuses.

g. *Use of Excessive Force and Violations of Humanitarian Law in Internal Conflicts.*—A mutual cessation of hostilities in March, a major agreement in September, and the signing of the final peace accord on December 29 that ended the 36-year-long civil war greatly reduced the number of human rights violations related to the conflict. However, instances of terrorist bombings conducted by unknown perpetrators occurred throughout the year. At least five explosive devices were detonated or deactivated in Guatemala City and two others outside the city, leaving at least two persons dead and several injured. Several of these devices were accompanied by URNG leaflets. Other bomb attacks were believed to be orchestrated by rightist groups opposed to the peace negotiations.

After reaching agreement on an accord with the Government on socioeconomic and agrarian issues on May 6, the guerrillas unilaterally stopped the collection of war taxes. Prior to this decision, however, MINUGUA had verified the accuracy of complaints of ranch owners against the URNG's practice of collecting war taxes in several departments. There were also complaints that either the URNG or criminal elements were still collecting "back taxes" at year's end.

Both the army and the guerrillas used antipersonnel land mines in civilian areas, particularly in San Marcos and Quiche departments. However, both sides cooperated with the U.N. and national authorities in the removal of mines. MINUGUA reported that three members of the military were killed, and one soldier and three civilians injured, in five mine explosions in the first half of the year. These incidents mainly occurred during attempts to remove the mines.

Throughout the year, guerrilla groups assembled captive audiences to listen to their political pronouncements. Armed guerrilla units occupied various towns throughout the country and the University of San Carlos campus in Guatemala City for several hours to disseminate propaganda. Local military zone commanders did not resist these incursions, and there were no confrontations or casualties. On July 30, press reports indicated that guerrillas took over a radio station in Mazatenango, forced personnel to play URNG propaganda tapes, and detonated a pamphlet bomb. There were no casualties in the incident.

On October 28, the Government announced it had captured a high ranking guerrilla commander in connection with the kidnaping of a wealthy 86-year-old woman. After negotiations, the authorities released the guerrilla in exchange for the victim's safe return. Guerrilla leaders later confirmed the commander's involvement in the kidnaping but claimed that he was acting without orders. There was widespread speculation of guerrilla involvement in other kidnapings.

The URNG claims it holds no prisoners, and there were no reports of any captives in URNG custody at year's end.

U.S. citizen lawyer Jennifer Harbury continued to search for the remains of her husband, guerrilla leader Efrain Bamaca Velasquez, who disappeared following a March 1992 clash between army and URNG forces. The military contends that Bamaca died in battle, but reliable information indicates the army captured Bamaca and held him for an undetermined period, interrogating and ultimately killing him. Several legal developments in ongoing Guatemalan court cases related to Bamaca's disappearance failed to shed additional light on his fate. In addition, the military frustrated at least two separate attempts to exhume a possible grave at the Las Cabanas military detachment in San Marcos by obtaining countermanding judicial orders. MINUGUA is assisting the Public Ministry in its investigation as part of its support for due process. In October the Constitutional Court denied legal recognition of the U.S. marriage of Harbury and Bamaca. The Inter-American Court of Human rights accepted a case against the Government over Bamaca's disappearance but gave no indication when a ruling may be issued.

Section 2. Respect for Civil Liberties, Including:

a. *Freedom of Speech and Press.*—The Constitution provides for freedom of expression. In addition to regular and open criticism of government policies, the media publicizes communiques from the URNG, leftist groups, and others opposed to the Government or its policies. Journalists admit, however, that in some particularly sensitive cases pressure and fears of reprisal result in self-censorship and limits on investigative reporting. Some journalists report they are reluctant to criticize the military or military officers or to discuss topics that could be perceived to affect the interests of powerful economic groups and individuals. Reports on human rights and narcotics trafficking are carefully written and sourced so that neither journalists nor their institutions are put at risk. Radio and television station owners observe that licensing procedures could give the Government powerful leverage over their editorial policies, but they have not cited any instances in which the Government attempted to use this power.

Continuing acts of political violence directed against journalists give credence to their complaints of pressure and coercion at the working level. The ODHAG reported 18 incidents of violence or threats against the media, including 3 murders, 2 bomb attacks, 1 case of torture, and 12 threats against reporters or editors. The ODHAG was unable to identify the perpetrators or determine the motives in most of these incidents but believes that many were related to the journalists' work.

On February 28, unknown men abducted radio reporter Vinicio Pacheco and physically abused him. They reportedly warned Pacheco to discontinue his aggressive coverage of drug trafficking and car theft. The authorities have not arrested anyone for this crime. On May 16, hand grenades were thrown at the car of newspaper editor Jose Ruben Zamora who, as editor of one of the major daily newspapers, had run articles sharply critical of the military and other powerful interests. The perpetrators were not apprehended.

The Constitution provides for academic freedom. There were no reports of professors or students being subject to violence or intimidation for their academic work.

b. *Freedom of Peaceful Assembly and Association.*—The Constitution provides for the right of peaceful assembly and association, and the Government respects this right in practice. Peaceful demonstrations were common, and demonstrators sometimes occupied government institutions, including the presidential palace, government ministries, Congress, and the Supreme Court building. In all these cases, the police acted with restraint, and the authorities negotiated a peaceful departure of the demonstrators. The Government did not interfere with political associations. The law requires organizations to obtain legal status, a cumbersome and expensive procedure.

c. *Freedom of Religion.*—The Constitution provides for religious freedom, and the authorities respect it in practice. However, personal and political enemies sometimes threatened or killed religious personnel because of their activism in human rights, indigenous rights, land reform, and related fields. During the year, both the ODHAG and the Council of Evangelical Churches denounced acts of intimidation and harassment directed against several members of the clergy, Evangelical pastors, and lay workers.

d. *Freedom of Movement Within the Country, Foreign Travel, Emigration, and Repatriation.*—The Government does not restrict foreign travel, nor does it revoke citizenship for political reasons. The authorities did not restrict movement inside the country except in some areas of conflict before the cessation of hostilities, where the army and PAC's limited travel.

Early in the year, guerrillas established roadblocks to rob private citizens, extort protection payments from businessmen, attack and drain petroleum trucks, and hinder travel in certain rural areas.

The Government cooperates with the office of the United Nations High Commissioner for Refugees (UNHCR) and other humanitarian organizations in assisting refugees from other countries. The issue of the provision of first asylum did not arise. There were no reports of forced expulsion of persons to countries where they feared persecution. Voluntary repatriation of refugees from Mexico continued. The UNHCR reported that 4,185 refugees returned to Guatemala in 1996, bringing the total to over 25,000 since initiation of the program in 1993.

Section 3. Respect for Political Rights: The Right of Citizens to Change Their Government

Citizens have the right to change their government by peaceful and democratic means, through secret ballot and universal suffrage for those 18 years of age and older. Members of the armed forces and police may not vote. Since the return to democracy and civilian rule in 1985, there have been seven free elections. International observers concluded that both the general elections for President, Vice President, Congress, and municipal offices, held on November 12, 1995, and the runoff presidential election held on January 7, 1996, were free and fair. In the runoff between Alvaro Arzu of the National Advancement Party (PAN) and Alfonso Portillo of the Guatemalan Republican Front (FRG), Arzu won with 51.2 percent of the vote to Portillo's 48.8 percent, and he took office on January 14.

Reflecting a greater opening for political activity, 24 parties, including a broad-front coalition composed of civic, human rights, and labor leaders, campaigned. The parties put forward 19 presidential candidates and thousands of candidates for congressional deputy and mayor. The election also was characterized by a greater participation by grassroots organizations and the left, incorporated into a newly formed coalition party called the New Guatemalan Democratic Front (FDNG). Although the URNG did not participate directly, in a radical departure from previous policy, it did call for voter participation in the election and agreed to a unilateral cease-fire for the last 2 weeks of both the first and second election periods in return for political parties' commitment to abide by those peace accords previously agreed to by the Government and the URNG.

Voters elect the 80-member Congress using a system of proportional representation based on population, with deputies elected both from districts and from a nationwide list. Congress has 64 deputies from districts and 16 from the national list. The last elections involved 24 political parties; 6 won seats in the legislature. Congress can and does act independently of the executive, but fragmentation along party lines and a weak support structure result in the Government being driven by the executive branch.

There are no legal impediments to women's participation in politics, but women are underrepresented in the political arena. Nevertheless, women do hold some prominent political positions, including a cabinet post. In the November 1995 elections, voters elected 11 women to the 80-member Congress. Two women also serve as Supreme Court justices, and one is a Constitutional Court justice.

Indigenous people are entitled to equal rights under the Constitution. Some have attained high positions as army officers (including one general), judges, and government officials, including eight members of Congress. In the November elections, 40 indigenous candidates won mayoral positions (out of 300 municipalities), including the mayor of Quetzaltenango, the second largest city. Nonetheless, they are still heavily underrepresented in politics due to limited educational opportunity and pervasive discrimination (see Section 5).

Section 4. Governmental Attitude Regarding International and Nongovernmental Investigation of Alleged Violations of Human Rights

The Government permits local human rights groups to operate freely. However, as noted by MINUGUA, a pervasive attitude continued among rightwing elements of the army, military commissioners, and civil defense patrol members that human rights activists were really subversives tied to the URNG.

A government-URNG accord led to the November 1994 introduction of MINUGUA into Guatemala. MINUGUA became fully staffed in 1995 and now numbers 305 personnel, with 8 regional and 5 subregional offices. MINUGUA's extensive international presence, its verification of alleged abuses, and other activities serve as a deterrent to human rights abuses. MINUGUA's two comprehensive 1996 reports documented both the Government's and the URNG's successes and failures in implementing the terms of the human rights agreement.

Relations between the Ombudsman's office and the executive branch were strained. The PDH reported that some security force agents intimidated and refused to cooperate with Ombudsman officials. Ombudsman Jorge Mario Garcia Laguardia also complained that the Government was neither funding his office adequately nor implementing his recommendations on human rights.

Other high-ranking officials working in the fields of human rights and jurisprudence complained publicly and privately of receiving threats stemming from their interest in resolving cases related to human rights violations, official corruption, and drug trafficking. ODHAG spokesmen reported that members of that office had received threats as well.

Several members of Congress, who are also leaders of human rights groups, reported receiving threatening letters at various times throughout the year. On April 11, unknown men broke into the house of Amilcar Mendez, FDNG congressional deputy and founder of the human rights group CERJ, and assaulted his adopted daughter. While the Government actively investigated the crime, there were no arrests. Other human rights activists also reported receiving threats throughout the year. For example, Federico Reyes Lopez, a member of the Guatemalan forensic anthropology team which is dedicated to uncovering mass graves—mainly resulting from human rights abuses in the 1980's—reported in June receiving threats presumably related to his work.

Both the PDH's office and the ODHAG continued to enjoy widespread public support and respect. Senior government officials also met with numerous foreign officials and human rights monitors. While many international human rights organizations and their workers do not enjoy formal legal status, they continue to operate openly.

Section 5. Discrimination Based on Race, Sex, Religion, Disability, Language, or Social Status

The Constitution states that all human beings are free and equal in dignity and rights and that the State must protect the life, liberty, justice, security, peace, and development of all Guatemalans. In practice, however, the Government is frequently unable or unwilling to enforce these provisions, due to inadequate resources, corruption, and a continuing atmosphere of impunity.

Women.—CONAVIGUA and the PDH reported that violence against women, including domestic violence, remains common among all social classes. There is no specific law against domestic violence, although it is considered to fall under other statutes. Victims rarely report criminal sexual violence, and relatively few rape cases go to court. The PDH reported that complaints of spousal abuse committed by husbands have continued to rise due to increased nationwide educational programs, which have encouraged women to seek assistance. There are family courts, and judges may issue an injunction against an abusive spouse or companion. The police are charged with enforcing such injunctions. There is also a Women's Rights Department of the PDH, and various nongovernmental organizations (NGO's) provide medical and legal assistance and information on family planning. In March the Constitutional Court overturned an adultery statute that applied only to women.

The Constitution asserts the principle of equality between the sexes. Nonetheless, women face job discrimination and on average receive significantly lower pay than men. They are primarily employed in low-wage jobs in the textile industry, agriculture, retail businesses, and the public sector. More working women than men are employed in the informal sector of the economy, where pay and benefits are generally lower. A 1989 survey reported that in Guatemala City women are underrepresented in high-income job categories and overrepresented among poorly paid workers. Women may own, manage, and inherit property on an equal basis with men.

Children.—The Constitution charges the Government with protecting the physical and mental health, as well as the moral well-being, of minors. These provisions notwithstanding, the Government consistently fails to devote sufficient resources to ensure adequate educational and health services for children. The abuse of street children (see Section 1.c.) is a serious problem in major cities. Estimates of the number of street children range between 1,500 and 5,000, with the majority of these youths concentrated in Guatemala City. Corrupt police and military personnel and criminals often recruit these children into thievery or prostitution rings. The Government and a number of NGO's operate youth centers, but the funds devoted to them are not sufficient to alleviate the problem.

The Presidential Human Rights Commission continued weekly meetings of the Permanent Commission for Children, composed of representatives from Casa Alianza and from the judicial and executive branches, with the aim of addressing the problems of street children. Relations between Casa Alianza and the National Police have often been strained.

People With Disabilities.—The Constitution provides that the State should protect disabled persons. Nonetheless, physically disabled persons are discriminated against in employment practices, and few resources are devoted to combat this problem or otherwise to assist people with disabilities. There is no legislation mandating provision of accessibility to public buildings or transportation for the disabled.

Indigenous People.—The Constitution states that Guatemala is composed of diverse ethnic groups and obliges the Government to recognize, respect, and promote the lifestyles, customs, traditions, forms of social organization, and manner of dress of indigenous people. Indigenous people constitute over one-half the population but remain largely outside of the country's political, economic, social, and cultural mainstream. Indigenous people suffered most of the serious human rights abuses described in Section 1.a. and throughout this report. Although the Constitution accords indigenous people equal rights, in practice they have only minimal participation in decisions affecting their lands, culture, traditions, and allocation of natural resources. In July the Congress ratified International Labor Organization (ILO) Convention 169, intended to safeguard the rights of indigenous people. The final peace accord reached between the Government and the URNG includes agreements on indigenous and socioeconomic issues which, together, should strengthen indigenous participation in society and increase government resources devoted to indigenous areas.

Rural indigenous people have limited educational opportunities and thus have fewer employment opportunities. Many indigenous people are illiterate and do not speak Spanish. Linguistic barriers hinder interaction with the Government and limit access to public services, including the judiciary, since few officials speak any of the 21 indigenous languages. Indigenous persons arrested for crimes are often at a disadvantage due to their limited comprehension of Spanish. The new Criminal

Procedures Code, which took effect in July 1994, states that, beginning in July 1996, the courts must provide interpretation for anyone requiring such services during criminal proceedings. The first programs aimed at implementing this provision began to function in May.

Section 6. Worker Rights

a. *The Right of Association.*—The Constitution and the Labor Code provide workers complete freedom of association and the right to form and join trade unions. The Government does not control unions. Major reforms to the Labor Code in 1992 mandated steps to improve worker rights by facilitating freedom of association, strengthening the rights of working women, increasing penalties for violations of labor laws, and enhancing the role of the Labor Ministry and labor courts in enforcing the statutes. All workers have the right to form or join unions, including public sector employees, with the exception of members of security forces.

At most, 8 percent of the work force, or 240,000 out of 3 million workers, are members of labor organizations. The 1,100 registered unions in the country are independent of government and political party domination. Labor Code amendments simplified the process for unions to obtain legal status. The Minister of Labor further revised the administrative process in May, reducing the number of steps within the Ministry for consideration of union applications and establishing strict timetables; the time for the procedure has been reduced to 20 days from 60. The Labor Ministry also initiated a program to assist unions with their applications, and the Minister warned officials that noncompliance with the timetable could lead to dismissal of those responsible for the delay. These new regulations accelerated the approval procedure and largely eliminated the backlog of union applications. The Labor Ministry granted legal status to 150 unions in the first half of 1996. Of the registered unions, 900 are in the private sector, and 250 are in the public sector.

Workers have the right to strike, but Labor Code procedures for having a strike recognized as legal are cumbersome. Labor organizers criticize the requirement that two-thirds of the workers must approve a vote to strike, the prohibition of strikes by agricultural workers at harvest time, and the right of the Government to prohibit strikes that it considers seriously harmful to the national economy. In June the Congress approved a law that further restricted the right to strike for workers employed in essential public services. The law was strongly opposed by unions and some members of Congress, who called the measure unconstitutional and contrary to commitments to the ILO. The law deems such services as urban and interurban transport, mail, and telegraph as essential. The law was under review by the Constitutional Court at year's end.

Those strikes that do occur are frequently in the public sector and almost always called without legal authorization. The Government declared illegal a strike by judicial workers in April and May; the workers eventually resumed their duties, and were paid for the time they were on strike. Previously, the Government had made no effort to intervene on the basis of a strike's illegality, but the new strike regulation law passed in June permits it to act more forcefully. Hence, the lack of legal approval for a strike can be used as a threat against strikers. Employers may suspend workers or fire them for absence without leave if the authorities have not legally approved their strike. The strike regulation law calls for binding arbitration if an impasse has been reached after 30 days of negotiations.

The law protects workers from retribution for forming and participating in trade union activities, but enforcement of these provisions is spotty. While an increasing number of employers accept unionization, many routinely seek to circumvent Labor Code provisions in order to resist union activities, which they view as historically confrontational and disruptive. An ineffective legal system and inadequate penalties for violations have hindered enforcement of the right to form unions and participate in trade union activities. While workers illegally fired for union activity should, under the Labor Code, be reinstated within 24 hours, employers often file a series of appeals, or simply defy judicial orders of reinstatement. Penalties for defying such orders were increased somewhat in the 1992 Labor Code reform.

In contrast to 1995, trade union leaders and members did not suffer labor-related violence, although written and telephone threats continued. Some public sector union leaders, as well as unionists in the high-profile in-bond export sector, reported receiving threats against themselves and their families. Investigations continued into previous years' cases of violence, including murder, against various labor leaders, although some of these investigations appear to have been suspended for lack of evidence.

An active "solidarity" movement claims approximately 250,000 members in over 475 companies. Unions may legally continue to operate in workplaces that have solidarity associations, and workers have the right to choose between the two or to belong to both. The Government views these associations as civic organizations that need not interfere with the functioning of trade unions. The amended Labor Code stipulates very clearly that trade unions have the exclusive right to bargain collectively over work conditions on behalf of workers. Unionists charge, however, that management promotes solidarity associations to avoid the formation of trade unions or to compete with existing labor unions. There are credible reports that some of these associations did not always adhere to democratic principles in their formation and management and that workers are unable to participate fully and freely in decisionmaking. Similar credible charges are made against some trade union organizations. At the request of trade union leaders, the independent Human Rights Ombudsman, through its Office for Economic and Social Issues, receives complaints related to trade union activities. Union leaders and workers filed some complaints with the PDH during the year, and the Ombudsman has spoken out in public statements about labor conditions in varying sectors of the economy. The PDH can investigate union complaints and issue a statement, but the office has no enforcement powers beyond attempting to ameliorate the situation through publicity and moral suasion.

Unions may and do form federations and confederations and join international organizations.

b. *The Right to Organize and Bargain Collectively.*—Workers have the right to organize and bargain collectively. However, the practice of collective bargaining is limited by the weak structure of the union movement, the requirement that 25 percent of the workers in a factory or business must be union members in order for collective bargaining to take place, the lack of experience with this practice, and the preference of management in many cases to avoid formal ties with trade unions. While both management and the unions honored some well-written collective contracts, in other instances both parties openly ignored and violated contracts. Most workers, even those organized by trade unions, do not have collective contracts to cover their wages and working conditions but do have individual contracts as required by law. Most workers receive the minimum wages established by bipartite commissions, which operate under the guidance of the Ministry of Labor.

Employers cannot dismiss workers for participating in the formation of a trade union; workers file complaints in this regard with the labor inspectors for resolution. The Labor Code provides for the right of employers to fire union workers for cause, permits workers to appeal their dismissal to the labor courts, and requires the reinstatement within 24 hours of any union worker fired without cause. The revised code prohibits employers from firing workers for union organizing and protects them for 60 days following the official publication of approval of the union. It also prohibits employers from firing any member of the executive committee of a union and protects them for an additional 12 months after they are no longer on the executive committee. An employer may fire a member of the union's executive committee for cause only after a trial and issuance of a court resolution.

Labor courts responsible for enforcing labor laws continued to be generally ineffective. Although two labor courts, the sixth and seventh, continued to function, efforts to restructure and modernize the labor court system made little headway. However, in November the president of the Supreme Court announced creation of eight new labor courts and two appeals courts, which are expected to open in early 1997. A heavy backlog of labor cases continues to clog the courts due to inefficiency and lack of resources. There is only spotty enforcement of the Labor Code, due to the scarcity of labor inspectors, corruption, the lack of adequate training and resources, and structural weaknesses in the labor court system. Nonetheless, enforcement is improving as new labor inspectors complete training and begin work outside the capital, allowing the Ministry of Labor to increase significantly its rate of inspections. The Ministry continued a series of inspections (initiated by the previous administration) at farms and plantations in rural areas, especially in Alta and Baja Verapaz, and cited those employers who were not paying the minimum wage. The number of ranches in these regions paying below minimum wage dropped from 42.6 percent of the total number inspected to 13.9 percent after the completion of the program.

The Ministry of Labor reorganized the Labor Inspector Corps to permit some complaints to be heard at the Ministry of Labor rather than requiring that inspectors travel to each work site. The Ministry increased the number of court cases filed for failure to comply with the Labor Code and has begun an educational campaign on worker rights (especially the rights of minors and women workers), including providing some documents in indigenous languages. In an effort to improve enforcement of the Labor Code outside the capital, the Ministry of Labor began an effort to decentralize its operations, beginning by opening a branch office in Coban, Alta Verapaz.

Labor laws and regulations apply throughout the country, including in the few export processing zones (EPZ's). The laws governing EPZ's are not discriminatory on the subject of organizing trade unions or collective bargaining. While union leaders often blame employer pressures and their unofficially restricted access to the EPZ's for their virtual inability to organize workers in these zones, labor conditions in the EPZ's are no different from those found outside the zones.

c. *Prohibition of Forced or Compulsory Labor.*—The Constitution bars forced or compulsory labor, and the practice does not exist. The Government repealed an old law that called for forced labor in prisons.

d. *Minimum Age for Employment of Children.*—The Constitution bars employment of minors under the age of 14 without written permission from the Ministry of Labor. However, children below this age are regularly employed. The laws prohibit minors from night work, extra hours (the legal workday for minors under the age of 14 is 6 hours; for minors 14 to 17 years of age, 7 hours), and from working in establishments where alcoholic beverages are served or in unhealthy or dangerous conditions. Laws governing the employment of minors are not effectively enforced, due to the shortage of qualified labor inspectors and structural weaknesses in the labor court system. While only 5,000 minors have permission from the Labor Ministry to work legally, thousands of others working without legal permission are open to exploitation, generally receiving no social benefits, social insurance, vacations, or severance pay, and below minimum salaries.

The Labor Ministry has a program to educate minors, their parents, and employers on the rights of minors in the labor market. Economic necessity, however, forces most families to have their children seek some type of employment to supplement family income. There are no export industries in which child labor is a significant factor. Child labor is largely confined to small or family enterprises, to agricultural work, and to the informal sectors of the economy.

The Constitution provides for compulsory education for all children up to the age of 12 or to the sixth grade. However, less than half the population actually receives a primary education. Children in rural and indigenous areas are less likely to complete primary school.

e. *Acceptable Conditions of Work.*—Although the law sets minimum wages, the legally mandated minimum wage for most unskilled and semiskilled workers is not always paid. A bilateral committee representing labor and management in specific economic sectors is named each year to make recommendations for increases in the minimum wage. In the event that agreement is not possible, the Government may decree such increases. The minimum wage was raised by 10 percent in December 1995, effective January 2, 1996. The new rate is $2.93 (17.60 quetzales) for industrial workers for an 8-hour workday, including a required hourly bonus, and is $2.66 (15.95 quetzales) per day plus mandatory productivity bonuses for agricultural workers. The minimum wage is not sufficient to provide even a minimum standard of living for a worker with a family. According to the U.N. Development Program, an estimated 80 percent of the population lives below the poverty line, including approximately 60 percent of those employed.

The legal workday is 8 hours, and the workweek is 44 hours, but a tradition of longer hours remains in place due to economic conditions. The amended Labor Code requires a weekly paid rest period of at least 24 hours. Trade union leaders and human rights groups charge that workers are sometimes forced to work overtime, often without premium pay, in order to meet work requirements. Labor inspectors report that numerous instances were uncovered of such abuses, but lack of stiff fines or strong regulatory sanctions, as well as inefficiencies in the labor court system, inhibit adequate enforcement of the law.

Occupational health and safety standards are inadequate. As with other aspects of the Labor Law, enforcement of standards that do exist is also inadequate. Workers have the legal right to remove themselves from dangerous workplace situations, and the law provides them with protection for their continued employment. However, few workers are willing to jeopardize their jobs by complaining about unsafe working conditions. When serious or fatal industrial accidents do occur, the authorities generally take no legal steps against those responsible. The Labor Ministry provides training courses for labor inspectors in health and safety standards but does not accord them a high priority due to scarce resources. The Government does not effectively enforce legislation requiring companies with more than 50 employees to provide on-site medical facilities for their workers, although most large employers do provide such facilities.

GUYANA

The Co-operative Republic of Guyana is a small, developing nation with a unicameral parliament chosen by direct elections in a multiparty political system. Dr. Cheddi Jagan of the Peoples' Progressive Party (PPP), which has a plurality in Parliament, is Executive President. The President appoints a Prime Minister and other cabinet ministers. The 1992 general election was considered the first free and fair poll since 1965. There is a constitutionally independent, albeit somewhat inefficient, judiciary.

The Guyana Defence Force (GDF) and the Guyana Police Force (GPF) are under civilian control. The GPF has the authority to make arrests and maintains law and order throughout the country. The GDF is a professional military responsible for national defense, internal security, and emergency response. The President deployed the GDF in 1996 to support police efforts against surging violent and drug-related crime. Some members of the police allegedly committed human rights abuses.

Guyana is a very poor country. Its mixed economy depends on the export of primary commodities from agriculture, fisheries, forestry, and mining. Sugar, rice, bauxite, and gold are the leading exports. The economy is slowly moving away from decades as a centrally directed, nationalized economy to one based on a mix of private and state enterprises. The standard of living for most citizens is low, with more than half living in poverty. External debt is high, there are severe shortages of skilled labor, and the economy is constrained by an inadequate and ill-maintained infrastructure for transportation, power distribution, flood control, and communications. The estimated economic growth rate for the first half of 1996 was about 6.3 percent, with per capita gross domestic product estimated around $632.

The Government's human rights record remained the same. Human rights problems continued to include police abuse of suspects, allegations of extrajudicial killings, poor prison conditions, delays in the inefficient judicial system, societal violence against women and children, and discrimination against women, minorities, and indigenous Amerindians. The authorities continued efforts to improve police training and prison conditions, especially in the areas of inmate training and rehabilitation, despite very limited resources. However, police abuses were often committed with impunity, and the Police Complaints Authority was largely ineffective because it lacks independent power. There are still some limitations on worker rights, but political control of trade union activity continued to diminish.

RESPECT FOR HUMAN RIGHTS

Section 1. Respect for the Integrity of the Person, Including Freedom From:

a. *Political and Other Extrajudicial Killing.*—There were no reports of political killings.

Some controversial cases led to allegations that police killed criminal suspects under questionable circumstances. The GPF's standing orders regulate police conduct in situations where firearms can be used. The principles guiding use of firearms permit police resort to weapons when other means are ineffective, for protection of property, and in self-defense.

In June the Guyana Human Rights Association (GHRA) reported an upsurge in violent incidents involving the police, asserting that there were 16 fatal shootings, 6 near-fatal shootings, 4 deaths in custody, and 30 cases of police assaults or brutality. The GHRA suggested that this trend in police practice is causing the public to be suspicious of and lose confidence in the GPF.

Cases alleging police abuse of power or unlawful use of deadly force are investigated by the statutorily independent Police Complaints Authority (PCA). Any police officer determined by the PCA to have acted unlawfully is reportedly disciplined, dismissed, or prosecuted. While critics admit that the PCA internal review process occurs in some cases, they don't believe that the authorities sufficiently investigate and punish many of the police officers responsible. Following a number of complaints against the police, the GPF introduced in July an internal affairs committee to review controversial cases in order to identify and discipline officers who act beyond their legal authority. The GPF also introduced a policy of a 48-hour response time to public complaints and inquiries, along with a special 24-hour hot line.

Allegations of police abuse are not new, but the controversial nature and public perception of some of these cases raised questions about the conduct of some GPF officers. On May 22, 20-year-old Jermain Wilkinson died from injuries he received during a police raid. Lance Corporal Robert Beresford allegedly helped beat Wilkinson and shot him in the leg. Wilkinson died hours later. Concerned citizens created the Justice for Jermain Committee (JFJC), which held public demonstrations that led to Beresford being charged with manslaughter. At the conclusion of a preliminary hearing in September, the magistrate raised Beresford's charge from manslaughter to murder, in view of sufficient doubt that the shooting was justified and inconsistent defense testimony. The court remanded Beresford to Georgetown prison to await trial, but he did not go to prison as ordered and left the court with police escorts. He was later reported to be ill and under guard at a hospital. The JFJC claimed that this conduct represents a double standard favoring police criminal suspects; and GPF officer involvement appeared designed to thwart the course of justice and disregard the court's authority. Beresford appealed the ruling that changed his charges to murder, and a hearing was set for early 1997. The Wilkinson case is representative of some of the principal concerns about police use of deadly force and the perceived failure of the authorities to respond adequately to grievances against the police.

Spontaneous community-based groups formed on three occasions as a result of police involvement in shootings: The Justice for Jermain Committee; the Bourda Market Group (BMK); and the Mahaica Justice Committee (MJC). The BMK formed after a July incident in one of the capital's major markets where city constable Oscar Cambridge shot Frankie Figueira in the chest and crippled him from the waist down due to a bullet lodged in his spine. The MJC grew out of a September incident in which two police officers were charged with manslaughter for allegedly shooting to death Ulrich Lynch, a GDF soldier, in a New Amsterdam disco. The MJC wants the joint GDF/GPF board of inquiry to upgrade the charges against the police to murder.

b. *Disappearance.*—There were no reports of politically motivated disappearances.

c. *Torture and Other Cruel, Inhuman, or Degrading Treatment or Punishment.*—The Constitution prohibits torture and there were no known incidents to suggest such an official policy or practice. However, there were credible reports that criminal suspects were beaten while in custody of the GPF. In addition, several cases of wounding by the police of citizens who were not necessarily criminal suspects were reported. In April police allegedly kicked and beat Kenworth Alleyne, and then shot him in both legs at close range. Alleyne had no criminal record nor was he charged with a crime; the officers were reportedly disciplined. Kamal Khan alleged that two police detectives shot him in the penis in a game of Russian roulette, and threatened him with death if he told what had happened. These officers were brought before the court charged with wounding with intent to commit grievous bodily harm. Rohoni Caceras alleged that police officers repeatedly kicked and struck her in the face after they responded to a traffic mishap involving a minibus and a car in which she was traveling. These officers were not disciplined for their conduct.

Although the PCA is the principal body charged with looking into complaints of police brutality or abuse, it has no power to interview police officers or witnesses and must rely on material submitted by the police. The PCA refers cases of alleged abuse to the Police Commissioner. Investigations of such charges sometimes result in serious disciplinary action. Officers charged as a result of complaints to the PCA are routinely suspended for a few days and sometimes fined, but rarely jailed. In 1995 the GPF reported that it received 113 complaints and answered 111 of them. Additionally, the authorities charged and tried 32 police officers for criminal offenses, dismissed 5 others from the force, and disciplined several others. Critics of this process complain that the police force is responsible for investigating itself.

Prison conditions are Spartan but generally meet minimum international standards. Periodic overcrowding is a problem; 5 prisons had a 1995 daily average of 896 inmates in space intended for 300. Eight people died in prisons, as distinguished from police lock-ups, in 1995. Seven died from medical conditions ranging from HIV to tuberculosis and pneumonia, among others. One reportedly died from hanging himself. The authorities note, however, that the incidence of communicable diseases among inmates is consistent with that of the general population.

In 1995 the GHRA cited poor diet, inadequate medical attention, underpaid and poorly trained staff, and lengthy trial delays as problems facing the prison system. The local press reported that due to overcrowding, tuberculosis, sexually transmitted diseases including HIV/AIDS, and other health problems are rising, posing serious public health risks for inmates when they are freed and return to their communities. Additionally, due to restricted budgets and other limitations, the large influx of prisoners in recent periods reduces efforts directed at rehabilitation and training.

Significant progress has been made in facilities improvements in recent years. In spite of severe financial shortages, infrastructure deficiencies, and inadequate human resources, prison officials have endeavored to train the relatively small staff and improve general conditions of diet, medical care, and academic and technical skills training for inmates. A successful part of the rehabilitation program is a literacy program, and there are options for inmates to achieve secondary school diplomas. Technical training in agricultural and construction skills is provided to help inmates obtain employment upon release from prison.

The GHRA participates as a member of the prison's visiting committee, which investigates prisoner complaints, inspects diets, reviews primary medical care services, and provides recommendations to prison authorities. The GHRA also participated in training and development programs for prison staff and a family visit program for children of female inmates in the New Amsterdam prison.

Groups concerned with conditions in police station temporary holding facilities report them to suffer often from poor sanitation and limited access to medical care. Some lock-ups are bare, overcrowded, damp, and uncomfortable. Few have beds, wash basins, furniture, or utensils. Diets and food preparation are of inconsistent quality. Each cell can have up to five persons, but rarely a toilet. Inmates are sometimes escorted by staff members outside of the cells to use holes in the floor for toilets. Inmates generally sleep on a thin pallet on the concrete floor. The East La Penitence police lock-up, where female prisoners are held until sentencing, is below standard compared to other lock-ups and prisons in the country. Intended as a temporary holding place before sentencing prisoners, the station has become a long-term home for many women whose cases are delayed by the overburdened judicial system.

d. *Arbitrary Arrest, Detention, or Exile.*—The Constitution provides that no person may be deprived of personal liberty except as authorized by law and requires judicial determination of the legality of detention, a mandate that the authorities generally respected in practice.

Arrest does not require a warrant issued by a court official. Police may arrest without a warrant when an officer witnesses a crime or at the officer's discretion in instances where there is good cause to suspect that a crime or a breach of the peace has been or will be committed. The law requires that a person arrested and held for more than 24 hours be brought before a court to be charged. Bail is generally available, except in capital offense cases. In narcotics cases, magistrates have limited discretion in granting bail before trial but must remand persons convicted on narcotics crimes into custody, even if an appeal is pending.

Exile is not practiced.

e. *Denial of Fair Public Trial.*—The Constitution provides for an independent judiciary, and the Government generally respects this provision in practice.

The court system is composed of a High (Supreme) Court, a national court of appeal, and a system of magistrate courts that have branches in the various regions of the country.

Magistrates are members of the civil service and are trained lawyers. The magistrate courts deal with both criminal and civil matters. The Ministry of Legal Affairs headed by the Attorney General is the principal legal advisor to the State. The Director of Public Prosecution is statutorily independent and can file legal charges against offenders. The Constitution provides that anyone charged with a criminal offense has the right to a hearing by a court of law. This right is respected in practice.

Delays in judicial proceedings are caused by shortages of trained court personnel and magistrates, inadequate resources, postponements at the request of the defense or prosecution, occasional alleged acts of bribery, and the slowness of police in preparing cases for trial. The inefficiency of the judicial system is so great as to undermine due process. The GHRA asserted that prisoners are often detained for 3 or 4 years while awaiting trial; however, the authorities denied that delays were this long. Defendants are granted public trials, and appeal may be made to higher courts. Appeals of some murder cases have experienced long delays. Trial postponements are routinely granted to both the defense and the prosecution. However, programs designed to improve legal structures, reform judicial procedures, upgrade technical capabilities, and improve efficiency of the courts are having a positive effect.

Although the law recognizes the right to legal counsel, in practice, with the exception of capital crimes, it has been limited to those who can afford to pay. The Georgetown Legal Aid Clinic, with public and private support, provides advice to people who cannot afford a lawyer, with a special interest in cases of violence against women and criminal cases related to civil cases in such matters (e.g., assault as part of a divorce case). The Government provides a small cash grant for the clinic as well as the services of a lawyer from the Attorney General's office. Apart from these efforts, very few lawyers provide free services in criminal cases. Defendants in murder cases who need a lawyer are assigned an attorney by the court. The Guyana Association of Women Lawyers provides free legal services for civil cases only.

There were no reports of political prisoners.

f. *Arbitrary Interference with Privacy, Family, Home, or Correspondence.*—The Government generally respects the right to privacy. The laws requiring judicially issued warrants for searches were generally respected.

Section 2. Respect for Civil Liberties, Including:

a. *Freedom of Speech and Press.*—The Government generally respects the constitutional provision for freedom of speech, and citizens freely criticize the Government and its policies.

The independent Stabroek News continued to publish seven times a week. Independent and opposition newspapers frequently criticized the Government in editorials and satirized it in cartoons. The government-owned Guyana Broadcasting Corporation operates two radio stations, Radio Roraima and Voice of Guyana. The Government also owns and operates one television station. There are no private radio stations, but 15 private television stations produce newscasts that are often critical of the Government.

The Government reallocated television channels in a manner that some critics assert favors the government-owned station to the disadvantage of the privately owned stations, which have been critical of the Government. Independent media organizations claim that government supporters have subjected them to telephone threats and other forms of intimidation. However, there is no proof that such harassment is directed or sanctioned by the Government.

The Government respects academic freedom.

b. *Freedom of Peaceful Assembly and Association.*—The Constitution provides for freedom of assembly, and the Government generally respects this right. The Public Order Act requires police permits for mass political meetings. The Police Commissioner has the authority to refuse permission for a public meeting if he believes that it will provoke a breach of the peace. In cases of refusal, applicants can appeal to the Minister of Home Affairs whose decision on the matter is final. Political parties and other groups held public meetings and rallies throughout the country without hindrance.

The Constitution also provides for freedom of association, and the Government generally respects this right.

c. *Freedom of Religion.*—The Constitution provides for freedom of religion, and the Government respects this right in practice. Members of all faiths are allowed to worship freely, and there are no restrictions on foreign religious proselytizing.

d. *Freedom of Movement Within the Country, Foreign Travel, Emigration, and Repatriation.*—The Constitution provides for freedom of movement within Guyana. Travel to Amerindian areas requires government permission, the result of a law dating from colonial times designed to protect the indigenous people from exploitation. In practice, however, most people travel throughout these areas without regard to the formality of a permit. Citizens are free to travel abroad, to emigrate, and to return.

The Government cooperates with the office of the United Nations High Commissioner for Refugees (UNHCR) and other humanitarian organizations in assisting refugees. The Government does not have a fixed policy on refugees or asylum but is studying draft model legislation prepared by the UNHCR. The issue of provision of first asylum did not arise; there were no reports of forced return of persons to a country where they feared persecution.

Section 3. Respect for Political Rights: The Right of Citizens to Change Their Government

Guyana has a unicameral Parliament chosen by direct election in a multiparty political system based on proportional representation. The leader of the party that obtains a plurality of seats in Parliament during national elections becomes President, with a 5-year term of office, unless the party loses control of Parliament or calls elections earlier. The President appoints a cabinet and a Prime Minister who, with the President, exercise executive power.

Citizens are free to join or support political parties of their choice and established nearly 20 new ones in 1996. The two major parties—the PPP and the People's National Congress (PNC)—are largely formed by Indo-Guyanese and Afro-Guyanese, respectively. The 1992 general election, considered free and fair by foreign observers, brought the former opposition party to power. Any citizen 18 years or older can register to vote, and about 80 percent cast votes in the 1992 election. In January a seven-member commission was sworn in to oversee the national elections expected in 1997 and which must take place no later than March 1998. The commission began its first task—preparation of voter registration lists—in June.

There are no legal impediments to participation of women or minorities in the political process, but historically, neither women nor Amerindians were encouraged to participate, other than by voting. The 17-person cabinet includes 2 women. The 72-member Parliament includes 12 women and 10 Amerindians, representing both major parties.

Section 4. Governmental Attitude Regarding International and Nongovernmental Investigation of Alleged Violations of Human Rights

The Guyana Human Rights Association, the most active local human rights group, functioned without government interference. The GHRA is a nongovernmental organization (NGO) formed in 1979 with the participation of trade unions, professional organizations, various ethnic groups, and churches. It issues periodic press releases and publishes an annual report on human rights in Guyana. The Government made no public statements in direct response to either GHRA or foreign human rights reports and appears willing to discuss human rights issues with international or domestic NGO's.

Section 5. Discrimination Based on Race, Sex, Religion, Disability, Language, or Social Status

The Constitution provides fundamental rights for all persons regardless of race, sex, religion, or national origin. However, the Government does not always enforce these provisions effectively.

Women.—Violence against women, including domestic violence, is a significant problem. Rape and incest are common. Lawyers say that more victims are reporting these crimes to the authorities although there is still a social stigma attached to them. The police are sometimes hesitant to interfere in cases of domestic disputes. Because of their economic circumstances and the lack of any family shelter or other place of solace, victims of domestic violence are often trapped in their homes with their abusers. A shelter for battered women, operated by a private organization, is expected to open in early 1997. Although the Government has not sponsored or funded programs for victims of violence, it provides a subsidy to an NGO working in this area.

The 1990 Equal Rights Act was intended to end discrimination based upon sex, but it is too restrictive to be an effective tool. There is no legal protection against sexual harassment in the workplace. Legislation prohibits dismissal on the grounds of pregnancy, and it does not occur in practice. The Women's Affairs Bureau of the Ministry of Labor, Human Services, and Social Security monitors the legal rights of women.

Legislation passed by parliament in 1990 protects women's property rights in common law marriages and entitles a woman who separates or divorces to one-half the couple's property if she had been working and one-third of the property if she had been a housewife. Divorce by consent remains illegal. Legislation also gives authority to the courts to overturn a man's will in the event that it does not provide for his wife, as long as she was dependent on him for financial support.

One of the few organizations that focus primarily on women's rights, other than those sponsored by political parties, is the Guyana chapter of the Caribbean Association for Feminist Research and Action.

Children.—An estimated 65 to 86 percent of the population lives in poverty, and children are more severely affected than any other group. Although the Government provides free education through secondary school, the severe deterioration of the public education and health care systems has stunted children's futures. The public health system is inadequate and for many children private health care is unaffordable. Children are often not given the opportunity to attend school because their families need them to contribute to running the household by working or providing child care.

The worst effects on children's lives come from migration. More than 3 percent of the population emigrates every year in search of a brighter economic future. Parents often leave behind their children to be raised by family members, friends, or by other children. Media reports of rape and incest indicate that violence against children is a significant problem. The administration of justice for children is characterized by a system that lacks social services needed by children fleeing sexual, physical, or emotional abuse.

People With Disabilities.—The lack of appropriate infrastructure to provide access to both public and private facilities makes it very difficult to employ the disabled outside their homes. There is no law mandating provision of access for people with disabilities.

There are several special schools and training centers for the disabled, but they lack trained staff and are in disrepair.

Indigenous People.—Most of the small Amerindian population, composed of nine tribal groups, live in reservations and villages in remote parts of the interior. Their standard of living is much lower than that of most citizens, and their ability to participate in decisions affecting their lands, cultures, traditions, and the allocation of natural resources is limited.

Amerindian life is regulated by the Amerindian Act, legislation dating from colonial times designed to protect indigenous people from exploitation. The act gives the Government the power to determine who is an Amerindian and what is an Amerindian community, to appoint Amerindian leaders, and to annul decisions made by Amerindian councils. It also prohibits the sale of alcohol to Amerindians and requires government permission before any Amerindian can accept formal employment, although these provisions generally are not enforced. Both individuals and Amerindian groups remain free to criticize the Government.

At a February conference sponsored by the World Bank, President Jagan assured the Amerindian population that the Government was committed to demarcating the lands to which they are entitled and to protecting Amerindian values from exploitation by foreign and local investors. However, Amerindians themselves did not select the Amerindian spokespersons at the conference. The Government chose them, and it did not invite the Guyanese Organization of Indigenous Peoples or the Amerindian People's Association, the two major NGO's representing indigenous people. These organizations mistrust the World Bank, which they claim has funded the construction of roads through tribal lands in the Rupununi savannahs. This activity has resulted in the decline of the Yanomami, Wapishana, Nimbigara, and Macushi nations, which live in areas southwest of the Rupununi river.

National/Racial/Ethnic Minorities.—Longstanding ethnic tensions, primarily between citizens of African and Indian descent, continued to influence society and political life. Historical patterns of social organization, formed during the colonial period, have resulted in social and political organizations coalescing around ethnic groups. This pattern of racial and ethnic grouping has become politicized over the years, polarizing society along ethnic lines. Discrimination and exclusion continue to occur.

Some Indo-Guyanese allege that the 1965–92 PNC government established a pattern of racial discrimination in favor of the Afro-Guyanese. However, many Afro-Guyanese now allege that they suffer racial discrimination and "political victimization" by the predominantly Indo-Guyanese PPP, which they say directs benefits and opportunities to its supporters. The civil service and defense and police forces are overwhelmingly staffed by Afro-Guyanese. Recruitment efforts targeted at Indo-Guyanese candidates for the uniformed services generally have met with an unenthusiastic response, with most qualified Indo-Guyanese candidates opting for a business or professional career over military, police, or public service. The chief of staff of the Guyana Defence Force is Indo-Guyanese and there are other Indo-Guyanese officers in both the GDF and the police force.

Section 6. Worker Rights

a. *The Right of Association.*—The Constitution provides for the right of association and specifically enumerates workers' rights to form or belong to trade unions. The law does not require employers to recognize a union in the workplace, even if a large majority of workers have indicated their desire to be represented by a union.

Approximately 34 percent of the work force is unionized. Most union members work in the public sector and in state-owned enterprises. Organized labor freely associates in one major national federation, the Guyana Trades Union Congress (TUC), which is composed of 22 unions. There is a tradition of close ties between the trade union movement and political parties.

Historically, the two major political parties wielded significant influence over the leadership of several unions, and trade union officials often served in dual roles as party officials. Although this still occurs, it is less common.

Workers have a generally recognized right to strike. Public employees providing essential services may strike if they provide the proper notice to the Ministry of Labor and leave a skeletal staff in place. A minority of strikes in 1996 were illegal, i.e., the union leadership did not approve them, or they did not meet the requirements specified in collective bargaining agreements. However, these strikes occurred in crucial sectors of the economy such as transportation.

There is no legislation prohibiting retaliation against strikers or of antiunion discrimination by employers. However, this principle is always included by the Government in the terms of resumption after a strike. Arbitration rulings, whenever agreed to by the contending parties, are legally enforceable.

Unions and their federations freely maintain relations with recognized Caribbean and international trade union and professional groups. All three of the major international trade union federations have affiliates in Guyana.

b. *The Right to Organize and Bargain Collectively.*—Public and private sector employees possess and utilize the generally accepted right to organize and to bargain collectively. The Ministry of Labour certifies all collective bargaining agreements and has never refused to do so. This right is not codified, however, and employers are not legally required to recognize unions or to bargain with them.

Individual unions directly negotiate collective bargaining status, pursuant to the 1993 repeal of a regulation that required that all collective bargaining be negotiated through the TUC. Unions are dissatisfied with a provision granting the Ministry of Finance veto power over wage contracts negotiated by other ministries.

The Chief Labour Officer and the staff of the Ministry of Labour provide consultation, enforcement, and conciliation services. The Ministry eliminated a backlog of pending cases, but insufficient manpower and transportation continued to limit the Ministry's ability to function.

There are no export processing zones.

c. *Prohibition of Forced or Compulsory Labor.*—The Constitution prohibits forced or compulsory labor, and there is no indication that it occurs.

d. *Minimum Age for Employment of Children.*—The Factories Act and the Employment of Young Persons and Children Act set out minimum age requirements for employment of children. Legally, no person under age 14 may be employed in any industrial undertaking and no person under age 16 may be employed at night, except under regulated circumstances. The law permits children under age 14 to be employed only in enterprises in which members of the same family are employed. However, it is common to see very young children engaged in street trading in the capital. While cognizant of the situation, the Ministry of Labor does not employ sufficient inspectors to enforce existing laws effectively.

e. *Acceptable Conditions of Work.*—The Labour Act and the Wages Councils Act allow the Labor Minister to set minimum wages for various categories of private employers. The minimum public sector wage is $2.20 (G$307.84) per day. Although enforcement mechanisms exist, it is difficult to put them into practice, and unorganized workers, particularly women and children, are often paid less than what is legally required. The legal minimum wage for the public sector is insufficient to provide an adequate standard of living for worker and family.

The Shops Act and the Factories Act set hours of employment, which vary by industry and sector. In general, work in excess of an 8-hour day or a 44-hour week requires payment of an overtime rate. However, if the initial contract stipulates a 48 hour workweek, then the overtime rate only applies for hours worked in excess of 48 hours. The law does not provide for at least a 24-hour rest period.

The Factories Act also sets forth workplace safety and health standards. The Occupation Health and Safety Division of the Ministry of Labour is charged with conducting factory inspections and investigating complaints of substandard workplace conditions. As with its other responsibilities, inadequate resources prevented the Ministry from effectively carrying out this function. Workers cannot remove themselves from dangerous work situations without jeopardizing continued employment.

HAITI

Haiti's second democratically elected President, Rene Preval, took office on February 7, continuing the significant progress in the transition to democracy that began with the restoration of deposed former president Jean-Bertrand Aristide in October 1994. The parliamentary democracy provided for in the 1987 Constitution was put into effect with the installation in 1995 of the bicameral, 110-member National Assembly. This body, for the first time, took up its responsibilities to direct government spending and serve as a counterweight to executive authority. Mayors and local councils, also elected in 1995, reflected broad, popular participation in democratic local government. Elections for some complementary local government bodies called for in the Constitution had not been organized by year's end. The judicial system—while theoretically independent—remained weak and corrupt after decades of government interference and corruption.

Then-president Aristide revoked the commissions of the majority of members of the former Haitian armed forces in January 1995, and he also asked parliament to take up a constitutional amendment to abolish the armed forces. The legislature will be constitutionally able to do so at the end of its term, in 1999. The newly deployed civilian Haitian National Police (HNP) is the first police force that meets constitutional provisions. The 5,200-officer force assumed full responsibilities on December 6, 1995, when then-President Aristide dissolved the interim police force and integrated its 1,598 members—699 former soldiers and 899 former migrants—into the

HNP. Other elements of the post-crisis security forces—the Presidential Security Unit, National Palace Residential Guard, and the Ministerial Security Corps—were gradually integrated into the national police structure. Over the course of the year, the HNP leadership, in cooperation with the international community, undertook a serious training and development effort to improve officers' skills, increase accountability, and bring the force into compliance with international standards. The United Nations Support Mission in Haiti (UNSMIH) has about 1,300 peacekeeping troops and 300 civilian police responsible for assisting the Government to maintain a secure and stable environment. Several mayors have created quasi-official forces to serve as municipal police. These groups lack legal standing, authority to carry weapons, or legitimate powers of arrest. The Port-au-Prince quasi-official force numbers about 60 men; that of Delmas, an adjoining suburb, about 30. The mayors of several other towns have much smaller corps. Some members of local government councils (CASEC's) have assumed arrest authority in defiance of the law. Members of the HNP, the other security forces, and the informal municipal police committed some serious human rights abuses.

Haiti is an extremely poor country, with a per capita income of about $260. It has a market-based economy with state enterprises controlling such sectors as telecommunications and utilities. The majority of the population works in subsistence agriculture, earns less than the average income, and lives in extreme poverty. A small, traditional elite controls much of the country's wealth. A small part of the urban labor force works in the industrial and assembly sectors. Assembled goods—textiles, leather goods, handicrafts, and electronics—are a major source of export revenue. Other important exports are mangoes, coffee, and sisal.

The Government generally respected the human rights of its citizens, continuing the overall improvement in the human rights climate since the end of the military regime. However, a significant number of serious abuses occurred, and cases of abuse remained steady in frequency and severity during the course of the year. Persons linked to palace security forces killed 2 opposition politicians, and the police killed at least 19 persons. Police officers shot and killed 16 persons while making arrests or controlling demonstrations and wounded more than 30 others in these situations. Police were also responsible for more than 86 cases of mistreatment of detainees, including repeated, severe beatings and psychological pressure during interrogations. The HNP Director General, following the recommendations of his Inspector General, fired at least 15 officers and placed 12 in detention pending prosecution for human rights abuses; he disciplined others for misconduct. The Inspector General, however, was slow in tackling politically sensitive cases. The police leadership made some progress in addressing management weaknesses which limit accountability for police misconduct, but many senior and midlevel positions remained unfilled.

hough independent in theory, in practice the judiciary is weak and corrupt. The Government plans sweeping judicial reforms, but Parliament had not passed a proposed reform law by year's end. The weak judicial system remained incapable of processing detainees in accordance with the law, and a large proportion of crimes, including some that may have had political motivations, remain unsolved. The authorities on occasion restricted freedom of assembly and illegally detained more than 30 persons who were members of the political opposition. Other arbitrary arrests, the clogged judicial docket, lengthy pretrial detention, poor prison conditions, illegal searches, and vigilante activity—including killings—also contributed to widespread human rights violations. Societal discrimination against women and abuse of children remain problems, particularly the widespread practice of rural families sending young children to the larger cities to work as unpaid domestics (restaveks).

The Government's limited effort to redress the legacy of human rights abuse from the 1991–94 period met largely with failure. The public prosecutor mishandled the trial of those suspected of killing former Justice Minister Guy Malary, and a jury acquitted the two suspects. Other important cases, such as those from the April 1994 Raboteau killings, languished in the courts. Judicial officials failed to begin processing many other complaints, although a few convictions were obtained. The Justice Ministry did not widely disseminate the report of the National Truth and Justice Commission and did not implement its recommendations, including that of compensation for victims.

RESPECT FOR HUMAN RIGHTS

Section 1. Respect for the Integrity of the Person, Including Freedom From:

a. *Political and Other Extrajudicial Killing.*—Political and extrajudicial killings by the authorities increased slightly in 1996 compared with 1995, while remaining far fewer in number than during the 1991–94 period, according to UNSMIH reports, the

HNP Inspector General, and other sources. In August persons linked to palace security forces killed two opposition politicians, Jacques Fleurival and pastor Antoine Leroy, apparently in the course of an illegal arrest. Separately, a member of the palace guard was reportedly linked to the June murder of the mayor of Chansolme, a small town in the northwest.

HNP members killed at least 19 persons. Police officers and ministerial security guards killed five persons in a chaotic police operation against armed gangs in Cite Soleil on March 6; they killed two other suspects who fired upon the police. In one June incident, police detained four suspects, drove them to a remote area, shot them, and left them for dead; two survived. In another incident in June, police at the Croix-de-Bouquets station shot two detainees, deposited one corpse in the latrine, and beat two other detainees to death. Police were also responsible for 16 additional deaths when officers used excessive force in making arrests or controlling demonstrations. Among them were five men shot when police caught them in a pickup truck filled with arms and ammunition in Delmas on November 5; one body examined later in the morgue had handcuffs on one wrist.

The quasi-official security force attached to the Port-au-Prince mayor's office probably was responsible for the summary execution of three persons suspected of theft in August.

Unknown perpetrators killed 11 police officers, including several cases in which political motives cannot be excluded. Estimates of the number of former soldiers killed by unknown persons in August and September—possibly in retaliation for the ex-soldiers' perceived role in antigovernment activity—range from 2 to 30. Instances of mob killings of suspected criminals continued to exceed 100. In one case in March in Morne Cabrit, a crowd stoned to death three suspected bandits, tortured a fourth, killed him with machetes, and hung the corpse upside down from a tree by the roadside. Except in the Morne Cabrit incident, the authorities rarely took action in these cases.

The public prosecutor (the Port-au-Prince Commissaire du Gouvernement) had the responsibility to investigate the deaths of Leroy and Fleurival. The Government suspended the chief of palace security, his deputy, and seven Presidential Security Unit guards allegedly at the scene and dismissed the member of the palace guard linked to the Chansolme mayor's death. The police Inspector General completed reports on several cases of summary execution or excessive force, and the Director General subsequently took disciplinary action—including 15 dismissals as well as suspensions and letters of reprimand. Due to weak or nonexistent mid-level supervisory leadership, however, some officers dismissed for misconduct returned to duty or continued to draw pay. The Government brought to trial two suspects in the 1993 political killing of Justice Minister Guy Malary. In part because of poor preparation by the prosecutor, the jury acquitted both suspects. As a result, the authorities postponed planned trials for other serious human rights abusers, including those suspected of the April 1994 killings at Raboteau.

There was no progress in resolving past killings such as those of Mireille Durocher Bertin, Jean Marie Vincent, and Claudy Musseau. The National Police's Special Investigative Unit continued to investigate notorious human rights abuses from previous years—including high-profile killings committed following then-President Aristide's return in 1994—but only the Malary case was brought to trial.

b. *Disappearance.*—There were no credible reports of politically motivated disappearances.

c. *Torture and Other Cruel, Inhuman, or Degrading Treatment or Punishment.*— The 1987 Constitution prohibits the use of unnecessary force or restraint, psychological pressure, or brutality by the security forces. However, training of police in human rights provisions of the Constitution is still limited, and members of the security forces frequently violated these provisions. Police officers used excessive—and often deadly—force in making arrests or controlling demonstrations and wounded more than 30 in such situations. The police also continued to beat demonstrators in a few instances.

The National Police tortured suspects in isolated incidents. In one particularly serious case, police chained several detainees suspected of drug trafficking to a tree and beat them over a period of 3 days. One victim was pregnant and shortly afterward miscarried. The U.N. mission noted unconfirmed reports that police in two stations used electricity to torture detainees.

Cases in which the National Police mistreated detainees—sometimes severely—increased dramatically in 1996. The UN/OAS International Civilian Mission (ICM) documented 86 instances of mistreatment in the first 5 months of 1996, and such violations of human rights continued throughout the year. Most often, police beat suspected members of armed gangs during the course of interrogation, sometimes with objects such as weapons or plastic pipe. Reported measures of psychological pressure during interrogations include blindfolding or using hoods on suspects, issuing death threats, and holding detainees under running water. Other victims had their heads shaved. The HNP is investigating the majority of cases documented in the ICM report.

Other abuses of police authority also resulted in cruel treatment of citizens. In July a police officer shot a female acquaintance in the vagina following a dispute. Police on leave were likely responsible for wounding seven persons during a public festival the same month. In sporadic cases, off-duty officers also used their weapons in disputes with taxi drivers or in nightclubs.

The quasi-official forces connected, respectively, to the Port-au-Prince and Delmas mayoralties on several occasions beat female vendors who allegedly were violating market rules.

Prison conditions remained poor. Prisoners and detainees, held in overcrowded and inadequate facilities, continued to suffer from inadequate basic hygiene, 24-qhour confinement to cells, and poor quality health care. Overcrowding in certain regional facilities worsened dramatically. In Gonaives, for example, the prisoner population increased fivefold, exacerbating already overcrowded conditions and posing a threat to the health and life of prisoners there. Prison observers noted that, on occasion, prisoners claimed that guards beat their charges.

The Government, with the help of the international community, made some progress in improving prison conditions. Prisoners nationwide generally received two adequate meals per day—a substantial improvement over 1995, when seven persons in the national penitentiary died of a vitamin deficiency. The International Committee of the Red Cross (ICRC) funded the installation of rudimentary clinics in the country's prisons. The Government failed, however, to keep these facilities adequately stocked with medicines and other health care supplies. It also failed to develop and enforce consistent standards of overall prisoner care.

Persons detained in politically sensitive cases were often kept in police station holding cells, rather than in regular prison facilities. These and other holding cell detainees depended largely on their families for food and medicine; the Government made no provision for their care. In some cases, police officers used their personal funds to buy food for such persons.

The authorities freely permit the ICRC, the Haitian Red Cross, the ICM, and other human rights groups to enter prisons and police stations, monitor conditions, and assist prisoners with medical care, food, and legal aid.

d. *Arbitrary Arrest, Detention, or Exile.*—The Constitution stipulates that a person may be arrested only if apprehended during the commission of a crime or if a judicial warrant has been issued. The authorities must bring the detainee before a judge within 48 hours of arrest. However, the authorities frequently ignored these provisions in practice.

Arbitrary arrests increased significantly. The ICM estimated that, at the end of September, 57 persons were awaiting trial on charges of threatening state security. In July and August, the Government arrested some 30 persons—members of the political opposition or former soldiers—on poorly substantiated charges of threatening state security. In two cases, police arrested family members—instead of the person sought—for antigovernment activity, despite the constitutional prohibition against arresting any person in place of another. Judicial officials or police subsequently released the family members. In another case, the brother of a former police chief continued to be kept in a police holding cell for "his own protection," according to the police officer in charge. Arbitrary arrests by those lacking arrest powers—some elements of the security forces, quasi-official forces, and local government councils (CASEC's)—occurred sporadically. The police also made arrests based on flawed warrants or in the presence of a justice of the peace, which is legally insufficient.

A jury acquitted two suspects in the killing of former Justice Minister Malary, but the authorities illegally kept the pair in detention while developing new charges against them for other murders.

Detainees who had never seen a judge or whose cases stagnated in the judicial system continued to crowd the prisons nationwide. An overburdened and inadequate judicial system frequently detained suspects well beyond the 48 hours permitted for arraignment, although respect for the 48-hour rule increased. Cases bound over to higher courts also languished. More than 80 percent of the inmates in the prison system were awaiting trial.

The Constitution prohibits involuntary exile of citizens. While some left the country for personal or political reasons, the Government did not make use of exile as punishment.

e. *Denial of Fair Public Trial.*—The Constitution provides for an independent judiciary, but the judiciary is not independent in practice. Years of rampant corruption and governmental neglect have left the judicial system poorly organized and virtually moribund. The judicial apparatus follows a civil law system based on the Napoleonic Code; the Criminal Code dates from 1832.

At the first level, the justices of the peace issue warrants, adjudicate minor infractions, take depositions, and refer cases to higher judicial officials. Investigating magistrates and public prosecutors cooperate in the development of more serious cases, which are tried by the judges of the first instance courts. Appeals courts judges hear cases referred from the first instance courts, and the Supreme Court deals with questions of procedure and constitutionality.

The Constitution provides for the right to a fair public trial, but this right was widely abridged. Unaddressed systemic weaknesses continued to contribute to a huge backlog of criminal cases, with some detainees waiting years in pretrial detention for a court date. Under the Code of Criminal Procedure, responsibility to investigate crimes is unclear, and authority to pursue cases is divided among police, prosecutors, and investigating magistrates. The code further stipulates two criminal court sessions per year, each lasting 2 weeks, to try all major crimes requiring a jury trial. Although the court system held more such sessions in more locations, the backlog continued to increase. Moreover, if an accused is ultimately tried and found innocent, he has no recourse against the Government for time served.

The Constitution expressly denies police and judicial authorities the right to interrogate persons charged with a crime unless the suspect has legal counsel present or waives this right. Nevertheless, most accused cannot afford legal counsel and the law does not require that the Government provide legal representation. Thus, despite the efforts of local human rights groups and the international community to provide legal aid, many interrogations without counsel continued to occur.

The Government devoted some effort to the task of reforming the judicial system. The Justice Ministry cooperated with international donors in providing training to sitting magistrates, improving the administration of the public prosecutors offices, strengthening judicial supervision, and establishing prison registries. In September the Government submitted to the National Assembly a draft law setting out sweeping judicial reforms, but the parliament had taken no action on the proposal by year's end.

There were no reports of political prisoners, although the Government detained some political opponents on charges of threatening state security (see Section 1.d.).

f. *Arbitrary Interference with Privacy, Family, Home, or Correspondence.*—The Constitution prohibits interference with privacy, family, home, or correspondence. Police and other security force elements did, however, conduct illegal warrantless searches, particularly in connection with a high-profile kidnaping case and with alleged destabilizing activities in August and September. Members of quasi-official forces also conducted illegal searches and seizures of property.

Section 2. *Respect for Civil Liberties, Including:*

a. *Freedom of Speech and Press.*—The Constitution provides for freedom of speech and the press, and the Government generally respects these rights; however, there were some exceptions. The press energetically exercised this freedom. Print media from opposite ends of the political spectrum often criticized the Government.

With an illiteracy rate of approximately 80 percent, broadcast media, especially Creole-language radio, have an unusual importance, and some 32 radio stations operate in the capital alone. Broadcast media tended to criticize the Government less than the press but freely expressed various political viewpoints. There were no reports of censorship, nor did the media appear to practice self-censorship. The government-sponsored daily newspaper remained closed following a 1995 dispute between the former information minister and the paper's editor.

Foreign journalists generally worked without hindrance, although the police did arrest one foreign reporter for photographing a corpse in the street. Police also clashed with domestic journalists at least four times, seizing cassettes and other journalistic records. Several journalists reported experiencing rough treatment at the hands of the police during these confrontations. Unknown armed individuals attacked two regional, privately owned radio stations in May, destroying transmitting equipment. Others shot at the government-owned national television headquarters in August.

b. *Freedom of Peaceful Assembly and Association.*—The authorities generally respected the constitutional rights of freedom of assembly and association. Political parties across the spectrum were able to meet and recruit members. New political organizations, including several dedicated to the rights of former soldiers, formed. In some instances, however, unrelated law enforcement actions may have restricted these rights. Late in the year, the authorities began to release some political detainees when investigations revealed no evidence of wrongdoing.

In August police arrested 15 former soldiers, 2 party activists, and 2 other persons meeting at the Port-au-Prince headquarters of an opposition political party, the Mobilization for National Development (MDN); in February, police had harassed MDN party members outside the capital. The authorities later charged those arrested in August with threatening state security. Over the next 2 months, police arrested several other MDN members and former soldiers on similar charges and issued a warrant for the arrest of the party's secretary general, Hubert de Ronceray. In September police also arrested a less well-known opposition political figure, Carmen Christophe, a former mayor of Port-au-Prince. The leader of the opposition political party Creddo, former military ruler Prosper Avril, likewise faced a warrant for his arrest on similar charges. The authorities also conducted illegal searches with the apparent intent of harassing opposition political figure Duly Brutus and members of his family.

c. *Freedom of Religion.*—The Constitution provides for the right to practice all religions and faiths, provided that practice does not disturb law and order, and the Government respected this right. The Government did not restrict missionary activities, affiliation with overseas coreligionists, or religious instruction or publishing.

d. *Freedom of Movement Within the Country, Foreign Travel, Emigration, and Repatriation.*—There are no legal restrictions on the movement of citizens within the country. An unknown number of undocumented migrants put to sea seeking better economic opportunities in other countries.

The Government operated a national migration office to assist citizens repatriated from other countries, notably the Bahamas and the Dominican Republic.

The Government has no policy regarding foreign nationals seeking refuge or asylum from third countries; no such cases were reported. The issue of provision of first asylum did not arise.

Section 3. Respect for Political Rights: The Right of Citizens to Change Their Government

The Constitution provides for regular elections for local and parliamentary offices and for the presidency. Voters elected officials to the national and local governments in a series of free and fair elections in 1995, although administrative incompetence marred the early rounds of the legislative and local elections. Elections for the Senate, where one-third of the seats were due to become vacant at year's end, and for some complementary local government bodies called for in the Constitution were months behind schedule. The Government constituted a new Provisional Electoral Council in November, and it scheduled Senate and local elections for March 1997.

No legal impediments to women's participation in politics or government exist. The generally lower status of women, however, limits their participation in these fields. Of the 83 members of the Chamber of Deputies, 3 are women. The 27-member Senate has none. President Preval named a few women to prominent positions in his Government, including the Women's Affairs Minister, the Secretaries of State for Tourism and Justice, and the Presidential spokesperson. The President also placed some female advisers on his palace staff.

Section 4. Governmental Attitude Regarding International and Nongovernmental Investigation of Alleged Violations of Human Rights

A wide variety of human rights groups operated without government restriction, commenting on human rights cases. The Government tolerated their views but was rarely responsive to their recommendations. About a dozen local human rights groups monitored conditions in the country, with some working on civic education and legal aid as well.

In August the Government requested and received an extension of the UN/OAS International Civilian Mission's mandate to December. The ICM investigated all reports of human rights violations, issued periodic reports and press releases, conducted civic education, and trained local human rights groups. The ICM also worked with the Government in a variety of ways to develop its institutional capacity to prevent and provide redress for human rights abuses.

The National Coalition for Haitian Rights (formerly the National Coalition for Haitian Refugees) was the only other international human rights organization to maintain a permanent presence. Representatives of other international human rights organizations visited freely from time to time. The ICRC was active throughout the year, particularly in prison renovation and assistance to prisoners.

The National Truth and Justice Commission, chartered by President Aristide in 1994 to document the abuses of the previous regime, presented its report to the Government in late January. The Justice Ministry did not disseminate the report widely, however, and the Commission's recommendations for redress and judicial reform remained unimplemented at year's end.

Section 5. Discrimination Based on Race, Sex, Religion, Disability, Language, or Social Status

The 1987 Constitution does not specifically prohibit discrimination on the grounds of race, sex, religion, disability, language, or social status. It does provide for equal working conditions regardless of sex, beliefs, or marital status. However, there is no effective governmental mechanism to administer or enforce these provisions.

Women.—Domestic violence against women and rape occur, but most victims and witnesses do not report these crimes to the police. The Haitian Center for Research and Action for the Promotion of Women published a preliminary report of a 1995 survey of 1,705 Haitian women. Of that group, 37 percent stated that they or someone they knew had been raped or otherwise sexually abused; in 42 percent of these cases, the assailant had no familial or other close connection with the victim. Of those interviewed, 33 percent reported that they or someone they knew had been the victim of other types of physical violence. Nearly two-thirds of the victims had never reported the abuse, most for fear of public shame or of retribution from their assailants, but some because they felt judicial penalties were insufficient. The law provides penalties for these crimes, but the authorities do not enforce these provisions adequately.

The Ministry of Women's Affairs is charged with promoting and defending the rights of women and ensuring that they attain an equal status in society, but it did little in this regard. In December Parliament proposed elimination of the Ministry.

Women do not enjoy the same social and economic status as men. In some social strata, tradition limits women's roles. Peasant women, often the breadwinner for their family, remain largely in the traditional occupations of farming, marketing, and domestic labor. Very poor urban women, who head their families and serve as its economic support, also often find their employment opportunities limited to traditional roles in domestic labor and marketing. Laws governing child support recognize the widespread practice of multiple-father families but are rarely enforced. Well-educated women have, however, occupied prominent positions in both the private and public sector in recent years.

Children.—The Government's programs do not promote or defend children's rights. Government health care and education programs for children are inadequate or nonexistent. Poorer families sometimes ration education money to pay school fees for male children only.

Rural families continued to send young children to serve as unpaid domestic labor for more affluent city dwellers, a practice cited by a 1991 U.N. study as an example of slavery in the 20th century. One international organization estimated in 1996 that 240,000 to 300,000 children are victims of this practice, called "restavek" (which means "lives with" in Creole). It is not limited to the wealthy class, as middle and lower class families also use restavek children. Employers compel the children to work long hours, provide them little nourishment, and frequently beat and abuse them. The Ministry of Social Affairs believes that many restavek children are mistreated.

Local human rights groups do not report on the plight of restavek children as an abuse or seek to improve their situation. The Ministry of Social Affairs believes that it can do little to stop this practice, regarding it as economically motivated; the Ministry assigned three monitors to oversee the welfare of restavek children. Society holds such children in little regard, and the poor state of the economy worsened their situation. Port-au-Prince's large population of street children includes many runaway restaveks.

People With Disabilities.—The Constitution provides that disabled persons shall have the means to ensure their autonomy, education, and independence. However, there is no legislation to implement these constitutional provisions or to mandate provision of access for people with disabilities. Although they do not face overt ill-treatment, given the severe poverty in which most Haitians live, those with disabilities face a particularly harsh existence.

National/Racial/Ethnic Minorities.—Some 99 percent of Haitians are descendants, in whole or in part, of African slaves who won their war of independence from France in 1804. The remaining population is of European, Middle Eastern, North American, or Latin American origin. The law makes no distinction based on race. Longstanding social and political animosities are often tied to cultural identification, skin color, and overlapping issues of class, in this starkly inegalitarian society. Some of these animosities date back to before Haiti's revolutionary period.

The Government recognizes two official languages: Creole, which is spoken by virtually all Haitians; and French, which is spoken by about 20 percent of the population, including the economic elite. The inability to communicate in French has long limited the political and economic opportunities available to the majority of the population. The Government prepared most documents only in French, and, despite the Justice Minister's order to use Creole in the courts, judges conducted most legal proceedings exclusively in French. Creole was, however, the language chosen for parliamentary debate in the lower house.

Section 6. Worker Rights

a. *The Right of Association.*—The Constitution and the Labor Code provide for the right of association and provide workers, including those in the public sector, the right to form and join unions without prior government authorization. The law protects union activities and prohibits a closed shop. The law also requires a union, which must have a minimum of 10 members, to register with the Social Affairs Ministry within 60 days of its formation.

Six principal labor federations represented about 5 percent of the total labor force, including about 2 to 3 percent of labor in the industrial sector. Each maintained some fraternal relations with various international labor organizations.

b. *The Right to Organize and Bargain Collectively.*—The Labor Code protects trade union organizing activities and stipulates fines for those who interfere with this right. Unions were generally free to pursue their goals, although the Government made little effort to enforce the law. Organized labor activity was concentrated in the Port-au-Prince area, in state enterprises, the civil service, and the assembly sector. The high unemployment rate and antiunion sentiment among some factory workers limited the success of union organizing efforts.

Collective bargaining continued to be nonexistent, and employers set wages unilaterally. The Labor Code does not distinguish between industries producing for the local market and those producing for export. Employees in the export-oriented assembly sector enjoyed better-than-average wages and benefits.

There are no export processing zones.

c. *Prohibition of Forced or Compulsory Labor.*—The Labor Code prohibits forced or compulsory labor. The Government failed to enforce this law, however, and children continued to be subjected to forced domestic labor (see Section 5).

d. *Minimum Age of Employment for Children.*—The minimum employment age in all sectors is 15 years. Fierce adult competition for jobs ensured that child labor is not a factor in the industrial sector. Children under the age of 15 commonly worked at informal sector jobs to supplement family income. The International Labor Organization criticized the Ministry of Social Affairs' enforcement of child labor laws as inadequate.

e. *Acceptable Conditions of Work.*—The legal minimum daily wage is about $2.40 (36 gourdes). Annually, a minimum wage worker would earn about $800, an income considerably above the national average but sufficient only to permit a worker and family to live in very poor conditions. The majority of Haitians work in subsistence agriculture, a sector where minimum wage legislation does not apply.

The Labor Code governs individual employment contracts. It sets the standard workday at 8 hours, and the workweek at 48 hours, with 24 hours of rest on Sunday. The code also establishes minimum health and safety regulations. The industrial and assembly sectors largely observed these guidelines. The Ministry of Social Affairs did not, however, enforce workhours or health and safety regulations.

With more than 50 percent of the population unemployed, workers were not able to exercise the right to remove themselves from dangerous work situations without jeopardy to continued employment.

HONDURAS

Honduras is a constitutional democracy with a President and unicameral Congress elected for 4-year terms and an independent judiciary headed by a Supreme Court of Justice. President Carlos Roberto Reina took office in January 1994 as the fourth democratically elected President since the reestablishment of democracy in 1982. Both major parties (Liberal and National) have now assumed power from the other after free elections.

The Honduran Armed Forces (HOAF) comprise the army, air force, navy, and the police (Public Security Force—FUSEP) as a fourth branch. In December, however, the Congress approved the second and final reading of a constitutional amendment to place FUSEP under civilian control. The armed forces operate with considerable institutional and legal autonomy, particularly in the realm of internal security and military affairs. The Government established an Ad Hoc Commission on Police and Judicial Reform in 1993, in response to credible allegations of extrajudicial killings by members of the FUSEP, particularly its Directorate of National Investigations (DNI). In January 1994, the Government established a new Public Ministry containing a new Directorate of Criminal Investigations (DIC) to replace the disbanded DNI; however, the DIC is not yet fully staffed or equipped. According to human rights organizations, including the Government's National Commission for the Protection of Human Rights, reports of abuses have steadily declined since the DNI was abolished. Nonetheless, members of both the armed forces and the FUSEP are reported to have committed human rights abuses.

The economy is primarily based on agriculture, with a small but increasingly important maquiladora (in-bond processing for export) industry that accounts for some 75,000 jobs. The armed forces or its pension fund play a role in the national economy, controlling enterprises usually associated with the private sector, including a bank, several insurance companies, and one of the two cement companies. Some entities (notably the merchant marine and the national telephone company) have passed from military to civilian control. Approximately 43 percent of workers engage in agriculture; about one-third of those work on large plantations. The principal export crops are coffee and bananas, which are the country's leading source of foreign exchange. Nontraditional products such as melons and shrimp also play an important role in the country's economy. Per capita income is about $670 annually, which provides most of the population with a low standard of living. The Government estimates that 65 percent of its citizens live in poverty.

The Government's human rights record improved somewhat, although serious problems remain in certain areas. Some members of the security forces allegedly committed extrajudicial killings. Reports of torture decreased significantly; however, police beatings and other abuse of detainees remained a problem. The Government administratively punished some abusers but took no judical action against them. Considerable impunity for members of the civilian and military elite, exacerbated by a weak, underfunded, and sometimes corrupt judicial system, contributes to human rights problems. Prison conditions remained harsh, and the judicial system is unable to provide prisoners awaiting trial with swift and impartial justice. No senior government official, member of the business elite, bureaucrat, or politician was convicted in 1996. However, the authorities arrested and jailed two officials of the former administration for fraud and abuse of power, and there are accusations against former President Callejas and members of his cabinet. There was an increase in the number of vigilante killings. Other human rights problems were societal discrimination and violence against women, discrimination against indigenous people, and abuse of street children.

RESPECT FOR HUMAN RIGHTS

Section 1. Respect for the Integrity of the Person, Including Freedom From:

a. *Political and Other Extrajudicial Killing.*—There were no reports of politically motivated killings. However, members of the security forces (notably District Command 7 of the police in Tegucigalpa) allegedly committed several extrajudicial killings.

The crime rate surged again in 1996, including a rise in the number of homicides. Random shootings were common; bombs were thrown at the President's home and at businesses of a human rights activist, at the courts, at Congress, and at government ministries. With the drastic increase in violent crime, it continued to be difficult to differentiate among homicides that may have been perpetrated by members of the various government security services, common criminals, or private vigilantes (these are privately hired, unlicensed guards or watchmen, as well as volunteer groups who patrol their neighborhoods or municipalities to deter crime).

Human rights groups have compiled credible evidence to indicate that at least 73 of these homicides were extrajudicial executions. In at least 21 of these cases, it is alleged that renegade elements of the security forces or civilian groups working with them (including vigilante elements) deliberately used unwarranted lethal force against supposed habitual criminals. Widespread frustration at the inability of the security forces to control crime and the well-founded perception that a corrupt police force is complicit in the high rate of crime, have led to considerable public support for vigilante justice. The Government did not take effective action to try, convict, or punish anyone for these offenses.

On July 23, residents discovered the body of a 20-year-old in a trash dump in El Segundo Anillo Periferico, a neighborhood in the northern city of San Pedro Sula. They found the victim, whose identity remains unknown, with his feet bound and his hands tied behind his back; he was shot twice in the head. Witnesses to the shooting claim that the victim was killed at the trash dump by several men who fled the scene. Police speculate that the killing was an act of vigilante justice but have not identified any suspects.

On July 1, the bodies of two men (Isauro Rene Rivera Salgado, age 25 and Ruben Omar Arambu Baile, age 21) were found in Cerro Grande, a neighborhood of Comayaguela, near Tegucigalpa. Both men, missing for 2 days, were found in a ditch with bullets in the head, the thorax, and both sides of the body. In a preliminary investigation, the police indicated that both appeared to be executions, adding that one or both were involved in some sort of illegal activities. There were no witnesses, and FUSEP has not interrogated or arrested any suspects.

Credible allegations of extrajudicial killings by members of the FUSEP, particularly its now-defunct Directorate of National Investigations, led to the creation in January 1994 of a new civilian-controlled Directorate of Criminal Investigations to replace the DNI within the new Public Ministry (which also includes a prosecutorial branch). Human rights groups, including the Attorney General's office, have noted a continuing drop in the number of reports of human rights abuses since the dissolution of the DNI. The new Ministry, responsible for investigating all cases of extrajudicial killings, has completed its initial program of training and organizing its staff. Although this process has been slow, the DIC did solve several high-profile cases, including two kidnapings where the DIC rescued the victims and arrested the kidnapers. The Ministry will lack the capability, however, to investigate adequately current or past criminal cases until the DIC reaches a higher level of operational capability. The DIC expects to reach this level in mid-1997, when it expects to have 1,500 fully trained and equipped agents. In 1996, the DIC had only 420 investigators and practically no communications equipment.

In June the stepdaughter of human rights activist Ramon Custodio, president of the Committee for the Defense of Human Rights in Honduras (CODEH), died under unclear circumstances; by year's end no final determination had been made whether the death was a murder or a suicide.

On January 5, the First Court of Appeals ruled that military officers accused of human rights abuses in the 1980's were covered by the 1991 amnesty decreed by the National Congress. However, in a decision announced January 19, the Supreme Court unanimously overruled the Appeals Court decision in the case of nine military officers accused of the illegal detention, torture, and attempted murder of six students in 1982. The case was returned to the criminal courts for action, which the appeals court had ruled did not have jurisdiction since past amnesty covered the military. The effect of this ruling was that courts of first instance will consider the application of amnesty on a case-by-case basis, subject to review by higher courts.

Following much-publicized investigations of human rights violations (past and present) by military personnel, judges in the civilian court system issued arrest warrants for 15 senior active and retired military and police officers, charging them with a number of serious crimes committed in 1982. These included the kidnaping, illegal detention, torture, and attempted murder of six students by the police; the illegal detention and murder of Nelson Mackay Chavarria and the attempted murder and illegal detention of Miguel Francisco Carias; and the illegal detention, robbery, murder, and threats to murder of Adan Aviles Funez and a Nicaraguan laborer named Amado Espinoza Paz, who disappeared together in Choluteca on June 12, 1982. Of the 15 with outstanding warrants, all but 2 remain fugitives and at large. (One of these turned himself in but was released after proving that he was not in the country at the time of the alleged crimes; the other is in prison serving a 5-year sentence for a narcotics conviction).

The Supreme Court on July 1 issued a special decree permitting officials associated with the criminal justice system (including the military, police, prison wardens and employees, criminal investigative agents, public prosecutors, judges, and magistrates), who are sought by the criminal courts, to serve their preventive detention at military bases and police centers rather than the central penitentiaries, as has been the case in the past. The decree is not mandatory and leaves the detention decisions up to the judge in each case. This ruling applies only to preventive detention and may encourage military officers sought for alleged human rights abuses in the 1980's to turn themselves in. The decree is designed as an interim measure, pending passage by the National Congress of a new penal procedures code that will modernize the now antiquated code.

There was no progress in investigation or prosecution of other alleged extrajudicial killings committed in previous years. These include the 1995 killings of four alleged criminals who had been detained by police of the 7th command of FUSEP in Tegucigalpa: Orlando Alvarez Rios, Diomedes Obed Garcia, Rony Alexis Betancourt, and Marco Antonio Serbellon; the 1995 killings of three alleged car thieves found tortured and shot to death outside the city of La Paz: Jose Alfredo Castro Urbina and Dennis Moises Castro Rosa (the third remains unknown); and a number of killings dating back to 1990.

b. *Disappearance.*—There were no reports of politically motivated disappearances.

The Attorney General continued investigations into the disappearances of 184 people in the 1980's. Various witnesses, survivors, and a few former members of the military have charged that a military intelligence group called Battalion 3-16 kidnaped, tortured, and murdered many of those who disappeared. The National Commissioner for Human Rights, Leo Valladares, also continued his investigation into the human rights abuses alleged to have been committed by members of Battalion 3-16 and the former DNI. The Attorney General had several clandestine grave sites excavated during the year, and forensic scientists identified several remains as those of persons on the list of those who disappeared. The Attorney General and the Human Rights Commissioner requested from the HOAF and the U.S. Government information they might have to aid this investigation. The HOAF claimed to have no relevant information. The U.S. Government reviewed documents from that period and released to the Attorney General and the Commissioner thousands of pages of declassified documents, including several hundred pages relating to the disappearance of a U.S. citizen Jesuit priest, Father James Carney.

In August the Government completed payment of indemnifications ordered by the Inter-American Court of Human Rights to the victims' families in the Velasquez Rodriguez and Godinez Cruz cases. The victims were students at the National Autonomous University in 1981 when DNI agents detained them; they were never seen again. The Inter-American Commission on Human Rights expressed its satisfaction with the Government's action and with the petitioners who testified.

c. *Torture and Other Cruel, Inhuman, or Degrading Treatment or Punishment.*—The Constitution prohibits torture, and there were only a few reports that officials employed such practices. However, police beatings and other alleged abuse of detainees remained a problem. The police also engaged in violence against street children (see Section 5).

The Office of Professional Responsibility (OPR), part of FUSEP, investigates cases of alleged torture and abuse; OPR officials recommend sanctions for police agents found guilty of such mistreatment. However, neither the FUSEP General Command nor the OPR is empowered to punish wrongdoers; only the commander of the accused agent has the authority to do so. Several human rights groups and the Public Ministry criticized the OPR for not being responsive to their requests for impartial investigations of FUSEP agents accused of abuses. The Public Ministry established the Office of Human Rights Inspector within the DIC to monitor the behavior of its agents. This office reports to the head of the human rights section and to the Attorney General. Investigations by this office resulted in the firing of 11 DIC agents in 1996.

Prison conditions are harsh. Prisoners suffer from severe overcrowding, malnutrition, and a lack of adequate sanitation. The 24 penal centers hold 9,342 prisoners, of which only 835 have been convicted and are serving sentences. The rest are still awaiting trial, some for as long as 5 years. More often than not, wardens house the mentally ill and those with tuberculosis and other infectious diseases together in the same cells with the general prison population. A new, larger detention facility for men located in Tamara lacks water and was not expected to open until sometime in 1997. Prisoners with money routinely buy private cells, decent food, and conjugal visitation rights, while prisoners without money often lack the most basic necessities as well as legal assistance. When the authorities arrest street children, they house many of them with adults who abuse them.

The Government permits prison visits by international human rights organizations.

d. *Arbitrary Arrest, Detention, or Exile.*—The law states that the police may arrest a person only with a court order, unless the arrest is made during the commission of a crime, and that they must clearly inform the person of the grounds for the arrest. (By law the FUSEP cannot investigate; it only detains suspects.) Police must bring a detainee before a judge within 24 hours; the judge then must issue an initial temporary holding order within 24 hours, release an initial decision within 6 days, and conduct a preliminary investigation to decide whether there is sufficient evidence to warrant further investigation. However, in practice, the authorities do not routinely observe these legal requirements. While bail is legally available, it is used primarily for ostensibly medical reasons, but procedures for granting it in such cases are confused and unclear. Poor defendants, even when represented by a public defender, are seldom able to take advantage of bail.

Under the 1984 Code of Criminal Procedures, a judge, the police, public officials, or any citizen may initiate criminal proceedings. Perhaps as many as 80 percent of the cases reported to the police are never referred to the criminal justice system but instead are settled administratively by the police or by municipal courts, which are separate from the regular judicial court system.

The Constitution prohibits the expatriation of a citizen to another country; exile is not used as a means of political control.

e. *Denial of Fair Public Trial.*—The Constitution provides for an independent judiciary and the right to a fair trial. While the Government respects these provisions in principle, historically in practice, adherence has been weak and uneven. A number of factors limit the effectiveness of the system: Both the judiciary and the Public Ministry suffer from inadequate funding; the civil law inquisitorial system functions very poorly; and powerful special interests still exercise their influence and often prevail in many lower courts. However, in landmark public sector cases (see Section 1.a.), the Supreme Court did show a significant degree of independence from powerful political and economic interests.

The court system is composed of a Supreme Court with 9 magistrates; 10 appeals courts; 67 courts of first instance of general jurisdiction; and 325 justice of the peace courts of limited jurisdiction. Congress elects the nine Supreme Court justices and names the president of the Court; the Supreme Court, in turn, names all lower court judges. The 4-year term for justices of the Supreme Court coincides with those of the Congress and the President.

Some progress was made in using a judicial career system to enhance qualifications of sitting judges, depoliticize the appointments process, and break the subcultures of corruption, clientism, patronage, and influence peddling within the judiciary. Nevertheless, many appeals courts and lower courts remain staffed by politically selected judges and unqualified clerks and are inefficienct and subject to influence by special interests.

An accused person has the right to a fair trial, which includes the right to an initial hearing by a judge, to bail, to an attorney provided by the State if necessary, and to appeal. Although the Constitution recognizes the principle of innocence, the Criminal Code is in practice often administered by ill-trained judges operating on a presumption of "guilty until proven innocent." Pretrial hearings and trials are written, and at the judge's discretion may be declared secret and not "public." Defendants and their attorneys are not always genuine participants in the process, despite rights accorded under law. Defendants may, through the judge, confront witnesses against them and present evidence on their own behalf. According to law, defendants and their attorneys have access to government-held evidence relevant to their cases, but in practice this is not always the case.

In the inquisitorial system, judges are legally in charge of the investigation as well as the trial and sentencing. Both the Public Ministry's public prosecutors and private prosecutors may bring criminal charges against citizens. A judge may jail an accused persons for 6 days before a determination is made of probable cause to admit the charge. If a judge sustains the criminal accusation, the accused remains in jail or may be released on bail while awaiting trial. Until recently, the same judge conducting the investigation was the trial and sentencing judge. By order of the Supreme Court, those jurisdictions are now separate.

A public defender program provides service to those unable to afford an adequate defense. There are 104 public defenders nationally providing free legal services for 37.4 percent of the prison population; however, public defenders are hard pressed to meet the heavy demands of a nonautomated, inadequately funded, and labor-intensive criminal justice system. Despite their best efforts, detention of criminal suspects pending trial averaged 2 years and remains a serious human rights problem. In a number of cases, poor prisoners remain in jail after being acquitted or completing their sentences, due to the failure by responsible officials to process release papers. A significant number of defendants serve the maximum possible sentence for the crime of which they are accused before their trials are ever concluded or even begun. In June government statistics showed that 89 percent of prisoners in jails had not been through a trial process or sentenced.

Pending consideration of proposed reforms, the Supreme Court issued an instruction that holds judges personally accountable for reducing the backlogged cases; separates judges into pretrial investigative judges, and trial and sentencing judges; and creates a program to monitor and enforce compliance with these measures. The instruction is intended to ensure that the rights of the accused to a timely and transparent defense are more effectively respected.

The 1994 Public Ministry Law and subsequent creation of the new ministry, with 196 public prosecutors assigned nationally, are also intended to strengthen a citizen's ability to seek redress from government abuses and to enjoy fair and public trials. The Public Ministry's independence from the other branches of the Government is also intended to reduce the opportunities for the politically and economically powerful to distort the investigative and prosecutorial process. After 2 years in full operation, the Public Ministry has taken decisive action in favor of human rights by investigating and accusing not only military officers of violations, but also investigating and accusing various high ranking officials of both the former and current government of abuses of power, fraud, and diversion of public funds and resources. These are crimes that seriously diminish the Government's ability to address fundamental economic issues affecting the human rights of the general population. Citizens can also seek redress through the National Human Rights Commissioner (Ombudsman), who is empowered to monitor and oversee the Government's performance on human rights matters. Despite the significant efforts of the Public Ministry, considerable independence shown by the Supreme Court on highly visible and different cases, and independent lower court judges, at year's end the justice system still tended to favor the rich and politically influential and remained weak, underfunded, marginally politicized, and generally inefficient.

Prior to 1994, the armed forces insisted that its members could only be tried through its own courts-martial. However, in 1993 Congress passed a resolution interpreting the jurisdiction of the military court system to be subordinate to the civilian system in cases of jurisdictional dispute. Since then both officer and enlisted military personnel accused of crimes against civilians have in fact been remanded to the civilian judicial system. Following much-publicized investigations of human rights violations (past and present) by military personnel, judges in the civilian court system brought criminal charges against a number of senior active and retired military officers for murder, attempted murder, and illegal detention (see Section 1.a.). The Public Ministry maintains civilian prosecutors accredited to 11 military courts as well as to the major courts of first instance in the country. Although the military continued to profess respect for civilian court jurisdiction over its members, only one military officer accused of human rights violations has turned himself in.

There were no reports of political prisoners.

f. *Arbitrary Interference with Privacy, Family, Home, or Correspondence.*—The Constitution specifies that a person's home is inviolable and that persons authorized by the State may enter only with the owner's consent or with the authorization of a competent authority. Entry may take place only between 6 a.m. and 6 p.m. or at any time in the event of an emergency or to prevent the commission of crime. However, as in previous years, there were credible charges that police and armed forces personnel failed at times to obtain the needed authorization before entering a private home. Despite a system of "duty judges" and "duty prosecutors" to issue search orders, coordination among the police, the court, and the Public Ministry remains weak. However, while these interagency liaison problems still undermine the effectiveness of the system, there was notable improvement during the year.

Section 2. Respect for Civil Liberties, Including:

a. *Freedom of Speech and Press.*—The Constitution provides for freedom of speech and the press, and the authorities largely respected these freedoms in practice. The media, while often openly critical of the Government and frequently willing to expose corruption, are themselves subject to high levels of corruption and politicization. Serious investigative journalism is still in its infancy. There were credible reports of powerful figures threatening the job security of reporters, as well as instances of self-censorship and payoffs to journalists to kill stories.

The Government respects academic freedom and has not attempted to curtail political expression on university campuses.

b. *Freedom of Peaceful Assembly and Association.*—The Constitution provides for these rights, and the Government respects them in practice.

c. *Freedom of Religion.*—The Constitution provides for all forms of religious expression, and the Government respects this right in practice.

d. *Freedom of Movement Within the Country, Foreign Travel, Emigration, and Repatriation.*—Citizens enter and exit the country without arbitrary impediment, and the Government does not restrict travel within the country's borders.

The Government cooperates with the United Nations High Commissioner for Refugees and other humanitarian organizations in assisting refugees. There were no reports of forced expulsion of those having a valid claim to refugee status. The Government provides first asylum and the granting of asylum or refugee status in accordance with the standards of the 1951 United Nations Convention and its 1967 Protocol Relating to the Status of Refugees.

Section 3. Respect for Political Rights: The Right of Citizens to Change Their Government

Citizens exercised the right to change their government through democratic and peaceful means in the November 1993 elections. International observers found the elections to be free and fair. The national government is chosen by free, secret, direct, and obligatory balloting every 4 years. Suffrage is universal, but the clergy and serving members of the armed forces are not permitted to vote. Any citizen born in Honduras or abroad of Honduran parentage may hold office except for members of the clergy and the armed forces. A new political party may gain legal status by obtaining 20,000 signatures and establishing party organizations in at least half the country's 18 departments. In December the major parties held vigorously contested primary elections—a first for the National Party—in preparation for elections in 1997.

There are no legal impediments to women or minorities participating in government and politics, but in practice, the proportion of women and minorities in political organizations and elective office is far lower than their overall representation in society. However, in the 1993 elections voters elected for the first time a woman, Guadalupe Jerezano, as one of the three vice presidents, and the losing opposition slate also had a female vice presidential candidate. Women hold a cabinet ministry and a Supreme Court position, as well as a number of vice ministerial positions. Of the 128 Deputies in Congress, 14 are women. There are few indigenous persons in leadership positions in government or politics. Five Deputies are indigenous persons, and the ambassador to the United Nations is a member of the Garifuna indigenous group.

Section 4. Governmental Attitude Regarding International and Nongovernmental Investigation of Alleged Violations of Human Rights

A wide variety of human rights groups operate without government restriction, investigating and publishing their findings on human rights cases. Government officials are generally cooperative and responsive to their views.

In March Congress ratified a presidential decree expanding the functions of the National Commission for the Protection of Human Rights and unanimously reelected Dr. Leo Valladares for a 6-year term as Commissioner. Under this new decree, and in fulfillment of his expanded functions, the Commissioner has free access to all civil and military institutions and centers of detention; he may enter without authorization or objection by anyone. The Commissioner performs his functions with complete immunity and autonomy from all persons.

Anonymous telephone callers continued to threaten several individuals active in human rights endeavors. Human Rights Commissioner Valladares received numerous telephone threats against himself and his family. Dr. Ramon Custodio, president of CODEH, and Berta Oliva de Nativi, coordinator for the Committee of the Relatives of the Detained and Disappeared in Honduras, also received numerous telephone threats. DIC director Wilfredo Alvarado has received death threats since his investigation into several high-profile scandals involving the illegal sales of Honduran diplomatic passports. Attorney General Edmundo Orellana reported threats against himself and his family due to his investigations of several cases of persons who disappeared in the 1980's.

Section 5. Discrimination Based on Race, Sex, Religion, Disability, Language, or Social Status

The Constitution bans discrimination based on race and sex. Although it also bans discrimination on the basis of class, in fact, both the military and the political and social elite generally enjoy impunity before the legal system. Members of these groups are rarely arrested or jailed. Some progress was made by the Government, however, with the arrest and incarceration of Jose Tomas Guillen Williams and Luciano Coello, two officials of the former Callejas government. Both remain in the central penitentiary in Tegucigalpa awaiting trial on charges of corruption and abuse of power.

In 1994 the Congress passed a constitutional amendment to end compulsory military service. This measure was designed to end the common practice of forcible recruitment into the armed forces of middle and lower class citizens. There were also allegations that the authorities do not adequately defend homosexuals from threats, harassment, or abuse and that some officials support, promote, or engage in such hostile activities.

Women.—Violence against women remains widespread, and serious weaknesses in the Penal Code severely impede efforts to combat it. The Honduran Women's Committee for Peace—Visitacion Padilla and the Center for Women's Rights have called for the passage of legislation now before the Congress that would strengthen penalties for crimes against women. Congress continues to resist addressing concerns of women's advocacy reform groups in this area. The majority of such violence takes place within the family. The courts do not take action in domestic violence cases unless the victim is badly injured and incapacitated for more than 10 days. Except in the case of children 12 years of age or under, rape is considered a private crime (meaning rape victims over age 12 must hire a private prosecutor, a luxury few can afford). The penalties for rape are relatively light, ranging from 3 to 9 years' imprisonment. There are few shelters specifically maintained for battered women. During the year, six new centers for battered women were opened offering legal, medical, and psychological assistance. Although the law offers some redress, few women take advantage of the legal process, believing that judges would be unwilling to apply the law vigorously. Sexual harassment in the workplace is also a problem.

Women are represented in at least small numbers in most of the professions, but cultural attitudes limit their career opportunities. In theory, women have equal access to educational opportunities, but family pressures often impede the ambitions of women intent on obtaining higher education. The law requires employers to pay women, who make up 51 percent of the work force, equal wages for equal work, but employers often classify women's jobs as less demanding than those of men, as a justification for paying them lower salaries.

Some organizations have begun to offer assistance to women, principally targeting those living in the rural sectors and marginal neighborhoods of cities. The Honduran Federation of Women's Associations, for example, provides home construction and improvement loans, offers free legal assistance to women, and lobbies the Government on women's causes. The human rights group CIPRODEH continues an education program to make women aware of their rights under the law.

Children.—Although the Government has committed itself to protecting children by allocating 27 percent of its 1996 budget to public education and health care, it is unable to prevent abuse of street children (see Section 1.c.) and child workers (see Section 6.d.). In Tegucigalpa there are about 4,000 street children, of whom 2,000 find shelter on any given day. Many of them have been sexually molested, and about 40 percent regularly engage in prostitution; approximately 30 percent of the street children in Tegucigalpa and San Pedro Sula are HIV positive. At least 40 percent are chronically addicted to glue sniffing. Over 75 percent of the street children find their way to the streets because of severe family problems; 30 percent are abandoned. Both the police and members of the general population engage in violence against street children. When the authorities arrest street children, they house many of them with adults who abuse them.

Casa Alianza worked with the police and courts to end the abuse of children who are arrested and incarcerated in adult prisons. As a result, juvenile centers in Tamara, El Carmen, and Hatillo (located in sections of Tegucigalpa and San Pedro Sula) were opened during the year. However, detention of children with adults, vigilante violence, and police abuse continue to be a problem due to a general lack of juvenile detention centers.

On September 10, new legislation covering children and adolescents took effect. The new code covers the rights, liberties, and protection of children, including the area of child labor, and establishes prison sentences of up to 3 years for persons convicted of abuse of children in any form. Given limited resources, the ability of the Government to enforce the new code is problematic.

People With Disabilities.—There are no formal barriers to participation by disabled persons in employment, education, and health care, but neither is there specific statutory or constitutional protection for them. There is no legislation that requires accessibility for disabled persons to government buildings or commercial establishments.

Indigenous People.—The small community of indigenous people have little or no ability to participate in decisions affecting their lands, cultures, traditions, or the allocation of natural resources. All indigenous land rights are communal. While the law permits persons to claim individual free holding titles, in practice this has been difficult. Tribal lands are often poorly defined in documents dating from the mid-19th century and in most cases lack legal title based on modern cadastral measurements. The Honduran Forestry Development Corporation makes decisions regarding exploitation of timber resources on indigenous lands, often over strenuous tribal objection. Nonindigenous farmers and cattle ranchers regularly usurp indigenous lands.

The courts commonly deny legal recourse to indigenous groups and show bias in favor of the nonindigenous parties, who are often people of means and influence. Failure to obtain legal redress frequently caused indigenous groups to attempt to regain land through invasions and other tactics, which usually provoked the authorities to retaliate forcefully. In April, 2 years after their 1994 pilgrimage, some 5,000 members of indigenous groups again threatened to march to Tegucigalpa to remind the Government of the promises it made (the "Plan of Presidential Action of 1994") and demand that their rights be respected. They called off the march after discussions with senior government officials but vowed to return if the Government does not fulfill these agreements.

Section 6. Worker Rights
  a. *The Right of Association.*—Workers have the legal right to form and join labor unions; the unions are independent of government and political parties. Although only about 14 percent of the work force is organized, trade unions exert some economic and political influence. During the year this influence diminished somewhat. Unions frequently participate in public rallies against government policies and make extensive use of the media to advance their views. There are also three large peasant associations directly affiliated with the trade unions. The Constitution provides for the right to strike, along with a wide range of other basic labor rights, which the authorities honor in practice. The Civil Service Code, however, stipulates that government workers do not have the right to strike. (This does not include those working in state-owned enterprises.) There were legal and illegal strikes during the year by workers in foreign-owned maquiladora (in-bond processing) plants exporting textiles and garments.
  A number of private firms have instituted "solidarity" associations, which are essentially aimed at providing credit and other services to workers and management who are members of the association. Organized labor, including the American Federation of Labor-Congress of Industrial Organizations and the International Confederation of Free Trade Unions, strongly opposes these associations on the grounds that they do not permit strikes, have inadequate grievance procedures, and neutralize genuine and representative trade unions.
  The trade union movement maintains close ties with various international trade union organizations.
  b. *The Right to Organize and Bargain Collectively.*—The law protects workers' rights to organize and to bargain collectively; collective bargaining agreements are the norm for companies in which workers are organized. However, although the Labor Code prohibits retribution by employers for trade union activity, it is a common occurrence. Some employers threaten to close down unionized companies, harass their workers, and in some cases fire them for trying to form a trade union. Employers actually dismiss relatively few workers for union activity once a union is recognized; these cases, however, serve to discourage other workers from attempting to organize. Workers in both unionized and nonunionized companies are under the protection of the Labor Code, which gives them the right to seek redress from the Ministry of Labor. The Ministry of Labor took action in several cases, pressuring employers to observe the code. Labor or civil courts can require employers to rehire employees fired for union activity, but such rulings are uncommon. Generally, however, agreements between management and unions contain a clause prohibiting retaliation against any worker who participated in a strike or union activity.
  The same labor regulations apply in export processing zones (EPZ's) as in the rest of private industry. Unions are active in the government-owned Puerto Cortes free trade zone (7 of the 11 maquiladora companies there are unionized), but factory owners have resisted efforts to organize the new privately owned industrial parks. The Maquiladora Association has sponsored several meetings and seminars between its membership and major labor groups. As a result, tensions declined, and some 20 plants unionized peacefully in the privately owned EPZ's. The attitude of the Government towards organized labor in the EPZ's is the same as for other industries.
  In a number of U.S.-owned plants, workers have shown little enthusiasm for unionizing since they believe that their treatment, salary, and working conditions are as good as or better than those in unionized plants. In the absence of a union and collective bargaining, several of the EPZ plants have instituted solidarity associations, which to some extent exist as company unions for the purpose of setting wages and negotiating working conditions. Others use the minimum wage to set starting salaries and adjust the wage scale by negotiating with common groups of workers and individuals depending on skill, years of employment, and other related criteria. Talks between unions and EPZ plants continue.
  Labor leaders blame the Government for permitting management to act contrary to the Labor Code, and say that this problem will continue until the Ministry of Labor is reorganized to make it more efficient. They criticize the Ministry for not enforcing the Labor Code, for taking too long to make decisions, and for being timid and indifferent to workers' needs. Under a November 1995 Memorandum of Understanding between the Minister of Labor and the United States Trade Representative's Office (calling for more forceful implementation of the Honduran Labor Code), the Ministry has made significant progress toward enforcing the code. In one case where the Ministry imposed a $10,000 (115,000 lempira) fine on a company for failure to rehire 16 workers fired for organizing a union, the company reinstated the workers the next day. The Ministry has increased its inspections of the

maquiladoras and the training of its inspectors; more needs to be done, however, to adhere completely to international labor standards.

The Labor Code clearly prohibits blacklisting; nevertheless, there was credible evidence that informal blacklisting occurred in the privately owned industrial parks. When unions are formed, organizers must submit a list of initial members to the Ministry of Labor as part of the process of obtaining official recognition. Before official recognition is granted, however, the Ministry must inform the company of the impending union organization. Ministry officials have consistently been unable to provide effective protection to workers. There are credible reports that, particularly in the EPZ sector, some inspectors have gone so far as to sell companies the names of employees involved in forming a union, which some companies used to dismiss union organizers before recognition was granted. There is also credible evidence that military intelligence maintains files on union activists.

c. *Prohibition of Forced or Compulsory Labor.*—The Constitution and the law prohibit forced or compulsory labor. Although there were no official reports of such practices, there were credible allegations of forced overtime in EPZ plants, particularly for women.

d. *Minimum Age for Employment of Children.*—The Constitution and the Labor Code prohibit the employment of minors under the age of 16, except that a child of 15 years is permitted to work with the permission of parents and the Ministry of Labor. The new Children's Code prohibits a child of 14 years of age or less from working (even with parental permission) and establishes prison sentences of 3 to 5 years for individuals who allow children to work illegally. An employer who legally hires a 15-year-old must certify that the young person has finished or is finishing compulsory schooling. The Ministry of Labor grants a number of work permits to 15-year-olds each year. It is common, however, for younger children to obtain these documents or to purchase forged permits that use the Labor Ministry's letterhead.

The Ministry of Labor cannot effectively enforce child labor laws, and violations of the Labor Code occur frequently in rural areas and in small companies. Many children work on small family farms, as street vendors, or in small workshops to supplement the family income. According to the Ministry of Labor, human rights groups, and organizations for the protection of children, the most significant child labor problem is in the construction industry. Employment of children younger than the legal working age in maquiladoras probably occurs but does not appear to happen on a large scale.

e. *Acceptable Conditions of Work.*—In December 1995, the Government decreed a 25 percent increase in the minimum wage. Daily pay rates vary by the sector of the economy affected and geographical zones: The lowest minimum wage is $2.00 (26 lempiras) per day in the agriculture sector. The highest minimum wage is in the mining sector at $3.48 (31.50 lempiras) daily. Urban workers earn slightly more than those in the countryside. The Constitution and the Labor Code stipulate that all labor be fairly paid, but the Ministry of Labor lacks the staff and other resources for effective enforcement. Even after the third consecutive annual increase, the minimum wage is considered insufficient to provide a decent standard of living for a worker and family. Labor leaders say that the Government has ignored those earning above the minimum wage (workers in the maquiladoras and organizations such as banks) and is calling for an across-the-board increase of 30 percent that they claim will benefit all.

The law prescribes a maximum 8-hour day and a 44-hour workweek. There is a requirement for at least one 24-hour rest period every 8 days. The Labor Code provides for a paid vacation of 10 workdays after 1 year and 20 workdays after 4 years. However, employers frequently ignore these regulations due to the high level of unemployment and underemployment and the lack of effective enforcement by the Ministry of Labor.

The Ministry of Labor is responsible for enforcing national health and safety laws, but does not do so effectively. Although fewer than in previous years, some complaints allege the failure of foreign factory managers to comply with occupational health and safety aspects of Labor Code regulations in factories located in free zones and industrial parks. There is no provision for a worker to remove himself from a dangerous work situation without jeopardy to continued employment.

JAMAICA

Jamaica is a constitutional parliamentary democracy and a member of the Commonwealth of Nations. Two political parties have alternated in power since the first elections under universal adult suffrage in 1944; a third major party was established in late 1995. The last general election, held in March 1993, was marred by political violence and fraud. The judiciary is independent but lacks adequate resources.

The Jamaica Constabulary Force (JCF) has primary responsibility for internal security, assisted by the Island Special Constabulary Force. The Jamaica Defence Force (army, air wing, and coast guard) is charged with supporting the JCF in maintaining law and order, although it has no powers of arrest. While civilian authorities generally maintain effective control of the security forces, some members of the security forces were charged with committing human rights abuses.

The economy is based on primary products (bauxite and alumina, sugar, bananas), services (tourism, finance), and light manufacturing (garment assembly). The Government promoted private investment to stimulate economic growth and modernization, pursuing in the process a sometimes painful program of structural adjustment. Annual per capita income is $1,850, but this figure is misleading as there is a large and widening gap between the wealthy and the impoverished.

The Government generally respects the human rights of its citizens; however, problems remained in certain areas. Although members of the security forces committed extrajudicial killings and beatings and carried out arbitrary arrests and detentions, the Government moved effectively to punish some of those involved. Prison and jail conditions remained poor, with overcrowding, brutality against detainees, dismal sanitary conditions, and inadequate diet the norm. The judicial system was overburdened and lengthy delays in trials were common. Political violence, largely absent since the 1993 election, reappeared. Economic discrimination and violence against women remained problems, as did mob violence against those suspected of breaking the law.

RESPECT FOR HUMAN RIGHTS

Section 1. Respect for the Integrity of the Person, Including Freedom From:

a. *Political and Other Extrajudicial Killing.*—The security forces frequently employed lethal force in apprehending criminal suspects, usually in the guise of shootouts. This resulted in the killing by police of 140 people during the year. While allegations of "police murder" were frequent, the validity of some of the allegations was suspect. This problem is the result of unresolved, long-standing antipathy between the security forces and certain communities, especially among the urban poor. The JCF conducted both administrative and criminal investigations into incidents involving fatal shootings by the police. The JCF policy statement on the use of force incorporates U.N.-approved language on basic principles on the use of force and firearms by law enforcement officials.

The authorities suspended four policemen and charged one with murder, after they allegedly beat to death a 22-year-old man in a West Kingston police station in April. Police are investigating the suspicious death in May of a man held in the Port Antonio jail.

In September a jury found a policeman charged with murder in connection with a July 1995 incident in Mandeville not guilty. In that incident, two policemen fired warning shots to disperse a crowd, killing one person and wounding two others. In March the authorities brought murder charges against another policeman, one who fired into a crowd of demonstrators in West Kingston in October 1995. The courts gave a constable in St. James a suspended 3-year sentence for unlawful wounding, following a 1994 incident in which he shot a detainee in the back during a struggle.

There were no developments in the murder trial of a JCF officer accused in two July 1993 killings. No action was reported in the civil lawsuits brought by relatives of two men who died in the Constant Spring jail in October 1992.

Political violence resurged in 1996. The former chairman of the opposition Jamaica Labour Party (JLP) resigned in 1995 and established a new party, the National Democratic Movement (NDM), late that year. Tensions between the JLP and NDM remained high, with frequent vilification of the NDM by JLP leaders. Beginning in January, strongly politicized areas of Kingston and Spanish Town were repeatedly wracked by political violence. According to police, this led to 10 deaths by mid-year, including murders of NDM and JLP supporters. The Government deployed strong police and military detachments to the affected areas in response to serious outbreaks of violence, which significantly dampened the level of political violence. However, the Government could not afford to maintain strong detachments in all affected areas at all times.

Vigilantism, involving spontaneous mob executions in response to crime, rose in 1996, both in rural areas and in Kingston. Mobs killed 10 persons in West Kingston between November 1995 and September 1996, 5 of whom were charged with murder at the time of their own deaths. Official investigations into the killings did not uncover any information. Mobs lynched four other persons suspected of robberies in rural St. Catherine in late 1995-early 1996. In May a crowd beat a man to death after he was allegedly caught sexually assaulting a 3-year-old girl in rural Hanover. In July crowds beat and slashed to death three other suspected robbers in rural St. Elizabeth (near Montego Bay). Police reported a total of 22 vigilante killings between November 1995 and August 1996.

b. *Disappearance.*—There were no reports of politically motivated disappearances.

c. *Torture and Other Cruel, Inhuman, or Degrading Treatment or Punishment.*—The law prohibits torture and other abuse of prisoners and detainees. However, reports of physical abuse of prisoners by guards continued, despite efforts by the Government to remove abusive guards and improve procedures.

Prison conditions remained poor, with overcrowding, inadequate diet, poor sanitary conditions, and insufficient medical care the norm. The Government continued to address these problems, allocating approximately $750,000 (75 percent of the correctional services budget) for the improvement of prison facilities.

The Government allowed private groups, voluntary organizations, international human rights organizations, and the media to visit prisons and monitor prison conditions.

d. *Arbitrary Arrest, Detention, or Exile.*—In 1994 Parliament repealed the Suppression of Crimes Act of 1974, which permitted warrantless searches and the arrest of persons "reasonably suspected" of having committed a crime. The Jamaica Constabulary Force Act, however, now contains several of these provisions, and there were continued reports that the police abused these provisions.

The law requires police to present a detainee in court within 48 hours of detention, but the authorities continued to detain suspects, especially those from poor neighborhoods, without presenting them before a judge within the prescribed period. Magistrates inquire at least once per week into the welfare of each person listed by the JCF as being detained. There is a functioning bail system.

Foreign prisoners must pay for their own deportation once they have completed their sentences. If they cannot afford to pay, they are jailed until relatives or consulates can arrange for transportation. In effect, this constitutes an additional prison term for indigents.

The Constitution prohibits exile, and no instances of exile occurred.

e. *Denial of Fair Public Trial.*—The Constitution provides for an independent judiciary, which exists in practice. However, the judicial system is overburdened and operates with inadequate resources. Trials in many cases are delayed for years, and other cases are dismissed because files cannot be located. The Government initiated a night court in September 1995, which has had some success in reducing the backlog of cases.

The Constitution allows the Court of Appeal and the Parliament to refer cases to the Judicial Committee of the Privy Council in the United Kingdom as a final court of appeal.

While the defendant's right to counsel is well-established, the courts appoint counsel for indigents only in cases of a serious offense (e.g., murder, rape, robbery, gun offenses). However, the law does not consider many offenses, including wounding with intent to cause great bodily harm, as "serious." Thus the courts try many defendants without benefit of counsel.

There were no reports of political prisoners.

f. *Arbitrary Interference with Privacy, Family, Home, or Correspondence.*—The Constitution prohibits arbitrary intrusion by the State into the private life of the individual. The revised Jamaica Constabulary Force Act continues to give security personnel broad powers of search and seizure similar to those granted by the former Suppression of Crimes Act.

Section 2. Respect for Civil Liberties, Including:

a. *Freedom of Speech and Press.*—The Constitution provides for freedom of speech and of the press, and the Government respects these rights in practice.

The Jamaica Broadcasting Company, largely deregulated in 1988, operates two radio stations and one of the island's two television stations. The Government's broadcasting commission has the right to regulate programming during emergencies. Foreign television transmissions are unregulated and available to tens of thousands of Jamaicans through satellite antennas. The four largest newspapers, all privately owned, regularly report on human rights abuses, particularly those involving the JCF. Foreign publications are widely available.

Physical intimidation was reportedly employed against journalists to halt stories unfavorable to certain politicians and political activists.

The Government does not restrict academic freedom.

b. *Freedom of Peaceful Assembly and Association.*—The Constitution provides for these rights, and the Government respects them in practice.

c. *Freedom of Religion.*—The Constitution provides for freedom of religion, and the Government respects this right in practice.

d. *Freedom of Movement Within the Country, Foreign Travel, Emigration, and Repatriation.*—The Constitution provides for these rights, and the authorities respect them in practice.

The Government cooperates with the U.N. High Commissioner for Refugees and other humanitarian organizations in assisting refugees. The Government provides first asylum, and provided it to approximately 40 persons in 1994. Similar but smaller numbers of first asylum cases, mainly Cubans and Haitians, were accepted in 1995 and 1996. There were no reports of forced return of persons to a country where they feared persecution. The Government established a committee and formal procedures to review claims to refugee status. This committee denied all claims to refugee status by Cubans and Haitians who had arrived in Jamaica since 1994. However, several Cuban applicants were granted permission to stay in Jamaica on other grounds.

Section 3. *Respect for Political Rights: The Right of Citizens to Change Their Government*

The Constitution provides citizens with the right to change their government peacefully. Periodic elections are held on the basis of universal suffrage. All citizens age 18 and over have the right to vote by secret ballot. The last general election, in March 1993, was marred by violence and fraud. The violence and fraud was most prevalent in so-called garrison communities, which are dominated by the major political parties. The People's National Party (PNP) holds a majority in the House of Representatives. The Jamaican Labour Party, which has alternated in power with the PNP since 1944, boycotted all by-elections since 1993, claiming that needed electoral reforms were not in place. Voter registration under an improved system was scheduled to begin island-wide on January 6, 1997.

There are no legal limits on the participation of women in politics. Women hold some 13 percent of all political offices and 30 percent of the senior civil service positions. Two of the 16 cabinet members are women, as is the PNP General Secretary.

Section 4. *Governmental Attitude Regarding International and Nongovernmental Investigation of Alleged Violations of Human Rights*

A number of human rights groups operate without government restriction, investigating and publishing their findings on human rights cases. The work of the Jamaica Council for Human Rights, the country's only formal organization concerned with all aspects of human rights, was severely hampered by a lack of adequate resources which required a substantial reduction in its staff. Government officials are generally cooperative and responsive to the views of human rights organizations.

Section 5. *Discrimination Based on Race, Sex, Religion, Disability, Language, or Social Status*

The Constitution prohibits discrimination on grounds of race, place of origin, political opinions, color, creed, or sex. The Government largely enforces these prohibitions in practice, except for widespread discrimination on the basis of political opinion in the distribution of scarce governmental benefits, including employment, especially in the garrison communities (see Section 3).

Women.—In practice, women suffer from economic discrimination, sexual harassment in the workplace, and social and cultural traditions that perpetuate violence against women, including spousal abuse. The Domestic Violence Act of 1995 came into effect in May 1996. It provides additional remedies for domestic violence, including restraining orders and other noncustodial sentencing. Violence against women is widespread, but many women are reluctant to acknowledge or report abusive behavior, leading to wide variations in estimates of its extent.

The Constitution and the 1975 Employment Act accord women full equality. The Bureau of Women's Affairs, in the Ministry of Labour, oversees programs to ensure the legal rights of women. These programs have had limited effect to date, but have raised the awareness of problems affecting women. In June the Government established a steering committee, charged with creating a Commission on Gender and Social Equity by the end of the year.

A number of active women's rights groups exist. They are concerned with a wide range of issues, including employment, violence against women, political representation, and the image of women presented in the media. Their effectiveness is mixed, but the groups were successful in advocating enactment of the Domestic Violence Act.

Children.—The Government is committed to improving children's welfare. Expenditure on education and health rose 50 percent, twice the rate of growth in the overall budget. The Ministry of Education, Youth, and Culture is responsible for implementation of the Government's programs for children.

The Juvenile Act of 1951 deals with several areas related to the protection of children, including prevention of cruelty, prohibition on causing or allowing juvenile begging, the power to bring juveniles in need of care or protection before a juvenile court, the treatment of juvenile offenders, the regulation and supervision of children's homes, and restrictions on employment of juveniles. In June the visiting Executive Director of the United Nations Children's Fund (UNICEF) said the Government had done very well in its efforts to improve the welfare and survival of children.

People With Disabilities.—No laws mandate accessibility for people with disabilities. Several government agencies and nongovernmental organizations provide services and employment to various groups of disabled citizens.

Section 6. Worker Rights

a. *The Right of Association.*—The law provides for the right to form or join a trade union, and unions function freely and independently of the Government. The Labor Relations and Industrial Disputes Act (LRIDA) defines worker rights. There is a spectrum of national unions, some of which are affiliated with political parties. Approximately 15 percent of the work force is organized.

The LRIDA neither authorizes nor prohibits the right to strike, but strikes do occur. Striking workers can interrupt work without criminal liability but cannot be assured of keeping their jobs. Workers in 10 broad categories of "essential services" are prohibited from striking, a provision the International Labor Organization (ILO) has repeatedly condemned as overly inclusive. The Government did not declare any strikes illegal in 1996.

Unions maintain a wide variety of regional and international affiliations.

b. *The Right to Organize and Bargain Collectively.*—The Government rarely interferes with union organizing efforts. Judicial and police authorities effectively enforce the LRIDA and other labor regulations. All parties are firmly committed to collective bargaining in contract negotiations, even in some nonunion settings. An independent Industrial Disputes Tribunal (IDT) hears cases where management and labor fail to reach agreement. Any cases not resolved by the IDT pass to the civil courts. The number of industrial disputes referred to the IDT declined. The IDT made decisions in a few cases, while others were settled by agreement or withdrawn. However, the majority of cases referred to the IDT remained unresolved. The LRIDA prohibits antiunion discrimination, and employees may not be fired solely for union membership. The authorities enforced this law effectively.

Domestic labor laws apply equally to the "free zones" (export processing zones). However, there are no unionized companies in any of the 3 zones—established in 1972, 1985, and 1988—which employ approximately 18,000 workers. Organizers attributethis to resistance by foreign owners in the zones to organizing efforts, but attempts to organize plants within the zones continue. Company-controlled "workers' councils" handle grievance resolution at most free zone companies, but do not negotiate wages and conditions with management. Management determines wages and benefits within the free zones; these are generally as good as or better than those in similar industries outside the zones. The Ministry of Labor has not performed factory inspections in the free zones since 1992.

c. *Prohibition of Forced or Compulsory Labor.*—The Constitution does not specifically address the matter of forced or compulsory labor. However, Jamaica is a party to both ILO conventions that prohibit compulsory labor, and there were no reports that this practice exists.

d. *Minimum Age for Employment of Children.*—The Juvenile Act provides that children under the age of 12 shall not be employed except by parents or guardians, and that such employment may only be in domestic, agricultural, or horticultural work. Enforcement, however, is erratic. Children under 12 peddle goods and services on city streets, but there is no evidence of widespread illegal employment of children in other sectors of the economy. The Educational Act stipulates that all children between 6 and 11 years of age must attend elementary school. Industrial safety, police, and truant officers are charged with enforcement. Under current economic circumstances, however, thousands of children are kept home to help with housework and avoid school fees. A 1994 UNICEF report stated that 4.6 percent of children below the age of 16 worked to help support their households.

e. *Acceptable Conditions of Work.*—The minimum wage, raised from $15.00 (J$500) to $22.50 (J$800) per week in July, is widely considered inadequate. Most salaried workers are paid more than the legal minimum. Work over 40 hours per week or 8 hours per day must be compensated at overtime rates, a provision that is widely observed.

The Labor Ministry's Industrial Safety Division sets and enforces industrial health and safety standards, which are considered adequate. Industrial accident rates, particularly in the bauxite/alumina industry, were once again low. Public service staff reductions in the Ministries of Labor, Finance, National Security, and the Public Service have contributed to the difficulties in enforcing workplace regulations. The law provides workers with the right to remove themselves from dangerous work situations without jeopardy to their continued employment if they are trade union members or covered by the Factories Act. The law does not specifically protect other categories of workers in those circumstances.

MEXICO

Mexico is a federal republic with an elected president, a bicameral legislature, and a constitutionally mandated independent judiciary. The Institutional Revolutionary Party (PRI) has won every presidential election since the party's founding in 1929, many of which involved credible allegations of fraudulent practices. Most national and international observers, however, regarded the August 1994 presidential elections as free and honest. The success of these elections carried over in 1995 into most state elections, with only one state election marred by allegations of serious fraud. In 1996 most state elections were fair and orderly. A few, such as the municipal race in Huejotzingo, Puebla, provoked serious postelectoral conflicts, most of which have been resolved. In November the Congress approved a package of further electoral reforms, including full autonomy for the Federal Electoral Institute and elections for Mexico City's local government. Due to disagreements on a number of issues, especially campaign spending limits and rules governing coalitions, however, the main opposition parties' legislators voted against the law. Despite opposition criticism of the PRI's decision to press for adoption of certain provisions on campaign financing in the reform package, the law includes the basic elements that had been agreed upon by the opposition.

Several southern states, most notably Guerrero, Tabasco, Oaxaca, and Chiapas, continued to suffer politically motivated violence. The Government and the Zapatista National Liberation Army (EZLN) remain committed to a negotiated settlement and peace talks continued throughout the year. On February 16, the parties signed an agreement on the rights of indigenous people. The army and the EZLN have not clashed since the Government unilaterally declared a cease-fire on January 12, 1994. A new group of uncertain origin and size, the Popular Revolutionary Army (EPR), made its appearance on June 28. The Government considers the EPR a terrorist organization and has vowed to bring the group to justice.

Police forces maintain internal security. The army is responsible for external security but also has domestic security responsibilities. The security forces, including the federal and state judicial police, federal highway police, and local police, are under the control of elected civilian officials. However, corruption is rife within police ranks. Members of the security forces continued to commit numerous human rights abuses.

Mexico has a market-based, mixed economy, which the Government has been progressively deregulating and opening. An ambitious program of privatization has reduced state-owned companies from more than 1,150 to less than 200. About 29 percent of gross domestic product (GDP) comes from manufacturing, 20 percent from commerce, 6 percent from agriculture, and 45 percent from service industries. There is significant subsistence agriculture, and 25 percent of the populace lives in rural areas. Leading exports include automobiles, manufactured and assembled products (including electronics and consumer goods), and petrochemicals. Although per capita GDP in 1994 was about $4,200, it fell to about $2,800 in 1995 as a consequence of currency devaluation and the recession. In 1996 there was steady improvement in macroeconomic indices such as GDP, external account balance, and foreign currency reserves and some modest recovery in employment. The microeconomic situation, however, did not improve significantly. Consumption, wages, and employment remain far below 1994 levels; this has produced higher levels of crime and social tension. There are severe and growing inequalities in income distribution, with large numbers of people living in extreme poverty in rural areas, shanty towns, and urban slums.

The Government generally respected the human rights of its citizens, although serious problems remained in some areas, and some states present special concerns. Major abuses included extrajudicial killings, torture, illegal arrests, arbitrary detentions, poor prison conditions, illegal searches, violence against women, discrimination against women and indigenous persons, some limits on worker rights, and extensive child labor in agriculture and in the informal economy. The Government continued, with limited success, its attempt to end the "culture of impunity" surrounding the security forces through reforms in the Federal Attorney General's office (PGR).These included the dismissal of over 1,250 corrupt officials, new recruitment and training procedures, and closer supervision of federal police and prosecutors. The Government also continued its support for the government-funded National Human Rights Commission (CNDH) and the implementation of a wide-ranging package of other police and judicial reforms.

RESPECT FOR HUMAN RIGHTS

Section 1. Respect for the Integrity of the Person, Including Freedom From:

a. *Political and Other Extrajudicial Killings.*—Police and vigilantes acting on behalf of local landowners continued to commit extrajudicial killings while dislodging peasant squatters from rural lands in several states. To expand communal land holdings, for decades peasants have invaded private lands and petitioned for government recognition of the seizures.

Some large landowners and local political bosses in Chiapas maintain private militias to defend their property from peasant land invasions and to intimidate local opposition. This problem is especially acute in some northern regions of the state, where the group Peace and Justice ("Paz y Justicia"), headed by autonomous local political bosses loosely affiliated with the PRI, is based. State authorities do not effectively impede the establishment of these militias, which reportedly often employ police and military personnel.

According to statistics compiled by the District Attorney's office for Chiapas state, approximately 500 peasants have been killed in the last 3 years as a result of violence in the northern municipalities of Tila, Sabanilla, Salto de Agua, and Tumbala. The Fray Bartolome de las Casas Center for Human Rights reported that at least 2,000 indigenous families have abandoned their lands for fear of violent attacks by the Peace and Justice group. Human Rights Watch/Americas similarly reported expulsions of peasants from Miguel Aleman, Nuevo Limar, Susuchumil, Tzaquil, and Usipa on account of the fact that they were supporters of the national Democratic Revolutionary Party (PRD).

On May 5, in Bachajon, Chiapas, an autonomous local paramilitary group also loosely affiliated with the PRI (the "Chinchulines"), was involved in violence with peasants arising out of longstanding land disputes. Members of the Chinchulines had arbitrarily detained villagers the day before. In retaliation for this and previous actions taken against them, the villagers attacked the house of the Chinchulines' leader and shot and killed him and another member of that group. Following the slayings, the Chinchulines pursued the peasants and in the resulting clash two more Chinchulines were killed, as well as two peasants. The Chinchulines then set fire to a number of houses belonging to the peasants. They also unsuccessfully attempted to burn a Jesuit residence in Bachajon. In total, 6 Chinchulines and peasants were killed, 23 houses and businesses burned to the ground, and 14 vehicles destroyed. State police were sent to the area and arrested 28 people for the violence.

According to the Miguel Agustin Pro Juarez Center for Human Rights, there were nine killings as a result of drug trafficking in the region of San Lucas Atoyaquillo, Oaxaca. Local political bosses ("caciques") have benefited not only from alleged narcotics ties but also from their ability to seize the lands deserted by peasants fleeing the violence. Drug traffickers also resorted to killings to intimidate the indigenous peoples of the Tarahumara region in the north.

In the Huasteca region of Northern Veracruz, citizens complain of a perceived militarization in the area caused by the presence of army troops. Police continued to evict, detain arbitrarily, and destroy the homes of peasant leaders in the state of Veracruz. Land disputes in the state, especially those involving ranchers and indigenous persons, are the principal cause of such violence. Police often fail to investigate killings of peasants by ranchers.

On April 10, citizens of Tepoztlan, Morelos, were marching on the "Emiliano Zapata Route" to Tlaltizapan in order to present a petition to President Zedillo protesting the planned development of a golf course on communal lands. The police stopped the protesters and fired shots; the protesters responded by fleeing and defending themselves with rocks. In the melee, police shot and killed one protester, Marcos Olmedo. The Governor of Morelos denounced the shooting, saying that police are under standing instructions not to use firearms against demonstrators. The authorities arrested one policeman in connection with the shooting, and he remained in custody at year's end.

There has been an increase in the number of public lynchings occurring throughout the country, primarily in rural communities with limited access to the criminal justice system. According to press reports, 21 people were killed by lynching from September 1995 to August 1996.

At the request of President Zedillo, a panel of three Supreme Court justices conducted an inquiry into the June 28, 1995 slaying of 17 peasants in Aguas Blancas, Guerrero. Guerrero state police killed the peasants while they were en route to protest the Government's failure to deliver promised herbicides. Many were members of the Peasant Organization of the Southern Sierra (OCSS), a small, leftist organization, formerly linked to the PRD. The justices rejected the conclusions of the Guerrero state attorney general's office that heavily armed policemen had acted in self-defense and that the peasants had fired first. The justices agreed with the conclusions of a CNDH investigation which determined that a film of the scene that officials had used to exonerate themselves had been tampered with, that at least one deliberate execution occurred, and that police placed weapons into the hands of the dead peasants in order to give the appearance that the peasants were armed and belligerent.

The justices also concluded that Guerrero Governor Ruben Figueroa shared responsibility for the massacre. Following the broadcast of an unedited, undoctored version of the film, clearly implicating the state police, and the start of the Supreme Court investigation, Governor Figueroa requested indefinite leave from his position. On March 13, the Guerrero state legislature named Angel Aguirre Rivero interim governor to replace Figueroa. In July, however, the Guerrero state legislature voted to exonerate Figueroa for any involvement he had in the Aguas Blancas killings. Nonetheless, he remains out of office. Then-CNDH president Jorge Madrazo called on the Guerrero state government to comply fully with the CNDH's recommendations, including a thorough reorganization of the state police. In accordance with CNDH recommendations, former special prosecutor Miguel Angel Garcia Dominguez (who later left his position to become a state supreme court justice in Guanajuato) brought criminal charges against some state officials and ordered the arrest of 10 policemen involved in the killings.

On December 29, an unknown killer murdered Rene Jaramillo Pineda, factional leader of the National Teachers' Union and chief of technical education in Guerrero, who was also a prominent supporter of former Governor Figueroa.

In January federal judicial police arrested 4 ex-officials and 18 state policemen in conjunction with the Aguas Blancas killings. They included the former state police operations director, Manuel Moreno Gonzalez, first deputy state attorney general Rodolfo Espino, former director general of state security Esteban Mendatt Ramos, and Gustavo Martinez Galeana, former chief of state security for the Costa Grande region of Guerrero. Then-CNDH president Madrazo said that in spite of the arrests of the four state government officials, other, higher ranking officials cited in the CNDH's recommendation as bearing responsibility for the crime remained free.

Raul Salinas de Gortari, brother of ex-President Carlos Salinas de Gortari, remains in prison pending trial as an alleged conspirator in the assassination of then-PRI Secretary General Jose Francisco Ruiz Massieu in September 1994. In addition to charges for the murder of Ruiz Massieu, Raul Salinas has also been charged with "unexplainable enrichment" (corruption) for allegedly amassing a fortune estimated in excess of $100 million during his brother's presidency.

Mario Ruiz Massieu, former Deputy Attorney General (and brother of Jose Ruiz Massieu), remains in the United States pending ongoing deportation efforts. The Government has charged him with obstruction of justice for concealing Raul Salinas' role in Jose Ruiz Massieu's murder.

Gaston Ayala Beltran, a former state judicial police officer, remains in custody for the May 10, 1995, murder of Jalisco state Attorney General Leobardo Larios Guzman. Three other alleged gunmen of the Tijuana drug cartel were arrested in connection with the murder, and they remain in custody.

On August 7, Othon Cortez Vazquez, the alleged second gunman in the March 1994 assassination of PRI presidential candidate Luis Donaldo Colosio, was released for lack of evidence. The PGR is appealing the decision.

On May 10, an appeals court overturned the conviction of police officer Jose Antonio Verduzco Flores for beating U.S. citizen Mario Amado to death in 1992 in a Baja California jail, allowing Verduzco to go free. No new charges have been brought. The state District Attorney's office was conducting a review of the Amado case.

There were no new developments in the 67 cases of violence (including murders) against PRD activists in which CNDH has issued recommendations since 1992. The authorities have fully complied with 28 recommendations but only partially complied with the remaining 39.

b. *Disappearance.*—There were credible reports by the media and NGO's of disappearances during sweeps by security and military forces in Oaxaca and Guerrero in attempts to round up EPR members. While denying that any individuals had been illegally detained, the Government offered to investigate each alleged disappearance. Many local NGO's report a disappearance when the authorities arbitrarily or illegally detain a person for questioning and release the suspect within days or weeks. In Oaxaca, for example, local human rights organizations indicated that all those reported as missing under such conditions were later accounted for.

According to the Miguel Agustin Pro Juarez Center for Human Rights, 18 persons in Sinaloa state and 1 person in Chihuahua disappeared in 1996, probably due to the actions of drug traffickers.

Amnesty International's 1996 report stated that two people who disappeared in 1995 still remain missing. On May 24, 1995, OCSS leader Gilberto Romero Vasquez disappeared after his organization had presented a series of demands to state authorities. Such demands later led to the Aguas Blancas massacre. Amnesty International also reported that in October 1995, Cuauhtemoc Ornelas Campos, a journalist and human rights activist, disappeared after receiving anonymous threats for publicly criticizing human rights abuses by local officials.

For the period of May 1995 to May 1996, the CNDH reported that it was able to conclude 38 cases of presumed disappearances. Of those cases, 33 of the people were found living, and the remaining 5 were found dead or with evidence of having died. This brings the total of cases of presumed disappearances investigated by CNDH to 153, of which 93 persons were found to be living and 36 dead or with evidence of having died.

c. *Torture and Other Cruel, Inhuman, or Degrading Treatment or Punishment.*—The Constitution prohibits torture; however, it continues to be a serious human rights problem. Members of the security forces continued to torture and abuse detainees. The most commonly used methods of torture were threats, beatings, asphyxiation, and electric shocks. Soldiers also reportedly used torture against members of the EPR (see Section 1.g.).

There are persistent reports by NGO's of widespread use of torture by police and security forces. Although the CNDH reported in May that torture dropped from the 15th to 17th most common type of complaint, the actual number of complaints of torture increased by 31 percent, with a total of 59 complaints during the year. Of the 59 complaints alleging torture received by the CNDH, it referred 16 to state human rights authorities having jurisdiction over such matters. Of those cases handled by the CNDH, 16 involved actions taken in 1996, 23 in 1995, and the remaining 4 occurred prior to 1995. As of publication of its 1995–96 report, the CNDH had issued recommendations in five of those cases, in all of which the authorities involved were in the process of taking corrective action.

The CNDH, however, does not maintain statistics on torture complaints made to state human rights commissions. Of the 31 states and the Federal District, only the states of Hidalgo and Puebla lack laws prohibiting torture. Poorly trained and equipped to investigate crimes, police officers continued to attempt to solve crimes by rounding up likely suspects and then exacting confessions from them. Many state human rights commissions received reports of torture allegedly committed by police. According to the Human Rights Commission for the Federal District, for the period from October 1995 to September 1996, torture had dropped to 33rd on its list of most common complaints, with 16 cases reported.

The authorities punish few officials for torture, which continues to occur mainly because confessions are the primary evidence in many criminal convictions. Many victims do not report, or do not follow through on, their complaints against the police for fear of reprisals.

On January 3, 1997, a Federal District appeals court freed seven alleged Zapatistas, convicted on August 20 on charges including possession of illegal weapons and explosives and sentenced to prison terms of 6 to 9 years. Police had arrested the seven and detained them since February 8, 1995, after their safe house was discovered in Yanga, Veracruz. Defense attorneys had protested the conviction and said their clients would appeal, stressing that the CNDH found that the defendants had been tortured by security forces.

In some cases police officers dismissed in one state find law enforcement employment in another. The CNDH discovered that even when the authorities censured some officers in one law enforcement job, they moved on to other positions and were subsequently charged again with human rights abuses. In an effort to remedy this situation, the CNDH publishes lists of censured public servants in its annual report and monthly newsletters. In addition, the Government has established a national security register to keep track of censured police officers and address this problem.

Prison conditions are poor. Many prisons are staffed by undertrained and corrupt guards, and some lack adequate facilities for prisoners and are overcrowded, despite an early release program endorsed by the CNDH and legal reforms reducing the number of crimes that carry mandatory prison sentences. Prisoners complain that they must purchase food, medicine, and other necessities from guards or bribe guards to allow the goods to be brought in from outside. Drug and alcohol use is rampant in prisons. Frequently, prisoners exercise authority within a prison, displacing prison officials. Conflicts between rival prison groups, often involved in drug trafficking, continued to spark lethal violence. While the authorities prosecuted a few prison officials for abusing prisoners, it was more common to dismiss them or to charge them with only minor offenses.

The penal system comprises 3 federal penitentiaries, 8 prisons within the Federal District, 274 state prisons, and 150 municipal jails for a total of 435 facilities. According to the Secretary of Government's Program for Prevention and Social Readaptation, 1995–2000, the prison population has increased annually by 25 percent, resulting in the space designed to hold 91,548 prisoners becoming overcrowded. As of December 1995, there was an excess of 2,026 prisoners for the space available.

According to a study conducted by the CNDH, from March 1994 to March 1996, over 50 prison riots occurred. Influence peddling, drug and arms trafficking, coercion, violence, sexual abuse, and protection payoffs are the chief methods of control used by prisoners against fellow prisoners in a form of self-government within the system.

A 5-day riot that began on July 3 at the Cereso One prison in Ciudad Victoria, Tamaulipas, resulted in 23 police injured, 12 prisoners injured, and 1 prisoner dead.

Some prisons, contrary to law, do not separate male and female populations. Officials sometimes encourage women to form sexual liaisons with male prisoners and guards. In some cases, officials coerce women into sexual relationships.

The CNDH has a program to inspect prisons (from May 1995 to May 1996, the CNDH made 77 visits to 54 prisons in 25 states) and to investigate prisoner complaints.

There is no specific law or regulation regarding the ability of NGO's to visit prisons. In practice, such prison visits are allowed and are common. For example, members of the Democratic Lawyers National Front represented prisoners alleged to be members of the EZLN and were allowed to visit them in prison. Similarly, representatives of the International Committee of the Red Cross were allowed to visit with the alleged EZLN members.

d. *Arbitrary Arrest, Detention, or Exile.*—The Constitution prohibits arbitrary arrest and detention; however, the police continued to arrest and detain citizens arbitrarily. The law provides that the District Attorney may not detain an accused person more than 48 hours before presenting the person before a judge, but it makes an exception for persons apprehended in the act of committing a crime. In November Congress amended the Penal Procedures Federal Code to apply this exception to acts committed up to 72 hours prior to detention. The Mexican Commission for Defense and Promotion of Human Rights strongly criticized this change. The Constitution provides that the authorities must try an accused person within 4 months if the alleged crime carries a sentence of less than 2 years, or within 1 year if the crime carries a longer sentence. The law requires that prisoners awaiting trial be housed separately from those convicted. In practice, judicial and police authorities frequently ignored these time limits. According to the CNDH and NGO's, the authorities often held criminal defendants with convicted prisoners and for longer than allowed by law before going to trial.

Arbitrary arrest and detention continued to be among the most common human rights abuses. For the period May 1995 to December 1996, the CNDH reported 303 findings of arbitrary detention and 36 cases in which it found that authorities held prisoners incommunicado. The Human Rights Commission for the Federal District reported 272 complaints of arbitrary detention for the period from October 1995 to September 1996. It found the most common complaint to be delay in the administration of justice, with 602 complaints. The Commission was critical of numerous arrest orders in the Federal District being ignored or unresolved.

In April 1995, the police arrested Mauricio Franco Sanchez for physically blocking efforts to build a golf course on an environmentally protected area in Tepoztlan, Morelos. In January 1996, a court sentenced Franco to a term of 10 years and 7 months, but he was released on July 8. The police also arrested several other members of the Tepoztlan United Committee who protested construction of the golf course and held them on charges of participating in a murder. Several human rights groups contend that the police are really holding these individuals because they protested construction of the golf course. In response to local protests, the developers of the proposed golf course and housing and resort complex canceled the project in April.

Detention of opposition political activists is neither widespread nor systematic but does occur frequently for short periods of time. Judges often failed to sentence indigenous detainees within legally mandated periods.

For the period from June 1994 to December 1996, the CNDH reviewed 7,823 files of indigenous persons detained in Mexican jails. The Commission recommended the immediate release of 1,887 persons. By year's end, the authorities had released 1,069 of them; 818 cases were still pending. Of those states with the largest numbers of indigenous prisoners, the CNDH reviewed 2,111 cases in Oaxaca, and recommended 403 releases, of which 272 have been accomplished; 1,106 cases in Veracruz, with 331 recommendations for release and 198 releases; and 639 cases in Puebla, with 154 releases recommended, and 63 releases took place.

Federal prosecutors continued to adhere to the recommendation by the National Indigenous Institute (INI) that they drop charges against first-time offenders accused of drug cultivation, as drug traffickers often forced indigenous defendants, who do not understand the legal significance of their actions, to grow the crops.

Many detainees report that officials ask them to pay bribes for release before formal arraignment; many of those arrested report that they are able to bribe officials to have them drop charges before they go before a judge. Corruption is rampant throughout the system.

In an effort to instill a greater sense of professionalism and root out corruption in the Mexico City police force, and in the aftermath of clashes between police and protesting teachers in May, President Zedillo replaced Police Commissioner David Garay with General Enrique Salgado Cordero. Salgado named about 40 military officers to key positions on the metropolitan police force. Many sectors of society, including human rights groups, expressed concern that this would result in increased militarization of the Mexico City police. Other broad sectors of society supported the move. Salgado announced a 22-point reform program, which includes human rights training for all police, a review of the institutional structure, and greater economic resources for the police.

Robberies committed by policemen are common. In a number of cases in northern border states, judges, police, and persons posing as attorneys extorted large sums of money ($3,000 to $10,000) from tourists to "fix" real or fabricated infractions. State human rights commission authorities in Coahuila widely published a toll-free telephone number for reporting police abuses, but, according to the Coahuila Human Rights Commission, there were few if any such calls.

Most citizens view the police as corrupt and unhelpful: 64 percent of crime victims in Mexico City did not report incidents to law enforcement authorities. According to a reliable 1995 poll, 75 percent of those surveyed felt that the justice system was riddled with corruption. Police academies in some states, such as Coahuila, Durango, and Sonora, sought to improve police conduct by offering special courses aimed at greater professionalization. However, such progress among the various police forces is highly uneven.

On August 16, then-Attorney General Antonio Lozano dismissed 737 federal judicial police officers as part of an effort to professionalize the police, control corruption, and combat organized crime and drug trafficking. These dismissals followed the gradual removal of over 500 PGR personnel since Lozano took office in December 1994. Lozano also announced creation of a technical administrative commission to establish guidelines and internal controls for federal police personnel. This commission will monitor the performance of federal police officers and determine if they should remain on the force.

These reforms are part of a wide-ranging package to reduce corruption and promote professionalism, which includes new training and recruitment procedures for the PGR, closer supervision of PGR officers, and a reorganization of the PGR's structure. In addition, CNDH president Madrazo launched, together with the Human Rights Commissions for the 31 states and the Federal District, a nationwide initiative to increase awareness of victims' rights. On December 2, Lozano resigned as Attorney General and was replaced by CNDH president Madrazo. President Zedillo emphasized that one of the new Attorney General's tasks was to complete the reform and cleanup of the PGR.

The law does not permit exile, and it is not practiced.

e. *Denial of Fair Public Trial.*—The judiciary is nominally independent but in the past has been influenced by the executive branch, and corruption and inefficiency were commonplace.

The federal court system is composed of 98 district courts, over which are 32 circuit courts of appeal and a Supreme Court. In 1995 President Zedillo proposed and Congress approved extensive judicial reform legislation. These reforms included: Selecting most lower and appellate federal court judges and law secretaries by competitive examinations; creating an independent judicial council to administer the federal courts (except the Supreme Court, which administers itself); and requiring two-thirds of the Senate to confirm the appointment of a Supreme Court justice. The reforms also provided the Supreme Court with the authority to strike down a law for unconstitutionality (one-third of the Congress, one-third of a state congress, or the Attorney General must ask the Supreme Court to review the constitutionality of a law before it can be declared unconstitutional). Significant efforts to implement these reforms were made in 1996. The first groups of federal judges chosen by examination entered the system.

The judicial trial system is based on the Napoleonic Code and consists of a series of fact-gathering hearings at which the court receives documentary evidence or testimony. In addition, officials may add notarized documents to the official case file without authentication. While the law requires that these hearings must be open to the public, in practice the courts ignore this law. Journalists covering judicial proceedings must rely on statements of attorneys outside the courtroom as to what occurred inside. A judge alone in chambers reviews the case file and makes a final written ruling based thereon. The record of the proceeding is not available to the public; only the parties and, by special motion, the victim may have access to the official file.

While there is a constitutional right to an attorney at all stages of criminal proceedings, in practice, the authorities often do not assure adequate representation for many poor defendants. Attorneys are not always available during the questioning of defendants; in some instances a defense attorney will attempt to represent several clients simultaneously by entering different rooms to certify that he was present although he did not actually attend the full proceedings. In the case of indigenous defendants, many of whom do not speak Spanish, the situation is often worse. The courts do not routinely furnish translators for them at all stages of criminal proceedings, and thus defendants may be unaware of the status of their case.

Some human rights groups claim that activists arrested in connection with land disputes and other civil disobedience activities are in fact political prisoners. The Government asserts that the system fairly prosecutes those charged in sometimes violent land invasions for common crimes, such as homicide and damage to property.

f. *Arbitrary Interference With Privacy, Family, Home, or Correspondence.*—The Constitution provides for the rights to privacy, family, home, and correspondence. The law requires search warrants, but there are credible claims that unlawful searches without warrants are common.

On November 21, 1995, Congress passed the General Law for the Coordination of the National System of Public Security, and the Government created a National Council for Public Security on March 7. It is composed of the heads of the Government's main offices related to internal security such as the Secretariats of the Interior, Defense, Navy, the PGR, and chief of the Mexico City police. It is also responsible for coordinating joint actions between local and federal police, assisting with international cooperation programs, and preparing legislation on security matters for the Congress.

On November 7, Congress passed the Federal Law against Organized Crime which, among other changes, allows for electronic surveillance with a judicial order. The law prohibits electronic surveillance in cases of electoral, civil, commercial, labor, or administrative matters.

g. *Use of Excessive Force and Violations of Humanitarian Law in Internal Conflicts.*—There were no reported clashes between troops stationed in Chiapas and the EZLN during 1996. The military continues to deny any responsibility for abuses committed during the early stages of the Chiapas rebellion in 1994. The military authorities who have jurisdiction have failed to punish any military personnel or government officials for committing abuses, although the CNDH issued an interim report in May 1994 finding that there was reason to believe that the military had injured or killed civilians in aerial attacks, and that there were summary executions, illegal detentions, and instances of torture.

Amnesty International reported that on February 9, 1995, soldiers kidnaped two indigenous men, Alfredo Jimenez Santis and Mario Alvarez Lopez. The soldiers tortured and beat the men for 5 days at a military installation in the state capital Tuxtla Gutierrez and then released them. The authorities took no disciplinary action against the soldiers.

The Chiapas women's rights organization, "Women of San Cristobal de Las Casas," has documented 50 cases of rape during 1995 in the municipalities of

Altamirano, San Andres Larrainzar, Amatenango, San Cristobal, and Ocosingo. They alleged that some were committed by security forces.

On February 9, 1995, the authorities arrested Javier Elorriaga Berdegue, a journalist covering the EZLN conflict, and charged him with terrorism, conspiring against the State, and rebellion. In May after his 1-year judicial proceeding was over, a court sentenced Elorriaga to 13 years' imprisonment. On June 7, however, an appeals court overturned Elorriaga's conviction and released him from prison.

Army troops were also deployed in Guerrero following the June 28 appearance of the EPR on the 1-year anniversary of the Aguas Blancas killings. Sweeps conducted by police and military personnel resulted in a number of arrests. Many NGO's expressed concern that the security forces tortured some of the detainees. There were reports of torture in connection with arrests by security forces searching for members of the EPR in the state of Guerrero. Soldiers detained Jose Nava Andrade, a member of the Organization of Towns and Settlers of Guerrero, on July 2 and allegedly tortured him in an attempt to force him to confess membership in the EPR. Information regarding this and similar cases was presented to the Inter-American Commission on Human Rights when the commission visited Mexico in July. Amnesty International also reported that the authorities arrested Hilario Mesino Acosta of the OCSS on July 3 and allegedly tortured him, accusing him of being an EPR member. At year's end, they were holding Mesino in the state prison in Acapulco, Guerrero.

On the night of August 28, the EPR carried out 18 small-scale actions in 7 states, ranging from attacks on municipal police stations in Guerrero and Oaxaca to handing out propaganda on roads in Chiapas. These attacks left 14 dead and 23 wounded. Police and military personnel deployed to search for the group in the states where there was reported EPR activity and arrested about 45 alleged EPR members. Many human rights groups reported that some of the persons detained were tortured or mistreated by the authorities. Following the emergence of the EPR, human rights groups noted an increase in the presence of army troops in the Huasteca area of Veracruz and in parts of Oaxaca.

The law does not require civil trial of soldiers involved in civil crimes, and the military continues to handle such cases. The Constitution provides for military jurisdiction for crimes or offenses involving any violation of military discipline. In cases in which a member of the military commits a crime and is arrested by civil authorities, the military has the right to immediately request transfer of the case to military jurisdiction. Several NGO's complained about the growing militarization of the country and expressed the fear that military abuses would not be subject to civil jurisdiction.

Section 2. Respect for Civil Liberties, Including:

a. *Freedom of Speech and Press.*—The Constitution provides for freedom of speech and the press, and the Government generally respects these rights in practice. Mass media are not subject to formal censorship from any element of government. Direct criticism of the Government, especially in print media in Mexico City, is severe and commonplace. Journalists and international scholars persuasively argue that editorial independence in many, if not most, of Mexico's news organizations is tilted towards the Government by a complex system that has developed over the years. The key elements of the system are: Coincidence of interest between media owners and the Government; broadcast licensing; official advertising (some of it disguised as news coverage); a state-run newsprint sales company; and a variety of cash and noncash payments to journalists from various levels of government. One important editor reports that he is the subject of government-inspired rumor mongering.

In June an appeals court overturned journalist Javier Elorriaga Berdegue's conviction on charges brought after he was arrested while covering the ELZN (see Section 1.g.).

The greatest concentration of official influence is in television. Television broadcasters give a contribution of air time—in the form of a 12.5 percent tax on advertising revenues —instead of actual cash payments. This system lowers effective tax rates of the broadcasters and gives the Government guaranteed access to this powerful medium. The giant Televisa chain dominates television, and its extremely close relation to the Government is openly acknowledged. The second national network, TV Azteca, has come under a cloud since the imprisoned Raul Salinas, brother of the former President, acknowledged loaning its principal shareholder part of the network's purchase price—although there is no evidence of criminality, and TV Azteca is clearly more distant from the Government than Televisa.

The Government has the power to grant or withdraw broadcast licenses. Media observers continue to allege privately that the Government delays issuance of broadcast licenses as an implicit control over broadcasters, but they have not proven any allegations of broadcast licensing delays by the Government. There have also been printed allegations of favoritism by the Government in granting broadcast licenses, but again, such allegations have never been proven. This possibility may lead to self-censorship by some broadcast media.

The CNDH reviews all reports of attacks on journalists that it receives. The CNDH received 17 allegations of attacks on journalists in the exercise of their profession during the latest reporting year (May 1995 to May 1996). There were 11 such complaints in the previous year. Most reports received by the CNDH were from outside Mexico City, and most alleged violent acts or intimidation. The 1995 murder of a newspaper reporter in Tijuana was still under investigation by state authorities in Baja California.

The Constitution recognizes academic freedom in higher education, and the Government respects this provision in practice.

b. *Freedom of Peaceful Assembly and Association.*—The Constitution provides for the right of assembly, and the Government respects this right in practice. The only requirement for holding demonstrations is that groups wishing to meet in public areas inform local police authorities; public demonstrations are held frequently.

The Constitution provides for the right to organize or affiliate with political parties, and the Government respects this right in practice. Opposition and independent associations functioned freely without government interference or restriction. The Federal Electoral Code recognizes national political associations. Such political associations can participate in elections through an agreement with one political party but are not allowed to use their names or symbols during the election campaigns. Private associations do not have legal status until they receive their official designation from the Federal Electoral Institute (IFE). In November the IFE recognized 24 citizen organizations.

c. *Freedom of Religion.*—The Constitution provides for the right to practice the religion of one's choice, and the authorities generally respect this right in practice. However, local authorities sometimes infringed on this right (see Section 5). The law bars clergy from holding public office and from advocating partisan political positions.

d. *Freedom of Movement Within the Country, Foreign Travel, Emigration, and Repatriation.*—The Constitution provides for the right of free movement, and the Government does not generally restrict movement of its citizens into, out of, or within the country.

The law provides protection for foreigners who face political persecution.

The Government cooperates with the office of the U.N. High Commissioner for Refugees (UNHCR) and other humanitarian organizations in assisting refugees. With the UNHCR, the Government assisted with the repatriation of Guatemalan refugees desiring to return home who had fled their country during the civil war in the 1980's and granted others wishing to stay in Mexico official immigrant residency status. The Government agrees, in practice, with the principle of first asylum and reviews each claim on a case-by-case basis with the assistance of the UNHCR.

During the first half of 1996, Mexico expelled 57,502 "undocumented" or illegal immigrants, the majority of whom were Guatemalans. After Guatemalans, the largest groups were Salvadorans and Hondurans. Many of those expelled were en route to the northern border with the United States. There were no reports of forced return of persons to a country where they feared persecution.

Illegal immigrants rarely file charges in cases of crimes committed against them. The authorities generally immediately deport illegal immigrants who come to their attention; therefore, a pending case brought by an illegal immigrant is subject to dismissal once the immigrant has been deported. In an effort to promote the human rights of migrants and to inform them of their rights, the CNDH and the Secretary of Government published in May a "Guide to Human Rights for Migrants." The Government is translating the guide into several indigenous dialects. Additionally, in August, the Interior Ministry established two additional Grupo-Beta type units (multiagency migrant protection units) along its southern border with Guatemala. In June and July, the Government negotiated agreements with Guatemala and Belize designed to make legal entry and exit more transparent and safer.

Until 1995 children who were in Mexico illegally did not have the right to matriculate in public schools. According to new Education Secretariat guidelines, any child may now be registered for public school with a Mexican or foreign birth certificate. Implementation of the new guidelines varies widely from state to state, however.

Section 3. Respect for Political Rights: The Right of Citizens to Change Their Government

The Constitution provides citizens with the right peacefully to change their government through periodic elections. The PRI dominates politics and has controlled the Government since the party was founded in 1929. It has won every presidential election since then and has maintained power, in part, by relying on public patronage, use of government and party organizational resources, and, in the past, electoral fraud. However, the Government no longer restricts the functioning of political opponents.

In 1996 state and municipal elections were held in the states of Baja California Sur, Coahuila, Guerrero, Hidalgo, Mexico, Nayarit, and Quintana Roo. These elections were generally peaceful and orderly.

An electoral reform agreement among the major political parties was approved in August. The ruling PRI and the opposition National Action Party (PAN), the PRD, and Labor Party agreed to a package of constitutional amendments that includes tighter financial regulation of election campaigns; a revised formula for public funding, including access to electronic media; a reduction in the number of congressional representatives allowed for any one party from 315 to 300; putting electoral law violations under the jurisdiction of the Supreme Court; full autonomy for the Federal Electoral Institute; and the first-ever direct popular election of a mayor for Mexico City. However, due to disagreements on issues such as campaign spending limits and rules governing coalitions, PAN and PRD legislators opposed the legislation implementing the accords. Since the PRI has a majority in both houses, Congress approved the reform package in a party-line vote in November.

The PAN protested manipulation of the electoral appeal process of the November 1995 municipal elections in Huejotzingo, Puebla, and on that basis had refused to participate in national electoral reform talks. Negotiations between the Government and the PAN resolved the dispute. On May 15, the PRI mayor of Huejotzingo stepped down from office, and pursuant to a vote in the state legislature was replaced by a PAN official. Shortly thereafter, national electoral reform talks resumed and resulted in the agreement described above.

A severe failure in the electoral process has been the lack of any meaningful prosecution of those accused of electoral crimes. Despite numerous accusations of fraud in various state races, the authorities declined to prosecute any electoral crimes. The placing of electoral law violations under the jurisdiction of the recently reformed Supreme Court is a step to address this problem.

Another continuing major obstacle to electoral reform is the deeply entrenched antidemocratic tradition of unchecked power exercised by local bosses over peasants in rural areas. These bosses often exercise some measure of control over virtually every aspect of peasants' lives, including how they vote. One NGO that studied the results of the August 21, 1994, elections in a remote district found that there were 30 percent more votes for the PRI in polling places where no independent observers were present.

Although there is no systematic exclusion of women and indigenous persons, they are underrepresented in politics. Women, however, hold numerous congressional seats and continue to increase their representation in political offices. At the beginning of his administration, President Zedillo appointed three women to his Cabinet: The Comptroller General, the Secretary of Tourism, and the Secretary of the Environment, Natural Resources, and Fisheries. In addition, there are 67 women in the 500-member Chamber of Deputies and 16 in the 128-member Senate.

Section 4. Governmental Attitude Regarding International and Nongovernmental Investigation of Alleged Violations of Human Rights

A wide variety of human rights groups operate largely without government restriction, investigating and publishing their findings on human rights cases. The number of NGO's dedicated to the defense of human rights has nearly doubled in the last 2 years. As of May, 376 NGO's monitor human rights problems, compared with 191 in November 1993. Government officials are generally cooperative and responsive to NGO views, and the Congress has established a citizen participation committee to act as a liaison with NGO's. In July the Inter-American Commission on Human Rights visited Mexico at the invitation of President Zedillo and met with over a hundred human rights groups.

However, many serious problems remain. For example, Amnesty International reported that leaders and members of numerous human rights NGO's received death threats for criticizing the human rights situation in the country. These included David Fernandez Davalos and Jose Lavanderos Yanez, director and lawyer respectively of the Miguel Agustin Pro Juarez Human Rights Center (PRODH) in Mexico City; Graciela Zavaleta Sanchez, president of the Mahatma Gandhi Regional Human Rights Commission in Oaxaca; Lourdes Saenz, member of the Citizens for Human Rights in Nuevo Leon; Francisco Goitia and Javier Nunez, president and lawyer respectively of the Human Rights Committee of Tabasco; Emelia Gonzalez Sandoval, founding member of the Human Rights Defense and Solidarity Commission of Chihuahua; and Maria Teresa Jardi and Julian Andrade Jardi of the Fund for Assistance, Promotion and Development in Mexico City. Death threats were also received by Pilar Noriega, Digna Ochoa, and Enrique Flota, lawyers for the PRODH representing alleged members of the EZLN.

To address human rights abuses, the Government established the CNDH in 1990. Since that time, the CNDH has received a total of 45,110 complaints of which it has concluded its investigations in 43,784 cases; it is still processing the remainder. Of those cases in which it made recommendations that appropriate action be taken against the offenders, its recommendations have been totally or partially followed 95 percent of the time. The CNDH cited 55 recommendations which authorities had been "negligent" in implementing during the past 6 years.

For the period of May 1995 to May 1996, the CNDH made 116 recommendations to government authorities. Of these, the authorities fully complied with 33, partially complied with 68, and rejected 4, while 18 were in various stages of processing. CNDH efforts resulted in sanctions against 282 public servants, as follows: 161 criminal actions; 10 dismissals; 17 declared incompetent for public service; 46 suspensions; 44 reprimands or warnings; and 4 fines. The CNDH publishes the names of all sanctioned public servants. In some cases, authorities applied multiple sanctions, but CNDH statistics list cases under the most severe sanction applied.

In its review of the various state human rights commissions' decisions, by September the CNDH had issued 78 recommendations for reconsideration or renewal of action. State commissions complied completely with 70 of the recommendations and partially with 8.

Some NGO's note that the CNDH lacks both autonomy and enforcement authority. Additionally, some contend that it has become too large and bureaucratic and that the state commissions are ineffectual.

In March 1995, the Federal District Attorney General's office announced the opening of a new subsection for human rights to address human rights abuses in Mexico City, by far the most populous jurisdicition. The office handled an average of two complaints per day against Federal District police officers, as well as other cases. In December the PGR also opened an office to strengthen communication with NGO's.

Then-Defense Minister General Antonio Riviello imprisoned General Jose Francisco Gallardo Rodriguez in November 1993 on a range of charges, including embezzlement and dishonoring the military. Gallardo claims that the embezzlement charges, which date back 7 years, had previously been abandoned for lack of evidence. He maintains that military authorities are persecuting him because of an academic dissertation calling for the establishment of a military human rights ombudsman's office. The army continues to hold Gallardo but has reduced the previous inordinately high level of security of his incarceration. The IACHR considered the Gallardo case in October, and the commission called for his immediate release and for the Government to indemnify him for damages suffered as a result of his imprisonment.

Section 5. Discrimination Based on Race, Sex, Religion, Disability, Language, or Social Status

The Constitution states that men and women are equal before the law. It also provides that education should sustain the ideals of "fraternity and equal rights of all mankind, avoiding privileges of race, sects, groups, sexes, or individuals." These provisions are not effectively enforced.

Amnesty International cites Mexico as one of the countries in which homosexual men and women are most likely to be victims of abuse and violence. Liborio Cruz, a 19-year-old male prostitute, was beaten to death by a group of men in Mexico City in June 1995. At least 12 homosexuals and 9 male prostitutes were killed in Tuxtla Gutierrez between 1991 and 1993. An independent prosecutor took over the investigation of the Tuxtla Gutierrez murders in April 1994 but had made no progress in solving them by the end of 1996.

Women.—The most pervasive violations of women's rights involve domestic and sexual violence, which is believed to be widespread and vastly underreported. Domestic assault is a crime, but in 10 states the "right to correct" a wife and children is not a crime unless this abuse involves cruelty or excessive frequency. Women are reluctant to report abuse or file charges, and, even when notified, the police are reluctant to intervene in what society considers to be a domestic matter. The municipality of Chimalhuacan, Mexico state, where the average time for police action on rape cases is 2 months, is a typical example of the difficulty rape victims experience. This is attributable to police inexperience in handling these cases, lack of investigative techniques, and unwillingness to get involved in what are often considered domestic affairs.

The Attorney General's office for the Federal District operates rape crisis centers around the city. Few women, however, avail themselves of the centers' services. Out of a municipal female population of more than 10 million, only 627 approached the centers. The majority were girls: 27 percent were between the ages of 13 and 17, and 25 percent were under the age of 13. Some women who availed themselves of the centers' services reported abusive, humiliating, and unprofessional behavior by police and medical examiners who work in the centers.

Although the Constitution provides for equality between the sexes, neither the authorities nor society in general respect this in practice. The legal treatment of women's rights is uneven. Women have the right to own property in their own names and to file for separation and divorce. However, in some states a woman may not bring suit to establish paternity and thereby obtain child support, unless the child was a product of rape or cohabitation; the child resides with the father; or there is written proof of paternity.

The Constitution and labor law provide that women shall have the same rights and obligations as men, and "equal pay shall be given for equal work performed in equal jobs, hours of work and conditions of efficiency." However, women are generally paid less and are concentrated in lower paying occupations. Labor law includes extensive maternity protection, including 6 weeks off before and 6 weeks off after childbirth, time off for breast feeding in adequate and hygienic surroundings provided by the employer, and, during pregnancy, full pay and no dismissals, heavy or dangerous work or exposure to toxic substances. There are reports that, in order to avoid these expensive requirements, some employers deliberately violate these provisions and expose pregnant women to difficult or hazardous conditions to make them quit; this reportedly occurs particularly in the low-wage, low-skill, high-turnover end of the in-bond export processing (maquila) industry. These reports claim that state and (for health and safety) federal labor authorities are unable or unwilling to enforce those provisions. Indeed, the number of maquila plants far outstrips what state and federal inspectors can handle. Discrimination in hiring does not seem to be addressed in labor law. Many lower wage employers discriminate in favor of women in hiring but against pregnant women because their benefits make them more expensive. Many employers require women to certify that they are not pregnant at the time of hiring. Others test applicants for pregnancy.

In 1995 the CNDH found that the largest number of complaints against health care institutions involved negligence or abuse during childbirth by medical personnel and charges of forced sterilization. It said that the number of such complaints had grown, in large part due to women's increased awareness of their rights. The Constitution states that all persons have the right to make free, responsible, and informed decisions on the number of children they choose to have. The 1984 General Health Law provides for criminal action against those who pressure a woman to undergo sterilization procedures or perform such procedures without the woman's consent. In a number of cases, charges have been brought against doctors for sterilizing a woman or inserting an IUD without her consent. The scope of this problem is difficult to quantify, although a number of NGO's and government agencies follow the issue, because women may not realize that these procedures have been performed on them or may be reluctant to come forward and file a complaint. The CNDH has recommended that medical administrators train their staffs to be more aware when dealing with such patients. The Government has instituted a number of mechanisms, including better training and medical review boards, to address the problem.

Children.—Children under the age of 18 make up over 40 percent of the population. While the Government is committed to children's health and education, it has failed to allocate sufficient resources to fulfill that commitment. Nine years of education are compulsory. There is no societal pattern of abuse against children, but children's advocates report many such cases. The United Nations Children's Fund (UNICEF) classifies Mexico as "lacking adequate strategies" to combat malnutrition among children, and reports that 30,000 children die each year of causes related to malnutrition. According to UNICEF, the Department of the Federal District, and the National System for the Integral Development of the Family, more than 13,000 children live on the streets of Mexico City, many the victims of family violence. The children themselves often become involved with alcohol, drugs, prostitution, and petty thievery. Police in Hermosillo, Sonora, conducted "sweeps" of street children, incarcerating many for short periods, in order to "clean up" the city.

While the Government and NGO's conduct a number of programs for street children, corrupt police exacerbate the problem by pressuring children to commit petty crimes and extorting profits from them. The CNDH has a program for protection of children's rights which includes educating children on their rights and reviewing legislation to ensure compliance with relevant international conventions. In January the Human Rights Commission for the Federal District opened the "Tree House," a space designed for children 8 to 11 years of age to help teach them about human rights and obligations. Over 26,000 children visited it.

People With Disabilities.—The law requires access for disabled persons to public facilities in Mexico City but not elsewhere in the country. In practice, however, most public buildings and facilities do not comply with the law. Recognizing that disabled persons often suffer employment discrimination, the Federal District instituted a new tax rebate program for businesses employing disabled persons. For the first time, the Public Education Sub-Secretariat for the Federal District mandated that all public and private schools grant access to physically (although not mentally) disabled children and that schools make the necessary arrangements (e.g., installation of ramps) to facilitate access. The National Public Education Secretariat printed 27,000 textbooks in Braille in 1995.

Indigenous People.—The indigenous population has long been victim of discriminatory treatment. The Chiapas uprising focused unprecedented attention on the demands of that state's indigenous persons for increased economic and social rights. Among its basic demands, the EZLN called on the Government to enact measures to protect indigenous cultures, provide more opportunity for employment, and invest in schools, clinics, and infrastructure projects. The Government, through the INI and the CNDH, operates programs to educate indigenous groups (many members of which do not speak Spanish) about their political and human rights, and it generally professes respect for their desire to retain elements of their traditional culture. The CNDH organized training courses on human rights for indigenous communities in Chiapas, Hidalgo, Mexico, Michoacan, Oaxaca, Chiapas and Nayarit. The courses were taught in the communities' indigenous languages.

More than 130 NGO's are dedicated to the promotion and protection of indigenous rights. Indigenous people do not live on independently governed reservations, although some indigenous communities exercise considerable local control over economic and social issues. These communities apply traditional law to resolve a variety of disputes, including allegations of crimes. However, these groups remain largely outside the country's political and economic mainstream, a result of longstanding patterns of economic and social development, and in many cases their ability to participate in decisions affecting their lands, cultural traditions, and allocation of natural resources is negligible.

The 1992 reforms in agrarian law were expected to promote economic development in the countryside, but indigenous groups generally perceived the reforms as intended to break up indigenous communal landholdings and prevent the groups from obtaining title to new lands. A 1991 amendment to the federal law requires that an interpreter be present at every stage of criminal proceedings against indigenous persons and stipulates that "their customs and traditions shall be taken into account." However, the courts continue to sentence indigenous people without the benefit of interpreters. The CNDH had reviewed the cases of 7,823 jailed indigenous persons and sought the release of 1,887. Of those, 1,069 have been released since June 1994, largely through CNDH efforts.

The General Education Act states that "teaching shall be promoted in the national language (i.e., Spanish) without prejudice to the protection and promotion of indigenous languages." However, many indigenous persons speak only their native languages. Non-Spanish speakers are frequently taken advantage of in commercial transactions involving bilingual middlemen, and have great difficulty finding employment in Spanish-speaking areas. Over 50 indigenous languages are currently spoken in Mexico.

Although the law provides some protection for the indigenous, and the Government provides indigenous communities support through social and economic assistance programs, legal guarantees and social welfare programs are not sufficient to meet the needs of all indigenous persons.

Religious Minorities.—In the highlands of Chiapas and other indigenous areas, traditional leaders sometimes acquiesced in, or actually ordered, the expulsions of Protestants belonging primarily to evangelical groups. In many cases the expulsions involved the burning of homes and crops, beatings, and, occasionally, killings.

In San Juan Chamula, Chiapas, where local authorities have expelled an estimated 30,000 evangelicals over the past 30 years, the evangelicals and the local authorities reached a truce in December 1995. Since that time, there have been no further expulsions of evangelicals from San Juan Chamula. The local authorities agreed that children of the evangelicals would be allowed to return to public school, from which they had been excluded for 3 years. However, in September, the children of evangelicals were once again excluded, and in retaliation, evangelical groups occupied these schools. By October the situation for the most part had been resolved, and at year's end the evangelicals' childen were attending public school in all but one community, Arvenza II, where the parents chose to keep their children at home.

In July the evangelicals began constructing a temple in the community of Arvenza I. Following protests by the local authorities, and in order to avoid a collapse of the December 1995 truce, the evangelicals agreed to halt temporarily construction of the temple. In September the traditional leadership in San Juan Chamula forced the mayor to step down and replaced him with a new leader opposing construction of the temple. By year's end, however, temple construction was allowed to resume.

Several evangelical members were jailed and fined in San Juan Yahe, Oaxaca. In addition, reliable press reports noted continued expulsions of evangelicals by that community because the evangelicals' faith violated the "customs and traditional practices" of the community.

The Federal Government Office of Religious Affairs actively promotes religious tolerance and held symposiums in July in the states of Oaxaca and Chiapas emphasizing the constitutional right of freedom of religion.

Section 6. Worker Rights

a. *The Right of Association.*—The Constitution and the Federal Labor Law (LFT) provide workers with the right to form and join trade unions of their choice. About 30 percent of the total work force is unionized, mostly in the formal sector, where about one-half the labor force is employed. This implies a formal sector unionization rate nearly twice that high.

No prior approval is needed to form unions, but they must register with the Federal Labor Secretariat (STPS) or state labor boards (JLCA) to obtain legal status in order to function. Registration requirements are not onerous. There are credible allegations, however, that the STPS or JLCA occasionally withhold or delay registration of unions hostile to government policies, employers, or established unions or register extortionists or labor racketeers falsely claiming to represent workers. To remedy this latter problem, STPS officials require evidence that unions are genuine and representative before registering them.

Like the Federal Labor Board (JFCA), the JLCA are tripartite. Although trade union presence on the boards is a generally positive feature, it can lead to unfair partiality in representation disputes; the member from an established union may work to dissuade a JLCA from recognizing a rival organization. The matter of trade union registration was the subject of followup activities in 1996, pursuant to a 1995 agreement reached in ministerial consultations under the North American Agreement on Labor Cooperation (NAALC), the side agreement on labor to the North American Free Trade Agreement (NAFTA).

Unions form federations and confederations freely without government approval. Most unions belong to such bodies. They too must register to have legal status. The largest trade union central is the Confederation of Mexican Workers (CTM), traditionally a sector of the ruling PRI, but affiliation is individual, and this is to be emphasized in new reforms, both within the PRI and in legislation under consideration in the Congress. The Federal Employee Union Federation (FSTSE), the Revolutionary Worker and Peasant Confederation, and most of the 35 separate national unions, smaller confederations, and federations in the Labor Congress (CT) are also allied with the PRI. However, several are not, including the large teachers' union, which severed its PRI ties several years ago, freeing its minority factions to cooperate openly with other parties, particularly the PRD. Rivalries within and between PRI-allied centrals are strong. There also are a few small labor federations and independent unions outside the CT which are not allied to the PRI. One is the small, left-of-center Authentic Labor Federation (FAT). Most FAT members sympathize with the PRD, but the FAT is independent and not formally tied to the PRD.

Union officers help select, run as, and campaign for, PRI candidates in federal and state elections and support PRI government policies at crucial moments. This gives unions considerable influence on government policies but limits their freedom of action to defend member interests in other ways, particularly when this might harm the Government or PRI. The CT, especially the CTM, is well represented in the PRI senatorial and congressional delegations.

The International Labor Organization (ILO) Conference Committee of Experts (COE) has found that certain restrictions in federal employee labor law, adopted at FSTSE request, violate ILO Convention 87 on freedom of association, which Mexico has ratified. These provisions allow only one union per jurisdiction, forbid union members to quit the union, and prohibit reelection of union officials. Again in 1996, the COE and the ILO Committee on Application of Standards (CAS) reiterated their criticism and asked the Government to amend these provisions. A Supreme Court decision invalidated similar restrictions in the laws of two states, but the decision applied only in the specific instances challenged.

There were developments regarding union representation in the new Environment Secretariat, an issue raised again in the CAS debate and in a submission under the NAALC. This Secretariat, formed late in 1994, merged the small former Fisheries Secretariat with much larger sections from the Agricultural and Social Development Secretariats. In early 1995, the Fisheries Union applied to the Federal Employee Labor Tribunal (TFCA) to change its name to union of the new secretariat. The TFCA denied the request. The TFCA is bipartite, with FSTSE as well as government members. Following the TFCA decision, the FSTSE, applying its statutes, convoked a convention, with delegates elected by secret ballot, to form a new union and elect its officers. The TFCA recognized the new union and withdrew recognition from the old. The new union thus benefited from the contractual relationship giving union delegates time off with pay for union work. The dissolved union appealed to a court, which upheld the appeal and returned the matter to the TFCA. The TFCA restored the Fisheries Union's registration and revoked that of the new union (again upholding the legal provision allowing registration of only one union per entity, violating ILO Convention 87). The unregistered union continued benefiting from time off and dues. The TFCA held a representation election ("recount"—see Section 6.b.) for employees to choose by secret ballot between the two unions. The Fisheries Union lost by a wide margin and challenged the validity of the election, charging irregularities, but the TFCA confirmed the election results.

In April the Federal District municipal government reached agreement with the jailed leaders of the SUTAUR-100 union of the bankrupt former public municipal bus company Ruta-100. The Government agreed to concede and allow the union to operate two of the new private bus companies to replace Ruta-100. The Government also agreed to appeal to the courts to release the leaders from jail while SUTAUR reached a settlement with the former members who had sued it to recover money from the union pension and other funds. The union leaders were released on bail in July and the first of the two union enterprises began operating at the end of August.

The Constitution and the LFT provide for the right to strike. The law requires 6 to 10 days' advance strike notice, followed by brief government mediation. If federal or state authorities rule a strike "nonexistent" or "illicit," employees must remain at work, return to work within 24 hours, or face dismissal. If they rule the strike legal, the company or unit must shut down totally, management officials may not enter the premises until the strike is over, and the company may not hire striker replacements. Provisions for maintaining essential services are not onerous. The law makes filing a strike notice an effective, commonly used threat, but few strikes actually occur, usually to protect a failing company's assets from creditors and courts until an agreement is reached on severance pay. On the other hand, informal stoppages are a fairly common tactic, but are uncounted in statistics and seldom last long enough to be recognized or ruled out of order.

The law permits public sector strikes, but formal public sector strikes are rare. Informal ones are more frequent. Informal stoppages by dissident factions of the national teacher union shut down many schools in several states and the Federal District in late May and June, and demonstrations disrupted traffic in the capital, until settlements were reached which included pay for strike days and unpaid overtime to make up lost work and complete the school year.

During the first 11 months of 1996, the JFCA reported that 7,690 strike notices were filed and 51 legal strikes occurred in federal jurisdiction, involving 54,394 workers and the loss of 653,020 work days. Although there were fewer legal strikes than during the same period in 1995, they involved more workers and resulted in more lost workdays. There were no reports that federal or state labor authorities stretched legal requirements to rule strikes nonexistent or illicit, or used delays to prevent damaging strikes and force settlements.

The Constitution and the LFT protect labor organizations from government interference in their internal affairs, including strike decisions. This can protect undemocratic or corrupt union leaders. The law permits closed shop and exclusion clauses, allowing union leaders to vet and veto new hires and force dismissal of anyone the union expels. Such clauses are common in collective bargaining agreements.

In 1995 employer organizations abandoned earlier efforts to push for labor law reform to limit union leaders' power and give employers a free hand. In effect, Government, employers, and unions had negotiated reforms through tripartite national agreements and collective bargaining at the enterprise level, and through cooperation in programs to increase, and compensate for, productivity. With government blessing, after nearly a year of negotiation, national labor and employer organizations agreed in August on a joint effort to build a new labor culture of mutual respect and cooperation to boost productivity, wages, and competitiveness.

Unions are free to affiliate with, and are often active in, trade union internationals.

b. *The Right to Organize and Bargain Collectively.*—The Constitution and the LFT strongly uphold the right to organize and bargain collectively. Interest by a few employees, or a union strike notice, compels an employer to recognize a union and negotiate, or ask the federal or state labor board to hold a union recognition election. LFT prounion provisions led some employers to seek out or create independent "white" or company unions as an alternative to mainstream national or local unions. Representation elections are traditionally open, not secret, although this seems to be changing. Traditionally, management and union officials are present with the presiding labor board official when workers openly declare their votes, one by one. Such open recounts are prevailing practice but are not required by law or regulation. Secret ballots are held when all parties agree.

As the economic crisis deepened in 1995, the Government, at union insistence, agreed to end the system of annual national pacts negotiated by the Government and major trade union, employer, and rural organizations, which had voluntarily limited free collective bargaining for the past decade. Wage restraints no longer exist, except for those caused by the economic recession and difficult situation of most employers. The Government and major employer and union organizations continue to meet occasionally to reaffirm the 1995 "Alliance for Economic Recovery" (in October they signed an "Alliance for Growth") and agree on new tax breaks or minimum wage increases, but the Government has kept its commitment to free collective bargaining without guidelines or government interference. Wages in most union contracts appeared to keep pace with inflation in 1996, after losing ground in 1995.

Mexico's record in internal union democracy and transparency is mixed. Some unions are democratic, but corruption or authoritarian and strong-arm tactics are common in others. The few protests alleging such practices this year included the hospital local of the Mexico City public sector municipal employees' union. The election seemed to have been conducted reasonably fairly, but the losers protested the results, seized union offices until driven out, and demonstrated in the streets, drawing blood from themselves to protest inadequate hospital supplies. Another protest involved factory committee leaders trying to improve conditions at a U.S.-owned maquila factory in Sonora. The committee leaders were fired with the complicity of an allegedly-CTM "leader" who had a protection contract. The telephone union, representing the fired former factory committee leaders, the Union of Goods and Services, and the Communications Workers of America filed a submission for review by the U.S. National Administrative Office, under provisions of the NAALC.

The public sector is almost totally organized. Industrial areas are heavily organized. Even states with little industry have transport and public employee unions, and rural peasant organizations are omnipresent. The law protects workers from antiunion discrimination, but enforcement is uneven in the few states with low unionization.

Unionization and wage levels in the in-bond export sector vary by area. Wages have been lower in this sector than in most of industry, especially in low technology facilities and in the west, but the gap has narrowed and may now be minimal. Some observers allege poor working conditions, inadequate wages, and employer and government efforts to discourage unionization in this sector. There is no evidence that the Federal Government opposes unionization of the plants, which tend to be under state jurisdiction, but some state and local governments in the west are said to help some employers discourage unions.

c. *Prohibition of Forced or Compulsory Labor.*—The Constitution prohibits forced labor. There have been no credible reports of forced labor for many years, with the exception of abuses of refugees and illegal immigrants in Chiapas (see Section 2.d.).

d. *Minimum Age for Employment of Children.*—The law bans child labor and sets the minimum legal work age at 14 years. The activities of those 14 and 15 years of age are so restricted as to be uneconomic (no night or hazardous work and limited hours). The ILO reported that 18 percent of children 12 to 14 years of age work, often for parents or relatives. Enforcement is reasonably good at large and medium-sized companies, especially in export industries and those under federal jurisdiction. Enforcement is inadequate at the many small companies and in agriculture. It is nearly absent in the informal sector, despite government efforts. Most child labor is in the informal sector (including myriad underage street vendors) or in agriculture and rural areas. The CTM agricultural union's success years earlier in obtaining free transport for migrant seasonal workers from southern states to fields in the north inadvertently led to a significant increase in child labor. The union and employers were unable to convince indigenous farm workers to leave their families at home, and many have settled near worksites in the north. The union has had some limited success in negotiating with employers to finance bilingual education near worksites and in obtaining social security child care centers, but it has had difficulty in persuading member families not to bring their children into the fields. Riots over pay delays in the San Quintin valley in Baja California drew media attention to the child labor and other problems of indigenous worker families there and spurred the state government to pledge action to end child labor and other social ills.

The Federal Government increased the number of obligatory school years from 6 to 9 in 1992 and made parents legally liable for their children's attendance, as part of a reform to upgrade labor force skills and long-term efforts to continue increasing educational opportunities for and participation by youth. It has a cooperative program with UNICEF.

e. *Acceptable Conditions of Work.*—The Constitution and the LFT provide for a daily minimum wage. The Tripartite National Minimum Wage Commission (government, labor, and employers) usually sets minimum wage rates each December, effective January 1, for the whole year, but any of the three parties can ask that the board reconvene during the year to consider a changed situation. As part of the Alliance, (see Section 6.b.) labor, employers, and the Government agreed in 1995 to ask their representatives on the Commission to increase the minimum wage 10 percent on December 1, 1995, instead of the usual January 1 increase, and another 10 percent on April 1, 1996. They later agreed to make the April increase 12 percent. In December the Wage Commission adopted a 17 percent increase, based in part on the Government's projection of a 15 percent annual inflation rate for 1997. Organized labor's unhappiness with the 17 percent increase (some labor organizations had demanded an increase of at least 25 percent) produced some suggestions that the official increase be challenged in court because it does not meet the constitutional requirement to be adequate to cover basic costs of living, including recreation. By year's end, however, no legal action of this sort had been filed.

In Mexico City and nearby industrial areas, Acapulco, southeast Veracruz state's refining and petrochemical zone, and most border areas, the minimum daily wage after April 1 was $3.01 (22.60 new pesos). However, employers actually paid minimum wage earners $3.42 (25.76 new pesos) due to a supplemental 14 percent fiscal subsidy (negative income tax or tax credit, which the Government refunds to employers). These income supplements to the minimum wage, agreed in annual tripartite pacts, are for all incomes less than four times the minimum wage, decreasing as wages and benefits rise. In Guadalajara, Monterrey, and other advanced industrialized areas, the minimum daily wage (before the fiscal subsidy) was $2.79 (20.95 new pesos). In other areas, it was $2.54 (19.05 new pesos). There are higher minimums for some occupations, such as building trades.

Few workers (only 14 to 18 percent of the workers covered by social security) earn only the minimum wage. Industrial workers average three to four times the minimum wage, earning more at bigger, more advanced and prosperous enterprises.

The law and contract arrangements provide workers with extensive additional benefits. Legally required benefits include free social security medical treatment and pensions, individual worker housing and retirement accounts, substantial Christmas bonuses, paid vacations, and profit-sharing. Employer costs for these benefits add from about 27 percent of payroll at marginal enterprises to over 100 percent at major firms with good union contracts.

The LFT sets 48 hours as the legal workweek, although with pay for 56 hours. Workers asked to exceed 3 hours of overtime per day or required to work overtime on 3 consecutive days must be paid triple the normal wage. For most industrial workers, especially under union contract, the true workweek is 42 hours, although they are paid for 7 full 8-hour days. This is why unions jealously defend the legal ban on hourly wages.

The law requires employers to observe occupational safety and health regulations issued jointly by STPS and the social security institute (IMSS), and to pay contributions that vary according to their workplace safety and health experience ratings. LFT-mandated joint management and labor committees set standards and are responsible for workplace enforcement in plants and offices. These meet at least monthly to consider workplace needs and file copies of their minutes with federal labor inspectors, who assumed jurisdiction for all such inspections in 1987, supplanting state inspectors and considerably strengthening inspection. The inspectors schedule visits largely in response to these workplace committees.

Individual employees or unions may also complain directly to inspectors or safety and health officials. Workers may remove themselves from hazardous situations without jeopardizing their employment. Plaintiffs may bring complaints before the Federal Labor Board at no cost to themselves.

STPS and IMSS officials report that compliance is reasonably good at most large companies. Federal inspectors are stretched too thin for effective enforcement if companies do not comply voluntarily and fulfill their legal obligation to train workers in occupational health and safety matters, although the number of inspectors was increased in 1995. There are special problems in construction, where unskilled, untrained, poorly educated, transient labor is common, especially at many small sites and companies. Many unions, particularly in construction, are not organized effectively to provide training, to encourage members to work safely and healthily, to participate in the joint committees, or to insist on their rights. The STSP completed work in 1996 on a comprehensive reform of regulations and procedures (resulting from extensive consultations through NAFTA cooperative mechanisms) concerning workplace health and safety.

NICARAGUA

Nicaragua is a constitutional democracy, with a directly elected President, Vice President, and a unicameral National Assembly. President Violeta Barrios de Chamorro was elected in a free and fair election in 1990, defeating the incumbent Sandinista National Liberation Front (FSLN) candidate, Daniel Ortega. In October Arnoldo Aleman defeated Ortega in free and fair presidential elections and took office January 10, 1997. The executive branch coexists with the activist National Assembly. The Supreme Electoral Council is an independent fourth branch of government. The judiciary is independent but weak.

The President is the supreme chief of national defense and security forces. President Chamorro served as nominal Minister of Defense; there was no Defense Ministry. President-elect Aleman named a civilian to be Defense Minister to head a civilian-led Defense Ministry in his Government. The Ministry of Government oversees the National Police, which are formally charged with internal security. However, they share this responsibility with the army in rural areas. The National Assembly's approval in August of a new Organic Police Law helped to strengthen civilian control of the National Police and established a new office of professional responsibility. Reflecting enhanced civilian control, the security forces' conduct improved, although some members continued to commit human rights abuses.

Nicaragua is an extremely poor country. The economy is predominantly agricultural, dependent on sugar, beef, coffee, and seafood exports, with some light manufacturing. The economy grew an estimated 5 percent in 1996—the third year of growth after a decade of contraction. Despite significant foreign debt relief negotiated during the year, the country continued to have a precarious balance of payments position and remained heavily dependent on foreign assistance. Although investment increased, the slow and complicated resolution of confiscated property claims continued to hinder private investment. The unemployment rate was officially estimated at 17 percent, while total unemployment and underemployment may have reached 50 percent. The inflation rate was about 11 percent. Estimated per capita annual income was $470.

The Government's human rights record improved measurably, but serious problems remain. Police use of excessive force resulted in instances of extrajudicial killing, but these diminished from previous years. Police beat and otherwise abused detainees, often to obtain confessions. Torture, once a major problem, was rare. Prison conditions are poor. Security forces arbitrarily arrested and detained citizens. The judiciary is weak, and large case backlogs, long delays in trials, and lengthy pretrial detention are problems. A weak and antiquated judiciary continued to hamper prosecution of human rights abusers. The authorities at times infringed upon citizens' privacy rights. Discrimination against women and indigenous people is a problem. Violence against women, including rape and domestic abuse, remained a serious problem, and public officials took little effective action to counter it. Murder and kidnaping by criminal bands in northern rural areas were common.

The Organization of American States' International Support and Verification Commission (OAS/CIAV) reported 26 deaths of members of the former Nicaraguan Resistance (RN) occurring during the year, none of which it attributed to the security forces, unlike previous years. However, the conviction rate among killers, particularly but not exclusively of ex-RN, was so low that a state of impunity could still be said to exist. The Tripartite Commission, composed of the Government, the Catholic Church, and the OAS/CIAV, formally ended its work on October 18 after finishing its 4-year-long review of slayings earlier in the decade of ex-RN members and other demobilized combatants and impunity enjoyed by their killers. The Commission sent 83 cases involving 164 murders, as well as 181 specific recommendations, to the Government for followup, but little action had been taken by year's end. Only 1 of 211 persons it cited as being involved in the slayings that occurred since

1990 was in jail during the year. In June the Supreme Court finished its review of judicial proceedings undertaken in 26 Tripartite Commission cases in which army and police officials stood accused, but in which the military court system had either issued acquittals or failed to prosecute. The Court found deficiencies in procedure in one-third of the cases and sent them back to the Government for prosecution or other appropriate action.

RESPECT FOR HUMAN RIGHTS

Section 1. Respect for the Integrity of the Person, Including Freedom From:

a. *Political and Other Extrajudicial Killing.*—There were no reports of political killings by government officials.

Then-National Police Commander Fernando Caldera stated publicly that policeman Roberto Sanchez used excessive force when he shot university student Donaldo Romero in the back on June 21 in Managua. Romero, suspected of car theft, was killed shortly after his companion attacked Sanchez and other police officers. Sanchez was immediately dismissed from the police force, and a Managua district court judge sentenced him to prison in July.

In September policeman Juan Isidro Flores shot and killed peasant Mario Amador Duarte in Nueva Guinea department while the latter was in detention on suspicion of having stolen vegetables. Flores claimed that he was attempting to disarm Duarte when he accidentally discharged the round that killed the suspect. Flores was detained by police.

Bandit leader Sergio Palacios ("El Charro") and his associate Ricardo Guzman ("Garza") were killed near Waslala on June 2. The Catholic Church, citing reports from area residents, asserted that a booby-trapped radio killed Palacios and Guzman when it exploded. The army claimed that its soldiers happened upon Palacios and Guzman by chance and killed them in an ensuing gunbattle. The Church, which had served as mediator in disarmament talks between Palacios and the army, publicly criticized the killing but did not directly accuse the army.

The civil war formally concluded in June 1990 with the demobilization of the Nicaraguan Resistance; however, society continued to be politically polarized and heavily armed. In particular, the rule of law and basic infrastructure and conditions to guarantee personal security and economic opportunity did not extend to rural areas. Reflecting these sources of instability, the level of violence, primarily criminal in nature, has remained high in the traditionally conflictive, poverty-stricken northern and north-central zones. According to the OAS/CIAV, a total of 26 demobilized ex-RN members were murdered during the period January-June (not including armed bandits who were ex-RN); bringing to 396 the number of demobilized RN members who died under violent circumstances since the beginning of the Chamorro administration. Of the 26 killed during 1996, according to OAS/CIAV, the security forces killed none, and rearmed resistance members (recontras) are known to have killed 10.

Armed bandit groups, some of which claimed political agendas, blocked highways, burned vehicles, and engaged in robbery, kidnaping for ransom, and murder in the lawless countryside of the northern and north-central zones. From January to June, 63 clashes between bandits and security forces resulted in 93 police and army casualties and an unknown number of bandit casualties. During the same period, the army and police arrested 218 bandits. The OAS/CIAV received an average of two reports per day of peasants fleeing their homes for fear of violence, and an average of 1.5 reports per day of homicide in these areas, a rate that has varied little during the past 6 years.

In response to coffee producers' concerns, the Government deployed soldiers and police to guard coffee transport routes and to protect farmers from extortion or kidnaping during the 1994-95 and 1995-96 harvest seasons. Local human rights groups reported very few cases of human rights abuses by the security forces deployed in the operation. The deployment effectively reduced the level of criminal violence in the affected areas. Army and police conducted another similar operation as an extension of troop reinforcements to ensure security of voters and election officials during the 1996 election campaign.

To address the issue of unresolved ex-RN deaths, President Chamorro established the Tripartite Commission in September 1992. The Commission concluded its review in October and turned 83 human rights cases involving 164 allegedly murdered excombatants, as well as 181 specific recommendations, over to the Government for followup, but the Government had taken no further action by year's end. The Commission issued three internal reports during 1993, covering investigations of 88 deaths and including 120 recommendations for followup action by the Government and security forces, ranging from arrest of known perpetrators to investigations of obstruction of justice. In September 1995, the Commission submitted to President Chamorro a fourth report covering an additional 33 cases plus an evaluation of the compliance level of all recommendations contained in the 3 earlier reports. The Commission verified that only 14 of the 120 recommendations contained in the first 3 reports had been fully implemented, while 40 had been partially implemented. Of 73 members of the police named in the 3 reports, the courts tried 36 on criminal charges and convicted 5. Of 38 military officials named, the courts tried 20 and convicted 2. According to the OAS/CIAV, none of those convicted served a complete sentence.

In June the Supreme Court finished a year-long review of judicial procedures employed in 26 Tripartite Commission cases undertaken at the direction of President Chamorro. Army commander Joaquin Cuadra and Minister of Government Sergio Narvaez, whose ministry controls the National Police, had requested the review in 1995. The Court's review focused on military court procedures followed in the prosecutions of army and police officials who were found not guilty, or cases of those named in the reports but never prosecuted. The Court found deficiencies in procedure in 4 cases, said that another 4 cases should be reopened should new evidence come to light, and found no fault with the other 18. Army and police officials arrested no one on related charges, but police officials ordered that searches be undertaken for officers cited by the court.

In June a jury found army major Ivan Gutierrez innocent of the September 1995 slaying of Carlos Jose Salinas. The Nicaraguan Center for Human Rights (CENIDH) suspected Gutierrez paid Salinas' mother to persuade the jury to exonerate him.

On December 13, 1995 a demonstration by university students and others outside the National Assembly resulted in a confrontation with police that left 2 protesters dead, 66 wounded (10 by gunfire according to police officials), and 8 police officers wounded. The police were not adequately prepared to control the violence. A new riot control unit has since been formed and equipped. A trial of police officers suspected of firing on the crowd was underway at year's end.

In August the Nicaraguan Association for Human Rights (ANPDH) participated in an exhumation of a mass grave found at Masaya national park. It said that this was one of 70 covert graves of persons allegedly murdered by Sandinista revolutionaries in 1978-79 found since the end of the civil war. The ANPDH reported that a total of 84 corpses had been exhumed from 8 covert graves, but said that it knew of more than 217 others that had not been exhumed. No government investigations were undertaken.

In November 1991, a special presidential commission charged with investigating the February 1991 killing of former RN commander Enrique Bermudez was dissolved after it claimed that there was a lack of evidence. A 1993 Scotland Yard investigation established no new leads with which to open the case, and no progress was made during the year.

In September the Inter-American Court of Human Rights heard testimony on a charge of obstruction of justice regarding the investigation of the 1990 killing of 16-year-old Jean Paul Genie. (Genie was slain following an incident involving members of the motorcade of then-army commander General Humberto Ortega.) The Court rejected the Government's argument that the Court lacked authority in the case because Nicaragua had not, at the time of the killing, accepted the Court's jurisdiction. The Government had previously said that all officials would testify if called, but neither army commander General Joaquin Cuadra nor General Ortega appeared when the Court called them in September. The Government's legal representative in the case separately told the Court that the Government opposed Cuadra's and Ortega's appearance because the Court had sufficient evidence to proceed to a judgment; a military tribunal headed by General Cuadra had already found General Ortega innocent in June 1994 (and he should not be subjected to double jeopardy); and, the Supreme Court had not yet ruled on the Genie family's appeal requesting that the it assert civilian jurisdiction in the case. At year's end, the Supreme Court had not yet ruled on the Genie family's petition.

On July 14, 1995, the Attorney General's office petitioned the Supreme Court to order the immediate arrest of former army Major Frank Ibarra. Ibarra was sentenced in absentia in 1993 to 20 years' imprisonment for the November 1992 murder of Dr. Arges Sequeira Mangas, president of the Association of Nicaraguan Confiscated Property Owners. Ibarra has remained a fugitive from justice since Sequeira's death.

b. *Disappearance.*—There were no reports of politically motivated disappearances.

The Government failed to respond to a request from the United Nations Working Group on Disappeared Persons for more information on the 1994 disappearance of Sandinista activist Mario Benjamin Mendez.

c. *Torture and Other Cruel, Inhuman, or Degrading Treatment or Punishment.*—Although use of torture is a punishable crime under the law, there were isolated instances of torture by the authorities. There were also credible reports that police beat and otherwise physically mistreated detainees, often to obtain confessions. Human rights groups attributed these abuses in part to the prevailing state of impunity. Another important contributing factor in such abuses by the police is the lack of professional training in sophisticated investigative techniques that would enable the police to avoid resorting to brutal methods. Inadequate budget support for professional training, salaries and benefits, and proper equipment and supplies also hampered efforts to improve police performance.

On May 22, a Boaco district court judge sentenced police officers Orlando Brizuela and Carlos Suazo to 1 year in prison each for abuse of authority, sexual assault, wounding, and wrongfully detaining a prisoner after the two beat and tortured Juan Pablo Reyes. They burned Reyes and threatened him with death after being arrested for committing a minor offense on May 2. The ANPDH reported that the police beat 15-year-olds Marco Antonio Gonzalez and Abelardo Rodriguez while in custody, the latter in Boaco department by police officer Venancio Obando. The police took no action to investigate these incidents. The ANPDH reported that prison guards subjected 15-year-old Juan Carlos Garcia to electrical shocks while in detention on Corn Island.

The Office of Civil Inspection for Professional Responsibility of the Ministry of Government is responsible for monitoring allegations of illegal detention and police abuse. Through September the office received 192 formal complaints involving 241 police officers. The office concluded that, of the 98 complaints that it had investigated through September, 25 were human rights cases. Of 45 policemen determined to be responsible for human rights violations, the authorities had administratively sanctioned 29 through September. The unit's small budget and staff hampered effective investigations and publicity. The Ministry of Government frequently does not follow up on the office's recommendations. Civil inspection officials said that police commanders often hindered their investigations by refusing to share pertinent information. The Ministry of Government took no action to improve police cooperation with the civil inspection unit.

Prison conditions are poor. The prison system remained overcrowded and underfunded, with medical attention virtually nonexistent and malnutrition a constant problem. According to government statistics, prisons had a total inmate population of 3,752 as of August, an average of 82 percent over capacity. The prisons of Esteli, Chinandega, and Bluefields housed more than double their intended capacity. The prison budget remained constant, although the inmate population increased by 14 percent during the year. Prison officials calculated that the daily expenditure on prisoners fell from $3.67 per prisoner in 1992 to $2.79 in 1996. Prison officials reported that the annual budget for food remained constant in spite of the growing prison population and that average daily caloric intake therefore fell to 750 to 800 calories, well below the 1,800 calories per day recommended by the United Nations. However, many prisoners received additional food from visiting family and friends. Medical care available to prisoners fell far short of the basic needs of all prisoners, while 200 chronically ill prisoners were in particularly bad condition. Lack of available medical care led prisons to release ill prisoners convicted of lesser offenses. Three prisoners charged with serious offenses died in prison in 1995 of malnutrition and lack of medical care.

As of August, 11.6 percent of the prison population was between the ages of 15 and 18. Youths were housed in the same prisons as adults for lack of juvenile detention centers, though in different wings of the prisons. While only Managua has a separate prison for women, there have been no reports of problems ensuing from mixed facilities. Women were also housed in separate wings in facilities outside the Managua area and were guarded by female custodians. Police station holding cells were overcrowded by an average of 30 percent. Officials claimed that suspects were often left in these cells during their trials, as budgetary shortfalls often restricted the use of fuel for frequent transfers from prison to distant courtrooms. As a result of overcrowding in both the cells and in prisons, police and penitentiary officials issued urgent calls for increased budgets to build more facilities and increase food purchases. Government officials responded that the budget could not be stretched to meet these demands.

Prison guards received human rights training from nongovernmental organizations (NGO's) and the Catholic Church, and generally treated prisoners well. However, there were instances of abuse, some of which involved minors.

d. *Arbitrary Arrest, Detention, or Exile.*—Arbitrary arrest and detention by the police were common. The Police Functions Law requires police to obtain a warrant prior to detaining a suspect and to notify family members within 24 hours of the detainee's whereabouts. However, the police rarely complied with this law. Detainees do not have the right to an attorney until they have been formally charged with a crime. Local human rights groups criticized the law for providing inadequate judicial oversight of police arrests.

The constitutional reforms instituted in July 1995 reduced from 72 to 48 hours the time police may legally hold a suspect before they must bring him before a judge to decide if charges should be brought. The judge must then either order the accused released or transferred to prison. Due to lack of prison space, there were over 1,000 prisoners in badly overcrowded police holding cells, most of whom were being held illegally beyond the 48-hour deadline. The CENIDH denounced one particularly egregious case, that of 13-year-old Dolores Juarez Salmeron, who was arbitrarily detained by police for 16 days. The new Organic Police Law passed in August allows the National Police to hold its own members suspected of wrongdoing up to 20 days while conducting initial investigations, which contravenes the constitutionally mandated 48-hour maximum period.

The ANPDH recorded 77 complaints of illegal or arbitrary detention by the National Police and army from January through June. The number represents a significant decline from previous years. As in past years, incidents of arbitrary detention were most common in the rural northern and north-central regions, where much of the civil war was fought.

Exile is not practiced. There were no reports of political violence against any citizens returning from civil war era self-imposed exile.

e. *Denial of Fair Public Trial.*—The judiciary is independent but weak. Human rights and lawyers' groups complained about the delay of justice caused by judicial inaction, sometimes for years.

The judicial system comprises both civil and military courts. The 12-member Supreme Court of Justice is the system's highest court and is also responsible for nominating all appellate and lower court judges. The Court is divided into specialized chambers on administrative, criminal, constitutional, and civil matters.

The 1994 Military Code requires the civilian court system to try members of the military charged with common crimes. From January to August the Attorney General for Penal Affairs' office received 136 complaints from civilians against members of the military. It referred 72 of these to civilian courts for trial. At the end of August, courts had sentenced members of the military to prison in 10 of the cases and found those involved in 6 cases innocent. The other 56 cases were in stages of judicial processing, which the Attorney General for Penal Affairs called "evidence of the worsening problem of backlog in the judicial system."

In criminal cases, the accused has the right to legal counsel, and defendants are presumed innocent until proven guilty. The presiding judge appoints attorneys from a standard list to represent indigent defendants, but, because they are not paid by the State, many attorneys pay a $1.50 fine rather than represent such clients. According to the ANPDH, approximately 90 percent of indigent defendants go to trial without an attorney to represent them. This contributes greatly to the slow pace of justice, and many prisoners spend more than a year in jail without a trial. The Permanent Commission for Human Rights (CPDH) has estimated that nearly half of all those incarcerated in the prison system have been awaiting trial for between 6 months and 2 years.

The Supreme Court removed Yali judge Federico Schneegan from office in August after he had been widely criticized by human rights organizations for accepting bribes and sexually abusing female prisoners. The CENIDH claims that Schneegan, in reaction to public denunciations made by the CENIDH's Yali representative, offered to pay bandit leader "El Ruco" 3,500 cordobas to kill the representative. "El Ruco" reported Schneegan's offer to police who then detained him. He was dead 2 hours after his detention; police contended he committed suicide. Schneegan was not charged with any crime.

There were no known political prisoners.

f. *Arbitrary Interference with Privacy, Family, Home, or Correspondence.*—The Constitution provides that all persons have the right to privacy of their family and to the inviolability of their home, correspondence, and communications. It also requires warrants for searches of private homes and excludes from legal proceedings illegally seized letters, documents, and private papers. The Government, however, did not always respect these rights in practice.

Section 2. Respect for Civil Liberties, Including:

a. *Freedom of Speech and Press.*—The Constitution provides for freedom of speech and a free press, and the Government respects these rights in practice. The privately owned print media, the broadcast media, and academic circles freely and openly discussed diverse viewpoints in public discourse without government interference.

The news medium with the largest audience is radio, but polls show that television is the primary source of news, particularly in the cities. Listeners receive a wide variety of political viewpoints, especially on Managua's 45 radio stations. There are five television stations, three of which carry news programming with partisan political content. There is no official state censorship, nor is self-censorship practiced.

Freedom of the press is potentially qualified, however, by several constitutional provisions. The Constitution stipulates that citizens have the right to "accurate information," thereby providing an exception by which the freedom to publish information that the Government deems inaccurate could be abridged. Although the right to information cannot be subject to censorship, there is retroactive liability established by law, defined as a "social responsibility," implying the potential for sanctions against irresponsibility by the press. The legislature did not modify these provisions in the constitutional reforms, but neither did the Government invoke these provisions to suppress the media.

The passage of a law in September that established a professional journalists' guild was perceived by some as a blow to freedom of expression. The law requires Nicaraguan journalists in the Managua area to have a bachelors degree in journalism or 5 years of journalistic experience in order to be accredited by a college of journalists and also requires media owners in the capital area to ensure that they employ only accredited journalists. The law was proposed by a journalists' association seeking to establish professional standards, but opposition forces claim that the law restricts the freedom of others to publish or state their views in the media. To mollify the opposition, the National Assembly amended the law to restrict its application to the national capital, where most of the media outlets are nonetheless located.

The Government does not restrict academic freedom.

b. *Freedom of Peaceful Assembly and Association.*—The Constitution recognizes the right to peaceful assembly without prior permission. It also recognizes the right to public assembly, demonstration, and mobilization "in conformity with the law." The Government generally respects the right of assembly, although the law requires demonstrators to obtain permission for a rally or march by registering its planned size and location with the police. The authorities routinely granted such permission, but many groups chose not to register because, they claimed, the process was too cumbersome. In most cases, the Government took no action against illegal demonstrations.

The Constitution provides for the right to organize or affiliate with political parties, and opposition and independent associations functioned freely without government interference or restriction. Private associations do not have legal status to conduct private fund raising or receive public financial support until they receive this authorization from the National Assembly, which it routinely confers.

c. *Freedom of Religion.*—The Constitution provides for freedom of religion, and the Government respects this right in practice.

Sporadic bombings of Catholic churches continued through August. Most of the attacks occurred in Masaya, Managua, and Leon, involved some small explosive devices, and caused minor damage to structures but no casualties. Church officials characterized the attacks as efforts by extremists to intimidate the Church and halt its civic education campaigns. In November a criminal court in Leon convicted 12 men for a number of the bombings and sentenced them to between 3 and 15 years in prison. Following the convictions, FSLN assembly deputies unsuccessfully tried to pass legislation pardoning the 12 persons. Cardinal Miguel Obando y Bravo and other church officials reported receiving anonymous telephone threats.

d. *Freedom of Movement Within the Country, Foreign Travel, Emigration, and Repatriation.*—The Constitution provides for the right to travel and reside anywhere in the country and to enter and exit the country freely. The law requires citizens and residents to obtain an exit visa to leave the country, but immigration authorities routinely granted these for a small fee. However, the law also allows a judge to order immigration officials to deny exit visas to those involved in court cases if there is reasonable suspicion that the accused may abscond. The right of citizens to return to Nicaragua is not established in the Constitution, but, in practice, the Government has not restricted anyone's return.

The Government cooperates with the office of the United Nations High Commissioner for Refugees and other humanitarian organizations in assisting refugees. The Constitution provides for asylum, and political refugees cannot be expelled to the country persecuting them. The issue of the provision of first asylum did not arise;

there were no reports of the forced return of persons to a country where they feared persecution.

Section 3. Respect for Political Rights: The Right of Citizens to Change Their Government

Citizens exercised their right peacefully to change their government in free and fair national elections in October, held under the auspices of the Supreme Electoral Council (CSE), an independent branch of government. Voters elected the Liberal Alliance's Arnoldo Aleman President from a field of 24 candidates with 51 percent of the vote, against 38 percent for FSLN candidate Daniel Ortega. Over 3,000 national and international observers declared the elections free and fair, despite some logistical and organizational problems. Observers from individual political parties monitored nearly all polling stations. The FSLN and some other losing parties claimed systematic irregularities in the process amounted to fraud, but the CSE's exhaustive, and closely monitored, vote tally verification process confirmed the final tallies. Nonetheless, at year's end the FSLN called the electoral process "legal but not legitimate."

The 1995 reforms to the 1987 Constitution established a more even distribution of power and authority among the four coequal branches of government. The executive branch is headed by the President and a cabinet appointed by the President, who is both head of state and head of government, as well as supreme chief of the defense and security forces. The Vice President has no constitutionally mandated duties or powers. Both the President and Vice President are elected to 5-year terms by direct popular vote, with the possibility of a runoff between the top two candidates if one does not obtain at least 45 percent of the vote on the first ballot. The Constitution does not permit reelection. Early in 1996, the Supreme Court dismissed challenges against the constitutionality of the prohibitions contained in the 1995 reforms against close relatives of an incumbent president, by blood or marriage, from running for election as president. Based on this and on constitutional prohibitions against candidates who had at any time given up their citizenship or were subject to legal prosecution, the CSE in July unanimously voted to disqualify 3 of the candidates running for the presidency.

A single-chamber National Assembly exercises legislative power. In October voters chose 93 members, including 20 deputies from nationwide lists, 70 from lists presented in each of the 15 departments and 2 autonomous regions, and 3 defeated presidential candidates who obtained a minimum percentage of the national vote. Members elected concurrently with the President and Vice President in 1996 are to serve 5-year terms.

There are no restrictions in law or practice against women, indigenous groups, or other minorities voting or participating in politics. Women served as President and Vice President, as well as president of the Supreme Electoral Council. Additionally, 3 of 12 Supreme Court justices are women; women hold ministerial, vice ministerial, and other senior positions in government; and voters elected 9 women to the National Assembly in October. Two members of the National Assembly were Miskito Indians; indigenous people are represented in government at both the local and national levels.

Section 4. Governmental Attitude Regarding International and Nongovernmental Investigation of Alleged Violations of Human Rights

Human rights groups operated without government interference, with rare exceptions. Major organizations included the Nicaraguan Center for Human Rights, the Permanent Commission for Human Eights, the Nicaraguan Association for Human Rights, the Episcopal Center for Development, and Cardinal Miguel Obando y Bravo's verification commission. The OAS's International Support and Verification Commission, which was established in 1990 to oversee the repatriation, disarmament, resettlement, and protection of the human rights of the members of the Nicaraguan Resistance, was scheduled to complete its mission in December, but its mandate was extended an additional 6 months. In June 1993, the OAS General Assembly expanded the mandate of the OAS/CIAV to monitor the human rights of, and provide assistance to, all those affected by the civil war, rather than just ex-RN, which had been its original task. OAS/CIAV and the Catholic Church helped create 45 "peace commissions" in the northern and central parts of the country, intended to give inhabitants of the area a means of dispute resolution, a means of monitoring human rights abuses, and a vehicle for expressing their concerns to government authorities.

The CENIDH complained that then-National Police Commander Fernando Caldera obstructed its investigations into alleged human rights abuses by police officers and severed all contact with the CENIDH for a short period during the year.

The Ministry of Government's civil inspection office also made similar complaints regarding lack of police cooperativeness (see Section 1.c.).

The ANPDH, the CENIDH, and the CPDH conducted numerous human rights workshops both at the police training academy and at various police headquarters throughout the country. The Catholic Church conducted human rights training for army units that were deployed to the northern and north-central regions in May to provide security to citizens and electoral workers during the June-July voter registration. The military distributed human rights manuals to its personnel. Some military officers received internationally sponsored human rights training.

Section 5. *Discrimination Based on Race, Sex, Religion, Disability, Language, or Social Status*

The Constitution prohibits discrimination on the basis of birth, nationality, political belief, race, gender, language, religion, opinion, national origin, economic condition, or social condition. In practice, however, the Government made little or no effort to combat discrimination. Few, if any, discrimination suits or formal complaints were filed with government officials.

Women.—The most prevalent violations of women's rights involved domestic and sexual violence, which were widespread and vastly underreported. The 528 reports of rape received by the National Police in 1993, the most recent year for which police statistics are available, represented only a fraction of the rapes that occurred. According to human rights activists, women are often reluctant to report abuse or file charges, in part due to social stigmas attached to victims of rape. Local human rights groups reported that while police sometimes intervened to prevent injury in cases of domestic violence, they rarely charged perpetrators. Those cases that actually reached the courts usually resulted in a not guilty verdict due to judicial inexperience with, and lack of legal training related to, proper judicial handling of such violence.

The police manage six "women's commissariats"—two in Managua, one in Esteli, one in Bluefields, one in Leon, and one in Masaya—supported in part by foreign assistance. The centers are annexes of local police stations and staffed by female police officers. They provide both social and legal help to women and mediate spousal conflicts. Through May 1995, the centers recorded 1,816 cases of violence against females, which included 705 cases of rape of girls from 4 to 15 years old. The National Assembly passed in August a new Law Against Aggression Against Women, designed to serve as the basis for prosecution of crimes against women.

Although the Constitution provides for equality between the sexes, some authorities and society in general often did not respect this in practice. While discrimination against women is technically illegal, reports of such discrimination were persistent throughout the year. Women are underrepresented in management positions in the private sector, and they constitute the majority of workers in the traditionally low-paid education, textile, and health service sectors.

According to government statistics, women have equal or somewhat better access to education than men. Net enrollment for girls in the primary grades is 79 percent, compared with 76 percent for boys. At the secondary level, 33 percent of girls and 26 percent of boys are enrolled.

Children.—Children 15 years of age and younger make up approximately 45 percent of the population. The Government expresses its commitment to children's human rights and welfare publicly but does not commit adequate funding levels for children's programs. Education is compulsory through the sixth grade, but this provision is not enforced. The United Nations Children's Fund (UNICEF), using 1993 statistics, estimated that 6,000 children have been abandoned by their families, some 2,000 live in orphanages, and approximately 1,800 are in foster homes. Every year the media carry stories of parents who abandoned or killed their children because they were too poor or otherwise unable to take care of them. UNICEF reported that 11.3 percent of all children from 6 to 14 years of age were employed or looking for work in the informal or agricultural sectors. Many children work during annual harvest, and approximately 30,000 children work in the streets of Managua as vendors or beggars. Child prostitution exists but is not common.

People With Disabilities.—The Government has not legislated or otherwise mandated accessibility for the disabled. However, through international NGO's, foreign governments, and the public health care system, the Government procured thousands of prostheses and other medical equipment for veterans and former resistance members. Through its clinics and hospitals, the Government provides care to war veterans and other disabled persons, but the quality of care is generally poor.

Indigenous People.—Comprising about 6 percent of the country's population, the indigenous people live primarily in the Northern Autonomous Atlantic Region (RAAN) and Southern Autonomous Atlantic Region (RAAS), created in 1987 out of the former department of Zelaya, which border the Caribbean sea and comprise 47 percent of the national territory. According to the Government's May 1995 census (which undercounted the population by as much as 25 percent in some rural areas), the four major identifiable tribes are the Miskito (with approximately 140,000 members), the Sumo (15,000), the Garifuna (1,500), and the Rama (1,000).

The indigenous people of the RAAN (principally the Miskito and the Sumo) have their own political party, the Yatama, with representation in regional and municipal councils. In an effort to encourage indigenous participation in the October elections, the CSE distributed electoral and civic education materials in four languages, including Miskito and Sumo. The 1987 Autonomy Law requires the Government to consult the indigenous regarding the exploitation of their areas' resources. The central Government often made decisions without adequate departmental or community consultation. As in previous years, some indigenous groups complained that central government authorities excluded the indigenous people of the Atlantic coast from meaningful participation in decisions affecting their lands, cultures, traditions, and the allocation of natural resources. Critics of government policy cited official statistics that unemployment approached 70 percent in the RAAS and was nearly 90 percent in the RAAN, far above national averages.

A 650-member tribe in the RAAN, the Awas Tigni, sued the Government, claiming that its decision to award a long-term lumber concession to a Korean firm on a portion of the land it claims as its own was a violation of the American Convention on Human Rights. The Government has worked with indigenous groups in the past to reach compromises, but in this case countered that the area the Awas Tigni claim, 392,500 acres, was excessive for a tribe of its size. At the root of the dispute was the Government's failure to demarcate the land. Other indigenous groups, squatters, ex-RN, and soldiers also have claims to the same area. At year's end, the courts had not yet ruled on the Awas Tignis' claim.

National/Racial/Ethnic Minorities.—Most Nicaraguans are of mixed background, and ethnicity is not a barrier to political or economic success. However, various indigenous groups from both the RAAN and the RAAS sometimes linked the Government's failure to expend resources in support of the Atlantic coast population to the existence of ethnic, racial, and religious (principally members of the Moravian church) minorities that predominate in that region.

Section 6. Worker Rights

a. *The Right of Association.*—The Constitution provides for the right of workers to organize voluntarily in unions, and this right was reaffirmed in the new Labor Code which entered into effect in November, replacing the antiquated 1944 code. Legally, all public and private sector workers, except those in the military and the police, may form and join unions of their own choosing, and they exercise this right extensively. New unions must register with the Ministry of Labor and be granted legal status before they may engage in collective bargaining. The new code legally recognizes cooperatives, into which many transportation workers are organized. Slightly less than half of the formal sector work force, including agricultural workers, is unionized, according to labor leaders. Union membership continued to fall during the year. The unions are independent of the Government, although some are affiliated with political parties.

The Constitution recognizes the right to strike. The Labor Code requires a majority vote of all the workers in an enterprise to call a strike. Workers may strike legally only after they have demonstrated that they have just cause to strike and have exhausted other methods of dispute resolution, including mediation by the Ministry of Labor and compulsory arbitration. The new Labor Code streamlines these procedures, often previously ignored because they were expensive and cumbersome. Union leaders reported being satisfied with the reformed mechanism for requesting legal authorization to strike. The Labor Code prohibits retribution against strikers and union leaders for legal strikes. However, this protection may be withdrawn in the case of an illegal strike. The new code provides protected status to union leaders, requiring that companies receive permission from the Labor Ministry after having shown just cause in order to fire union executive board members. Such protection is limited to nine individuals per union.

Unions freely form or join federations or confederations and affiliate with and participate in international bodies.

b. *The Right to Organize and Bargain Collectively.*—The Constitution provides for the right to bargain collectively, and this right was reaffirmed in the new Labor Code. The Government generally sought to foster resolution of pressing labor conflicts (usually in the public sector) through informal negotiations rather than through formal administrative or judicial processes. According to the reformed code, companies engaged in disputes with employees must negotiate with the employees' union if the employees have thus organized themselves.

Eighteen firms, employing some 10,000 workers, operate in the government-run export processing zone (EPZ), and a private EPZ contains another firm with 500 employees. Three additional zones were authorized but had not been opened by year's end. While EPZ officials maintain that labor laws are more strictly enforced in the EPZ than elsewhere, Managua-based representatives of the American Institute for Free Labor Development and union representatives have long maintained that the Labor Ministry is doing a poor job of enforcing the Labor Code in the EPZ's. Of the 19 EPZ enterprises, only 2 are unionized. EPZ officials claimed that, due to memories of the corrupt and ineffective unions of the 1980's, workers in the other 17 EPZ enterprises simply have no interest in unionizing. They also claim that wages and working conditions in EPZ enterprises are better than the national average.

c. *Prohibition of Forced or Compulsory Labor.*—The Constitution prohibits forced or compulsory labor, and there is no evidence that it is practiced.

d. *Minimum Age for Employment of Children.*—The Constitution prohibits child labor that can affect normal childhood development or interfere with the obligatory school year. The new Labor Code raised the age at which children may begin working with parental permission from 12 to 14 years. Parental permission to work is also required for 15- and 16-year-olds. The law limits the workday for such children to 6 hours and prohibits night work. However, because of the economic needs of many families and lack of effective government enforcement mechanisms, child labor rules are rarely enforced except in the small, modern sector of the economy. A UNICEF study, citing 1993 statistics, estimated that some 108,000 children under the age of 15 are involved in some sort of labor in the formal and informal sectors of the economy. The same report estimated that 72,000 children under the age of 15 help with planting and harvesting crops such as coffee, cotton, bananas, tobacco, and rice. Children the age of 10 or older often worked for less than $1.00 per day on the same banana plantations and coffee plantations as their parents. Many small children work in the streets of Managua hawking merchandise, cleaning automobile windows, or begging. Working children averaged a 47-hour workweek, according to UNICEF.

e. *Acceptable Conditions of Work.*—A 1991 executive branch decree established minimum wage rates, but they have not been adjusted for inflation since then. As a result, the purchasing power of the minimum wage has fallen some 50 percent over the past 5 years. Minimum wages vary by sector. Examples of monthly rates are: Agriculture, $17.44 (150 cordobas); construction, $22.09 (190 cordobas; government, $27.21 (234 cordobas); manufacturing, $29.07 (250 cordobas); and banking, $34.88 (300 cordobas). The minimum wage falls far below government estimates of what an urban family must spend each month for a basic basket of goods ($140.70, or 1,210 cordobas). In reality, the vast majority of urban workers earn well above the minimum rates.

The new Labor Code maintains the constitutionally mandated 8-hour workday; the standard legal workweek is a maximum of 48 hours, with 1 day of rest weekly. The new code establishes that severance pay shall be from 1 to 5 months' duration, depending on the duration of employment and the circumstances of firing. It also establishes an obligation of an employer to provide housing to employees who are temporarily assigned to areas beyond commuting distance. The new Labor Code seeks to bring the country into compliance with international standards and norms of workplace hygiene and safety, but the Ministry of Labor's office of hygiene and occupational security lacks adequate staff and resources to enforce these provisions. The new code gives workers the right to remove themselves from dangerous workplace situations without jeopardy to continued employment.

PANAMA

Panama is a representative democracy with an elected executive composed of a president and two vice presidents, an elected 72-member legislature, and an appointed judiciary. President Ernesto Perez Balladares, elected in May 1994 at the head of a multiparty coalition, is the chief executive. The judiciary is independent, but subject to corruption.

Panama has had no military forces since 1989. The Legislative Assembly amended the Constitution in 1994 to abolish a standing military. The amendment contains a provision for the temporary formation of a "special police force" to protect the borders in case of a "threat of external aggression." The Panamanian National Police (PNP), under the executive branch's Ministry of Government and Justice, are responsible for law enforcement. The Judicial Technical Police (PTJ), under the judicial branch's Public Ministry, perform criminal investigations in support of public prosecutors. National Maritime Service and National Air Service forces also perform police functions along the coasts and at the Tocumen International Airport, respectively. Credible reports of corruption within both the PNP and PTJ contributed to some police dismissals. All police forces are responsive to civilian authority and are headed by appointed civilian directors. There were reports of instances of abuse by some members of the security forces.

The service-oriented economy uses the U.S. dollar as currency although it is called the Balboa. Gross domestic product grew less than 2 percent in 1996, the seventh consecutive year of growth, although the growth rate has declined each of the past 4 years. Poverty is pervasive, with great and increasing income disparities between rich and poor. A year-end survey estimated unemployment at 14.7 percent and underemployment at 19.6 percent, together affecting over one-third of the population.

Principal human rights abuses continued to be prolonged pretrial detention; an inefficient and often corrupt criminal justice system, undermined by low wages and poor working conditions; illegal searches; and overcrowded, decrepit prisons. The police generally performed in a professional and restrained manner, even during numerous student and worker protests that sometimes turned violent. However, there were reports that police used excessive force against detainees; prison guards also beat prisoners. There were instances of political pressure on the media. Discrimination against women and indigenous people persists. Violence against women remained a serious problem, compounded by society's unwillingness to recognize it. The Government modified a decree that had initially severely restricted worker rights in export processing zones, but the decree still makes no specific reference to unions and requires mandatory arbitration of disputes.

The Government continued to prosecute some persons responsible for abuses committed during the 21 years of dictatorship from 1968 to 1989. In November 1995, a jury convicted a former military noncommissioned officer for the murder of two unarmed civilians during the 1989 U.S. Operation Just Cause. The Government's determination to mete out justice for past human rights violations was called into question during a rancorous debate over an amnesty bill in May. The proposed beneficiaries included human rights violators, common criminals, and even convicted murderers; eventually, the Legislative Assembly postponed consideration of the bill indefinitely. On December 29, the Assembly approved a bill to create the first office of the Defender of the People, or human rights ombudsman.

RESPECT FOR HUMAN RIGHTS

Section 1. Respect for the Integrity of the Person, Including Freedom From:

a. *Political and Other Extrajudicial Killing.*—There were no reports of political or extrajudicial killings.

The Construction Workers Union continued to claim that one of the four citizens killed during labor protests in 1995 was a victim of police brutality. According to the PNP, evidence to date indicates that the man was shot, but it cannot be determined with certainty that it was a police gun that fired the fatal bullet.

After an investigation of the July 1995 shooting of a police officer by two fellow officers, the PNP discharged the two in October and at year's end they faced trial on charges of murder.

The Government continued to prosecute approximately 20 cases of persons responsible for abuses committed during the 21 years of dictatorship from 1968 to 1989. In a few cases that ended in acquittal, the Government appealed the decisions to a higher court. In one of three known cases that had yet to go to trial, a former member of the Panama Defense Forces (PDF) charged with a 1985 kidnaping asked the authorities to speed up his trial, after more than 7 years in detention.

In November 1995, two related, high-profile murder cases finally came to trial: Those of Raymond Dragseth, a U.S. citizen school teacher, and Fernando Brathwaite, a Panamanian contract employee of the U.S. Embassy—unarmed civilians killed by former strongman Manuel Noriega's PDF during Operation Just Cause. On the night of December 20, 1989, members of a PDF antiterrorist unit (UESAT) forced Dragseth from his home in a private residential area; police officers grabbed Brathwaite, identified only by his embassy badge, at gunpoint on the street in another part of town. Both men were taken to a police station where they were beaten and kept bound and gagged through the following day. On the night of December 21, PDF sergeant Juan Barria Jimenez drove the two men into the country and shot them. In November 1995 a jury convicted Barria of the two murders and sentenced him to 20 years' imprisonment. The jury also convicted Cesar Augusto Roldan, a

UESAT squad member, of illegal detention. However, the authorities released Roldan some months later because, as provided under the law in certain cases, he had already served a majority of his sentence while in pretrial detention.

The Government's determination to mete out justice for past human rights violations was called into question during a rancorous debate over an amnesty bill in May. A list of 951 proposed beneficiaries put forward by the ruling party included the names of human rights violators, common criminals, and even convicted murderers. The University of Panama closed for almost a week as students took to the streets to protest the amnesty bill. In quelling the disturbances police responded in measured fashion, although some students were injured, mainly from exposure to tear gas. Amnesty International, opposition parties, and the general public also rejected the bill, leading the Legislative Assembly to postpone consideration of it indefinitely.

b. *Disappearances*There were no reports of politically motivated disappearances.

c. *Torture and Other Cruel, Inhuman, or Degrading Treatment or Punishment.*—The Constitution prohibits use of measures that could harm the physical, mental, or moral integrity of prisoners or detainees.The police generally performed in a professional and restrained manner, although on occasion there were reports of incidents involving excessive use of force. There also were reports that police still use physical violence to control detainees, particularly during the initial arrest, interrogation, and holding phases.

Corruption among police officers continues to be a problem, although the Director of the PNP vowed he would not tolerate it and has made public some occasional firings of police involved in corruption. The authorities fired four police officers who failed to turn in $60,000 from a robbery and held them for trial. Another officer was fired in October for unspecified criminal acts, and the authorities dismissed 90 recruits from the Police Academy earlier in the year when background checks revealed they had prior ties to criminal youth gangs or organized crime.

In November a court tried 12 defendants, including 2 former PTJ agents and 1 former PNP officer, for attempting to steal 225 kilograms of cocaine from drug traffickers in June 1995. This case notwithstanding, the head of the Office of Professional Responsibility of the PTJ says her office has seen a decline in misconduct cases, which she attributes to an influx of higher quality agents. There were no documented cases of physical abuse of citizens by the PTJ.

The PTJ and the PNP have offices of professional responsibility that act as internal affairs organs to hold officers accountable for their actions. Both have staffs of independent investigators and administrative authority to open internal investigations which, upon completion, go to their respective inspectors general for submission to review boards. The review boards, in turn, recommend to the service's director the appropriate action; the service director has the final authority to determine the disposition of each case. Penalties may include reduction in rank, dismissal, and in severe cases, criminal prosecution.

Through November the PTJ investigated 85 cases of all categories of misconduct; there were no dismissals. The PNP through October opened 510 investigations into misconduct by police and forwarded 5 cases to the courts for possible action. Of the 709 cases closed through October (including 199 cases still open from previous years), 38 resulted in dismissals, 46 in other disciplinary action, and 11 in reprimands. The rest of the cases were either dismissed administratively, or the police in question were absolved of any wrongdoing.

In early August, the PNP clashed with Kuna Indians in the eastern part of Panama province in a dispute concerning land rights. Demanding that the Government remove non-Indian farmers from land claimed by the tribe, an armed group of Kunas blocked the Pan American Highway. The authorities called in the PNP to reopen the road, and they exchanged fire with some of the protesters. Police claim four officers were wounded, while the Kuna say three of the protesters were injured.

In October police wounded and captured two members of the Ngobe-Bugle tribe who were sniping at cars on a road in Chiriqui province. The snipers seriously wounded at least one motorist, and the incident likely was connected to a protest against an exploratory copper mining project in the area. The two accused snipers, while recovering under detention in a hospital, alleged that police denied them visits from family members and lawyers (see Section 5).

In December the National Assembly began consideration of a bill to established an Organic Law for the National Police. The bill includes specific guidelines for PNP use of force, including deadly force; sets up norms for selection and promotion of officers, contributing to PNP professionalization; and seeks to depoliticize the PNP by prohibiting officers' participation in certain political activities. (The police have been operating under a legal code dating from the Noriega years and a 1991 presidential decree regulating the use of force.) Local human rights organizations welcomed the proposed clarifications, noting they had received calls during the year from police officers unsure of proper uses of force in controlling and subduing suspects. Some police officers, however, opposed a clause in the bill which would require the PNP director to be a civilian.

Conditions in many prisons throughout the country remain deplorable and a threat to prisoners' health. Most prisons were built in the 1950's or before and are dilapidated and overcrowded; medical screening or care is inadequate; escape attempts are frequent; and riots and murders are common. The Government opened three new prisons in 1996 and closed and demolished the notorious La Modelo prison. The prison system has so many problems that the Government had a hard time filling the position of Director of National Corrections, which was vacant for several months until a new director took office in September.

The National Corrections Department (DNC), under the Ministry of Government and Justice, still largely depends on PNP officers, who are not properly trained for prison duty, to supply its guard force. Civilian correction officers or "custodians" handle inmates within La Joya, Renacer, and the Central Women's Prison. (The latter facility uses only female guards.) The DNC has authority to discipline its own prison guards with either criminal or civil sanctions, depending on the severity of the abuse. In practice, however, few prisoners or detainees have sought redress for alleged abuse by prison guards. DNC authorities have no direct control over PNP officers at prisons, however, creating a serious command and coordination problem. For example, in a widely publicized beating of prisoners by PNP guards at La Modelo prison in July, guards reportedly acted on outside command from police supervisors, bypassing DNC officials entirely.

The number of trained guards is inadequate to ensure proper security, given the large number of prisoners and generally overcrowded conditions. The first formal training class of approximately 140 corrections officers graduated from the PNP Police Academy. In its 1996 budget request, the DNC asked for funding for 277 new guard positions, but none were approved. Effective prison management also is hampered by the lack of consistent national operating guidelines; individual prison directors are free to establish their own procedures without effective central control or oversight. Given the high turnover rate among directors, this system leads to internal administrative confusion and increases directors' susceptibility to corruption and abuse of authority.

There were credible reports of corruption and abuse of prisoners by guards. Former inmates and family members of inmates of La Modelo prison alleged that some prison guards participated in selling and distributing illicit drugs within the prison. They also alleged that guards accepted bribes to allow knives to be smuggled in to prisoners for use in battles among rival gangs. There were reports from nearly every prison of riots or gang battles; in numerous such incidents prisoners were killed or wounded. Guards frequently used buckshot and tear gas, fired at close range, to quell prisoner disturbances or halt escape attempts. Use of buckshot injured numerous prisoners and, in at least one case, other guards.

While a new case tracking system has shown a decrease in case delays in the courts and with the public prosecutors, the DNC's own statistics indicate that a majority of prisoners have yet to be sentenced. Through November, of 5,907 inmates nationwide for whom information was available, 1,586 had received final sentences; 99 others had been sentenced but were on appeal. The remaining 4,222 were awaiting trial or final sentencing. Total reported prison population as of December 2 was 7,308 inmates, compared with a total prison design capacity of 5,151.

The Government enacted measures in 1995 to speed the pace of prosecutions, including allowing prisoners to waive their preliminary hearing and go directly to trial if they wish (thus avoiding the often months-long wait between the two proceedings). However, these measures appear to have been largely ineffective in moving cases more expeditiously. In public statements during the year, both the Minister of Government and Justice and the President highlighted this area as one in dire need of additional reform.

Until its closing at the end of November, La Modelo prison continued to have a prison population many times greater than its designed capacity. Conditions were reportedly so overcrowded that prisoners literally were living in the bathrooms, some with overflowing toilets. In the main gallery, hammocks were stacked five high. On July 27, a deadly battle between rival gangs in La Modelo provoked severe beatings by prison guards, some of which were filmed and publicized. President Perez Balladares reacted by ordering La Modelo emptied and demolished; the Minister of Government and Justice fired La Modelo's director, as well as 12 guards identified as taking part in the beatings.

La Modelo prison, condemned by the Catholic Archbishop as a "cemetery of the living," was opened to the public and media for tours December 3-5. In a ceremony on December 10, International Human Rights Day, President Perez Balladares pushed the plunger to blow up the vacant structure. In his remarks, the President termed the prison a national disgrace, acknowledging that it had been the site of grave human rights abuses of common criminals and political prisoners alike.

The prison situation in Colon remained grim, with high crime and incarceration rates mirroring the lack of economic opportunity in Colon city and province. The President inaugurated Nueva Esperanza prison in April, a former cold storage facility converted to a prison to relieve the terrible overcrowding in Colon prison. However, rival prisoner gang members were not properly separated upon transfer to the new facility, and in June violence among prisoners provoked a riot that left four dead, many injured, and extensive damage to the new facility.

Transfer of La Modelo prisoners to other facilities worsened the conditions at those facilities. The Government expanded the maximum security cellblocks at La Joya prison to allow it to absorb inmates from other overcrowded prisons, principally those formerly in La Modelo. As of November, this relatively new 1,000-bed facility housed 1,194 inmates and detainees; an additional 1,041 inmates were housed in an adjacent minimum- to medium-security facility. The DNC also put in place a classification program to categorize inmates according to risk, an important step in light of the transfer of dangerous maximum security inmates from La Modelo, a system which the DNC plans to extend to all prisons nationwide.

Conditions on Coiba Island Penal Colony continued to be deplorable. Of the 679 prisoners, 451 await trial or final sentencing, and the majority reportedly will have served almost two-thirds of their potential sentences before reaching trial. Prisoners suffer from malnutrition and shortages of potable water, and medical care is practically nonexistent. Coiba has a civilian administrator, but its guard force still consists of police guards instead of civilian corrections officers. Geographic isolation and lack of communications have separated detainees from their attorneys and caused many to miss trials. Escapes from Coiba are reported common. The Government began transferring prisoners out of Coiba as a preliminary step to closing it, but following the decision to close La Modelo prison, Coiba has become a key holding facility for transferred La Modelo inmates. The Government acknowledges it must keep Coiba open, but as yet has made no provisions to upgrade or maintain the facility.

Conditions at women's prisons in Panama City and Chiriqui province were noticeably better. Even so, female prisoners, especially those in the primary detention area, reportedly suffered from overcrowding, poor medical care, and lack of basic supplies for personal hygiene.

At the Juvenile Detention Center, the Attorney General in September ordered an investigation into conditions after the Center fired an official who alleged that there were incidents of abuse of juvenile detainees. Both male and female minors are housed in the same facility, although in separate buildings.

d. *Arbitrary Arrest, Detention, or Exile.*—The Constitution stipulates that arrests must be carried out with a warrant issued by the appropriate authorities. Exceptions are permitted when an officer apprehends a person during the commission of a crime, or when disrespect by the individual toward the officer prevents the officer from carrying out his duty. The law requires the arresting officer to inform the detainee immediately of the reasons for arrest or detention and of the right to immediate legal counsel, to be provided by the State for the indigent.

The Constitution also provides for judicial review of the legality of detention and mandates the immediate release of any person detained or arrested illegally. The Constitution prohibits police from detaining suspects for more than 24 hours without bringing them before a competent judicial authority. In practice, the authorities often violated the 24-hour time limit by several days. Under law the preliminary investigation phase may last 8 days to 2 months, and the follow-on investigation phase another 2 to 4 months, depending on the number of suspects. However, extensions of these limits are frequently granted by the courts, leaving the accused in detention for an extended period without having been formally charged.

Extended pretrial detention continued to be one the most serious human rights problems, in part a consequence of the elaborate notification phase in criminal cases. According to DNC statistics, pretrial detainees composed approximately 71 percent of the prison population, down slightly from 78 percent in 1995. Almost 25 percent of the total prison population is under detention beyond legally permissible time limits. According to public defenders, the average period of pretrial custody for a defendant was approximately 16 months; pretrial detention in excess of the maximum sentence for the alleged crime was common. A legal mechanism exists to hold the Government financially accountable in cases where a detainee spends more than 1 year in jail but subsequently has all charges dismissed at a preliminary hearing. The dismissal must be either because the act of which the detainee was accused is not ruled a crime or because there is no evident to link the suspect to the crime.

Although this redress procedure is not extremely complicated, few former detainees have sought redress for their time in detention.

In October the authorities arrested a group of 134 protesters from the radical Colon civic action group "Reaction Three," who staged a violent protest at the Ministry of Housing, causing extensive damage. A judge sentenced the protesters to 20 days' confinement; 89 men were sent to Coiba Island prison, while 45 women were detained at the Central Women's prison. Human rights groups denounced the Government's decision to send the male detainees to Coiba, given the atrocious living conditions and its inaccessibility to family members and lawyers. The Supreme Court declared that the detention was legal but that the Government had acted improperly in sending the male detainees to Coiba. The authorities deported one "Reaction Three" leader to Colombia; he subsequently accused police of having beaten him and taken his money, but the charges could not be substantiated.

The Constitution prohibits exile, and there were no reports of forced exile.

e. *Denial of Fair Public Trial.*—The Constitution provides for an independent judiciary; however, the judiciary is susceptible to corruption. The President appoints nine Supreme Court magistrates to 10-year terms, subject to Legislative Assembly confirmation. The Supreme Court magistrates appoint appellate (Superior Tribunal) judges, who, in turn, appoint circuit and municipal court judges in their respective jurisdictions. The Attorney General, who heads the Public Ministry jointly with the Solicitor General, appoints the superior and circuit-level prosecutors. Appointments are supposed to be made under a merit-based system, but the top-down appointment system lends itself to political tinkering and undue interference by higher-level judges in lower-level cases in which they have no jurisdiction.

At the local level, mayors appoint administrative judges who exercise jurisdiction over minor civil and criminal cases in which they may impose fines or sentences of up to 1 year. This system has serious shortcomings. For example, defendants lack adequate procedural safeguards, the officials need not be (and normally are not) attorneys, and some engage in corrupt practices. In reality, appeal procedures are nonexistent. More affluent defendants tend to pay fines while poorer defendants go to jail, one of the chief factors leading to current prison overcrowding.

The Constitution provides that persons charged with crimes have the right to counsel, to be presumed innocent until proven guilty, to refrain from incriminating themselves or close relatives, and to be tried only once for a given offense. If not under pretrial detention, the accused may be present with counsel during the investigative phase of the proceeding. Judges can order the presence of pretrial detainees for the rendering or amplification of statements, or for confronting witnesses. Trials are conducted orally with the accused present, but with little new evidence presented beyond that in the case file compiled by the public prosecutor. The Constitution and Criminal Procedure Code provide for trial by jury at the defendant's election, but only in criminal cases where at least one of the charges is murder.

The Constitution obliges the Government to provide public defenders for the indigent. Many public defenders are not appointed until after the investigative phase of the case, a serious disadvantage for the defendant since it is during this stage that the prosecutor produces and evaluates the bulk of the evidence and decides whether to recommend trial or the dismissal of charges. Nevertheless, many more public defenders than in past years were assigned to cases prior to commencement of the investigative phase, significantly improving the defense's opportunity to present exculpatory evidence. Public defenders' caseloads remained staggering, averaging 410 cases per attorney in 1995. Only 1 new public defender has been hired since 1992, making a total of 36 nationwide, while the caseload increased 74 percent since then. This heavy workload undermined the quality of representation, with many prisoners meeting their public defender for the first time on the day of their trial.

Trial activity was hampered by budgetary shortfalls. Additionally, according to various independent sources, the judicial system was undercut by narcotics-related judicial corruption. Citizen complaints about corrupt practices by Supreme Court Justice Jose Manuel Faundes led to formal charges by the Attorney General that he improperly influenced cases. The Legislative Assembly investigated wrongdoing by Faundes during special Judicial Sessions in August and September, which resulted in a decision to initiate impeachment proceedings against him. The case against Faundes included charges that he abused his authority and accepted cash payments in exchange for lenient sentencing and treatment of certain prisoners, including narcotics traffickers.

The Attorney General also investigated other judicial branch and Public Ministry officials for improprieties. In November President Perez Balladares made sweeping public accusations of corruption in the judicial branch, alleging that a majority of citizens believe justice is "bought and sold" in the country; the President proposed the creation of a new office to review court decisions. Two Supreme Court Justices denounced the President's broad accusations and challenged the executive to present concrete evidence of specific cases of corruption.

In June the lawyer for an accused narcotics trafficker revealed that two narcotics-tainted donations had reached President Perez Balladares' 1994 election campaign. The President promptly and publicly admitted the funds had entered his campaign but insisted that he was personally unaware of their origin at the time. At the President's behest, the Attorney General conducted an investigation, subsequently declaring that no evidence of criminal wrongdoing had been found.

There were no reports of political prisoners. Advocates of the amnesty bill (see Section 1.a.) claimed that its beneficiaries were political prisoners and others charged with, or convicted of, political crimes. Closer scrutiny, however, revealed that many potential beneficiaries were common criminals (including some violent offenders). The Attorney General, who opposed the legislative amnesty, declared at the time that there were no political prisoners or politically motivated prosecutions pending.

f. *Arbitrary Interference with Privacy, Family, Home, or Correspondence.*—The Constitution provides for the inviolability of the home, private papers, and telephonic communications. The authorities may not enter private residences except with the owner's permission, or by written order from the appropriate authority for specific purposes. (These may include entry to assist the victims of crime or disaster, or to conduct lawful health and safety inspections.) In practice, however, there were credible complaints that the police failed to follow legal requirements and instead conducted indiscriminate searches of private residences. The authorities may not examine private papers and correspondence, except as properly authorized by competent legal authority and in the presence of the owner, a family member, or two neighbors.

Despite the view of some that the Constitution prohibits all wiretapping, the Government maintains that wiretapping with judicial branch approval is legal. Under the guidelines established by antinarcotics legislation passed in July 1994, the Public Ministry may engage in undercover operations, including "videotaping and recording of conversations and telephonic communications." The Supreme Court may ultimately decide whether wiretapping is constitutional and, if so, under what circumstances. However, media publication of unauthorized taped phone conversations during the Faundes impeachment hearings suggest that wiretapping is not unknown.

Section 2. Respect for Civil Liberties, Including:

a. *Freedom of Speech and Press.*—The Constitution provides for freedom of speech and the press, and the Government generally respects these rights in practice. Six national daily newspapers, 3 commercial television stations, 2 educational television stations, and over 95 radio stations provide a broad choice of informational sources; all are privately or institutionally owned. Close relatives of the President control one major television station and have close political and economic ties with the management of another. While many media outlets took identifiable editorial positions, the media carried a wide variety of political commentaries and other perspectives, both local and foreign.

Panamanian and foreign journalists worked and traveled freely throughout the country, and the population had access to foreign media. After tense verbal sparring with journalists over coverage of narcotics traffickers contributing to political campaigns, the President eventually accepted the legitimacy of tough investigative journalism on this issue. In August he forced Second Vice President Virzi to apologize publicly after calling journalists "clowns."

There were some cases of government harassment of journalists, such as barring individual journalists from covering government events and pressure on the management of certain television stations to modify their programming. After the scandal caused by the July filming of prisoner beatings at La Modelo prison, some journalists reported being harassed by police who wanted to prevent them from entering adjacent apartment buildings to do additional filming. The Government has legal authority to prosecute media owners and reporters for criminal libel and calumny, but has not used it. Informal pressure on the media was more common.

A special executive branch authority has discretionary powers to administer the libel laws, which provide for fines and up to 2 years in prison. Under the statute, opinions, comments, or criticism of government officials acting in their official capacity are specifically exempted from libel prosecution, but a section of the law allows for the immediate discipline of journalists who show "disrespect" for the office of certain government officials. While this section of the law was not used during the year, its existence inhibits some writers' self-expression.

In November a court cleared the associate director of daily La Prensa of libel charges brought by President Perez Balladares over remarks in a November 1993 newspaper column about party leaders, including Perez Balladares. Also in November, the Public Prosecutor's office summoned another La Prensa journalist to make sworn statements in a libel case brought by the Minister of Public Works over allegations of wrongdoing in 1991 reported in a La Prensa article.

The press laws provide for the establishment of a censorship board. There were no reports of the board taking any restrictive actions in 1996, although one legislator publicly complained that the board has not done enough to control allegedly offensive content of radio and television programs.

The law provides for academic freedom, which was freely exercised in both public and private universities.

b. *Freedom of Peaceful Assembly and Association.*—The Constitution provides for the rights of peaceful assembly and association, and the Government generally respects these rights in practice. No authorization is needed for outdoor assembly, although prior notification for administrative purposes is required.

Several times during the year the Government responded to student unrest at the University of Panama by sending PNP riot police to the campus periphery. In October the police entered the campus directly to deal with protesters. Students and some university staff reacted angrily to the police presence and accused them of excessive use of force. Overall, police response to student protests was restrained, despite considerable interference with public order when the protests spill over onto major thoroughfares, blocking vehicle traffic and threatening passersby. Police showed similar restraint while monitoring large protest marches during the year by civil servants and members of indigenous tribes.

Citizens have the right to form associations and professional or civic groups without government interference. They may form and organize political parties freely, although new parties must meet strict membership and organizational standards in order to gain official recognition and participate in national campaigns. On December 8, the presidents of eight small parties in the process of formation jointly denounced the Electoral Tribunal for allegedly creating intentional obstacles to impede new parties.

c. *Freedom of Religion.*—The Constitution, although specifically recognizing Catholicism as "the religion of the majority of Panamanians," provides for free exercise of all religious beliefs, provided that "Christian morality and public order" are respected. The Government imposes no limitations in practice. Clerics are constitutionally prohibited from holding public office, except as related to social assistance, education, or scientific research.

d. *Freedom of Movement Within the Country, Foreign Travel, Emigration, and Repatriation.*—The Constitution provides for these rights, and the Government respects them in practice. A 9:00 p.m. curfew for minors under 18 years of age in the Panama City and San Miguelito districts of Panama province, imposed in 1992, remained in effect. Police enforcement of the curfew was uneven, with strictest compliance focused on high-crime areas.

The immigration authorities in November deported to Colombia a group of 88 migrants (mostly women and children), who reportedly had fled into the border province of Darien to escape killings and harassment by paramilitary groups and leftist guerrillas. The authorities determined that the Colombians were not entitled to refugee status because they could be resettled in other regions of Colombia and repatriated the group. Subsequently, however, Amnesty International criticized the move and called on the Government to halt any further deportations, claiming that the Colombians were indeed entitled to refugee status and merited protection.

The Government cooperates with the office of the United Nations High Commissioner for Refugees and other humanitarian organizations in assisting refugees. The Government honors the principle of first asylum, but the issue did not arise in 1996.

Section 3. Respect for Political Rights: The Right of Citizens to Change Their Government

The Constitution provides for a representative democracy with direct popular election by secret ballot of the President, two vice presidents, legislators, and local representatives every 5 years. The President is currently limited to a single term, although President Perez Balladares' supporters have suggested he may be interested in having the Constitution amended to permit him to run for a second term. The independent National Electoral Tribunal arranges and supervises elections. The Government respected the rights of its citizens to join any political party, propagate their views, and vote for candidates of their choice.

There are no legal barriers to participation by women or people of African, Asian, or indigenous descent, but their presence in senior leadership positions in government or political parties is not proportionate to their numbers within society. Women hold 5 of 72 Legislative Assembly seats and 1 of 11 Cabinet positions. The Legislative Assembly's vice president is a woman; as are the provincial governors of Panama and Colon, and the mayor of Panama City. In 1994 a woman ran for President and finished second with over 28 percent of the vote.

The Government provides semiautonomous status to several indigenous groups in their homelands, including the San Blas, Madugandi, and Darien Embera-Wounaan reserves. The San Blas groups have two representatives in the Legislative Assembly, proportionate to their share of the population. Locally, the reserve is governed by tribal chiefs, who meet in a general congress twice a year. Neither the Madugandi nor the Embera-Wounaan reserve has its own dedicated legislators, but each has a separate governor.

Section 4. Governmental Attitude Regarding International and Nongovernmental Investigation of Alleged Violations of Human Rights

Human rights organizations, including both religious and secular groups, generally operated without government restrictions. These organizations carried out a full range of activities, including investigations and dissemination of their findings. Human rights advocates generally had free access to government officials while investigating complaints. Amnesty International's criticism of the ruling party's proposed amnesty bill was widely publicized.

On December 29, the Legislative Assembly approved a bill to create an office of "Defender of the People," or a human rights ombudsman. The new office is to be an appendage of the Legislative Assembly, with privileges and immunities comparable to those of a legislator. The ombudsman has broad powers to investigate complaints of human rights abuses, but no coercive authority, depending instead on moral suasion. The Assembly modified the original bill to require that the successful ombudsman candidate be approved by only a simple majority vote, not by two-thirds as originally contemplated. While this will likely simplify the approval process, opposition critics say it could make the incumbent susceptible to political manipulation by the ruling party.

Section 5. Discrimination Based on Race, Sex, Religion, Disability, Language, or Social Status

The Constitution prohibits either special privileges or discrimination on the basis of race, birth status, social class, sex, religion, or political views. Nevertheless, society, particularly the upper class, still harbors many prejudices based primarily on race, sex, and social status.

Women.—Domestic violence against women continued to be a serious problem, and local justices processed thousands of domestic violence cases. The reputable Center for the Development of the Woman estimated that victims report as few as 20 percent of sexual assaults to judicial or law enforcement authorities. The Foundation for the Promotion of the Woman, among other women's advocacy groups and government agencies, operated programs to assist victims of such abuse.

In addition to domestic violence, sexual harassment is a serious threat to the equal status of women in society. A reliable report from the Latin American Committee for the Defense of Women revealed in 1995 that up to 70 percent of female government employees had been sexually harassed in the workplace, 42 percent by their immediate supervisors and 18 percent by even more senior supervisors. In 1995 officials relieved several academics and administrators of their positions at the University of Panama for sexual harassment.

Women generally do not enjoy the same economic opportunities as men. Until 1995 the law did not recognize property in common, and divorced or deserted women are often left destitute. The new Family Code promulgated in 1995 recognizes for the first time joint or common property in marriages. However, the Government has not committed sufficient funding to provide enough judges and administrative resources to enforce the new code's provisions.

The Constitution mandates equal pay for equal work, but wages paid to women are often lower than those for equivalent work performed by men and increase at a slower rate. A 1994 U.N. report noted that women occupy only 4 percent of the managerial positions in Panama. Although statistics are lacking, there are credible reports of hiring practices based on age and "attractiveness." A Government Employees Union leader claimed in September that the Government fired 150 women from their civil service jobs because they were pregnant, and had only reinstated 10 of them.

A number of private women's rights groups, including groups for indigenous women, concentrate on disseminating information about women's rights, countering domestic abuse, enhancing employment and other skills, and pressing for legal reforms. Indigenous women vocally criticized male government administrators and politicians for overlooking their rights. At a formal gathering of Kuna women in San Blas in October, participants complained that male tribal leaders ignore the interests and opinions of women, and alleged that domestic abuse of Kuna women is a serious but underreported problem.

Children.—Education of children is compulsory through the equivalent of ninth grade. The Government furnishes basic health care for children through local clinics run by the Ministry of Health; a central Children's Hospital in Panama City operates on government funds as well as private donations.

The Superior Tribunal for Minors and Superior Tribunal for Families are judicial authorities charged with overseeing the protection and care of minors, but the Government has no specific office charged with protecting children's rights. A women's advocacy group reported in 1994 that 72 percent of children are born from nonstable, short-term relationships. Many children suffer from malnutrition, neglect, and inadequate medical care. A government nutrition survey released in November found that among children entering first grade nationwide in 1994, 24 percent were malnourished. Urban areas showed the lowest levels of malnourishment, while the highest levels were registered among indigenous groups, led by a 71.2 percent rate for Kuna children in San Blas.

Juvenile courts report a high incidence of juvenile delinquency in major urban areas. The Family Code, in force since 1995, placed juvenile court authority, including rehabilitation programs, orphan care authority, and juvenile detention authority, under the Supreme Court. It also clarified reporting authority and strengthened preventive protection powers in suspected juvenile-abuse cases. While it also aimed to create a mechanism to record and report suspected domestic violence cases involving minors, budgetary shortfalls hampered the new bureaucracy's efforts to implement the reporting program.

People With Disabilities.—The Workers with Disabilities Office of the Department of Labor and Social Welfare is responsible for government policy and support for citizens with disabilities and for placing qualified disabled workers with employers. The office was in charge of implementing a June 1993 executive order that provided employers with tax incentives for hiring people with disabilities but has had only minimal success. Although some public buildings and retail stores have access ramps for disabled people, no law or regulation compels the installation of ramps or other facilitated-access features in public or private buildings.

Indigenous People.—Indigenous people number approximately 194,000 (8 percent of the population) and theoretically have the same political and legal rights as other citizens. The Constitution protects the ethnic identity and native languages of indigenous people, requiring the Government to provide bilingual literacy programs in indigenous communities. Indigenous people have legal rights and take part in decisions affecting their lands, cultures, traditions, and the allocation of natural resources. The Family Code recognizes traditional indigenous cultural marriage rites as the equivalent of a civil ceremony. The Ministry of Government and Justice maintains a Directorate of Indigenous Policy. The Legislative Assembly also has an Indigenous Affairs Commission to address charges that the Government has neglected indigenous needs.

Despite legal protection and formal equality, indigenous people generally endure relatively higher levels of poverty, disease, malnutrition, and illiteracy than the rest of the population. Discrimination is widespread. Since indigenous populations infrequently master Spanish well enough to use appropriate legal terminology, they often have difficulty understanding their rights under the law and defending themselves in court. The indigenous population, particularly Ngobe-Bugle, has grown increasingly vocal in requesting that the Government grant it more autonomy by creating more indigenous reserves or expanding existing ones. A general standoff has existed between Government and indigenous reserve status negotiators. Ngobe-Bugle groups complained that private landholders restricted access to claimed tribal lands. The Government supported the landholders' claims that legal leases were still in effect based on prior indigenous members' sales of the property to private individuals. In August police clashed with Kuna Indian protesters over demarcation of indigenous lands in the eastern part of Panama province; several protesters and police officers were injured (see Section 1.c.).

Members of the Ngobe-Bugle tribe continued to pressure the Government into granting them official demarcation of a semiautonomous tribal reserve, a demand that the tribe has pursued unsuccessfully over the last 20 years. The Ngobe-Bugle also demanded that the Government cancel a concession for exploratory copper mining on indigenous lands in Chiriqui province, holding several demonstrations there followed by a symbolic march to Panama City to press their demands in October. The protesters met with government officials, including President Perez Balladares, but refused to participate in separate government-appointed commissions to study the demarcation issue and the mining concession, claiming that the Government was not bargaining in good faith. Under heavy media pressure to resolve the dispute, the Executive Branch on December 2 presented a bill to the Legislative Assembly to create a Ngobe-Bugle semiautonomous region covering approximately 694,000 hectares spread across Chiriqui, Bocas del Toro, and Veraguas provinces. Ngobe-Bugle activists originally denounced the bill because it reduced their original land claim and left the mining concession intact, but protests subsided after an Assembly committee approved the first few articles of the bill.

National/Racial/Ethnic Minorities.—The law prohibits discrimination against any social, religious, or cultural group; however, naturalized citizens may not hold certain categories of elective office. There is some evidence that a constitutional provision reserving retail trade to Panamanian citizens originally was directed at Chinese immigrants, but government officials have stated that it serves as a barrier to prevent foreign retail chains from operating in the country. The measure is not enforced in practice, however. Chinese, Middle Eastern, and Indian residents, as well as citizens of Chinese and Indian descent, operate much of the retail trade, particularly in urban areas.

Leaders of the over 100,000-member East Asian and South Asian communities credibly claimed that Panamanian elites treat Panamanian-resident Chinese and Indians as well as citizens of Asian origin as second-class citizens.

Section 6. Worker Rights

a. *The Right of Association.*—Private sector workers have the right to form and join unions of their choice, subject to registration by the Government. A Labor Code reform package signed in 1995 significantly increased workers' ability to establish unions. The reforms streamline the accreditation and registration process for unions, reduce the minimum size from 50 to 40 workers and cut the Government's required response time on applications from 2 months to 15 days. In the event the Government does not respond within this time frame, the union will automatically be recognized and accorded all rights and privileges under the law.

Neither the Government nor the political parties control or financially support any unions. During debate on the Labor Code, militant labor unions took to the streets to agitate against its passage. The unions claimed that one of their number who was killed during the unrest was a victim of police abuse. The police said that available evidence did not show that the fatal bullet was fired from a police weapon (see Section 1.a.).

According to Ministry of Labor statistics, approximately 10 percent of the total employed labor force is organized. There are 257 active unions, grouped under 6 confederations and 48 federations representing approximately 73,300 members in the private sector.

The 1994 Civil Service Law permits most government workers to form public employee associations and federations and establishes their right to represent members in collective bargaining with their respective agencies. It also provides most workers with the right to strike, except for certain government workers in areas vital to public welfare and security, such as the police and health workers and those employed by the U.S. military forces and the Panama Canal Commission. The Government fired striking air traffic controllers in November, on the grounds that they had abandoned their positions and left the public in danger. Public sector workers are lobbying the Government to have their associations accorded formal "union" status.

The new Labor Code addressed some longstanding concerns of the International Labor Organization (ILO). The code no longer makes labor leaders automatically ineligible to keep their union positions if they are fired from their jobs.

There were fewer private sector strikes in 1996, although unions protested and challenged in court a series of cabinet decrees governing labor and management relations in Export Processing Zones (EPZ's—see Section 6.b.).

Union organizations at every level may and do affiliate with international bodies.

b. *The Right to Organize and Bargain Collectively.*—The Labor Code provides most workers with the right to organize and bargain collectively, and unions widely exercise it. The law protects union workers from antiunion discrimination and requires employers to reinstate workers fired for union activities. The Ministry of Labor has mechanisms to resolve complaints against antiunion employers. The Civil Service Law allows most public employees to organize and bargain collectively and grants them a limited right to strike. The Labor Code establishes a conciliation board in the Ministry of Labor to resolve labor complaints and provides a procedure for arbitration.

Employers commonly hire temporary workers to circumvent onerous labor code requirements for permanent workers; such temporary workers receive neither pensions nor other benefits. The practice of blank contracts is, according to union sources, becoming more widespread. The new labor legislation addresses this problem by requiring all companies to submit copies of all labor contracts for permanent workers to the Labor Ministry and by requiring the Labor Ministry to conduct periodic inspections of companies' work forces and review all contracts to ensure that they are in order. The new code also authorizes the Labor Ministry to levy fines against companies not in compliance with the law.

In January and February, the Government issued cabinet decrees governing labor relations in export processing zones (EPZ's), as a means of attracting investment into areas vacated under the terms of the Panama Canal Treaty. The original decree limited a broad swath of labor rights, including the right to strike and to bargain collectively. The second decree modified the first, and restored most worker rights in EPZ's. However, it provides for collective bargaining with "representatives of employees" but makes no specific mention of trade unions; it requires mandatory arbitration of disputes, and allows for participation on the tripartite (government, labor, and industry) arbitration commission by an unrepresentative worker delegate.

c. *Prohibition of Forced or Compulsory Labor.*—The Labor Code prohibits forced or compulsory labor, and neither practice was reported.

d. *Minimum Age for Employment of Children.*—The Labor Code prohibits the employment of children under 14 years of age as well as those under 15 years if the child has not completed primary school; children under age 16 cannot work overtime; those under 18 years cannot perform night work. Children between the ages of 12 and 15 may perform farm or domestic labor as long as the work is light and does not interfere with the child's schooling. The Ministry of Labor enforces these provisions in response to complaints and may order the termination of unauthorized employment. The Government has not enforced child labor provisions in rural areas, claiming insufficient staff. According to an ILO report, 11,600 children between the ages of 10 and 14 are in the labor force—primarily in farm or domestic labor.

e. *Acceptable Conditions of Work.*—The Labor Code establishes a standard work week of 48 hours and provides for at least one 24-hour rest period weekly. It also establishes minimum-wage rates for specific regions and for most categories of labor. The minimum wage, last increased in January 1993, is $1.00 per hour in the districts of Panama, Colon, and San Miguelito, and for workers in financial services. It is not enough to support a worker and family above the poverty level in the relatively high-cost economy. Most workers formally employed in urban areas earn the minimum wage or above, but most workers in the large informal sector earn below the minimum wage. Unions have repeatedly alleged that contractors operating in the Panama Canal area pay less than the required minimum wage. The Ministry of Labor does not adequately enforce the minimum wage law, due to insufficient personnel and financial resources.

The Government sets and enforces occupational health and safety standards. An occupational health section in the Social Security System is responsible for conducting periodic inspections of especially hazardous employment sites, such as those in the construction industry, as well as inspecting health and safety standards in response to union or worker requests. The law protects from dismissal workers who file requests for health and safety inspections. Workers also have the right to remove themselves from situations that present an immediate health or safety hazard without jeopardizing their employment. They are generally not allowed to do so if the threat is not immediate, but may request a health and safety inspection to determine the extent and nature of the hazard. The Ministry of Labor is responsible for enforcing health and safety violations and generally does so. The standards are fairly encompassing and generally emphasize safety over long-term health hazards, according to organized labor sources. Health problems, however, continue in the banana industry as well as in the cement and milling industries.

PARAGUAY

Paraguay is a constitutional republic with a strong executive branch and an increasingly important bicameral legislature. The President is the head of government and cannot succeed himself. In 1993 Juan Carlos Wasmosy became the country's first freely elected civilian president. (Authoritarian regimes had ruled the country until 1989, when dictator Alfredo Stroessner was overthrown by General Andres Rodriguez, who was elected president later that year.) There are three major political parties and a number of smaller ones. The opposition's power has increased as a result of the changes brought about by the 1992 Constitution and the subsequent election of a civilian President and an opposition-controlled Congress. The Constitution provides for an independent judiciary, and the Supreme Court completely restaffed judicial and prosecutorial positions during the course of the year.

President Wasmosy has worked to consolidate the nation's democratic transition, and in April he resisted an attempted coup by the then-army commander. The military no longer plays an overt political role, and the national police force, under the overall authority of the Ministry of the Interior, has responsibility for maintaining internal security and public order. The civilian authorities maintain effective control of the security forces. The police committed some human rights abuses.

Paraguay has a market economy with a large informal sector. The formal economy is oriented towards services, with less than half of the $8 billion gross domestic product resulting from agriculture and industry. Over 40 percent of the population is engaged in agricultural activity. Wealth continues to be concentrated, with both urban and rural areas supporting a large subsistence sector. Agricultural commodities (soybeans, cotton, lumber, and cattle) continue to be the most important export items. Due to the lingering effects of a 1995 financial crisis, the economy grew 2 percent in 1996, down from an average of 3 to 3.5 percent over the previous 5 years. Annual per capita income is approximately $1,500.

The Government's human rights record improved somewhat, but serious problems remain in certain areas. Principal human rights problems included instances of extrajudicial killings, torture and mistreatment of criminal suspects and prisoners, poor prison conditions, detention of suspects without judicial orders, lengthy pretrial detention, general weaknesses within the judiciary, infringements on citizens' privacy, and firings of labor organizers. Discrimination against women and indigenous people and violence against women are also problems. The Government used violent force to repress one general strike but acted with relative restraint during two others. The Government continued its efforts to convict and punish those who committed human rights abuses during the Stroessner era, bringing several cases to a successful conclusion.

RESPECT FOR HUMAN RIGHTS

Section 1. Respect for the Integrity of the Person, Including Freedom From:

a. *Political and Other Extrajudicial Killing.*—There were at least three politically related killings prior to the November 17 municipal elections. The authorities arrested the opposition Liberal party mayor of Lambare, Celso Cabral, in connection with the November 1 slaying of Agustin Veron Prieto, a member of the ruling Colorado party, during a late-night barroom argument over politics. Cabral has been charged and is to be tried for the killing. The police arrested policeman Teofilo Sanabria for fatally shooting Colorado party activist Raul Bittar November 5, when Sanabria was trying to break up a fracas between Colorado and Liberal party members. Sanabria claimed the shooting was accidental; by year's end the prosecutor had not yet decided whether to file charges. The authorities arrested Tiburcio Nunez, a Colorado party member, for the November 6 killing of Arnaldo Gonzalez, an Encuentro Nacional supporter shot during a political gathering in the town of Capitan Bado. Another killing that may have been politically motivated was the November 3 slaying of Ramon Alvarenga, a campaign manager for Encuentro Nacional, whom an unknown assailant shot twice outside his party office. The police were investigating this incident at year's end.

There were two instances of possible extrajudicial killings by law enforcement officials while performing their duties. On July 1, a guard shot in the back and killed Lourdes Estigarribia Velazquez, a pregnant inmate of the Buen Pastor women's prison, during an escape attempt. The prison guard who fired the shot claimed that it was a warning shot not aimed at the deceased. The case remained under judicial investigation at year's end. On November 2, police officer Oscar Raul Miranda Mazacote shot and killed Gilberto Ramon Diaz, a transvestite prostitute. Miranda, under arrest pending an investigation, said that the fatal round was a warning shot fired after Diaz and several other transvestites began throwing rocks at his police car.

There were numerous allegations of mistreatment of military recruits by noncommissioned and commissioned officers, and several conscripts died in unclear circumstances. Investigations into these incidents were still in progress at year's end. In February the Supreme Court of Military Justice sentenced a noncommissioned officer to 8 years in jail for murdering a conscript in 1994. The military formally charged another noncommissioned officer for the 1995 killing of a naval recruit.

Two of the three judges who were in the process of trying the sedition case against former army commander Lino Oviedo received death threats; there were also allegations of bribery. The tribunal ruled that Oviedo had not committed sedition, a decision very favorable to the defendant.

There were no major developments in the investigations into the 1995 killing of peasant protester Pedro Jimenez or the 1994 killings of peasant leaders Sebastian Larrosa and Esteban Balbuena.

b. *Disappearance.*—There were no reports of politically motivated disappearances.

c. *Torture and Other Cruel, Inhuman, or Degrading Treatment or Punishment.*—The Constitution prohibits torture, as well as cruel, inhuman or degrading punishment or treatment; however, torture and brutal and degrading treatment of convicted prisoners and other detainees continued. A human rights group, the Committee of Churches, reported several cases of torture and other abusive treatment of persons, including women and children, designed to extract confessions, punish escape attempts, or intimidate detainees.

The Public Ministry (Attorney General's office) and the Committee of Churches have filed several criminal complaints on behalf of prisoners, and these cases remained pending in the courts at year's end. The Justice and Labor Ministry suspended and commenced administrative disciplinary proceedings against four juvenile prison guards charged with mistreating detained minors. These cases were pending at year's end. Mistreatment of conscripts was also a problem, and several conscripts died under unclear circumstances (see Section 1.a.).

There were charges that the police used excessive force during the May 2–3 general strike, when 130 people were injured—including 15 policemen—and more than 20 persons were hospitalized. Police reportedly used truncheons against the demonstrators; none of the injuries were life-threatening.

Credible reports continued that landowners, many of them Brazilians living near the border in the Alto Parana, Canindeyu, and Amambay departments, acted without court orders and armed their employees for the purpose of removing squatters from their property. Some of the evictions reportedly were violent, and there were unsubstantiated reports of fatalities. However, the authorities undertook no effective action in response to these reports.

On December 31, the Supreme Court overturned the 1963 murder conviction of Captain Napoleon Ortigoza, who had been released from prison in 1988. The Court ruled that the conviction was based on a confession obtained under torture. Ortigoza, an opponent of dictator General Stroessner, was reportedly subjected to beatings, electroshocks, and 6 months' confinement in a 2-by-1 meter cell during his years in prison. A delegation from the Inter-American Human Rights Commission called the Court's decision "a very positive action that speaks well of the judicial branch."

Prison conditions are extremely poor. Overcrowding and unsanitary living conditions were the most serious problems affecting all prisoners. Mistreatment of prisoners is also a serious problem. Tacumbu prison, the largest in Asuncion, was built to hold 800 inmates but currently houses over 1,400. Similar cases of overcrowding exist at other facilities. At the prison in Encarnacion there is one latrine for 280 detainees.

President Wasmosy was shocked by conditions in the Panchito Lopez juvenile detention center during an October visit, and directed the prompt installation of roofing and a new sewage system, which was completed before the end of that month. In December the Supreme Court upheld a lower court decision that ordered the Ministry of Justice and Labor (responsible for prison operations) to report on the status of the criminal cases against, and the physical condition and needs of, each minor being held at Panchito Lopez. The Ministry had sought to overturn the decision, which responded to a habeas corpus suit filed by Fundacion Tekojoja, a nongovernmental organization (NGO) dedicated to the protection of children's rights.

The Government permits independent monitoring of prison conditions by interested NGO's.

d. *Arbitrary Arrest, Detention, or Exile.*—The Constitution prohibits detention without an arrest warrant signed by a judge and stipulates that any person arrested must appear before a judge within 48 hours to make a statement. The police can arrest persons without a warrant if they catch them in the act of committing a crime, but must bring them before a judge within 24 hours. However, the authorities often violated these provisions.

More than 95 percent of an estimated 3,052 prisoners are being held pending trial, many for months or years after their arrest. Only 4 of 224 jailed juveniles have been convicted. While the law encourages speedy trials, the Constitution permits detention without trial until the accused completes the minimum sentence for the alleged crime, which often occurs in practice. A bail system exists for most crimes, but does not apply to juveniles. Judges frequently set relatively high bail, and many accused are unable to post bond. The Supreme Court, the Public Ministry, and a judicial working group took steps to reduce the large number of detainees held without being sentenced or without cause, but achieved only modest results. The Supreme Court and many criminal court judges also make quarterly visits to the prisons to identify and release improperly held individuals.

The Constitution expressly prohibits employing exile as a punishment.

e. *Denial of Fair Public Trial.*—The Constitution provides for an independent judiciary, and the nine-member Supreme Court is independent in practice.

There are four types of appellate tribunals: Civil and commercial, criminal, labor, and juvenile. Several minor courts and justices of the peace fall within these four functional areas. Based on recommendations from the Magistrates Council, the Supreme Court named some 215 lower court judges and magistrates. While judges traditionally have been subject to political and economic influence, the new Supreme Court acted promptly in several cases to investigate and sanction judges and prosecutors suspected of improper activity. It prosecuted three judges and four more are under investigation. The judicial system remains relatively inefficient, however, due to outdated penal and criminal procedure codes, insufficient resources, and delays as the new judicial officials learn their tasks.

The 1992 Constitution stipulates that all defendants have the right to an attorney, at public expense if necessary, but this right often is not respected in practice. Many destitute suspects receive little legal assistance, and few have access to an attorney sufficiently in advance of the trial to prepare a defense. There are only 31 public defenders available to assist the indigent. Moreover, the public defenders lack the resources to perform their jobs adequately. For example, it is reported that no public defender visited the Emboscada prison from January until September because none could obtain access to an official vehicle.

Trials are conducted almost exclusively by presentation of written documents to a judge who then renders a decision. A Public Ministry official is responsible in most cases for bringing charges against accused persons. Defendants and the Public Ministry can present written testimony of witnesses as well as evidence. All interested parties have access to all documents reviewed by the judge, and defendants can rebut witnesses. Defendants enjoy a presumption of innocence. The judge alone determines guilt or innocence and decides punishment. During the pretrial phase, the judge receives and may request investigative reports. In this phase, the judge is also likely to make a personal inspection of the scene of the crime and of the available physical evidence. The accused often appears before the court only twice: To plead and to be sentenced. An appellate judge automatically reviews all verdicts, and the law provides for appeals to the Supreme Court. The military has its own judicial system.

A separate documentation center and repository holds the government archives discovered in December 1992, which document various human rights abuses and implicate many former government officials of the Stroessner regime. The appellate court affirmed the convictions for human rights abuses of five Stroessner-era officials (former police investigations director Pastor Coronel and police officers Lucilo Benitez Santacruz, Agustin Bellotto Vouga, Camilo Almada Morel, and Juan Aniceto Martinez), as well as their sentences from 9 to 25 years in prison.

There were no reports of political prisoners.

f. *Arbitrary Interference with Privacy, Family, Home, or Correspondence.*—While the Government and its security forces generally did not interfere in the private lives of citizens, there were exceptions in which local officials and police officers abused their authority by entering homes or businesses without warrants and harassing private citizens. The Constitution provides that police may not enter private homes except to prevent a crime in progress or when the police possess a judicial warrant. There were allegations that the Government occasionally spied on individuals and monitored communications for political and security reasons. There also were credible allegations that some government agencies required or pressured their employees to join or campaign on behalf of the ruling Colorado party.

Section 2. Respect for Civil Liberties, Including:

a. *Freedom of Speech and Press.*—The Constitution provides for freedom of expression and the press, and the Government respects these rights in practice. The public and the press exercised these rights more freely than at any time in the nation's recent history.

The print and electronic media are independently owned. The media commonly criticized the Government and freely discussed opposition viewpoints. Although the authorities made several attempts to use the judicial system to silence the press, the courts dismissed them at the trial or appellate level. An appellate court reversed a lower court decision that found a columnist for the afternoon daily Ultima Hora guilty of libeling a prominent Colorado party politician in 1992. The appellate court ruling stated that, although a free press may at times offend, its overall value in democracy outweighs its costs. Vladimir Jara, a journalist for the ABC Color newspaper, had his residence broken into and received death threats after he published reports on suspected law enforcement corruption.

The Government does not restrict academic freedom

b. *Freedom of Peaceful Assembly and Association.*—The Constitution provides for the right of all citizens to free association and peaceful assembly. A law regulating demonstrations in Asuncion limits the areas where and the hours when demonstrations may take place, and requires that organizers notify the Asuncion police 24 hours before any rally in the downtown area. The police may ban a protest but must provide written notification of such a ban within 12 hours of receipt of the organizers' request. The law permits a police ban only if a third party has already given notice of plans for a similar rally at the same place and time. In addition, the law prohibits public meetings or demonstrations in front of the Presidential Palace and outside military or police barracks.

Most political and social demonstrations and rallies occurred without major incidents, including the March 15 peasant march, and the March 28 and August 28 general strikes. However, there was violence during the May 2–3 general strike, which resulted in the arrest of several union leaders, 130 injuries, and charges of excessive use of force by the police (see Section 1.c.).

c. *Freedom of Religion.*—The Constitution provides for freedom of conscience for all persons and recognizes no official religion; the Government continued to respect this freedom. Roman Catholicism is the predominant religion, but all denominations are free to worship as they choose. Adherence to a particular creed confers no legal advantage or disadvantage, and foreign and local missionaries proselytize freely. All religious groups must be registered with the Ministry of Education and Worship, but the Government imposes no controls on these groups.

d. *Freedom of Movement Within the Country, Foreign Travel, Emigration, and Repatriation.*—All citizens may travel freely within the country with virtually no restrictions, and there are no restrictions on foreign travel or emigration.

The Government cooperates with the office of the United Nations High Commissioner for Refugees and other humanitarian organizations in assisting refugees. There are no established provisions to grant asylum or refugee status; the Immigration Department determines each request on a case-by-case basis in consultation with the Ministries of Foreign Relations and the Interior and the Committee of Churches (an NGO that investigates claims to refugee status). The issue of the provision of first asylum has never arisen. There were no reports of the forced return of persons to countries where they feared persecution.

Section 3. *Respect for Political Rights: The Right of Citizens to Change Their Government*

Citizens have the right and ability to change their government through democratic means. Multiple parties and candidates contest the nation's leadership positions. Four parties are represented in the Congress, and nine candidates ran for the presidency in 1993. The Constitution and the Electoral Code mandate general elections every 5 years, voting by secret ballot, and universal suffrage. The executive and legislative branches govern the country; opposition political parties control the Congress. Debate is free and frank. The Congress often rejects important government proposals and overrides presidential vetoes.

The Government survived a test in April, when army commander General Lino Oviedo threatened to remove President Wasmosy. Strong public reaction and prompt international condemnation convinced him to back down and accept appointment as Defense Minister, a post not in the chain of command. However, President Wasmosy rescinded that offer, in the face of continued public demonstrations, after Oviedo retired from the army.

Vestiges remain, however, of the Stroessner-era merging of the State, the armed forces, and the Colorado party. The press has reported the use of state resources, particularly vehicles, to support party political rallies. There were also credible reports of government officials requiring public employees to attend Colorado party functions and contribute to party coffers. Since the failure of the April coup attempt, military influence over political activity diminished markedly.

There are no formal legal impediments to women seeking to participate in government and politics. Voters elected 5 women to the Congress (3 of 45 Senators, 1 of whom died in October, and 2 of 80 national Deputies), and there is 1 woman, the Secretary for Women's Affairs, in the Cabinet. The new Electoral Code requires that, in their internal primaries, 20 percent of each party's candidates for elective office be women. Women are well-represented in the judicial system as judges and prosecutors.

Members of indigenous groups are entitled to vote, and the percentage of indigenous people who exercised this right grew dramatically in recent years. Nevertheless, the inhabitants of some indigenous communities report being threatened and inhibited from fully exercising their political rights.

Section 4. *Governmental Attitude Regarding International and Nongovernmental Investigation of Alleged Violations of Human Rights*

Several human rights groups operate in Paraguay, including the Committee of Churches (an interdenominational group that monitors human rights and provides legal assistance), Prodemos (a group linked to the Catholic church), Tekojoja (a group dedicated to protection of children's rights), SERPAJ (a group that defends conscientious objectors), and the local chapter of the Association of Latin American Lawyers for the Defense of Human Rights. The Government did not restrict the activities of any human rights group.

The Director General of Human Rights, located in the Ministry of Justice and Labor, chairs the National Commission on Human Rights, which is drafting a national plan on human rights and sponsors seminars to promote human rights awareness. This office has access to congressional, executive, and judicial authorities. It does not have subpoena or prosecutorial powers, but may forward information concerning human rights abuses to the Attorney General for action. It also serves as a clearing house for information on human rights and has trained thousands of educators in human rights law.

Section 5. *Discrimination Based on Race, Sex, Religion, Disability, Language, or Social Status*

Although the Constitution and other laws prohibit discrimination, certain groups faced significant discrimination in practice.

Women.—Spousal abuse is common. In 1994 primary care centers treated over 5,000 women for injuries linked to domestic violence, and greater numbers are estimated for 1996. Official complaints are rarely filed, or when filed are soon withdrawn due to spousal reconciliation or family pressure. The Public Ministry is prosecuting just two cases of spousal abuse, both of which are pending before the courts. To date the courts have not yet convicted any perpetrators of domestic violence against women. The Secretariat of Women's Affairs chairs a national committee, made up of other government agencies and NGO's, that has developed a national plan to prevent and punish violence against women. Pursuant to the plan, an office of care and orientation receives reports on violence against woment and coordinates responses with the National Police, primary health care units, the Attorney General's office, and NGO's. The Secretariat also conducts training courses for the police, health care workers, prosecutors, and others.

The law prohibits trafficking and sexual exploitation of women, but the authorities do not enforce it effectively. Exploitation of women, especially teenage prostitutes, remains a serious problem. Law enforcement officials regularly stage raids on houses of prostitution, and several brothel owners were being tried for employing minors, although there were no convictions in these cases by year's end.

The Secretary for Women's Affairs continued to sponsor programs intended to enable women to have free and equal access to employment, social security, housing, ownership of land, and business opportunities. However, sex-related job discriminationcontinues to be common and widely tolerated. Some women complained that job promotions were conditioned upon their granting sexual favors.

Several groups work to improve conditions for women. One is SEFEM, which highlights such issues as women and public policy, women and social policy, participation of women in local development, and women in the Americas. Other groups include Sumando, an NGO promoting educational reform policy and voter participation in elections, and Women for Democracy, which is active in civic and electoral education. These groups are effective advocates for change.

Children.—The Constitution protects certain children's rights, and stipulates that parents and the State should care for, feed, educate, and support children. Boys and girls are entitled to equal treatment in education and health care.

There is no societal pattern of abuse of children. However, approximately 26,000 children work in urban areas as street vendors or as prostitutes. The majority of these children suffer from malnutrition, lack of access to education, and disease. The employers of some young girls working as domestic servants or nannies deny them access to education and mistreat them. Employers sometimes falsely charge those who seek to leave domestic jobs with robbery and turn them over to the police.

Baby trafficking continued to be a serious problem, as foreign adoptive parents were willing to pay from $20,000 to $40,000 in adoption fees and costs to adopt a healthy baby. In order to develop new legislation to address the problem, in 1995 the Government suspended international adoptions for 1 year; Congress extended this suspension for an additional 6 months in September.

President Wasmosy and the armed forces chief of staff have ordered all officers responsible for recruiting to ensure that all conscripts meet the constitutionally mandated minimum age of 17 years for military service. There were several reported violations, including allegations of military recruiters forcing underage recruits to join units. The military took no significant disciplinary action against those responsible for underage recruits.

People With Disabilities.—The 1992 Constitution provides for equal opportunity for people with disabilities and mandates that the State provide them with health care, education, recreation, and professional training. It further requires that the State formulate a policy for the treatment, rehabilitation, and integration into society of people with disabilities. Congress has never enacted, however, legislation to establish such programs. Many people with disabilities face significant discrimination in employment; others are unable to seek employment because of a lack of accessible public transportation. Accessibility for the disabled has not yet been mandated through law; the vast majority of the nation's buildings, both public and private, are inaccessible to people with disabilities.

Indigenous People.—The unassimilated and neglected indigenous population is estimated at 75,000 to 100,000. Weak organization and lack of financial resources limit access by indigenous people to the political and economic system. Indigenous groups relied primarily upon parliamentary commissions to promote their particular interests, notwithstanding the fact that the Constitution provides indigenous people with the right to participate in the economic, social, political, and cultural life of the nation. The Constitution also protects their property interests, but these rights are still not fully codified. The Constitution provides that Public Ministry officials may represent indigenous people in matters involving the protection of life and property. The Public Ministry has charged landowners with exploiting and killing Indians on their estates. These cases remained under judicial investigation at year's end.

The Government's National Indigenous Institute has the authority to purchase land on behalf of indigenous communities and to expropriate private property under certain conditions to establish tribal homelands. However, many indigenous people find it difficult to travel to the capital to solicit land titles or process the required documentation associated with land ownership.

The main problems facing the indigenous population are lack of education, malnutrition, lack of medical care, and economic displacement resulting from development and modernization. Scarce resources and limited government attention resulted in little progress in dealing with these problems.

Section 6. Worker Rights

a. *The Right of Association.*—The Constitution allows both private and public sector workers (with the exception of the armed forces and the police) to form and join unions without government interference. The Constitution contains several provisions that protect fundamental worker rights, including an antidiscrimination clause, provisions for employment tenure, severance pay for unjustified firings, collective bargaining, and the right to strike. Approximately 10 percent (150,000) of workers are organized.

In general, unions are independent of the Government and political parties. However, one of the nation's three labor centrals, the Confederation of Paraguayan Workers (CPT), has traditionally been closely aligned with the ruling Colorado party. These ties appear to be loosening, as the CPT supported all three general strikes.

All unions must be registered with the Ministry of Justice and Labor. The registration process is cumbersome and can take several months. Employers who wish to oppose the formation of a union can further delay union recognition by filing a writ opposing it. However, virtually all unions that request recognition eventually receive it, and the Ministry recognized 29 new unions through October. The Constitution provides for the right to strike, bans binding arbitration, and prohibits retribution against strikers and leaders carrying out routine union business, a prohibition often violated by employers. Voluntary arbitration decisions are enforceable by the courts, but this mechanism is still rarely employed. High-level labor ministry officials are available to mediate disputes, and helped resolve over 50 cases.

The International Labor Organization (ILO) Committee on Freedom of Association criticized the Government for failing to protect worker rights in five cases dealing with minimum-wage fixing machinery, the right to organize, abolition of forced labor, discrimination in employment and occupation, and employment policy.

Unions are free to form and join federations or confederations and affiliate with and participate in international labor bodies.

b. *The Right to Organize and Bargain Collectively.*—The law provides for collective bargaining, and many collective contracts were successfully concluded. The number of negotiated collective contracts continued to grow; however, they were still the exception rather than the norm in labor-management relations and typically reaffirmed minimum standards established by law. When wages are not set in free negotiations between unions and employers, they are made a condition of individual offers of employment made to employees.

While the Constitution prohibits antiunion discrimination, the firing and harassment of some union organizers and leaders in the private sector continued. Fired union leaders can seek redress in the courts, but the labor tribunals have been slow to respond to complaints and typically favored business in disputes. The courts are not required to order the reinstatement of workers fired for union activities. As in previous years, in some cases where judges ordered reinstatement of discharged workers, the employers disregarded the court order with impunity. There are a number of cases in which trade union leaders, fired as long as 5 years ago, have not yet received a decision from the courts.

There were more than 30 strikes by unions affiliated with the Unitary Workers Central alone. The vast majority of these were directly related to the firing of union officials (over 100 cases reported), to management violations of a collective contract, to management efforts to prevent the free association of workers, or to demands for benefits such as payment of the minimum wage or contribution to the social security system. The failure to meet salary payments also frequently precipitated labor disputes. Principal problems included bottlenecks in the judicial system and the inability or unwillingness of the Government to enforce labor laws. There were also complaints of management creating parallel or "factory" unions to compete with independently formed unions. There were several cases of workers who chose not to protest because of fear of reprisal or anticipation of government inaction.

The major labor centrals and peasant organizations organized general strikes on March 15, May 2–3, and August 28. The strikes were relatively peaceful, with scattered incidents of violence, demonstrations, and vandalism, but no deaths or serious injuries were reported (see Section 1.c.). Police arrested several labor leaders during the May strike, but quickly released them.

c. *Prohibition of Forced or Compulsory Labor.*—The law prohibits forced labor. However, cases of abuse of national service obligations occurred. There were several reports of conscripts forced to work as servants or construction workers for military officers in their residences or privately owned businesses. Apart from abusing national service obligations, the authorities appear to effectively enforce the law.

d. *Minimum Age for Employment of Children.*—The Director General for the Protection of Minors in the Ministry of Justice and Labor is responsible for enforcing child labor laws. Minors between 15 and 18 years of age may be employed only with parental authorization and cannot be employed in dangerous or unhealthy conditions. Children between 12 and 15 years of age may be employed only in family enterprises, apprenticeships, or in agriculture. The Labor Code prohibits work by children under 12 years of age, and all children are required to attend elementary school. In practice, however, many thousands of children, many of them younger than 12 years of age, may be found in urban areas engaged in informal employment such as selling newspapers and sundries, shining shoes, and cleaning car windows. In rural areas, it is not unusual for children as young as 10 years of age to work beside their parents in the field. Local human rights groups do not regard families harvesting the crop together as an abuse of child labor.

e. *Acceptable Conditions of Work.*—The executive, through the Ministry of Justice and Labor, has established a private sector minimum wage sufficient to maintain a minimally adequate standard of living. The minimum salary is adjusted whenever annual inflation exceeds 10 percent and was $240 per month (480,069 guaranies) at year's end. The Ministry is unable to enforce the minimum wage, however, and most analysts agree that from 50 to 70 percent of workers earn less than the decreed minimum.

The Labor Code allows for a standard legal workweek of 48 hours (42 hours for night work), with 1 day of rest. The law also provides for an annual bonus of 1 month's salary and a minimum of 6 vacation days a year. The law requires overtime payment for hours in excess of the standard, but there are no prohibitions on excessive compulsory overtime. Many employers violate these provisions. Workers in the transport sector routinely stage strikes to demand that their employers comply with the Labor Code's provisions on working hours, overtime, and minimum wage payments.

The Labor Code also stipulates conditions of safety, hygiene, and comfort. The Ministry of Justice and Labor and the Ministry of Health did not effectively enforce these provisions, due in part to a lack of inspectors and other resources. This led the labor movement to sponsor inspector training programs designed to ensure that unsafe or unhealthy conditions were registered. Workers have the right to remove themselves from situations that endanger health or safety without jeopardy to their continued employment, but may not do so until such conditions are formally recognized by the Ministries of Labor and Health. Although workers who file complaints about such conditions are protected by law, many employers reportedly took disciplinary action against them.

PERU

Peru is a multiparty republic with a dominant executive branch. President Alberto Fujimori was reelected to a second 5-year term in 1995 under provisions of a Constitution enacted in 1993. The President's party also controls Congress, which passed a law permitting the President to run for an unprecedented third term (opposition parties were challenging the law at year's end). The Constitution also provided for several new judicial institutions to help create a more effective and independent system of justice and, with a view to reform, the entire legal system is undergoing a review directed and controlled by the executive branch.

The police and military share security duties. Civilian authorities generally maintain effective control of the security forces. Since 1980 much of the security forces' effort has been directed against the Sendero Luminoso and the Tupac Amaru Revolutionary Movement (MRTA) terrorist groups. They continue to pose a threat in some areas, but at a much reduced level than in previous years, despite the MRTA's hostage taking attack in December. Members of the security forces committed some human rights abuses.

Over the past 5 years, the Government implemented major economic reforms, moving from heavy regulation to one of the most market-oriented economies in the hemisphere. Government controls on capital flows, prices, and trade have been eliminated. The Government has privatized most state enterprises, and those remaining are scheduled to be sold by the end of 1997. As a result, inflation was brought under control, and growth and foreign investment soared. Gross domestic product was estimated at $51.5 billion. Major exports include minerals (principally copper), fishmeal, and textiles. Illegal exports of processed coca are thought to have earned about $600 to $800 million in past years. Unemployment is around 8 percent, but more than half of the economically active population works in the informal sector of the economy, which largely operates beyond government supervision and taxation. The poor account for 45 percent of the population, of which half live in extreme poverty.

Although the human rights situation improved somewhat, serious problems remain. Security forces were responsible for extrajudicial killings, disappearances, torture, and beatings. Although individual prison directors made some efforts to improve conditions in their own prisons, overall prison conditions remain extremely harsh, particularly in the case of prisoners jailed for terrorism offenses. Arbitrary detention, accountability, lack of due process, lengthy trial delays, and prolonged pretrial detention remain problems. The authorities at times infringed upon citizens' privacy rights. Violence against women and children and discrimination against the disabled, indigenous people, and minorities are continuing problems. Child labor is also a problem.

In April a Human Rights Ombudsman was sworn in, and in August Congress established an ad hoc commission to review and recommend for presidential pardon those unjustly detained for terrorism or treason. However, Congress extended yet again "faceless" tribunals, considered a major reason for the unjust imprisonment of an estimated 700 to 1,000 individuals on terrorism and treason charges, and it also extended the processing by military judges of civilians accused of the most serious terrorism offenses.

Sendero Luminoso and MRTA terrorists were responsible for the vast majority of the killings and other violence. Sendero Luminoso used torture and other forms of brutality, infringed upon citizens' privacy rights, intimidated religious workers, and violated the rights of indigenous people. In December the MRTA attacked the Japanese ambassador's residence, initially holding hundreds of people hostage, an event not resolved by year's end.

RESPECT FOR HUMAN RIGHTS

Section 1. Respect for the Integrity of the Person, Including Freedom From:

a. *Political And Other Extrajudicial Killings*There were no political killings attributed to security forces. However, there continued to be reports of deaths caused by police beatings of detainees. On March 22, police picked up engineer Mario Palomino on a Lima street and beat him to death in a police station after he allegedly complained about the police publicly mistreating a detainee. The Government is currently prosecuting five officers for Palomino's death.

Armed forces personnel also beat citizens to death. According to human rights monitors, on August 23 soldiers detained Nicolas Carrion Escobedo, a resident of Uruspampa village in Sanchez Carrion, La Libertad, and took him to the military base at Sarin. Later that day, Escobedo was found dead. An autopsy revealed that he had received heavy blows to the head as well as other parts of his body. Relatives of Alberto Flores Montejo reported that soldiers based in the town of Aucayacu detained him on March 24; he was never seen again. The judicial investigation into the case determined that Montejo was killed in Madre Mia, San Martin department, and referred the case to the prosecutor's office in Tocache for further investigation. In August military personnel also reportedly beat and killed one soldier who lost a rifle at the Monzon base. On August 30, military personnel killed farmer Jorge Chavez, who was suspected of a role in the rifle's disappearance, and then—according to witnesses—drank Chavez's blood.

In the case of Jhoel Huaman Garcia, who was killed while in police detention in 1995, a court sentenced two police officers in July to 5 and 6 years in prison. A third police officer is charged but has fled.

A 1995 law granted amnesty from prosecution to those who committed human rights abuses during the war on terrorism from May 1980 to June 1995. When lower court judge Antonia Sacquicuray declared the Amnesty Law unconstitutional, Congress immediately passed a second law blocking any judicial review of the law's constitutionality. Subsequently, a split decision by a superior court overturned the Sacquicuray decision. These events created considerable concern over military and police impunity for past abuses. The Amnesty Law also cleared the records of security force personnel who had already been convicted of human rights abuses, including the eight military perpetrators of the 1992 La Cantuta massacre, who were sentenced in 1994 but released by military authorities a few days after the Amnesty Law's passage.

In July the United Nations Human Rights Committee severely criticized the Amnesty Law and called for its repeal. Committee members considered the Amnesty Law a violation of the Constitution, reflecting the earlier Sacquicuray decision. The Amnesty Law demonstrates a lack of serious commitment to accountability and the protection of human rights.

Sendero Luminoso, whose insurgency has led to the deaths of over 25,000 persons since 1980, continued to kill civilians. During the year, Sendero killed a total of 124 persons, including security force personnel and civilians, according to statistics compiled by Peruvian nongovernmental organizations (NGO's). Among the civilians killed by Sendero was Pascuala Rosado, a community leader in Huaycan known for her opposition to Sendero. On July 30, Sendero killed community leader Epifanio Santarria in Los Olivos, near Lima. In February Sendero killed a community leader and his two sons in Angashyacu, Huanuco. On August 22, Sendero murdered the brother of the mayor of Delicias, Huanuco.

b. *Disappearance.*—Disappearances continued to be reported. A human rights group working in the Huallaga valley reported nine disappearances. The army is believed responsible for two of them. On July 27, the army detained Maria Cardenas Espinoza in Chinchabito, Huanuco. While the army denied that it is holding her, other detainees reported seeing her at the Tingo Maria army base.

On February 13, Belen Zavallos Masgo disappeared from his home in La Esperanza, Huanuco. According to members of his family, three masked and armed men took him away when they raided his house. They beat him badly and dragged him into a waiting car. Two days later, Belen Zavallos' wife reported her husband's disappearance to the human rights prosecutor's office in Huanuco. On March 15, the prosecutor's office reported that it had evidence that members of the armed forces carried out the kidnaping.

A human rights group working in the Huallaga valley blamed Sendero for the disappearance of Rufino Velasquez Pujay on July 28 from Moyuna near Aucayacu, Huanuco.

c. *Torture and Other Cruel, Inhuman, or Degrading Treatment or Punishment.*— Although the Constitution prohibits torture and inhuman or humiliating treatment, security force torture and brutal treatment of detainees remains common. This is as true for common criminals as it is for alleged subversives. Torture most often took place in the period immediately after detention. The law permits police to hold terrorism suspects incommunicado for 10 days, and for another 15-day period in cases of treason. Human rights groups report that the incidence of torture is high during this time, partly because detainees are normally not allowed access to family or an attorney except when giving sworn statements to the public prosecutor.

Eyewitnesses and human rights monitors credibly reported that government security forces still routinely torture suspects at military and detention centers in some emergency zones, where certain constitutional guarantees are suspended due to high levels of terrorist activity. In Tocache 17-year-old Juan Gutierrez Silva was tortured repeatedly on July 6, when he refused to sign a confession for allegedly shooting at the girlfriend of a military officer. When hospitalized after 10 hours of beatings, Gutierrez's skull was cracked, he had been stabbed with a thin rod 10 times in the chest area, and suffered cuts in the neck and left arm. Near death, Gutierrez was transported to Lima for medical treatment. At that point, the police offered to pay for his medical treatment if Gutierrez's family would sign a statement that his injuries were self-inflicted. The family refused. The police in Tocache nevertheless issued a statement asserting that Gutierrez's injuries were self-inflicted. Human rights workers claim that incidents similar to Gutierrez's are not rare in Tocache. However, most detainees who are tortured or beaten do not speak out for fear of reprisal.

Army personnel at the Monzon army base in the Huallaga Valley have been implicated in the torture of a 5-year-old girl, who was beaten in an effort to obtain her mother's confession. Human rights groups received numerous reports of torture and beatings by soldiers in emergency zones. In Pucallpa on April 11, three police officers detained and beat the 21-year-old son of a former police officer. One of the officers allegedly tried to rape the detainee, who was never told why he was being held. The young man was released April 13 as a result of his father's intervention. Reports also continue of rape of female detainees by the security forces or prison personnel. In one high-profile case in Lima, a woman reported that she was drugged by a male prison nurse and raped. As a result, the nurse was arrested and charged with a crime; however, the charges were dismissed, and he returned to his job. Legal action against those who commit prison rapes is rare.

Besides beatings, common methods of torture included electric shock, water torture, asphyxiation, and the hanging of detainees by a rope attached to their hands tied behind the back. Common forms of psychological torture included sleep deprivation and death threats against both detainees and their families. Interrogators frequently blindfolded their victims during torture to prevent them from later identifying their abusers. The authorities rarely if ever bring the perpetrators of such acts to trial in court.

Many victims of Sendero Luminoso terrorism also showed signs of torture. Credible accounts indicate that Sendero tortured people to death by slitting throats, strangulation, stoning, and burning.

Prison conditions are extremely harsh. Prisoners in many facilities experienced unsanitary conditions, poor nutrition and health care, and occasionally harsh treatment by both prison staff and fellow inmates. Human rights groups report that prisoners jailed for terrorist acts are singled out for particularly inhuman treatment. This includes years of incarceration in cells 2 meters square, unusually short exercise periods (30 minutes per day), and infrequent, brief family visits (30 minutes per month by adults, but 30 minutes every 3 months by children), as well as refusal by prison authorities to allow prisoners to touch their visiting children. At least some of the prisons where those convicted of terrorist acts are jailed, such as Yanomayo in Puno, are located at very high altitudes where the cold temperature and inadequate supply of oxygen negatively affect the health of inmates. Illegal drugs are available in abundance, and tuberculosis and AIDS are reportedly at near-epidemic proportions in Lima's Lurigancho prison, the country's largest, containing just over 24 percent of the male prison population. The police chief at Lurigancho prison admitted that some of the prisoners there had contracted AIDS or tuberculosis while in prison. There were reports of prisoners suffering from severe depression, advanced neuroses, and schizophrenia, but there was no mental health assistance available.

Corruption continued to be a problem among prison staff, who were implicated in offenses such as sexual blackmail, selling narcotics and weapons, and arranging escapes. Prisoners often have to bribe guards to get a mattress and report that guards subject inmates to beatings, torture, and degrading treatment. In an effort to improve prison staff, the National Penitentiary Institute (INPE) began to evaluate the work performance and ethics of its personnel and dismissed 222 INPE employees in August. As part of its anticorruption drive, INPE announced in September the arrest of an employee in Callao for taking a bribe from a relative of a detainee. INPE, as part of its efforts to improve prison management, moved all female prisoners from facilities in Callao to the Chorrillos prison in Lima, leading to increased overcrowding. Public phones for use by inmates were installed in both Callao and Chorrillos.

Detainees held temporarily in windowless cells in Lima's Palace of Justice are not allowed outside for exercise and fresh air and are taken to the bathroom only once a day. Adequate food, health care, and bedding are often not provided by the prison authorities, requiring families of prisoners to provide for these basic needs. In some prisons, female inmates are allowed to see their children only once every 3 months. While conditions for many prisoners remained inadequate, the Government continued to make a costly and extensive effort to improve existing penal facilities, construct new penitentiaries, and ameliorate the physical conditions of detention.

The authorities were able to quell peacefully a June 14 riot by 5,000 prisoners at Lurigancho prison protesting new restrictions on family visits, unlike in 1986, when security forces killed over 120 prisoners after a riot at that facility. The authorities suspended the prison director and security chief, but later reinstated the prison director. The Inter-American Court of Human Rights ruled in September that the Government should pay $154,000 in compensation to the families of three prisoners who died in a similar 1986 El Fronton prison riot.

Many rural communities lack appropriate detention facilities. For example, in Tocache, all male and female detainees are held separately in two large rooms with no privacy, sometimes for up to 2 years. Detainees who are minors are held with adults in the same room, even though this contravenes the law.

The authorities continued to permit International Committee of the Red Cross (ICRC) representatives to visit detainees in any place of detention, including prisons, jails, police stations, and military bases. However, in late December, in the wake of the MRTA's seizure of the Japanese ambassador's residence (see Section 1.g.), the Government suspended an agreement that allowed the ICRC to visit over 4,000 accused or convicted terrorists, among them MRTA members, in the prisons of the Ministry of Justice. During the year, the Government prohibited many human rights monitors from other groups from visiting some prisons.

d. *Arbitrary Arrest, Detention, or Exile.*—The Constitution, Criminal Code, and antiterrorist legislation delineate the arrest and detention process. However, a number of constitutional protections are suspended in emergency zones. For example, security forces do not need an arrest warrant; they may legally hold incommunicado those detained for treason or terrorism and deny them access to an attorney during the 10-day interrogation period, except when giving formal statements.

In areas not subject to a state of emergency, the law requires a judicial warrant for arrest, unless a perpetrator is caught in the act. However, the Organic Law of the National Police permits detention of an individual for any investigation, which is contrary to constitutional provisions. The authorities must arraign persons arrested within 24 hours (a law they frequently violate, according to informed observers), except in cases of terrorism, drug trafficking, or espionage, for which the limit is 15 to 30 days. If the military is the detaining authority, it must turn over detainees to the civilian police within 24 hours (or as soon as practicable in remote areas). However, the military regularly disregard this law.

A 1993 modification to antiterrorism legislation authorized lower court and superior court judges to order the unconditional release of terrorist defendants if there was insufficient evidence to bring a case against them. However, in practice, judges have rarely applied this law; rather, persons accused of terrorism sometimes must wait until their cases have been reviewed and dismissed by the Supreme Court before they are freed, a process that often lasts more than a year. Another 1993 modification to the antiterrorist laws restored a detainee's right to a prompt judicial determination of the legality of the detention ("habeas corpus"). In practice, however, this provision has gone unheeded. According to human rights attorneys, judges have denied most requests for such hearings.

According to INPE statistics, almost 76 percent of the country's prison population—about 16,700 of the almost 22,000 detainees—consisted of accused prisoners awaiting the conclusion of their trial. The average delay between arrest and trial in civil cases as well as in criminal or terrorism cases was between 26 and 36 months. However, those tried on treason charges by military courts generally wait no longer than 40 days between the time of detention and the beginning of the trial.

In November retired General Rodolfo Robles was violently abducted on a street and placed under arrest. For 2 hours, his family had no news of his whereabouts, until a government Congressman announced that Robles was being held in a military prison on charges of disobedience, insulting a superior officer, insulting the military, and giving false testimony. Robles's arrest took place after he had charged in a televised interview that the military had reactivated a death squad and was responsible for the October bombing of a television transmitter. (In 1993, Robles had publicly confirmed the existence of a military death squad whose members were later convicted of killing nine students and a professor at La Cantuta University.) After widespread criticism of the arrest, on December 3 President Fujimori sent to Congress a bill for an amnesty of retired military officers under trial for criticizing the military. Congress passed the law on December 5, and Robles was released from custody 2 days later. After his release, Robles publicly charged that his arrest was a bungled attempt by the military to kill him disguised as a terrorist assassination.

The law which amnestied Robles also applied to the military judge and prosecutor who had refused to accept a civilian court judge's habeas corpus ruling in favor of Robles. The authorities initially had transferred that judge—Greta Minaya—from her job after she issued the habeas corpus decree, but they transferred her back after Congress approved the Robles amnesty.

The Constitution does not permit exile, and the Government does not practice involuntary exile of its citizens.

e. *Denial of Fair Public Trial.*—The judicial branch is not fully independent of the executive. The 1993 Constitution provides for an improved system for naming judges, which was intended to produce a significantly more independent judiciary. It also provides for several new judicial institutions that would theoretically enhance the professionalism and independence of the judiciary: An Office of the Defender of the People (a human rights ombudsman); a Tribunal of Constitutional Guarantees (to rule on the constitutionality of legislation and government actions); the National Judiciary Council (a permanent, independent entity designed to test, name, confirm, and periodically evaluate and discipline the country's judges and prosecutors); and a Judicial Academy (to train judges and prosecutors).

In June Congress finally agreed upon seven members to form the Tribunal of Constitutional Guarantees, and they were installed in August. However, many critics have already questioned the independence of this tribunal: While three of its members are in some way associated with the President and his party, it only takes two to prevent any law or government action from being declared unconstitutional. In addition, these critics point to recent legislation that limits the window of opportunity for challenging the constitutionality of a particular law to a brief 6-month period immediately following promulgation.

In order to improve the entire judicial branch's performance, the President created a Judicial Coordination Commission, which serves as an umbrella over a number of important judicial institutions. However, in what government opponents say was an effort to ensure executive control of the justice system, the President appointed as head of this commission a retired Navy commander who reports directly to him.

The judicial structure consists of lower courts, superior courts, and appellate courts, with the Supreme Court at its apex.

The justice system is generally based on the Napoleonic Code. Judicial proceedings have three stages. The first is before an examining judge in a lower court; the second is conducted by a superior court which tries and sentences the defendant; and the third is before an appeals court. A Public Ministry prosecutor investigates criminal cases and submits an opinion to a lower court judge, who decides whether to indict. Following study of the case, the judge renders a verdict, which must then be reviewed by a superior court prosecutor. The superior court prosecutor submits an advisory opinion to a superior court judge, who holds a trial. Virtually all civilian court convictions are appealed to the Supreme Court. Defendants have the right to be present at their trial. A 1993 modification to antiterrorism laws eliminated convictions in absentia. Defendants have the right to counsel, but the Government often does not provide indigents with qualified attorneys.

Jorge Santistevan de Noriega was sworn in as the first human rights ombudsman in April. The Ombudsman's office opened in mid-September in Lima, and there are plans for additional offices throughout the country. In August the Ombudsman was named along with the Justice Minister and a representative of the President, Father Hubert Lanssiers, as members of a congressionally mandated ad hoc commission to recommend presidential pardons for detainees believed to have been unjustly accused of terrorism or treason. According to human rights groups, there are more than 1,000 such individuals. The commission's mandate lasts 6 months and can be renewed for an additional 6-month period. On September 30, President Fujimori granted the first 3 pardons; by the end of the year 110 persons had received such pardons. The Government suspended the granting of pardons after the MRTA terrorist takeover of the Japanese ambassador's residence on December 17, but the process was expected to resume after the hostage crisis is over.

President Fujimori acknowledged the problem of those unjustly detained for terrorism in a speech on July 1, in which he spoke about the work of a team of attorneys which, with government support and under the guidance of Father Lanssiers, had obtained the release of 150 such individuals during the previous 2 years. In his July 28 state of the union message, President Fujimori also referred to the problem of those unjustly imprisoned and asserted that the abuses resulted from the "repentant terrorist" law, which expired in November 1994. Although human rights groups have welcomed the review of the cases of those unjustly incarcerated for terrorist acts, they claim that those unjustly accused should be released and declared innocent rather than pardoned and should be compensated for the years that they have spent in jail.

Proceedings in military courts that hear terrorism and treason cases do not meet internationally accepted standards for due process. Military trials are closed to the public and are carried out in secrecy by military judges whose identities are not revealed in court. Defense attorneys do not have access to evidence, nor can they interview police or military witnesses (to protect their identities) prior to or during the trial. There are reports that many of the judges are active duty line officers with no legal background. Military tribunals in theory must pass judgment within 10 days. Defendants may appeal a verdict to the Superior Military Council, which has 10 days to make a decision. The Supreme Council of Military Justice must act on a final appeal within 5 days, although this calendar is subject to delays. Human rights groups charge that military judges have sentenced some defendants before their lawyers were even notified that the trial phase had begun.

According to Supreme Council of Military Justice statistics, between 1992 and August 1996, these faceless military tribunals tried 1,498 cases of treason. In those cases in which a verdict was reached, the tribunals sentenced 346 individuals to life sentences, 338 persons to 30 years or less, sent 256 cases to civilian court terrorism trials, and absolved 40 persons of all charges. From January to August, the Supreme Council of Military Justice reached verdicts in 124 treason cases, leading to 41 life sentences, 59 sentences of 30 years or less, 23 cases sent to civilian courts for trial, and 1 individual found not guilty.

The sentencing in January to life imprisonment of U.S. citizen Lori Berenson on treason charges focused additional international attention on the lack of due process in the faceless military tribunals. The authorities ignored requests on Berenson's behalf for an open trial in a civilian court on charges stemming from her involvement with the MRTA.

In October Congress extended for another year trials by faceless superior court tribunals of terrorism cases, thereby further undermining fairness, due process, and accountability. Human rights groups remain concerned about persons found not guilty by the faceless military courts but remanded to faceless civilian courts where a new trial is initiated. There were fewer reports of such problems in 1996 than in 1995. In July the United Nations Human Rights Committee, which monitors compliance with the International Covenant on Civil and Political Rights, called for an end to the faceless tribunal system because of its lack of due process guarantees. In September United Nations Special Rapporteur Dato'param Cumaraswamy visited Peru and repeated this call.

The President did not sign criminal procedures code legislation passed by Congress in December 1995 and returned it to Congress for revision. This legislation was designed to institute new accusatorial, investigative, and trial procedures; to grant more investigative authority to civilian prosecutors; and to allow prosecution of military personnel in civilian courts for crimes that do not come under the Military Code of Justice. Informed observers noted that the police opposed increased authority for civilian prosecutors, and the armed forces opposed civilian prosecution of military personnel.

There were no reports of political prisoners. Members of Sendero Luminoso and MRTA charged with terrorism—however arbitrarily in some instances—are not considered political prisoners.

f. *Arbitrary Interference with Privacy, Family, Home, or Correspondence.*—The Constitution requires security forces to have a judicial warrant to enter a private dwelling, but this requirement is suspended in the emergency zones. Security forces in those areas routinely conduct searches without a warrant. There were frequent credible reports of illegal telephone monitoring.

A number of rural communities—with arms, training, and encouragement from the army—have organized self-defense forces (or "rondas") to protect local communities against terrorism and banditry. These have had a noticeable impact on curbing Sendero's activity in certain areas of the country. In some parts of the country, rondas have existed for centuries as a form of social organization to protect communities from invaders and rustlers. However, military authorities organized many of the newer rondas and sometimes coerced peasants into participating.

As a regular practice and to a far greater degree, Sendero and the MRTA forced peasants to join their military ranks, often for extended periods, and to participate in terrorist attacks and executions.

g. *Use of Excessive Force and Violations of Humanitarian Law in Internal Conflicts*With the internal conflict winding down, reports of use of excessive force by the military declined significantly from previous years. However, there were reports of excessive use of force by the military in counterinsurgency operations against terrorists in San Martin and Huanuco departments. During operations in these departments, reports continued of arbitrary detention by the military in communities where Sendero Luminoso had entered and terrorized residents.

Although both the army and Sendero Luminoso committed serious human rights abuses in Peru's internal conflict, the latter was responsible for many more heinous acts. Sendero frequently used arbitrary violence against civilians and nonmilitary targets. It continued to detonate powerful bombs in public places, indiscriminately killing and injuring bystanders, and persisted in its practice of entering villages and killing residents. Victims included unarmed women and children. Sendero Luminoso terrorists were responsible for 124 killings, including 6 current or former members of that organization. A Sendero car bomb on July 26 killed one civilian and seriously injured a police officer in front of a police station in central Lima. A Sendero car bomb next to a Shell warehouse in Lima on May 16 injured 10 persons. In armed confrontations, Sendero never took prisoners or attended to the wounded. Sendero also practiced forced military conscription of children. In Delicias, Huanuco department, Sendero terrorists forcibly recruited eight adolescents in August. There were also reports that Sendero forced Ashaninka tribesmen in the Satipo area of Junin department to join its ranks.

On December 17, MRTA terrorists took control of the Japanese Ambassador's residence during a national day reception and initially took over 600 hostages. The hostage takers gradually released most of the hostages, however, and by the end of the year there were fewer than one hundred hostages, including the Foreign Minister and Ambassadors from Japan and Bolivia. The hostage takers' key demand was the release of over 400 imprisoned MRTA terrorists. Through November MRTA terrorists were blamed for the deaths of three persons, including a soldier and a police officer.

Section 2. *Respect for Civil Liberties, Including:*

a. *Freedom of Speech and Press.*—The Constitution provides for freedom of speech and of the press. The Government generally respects these provisions, although the Government uses its economic power in the form of newspaper advertising to influence the press. The Government selectively disseminates information in order to exert some control over the views expressed. Government press offices have refused to send news releases and other information to some magazines and often limited opposition media access to official transportation when the President visited remote parts of the country or traveled abroad.

The media represent a wide spectrum of information and opinion, with 22 daily newspapers, 10 television stations, 2 cable systems, and 120 radio stations in Lima alone. The media regularly criticize the Government and its policies. The Government owns a daily newspaper, a television network, and two radio stations, none of which are especially influential.

Opposition political parties have access to the media. Television stations, although generally progovernment, provide regular access to opposition figures on a variety of news and public affairs programs. The print press is divided between popular, largely apolitical tabloids and more comprehensive editorial-bearing papers, which at times articulate positions in opposition to the Government's policies.

The authorities detained and prosecuted three military intelligence officers for their involvement in the October 17 bombing of the television transmitter of a station in Puno that broadcasts a Lima program hosted by an outspoken critic of the Government. One of those arrested, Angel Sauni Pomaya, had been investigated for his involvement with the military death squad responsible for the 1991 Barrios Altos massacre.

As part of the newly enacted legislation to review terrorism cases, the Government pardoned on September 30 and released from detention journalist Jesus Alfonso Castiglione and two other detained journalists. Castiglione, the former director of Radio Amistad in Huacho, was serving a 20-year sentence for terrorism despite a lack of evidence. Another well-known case of a detained journalist, Javier Tuanama Valera, remains unresolved. The authorities have detained Tuanama, the former managing editor of the Tarapoto daily newspaper Hechos, for 6 years on various terrorism charges, despite two acquittals, one on a charge that he took part in a terrorist act committed after his detention in 1990.

The Government exercised substantial influence over the media through the placement of advertisements. Some media owners claimed that the Government also encourages private advertisers to boycott opposition publications and uses tax investigations to harass them. Many media owners are involved in other economic activities that require government licensing or involve bidding on government contracts. Opposition media access to government information has been restricted.

b. *Freedom of Peaceful Assembly and Association.*—The Constitution expressly provides for the right of peaceful assembly and association, and the authorities normally respect these rights in practice, except in areas under a state of emergency (where the right of assembly is suspended). Public meetings in plazas or streets require advance permission, which may be denied only for reasons of public safety or health. Municipal authorities usually approved permits for demonstrations in Lima and nonemergency zones.

c. *Freedom of Religion.*—The Constitution provides for freedom of religion, and the Government respects this provision in practice. The Constitution recognizes Roman Catholicism "as an important element in the historical, cultural, and moral development of the nation" but also establishes the separation of church and State. Conversion to other religions is respected, and missionaries are allowed to enter and proselytize.

Sendero Luminoso rejects religion and continues to threaten and intimidate religious workers. Members of the Mormon Church, in particular, continued to receive threats and were victims of extortion by Sendero.

d. *Freedom of Movement within the Country, Foreign Travel, Emigration, and Repatriation.*—The Constitution provides for the right of free movement, and there are no political or legal constraints on foreign travel or emigration. However, the authorities can restrict people with pending criminal and, in some cases, civil charges from leaving the country. The Constitution prohibits the revocation of citizenship; repatriates (both voluntary and involuntary) are not treated any differently from other citizens. Freedom of movement is suspended in the emergency zones but is generally permitted under the army's supervision. Nonetheless, the authorities may detain travelers in an emergency zone at any time. Passengers on public transportation are controlled at check points throughout the country.

Sendero still occasionally tries to interrupt free movement within the country. Sendero roadblocks were reported to be commonplace in sections of the Huallaga valley.

The Government cooperates with the office of the United Nations High Commissioner for Refugees and other humanitarian organizations in assisting refugees. There are provisions for granting asylum and refugee status, although the procedures have been used by only a few persons in recent years, principally Cubans. The issue of the provision of first asylum did not arise in 1996. There were no reports of forced return of persons to countries where they feared persecution.

Section 3. *Respect for Political Rights: The Right of Citizens to Change Their Government*

The Constitution provides for the right of citizens to change their government, and citizens exercise this right in practice. The law bars only groups that advocate violent overthrow of the Government from participating in the political process. Voting by secret ballot is mandatory for all citizens between the ages of 18 and 70; however, prisoners and members of the armed forces and the police are ineligible to vote. Legal opposition parties represent a wide variety of opinion and ideology, although the degree of grassroots support and organization of some parties is often not significant.

Running for a second term under provisions of the 1993 Constitution, President Fujimori was reelected to a 5-year term in 1995 over 12 other candidates, with 65 percent of the valid vote. Voters also elected 120 members of the unicameral Congress. Fujimori's Cambio 90/Nueva Mayoria party won 67 seats in Congress; 12 opposition parties won the remaining 53 seats. In August Congress passed a law, over considerable opposition, permitting the President to run for a third term. This law states that the President could run again in 2000 because he would be running for his second term under the 1993 Constitution. The opposition embarked on a petition drive for a referendum on this issue. However, on October 10, Congress approved a law declaring that, for a referendum to take place, not only must the proponents gather 1.2 million signatures (as was the original requirement), but at least 48 members of Congress must also vote to hold it. In a 4-to-1 decision on October 31, the National Elections Commission (JNE) ruled that the new law could not be applied retroactively. The JNE's decision not only put the petition drive for a referendum on the third term back on track, but also that for another referendum on the privatization of the state oil company, PetroPeru.

Women and minorities participate fully in government and politics. There are 11 female members of Congress. In addition, 3 of the 15 cabinet ministers and several vice ministers are women, as are the Attorney General and a Supreme Court justice.

Peruvians of Asian descent hold leadership positions in government; President Fujimori is from an Asian ethnic minority. There are several indigenous congressmen, and a recent vice president was a Quechua speaker. However, it is rare for indigenous people, who represent 30 percent of the population, to reach the highest leadership levels in the public sector. Until recently, discrimination has often led to exclusion of members of these groups from leadership positions in government. Members of the black minority have no leadership role in government, and there are no black members of Congress.

Section 4. Governmental Attitude Regarding International and Nongovernmental Investigation of Alleged Violations of Human Rights

The Government allowed numerous nongovernmental organizations dedicated to monitoring and advancing human rights to operate freely, although government officials continued to criticize them. The military often restricted the ability of local and international human rights workers to investigate human rights abuses; the Government usually ignored human rights groups' requests for information. It prohibited many human rights monitors—except those from the ICRC (until late December)—from visiting some prisons. Public attacks by the Government against both domestic and international human rights monitors lessened in 1996. Legitimate fears of physical attack by Sendero severely limited the ability of human rights monitors to carry out their work in some parts of the country.

A human rights attorney fled Peru for 3 months early in 1996 due to threats that she received. On February 18, three masked men entered the home of human rights attorney Edith Luquillas Gonzalez, who was investigating the case of Jhoel Huaman Garcia (see Section 1.a.). When they did not find Luquillas, the men threatened her family members that she could be killed at any moment.

Most Peruvian human rights NGO's are independent and generally objective in their views. Several private human rights groups joined in 1985 to form an umbrella organization known as the National Coordinating Committee for Human Rights, or Coordinadora. The Coordinadora maintains a policy of not mixing politics with human rights (its individual members may do so, but not in the Coordinadora's name). Its members, although widely recognized by the general public as thorough and impartial observers, are privately criticized by military, judicial, and police officials as biased against the authorities. The Coordinadora has begun to work closely with the newly established Human Rights Ombudsman in addressing key areas of mutual concern.

Human rights groups repeatedly denounced Sendero Luminoso as the greatest violator of human rights in Peru, while simultaneously documenting violations by the security forces. Documentary evidence indicates that Coordinadora members have been balanced in their denunciations of abuses by both sides. In its annual report, the Coordinadora regularly reported and denounced political violence by Sendero as well as by the MRTA and has issued press communiques denouncing violence by terrorist groups.

Section 5. Discrimination Based on Race, Sex, Religion, Disability, Language, or Social Status

The Constitution provides for equal rights for all citizens and specifically prohibits discrimination based on ethnic origin, race, gender, language, religion, opinion, or economic condition. Nevertheless, discrimination against women, the disabled, and minorities continued.

Women.—Violence against women, including rape and spousal abuse, is a chronic problem, according to local women's groups and law enforcement offices. According to official statistics, nationwide there were approximately 5,900 complaints of violence against women in 1995. Of these, 50 percent were due to marital problems, 20 percent for other family causes, and 18 percent due to economic problems. In 40 percent of the cases the aggressor was under the influence of alcohol, and in 10 percent he was under the influence of drugs. Despite this large number of complaints, many cases go unreported. Rape is also believed to occur frequently, and high-profile cases of minor girls who were raped and killed has led to calls for drastic sentences to punish those responsible. In July Congress formed its first committee to look specifically at women's issues, and among the new legislation it studied was a bill providing for mandatory prison sentences of up to 12 years for those who attack women. Rape victims frequently are reluctant to come forward, and there are no accurate statistics of rape victims. Women's groups complain of police indifference and the pervasive assumption that if a women was raped she probably enticed her attacker.

In order to address the special concerns of women, President Fujimori announced creation in October of a new Ministry of Women's Issues and Human Development and appointed Miriam Schenone to head it. In addition, Human Rights Ombudsman Santistevan named a deputy in November specifically to handle women's rights. Partially in reaction to a lack of response by regular policemen to domestic abuse cases, the authorities established special police stations in Lima and other major cities where policewomen deal directly with abused women. They report a rising number of complaints of domestic violence. In addition, women's groups have established legal aid and health centers for women. Judicial authorities take legal action against perpetrators of domestic violence. Although the Government has passed strong legislation against domestic violence, it is not always implemented, especially outside the major cities.

Sexual harassment in the workplace continues to be a common problem. One study by a women's rights organization showed that 62 percent of working women knew of cases of sexual harassment in the workplace.

The Constitution grants women equality, and laws on marriage, divorce, and property rights do not discriminate against women. Nevertheless, tradition often impedes access by women to leadership roles in major social and business institutions. The 1995 employment law treats both men and women equally and supersedes earlier legislation that had provided special working conditions for women. Among the benefits female workers lost were the guarantee of an hour each day for breast-feeding of children up to 1 year of age and the requirement that employers with more than 25 female employees provide a nursery.

Children.—The Government made efforts to address children's human rights and welfare; however, much work still needs to be done. The Government provides free, compulsory education through primary school. The President frequently emphasized the need to improve education at all levels, but the Government does not have sufficient funds for public schools, and school enrollment actually declined in 1996. A 1993 government survey reported that only 59 percent of children between the ages of 6 and 11 attend school, and only 27 percent of those between the ages of 12 and 17. Millions of children continue to suffer from malnutrition and live in extreme poverty. There were frequent press reports highlighting issues relating to child labor and children living in poverty.

In Lima there are thousands of orphaned, homeless, and abandoned children, and many of them are forced to work in the informal economy to support themselves. Estimates vary, but most experts believe almost 1 million children between the ages of 6 and 17 work; 55 percent of them live in rural areas.

Violence against children is a serious problem. According to some estimates, approximately half of all rapes are perpetrated against minors. Almost 70 percent of homeless children reported that they left their homes because of mistreatment, whereas only 16 percent said that they left their homes because of economic problems.

New legislation in 1995 discontinued the practice of adult terrorism trials for those under the age of 18 and ordered that underage prisoners be moved to juvenile detention facilities. In 1996, however, new cases continued to come to light of persons under 18 years of age being held in adult prisons.

People With Disabilities.—Although the Constitution states that disabled persons "have the right to respect of their dignity and to a regime of protection, care, rehabilitation, and security," the Government has few resources available for assisting the disabled or preventing discrimination against them. There is no law mandating access to buildings for people with disabilities, and few accommodations (such as wheelchair ramps on streets and in buildings) exist for them.

The number of those disabled is believed to have increased as a result of the years of violence during the Sendero and MRTA insurgencies. Although according to the 1993 census, 1.3 percent of the population (288,526 persons) are disabled in some form, nongovernmental experts believe that the figure is in reality much higher. Disabled persons face discrimination when seeking employment, and many are reduced to begging in the streets. The publicity surrounding the performance of Peru's medal-winning team to the 1996 Special Olympics again focused public attention on the problems of the disabled.

The Rehabilitation Center for the Blind, a private institute, has operated in Lima for 29 years providing job skill training and other useful guidance to thousands. There are several schools for blind children throughout the country.

Indigenous People.—The 1993 Constitution prohibits discrimination based on race and provides for the right of all citizens to speak their native language. Nevertheless, the large indigenous population faces pervasive discrimination and social prejudice. Because of geographic isolation, government centralization, lack of organization, and social marginalization, indigenous people in general are unable to participate in, or are excluded from, decisions affecting their lands, cultures, traditions, and the allocation of natural resources. In jungle areas, colonists, coca growers, guerrillas, and business interests steadily encroach on native lands, many seeking to exploit natural resources. Indigenous people lack access to public services in many inland areas while business investment is concentrated on the coast.

The largest indigenous groups are those speaking Quechua and Aymara, which are recognized as official languages. These languages are not taught in schools, however, and efforts to introduce Quechua and Aymara curriculums have so far failed. There are also dozens of smaller native language groups.

The 45,000 Aguaruna-Huambisa people inhabit areas near the Upper Cenepa Valley where the 1995 Peru-Ecuador border conflict took place. Aguaruna-Huambisa leaders have complained about poor living conditions and the lack of consultation by the Government on matters affecting their welfare, including land tenure.

The Confederation of Amazonian Nationalities of Peru (CONAP) is one of eight NGO's representing the more than 50 ethnolinguistic groups—nearly 200,000 people—from the Peruvian Amazon, and does not necessarily speak for the entire indigenous population. CONAP is critical of the 1995 land law which, according to its interpretation, allows Amazonian land to be bought and sold if no one is using it or living on it. Land as a marketable commodity is an alien concept to some indigenous people, who have a religious way of relating to it. Moreover, some indigenous people are nomadic, moving from one part of their lands to another, and do not use all their land all the time. Recognizing that mining and other development activity is inevitable, CONAP says that indigenous people want to benefit from it, rather than die out because of it. Consultation and negotiation about the disposition of their lands is key, however, and CONAP claims that the Government's Indigenous Institute has failed to provide such an opportunity.

Amazon tribes, particularly the over 10,000 Conipo-Shipibo people of the Ucayali region, are also struggling to obtain government recognition of their economic problems and to obtain development projects to improve their living standards. The Conipo-Shipibo people have started their own radio program, "the indigenous voice of the Ucayali," which is broadcast in their native language. Amazon tribes in areas of oil exploration and extraction have complained that environmental damage has negatively affected the health of their members and sometimes led to deaths. These tribes assert that the Government does not take their concerns seriously.

Sendero Luminoso has been the most egregious violator of indigenous rights. At the end of the year, thousands of Ashaninkas in the central jungle area remained displaced, and many were in areas under Sendero control, although some displaced groups of Ashaninkas reincorporated into their original communities. Reports continued, however, of forcible recruitment of Ashaninkas by Sendero.

National/Racial/Ethnic Minorities.—Peru's population includes several small racial minorities, the largest of which are blacks of African descent and Asians. Blacks, who tend to be concentrated along the coast, face particularly pervasive discrimination and social prejudice and are among the poorest groups in the country. They are excluded from leadership roles in government, military, and business institutions. Both the navy and the air force reportedly have unwritten policies that exclude blacks from the officer corps. According to Peru's two black human rights groups, police routinely detain persons of African descent on suspicion of committing crimes for no other reason than the color of their skin, and police rarely act on complaints of crimes against blacks. The Government has taken no action to remedy these problems.

Although Peruvians of Asian descent have traditionally been subjected to discrimination, this has changed during the past decade as Peru has looked toward Asia as a growth model and as the Asian community has achieved financial success. Apart from President Fujimori, who is of Japanese descent, many other Asians now hold prominent leadership positions in business and government.

Section 6. Worker Rights

a. *The Right of Association.*—It is estimated that only 5 percent of the total work force of 8.5 million belong to organized labor unions. More than half of all workers are in the informal sector of the economy. Workers do not need prior authorization to form a trade union, nor, by law, can employment be conditioned on union membership or nonmembership. Existing unions represent a cross section of political opinion. Although some unions have been traditionally associated with political groups, the law prohibits unions from engaging in explicitly political, religious, or profitmaking activities. The several union leaders who ran unsuccessfully for Congress in 1995 all did so as individuals, without union sponsorship.

In 1995 Congress approved a new employment law, which all of the main union confederations publicly criticized for violating the rights of unions, including freedom to bargain collectively and the right to work. Unions also complained that the new law eliminated the compulsory reinstatement of dismissed workers when it is proven that they were unjustly dismissed. At present such workers only have the right to a year's pay as indemnification. In practice, the new Labor Code has had a negative impact on the right of association by making it easier for companies to fire workers involved in union activities.

The International Labor Organization (ILO) in June called on the Government to adopt new legislation to enhance freedom of association, including a guarantee that reduction of personnel not be used as an antiunion measure and permitting new probationary workers the right to join a union.

There are no restrictions on membership in international bodies. Several major labor unions and confederations are affiliates of international labor groups, including the ILO and the International Confederation of Free Trade Unions.

b. *The Right to Organize and Bargain Collectively.*—The 1993 Constitution recognizes the right of public and private workers to organize and bargain collectively. However, it states that these rights must be exercised in harmony with broader social objectives. Labor regulations promulgated prior to the 1993 Constitution provide that workers can form unions based on profession, employment, or geographic location. The regulations exclude temporary, probationary, apprentice, or management employees from union membership. They require a minimum of 100 members to form trade unions by branch of activity, occupation, or for various occupations; and a minimum of 20 workers to form a union within a company. They also limit the number of union officials, the amount of time they may devote to union business on company time, and require them to be active members of the union. No legal provisions require employers who commit antiunion discrimination to reinstate workers fired for union activities.

Labor regulations set the number of union representatives who can participate in collective bargaining negotiations (a minimum of 3, a maximum of 12) and establish the negotiating timetable. The management negotiating team cannot exceed the size of the workers' team; both sides may have attorneys and professional experts in attendance as advisers. A majority of all workers in a company, whether union members or not, must approve a strike by a secret ballot. A second vote must be taken upon petition of 20 percent or more of the workers. The labor movement criticized provisions of the new Labor Code that facilitate an employer's ability to dismiss employees as impeding workers' right to bargain collectively. However, there are apparently no restrictions that would prohibit unions from negotiating a higher standard than the base line of protection provided for workers by the law. To become an official collective bargaining representative, a union must represent 20 workers.

In response to a complaint regarding the right to organize and bargain collectively, an ILO committee noted that the 1995 Labor Code fails to ensure the protection of workers against acts of antiunion discrimination and to protect workers' organizations against acts of interference by employers. In addition, the ILO found obstacles to voluntary negotiation resulting from the requirement of a majority not only of a number of workers, but also of enterprises, in order to conclude a collective agreement for a branch of activity or occupation.

Labor regulations also permit companies unilaterally to propose temporary changes of work schedules, conditions, and wages and to suspend for up to 90 days collective bargaining agreements if obliged to do so by an unexpected event or economic conditions, provided that they give 15 days' notice to employees. If workers dispute the proposed changes, the Labor Ministry must resolve the dispute based upon criteria of "reasonableness" and "economic necessity." In such cases, employers must authorize vacation time and in general adopt measures that avoid aggravating the employment situation.

A conciliation and arbitration system resolves disputes, but union officials complain that their proportionate share of the cost of arbitration can exceed their resources. (In the past, business and government entities had covered these costs.) Union officials also state that a growing number of companies utilize a policy of hiring workers on temporary, personal services contracts to prevent union affiliation. The new law restricts such hiring to 20 percent of a company's work force. The Labor Ministry is still formulating regulations on this point. This is a subject of continuing contention between organized labor and employers and is one of the concerns that labor continues to raise in international forums. Employers deny the accusation of antiunion bias and assert that labor stability provisions of the law have made long-term commitments to workers too expensive.

Special regulations permitting greater flexibility in application of the Labor Code in export and duty free zones provide for the use of temporary labor as needed, flexibility in labor contracts, and a wage system based upon supply and demand. As a result, workers in duty free zones are unable to unionize. Duty free zone employers do not engage in illegal activities to prevent unionization.

c. *Prohibition of Forced or Compulsory Labor.*—The Constitution prohibits forced or compulsory labor. However, there are periodic reports of the practice of forced labor in remote Andean mountain and Amazonian jungle regions of the country. In response to a complaint filed with the ILO, the Government in 1994 acknowledged the existence of such practices and asserted that it had taken measures to end these abuses. However, reports of forced labor, including that of children in gold mines in the remote Madre de Dios department, continued to emerge. Forced labor is not a problem in urban areas.

d. *Minimum Age for Employment of Children.*—Education through primary school is compulsory and free. A high percentage of school-age children nevertheless work rather than attend daytime classes, with only a small number of such children attending classes at night. Given widespread poverty, children work in the informal economy without government supervision of wages or conditions from a very early age to help support their families. A recent government labor study found that 8 percent of the work force was between the ages of 6 and 14. The Government's National Institute of Family Welfare cooperates with the United Nations Children's Fund and the Inter-American Development Bank to assist street children and other child laborers.

The minimum legal age for employment is 16. The new Labor Code raised the age from 21 to 25 years for the special youth labor provisions, which allow employers to pay lower salaries as part of a program to provide new workers with specialized training. The new code also increased the period of apprenticeship from 18 to 36 months. In addition, workers covered by these provisions now may make up 30 percent (increased from 15 percent) of a company's work force.

Child labor is heavily used in the agricultural sector and in informal gold mining, but not in other major export industries, such as petroleum and fisheries. Recent studies by NGO's found that approximately 4,500 workers younger than 18 years of age work in harsh conditions in the informal Madre de Dios gold mines. Many of these workers are under the age of 15, and some are as young as 11. These child laborers were recruited from their families through a system known as "enganche" in Puno, Juliaca, Sicuani, Abancay, and Cuzco, through which they are provided free transportation to the mine and reportedly agree to work for at least 90 days before being paid. The Government has not exercised control over these employment agencies, and employers do not comply with labor code provisions relating to juveniles. Children who work in the informal gold mines lack proper medical care, must work long hours, and are often subjected to beatings, mistreatment, and rape. There are also reports of these mine workers not being paid.

More than 20 children between the ages of 4 and 14 work in harsh conditions at Cerro de Belen caves near Arequipa collecting pumice stones, which are used in the manufacture of stonewashed jeans. These children work alongside their parents and other family members and suffer from various illnesses including tuberculosis and atrophy of the respiratory tract.

e. *Acceptable Conditions of Work.*—The Constitution provides that the State promote social and economic progress and occupational education. It states that workers should receive a "just and sufficient" wage, to be determined by the Government in consultation with labor and business representatives and "adequate protection against arbitrary dismissal." The current minimum wage is about $87 (S/217) per month and is generally considered inadequate to support a worker and family. A considerable portion—one-half according to some estimates—of the country's work force makes only the minimum wage.

The Constitution also provides for a 48-hour workweek, a weekly day of rest, and a yearly vacation. It prohibits discrimination in the workplace. In December President Fujimori vetoed legislation passed by Congress in September that would have improved benefits and working hours for household maids. While occupational health and safety standards exist, the Government lacks the resources to monitor or enforce compliance. Employers and workers generally agree upon compensation for industrial accidents on an individual basis. The Government introduced reforms in 1993 eliminating the need to prove culpability in order to obtain worker's compensation for injuries. There are no provisions for workers to remove themselves from dangerous work situations without jeopardy to continued employment.

ST. KITTS AND NEVIS

St. Kitts and Nevis is a multiparty, parliamentary democracy and a member of the Commonwealth of Nations. The Constitution provides the smaller island of Nevis considerable self-government, as well as the right to secede from the Federation in accordance with certain enumerated procedures. A Prime Minister, a Cabinet, and a bicameral Legislative Assembly comprise the Government. A Governor General, appointed by the British Monarch, is the titular head of state, with largely ceremonial powers. After national elections in June 1995, Dr. Denzil Douglas of the St. Kitts and Nevis Labour Party became Prime Minister and formed a government with 7 of 11 seats in the legislature. The judiciary is independent.

Security forces consist of a small police force, which includes a 50-person Special Services Unit that receives some light infantry training, and a small coast guard.

The mixed economy is based on sugar cane, tourism, and light industry. Most commercial enterprises are privately owned, but the sugar industry (the country's largest economic enterprise) and 85 percent of arable land are owned by a state corporation.Per capita gross domestic product was about $3,500 in 1994.

Human rights were generally respected, although the Government continued to restrict access by the opposition to government-controlled media. Violence against women is a problem.

RESPECT FOR HUMAN RIGHTS

Section 1. Respect for the Integrity of the Person, Including Freedom From:

a. *Political and Other Extrajudicial Killing.*—There were no political or other extrajudicial killings.

b. *Disappearance.*—There were no reports of politically motivated disappearances.

c. *Torture and Other Cruel, Inhuman, or Degrading Treatment or Punishment.*—Law enforcement authorities abide by the constitutional prohibitions against the use of torture or other forms of inhuman or degrading treatment or punishment. Family members, attorneys, and clergy are permitted to visit detainees regularly.

St. Kitt's prison was built in the 1830's. Prisoners suffer from severe overcrowding, poor food, and lax security. These conditions have contributed to riots in the past, although none occurred in 1996.

d. *Arbitrary Arrest, Detention, or Exile.*—The Constitution prohibits arbitrary arrest and detention, and this provision is respected in practice. The law requires that persons detained be brought before a court within 48 hours. There were no reported cases of exile.

e. *Denial of Fair Public Trial.*—The Constitution provides that every person accused of a crime must receive a fair, speedy, and public trial, and these requirements are generally observed.

The judiciary is highly regarded and independent. The court system comprises one high court and four magistrates' courts at the local level, with the right of appeal to the Organization of Eastern Caribbean States Court of Appeal. Final appeal may be made to the Privy Council in the United Kingdom. There are no military or political courts. Legal assistance is available for indigent defendants.

There were no reports of political prisoners.

f. *Arbitrary Interference With Privacy, Family, Home, or Correspondence.*—There were no reports of arbitrary government or police interference in the private lives of individuals. The law requires judicially issued warrants to search private homes.

Section 2. Respect for Civil Liberties, Including:

a. *Freedom of Speech and Press.*—The Constitution provides for freedom of speech and the press, and, for the most part, the authorities respected these provisions in practice. However, the Government owns the only radio and television station on St. Kitts, and these media generally did not adequately publicize rallies and conventions held by the opposition political party. There is a religious television station and a privately owned radio station on Nevis.

St. Kitts and Nevis does not have a daily newspaper; each of the major political parties publishes a weekly or biweekly newspaper. A third weekly newspaper is nonpartisan. The papers are free to criticize the Government and do so regularly and vigorously. The nonpartisan paper claims that politicians both in opposition and the Government have threatened to close it down; however, the paper recently celebrated its second anniversary without interruption of its publication. International news publications are readily available.

The Government does not restrict academic freedom.

b. *Freedom of Peaceful Assembly and Association.*—The Constitution provides for the right of peaceful assembly. Political parties organized demonstrations, rallies, and public meetings during the 1995 election campaign without significant government interference. Many meetings sponsored by the Nevis Island administration and opposition parties were held in Nevis to discuss the secession question.

c. *Freedom of Religion.*—The Constitution provides for the free exercise of religion, and religious practices are not restricted. All groups are free to maintain links with coreligionists in other countries.

d. *Freedom of Movement Within the Country, Foreign Travel, Emigration, and Repatriation.*—The Government does not restrict travel within or departure from the country.

No formal government policy toward refugee or asylum requests exists. The issue of provision of first asylum did not arise. There were no reports of forced expulsion of anyone having a valid claim to refugee status; however, government practice remains undefined.

Section 3. Respect for Political Rights: The Right of Citizens to Change Their Government

Citizens are free to change their government by peaceful means. A vigorous multiparty political system exists in which political parties are free to conduct their activities. Periodic elections are held in which all citizens 18 years of age and older may register and vote by secret ballot.

The Legislative Assembly has 11 elected seats; 8 for St. Kitts and 3 for Nevis. In the June 1995 elections, Dr. Denzil Douglas' St. Kitts and Nevis Labour Party won seven of eight seats at stake in St. Kitts with 60 percent of the popular vote, and Douglas became Prime Minister. The People's Action Movement (PAM), the former ruling party, took only one seat, but received 40 percent of the vote. The Concerned Citizens Movement won two of the three Nevis seats; the Nevis Reformation Party won the remaining one. The island of Nevis has considerable self-government and its own legislature.

In accordance with its rights under the Constitution, the Nevis Island Assembly in July initiated steps towards secession from the Federation when a bill of secession passed unanimously on first reading. On second reading in November, however, two opposition members abstained and the bill failed to obtain the required two-thirds majority of the five-seat Assembly. The bill would have authorized drafting a new constitution and, after a 6-month period to allow the citizenry time to debate, the holding of a Nevis-wide referendum. The secession referendum would require two-thirds of the votes cast on Nevis in favor for secession to be ratified. All parties involved have been following constitutional procedures, and no acts of violence have been recorded in connection with the secession question.

Although the Constitution prohibits discrimination on grounds of political opinion or affiliation, the opposition PAM alleges widespread employment discrimination by the St. Kitts Labour Party against public sector employment of persons perceived to be opposition supporters. PAM alleges that the ruling party dismissed or demoted many PAM supporters from their jobs in order to replace them with its own supporters. A government official confirmed that opposition members of Parliament voted out of office and entitled to pension benefits did not receive those payments.

There are no impediments in law or in practice to the participation of women in leadership roles in government or political parties. St. Kitts and Nevis' sole female member of Parliament chose not to run for reelection in the June 1995 elections, and there were no other female candidates. However, women do hold such high government offices as permanent secretary and are active within the political parties.

Section 4. Governmental Attitude Regarding International and Nongovernmental Investigation of Alleged Violations of Human Rights

While there are no governmental restrictions, no local human rights groups have been formed. There were no requests for investigations or visits by international human rights groups.

Section 5. Discrimination Based on Race, Sex, Religion, Disability, Language, or Social Status

The Constitution prohibits discrimination on grounds of race, place of origin, birth out of wedlock, political opinion or affiliation, color, sex, or creed, and the Government generally respects these provisions in practice.

Women.—The role of women in society is not restricted by law but is circumscribed by culture and tradition. According to a government official, violence against women is a problem, but many women are reluctant to file complaints or pursue them in the courts. Despite this reluctance, there were publicly reported cases of both domestic violence and rape, and a few convictions. A special police unit works closely with the Ministry of Women's Affairs to investigate domestic violence and rape cases.

Children.—The Government is committed to children's rights and welfare and has incorporated most of the provisions of the U.N. Convention on the Rights of the Child into domestic legislation.

People With Disabilities.—Although there is no legislation to protect the disabled or to mandate accessibility for them, the Government and the Constitution prohibit discrimination in employment, education, and other state services.

Section 6. Worker Rights

a. *The Right of Association.*—The Constitution provides for the right of all workers to form and belong to trade unions. The law permits the police, civil service, and other organizations to have associations which serve as unions. The major labor union, the St. Kitts Trades and Labour Union, is affiliated with the St. Kitts and Nevis Labour Party and is active in all sectors of the economy. There is also an independent teachers' union, a union representing dockworkers in the capital city, and two taxi drivers' associations.

The right to strike, while not specified by law, is well established and respected in practice. There were no major strikes. Unions are free to form federations or confederations and to affiliate with international organizations.

The islands' unions maintain a variety of international ties. St. Kitts and Nevis became a member of the International Labor Organization in June and assumed all its obligations for enforcement of labor standards.

b. *The Right to Organize and Bargain Collectively.*—Labor unions are free to organize and to negotiate for better wages and benefits for union members. The law prohibits antiunion discrimination but does not require employers found guilty to rehire employees fired due to antiunion discrimination. However, the employer must pay lost wages and arrange for severance pay. There is no legislation governing the organization and representation of workers, and employers are not legally bound to recognize a union, but in practice employers do so if a majority of workers polled wish to organize. Collective bargaining takes place on a workplace by workplace basis, not industrywide. The Labour Commission mediates all types of disputes between labor and management on an ad hoc basis. In practice, however, few disputes actually go to the Commission for resolution. If neither the Commission nor the Minister of Labour can resolve the dispute, legislation allows for a case to be brought before a civil court.

There are no export processing zones.

c. *Prohibition of Forced or Compulsory Labor.*—The Constitution forbids slavery and forced labor, and they do not occur in practice.

d. *Minimum Age for Employment of Children.*—The minimum legal working age is 14 years. The Labour Ministry relies heavily on school truant officers and the community affairs division to monitor compliance, which they do effectively. Local law mandates compulsory education up to the age of 16.

e. *Acceptable Conditions of Work.*—A 1984 law, updated in 1994, establishes minimum wage rates for various categories of workers, such as domestic servants, retail employees, casino workers, and skilled workers. The minimum wage varies from $56.18 (EC$ 150) per week for full-time domestic workers to $74.91 (EC$ 200) per week for skilled workers. These provide an adequate, though Spartan, living for a wage earner and family; many workers supplement wages by keeping small animals such as goats and chickens. The Labour Commission undertakes regular wage inspections and special investigations when it receives complaints; it requires employers found in violation to pay back wages.

The law provides for a 40-q to 44-hour workweek, but the common practice is 40 hours in 5 days. Although not required by law, workers receive at least one 24-hour rest period per week. The law provides that workers receive a minimum annual vacation of 14 working days. While there are no specific health and safety regulations, the Factories Law provides general health and safety guidance to Labour Ministry inspectors. The Labour Commissioner settles disputes over safety conditions. Workers have the right to report unsafe work environments without jeopardy to continued employment; inspectors then investigate such claims.

SAINT LUCIA

St. Lucia is a multiparty, parliamentary democracy and a member of the Commonwealth of Nations. The Government comprises a prime minister, a cabinet, and a bicameral legislative assembly. A Governor General, appointed by the British monarch, is the titular head of state, with largely ceremonial powers. In an intraparty transfer of power in March, John Compton of the United Workers Party

(UWP) stepped down as Prime Minister and party leader in favor of Dr. Vaughan Lewis. (Compton had served as Prime Minister from 1964 to 1979, and from 1982 until his resignation.) The UWP holds 12 of 17 seats in the House of Assembly.

The Royal Saint Lucia Police is the only security force and includes a small unit called the Special Services Unit (which has some paramilitary training) and a coast guard unit. Although the police have traditionally demonstrated a high degree of respect for human rights, there were allegations of abuse by police and prison officials.

The economy is based on tourism and on the export of bananas, which represent the principal sources of foreign exchange earnings. Saint Lucia is diversifying its economy into other types of agriculture, light manufacturing, and construction. Unemployment, estimated at 20 percent, remains a source of potential instability.

The authorities generally respected human rights. Government criticism of the media, occasional credible allegations of physical abuse of suspects or prisoners, poor prison conditions, domestic violence against women, child abuse, and a lack of effective government children's rights programs continued to be problems.

RESPECT FOR HUMAN RIGHTS

Section 1. Respect for the Integrity of the Person, Including Freedom From:

a. *Political and Other Extrajudicial Killing.*—There were no reports of political or other extrajudicial killings.

b. *Disappearance.*—There were no reports of politically motivated disappearances.

c. *Torture and Other Cruel, Inhuman, or Degrading Treatment or Punishment.*— The Constitution specifically prohibits torture, and there were no reports of such abuse. However, many criminal convictions in recent years have been based on confessions, which may reflect an effort by police to force confessions rather than use investigative approaches.

Poor prison conditions stem from a lack of resources. The island's only prison, built in the 1800's to house a maximum of 101 prisoners, has over 400 prisoners, resulting in severe overcrowding. Prison guards are generally well-trained.

The Government permits prison visits by human rights monitors.

d. *Arbitrary Arrest, Detention, or Exile.*—The Government adheres to the constitutional provisions prohibiting arbitrary arrest or imprisonment and requiring a court hearing within 72 hours after detention. However, the authorities have frequently held prisoners for years "on remand" after charging them (there is no constitutional requirement for a speedy trial).

There were no reports of forced exile.

e. *Denial of Fair Public Trial.*—The Constitution provides for an independent judiciary, and it is independent in practice.

There are two levels of courts: Courts of summary jurisdiction (magistrate's courts) and the High Court. Both levels have civil and criminal authority. The lower courts accept civil claims up to about $1,900 (EC$5,000) in value, and criminal cases generally classified as "petty." The upper court has unlimited authority in both civil and criminal cases. All cases can be appealed to the Organization of Eastern Caribbean States Court of Appeal. From there, cases may be appealed to the Privy Council in London as the final court of appeal.

The Constitution requires public trials before an independent and impartial court and, in cases involving capital punishment, provision of legal counsel for those who cannot afford a defense attorney. In criminal cases not involving capital punishment, defendants must obtain their own legal counsel. Defendants are entitled to select their own legal counsel, are presumed innocent until proven guilty in court, and have the right of appeal. The authorities observe both constitutional and statutory requirements for fair public trials.

There were no reports of political prisoners.

f. *Arbitrary Interference with Privacy, Family, Home, or Correspondence.*—The Constitution prohibits such practices. Government authorities generally respect these prohibitions, and violations are subject to effective legal sanctions.

Section 2. Respect for Civil Liberties, Including:

a. *Freedom of Speech and Press.*—Although the Government generally respects constitutional provisions for free speech and press, it occasionally has demonstrated open hostility toward both the print media and radio. However, the Government's attitude toward the press does not appear to affect press freedoms in Saint Lucia.

Five privately owned newspapers, two privately owned radio stations, and one partially government-funded radio station operate in St. Lucia. They carry a wide spectrum of political opinion and are often critical of the Government. The radio stations have discussion and call-in programs that allow people to express their views. The two local television stations are also privately owned and cover a wide range of views. In addition, people can subscribe to cable television service, which provides programming from a variety of sources.

The Government does not restrict academic freedom.

b. *Freedom of Peaceful Assembly and Association.*—The Constitution provides for freedom of association and assembly, and the Government generally respects these rights in practice. The law requires permits for public meetings and demonstrations if they are to be held in public places, such as on streets or sidewalks or in parks. The police routinely grant such permits; the rare refusal generally stems from the failure of organizers to request the permit in a timely manner, normally 48 hours before the event. Police used tear gas and rubber bullets to disperse strikers during an October strike by banana farmers, resulting in several serious injuries.

c. *Freedom of Religion.*—The Constitution provides for freedom of religion, and the Government respects this right in practice.

d. *Freedom of Movement Within the Country, Foreign Travel, Emigration, and Repatriation.*—The Constitution provides for these rights, and the Government respects them in practice.

No formal government policy toward refugee or asylum requests exists. The issue of the provision of first asylum did not arise. There were no reports of forced expulsion of anyone having a valid claim to refugee status; however, government practice remains undefined.

Section 3. Respect for Political Rights: The Right of Citizens to Change Their Government

Citizens have the right to change their government. Saint Lucia's parliamentary system provides for genuine choices among parties, policies, and officials. The 1996 merger of the smaller parties—the Concerned Citizens' Movement, St. Lucia Freedom Party, and Citizens' Democratic Party—with the opposition St. Lucia Labour Party (SLP) leaves St. Lucia with two major parties: The SLP and the ruling United Workers Party (UWP). Under the Constitution, general elections must be held by April 1997, but could be called at any time before then by the Government. Elections are held at least every 5 years by secret ballot. The SLP plays a significant role in the country's political life and holds 5 of the 17 seats in the Legislative House of Assembly. Two members of the Senate are independent, appointed by the Governor General.

There are no legal impediments to participation by women and minorities in government. Both the Attorney General and the Deputy Leader of the Senate are women. However, women and minorities are not represented in numbers proportional to their percentage of the population.

Section 4. Governmental Attitude Regarding International and Nongovernmental Investigation of Alleged Violations of Human Rights

While there are no local human rights groups, there are no governmental restrictions that would prevent their formation.

Section 5. Discrimination Based on Race, Sex, Religion, Disability, Language, or Social Status

Government policy is nondiscriminatory in the areas of housing, jobs, education, and opportunity for advancement. There are no legal restrictions on the role of women or minorities.

Women.—There is increased awareness of the seriousness of violence against women. The Government does not prosecute crimes of violence against women unless the victim herself presses charges. If the victim chooses for any reason not to press charges, the Government cannot bring a case. Charges must be brought under the ordinary civil code. The police force conducts some training for police officers responsible for investigating rape and other crimes against women. Police and courts enforce laws to protect women against abuse, although police are hesitant to intervene in domestic disputes, and many victims are reluctant to report cases of domestic violence and rape or to press charges.

The 1994 Domestic Violence Act allows a judge to issue a protection order prohibiting an abuser from entering or remaining in the place where the victim is. It also allows the judge to order that an abuser's name be removed from housing leases or rental agreements, with the effect that the abuser would no longer have the right to live in the same residence as the victim.

The Saint Lucia Crisis Center monitors cases of abuse (physical and emotional) and helps its clients deal with such problems as incest, nonpayment of child support, alcohol and drug abuse, homelessness, custody, and visitation rights. The group has publicized the plight of battered women and has protested the rare deaths of women who were victims of domestic violence. The Crisis Center is also working to establish a shelter for battered women and homeless girls. Some secondary schools address the problem of sexual harassment and battering in their curriculum topics.

The Minister for Women's Affairs is responsible for protecting women's rights in domestic violence cases and preventing discrimination against women, including equal treatment in employment.

Children.—Despite the 1992 Children's Rights Act, which details a strong commitment to children's rights, the Government has not fulfilled that commitment with effective programs. Domestic violence and incest continued to be among the problems most affecting the welfare of children in Saint Lucia. The St. Lucia Crisis Center reported that incidents of child abuse increased substantially compared to 1995.

People With Disabilities.—There is no specific legislation protecting the rights of the disabled, nor mandating provision of access to buildings or government services for them. There is no rehabilitation facility for the physically disabled, although the Health Ministry operates a community-based rehabilitation program in residents' homes. There are schools for the deaf and for the blind up to the secondary level.

Section 6. Worker Rights

a. *The Right of Association.*—The Constitution specifies the right of workers to form or belong to trade unions under the broader rubric of the right of association. Most public sector employees are unionized; about 20 percent of the total work force is unionized. Unions are independent of government, and are free to choose their own representatives in often vigorously contested elections. However, there have been recent, unsubstantiated reports of government obstruction of attempts to have union views publicized. There are no restrictions on the formation of national labor federations. In 1994 several of the major unions formed an umbrella grouping called the "Industrial Solidarity Pact." Unions are free to affiliate with international organizations, and some have done so.

Strikes in both the public and private sectors are legal, but there are many avenues through collective bargaining agreement and government procedures which may preclude a strike. The law prohibits the police and fire departments from striking. Other "essential services" workers—water and sewer authority workers, electric utility workers, nurses, and doctors—must give 30 days' notice before striking. Banana farmers conducted a 12-day strike in October to protest a government charge for cartons.

b. *The Right to Organize and Bargain Collectively.*—Unions have the legal right to engage in collective bargaining, and they fully exercise this right. Union representatives have reported attempts by Government and other employers to undermine this process.

The law prohibits antiunion discrimination by employers, and there are effective mechanisms for resolving complaints. It also requires that employers reinstate workers fired for union activities.

Labor law is applicable in the export processing zones (EPZ's), and there are no administrative or legal impediments to union organizing or collective bargaining in those zones. In practice, however, many firms resist union efforts to organize in the EPZ's, even to the point of closing operations.

c. *Prohibition of Forced or Compulsory Labor.*—Forced or compulsory labor is illegal and does not exist.

d. *Minimum Age for Employment of Children.*—The Women's and Young Persons Act stipulates a minimum legal working age of 14 years. Ministry of Labour officials are responsible for enforcing the law. There were no reports of violations of child labor laws.

e. *Acceptable Conditions of Work.*—The Wages Regulations (Clerks) Orders, in effect since 1985, set out minimum wage rates only for clerks. These office workers receive a legislated minimum wage of about $300 (EC$800) per month. The minimum wage is not sufficient to provide a decent standard of living for a worker supporting a four-person family, but some categories of workers receive more than the legal minimum for clerks, which is used only as a guide for setting pay for other professions.

There is no legislated workweek, although the common practice is to work 40 hours in 5 days. Special legislation covers hours which shop assistants, agricultural workers, domestics, and young people in industrial establishments may work.

Occupational health and safety regulations are relatively well developed. The Labor Ministry periodically inspects health and safety conditions at places of employment under the Employees' Occupational Safety and Health Act of 1985. The Ministry enforces the act through threat of closure of the business if it discovers violations and the violator does not correct them. Workers are free to leave a dangerous workplace situation without jeopardy to continued employment.

SAINT VINCENT AND THE GRENADINES

St. Vincent and the Grenadines is a multiparty, parliamentary democracy and a member of the Commonwealth of Nations. A prime minister, a cabinet, and a unicameral legislative assembly compose the Government. A Governor General, appointed by the British monarch, is the titular head of state, with largely ceremonial powers. Prime Minister Sir James F. Mitchell and his New Democratic Party returned to power for an unprecedented third term in free and fair elections held in February 1994.

The Royal St. Vincent Police, the only security force in the country, includes a coast guard and a small Special Services Unit with some paramilitary training. The force is controlled by and responsive to the Government, but there continued to be occasional allegations of police brutality and the use of force and other extralegal means to elicit confessions from suspects.

St. Vincent has a market-based economy. Much of the labor force is engaged in agriculture, in particular, banana production. Bananas are the leading export and the major source of foreign exchange earnings. The tourism sector is growing. However, unemployment remains high at over 30 percent, and per capita gross domestic product is low, at approximately $2,517.

Human rights are generally well respected. The principal human rights problems continued to include occasional instances of excessive use of force by police, the Governments's failure to punish those involved in such abuse, inadequate and overcrowded prisons, and an overburdened court system.

RESPECT FOR HUMAN RIGHTS

Section 1. Respect for the Integrity of the Person, Including Freedom From:

a. *Political and Other Extrajudicial Killing.*—There were no reports of political or other extrajudicial killings.

b. *Disappearance.*—There were no reports of politically motivated disappearances.

c. *Torture and Other Cruel, Inhuman, or Degrading Treatment or Punishment.*—The Constitution prohibits torture and other forms of cruel, inhuman, or degrading treatment or punishment. However, a very high percentage of convictions (estimated at 90 percent by the regional human rights group, Caribbean Rights) continue to be based on confessions. A local human rights group claims that some of these confessions resulted from unwarranted police practices, including the use of physical force during detention, illegal search and seizure, and not properly informing those arrested of their rights. The Police Commissioner has dismissed or demoted officers involved in extralegal activity. The authorities charged one police officer with manslaughter; his trial had not concluded by the end of the year.

There is no independent review board to monitor police activity and to hear public complaints about police misconduct. Caribbean Rights has advocated such a board to protect the rights of citizens complaining of these activities.

In a shocking case of police brutality, the local press reported that on April 8 two police officers allegedly burned McCarthy Patterson, a 12-year-old boy accused of stealing a radio, on the chest, thighs, back, and penis. The authorities dismissed the case against the two officers, however, after the child and his mother refused to testify. Following an investigation, the Police Commissioner dismissed the two officers from the force, demoted another officer, and accepted the resignation of a fourth. In a March 22 letter to the editor, the president of the local human rights association called on the Police Commissioner to investigate two other incidents of police brutality. A plain clothes policeman allegedly pistol whipped Everard Knights in the face and struck him in the back as another officer held him. In addition, a police officer allegedly assaulted a 15-year-old boy.

Inadequate and overcrowded prisons remain a serious problem. These conditions are particularly harsh for juvenile offenders. There is a small facility for delinquent boys, but it is seriously inadequate and is generally used for those already convicted through the criminal system. Although separate legal statutes exist for youthful offenders, there are no separate magistrates or prosecutors to handle such cases.

d. *Arbitrary Arrest, Detention, or Exile.*—The Constitution provides for persons detained for criminal offenses to receive a fair hearing within a reasonable time by an impartial court. Although there are only two official magistrates, the registrar of the High Court and the presiding judge of the family court now effectively serve as magistrates when called upon to do so. While this reduced the backlog, complaints remain regarding police practices in bringing cases to court. Some defense attorneys claim this has caused 6- to 12-month delays in preliminary inquiries for serious crimes.

There were no reports of instances of arbitrary arrest, detention, or exile.

e. *Denial of Fair Public Trial.*—The Constitution provides for public trials before an independent and impartial court. The court appoints attorneys for indigent defendants only when the defendant is charged with a capital offense. Defendants are presumed innocent until proven guilty and may appeal cases to a regional high court system and ultimately to the Privy Council in the United Kingdom. There are no separate security or military court systems. There were no reports of political prisoners.

f. *Arbitrary Interference with Privacy, Family, Home, or Correspondence.*—The Constitution prohibits arbitrary search and seizure or other government intrusions into the private life of individual citizens, and there were no reports of such abuses.

Section 2. Respect for Civil Liberties, Including:

a. *Freedom of Speech and Press.*—The Constitution provides for freedom of speech and the press. There are two major newspapers and numerous smaller, partisan publications; all are privately owned, and most are openly critical of the Government's policies. There were no reports of government censorship or interference with the operation of the press.

The lone television station in St. Vincent is privately owned and operates without government interference. Satellite dishes are popular among those who can afford them. There is also a cable system with mainly North American programming that has approximately 300 subscribers. The Government controls programming for the government-owned radio station. There are no call-in talk shows; the Government canceled such a show in 1988, claiming it was politically slanted.

The Government does not restrict academic freedom.

b. *Freedom of Peaceful Assembly and Association* The Constitution provides for these rights, and the Government respects them in practice.

c. *Freedom of Religion.*—The Constitution provides for freedom of religion, and the Government respects this right in practice.

d. *Freedom of Movement Within the Country, Foreign Travel, Emigration, and Repatriation.*—The law provides for these rights, and the Government respects them in practice.

No formal government policy toward refugee or asylum requests exists. The issue of the provision of first asylum did not arise. There were no reports of forced expulsion of anyone having a valid claim to refugee status; however, government practice remains undefined.

Section 3. Respect for Political Rights: The Right of Citizens to Change Their Government

Citizens have the right to change their government through regularly scheduled free and fair elections. St. Vincent has a long history of multiparty parliamentary democracy. During the last elections in 1994, the two opposition parties united to challenge the ruling New Democratic Party. The effort was successful to the extent that the "Unity" coalition won 3 of 15 parliamentary seats—the NDP held all 15 prior to the election. The opposition continues to charge that the ruling party has not complied with what the opposition asserts is a constitutional obligation to answer questions it puts forth.

Two of the 15 members of Parliament are women. The same two women hold ministerial portfolios in the current Government.

Section 4. Governmental Attitude Regarding International and Nongovernmental Investigation of Alleged Violations of Human Rights

Opposition political groups and the Vincentian press often comment on human rights matters of local concern. The St. Vincent and Grenadines Human Rights Association, affiliated with the regional Caribbean Human Rights Network, closely monitors government and police activities, especially with respect to treatment of prisoners, publicizing any cases of abuse. The Government is generally responsive to public and private inquiries about its human rights practices.

Section 5. Discrimination Based on Race, Sex, Religion, Disability, Language, or Social Status

The Constitution provides for equal treatment under the law regardless of race, sex, or religion, and the Government adheres to this provision.

Women.—A local human rights group reports that violence against women (particularly domestic violence) is a major problem. The Government has failed to take steps to determine the seriousness of the problem. To speed up the judicial handling of such cases, the Government established a family court under the Domestic Violence Act of 1995.

Depending on the magnitude of the offense and the age of the victim, the penalty for rape is generally 10 or more years in prison. In May 1995, the legislature amended the Child Support Law to allow for payments ordered by the courts even though notice of an appeal has been filed. Previously, fathers who had been ordered to pay child support could appeal decisions and not pay while the appeal was being heard. This resulted in a huge backlog of appeal cases and effectively reduced the number of mothers and children receiving support payments.

The Ministry of Education, Youth, and Women's Affairs has a women's desk which assists the National Council of Women with seminars, training programs, and public relations. The minimum wage law specifies that women should receive equal pay for equal work.

Children.—The Social Welfare Office is the government agency responsible for monitoring and protecting the welfare of children. The police are the enforcement arm—the Social Welfare Office refers all reports of child abuse to the police for action. Marion House, a social services agency established by the Catholic Church in 1989, provides counseling and therapy services.

People With Disabilities.—There is no specific legislation covering those with disabilities. Most severely disabled people rarely leave their homes because of the poor road system and lack of affordable wheelchairs. The Government partially supports a school for the disabled which has two branches. A separate, small rehabilitation center treats about five persons daily.

Section 6. Worker Rights

a. *The Right of Association.*—The Constitution provides citizens the right to form unions, organize employees, and strike. There are no laws to complement this constitutional provision, however, and employers often ignore it by claiming it is their constitutional right not to recognize a trade union. Some employers, however, seek a good industrial relations environment, and cooperate with trade unions. There were no major strikes. Unions have the right to affiliate with international bodies.

b. *The Right to Organize and Bargain Collectively.*—There are no legal obstacles to organizing unions; however, no law requires employers to recognize a particular union as an exclusive bargaining agent. Some companies offer packages of benefits with terms of employment better than, or comparable to, what a union can normally obtain through negotiations. The law prohibits antiunion discrimination by employers against union members and organizers. Generally effective mechanisms exist for resolving complaints. The authorities can order employers found guilty of antiunion discrimination for firing workers without cause (including for participation in union activities) to reinstate the workers or give them severance pay.

There are no export processing zones.

c. *Prohibition of Forced or Compulsory Labor.*—Forced or compulsory labor is illegal and does not exist.

d. *Minimum Age for Employment of Children.*—The law sets the minimum working age at 16 years of age, although a worker must be 18 years of age to receive a national insurance card. The labor inspection office of the Ministry of Labour monitors and enforces this provision, and employers generally respect it in practice. The age of leaving school at the primary level is 15 years; when these pupils leave school they are usually absorbed into the labor market disguised as apprentices. There is no known child labor except for children working on family-owned banana plantations, particularly during harvest time, or in family-owned cottage industries.

e. *Acceptable Conditions of Work.*—The law sets minimum wages, which were last promulgated in 1989. They vary by sector and type of work and are specified for several skilled categories, including attendants, packers, cleaners, porters, watchmen, and clerks. In agriculture the wage for workers provided shelter is $0.82 (EC$2.25) per hour; skilled industrial workers earn $7.36 (EC$20) per day, and unskilled workers earn $3.68 (EC$10) per day. In many sectors the minimum wage is not sufficient to provide a decent standard of living for workers and their families, but most workers earn more than the minimum. The Wages Council, according to law, should meet every 2 years to review the minimum wage. However there has been no meeting of the council for the last 7 years. There is no legislation concerning the length of the workweek; however, the general practice is to work 40 hours in 5 days. The law provides workers a minimum annual vacation of 2 weeks.

According to the Ministry of Labour, legislation concerning occupational safety and health is outdated. The most recent legislation, the Factories Act of 1955, has some regulations concerning only factories, but enforcement of these regulations is ineffective. Workers enjoy a reasonably safe working environment; however, the trade unions have dealt with some violations relating to safety gear, long overtime hours, and the safety of machinery. There were some reports of significant visual deficiency by visual display unit workers, and some reports of hearing impairment by power station and stone crushing employees.

SURINAME

After over a decade of predominantly military rule, Suriname installed a freely elected Parliament and inaugurated a democratically chosen President in 1991. Since then the Government has made fitful progress in consolidating democracy and slow but steady progress toward professionalizing and depoliticizing the military and reestablishing civilian authority over it. In 1992 the Government concluded a peace accord with members of insurgent groups that fought a domestic armed conflict between 1986 and 1991. Elections were completed on May 23 without incident and were deemed free and fair by observers from the Organization of American States. A People's Assembly elected Jules Wijdenbosch President in September and he formed his Cabinet from members of the National Democratic Party (NDP) and several other political parties. Former military strongman Desi Bouterse, president of the NDP, does not hold a position in the new Government, but exerts considerable influence through his party role.

The Government of former President Ronald Venetiaan took positive steps toward reforming the military during 1995 and early 1996. The purging of Bouterse supporters, including the armed forces commander in 1995 and the army commander in February, both of whom were reportedly close to Bouterse, extended somewhat democratic civilian control over the military. This positive trend may be affected, however, with the return of the Bouterse-led NDP to government. Cooperation between the military and the civilian police improved as respective roles have been clarified. Some aspects of the relationship between the Government and the military remain to be defined. Civilian police bear primary responsibility for the maintenance of law and order, but they continue to be responsible for some human rights abuses.

The market-oriented economy is largely agricultural, but with an important bauxite and alumina export sector. There is a high degree of state involvement and regulation; the Government and state-owned companies employ over half the working population. For the last several years, depressed world prices for bauxite and alumina, the damaging effects of the country's domestic armed conflict, and rapid growth of the money supply resulted in high inflation and reduced economic growth. Previously high inflation, which reached 586 percent in 1994 and 37 percent in 1995 according to the Surinamese Statistics Bureau, dropped to less than 1 percent in the first half of 1996. The estimated real economic growth rate was about 4 percent, and per capita annual income is about $1,400. The recent stabilization of the currency following the July 1995 unification of the exchange rate is cited by some as an indication that the economy is beginning to respond to government efforts at structural reform. There are indications that the new Government, despite its populist base, is continuing efforts to limit expenditures and to support the local currency.

Both the Wijdenbosch and the Venetiaan governments generally respected the human rights of their citizens; however, problems remained in some areas. These are police mistreatment of detainees, abuse of prisoners, overcrowding of jails, societal discrimination and violence against women, and marginalization of indigenous people. Both governments failed to call to account those responsible for human rights abuses in previous regimes.

RESPECT FOR HUMAN RIGHTS

Section 1. Respect for the Integrity of the Person, Including Freedom From:

a. *Political and Other Extrajudicial Killing.*—There were no reports of political or other extrajudicial killings. There was, however, one report of a Molotov cocktail attack on the home of a human rights activist. The victim was pressing for an investigation of the 1982 murders of 15 opposition leaders.

The authorities took no action against prison guards who allegedly beat a prisoner to death in 1993. The Government also took no action to investigate past human rights violations, such as the 1982 executions by the military regime of 15 opposition leaders or the 1986 massacre of civilians at the village of Moiwana. The human rights group Moiwana '86 unsuccessfully challenged in the lower court of Paramaribo the validity of the amnesty law passed in 1992, which pardoned members of the military and the insurgents for crimes (except crimes against humanity) committed between January 1985 and August 1992.

The Inter-American Court of Human Rights rendered a judgment in 1993 that required the Government to pay compensation to the survivors of seven Maroons (descendants of escaped slaves who fled into the interior to avoid recapture) killed near the village of Pokigron in 1987. The Government responded by establishing a fully funded foundation to pay compensation to relatives of the victims. The foundation is actively disbursing compensation and has also funded a school and clinic in the village.

b. *Disappearance.*—There were no reports of politically motivated disappearances. The Government, however, took no action to investigate earlier allegations of disappearances that occurred under previous regimes.

c. *Torture and Other Cruel, Inhuman, or Degrading Treatment or Punishment.*— The Constitution prohibits inhuman treatment or punishment, but human rights monitors continued to express concern about official mistreatment of detainees and prisoners. The authorities fired two prison guards and suspended a third for reportedly beating prisoners and using unnecessary force in attempting to quell a riot at the Latour jail in February. The Government has not released the results of an inquiry into charges that guards beat several recaptured prisoners in 1993.

The completion of a new prison and renovation of existing jails have somewhat reduced overcrowding and improved overall health and safety conditions. However, the new prison, at Duuisberglaan, is operating at only half its capacity, in large part due to difficulty in recruiting and training additional prison guards. Older jails remain seriously overcrowded with as many as four times the number of detainees they were designed for; they are also unsanitary. At police stations, guards allow detainees no exercise and only rarely permitted them to leave the cells. Detainees also suffer from inadequate nutrition, although families are permitted and encouraged to provide food to incarcerated relatives. Female prisoners were housed exclusively in an older jail and were not eligible for transfer to the new facility. According to local women's groups, there were no reports of sexual abuse of female prisoners by police officers.

The Government permits independent monitoring of prison conditions.

d. *Arbitrary Arrest, Detention, or Exile.*—The law provides that the police may detain for investigation up to 14 days a person suspected of committing a crime for which the sentence is longer than 4 years. Within the 14-day period, the police must bring the accused before a prosecutor to be formally charged. If additional time is needed to investigate the charge, a prosecutor may authorize the police to detain the suspect for an additional 30 days. Upon the expiration of the initial 44 days, a "judge of instruction" may authorize the police to hold the suspect for up to 120 additional days, in 30-day increments (for a total of 164 days), before the case is tried. The judge of instruction has the power to authorize release on bail, but that power is rarely, if ever, used. There were no reports of detentions in contravention of these standards.

Pretrial detainees constitute a large percentage of inmates and are often held in overcrowded detention cells at local police stations. Of those held in police custody, 15 percent had already been convicted.

The military police observed the requirement to hand over to the civil police civilians arrested for committing a crime in their presence. The military police continued to perform the immigration control function at the country's borders and airports but no longer investigated civilian crimes.

While not specifically forbidden by law or the Constitution, exile is not practiced as a means of political control.

e. *Denial of Fair Public Trial.*—Although the Constitution provides for an independent judiciary and the right to a fair public trial in which defendants have the right to counsel, the effectiveness of the civilian and military courts is limited. The courts assign lawyers in private practice to defend prisoners and pay them from public funds. The courts must, and in practice do, free a detainee who is not tried within the 164-day period. Trials are before a single judge, with right of appeal. There is little firm evidence of the extent to which corruption affects the court system, but the entire criminal justice system was subjected to severe strain during the period when the military controlled the Government and prominent members of the judiciary were involved with, or afforded protection to, drug traffickers. Recent escapes of high-profile prisoners were linked to corruption of prison guards.

The 1987 Constitution calls for the establishment of an independent constitutional court. However, as no steps have been taken to set up such a court, it remains unclear when the Government will create this institution.

Military personnel are generally not subject to civilian criminal law. A soldier accused of a crime immediately comes under military jurisdiction and military police are responsible for all such investigations. Military prosecutions are directed by an officer on the public prosecutor's staff, and take place in separate courts before two military judges and one civilian judge. The military courts follow the same rules of procedure as the civil courts. There is no appeal from the military to the civil system.

Since the change in military leadership in 1993, coordination between the military police and the civil police has improved, and there were no further instances of military interference in civilian police investigations. The pervasive climate of fear and intimidation that previously prevented cases involving military personnel or drug traffickers from being tried began to dissipate, and prospects for the impartial administration of justice have improved. Fear of possible reprisals by the ex-military strongman Desire Bouterse, however, appears to affect judicial decisionmaking in cases involving persons close to Bouterse.

Foreign military instructors conducted human rights and military justice seminars in July 1995 and in March 1996. These seminars provided unprecedented opportunities for civilian government and private sector representatives and military personnel to discuss human rights and the role of the military in a democracy.

There were no reports of political prisoners.

f. *Arbitrary Interference with Privacy, Family, Home, or Correspondence.*—The Constitution provides for the right to privacy. The law requires warrants for searches, which are issued not by judges but by quasi-judicial officers who supervise criminal investigations. The police obtain them in the great majority of investigations. The military command curbed invasions of privacy by the military such as the illegal monitoring of telephone calls, monitoring of the movements of human rights advocates, and threatening government officials, policemen, politicians, human rights workers, and journalists.

Section 2. Respect for Civil Liberties, Including:

a. *Freedom of Speech and Press.*—The Constitution provides for freedom of speech and of the press, and the Government generally respects these rights.

The parliamentary and extraparliamentary opposition criticize the Government freely. Media members continue to practice some self-censorship, because of the recent history of intimidation and reprisals by certain elements of the former military leadership.

The two daily newspapers and most of the radio stations are privately owned. The two television stations and one of the radio stations are publicly owned. The Government did not attempt to interfere with publications or to abridge academic freedom.

b. *Freedom of Peaceful Assembly and Association.*—The Constitution provides for these rights, and the Government respects them in practice.

c. *Freedom of Religion.*—The Constitution provides for freedom of religion, and the Government respects this right in practice.

d. *Freedom of Movement Within the Country, Foreign Travel, Emigration, and Repatriation.*—Citizens may change their residence and work places freely and travel abroad as they wish. Political dissidents who emigrated to the Netherlands and elsewhere during the years of military rule are welcome to return. Few of them have chosen to do so. Citizenship is not revoked for political reasons.

The Government cooperates with the U.N. High Commissioner for Refugees and other humanitarian organizations in assisting refugees. The issue of the provision of first asylum did not arise. There were no reports of forced return of persons to a country where they feared persecution.

Section 3. Respect for Political Rights: The Right of Citizens to Change Their Government

The Constitution provides for this right, but in the past the military prevented its effective exercise. Although the military has twice handed over power to elected civilian governments following coups, 1996 marked the first time since independence from the Netherlands in 1975 that one elected government succeeded another in accordance with constitutional provisions. However, the Government is still in the process of institutionalizing democratic, constitutional rule.

The Constitution stipulates that power and authority rest with the people and provides for the right to change the government through the direct election by secret ballot of a National Assembly of 51 members every 5 years. The National Assembly then elects the President by a two-thirds vote. If the legislature is unable to do so, as has been the case both in the 1991 and 1996 national elections, the Constitution provides that a national People's Assembly, comprising Members of Parliament and regional and local officials, shall elect the President.

The Constitution provides for the organization and functioning of political parties, and many parties and political coalitions are represented in the National Assembly.

There are historical and cultural impediments to equal participation by women in leadership positions in government and political parties. In the past, most women expected to fulfill the role of housewife and mother, thereby limiting opportunities to gain political experience or position. Participation by women in politics (and other fields) was generally considered inappropriate. While women have made limited gains in attaining political power in recent years, political circles remain under the influence of traditional male-dominated groups, and women are disadvantaged in seeking high public office. In May voters elected six women to the National Assembly, compared with three who held seats in the previous assembly, and the Assembly appointed one of them as chairperson. The Wijdenbosch Cabinet includes a woman as Minister of Regional Development.

Although the Constitution proscribes racial or religious discrimination, several factors limit the participation of Maroons and Amerindians in the political process. Most of the country's political activity takes place in the capital and a narrow belt running east and west of it along the coast. The Maroons and Amerindians are concentrated in remote areas in the interior and therefore have limited access to, and influence in, the political process. There is a small Maroon political party, which holds three seats in the National Assembly and belongs to an opposition coalition. Although there is no Amerindian political party, voters elected the first Amerindian to the National Assembly in May. There are seven Maroons in the National Assembly. There are no Maroons or Amerindians in the Cabinet.

Section 4. Governmental Attitude Regarding International and Nongovernmental Investigation of Alleged Violations of Human Rights

Human rights groups operate without government restriction, investigating and publishing their findings on human rights cases. Government officials are, however, generally not cooperative or responsive to their views. In April the Government refused a request by Amnesty International to allow a video crew to make a film about the December 1982 murders (see Section 1.a.) on the grounds that the timing would upset the elections. In May a Surinamese organization, the Organization for Justice and Peace, approached the Government with the idea of establishing a "truth commission" to investigate past human rights abuses. However, the Government turned down the idea again citing the fear that any findings would have an adverse impact on the election process. The National Institute of Human Rights, which had been initiated by the Government but authorized to act independently, was dissolved in 1994, after the expiration of the first members' 10-year term.

The Venetiaan Government reacted negatively to calls for investigations into past human rights violations and refused to initiate such studies. By year's end, the new Wijdenbosch Government had taken no concrete steps to initiate any investigations.

Section 5. Discrimination Based on Race, Sex, Religion, Disability, Language, or Social Status

The Constitution and laws do not differentiate among citizens on the basis of their ethnic origins, religious affiliations, or other cultural differences. In practice, however, several groups within society suffer various forms of discrimination.

Women.—The law does not differentiate between domestic violence and other forms of assault, and the Government has not specifically addressed the problem of violence against women. According to a national women's group, victims reported approximately 500 cases of violence against women, and complained of an inadequate response from the Government and society to what appears to be a trend of increasing family violence. Police are reluctant to intervene in instances of domestic violence. It remains a problem at all levels of society.

There are no specific laws to protect women against trafficking and sexual exploitation. A local women's group is investigating several cases of arranged marriages to foreigners where the women were subsequently forced into prostitution. There are also credible reports of trafficking in Brazilian women for prostitution. Neither medical nor legal assistance is available to victims. Victims are not discouraged from filing complaints and do not face legal or other penalties.

Women have a legal right to equal access to education, employment, and property. Nevertheless, social pressures and customs inhibit their full exercise of these rights, particularly in the areas of marriage and inheritance. Women, notably those who were heads of families, were adversely affected by deteriorating economic conditions. Women experience economic discrimination in access to employment and in rates of pay for the same or substantially similar work. The Government has not made specific efforts to combat economic discrimination.

The National Women's Center is a government agency devoted to women's issues; there is also a women's policy coordinator. Their effectiveness is severely limited by financial and staffing constraints. There are several active women's rights groups. Their principal concerns are political representation, economic vulnerability, violence, and discrimination. These groups are somewhat effective.

Children.—The Government makes only limited efforts to ensure safeguards for the human rights and welfare of children. The steady increase in the number of cases of malnutrition, by some estimates reaching upwards of 20 percent of schoolchildren in the Paramaribo area, has been cause for concern. In the capital, where most of the country's population is concentrated, there are some orphanages, and a privately funded shelter for sexually abused children opened in 1993. Elsewhere, distressed children must usually rely on the resources of their extended families. There is no societal pattern of abuse directed against children. Both in the capital and in the country's interior, some school-age children do not have access to education because of a lack of transportation, facilities, or teachers. There is no difference in the treatment of girls and boys in education or health care services. Children face increasing economic pressure to discontinue their education in order to work.

People With Disabilities.—There are no laws concerning disabled people and no provisions for making private or public buildings accessible to them. There are also no laws mandating that they be given equal consideration when seeking jobs or housing. However, there are some training programs for the blind and others with disabilities.

Indigenous People.—Most Amerindians and Maroons suffer a number of disadvantages and have only limited ability to participate in decisions affecting their lands, cultures, traditions, and natural resources. The nation's political life, educational opportunities, and jobs are concentrated in the capital and its environs, while the majority of Amerindians and Maroons live in the interior. Government services in the interior became largely unavailable and much of the infrastructure was destroyed during the 1986–91 domestic insurgencies; progress in reestablishing services and rebuilding the infrastructure has been very slow.

The Government appointed the Consultative Council for the Development of the Interior in September 1995. This Council, provided for in the 1992 peace accords ending the insurgencies, includes representatives of the Maroon and Amerindian communities. The Government did not, however, consult with representatives of these communities about the granting of gold and timber concessions.

In May the World Council of Churches condemned the mining activity of two Canadian mining companies, claiming that they violate the human rights of the indigenous people who live within the mining concession areas. Organizations representing Maroon and Amerindian communities complained that the companies dig trenches that cut residents off from their agricultural land and threaten to drive them away from their traditional settlements. In December the Minister of Natural Resources met with the leaders of Nieuw Koffiekamp, one of the principal villages involved in the indigenous community conflicts with mining concessionaires, to discuss the village's concerns and options to resolve this particular dispute.

Although a special mission from the Organization of American States has embarked on a number of initiatives related to the determination of indigenous rights and the division of interior districts, implementation has been delayed by the cumbersome government bureaucracy and its reluctance to tackle sensitive political issues.

Maroon and Amerindian groups are beginning to cooperate in order to exercise their rights more effectively. The second summit, or "gran krutu," in as many years between Maroon and Amerindian tribal leaders took place in September. The leaders reiterated their demands for the right to participate in decisions concerning the use of natural resources and for greater autonomy from the Government.

Section 6. Worker Rights

a. *The Right of Association.*—The Constitution protects the right of workers to associate and to choose their representatives democratically. Nearly 60 percent of the work force is organized into unions, most of which belong to one of the country's six major labor federations. Unions are independent of the Government and play an active role in politics. The small Labor Party, which is independent of the labor movement, has historically been a very influential force in government.

The Constitution provides for the right of nongovernment employees to strike. Civil servants have no legal right to strike or mount other labor actions, but in practice do so. Strikes in both the public and private sectors were common as workers tried to secure wage gains to protect their earning power from rapid inflation.

Suriname was elected to the governing body of the International Labor Organization in March. There are no restrictions on unions' international activities. Several labor federations were reaccepted as affiliates of international trade union organizations in the late 1980's, after having been suspended for collaboration with the military regime.

b. *The Right to Organize and Bargain Collectively.*—The Constitution explicitly recognizes these rights, and the authorities respect them in practice. Collective bargaining agreements cover approximately 50 percent of the labor force. The law prohibits antiunion discrimination by employers, and there are effective mechanisms for resolving complaints of such discrimination. Employers must have prior permission from the Ministry of Labor to fire workers, except when discharging an employee for cause. The Labor Ministry individually reviews dismissals for cause; if it finds a discharge unjustified, the employee must be reinstated.

There are no export processing zones.

c. *Prohibition of Forced or Compulsory Labor.*—The Constitution prohibits forced or compulsory labor, and there were no known instances of it.

d. *Minimum Age for Employment of Children.*—The law sets the minimum age for employment at 16 years. However, the Ministry of Labor and the police enforce this law only sporadically. Those under 16 years of age often work as street vendors, newspaper sellers, or shop assistants. Working hours for youths are not limited in comparison with the regular work force. School attendance is compulsory until 12 years of age.

e. *Acceptable Conditions of Work.*—There is no minimum wage legislation. Following a 40 percent pay hike instituted during election time, the lowest wage for civil servants was about $41.79 (SF 16,800) per month. This salary level makes it very difficult to provide a decent living for a worker and family. Government employees, who comprise close to 50 percent of the work force of 100,000, frequently supplement their salaries with second or third jobs, often in the informal sector. The Government sets civil service wages and the National Assembly approves them.

Work in excess of 9 hours per day or 45 hours per week on a regular basis requires special government permission, which is routinely granted. Such overtime work earns premium pay. The law requires one 24-hour rest period per week.

A 10- to 12-member inspectorate of the Occupational Health and Safety Division of the Ministry of Labor is responsible for enforcing legislated occupational safety and health regulations. Resource constraints and lack of trained personnel preclude the division from making regular inspections of industry. Accident rates in local industry do not appear to be high, and the key bauxite industry has an outstanding safety record. There is, however, no law authorizing workers to refuse to work in circumstances they deem unsafe. They must appeal to the inspectorate to declare the workplace situation unsafe.

TRINIDAD AND TOBAGO

Trinidad and Tobago, a member of the Commonwealth of Nations, is a parliamentary democracy in which there have been free and fair general elections since independence from the United Kingdom in 1962. A bicameral Parliament and a Prime Minister govern the country. Parliament elects the President, whose office is largely ceremonial. A 12-member elected House of Assembly handles local matters on the island of Tobago.

The Ministry of National Security controls the police service and the defense force, which are responsive to civilian authority. An independent body, the Police Service Commission, makes all personnel decisions in the police service, and the Ministry has little direct influence over changes in senior positions.

The country's mixed economy is based primarily on the petroleum and natural gas industries, but efforts are being made to diversify the economy into services, manufacturing, and tourism. The Government has historically owned many businesses wholly or partially; however, under a major divestment program a number of state-owned corporations have been privatized either partially or completely. The rate of real economic growth was about 3.1 percent, and annual per capita income was about $4,391.

Citizens enjoy a wide range of civil liberties and individual rights. Nonetheless, increased violent crime and narcotics trafficking strained the justice system, which was severely bogged down by excessive delays. Human rights abuses also included overcrowded prisons and violence against women.

RESPECT FOR HUMAN RIGHTS

Section 1. Respect for the Integrity of the Person, Including Freedom From:

a. *Political and Other Extrajudicial Killing.*—There were no reports of political or other extrajudicial killing.

b. *Disappearance.*—There were no reports of politically motivated disappearances.

c. *Torture and Other Cruel, Inhuman, or Degrading Treatment or Punishment.*—The Constitution prohibits the imposition of cruel or unusual treatment or punishment, and there were no allegations of police brutality in 1996.

Courts frequently order the flogging of prisoners, but this is not actually carried out in practice. The relevant statute requires that the punishment be carried out within 6 months of sentencing; defendants appeal all flogging sentences, and courts do not hear the appeals before the 6-month deadline.

Overcrowding is a serious problem in men's prisons, where shortages of guards and unsanitary conditions have led to serious social and health problems. Conditions are most serious in the older facilities: Port of Spain prison, for example, was designed for 250 inmates, but houses 977. Diseases such as chicken pox, tuberculosis, AIDS, and other viruses spread easily, and prisoners generally must purchase their own medication. A new maximum security facility was supposed to open but had not been completed at year's end. Facilities for, and treatment of, women prisoners appear to be better, with a strong and successful orientation toward rehabilitation.

The Government admits independent human rights monitors into prisons, according to the Ministry of National Security.

d. *Arbitrary Arrest, Detention, or Exile.*—The Constitution prohibits arbitrary detention, imprisonment, or exile of any person. A police officer may arrest a person either based on a warrant issued or authorized by a magistrate or without a warrant when the officer witnesses commission of the alleged offense. For less serious offenses, the authorities typically bring the accused before a magistrate within 24 hours; for indictable offenses, the accused must appear within 48 hours. At that time the magistrate reads the charge and determines whether bail is appropriate. Magistrates may deny bail to violent or repeat offenders. If for some reason the accused does not come before the magistrate, the case comes up on the magistrate's docket every 8 to 10 days until a hearing date is set. The courts notify persons of their right to an attorney and allow them access to an attorney once they are in custody and prior to any interrogation. The authorities do not always comply with these standards, however.

The Minister of National Security may authorize preventive detention in order to prevent actions prejudicial to public safety, public order, or national defense, and the Minister must state the grounds for the detention. A detainee under this provision has access to counsel and may have his detention reviewed by a three-member tribunal established by the Chief Justice and chaired by an attorney. The Minister must provide the tribunal with the grounds for the detention within 7 days of the detainee's request for review, which shall be held "as soon as reasonably practicable" following receipt of the grounds. There have been no reports that the authorities abused this procedure.

As noted, exile is forbidden by the Constitution and is not practiced.

e. *Denial of Fair Public Trial.*—The judiciary is independent in practice and is not influenced by the executive or legislative branches or the military.

The court system consists of high courts, a system of magistrate's courts, and a national court of appeal. The high courts handle all civil cases and most "serious" offenses, such as capital crimes. All criminal cases are first sent to a magistrate's court, but for serious offenses, the magistrate only hears the case to record whether the defendant pleads guilty or innocent. Appeals may be made to the national court of appeal and then to the Privy Council in London.

The Constitution provides the right to a fair public trial for persons charged with criminal offenses. It also provides for presumption of innocence, reasonable bail, fair and public hearing by an independent and impartial tribunal, and an interpreter for non-English speakers. The authorities generally respected these rights in practice. All criminal defendants have the right to an attorney. In practice, the courts sometimes appoint attorneys for those persons charged with indictable offenses (serious crimes) if they cannot retain one on their own behalf. The law requires a person accused of murder to have an attorney. An indigent person may refuse to accept an assigned attorney for cause and obtain a replacement. In spite of these provisions, however, there were several allegations by prisoners charged with narcotics trafficking offenses that the authorities did not provide them with attorneys even after they specifically requested counsel.

Despite serious efforts to improve the judiciary, severe inefficiency remains in many areas. Several criminal cases were dismissed due to judicial or police inefficiency. On October 11, the courts acquitted a defendant charged with murdering a police officer in March 1982; the authorities had held him in custody for over 14 years. Over 20,000 criminal cases introduced since 1986 await trial.

The limited availability of transport to take defendants from prisons to courts is a serious problem contributing to the delay in trials. Despite efforts to provide more transportation, prisoners continue to miss court dates because of a lack of vehicles, and there have been charges by inmates that transport operators demand bribes in order to transport prisoners.

There were no reports of political prisoners.

f. *Arbitrary Interference with Privacy, Family, Home, or Correspondence.*—The law prohibits such practices, government authorities generally respect these prohibitions, and violations are subject to effective legal sanction. Police must obtain search warrants to enter private property.

Section 2. Respect for Civil Liberties, Including:

a. *Freedom of Speech and Press.*—The Constitution provides for freedom of the press, and the Government respects this right in practice. An independent press and a functioning democratic political system combine to ensure freedom of speech and of the press, including academic freedom.

The three major daily newspapers freely and often criticize the Government in editorials. Widely read weekly tabloids tend to be extremely critical of the Government. All newspapers are privately owned. The two local television newscasts, one of which appears on a state-owned station, are sometimes critical of the Government but generally do not editorialize.

In April a reporter with the Trinidad Guardian newspaper said that plainclothes police grabbed him after he photographed the arrest of a robbery suspect. The reporter said that a police officer forced him to open the camera, took out the film, and exposed it. He reported the matter to the San Fernando police, but the authorities took no action.

A Board of Film Censors is authorized to ban films it considers to be against public order and decency or contrary to the public interest. This includes films which it believes may be controversial in matters of religion, seditious propaganda, or race. In practice, films are rarely prohibited.

b. *Freedom of Peaceful Assembly and Association.*—The Constitution provides for the rights of freedom of assembly and association, and the Government respects these rights in practice. Registration or other governmental permission to form private associations is not required. The police routinely grant the required advance permits for street marches, demonstrations, or other outdoor public meetings.

Political activity by trade associations or professional bodies is not restricted, and these organizations affiliate freely with recognized international bodies in their fields.

c. *Freedom of Religion.*—The Constitution provides for freedom of religion, and the authorities respect this right in practice.

d. *Freedom of Movement Within the Country, Foreign Travel, Emigration, and Repatriation.*—The Constitution provides for these rights, and the Government respects them in practice. Residents are free to emigrate, return, and travel within or outside the country, as well as to change residence and workplace.

There is no provision for persons to claim or be classified as refugees or asylum seekers; any such cases are handled on a case-by-case basis by the Ministry of National Security's Immigration Division. The issue of the provision of first asylum did not arise. There were no reports of forced return of persons to a country where they feared persecution.

Section 3. Respect for Political Rights: The Right of Citizens to Change Their Government

Citizens choose their government by secret ballot in free and fair multiparty elections held at intervals not to exceed 5 years. Elections for the 12-member Tobago House of Assembly are held every 4 years. The Constitution extends the right to vote to citizens as well as to legal residents with citizenship in other Commonwealth countries who are at least 18 years of age.

In November 1995 general elections, the former opposition United National Congress (UNC) and the ruling People's National Movement (PNM) each won 17 seats in Parliament. The National Alliance for Reconstruction (NAR) won two seats and joined with the UNC in forming a new government. Basdeo Panday became the country's first Prime Minister of East Indian descent. The PNM is primarily but not exclusively Afro-Trinidadian; the UNC is primarily but not exclusively Indo-Trinidadian.

There are no specific laws that restrict the participation of women or minorities in government or the political parties. Women hold many positions in the Government and political party leadership. Four out of 36 elected members of the House of Representatives and 9 out of 31 appointed Senators are female, with 3 serving as ministers. Prime Minister Panday appointed a woman as Attorney General. She was the first female Attorney General, and she has since moved to the position of Minister of Legal Affairs.

Section 4. Governmental Attitude Regarding International and Nongovernmental Investigation of Alleged Violations of Human Rights

Several small nongovernmental human rights groups operate freely without government restriction or interference. An independent Ombudsman receives complaints relating to governmental administrative issues and investigates complaints of human rights abuse. The Ombudsman can make recommendations but does not have authority to force government offices to take action.

Section 5. Discrimination Based on Race, Sex, Religion, Disability, Language, or Social Status

The Government respects in practice the constitutional provisions of fundamental human rights and freedoms to all without discrimination based on race, origin, color, religion, or sex.

Women.—Physical abuse of women continued to be an extensive problem; murder, rape, and other crimes against women are frequently reported. There are several shelters for battered women, and a rape crisis center offers counseling for rape victims and perpetrators on a voluntary basis; as of September 30, 154 people had voluntarily requested counseling, and 54 incidents of rape had been reported. Law enforcement officials and the courts are generally not sensitive to family violence problems.

Many women hold positions in business, the professions, and government, but men tend to hold the most senior positions. There is no law or regulation requiring equal pay for equal work.

The Division of Women's Affairs in the Ministry of Community Development, Women's Affairs, and Culture is charged with protecting women's rights in all aspects of government and legislation. Several active women's rights groups also exist.

Children.—The Government's ability to protect children's welfare is limited by a lack of funds and expanding social needs. Some parts of the public school system seriously fail to meet the needs of the school age population due to overcrowding, substandard physical facilities, and occasional classroom violence by gangs. There is no societal pattern of abuse directed at children. The Domestic Violence Act provides protection for children abused at home. Abused children are usually placed with relatives if they are removed from the home. If there is no relative who can take them, there are several government institutions and nongovernmental organizations (NGO's) which accept children.

People With Disabilities.—There is no legislation that specifically enumerates or protects the rights of disabled persons nor mandates the provision of access to buildings or services, although NGO's lobbied Parliament to pass such legislation. Lack of access to transportation, buildings, and sidewalks is a major obstacle for the disabled. Only two vans in the country are equipped with hydraulic lift devices for access by disabled persons. One such van broke down in 1995 and was not repaired; the other broke down in 1996. The Government provides some public assistance and partial funding to a variety of NGO's which, in turn, provide direct services to disabled members or clients.

Indigenous People.—Members of a very small group in the population identify themselves as descendants of the original Amerindian population of the island. They maintain social ties with each other and other aboriginal groups and are not subject to discrimination.

National/Racial/Ethnic Minorities.—Various ethnic and religious groups live together peacefully, generally respecting each other's beliefs and practices. However, at times racial tensions appear between Afro-Trinidadians and Indo-Trinidadians. Each group comprises about 40 percent of the population. The private sector is dominated by Indo-Trinidadians and people of European, Middle Eastern, or Asian descent. Indo-Trinidadians also predominate in agriculture. Afro-Trinidadians tend to find employment in disproportionate numbers in the civil service, police, and military. Some Indo-Trinidadians assert that they are excluded from equal representation in the civil service due to racial discrimination. Since Indo-Trinidadians constitute the majority in rural areas and Afro-Trinidadians are in the majority in urban areas, competition between town and country for public goods and services often takes on racial overtones.

In October there were reports that several popular recreational clubs were refusing entry to Afro-Trinidadians and dark skinned Indo-Trinidadians. The reports created a great outcry in the local press against racism, and the Government pledged to implement a law banning racial discrimination in entry policies for private clubs.

Section 6. Worker Rights

a. *The Right of Association.*—The 1972 Industrial Relations Act provides that all workers, including those in state-owned enterprises, may form or join unions of their own choosing without prior authorization. Union membership has declined, with an estimated 20 to 28 percent of the work force organized in 14 active unions. Most unions are independent of the Government or political party control, although the Sugar Workers' Union is historically allied with the UNC. The Prime Minister was formerly president of the Sugar Workers' Union.

The law prohibits antiunion activities before a union is legally registered, and the Ministry of Labor enforces this provision when it receives a complaint. A union may also bring a request for enforcement to the Industrial Court. All employees except those in "essential services," such as government employees and police, have the right to strike.

In August junior doctors at Port of Spain and San Fernando general hospitals began a series of sick-outs and work-to-rule actions to protest poor working conditions and insufficient pay. During these actions, several wards were frequently out of service at Port of Spain general hospital, including the intensive care ward. In late October, some of the junior doctors stopped their work-to-rule policy and began settlement negotiations with the Ministry of Health and the regional health authority. In September public school teachers began a series of work-to-rule actions and sick-outs. The Trinidad and Tobago Unified Teachers Association called for salary increases and improved working conditions.

The Labor Relations Act prohibits retribution against strikers and provides for grievance procedures if needed. A special section of the Industrial Court handles mandatory arbitration cases. Arbitration agreements are enforceable and appealable only to the Industrial Court.

Unions freely join federations and affiliate with international bodies. There are no restrictions on international travel or contacts.

b. *The Right to Organize and Bargain Collectively.*—The Industrial Relations Act establishes the right of workers to collective bargaining. The Ministry of Labor conciliation service maintains statistical information regarding the number of workers covered by collective bargaining agreements and the number of antiunion complaints filed.

The Industrial Court may order employers found guilty of antiunion activities to reinstate workers and pay compensation, or it can impose other penalties including imprisonment. When necessary, the conciliation service also determines which unions should have senior status.

There are several newly organized export processing zones (EPZ's). The same labor laws apply in the EPZ's as in the country at large.

c. *Prohibition of Forced or Compulsory labor*—*The law does not explicitly prohibit forced or compulsory labor, but there were no reports that it was practiced.*

d. *Minimum Age for Employment of Children.*—The minimum legal age for workers is 12 years. Children from 12 to 14 years of age may only work in family businesses. Children under the age of 18 may legally work only during daylight hours, with the exception of 16- to 18-year-olds, who may work at night in sugar factories. The probation service in the Ministry of Social Development and Family Services is responsible for enforcing child labor provisions, but enforcement is lax. There is no organized exploitation of child labor, but children are often seen begging or working as street vendors. Some are used by criminals as guards and couriers.

e. *Acceptable Conditions of Work.*—There is no national minimum wage. The Government has set minimum wages for 53 job categories in 5 nonunionized occupational groupings. The minimum pay ranges from $26 (TT$130.45) per week to $57 (TT$285) per week. These rates were to be adjusted for cost-of-living increases at regular intervals, but Parliament has never considered an adjustment since passing the laws. The Ministry of Labor enforces the minimum wage regulations. A minimum wage is not sufficient to support a worker and family, but most workers earn more than the minimum.

The standard workweek is 40 hours. There are no restrictions on overtime work. Daily rest periods and paid annual leave form part of most employment agreements. For those sectors covered, the minimum wage laws also stipulate holiday pay, 2 weeks' vacation, and 14 days' sick leave per year.

The Factories and Ordinance Bill of 1948 sets requirements for health and safety standards in certain industries and provides for inspections to monitor and enforce compliance. The Industrial Relations Act protects workers who file complaints with the Ministry of Labor regarding illegal or hazardous working conditions. Should it be determined upon inspection that hazardous conditions exist in the workplace, the worker is absolved in refusing to comply with an order that would have placed him or her in danger.

URUGUAY

Uruguay is a constitutional republic with an elected president, a bicameral legislature, and an independent judicial branch. In November 1994, former President Julio Maria Sanguinetti won a narrow election victory. He began his 5-year term in March 1995.

The Interior Ministry administers the country's police departments and the prison system and is responsible for domestic security and public safety. The police continued to commit human rights abuses.

The economy is a mixture of private and state enterprises and is heavily dependent on agricultural exports and agroindustry. The Government respects private property rights. The economy contracted 2.4 percent in 1995, but estimated growth for 1996 was 1.0 percent. Annual per capita income was about $5,767 in 1995.

The Government generally respected the human rights of its citizens, and the law and judiciary generally provide effective means of dealing with instances of individual abuse. However, there were problems in some areas, principally continued police abuse and mistreatment of detainees, and poor prison conditions. Low pay and consequent lack of professionalism in police ranks continue to be a problem. Court cases sometimes last many years, resulting in lengthy pretrial detention. Other problems include continued societal discrimination against women and the black minority, violence against women, and one case of abridgment of freedom of the press.

RESPECT FOR HUMAN RIGHTS

Section 1. Respect for the Integrity of the Person, Including Freedom From:

a. *Political and Other Extrajudicial Killing.*—There were no reports of political or other extrajudicial killings.

An earlier case resurfaced in June when the authorities identified a body, discovered in 1995 buried at a beach resort, as that of Eugenio Berrios, a Chilean chemist. He had disappeared from Chile in 1992 after he was called to testify concerning the assassination of former Chilean Foreign Minister Orlando Letelier. Berrios reportedly entered Uruguay illegally under protective military custody. He was last seen alive on November 15, 1992, when he showed up at a Canelones police station claiming that he had escaped from his captors. The police claimed that they returned Berrios to the custody of military officers. The Canelones chief of police destroyed the police station records and later had to resign because of that action. The Ministry of Interior conducted an internal investigation and determined that Berrios left for Brazil the day after the incident. The case was ignored until August 1995, when the presidents of Uruguay and Chile both agreed that the matter would be placed in the hands of the Uruguayan court, thus reopening the case.

b. *Disappearance.*—There were no reports of politically motivated disappearances.

There were substantial calls for investigation into past disappearances, despite the 1985 amnesty which was confirmed by a 1989 plebiscite. In April a Senator whose father was tortured and killed in Argentina in 1976 called on the Government to investigate the fate of those who had disappeared in Uruguay. Also in April, a former navy officer acknowledged to the press that he had "acted inhumanely" but asserted that had not killed anyone nor known about the fate of those who had disappeared. He said that he assumed full responsibility and called on others to do the same. This was followed in May by a silent march in honor of the disappeared persons in which 50,000 people participated.

The press and a number of opposition political leaders called for an official investigation under the Amnesty Law, which obliges the executive branch to investigate cases of citizens who were detained and then disappeared. The Government and the traditional parties supported the military's insistence that there be no investigation and argued that the 1989 plebiscite resolved the issue. Since the return to democracy, three administrations have consistently refused to open official investigations into the fate of those who disappeared under the military regime.

c. *Torture and Other Cruel, Inhuman, or Degrading Treatment or Punishment.*—The Constitution prohibits brutal treatment of prisoners, but the police continued to commit abuses. The Ministry of Interior did not receive any accusations of prisoner abuse or torture under the Sanguinetti administration, which replaced all the prison authorities.

The judicial and parliamentary branches of government are responsible for investigating specific allegations of abuse. A recently formed internal police investigative unit, staffed by attorneys, receives complaints from any person concerning possible noncriminal police abuse of power. While the courts seldom convicted and punished law enforcement officials for such abuse in the past, such prosecutions are occurring more frequently: For example, a tribunal upheld the prosecution of four police officers (who were disciplined but not sent to prison) involved in the August 1994 Filtro hospital demonstrations in which police killed 1 person and injured 50. The court stated that the police had committed excesses and that their use of firearms was not justified. In a separate case, a court convicted and sent to prison two officers accused of robbing a bill collector.

Police officers charged with less serious crimes may continue on active duty; those charged with more serious crimes are separated from active service until the court resolves their cases. A Ministry of Interior report stated that 440 police officers on active duty had a prior criminal record; of those, 232 had committed crimes while on duty. The 1995 Public Security Law, now completely implemented, requires a proportional use of force by the police and the use of weapons only as a last resort, in accordance with United Nations codes regarding the use of force.

Conditions in prisons and juvenile detention facilities remain poor but not life threatening. As part of the new Public Security Law, a commission formed to study prison conditions and update legislation on penal institutions to bring them into compliance with international standards presented its report to the Government in June. It criticized the treatment of prisoners as contrary to minimal U.N. standards; cited overcrowding, lack of staff training, corruption, and physical violence as problems; and recommended the immediate closure of seven penal institutions.

The Government permits prison visits by human rights monitors.

d. *Arbitrary Arrest, Detention, or Exile.*—The Constitution requires the police to have a written warrant issued by a judge before making an arrest. The only exception is when the police apprehend the accused during commission of a crime. The Constitution also provides the accused with the right to a judicial determination of the legality of detention and requires that the detaining authority explain the legal grounds for the detention. Police may hold a detainee incommunicado for 24 hours before presenting the case to a judge, at which time the detainee has the right to counsel. It is during this 24-hour period that police sometimes abuse prisoners, occasionally resulting in forced confessions.

A 1980 law stipulates that police confessions obtained before a prisoner appears before a judge and attorney (without the police present) have no validity. Further, should a prisoner claim that he has been mistreated, by law the judge must investigate the charge.

If the detainee cannot afford a lawyer, the courts appoint a public defender. If the crime carries a penalty of at least 2 years in prison, the accused person is confined during the judge's investigation of the charges unless the authorities agree to release the person on bail. This seldom happens. As a result, approximately 93 percent of all persons currently incarcerated are awaiting a final decision in their case. Because of the slowness of the judicial process, the length of time prisoners spend in jail before being sentenced may exceed the maximum sentence for their crime. Human rights groups claim that the uncertainty as to how long one will be imprisoned is a factor creating tension within the country's prisons.

The Government does not use forced exile as a means of punishment.

e. *Denial of Fair Public Trial.*—The Constitution provides for an independent judiciary, and the Government respects this provision in practice.

The Supreme Court heads the judiciary system and supervises the work of the lower courts. A parallel military court system operates under a Military Justice Code. Two military justices sit on the Supreme Court but participate only in cases involving the military. Military justice applies to civilians only during a state of war or insurrection.

Trial proceedings are usually based on written arguments to the judge, which are not routinely made public. Only the prosecutor and defense attorney have access to all documents that form part of the written record. The courts introduced oral argument in 1990, but individual judges use it at their option. Most judges choose to retain the written method, a major factor slowing down the judicial process. There is no legal provision against self-incrimination, and judges may compel defendants to answer any question they pose. The defense attorney or prosecutor may appeal convictions to a higher court, which may acquit the person of the crime, confirm the conviction, or reduce or increase the sentence.

There were no reports of political prisoners.

f. *Arbitrary Interference with Privacy, Family, Home, or Correspondence.*—The Constitution provides for the right to privacy, and the Government generally respects constitutional provisions and safeguards in practice.

Section 2. *Respect for Civil Liberties, Including:*

a. *Freedom of Speech and Press.*—The Constitution provides for freedom of speech and the press, but the authorities may abridge these rights if persons are deemed to be inciting violence or "insulting the nation."

All elements of the political spectrum freely express their viewpoints in both print and broadcast media. Montevideo alone has 8 daily newspapers and 6 important weeklies; there are also approximately 100 other weekly and a few daily newspapers throughout the country. Montevideo has one government-affiliated and three commercial television stations. There are about 110 radio stations and 20 television stations in the country.

A 1989 law stipulates that expression and communication of thoughts and opinions are free, within the limits contained in the Constitution, and it outlines methods of responding to "inexact or aggravating information." The law calls for 3 months' to 2 years' imprisonment for "knowingly divulging false news that causes a grave disturbance to the public peace or a grave prejudice to economic interests of the State" or for "insulting the nation, the State, or their powers." The authorities use this law intermittently to set and enforce certain limits on freedom of the press.

The Government closed a radio station after an August 1994 riot; it remains closed, and the authorities never brought specific charges against the station or its owners.

In May a court sentenced the director and the editor of a leftist daily to 2 years in prison on charges of offending the honor of a head of state (the President of Paraguay). The judge based the sentence on the national press law and the Constitution rather than on whether or not the information in the newspaper was correct. The two were later conditionally released from jail, but the case is still pending. The sentence drew the attention and criticism of human rights groups around the world. In October a judge rejected another case involving a libel suit filed by a former president, on the grounds that freedom of the press was an essential pillar and indispensable condition of democracy.

A June decree requires the Government's prior authorization for the import of newsprint. The Inter-American Press Association urged the Government to repeal this decree, calling it a "serious threat to the preservation of freedom of the press," inasmuch as it stipulates prior government authorization and grants the power to establish quotas.

The national university is autonomous, and the authorities generally respect academic freedom.

b. *Freedom of Peaceful Assembly and Association.*—The law provides for these rights, and the Government respects them in practice.

c. *Freedom of Religion.*—The Constitution provides for freedom of religion, and the Government respects this right in practice.

d. *Freedom of Movement Within the Country, Foreign Travel, Emigration, and Repatriation.*—The Constitution provides for these rights, and the Government respects them in practice.

The Government grants refugee status in accordance with the 1951 U.N. Convention Relating to the Status of Refugees and its 1961 Protocol. The Government grants asylum only for political crimes as set forth in the 1928 Treaty of Havana, the 1889 Treaty of Montevideo, and the 1954 Caracas Convention. The Government cooperates with the United Nations High Commissioner for Refugees (UNHCR) and other humanitarian organizations in assisting refugees. The issue of the provision of first asylum did not arise in 1996. There were no reports of forced return of persons to a country where they feared persecution.

In December an appellate court decided not to extradite to Peru two members of the Tupac Amaru Revolutionary Movement (MRTA) and released them from custody. The two then applied to the UNHCR for refugee status. At year's end, the UNHCR had not determined if the two MRTA members met the conditions for such status.

Section 3. Respect for Political Rights: The Right of Citizens to Change Their Government

Citizens have the right and ability peacefully to change their government. Uruguay is a multiparty democracy with mandatory universal suffrage for those 18 years of age or older, and there are no restrictions regarding race, sex, religion, or economic status. The Colorado party, the National (Blanco) party, the Broad Front coalition, and the New Space party are the four major political groupings.

A constitutional reform approved by plebiscite on December 8 did away with the old "law of lemas," by which a party could run multiple presidential and legislative candidates for the same offices. The candidate receiving the most votes from the party receiving the most votes filled the presidency, and each party gained seats in the Senate and Chamber of Deputies according to the percentage of votes that it received. The reform limits parties to one candidate, determined by internal party primaries, per elected office. The top two presidential candidates face a runoff election if no one wins a first-round majority vote.

Women and blacks face impediments to high-level participation in politics and employment in government. Only 1 of 12 cabinet ministers is a woman. In the legislature that was installed in February 1995, 2 of 30 Senators are women (the first since 1973), and 8 of 99 Deputies are women. There are no minority representatives or cabinet officials.

Section 4. Governmental Attitude Regarding International and Nongovernmental Investigation of Alleged Violations of Human Rights

A number of human rights groups operate without government restriction, investigating and publishing their findings on human rights cases. Government officials are generally cooperative and responsive to their views.

Section 5. Discrimination Based on Race, Sex, Religion, Disability, Language, or Social Status

The Constitution and the law prohibit discrimination based on race, sex, religion, or disability. Despite these provisions, discrimination against some groups exists.

Women.—Violence against women continues to be a serious problem. There were more than 400 reported cases of family violence, reflecting both an increased public awareness of the problem as well as a growing change in attitude among women. Previously, a woman's ability to file and sustain a complaint was hampered by the legal requirement to show lesions. The new Public Security Law provides for sentences of 6 months to 2 years in prison for a person found guilty of committing an act of violence or of making continuing threats to cause bodily injury to persons related emotionally or legally to the perpetrator. The Montevideo city hall has a hot line for victims of violence.

The Government has established an office of assistance for victims of domestic violence which trains police how to receive complaints of violence against women. The Government also asked the United Nations to resume a project, begun in 1990 but abandoned for lack of funds, designed to train judges, police, and prison officials how to handle crimes against women.

Women enjoy equality under the law but face discrimination stemming from traditional attitudes and practices. The work force exhibits segregation by gender. Women, who make up almost one-half the work force, tend to be concentrated in lower paying jobs. However, one-half the students now entering universities are women. They often pursue professional careers but are underrepresented in traditionally male-dominated professions. Human rights groups have criticized the Government because it still has not implemented a 1989 law for equality in the workplace. The Liceo Militar, a military-run secondary school that prepares officer-candidates for all the services, admitted 110 women, an indication of the military's movement toward integrating women into the military officer corps.

A small institute in the Ministry of Education coordinates government programs for women. There are a number of active women's rights groups, and many of their activities in 1996 centered on followup to the platform of action of the 1995 U.N. Conference on Women.

Children.—The Government is generally committed to protecting children's rights and welfare. An institute in the Ministry of Interior oversees implementation of the Government's programs for children but receives only limited funding for programs. The Government regards the education and health of children as a top priority and believes it should do more to ensure free education and proper health care for all children. Since 40 percent of children under the age of 5 live in 20 percent of the poorest homes, the Government is attempting to extend proper health and education to them with the help of the United Nations Children's Fund.

There are no societal patterns of abuse of children. Minors under the age of 18 are not subject to criminal trial, but receive special treatment with special judges and, when sentenced, stay in institutions run by the National Institute for Minors (INAME) for the set period determined by the judge. The Government currently houses all its problem minors in INAME. The most controversial aspect of the 1995 Public Security Law would allow the Government to put minors with a record of violent crimes in adult prisons if INAME has no room in its own institutions. Even though the law stipulates that minors would occupy separate facilities within the prisons, human rights groups adamantly oppose this provision. As a result, INAME has decided that it will not send minors to adult prisons.

People With Disabilities.—The legislature passed a law covering the rights of the disabled in 1989. A national disabilities commission oversees implementation of the law. Although the law mandates accessibility only to new buildings or public services for people with disabilities, the Government is providing access to a number of existing buildings. The law reserves 4 percent of public sector jobs for the disabled.

In general the country has an excellent mental health system and an interest in the rights of people with mental disabilities. Nevertheless, a 1995 study of mental health institutions found that conditions violated a broad range of rights codified in United Nations principles for the protection of persons with mental disabilities. It found that treatment was limited almost exclusively to psychotropic medication and electroconvulsive therapy; commitment could occur with a vague diagnosis of "mentally ill;" there were no practical limitations on the length of commitments; once admitted, patients often found it very difficult to get released; there was little or no psychotherapy, rehabilitation, or vocational training; and there was little or no respect for the dignity or privacy of residents.

National/Racial/Ethnic Minorities.—The country's black minority, estimated at 6 percent of the population, continues to face societal discrimination. The Government lacks adequate statistics on blacks, which contributes to a lack of awareness that problems exist. The latest report (1993) put the number of black university graduates at 65, and black professionals at fewer than 50. Blacks are practically unrepresented in the bureaucratic, political, and academic sectors of society. They lack the social and political connections necessary for entry into these groups. In a February 1995 public opinion poll, more than three-quarters of the persons interviewed admitted that racial prejudice existed, and two-thirds of them named blacks as the group that faced most discrimination. The Government is working with local minority organizations to address this problem and invited the leading black minority organization to help prepare an official report on racial discrimination.

A broader concern expressed by minority groups is that the high level of unemployment in other neighboring countries will prompt increased migration of workers from one country to another, giving rise to discrimination against blacks.

Section 6. Worker Rights

  a. *The Right of Association.*—The Constitution states that laws should promote the organization of trade unions and the creation of arbitration bodies. In spite of this provision, there is almost no legislation concerning union activities. Unions traditionally organize and operate free of government regulation. Civil servants, employees of state-run enterprises, and private enterprise workers may join unions. An estimated 12 percent of the work force is unionized. Labor unions are independent of political party control but have traditionally associated more closely with the Broad Front, the leftist political coalition.

The Constitution provides workers with the right to strike, and there were numerous strikes during the year. The Government may legally compel workers to work during a strike if they perform an essential service which, if interrupted, "could cause a grave prejudice or risk, provoking suffering to part or all of the society."

There are mechanisms for resolving workers' complaints against employers, but unions complain that these mechanisms are sometimes applied arbitrarily. The law generally prohibits discriminatory acts by employers, including arbitrary dismissals for union activity. Unions maintain that organizers are dismissed for other fabricated reasons, thus avoiding penalty under the law.

There are no restrictions on the right of unions to form confederations or to affiliate with international trade union groups; however, the one national confederation has chosen not to affiliate officially with any of the world federations. Some individual unions are affiliated with international trade secretariats.

  b. *The Right to Organize and Bargain Collectively.*—Collective bargaining between companies and their unions determines a number of private sector salaries. The executive branch, acting independently, determines public sector salaries. There are no laws prohibiting antiunion discrimination, but a 1993 executive decree established fines for employers engaging in antiunion activities. The law does not require employers to reinstate workers fired for union activities. However, in cases of legal challenges by union activists, courts tend to impose indemnization levels that are higher than those normally paid to dismissed workers.

Union members continued to file claims of discrimination with the Ministry of Labor, which has a labor commission that investigates all claims. In some of the cases, employers agreed to reinstate workers, but other cases remained unresolved at year's end.

All labor legislation fully covers workers employed in special export zones. There are no unions in any of these zones, but the few workers in these zones are not in traditionally organizable occupations. Because of the protected status given many of the companies in the free zones and the lack of union presence, occasionally companies will implement labor practices in violation of the law.

c. *Prohibition of Forced or Compulsory Labor.*—The Constitution prohibits forced or compulsory labor, and there is no evidence of its existence.

d. *Minimum Age for Employment of Children.*—The Child Labor Code protects children; the Ministry of Labor and Social Security is responsible for enforcing the laws. Illegal child labor is not a problem. The law generally does not permit children under 15 years of age to work, but 12-year-olds may work if they have a special permit. Children under the age of 18 may not perform dangerous, fatiguing, or night work. Controls over salaries and hours for children are more strict than those for adults. Children over the age of 16 may sue in court for payment of wages, and children have the legal right to dispose of their own income. However, many children work as street vendors in the expanding informal sector or in the agrarian sector, which are generally less strictly regulated and where pay is lower.

e. *Acceptable Conditions of Work.*—The Ministry of Labor effectively enforces a legislated minimum monthly wage which is in effect in both the public and private sectors. The Ministry adjusts the minimum wage whenever it adjusts public sector wages, usually once every 4 months. The minimum wage, which was about $95 (793 pesos) per month, functions more as an index for calculating wage rates than as a true measure of minimum subsistence levels, and it would not provide a decent standard of living for a worker and family.

The standard workweek is 48 hours in industry and 44 hours in commerce, with a 36-hour break each week. The law stipulates that industrial workers receive overtime compensation for work in excess of 48 hours and that workers are entitled to 20 days of paid vacation after a year of employment.

The Ministry of Labor and Social Security enforces legislation regulating health and safety conditions in a generally effective manner. However, some of the regulations cover urban industrial workers more adequately than rural and agricultural workers. Workers have the right to remove themselves from what they consider hazardous or dangerous conditions.

VENEZUELA

Venezuela is a republic with an active multiparty democratic system, a bicameral Congress, and a popularly elected president. Over three decades of two-party dominance ended in 1994 when former president Rafael Caldera was sworn in as President with the support of a coalition of small and medium sized parties. Five major political groupings now comprise the Congress. In July 1995, the Government reinstated most of the constitutional protections for citizens' rights that it had suspended in June 1994 ostensibly to combat subversion and to address the country's financial crisis. In some border areas, suspension of the freedom from arbitrary arrest and detention and search without warrant, as well as freedom to travel, remained in effect. The judiciary is legally independent, but judges are subject to influence.

The security apparatus comprises civilian and military elements, both accountable to elected authorities. The Justice Ministry controls the Judicial Technical Police (PTJ), which conducts most criminal investigations. The Interior Ministry controls the State Security Police (DISIP), which is primarily responsible for protecting public officials and investigating cases of subversion and arms trafficking. The General Directorate for Military Intelligence (DIM), under the Defense Ministry, is responsible for collecting intelligence related to national security and sovereignty. The National Guard, a branch of the military, has arrest powers and is largely responsible for guarding the exterior of prisons and key government installations, maintaining order during times of civil unrest, monitoring frontiers, and providing law enforcement in remote areas. It also supplies the top leadership for the Metropolitan Police, the main civilian police force in and around Caracas, and for various state and municipal police forces. Both police and military personnel were responsible for human rights abuses.

The public sector, including the petroleum industry which accounts for some 24 percent of gross domestic product, dominates the economy. In response to a financial crisis in 1994, the Government instituted price and exchange controls, which exacerbated the economic recession and the Government's fiscal and monetary difficulties. To stabilize and revive the economy, the Government implemented a reform program and virtually eliminated controls in April. High inflation negatively affected the poor and a shrinking middle class. The Government estimates unemployment at 12 percent, but does not include the informal sector, which represents about 50 percent of the labor force.

The Government's human rights record continued to be poor in certain areas, and includes extrajudicial killings by the police and military, torture and abuse of detainees, failure to punish police and security officers accused of abuse, arbitrary arrests and excessively lengthy detentions, illegal searches, corruption and severe inefficiency in the judicial and law enforcement systems, and extremely harsh prison conditions. Violence against women, abuse of children, and discrimination against the disabled continue to be problems. The Government does not rigorously defend the rights of indigenous people. In an effort to address these problems and better coordinate human rights policy, the Government created an intergovernmental Human Rights Commission in December.

RESPECT FOR HUMAN RIGHTS

Section 1. Respect for the Integrity of the Person, Including Freedom From:

a. *Political and Other Extrajudicial Killing.*—There were no reports of targeted political killings, but extrajudicial killings, primarily of criminal suspects, by the security forces continued. The Venezuelan Program of Action and Education in Human Rights (PROVEA), a highly respected nongovernmental human rights organization, documented 146 extrajudicial killings from October 1995 through September 1996. The killings involved summary executions, indiscriminate or excessive use of force, death resulting from torture and mistreatment while in custody, and death resulting from abuse during military or public service. According to PROVEA, the State Police carried out 47 of the killings; the Metropolitan Police of the Federal District, 26; the Municipal Police, 18; the PTJ, 15; the National Guard, 12; the armed forces, 12; the DISIP, 11; and other branches of the security apparatus or a combination of branches, 5.

The perpetrators of extrajudicial killings act with near impunity, as the Government rarely prosecutes such cases. The police often fail to investigate crimes allegedly committed by their colleagues and characterize incidents of extrajudicial killings as "confrontations," even though eyewitness testimony and evidence strongly indicate otherwise. In addition, the civilian judicial system remains highly inefficient and sometimes corrupt, and military courts are often strongly biased in favor of members of the armed forces accused of abuse. A special pretrial summary phase called "nudo hecho," which is used in cases involving public officials and is conducted in secret, often shields members of the security forces from prosecution, since cases can languish in that phase for several years. In the small number of prosecutions in which the courts convict perpetrators of extrajudicial killings and other abuses, the sentences issued are frequently light or the convictions are overturned on appeal. Unlike common criminals, members of the security forces charged with crimes rarely spend much time in prison.

In February several agents of the National Guard in Maracaibo detained Danny Ojeda Arrieta ostensibly for failure to carry proper identification. Two hours later they delivered him to a hospital with severe head injuries. He died 2 days later. The guardsmen involved claimed that Ojeda Arrieta jumped from their moving car. The Zulia state legislative assembly has requested an investigation. In April several members of the Caracas Metropolitan Police took Ramses Zambrano from his home to question him about a burglary. Less than an hour later they took him to a hospital with severe bruises to his chest, neck, and face. Zambrano died a short time later; the case was under investigation. In June following a robbery and shooting in a Caracas bakery in which a policewoman and a suspect were killed, members of the Metropolitan Police captured uninjured two other suspects whom they handcuffed and took away. A few hours later the police delivered the two suspects to the morgue, dead from bullet wounds. The authorities charged seven policemen with the killings, but a judge released all of them in September on the grounds that the case as filed was technically deficient.

In October during a dispute with some inmates, members of the National Guard fired tear gas canisters into a closed cellblock of La Planta prison in Caracas, which started a fire that killed 25 trapped inmates. The authorities charged three National Guard members and one prison guard with manslaughter. The prison guard, who applied the lock, testified that the National Guard prevented him from opening the cell when the fire started. Their trial had not been held by year's end.

A prosecutor charged with investigating the 1995 disappearance of Marcos Tulio Briceno Escalona told his family members that Briceno had been killed and his body dumped in a reservoir. Although witnesses claimed that PTJ members detained Briceno just before his disappearance, the prosecutor's office found insufficient evidence to charge any official. PROVEA included his death in its list of extrajudicial killings. There has been no trial or other resolution of the August 1995 execution-style killing of 21-year-old Hector Rojas, although the authorities have imprisoned four members of the PTJ.

There were no prosecutions or new revelations surrounding the discovery of a common grave in April 1994 in the Sierra de Perija region of Zulia state. Forensic experts provided no count of the number of bodies found in the grave, but human rights groups placed the number at around 15. At least one of the bodies showed signs of execution-style killing. Although members of a special rural contingent of the Zulia state police were alleged to have committed the killings, there were no arrests. A number of persons have come forward with credible testimony in recent years that there are additional common graves in the Sierra de Perija and Catatumbo regions as a result of killings by security forces, although subsequent government investigations were inconclusive. Human rights groups reported that local farmers and indigenous people are afraid to come forward with additional information for fear of reprisals.

The authorities also never prosecuted or held anyone responsible for the November 1992 killing of at least 63 prisoners at Catia prison. The National Guard—erroneously claiming that coup leaders had distributed arms there—stormed the prison, opened cells, and fired on inmates. The majority of bodies found were reportedly shot at close range, suggesting summary executions. Apart from the officially recorded 63 prisoners killed, the fate of 25 others remains unknown—either their bodies were not found or they escaped during or near the time of the killings. The Committee of Family Members of the Victims of the Unrest (COFAVIC) continued to seek prosecutions and a thorough investigation of the Catia prison killings.

There were no prosecutions for the 1992 killing of reporters Maria Veronica Tessari and Virgilio Fernandez by members of the security forces. Tessari had been covering a student demonstration and Fernandez a coup attempt.

Minimal progress was made towards resolving some 300 alleged extrajudicial killings by security forces during and after the civil unrest of February-March 1989. There has been only one prosecution: A police officer was found guilty in 1991 of killing 18-year-old Eleazar Ramon Mavares, shot by several police officers some 18 times at close range. The courts released the officer from prison 1 year later. In negotiations held with the Inter-American Commission on Human Rights (IACHR) in 1995, the Government agreed to initiate a new investigation of the Mavares case, punish those responsible, and provide indemnities to the victim's family. The Government's offer to pay $14,737 (7 million bolivars) in damages was judged inadequate by the family. COFAVIC referred 44 cases surrounding the 1989 killings to the IACHR, asserting that the Government had not ensured justice.

In September the Inter-American Court of Human Rights awarded $722,332 in damages to two survivors and the families of 14 fishermen killed in 1988 by military and police officers near the border town of El Amparo, Apure state. The military originally claimed that the deaths were the result of action taken against Colombian guerrillas, but the Government later acknowledged responsibility and said that it would pay indemnities to the survivors and the victims' families. In August 1994, a military tribunal overturned the conviction of 16 defendants in the case despite strong evidence that they had participated in a planned ambush.

Mob lynchings of supposed criminals is a growing problem. The victims are almost always known criminals who prey on residents of poor neighborhoods. Between October 1995 and September 1996, PROVEA recorded 14 lynchings resulting in death and 24 attempted lynchings.

b. *Disappearance.*—There were no reliable reports of persons who disappeared after being detained by the police or the armed forces.

There were no developments in connection with the 1995 disappearances of Julio Rafael Tovar, Fidel Ernesto Croes Aleman, Luis Martin Sanches Vargas, Juan Daniel Monsalve, or Jose Ramos; or the 1994 disappearances of Elsida Ines Alvarez, Benjamin Vasquez, or Fidel A. Sanabria. All had reportedly been detained by security force members prior to their disappearances. A family member of Yolanda Landino, who disappeared in 1993, claims that she is living in Colombia.

c. *Torture and Other Cruel, Inhuman, or Degrading Treatment or Punishment.*—The law prohibits torture, but credible human rights groups report that security forces continue to abuse detainees physically. This abuse most commonly comprises beatings during arrest or interrogation, but there have been incidents when the security forces used near suffocation and other forms of torture that leave no telltale signs. Most victims come from the poorest and least influential parts of society. There were also cases of torture of political activists and student leaders, after they were arrested and held on charges such as assault or destruction of property.

PROVEA documented 63 cases of torture from October 1995 through September 1996. A large number of cases were never reported because the victims feared retribution. According to PROVEA, the PTJ were responsible for 31 of the reported torture incidents; the State Police, 6; the Metropolitan Police, 5; the DIM, 4; the armed forces, 3; the DISIP, 2; the National Guard, 1; and unknown branches of the security apparatus or a combination of branches, 11. Many of these cases were in border areas where constitutional protections were suspended.

Torture, like extrajudicial killings, continues because the Government does not ensure the independent investigation of complaints needed to bring those responsible to justice. In addition to lack of vigor by the judiciary, the fact that the Institute of Forensic Medicine is part of the PTJ also contributes to a climate of impunity, since its doctors are unlikely to be impartial in their examinations of cases that involve torture by members of the PTJ. Very few instances of torture have resulted in convictions.

In January and twice in April plainclothes Caracas police detained and tortured Luis Escobar Ugas, an activist with the Bolivarian Revolutionary Movement. During the last detention Escobar suffered eight cigarette burns on his left arm and was forced to kneel for a mock execution. In May members of the PTJ suspended bank robbery witness Ramon Molina Castro from the ceiling by his hands, which were handcuffed behind his back. He stayed in that position for 3 hours, and he no longer has use of his hands or arms. He was released from detention after 8 days with the threat of death if he reported what had happened. In June while investigating an arson burning of 13 buses, members of the PTJ allegedly beat, suspended from the ceiling, and threatened with death eight suspects in order to extract confessions. The prosecutor ordered medical examinations in order to determine whether the suspects had been tortured; the results were negative, and no charges were filed.

In the border area where constitutional protections have been suspended, the National Guard and army commit abuses with near impunity. The Support Network for Justice and Peace has documented many such cases by amassing detailed witness testimony. For example, in February in the Anaru district of Apure state two drunken guardsmen reportedly entered the house of two women and a baby and sexually assaulted one of the women. Later in the same day 10 guardsmen went to the house to threaten the women if they filed a complaint. They nevertheless did so, but the guardsmen were not detained.

There has been no resolution of the border-area cases from 1995, in which members of the military tortured 23 rural workers near Cararabo and 19 peasant farmers in La Victoria, both in Apure state.

Prison conditions continued to be extremely harsh due to underfunding, poorly trained staff, corruption among prison staff and National Guard members, and overcrowding so severe as to constitute inhuman and degrading treatment. As of December 5, the 31 prisons administered by the Ministry of Justice held 25,369 inmates, of whom the courts had sentenced only 6,513. The prisons operate on average at twice their designed capacity. Inadequate diet, minimal health care, a prisoner to guard ratio as high as 40 to 1, and physical abuse by guards and by other inmates led to many prison riots. At least two deaths were attributed to guards: That of a prisoner shot in the face in Catia prison, and a prisoner tortured to death by fellow inmates instigated by National Guard members in Tocoron prison. In October guards fired tear gas canisters that started a fire that killed 25 inmates in a locked cellblock (see Section 1.a.). Inmates often have to pay guards as well as each other to obtain necessities such as space in a cell, a bed, and food. Guns, knives, and illegal drugs are easily smuggled into most prisons, and violence between prisoners is very common.

In March a 6-hour-long pitched battle between rival inmate groups in La Pica prison in Monagas state left at least 12 persons dead and 25 injured. In April a riot in Santa Ana prison in Tachira state left six dead and two injured. PROVEA registered a total of 220 prisoners killed and another 1,333 wounded as a result of violence from October 1995 through September 1996. According to the Ministry of Justice, 207 inmates were killed, mostly by firearms or knives, and 1,133 were wounded during the year. In addition, hundreds of others died as a consequence of filth, poor diet, and inadequate medical care.

There were no prosecutions of public officials for the corruption and neglect that contributed to the January 1994 riot at Sabaneta prison in Maracaibo, in which inmates killed 105 fellow prisoners and wounded scores of others. Prison staff and the

National Guard were generally unwilling to enter the facility in the months leading up to the riot, allowing a state of near anarchy to develop. In addition, during the riot, the National Guard allegedly waited for at least 2 hours before entering to restore order. As a result, the number of casualties increased unnecessarily.

The Government permits prison visits by human rights monitors. Delegations from Amnesty International, Human Rights Watch, and the IACHR visited several prisons in 1996 and came to similar conclusions regarding the inhuman conditions. The Government acknowledged the poor state of the prisons and made plans to improve the situation. The President inaugurated two prison expansions in December, designed to replace Caracas' violence-prone Catia prison, and the Government announced plans to build three new prisons in 1997. Nonetheless, funding for prisons remained extremely low, preventing significant improvement in most penitentiaries.

d. *Arbitrary Arrest, Detention, or Exile.*—In 1995 the Government reinstated the constitutionally protected freedom from arbitrary arrest and detention in all but 16 municipalities along the Colombian border where guerrilla activity was a continuing problem. However, the press and human rights groups continued to report a large number of arbitrary detentions during anticrime sweeps in impoverished areas by the Metropolitan Police, the DISIP, the National Guard, and the PTJ. The authorities detained persons during the sweeps for up to 2 days while they checked criminal records; most were released without charges. PROVEA documented 8,888 persons detained in sweeps from October 1995 through September 1996.

The law provides for the right to judicial determination of the legality of detention; however, the police may hold persons without an arrest warrant for up to 8 days, and the courts may hold them for up to an additional 8 days in court custody. In many cases, the police abused detainees physically and psychologically during the initial 8-day period and illegally held them incommunicado. During the second 8-day period a judge may, on the basis of the police investigation, order either the formal arrest or the release of the suspect. Arbitrary arrests are common, and authorities sometimes exceed the time limits for holding suspects. Prison officials often illegally demand payment from prisoners for transportation to judicial proceedings at which formal charges are made. Those who are unable to pay are often forced to forgo their judicial hearings.

The 1939 Vagrancy Law permits the detention for up to 5 years, without warrant, trial, or judicial appeal, of people deemed by the police to be a danger to society even though there is no evidence that they committed a punishable crime. This law is used chiefly against people with previous criminal records who are detained during police sweeps. In October the governor of Carabobo decreed that the Vagrancy Law would be applied to squatters on public and private land. PROVEA documented the application of this law against 552 detainees from October 1995 through September 1996.

Forced exile is illegal and is not practiced.

e. *Denial of Fair Public Trial.*—The civilian judiciary is legally independent, but judges are subject to influence from a number of sources.

The judicial sector consists of the Supreme Court, which is the court of final appeal; the prosecutor general, who provides opinions to the courts on prosecution of criminal cases and acts as public ombudsman to bring public employee misconduct or violations of the constitutional rights of prisoners or accused to the attention of the proper authorities; the Ministry of Justice, which manages the national police force and prisons and files complaints in criminal courts; and the Judicial Council, which oversees the lower courts as well as the selection and training of judges. The lower court system includes district and municipal courts as well as trial and appeal courts which deal with civil and criminal matters.

The law provides for the right to a fair trial and considers the accused innocent until proven guilty in a court. The justice system, however, is overburdened and inefficient, suffers from widespread corruption, and lacks public credibility. Judges are underpaid, poorly disciplined, and susceptible to political influence. The judicial process is paper intensive, requiring the costly and time-consuming production of voluminous reports at every stage by judges, attorneys, and witnesses. Case backlogs and lengthy pretrial detention averaging 4½ years are the norm.

The law provides for public defenders for those unable to afford an attorney, but there are not enough public defenders to handle the caseload. The Judicial Council reported that there are 159 public defense attorneys for the entire country.

Military courts can try civilians in cases of armed subversion and whenever armed forces members are involved. Military courts are subject to a requirement for a speedy trial and a statute of limitations similar to that of civilian courts. Persons convicted by a military court have the same right of appeal to the Supreme Court as do those convicted by the civilian system. Military courts, however, are significantly different from civilian courts in that by law the President must review every case after the initial investigation stage and decide if that case will go to trial. Human rights groups assert that this gives the executive excessive power to intervene in military cases. In addition, the Supreme Court selects military judges from a list of candidates provided by the Minister of Defense, a process that links the careers of military judges to the high command. The tendency of military judges to be responsive to the views of their military leaders, to maintain procedural secrecy, and to act slowly in high-profile cases in which the military is implicated make impartial or timely trials for defendants unlikely. As a result, military offenders evade punishment for extrajudicial killings and other human rights abuses.

There were no reports of political prisoners.

f. *Arbitrary Interference with Privacy, Family, Home, or Correspondence.*—Constitutional provisions prohibit arbitrary interference with privacy, family, home, and correspondence. However, from June 1994 to July 1995, the Government suspended the constitutional protection of freedom from search without a warrant, along with other freedoms. This suspension remained in effect in some border areas throughout 1996. Even after reinstatement of the provision in urban areas, security forces often conducted searches of homes without warrants, especially during anticrime sweeps in impoverished neighborhoods. In recent years, there have been some complaints of telephone surveillance, and human rights monitors accused the security forces of illegal telephone monitoring.

Section 2. *Respect for Civil Liberties, Including:*

a. *Freedom of Speech and Press.*—The Constitution provides for freedom of speech and the press, and the Government generally respects these rights in practice. Individuals criticize the Government publicly, although there were a few instances of reprisal. In February an artist was detained after exhibiting on a street corner his painting of the President and the Pope together with starving people. In October the DISIP detained an astrologer overnight and questioned him because he had predicted that the President would die in 1997. In December a judge sentenced the author of a 1995 book to 1 year in prison for criminal defamation. The book, titled "How much does a judge cost?" (Cuanto vale un juez?), is a compilation of accusations of judicial corruption; the judge also ordered confiscation of the book.

The print and electronic media are independent. However, a 1994 law forbids persons without journalism degrees to practice and requires journalists to be members of the National College of Journalists. Media owners, under the name Venezuelan Press Bloc, brought a case to the Supreme Court in November 1995 challenging the law as a violation of the freedom of expression provided for in the Constitution and international agreements on human rights that have the force of law. The Court had not ruled by year's end.

Some newspapers claimed that the Government restricted their access to foreign exchange to pay for newsprint because they took an antigovernment editorial line. Courts used restraining orders to limit reporting on certain cases. The police harassed television reporters who had filmed the arrest of two robbery suspects just before the police shot and killed them. The authorities never prosecuted security force members who killed two reporters in 1992 (see Section 1.a.).

The Government respects academic freedom.

b. *Freedom of Peaceful Assembly and Association.*—The Government generally respects the constitutional provision for freedom of peaceful assembly and association. Public meetings, including those of all political parties, are generally held unimpeded. The Government requires permits for public marches but does not deny them for political reasons.

As in earlier years, many demonstrations turned violent and were quelled by security forces. In January and February there were a number of violent protests against bus fare increases throughout the country. Hooded youths known as "encapuchados" frequently fomented the violence. In June groups of encapuchados set fire at night to a total of 13 minibuses used to transport workers from the Caracas suburbs. The fire killed a couple sleeping in one of the buses. In November violence broke out at the Central University of Venezuela and the Pedagogic University Institute of Caracas after the Government turned down a request to hold a march to protest a higher education bill in Congress. There were also a number of incidents where security forces contained or stopped peaceful protests. According to PROVEA, 181 people were injured during demonstrations and 756 detained from October 1995 through September 1996.

The Government generally respects the constitutional provision for freedom of association. Professional and academic associations operate without interference.

c. *Freedom of Religion.*—The Constitution provides for freedom of religion, provided that a faith does not threaten public order or violate good custom. The authorities respect this right in practice; all religious groups enjoy freedom of worship.

d. *Freedom of Movement Within the Country, Foreign Travel, Emigration, and Repatriation.*—The Constitution provides for the right of citizens and legal residents to travel within the country and to go abroad and return. The Government, however, can suspend the freedom to travel, as it did from June 1994 to July 1995. The Government also restricts foreign travel for persons being investigated for criminal activities.

Venezuela traditionally has been a haven for refugees, exiles, and displaced persons from many European, Caribbean, and Latin American countries. The Government cooperates with the office of the United Nations High Commissioner for Refugees and other humanitarian organizations in assisting refugees. Government policy does afford first asylum, but precise data were not available. There were a total of 337 applicants for asylum, of which 45 were accepted; about 90 percent of these cases involved first asylum. There were no reports of forced return of persons to a country where they feared persecution.

Section 3. Respect for Political Rights: The Right of Citizens to Change Their Government

The Constitution provides citizens with the right peacefully to change their government, and citizens exercise this right through periodic, free, and fair elections held on the basis of universal suffrage. An antiquated and inefficient system for counting votes, however, gives rise to numerous and, in some cases, credible allegations that the political parties that dominate electoral councils commit fraud.

Women and nonwhites participate fully in government and politicsbut remain underrepresented in senior leadership positions. Women hold 12 seats as Deputies in the 203-member lower house of Congress, 3 seats in the 53-person Senate, and 1 of 27 ministerial positions. Indigenous people have traditionally not been fully integrated into the political system due to their lack of knowledge of how it works, low voter turnout, and residency in areas far from the capital and other cities. Few indigenous people are in the Government, and only one is in Congress as an alternate deputy.

Section 4. Governmental Attitude Regarding International and Nongovernmental Investigation of Alleged Violations of Human Rights

A wide variety of human rights groups generally operate without government restriction, investigating and publishing their findings on human rights cases. Both international and local human rights organizations were provided ready access to the prison system. However, government officials were often critical of human rights groups, accusing them of seeking to discredit the State and undermine the country's image. In July the Minister of the Presidency met with Amnesty International (AI) chairman Pierre Sane, who had come to present AI's report on prison conditions. The Minister later asserted that Sane had his mind made up on the subject in advance of the meeting. Subsequently, the Minister of Interior opened a dialog with the local AI representative in an effort to establish a channel to allow information about human rights abuses to reach the Ministry for investigation.

In July and October, several human rights monitors operating in the militarized zone of Apure state were jailed briefly without justification. In December the President named a national human rights commission, whose functions include advising the executive branch on human rights issues, making recommendations to improve respect for human rights, and facilitating cooperation with international and nongovernmental bodies concerned with human rights.

Section 5. Discrimination Based on Race, Sex, Religion, Disability, Language, or Social Status

The law prohibits discrimination based on ethnic origin, sex, or disability. The Government, however, does not sufficiently enforce laws that safeguard the rights of indigenous people, protect women against societal and domestic violence, and ensure disabled people's access to jobs and public services. Very few resources are devoted to children's welfare; young delinquents are locked in institutions that are unsafe and dangerous.

Women.—Women face substantial institutional and societal prejudice with respect to rape and domestic violence. The law makes rape extremely difficult to prove, requiring at a minimum medical examination within 48 hours of the violation. Few police officers are trained to deal responsibly with rape victims. A total of 7,816 sexual assaults, including rape, were reported to the authorities in 1995; data for 1996 were not yet available at year's end. Women's organizations, however, assert that such figures are very low and do not accurately portray the problem of rape and sexual assault. The overwhelming majority of victims do not report the incident or press charges due to societal pressure and their own feelings of guilt.

Domestic violence against women is very common and has been aggravated by the country's economic difficulties. According to local monitors, the police are generally unwilling to intervene to prevent domestic violence, and the courts rarely prosecute those accused of such abuse. In addition, poor women are generally unaware of legal remedies and have little access to them.

The Congress reformed the Civil Code in the 1980's to make women and men legally equal in marriage. Women account for roughly half the student body of most universities, have advanced in many professions, including medicine and law, and have gradually surmounted many of the barriers to their full participation in political and economic life. Nonetheless, women are still underrepresented in the higher ranks of labor unions and private industry.

The Labor Code specifies that employers must not discriminate against women with regard to pay or working conditions, must not fire them during pregnancy and for a year after giving birth, must grant them unpaid leave and benefits for 6 weeks before the birth of a child and 12 weeks after, and must provide them with 10 weeks of unpaid leave if they legally adopt children under 3 years of age. According to the Ministry of Labor and the major labor federation, these regulations are enforced in the formal sector, although social security payments are often delayed.

Children.—The Government scaled back its expenditure on education, health, and social services. While the law provides for universal free education, the Government dedicates very little funding to primary and secondary education. According to a study by two reputable nongovernmental organizations (NGO's), one in four children is malnourished. Many government agencies responsible for the welfare of children are plagued by corruption, and government funding often does not reach the children it is intended to help. In addition, a large number of children are not eligible to receive government assistance because their birth is not properly documented.

A survey by the National Institute for Minors determined that 206,000 children were involved in illicit activities, principally begging but also petty theft, prostitution, and drug trafficking. Some 40,000 children were exploited sexually, according to a 1994 study. The preliminary results of a national epidemiological survey conducted in April-June showed that heroin, along with other drugs, has been introduced to public and private schools. The authorities in the metropolitan Caracas area, the states of Carabobo and Lara, and in some municipalities in Guarico, Merida, and Portugesa instituted a 10 p.m. to 5 a.m. curfew for unsupervised minors. Children's rights advocates claim that curfews permit the police to act arbitrarily in detaining persons who have committed no crime.

Because reform institutions are filled to capacity, hundreds of children accused of infractions are confined in jails. Crowded into small cells, child inmates often live in filth, are fed only once a day, and sleep on bare concrete floors. The Coche facility near Caracas was temporarily emptied of its 53 inmates in September after press exposure of the harsh conditions there. The authorities have not formally charged most of the children in jails with any crimes.

The recent increase in poverty has raised the level of stress within families and led to a rise in the number of abandoned children and to more child abuse. Moreover, neighbors often hesitate to report cases of child abuse, due to a fear of entanglement with the authorities and ingrained attitudes regarding family privacy. The overburdened judicial system, though very slow, generally ensures that in most situations children are removed from abusive households once a case has been reported. Public facilities for such children, however, are inadequate and have poorly trained staff.

People With Disabilities.—The physically disabled have minimal access to public transportation, and ramps are practically nonexistent, even in government buildings. According to local advocates, the disabled are discriminated against in many sectors, including education, health care, and employment.

In 1993 the Government passed the first comprehensive law to protect the rights of the disabled. That law requires that all newly constructed or renovated public parks and buildings provide access for the disabled. Among other important provisions, the law forbids discrimination in employment practices and in the provision of public services. However, the Government did not make a significant effort to implement the new law, to inform the public of it, or to try to change societal prejudice against the disabled.

Indigenous People.—Although the law prohibits discrimination based on ethnic origin, members of the country's indigenous population frequently suffer from inattention to and violation of their human rights. There are about 316,000 indigenous people comprising 28 ethnic groups, according to a special 1992 census.

The Constitution provides for special laws governing "the protection of indigenous communities and their progressive incorporation into the life of the nation." Nonetheless, local political authorities seldom take account of the interests of indigenous people when making decisions affecting their lands, cultures, traditions, and the allocation of natural resources. In March a judge in Puerto Ayacucho stopped the state government of Amazonas from building a road without undertaking an environmental impact assessment. As farmers and miners intrude on their habitat, indigenous communities are threatened by deforestation and water pollution. Few indigenous people hold title to their land. Since 1994 the Panare indigenous group of Bolivar state has unsuccessfully tried to defend its land from encroachment by cattle ranchers. In September a land dispute involving 28 families of the Wayuu indigenous group of Zulia state resulted in their being forcibly removed from their homes.

In 1995 representatives of the 19 indigenous groups of Amazonas state brought a case to the Supreme Court challenging the constitutionality of the law that defines political boundaries in their state. They claimed that the law, promulgated in 1994, jeopardized their collective possession of ancestral lands and did not respect traditional indigenous systems of decisionmaking. In December the Supreme Court ruled in their favor, declaring the law null because it was passed without the required consultations with the affected population.

Many of the country's indigenous people live isolated from modern civilization and lack access to basic health and educational facilities. High rates of cholera, hepatitis-B, malaria, and other diseases plague their communities. An outbreak believed to be leptospirosis killed 15 people in the Yanomami village of Manotheri between November 1995 and January 1996. Severe flooding in July destroyed indigenous homes and gardens in Amazonas state, causing a dramatic increase in malnutrition, diarrheal diseases, and other health problems.

The Yanomami, among the most isolated of the indigenous people, have been subject to persistent incursions into their territory by illegal gold miners. The miners have not only introduced new diseases but social ills as well. In August 1993, Brazilian miners killed at least 16 Yanomami in a remote area of Amazonas state and then retreated into Brazilian territory. The Government failed to seek their prosecution forcefully, and the Brazilian authorities released the miners after 3 months' detention. In August and September, the Government undertook a massive military operation in southern Amazonas state to dislodge illegal miners; about 80 were arrested, but several hundred more were believed to be still operating.

In February 1994, members of the army shot and killed three members of the Yucpa ethnic group after women in the group tried to block the soldiers from taking wood they had cut. The military allegedly responded by firing indiscriminately. There were no arrests of those responsible for the killings.

Section 6. Worker Rights

a. *The Right of Association.*—Both the Constitution and labor law recognize and encourage the right of unions to organize. The comprehensive 1990 Labor Code extends to all private sector and public sector employees (except members of the armed forces) the right to form and join unions of their choosing. The Code mandates registration of unions with the Ministry of Labor, but it reduces the Ministry's discretion by specifying that registration may not be denied if the proper documents (a record of the founding meeting, the statutes, and the membership list) are submitted. Only a judge may dissolve a union, and then only for reasons listed in the law, such as the dissolution of a firm or by agreement of two-thirds of the membership.

One major union confederation, the Venezuelan Confederation of Workers (CTV), and three small ones, as well as a number of independent unions, operate freely. About 25 percent of the national labor force is unionized. The CTV's top leadership includes members of several political parties. The majority are affiliated with the country's largest party, Democratic Action (AD). The CTV and the AD exercise reciprocal influence on each other.

The law recognizes the right of public and private sector employees to strike. However, public servants may only exercise it if it does not cause "irremediable damage to the population or to institutions." The Labor Code allows the President to order public or private sector strikers back to work and to submit their dispute to arbitration if the strike "puts in immediate danger the lives or security of all or part of the population." During 1996 most strikes occurred among government employees such as teachers, whose strike lasted more than 6 weeks; judicial workers, who were on strike for over 2 weeks; and physicians in public hospitals and clinics, whose strike included emergency care. In addition, there were a number of work stoppages by public sector employees to protest the Government's delay in paying negotiated and agreed-upon salary increases and bonuses.

There are no restrictions on affiliation with international labor organizations, and many union organizations are active internationally.

b. *The Right to Organize and Bargain Collectively.*—The Labor Code protects and encourages collective bargaining, which is freely practiced. According to the code, employers "must negotiate" a collective contract with the union that represents the majority of their workers. The code also contains a provision stating that wages may be raised by administrative decree, provided that the Congress approves the decree.

The law prohibits employers from interfering with the formation of unions or with their activities and from stipulating as a condition of employment that new workers must abstain from union activity or must join a specified union. Ministry of Labor inspectors hear complaints regarding violations of these regulations, and can impose a maximum fine of twice the minimum monthly wage for a first infraction. Under the code, union officials enjoy special protection from dismissal. If a judge determines that any worker was fired for union activity, the worker is entitled to back pay plus either reinstatement or payment of a substantial sum of money, which varies according to his years of seniority.

Labor law and practice is the same in the sole export processing zone as in the rest of the country.

c. *Prohibition of Forced or Compulsory Labor.*—The Labor Code states that no one may "obligate others to work against their will." However, there are credible reports of prison labor being administratively imposed on persons detained under the Vagrancy Law.

d. *Minimum Age for Employment of Children.*—The Labor Code allows children between the ages of 12 and 14 years to work only if the National Institute for Minors or the Labor Ministry grant special permission. It states that children between the ages of 14 and 16 years may not work without permission from their legal guardians. Minors may not work in mines or smelters, in occupations "that risk life or health" or could damage intellectual or moral development, or in "public spectacles."

Those under 16 years of age must by law work no more than 6 hours a day or 30 hours a week. Minors under the age of 18 years may work only during the hours between 6 a.m. and 7 p.m. The Ministry of Labor and the National Institute for Minors enforce the law effectively in the formal sector of the economy but much less so in the informal sector, which accounts for about half of total employment. According to a 1992 survey of sample households, more than 1 million children work in the informal sector, mostly as street vendors; large numbers of children also work as beggars and bootblacks.

e. *Acceptable Conditions of Work.*—There is a national urban minimum wage and a national rural minimum wage. The monthly minimum wage was $32 (15,000 bolivars) in the private sector for urban workers and $26 (12,500 bolivars) for rural workers. In addition, minimum wage workers in the private sector received mandatory food and transport bonuses amounting to $80 (37,800 bolivars). Total take-home pay in the public sector, the product of collective bargaining, was at least equal to that received by private sector minimum wage workers. Fringe benefits are added to these minimum figures; they vary with the workers' individual circumstances, but in general increase wages by about one-third. However, even with bonuses and benefits, the minimum wage is not sufficient to provide a decent standard of living for a worker and family. Unions point out that this combined income is far less than the cost of a family's basic food basket, estimated in September at $247 (116,395 bolivars).The law excludes only domestic workers and concierges from coverage under the minimum wage decrees. Under the Labor Code, the rates are set by administrative decree, which Congress may either suspend or ratify but may not change. The Ministry of Labor enforces minimum wage rates effectively in the formal sector of the economy but generally does not enforce them in the informal sector.

The 1990 Labor Code reduced the standard workweek to a maximum of 44 hours, and requires 2 "complete days of rest each week." Some unions, such as the petroleum workers, have negotiated a 40-hour week. Overtime may not exceed 2 hours daily, 10 hours weekly, or 100 hours annually, and may not be paid at a rate less than time and a half. The Ministry of Labor effectively enforces these standards in the formal sector.

The 1986 health and safety law is still awaiting implementation regulations and is not enforced. The delay is due largely to concern that the law provides penal sanctions against management when violations of health and safety occur and to ambiguity in the law over what constitutes a violation. The Labor Code states that employers are obligated to pay specified amounts (up to a maximum of 25 times the minimum monthly salary) to workers for accidents or occupational illnesses, regardless of who is responsible for the injury.

It also requires that workplaces must maintain "sufficient protection for health and life against sicknesses and accidents," and it imposes fines of from one-quarter to twice the minimum monthly salary for first infractions. In practice, however, unsafe job sites are seldom closed down by Ministry of Labor inspectors. Under the law, workers can remove themselves from dangerous workplace situations without jeopardy to continued employment.

EAST ASIA AND THE PACIFIC

AUSTRALIA

Australia has a federal system of government and a long history as a multiparty parliamentary democracy. The judiciary is independent.

Federal, state, and local police are under the firm control of civilian authorities and carry out their functions in accordance with the law.

A highly developed economy, which includes manufacturing, mining, agriculture, and services, provides most people with a high per capita income. A wide range of government programs offers assistance for disadvantaged citizens.

The Government respected the human rights of its citizens, and the law and judiciary provide effective means of dealing with instances of individual abuse. The Government administers many programs to improve the socioeconomic conditions of Aboriginals and Torres Straits Islanders, who together form about 2 percent of the population, and to address longstanding discrimination against them. Societal discrimination and violence against women are problems, that are being actively addressed.

RESPECT FOR HUMAN RIGHTS

Section 1. Respect for the Integrity of the Person, Including Freedom From:

a. *Political and Other Extrajudicial Killing.*—There were no reports of political or other extrajudicial killings.

b. *Disappearance.*—There were no reports of politically motivated disappearances.

c. *Torture and Other Cruel, Inhuman, or Degrading Treatment or Punishment.*—The law prohibits all such practices.

Human rights observers allege a pattern of mistreatment and abuse of indigenous people by police (see Section 5).

Prison conditions meet international standards, and the Government permits visits by human rights monitors.

d. *Arbitrary Arrest, Detention, or Exile.*—The law prohibits arbitrary arrest, detention, or exile, and the Government observes this prohibition.

e. *Denial of Fair Public Trial.*—The Constitution provides for an independent judiciary, and the executive and legislative branches respect its provisions. There is a well-developed system of federal and state courts, with the High Court at its apex. Almost all criminal trials are conducted by courts established under state and territorial legislation. The Federal Court and the High Court have very limited roles to play. When trials are conducted in local courts, the magistrates sit alone. In the higher courts, namely the state district or county courts and the state or territory supreme courts, trials are usually conducted by judge and jury. The jury decides on the facts and verdict after a trial conducted by a judge. The law provides for the right to a fair trial, and the judiciary vigorously enforces this right. There were no reports of political prisoners.

f. *Arbitrary Interference with Privacy, Family, Home, or Correspondence.*—The law prohibits such practices, government authorities generally respect these prohibitions, and violations are subject to effective legal sanction.

Section 2. Respect for Civil Liberties, Including:

a. *Freedom of Speech and Press.*—Australia does not have a bill of rights. In two decisions, the High Court has indicated that freedom of political discourse is implied in the Constitution. The Government respects these rights in practice. An independent press, an effective judiciary, and a functioning democratic political system combine to ensure freedom of speech and of the press, including academic freedom.

b. *Freedom of Peaceful Assembly and Association.*—Although these rights are not codified in law, citizens exercise them without government restriction.

c. *Freedom of Religion.*—Citizens have complete freedom of religion. A provision of the Constitution precludes the adoption of a state religion.

d. *Freedom of Movement Within the Country, Foreign Travel, Emigration, and Repatriation.*—The law provides for these rights, and the Government respects them in practice.

The Government cooperates with the United Nations High Commissioner for Refugees and other humanitarian organizations in assisting refugees. There is no provision for first asylum. The Government either grants a protection visa, with full residence and employment rights in Australia, or refuses it, with no in-between measures. The Government has continued to forcibly expel persons who it has determined do not have a valid claim to refugee status. Human rights and refugee lobby groups maintain that the Government's refugee and asylum adjudication process is applied inconsistently.

Under the Migration Reform Act of 1994, asylum seekers who arrive at the border without prior authorization to enter the country are automatically detained, but may be released from detention if they meet certain criteria—including age, ill-health, and experiences of torture or other trauma. The majority of asylum seekers are detained for the duration of the often-prolonged review process. The detention policy has led to extensive litigation initiated by human rights and refugee lobbies charging that the sometimes lengthy detentions violate the human rights of the asylum seekers. In 1994–95, Australia accepted 13,362 migrants under the humanitarian program, which accepts refugees and those in refugee-like situations in urgent need of resettlement. In addition, 1,407 persons (out of 8,802 applicants) already in Australia were granted refugee status in the same period. Regular migration figures for this period were 44,500 in the family category and 30,400 in the skills category.

Section 3. Respect for Political Rights: The Right of Citizens to Change Their Government

The Constitution provides citizens with the right to change their government peacefully, and citizens exercise this right in practice through periodic, free, and fair elections held on the basis of universal suffrage and mandatory voting. On March 2, 13 years of Labor Party government at the federal level ended when voters returned a Liberal-National Party coalition Government to power in the House of Representatives.

No legal impediments prevent women and indigenous people from holding public office. However, historical patterns of bias against women and the deleterious effects of poor educational achievement and a generally inferior socioeconomic status for indigenous people have contributed to their underrepresentation among political leaders. Approximately 22 percent of Members of Parliament (M.P.'s) are women. The percentage increased from 14 percent as a result of the 1996 election. There are no Aboriginals serving as M.P.'s.

Section 4. Governmental Attitude Regarding International and Nongovernmental Investigation of Alleged Violations of Human Rights

A wide variety of human rights groups operate without government restriction (and in some instances with government funding), investigating and publishing their findings on human rights cases. Government officials are cooperative and responsive to their views.

Section 5. Discrimination Based on Race, Sex, Religion, Disability, Language, or Social Status

The law prohibits discrimination based on the above listed factors, and the Government and an independent judiciary vigorously enforce the prohibition.

Women.—Social analysts and commentators estimate that domestic violence may affect as many as one family in three or four. The Government recognizes that domestic violence and economic discrimination are serious problems, and the statutorily independent Sex Discrimination Commissioner actively addresses these problems and other areas of discrimination. Government statisticians state that, because of underreporting and the lack of an agreed method for collecting statistics, it is impossible to provide an accurate national profile of the number of women who are victims of domestic violence.

Women have equal status under the law, and the law provides for pay equity. There are highly organized and effective private and public women's rights organisations at the federal, state, and local levels. There is a federal-level Office of the Status of Women which monitors women's rights. The Federal Sex Discrimination Commissioner receives complaints and attempts to resolve those that are deemed valid. A 1994 U.N. report estimated that women receive approximately 90 percent of wages paid to men for substantially similar work.

Children.—The Government demonstrates its strong commitment to children's rights and welfare through its well-funded systems of public education, day care, and medical care. The Federal Human Rights and Equal Opportunity Commission receives complaints and attempts to resolve those it finds valid. Similarily, the six states and two territories investigate complaints of neglect or child abuse and institute practical measures aimed at protecting the child when such complaints prove founded. The Government has enacted strict new legislation aimed at restricting the trade in, and possession of, child pornography and which further allows suspected pedophiles to be tried in Australia regardless of where the crime was committed. There is no societal pattern of abuse.

People With Disabilities.—Legislation prohibits discrimination against disabled persons in employment, education, or other state services. The Disability Discrimination Commissioner promotes compliance with federal laws prohibiting discrimination against disabled persons. The Commissioner also promotes energetic implementation and enforcement of state laws that require equal access and otherwise protect the rights of disabled persons.

There is no federal legislation mandating the uniform provision of accessibility for the disabled. It is lawful to deny employment or services to those with disabilities if there are reasonable grounds for believing that the disabled person would be unable to carry out the work or would require the employer or service provider to furnish services or facilities which could not reasonably be provided.

Indigenous People.—The Racial Discrimination Act of 1975 prohibits discrimination on grounds of race, color, descent, or national or ethnic origin. The Ministry for Aboriginal Affairs, in conjunction with the Aboriginal and Torres Straits Islander Commission (ATSIC), has the main responsibility for initiating, coordinating, and monitoring all governmental efforts to improve the quality of life of indigenous people. A wide variety of government initiatives and programs seek to improve all aspects of Aboriginal and Torres Straits Islander life.

In practice, however, indigenous Australians continue to experience significantly higher rates of imprisonment, inferior access to medical and educational infrastructures, greatly reduced life expectancy rates, elevated levels of unemployment, and general discrimination which contribute to an overwhelming feeling of disenfranchisement.

Nationally, indigenous people are imprisoned at over 15 times the rate of nonindigenous people. Over 45 percent of Aboriginal men between the ages of 20 and 30 have been arrested at some time in their lives. The incarceration rate for indigenous juvenile offenders is 21 times that of nonindigenous juveniles. Indigenous groups claim that the Government's lack of response to a series of recommendations by the 1991 Royal Commission into Aboriginal Deaths in Custody contributes to these disturbing statistics. Human rights observers claim that socioeconomic conditions give rise to the common precursors of indigenous crime, e.g., unemployment, homelessness, and boredom.

During a 12-month reporting period ending in July, 21 Aboriginal people were reported to have died in custody or during police operations. The five Aborigines who died "under the custodial authority of the police" all died of injuries which were not inflicted by the police. Injuries were suffered in fights or accidents before the prisoners were taken into custody. The 16 Aborigines who died in prison died of hanging (7), natural causes (7), and injuries (2). Of the seven who died of natural causes, five died of cardiovascular disease. This is the highest number of Aboriginal deaths in custody in a single 12-month period since records were first collected in 1980. Each death in custody is subject to a full and complete coroner's inquiry; no police have been charged with causing deaths in custody since 1980. Although indigenous people make up only 1.3 percent of the total adult population over 14 years of age, they account for almost 14 percent of the prison population and approximately a quarter of custody-related deaths. During the same time frame, 65 non-Aborigines died in police custody or during police operations.

Indigenous groups charge that police harassment of indigenous people is pervasive and that racial discrimination among police and prison custodians persists. A human rights delegation that visited Australia in March alleged a pattern of ill-treatment and arbitrary arrests occurring against a backdrop of systematic discrimination. In one study, 85 percent of juvenile indigenous suspects reported being hit, punched, kicked, or slapped by police. Most of the juveniles interviewed had complained about violence occurring after apprehension and during questioning about alleged offenses. Government statistics confirm the common perception among indigenous people that they are systematically ill-treated by police. Government reports have suggested that the pursuit of economic self-determination for indigenous people would greatly assist in solving the crime problems in indigenous communities and the inequitites in rates of imprisonment.

The average life expectancy of an indigenous person is 17 years less than that of a nonindigenous person. The infant mortality rate for indigenous children is 3 times that of nonindigenous children. The maternal mortality rate for indigenous women is 5 times that of nonindigenous women. The incidence of illnesses such as tuberculosis, leprosy, hepatitis, and of sexually transmitted diseases is 10 times greater among indigenous people than nonindigenous people. Data indicate that 22.5 percent of indigenous children complete secondary education versus 76.2 percent of nonindigenous children. Calendar year 1995 figures from the Department of Education, Employment and Training show that the participation rate in university education for Aborigines is 2.4 percent (up from 1.8 percent in 1991) compared to 2.7 percent for non-Aborigines.

Government programs, including a $750 million Indigenous Land Fund and a Federal Social Justice Package, aim at ameliorating the real challenges faced by indigenous Australians. The Government is also seeking ways to improve upon 1993 Native Title Legislation which has been largely unsuccesful in assisting Aborigines to establish and pursue title to land.

Section 6. Worker Rights

a. *The Right of Association.*—The law and practice provide workers, including public servants, freedom of association domestically and internationally. Approximately 35 percent of the work force is unionized.

Unions carry out their functions free from government or political control, but most local affiliates belong to state branches of the Australian Labor Party (ALP). Union members must make up at least 50 percent of the delegates to ALP congresses, but unions do not participate or vote as a bloc.

There are no restrictions on the right to strike. Legislation that went into force on March 30, 1994, for the first time legalized what had always been a de facto right to strike.

Laws and regulations prohibit retribution against strikers and labor leaders, and they are effectively enforced. In practice, employers tend to avoid legal remedies (e.g., secondary boycott injunctions) available to them in order to preserve a long-term relationship with their unions.

Unions may freely form and join federations or confederations, and they actively participate in international bodies.

b. *The Right to Organize and Bargain Collectively.*—The law and practice provide workers with the right to organize and bargain collectively, and the law protects them from antiunion discrimination.

Federal and state governments administer centralized minimum-wage awards and provide quasi-judicial arbitration, supplemented by industrywide or company-by-company collective bargaining.

Legislation has aimed to facilitate decentralized collective bargaining, keyed to individual enterprises, in order to relate wage increases more directly to gains in productivity. Workers can trade fringe benefits for greater wage increases but must register their agreement with the Australian Industrial Relations Commission, which insures that they suffer no net disadvantage. Legislation also provides for an industrial relations court to adjudicate disputes, especially the failure to bargain in good faith, arising from the increased use of enterprise bargaining.

There are no export processing zones.

c. *Prohibition of Forced or Compulsory Labor.*—Although there are no laws prohibiting it, forced labor is not practiced.

d. *Minimum Age for Employment of Children.*—There is no federally mandated minimum age for employment, but state-imposed compulsory education requirements, monitored and enforced by state educational authorities, effectively prevent most children from joining the work force until they are 15 or 16 years of age. Federal and state governments monitor and enforce a network of laws, which vary from state to state, governing minimum school-leaving age, minimum age to claim unemployment benefits, and minimum age to engage in specified occupations.

e. *Acceptable Conditions of Work.*—Although a formal minimum wage exists, it has not been relevant in wage agreements since the 1960's. Instead, 80 percent of workers are covered by differing minimum wage rates for individual trades and professions, all of which are sufficient to provide a decent standard of living for a worker and family.

Most workers are employees of incorporated organizations. For them, a complex body of government regulations, as well as decisions of applicable federal or state industrial relations commissions, prescribe a 40-hour or shorter workweek, paid vacations, sick leave, and other benefits, including at least one 24-hour rest period per week.

Federal or state safety laws apply to every workplace.

The Occupational Health and Safety (Commonwealth Employment) Act of 1991 provides federal employees with the legal right to cease work if they believe that particular work activities pose an immediate threat to individual health or safety. Most states and territories have laws that grant similar rights to their employees. At a minimum, private sector employees have recourse to state health and safety commissions, which will investigate complaints and demand remedial action.

BRUNEI

Brunei Darussalam, a small, wealthy monarchy located on the north coast of Borneo, is a sultanate ruled by the same family for 600 years.

The 1959 Constitution provided for the first delegation of political power by former Sultan Omar Ali Saifuddin to an appointed council of state, but in 1962 the Sultan invoked an article of the Constitution that allowed him to assume emergency powers for 2 years. These powers have been regularly renewed, most recently by the current Sultan in July. Although not all of the articles of the Constitution are suspended, the state of emergency places few limits on the Sultan's power. He also serves as Prime Minister, Minister of Defense, chancellor of the national university, superintendent general of the Royal Brunei Police Force, and leader of the Islamic faith.

The police force, which has responsibility for internal security, reports to the Prime Minister's office and is firmly under the control of civil authorities.

Brunei's large oil and natural gas reserves, coupled with its small population, give it one of the world's highest per capita gross national products.

Human rights remain broadly circumscribed. In practice citizens do not have the right to change their government, and they generally eschew political activity of any kind, knowing that the Government and ruler will disapprove such activity and may punish them. Nor, constitutional provisions notwithstanding, do they genuinely exercise the freedoms of speech, press, and association. Other human rights abuses, including discrimination against women and restriction of religious freedom, continued.

RESPECT FOR HUMAN RIGHTS

Section 1. Respect for the Integrity of the Person, Including Freedom From:

a. *Political and Other Extrajudicial Killing.*—There were no reports of political or other extrajudicial killings.

b. *Disappearance.*—There were no reports of politically motivated disappearances.

c. *Torture and Other Cruel, Inhuman, or Degrading Treatment or Punishment.*—The media occasionally report allegations of police mistreatment of prisoners, but these reports cannot be verified. Reports of police mistreatment of prisoners are investigated as violations of Brunei law. In 1988 caning became mandatory punishment for 42 drug-related and other criminal offenses and for vandalism. Since then, sentences of caning have been handed down and carried out in the presence of a doctor who monitors implementation and has the authority to interrupt and postpone the punishment for medical reasons. It is not known how many persons are sentenced to caning each year.

In October the authorities arrested two policemen for the rape of a waitress from the Philippines (see Section 5).

Prison conditions range from fair to good. There is no overcrowding, and prisoners usually have a cell to themselves. Prisoners receive regular medical checkups. Remand cells at police stations are Spartan but adequate.

d. *Arbitrary Arrest, Detention, or Exile.*—The law provides for a prompt judicial determination of the validity of an arrest. However, those provisions, like the Constitution itself, may be superseded, either partially or wholly, through invocation of the emergency powers. The Internal Security Act (ISA) permits the Government to detain suspects without trial for renewable 2-year periods. The Government occasionally has used the ISA to detain persons suspected of antigovernment activity; however, information on the detainees is only published after they are released. Two former rebel leaders were pardoned and released, after undergoing "political retraining" and swearing loyalty to the Sultan. The authorities assert they are holding one or two other former rebel leaders in detention under the ISA.

Police officers have broad powers to make arrests without warrants. However, under normal circumstances, a magistrate must endorse a warrant for arrest. Warrants are issued without this endorsement on rare occasions, such as when police are unable to obtain the endorsement in time to prevent the flight of a suspect.

Under the colonial era Banishment Act of 1918, any person deemed to be a threat to the safety, peace, or welfare of Brunei, may be forcibly exiled either permanently or temporarily by the Sultan. Since independence, there have been no cases of banishment of citizens.

e. *Denial of Fair Public Trial.*—The Constitution does not specifically provide for an independent judiciary. In mid-September, in a landmark legal decision, however, the appellate-level, High Court ruled that the Court has powers independent of the prosecution, and ordered a discharge in a car theft case under review, which amounted to an acquittal under the Criminal Procedure Code. So far the Government has not challenged the court's finding that magistrates have the legal power to discharge and acquit a defendant, even when the discharge is not requested by the prosecution.

The judicial system consists of five levels of courts, with final recourse in civil cases available through the Privy Council in London. In January 1995, Brunei terminated appeal to the Privy Council in criminal cases. Procedural safeguards include the right to defense counsel, the right to an interpreter, the right to a speedy trial, and the right to confront accusers. There were no known instances of government interference with the judiciary and no trials of political opponents.

The civil law, based on English common law, provides citizens with a fair and efficient judicial process. Shari'a (Islamic law) supersedes civil law in a number of areas, including divorce, inheritance, and sexual crimes.

Two "returnees" (individuals accused or convicted of participating in the 1962 rebellion, who fled or escaped the country, and subsequently returned) were released after going through "political retraining," and swearing loyalty to the Sultan, and government officials assert that only one or two such political prisoners are still in prison because of their role in the 1962 rebellion and their alleged refusal to renounce violence and pledge loyalty to the Sultan.

f. *Arbitrary Interference with Privacy, Family, Home, or Correspondence.*—Although the law permits government intrusion into the privacy of individual persons, families, or homes, this rarely happens. There are occasional reports of mail having been opened prior to delivery.

Section 2. Respect for Civil Liberties, Including:

a. *Freedom of Speech and Press.*—There is no law restricting freedom of speech and freedom of the press. However, the Government on a few occasions censored international newspapers and periodicals by removing or blacking out articles or photographs found to be objectionable, particularly those potentially embarrassing to the royal family, critical of the Government or the Sultan, or those judged sexually improper by censors. Magazine articles with a Christian theme are reportedly invariably censored. However, the growing use of fax machines, the Internet, and access to satellite transmissions make it increasingly difficult to keep such material from entering. There appears to be less evidence that authorities are trying to prevent the entry of such material. The independently owned local newspaper appears to practice self-censorship in its choice of topics so as not to anger the Government but it has instituted a new feature of letters to the editor by which citizens—some by name and some anonymously—criticize the Government's handling of certain social, economic, and environmental issues.

Although the only Brunei-based television station is government-owned, two Malaysian television channels are also received locally. A 10-channel cable network of television stations is widely available. This network includes the Cable News Network, the British Broadcasting Corporation World News, and several entertainment channels.

The Government's tolerance of political criticism has not been tested recently because there is no organized opposition. Moreover, citizens generally make almost no criticism of their government. In the past, the Government has not hesitated to arrest those who attempted to propagate unwelcome political views.

b. *Freedom of Peaceful Assembly and Association.*—Freedom to assemble for political purposes also has not been seriously tested in recent years. Following a 1967 ban on political parties, the Government allowed two parties to form in 1985 and 1986. The Government severely restricted membership in both, and disbanded one of them in 1988.

The remaining party, the Brunei Solidarity National Party, which had been inactive for several years, held an assembly in February 1995, reportedly with the consent of the Government. About 50 people attended. In May 1995, the party president resigned. In a September 1995 interview in a local newspaper, he said that he had resigned after the Home Affairs Ministry warned him not to involve himself in political activity because he is a former political detainee. He told the interviewer that he was seeking authorization from the Government to resume political activity. There has been no public party activity since the February 1995 assembly.

The activities of international service organizations such as Rotary, Kiwanis, and the Lions, continue to be constrained by the Government, which in 1995 reminded local leaders of these organizations that Muslims may not be members.

c. *Freedom of Religion.*—The Constitution states that, "The religion of Brunei Darussalam shall be the Muslim religion according to the Shafeite sect of that religion: Provided that all other religions may be practiced in peace and harmony by the person professing them in any part of Brunei Darussalam." In recent months, the Government has sporadically voiced alarm about "outsiders" preaching radical Islamic fundamentalist or unorthodox beliefs. Citizens deemed to have been influenced by such preaching (usually students returning from overseas study) have been "shown the error of their ways" in study seminars organized by orthodox Islamic religious leaders. The Government seems more concerned about these so-called Islamic "opportunists" than unwelcome political views. Moreover, the Government does not hesitate to investigate and to use its internal security apparatus against these purveyors of radical Islam.

In 1991 the Government began to reinforce the legitimacy of the hereditary monarchy and the observance of traditional and Muslim values by reasserting a national ideology known as the Malaya Islam Beraja (MIB) or "Malay Muslim monarchy," the genesis of which reportedly dates back to the 15th century. The Government in 1993 participated in issuing the Kuala Lumpur Declaration, which confirms the right of all persons to a wide range of human rights, including freedom of religion. Despite this and constitutional provisions providing for the full and unconstrained exercise of religious freedom, the Government routinely restricts the practice of non-Muslim religions by: Prohibiting proselytizing; occasionally denying entry to foreign clergy or particular priests, bishops, or ministers; banning the importation of religious teaching materials or scriptures such as the Bible; and refusing permission to expand, repair, or build new churches, temples, and shrines.

The Ministry of Education has also restricted the teaching of the history of religion or other courses in religion in non-Islamic schools while requiring courses on Islam or the MIB in all schools. Currently only the Bandar Seri Begawan International School, which citizens or permanent residents generally are not permitted to attend, is exempted from these restrictions.

d. *Freedom of Movement Within the Country, Foreign Travel, Emigration, and Repatriation.*—The Government restricts the movement of former political prisoners during the first year of their release. Otherwise, it generally does not restrict freedom of movement for most citizens, visitors, and permanent residents. The Government places some contractual restrictions on foreign travel for certain expatriate employees, but this is limited to the first year of the contract. Brunei has no legal provision for granting temporary refuge, first asylum, or refugee status to those seeking such refuge or asylum. Under the law, persons arriving without valid entry documents and means of support are considered illegal immigrants and are deported. There were no known cases of individuals seeking temporary refuge in 1996. Brunei has agreed in principle, and subject to certain reservations, to the Comprehensive Plan of Action adopted by the 1989 International Conference on Indochinese Refugees.

Section 3. Respect for Political Rights: The Right of Citizens to Change Their Government

Citizens are unable to change their government through established democratic processes. Under the continuing state of emergency, there is no parliament, and political authority and control rests in the hands of the ruling monarch. Individual citizens may seek to express their views or to influence government decisions and policies by petitioning the Sultan or handing him letters when he appears in public.

A form of popular representation lies in a traditional system of village chiefs who, since 1992, are elected by secret ballot by all adults. These leaders communicate constituents' wishes through a variety of channels, including periodic meetings chaired by the Home Affairs Minister, with several officials appointed by the Sultan. In May the Sultan officiated at the first General Assembly of the "mukim" (a group of villages) and village consultative council. Over 1,000 village chiefs from 150 villages and 35 mukim participated as delegates. The delegates were elected from among individual villagers, and the Government described the Assembly as "a grass roots level political system." The council's advisers, however, are all appointed by the Sultan. The Government insists that ordinary citizens actually use these councils to present their grievances and to obtain redress.

Substantial numbers of women serve at the junior and middle levels of the large government bureaucracy. At higher levels of the bureaucracy, a clear pattern of discrimination exists. Since independence, no woman has been appointed to head a ministry, and women continue to be passed over despite the presence of a number of well-qualified candidates for promotion to positions at permanent secretary and deputy minister levels. A woman now serves as an intermediate court judge, the highest judicial position held by citizens, and a sister of the Sultan has the rank of ambassador-at-large and is the second highest ranking official in the Foreign Ministry.

Section 4. Governmental Attitude Regarding International and Nongovernmental Investigation of Alleged Violations of Human Rights

There are no government or private organizations that deal specifically with the protection of human rights. Given the tight restrictions on freedom of speech and press and the Government's unwillingness to tolerate criticism, any group or individual attempting to investigate and report publicly on human rights issues would face severe constraints. There were no known allegations of abuses or requests to visit by international human rights groups.

Section 5. Discrimination Based on Race, Sex, Religion, Disability, Language, or Social Status

Except for religion (see Section 2.c.), the Constitution does not contain specific provisions prohibiting discrimination based on the factors listed above.

Women.—The extent to which spousal abuse may occur and go unreported is not known. However, in response to a growing perception that domestic violence is a serious problem, the police established a special unit to investigate allegations of spousal abuse in October 1994. Approximately 16 cases of domestic abuse were reported to police in the first half of 1995. The Government has established a shelter for abused women, and reportedly there were four residents there in 1995. In general Islamic religious authorities oppose divorce and encourage spouses to return even to flagrantly abusive husbands. However, they recognize wife beating as grounds for divorce. In 1995 the Government initiated a well-publicized telephone hot line to report abusers.

The criminal penalty for a minor domestic assault is 1 to 2 weeks in jail and a fine. An assault resulting in serious injury would be punished by caning and a longer jail sentence. One area of apparent abuse involves female domestic servants. While the level of violence in society is low, beating of servants—or refusing them the right to leave the house on days off, sometimes on grounds that they "might encounter the wrong company"—is less socially unacceptable behavior. Since most female domestics are foreign workers who are highly dependent on their employers, those subject to abuse may be unwilling or unable to bring complaints, either to the authorities or to their governments' embassies. When such complaints are brought, however, the Government is generally quick to investigate allegations of abuse and impose fines and punishment as warranted. In October the Government moved quickly to arrest and charge two policemen who viciously raped a 30-year-old waitress from the Philippines. If convicted they could face up to 30 years' imprisonment for aggravated rape involving threat and hurt. The victim of the alleged rape immediately sought refuge with her embassy, which lodged a police report. She was also taken for a medical examination.

In accordance with Koranic precepts, women are denied equal status with men in a number of important areas, such as divorce, inheritance, and custody of children. Under the Brunei Nationality Act, citizenship is transmitted through males only. Female citizens who are married to foreigners or bear children by foreign fathers cannot transmit citizenship to their children, even when such children are born in Brunei. This has resulted in creation of a sizable population of stateless children, estimated at more than 5,000 residents, who are entitled to live in Brunei and be documented for travel by the Government, but who cannot enjoy the full privileges of citizenship, including the right to own land.

Although men are eligible for permanent positions in government service whether or not they hold university degrees, women who do not have university degrees are eligible to hold government positions only on a month-to-month basis. While recent changes eliminated some previous inequities, women in month-to-month positions continue to receive slightly less annual leave and fewer allowances than their male and female counterparts in permanent positions.

Religious authorities strongly encourage Brunei Muslim women to wear the tudong, a traditional head covering, and many women do so. Some Muslim women do not, however, and there is no official pressure on non-Muslim women to do so. All female students in government-operated schools are required to wear the tudong; students in nongovernment schools are encouraged to wear it.

There are no separate pay scales for men and women, and in recent years there has been a major influx of women into the work force. Women serve in a wide variety of capacities in the armed forces, although they may not serve in combat. The number of female university graduates is increasing, and nearly two-thirds of Brunei University's entering class is female.

Children.—There are no published statistics regarding the welfare of children. The strong commitment to family values within society, the high standard of living, and government funding for children's welfare provides most children a healthy and nurturing environment. With a few exceptions involving small villages in extremely remote areas, nutritional standards are high, and poverty is almost unknown. There were 18 reported cases of child abuse in the first half of 1995. In 1996 Brunei became a signatory to the U.N. Convention on the Rights of the Child. In October the Brunei High Court convicted a father of 11 of child abuse. The Chief Justice sentenced him to 20 years in prison and ordered him caned with 20 strokes of the rattan for causing the death of his 3-year-old daughter and grievous hurt to another 2 of his children.

People With Disabilities.—No legislation mandating accessibility or other assistance for disabled persons has been passed. The Government is attempting to provide educational services for children with disabilities, although these efforts are not yet adequate to address the situation. Teachers are still being trained to deal with disabled children and some children have no educational opportunities. A special facility with trained educators is needed to accommodate the disabled children who cannot be assimilated into normal classrooms.

Indigenous People.—The 6 percent of the population that is composed of indigenous peoples has long been integrated into society, and enjoys the same rights as other citizens.

National/Racial/Ethnic Minorities.—Some members of non-Malay minorities, such as ethnic Chinese, including those born and raised in Brunei, are not automatically accorded citizenship and must travel abroad as stateless persons. Brunei's colonial-era naturalization laws are widely viewed as out of date and in need of reform.

Section 6. Worker Rights

a. *The Right of Association.*—Trade unions are legal in Brunei but must be registered with the Government. There are three registered trade unions, one passive and two generally inactive, all of them in the oil sector, and with a total membership amounting to less than 5 percent of that industry's work force. All workers, including civil servants other than those serving in the military and police, may form or join trade unions. Unions are independent of the Government. The Trade Unions Act of 1962 permits the formation of trade union federations, but forbids affiliation with labor organizations outside Brunei. An individual contract is required between an employer and each employee, but legal trade union activities cannot be deemed to violate employee contracts. Local legal experts interpret this provision as conferring the right to strike, but there have been no strikes. Brunei is not a member of the International Labor Organization.

b. *The Right to Organize and Bargain Collectively.*—The Government has not prevented the legal registration of trade unions, nor has it dissolved any. The Government did not interfere with lawful union activity. It is illegal to refuse employment or discriminate against an employee on the basis of membership or nonmembership in a trade union. While unions are legal and easy to register, conditions are not conducive to the development of trade unions. There is little interest on the part of workers in forming trade unions, and existing unions are not very active. The law is silent on collective bargaining, and it occurs in only a few industries. There are few industries of the kind in which unions have traditionally developed. Also, cultural tradition favors consensus over confrontation. Wage and benefit packages are based on market conditions and tend to be generous.

There is a free trade zone in Muara Port, known as the Muara Export Zone (MEZ), established in May 1994.

c. *Prohibition of Forced or Compulsory Labor.*—The law prohibits forced labor, and it is not practiced.

d. *Minimum Age for Employment of Children.*—The Labor Enactment Laws of 1954 prohibits employment of children below the age of 16. Parental consent and approval by the Labor Commission is required for those below the age of 18. Women under age 18 may not work at night or on offshore oil platforms. The Department of Labor (DOL), which is a part of the Ministry of Home Affairs, effectively enforces laws on the employment of children. There were no reports of violations of the child labor laws.

e. *Acceptable Conditions of Work.*—Skilled labor is in short supply, and market forces enable most citizens to command good salaries. There is no minimum wage. The standard workweek is Monday through Thursday and Saturday, with Friday and Sunday off, allowing for two 24-hour rest periods each week. Overtime is paid for work in excess of 48 hours a week, and double time is paid for work performed on legal holidays. Occupational health and safety standards are established by government regulations. The DOL inspects working conditions on a routine basis and in response to complaints. The DOL generally enforces labor regulations effectively. However, in the unskilled labor sector enforcement is lax, especially for foreign laborers (see also the subsection on Women in Section 5). The DOL is empowered to close any workplace where health, safety, or working conditions are unsatisfactory, and it has done so in the past.

BURMA

Burma continued to be ruled by a highly authoritarian military regime widely condemned for its serious human rights abuses. The military Government, known as the State Law and Order Restoration Council (SLORC), headed by armed forces commander General Than Shwe and composed of top military officers, seized power in September 1988 after harshly suppressing massive prodemocracy demonstrations. Retired dictator General Ne Win, whose idiosyncratic policies had isolated Burma and driven the country into deep economic decline, is believed by many to continue to wield considerable influence. The judiciary is not independent of the executive.

The SLORC permitted a relatively free election in 1990, but it failed to honor the results—which were an overwhelming rejection of military rule—nor to cede power to the victorious prodemocracy forces. Instead, the SLORC attacked the coalition of winning parties and their leaders through intimidation, detention, and house arrest. In January 1993, the SLORC established the "National Convention," a body ostensibly tasked with drafting a new constitution. Overwhelmingly made up of delegates handpicked by the military forces, the SLORC has carefully stage-managed the Convention's proceedings and ignored even limited opposition views. Despite having no legal mandate, the SLORC appears determined to draft a constitution that would ensure a dominant role for the military forces in the country's future political structure.

The Government reinforces its rule via a pervasive security apparatus led by military intelligence, the Directorate of Defense Services Intelligence (DDSI). Control is buttressed by selective restrictions on contact by citizens with foreigners, surveillance of government employees and other private citizens, harassment of political activists, intimidation, arrest, detention, and physical abuse. The Government justifies its security measures as necessary to maintain order and national unity, although most major insurgent groups have reached accommodation with the SLORC in recent years. Members of the security forces committed numerous serious human rights abuses.

Burma is a poor country, with an average per capita income of an estimated $200 to $300 per year on a cash basis or about $600 to $800 on a purchasing power parity basis. Primarily an agricultural country, Burma also has substantial mineral, fishing, and timber resources. Since 1988 the Government has partly opened the economy to permit expansion of the private sector and to attract foreign investment. Some economic improvement has ensued, but major obstacles to economic reform persist. These include extensive overt and covert state involvement in economic activity, excessive state monopolization of leading exports, a bloated bureaucracy prone to arbitrary and opaque governance, poor human and physical infrastructure, and disproportionately large military spending.

The Government's severe repression of human rights increased during 1996, even as increased economic activity fostered the appearance of greater normalcy. Out of sight of most visitors, citizens continued to live subject at any time and without appeal to the arbitrary and sometimes brutal dictates of the military dictatorship. Citizens do not have the right to change their government. There continued to be credible reports, particularly from ethnic minority-dominated areas, that soldiers committed serious human rights abuses, including extrajudicial killing and rape. Disappearances continued, and members of the security forces beat and otherwise abused detainees. Prison conditions remained harsh. Arbitrary arrests and detentions continued for expression of dissenting political views. Several hundred, if not more, political prisoners remained in detention, including approximately 20 Members of Parliament (M.P.'s) elected in 1990. The judiciary is subject to executive influence, and the Government infringes on citizens' rights to privacy.

The SLORC intensified restrictions on basic rights to free speech, press, assembly, and association. Political party activity remained severely restricted. Although the authorities recognize the chief opposition party, the National League for Democracy (NLD), as a legal entity, they detained more than 260 NLD M.P.'s elected in 1990 in connection with the Party's Convention in May. While most were released shortly thereafter, seven remain in custody. The SLORC's relentless harassment of the NLD continued with the arrest in August and later conviction of 26 NLD activists on charges of spreading disinformation and threatening the stability of the State. In September the SLORC again prevented the NLD from holding its first All-Burma Congress and detained more than 560 NLD members and supporters, most of whom they released after questioning. In December, in the wake of student demonstrations, the SLORC detained more than 200 NLD activists and supporters whom they accused of aiding and abetting the student protests. At year's end, more than 147 NLD activists and supporters who had been arrested during the year remained in detention.

The SLORC restricted the political activities of opposition leader Aung San Suu Kyi (it held her under house arrest from 1989 until July 1995). Beginning in late September, it prevented her from addressing public gatherings of her supporters, and confined her to her compound from December 6 to December 29.

Although more than 220,000 Rohingyas, Burmese Muslims from Arakan state, who fled to Bangladesh in 1992 had returned by year's end, about 33,000 remained in camps across the border. An estimated 10,000 new asylum seekers entered Bangladesh this year. A few thousand students and dissidents remained in exile in Thailand. Approximately 90,000 citizens were residing in ethnic minority camps along the Thai-Burma border, among these thousands of new arrivals driven out by army attacks in the areas controlled by the Karen and Karenni ethnic minorities. Discrimination against women and ethnic minorities, violence against women, and child prostitution remained problems. The Government restricts worker rights and uses forced labor. The use of porters by the army—with attendant mistreatment, illness, and even death for those compelled to serve—remained a common practice. The military authorities continued to force ordinary citizens (including women and children) to "contribute" their labor on a massive scale, often under harsh working conditions, on construction projects throughout the country. During the year, the military began using soldiers instead of civilians at certain infrastructure projects, following the issuance of directives in 1995 to end the practice of forced civilian labor. Child labor is also a problem.

The SLORC has given no sign of willingness to cede its hold on absolute power. The generals have continued to refuse to negotiate with prodemocracy forces and ethnic groups for a genuine political settlement to allow a return to the rule of law and respect for basic human rights.

RESPECT FOR HUMAN RIGHTS

Section 1. Respect for the Integrity of the Person, Including Freedom From:

a. *Political and Other Extrajudicial Killing.*—There was no evidence of an explicit or systematic government policy encouraging summary killings. However, there continued to be credible reports of instances of brutality and killings of civilians by the military, particularly in areas dominated by ethnic minorities and among those impressed as porters. The Government's general disregard for human rights has created a climate clearly conducive to such abuses.

b. *Disappearance.*—As in previous years, private citizens and political activists continued to "disappear" temporarily, for periods ranging from several hours to several weeks. DDSI officials usually apprehended individuals for questioning without the knowledge of their family members. In many, though not all, cases they released them soon afterward. At the same time, large numbers of people continued to be conscripted by the military for porterage or other duties, often without the knowledge of their family members. The whereabouts of those conscripted, as well as of prisoners transferred for labor or porterage duties, remained difficult to determine (see Sections 1.g. and 6.c.).

c. *Torture and Other Cruel, Inhuman, or Degrading Treatment or Punishment.*—Political detainees continued to be held incommunicado for long periods. The authorities routinely subjected detainees to harsh interrogation techniques designed to intimidate and disorient. The most common forms of mistreatment were sleep and food deprivation, coupled with round-the-clock questioning; some detainees were also kicked and beaten. In recent years, there have been credible reports that prisoners were forced to squat or assume unnatural positions for lengthy periods.

There continued to be credible reports that security forces subjected ordinary citizens to harassment and physical abuse. The military forces routinely confiscated property, cash and food, and used coercive and abusive recruitment methods to procure porters. Those forced into porterage or other duties faced extremely difficult conditions and mistreatment that sometimes resulted in death. There were many reports that soldiers raped women who were members of ethnic minorities.

Prison conditions are harsh. The regimen at Insein prison near Rangoon remained extremely harsh, including widespread use of solitary confinement, use of dirt-floored "doggie cells." It also involves little or no exercise, no mosquito nets, no reading or writing materials for many prisoners, poor nutrition, and inadequate medical care. A handful of prominent political prisoners were housed in separate bungalow accommodations on the prison compound. Most prisoners were permitted to receive medicine as well as supplemental food brought by their families during the 15-minute visits permitted every 2 weeks.

Conditions for political prisoners were reliably reported to be much worse at some upcountry prisons. NLD M.P.-elect, U Hla Than, a political prisoner serving a 20-year sentence in Insein, died on August 2, after being transferred from the prison to Rangoon General Hospital with a terminal illness. His family had sought permission to allow him to die at home, but the Government insisted that he renounce his mandate as an NLD parliamentarian, a condition that the family and the Party rejected. His family at first understood that Hla Than died of tuberculosis, but later the Government said that he had died of AIDS. Responding to foreign journalists at a press conference in September, the Government asserted that Hla Than had been well-cared for in prison, but that the AIDS diagnosis had only been made in July. It is clear that Hla Than did not receive proper medical treatment throughout his illness because the Government had made the AIDS diagnosis too late.

d. *Arbitrary Arrest, Detention, or Exile.*—There is no provision in the law for judicial determination of the legality of detention. The SLORC routinely practiced arbitrary arrest and incommunicado detention. Prior to being charged, detainees rarely have access to legal counsel or their families, and political detainees have no opportunity to obtain release on bail.

With the increase in political activism in the wake of Aung San Suu Kyi's release from house arrest in July 1995, the number of cases of arbitrary arrest and detention increased. The most egregious cases involved the detention during the week of May 19 of approximately 260 NLD M.P.'s-elect in conjunction with the Party's May 26–28 convention. Although all but a few are believed to have been released, elected M.P.'s in the group have been subjected by the SLORC to intense pressure to relinquish their electoral mandates. As of year's end, 25 had done so, primarily as the result of threats against their family members or business interests. Again in September, the SLORC cracked down on the NLD, arresting more than 560 NLD activists and supporters to prevent the convening of its first All-Burma Congress. Although the SLORC claims to have released all those detained, the NLD believes that many persons remain in detention. Yet again in December, in the wake of student demonstrations, the SLORC detained more than 200 activists, supporters, and others, in addition to at least 263 students whom they had detained and released, and whom they accused of aiding and abetting the student protests.

Authorities confined Aung San Suu Kyi to her compound from December 6 to December 29. Since mid-December, she has been severely restricted in her ability to receive visitors.

The number of NLD members and activists arrested since May 19 and still in detention at the end of the year totaled at least 147, including at least 17 M.P.'s-elect. None of those arrested can reasonably be considered to have engaged in activities violently threatening to the State. U Win Htein, Aung San Suu Kyi's personal secretary, was arrested in June (along with two other NLD activists) and sentenced on August 15 to a 7-year prison term for "knowingly disseminating false information." The charges related to statements made by him on an Australian television program earlier in the year. On August 26, he was sentenced to an additional 7 years for undermining the economy by having assisted in the production of a videotape of rice fields in the Delta region.

In June, 19 NLD activists—including two M.P.'s-elect from Mandalay-Sagaing, and Chin state—were arrested on charges of possessing "subversive" literature on passive resistance. The 19 were each sentenced to 7 years in prison.

The SLORC was prepared to go to considerable lengths in its campaign to harass and intimidate the NLD. For example, in March a party benefactor from Mandalay, Sein Hla Aung, was sentenced to 3 years' imprisonment for selling videotapes of NLD weekend rallies; two comedians from Mandalay, Par Par Lay and Lu Zaw, who performed skits critical of the SLORC on the Nobel Laureate's compound, were sentenced along with two others to 7-years' imprisonment; and Leo Nichols, a friend and benefactor of Aung San Suu Kyi, was arrested in April for possessing unauthorized telephones and a facsimile machine. He received a maximum 3-year sentence, suffered a cerebral hemorrhage on June 22 while in custody, and died a few hours later in Rangoon General Hospital. The harsh treatment he received in prison almost certainly hastened his death.

Forced exile is not used as a method of political control. However, in 1990, when the SLORC refused to recognize the results of the elections and pressured successful candidates to resign, some of them responded by going into exile.

e. *Denial of Fair Public Trial.*—The judiciary is not independent of the executive. The SLORC names justices to the Supreme Court who, in turn, appoint lower court judges with the approval of the SLORC. Pervasive corruption further serves to undermine the impartiality of the justice system.

The court system, as inherited from the United Kingdom and subsequently restructured, comprises courts at the township, district, state, and national levels.

Throughout the year, the Government continued to rule by decree and was not bound by any constitutional provisions guaranteeing fair public trials or any other rights. Although remnants of the British-era legal system were formally in place, the court system and its operation remained seriously flawed. Particularly in the handling of political cases, ongoing unprofessional behavior by some court officials, the misuse of overly broad laws, and the manipulation of the courts for political ends continued to deprive citizens of the right to a fair trial and the rule of law.

Some basic due process rights, including the rights to a public trial and to be represented by a defense attorney, were generally respected except in sensitive political cases. Defense attorneys are permitted to call and cross-examine witnesses, but their primary role is to bargain with the judge to obtain the least severe possible sentence for their clients. Most court proceedings are open to the public. However, in political cases, trials are held in courtrooms located in prison compounds and are not open to the public. In these instances, defense counsel appears to serve no other purpose than to provide moral support, since reliable reports indicate that verdicts are dictated by higher authorities. In the case of Win Htein, defense counsel was prevented from attending his trials because the authorities withheld permission.

In contrast with past years, there have been virtually no publicly announced releases of prisoners believed to be held for political reasons. To date, only one such announcement involving four persons appeared in the press. At year's end, at least several hundred—if not many more—political prisoners remained incarcerated.

f. *Arbitrary Interference with Privacy, Family, Home, and Correspondence.*—Military authorities ruled unchecked by any outside authority, and the State continued to interfere extensively and arbitrarily with the lives of private citizens. Through its extensive intelligence network, the Government closely monitored the travel, whereabouts, and activities of many citizens, particularly those believed to be politically active. Security personnel selectively screened private correspondence and telephone calls and conducted warrantless searches of private premises. At times the Government attempted to jam foreign radio broadcasts, and private citizens were generally unable to subscribe directly to foreign publications (see Section 2.a.). Government employees were required to obtain advance permission before meeting with foreigners.

The SLORC continued to move citizens out of cities to peripheral new town settlements, though not on the same scale as in the early 1990's. While facilities in some of these areas have improved over time, residents targeted for displacement continued to be given no option but to move, usually on short notice. In Hlaing Thaya township near Rangoon, residents were relocated again after having been moved in 1992. The military forces also continued to relocate by force hundreds of rural villages, especially in ethnic minority areas. Approximately 30,000 Karenni were displaced, as were tens of thousands of Shan villagers.

Those in established cities and towns were subject to arbitrary seizure of their property. In a number of urban areas, residents were compelled to cede land for road-widening projects decided upon without any public consultation nor endorsement. Other long-term city residents were required to cede land for commercial redevelopment and were compensated at only a fraction of the value of their lost homes. In rural areas, military personnel at times confiscated livestock and food supplies. Even the resting places of the dead were not spared as the Government took over several cemeteries for development and gave families only a few weeks to relocate their ancestors' remains.

g. *Use of Excessive Force and Violations of Humanitarian Law in Internal Conflicts.*—For more than four decades the army has battled diverse ethnic insurgencies. These ethnic minority insurgent groups have sought to gain greater autonomy from the dominant ethnic Burman majority. In 1989 the SLORC began a policy of seeking cease-fire agreements with most ethnic insurgent groups along the borders. In late 1995, government troops attempted to move into Karenni-held areas of Kayah state, leading to the breakdown of the cease-fire with the Karenni National Progressive Party (KNPP) that the SLORC had negotiated in June 1995.

In January the army began an offensive against the KNPP, which continued throughout the year. In June the military forcibly relocated 96 Karenni villages having an estimated population of 20,000 to 30,000 as part of its campaign to deny the guerrillas local support. Also in January, the SLORC negotiated a cease-fire with alleged drug trafficker Khun Sa and his Mong Tai Army. Although the cease-fire succeeded in breaking up the majority of Khun Sa's forces, dissident elements continued to fight the Government, which prompted a campaign of relocation against the Shan people. As many as 50,000 persons may have been forced to move from their villages.

In conjunction with the military's campaigns against the Karen, Karenni, and the remnants of Khun Sa's Mong Tai Army, it was standard practice for the military authorities to coerce thousands of civilians living in jungle areas in or near combat zones into working as porters. There were also many reports that soldiers raped female members of ethnic minorities. In the regions controlled by insurgent groups involved in the illegal narcotics trade, civilians were reliably reported to have been subjected by the army to forced labor as well.

Antigovernment insurgent groups were also responsible for violence, including the use of mines, causing both civilian and military deaths.

Section 2. Respect for Civil Liberties, Including:

a. *Freedom of Speech and Press.*—The Government continued to impose severe restrictions on freedom of speech and the press. The security services continued to repress those attempting to express opposition political views, and many more refrained from speaking out for fear of arrest and interrogation. The major exceptions were Aung San Suu Kyi and NLD vice-chairmen Tin Oo and Kyi Maung, who gave speeches every weekend in front of Aung San Suu Kyi's residence to those willing to risk being detained by military intelligence authorities. However, in September the authorities prohibited the weekend speeches as part of the Government's campaign to prevent the NLD from holding its Party Congress. The barriers in front of Aung San Suu Kyi's house remained in place, and the weekend speeches were barred at year's end.

All forms of domestic public media were officially controlled and/or censored. This strict control in turn encouraged self-censorship on the part of writers and publishers. Private citizens were generally unable to subscribe directly to foreign publications, but a limited selection of foreign newspapers could be purchased in a few hotels in Rangoon. A limited supply of secondhand copies of international news magazines and a sizable number of private publications on nonpolitical issues were available to the public, but censors frequently banned issues or deleted articles deemed unwelcome by the Government.

The government-monopoly television, radio, and newspaper media remained propaganda instruments. With the exception of reporting on some limited aspects of the National Convention, these official media did not report opposing views except to criticize them. Editors remained answerable to military authorities. While the English-language daily New Light of Myanmar continued to include many international wire service reports of foreign news, domestic news hewed strictly to and reinforced government policy.

Many foreign journalists, including television crews, were able to visit and report on developments, though the Government sometimes restricted and monitored their movements. At the same time, it denied visas to other journalists, or their issuance was so delayed as to render a planned visit impossible. It harassed journalists during the abortive September NLD Party Congress and subsequently during student demonstrations.

Foreign radio broadcasts, such as those of the British Broadcasting Corporation, Voice of America, and Norway-based Democratic Voice of Burma, remained prime sources of uncensored information. The authorities at times attempted to jam or otherwise interfere with the reception of these broadcasts (see Section 1.f.). The Government allowed some official foreign news services to conduct a range of programs.

The authorities continued to restrict the reception of satellite television broadcasts. Penalties of up to 3 years' imprisonment for operation of an unlicensed satellite television receiver can be imposed. Licenses, however, were almost impossible to obtain by ordinary citizens.

During the year, the Government issued a series of Orwellian decrees designed to strengthen its control over all forms of political expression and its citizens' access to information. In June the SLORC issued Order 5/96, which prohibited speeches or statements that "undermine national stability" as well as the drafting of alternative constitutions. In July the Government amended the television and video law to impose additional restrictions and stiffer penalties on the distribution of videotapes not approved by the censor. In September the Government decreed that all privately owned computers, software, and associated telecommunications devices would be subject to government registration. The law required government permission for all communications by computer.

University teachers and professors remained subject to the same restrictions on freedom of speech, political activities, and publications as other government employees. These included warnings against criticism of the Government; instructions not to discuss politics while at work; and strictures against joining or supporting political parties, engaging in political activity, or meeting foreigners. Teachers continued to be held responsible for propagating SLORC political goals among their students and for maintaining discipline and preventing students from engaging in any unauthorized political activity.

b. *Freedom of Peaceful Assembly and Association.*—The Government does not respect these rights. The Government's prohibition on unauthorized outdoor assemblies of more than 5 people remained in effect, albeit unevenly enforced. For example, 3,000 to 4,000 persons regularly gathered in front of Aung San Suu Kyi's residence to listen to her speak at weekly talks until authorities stopped the speeches in September. At the time when the Government prevented the NLD Congress, it also erected barricades at her residence and imposed additional restrictions on her freedom to leave the premises. Aung San Suu Kyi has been unable to speak to the public since September, except briefly on two occasions.

The Government curtailed student demonstrations in December. It did, however, permit students to demonstrate for several days early in the month. Riot police eventually curtailed the demonstrations, using water cannons and batons. After detaining and releasing hundreds of students, the Government closed the universities to prevent further demonstrations.

Legal political parties remained formally required to request permission from the authorities to hold internal meetings of their members, although some members still met without official permission. These persons, like those attending Aung San Suu Kyi's addresses, remained liable to arrest for these activities. In the NLD's attempt to hold a Party Congress, the authorities temporarily detained hundreds of supporters; several dozen remain in jail. The Government's own mass mobilization organization, the Union Solidarity and Development Association (USDA), continued to hold large-scale rallies in support of government policies. In many cases, it coerced attendance, using explicit threats of penalties for those who contemplated staying away. Religious groups, by contrast, sometimes encountered problems holding outdoor gatherings.

Aside from officially sanctioned organizations such as the USDA, the right of association existed only for the few organizations, such as trade associations and professional bodies, permitted by law and duly registered with the Government. Only a handful continued to exist, and even those were subject to direct government intervention or took special care to act in accordance with government policy. This included such benign organizations as the Myanmar Red Cross and the Myanmar Medical Association.

c. *Freedom of Religion.*—Adherents of all religions that were duly registered with the authorities generally enjoyed freedom to worship as they chose, although Buddhists continued to enjoy a privileged position. In recent years, the Government made special efforts to link itself with Buddhism as a means of asserting its own popular legitimacy. For example, the SLORC continued its construction of two pagodas to house a venerated Buddha tooth relic from China, which is expected to be available for loan for periodic visits. The SLORC also renovated the Shwedagon Pagoda to commemorate its eighth anniversary in power.

The Government monitored the activities of members of all religions, in part because such members have, in the past, become politically active. The Muslim and Christian religious minorities continued to be regarded with suspicion by authorities. Moreover, there is a concentration of Christians among the particular ethnic minorities against whom the army has fought for decades. Religious publications, like secular ones, remained subject to control and censorship. Christian bibles translated into indigenous languages could not legally be imported or printed. It remained extremely difficult for Christian and Muslim groups to obtain permission to build new churches and mosques. There were credible reports of incidents in which the Government removed cemeteries in constructing infrastructure projects in urban areas. In December the Government ordered the removal of Christian, Chinese, and Buddhist graves from the Kyandaw Cemetery in Rangoon to make way for a planned real estate development.

Religious groups have established links with coreligionists in other countries, although these activities were reportedly monitored by the Government. Foreign religious representatives were usually allowed visas only for short stays but in some cases were permitted to preach to congregations. Permanent foreign missionary establishments have not been permitted since the 1960's, but seven Catholic nuns and four priests working in Burma since before independence in January 1948, continued their work.

d. *Freedom of Movement Within the Country, Foreign Travel, Emigration, and Repatriation.*—Although citizens have the right to live anywhere, both urban and rural residents were subject to arbitrary relocation (see Section 1.f.). Except for limitations in areas of insurgent activity, citizens could travel freely within the country but were required to notify local authorities of their whereabouts. Those residents unable to meet the restrictive provisions of the citizenship law (e.g., Chinese, Arakanese Muslims, etc.), were required to obtain prior permission to travel.

The Government carefully scrutinized all prospective travel abroad, and rampant corruption resulted in many applicants having to pay bribes to obtain passports to which they were legally entitled. The official board that reviews passport applications denied passports in some cases on apparent political grounds. In January the Government began restricting the issuance of passports to young female applicants seeking work abroad. The new procedures are reportedly intended to prevent young women from being enticed to travel abroad to jobs that in fact are in the commercial sex industry. All college graduates obtaining a passport (except for certain government employees) were required to pay a special education clearance fee to reimburse the Government. Citizens who emigrated legally were generally allowed to return to visit relatives. Even some citizens who had lived abroad illegally and acquired foreign citizenship were able to return to visit.

In anticipation of the Government's planned "Visit Myanmar Year 1996," restrictions on foreign travelers were eased. Burmese embassies issued tourist visas, valid for 1 month, within 24 hours of application. However, select categories of applicants, such as some human rights advocates and political figures, continued to be denied entry visas unless traveling under the aegis of a sponsor acceptable to the Government. Although some areas of the country remained off-limits to foreigners for security reasons, the authorities allowed travel to most destinations.

In 1996 approximately 23,000 of the Rohingya Muslims who fled to Bangladesh in 1992 returned to Burma, bringing the total number of returnees to about 220,000. In comparison with 1995, the pace of repatriation slowed, with over 30,000 still in camps across the border at year's end. The U.N. High Commissioner for Refugees reported that the authorities cooperated in investigating the isolated incidents of renewed abuse that were reported. However, returnees complained of restrictions imposed by the Government on their ability to travel and to engage in economic activity. Since February an estimated 10,000 new asylum seekers entered Bangladesh to escape economic hardship and the abusive regime.

The Government does not allow refugees or displaced persons from abroad to resettle or seek safe haven. The Government has not formulated a policy concerning refugees, asylees, or first asylum, and it is not a party to the 1951 U.N. Convention or its 1967 protocol relating to the status of refugees.

Section 3. Respect for Political Rights: The Right of Citizens to Change Their Government

Despite the overwhelming desire that citizens demonstrated in the 1990 elections for a return to democracy, they continued to be denied the right to change their government. Despite the appointment of several civilians to the Cabinet in 1992, the process of placing military or recently retired military officers in most key senior level positions in the economic ministries has continued.

Following the NLD's victory in the 1990 elections, the SLORC set aside the election results and disqualified, detained, arrested, or drove into exile many successful candidates. Since then, 216 of the 485 Deputies elected have either been disqualified, resigned under pressure, gone into exile, been detained, or died. An estimated 28 successful candidates from the election remain in prison.

Rather than accept the will of the citizenry, the SLORC convened a National Convention in January 1993 to draw up principles for a new constitution. The SLORC handpicked most delegates and carefully orchestrated the proceedings; even limited opposition views were ignored. Despite having no mandate from the people, the SLORC tasked the Convention with drafting principles for a new constitution designed to provide a dominant role for the military services in the future political structure. Representatives of the SLORC leadership met with prodemocracy leader Aung San Suu Kyi on two occasions in late 1994, but did not engage in a genuine dialog on the country's political future. It instead proceeded with its own controlled "consultations" on a new constitution. In November 1995, the NLD delegates withdrew from the Convention pending agreement by the authorities to discuss revising the Convention's working procedures. Two days later they were formally expelled. The National Convention continued its deliberations until it adjourned in March. The specific provisions adopted to date were designed to ensure the major involvement of the military services in all levels of government—to the point of reserving 25 percent of seats in the Parliament to appointed, rather than elected, members of the military services. In addition, provisions have been adopted prohibiting, among other things, anyone "under acknowledgement of allegiance" to a foreigner or who has received any type of assistance from a foreign source, from participating in the Government. These provisions are apparently designed to exclude Aung San Suu Kyi who is married to an Englishman and who won the Nobel Peace Prize in 1991.

Women and minorities are underrepresented in the top ranks of government service and excluded from military leadership. Members of certain minority groups continue to be denied full citizenship (see Section 5).

Section 4. Governmental Attitude Regarding International and Nongovernmental Investigation of Alleged Violations of Human Rights

The Government does not allow domestic human rights organizations to exist, and it remained generally hostile to outside scrutiny of its human rights record. During 1995 the U.N. Human Rights Commission (UNHRC) adopted a resolution severely criticizing the Government for the human rights situation. The resolution was based on a report by Professor Yozo Yokota, the UNHRC's Special Rapporteur for Burma. The Burmese representative at the Commission in turn rejected the criticism as "inaccurate, intrusive, and politically motivated." In keeping with the Special Rapporteur's mandate, in October 1995, the Government permitted Professor Yokota to undertake another survey trip to Burma, after which he delivered a highly critical review of the human rights situation to the U.N. General Assembly's Third Committee. In December 1995, the U.N. General Assembly adopted another consensus resolution deploring the continued violation of human rights in Burma. Upset by this severe criticism, the authorities refused to meet with UNHRC representatives during 1996. The UNHRC Commissioner, Jose Ayala Lasso, and the new Special Rapporteur for Burma, Rajsoomer Lallah, tried unsuccessfully to arrange visits.

Approximately 12 nonpolitical international nongovernmental organizations (NGO's) continued project work, while a few more established a provisional presence while undertaking the protracted negotiations necessary to set up permanent operations in the country.

Section 5. Discrimination Based on Race, Sex, Religion, Disability, Language, or Social Status

The Government continued to rule by decree and was not bound by any constitutional provisions concerning discrimination.

Women.—Violence against women, including spousal abuse, is infrequent. Married couples often do not live by themselves but rather in households with extended families, where social pressure tends to protect the wife from abuse. Trafficking in women and girls remains a serious problem. There were reliable reports that many women and children in border areas, where the Government's control is limited, were forced or lured into working as prostitutes in Thailand. It is unknown how many young women have been deceived into working as prostitutes, but a common practice is to lure young women to Thailand with promises of employment as a waitress or domestic servant (see country report for Thailand). In addition, the military forces continued to impress women for military porterage duties, and there were many reports of rape of ethnic minority women by soldiers (see Sections 1.c. and 1.g.).

In general women have traditionally enjoyed a high status, exercising most of the same basic rights as men and taking an active role in business. Consistent with traditional culture, they keep their own names after marriage and often control family finances. However, women remained underrepresented in most traditionally male occupations, and a few professions continued to be entirely barred to women. The burden of poverty, which is particularly widespread in rural areas, fell disproportionately on women.

Women did not consistently receive equal pay for equal work. There were no independent women's rights organizations, and no government ministry was specifically charged with safeguarding women's interests. The Myanmar Maternal and Child Welfare Association, a government-controlled agency, provided assistance to mothers. A professional society for businesswomen, the Myanmar Women Entrepreneurs' Association, formed in 1995, provided loans to new businesses.

Children.—Despite the establishment of various child welfare programs, the Government allocated little funding to programs that aid children. According to government data, education's share of central government operating expenditures continued its decline to 12 percent in 1994–95, the latest year for which such data was available. Although education is compulsory, almost 40 percent of children never attend school, and almost three-fourths fail to complete 5 years of primary education. Child prostitution of young females forced or lured into the commercial sex trade in Thailand continued to be a major problem. The rising incidence of HIV infection has increased the demand for supposedly "safer" younger women.

People With Disabilities.—Official assistance to persons with disabilities is extremely limited. There is no law mandating accessibility to buildings, government facilities, or public transportation. While several small-scale organizations have programs to assist the disabled, most disabled persons must rely on traditional family structures to provide for their welfare. Disabled veterans receive available benefits on a priority basis. Because of land mine detonations, Burma has a very high rate of amputee injuries.

National/Racial/Ethnic Minorities.—Burma's myriad ethnic minorities have long resented the dominance of the Burman majority. Members of these minorities, largely excluded from the military leadership, have been underrepresented in the Government. Over the last few years and continuing in 1996, the SLORC, in the name of national solidarity, sought to pacify ethnic groups by means of negotiated cease-fires, grants of limited autonomy, and promises of development assistance.

The Government included a large number of ethnic minority representatives in the National Convention and permitted extended debate on the issue of minority autonomy. However, the ethnic minority populations complained that their concerns have not been addressed adequately by the Government, and none is satisfied with the provisions on limited "self-administration," which the authorities plan to accord to a few groups under the new constitution.

Government investment in the border areas in road, hospital, and school construction has been modest, and economic development among minorities continued to lag, leaving many living at barely subsistence levels. Since the focus of the hostilities against armed insurgencies has been in the border areas where most minorities are concentrated, those populations have been disproportionately victimized by the general brutalization associated with the military forces' activities.

Since only people who can prove long familial links to Burma are accorded full citizenship, ethnic populations such as Muslims, Indians, and Chinese, continued to be denied full citizenship and to be excluded from government positions. People without full citizenship are not free to travel domestically and are barred from certain advanced university programs in medicine and technological fields. Anti-Chinese and anti-Muslim sentiment remained pervasive.

Section 6. Worker Rights

a. *The Right of Association.*—Free trade unions do not exist, and even former government-controlled ones were dormant. Workers continued to be unable to strike. There were no reported instances in which workers attempted to strike, although there was an unconfirmed report that workers in a government jute factory on occasion failed to come to work. In July 1989, the United States suspended Burma's eligibility for trade concessions under the Generalized System of Preferences program, pending steps to afford its labor force internationally recognized worker rights.

Because of its longstanding violation of International Labor Organization (ILO) Convention 87 on Freedom of Association, the Government received unusually harsh criticism at the ILO Conference in June where the Committee on the Application of Standards devoted a "special paragraph" to Burma in its General Report. This action followed the last minute cancellation in May of a visit by a high-level ILO technical assistance mission while it was en route to Rangoon at the invitation of the Government.

b. *The Right to Organize and Bargain Collectively.*—Workers do not have the right to organize and bargain collectively to set wages and benefits. The Government's Central Arbitration Board, which theoretically provides a means for settling major labor disputes, nominally continued to exist, but in practice was dormant. Township-level labor supervisory committees remained in place to address various minor labor concerns.

The Government unilaterally sets wages in the public sector. In the private sector, wages are set by market forces. The Government pressures joint ventures not to pay salaries greater than those of ministers or other senior employees. Joint ventures circumvent this with supplemental pay, including remuneration paid in foreign exchange certificates, as well as through incentive and overtime pay and other fringe benefits. Foreign firms generally set wages near those of the domestic private sector but follow the example of joint ventures in awarding supplemental wages and benefits.

There are no export processing zones.

c. *Prohibition of Forced or Compulsory Labor.*—In September, following an investigation of the country's forced labor practices, the European Union Commission proposed to withdraw benefits under the Generalized System of Preferences. In recent years, the Government has increasingly supplemented declining investment with uncompensated people's "contributions," chiefly of forced labor, to build or maintain irrigation, transportation, and tourism infrastructure projects.

The army continued to force citizens to work as porters, which led to mistreatment, illness, and death. Citizens, including women and children, were forced to labor under harsh working conditions on construction projects throughout the country (see Sections 1.c. and 1.g.).

The Government's statistics on these contributions and infrastructure projects suggest that the market value of these uncompensated "contributions" has increased since 1992. According to the Prison Department exhibit in the Defense Services Museum in Rangoon, the quantity of stone quarried by prisoners increased more than fourfold between fiscal year 1988/89 and fiscal year 1994/95.

In June 1995, the Government issued a directive prohibiting unpaid labor in national government projects. In June 1996, the Government introduced an initiative to use military personnel for infrastructure projects. The scale of these initiatives and their impact on the use of civilian forced labor have yet to be determined. Nonetheless, there were credible reports that forced labor continued in a variety of projects throughout the country.

During 1996 there were repeated allegations that forced labor was used in a project to build a pipeline across the Tenasserim Division. The preponderance of evidence indicates that the pipeline project has paid its workers at least a market wage.

In June 1995, the ILO Conference Committee on the Application of Standards cited Burma in a second special paragraph for its violation of ILO Convention 29 on forced labor. In November of this year, the governing board of the ILO took action on an Article 26 complaint, accusing the Government of systematic use of forced labor, which could eventually lead to the appointment of a Commission of Inquiry on the problem.

d. *Minimum Age for Employment of Children.*—Although the law sets a minimum age of 13 years for the employment of children, in practice the law is not enforced. Working children are highly visible in cities, mostly working for small or family enterprises. Children are hired at lower pay rates than are adults for the same kind of work, and economic pressure forces children to work not only for their survival but also to support their families. Arts and crafts is the only sector producing for the export market that employs a significant number of children. Despite a compulsory education law, almost 40 percent of children never enroll in school, and only 27 percent complete the 5-year primary school course.

e. *Acceptable Conditions of Work.*—Surplus labor conditions and lack of protection by government authorities continue to dictate substandard conditions for workers, despite recent annual economic growth of at least 5 percent. The Law on Fundamental Workers Rights of 1964 and the Factories Act of 1951 regulate working conditions. There is a legally prescribed 5-day, 35-hour workweek for employees in the public sector and a 6-day, 44-hour workweek for private and public sector employees, with overtime paid for additional work. The law also allows for a 24-hour rest period per week, and workers have 21 paid holidays a year. Such provisions actually affect only a small portion of the country's labor force.

Only government employees and employees of a few traditional industries are covered by minimum wage provisions. The minimum monthly wage for salaried public employees is $3.75 (600 kyat), but this sum is supplemented by various subsidies and allowances. The low level of pay in public employment fostered widespread corruption. The government minimum wage for day labor is $0.12 (20 kyat). The minimum wage does not a provide a worker and family with a decent standard of living. Workers in the private sector are much better paid. The actual average wage rate for casual laborers in Rangoon was six times the official minimum. Wage increases continued to lag far behind inflation.

Numerous health and safety regulations exist, but in practice the Government has not made the necessary resources available to those charged with their enforcement. Although workers may in principle remove themselves from hazardous conditions, in practice workers cannot expect to retain their jobs if they do so.

CAMBODIA

Cambodia completed its third year under democratic rule after 20 years of civil war and authoritarian or totalitarian regimes. The transition to a democratically elected government followed the signing of the Paris Peace Accords by Cambodia's rival factions in 1991, which led to free and fair elections administered by the United Nations in May 1993 and the promulgation of a constitution in September 1993. The Royal Government of Cambodia (RGC) is a coalition composed primarily of the FUNCINPEC party, which won the largest number of votes in the 1993 election and the Cambodian People's Party (CPP), which had ruled the country since the ouster of the Khmer Rouge (KR) by the Vietnamese army in 1979. The leader of FUNCINPEC, Prince Norodom Ranariddh, and former State of Cambodia Prime Minister Hun Sen of the CPP are first and second Prime Ministers, respectively. King Norodom Sihanouk is the constitutional monarch and Head of State. Most power lies with the executive branch; the judiciary is not independent in practice.

The Khmer Rouge, which signed the Paris Accords but refused to implement them, continued to wage a mostly low-level guerrilla insurgency against the Government. However, the Khmer Rouge appeared to be seriously weakened by an internal split when top official Ieng Sary entered into defection negotiations with the Government on behalf of a breakaway KR faction in August. In September King Sihanouk acted upon a request from the co-Prime Ministers and granted amnesty to Ieng Sary. The amnesty applied to a death sentence issued by a 1979 war crimes tribunal in Cambodia and a 1994 law outlawing the Khmer Rouge.

The police have primary responsibility for internal security, but the Royal Cambodian Armed Forces (RCAF), including the military police, also have domestic security responsibilities. The Government continued to integrate former FUNCINPEC and Buddhist Liberal Democratic Party personnel into the police force. The Government also continued to implement a reform plan to improve RCAF and police performance. Members of the security forces committed human rights violations, for which they were rarely prosecuted.

Cambodia has a market economy in which approximately 80 percent of the population engages in subsistence farming, with rice as the principal crop. The country has a small, but growing, garment industry. Foreign aid is an important source of national income. Cambodia's annual per capita gross domestic product is $260.

Significant problems remained in many human rights areas. There continued to be reports of numerous abuses. The security forces committed extrajudicial killings, and there were credible reports that members of the security forces tortured, beat, and killed detainees. Prison conditions remained poor, and arbitrary arrest, prolonged detention, and infringement on citizens' privacy rights were problems. Political intimidation of journalists and members of the political opposition also occurred. The Government lacked the resources or the political will to act aggressively against individuals, particularly members of the military services who were suspected of being responsible for such abuses.

The Government sometimes limits press freedom; it prosecuted several journalists critical of the Government, although all eventually received royal pardons. Fear of government-directed violence against the press and government pressure created a climate that encouraged self-censorship by some journalists. A prominent opposition party was harassed by security forces, leading to concern about government intolerance toward opposing political viewpoints. Emerging democratic institutions, particularly the judiciary, remain weak. The judiciary is subject to influence by the executive and marred by inefficiency, a lack of training, a shortage of resources, and corruption related to low wages. Irregularities in the legal system continued, and citizens were effectively denied the right to a fair trial. Domestic violence against women and children is common. The ethnic Vietnamese minority faced widespread social discrimination and some violence from the Khmer Rouge; people with disabilities also faced societal discrimination. The Government does not adequately enforce existing legal prohibitions against antiunion discrimination, nor provisions outlawing forced labor.

Citizens living in areas controlled by the Khmer Rouge were denied virtually all political rights and were subject to serious human rights abuses by the KR leadership. KR forces committed numerous extrajudical killings and were responsible for disappearances, forced labor, and restriction of freedom of speech, the press, assembly, association, religion, and movement.

RESPECT FOR HUMAN RIGHTS

Section 1. Respect for the Integrity of the Person, Including Freedom From:

a. *Political and Other Extrajudicial Killing.*—There was no evidence of a government-sponsored campaign of violence. However, there were more than 30 reported cases of police, local government, or military involvement in killings of civilians, possibly including the deaths of a journalist, provincial political workers, and other civilians. The authorities made few arrests in connection with these crimes, due to a combination of ineffective law enforcement, intimidation of civilian authorities by military personnel, and in some cases a lack of prosecutorial vigor. Elements of the police and military forces were associated with a large number of violations, especially in Battambang province. Victims of extrajudicial killings were often young male civilians accused of crimes and subsequently killed while in police custody.

In January police in Kompong Cham province tortured and killed Liv Peng An, a suspect in a rape case. According to human rights investigators, Peng An was handcuffed, starved, and beaten for 3 days before dying. Family members who had come to visit him were only allowed to see Peng An after he was killed. Although the police claimed Peng An committed suicide by hanging, an abbot who prepared the body for burial said that it showed evidence of beating, including broken ribs. Following intervention by a human rights nongovernmental organization (NGO) and Peng An's family, the Ministry of Interior allowed Peng An's body to be exhumed. Investigators determined that he had been killed by torture. No one has been charged.

In May, Am Han, a resident of Svay Por district in Battambang province, died after 3 days in police custody. Han was arrested on suspicion of supporting the Khmer Rouge and was tortured, and eventually killed, in an attempt to force him to confess to crimes he did not commit, according to human rights workers. Police officials asserted that Han committed suicide by hanging. Seven men suspected in Han's killing have been charged and face trial.

In May journalist Thun Bunly, editor of the Khmer Ideal newspaper and a member of the opposition Khmer Nation Party (KNP), was shot to death by two men while riding a motorcycle taxi in central Phnom Penh. A government investigation has thus far failed to identify the murderers. Also in May, Khem Khin, a KNP member, sustained a fatal beating by an unknown assailant while walking to his house in Siem Reap province. No one has been charged in the killing. In June local KNP leader Soeun Sim was shot and killed by six armed men while he and his wife were sitting in front of their home in Chrey village, Siem Reap province. No suspects have been detained. In November Ros Chhem, a FUNCINPEC party candidate for provincial office, was killed by unidentified gunmen in Kandal province. A police identification has not yet identified any suspects. Koy Samuth, a Ministry of Interior official and the brother-in-law of Second Prime Minister Hun Sen, was shot and killed in November by two gunmen in Phnom Penh. Police were investigating the case at year's end, but had brought no charges.

Alleged connections with the Khmer Rouge were used as justification in at least two fatal incidents involving police and local villagers. In May local police killed a child and injured 15 adults when they arrested a group of villagers accused of being Khmer Rouge members in Lobeuk village, Kampot. In June, three farmers in Mong Russey district, Battambang province, were killed by three soldiers who accused them of being Khmer Rouge members. The Ministry of Interior suspended three policemen involved in the Lobeuk case; no government action was taken in the Mong Russey case.

In May military police killed two residents of Bong Rey village, Svay Rieng province, in a revenge killing. They claimed that thieves had killed their relatives and asked local villagers to identify the murderers. The military police killed one villager identified by his neighbors, then killed another under similar circumstances the next day. No government action was taken.

Eight civilians were killed by a communal chief and six communal militiamen in a February incident at Andeuk Island in Koh Kong province. Nine armed bandits who burglarized the house of a village chief in Koh Kong were followed into the jungle by several armed villagers, who killed one of the bandits in a gunfire exchange. Two days later, local police led by communal chief Seng Sao arrested six of the eight thieves, as well as two log cutters who happened to be in the vicinity. The two remaining thieves escaped. Those arrested were then detained in the district jail, where district chief Phai Thuon Phlamkesorn apparently instructed Seng Sao and six communal militiamen to kill the six persons in custody.

Local fishermen discovered the eight bodies in a cave at Andeuk Island. Seng Sao was then arrested on orders from the first deputy governor of the province, but the six militiamen escaped to Thailand. Officials from the Ministries of Interior and Defense investigated the killings but did not release any findings. Seng Sao was finally released from the Koh Kong provincial jail in late February, allegedly following the intervention of Koh Kong governor Rung Plam Kesorn. Seng Sao has since escaped to Thailand.

Colonel Sath Soeun, charged by the provincial court in Kompong Cham for the killing of a journalist and a boy in two separate incidents in 1994 and 1995, continues to serve in the provincial army. Soeun was tried and acquitted for the murder of journalist Chan Dara in 1994. A warrant was issued for his arrest following his 1995 killing of a 16-year-old boy, but he has not been apprehended.

The Khmer Rouge continued to abduct and kill civilians. One of the most serious incidents occurred in June, when a group of 37 KR guerrillas abducted approximately 50 wood cutters in Kampot province. Although 31 of the workers were later released in exchange for ransom money, the KR reportedly murdered 14 of the hostages. In July Khmer Rouge forces abducted 25 villagers in Siem Reap province; they later killed 21 of them. The KR also targeted ethnic Vietnamese, killing 25 citizens of Vietnam in August (see Section 5).

b. *Disappearance.*—There were no reports of politically motivated disappearances. However, there were at least a dozen cases in which the Khmer Rouge reportedly abducted local villagers, often for periods of 2 weeks to 1 month. Abductees were typically required to provide forced labor.

In March a group of 26 demining workers were kidnaped by KR soldiers in Siem Reap province. The KR later released all but two of the hostages: Christopher Howes, a British citizen, and his Cambodian interpreter Houn Hoerth. It is not known whether Howes and Hoerth are still alive.

Also in March, nine soldiers and military police charged in the 1995 kidnaping of casino executive Lim Kim Hock received jail sentences for the crime. Hock was kidnaped and held for 2 days before being released unharmed.

c. *Torture and Other Cruel, Inhuman, or Degrading Treatment or Punishment.*— The 1993 Constitution prohibits torture and physical abuse of prisoners. The Government does not systematically use torture, but there were credible reports that security officials occasionally used torture and often beat criminal detainees severely, particularly during interrogation. One Cambodian human rights NGO documented 14 cases of torture committed by police, military, or local authorities between March and August. Another Cambodian human rights NGO investigated 36 cases of torture committed under similar circumstances between January and June. In at least two instances, such torture resulted in the deaths of suspects by beatings.

Conditions in many prisons remain poor. The Government continued efforts to improve prison conditions but has been hampered by lack of funds. The U.N. Center for Human Rights, the U.N. Secretary General's Special Representative for Human Rights, and an international NGO cited a number of serious problems, including overcrowding, food and water shortages, malnutrition, and poor security. Human rights workers reported that the practice of using shackles and holding prisoners in small, dark cells, a practice thought virtually eliminated by the U.N. Transitional Authority in Cambodia (UNTAC), continued in some prisons. Government ration allowances for purchasing prisoners' food have not increased for 2 years and are increasingly inadequate.

The Government continued to allow human rights groups to visit prisons and to provide human rights training to prison guards.

Although an alleged illegal detention facility in Battambang province was closed in 1994, there were unconfirmed reports of the existence of small, illegal detention facilities in several provinces.

d. *Arbitrary Arrest, Detention, or Exile.*—The Constitution prohibits arbitrary arrest, detention, and exile. A Penal Code drafted by UNTAC and approved by the interim Supreme National Council remains in effect, as does a criminal procedure law dating from the State of Cambodia period. The Criminal Procedure Law in theory provides adequate protection for criminal suspects, but in practice the Government frequently ignored these provisions. Cambodian human rights investigators documented at least 23 cases of illegal detention and arrest committed by police, military, or local government authorities through November.

While lengthy detention without charge is illegal, suspects are often held by authorities for long periods before being charged. Accused persons are legally entitled to a lawyer, although in practice they often have no access to legal representation. Many judges believe that lawyers must be appointed only in criminal felony cases. In family cases, parties are frequently not informed about their legal rights by the courts. Prisoners are routinely held for several days before gaining access to a lawyer or family members. Although there is a bail system, many prisoners, particularly those without legal representation, often have no opportunity to seek release on bail. The introduction into the legal system of a corps of defenders who work without fee, and who are trained by NGO's, resulted in significant improvements for those defendants who were provided with counsel, including a reduction in their pretrial detention period and improved access to bail. For example, 34 percent of defendants were acquitted in 242 legal cases involving such nonlawyer defenders trained by one international NGO. Human rights groups report that judges made progress in informing suspects of their rights.

The Government generally did not use detention without charge as a means of political control; however, there were several instances of detention used against the opposition KNP. In January police conducted a raid on KNP headquarters in Phnom Penh as part of a search for two witnesses to a car theft who were alleged to be inside the headquarters building. Journalists, human rights workers, and KNP staff members were detained in the headquarters building for 4½ hours before the police allowed them to leave. In March two KNP party workers were arrested by the police in Siem Reap province and accused of distributing propaganda on behalf of the KNP. Provincial authorities determined that the two party workers had not broken any law; they were released from custody after 1 day's detention; the case was dropped. In May three KNP workers in Kandal province were arrested and held for 2 days by local police on charges of illegally recruiting members for the KNP. The three were released following intervention by human rights groups.

It remained easy for the Government to obtain detention warrants from the courts quickly.

Exile is prohibited by the Constitution and is not practiced.

No legal system is known to exist in Khmer Rouge zones. Khmer Rouge forces often seize hostages in order to intimidate villagers into cooperating with them.

e. *Denial of Fair Public Trial.*—The Constitution provides for an independent judiciary. However, in practice, the Government does not ensure an independent judiciary. The courts are subject to influence by the executive, and there is widespread corruption among judges, virtually none of whom receives a living wage.

The court system consists of lower courts, an appeals court, and a Supreme Court. The Constitution also mandates a Constitutional Council, which is empowered to review the constitutionality of laws and a Supreme Council of Magistrates, which appoints and disciplines judges. These two bodies have not yet been established due to disputes between the two major parties concerning their composition. Human rights workers indicate that there has been incremental progress in establishing judicial independence, however. Civilian courts are often unable to try members of the military forces. Courts must obtain Ministry of Justice permission to prosecute members of the civil service, including the police. Human rights groups report that in practice ministries often decline to respond to the courts or refuse their requests for prosecution. Delays in responding to the courts' requests sometimes allow those accused of crimes to flee in order to escape prosecution.

A serious lack of resources and poor training contribute to inefficiency in the judicial branch, and in practice the Government does not ensure due process. For example, judges often lack copies of the laws on which they are expected to rule. As a result of these weaknesses, citizens were often effectively denied the right to a fair trial.

There is also a military court system, which suffers from deficiencies similar to those of the civilian court system.

The Government continued its ongoing work with a variety of foreign donors and NGO's to improve the functioning of the legal system.

The courts often pressure victims of crimes to accept small cash settlements from the accused. When a case does make its way to court, the verdict is often determined by a judge before the case is heard, sometimes on the basis of a bribe paid by the accuser or the defendant. Sworn, written statements from witnesses and the accused are usually the extent of evidence presented in trials. Often these statements result from beatings or threats by investigating officials, and illiterate defendants are often not informed of the content of written confessions that they are forced to sign. In cases involving military personnel, military officers often exert pressure on judges to have the defendant released.

Trials are public. Defendants have the right to be present and to consult with an attorney, to confront and question witnesses against them, and to present witnesses and evidence on their own behalf. However, trials are typically perfunctory, and extensive cross-examination usually does not take place. The serious shortage of attorneys is somewhat alleviated by the provision of nonlawyer defenders trained by international human rights organizations. Defendants are also legally entitled to the presumption of innocence and the right of appeal. Because of extensive corruption, however, defendants are often expected to bribe the judge for a favorable verdict and are therefore effectively denied the presumption of innocence.

There were no reports of political prisoners.

f. *Arbitrary Interference with Privacy, Family, Home, or Correspondence.*—The Constitution contains provisions protecting the privacy of residence and correspondence and includes a provision against illegal search. There were, however, unconfirmed reports that the Government arbitrarily monitored private electronic communications. According to human rights observers, the police routinely conducted warrantless searches and seizures. Although people were largely free to live where they wished, there were charges that in September the Government forcibly removed hundreds of residents of Phnom Penh's "Borei Keila" district without adequate compensation.

The Government does not coerce or forbid membership in political organizations. However, membership in the Khmer Rouge, which is conducting an armed insurgency against the Government, is illegal.

g. *Use of Excessive Force and Violations of Humanitarian Law in Internal Conflicts.*—Fighting between government and Khmer Rouge forces continued; however, negotiations between the Government and various Khmer Rouge commanders secured the defection of thousands of Khmer Rouge soldiers and civilians in the northwest and contributed to a reduction in armed conflict during the second half of the year. Government soldiers used alleged connections with the Khmer Rouge as justification for attacks on civilians in areas near Khmer Rouge zones (see Section 1.a.)

As in previous years, many civilians were killed or wounded by indiscriminate shelling and by land mines laid by both sides. Villages were subjected to burning and looting by the Khmer Rouge. These attacks had escalated following an October 1994 Khmer Rouge policy decision to harass local officials and terrorize the local population, although recent defections and the ongoing cease-fire in the northwest decreased the level of violence in many areas during the year.

Section 2. *Respect for Civil Liberties, Including:*

a. *Freedom of Speech and Press.*—The Constitution provides for freedom of expression, press, and publication, but the Government sometimes limits press freedom in practice. The Constitution implicitly limits free speech by requiring that speech not adversely affect public security. The Constitution also declares that the King is "inviolable." A press law in effect since 1995 provides journalists with a number of rights, including a prohibition on prepublication censorship and protection from imprisonment for expressing opinion.

However, the law includes a vaguely worded prohibition on publishing articles that affect national security and political stability. These provisions were strongly criticized by human rights groups and journalists. A draft government subdecree on this matter in May was criticized by human rights groups and journalists because it did not provide specific definitions of "national security" and "political stability," and because it added a training requirement for those interested in becoming journalists. The Government continued to revise the draft subdecree; however, it banned the establishment of new newspapers until the subdecree was completed. This ban was in contradiction of the press law. Three new newspapers have been established since July, including one opposition newspaper.

Cambodia's news organizations, including over 50 newspapers, remained active, and many frequently criticized the Government. Most newspapers were nominally independent, but many received financial support from political parties. The Government, the military forces, and political parties continued to dominate the broadcast media. The Government refused to allow the KNP, which has not been legalized by the Government, to have its own television and radio stations. Although many newspapers remained critical of the Government, fear of violence against the press and government pressure created a climate that encouraged self-censorship by some journalists. There are three journalists' associations; they lobbied for more liberal press regulations and against the detention of journalists.

The Government continued its intimidation of newspapers which were overtly critical of government actions, although this intimidation was not so extensive as in past years. There have been no arrests in the killing of KNP politician and journalist Thun Bunly in Phnom Penh, who was shot by unknown attackers (see Section 1.a.). Journalist Sum Dara of the New Angkor newspaper was detained and beaten by two armed men in Phnom Penh in August. The police interrogated Dara about the activities of other journalists before releasing him. Using the press law, the Government suspended publication of the antimonarchy Republic News for 78 days. The newspaper reopened following intervention by the League of Cambodian Journalists and continued its critical viewpoint. Journalists Chan Rotana and Hen Vipheak, sentenced to prison terms in 1995 for separate violations of press regulations, were pardoned and released from prison in July and August, respectively. Both served less than 1 week of their prison terms. Their newspapers continued to publish and remained critical of the Government. There were seven reports that journalists received threatening telephone calls from political interests opposed to their newspapers' editorial views.

The media reported that the Government issued a directive instructing teachers, including private school teachers, not to talk about politics in class. There continues to be inhibition of discussion of some political issues at the University of Phnom Penh.

The Khmer Rouge do not allow freedom of speech or press in zones they that control.

b. *Freedom of Peaceful Assembly and Association.*—The Constitution provides for freedom of peaceful assembly and freedom of association.

In May heavily armed government security forces confronted the funeral procession of slain journalist Thun Bunly (see Section 1.a.) when it attempted to divert from its authorized course through central Phnom Penh. There was no violence, and the funeral procession proceeded along its authorized route without incident.

Provincial farmers protesting poor agricultural conditions were turned away from the royal palace and the Ministry of Interior by security personnel in June.

Although several provincial offices of the KNP remain open, others had their opening ceremonies disrupted by local police or were otherwise harassed after opening.

An October demonstration organized by the KNP against the state visit of General Than Shwe, leader of Burma's State Law and Order Restoration Council, was not approved by government officials. KNP protesters were diverted by police and dispersed peacefully. Two policemen were injured when a car occupied by KNP leader Sam Rainsy's driver and bodyguard attempted to pass a police roadblock. Police reportedly beat the driver and detained him briefly before releasing him. Rainsy's bodyguard was arrested, convicted of destroying government property, and imprisoned 23 days. In November KNP protests took place without incident.

The Government requires local NGO's to register with the Ministry of Interior. No action has been taken against unregistered NGO's, however. A draft NGO law, prepared with assistance from the U.N. Center for Human Rights, has not yet been passed by the National Assembly.

In Khmer Rouge-controlled areas, freedom of assembly and association do not exist.

c. *Freedom of Religion.*—The Constitution provides for freedom of religion and prohibits discrimination based on religion. The Government respects this right in practice. Buddhism is the state religion.

The Khmer Rouge have traditionally banned or discouraged religion.

d. *Freedom of Movement Within the Country, Foreign Travel, Emigration, and Repatriation.*—The Government does not restrict international travel or within the parts of the country that it controls, although the presence of land mines and bandits make travel in some areas perilous.

Government security forces operate numerous security checkpoints along major highways. There were reports that Vietnamese citizens were routinely harassed by these soldiers and forced to pay bribes on Route 5 near Kompong Chang.

Tens of thousands of citizens who are ethnic Vietnamese fled Cambodia in early 1993 due to racial violence directed at Vietnamese. Many returned after the elections. However, the authorities stopped and forbade entry to occupants of several thousand boats on the Mekong River. Most of these people have been allowed to return, while others entered informally.

The Government allows noncitizens to apply to the United Nations High Commissioner for Refugees (UNHCR) for refugee status in Cambodia. However, in December, the Government expelled 19 ethnic Vietnamese to Vietnam after detaining them for alleged involvement in a political organization called the People's Action Political Party of the Vietnamese People. The Government asserted that this organization was part of the illegal Free Vietnam Movement. Nine of the 19 had already requested political asylum from the UNHCR office in Phnom Penh.

The Government did not provide first asylum in 1996. The small number of requests made were still pending by year's end. The Government did, however, provide first asylum in 1995. The Government has not yet fully formulated a policy regarding refugees, asylees, or first asylum.

The Khmer Rouge, who refused to comply with the Paris Accords by opening the areas they control, continued to restrict access to, from, and within these zones.

Section 3. Respect for Political Rights: The Right of Citizens to Change Their Government

The Constitution provides for the right of citizens to change their government, and most citizens exercised this right by participating in the 1993 U.N.-administered elections. In those areas of the country controlled by the Khmer Rouge, citizens cannot exercise this right.

In the 1993 election, each province elected National Assembly members through proportional representation. Some 20 parties took part; 4 won seats. The United Nations certified the election as free and fair. After the drafting of a constitution, the constituent assembly became the National Assembly. Members of all four parties that won seats in the Assembly entered a coalition government, which remained in power through 1996.

The legislature was weak in comparison with the executive branch. All legislation considered or adopted by the National Assembly originated in the ministries. The Government appointed the provincial governors and their deputies, who are divided between the two coalition parties. District and commune officials are also appointed by the executive branch; most of these officials are People's Republic of Kampuchea or State of Cambodia appointees. FUNCINPEC has complained that district chief positions are not equally divided between the two major coalition parties. Communal elections are scheduled for late 1997. The Government has prepared a draft communal electoral law, but it has not been presented to the National Assembly.

International election advisers were received by government officials, including the Prime Ministers.

Traditional cultural practices inhibit the role of women in Government. There are 7 women among the 120 members of the National Assembly. Although there are no female Governors or Cabinet ministers, there are a few women at the state secretary and deputy governor levels. There are several members of ethnic and religious minorities in the Cabinet and the National Assembly.

Section 4. Governmental Attitude Regarding International and Nongovernmental Investigation of Alleged Violations of Human Rights

Cambodia's large international and domestic human rights community, which first began operating under UNTAC, remained active and engaged in diverse activities. Numerous human rights organizations and the U.N. Center for Human Rights conducted highly effective human rights training for military officers, villagers, the legal community, and other groups. There are approximately 40 NGO's involved in human rights activities, some of which carried out investigations of abuses.

According to a study made by an international NGO, however, only 9 of the 40 NGO's have a primary focus on human rights and civic education. According to NGO leaders, communication between human rights NGO's and the executive branch of the government continued to improve. Most NGO's reported little overt intimidation, although many felt that the sensitive issues that they covered required them to exercise caution in carrying out their activities.

The National Assembly's Human Rights Commission, headed by a former NGO leader, served as a liaison between the Assembly and the human rights community. The Commission began using its own investigators during the year and conducted high profile human rights investigations in the provinces.

One domestic human rights organization reported limited cooperation from some provincial authorities in conducting inspections of prison conditions.

Following the signing of a memorandum of understanding with the Government in March, the U.N. Center for Human Rights extended its mandate for 2 additional years. The U.N. Secretary General's Special Representative for Human Rights, Thomas Hammarberg, was received by both of the co-Prime Ministers.

The Khmer Rouge do not permit any investigation of human rights violations in their zones. Many international and indigenous NGO's have made plans to enter the Khmer Rouge defector zones in the northwest as soon as the area is fully secured by the Government.

Section 5. Discrimination Based on Race, Sex, Religion, Disability, Language, or Social Status

The Constitution prohibits discrimination based on race, color, sex, language, religious beliefs, or political views. Although the Government does not systematically engage in discrimination, it often fails to protect these rights in practice.

Women.—International and Cambodian NGO workers report that violence against women, including rape and domestic violence, is common. There were reports of rape, but there were no statistics available on this problem. A study by an international NGO released in July estimates that one in six wives is physically abused by her husband, and half of those are injured. Authorities normally decline to become involved in domestic disputes. There are some indications that stress and other psychological problems originating during the Khmer Rouge period of the 1970's contribute to the problem of violence against women. NGO's reported that prostitution and trafficking in women were serious problems. The Government passed a law against prostitution and trafficking in January, but human rights groups indicate that it is not adequately enforced.

According to an international labor NGO's report, women now comprise 55 percent of the population, but 60 percent of agricultural workers, 85 percent of the business work force, 70 percent of the industrial work force, and 60 percent of all service sector workers. Women are often concentrated in low-paying jobs in these sectors and are largely excluded from management positions, which remain dominated by men.

The Constitution contains explicit language providing for equal rights for women, equal pay for equal work, and equal status in marriage. In practice, women have equal property rights with men, have the same status in bringing divorce proceedings, and have equal access to education and some jobs. However, cultural traditions continued to limit women's ability to reach senior positions in government, business, and other areas. There are a large number of women's NGO's, which concentrated on training poor women and widows and addressing social problems such as spousal abuse and prostitution. Within the Government, the Secretariat of State for Women's Affairs is responsible for women's issues.

Children.—The Constitution provides for children's rights, and ensuring the welfare of children is a specific goal of the Government's political program. However, the Government relies on international aid to fund most social welfare programs targeted at children, resulting in only a modest flow of resources to ameliorate problems affecting children. Children frequently suffer from the inadequacy of the health care system. Infant mortality is reported at 115 per thousand and nearly 20 percent of children do not live to the age of 5. Child mortality from preventable diseases is high.

Children are also adversely affected by the inadequate educational system. Only around 1 percent of primary school teachers have completed high school. Schools are overcrowded and short of equipment. The Government does not deny girls equal access to education, but in practice, families with limited resources often give priority to educating boys.

Child abuse is believed to be common, although there are no statistics on the extent of the problem. Studies conducted by human rights organizations indicate that child prostitution became increasingly widespread during the year, although it is difficult to gauge the extent of the problem. There were reliable reports that girls were kidnaped in several provinces and forced into the illegal sex trade, both in Cambodia and abroad.

People With Disabilities.—The Government does not mandate accessibility for people with disabilities to buildings or government services. According to international human rights groups, 1 in 236 Cambodians is missing at least one limb. This figure reflects the continuing effects of land mines on the population. Programs administered by various NGO's have brought about dramatic improvements in the treatment and rehabilitation of amputees. However, they face considerable societal discrimination, particularly in obtaining skilled employment.

National/Racial/Ethnic Minorities.—Citizens of Vietnamese and Chinese ethnicity have long comprised the largest ethnic minorities. Ethnic Chinese are well accepted. However, fear and animosity continue toward ethnic Vietnamese people, who are seen as a threat to the Cambodian nation and culture.

The rights of minorities under the nationality law passed in August are not explicit; constitutional protections are extended only to "Khmer People," that is, Cambodians.

There were reports that Vietnamese nationals were singled out for harassment at illegal government security force checkpoints (see Section 2.d.).

Ly Chandara, a Cambodian national of Vietnamese ethnicity, was arrested and expelled to Vietnam in March after being accused of serving as the deputy Commander-in-Chief of the Free Vietnam Movement, which the Government charges carried out illegal activities against the Government of Vietnam. Two others, a Cambodian and a Vietnamese resident of Cambodia, were expelled with Chandara on the basis of similar charges. Chandara was the editor of the Vietnamese Language newspaper Tudo, which was closed by the Government in December 1995. Chandara was later released by the Government of Vietnam and allowed to return to Cambodia.

Several thousand ethnic Vietnamese fled to the Vietnam-Cambodia border following massacres in early 1993. By the end of the year, many had in fact returned to their homes, while a few remained stranded on the border (see Section 2.d.).

The Khmer Rouge continued a calculated campaign of inflammatory propaganda directed against ethnic Vietnamese, and there were reports that 25 citizens of Vietnam were killed as part of a Khmer Rouge ethnic cleansing campaign in August. In May a group of 20 armed men killed 11 Vietnamese and 1 Cambodian, and wounded 15 others, in an ethnically motivated attack on a village in Pursat province.

Section 6. Worker Rights

a. *The Right of Association.*—The Government finalized its draft of a new labor law with assistance from the International Labor Organization (ILO) and the Asian American Free Labor Institute (AAFLI). The legislation provides for internationally accepted labor rights, including the right to organize and bargain collectively. The National Assembly passed the new law in January 1997.

The 1992 Labor Law dates from the State of Cambodia period. Workers have the right to form worker organizations of their choosing without previous authorization, and employees in each workplace are required to select a single worker representative. In practice, management or the Government usually controls the selection process for the worker representative. Worker organizations are not required to join a single trade union structure under the 1992 law.

There were few active independent trade unions. The majority of salaried workers are employed by the State, although there is a growing services sector. A large proportion of the urban population is engaged in low-level commerce or self-employed skilled labor. The code does not apply to workers in the public sector.

b. *The Right to Organize and Bargain Collectively.*—The 1992 Labor Law provides for collective bargaining, although any agreement reached between workers and employees is subject to government approval. In practice, collective bargaining does not take place. The Government sets wages for civil servants. Wage rates in other sectors are based largely on market conditions and are set by employers. The 1992 Labor Law prohibits antiunion discrimination by employers, but there is no mechanism for enforcing this provision.

Opposition politician Sam Rainsy announced the formation of the Free Trade Union of Cambodian Civil Servants in November. Hundreds took part in a demonstration without incident. Another union, the Free Trade Union of Khmer Workers, formed in December and organized a walkout from a foreign-owned garment factory.

There are no export processing zones.

c. *Prohibition of Forced or Compulsory Labor.*—The 1992 Labor Law prohibits forced or compulsory labor and contains penal sanctions for offenders. However, the Government does not adequately enforce these provisions. There were credible reports that workers have been coerced into working overtime, and there were some reports of women being forced to work as prostitutes.

The Khmer Rouge compel people under their control to serve as porters for military and other supplies and to clear land for farming (see Section 1.b.).

d. *Minimum Age for Employment of Children.*—The 1992 Labor Law states that the minimum age for employment is 16 years, except for those workers in family enterprises. Although penalties exist for violation of these provisions, the Government has not established an apparatus to enforce them. Youth under the age of 16 years routinely engage in a variety of jobs, including street trading, construction, agriculture, and manufacturing.

e. *Acceptable Conditions of Work.*—The 1992 Labor Law does not provide for a nationwide minimum wage but requires a wage that assures a decent living standard. The Government does not enforce this requirement. In practice, the wage is often set by employers. Market-determined wage rates at lower levels are not sufficient to provide a decent living for a worker and family.

The new labor legislation requires the Government to set and periodically revise a minimum wage, and at year's end the Government was in the process of preparing a decree that would set the Kingdom's first minimum wage.

The 1992 Labor Law provides for a standard legal workweek of 48 hours and a 24-hour rest period, and requires overtime pay. The Government does not enforce these standards, and workers commonly work more than 48 hours per week. Some workers incur salary deductions if they do not perform overtime or holiday work. The Law states that the workplace should have health and safety standards adequate to ensure workers' well-being. However, the Government has not yet set specific standards, and work-related injury and health problems are common. Penalties are specified in the law, but there are no provisions to protect workers who complain about unsafe and unhealthful conditions. Conditions in factories and small-scale industries are generally poor and often do not meet international standards.

CHINA

The People's Republic of China (PRC) is an authoritarian state in which the Chinese Communist Party (CCP) is the paramount source of power. At the national and regional levels, party members hold almost all top civilian, police, and military positions. Ultimate authority rests with the members of the Politburo, who often consult with still-influential past members of that body on major decisions. These leaders stress the need to maintain stability and social order and are committed to perpetuating rule of the CCP and its heirarchy. Citizens lack the freedom to peacefully express opposition to the party-led political system and the right to change their national leaders or form of government. Socialism continues to provide the theoretical underpinning of Chinese politics, but Marxist ideology has given way to economic pragmatism in recent years. Economic decentralization has increased the authority of regional officials. The party's authority rests primarily on the success of economic reform, its ability to maintain stability, appeals to patriotism, and control of the security apparatus.

The security apparatus comprises the Ministries of State Security and Public Security, the People's Armed Police, the People's Liberation Army and the state judicial, procuratorial, and penal systems. Security policy and personnel were responsible for numerous human rights abuses.

China has a mixed economy that is expanding rapidly. Economic reforms are raising living standards for many, strengthening entrepreneurs, diminishing central control over the economy, and creating new economic opportunities. Although there are problems in the state sector, individual economic opportunities continue to expand rapidly with increased freedom of employment and mobility. As the Government continues to adopt market-based policies, both state-owned and nonstate enterprises are benefiting from increased freedom to compete in domestic and overseas markets. As economic opportunities grow, however, income disparities between coastal and inland areas continue to widen. The number of citizens living in absolute poverty continues to decline, although estimates of those in poverty range from official figures of 65 million to estimates as high as 350 million out of a total population of 1.2 billion. Tens of millions of peasants have left their homes in search of better jobs and living conditions. According to estimates, as many as 100 million people make up this "floating population," with many major cities counting 1 million or more such people. Urban areas are also coping with workers idled by industrial reforms. An estimated 10 million state workers have been laid off, or not paid. Millions more have been idled on partial wages.

The Government continued to commit widespread and well-documented human rights abuses, in violation of internationally accepted norms, stemming from the authorities' intolerance of dissent, fear of unrest, and the absence or inadequacy of laws protecting basic freedoms. The Constitution and laws provide for fundamental human rights, but they are often ignored in practice. Abuses included torture and mistreatment of prisoners, forced confessions, and arbitrary and lengthy incommunicado detention. Prison conditions remained harsh. The Government continued severe restrictions on freedom of speech, the press, assembly, association, religion, privacy, and worker rights. Some restrictions remained on freedom of movement. In many cases, the judicial system denies criminal defendants basic legal safeguards and due process because authorities attach higher priority to maintaining public order and suppressing political opposition than to enforcing legal norms.

Although the Government denies that it holds political prisoners, the number of persons detained or serving sentences for "counterrevolutionary crimes" or "crimes against the state," or for peaceful political or religious activities are believed to number in the thousands. Persons detained during 1996 included activists arrested for issuing petitions or open letters calling for reforms and greater democracy.

Overall in 1996, the authorities stepped up efforts to cut off expressions of protest or criticism. All public dissent against the party and government was effectively silenced by intimidation, exile, the imposition of prison terms, administrative detention, or house arrest. No dissidents were known to be active at year's end. Even those released from prison were kept under tight surveillance and often prevented from taking employment or otherwise resuming a normal life. Nonapproved religious groups, including Protestant and Catholic groups, also experienced intensified repression as the Government enforced 1994 regulations that require all such groups to be registered with government religious affairs bureaus and come under the supervision of official "patriotic" religious organizations. Discrimination against women, minorities, and the disabled, violence against women, and the abuse of children remain problems. Serious human rights abuses persist in minority areas, including Tibet, Xinjiang, and Inner Mongolia. Controls on religion and on other fundamental freedoms in these areas have also intensified.

During 1996 the National Peoples' Congress (NPC) passed new laws designed to reform criminal procedures and the legal profession. The Government's village elections program conducted closely supervised multicandidate elections in villages inhabited by hundreds of millions of rural citizens. Although these offer some opportunity for local clans and other groups to work out differences democratically, they are tightly controlled and do not threaten the leading role of the Communist Party. In 1996 China had limited human rights discussions and exchanges on the rule of law with foreign interlocutors and hosted a meeting of the Interparliamentary Union at which a human rights resolution was drafted.

In many respects, Chinese society continued to open further. Greater disposable income, looser ideological controls, and freer access to outside sources of information led to greater room for individual choice, more diversity in cultural life, and increased media reporting. Although the sale and use of satellite dishes are tightly regulated, satellite television broadcasts are widely available, particularly in coastal areas. Increasing numbers of citizens have access to the Internet although the Government closed down some World Wide Web sites, including Chinese-language sites in Hong Kong and Taiwan, those of Western news organizations, and attempted to control the political and social content of the material available through the Internet. Controls on reporting economic information imposed in 1995 continued, and the Government placed new restrictions on the news media.

RESPECT FOR HUMAN RIGHTS

Section 1. Respect for the Integrity of the Person, Including Freedom From:

a. *Political and Other Extrajudicial Killing.*—There were reports of extrajudicial killings, including some carried in the Chinese press. There is, however, no reliable information about the number of such killings or the adequacy of the government response. There have been numerous executions carried out immediately after mass summary trials. Often these "trials" occur under circumstances where the lack of basic due process protections borders on extrajudicial killing (see Section 1.e.).

In April the official press reported that a guard assigned to maintain public order in Shenzhai village, Anhui province, was executed for murdering one farmer and wounding two others after they refused to pay illegal levies imposed on local residents. The village chief was given a suspended death sentence for his role in the incident. In March the parents of 33-year-old Wang Jingbo released a statement claiming that their son was beaten to death while illegally detained by the Public Security Bureau in Beijing's Chaoyang District. The victim's parents demanded an impartial investigation after an autopsy reportedly showed that their son suffered a brain hemorrhage and 12 broken ribs while detained. At least three Buddhist monks died as a result of mistreatment while in prison in Tibet (see Tibet addendum).

b. *Disappearance.*—In January the United Nations Working Group on Enforced or Involuntary Disappearances reported on three new cases of disappearances that allegedly occurred in 1995. Most of the 56 cases which the Working Group has under review occurred between 1988-90. The majority were Tibetans, the others were political activists. The Government still has not provided a comprehensive, credible public accounting of all those missing or detained in connection with the suppression of the 1989 Tiananmen demonstrations. Long incommunicado detentions continued (see Section 1.d.).

c. *Torture and Other Cruel, Inhuman, or Degrading Treatment or Punishment.*— The law prohibits torture, however, both official Chinese sources and international human rights groups continued to report many cases in which police and other elements of the security apparatus employed torture and degrading treatment in dealing with detained and imprisoned persons. Former detainees have credibly reported that officials used cattle prods, electrodes, thumb cuffs, prolonged periods of solitary confinement and incommunicado detention, beating, shackles, and other forms of abuse against detained men and women. Persons detained pending trial were particularly at risk as a result of government failure to correct obvious systemic weaknesses in design and operation of pretrial detention. These weaknesses include a reliance on confessions as a basis for convictions and the lack of access to prisoners by legal counsel and family members until after authorities file formal charges, a step that often takes months. Some, but not all, of these problems were addressed in March, when the National People's Congress enacted amendments to the Criminal Procedures Law. The amendments, which were to become effective on January 1, 1997, are a positive step toward bringing China's criminal justice process into conformity with international norms (see Sections 1.d. and 1.e.).

In April a Chinese delegate to the United Nations Commission on Human Rights stated that "the Chinese judiciary deals with every complaint of torture promptly after it is filed, and those found guilty are punished according to law." The Government also claimed in its report to the United Nations Committee against Torture that "the State, taking an extremely serious view of any incident of torture, has adopted commensurate measures through administrative and judicial means to punish by law anyone guilty of such an act." However, because prisoners remain inaccessible to international humanitarian organizations, such as the International Committee of the Red Cross (ICRC), these claims are impossible to verify independently.

In March the Supreme People's Procuratorate reported that it had investigated 412 cases in which torture was used to extract confessions in 1995, but it provided no information on convictions or punishments. The number of actual incidents of torture and mistreatment by government officials is almost certainly greater than reflected in published government statistics.

Conditions in penal institutions are generally harsh and frequently degrading, and nutritional and health conditions are sometimes grim. Adequate medical care for prisoners continues to be a problem, despite official assurances that prisoners have the right to prompt medical treatment if they become ill. Political prisoners who reportedly had difficulties in obtaining timely and adequate medical treatment during 1996, despite repeated appeals on their behalf by their families and the international community, included Xi Yang, Zhou Guoqiang, Wei Jingsheng, Wang Dan, Bao Tong, Liu Nianchun, and Gao Yu. Chen Ziming, who has been diagnosed with cancer, was released for a second time on medical parole in November. The terms of his parole were highly restrictive, and he was placed under tight police surveillance. China's 1994 Prison Law was designed, in part, to improve treatment of detainees and respect for their legal rights. The Government's stated goal is to convert one-half of the nation's prisons and 150 reeducation-through-labor camps into "modernized, civilized" facilities by the year 2010. In 1995 Government officials claimed that the Procuratorate had assigned officials to virtually all the prisons, houses of detention, and centers for reeducation through labor, in order to supervise prison management and enforce laws on treatment of prisoners. No information about the number of personnel assigned or the effectiveness of this step was available at year's end.

The official press reported in February 1995 that the Government has established 157 psychological treatment centers and 54 consultation clinics in the nation's 685 prisons. Official sources also claimed that more than 17,000 prisoners were treated at those facilities over the past 10 years. Mental hospitals have reportedly been used on occasion to control political dissidents. The foreign press reported in September that dissident writer Wang Wanxing, who was arrested in 1992 for protesting in Tiananmen Square on the third anniversary of the 1989 demonstrations, was in good mental health but remained detained against his will at the An Kang psychiatric hospital in Shanghai. Neither conditions at such institutions nor treatment of prisoners at these centers could be verified because of lack of access by independent observers.

Conditions of imprisonment and detention for political prisoners vary widely. Bao Tong remained detained at a government residential compound after his 7-year prison term expired in May. Other political prisoners, including Wei Jingsheng, Chen Ziming, and Gao Yu were incarcerated with common criminals. Fellow inmates reportedly beat Liu Nianchun at a prison in Heilongjiang province. Imprisoned dissident Chen Longde reportedly attempted to commit suicide in August by jumping from a multistory prison building after he was kicked, punched, and beaten with electric prods. He survived the fall, but suffered serious injuries. According to nongovernmental organization (NGO) reports, Wang Hui, wife of jailed labor activist Zhou Guoqiang was detained in May, reportedly for pressing her husband's case. As a result of her treatment, including the withholding of liquids, she attempted suicide. Her attempt was punished with a severe beating. She was released sometime prior to November. According to NGO reports, dissident Yao Zhenxiang also was beaten after his detention in April.

China does not permit independent monitoring of prisons or reeducation-through-labor camps. The Procuratorate is charged with law enforcement in the corrections system. The official press reported in July that 50,000 reprimands were issued to prison personnel during the first 5 months of 1996 for inappropriate conduct. Negotiations with the ICRC regarding access to prisoners have not been resumed since the Government suspended discussions in March 1995.

d. *Arbitrary Arrest, Detention, or Exile.*—Under the Criminal Procedure Law, officials may hold detainees for up to 10 days before the Procuratorate must approve a formal arrest warrant. In theory, the Administrative Procedure Law permits a detainee to challenge the legality of his detention. In practice, however, lack of access to legal counsel inhibits the effective use of this law to obtain prompt judicial decisions on the issue. In known cases involving political dissidents, authorities have interpreted the law in the Government's favor and strictly against detainees.

Activist Wang Dan was held in incommunicado detention for 17 months in connection with the issuance of a prodemocracy petition before being charged, tried, and sentenced in October to 11 years in prison. He is appealing his sentence to the Supreme Court, having lost a lower level appeal.

There is no system of bail, but at the discretion of public security officials some detainees can be released pending further investigation. The authorities must notify the detainee's family or work unit of his detention within 24 hours; in practice, however, authorities seldom give timely notification. Under a sweeping exception to the law, officials need not provide notification if it would "hinder the investigation" of a case. The Government held dissident Liu Nianchun incommunicado for more than a year without charges before his wife was notified of his whereabouts and permitted to visit him in July. His suit contesting his detention was initially dismissed in mid-1996 for reasons that included the fact that his legal papers were written with a ballpoint pen, a minor detail usually overlooked in Chinese courts.

The State Compensation Law provides a legal basis for citizens to recover damages for illegal detentions. Although the majority of Chinese remain unaware of this 1995 law, there is evidence that it is having some impact. The Chinese press reported several cases involving Guangdong and Fujian residents who sued officials for malfeasance and won damage awards. In Hebei a woman was awarded over $2,000 for wrongful detention.

Amendments to the Criminal Procedures Law enacted by the National People's Congress in March, and effective January 1, 1997, are designed to address some of the problems related to detention. During the year, the Government initiated efforts to educate the Chinese legal community on the nature and function of the new amendments. Human rights activists and legal scholars in China and abroad acknowledged the positive reforms introduced by the new law, but they noted that they do not fully bring Chinese criminal procedure practices into conformity with international standards and may be difficult to implement. The amendments do not apply retroactively.

Because the Government tightly controls information, it is impossible to estimate accurately the total number of people subjected to new or continued arbitrary arrest or detention. Nevertheless, Procurator General Zhang Siqing reported in March to the NPC that during 1995 the Supreme Procuratorate investigated 4,627 illegal detention cases. These figures likely include illegal detentions of those involved in commercial disputes as well as those detained for other reasons. Local officials and business leaders frequently conspire to use detentions as a means of exerting pressure in commercial disputes. In June the Chief Procurator of Hebei province reported that 600 persons were rescued in 345 cases of illegal hostage-taking in 1995. Such incidents often involve commercial disputes. There were similar cases involving detained foreign businessmen whose passports were confiscated during business disputes. Australian businessman James Peng, whom Chinese public security officials kidnaped in Macau in 1994 and brought to China for trial, was tried in November 1994 and sentenced to a lengthy prison term in September 1995. He remained imprisoned despite continued official and unofficial appeals on his behalf.

In practice, authorities often disregarded or circumvented limits on detention by using regulations on "taking in for shelter and investigation," "supervised residence," and other methods not requiring procuratorial approval. According to Chinese legal experts, the new Criminal Procedures Law amendments are designed to eliminate taking in for shelter and investigation. Recent reforms do not affect the reeducation-through-labor system, which permits authorities to extrajudicially sentence detainees to terms as long as 3 years in labor camps. Liu Xiaobo was detained on October 8 and within hours sentenced to 3 years' reeducation through labor under this system. Numerous other dissidents, including Liu Nianchun, Zhou Guoqiang, Bishop Zeng Jingmu, Chen Longde, Zhang Lin, and Bao Ge were held in reeducation-through-labor camps in 1996.

Authorities detained political and labor activists without cause at "sensitive" times during the year and also used parole regulations to control their activities. Guangzhou authorities detained dissident Wang Xizhe for 15 days in June, ostensibly because he violated his parole by attending a family dinner in an area outside of Guangzhou City. (Wang fled the country in October, see also Section 2.d.) Wang's arrest coincided with the anniversary of the 1989 Tiananmen demonstrations. At the height of a period of increased political tension in mid-1996 between China and Japan regarding sovereignty over the Diaoyu/Senkaku islands, the Government forced longtime anti-Japanese activist Tong Zeng to depart Beijing for a 2-week trip to Gansu province.

The Government continued to impose restrictions on reentry into China by dissidents and activists (see Section 2.d.). There were no reports of the Government forcibly exiling citizens.

e. *Denial of Fair Public Trial.*—According to the Constitution, the court system is equal in authority to the State Council and the Central Military Commission, the two most important government institutions. All three organs are nominally under the supervision of the NPC. Officials state that China's judiciary is independent but acknowledge that it is subject to the Communist Party's policy guidance. All of these state organs are given policy direction by the high-level Party Political and Legal

Commission. Party and government leaders use a variety of means to direct the courts on verdicts and sentences. Corruption and conflicts of interest also affect judicial decisionmaking. Supreme Court President Ren Jianxin reported in March to the NPC that in 1995 the judiciary cited some 962 court staff members for violations of discipline and law, and 61 judicial officers received criminal penalties.

The Supreme People's Court stands at the apex of the court system, followed in descending order by the higher, intermediate, and basic people's courts. Judges are appointed by the people's congresses at the corresponding level. There are special courts for handling military, maritime, and railway transport cases.

In February 1995, the NPC passed three new laws designed to professionalize judges, prosecutors, and policemen; the laws came into effect in July 1995.

In May the NPC passed a new lawyers' law designed to professionalize the legal profession. The law replaced temporary regulations adopted in 1980, 1 year after China permitted lawyers to resume the practice of law following a 20-year period when the practice of law was prohibited. The new law recognized for the first time that lawyers represent their clients, not the State. The bill also granted lawyers formal permission to establish private law firms, established educational requirements for legal practitioners, encouraged free legal services for the general public, and provided for the discipline of lawyers.

Officials often ignore the due process provisions of the law and of the Constitution. Both before and after trial, authorities subject prisoners to severe psychological pressure to confess. Defendants who fail to "show the right attitude" by confessing their crimes are typically sentenced more harshly. Criminal trials remain essentially sentencing hearings, despite official denials. Confessions without corroborating evidence are insufficient for a conviction under law, but coerced confessions are frequently introduced into evidence. International observers were especially concerned that the Government's "strike hard" anticrime campaign, which extended throughout most of the year, further encouraged law enforcement personnel to arrest, convict, and punish suspects without according full due process rights.

Under the 1979 Criminal Procedure Law, which was in effect in 1996, the authorities give accused persons virtually no opportunity to prepare an adequate defense while their cases are being investigated, the phase during which the question of guilt or innocence is essentially decided. The law provides that defense lawyers may be retained no earlier than 7 days before the trial. However, in some cases even this brief period is shortened under regulations issued in 1983 to accelerate the adjudication of certain serious criminal cases. Under the law, there is no requirement that the court appoint a defense attorney for the defendant unless the defendant is hearing impaired or a minor, although the court may appoint defense counsel if it feels an attorney is necessary. When attorneys do appear, they have little time to prepare a defense and rarely contest guilt; their function is generally confined to requesting clemency. The conviction rate is over 90 percent. The court's permission is required before the accused or his representative can interrogate witnesses, produce new witnesses, or review evidence.

The Criminal Procedure Law requires that all trials be held in public, except those involving state secrets, juveniles, or "personal secrets." Under this provision, details of cases involving "counterrevolutionary" charges have frequently been kept secret, even from defendants' relatives. The 1988 Law on State Secrets affords a ready basis for denying a public trial. There is an appeals process, but appeals generally do not reverse arbitrary or erroneous verdicts. Under the Criminal Procedure Law, persons "exempted from prosecution" by procurators may still be deemed to have a criminal record, despite the lack of a judicial determination of guilt. Such provisions can be applied in counterrevolutionary crimes as well as for ordinary criminal offenses.

Amendments to the Criminal Procedure Law, passed in March and effective January 1997, are designed to encourage adversarial criminal proceedings and thereby change the traditional practice of holding trials that have essentially been sentencing hearings. The amendments state that criminal suspects may, after being first interrogated by an investigative organ or from the day coercive measures are first taken, retain a lawyer to offer legal advice. Defense attorneys may conduct limited investigations, call defense witnesses, and argue their clients cases in open court. Moreover, courts are prohibited from treating suspects as criminals until they are convicted. Coerced confessions are expressly forbidden. The "exempted from prosecution" provision is barred. Throughout 1996 scholars and government officials took steps to educate legal, procuratorate, and court personnel about these amendments.

Government officials state that China has an insufficient number of lawyers to meet the country's growing needs. A key element in Justice Ministry efforts to encourage legal reform is a plan to have 150,000 lawyers, 30,000 notaries, and 40,000 grassroots legal service centers by the year 2000. Minister of Justice Xiao Yang stated in January that China currently has 89,000 lawyers, 16,548 notarial personnel, and more than 100,000 grassroots legal service workers. China has more than 7,200 law firms including 73 foreign law offices. In many cities, lawyers are organizing private law firms outside the framework of established government legal offices. These firms are self-regulating and do not have their personnel or budgets determined directly by the State. A foreign press report quoted Justice Ministry officials as stating that there were approximately 1,000 such firms in early 1995. Only a small percentage of lawyers practice criminal law. Political dissidents have frequently found it difficult to find an attorney willing to handle the most sensitive political cases. One explanation for the problem is that authorities have retaliated in the past by revoking the legal licenses of lawyers representing such defendants. Like other citizens, many defense lawyers still depend on an official work unit for employment, housing, and other benefits. Some lawyers are therefore reluctant to be seen as overzealous in representing certain defendants.

The impact of the lack of due process is particularly egregious in death penalty cases. China's 1979 Criminal Code contained 26 crimes punishable by death; 1995 legislation raised this number to 65, including financial crimes such as counterfeiting currency, passing fake negotiable notes and letters of credit, and illegal "pooling" of funds. In May the Supreme Court called for wider use of capital punishment, including in the case of crimes that result in death. It stated that persons whose crimes result in death should be punished by death regardless of extenuating circumstances or lack of a prior criminal record. National figures on the number of executions are not available, but in 1996 it has been estimated that several thousand executions were carried out. The Chinese press confirms that large numbers of speedy executions were carried out in 1996 as part of the "Strike-Hard" national anticrime campaign. A high court nominally reviews all death sentences, but the time between arrest and execution is often a matter of days, and reviews have consistently resulted in a confirmation of sentence. In June the Jilin Provincial Court held a news conference to report that, during a crackdown on crime in the preceding month, provincial authorities held 46 public rallies to "sternly and rapidly" sentence serious criminals. Defendants sentenced included three persons who were caught, tried, and executed within 10 days after they allegedly looted a car, and within 7 days of their arrest. In February the Shanghai Municipal No. 1 Intermediate Court held three separate rallies within 2 days to sentence and execute 18 criminals found guilty of murder, robbery, or other crimes. No executions for political offenses are known to have occurred in 1996.

In recent years, credible reports have alleged that organs from some executed prisoners are removed and transplanted. Officials have confirmed that executed prisoners are among the sources of organs for transplant. There is no national legislation governing organ donations, but officials assert that consent is required from prisoners or their relatives before organs are removed.

Only courts can sentence prisoners to facilities managed by the criminal justice system. Justice Ministry statistics issued in January 1995 showed that China has imprisoned and released approximately 10 million prisoners since 1949; there were 1,285,000 prisoners in prisons or reform-through-labor camps at the end of 1994. Government authorities can, however, assign persons accused of "minor" public order offenses to reeducation-through-labor camps in an extrajudicial process. Terms of detention run from a normal minimum of 1 year to a maximum of 3 years. The labor reeducation committee, which determines the term of detention, may extend an inmate's sentence for an additional year. According to prison officials, 200,000 detainees were in reeducation-through-labor facilities at the end of 1995, up from 153,000 at the end of 1993. Other estimates of the number of such inmates are considerably higher.

Since 1990 defendants have been able to challenge reeducation-through-labor sentences under the Administrative Procedure Law. While some persons have gained a reduction in or suspension of their sentences after reconsideration or appeal, in practice these procedures are not widely used, and such problems as short appeal times and lack of access to lawyers weaken their effectiveness in preventing or reversing arbitrary decisions. Liu Nianchun unsuccessfully appealed the reeducation-through-labor sentence that he received in mid-1996. Irregular appellate procedures in his case included inadequate notice of the hearing and insufficient time and resources to prepare the appeal.

Government officials deny that China holds any political prisoners, asserting that authorities detain persons not for the political or religious views they hold, but because they have taken some action that violates the Criminal Law. However, the authorities continue to confine citizens for political reasons. Perhaps thousands of political prisoners remain imprisoned or detained.

Political dissidents are often detained or charged with having committed counterrevolutionary crimes under Articles 90 through 104 of the Criminal Law. Counterrevolutionary offenses range from treason and espionage to spreading counterrevolutionary propaganda. The authorities have also used these articles to punish persons who organized demonstrations, disrupted traffic, disclosed official information to foreigners, or formed associations outside of state control. Efforts are under way, through revisions to the Criminal Law, to redefine counterrevolutionary offenses as treasonous acts designed to threaten national security, but it is not clear whether such a change would make a significant difference in how political cases are treated. Labor rights activists Li Wenming and Guo Baosheng, who were arrested in May and June of 1994 on the charge of "counterrevolutionary propaganda and incitement," were tried and found guilty in November on the more serious charge of "conspiracy" to subvert the Government for spreading information among workers about their rights. By year's end, they had not been sentenced. Of the 12 others who were indicted with Li and Guo, 2 have been sentenced to 1-year terms of reeducation through labor, 2 are being tried in Beijing, and the rest were released.

In January 1995, a Justice Ministry official said that there were 2,678 people serving sentences for counterrevolutionary crimes at the end of 1994. These figures include people convicted of espionage or other internationally recognized criminal offenses, but they do not include political prisoners detained but not charged; political or religious activists held in reeducation-through-labor camps; and persons detained or convicted for criminal offenses solely involving nonviolent political or religious activities.

The 1988 Law on State Secrets provides justification for denying a public trial. Details regarding cases falling under this provision are frequently kept secret, even from defendants' relatives. At least 14 persons were imprisoned on "state secrets" charges in 1996. In May, after being detained for exactly 1 year, dissident Li Hai was tried for stealing unspecified state secrets. Li's family was not permitted to attend the trial. In December authorities announced Li had been convicted and sentenced to a 9-year prison term for "prying into and gathering the following information about people sentenced for criminal activities during the June 4, 1989 period: name, age, family situation, crime, length of sentence, location of imprisonment, treatment while imprisoned." The verdict stated that these data constitute state secrets.

The Government released certain prisoners detained for their political or religious beliefs, including Ren Wanding, Fu Shenqi, and Zhang Xianliang. Fu and Zhang departed China in September. Others were released and then detained again. Tong Yi was released in June after serving her full sentence but was briefly detained again shortly thereafter for traveling without official authorization. Bao Tong was also released from prison in May but remained held in custody in a government facility at year's end (see Section 1.c.). Liu Xiaobo was released in January but was rearrested on October 7 and administratively sentenced to a 3-year term of reeducation through labor the next day. Many others, including Wei Jingsheng, Xi Yang, Hu Shigen, Kang Yuchun, Liu Jingsheng, Jampa Ngodrup, and Ngawang Phulchung remained imprisoned or under other forms of detention during the year. Ngawang Sangdrol, a 19-year-old Tibetan nun serving a 9-year sentence for taking part in a proindependence demonstration and for singing nationalistic songs in prison had her sentence doubled in July (see Tibet addendum).

The Government subjects many prisoners—including political prisoners—to "deprivation of political rights" even after they have served their sentences. This status explicitly limits rights of free speech and association. Former prisoners often find their status in society, ability to find employment, freedom to travel, and access to social services severely restricted. Economic reform and social change have ameliorated these problems for nonpolitical prisoners to some extent in recent years. Former political prisoners and their families, however, are frequently subjected to police surveillance and harassment and also may encounter difficulty in obtaining or keeping employment and housing. Dissident Liu Gang cited constant police harassment, his inability to work, rent an apartment, or accept help from friends as reasons for his decision to flee China in April and seek resettlement abroad. Government harassment has prevented relatives of Chen Ziming, Liu Nianchun, Qin Yongmin, and other dissidents from obtaining and keeping steady employment.

f. *Arbitrary Interference with Privacy, Family, Home, or Correspondence.*—Economic liberalization is creating diverse employment opportunities and introducing market forces into the economy, thus loosening governmental monitoring and regulation of personal and family life, particularly in rural areas. In urban areas, however, most people still depend on their government-linked work unit for housing, permission to have a child, approval to apply for a passport, and other aspects of ordinary life. The work unit, along with the neighborhood committee, are charged with monitoring activities and attitudes, although these institutions have become less important as means of social or political control in urban areas.

Although the law requires search warrants before security forces can search premises, this provision is often ignored in practice. In addition the Public Security Bureau and the Procuratorate issue warrants on their own authority.

The 1982 Constitution states that "freedom and privacy of correspondence of citizens are protected by law." In practice, however, authorities frequently monitor telephone conversations, fax transmissions, electronic mail, and Internet communications of foreign visitors, businessmen, diplomats, residents, and journalists as well as Chinese dissidents, activists, and others. Authorities also open and censor domestic and international mail. In March Procurator General Zhang Siqing reported to the National People's Congress that in 1995 the Supreme People's Procuratorate investigated 1,739 cases of illegal searches of residences or surveillance and 87 cases of hindering postal and telecommunications and encroaching on freedom of communications. Government security organs monitor and sometimes restrict contact between foreigners and citizens, particularly dissidents. Rules implementing the State Security Law define as a violation of the law "activities of individuals outside the country (including non-Chinese citizens resident in China) who disregard dissuasion and meet with personnel in the country who have endangered state security or who are seriously suspected of endangering state security."

The Government encouraged expansion of Internet and other communications infrastructure. The Ministry of Posts and Telecommunications licensed more than 20 companies as "agents" authorized to offer Internet access, and access is becoming easier. There are no reliable statistics on the number of Chinese Internet users, but the number in Beijing alone is thought to exceed 10,000. Nevertheless, authorities dedicated increased attention and resources to efforts to control Internet content and usage. In January authorities issued regulations requiring Internet users to register and sign a vaguely worded pledge not to use the Internet to endanger security. In September the Government blocked access to more than 100 news sites on the World Wide Web, including many Chinese language sites in Hong Kong and Taiwan and the sites of major Western news organizations. Sites hosted by dissidents were also blocked. During the year, China's Ministry of State Security was tasked with controlling material on line. Regulations allegedly adopted to preserve public security were used to implement Internet censorship.

In April the Government issued regulations requiring foreign wire service providers of economic information and financial market data to register, pay substantial fees, and face penalties for the transmission of information deemed "harmful to Chinese national interests." Providers were further required to provide equipment allowing Chinese authorities to simultaneously monitor information provided to customers. All operations, customers, and contracts also were subject to government preapproval. Foreign wire services in China strongly protested and began discussions with the authorities to resolve concerns over the nature and scope of the new regulations. No foreign wire service had completed registration procedures by the end of the year.

The authorities continue to jam Voice of America (VOA) broadcasts, but the effectiveness of this interference varies considerably by region, with audible signals of VOA and other broadcasters reaching most parts of China, including the capital. The British Broadcasting Corporation monitoring service noticed in May that the government-owned China Radio International (CRI) was using English-language programming purchased from an Australian entertainment company to jam the "Voice of Tibet," a Tibetan dissident radio station which is produced outside China.

Radio Free Asia began operation in Chinese in September and in Tibetan in December. Reception has been good to fair, and there are no reports of jamming.

The Government continued to implement comprehensive and highly intrusive one-child family planning policies first adopted in the late 1970's. The State Family Planning Commission formulates and implements government policies with assistance from the Family Planning Association, which has 83 million members in 1.02 million branches. China's population policy most heavily affects ethnic Han Chinese in urban areas. Urban couples seldom obtain permission to have a second child. Exceptions are allowed for many of the 70 percent of Han who live in rural areas, and ethnic minorities are subject to less stringent population controls. In special circumstances, minorities in some rural areas are permitted to have as many as four children.

Population control policy relies on education, propaganda, and economic incentives, as well as on more coercive measures, including psychological pressure and economic penalties. Rewards for couples who adhere to the policy include monthly stipends and preferential medical and educational benefits. Disciplinary measures against those who violate the policy include fines, withholding of social services, demotion, and other administrative punishments that sometimes result in loss of employment. Penalties for excess births can be levied against local officials and the mothers' work units providing multiple sources of pressure. Fines for giving birth without authorization vary, but they can be a formidable disincentive. In Fujian, for example, the standard fine has been calculated to be twice a family's gross annual income or twice the calculated average income of rural families with no quantifiable cash income; additional, unauthorized births incur fines assessed in increments of 50 percent per child. In Guangzhou the standard fine is calculated to be 30 to 50 percent of 7 years' income for the average resident. Unpaid fines have sometimes resulted in confiscation or destruction of personal property. There were also reports that teams of village officials expelled women and their families from their homes and then destroyed the houses. According to a 1995 government white paper, more than 200 million married couples of childbearing age, or about 80 percent of all couples in that age group, use contraception. The Government does not authorize the use of force to compel persons to submit to abortion or sterilization, but officials acknowledge that there are instances of forced abortions and sterilizations. Officials maintain that, when discovered, the responsible officials are disciplined and undergo retraining, but they have not provided any data or examples to verify this assertion. Officials admit, however, that more severe punishment is rare. The State Family Planning Commission has limited ability to punish lower level offenders. Individuals can sue officials who have exceeded their authority in implementing family planning policy, but there are no known successful suits on these grounds.

Poor supervision of local officials who are under intense pressure to meet family planning targets results in instances of abuse, including forced abortion and sterilization. During an unauthorized pregnancy, often a woman is visited by family planning agents and pressured to terminate the pregnancy. There were credible reports that several women were forced to undergo abortions of unauthorized pregnancies in Fujian. The press sometimes reports instances of abuse. For example, a newspaper in Shenyang reported that family planning agents convinced a woman, 7-months pregnant, to take "appropriate measures." A well-documented incident of a 1994 forced 8-month abortion has been reported in the coastal province of Guangdong. A 1995 incident involving a forced sterilization was also reported in Guangzhou.

Regulations forbid the termination of pregnancies based on the sex of the fetus, but because of the traditional preference for male children, particularly in rural areas, some families have used ultrasound to identify female fetuses. Use of ultrasound for this purpose is specifically prohibited by the new Maternal and Child Health Care Law, which calls for punishment of medical practitioners who violate this provision. According to the State Family Planning Commission, a handful of doctors have been charged under this law. The Chinese press has reported that the national ratio of male to female births is 114 to 100. One October 1994 survey of births in rural areas put the ratio as high as 117 male births to 100 female. The statistical norm is 106 male births to 100 female. Official statistics may exclude many female births, especially the second or third in a family. Such births are unreported so that the parents can keep trying to conceive a boy. These statistics also probably reflect, however, the abuse of sonography and the termination of pregnancies based on the sex of the fetus. Female infanticide or neglect of baby girls may also be a factor in some areas.

The Maternal and Child Care Law, which came into effect in June 1995, calls for premarital and prenatal examinations to determine whether couples have acute infectious diseases, certain mental illnesses (not including mental retardation), or are at risk for passing on debilitating genetic diseases. The Ministry of Health, not the State Family Planning Commission, implements the law, which mandates abortion or sterilization in some cases, based on medical advice. The law also provides for obtaining a second opinion and states that patients or their guardians must give written consent to procedures (see also Section 5). At least five provincial governments have implemented regulations seeking to prevent people with severe mental disabilities from having children.

Section 2. Respect for Civil Liberties, Including:

a. *Freedom of Speech and Press.*—Although the Constitution states that freedom of speech and freedom of the press are fundamental rights enjoyed by all citizens, the Government interprets the Communist Party's "leading role" as circumscribing these rights. It does not permit citizens to publish or broadcast criticism of senior leaders or opinions that contradict basic Communist Party doctrine providing for a Socialist state under the party's leadership. During the year the Government and party further intensified control over expression of unauthorized political views. The formal charges brought against dissident and prodemocracy advocate Wang Dan were based on public criticisms of the Government. These criticisms together with his publication of articles and his activities in support of democracy advocates resulted in his November conviction and sentence to 11 years in prison, a much harsher sentence than he received for his prodemocracy activities in 1989. The case was not reported in the Chinese language press. Liu Nianchun, who was denied permission in 1994 to register the Association for Protection of Labor Rights, was sentenced in July to 3 years' reeducation through labor after having been held in detention since his 1995 arrest for involvement with a prodemocracy petition drive (see Section 1.d.).

The party and the Government continue to control print and broadcast media and compel them to propagate the current ideological line. All media employees are under explicit, public orders to follow CCP directives, and to "guide public opinion" as directed by political authorities. This greatly restricts the freedom of newspapers and broadcast journalists to report the news. Both formal and informal press guidelines continued to require reporters to avoid coverage of sensitive subjects and to protect "state secrets." Under the State Security Law, state secrets are broadly defined, and interpretation of the law is left to the Ministries of State Security and Public Security.

In June authorities fired the director of the Beijing Youth Daily after the newspaper printed a factual story about the poisoning deaths of three children who drank "Wahaha," a popular beverage produced by a state-owned enterprise. The Party Propaganda Department also forced all those involved with publishing the article to engage in self-criticism, a move that highlighted the absence of laws protecting journalists and consumers. After the fall Communist Party plenum the Propaganda Department reportedly issued a directive forbidding the publication of negative stories, including any major cases of corruption and unrest. It also censored several authors and called for strict supervision over articles on the reversion of Hong Kong. Shanghai customs officials impounded the May 21 editions of the International Herald Tribune and the Asian Wall Street Journal because they carried reports and pictures of the Lee Teng-hui inauguration in Taiwan. Shanghai officials also expurgated foreign English-language newspapers and clamped down on "Hong Kong" style political magazines. Government regulators permit transmission of Hong Kong television broadcasts to Guangzhou but occasionally censor program content.

A Western press report stated that 38 newspapers have been shut down since 1994 either due to poor management or "political problems." According to reports other papers and magazines have been shut down for publishing sensitive articles on the plight of state farms, the cultural revolution, and debates on Deng Xiaoping's reform program.

Articles published by foreign journalists are monitored. The Government has withheld visas from journalists who have written stories critical of China. Foreign journalists working in China have also been subjected to surveillance and, on occasion, harassment. French journalist Christine Ockrent, who visited China in July, was prevented from meeting with any Chinese dissidents and was under surveillance by a team of more than 10 plainclothes officials.

Despite these government controls, uncontrolled information about the nation is flowing into China at an increasing rate. Residents in Guangdong and other parts of southern China have access to Hong Kong television programs and newspapers. Throughout China, a lively tabloid sector continues to flourish. Radio talk shows remain popular, and, while generally avoiding politically sensitive subjects, they provide opportunities for citizens to air grievances about public issues. Despite licensing requirements, a small but rapidly growing segment of the population has access to satellite television broadcasts and most sites on the Internet. Most citizens have the means to own and use shortwave radios, and the Government does not place any restrictions on their use.

Fierce competition and dwindling government subsidies have increased opportunities for private publishers and booksellers, but the Government moved to tighten its control over the production and dissemination of publications during the year. In 1995 the China Press and Publications Administration announced that it would limit the number of books published by controlling book registration numbers issued to officially approved publishing houses. Despite this effort, books continued to be published through unsanctioned channels.

Fear of government retaliation limited artistic freedom of expression. Security personnel have effectively eliminated an artist community near Beijing University at Yuanmingyuan through harassment and arrests. The crackdown, which began in 1995, appeared to be the result of official irritation over the artists' antigovernment views.

The Government has continued to impose heavy ideological controls on political discourse at colleges, universities, and research institutes. In September, for example, authorities closed computer bulletin boards at universities in Beijing when students began using the Internet to urge government action in defense of Chinese sovereignty claims over the Diaoyu/Senkaku islands. As a result of official controls, many intellectuals and scholars, fearing that books or papers on political topics would be deemed too sensitive to be published, feel compelled to exercise self-censorship. In areas such as economic policy or legal reform, there was far greater official tolerance for comment and debate.

b. *Freedom of Peaceful Assembly and Association.*—While the Constitution has provisions for freedom of peaceful assembly and association, the Government severely restricts these rights in practice. The Constitution provides, for example, that such activities may not infringe upon the "interests of the State." Protests against the political system or its leaders are prohibited.

Authorities deny permits and quickly move to suppress demonstrations involving expression of dissident political views. On the June 4 anniversary of the 1989 Tiananmen crackdown, police arrested a woman who attempted to commemorate the event by leaving flowers at the Memorial to People's Heroes in Tiananmen Square. In June authorities in Shanghai prevented a Greenpeace ship on an antinuclear mission from calling at the port. In September a group of students from several Beijing universities were detained for attempting to stage a demonstration outside the Japanese Embassy. The Government tolerates some small-scale demonstrations about nonpolitical grievances, and unauthorized protests on nonpolitical subjects are not automatically disrupted. In July some 200 Beijing residents protested in front of the Beijing Municipal Office the Government's failure to provide promised housing and to pay owed factory wages. Police did not interfere with the protest, but no government officials agreed to the group's request for a meeting to discuss its concerns. Such incidents were not uncommon in Beijing and other areas during the year.

The Communist Party organizes and controls most professional and social associations. Regulations require all organizations to be officially registered and approved. Authorities can detain violators for up to 15 days and impose fines up to $23 (RMB200). Ostensibly aimed at secret societies and criminal gangs, the regulations also deter the formation of unauthorized political, religious, or labor organizations. Political activists including Liu Nianchun and Yang Zhou, were denied permission to register their labor and human rights associations.

In March the Government cited the organizers' failure to preregister with authorities to justify a Beijing police raid of a charity banquet to raise funds for Chinese orphans. The police initially demanded that the event be canceled but relented when the organizers agreed to separate guests into subgroups, to cancel speeches by scheduled speakers, remove banners, and do no fundraising. The 447 guests in attendance included Chinese officials, foreign ambassadors, and foreign business leaders, journalists, and teachers.

c. *Freedom of Religion.*—Although the Constitution affirms toleration of religious beliefs, the Government seeks to restrict all religious practice to closely controlled and government-sanctioned religious organizations and registered places of worship. At the annual national religious affairs conference in January religious policy was "readjusted" to emphasize harder line aspects. During the year many religious groups were subjected to increased restrictions although the degree of restriction varied significantly in different regions of China. Despite these increased restrictions, the number of religious adherents continues to grow. The annual conference gave special attention to appointing a new generation of party loyalists to lead the work of official religious bodies and to the issue of registering unofficial religious groups.

Although there is no legislation governing religious affairs, State Council regulations require all religious groups to register with government religious affairs bureaus and come under the supervision of official "patriotic" religious organizations. In 1996 some groups registered while others were refused registration. Many, however, have been reluctant to comply out of principled opposition to state control of religion or for fear of adverse consequences if they reveal, as required, the names and addresses of members and details about leadership activities, finances, and contacts in China or abroad. The campaign to shut down unauthorized groups is in the hands of the police and religious affairs officials and is being conducted concurrently with other police actions against criminals and underground separatists, prodemocracy, and labor groups. The national goal for 1996 was to register or close down all unregistered religious groups.

In 1996 police closed dozens of "underground" mosques, temples, and seminaries and hundreds of Protestant "house church" groups, many with significant memberships, properties, financial resources, and networks. Leaders of such groups, including itinerant teachers and evangelists, increasingly have been detained for lengthy investigation. There are NGO reports of deaths of detainees by beating. Some congregations have been hit with heavy fines. In Shanghai, home of the patriotic Protestant headquarters, authorities have been particularly tough.

Official Chinese media carried warnings of the "threat of religious infiltration." In August the Communist Party newspaper People's Daily said that "hostile international forces resort to ethnic and religious issues to 'Westernize' and 'split' Socialist countries and step up religious infiltration." The publication also quoted a senior Communist official as saying that religion had "interfered in government administration, judicial matters, education, and marriages."

The State Council's Religious Affairs Bureau and the CCP United Front Work Department, which are staffed by officials who rarely are religious adherents, provide "guidance and supervision" over implementation of government regulations on religion and on the role of foreigners in religious activity. Communist Party officials state that party membership and religious belief are incompatible. This places a serious limitation on religious believers, since party membership is required for almost all high-level positions in government and state-owned businesses. According to a 1995 government survey, 20 percent of Communist Party members engage in some form of religious activity. In January 1995, the CCP circulated a document to party organizations at the provincial level ordering expulsion of party members belonging to open or clandestine religious organizations. In November the People's Liberation Army Daily's report on military "spiritual civilization" stated that "it is necessary to conduct education in atheism so that they (the military) believe in science and oppose superstition. Participation in religious activities is forbidden."

After forcefully suppressing all religious observances and closing all seminaries during the 1966–76 Cultural Revolution, the Government began in the late 1970's to restore or replace damaged or confiscated churches, temples, mosques, and monasteries and allowed seminaries to reopen. According to the Government, there are now 68,000 religious sites in China and 48 religious colleges. The Government also adopted a policy of returning confiscated church property. Implementation of this policy has varied from locality to locality. The official religious organizations administer local Bible schools, more than a dozen Catholic and Protestant seminaries, nine institutes to train imams and Islamic scholars, and institutes to train Buddhist monks. Students who attend these institutes must demonstrate "political reliability," and all graduates must pass an examination on their theological and political knowledge to qualify for the clergy. The Government permitted some Catholic seminarians, Muslim clerics, and Buddhist clergy to go abroad for additional religious studies in 1996. Unofficial churches, however, have significant problems training clergy.

The authorities permit officially sanctioned religious organizations to maintain international contacts as long as these do not entail foreign control. The January 1994 regulations codified many existing rules involving foreigners, including a ban on proselytizing by foreigners, but allow foreign nationals to preach to foreigners, bring in religious materials for their own use, and preach to Chinese at churches, mosques, and temples at the invitation of registered religious organizations. Chinese authorities strictly enforced the 1994 regulations in several cities. Some regularly scheduled expatriate religious services were shut down by police, who asserted that the meetings did not comply with regulations that require registration of religious gatherings. Meetings were subsequently allowed to resume in some cases.

Buddhists make up the largest body of religious believers in China. The Government estimates that there are 100 million Buddhists, most of whom are from the dominant Han ethnic group. The Government says that there are 9,500 Buddhist temples and monasteries in China and more than 170,000 nuns and monks. Some local authorities have called for controls on Buddhist places of worship, especially newly established sites. The Zhejiang provincial government, for example, said that from April to June, 17,900 shrines and churches, which had been illegally erected, had been "rectified" which can mean destroyed, registered, or transferred to another group. Religious shrines in other areas of China were also destroyed. In November the Guangming Daily reported that 1,600 "pagan shrines" were destroyed in Hubei province in a nationwide crackdown on superstition. The newspaper reported that the shrines covered approximately 35 acres of land and cost approximately $700,000 to construct. The Guangming Daily reported that in November nine temples were closed in Guizhou province. In December Beijing Central Television reported that farmers had destroyed 400 temples and ancestral halls in Jiangxi province. The report stated that 200 new schools would be built on the land previously occupied by the temples. (A discussion of government restrictions on Tibetan Buddhism can be found in the addendum to this report.)

According to government figures, there are 17 million Muslims. In some areas with large Muslim populations, officials continue to restrict the building of mosques and the religious education of youths under the age of 18. Following unrest in 1990 in Xinjiang, which has a large Muslim population, the authorities issued regulations further restricting religious activities and teaching. There were several reports of unrest in Xinjiang, prompting the leadership to issue statements on the need to control religion there. During a trip to Xinjiang on September 11, Premier Li Peng said that relevant Chinese departments should "step up the control of religious affairs." Li also stated that China upholds freedom of religious belief, but added that religion "should serve the aims of socialism."

Authorities in Ningxia Hui Autonomous Region, another province with a large Muslim population, issued regulations in July 1994, forbidding religious bodies from interfering in administrative affairs, including education, marriage, and family planning. China permits Muslim citizens to make the hajj to Mecca, and the number of those making the pilgrimage has increased significantly in recent years.

The number of Christians continues to grow rapidly. However, the Government permits only those Christian churches affiliated with either the Catholic Patriotic Association or the (Protestant) Three Self Patriotic Movement to operate openly. The Government established both organizations in the 1950's to eliminate perceived foreign domination of local Christian groups.

In some areas there is tacit cooperation between official and unofficial churches, but active, unofficial religious movements are viewed as posing a challenge as well as an alternative to the state-regulated churches. The unofficial, Vatican-affiliated Catholic Church claims a membership far larger than the 4 million persons registered with the official Catholic Church, although actual figures are unknown. While government officials estimate that there are about 15 million Protestant worshipers in China, other estimates indicate that there are at least 10 million people who belong to the official Protestant church, while perhaps 30 million worship privately in house churches that are independent of government control. As a result of the increase in Protestant worshipers, there has been a corresponding demand for Bibles. This year, the Government supervised the publication of about 3 million Bibles—a two-fold increase over 1995.

There was evidence that authorities in some areas, guided by national policy, made strong efforts to crack down on the activities of the unapproved Catholic and Protestant movements. Local authorities have used threats, demolition of unregistered property, extortion of "fines," interrogation, detention, and reform-through-education sentences. Unofficial religious groups have been hard hit in Beijing and nearby provinces of Henan, where there are rapidly growing numbers of unregistered Protestants, and Hebei, a center of unregistered Catholics. In Henan police closed down several hundred house churches that were part of a nationwide network claiming 10 million members affiliated with Xu Yongzhe, a religious leader who has been subjected to decades of persecution, including detention and imprisonment. In Hebei repression focused on the location of an annual spring pilgrimage to Donglu that was banned this year after attracting 10,000 unofficial Catholics in 1995. Hebei's underground church seminary was also closed down.

In Jiangxi, Zhejiang, and Fujian, police reportedly raided underground masses, destroyed altars, confiscated books, roughed up congregations, and detained some worshipers. During November, according to credible reports, approximately 80 underground Catholics from Linchuan, Jiangxi province, were arrested without warrants, beaten, and jailed. One source reported that several unofficial priests "disappeared" in Shanghai and Hebei.

A Western news report said that Chinese authorities in Fujian refused in August to provide medical care for 76-year-old Catholic Bishop Zeng Jingmu, who had contracted pneumonia. Zeng has been detained since March for holding illegal church services in his home. In May Beijing police detained Fu Xiqiu and his wife, Cai Bochun, for their work in establishing a Christian training center near Beijing. The couple were released in July, apparently after police could not find any evidence against them, but they were kept under close surveillance and lost their employment and housing.

Nonmainstream sects are often singled out for particularly heavy-handed treatment. In 1996 police continued to put pressure on an underground evangelical sect called the "Shouters." The Shouters sect has been deemed counterrevolutionary by the Government, and its members have been repeatedly detained, fined, and imprisoned since its establishment over 16 years ago. In August authorities arrested well-known writer Bei Cun, along with 39 others in Fujian Province, for seeking converts to the outlawed sect. In February Public Security Bureau officers in Fujian detained Zhang Ruiyu, a member of the New Testament Church, and in March arrested church member Cai Lifen.

d. *Freedom of Movement Within the Country, Foreign Travel, Emigration, and Repatriation.*—The effectiveness of the Government's identification card system, used to control and restrict the location of individual residences within China, continued to erode. Estimates of the "floating population" of economic migrants leaving their home areas to seek work elsewhere in China range from tens of millions to as many as 100 million. This itinerant population enjoys increased economic opportunities but lacks official residence status which provides full access to social services and education. Unless they obtain resident status, they must pay a premium for these services.

Authorities have denied some former inmates permission, under the "staying at prison employment" system, to return to their homes, a provision applicable to recidivists incarcerated in reform-through-labor camps. Those inmates sentenced to more than 5 years in reeducation-through-labor camps also may lose their legal right to return home. For those assigned to camps far from their residences, this constitutes a form of internal exile. The number of prisoners subject to this restriction is unknown. Authorities have reportedly forced others to accept jobs in state enterprises where they can be more closely supervised after their release from prison or detention.

Other released or paroled prisoners returned home but were not permitted freedom of movement. Chen Ziming, who was paroled on medical grounds in November, is confined to his home except for police-escorted visits to doctors. Bao Tong has been held in custody at a government facility in Beijing since his May release from Qincheng prison upon completion of his sentence (see also Sections 1.c. and 1.e.).

The Government routinely permits legal emigration and most foreign travel. In November the Government announced streamlined and standardized procedures for Chinese citizens to obtain exit permits. In September dissident Zhang Xianliang departed China after his release from prison earlier in the year. In the same month, authorities issued a passport to the father of Tiananmen activist Chai Ling but reportedly denied the passport application of Guangzhou dissident Wang Xizhe. Wang fled China in October (see Section 1.d.). Some have reported that their passports have been held by the Ministry of State Security.

Students wishing to go abroad still routinely were able to obtain passports. Permission for couples to travel abroad was sometimes conditioned on agreement to delay childbirth; noncompliance triggered fines for the couple or their work unit. The Government continued to use political attitudes as a major criterion in selecting people for government-sponsored study abroad, but it did not similarly control privately sponsored students, who currently constitute the majority of students studying abroad. The Government continued efforts to attract persons who have studied overseas back to China. Official media have said that people who have joined foreign organizations hostile to China should quit them before returning home and refrain while abroad from activities that violate Chinese law.

In June a Xinhua News Agency official told a journalist that Chinese border control stations generally kept background records of certain citizens so that officials could decide whether to admit them to China. The following month, a Foreign Ministry spokesman dismissed reports that China "blacklists" political activists as "sheer rumor." International observers reported in 1995 that they had documents that substantiated their claims that such lists exist. Perhaps the most prominent case of a dissident refused reentry is labor activist Han Dongfang, whose passport was revoked in 1993 because he allegedly engaged in activities hostile to China while overseas. He remains in Hong Kong. The were instances during 1996 when the authorities refused visas or entry to China on apparent political grounds. In July eight Hong Kong members of the United Front Against the Provisional Legislature, who had hoped to hand a protest petition to the authorities, were denied entry at the Beijing airport.

The Government continued to accept the repatriation of citizens who had entered other countries or territories illegally. In 1996, in addition to the routine return of Chinese illegal immigrants found in Hong Kong, the Government continued accepting the return of several groups of illegal immigrants from other countries. Citizens illegally smuggled to other countries were often detained upon their return for a short time to determine identity and any past criminal record or involvement in smuggling activities. As a deterrent and to recover local costs incurred during the repatriation, the authorities in some areas levied fines of varying amounts up to a maximum of $1,000 on returnees. Exact amounts depended upon the extent to which returnees actively cooperated with the smugglers. Leaders of the alien smuggling rings are sometimes fined more than $1,000 and also face prison sentences.

Since the late 1980's, China has adopted a de facto policy of tolerance toward the small number of persons—fewer than 100 annually—from other nations who have registered with the Beijing office of the United Nations High Commissioner for Refugees (UNHCR) as asylum seekers. China has permitted these persons to stay in China while the UNHCR makes determinations as to their status and—if the UNHCR determines that they are bona fide refugees—while they await resettlement in third countries. Treatment of asylum seekers who present themselves initially to Chinese authorities is unknown. As yet China has no law or regulations that authorize the authorities to grant refugee status, but the Government is reportedly drafting working rules on granting such status.

The Government provided local resettlement to almost 300,000 asylum seekers, overwhelmingly ethnic Chinese, who left Indochina for China during the late 1970's and the 1980's. The authorities have accepted the return to China of would-be illegal emigrants to Hong Kong and Australia from among these individuals, provided that China can verify their identity and willingness to return voluntarily. China has successfully worked with Laos and Cambodia to facilitate the return of resettled individuals who have decided to return to their home countries, and it is now using the UNHCR's good offices to negotiate Vietnamese agreement to accept 9,000 persons seeking to repatriate to Vietnam. The Government denies having tightened its policy on accepting Vietnamese asylum seekers. In recent years very few such asylum seekers have found resettlement in China.

Section 3. Respect for Political Rights: The Right of Citizens to Change Their Government

Citizens lack the means to change their government legally and cannot freely choose or change the laws and officials that govern them. Citizens vote directly only for party-reviewed candidates for delegate positions in county-level people's congresses and for village-level officials. People's congress delegates at the provincial level, however, are selected by county-level people's congresses, and in turn provincial-level people's congresses select delegates to the National People's Congress (NPC). NPC seats are allocated on the basis of 1 per 220,000 urban residents and 1 per 880,000 rural residents. Although the CCP approves the candidates, many county and provincial elections are competitive, with more candidates running than there are seats available.

According to the 1982 Constitution, the NPC is the highest organ of state power. Formally it elects the President and Vice President, selects the Premier and Vice Premiers, and elects the Chairman of the Government's Central Military Commission. At the 1996 session of the NPC nearly 30 percent (799) of the delegates attending took the unusual step of either voting against, abstaining, or failing to vote on the Supreme People's Procuratorate work report. The Supreme Court work report received 514 negative votes. Most observers interpret these votes as expressions of delegate unhappiness about the problems of crime and corruption. The NPC has not in practice demonstrated the power to set policy or remove government or party leaders.

The election and agenda of people's congresses at all levels remain under the firm control of the Communist Party, the paramount source of political authority in China. A number of small "democratic" parties that date from before the Communist takeover in 1949 play only a minor consultative role, and they pledge their allegiance to the Communist Party. The party retains a tight rein on political decisionmaking. Efforts to form new political parties are suppressed.

Direct elections for basic level or village government are legally sanctioned for all of China's approximately 1 million villages. Foreign observers estimate that more than 80 percent of these villages have already participated in elections for local leaders. Although many have yet to hold truly competitive elections, central government officials have expressed their intent to further expand the competitive election process, and efforts to make these elections more competitive and fair continued. Successful village elections have included campaigning by multiple candidates, platforms, and the use of secret ballots. The Ministry of Civil Affairs, which administers the village election program, plans to set up an election training center in Beijing that will train local and provincial officials to teach others the basic techniques of running democratic elections. In some cases, candidates most favored by the authorities were defeated in village elections. Although there have been reports of "vote buying" in some locales, elections have reportedly reduced corruption and brought better management to some villages. Many local observers do not, however, take village elections seriously. Political controls are tight, and village elections do not threaten to undermine implementation of unpopular central policies or endanger the leading role of the Communist Party.

The official requirement that associations register and be approved discourages independent interest groups from forming and affecting the system. Social organizations registered in recent years include groups promoting environmental protection, consumer rights, charitable work, and the rights of the disabled, but the Government monitors their activities to ensure that they remain apolitical. Political activities are quickly suppressed. Liu Xiaobo, Wang Xizhe, and other activists submitted proreform petitions to government authorities. Liu was arrested in October and sentenced in a matter of hours to 3 years at a reeducation-through-labor camp. Shortly thereafter, Wang escaped China and is now living abroad.

The Government places no formal restrictions on the participation of women or minority groups in the political process. The Government and party organizations include approximately 12 million female officials. In September the press reported that women and ethnic minorities constituted 21.03 percent and 14.7 percent of National People's Congress delegates, respectively. All of China's 56 nationalities are represented in the NPC membership. Women and minorities, however, hold relatively few positions of significant influence within the party or government structure. There are currently no women in the Politburo, but women hold 3 out of 41 ministerial-level positions.

Section 4. Governmental Attitude Regarding International and Nongovernmental Investigation of Alleged Violations of Human Rights

There are no independent Chinese organizations that publicly monitor or comment on human rights conditions in China. Shanghai officials, for example, have refused to register the Chinese Human Rights Association. Founders of the group were detained, but it is not clear whether their detentions resulted solely from their involvement in the group. The detention or incarceration of all active, prominent human rights activists confirms the Government's intolerance of such groups. For example, Wang Dan—the Tiananmen-era activist who announced in 1994 his intention to investigate China's human rights situation—was sentenced to 11 years' imprisonment in October after having been held in incommunicado detention for 17 months.

Since 1991 the Government has promoted limited academic study and discussion of concepts of human rights, although activity in these areas has been less frequent since 1994. In 1993 the Government formed the China Society for Human Rights Studies as a "nongovernmental organization." Its efforts have focused largely on improving China's image abroad and responding to criticism of China's human rights record. The Society was widely regarded as the author of a March commentary published in various official newspapers and magazines entitled "A Comparison of Human Rights in China with Those in the United States." The article purported to refute alleged U.S. "distortions" of China's human rights record while arguing that China's human rights performance was better than that of the United States. In March the State Council's Information Office issued a White Paper entitled "Safeguarding Human Rights or Interfering in Internal Affairs of China," which criticized foreign criticism of China's human rights record.

In September the Government hosted a meeting of the Interparliamentary Union (IPU), an international organization of legislators. China played a role in efforts to draft an IPU human rights resolution, displayed greater openness on human rights issues, and agreed to a final resolution text that recognized the universality of human rights. Despite this public acknowledgment of universal human rights principles, however, Chinese officials reject in theory the universality of human rights. They argue instead that a nation's political, economic, and social system and its unique historical, religious, and cultural background determine its concept of human rights.

The Government remains reluctant to accept criticism of China's human rights situation by other nations or international organizations and often criticized reports by international human rights monitoring groups. To deflect attempts to discuss its human rights record, the Government strongly opposed and vigorously lobbied against a resolution on China's human rights record at the 1996 session of the U.N. Commission on Human Rights (UNHRC). The Government also introduced a procedural motion, as it has every year the resolution is introduced, to take no action on the resolution. The motion was passed by the Commission, and the resolution was not debated by the Commission.

Nevertheless, officials no longer dismiss all discussion of human rights as interference in China's internal affairs. Chinese authorities continued to discuss human rights issues with foreign governments during bilateral visits. The Government sought to limit the Dalai Lama's influence by threatening leaders of several nations with serious diplomatic and economic consequences if they met with him (see Tibet addendum). China's displeasure with those who cosponsored the UNHRC resolution in April led it to refuse some foreign governments' requests to hold a human rights dialog.

Section 5. *Discrimination Based on Race, Sex, Religion, Disability, Language, or Social Status*

There are laws designed to protect women, children, the disabled, and minorities. In practice, however, societal discrimination based on ethnicity, gender, and disability has persisted. The concept of a largely homogeneous Chinese people pervades the thinking of the Han majority.

Women.—Violence against women can be grounds for prosecution under the law. Nationwide statistics on the extent of physical violence against women are not available, but the public discussion of the establishment of abuse hot lines and women's centers has focused attention on the problem. In April 1995, the Chairman of the China Academy of Management Science Institute of Women's Studies stated that domestic incidents have become both more violent and more frequent in recent years. In 1994 the Beijing Society for Research on Marriage and the Family published a survey of 2,100 families showing that one-fifth of the wives surveyed had been abused by their spouses.

In recognition of the seriousness of spousal abuse, some areas took measures to address the problem. In February the city of Changsha, Hunan province, implemented China's first provincial regulation on controlling and preventing family violence. The regulation called on grassroots governments and party committees to assist efforts to decrease domestic violence. In March a women's legal hot line was set up in Beijing to provide legal advice for women who cannot afford regular attorneys' fees. In May Shanghai opened its first shelter for battered women. A women's legal center, which was opened near Beijing in 1995, was active in educating women about their legal rights and offering free or inexpensive legal aid to women and children in need and unable to escape family violence and abuse. The women served were poor, uneducated rural women. Some were not even aware that they could leave home without their husband's permission. The center has been highly successful and has developed a cooperative relationship with police, who have started bringing battered women to the center.

No statute outlaws sexual harassment in the workplace, a problem that is often unaddressed in society and the legal system. A 1996 case highlighted the obstacles that victims of sexual harassment and abuse face in Chinese courts. A woman who complained to peers about sexual harassment by her boss, was sued by him for criminal defamation, found guilty, fined, and sentenced to 2 years in prison. She served 7 months of her sentence before an appeal to a provincial supreme court reversed the decision in her case and found her innocent.

The increased commercialization of sex and related trafficking in women has trapped tens of thousands of women in a cycle of crime and exploitation. These women face a high risk of drug addiction, AIDS, and other sexually transmitted diseases. According to media reports, 80 percent of Beijing's massage parlors offer sex service. In July the Beijing municipal government announced a crackdown on massage parlors in the capital, but the long-term effectiveness of the crackdown on this lucrative business, which involves organized crime groups, businesspeople, and even the military is uncertain. Unsafe working conditions are rampant among the saunas, massage houses, and hostess bars that have sprung up in large numbers.

The abduction of women is a serious and growing problems. The Government continued to condemn and to take steps to prevent and punish the abduction and sale of women for marriage or prostitution. The press reported in March that 10 Xinjiang farmers, who were part of a gang, were convicted for abducting and selling as many as 75 women. In June, 24 gang members from Guangdong province were arrested for allegedly abducting and selling 230 young women in southern China. According to figures announced by the Ministry of Public Security in January 1994, there were over 15,000 cases of abduction and trafficking in women and children in 1993. In October police broke up China's largest female abduction racket, arresting 62 alleged traffickers and freeing 344 young women after a gunfight in the small village of Maoyanghao in Anhui province. According to a Chinese media report, more than 80 percent of the village's population was implicated in supporting the racket. The group had sold girls as young as 12 years old. In November police arrested 61 kidnapers in Fujian province and set free 79 women and children in a raid.

Some research indicates that a key reason for the abduction and sale of women is a serious imbalance in sex ratios in certain localities. Male/female birth ratios and the traditional preference for boys contribute to this situation (see Section 1.f.). This has created a situation where the demand by men for marriageable women cannot be met by local brides. Some families address the problem by recruiting women in economically less advanced areas. Others seek help from criminal gangs, which either kidnap women or trick them by promising them jobs and an easier way of life and then transport them far from their home areas for delivery to buyers. Once in their new "family," these women are. "married" and raped. Some accept their fate and join the new community; others struggle and are punished.

The authorities have enacted laws and conducted educational campaigns in an effort to eradicate the traditional preference for sons; however, this preference remains strong in rural China. A number of provinces have sought to reduce the perceived higher value of boys in providing old-age support for their parents by establishing or improving pensions and retirement homes.

The 1982 Constitution states that "women enjoy equal rights with men in all spheres of life," including ownership of property, inheritance rights, and access to education. In 1992 the NPC enacted legislation on the protection of the rights and interests of women, which was designed to assist in curbing gender-based discrimination. Women have continued, however, to report discrimination, sexual harassment, unfair dismissal, demotion, and wage discrepancies.

Women are also sometimes the unintended victims of reforms designed to streamline enterprises and give workers greater job mobility. The press reported that, according to a 1995 survey by the Women's Research Institute of the Chinese Academy of Management Science, women constituted 70 percent of persons fired or likely to be fired as a result of restructuring unprofitable state enterprises. Women under the age of 35 or over the age of 45 were the most affected, and the least likely to be retrained. In addition, female employees were more likely to be chosen to take pay cuts when a plant or company was in financial trouble.

Many employers prefer to hire men to avoid the expense of maternity leave and child care, and some even lower the effective retirement age for female workers to 40 years of age. (The official retirement age for men is 60 years and for women 55 years.) Although the law promises equal pay for equal work, a 1990 survey found that women's salaries averaged 77 percent of men's. Those statistics still appear to be accurate. Most women employed in industry work in lower skilled and lower paid jobs.

While the gap in the education levels of men and women is narrowing, men continue to constitute the majority of the relatively small number of Chinese who receive a university-level education. In 1994, 830,000 Chinese graduated from undergraduate institutions. According to the State Education Commission, women made up 35.6 percent of college students and 30.3 percent of postgraduate students. Educators in China's large cities have reported, however, that there is a trend toward greater gender balance in universities. Some academics have reported that in some departments, women are beginning to outnumber men—even in some graduate schools. However, women with advanced degrees report an increase in discrimination in the hiring process as the job distribution system has opened up and become more competitive.

In March the Government outlined its 5-Year Plan for the Advancement of Women in China. The main priority is to increase literacy of rural women, 80 percent of whom are illiterate or nearly illiterate. Overall, women make up about 70 percent of illiterates in the country. The All-China Women's Federation, the country's largest organization devoted to women's issues, stated that one of the goals of the plan was to decrease the number of female illiterates by 3 million every year. Some Chinese women's advocates, however, were skeptical that the goal could be realized because of a lack of resources.

Children.—According to a government white paper on children released in April, "The Constitution of China * * * promotes the all-around moral, intellectual and physical development of children and young people," and prohibits maltreatment of children. The white paper also states that "China's legal framework for the protection of children's rights and interests and its social guarantee mechanisms are effective in practice." China ratified the United Nations Convention on the Rights of the Child in 1995.

The Constitution provides for 9 years of compulsory education for children (see Tibet addendum). The extensive health care delivery system has led to improved child health and a sharp decline in national infant mortality rates. According to the April Child Welfare White Paper, the infant mortality rate has decreased to 37.79 per 1,000 from approximately 200 per 1,000 in the early 1950's. There were credible reports of female infanticide and the use of ultrasound tests to terminate pregnancies of female fetuses, but no reliable statistics were available to demonstrate the extent of the problem. The Chinese press has reported in the past that the national ratio of male to female births is 114 to 100, while the worldwide statistical norm is 106 to 100 (see Section 1.f.).

Physical abuse of children can be grounds for criminal prosecution. The 1992 Law on the Protection of Juveniles forbids infanticide, as well as mistreatment or abandonment of children. This law also prohibits discrimination against disabled minors, emphasizes the importance of safety and morality, and codifies a variety of judicial protections for juvenile offenders. In January the press reported that a couple in Dongguan was fined the equivalent of a month's wages for abandoning their newborn son at a hospital; the child was born with a deformed liver, kidneys, and intestines.

Despite government efforts to prevent the kidnaping and buying and selling of children, the problem persists in some rural areas. In March 1995, authorities in Guangxi province reported that, as a result of three campaigns in the past 2 years against trading of children and women, police arrested 3,886 criminals, smashed 595 criminal gangs, and released 134 children and 2,861 women. In December 1995, the press reported that six boys, some of whom were taken from their parents soon after birth, were returned from central Henan province to their original families in neighboring Sichuan province (see also section on Women above).

According to a 1994 Beijing University demographics study, the number of children abandoned in China each year is approximately 1.7 million, despite the fact that under the law child abandonment is punishable by fines and a 5-year prison term. The vast majority of those eventually admitted to Chinese orphanages every year are female or disabled and are in poor health. The treatment of children at orphanages varies from deplorable to adequate. There have been reports of children being restrained for long periods of time and being denied basic care and feeding. Differences among available statistics make accurate determination of infant mortality rates in orphanages difficult, but rates appear to be very high at many orphanages, especially among new arrivals. Human Rights Watch cites Ministry of Civil Affairs statistics for 1989–90 that put infant mortality in orphanages in 10 provinces at over 50 percent.

According to several sources, orphanage workers practice triage and reserve basic medical care and even nutrition for children who are deemed to have the best chances for survival. Some sources report that children whose prospects of survival are determined to be poor are placed in rooms separate from other children and subjected to extreme neglect. Claims that government policies, as opposed to lack of resources, were to blame for the lack of care of children placed in orphanages could not be verified. Human Rights Watch reported in January, however, that many orphanages, including those with the highest death rates, have budgets that provide for adequate wages, bonuses, and other personnel-related costs, but that budgets for children's food, clothing, and other necessities are low in institutions throughout the country. The Government denies that orphans are mistreated or refused medical care but acknowledges that the orphanage system is hard pressed to provide for those children who are admitted with serious medical problems.

People With Disabilities.—In 1990 the Government adopted legislation protecting the rights of the country's approximately 60 million disabled persons. According to the official press, all local governments subsequently drafted specific measures to implement the law. The Government reported in July that, in the 3 preceding years, the NPC Standing Committee conducted nationwide inspections to verify compliance with the law; it "found that the handicapped generally received good services and help in both their dealings with officials and in public life."

However, reality for the disabled lags far behind legal dictates. Misdiagnosis, inadequate medical care, pariah status, and abandonment remain common problems for the disabled population. Moreover, statistics compiled in 1993 and published in the official press as recently as March show that approximately 50 percent of the disabled lack adequate food and clothing. The same figures show that 68 percent of the disabled are illiterate; 67 percent require family support; 49 percent are unemployed; only 6 percent of blind and deaf children enter school; and only 0.33 percent of mentally retarded children enter school.

Deng Pufang, son of retired senior leader Deng Xiaoping, heads the China Welfare Fund for the Handicapped, the government organization tasked with assisting the disabled. In July the official press reported that the State Council had completed the outline of a government program for the disabled. The program, which is a part of the Government's ninth 5-year plan for 1996–2000, is designed to solve food and clothing problems for the 15 million disabled persons able to work, and to guarantee the basic needs of 3 million disabled individuals believed to be living in extreme poverty. The program also confirms goals previously established to provide rehabilitation services to 3 million people, raise school enrollment rates for disabled persons to 80 percent, and increase their employment rate to 80 percent. The Government requires all state enterprises to hire a certain number of disabled workers, but authorities estimate that nearly half of all disabled persons are jobless.

Standards adopted in 1994 for making roads and buildings accessible to the disabled are subject to the 1990 Law on the Handicapped, which calls for their "gradual" implementation. To date lax compliance with the law has resulted in only limited access to most buildings.

The new Maternal and Child Health Care Law forbids the marriage of persons with certain specified contagious diseases or certain acute mental illnesses such as schizophrenia. If doctors find that a couple is at risk of transmitting disabling congenital defects to their children, the couple may marry only if they agree to use birth control or undergo sterilization. This law mandates premarital and prenatal examination for genetic or contagious diseases, but it specifies that medically advised abortion or sterilization requires the signed consent of the patients or their guardians.

National/Racial/Ethnic Minorities.—The State Statistical Bureau reported in February that, according to an October 1, 1995, census, the total population of China's 55 ethnic minorities was 108.46 million, or 8.98 percent of the national population. Most minority groups reside in areas they have traditionally inhabited, many of which are mountainous or remote. China's policy on minorities calls for preferential treatment in marriage regulations, family planning, university admission, and employment. The Government has programs to provide low interest loans, subsidies, and special development funds for minority areas.

Government development policies have helped improve minority living standards in recent years. According to government statistics, between 1991 and 1995 the economies in minority regions grew by 11 percent annually. However, incomes for members of minorities in minority areas remain well below the national average. Development programs have disrupted traditional living patterns of minority groups, including Tibetans and the Muslim Uighur majority of western Xinjiang. Recent plans to develop tourism in Xinjiang have often, for example, focused on marketing and investment opportunities but paid little attention to how minority cultures and the environment might be adversely affected. However, some projects have been dropped for environmental reasons, for example, a proposal to build a railroad track around Lake Tianchi near Urumqi.

In the area of education, the Government has tried to design policies responsive to minority concerns. According to government statistics, 15.34 million minority students have attended schools since 1994. In many areas with a significant population of minorities, there are two-track school systems using either standard Chinese or the local minority language. Students can choose to attend schools in either system. One acknowledged side effect of this policy designed to protect and maintain minority cultures has been reinforcement of a segregated education system. Under this divided education system, those graduating from minority schools are at a disadvantage in competing for jobs in government and business, which require good spoken Chinese. These graduates must take Chinese-language instruction before attending universities and colleges (see also Tibet addendum).

The Communist Party has an avowed policy of boosting minority representation in the Government and the party. In March the official press reported that there were 2.4 million minority cadres. Many members of minorities occupy local leadership slots, and a few have positions of influence at the national level. However, in most areas, ethnic minorities are shut out of positions of real political and decision-making power. Minorities often resent Han officials holding key positions in minority autonomous regions. Ethnic minorities in Tibet, Xinjiang, and elsewhere have at times demonstrated against Han Chinese authority.

In 1996 tensions between ethnic Hans and Uighurs in Xinjiang intensified, and incidents of violence occurred. According to some estimates, the migration of ethnic Han into the area in recent decades has caused the Han-Uighur ratio in Urumqi to shift from 20:80 to 80:20 and has created Uighur resentment. Chinese officials' control of the region's political and economic institutions has also been a factor in the growth of tension. Although Chinese policies have brought tangible economic improvements, Uighurs maintain that they receive only a small share of the benefits. Authorities have maintained tight control over separatist activities. Possession of separatist publications is not permitted, and according to reports, possession of such materials has resulted in lengthy prison sentences. In general, central authorities have made it clear that they will not tolerate opposition to Communist Party rule in minority regions and have responded to unrest with force and heightened security measures.

Section 6. Worker Rights

a. *The Right of Association.*—The 1982 Constitution provides for "freedom of association," but qualifying language makes it clear that this right is subject to the interests of the State and the leadership of the Communist Party. The country's sole officially recognized workers' organization, the All-China Federation of Trade Unions (ACFTU), is controlled by the Communist Party. Independent trade unions are illegal. Although ACFTU officials recognize that workers' interests may not always coincide with those of the Communist Party, the ACFTU's primary goals and functions remain to improve labor discipline, mobilize workers to achieve party and government objectives, and to dispense social welfare funds. The 1993 Trade Union Law required that the establishment of unions at any level be submitted to a higher level trade union organization for approval. The ACFTU, the highest level organization, has not approved the establishment of independent unions. Attempts to form or register independent unions have been severely repressed.

The ACFTU's primary attention remains focused on state-sector workers. The Trade Union Law mandates that workers may decide whether to join the union in their enterprise. By official estimate, approximately 8 percent of workers in collective and state-owned enterprises have chosen for their own reasons not to join. There have been no reports of repercussions for workers who have not joined ACFTU unions. Diversification in types of enterprises over the last decade of reform has vastly increased the number of workers outside the traditional sphere of the ACFTU.

Over half of China's nonagricultural work force is now largely unorganized and outside the state industrial structure, employed in collectives, township and village enterprises, private and individual enterprises, and foreign investment enterprises. In township and village enterprises, one of the fastest growing sectors of the economy, only a tiny percentage of workers are organized in ACFTU affiliates. Workers in companies with foreign investors, even when such companies are located in special economic zones (SEZ's), have the right to form unions provided that the unions are affiliated with the ACFTU. The ACFTU estimates that, as of the end of 1995, 91 percent of foreign investment enterprises had union branches. Anecdotal evidence, however, indicates that union influence in such enterprises is weak.

Credible reports indicate the Government has attempted to stamp out illegal union activity. Veteran labor activist Liu Nianchun, who was detained in May 1994 after he tried to register the "League for the Protection of the Rights of the Working People," and again in May 1995 after he had signed a petition calling for labor rights, was sentenced to 3 years of reeducation through labor in July. Labor rights activist Li Wenming and Guo Baosheng were tried in November but by year's end had not yet been sentenced (see Section 1.e.).

In March 1994, a petition calling for workers to have "freedom from exploitation," the right to strike, and the right to organize nonofficial trade unions was circulated in Beijing. The authorities detained Zhou Guoqiang, Yuan Hongbing, and Wang Jiaqi after they presented the petition. Zhou is an associate of Han Dongfang, the leader of the Beijing Autonomous Workers' Federation. Zhou was sentenced in September 1994 to 3 years' reeducation through labor, although the charges against him were reportedly not linked to the petition. According to reports, he was sentenced in 1995 to a fourth year for an alleged escape attempt. Accurate figures are not available on the number of Beijing Autonomous Workers' Federation detainees still being held for their participation in the 1989 Tiananmen Square demonstrations.

The Government was cited by the International Labor Organization (ILO) during 1996 for its failure to protect the human and trade union rights of Chinese seafarers serving on foreign-flag ships (ILO complaint number 1819). The case stemmed from a complaint brought against China by the International Confederation of Free Trade Unions (ICFTU) in January 1995, regarding the Government's arrest of Chinese seafarers who had requested the assistance of the International Transport Workers' Federation (ITF) to improve their wages and working conditions. The Government detained three of the seafarers for 2½ years and confiscated their seamen's documentation and evidence of qualifications. The ILO's Committee on Freedom of Association (CFA) in its subsequent recommendations urged the Chinese Government to "refrain in the future from having recourse to any act of antiunion discrimination, especially the arrest and detention of Chinese seafarers who pursue their legitimate grievances through the organizations of their choice."

The right to strike, which had been included in China's 1975 and 1978 constitutions, was removed from the 1982 Constitution on the ground that the Socialist political system had eradicated contradictions between the proletariat and enterprise owners. The Trade Union Law assigns unions the role of mediators or go-betweens with management in cases of work stoppages or slowdowns. Beginning in 1993, the Ministry of Labor stopped officially denying the existence of strikes, but strikes are still not officially sanctioned, and accurate statistics on strike incidents are not available. One unofficial, yet credible 1995 estimate put the number of work stoppages at 1,870. In March 600 workers went on strike to protest unpaid back wages and excessive overtime at a joint venture hardware manufacturing factory in the Shenzhen SEZ. In Wuhan, according to reports, unemployed workers have repeatedly staged sit-down protests in front of the entrances of the Wuhan government and Hubei provincial government offices. Six hundred people participated in the largest demonstration.

A dispute settlement procedure has been in effect since 1987. The procedure provides for mediation, two levels of arbitration committees, and a final appeal to the courts. According to official statistics based on National Mediation Center and Labor Bureau records, labor disputes increased by approximately 73 percent in 1995. This followed a 65 percent increase during 1994. Most cases are solved through arbitration, and very few reach the courts. According to Ministry of Labor officials, the majority of arbitration cases are filed by contract workers or their employers. During 1995, 23,000 labor disputes were brought before arbitration committees.

There are no provisions allowing for individual workers or unofficial worker organizations to affiliate with international bodies.

b. *The Right to Organize and Bargain Collectively.*—The National Labor Law, which took effect on January 1, 1995, permits workers in all types of enterprises to bargain collectively. This law supersedes a 1988 law that allowed collective bargaining only by workers in private enterprises. The Labor Law provides for workers and employers at all types of enterprises to sign individual as well as collective contracts. Collective contracts are to be worked out between ACFTU or worker representatives and management and specify such matters as working conditions, wage distribution, and hours of work. Individual contracts are then to be drawn up in line with the terms of the collective contract. Collective contracts must be submitted to local government authorities for approval within 15 days. As of August, approximately 44 percent of China's industrial work force were officially on collective contracts.

To date, union and labor officials report the initiation of only a few experiments in collective bargaining. Official sources have explained that sufficient ideological and practical difficulties remain to preclude drawing clear distinctions between labor and capital in China's state-owned enterprise sector. According to the ACFTU, collective bargaining is being implemented first in foreign investment enterprises where capital interests are clearly delineated.

The Ministry of Labor sets a total wage bill for each collective and state-owned enterprise according to four criteria: 1) as a percentage of profits, 2) as a contract amount with the local labor bureau, 3) for money losing enterprises, according to a state-set amount, or 4) as an enterprise-set amount subject to Labor Ministry review. Individual enterprises determine how to divide the total among workers, a decision usually made by the enterprise manager in consultation with the enterprise party chief and the ACFTU representative.

Worker congresses are authorized to review plans for wage reform, although these bodies serve primarily as rubber-stamp organizations. Wages are generally equal for the same type of work within enterprises. Incentives are provided for increased productivity. Under the National Labor Law, wages may be set according to conditions stipulated in collective contracts negotiated between ACFTU representatives and management. In practice, however, only the small number of workers with high technical skills can negotiate effectively on salary and fringe benefits.

Worker congresses theoretically have the authority to remove incompetent managers and approve major decisions affecting enterprises, notably wage and bonus distribution systems. The congresses generally, however, take place only once a year and serve essentially to approve agreements worked out among factory managers, party secretaries, and ACFTU representatives. In smaller enterprises it is not unusual to find these three posts held by the same person. The Trade Union Law prohibits antiunion discrimination and specifies that union representatives may not be transferred or terminated by enterprise management during their term of office. Unionized foreign businesses generally report pragmatic relations with ACFTU representatives.

Laws governing working conditions in SEZ's are not significantly different from those in the rest of the country. Wages in the SEZ's, however, and in southeastern China generally, are significantly higher than in other parts of the country because high investment has created a great demand for available labor. As in other areas of China, officials admit that some foreign investors in SEZ's are able to negotiate "sweetheart" deals with local partners that effectively bypass labor regulations.

c. *Prohibition of Forced or Compulsory Labor.*—Some penal facilities contract with regular industries for prisoners to perform light manufacturing and assembly work. In 1991 the Government published a reiteration of its regulations barring the export of prison-made goods.

On August 7, 1992, the U.S. and Chinese Governments signed a Memorandum of Understanding (MOU) prohibiting trade in prison labor products. A statement of cooperation (SOC) detailing specific working procedures for implementation of the MOU was signed on March 14, 1994. Although the signing of the SOC initially helped to foster a more productive relationship with the authorities, cooperation has been limited recently. In 1996 the authorities granted access to only one prison labor facility requested by U.S. Customs. Repeated delays in arranging prison labor site visits called into question the Government's intentions regarding the implementation of the MOU and SOC.

In addition to prisons and reform through labor facilities, which hold inmates sentenced through judicial procedures, the Government also maintains a network of reeducation-through-labor camps, where inmates are sentenced through nonjudicial procedures (see Section 1.e.). Inmates of reeducation-through-labor facilities are generally required to work, but the authorities assert that the facilities are not prisons and have denied access to them under the 1992 prison labor MOU with the United States. Reports from international human rights organizations and the foreign press indicate that at least some persons in pretrial detention are also required to work.

Most anecdotal reports conclude that work conditions in the penal system's light manufacturing factories are similar to those in other factories, but conditions on the penal system's farms and in mines can be very harsh. As in many Chinese workplaces, safety is a low priority. There are no available figures for casualties in prison industry.

d. *Minimum Age for Employment of Children.*—The National Labor Law specifies that "no employing unit shall be allowed to recruit juveniles under the age of 16." Administrative review, fines, and revocation of business licenses of those businesses that hire minors are specified in Article 94 of the Labor Law. The law also provides for children to receive 9 years of compulsory education and to receive their subsistence from parents or guardians. Laborers between the ages of 16 and 18 are referred to as "juvenile workers" and are prohibited from engaging in certain forms of physical work, including labor in mines.

The Ministry of Labor is responsible for the enforcement of labor-related regulations. The Labor Law mandates the establishment of labor inspection corps at all administrative levels above county government. The rapid growth of the nonstate sector, however, has outpaced the evolution of government regulatory structures and resulted in inadequate labor inspection and enforcement regimes. In poorer, isolated areas, child labor in agriculture is widespread, given the few options available to minors who have completed their primary school education at approximately 13 years of age.

The vast reserve of surplus adult labor, however, minimizes the incentive to employ children. Most independent observers agree with Chinese officials that urban child labor is a relatively small problem in formal, monetized sectors of the economy. Rising dropout rates at secondary schools in some provinces and anecdotal reports suggest that children may increasingly be entering unregulated sectors of the economy. It has been reported that the Government puts the number of children between the ages of 6 and 14 who did not attend school in 1995 between 13 and 24 million. Using this report, there is one estimate that approximately 12 million children are in the work force full time. No specific industry is identifiable as a significant violator of child labor regulations.

e. *Acceptable Conditions of Work.*—The Labor Law codifies many of the general principles of labor reform, setting out provisions on employment, labor contracts, working hours, wages, skill development and training, social insurance, dispute resolution, legal responsibility, supervision, and inspection. There is no national minimum wage. Rather, the Labor Law allows local governments to determine their own standards on minimum wages. In general, minimum wage level determinations are higher than the local poverty relief ceiling but lower than the current wage level of the average worker.

In December the monthly minimum wage in Beijing was raised to $32.50 (RMB 270) from $29. In the Shenzhen and Zhuhai SEZ's in south China, the monthly minimum wage was approximately $48 (RMB 398). Minimum wage levels were raised in 12 provinces in December. Although these wage levels may be slightly greater than average living expenditures according to some official statistics, they would provide only a very basic standard of living for a worker and family. Minimum wage figures do not, however, include free or heavily subsidized benefits that some state-sector employers may provide in kind, such as housing, medical care, and education. In poorer, rural areas monthly minimum wage levels are as low as $14 (RMB 120). Official government estimates put the number of people living in absolute poverty at 65 million; other estimates range to 350 million.

China reduced the national standard workweek in May 1995 from 44 hours to 40 hours, excluding overtime. The Labor Law mandates a 24-hour rest period weekly and does not allow overtime work in excess of 3 hours a day or 36 hours a month. It also sets forth a required scale of remuneration for overtime work. Enforcement of regulations regarding overtime work varies according to region and type of enterprise. The official press regularly reports cases of workers forced to work long overtime hours at small-scale foreign investment enterprises, particularly in southern China and the SEZ's. Abuses at private enterprises are sometimes also given coverage.

Occupational health and safety are constant themes of posters and campaigns. Every work unit must designate a health and safety officer, and the ILO has established a training program for these officials. Although the 1982 Constitution does not provide for the right to strike, the Trade Union Law explicitly recognizes the right of unions to "suggest that staff and workers withdraw from sites of danger" and participate in accident investigations. It is unclear, however, to what extent workers can actually remove themselves from such dangerous situations without risking loss of employment.

Pressures for increased output, lack of financial resources to maintain equipment, lack of concern by management, and a traditionally poor understanding of safety issues by workers have contributed to a continuing high rate of accidents. According to one official survey, 18,160 people died, and 6,005 people were injured in 1995 due to work-related accidents, a decrease from 1994. Over 10,000 of the deaths occurred as a result of mine accidents. According to the Ministry of Public Health, over 75 million workers are at risk from occupational respiratory diseases such as pneumoconiosis due to poor working conditions. Less than half of rural enterprises meet national dust and poison standards. Many factories using harmful products, such as asbestos, fail not only to protect their workers against the ill effects of such products, but also fail to inform them about the potential hazards.

Poor enforcement by local officials of occupational safety and health regulations continues to put the lives of workers at risk. Work safety issues have, however, attracted the attention of senior government leaders. In August the National People's Congress sent seven inspection teams to various provinces to investigate poor enforcement of work safety standards and other labor abuses. The Ministry of Labor is also trying to draft a more rigorous national system of occupational health and safety standards. It is unlikely, however, that supervision of small-scale private and township and village enterprises, where many accidents occur, will improve substantially in the near future.

TIBET

(This section of the report on China has been prepared pursuant to Section 536 (b) of Public Law 103–236. The United States recognizes the Tibet Autonomous Region—hereinafter referred to as "Tibet"—to be part of the People's Republic of China. Preservation and development of Tibet's unique religious, cultural and linguistic heritage and protection of its people's fundamental human rights continue to be of concern.)

Respect for the Integrity of the Person.—Because the Chinese Government strictly controls access to and information about Tibet, the scope of human rights abuses cannot be precisely determined. However, according to credible reports, during 1996 Chinese government authorities continued to commit widespread human rights abuses in Tibet, including instances of death in detention, torture, arbitrary arrest, detention without public trial, long detention of Tibetan nationalists for peacefully expressing their religious and political views, and intensified controls on religion and on freedom of speech and the press, particularly for ethnic Tibetans.

The authorities permit many traditional religious practices. Those seen as a vehicle for political dissent, however, are not tolerated and are promptly and forcibly suppressed. Individuals accused of political activism faced increased persecution during the year, as the Government moved to limit the power of religious persons and secular leaders who openly sympathized with the Dalai Lama. In February the Government issued orders to close all politically active monasteries, and during the year authorities increased repression, imprisonment, and abuse or torture of monks and nuns accused of political activism. According to authoritative Chinese press reports, in May Beijing launched a campaign to "limit criminal activity in the guise of religious practice." The crackdown appears to have three goals: To stop acts of defiance, to break the political power wielded by lamas, and to remove officials loyal to the Dalai Lama.

There have been reports of bomb blasts in Lhasa. There is no information about casualties. Chinese officials claim Tibetan separatist groups are responsible for the bombings, which they characterize as "terrorist acts." However, no group has claimed responsibility.

During 1996 small-scale protests occurred at the Ganden, Sera, Drepung, Jokhang, and Tashilhunpo monasteries, resulting in swift detention for many participants. In April the Government banned photographs of the Dalai Lama in monasteries and private homes, extending and widening a 1994 prohibition on the sale of the Dalai Lama's photograph in shops and on officials displaying his photograph in their homes or offices. Police reportedly conducted house-to-house searches to enforce the ban. This ban prompted some of the protests in monasteries. In May and June, approximately 90 monks openly sympathetic to the Dalai Lama protested and were detained at Lhasa's Ganden monastery. During a May incident at Ganden, security personnel reportedly shot three monks. One of the monks, 40-year-old Kelsang Nyendrak, reportedly died of a bullet wound. According to press reports, a Chinese official admitted that monks were arrested but denied the murder.

Legal safeguards for ethnic Tibetans detained or imprisoned mirror those in the rest of China and are inadequate in design and implementation. Lack of independent outside access to prisoners or prisons makes it difficult to assess the extent and severity of abuses and the number of Tibetan prisoners.

International human rights organizations reported that a 49-year-old Tibetan monk, Kelsang Thutob, died in July at Drapchi prison in Lhasa. He was reportedly imprisoned in 1989 and sentenced to 18 years for forming a prodemocracy group and distributing antigovernment material that included a Tibetan translation of the Universal Declaration of Human Rights. The monk reportedly suffered from high blood pressure and other ailments but received no medical care. Tibetan exile sources reported that a 19-year-old monk, Sangye Tenphel, also died in Drapchi as a result of beatings by prison guards. In September Tenchok Tenphel, a 27-year-old monk, died in Sakya detention center, 2 weeks after being detained during a ritual dance performance, according to an NGO report. Chinese officials claimed the death was suicide, but, according to local sources, he died of abuse while in detention. His body reportedly was cremated before the family could view it, and no autopsy was performed. Yongdrung, a 27-year-old artist who specialized in painting portraits of the Dalai Lama was found in shock in Lhasa in October after having been released from 58 days in a detention center, where he was reportedly tortured. In July Ngawang Sandrol, who has been in jail since she was 15, reportedly had her sentence doubled for protesting a political reeducation campaign aimed at monks and nuns.

There were credible reports that Chinese authorities also detained foreigners visiting Tibet, searched them, and confiscated materials deemed politically sensitive. Ngawang Choephel, a 29-year-old Tibetan ethnomusicologist and former Fulbright scholar, was held in incommunicado detention in Tibet throughout 1996. He is believed to have been detained in Shigatse in August 1995 while making a film documentary about Tibetan performing arts. In December Ngawang Choephel was sentenced to 18 years in prison for "espionage" under the State Security Law. A New Zealand tourist was detained, interrogated, and forced to make a confession after sending a fax to New Zealand that included a reference to what he thought might be a bomb explosion in Lhasa.

Freedom of Religion.—The Government does not tolerate religious manifestations that advocate Tibetan independence. The Government condemns the Dalai Lama's political activities and his leadership of a "government in exile." The official press intensified the rhetoric against him and repeatedly described him as a "criminal" determined to "split" China. The Government sought to limit the Dalai Lama's international influence by threatening leaders of Britain, Germany, Australia, and other nations with serious diplomatic and economic consequences if they met with him during his visits to those countries. International leaders generally ignored China's threats and welcomed meetings with the Tibetan Buddhist religious leader and Nobel laureate.

Tibetan Buddhism and proindependence activism are closely associated in Tibet, and already tense relations between Buddhists and secular authorities worsened during the year in some areas, although nonpolitical forms of worship were tolerated. In May the Government reportedly began a campaign to "register" and "reeducate" dissident monks at Tibet's three main monasteries, Drepung, Sera, and Ganden. Hundreds of officials participated in the campaign, during which monks were forced to attend sessions on law, patriotism, and support for national unity and were coerced to sign statements criticizing the Dalai Lama. According to reports, some monks fled their places of worship and feigned illness to avoid attending the sessions, but the management committees of the involved monasteries imposed deadlines for participation forcing monks to cooperate or be stricken from the roles of the monastery.

Chinese officials claim that some 46,000 Buddhist monks and nuns live in approximately 1,400 Tibetan monasteries, and some travelers to Tibet have reported seeing increased numbers of monks and nuns. The Government, however, has moved to curb the proliferation of Tibetan Buddhist monasteries, which are seen as a drain on local resources and a conduit for political infiltration by the Tibetan exile community. In March 1995, the Government acknowledged that it strictly enforces limits on the number of monks in major monasteries. In April the Tibetan press reported that the Tibet Autonomous Region Religious Affairs Bureau had issued regulations that restricted leadership of management committees of temples to "patriotic and devoted monks and nuns." To bolster loyalty to the party, the Government stepped up efforts to ensure that party cadres in Tibet, over 70 percent of whom are ethnic Tibetans, adhere to the party's code of atheism.

In November the official Tibet Daily newspaper called for "large-scale" reform of religious policy. "Buddhism must conform to socialism, not socialism to Buddhism * * * Some people are seeking to expand the role and influence of religion, without recognizing its negative influence." The article published statistics that it said provided indications of the negative influence of religion on Tibet's economic development: There were 1,787 temples in Tibet at the beginning of 1996, "exceeding the number of towns and cities," while 46,000 monks and nuns "outnumbered middle school students." Temples compete for scarce resources hurting other areas, the article claimed. "We must adopt an offensive strategy to protect the paramount interests of the state. * * *"

The Government continues to oversee the daily operations of monasteries. Although the Government generally only contributes a small percentage of the monasteries' operational funds, it retains management control of the monasteries through the government-controlled democratic management committees and the local religious affairs bureaus.

The Government continued to insist that a boy it selected and enthroned in 1995 is the Panchen Lama's eleventh reincarnation. The boy appeared publicly on at least two occasions, including Chinese National Day in October. At all other times, he was held incommunicado by Chinese authorities. Meanwhile, the Government also detained the boy selected by the Dalai Lama as the Panchen Lama's reincarnation. The boy's family was also detained. The Government refused to provide access by unofficial observers to either of the boys or their families, whose exact locations were unknown. Tibetan monks have claimed that they were forced to sign statements pledging allegiance to the boy selected as the reincarnation of the Panchen Lama by the Government.

Buddhist sites, many of which were destroyed during the Cultural Revolution, continue to be restored. Despite government attempts to curb their proliferation, the monasteries continue to house and train young monks, making possible the transmission of Tibetan Buddhist traditions to future generations.

Economic Development and Protection of Cultural Heritage.—Like China's 54 other minority ethnic groups, Tibetans receive nominal preferential treatment in marriage policy, university admission, and employment. However, in practice, discrimination against Tibetans is widespread, especially in the area of employment. In addition, ethnic Han and Hui immigrants from other parts of China, encouraged by government policies and new opportunities are competing with—and in some cases displacing—Tibetan enterprises and labor. Overall, government development policies have helped raise the economic living standards of many ethnic Tibetans. However, rapid and ecologically inappropriate growth has also disrupted traditional living patterns and thereby threatened traditional Tibetan culture.

Chinese officials moved on several fronts to downgrade the use of Tibetan in education. According to NGO reports Tibet University dropped its Tibetan language entrance requirement and switched to Chinese to teach a course in Tibetan history in the Tibetan Language Department. All but 1 of 17 courses there are now taught in Chinese, although the University was established in 1985 to increase the study of Tibetan language and culture in Tibetan. There was a suggestion late in the year to suspend entry of the 1997 freshman class entirely while new materials were developed and resume operation with a class to enter in 1998. Four highly successful experimental Tibetan language middle schools are being closed down or phased out. A new project has started to provide bilingual Chinese and Tibetan instruction from grade one on to increase children's fluency in Chinese.

Primary schools at the village level teach in Tibetan, but those usually have only two or three grades. Illiteracy levels are high—the current rate for all Tibetans is over 44 percent—and in some areas it reaches 80 percent. Approximately 70 percent of eligible children attend primary school, but most pupils end their formal education after graduating from village schools. Most of those who attend regional high schools continue to receive some of their education in Tibetan, but knowledge of Chinese is necessary to receive a higher education.

The Dalai Lama continued to express concern that development projects and other central government policies encourage a massive influx of Han Chinese into Tibet, which has the effect of overwhelming Tibet's traditional culture and diluting Tibetan demographic dominance. In recent years, freer movement of people throughout

China, government-sponsored development, and the prospect of economic opportunity in Tibet have led to a substantial increase in the non-Tibetan population (including China's Muslim Hui minority as well as Han Chinese) in Lhasa and other urban areas. Most of these migrants profess to be temporary residents, but small businesses run by ethnic Han and Hui peoples (mostly restaurants and retail shops) are becoming more numerous in or near some Tibetan towns and cities. In Lhasa roughly one-third of the population is Han Chinese; elsewhere, the Han percentage of the population is significantly lower. Chinese officials assert that 95 percent of Tibet's officially registered population is Tibetan, with Han and other ethnic groups making up the remainder. Ongoing economic development raises the prospect of the temporary or permanent transfer to Tibet of increased numbers of non-Tibetan technical personnel. Since 1994, 50 major investment projects have been completed at a cost of $400 million. An increased number of immigrants from China's large transient population is seeking to take advantage of new economic opportunities.

Economic development, fueled by central government subsidies, is modernizing parts of Tibetan society and changing traditional Tibetan ways of life. While the Government has made efforts in recent years to restore some of the physical structures and other aspects of Tibetan Buddhism and Tibetan culture damaged or destroyed during the Cultural Revolution, repressive social and political controls continue to limit the fundamental freedoms of ethnic Tibetans.

TAIWAN

With the popular election of President Lee Teng-hui in March, Taiwan completed its transition to an open, democratic system. Lee, who is also the chairman of the Nationalist Party (KMT), appoints the Premier, who heads the Executive Yuan (EY), or cabinet; the Legislative Yuan (LY) must confirm the appointment of the Premier. Current LY members were elected in a free and fair election in December 1995. While the ruling KMT remains the single most powerful political force, it enjoys only a two-vote LY majority, and two opposition parties play important roles in the LY. The Judicial Yuan (JY) is constitutionally independent of the other branches of the political system, but corruption and political influence remain serious problems.

The National Police Administration (NPA) of the Ministry of Interior (MOI), the NPA's Criminal Investigation Bureau, and the Ministry of Justice (MOJ) Investigation Bureau are responsible for law enforcement relating to internal security. The National Security Bureau and Ministry of National Defense military police units also play limited law enforcement roles. These police and security agencies are under effective civilian control. Some members of the defense and security forces committed a number of human rights abuses.

Taiwan has a dynamic, export-oriented, free-market economy. Liberalization of the economy has undercut the dominant role that state-owned and party-run enterprises played in such major sectors as finance, transportation, utilities, shipbuilding, steel, telecommunications, and petrochemicals. As the economy has evolved, services and capital- and technology-intensive industries have become the most important sectors. Major exports include computers, electronic equipment, machinery, and textiles. Citizens generally enjoy a high standard of living.

The authorities generally respect the human rights of citizens; however, occasional problems remain in some areas. Principal problems include police abuse of detainees; physical abuse of military personnel, which appears to be declining; political and personal pressures on the judiciary; some restrictions on freedom of assembly, and association; prison overcrowding; discrimination and violence against women; child prostitution and abuse; restrictions on workers' freedom of association and on their ability to strike.

RESPECT FOR HUMAN RIGHTS

Section 1. Respect for the Integrity of the Person, Including Freedom From:

a. *Political and Other Extrajudicial Killing.*—There were no reports of political or other extrajudicial killings. Ten jailers charged with the beating death of a prisoner in Chia-i County in September 1995 were convicted and sentenced to prison terms ranging from 8 months to 8½ years. The High Court has not yet ruled on the appeal of five policemen found guilty of the 1994 murder of a prisoner in Tainan.

b. *Disappearance.*—There were no reports of politically motivated disappearances.

c. *Torture and Other Cruel, Inhuman, or Degrading Treatment or Punishment.*—The Constitution does not directly address the issues of torture and punishment.

The Code of Criminal Conduct, however, stipulates that no violence, threat, inducement, fraud, or other improper means shall be used against accused persons. There were credible reports that police occasionally physically abused persons in their custody. The law allows suspects to have attorneys present during interrogations, primarily to ensure that abuse does not take place (see Section 1.d.). The MOJ says that each interrogation is recorded and that any allegation of mistreatment is investigated. Lawyers and legal scholars note that abuses most often occur in local police stations where interrogations are not recorded and when attorneys are not present. Informed observers note that police forces are weak in scientific investigative skills, so that when political leaders demand that cases be solved, there is great pressure on the police to coerce confessions. International observers have also noted that the judicial system seems preoccupied with obtaining confessions, which are sometimes accepted by the legal system even when they contradict available physical evidence or logic. Detainees who are physically abused have the right to sue the police for torture, and confessions shown to have been obtained through torture are inadmissible in court proceedings. There were no such suits reported during the year.

The authorities made efforts to investigate, prosecute, and punish officials responsible for torture and other mistreatment. Although the basic responsibility for investigating mistreatment lies with prosecutors, the Control Yuan (CY), a coequal branch of the political system which investigates official misconduct, also investigates such cases. Women's and children's rights groups also monitor police and judicial performance and periodically mount campaigns to correct abuses.

Although corporal punishment is forbidden under military law, there continued to be reports of physical abuse of military personnel. Following the beating death of a marine recruit in 1995, the CY began unannounced inspections of military facilities to question young servicemen regarding conditions of service in the military and allegations of abuse. The authorities also established a national telephone hot line to report alleged abuses within the military. The Ministry of National Defense has attributed some of the blame for abuse of recruits to a supposed softening of youth, which makes them incapable of accepting the rigors of combat training. However, the Ministry also has recognized that some trainers have used inappropriate methods to address these deficiencies. In order to standardize, rationalize, and make transparent the military basic training program, the Ministry appointed three professional researchers to design practical training and curriculums for all military personnel who have contact with new recruits. Recently, physical abuse of recruits appears to be diminishing. Pressure from parents of recruits and a program to retain recruits have also contributed to this apparent reduction.

Overcrowding at the 45 prisons and detention centers remained a problem despite some expansion of existing facilities and a 1994 Criminal Code amendment allowing prisoners to be paroled after serving one-third, rather than one-half, of their sentences. The 48,942 inmates detained as of July 1 exceeded the facilities' planned capacity by 9,886. According to the MOJ, the number of prisoners has grown rapidly in recent years because of increased arrests of narcotics law violators. These violators now make up more than 50 percent of the overall inmate population. The MOJ has set up drug treatment facilities to reduce the number of addicts in the prison population. Conditions in illegal immigrant detention centers are poor (see Section 2.d.).

The authorities permit prison visits by human rights monitors, and the China Human Rights Association has made prison visits.

d. *Arbitrary Arrest, Detention, or Exile.*—The law prohibits arbitrary arrest, detention, or exile, and the authorities generally observe this prohibition. Police may legally arrest without a warrant anyone they suspect of committing a crime for which the punishment would be imprisonment of 5 years or more and may question persons without a formal summons. However, the authorities must, within 24 hours after detention, give written notice to the detainee or a designated relative or friend, stating the reason for the arrest or questioning. Indicted persons may be released on bail at judicial discretion.

The Criminal Procedure Code specifies that the authorities may detain a suspect for up to 2 months during the investigative phase before filing a formal indictment. The prosecutor's office may extend the investigative detention for an additional 2-month period. A suspect may be held for up to 3 months during trial proceedings, and the court may extend the trial detention for two additional 3-month periods. The authorities generally have followed these procedures, and trials usually take place within 3 months of indictment.

The authorities generally respect a detainee's request to have a lawyer present during the investigation phase, but defense lawyers continue to complain that people often are not advised of their right to have legal representation during police interrogation. While there is no legal requirement that the police advise suspects of their right to counsel, arresting officers' checklists do provide for such notification. There is no legal requirement that indigent people be provided counsel during police interrogation, although such counsel is provided during trials.

The "Antihoodlum" Law of 1985 was a departure from international standards of due process in that it included a secret witness system that allowed police to conduct "sweeps" of suspected "hoodlums" and to use the testimony of unidentified informants in detaining the suspects. Lawyers for the alleged hoodlums were not permitted to cross-examine these informants. While defense lawyers have been given the right to examine documentary evidence, critics charge that evidence in these cases was often weak or fabricated. In 1995, however, the Council of Grand Justices (CGJ) declared unconstitutional the administrative procedures that had been used to sentence hoodlums to reformatory education. The authorities have drafted new antigang legislation, which was passed by the LY on December 30.

The authorities do not use forced exile.

e. *Denial of Fair Public Trial.*—The Constitution provides for an independent judiciary and for equality before the law. In the past, some observers have characterized the judiciary as not fully independent and as susceptible to political and personal pressure and influence.

Dissatisfaction exists among judges and others about the slowness of strengthening the rule of law. Corruption within the judiciary remains a problem. During the year, there were a number of indictments of judges for accepting bribes in exchange for favorable judgments. A number of judges have called for significant reforms, such as an end to the process of automatic review by senior judges of decisions by junior judges.

The Judicial Yuan is one of the five coequal branches of the political system. The JY is headed by a president and a vice president and also contains the 16-member CGJ, which interprets the Constitution as well as laws and ordinances. Subordinate JY organs include the Supreme Court, high courts, district courts, the Administrative Court, and the Committee on the Discipline of Public Functionaries.

The law provides for the right of fair public trial, and this is generally respected in practice. Judges, rather than juries, decide trials, and all judges are appointed by, and responsible to, the JY. In a typical court case, parties and witnesses are interrogated by a single judge but not directly by a defense attorney or prosecutor. The judge may decline to hear witnesses or to consider evidence a party wishes to submit if the judge considers it irrelevant; refusal to hear evidence may be a factor in an appeal. Trials are public, but attendance at trials involving juveniles or potentially sensitive issues that might attract crowds may require court permission. In addition, as the result of a CGJ ruling, judges will have the sole authority, once implementing legislation has been passed by the LY, to order pretrial detention of suspects, a power now shared by prosecutors. Such implementing legislation had not been passed by year's end.

A defendant has the right to an attorney. If the defendant is suspected of committing a crime for which the penalty is 3 or more years' imprisonment, or if the defendant is disabled or elderly, the judge may assign an attorney. Criminal law specifically provides the defendant with protection from self-incrimination. Persons convicted in cases in which the sentence exceeds 3 years have the right to appeal to a high court and to the Supreme Court. The Supreme Court automatically reviews life imprisonment and death sentences. Under the law, prosecutors have the right to appeal verdicts of not guilty.

There were no reports of political prisoners.

f. *Arbitrary Interference with Privacy, Family, Home, or Correspondence.*—The Constitution and sections of the Criminal and Civil Codes contain provisions protecting privacy. A warrant, issued by a prosecutor or a judge, must be obtained before a search, except when "incidental to arrest." Critics, however, claim that the incidental to arrest provision is not only unconstitutional but often interpreted broadly by police to justify searches of locations other than actual arrest sites. Moreover, police continue to search cars routinely at roadblocks. According to the National Police Administration, warrantless searches are allowed only in special circumstances, such as to arrest an escapee or if facts indicate a person is in the process of committing a crime. In any such case, the police must file a report with the prosecutor or court within 24 hours. Evidence collected without a warrant is not excluded from introduction during a trial; however, a policeman who carries out an illegal search may be sued for illegal entry and sentenced to up to 1 year's imprisonment.

According to Executive Yuan regulations, judicial and security authorities may file a written request to a prosecutor's office to monitor telephone calls to collect evidence against a suspect involved in a major crime.

Section 2. Respect for Civil Liberties, Including:

a. *Freedom of Speech and Press.*—The Constitution provides for freedom of speech and of the press, and the authorities generally respect these rights in practice. However, these rights are formally circumscribed by a statute prohibiting advocacy of communism or division of national territory; these provisions are not enforced in practice.

While print media represent the full spectrum of views within Taiwan society, residual political influence still exists over the electronic media, particularly television stations, as the KMT, the Taiwan Provincial Government, and the military continue to be the largest shareholders in the three island-wide broadcast television stations. Although considerable progress has been made toward loosening KMT control of the broadcast media, some critics still claim that coverage has been biased in favor of the KMT and against opposition parties. The planned fourth island-wide broadcast television station, to be based in Kaohsiung, is associated with the largest opposition party, the Democratic Progressive Party (DPP). The opening of this station would eliminate the KMT's monopoly on broadcast television, and represent a significant move toward more complete media independence. Experts expect, however, that due to lack of funds it might take some time for this new network to begin operation. In any event, the proliferation of cable television stations, some of which carry programming openly hostile to the ruling party, has greatly diminished the importance of KMT control over the three established stations. Over 70 percent of households receive cable television, which includes local, privately financed channels as well as many major international networks. Several mainland China and Japanese channels are also widely carried on cable.

Controls over radio stations were more limited than those over television stations and are being further liberalized. Until recently more than three-fourths of the 33 authorized radio frequencies were held by the authorities, the KMT, and other noncommercial entities. Past refusals to approve new television and radio stations led to the establishment of "underground" cable television and radio operations. In 1996 the authorities continued a multiyear process, started in 1993, to loosen controls using a five-stage licensing procedure for new radio stations. From 1993 to April 1996, the Government Information Office (GIO) received 529 applications. A total of 169 frequencies were made available and 107 of these were apportioned and construction permits granted. The new radio stations have limited broadcast ranges, however, leading critics to charge that the stations do not constitute a genuine counterweight to the authorities' monopoly on island-wide broadcasting.

Several underground radio stations associated with opposition parties remain unlicensed. Observers have noted that licensing requirements oblige prospective radio station owners to have more capital than is required to actually operate a station. This in itself inhibits individuals or groups from applying for radio station licenses.

In 1992 the authorities revised sedition statutes to limit the purview of the Sedition Law and the National Security Law (NSL) and to remove prohibitions on "actions against the Constitution." However, the NSL and related statutes such as the Civic Organizations Law and the Parade and Assembly Law still retain prohibitions against advocating communism or espousing the division of national territory, even though these provisions are not enforced in practice.

There is a vigorous and active free press despite the Publications Law, which empowers the police to seize or ban printed material that is seditious, treasonous, sacrilegious, interferes with the lawful exercise of public functions, or violates public order or morals. There were no reports of censorship of the print media during the year nor were there any seizures of materials on political grounds. The police do sometimes conduct raids to seize pornographic materials.

The GIO has demanded that any publications imported from mainland China be sent to the GIO publications department for screening before sale or publication in Taiwan. The GIO still seeks to ban the importation of publications that advocate communism or the establishment of united front organizations, endanger public order or good morals, or violate regulations or laws. However, few local publishing companies observe this regulation, and substantial People's Republic of China-origin material is imported every year. Moreover, cable television systems broadcast uncensored television channels from mainland China.

Among other restrictions regulating the media are those precluding people previously convicted of sedition from owning, managing, or working in television and radio stations. Major opposition leaders, many of whom were convicted of sedition after the December 1979 Kaohsiung incident, are nevertheless not affected because their rights were restored through presidential amnesties.

There are few restrictions on academic freedom. The expression of dissenting political views is common.

b. *Freedom of Peaceful Assembly and Association.*—The Constitution provides for freedom of assembly and association, but the authorities restrict these rights somewhat in practice. The Parade and Assembly Law permits peaceful demonstrations as long as they do not promote communism or advocate Taiwan's separation from mainland China and are approved in advance by the authorities. In practice the authorities do not interfere with demonstrators advocating independence for Taiwan. The authorities indicted a telecommunications union leader, Chang Shi-chung, under the Parade and Assembly Law as a result of a peaceful demonstration, which authorities charged was excessively noisy, held outside the Legislative Yuan in January (see Section 6.a.). Two Aborigine demonstrators were prosecuted under the law for an unauthorized demonstration in 1995, and prosecution continues of four senior leaders of the opposition DPP for leading unauthorized demonstrations in 1992.

The Civic Organization Law requires all civic organizations to register; however, the authorities have refused to approve registration of some groups—such as the Taiwan Association for Human Rights (TAHR), the Taiwan Association of University Professors, and the Taiwan Environmental Protection Alliance—which use the word "Taiwan" in their titles (a usage that is regarded by the authorities as promoting Taiwan independence). The lack of registration entails some inconvenience to the operations of these groups. For example, they may not solicit donations from the public and contributors may not take income tax deductions for their contributions. Nonetheless, they operate actively, freely, and effectively.

A 1992 revision of the Civic Organization Law removed from the Executive Yuan the power to dissolve political parties. This power now resides in the Constitutional Court. Grounds for dissolution include objectives or actions that are deemed to jeopardize the existence of the "Republic of China." The Constitutional Court heard no cases under this law in 1996.

c. *Freedom of Religion.*—The Constitution provides for freedom of religion, and the authorities respect this right in practice.

d. *Freedom of Movement Within the Country, Foreign Travel, Emigration, and Repatriation.*—The authorities do not restrict freedom of internal travel. Foreign travel by Taiwan passport holders is common.

Nonresident Taiwan passport holders are usually issued "overseas Chinese" passports and require entry permits to travel to Taiwan. According to 1992 revisions to the National Security Law, entry permits may be refused only if there are facts sufficient to create a strong suspicion that a person is engaged in terrorism or violence. Reasons for entry and exit refusals must be given, and appeals may be made to a special board. No exit or entry permit refusals were reported during 1996.

Since 1988 Taiwan has substantially relaxed strictures against travel by Taiwan residents to the Chinese mainland, and such travel is common. In 1993 new measures provided that holders of Taiwan passports who normally reside abroad may return and regain their household registration, a document required to vote or participate as a candidate in an election. Relatively tight restrictions on the entry of Chinese from the mainland remain in force.

There is no law under which noncitizens may ask for asylum, and there were no applications for refugee status in 1996. While the authorities have been reluctant to return to the mainland those who might suffer political persecution there, they regularly deport to the mainland, under provisions of the Mainland Relations Act, those mainlanders who illegally enter the island for economic reasons. There were no reports of forced return of persons to a country where they feared persecution.

Conditions at detention camps for illegal immigrants (most from mainland China) continued to be criticized by local media. The Entry and Exit Bureau admitted that the three detention camps are overcrowded but blamed mainland Chinese authorities, who insist on extensive background checks, for delays in accepting the timely repatriation of illegal immigrants.

Section 3. Respect for Political Rights: The Right of Citizens to Change Their Government

During the year, Taiwan for the first time carried out the direct, popular election of its president, thus completing its transition to a democratic, multiparty political system. The transition began with the lifting of martial law in 1987. After generally free and fair popular elections for the LY in 1992, the second direct election of all LY members took place in December 1995. Previously, the President and Vice President had been indirectly elected by the National Assembly (NA), which now stands for popular election every 4 years and is charged mainly with amending the Constitution.

The KMT remains the largest political party, with 2 million members, although voters gave it only a slim majority in the December 1995 elections for the LY. The KMT has 85 seats in the 164-member LY. The Democratic Progressive Party, which advocates independence for Taiwan, holds 54 seats. The DPP also holds 7 of 23 mayor and county magistrate posts, including mayor of Taipei and the magistrate of Taipei County, and has an estimated 70,000 members. The New Party was established in 1993 by younger KMT members who opposed the party's domination by "mainstream" ethnic Taiwanese supporters of President and party chairman Lee Teng-hui. The New Party holds 21 seats in the LY and claims a membership of 86,000.

The KMT benefits from its ownership of the major television channels and of enterprises and business holdings estimated to be worth in excess of $6 billion, and from the fact that its members still hold most key positions in the political system, sometimes concurrently with important party positions. In recent years, opposition parties have grown rapidly, however, and freely contest elections, criticize the authorities, and influence national policy through the legislative process. In 1994 a member of the DPP was elected mayor of Taipei, a position that makes him a member of the Cabinet.

The Constitution provides for equal rights for women, but their role in politics, while increasing, remains limited. Nevertheless, a number of women hold senior administrative and KMT positions, including National Health Administration Director General Dr. Chang Po-ya, Minister without Portfolio and KMT Central Standing Committee (CSC) member Shirley Kuo (a former Finance Minister), CSC member Hou Tsai-feng, and one major general in the armed forces. In addition, 23 of 164 LY members, 61 of 334 National Assembly members, 16 of 79 Provincial Assembly members, 2 of 26 Control Yuan members, and 255 of 1,300 judges are women.

Aborigine representatives participate in most levels of the political system, partially through 6 reserved seats in the NA and LY and 2 seats in the Provincial Assembly—half of each elected by the plains Aborigines and half by mountain Aborigines. An Aborigine serves as Chief of the Ministry of Interior's Aborigine Affairs Section. The magistrate of Taitung county is an Aborigine elected in 1993.

Section 4. Governmental Attitude Regarding International and Nongovernmental Investigation of Alleged Violations of Human Rights

The principal human rights organizations are the establishment-oriented Chinese Association of Human Rights (CAHR) and the opposition-aligned Taiwan Association for Human Rights (TAHR). Coordination between the two bodies is limited. Despite the authorities' refusal to register it (see Section 2.b.), the TAHR continues to operate freely. Both organizations investigate human rights complaints, many of which come to public attention through the media and statements by lawmakers from all political parties. The authorities permit representatives of international human rights organizations to visit and meet with citizens freely.

Section 5. Discrimination Based on Race, Sex, Religion, Disability, Language, or Social Status

The Constitution provides for equality of citizens before the law "irrespective of sex, religion, race, class, or party affiliation." Other laws provide for the rights of disabled persons. While the authorities are committed to protecting these rights, some areas of discrimination continue to exist.

Women.—Domestic violence, especially wife beating, is a serious problem. According to a 1994 survey by the Taiwan Provincial Social Affairs Department, 17.8 percent of married women had been beaten by their husbands. The DPP Women's Development Committee said that other statistics showed that 35 percent of married women were victims of spousal abuse. According to the law, a prosecutor may not investigate domestic violence cases until a spouse files a formal lawsuit. Although some cases are prosecuted, strong social pressure discourages abused women from reporting incidents to the police in order to avoid disgracing their families. Rape also remains a serious problem, and its victims are socially stigmatized. One expert believes that only 10 percent of the estimated 7,000 rapes occurring annually are reported to the police. Because rape trials are public, women have been reluctant to prosecute their attackers. Support from feminist and social welfare organizations, however, has made victims more willing to come forward and press charges. Under the law, the authorities may not prosecute for rape without the victim's complaint. The Criminal Code establishes the punishment for rape as not less than 5 years' imprisonment, and those convicted are usually sentenced to from 5 to 10 years in prison.

Prostitution, including coerced prostitution and child prostitution, is also a problem although there is little public concern about adult prostitution. When the police discover illegal prostitution, the cases are prosecuted according to the Criminal Code. However, under the "prostitute management regulations," prostitution is legal in registered houses of prostitution in specified urban areas, mainly in Taipei and Kaohsiung.

The law prohibits sex discrimination, and the LY has in recent years begun a systematic review and revision of those portions of the Legal Code relating to divorce, property, and child custody. As a result, recent legislation has eliminated many discriminatory sections of the code. In 1994 the CGJ declared unconstitutional a Civil Code provision dating back to the 1930's that gave fathers priority in child custody disputes. In September the LY passed bills eliminating the assumption that custody would go to the father and providing for equal distribution of assets in divorce cases.

There is no equal employment rights law, and enforcement of existing sex discrimination laws remains a problem. Labor laws provide for maternity leave, but employers do not always grant it. Women also have complained of being forced to quit jobs upon marriage or because of age or pregnancy. Women often complain of less frequent promotions and lower salaries than their male counterparts. According to the Council on Labor Affairs, salaries for women average 85 percent of those of men performing roughly equal jobs.

In the past, many women married to foreigners claimed that their husbands had a more difficult time obtaining residency than the foreign wives of Taiwan citizens. They also complained that their children were not allowed to enter public schools. In 1995 the Ministry of Foreign Affairs announced a relaxation of the regulations governing foreign husbands' residence permits that allows the foreign husbands of citizens to remain in Taiwan for 6 months at a time rather than the shorter periods granted previously. The LY also passed new legislation permitting the children of foreign fathers to attend public schools. However, the Citizenship Law continues to stipulate that the transmission of citizenship may occur exclusively through the father. A Taiwan mother with a foreign husband thus cannot apply for a Taiwan passport for her child.

Children.—The Constitution has provisions to protect children's rights, and the authorities are committed to supporting them. Education for children between 6 and 15 years of age is compulsory and enforced. The Constitution provides that spending on education shall be no less than 15 percent of the central budget, 25 percent of the provincial and special municipality budgets, and 35 percent of the county and city budgets.

Child abuse is a significant problem. The 1993 revision of the Child Welfare Act mandates that any persons discovering cases of child abuse or neglect must notify the police, social welfare, or child welfare authorities, that child welfare specialists must do so within 24 hours, and that the authorities involved must issue an investigation report within 24 hours. Both the Ministry of Interior Social Affairs Department and private organization specialists assert that these requirements are followed.

Child prostitution is a serious problem involving between 40,000 and 60,000 children, an estimated 5 percent of whom are Aborigines, according to reports by police and social workers. Most child prostitutes range from 12 through 16 years of age. The Juvenile Welfare Law enables juvenile welfare bodies, prosecutors, and victims to apply to courts for termination of guardianship of parents and the appointment of qualified guardians if parents have forced their children into prostitution. If children are engaged in prostitution of their own free will, and the parents are incapable of providing safe custody, the courts may order competent authorities to provide counseling for not less than 6 months and not more than 2 years. However, legal loopholes and cultural barriers remain obstacles to enforcement. For example, if both parents have sold a child into prostitution, a problem associated mostly with Aborigine families, the law requires the child to lodge a complaint before prosecution is undertaken. In many cases, the child is reluctant or afraid to do so.

According to some reports, violence, drug addiction, and other forms of coercion are used by brothel owners to prevent child prostitutes from escaping. In 1995 the LY passed legislation providing for as much as 2 years' incarceration for customers of any prostitute who is under the age of 18. The legislation also requires the publication of the names of violators in newspapers. At year's end several hundred cases were being prosecuted under that law, although only a handful of convictions had been obtained.

People With Disabilities.—The Disabled Welfare Law was revised and strengthened in 1990. It prohibits discrimination against the disabled and sets minimum fines at approximately $2,400 for violators. Under these revisions, new public buildings, facilities, and transportation equipment must be accessible to the disabled, while existing public buildings were to be brought into conformity by 1995. Although new buildings appear to meet many accessibility requirements, there does not as yet appear to be substantial effort aimed at refitting older buildings to accommodate disabled people.

A leading expert in the field estimates that the number of disabled is between 400,000 and 500,000—possibly as high as 700,000. One-third of the total are severely disabled and receive shelter or nursing care from the authorities. The Disabled Welfare Law requires large public and private organizations to hire disabled persons, 2 and 1 percent of their work forces respectively. Organizations failing to do so must pay, for each disabled person not hired, the basic monthly salary (approximately $570) into the Disabled Welfare Fund, which supports institutions involved in welfare for the disabled. Many organizations complain that it is difficult to find qualified disabled workers and appear to prefer to pay the fines involved. The authorities have noted the impact of a traditional belief that the disabled lack the ability to do real work. During the year, several disabled students received extraordinarily high scores on the university entrance examinations. This performance was well publicized and may serve to lessen the negative impression many residents have of disabled people.

Indigenous People.—Taiwan's only non-Chinese minority group consists of the Aboriginal descendants of Malayo-Polynesians already established in Taiwan when the first Chinese settlers arrived. According to MOI statistics, there are 357,000 Aborigines. More than 70 percent are Christian while the dominant Han Chinese group is largely Buddhist or Taoist. The civil and political rights of Aborigines are fully protected under law. The National Assembly amended the Constitution in 1992 to upgrade the status of Aboriginal people, protect their right of political participation, and ensure cultural, educational, and business development. In addition, the authorities have instituted social programs to help the Aborigines assimilate into the dominant Chinese society. As part of its efforts to preserve ethnic identities, the Ministry of Education now includes some Aboriginal-language classes in primary schools.

Although they face no official discrimination, Aborigines have had little impact, over the years, on major decisions affecting their lands, culture, traditions, and the allocation of their natural resources. In addition, they complain that they are prevented from owning ancestral lands in mountain areas under the authorities' control, some of which have been designated as national parks or conservation areas. According to MOI statistics, only about 50 percent of Aborigine children complete elementary school. Researchers have found alcoholism to be a significant problem among the Aborigines, with alcohol addiction rates exceeding 40 percent among adult members of three of the nine major tribes. In the past, Aborigines were not allowed to use non-Chinese personal names on legal documents, but this was changed by legislation in 1996.

The sale of Aboriginal girls into prostitution by their parents is a serious social problem (see Children above). However, recent reports have indicated that in the period from June 1994 to July 1995, the percentage of all arrested child prostitutes who were of Aboriginal origin dropped from 15 percent to 5 percent. This reduction may have come about due to intensive efforts on the part of social workers and nongovernment organizations to combat the practice of selling female children into prostitution.

Section 6. Worker Rights

a. *The Right of Association.*—In 1995 the Judicial Yuan decided that the right to organize trade unions is protected by the Constitution. But, until new legislation implementing this decision is passed, teachers, civil servants, and defense industry workers are still not permitted to form labor unions. Even with this ruling, there are a number of laws and regulations limiting the right of association. Labor unions may draw up their own rules and constitutions, but they must submit these to the authorities for review. Unions may be dissolved if they do not meet certification requirements or if their activities disturb public order. However, there were no instances of the authorities dissolving local labor groups or denying new unions certification.

The Labor Union Law requires that union leaders be elected regularly by secret ballot, and, in recent years, workers have sometimes rejected KMT- or management-endorsed union slates.

Unions may form confederations, but no administrative district, including a city, county, or province, can have competing labor confederations. There is only one Taiwan-wide labor federation, the Chinese Federation of Labor (CFL) which is closely associated with the ruling KMT. The Chairman of the Council of Labor Affairs (CLA—equivalent to a ministry of labor but not a cabinet department) was formerly head of the CFL. Ho Tsai-fong, a standing member of the CFL's board of directors, is also a member of the KMT's Central Standing Committee.

The restriction on island-wide unions was challenged in 1994 when 12 unions from state-run enterprises announced that they would withdraw from the CFL and establish a new national federation of labor unions of state-run enterprises. The CLA turned down their application, as well as the appeal of that rejection. In the meantime, the trade unions have retained their seats in the CFL. In general, the drive for independent labor unions has lost momentum in recent years due to the extremely low unemployment rates, higher wages, the shift from manufacturing to service industries, the small scale and poor organization of most unions, and prosecution of labor activists by the authorities in the past. Chang Shi-chung, leader of an independent group under the Union of the Telecommunications Industry, was charged under the Parade and Assembly Law for protesting a revision of the Telecommunications Law in January (see Section 2.b.).

The law governing labor disputes recognizes the right of unions to strike but imposes restrictions that make legal strikes difficult and seriously weaken collective bargaining. For example, the authorities require mediation of labor/management disputes when they deem the disputes to be sufficiently serious or to involve "unfair practices." The law forbids both labor and management from disrupting the "working order" when either mediation or arbitration is in progress. The law mandates stiff penalties for violations of no-strike/no-retaliation clauses. Employers in the past sometimes ignored the law and dismissed or locked out workers without any legal action being taken againt them, although there were no such cases reported in 1996. The CLA reported that from 1990 to August 1995, there were 31 strikes, of which 22 involved workers at bus companies asking for increased pay and reduced hours. There were no strikes recorded in 1996.

Taiwan was expelled from the International Labor Organization in 1971 when the People's Republic of China replaced it in the United Nations. The CFL is affiliated with the International Confederation of Free Trade Unions.

b. *The Right to Organize and Bargain Collectively.*—Except for the categories of workers noted in Section 6.a., the Labor Union Law and the Settlement of Labor Disputes Law give workers the right to organize and bargain collectively. As of March, some 3.1 million workers, approximately 33.5 percent of Taiwan's 9.2-million person labor force, belonged to 3,763 registered labor unions.

Under the Labor Union Law, employers may not refuse employment to, dismiss, or otherwise unfairly treat workers because they are union members. In practice, however, union leaders have sometimes been dismissed without reasonable cause by employers, and observers point out that the law sets no specific penalties for violations. According to the illegal National Federation of Independent Trade Unionists, a federation of 20 legal unions with a combined total of 4,000 members, about 400 trade unionists and supporters have been fired since Taiwan's labor movement began to expand after the 1987 lifting of martial law.

The Collective Agreements Law provides for collective bargaining but does not make it mandatory. Since such agreements are made only in large-scale enterprises, and less than 5 percent of Taiwan's enterprises fall into this category, the proportion of workers covered remains small. Employers set wages generally in accordance with market conditions.

Firms in export processing zones are subject to the same laws regarding treatment of labor unions as other firms and follow normal practices including collective bargaining agreements with their unions.

c. *Prohibition of Forced or Compulsory Labor.*—The Labor Standards Law prohibits forced or compulsory labor. There were no reports of these practices.

d. *Minimum Age for Employment of Children.*—The Labor Standards Law stipulates age 15, after compulsory education required by law ends, as the minimum age for employment. County and city labor bureaus enforce minimum age laws.

e. *Acceptable Conditions of Work.*—The Labor Standards Law (LSL) mandates labor standards. According to the CLA, the law covers 3.5 million of Taiwan's 6.3 million salaried workers. The law is not well enforced in areas such as overtime work and pay or retirement payments.

The Executive Yuan approved a raise in the minimum wage of 3.23 percent to about $570 (NT$ 15,360) per month effective September 1. While sufficient in cheaper areas, this is less than what is needed to assure a decent standard of living for a worker and family in metropolitan areas such as Taipei. However, the average manufacturing wage is more than double the legal minimum wage, and the average for service industry employees is even higher. The law limits the workweek to 48 hours (8 hours per day, 6 days per week) and requires 1 day off in every 7 days.

The 1991 Revised Occupational Safety and Health Law enlarged coverage to include workers in agriculture, fishing, and forestry industries and appeared to strengthen penalties for safety violations. It nevertheless still provides only minimal standards for working conditions and health and safety precautions. The Occupational Safety and Health Law gives workers the right to remove themselves from dangerous work situations without jeopardy to continued employment. Some critics, however, see the law as a step backward; for example, they note that, under the revised law, general contractors are not responsible for the safety of those working for subcontractors.

The 1993 Labor Inspection Law was designed to strengthen the enforcement of labor standards and health and safety regulations. It increased the number of enterprises and types of safety issues to be inspected; gave inspectors quasi-judicial powers; required preexamination of dangerous working places such as naphtha-cracking plants, pesticide factories, and firecracker factories; and raised penalties for violations. Critics allege that the CLA does not effectively enforce workplace laws and regulations because it employs too few inspectors. There are slightly over 200 inspectors for the approximately 300,000 enterprises covered by the Occupational Safety and Health Law. Because the new law expanded coverage to include more enterprises, the inspection rate actually declined. Since many enterprises are small, family-owned operations employing relatives unlikely to report violations, actual adherence to the hours, wage, and safety sections of various labor laws is hard to document but is thought to be minimal in these smaller enterprises.

Because of Taiwan's acute labor shortage, there has been a legal influx of foreign workers in the last several years. The law stipulates that foreign workers who are employed legally receive the same protection as local workers. However, authorities say that in many cases illegal foreign workers, many from Thailand and the Philippines, receive board and lodging from their employers, but no medical coverage, accident insurance, or other benefits enjoyed by citizens. In addition, observers say that conditions in many small and medium-sized factories that employ illegal foreign labor are dangerous, due to old and poorly maintained equipment. Illegal foreign workers remain vulnerable to exploitation, including confiscation of passports, imposition of involuntary deductions from wages, and extension of working hours without overtime pay. There are also occasional reports of mistreatment of legal foreign workers. According to available statistics, there are almost 230,000 legal foreign workers in Taiwan, including approximately 143,000 workers from Thailand and 72,000 workers from the Philippines. As the unemployment rate began to rise in mid-1996, reaching a decade-long high of 3.1 percent in August, the CLA has moved to impose stricter limits on the number of foreign workers entering Taiwan.

FIJI

Fiji's system of parliamentary government, inherited when the country gained independence from Great Britain in 1970, was interrupted in 1987 with the installation of a military-led regime following two bloodless coups. Fiji returned to elected government in 1992, and Prime Minister Sitiveni Rabuka was re-elected in 1994.

An independent, multiethnic Constitutional Review Commission presented its long-awaited report to the President in September. The 1990 Constitution reflected the proindigenous Fijian bias of the two coups; the Constitutional Review Commission's report proposes a more representative system. The report aims to encourage multiethnic government through heterogeneous electoral districts and a preferential voting scheme, while preserving ethnic Fijian veto power over legislation affecting interest in land or customs. The proposal, if approved, would be a major step toward an improved political and business climate.

Ethnicity plays a major role in Fiji's politics, economy, and society. Fiji's more than 775,000 people constitute a multiracial society in which indigenous Fijians and ethnic Indians, in roughly equal numbers, account for 96 percent of the population. The rest are Asian and Caucasian. Indo-Fijians dominate the commercial sector and professions and are well represented in the lower and middle levels of the Government. Ethnic Fijians control the bureaucracies and dominate the military.

The small but professional Fiji Military Forces (FMF) and a separate police force report to and are under the control of the Minister for Home Affairs and, ultimately, the President. The Constitutional Review Commission report recommends that the army's legal basis be legislative, not constitutional. In 1990 the Government established the Fiji Intelligence Service, with limited statutory powers to search people and property, monitor telephones, and access mail correspondence and financial records. There continue to be credible reports of human rights abuses by individual police officers.

Sugar and tourism constitute the mainstays of the economy, accounting for almost half of the nation's foreign exchange earnings. The Government is promoting light manufacturing for export. Due to political uncertainty, private investment as a percentage of gross domestic product dropped from 12 percent in 1987 and was 5 percent in early 1996.

The principal human rights problem remains constitutionally imposed and ethnically based political discrimination, which abridges the right of citizens to change their government. The Government and people are seeking to redress this problem through the constitutional review process. Other human rights problems include overt bias in land tenure and government policies favoring ethnic Fijians, occasional police brutality, potential constraints on the exercise of freedom of the press, continued delays in bringing criminal and civil cases to trial, discrimination and cases of violence against women, and instances of abuse of children.

RESPECT FOR HUMAN RIGHTS

Section 1. Respect for the Integrity of the Person, Including Freedom From:

a. *Political and Other Extrajudicial Killing.*—There were no reports of political or other extrajudicial killings.

b. *Disappearance.*—There were no reports of politically motivated disappearances.

c. *Torture and Other Cruel, Inhuman, or Degrading Treatment or Punishment.*—Police sometimes physically abuse detainees; the authorities have punished some of the offending officers, but these punishments have not been sufficient to deter all police abuses. The Police Department's internal affairs unit investigates complaints of police brutality and is working with the Ombudsman's office to ensure impartial observers in the investigation of complaints about police conduct.

Prison authorities strive to meet minimum international standards, within the limits of local financial restraints. Prison conditions are Spartan and food and sanitation limited. The Government permits visits to prisons by church groups and family members.

The law permits corporal punishment as a penalty for criminal acts, but this provision is seldom invoked.

d. *Arbitrary Arrest, Detention, or Exile.*—The Law of Arrest and Detention provides that a person may be arrested only if police believe that a breach of the criminal law has been or is about to be committed. Arrested persons must be brought before a court without "undue delay." This is taken to mean within 24 hours, with 48 hours as the exception (such as when an arrest is made over the weekend). Rules governing detention are designed to ensure fair questioning of suspects. Defendants have the right to a judicial review of the grounds for arrest; in urgent cases defendants may apply to a judge at any time, whether he is sitting or not. Incommunicado and arbitrary detention, both illegal, did not occur.

Exile is not practiced.

e. *Denial of Fair Public Trial.*—The judiciary is independent under the Constitution and in practice. There were no credible reports in 1996 of courts having been influenced by the executive. The 1996 Constitutional Review Commission report recommended continuation of an independent judiciary.

The judicial structure is patterned on the British system. The principal courts are the magistrate courts, the High Court, the Court of Appeal, and the Supreme Court. There are no special courts; military courts try only members of the armed forces. Magistrate courts continue to try the large majority of cases. In addition to its jurisdiction in serious civil and criminal cases, the High Court is granted special interest jurisdiction on behalf of the public and is empowered to review alleged violations of individual rights provided by the Constitution.

Defendants have the right to a public trial and to counsel. Trials in the High Court provide for the presence of assessors (citizens randomly selected to represent the community); cases in magistrate court do not. In litigation involving lesser complaints, a public legal advisor assists indigent persons in domestic or family law cases. The right of appeal exists but is hampered by continuing delays in the appeals process. Bail procedures mean that most defendants do not experience any pretrial detention.

The law sometimes treats women differently from men. In some instances there is a presumption of reduced competence and thus reduced responsibility. For example, only women can be charged with infanticide (if a man kills an infant the act is treated as murder, a more serious charge). A woman in an infanticide case is presumed to have diminished mental capacity, and sentences are reduced or suspended accordingly.

There were no reports of political prisoners.

f. *Arbitrary Interference with Privacy, Family, Home, or Correspondence.*—In general, the Government respects the privacy of the home. However, the Intelligence Service has powers, within specific operational guidelines, to search people and property, access private financial records, and monitor mail and telephones when a warrant is issued by the National Security Council. The Intelligence Service does conduct surveillance of persons it believes represent a security threat. Some political dissidents believe their telephones and mail are monitored, but they have not produced substantiating evidence.

Section 2. Respect for Civil Liberties, Including:

a. *Freedom of Speech and Press.*—Freedom of speech is generally respected. The Government at times criticizes the media for its coverage of sensitive issues, particularly if the Government perceives the coverage as resulting in a diminution of respect for authority.

Nevertheless, political figures and private citizens can and do speak out against the Government. Although the Public Order Act and other acts prohibit actions that are likely to incite racial antagonism, there were no reported arrests for such public statements.

Legislation pertaining to the press is contained in the Newspaper Registration Act (NRA) and the Press Correction Act (PCA). Under the NRA, all newspapers must be registered with the Government before they can begin publishing. Although the Government has never used the PCA, the act gives the Minister of Information sole discretionary power to order a newspaper to publish a "correcting statement" if, in the Minister's opinion, a false or distorted article has been published. Should the newspaper refuse to publish the Minister's correction, it can be taken to court, and if found guilty, fined approximately $700 (individual persons convicted under the act may be fined approximately $150 or imprisoned for 6 months or both). The PCA allows the Government to arrest anyone who publishes "malicious" material. This includes anything the Government considers false news that could create or foster public alarm or result in "detriment to the public."

The media operate without prior censorship but with considerable self-censorship. Newspapers occasionally print editorials critical of the Government but rarely do investigative reporting. They widely report statements about the political situation by opposition figures and foreign governments. The letters-to-the-editor columns of the two daily newspapers also frequently carry political statements from a wide cross section of society, including members of the deposed precoup government, which are highly critical of the Government, its programs, and the Constitution. Criticism, albeit muted, of the once sacrosanct traditional chiefly system is appearing more frequently. However, the Government still views comments about individual chiefs with disfavor.

An active local organization, the Fiji Islands Media Association (FIMA), is an affiliate of the regional Pacific Islands News Association (PINA). Both FIMA and PINA are pressing for better training and the establishment of codes of ethics for journalists. In a show of tangible support for strengthening the media, the Government has unconditionally provided space for housing the Fiji Journalism Training Institute.

Fiji's television news production is owned and operated by Fiji One, the only noncable television station. Fiji One, in turn is owned by a variety of private individuals and interests, and 51 percent by a trust operating on behalf of Fiji's provincial governments. While academic freedom is respected, the Government has effectively deterred university employees from participation in domestic politics. Since 1991 staff members of the Fiji-based University of the South Pacific must take leave if they run for public office and must resign from their university positions if elected. Senior staff cannot hold office in political parties. Student groups are free to organize and do so.

b. *Freedom of Peaceful Assembly and Association.*—The Constitution provides the right to assemble for political purposes, subject to restrictions in the interest of public order. Permits for public gatherings must be obtained from the district officer. The Government does not always grant permits for large outdoor political meetings or demonstrations, particularly if the police advise of difficulties with the anticipated crowd size or their ability to assure public safety.

The Government routinely issued permits for rallies organized by political parties, religious groups, and groups opposed to government policies.

All opposition party headquarters operate without government interference. Political organizations operate and issue public statements and did so repeatedly and openly throughout the year.

c. *Freedom of Religion.*—The Constitutional provision of freedom of religion is honored in practice. The Government does not restrict foreign clergy and missionary activity or other typical activities of religious organizations.

d. *Freedom of Movement Within the Country, Foreign Travel, Emigration, and Repatriation.*—The Government does not restrict freedom of movement within the country or abroad. Occasional detentions at the airport occur, but the courts order redress where this is warranted. Citizens are free to emigrate, and an estimated 40,000 have done so since 1987. The Government does not restrict their return if

they choose to do so, and has, in fact, encouraged those who left after the coups to return.
The Government cooperates with the office of the United Nations High Commissioner for Refugees (UNHCR) and other humanitarian organizations in assisting refugees. However, authorities were reluctant to grant first asylum to two Iranian Christians who entered Fiji via Malaysia. Only after receiving assurances from the UNHCR that the two would ultimately be moved to a third country did the authorities permit them to remain.

Section 3. Respect for Political Rights: The Right of Citizens to Change Their Government

The Constitution ensures political dominance by ethnic Fijians, primarily through race-based voting registration and representation in Parliament, thus abridging the right of citizens to change their government. The Constitutional Review Commission report recommends heterogeneous voting districts and a preferential voting scheme on the Australian model. The Government has respected scrupulously the independence of the Review Commission.

The Constitution provides ethnic Fijians with 37 of 70 seats in the elected lower house of Parliament, Indo-Fijians are accorded 27 seats, Rotumans (culturally distinct Polynesians) 1, and all others 5. In the Senate (an appointed body with essentially review powers), ethnic Fijians hold 24 of the 34 seats, Rotumans 1, and the other groups 9. The Review Commission report proposes that the House of Representatives still total 70, but with 45 seats (64 percent) distributed among 15 three-member districts of approximately equal population and multiethnic makeup. Voters would elect representatives from those districts based on a general registration; there would be no ethnic seats. For the short term, however, 25 seats would remain allocated on ethnic lines. The Review Commission report also proposes a mostly elected senate.

The Constitution requires that the Prime Minister be an ethnic Fijian; selection procedures virtually ensure that the President will also be an ethnic Fijian. The President chooses the Prime Minister (who, along with the Cabinet, holds most of the executive authority) from among the ethnic Fijian members of the lower house on the basis of ability to command majority support within that body.

The Constitutional Review Commision strongly endorsed maintaining a bill of rights, providing for freedom of speech, assembly, religion, and other universally accepted rights and freedoms. The Commission recommended restricting Parliament's emergency powers, specifically repeal of a 1990 provision permitting Parliament to legislate contrary to the Bill of Rights in an emergency.

Fiji has about 10 political parties. The ethnic Fijian SVT (or Fijian Political Party) forms the core of the parliamentary majority. Two predominantly Indo-Fijian parties, the National Federation Party (NFP) and the Fiji Labour Party (FLP) are joined on the opposition side of the legislature by an ethnic Fijian party (the Fijian Association). Two small parties representing primarily Caucasians and Asians, the General Electors and General Voters parties, are each represented by a minister in the Cabinet.

The Constitutional Review Commision's proposals will be studied by a select committee composed of the variety of parties. This committee will be charged with making recommendations for an "act to amend the Constitution," which is to be signed into law by July 1997.

Women in both the Fijian and Indian communities have functioned primarily in traditional roles, although some women achieve responsible positions in public service, politics, and business. Two women sit in Parliament; one is a cabinet minister. Women can also attain high status in Fiji's traditional chiefly system. The President's wife is, in her own right, one of Fiji's three highest ranking chiefs.

Section 4. Governmental Attitude Regarding International and Nongovernmental Investigation of Alleged Violations of Human Rights

There are no local groups that focus solely on human rights matters, but the women's rights movement, the labor movement, and various political groups (including organized political parties) are engaged in promoting human rights. There are also several small, not very active, foreign-based organizations that concentrate on human rights causes in Fiji, including the Coalition for Democracy in Fiji (with offices in New Zealand and Australia) and two United Kingdom-based groups, the International Fiji Movement and the Movement for Democracy in Fiji.

Section 5. Discrimination Based on Race, Sex, Religion, Disability, Language, or Social Status

The Constitution prohibits discrimination on the basis of race, sex, place of origin, political opinion, color, religion, or creed, and provides specific affirmative action provisions for those disadvantaged as a result of such discrimination. Enforcement of these constitutional provisions is attenuated by the Government's policy of using "affirmative action" to advance ethnic Fijians and by traditional mores as to the roles and rights of women and children.

Women.—Women in Fiji are actively addressing the problem of domestic violence. Reliable estimates indicate that 10 percent of women have been abused in some way, and this abuse is a major focus of the women's movement. Over the last year, Fiji police have adopted a "no drop" rule, according to which they will prosecute cases of domestic violence even when the victim does not wish to press charges.

There is a small but active women's rights movement, which has pressed for more serious punishment for rape convictions. Courts have imposed sentences that vary widely but are generally lenient. Women have sought to have all rape cases heard in the High Court where sentencing limits are higher.

Suva, the capital, and Ba, the regional center, have privately funded women's crisis centers, which offer counseling and assistance to women in cases of rape, domestic violence, and other problems, such as child support payments. There is, overall, a growing awareness of the abuse of women's rights.

Despite constitutional provisions, the Government practiced a form of sexual discrimination in the recognition of spousal and offspring rights. For example, spouses of female citizens are not automatically granted residence, whereas spouses of male citizens are. Children of female ethnic Fijians married to nonethnic Fijians are not entitled to registry in the document governing which persons share in income from communal ownership of native lands, and which persons who have the right to vote as an ethnic Fijian and hold ethnic Fijian-designated seats in Parliament. Men, however, confer ethnic Fijian status on their offspring regardless of the mother's ethnic background. In a high-profile 1992 court challenge to the registration restrictions, the son of a Chinese father and ethnic Fijian mother won his appeal to be registered as an ethnic Fijian. The long-term effects of the decision on registration restrictions and, thus, a woman's right to pass on her ethnic status remain unclear.

In general, women in the Fijian community are more likely to rise to prominence in their own right than are women in the Indo-Fijian community. Women have full rights of property ownership and inheritance, and a number have become successful entrepreneurs. Women are generally paid less than men, a discrepancy that is especially notable in the garment industry. Garment workers, most of whom are female, are subject to a special minimum wage considerably lower than that in other sectors.

Children.—The Government is committed to childrens' rights and welfare but has limited financial resources to carry out the commitment. In addition, the legal system is at times inadequate to protect the rights of children, as children's testimony is inadmissable unless corroborated by an adult. Societal changes have undermined the traditional village and extended family based social structures—an outgrowth of this has been a child abuse problem. The Government in 1993 created a Child Welfare Committee to address these problems, but it is likely to remain reluctant to become directly involved in what are generally perceived to be "family matters."

Corporal punishment is widely administered in schools and at home. The Ministry of Education has guidelines for the administration of such punishment by principals and head teachers. In 1993 one principal was fired for overstepping these guidelines. There is credible information that not all abuses are reported or punished.

People With Disabilities.—Legal discrimination against physically disabled persons in employment, education, and the provision of other state services does not exist. However, there is no legislation or mandated provision for accessibility for the disabled. Several small voluntary organizations promote greater attention to the needs of the disabled.

National/Racial/Ethnic Minorities.—The stated purpose of the 1987 military coups was to ensure the political supremacy of the indigenous Fijian people and to protect their traditional way of life and communal control of land. To this end, the Government initiated a number of constitutional and other measures to ensure ethnic Fijian control of the executive and legislative branches (see Section 3). The Government also successfully raised the proportion of ethnic Fijians and Rotumans in the public service to 50 percent or higher at all levels, but most dramatically at the senior level: Indo-Fijians now represent only 10 percent of the highest levels of the civil service. As a result, some Indo-Fijians justifiably complain of a "glass ceiling" whereby, despite their experience and higher educational achievements, they are promoted only to middle management levels of the civil service.

Control of land is a highly sensitive issue. Ethnic Fijians currently hold, communally, about 83 percent of land, the State holds another 8 percent, and only the remaining 9 percent is in the hands of nonethnic Fijians. The British colonial administration instituted the present land ownership arrangements to protect the interests of the indigenous Fijians whose traditional beliefs, cultural values, and self-identity are tied to the land. Most cash crop farmers are Indo-Fijians, who lease land from the ethnic Fijian landowners through the Native Land Trust Board. Many Indo-Fijians, particularly farmers, believe that the absence of secure land tenure discriminates against them. Between 1997 and 2000, most current leases will expire. A review of the current land tenure and leasing arrangements is under way, with all indications that the Government will make few changes to the existing system. Some landowners are likely to decline to renew leases; the Government has acknowledged its responsibility to help relocate displaced Indo-Fijian farmers, although it has few resources to offer.

Indo-Fijians are subject to occasional harassment and crime based on race, which is compounded by inadequate police protection. There have been no credible allegations of government involvement in such incidents, which the police have investigated, sometimes resulting in arrests.

Section 6. Worker Rights

a. *The Right of Association.*—The law protects the right of workers to form and join unions, elect their own representatives, publicize their views on labor matters, and determine their own policies, and the authorities respect these rights in practice. However, the law permits restrictions to be applied in government employment and in the interests of defense, public safety, public order, public morality, or public health, or to protect the rights and freedoms of other persons. An estimated 20 percent of the labor force is unionized.

All unions must register with, but are not controlled by, the Government. The only central labor body is the Fiji Trade Union Congress (FTUC), which was closely associated with the opposition Fiji Labour Party until mid-1992. It currently takes a more independent political stance. The FTUC is free to associate internationally and does so. The labor movement is led largely by Indo-Fijians, with ethnic Fijians beginning to assume leadership roles. Persons with close ties to the Government have organized rival unions primarily for ethnic Fijians; these unions are more amenable to cooperation with the Government.

In 1994 Parliament completed a 2-year process of reforming labor legislation by amending several acts. The changes include the elimination of a ban on a person holding multiple union officer positions and the elimination of restrictions on seeking international support on labor issues. Although the FTUC thereafter returned to participate in the Government's Tripartite Economic Strategies Committee, it subsequently suspended its participation pending additional reforms.

Strikes are legal, except in connection with union recognition disputes. The Government remains involved in certifying union strike balloting, which can be an elaborate process given the distance between some of the island locations. The failure of the National Bank of Fiji sparked labor unrest. Furloughed bank employees eventually won a settlement package that they, and their union, deemed fair.

b. *The Right to Organize and Bargain Collectively.*—The law recognizes the right to organize and bargain collectively. Employers are required to recognize a union if more than half the employees in a workplace have joined it. Recognition is determined by union membership rather than by an election. The Government has the power to order recalcitrant employers to recognize unions and has done so. Key sectors of the economy, including sugar and tourism, are heavily organized. Following the May 1992 return to accountable government, the Government lifted wage guidelines, and unrestricted collective bargaining on wages is now the norm.

Wage negotiations are conducted on an individual company or enterprise basis rather than on an industrywide basis. A government proposal to introduce such negotiations has been supported by employers but opposed by unions.

The law specifically prohibits antiunion discrimination. In practice, the unions are generally successful in preventing discrimination against workers for union activities, but the law does not mandate that fired workers be reinstated.

Export processing zones (EPZ's) are subject to the same law as the rest of the country, and unions have negotiated collective bargaining agreements with many EPZ firms.

c. *Prohibition of Forced or Compulsory Labor.*—The Constitution specifically prohibits forced labor, and there is no indication that it is practiced.

d. *Minimum Age for Employment of Children.*—Children under the age of 12 may not be employed in any capacity. "Children" (under age 15) and "young persons" (ages 15 to 17) may not be employed in industry or work with machinery. Enforcement by the Ministry for Labour and Industrial Relations generally is effective, except for family members working on family farms or businesses and "self-employed" homeless youths. School is not mandatory.

e. *Acceptable Conditions of Work.*—There is no national minimum wage. Certain sectors have minimum wages set by the Ministry for Labour and Industrial Relations, which effectively enforces them. Minimum wage levels will generally support a barely adequate standard of living for a worker and family in all sectors except for the garment industry, in which the starting hourly wage, $0.50 (FJ$0.72) for learners and $0.65 (FJ$0.94) for others, is based on the assumption that workers are young adults or married women living at home and not supporting a household.

There are no regulations specifying maximum hours of work for adult males. Women can do night work in factories and overtime but are prohibited from underground work in mines. Certain industries, notably transportation and shipping, have problems with excessive hours of work. Indo-Fijians, who generally require a cash income to survive, are more vulnerable to pressure to work long hours than are ethnic Fijians. Many ethnic Fijians can and do return to their villages rather than work what they consider excessive hours.

There are workplace safety regulations, a Workmen's Compensation Act, and an accident compensation plan. Awards for workers injured on the job are set by a tribunal. Government enforcement of safety standards under the direction of the Labour Ministry suffers from a lack of trained enforcement personnel, but unions do a reasonable job of monitoring safety standards in organized workplaces. The International Labor Organization's (ILO) 1992 recommendations cited the need to improve working conditions, particularly in the garment industry. In June the Government passed legislation to address some of these shortcomings, and the ILO is assisting with implementation.

INDONESIA

Despite a surface adherence to democratic forms, the Indonesian political system remains strongly authoritarian. The Government is dominated by an elite comprising President Soeharto (now in his sixth 5-year term), his close associates, and the military. The Government requires allegiance to a state ideology known as "Pancasila," which stresses consultation and consensus, but is also used to limit dissent, to enforce social and political cohesion, and to restrict the development of opposition elements. The judiciary is subordinated to the executive and the military.

The primary mission of the 450,000-member armed forces, which includes 175,000 police, is maintenance of internal unity and stability. Military spending is approximately 1.4 percent of the gross national product. Despite a decrease in the number of active or retired military officers in key government positions, the military retained substantial nonmilitary powers under a "dual function" concept that accords it a political and social role in "developing the nation." There continued to be numerous, credible reports of human rights abuses by the military and the police.

Indonesia has a vigorous and rapidly growing economy. The benefits of economic development are widely dispersed, but pervasive corruption remains a problem. Pressures for change and sporadic unrest led to stronger demands that the Government act more effectively to address social and economic inequities. In rural areas, discontent often focused on the grievances of small land owners—especially those forced off their land by powerful economic and military interests. In some regions, exploitation of natural resources has entailed environmental degradation with adverse social consequences.

The Government continued to commit serious human rights abuses. Rising pressures for change, including those by political activists and opponents, triggered tough government actions that further infringed on fundamental rights. The authorities maintained their tight grip on the political process, which denies citizens the ability to change their government democratically. In other areas, such as increased police and army accountability for abuses, the decline in extra-legal executions, access to prisoners, the variety of information sources, and tolerance of public criticism, there were encouraging signs along with substantial grounds for continuing concern. Reports of extrajudicial killings—including killings of unarmed civilians, disappearances, and torture and mistreatment of detainees by security forces continued. In practice, legal protections against torture are inadequate, and security forces continued to torture and mistreat detainees, particularly in regions such as Irian Jaya and East Timor. There were persistent reports that some of the detainees seized by the Government during unrest in Jakarta sparked by the government-backed seizure of an opposition party headquarters on July 27 and during the subsequent crackdown on political opponents were subjected to mistreatment. Reports of arbitrary arrests and detentions and the use of excessive violence (including deadly force) continued. Prison conditions remained harsh, and security forces regularly violated citizens' right to privacy.

The Government continued to impose severe limitations on freedom of assembly and association. In anticipation of the 1997 parliamentary elections, the Government took a number of actions to intimidate political opponents. Notably, the Government crudely engineered the removal of a popular opposition party leader and the forcible takeover of the party headquarters. The headquarters-takeover and the subsequent rioting in Jakarta, the worst in decades, resulted in at least 5 dead, over 20 missing, scores of injuries, and over 200 arrests. Some witnesses testified in court that one person was killed during the takeover of the party headquarters. The Government, invoking limited use of the controversial Antisubversion Law, responded with a wave of arrests, interrogations, and expanded surveillance aimed at reining in nongovernmental organizations (NGO's) and political activists. The International Committee of the Red Cross (ICRC) and the National Human Rights Commission were able to visit many of those detained or hospitalized after the takeover and riot, although access has been sporadic.

An independent election monitoring committee, formed by private organizations, prompted a mixed government response. Its head was called in for questioning during the Government's crackdown on political opponents and NGO's after the July 27 incident. On the other hand, the Indonesian National Human Rights Commission, despite limited resources, and occasional government pressure and intimidation, vigorously undertook investigations and publicized its independent findings and recommendations. In some but not all cases, the Government acted on these findings.

The judiciary is still subservient to the executive branch and subject to widespread corruption. A justice's criticism of judicial corruption focused increased attention on the need to reform the judicial system. In a controversial and much criticized action, the Supreme Court reimposed a prison sentence on Indonesia's most prominent independent labor leader, Muchtar Pakpahan, reversing its own 1995 decision to overturn the conviction. Reversing lower court decisions, the Supreme Court also upheld the legality of the Government's closure of three magazines in 1994.

The Government continued to exercise indirect control over and intimidation of the press. Criticism of the Government was tolerated, but critics of the President, senior officials, or powerful local interests risked harassment, arrest, or intimidation. Despite these problems and government pressure on the media in the wake of the July 27 events, observers considered the print media more open and outspoken than in recent years. The Government continued to impose some restrictions on freedom of religion and movement. Discrimination against women and the disabled and violence against women are endemic problems.

Security forces displayed improved discipline in responding to several incidents of unrest in Irian Jaya, where newly issued human rights guidelines were in effect, but brutality in handling unruly demonstrations in Pontianak and Ujung Pandang resulted in civilian deaths. In the July rioting in Jakarta, the police beat demonstrators and onlookers. Higher authorities punished increased numbers of police and military personnel, including officers, for infractions of the law or indiscipline. Punishment, however, usually failed to match the severity of the abuse.

The Government maintained its opposition to alternatives to the government-sponsored labor movement and to the development of a free trade union movement. Members of the principal unauthorized labor organization cited continued instances of harassment. Government pressure on this organization—widely viewed as an attempt to discredit or destroy it—has increased since the July 27 violence in Jakarta. In a move that has elicited considerable domestic and foreign criticism, the Government detained and brought subversion charges against the leader of this organization (the same man against whom the Supreme Court had reinstated a conviction it had earlier overturned) for alleged political activities. Abuses, including the use of child labor, mistreatment of labor, and inadequate remuneration continued. On the positive side, the Government raised the minimum wage again and, for the first time, allowed unions to collect and distribute their own dues.

In East Timor, still troubled by a low-level insurgency and a disaffected indigenous population that generally resents Indonesian rule and has inadequate opportunity to determine its own affairs, there were further instances of killings, disappearances, torture, and excessive use of force by the military and insurgents. Respected observers noted a decrease in serious incidents, but 1996 Nobel Peace Prize co-laureate Bishop Belo said that it would be a mistake to conclude that the human rights environment in East Timor was improving. No progress was made in accounting for the missing persons following the 1991 Dili incident or the others who disappeared in 1995–96. Troop levels remained unjustifiably high. The Government granted limited access to the area to foreign journalists but banned travel by all foreign human rights NGO's except the ICRC. In several cases, the Indonesian military punished abuses by its personnel. The National Human Rights Commission in a small, symbolically important step—whose practical effect remains to be seen—opened a branch office in Dili. Young disgruntled East Timorese mounted repeated intrusions into embassies in Jakarta seeking asylum and publicity for their cause.

In Irian Jaya, tribal resentment against government and private companies' policies viewed as heavyhanded and arbitrary remained. Real and perceived discrimination against native Irian people led to several outbreaks of violence and a strengthened military presence in Timika. Guerrilla terrorists seeking separation or autonomy for Irian Jaya took hostages in four incidents and murdered several of their captives.

RESPECT FOR HUMAN RIGHTS

Section 1. Respect for the Integrity of the Person, Including Freedom From:

a. *Political and Other Extrajudicial Killings.*—Historically, politically related extrajudicial killings have occurred most frequently in areas where separatist movements were active, such as East Timor, Aceh, and Irian Jaya. Security forces continued to employ harsh measures against separatist movements in East Timor and Irian Jaya. Although the Government claims that the "Aceh Merdeka" movement has been eliminated, Aceh is still officially listed as one of Indonesia's three "trouble spots" (along with East Timor and Irian Jaya), and the Government has issued public calls for the "rebels" to come home to their families. There are credible reports that the Aceh Merdeka movement still exists, but its activities are now underground. Security forces in East Timor killed two unarmed civilians in April in separate unrelated incidents. On April 25, near Baucau an unarmed East Timorese civilian allegedly attempted to escape questioning by security personnel and was killed when one of them fired what was described as a warning shot. A military officer was convicted of accidentally killing the victim. On April 28, in Dili a member of the security forces fired on and killed an unarmed civilian during an altercation caused because the victim was allegedly burning an Indonesian flag. In early August, a student was killed after quarreling with soldiers and them seeking to escape arrest.

Four soldiers received 1- to 3-year prison terms in February as a result of the killing of three civilians in Irian Jaya in the spring of 1995. These convictions resulted from reports by the National Human Rights Commission, the Catholic Church, and NGO's about the killings of 16 or more civilians in Irian Jaya between mid-1994 and mid-1995. However, these convictions resulted from one case only, and the military court addressed only charges of murder and did not address charges of rape of indigenous women. Five other cases of alleged human rights violations in Irian Jaya, cited in a September 1995 report by the National Human Rights Commission, have languished. Moreover, in the one prosecuted Irian Jaya case, many court documents were declared to be "state documents," precluding their release to the public.

The killing of unarmed civilians by security forces was not limited to the areas with active separatist movements. Military personnel abducted and allegedly tortured an unarmed civilian in West Kalimantan in April following a minor traffic accident. One civilian was killed and at least four were injured when military personnel fired upon unarmed civilians who attacked the local military headquarters in protest. Six military personnel were tried and convicted and received sentences ranging from 3 to 11 months for involvement in this incident. Six others, who had originally been named by the military authorities as suspects in the case, were punished for disciplinary infractions but not tried.

At least three civilian deaths occurred when security personnel in Ujung Pandang responded to student demonstrations in April. The Government acknowledged that three deaths occurred, claiming that the students drowned in a river while fleeing security forces. However, photos of the three bodies of the dead students showed bruises and what may have been knife wounds. The investigation by the National Human Rights Commission confirmed the number of deaths but identified excesses by the troops. Some student groups asserted at the time that the number killed was higher. Twelve soldiers were subsequently charged in the case. Six low-ranking officers were tried and convicted in October receiving sentences of 90 to 105 days.

The Government assisted the forcible takeover of the Indonesian Democratic Party's (PDI) headquarters on July 27, and the harsh treatment of demonstrators later in the day by security forces, sparked Jakarta's most serious rioting in years. The Government acknowledged that four deaths occurred. A report released on October 12 by the National Human Rights Commission—which cited government intervention as a factor in the violence—put the casualties at 5 dead, 149 injured, and 23 missing. No members of the military or police have been held accountable by the Government in connection with this violence, which included police caning of individuals in a crowd who fell during a police charge. PDI witnesses testified in court that one person was killed during the government-backed assault against the party headquarters.

The police employed excessive and sometimes deadly force in apprehending suspects or coping with alleged criminals. In response to protests that the methods used were unjustifiably harsh and amounted to execution without trial, police generally claimed that the suspects were fleeing, resisting arrest, or threatening the police. Accurate statistics about the number of such cases are not available. In December police in Jakarta shot and killed a robbery suspect who they said was trying to escape from custody, and in November they did the same to a crime suspect in West Java. Also in November, a human rights organization charged that security forces, during a crackdown on street vendors, beat and kicked vendors, and that one of the vendors fell into a river and drowned while he was fleeing.

In the past higher authorities rarely punished the military or police for using excessive force. There were some indications that this situation was improving, although the action taken by the authorities is usually not commensurate with the gravity of the security force abuses.

Irian Jaya rebels, including some from the Free Papua Organization (OPM), abducted civilian hostages on four occasions in Irian Jaya. In two of these incidents hostages were killed by their abductors. A rescue attempt by Indonesian special forces May 15, succeeded in freeing nine hostages, but two others died of slash wounds inflicted by their abductors. Government troops killed eight of the abductors in a fight that also involved armed local villagers who supported the rebels. Earlier in this hostage taking, government forces sought to bring an end to the incident through ICRC mediation, which eventually failed due to bad faith on the part of the abductor leader, Kelly Kwalik. On September 18, Armed Forces of the Republic of Indonesia (ABRI) elements in pursuit of Irian Jaya rebels, who had taken 14 logging company employees hostage August 14, reported that two of the hostages had been found murdered. Government reports claimed the two had been tortured before they were killed by their abductors, though a knowledgeable source later shed doubt on this claim. The armed forces conducted operations to hunt down the OPM guerrillas. On at least two occasions OPM and government forces exchanged fire with reports of casualties. Access to the general area was restricted by the Government to prevent additional hostage-taking. There were unconfirmed claims from government critics that military campaigns to capture the hostage takers had resulted in civilian losses.

ABRI reportedly suffered casualties in East Timor during a clash with guerrillas in August. In ensuing military operations, five East Timorese reportedly were arrested. ABRI does not release its casualty statistics, but reliable reports indicate soldiers have been killed throughout the year. Guerrillas carried out attacks against immigrants and progovernment Timorese, and suspected informers that resulted in several deaths according to government and Indonesian press sources.

On December 24, in Dili an out-of-uniform police officer was beaten to death by a crowd when he was discovered to be carrying a pistol and a hand radio. Several other policemen including the Dili chief of police were injured, some seriously.

b. *Disappearance.*—Following the July 27 violence and its aftermath, the National Human Rights Commission on October 12 released a report that listed 23 missing, 149 injured, and 5 dead, of whom had been shot. The Commission's attention to the number of missing reflected persistent reports from human rights groups that people remain unaccounted for following the July 27 violence. In contrast, the Government did not acknowledge that any people were missing. Security forces in Indonesia sometimes held suspects incommunicado before acknowledging their detention. In certain cases, including after the July 27 violence, suspects were held for substantial periods of time before formal charges were brought; in some cases charges were not brought, and they were simply released. A respected international human rights NGO reported to the United Nations the disappearance of a Timorese man from Same, on or around May 13.

There were no new efforts by the Government to account for the missing and dead from the November 12, 1991 military shooting of civilians in Dili, East Timor. Of those still listed as missing in a report that the military gave to Human Rights Watch/Asia, no additional cases were resolved during the year. Knowledgeable observers continued to believe that most of the missing are dead and that members of the armed forces know where their bodies are located.

c. *Torture and Other Cruel, Inhuman, or Degrading Treatment or Punishment.*— The Criminal Code makes it a crime punishable by up to 4 years in prison for any official to use violence or force to elicit a confession. It establishes pretrial procedures to give suspects or their families the right to challenge the legality of an arrest or detention. In practice, however, legal protections are both inadequate and widely ignored, and security forces continued to employ torture and other forms of mistreatment, particularly in regions where there were active security concerns, such as Irian Jaya and East Timor. Police often resort to physical abuse, even in minor incidents.

In East Timor, military units regularly detain civilians for interrogation; often these civilians are mistreated for several days and then released. According to credible reports, in January security forces seized nine East Timorese from their homes in the Zumlai "Kecamatan" because they were suspected of cooperating with guerrilla forces. One of the detainees alleged that they had been beaten and mistreated, including being placed in a small underground hole. There were other reports that military and police units make frequent use of random torture against young men to maintain order in urban areas of East Timor. Credible sources reported that on November 27, following the stoning of police hut in Baucau, police entered a high school student dormitory and arbitrarily detained and severely beat two students.

In Irian Jaya, after an investigation, reliable sources concluded that all 130 persons detained during the March 18–20 demonstrations and rioting in Jayapura were mistreated and that some were tortured.

The Government continued to maintain an excessive military presence in East Timor. Taking advantage of high unemployment among young men ABRI recruited local East Timorese to constitute an East Timorese force subordinate to ABRI. Some East Timorese sources charged this force with human rights abuses as well. The Government, as it does elsewhere, also relied on bands of youths, organized and directed by the Government, to intimidate and harass its opponents in East Timor.

There were persistent assertions that some of the prisoners and detainees seized on July 27 and during the subsequent crackdown were subjected to mistreatment. This included both prisoners who were awaiting trial and detainees who were questioned and then released. Examples of the alleged mistreatment included kicking, beating, and electric shocks, notably while in the custody of military intelligence or the police. The ICRC and National Commission on Human Rights were unable to confirm these allegations. One case of alleged mistreatment involved five students who were said to have been beaten in Yogyakarta while in police detention in early August. Another case involved a raid on the headquarters of an Indonesian NGO. One of the staff members, the relative of a member of a small unauthorized political party that the authorities consider subversive (the People's Democratic Party or PRD), was detained and subjected to beatings and electric shocks. Regarding the arrests of PRD members following July 27, Human Rights Watch/Asia stated that "a clear pattern has emerged where students are taken first to military intelligence for interrogation and often subjected to severe physical abuse, including electric shocks, for a period that can last up to a week." Lawyers for three of the PRD defendants publicly charged in October to the Human Rights Commission that their clients had been tortured.

In West Java, Tjetje Tadjudin died while in police custody in October. Initially the police claimed that his death was caused by respiratory problems. However, his examination at the hospital showed that injuries had been inflicted upon him, indicating that he had been tortured. The national police chief held the detective who had conducted the interrogation responsible and relieved him from duty. The police chief has promised to investigate the case thoroughly and take disciplinary action. Before Tjetje died, he had been "lent" to the military police for questioning because there were allegations that military personnel were involved in the initial crime. However, high level military officials insisted that the military had no role in his death.

A foreign human rights group reported that in January security forces detained 14 people in East Kalimantan. Several of the detainees were representing their village, Menemang in Kutai Regency, in a longstanding dispute with a company that had been clear-cutting land of disputed ownership in the area of the village. According to this report, the 14 were severely mistreated by the security forces, including being stripped, repeatedly beaten, kicked and pistol whipped, and some were burned with cigarettes.

In December in Cibentang, West Java, security forces reportedly clashed with villagers on two occasions. The villagers were resisting the installation of electric cables by a state-run company, which involved the expropriation of their land, because they believed they had been inadequately compensated. During one of the clashes, which reportedly occurred on December 26, the villagers claim that 200 security force personnel were involved, and five villagers alleged that they had been mistreated. The security forces claim that only 30 personnel were involved.

Prison conditions are harsh with violence among prisoners and mistreatment and extortion of inmates by guards common. In November a thirteen-year-old boy died of respiratory problems while serving a murder sentence. His lawyer publicly charged that the boy died because of poor conditions in the detention center, and this claim was supported publicly by some of the defendants in the July 27 violence case who were detained in that facility as well. The incidence of mistreatment by prison officials dropped sharply once a prisoner had been transferred from police or military intelligence (BIA) custody into the civilian prison system or into the custody of the Attorney General. Officials publicly condemned police brutality and harsh prison conditions and occasionally took disciplinary action, including transfer, dismissal, and trials leading to prison. Political prisoners were usually mixed with the general prison population, although in the Cipinang prison in Jakarta high-profile political prisoners were segregated.

The Government allowed the ICRC access on one occasion to those detained on antisubversion charges by the Attorney General following the July 27 violence. Authorities denied a visiting foreign official access to imprisoned East Timorese guerrilla leader Xanana Gusmao in Jakarta, although he was permitted to visit East Timor. In September the Attorney General's office invited a senior-level foreign government delegation to visit two individuals detained in connection with the July 27 violence.

d. *Arbitrary Arrest, Detention, or Exile.*—The Criminal Procedures Code contains provisions against arbitrary arrest and detention, but it lacks adequate enforcement mechanisms and is routinely violated. The code specifies that prisoners have the right to notify their families and that warrants must be produced during an arrest except under specified conditions, such as when a suspect is caught in the act of committing a crime. The law also requires that families of detainees be notified promptly. The law authorizes investigators to issue warrants to assist in their investigations or if sufficient evidence exists that a crime has been committed. However, authorities sometimes made arrests without warrants.

The law presumes defendants innocent and permits bail. They or their families may also challenge the legality of their arrest and detention in a pretrial hearing and may sue for compensation if wrongfully detained. However, it is virtually impossible for detainees to invoke this procedure, or to receive compensation, after being released without charge. In both military and civilian courts, appeals based on claims of improper arrest and detention are rarely, if ever, accepted. The Criminal Procedures Code also contains specific limits on periods of pretrial detention and specifies when the courts must get involved to approve extensions, usually after 60 days. In addition, suspects charged under the 1963 Antisubversion Law are subject to special procedures outside the code. These give the Attorney General the authority to hold a suspect up to 1 year before trial. He may renew this 1-year period without limit. In the case of individuals held by the Attorney General's Office in connection with the July 27 violence in Jakarta, the Attorney General's Office waived authority under the Antisubversion Law to hold suspects indefinitely, and sought judicial approval of continued detention as provided for under criminal law.

The authorities routinely approve extensions of periods of detention. In areas where active guerrilla movements exist, such as East Timor and Irian Jaya, there are instances of people being detained without warrants, charges, or court proceedings. This was also the case following the July 27 violence in Jakarta. Bail is rarely granted, especially in political cases. The authorities frequently prevent access to defense counsel while suspects are being investigated and make it difficult or impossible for detainees to get legal assistance from voluntary legal defense organizations. Special laws on corruption, economic crimes, and narcotics do not come under the code's protections.

The Agency for Coordination of Assistance for the Consolidation of National Security (BAKORSTANAS) operates outside the legal code and has wide discretion to detain and interrogate persons thought to threaten national security. Despite the existence of this agency, ABRI began discussing publicly in September the need for a new internal security act to give the Government greater power to suppress dissent prior to the 1997 parliamentary elections. There is no reliable data on which to quantify the number of arbitrary arrests or detentions without trial, particularly in East Timor and Irian Jaya.

In the period March 10–13, Irianese with grievances against the Government and the policies and practices of a foreign mining company rioted in the Timika-Tembagapura area. There was also rioting in a suburb of Jayapura March 18–19. Fatalities were reported in both instances though not, apparently, at the hands of security forces. Approximately 7 persons were detained in the wake of the Timika-Tembagapura rioting while over 100 reportedly were detained in the wake of the Jayapura rioting.

According to credible reports, numerous individuals were seized from their homes in Dili and arbitrarily detained in February. There were similar reports of persons being arbitrarily detained in Baucau in November, and in Viqueque in December. According to a report from a foreign human rights group, four Irianese were detained in March due to a peaceful protest they carried out in Jakarta. Without being informed of the charges, they were held incommunicado for over a week and then released. Documents confiscated from one of these individuals were not returned.

According to the Government, 206 people were arrested on the weekend of July 27 in connection with the violent, government-assisted takeover of PDI headquarters and the ensuing disturbances. Scores of persons were detained by the Government on July 27 for refusing to shut down a "free speech forum" organized by supporters of ousted PDI leader Megawati Sukarnoputri and for continuing to occupy the PDI headquarters. Plain clothes police clandestinely tape recorded speeches given at the forum that were generally critical of the Government. On November 27 the central Jakarta district court ordered the release of 124 of that group who had been charged with assault and resisting orders. Judges acquitted 9 of the accused and sentenced the other 115 to time already served. Assault charges were dropped. Many of those convicted plan to appeal. In addition, the leader of an unsanctioned labor union, Muchtar Pakpahan, and 12 members of the People's Democratic Party (PRD), including its leader Budiman Sudjatmiko, had been arrested. The trials of nine of the PRD members for subversion began in Jakarta in December, as did the trial of Pakpahan who was also charged with subversion. Outside of Jakarta there were numerous arrests and detentions, some temporary, of those suspected of having a connection to the PRD or responsibility for the July 27 riots. For example, five students were detained in Yogyakarta in early August. At least two PRD members were detained in Semarang in September, and held incommunicado for at least 2 weeks. In a raid conducted against a Jakarta NGO, detaining forces failed to provide identification or misidentified themselves. In response to instances of illegal military detention of suspects, the National Human Rights Commission issued a public caution that only police were empowered to carry out arrests.

In February, 15 women reportedly protested the 5-month detention of their husbands and sons to the local Lampung legislature. They claimed that their family members had not received due process, that one of the detainees had been killed in prison, and that another had been severely injured.

The Government does not use forced exile.

e. *Denial of Fair Public Trial.*—The Constitution stipulates the independence of the judiciary, but in practice the judiciary is subordinated to the executive and the military. In many cases procedural protections, including those against coerced confessions, particularly those coerced by the police and military intelligence (BIA), are inadequate to ensure a fair trial. Several court challenges to the Government's transparent manipulation of the PDI leadership structure have been dismissed, results that were widely expected given the judiciary's subservience to the executive and military on key issues.

A quadripartite judiciary of general, religious, military, and administrative courts exists below the Supreme Court. The right of appeal from district court to high court to Supreme Court exists in all four systems of justice. The Supreme Court does not consider factual aspects of a case, only the lower courts' application of law. The Supreme Court theoretically stands coequal with the executive and legislative branches, but it does not have the right of judicial review over laws passed by Parliament. The Supreme Court has not yet exercised its authority (held since 1985) to review ministerial decrees and regulations. In 1993 Chief Justice Purwoto Gandasubrata laid out procedures for limited judicial review. Judges are civil servants employed by the executive branch, which controls their assignments, pay, and promotion. They are subject to considerable pressure from military and other governmental authorities that often determines the outcome of a case. The Supreme Courts's unprecedented reversal of its own 1995 decision freeing labor leader Muchtar Pakpahan from prison throws its lack of independence into sharp relief. Corruption is a common feature of the legal system and the payment of bribes can influence prosecution, conviction, and sentencing in civil and criminal cases. A Supreme Court justice who alleged widespread corruption and collusion within the court system was the subject of efforts by the Chief Justice to secure his dismissal from the court. The Government did not act on this recommendation.

A panel of judges conducts trials at the district court level, poses questions, hears evidence, decides guilt or innocence, and assesses punishment. Initial judgments are rarely reversed in the appeals process, although sentences can be increased or reduced. Both the defense and the prosecution may appeal.

Defendants have the right to confront witnesses and to produce witnesses in their defense. An exception is allowed in cases in which distance or expense is deemed excessive for transporting witnesses to court. In such cases, sworn affidavits may be introduced. However, the Criminal Procedures Code does not provide for witnesses' immunity or for defense power of subpoena. As a result, witnesses are sometimes too afraid of retribution to testify against the authorities. The courts commonly allow forced confessions and limit the presentation of defense evidence. Defendants do not have the right to remain silent and can be compelled to testify against themselves. The Criminal Procedures Code gives defendants the right to an attorney from the moment of their arrest, but not during the prearrest investigation period, which may involve prolonged detention. Persons summoned to appear as witnesses in investigations do not have the right to be assisted by lawyers even though information developed in the course of rendering testimony can subsequently become the basis of an investigation of the witness. The law requires that a lawyer be appointed in capital cases and those involving a prison sentence of 15 years or more. In cases involving potential sentences of 5 years or more, a lawyer must be appointed if the defendant desires an attorney and is indigent. In theory, destitute defendants may obtain private legal help, such as that provided by the Legal Aid Institute (LBH). In practice, however, defendants are often persuaded not to hire an attorney, or access to an attorney of their choice is impeded.

Signs of nascent judicial independence were less evident in 1996. In June the Supreme Court overturned rulings by the lower courts and maintained the ban on the periodical Tempo and two other publications. In 1995 an administrative court in Jakarta had found in favor of the plaintiffs, employees of Tempo, in their civil suit against the Minister of Information for revoking Tempo's publication license in 1993. The High Court unanimously upheld this decision in November 1995, stating that the ministerial regulations permitting publications to be banned were in conflict with press freedoms contained in the Constitution. The Government appealed the High Court ruling to the Supreme Court, which found in favor of the Government. In November the Supreme Court revealed that it had reversed its earlier decision to overturn the 1994 verdict against independent labor leader Muchtar Pakpahan. This reversal prompted broad criticism by legal scholars and by one highly regarded Supreme Court justice who had chaired the panel which overturned the 1994 decision.

The Antisubversion Law, which carries a maximum penalty of death (which has never been invoked in recent years), makes it a crime to engage in acts that could distort, undermine, or deviate from the state ideology or broad outlines of state policy, or which could disseminate feelings of hostility or arouse hostility, disturbances, or anxiety among the population. The excessively vague language of this law makes it possible to prosecute people merely for peaceful expression of views contrary to those of the Government. Independent labor leader Muchtar Pakpahan and PRD members were charged with subversion in trials that opened in December.

Various sources estimate that several hundred people are serving sentences for subversion, including members of the banned Communist Party of Indonesia (PKI), Muslim militants, and those convicted of subversion in Irian Jaya, Aceh, and East Timor. Following the July 27 violence, the Government in December charged 10 individuals under the Antisubversion Law. Scores, and possibly hundreds, more were believed to be serving sentences under the Hate-Sowing or Sedition laws. Some of these persons advocated or employed violence, but others are political prisoners who were convicted for attempting to exercise such universally recognized human rights as freedom of speech or association, or who were convicted in manifestly unfair trials.

f. *Arbitrary Interference with Privacy, Family, Home, or Correspondence.*—Judicial warrants for searches are required except for cases involving suspected subversion, economic crimes, and corruption. However, security agencies regularly made forced or surreptitious entries. A Jakarta NGO was raided by security personnel who misidentified themselves as police. The intruders reportedly tortured one staff member and confiscated documents (see Section 1.c.). The NGO has not been able to regain the confiscated documents because the intruding officials neither presented a warrant nor properly identified themselves. Security forces also engaged in surveillance of persons and residences and selective monitoring of local and international telephone calls without legal restraint.

Following the July 27 violence, the authorities charged that a small, unauthorized, leftist-oriented group, the Democratic People's Party (PRD) had incited the violence and was a Communist organization bent on forcibly overthrowing the Government. They launched a nationwide search for PRD members and promised to capture the leaders. PRD leader Budiman Sudjatmiko has been detained since early August. The Government intimidated political activists through a campaign of police questioning. Ousted PDI Chair Megawati Sukarnoputri was questioned several times as a witness in several cases, and prominent human rights, environmental, labor, and democracy activists faced similar treatment. Soerjadi, who replaced Megawati as PDI chair, was also questioned. The questioning sessions by the police or Attorney General's Office were lengthy, lasting a full day in some cases. Most of those questioned were not named as suspects, but the Government stated publicly that witnesses could become suspects. Following up on this threat, in late September, the Government called a PDI legislator in for questioning as a suspect, claiming that he had "insulted the President" at the "free speech forum."

Government security officials monitor the movements and activities of former members of the Communist Party of Indonesia (PKI) and its front organizations, especially persons the Government believes were involved in the abortive 1965 Communist-backed coup. These persons and their relatives sometimes are subject to surveillance, required check-ins, periodic indoctrination, and restrictions on travel outside their city of residence. One of the methods the Government has used to monitor the activities of these people has been to require that the initials "E.T." ("Ex-Tapol" or political prisoner) be stamped in their identification cards. This allows the government and prospective employers to identify former Communist Party members, and subjects them to official and unofficial discrimination. Although the requirement that E.T. be stamped in identification cards is being phased out, many individuals still carry such cards.

In recent years the Government significantly reduced its transmigration program, which moves large numbers of people from overpopulated islands to more isolated and less developed ones. Human rights monitors say that the program violates the rights of indigenous people and dupes some transmigrants into leaving their home villages without any means of return. Transmigrants and migrants outside the government transmigration program received indirect government support in the form of developmental assistance programs and contracts with ABRI or local government officials. This practice, particularly in East Timor and Irian Jaya, led to resentment among indigenous populations. The resulting communal tensions led to rioting in both locations.

The Government prohibits the import of Chinese-language publications (see Section 5).

Section 2. Respect for Civil Liberties, Including:

a. *Freedom of Speech and Press.*—Although the 1945 Constitution and the 1982 Press Law provide for freedom of the press, the Government continued to restrict press freedom in practice. Following the revocation of the publishing licenses of three well-known newsmagazines in 1994, in June the Supreme Court overturned lower court rulings and upheld the 1994 ban on Tempo magazine.

The Government uses the issuance of publishing licenses under a 1984 ministerial decree to control the press. Other means of control include regulation of the amount of advertising permitted and of the number of pages allowed in newspapers. In sensitive areas, the authorities continued to provide guidance to local journalists and editors on what they should print, although there were many cases where such guidance was ignored.

Vigorous debate on a number of sensitive topics, such as corruption, the role of the first family in business, and lack of government fiscal accountability, continued, particularly in the English-language press. Major Indonesian-language newspapers were more cautious in covering controversial subjects.

While public dialogue is freer than it was a number of years ago the Government continues to impose restrictions on free speech. For example, the violent expulsion of Megawati Sukarnoputri supporters from the PDI headquarters in Jakarta on July 27 effectively shut down the "free speech forum" that had been held at the headquarters for several weeks. In May a Jakarta district court supported the Government's position when it convicted former Member of Parliament Sri Bintang Pamungkas of insulting President Soeharto during an April 1995 lecture in Berlin. He was sentenced to 2 years and 10 months, but has not yet started serving his sentence pending appeal.

Nobel Prize co-laureate Bishop Belo was subjected to intense government pressure to retract published remarks critical of some government and military actions in East Timor. He eventually did so, after being the target of government-organized demonstrations when he travelled to Jakarta and issued a partial repudiation of some parts of the article in which he had been quoted. A number of students were detained after a November 25 demonstration in Dili, apparently for displaying anti-Soeharto banners; all but one were eventually released. A journalist in Yogyakarta was attacked in his home by unidentified intruders, possibly in connection with articles he had written that were critical of local government officials' actions in land cases. He died several days later as a result of the injuries sustained during the attack. The investigation into the case was taken out of the hands of the local police several weeks after the incident. The police arrested a suspect in the crime, but the Human Rights Commission expressed concerns about the process in which the suspect was detained and there was widespread public doubt as to whether the right person had been apprehended. The suspect was released from custody in December, but remains under suspicion.

In addition, there were several cases of violent attacks on, and intimidation of the news media during and after the PDI related disturbances in Jakarta. During a June 20 clash between PDI demonstrators and security forces, an employee of a foreign news organization was hit by security personnel, and there were reports that other foreign and local news personnel suffered injuries that day as well. During the July 27 incident, at least three foreign journalists had minor injuries inflicted by the police. At least two local journalists suffered police beatings that required hospitalization. Two journalists in Surabaya were reportedly detained during a protest against the takeover of PDI headquarters. Although they identified themselves as journalists, they were beaten while in custody. A group of Western journalists was threatened with a drawn pistol by a police officer while witnessing the violent breakup of a PDI demonstration by security forces on July 28. On October 28, security forces raided a printing house used to produce the October edition of the Alliance of Independent Journalists' (AJI) unlicensed magazine Suara Independen. They seized 5,000 copies of the magazine and arrested a print shop technician and an AJI activist who was picking up the magazine. The two were charged with distributing printed material defaming the President, and if convicted could each be imprisoned for 6 years.

The electronic media remained more cautious in their coverage of the Government than the print media. The Government operates a nationwide television network with 12 regional stations. Private commercial television companies, many with ownership by, or management ties to, the President's family, continued to expand. All are required to broadcast government-produced news, but many also produce public affairs style programming with news content.

Over 600 private radio broadcasting companies exist in addition to the Government's national radio network. They all were required to belong to the government-sponsored Association of Private Radio Stations (PRSSNI) to receive a broadcasting license. The government radio station produces the program "National News," which is the only news permitted by law to be broadcast in Indonesia. It is relayed throughout the country by private stations and 49 regional affiliates of the Government station. By law, the private radio stations may produce only "light" news, such as human interest stories, and may not discuss politics. In practice, however, many broadcast interviews and foreign news as well.

Foreign television and radio broadcasts were readily accessible. Satellite dishes have proliferated throughout the country, and there was access to the Internet. The Government made no effort to restrict access to this programming, and has proclaimed an "open skies" policy. Some signals have been scrambled by broadcasters for commercial reasons.

The Government closely regulates access to Indonesia, particularly to certain areas of the country, by visiting and resident foreign correspondents. It occasionally reminds the latter of its prerogative to deny requests for visa extensions. Numerous foreign journalists were still in Jakarta on July 27, following the Association of Southeast Asian Nations (ASEAN) meetings the week before, and were able to cover the incident for an international audience. The Government requires a permit for the importation of foreign publications and video tapes, which must be reviewed by government censors. Importers sometimes avoided foreign materials critical of the Government or dealing with topics considered sensitive, such as human rights. Foreign publications are widely available.

Publishers sometimes refused to accept manuscripts dealing with controversial issues. Most books by the prominent Indonesian novelist and former political prisoner Pramoedya Ananta Toer are banned. The Attorney General's Office reported publicly that two publications were banned in 1996.

Special permission is necessary for foreign journalists to travel to East Timor, Aceh, and Irian Jaya. With a few exceptions (including permission for journalists to accompany a diplomatic delegation in April, to cover President Soeharto's visit in October, and to attend a press conference by Bishop Belo in November) press access to East Timor was restricted. A number of journalists repeatedly requested permission to go to East Timor without success.

While the law provides for academic freedom, constraints exist on the activities of scholars. Political activity and discussions at universities, while no longer formally banned, remained constrained. Some scholars displayed caution in producing or including in lectures and class discussions materials that might provoke government displeasure.

b. *Freedom of Peaceful Assembly and Association.*—The Constitution provides for freedom of assembly and association; however, the Government places significant controls on the exercise of these rights. Until 1995 public meetings of five or more persons, as well as academic or other seminars and marches and demonstrations, required permits from the police and several government agencies. While obtaining such approval was usually routine, the authorities occasionally arbitrarily and inconsistently withheld permission or broke up peaceful gatherings for which no permit had been obtained. The Government promulgated regulations in December 1995 that eliminated the permit requirements for some types of public meetings. A requirement to notify the police remained. Some meetings continued to be prevented or broken up. Meetings by the Indonesian Prosperity Union (SBSI) were broken-up in October and December, despite the fact that it had given the police notification. Various NGO's had difficulty obtaining approval to hold meetings following the July 27 violence.

The 1985 Social Organizations Law (ORMAS) requires the adherence of all organizations, including recognized religions and associations, to the official ideology of Pancasila. This provision, which limits political activity, is widely understood as designed to inhibit activities of groups seeking to engage freely in democratic political competition, make Indonesia an Islamic state, revive communism, or return the country to a situation of partisan ideological division. This law empowers the Government to disband any organization it believes to be acting against Pancasila and requires prior government approval for any organization's acceptance of funds from foreign donors, thereby hindering the work of many local humanitarian organizations. Nevertheless, a significant number of organizations, including the independent labor organization Serikat Buruh Sejahtera Indonesia (SBSI), continued to be active without official recognition under this law. Sri Bintang Pamungkas established the Democratic Union Party (PUDI) in May. As only three political parties are permitted in Indonesia, it was not recognized by the Government but was not banned. However, after the July 27 violence, the Government cited the unauthorized PRD as a subversive, neo-Communist organization and has sought to arrest its membership (see Section 1.f.).

In the past few years, NGO's have proliferated in such fields as human rights, the environment, development, and consumer protection. Until 1996 the Government gave them rather wide latitude to pursue their aims, including public criticism of government policies and in some cases lawsuits against the Government. Following the July 27 violence, the Government moved to monitor activities by certain NGO's and activists more closely, which had an intimidating effect. In November high level government officials threatened publicly that legal action could be taken against selected NGO's deemed to be "trouble-making." Even before July, there were signs of government concern over political activism. The establishment of the Independent Election Monitoring Committee (KIPP) by political activists in March met with a mixed response from the Government and sporadic harassment. KIPP's national leader was called in for questioning after the July 27 violence. On April 21, the Legal Aid Foundation's (LBH) Medan office was stoned by unidentified individuals during a gathering of local activists preparing to form a local chapter of KIPP. Several police officers were nearby but took no action to stop the attack. Early the next morning, the LBH office was burned and completely destroyed.

c. *Freedom of Religion.*—The Constitution provides for religious freedom and belief in one Supreme God. The Government recognizes Islam, Catholicism, Protestantism, Buddhism, and Hinduism, and permits the practice of the mystical, traditional beliefs of "Aliran Kepercayaan." Although the population is over 85 percent Muslim, the practice and teachings of the other recognized religions are generally respected, and the Government actively promotes mutual tolerance and harmony among them. However, some restrictions on certain types of religious activity, including unrecognized religions, exist.

Because the first tenet of Pancasila is belief in one Supreme God, atheism is forbidden. The legal requirement to adhere to Pancasila extends to all religious and secular organizations. The Government strongly opposes Muslim groups that advocate establishing an Islamic state or acknowledging only Islamic law. The Government banned some religious sects including Jehovah's Witnesses, Baha'i, and in some provinces the messianic Islamic sect Darul Arqam. The Government closely monitors Islamic sects considered in danger of deviating from orthodox tenets, and in the past has on occasion dissolved such groups.

High-level officials continued to make public statements and emphasize by example the importance of respect for religious diversity in the country. Lower-level officials, however, were frequently alleged to be reluctant to facilitate and protect the rights of religious minorities.

The law allows conversion between faiths, and such conversions occur. The Government views proselytizing by recognized religions in areas heavily dominated by another recognized religion as potentially disruptive and discourages it. Foreign missionary activities are relatively unimpeded, although in East Timor and occasionally elsewhere missionaries have experienced difficulties and delays in renewing residence permits, and visas allowing the entrance of new foreign clergy are difficult to obtain. Laws and decrees from the 1970's limit the number of years that foreign missionaries can spend in Indonesia, with some extensions granted in remote areas like Irian Jaya. Foreign missionary work is subject to the funding stipulations of the ORMAS Law. Citizens practicing the recognized religions maintain active links with coreligionists inside and outside the country and travel abroad for religious gatherings.

d. *Freedom of Movement Within the Country, Foreign Travel, Emigration, and Repatriation.*—Although in 1993 the Government drastically reduced the number of people barred either from entering or departing Indonesia from a publicly announced figure of 8,897 "blacklisted" people to a few hundred, such restrictions still exist. The Government also restricts movement by citizens and foreigners to and within parts of the country. In addition, it requires permits to seek work in a new location in certain areas, primarily to control further population movement to crowded cities. Special permits are required to visit certain parts of Irian Jaya. The authorities require former political detainees, including those associated with the abortive 1965 coup, to give notice of their movements and to have official permission to change their place of residence (see Section 1.f.). Following the July 27 incident, a travel ban was imposed on Budiman Sudjatmiko and other PRD members sought by government authorities.

In past years, the Government offered first asylum to over 125,000 Indochinese boat people. In September Indonesia's Galang Island camp was closed as the last remaining asylum seekers were repatriated. There remain, however, some 18 persons awaiting a third country resettlement opportunity. While providing first asylum for Vietnamese and Cambodian boat people, the Government has not formulated a policy regarding asylum seekers of other nationalities. In 1996 the United Nations High Commissioner for Refugees (UNHCR) assisted 21 non-Indochinese who were recognized as refugees under the UNHCR mandate. The Government has refused to grant these refugees asylum or legal permission to stay in Indonesia. Some have been accepted for resettlement in third countries, while others have been held in detention or allowed to stay in Indonesia without legal status. There were no reports of forced return of persons to a country where they feared persecution.

A number of East Timorese asylum seekers who took refuge in various embassies in Jakarta were permitted to emigrate after negotiations.

Section 3. Respect for Political Rights: The Right of Citizens to Change Their Government

Citizens do not have the ability to change their government through democratic means. In June the Government engineered the ouster of the popular leader of the Indonesian Democratic Party (PDI)—Megawati Sukarnoputri, who had become the subject of public speculation as a possible candidate for president in 1998—and the subsequent violent removal of her supporters from PDI headquarters in July. So far there has never been an electoral challenge to President Soeharto.

The 1,000-member People's Consultative Assembly (MPR), is constitutionally the highest authority of the State. It meets every 5 years to elect the President and Vice President and to set the broad outlines of state policy. The MPR is effectively controlled by President Soeharto and his government, therefore, the election of any candidate other than one of his choosing is essentially impossible. Five hundred members of the MPR come from the National Parliament (DPR), 425 of whose members will be elected in elections in 1997 (up from 400 elected members in 1992). The remaining 75 members will be military appointees. In 1993 the MPR elected Soeharto to his sixth uncontested 5-year term as President. Legally the President is constitutionally subordinate to the Parliament, but actually he and a small group of associates exercise governmental authority.

Under a doctrine known as dual function, the military assumes a significant sociopolitical as well as a security role. Members of the military were allotted 100 unelected seats in the DPR, in partial compensation for not being permitted to vote. In 1995 the Government legislated a reduction in the number of these seats from 100 to 75, or 15 percent of a total of 500, effective in 1997. This reduction has already taken place through attrition. The military will continue to hold an unelected 20 percent of the seats in provincial and district parliaments, and to occupy numerous key positions in the administration. The other 85 percent of national and 80 percent of local parliamentary seats are filled through elections held every 5 years. All adult citizens, except active duty members of the armed forces, convicted criminals serving prison sentences, and some 36,000 former members of the Communist Party, are eligible to vote. Voters choose by secret ballot between the three government-approved political organizations, which field candidate lists in each electoral district. Those lists must be screened by BAKORSTANAS, which determines whether candidates were involved in the abortive 1965 Communist coup or pose other broadly defined security risks. Critics charge that these screenings are unconstitutional, since there is no way to appeal the results, and note that they can be used to eliminate critics of the Government from Parliament.

Strict rules establish the length of political campaigns, access to electronic media, schedules for public appearances, and the political symbols that can be used. The Government formally permits only three political organizations to exist and contest elections (see Section 2.b.). The largest and most important of these is GOLKAR, a government-controlled organization of diverse functional groups that won 68 percent of the seats in the 1992 elections. The President strongly influences the selection of the leaders of GOLKAR. The other two small political organizations, the United Development Party (PPP) and the Indonesian Democratic Party (PDI), gained 17 and 15 percent respectively of the remaining vote. The two smaller parties are not permitted to maintain party offices below the district level, placing them at a disadvantage to the government-supported GOLKAR. The law requires all three political organizations to embrace Pancasila, and none of the organizations is considered an opposition party. (After the July violence in Jakarta, the Government cracked down on the PRD, a small leftist organization that it charged was an unauthorized political party bent on subverting the Government (see Section 1.f.). Government authorities closely scrutinize and often guide the activities of the three political organizations, as evidenced by the blatant intervention in the internal affairs of the PDI in 1996. Members of the DPR and the provincial assemblies may be recalled from office by party leaders.

GOLKAR maintains close institutional links with the armed forces and KORPRI, the association to which all civil servants automatically belong. Civil servants may join any of the political parties with official permission, but most are members of GOLKAR. Former members of the PKI and some other banned parties may not run for office or be active politically. The DPR considers bills presented to it by government departments and agencies but does not draft laws on its own, although it has the constitutional authority to do so. The DPR does make technical, and occasionally substantive alterations to bills it reviews. In practice, it remains clearly subordinate to the executive branch, but recently it has become more active in scrutinizing government policy, and exercising oversight of government budgetary expenditures and program implementation through hearings at which members of the Cabinet, military commanders, and other high officials are asked to testify. The Speaker of the DPR has publicly called for a larger role for the body. The DPR has also become increasingly a focal point of appeals and petitions from students, workers, displaced farmers, and others protesting alleged human rights abuses and airing other grievances. It rarely is the source of any relief to petitioners other than providing a channel through which their complaints can be aired.

While there are no legal restrictions on the role of women in politics, they are underrepresented in government. About 11 percent (55 of 500) DPR members are women; 2 women are cabinet members. During the selection process of candidates for Parliament, discussion of the underrepresentation of women has arisen. The State Minister for Women's Roles complained publicly that GOLKAR was nominating fewer women than had been promised.

Section 4. Governmental Attitude Regarding International and Nongovernmental Investigation of Alleged Violations of Human Rights

Domestic human rights organizations and other NGO's have been subjected to a systematic government crackdown since the July 27 violence at PDI headquarters. The Government has used the violence associated with the July 27 incident as a pretext to intimidate, arrest, and otherwise pressure human rights and other activists into limiting their activities. NGO's faced government harassment including police raids on their offices, surveillance by police or military intelligence, interrogations at police stations, or cancellations of private meetings; in some cases high level government officials threatened that legal action would be taken against them because they were considered to be trouble-making. While no NGO's had been banned or subject to formal legal action as of the end of the year, the harassment and intimidation continued. Moreover, some small NGO's were effectively forced to close their doors after July 27.

The Government has resisted a proposal by the United Nations Human Rights Commission to open an office in Jakarta that would have the capacity to monitor human rights developments. The Government had indicated a willingness to permit an office to open in Jakarta only if its mission was restricted to technical operations such as conducting seminars without any monitoring function.

The Government considers outside investigations or foreign-based criticism of alleged human rights violations to be interference in its internal affairs. It emphasizes its belief that linking foreign assistance or other sanctions related to its human rights observance constitutes interference in its internal affairs and is therefore unacceptable.

Sources in Irian Jaya claim that the Government has obstructed NGO and church efforts to investigate ABRI actions in the Mapenduma area, where hostage taking had occurred early in the year, which, according to unconfirmed reports from government critics, had resulted in losses among the civilian population. The Government claims that it has limited access to the area for all nonresidents as a security measure.

The ICRC continued to operate in East Timor, Irian Jaya, and Aceh, and to visit prisoners convicted of participation in the abortive, Communist-backed coup in 1965, convicted Muslim extremists, and East Timorese prisoners. The Government also permitted the ICRC to visit 10 detainees in the custody of the Attorney General's Office who had been arrested in connection with the July 27 violence in Jakarta. The Government also invited senior foreign government officials to visit with two of these detainees on one occasion.

While receiving support for its work from the Government in principle, the ICRC periodically faced difficulty in implementing its humanitarian program in East Timor. The ICRC no longer maintains an office in Irian Jaya, but it visits that province from Jakarta several times a year. The ICRC was deeply involved in the attempt to negotiate an end to the January-May hostage crisis in Irian Jaya, working in close collaboration with the Government to achieve a nonviolent end to that crisis. The ICRC also visits Aceh regularly, but the Government has not approved the ICRC's request to open an office there. Travel to East Timor by foreign human rights NGO's has not been approved. Domestic human rights organizations are able to visit East Timor.

The Government-appointed National Human Rights Commission, in its third year of operation, continued to be active in examining reported human rights violations and continued to show independence and a willingness to criticize government actions and policies. It investigated the April deaths of students in Ujung Pandang, issued a forthright statement in June condemning the Government's interference in internal PDI affairs, and launched an investigation of the July 27 incident, which was widely considered to be its greatest challenge yet. Its report on the July 27 incident, released October 12, found the Government and its security apparatus partially responsible for the violence. The Government has not responded to the Commission's report or taken any steps to punish those government and government-backed personnel responsible for the violence.

Lacking enforcement powers, the Commission attempts to work within the system, sending teams where necessary to inquire into possible human rights problems and employing persuasion, publicity, and moral authority to highlight abuses, make recommendations for legal and regulatory changes, and encourage corrective action. The Commission now occupies its own permanent facilities, but still continues to have very limited staff support.

Although the Government appointed the original Commission members, the Commission fills vacancies in its ranks independently by internal election. A new chairman and four new members, replacing those who had died while in office, were elected in the fall.

The Commission opened an East Timor office in June. This was widely regarded as a positive step in the ongoing effort to address and resolve human rights abuses in East Timor. However, many observers also had doubts about the potential effectiveness of the East Timor office because of its location next to the local military headquarters, its leadership by a non-Timorese, its reliance on government-provided staffing, and the fact that it could only receive complaints and send them back to Jakarta, but not take action itself. The initial flow of citizens to the facility tended to comprise people who did not make complaints regarding the Government, the military, or local authorities, conveying the impression that the local population were reluctant to approach the facility. As of year's end, the office had limited itself to dealing only with nonpolitical cases and therefore had made little impact with regard to the more serious human rights problems in East Timor. The Commission is trying to address some of the problems that have impeded the effectiveness of the office.

Findings issued by the Commission that were critical of the Government or disagreed with the government perspective, notably with regard to the interim report on the July 27 rioting in Jakarta, have drawn thinly veiled government rebukes and warnings. Moreover, the Government has tended to ignore some commission findings or, in some instances, has moved lethargically in reaction to them. The Government has not responded to the Commission's final report on the July 27 violence issued October 12. Of six cases of ABRI abuse of indigenous people in Irian Jaya identified by the Commission in September 1995, only one had led to court action by year's end.

Section 5. Discrimination Based on Race, Sex, Religion, Disability, Language, or Social Status

The Constitution does not explicitly forbid discrimination based on gender, race, disability, language, or social status. However, the Constitution stipulates equal rights and obligations for all citizens, both native and naturalized. Chapter 4 of the 1993 Guidelines of State Policy (legal statutes adopted by the People's Consultative Assembly) explicitly states that women have the same rights, obligations, and opportunities as men. However, marriage law dictates that men are the head of the family. The Constitution grants citizens the right to practice their individual religion and beliefs; however, the Government imposes some restrictions on religious activity.

Women.—Violence against women remains poorly documented. However, the Government has acknowledged the problem of domestic violence in society, which some say has been aggravated by social changes brought about by rapid urbanization. Longstanding traditional beliefs that the husband may "teach" or "control" the wife through several means, including violence, also contribute to the problem. Rape by a husband of a wife is not a crime, although women's groups are trying to change this law. While police could bring assault charges against a husband for beating his wife, due to social attitudes they are unlikely to do so. Cultural norms dictate that problems between husband and wife are private problems, and violence against women in the home is rarely reported. The Government provides some counseling, and several private organizations exist to assist women. Many of these organizations focus on reuniting the family rather than on providing protection to the women involved. Many women rely on extended family systems for assistance in cases of domestic violence. In 1995 the first drop-in center for battered women was founded in Jakarta by an NGO. Another drop-in center was founded in Jakarta by the official, government-sponsored National Women's Organization (KOWANI). There is one crisis center for women in Yogyakarta run by an NGO. There are NGO plans for training volunteer counselors to work at a women's crisis center/shelter, which is also to have a hot line, which is expected to open as soon as funds are available.

Rape is a punishable offense in Indonesia. Men have been arrested and sentenced for rape and attempted rape although reliable statistics are unavailable. Mob violence against accused rapists is frequently reported. Women's rights activists believe that rape is grossly underreported owing to the social stigma attached to the victim. Some legal experts state that if a woman does not go immediately to the hospital for a physical examination that produces physical evidence of rape, she will not be able to bring charges. A witness is also required in order to bring charges, and only in rare cases is there a witness. Some women reportedly fail to report rape to police, because the police do not take their allegations seriously.

There is no sexual harassment law, only an indecent behavior law. Sexual harassment charges, however, can damage a civil service career. The current law reportedly covers physical abuse only, and requires two witnesses. Women job applicants and workers have complained of being sexually victimized by foremen and factory owners.

According to the Constitution, women are equal to and have the same rights, obligations, and opportunities as men. However, in practice women face some legal discrimination. Marriage law, based on Islamic law, allows men to have up to four wives if the first wife is unable "to fulfill her tasks as a wife." Permission of the first wife is required, but reportedly most women cannot refuse. A civil servant who wishes to marry a second woman also must have the consent of his supervisor. To set an example, the President has forbidden cabinet officials and senior military officers from having second wives. In divorce cases women often bear a heavier evidentiary burden than men, especially in the Islamic-based family court system. Alimony is rarely received by divorced women, and there is no enforcement of alimony payment. By law, a woman cannot pass citizenship to her child, born inside or outside Indonesia, if the father of the child is not a citizen. The child must obtain residency visas to remain in Indonesia, and can only apply for citizenship when he or she reaches the age of 18. A case in which the court ordered the deportation of a 4-year-old child of an Indonesian woman and non-Indonesian man attracted considerable media attention during the year.

Although some women enjoy a high degree of economic and social freedom and occupy important mid-level positions in both the public and private sectors, the majority of women do not experience such social and economic freedoms and are often disproportionately represented at the lower end of the socioeconomic scale. Although women constitute one-quarter of the civil service, they occupy only a small fraction of the service's top posts. Income disparity between men and women diminishes significantly with greater educational attainment.

Female workers in manufacturing generally receive lower wages than men. Many female factory workers are hired as day laborers instead of as full-time permanent employees, and companies are not required to provide benefits, such as maternity leave, to day laborers. Female activists report that a growing trend in manufacturing is the hiring of women to do work in their homes for less than minimum wage. Unemployment rates for women are approximately 50 percent higher than for men. Women are often not given the extra benefits and salary that are their due when they are the head of household, and in some cases do not receive employment benefits for their husband and children, such as medical insurance and income tax deductions.

Despite laws that provide women with a 3-month maternity leave, the Government has conceded that pregnant women are often dismissed or are replaced while on leave. Some companies require that women sign statements that they will not become pregnant. The employment law mandates 2 days of menstrual leave per month for women.

Women disproportionately experience illiteracy, poor health, and inadequate nutrition. The President has called for expanded efforts to reduce the maternal mortality rate, which at 425 per 100,000 live births is very high. The Government, with the help of international donors, launched a major effort in December to reduce the maternal mortality rate. Women's educational indicators have improved in the last decade. For example, the number of girls graduating from high school tripled from 1980 to 1990. A number of voluntary private groups work actively to advance women's legal, economic, social, and political rights and claim some success in gaining official cognizance of women's concerns.

Women's NGO's have felt pressure from increased government scrutiny of all NGO's in the wake of the July 27 violence in Jakarta.

Children.—The Government is committed to children's rights and welfare, but is hampered by a lack of resources that prevents it from translating this commitment into practice. A 1979 law on children's welfare defines the responsibility of the State and parents to nurture and protect children. However, implementing regulations have never been developed, and the law's provisions have yet to go into effect. The Government has made particular efforts to improve primary education and maternity services. Although primary education is in principle universal, the United Nations Children's Fund (UNICEF) estimates that more than 1 million children drop out of primary school every year due mainly to the cost of supplies, uniforms, and other expenses, in addition to the professed need for the children to supplement family income. Government figures put the number of working children between the ages of 10 and 14 at 8 percent of the total, half of whom go to school and also work and half of whom work exclusively. Unofficial estimates are higher.

According to the Ministry of Social Affairs, there are between 20,000 and 30,000 street children in Jakarta. Thousands more live in other cities. They sell newspapers, shine shoes, help to park or watch cars, and otherwise earn money. Many thousands more work in factories and fields (see Section 6.d.). According to NGO sources, there are thousands of children working on fishing platforms off the coast of North Sumatra for average monthly salaries of $12 to $18. There are reports of harsh living conditions and virtual abduction of children from parents who are misled into thinking the children will be paid and treated well.

There is reportedly growing Government concern about street children, because in some cities they have become well organized and more interested in protecting their rights.

NGO's criticize government efforts to help street children and working children as inadequate, although the Government is beginning to address the problems. The Ministries of Manpower, Education, Welfare, and Foreign Affairs, along with the Regional Planning Board, the United Nations Development Program, and four indigenous NGO's are designing a program to address the needs of working children. The project incorporates many ideas generated by the NGO community, including establishing "open houses" in targeted areas which will provide vocational training and basic education to street children. The project has begun on a pilot basis in Jakarta and Surabaya, and is planned for Bandung, Yogyakarta, Semarang, Ujung Pandang, and Medan.

Another approach being taken to the street children problem utilizes the National Program for Discipline and Clean Cities Decree. The street children are physically removed from cities by bus. Usually, they are taken outside the city and left there. Sometimes they are taken to "holding houses" where they are first interrogated and later released. One NGO reported that in the latter part of the year, Bandung city expanded efforts to "clean" the streets of street children, and was busing them out of the city several times a week.

NGO's working for the rights of children experienced increased harassment by the authorities. Several groups have reported that it became more difficult to obtain the required government permission for their activities. An exhibition and seminar about street children and violence planned by an NGO was canceled by the authorities the day before it was to open. Visiting street children were put in buses and escorted out of the region by the military.

Child prostitution and other sexual abuses occur, but data on their incidence are lacking. While there are laws designed to protect children from indecent activities, prostitution, and incest, the Government has made no special enforcement efforts in these areas. Greater attention was paid to the problem of child prostitution in the press, which may have resulted in increasing awareness of a problem that is poorly documented.

A separate criminal justice system for juveniles does not exist. Police officials admit that juveniles are often imprisoned with adult offenders. Currently juvenile crime is handled by ordinary courts. A juvenile justice law was passed December 19. It defines juveniles as children between the ages of 8 and 18, and establishes a special court system and criminal code for them. The draft bill had been controversial because four articles were seen as not in line with Islamic law and doctrine. They covered custody, adoption, neglected children, and care of delinquents, and among other things would have permitted the adoption of Muslim children by non-Muslims. The Government removed the contentious article to secure passage of the bill.

A form of female genital mutilation (FGM), which is widely condemned by international health experts as damaging to both physical and psychological health, is practiced in some parts of Indonesia. There are no statistics available; the only information available is anecdotal. Usually a small section of the tip of the clitoris is cut or a small incision is made with the purpose of drawing a few drops of blood. Total removal of the clitoris is not the objective of the practice, although it does occur if ineptly performed. It usually takes place within the first year after birth, often on the 40th day, though it can be done up to age seven. It is performed either at a hospital or, especially in rural areas, by a local traditional practitioner or "dukun." More severe forms of FGM are reportedly practiced in certain areas.

People With Disabilities.—The Constitution stipulates that the Government provide care for orphans and the disabled, but does not specify how the term "care" should be defined, and the provision of education to all mentally and physically disabled children has never been inferred. Regulations specify that the Government establish and regulate a national curriculum for special education by stipulating that the "community" provide special education services to its children.

There are no accurate statistics on the numbers of disabled in the general population. Families often hide their disabled family members to avoid social stigma or embarrassment. The disabled face considerable discrimination in employment, although there are factories that have made special efforts to hire disabled workers. In several provinces there are "rehabilitation centers" for the disabled. Disabled people are reportedly taken off the streets by the authorities and brought to these centers for job training.

NGO's are the primary providers of education for the disabled. There are currently 1,084 schools for the disabled; 680 are private, and 404 are government schools. Of the government schools 165 are "integrated," serving both regular and special education students. In Jakarta there are 98 schools for the disabled, 2 of which are government-run, and 96 of which are private. The Government also runs three national schools for the visually, hearing, and mentally disabled. These schools accept children from throughout Indonesia.

There is no law that mandates accessibility to buildings and public transportation for the disabled, and virtually no buildings or public transportation are designed with such accessibility in mind.

Indigenous People.—The Government considers the term "indigenous people" to be a misnomer, because it considers all Indonesians to be indigenous. Nonetheless, it publicly recognizes the existence of several "isolated communities," and that they have a right to participate fully in political and social life. The Government estimates the number of people in isolated communities is 1.5 million. This includes, but is not limited to, groups such as the Dayak population in Kalimantan who live in remote forest areas, indigenous communities throughout Irian Jaya, and economically disadvantaged families living as sea nomads on boats near Riau in east Sumatra and near Ujung Pandang in Southern Sulawesi. Critics maintain that the Government's approach is basically paternalistic and designed more to integrate indigenous people more closely into Indonesian society than to protect their traditional way of life. Human rights monitors criticize the Government's transmigration program for violating the rights of indigenous people (see Section 1.f.).

A majority of the cases brought to legal aid organizations throughout Indonesia concern complaints about land seizure. According to a law derived from Dutch practices, all subsurface mineral resources belong to the Government. The Basic Agrarian Law states that land rights cannot be "in conflict with national and state interests," which provides the Government with a broad legal basis for land seizures. When disputes cannot be settled the Government has the authority to define fair compensation for land. There are a number of reports of the use of intimidation, sometimes by the authorities, for land acquisition. In East Kalimantan, according to a foreign human rights group, 14 men were severely mistreated by military personnel after failed negotiations over a land dispute between villagers and a logging company (see Section 1.c.). In West Kalimantan reliable sources reported that local military accompanied plantation owners during negotiations with local land owners for land acquisition. In this case, although intimidation was used, two villages still refused to relinquish their land.

Where indigenous people clash with development projects, the developers almost always win. Decisions regarding development projects, resource-use concessions, and other economic activities are generally carried out without the participation or informed consent of the affected communities. Indonesian environmental NGO's that have sought to aid these communities have been subjected to verbal attacks, raids, and other forms of intimidation by government security forces.

Tensions with indigenous people in Irian Jaya, including in the vicinity of a foreign mining concession area near Timika, continued, highlighted by large-scale rioting by Irianese tribesmen in March. The Government and the foreign mining company alleged that Indonesian environmental NGO's and international NGO's had prodded the tribesmen to action. The Government and the foreign mining company have since tried to reach a financial settlement with tribal representatives. Indigenous Irian Jaya residents complain of racism, religious bias, paternalism, and condescension as constant impediments to better relations with non-Irian people, including members of the Government, the military, and the non-Irian business community. They also complain of abusive behavior by the Indonesian security forces (see Section 1.a.). Rioting in numerous Irian Jaya towns, including Timika/Tembagapura, Nabire, Jayapura, and Wamena, resulted in several deaths and many injuries. The riots tended to pit newly arrived nonindigenous peoples against indigenous groups who claimed that the "outsiders" were monopolizing jobs, exploiting local labor, and illegally expropriating indigenous lands. As a result of the deaths of civilians and other violent human rights abuses brought to light in 1995, four soldiers received prison terms in February (see Section 1.a.) Irianese have expressed anger that the Government has prosecuted only one of six cases identified in a September 1995 Human Rights Commission report as warranting government prosecution. In the one case that was prosecuted, the military court addressed only charges of murder and did not take up charges of rape of indigenous women.

Human rights monitors have expressed concern about the practices of some logging companies that recruit indigenous people for work. According to Human Rights Watch/Asia, this activity in Irian Jaya has separated these people from their traditional economies. In many cases, these new recruits for development projects are ill-prepared for the modern world, leading to their being forced into debt and then indentured (see Section 6.c.). Most civil servants in local governments in Irian Jaya and other isolated areas continue to come primarily from Java, rather than from the local indigenous population.

Religious Minorities.—There were several instances of religion-related mob violence. In July several Christian churches were burned in Surabaya. On October 10, Muslim rioters associated with the National Ulama (NU) Islamic organization burned or ransacked and destroyed 24 churches and a Buddhist temple on the East Java coast. A Protestant minister, his wife and child, and a church worker were burned to death. The riot was triggered by perceived insufficiency of a sentence meted out by a court for a man's alleged blasphemy against Islam. NU leader Abdurrahman Wahid, in an effort to maintain calm after the riot, expressed regrets for the riot. The reported police beating of Islamic teachers on December 23, along with the false rumor that one of the teachers had been killed, apparently was the cause of serious rioting in Tasikmalaya, West Java on December 26, involving thousands of people. Although sparked by anger over police abuse, the rioting reportedly targeted businesses, factories, and shops, including those owned by members of the Chinese community, churches, and police offices. The incident was being investigated by the National Human Rights Commission and the Legal Aid Foundation (LBH) as the year ended. In September a group of young people burned a Catholic church in east Jakarta. The group was apparently Muslim, and was seeking to eliminate non-Muslim influences in the area. In August, in Viqueque, East Timorese demonstrated against government-sponsored Muslim migrants to the area, and burned a number of shops owned by these migrants. In June, also in East Timor, the desecration of either a picture or statue of the Virgin Mary in Baucau sparked rioting on the part of the Catholic East Timorese. This led to numerous arrests and at least one serious injury.

National/Racial/Ethnic Minorities.—The Government officially promotes racial and ethnic tolerance. Ethnic Chinese, at approximately 3 percent of the population by far the largest nonindigenous minority group, are the target of both official and societal discrimination. Since 1959 noncitizen ethnic Chinese have been denied the right to run businesses in rural Indonesia. Regulations prohibit the operation of all Chinese schools, formation of exclusively Chinese cultural groups or trade associations, and public display of Chinese characters. Since August 1994, firms working in the tourist industry have been allowed to produce Chinese-language brochures, programs, and similar material for Chinese-speaking tourists. However, Chinese-language publications, with the exception of one government-owned daily newspaper, may neither be imported nor produced domestically.

Private instruction in Chinese is generally prohibited but takes place to a limited extent, and since 1994 has been allowed to train employees in the tourism industry. The University of Indonesia has Chinese-language courses. State universities have no formal quotas that limit the number of ethnic Chinese. The law forbids the celebration of the Chinese New Year in temples or public places, but its enforcement is limited.

East Timorese and various human rights groups charge that the East Timorese are underrepresented in the civil service in East Timor. The Government has made some efforts to recruit more civil servants in both East Timor and Irian Jaya, and there has been some increase in the number of civil servant trainees for these two provinces, despite a "no growth" policy for the civil service as a whole. East Timorese and Irianese, however, have been very reluctant to accept government jobs outside their own provinces. East Timorese have expressed concerns that the transmigration program (see Section 1.f.) could lead to fewer employment opportunities and might eventually destroy East Timor's cultural identity. However, transmigration projects in Timor have been reduced in recent years and are limited to Hindus and Christians to avoid religious friction. In 1995 a government official claimed that 75 percent of the transmigrants were from other parts of East Timor, and only 25 percent from other areas. In the last several years, informal predominantly Muslim migration to the province has sparked socioeconomic tension in urban areas, proving an even greater concern than the formally sponsored transmigration program.

Section 6. Worker Rights

a. *The Right of Association.*—Private sector workers are by law free to form worker organizations without prior authorization. However, government policies and current numerical requirements for union recognition constitute a significant barrier to freedom of association and the right to engage in collective bargaining. The Department of Manpower uses a regulation that requires that a union be set up "by and for workers" to deny recognition to groups that include people it considers nonworkers, such as lawyers or human rights activists, who are involved as labor organizers. Until 1994 only the government-sponsored Federation of All-Indonesian Trade Unions (SPSI) could legally bargain on behalf of employees or represent workers in the Department of Manpower's labor courts. However, single company unions were widespread in practice. A 1994 regulation provides that workers in a single company with more than 25 employees can join together as a "plant-level union" and negotiate a legally binding agreement with their employer outside the SPSI framework, although the Government encourages these plant-level unions to join the SPSI. According to the Department of Manpower, 1,144 plant-level unions had been established by year's end. Nongovernmental organizations have charged, however, that many of these unions are "yellow unions" formed by company management with little or no worker participation. There are also credible reports that local Department of Manpower officials accept payments from employers to set up plant-level unions in their factories because they are considered even weaker than SPSI. On the other hand, there are numerous reports of successful strikes by these single company unions, particularly against foreign ventures.

There is a de facto single union system, the SPSI and its 13 federated sectoral unions. The SPSI completed in 1995 a transformation from a unitary (centralized) to a federative (decentralized) structure. Its 13 industrial sectors are now registered as separate national unions; the SPSI is the only trade union federation recognized by the Department of Manpower. The Minister of Manpower has stated that any unions that are formed should affiliate with the SPSI federation, and that the Government will not recognize any unions outside the federation. The Government's stated policy is to improve effectiveness of the recognized SPSI unions rather than to allow the formation of alternative organizations.

The Government may dissolve a union if it believes that the union is acting against Pancasila, although it has never actually done so, and there are no laws or regulations specifying procedures for union dissolution.

Two labor groups other than SPSI are active but not recognized by the Government: the Serikat Buruh Sejahtera Indonesia (SBSI, Indonesian Prosperity Trade Union), and the Alliance of Independent Journalists (AJI). The SBSI, created in 1992, claims that it has formed the necessary number of factory-level units to meet the legal requirements for registration as a labor union, but its most recent request (in November 1994) for registration as a trade union was denied. The Department of Manpower has also blocked SBSI attempts to register with the Department of Home Affairs as a social organization under the ORMAS Law. The Government considers the SBSI to be illegal. Although the Government has not disbanded it, it continues to harass the SBSI, by means such as disbanding its meetings and training seminars. Specific government actions against the SBSI included the detention of Roliati Harefa, an SBSI organizer in Binjai, North Sumatra, for a month in January and again in April. Assault charges were filed against her after she had complained to the police that her supervisor had assaulted her. SBSI leader Muchtar Pakpahan was arrested on July 30. His trial on charges of subversion and sowing hatred against the Government began on December 12 and was still proceeding at year's end. Before his trial, the Government stated that he was being held for political activities, not labor activities. However, the Government's indictment against Pakpahan refers to his activities as head of the SBSI, states that he undertook activities together with fellow board members of the SBSI, and lists specific labor activities (e.g., a labor rally) as the basis for the charges against him. In October the Supreme Court, in an unprecedented decision, reinstated an old conviction against Pakpahan for fomenting labor unrest, thus requiring him to serve out a 4-year sentence that it had previously overturned.

Government pressure on the SBSI intensified after the July 27 violence in Jakarta, as the Attorney General's Office has questioned members of the union's Central Leadership Council and SBSI organizers around the country. Police confiscated SBSI archives from the union's central office in Jakarta, and closed down the union's office in Garut, West Java. In November a senior official of the Ministry of Home Affairs stated that the SBSI was one of the trouble-making NGO's the Government would investigate (see Section 4). It is widely believed that the Government's actions against the SBSI leadership were intended to discredit or destroy the organization.

The Association of Indonesian Journalists (PWI) is the only government-sanctioned organization representing journalists. Although press laws stipulate that all journalists must belong to PWI, a few journalists have avoided membership. In the wake of the 1994 banning of three publications approximately 80 journalists formed the Alliance of Independent Journalists (AJI) as an alternative to the government union. A government crackdown in March 1995 resulted in the imprisonment of three AJI members charged with "sowing hate." Despite occasional pressure on publications employing AJI members, the Government allows AJI a continued underground existence.

Because of past Department of Manpower regulations, many SPSI factory units are led by persons who have little credibility with their units' members because they were selected by employers. A 1995 regulation states that employees must only notify their employer that they wish to form a union and that they may proceed if they do not receive a response from their employer within 2 weeks. Despite this provision, strikes continue to occur when employers attempt to prevent the formation of union branches. These strikes are generally successful, and the formation of an SPSI unit follows shortly thereafter. However, workers who are active in the formation of the union are frequently dismissed and have no practical protection by either law or government practice.

Civil servants are not permitted to join unions and must belong to KORPRI, a nonunion association whose Central Development Council is chaired by the Minister of Home Affairs. State enterprise employees, defined to include those working in enterprises in which the State has a 5-percent holding or greater, usually are required to join KORPRI, but a small number of state enterprises have SPSI units. Teachers must belong to the Teachers' Association (PGRI). While technically classed as a union, the PGRI continues to function more as a welfare organization and does not appear to have engaged in trade union activities such as collective bargaining. Mandatory KORPRI and PGRI contributions are automatically deducted from teachers' salaries.

Unions may draw up their own constitutions and rules and elect their representatives. However, the Government has a great deal of influence over the SPSI and its federated unions. The head of SPSI and many members of the Executive Council are also members of GOLKAR and its constituent functional groups. These persons have been given positions in the federated industrial sector unions. The Minister of Manpower is a member of the SPSI's Consultative Council.

The Government announced late in 1995 its intention to relax a regulation requiring police approval for all meetings of five or more people of all organizations outside offices or normal work sites (see Section 2.b.). However, in practice this regulation continues to apply to union meetings. Permission was routinely given to the SPSI but not to rival organizations such as the SBSI.

In 1994 the International Confederation of Free Trade Unions lodged a formal complaint against Indonesia with the ILO, accusing the Government of denying workers the right to set up unions of their own choosing, harassing independent workers' organizations, and of taking other actions contrary to ILO standards on freedom of association and the right to collective bargaining. In considering this complaint, the ILO's Committee on Freedom of Association in November "deeply deplored" the fact that "virtually no remedial action was taken by the Indonesian authorities" in response to old and new allegations against it. The Committee found that "Indonesian legislation comprises requirements that are so stringent as to constitute a major limitation to freedom of association." The Committee urged the Government to "take all the necessary measures" to ensure that the SBSI be registered "without delay." The Committee also concluded that "there exists a strong presumption, which the Government has not reversed, to the effect that under the cover of allegations of subversive activity, the charges brought and the measures taken against Mr. Pakpahan are linked to his trade union activities." It urged the Government to "take without delay the necessary measures for Mr. Pakpahan's release (and) to drop the charges related to the July 1996 events."

While Pancasila principles call for labor-management differences to be settled by consensus, all organized workers except civil servants have the legal right to strike. While state enterprise employees and teachers rarely exercise this right, private sector strikes are frequent. Before a strike can occur legally in the private sector, the law requires intensive mediation by the Department of Manpower and prior notice of the intent to strike. However, no approval is required. In practice, dispute settlement procedures are not followed, and formal notice of the intent to strike is rarely given because Department of Manpower procedures are slow and have little credibility with workers. Therefore, sudden strikes tend to result from longstanding grievances or recognition that legally mandated benefits or rights are not being received. Strike leaders often lose their jobs and have no legal recourse for reinstatement. The number of strikes during the year increased to 346 from 276 in 1995, but most of the increase occurred before the July 27 violence and the subsequent crackdown on NGO's. NGO's believe that the actual number of strikes is higher, but agree with the general trend. The largest-scale labor protests occurred in Surabaya on July 8–9, involving thousands of workers. Police arrested 26 persons in connection with this incident.

The SPSI maintains international contacts but its only international trade union affiliation is the ASEAN Trade Union Council.

b. *The Right to Organize and Bargain Collectively.*—Collective bargaining is provided for by law, and the Department of Manpower promotes it within the context of the national ideology, Pancasila. Until 1994 only recognized trade unions—the SPSI and its components—could legally engage in collective bargaining. Since early 1994, government regulations also permit unaffiliated plant-level workers' associations to conclude legally binding agreements with employers, and some 24 had done so by mid-1995, according to government figures. Agreements concluded by any other groups are not considered legally binding and are not registered by the Department of Manpower. Once notified that 25 employees have joined a registered SPSI or independent plant-level union, an employer is obligated to bargain with it.

In companies without unions, the Government discourages workers from utilizing nongovernment outside assistance, e.g., during consultations with employers over company regulations. Instead, the Department of Manpower prefers that workers seek its assistance and believes that its role is to protect workers. There are credible reports that for many companies, consultations are perfunctory at best and usually with management-selected workers; there are also credible reports to the contrary from foreign companies. Over half of the factory-level SPSI units have collective bargaining agreements. The degree to which these agreements are freely negotiated between unions and management without government interference varies. By regulation, negotiations must be concluded within 30 days or be submitted to the Department of Manpower for mediation and conciliation or arbitration. Most negotiations are concluded within the 30-day period. Agreements are for 2 years and can be extended for 1 year. According to NGO's involved in labor issues, the provisions of these agreements rarely go beyond the legal minimum standards established by the Government, and the agreements are often merely presented to worker representatives for signing rather than being negotiated. Although government regulations prohibit employers from discriminating or harassing employees because of union membership, there are credible reports from union officials of employer retribution against union organizers, including firing, which is not effectively prevented or remedied in practice. Some employers reportedly have warned their employees against contact with union organizers from the unrecognized SBSI organization. Charges of antiunion discrimination are adjudicated by administrative tribunals. However, because many union members believe the tribunals generally side with employers, many workers reject or avoid the procedure and present their grievances directly to the National Human Rights Commission, Parliament and other agencies. Administrative decisions in favor of dismissed workers tend to be monetary awards; workers are rarely reinstated. The provisions of the law make it difficult to fire workers, but the law is often ignored in practice.

Commenting on antiunion discrimination and restrictions on collective bargaining in the context of ILO Convention 98 on the right to organize and bargain collectively, the ILO's Committee on the Application of Conventions and Recommendations' June report expressed "the firm hope that the Government will provide it in its next report with information with regard to the measures actually taken in order to bring law and practice more in line with the provisions of the Convention, and in particular to strengthen the protection of workers against acts of antiunion discrimination accompanied by effective and dissuasive sanctions, to adopt specific provisions to protect workers' organizations against acts of interference by employers or their organizations and to eliminate the restrictions imposed on free collective bargaining."

On June 1, the Minister of Manpower issued a new regulation permitting unions affiliated with the SPSI to collect union dues directly through the checkoff system, rather than having the Department of Manpower collect dues and transfer them to the SPSI. Dues are to be collected at the local level and then transmitted up the union chain.

The armed forces, which include the police, continue to involve themselves in labor issues, despite the Minister of Manpower's revocation in 1994 of a 1986 regulation allowing the military to intervene in strikes and other labor actions. However, a 1990 decree giving the Agency for Coordination of National Stability (BAKORSTANAS) authority to intervene in strikes in the interest of political and social stability remains in effect. There are some indications that military involvement in labor matters decreased from 1995 to mid-1996, but not all observers agree that this has occurred. Workers charge that members of the security forces attempt to intimidate union organizers and strike leaders and have been present in significant numbers during some strikes, even when there has been no destruction of property or other violence. Military officials occasionally have been present during negotiations between workers and management and other union activities. Their presence has been described as intimidating by plant-level union officials.

Labor law and practice are the same in export processing zones as in the rest of the country.

c. *Prohibition of Forced or Compulsory Labor.*—The law forbids forced labor, and the Government generally enforces it. However, there are credible reports of teenage children being forced to work under highly dangerous conditions on fishing platforms off the coast of northeastern Sumatra. These platforms are miles off shore, with access controlled by the employers, and in many cases the children are virtual prisoners on the platforms and forced to work for up to 3 months at a time for well below the minimum wage. According to knowledgeable sources, hundreds of children may be involved. The Government has done little to address the problem. There are also allegations that indigenous people who take jobs in the modern sector sometimes end up indebted to their employers, and exploited as indentured labor (see Section 5 Indigenous People).

d. *Minimum Age for Employment of Children.*—Child labor exists in both urban and rural areas, and in both the formal and informal sectors. According to a 1995 report of the Indonesian Central Bureau of Statistics, 4 percent of Indonesian children between the ages of 10 and 14 work, and another 4 percent work in addition to going to school. Indonesia was one of the first countries to be selected for participation in the ILO's International Program on the Elimination of Child Labor (IPEC), and it signed a memorandum of understanding with the ILO in 1992 to guide collaboration under this program. Recommendations for an action plan were developed at a national conference in Bogor in 1993. By the end of the year, 130 government labor inspectors had received ILO-sponsored training on child labor matters under the IPEC program. However, enforcement remains lax.

The Government acknowledges that there is a class of children who must work for socioeconomic reasons, and in 1987 the Minister of Manpower issued regulation per-0l/men/1987, "Protection of Children Forced to Work," to regulate this situation. This regulation legalizes the employment of children under the age of 14 who must work to contribute to the income of their families. It requires parental consent, prohibits dangerous or difficult work, limits work to 4 hours daily, and requires employers to report the number of children working under its provisions. It does not set a minimum age for children in this category, effectively superseding the colonial-era government ordinance of December 17, 1925, on "Measures Limiting Child Labor and Nightwork of Women," which is still the current law governing child labor and sets a minimum age of 12 for employment. The 1987 regulation is not enforced. No employers have been taken to court for violating its restrictions on the nature of employment for children, and no reports are collected from establishments employing children.

Act No. 1 of 1951 was intended to bring into force certain labor measures, including provisions on child labor that would replace those of the 1925 legislation. However, implementing regulations for the child labor provisions have never been issued. Thus the child labor provisions in the 1951 Act have no validity.

e. *Acceptable Conditions of Work.*—There is no national minimum wage. Rather, area wage councils working under the supervision of the national wage council establish minimum wages for regions and basic needs figures for each province—a monetary amount considered sufficient to enable a single worker to meet the basic needs of nutrition, clothing, and shelter. While Indonesia has succeeded in dramatically lowering the level of poverty throughout the country, the minimum wage rates until recently have usually lagged behind inflation and even the basic needs figures. The Government raised minimum wage rates each of the last 3 years, and in 1996 required employers to pay workers for 30 days during a month. In Jakarta the minimum wage is about $2.28 (Rp 5200) per day. An additional increase is planned for early 1997.

There are no reliable statistics on the number of employers paying at least the minimum wage. Independent observers' estimates range between 30 and 60 percent. Several SPSI sector chairmen signed agreements with industry leaders delaying implementation of the minimum wage in their sectors. According to Department of Manpower figures, the Department investigated 75 cases of violations of labor laws during the year. Of the 28 cases decided by the end of the year, 6 cases resulted in prison sentences for company management, and 21 in fines; 1 employer was found not guilty. The Department of Manpower increased the number of labor inspectors and announced a scheme of "blacklisting" offending companies, but enforcement of minimum wage and other labor regulations remains inadequate, and sanctions too light. Over 200 companies have applied for and been granted relief from the latest minimum wage increases on the ground that the companies would otherwise close. In December the State Secretariat submitted a draft basic labor law which, among other things, would raise statutory fines, which have been devalued by inflation, to more appropriate levels. Some observers believe that increased government pressures on employers and memories of the 1994 Medan riots have improved minimum wage compliance.

Labor law and ministerial regulations provide workers with a variety of other benefits, such as social security, and workers in more modern facilities often receive health benefits, free meals, and transportation. The law establishes 7-hour workdays and 40-hour workweeks, with one 30-minute rest period for each 4 hours of work. The law also requires 1 day of rest weekly. The daily overtime rate is 1½ times the normal hourly rate for the first hour, and 2 times the hourly rate for additional overtime. Regulations allow employers to deviate from the normal work hours upon request to the Minister of Manpower and with the agreement of the employee. Workers in industries that produce retail goods for export frequently work overtime to fulfill contract quotas. Observance of laws regulating benefits and labor standards varies from sector to sector and by region. Employer violations of legal requirements are fairly common and often result in strikes and employee protests. The Ministry of Manpower continues publicly to urge employers to comply with the law. However, in general, government enforcement and supervision of labor standards are weak.

In December the Government submitted to Parliament a draft basic labor law designed to update, clarify, and codify laws and regulations affecting labor. Some NGO representatives have criticized the draft for not going far enough to protect worker rights.

Both law and regulations provide for minimum standards of industrial health and safety. In the largely Western-operated oil sector, safety and health programs function reasonably well. However, in the country's 100,000 larger registered companies outside the oil sector, the quality of occupational health and safety programs varies greatly. The enforcement of health and safety standards is severely hampered by the limited number of qualified Department of Manpower inspectors as well as by the low level of employee appreciation for sound health and safety practices. Allegations of corruption on the part of inspectors are common. Workers are obligated to report hazardous working conditions. Employers are forbidden by law from retaliating against those who do, but the law is not effectively enforced.

JAPAN

Japan is a parliamentary democracy based on a 1947 Constitution. Sovereignty is vested in the people, and the Emperor is defined as the symbol of state. Executive power is exercised by a cabinet, composed of a prime minister and ministers of state, responsible to the Diet, a two-house Parliament. The Diet, elected by universal suffrage and secret ballot, designates the Prime Minister, who must be a member of that body. The Government, formed in November, is a loose coalition led by the Liberal Democratic Party (LDP), in which the Social Democratic Party and the New Party Sakigake cooperate with the LDP from outside the Cabinet. The judiciary is independent of the Government.

A well-organized and disciplined police force generally respects the human rights of the populace and is firmly under the control of the civil authorities. However, there continued to be credible reports of harsh treatment of some suspects in custody.

The industrialized free market economy is highly efficient and competitive in world markets and provides residents with a high standard of living. In 1996 economic growth picked up from the slow pace of the previous 4 years.

A just and efficient legal system generally assures observance of constitutionally provided human rights. However, there continue to be some reports of physical and psychological abuse of prisoners or detainees. Officials are sometimes dismissed for such abuse but are seldom tried, convicted, and imprisoned. The Burakumin (a group historically treated as outcasts), the Ainu (Japan's indigenous people), women, and alien residents experience varying degrees of societal discrimination, some of it severe and longstanding.

RESPECT FOR HUMAN RIGHTS

Section 1. Respect for the Integrity of the Person, Including Freedom From:
a. *Political and Other Extrajudicial Killing.*—There were no reports of political or other extrajudicial killings.
b. *Disappearance.*—There were no reports of politically motivated disappearances.
c. *Torture and Other Cruel, Inhuman, or Degrading Treatment or Punishment.*—The Constitution provides for freedom from torture and cruel, inhuman, or degrading treatment or punishment. However, reports by several Japanese bar associations, human rights groups, and some prisoners indicate that police sometimes use physical violence, including kicking and beating, as well as psychological intimidation, including threats and name calling, to obtain confessions from suspects in custody or to enforce discipline. In Japan confession is regarded as the first step in the rehabilitative process. Although under the Constitution no criminal suspect can be compelled to make a self-incriminating confession, roughly 90 percent of all criminal cases going to trial include confessions, reflecting the priority that the system places on admissions of guilt. The Government points out that the high percentage of confessions, like the high conviction rate, is reflective of a higher standard of evidence needed to bring about indictment in the Japanese system. Since a system of arraignment does not exist in Japan, a suspect, if indicted, will be brought to trial even if that person has confessed to the crime. This results in a higher conviction rate than would otherwise be the case.

Appellate courts have overturned several convictions in recent years on the ground that they were obtained as a result of forced confession. In addition, civil and criminal suits have been brought against some police and prosecution officials, alleging abuse during interrogation and detention. Finally, there were scattered allegations of beatings of detainees in immigration detention facilities.

The Japanese Federation of Bar Associations and human rights groups have criticized the prison system, with its emphasis on strict discipline and obedience to numerous rules. Guards sometimes selectively enforce rules and impose punishment, including "minor solitary confinement," which may be imposed for at least 1 and not more than 60 days and in which the prisoner is made to sit (for foreigners) or kneel (for Japanese) motionless in the middle of an empty cell.

Some human rights groups allege that physical restraints, such as leather handcuffs, have been used as a form of punishment and that prisoners have been forced to eat and relieve themselves unassisted while wearing these restraints. Ministry of Justice officials state that restraints are used inside the prison only when prisoners have been violent and pose a threat to themselves and others, or when there is concern that a prisoner might attempt to escape.

d. *Arbitrary Arrest, Detention, or Exile.*—Constitutional provisions for freedom from arbitrary arrest or imprisonment are respected in practice. The law provides for judicial determination of the legality of detention. People may not be detained without charge, and prosecuting authorities must be prepared to demonstrate before trial that probable cause exists in order to detain the accused. Under the Code of Criminal Procedure, a suspect may be held in police custody for up to 72 hours without judicial proceedings. Preindictment custody may be extended by a judge for up to 20 additional days. If an indictment follows, the suspect is transferred to a criminal detention facility. Bail is available in only about 25 percent of cases.

The bar associations and human rights groups have criticized the practice of "substitute detention." Although the law stipulates that suspects should be held in "houses of detention" between arrest and sentencing, a police detention facility may be substituted at the order of the court. This provision was originally added to cover a shortage of normal detention facilities. According to the most recent Ministry of Justice White Paper on Crime, published in 1995, normal detention facilities were filled to 53 percent of capacity in 1994. Critics charge that allowing suspects to be detained by the same authorities who interrogate them heightens the potential for abuse and coercion. The Government counters that adequate safeguards to prevent abuse, including strong judicial oversight, have been built into the system. Preventive detention does not exist.

The length of time before a suspect is brought to trial depends on the nature of the crime but rarely exceeds 3 months from date of arrest; the average is 1 to 2 months. Critics charge that access to counsel is limited both in duration and frequency, although the Government denies that this is the case. The Criminal Procedure Code grants the prosecution and investigating police officials the power to control access to attorneys before indictment when deemed necessary for the sake of the investigation. As a court-appointed attorney is not approved until after indictment, suspects must rely on their own resources to hire an attorney for counseling before indictment. In addition, counsel may not be present during interrogation at any time before or after indictment. Beyond this, the Government affirms that the right of the accused to seek legal counsel is fully respected and that attorneys are almost always able to see clients without obstruction. Local bar associations provide detainees with a free counseling session prior to indictment. Counsel is provided at government expense after indictment if the arrested person cannot afford one.

The Government does not use forced exile.

e. *Denial of Fair Public Trial.*—The judiciary is independent and free from executive branch interference. The Cabinet appoints judges for 10-year terms, which can be renewed until judges have reached age 65. Justices of the Supreme Court can serve until the age of 70 but face periodic review through popular referendum. A defendant who is dissatisfied with the decision of a trial court of first instance may, within the period prescribed by law, appeal to a higher court. There are several levels of courts, with the Supreme Court serving as the highest judicial authority. There is no trial by jury.

The Government respects in practice the constitutional provisions for the right to a speedy and public trial by an impartial tribunal in all criminal cases. The defendant is informed of charges upon arrest and assured a public trial by an independent civilian court with defense counsel and the right of cross-examination. The Constitution provides defendants with the right not to be compelled to testify against themselves as well as to free and private access to counsel, although the right to such access is sometimes abridged in practice. For example, the law allows prosecutors to control access to counsel before indictment, and there are persistent allegations of coerced confessions. Defendants are also protected from the retroactive application of laws and have the right of access to incriminating evidence after a formal indictment has been made. However, the law does not require full disclosure by the prosecutor, and material that the prosecution will not use in court may be suppressed.

There were no reports of political prisoners.

f. *Arbitrary Interference with Privacy, Family, Home, or Correspondence.*—Under the Constitution, each search or seizure must be made upon separate warrant issued by a judge. Standards for issuing such warrants exist to guard against arbitrary searches. There were no reports that the Government or any other organization arbitrarily interfered with privacy, family, home, or correspondence.

Section 2. *Respect for Civil Liberties, Including:*

a. *Freedom of Speech and Press.*—The Constitution provides for freedom of speech and of the press, and the Government respects these rights in practice. An independent press, an effective judiciary, and a functioning democratic political system combine to ensure freedom of speech and of the press, including academic freedom.

b. *Freedom of Peaceful Assembly and Association.*—These freedoms are provided for in the Constitution and respected in practice.

c. *Freedom of Religion.*—Freedom of religion is provided for in the Constitution and is respected in practice. While Buddhism and Shintoism are the two major religions, there are many others, including several Christian denominations. Some temples and shrines receive public support as national historic or cultural sites.

The Government does not require that religious groups be licensed. However, to receive official recognition as a religious organization, which brings tax benefits and other advantages, a group must register with local or national authorities as a "religious corporation." In practice, almost all religious groups register, and until this year the procedure was little more than a formality. In response to a series of crimes committed by the Aum Shinrikyo religious sect, the Diet amended the Religious Corporation Law to give governmental authorities increased oversight of religious groups and to require greater disclosure of financial assets by religious corporations. These amendments entered into force on September 15.

d. *Freedom of Movement Within the Country, Foreign Travel, Emigration, and Repatriation.*—Citizens have the right to travel freely both within Japan and abroad, to change their place of residence, to emigrate, and to repatriate voluntarily. Japanese nationality may be lost by naturalization in a foreign country, or by failure of people born with dual nationality to elect Japanese nationality at the required age.

The Government has granted asylum in only a small number of cases to those claiming fear of persecution if they return to their homeland. It believes that most people seeking asylum in Japan do so for economic reasons. According to the Justice Ministry, from 1982 to August 1996, it was determined that 208 of 1,255 applicants met the required standard for asylum. None of the 93 applications for asylum filed between August 1995 and August 1996 was approved. The Government has shown flexibility in dealing with visa extensions for Chinese student dissidents, although it continues to be reluctant to grant permanent asylum.

Strict administrative procedures contribute to the roughly 20-percent rate of approval of asylum applications. For example, appeals of initial denials are reviewed by a separate authority of the same body, and decisions are rarely overturned. Asylum seekers and some critics claim that the processing of asylum applications is not readily understandable, making it difficult for applicants to comply with government procedures. Also, the Government's "60-day rule" requires applicants to appear at an immigration office within 60 days of arrival or within 60 days of the time they learn they are likely to be persecuted in their home country; most asylum seekers arrive in Japan without knowledge of this requirement and can inadvertently waive their claim by not acting promptly. In an effort to make procedures clearer to applicants, the Government has revised the English-language pamphlet it distributes to those interested in the asylum process.

In September 155 Vietnamese asylum seekers were returned to Vietnam from Japan. The Vietnamese put up minimal resistance to boarding the flight although three individuals had to be carried on board. One immigration official was slightly injured. An additional 14 Vietnamese asylum seekers remain in Japan. They have been determined to be refugees and are being considered for eventual third country resettlement.

Section 3. *Respect for Political Rights: The Right of Citizens to Change Their Government*

Citizens have the right peacefully to change their government and are able to exercise this right in practice through frequent, free, and fair elections on the basis of universal suffrage by secret ballot. A parliamentary democracy, Japan is governed by the political party or parties able to form a majority in the lower house of its bicameral Diet. From 1955 until 1993, all prime ministers and almost all cabinet ministers were members of the Liberal Democratic Party (LDP), which enjoyed a majority in the lower house throughout this period. Since 1993, except for a brief period of non-LDP coalition government from August 1993 to June 1994, the LDP has been part of successive coalition governments. Local and prefectural governments are often controlled by coalitions.

There are no legal impediments to women's participation in government and politics, but cultural attitudes are not favorable to their participation. Women hold 23 seats in the 500-member lower house of the Diet, and 19 seats in the 252-member upper house. As of November, the 21-member Cabinet had 1 female member. Women make up 21.8 percent of all national government workers, but hold less than 0.9 percent of top (director level and higher) government posts. In 1991 the Prime Minister's Office promulgated an action plan to increase the number of women in leadership positions on government advisory panels to 30 percent by the end of fiscal year 1995. However, the target was later cut to 15 percent, a step apparently reflecting slower than anticipated progress. Only 117 of the 205 existing panels have met the 15-percent target.

There is one Ainu member of the Diet (see Section 5).

Section 4. Governmental Attitude Regarding International and Nongovernmental Investigation of Alleged Violations of Human Rights

A number of local and international human rights organizations function freely, without governmental restrictions or impediments, investigating and publishing their findings on human rights cases. Government officials are generally cooperative and responsive to their views, although the Government restricts access to prisons and detention facilities by human rights groups.

Section 5. Discrimination Based on Race, Sex, Religion, Disability, Language, or Social Status

The Constitution prohibits discrimination on the basis of race, creed, sex, social status, or family origin, and, in general, the Government respects these provisions.

Women.—According to the National Police Agency, 474 incidents of spousal abuse against women were reported to authorities in 1994. However, violence against women, particularly domestic violence, often may go unreported due to social and cultural concerns about shaming one's family or endangering the reputation of one's spouse or offspring. Typically, victimized women often return to the home of their parents rather than file reports with authorities. Therefore, National Police Agency statistics on violence against women undoubtedly understate the scope of the current situation. Many local governments are responding positively to a need for confidential assistance by establishing special women's consultation departments in police and prefectural offices.

There is no specific law on sexual harassment. Although a woman may sue for "unlawful conduct" against an individual, the employing company's responsibility is not at issue in such a suit. Sexual harassment in the workplace is widespread, as evidenced by a May survey by the Japanese Trade Union Confederation, RENGO, which revealed that over 40 percent of working women have experienced sexual harassment. Women in this survey complained about a range of actions including sexually charged jokes, comments about physical features such as breast size, the display of pornographic photos, molestation, and direct requests for sexual favors. The Tokyo Rape Crisis Center stated that office rapes account for a "substantial share" of rape cases. In Japan media attention has focused on sexual harassment following an April equal employment opportunity complaint action against a U.S. subsidiary of Mitsubishi Motors Corporation.

The number of illegal female workers decreased in 1995, paralleling the decrease in illegal male workers that began in 1993. According to the Ministry of Justice, 3.4 percent of illegal female immigrants work in occupations involving prostitution. However, human rights groups estimate that the figure is actually much higher. The Government is working to reduce the foreign prostitution problem by enforcing existing antiprostitution laws as well as provisions in the Immigration Control and Refugee Recognition Act directed against anyone "encouraging a person to engage in illegal work." In recent years, police, especially in Tokyo, have conducted a number of sweeps against both foreign prostitutes and their employers.

The position of women in society, although significantly improved during the last few decades, continues to reflect deep-seated traditional values that assign women a subordinate role in the workplace. Although discrimination by private employers against women is prohibited by the Constitution, it persists. Legislation has been enacted over the past 30 years to accord women the same legal status as men. The Equal Employment Opportunity Law of 1986 was aimed at eliminating sex discrimination in such areas as recruitment, promotion, and vocational training. Yet the law does not expressly forbid discrimination in recruitment, hiring, assignment, and promotion of workers; it merely states that "employers should endeavor" to avoid it. Under this law and other regulations, the Ministry of Labor attempts to encourage corporate compliance with its objectives by positive inducements; it does not enforce compliance through fines or other punitive measures.

Although the Equal Employment Opportunity Law prohibits discrimination against women in wages, female workers on average earned only 62 percent of average male earnings. Much of this disparity results from the "two-track" personnel administration system found in most larger companies. Under this system, newly hired employees are put into one of two categories: managerial track (those engaged in planning and decisionmaking jobs and with the potential to become top executives), or clerical track (those engaged in general office work). According to a 1995 Ministry of Labor survey, 72 percent of companies responding said they hired only male workers for managerial track jobs. Female workers have also suffered disproportionately from the continued sluggishness of the economy: in 1995 only 28 percent of companies hired both male and female managerial track workers, down from the 46 percent that did so in 1992.

Public awareness of discrimination against women and sexual harassment in the workplace has increased. A growing number of government entities are establishing hot lines and designating ombudsmen to handle complaints of discrimination and sexual harassment. Nevertheless, sexual discrimination and stereotyping in the workplace continue to be major problems for women.

In 1993 the Prime Minister publicly acknowledged and apologized for the former Imperial Government's involvement in the army's practice of forcing an estimated 200,000 women (including Koreans, Filipinas, Chinese, Indonesians, Burmese, Dutch, and Japanese) to provide sex to soldiers between 1932 and 1945. Five cases concerning the "comfort women" problem are pending in the Tokyo District Court. In four cases the plaintiffs are seeking monetary compensation; in one case the plaintiff is seeking an official apology from the Government.

The Asian Women's Fund was established in July 1995 as a private, government-sponsored fund to compensate former comfort women. The fund will support three projects. The first will provide direct compensation payments to individual victims and will be financed entirely through private donations. A second project will provide medical and welfare assistance to individual comfort women. A third will fund projects to improve the general status of women and girls in Asia. The second and third projects will be funded by the Government and administered by the fund. The Asian Women's Fund is having trouble reaching its funding goals and finding former comfort women willing to accept compensation payments. In August four former comfort women from the Philippines agreed to accept compensation payments from the fund. Each received a lump-sum payment of $18,600 (2 million yen) and a letter of apology signed by Prime Minister Hashimoto.

Children.—The Government is committed to children's rights and welfare, and in general, the rights of children are adequately protected. Boys and girls have equal access to health care and other public facilities. There is no societal pattern of abuse against children.

In recent years, the problem of severe bullying, or "ijime," received greater public attention. It involves verbal or physical abuse in middle and high schools. In 1995, 56,601 cases of bullying in elementary and secondary schools were reported to the Education Ministry, but many cases go unreported. The Education Ministry also reported five suicides among elementary and secondary school students related to bullying in 1995, but the actual number of cases was probably higher. In August 1994, the Ministry of Justice established the Office of Ombudsman for Children's Rights to cope with bullying and other children's issues. In addition to compiling statistics on bullying and consulting with various groups concerned with children's welfare, the Office of Ombudsman provides counseling services for children 18 years of age and younger who have been victims of bullying.

People With Disabilities.—Although not generally subject to overt discrimination in employment, education, or in the provision of other state services, the disabled face limited access to public transportation, "mainstream" public education, and other facilities. Japan has no national law protecting the rights of the disabled, including access and employment, but some prefectures and cities have enacted their own legislation addressing the issue. Despite the disabled's lack of legal protection, there is growing societal awareness of the issue.

Indigenous People.—The Ainu, a people descended from the first inhabitants of Japan, now probably number fewer than 100,000; almost all of them live on

Hokkaido, the northernmost of Japan's four main islands. Their primary occupations are fishing, small-scale farming, and jobs in the tourism industry. As a result of a law passed in 1899, the Former Aborigines Protection Act, the Ainu today control only approximately 0.15 percent of their original landholdings. Ainu leaders continue to express grievances about this situation. Meanwhile, the Ainu continue to face societal discrimination while engaging in an uphill struggle against complete assimilation.

The Government has done little in response to Ainu grievances. An interagency study group opened hearings in January 1990 with the stated goal of reviewing Ainu history and making recommendations, but it has not been active. In March a special advisory council headed by former Supreme Court Justice Masami Ito, which was appointed during the Murayama administration, issued a report calling for new legislation to address the situation of Japan's Ainu minority. Some Ainu activists are critical of the report because it did not recommend that the Ainu be formally designated as an indigenous people. Other Ainu leaders, however, are satisfied with the report and believe that pushing harder for special recognition will be counterproductive. The Hashimoto Administration has set up an interagency committee to study the Ito report and possible new Ainu legislation. The committee plans to have its proposals ready for Diet consideration in 1997.

In 1994 Shigeru Kayano became the first Ainu member of the Diet when he gained a seat in the upper house. Kayano has drawn attention to Ainu issues.

National/Racial/Ethnic Minorities.—The ethnocentric nature of Japanese society, reinforced by a high degree of cultural and ethnic homogeneity and a history of isolation from other cultures, has impeded the integration of minority groups. This primarily affects Burakumin, Koreans, and alien workers.

The Burakumin (descendants of feudal era "outcasts" who practiced "unclean" professions such as butchering and undertaking), although not subject to governmental discrimination, are frequently victims of entrenched societal discrimination including restricted access to housing and employment opportunities. They are estimated to number approximately 3 million, but most prefer to hide their identity. Beginning in 1969, the Government introduced with some success a number of social, economic, and legal programs designed to improve conditions for the Burakumin and hasten their assimilation into mainstream society. In recent years, however, some within the Burakumin community have questioned whether assimilation is an appropriate goal. The Government has extended basic legislation to provide funding for Burakumin programs until 1997, but the Burakumin continue to lobby for a new law that will expand current programs.

Despite improvements in Japan's legal safeguards against discrimination, Korean permanent residents (most of whom were born, raised, and educated in Japan and who are estimated to number approximately 700,000) are still subject to various forms of deeply entrenched societal discrimination. In 1993 the Government halted the fingerprinting of permanent foreign residents. Instead of fingerprinting, the Government has established a family registry system that uses the resident's picture and signature and contains information on parents and spouses living in Japan, a system similar to that used for Japanese nationals. The current law leaves intact the requirement that all foreign residents carry alien registration certificates at all times.

In recent years, the Government has enacted several laws and regulations providing permanent resident aliens with equal access to public housing and loans, social security pensions for those qualified, and certain public employment rights. Some immigrants reportedly face police harassment and discrimination in obtaining housing, jobs, and health care. In recognition of the difficulties faced by foreigners in these areas, the city of Tokyo has issued a law to prevent housing discrimination against foreigners.

The January 1991 Memorandum Between the Japanese and South Korean Governments extended employment rights to local government positions, giving each locality the authority to decide which jobs may be held by non-Japanese nationals. Local governments are also being urged by the Government to allow Korean residents to take the Teacher Entrance Examination and to employ them on a full-time basis. Private-sector employment and societal discrimination are still common. Antidiscrimination laws affecting Korean residents were initiated as government guidance and are not supported by penalty provisions. In May, in the first court test of the antidiscrimination laws, the Tokyo District Court ruled against a second-generation Korean nurse who sued the Tokyo Metropolitan Government on the grounds that she had been refused consideration for promotion because she is not Japanese. The Court held that constitutional guarantees of freedom to choose one's career do not apply to the employment of foreigners in local civil services. The nurse has appealed to a higher court.

In May the Kawasaki city government and several other local governments agreed to allow resident foreigners, most of whom are Koreans, to take civil service exams for nonsupervisory jobs. In response to this development, the Home Affairs Ministry sent a letter to all prefectural and municipal governments on June 3, citing the Tokyo District Court ruling and urging these governments not to drop a Japanese nationality requirement for their employees. However, the Home Affairs Ministry has no legal authority to interfere in the personnel decisions of local governments, and there is no law stipulating Japanese nationality for jobs with prefectural or local governments. Apparently in response to pressure from the Home Affairs Ministry, the Kochi prefectural government and the Osaka city government dropped plans to allow foreigners to apply for civil service jobs.

By law, aliens with 5 years of continuous residence are eligible for naturalization and the simultaneous acquisition of citizenship rights, including the right to vote. In fact, however, most eligible aliens choose not to apply for citizenship, in part due to fears that their cultural identity would thereby be lost. De facto obstacles to naturalization include broad discretion available to adjudicating officers and great emphasis on Japanese language ability. In February 1995, the Supreme Court ruled that the Constitution does not bar permanent foreign residents from voting in local elections. However, the court also ruled that existing laws denying voting rights to foreign residents are not unconstitutional.

The Immigration Bureau of the Justice Ministry estimated that, as of May 1, there were 284,500 foreign nationals residing illegally in Japan, a decrease of 0.8 percent from the previous year. Illegal immigrants come primarily from: South Korea, the Philippines, Thailand, China, Peru, Iran, Malaysia, and Taiwan.

While many illegally resident foreigners came in search of better paying manufacturing and construction jobs, these opportunities decreased during the economic slowdown. Thus, more of the foreign workers are unemployed or marginally employed. Some illegal alien workers have been exploited. Activist groups claim that employers can easily discriminate against foreign workers, who often have little or no knowledge of the Japanese language or their legal rights. The Government attempts to deal with the problem of illegal workers within the bounds of existing law. It has tried to reduce the inflow of illegal foreign workers by prosecuting employers. Recent revisions of the Immigration Law provide for penalties against employers of undocumented foreign workers. Suspected foreign workers may also be denied entry for passport, visa, and entry application irregularities. The Government continues to study the foreign worker issue, and several citizens' groups are working with illegal foreign workers to improve their access to information on worker rights.

Section 6. Worker Rights

a. *The Right of Association.*—The Constitution provides for the right of workers to associate freely in unions. Approximately 24 percent of the active work force belongs to unions. Unions are free of government control and influence. Most unions are involved in political activity as well as labor relations, but they are not controlled by political parties. The Japanese Trade Union Confederation (RENGO), which represents 7.8 million Japanese workers and was formed in 1989 through the merger of several confederations, is the largest labor organization. There is no requirement for a single trade union structure, and there are no restrictions on who may be a union official. Members of the armed forces, police, and firefighters are not permitted either to form unions or to strike. These restrictions have led to a long-running dispute before the International Labor Organization's (ILO) Committee on the Application of Conventions and Recommendations over observance of ILO Convention 98 concerning the right to organize and bargain collectively. The Committee has observed that these public employees have a limited capacity to participate in the process of determining their wages and again in June asked the Government to consider any measures it could take to encourage negotiations with public employees.

Unions are active in international bodies, most notably the International Confederation of Free Trade Unions and maintain extensive international contacts. The right to strike, implicit in the Constitution, is exercised. During 1994, 85,000 worker days were lost to strikes. The law prohibits retribution against strikers and is effectively enforced. Public employees do not have the right to strike, although they do have recourse to mediation and arbitration. The Government determines the pay of government employees based on a recommendation by the independent National Personnel Authority.

b. *The Right to Organize and Bargain Collectively.*—The Constitution provides unions with the right to organize, bargain, and act collectively. These rights are exercised freely, and collective bargaining is practiced widely. The annual "Spring Wage Offensive," in which individual unions in each industry conduct negotiations simultaneously with their firms, involves nationwide participation. Management usually consults closely with its enterprise union. However, trade unions are independent of management and aggressively pursue the interests of their workers. Antiunion discrimination is prohibited by law, and adequate mechanisms exist for resolving such cases as do exist. As noted above, the collective bargaining rights of public employees are limited.

There are no export processing zones.

c. *Prohibition of Forced or Compulsory Labor.*—The Labor Standards Law prohibits the use of forced labor, and there are presently no known cases of forced or compulsory labor.

d. *Minimum Age for Employment of Children.*—Under the revised Labor Standards Law of 1987, minors under 15 years of age may not be employed, and those under the age of 18 years may not be employed in dangerous or harmful work. The Labor Inspection Division of the Ministry of Labor rigorously enforces child labor laws.

e. *Acceptable Conditions of Work.*—Minimum wages are set on a regional (prefectural) and industry basis, with the input of tripartite (workers, employers, public interest) advisory councils. Employers covered by a minimum wage must post the concerned minimum wages, and compliance with minimum wages is considered widespread. Minimum wage rates, which averaged approximately $50 (5,388 yen) per day in 1995, are considered sufficient to provide workers and their families with a decent living. The Labor Standards Law provides for a 40-hour workweek for most industries and mandates premium pay for hours worked over 40 in a week, or 8 in a day.

The Ministry of Labor effectively administers various laws and regulations governing occupational health and safety, principal among which is the Industrial Safety and Health Law of 1972. Standards are set by the Ministry of Labor and issued after consultation with the Standing Committee on Safety and Health of the Tripartite Labor Standards Commission. Labor inspectors have the authority to suspend unsafe operations immediately, and the law provides that workers may voice concerns over occupational safety and remove themselves from unsafe working conditions without jeopardizing their continued employment.

KIRIBATI

Kiribati comprises some 78,400 people occupying 33 small islands widely scattered across 3.5 million square kilometers of the central Pacific. The population is primarily Micronesian, with a significant component of Polynesian origin. Kiribati gained full independence from the United Kingdom in 1979 and became a republic within the Commonwealth of Nations. It has a popularly elected president and a legislative assembly with 39 members elected by universal adult suffrage, and 2 who are members by virtue of their office.

A police force of about 250 personnel is effectively controlled by civilian authority.

Economic activity consists primarily of subsistence agriculture and fishing. The islands' isolation and meager resources, including poor soil and limited arable land, severely limit prospects for economic development.

Society is egalitarian, democratic, and respectful of human rights. There were no reports of specific human rights abuses, but in the traditional culture women occupy a subordinate role with limited job opportunities.

RESPECT FOR HUMAN RIGHTS

Section 1. Respect for the Integrity of the Person, Including Freedom From:

a. *Political and Other Extrajudicial Killing.*—There were no reports of political or other extrajudicial killings.

b. *Disappearance.*—There were no reports of politically motivated disappearances.

c. *Torture and Other Cruel, Inhuman, or Degrading Treatment or Punishment.*—Although torture and inhuman or degrading treatment or punishment are forbidden by the Constitution, corporal punishment is permitted under traditional mores for criminal acts and other transgressions. On some outer islands, the island councils occasionally order strokes with palm fronds to be administered for public drunkenness and other minor offenses such as petty thievery.

The authorities strive to meet minimum international standards for prisons but have limited financial resources. Food and sanitation are limited. Family members and church representatives are allowed access to prisoners. The question of monitoring of prison conditions by local human rights groups has not arisen, and no policy concerning such monitoring has been formulated.

d. *Arbitrary Arrest, Detention, or Exile.*—The Constitution prohibits arbitrary arrest, detention, or exile, and the Government observes this prohibition.

e. *Denial of Fair Public Trial.*—The judiciary is independent and free of governmental interference. The right to a fair public trial is provided by law and observed in practice. The Constitution provides that an accused person be informed of the nature of the offense for which he is charged and be provided adequate time and facilities to prepare a defense. The right to confront witnesses, present evidence, and appeal convictions is enshrined in law. Procedural safeguards are based on English common law.

There are no political prisoners.

f. *Arbitrary Interference with Privacy, Family, Home, or Correspondence.*—The law prohibits such practices. Government authorities respect these provisions, and violations are subject to effective legal sanctions.

Section 2. Respect for Civil Liberties, Including:

a. *Freedom of Speech and Press.*—The Constitution provides for freedom of speech and the press, and the Government respects this right in practice. The radio station and the only newspaper are government owned but offer a variety of views. Churches publish newsletters and other periodicals. Academic freedom is respected.

b. *Freedom of Peaceful Assembly and Association.*—The Constitution provides for freedom of assembly and association, including the right to form or belong to associations for the advancement or protection of a group's interests, and the Government does not impose any significant restrictions in practice.

c. *Freedom of Religion.*—Freedom of religion prevails. There is no state or preferred religion. Missionaries are free to seek converts.

d. *Freedom of Movement Within the Country, Foreign Travel, Emigration, and Repatriation.*—The law provides for these rights, and the Government respects them in practice. There were no reports of refugees. The Government has not formulated a policy regarding refugees, asylees, or first asylum.

Section 3. Respect for Political Rights: The Right of Citizens to Change Their Government

The Government is chosen by the people in periodic free and open elections. Executive authority is exercised by the President, who is elected for a 4-year term. No less than three and no more than four presidential candidates are nominated by the elected Legislative Assembly from among its members. Under the Constitution the President is limited to three terms.

The snap general election of August 1994 saw the formation of Kiribati's first real political party, the Maneaban Te Mauri Party (MTM), as opposition forces united to bring down the National Progressive Party (NPP). (The NPP, the group which had led Kiribati since independence in 1979, has never been organized as a political party.) In those elections, the MTM won 19 of the 39 seats (2 more are ex officio), and an MTM leader, Teburoro Tito, was elected President.

Women are underrepresented in politics and government. No women hold ministerial or permanent secretarial positions, and none hold national elective office.

Section 4. Governmental Attitude Regarding International and Nongovernmental Investigation of Alleged Violations of Human Rights

There are no restrictions on the formation of local nongovernmental organizations that concern themselves with human rights, but to date none has been formed. There have been no reported allegations of human rights violations by the Government and no known requests for investigations. Kiribati is not a member of the United Nations.

Section 5. Discrimination Based on Race, Sex, Religion, Disability, Language, or Social Status

The Constitution prohibits discrimination on the basis of race, creed, national origin, or sex, and the Government generally observed this prohibition in practice. Kiribati society, fundamentally egalitarian, has no privileged chiefly class.

Women.—Violence against women does not appear to be a major problem in this isolated, rural society. Rape is a crime under the law, and the law is enforced when charges are brought to court. To the extent that it exists, wife beating is dealt with informally and in a traditional way; frequently, communal pressure is brought to bear.

The traditional culture in which men are dominant has been an impediment to women taking a more active role in the economy. This is slowly changing, and more women are finding work in unskilled and semiskilled occupations. There are also signs of increased government hiring and promotions to redress this culturally based inequity. Women have full and equal access to education.

Statistics on the participation of women in the work force and on comparative wages are unavailable. Women have full rights of ownership and inheritance of property.

Children.—Within the limited resources of the Government, adequate expenditures are made for child welfare. If child abuse exists, it is rare and has not become a source of societal concern.

People With Disabilities.—There is no evidence or complaint of discrimination in employment, education, or provision of other state services. Accessibility for the disabled has not been mandated.

Section 6. Worker Rights

a. *The Right of Association.*—Freedom of association is provided for in the Constitution. Workers are free to organize unions and choose their own representatives. The Government does not control or restrict unions. Over 90 percent of the work force is occupied in fishing or subsistence farming, but the small wage sector has a relatively strong and effective trade union movement. In 1982 the seven registered trade unions merged to form the Kiribati Trade Union Congress (KTUC). It has approximately 2,500 members, mostly from the public service sector. The KTUC is affiliated with the International Confederation of Free Trade Unions. The law provides for the right to strike. However, strikes are rare, the last one having taken place in 1980.

b. *The Right to Organize and Bargain Collectively.*—Collective bargaining is provided for under the Industrial Relations Code. The Government sets wages in the large public sector. However, in a few statutory bodies and government-owned companies, employees may negotiate wages and other conditions. In the private sector employees may also negotiate wages with employers. Negotiations are generally nonconfrontational, in keeping with Kiribati tradition. There have been no reports of antiunion discrimination. However, mechanisms exist for resolving any such complaints.

There are no export processing zones.

c. *Prohibition of Forced or Compulsory Labor.*—The Constitution prohibits forced or compulsory labor, and it is not practiced.

d. *Minimum Age for Employment of Children.*—The law prohibits the employment of children under the age of 14. Children through the age of 15 are prohibited from industrial employment and employment aboard ships. Labor officers from the Ministry of Commerce, Industry, and Employment normally enforce these laws effectively, given the rudimentary conditions of the economy and its industrial relations system. Children are rarely employed outside the traditional economy.

e. *Acceptable Conditions of Work.*—The Government has taken no concrete action to implement longstanding legislation authorizing establishment of minimum wages. There is no legislatively prescribed workweek. The Government is the major employer in the cash economy.

Employment laws provide rudimentary health and safety standards for the workplace. Employers must, for example, provide an adequate supply of clean water for workers and ensure the existence of sanitary toilet facilities. Employers are liable for the expenses of workers injured on the job. The Government's ability to enforce employment laws is hampered by a lack of qualified personnel. Women may not work at night except under specified circumstances (generally in service jobs such as hotel clerks).

DEMOCRATIC PEOPLE'S REPUBLIC OF KOREA*

The Democratic People's Republic of Korea (DPRK) is a dictatorship under the absolute rule of the Korean Workers' Party (KWP). Kim Il Sung ruled the DPRK from its inception until his death in July 1994. Since then his son Kim Jong Il appears to have had unchallenged authority, although he has not assumed his father's positions of President of the DPRK and Secretary General of the KWP. Both Kim Il

---

*The United States does not have diplomatic relations with the Democratic People's Republic of Korea. North Korea does not allow representatives of foreign governments, journalists, or other invited visitors the freedom of movement that would enable them to fully assess human rights conditions there. This report is based on information obtained over more than a decade, updated where possible by information drawn from recent interviews, reports, and other documentation. While limited in detail, this information is nonetheless indicative of the human rights situation in North Korea today.

Sung and Kim Jong Il continue to be the objects of intense personality cults. The regime emphasizes "Juche," a national ideology of self-reliance.

The Korean People's Armed Forces is the primary organization responsible for external security. It is assisted by a large military reserve force and several quasi-military forces, including the Worker-Peasant Red Guards and the People's Security Force. These organizations assist the Ministry of Public Security and cadres of the KWP in maintaining internal security. Members of the security forces committed serious human rights abuses.

The State directs all significant economic activity, and only government-supervised labor unions are permitted. The North Korean economy contracted in 1996, as it has each year since the beginning of the decade. This decline is due in part to the collapse of the Soviet bloc and the elimination of Soviet and Chinese concessional trade and aid. It is also due to distribution bottlenecks, inefficient allocation of resources, lack of access to international credit stemming from the DPRK's default on much of its foreign debt, and the diversion of a quarter of the gross national product to military expenditures. For the last 2 years, flooding damaged crops, forced thousands from their homes, and aggravated an already difficult economic situation. Significantly, North Korea admitted publicly for the first time that it was suffering from food shortages and sought international food aid as well as other forms of assistance. While the Government attributed the food shortages only to flooding, the flood apparently exacerbated structural shortages that have existed for years. Food, clothing, and energy are rationed throughout the country.

The Government continues to deny its citizens human rights. Citizens do not have the right peacefully to change their government. There continued to be reports of extrajudicial killings and disappearances. Citizens are detained arbitrarily, and many are held as political prisoners; prison conditions are harsh. The constitutional provisions for an independent judiciary and fair trials are not implemented in practice. The regime subjects its citizens to rigid controls. The state leadership perceives most international norms of human rights, especially individual rights, as illegitimate and alien social artifacts subversive to the goals of the State and party. The Penal Code is draconian, stipulating capital punishment and confiscation of all assets for a wide variety of "crimes against the revolution," including defection, attempted defection, slander of the policies of the party or State, listening to foreign broadcasts, writing "reactionary" letters, and possessing "reactionary" printed matter. The Government prohibits freedom of the press and association, and all forms of cultural and media activities are under the tight control of the party. Radios sold in North Korea are constructed to receive North Korean radio broadcasts only; radios obtained from abroad must be altered to work in a similar manner. Under these circumstances, little outside information reaches the public except that approved and disseminated by the Government. The Government restricts freedom of religion, citizen's movements, and worker rights.

RESPECT FOR HUMAN RIGHTS

Section 1. Respect for the Integrity of the Person, Including Freedom From:

a. *Political and Other Extrajudicial Killing.*—Defectors report that the regime continued executions of political prisoners, opponents of the regime, repatriated defectors, and others (reportedly including military officers suspected of plotting against Kim Jong Il). The criminal law makes the death penalty mandatory for activities "in collusion with imperialists" aimed at "suppressing the national liberation struggle." Some prisoners are sentenced to death for such ill-defined "crimes" as "ideological divergence," "opposing socialism," and other "counterrevolutionary crimes." In some cases, executions reportedly were carried out at public meetings attended by workers, students, and school children. Executions have also been carried out before assembled inmates at places of detention.

Many prisoners have reportedly died from torture, disease, starvation, or exposure (see Section 1.c.).

In September a North Korean submarine attempting to infiltrate an armed reconnaissance team into South Korean territory ran aground off the South Korean coast. The 26 North Korean personnel onboard abandoned the vessel. Eleven crew members were apparently killed by the submarine's complement of highly trained infiltrators. In addition, the North Korean commandos killed nine members of the South Korean military, a police officer engaged in the search, and three civilian bystanders.

On December 30, the DPRK made a formal announcement of regret for the incident. The South Korean Government later returned the remains of the North Korean personnel to the DPRK through the Military Armistice Commission in Panmunjom.

b. *Disappearance.*—There is no reliable information on disappearances. However, the Government is reportedly responsible for such cases. According to defector reports, individuals suspected of political crimes are often taken from their homes by state security officials late at night and sent directly, without trial, to camps for political prisoners. There are also many reports of DPRK involvement in the kidnaping abroad of South Koreans, Japanese, and other foreign nationals. The Japanese press estimates that, over the last 30 years, as many as 20 Japanese may have been kidnaped and are being detained in North Korea. In addition, several cases of kidnaping, hostage-taking, and other acts of violence apparently intended to intimidate ethnic Koreans living in China and Russia have been reported. For example, there is credible evidence that North Korea may have been involved in the abduction of a South Korean citizen working in China as a missionary. The DPRK denies this and other similar reports.

Amnesty International (AI) reports detail a number of cases of disappearances including that of Japanese citizen Shibata Kozo and his wife Shin Sung Suk, who left Japan in 1960 and resettled in North Korea. Shibata was reportedly arrested in 1962 after encouraging a demonstration by former Japanese residents against the poor treatment given them. In 1993 AI claimed that he was still in custody, and in poor health, and that there had been no word about his wife and three children since 1965. In June 1995, AI was informed by North Korean officials that Shibata Kozo, his wife, and children had died in a train accident in early 1990, a few weeks after he was released from nearly 30 years in prison. However, AI reports that Shibata Kozo was still in custody at the time of the alleged accident.

In a case cited by AI in 1993, North Korean officials informed Amnesty in April 1995 that Japanese citizens Cho Ho Pyong, his ethnic Japanese wife Koike Hideko, and their three young children were killed in 1972 while attempting to leave the country. The authorities told AI that Cho had escaped from a detention center where he was being held for spying, killing a guard in the process. The cases of three ethnic Korean residents of Beijing, China (16, 18, and 20 years of age), reported by AI in 1995 to have been taken to North Korea against their will, remained unresolved. The three were taken in apparent retaliation for criticism of North Korean human rights violations made by their father, a former prisoner in North Korea, on Japanese television and in the Japanese press. The North Korean authorities deny this allegation, claiming that the three brothers had been deported to North Korea for breaking Chinese law, and that they are now living with relatives. AI has been unable to confirm this account, and at year's end was still concerned about the welfare of the three brothers.

Numerous reports indicate that ordinary citizens are not allowed to mix with foreign nationals, and AI has reported that a number of North Koreans who maintained friendships with foreigners have disappeared. In at least one case, AI reported that a citizen who had disappeared was executed for maintaining a friendship with a Russian national.

c. *Torture and Other Cruel, Inhuman, or Degrading Treatment or Punishment.*—While there is no information on recent practices, credible reports indicate that prisoners are ill-treated and that many have died from torture, disease, starvation, or exposure.

Prison conditions are harsh. According to international nongovernmental organizations (NGO) and defector sources, whole families, including children, are imprisoned together. "Reeducation through labor" is common punishment, consisting of forced labor, such as logging and tending crops, under harsh conditions. A small number of people who claim to have escaped from detention camps report that starvation and executions are common. In one prison, clothing was reportedly issued only once in 3 years. Former inmates have produced photographs of an inmate wearing specially designed leg irons that permit walking but make running impossible. AI reports the existence of "punishment cells," too low to allow standing upright and too small for lying down flat, where prisoners are kept for up to several weeks for breaking prison rules. Recent visitors to North Korea report observing prisoners being marched in leg irons, metal collars, or shackles. AI representatives recently were permitted to visit one model "rehabilitation center," but the Government does not normally permit inspection of prisons by human rights monitors.

d. *Arbitrary Arrest, Detention, or Exile.*—There are no restrictions on the ability of the Government to detain and imprison persons at will and to hold them incommunicado.

Little information is available on North Korea's criminal justice procedures and practices, and outside observation of its legal system has been limited to "show trials" for traffic violations and other minor offenses.

Family members and other concerned persons find it virtually impossible to obtain information on charges against detained persons. Judicial review of detentions does not exist in law or in practice.

Defectors claim that North Korea detains about 150,000 persons for political reasons, sometimes along with their family members, in maximum security camps in remote areas. An October 1992 report by two former inmates made reference to severe living conditions in what they called "concentration camps." North Korean officials deny the existence of such prison camps but admit that there are "education centers" for people who "commit crimes by mistake."

One credible report lists 12 such prison camps in the DPRK. It is believed that some former high officials are imprisoned in the camps. Visitors were formerly allowed, but currently any form of communication with detainees, including visitors, is said to be prohibited.

In July 1991, a North Korean defector who had been a ranking official in the DPRK Ministry of Public Security, said that there were two types of detention areas. One consists of closed camps where conditions are extremely harsh and from which prisoners never emerge. In the other, prisoners can be "rehabilitated."

The Government is not known to use forced exile abroad. However, the Government routinely uses forced resettlement and has relocated many tens of thousands of people from Pyongyang to the countryside. Often, those relocated are selected on the basis of family background. Nonetheless, there is some evidence that class background is less important than in the past because of the regime's emphasis on the solidarity of the "popular masses."

e. *Denial of Fair Public Trial.*—The Constitution states that courts are independent and that judicial proceedings are to be carried out in strict accordance with the law. The Constitution contains elaborate procedural guarantees, and it states that "cases are heard in public, and the accused is guaranteed the right to defense; hearings may be closed to the public as stipulated by law." However, an independent judiciary and individual rights do not exist in the DPRK. The Public Security Ministry dispenses with trials in political cases and refers defendants to the Ministry of State Security for imposition of punishment.

When trials are held, lawyers are apparently assigned by the Government. Reports indicate that defense lawyers are not considered representatives of the accused; rather, they are are expected to help the court by persuading the accused to confess guilt. Some reports note a distinction between those accused of political crimes and common criminals and state that the Government affords trials or lawyers only to the latter. The Government considers critics of the regime to be "political criminals."

Numerous reports suggest that political offenses have in the past included such behavior as sitting on newspapers bearing Kim Il Sung's picture, or (in the case of a professor reportedly sentenced to work as a laborer) noting in class that Kim Il Sung had received little formal education. A foreigner hired to work on foreign broadcasts for the regime was imprisoned for 1 year without trial for criticizing the quality of the regime's foreign propaganda. He was then imprisoned for 6 more years (with trial) shortly after his release for claiming in a private conversation that his original imprisonment was unjust. While AI has listed 58 political prisoners by name, the total number of political prisoners being held is unknown. Several defectors and former inmates reported that the total figure is approximately 150,000.

f. *Arbitrary Interference with Privacy, Family, Home, or Correspondence.*—The constitutional stipulation that "citizens are guaranteed the inviolability of person and residence and the privacy of correspondence" does not reflect reality. The regime subjects its citizens to rigid controls. The state leadership perceives most international norms of human rights, and especially individual rights, as illegitimate and alien social artifacts subversive to the goals of the State and party. The Government relies upon an extensive, multilevel system of informers to identify critics and potential troublemakers. Whole communities are sometimes subjected to massive security checks. According to Kim Jong Il, North Korean society represents "a new way of thinking" that cannot be evaluated on the basis of "old yardsticks" of human rights imported from abroad. In this context, the DPRK celebrates the closed nature of its society. The possession of "reactionary material" and listening to foreign broadcasts are both considered crimes that may subject the transgressor to harsh punishments. In some cases, entire families are punished for alleged political offenses committed by one member of the family.

The regime justifies its dictatorship with arguments derived from Marxist-Leninist concepts of collective consciousness and the superiority of the collective over the individual, appeals to nationalism, and citations of "the Juche idea," a national ideology of self-reliance promulgated by Kim Il Sung. The North Koreans emphasize that the core concept of Juche is "the ability to act independently without regard to outside interference." Originally described as "a creative application of Marxism-Leninism" in the Korean context, Juche is a malleable philosophy reinterpreted from time to time by the regime as its ideological needs change and used by the regime as a "spiritual" underpinning for its rule.

As defined by Kim Il Sung, Juche is a quasi-mystical concept in which the collective will of the people is distilled into a supreme leader whose every act exemplifies the State and society's needs. Opposition to such a leader, or to the rules, regulations, and goals established by his regime, is thus in itself opposition to the national interest. The regime therefore claims a social interest in identifying and isolating all opposition.

Since the late 1950's the regime has divided society into three main classes: "core," "wavering," and "hostile." These 3 classes are further subdivided into over 50 subcategories based on perceived loyalty to the party and the leadership. Security ratings are assigned to each individual; according to some estimates, as much as 50 percent of the population is designated as either "wavering" or "hostile." These loyalty ratings determine access to employment, higher education, place of residence, medical facilities, and certain stores. They also affect the severity of punishment in the case of legal infractions. While there are signs that this rigid system has been relaxed somewhat in recent years—for example, children of religious practioners are no longer automatically barred from higher education—it remains a basic element of North Korean society.

Citizens with relatives who fled to South Korea at the time of the Korean War appear to be still classified as part of the "hostile class" in the DPRK's elaborate loyalty system. This subcategory alone encompasses a significant percentage of the North Korean population. One defector estimated that the class of those considered potentially hostile may comprise 25 to 30 percent of the population; others place the figure at closer to 20 percent. Members of this class are still subject to discrimination, although a defector has claimed that their treatment has improved greatly in recent years.

The authorities subject citizens in all age groups and occupations to intensive political and ideological indoctrination. Even after Kim Il Sung's death, his cult of personality and the glorification of his family and the official Juche ideology remained omnipresent. The cult approaches the level of a state religion. The goal of indoctrination remains to ensure loyalty to the Kim Il Sung system and his son and heir Kim Jong Il, as well as conformity to the State's ideology and authority. The necessity for the intensification of such indoctrination is repeatedly stressed in the writings of Kim Jong Il, who attributes the collapse of the Soviet Union largely to insufficient ideological indoctrination, compounded by the entry of foreign influences.

Indoctrination is carried out systematically, not only through the mass media, but also in schools and through worker and neighborhood associations. Kim Jong Il has stated that ideological education must take precedence over academic education in the nation's schools, and he has also called for the intensification of mandatory ideological study and discussion sessions for adult workers.

Another aspect of the State's indoctrination system is the use of mass marches, rallies, and staged performances, sometimes involving hundreds of thousands of people. Celebrations of the 50th anniversary of the founding of the Korean Workers' Party included hours of carefully choreographed demonstration of mass adulation of the leadership, reportedly involving virtually the entire population of Pyongynag and outlying communities. Foreign visitors have been told that nonparticipation by Pyongyang residents in this event was unthinkable.

The Government monitors correspondence and telephones. Telephones essentially are restricted to domestic operation although some international service is available on a very restricted basis (see Section 2.a.).

Section 2. *Respect for Civil Liberties, Including:*

a. *Freedom of Speech and Press.*—Articles of the Constitution that require citizens to follow "Socialist norms of life" and to obey a "collective spirit" take precedence over individual political or civil liberties. Although the Constitution provides for freedom of speech and the press, the Government prohibits the exercise of these rights in practice. The regime permits only activities that support its objectives.

The Government strictly curtails freedom of expression. The authorities may punish persons for criticizing the regime or its policies by imprisonment or "corrective labor." One defector reported in 1986 that a scientist, whose home was bugged through his radio set, was arrested and executed for statements made at home critical of Kim Il Sung. In another case, AI reports that a family formerly resident in Japan was sent to a "reeducation through labor" center because one member of the family allegedly made remarks disparaging the Government.

The Government attempts to control all information. It carefully manages the visits of Western journalists. In July Cables News Network was allowed to broadcast live, unedited coverage of the second year memorial service for the death of Kim Il Sung. Domestic media censorship is strictly enforced, and no deviation from the official government line is tolerated.

The regime prohibits listening to foreign media broadcasts except by the political elite, and violators are subject to severe punishment. Radios and television sets are built to receive only domestic programming; radios obtained from abroad must be submitted for alteration to operate in a similar manner. Private telephone lines operate on an internal system that prevents making and receiving calls from outside the country. International phone lines are available under very restricted circumstances.

The Government severely restricts academic freedom and controls artistic and academic works. Visitors report that one of the primary functions of plays, movies, operas, children's performances, and books is to contribute to the cult of personality surrounding Kim Il Sung and Kim Jong Il.

b. *Freedom of Peaceful Assembly and Association.*—Although the Constitution provides for freedom of assembly and association, the Government does not respect these provisions in practice. The Government prohibits any public meetings without authorization. There are no known organizations other than those created by the Government. Professional associations exist primarily as another means of government monitoring and control over the members of these organizations.

c. *Freedom of Religion.*—The 1992 Constitution provides for the "freedom of religious belief," including "the right to build buildings for religious use." However, the same article adds that "no one can use religion as a means to drag in foreign powers" or to disrupt the social order. In practice, the regime discourages all organized religious activity except that which serves the interests of the State.

As late as the early 1980's, foreign visitors were told that there were no churches in the country and only a handful of Buddhist temples. However, in recent years, the regime has allowed the formation of several government-sponsored religious organizations. These serve as interlocutors with foreign church groups and international aid organizations. Some foreigners who have met with representatives of these organizations are convinced that they are sincere believers; others claim that they appeared to know little about religious dogma, liturgy, or teaching.

There are a few Buddhist temples where religious activity is permitted, and three Christian churches—two Protestant and one Catholic—have been opened since 1988 in Pyongyang. Many visitors say that church activity appears staged. Foreign Christians who have attempted to attend services at these churches without making prior arrangements with the authorities report finding them locked and unattended, even on Easter Sunday.

The DPRK claims that there are 10,000 Christians who worship in 500 house churches, and the Chondogyo Young Friends Party, a government-sponsored group based on a native Korean religious movement, is still in existence. The authorities have told foreign visitors that one Protestant seminary exists, accepting six to nine pupils every 3 years.

d. *Freedom of Movement Within the Country, Foreign Travel, Emigration, and Repatriation.*—The regime strictly controls internal travel, requiring a travel pass for any movement outside one's home village. These passes are granted only for official travel or attendance at a relative's wedding or funeral. Long delays in obtaining the necessary permit often result in denial of the right to travel even for these limited purposes. There are reports that North Korea's recent food shortages have forced the regime to allow citizens increased mobility in order to seek food. As an additional means of control, travelers must produce special "travelers coupons" to buy food on trains or at restaurants or shops. Only members of a very small elite have vehicles for personal use. The regime tightly controls access to civilian aircraft, trains, buses, food, and fuel.

Reports, primarily from defectors, indicate that the Government routinely uses forced resettlement, particularly for those deemed politically unreliable. The Government strictly controls permission to reside in, or even enter, Pyongyang. This is a significant lever, since food, housing, health, and general living conditions are much better in Pyongyang than in the rest of the country.

The regime limits foreign travel to officials and trusted artists, athletes, academics, and religious figures. It does not allow emigration. In recent years, the number of defectors has increased. The regime reportedly retaliates harshly against the relatives of those who manage to escape. According to the Penal Code, defection and attempted defection (including the attempt to gain entry to a foreign embassy for the purpose of seeking political asylum) are capital crimes. Defectors and other sources report that involuntarily repatriated defectors are routinely executed. Following the collapse of European communism, the regime pulled back several thousand students from overseas. It no longer allows students to study abroad except in China and a few other places.

From 1959 to 1982, 93,000 Korean residents of Japan, including 6,637 Japanese wives, voluntarily repatriated to North Korea. Despite DPRK assurances that the wives, more than a third of whom still had Japanese citizenship, would be allowed to visit Japan every 2 or 3 years, none is known to have done so. Many have not been heard from since, and their relatives and friends in Japan have been unsuccessful in their efforts to gain information about their condition and whereabouts.

Although the DPRK has permitted an increasing number of overseas Korean residents of North America, Japan, China, and other countries to visit their relatives in North Korea over the past decade, most requests for such visits are still denied. Many foreign visitors to the April 1995 International Pyongyang Sports Festival reported that they were denied permission to visit or otherwise contact their relatives, even those who lived only a few miles from Pyongyang.

Although the DPRK is a member of the United Nations, it does not participate in international refugee forums, and it is not in contact with the U.N. High Commissioner for Refugees.

Section 3. Respect for Political Rights: The Right of Citizens to Change Their Government

Citizens have no right or mechanisms to change their leadership or government. The political system is completely dominated by the KWP, with Kim Il Sung's heir Kim Jong Il in full control. There is very little reliable information available on intraregime politics following Kim Il Sung's death. The legislature, the Supreme People's Assembly, which meets only a few days a year, serves only to rubber-stamp resolutions presented to it by the party leadership.

In an effort to create the appearance of democracy, the DPRK has created several "minority parties." Lacking grass roots organizations, they exist only as rosters of officials with token representation in the Supreme People's Assembly. Their primary purpose appears to be promoting government objectives abroad as touring parliamentarians. Free elections do not exist, and Kim Jong Il has criticized the concept of free elections and competition among political parties as an artifact of capitalist decay.

Elections to the Supreme People's Assembly and to provincial, city, and county assemblies are held irregularly. In all cases there is only one government-approved candidate in each electoral district. According to the media, over 99 percent of the voters turn out to elect 100 percent of the candidates approved by the KWP. The vast majority of the KWP's estimated 3 million members (in a population of 22 million) work to implement decrees formulated by the party's small elite.

Few women have reached high levels of the party or the Government.

Section 4. Governmental Attitude Regarding International and Nongovernmental Investigation of Alleged Violations of Human Rights

The Government does not permit any independent domestic organizations to monitor human rights conditions or to comment on violations of such rights. Although a North Korean Human Rights Committee was established in 1992, it denies the existence of any human rights violations in North Korea and is merely a propaganda arm of the regime. However, by offering international human rights organizations an identifiable official interlocutor, the Committee has helped increase their ability to enter into two-way communication with the regime.

In April a delegation from AI visited the DPRK and discussed legal reforms and prisoner cases with senior government officials. The Government has ignored requests for visits by other international human rights organizations.

Section 5. Discrimination Based on Race, Sex, Religion, Disability, Language, or Social Status

The Constitution grants equal rights to all citizens. However, in practice the Government denies its citizens most fundamental human rights.

Women.—There is no information available on violence against women.

The Constitution states that "women hold equal social status and rights with men." However, although women are represented proportionally in the labor force, few women have reached high levels of the party or the Government. In many small factories, the work force is predominantly female. Like men, working-age women must work. They are thus required to leave their preschool children in the care of elderly relatives or in state nurseries. However, according to the Constitution, women with large families are guaranteed shortened working hours.

Children.—Social norms reflect traditional, family centered values in which children are cherished. The State provides compulsory education for all children until the age of 15. There is no evidence of societal or familial abuse of children. However, some children are denied educational opportunities and subjected to other punishments and disadvantages as a result of the loyalty classification system and the principle of "collective retribution" for the transgressions of their parents (see Section 1.f.).

Like others in society, children are the object of intense political indoctrination; even mathematics textbooks propound the party line. In addition, foreign visitors and academic sources report that children are subjected to several hours a week of mandatory military training and indoctrination at their schools from an early age. School children are sometimes sent to work in factories or in the fields for short periods to assist in completing special projects or in meeting production goals.

People With Disabilities.—Traditional social norms condone discrimination against the physically disabled. Disabled persons are almost never seen within the city limits of Pyongyang, and several defectors and other former North Korea residents report that disabled persons are routinely assigned to the rural areas. According to one report, authorities check every 2 to 3 years in the capital for persons with deformities and relocate them to special facilities in the countryside. There are no legally mandated provisions for accessibility to buildings or government services for the disabled.

Section 6. Worker Rights

a. *The Right of Association.*—Nongovernmental labor unions do not exist. The Korean Workers' Party purports to represent the interests of all labor. There is a single labor organization, called the General Federation of Trade Unions of Korea, which is affiliated with the formerly Soviet-controlled World Federation of Trade Unions. Operating under this umbrella, unions function on the classic "Stalinist model," with responsibility for mobilizing workers behind production goals and for providing health, education, cultural, and welfare facilities. They do not have the right to strike. North Korea is not a member of, but has observer status with, the International Labor Organization.

b. *The Right to Organize and Bargain Collectively.*—Workers have no right to organize or to bargain collectively. Wages are set by government ministries. The State assigns all jobs. Ideological purity is as important as professional competence in deciding who receives a particular job, and foreign companies that have established joint ventures report that all their employees must be hired from lists submitted by the KWP. Factory and farm workers are organized into councils, which do have an impact on management decisions.

c. *Prohibition of Forced or Compulsory Labor.*—There is no prohibition on the use of forced or compulsory labor, and the Government routinely uses military conscripts for construction projects. "Reformatory labor" and "reeducation through labor" are common punishments for political offenses. AI reports that forced labor, such as logging and tending crops, is common among prisoners. School children are assigned to factories or farms for short periods to help meet production goals (see Section 5).

d. *Minimum Age for Employment of Children.*—According to the Constitution, the State prohibits work by children under the age of 16 years. As education is universal and mandatory until the age of 15, it is believed that this regulation is enforced; however, as noted above school children are assigned to factories or farms for short periods to help meet production goals.

e. *Acceptable Conditions of Work.*—The Constitution states that all working-age citizens must participate in work and "strictly observe labor discipline and working hours." The Penal Code states that anyone who hampers the nation's industry, commerce, or transportation by intentionally failing to carry out a specific assignment "while pretending to be functioning normally" is subject to the death penalty; it also states that anyone who "shoddily caries out" an assigned duty is subject to no less than 5 years' imprisonment.

Even persistent tardiness may be defined as "anti-Socialist wrecking" under these articles, although as a result of food shortages absenteeism has reportedly become widespread as more time is spent finding food. A DPRK official described the North Korean labor force to an audience of foreign business executives by noting that "there are no riots, no strikes, and no differences of opinion" with management.

The minimum wage for workers in North Korea's Free Economic and Trade Zone (FETZ) is $80 (about 168 won) a month; in foreign-owned and joint venture enterprises outside the FETZ the minimum wage is reportedly $110 (about 231 won) per month; no data is available on the minimum wage in state-owned industries. Until the increasing food shortages of recent years, wages and rations appeared to be adequate to support workers and their families at a basic subsistence level. Wages are not the primary form of compensation since the State provides all educational and medical needs free of charge, while most goods are distributed according to a rationing system, and only token rent is charged.

In 1994 new labor regulations for enterprises involving foreign investments were reportedly adopted by the Administration Council. The regulations on labor contracts set out provisions on the employment and dismissal of workers, technical training, workhours, rest periods, remuneration, labor protection, social security, fines for violations of regulations, and settlement of disputes.

The Constitution stipulates an 8-hour workday; however, several sources report that most laborers work 12 to 16 hours daily. Some of this additional time may represent mandatory study of the writings of Kim Il Sung and Kim Jong Il. The Constitution provides all citizens with a "right to rest," including paid leave, holidays, and access to sanitariums and rest homes funded at public expense. Many worksites are hazardous, and the rate of industrial accidents is high.

REPUBLIC OF KOREA

The Republic of Korea is governed by a directly elected president and a unicameral legislature selected by both direct and proportional voting. The judiciary operates independently of the executive branch. The Government held legislative elections in April and continued to reform the political system, creating a special legislative committee composed of assembly members from ruling and opposition parties to revise election laws and investigate campaign irregularities.

Responsibility for maintaining internal security lies with the National Security Planning Agency (NSP), the Korean National Police (KNP), and the Defense Security Command (DSC). Legislation passed in 1993 restricted the NSP from interfering in domestic politics; and gave it investigative authority only in cases involving terrorism, espionage, and international crime organizations. In December the Government revised this law to allow the NSP to investigate domestic organizations that are viewed as supporting the North Korean Government. There continued to be credible reports of some infringements of suspects' rights by NSP officials during the interrogation process.

After a period of sustained economic growth averaging about 9 percent per year, the economy has slowed somewhat, with 1996 economic growth projected at 7 percent. This slowdown in the rate of growth is attributable to dampened demand for key exports, declining terms of trade, and lower investment growth. While economic growth is still robust, Korea continues to face issues of declining competitiveness, a labor shortage, an inefficient agricultural sector, and inadequate infrastructure.

The Government generally respects the human rights of its citizens; however, there were problems in some areas. The use or threatened use of the National Security Law (NSL) continued to infringe upon citizens civil liberties, including the right to free expression. There was no progress toward reform of the NSL, although judges appointed since the onset of democratic government demonstrated their independence in several cases in which they refused to authorize prosecution of dissidents under the NSL or acquitted defendants charged under its provisions. The Ministry of Justice continued to implement guidelines requiring that suspects be told at the time of arrest of their right to remain silent and their right to a lawyer. Nevertheless, there continued to be credible reports that, in some instances, police deprived suspects of timely access to counsel or subjected detainees to verbal threats, physical abuse, and sleep deprivation. Some human rights groups alleged that police used excessive violence in confrontations with student demonstrators. Women continued to face legal and societal discrimination. Violence against women and physical abuse remain serious problems. There is still insufficient legal redress for these problems. Ethnic minorities face legal and societal discrimination. In December labor statutes were amended in an effort to meet international standards for worker rights and to increase labor flexibility. However, key worker rights provisions were either delayed or deleted from the final legislation, while promanagement labor market changes are to become effective March 1997. The labor bill encountered strong opposition from Korean labor organizations, which launched demonstrations and strikes to protest its passage. After opposition legislators physically prevented a vote on this bill, it, as well as the revised NSP statute, was passed in a secretive, predawn National Assembly session with no opposition legislators present.

The Government continued its surveillance of some released political prisoners and continued to require released political prisoners to make regular reports to the police under the Social Surveillance Law. However, the Government still has not authorized independent investigations of the cases of some prisoners who received sentences on charges believed to have been fabricated by previous governments. Some of these prisoners reportedly were subjected to torture to extract confessions and to trials that did not meet international standards of fairness.

RESPECT FOR HUMAN RIGHTS

Section 1. Respect for the Integrity of the Person, Including Freedom From:

　a. *Political and Other Extrajudicial Killing.*—There were no reports of political or extrajucicial killings by the police or military. One student and a policeman died during demonstrations. No Su Sok, a student at Seoul's Yonsei University who participated in a demonstration during the spring near the campus, was stricken by heart failure while fleeing from police. Activists maintained that bruises on No's body suggested that the heart attack may have been induced by police violence. However, medical authorities who examined the body attributed No's death to a heart attack. A policeman trying to control a demonstration at Yonsei University in August died after rocks thrown by students struck him in the head (see Section 2.b.).

　On September 18, a North Korean submarine attempting to infiltrate an armed reconnaissance team into South Korean territory ran aground off the South Korean coast. The 26 North Korean personnel onboard abandoned the vessel. Eleven crew members were apparently killed by the submarine's complement of highly trained infiltrators in order to prevent their capture. Of the surviving infiltrators, 13 were killed in enounters with South Korean security forces, 1 was captured alive, and 1 remains unaccounted for. Nine members of the South Korean military and a police officer were killed in the search for the infiltrators. Three civilian bystanders were murdered by the infiltrators. One civilian was killed accidentally by South Korean military personnel.

　b. *Disappearance.*—There were no reports of politically motivated disappearances.

　c. *Torture and Other Cruel, Inhuman, or Degrading Treatment or Punishment.*—The Government has ordered investigating authorities to protect the human rights of suspects, and allegations of abuse by authorities of those in custody for questioning continued to decline. Nonetheless, prosecutors continued to place much emphasis on securing convictions through confessions. In spite of government directives discouraging sleep deprivation as a technique for obtaining confessions, there continued to be reports of police questioning suspects through the night and, reportedly in some cases, verbally or physically abusing suspects, including beatings, threats, and sexual intimidation in the course of arrest and police interrogation. Some human rights groups alleged that police used excessive violence in quelling disturbances that resulted from student demonstrations in August (see Section 2.b.).

　The Government continued to consider cases in which former detainees argued that they deserved redress for torture suffered in the past. However, the Government has failed to provide an effective mechanism for redress, such as an independent body to investigate complaints of past human rights violations. It remained relatively rare for officials accused of abuse or harassment of suspects to be prosecuted.

　Prison conditions are Spartan. Prison diets are adequate, but the prisons offer little protection against cold in winter and heat in the summer. Consequently, some prisoners claim that the conditions have damaged their health. There have been a few claims that prison guards have used excessive force or have needlessly put prisoners in manacles and that medical care for prisoners has been inadequate. Prisoner access to reading materials and television broadcasts has improved significantly in recent years. There is little independent monitoring of prison conditions, although representatives of human rights groups may visit certain prisoners at the discretion of the prison warden.

　d. *Arbitrary Arrest, Detention, or Exile.*—Korean law is often vague, and prosecutors have wide latitude to interpret the law. The NSL defines espionage in broad terms, and permits the authorities to detain and arrest persons who commit acts viewed as supportive of North Korea and therefore dangerous to the Republic of Korea. Authorities arrested persons not only spying on behalf of North Korea but also those who praised North Korea, its former leader Kim Il Sung, or the DPRK's self-reliance" ("juche") political philosophy. The United Nations Human Rights Committee has termed the NSL "a major obstacle to the full realization of the rights enshrined in the International Covenant on Civil and Political Rights." The Government arrested over 200 dissidents under the NSL during the year, accusing most of them of trying to undermine democracy by aiding North Korea.

　Article 7 of the NSL permits the imprisonment for up to 7 years of anyone who "with the knowledge that he might endanger the existence or security of the State or the basic order of free democracy, praised, encouraged, propagandized for, or sided with the activities of an antistate organization." The legal standard for knowing what might endanger the existence of the State is vague. Consequently, a number of Koreans have been arrested for what appeared to be peaceful expression of opposing views. For example, in February singer Lee Run Jin and publisher Won Yong Ho were arrested for publishing a songbook that allegedly praised North Korea.

The Government's rationale for retaining the NSL is that North Korea is actively trying to subvert the Government and society and that special circumstances call for limiting some forms of expression to block the greater danger to freedom and democracy posed by totalitarianism. The effect sometimes is to relieve the Government of the burden of proof in a court of law that any particular speech or action does, in fact, threaten the nation's security. Citizens continued to be prosecuted for unauthorized travel to North Korea (see Section 2.d.).

The Criminal Code requires warrants to be issued by judges in cases of arrest, detention, seizure, or search, except if the person is apprehended while committing a criminal act, or if a judge is not available and the authorities believe that the suspect may destroy evidence or escape capture if not quickly arrested. In such emergency cases, judges must issue arrest warrants within 48 hours after apprehension, or, if a court is not located in the county, in 72 hours. Police may detain suspects who voluntarily come in for questioning for up to 6 hours but must notify the suspects' families. The police generally respected these legal requirements.

Upon issuance of an arrest warrant, the security services normally must release suspects after 30 days unless an indictment is issued. Hence, detainees are a relatively small percentage of the total prison population.

The Constitution specifically provides for the right to representation by an attorney, but attorneys are not allowed to be present during a police interrogation. The Government began in 1993 to permit suspects to consult with "duty lawyers" during breaks in the interrogation. The Justice Ministry also issued guidelines last year requiring police to inform suspects at the time of arrest about their right to be represented by a lawyer. However, there continued to be complaints that access to a lawyer was restricted during this phase. There is a functioning system of bail, but human rights lawyers say that bail is generally not granted in cases involving serious offenses, and, even when the offense is relatively minor, bail often will not be granted unless the victim of the alleged crime agrees to the bail request.

The Government does not use forced exile.

e. *Denial of Fair Public Trial.*—The Constitution provides for an independent judiciary. The President appoints the Chief Justice and most justices of the Constitutional Court. Although judges do not receive life appointments, in recent years the judiciary has shown increasing independence. Judges cannot be fired or transferred for political reasons. In a notable instance of judicial independence, a district court judge in Pusan ruled in January that a student activist's exchange of faxes with North Korean students and chanting of slogans at demonstrations that echoed North Korean propaganda were not sufficient grounds to convict him of violating the NSL. In July a Seoul District Criminal Court rejected an arrest warrant request for Catholic Priest Moon Chong Hyon, who met with North Korean figures in Poland. The Court ruled that authorities had not presented evidence that Moon's actions undermined freedom or democracy in the South Korea.

The judicial system has local courts presided over by judges who render verdicts in all cases. There is no trial by jury. Defendants can appeal a verdict to a district appeals court and to the Supreme Court. Constitutional challenges can be taken to the Constitutional Court. The Constitutional Court, which began operation in 1988, continued to grow in its role of interpreting the Constitution.

The Constitution provides defendants a number of rights in criminal trials, including presumption of innocence, protection against self-incrimination, freedom from retroactive laws and double jeopardy, the right to a speedy trial, and the right of appeal. When a person is physically detained, the initial trial must be completed within 6 months of arrest. These rights are generally observed. Trials are open to the public, but the judge may restrict attendance if he believes spectators may seek to disrupt the proceedings.

Judges generally allow considerable scope for examination of witnesses by both the prosecution and defense. Cases involving national security and criminal cases are tried by the same courts. Although convictions are rarely overturned, appeals often result in reduced sentences. Death sentences are automatically appealed.

Human rights groups believe that many dissidents tried under past military governments were sentenced to long prison terms during the 1970's and 1980's on trumped up charges of spying for North Korea. Furthermore, these persons, dozens of whom are still in jail, reportedly had been held incommunicado for up to 60 days after their arrest, subjected to extreme forms of torture, forced to make "confessions," and convicted after trials that did not conform to international standards for a fair trial. Political prisoners have been denied early parole because they refused to renounce real or alleged communist beliefs. Some released political prisoners were required to report their activities regularly to the police.

In a landmark decision this year, former presidents Chun Doo Hwan and Roh Tae Woo and several of their close associates were convicted for their roles in the military takeover of the Government in 1979 and 1980. Chun, who argued that the court proceedings were unconstitutional because the statute of limitations had expired for these offenses, was sentenced to death. Roh was sentenced to a prison term of more than 20 years. These sentences were subsequently reduced to life in prison and 17 years respectively.

It is difficult to estimate the number of political prisoners, because it is not clear whether particular persons were arrested for merely exercising the rights of free speech or association or were detained for committing acts of violence or espionage. Some human rights monitors estimate the number of political prisoners at over 400. However, these monitors' definition of political prisoner often includes all persons imprisoned for acts that were politically motivated, without distinction as to whether the acts themselves included violence or other criminal behavior. The number of political prisoners and detainees as defined by international standards appears to number under 200.

f. *Arbitrary Interference with Privacy, Family, Home, or Correspondence.*—In general the Government honors the integrity of the home and family. In the past, the security services conducted varying degrees of surveillance, including wiretaps, of political dissidents. The Antiwiretap Law and the law to reform the NSP were designed to curb government surveillance of civilians and appear largely to have succeeded. The Antiwiretap Law lays out the conditions under which the monitoring of telephone calls, mail, and other forms of communication are legal. It requires government officials to secure a judge's permission before placing wiretaps, or, in the event of an emergency, soon after placing them, and it provides for jail terms for those who violate this law. Some human rights groups argue that a considerable amount of illegal wiretapping is still taking place and assert that the lack of an independent body to investigate whether police have employed illegal wiretaps hinders the effectiveness of the Antiwiretap Law.

Citizens are not allowed to listen to North Korean radio in their homes or read books published in North Korea if the Government determines that they are doing so for the purpose of helping North Korea. Student groups make plausible claims that government informants are posted around university campuses. Persons with backgrounds as political or labor activists may find it difficult to obtain some forms of employment or advance in such fields as government, broadcast media, and education.

Section 2. Respect for Civil Liberties, Including:

a. *Freedom of Speech and Press.*—While most political discourse is unrestricted, under the NSL the Government limits the expression of ideas that authorities consider Communist or pro-North Korean. Broad interpretations of the NSL allow for restrictions on the peaceful expression of dissenting views.

While the Government has abandoned direct control over the news media, it continues to exercise considerable indirect influence. Some officials reportedly lobby journalists aggressively to discourage them from writing stories critical of the Government. In addition, the latent threat of tax investigations against parent media companies is widely believed to encourage newspapers and broadcasters to soften criticism. Moreover, while the Government's anticorruption campaign curtailed politicians' payments of money to reporters, it did not eliminate these payments. Nevertheless, press criticism of the Government is extensive in all fields, and authorities have not used repressive measures to stop media reporting. Although most radio and television stations are state-supported, the stations maintain a considerable degree of editorial independence in their news coverage.

Journalists allege that the libel laws are used to harass publications for articles that are unflattering but not necessarily untrue. In January a Seoul district court ordered the Hangyoreh Sinmun newspaper to pay a libel award of approximately $500,000 to President Kim's son, Kim Hyun Chul. The court maintained that the paper had not adequately checked its facts before reporting that the President's son had accepted bribes. Many reporters criticized the award, saying that the court had been influenced by government pressure. However, other credible observers noted that Korean journalism suffers from sensationalism and insufficient fact checking, and they argued that the judge in this case appropriately penalized the reporter for basing serious defamatory charges on a single source whose allegations could have been refuted by checking with other principals involved.

Prosecutors continued to indict dissidents under the NSL for producing, selling, or distributing pro-North Korean or pro-Communist materials. Court precedents allow Koreans to possess these kinds of publications for purely academic use, profit, or curiosity, but not with the intent of subverting the State. Prosecutors are given wide discretion in determining motives for possessing or publishing such material.

The Government continued to allow, within its guidelines, an increase in media coverage of North Korea. Television networks continued to broadcast edited versions of North Korean television programs. The media extensively reported on United States and South Korean talks with North Korean officials.

The Government Censorship Board, which screens movies for sexual or violent content before release, has followed more liberal guidelines in recent years. Consequently, a broader range of films has been released to the public.

In 1994 authorities began investigating eight Kyongsang University professors on the grounds that their textbook on Korean society endorsed North Korean ideology. This investigation was regarded by much of the scholarly community as a serious infringement on academic freedom. However, prosecutors who sought to arrest several of the professors under the NSL were denied warrants by a judge who decided that authorities had not provided evidence of the scholars' pro-Communist activities. This investigation has been closed, and no instances of prosecution for scholarly writing were reported in 1996. However, student groups plausibly report the presence of government informants on university campuses (see Section 1.f.).

b. *Freedom of Peaceful Assembly and Association.*—The Law on Assembly and Demonstrations prohibits assemblies considered likely to undermine public order. The law forbids outside interference in peaceful assemblies approved by the authorities and requires that the police be notified in advance of demonstrations of all types, including political rallies. Police must notify organizers if they consider the event impermissible under this law. The Government forbade some demonstrations, such as a rally of students at the border of North and South Korea, that authorities believed were orchestrated by North Korea to undermine the State.

In August thousands of student demonstrators, led by the National Federation of Student Councils, occupied buildings on the Yonsei University campus after being denied permission to hold a rally at the border of North and South Korea. Departing from its usual practice of not intervening in protests contained within university campuses, the Government sent a massive police force onto the campus to remove demonstrators. The students resisted using steel pipes, rocks, and firebombs. In the confrontations at the university, which lasted for more than a week, one policemen was killed and scores of students and police were injured. Some human rights groups alleged that police used excessive violence in quelling the disturbance. However, most observers also acknowledged that the tactics of protesting students were violent and provocative. Associations, except those whose aim is deemed by the Government to be the overthrow of the State, operate freely.

c. *Freedom of Religion.*—The Constitution provides for freedom of religion, and the Government respects this provision in practice.

d. *Freedom of Movement Within the Country, Foreign Travel, Emigration, and Repatriation.*—Most citizens are allowed to move freely throughout the country. However, police may restrict the movements of some former prisoners. Foreign travel is generally unrestricted, but travel to North Korea must be approved by the Government. To obtain approval, potential visitors must demonstrate to authorities that their trip does not have a political purpose—that is, to praise North Korea or criticize the South Korean Government. Travelers to North Korea who do not receive government permission are likely to be arrested upon their return to South Korea. For example, Chong Win Ju, a student at Inchon University, and Lee Hye Jong, a student at Catholic University, were sentenced in the spring to 3 years in jail for visiting North Korea in August 1995 to attend a "unification rally."

In the past, the Government forbade some Koreans convicted of politically related crimes from returning to Korea, and some citizens still face sanctions if they return. In 1994 the NSP lifted the entry ban on composer Yun I Sang, a dissident who had been living in Berlin for a number of years. However, the Government required that he refrain from any political activity while in Korea and that he give an accounting of his political activities overseas before authorities would allow him into the country. Yun refused these conditions and decided against returning to South Korea.

The Government cooperates with the U.N. High Commissioner for Refugees and other humanitarian organizations in assisting refugees. Government guidelines provide for offering temporary refuge in the case of a mass influx of asylum seekers (sometimes referred to as "first asylum"). However, the issue of provision of first asylum did not arise in 1996, and there were no reports of forced return of persons to a country where they had a fear of persecution.

Section 3. Respect for Political Rights: The Right of Citizens to Change Their Government

Citizens have the right to elect their own government. The Constitution, as amended in 1987, provides for the direct election of the President and for a mixed system of direct and proportional election of legislators to the unicameral National Assembly. The President serves a single 5-year term and may not be reelected. National Assembly members serve 4-year terms. All citizens 20 years of age or above have the right to vote, and elections are held by secret ballot. Kim Young Sam, who took office in February 1992, is Korea's first chief executive in nearly 30 years not to have a career military background.

Because of cultural traditions and discrimination, women occupy few important positions in government. In the current and past governments, the only woman in the Cabinet has been the Second Minister for Political Affairs, whose portfolio is Women's Affairs. In addition, in 1995 a woman was elected mayor of Kwangmyong City, and a female legislator chairs one of the special committees of the National Assembly.

Section 4. Governmental Attitude Regarding International and Nongovernmental Investigation of Alleged Violations of Human Rights

Several nongovernmental private organizations are active in promoting human rights, and they operate without government restriction. Chief among these groups are the Lawyers for a Democratic Society, Sarangbang, the Human Rights Committee of the National Council of Churches in Korea, the Korean Bar Association, and "Mingahyup," an association of the families of political prisoners. These groups publish reports on the human rights situation in Korea and make their views known both inside and outside the country. Government and ruling party officials generally have been willing to meet with international human rights groups.

Section 5. Discrimination Based on Race, Sex, Religion, Disability, Language, or Social Status

The Constitution and equal opportunity statutes forbid discrimination on the basis of race, sex, religion, disability, or social status, and the Government respects these provisions. However, traditional attitudes limit opportunities for women and the disabled. Ethnic minorities face both legal and societal discrimination.

Women.—Violence against women remains a problem, and some women's rights groups maintain that such violence, including spousal abuse, has worsened in the past few years. The law does not provide adequate protection to victims of abuse.

Rape remained a serious problem, with 6,173 cases reported in 1994 (the last year for which statistics are available). Many incidents of rape go unreported because of the stigma associated with being a rape victim. The activities of a number of women's groups have increased awareness of the importance of reporting and prosecuting rapes as well as offenses such as sexual harassment in the workplace. According to women's rights groups, cases involving sexual harassment or rape generally go unprosecuted, and perpetrators, if convicted, often receive very lenient sentences.

The amended Family Law, which went into effect in 1991, permits women to head a household, recognizes a wife's right to a portion of the couple's property, and allows a woman to maintain greater contact with her children after a divorce. Although the revisions helped abused women, divorce remains a social taboo, and there is little government or private assistance for divorced women. These factors, plus the fact that divorced women have limited employment opportunities and have difficulty remarrying, lead some women to stay in abusive situations. The Government has created some shelters for battered women and increased the number of child care facilities, providing women in abusive situations with more options, but women's rights groups say that they fall far short of dealing effectively with the problem.

A conservative Confucian tradition has left women subordinate to men socially and economically. There has been some limited and gradual change in social mores and attitudes affecting women; for example, women have full access to education, and a few have become government officials and hold elected office. Despite the passage of equal employment opportunity legislation in 1988, however, few women work as company executives or leading officials in government. The Women's Affairs Ministry continued its efforts to expand employment opportunities for women, and during the year the air force implemented a program to encourage women to become pilots and seek other senior positions.

Children.—The Government continued to devote an increasing share of the overall budget to social expenditures, which includes those related to the welfare of children. High quality elementary education is available to all Korean children free of charge, and most obtain a good quality secondary education. High quality health care facilities are widely available to children.

Child abuse does not appear to be a significant problem or policy issue. Child abuse has not been studied extensively, and statistics on such abuse are limited. About 150 cases were reported during the year. Although experts believe that a number of cases go unreported, instances of child abuse still appear to be relatively rare. The Seoul metropolitan government runs a children's counseling center, which investigates reports of abuse, counsels families, and cares for runaway children. In the absence of a specific law against child abuse, however, it is not possible to prosecute and punish child abusers unless they commit a crime punishable under a separate law.

The traditional preference for male children continues, although it is less evident among people in their twenties and thirties. Although the law bans fetal sex testing, such testing and the subsequent termination of pregnancies with female fetuses frequently occur. The Government has expressed concern at the widening disparity between male and female birth rates.

People With Disabilities.—Although new measures aimed at creating opportunities for the disabled have been taken, public facilities for their everyday care and use remained inadequate. However, there is no legal discrimination against disabled persons in employment, education, or in the provision of other state services.

In 1995 the Government expanded job training programs, medical benefits, and welfare facilities for disabled citizens. Since 1991 firms with over 300 employees have been required by law either to hire disabled workers or pay a fee. After human rights groups publicized a survey indicating that most companies either paid the fee or evaded the law, the Labor Ministry announced it would increase the subsidies provided to companies that hire the disabled. New public buildings are required to include facilities for the disabled, such as ramp access to entrances, a wheelchair lift, and special parking spaces.

National/Racial/Ethnic Minorities.—The Republic of Korea is a racially homogeneous country with no ethnic minorities of significant number. Citizenship is based on blood, not location of birth, and Koreans must show as proof their family genealogy. Ethnic Chinese born and resident in Korea cannot obtain citizenship or become public servants and may have difficulty being hired by some major corporations. Due to legal as well as societal discrimination, many formerly resident ethnic Chinese have emigrated to other countries since the 1970's. Amerasian children are usually able to obtain Korean citizenship, and no legal discrimination against them exists. Informal discrimination, however, is prevalent, making it more difficult for Amerasians to succeed in academia, business, or government.

Section 6. Worker Rights

a. *The Right of Association.*—The Constitution gives workers, with the exception of public sector employees and teachers, the right to free association. There are some blue-collar public sector unions in railroads, telecommunications, the postal service, and the national medical center. The Trade Union Law specifies that only one union is permitted at each place of work and that all unions are required to notify the authorities when formed or dissolved. About 10 percent of workers belong to a union.

In the past, the Government did not formally recognize labor federations that were not affiliated with the country's two legally recognized labor groupings—the Federation of Korean Trade Unions (FKTU) and the Independent Korean Federation of Clerical and Financial Workers. In the past several years, however, the Labor Ministry officially recognized some independent white-collar federations representing hospital workers, journalists, and office workers at construction firms and government research institutes. The courts ruled in 1992 that affiliation with the FKTU is not required to be registered as a legal labor federation. In practice, labor federations not formally recognized by the Labor Ministry exist and work without government interference, unless authorities considered their involvement in labor disputes disruptive. In May the President created a presidential commission to consider additional changes in the labor laws, including granting legal recognition to the dissident Korean Confederation of Trade Unions (KCTU). In October, however, in connection with a pending decision on its application for membership in the Organization for Economic Cooperation and Development (OECD) and in anticipation of specific recommendations from the Commission, the Government pledged to reform its labor legislation so as to achieve greater conformity with internationally recognized labor standards.

In December the National Assembly passed labor reform legislation with provisions designed both to enhance worker rights and increase labor market flexibility. However, last-minute changes to the legislation by the National Assembly delayed the legalization of multiple trades unions by at least 3 years and deleted provisions that would have allowed teachers to form associations, thus limiting the worker rights enhancements. The new law also maintained certain restrictions preventing unauthorized "third-parties" from becoming involved in labor disputes and did not address organizing rights for white-collar government employees. In contrast, the promanagement changes concerning Korea's labor market flexibility changes (including provisions making layoffs easier, increasing employer flexibility in establishing employee work schedules, and permitting the replacement of strikers) are to become effective March 1, 1997. The bill encountered strong opposition from labor which launched demonstrations and strikes to protest its passage.

The Government arrested and tried unionists it viewed as acting as "third parties" in instigating labor disputes. Cho Myung Lae and Kim Seung Hyun, officers of the Korean Federation of Metalworkers Unions, were arrested in June for their alleged role in fomenting a dispute at the Korea Textile Company. Kwon Yong Kil and Yang Kyu Hun, respectively Chairman and Vice President of the KCTU, both were tried for their role as "third parties" in the 1994 subway and railroad strikes. Authorities charged that they had incited illegal and violent strikes in the public sector. Human rights groups argued that Kwon was arrested for attempting to exercise the legitimate functions of a trade union federation leader. Several dozen workers were arrested for "interference with business" and for committing criminal violence during strikes. The International Confederation of Free Trade Unions (ICFTU) alleges that over 40 trade unionists were imprisoned for prolonged periods for various trade union activities during the year.

The Government continued the ban on labor union activities by public and private schoolteachers, arguing that the teachers' union (Chonkyojo) is essentially a political organization with radical aims. The Government continued its program of reinstating those among the 1,500 fired teachers who agreed to resign from Chonkyojo.

Only two members are required to form a union. Election and labor laws forbid unions from donating money to political parties or participating in election campaigns. However, trade unionists have circumvented the ban by temporarily resigning from their union posts and running for office on the ticket of a political party or as independents.

Strikes are prohibited in government agencies, state-run enterprises, and defense industries. By law, unions in enterprises determined to be of "public interest," including public transportation, utilities, public health, banking, broadcasting, and communications, can be ordered to submit to government-ordered arbitration in lieu of striking. In practice, however, the Government rarely imposes arbitration. The number of labor disputes has declined in recent years. According to Labor Ministry statistics, 88 strikes occurred in 1995, the last year for which complete data are available. The Labor Dispute Adjustment Act requires unions to notify the Labor Ministry of their intention to strike, and it mandates a 10-day "cooling-off period" before a work stoppage may legally begin. (The cooling-off period is 15 days in public interest sectors.) Labor laws prohibit retribution against workers who have conducted a legal strike and allow workers to file complaints of unfair labor practices against employers.

Both the FKTU and the KCTU are affiliated with the ICFTU. Most of the FKTU's 20 constituent federations maintain affiliations with international trade secretariats, as does the KCTU Metalworkers Council. In response to freedom of association complaints lodged by dissident and independent unions, the International Labor Organization (ILO) Committee on Freedom of Association issued a report at midyear recommending that the Government bring Korean labor law and policy up to international worker rights standards in accordance with the principle of free association.

In recent years, the Government has cultivated a more neutral stance in labor disputes. Authorities rarely sent police to quell labor disturbances, and there were no reports of employer-hired squads assaulting workers in 1996.

Since July 1991, South Korea has been suspended from the U.S. Overseas Private Investment Corporation (OPIC) insurance programs because of the Government's infringements on freedom of association and other worker rights.

b. *The Right to Organize and Bargain Collectively.*—The Constitution and the Trade Union Law provide for the right of workers to collective bargaining and collective action. This law also empowers workers to file complaints of unfair labor practices against employers who interfere with union organizing or practice discrimination against union members. Employers found guilty of unfair practices can be required to reinstate workers who were fired for union activities.

Extensive collective bargaining is practiced, even with unions whose federations are not legally recognized by the Government. The labor laws do not extend the right to organize and bargain collectively to government employees, including employees of state or public-run enterprises, defense industries, and public and private schoolteachers.

Korea has no independent system of labor courts. The central and local labor commissions form a semiautonomous agency of the Labor Ministry that adjudicate disputes in accordance with the Labor Dispute Adjustment Law. Each labor commission is composed of equal representation from labor (represented by the FKTU), management, and "the public interest." Local labor commissions are empowered to decide on remedial measures in cases involving unfair labor practices and to mediate and, in some situations, arbitrate labor disputes. Arbitration can be made compulsory in sectors of the economy (e.g., utilities and transportation) that are deemed essential to public welfare.

The Trade Union Law and Labor Dispute Adjustment Law forbid third-party intervention in union and labor disputes by federations not recognized by the Government (such as the dissident federation, the KCTU), but they allow recognized labor federations, principally the FKTU, its affiliates, and some independent white-collar federations, to assist member unions. The ban on third-party intervention also applies to mediation efforts by lawyers, experts, and others who have the consent of both labor and management.

Enterprises in Korea's two export processing zones (EPZ's), had been designated by the Government as public interest enterprises. Workers in these enterprises, whose rights to organize were formerly restricted, have gradually been given the rights enjoyed by workers in other sectors of the economy.

c. *Prohibition of Forced or Compulsory Labor.*—The Constitution provides that no person shall be punished, placed under preventive restrictions, or subjected to involuntary labor, except as provided by law and through lawful procedures. Forced or compulsory labor is not condoned by the Government and is not practiced.

d. *Minimum Age for Employment of Children.*—The Labor Standards Law prohibits the employment of persons under the age of 13 without a special employment certificate from the Labor Ministry. Because there is compulsory education until the age of 13, few special employment certificates are issued for full-time employment. Some children are allowed to hold part-time jobs such as selling newspapers. To gain employment, children under 18 years of age must have written approval from their parents or guardians. Employers may require minors to work only a limited number of overtime hours and are prohibited from employing them at night without special permission from the Labor Ministry. Child labor laws and regulations are clear and usually enforced when violations are found, but the Government employs too few inspectors to carry out regular inspections.

e. *Acceptable Conditions of Work.*—The Government implemented a minimum wage law in 1988. The minimum wage level is reviewed annually. In September the minimum wage was raised to approximately $1.70 (1,400 won) per hour. Companies with fewer than 10 employees are exempt from this law. Due to Korea's tight labor market, however, most firms pay wages well above the minimum to attract and retain workers. The FKTU and other unions continue to claim that the current minimum wage does not meet the minimum requirements of urban workers. In fact, a worker earning the minimum wage would have difficulty in providing a decent standard of living for himself and his family, despite the fringe benefits such as transportation expenses with which Korean companies normally supplement salaries. (The Government notes that the money an average blue-collar worker takes home in overtime and bonuses significantly raises the total compensation package.) According to the Ministry of Labor, 3.3 percent of the population lived below the poverty level in 1995.

Foreign workers, most of whom come from China, the Philippines, Bangladesh, Nepal, and Pakistan, often face difficult working conditions. The Government has sought to ameliorate the problems of illegal workers by creating a program whereby about 60,000 foreign workers were allowed to enter Korea legally to work at established wages and with legal safeguards. Illegal foreign workers, who probably number more than 100,000, still suffer significant hardships in the workplace. It is difficult for illegal workers to seek relief for loss of pay or unsatisfactory living and working conditions because they always face the threat of being deported. The Government has, however, established counseling centers that hear complaints from illegal foreign workers facing deportation proceedings about such issues as overdue wages and industrial accidents. Other foreigners working as language teachers have complained that language institutes that hired them frequently violated employment contracts and that the legal system provided insufficient redress for such abuses.

Amendments to the Labor Standards Law passed in 1989 brought the maximum regular workweek down to 44 hours, with provision for overtime to be compensated at a higher wage. The law also provides for a 24-hour rest period each week. However, labor groups claim that the Government does not adequately enforce these laws, especially with regard to small companies.

The Government sets health and safety standards, but South Korea suffers from unusually high accident rates. The accident rate continues to decline gradually, due to public and union pressure for better working conditions. However, the number of deaths resulting from work-related accidents remains very high by international standards. The Labor Ministry has improved enforcement of safety standards but still lacks enough inspectors to enforce the laws fully. The Industrial Safety and Health Law does not guarantee job security for workers who remove themselves from dangerous work environments.

LAOS

The Lao People's Democratic Republic (LPDR) is an authoritarian one-party state ruled by the Lao People's Revolutionary Party (LPRP).

The Ministry of Interior (MOI) remains the main instrument of state control. MOI police maintain order and monitor Lao society and foreign nationals, including foreign officials and diplomats. The degree of surveillance varies by locality, but overall has diminished considerably in recent years.

Laos is an extremely poor country. After the LPRP came to power in 1975, at least 350,000 people fled the country to escape the Government's harsh political and economic policies. Since 1986 the Government has largely abandoned its Socialist economic agenda. Economic reforms have moved the country from a moribund, centrally planned system to a growing, market-oriented economy open to foreign investment.

There has been a general trend away from the harsh conditions that existed after the LPRP assumed power in 1975, but serious problems remain. Citizens do not have the right to change their government. Even with ongoing economic liberalization, the adoption of a Constitution in 1991, and National Assembly elections in 1993, the Government has only slowly eased restrictions on basic freedoms and begun codification of implementing legislation for rights stipulated in the Constitution. Many of the rights provided for in the Constitution have not been codified with implementing legislation. In practice, the Government restricts the freedoms of speech, assembly, and, to a lesser extent, religion, even though they are provided for in the Constitution. Citizens do not have the right to privacy and do not enjoy a free press, although most citizens have ready access to a variety of foreign media. Prison conditions remain harsh, and some societal discrimination against women and minorities persists.

RESPECT FOR HUMAN RIGHTS

Section 1. Respect for the Integrity of the Person, Including Freedom From:

a. *Political and Other Extrajudicial Killing.*—There were no reports of political or other extrajudicial killings.

While there continued to be occasional killings by armed bands, who ambushed and robbed persons in vehicles north of Vientiane, it remains unclear whether these killings were politically motivated. There were three such incidents reported in September. Similar attacks occurred in this area prior to the formation of the current Government. However, since passengers are assaulted as well as robbed, this may indicate that a vestige of the low level insurgency of the 1980's remains.

The Government does not ordinarily publicize lethal incidents. In September, however, following an attack on passengers in a tour agency's minivan which resulted in the deaths of a well-known expatriate businessman and four others, the media not only reported the incident but included a warning that the area in which the attack occurred is not considered safe.

b. *Disappearance.*—There were no reports of politically motivated disappearances.

In September 1993, Vue Mai, a Hmong leader who in November 1992 returned voluntarily to Laos from a refugee camp in Thailand, disappeared in Vientiane. No new information relevant to the case came to light during the year.

c. *Torture and Other Cruel, Inhuman, or Degrading Treatment or Punishment.*— The Penal Code prohibits torture or mistreatment of prisoners, and the Government generally observed these principles in practice.

Prison conditions are harsh but not life threatening. Prison authorities deny some prisoners regular family visits, and medical care ranges from inadequate to nonexistent. Inmates sometimes resort to bribing guards to obtain food and medicines. Prison conditions for women are similar to those for men. The extent of sexual harassment in prison is unknown, but it is not believed to be a serious problem. There is no independent monitoring of prison conditions.

d. *Arbitrary Arrest, Detention or Exile.*—The Constitution and Penal Code provide some protection, including a statute of limitations for those accused of crimes, but the Government does not fully respect these provisions. Those accused of hostility toward the regime are subject to arrest and confinement for long periods. There have been no reports of this type of arrest in the past 4 years.

There continued to be allegations that the Government has detained three Hmong males since 1992 because of their association with the United States Government prior to 1975. The Lao Government has thus far not responded directly to repeated inquiries about these allegations.

While citizens have the protection of due process, authorities have reportedly arrested some persons based on unsupported accusations and without informing them of the charges, the accusers' identities, or their legal rights. Due process rights are unevenly upheld across the country.

The Government does not use forced exile.

e. *Denial of Fair Public Trial.*—The Constitution provides for the independence of judges and prosecutors and protects their decisions from outside scrutiny. In practice, however, the courts, which are understaffed and poorly trained, appear to accept recommendations of other government agencies, especially the Ministry of Interior, in making their decisions.

The judiciary is composed of district courts, provincial courts, and the Supreme Court.

Although regulations provide for public trial, widespread ignorance of constitutional rights among both citizens and law enforcement authorities often results in trials that are little more than public announcements of predetermined verdicts. Politically sensitive trials have not been open to the public, although trials of civil crimes appeared to be open; these are increasingly publicized in the media.

There is provision for appeal to the provincial courts and the Supreme Court. Senior government and party officials reportedly may also review politically sensitive cases.

The Constitution provides that all accused persons have the right to defend themselves in court. A board of legal advisors formed in 1991 was suspended in 1992, pending enactment of a legally clarified body of governing regulations. The Government strengthened the legal profession and individual rights to counsel in August by establishing a formal bar association. According to the Criminal Code, defendants in criminal cases are entitled, at their own expense, to representation by a "rights protector" who may be a practicing attorney. However, because citizens are largely unaware of their rights and legal authorities are not required by law to enlighten them, few defendants seek or have legal representation.

Arrests, trials and convictions are usually unannounced, thereby complicating efforts to estimate accurately the number of political prisoners. Three former government officials are serving 14-year sentences handed down in 1992 for advocating a multiparty system and criticizing restrictions on political liberties. Also in 1992, three men detained since 1975 were sentenced to life terms for crimes allegedly committed during their tenure as officials of the previous regime. The Government claims that three other officials of the former government released in 1992 have chosen to remain in the same remote province where they and the six prisoners mentioned above were held. There have been no reports of other political prisoners in the last few years.

f. *Arbitrary Interference with Privacy, Family, Home, or Correspondence.*—At the same time that it sought to liberalize the economy, the Government relaxed some elements of state control, including its rigorous police monitoring of personal and business activities and enforcement of the nighttime curfew. However, while the Constitution prohibits arrests or searches in homes without a warrant or authorization, the security bureaus may authorize search and seizure by themselves rather than by judicial authority. The Government and the Party continue to monitor citizens sporadically through a system of neighborhood and workplace committees. The neighborhood committees also have responsibility for maintaining public order and reporting "bad elements" to the police. These committees usually concern themselves more with street crime and instances of moral turpitude than with political activism. The degree of surveillance and control varies from province to province, but overall has diminished considerably in recent years.

The Penal Code forbids telephone monitoring without proper authorization, but the security bureaus are believed to authorize such monitoring themselves. The Government continued to monitor international mail and telephone calls, probably including some faxes, although the increasing number of such calls limited the scope of such surveillance.

The Constitution stipulates that the "national community" owns all land. Private "ownership" is in the form of land use certificates, which can be bought, sold, and transferred to heirs. Many citizens who fled the country after 1975 have regained confiscated land and property after demonstrating their intent to repatriate.

Contact between ordinary citizens and foreigners has increased in recent years as restrictions such as the requirement for government approval of invitations to most foreigners' homes are no longer enforced. The Government has eased the prohibition against foreigners staying with Lao families in urban areas, and allows citizens to marry foreigners but only with prior government approval. Marriages without government approval may be annulled, with both partners subject to fine and arrest.

Section 2. *Respect for Civil Liberties, Including:*

a. *Freedom of Speech and Press.*—Despite the constitutional provisions for freedom of speech and the press, the Government exerts broad control over the exercise of these freedoms and has reacted harshly to expressions of political dissent. Three persons arrested in 1990 after persisting in public criticism of party policies and calling for fundamental political and economic change, each received 14-year sentences in 1992 (see Section 1.e.). The Penal Code forbids slandering the State, distorting party or state policies, and spreading false rumors conducive to disorder. It also prohibits disseminating books and other materials that authorities deem indecent or that would assail the national culture.

All domestically produced newspapers and radio and television are controlled by the Government. Local news in all media reflect government policy; however, foreign news reports, including those from Western sources, are usually translated without bias. In recent years, the Government has relaxed its control of the flow of information from abroad, and Thai and Western newspapers and magazines have been sold in the towns where there is demand for them. The Government makes no effort to discourage reception of Thai radio or television broadcasts. These are widely received in the Mekong River valley, where the majority of the population lives.

The Government requires registration of satellite television receiving dishes and payment of a one-time licensing fee for their installation, but otherwise makes no effort to restrict their use. In 1996 the number of such dishes continued to increase, both in major urban areas and in remote provincial and district towns. The Cable News Network (CNN), the British Broadcasting Corporation (BBC), and several stations in Thailand are among the many channels available to satellite dish owners.

The Government prohibits pornographic or politically inflammatory videocassettes. In late 1994 the Vientiane Municipality imposed restrictions governing the content of music played in night clubs and outlawed karaoke in order to strengthen Lao culture against its perceived erosion by foreign influences. Enforcement of these restrictions has been lax.

The Government restricts academic freedom. The Government has at times in the past denied permission to Lao academicians to travel abroad for conferences or training. Invitations to visit and collaborate with foreign colleagues must be approved by the Lao employer and the Ministry of Foreign Affairs. The Ministry of Education must approve grants, including those for research and study abroad. The Government also monitors and may restrict the activities of Western scholars doing research in Laos.

b. *Freedom of Peaceful Assembly and Association.*—The Penal Code prohibits demonstrations or protest marches aimed at causing turmoil and social instability, prescribing penalties of from 1 to 5 years' imprisonment. Although the Constitution provides citizens with the right to organize and join associations, all associations are party-controlled, and their products reflect official policy. Foreigners are not allowed to engage in political activity.

c. *Freedom of Religion.*—The Constitution contains provisions for religious freedom. In practice, the Government continues to restrict freedom of religion, especially for some Christian denominations.

Links with coreligionists and religious associations in other countries require government approval. Although the Government permits foreign nongovernmental organizations with religious affiliations to work in the country, it prohibits foreigners from proselytizing. The Government also restricts the import of foreign religious publications and artifacts.

The enforcement of these regulations varies by province. For example, the Catholic Church is unable to operate in the highlands and much of the north, but Catholics can openly attend churches and chapels in central and southern Laos. Several Protestant denominations operate more than 100 churches throughout the country. There continued to be credible reports that local authorities detained some clergy for allegedly criticizing other religions and harassed, arrested, and jailed other religiously active clergy. The persistence of such reports underscores the continuing suspicion on the part of authorities toward some parts of the Lao Christian community. There were also unconfirmed reports that Lao Christians were sometimes barred from the Party or from government employment and that some rural Lao were not allowed to convert to the Baha'i faith.

By comparison, the Government openly encourages Buddhism and supports Buddhist organizations. High-ranking government officials routinely attend religious functions, and Buddhist clergy are prominently featured at important state and party functions. The Government permits Buddhist festivals without hindrance.

Two mosques and a Baha'i center operate openly in Vientiane.

d. *Freedom of Movement Within the Country, Foreign Travel, Emigration, and Repatriation.*—There are no domestic travel restrictions for citizens and private foreign visitors except in areas considered unsafe. Most citizens can easily obtain passports and exit permits from the Ministry of Foreign Affairs for personal travel abroad. Border crossing permits to visit Thailand are routinely available from local village committees for a modest issuance fee, and the Government does not appear to interfere with persons desiring to emigrate. Except for around 30 persons convicted in absentia in 1975 for antigovernment activities, citizens have the right of return.

The stated government policy since 1977 is to welcome back the approximately 10 percent of the population that fled after the change of government in 1975. In recent years, an increasing number of ethnic Lao living abroad returned to visit; several remained to operate businesses.

Laos, Thailand, and the U.N. High Commissioner for Refugees (UNHCR) are cooperating on the return of the Lao asylum seekers in camps in Thailand who volunteer to return to Laos. This program includes provisions for monitoring returnees to ensure that they are given the same rights and treatment as resident Lao. According to the UNHCR and voluntary agencies, returnees are not subject to discrimination or persecution, and returnees are allowed to return with all the belongings they accumulated while outside the country. There were no forcible repatriations to Laos in 1996; however, nine Lao were voluntarily repatriated to Laos by the UNHCR during the year. No new Lao asylum seekers arrived in Thailand.

Section 3. Respect for Political Rights: The Right of Citizens to Change Their Government

Citizens do not have the ability to change their government, despite constitutional provisions for the public election of National Assembly members. While the Constitution does not explicitly exclude formation of multiple political parties, it assigns to the ruling LPRP the leading role in the political system. All candidates needed the approval of the LPRP before they could stand for the December 1992 National Assembly elections; no other parties were allowed, and voting was mandatory. However, not all candidates were LPRP members, and a few nonparty candidates won seats.

Women are underrepresented in government and politics. Of the 85 members of the National Assembly 8 are women. While three members of the 49-member LPRP Central Committee are women, there are no women in the Politburo or the Council of Ministers.

Men of lowland Lao origin dominate the upper echelons of the party and the Government. Nonetheless, the Prime Minister, the Deputy Prime Minister, the Minister of Interior and 23 members of the National Assembly are believed to be members of ethnic minority groups. Members of these minorities often adopt lowland Lao names as they are increasingly assimilated into mainstream society, thus making it difficult to ascertain accurately the number of ethnic minority members in any organization.

Section 4. Governmental Attitude Regarding International and Nongovernmental Investigation of Alleged Violations of Human Rights

There are no domestic human rights groups. Any organization wishing to investigate and publicly criticize the Government's human rights policies would face serious obstacles if it were permitted to operate at all. The Government generally does not cooperate with international human rights organizations. It has, however, permitted U.N. human rights observers to monitor the treatment of returning refugees without interference and responded to inquiries about specific human rights problems.

Section 5. Discrimination Based on Race, Sex, Religion, Disability, Language, or Social Status

The Constitution provides for equal treatment under the law for all citizens without regard to sex, social status, education, faith, or ethnicity. Although the Government took action when cases of discrimination came to the attention of high-level officials, the legal mechanism whereby a citizen may bring charges of discrimination against an individual or organization is neither widely developed nor widely understood among the general population.

Women.—There are reports that domestic violence against women occurs, although it is not widespread. Sexual harassment and rape are reportedly rare. In cases of rape that are tried in court, defendants are generally convicted. The Government relies on the Women's Union, a party-sanctioned organization, and youth organizations to educate girls and young women about the schemes of recruiters for brothels and sweatshops in Thailand and elsewhere. In the past, the Government has prosecuted some persons for involvement in such recruiting activities. During the year, law enforcement agencies conducted several raids of entertainment establishments accused of fostering prostitution.

The Constitution provides for equal rights for women, and the Lao Women's Union operates nationally to promote the position of women in Lao society. However, traditional culturally based discrimination persists, especially among lowland Lao and some hill tribes. Many women occupy responsible positions in the civil service and private business, and in urban areas their incomes are often higher than those of men. The Family Code prohibits legal discrimination in marriage and inheritance.

Children.—Government resources are inadequate to provide fully for children's basic health and educational needs. Education is compulsory through the fifth grade, but children from rural areas and poor urban families rarely comply with this requirement. Violence against children is prohibited by law. Reports of the physical abuse of children are rare.

People With Disabilities.—With donor assistance, the Government is implementing limited programs for the disabled, especially amputees. The law does not mandate accessibility to buildings or government services for disabled persons.

National/Racial/Ethnic Minorities.—The Constitution provides for equal rights for all minorities, and there is no legal discrimination against them. However, societal discrimination persists.

Approximately half the population is ethnic Lao, also called "lowland Lao." Most of the remainder is a mosaic of diverse upland hill tribes whose members, if born in Laos, are Lao citizens. There are also ethnic Vietnamese and Chinese minorities, particularly in the towns. There is a small community of South Asian origin. The implementation in 1994 of the 1990 Law on Nationality provided a means for these Vietnamese and Chinese minorities to regularize their Lao citizenship. While the Government encourages the preservation of minority cultures and traditions, minority tribes have little voice in government decisions affecting their lands and the allocation of natural resources. Hill tribe interaction with the Government is limited by poor transportation and communication links and a shortage of government resources.

The Hmong are one of the largest and most prominent highland minority groups. They split along clan lines during the U.S. war with Vietnam; many were strongly anti-Communist while others sided with the Lao and Vietnamese Communists. The Government repressed many who had fought against it, especially those still perceive to be resisting its authority. In recent years, the Government has initiated projects designed to integrate the Hmong into the general society, and an increasing number of those who fled the country after 1975 have repatriated to Laos without suffering persecution. Two U.N. observers who monitored repatriation efforts reported no incidents of abuse or discrimination during the year.

Section 6. Worker Rights

a. *The Right of Association.*—Although the Constitution provides citizens with the right to organize and join associations, the party controls all associations, and all conform to official party policy (see Section 2.b.).

Subsistence farmers comprise an estimated 85 percent of the work force. The State employs the majority of salaried workers, although this situation is changing as the Government reduces the number of its employees and privatizes state enterprises, and as foreign investors open new factories and businesses. Under the 1990 Labor Code, labor unions can be formed in private enterprises as long as they operate within the framework of the officially sanctioned Federation of Lao Trade Unions (FLTU), which in turn is controlled by the LPRP. Most of the FLTU's 80,000 members work in the public sector, overwhelmingly as public servants.

Strikes are not prohibited under the law, but the Government's ban on "destabilizing subversive activities" makes a strike unlikely, and none was reported this year (see Section 2.a.).

With advice from the International Labor Organization (ILO), including a foreign expert provided by the ILO to work with the Ministry of Labor and Social Welfare, the Government has revised the Labor Code in an effort to clarify rights and obligations of workers and employers.

The extent to which the FLTU is free to engage in contacts and affiliate with foreign labor organizations is unknown.

  b. *The Right to Organize and Bargain Collectively.*—There is no right to organize and bargain collectively. The Labor Code stipulates that disputes be resolved through workplace committees composed of employers, representatives of the local labor union, and representatives of the FLTU, with final authority residing in the Ministry of Labor and Social Welfare. Labor disputes are infrequent. The Government sets wages and salaries for government employees, while management sets wages and salaries for private business employees.

The Labor Code stipulates that employers may not fire employees for conducting trade union activities, for lodging complaints against employers about labor law implementation, or for cooperating with officials on labor law implementation and labor disputes. Workplace committees are one mechanism used for resolving complaints.

There are no export processing zones.

  c. *Prohibition of Forced or Compulsory Labor.*—The Labor Code prohibits forced labor except in time of war or national disaster, when the State may conscript laborers.

  d. *Minimum Age for Employment of Children.*—Under the Labor Code, children under the age of 15 may not be recruited for employment. However, many children help their families on farms or in shops. The Labor Code accordingly provides that children may work for their families, provided that such children are not engaged in dangerous or difficult work. Such employment of children is common in urban shops, but rare in industrial enterprises. The Ministries of Interior and Justice are responsible for enforcing these provisions, but enforcement is ineffective due to a lack of inspectors and other resources. Education is compulsory through the fifth grade, but this requirement is rarely observed in the rural areas or among the urban poor.

  e. *Acceptable Conditions of Work.*—The Labor Code provides for a broad range of worker entitlements, including a workweek limited to 48 hours (36 in dangerous activities), safe working conditions, and higher compensation for dangerous work. The code also provides for at least 1 day of rest per week. Employers are responsible for all expenses for a worker injured or killed on the job, a requirement generally fulfilled by employers in the formal economic sector. The daily minimum wage is $1.09 (1,000 kip), which is insufficient to provide a decent standard of living for a worker and family. Most civil servants receive inadequate pay. However, few families in the wage economy depend on only one breadwinner. Some piecework employees, especially on construction sites, earn less than the minimum wage. Many are illegal immigrants, particularly from Vietnam, and are more vulnerable to exploitation by employers. Although workplace inspections have reportedly increased, the Ministry of Labor and Social Welfare lacks the personnel and budgetary resources to enforce the Labor Code effectively. The Labor Code has no specific provision allowing workers to remove themselves from a dangerous situation without jeopardizing their employment.

MALAYSIA

Malaysia is a federation of 13 states with a parliamentary system of government based on periodic multiparty elections, but in which the ruling National Front coalition has held power since 1957. The coalition headed by Prime Minister Mahathir bin Mohamed increased its majority in a general election held in 1995. Opposition parties actively contest elections, although they hold only 11.5 percent of the seats in the Federal Parliament; an opposition party controls one state government.

The Royal Malaysian Police has primary responsibility for internal security matters; it reports to and is under the effective control of the Minister of Home Affairs. The Prime Minister also holds the Home Affairs portfolio. There are allegations that some members of the police committed human rights abuses.

Rapidly expanding exports of manufactured goods, now over 50 percent of gross domestic product, continue to maintain high annual rates of economic growth. Crude oil exports and traditional commodities (tropical timber, palm oil, and rubber) add to trade revenues. Strong economic performance in recent years has led to significant reductions in poverty, an improved standard of living, and more equal income distribution.

The Government generally respected the human rights of its citizens; however, there were problems in some areas. The Government continued to arrest and detain citizens without trial and to impose long-term restrictions on movement without due process hearings. The Government sometimes limits freedom of assembly, association, speech, the press, and judicial independence. These limits make it very difficult for opposition parties to compete on equal terms with the long-ruling governing coalition. Religious minorities are subject to some restrictions. Domestic violence against women and child abuse continued to be problems. In a development welcomed by women's groups, the Government began to implement the Domestic Violence Act, which covers violence against women and children, after a long delay. Some discrimination against indigenous people and restrictions on worker rights persist. In November the authorities terminated an international conference about East Timor because of the disorder created by demonstrators from the youth wings of the ruling coalition parties. Although nongovernmental organizations (NGO's) are normally free to criticize the Government, the authorities filed criminal charges under the Publications Act against a prominent human rights activist who alleged mistreatment of illegal aliens in detention centers. The authorities punished law enforcement officers implicated in a police brutality case.

RESPECT FOR HUMAN RIGHTS

Section 1. Respect for the Integrity of the Person, Including Freedom From:
 a. *Political and Other Extrajudicial Killing.*—There were no reports of political killings.
 Following investigations by the Attorney General's office and the police into the circumstances surrounding the 1995 death of a criminal suspect, the High Court sentenced two police officers to 3 years' imprisonment for misconduct during the suspect's interrogation. The deceased, who was a suspect in a burglary case, died while in police custody from "hemorrhage caused by blunt trauma in most parts of his body," raising suspicions of police brutality. The other police officers implicated in the case were subjected to internal discipline.
 The Government continued to deny allegations of mistreatment and corruption in illegal alien detention centers. Stating that the death of approximately 50 illegal aliens in the centers last year was not due to misconduct, the Government brought criminal charges against human rights activist Irene Fernandez for publishing a report containing allegations about conditions in the detention centers. The case is currently pending in a magistrate's court (see Sections 1.c., 1.d., and 1.e.).
 b. *Disappearance.*—There were no reports of politically motivated disappearances.
 c. *Torture and Other Cruel, Inhuman, or Degrading Treatment or Punishment.*—There continued to be allegations that police officers abused criminal suspects during interrogation, including strong psychological pressure and sometimes physical abuse. In some cases, government authorities have investigated police officials for such abuses, but because they refuse to release information on the results of the investigations, it cannot be determined whether those responsible for any such abuses are punished.
 In one case, however, police officers were sentenced to 3 years' imprisonment for misconduct in the 1995 death of a criminal suspect in custody (see Section 1.a.). This was the first reported instance in recent years of police officials being tried, convicted, and sentenced for abuse of prisoners. In another case, a civil suit filed by a former suspect, a sessions court ordered police officers to pay compensation to the plaintiff for assaulting him in 1995 while in custody.
 Responding to public criticism of police professionalism, the Inspector General of Police has stated that he would punish those who abuse their power or use violence in carrying out their duties. Several police officers also were arrested for various criminal offenses including extortion, drug abuse, and murder.
 A number of law enforcement officials were arrested on narcotics-related charges. The Prisons Department revealed that at least 12 prison officers were arrested for drug-related activities. A total of 78 prison officers have been arrested for drug-related offenses since 1990.
 Criminal law prescribes caning as an additional punishment to imprisonment for those convicted of some nonviolent crimes such as narcotics possession and criminal breach of trust. Early in the year, the Government amended the Immigration Act to make caning a mandatory part of the sentence for those convicted of using forged passports. Judges routinely include caning in sentencing those convicted of such crimes as kidnaping, rape, and robbery. The caning, which is normally carried out with a ½-inch-thick wooden cane, commonly causes welts and sometimes scarring.
 Prison conditions generally meet international standards. Basic human needs, including medical care, sanitation, nutrition, and family access, are met. Overcrowd-

ing is a problem in some large prisons. However, a new prison complex has eliminated the overcrowding problem in the Kuala Lumpur area.

Prison guards have been accused and convicted of criminal wrongdoing, mostly in nonviolent narcotics-related cases. While acknowledging that prison guards have been arrested for such activities, the Director General of the Prisons denied a well publicized allegation by a former inmate that heroin was readily available in the prisons. "Security" prisoners (see Section 1.d.) are detained in a separate detention center. Conditions there are not significantly different from those of the regular prison population.

The Government does not permit visits by human rights monitors.

The Government denied allegations that the 1995 death of approximately 50 illegal aliens was due to inhuman conditions in illegal alien detention centers (see Sections 1.a., 1.d., and 1.e.). Stating that every allegation made in human rights activist Irene Fernandez's report on the centers is false, the Government prosecuted her for publishing a false report. The case was pending in a magistrate's court at year's end. Fernandez alleged that migrants in the camps were denied proper food and water, lacked medical attention, and were subjected to abuse by camp guards. An Independent Board of Visitors appointed by the Government to investigate the allegations of misconduct found no evidence of ill-treatment or abuse of migrant workers. In a report submitted to the Government in December, the board recommended that improvements be made in health and sanitation facilities, and, noting that beriberi was common in the centers, that a more nutritious diet be provided. The Ministry of Home Affairs announced that the Government would seek additional funds to make the improvements.

d. *Arbitrary Arrest, Detention, or Exile.*—Three laws permit the Government to detain suspects without judicial review or filing formal charges: The 1960 Internal Security Act (ISA), the Emergency (Public Order and Prevention of Crime) Ordinance of 1969, and the Dangerous Drugs Act of 1985. The Government continued to use long-term detention without trial in cases alleged to involve national security, as well as in narcotics trafficking and other cases. According to the Home Affairs Ministry, there are 2,008 people being detained without trial under these laws; most are being held under the Dangerous Drugs Act.

Passed more than 30 years ago when there was an active Communist insurgency, the ISA empowers the police to hold any person who may act "in a manner prejudicial to the security of Malaysia" for up to 60 days initially. The Minister of Home Affairs may authorize, in writing, further indefinite detention for periods of up to 2 years. Those released before the end of their detention period are subject to "imposed restricted conditions," which are in effect for the balance of their detention periods. These conditions limit their rights to freedom of speech, association, and travel outside the country. According to the Government, the goal of the ISA is to control internal subversion, although many observers believe that the act is now sometimes used for other purposes. The Government also uses the ISA against passport and identity card forgers. According to the Home Affairs Ministry, there were 76 ISA detainees at year's end, compared with 34 in 1995. Most of the detainees currently in custody under the ISA are forgers. Since the authorities exposed a criminal syndicate involved in selling forged Malaysian identity cards to illegal aliens last year, 67 suspects have been arrested under the ISA. Of these, the Government has thus far authorized 2-year detentions for 50, including several government officials.

Several members of the outlawed Islamic fundamentalist movement Al Arqam were arrested under the ISA for attempting to revive the movement. The Government authorized 2-year detentions for seven upon expiration of their 60-day remand orders. The wife of the movement's founder was placed under restricted residence under the act. In 1994 the Government outlawed the movement as deviationist and detained its founder under the ISA. After a brief period of detention, the founder apologized for his deviationist teachings and vowed to stop the movement.

Security authorities sometimes wait several days after a detention before informing a detainee's family. Even when there are no formal charges, the authorities must inform detainees of the accusations against them and permit them to appeal to an advisory board for review every 6 months. Advisory board decisions and recommendations, however, are not binding on the Home Affairs Minister, are not made public, and are often not shown to the detainee. A number of ISA detainees have refused to participate in the review process under these circumstances.

Amendments to the ISA severely limit judicial review of detentions, contravening international standards of due process. Opposition leaders and human rights organizations continued to call on the Government to repeal the ISA and other legislation that deprive people of the right to defend themselves in court. The Deputy Home Affairs Minister announced in February that the Government had prepared proposed amendments to the ISA; these proposals reportedly are designed to make the ISA "less ominous."

In a civil lawsuit, the High Court ruled in September in favor of a former ISA detainee who had alleged that the Government's extension of his detention period was improper. After his initial 2-year detention, the Government extended his detention for another 2 years, but without specifying the grounds for detention. Although the court ruled in the plaintiff's favor, it awarded him damages of only about $0.40 (one ringgit). The judge noted that the plaintiff had been set free because of a technical error and should have rested on his good fortune.

In December senior government officials warned that the ISA would be used against NGO's if they continued to "bait" the Government. Expressing irritation at NGO plans to hold a conference on police abuse in January 1997, the Home Affairs Minister said that the Government may have to use the act if the "situation becomes bad." The Minister added, however, that the Government would not bar the organizations from holding the meeting if they do not break any laws. The Government would take action only if the organizers make it into a public meeting by inviting non-NGO's or the press.

Under the 1969 Emergency Ordinance, which was instituted after intercommunal riots in that year, the Home Affairs Minister can issue a detention order for up to 2 years against a person if he deems it necessary to protect public order or for the "suppression of violence or the prevention of crimes involving violence." According to the Home Affairs Ministry, there were 56 people in detention under the Emergency Ordinance, compared with 447 in 1995.

Provisions of the 1985 amendments to the Dangerous Drugs Act give the Government specific power to detain suspected drug traffickers. The suspects may be held up to 39 days before the Home Affairs Minister must issue a detention order. Once the Ministry has issued an order, the detainee is entitled to a habeas corpus hearing before a court. In some instances, the judge may order the detainee's release. Suspects may be held without charge for successive 2-year intervals, with periodic review by an advisory board, whose opinion is binding on the Home Affairs Minister. However, the review process contains none of the due process rights that a defendant would have in a court proceeding. As of September, 1,876 drug suspects remained under detention or under restrictions equivalent to house arrest under this statute, compared with 1,810 in 1995. The police frequently rearrest suspected narcotics traffickers and firearms offenders under the preventive measures clauses of the Dangerous Drugs Act or the ISA, after an acquittal in court on formal charges under separate provisions of those acts.

Immigration laws are used to detain possible illegal aliens without trial or hearing. Approximately 8,500 migrant workers who were unable to prove their legal status have been placed in temporary detention under immigration laws. The detainees are not accorded any administrative or legal hearings and are released only after their employers prove their legal status. Those who can produce legal documents are normally released immediately; those who cannot prove their legal status may be held for extended periods before deportation. Illegal aliens are kept in detention centers which are separate from prisons. There are currently an estimated 1 million or more illegal workers in Malaysia.

Following the death of approximately 50 illegal aliens in detention centers in 1995, human rights organizations and opposition leaders accused the authorities of mistreatment and corruption and called for a thorough investigation. After its investigation, however, the Government denied the allegations and brought criminal charges under the Printing and Publications Act against the human rights activist who first brought the controversy to light. She is accused of publishing false information regarding the centers' conditions. The case, which was proceeding in a magistrate's court at year's end, is being monitored by international observers and human rights groups. NGO's report that the conditions in the centers have marginally improved, and an independent board appointed by the Government found no evidence of ill-treatment and noted that it was satisfied with living conditions in the camps (see Section 1.c.).

Law enforcement authorities also continued to utilize the Restricted Residence Act to restrict movements of criminal suspects for an extended period. The act allows the Home Affairs Ministry to place criminal suspects under restricted residence in a remote district away from home for a period of 2 years. The Ministry is authorized to issue the "banishment" orders without any judicial or administrative hearings. Several professional soccer players and coaches, who were banished in 1995 for alleged involvement in match fixing and bribery, remain under restricted conditions. The restricted residence practice violates due process and is viewed in the same light as detention without trial. Human rights activists have questioned the need for a law that was passed 60 years ago to deal with gambling under very different circumstances and have called for its repeal. The Government continued to justify the act as a necessary tool in dealing with vice and gambling activities. (See also Sections 1.f. and 2.d.)

The Government does not use forced exile.

e. *Denial of Fair Public Trial.*—Past government action, a constitutional amendment, and legislation restricting judicial review undermine judicial independence and strengthen executive influence over the judiciary in politically sensitive cases. A series of election-related decisions and high-profile commercial cases in 1995 intensified the debate on judicial impartiality and independence. Members of the bar and other observers continued to express serious concern about this issue.

The legal system is based on English common law. High courts have original jurisdiction over all criminal cases involving serious crimes and most civil cases. Civil suits involving automobile accidents and landlord-tenant disputes are heard by sessions courts. Magistrate's courts hear criminal cases in which the maximum term of sentence does not exceed 12 months. The Court of Appeal has appellate jurisdiction over high court and session court decisions. The Federal Court hears appeals of Court of Appeal decisions. Islamic religious laws administered by state authorities through Islamic courts bind ethnic Malays in some civil matters, such as family relations and diet.

Most civil and criminal proceedings are generally fair and open. The accused must be brought before a judge within 24 hours of arrest, and charges must be levied within 10 days. Defendants have the right to counsel, bail is available, and strict rules of evidence apply in court. Defendants may appeal court decisions to higher courts and, in criminal cases, may also appeal for clemency to the King or local state rulers as appropriate. All criminal trials, including murder trials, are heard by a single judge. Parliament voted in 1994 to amend the Criminal Procedure Code to abolish jury trials in death penalty cases. The defense in both ordinary criminal cases and the special security cases described below is not entitled to a statement of evidence before the trial.

The right to a fair trial is restricted in criminal cases in which the Attorney General invokes the Essential (Security Cases) Regulations of 1975. These regulations governing trial procedure normally apply only in firearms cases. In cases tried under these regulations, the standards for accepting self-incriminating statements by defendants as evidence are less stringent than in normal criminal cases. Also, the authorities may hold the accused for an unspecified period of time before making formal charges. The Attorney General has the authority to invoke these regulations in other criminal cases if the Government determines that the crime involves national security considerations, but such cases are rare. There were no cases involving this restriction in 1996.

A letter alleging gross judicial misconduct led to an investigation by the Government and the abrupt resignation of a high court judge who was widely assumed to have authored the letter. The Attorney General proposed that the Bar Council's membership include law lecturers and government lawyers, in addition to private attorneys. Members of the Council, however, view this proposal as an attempt to dilute the Council's effectiveness and independence, and have vowed to fight it.

There were no reports of political prisoners.

f. *Arbitrary Interference with Privacy, Family, Home, or Correspondence.*—The law provides for these rights and the Government generally respects them. Provisions in the security legislation (see Section 1.d.), however, allow the police to enter and search without a warrant the homes of persons suspected of threatening national security. Police may also confiscate evidence under these acts. In some cases each year, police have used this legal authority to search homes and offices, seize books and papers, monitor conversations, and take people into custody without a warrant. The law permits the Home Affairs Ministry to place criminal suspects under restricted residence in a remote district away from home for a 2-year period.

Section 2. *Respect for Civil Liberties, Including:*

a. *Freedom of Speech and Press.*—Although the Constitution provides for freedom of speech and the press, some important limitations exist, and over the years the Government has restricted freedom of expression of media organizations and individuals. The Constitution provides that freedom of speech may be restricted by legislation "in the interest of security * * * (or) public order." Thus, the Sedition Act prohibits public comment on issues defined as sensitive, such as citizenship rights for non-Malays and the special position of Malays in society.

The Government used the Sedition Act and the Publications Act to file criminal charges against opposition member of parliament Lim Guan Eng before the 1995 general election. The charges were based on Lim's public comments about a statutory rape case involving a former chief minister of Malacca. The trial was still pending at year's end following several continuances. Lim has argued that the case against him is politically motivated. Amnesty International also considers the charges against Lim to be politically motivated, and has called on the Government to dismiss the case. Lim was reelected in the general election, but could lose his parliamentary seat if he is convicted and sentenced to more than 1 year in prison or fined more than $800 (2,000 ringgits).

The Printing Presses and Publications Act of 1984 contains important limitations on press freedom. Domestic and foreign publications must apply annually to the Government for a permit. The act was amended in 1987 to make the publication of "malicious news" a punishable offense, expand the Government's power to ban or restrict publications, and prohibit court challenges to suspension or revocation of publication permits. Government policies create an atmosphere that inhibits independent or investigative journalism and result in self-censorship of issues government authorities might consider sensitive. Government displeasure with press reporting is often conveyed directly to a newspaper's board of directors.

In practice press freedom is also limited by the fact that leading political figures, or companies controlled by leading political figures in the ruling coalition, own most of the major newspapers and all radio and television stations. These mass media provide generally laudatory, noncritical coverage of government officials and policies, and give only limited and selective coverage to political views of the opposition or political rivals. Editorial opinion in these mass media frequently reflects government positions on domestic and international issues. Chinese-language newspapers are generally more free in reporting and commenting on sensitive political and social issues.

Small-circulation publications of opposition parties, social action groups, unions, and other private groups actively cover opposition parties and frequently print views critical of government policies. However, the Government retains significant influence over these publications by requiring annual renewal of publishing permits.

Although there were no cases of denial of renewal requests in 1996, the Government has in the past used this requirement to place limitations on opposition and other publications critical of the Government. The Official Secrets Act also can be used to restrict freedom of the press. Pointing out the dangers of abuse to restrict press freedom, the Bar Council and NGO's have called for a review of certain provisions that grant considerable discretion to the authorities. In 1995 the authorities arrested two journalists under the act, but released them without bringing formal charges.

The government-controlled Malaysian News Agency (Bernama) is by law the sole distributor of foreign news, although the Government has not to date used this law to restrict foreign news coverage or availability. NGO's currently enjoy considerable freedom to speak out against Government policies. The Government's case against NGO activist Irene Fernandez under the Printing Presses and Publications Act is being closely monitored by NGO's and others as a test case of the Government's willingness to permit public criticism.

The Government generally respects academic freedom in the areas of teaching and publication. Academics are often publicly critical of the Government. However, there is a degree of self-censorship among public university academics whose career advancement and funding are prerogatives of the Government. Private institution academics also practice a limited degree of self-censorship for fear that the Government may revoke licenses for their institutions. Legislation also imposes limitations on student associations and student and faculty activity (see Section 2.b.).

b. *Freedom of Peaceful Assembly and Association.*—The Constitution provides for the rights of freedom of peaceful assembly and association, but there are significant restrictions. These rights may be limited in the interest of security and public order, and the 1967 Police Act requires police permits for all public assemblies with the exception of workers on picket lines. Spontaneous demonstrations occur periodically without permission, but they are limited in scope and generally occur with the tacit consent of the police.

In the aftermath of the intercommunal riots in 1969, the Government banned political rallies. The Government continued that policy during the 1995 general election. However, both government and opposition parties held large indoor political gatherings dubbed "discussion sessions" during the campaign period. The ruling coalition also held several large-scale events that very much resembled political rallies.

Government and opposition candidates campaign actively. There are, however, some restrictions on freedom of assembly during campaigns. During the actual campaign period, political parties submit lists of times and places for their discussion sessions. Some opposition discussion group meetings in past campaigns have been canceled for lack of a police permit. An opposition meeting during the 1996 Sarawak state election campaign was canceled for lack of a permit. Outside of the campaign period, a permit also is required, with most applications routinely approved. These restrictions and the ban on political rallies handicap the opposition's ability to campaign effectively.

Other statutes limit the right of association, such as the Societies Act of 1966, under which any association of seven or more members must register with the Government as a society. The Government may refuse to register a new society or may impose conditions when allowing a society to register. The Government also has the power to revoke the registration of an existing society for violations of the act, a power it has selectively enforced against political opposition groups. This threat of possible deregistration inhibits political activism by public or special interest organizations.

Another law affecting freedom of association is the Universities and University Colleges Act; it mandates government approval for student associations and prohibits student associations, as well as faculty members, from engaging in political activity. Campus demonstrations must be approved by a university vice chancellor. Human rights organizations have called for a repeal of the act on the grounds that it inhibits the free flow of ideas and exchange of views.

The authorities terminated an international conference about East Timor in November because of the disorder created by demonstrators from the youth wings of the ruling coalition parties. Both the demonstrators and the organizers of the event were arrested and held for several days. They were all released on bail, and no formal charges have yet been brought against them.

c. *Freedom of Religion.*—Islam is the official religion. Religious minorities, which include large Hindu, Buddhist, Sikh, and Christian communities, generally are permitted to worship freely but are subject to some restrictions. Adherence to Islam is considered intrinsic to Malay ethnic identity, and therefore Islamic religious laws administered by state authorities through Islamic courts bind all ethnic Malays in some civil matters, such as family relations and diet. Government funds support an Islamic religious establishment, and it is official policy to "infuse Islamic values" into the administration of the county. At the same time, the Constitution provides for freedom of religion, and the Government has refused to accede to pressures to impose Islamic religious law beyond the Muslim community.

The Government opposes what it considers extremist or deviant interpretations of Islam. In the past, the Government has imposed restrictions on certain Islamic sects. In August 1995, the Government banned the Al Arqam religious movement for what it termed "deviationist teachings," and it remained banned at year's end. The Government continues to monitor the activities of the Shi'ite minority.

Government authorities continued to emphasize the importance of controlling deviationist groups, and arrested followers of the banned Al Arqam movement for attempting to revive the deviationist sect (see Section 1.d.). The Government announced that the authorities were investigating another 50 or so "deviationist" groups. In most cases, the Government expected to provide "counselling and hold dialogs" to encourage them to return to "the right path." The authorities have warned that such groups would not be allowed to take advantage of freedom of religion to spread discord among the people.

There continued to be allegations that some state governments are slow in approving building permits for non-Muslim places of worship or land for cemeteries for non-Muslims.

The Government discourages the circulation of a popular Malay-language translation of the Bible. Some states have laws prohibiting the use of Malay-language religious terms by Christians, but the authorities do not actively enforce them.

The Government permits but discourages conversion to religions other than Islam. Some states have long proscribed by law proselytizing of Muslims, and other parts of the country strongly discourage it as well. In a March 1990 decision, the Supreme Court upheld the primacy of the Constitution over inconsistent state laws by ruling that parents have the right to determine the religion of their minor children under the age of 18. The decision eased fears in the non-Muslim community over state laws that in religious conversion cases set the age of majority at puberty based on Islamic law.

d. *Freedom of Movement Within the Country, Foreign Travel, Emigration, and Repatriation.*—Citizens generally have the right to travel within the country and live and work where they please, but the Government restricts these rights in some circumstances. The east Malaysian states of Sabah and Sarawak have the independent right to control immigration into their territories; citizens from peninsular west Malaysia and foreigners are required to present passports or national identity cards for entry. The Government regulates the internal movement of provisionally released ISA detainees. It also limits the movement of some released ISA detainees to a designated city or state (see Section 1.d.). The Government also uses the Restricted

Residence Act to limit movements of those suspected of gambling or vice activities (see Section 1.d.).

The Police Inspector General in late 1995 announced that over 400 former communists had been "rehabilitated" by the security authorities and resettled since December 1989. This rehabilitation consists of detention without trial under the ISA at the Kamunting Detention Center in Perak state. In addition, rehabilitated former Communist Party of Malaya members who have reintegrated into society are restricted to certain areas where security authorities watch them carefully for up to 6 years. These rehabilitated persons cannot resume full participation in political life until this period of surveillance demonstrates to the satisfaction of the police that they have abandoned their former ideology.

The Government generally does not restrict emigration. Citizens are free to travel abroad, although in some cases the Government has refused to issue or has withheld passports on security grounds or in the belief that the trip will be detrimental to the country's image. In 1995 the Government prevented an environmental activist from traveling overseas to attend a conference. Most such government actions are taken because of suspected drug trafficking offenses or other serious crimes.

Citizens must apply for the Government's permission to travel to Israel. Travel to Jerusalem for religious purposes is explicitly allowed.

There are 1 million or more foreign workers, concentrated primarily in low-skill jobs, the Human Resources Ministry estimates that as much as 90 percent of the labor force in the plantation sector is foreign. Nearly half of the foreign workers may be in the country illegally. Some illegal workers eventually are able to regularize their immigration status, others depart voluntarily after a few months, and some are formally deported as illegal migrants. The Government instituted a second illegal worker registration program in July, which had regularized the status of 200–300,000 workers by fall, and ran through the end of the year. After a similar registration program ended 3 years ago, the Government launched combined police and military operations to enforce immigration and passport laws. As a result, the authorities detained more than 130,000 foreign workers and deported 50,000 of them in 1994.

Following a report of numerous deaths in the detention centers in 1995, human rights groups and opposition politicians accused the authorities of mistreatment and corruption and called for an independent investigation. A government-appointed independent board reported that a total of 90 illegal immigrants had died in the detention centers, 22 since September 1995; all reportedly died of natural causes (see Sections 1.a., 1.c., and 1.d.).

The Government cooperates with the office of the United Nations High Commissioner for Refugees and other humanitarian organizations in assisting refugees. There were no reports of forced expulsions of those having a valid claim to refugee status. Over the past 21 years, Malaysia gave first asylum to approximately 254,000 Vietnamese; on June 25, it closed its last camp for Vietnamese refugees. Approximately 249,000 Vietnamese were resettled in third countries, with over half going to the United States. As of December 31, 23 asylum seekers from the closed Vietnamese refugee camp remained in custody, the two largest subgroups being screened-in Vietnamese who are awaiting resettlement in third countries (8) and purported "stateless" individuals who claim ties with Taiwan (11).

Section 3. Respect for Political Rights: The Right of Citizens to Change Their Government

By law citizens have the right to change their government through periodic elections, which are procedurally free and fair, with votes recorded accurately. In practice, however, it is difficult for opposition parties to compete on equal terms with the governing coalition (which has held power at the national level since 1957) because of legal restrictions on campaigning, as well as restrictions on freedom of association and of the press. Nevertheless, opposition candidates campaign actively and agree that the voting and counting of votes are relatively free and fair. The government coalition controls 12 of 13 states. An Islamic opposition party controls the northern state of Kelantan.

Malaysia has a Westminster-style parliamentary system of government. National elections, required at least every 5 years, have been held regularly since independence in 1957. In the 1995 general election the ruling coalition won an overwhelming victory, increasing its seats in the Parliament to 82 percent. Several members of the opposition camp have since joined the coalition, increasing the coalition's representation in the Parliament to approximately 88 percent. The Malay-based United Malay National Organization (UMNO) party dominates the ruling National Front coalition. Within the UMNO there is active political debate, and there was intense competition in the October UMNO party elections.

The Parliament in 1995 passed amendments to its rules that strengthen the power of the Speaker and curb parliamentary procedures heavily used by the opposition. The amendments empowered the Speaker to ban obstreperous opposition Members of Parliament for up to 10 days, imposed limits on their ability to pose supplementary questions and revisit nongermane issues, and established restrictions on the tabling of questions of public importance. The amendments have restricted the opposition's ability to criticize the Government in Parliament.

Women face no legal limits on participation in government and politics, but there are practical impediments. Women are represented in senior leadership positions in the Government in small numbers, including two cabinet-level ministers. Women hold 15 of 192 seats of the elected lower house of Parliament and 13 of 69 seats in the appointed upper house. Women also hold high-level judgeships.

Ethnic minorities are represented in cabinet-level positions in government, as well as in senior civil service positions. Nevertheless, the political dominance of the Malay majority means in practice that ethnic Malays hold the most powerful senior leadership positions. Non-Malays fill 8 of the 28 cabinet posts. Ethnic Chinese leaders of a component party of the ruling coalition hold executive power in the state of Penang.

Section 4 Governmental Attitude Regarding International and Nongovernmental Investigation of Alleged Violations of Human Rights

The National Human Rights Association publicly criticizes the Government, as do other NGO's, although it does not investigate except in response to individual complaints. It seeks repeal of the ISA and is reviewing opposition-controlled Kelantan's efforts to impose Islamic restrictions in that state.

A number of other organizations, including the Bar Council and public interest groups, devote considerable attention to human rights activities. The Government tolerates their activities but rarely responds to their inquiries or occasional press statements. Officials criticize local groups for collaborating with international human rights organizations.

NGO's are becoming increasingly active and critical of the Government. However, the authorities still accuse some NGO's of painting a negative picture of the country to the outside world. Although the Government did not place any restrictions on their activities, the Government announced that it would draw up clearer guidelines for registration of NGO's. Human rights monitors called on the Government to impose guidelines that make it easier for NGO's to operate.

Observers are concerned that the Government's case against a prominent NGO activist under the Publications Act may inhibit the willingness and ability of NGO's to speak out against the Government.

The Government has not acceded to any of the major international treaties on human rights, generally maintaining that such issues are internal matters. It rejects criticism of its human rights record by international human rights organizations and foreign governments, and has blocked registration of a local chapter of a prominent international human rights organization.

Section 5. Discrimination Based on Race, Sex, Religion, Disability, Language, or Social Status

The Constitution provides for equal protection of the law and prohibits discrimination against citizens on the basis of religion, race, descent, or place of birth. Although neither the Constitution nor laws explicitly prohibit discrimination on the basis of sex or disabilities, the Government has made efforts to eliminate discrimination against women and the disabled. Government policies include affirmative action programs for Bumiputras (i.e., Malays and Muslims).

Women.—Government leaders have identified domestic violence as a continuing social ill. Between January and August, there were 514 reported cases of domestic violence. In a development welcomed by women's organizations, the Government began to implement the 1994 Domestic Violence Act. It offers a broad definition of domestic violence, gives powers to the courts to protect victims, and provides for compensation and counseling for victims. Those covered under the bill include a spouse, a former spouse, a child, an incapacitated adult, or any other member of the family. Cases of wife beating or child abuse, which had been tried under provisions of the Penal Code governing assault and battery, are now expected to come under the Domestic Violence Act.

NGO's concerned about women's issues advocate legislative and social reforms to improve the status of women. These groups raise issues such as violence against women, trafficking in women and young girls, employment opportunities with equal pay, and greater participation by women in decisionmaking positions. Women's issues continued to receive prominent coverage in public seminars and the media.

The cultural and religious traditions of the major ethnic groups heavily influence the condition of women in society. In family and religious matters, Muslim women are subject to Islamic law. Polygyny is allowed and practiced to a limited degree, and inheritance law favors male offspring and relatives. The Islamic Family Law was revised in 1989 to provide better protection for the property rights of married Muslim women and to make more equitable a Muslim woman's right to divorce.

Non-Muslim women are subject to civil law. Changes in the Civil Marriage and Divorce Act in the early 1980's increased protection of married women's rights, especially those married under customary rites.

Government policy supports women's full and equal participation in education and the work force. Women are represented in growing numbers in the professions, but women's groups argue that the level of participation is still disproportionately low. According to various studies, only about 1.4 percent of women currently hold decisionmaking posts. The studies also estimate that only about 5 percent of political decisionmakers are women. In the scientific and medical fields, women make up more than half of all university graduates and the total intake of women into universities increased from 29 percent in 1970 to one-half of the student population in recent years. The participation of women in the labor force increased from 37 percent in 1970 to almost one-half in 1996.

In the opposition-controlled state of Kelantan, the state government has imposed restrictions on all female workers, including non-Muslims. Female workers cannot work at night and are restricted in the dress they may wear in the workplace. The state government justifies these restrictions as reflecting Islamic values.

Children.—The Government is committed to children's rights and welfare; it spends roughly 20 percent of its budget on education. The Government has taken some steps to deal with the problem of child abuse. Parliament passed the Children's Protection Act in 1991, effective in 1993. The Domestic Violence Act, which covers children, is also expected to provide protection against child abuse. In 1995 the Justice Minister announced that the Government was considering imposing a mandatory death sentence for those found guilty of child abuse that resulted in death, but the Government has not instituted changes to that effect.

Statistics on the extent of child prostitution are not available, but women's organizations have highlighted the problem of trafficking in underage girls. The Health Ministry announced that it would work closely with the police to stamp out child prostitution. Brothels are frequently raided, and some brothel owners are prosecuted.

People With Disabilities.—The Government does not discriminate against physically disabled persons in employment, education, and provision of other state services. However, public transportation, public buildings, and other facilities are not adapted to the needs of the disabled, and the Government has not mandated accessibility for the disabled, through legislation or otherwise. Special education schools exist, but they are not sufficient to meet needs. Nevertheless, the Government as well as the general public are becoming more sensitive to the needs of the physically disabled. New commuter trains are being made wheelchair accessible. The Government also provides incentives for employers to offer employment opportunities for the disabled. The Health Minister announced plans to restructure the health care system to place greater emphasis on rehabilitation of the disabled.

Disabled persons work in all sectors of the economy, but the prevalent feeling in society remains that disabled people cannot work. The Government continued its effort to register those with disabilities under four categories—blind, deaf, physical, and mental. As of August, however, the Government had registered only 57,844 of the estimated 200,000 persons with disabilities in the country. The Social Development Minister encouraged all disabled persons to register, as the registration process is a part of the Government's efforts to provide training to the disabled.

In 1994 the Deputy Prime Minister signed the Economic and Social Commission for Asia and the Pacific proclamation on full participation and equality for people with disabilities in the region, and in response to that commitment the Government has taken initiatives to make public facilities more accessible to disabled persons, and has increased budgetary allotments for programs aimed at aiding them.

Indigenous People.—Indigenous groups and persons generally enjoy the same constitutional rights—along with the same limitations—as the rest of the population. In practice, federal laws pertaining to indigenous people vest almost total power in the Minister of National Unity and Social Development to protect, control, and otherwise decide issues concerning them. As a result, indigenous people have very little ability to participate in decisions. Under the Aboriginal People's Act, indigenous people (known as Orang Asli) have no right to own land. The law does not permit Orang Asli in peninsular Malaysia, who have been granted land on a group basis, to own land on an individual basis or to receive titles to the land. In a development welcomed by the Orang Asli community, the Social Development Ministry announced in March that state governments, which make decisions affecting land rights, had agreed to issue titles to Orang Asli. Amendments were being drafted to enable Orang Asli to hold titles on an individual basis.

In east Malaysia, although state law recognizes indigenous people's right to land under "native customary rights," the definition and extent of these lands are in dispute. Indigenous people in the state of Sarawak continued to protest the alleged encroachment by the State or private logging companies onto land that they consider theirs by virtue of customary rights. A large project (Bakun dam) in Sarawak, which will involve resettlement of a large number of residents in the area, has raised several controversial questions regarding land disputes as well as potential environmental problems. NGO's and opposition politicians have called on the Government to address these issues before proceeding with the project.

The indigenous people in peninsular Malaysia, who number fewer than 100,000, are the poorest group in the country. However, according to government officials, Orang Asli are gradually catching up to other citizens in their standard of living, and the percentage of Orang Asli who were still leading a nomadic lifestyle has dropped to less than 40 percent. The Government also has pointed out that the changes allowing Orang Asli to own land in peninsular Malaysia are expected to enhance their economic standing.

National/Racial/Ethnic Minorities.—The Government implements extensive affirmative action programs designed to boost the economic position of the ethnic Malay majority, which remains poorer on average, than the Chinese minority despite the former's political dominance. Such government affirmative action programs and policies do, however, limit opportunities for non-Malays in higher education, government employment, business permits and licenses, and ownership of newly developed agricultural lands. Indian Malaysians continue to lag behind in the country's economic development, although the national economic policies target less advantaged populations regardless of ethnicity. According to the Government, these programs have been instrumental in ensuring ethnic harmony and political stability. Early in the year, senior government officials reiterated the need for the programs despite significant improvements in economic standing of the Malay population.

Section 6. Worker Rights

a. *The Right of Association.*—By law most workers have the right to engage in trade union activity, and approximately 10 percent of the work force belong to trade unions. Exceptions include certain limited categories of workers labeled "confidential" and "managerial and executives," as well as defense and police officials. Within certain limitations, unions may organize workplaces, bargain collectively with employers, and associate with national federations.

The Industrial Relations Act prohibits interfering with, restraining, or coercing a worker in the exercise of the right to form trade unions or in participating in lawful trade union activities. The Trade Unions Act, however, restricts a union to representing workers in a "particular establishment, trade, occupation, or industry or within any similar trades, occupations, or industries," contrary to International Labor Organization (ILO) guidelines. The Director General of Trade Unions may refuse to register a trade union and, in some circumstances, may also withdraw the registration of a trade union. When registration has been refused, withdrawn, or canceled, a trade union is considered an unlawful association. The Government justifies its overall labor policies by positing that a "social compact" exists wherein the Government, employer, and worker are part of an overall effort to create jobs, train workers, boost productivity and profitability, and ultimately provide the resources necessary to fund human resource development and a national social safety net.

Trade unions from different industries may join together in national congresses, but must register as societies under the Societies Act (see Section 2.b.). On international Labor Day, May 1, the Malaysian Labor Organization (MLO), which had split from the MTUC in 1990, officially merged with it again, thus reunifying the principal labor centers.

Government policy discourages the formation of national unions in the electronics sector; the Government believes enterprise-level unions are more appropriate for this sector. In mid-1996, there were six such enterprise-level unions registered in the electronics industry. An enterprise union can be recognized voluntarily by its company, or it can be certified by the Government when it is confirmed as having the support of 50 percent plus one of the workers in that company. Four unions have been recognized through certification, and two of them have negotiated collective bargaining agreements with their employers. Restrictions on freedom of association in the electronics industry have been the subject of complaints to the ILO.

In one case in 1990, a company dismissed all members of one union. The union charged the company with union-busting and wrongful dismissal in industrial court in September of that year. The union appealed a May 1994 industrial court decision that found for the company. In August 1994, a high court remanded the case to an industrial court on procedural grounds for reajudication, but the company appealed the decision for retrial to the higher Court of Appeals. In September the Court of Appeals ruled in favor of the plaintiffs (the union), ordering reinstatement of all dismissed employees with back wages by October 1. Although the company reinstated the plaintiffs as ordered, it appealed the ruling on the issue of back wages. In July 1995, in a case involving the Metal Industry Workers Union, the Ministry of Human Resources went to court to force an employer to disclose information necessary to resolve a claim of recognition—the first action of its kind.

Unions maintain independence both from the Government and from political parties, but individual union members may belong to political parties. Although union officers are forbidden to hold principal offices in political parties, individual trade union leaders have served in Parliament as opposition members. Trade unions are free to associate with national labor societies that exercise many of the responsibilities of national labor unions, although they cannot bargain for local unions.

Relations between the Government and the Malaysian Trade Union Congress (MTUC) remain cool. The low point was reached in 1994 when MTUC President Zainal Rampak and former MTUC Secretary General Dr. V. David were arrested and charged, along with two other labor figures, with criminal breach of trust. Some groups claimed that the arrests (based on events in the 1980's) and the high bail amount were an attempt to keep Rampak from attending international labor forums. Ultimately, however, Rampak was given permission to travel to the ILO conference in Geneva. The accused labor figures appeared in a sessions court on November 21, 1994 and pled not guilty to all charges. The case was postponed several times and is still pending. There is still considerable MTUC and international observer concern about the outcome of this trial.

Although strikes are legal, the right to strike is severely restricted. The law contains a list of "essential services" in which unions must give advance notice of any industrial action. The list includes sectors not normally deemed essential under ILO definitions. There were 13 strikes in 1995 resulting in a loss of 4,884 workdays; the majority of the strikes (8) were in the manufacturing sector. The number of workers involved in strikes in 1995 was 1,748, down 15 percent from 1994.

The Industrial Relations Act of 1967 requires the parties to notify the Ministry of Human Resources that a dispute exists before any industrial action (strike or lockout) may be taken. The Ministry's Industrial Relations Department may then become actively involved in conciliation efforts. If conciliation fails to achieve a settlement, the Minister has the power to refer the dispute to the industrial court. Strikes or lockouts are prohibited while the dispute is before the industrial court. According to 1994 data, the industrial court found for labor in 62 percent of its cases and for management in 14 percent. The remaining 24 percent were settled out of court. Figures for 1995 and 1996 are not available. The Industrial Relations Act prohibits employers from taking retribution against a worker for participating in the lawful activities of a trade union. Where a strike is legal, these provisions would prohibit employer retribution against strikers and leaders. Although some trade unions question their effectiveness, it is not possible to assess fully whether these provisions are being effectively enforced, given the limited number of cases of alleged retribution.

There are three national labor organizations currently registered: One for public servants, one for teachers, and one for employees of state-based textile and garment companies. Public servants have the right to organize at the level of ministries and departments. There are three national joint councils representing management and professional civil servants, technical employees, and nontechnical workers.

Enterprise unions can associate with international labor bodies and actively do so.

b. *The Right to Organize and Bargain Collectively.*—Workers have the legal right to organize and bargain collectively, and collective bargaining is widespread in those sectors where labor is organized. The law prohibits antiunion discrimination by employers against union members and organizers. Charges of discrimination may be filed with the Ministry of Human Resources or the industrial court. When conciliation efforts by the Ministry of Human Resources fail, critics say that the industrial court is slow in adjudicating worker complaints; however, other critics point out that the industrial court almost always sides with the workers in disputes.

Companies in free trade zones (FTZ's) must observe labor standards identical to those in the rest of the country. Many workers at FTZ companies are organized, especially in the textile and electrical products sectors. During 1993 the Government proposed amendments to the Industrial Relations Act to remove previous restrictions on concluding collective agreements about terms and conditions of service in "pioneer industries." Legislation to address this issue was introduced and subsequently withdrawn in late 1994 by the Ministry of Human Resources to take into account other developments in the labor sector. The legislation was not reintroduced. The Government took these measures in part to respond to ILO criticism of its previous policy with respect to pioneer industries. The ILO continues to object to other legal restrictions on collective bargaining. Some labor leaders criticized amendments to the Labor Law in 1980, designed to curb strikes, as an erosion of basic worker rights. The labor critics contend that these changes do not conform to ILO standards.

c. *Prohibition of Forced or Compulsory Labor.*—There is no evidence that forced or compulsory labor occurs. In theory, certain laws allow the use of imprisonment with compulsory labor as a punishment for persons expressing views opposed to the established order or who participate in strikes. The Government maintains that the constitutional prohibition on forced or compulsory labor renders these laws without effect.

d. *Minimum Age for Employment of Children.*—The Children and Young Persons (Employment) Act of 1966 prohibits the employment of children younger than the age of 14. The Act permits some exceptions, such as light work in a family enterprise, work in public entertainment, work performed for the Government in a school or training institution, or work as an approved apprentice. In no case may children work more than 6 hours per day, more than 6 days per week, or at night. Ministry of Human Resources inspectors enforce these legal provisions. In December 1994, a Japanese electronics firm was fined $5,400 for violating the Children and Young Persons Act. This was the first time that a large firm had been fined under the act.

According to credible reports, child labor is still occurring in certain sectors of the country. A joint report by the International Confederation of Free Trade Unions and the Asian and Pacific Regional Organization put the child work force at 75,000. However, government officials maintain that the figure is outdated as it was based on a nationwide survey of child labor undertaken in 1980, which estimated that more than 73,400 children between the ages of 10 to 14 were employed full-time. NGO surveys indicate that most child laborers are employed on agricultural estates, but there are indications that some are being employed in small factories. Government officials do not deny the existence of child labor but maintain that child laborers have largely been replaced by foreign workers and that the Government vigorously enforces child labor provisions.

e. *Acceptable Conditions of Work.*—There is no national minimum wage, but the Wage Councils Act provides for a minimum wage in those sectors or regions of the country where a need exists. Under the law, workers in an industry who believe that they need the protection of a minimum wage may request that a "wage council" be established. About 150,000 workers of the 8-million-member labor force are covered by minimum wages set by wage councils. Representatives from labor, management, and the Government sit on the wage councils. The minimum wages set by wage councils generally do not provide for an adequate standard of living for a worker and family. However, prevailing wages, even in the sectors covered by wage councils, are higher than the minimum wages set by the wage councils and do provide an adequate living.

Under the Employment Act of 1955, working hours may not exceed 8 hours per day or 48 hours per workweek of 6 days. Each workweek must include one 24-hour rest period. The act also sets overtime rates and mandates public holidays, annual leave, sick leave, and maternity allowances. The Labor Department of the Ministry of Human Resources enforces these standards, but a shortage of inspectors precludes strict enforcement. In 1993 Parliament adopted a new Occupational Safety and Health Act (OSHA), which covers all sectors of the economy, except the maritime sector and the military. The act established a national Occupational Safety and Health Council, composed of workers, employers, and government representatives, to set policy and coordinate occupational safety and health measures. It requires employers to identify risks and take precautions, including providing safety training to workers, and compels companies having more than 40 workers to establish joint management-employee safety committees. The act requires workers to use safety equipment and to cooperate with employers to create a safe, healthy workplace. Trade unions maintain that relatively few committees have been established and, even in cases where they exist, that they meet infrequently and are generally ineffective.

There are currently no specific statutory or regulatory provisions that provide a right for workers to remove themselves from dangerous workplace conditions without arbitrary dismissal. Employers or employees violating the OSHA are subject to substantial fines or imprisonment for up to 5 years.

Significant numbers of contract workers, including numerous illegal immigrants, work on plantations and in other sectors. Working conditions on plantations for these laborers compare poorly with those of direct hire plantation workers, many of whom belong to the National Union of Plantation Workers. Moreover, immigrant workers in the construction and other sectors, particularly if they are illegal entrants, generally do not have access to the system of labor adjudication. Government investigations into this problem have resulted in a number of steps to eliminate the abuse of contract labor. For example, in addition to expanding programs to regularize the status of immigrant workers, the Government investigates complaints of abuses, endeavors to inform workers of their rights, encourages workers to come forward with their complaints, and warns employers to end abuses. Like other employers, labor contractors may be prosecuted for violating the labor laws.

The Government admitted that approximately 50 foreign workers died while in detention in 1995 but vigorously denied allegations by NGO's that detainees are tortured, are living in inhuman conditions, and are not given proper medical care. The Government issued new guidelines on foreign worker recruitment, and took action against labor contractors who violate the law. The minimum fine assessed by law is $8,000. In principle, serious violators can be jailed, but, in practice, such punishments are rare.

MARSHALL ISLANDS

The Republic of the Marshall Islands, a self-governing nation under the Compact of Free Association with the United States, is composed of 34 atolls in the central Pacific, with a total land area of about 70 square miles. The approximately 56,000 inhabitants are of Micronesian origin and concentrated primarily on Majuro and Kwajalein atolls.

The Constitution provides for free and fair elections, executive and legislative branches, and an independent judiciary. The legislature consists of the Nitijela, a 33-member Parliament, and a Council of Chiefs (Iroij), which serves a largely consultative function dealing with custom and traditional practice. The President is elected by majority Nitijela vote and he appoints his Cabinet from its membership.

Under the Compact of Free Association, the United States is responsible for defense and national security, and the Marshall Islands has no external security force of its own. The national and local police forces have responsibility for internal security. These agencies honor constitutional and legal civil rights protections in executing their responsibilities.

The economy depends mainly on transfer payments from the United States. Coconut oil and copra exports, a small amount of tourism, and the fishing industry generate limited revenues.

The Government fully respects the human rights of its citizens, but its influence leads to occasional instances of media self-censorship in sensitive political or cultural areas.

RESPECT FOR HUMAN RIGHTS

Section 1. Respect for the Integrity of the Person, Including Freedom From:

a. *Political and Other Extrajudicial Killing.*—There were no reports of political or other extrajudicial killings.

b. *Disappearance.*—There were no reports of politically motivated disappearances.

c. *Torture and Other Cruel, Inhuman, or Degrading Treatment or Punishment.*—The Constitution expressly forbids such practices, and there were no reports that officials employed them. Prison conditions, while Spartan, meet minimal international standards. The Government permits visits by human rights monitors.

d. *Arbitrary Arrest, Detention, or Exile.*—The Constitution prohibits arbitrary arrest, detention, or exile, and the Government observes this prohibition.

e. *Denial of Fair Public Trial.*—The Constitution provides for the right to a fair trial, and the Government generally respects this right.

The Constitution provides for an independent judiciary. However, the Government has injected itself into judicial matters. The President assumed and retained the Ministry of Justice portfolio following his January reelection until his death on December 20. The Acting President has now assumed the Justice portfolio. Government interest in an allegedly improper probate procedure involving the relative of an influential local leader led to the resignations of the Chief Justices of both the Supreme Court and the High Court. In another action, legislation, followed by direct instructions from the Cabinet, caused the Attorney General to remove from the Social Security Administration a private counsel who had upset influential individuals by his efforts to collect outstanding debts from them. In a further action, the legislature passed a bill denying the application of certain foreign court money judgment decisions in the Marshall Islands.

There were no reports of political prisoners.

f. *Arbitrary Interference With Privacy, Family, Home, or Correspondence.*—The Constitution provides for freedom from such practices, government authorities respect these prohibitions, and violations are subject to effective legal sanction.

Section 2. Respect for Civil Liberties, Including:

a. *Freedom of Speech and Press.*—The Constitution provides for freedom of speech and the press, and the Government generally honors these rights in practice. However, government influence leads to occasional self-censorship by the media in areas of political or cultural sensitivity. There are four operating radio stations, one government owned and three privately owned, including one owned by a prominent member of the opposition. There is a cable television company which normally shows U.S. programming but occasionally covers local events. The cable company is owned and operated by members of the political opposition.

A U.S. citizen and longtime resident operates the country's sole privately owned newspaper. The editor and two reporters are U.S. citizens as well.

The Government publishes a monthly gazette containing official news and notices only.

The Government respects academic freedom.

b. *Freedom of Peaceful Assembly and Association.*—The Constitution provides for freedom of peaceful assembly and association, and this is observed in practice.

c. *Freedom of Religion.*—The Constitution provides for freedom of religion, and the Government respects this right in practice.

d. *Freedom of Movement Within the Country, Foreign Travel, Emigration, and Repatriation.*—The Constitution provides for these rights, and the Government respects them in practice.

There are no recent reports of refugees. The Government has not formulated a policy regarding refugees, asylees, or first asylum.

Section 3. Respect for Political Rights: The Right of Citizens to Change Their Government

The Constitution provides citizens with the right to change their government peacefully, and citizens exercise this right through periodic, free, and fair elections held on the basis of universal suffrage for citizens 18 years of age and older. The Government is chosen by secret ballot in free and open elections every 4 years. There are no restrictions on the formation of political parties, although political activity by foreigners is prohibited. Until his death in December, the country had the same President since 1979 due primarily to traditional loyalties and concentrated political influence. The election of a new President took place January 14, 1997.

There are no legal impediments to women's participation in government and politics. Two women hold deputy minister positions. The mayor of Majuro, the country's capital and principal urban center, also is a woman. Society is matrilineal, and those men and women who exercise traditional leadership and land ownership powers base their rights either on their own positions in the family, or on relationships deriving from their mother's and sister's lineage. Although women have an increasing role in government, their cultural responsibilities and roles are not seen to be managerial or executive in nature, and they remain underrepresented in Parliament and other government positions.

Section 4. Governmental Attitude Regarding International and Nongovernmental Investigations of Alleged Violations of Human Rights

While there are no official restrictions, no local nongovernmental human rights organizations have been formed. No international human rights organization has expressed interest or concern or visited the country.

Section 5. Discrimination Based on Race, Sex, Religion, Disability, Language, or Social Status

The Constitution prohibits discrimination on the basis of sex, race, color, language, religion, political or other opinion, national or social origin, place of birth, family status or descent, and the Government respects these provisions.

Women.—There are allegations of violence against women, mainly related to domestic abuse. Wife beating is not condoned in society, and most assaults occur while the assailant is under the influence of alcohol. The Government's health office advises that few such cases are reported to the authorities, but many more are believed to go unreported. Assault is a criminal offense, but women involved in domestic violence are reluctant to prosecute spouses in the court system, and disputes are usually resolved through traditional methods involving apology and reparation to the members of the aggrieved party's family. Women's groups have been formed to publicize women's issues and to create a greater awareness of the rights of women. Violence against women outside the family is not considered a growing problem, although women in the urban centers would assume a risk by going out alone after dark.

Inheritance of property and of traditional rank is matrilineal, with women occupying positions of importance within the traditional system. No instances of unequal pay for equal work or sex-related job discrimination were reported.

Children.—The Government is committed to children's welfare through its programs of health care and education, but these have not been adequate to meet the needs of the country's sharply increasing population. Marshall Islands is working to incorporate the provisions of the Convention of the Rights of the Child into law. The Domestic Relations Amendment of 1993 defines child abuse and neglect and makes them criminal offenses. Other legislation requires teachers, caregivers, and other persons to report instances of child abuse and exempts them from civil or criminal liability as a consequence of making such a report. Child abuse is thought to be neither common, widespread, nor a growing problem, and there have been few child abuse prosecutions.

People With Disabilities.—There is no apparent discrimination against disabled persons in employment, education, or in the provision of other state services. There are no building codes, and there is no legislation mandating access for the disabled.

Section 6. Worker Rights

a. *The Right of Association.*—The Constitution provides for the right of free association in general, and the Government interprets this right as allowing the existence of labor unions, although none has been formed to date. The Constitution does not provide for the right to strike, and the Government has not addressed this issue.

b. *The Right to Organize and Bargain Collectively.*—There is no legislation concerning collective bargaining or trade union organization. However, there are no impediments to the organization of trade unions or to collective bargaining. Wages in the cash economy are determined by market factors in accordance with the minimum wage and other laws.

c. *Prohibition of Forced or Compulsory Labor.*—The Constitution prohibits involuntary servitude, and there is no evidence of its practice.

d. *Minimum Age for Employment of Children.*—The law does not prohibit the employment of children. Children are not typically employed in the wage economy, but some assist their families with fishing, agriculture, and other small-scale domestic enterprises. The law requires compulsory education for children from 6 to 14 years of age; but the Government does not enforce this law due to a lack of classrooms and teachers. There is no law or regulation setting a minimum age for employment of children.

e. *Acceptable Conditions of Work.*—There is a government-specified minimum wage established by law, and it is adequate to maintain a decent standard of living in this subsistence economy where extended families are expected to help less fortunate members. The minimum wage for all government and private sector employees is $2.00 per hour. (The U.S. dollar is the local currency.) The Ministry of Resources and Development oversees minimum wage regulations, and its oversight has been deemed adequate. Foreign employees and Marshallese trainees of private employers who have invested in or established a business in the country are exempt from minimum wage requirements. This exemption does not affect a significant segment of the work force.

There is no legislation concerning maximum hours of work or occupational safety and health. Most businesses are closed and people generally refrain from work on Sunday.

A government labor office makes recommendations to the Nitijela on working conditions, i.e., minimum wage, legal working hours and overtime payments, and occupational health and safety standards in accordance with International Labor Organization conventions. The office periodically convenes board meetings that are open to the public. There is no legislation specifically giving workers the right to remove themselves from situations which endanger their health or safety without jeopardy to their continued employment, and there is no legislation protecting workers who file complaints about such conditions.

FEDERATED STATES OF MICRONESIA

The Federated States of Micronesia (FSM) is composed of 607 small islands extending over a large area of the central Pacific. Four states—Chuuk (formerly Truk), Kosrae, Pohnpei, and Yap—make up the federation. The population is estimated at 106,000, mostly of Micronesian origin. The four states were part of the Trust Territory of the Pacific Islands and were administered by the United States from 1947 to 1986 pursuant to an agreement with the United Nations.

Political legitimacy rests on the popular will expressed by a majority vote through elections in accordance with the Constitution. There are three branches of government: An executive branch led by a president who also serves as head of state, a unicameral legislature elected from the four constituent states, and a judicial system that applies criminal and civil laws and procedures closely paralleling those of the United States.

Under the Compact of Free Association, the United States is responsible for defense. The FSM has no security forces of its own, aside from local police and other law enforcement officers, all of whom are firmly under the control of the civil authorities.

The economy depends heavily on transfer payments from the United States, fishing, tourism, and subsistence agriculture.

The Government generally respects the human rights of its citizens. However, traditional customs sustain a value system that distinguishes between people on the basis of social status and sex. There is evidence of some increase in both spousal abuse and child neglect. So far neither the Government nor other organizations have successfully filled the role of the traditional extended family in protecting and supporting its members.

RESPECT FOR HUMAN RIGHTS

Section 1. Respect for the Integrity of the Person, Including Freedom From:

a. *Political and Other Extrajudicial Killing.*—There were no reports of political or other extrajudicial killings.

b. *Disappearance.*—There were no reports of politically motivated disappearances.

c. *Torture and Other Cruel, Inhuman, or Degrading Treatment or Punishment.*—There was no known incidence of torture or other cruel, inhuman, or degrading treatment or punishment.

Prison conditions meet minimum international standards. There are no local organizations concerning themselves solely with human rights, and the question of visits by human rights monitors has not arisen.

d. *Arbitrary Arrest, Detention, or Exile.*—Legal procedures, for the most part patterned after U.S. law, provide for due process, which is carefully observed. There is no governmental use of exile for political purposes.

e. *Denial of Fair Public Trial.*—The Constitution provides for an independent judiciary, and it is independent in practice.

The Chief Justice of the Supreme Court is appointed by the President, with the advice and consent of the Congress.

Public trial is provided for in the Bill of Rights, and trials are conducted fairly. Juveniles may have closed hearings. Despite these provisions, cultural resistance to litigation and incarceration as methods of maintaining public order have allowed some to act with impunity. Serious cases of sexual and other assault and even murder have not gone to trial, and suspects are routinely released indefinitely.

There were no reports of political prisoners.

f. *Arbitrary Interference with Privacy, Family, Home, or Correspondence.*—The law prohibits such arbitrary interference, and in practice there is none.

Section 2. Respect for Civil Liberties, Including:

a. *Freedom of Speech and Press.*—The Constitution provides for these rights, and the Government respects them in practice. Each of the four state governments controls a radio station broadcasting primarily in the local language. Local television programming in some states shows videotaped and occasionally live coverage of local sports and political and cultural events. Subscription cable television, showing major U.S. programming, is available in Chuuk and Pohnpei. Religious groups operate private radio stations. The national Government and the four states publish newsletters.

Academic freedom is respected.

b. *Freedom of Peaceful Assembly and Association.*—The Bill of Rights provides for freedom of peaceful assembly and association, and the Government respects these in practice. During political campaigns, citizens often question candidates at public meetings. Formal associations are uncommon in Micronesia, but student organizations exist.

c. *Freedom of Religion.*—The Bill of Rights forbids establishment of a state religion and governmental restrictions on freedom of religion. The Government respects this freedom in practice; it is hospitable to diverse religions, and missionaries of many faiths work within the nation.

d. *Freedom of Movement Within the Country, Foreign Travel, Emigration, and Repatriation.*—The Constitution has specific provisions for freedom of movement within the FSM. It is silent on foreign travel, emigration, and repatriation, but in practice none of these is restricted. There have been no refugees or asylum seekers in the FSM, and the Government has not formulated a policy regarding refugees, asylees, or first asylum.

Section 3. *Respect for Political Rights: The Right of Citizens to Change Their Government*

The Congress is elected by popular vote from each state; the Congress then chooses the President and Vice President from among its four at-large senators by majority vote. State governors, state legislators, and municipal governments are all elected by direct popular vote. Political campaigning is unrestricted, and, as there are no established political parties, political support is generally courted from among family and allied clan groupings.

Although there are no restrictions on the formation of political groups, there have been no significant efforts to form political parties.

Cultural factors in the male-dominated society have limited women's representation in government and politics. Although women are represented in mid-level positions at both the federal and state level, there are no women in leadership roles at the highest government levels.

Section 4. *Governmental Attitude Regarding International and Nongovernmental Investigation of Alleged Violations of Human Rights*

There were no known requests for investigations of alleged human rights violations. While there are no official restrictions, there are no local groups exclusively concerned with human rights. There are, however, women's groups which concern themselves with rights for women and children.

Section 5. *Discrimination Based on Race, Sex, Religion, Disability, Language, or Social Status*

Although the Constitution provides explicit protection against discrimination based on race, sex, language, or religion, there is extensive societal discrimination, notably discrimination and violence against women. Government enforcement of these constitutional protections is weak.

Women.—Most violence against women occurs in the family context. In the traditional Micronesian extended family unit, spouses and children were accorded strong protections from violence, abuse, and neglect. These were deemed offenses against the family, not just the individuals, and were dealt with by a complex system of familial sanctions. With increasing urbanization and monetarization of the FSM economy, however, more and more emphasis has been placed on the nuclear family, and the traditional methods of coping with family discord are breaking down. So far, no government agency, including the police, has been successful in replacing that extended family system or in addressing the issue of familial violence directly.

Incidents of both reported and unreported spousal abuse, often of increasing severity, are on the rise. Effective prosecution of such offenses is rare. In many cases the victim is pressured by family, or fears of further assault, or is convinced that the police will not actively involve themselves in what is seen as a private, family problem, and decides against pressing legal charges. There are no laws against domestic abuse, and no governmental or private facilities to shelter and support women in abusive situations.

There are also a growing number of cases of physical and sexual assaults against women outside the family context. These assaults are perpetrated against both citizens and foreigners. Unmarried women are sometimes considered to have invited such violence by living, traveling, or socializing alone.

Women have equal rights under the law, and there are no cultural or institutional barriers to education and employment. Women receive equal pay for equal work; they are well-represented in the lower and middle ranks of government, although there are no women at the highest levels of government. Women are active and increasingly successful in private business and enterprise. There has been a National Women's Advisory Council in existence since 1992, and there are several small nongovernmental groups interested in women's issues, particularly ones associated with spousal and family violence and abuse.

Children.—The Government is committed to children's welfare through its programs of health care and education, but these have not been adequate to meet the needs of the country's sharply growing population in an environment in which the extended family is breaking down.

People With Disabilities.—Neither laws nor regulations mandate accessibility to public buildings and services for the disabled. Schools have established special education classes to address problems encountered by those who exhibit learning disabilities, although such classes are reportedly in jeopardy due to the cutoff of the grant funds under which they were established.

National/Racial/Ethnic Minorities.—The FSM prohibits non-Micronesians from purchasing land in the FSM, and the national Congress grants citizenship to non-Micronesians only by individual acts. For the most part, however, non-Micronesians share fully in the social and cultural life of the FSM.

Section 6. Worker Rights

a. *The Right of Association.*—Under the Bill of Rights, citizens have the right to form or join associations, and national government employees by law may form associations to "present their views" to the Government. However, as yet, neither associations nor trade unions have been formed in this largely nonindustrial society.

b. *The Right to Organize and Bargain Collectively.*—There is no law dealing specifically with trade unions or with the right to collective bargaining. Wages are set by individual employers, the largest of which are the national and state governments. The Government is not a member of the International Labor Organization. There are no export processing zones.

c. *Prohibition of Forced or Compulsory Labor.*—The Constitution specifically prohibits involuntary servitude, and there is no evidence of its practice.

d. *Minimum Age for Employment of Children.*—There is no law establishing a minimum age for employment of children. While in practice there is no employment of children for wages, they often assist their families in subsistence farming activities. The FSM does have a compulsory education law which requires that all children begin school at the age of 6. Children may leave school when they reach the age of 14 or after completing the eighth grade, whichever comes first.

e. *Acceptable Conditions of Work.*—The four state governments have established minimum wage rates for government workers. Pohnpei has a minimum hourly wage rate of $2.00 for government and $1.35 for private workers effective as of January. The other three states have established minimum hourly rates for only government workers, $1.25 for Chuuk; $1.35 for Kosrae; and $0.80 for Yap. These minimum wage structures and the wages customarily paid to skilled workers are sufficient to provide an acceptable standard of living under local conditions.

There are no laws regulating hours of work (although a 40-hour workweek is standard practice) or prescribing standards of occupational safety and health. A federal regulation requires that employers provide a safe place of employment. The Department of Health has no enforcement capability; working conditions vary in practice.

The FSM does not have any law for either the public or private sector which would permit workers to remove themselves from dangerous work situations without jeopardy to their continued employment.

MONGOLIA

Mongolia continued its transition from a highly centralized Communist-led state to a full-fledged multiparty democracy. The Prime Minister is nominated by the President and approved by the State Great Hural, the national legislature. Mongolia's progress in the development of democratic institutions was demonstrated by the overwhelming, and unexpected, June 28 election defeat of the Mongolian People's Revolutionary Party (MPRP), which had been in power since 1921. A coalition of democratic, reform-minded parties took 50 of 76 seats in the unicameral legislature. The coalition won despite the MPRP-designed single member districts, which the MPRP apparently calculated would give it a far greater majority in the Hural than it anticipated it would get under proportional representation or a mixed system. The MPRP accepted its defeat and entered into its new role in opposition.

Security forces are under civilian control; the newly appointed Minister of Defense is the first civilian to hold this post. Reduced government spending continues to downsize the military. The Mongolian Central Intelligence Agency (MCIA) is responsible for internal security; its head has ministerial status and reports directly to the

Prime Minister. Some members of the security forces committed occasional human rights abuses.

Despite post-1990 reforms, most large economic entities remain under state control; the new Government plans to privatize 60 percent of these entities by 2000. The economy continued to expand and strengthen, despite annual inflation rates of about 40 to 50 percent. However, Mongolia remains a very poor country, with per capita income at approximately $340 a year. The mainstays of the economy continue to be copper production and other mining, livestock raising done by a majority of the rural population, and related food-, wool-, and hide-processing industries, which meet both local needs and produce goods for export. A growing trade and small entrepeneurial sector in the cities provides basic consumer goods. Minerals, especially copper, provide the bulk of export earnings; foreign exchange earnings were hurt badly by the drop in world copper prices. An unreliable energy system, the lack of transportation and other infrastructure, and a small domestic market discourage foreign investment.

The Government generally respected the human rights of its citizens. Problems remain, however, including occasional beatings of detainees and prisoners by security forces, poor prison conditions, restrictions on due process for detainees, and violence against women.

RESPECT FOR HUMAN RIGHTS

Section 1. Respect for the Integrity of the Person, Including Freedom From:

a. *Political and Other Extrajudicial Killing.*—There were no reports of political killings.

Several dozen prisoners died in custody, at least partially due to inadequate management and oversight by the authorities (see Section 1.c.).

b. *Disappearance.*—There were no reports of politically motivated disappearances.

c. *Torture and Other Cruel, Inhuman, or Degrading Treatment or Punishment.*—Although the Constitution forbids such practices, there were credible reports that police and prison officials sometimes beat or otherwise physically abused prisoners and detainees.

Prison conditions are poor—including insufficient food and heat—and threaten the health of detainees. With the continuing rise in crime and subsequent rise in the prison and pretrial detainee population, severe crowding in both prisons and detention facilities is common, aggravating management and resource issues.

The deaths of several dozen prisoners from unclear health-related causes appears at least partially attributable to negligence and inadequate oversight. However, there is no evidence of a pattern of deliberate abuse or of a policy of withholding food or other necessities as punishment.

d. *Arbitrary Arrest, Detention, or Exile.*—The Constitution provides that no person shall be searched, arrested, detained, or deprived of liberty except by law, but these protections have not been fully codified. Under the Criminal Procedures Code, police may arrest those caught committing a crime and hold them up to 72 hours before the decision is taken to prosecute or release. A warrant must be issued by a prosecutor for incarceration of longer duration or when the actual crime was not witnessed. A detainee has the right to see a defense attorney during this period and during any subsequent stage of the legal process. If a defendant cannot afford a private attorney, a state-appointed attorney will be appointed.

The Government does not use forced exile.

e. *Denial of Fair Public Trial.*—The Constitution provides for an independent judiciary. The courts are independent, and there is no evidence that they discriminate against any group, or that decisions are made for political reasons.

The court system consists of local courts, provincial courts, and the Supreme Court. The 9-member Supreme Court is at the apex of the judicial system, hearing appeals from lower courts and cases involving alleged misconduct by high-level officials. Local courts hear mostly routine criminal and civil cases; provincial courts hear more serious cases such as rape, murder, and grand larceny and also serve as the appeals court for lower court decisions. A Constitutional Court, separate from the criminal court system, has sole jurisdiction over constitutional questions. The General Council of Courts, an independent administrative body, nominates candidates for vacancies on both the Supreme and lower courts; the President has the power to ratify or refuse to approve such nominations. The Council also is charged with ensuring the rights of judges and guaranteeing the independence of the judiciary.

All accused persons are guaranteed due process, legal defense, and a public trial, although closed proceedings are permitted in cases involving state secrets, rape cases involving minors, and other cases provided by law.

There were no reports of political prisoners.

f. *Arbitrary Interference with Privacy, Family, Home, or Correspondence.*—The Constitution provides that the State shall not interfere with the private beliefs and actions of citizens, and the Government generally respects these rights in practice. The head of the MCIA may, with the knowledge and consent of the Prime Minister, direct the monitoring and recording of telephone conversations. The extent of such monitoring is unknown.

Section 2. Respect for Civil Liberties, Including:

a. *Freedom of Speech and Press.*—The Constitution provides for the rights of freedom of speech, press, and expression. The Government generally respects these rights in practice.

A growing range of newspapers and other publications represent major political party viewpoints as well as independent views. Although in the past the Government controlled access to newsprint, all newspapers now buy newsprint directly from private suppliers, and neither party-affiliated nor independent news media report difficulty securing an adequate supply. Due to transportation difficulties, uneven postal service, and fluctuations in the amount of newsprint available, access to a full range of publications is somewhat restricted in outlying regions.

There is a government-financed television station with countrywide reception, as well as a new, limited operation private television channel, and several radio stations. The latter are particularly important as the major sources of news in the countryside. Both official and private media present opposition and government views. Residents also have access to foreign broadcasts from the United States, China, Russia, Japan, the United Kingdom, and other countries on commercial satellite and cable television systems.

The Government respects academic freedom.

b. *Freedom of Peaceful Assembly and Association.*—The Constitution provides for these rights, and the Government respects them in practice.

c. *Freedom of Religion.*—The Constitution provides for the right both to worship and not to worship and explicitly recognizes the separation of church and state. The Government generally respects these provisions in practice. Although Mongolia has no official state religion, the Government has contributed to the restoration of several Buddhist sites important as religious, historical, and cultural centers.

Although under the provisions of a 1993 law on relations between church and state, the Government may supervise and limit the numbers of both places of worship and clergy for organized religions, there are no reports that it has done so. Religious groups, however, must register with the Ministry of Justice. Proselytizing is allowed, although a Ministry of Education directive bans the mixing of foreign language or other training with religious teaching or instruction. Contacts with coreligionists outside the country are allowed.

d. *Freedom of Movement Within the Country, Foreign Travel, Emigration, and Repatriation.*—The Constitution provides for freedom of movement within the country as well as the right to travel and return without restriction, and the Government generally respects these rights in practice. By regulation, some categories of foreigners who wish to travel for more than a week must notify the police in their projected destination of their plans.

The Government cooperates with the U.N. High Commissioner for Refugees and other humanitarian organizations in assisting refugees in the small number of cases reported in which such status has been claimed. There were no reports of forced expulsion of those having a valid claim to refugee status.

Section 3. Respect for Political Rights: The Right of Citizens to Change Their Government

The Constitution provides citizens with the right to change their government through periodic, free elections by secret ballot, with universal suffrage. Presidential, national legislative, and local elections are held separately. The MPRP, which had ruled since 1921, had hoped to continue its domination of the Hural through the establishment of 76 single member, electoral districts in which a plurality could determine the winner. However, the MPRP was beaten by a coalition of democratic parties in June legislative elections. About 90 percent of eligible voters cast ballots; international observers judged the elections to be free and fair. The MPRP handed over power and stepped down, in the first transition of power between political parties in Mongolian history. In October 6 local elections, the MPRP succeeded in capturing 14 of 21 provincial assemblies. There are currently 12 registered political parties.

There are no legal impediments to the participation of women in government and politics, but they are underrepresented in the highest levels of the Government and in the highest echelons of the judiciary. Only 7 of 76 Hural members are women. Although there are significant numbers of women in various midlevel ministry positions, there are no women in the Cabinet or the Supreme or Constitutional Courts. Underrepresentation of women at the highest levels of government and in the professions has several causes, including tradition and some degree of discrimination by the virtually all-male web of leadership.

Section 4. Governmental Attitude Regarding International and Nongovernmental Investigation of Alleged Violations of Human Rights

A number of human rights groups operate without government restriction, investigating and publishing their findings on human rights cases. Government officials are generally cooperative and responsive to their views.

Section 5. Discrimination Based on Race, Sex, Religion, Disability, Language, or Social Status

The Constitution states that "* * * No person shall be discriminated against on the basis of ethnic origin, language, race, age, sex, social origin, or status" and that "* * * Men and women shall be equal in political, economic, social, cultural fields, and family affairs." The Government generally enforces these rights in practice.

Women.—There is increasing public discussion of domestic violence, including spousal and child abuse, after many years of government and societal denial. Although there are no reliable or exact statistics as to the extent of such abuse, human rights groups believe that it is a common phenomenon. The large economic and societal changes under way have created new stresses on the family, including loss of jobs, inflation, and lowered spending on social and education programs. These factors, coupled with the serious problems caused by extremely high rates of alcohol abuse, have led to increased instances of abuse and abandonment and have added to the ranks of single-parent families, most of which are headed by women. Although women's groups are advocating new statutes to cope with domestic violence, at present there is no known police or government intervention in cases involving violence against women beyond prosecution under existing assault laws when formal charges have been filed.

The Constitution provides men and women with equal rights in all spheres, and, both by law and practice, women receive equal pay for equal work and have equal access to education. Women represent about half of the work force, and a significant number are the primary earners for their families. Although many women occupy midlevel positions in government and the professions and many are involved in the creation and management of new trading and manufacturing businesses, women are almost completely absent from the highest leadership ranks of both the public and private sectors. There is no government agency overseeing women's rights, nor are there any notable efforts by the Government to encourage greater representation by women in policymaking positions.

A small number of women's rights groups concern themselves with such issues as maternal and children's health and domestic violence. The law prohibits women from working in certain occupations that require heavy labor or exposure to chemicals that could affect infant and maternal health.

Children.—Increased stress on the family structure and in society has had direct effects on many children, and the Government has been unable to keep pace with all of the educational, health, and social needs of the most rapidly growing segment of its population. Children of both sexes are guaranteed free public education through the age of 16, although family economic needs and state budgetary difficulties make it difficult for some children to attend school. In addition there continues to be a severe shortage of teaching materials at all educational levels.

There are growing numbers of infants and small children orphaned by maternal deaths and desertion and, in Ulaanbaatar and major urban centers, growing numbers of street children; one unconfirmed estimate has the national street children population at 3,000. The Government is committed in principle to children's rights and welfare, but it provides only minimal support for the shelters and orphanages that do exist; those facilities must turn to private sources to sustain their activities.

Mongolia has a long tradition of support for, and often communal raising of, children. The Government has been reluctant to admit the extent of the problem and slow to take steps to improve the welfare of children who have become the victims of larger societal and familial changes.

People With Disabilities.—There is no discrimination against disabled persons in employment and education, and the Government provides benefits to the disabled according to the nature and severity of the disability. Those who have been injured in industrial accidents have the right to be reemployed when ready to resume work. The Government also provides tax benefits to enterprises that hire the disabled, and some firms do so exclusively. There is no legislation mandating access for the disabled.

Section 6. Worker Rights

a. *The Right of Association.*—The Constitution entitles all workers to form or join union and professional organizations of their own choosing. Union officials estimate that union membership now totals over 400,000, somewhat less than half the work force. Union membership rolls are decreasing as the economy shifts from large enterprises and as increasing numbers of workers become either self-employed or work at small, nonunionized firms. No arbitrary restrictions exist on who may be a union official, and such officers are elected by secret ballot.

Union members have the right to strike. Those employed in essential services, which the Government defines as occupations critical for national defense and safety, e.g., police, utility, and transportation workers do not have the right to strike.

Most union members are affiliated with the Mongolian Trade Unions Confederation (MTUC), but some are affiliated with the newer Association of Free Trade Unions (AFTU). Both organizations have ties with international labor organizations and confederations in other countries.

b. *The Right to Organize and Bargain Collectively.*—In theory wage levels and other employment issues are decided in tripartite contract negotiations between employer, union, and government representatives. The Government's role is limited to ensuring that the contract meets legal requirements as to hours and conditions of work. In practice wages and other conditions of employment are set mainly by the employer, whether that employer is a private firm or the Government.

There are no export processing zones.

c. *Prohibition of Forced or Compulsory Labor.*—The law specifically prohibits forced or compulsory labor. However, most members of the military are required to help with the fall harvest. Many members of the military, along with prisoners, joined in the fight against the massive steppe and forest fires that struck Mongolia in the spring.

d. *Minimum Age for Employment of Children.*—The law prohibits children under the age of 16 from working, although those 14 and 15 years of age may do so with parental consent. Those under 18 years of age may not work at night, engage in arduous work, or work in dangerous occupations such as mining and construction. Enforcement of these prohibitions, as well as all other labor regulations, is the responsibility of state labor inspectors assigned to regional and local offices. These inspectors have the authority to compel immediate compliance with labor legislation, but enforcement is limited due to the small number of labor inspectors and the growing number of independent enterprises.

e. *Acceptable Conditions of Work.*—The monthly legal minimum wage is $13 (7,680 tugriks) per month, or $0.06 (37 tugriks) per hour. This level applies to both public and private sector workers and is enforced by the Ministry of Population Policy and Labor. This is the lowest wage for manual labor, such as janitorial work; virtually all civil servants make more than this amount, and many in private businesses earn considerably more. The minimum wage alone is insufficient to provide a decent standard of living for a worker and family.

The law sets the standard legal workweek at 46 hours and establishes a minimum rest period of 24 hours between workweeks. For those under 18 years of age, the workweek is 36 hours, and overtime work is not allowed. Overtime work is compensated at either double the standard hourly rate or by giving time off equal to the number of hours of overtime worked. Pregnant women and nursing mothers are prohibited by law from working overtime.

Laws on labor, cooperatives, and enterprises set occupational health and safety standards, and the Ministry of Health and Welfare provides enforcement. According to labor law, workers have the right to remove themselves from dangerous work situations and still retain their jobs. Mongolia's near total reliance on outmoded machinery and problems with maintenance and management lead to frequent industrial accidents, particularly in the mining, power, and construction sectors. Effective enforcement of existing occupational health and safety standards is difficult because the Government has less than 40 full-time inspectors to cover all firms, including a growing number of small enterprises. Some of the major industrial sectors, however, have part-time inspectors.

NAURU

The Republic of Nauru, a small Pacific island with about 10,500 inhabitants, gained independence in 1968, at which time it adopted a modified form of parliamentary democracy. Nauru has two levels of government, the unicameral Parliament and the Nauru Island Council (NIC). Parliamentary elections must be held at least triennially. The Parliament, consisting of 18 members from 14 constituencies, is responsible for national and international matters. It elects the President, who is both Head of State and Head of Government, from among its members. The NIC acts as the local government and is responsible for public services. The judiciary is independent.

Nauru has no armed forces although it does maintain a small police force (less than 100 members) under civilian control.

The economy depends almost entirely on the country's rapidly depleting phosphate deposits, mined by the government-owned Nauru Phosphate Corporation (NPC). The Government places a large percentage of the NPC's earnings in long-term investments meant to support the citizenry after the phosphate reserves have been exhausted, which, using current extraction techniques, will probably occur by the year 2000. The Governments of Nauru and Australia reached a $70.4 million out-of-court settlement in 1993 for rehabilitation of the Nauruan lands ruined by Australian phosphate mining.

Fundamental human rights are provided for in the Constitution and generally respected in practice. There were no reports of specific human rights abuses, but in the traditional culture women occupy a subordinate role, with limits on their job opportunities. Complaints of discrimination against workers from Kiribati, Tuvalu, and Vanuatu, particularly in treatment by police and in housing, continued.

RESPECT FOR HUMAN RIGHTS

Section 1. Respect for the Integrity of the Person, Including Freedom From:

a. *Political and Other Extrajudicial Killing.*—There were no reports of political or other extrajudicial killings.

b. *Disappearance.*—There were no reports of politically motivated disappearances.

c. *Torture and Other Cruel, Inhuman, or Degrading Treatment or Punishment.*—The Constitution prohibits these practices, and the Government respects these prohibitions in practice.

The Government attempts to provide internationally accepted minimum prison conditions within its limited financial means and in accordance with local living standards. Prison conditions, however, are basic, and food and sanitation are limited. There are no local human rights groups, and the question of visits to prisons by human rights monitors has not been raised. Visits by church groups and family members are permitted.

d. *Arbitrary Arrest, Detention, or Exile.*—The constitutional prohibition against arbitrary arrest and detention is honored. The police may hold a person for no more than 24 hours without a hearing before a magistrate. The Government does not practice forced exile.

e. *Denial of Fair Public Trial.*—The judiciary is independent, and constitutional provisions for both a fair hearing and a public trial are respected. Defendants may have legal counsel, and a representative will be appointed when required "in the interest of justice." However, many cases never reach the formal legal process, as traditional reconciliation is used—usually by choice but sometimes under communal (not government) pressure. Workers from Kiribati and Tuvalu are particularly at a disadvantage in complaints against citizens. There are only two trained lawyers, and many people are represented in court by "pleaders," trained paralegals certified by the Government.

There were no reports of political prisoners.

f. *Arbitrary Interference With Privacy, Family, Home, or Correspondence.*—The Constitution generally prohibits these abuses. Searches not sanctioned by court order are prohibited, and there is no surveillance of individuals or of private communications. Citizenship and inheritance rights are traced through the female line. Until very recently, laws restricted intermarriage with non-Nauruans. Although the laws have changed, intermarriage between women and foreign males still draws substantial social censure. The foreign spouses—male or female—of citizens have no automatic right of abode. They are, however, normally granted short-term "visits" sponsored by the citizen spouse, or they may apply for longer term work permits. Foreign spouses are not eligible for citizenship.

Section 2. Respect for Civil Liberties, Including:

   a. *Freedom of Speech and Press.*—The Constitution provides for freedom of expression. News and opinion circulate freely, rapidly, and widely by the press and word of mouth. The country has two regular publications: The private, fortnightly newspaper, the Central Star News, which operates and editorializes freely; and the Government Gazette, which contains mainly official notices and announcements. The sole radio station, also owned and operated by the Government, broadcasts Radio Australia and British Broadcasting Corporation news reports but not local news. Pay television broadcast from New Zealand is received by satellite. Foreign publications are widely available.

   There are no prohibitions or restrictions on academic freedom.

   b. *Freedom of Peaceful Assembly and Association.*—The Government respects the constitutional right of peaceful assembly and association. There are no limitations on private associations, and no permits are required for public meetings.

   c. *Freedom of Religion.*—The Constitution provides for freedom of religion, and the Government respects this right in practice.

   d. *Freedom of Movement Within the Country, Foreign Travel, Emigration, and Repatriation.*—The law provides for these rights for citizens, and the Government respects them in practice.

   Foreign workers must apply to their employers for permission to leave during the period of their contracts. They may break the contract and leave without permission but would lose their positions and often a sizable bond as a result. In most cases, foreign employees whose contracts are terminated by their employers must leave Nauru within 60 days.

   The Government cooperates with the office of the United Nations High Commissioner for Refugees and other humanitarian organizations in assisting refugees. No person in recent memory has applied for refugee status, and the Government has not formulated a formal policy regarding refugees, asylees, or first asylum.

Section 3. Respect for Political Rights: The Right of Citizens to Change Their Government

   Citizens have, and exercise, the right to change their government. Although Nauru has no organized political parties, persons with diverse points of view run for and are elected to Parliament and to the NIC.

   Parliament elects the President. Nauru has had eight changes in presidential leadership since independence in 1968. Power has always been transferred peacefully and in accordance with the Constitution. Voting by secret ballot is compulsory for all citizens over the age of 20 for parliamentary elections. There have been multiple candidates for all parliamentary seats during recent elections. The approximately 3,000 guest workers have no voice in political decisions.

   There are no legal impediments to participation in politics by women, and currently there is one female Member of Parliament.

Section 4. Governmental Attitude Regarding International and Nongovernmental Investigation of Alleged Violations of Human Rights

   There are no restrictions on establishing local groups that concern themselves specifically with human rights, but to date none has been formed. There have been no allegations by outside organizations of human rights violations in Nauru nor any requests for investigations.

Section 5. Discrimination Based on Race, Sex, Religion, Disability, Language, or Social Status

   The Constitution prohibits discrimination on the basis of race, sex, religion, disability, language, or social status. The Government generally observes this in practice; however, women do not receive the same degree of freedom and protection as men.

   Women.—Previous governments have shown little interest in the problems of women. While the authorities give high priority to improved health care and education, the island has no gynecologists, and the Government has not addressed the physical abuse of women and does not collect statistics on it. Some credible reports indicate that sporadic abuse, often aggravated by alcohol abuse, occurs. Families usually attempt to reconcile such problems informally as is standard islander practice. Major and unresolved family disputes are treated seriously by the courts and the Government.

   Constitutional provisions assuring women the same freedoms and protections as men are not fully observed in practice. The Government provides equal opportunities in education and employment, and women are free to own property and pursue private interests. However, both the Government and society still give women clear signals that their ultimate goal should be marriage and raising a family. The population has been almost eliminated on several occasions, first by disease and drought, and then during World War II as a result of massive removals by the Japanese. The Government has gone to great lengths to encourage large families, and women complain that emphasis on their reproductive role reduces their opportunities. For example, young women studying abroad on scholarship and contemplating marriage face possible termination of their educational grants as it is assumed that they will leave the work force and thus not require additional academic training.

Children.—The Government devotes considerable attention to the welfare of children, with particular stress on their health and educational needs. Child abuse statistics do not exist, but alcohol abuse sometimes leads to child neglect or abuse. The NIC treats child abuse as a serious communal matter. There were no reported cases of child abuse during the year.

People With Disabilities.—There is no reported discrimination in employment, education, and the provision of state services to persons with disabilities. There is, however, no legislation mandating accessibility to public buildings and services for the disabled.

National/Racial/Ethnic Minorities.—Foreign laborers, mainly from Vanuatu, Kiribati, and Tuvalu, experience some discrimination. While guest workers are provided free housing, the shelters they are given are often poorly maintained and overcrowded. Some guest workers have alleged that the police rarely act on complaints they make against citizens.

Section 6. Worker Rights

a. *The Right of Association.*—The Constitution provides for the right of citizens to form and belong to trade unions or other associations. However, Nauru has virtually no labor laws, and there are currently no trade unions. Past efforts to form unions were officially discouraged. The transient nature of the mostly foreign work force and the relative prosperity of the citizenry also have served to hamper efforts to organize the labor force. The right to strike is neither protected, prohibited, nor limited by law. No strikes took place in 1996. Nauru is not a member of the International Labor Organization. There are no provisions which would prohibit or limit the right of unions to affiliate with international bodies.

b. *The Right to Organize and Bargain Collectively.*—While there are no legal impediments, collective bargaining does not take place, and, as noted above, has been unsuccessful. The private sector employs only about 1 percent of salaried workers. For government workers, public service regulations determine salaries, working hours, vacation periods, and other employment matters. There are no export processing zones.

c. *Prohibition of Forced or Compulsory Labor.*—The Constitution forbids forced or compulsory labor, and there have been no instances of either.

d. *Minimum Age for Employment of Children.*—Education is compulsory until the age of 16; the law sets 17 as the minimum age of employment. This is honored by the only two large employers, the Government and the NPC. Some children under the age of 17 years work in the few, small, family-owned businesses.

e. *Acceptable Conditions of Work.*—Minimum wages vary considerably between office workers and manual laborers, but they suffice to provide an adequate, if modest, standard of living. Thanks to yearly dividends paid by the NPC, most families live in simple but adequate housing, and almost every family owns at least one car or truck. The Government sets the minimum yearly wage administratively for both public and private sectors. Since November 1992, that rate has been $6,562 ($A9,056) for those 21 years of age or older. The rate is progressively lower for those under 21 years of age. Employers determine wages for foreign contract workers based on market conditions and the consumer price index. Usually foreign workers and their families receive free housing, utilities, medical treatment, and often a food allowance. By regulation the workweek for office workers is 36 hours and for manual laborers 40 hours in both the public and private sectors. Neither law nor regulations stipulate a weekly rest period; however, most workers observe Saturdays and Sundays as holidays.

The Government sets health and safety standards. The NPC has an active safety program that includes worker education and the use of safety helmets, safety shoes, respirators for dusty conditions, and other safety measures. The NPC has a safety officer who is specifically responsible for improving safety standards and compliance throughout the company.

NEW ZEALAND

New Zealand is a parliamentary democracy, with executive authority vested in a 20-member cabinet led by a prime minister. Five seats in the 120-member Parliament are reserved for the native Maori minority population. The judiciary is independent.

The Cook Islands, and Niue are self-governing states in free association with New Zealand. Tokelau is a New Zealand territory. Their local laws are compatible with New Zealand and British common law.

The police and defense forces are responsible to and firmly controlled by civilian officials.

New Zealand is a highly efficient producer of agricultural products. The mainstay of its market-based economy is the export of wool, meat, and dairy products. An expanding manufacturing sector is engaged primarily in food processing, metal fabrication, and the production of wood and paper products. Tourism is also a significant sector of the economy, and niche industries are developing in such high technology sectors as software production. Disparities in wealth are small but increasing. Most citizens enjoy a comfortable standard of living.

The Government fully respects the human rights of its citizens, and the law and judiciary provide effective means of dealing with instances of individual abuse. The Government has taken steps to address the problems of overcrowded prisons, domestic violence, and societal discrimination against indigenous people.

RESPECT FOR HUMAN RIGHTS

Section 1. Respect for Integrity of the Person, Including Freedom From:

a. *Political and Other Extrajudicial Killing.*—There were no reports of political or other extrajudicial killings.

b. *Disappearance.*—There were no reports of politically motivated disappearances.

c. *Torture and Other Cruel, Inhuman, or Degrading Treatment or Punishment.*—The law prohibits torture and other forms of mistreatment, and the Government respects these prohibitions in practice.

Prison conditions generally meet minimum international standards, and the Government permits visits by human rights monitors. Officials were increasingly concerned about overcrowding in some prisons. The Office of the Ombudsman was critical of facilities in which prisoners were kept three to a cell and had to use buckets for toilets. The Department of Corrections acknowledged that there was a problem, which it described as "temporary," noting that new prisons scheduled to open later in the year were expected to ease the situation.

A study released in August showed that Maori and Pacific Islander inmates had a suicide rate many times that of their counterparts of European heritage. However, it was also noted that the number of suicides in police custody has dropped considerably since 1991. This decline was attributed to increased training for police officers, who had been taught to recognize and monitor prisoners at risk.

d. *Arbitrary Arrest, Detention, or Exile.*—The law prohibits arbitrary arrest, detention, or exile, and the Government observes these prohibitions.

e. *Denial of Fair Public Trial.*—The law provides for the right to a fair trial and an independent judiciary, and the Government respects this provision in practice. The judiciary provides citizens with a fair and efficient judicial process. A three-tiered impartial judiciary is in place, with the right to take an appeal to the Privy Council in London, though this privilege is rarely invoked.

There were no reports of political prisoners.

f. *Arbitrary Interference with Privacy, Family, Home, or Correspondence.*—The law prohibits such practices, government authorities respect these prohibitions, and violations are subject to effective legal sanction.

Section 2. Respect for Civil Liberties, Including:

a. *Freedom of Speech and Press.*—The law provides for freedom of speech and of the press, and the Government respects these rights in practice. An independent press, an effective judiciary, and a functioning democratic political system combine to ensure freedom of speech and of the press.

Academic freedom is not limited.

b. *Freedom of Peaceful Assembly and Association.*—The law provides for these rights, and the Government respects them in practice.

c. *Freedom of Religion.*—The law provides for freedom of religion, and the Government generally respects this right in practice. In April the court ruled on the 1995 case of a family of Jehovah's Witnesses. The parents had appealed a court order that their son be given a blood transfusion in contravention of their religious beliefs;

the family lost the appeal. Several other families also have sought the right to refuse medical treatment for their children on religious grounds. These cases were still being reviewed by the courts at year's end.

d. *Freedom of Movement Within the Country, Foreign Travel, Emigration, and Repatriation.*—The law provides for these rights, and the Government respects them in practice. The Government cooperates with the United Nations High Commissioner for Refugees and other humanitarian organizations in assisting refugees. New Zealand provides first asylum and conferred this status on approximately 850 persons in 1996. There were no reports of persons forced to return to a country where they feared persecution.

Section 3. Respect for Political Rights: The Right of Citizens to Change Their Government

The law provides citizens with the right to change their government peacefully, and citizens exercise this right in practice through periodic, free, and fair elections held on the basis of universal suffrage. A new electoral system, mixed-member proportional representation, was used in the October 12 general election with 27 political parties participating.

Women and minorities are accorded full opportunity to participate in political life. In the 120-member Parliament, 35 seats are held by women; 15 by Maori; 2 members are of Pacific Island origin; and 1 is of Asian heritage. The current Executive Council (cabinet) has 20 ministers including 3 Maori and 1 woman. There are also six ministers outside the Cabinet, three of whom are women.

Section 4. Governmental Attitudes Regarding International and Nongovernmental Investigation of Alleged Violations of Human Rights

A number of human rights groups operate without government restriction, investigating allegations and publishing their findings on human rights cases. Government officials are cooperative and responsive to their views.

Section 5. Discrimination Based on Race, Sex, Religion, Disability, Language, or Social Status

The law prohibits discrimination on the basis of all the above listed factors, and the Government effectively enforces it.

Women.—A 1995 government-commissioned survey found widespread physical and psychological abuse by men of their partners, and the Government is making a concerted effort to stop violence against women; initiatives include the issuance of nonmolestation and nonviolence orders against abusive partners, civil protection orders issued in family courts, and suits for compensation for some forms of negligent harm. The law penalizes spousal rape.

In addition, the Domestic Violence Act went into effect in July. This law broadened the definition of violence to include psychological abuse, threats, intimidation, harassment, and allowing children to witness psychological abuse. The law also provided some relief from the costs of legal aid and mandated stricter penalties for offenders.

Discrimination in employment and rates of pay for equal or similar work is prohibited by law. There are effective legal remedies available for women who experience discrimination.

Children.—The law provides specific safeguards for children's rights and protection. The Government demonstrates its commitment to children's rights and welfare through its well-funded systems of public education and medical care. While female genital mutilation (FGM) is not known to be practiced in New Zealand, the Government recognizes that the procedure is widely condemned by international health experts as damaging to both physical and psychological health. As New Zealand receives increasing numbers of migrants and refugees from regions where FGM is practiced, the Government is conducting an education program to enable health care professionals to inform their patients about the consequences of FGM. As of January 1, it is expressly illegal to perform FGM or to make arrangements for a child to be removed from New Zealand in order to have the procedure.

While no societal pattern of abuse of children exists, the Government recognizes the problem of violence within the family. Both government-sponsored and charitable organizations work to prevent child abuse in the home.

People With Disabilities.—The law prohibits discrimination against people with disabilities in employment, education, and the provision of other state services. Compliance with access laws, mandated by the Disabled Persons Community Welfare Act, varies as business owners and others strive to make necessary adaptations.

The 1996 census included questions regarding disabilities for the first time. In addition a sample of the population was asked for more detailed information on disabilities and the barriers faced by the disabled.

Following a 1994 decision by the government Human Rights Commission that Stagecoach Wellington, the city bus company, had discriminated against the disabled, the bus company, in cooperation with the Commission and a coachbuilding company, reached agreement on a design for wheelchair-accessible buses, and began test driving the buses in August.

Indigenous People.—Approximately 13 percent of the population claim at least one ancestor from the country's indigenous Maori or Moriori minorities. The law prohibits discrimination against the indigenous population, yet a disproportionate number of Maori are included in the unemployment and welfare rolls, the prison population, school dropouts, infant mortality statistics, and single-parent households. Government policy recognizes a special role for indigenous people and their traditional values and customs, including cultural and environmental issues that have an effect on issues of commercial development. The Ministry of Maori Development, in cooperation with several Maori nongovernmental organizations, seeks to improve the status of indigenous people. A special tribunal continues to hear Maori tribal claims to land and other natural resources stemming from the Treaty of Waitangi.

National/Racial/Ethnic Minorities.—Pacific Islanders, who make up 5 percent of the population, are not an indigenous people, but they experience difficulties similar to Maori.

Section 6. Worker Rights

a. *The Right of Association.*—Workers have unrestricted rights to establish and join organizations of their own choosing and to affiliate these organizations with other unions and international organizations. The principal labor organization, the New Zealand Council of Trade Unions, is affiliated with the International Confederation of Free Trade Unions. A second, smaller national labor federation, the New Zealand Trade Union Federation, was established in 1993. There are also a number of independent labor unions.

Labor organization is rudimentary in the territory of Tokelau (population 1,800) and in the Freely Associated State of Niue (population 2,000). In the more developed Associated State of the Cook Islands (population 18,000), most workers in the public sector, the major employer, belong to independent local unions inspired by New Zealand models. Industrial relations in the Cooks are governed by a simplified version of older national legislation.

The law protects unions from governmental interference, suspension, and dissolution. Unions, in fact, influence legislation and government policy. Some unions are affiliated with the Labour Party; others operate independently of political parties; all are free to support parties whose policies they favor. They freely exercise the right to strike.

The law prohibits strikes designed to force an employer to become party to a multicompany contract. Under the Police Act of 1958 and amendments, "sworn police officers," i.e., all uniformed and plainclothes police but excluding clerical and support staff, are barred from striking or taking any form of industrial action. Police, however, have freedom of association and the right to organize and to bargain collectively. Issues which cannot be settled between the Police Association and management through negotiation are subject to compulsory, final-offer arbitration.

b. *The Right to Organize and Bargain Collectively.*—The law provides for the right of workers to organize and bargain collectively, and this is observed in practice in the country and its dependencies. The law prohibits uniformed members of the armed forces from organizing unions and bargaining collectively.

Unions now represent fewer than half of all wage earners. Under the Employment Contracts Act, employment relationships are based on contracts. Individual employees and employers may choose to conduct negotiations for employment contracts on their own behalf, or they may authorize any other person or organization to do so on their behalf. Although choosing a union is entirely voluntary, unions have remained the most common agent used by workers to negotiate with employers. Employers must recognize a representative authorized by an employee or employees. Neither employers or employees, however, are required to negotiate or to agree to a contract.

The Government does not control mediation and arbitration procedures. The employment court hears cases arising from disputes over the interpretation of labor laws. A less formal body, the employment tribunal, is available to handle wage disputes and assist in maintaining effective labor relations. Firing an employee for union activities is grounds for a finding of unjustified dismissal and may result in reinstatement and financial compensation.

There are no export processing zones in New Zealand, the Cook Islands, Niue, or Tokelau.

c. *Prohibition of Forced or Compulsory Labor.*—The law prohibits forced or compulsory labor. Inspection and legal penalties ensure respect for the provisions.

d. *Minimum Age for Employment of Children.*—Department of Labour inspectors effectively enforce a ban on the employment of children under the age of 15 years in manufacturing, mining, and forestry. Children under the age of 16 may not work between the hours of 10 p.m. and 6 a.m. In addition to explicit restrictions on the employment of children, compulsory education ensures that children under the minimum age for leaving school (now 16 years) are not employed during school hours. By law children enrolled in school may not be employed, even outside school hours, if such employment would interfere with their education.

e. *Acceptable Conditions of Work.*—The law provides for a 40-hour workweek, with a minimum of 3-weeks annual paid vacation, and 11 paid public holidays. Under the Employment Contracts Act, however, employers and employees may agree to longer hours than the 40 hours per week standard. While the law does not specifically provide for a 24-hour rest period weekly, the practice is accepted by management and labor, and it is the norm. The government-mandated hourly minimum wage of approximately $4.40 ($NZ 6.375) applies to workers 20 years of age and older. Combined with other regularly provided entitlements and welfare benefits for low-income earners, this wage is adequate to provide a decent standard of living for a worker and family. In 1994 a minimum wage for younger workers was introduced at 60 percent of the adult minimum. A majority of the work force earns more than the minimum wage.

An extensive body of law and regulations govern health and safety issues, notably the Health and Safety in Employment Act of 1992. Under this legislation, employers are obliged to provide a safe and healthy work environment, and employees are responsible for their own safety and health as well as ensuring that their actions do not harm others. The New Zealand Council of Trade Unions has criticized the act, however, for not providing sufficient employee involvement in workplace decisions affecting health and safety. Under the Employment Contracts Act, workers have the legal right to strike over health and safety issues. Unions and members of the general public may file safety complaints on behalf of workers. Department of Labour inspectors enforce safety and health rules, and they have the power to shut down equipment if necessary. The Department of Labour standard is to investigate reports of unsafe or unhealthy working conditions within 24 hours of notification. Workers have the right to withdraw from a dangerous work situation without jeopardy to continued employment.

PALAU

Formerly a United Nations trusteeship administered by the United States, Palau became an independent nation in free association with the United States on October 1, 1994. Under the Compact of Free Association, the United States is responsible for Palau's defense. An archipelago of more than 300 islands in the Western Pacific, Palau has a total land area of 188 square miles and is politically divided into 16 states, more than two-thirds of its approximately 18,000 population resides in or near the capital, Koror.

The democratically elected Government is modeled after that of the United States. The Constitution, which took effect on January 1, 1981, provides for free and fair elections, executive and legislative branches, and an independent judiciary. The legislature, the Olbil Era Kelulau, is composed of two equal houses, the 14-member Senate and the 16-member House of Delegates.

Palau has no security forces of its own, aside from local police and other civilian law enforcement personnel, all of whom are under the firm control of civil authorities.

With a household median income of $12,791, Palau is a medium income country with a small, market-based economy largely sustained by transfer payments from the United States. Nearly half the work force is employed by government entities. Tourism and other service sectors account for most other paid employment. Tuna, harvested by foreign operated fleets, is the dominant export. Several small-scale operations, employing foreign workers, assemble clothing for export from imported materials. Most of the population still work in traditional subsistence agriculture and fishing.

Traditional customs sustain a value system that distinguishes between people on the basis of social status and sex. The weakening of those customs, including the breakdown of the extended family and the increasing abuse of alcohol and other drugs, has contributed to violence against women and instances of child neglect, the principal human rights problems. Societal discrimination against certain foreign workers, who account for nearly one-fifth of the population and one-half of the paid work force, is also a serious problem.

RESPECT FOR HUMAN RIGHTS

Section 1. Respect for the Integrity of the Person, Including Freedom From:

   a. *Political and Other Extrajudicial Killing.*—There were no reports of political or other extrajudicial killings.

   b. *Disappearance.*—There were no reports of politically motivated disappearances.

   c. *Torture and Other Cruel, Inhuman, or Degrading Treatment or Punishment.*—The Constitution prohibits such practices, and there were no reports that officials employed them.

   Prison conditions meet minimum international standards, and the Government permits visits by human rights monitors.

   d. *Arbitrary Arrest, Detention, or Exile.*—The Constitution prohibits arbitrary arrest, detention, or exile, and the Government observes this prohibition.

   e. *Denial of Fair Public Trial.*—The Constitution provides for an independent judiciary, and the Government respects this provision in practice. The Government includes an independent special prosecutor and an independent public defender system. The Constitution provides for the right to a fair trial, and an independent judiciary vigorously enforces this right.

   There were no reports of political prisoners.

   f. *Arbitrary Interference with Privacy, Family, Home, or Correspondence.*—The Constitution prohibits such practices, government authorities generally respect these prohibitions, and violations are subject to effective legal sanction.

Section 2. Respect for Civil Liberties, Including:

   a. *Freedom of Speech and Press.*—The Constitution provides for freedom of speech and of the press, and the Government respects these rights in practice. An independent press, an effective judiciary, and a functioning democratic political system combine to ensure freedom of speech and of the press, including academic freedom.

   b. *Freedom of Peaceful Assembly and Association.*—The Constitution provides for these rights, and the Government respects them in practice.

   c. *Freedom of Religion.*—The Constitution provides for freedom of religion, and the Government respects this right in practice.

   d. *Freedom of Movement Within the Country, Foreign Travel, Emigration, and Repatriation.*—The Constitution provides for these rights, and the Government respects them in practice.

   The Government has not formulated a policy regarding refugees, asylees, or first asylum and government practice remains undefined. However, there were no reports of forced expulsion of anyone having a valid claim to refugee status.

Section 3. Respect for Political Rights: The Right of Citizens to Change Their Government

The Constitution provides citizens with the right to change their government peacefully, and citizens exercise this right in practice through periodic, free, and fair elections held on the basis of universal suffrage.

There are no legal impediments to women participating in government and politics. As a result of the October general elections, a women will take a seat in the Senate for the first time. Women hold office in 10 of the 16 state legislatures where they constitute 7 percent of the membership.

Section 4. Governmental Attitude Regarding International and Nongovernmental Investigation of Alleged Violation of Human Rights

Palau has a history of openness to a variety of human rights groups without government restriction. Government officials have met with representatives of these groups and foreign officials regarding the issues of civil rights of foreign minority workers. Government officials are generally cooperative and responsive to their views. The Palau Red Cross Society opened its office in April; the local society is seeking full membership in the International Federation of Red Cross and Red Crescent Societies.

Section 5. Discrimination Based on Race, Sex, Religion, Disability, Language, or Social Status

The Constitution prohibits discrimination on the basis of sex, race, place of origin, language, religion or belief, social status or clan affiliation, and the Government generally respects these provisions.

Women.—There are occasional allegations of violence against women, mainly related to domestic abuse. Alcohol and other drug abuse increasingly contribute to this problem. According to the Attorney General's Office, the Government's Public Health Office, and women's groups, only a few such cases are reported to the authorities every year, but many more are believed to go unreported. Although assault is a criminal offense, women are reluctant to prosecute their spouses.

Inheritance of property and of traditional rank is matrilineal, with women occupying positions of importance within the traditional system. Women are serving under presidential appointment as bureau directors for women's interests, human resources, and clinical services. No instances of unequal pay for equal work or sex-related job discrimination were reported to the Office of the Attorney General.

Children.—The Government demonstrates its strong commitment to children's rights and welfare through its well-funded systems of public education and medical care. There is no societal pattern of abuse directed against children. Child prostitution and female genital mutilation are neither accepted within the culture nor practiced. There is no difference in the treatment of girls and boys in educational opportunities offered in Palau, nor in availability of scholarships to attend postsecondary education abroad. Girls and boys receive equal treatment in health care services.

Child abuse is thought to be uncommon, and there have been few child abuse prosecutions. While children's rights are generally respected, there were reports of several instances of child neglect, a byproduct of the breakdown of the extended family.

People With Disabilities.—The National Code includes a Disabled Persons Antidiscrimination Act and a Handicapped Children Act. There were no reported instances of discrimination against the disabled. There are no building codes or legislation requiring access for the disabled. The public schools have established special education programs to address problems encountered by those with disabilities.

National/Racial/Ethnic Minorities.—Non-Palauans are prohibited from purchasing land or obtaining citizenship. The rapidly increasing numbers of foreign workers, who now represent nearly half the work force and over 20 percent of the population, are viewed negatively by a majority of the citizens. Foreign residents can be subject to some forms of discrimination and are targets of petty, and sometimes violent, crimes as well as other random acts against person and property. There have been credible complaints by foreign nationals that the authorities do not pursue crimes against non-Palauans with the same vigor as crimes against nationals. Certain nationalities are the focus of systemic discrimination in employment, pay, housing, education, and access to social services, although such discrimination is prohibited by law. Instances of abuse of workers' civil rights are predominately found perpetrated against domestic helpers, bar girls, construction laborers, and other lower skilled workers, the majority of whom are from the Philippines, China, and Bangladesh. Foreign workers are often reluctant to seek legal redress for fear of losing their employment and, thus, their right to remain in the country.

Section 6. Worker Rights

a. *The Right of Association.*—The Constitution provides for the right of all persons to assemble peacefully or to associate with others for any lawful purpose, including the right to organize and to bargain collectively. There are no active employee organizations.

b. *The Right to Organize and Bargain Collectively.*—The Constitution does not provide for the right to strike, and the Government has not addressed this issue. There is no legislation concerning collective bargaining or trade union organizations, although there are no legal impediments to either. Wages in the cash economy are determined by market factors.

There are no export processing zones.

c. *Prohibition of Forced or Compulsory Labor.*—The Constitution prohibits slavery or involuntary servitude except to punish crime. There were reported instances of foreign workers, especially domestic helpers and unskilled laborers, being forced to do jobs different from those for which they were recruited. Freedom of foreign workers to leave employment situations not to their liking may be hindered by physical barriers and/or the withholding of passports and return tickets to their country of recruitment.

d. *Minimum Age for Employment of Children.*—The Constitution states that the Government shall protect children from exploitation. There is no minimum age for employment. Children are not typically employed in the wage economy, but some assist their families with fishing, agriculture, and other small-scale family enterprises. The law requires compulsory education for children between 6 to 14 years of age, and the Government generally enforces this law.

e. *Acceptable Conditions of Work.*—There is no minimum wage law. However, the Foreign Investment Law (which is being revised) states that foreign companies must pay a minimum wage equivalent to the lowest wage paid a government worker—$2.75 per hour. This amount appears to be sufficient, given the level of economic development, to provide a worker and his family with a decent standard of living. Anecdotal evidence indicates that unskilled workers for commercial firms are paid only $1.50 to $2.00 per hour. However, foreign workers are usually provided, in addition to their wages, basic accommodations and food at no or nominal cost. Although these wages are low, Palau continues to attract large numbers of foreign workers from the Philippines, China, and Bangladesh.

There is no legislation concerning maximum hours of work, although most businesses are closed on either Saturday or Sunday. The Division of Labor has prepared some regulations regarding conditions of employment for nonresident workers. The Division may inspect the conditions of the workplace and employer-provided housing on specific complaint of the employees, but actual enforcement is sporadic; working conditions vary in practice. There is no legislation specifically giving workers the right to remove themselves from situations which endanger their health or safety without jeopardy to their continued employment, and there is no legislation protecting workers who file complaints about such conditions.

PAPUA NEW GUINEA

Papua New Guinea (PNG) comprises some 1,000 tribes and over 800 distinct languages in a population of about 4 million. It has a federal parliamentary system, based on universal adult suffrage with periodic free and fair elections, and has an independent judiciary.

The Government has constitutional authority over the Defense Force (PNGDF), the Royal Papua New Guinea Constabulary (RPNGC) and intelligence organizations. Government security forces committed serious human rights abuses.

Exploitation of such natural resources as minerals, hydrocarbons, and tropical timber, and production of tree crops such as coffee, cocoa, and copra, generate significant export and tax revenues. However, 85 percent of the population resides in isolated villages, and engages in subsistence and smallholder agriculture. For a majority of the citizens, income and literacy are at a low level, and infant and maternal mortality rates are high.

The 8-year-old secessionist movement on the island of Bougainville continued. While human rights abuses by both sides decreased following the September 1994 cease-fire, the secessionist Bougainville Revolutionary Army (BRA) later repudiated the cease-fire and, following repeated BRA attacks, the Government also renounced it in March and launched an unsuccessful offensive in June-July. Human rights abuses by both sides, including extrajudicial killings and physical abuse, increased with the greater level of hostilities. Some human rights abusers have been prosecuted in the courts.

Besides the conflict with the BRA, there continued to be credible reports that security forces committed extrajudicial killings, were responsible for disappearances, abused prisoners and detainees, and employed harsh enforcement measures against civilians. The Government on occasion investigated alleged instances of abuse and prosecuted those believed responsible. Prison conditions remain poor, there are lengthy pretrial detentions, and the Government limits freedom of assembly. Extensive discrimination and violence against women, discrimination against the disabled, and ethnically motivated tribal violence remain serious problems.

RESPECT FOR HUMAN RIGHTS

Section 1. Respect for the Integrity of the Person, Including Freedom From:

a. *Political and Other Extrajudicial Killings.*—The PNGDF on Bougainville, as well as the progovernment militia allied with it, and the RPNGC when taking police actions, committed a number of extrajudicial killings. While no defense force or militia members have yet been prosecuted, the authorities on occasion punished some RPNGC officers, fulfilling a promise by police officials to bring police officers accused of serious misconduct to trial.

According to the United Nations Special Rapporteur, who visited in late 1995 at the invitation of the Government, the PNGDF was believed to have extrajudicially executed 64 people between 1991 and 1995. The Government reportedly made no response to the allegations of human rights violations that the Special Rapporteur transmitted to it. Although reports of extrajudicial killings have lessened, PNGDF soldiers and allied militia members, called in to mediate a local dispute, were suspected to have killed eight ex-BRA members in June, after leading them away from a village near Torokina. Although the PNGDF leadership vowed to investigate the allegation and take tough measures against those involved, no report was publicly released and no corrective action was taken. Following a month-long research mission to PNG, two representatives from Amnesty International (AI) told the media that relatives had reported several killings that had taken place on Buka island, the administrative center of Bougainville province.

In August the Prime Minister stated that human rights abuses on Bougainville were inevitable, but reaffirmed the Government's commitment to investigate and prosecute those on all sides who commit serious abuses. The Government has begun an investigation into the murder of the Premier of Bougainville in which Defense Force members have been implicated. No other reported human rights abuses by security forces on Bougainville have been investigated. With the Prime Minister's announced general amnesty in May 1995 for BRA crimes committed up to that time, which was extended to include security force actions on Bougainville, it is unlikely that the Government will investigate past abuses, the worst of which took place in 1989 and 1990.

RPNGC overreaction on occasion resulted in extrajudicial killings. In an incident in July, which witnesses described as an execution-style murder, a policeman called to investigate harassment reports shot a young man at point-blank range with a police-issued assault rifle on a street in Port Moresby in front of a crowd of onlookers. The victim was an innocent bystander. The policeman was later arrested and charged with willful murder. In March a pregnant woman, who was a passenger along with several children in a car driven by her husband, was shot by police who thought the car was stolen. The policeman responsible was arrested and later charged with murder, after the woman died in the hospital. Other examples of actions taken against police officers for extrajudicial killings include: A constable sentenced to 5 years in prison for killing a man when police attempted to quell a brawl at a convenience shop in Port Moresby; three policemen charged with murder for the November 1994 death of a man whom they had struck several times in the course of arresting him for running a black market beer operation in Enga province; and in October the police commander in Lae, the country's second largest city, was arrested and charged with willful murder for the shooting death of a man during a riot at a sporting event in September. There were also reports that detainees died under suspicious circumstances while in police custody, as well as during arrests. The country's Chief Magistrate expressed concern in April about the long delays in internal investigations of police shootings, saying that police investigators appeared "suspiciously reluctant" to complete their investigations.

The BRA killed and terrorized civilians in areas it controls. The BRA reportedly killed six civilians including an elderly woman on Bougainville's west coast in June, a civilian in southwest Bougainville in April, two civilians in south Bougainville also in April, three civilians including an old woman in northwest Bougainville in February, two civilians in southwest Bougainville also in February, and three civilians outside Bougainville's main town of Arawa in January. In September the BRA reportedly killed five civilians and wounded several others in an ambush in Buin, southern Bougainville, and killed two villagers, who were described as dedicated peace workers, near Tinputz in the northern part of the island. Frequently the BRA ambushes civilians after they leave government-controlled care centers to tend their fields and gardens at their abandoned villages. The Red Cross field office in Arawa, which coordinates operations on the island, temporarily closed in July after rebels fired on it, the third such BRA attack since the Red Cross resumed operations on Bougainville. Both the visiting U.N. Special Rapporteur and the AI team heard reports that the BRA was responsible for atrocities, executions, and unlawful detentions.

In October Theodore Miriung, the Premier of the progovernment Bougainville Transitional Government and an advocate for peace was killed by unidentified gunmen while dining with his family at their home village. Miriung had been strongly critical of both the Government and the rebels for using force to resolve the Bougainville crisis. To ensure the objectivity of the investigation, at the Prime Minister's request an independent inquest was conducted, headed by a distinguished jurist appointed by the Commonwealth Secretariat. Prior to departing the country following a 3-week investigation, the Sri Lankan judge who conducted the inquest told the press that some Defense Force members along with resistance members were involved in the killing. The Government was awaiting a full report at year's end.

b. *Disappearance.*—There were several reports that people disappeared on Bougainville while they were under the control of the PNGDF and its allied militia. In February the chief provincial officer publicly expressed concern over allegations that nine people had disappeared in various parts of Bougainville while detained by security forces. In September the chief coordinator of the Kangu Beach care center disappeared after being detained by PNGDF soldiers.

The BRA also was suspected of involvement in several disappearances, including one case in July in which a man disappeared after being picked up by the BRA in Kieta. According to one report, scores of patients removed by the BRA from the Longata health center could have died when taken to BRA-controlled areas where health care was not available.

c. *Torture and Other Cruel, Inhuman, or Degrading Treatment or Punishment.*—The Constitution forbids torture and other cruel or degrading treatment or punishment. Nonetheless, some PNG soldiers, allied militia and police, as well as BRA insurgents, continued to engage in such practices. In April PNGDF members reportedly detained several Buka villagers without charges, forcing some to run extended distances or sit unsheltered at gunpoint under the scorching sun for long periods of time. In May a PNGDF officer detained a senior provincial political leader overnight and threatened him at gunpoint for reporting directly to authorities in Port Moresby.

RPNGC members used excessive force, particularly when dealing with tribal fighting in the highlands region of the country. In a particularly egregious incident, police mobile squads reportedly shot several villagers and left over 200 families homeless when they burned homes and destroyed other property in the Markham Valley following tribal violence in February. During the 2-month-long coroner's inquest, the Police Commissioner admitted that the police had overreacted and caused massive destruction.

Members of the police have been accused of being ill-disciplined and quick to use violence to obtain information, to punish perceived slights, or to punish those in police custody. In June police beat students and a reporter at a demonstration (see Section 2.b.). During a joint police-electoral commission workshop in May, the Prime Minister called on police to refrain from unnecessary and rough behavior when carrying out their duties. The Police Commissioner has publicly vowed to discipline police members who use brutal tactics.

Police officers have been charged before the courts for criminal offenses (see Section 1.a.). In April two officers were sentenced to 7 years' imprisonment for the December 1994 rape of a teenage girl at the police barracks in Port Moresby. In February a policeman was charged with raping a girl at a police station in the Western Highlands province earlier that month. In a case in May involving the beating of a prisoner, the courts fined the four prison wardens involved, in addition to setting a judgment against the State.

A BRA rebel, accused of participating in a reign of terror in the Tinputz district of Bougainville in late 1995, was convicted in September and sentenced to an 8-year jail term on arson, armed robbery, and theft charges. Up to 18 other BRA insurgents are awaiting prosecution on charges including murder, rape, and armed robbery. Following numerous complaints, in September police on Buka arrested on assault charges one militia member and announced plans to arrest others believed responsible for harassing several villagers, who were illegally detained for several days in a militia camp, and reportedly forced to crawl naked, and drink urine.

Prisons are severely overcrowded and understaffed, and are unable to provide adequate medical care or even food due to the Government's financial problems. Although the Correctional Services Act, which came into effect in February, attempted to address humane custody of prisoners, the Minister responsible for prisons stated publicly that most inmates were being held in "appalling conditions." He called upon the Government to either fund the system adequately or close the prisons. The acting Prison Commissioner admitted in May that prison conditions throughout the country had deteriorated, especially due to overcrowding. Many prisoners as well as guards do not have uniforms, making it difficult for outsiders to distinguish between the two. The prison in Daru, Western Province, was closed in 1993, with only those convicted of the most serious offenses such as rape and murder being held in the local jail. All other convicts were released into society, which led to the expression of great concern by the country's Chief Justice in September.

The Government permits visits by human rights monitors.

d. *Arbitrary Arrest, Detention, or Exile.*—The courts generally enforce constitutional protections against arbitrary arrest and detention. However, these protections were weakened by the 1993 Internal Security Act (ISA) and amendments to existing anticrime legislation that provide that judicially issued warrants are no longer required when authorities suspect that a person has committed an ISA offense or certain other offenses. Under 1993 amendments to the Bail Act and the Criminal Code, only National or Supreme Court judges may grant bail in certain criminal cases involving firearms. In all other cases, bail may be granted unless the judge rules otherwise. Those under arrest have the right to legal counsel, to be informed of the charges against them, and to have their arrests subjected to judicial review.

Given the relative shortage of police and judicial resources and an exceptionally high crime rate, pretrial detention periods can be long, particularly in rural areas. However, pretrial remand is subject to strict judicial review through continuing pretrial consultations, especially at the National Court level. Nonetheless, cases are frequently delayed for months awaiting the results of police investigations.

The Constitution prohibits exile and it is not practiced.

e. *Denial of Fair Public Trial.*—The Constitution provides for an independent judiciary, and the courts are independent of executive, legislative, and military authorities. The legal system is based on English common law. The Supreme Court is the final court of appeal and holds original jurisdiction on constitutional matters. The National Court hears most cases and appeals from the lower district courts established at the provincial level. There are also village courts headed by lay persons, who judge minor offenses under both customary and statutory law.

The Constitution provides for due process, including a public trial, and the court system generally enforces these provisions. Defendants have the right to an attorney. Legal counsel is provided either by the public solicitor's office or by the Law Society on recommendation of the public solicitor's office for those accused of serious offenses and unable to afford counsel. "Serious offenses" are generally defined as felony charges or any case heard in either the National or district court (as opposed to the village or magistrate courts). Defendants and their attorneys may confront witnesses, present evidence, plead cases, and appeal convictions. Despite these safeguards, justice was delayed for many remandees throughout the country in September when Supreme and National Court circuit schedules were disrupted due to a financial crisis.

There were no reports of political prisoners.

f. *Arbitrary Interference with Privacy, Family, Home, or Correspondence.*—While the authorities generally respect privacy rights, police—especially in the highlands—have burned homes to quell intertribal conflict and punish communities suspected of harboring suspected criminals.

Some communities have sought redress through civil suits, a practice that provides compensation to victims but does not result in criminal prosecution of the perpetrators. Over the past 2 years, the State has paid nearly $5 million following court-ordered judgments for wrongful police raids. In a court case in August, the judge not only ordered the state to pay sizable monetary compensation to villagers in the southern highlands for a police raid in 1990, but also ordered the former police minister and three police officers personally to pay compensation for their roles in committing abuses, which included assault, false arrest, and inhuman treatment of suspects.

In spite of constitutional provisions requiring warrants, the police continued to conduct warrantless searches.

g. *Use of Excessive Force and Violations of Humanitarian Law in Internal Conflicts.*—Following the September 1994 cease-fire agreement with the BRA, the armed conflict decreased significantly. However, the BRA boycotted an October 1994 peace conference, and continued insurgent activities in 1995–96. The Government repudiated the cease-fire in March, and launched an unsuccessful military operation against the BRA in June-July.

Prior to commencing the operation, the Government warned all civilians in BRA-held areas to move to government-supported care centers for their own protection. Many thousands did, but found that the authorities were not able to feed or care for the new arrivals. Many subsequently returned to their villages after the operation ended. Others, who either chose not to go to the care centers or whom the BRA prohibited from doing so, risked being caught in the fighting. In one incident, four members of a family were reportedly killed by a government mortar round which exploded in their village, Kurai, in central Bougainville. Without confirming the incident, the security forces apologized, but stressed that civilians had been warned to leave the area.

PNGDF abuse of the local population is blamed for provoking the Kangu Beach massacre in September, in which 12 soldiers and policemen were killed and five others taken prisoner. The Government released a report in October blaming members of the Resistance Force (a progovernment militia) and the BRA for the killings, but criticized PNGDF "severe provocations" including: Troop indiscipline; drunkenness; drug use; fraternization with local women; and mistreatment of Resistance Force personnel.

The BRA in July reportedly burned two villages and a community school in retaliation against villagers who had departed for government care centers. The BRA also reportedly prevented people in areas it controlled from traveling to government-controlled areas for medical treatment.

Section 2. Respect for Civil Liberties, Including:

a. *Freedom of Speech and Press.*—The Constitution provides for free speech, including freedom of the media, and the Government generally respects this freedom in practice.

The media provided independent coverage and analysis of major controversies, including the ongoing insurrection on Bougainville and the legal problems of government and opposition politicians.

The two daily newspapers and the two weeklies compete aggressively in Port Moresby, but have limited circulation in other urban areas. One of the dailies is owned by a Malaysian firm, which has invested heavily in PNG's timber industry; the newspaper publishes little on the controversial subjects of logging and forestry, but is generally independent and unbiased on other issues. The television broadcasting company, EM-TV, is also independent, although there is limited television reception outside Port Moresby. The government-owned National Broadcasting Corporation (NBC) owns two radio networks that potentially could reach the country's entire population, but the networks are limited by poor funding and the deteriorating state of their equipment. A privately owned radio network, NAU-FM, is popular in Port Moresby and is expanding into other areas of the country.

Journalists are required to obtain permission from the Prime Minister's office and from the defense force commander before traveling to Bougainville. Requests are frequently denied under the rationale that the PNGDF cannot guarantee the reporters' safety (see Section 2.d.).

In January the Constitutional Review Commission (CRC), a parliamentary body, began a review of ways to make the media "more accountable" and to ensure that persons "aggrieved by media abuses have accessible redress." However, media and general public representatives reacted strongly, viewing the CRC effort as an attempt to control the media. The CRC initially reported in June that no new restrictions needed to be enacted, and recommended instead that an independent media commission be established charged with self-regulation, an approach that the media representatives supported. However, media representatives again became concerned when the CRC chairman stated in October that the CRC had been directed to draft legislation to make the media more accountable and to establish an independent body, in addition to the media commission, that would look into complaints against the media.

The Government showed itself acutely sensitive to media criticism on several occasions. In February the Prime Minister attacked as "totally unfounded" and "damaging to the country" a media report, later confirmed, relating to strained meetings between a World Bank team and the Government. The Prime Minister sought consideration of barring the media representatives involved from reporting on parliament. The Forestry Minister admitted to having placed four telephone calls in an unsuccessful attempt in September to convince EM-TV management to stop showing a documentary on Bougainville, while it was being broadcast. The Minister defended his actions by saying the program was not in the people's interest. Such government sensitivities have apparently affected reporting. The editor of a Port Moresby newspaper stated publicly in February that the media have deliberately chosen not to report on certain areas that would be open subjects in Western societies, such as the private lives of political leaders and allegations of corruption.

The courts occasionally tried citizens and foreigners under those provisions of the Censorship Act that ban the import, broadcast or publication of materials deemed pornographic according to Papua New Guinea's Censorship Code. The usual sentence for violations is confiscation and destruction of restricted goods, although the courts can legally impose a fine of $17 or more, or a prison sentence of up to 2 years. Cosmopolitan and Cleo magazines were banned in 1995 for having "gone against the nature of decency" in several of their issues.

The BRA reportedly on occasion jammed the broadcasts of the progovernment provincial station, Radio United Bougainville.

The Government respects academic freedom.

b. *Freedom of Peaceful Assembly.*—Public assemblies and private associations are legal. Public demonstrations require police approval and 7 days' prior notice. Such permission is frequently denied on the grounds that such activities encourage bystanders to engage in vandalism and violence. Students protesting university fees staged unapproved demonstrations. In one such demonstration in June, police fired tear gas and warning shots over the heads of protesting students at the university campus in Port Moresby, and beat several students as well as a television reporter after the students allegedly threw rocks. The police commander defended the police action, and stated that students must give the required 7 days' notice to hold demonstrations.

The Government does not require registration of associations. International affiliation of church and civic groups is also freely permitted.

c. *Freedom of Religion.*—The Constitution contains provisions for freedom of religion, and the Government respects them in practice.

d. *Freedom of Movement Within the Country, Foreign Travel, Emigration, and Repatriation.*—Government approval is required to travel to Bougainville. Following the September 1994 cease-fire on Bougainville PNG security forces no longer required travellers to Buka to obtain permits. However, following a series of lethal BRA attacks around the island in March, all scheduled flights were cancelled and the airport closed for a short period. Even officials of the progovernment Bougainville Transitional Government have on occasion been restricted from travelling from the administrative center on Buka to Bougainville. The PNGDF occasionally imposed sea travel restrictions on villagers living on small islands off Bougainville due to concerns over potential BRA attacks.

Otherwise, the Government does not restrict freedom of movement within and outside the country. The Government has not applied sections of the ISA that authorize the Government to exclude from any part of the country anyone convicted under the act or likely to commit an offense under its provisions. It has on occasion used its immigration powers to prohibit entry of noncitizens with whose views its disagrees. In June it refused to issue a visa to a Tongan human rights monitor invited to participate in a government-hosted U.N. Decolonization Committee meeting taking place in Port Moresby.

The BRA reportedly restricted people from moving from its areas into government areas. The BRA also prevented several church groups from entering its areas to conduct peace vigils, although it did permit entry to a three-woman religious group in May.

The Government provides first asylum for approximately 3,000 people who have fled from the neighboring Indonesian province of Irian Jaya. The Government cooperates with the United Nations High Commissioner for Refugees (UNHCR) in assisting the Irian Jayans who live in the East Awin refugee camp in Western Province. Until June this camp was administered by the UNHCR, but its functions were transferred to the Government when the UNHCR closed its office. Just prior to the closing, the Government announced a new policy of limited integration of Irian Jayans having certain skills or other qualifications, who could be accorded permissive residency status and permitted to leave the refugee settlement. A government committee is being formed to review applicants for such permission; it can also authorize repatriation of Irian Jayans who violate the conditions of their refugee status. There were no known forced repatriations of Irian Jayans to Indonesia in 1996. Several thousand traditional border-crossers live just within the country's border and move more or less freely between the two countries.

Section 3. *Respect for Political Rights: The Right of Citizens to Change Their Government*

Citizens freely exercise the right to change their government through direct elections with a secret ballot and universal adult suffrage. The voters elect a unicameral parliament of 109 members from all 19 provinces and the Port Moresby National Capital District. Any citizen can stand for election; several foreign-born citizens sit in Parliament and one sits in the Cabinet. With a multiplicity of small parties, coalition governments tend to be weak and shifting; none has yet survived its 5-year electoral mandate in the 20 years of PNG independence. The next general election will be held in July 1997.

Although there are no legal barriers to their participation in political life, women are underrepresented in senior positions in government and in politics. There are no women in the Cabinet or in Parliament. Although 3 women have been elected to parliament since independence in 1975, none has been elected in the past 15 years.

Section 4. *Governmental Attitude Regarding International and Nongovernmental Investigation of Alleged Violations of Human Rights*

There are no official barriers to the formation of human rights groups. While the PNG Association for Human Rights, formed in 1992, has been inactive, the Individual and Community Rights Advocacy Forum (ICRAF), a nongovernmental organization (NGO), has become increasingly active since its formation in 1993. ICRAF concentrated its efforts on human rights and the environment. NGO's exercised their right to comment on human rights issues in the media without any known governmental interference or retribution. ICRAF leaders participated in a peaceful demonstration by Irian Jayan supporters who presented a petition to members of the U.N. decolonization meeting in Port Moresby in June.

The Government permitted a month-long visit by representatives of Amnesty International, who were investigating human rights problems, especially those relating to Bougainville. The team completed its visit, which included a stop in Buka, in July.

Section 5. Discrimination Based on Race, Sex, Religion, Disability, Language, or Social Status

The Constitution provides for equal protection under the law irrespective of race, tribe, place of origin, political opinion, color, creed, religion, or sex. Despite these constitutional and other legal guarantees, women often face discrimination.

Extreme ethnic and geographic diversity prevents any tribe or clan from dominating the country. The democratically elected government, based on loose coalitions, has consistently avoided favoring any group.

Women.—Violence against women, including domestic violence and gang rape, is a serious and prevalent problem. While ostensibly protected by their families and clans, women are nonetheless often victims of violence. Traditional village deterrents are breaking down, and the number of gang rapes is believed to have risen. Although rape is punishable by imprisonment, and sentences are levied when assailants are found guilty, few assailants are apprehended. Domestic violence such as wife beating is also common, but is usually viewed by police and citizenry alike as a private, family matter. According to a 1992 report of the Law Reform Commission, two-thirds of wives have been beaten by their husbands.

Violence committed by women against women frequently stems from domestic problems, and, where polygynous marriages are still customary, there has been an increase in the number of women charged with the murder of another of their husband's wives. According to one report, 65 percent of women in prison are there for attacking or killing another woman. In view of the number of such incidents, a senior police official in the highlands region in April called for legislation to make a man who has married more than one wife responsible if one of the wives dies as a result of a fight among the wives.

The Constitution and laws have provisions for extensive rights for women dealing with family, marriage, and property issues. Some women in the modern sector have achieved senior positions in the professions, business, and civil service. However, traditional patterns of discrimination against women persist. Despite constitutional and legal provisions, most women, even those in urban areas, are considered second-class citizens. For example, village courts tend to be overly severe on women, imposing jail terms on those found guilty of adultery, while penalizing men lightly or not at all. Circuit-riding National Court justices frequently annulled such village court sentences. In April the Government approved amendments to the Village Courts Act requiring that orders for imprisonment be endorsed by a district court before they take effect. Polygyny, a customary practice among some tribes, particularly in the highlands, and the custom of paying bride-price serve to reinforce a view of women as property. This view was carried to the extreme when tribesmen from a western highlands village, in pressing compensation claims for the death of a relative, demanded that a young woman be included as part of a compensation package of goods and money. ICRAF brought the matter to the National Court which in June issued a protective custody order to prevent the villagers from threatening the woman.

According to U.N. Children's Fund (UNICEF) figures released in June, Papua New Guinea has a very high maternal mortality rate. Only 40 percent of women are literate, trailing men by nearly 10 percent. According to another U.N. report, 33 percent of girls are not attending primary school, compared to 21 percent of the boys, thus perpetuating their disadvantage. Both the Government and NGO's are working to improve the status and conditions of women, but have had limited results. The Government provides a grant to the National Council of Women. A Division of Women's Affairs exists in the Department of Youth, Home Affairs, and Religion.

Children.—The Government did not dedicate significant resources to protect the rights and welfare of children. Most programs to protect and develop youth are operated by NGO's and religious organizations. Many government programs are severely underfunded. In PNG's traditional clan system, children are generally cared for within the extended family, in accordance with financial resources and the tribe's access to services. Because of the geographic isolation and remoteness of many villages, malnourishment and infant mortality rates are very high. More than 60 infants out of every 1,000 die during their first year of life. Although statistics are not available, welfare officers believe that child abuse is increasing as village life and the extended family give way to the influences of modern society. Although PNG ratified the U.N. Convention on the Rights of the Child (CRC) in 1993, it has not yet completed the report due in 1995 on CRC implementation, nor prepared the national program of action.

People With Disabilities.—Through the National Board for the Disabled, the Government provides limited funding to more than a dozen NGO's that provide services to the disabled. The Government does not provide direct programs or services. Services and health care for the disabled, except for that provided by the traditional family and clan system, do not exist in several of the country's provinces. No legislation mandates accessibility for the disabled. Disabled persons face discrimination in education, training, and employment.

Section 6. Worker Rights

a. *The Right of Association.*—The right to form and join labor unions is provided by law, subject to registration by the Department of Industrial Relations. While the Government does not use registration as a form of control over unions, an unregistered union has no legal standing with the Department of Labor or before the courts and, accordingly, cannot operate effectively. Unionized workers account for about one-half of the 250,000 wage-earners in the formal economy and are organized into some 50 trade unions. Most of the unions representing private-sector workers are associated with the Trade Unions Congress. Unions are independent of the Government and of political parties. They may freely affiliate with international organizations.

Both public- and private-sector unions exercised their legal right to strike in 1996.

b. *The Right to Organize and Bargain Collectively.*—The Constitution provides for the right to engage in collective bargaining and to join industrial organizations. These rights are exercised freely. The Government did not take action to amend a law criticized by the International Labor Organization in 1994 that gives it discretionary power to cancel arbitration awards or declare wage agreements void when they are contrary to government policy. Antiunion discrimination by employers against union members and organizers is prohibited by law. The Department of Industrial Relations and the courts are involved in dispute settlement. Wages over the minimum wage are set through negotiations between employers and employees or their respective industrial organizations.

There are no export processing zones.

c. *Prohibition of Forced or Compulsory Labor.*—The Constitution forbids slavery and all forms of forced or compulsory labor, and there were no reports of such practices.

d. *Minimum Age for Employment of Children.*—The minimum working age, as established in the Employment Act, is 18 years. However, children between the ages of 11 and 18 may be employed in family-related work provided they have parental permission, a medical clearance, and a work permit from a labor office. Such employment is rare, except in subsistence agriculture.

e. *Acceptable Conditions of Work.*—Minimum wages for the private sector are set by the Minimum Wage Board, a quasi-governmental body with worker and employer representation. A 1992 determination, which is still valid, reduced the minimum wage for newly hired urban workers significantly, to equal the minimum wage for rural workers. The minimum wage of about $17.00 (22.96 kina) per week does not provide a decent standard of living for a worker and family who exist solely on the cash economy. At the same time, the national youth wage, for new entrants into the job market of 16 to 21 years of age, was set at 75 percent of the adult minimum wage. The Department of Labor and Employment and the courts take steps to enforce the minimum wage law, but enforcement is not effective because of the lack of resources. The depreciation of the kina against the U.S. dollar, about 30 percent since September 1994, has reduced the real wage received by most workers. Minimum wage levels, allowances, rest periods, holidays, leave, and overtime are regulated by law. The workweek is limited by law to 42 hours (44 in rural areas). The law provides for at least one rest period of 24 consecutive hours in every week.

Enforcement of the Industrial Health and Safety Law and related regulations is the responsibility of the Department of Labor and Employment. The law requires that inspections take place on a regular basis, but, due to a shortage of inspectors, they occur only when requested by workers or unions. The ability of workers to remove themselves from hazardous conditions varies by workplace. Where workers are unionized there is some measure of protection in such situations.

PHILIPPINES

The Philippines is a democratic republic with an elected president, a fully functioning political party system, a bicameral legislature, and an independent judiciary. Political corruption remains endemic, however, particularly in the electoral and judicial systems. The Government achieved significant gains in peace talks with insurgent groups.

The Department of National Defense controls the Armed Forces of the Philippines (AFP), and the Department of Interior and Local Government supervises the civilian Philippine National Police (PNP). The two forces share responsibility for fighting a declining Communist insurgency, terrorists, and Muslim separatists. Military forces, including local civilian militias and the police, committed human rights abuses.

The Government is implementing a far-reaching reform program, "Philippines 2000," to convert its agrarian-based, paternalistic economy into an industrial, market-driven one. Although "nationalist" blocs and vested interests continue to pose obstacles, the Government has succeeded in liberalizing the investment, trade, and foreign exchange regimes. This program has opened formerly restricted sectors, which had included banking, insurance, aviation, telecommunications, and oil; "reprivatized" state-controlled firms; and addressed infrastructure complaints. Long-term fiscal stability is a major concern. The Government has proposed for Congressional approval a comprehensive tax reform program. Exports and investment spurred a 5.5 percent real gross national product expansion in 1995 and 7.1 percent in 1996. Garments and electronics make up more than half of merchandise export receipts and are significantly complemented by overseas worker remittances. While the Government has accelerated market reforms, poverty and inequitable income distribution remain. More than 40 percent of the population of 70 million are unable to meet basic nutritional and other needs, while the richest 10 percent of families receive 36 percent of aggregate personal income. Annual per capita national income is estimated at $1,184.

The Government generally respected the human rights of its citizens; however, there were problems in some areas. A general decline in the number of abuses was partially offset by encounters between government and insurgent forces in Mindanao that resulted in an increase in the number of civilian casualties. Members of the security forces were responsible for extrajudicial killings, disappearances, torture, and arbitrary arrest and detention. According to the Commission on Human Rights (CHR), an independent government agency, the police continued to be the leading abusers of human rights. Some abuses were committed by personnel of the police and military forces involved in illegal activities such as coerced protection, political gangsterism, kidnap-for-ransom syndicates, and assistance to illegal loggers. The authorities rationalized other abuses as necessary shortcuts to fighting crime in a criminal justice system that is slow, cumbersome, and disposed to freeing criminals or treating them leniently. There continued to be increased public concern for due process and equal justice, however, as personal ties undermined the commitment of some government institutions to ensuring fairness and justice.

The courts remained hobbled by backlogs, limited resources, and venality. Long delays in trials are common, and prison conditions remained poor. An estimated 4 million citizens living abroad remained disenfranchised because Congress has not yet enacted absentee voting, as required by the Constitution. Violence and discrimination against women and abuse of children continued to be serious problems. Discrimination against indigenous people and Muslims persists. Child labor is a problem. The Government often relies on the more than 5,000 local nongovernmental organizations (NGO's) to help change public attitudes and pressure local authorities to address abuses.

Communist and Muslim insurgent groups also committed human rights abuses, including extrajudicial killings, kidnapings, torture, arbitrary arrests and detentions, and the use of summary justice in informal courts.

RESPECT FOR HUMAN RIGHTS

Section 1. Respect for the Integrity of the Person, Including Freedom From:

a. *Political and Other Extrajudicial Killing.*—The CHR reported 64 incidents of extrajudicial killing during the first quarter. It reported 172 such killings for all of 1995. Task Force Detainees of the Philippines (TFDP), a prominent NGO, reported 14 people killed extrajudicially in the first 6 months of 1996, compared with 38 in 1995. The numbers given by the CHR are greater, in part because the CHR includes violations by both government and insurgent groups, including the Communist Party of the Philippines and its armed wing, the New People's Army (CPP/NPA), while the TFDP lists only offenses attributed to government authorities. In addition, the TFDP's ability to gather human rights violation statistics was adversely affected in 1995 (and to a lesser extent in 1996) by an internal organizational dispute that limited reporting from some of its provincial affiliates.

Both the CHR and the TFDP attribute the majority of human rights abuses, including extrajudicial killings, to the police and military forces, including civilian militia units. The CHR reported that in 1995, the PNP accounted for nearly half the complaints filed. According to the TFDP, the rate of PNP involvement increased during the year. This statistic conformed to a pattern dating from 1989, when the PNP overtook Communist rebels as the Philippines' main institutional violator of human rights.

As in 1995, extrajudicial killings and other security force abuses increased press and public concern for due process. However, personal ties undermined the commitment of some government institutions to ensuring due process and equal justice, resulting in impunity that absolved the entrenched and powerful.

Civilian militia units or Citizens Armed Forces Geographical Units (CAFGU's) also committed extrajudicial killings. Organized by the police and the AFP to secure areas cleared of insurgents, these nonprofessional units have inadequate training, poor supervision, and a propensity for violent behavior. Improved training and supervision have corrected some of these flaws, but continued fighting in Mindanao and resistance from some governors, particularly in northern Luzon, who feared a renewed Communist threat, substantially frustrated efforts to lower force levels. The TFDP attributes eight human rights violations in the first 6 months of the year to CAFGU involvement, of which two were extrajudicial killings.

With the upsurge in counterinsurgency fighting in Mindanao (see also Section 1.g.), the TFDP attributed 14 deaths from the first half of 1996 to AFP personnel. The TFDP did not include in this count the April 12 killing of three members of the League of Filipino Students in Camarines Norte who, according to military reports, were also members of the New Peoples' Army (NPA).

Problems of corruption and impunity hindered the prosecution of cases of killings from previous years (see Section 1.e.).

Private security forces maintained by local landowners, political figures, and criminal gangs also committed many killings. Despite a continuing government effort to dismantle "private armies," House of Representatives Speaker Jose de Venecia stated in June that 562 such groups remained. PNP officials estimated that approximately 24,000 persons took part in these groups; the PNP confiscated and disposed of more than 11,000 firearms.

Although the NPA insurgency was greatly reduced from its height in the 1980's, NPA insurgents committed numerous killings, including civilians in mountainous or jungle areas far from Manila, including Mindanao, Negros Island, and the Cordelleria region in northern Luzon. The CHR charged 12 NPA members with human rights violations during the year; the total number of deaths from NPA violence is not known. The NPA also extorted funds and supplies from businessmen, government officials, uncooperative nongovernmental organizations, and families in communities where it operated. Both the NPA and the breakaway Communist Alex Boncayao Brigade (ABB) targeted and killed police officials and former ("traitor") party members. The ABB claimed credit for the June 13 daytime ambush and killing of former Ilocos Norte Vice Governor Rolando Abadilla on a busy Manila street. Abadilla was the former leader of a martial law security group.

Members of the Muslim extremist Abu Sayyaf Group (ASG) were the suspected killers of two Christian clergymen in Negros Island and Northern Luzon areas. Authorities also suspected that the ASG was responsible for a series of attacks directed against teachers and schools in Basilan.

b. *Disappearance.*—The CHR cited five cases of disappearance in the first nine months of the year, compared with 15 cases for all of 1995. The courts and police have failed to address complaints of families covering disappearances over the past decade. An advocacy group, Families of Victims of Involuntary Disappearance, has presented to the Government records of more than 1,500 such missing individuals.

According to Citizens Action Against Crime, an NGO that closely monitors kidnapings, there was an increase in kidnapings-for-ransom to 147 incidents during the year, involving more than 241 victims, of whom more than 30 were killed. Victims came from the middle to upper-middle class (the wealthiest members of society, being protected by hired bodyguards, were targeted less frequently). Many of the victims were members of the Chinese-Filipino community, which numbers perhaps 1 to 2 percent of the total population and is commonly perceived as wealthy. Fearing retribution, victims and their families typically refused to cooperate with the authorities or to identify their captors, when known. The most prominent victims included renowned architect Gilbert Yu and Leo Ongpin, the nephew of two former Cabinet Secretaries. Ongpin's kidnapers killed him even though they demanded a ransom. Random kidnapings also took place in some Manila neighborhoods, as criminals intercepted cars bearing one or two passengers and held them there while negotiating with their families.

While criminal elements were responsible for some kidnaping incidents, evidence (including the precision with which victims were abducted, and the high powered firearms and sophisticated communication equipment used) along with several court convictions, supported public perceptions that kidnapers often included persons with previous police and military service, as well as active duty personnel.

c. *Torture and Other Cruel, Inhuman, or Degrading Treatment or Punishment.*—The Constitution prohibits torture, and evidence obtained through its use is legally inadmissible. However, members of the security forces continued to use torture and otherwise abused suspects and detainees. In July the Department of Interior and Local Government (DILG) distributed a 10-page primer to police on the rights of suspects, from the time of arrest through investigation, detention, and trial. The primer, which the DILG prepared in coordination with the CHR, reiterated standing directives to law enforcement agencies to avoid unnecessary force in all these phases. Nonetheless, abuses continued.

Four cases of torture were reported to the CHR in the first 8 months of 1996, compared with two in 1995. The TFDP cited 3 cases in the first 6 months of 1996, compared with 17 for all of 1995. The CHR maintained its program of human rights awareness training in the military and provided AFP promotion panels with "certificates of clearance" on officers' human rights performance. No comparable program exists for police and custodial officials in charge of the country's jails and prisons, where physical punishment is common. A study commissioned by the NGO LawAsia identified the most common forms of abuse during arrest and interrogation as mauling, slaps, strangulation, hitting with rifle butts or wooden clubs, poking with a gun, enclosing a victim's head in cellophane, and applying electrical current to the genitals. Police also reportedly burn or drag suspects behind cars to coerce confessions.

Newspaper editorials and the CHR questioned the March appointment to an elite National Bureau of Investigation (NBI) unit of an officer implicated in a well-publicized 1995 incident in which NBI agents "interrogated" an 18-year-old university student who had intervened to help a jeepney driver being mauled on a Manila street. The assailant was an NBI agent who, along with several companion agents, beat the student severely, then handcuffed, blindfolded, and locked him in a small cell for more than 24 hours. The matter provoked a Senate inquiry and led to the NBI commanding officer's reassignment in a provincial post. Notwithstanding the public record, the Ombudsman dismissed charges of misbehavior for lack of evidence, paving the way for NBI superiors to restore the questioned officer to his position.

Prison conditions are poor. Jails and prisons are overcrowded, have limited exercise and sanitary facilities, and provide prisoners with unhygienic and unpalatable food rations. Guards routinely abuse prisoners; female prisoners are at particular risk of sexual assault. A CHR report on jail facilities throughout the country indicated that of 613 jails visited, only 64 had adequate facilities and were in good condition. Some prominent prisoners and celebrities, however, are treated far better. In June newspapers reported that a detained "drug lord" received not only food but drugs inside his Manila jail cell. Popular movie star Robin Padilla, jailed in 1995 for illegal possession of high-powered firearms, acted in a film and was married in a celebrity wedding ceremony conducted on prison grounds. The May recapture of Rolito Go, a convicted murderer who escaped from jail 3 years earlier, highlighted the fact that prisoners with wealth and connections not only are able to get special privileges but on occasion can bribe their way out of detention.

International monitoring groups, the International Committee of the Red Cross, and foreign embassy officials are allowed free access to jails and prisons.

d. *Arbitrary Arrest, Detention, or Exile.*—Although the Constitution requires a judicial determination of probable cause before issuance of an arrest warrant and prohibits holding prisoners incommunicado or in secret places of detention, authorities continue to arrest arbitrarily and detain citizens.

Detainees have the right to a judicial review of the legality of their detention and, except for offenses punishable by a life sentence or death (when evidence of guilt is strong), the right to bail. Authorities are required to file charges within 12 to 36 hours of a warrantless arrest, depending upon the seriousness of the alleged crime. The CHR listed 54 cases of illegal arrest and detention for the first quarter of 1996, compared with 129 for all of 1995. The TFDP found that 60 persons were arrested illegally in the first 6 months of 1996, compared with 272 such arrests in the previous year.

The decline in arbitrary arrests and detentions is attributable in part to the Government's domestic peace process, involving talks with Communist, Muslim, and military rebels. The Government in 1995 offered amnesty to former rebels and members of government security forces up to a June 1, 1995, deadline. In the case of rebels, crimes covered by the amnesty must have been committed in pursuit of political beliefs; for members of government forces, the crimes covered had to be those committed in the performance of duty. Members of government security forces who committed serious human rights violations (arson, torture, extrajudicial killings, massacres, rape, torture, and robbery) were excluded from the program. A quasi-judicial National Amnesty Commission (NAC), whose decisions are subject to review only by the Court of Appeals, was established to process amnesty applications. The TFDP reported that the NAC processed and oversaw the release of 14 political prisoners during the year. Communist groups rejected the amnesty offer, arguing that it should have stemmed from peace negotiations and not arbitrary action of the Government.

A 1995 LawAsia Human Rights Committee study on administrative detention determined that a majority of interviewed detainees had been arrested without warrant; they were merely "invited" in for police questioning, but subsequently held. The law provides, however, that anyone under custodial investigation, whether or not "invited," is entitled to counsel. The LawAsia study cited numerous violations of constitutional and human rights, such as lack of access to counsel during investigation and interrogation, as well as physical mistreatment during detention.

Several well-publicized incidents illustrated the frequency with which police ignored proper arrest procedure and the complications this posed for other parts of the criminal justice system. In February police responding to a Manila bank robbery arrested a sloppily dressed suspect who, in reality, was a photojournalist who had arrived at the crime scene before the police. Manila's press and the National Union of Journalists provided detailed reporting of police violation of detention laws in arresting and manhandling the "suspect," leading senior police authorities to discipline the officers involved. The June murder of former Ilocos Norte Vice Governor Rolando Abadilla (see Section 1.a.) led to the arrest of several suspects who, the CHR subsequently determined, had been denied counsel and visitorial rights. The CHR was unable to determine if the evidence was sufficient to sustain claims of torture and warrantless arrests, leaving these issues for courts to decide. Police mishandling of the Abadilla case also led the authorities to discipline the officers involved. In August a regional trial court judge acquitted for lack of sufficient evidence five suspects in a murder and rape trial; prosecutors had relied on extrajudicial confessions made without the presence of counsel, which were not admissible in court. DILG Secretary Robert Barbers publicly acknowledged that the trial court judge was observing provisions of the Constitution and advised police to follow authorized procedures when making arrests.

According to the TFDP, the Government continued to detain more than 100 persons who have not been convicted of any offense (see Section 1.e.).

The NPA is responsible for some arbitrary arrests and detentions, often in connection with informal courts set up to try civilians and local politicians for "crimes against the people." Many defendants in such trials are tortured or summarily executed. Breakaway leaders of the CPP have been at particular risk for such "people's court" trials.

Forced exile is illegal and is not practiced.

e. *Denial of Fair Public Trial.*—The Constitution provides for an independent judiciary, but the judicial system suffers from corruption and inefficiency.

The national court system consists of four levels: local and regional trial courts, a national Court of Appeals divided into 15 divisions, a 15-member Supreme Court, and an informal local system for arbitrating or mediating certain problems, and which operates outside the formal court system.

The Constitution provides that those accused of crimes be informed of charges against them, have the right to counsel, and be provided with a speedy and public trial. Defendants are presumed innocent and have the right to confront witnesses against them, to present evidence, and to appeal convictions. The authorities generally respect the right of defendants to be represented by a lawyer. There is no jury system under the law; all cases are heard by judges. The judiciary is perceived as biased in favor of the rich and influential. Corruption extends to jails and prisons.

According to the NGO Alterlaw, personal connections, patronage, influence peddling, and bribery are some of the most common "unorthodox" methods used in the practice of law. Legal experts in and outside the justice system also criticize personal and professional relationships between judges and the individuals and corporations whose cases they are assigned. Some law firms, known in that profession as case fixers, gain the favor of judges and other court officials, and bribe some witnesses. While it is technically illegal to settle criminal cases out of court, the practice of reaching an "amicable settlement" is routine; without key victims or witnesses to testify, the authorities are forced to abandon their case. The Government has been unable, for the most part, to take effective action to intervene in these situations.

The pace of justice is slow. The court system is unable to assure detained persons expeditious trials. In July a Manila newspaper published the appeal of a man who had been wrongfully imprisoned for 20 years. He had been imprisoned from 1974 to 1991 on an illegal sentence imposed by a military court. He was released following intervention by the U.N. Human Rights Commission and the CHR.

There is a widely recognized need for more prosecutors, judges, and courtrooms. According to the Constitution, cases are to be resolved within set time limits once submitted for decision: 24 months for the Supreme Court; 12 for the Court of Appeals, and 3 months for lower courts. There are no time limits for trials. Because of numerous technical delays and frequent failures of judges and prosecutors to appear, trials can last many months. Police who cut short the investigative process by extracting forced confessions contribute to lengthy court dockets, as judges reject such breaches of due process. In July a regional trial court acquitted six Pakistanis who had been accused of terrorism; the evidence suggested that the police may have planted evidence against the defendants.

In May President Ramos appointed a new DILG Secretary, Robert Barbers, to counter growing criticism of failures in law enforcement. In a high profile case, Barbers personally arrested a town mayor suspected of murdering political rival and human rights activist Clarence Agarao in an attempt to show that an official was not above the law.

In July the NBI filed rape charges against a provincial police chief, the type of powerful local official who in earlier years might have been immune to prosecution. The "Vizconde Massacre" murder trial, whose defendants included an ex-policeman accused of destroying evidence and the sons of several prominent persons, including a sitting Senator, proceeded routinely—with all defendants remaining incarcerated for the duration. Barbers announced late in the year that he had dismissed more than 2,300 members of the police force for dereliction of duty.

Other developments, however, provided further examples of continued corruption in the police and judicial system and of impunity for the rich and powerful. The CHR indicated that 250 members of the PNP were involved in human rights violations in the first 6 months of the year. In October DILG Secretary Barbers and Justice Secretary Guingona quarreled over their respective agencies' failings. Barbers pointed to widespread inaction by prosecutors who fail to bring cases to court, despite clear evidence of criminality. Guingona in turn accused the Manila police of having failed to serve 3,500 warrants issued by judicial authorities. Guingona estimated that there were 30,000 unserved warrants nationwide and more than 50 cases of police refusal to testify in court.

After the May recapture of escaped murderer Rolito Go, it became clear that his ability to elude capture for years was due to help provided by many influential persons, including business associates, law enforcers, mayors, governors, journalists, entertainers, and government officials who could have helped return him to prison. A July Supreme Court decision criticized the performance of a provincial governor, police director, regional trial court judge, and jail warden, whose "connivance or inexcusable negligence" allowed three policemen convicted of murder to escape punishment. Also in July, a large police force assigned to arrest fugitive policemen who had killed four alleged car thieves who came from poor families failed to capture the fugitives; the hunted men reportedly slipped out of their hideaway 2 hours before the police force arrived. In July a 63-year-old woman complained that she had been violently assaulted and robbed at home by her daughter's 28-year-old friend. The alleged assailant was the youngest son of Vice President Joseph Estrada, head of the Presidential Anti-Crime Commission (PACC). Subsequently, the press reported the authorities' inability or unwillingness to prosecute the case. One month after the incident, the victim withdrew her complaint.

Corruption and impunity also tarnished the proceedings in older cases. For example, a case that began with the killing of 11 suspected bank robbers in May 1995 led to a Senate investigation and a conclusion that the police had deliberately and summarily executed the victims. After charges of procrastination, in November 1995 the Ombudsman's office finally indicted 27 policemen, including all four implicated senior officers. Despite this progress, the case had not come to trial by year's end. In February a Kuratong prosecutor reported receiving death threats, then withdrew from the case. A police witness placed under the Government's witness protection program said that a lawyer for the defense had offered him a bribe to clear the top officers. After newspaper criticism, prosecution witnesses charged that some investigators, including the Ombudsman, had links to the accused or their associates. In March the Ombudsman filed a revised indictment, reducing the charges against senior officers from the status of principals in the crime to that of accessories. The downgrading removed the case from the Sandiganbayan, a court for combating corruption, whose jurisdiction is limited to high ranking officials. The Ombudsman's decision sparked protests by key congressmen and human rights groups, calls for his impeachment, and efforts to restore the prior charges and status of the case. In October the U.N. Special Rapporteur on Summary and Arbitrary Execution criticized the Government's slow progress in the case. The Government claimed that it could not respond to the U.N.'s question because the case was still in the judicial process; at year's end, the case is unresolved.

The TFDP claims that the slow pace of justice resulted in about 175 political prisoners still being held illegally, of whom more than 100 have yet to be convicted of any offense. The Government disputes this charge, contending that it has released all political prisoners and that those held for allegedly political reasons are being detained for common crimes. It is likely that some of the prisoners in question have committed common crimes, such as illegal possession of firearms, in the pursuit of their political beliefs. It also is possible that some are actual or suspected Communists who were wrongfully convicted of common crimes. Proving this is difficult, however, and the burden of proof of unjust punishment or imprisonment is placed on the prisoner.

f. *Arbitrary Interference with Privacy, Family, Home, or Correspondence.*—The Constitution provides that search warrants may be issued by a judge on a finding of probable cause. Restrictions on search and seizure within private homes are generally observed, although searches without warrants do occur. Judges have declared evidence obtained illegally to be inadmissable.

The Government does not interfere with the free personal use of the mail or other public communications except upon issuance of a court order in the course of an investigation.

Contradictions remain in the law regarding squatters. Since 1992 forced eviction of squatters has been illegal, unless adequate notice and resettlement sites are provided. However, another law still in force makes squatting a criminal offense. Squatters' rights organizations call for this law's repeal on the grounds that classifying squatters as criminals is unfair, and that the law encourages the police to use violence when responding to a challenge to their authority. Although President Ramos has joined calls for repeal, others argued that repeal would make the practice legitimate.

Human rights NGO's have criticized government efforts to resettle tenant farmers and urban squatters to make way for infrastructure projects, and commercial and housing developments. The U.N. Committee on Economic, Social, and Cultural Rights expressed concern over reports of forced evictions. Government efforts to resettle squatters have been complicated by extensive poverty, the limited availability of affordable housing for the urban poor, and squatter syndicates that exploit human misery and legal safeguards for pecuniary or political ends. In some instances, government authorities have resorted to forced evictions when faced with repeated, organized squatter occupations of previously cleared land. Critics charged that accelerated government efforts to clear squatters out of areas in Manila, along key highways and railroad rights-of-way, were designed to improve the city's appearance before Asia-Pacific Economic Cooperation (APEC Summit) leaders met in Manila in November. Land rights problems are made more difficult by the slow process of the Government's exercise of eminent domain and complex zoning regulations.

g. *Use of Excessive Force and Violations of Humanitarian Law in Internal Conflicts.*—Despite an historic September peace agreement between the Government and the Moro National Liberation Front, a major Islamic insurgent group, occasional clashes between government and insurgent forces continued to inflict hardship on civilians. Most of the fighting took place in the Mindanao provinces, particularly North Cotabato, Maguindanao, Sultan Kudarat, and Basilan. According to the Ecumenical Commission for Displaced Families and Communities, 10 incidents of armed clashes in the first half of the year displaced some 7,400 families, or nearly 45,000 persons. Civilian casualties reportedly resulted from cannon and rocket fire, despite AFP efforts to limit the use of artillery in civilian areas.

Section 2. Respect for Civil Liberties, Including:

a. *Freedom of Speech and Press.*—The Constitution provides for freedom of speech and of the press, and the Government generally respects these rights in practice. A number of government officials and private persons either filed or threatened to file libel suits after being embarrassed by press reports. In August leaders in the House of Representatives threatened a libel suit against a newspaper critical of apparent bias by prominent members in favor of their own constituencies. They dropped the threat. Court decisions consistently rejected these suits. Columnist Herman Laurel was arrested in March, based on a complaint filed by the chairman of the autonomous Commission on Elections (Comelec) that he had falsified his citizenship when seeking public office in 1995. The complaint came in the wake of columns written by Laurel in which he criticized actions taken by Comelec and its chairman.

The hazards of reporting on corruption or exposing illegal activities such as gambling, logging, prostitution, and the drug trade among powerful individuals or vested interests are greatest outside Manila. Provincial editor and publisher Ferdinand Reyes, against whom some 30 libel cases had been filed, was killed on February 12 and, despite multiple police claims to have solved the case, his murderer remained at large. No arrest was made. Other provincial journalists and radio broadcasters, whose public affairs programs reach a much wider audience than either newspapers or television, were threatened by local police and government officials. In March two correspondents for national dailies were wounded by shots fired by an unidentified assailant.

In December a television reporter was killed at his home in Cavite after investigating drug trafficking; there were no arrests by year's end.

Despite a 1995 change in leadership, the government-appointed Movie and Television Review and Classification Board continued to censor films on the grounds that certain sexually related scenes were contrary to Philippine cultural values, customs, and morals. Electronic media access is unhindered.

The Government respects academic freedom.

b. *Freedom of Peaceful Assembly and Association.*—The Constitution provides for these rights, and the Government respects them in practice.

c. *Freedom of Religion.*—The Constitution provides for freedom of religion, and the Government respects this right in practice.

d. *Freedom of Movement Within the Country, Foreign Travel, Emigration, and Repatriation.*—Citizens enjoy the freedom to change their places of residence and employment. Travel abroad is limited only in rare circumstances, such as pending court cases or when government authorities try to discourage travel by vulnerable workers such as young women traveling to areas where they face personal risk (see Section 5).

The Government continued to allow approximately 1,910 asylum seekers from Vietnam to remain in the Philippines after the termination of the Comprehensive Plan of Action (CPA) on June 30. All these asylum seekers have been "screened out" from refugee status in accordance with CPA provisions. Approximately 1,020 of these remain in a first asylum camp in Palawan, while approximately 890 have fled into the population.

The Government continued to encourage voluntary repatriation of the screened out asylum seekers and has ruled out forcible repatriation. There is significant government and nongovernmental support (particularly from the Catholic Church) for allowing the screened out asylum seekers who do not wish to repatriate and who are ineligible for resettlement in third countries to remain in the Philippines permanently.

Section 3. Respect for Political Rights: The Right of Citizens to Change Their Government

The Constitution provides citizens with the right to change their government peacefully, and citizens exercise this right through periodic elections. Congress has yet to enact, however, a system for absentee voting, as required by the Constitution. This provision affects an estimated 4 million potential voters or about 10 percent of the electorate, most of whom are expatriates. In June Congress passed a measure easing domestic registration requirements.

An estimated 70 to 75 percent of registered voters participated in 1995 national and local elections that confirmed the control of a loose progovernment coalition in both the House of Representatives and the Senate. The hand-counting of millions of paper ballots delayed the official announcement of election results and contributed, according to the National Movement for Free Elections, to cheating that distorted the tallies in certain Senate races.

Additional details of 1995 election fraud became public in 1996 as a result of an election protest filed by former Senator Aquilino Pimentel with the Senate Electoral Tribunal. Pimentel alleged that he was victimized by a systematic campaign of vote tampering, "Operation Dagdag-Bawas" (literally "Addition-Subtraction"), which boosted the votes of rivals at his expense. While several Senators warned that delay in resolving the matter would adversely affect the Senate's credibility, and newspaper editorials criticized Comelec for errors in its slow operation, the most effective protest emerged from within Comelec itself. In June senior Commission staffers protested the Chairman's indecision and delay in resolving major issues and the Commission's failure to prosecute those responsible for the Dagdag-Bawas operation and other irregularities.

In 1996 the Government achieved significant gains in peace talks with insurgent groups, which had begun in 1995. In September government negotiators reached a peace agreement with the largest Muslim insurgent group, the Moro National Liberation Front (MNLF), which settled several basic disputes. These included the establishment of a transitional regional council for peace and development in Mindanao, headed by the MNLF, and MNLF participation in elections for the government of the Autonomous Region of Muslim Mindanao (ARMM). After 3 years, a new regional government is to be created and a plebiscite held to determine which provinces will form part of the reconstituted autonomous zone.

In July the Government resumed negotiations with the Joma Sison-led faction of the CPP. These talks had stalled in 1995 over the release of a captured NPA leader. Progress remained slow, however, with Communist negotiators insisting on receiving "belligerency" status.

There are no restrictions in law or practice on participation by women and minorities in politics. Three women head cabinet departments, 4 of the 24 Senators are women, 23 of the 204 elected members of the House are women, and 2 additional women serve as appointed "sectoral" members of the House.

Section 4. Governmental Attitude Regarding International and Nongovernmental Investigation of Alleged Violations of Human Rights

A wide variety of human rights groups operate without government restriction, investigating and publishing their findings on human rights cases. Government officials are generally cooperative and responsive to their views. The Philippine Alliance of Human Rights Advocates (PAHRA), a leading NGO network, reported that official harassment of human rights workers continued, but on a reduced scale. They cited the initiative of local military or police commanders.

The Manila office of Amnesty International hosted a September conference on Human Rights in China. A major coalition of human rights and labor groups hosted the Asia Pacific regional conferences during the November APEC meetings.

Section 5. Discrimination Based on Race, Sex, Religion, Disability, Language, or Social Status

The Constitution prohibits discrimination against women, children, and members of minorities. Implementation of constitutional protections is at times hindered by lack of implementing legislation and by budgetary constraints.

Women.—Violence against women, particularly domestic violence, is a serious problem. The Women's Crisis Center, an NGO assisting abused and battered women, reported that it receives over 100 calls per week from battered women in the metropolitan Manila area. Women's advocates cite the lack of laws on domestic violence, double standards of morality, and a traditional societal reluctance to discuss private family affairs as some of the reasons for domestic violence. The absence of divorce under the law and the lack of job opportunities combine to limit the ability of both poor and wealthy women to escape destructive relationships.

Nonetheless, women's rights advocates describe the greater willingness of women to speak out, despite a sense of shame, fear, and a desire to preserve "family honor," as a positive movement toward gender equality. Working in conjunction with NGO's, the Government's Bureau of Women's Welfare supports temporary shelters to protect female victims from further harm and high risk situations. Bureau officials believe that these programs, along with changing attitudes, accounted for the increase in batterings reported to authorities, which more than doubled between 1994 and 1995 and continued to increase in 1996. Both the Bureau and the PNP maintain a Women's Help Desk to protect women and encourage the reporting of crimes. PNP stations include female as well as male officers who, with help from NGO's, receive gender-sensitivity training in dealing with victims of sexual crimes and domestic violence.

Rape continues to be a major problem, and reports of rape continued to increase. Public pressure on Congress to enact reform legislation mounted. Both houses passed a measure introduced in 1994 to change the definition of rape, classifying it as a crime against a person instead of a crime against chastity, which is punishable only under the civil code. Controversial provisions in the bill would make marital rape a crime, expand the definition of rape, rule out sexual history as an issue in rape prosecution, and allow a rape victim's family or the State to file a complaint on the victim's behalf. It awaited conference committee agreement at year's end.

As with battering, government officials attributed the increase in reported rape to changing attitudes. Women's groups charge that the male-dominated law enforcement and judicial systems treat accused rapists leniently. For example, they cited the August dismissal of a rape complaint brought by the 42-year-old executive director of the Davao Chamber of Commerce against a 61-year-old local businessman and past president of that organization. Judicial authorities held that the alleged victim's complaint was not credible because, as a highly educated career woman, it was not possible for her to have been cowed into submission. Such paralysis and refusal to fight back, they asserted, could be an expected response only of a young, immature, and unlettered female.

While rape trials entailed the risk of the victim's own behavior, the restored death penalty emerged as a further factor inhibiting victims from pressing charges. Convictions for rape could and often did result in imposition of a death sentence (approximately half of all capital punishment convictions involved rape).

Women and girls in the lower economic stratums seek economic improvement through employment overseas. They are particularly vulnerable to exploitation by unethical recruiters who promise jobs abroad or, in some cases, arrange marriages with foreign men. Some find work only as prostitutes or suffer abuse at the hands of their foreign employers or husbands. Those recruited to work as maids, entertainers, or models may, while overseas, be forced to participate in public shows or dances where nudity and the prospect of sex is the principal attraction. Others knowingly accept questionable jobs to support parents, children, or siblings with their remittances. To curb such abuses, the Government campaigned to end illegal recruiting and, by raising age, educational, and professional standards for young women seeking jobs abroad, tried to discourage employment migration. The Migrant Workers and Overseas Filipinos Act of 1995 sought to provide the Government with greater financial resources and improved authority to combat these problems. NGO's agreed unanimously that these measures were not adequate.

Prostitution remains illegal, but widespread, and a fact of life for many poorer Filipinos with otherwise limited economic and job opportunities. While penalties for prostitution are light, detained prostitutes are subjected to administrative indignities. Public pressure mounted for legal action to be directed not only against prostitutes but also against their employers and clients seeking their services.

In law but not in practice, women have most of the rights and protections accorded men. The Women in Development and Nation Building Act of 1992 terminated previous restrictions on women's rights to buy and sell property. Lack of public awareness and limited governmental implementing machinery limit the effectiveness of this reform.

Church opposition to divorce in this overwhelmingly Catholic nation is strong. Changes in the Legal Code have made marriage annulment fairly easy, and the practice has become more frequent. The legal cost, however, precludes this option for many women. The practice of "unofficial divorce" (permanent separation) is common among lower income families; in these cases the wife is usually left with the children, and the husband provides little or no financial support.

Except for government service and jobs in Government-owned or controlled corporations, women face discrimination in employment. Among administrative, executive, and managerial workers, the average woman's salary is only one-third that of her male counterparts.

Sexual harassment is also a problem. A recent survey by the Institute of Labor Studies found workplace sexual harassment to be widespread, yet underreported due to victims' reticence and fear of losing their jobs. In February a city health officer in Cagayan de Oro was forced to take a leave of absence after nine women complained that he had harassed them. In July the Supreme Court dismissed a regional trial court judge after a series of accusations of harassment.

Children.—Several government agencies have programs devoted to the education, welfare, and development of children. The CHR's Child Rights Center (CRC), which opened in 1994, is designed to monitor and investigate violations of children's rights. Reflecting generally increased societal awareness of abuse against women and children, the CRC's case load rose more than 50 percent above its 1995 level. Lack of funding, incomplete interagency coordination, and failure to institutionalize sensitivity to children's needs among the agencies tasked to carry out enforcement limit the Government's ability to achieve its protection objectives.

The Intercountry Adoption Act of 1995, which strengthened safeguards against the sale and trafficking of children abroad, expanded on children's rights legislation enacted in 1992 and 1993. In June the Philippines ratified the Hague Convention on the Protection of Children and Cooperation in Respect of Intercountry Adoption. Children's rights advocates criticized the Congress' failure to pass previously introduced legislation that would have created children's and family courts to handle juvenile and domestic relations cases. As traditional societal values define children as extensions and property of the parents, ordinary courts favor parental authority over the rights of a child.

A conference on children's rights and the media was held in Manila in July. Members of the media, the academic community, government officials, and NGO's discussed the often adverse media effect on children, prostitution of children, and sex tourism. Subsequently, two foreigners accused of pedophilia were tried, convicted, and jailed.

Widespread poverty hindered government efforts to eradicate organized abuses involving the commercial sexual exploitation of children. A disastrous fire in March in a fashionable Manila discotheque, which resulted in the death of over 150 people, highlighted the appeal that illegal employment holds for some minors. The victims included "guest relations officers" who, as with other teenagers working in brothels, bars, and massage parlors, were lured to commercial sex jobs by the prospect of high incomes. Manila municipal officials shut down some sexually oriented establishments employing minors. Notwithstanding such efforts, 60,000 children according to UNICEF estimates, remained as prostitutes and victims of pedophilia.

As with women's issues, greater public awareness eroded traditional reticence to report abuses against children. Reports of rape, incest, and other forms of abuse mounted, with trials leading to conviction and harsh sentences, usually life imprisonment or death. As in 1995, of some 200 men sentenced to die by year's end, over half had been found guilty of rape and, of these, most had abused children under 15 years of age.

Rape figured in another area of child abuse highlighted during the year. Fifteen-year-old Sarah Balabagan, sent in 1994 to work as a domestic in Abu Dhabi, killed her 58-year-old employer as he sexually assaulted her. The Philippine press and public strongly criticized the decision of a Muslim court in Abu Dhabi, which tried and sentenced her to death. With her release from prison and return home in August, government authorities had to face other distressing aspects of her experience: the connivance between parents, recruiters, and corrupt government officials that produced falsified documents giving her age as 27. There were also similar cases in which parents knowingly conspired to exploit their children by sending them abroad to work.

Street begging and truancy are common in large cities. The CHR estimates the number of street orphans in metropolitan Manila at fewer than 1,000, but up to 100,000 destitute children spend most of their waking hours on the streets. The insurgency in Mindanao and other southern islands added to Manila's street children problem.

People With Disabilities.—A 1983 law provides for equal physical access for the disabled to all public buildings and establishments, and a law passed in 1992 provides for "the rehabilitation, self-development, and self-reliance of disabled persons and their integration into the mainstream of society." Advocates for the rights of the disabled contend that these laws have been ineffective, as implementing regulations have not been published, and government programs are palliative rather than focused on reintegration.

Indigenous People.—Indigenous people live throughout the Philippines but primarily in the mountainous areas of northern Luzon and Mindanao. They account for 10 to 15 percent of the population. Although no specific laws discriminate against indigenous people, the remoteness of the areas many inhabit and cultural bias prevent their full integration into society. Their ability to participate meaningfully in decisions affecting their lands, cultures, traditions, and the allocation of natural resources is minimal. Because they inhabit mountainous areas also favored by guerrillas, indigenous people suffer disproportionately from counterinsurgency operations. In particular, indigenous children suffer disproportionately from a lack of basic services, health, and education.

Although the 1987 Constitution provides for the protection of the ancestral lands and cultures of indigenous people, the Government had not actively supported legislation to enforce these rights until late in the year. In the absence of such legislation, the Government has issued "certificates of ancestral land claims." Other measures affect ancestral lands in less benign ways. For example, development projects infringed on indigenous lands and rights. The Philippine Mining Act of 1995 continued a legislative trend promoting mining operations, hydroelectric dams, and other large-scale projects that force indigenous communities to relocate and abandon farming and hunting lands used for generations. In an August meeting with northern and southern Philippine indigenous group representatives, President Ramos stressed that "if development is to be for all Filipinos and not just for a privileged and powerful few, then we must assume the burdens of our ethnic people as a special and urgent concern." The Government's inability to strike an acceptable balance between protection of ancestral lands and economic development again hindered efforts to pass an Autonomy Act for northern Luzon's Cordillera region. The 1991 eruption of Mount Pinatubo displaced several thousand indigenous Aeta families as well as other residents of central Luzon.

Religious Minorities.—Muslims, who comprise about 5 percent of the population and reside principally in Mindanao and nearby islands, constitute the largest minority group in the country. They historically have been alienated from the dominant Christian majority, and government efforts to integrate Muslims into the political and economic fabric of the country have met with only limited success. Distrust of Muslim loyalty has occasionally led to police raids, such as that which occurred on March 18 in Tagig (suburban Manila), when able-bodied men were rounded up as suspected members of the ASG, MILF, or MNLF.

Philippine culture, with its emphasis on familial, tribal, and regional loyalties, creates informal barriers whereby access to jobs or resources is provided first to those of one's own family or group. Many Muslims claim that they continue to be underrepresented in senior civilian and military positions.

In June government negotiations with the MNLF dramatically improved prospects for better Christian-Muslim relations. In accordance with their agreement, a Southern Philippines Council on Peace and Development (SPCPD) was established to coordinate economic growth in 14 provinces in Mindanao. MNLF leaders were granted key leadership positions in the SPCPD, with provision for a Muslim religious council to advise it. The accord also provided for integrating MNLF fighters into the armed forces and police. The two sides expect this initiative to ease Christian and Muslim suspicions of each other and, by improving ethnic harmony and promoting economic growth, to bring the region political stability. Demonstrating his acceptance of the Philippine political system, MNLF Chairman Nur Misuari agreed to chair the SPCPD and run for governor of the ARMM, which was established in 1990 to meet the demand of Muslims for local autonomy in areas where they are a majority or a substantial minority. While portions of Mindanao's Christian population expressed fear of Muslim domination, both the Government and MNLF sought to allay these concerns.

Section 6. Worker Rights

a. *The Right of Association.*—The Constitution and laws provide for the right of workers, including public employees, to form and join trade unions. Although this right is exercised in practice, aspects of the public sector organization law restrict and discourage organizing. Trade unions are independent of the Government and generally free of political party control. Unions have the right to form or join federations or other labor groups.

Subject to certain procedural restrictions, strikes in the private sector are legal. However, a 1989 law stipulates that all means of reconciliation must be exhausted and that the strike issue has to be relevant to the labor contract or the law.

In February 1995, the Committee of Experts of the International Labor Organization (ILO) noted that certain amendments have been proposed to legislation that the Committee had previously criticized for placing undue restrictions on the right to strike in nonessential services. The Committee remains concerned by the imposition of penalties in cases where strikes have been deemed illegal, by restrictions on the right of government workers to strike, by some restrictions on the right to organize and form a bargaining unit which are in conflict with ILO Convention 87 on freedom of association, and by limitations on the right to elect workers' representatives freely.

The number of strikes declined in the first 6 months of 1996, with 44 cases reported (as compared with 63 during the same period in 1995). Workdays lost to work stoppages declined even further, from 266,000 to 131,000. Workers involved in industrial disputes decreased from 38,670 to 8,564.

In March the ILO's Committee on Freedom of Association issued a finding that substantiated Trade Union Congress of the Philippines (TUCP) and International Confederation of Free Trade Union (ICFTU) charges of worker rights violations at the Danao (Cebu province) plant of Japanese manufacturer Mitsumi. The case, which began with a February 1994 petition by local union officials to the Department of Labor and Employment (DOLE) to hold a certification election, included the arrest of top union officials on spurious criminal (drug) charges, the repeated setting and postponing of elections, and management efforts to prevent workers from participating, or voting freely, in such elections.

According to the Center for Trade Union and Human Rights (CTUHR), which publicizes allegations of worker rights violations, attacks on striking workers declined from earlier years. The CTUHR documented 39 incidents in the first 6 months of 1996, involving 779 worker-victims. This contrasts with 107 incidents and 7,673 victims in 1995. Although the police continued to be involved in many of these cases, the CTUHR noted an upsurge of incidents initiated by management.

Unions have the right to affiliate with international trade union confederations and trade secretariats. Two of the largest trade union centrals, the TUCP and the FFW, are affiliated with the ICFTU and the World Confederation of Labor (WCL) respectively.

b. *The Right To Organize and Bargain Collectively.*—The Constitution provides for the right to organize and bargain collectively. The Labor Code provides for this right for private sector employees and for employees of government-owned or controlled corporations, but current law limits the rights of government workers. Although unions claim to have organized some 12 percent of the total work force of 29.1 million, fewer than 600,000 workers (2 percent) are covered by collective bargaining agreements. Unions oppose government efforts to loosen prohibitions against "labor only" subcontracting. Unions prefer to criminalize this practice, which they claim allows unscrupulous employers to use subcontractors to evade obligations to their employees and to break unions.

Some employers intimidated workers trying to form a union with threats of firing, factory closure or, as happened at Mitsumi, the filing of criminal charges against labor leaders. Allegations of intimidation and discrimination in connection with union activities are grounds for review as possible unfair labor practices before the National Labor Relations Commission (NLRC). Before disputes reach the time-consuming, quasi-judicial NLRC, the DOLE provides the services of the National Conciliation and Mediation Board (NCMB). The NCMB settles most of the unfair labor practice disputes raised as grounds for strikes before such strikes can be declared.

Labor law is uniform throughout the country, including export processing zones (EPZ's). However, local officials in most of the EPZ's and the Special Economic Zones have tried to frustrate organizing efforts by maintaining "union free/strike free" policies. The 1995 election defeat of one such official, the Governor of Cavite, opened the way for significant union organizing gains both in the EPZ and Cavite province itself.

c. *Prohibition of Forced or Compulsory Labor.*—Forced labor is prohibited, and the Government effectively enforces this prohibition.

The Government's efforts to protect workers from abuse also extends to the large number of Philippine workers overseas. By raising the issue in bilateral contacts and international forums, it attempts to secure firmer guarantees of basic rights for guest workers and otherwise provides assistance through its diplomatic missions.

d. *Minimum Age for Employment of Children.*—The law prohibits the employment of children below the age of 15, except under the direct and sole responsibility of parents or guardians or where employment in cinema, theater, radio, or television is essential. The Labor Code allows employment for those between the ages of 15 and 18 for such hours and periods of the day as are determined by the Secretary of Labor, but it forbids employment of persons under 18 years of age in hazardous or dangerous work. However, a significant number of children under the legal are are employed in the informal sector of the urban economy or as unpaid family workers in rural areas. In the formal sector, instances of child labor are few. Some children continued to be employed in a dangerous form of coral reef fishing, which exposes them to shark and needlefish attacks and increases their vulnerability to disease.

In addition to projects undertaken with the U.N. Children's Fund and the ILO's International Program for the Elimination of Child Labor (IPEC), the DOLE investigated and attempted to reduce violations of child labor laws outside the agricultural sector through publicized raids on reported violators. The DOLE's raids were coordinated with police and, at times, with personnel from concerned NGO's, especially the Kamalayan Development Foundation. Heightened public awareness led to greater cooperation by local authorities, increased involvement by government agencies, and prosecution of violators. By year's end, however, none of these prosecutions had led to a conviction and sentencing. Kamalayan also complained of shortcomings in government efforts to rehabilitate and reintegrate rescued children into society.

e. *Acceptable Conditions of Work.*—Tripartite regional wage boards set minimum wages. The latest round of wage increases occurred in late 1995 and early 1996, with the highest rates set in the National Capital region (NCR) and the lowest in rural regions. The minimum wage for NCR nonagricultural workers is approximately $6.30 (P165) per day. This wage represents a 13.8 percent nominal increase over the previous minimum for the region. With this amount, at least two family members would have to work (one full-time, one part-time) to support a family of six above the Government's "poverty threshold." Regional board wage orders cover all private sector workers except domestic helpers and those employed in the personal service of another. Boards outside the NCR exempted some employers because of factors such as establishment size, industry sector, involvement with exports, financial distress, and level of capitalization. These exemptions excluded substantial additional numbers of workers from coverage under the law. DOLE surveys in the first several months of 1996 showed that some 22 percent of inspected establishments violated the minimum wage law. Given the difficulty of prosecuting cases through the courts, the DOLE relies on administrative procedures and moral suasion to encourage voluntary employer correction of violations.

The standard legal workweek is 48 hours for most categories of industrial workers and 40 hours for government workers, with an 8 hour per day limit. An overtime rate of 125 percent of the hourly rate is mandated on ordinary days and 130 percent on rest days and holidays. The law mandates a full day of rest weekly. Enforcement of workweek hours is managed through periodic inspections by the DOLE.

A comprehensive set of occupational safety and health standards exists in law. Although policy formulation and review of these standards is the responsibility of the DOLE, actual enforcement is carried out by an inspectorate corps of some 260 labor and employment officers in 14 regional offices. Statistics on actual work-related accidents and illnesses are incomplete, as incidents (especially in regard to agriculture) are underreported. Workers do not have a legally protected right to remove themselves from dangerous work situations without jeopardy to continued employment.

SINGAPORE

Singapore, a city-state of 3.4 million people, is a parliamentary republic in which politics is dominated by the People's Action Party (PAP), which has held power since Singapore gained autonomy from the United Kingdom in 1959. The PAP holds 77 of the 81 elected seats in Parliament. Goh Chok Tong completed his sixth year as Prime Minister. Lee Kuan Yew, who served as Prime Minister from independence in 1965 until 1990, remains active politically, holding the title of Senior Minister. The majority of the population is ethnic Chinese (78 percent), with Malays and Indians constituting substantial minorities.

The Government maintains active internal security and military forces to counter perceived threats to the nation's security. It has frequently used security legislation to control a broad range of activity. The Internal Security Department (ISD) is responsible for enforcement of the Internal Security Act (ISA), including its provisions for detention without trial. All young males are subject to national service (mostly in the military).

Singapore has an open free market economic system. The construction and financial services industries and manufacturing of computer-related components are key sectors of the economy, which has achieved remarkably steady growth since independence. Gross domestic product rose a projected 8.8 percent in 1996, and citizens have an annual per capita gross domestic product of more than $24,000. Wealth is distributed relatively equally in what is essentially a full-employment economy.

Although there were problems in some areas, the Government generally respected the human rights of its citizens. The Government continued to intimidate opposition parties and their candidates and to restrict the independence of the judiciary in cases with political implications or affecting members of the ruling party. The Government has wide powers to detain people arbitrarily and subsequently restrict their travel, freedom of speech, and right to associate freely, and to handicap political opposition. There was no evidence of a change in the Government's willingness to restrict these human rights when it deemed that necessary in pursuit of its policy goals. The Government restricts press freedom and intimidates journalists into practicing self-censorship. There is some legal discrimination against women, which affects only a small percentage of the population. The Government has moved actively to counter societal discrimination against women and minorities. While freedom of religion is generally respected, the Jehovah's Witness organization has been banned since 1972.

RESPECT FOR HUMAN RIGHTS

Section 1. Respect for the Integrity of the Person, Including Freedom From:

a. *Political and Other Extrajudicial Killing.*—There were no reports of political or other extrajudicial killings.

Three prison officers pleaded guilty to manslaughter for causing the death of a prisoner in August 1995 (see Section 1.c.).

b. *Disappearance.*—There were no reports of politically motivated disappearances.

c. *Torture and Other Cruel, Inhuman, or Degrading Treatment or Punishment.*—The law prohibits torture, and government leaders have stated that they oppose its use. However, there have been credible reports in past years of police mistreatment of detainees. Reliable reports indicate that police have sometimes employed sleep deprivation or interrogation of detainees in very cold rooms where the prisoners may be stripped of their clothes and doused with water. In 1993, the last year for which statistics are available, of the 94 complaints of police abuse investigated, 14 were substantiated.

The Government reserves the right to use indefinite detention without trial to pressure detainees to "rehabilitate" themselves as well as to make admissions of wrongdoing. In the past, the Government has acknowledged that, in the case of detentions without trial under the Criminal Law (Temporary Provisions) Act (CLA), the indefinite nature of the detentions served to pressure the detainees. Persons alleging mistreatment under detention may bring criminal charges against government officials who are alleged to have committed such acts, but they may be discouraged from making accusations for fear of official retaliation (see Sections 1.d. and 1.e.).

The Penal Code mandates caning, in addition to imprisonment, as punishment for some 30 offenses involving the use of violence or threat of violence against a person, such as rape, robbery and extortion. The law also mandates caning in other areas, such as for certain convictions under the Vandalism Act and for specific immigration and drug-trafficking offenses.

Caning is discretionary for convictions on other charges involving the use of criminal force, such as kidnaping, or voluntarily causing grievous hurt. The law prescribes a maximum or minimum number of cane strokes in many of these cases, although the court does not always abide by these guidelines. Women are exempted from caning, as are men over 50, under 16, and those determined unfit by a medical officer. In 1993, the last year for which statistics are available, the courts included a caning sentence in 3,244 cases.

Prison conditions are generally good and meet minimum international standards. Some abuses have occurred and have been reported in the press. In March, for example, three prison officials pleaded guilty to manslaughter for causing the death of a prisoner in August 1995. The Government had responded quickly to the abuse and publicly denounced all abuses of power by prison officials. The Government does not allow human rights monitors to visit prisons.

d. *Arbitrary Arrest, Detention, or Exile.*—The Internal Security Act, the Criminal Law (Temporary Provisions) Act, the Misuse of Drugs Act (MDA), and the Undesirable Publications Act all have provisions for arrest without warrant. Those arrested must be charged before a magistrate within 48 hours. At that time, those detained under criminal charges may obtain legal counsel. A functioning system of bail exists for those charged, and there were no reported abuses of it.

The ISA, the CLA, and the MDA authorize detention without trial. The CLA is used almost exclusively in cases involving narcotics and secret criminal societies and has not been used for political purposes. According to the Government, the cumulative number of persons currently detained under the CLA as of July 1995, the last period for which statistics are available, was 570, of whom 248 were for secret society activities and 322 for drug trafficking. Under the MDA, the Director of the Central Narcotics Bureau may also commit—without trial—suspected drug users to a drug rehabilitation center for up to 6 months, with subsequent extensions, in cases of positive urinalysis tests.

Those persons detained without trial under the ISA are entitled to counsel but have no legal recourse through the courts to challenge the substantive basis for their detention. Persons detained without trial under the CLA are also entitled to counsel but may only challenge the substantive basis for their detention to the committee advising the Minister for Home Affairs on detention issues. The ISA gives broad discretion to the Minister of Home Affairs to order detention without charges if the President determines that a person poses a threat to national security. The President may authorize detention for up to 2 years; the detention order may be renewed for 2-year periods with no limitation on renewal. An advisory board reviews each detainee's case periodically, and detainees may make representations to it. The board may make nonbinding recommendations that a detainee be released prior to expiration of the detention order. If the Minister wishes to act contrary to a recommendation for release by the board, he must seek the agreement of the President.

The ISA empowers the police to detain a person for up to 48 hours; any police officer at or above the rank of superintendent may authorize that the detainee be held for up to 28 days longer. Once initial interrogation has been completed, the authorities have generally allowed ISA detainees access to lawyers and visits by relatives.

No one has been jailed under formal ISA detention since 1990. However, the Government has maintained some restrictions on the rights of two former ISA detainees to travel abroad, make public statements, and associate freely. Chia Thye Poh, a former Member of Parliament, was released from prison in 1989 after 23 years in preventive detention under the ISA but was confined to a small island adjacent to Singapore during evening and night hours until 1992. Now resident in Singapore proper, he cannot be employed, travel abroad, issue public statements, or associate with other former detainees without ISD approval. Vincent Cheng, a detainee released in 1990, could not issue public statements, publish, or travel abroad without ISD consent until July 1995, when the ISD removed the restriction order against him.

The Constitution prohibits exile, and the Government respects the prohibition in practice.

e. *Denial of Fair Public Trial.*—The Constitution provides for an independent judiciary, but the Government restricts the independence of the judiciary in practice through its control over the assignment of judges and through laws limiting judicial review. In 1989 the Government amended the Constitution and the ISA to eliminate judicial review of the objective grounds for detentions under the ISA and subversion laws. This allows the Government to restrict, or even eliminate, judicial review in such cases and thereby restrict, on vaguely defined national security grounds, the scope of certain fundamental liberties provided for in the Constitution.

The judicial system has two levels of courts: The Supreme Court, which includes the High Court and the Court of Appeal; and the subordinate courts. The President appoints judges to the Supreme Court on the recommendation of the Prime Minister in consultation with the Chief Justice. The President also appoints subordinate court judges on the recommendation of the Chief Justice. The term of appointment is determined by the Legal Service Commission of which the Chief Justice is the chairman. Subordinate court judges and magistrates, as well as public prosecutors, are civil servants whose specific assignments are determined by the Legal Service Commission, which can decide on job transfers to any of several legal service departments. Supreme Court Justices may remain in office until the mandatory retirement age of 65, after which they may continue to serve at the Government's discretion for brief, renewable terms at full salary. Judicial officials, especially in the Supreme Court, have close ties to the ruling party and its leaders.

In February 1994, completing a transition begun in 1989, Parliament approved a bill abolishing all appeals to the Privy Council in London. The single Court of Appeal, established in 1993, combining the former Court of Appeal (for civil cases) and Court of Criminal Appeal, therefore became the highest court of review in Singapore.

The judicial system provides citizens with an efficient judicial process. In normal cases the Criminal Procedures Code provides that a charge against a defendant must be read and explained to him as soon as it is framed by the prosecution or the magistrate. Defendants enjoy a presumption of innocence and the right of appeal, in most cases. They normally have the right to be present at their trials, to be represented by an attorney, to confront witnesses against them, to provide witnesses and evidence on their own behalf, and to review government-held evidence relevant to their cases.

The Constitution extends the above rights to all citizens. However, persons detained under the ISA and the MDA are not entitled to a public trial (see Section 1.d.). In all remaining cases, trials are public and by judge; there are no jury trials. There were no reports of political prisoners.

f. *Arbitrary Interference with Privacy, Family, Home, or Correspondence.*—The Government can use its wide discretionary powers under the ISA if it determines that national security is threatened. In most cases, the law requires search warrants, normally issued by the magistrate court, for intrusion into the home. Law enforcement officers may, however, search a person, home, or property without a warrant if they decide that searches are necessary to preserve evidence.

The CLA and the MDA Act also permit warrantless searches in dealing with drug and secret society-related offenses. The courts may undertake judicial review of such searches at the request of the defendant. Divisions of the Government's law enforcement agencies, including the Internal Security Department and the Corrupt Practices Investigation Board (CPIB), have wide networks for gathering information. The authorities have the capability to monitor telephone and other private conversations and conduct surveillance. While there were no proven allegations that they did so in 1996, it is widely believed that the authorities routinely conduct surveillance on some opposition politicians and other critics of the Government.

Section 2. Respect for Civil Liberties, Including:

a. *Freedom of Speech and Press.*—The Constitution permits official restrictions on the freedom of expression and, in practice, the Government restricts the freedoms of speech and the press and intimidates journalists into practicing self-censorship.

The ISA permits the Government to prohibit or to place conditions on publications that incite violence, that counsel disobedience to the law, that might arouse tensions among the various classes (races, religions, and language groups), or that might threaten national interests, national security, or public order. The Government uses a broad definition of these laws to restrict political opposition and criticism. It is clear from recent events that the Government will not tolerate discussions in the press of alleged government corruption, nepotism, or a compliant judiciary.

All general circulation newspapers in all four official languages—English, Chinese, Malay, and Tamil—are owned by Singapore Press Holdings Ltd. (SPH), a private corporation that has close ties to the national leadership. SPH also owns 20 percent of Singapore Cablevision, which operates the expanding cable television system. SPH is required by law to issue ordinary and management shares; holders of management shares have the power to control all SPH personnel decisions. The Government must approve, and can remove, holders of management shares. Hence, while Singapore newspapers print a large and diverse selection of articles from their domestic and a variety of foreign sources, editorials and coverage of domestic events closely parallel government policies and the opinions of government leaders. Government leaders often criticize what they call the "Western model" of journalism, in which the media are free to report the news as they see it. Government officials argue that the role of the domestic media is to support the goals of the elected leadership.

A wide range of international magazines and newspapers may be purchased uncensored, although newspapers printed in Malaysia may not be imported. A 1990 law requires foreign publications that report on politics and current events in Southeast Asia to register, post a bond the equivalent of $141,100, and name a person in Singapore to accept legal service. These requirements strengthen government control over foreign media. The Government may ban the circulation of domestic and foreign publications under provisions of the ISA and the Undesirable Publications Act. Under amendments to the Newspaper and Printing Presses Act, it may limit the circulation of foreign publications which, by the Government's broad determination, interfere in Singapore's domestic politics. It has done so on occasion in the past.

The Asian Wall Street Journal (AWSJ), Asiaweek, and the Far Eastern Economic Review (FEER) are "gazetted" (limited in circulation). In July the Government relaxed restrictions and raised the limits for the FEER from 4,000 per issue to 6,000 per issue and the AWSJ from 7,000 per issue to 9,000 per issue. The limit for Asiaweek remained at 15,000 per issue.

Some publications are barred from importation, and the authorities censor movies, television programs, video materials, and music. Censorship of materials and the decision to deny the importation of specific publications are based on a determination that such materials would undermine the stability of the state, are pro-Communist, contravene moral norms, are pornographic, show excessive or gratuitous sex and violence, glamorize or promote drug use, or incite racial, religious, or linguistic animosities. The authorities report that there is strong public support for continued censorship of sex and violence in films.

The Singapore Broadcasting Authority (SBA) was established in 1994 to regulate and promote the broadcasting industry. The SBA develops censorship standards with the help of advisory panels whose membership represents a cross section of society. In July the SBA assumed responsibility for regulating access to the Internet. While the Government does not classify regulation of the Internet as censorship, access to web pages that undermine public security, national defense, racial and religious harmony, and public morals is banned. In addition, content that tends to bring the Government into hatred or contempt, or that excites disaffection against the Government is forbidden. In September Internet service providers were required to filter Internet access for the more than 120,000 Internet subscribers through proxy servers. These proxy servers are designed to prevent subscribers from seeing about a dozen sites, deemed to violate the government's ban. The list of banned sites is not a matter of public record.

The government-linked holding company, Singapore International Media PTE Ltd, has a near monopoly on broadcasting. Its 4 main subsidiaries operate all 4 free television channels and 10 of the 15 domestic radio stations. Of the five remaining radio stations, two are owned by the Ministry of Defense and two by the National Trade Union Conference (NTUC), which is closely affiliated with the Government. The only radio station not under government control is the British Broadcasting Corporation (BBC) World Service, which is available 24 hours a day. In addition to the BBC, Malaysian and Indonesian television and radio broadcasts are available. An expanded cable service, Singapore Cable Vision (SCV), jointly held by government-linked corporations and the U.S.-owned Continental Cablevision Company, began operation in June 1995. The island nation currently is being wired for a fiber-optic network. When the project is complete by the year 2000, more than 30 channels, including BBC and other international news and entertainment programs, will be available to subscribers. Cable News Network International, carried live, is available 24 hours a day on SCV's pay television. Satellite dishes are banned with few exceptions.

Journalists from foreign publications are required by law to apply annually for renewal of the employment pass that allows them to operate in Singapore. The Government continued to limit the amount of time that some foreign correspondents could remain in the country by denying requests for renewal of their employment passes, usually beyond a period of 3 years. The Government has denied requests in the past from several major publications to station correspondents in Singapore. Tension between the Government and foreign correspondents remained because of earlier government allegations that the "liberal western media" had carried out a "conspiracy" to undermine PAP rule and had engaged in irresponsible reporting in Singapore and abroad.

Government leaders sometimes use defamation suits or the threat of such actions to discourage public criticism. In July 1995, Prime Minister Goh Chok Tong, Senior Minister Lee Kuan Yew, and his son, Deputy Prime Minister Lee Hsien Loong, won a libel suit against the International Herald Tribune (IHT) for an article, published in August 1994, allegedly suggesting that the younger Lee was appointed to his post on account of his father. The plaintiffs sought damages in addition to a printed apology, which appeared in the newspaper on August 31, 1994. In June 1995, during a widely publicized public hearing to determine the scope of the judgment against the IHT, all three plaintiffs testified that the IHT did not apologize in good faith and demanded aggravated damages for the harm caused to their reputations. In July 1995, the High Court awarded a record defamation judgment of $678,000.

In January 1995, Dr. Christopher Lingle, an American academic who had been a visiting lecturer at the National University of Singapore, the IHT, and the Singapore printer were fined for contempt of court following the publication of an article about Asian governments by Lingle on October 7, 1994. Although Singapore was not mentioned in the article, the court focused on the article's reference to some governments as being "more subtle: Relying upon a compliant judiciary to bankrupt opposition politicians or buying out enough of the opposition to take control democratically" as a reference to Singapore. Although the IHT published an apology for the article in December 1994, Senior Minister Lee Kuan Yew filed a civil libel suit. The IHT agreed in November 1995, to pay the Senior Minister $213,000 in damages plus costs for the civil suit. Lingle was separately ordered by the courts in April to pay $71,000 in damages, plus costs, to the Senior Minister. In at least the two incidents cited above, the use of libel suits appears to have intimidated the press successfully.

Faculty members at public institutions of higher education are government employees. A number of university lecturers are concurrently PAP Members of Parliament (M.P.'s). Academics sometimes criticize government policies, but they avoid public criticism of individual government leaders and sensitive social and economic policies because of possible sanctions, such as in the cases of Christopher Lingle and Chee Soon Juan (see also Section 3). Publications by local academics and members of think tanks rarely deviate substantially from government views.

b. *Freedom of Peaceful Assembly and Association.*—The Constitution grants citizens the freedom of peaceful assembly and association but permits Parliament to impose restrictions "as it considers necessary or expedient in the interest of the security of Singapore." The Government restricts those rights in practice. Assemblies of more than five persons in public, including political meetings and rallies, must have police permission. Persons wishing to speak at a public function, excluding functions provided by or under the auspices of the Government, must obtain permission from the public entertainment licensing unit, a division of the Criminal Investigation Department. Opposition politicians routinely experience delays of 3 to 4 weeks before being notified of the disposition of their applications.

The Government closely monitors political gatherings regardless of the number present. Most associations, societies, clubs, religious groups, and other organizations with more than 10 members must be registered with the Government under the Societies Act. The Government denies registration to groups it believes likely to be used for unlawful purposes or for purposes prejudicial to public peace, welfare, or public order (see Section 2.c.). The Government has absolute discretion in applying this broad and vague language to register or dissolve societies. It prohibits organized political activities, except by organizations registered as political parties. This prohibition effectively limits opposition activities (see Section 3). It has less of an effect on the PAP, which enjoys the support of residential committees and neighborhood groups ostensibly organized for nonpolitical purposes but whose leadership contains many grassroots PAP members.

c. *Freedom of Religion.*—Freedom of religion is provided for in the Constitution and usually respected in practice. There is no state religion. The Government has determined that all residents of public housing should have access to religious organizations traditionally associated with their ethnic groups. It therefore provides some financial assistance to build and maintain mosques. The Government also facilitates contributions to the construction of Indian and Chinese temples.

Missionaries are permitted to work and to publish religious texts. However, all religious groups are subject to government scrutiny and must be legally registered. The Government restricts some religious groups by application of the Societies Act and has banned others, such as Jehovah's Witnesses and the Unification Church. The Government banned the former in 1972 on the grounds that it opposes military service, and its roughly 2,000 members refuse to perform military service, salute the flag, or swear oaths of allegiance to the State. In July a 72-year-old grandmother was arrested and convicted for possession of banned Jehovah's Witness literature. She was sentenced to a $500 fine. She refused to pay and was ordered to jail for 7 days. She was first arrested in February 1995, along with 69 other suspected Jehovah's Witnesses, at which time the police seized books, magazines, periodicals, and other materials believed to be related to the group. Of the 69 persons arrested, 28 were tried and found guilty of holding a meeting of a "banned society" and were fined between $500 and $2,000.

The 1990 Maintenance of Religious Harmony Act made illegal what the Government deems to be the inappropriate involvement of religious groups and officials in political affairs. The act also prohibits judicial review of any possible denial of rights arising from the act, and it specifically denies judicial review of its enforcement.

d. *Freedom of Movement Within the Country, Foreign Travel, Emigration, and Repatriation.*—The Constitution grants citizens the right to move freely throughout the country, though Parliament may pass laws restricting that right on the basis of "the security of Singapore * * * the public order, public health, or the punishment of offenders." The Government requires all citizens and permanent residents over the age of 12 to register and to carry identification cards. After the completion of national service, enlisted men are required to participate in reserve training until age 40 and officers to age 50. Reservists who plan to travel overseas for less than 6 months must advise the Ministry of Defense; for trips longer than 6 months, reservists must obtain an exit permit. Beginning at age 11, boys' passports are restricted to 6 months. Males approaching national service age must obtain an exit permit in order to study outside the country. Boys over the age of 17 1/2, who have not already obtained a deferment, cannot obtain an exit permit until they have at least begun their national service. The Goverment may refuse to issue a passport and has done so in the case of former ISA detainees.

The ISA allows the Ministers for Law and Home Affairs to suspend or revoke a detention order or to impose restrictions on former detainees' activities, places of residence, and travel abroad (see Section 1.d.). The right of voluntary repatriation is extended to holders of Singaporean passports. In 1985 Parliament provided for the loss of citizenship by Singaporeans who reside outside the country for more than 10 years consecutively. Action under this law is discretionary and has been taken in at least one case involving a well-known government opponent, Tan Wah Piaow.

The law stipulates that former Singaporean members of the Communist Party of Malaya (CPM) residing outside must apply to the Government to be allowed to return. They must renounce communism, sever all organizational ties with the CPM, and pledge not to take part in activities prejudicial to the State's internal security. In addition, the law requires them to be subject to interview by the ISD and to any restrictive conditions imposed on them.

Singapore neither accepted the Comprehensive Plan of Action for Indochinese seeking refugee status nor offered first asylum to refugees. Prior to 1991, the Government permitted Indochinese asylum seekers to disembark if a resettlement country promised to remove them within 90 days and if the rescuing vessel was in Singapore on a scheduled port of call. In June 1991, the Government halted disembarkation on the grounds that resettlement countries had not honored their guarantees of removal. Approximately 140 Vietnamese boat people were placed in an open camp in Singapore. All were interviewed to determine refugee status and a number were resettled in resettlement countries. Ninety-nine Vietnamese boat people were repatriated on June 29, under the United Nations High Commissioner for Refugees (UNHCR) voluntary repatriation program. Five other Vietnamese asylum seekers have been allowed to remain in Singapore. The authorities permit persons of other nationalities who make claims for asylum to have their status determined by the UNHCR for possible resettlement elsewhere.

Section 3. Respect for Political Rights: The Right of Citizens to Change Their Government

The Constitution provides citizens with the right to change their government peacefully through democratic means, and the voting and vote-counting systems in elections are fair, accurate, and free from tampering. In practice, however, the Government uses its extensive powers to place formidable obstacles in the path of political opponents. It also attempts to intimidate the opposition through the threat of libel suits and potential loss of employment or professional licenses. Parliamentary elections may be called at any time but must be held no later than 5 years from the date Parliament first sits.

Opposition parties have been unable seriously to challenge the PAP since the late 1960's. Consequently, the PAP's domination of the political system continues as it has for 3 decades under Lee Kuan Yew. Opposition politicians hold 4 seats in the 81-member elected Parliament, 3 for the Social Democratic Party and 1 for the Workers' Party. In addition to the 81 elected members, the President appoints 6 "prominent citizens" to serve as nominated M.P.'s for 2-year terms. The PAP's political success in part results from restrictions on opposition political activities, but also from government policies that helped Singapore achieve rapid economic growth, thereby enabling the Government to provide a wide array of public services. The PAP has a broad base of popular support, sustained in part through neighborhood, youth, and labor groups.

Although political parties are legally free to organize, the authorities impose strict regulations on their constitutions, fundraising, and accountability. While the PAP has been able to enjoy the support of ostensibly nonpolitical organizations, the Government has used its broad discretionary powers to hinder the creation of comparable support organizations for opposition parties. Singapore's economic success under the PAP has strengthened the party's leadership role. However, its grip on power has also been enhanced by: Patronage; political control of the press and the courts; strong party discipline; and access to the instruments of power. For example, during the December election campaign senior government officials pointedly warned voters that precincts that elected opposition candidates would have the lowest priority in extensive government plans to upgrade public housing facilities, heightening concerns among some observers about the degree of freedom of choice within the electorate. Government regulations also hinder attempts by opposition parties to rent office space in government housing or to establish community foundations for, among other purposes, running private kindergartens. In August the Government denied an opposition party request to produce and distribute video tapes on the grounds that visual images can be used to evoke emotional rather than rational responses. Moreover, according to the Government, the use of videos could allow political parties to sensationalize or distort information to capture the maximum attention of the viewer. The PAP claims that the lack of an effective opposition is due to disorganization, lack of leadership, and lack of alternative policy programs.

In August 1993, citizens elected their first president. The presidency has some powers over civil service appointments, government and statutory board budgets, and internal security affairs. Presidential aspirants must be certified by the Presidential Elections Committee (PEC), a body composed of the Chairman of the Public Service Commission, the Chairman of the Public Accountants Board, and a member of the Presidential Council for Minority Rights. The PEC was responsible for screening applicants on the basis of integrity, character, reputation, ability, and experience in managing the financial affairs of a large institution. Eligibility was considered automatic if the candidate had 3 years' experience as a high-ranking public servant or chief executive officer of a large corporation. These requirements limit the pool of potential presidential candidates. The Committee rejected the applications of two opposition figures—J.B. Jeyaretnam, Secretary General of the Workers' Party (WP) and a former M.P., and another WP member—for not satisfying the eligibility criteria regarding character and financial expertise.

The threat of civil libel or slander suits continues to discourage criticism or challenges by opposition leaders. The Legal Code also provides for criminal defamation offenses, but these provisions are seldom used.

The most recent example of the use of libel or slander suits by government entities to intimidate prominent opposition politicians was that of Chee Soon Juan, a lecturer at the National University of Singapore and Secretary General of the Singapore Democratic Party (SDP). Chee was dismissed from his teaching position in March 1993 for alleged irregularities involving his use of research funds and sued by his department chairman, S. Vasoo, a PAP M.P., for making allegedly defamatory remarks. Chee had to pay $200,000 in damages to Vasoo and two other university employees as compensation for his allegedly defamatory remarks.

The Government uses parliamentary censure or the threat of censure to humiliate or intimidate opposition leaders. For example, Parliament censured Chee Soon Juan and the SDP in November 1995 for allegedly endorsing attacks on the judiciary made by Chee's fellow panelists, dissident Francis Seow and academic Christopher Lingle, at a forum held in the United States at Williams College in September 1995. The Government did not attribute any statement directly attacking the judiciary or endorsing the views of Seow and Lingle to Chee or the SDP. Instead, government parliamentary leaders said that the failure of Chee and other SDP leaders to contradict the attacks made by Seow and Lingle constituted positive assent by "clever omission." In December Parliament levied fines in excess of $36,000 against Chee and three other SDP members, claiming that they had committed perjury and other offenses during the proceedings of a special parliamentary committee examining government health care subsidies. Parliament accused the opposition party of fabricating statistics about the extent of these subsidies in a written submission and subsequent testimony to the committee. Chee and his colleagues claimed that they had submitted some incorrect figures to the committee in error but that they had not intended to mislead anyone.

Although there is no legal bar to the participation of women in politics, they are underrepresented in Parliament. There are no female cabinet members, and only 2 of the 81 elected parliamentary seats are occupied by women. Two of the six nominated Members of Parliament are women. Women occupy 128 of 560 positions at the senior levels of the civil service, although they occupy none of the top 29 positions.

There is no restriction in law or practice against minorities voting or participating in politics. Malays comprise 14 percent of the general population and currently hold 12 percent of the seats in Parliament. Indians make up 7 percent of the general population and hold 9 percent of the seats in Parliament. Minority representation in Parliament is in part the result of laws requiring a minority representative in selected group constituencies.

Section 4. Governmental Attitude Regarding International and Nongovernmental Investigation of Alleged Violations of Human Rights

There are no nongovernmental organizations, with the exception of the opposition political parties, that actively and openly monitor alleged human rights violations. While the Government does not formally prohibit them, efforts by any independent organization to investigate and criticize publicly government human rights policies would face the same obstacles as those faced by political parties. The Government denies that international organizations have any competence whatsoever to look into human rights matters in Singapore. Visa regulations do not recognize monitoring human rights as a "business purpose" for visiting the country, but neither is such activity regarded as a "social visit." Amnesty International is not allowed to operate in, or to visit, Singapore. The Government continued to allege a "conspiracy" between the "liberal Western media" (see Section 2.a.) and international human rights organizations and other institutions which it claimed were intent on undermining its rule.

Section 5. Discrimination Based on Race, Sex, Religion, Disability, Language, or Social Status

The Constitution contains no explicit provision providing equal rights for women and minorities; instead, it states that all persons are equal before the law and entitled to the equal protection of the law. Mindful of Singapore's history of intercommunal tension, the Government takes affirmative measures to ensure racial, ethnic, religious, and cultural nondiscrimination. Social, economic, and cultural facilities are available to all citizens regardless of race, religion, or sex. Minorities actively participate in the political process, and are well represented throughout the Government.

Women.—There is no evidence of any widespread practice of violence or abuse against women. Laws such as the Penal Code and the Women's Charter protect women against domestic violence and sexual or physical harassment. A battered wife can obtain court orders barring the spouse from the home until the court is satisfied that he will stop his aggressive behavior. The Penal Code prescribes mandatory caning and a minimum imprisonment of 2 years for conviction on a charge of "outraging modesty" that causes the victim fear of death or injury.

Women enjoy the same legal rights as men in most areas, including civil liberties, employment, commercial activity, and education. The Women's Charter, enacted in 1961, gives women, among other rights, the right to own property, conduct trade, and receive divorce settlements. Muslim women enjoy most of the rights and protections of the Women's Charter. Muslim men may practice polygyny; they also may divorce unilaterally, whereas Muslim women may not. Polygyny occurred in 104 of 4,412 marriages registered in 1995.

In 1962 the Government instituted the principle of equal pay for equal work in the civil service and abolished separate salary scales in 1965. Women make up 39 percent of the labor force and are well represented in many professional fields, but they still hold the preponderance of low-wage jobs such as clerks and secretaries. As a result, their average salary levels are only 74 percent those of men. Women hold few leadership positions in the private sector.

Other areas of discrimination remain. For example, children born overseas to female citizens are not granted citizenship automatically, while those of male citizens are. Female civil service employees who are married do not receive health benefits for their spouses and dependents as do male government employees.

Children.—The Government demonstrated its strong commitment to children's rights and welfare through its well-funded systems of public education and medical care. Access to public education and medical care is equal for all children in society. In 1993 the Government updated and reenacted the Children and Young Persons Act. This revised act establishes protective services for those children who are orphaned, abused, disabled, or refractory, and it creates a juvenile court system. The Ministry of Community Development works closely with the National Council for Social Services to oversee children's welfare cases. Voluntary organizations operate most of the homes for children, while the Government funds up to 50 percent of all child costs, which includes normal living expenses and overhead, as well as expenses for special schooling, health care, or supervisory needs. There is no societal pattern of abuse directed against children.

People With Disabilities.—The Government implemented a comprehensive code on barrier-free accessibility in 1990, which established standards for facilities for the physically disabled in all new buildings and mandated the progressive upgrading of older structures. Although there is no legislation that addresses the issue of equal opportunities for the disabled in education or employment, the National Council of Social Services, in conjunction with various voluntary associations, provides an extensive job training and placement program for the disabled. Informal provisions in education have permitted university matriculation for visually impaired, deaf, and physically disabled students. The Government allows the equivalent of a $2,400 tax deduction for families with a disabled person.

National/Racial/Ethnic Minorities.—The Indian and Eurasian communities have achieved economic and educational success rates on a par with the majority Chinese. Malay Singaporeans, however, still have a lower standard of living, although the gap has diminished in recent years. Malays remain underrepresented at the uppermost rungs of the corporate ladder, and, some have claimed, in certain sectors of the Government, a reflection of their historically lower education and economic position, but also a result of employment discrimination. Advertisements sometimes specify ethnicity and gender requirements or require fluent Mandarin speakers.

The Constitution acknowledges the "special position" of Malays as the indigenous people of Singapore and charges the Government to support and promote their "political, educational, religious, economic, social, and cultural interests." A Presidential Council on Minority Rights examines all pending bills to ensure that they are not disadvantageous to a particular group. It also reports to the Government on matters affecting any racial or religious community and investigates complaints.

Section 6. Worker Rights

a. *The Right of Association.*—The Constitution provides all citizens with the right to form associations, including trade unions. Parliament may, however, impose restrictions based on security, public order, or morality grounds. The right of association is delimited by the Societies Act and by labor and education laws and regulations. The Trade Unions Act authorizes the formation of unions with broad rights, albeit with some narrow restrictions, such as prohibitions on the unionization of uniformed employees. The national labor force comprises about 1.75 million employees, more than 237,000 of whom are organized into 84 employee unions. Seventy-five of these unions, representing almost 73 percent of all unionized workers, are affiliated with the National Trades Union Congress (NTUC), an umbrella organization that has a close relationship with the Government.

The NTUC unabashedly acknowledges that its interests are closely linked with those of the ruling PAP, a relationship often described by both as "symbiotic." For example, President Ong Teng Cheong served simultaneously as NTUC Secretary General and Second Deputy Prime Minister before assuming his current position as President in 1993. His successor at the NTUC, Lim Boon Heng, was formerly Second Minister for Trade and Industry and continues as Minister Without Portfolio. In addition, several other high-ranking NTUC officials are PAP M.P.'s. NTUC policy prohibits union members who actively support opposition parties from holding office in affiliated unions. While the NTUC is financially independent of the PAP, with income generated by NTUC-owned businesses, the NTUC and PAP share the same ideology.

Workers, other than those in essential services, have the legal right to strike but rarely do so; no strikes have occurred since 1986. Most disagreements are resolved through informal consultations with the Ministry of Labor. If conciliation fails, the disputing parties usually submit their case to the Industrial Arbitration Court, which has representatives from labor, management, and the Government. These labor dispute mechanisms, along with the PAP/NTUC nexus, have played important roles in creating nonconfrontational labor relations. The Government also attributes the rarity of strikes to a cultural aversion to confrontation, high economic growth rates, labor shortages in recent years that have sustained regular wage increases, and the popular conviction that strikes would undermine Singapore's attractiveness to investors.

The NTUC is free to associate regionally and internationally.

b. *The Right to Organize and Bargain Collectively.*—Collective bargaining is a normal part of management-labor relations, particularly in the manufacturing sector. Agreements between management and labor are renewed every 2 to 3 years, although wage increases are negotiated annually. Collective bargaining agreements generally follow the guidelines issued by the National Wages Council, a group composed of labor, management, and government representatives, that makes annual recommendations regarding salary and bonus packages. The Industrial Relations Act makes it an offense to discriminate against anyone who is or proposes to become a member or an officer of a trade union. The offense is punishable by a fine equivalent to $1,414 and/or a 6-month prison sentence. Labor laws and regulations are enforced uniformly.

There are no export processing zones.

c. *Prohibition of Forced or Compulsory Labor.*—Under sections of the Destitute Persons Act, any indigent person may be required to reside in a welfare home and engage in suitable work. The International Labor Organization (ILO) has criticized the coercive terms of this act, which includes penal sanctions as not in compliance with the ILO Convention on Forced Labor, ratified by Singapore in 1965. The Government maintains that the act is social legislation providing for the shelter, care, and protection of destitute persons; and that work programs are designed to reintegrate individuals into society.

d. *Minimum Age for Employment of Children.*—The Government enforces the Employment Act, which prohibits the employment of children under age 12. A child over age 12 and under age 14 must receive written permission from the Commissioner for Labor for "light work suited to his capacity." There are few such applications, and the Commissioner for Labor has never approved one. Employers must notify the Ministry of Labor within 30 days of hiring a child between the ages of 14 and 16 and must forward medical certification to the Commissioner. The incidence of children taking up permanent employment is also low, and abuses are almost nonexistent.

Ministry of Labor regulations prohibit night employment of children and restrict industrial work to no more than 7 hours a day. Children may not work on commercial vessels, with any machinery in motion, on live electrical apparatus lacking effective insulation, or in any underground job. The Ministry of Labor effectively enforces these laws and regulations.

e. *Acceptable Conditions of Work.*—There are no laws or regulations on minimum wages or unemployment compensation. The labor market offers relatively high wages and good working conditions. The Employment Act sets the standard legal workweek at 44 hours and provides for 1 rest day each week. The Ministry of Labor effectively enforces laws and regulations establishing working conditions and comprehensive occupational safety and health laws. Enforcement procedures, coupled with the promotion of educational and training programs, have reduced the frequency of job-related accidents by a third over the past decade. While a worker has the right under the Employment Act to remove himself from a dangerous work situation, his right to continued employment depends upon an investigation of the circumstances by the Ministry of Labor.

Because of the domestic labor shortage, over 350,000 foreign workers are employed legally in Singapore, 20 percent of the total work force. Most are unskilled laborers and household servants from other Asian countries. Foreign workers face no legal wage discrimination, however, they are concentrated in low-wage, low-skill jobs and are often required to work long hours. Foreign construction workers often live in substandard housing on construction sites. About 85,000 foreign maids, mainly from the Philippines, Indonesia, and Sri Lanka, are employed in Singapore.

Maids, foreign or domestic, are not covered under the Employment Act. Most work 6 days per week from very early morning until late in the evening. Many contracts allow only 1 day off per month. Contracts often stipulate that a maid must remain on the premises except for official duties or on her day off. Wages average around $210 per month (not including free room and board). Maids often work for several months without pay because they must reimburse their placement agents. Labor law requires that employers contribute to a central provident fund for maids. Work permits for low-wage workers stipulate that their work permit will be cancelled if they apply to marry or marry a Singapore citizen or permanent resident. Maids only occasionally complain since they find the wages and working conditions to be generally acceptable. Although many lower-paid workers not covered under the Employment Act are ineligible for the limited free legal assistance that is available to citizens, the Government does not bar complainants from seeking legal redress and takes a firm stand against employers who abuse their domestic servants. The authorities have fined or imprisoned employers who have abused domestics, often with great publicity.

SOLOMON ISLANDS

Solomon Islands, with its approximately 400,000 people, is an archipelago stretching over 840 miles in the South Pacific. Its government is a modified parliamentary system consisting of a single-chamber legislative assembly of 47 members. Executive authority lies with the Prime Minister and his Cabinet. The Prime Minister, elected by a majority vote of Parliament, selects his own Cabinet. Political legitimacy rests on direct election by secret ballot. There have been four general elections since independence in 1978, most recently in June 1993.

A police force of about 500 men under civilian control is responsible for law enforcement. There were occasional reports of police abuse of human rights.

About 85 percent of the population engages to some extent in subsistence farming, obtaining food by gardening and fishing, and has little involvement in the cash economy. Approximately 10 to 15 percent of the working population (15 years and older) are engaged in nonsubsistence production. Although exports, particularly of unprocessed logs, have boomed, the number of wage earners has remained unchanged for the past several years, despite high population growth.

Most basic individual rights are provided for in the Constitution, respected by authorities, and defended by an independent judiciary. Discrimination and violence against women remain problems, and the Government on occasion has imposed restrictions on the media. There is a constitutionally provided ombudsman to look into and provide protection against improper or unlawful administrative treatment.

RESPECT FOR HUMAN RIGHTS

Section 1. Respect for the Integrity of the Person, Including Freedom From:

   a. *Political and Other Extrajudicial Killing.*—There were no reports of political or other extrajudicial killings.

   b. *Disappearance.*—There were no reports of politically motivated disappearances.

   c. *Torture and Other Cruel, Inhuman, or Degrading Treatment or Punishment.*—These practices are prohibited by law. There were a few complaints of excessive use of force by police in making arrests. These are handled either by the police's internal investigations office or by the courts. In one instance, the Honiara magistrate's court in August fined a police constable for striking a drunk with his baton when arresting him.

   Prison conditions meet minimum international standards. Prisons are overcrowded, and new facilities are under construction at the central prison in Rove. The new prison complex, due to open in 1997, is designed to provide separate facilities for short-, medium-, and long-term prisoners, as well as for juvenile offenders. Since there are no human rights organizations in Solomon Islands, the question of whether the Government would permit visits by human rights monitors has never arisen. A government-appointed Committee of Mercy, comprised of church and social leaders, recommends pardons for rehabilitated prisoners.

   d. *Arbitrary Arrest, Detention, or Exile.*—There was no evidence of politically motivated arrests or detentions. Exile is not practiced.

   e. *Denial of Fair Public Trial.*—The Constitution provides for an independent judiciary and it is independent in practice.

   The judicial system consists of a High Court and magistrates' courts. Accused persons are entitled to counsel. The law provides for a judicial determination of the legality of arrests. Officials found to have violated civil liberties are subject to fines and jail sentences.

There were no reports of political prisoners.

f. *Arbitrary Interference with Privacy, Family, Home, or Correspondence.*—In addition to legal provisions, the traditional culture provides strong protection against these types of abuses. A constitutionally provided ombudsman, with the power of subpoena, can investigate complaints of official abuse, mistreatment, or unfair treatment. While the Ombudsman's office has potentially far-ranging powers, it is limited by a shortage of investigators and other resources.

Section 2. Respect for Civil Liberties, Including:

a. *Freedom of Speech and Press.*—The Government generally respects the constitutional provisions for freedom of speech and of the press. The media comprise the Solomon Islands Broadcasting Corporation (SIBC), a statutory body that comes directly under the Prime Minister's office and whose radio broadcasts are heard throughout the country; a privately owned FM radio station; and three privately owned weekly or semiweekly newspapers. Given the high rate of illiteracy, the SIBC is more influential than the print media. The Department of Information in the Prime Minister's office publishes a monthly newspaper which is strongly progovernment. At least two nongovernmental organizations (NGO's) publish periodic news journals; their environmental reporting frequently is critical of the Government's logging policy and foreign logging companies' practices. In addition to the three established newspapers, a newspaper in Solomon Islands Pidgin, the language understood by most of the population, began semiweekly publication in late 1996. A private company has been given a license to begin limited television operations in 1997.

The state-owned SIBC is relatively bias free. In April the Prime Minister banned SIBC from broadcasting any statements by the Honiara-based spokesman of the Papua New Guinea secessionist movement, the Bougainville Revolutionary Army (BRA). This action followed demands from the Papua New Guinea Government that the Solomon Islands not allow BRA rebels to operate in its territory. In May, following a news report that the Government believed unfounded and prejudicial to the national security, the SIBC governing board directed that all news and current affairs programs have executive management clearance before being broadcast. Several SIBC newswriters and producers subsequently staged a short sit-in in protest against management statements that adversely reflected on their professionalism. The Solomon Islands Media Association also reacted strongly, saying that the prescreening of news broadcasts necessary.

The Government is acutely sensitive to international media coverage of the politically sensitive logging issue. Although journalists do not require visas, the Government must clear any filming, and Australian broadcast media representatives were initially denied permission to enter the country on the grounds that the logging subject already had been thoroughly covered. Two journalists later entered as tourists and used small video cameras. Their report, which was broadcast in Australia in August, highlighted an apparent conflict of interest in that the Prime Minister's logging company had received 100 percent tax exemptions on its exports. The Government reacted angrily to the apparent violation of immigration law.

b. *Freedom of Peaceful Assembly and Association.*—The Constitution provides for the right of association, and this right is freely exercised. Demonstrators must obtain permits, but permits are not known to have been denied on political grounds.

c. *Freedom of Religion.*—The law provides for freedom of religion, and the Government respects this provision in practice.

d. *Freedom of Movement Within the Country, Foreign Travel, Emigration, and Repatriation.*—The Government places neither legal nor administrative restrictions on the movement of citizens within or out of the country. Native-born citizens may not be deprived of citizenship on any grounds. Following several instances of attempted illegal immigration, the Government banned individuals from all Caribbean and African countries, and from the Pacific Island nations of Kiribati and Nauru, from visiting without prior approval of the Director of Immigration.

The Government provides first asylum to approximately 1,000 to 2,000 people from Papua New Guinea's Bougainville Island, who fled the conflict there several years earlier. Although they have not been granted formal refugee status, they have been allowed to remain. Most reside in Honiara with friends, while several hundred live in Red Cross-administered care centers elsewhere. The Government cooperated with the United Nations High Commissioner for refugees in locating asylum in the Netherlands for the Honiara-resident spokesman for the Bougainville rebels in May when his safety could no longer be assured.

Section 3. Respect for Political Rights: The Right of Citizens to Change Their Government.

Citizens have the right to change their government through periodic free elections. Since independence in 1978, there have been four parliamentary elections, most recently in June 1993, and several elections for provincial and local councils. On four occasions changes of government resulted from either parliamentary votes of no confidence or the resignation of the Prime Minister. Suffrage is universal over 18 years of age.

While the country's democratic commitment appears to remain strong, it was brought into question when the Deputy Prime Minister publicly stated in July that party politics destabilizes the country and causes disunity among the people. He favored instead a one-party system that would rule the country "intelligently."

Traditional male dominance has limited the role of women in government. Only 1 of the 47 members of Parliament is a woman.

Section 4. Governmental Attitude Regarding International and Nongovernmental Investigation of Alleged Violations of Human Rights

While there are no restrictions on the formation of local organizations to monitor and report on human rights, none has been established to date. There were no known requests for investigation by outside human rights organizations.

Section 5. Discrimination Based on Race, Sex, Religion, Disability, Language, or Social Status

The Constitution provides that no person—regardless of race, place of origin, political opinions, color, creed, or disabilities—shall be treated in a discriminatory manner in respect of access to public places. The Constitution further prohibits any laws which would have discriminatory effects, and provides that no person should be treated in a discriminatory manner by anyone acting in an official capacity. Despite constitutional and legal protections, women remain the victims of discrimination in this tradition-based society. Due to high rates of unemployment, there are a limited number of jobs available to the disabled.

Women.—While actual statistical data are scarce, incidents of wife beating and wife abuse appear to be common. In the rare cases that are reported, charges are often dropped by the women before the court appearance or are settled out of court. Police are reluctant to interfere in what they perceive as domestic disputes. In addition, many of the laws benefiting women derive from the British tradition and are viewed by many Solomon Islanders as "foreign laws" not reflective of their own customs and traditions. The magistrates' courts deal with physical abuse of women as with any other assault, although prosecutions are rare.

The law accords women equal legal rights. However, in this traditional society men are dominant, and women are limited to customary family roles. This situation has prevented women from taking more active roles in economic and political life. A shortage of employment opportunities throughout the country has inhibited the entry of women into the work force. The majority of women are illiterate; this is attributed in large part to cultural barriers. According to a 1995 United Nations Development Program (UNDP) report on human development, Solomon Islands ranked very low on the gender empowerment measure that examines women's ability to participate in economic and political life. The National Council of Women and other NGO's attempt to make women more aware of their legal rights through seminars, workshops and other activities. The government's Women Development Division also addresses women's issues.

Children.—Within the limits of its resources, the Government is committed to the welfare and protection of the rights of children. There is no compulsory education, and, according to some estimates, only 60 percent of school age children have access to primary education; the percentages of those attending secondary and tertiary institutions are much smaller. Children are respected and protected within the traditional extended-family system, in accordance with a family's financial resources and access to services. As a result, virtually no children are homeless or abandoned. Although some cases of child abuse are reported, there is no societal pattern of abuse. The Constitution grants children the same general rights and protection as adults. Existing laws are designed to protect children from sexual abuse, child labor, and neglect.

People With Disabilities.—There is no law or national policy on the disabled, and no legislation mandates access for the disabled. Their protection and care are left to the traditional extended family and nongovernmental organizations. With high unemployment countrywide and few jobs available in the formal sector, most disabled persons, particularly those in rural areas, do not find work outside the family structure. The Solomon Islands Red Cross society led private fund-raising efforts to build a new national center for disabled children, completing the first phase in this campaign by year's end.

Section 6. Worker Rights

a. *The Right of Association.*—The Constitution implicitly recognizes the right of workers to form or join unions, to choose their own representatives, to determine and pursue their own views and policies, and to engage in political activities. The courts have confirmed these rights. Only about 10 to 15 percent of the population participate in the formal sector of the economy. Approximately 60 to 70 percent of wage earners are organized (90 percent of employees in the public sector and about 50 percent of those in the private sector).

The law allows strikes, but there were none of note in 1996. The unions seldom resort to strikes, preferring instead to negotiate. Disputes are usually referred quickly to the Trade Disputes Panel (TDP) for arbitration, either before or during a strike. In practice, the small percentage of the work force in formal employment means that employers have ample replacement workers if disputes are not resolved quickly. Employees, however, are protected from arbitrary dismissal or lockout while the TDP is deliberating.

Unions are free to affiliate internationally, and the largest trade union, the Solomon Islands' National Union of Workers, is affiliated with the World Federation of Trade Unions, the South Pacific Oceanic Council of Trade Unions, and the Commonwealth Trade Union Congress.

b. *The Right to Organize and Bargain Collectively.*—The Trade Disputes Act of 1981 provides for the rights to organize and to bargain collectively and unions exercise these rights frequently.

Wages and conditions of employment are determined by collective bargaining. If a dispute between labor and management cannot be settled between the two sides, it is referred to the TDP for arbitration. The three-member TDP, comprising a chairman appointed by the judiciary, a labor representative, and a business representative, is independent and neutral.

The law protects workers against antiunion activity, and there are no areas where union activity is officially discouraged.

There are no export processing zones.

c. *Prohibition of Forced or Compulsory Labor.*—The Constitution prohibits forced labor, except as part of a court sentence or order, and this prohibition is observed.

d. *Minimum Age for Employment of Children.*—The law forbids child labor by children under the age of 12, except light agriculture or domestic work performed in the company of parents. Children under age 15 are barred from work in industry or on ships; those under age 18 may not work underground or in mines. The Labor Division of the Ministry of Commerce, Trade, and Industry is responsible for enforcing child labor laws. Given low wages and high unemployment, there is little incentive to employ child labor.

e. *Acceptable Conditions of Work.*—The minimum hourly wage rate was raised in 1996 from its 1988 rate of $0.22 (0.74 Solomon Islands dollars) to $0.42 (1.50 Solomon Islands dollars) for all workers except those in the fishing and agricultural sectors, who now receive $0.34 (1.20 Solomon Islands dollars). Even at the new rate, the legal minimum wage is not sufficient to support an urban family living entirely on the cash economy. However, most families are not dependent solely on wages for their livelihoods.

The Labor Act of 1969, as amended, and the Employment Act of 1981, as well as other laws, regulate premium pay, sick leave, the right to paid vacations, and other conditions of service. The standard workweek is 45 hours and is limited to 6 days per week. There are provisions for premium pay for overtime and holiday work and for maternity leave.

Both an active labor movement and an independent judiciary ensure widespread enforcement of labor laws in major state and private enterprises. The Commissioner of Labor, the Public Prosecutor, and the police are responsible for enforcing labor laws. However, they usually react to complaints rather than routinely monitoring adherence to the law. The extent to which the law is enforced in smaller establishments and in the subsistence sector is unclear. Safety and health laws appear to be adequate. Malaria is endemic in Solomon Islands and affects the health of many employees. Agricultural workers have a high risk of contracting malaria.

THAILAND

Thailand is a democratically governed constitutional monarchy with a history of military coups and powerful bureaucratic-military influence over political life. The King exerts strong informal influence on carefully selected issues and has the constitutionally mandated power, to date never used, to veto legislation (requiring two-thirds of Parliament to override) or dissolve the elected house of representatives. The coalition government of Prime Minister Banharn Silpa-Archa, elected in July 1995, was dissolved in the wake of a no-confidence vote in September. In general elections held on November 17, General Chavalit Yongchaiyudh's New Aspiration Party narrowly won the most number of seats and formed a coalition government with five other parties. The judiciary is independent but subject to corruption.

The security apparatus has wide-ranging legal powers, derived primarily from past militarily controlled administrations. Military leaders still have an informal but influential role in internal politics. Since 1992 military influence in politics has been substantially reduced, however, and progress has been made toward establishing civilian control over the armed forces, which are becoming increasingly professional. The police have primary responsibility for internal security and law enforcement. Elements of both the armed forces and the Royal Thai Police have a reputation for corruption. Some members of the security forces continue to commit serious human rights abuses.

Thailand, a newly industrializing country with a flourishing free enterprise system, continues to enjoy a high rate of economic growth. Per capita income is estimated at $3,000 per year. The political system generally provides protection for individual economic interests, including property rights. A lack of transparency in many government processes threatens some economic interests. Although the industrial and services sectors are expanding rapidly—contributing over half the gross national product—about 60 percent of the population is rural and agrarian. Government efforts to close the economic gap between urban and rural areas have been ineffective. Thailand's regional income disparities have grown, and income distribution has become wider; the income gap between segments within urban areas is also growing. Government land appropriation by eminent domain in large development projects and unresolved grievances by farmers, workers, and slum dwellers led to a demonstration in April by more than 10,000 protesters—mostly from rural areas—who set up a "Village of the Poor" in Bangkok.

The Government generally respects the human rights of its citizens, but some significant problems remain. Some police officers committed extrajudicial killings, and the incidence of political and other extrajudicial killings increased. Police occasionally tortured and beat suspects. Members of the armed forces were responsible for sporadic brutality against the lower ranks and aliens under their control in border areas. The Government investigated and prosecuted few police or military officers accused of abuse or extrajudicial killings. Conditions in immigration detention facilities are poor, and the prolonged detention of aliens is a problem. An ingrained culture of corruption in the bureaucracy, police, and military services plagues society. Some members of both police and military services used their positions to facilitate the trade in prostitution.

Bribes or "tea money," demanded on a regular basis, undermine the rule of law, permitting a climate of impunity for illegal practices such as income tax evasion, gambling, immigrant trafficking, goods smuggling, and prostitution. Enforcement of a broad range of laws and regulations by police continues to be noticeably lax.

There were isolated attempts by some officials to limit press freedom through police "warnings," to restrict some activities of human rights nongovernmental organizations (NGO's), and to harass an academic researcher. Legal and societal discrimination against women, violence against women and children, and illegal child labor persist. Societal discrimination against religious and ethnic minorities is a problem. The Government imposes restrictions on the movement of tribal people.

At year's end, the Government had not yet established institutions—government ombudsmen and an independent election commission—almost 2 years after their formal adoption in the Constitution. An earlier government's commitment in 1992 to establish a human rights commission has not been pursued.

RESPECT FOR HUMAN RIGHTS

Section 1. Respect for the Integrity of the Person, Including Freedom From:

a. *Political and Other Extrajudicial Killing.*—There were two reported political killings in 1996. In January Thong-in Kaew-Wattha, a leader of protests against a toxic waste treatment plant in an agricultural community, was shot and killed by a gunman and his accomplice. Two suspects, identified by eyewitnesses, are in custody and awaiting trial. NGO's, academic researchers, and other professional groups believe that the suspects were hired by a local businessman whose interests were adversely affected by Thong-in's environmental activism. The police abandoned further investigation, despite self-incriminating statements by the main suspect.

In July Joon Bhoonkhuntod, a farmer activist in Chaiyaphum, was shot and killed by a police private. Police stated that the victim was resisting arrest on charges of cultivating marijuana, later adding that the shooting was accidental. NGO's claimed that Joon was targeted based on his political activities. Some allege that the use of force was not only excessive but may have been part of a carefully planned ambush. The accused policeman was arrested and released on bail pending further investigation.

Legal organizations, reputable NGO's, and the press continued to provide credible reports that some police officers summarily executed criminal suspects, particularly in areas outside the capital. The police information center reported a total of 23 suspects killed during attempted arrest in 1995, with 16 such killings in the first half of 1996. It appears that a number of the deaths during arrests occurred when police returned fire by armed suspects. In November news media documented the arrest of six suspects in Suphan Buri who were led away handcuffed by police; the six were found dead minutes later. Police claim that they acted in self-defense since one of the suspects attempted to seize a weapon, but responsible sources questioned the credibility of the official explanation. According to data from the Attorney General's office released in Seprember, 90 cases of killings by all civil officials (including police and other agency officials, such as forestry and district officials) during 1995 resulted in 89 cases being dismissed by the courts and one case continuing. During the first half of 1996, all 21 cses of killings by officials were dismissed by the courts.

The Attorney General's office reported that a total of 324 suspects and detainees died while in the "custody of government officials" in 1995, with another 205 dying in the first 9 months of 1996. According to police, there were 98 deaths in custody after initial detention during 1995 and the first 6 months of 1996. Of these, 63 were reported as apparent suicides. However, specific case reports from regional authorities indicated that the figure may be as high as 140 deaths in custody.

Political activists allege that the October 1995 killing of conservationist Winai Chantamano in Satun province was the result of his opposition to encroachment on national forest lands by an influential group of investors. Two of four alleged assailants have been detained, and the case remains under investigation.

The Government prosecutes few police or military officers accused of extrajudicial killings. Courts rarely convict police officers involved in summary executions, in part because witnesses are often intimidated or bribed to withhold evidence. The resulting climate of impunity is the single largest factor preventing any significant change in police behavior. None was convicted in 1996. The law allows personal suits against police officers for criminal actions taken while making an arrest. However, due to flaws in the legal process and ingrained cultural attitudes, victims or their families rarely file suits against the police. During the initial police inquiry, most police investigations routinely determine that no wrongful action was taken on the part of the police; judges generally follow the prosecutor's recommendations. If pursued by the family, the case is handled by the same office, in some instances by the same prosecutor, who has already ruled that no criminal action occurred. There is no information to determine how many cases are settled out of court, but in cases in which suits are filed, the official charged often compensates the family of the deceased, and the suit is dropped.

b. *Disappearance.*—There were no reports of politically motivated disappearances.

There were no developments in the 1994 disappearance of environmental activist Suchada Khamfubutra or the 1991 disappearance of Labor Congress of Thailand President Thanong Po-an.

There were no developments in investigations into the whereabouts of the remaining 39 prodemocracy protesters listed as missing following the military's suppression of demonstrations in May 1992. Most, if not all, are presumed by family members and NGO's to be dead. A civil case brought by family members remains before the courts.

c. *Torture and Other Cruel, Inhuman, or Degrading Treatment or Punishment.*— The Criminal Code forbids cruel, inhuman, or degrading treatment or punishment. However, there continued to be credible reports that police sometimes tortured and beat prisoners and detainees. Credible reports from nongovernmental organizations (NGO's), academic institutions, and professional groups indicate that some police occasionally tortured and beat suspects and obtained coerced confessions through the use of physical abuse. Criminal suspects occasionally complained of police attempts to secure confessions or evidence through the use of torture such as electric shock. Similar, isolated complaints have been heard about treatment by the military personnel in armed forces detention centers or in border areas under martial law. Police and military personnel officially deny these allegations, but some police officials acknowledged that torture is occasionally carried out in police custody, with the implicit backing of some senior police officers. The Government made no visible efforts to prosecute, convict, and appropriately punish those who committed these abuses.

Prison conditions are Spartan but do not in general threaten the life or health of inmates. Sleeping accommodations and access to medical care are areas of concern that require continued attention to meet minimum international standards.

Some prison guards resort to physical abuse of both Thai and foreign prisoners in response to disciplinary problems. A number of credible sources reported that prisoners caught in escape attempts are often beaten and sometimes beaten to death. Solitary confinement and heavy leg irons are sometimes used to punish difficult prisoners. Medical care in prisons is inadequate. To care for a total prison population of 100,000, the Corrections Department employs only 12 full-time and 2 part-time doctors and 4 dentists.

Access to prisoners is not restricted, and the Government permits visits by human rights monitors.

Conditions at the Suan Phlu Immigration Detention Center (IDC), were poor, although an increased budget resulted in some modest improvements. There were periods during which as many as 200 IDC detainees were kept in holding areas of about 1,200 square feet, allowing only about 6 square feet for each prisoner to sleep in packed, wall-to-wall formation. Overcrowding, poor sanitation and ventilation, and inability to exercise are recurring problems. Additional detention centers were under construction. Except for medical care provided under the auspices of the U.N. and private institutions, there is no governmental medical care available in the IDC. Consistent with nationwide treatment of illegal immigrants, children are detained with their parents, and a food ration is provided only for parents, not the accompanying children.

Immigration detention facilities are not administered by the Department of Corrections and are not subject to many of the regulations found in the regular prison system. Citizens of countries that will not accept deportees because of uncertainties over citizenship face an extended stay in the IDC. While the law requires that prosecutors formally charge criminal suspects in court within 91 days of their detention, some IDC detainees have been held for up to 2 years. In June a royal pardon resulted in the release and repatriation of about 1,300 IDC detainees.

d. *Arbitrary Arrest, Detention, or Exile.*—Except in cases of crimes in progress, the law generally requires arrest warrants, and authorities respect this provision in practice. Arrested persons must be informed of the likely charges against them immediately after arrest. Police have the authority to extend the detention period to 7 days in order to complete an investigation. After 7 days, the police must present the case to the public prosecutor to determine if the case should be pursued. While detainees have a right to have a lawyer present during questioning, they are often not informed of this right. Foreign prisoners are often forced to sign confessions and stand trial without benefit of a translator, although the Government is studying provision of translation services for court hearings.

There is a functioning bail system, but judges have considerable discretion in determining eligibility for bail, with no means of appeal. The only legal basis for detention by the police without specific charges for long periods (up to 480 days) is the Anti-Communist Activities Act, which was not invoked in 1996 (see Section 1.e.).

As of October, there were 103,202 prison inmates in Thailand. Of that number, about 9,500 were persons appealing their sentences, and approximately 25,000 were pretrial detainees. These two groups are not usually segregated from the general prison population, although sometimes an effort is made to confine those facing narcotics charges in a separate facility. The June a royal pardon resulted in the release of about 24,000 prisoners.

In March two Amnesty International (AI) representatives were detained at Bangkok's Bang Rak police station for 90 minutes while police inspected their passports and travel documents. The detention, which the police later labeled an "invitation" to the police station, coincided with the time during which AI had planned to release publicly a report highly critical of human rights practices in China.

A group of 12 Burmese student political activists of concern to the United Nations High Commissioner for Refugees remained in the Special Detention Center (SDC). In addition, four of these Burmese refugees, originally detained in the safe area camp, have been held in the SDC from periods ranging from 22 to 30 months for staging protests at a Burmese refugee camp or for minor infractions of the camp rules. None of the four was formally charged or sentenced. At year's end, they were still being held without charges in Bangkok's special detention center, after initially being apprehended for their political activities.

Exile is not used as a means of political control.

e. *Denial of Fair Public Trial.*—The Constitution provides for an independent judiciary, and, although generally regarded as independent, the judiciary has a reputation for venality.

The civilian judicial system has three levels of courts: courts of first instance, courts of appeal, and the Supreme Court. A separate military court hears criminal and civil cases pertaining to military personnel as well as those brought during periods of martial law. A serious flaw in providing due process rights is the lack of appeal from decisions of a military court. Islamic (Shari'a) courts provide due process and hear only civil cases concerning members of the Muslim minority.

The Constitution provides for presumption of innocence. Access to courts or administrative bodies to seek redress is provided for and practiced.

There is no trial by jury. Trials for misdemeanors are decided by a single judge, and more serious cases require two or more judges. While most trials are public, the court may order a trial closed. This is done most often in cases touching on national security or the royal family. Career civil service judges preside over the courts. Judicial appointments and structures are not subject to parliamentary review.

Defendants tried in ordinary criminal courts enjoy a broad range of legal rights, including access to a lawyer of their choosing. A government program provides free legal advice to the poor, but indigent defendants are not automatically provided with counsel at public expense. Most free legal aid comes from private groups, including the Thai Lawyers' Association and the Thai Women Lawyers' Association.

Credible legal sources say that, aside from nine Muslim activists, there were no political prisoners at year's end, the last few prisoners serving prison sentences under the Anti-Communist Activities Act having been released under a general pardon granted by the King in June. Muslim groups claimed that nine prisoners are jailed on criminal convictions because of their political views. Some have been imprisoned since 1990; their unduly harsh sentences were imposed for participating in a protest rally in Pattani.

f. *Arbitrary Interference with Privacy, Family, Home, or Correspondence.*—The law in most instances requires police to obtain a warrant prior to a search. Warrants are issued by the police with prior Ministry of Interior or provincial governor approval and are not subject to judicial review. There were some credible reports that officers sometimes endorse warrants in advance, then allow their noncommissioned subordinates to apply them as needed. According to human rights lawyers, search warrants were sometimes abused by police to engage in ill-defined and intrusive searches outside the stated evidentiary domain, aimed at uncovering any incriminating item, even if unrelated to the crime originally alleged in the warrant. The Anti-Communist Activities Act allows officials engaged in "Communist suppression operations" to conduct searches without warrants, but these powers have rarely been invoked in recent years and were not invoked during the year.

Security services monitor persons espousing leftist or controversial views, including some foreign visitors (see Sections 2.d. and 4).

Section 2. Respect for Civil Liberties, Including:

a. *Freedom of Speech and Press.*—The Constitution provides for, and citizens generally enjoy, a large measure of freedom of speech. However, the law prohibits criticism of the royal family (lese majeste), threats to national security, or speaking in a manner likely to incite disturbances or insult Buddhism.

Newspapers and periodicals practice some self-censorship, especially with regard to the monarchy and national security issues. However, strong media criticism of political parties, public figures, and the Government is common and vigorous. Journalists are generally free to comment on government activities without fear of reprisal, although there were credible reports of occasional harassment of journalists by individual politicians and military personnel. Also, journalists are reluctant to criticize the judiciary out of fear that they would not be treated fairly by judges during libel proceedings.

Under the Printing and Advertisement Act of 1941, the Royal Thai Police Special Branch issues warnings to publications for various violations such as disturbing the peace, interfering with public safety, or offending public morals. In 1995 police issued 13 such warnings. In 1996 the total reached 22, including 6 warnings issued to newspapers and weeklies for reports on the May censure debate in Parliament against the Government. Punishments were restricted to small fines, but could have included imprisonment of the owner, publisher, editor, and journalist for up to 3 months. Police closure of newspapers or printing presses is also permitted under the 1941 act but only in time of war or national emergency.

Radio and television stations are licensed by the Government and operated under the direct or indirect oversight of the Government and the military forces. Radio stations must renew their licenses each year, and their signals are broadcast via government transmitters. They are required by law to broadcast government-produced newscasts twice daily, 30 minutes each in the morning and evening.

Although programmers are generally free to determine the content and nature of television broadcasts, a government internal censorship board commonly edits or "blacks out" portions of programming deemed politically sensitive or pornographic. Self-censorship this year tended to be more prevalent in television stations directly controlled by the Government, although subcontracted stations remained mindful that they operate under 30-year government concessions.

There are also three cable television networks, which enjoy almost complete autonomy under the indirect oversight of the Mass Communications Authority of Thailand. The first ultra high frequency station, managed by a private consortium including the outspoken Nation Publishing Group, was launched in July under a 30-year concession from the Office of the Prime Minister. Touted as the country's first independent television station, its status is similar to that of other subcontracted stations, with free, daily, direct broadcasting.

Domestic publications continued to present a wide range of political and social commentary. Unless critical of the royal family or the monarchy, foreign and domestic books normally are not censored and circulate freely. Police had the power to ban the import of publications until late 1990; the list of publications previously banned, mainly pornographic material but also including books written by Communists, remains in effect.

An antipornography law allows police to restrict or confiscate publications and other materials deemed obscene; the interpretation given usually covers hard-core pornographic materials.

Although academic and technical research is generally conducted freely, the Government in August used unusually strong measures to rebut a university researcher's academic paper on alleged police bribe-taking in connection with illegal gambling. Unsolicited, police-ordered security for the researcher induced the researcher and his family to go into hiding due to fear of the police, and led political activists and labor leaders to charge the police with harassment and intimidation. With the Prime Minister's approval, the police lodged a defamation complaint against the researcher, who had cited police sources in his study. The police later withdrew the lawsuit, but only after the Prime Minister brokered a meeting between the researcher and his university superiors in which they apparently negotiated alterations to the paper.

b. *Freedom of Peaceful Assembly and Association.*—The legal system recognizes the right of peaceful assembly, and the Government respects this right in practice. Private associations must register with the Government, but permits are not required for private meetings or gatherings unless held on public property; these are routinely granted.

c. *Freedom of Religion.*—Freedom of religion is protected by law, and the Government generally respects this right in practice. The de facto state religion is Theravada Buddhism, but other religions are not restricted.

Members of minority religious movements are occasionally subjected to legal action. Dissident Buddhist leader Phra Potirak and 79 followers, convicted and sentenced to 2 years' probation for violating the civil law governing the Buddhist hierarchy and impersonating Buddhist monks or nuns, appealed their convictions. At year's end, all remained free and continued their official religious activities.

Dissemination by the Government of school textbooks containing religious information, but only on Buddhism, was reportedly a source of annoyance among religious minorities.

d. *Freedom of Movement Within the Country, Foreign Travel, Emigration, and Repatriation.*—The right, provided for by the Constitution of citizens to change their residence or workplace was unabridged. Travel was restricted in certain border areas where foreign or vestigial domestic insurgent groups remain active. Long-standing restrictions on the travel and place of residence of certain Vietnamese aliens who immigrated to Thailand in 1945–46 and Chinese who immigrated between 1953 and 1961 remained in place. In addition, some long-term noncitizen residents of Thailand, including several hundred thousand tribal people, are required to seek permission from local authorities or the army for foreign or domestic travel. In practice, authorities rarely enforced these restrictive measures, and registered resident aliens were able to move freely within the country (see Section 5).

Under a new regulation operative in September, illegal alien workers already in the country and working in specified manual labor jobs were allowed to register and work in 43 of the 76 provinces. These illegal aliens are allowed to work for up to

2 years while awaiting formal deportation. The new measure had the effect of regularizing many illegal aliens, allowed them to move freely so long as their employer registered them with local authorities, and generally enhanced their prospects to seek redress for human rights abuses (see Section 6.e.).

Several regulations intended and used to help reduce trafficking in women and children for purposes of prostitution could also be used to infringe on the right of women and children to travel freely. One rarely used statute, dating to the last century, requires a woman to obtain her husband's permission before traveling outside Thailand. Also, female passport applicants under the age of 36 must sit through a series of interviews regarding their employment records and finances. Passport applications by single women and children under the age of 14 must also be approved by the Department of Public Welfare.

Thailand continued to provide first asylum to Vietnamese and Lao asylum seekers. It did not officially recognize the refugee status of some Vietnamese mandated by the U.N. High Commissioner for Refugees (UNHCR), but neither did it compel them to leave Thailand. Host government screening for Vietnamese and Lao continued, as set out under the Comprehensive Plan of Action (CPA) agreed to in Geneva in 1989, until the CPA's termination on June 30. After that time, extensions of CPA policies or ad hoc measures consistent with the spirit of the CPA were employed. There were no credible reports of forced repatriation of Lao asylum seekers. Nor were there reports that Lao asylum seekers were denied entry at the border. There was an unconfirmed but credible report in May that provincial Thai authorities in Nan arrested and turned over to the Lao Government 13 Hmong men on December 26, 1995. These Hmong had removed themselves from UNHCR protection and had been living illegally in Thailand.

Repatriation of screened-out (i.e. nonrefugee) Vietnamese both voluntarily and involuntarily through the CPA-mandated orderly return program, continued throughout the year. From late June to mid-November, nearly 1,900 screened-out Vietnamese at Sikhiu camp were repatriated involuntarily in 13 movements. About 265 Vietnamese, including those on repatriation manifests as well as sympathizers in the camp, sustained self-inflicted injuries, chiefly superficial skin lacerations. These acts in protest of involuntary return were an attempt to postpone repatriation.

Some Vietnamese complained that Thai authorities handled them roughly during their involuntary repatriation by airplane. One Vietnamese man climbed up on a roof to avoid repatriation, and later jumped off; his injuries from the fall proved fatal.

The Government cooperated with the UNHCR in administering the sole camp for Lao refugees at Ban Napho, Nakhon Phanom, in assisting with voluntary repatriation, and in expediting the resettlement of about 3,000 highland and lowland Lao refugees to the United States. Under the law, most Burmese (and other, non-Indochinese) asylum seekers are considered illegal immigrants subject to deportation, but the Government continued to permit Burmese asylum seekers to remain in camps along the Thai-Burma border and near Bangkok. While Burmese outside of camps were arrested periodically as illegal aliens, the Government did not deport any Burmese recognized by the UNHCR as a "person of concern." There was a confirmed report that Thai authorities ordered the refoulement of at least 100 members of minority hill tribes on October 11. The Shan members appeared to have been fleeing repression, including forced porterage, by the Government of Burma. Unlike other Burmese minority groups seeking refuge in Thailand, Shan asylum seekers have no access to recognized temporary camps at which they could seek assistance or protection.

At year's end, a number of Burmese dissidents, detained as illegal immigrants, remained in immigration detention centers in central Thailand (see Section 1.d.).

Residents of the Safe Area first asylum camp for Burmese dissidents in Ratchaburi province had regular access to the UNHCR, which concluded that conditions at the safe area meet broadly accepted international standards for the protection and welfare of asylum seekers. As a general rule, the Government restricts entry to the Safe Area to asylum seekers from Burma whom the UNHCR had found to be "persons of concern" prior to mid-1996. By year's end, about 800 Burmese persons of concern resided there.

More than 100,000 ethnic minority Burmese and almost 2,000 Burmese students and dissidents continued to reside in some 34 camps along the Burma border. Several camps were evacuated temporarily or relocated because of cross-border attacks from Burma. The Government continued to permit voluntary agencies to provide food, medical, and sanitation assistance along the border. Adequate access to the camps by NGO's, to ensure adequate provision of health care and sanitation, remains a concern.

Beginning in May, the Government allowed more than 4,000 Karenni asylum seekers refuge following widespread Burmese government forced relocations of a number of Karenni villages throughout Kayah state in Burma. During the year, a Burmese government-supported Karen faction, the Democratic Karen Buddhist Army, conducted isolated attacks on Karen refugee camps within Thailand, as well as on Thai villages, killing and abducting several persons, including members of the Thai security forces. The number of security incidents decreased during the rainy season beginning in June but increased again late in the year. Reports from NGO's and other credible sources strongly suggested that government-provided security of refugee camps along the Burma border was not sufficient to protect against raids into the country by Burmese armed forces or their armed supporters; however, the government increased the number of regular and paramilitary forces stationed in the border regions later in the year. In an attempt to provide better security, the Government has proposed to consolidate refugee camps and move them further from the border.

In the east, at various times during the year, the Government accepted small numbers of Cambodian civilians seeking temporary refuge from low-scale conflicts between the Khmer Rouge and Cambodian government forces in Cambodia. These temporary asylum seekers were allowed to choose the time and place of their repatriation.

Section 3. Respect for Political Rights: The Right of Citizens to Change Their Government

The Constitution provides for the right of citizens to choose or change their government through free and fair elections based on universal suffrage, and citizens exercised this right in November 1996. In that election, one elected government replaced another through a free election, and served to strengthen democratic institutions. The military services generally showed further evidence of acceptance of civilian control. In April the Prime Minister appointed 260 members to the Senate, the first Senators appointed by an elected official in the 1990's. The new Senate replaced a body that had been appointed by a military government and reflects a substantial decline in the number of seats held by active duty or retired military officers.

The widespread practice of vote-buying was again present during 1996 parliamentary by-elections and general elections, supporting critics' contentions that some elections, although free, were fraudulent. At year's end, the Government had not yet established the Election Commission called for in constitutional amendments of February 1995. A draft bill submitted by the new Chavalit Government in December passed the first of three readings in Parliament. Under this bill, the Interior Ministry would continue to handle most of the important election supervision functions.

While there are no legal restrictions on their political participation, women are generally underrepresented in national politics, especially at the senior levels. Although the number of women in national politics continued to increase, only 22 of the 393 Members of Parliament are women. In April Prime Minister Banharn appointed 21 women to the 260-member Senate. Two women held cabinet portfolios until their party withdrew from the coalition government: a Deputy Minister of the Interior and a Deputy Minister of Transport and Communications. There were no women appointed to the first Cabinet of Prime Minister Chavalit which took office in December.

In the civil service, 46 women were reported to hold a rank at or above Director General. In April the military services for the first time appointed six women to the rank of General, although women are still not allowed to attend military academies or the army, navy, or air force staff colleges. An additional five women were appointed to flag rank in October.

No laws prohibit the participation of ethnic minorities, but few hold positions of authority in national politics or the civil service. Ethnic minorities in the north often lack documentation of citizenship, effectively barring their participation in the political process (see Section 5). Muslims from the south hold significant posts in the Government, although they continue to be underrepresented in local and provincial government positions (which are appointed by the central Government).

Section 4. Governmental Attitude Regarding International and Nongovernmental Investigation of Alleged Violations of Human Rights

Local human rights organizations operate without government restriction. International human rights NGO's generally work freely on controversial issues, investigating and publishing their findings without hindrance. The Government sometimes criticized these groups for being politically motivated and biased, but in most cases it did not penalize or hinder human rights observers.

Before and during the 25-nation Asia-Europe Meeting in February, the Government imposed entry visa bans on some political activists and NGO leaders whom the Government believed would stage protests.

The brief detention of Amnesty International (AI) human rights monitors in March, immediately prior to a planned AI press conference on human rights in China, was openly described by local authorities as an attempt to prevent the press conference from taking place (see Sections 1.d. and 2.a.). However, other AI members who remained at liberty held a press conference at a previously publicized location without hindrance from the police.

Section 5. Discrimination Based on Race, Sex, Religion, Disability, Language, or Social Status

The Constitution provides for equal treatment under the law without respect to race, sex, religion, disability, language, or social status. In practice, some discrimination exists, and government enforcement of equal protection statutes is uneven.

Women.—Domestic abuse continues to be a serious problem affecting the welfare of many women; reliable reports indicate that domestic abuse crosses all social classes. One NGO estimates that as many as 50 percent of women in Bangkok's slum areas are victims of abuse. Police do not enforce laws against such violence vigorously, and domestic violence often goes unreported. Under the Criminal Code, spousal and child abuse is covered under assault provisions, but rules of evidence often make prosecuting such cases difficult. Since 1994 a pilot project in three Bangkok police stations, which has yet to be expanded, included female team to handle rape and abuse cases in order to encourage more victims to report these abuses.

Prostitution, although illegal, flourishes and is deeply ingrained. Estimates of the numbers of women and children engaged in prostitution vary widely because of temporary sex workers and the migratory nature of prostitution. Reliable NGO's estimate the number of adult female prostitutes at around 250,000.

Prostitution exposes women to a number of human rights abuses, as well as a much higher risk of contracting AIDS. Some women are forced into prostitution, although the number of such cases is difficult to determine. Incidents of coerced prostitution most commonly involve women who are not ethnic Thai from hill tribes or are from neighboring countries; the number of such women entering the country to work as prostitutes continued to rise. Because they cannot speak Thai, and are considered illegal immigrants, these women are particularly vulnerable to physical abuse, confinement, and exploitation. Some women are lured with promises of jobs as waitresses or domestic helpers, but are then forced to work as prostitutes. As illegal immigrants, these women have no right to legal counsel or health care if arrested, and this group is not protected under new regulations concerning illegal alien workers.

Human rights monitors believe that the majority of those who engage in prostitution are not kept under physical constraint, but that a large number labor in debt bondage. Brothel procurers often advance parents a substantial sum against their daughter's future earnings, often without the consent of the young woman involved. The women are then obligated to work in a brothel in order to pay back the loan. On the border with Cambodia, procurers provide women and girls as young as the age of 14 who were trafficked from Vietnam or China and live under slave-like circumstances in Cambodia. Observers believe that their illegal border crossing for the purposes of prostitution is accomplished with the complicity of local officials.

During the year, the Government stepped up efforts against prostitution. In August the Government endorsed an operational plan against commercial sex services, calling for such measures as further compulsory education, more vocational education, an enhanced public information campaign, and professional training, especially of teachers and health care workers. In addition, under the Chavalit Government, the Labor Permanant Secretary chairs a Committee for Protection and Vocational Development aimed a combating prostitution.

The Government and NGO's have already established vocational training and education programs to combat the lure of prostitution for young Thai women and their families. As a result of the strengthened national antiprostitution policy, the Government is expanding these programs, which are part of a 5-year program that started in October. Despite occasional highly publicized raids on brothels, however, the Government has failed to enforce effectively laws against prostitution, and, in many cases, brothel operators bribe local government representatives and police. There continue to be credible reports of involvement by some corrupt police, military, and other officials in trafficking schemes.

Until recently, prostitutes were considered criminals, whereas brothel owners, procurers, and clients were not subject to criminal statutes. A new law passed in

September further criminalizes those involved in the trafficking of women and children for the purpose of prostitution or slave labor.

Women generally have equal legal rights, but inequalities remain in domestic law. Whereas a man may sue for divorce on the grounds that his wife has committed adultery, a woman faces the additional legal burden of proving that her husband has maintained or honored another woman in a manner equal to his wife. Women face more stringent requirements to obtain passports than do men (see Section 2.d.).

Statistics compiled by the Government and NGO's concerned with women's issues note that women represent 47 percent of the economically active population and that their numbers have increased in professional positions. Government regulations require employers to pay the same wages and benefits for similar work regardless of sex. However, there is a significant gap between average salaries earned by men and women as a result of the concentration of women in traditionally lower paying jobs. In addition, women tend to receive lower pay for equal work in virtually all sectors of the economy, a fact already documented in studies of manufacturing, services, and agriculture.

Women generally have access to higher education; more than half the university graduates are women.

Despite improvements in the Government's performance regarding women's rights, including well-received proposed amendments to the Family Act, many women's rights NGO's remain skeptical that women will soon be able to enjoy equal income opportunities or obtain opportunities equal to men to enter decisionmaking positions in high-ranking government appointments, the civil service, or in the private sector.

Children.—The Government is committed to the rights and welfare of children, although child labor, a relatively short compulsory education system, and child prostitution remain areas of concern. "Human Development" was a major theme of the Eighth National Economic and Social Development Plan, released in midyear. Key among the human development proposals is an increased emphasis on extending compulsory education from grade 6 to grade 9 and to alleviating poverty. There are no reliable statistics on the number of children involved in the sex industry, but official estimates by the Government's National Commission on Women's Affairs indicate that 15 to 20 percent of prostitutes are children under the age of 18. Applying this official estimate to the NGO's count, there are probably from 20,000 to 40,000 child prostitutes.

While the Government did take several significant steps to combat child prostitution, it is unclear how effectively new laws will be enforced and new policies implemented. Clients of child prostitutes are now subject to criminal prosecution and strong penalties, including up to 6 years' imprisonment. Credible NGO's reported at year's end that efforts by police to enforce the new antiprostitution law were only moderately successful in curbing the trade in children for commercial sex.

In August the Banharn Government's Cabinet approved draft legislation that would revise the Criminal Code to toughen the laws regarding abuse of children under 18 years of age; the draft includes especially severe penalties for violations perpetrated against children under the age of 15. The bill, under consideration by the Chavalit Cabinet since December, would provide a fund to assist such children and initiate a parenting education program.

The Criminal Code provides for the protection of children from abuse, and laws on rape and abandonment provide for harsher penalties when the victim is a child. As in the case of domestic violence against women; however, police are often reluctant to pursue abuse cases, and rules of evidence make prosecution of child abuse cases difficult.

People With Disabilities.—The Government again took few steps to implement provisions in the Disabled Rehabilitation Law that established a quota system and employer incentives for hiring the disabled. Another regulation requiring factories to hire one disabled person for every 200 nondisabled employees was also not enforced. There are no laws mandating access to public facilities for disabled persons.

Religious Minorities.—Muslims represent a significant minority within the country as a whole and constitute the majority in the four southernmost provinces that border Malaysia. Although the Government has attempted to integrate the Muslim community into society through developmental efforts and expanded educational opportunities, societal discrimination remains widespread.

National/Racial/Ethnic Minorities.—Progress in integrating ethnic minorities into society is limited. Only half the estimated 500,000 to 600,000 members of hill tribes reportedly possess documentation that either lists them as citizens or places them on the record as being eligible for future citizenship. The rest lack documentation, and thus access to adequate education and health care. Noncitizens are also barred from participating in the political process. Undocumented hill tribe people cannot own land and are not subject to labor laws, including minimum wage requirements. In August the Government ran a pilot test of new criteria to establish alien resident status for highlanders, but the lack of legal status for this group persists. Under the 1992 Thai Nationality Law, children born in Thailand to two permanent residents have the right to citizenship.

Approximately 45,000 Vietnamese who fled Indochina in the 1940's and 1950's reside in northeastern Thailand and live under a set of laws and regulations restricting their movements, residences, education, and occupations. The Government has slowly pursued a more lenient policy toward longtime Vietnamese residents in recent years and in August announced that it is reviewing a process for granting citizenship to all members of this group. There are also approximately 40,000 noncitizen Chinese and their descendants who live in border areas. Very few of these people have citizenship, and the vast majority must seek permission from local authorities in order to travel outside their districts (see Section 2).

Under a quota system, only 100 persons per nationality per year may be naturalized as citizens. However, in addition to the review of citizenship for Vietnamese in the northeast, the Interior Ministry is considering a measure to speed up naturalization of the 10,000 Chinese and 8,000 Vietnamese that it reports are currently seeking citizen status.

Section 6. Worker Rights

a. *The Right of Association.*—The law grants freedom of association to private sector workers. Workers have the right to form and join unions of their choosing without prior authorization; to decide on the constitutions and rules of these associations and unions; to express their views without government or employer interference; to confederate with other unions; to receive protection from discrimination, dissolution, suspension, or termination by any outside authority because of union activities; and to have employee representation in direct negotiations with employers. However, no law explicitly protects workers from discrimination due to their participation in organizing new unions that have not yet been officially registered. Union leaders report that employers often discriminate against workers seeking to organize unions.

Workers in the public sector do not have the right to form unions. In state enterprises, the law allows workers in each state enterprise to form a single "association" after at least 30 percent of the enterprise's employees submit a petition to the Ministry of Labor to register such an association. These associations submit employee grievances to management and propose changes in benefits and working conditions but may not negotiate wages. Associations do not have the right to confederate or to join private sector federations. Unofficial contacts between public and private sector unions continue, however, and the Government has not interfered with these relationships.

The law denies all state enterprise workers the right to strike. In the private sector, to be considered legal a proposed strike must be approved by a majority of the union members in a secret ballot and be registered beforehand with the Ministry of Labor.

In 1991 the International Labor Organization (ILO) criticized labor law amendments adopted by a military-appointed legislature in March 1991 that dissolved state enterprise unions, transferred their assets, limited the number of associations that may be formed in each state enterprise, set relatively high minimum membership requirements for associations, denied associations the right to affiliate with private sector unions, and completely forbade strikes in state enterprises. Although the Government has not vigorously enforced these restrictions, it pledged to pass a new version of the law that would restore for the most part the rights enjoyed by state enterprise workers prior to the 1991 changes. A draft bill which failed to become law during the 1995–96 Banharn Government was resubmitted to Parliament by the Chavalit Government in December and passed the first of three readings needed to move the bill out of the House of Representatives.

The Government has the authority to restrict private sector strikes that would "affect national security or cause severe negative repercussions for the population at large." The Government seldom invokes this provision and did not do so in 1996. Labor law also forbids strikes in "essential services," defined much more broadly than the ILO criteria for such services. No strikes were disapproved on those grounds in 1996. The number of legal strikes has averaged fewer than 10 annually for the past 10 years.

Over half of the work force is employed in the unorganized agricultural sector. Less than 2 percent of the total work force, though nearly 11 percent of industrial workers, is unionized. Cultural traditions and unfamiliarity with the concept of industrial relations are often cited as the reasons for low rates of labor organization.

While violence against labor leaders is rare, the 1991 mysterious disappearance of outspoken labor leader Thanong Po-an remains unsolved (see Section 1.b.).

There is a legacy of corrupt public sector union leaders who were exploited by the military forces, politicians, or employers for their own purposes, but private unions generally operate independently of the Government and other outside organizations.

Unions are free to associate internationally with other trade union organizations, and they maintain a wide variety of such affiliations.

b. *The Right to Organize and Bargain Collectively.*—The 1975 Labor Relations Act recognizes the right of private sector workers to organize and bargain collectively and defines the mechanisms for such negotiations and for government-assisted conciliation and arbitration in cases under dispute. In practice, genuine collective bargaining occurs only in a small fraction of workplaces and in most instances continues to be characterized by a lack of sophistication on the part of employee groups and autocratic attitudes on the part of employers. Wage increases for most workers come as a result of increases in the minimum wage, rather than as a result of collective bargaining.

The Government sets wages for both civil servants and state enterprise employees. A system of labor courts created in 1980 exercises judicial review over most aspects of labor law for the private sector. Workers may also seek redress for their grievances from the Tripartite Labor Relations Committee. Redress of grievances for state enterprise workers is handled by the State Enterprise Labor Relations Committee. Labor leaders did not indicate dissatisfaction with the treatment that their concerns received in these forums, except that union leaders dismissed unjustly usually are awarded only monetary compensation.

No separate labor legislation applies to export processing zones, where wages and working conditions often are better than national norms because of the preponderance of Western and Japan-based multinational firms.

c. *Prohibition of Forced or Compulsory Labor.*—The Constitution prohibits forced or compulsory labor, except in the case of national emergency, war, or martial law. However, there are reports of sweatshops in the informal sector that physically restrain workers from leaving the premises. There are no estimates of how many such workshops exist, but the growing number of illegal aliens from Burma, Cambodia, and Laos increases the opportunities for such abuse. In one notable case, a Bangkok industrial glove making factory employed six girls 13 to 14 years of age working 15-hour days. The owner allegedly used a hot iron to inflict burns on three girls—two of whom were from Laos—as punishment for falling asleep on the job. In July authorities raided the shop and arrested the owner.

For several years, the ILO has cited Thailand for violations of Convention 29 on forced labor. In 1995 Thailand was the subject of a country "observation," but the ILO declined to make Thailand the subject of a special paragraph. The primary focus of ILO criticism is forced child labor, especially child prostitution. Since the ILO raised these concerns, the Government has cooperated in setting up important institutional links, particularly with the International Program on the Elimination of Child Labor, to help address the problem (see Section 5).

d. *Minimum Age for Employment of Children.*—The legal minimum age for employment is 13 years. Nearly 90 percent of children complete six grades of compulsory education at age 12; only 60 percent of 13-year-olds are enrolled in seventh grade, but this percentage is increasing. The law permits the employment of children between the ages of 13 and 15 only in "light work," where the lifting of heavy loads and exposure to toxic materials or dangerous equipment or situations is restricted. The employment of children at night (10 p.m. to 6 a.m.), or in venues where alcohol is served, is prohibited by law. An analysis based on population and school enrollment data shows that between 850,000 and 1,480,000 children work in Thailand, mostly on family farms. Between 240,000 and 410,000 (2 to 4 percent of the 6 to 14 age group) are estimated to be in urban employment at particular risk of labor abuse.

The Ministry of Labor has increased the number of inspectors specifically responsible for child labor issues, although not all these officers are engaged in full-time inspection work. Enforcement of child labor laws is not rigorous. The inclination when dealing with violators is to negotiate promises of better future behavior, rather than to seek prosecution and punishment.

The Government is also addressing the problem of child labor by proposing to extend compulsory education from 6 to 9 years.

e. *Acceptable Conditions of Work.*—A tripartite wage committee consisting of government, employer, and worker representatives increased the daily legal minimum wage by 7.6 percent in September. Minimum wage rates now range between $5.05 (128 baht) and $6.20 (157 baht) per day depending upon the cost of living in various provinces. This wage is not adequate to provide a decent standard of living for an urban worker and family. With extended family members' financial contributions, the minimum wage provides the basis for a marginally adequate overall standard of living. However, more than half of workers countrywide receive less than the minimum wage, especially in rural provinces. Unskilled migrant workers, as well as illegal aliens, often work for wages significantly less than the minimum wage. The minimum wage does not apply to undocumented hill tribe people. The Ministry of Labor is responsible for ensuring that employers meet minimum wage requirements. Despite encouragement of employees to report violations to labor inspectors, enforcement of minimum wage laws is mixed.

The Government has not mandated a uniform workweek for the entire labor force. By regulation, commercial employees work a maximum of 54 hours per week, employees in industry work 48, and those in "dangerous" work such as in the chemical, petroleum, mining, or other industries involving heavy machinery, 42. Transportation workers are restricted to no more than 8 hours per day. Enforcement of these standards is weak. There is no 24-hour rest period mandated by law.

Working conditions vary widely. In medium-sized and large factories, government health and safety standards are often maintained, but lax enforcement of safety standards is common. In the large informal sector, the health and safety environment is substandard. Employers are able to ignore safety regulations in part because nonunionized workers often do not understand safety and health standards and do not report violations. When 188 workers died in the May 1993 Kader Toy Factory fire near Bangkok, the Government brought suit against eight persons, including the managing director. The case commenced in June 1994 and continued throughout 1996 in once-weekly sessions without conclusion. There is no law affording job protection to employees who remove themselves from dangerous work situations. The Ministry of Labor and Social Welfare promulgates health and safety regulations regarding conditions of work. Labor inspectors are responsible for enforcement of health and safety regulations; the strictest penalty is 6 months in jail.

TONGA

The Kingdom of Tonga comprises 169 small islands scattered over a wide area of the South Pacific. Most of the approximately 105,000 inhabitants are Polynesian. Tonga is a constitutional monarchy in which political life is dominated by the King, the nobility, and a few prominent commoners. It is fully independent and a member of the Commonwealth of Nations.

The security apparatus is composed of the Tonga Defense Services (TDS) and a police force. The 350-man TDS force is responsible to and controlled by the Minister of Defense.

The economy is based primarily on the cultivation of tropical and semitropical crops. An increasing demand for imported manufactured goods and products unavailable locally has led to a substantial trade deficit. This has been offset largely by remittances from Tongans employed abroad, overseas aid, and to a lesser degree tourism. Remittances continued to diminish due in part to recessionary economic conditions in those overseas countries and in part to a weakening of emigrant ties to Tonga.

The principal human rights abuses remain severe restrictions on the right of citizens to change their government and discrimination against women. The Constitution, dating from 1875, has been increasingly challenged by commoners, whom it disadvantages.

RESPECT FOR HUMAN RIGHTS

Section 1. Respect for the Integrity of the Person, Including Freedom From:

a. *Political and Other Extrajudicial Killing.*—There were no reports of political or other extrajudicial killings.

b. *Disappearance.*—There were no reports of politically motivated disappearances.

c. *Torture and Other Cruel, Inhuman, or Degrading Treatment or Punishment.*— The Constitution forbids torture and inhuman or degrading punishment or other such treatment, and there were no reports of such practices. Prison conditions are basic, especially as regards food and sanitation, but in accordance with local living standards. Church representatives and family members are permitted to visit prisoners. As there are no local human rights groups, the question of visits by human rights monitors has not arisen.

d. *Arbitrary Arrest, Detention, or Exile.*—The Constitution proscribes arbitrary arrest or detention, and provides for the right to judicial determination of the legality of arrest; these are observed in practice. There is no preventive detention, although there are no statutory limits to the length of time a suspect may be held prior to being charged. The law does not limit access by counsel and family members to detained persons. There is no exile, internal or external.

e. *Denial of Fair Public Trial.*—The judiciary, whose top judges are expatriates, is independent of the King and the executive branch. The Court of Appeals, as the appellate court of last resort, is the highest court. The King's Privy Council presides over cases relating to disputes over titles of nobility and estate boundaries. The King has the right to commute a death sentence in cases of murder or treason. In addition, the court system consists of the Supreme Court (which has original jurisdiction over all major cases), the police magistrates' courts, a general court, a court martial for the TDS, a court tribunal for the police force, and a court of review for the Inland Revenue Department.

The law provides for the right to a fair public trial, and the Government honors it in practice. A court may not summon anyone without providing the person a written indictment stating the offenses it charges the person committed. Defendants are entitled to counsel, and lawyers have free access to defendants.

There were no reports of political prisoners.

f. *Arbitrary Interference with Privacy, Family, Home, or Correspondence.*—By law and in practice, no one may enter or search the home of another or remove any item of property unless in possession of a warrant issued by a magistrate. Neither the State nor political organizations intrude arbitrarily into a person's private life.

Section 2. Respect for Civil Liberties, Including:

a. *Freedom of Speech and Press.*—The Constitution provides for freedom of speech and the press. Tonga has five newspapers (one of which is government owned) and one national magazine. The Government owns the only radio station. While there is generally little editorializing in the government-owned media, opposition opinion appears regularly alongside government statements and letters. A privately owned newspaper, Kele'a, openly criticizes the Government without government interference. A Catholic monthly, Taumu'a Lelei, also speaks out freely.

However, infringements of freedom of the press do occur. The Minister of Police has on occasion threatened action against the independent media. Specific infringements are usually tied to a particular event. An Australian journalist who had written critically (and, the Government alleged, not factually) about the Tongan royal family was barred from attending the July Pacific Island Media Association convention. In September two journalists, one a Tongan-American, were arrested and sentenced to 30 days in prison by the Parliament for publishing a notice of impeachment submitted to Parliament against the Justice Minister for having traveled to the Atlanta Olympics. The Member of Parliament who submitted the notice of impeachment also was jailed.

b. *Freedom of Peaceful Assembly and Association.*—The law provides for peaceful assembly and association. There are no significant restrictions.

c. *Freedom of Religion.*—The Constitution provides for freedom of religion, and the Government respects this right in practice.

d. *Freedom of Movement Within the Country, Foreign Travel, Emigration, and Repatriation.*—Citizens are free to travel anywhere within the Kingdom and abroad. The law places no restrictions on repatriation.

The Government cooperates with the office of the United Nations High Commissioner for Refugees and other humanitarian organizations in assisting refugees. No person in recent memory has applied for refugee status, and the Government has not formulated a formal policy regarding refugees, asylees, or first asylum.

Section 3. Respect for Political Rights: The Right of Citizens to Change Their Government

Citizens do not have the ability to change their leaders or the system of government. The King and a small group of hereditary nobles dominate political life. They assert authority largely through their control of substantial landholdings and their predominant role in the Legislative Assembly. The Constitution allows the monarch broad powers, many of which do not require the endorsement of the legislative branch. The King appoints and presides over the Privy Council, which makes major policy decisions. (When the King is not presiding, the Privy Council is called the Cabinet.) The King also selects the Prime Minister and other Cabinet ministers, who hold office at his pleasure.

The unicameral legislature, the Legislative Assembly, consists of 12 Cabinet ministers, 9 nobles elected by their peers, and 9 people's representatives. All literate Tongans 21 years of age or older are eligible to vote. The King appoints the Speaker from among the representatives of the nobles. Government ministers generally vote with the nobles' representatives as a bloc. People's representatives sometimes vote against the Government.

Throughout the 1990's, people inside and outside the government establishment have called for democratic change. The Prodemocracy Movement, formally established in 1993, is dedicated to educating the people about their democratic rights. Following its election victory in February 1993, the movement turned to drafting proposals for revision of the 1875 Constitution, most notably proposals for popular election of all 30 members of the Assembly and election of the House Speaker from among Assembly members. As a result of January parliamentary elections, all of the nine people's representative seats are now held by legislators who advocate democratic reform.

Section 4. Governmental Attitude Regarding International and Nongovernmental Investigation of Alleged Violations of Human Rights

While there are no known barriers to the formation of local nongovernmental organizations that concern themselves with human rights, no such organizations exist. No outside organizations are known to have made requests to investigate alleged human rights violations. Tonga is not a member of the United Nations.

Section 5. Discrimination Based on Race, Sex, Religion, Disability, Language, or Social Status

Social, cultural, and economic facilities are available to all citizens regardless of race or religion. However, members of the hereditary nobility have substantial advantages. These include control over most of the land and a generally privileged status. Nonetheless, it is possible for commoners to rise to cabinet positions in government and to accumulate great wealth and status in the private sector.

Women.—Domestic violence is infrequent. Incidents of wife beating that do occur are generally dealt with in traditional ways between the families and village elders; abused wives sometimes return to their families if mediation fails.

In this male-dominated society, women generally occupy a subordinate role. While the strong Polynesian cultural tradition has discouraged the rise of women to positions of leadership, a few have nonetheless become members of the legislature and have served in responsible positions in various occupations. However, these women needed connections with the nobility or extraordinary luck, and they face severe limits on their upward mobility in this tradition-bound society. Some village women are breaking the mold of passive, docile followers by leading village-based development projects. The Government has sought to direct the efforts of women's nongovernmental organizations (NGO's) by establishing a women's unit within the Prime Minister's office. However, women's groups view this as an attempt to co-opt them and their programs. They criticize the Government's emphasis on organization, process, and control, with few programs of substance. The NGO's and the women's unit disagree on the need for and potential composition of a government-sponsored National Council of Women.

Children.—The Government is committed to children's human rights and welfare and provides commensurate funding for children's welfare within the context of the total resources available to the State. Child abuse, if it occurs, is rare and has not become a source of societal concern.

People With Disabilities.—No mandated provisions for accessibility for the disabled exist. There were no known complaints of discrimination in employment, education, or provision of other state services. Education of children with special needs has been a longstanding priority of the Queen.

Section 6. Worker Rights

a. *The Right of Association.*—Workers have the right to form unions under the 1964 Trade Union Act, but to date no unions have been formed, presumably because of the small size of the wage economy and the lack of a perceived need for unions. The lack of unions makes the question of the ability of unions to affiliate with international bodies moot; however, such a right is neither protected, prohibited, nor limited by the Government.

b. *The Right to Organize and Bargain Collectively.*—Since no unions have been formed, collective bargaining is not practiced. There is no legislation permitting and protecting collective bargaining or the right to organize. Labor laws and regulations are enforced in all sectors of the economy, including in the two small export enhancement zones.

c. *Prohibition of Forced or Compulsory Labor.*—The law prohibits forced labor, and it is not practiced.

d. *Minimum Age for Employment of Children.*—Child labor is not used in the wage economy, although there is no legislation prohibiting it. Education has been compulsory since 1882. Although it is sometimes criticized as being of poor quality, education is provided for all children through Form 6 (high school). Compliance rates are good.

e. *Acceptable Conditions of Work.*—There is no minimum wage law. Labor laws and regulations, enforced by the Ministry of Labor, Commerce, and Industry, limit the workweek to 40 hours. The Ministry of Labor enforces laws and regulations reasonably well in the wage sector of the economy, particularly on the main island of Tongatapu. Enforcement in agriculture and on the outer islands is limited by isolation.

Industrial accidents are rare, as few industries exist that would expose workers to significant danger. Due to these factors, there has been little or no work done on industrial safety standards.

TUVALU

Tuvalu, with about 10,000 primarily Polynesian people, occupies a land surface area of 26 square kilometers on 9 atolls in the central South Pacific. It became independent from the United Kingdom on October 1, 1978, and is a member of the Commonwealth of Nations. Its Constitution provides for a Westminster-style parliamentary democracy. Tuvalu's Head of State is the British Queen, represented by the Governor General who must be a Tuvaluan citizen.

A 32-member police constabulary, the only security apparatus, is responsible to and effectively controlled by civilian authority.

The primarily subsistence economy relies mainly on coconuts, taro, and fishing. Tuvalu depends heavily on foreign aid, mainly from Australia, New Zealand, Japan, and Taiwan. Remittances from Tuvaluans working abroad as well as the sale of commemorative and thematic postage stamps and of fishing licenses to foreign vessels provide additional sources of foreign exchange. Tuvalu's isolation and meager natural resources limit prospects for economic development.

Tuvaluan society is egalitarian, democratic, and respectful of human rights. Social behavior, as determined by custom and tradition, however, is considered as important as the law and is ensured by the village elders. Land is also key to much of the structure of Tuvaluan society. There were no reports of specific human rights abuses. However, in the traditional culture of the islands, women occupy a subordinate role, with limits on their job opportunities, although recently there has been substantial effort to accord women equality in employment and decisionmaking.

RESPECT FOR HUMAN RIGHTS

Section 1. Respect for the Integrity of the Person, Including Freedom From:

a. *Political and Other Extrajudicial Killing.*—There were no reports of politically motivated or other extrajudicial killings.

b. *Disappearance.*—There were no reports of politically motivated disappearances.

c. *Torture and Other Cruel, Inhuman, or Degrading Treatment or Punishment.*—The Constitution forbids torture and inhuman or degrading punishment, and there were no reported instances of such practices. Local hereditary elders exercise considerable traditional authority—including the seldom invoked right to inflict corporal punishment for infringing customary rules—which can be at odds with the national law.

Prison facilities in this tiny island nation with less than 10,000 population consist of several holding cells at the back of the police station. There have been no serious crimes within the memory of local officials. It is rare for a prisoner to spend as long as a week in a cell; more commonly, a person is incarcerated overnight because of drunkenness. While prison conditions are somewhat Spartan as regards food and sanitation, the level of complaints seems to be minimal or nonexistent. Since there are no local human rights groups, the question of prison monitoring by them has not arisen. Visits by church groups and family members are permitted.

d. *Arbitrary Arrest, Detention, or Exile.*—The Constitution prohibits arbitrary arrest, detention, or exile, and the Government observes this prohibition.

e. *Denial of Fair Public Trial.*—The judicial system consists of the higher courts, namely, the Privy Council, the Court of Appeal, and the High Court; and the lower courts, i.e., those of the senior and resident magistrates, the island courts, and the land courts. The Chief Justice, who is also Chief Justice of Nauru, sits on the High Court about once a year.

The right to a fair public trial is ensured by law and observed in practice. The Constitution provides that accused persons must be informed of the nature of the offenses with which they are charged and be provided the time and facilities required to prepare a defense. An independent people's lawyer is ensured by statute. The services of this public defender are available to all Tuvaluans free of charge. The right to confront witnesses, present evidence, and appeal convictions is provided by law. Procedural safeguards are based on English common law. The judiciary is independent and free of governmental interference. There were no reports of political prisoners.

f. *Arbitrary Interference with Privacy, Family, Home, or Correspondence.*—The Government adheres in practice to the legal protection of privacy of the home. It does not arbitrarily intrude into the private life of the individual.

Section 2. Respect for Civil Liberties, Including:

a. *Freedom of Speech and Press.*—The Government respects in practice freedom of speech and press. The one radio station is under government control.

b. *Freedom of Peaceful Assembly and Association.*—The Constitution provides for freedom of assembly and association, and there are no significant restrictions in practice.

c. *Freedom of Religion.*—The Constitution provides for separation of church and state and imposes no restrictions on freedom of religion, and the Government respects these provisions.

d. *Freedom of Movement Within the Country, Foreign Travel, Emigration, and Repatriation.*—Citizens are free to travel within the country and abroad.

The Government does not restrict repatriation. The Government cooperates with the United Nations High Commissioner for Refugees and other humanitarian organizations in assisting refugees. No person in recent memory has applied for refugee status, and the Government has not formulated a formal policy regarding refugees, asylees, or first asylum.

Section 3. Respect for Political Rights: The Right of Citizens to Change Their Government

The people freely and directly elect a 12-member unicameral Parliament whose normal term is 4 years. Each of Tuvalu's nine atolls is administered by a six-person council, also elected by universal suffrage to 4-year terms. The minimum voting age is 18 years.

The Cabinet consists of the Prime Minister, elected by secret ballot from among the Members of Parliament, and up to four other ministers, appointed and removed from office by the Governor General with the advice of the Prime Minister. The Prime Minister may appoint or dismiss the Governor General on behalf of the British Monarch. There are no formal political parties in Tuvalu. The Prime Minister may be removed from office by a parliamentary vote of no confidence.

For cultural reasons, women are underrepresented in politics. The Parliament has one female member. She had served as Minister of Health in a previous government but stepped aside in favor of her husband's successful bid to become Prime Minister.

Section 4. Governmental Attitude Regarding International and Nongovernmental Investigation of Alleged Violations of Human Rights

There have been no reported allegations of human rights violations by the Government and no known requests for investigations. While no known barriers block their establishment, there are no local nongovernmental organizations that concern themselves with human rights. Tuvalu is not a member of the United Nations.

Section 5. Discrimination Based on Race, Sex, Religion, Disability, Language, or Social Status

The Constitution prohibits discrimination on the basis of race, creed, sex, or national origin, and the Government generally respects these prohibitions. However, the traditional culture has limited women's job opportunities.

Women.—Violence against women is rare. If wife beating occurs, it is infrequent and has not become a source of societal concern.

Women increasingly hold positions in the health and education sectors. This trend was partly due to former Prime Minister Paeniu, who favored greater opportunities for women. Paeniu named women among his senior advisers and included them in his Cabinet. Although the current Prime Minister has not appointed any women to his Cabinet, he has encouraged the participation of women in other areas of the Government, especially in the Tuvaluan Education for Life program.

Children.—The Government is committed to children's human rights and welfare and provides commensurate funding for children's welfare within the context of the total resources available to the State. There are no reports of child abuse.

People With Disabilities.—Although there are no mandated accessibility provisions for the disabled, there are no known reports of discrimination in employment, education, or provision of other state services.

Section 6. Worker Rights

   a. *The Right of Association.*—Workers are free to organize unions and choose their own labor representatives, but most of the population lacks permanent employment and is engaged in subsistence activity. The law provides for the right to strike, but no strike has ever been recorded.

   In the public sector, the country's civil servants, teachers, and nurses—who, taken together, total less than 1,000 employees—are grouped into associations which do not presently have the status of unions. The only registered trade union, the Tuvalu Seamen's Union, has about 600 members, who work on foreign merchant vessels. Unions may affiliate with international bodies. The Seamen's Union is a member of the International Transportation Workers' Federation.

   b. *The Right to Organize and Bargain Collectively.*—The Industrial Relations Code (1978) provides for conciliation, arbitration, and settlement procedures in cases of labor disputes. Although there are provisions for collective bargaining, the practice in the private sector is for wages to be set by employers. For both the private and public sectors, the legal procedures for resolving labor disputes are seldom used; instead, the two sides normally engage in nonconfrontational deliberations in the local multipurpose meeting hall.

   Tuvalu is not a member of the International Labor Organization.

   There are no export processing zones.

   c. *Prohibition of Forced or Compulsory Labor.*—The Tuvalu Employment Ordinance (1978) prohibits forced or compulsory labor, and there have been no reports of either being practiced.

   d. *Minimum Age for Employment of Children.*—The Employment Law prohibits children under the age of 14 from working. Education is compulsory for children from 6 through 13 years of age. The Law also prohibits children under 15 years of age from industrial employment or work on any ship and stipulates that children under the age of 18 years are not allowed to enter into formal contracts, including work contracts. Children are rarely employed outside the traditional economy.

   e. *Acceptable Conditions of Work.*—The modest minimum wage, set administratively by the Government, is sufficient to allow a worker and family in the wage economy to maintain a decent standard of living. The present minimum wage in the public (government) sector is $0.40 per hour ($A0.55) per hour. This rate applies regardless of sex and age. In most cases, the private sector adopts the same minimum wage rate.

   The Labor Office may specify the days and hours of work for workers in various industries. The workday is legally set at 8 hours. The majority of workers are outside the wage economy. The law provides for rudimentary health and safety standards. It requires employers to provide an adequate potable water supply, basic sanitary arrangements, and medical care. Specific provisions of the law provide for the protection of female workers. The Ministry of Labor, Works and Communications is responsible for the enforcement of these regulations, but it is able to provide only minimum enforcement.

VANUATU

Vanuatu, a small South Pacific island nation of approximately 170,000 people which was jointly administered by Britain and France prior to its independence in 1980, has a parliamentary form of government with a 50-member Parliament, a Prime Minister, and a President. The latter's powers are largely ceremonial, except when acting on the advice of the Council of Ministers. Political legitimacy is based on majority rule.

The civilian authorities normally control the small police and paramilitary Vanuatu Mobile Force, however, a brief mutiny in October by elements of the VMF over pay issues shook the principle of civilian control. The mutiny was resolved without bloodshed.

Subsistence and small-scale agricultural production and fishing support more than 80 percent of the population. Copra, cocoa, and beef cattle are the main cash crops. The service sector—government, tourism, and an offshore financial center—provides most formal employment and represents the largest component of the country's gross domestic product.

Government control over much of the country's media, attempts to interfere with the independence of the judiciary, together with discrimination and violence against women, remain the major human rights problems.

RESPECT FOR HUMAN RIGHTS

Section 1. Respect for the Integrity of the Person, Including Freedom From:

a. *Political and Other Extrajudicial Killing.*—There were no reports of political or other extrajudicial killings.

b. *Disappearance.*—There were no reports of politically motivated disappearances.

c. *Torture and Cruel, Inhuman, or Degrading Treatment or Punishment.*—Constitutional provisions against torture and cruel, inhuman, or degrading treatment are observed in practice and enforced by the courts. The law provides that prisoners shall have recourse to the Ombudsman, a constitutional position.

Prison conditions meet minimum international standards, and the Government permits visits by human rights monitors, if requested.

d. *Arbitrary Arrest, Detention, or Exile.*—There were no reports of arbitrary arrests. Arrest is by warrant. The Constitutional provision that suspects must be informed of the charges and given a speedy hearing before a judge is observed in practice. There is no exile.

e. *Denial of Fair Public Trial.*—The courts are normally free of military or executive interference. The courts uphold constitutional provisions for a fair public trial, presumption of innocence until guilt is proven, prohibition against double jeopardy, the right of judicial determination of the validity of arrest or detention, and appeal to the Supreme Court. However, the executive has tried to pressure the largely expatriate judiciary in cases with political implications (see Section 2.d.).

There were no reports of political prisoners.

f. *Arbitrary Interference with Privacy, Family, Home, or Correspondence.*—There were no reports of arbitrary interference with privacy, family, home, or correspondence.

Section 2. Respect for Civil Liberties, Including:

a. *Freedom of Speech and Press.*—The Constitution provides for freedom of speech and the press; however, these provisions have not always been honored in practice. The Government controls much of the country's media, including a weekly newspaper, one AM and one FM radio station, and a limited-service television station confined to the capital, Port Vila, which provides English and French news service three times a week. In late 1994, an independent weekly, which has since expanded into semiweekly editions, began publishing. Opposition political parties and groupings occasionally publish newsletters, one of which developed into a newsweekly by mid-year.

The December 1995-February 1996 coalition government headed by Prime Minister Serge Vohor continued the previous government's policy of pressuring both government-owned and private media to limit the presentation of views with which it did not agree. A minister implicitly threatened to revoke the residency permit of the expatriate publisher of the independent semiweekly newspaper for allegedly irresponsible reporting. As the political crisis intensified just prior to the parliamentary vote that unseated the Vohor government in late February, Vohor ordered a broadcast ban on all information relating to his resignation revocation and the forthcoming extraordinary session of Parliament. The Pacific Islands News Association (PINA) condemned the ban.

Some pressures on the media lessened following Parliament's selection of Maxime Carlot Korman to replace Vohor in February. However, the Carlot Korman government continued to restrict news disseminated by the government-controlled media. In May it banned Radio Vanuatu from broadcasting a Vohor press statement criticising the Supreme Court decision upholding the legality of the parliamentary vote which had unseated him. The Government reportedly also instructed Radio Vanuatu to submit all political statements and news items for prior review.

Following a shift in political alliances, in September Parliament voted no confidence in the Carlot Korman government, and reelected Vohor as Prime Minister. Immediately following his reelection, Vohor promised to support press freedom.

Vanuatu governments have not been as concerned over media reports directed to external audiences. PACNEWS, a Pacific regional news agency located in Vanuatu since 1994, continued to transmit stories throughout the region even when they included criticism of the country's leaders. Correspondents for international media are also allowed to report without interference.

b. *Freedom of Peaceful Assembly and Association.*—Permits must be obtained to hold public demonstrations and rallies; usually they are routinely granted.

The Government does not restrict the forming of political parties and other groups.

c. *Freedom of Religion.*—The law provides for freedom of religion, and the Government generally respected it in practice. Missionaries of various Christian denominations work without restriction. The Government apparently has not attempted to enforce the 1995 Religious Bodies Act, which the President refused to sign on constitutional grounds. The act gives the Government the right to register and potentially to control the activities of religious organizations.

d. *Freedom of Movement Within the Country, Foreign Travel, Emigration, and Repatriation.*—All citizens are free to travel internally and externally and to return from abroad without restrictions.

The Government has not formulated a policy regarding refugees, asylees, or first asylum. The issue of the provision of first asylum has never arisen.

Various governments have used their immigration powers to expel, or try to expel, as undesirable immigrants, expatriates with whom they were displeased. A minister in the first Vohor government (December 1995-February 1996) implicitly threatened to revoke the residency permit of the expatriate publisher of an independent, semiweekly newspaper for allegedly irresponsible reporting (see Section 2.a.). The Carlot Korman government, in power from February to September, declared two expatriate jurists associated with the previous Vohor government undesirable immigrants. One was an Australian lawyer, who had unsuccessfully contested in court the legality of the February parliamentary session that elected Carlot Korman as prime minister. The other was a jurist, who the Vohor government had brought to Vanuatu before its ouster with the intention of appointing him a Supreme Court justice. Both departed the country in March. The second Vohor Government in October threatened to fire and expel the Supreme Court Chief Justice, who had sought to use the Court's judicial powers to issue warrants against leaders of a VMF mutiny in contravention of a cabinet promise that the mutineers would not be punished. His expulsion was suspended while the Court heard his appeal of the immigration order.

Section 3. Respect for Political Rights: The Right of Citizens to Change Their Government

The Constitution provides for parliamentary elections every 4 years, through which citizens can freely change their government. The general elections held in November 1995 did not give a majority to any of the three main political parties. Since the election, two short-lived coalition governments have held office. The present Government, also a coalition led by Prime Minister Serge Vohor, assumed office in October.

While outside observers generally consider the November 1995 voting to be fair, the Government's influence on the media prevented opposition parties from fully publicizing their views. That government, as well as successor governments, have also been accused of politically biased employment practices.

Traditional attitudes, in which males are dominant and females are frequently limited to customary family roles, hamper women from taking a more active role in economic and political life. One member of parliament is a woman, who also served briefly as a cabinet minister in the current government. A woman is mayor of the second largest town.

Section 4. Governmental Attitudes Regarding International and Nongovernmental Investigation of Alleged Violations of Human Rights

There are no restrictions on the formation of local human rights organizations, and Vanuatu's first, the Human Rights Forum, was founded in 1994.

Section 5. Discrimination Based on Race, Sex, Religion, Disability, Language, or Social Status

The 1980 Constitution provides fundamental rights and freedoms to "all persons * * * without discrimination on the grounds of race, place of origin, religious or traditional beliefs, political opinions, language, or sex." Despite constitutional and legal protections, women remain victims of discrimination in this tradition-based society. Due to high rates of unemployment, there are few jobs available to the disabled.

Women.—Violence against women, particularly wife beating, is believed to be common, although no accurate statistics exist. Courts occasionally prosecute offenders using common law assault as a basis for prosecution since there are no specific laws against wife beating. However, most cases of violence against women, including rape, go unreported because women, particularly in rural areas, are reluctant to report them for fear of further abuse. In addition police are frequently reluctant to intervene in what are considered to be domestic matters.

While women have equal rights under the law, they are only slowly emerging from a traditional culture characterized by male dominance, a general reluctance to educate women, and a widespread belief that women should devote themselves primarily to childbearing. In announcing Vanuatu's ratification of the U.N. Convention on Elimination of all Forms of Discrimination Against Women (CEDAW) at the 1995

U.N. Conference on Women in Beijing, the then-Deputy Prime Minister stated that it would take time to implement the laws giving equal rights to women.

The majority of women enter into marriage through "bride-price payment," a practice that encourages men to view women as property. Women are also inhibited by tradition from owning land, and at least one women's advocate believes this limitation serves to underpin their secondary status. Many female leaders view village chiefs as a major obstacle to attaining social, political and economic rights for women. The National Council of Women organized seminars prior to the November 1995 general elections to increase women's awareness of their political rights.

Children.—Although the Government has made education a priority, access to education is limited and school attendance is not compulsory. Children are protected within the traditional extended-family system. Members of the extended family, particularly paternal uncles, play an active role in a child's development. As a result, virtually no children are homeless or abandoned. There is no societal pattern of abuse, although cases of child abuse are occasionally reported.

People With Disabilities.—There is no known governmental or national policy on the disabled and no legislation mandating access for them. Their protection and care is left to the traditional extended family and to voluntary nongovernmental organizations.

National/Racial/Ethnic Minorities.—Most of the population is made up of Melanesians. Small minorities of Chinese, Fijians, Vietnamese, Tongans, and Europeans are generally concentrated in two towns and on a few plantations; they experience discrimination with regard to land ownership. There is no evidence to suggest a pattern of ethnic discrimination in the provision of the limited basic services which the Government provides.

Section 6. Worker Rights

a. *The Right of Association.*—The law provides workers with the right to organize unions. Unions may not affiliate with international labor federations without government permission.

Approximately 29,000 persons participate in the formal economy as wage earners. There are five trade unions. The unions are grouped under an umbrella organization, the Vanuatu Council of Trade Unions, a member of the International Confederation of Free Trade Unions. The trade unions are independent of the Government and ran a number of candidates under the Labor Party banner in the November 1995 general elections, although no Labor candidate was elected to Parliament or received more than a small percentage of the votes.

The high percentage of the population still engaged in subsistence agriculture and fishing deters extensive union activity. In addition membership in the Vanuatu Public Servants Union fell dramatically following the Government's wholesale dismissal of hundreds of full-time public servants during a protracted general strike in 1994. The Supreme Court in February 1994 ruled that the union had not complied with its own rules when it undertook the general strike and declared the strike illegal. Combined union membership in the private and public sectors reportedly has fallen from more than 4,000 to less than 1,000 in the aftermath of the 1994 strike.

The law prohibits retribution if the strike is legal. In the case of private-sector employees, violations would be referred to the Labor Department for conciliation and arbitration. In the public sector, violations would be handled by the Public Service Commission.

In August 1995, Parliament passed a law requiring unions to give 30 days' notice of intent to strike, with a list of the names of intending strikers.

There was no significant strike activity in 1996.

b. *The Right to Organize and Bargain Collectively.*—Unions exercise the right to organize and bargain collectively. Labor unions negotiate wages and conditions directly with management. If the two sides cannot agree, the matter is referred to a 3-member arbitration board appointed by the Minister of Home Affairs. The board consists of one representative from organized labor, one from management, and the senior magistrate of the magistrate's court. While a dispute is before the board, labor may not strike and management may not dismiss union employees. Unions and management, however, generally reach agreement on wages without having to refer the matter to arbitration. Complaints of antiunion discrimination are referred to the Commissioner of Labor. While the law does not require union recognition, once a union is recognized, it does prohibit antiunion discrimination.

There are no export processing zones.

c. *Prohibition of Forced or Compulsory Labor.*—The law prohibits forced or compulsory labor, and there were no reports that either is practiced.

d. *Minimum Age for Employment of Children.*—The law prohibits children under 12 years of age from working outside of family-owned agricultural production, where many children assist their parents. Employment of children from 12 to 18 years of age is restricted by occupational category and conditions of labor, for example, restrictions on employment in the shipping industry and on night-time employment. The Labor Department effectively enforces these laws.

e. *Acceptable Conditions of Work.*—Vanuatu has a legislated minimum wage, effectively enforced by the Labor Department. In February 1995, it was raised to a flat rate of approximately $143 (16,000 vatu) per month for both urban and rural workers. The previous minimum wage was approximately $93 for rural workers and $107 (13,200 vatu) for urban workers. The minimum wage would not support an urban family living entirely on the cash economy. Most families are not dependent solely on wages for their livelihoods.

Various laws regulate the rights to sick leave, annual vacations, and other conditions of employment, including a 44-hour maximum workweek, with at least one 24-hour rest period weekly. Vanuatu's Employment Act, enforced by the Labor Department, includes provisions for safety standards. However, the 1987 safety and health legislation is inadequate to protect workers engaged in logging, agriculture, construction, and manufacturing, and the single inspector attached to the Labor Department is hard pressed to enforce the act fully. Workers have the right to remove themselves from dangerous work situations without jeopardy to their continued employment.

VIETNAM

The Socialist Republic of Vietnam (SRV) is a one-party state controlled by the Vietnamese Communist Party (VCP). The VCP's constitutionally mandated leading role and the occupancy of all senior government positions by Party members ensures the primacy of Politburo guidelines. The National Assembly, chosen in elections in which all candidates are approved by the Party, remains largely subservient to the VCP, as does the judiciary. Most Assembly members belong to the VCP. The National Assembly played a stronger role than in the past by seriously debating and revising proposed legislation. The Government is working to reduce formal involvement of the Party in government operations, and government officials have some latitude in implementing policies. The Government continued to restrict significantly civil liberties on national security grounds.

The military services are responsible for external defense, including the border defense force. While they have no direct responsibility for maintaining internal security, the military forces are seeking to establish for themselves a role in public education and campaigns against perceived threats to society. The Ministry of Interior is responsible for internal security. It controls the police, a special national security investigative agency, and other units that maintain internal security. Acting under the control of the Party and the Government, the Ministry enforces laws and regulations that significantly restrict individual liberties and violate other human rights. The Ministry of Interior also maintains a system of household registration and block wardens to monitor the population, concentrating on those suspected of engaging, or being likely to engage, in unauthorized political activities. Members of the security forces committed human rights abuses.

Vietnam is a very poor country undergoing a transition from a centrally planned to a more market-oriented economy. Agriculture, primarily rice cultivation, employs two-thirds of the work force and accounts for one-third of gross domestic product (GDP). As a result of reforms, the country has experienced rapid growth in many industries, including construction, petroleum, textiles, and light manufacturing. Exports, led by crude oil, rice, marine products, textiles, and foodstuffs, have increased sharply. Estimated annual GDP per capita has increased to approximately $300. Particularly in urban areas, economic reforms have raised the standard of living and reduced party and government control over, and intrusion into, people's daily lives.

The Government's human rights record continued to be poor. The Government continued to repress basic political and some religious freedoms and to commit numerous abuses. While the VCP moved to reform procedures and debate within itself, the Government denied citizens the right to change their government and significantly restricted freedom of speech, the press, assembly, association, privacy, and religion. The Government arbitrarily arrested and detained citizens, including detention for peaceful expression of political and religious objections to government policies, and denied them the right to a fair and expeditious trial. The Government continued its longstanding policy of not tolerating most types of public dissent and of prohibiting independent religious, political, and labor organizations. There were credible reports that security officials beat detainees. Prison conditions were harsh.

Societal discrimination and violence against women remained problems. Trafficking in children for prostitution within Vietnam and to other countries grew, although the Government moved to combat the problem.

Within still narrow parameters, the National Assembly and the press engaged in increasingly vigorous debate on legal, economic, and social issues, and there was continued progress in building a legal infrastructure. In July a new Civil Code took effect that included an administrative court system to deal with complaints about abuse and corruption by state officials. The trend toward reduced government interference in people's daily lives continued, as did the trend toward economic liberalization. The Government allowed people slightly greater freedom of expression and assembly to protest grievances, but intermittently restricted some activities of clergy. There were credible reports that some political prisoners were denied visitation rights and that certain prisons employ the use of forced labor, sometimes as part of commercial ventures.

RESPECT FOR HUMAN RIGHTS

Section 1. Respect for the Integrity of the Person, Including Freedom From:

a. *Political and Other Extrajudicial Killing.*—There were no known politically motivated extrajudicial killings. Little information is available on the extent of deaths in police custody or on official investigations into such incidents. The Government is investigating a case reported in the domestic media wherein police may have tried to cover up the death of a man in police custody by attempting to depict his death as a suicide.

b. *Disappearance.*—There were no reports of politically motivated disappearances.

c. *Torture and Other Cruel, Inhuman, or Degrading Treatment or Punishment.*—The law prohibits physical abuse. However, there is evidence that security officials beat detainees and used threats and other psychological coercion to elicit confessions. There were no known reports of torture of detainees. Little information is available on the extent of police brutality during interrogations. In September police beat and detained a foreign journalist reporting on a political demonstration in the capital.

Prison conditions are harsh. Conditions generally do not threaten the lives of prisoners, but some released prisoners reported that the death rate among male prisoners due to disease and violence was high. Overcrowding, insufficient diet, and poor sanitation remain serious problems. Conditions in pretrial detention are particularly harsh, and there were credible reports that detainees were sometimes denied access to sunlight, exercise, and reading material. Most prisoners have access to basic health care and, for those with money, to supplemental food and medicine. However, there were credible reports that some political prisoners were denied visitation rights and that some prisons employ the use of forced labor, sometimes as part of commercial ventures (see Section 6.c.). Prisoners sentenced to hard labor complained that the diet and health care were insufficient to sustain their health, especially when they were detained in remote, disease-ridden areas.

Several political prisoners with serious medical conditions are being held in harsh conditions in remote prisons with little access to medical care. For example, Dr. Doan Viet Hoat (see Section 1.e.) continued to serve a 15-year sentence at the Thanh Cam camp, in a remote and malaria-ridden area of Thanh Hoa province, 1,400 kilometers from his home and relatives. His location has made it difficult for his family to provide medicine for his kidney disorder. Similarly, Do Van Thac, imprisoned for 14 years (reduced to 12 years) on charges of attempting to overthrow the Government, remains imprisoned in remote Nam Ha province despite having suffered a stroke and suffering from heart disease. Dr. Nguyen Dan Que has been held in isolation in Camp Z30A-K3 in Xuan Loc, Dong Nai province for nearly 3 years. Reports indicate Thich Hai Tang, a Buddhist monk convicted of involvement in a demonstration by Buddhists in Hue in 1993 and sentenced to 4 years in prison, is ill and being held in solitary confinement.

The Government does not permit independent monitoring of its prison and detention system, although it did allow an Australian parliamentary delegation to visit one prison in 1995. The United Nations Working Group on Human Rights visited several prisons in October 1994.

d. *Arbitrary Arrest, Detention, or Exile.*—The Government continued to arrest people arbitrarily. Although the 1990 Criminal Procedure Code provides various rights for detainees, including time limits on pretrial detention and the right of the accused to have a lawyer present during interrogation, in practice the authorities often ignore these legal safeguards.

Law enforcement officials appear able to arrest and incarcerate people without presenting arrest warrants. In cases where a warrant is presented, the procurator rather than an independent judiciary approves issuance of warrants. Once arrested, detainees often are held for lengthy periods without formal charges or trial. Nguyen Xuan Tu, also known as Ha Si Phu, and Le Hong Ha were held without trial from December 5, 1995 until their 1-day trial on August 22. Ha was released on December 9.

Those arrested for peaceful expression of their views are likely to be charged under any one of several provisions in the Criminal Code outlawing acts against the State.

No official statistics are available on what percentage of the prison population consists of pretrial detainees or the average period of time such detainees have been held. It is difficult to determine the exact number of political detainees in part because the Government does not usually publicize such arrests and frequently conducted closed trials and sentencing.

The Government does not use exile as a means of political control but has employed internal exile to restrict the movement of certain political or religious dissidents. For example, credible reports indicate that the leader of the United Buddhist Church of Vietnam (UBCV), Thich Huyen Quang, remains in a remote area of Quang Ngai province, where he was involuntarily moved from his pagoda in 1995. Similarly, two Buddhist monks, released in 1995 after serving sentences, were removed from their base pagoda in Hue in November and restricted to their home villages.

e. *Denial of Fair Public Trial.*—While the Constitution provides for the independence of judges and jurors, in practice the VCP controls the courts closely at all levels, selecting judges primarily for political reliability. Credible reports indicate that party officials, including top leaders, instruct courts on how to rule on politically important cases. The President appoints judges.

The court system consists of local people's courts, military tribunals, and the Supreme People's Court. The Supreme People's Court can review cases from the lower courts or tribunals. In addition, local mass organizations are empowered to deal with minor breaches of law or disputes. Economic courts handle commercial disputes, and administrative courts deal with complaints by citizens about official abuse and corruption; they have addressed few cases since their creation in 1993. In July the 838-article Civil Code came into effect, a major step in efforts to strengthen the rule of law.

The People's Procuracy has unchecked power to bring charges against the accused and serves as prosecutor during trials. A judging council, made up of a judge and one or more people's jurors (lay judges), determines guilt or innocence and also passes sentence on the convicted. The relevant people's council appoints people's jurors, who are required to be people of high moral standards but who are not required to have legal training.

Trials are generally open to the public, although judicial authorities sometimes closed trials or strictly limited attendance in sensitive cases. For example, the 1-day trial of Ha Si Phu, Le Hong Ha, and Nguyen Kien Giang on August 22 was closed to the public. The Government did not respond to requests by foreign diplomats to attend the trial. Defendants have the right to be present at their trial and to have a lawyer, and the defendant or the defense lawyer has the right to cross-examine witnesses. In political cases, however, there are credible reports that defendants were not allowed access to government evidence in advance of the trial, to cross-examine witnesses, or to challenge statements. Little information is available on the extent to which defendants and their lawyers have time to prepare for trials. Those convicted have the right to appeal. Although Vietnam has made some progress in developing a legal system, many judges and other court officials lack adequate legal training. Government efforts to develop a fair, effective judicial system were undermined by the lack of openness in the judicial process and the continuing subservience of the judiciary to the Party.

The Government continued to hold a number of political prisoners incarcerated for the peaceful expression of dissenting religious or political views. For example, Doan Viet Hoat is serving a 15-year sentence for publishing a reformist newsletter. His family reports that the Government has withheld food, medicine, and letters that they have sent him, and denied him reading materials. Others arrested with him, including Pham Duc Kham, Nguyen Van Thuan, and Le Duc Vuong, are also serving lengthy prison sentences. Human rights activist Nguyen Dan Que, sentenced to 20 years' imprisonment in 1991 for publicly supporting political reform and respect for human rights, remains in isolation in prison despite being in poor health. Nine people, including Nguyen Dinh Huy, remain in prison for trying to organize a conference on democracy in Ho Chi Minh City in 1993. At least seven Catholic priests of the Congregation of the Mother Co-redemptrix remain in prison under long sentences imposed after their 1987 arrest and conviction on charges of "sowing disunity between the people and State." Following diplomatic appeals, in February the SRV released political prisoner Doan Thanh Liem from prison and allowed him and his family to emigrate for humanitarian reasons.

Hoang Minh Chinh was released on June 14 upon completion of his 12-month sentence. Chinh was arrested with Do Trung Hieu in 1995 for spreading "antisocialist propaganda," apparently for writings that urged the party to admit past mistakes and move toward national reconciliation (see Section 2.a.). Chinh and Hieu were convicted of "abusing democratic privileges" and sentenced to 12 and 18 months' imprisonment, respectively. Ha Si Phu was released December 9 after completion of his 12-month sentence, including 8 months detention (see Section 2.a.).

Vietnamese exile groups have claimed that there are as many as 1,000 political prisoners in the country; other reliable sources put the figure closer to 200. Amnesty International lists 70 prisoners held for political reasons, but suggests that the number may be higher. The Government continued to release prisoners as part of regular amnesties to commemorate important national holidays.

f. *Arbitrary Interference with Privacy, Family, Home, or Correspondence.*—The Constitution provides for the right to privacy of home and correspondence. The Government continued, however, to operate a nationwide system of surveillance and control through household registration and block wardens who use informants to keep track of individuals' activities. Citizens must register when they change locations. However, many foreign observers believe that this monitoring was done with less vigor and efficiency than in the past, as the authorities focused on those suspected of involvement in unauthorized political or religious activities. Anecdotal evidence suggests that government monitoring is stricter in the south, especially in Ho Chi Minh City. In urban areas, most citizens were free to maintain contact and work with foreigners.

The Government continued to open and censor mail, confiscate packages, and monitor telephone, electronic mail, and fax transmissions. The Party now exerts less pressure on people than it has in the past to belong to one or more mass organizations, which exist for villages, city districts, schools, workers (trade unions), youth, and women. Membership in the VCP remains an aid to advancement in the Government or in state companies and is vital for promotion to senior levels of the Government. At the same time, diversification of the economy has made membership in mass organizations and the VCP less essential to financial and social advancement.

The Government continued to implement a family planning policy that urges all families to have no more than two children. In principle the Government can deny promotions and salary increases to government and party employees with more than two children. In practice the penalty is not applied to employees in good standing. For others, there are no penalties for those with more than two children, but local regulations permit fines based on the cost of extra social services incurred by the larger family, or reductions in state subsidies for those services. These penalties are not uniformly or universally applied.

While foreign language periodicals are widely available in the cities, the Government regularly censors articles about the country in foreign periodicals for sale within the country. The Government has not allowed citizens free access to the Internet, citing concerns for national security and cultural preservation. It formally restricted access to satellite television to top officials, foreigners, hotels, and the press by a November edict.

Section 2. Respect for Civil Liberties, Including:

a. *Freedom of Speech and Press.*—The Constitution provides for freedom of speech and the press, but in practice the Government severely limits these freedoms, especially concerning political and religious subjects.

Both the Constitution and the Criminal Code include broad national security and antidefamation provisions that the Government uses to strictly limit such freedoms. The Party and Government tolerated public discussion and even criticism somewhat more than in the past, although less than in the period from 1987 to 1989. For example, citizens could and did complain openly about bureaucratic lethargy, administrative procedures, corruption, and even economic policy. However, the Government continued to clamp down on free speech that strayed outside narrow limits to question the role of the Party, criticize individual SRV leaders, promote pluralism, multiparty democracy, or question the regime's policies on sensitive matters such as human rights. There continued to be an ambiguous line between what constituted private speech about sensitive matters, which would be tolerated, and public speech in those areas, which would not. On August 22, the authorities tried and convicted two dissidents, Ha Si Phu and Le Hong Ha, a former security official, on charges of illegally possessing secret government documents (see Section 1.e.). Ha Si Phu was arrested on December 6, 1995 for criticizing the regime. Le Hong Ha was arrested at the same time for involvement with efforts to convince the Party to address past mistakes.

The Party, Government, and Party-controlled mass organizations control all print and electronic media. The Government exercises oversight through the Ministry of Culture, supplemented by pervasive party guidance and national security legislation sufficiently broad to ensure effective self-censorship in the domestic media. In July the Government threatened to prosecute three state- or party-owned newspapers for "disclosing state secrets" after they criticized government actions in the nation's aviation and oil industries.

The Government also approved a number of new newspapers for publication; none are privately owned. With apparent party approval, several newspapers engaged in investigative reporting on corruption and mismanagement as well as in open and sometimes heated debate on economic policy. The Government made no effort to limit access to international radio, to which many citizens listen regularly, although it restricted access to the Internet and censored foreign publications (see Section 1.f.).

Foreign journalists must be approved by the Foreign Ministry's Press Center and must be based in Hanoi, and the number of foreign staff allowed each foreign press organization is limited. The Center monitors journalists' activities and decides on a case-by-case basis whether to approve their interview, photograph, film, or travel requests. A Foreign Ministry official accompanies foreign journalists during all interviews with Vietnamese. The Government censors television footage and delays export of footage by several days.

On September 9, uniformed and plain clothes police beat, kicked, and detained a foreign journalist for taking photographs of a small protest demonstration in Hanoi. The Foreign Ministry announced on September 13 that it would investigate the incident, the first physical assault on a journalist about which information is publicly available. In September the Government refused to extend the visa of a correspondent working for an international business magazine, effectively expelling him for articles that he had written which displeased the Government.

A general trend toward increased information flow appeared to extend into the university system. Foreign academic visitors working temporarily at universities said that they were able to discuss nonpolitical issues widely and freely in the classroom, but government monitors regularly attended classes taught by foreigners and Vietnamese without official notification. Academic publications usually reflect the views of the Party and the Government.

b. *Freedom of Peaceful Assembly and Association.*—The right of assembly is restricted in law and practice. People wishing to gather in a group are required to apply for a permit, which local authorities can issue or deny arbitrarily. However, people routinely gathered in informal groups without government interference. The Government does not permit demonstrations that could be seen as having a political purpose, but was more tolerant than in the past of occasional popular demonstrations about specific grievances against local officials. Nonetheless, the Government did not tolerate extended demonstrations. For example, authorities arrested several leaders and suppressed a protest over expropriation of land for a golf course financed abroad.

With a few exceptions, the Government prohibits the establishment of private, independent organizations, insisting that individuals work within established, party-controlled organizations. Citizens may not establish any sort of independent organization, including political parties, labor unions, religious, or veterans organizations.

c. *Freedom of Religion.*—Both the Constitution and government decrees provide for freedom of worship, but the Government continued to restrict severely religious activities it defined as at variance with state laws and policies. The Government generally allowed people to practice the religion of their choice, and participation in religious activities throughout the country continued to increase. However, the Government also maintained policies designed to control religious hierarchies and organized religious activities, in part because it fears that organized religion may undermine the Party's authority and influence.

Religious organizations must obtain government permission to hold training seminars, conventions, and celebrations outside the regular religious calendar, to build or remodel places of worship, to engage in charitable activities or operate religious schools, and to ordain, promote, or transfer clergy. All religious groups continued to face difficulty in obtaining teaching materials, expanding training facilities in response to increasing demand for clergy, and publishing religious materials.

The Government requires all Buddhist monks to work under the party-controlled Buddhist umbrella organization. The Government has actively continued to suppress efforts by the UBCV to operate independently. The tension between the Government and the UBCV, which resurfaced in 1992 and increased in 1993–94, continued in 1996. Despite SRV claims to the contrary, credible reports indicate that the UBCV's leader, the Venerable Thich Huyen Quang, remains under house arrest or other confinement in a remote area of Quang Ngai Province. Worshipers in several Buddhist, Catholic, and Cao Dai sect centers of worship regularly report that undercover government observers attend worship services and monitor the activities of the congregations and clergy.

The Government has sought to control the Catholic Church hierarchy, in part by requiring that all clergy to belong to the government-controlled Catholic Patriotic Association. It has also insisted on approving Vatican appointments. The Church hierarchy remained frustrated with the Government's restrictions. In a February 2 letter to the Archbishop of Hanoi, Prime Minister Vo Van Kiet prohibited elder Bishop Huynh Van Nghi from being assigned to any post. The Government prohibits the Catholic Church from educational and charitable activities because it will not accept government supervision and authority, as Buddhist congregations do.

The Government allowed bishops and priests to travel freely within their dioceses, but continued to restrict their travel outside these areas. The Government has limited the Church to operating 6 major seminaries throughout the country, totaling approximately 700 students. The Government allows the Church to recruit new students only every 2 years. All students must be approved by the Government, both upon entering the seminary and prior to ordination as priests. The number of graduating students was insufficient to support the growing Catholic population, estimated at 5 million. In his February 2 letter, the Prime Minister reiterated that local officials have the right to approve or disapprove the selection of candidates for training, continuation of study, and ordination. This power lies principally with the People's Committee of the province or city where the candidate lives.

In November the Government reported that it had closed a Zen Buddhist center in Dalat, alleging that its leader was not a real monk and had been sexually abusing his followers. There is evidence that the monk and the center had been legally registered as a Buddhist center since before 1975. There are reports that the followers allegedly abused by the monk have denied the reports and are seeking to sue government newspapers for spreading false reports. Witnesses reported that police destroyed the center.

The Christian Missionary Alliance of Vietnam, the only government-approved Protestant organization in the country, enjoyed slightly greater freedom to operate. Church attendance grew despite continued government restrictions on proselytizing activities. Nongovernmental organizations (NGO's) reported continued arrests and government harassment of some ethnic Hmong Protestants for proselytizing in northern Vietnamese villages. In February police in Ho Chi Minh City and Pleiku disbanded meetings held by Christians that included expatriates. Police interrogated, then released, the participants. The authorities in Hanoi questioned, harassed, and fined a U.S. citizen for distributing pens bearing a Christian religious symbol. According to reports, police interrogated her repeatedly during October and November, before fining and expelling her. There have been reports that members of the Cao Dai religion have also been subject to arbitrary detention and persecution.

There is no officially sanctioned umbrella organization for Protestants. Reports indicate that Protestant congregations are not allowed to cooperate on joint religious observances or other activities.

The Government restricts exit permits for Muslims seeking to make the hajj (see Section 1.d.).

d. *Freedom of Movement Within the Country, Foreign Travel, Emigration, and Repatriation.*—Most citizens enjoy freedom of movement within the country. However, there were credible reports that local authorities required members of ethnic minority groups to obtain permission to travel outside certain highland areas. Officially, citizens must obtain permission to change their residence. In practice many people continued to move without approval, although this prevented them from obtaining legal work permits. Foreigners are generally free to travel throughout the country. Although the Government retains the right to approve travel to border areas, to some areas in the central highlands, and to some islands, in practice foreigners can easily travel to most border areas without approval.

The Government still requires citizens traveling abroad, including government officials, to obtain exit and reentry visas. Both law and regulation provide for the right of all citizens to obtain an exit permit, except for: Members of the small Muslim community seeking to make the hajj; political activists; certain Buddhist clerics; the mentally ill; those serving prison sentences; under criminal investigation; holding state secrets; suffering serious health problems; involved in tax or real estate disputes; or whose sponsors are engaged abroad in activities opposed to the Government. The Government maintains the right to reject exit visa applications in these categories.

The Government continued to permit limited departure for some Vietnamese seeking to emigrate. The U.S. Orderly Departure Program (ODP) continued to resettle immigrant and refugee beneficiaries in the United States, including Amerasians, former reeducation camp detainees, and family unification cases, at the rate of about 2,000 persons per month. Other nations operate smaller resettlement programs for Vietnamese citizens. There are some concerns that members of minority ethnic groups, particularly highland peoples, such as the Montagnards, may not have ready access to these programs. The Government continued to deny exit permits for certain Montagnard applicants for emigration to the United States. Former political prisoner Doan Thanh Liem emigrated to the United States through the ODP in February.

Citizens' access to exit permits is frequently constrained by factors outside the law. Refugee and immigrant visa applicants to the ODP sometimes encounter local officials who arbitrarily deny exit permits based on personal animosities or the official's perception that an applicant does not meet program criteria.

In May Vietnam and the United States reached an agreement in principle to allow several thousand Vietnamese living in refugee camps in Southeast Asia to apply for resettlement in the United States, provided that they first return to Vietnam and apply in writing. The two governments are consulting on implementation of the agreement.

The Government generally permits Vietnamese who emigrate to return to visit, but it considers them Vietnamese citizens and therefore subject to the obligations of a Vietnamese national under the law even if they have adopted another country's citizenship. However, Vietnamese who have emigrated are not able to obtain Vietnamese passports. Because overseas Vietnamese are both a valuable potential source of foreign exchange and expertise and a potential security threat, the Government generally encourages them to visit Vietnam but monitors many of them carefully.

In 1988 Vietnam signed a memorandum of understanding with the United Nations High Commissioner for Refugees (UNHCR) to increase acceptance of voluntary repatriates, provided that there was financial assistance. The agreement included a commitment to waive prosecution and punitive measures for illegal departure from Vietnam of persons who return under the UNHCR Voluntary Repatriation Program. Vietnam also agreed to permit the UNHCR to monitor the returnees through direct visits. More than 106,000 Vietnamese have returned voluntarily. The UNHCR, which extensively monitors those who have repatriated voluntarily, reports that they do not face retribution or discrimination. There was no credible evidence to substantiate claims that refugees returning under UNHCR auspices were harassed because of their status as returnees.

The Constitution allows consideration of asylum for foreigners persecuted abroad under certain circumstances. Otherwise, Vietnam is not signatory to, and does not have provisions for, the granting of asylum or refugee status in accordance with the standards of the 1951 U.N. Convention Relating to the Status of Refugees and its 1967 Protocol. There were no reports of individuals requesting asylum in Vietnam. In the past, Vietnam admitted refugees from Cambodia, most of whom were ethnic Vietnamese, most recently 30,000 persons between 1993 and 1995. The Government cooperates with the UNHCR and other humanitarian organizations in assisting refugees. There were no reports of forced return of persons to a country where they feared persecution.

Section 3. Respect for Political Rights: The Right of Citizens to Change Their Government

Citizens are not free to change their government. All authority and political power is vested in the VCP; political opposition and other political parties are not tolerated. The VCP Central Committee is the supreme decisionmaking body in the nation, and the Politburo is the locus of policymaking. The Eighth Congress of the VCP in June replaced the Secretariat of the Central Committee with a standing board, consisting of five members of the Politburo, to oversee day-to-day implementation of leadership directives. Debate and criticism are limited to certain aspects of individual, state, or party performance determined by the VCP itself. No public challenge to the legitimacy of the one-party state or even debate on the subject is permitted (see Section 2.a.).

Citizens elect the members of the National Assembly, ostensibly the main legislative body, but the Party approves all candidates, almost all of whom are VCP members. During its semi-annual month-long sessions in April and October, the National Assembly engaged in increasingly vigorous debate on economic, legal, and social issues, including corruption, management of the budget, and foreign investment. Legislators questioned and criticized ministers. However, the National Assembly remained subservient to the VCP. It does not initiate legislation and may not pass legislation that the Party opposes. Party officials occupied most senior government and National Assembly positions and continued to have the final say on key issues.

The law provides the opportunity for equal participation in politics by women and minority groups, but in practice they are underrepresented. Most of the top leaders are male. In June the Party for the first time elected a woman to the Politburo. Women hold a few important positions, including vice president and several vice ministerships or equivalent positions. The president of the National Assembly, who is also a Politburo member, is a member of an ethnic minority.

Section 4. Governmental Attitude Regarding International and Nongovernmental Investigation of Alleged Violations of Human Rights

The Government does not permit private human rights organizations to form or operate. It generally prohibits private citizens from contacting international human rights organizations. The Government permitted international visitors to monitor implementation of its repatriation commitments under the Comprehensive Plan of Action and carried on a limited dialog with foreign human rights organizations based outside Vietnam. The Government continued to refuse entry to some major international human rights NGO's. However, the Government did permit the September visit by a delegation from the Committee to Protect Journalists.

The Government has shown increased willingness to discuss human rights issues bilaterally with other governments if such discussions take place under the rubric of "exchanges of ideas" rather than as "investigations." Several foreign governments held official talks concerning human rights issues.

Section 5. Discrimination Based on Race, Sex, Religion, Disability, Language, or Social Status

The Constitution prohibits discrimination based on gender, ethnicity, religion, or social class. Enforcement of these prohibitions has been uneven. People released from reeducation camps over the years have reported varying levels of discrimination in the areas of housing and education. They are generally not eligible to regain their citizenship rights until 1 year after their release. They and their families are not allowed employment with the Government, although this prohibition was less problematic than in the past because of the growth of private sector job opportunities.

Women.—Although the law addresses the issue of domestic violence, there is credible evidence that the problem is on the rise, and that the laws are not enforced adequately. International NGO workers and many women have stated that domestic violence against women is common. Most divorces are due to domestic violence, although many women remain in abusive marriages rather than confront the stigma of divorce. Domestic abuse appears to be more prevalent in rural areas.

The Government, international NGO's, and the press reported a marked increase in recent years in the trafficking of women both domestically and abroad for purposes of prostitution. Organized rings reportedly lure poor, often rural, women with promises of jobs or marriage and force them to work as prostitutes. Some are kidnapped and sold as wives to men in other countries. The press and anecdotal sources indicate that the problem of sex tourism is growing, with increasing prostitution of children. The Government is working with NGO's to supplement law enforcement measures in these areas.

While there is no legal discrimination, women face deeply ingrained social discrimination. Despite extensive provisions in the Constitution, in legislation, and in regulations that mandate equal treatment, and although some women occupy high government posts, in general few women are able to compete effectively for higher status positions. The Government has not enforced the constitutional provision that women and men must receive equal pay for equal work. The large body of legislation and regulations devoted to the protection of women's rights in marriage as well as in the workplace and the new labor law calling for the preferential treatment of women are distant from the reality of many, if not most, women.

The party-controlled Women's Union has a broad agenda to promote women's rights, including political, economic, and legal equality, and protection from spousal abuse. NGO's and international organizations regard the Union highly, but they and Women's Union representatives believe that it will take some time to overcome societal prejudices. The Government also has a Committee for the Advancement of Women, led by the Vice President, who is a woman.

Children.—Reputable international organizations, including the U.N. Children's Fund (UNICEF), commend the Government's interest in children's issues and its promotion of child welfare. While education is compulsory, the authorities do not enforce the requirement, especially in rural areas (see Section 6.d.). The Government has continued a nationwide immunization campaign, and the government-controlled press regularly stresses the importance of health and education for all children. Despite some success, UNICEF estimates that there are still 3 million children living in "especially difficult" circumstances.

Widespread poverty has contributed to the reported increase in trafficking of minors domestically and to foreign destinations as prostitutes. UNICEF reported that responsible government agencies are seriously engaged in combatting this abuse. There is no information publicly available on the extent of child abuse (see Section 6.c.).

People With Disabilities.—The Government provides little official protection or support for the disabled, and there are no laws mandating physical access to buildings. However, the 1994 Labor Law requires the State to protect the rights and encourage the employment of the disabled. It includes provisions for preferential treatment for firms that recruit disabled persons for training or apprenticeship and a special levy on firms that do not employ disabled workers. It is uncertain whether the Government enforces these provisions. The Government has permitted international groups to assist those who have been disabled by war or by subsequent accidents involving unexploded ordnance.

National/Racial/Ethnic Minorities.—Although the Government says that it is opposed to discrimination against ethnic minorities, there continued to be credible reports that local officials sometimes restricted ethnic minority access to education, employment, mail services, and travel, both domestic and foreign. The Government continued to implement policies designed to narrow the gap in the standard of living between ethnic groups living in the highlands and lowland ethnic Vietnamese by granting preferential treatment to domestic and foreign companies investing in highland areas. There were anecdotal reports that the Government continued to repress some highland minorities for suspected ties with resistance groups.

Section 6. Worker Rights

a. *The Right of Association.*—All unions are Party-controlled. Workers are not free to form or join unions of their choosing unless they have obtained approval from the local office of the Party-controlled Trade Union Federation of Vietnam (VGCL). The VGCL is the umbrella organization under which all local trade unions must operate. The 1994 Labor Law requires provincial trade union organizations to establish unions at all new enterprises with more than 10 employees as well as at existing enterprises that currently operate without trade unions. Management of those companies is required to accept and cooperate with those unions. However, many joint ventures and small, private companies, especially at the retail level, do not have unions.

The Labor Law provides for the right to strike under certain circumstances. It calls for management and labor to resolve labor disputes through the enterprise's own labor conciliatory council. If that fails, the matter goes to the provincial labor arbitration council. On July 1, new labor courts within the people's court system came into being. The new courts have begun to hear a small number of cases, but still are in the early stages of development. Unions have the right to appeal a council decision to the provincial people's court and to strike. However, the law prohibits strikes at enterprises that serve the public and those that are important to the national economy or national security and defense; these functions are defined by the Government. The law also grants the Prime Minister the right to suspend a strike considered detrimental to the national economy or public safety. On August 29, the Prime Minister prohibited strikes in 54 occupational sectors and businesses including public services, businesses producing "essential" goods, and businesses serving national defense under the Ministries of Interior and National Defense.

The number of strikes increased in 1996, primarily against foreign-owned companies but also involving state-owned and private firms. The Government tolerated these strikes, which were mostly illegal. None was organized by the VGCL or its affiliate unions. The Labor Law prohibits retribution against strikers, and there have been no credible reports of such retribution. In the wake of several highly publicized strikes, the SRV has promulgated new procedures for settlement of strikes as well as individual claims related to labor problems. The new procedures took effect on July 1.

Unions are not legally free to, and do not in practice, join, affiliate with, or participate in international labor bodies.

b. *The Right to Organize and Bargain Collectively.*—Workers have the right to organize unions in their enterprises, but they must be approved by the provincial or metropolitan branch of the VGCL. They also can bargain collectively through the party-approved unions at their enterprises. In the past, the State generally set wages, since most employees worked for state companies. With the growth of the private sector and the increased autonomy of state firms, a growing percentage of companies are setting wages through collective bargaining with the relevant unions. Market forces also play a much more important role in determining wages. The Labor Code prohibits antiunion discrimination on the part of employers against employees seeking to organize.

The Government has approved formation of a number of export processing zones and new industrial zones, which are governed by the same labor laws as the rest of the country.

c. *Prohibition of Forced or Compulsory Labor.*—The Labor Law prohibits all forms of forced labor. However, there were credible reports that some prisons employ the use of forced labor, sometimes as part of commercial ventures.

d. *Minimum Age for Employment of Children.*—The Labor Law sets the minimum age for employment at 15 years. Children as young as 13 can register at trade training centers, which are a form of vocational training. There are compulsory education laws, but they are not effectively enforced, especially in rural areas where children are needed in agriculture. However, the culture's strong emphasis on education leads people who can afford it to send their children to school rather than to work.

e. *Acceptable Conditions of Work.*—The Labor Law requires the Government to set a minimum wage, which changes with inflation and other economic changes. The monthly minimum wage for foreign-investment joint ventures is $35 (385,000 dong) in Hanoi and Ho Chi Minh city and $30 (330,000 dong) elsewhere. The minimum monthly wage for Vietnamese-owned companies is $11 (120,000 dong). This minimum wage alone is insufficient to provide a worker and family with a decent standard of living. Many workers receive bonuses and supplement their incomes by engaging in entrepreneurial activities. A decreasing number of workers receive government-subsidized housing. The Government enforces the minimum wage at foreign and major Vietnamese firms.

The Labor Law sets working hours at a maximum of 8 hours per day and 48 hours per week, with a mandatory 24-hour break each week. Any additional hours require overtime pay, and the law limits compulsory overtime. It is uncertain how well the Government enforces these provisions.

The Labor Law requires the Government to promulgate rules and regulations to ensure worker safety. The Ministry of Labor, in coordination with local people's committees and labor unions, is charged with enforcing the regulations. In practice, enforcement is inadequate because of the Ministry's inadequate funding. Anecdotal evidence indicates that workers, through labor unions, have been more effective in forcing changes in working conditions than has the Government. There was no information on the ability of workers to remove themselves from work situations that endanger health or safety without jeopardy to their continued employment.

WESTERN SAMOA

Western Samoa, a small Pacific island country with a population of approximately 162,000, is a parliamentary democracy but with certain concessions to Samoan cultural practices. The Constitution provides for a Samoan head of state, a unicameral legislature composed of Matai (family heads) elected by universal suffrage, an independent judiciary, protection of Samoan land and traditional titles, and guarantees of fundamental rights and freedoms. Executive authority is vested in the Head of State, with the Government administered by the Cabinet, consisting of the Prime Minister and 12 ministers chosen by him. All laws passed by the Legislative Assembly need the approval of the Head of State, Malietoa Tanumafili II, who holds the position for life. His successors will be elected by the Legislative Assembly for 5-year terms.

The country does not have a defense force. The small national police force is firmly under the control of the Government but has little impact beyond Apia, the capital city. Enforcement of rules and security within individual villages is vested in the fono (Council of Matai), which settles most internal disputes. Judgments by the fono usually involve fines or, more rarely, banishment from the village.

Western Samoa is a poor country with a market-based economy in which over 60 percent of the work force is employed in the agricultural sector. Coconut products and kava are the principal exports. The small industrial sector is dominated by a Japanese factory which assembles automotive electrical parts for export. The Government has initiated a major push for tourism. Per capita gross domestic product is $1,100 per year. The country is heavily dependent on foreign aid and on remittances sent to family members by the more than 100,000 Samoans living overseas, mostly in Australia, New Zealand, and the United States.

The Government generally respected the human rights of its citizens. Principal human rights abuses arise out of political discrimination against women and nonmatai, and violence against women and children. Societal pressures and customary law may interfere with the ability to conduct fair trials, and there are some restrictions on freedoms of speech, press, and religion.

RESPECT FOR HUMAN RIGHTS

Section 1. Respect for the Integrity of the Person, Including Freedom From:

a. *Political and Other Extrajudicial Killing.*—There were no reports of political or other extrajudicial killings.

b. *Disappearance.*—There were no reports of politically motivated disappearances.

c. *Torture and Other Cruel, Inhuman, or Degrading Treatment or Punishment.*—The law prohibits such practices, and there were no reports that officials practiced them. However, villages are controlled by customary law, and the fono may mete out banishment when deemed necessary. This is one of the harshest forms of punishment in this collective society.

Although jail conditions are fairly basic so far as food and sanitation are concerned, there have been no reports of abuses in prisons. While there are human rights groups, the question of monitoring of prison conditions by them has not arisen. Prison visits by family members and church representatives are permitted.

d. *Arbitrary Arrest, Detention, or Exile.*—The law prohibits arbitrary arrest, detention, or exile, and the Government observes this prohibition.

e. *Denial of Fair Public Trial.*—The law assures the right to a fair public trial, and this is honored by the official court system. However, many civil and criminal matters are not handled by courts but by village fono, which differ considerably both in their decisionmaking style and in the number of matai involved in the decisions. The Village Fono Act of 1990 gives legal recognition to the decisions of the fono and provides for limited recourse of appeal to the Lands and Titles Courts and to the Supreme Court. In a 1993 court case, a village fono ordered the property of a villager to be burned after he had disobeyed and flouted village rules. An angry mob killed the villager and burned all his belongings. The villager who actually shot the victim was tried in 1994 and sentenced to death by the Supreme Court. The six matai members, although originally charged by the Supreme Court with inciting murder, were subsequently charged only with willful damage and received a minimal fine and no jail sentence. The Attorney General lodged an appeal in 1994 on the grounds that the sentence was "inadequate and inappropriate." A ruling on this appeal is still pending.

There were no reports of political prisoners.

f. *Arbitrary Interference with Privacy, Family, Home, or Correspondence.*—The law provides for protection from invasion of the home or seizure of property without substantive and procedural safeguards, including search warrants, which are issued by the judicial branch. Practically, however, there is little or no privacy in the village. Village officials by law must have permission to enter homes, but there can be substantial social pressure to grant such permission.

Section 2. Respect for Civil Liberties, Including:

a. *Freedom of Speech and Press.*—The Constitution provides for freedom of speech and of the press, and the Government generally respects these rights in practice. In 1995 the Government charged two senior members of Tumua and Pule, the traditional leadership organization of Samoa, with sedition stemming from statements they made during a 1994 protest rally. The two were leaders of a protest movement against a highly unpopular value-added tax imposed by the Government. The judiciary dismissed all charges when the Government failed to present any evidence against the defendants.

The Newspapers and Printers Act and the Defamation Act require journalists to reveal their sources in the event of a defamation suit against them. There has been no court case requiring that these acts be invoked.

Two English-language newspapers and numerous Samoan-language newspapers are printed regularly in the country. The Government operates a radio station and the country's sole television station. There are two private radio stations. Television from American Samoa is readily available.

The Government respects academic freedom.

b. *Freedom of Peaceful Assembly and Association.*—The Constitution provides for these rights, and the Government respects them in practice.

c. *Freedom of Religion.*—The Constitution provides for freedom of religion, along with freedom of thought and conscience. Nearly 100 percent of the population is Christian. While the Constitution grants each person the right to change religion or belief and to worship or teach religion alone or with others, in practice the matai often choose the religious denomination of the aiga (extended family). There is strong societal pressure to support church leaders and projects financially. Such contributions often total more than 30 percent of personal income.

d. *Freedom of Movement Within the Country, Foreign Travel, Emigration, and Repatriation.*—The Constitution provides for freedom of internal movement, but in practice some citizens have been banished either from village activities or completely from the village. The Government actively supports emigration as a "safety valve" for pressures of a growing population, especially for potentially rebellious youths, and because it generates foreign income through remittances. The Government does not restrict foreign travel arbitrarily or the right of citizens to return from abroad.

Western Samoa has not had any refugees or asylum seekers, and it is not a party to any international protocol on them. However, the authorities have indicated that they would conform to international norms if such cases should arise.

Section 3. Respect for Political Rights: The Right of Citizens to Change Their Government

Citizens have the right to change their government through direct, multiparty elections, but women's political rights are restricted by the fact that few of them are matai. While all citizens above the age of 21 may vote, the right to run for 47 of the 49 seats in the Legislative Assembly remains the prerogative of the approximately 25,000 matai, 95 percent of whom are men. The remaining two seats are reserved for citizens not of Samoan heritage. While all adult Samoans may vote for the Legislative Assembly, matai continue to control local government through the village fono which are open to them alone.

The political process is more a function of personal leadership characteristics than of party. In the April general elections, the Human Rights Protection Party (HRPP) led by Prime Minister Tofilau Eti Alesana, retained the majority of seats in the Legislative Assembly. Tofilau and the HRPP have dominated the political process, winning five consecutive elections since 1982. Although candidates are free to propose themselves for electoral office, in practice, they require the blessing of the village high chiefs. Those who ran in the 1996 elections in spite of fono objections faced ostracism and even banishment from their village. Following the elections there were multiple charges of fraud and bribery. Four elections were subsequently overturned by the Supreme Court, and by-elections were held.

Women occasionally reach high public office. The 12-member Cabinet has 1 female member, and women hold 3 of the 49 seats in Parliament. The first female judge was named in 1994.

Section 4. Governmental Attitude Regarding International and Nongovernmental Investigation of Alleged Violations of Human Rights

A number of human rights groups operated without government restriction, investigating the Tumua and Pule sedition case and publishing their findings about it. Government officials are usually cooperative.

Section 5. Discrimination Based on Race, Sex, Religion, Disability, Language, or Social Status

The Constitution prohibits discrimination based on race, sex, religion, disability, language, or social status. This is a homogeneous society with no significant ethnic minorities. Politics and culture are the product of a heritage of chiefly privilege and power, and members of certain families have some advantages. While there is discrimination against nonmatai and women, women (and particularly female matai) play an important role in society and may occasionally reach high office.

Women.—The traditional subordinate role of women is changing, albeit slowly, especially in the more conservative parts of society. While abuse of women is prohibited by law, social custom tolerates physical abuse of women within the home. The role and rights of the village fono and tradition would prevent police from interfering in instances of domestic violence, barring a complaint from the victim—which village custom strongly discourages. While police do receive some complaints from abused women, domestic violence offenders are typically punished by village councils, but only if the abuse is considered extreme. ("Extreme abuse" would be visible signs of physical abuse.) The village religious leader may also intervene in domestic disputes.

Many cases of rape may still go unreported because tradition and custom discourage such reporting. In spite of this, the authorities note a greater number of reported cases of rape, as women are slowly becoming more forthcoming with the police. Rape cases that do reach the courts are treated seriously. Convicted offenders are often given relatively stiff sentences of several years' imprisonment.

The Ministry of Women's Affairs oversees and helps ensure the rights of women.

Children.—The Government has made a strong commitment to the welfare of children through the implementation of various youth programs by the Ministry of Education and the Ministry of Health. Law and tradition prohibit severe abuse of children, but tradition tolerates corporal punishment. The police noted an increase in reported cases of child abuse, attributed to Samoans becoming more aware of the need to report physical, emotional, and sexual abuse of children.

People With Disabilities.—The Government has passed no legislation pertaining to the status of handicapped or disabled persons or regarding accessibility for the disabled. Samoan tradition dictates that handicapped persons be cared for by their family, and this custom is widely observed in practice.

Section 6. Worker Rights

a. *The Right of Association.*—Workers have legally unrestricted rights to establish and join organizations of their own choosing. To date, two trade unions have been organized. The Western Samoa National Union, organized in 1994, is a six-member association which includes workers from the three major banks. A second union represents members at the sole factory in the country. Both unions are independent of the Government and political parties. There are no laws specific to union activity. The Commissioner of Labor would adjudicate any cases of retribution against strikers or union leaders on a case by case basis.

The Public Service Association, representing government workers, an increasingly important sector of the work force, also functions as a union. The Supreme Court has upheld the right of government workers to strike, subject to certain restrictions imposed principally for reasons of public safety. Workers in the private sector have the right to strike, but in 1996 there were no strikes. The Public Service Association freely maintains relations with international bodies and participates in bilateral exchanges.

b. *The Right to Organize and Bargain Collectively.*—While workers have the legal right to engage in collective bargaining, they have seldom practiced it, due to the newness of union activity and the inexperience of union leaders. However, the Public Service Association engages in collective bargaining on behalf of government workers, including bargaining on wages. Minimum wages are set by an advisory commission to the Minister of Labor. Wages in the private sector are determined by competitive demand for the required skills. Any antiunion discrimination case would be reported to and adjudicated by the Commissioner of Labor. Arbitration and mediation procedures are in place to resolve labor disputes, although these rarely arise.

Labor law and practice in the one export processing zone are the same as in the rest of the country.

c. *Prohibition of Forced or Compulsory Labor.*—While the Government does not demand compulsory labor and it is prohibited by law, in this collective society people are frequently called upon to work for their villages. Most people do so willingly, but if not, the matai can compel them to do so.

d. *Minimum Age for Employment of Children.*—Under the Labor and Employment Act (LEA) of 1972 as amended, it is illegal to employ children under 15 years of age except in "safe and light work." The Commissioner of Labor refers complaints about illegal child labor to the Attorney General for enforcement. Children are increasingly seen selling goods and foodstuffs on Apia street corners. Although a violation of the LEA, local officials mostly tolerate and overlook the child vendors. The law does not apply to service rendered to the matai, some of whom require children to work, primarily on village farms.

e. *Acceptable Conditions of Work.*—The LEA established for the private sector a 40-hour workweek and an hourly minimum wage of $0.50 (Tala 1.25). This minimum wage suffices for a basic standard of living when supplemented by the subsistence farming and fishing in which most families engage. The act provides that no worker should be required to work for more than 40 hours in any 1 week.

The act also establishes certain rudimentary safety and health standards, which the Attorney General is responsible for enforcing. Independent observers report, however, that the safety laws are not strictly enforced except when accidents highlight noncompliance. Many agricultural workers, among others, are inadequately protected from pesticides and other dangers to health. Government education programs are addressing these concerns. The act does not apply to service rendered to the matai. While the act does not specifically address the right of workers to remove themselves from a dangerous work situation, a report of such a case to the Commissioner of Labor would prompt an investigation, without jeopardy to continued employment. Government employees are covered under different and more stringent regulations, which are adequately enforced by the Public Service Commission.

EUROPE AND CANADA

ALBANIA

Albania is a parliamentary republic with a Parliament elected in a seriously flawed process. Pending a new constitution, the Law on Major Constitutional Provisions, which includes a Law on Fundamental Human Rights and Freedoms, serves in its place. The governing Democratic Party won 122 out of the 140 parliamentary seats, an 87.1 percent majority, in flawed multiparty elections in May. The major opposition party, the Socialist Party, together with some small center parties, staged a boycott of the election process several hours before the polls closed, citing reports of widespread Government-sponsored fraud, beatings, and intimidation. They refused to recognize the newly elected Parliament's legitimacy. President Sali Berisha, elected by Parliament in 1992, continued his 5-year term. The law provides for the separation of powers and an independent judiciary. However, the judicial branch remains subject to strong executive pressure and corruption.

Local police detachments reporting to the Ministry of the Interior are principally responsible for internal security. In addition to their usual tasks, police were responsible for securing order during the parliamentary and local elections in May and October respectively. There were numerous allegations of police abuse before, during, and after the May elections. In September Parliament passed new legislation governing police conduct during the October elections. The Albanian National Intelligence Service (SHIK) is legally responsible for both external and domestic intelligence collection and counterintelligence functions. SHIK's internal responsibilities include gathering information on government corruption and anticonstitutional activities in support of law enforcement agencies. Given the activities of the former security service (Sigurimi) under the Communists, some citizens perceive SHIK as a similar organization and fear it accordingly.

Albania is a poor country experiencing the painful transition of reform after nearly 50 years of a Stalinist, centrally planned economy. Its economy remains based on agriculture, but a rapidly growing commercial and trade sector has taken root in cities and larger towns. Construction is the fastest growing sector. There is some mining and light manufacturing (clothes, shoes, beverages, and consumer products). Most state-owned heavy industry is moribund. The Government continued privatizing medium and large state enterprises, a process begun in 1994. Privatization has expanded to many sectors of the economy and continues in the mining, energy distribution network, telecommunications, and textiles sectors. Remittances from Albanians working abroad and foreign assistance remain major sources of income. With the lifting of sanctions against Serbia and Montenegro at the end of 1995, the country lost a significant source of hard currency from organized fuel smuggling to those countries. Prices for key consumer items such as bread, electricity, and kerosene were freed from state control at midyear, creating additional hardships for public sector workers and pensioners on fixed incomes, but moving the overall economy toward greater efficiency. Salary increases and subsidies for public sector workers and those receiving pensions helped offset these increases. Overall economic growth remained strong, about 6 percent for the second year in a row. Inflation, which was near zero at the end of 1995, was expected to exceed to 20 percent in 1996, largely as a result of growing government budget deficits. While per capita gross domestic product reached approximately $650, more than double that in 1992, the economic transformation has created an emerging middle class as well as widening income disparities. Organized crime has surged. A number of large pyramid type schemes operate throughout the country, and a significant number of people have deposited money in them. Several of these schemes, including some larger ones, collapsed in 1996, causing depositors to lose their funds.

The Government's human rights record worsened during the year. The flawed May elections, coming at a time of further government pressure on the judiciary and the press were major steps backwards for democracy. There were numerous serious human rights abuses during the May 26 parliamentary elections and the May 28 opposition demonstration in protest of those elections. Other serious problems included police killings and beatings; poor prison and pretrial detention conditions; harassment of the press; a judiciary that is subject to widespread corruption and executive pressure and lacking in resources, training, and experience; and discrimination and violence against women. However, the Government took some positive steps by ratifying the European Convention on Human Rights, amending the law on public meetings, and exempting city and district council candidates from the antigenocide and lustration laws for the local elections in October. The Government made physical improvements in some prisons, set up courses for prison officials to improve treatment of prisoners, introduced training programs and new regulations for local police, and prosecuted those who committed abuses against prisoners. The Government is working with the Greek Government to assure improved conditions for the Greek minority.

RESPECT FOR HUMAN RIGHTS

Section 1. Respect for the Integrity of the Person, Including Freedom From:

a. *Political and Other Extrajudicial Killing.*—There was one report of a killing in custody.

Authorities arrested former president Ramiz Alia in February and charged him with the internment and imprisonment in concentration camps of thousands of citizens during the Communist regime. After pretrial detention, the prosecutor added other charges: Ordering the killing of people who attempted to leave the country; ordering troops and police to fire on the people who toppled the Hoxha monument in Tirana; ordering the arming of military students who subsequently killed some civilians; and ordering the shootings on April 2, 1991, in Shkodra that left four dead. Estimates are that another 6 months of investigation will be needed before Alia is brought to trial.

Unknown persons beat and burned to death a 15-year-old Romani boy (see Section 5).

The Government has yet to respond to queries about the status of charges against police and prison guards in 1994 deaths in custody of Enrik Islami and Irfan Nano.

b. *Disappearance.*—There were no reports of politically motivated disappearances.

c. *Torture and other Cruel, Inhuman, or Degrading Treatment or Punishment.*— The Law on Fundamental Human Rights and Freedoms states that "no one can be subject to torture, punishment, or cruel and brutal treatment." The Penal Code makes the use of torture a crime punishable by up to 10 years in prison and prohibits the use of physical or psychological force during criminal proceedings, with penalties for those found guilty of abuse. Police nevertheless continued to beat detainees, journalists, and political opposition party members, most noticeably around the time of the May election campaigns and post-election demonstrations (see Section 3). Except for incidents during the election, many of the beatings appear to be random or based on revenge or family blood feuds (usually more common in the north but now occurring throughout the country). The Interior Minister opened offices in the Ministry and local police stations to deal with citizen complaints and instituted human rights training courses for police. The impact of these measures remains to be seen.

Prison conditions do not meet minimum international standards; some are well below those levels, but the Government has made a serious effort to improve conditions in all prisons. Pretrial detention conditions are still poor, particularly hygiene and sanitation. The Government transferred responsibility for prisons from the Ministry of Interior to the Ministry of Justice. Two new prisons are under construction and were designed using international standards. The Government invested $1.8 million in improvements at two of the seven existing prisons. The European Union (EU) gave the Government 800,000 Ecu to modernize and increase the capacity of the prison in Lezha. All prisons now offer water 24 hours a day and allow personal furniture. However, severe budget restraints limit the Government's abilities to address all the problems.

The Ministry instituted new rules for treatment of prisoners and started training courses for prison officials and guards, some of whom received additional short-term training in Western Europe. There were no reported cases of torture in the prisons. Officials now attempt to house those sentenced for violent crimes apart from those in prison for minor offenses as well as from those under age 18, but such separation is not always possible. According to the Penal Code, military and civilian prisoners should be in separate facilities; again, this division is not always followed. New visitation rules allow a prisoner to meet family members once a week for 30 minutes per session, or twice a month in maximum security prison. One conjugal meeting a month is granted for married prisoners. Prisoners can receive items from visitors, e.g., food, televisions, radios, or books and newspapers, and use them in their cells. Prisoners receive approximately 1 hour of daily physical activity. There is no confirmation that these new regulations are as yet applied throughout the prison system. Reportedly those prisoners with money still can bribe prison officials for better treatment and more food.

According to ministry figures, 35 women are in prison. They are housed in a separate prison in Tirana, and their living conditions are reportedly much better than conditions in other prisons, due to funds provided by an Italian charity.

Official state or nongovernmental organization (NGO) personnel can have unlimited visitation rights but must first secure permission from the general director of prisons. Local NGO's usually receive permission.

d. *Arbitrary Arrest, Detention, or Exile.*—The Parliament approved new penal and penal procedure codes based on European standards in 1995 and modified them in 1996. The Penal Procedures Code mandates improved rights for detained and arrested persons, but the extent to which they are followed in practice remains unclear. According to the code, a police officer or prosecutor may order a suspect into custody. Detained persons must be informed of the charges against them and their rights, and, if detained by the police, a prosecutor must be notified within 12 hours. Within 24 hours from the time of arrest or detention a court must decide, in the presence of the prosecutor, the suspect, and the suspect's lawyer, if the detainee is to be released or charged. Legal counsel must be provided free of charge if the defendant is unable to afford a private attorney.

Bail in the form of money or property may be required if it is believed the accused may not appear for the hearing, or a suspect may be placed under house arrest. The court may order pretrial confinement in cases where there is reason to believe that the accused may leave the country or is a danger to society.

The Penal Procedures Code requires completion of pretrial investigations within 3 months. The prosecutor may extend this period by 3-month intervals in especially difficult cases. The accused and the injured party have the right to appeal these extensions to the district court.

The Albanian Helsinki Committee (AHC) reports increased complaints received in 1996 of police violating the law pertaining to search and seizure, detention, interrogation, advice of rights, timely court appearance, and adequate access to defense counsel.

The appeals court has reduced more than a dozen of the sentences given to high-level officials found guilty of crimes against humanity in connection with the vast network of prisons and labor camps under the Communist regime. The court reduced former chief of the Supreme Court Aranit Cela's and former general prosecutor Rrapu Mino's death sentences to 25 years in prison each and former head of the secret police Zylyflar Ramizi's to life in prison. The Appeals Court also reduced or commuted several other Communist officials' sentences, although the head of the Tirana Communist Party Llambi Gegprifti's sentence remains at 20 years. On December 29, the President issued a decree reducing in part or all of the sentences of 102 persons in prison for various charges. The times reduced ranged from 6 months to 6 years off an individual's sentence. Former prime minister Fatos Nano's sentence was reduced by 6 months under this decree (see Section 1.e.).

The law does not provide for and the Government does not employ exile as a form of punishment or political control.

e. *Denial of Fair Public Trial.*—The Law on Major Constitutional Provisions provides for an independent judiciary, but the judiciary is hampered by political pressures, insufficient resources, inexperience, patronage, and corruption. The Parliament approved new civil, penal, and labor codes and new penal procedures in 1995.

The judicial system comprises the courts of first instance (also known as district courts), the Courts of Appeals, and the Court of Cassation (also known as the High Court or Supreme Court). Each of these courts is divided into three jurisdictions: Criminal, civil, and military. The Court of Cassation hears appeals from the Court of Appeals, while a Constitutional Court decides those cases requiring interpretation of constitutional legislation or acts.

The Law on Fundamental Human Rights and Freedoms provides for the right to a fair and speedy trial. However, there have been delays in bringing some cases to court. The law also mandates public trials, except in cases in which the interests of public order, morality, national security, the private lives of the parties, or justice require restrictions. If convicted, the accused has the right to appeal the decision within 5 days to the Court of Appeals and again to the Court of Cassation, which renders the final verdict. The law does not specify any time period within which the Court of Appeals or the Court of Cassation must hear appeals.

The Parliament has the authority to approve and dismiss judges of the Constitutional Court (9 members, of which the Parliament nominates 5 and the President 4) and the Cassation Court (11 members, which Parliament nominates. The President nominates the chairman and the two deputies subject to parliamentary approval. Cassation judges may be dismissed only for mental incompetence or conviction of a serious crime. Constitutional Court justices serve maximum 9-year terms, rotating in three new justices every 3 years. Cassation Court judges are elected for 7-year terms. The President heads the Supreme Judicial Council which appoints and dismisses all other judges. According to its internal statute, the Supreme Judicial Council has broad powers to fire, demote, transfer, and otherwise discipline district and appeals court judges for incompetence, commission of a serious crime, or questionable morality. The composition of the Supreme Judicial Council and its broad authority subjects the courts to direct executive branch control. Judges are not always notified in advance of disciplinary proceedings underway against them and often are not given the opportunity to present facts in their defense.

In 1996 the Council removed 17 judges from their positions for disciplinary reasons based on the 1992 law "On the Organization of the Judiciary," which sanctions removal on the decision of the Supreme Judicial Council for violation of the law, rules and procedures, corruption, and meting out light sentences for serious crimes. Reasons cited for removing the 17 included falsifying documents, delaying procedures, giving light sentences, and taking bribes. Judges may also be removed for poor health, failure to pass the periodic professional test, or discipline or moral problems. Many lawyers report that loyalty to the ruling Democratic Party is a key prerequisite in selecting replacements. Judges' salaries are low, and there are widespread accusations of corruption. The Justice Ministry claims that it investigates all charges.

The Parliament approves the court budgets. Administration of courts' budgets was transferred from the Ministry of Justice to the courts, although the Ministry still provides and approves administrative and support personnel.

The Parliament appoints the chief prosecutor and the two deputies on the recommendation of the President. They may be dismissed only for mental incompetence or conviction of a serious crime. To improve the judicial system, the Parliament passed a law in July to establish a magistrates' school, a government-subsidized institution to assure the professional training of judges and prosecutors. The program is expected to include mandatory initial training of candidates for magistrate positions as well as a program for the continuing education of magistrates. One seminar took place in November. Regular classes are scheduled to begin in October 1997.

The Council of Europe and foreign NGO's are working with the Government to print and distribute the penal codes and laws from Parliament throughout the country. Many courtrooms, however, are still without updated versions of many of the laws and codes.

On February 14, the Constitutional Court ruled that the September 1995 dismissal by the Parliament of the former Chief Justice of the Court of Cassation, Zef Brozi—which became a major political issue—was legal, because Brozi had committed serious criminal offenses. Although Brozi had not been charged with a specific crime, the court held in its decision that the Parliament acted reasonably and that the unconstitutionality of Brozi's actions, e.g., in suspending the execution of certain decisions, was sufficient to constitute a serious criminal offense. Numerous domestic and international observers believe that Brozi's actions did not provide legal grounds for removal, that he was removed to subordinate the Court to the executive, and that the Government falsified the parliamentary vote to do so, actions all motivated by political reasons, including Brozi's attempt to reopen the Fatos Nano case. Nano, Socialist Party chairman and former prime minister, was convicted on charges of corruption. However, many observers believe Nano was imprisoned because he was President Berisha's principal political opponent.

Members of the opposition and human rights NGO's claimed that some persons being held on criminal charges are actually political prisoners.

f. *Arbitrary Interference With Privacy, Family, Home, or Correspondence.*—The Law on Fundamental Human Rights and Freedoms Provides for the inviolability of dwellings and the individual person, as well as the privacy of correspondence. There have been credible reports of government-sanctioned tampering with correspondence and wiretapping or interference with telephone service.

In January the Constitutional Court ruled that the genocide law and the law on the verification of the character of officials (lustration law) were legal. The law had the effect of exempting President Berisha and many of his chief aides, also former Communists.

Under the provisions of the genocide and lustration laws, the Government examined the files of political candidates in the May parliamentary elections. The 1995

Law on Genocide and Crimes against Humanity Committed during the Communist Regime prohibits any persons who were senior government officials, members of the secret police, or secret police collaborators before March 1991 from holding high-ranking state positions or being elected as Members of Parliament until the year 2002. The lustration law allows examination of the former secret police files to determine the rights of individuals under the genocide law. The Special Commission (Verification Committee) set up to review these files consists of 7 individuals: The Council of Ministers appointed two members; the Minister of Justice, the Minister of Defense, Minister of the Interior, and the head of the National Intelligence Service each appointed one member; and the Parliament elected the chairman. The opposition parties were able to participate only in a limited and inadequate way, through their minority in the Parliament, in the selection of and actions of the Commission. The executive branch effectively controlled the Commission and gave it the powers to judge, in closed session, decisions based on secret files that were not open for review to the general public, but that were available to the candidates and their lawyers for examination. The executive branch also had the final say in the decisions; the Prime Minister, Minister of Interior, and the head of SHIK had the right to appear before the Commission and take part in the decision in any case on the basis of state security interests.

Under these laws, the Commission banned 139 individuals from participating in the May parliamentary elections. Of those banned, 45 were members of the Socialist Party, 23 were Social Democrats, 11 were from the Democratic Alliance, 13 from the Republican Party, 3 from the Democratic Party, and the rest from minor parties. According to the law, these individuals had the right to appeal the Commission's decision to the Court of Cassation. Only 57 appealed and the Court overturned 7 decisions. The Albanian Helsinki Committee contends that the entire process violated Albanian and international law by failing to grant prospective candidates the right to due process. All court sessions were closed to observers and the media. There were complaints that the time for appeal was too limited, and several decisions came after the time limit had passed for candidates to file for the election.

Section 2. Respect for Civil Liberties, Including:

a. *Freedom of Speech and Press.*—The Law on Fundamental Human Rights and Freedoms provides for freedom of speech and the press. In practice, however, the Government sometimes restricted freedom of speech, including the freedom to criticize the Government and its officials. In some cases, the Government used laws against slander, insult, incitement to national hatred, and distribution of anticonstitutional literature to prosecute persons, especially journalists, for critical commentary.

Although financial and judicial harassment of journalists increased, particularly at the time of the May elections, the print media remain willing and able to criticize the Government. Publications in general, however, are hampered by small circulation and limited revenue. Taxes on publications, in addition to rising printing costs, made it difficult for independent media to be economically viable without subsidies or loans from their patrons, e.g., political parties, trade unions, social organizations, or private businesses. Their dependence on outside sources for revenue leads to pressures that limit the independence of reporting. Some journalists believe that the Government is using excessive taxation as a deliberate means to cripple the independent and opposition press. On December 24 President Berisha told the heads of the main newspapers that he would lower some taxes and levies. At year's end, the reductions had not yet been implemented. Between 150 to 250 different publications are nevertheless available. Three Greek minority newspapers are published in southern Albania.

A 1993 press law assesses large fines for publishing material that the Government considers secret or sensitive, permits confiscation of printed matter or property by judicial order, and allows for criminal punishment under certain circumstances. The media and the AHC denounce the press law as being too imprecise and too harsh for a country with poorly developed legal institutions. Under this law and general criminal laws journalists have been beaten, detained, arrested, fined, and jailed, although most sentences are reduced to fines.

Government officials invoked libel laws as well as the press law against journalists. The Government prosecuted one reporter and teacher, Ylli Polovina, accusing him on state television of provoking a car bombing through an article he wrote following the October 3, 1995, assassination attempt on the president of the former Yugoslav Republic of Macedonia. The article deplored the attack and stated that in the Balkans corruption and political oppression are dangerous and should be fixed before they lead to another such extreme result. In January there was an assassination attempt against Tirana's head judge. In February a car bomb exploded in front of a Tirana grocery store killing four people. Polovina was taken from his home 6 hours after the bombing incident, held for 12 days, brought to trial, and convicted of instigating the violence through his article, fined $300, and released. He was fired from his teaching job but was later given another teaching job in a small village after he wrote a public letter to the President.

The newspaper Koha Jone (KJ), which has the country's largest circulation, as well as other opposition papers, accused the Government of systematic harassment, e.g., through higher taxes and increased printing charges. Reporters claim regular harassment from police and threats from unknown individuals. Police confiscated eight of KJ's cars for various reasons, such as no license, no documentation, or having tinted windows. Police later returned six cars to the newspaper. KJ's telephones were disconnected from April 14 to December 8, ostensibly for technical reasons. Allegedly based on two separate eyewitnesses who placed a KJ employee near the scene of the February car bombing in Tirana, police detained the entire KJ staff, including drivers and janitorial staff. Koha Jone reporters say that they suffered physical harassment, including a relatively serious beating of one KJ reporter by persons unknown early in the May election campaign. Several newspapers complained that telephone/fax lines were cut for 2 or more months during the campaign. Opposition newspapers reported that police blocked cars and impounded copies of their newspapers before the May elections.

Police clubbed several journalists, including some foreign reporters, and confiscated cameras and film during the post-parliamentary election demonstration in Tirana on May 28. Assailants almost killed one independent journalist, Bardhok Lala, who was still in serious condition at year's end from the beating he received.

State-run radio and television are the main sources of domestic news for the vast majority of people, giving the Government a near-monopoly on domestic news. State-owned television relays international entertainment and news broadcasts in some cities. Home satellite dishes are common, and most Albanians, even in remote villages, have access to international broadcasts. There is still no law on private radio and television broadcasting, but there are at least four "pirate" private radio stations. The Government has temporarily closed some stations but generally allows stations to operate provided they do not heavily criticize the Government.

Since November 1991, the Parliament has exercised direct control over television, delegating some oversight duties to an Executive Committee of Radio and Television, which it appoints. The Executive Committee comprises 11 members from outside the Parliament and meets occasionally to review programming and the content of news broadcasts. This gives control of programming effectively to the Democratic Party. International observers and opposition critics noted, for example, that the Government-run television was used to serve the interests of the Democratic Party during the May parliamentary election campaign and its aftermath. Parliament amended the local election law in September to provide a new formula for equal media time dedicated to the campaign (50 percent for the Government and 50 percent for all opposition parties) during the October local elections.

Local radio in the south broadcasts some Greek-language programming, with its content translated directly from Albanian language reporting. Also widely listened to are stations from Greece, the FYROM, the British Broadcasting Corporation, and Voice of America radio.

The AHC has criticized the Government's infringement of academic freedom. Although student newspapers do not exist, there is a relatively new independent student union. However, the university system still operates with a number of its former faults intact. Grade corruption is widespread, a large percentage of the student body bypasses exams and enters university via political means, and decisions are thoroughly centralized. There are reports that political criteria figure prominently in the tenuring and promotion of professors. Ten professors who were opposition members of the 1992-96 parliament have not been allowed to return to their jobs after they lost their seats in the May elections.

Local and foreign observers reported a growing climate of apprehension in the universities in the last quarter of the year. In November a number of foreign professors were removed from their teaching positions, ostensibly for lack of contracts of formal sponsorship by a foreign university. Efforts to return these teachers to the classroom continued at year's end. There is no change in the status of the eight educators fired last year under an amendment to the Labor Code permitting the release of employees accused of obstructing democratic and economic reforms.

b. *Freedom of Peaceful Assembly and Association.*—The Law on Fundamental Human Rights and Freedoms provides for the right of peaceful assembly. However, the Government places some limitations on this right. Many in the opposition parties complained about restrictions on campaign rallies and gatherings before and after the May 26 parliamentary elections. To address those complaints, in September the Parliament passed a new law to replace the 1991 decree on public gatherings.

However, there are still some limitations on the right of assembly. For gatherings in public places, organizers must request permission from the chief of police in the locality of the planned rally at least 3 days prior to the event. The chief of police must issue his decision, with explanations for any refusal, no later than 24 hours prior to the event. The police may refuse the permit in cases when the rally may violate human rights and freedoms; traffic obstruction may become a problem; there is sufficient evidence that violent or criminal acts may occur; if another rally is planned for the same time; or if it would interfere with a national event, e.g, a Presidential speech. No advance official permission is now required for meetings held in closed nonpublic places. The police no longer have the authority to preapprove speech or slogan content.

Under the September law, police have the authority to be present during any lawful rally in a public place and are authorized to disperse the participants if the rally calls for anticonstitutional actions or incites calls for violence. If the participants do not disperse, the chief of police or authorized representative may order their dispersion by force after the police issue a warning. The law provides that the police should avoid the use of force wherever possible, but if force is used, it should be limited to the minimum necessary for the situation. Under the new laws, the opposition parties freely organized rallies during the October local election campaign, although some problems were reported.

The Socialist Party applied for permission under the 1991 meetings law to hold a gathering in Tirana's main square on May 28 to protest the conditions of the May 26 parliamentary elections but was refused by the police. The opposition parties nevertheless called for the meeting to be held in the square and urged members to attend.

The Government contends the resultant rally was illegal. The police severely beat a number of opposition leaders and their supporters as well as journalists and onlookers in the square. Some were arrested and mistreated at police stations. The Government admitted that the police actions were excessive, but the Interior Ministry blamed the opposition for inciting the initial police reactions. After conducting an investigation, the Ministry claimed that two high ministry officials and five police officials were fired. The police also took disciplinary action against officers who used excessive violence, and the prosecutor has filed criminal charges against a large number of these officers, although the disposition of these cases has not been ascertained.

The Law on Fundamental Human Rights and Freedoms provides for the right of association and states that "no one may be denied the right to collective organization for any lawful purpose." A political party must apply to the Ministry of Justice for official certification. It must declare an aim or purpose that is not anticonstitutional or contrary to law, and it must describe its organizational structure and account for all public and private funds that it receives. In 1995 the Ministry of Justice denied such certification for the Party of the Democratic Ideal, using the argument that the party's program "is no different from the programs of other parties * * * it is not likely that the problems in these areas (economic and political) will be solved with other alternatives outside of those of the parties already registered in any fundamental way." The Ministry of Justice also confirmed that it refused certification because it considered some of the points in the party's program against the national interest, e.g., advocating a greater Albania by all means necessary, including force. The party appealed its case to the Court of Cassation, which invalidated the Ministry's decision. There were no other cases in 1996.

c. *Freedom of Religion.*—The Law on Fundamental Human Rights and Freedoms states that "the freedom of thought, conscience, and religion may not be violated. Citizens may change freely change their religion or beliefs and may manifest them alone or in community with others, and in public or in private life, in worship, teaching, practice, and observance." The Government respects these provisions in practice.

The majority of Albanians are secular in orientation after nearly 45 years of severe religious persecution and 25 years of rigidly enforced atheism. The largest traditional religious group, Muslims, follow moderate forms of Islam. The other large traditions are the Albanian Autocephalous Orthodox and Roman Catholic. The Albanian Orthodox Church split from the Greek Orthodox Church in 1922, and there is a strong identification with the national church as distinct from the Greek church. The current archbishop is Greek because there are no Albanian monks qualified for this position, and two Greek priests serve as his assistants. One Greek priest travels to Gjirokaster on a regular basis to teach. Other priests from Greece come on a rotating basis to teach and augment the indigenous clergy of the Albanian Orthodox Church in the Greek-speaking congregations primarily in the south. There are three Greek nuns in Tirana. Foreign clergy, including Muslim clerics, Christian, and Baha'i missionaries, freely carry out religious activities. The Minister of Culture estimates that 15 different Muslim societies and sects and approximately 80 Christian societies and sects are active in Albania. The Government considers some of these groups to be of dubious origins, and some Orthodox Church leaders have accused certain groups of being responsible for a number of suspicious activities such as destroying Orthodox icons, spying, or setting fire to a Greek school. No substantiating evidence is available in any of those cases. The Government lacks control over these groups and has little accurate information about most of them.

A small but growing Protestant evangelical community desires official government recognition and representation in the religious affairs section of the Council of Ministers. A Protestant umbrella organization, the Albanian Evangelical Alliance, complains that Protestant groups have encountered some administrative obstacles to building churches and obtaining access to the national media.

A religious affairs section in the Council of Ministers oversees the activities of the religious communities. The ministers decided in January that 21 religious sites (18 orthodox Churches, 2 mosques and 1 Catholic Church) were cultural properties that required special protection. These sites are from a list of 175 religious cultural objects and edifices, of which 140 are churches (mostly Orthodox). According to the decision, each religious community must negotiate an agreement with the Institute for Cultural Monuments to decide how often religious services will be allowed in each of the 21 old buildings to protect them from deterioration and the theft of icons and other artistic treasures. The director of the Institute said that the Government retains many icons for safekeeping. It returned some objects to the churches, but some churches also asked the Government to keep them because they had no way to secure them safely. The Orthodox Church, however, has complained to the Government because the authorities have dragged their heels on returning some objects turned over for restoration and safekeeping. President Berisha promised to return to churches and mosques the land they owned prior to state confiscation or, in cases where it is impossible to return the original land, to compensate the church with money or another piece of land. The Government has not yet returned all lands but this spring successfully completed the turnover of all the buildings at Ardenitsa to the Albanian Orthodox Church. Restitution of religious properties to the respective religions is a long, difficult, and delicate process. Each religion is slowly recovering old properties, but in cases where the monuments were "cultural monuments protected by the state" or military objects, transfer of ownership is problematic and slow.

d. *Freedom of Movement Within the Country, Foreign Travel, Emigration, and Repatriation.*—There are no restrictions on freedom of movement within the country. Albanian-born citizens in all foreign countries are eligible to apply for dual citizenship. Since the downfall of the Communist regime, hundreds of thousands of economic migrants have left. Most go to Greece or Italy, many entering those countries illegally. Their remittances are an important economic factor. Albanians who fled the country during the Communist dictatorship are welcomed back with citizenship restored.

There is a significant influx of refugees from Kosovo. Young men from Kosovo come to Albania and stay to avoid the Serbian draft. The Government has no formal refugee policy. The transit of refugees without visas is also problematic, especially of Kurds, Pakistanis, Chinese, Turks, and others from the Middle East and Asia on their way to Western Europe, usually through the port at Vlora. The Government did not forcibly expel anyone who had a valid claim to refugee status. The United Nations High Commissioner for Refugees (UNHCR), in conjunction with the Albanian Red Cross, runs a "care and maintenance" program for what they consider "vulnerable" groups, i.e., those who arrive in Albania and cannot return to where they came from or continue further. The UNHCR office in Tirana assesses refugee cases and approves grants of money, shelter, and food for those considered to meet refugee criteria.

Section 3. Respect for Political Rights: The Right of Citizens to Change Their Government

The Law on Major Constitutional Provisions states that citizens have the right to change their government "by free, general, equal, direct, and secret ballot." Parliamentary elections were held on May 26, and local elections, which were not nearly as politically significant, were held on October 20. International observers judged the May parliamentary elections to be seriously flawed. The opposition parties, claiming massive fraud and manipulation, withdrew from the elections several hours before the polls closed and subsequently boycotted the second round of elections June 2 and the reruns of individual races held on June 16.

Numerous irregularities marred the elections and represent a significant step backward from the previous parliamentary elections in 1992. Various observers witnessed instances in which the authorities violated the electoral laws, including the manipulations of vote counts and the casting by single voters of multiple ballots. The intimidating presence of armed guards at some polling stations also has been reported. Irregularities have been acknowledged by the authorities themselves.

However, the premature withdrawal of opposition party candidates and their members of the electoral commissions—who claimed they were threatened with violence—also made it difficult to gauge the true dimension of problems subsequently observed during the vote count. The Council of Europe (COE) and the Organization for Security and Cooperation in Europe (OSCE) asked for a repeat of the flawed parliamentary elections.

The OSCE parliamentary report concluded that "Albanian legislation provides conditions for free and fair elections. However, the law on genocide includes procedures which cannot be considered fair and transparent. It also includes stipulations which limit the electorate's options to freely choose their candidates. During the campaign authorities did not always act in an unbiased manner. There also appeared to be confusion concerning some decisions, or lack of decisions, on behalf of the Central Election Commission in the management of the process. Procedures in the polling stations were, in general, in accordance with the law. There were, however, a number of irregularities and technical shortcomings. The state-owned media was not entirely unbiased." The OSCE report also said that "The political environment appeared to have deteriorated after the first round of the elections. This diminished the integrity of the second round and also undermines the credibility of the democratic process in the country.* * *"

The OSCE's Office for Democratic Institutions and Human Rights (ODIHR) published a separate final statement on the May elections. It concluded that "although the lawfulness of the newly elected Albanian Parliament cannot be questioned, the electoral process included several aspects and incidents which severely question the credibility of the democratic process in the country. The Government and all parties alike share responsibility in this matter." The OSCE and ODIHR each offered a list of recommendations to improve the electoral procedure.

The Albanian Helsinki Committee also issued a critical report on the parliamentary election process. It outlined the obstacles facing the opposition during the campaign, especially government control of the media and actions against the opposition when it attempted to hold rallies, leading to the problems on election day. The Government did not give official permission for the AHC to monitor the elections. The Government made it difficult for other domestic observers, particularly those from the Society for Democratic Culture (SDC), to get credentials. Some government officials claim that the AHC and the SDC submitted some names and information about potential observers too late for processing. The AHC said that the progovernment press tried to discredit the committee as "a tool in the hands of the Socialist Party." The AHC reported that the police intimidated and beat opposition party local electoral commission members as well as some voters, forcibly removed opposition party observers from polling stations, and harassed or attacked some opposition candidates. In addition the AHC accused "secret agents and government appointees of the electoral commissions" of "brutally" violating the electoral law. The AHC and the International Helsinki Federation for Human Rights (IHF) issued a joint evaluation on June 6. They called for the Government, the OSCE, the COE, and the United Nations to declare the elections invalid. They recommended new elections, an investigation of electoral fraud and police violence, and a separation of powers within the Government. The report condemned government control of the media, government interference in the work of NGO's in the country, and the violent actions of police forces during the May 28 demonstration and during other attempts of the opposition to meet. Committee members wrote that "human rights violations before, during, and after the Albanian parliamentary elections on 26 May and 2 June 1996 have seriously compromised free and fair elections and significantly undermined the development of just democratic institutions in transition Albania. Ballot stuffing, multiple voting, voter list manipulation and police intimidation and violence have all contributed to violating the constitutional right of the Albanian people to freely and fairly elect their political representatives. These violations call into question the willingness of the Government to abide by the rule of law and ensure that political processes occur in conformity to Albanian and international law.* * *"

During the campaign numerous opposition party members and credible eyewitnesses reported police restrictions on their campaign activities, e.g., preventing rallies and beatings. The worst violence occurred on May 28 during a post-election opposition party rally (see Section 2.b.).

The Democratic Party won 122 of 140 seats in the Parliament. President Sali Berisha insists that the election was valid and that the current Parliament is representative of the will of the people. The Socialist Party won only 10 parliamentary seats and refused as a party to enter Parliament, which it considers illegitimate. One of the Socialist candidates nevertheless took his seat, but the Party states that individual does not represent it.

International observers judged the October 20 local elections to be an improvement over the May 26 parliamentary elections, although some irregularities were observed. The major political parties met in roundtable discussions prior to the local elections, and these sessions led to significant changes in the local election law, the rules governing the conduct of the police during the voting, and in access to television time during the campaign. Enactment of a new law on meetings and gatherings, designed to eliminate the abuses encountered in the May parliamentary campaign, was largely successful.

The Government took a number of steps apparently designed to hamper both local and international monitoring efforts. Age qualifications for monitors were raised from 18 to 25. This had the effect of eliminating the vast majority of university students as monitors. It also created a situation in which persons old enough to vote, serve on election commissions, and hold elective office were disqualified as observers. Due to disagreement with some provisions in ODIHR's report on the May elections, the Government initially refused to allow ODIHR to send any monitors for the October elections. The Government later modified its decision, but sought to vet the names of the observers and limit their number to 15, a number ODIHR considered insufficient to do the job effectively. As a result, ODIHR did not send any observers. The EU denounced the lack of Government cooperation with ODIHR. The COE and several EU-member governments sent monitors for the local elections.

The COE described the elections as "sufficiently free and fair to be accepted as a reliable expression of the inhabitants' preference for their future mayor or head of commune, and agreed that these elections are a definite step in the right direction." Other international observer groups issued similar statements. While opposition politicians did not explicitly accept the elections as "free and fair," they generally acknowledged that the Government's actions before, during, and after the October elections were a substantial improvement over its actions in regard to the May elections. Some of the problems included accuracy of the voting lists, ballot box stuffing, and altered vote counts. The Democratic Party won more than 80 percent of the local offices. The opposition acknowledged the victory, although it did not concede all the vote totals. The Government never published the voting protocols as required by the election law. The opposition cited as an additional problem low turnout among its supporters because of lack of confidence in the process due to the events in May.

Although there are no legal impediments to their participation and their numbers are slowly increasing, women are still underrepresented in politics and government. According to women's groups, 18 women are members of Parliament, 2 are Ministers, 2 are State Secretaries, at least 1 is a Deputy Minister. The major political parties have women's organizations, and a few women sit on the parties' leadership committees. Reportedly some women discovered that their names were printed on ballots in the May elections without their knowledge or consent.

The 1992 Law on Political Parties prohibits the formation of any party or organization with an antinational, chauvinistic, racist, totalitarian, Fascist, Stalinist, "Enverist" or Communist, or Marxist-Leninist character or any political party with an ethnic or religious basis. The Unity for Human Rights Party, founded by ethnic Greeks but representing several ethnic minorities, is most popular in the south where the majority of the Greek minority resides. There are three Human Rights Party members of Parliament.

Section 4. Governmental Attitude Regarding International and Nongovernmental Investigation of Alleged Violations of Human Rights

The Government generally permitted various human rights and related organizations to function freely. Some organizations noted that while they were able to operate and on occasion cooperate with the Government, they were harassed and intimidated once they had made direct criticisms of the Government. Some groups complained that the Government failed to respond to written requests for information or data that would normally be considered of a public nature. The AHC, the major human rights monitoring organization, took an active role in defending human rights in certain areas, particularly during and after the May parliamentary elections. The AHC believes that it was unable to function this year as freely and indiscriminately as in the past. Representatives complain that the Committee has become the target of criticism in progovernment newspapers and verbal attacks by government officials. Besides the election, the AHC focuses on the status of minorities, rule of law issues, the importance of a new constitution and is pressing for amendments to the law on the organization of the national intelligence service.

Several new domestic NGO's focus on the rights of women and children. The Albanian Human Rights Documentation Center continues to be active in preparing human rights educational materials to be used in elementary and secondary schools. It has a library that attempts to keep current on the most important human rights issues. Like most domestic NGO's, the Center's work is hampered by a lack of sufficient funds and equipment. The Society for Democratic Culture works on civic education, monitoring elections, and women's issues. Progovernment newspapers criticized the SDC's director, and several individuals, including a member of the Central Election Commission, reportedly verbally threatened her following the release of the Society's report critical of the May 26 elections.

Delegations from the COE, the OSCE, OSCE's ODIHR, and the European Parliament made several visits to observe and evaluate the May parliamentary elections and assist in preparation for the October local elections. Representatives of the OSCE's Office of the High Commissioner for National Minorities also visited to confer with political officials and representatives of the ethnic Greek community.

Section 5. Discrimination Based on Race, Sex, Religion, Disability, Language, or Social Status

The Law on Major Constitutional Provisions prohibits discrimination based on sex, race, ethnicity, language, or religion, but women and some minority groups complained of discrimination in practice.

Women.—Women's groups report that spousal abuse in this traditional, male-dominated society continued to be common and is generally treated by police as a family matter. However, there was an increase in cases reported to the authorities. There is no government-sponsored program that protects the rights of women, nor are there any shelters for abused women. Many men, especially those from the north, still follow the old traditions of law in which women are considered as chattel and treated as such. The concept of marital rape is still foreign to many; it is not considered a crime and is not reported. A recent report indicated that divorce is on the rise, and that women now initiate around 70 percent of the divorce cases.

Some women, either voluntarily or by force, participate in prostitution rings and other criminal activities.

The situation of women improved during the last year, but overall it remains inadequate. There are currently 26 NGO's devoted to women's issues, and some are starting to coordinate with each other. They organize seminars, training courses, and counseling for women throughout the country. Although most are located in Tirana, the larger groups are starting to establish branches outside the major cities. International foundations and NGO's provide expertise and support, and as a result the women's NGO's are getting stronger. Some women have organized their own roundtables for discussion of issues. Women are now doing research on a number of problems, e.g., the need for a law on domestic violence and the position of women in society in relation to land ownership. They plan to lobby the Parliament to pass laws on these and other issues and have already successfully lobbied legislators to pass a law relating to land inheritance. In January the Parliament passed a law on reproductive rights.

Women involved in these groups believe that communications have improved between the Government and the NGO's, but old prejudices and attitudes still remain. In January the Government established a "Women and Family Department" in the Ministry of Labor and Social Affairs with the intent to create a network of offices to address social problems around the country. Some women claim, however, that the department is not really focused on women's rights so much as social protection in general and that it has not produced any concrete results. The Government also created a new Department for Women's Issues in the Ministry of Culture, Sports, and Youth, but women say that its aims are unclear. Female members of Parliament do not usually independently contact women's NGO's, but some have been responsive when NGO's take the initiative.

Women are not restricted, either by law or practice, from any occupations but do not typically rise to the top of their fields. The Labor Code mandates equal pay for equal work. While no data are available on whether women receive equal pay for equal work, public sector wage scales are based on rank and duties, not sex. Women have suffered more from unemployment and discrimination in seeking jobs. Although women enjoy equal access to higher education, they are not accorded full, equal opportunity and treatment with men in their careers. An increasing number of women is beginning to open shops and small businesses. Many are migrating along with men to Greece and Italy to seek employment.

Children.—The Government's commitment to children's rights and welfare is based on domestic law and international agreements. Attendance at school is mandatory through the eighth grade (or age 18, whichever comes first); the Government has adopted measures to discourage truancy, but these measures in many areas are not very successful.

Child abuse is a little-reported problem, but the authorities and NGO's believe that it exists. There have been two publicized cases in which men were convicted of the sexual abuse of children. One was sentenced to 18 months and the other to 2 years in prison. There are numerous reports that organized criminal elements kidnap children, especially young girls, and send them to Italy and elsewhere to work as beggars and prostitutes. Romani children in particular are used as beggars, in full view of the police who take no action either to assist the children or against the adults who use them. Child Hope, an international NGO, operates a center for street children.

People With Disabilities.—There is no law mandating accessibility to public buildings for people with disabilities, and little has been done on their behalf.

Widespread poverty and the poor quality of medical care account for a large number of disabled persons. The disabled are eligible for various forms of public assistance, but budgetary constraints limit the amount received. The public care section of the Ministry of Labor and Social Affairs has set up a network of social service administrators throughout the country whose goal is to improve the quality of services to disabled persons and promote their social integration rather than institutionalization. Donations from abroad have led to improvements in living conditions in some institutions, especially in Korca and Durres. In Lezha a daycare center for the disabled was opened. This center works to help integrate the disabled into their families. Oxfam, a British NGO, helped open a workshop to employ the disabled.

National/Racial/Ethnic Minorities.—While no recent official statistics exist regarding the size of the various ethnic communities, ethnic Greeks are the most organized and receive the most attention and assistance from abroad. The Greek minority, which according to the AHC "is an integral part of the Albanian society," is concentrated in the south and numbers, by official estimates, 80,000 people. Greek minority sources' estimates run as high as 200,000 people. The numbers are always varying because of the continuous movement of a portion of the population back and forth between Albania and Greece. In the eastern part of the country are a few thousand ethnic Macedonians and in the north a small group of ethnic Montenegrins. There are no reports of discrimination against the Vlach, who speak Romanian as well as Albanian, or against the Cams (ethnic Albanians from northern Greece).

Relations between Albania and Greece improved, and in March the two Governments signed a treaty of cooperation and friendship. This treaty led to a number of agreements on the key issues of Albanian immigration to Greece and Greek language education in Albania, as well as agreements on other issues. The Government opened three new first-year classes in the Greek language in the southern cities of Saranda, Gjirokaster, and Delvina when the new school year started in September. The AHC concluded in a recent report that the rights of the ethnic Greek minority had "reached a new (positive) dimension," and that the Greek minority was "an integral part" of Albanian society.

There is an association which claims to represent more than 100,000 Roma throughout Albania. There was one reported incident in July in which a group of young men of unknown ethnicity beat and then burned to death a 15-year-old Romani boy. The AHC strongly condemned the incident and asked the general prosecutor to undertake a full investigation. Action remained pending at year's end. The AHC fears any revival of racism, which is now uncommon.

Section 6. Worker Rights

a. *The Right of Association.*—Workers have the right to create independent trade unions, and the Independent Confederation of Trade Unions of Albania (BSPSH) acts as the umbrella organization for a number of smaller unions. A separate rival federation continues to operate in close cooperation with the Socialist Party. There are also some independent unions not affiliated with either federation. The private sector employs more than 800,000 workers, mostly in agriculture, small shops, enterprises, and restaurants, but very few of them have formed unions to represent themselves.

According to the Law on Major Constitutional Provisions and other legislation, all workers, with the exception of uniformed military, police, and some court authorities, have the right to strike. The law forbids strikes that are openly declared to be political, or so judged by the courts. Public workers staged a peaceful 1-hour "warning" strike on September 16 to protest a lack of government subsidies to compensate for the new, higher prices of essential goods such as bread, gas, and kerosene. The Government previously offered to pay public sector employees and pensioners a supplement to cover the rising costs, but the amount was deemed inadequate. The average family spends $20 to 25 per month on bread, which remains the diet staple. Workers staged a peaceful 1-day walkout on October 4 and threatened an indefinite walkout in the future if the Government did not increase wages or subsidies. In December, Prime Minister Meksi signed an agreement with the largest confederation of independent trade unions to index wages to inflation.

Labor federations are free to maintain ties with international organizations.

b. *The Right to Organize and Bargain Collectively.*—Citizens in all fields of employment, except uniformed members of the armed forces, police officers, and some court employees, have the right to organize and bargain collectively. In practice, unions representing public sector employees negotiate directly with the Government. Wages for all state employees are defined by the wage pyramid, legislated in 1992, which comprises 25 wage levels organized by trade.

Parliament passed a law establishing free-trade zones between Tirana and Durres and elsewhere in the country. These are to become export processing zones, but the zones are not yet functioning due to the lack of implementing regulations.

c. *Prohibition of Forced or Compulsory Labor.*—The Law on Major Constitutional Provisions and the Labor Code prohibit forced labor, and there were no cases reported.

d. *Minimum Age for Employment of Children.*—The Labor Code sets the minimum age of employment at 14 years of age and limits the amount and type of labor that can be performed by persons between the ages of 14 and 18. The Labor Code covers working conditions for those over the age of 16. The Ministry of Labor enforces the minimum age requirement through the courts. In rural areas, children continue to be required to assist their families in farm work.

e. *Acceptable Conditions of Work.*—The minimum wage for all public sector workers over the age of 16 is approximately $35 (3,500 lek) per month, which is not sufficient to maintain a decent standard of living for a worker and family. Most workers must find second or part-time jobs to supplement their incomes or rely on remittances from family members residing abroad. The law guarantees social assistance (income support) and unemployment compensation. However, this is extremely limited, both in the numbers of unemployed who receive it and in the amount that they receive. The average monthly wage for workers in the public sector is approximately $100 (10,000 lek), an increase of around 60 percent over last year. No data are available for private sector wages, but they are perceived to be considerably higher than the public sector. A draft law was under consideration at the end of 1996 that would set a minimum wage for private sector employees.

Workers are limited by law to a 48-hour workweek, and many workers normally work 6 days a week; the Council of Ministers must approve exceptions. The Ministry of Labor enforces this law whenever possible. Women may not work at night in some professions, and pregnant women may not perform any night work.

The Government sets occupational health and safety standards but has limited funds to make improvements in the remaining state-owned industries; health and safety are generally very poor. The 1995 Labor Code spells out the obligations of employers and their employees with regard to workplace safety. The law, however, does not provide specific protection to workers who choose to leave the workplace for fear of hazardous conditions.

ANDORRA

The principality of Andorra became a parliamentary democracy in 1993 when its Constitution was approved by popular referendum. Two Co-Princes representing secular and religious authorities have governed since 1278. Under the Constitution, the two Co-Princes—the President of France and the Spanish Bishop of Seu d'Urgell—serve equally as Heads of State and are each represented in Andorra by a delegate. Elections were held in December 1993 to choose members of the Consell General, the Parliament, which selects the Head of Government. The judiciary functions independently.

Andorra has no defense force. The national police have sole responsibility for internal security.

The market-based economy is dependent on those of its neighbors France and Spain. With creation of the European Union internal market Andorra lost its privileged duty-free status and is suffering an economic recession. Tourism is still an important source of income. Because of banking secrecy laws, the financial services sector is growing in importance.

The Government fully respected the human rights of its citizens, and the law and the judiciary provide effective means of dealing with instances of abuse.

RESPECT FOR HUMAN RIGHTS

Section 1. Respect for the Integrity of the Person, Including Freedom From:

a. *Political and Other Extrajudicial Killing.*—There were no reports of political or other extrajudicial killings.

b. *Disappearance.*—There were no reports of politically motivated disappearances.

c. *Torture and Other Cruel, Inhuman, or Degrading Treatment or Punishment.*—The Constitution prohibits such practices, and there were no reports that officials employed them.

Prison conditions meet minimum international standards, and the Government permits visits by human rights monitors.

d. *Arbitrary Arrest, Detention, or Exile.*—The Constitution prohibits arbitrary arrest, detention, or exile, and the Government observes this prohibition.

e. *Denial of Fair Public Trial.*—The Constitution provides for an independent judiciary, and the Government respects this provision in practice. The highest judicial body is the five-member Superior Council of Justice. One member each is appointed by: The two Co-Princes; the Head of Government; the President of the Parliament; and, collectively, members of the lower courts. Members of the judiciary are appointed for 6-year terms. The judiciary provides citizens with a fair and efficient judicial process.

There were no reports of political prisoners.

f. *Arbitrary Interference With Privacy, Family, Home, or Correspondence.*—The Constitution provides citizens with safeguards against arbitrary interference with their "privacy, honor and reputation," and government authorities generally respect these prohibitions. Private dwellings are considered inviolable. No searches of private premises may be conducted without a judicially issued warrant. Private communications also are protected by law.

Section 2. Respect for Civil Liberties, Including:

a. *Freedom of Speech and Press.*—The Constitution provides for freedom of speech and of the press, and the Government respects these rights in practice. An independent press, an effective judiciary, and a functioning democratic political system combine to ensure freedom of speech and of the press, including academic freedom.

b. *Freedom of Peaceful Assembly and Association.*—The Constitution provides for these rights, and the Government respects them in practice. Since adoption of the 1993 Constitution, the Government has registered seven political parties.

c. *Freedom of Religion.*—The Constitution provides for freedom of religion, and the Government respects this right in practice. The Constitution acknowledges a special relationship between the Roman Catholic Church and the State, "in accordance with Andorran tradition." The Catholic Church receives no subsidies from the Government.

d. Freedom of Movement Within the Country, Foreign Travel, Emigration, and Repatriation.—The Constitution provides for these rights, and the Government respects them in practice.

The Government cooperates with the United Nations High Commissioner for Refugees and other humanitarian organizations in assisting refugees. It is government policy not to expel persons having valid claims to refugee status, and there were no reports of such expulsions.

Section 3. Respect for Political Rights: The Right of Citizens to Change Their Government

The Constitution provides citizens with the right to change their government peacefully, and citizens exercise this right in practice through periodic, free, and fair elections held on the basis of universal suffrage.

Women have enjoyed full suffrage since 1970, but they continue to play a relatively minor role in politics. Notwithstanding the absence of formal barriers, few women have run for office; only 1 of 28 Members of Parliament is a woman, and only 2 women have occupied cabinet level positions.

Section 4. Governmental Attitude Regarding International and Nongovernmental Investigation of Alleged Violations of Human Rights

While there are no restrictions to prevent their formation, no formal human rights organizations operate in Andorra.

Section 5. Discrimination Based on Race, Sex, Religion, Disability, Language, or Social Status

The Constitution declares that all persons are equal before the law and prohibits discrimination on grounds of birth, race, sex, origin, religion, opinions, or any other personal or social condition, although the law grants many rights and privileges exclusively to citizens. The Government effectively enforces these provisions.

Women.—No data exists on the incidence and handling of domestic violence cases, but spousal abuse appears to be virtually nonexistent. There is no legal discrimination against women, either privately or professionally.

Children.—There is no evidence of any special commitment by the Government to children's rights and welfare, although there is no indication of any problems in this area. Over the past 12 years there has been only one known case of child abuse.

People With Disabilities.—There is no discrimination against disabled persons in employment, education, or in the provision of other state services. The law mandates access to new buildings for people with disabilities, and the Government enforces these provisions in practice.

National/Racial/Ethnic Minorities.—Spanish nationals are the largest group of foreign residents, accounting for 47 percent of the population. Other sizable foreign groups are Portuguese, French, and British. A small number of North African and African immigrants work mostly in agriculture and construction.

Although the Constitution states that legal residents enjoy the same rights and freedoms as Andorran citizens, immigrant workers do not believe that they have the same rights and security. They lack many social benefits paid to residents and often live in difficult and crowded conditions. The cost of living is high, and workers employed in low-wage industries often cannot afford normal housing costs. Many of them live in trailers or crowded apartments, with as many as 8 or 10 people sharing quarters designed for 4. Many such workers are on temporary work permits. These permits are valid only as long as the job for which the permit was obtained exists. A worker hired on a temporary contract loses his work permit when the contract expires. If unable to find new employment, the worker quickly becomes an undocumented alien with no visible means of support and may be deported.

Section 6. Worker Rights

a. *The Right of Association.*—The Constitution recognizes the right of all persons "to form and maintain managerial, professional, and trade union associations without prejudice." The Constitution provides that a registry of associations be established (through future legislation) and maintained. Strikes were illegal under the old system, and the new Constitution does not state explicitly that strikes are permitted.

b. *The Right to Organize and Bargain Collectively.*—The Constitution states that both "workers and employers have the right to defend their own economic and social interests." Parliament is charged with adopting legislation to regulate this right in order to guarantee the provision of essential services. The threat of immediate dismissal (see Section 6.e.) is a powerful deterrent to complaints from workers, especially since there is very limited unemployment insurance. This inhibits workers from organizing effectively to press their cases. Antiunion discrimination is not prohibited under current law.

There are no export processing zones.

c. *Prohibition of Forced or Compulsory Labor.*—Forced labor is not specifically prohibited by law, but it does not occur.

d. *Minimum Age for Employment of Children.*—Children under the age of 18 are normally prohibited from working although in exceptional circumstances children ages 16 and 17 may be allowed to work. Child labor regulations are enforced by the Labor Inspection Office in the Ministry of Social Welfare, Public Health, and Labor. That office does not routinely inspect work places but responds to complaints.

e. *Acceptable Conditions of Work.*—The workweek is limited to 40 hours, although longer hours may be required. The legal maximums for overtime hours are 66 hours per month and 426 hours per year. There is an official minimum wage, set by government regulations. Other, higher wages are established by contract. The minimum wage is approximately $4.50 (Ptas 600) per hour. In principle it is enforced by the Labor Inspection Office, but self-enforcement is the norm. Living costs are high, and the current minimum wage is inadequate for a worker and family.

Worker complaints center on the lack of job security. Workers may be dismissed without prior notice and receive social security and health benefits for only 25 days; thereafter, there is no unemployment insurance. Foreign workers who contribute to the social security system are ineligible to receive retirement benefits if they do not remain in Andorra after retirement; however, they may apply for a lump-sum reimbursement of social security contributions when they leave the country. Retirement benefits are controlled by a board composed of Andorran nationals although they represent only a small portion of the work force. There is no special court or board to hear labor complaints.

The Government sets occupational health and safety standards, but enforcement is loose as there are no routine inspections. There is no legislation giving workers the right to remove themselves from dangerous work situations without jeopardy to their continued employment.

ARMENIA

Armenia has a constitutional government in which the President has extensive powers and the role of the legislature relative to the executive branch is severely circumscribed. The President appoints the Prime Minister, who is now in charge of the Cabinet. President Levon Ter-Petrossian was reelected in a controversial multicandidate election in September, which was flawed by numerous irregularities and serious breaches of the election law. The opposition rejected the official election results and asked the Constitutional Court to invalidate the Central Election Commission (CEC) decision on the results and to order a new election. The Court's handling of the case did not assuage doubts about the credibility of the official election results. A transitional National Assembly in which ruling party loyalists hold about 88 percent of the seats was elected in July 1995; local and international observers characterized the 1995 elections as "generally free, but not fair." Elections for a new National Assembly are scheduled for 1999. The Constitution provides for an independent judiciary; however, in practice judges are subject to political pressure from both the executive and legislature.

In October the Ministry of the Interior and the Ministry of National Security combined to form the Ministry of Internal Affairs and National Security which is responsible for domestic security, intelligence activities, border control, and supervises the national police force. The Ministry of Defense assists in domestic security during serious internal disorders. Some of the security forces committed serious human rights abuses.

Economic reforms continued to move forward in the face of many obstacles: The collapse of external trade links and sources of raw material that followed the Soviet Union's demise; the lingering effects of the massive 1988 earthquake; and the threat of a renewed conflict in Nagorno-Karabakh. Despite these problems, gross domestic product (GDP) increased by 6 percent in 1996. Per capita annual GDP rose by about 14 percent to $533. Inflation remained low, and the currency was stable. The Government passed a property law and is currently in the process of issuing titles to real estate owners.

The Government's human rights record remained uneven, improving incrementally in some areas, while serious problems remained in others. Its manipulation of the September presidential election continued to restrict citizens' ability to change their government. Although the Government passed an improved election law and selected new members of the CEC, including a new chairman, international observers reported that serious breaches of the election law and numerous irregularities resulted in a lack of confidence in the integrity of the overall election process. International observers urged that the Government implement recommendations of international experts to address the flaws and rebuild public confidence in the electoral process. Members of the security forces beat detainees during arrest and interrogation and also beat passersby in areas adjoining demonstrations. These violations of the law by internal security personnel, notably the sixth directorate of the Ministry of Internal Affairs in Yerevan, continued in a climate of impunity from government sanction. Security forces continued to arbitrarily arrest and detain citizens. During the government crackdown following a violent demonstration after the presidential election, authorities beat and detained members of the opposition and demonstrators.

The Government signed an agreement with the International Committee of the Red Cross (ICRC) giving general and private access to detainees; however, the Government's cooperation in implementing the agreement was uneven. Security forces also infringed on citizens' privacy rights. The judiciary is subject to political pressure; however, in one notable case a court reversed the illegal actions of government officials; a district court judge overturned the decision of the Minister of Justice to dismiss the leadership and transfer ownership of a prominent independent newspaper. The Government continued to place some restrictions on freedom of the press; security forces beat and detained journalists after the September election, and journalists practice some self-censorship. Although reduced from previous years, credible reports of harassment and intimidation of journalists and editors continued. The number of local independent television and radio stations grew and, together with the press, were increasingly vocal and critical. However, the Government continued to dominate nationwide television and radio broadcasting. The Government imposed some limits on freedom of assembly and association especially during the post-election crackdown. A previously suspended prominent political party, the Armenian Revolutionary Federation (ARF/Dashnaks), was not reinstated, although the authorities tolerated its gatherings, news conferences and activities, and the Prime Minister initiated meetings with its representatives. The National Democratic Union's (NDU) party office in Yerevan was closed for about 2 months following the postelection violence and not reopened until after the Constitutional Court ruling on the NDU's election grievances. The Government retains some limits on freedom of religion. Discrimination against women and minorities is a problem.

RESPECT FOR HUMAN RIGHTS

Section 1. Respect for the Integrity of the Person, Including Freedom From:

a. *Political and Other Extrajudicial Killings.*—There were no reported cases of political or extrajudicial killings.

b. *Disappearance.*—There were no reported cases of political disappearance.

c. *Torture and Other Cruel, Inhuman, and Degrading Treatment or Punishment.*—The Constitution and the law prohibit torture. However, the practice of security personnel beating detainees during arrest and interrogation continued. For example, Aramazd Zakaryan, an opposition National Assembly deputy with immunity, was beaten badly and detained for 2 days before being released to a hospital with broken ribs and a concussion. There were credible reports of threats to detainees' family members. In the first days of the postpresidential election crackdown, while a ban on meetings was in effect, nonuniformed internal security forces beat and harassed passersby in the area where a demonstration was held. Two cases of police brutality were registered in the first half of the year. In each case, a detainee committed suicide in detention after having been severely beaten by police. Both cases are under consideration in the Supreme Court. Most cases of police brutality go unreported.

The office of the Prosecutor General (Attorney General) investigates allegations of mistreatment. If the investigation reveals evidence to support the allegations and if there is a serious violation of the law, the prosecutor's office files criminal charges. Less serious cases are referred to the Ministry of Internal Affairs for administrative action.

There is no available information on whether or not the five cases of police brutality reported in 1995 were ever prosecuted.

Prison conditions are Spartan and often overcrowded. According to reliable reports, prisoners in "kartser" receive food every other day. There are not adequate medical and sanitary facilities in prisons, communicable disease is common, and some prisoners reportedly have died of treatable diseases.

In January the Government agreed to permit independent monitoring of prisoners by the ICRC. The ICRC was granted unaccompanied access to many political detainees. However, while the Ministry of National Security honored the terms of the ICRC agreement, often the Ministry of Interior was not cooperative. The ICRC experienced significant difficulties in gaining access to prisoners detained by the Ministry of the Interior after the September 25 assault on Parliament by some members of the opposition, and ICRC representatives were compelled to wait for more than 3 weeks for access to these prisoners. Only occasional visits were allowed. The Prosecutor General's cooperation in carrying out the agreement was uneven.

d. *Arbitrary Arrest, Detention, or Exile.*—Authorities continued to arbitrarily arrest and detain citizens without legal warrants. Those arrested are frequently brought to prison without notification of family members. It is often several days before family members obtain information as to whether someone has been arrested and their location. Access of lawyers and family members to prisoners is often restricted, particularly in the weeks after arrest.

During the Government crackdown on the opposition after the flawed presidential elections, international and domestic observers reported that 17 prominent opposition figures and over 100 participants in the September 25 demonstration were detained for violation of Article 74 of the Criminal Code, "participation in mass disorder". Sixteen of the latter group were still being held on this charge at year's end. Many detainees were held for 15 days of "administrative detention," during which several were reportedly beaten, and access by international humanitarian groups was delayed or denied.

In addition four opposition deputies were detained before being stripped of their immunity by the National Assembly on September 26. During that National Assembly session, progovernment members of parliament assaulted some of these opposition deputies in front of national television cameras.

The transitional provisions of the Constitution provide that Soviet-era procedures for searches and arrests are to be maintained until the Soviet-era Criminal Code and Criminal Procedure Code are redrafted and brought into line with the Constitution. A suspect may be jailed for up to 12 months pending trial and completion of the investigation. If no sentence is passed during the period of detention, the suspect must be released. In spite of this provision, three suspects in a "satellite" case of the "Dro" trial were held for almost two years without trial. Informed sources stated that the three were charged with not reporting a state crime. After having been held almost a year beyond that allowed by law, they were released on their own recognizance pending the appeals in the "Dro" trial.

The long-running "Dro" trial concluded on December 10 with the judge pronouncing all defendants guilty and imposing three death sentences. The highest ranking Dashnak defendant, Hrant Markaryan, was found guilty of only minor crimes, leading Dashnak Party representatives to claim that the judge had found no link between the Dashnak Party and the "Dro". The existence of such a link had been the government's justification for suspending the Dashnak Party and related media outlets in 1994. The verdict has been appealed by both sides in the case. A second case, the "Trial of 31", opened on March 15, and at year's end had completed only its first stage. The main defendant, Dashnak leader Vahan Hovannisyan, went on a hunger strike in early November to protest delays in the proceedings. He stopped his strike 2 weeks later, reportedly at the request of the Dashnak Party. Most defendants in the case alleged they had been tortured and pressured into giving false testimony. Defense lawyers have filed numerous motions to investigate these allegations, but thus far the judge has denied the motions.

There is no provision for bail although detainees may sign a document and remain at liberty under their own recognizance pending trial.

On May 19, the Government released all known prisoners in custody at that time in conjunction with the Nagorno-Karabakh conflict. Subsequently, there were reports of the capture of other POW's who had not been released at year's end.

There were no reports of forced exile.

e. *Denial of Fair Public Trial.*—Although the Constitution nominally provides for an independent judiciary, in practice courts are subject to political pressure from both the executive and the legislature. The provisions of the Constitution do not appear designed to insulate the courts from political pressure. Under the Constitution, the Justice Council, headed by the President, the Prosecutor General, and the Justice Minister, appoints and disciplines judges for the tribunal courts of first instance, review courts, and the Court of Appeals. The President appoints the other 14 members of the Justice Council and 4 of the 9 Constitutional Court judges. This gives the President dominant influence in appointing and dismissing judges at all levels. Judges are subject to review by the President through the Council of Justice after 3 years, whereupon they serve until they reach the age of 65.

The judicial system is in transition. A reform effort is now underway to completely revamp the judiciary, but has only just begun. Judges during the transition period must use a confusing array of Soviet-era laws and some new civil and criminal laws. However, civil and criminal codes are still under preparation. Adoption of new civil and criminal codes and enabling legislation to implement them is critical to the success of judicial reform.

According to the transitional provisions of the Constitution, the existing courts are to retain their powers until the new judicial system is established. The existing court system comprises a number of district courts, arbitration courts, a lame duck supreme court, a newly created Constitutional Court, and a military tribunal. District courts try the overwhelming majority of cases. There is no provision for a supreme court in the new Constitution, and the powers of the current court expire after a 3-year transition period. The Constitution envisages the creation of review courts and a court of appeals to handle cases previously sent to the Supreme Court. The Constitutional Court has jurisdiction over ensuring conformity of legislation with the Constitution and approves international agreements. The Court's nine members are appointed either by the President or the parliament, the majority of which consists of progovernment members. It can only accept those cases proposed by the President, one-third of all National Assembly deputies, or election related cases brought by candidates for parliament or the presidency. The inherited Soviet prosecutorial system views the court largely as a rubber stamp for the procurator and not a defender of citizens' rights.

Many corrupt and inefficient judges were replaced during the year. Early in the year, in accordance with constitutional provisions, the President issued a decree appointing numerous new judges, replacing over 60 percent of Soviet-era judges.

The military tribunal operates essentially as it did in the Soviet era. Military prosecutors perform the same functions as their civilian counterparts, operating in accordance with the Soviet-era legal code.

Trials are public except when government secrets are at issue. Defendants are required to attend their trials unless they have been accused of a minor crime not punishable by imprisonment. Defendants have access to a lawyer of their own choosing. The court appoints an attorney for any defendant who needs one. Defendants may confront witnesses and present evidence. The Constitution provides that those accused of crimes shall be informed of charges against them. Defendants and prosecutors have the right of appeal.

The Dashnak-related "Dro" trial concluded in December with all 11 defendants receiving a guilty verdict. Throughout, the trial was marred by procedural irregularities, allegations of torture, recanted testimony, and accusations of deliberate delay by the authorities in prosecuting the case. However, prominent Dashnak Hrant Markarian was acquitted of the charge of murder, discrediting the Government's charge of criminal conspiracy between the "Dro Terrorist Organization" and the banned Armenian Revolutionary Federation (ARF or "Dashnaks").

The government reportedly held some political prisoners.

Credible human rights organizations reported that the Ministry of Justice refused to register the nongovernmental organization Committee for the Defense of Political Prisoners on the grounds that there were no political prisoners, and such an organization was therefore unnecessary.

f. *Arbitrary Interference With Privacy, Family, Home, or Correspondence.*—The Constitution prohibits unauthorized searches and preserves citizens' rights to privacy and confidentiality of correspondence, conversations, and other messages. Procedurally, the security ministries must petition the prosecutor's office for permission to tap a telephone or intercept correspondence. The prosecutor's office purportedly must find a compelling need for the wiretap before it will grant the agency permission to proceed.

The law requires security forces to obtain a search warrant from a prosecutor before conducting a search; in practice, searches continue to be made without a warrant. During the postelection crackdown in September, the offices of the NDU and NSDU and homes of prominent NDU and NSDU members were searched without warrant. The Government subsequently permitted the reopening of these offices and promised compensation to the NSDU office.

There continued to be violations of the right to privacy during army conscription drives. There were several cases in which armed forces recruiters took hostages, in order to compel the surrender of draft-evading or deserting relatives. There are credible reports of forced conscription of several refugees from Nagorno-Karabakh and Azerbaijan.

Section 2. Respect for Civil Liberties, Including:

a. *Freedom of Speech and Press.*—The Constitution provides for freedom of speech and the press; however, while the Government generally respects freedom of speech, it has placed some significant restrictions on freedom of the press. Most independent and opposition newspapers operate with extremely limited resources and depend on the Government for publication and distribution facilities—an arrangement that has continued intact from the Soviet period. However, the Government has begun to divest itself of the state publishing apparatus and has disbanded the Ministry of Information.

A growing number of printed publications present lively debate and a variety of views. The opposition press regularly criticizes government officials and policies; however, those who report on major corruption or national security issues risk government and other reprisal such as detention, beatings, threats, false prosecutions, and harassing tax audits. The Government provides a list of "forbidden subjects," and accordingly journalists practice some self-censorship.

During the period following the postelection government crackdown in late September (see Section 2.b.), the opposition press continued to print articles critical of the Government, including reports and analyses written by released opposition figures. However, security forces beat and detained some members of the press after the election. There was no access for the opposition to television or radio after the elections. Troops cordoned off state broadcasting outlets and independent HAI–FM radio station took itself off the air. The opposition's Hairikhyan was given 10 minutes of airtime in October to announce the postponement of an opposition rally. The new Yerevan Press Club objected strongly to the Government's restrictive draft press law, which was pulled back for renewed consideration. Armenian media organizations have submitted a new draft press law for government consideration. However, Dashnak party-affiliated media outlets, which were shut down in December 1994, remained closed.

Television and radio broadcasting is largely controlled by the Government. There are 3 functioning independent radio stations and 10 small independent television stations, the latter of which operate largely in the regions outside of Yerevan.

Broadcast media coverage of presidential candidates prior to the September election gave an overwhelming advantage to incumbent President Ter-Petrossian. The Organization for Security and Cooperation in Europe (OSCE) election observer mission noted in its September 24 statement that Ter-Petrossian had 16 times more editorial coverage on state television than his nearest challenger in the weeks prior to the election. According to the OSCE, this "far exceeded what is normal in such contests elsewhere in the world." State television did, however, provide 90 minutes of free airtime per presidential candidate during the campaign, and provided more balanced coverage than during the 1995 parliamentary elections.

The judge in a court case involving the ownership of the independent newspaper Azg ruled in favor of the local operators and against the Ministry of Justice, which was attempting to unilaterally transfer ownership to parties more supportive of the current Government.

There is no evidence that the Government inhibits or censors importation of international newspapers and magazines. The Internet and electronic mail have greatly increased the amount of foreign and domestic information available to both governmental and nongovernmental outlets. Middle and upper class Armenians have access to international satellite television from abroad, including Russian and Turkish television, which erodes the Government's near monopoly on television.

The Government respects academic freedom. Over 50 private institutions of higher education have been established since independence in 1991.

b. *Freedom of Peaceful Assembly and Association.*—The Constitution provides for freedom of assembly, and the Government generally respects this right in practice, with some important exceptions. On September 24 and 25, massive peaceful demonstrations were held in Yerevan protesting the results of the September presidential elections. However, some of the demonstrators turned violent on September 25, leading successively to a break-in at the parliament building, the beating of the Speaker and Deputy Speaker, and a government crackdown which involved banning public meetings for 2 weeks. Peaceful demonstrations then resumed.

The Constitution provides for freedom of association, and the Government generally respects this right in practice with some important exceptions. There are registration requirements for all parties, associations, and organizations. No political parties were refused initial registration in 1996.

During the postelection crackdown, although parties were not banned, opposition offices were closed and one, the NDU office, remained closed until after the Constitutional Court ruling on its election grievances in November.

The ARF/Dashnak party, suspended since 1994, had an application for reinstatement pending with the Ministry of Justice. The Ministry of Justice by year's end had yet to provide a written response to the application, although the law requires an answer within 30 days of filing. Although the activities of the party are still officially suspended, officials have not interfered while the party held a 2-week congress, elected a new governing body, held news conferences, and actively supported the opposition's National Alliance, forming a part of the Alliance's five-party leadership. The authorities charge that the presence of foreign members in the ARF's ruling body, the International Bureau, violates the law on public political organizations. The party reconstituted its ruling bodies during the year and claims to have created purely indigenous local structures.

c. *Freedom of Religion.*—The Constitution provides for freedom of religion; however, in practice the law imposes restrictions on religious freedom.

The 1991 Law on Religious Organizations establishes the separation of church and state, but grants the Armenian Apostolic Church (the Armenian Orthodox Church) special status. A variety of religious organizations, including Protestants, Mormons, and others hold services. The Armenian Orthodox clergy resent the inroads made by nonapostolic religions in recent years.

The law forbids proselytizing and requires all nonapostolic religious denominations and organizations to register with the Ministry of Justice. Petitioning organizations must "be free from materialism and of a purely spiritual nature," and must subscribe to a doctrine based on "historically recognized holy Scriptures." A presidential decree issued in 1993 supplemented the 1991 law and strengthened the position of the Armenian Apostolic Church. The decree enjoins the Council on Religious Affairs to investigate the activities of the representatives of registered religious organizations and to ban missionaries who engage in activities contrary to their status. No action was taken against missionaries in 1996.

A religious organization refused registration cannot publish a newspaper or magazine, rent a meeting place, have its own program on television or radio, or officially sponsor the visas of visitors. One nonapostolic religious organization was denied registration by the Ministry of Justice during the year the grounds that it does not permit military service. Three religious organizations were registered, bringing the total of churches and religious organizations registered to 43.

Despite the Government's pledge to apprehend those who staged a series of attacks against a dozen nonapostolic religious groups in 1995, the authorities have made no arrests. No attacks were reported in 1996.

d. *Freedom of Movement Within the Country, Foreign Travel, Emigration, and Repatriation.*—The Constitution provides for freedom of movement within the country, foreign travel, emigration, and repatriation, but the Government places restrictions on some of these rights. According to informed estimates, up to one-third of the population has temporarily or permanently emigrated during the last 7 years. Travel passports may be denied to persons possessing state secrets and to those whose relatives have made financial claims against them. The Office of Visas and Registrations (OVIR) has eased travel and emigration procedures by discontinuing the requirement for exit visas. The Government publicly appeals to Armenians who have emigrated to return, and a small flow of repatriates has begun. The Government does not restrict internal movement; citizens have the right to change freely their residence or work place.

The 1988–89 anti-Armenian pogroms in Azerbaijan caused an exchange of populations between the two republics. The ethnic minorities on both sides were subject to discrimination and intimidation, often accompanied by violence intended to drive them from the country. All of the ethnic Azeris living in Armenia at the time, some 185,000 persons, fled to Azerbaijan. Of the 400,000 ethnic Armenians then living in Azerbaijan, 330,000 fled to and were granted refugee status in Armenia. The majority of the rest took refuge in Russia with small numbers remaining in Azerbaijan.

Armenia is a signatory to the 1951 U.N. Convention on Refugees and its 1967 Protocol. The National Assembly passed a Law on Citizenship, Article 10 of which provides for refugees to gain citizenship, provided they are stateless and have resided in the country for the past 3 years. Implementing regulations for the law and naturalization procedures are being worked out with the United Nations High Commissioner for Refugees. The status of those who remain refugees will continue to be unclear until a Law on Refugees is passed. Currently, there is a 5-year state program on refugees (1994–1999). The program's goal is to help the refugees integrate into the community. This program deals exclusively with refugees of Armenian nationality who have fled states in the region.

The Government cooperates with the Office of the UNHCR and other humanitarian organizations in assisting refugees. The Government provides first asylum and provided it to fewer than 50 persons in 1996. There were no reports of forced return of persons to a country where they feared persecution.

Section 3. *Respect for Political Rights: The Right of Citizens to Change Their Government*

The Government's manipulation of the presidential election continued to restrict the Constitutional ability of citizens to change their government peacefully.

The outcome of the September presidential elections, in which incumbent President Ter-Petrossian officially was declared the victor in the first round of balloting with 51.75 percent, was contested by his leading challenger Vazgen Manukyan, who officially garnered 41.29 percent of the vote. Fifty percent of the vote by one candidate was required to avoid a second round of elections. Manukyan's National Alliance filed an appeal to the Constitutional Court. An OSCE election observer mission noted "irregularities," "discrepancies," and "very serious breaches of the election law" which caused "concern for the overall integrity of the election process." The final report of the OSCE mission concluded that the breaches in the election law "can only contribute to a lack of confidence in the integrity of the overall election process." Specific problems during the election process included intimidation; unauthorized persons in polling stations; irregularities in military voting, especially instructions by officers to troops on their voting choice; vote tabulation; verification; and the aggregation of results. Local organizations that observed the 1995 parliamentary elections were not explicitly permitted to observe under the new presidential electoral law. Citing the law's silence, the CEC refused to allow such observers.

In response to the official election results, opposition candidates Manukyan and Manucharian claimed fraud and appealed directly to the Constitutional Court in late October for new elections. The Court upheld the official election results in late November. Major questions were raised regarding the Court's procedures in this case. The Central Election Commission refused requests by the opposition and international experts to release the detailed election protocols (voting results) from all voting precincts. The Constitutional Court denied the opposition's request to publish all precinct results nationwide, confining its review to those precinct results presented by the appellants; 1,155 of a total of 1,596 precinct results were reviewed. To protest this and other aspects of the Court's treatment of their case, the opposition walked out of the Court's proceedings prior to its ruling. The Court's decision rejecting the opposition's appeal did not dispel doubts about the credibility of the official election results.

Although the Presidential election was flawed, observers agreed that the conduct of the preelection campaign—excluding opposition party media access—was an improvement over the 1995 parliamentary elections. All candidates with sufficient signatures were registered by the CEC. Opposition representatives participated as minority members of electoral commissions in all regional and most precinct and community levels. The opposition campaigned effectively and drew an impressive response from the voters. Checks and balances were enacted into law, which, if implemented, might have addressed many of the suspicions about vote manipulation. Multiple irregularities in the balloting and tabulation process undermined the credibility of the vote and remain a problem. The Government's failure to address effectively these flaws eroded public confidence in the integrity of the electoral process and remains a source of deep polarization within the country.

Under the Constitution, the President appoints the Prime Minister and has considerable influence in appointing judges. The Constitution provides for independent legislative and judicial branches, but in practice these branches are not insulated from political pressure from the executive branch.

The Government appoints the 10 regional governors (marzpets). The Constitution gives local communities the right to elect local authorities. In November the first elections for municipal councils and mayors were held. The municipal elections were also characterized by extensive irregularities, notwithstanding the initial observation by Council of Europe observers that elections were "free and fair" at the precincts that they visited. In addition some opposition parties officially boycotted the elections in protest over the conduct of the presidential elections.

The National Assembly is to operate as a part-time institution for the duration of its first term. Approximately one-third of the parliamentarians have been designated full-time deputies. Parliament also has a truncated work schedule for its first term. Sessions may be called, but may not last more than 6 days.

There are no legal restrictions on the participation of women and minorities in government and politics. However, due to traditional social attitudes, both are underrepresented in all branches of government. There is one woman in Cabinet (Minister of Social Welfare), but no minorities. Only 11 of the 190 deputies in the Parliament are women.

Section 4. Governmental Attitude Regarding International and Nongovernmental Investigation of Alleged Violations of Human Rights

There are several fledgling nongovernmental human rights organizations that are active and operate openly, criticizing publicly and publishing their findings on government human rights violations. The Government at times impeded investigations into alleged violations of human rights by international human rights organizations.

The Government accepted an OSCE election observer mission for its presidential elections and provided international observers with countrywide access. However, local observer organizations, which had been given access during the 1995 parliamentary elections, were not allowed to observe the presidential elections (see Section 3).

The Government was generally cooperative in granting the ICRC access to prisoners of war and civilian detainees held by Armenia in connection with the Nagorno-Karabakh conflict. Prisoners on the ICRC lists were released in a prisoner exchange in May. The ICRC was also provided access to detainees facing politically motivated charges in connection with the "Dro," "Trial of 31," and other cases. However, the ICRC had significant difficulties in meeting with the prisoners detained by the Ministry of Interior following the government crackdown in September after the presidential election (see Section 1.c.).

Section 5. Discrimination Based on Race, Sex, Religion, Disability, Language, or Social Status

Discrimination based on race, sex, religion, disability, language, or social status is prohibited by the Constitution, but cultural and economic factors prevent women, ethnic and religious minorities, and persons with disabilities from participating fully in public life.

Women.—The Legal Code (the old Soviet code) cites specific punishments for rape, forced abortion, forbidding a woman from marrying, and discrimination in hiring due to pregnancy. There is no specific law banning violence against women. Few cases of rape, spouse abuse, or other violence against women are reported in this conservative, patriarchal society, although their number is likely higher than the statistics indicate. Between January and September, the Interior Ministry registered 32 cases of rape and attempted rape.

In the workplace, women receive equal pay for equal work, but are generally not afforded the same professional opportunities given to men and are often relegated to more menial or low-skill jobs. The 1992 law on employment prohibits discrimination in employment, but the extremely high unemployment rate makes it difficult to gauge how effectively the law has been implemented to prevent discrimination.

Currently there are more women receiving university and postgraduate education than men.

Children.—The Government does not have the economic means to provide fully for the welfare of children. The family tradition is strong, and child abuse does not appear to be a serious problem. The Government focuses its efforts on children's rights and welfare with measures to insulate large families—four or more children—from the effects of the country's current difficult circumstances. The Government similarly targets foreign humanitarian aid programs at large families.

Girls and boys receive equal educational educational opportunities as education is highly prized for both men and women.

People With Disabilities.—The Constitution provides for right to social security in the event of disability. The 1993 Law on Invalids provides for the social, political, and individual rights of the disabled but does not mandate the provision of accessibility for the disabled. In its current economic circumstances, the Government has difficulty making good on its commitments in this area. The Government's enforcement of the rights of the disabled remains rudimentary. There is societal discrimination against the disabled.

Religious Minorities.—In June the Catholicos of all Armenians, Karekin I, who heads the Armenian Apostolic Church, received a large delegation of the Armenian Evangelical Church (AEC), which is the second largest Armenian religious body. The two set in motion a new ecumenical spirit that had been lacking since the AEC was established 150 years ago. This process is expanding to include Orthodox-Protestant cooperation in religious education. Although minority religious groups, especially new religious movements, are not widely accepted in society, there was no violence against minority religious groups.

National/Racial/Ethnic Minorities.—The Government does not discriminate against the small communities of Russians, Jews, Kurds, Yezids, Georgians, Greeks, and Assyrians in employment, housing, or health services. Following the protracted conflict (see Section 2.d.), there is no significant Azeri minority. There are several hundred Azeris or persons of mixed Azeri heritage still living in Armenia, but they are isolated from one another and maintain a low profile. Although there have been no reported cases of persecution, they face societal discrimination.

The Constitution grants national minorities the right to preserve their cultural traditions and language, and the 1992 law on language provides linguistic minorities the right to publish and study in their native language. There are publications in minority languages, but the Government has not devoted sufficient resources to organizing minority language schools. In practice, virtually everyone, including members of the Yezid, Greek, and Jewish communities, speaks Armenian. There are no known allegations of persecution based on minority group among the non-Azeri minority groups.

Section 6. Worker Rights

a. *The Right of Association.*—The Constitution provides employees with the right to form and join trade unions and the right to strike. The Constitution stipulates that the right to form associations—including political parties and trade unions—may be limited with respect to persons serving in the armed services and law enforcement agencies. A 1993 presidential decree prohibits the Government and other employers from retaliating against strikers and labor leaders. In practice labor organization remains weak due to high unemployment and stalled industry.

Unions are free to affiliate with international organizations.

b. *The Right to Organize and Bargain Collectively.*—Collective bargaining is not practiced. The Constitution provides all citizens with the right to a just wage no lower than the minimum set by the Government. Although the 1992 Law on Employment provides for the right to organize and bargain collectively, voluntary and direct negotiations do not take place between unions and employers without the participation of the Government because nearly all enterprises, factories, and organizations remain under state control. The near collapse of major industrial production has undercut the organization of labor unions.

The Government encourages profitable factories to establish their own pay scales. Factory directorates generally set the pay scales, without consultation with employees. Wage and other labor disputes are adjudicated through the Arbitration Court.

There are no export processing zones.

c. *Prohibition of Forced or Compulsory Labor.*—The Constitution and the 1992 law on employment prohibit forced labor, and it is not practiced. This provision is enforced by the local councils of deputies, unemployment offices, and, as a final board of appeal, the Arbitration Commission.

d. *Minimum Age for Employment of Children.*—Child labor is not practiced. According to the 1992 Law on Employment, 16 years is the minimum age for employment. Children may work from the age of 14 with the permission of a medical commission and the relevant labor union board. The Law on Employment is enforced by the local councils of deputies, unemployment offices, and, as a final board of appeal, the Arbitration Commission.

e. *Acceptable Conditions of Work.*—The Government sets the minimum wage by decree. In July the national minimum wage was set at $2 dollars (820 drams) per month. The standard legal workweek is 41 hours.

Given the cost of living, employees paid the minimum wage cannot support either themselves or their families on their pay alone. The overwhelming majority of the population lives below the officially recognized poverty level as a result of the economic dislocations caused by the breakup of the Soviet Union, the 1988 earthquake, the conflict in Nagorno-Karabakh, and the resulting blockade and disruptions in trade. The vast majority of enterprises are either idle or operating at only a fraction of their capacity. Some furloughed workers are still receiving minimal partial compensation from their enterprises, but most are no longer receiving any payment if they are not working.

The Constitution provides citizens with the right to clean and safe work places, but Soviet-era occupational and safety standards remain in force. Labor legislation from 1988 places responsibility on the employer and the management of each firm to ensure "healthy and normal" labor conditions for employees, but it provides no definition of healthy and normal. The employment situation is such that workers would be afraid of the risk of losing their jobs and, therefore, it is unlikely that they would attempt to remove themselves from hazardous working conditions.

AUSTRIA

Austria is a constitutional democracy with a federal parliamentary form of government and an independent judiciary. Citizens choose their representatives in periodic, free, and fair multiparty elections.

The police are subordinated to the executive and judicial authorities. The national police maintain internal security. The army is responsible for external security.

Austria's highly developed, market-based economy, with its mix of technologically advanced industry, modern agriculture, and tourism affords its citizens a high standard of living.

The Government fully respected the human rights of its citizens, and the law and judiciary provide effective means of dealing with instances of individual abuse. There were occasional reports of abuse by police. The Government is taking serious steps to address violence against women.

RESPECT FOR HUMAN RIGHTS

Section 1. Respect for the Integrity of the Person, Including Freedom From:

a. *Political and Other Extrajudicial Killing.*—There were no reports of political or other extrajudicial killings.

b. *Disappearance.*—There were no reports of politically motivated disappearances.

c. *Torture and Other Cruel, Inhuman, or Degrading Treatment or Punishment.*—Although the Constitution prohibits such practices, government statistics for 1995 showed 615 complaints against police officials for illegitimate use of force, a decrease of 61 compared with 1994. In six cases, police officials were convicted and required to pay fines. In nine cases, officers faced disciplinary proceedings, and in one case, the disciplinary proceeding was terminated. Of the people who filed complaints against the police, 23 were sued for slander and 15 were sued for resisting arrest.

Prison conditions meet minimum international standards. The Government is a party to the European Convention for the Protection of Human Rights and Fundamental Freedoms, which includes a provision for human rights monitoring missions. In individual cases, investigating judges or prison directors have jurisdiction over questions of access to the defendant.

d. *Arbitrary Arrest, Detention, or Exile.*—The Constitution prohibits arbitrary arrest, detention, or exile, and the Government observes this prohibition.

In criminal cases the law provides for investigative or pretrial detention for up to 48 hours, except that in cases of charges of "aggressive behavior" an investigative judge may within that period decide to grant a prosecution request for detention up to 2 years pending completion of an investigation. The grounds required for such investigative detention are specified in the law, as are conditions for bail. The investigative judge is required to evaluate an investigative detention at 2 weeks, 1 month, and every 2 months after the arrest.

e. *Denial of Fair Public Trial.*—The Constitution provides for an independent judiciary, and the Government respects this provision in practice. The judiciary provides citizens with a fair and efficient judicial process. There were no reports of political prisoners.

f. *Arbitrary Interference With Privacy, Family, Home, or Correspondence.*—The Constitution prohibits such practices, government authorities generally respect these prohibitions, and violations are subject to effective legal sanction.

Section 2. Respect for Civil Liberties, Including:

a. *Freedom of Speech and Press.*—The Constitution provides for freedom of the press, and the Government generally respects this right in practice, although stringent slander laws tend to discourage reports of police brutality. Publications may be removed from circulation if they violate legal provisions concerning morality or public security, but such cases are extremely rare.

Television and national radio are government monopolies, but they present diverse points of view. A law passed in 1993 permits regional private radio stations, but implementation of the law was delayed due to legal challenges by unsuccessful applicants for licenses. After the Constitutional Court ordered the revision of radio frequencies and after complaints against the law were dropped in Styria and Salzburg, two stations opened. The text of the law, with rewritten radio frequency rules, is under revision.

Academic freedom is respected.

b. *Freedom of Peaceful Assembly and Association.*—The Constitution provides for freedom of assembly and association, except for Nazi organizations and activities (an exception stipulated also in the Austrian State Treaty of 1955). The law on the formation of associations states that permission to form an organization may be denied if it is apparent that the organization will pursue the illegal activities of a prohibited organization.

c. *Freedom of Religion.*—The Constitution generally provides for freedom of religion of individuals, as laid down by the Treaty of St. Germain. The status of religious organizations, however, is governed by the 1874 "Law on Recognition" of churches. Religious recognition has wide-ranging implications, e.g., the authority to participate in the state-collected religious taxation program, engage in religious education, and import religious workers to act as ministers, missionaries, or teachers. Officially, 75.3 percent of the populace is Roman Catholic, and there are 12 other recognized religious organizations. For non-European Union missionaries or pastors, recognition is the key to residence and work. Some foreign Protestant churches have not qualified for religious recognition and have had to withdraw or scale back their services.

d. *Freedom of Movement Within the Country, Foreign Travel, Emigration, and Repatriation.*—The Government does not restrict movement, including emigration. Citizens who leave the country have the right to return at any time.

Austria has signed the 1951 United Nations Convention on Refugees and its 1967 Protocol Relating to the Status of Refugees, but it subscribes to the "safe country" concept. Asylum seekers who have entered illegally are required to depart and seek refugee status from outside the country (a provision which is not always enforced). Individuals found to be true refugees by government authorities are not sent back to the countries from which they have fled.

According to one NGO report, conditions in refugee detention centers are very poor. Suicide attempts and hunger strikes have been reported in these centers where detainees may spent up to 6 months in custody. The Government cooperates with the Office of the United Nations High Commissioner for Refugees (UNHCR) relying on UNHCR information to determine "safe" countries." Before the 1992 legal reforms the UNHCR played a more direct role in Austrian refugee decisions; today the UNHCR has withdrawn to a more advisory and monitoring role. In this role, the UNHCR continues to chide the Government over the safe country concept and the legal applicant rules, both of which appear to represent diversions from the Convention and its Protocol.

At present Austria provides a "temporary protected status" which, although limited in scope by time and nationality, could be considered "first asylum."

Refugees from the former Yugoslavia arriving between April 1992 and July 1993 were granted protected status, but this window has now closed. Since 1992 the Government has granted refugee status only to several hundred individuals from the former Yugoslavia. The rest have remained under protected status, been absorbed through the normal immigration process, or remained illegally. Outside the influx from the former Yugoslavia, since passage of the 1992 law, the Government has granted refugee status to an average of 600 applicants yearly.

Section 3. Respect for Political Rights: The Right of Citizens to Change Their Government

The Constitution provides citizens with the right peacefully to change their government. Citizens exercise this right in practice through periodic, free, and fair elections held on the basis of universal suffrage.

Approximately 26 percent of the members of Parliament and 4 of 16 cabinet members are women.

Section 4. Governmental Attitude Regarding International and Nongovernmental Investigation of Alleged Violations of Human Rights

A number of human rights groups operate without government restriction, investigating and publishing their findings on human rights cases. In some cases, they have been dissatisfied with the information authorities have supplied in response to specific complaints.

Section 5. Discrimination Based on Race, Sex, Religion, Disability, Language, or Social Status

The law provides for protection against any of these kinds of discrimination in employment, provision of welfare benefits, and other matters, and the Government generally enforces its provisions effectively.

Women.—Official data for 1995 (the latest statistics available) show 12,554 reported cases of violence against women, of which 500 were rapes and 279 other sexual assaults. Police and judges enforce laws against violence; however, only about 10 percent of abused women file complaints. The Government plans to expand police authority to enforce measures banning an abusive spouse from a previously jointly owned home or other places where the victim might be stalked.

Most legal restrictions on women's rights have been abolished. Women are still prohibited by law from night work in most occupations. Although this ban is sometimes used as a pretext for not hiring women, it is supported by the Women's Affairs Ministry and women's organizations. (Nurses, taxi drivers, and a few other occupations are exempted from this ban.) According to a 1994 ruling by the European Court of Justice, a sex-based prohibition of nighttime work is not permissible. The Government has been granted a transition period until 2001 to adapt its legislation to gender-neutral European Union regulations and is due to report in 1997 on its progress.

In addition to the federal Women's Affairs Ministry, a federal Equality Commission and a federal Commissioner for Equal Treatment oversee laws prescribing equal treatment of men and women. Sixty percent of women between the ages of 15 and 60 are in the labor force. Despite substantial gains in women's incomes, they average 20 percent lower than those of men. Women are not allowed in the military.

Although labor laws providing for equal treatment extend to women in the civil service, they remain underrepresented there. To remedy this, a 1993 law requires hiring women of equivalent qualifications ahead of men in civil service areas in which less than 40 percent of the employees are women; but there are no penalties for failure to attain the 40 percent target.

Women may be awarded compensation of up to 4 months' salary if discriminated against in promotions because of their sex. The Labor Court can also award compensation from employers to victims of sexual harassment.

Women's rights organizations are partly politically affiliated, and partly autonomous groups. In voicing their concerns, they receive wide public attention.

Children.—Laws protect the vast majority of children's rights established in international conventions and in some respects go beyond them. Each provincial government and the federal Ministry for Youth and Family Affairs has an "Ombudsperson for Children and Adolescents" whose main function is to resolve complaints about violations of rights of children. There is no societal pattern of abuse against children.

Allegations concerning a suspected Austrian-Slovak child pornography ring in August led to strong public and political pressure to further tighten Austrian legislation on child pornography. Pertinent legislation was last amended in 1994, when possession of child pornography videos was made a criminal offense.

People With Disabilities.—Disabled individuals are protected by law from discrimination in housing, education, and employment. The law requires all private enterprises and state and federal government offices to employ 1 disabled person for every 25 to 45 employees, depending on the type of work. Employers who do not meet this requirement must pay a fee to the Government, and the proceeds help finance services for the disabled such as training programs, wage subsidies, and workplace adaptations. No federal law mandates access for the physically disabled; some public buildings are virtually inaccessible for those unable to climb stairs.

National/Racial/Ethnic Minorities.—The Interior Ministry issued a report on rightwing extremism, which showed that in 1995 the number of complaints and reports of incidents of rightwing extremism, xenophobia, and anti-Semitism rose to 621, which was 20 cases higher than in 1994. Eighty-nine cases resulted in court sentences.

Small, loosely organized, rightwing groups are increasing their use of computers and international electronic networks. In 1995 criminal investigations were launched against three Austrians for spreading fascist and extreme rightwing propaganda through the Internet. At year's end, the cases are still pending with no arrests, prosecutions, or convictions. In late 1995, the Justice and Interior Ministries developed a joint proposal for legislation to expand the use of investigative tools, such as electronic eavesdropping and merging of databases, and to introduce protection for defendants and witnesses who cooperate with investigative authorities. The proposal was controversial, and it is estimated that changes in the law will not occur before mid-1997.

Religious Minorities.—In May a Jewish cemetery in Rechnitz was vandalized. In November unidentified vandals desecrated a Jewish cemetery in Hollabrunn. On December 18, "Wolfgang T" was convicted of desecrating the Jewish cemetery in Eisenstadt in 1993. A second suspect remains at large.

Jewish community leaders praised the Government's auction of the "Mauerbach" collection, a compilation of art works originally owned by Austrian Jews, then seized by the Nazis, and later held by the Government. Following efforts to find the original owners, the Government auctioned about 8,000 art works with 88 percent of the proceeds going to the Austrian Jewish community for use in social projects.

Section 6. Worker Rights

a. *The Right of Association.*—Workers have the right to form and join unions without prior authorization, under general constitutional guarantees of freedom of association. In practice, trade unions have an important and independent voice in the political, social, and economic life of the country. Fifty-two percent of the work force was organized in 14 national unions, all belonging to the Austrian Trade Union Federation (OGB), which has a highly centralized leadership structure. Individual unions and the OGB are independent of government or political party control, although formal factions within these organizations are closely allied with political parties.

Although the right to strike is not explicitly provided for in the Constitution or in national legislation, it is universally recognized. Historically, strikes have been comparatively few and usually of short duration. There were no strikes during the year. A major reason for the record of labor peace is the unofficial system of "social partnership" among labor, management, and government. At the center of the system is the Joint Parity Commission for Wages and Prices, which has an important voice on major economic questions.

b. *The Right to Organize and Bargain Collectively.*—Unions have the right to organize and bargain collectively. Almost all large companies, private or state-owned, are organized. Worker councils operate at the enterprise level, and workers are entitled by law to elect one-third of the members of the supervisory boards of major companies. Collective agreements covering wages, benefits, and working conditions are negotiated by the OGB with the National Chamber of Commerce and its associations, which represent the employers. Wage and price policy guidelines are set by the Joint Parity Commission. A 1973 law obliges employers in enterprises with more than five employees to prove that job dismissals are not motivated by antiunion discrimination. Employers found guilty of this are required to reinstate workers. Labor and business representatives remain in disagreement over how to comply with the obligation under the International Labor Organization's Convention 98 to provide legal protection to employees against arbitrary dismissals in firms with five employees or fewer.

Typically, legal disputes between employer and employees regarding job-related matters are handled by a special arbitration court for social affairs. The OGB is exclusively responsible for collective bargaining. The leadership of the Chamber of Labor, the Chamber of Commerce, and the OGB are elected democratically.

There are no export processing zones.

c. *Prohibition of Forced or Compulsory Labor.*—Forced labor is prohibited by law and is not practiced.

d. *Minimum Age for Employment of Children.*—The minimum legal working age is 15 years. The law is effectively enforced by the Labor Inspectorate of the Ministry of Social Affairs.

e. *Acceptable Conditions of Work.*—There is no legislated national minimum wage. Instead, nationwide collective bargaining agreements set minimums by job classification for each industry. The generally accepted unofficial minimum gross income is $14,000 per year. Every worker is entitled to a variety of generous social benefits. The average citizen has a high standard of living, and even the minimum wages are sufficient to permit a decent living for workers and their families.

Although the legal workweek has been established at 40 hours since 1975, more than 50 percent of the labor force is covered by collective bargaining agreements that set the workweek at 38 or 38½ hours.

Extensive legislation, regularly enforced by the Labor Inspectorate of the Ministry of Social Affairs, provides for mandatory occupational health and safety standards. Workers may file complaints anonymously with the Labor Inspectorate, which may bring suit against the employer on behalf of the employee, but this option is rarely exercised, as workers normally rely instead on the Chambers of Labor, which file suits on their behalf.

The Labor Code provides that workers have the right to remove themselves from a job if they fear "serious, immediate danger to life and health" without incurring any prejudice to their job or career.

AZERBAIJAN

Azerbaijan is a republic with a presidential form of government. Heydar Aliyev, who assumed presidential powers after the overthrow of his democratically elected predecessor, was elected President in 1993. He and his supporters, many from his home region of Nakhichevan, dominate the Government and the multiparty, 125-member Parliament chosen in the November 1995 elections. The Constitution, adopted in a November 1995 referendum, established a system of government based on division of powers between a strong presidency, a legislature with the power to approve the budget and impeach the President, and a judiciary with limited independence. After years of interethnic conflict between Armenians and Azerbaijanis, Armenian forces affiliated with the self-styled "Republic of Nagorno-Karabakh" (which is not recognized by any government) occupy 20 percent of Azerbaijan's territory. Although both sides largely continue to observe the cease-fire concluded in May 1994 and the peace process continues, there are continued reports of cease-fire violations from both sides and military operations continued to affect the civilian population. There are about 780,000 Azerbaijani refugees and internally displaced persons (IDP's) who cannot return to their homes. In the part of Azerbaijan that the Government controls, government efforts to hinder the opposition continue to impede the transition to democracy. In the part of Azerbaijan that Armenians control, a heavily militarized ruling structure prevents ethnic Azerbaijanis from returning to their homes.

Police and the Ministry of National Security are responsible for internal security. Members of the security forces committed numerous human rights abuses.

Azerbaijan has a state-dominated economy rich in oil, natural gas, and cotton. An informal private sector, operating outside official channels but often with ties to persons in the Government, plays an important role in the economy. In June and December, the Government signed contracts for third and fourth international consortiums to develop additional oil fields. Oil bonus payments from these consortiums contributed importantly to the Government's budget and fiscal stability. However, the economy continued to suffer from the lack of significant economic reform and the slow pace of privatization. The Parliament passed a revised mass privatization law in November 1995, but to date the Government has only privatized about 3,000 small service enterprises. Russian measures to restrict transport flows at the northern border hamper trade. The loss of the Nagorno-Karabakh region and surrounding territories, which took significant amounts of agricultural land out of production, led to reduced agricultural output. Widespread corruption is an obstacle to economic development. The overall economic situation of the average citizen remains precarious, although in urban areas a growing monied class with trade and oil-related interests has emerged. Both underemployment and unemployment are extremely high.

The Government's human rights record continued to be poor, and the Government continued to commit serious abuses. The security forces beat persons and some beatings resulted in deaths. Security forces also arbitrarily arrested, and detained persons; conducted searches and seizures without warrants; and suppressed peaceful demonstrations. In a variety of separate incidents, the Government arrested 25 members of the opposition Azerbaijan Popular Front Party and 9 members of the Islamic Party. In May one member of the Islamic Party died after being arrested and beaten by security force officials. The Government did not take effective action to punish any abusers. Prison conditions remained harsh. The judiciary is corrupt, inefficient, and subject to executive influence. The Government tolerated the existence of many opposition political parties, although it continued to refuse to register some of them. The Government restricts citizens' ability to change their government peacefully. Government efforts to hamper opposition candidates marred parliamentary runoff elections in February. The Government restricted freedom of speech, press, assembly, association, religion, and privacy when it deemed it in its interest to do so. Press censorship continued, and the Government closed a leading independent newspaper for 1 month. However, scores of opposition and independent newspapers continued to publish and discuss a wide range of sensitive domestic and foreign policy issues. Discrimination against ethnic minorities and societal discrimination and violence against women are problems.

Nevertheless, there were some positive signs. The Government was open to increased dialogue with domestic and international human rights organizations; undertook to investigate the alleged beating of a journalist; and was responsive to interventions on individual cases. For example, the Government released from custody a former Foreign Minister and an opposition leader.

Cease-fire violations by both sides in the Nagorno-Karabakh conflict resulted in civilian injuries and deaths and the taking of prisoners. Insurgent Armenian forces in Nagorno-Karabakh and the occupied territories continued to prevent the return of IDP's to their homes. This restriction resulted in significant human suffering for hundreds of thousands of people.

RESPECT FOR HUMAN RIGHTS

Section 1. Respect for the Integrity of the Person, Including Freedom From:

a. *Political and Extrajudicial Killings.*—A member of the Islamic Party of Azerbaijan, Haci Qablaqa Quliyev, died in May after severe beatings by guards in prison. Rafiq Ismaylov, a barber not involved in politics, died after being beaten while in police custody in Massali province at the end of 1995. Ilqar Samedov died in pretrial detention on July 29 as a result of injuries sustained during beatings by police. A Human Rights Watch report states that, according to a coroner's report, he died of "blows to the head with a blunt object." The Government took no action against offenders in any of these cases.

There has been no action by the Government in the murder of opposition Azerbaijan Popular Front (APF) MP Shakhsultan Jafarov in July 1995.

b. *Disappearance.*—There were no reports of politically motivated disappearances. All sides to the Nagorno-Karabakh conflict still detain prisoners. The International Committee of the Red Cross (ICRC) visited 122 people held in relation to this conflict. In July the parties freed a total of 109 in a prisoner exchange: 39 by Azerbaijan, 11 by Armenia, and 59 by the authorities in Nagorno-Karabakh. Subsequently, 21 additional people have been detained: 17 Armenians held by Azerbaijan, including 2 women and one child, and 4 Azerbaijanis held by the authorities in Nagorno-Karabakh. The ICRC repeatedly asked the concerned parties for notification of any person captured in relation to the conflict, access to all places of detention connected with the conflict, and release of all such persons. The ICRC also urged the parties to provide information on the fate of persons reported missing in action. The Government presented to the ICRC a list of 856 persons allegedly held by the Armenians.

The Human Rights Center of Azerbaijan, together with other local human rights organizations, successfully negotiated with the Ministry of Justice to visit a woman's prison.

c. *Torture and Other Cruel, Inhuman, or Degrading Treatment or Punishment.*— Torture is illegal; however, the security forces' practice of beating prisoners during arrest and interrogation was widespread. Ministry of National Security officials arrested, beat, and then released Mirsaleh Jafarov, a member of the Islamic Party in April/May. Two persons died after beatings by security force officials, one while in police custody, and another while in prison (see Section 1.a.).

Prison conditions are harsh, especially in the special security prisons. The quality of food, housing, and medical care is poor. Prisoners often must rely on their families to procure food and medicine. There are widespread reports that authorities deny, or give inadequate, medical treatment to prisoners for serious medical conditions. The family of Kenan Gurel, on trial for participating in a coup attempt, reported that he receives inadequate treatment for a kidney ailment. Authorities severely limit opportunities for exercise for prisoners in security prisons.

Despite Government assurances that former Interior Minister Iskendar Hamidov is receiving medical care, Hamidov's relations say that his medical care is inadequate and that he continues to suffer from ill health in prison. Hamidov remains in the central Ministry of National Security prison, despite a sentence to a regular prison. The Government claims that incarceration of Hamidov in a regular prison would be dangerous for Hamidov, who as Interior Minister was responsible for placing many of the prisoners in jail.

On two occasions, police beat a journalist (see Section 2.a.). Police also dispersed demonstrators by force (see Section 2.b.).

There were no further developments in the 1995 arrest and beating of Farrukh Agaev for allegedly reading (opposition-oriented) bulletins on a wall in Lenkoran.

Various foreign embassies have petitioned the Government for permission to visit all prisons. In general, when asked, the authorities grant foreign officials access to regular prisons to visit imprisoned nationals of their countries. However, the Government denies access to detainees held in security prisons.

Human rights organizations were able to visit prisons on at least one occasion. The ICRC visits most prisons in the country.

d. *Arbitrary Arrest, Detention, or Exile.*—Arbitrary arrests without legal warrant occur. Often authorities do not notify family members after arrests. Frequently, it is days before family members are able to obtain information as to whether authorities have arrested someone and where authorities are holding the detainee. Family members do not enjoy the right of visitation. Authorities generally deny bail to detained individuals and often do not inform detainees of the charges against them. Access to lawyers is often poor.

Authorities arrested Kemal Talibov in Nakhichevan after he published a newspaper article criticizing political and economic conditions in the Nakhichevan Autonomous Republic. Police arrested, beat, and then released Turkish journalist Yashar Tezel, who was found in the company of former Prime Minister Penah Huseynov. In the course of the year, the police arrested 25 members of the opposition Azerbaijan Popular Front Party. Among them was former Prime Minister Panah Huseynov. Security forces also arrested 9 members of the Islamic Party.

Despite such actions, the Government did release some detainees. The Government freed former Foreign Minister Tofiq Qasimov from detention in February and allowed him to remain at home with his family to seek medical treatment after Qasimov suffered medical problems during incarceration. The court postponed Qasimov's trial pending his recovery. In July the Government released deputy chair of the Azerbaijan Popular Front Party Arif Pashayev after 25 months in prison. In both cases, international and local human rights organizations, and foreign embassies, intervened on behalf of the prisoners.

Various local estimates put the number of political detainees currently under arrest on politically motivated charges at approximately 35. Authorities charged them with common crimes or with treason.

The Government does not practice forced exile.

e. *Denial of Fair Public Trial.*—The Constitution provides for a judiciary with limited independence. The President appoints Supreme and Constitutional Court judges, subject to confirmation by Parliament. The President directly appoints lower level judges with no requirement for confirmation. Constitutional provisions for judicial independence to the contrary, judges do not function independently of the executive branch. The judicial system is subject to the influence of executive authorities and has been widely seen as corrupt and inefficient.

Courts of general jurisdiction may hear criminal, civil, and juvenile cases. District and municipal courts try the overwhelming majority of cases. The Supreme Court may also act as the court of first instance, depending on the nature and seriousness of the crime.

The government organizes prosecutors into offices at the district, municipal, and republic levels. They are ultimately responsible to the Minister of Justice, are appointed by the President, and confirmed by Parliament. The Constitution prescribes equal status for prosecutors and defense attorneys before the courts. In practice, however, prosecutorial prerogatives still generally outweigh those of defense attorneys. Investigations often rely on obtaining confessions rather than obtaining evidence against suspects.

Cases at the district court level are tried before a panel consisting of one judge and two lay assessors. Judges frequently send cases unlikely to end in convictions back to the prosecutor for "additional investigation." Such cases may be either dropped or closed, occasionally without informing the court or the defendant.

The Constitution provides for public trials except in cases involving state, commercial, or professional secrets, or matters involving confidentiality of personal or family matters. The Constitution provides for the presumption of innocence in criminal cases, and numerous other rights, including an exclusionary rule barring the use of illegally obtained evidence, a suspect's right to legal counsel, to be informed immediately of his legal rights, and of the charges against him. The Government has not made significant efforts to enforce these rights throughout the criminal justice system. Defendants may confront witnesses and present evidence. The court appoints an attorney for indigent defendants. Defendants and prosecutors have the right of appeal. The Government has generally observed the constitutional provision for public trial. Foreign and domestic observers were able to attend trials, including sensitive trials involving high-profile political figures.

The Government held approximately 100 political prisoners at year's end, a figure comparable with 1995 levels.

f. *Arbitrary Interference With Privacy, Family, Home, or Correspondence.*—The population widely believes that the Ministry of National Security monitors telephones, especially those of foreigners and prominent political and business figures. The police have periodically raided the offices of opposition political parties and the homes of their members, allegedly searching for illegal weapons or other materials. These searches are usually conducted without a warrant, and investigations can result in confining the individuals to their city of residence or a brief jail sentence for questioning. There were no reported cases of such limitations being imposed in 1996.

g. *Use of Excessive Force and Violations of Humanitarian Law in Internal Conflicts.*—There were continued reports of civilian deaths and injuries due to shelling by Armenian forces. The Armenian press reported deaths and injuries to Armenian civilians from Azerbaijani shelling. Foreign diplomats who visited areas in Azerbaijan near the front lines met individuals who claimed that they or family members were injured in shellings by Armenian forces. These sources reported civilian deaths from Armenian shelling. According to the Government, six persons were wounded by Armenian activity in the first 2 months of 1996. No annual figures were available on civilian and military casualties.

Section 2. Respect for Civil Liberties, Including:

a. *Freedom of Speech and Press.*—The Constitution provides for freedom of speech and the press, and specifically outlaws press censorship; however, the Government often did not respect these rights in practice. While the press debated a wide variety of sensitive topics, censorship limited the public's ability to be informed about and discuss political issues. Censorship continued at approximately 1995 levels, although the Government did not prevent independent and opposition press from continuing to play an active, influential role in politics. Officially, the Government limited censorship to military topics. In practice, however, censorship of political topics continued. The Ministry of Information can legally close a newspaper for 1 month for violating censorship rules. Censors deleted portions of newspaper articles or entire articles. Journalists often exercised self-censorship and are forbidden to write about censorship. A major opposition newspaper claimed to have been subjected to 105 cases of censorship in the course of the year. Censors banned an entire issue of one opposition newspaper for having previously published a mildly satirical article about the President. The Ministry of Information took another independent newspaper to court and had it closed for 1 month due to previously published articles on sensitive foreign policy subjects. The President's office rescinded this order 1 week later. On two occasions, the Speaker of Parliament banned a journalist from entering Parliament. In one of those cases, a court rendered an apparently prearranged verdict that confirmed the ban and ruled that the journalist had slandered Parliament. Authorities in the Nakhichevan Autonomous Republic banned an opposition journalist from Nakhichevan after she published an article critical of conditions there. On two occasions, police beat a journalist attempting to cover demonstrations that the Government had not authorized. In one of these cases, when the journalist filed a complaint about police behavior, the prosecutor's office opened an investigation of police behavior. The investigation was ongoing at year's end.

Despite government censorship, articles critical of government policy and high government figures appeared routinely in the print media. Newspapers were able to publish articles opposing government views in sensitive areas such as Azerbaijan's relations with Russia and Iran, the Nagorno-Karabakh peace process, conflicts within the President's political party, and government failures in economic reform.

A large number of newspapers continued to publish. One reliable source put the number at more than 300. These include independent newspapers and newspapers with links to major and minor opposition parties. Government-run kiosks and independent news distributors distributed opposition and independent newspapers. Most independent newspapers, many of which operated with precarious finances, remained dependent on the Government for printing facilities.

The Government tightly controlled most radio and television. Opposition parties had virtually no access to the official electronic media. The Government appointed a new director of state television, who said that it was the duty of state television to implement the policies of the President. There is a limited range of private television stations, and some of them are accessible only to those local residents who own modern, foreign-produced television sets. Independent radio, the choice of the overwhelming majority of listeners, is almost entirely entertainment oriented. Independent television and radio broadcasters are reluctant to air controversial political topics for fear of Government retaliation.

An order from the Ministry of Justice in June ordered the closing of all independent television stations pending the passage of a national law regulating independent television. The authorities closed three stations, pending receipt of applications for broadcast licenses. Authorities closed another station after it interviewed a leader of an opposition party. Six independent television stations continue to operate in Baku and other regions. Broadcasts of several foreign television stations can be seen in Azerbaijan, and there are no restrictions on reception of foreign stations via satellite.

The Government did not pursue a case against those responsible for beating the head of an independent TV station in Baku in 1995. There is no evidence that the individual filed a complaint with the police.

Appointments to government-controlled academic positions are heavily dependent on political connections. Nevertheless, several professors with tenure are active in opposition parties. There were no complaints of violation of academic freedom or of censorship of books or academic journals.

b. *Freedom of Peaceful Assembly and Association.*—The Constitution provides for these rights; however, the Government restricts the right of peaceful assembly and association when it decides that it is in its interest to do so. The Government permitted demonstrations on some occasions, but on others it restricted citizens' rights to assemble freely. Although the authorities allowed a demonstration by opposition political parties at a foreign embassy, they denied permits for demonstrations in the capital on at least three occasions, and dispersed demonstrators by force when they attempted to gather. Security forces broke up two demonstrations near the Russian embassy protesting the treatment of Azerbaijanis in Russia in July and August. In the Nakhichevan Autonomous Republic, the police seized the local headquarters of the opposition Azerbaijan Popular Front Party.

The Government cited no clear criteria when it denied permission to assemble. Police broke up a demonstration called by a former leader of an opposition party. Authorities evicted Azerbaijan Popular Front Deputy Chairman and Member of Parliament Ali Kerimov from a hall in which he was addressing supporters in his electoral district. In the latter part of the year, opposition parties began active preparations for mounting campaigns for the 1998 presidential elections. As of year's end, there had been no government effort to obstruct these activities.

The Government requires political parties to register. There are over 40 registered political parties. Some of these are affiliated with or support the President's party. At least 10 registered parties are considered opposition parties. There are at least three opposition parties that the Government has refused to register.

The Government generally allowed associations other than political parties to function freely. However, the Ministry of Justice requires private organizations to register. It denied or unduly delayed registration for numerous private voluntary organizations, including one private human rights organization. Reports of harassment of political figures continued. Individuals and groups involved in human rights activities reported a mixed record—while the Ministry of Justice declared that the operation of unregistered human rights organizations might be illegal, the Ministry also worked with these groups on specific human rights issues.

c. *Freedom of Religion.*—The Constitution provides for no state religion and allows people of all faiths to practice their religion without restrictions. The Government respects this provision in practice for Shi'a and Sunni Muslims, Russian Orthodox Christians, and Jews. However, a new law on foreigners and stateless persons contains language which prohibits religious proselytizing by foreigners. In July Parliament passed an amendment to the law on religion that subordinated all Islamic religious organizations to the Azerbaijan-based Directorate of Caucasus Muslims. This law permits the production, importation, and dissemination of religious literature only with the agreement of local government authorities. The Ministry of Justice denied registration to a foreign Christian group, but has allowed it to continue to function. Two non-Orthodox Christian groups were evicted from facilities in which they held religious services and prevented from renting other facilities, but both groups had found facilities and continued to operate by year's end. Non-Orthodox Christian groups have complained of official harassment. Numerous articles in Government and progovernment newspapers crudely depicted various religious groups including some non-Orthodox Christian groups as a threat to national identity, traditions, and morals. Some opposition newspapers also attacked Christian missionary activity. Because of anti-Armenian sentiment and the forced departure of most of the Armenian population, Armenian churches remained closed. Azerbaijan's Jewish community has freedom to worship and conduct educational activities.

   d. *Freedom of Movement Within the Country, Foreign Travel, Emigration, and Repatriation.*—The Constitution provides for the right of citizens to choose freely their place of domicile and to travel abroad and return. Residents of border areas in both Azerbaijan and Iran travel across the border in this restricted zone without visas. The Government no longer tried to require foreigners to obtain visas to travel outside of Baku. Foreigners and citizens require a visa to travel to the Autonomous Republic of Nakhichevan.

   There continue to be bans on travel outside of Baku on some prominent political leaders who are under criminal investigation. However, two opposition leaders under such restrictions—Isa Gambar of the Musavat Party (charged with using military force in the context of a rebellion leading to the overthrow of the Elcibey government in 1993); and Ali Kerimov of the Azerbaijan Popular Front (charged with concealing hand grenades in his pockets)—were permitted to travel outside of Azerbaijan.

   The Government officially recognizes freedom of emigration. Jewish emigration to Israel is unrestricted. However, with the majority of those who wish to emigrate already having left, the number of Jewish emigrants is now small. The remaining Armenian population in Azerbaijan (other than Armenians residing in the Nagorno-Karabakh region of Azerbaijan) is approximately 10,000 to 20,000, mostly people of mixed descent or in mixed marriages. While official government policy is that Armenians are free to travel, low-level officials seeking bribes have harassed Armenians wishing to emigrate.

   There were no draft notifications that restricted movement this year. Draft-age men must obtain documents from military officials before they can leave for international travel.

   The number of refugees and displaced persons in Azerbaijan is approximately 780,000. Armenians have begun to settle in parts of the occupied territories. However, the Armenians have not allowed the hundreds of thousands of Azerbaijanis who were forced out of the now-occupied territories to return to their homes. Most of these people continue to live in camps and other temporary shelters, often at below-subsistence levels, without adequate food, housing, education, or medical care. The parties to the conflict have cut normal trade and transportation links to the other side, causing severe hardship to civilians in Nagorno-Karabakh, Armenia, and the Azerbaijani exclave of Nakhichevan.

   The Constitution provides for political asylum consistent with international norms. The Government is receptive to international assistance for refugees and internally displaced persons. It cooperates with international organizations to provide aid for them. The Government cooperates with the Office of the United Nations High Commissioner for Refugees (UNHCR) and other humanitarian organizations in assisting refugees. The issue of the provision of first asylum did not arise. There were no reports of forced expulsion of those having a valid claim to refugee status. However, the Government ordered at least two Iraqis whose claims to refugee status were still under consideration by the UNHCR to leave the country, but did not act to expel or repatriate them to Iraq. They remained in the country at year's end.

Section 3. Respect for Political Rights: The Right of Citizens to Change Their Government

In theory the election law and Constitution allow citizens to change their government by peaceful means. However, Government interference in elections restricted citizens' ability to change their government peacefully.

The Government held the third round of runoff elections for the national Parliament in February. It was flawed by many of the same irregularities that marked the first and second rounds in 1995. The most serious irregularities involved reported turnouts much higher than those observed at the polls. A continuing problem was multiple voting, with one person voting for a group. Most often, male heads of household voted for entire families. Foreign observers noted a greater tendency for local election officials to inflate voter turnout than in the first election round in November 1995. The Government attempted to hinder international monitoring of these elections by not inviting some foreign observers until the evening before the election.

In this special election round, the Government made a major effort to prevent the election of opposition Musavat Party candidate Isa Gambar, who ran in a district in Sumgait. Gambar was able to campaign and hold speeches and rallies in Sumgait, despite his being confined to the city limits of Baku by court order as part of an ongoing investigation. However, police seized the Sumgait headquarters of the Musavat Party the week before the election and detained several Musavat party workers. There were numerous reports of government officials urging local election officials to prevent a victory by the Musavat Party leader.

A parliamentary by-election in July was flawed by multiple voting, failure to check voters identities, and a reported voter turnout (90 percent) far greater than election monitors observed. Election observers had access to polling stations. They were also able to observe the ballot counting process, which appeared fair.

As a result of the flawed 1995 parliamentary election, the New Azerbaijan Party led by President Aliyev and nominally independent deputies loyal to the President occupy the overwhelming majority of seats in the 125-member Parliament. Parties considering themselves part of the opposition hold only 9 seats. Opposition parties continued to be active outside the Parliament, agitating for their views in their newspapers and through public statements. However, the Government continued to deny registration to at least three opposition parties not represented in Parliament. Explicitly ethnically or religiously based parties were prohibited from participating in elections, including the February 1995 election. A candidate from the Talysh Party stood in the 1995 election as an independent.

Parliamentary activity revealed the severe limits on the legislature's independence from the executive. The President's New Azerbaijan Party mounted a public attack on the Speaker of Parliament (who had expressed views critical of the Government) that resulted in his orchestrated ouster from office. A confrontation between Parliament and the Government over the state budget showed that the Parliament's powers to question government ministers are limited in practice. The Parliament exercises little legislative initiative independent of the executive.

The Constitution allows citizens to file court proceedings to challenge illegal actions of government officials. However, citizens rarely make use of this provision, preferring to appeal to higher levels of authority, up to and including the President.

There are no legal restrictions on women's participation in politics. However, traditional social norms restrict women's roles in politics. Men continued to cast votes for their wives and other female members of their families, an abuse that was widely noted in the Parliamentary runoff election held this year. There are 11 female members of Parliament and 2 women with ministerial rank.

There are no restrictions on the participation of minorities in politics as individuals. However, explicitly ethnically or religiously based parties were prohibited from participating in the February election. Indigenous ethnic minorities such as Talysh and Lezghis occupy some senior government positions; the Deputy Minister of Defense is Lezghi; the head of the Central Election Commission is Talysh.

Section 4. Government Attitude Regarding International and Nongovernmental Investigation of Alleged Violations of Human Rights

Several human rights organizations monitor the human rights situation in the country. The Government posed no objections to international human rights groups monitoring the situation. Some of these groups investigate human rights abuses and disseminate their findings through the media. Eighteen women's groups are active.

The Government has demonstrated a willingness to discuss human rights problems with international government and nongovernmental organizations. Ministry of Interior and Justice officials conducted discussions with a local nongovernmental organization, the Institute for Peace and Democracy, on human rights issues. The

Prosecutor General and large numbers of law enforcement personnel participated in a seminar in December discussing legal aspects of human rights in Azerbaijan organized by the OSCE Office for Democratic Institutions and Human Rights. The International Committee of the Red Cross conducted education programs on international humanitarian law for officials of the Ministries of Interior and Defense, and for university and secondary school students. Government officials participated in a UNHCR-organized training seminar in December aimed at reforming the Law on Refugees and Displaced Persons.

The Ministry of Justice announced that several human rights groups were not registered and warned that their continued operation might be illegal. However, the Government has taken no action to halt their activities. A local nongovernmental organization monitored the activities of political parties and published a newsletter with statements by opposition party leaders critical of the Government and the political system.

The Government did not facilitate foreign monitoring of the February runoff elections, but welcomed foreign embassy monitoring of the July parliamentary by-election and provided monitors with district-wide access. The ICRC has had access to prisoners of war as well as civilians held in relation to the conflict over Nagorno-Karabakh. However, the ICRC has requested and been denied access to prisoners not related to the Nagorno-Karabakh conflict being held in special security prisons.

Section 5. Discrimination Based on Race, Sex, Religion, Disability, Language, or Social Status

The Constitution provides for equal rights irrespective of gender, race, nationality or national origin, religion, language, social status, or membership in political parties, trade unions, or other public organizations. In the wake of the conflict over Nagorno-Karabakh, there are widespread anti-Armenian sentiments in society. Preventing discrimination is not a major government priority.

Women.—Discussion of violence against women is a taboo subject in Azerbaijan's patriarchal society. In rural areas, women have no real recourse against violence by their husbands, regardless of the law. Rape is severely punishable, but, especially in rural areas, only a small fraction of offenses against women are reported or prosecuted. Police statistics note 72 cases of rape this year. These figures probably reflect underreporting, especially from the conservative rural areas.

Women nominally enjoy the same legal rights as men, including the right to participate in all aspects of economic and social life. In general women have extensive opportunities for education and work. However, traditional social norms continue to restrict women's roles in the economy. Representation of women is sharply lower in higher levels of the work force. There are few women in executive positions in leading businesses.

The Association for the Defense of Rights of Azerbaijani Women spends most of its time fighting uniquely post-Soviet problems. It has helped divorced women, widows, and wives whose husbands are in prison, all of whom have become socially and legally vulnerable since the fall of the Soviet Union. It assisted widows whose landlords privatized their apartments and then evicted them. It also worked with divorced women who feel unfairly treated by divorce courts.

Children.—The Constitution and laws commit the Government to protecting the rights of children to education and health. Difficult economic circumstances limit the Government's ability to carry out these commitments. Education is compulsory through the eleventh grade, that is, until age 17. The Constitution places children's rights on the same footing as adults. The Criminal Code prescribes severe penalties for crimes against children. The Government has authorized subsidies for children in an attempt to shield families against economic hardship in the wake of price liberalization. The subsidies do not come close to covering the shortfall in family budgets, and the Government does not have the financial means to meet its new commitments. There are a large number of refugee and displaced children living in substandard conditions in refugee camps and public buildings. Children beg on the streets of Baku and other towns.

People With Disabilities.—The law on support for the disabled, enacted in late 1993, prescribes priority for invalids and the disabled in obtaining housing, as well as discounts for public transport, and pension supplements. The Government does not have the means in its current financial crisis to make good on its commitments. There are no special provisions in the law mandating accessibility to buildings for the disabled.

National/Racial/Ethnic Minorities.—The outbreak of hostilities and anti-Armenian riots in the final years of the Soviet Union led to the expulsion of many Armenians and the departure of others. An estimated 10,000 to 20,000 Armenians still live in Azerbaijan, mostly in mixed Azerbaijani-Armenian families. Some have changed their nationality, as reported in their passports, to Azerbaijani. With the nearly complete departure of the Armenian population, the number of problems reported by this ethnic minority has decreased. Armenians have complained of discrimination in employment and harassment at schools and workplaces, and of refusal of local government authorities to grant Armenians passports or pay pensions. Armenian widows have had permits to live in Baku revoked. In July a State television news program accused by name a Baku Armenian family of making inflammatory anti-Azerbaijani statements. However, some persons of mixed Armenian-Azerbaijani descent continue to occupy government positions. In a speech in August, the President urged Azerbaijanis not to accuse or behave negatively towards Armenians in mixed families.

Indigenous ethnic minorities such as the Talysh, Lezghis, Avars, and Georgians do not suffer discrimination. However, Meskhetian Turks displaced from Central Asia as well as Kurdish displaced persons from the Lachin region complain of discrimination.

In the area of the country controlled by insurgent (Armenian) forces, the Armenians forced about 500,000 ethnic Azerbaijanis to flee their homes. The regime that now controls these areas has effectively banned ethnic Azerbaijanis from all spheres of civil, political, and economic life.

Section 6. Worker Rights

a. *The Right of Association.*—Most labor unions still operate as they did under the Soviet system and remain tightly linked to the Government. The Constitution provides for freedom of association, including the right to form labor unions. However, one or another subbranch of the government-run Azerbaijani Labor Federation organizes most industrial and white-collar workers. Most major industries remain state-owned. There is at least one independent labor union, the Independent Oil Workers Union, which voices the demands of oil workers. In September a group of oil workers, including some fired after a strike in April, founded an independent association, the Committee to Defend the Rights of Azerbaijani Oil Workers. This organization operates outside established trade union structures.

The Constitution provides for the right to strike, and there are no legal restrictions on strikes nor provisions for retribution against strikers. Oil workers conducted several short strikes demanding back pay amounting to several months' arrears. After at least one of these strikes, management fired several strike organizers. Employers did not meet assurances to restore back pay. There are no established mechanisms to avoid such wildcat strikes.

Unions are free to form federations and to affiliate with international bodies, however, none has done so.

b. *The Right to Organize and Bargain Collectively.*—There is effectively no system of collective bargaining. Government-appointed boards and directors run the major enterprises and set wages. Unions do not participate in determining wage levels. In a carryover from the Soviet system, both management and workers are considered members of the professional unions.

There are no export processing zones. Although there has been a United Nations Development Program-supported effort underway to create an economic zone in Sumgait since 1995, Parliament has not yet considered legislation to create such a zone.

c. *Prohibition of Forced or Compulsory Labor.*—The Constitution allows forced or compulsory labor only under states of emergency or martial law, or as the result of a court decision affecting a condemned person. The Government has not invoked this clause. Two departments in the General Prosecutors Office (the Department of Implementation of the Labor Code and the Department for Oversight Over Minors) enforce the prohibition on forced or compulsory labor. During the fall, there were widespread, but unconfirmed, reports that local government authorities in rural areas forced children, teachers, and other adults to harvest cotton without payment.

d. *Minimum Age for Employment of Children.*—The minimum employment age is 16 years. The law allows children of age 14 to work during vacations with the consent of their parents and certification of a physician. Children of age 15 may work if the workplace's labor union does not object. There is no explicit restriction on the kinds of labor that children of age 15 may perform with union consent. The Labor Ministry has primary enforcement responsibility for child labor laws. With high adult unemployment, there have been few, if any, complaints of abuses of child labor laws. However, in the fall there were widespread, but unconfirmed, reports that some rural authorities forced children between the ages of 11 and 16 to harvest cotton without payment (see Section 6.c.).

e. *Acceptable Conditions of Work.*—The Government sets the nationwide administrative minimum wage by decree. It is $1.30 (5,500 manat) per month. The wage is not sufficient to provide a decent standard of living for a worker and family. The recommended monthly wage level to meet basic subsistence needs was estimated to be $72 (310,000 manat). There seems to be no active mechanism to enforce the minimum wage. However, since most people who work earn more than the minimum wage, its low level is not a major issue in labor or political debate.

The disruption of economic links with the rest of the former Soviet Union continues to affect employment in many industries. Idle factory workers typically receive less than half of their former wage. Under these conditions, many workers rely on the safety net of the extended family. More workers and unemployed persons turn to second jobs and makeshift employment in the informal sector, such as operating the family car as a taxi, selling produce from private gardens, or operating small roadside shops. Combinations of these and other strategies are the only way for broad sectors of the urban population to reach the subsistence income level.

The legal workweek is 41 hours. There is a 1-hour lunch break per day and shorter breaks in the morning and afternoon. The Government does not enforce these rules in the informal sector.

Health and safety standards exist, but they are mostly ignored in the workplace. Workers cannot leave dangerous work conditions without fear of losing their jobs.

BELARUS

Belarus has a constitutional government with executive, legislative, and judicial branches, but the President exercised total control over most aspects of the Government by the end of the year. Since his election as the first President in July 1994, Aleksandr Lukashenko has steadily amassed power in the executive branch. The President appoints the Cabinet of Ministers and all executive heads of the country's six provinces. Presidential decrees have the force of law, except—in theory—in those cases restricted by the Constitution and Parliament. A new Parliament was seated in January, but the President restricted it from carrying out nearly all of its constitutional duties and dissolved it following a controversial constitutional referendum in November. The Troika of Foreign Ministers of the Organization for Security and Cooperation in Europe concluded that the circumstances of the referendum deprived it "of any legitimacy." The President repeatedly ignored limits on the authority of the executive branch. The judiciary is not independent.

The Committee for State Security (KGB) and Ministry of Internal Affairs (MVD), both answerable to the President, remained the chief law enforcement and police organs. Under President Lukashenko's direction, the Presidential Guard (initially created to protect senior officials) expanded its role and used force against the President's political enemies with no judicial or legislative oversight. Members of the security forces committed numerous human rights abuses.

The economy is still largely state controlled and continued its steady decline since the breakup of the Soviet Union. Only limited, small-scale privatization has occurred, and although most prices were liberalized, the prices of staple food products are controlled by the Government. Most state enterprises have not been restructured, and many are operating at a fraction of their capacity. Industry and construction employ 40 percent of the labor force; agriculture employs 20 percent. According to official statistics, per capita gross domestic product (GDP) at the end of 1995 was $1,000; however, actual per capita GDP probably is higher since many economic activities are unreported. Major exports include machinery, transport equipment, and chemicals.

The Government's human rights record worsened significantly as the President continued to lead Belarus back toward Soviet-era authoritarian practices. The Government severely limits citizens' right to change their government. Lukashenko used a November constitutional referendum, which the international community generally regarded as illegitimate, to consolidate and extend his power. He used the results of the referendum to disband the Parliament (Supreme Soviet) and form a new legislature subordinate to his rule. The constitutional referendum, which was riddled with violations of democratic norms, also extended his term of office by 2 years and further subordinated the judiciary to his rule. He also announced that he would be a cabinet member for life.

The constitutional referendum occurred in a repressive political environment and with pervasive government control of the media. Through this control, the Government denied the voters access to the views of the opposition—including members of Parliament and of the Constitutional Court. The judiciary is not independent, and is largely unable to act as a check on the executive branch and its agents.

Executive branch abuse of its monopolies on the security apparatus and on the mass media increased. Security forces reportedly regularly beat detainees and prisoners. On occasion security forces arbitrarily arrested and detained citizens. The security services monitored the activities of opposition politicians and other segments of the population closely. Formations of MVD troops used force to break up political demonstrations and made mass arrests following one protest. Severe hazing continued in many military units. Prison conditions are poor. Prolonged detention and delays in trials were common. Restrictions on freedoms of speech, the press, and peaceful assembly all increased. Although the Government generally respected freedom of association, there were serious exceptions. Restrictions on the freedoms of religion and of movement continued. Discrimination and domestic violence against women remained significant problems. The Government sharply curtailed the rights of workers to organize and bargain collectively.

RESPECT FOR HUMAN RIGHTS

Section 1. Respect for the Integrity of the Person Including Freedom From:
  a. *Political and Extrajudicial Killing.*—There were no reports of political or other extrajudicial killings. The Government did not apologize for the September 1995 downing of a sport balloon by the Belarusian Air Defense Force, which resulted in the deaths of two American citizens, despite the May conclusion of the International Civil Aviation Organization's investigation that the tragedy was the result of a variety of factors, including failures and errors by Belarusian civil aviation and military authorities.
  b. *Disappearance.*—There were no reports of politically motivated disappearances.
  c. *Torture and Other Cruel, Inhuman, or Degrading Treatment or Punishment.*—Both the 1994 Constitution and the new Constitution adopted as a result of the November referendum provide for the inviolability of the person and specifically prohibit torture, as well as cruel, inhuman, or degrading punishment. However, police and prison guards reportedly regularly beat detainees and prisoners. Law enforcement and prison officials may use physical force against detainees and prisoners if the latter are violent, have refused to obey the instructions of the prison administration, or have "maliciously violated the terms of their sentences." Law enforcement sources as well as former detainees report that investigators physically abused detainees in order to secure confessions. Although such behavior is against the law, the Government seldom, if ever, punishes people who commit such abuses.
  Police beat and detained journalists covering an April 26 antigovernment rally (see Sections 1.d. and 2.a.).
  The Ministry of Defense announced that "dedovshchina," the practice of hazing new recruits, would no longer be tolerated. This practice of severe harassment and abuse of new draftees by senior soldiers to maintain strict discipline has abated somewhat, but there are reports that hazing continues in many units.
  Prison conditions are poor, marked by severe overcrowding, shortages of food and medicine, and the spread of diseases such as tuberculosis and syphilis. Conditions at prison hospitals are similarly poor.
  Human rights monitors were not granted sufficient access to prisoners.
  d. *Arbitrary Arrest, Detention, or Exile.*—Belarus has only slightly amended its Soviet-era law on detention. On occasion security forces arbitrarily arrested and detained citizens. The Criminal Procedure Code provides that police authorities may detain a person suspected of a crime for 3 days without a warrant. This period may be extended for up to 10 days, pending further investigation of a crime. On the basis of a local prosecutor's authority, detainees may be kept in pretrial detention for up to 3 months. Regional and republic level prosecutors may request extensions up to a maximum of 18 months. The law permits citizens to appeal the legality of an arrest either to the court or to the prosecutor's office. According to judicial sources, nearly 90 percent of all arrests are now contested.
  By law a judge must initiate a trial within 3 weeks from the time charges are filed. However, the overloaded court system often does not meet this requirement, and months may pass before a defendant is finally brought to court.
  Detainees may be allowed unlimited access to their legal counsel, and, according to the 1994 Constitution, if they cannot afford counsel, a lawyer is to be appointed free of charge. Lawyers are not appointed free of charge in "minor" cases, however, and prisoners without the means to hire their own counsel have received sentences of up to 5 years without consulting an attorney.
  Prisoners and lawyers both report restrictions on consultations, and investigators may prohibit consultations between a lawyer and a client. Some detainees reported that investigators coerced them to sign statements waiving the right to an attorney during interrogation. The Government has failed to budget sufficient funds for de-

fense attorneys representing the indigent, and defense attorneys' fees are prohibitively expensive for many defendants. The law does not provide for the right to a prompt judicial determination of the legality of detention. Since there are no legal provisions for bail and because there is no effective judicial oversight of prosecutors' actions, pretrial detention has in some instances lasted longer than 3 years, sometimes without the accused knowing the charge against him. Two opposition leaders detained for activities in conjunction with the April 26 protest were released on their own recognizance to await trial after their month-long hunger strike threatened their lives (see Section 1.e.).

The constitutional right of access to counsel and the requirement to charge detainees are frequently ignored. Witnesses at criminal trials who gave evidence to police without access to an attorney were subsequently charged based on their testimony.

On April 26, opposition Member of Parliament Pavel Znavets was detained after a raid on Belarusian Popular Front headquarters and held incommunicado for more than 24 hours despite parliamentary immunity from arrest. Security forces refused to answer parliamentary inquiries about the circumstances surrounding his detention. The Supreme Soviet formed a commission to investigate the matter. It determined that Znavets had parliamentary immunity and should not have been detained. The matter has been dropped.

Ukrainian nationalists detained in conjunction with an April 26 antigovernment rally were publicly criticized on national television before their trial began. A state-employed cameraman, posing as an interrogator, questioned the detainees, and official television broadcast their interrogation as part of the Government's campaign to justify the extreme police reaction to the protest.

On the evening of April 26, hours after the conclusion of the "Path of Chernobyl" antigovernment protest, police arbitrarily rounded up groups of youths on the streets of Minsk. Anatoly Lisun, who has been deaf and mute since birth, was detained for 3 days for "shouting antipresidential slogans." In all police rounded up over 100 people on the streets of Minsk. Detainees were held in a Minsk prison with no facilities for consulting lawyers or visits from family members. For more than 30 days, foreign diplomats were refused access to their citizens detained in conjunction with the April 26 protest.

In October authorities reportedly detained miners who sought to attend an opposition congress (see Section 2.b.).

Two leaders of the opposition Belarusian Popular Front, who had played a prominent role in organizing protest demonstrations in March and April, evaded a security forces dragnet and fled the country. Both were granted political asylum abroad.

Beginning in 1996, there were reports of people being apprehended by unidentified individuals and held incommunicado for varying periods. Those conducting the apprehensions were presumed to be members of the government security services, since the detentions occurred during opposition demonstrations.

Exile is not practiced.

e. *Denial of Fair Public Trial.*—The judiciary is not independent and is largely unable to act as a check on the executive branch and its agents. The Supreme Council passed legislation to support the independence of the judiciary in 1995, but these reforms were not implemented. Without the implementation of major structural reforms, the independence of the judiciary from outside pressure cannot be realized. The November constitutional referendum further subordinated the judiciary to Lukashenko's rule by giving the President the power to appoint 6 of the 12 members of the Constitutional Court, including the chairman. The remaining 6 are appointed by the Senate, which itself is at least partially under the control of the President by virtue of his power to directly appoint 8 of the 64 Senators and indirectly to influence the election of the remainder.

The criminal justice system, following the former Soviet model, has three tiers: district courts, regional courts, and the Supreme Court. Several modifications have been made, brought about by passage of the new Constitution, including direct presidential appointment of all district level and military judges. The President also appoints the chairmen of the Constitutional Court, the Supreme Court, and the Supreme Economic Court. A Constitutional Court was established in 1994 to adjudicate serious constitutional issues, but it has no means to enforce its decisions.

Parliament selects judges for republic-level courts on the basis of recommendations from the Ministry of Justice, based in part on examination results. However, many current judges and prosecutors were appointed in Soviet times when political influence pervaded the criminal justice system as it does today. Judges are dependent on the Ministry of Justice for sustaining the court infrastructure and on local executive branch officials for providing their personal housing. Organized crime has had a significant impact on court decisions. There have been reports of judges granting lenient sentences to defendants "connected" with organized crime.

Prosecutors, like the courts, are organized into offices at the district, regional, and republic levels. They are ultimately responsible to, and serve at the pleasure of, the Procurator General, who according to the Constitution adopted by the November referendum is appointed by the Senate. The previous Constitution also gave the legislature authority to appoint the Prosecutor General.

By law trials are public, although they may be closed on grounds of national security. Defendants have the legal right to attend proceedings, confront witnesses, and present evidence on their own behalf. These rights are not always respected in practice. Defendants also have the right to be represented by counsel, another right not always respected in practice (see Section 1.d.). Trials for those detained on misdemeanor charges following the April 26 protests were held assembly-line style at the prison, and some defendants did not have the opportunity to call witnesses on their behalf.

While the Constitution establishes a presumption of innocence, conviction rates have not changed from the Soviet era. Nearly 99 percent of completed cases result in convictions. Judges frequently send cases unlikely to end in convictions back to the prosecutor for "additional investigation," and prosecutors also withdraw cases not likely to result in conviction.

Both defendants and prosecutors have the right of appeal, and now nearly 60 percent of all criminal cases are appealed. On appeals, neither defendants nor witnesses appear before the court; the court merely reviews the protocol and other documents from the lower court's trial, and appeals rarely result in reversals of verdicts.

Two leaders of the Belarusian Popular Front, Yuri Khadyko and Vyacheslav Sivchik, were detained on April 26 and charged with two felonies: Creating a public disturbance and interfering with the actions of police officers. After a hunger strike that lasted nearly a month and broad appeals for their release, both were released on condition that they remain in Minsk until their trial, which has been repeatedly postponed.

Andrei Romashevsky, Vice President of the Belarusian Beer Lovers' Party, was detained following the April 26 demonstration and charged with "malicious hooliganism" for desecrating state symbols. Following the May 1995 referendum that approved the "new," Soviet-style Belarusian flag, Romashevsky burned that banner, yet he was only detained 1 year later, following his participation in a student antigovernment rally in May. After serving nearly 3 months in pretrial detention, Romashevsky was given 1-year probation and a 2-year suspended sentence.

The nationalist poet Slavomir Adamovich was detained on April 18 for publishing a poem titled "To Kill a President" and charged with inciting a terrorist act. His trial was continuing in criminal court at year's end.

Vladimir Dzyuba, news editor of Belarusian Radio 2, was detained after the April 26 rally and served a 3-day sentence for "petty hooliganism." Immediately after his release, he was again detained and given a second sentence of 15 days, reportedly after the judge was pressured by the executive branch for giving Dzyuba too lenient a sentence.

There were no reports of political prisoners at year's end.

f. *Arbitrary Interference With Privacy, Family, Home or Correspondence.*—Government monitoring of residences and telephones increased. The KGB is widely believed to enter homes without warrants, conduct unauthorized searches, and also to read mail. Human rights organizations believe that their correspondence is routinely monitored by the security services. The KGB, the MVD, and certain border guard detachments have the right to request permission to install wiretaps but legally must obtain a prosecutor's permission before installation. The Presidential Guard formed in 1995 reportedly conducted surveillance activities of the President's political opponents. There is no judicial or legislative oversight of the Presidential Guard's budget or activities, and the executive branch has repeatedly thwarted attempts to exercise such oversight.

The Government makes no secret of the security service's activities or capabilities and conducts active surveillance of opponents of the Lukashenko Government. In February a telephone installed in the residence of the newly elected Speaker of the Parliament was found to be wiretapped. In September the Chairman of the Constitutional Court announced that he had received information from a source within the Presidential Guard that President Lukashenko had given instructions to record the Justice's telephone conversations, both at home and at work, as well as to collect "compromising materials" on the leader of the country's highest court.

In a February 26 address to government and industry leaders, the President openly referred to a "special services" report detailing trade union meetings with international labor organizations. The President attempted to discredit trade union leaders, accusing them of plotting to "destabilize the domestic political situation."

Nearly all opposition political figures assumed that the Government monitors their activities and conversations. The Lukashenko Government did nothing to refute these assumptions. Indeed, government officials do not appear to be exempt from monitoring. Lukashenko declared to a television audience that he was confident of then-Prime Minister Chigir's loyalty because he knew what Chigir said in private to his wife.

Section 2. Respect for Civil Liberties, Including:

a. *Freedom of Speech and Press.*—The Constitution provides for freedom of speech, but the Government does not respect this right in practice. The executive branch, through the head of the President's Chief Directorate for Public Information, further increased direct suppression of freedom of expression through its near total monopoly on the means of production and distribution of mass media and by restricting the access of independent media to official sources of information. The Government increased economic pressure on the independent media by pressuring advertisers to withdraw advertisements and by ordering intrusive, prolonged inspections of their financial activities.

The defamation law makes no distinction between private and public persons for the purposes of lawsuits for defamation of character. A public figure who has been criticized for poor performance in office may ask the public prosecutor to sue the newspaper that printed the criticism.

In January the President signed a decree ordering that all editors in chief of state-supported newspapers would henceforth be official state employees and would become members of the appropriate level government council. Another decree granted the Ministry of Press authority to assign graduates of state-supported journalism schools to work in state-owned media organizations as a means of payment for their schooling.

In December 1995, on instructions from President Lukashenko, the state publishing house refused to renew printing contracts with the four leading independent newspapers. These publications continued to circulate in Belarus, but they are still denied access to the state-controlled system of distribution and publishing facilities.

The Belarusian Television and Radio Company (B–TR) maintained its total monopoly as the only nationwide television station. B–TR Director Grigory Kisel instructed the state television company to cease broadcasting the opening session of Parliament. Despite parliamentary resolutions calling for time on state television, B–TR did not broadcast the Constitutional Court's annual address to the nation, which was highly critical of many of President Lukashenko's actions. On April 18, the Parliament adopted a resolution that claimed that the B–TR "regularly broadcast information which discredited the activities of the highest legislative body." On September 27, in response to what it termed consistently tendentious coverage, Parliament withdrew B–TR's press accreditation. (Russian television networks continue to have access to Supreme Council sessions.)

The Government regularly restricted the access of independent media to official sources of information. On many occasions, representatives of the independent media were not granted accreditation to government press conferences. The Cabinet of Ministers announced on February 8 that the Russian news agency Interfax would not be granted further access to information for "grossly distorting" the meaning of testimony by the Prime Minister before Parliament. In accordance with a presidential decree, the Government broke the lease on the editorial offices of the independent news agency "Belapan" and the opposition newspaper "Svaboda" and forced them to move without compensation.

Police beat journalists attempting to cover the April 26 antigovernment rally during the melee that followed the rally, and detained two journalists. Radio Liberty correspondent Eduard Terlitsky and Cezary Golinski of the Polish daily "Gazeta Wyborcza" were seriously injured.

Journalists covering a peaceful May Day rally were harassed and roughly handled by unidentified security officers in civilian clothing, reportedly members of the Presidential Guard service. The film of two journalists was exposed and videotapes were removed from the camera of the Moscow-based NTV correspondent. The prosecutor's office initiated an investigation, but it has not produced results. Journalists claimed that the incidents were an attempt to intimidate them and influence their coverage of future civil disturbances.

On the night of June 20–21, two men reportedly broke into the apartment of Radio Liberty correspondent Yuri Drakokhrust and physically abused his wife Galina. Drakokhrust, who was away on a business trip, was a vocal critic of the Lukashenko administration. Galina Drakokhrust claimed that the men used a key to enter the apartment, stole nothing, and insisted that she "tell her husband" what happened.

The Government used the State Tax Inspectorate and the "President's Control Board" to harass the independent media. The publisher of Belarus' leading independent newspapers claimed that the tax inspectorate had received instructions to "keep looking through the books until they find a reason to close them down." The bank accounts of five independent newspapers were frozen for period of about 1 month but were no longer frozen at year's end.

The Government closed down Radio 101.2, Minsk's only independent Belarusian language radio station, on September 1. After the Government initially claimed that the antenna interfered with security force communications, the President admitted that "a government transmitter and government frequencies * * * would not be used for antigovernment policies." In fact Radio 101.2 purchased the transmitter and antenna, but due to government prohibitions on private ownership of broadcast equipment, transferred title of the equipment to the Ministry of Communications and was renting the equipment back from the Government. In October Belarusian authorities closed down Radio NBK, the only independent station in Grodno, for alleged financial irregularities. State television and radio consistently denied access to the opposition, including the Speaker of the Supreme Soviet, prior to the November referendum despite repeated appeals by the Parliament. An analysis of media coverage during the November 9–24 referendum by the European Institute for Media concluded that of the 2,000 minutes devoted to referendum reporting on television, 90 percent openly supported the President's position; the other 10 percent was considered nonbiased. Radio coverage during the same period similarly contained no coverage that could be considered supportive of the opposition to the referendum or the Parliament.

The observance of academic freedom is mixed. University students and academics alike are free to pursue virtually any course of study or research. After enjoying considerable freedom to develop curricula in the first years following independence, educators are now more restrained.

On February 26, Vladimir Zametalin, President Lukashenko's Chief of Socio-Political Information, sent a letter to all academic institutions requiring a full report on all educators' publications, membership in social organizations (including political party affiliation), and any prizes and grants won from both foreign and domestic organizations.

During an April 4 press conference, President Lukashenko accused educators of inciting students to oppose his Government's plans for closer integration with Russia. Lukashenko warned academics that "we know who you are," and not to hide behind the youths whom they "throw out" to the demonstrations. Addressing teachers on October 5, the President called for the reintroduction of "ideological education," without which, he claimed, students were more disposed to participate in "nationalist riots."

b. *Freedom of Peaceful Assembly and Association.*—The Government restricts freedom of assembly. The Soviet Law on Demonstrations, which is still valid, requires an application to be made at least 10 days in advance to local officials. The local government must respond either positively or negatively not later than 5 days prior to the scheduled event. Public demonstrations occurred frequently but always under strict government control. Throughout a series of antigovernment demonstrations in the spring, the Government appeared to be following a policy of seeking confrontation with protestors, and police regularly used force to disperse crowds. The Government continued to restrict citizens' right to assemble throughout the year, but beginning with a May 1 demonstration, authorities instituted a more balanced policy—reinforced, at times, by a heavy police presence, and no further serious clashes with demonstrators occurred.

The Government issued permits for rallies on March 24 and April 26, but (according to opposition members) placed unreasonable restrictions on the location and path of the rallies. The Government placed formations of internal troops dressed in riot gear in the likely path of the marchers and used truncheons and tear gas in attempts to repel crowds. During the April 26 demonstration, the crowd responded with rocks and bottles and overturned two police cars. After the rally, police rounded up over 100 people on the streets of Minsk and raided the headquarters of the Belarusian Popular Front.

For most of the year, the Government denied permission for rallies to be held near Minsk's Independence Square and the President's office building; however, during the November referendum authorities allowed both opposition and propresidential demonstrators to remain in the square for a week-long vigil. In June the Association of Independent Industrial Trade Unions was denied permission to picket the President's office building but was granted permission to picket the Parliament.

Members of the Independent Miners' Union who attempted to walk from Soligorsk to Minsk to attend an October 18–19 opposition congress were repeatedly detained en route. After being released on October 21, 5 of the original 17 miners who set out reached Minsk on October 23. University instructors were told not to let students leave after class in order to hold down participation in an October 19 demonstration held in opposition to the concurrent All-Belarusian People's Congress organized by President Lukashenko.

Both the 1994 Constitution and the Constitution adopted by the November referendum provide for freedom of association; however the Government did not fully respect this right in practice. According to members of parties in opposition to the President, opposition groups frequently are denied permission to meet in public buildings. Employees at state-run enterprises are discouraged from subscribing to independent journals and were bused to rallies in support of the President. The Government regularly used the nationalist Belarusian Popular Front as a scapegoat, raided its headquarters, confiscated leaflets that would have publicized "unsanctioned rallies," and in June froze the organization's bank account. In addition the Government's suspension of the Free Trade Union of Belarus continued (see Section 6.a.).

At year's end there were 34 registered political parties. A 1995 decision by the Ministry of Justice required existing public associations to reregister. During the reregistration process, the Ministry frequently found cause to deny reregistration to many organizations, effectively reducing the number of public associations in Belarus from 700 to 400 by year's end. According to the Belarus League for Human Rights, some government officials admitted that the process was illegal and, therefore, allowed some groups to continue operating under their original registration. Nongovernmental organizations can legally be established, but the Ministry of Justice scrutinizes their registration applications and frequently finds cause not to register them.

c. *Freedom of Religion.*—The Constitution provides for freedom of religion, and the Government generally respects this right in practice. However, a July 1995 Cabinet of Ministers directive sharply limits the activity of foreign religious workers. Citizens are not prohibited from proselytizing, but foreign missionaries may not engage in religious activities outside the institutions that invited them. Only religious organizations already registered in Belarus may invite foreign clergy. This new directive hampered foreign religious workers' efforts to proselytize; it seeks to limit them to providing humanitarian aid only.

The Cabinet of Ministers regulation is seen as a means of enhancing the position of the Orthodox Church with respect to the faster-growing Roman Catholic and Protestant churches and also as a means of preventing religious movements outside the mainstream from spreading. The President granted special tax and other financial advantages to the Orthodox Church, which other denominations do not enjoy, and has declared the preservation and development of Orthodox Christianity a "moral necessity." In 1995, 50 Polish Roman Catholic priests were reportedly denied registration as foreign religious workers. There were no reports of such denial of registration in 1996. Bishops must receive permission from the State Committee on Religious Affairs before transferring a foreign priest to another parish. The head of the Orthodox Church, who is closely associated with the President, frequently speaks critically of missionaries.

Some difficulties still exist in transferring church property from state control back to the former owners. There has been very limited and inconsistent progress on the repatriation of former Jewish property.

d. *Freedom of Movement Within the Country, Foreign Travel, Emigration, and Repatriation.*—According to the Constitution, citizens are free to travel within the country and to live and work where they wish. All adults are still issued internal passports, which serve as primary identity documents and are required for travel, permanent housing, and hotel registration.

The right to choose one's place of residence, although provided by law, remains restricted in practice. Despite its formal abolition by the Soviet government in October 1991, the "propiska" (pass) system survives in Belarus. All citizens are required to register their places of residence and may not change them without official permission. The authorities no longer explicitly limit the number of residence permits in Minsk and the five regional centers of Brest, Grodno, Mogilev, Vitebsk, and Gomel. However, in order to register, a citizen must already have employment in the city. To be employed in the city, however, one must already be registered.

Police checkpoints at the approaches to all major cities are manned by police and, at times, by soldiers in full combat gear who randomly inspect vehicles. Citizens who appear to be of Central Asian descent report that they are stopped much more frequently than others.

Government regulations on entry and exit require citizens who wish to travel abroad to first receive an overseas passport and a "global" exit visa, which is valid for from 1 to 5 years. Once a traveler has these documents, the law does not restrict travel. However, a severe shortage of overseas passports has led to a backlog in issuance. In an address on June 20, President Lukashenko announced that "from July 1 forward, not one citizen will travel beyond the borders of our State without notifying the authorities," but no new restrictions on travel were introduced. At the end of the year, the Government took measures aimed at limiting the travel of opposition politicians. The Ministry of Foreign Affairs announced in December that those parliamentarians who did not join the new legislature could no longer travel on their diplomatic passports. Although the diplomatic passports were not confiscated, the border guards reportedly had a "black list" of opposition members who were to be denied exit from the country if using a diplomatic passport.

According to government data, no citizen was denied permission to emigrate. However, legislation restricting emigration by those with access to "state secrets" remained in effect, and any citizen involved in a criminal investigation was also ineligible to emigrate. Prospective emigrants who have been refused the right to emigrate may appeal to the courts.

The Government cooperates with the United Nations High Commissioner for Refugees (UNHCR) and other humanitarian organizations in assisting refugees. However, there is no law regulating the status of refugees, and the Government has no policy on first asylum. The Government does little to assist refugees. The Constitution states that the State "may grant refuge to persons being persecuted in other states for their political and religious convictions or on account of their nationality." The UNHCR estimates that there are 170,000 refugees in Belarus. Although the UNHCR reports that the delay in establishing a state migration service has made the life of these individuals "very difficult," there were no reports of forced expulsion of those having a valid claim to refugee status or of persons to countries where they feared persecution.

Section 3. Respect for Political Rights: The Right of Citizens to Change Their Government

The Government severely limits the right of citizens to change their government. The 1994 Constitution calls for a republic with strong executive and legislative branches as well as an independent judiciary. The President controls the Cabinet of Ministers and appoints province governors, who in turn appoint local authorities. Presidentially appointed local officials, not the elected city councils, exercise power in municipalities. In practice the President restricted the activity and authority of the Parliament and the Constitutional Court and successfully resisted repeated attempts to confine his authority to constitutionally prescribed bounds.

During the November 9–24 period, the executive branch held a controversial constitutional referendum that was neither free nor fair. Many members of Parliament and of the Constitutional Court actively opposed Lukashenko's proposals for both substantive and procedural reasons. They asserted substantively that the referendum gave Lukashenko control over the legislative and judicial branches of government and extended his term in office; and procedurally that it was an unconstitutional means for eliminating the Constitution's checks and balances and granting the President virtually unlimited powers.

In the period leading up to the referendum, opponents of Lukashenko's proposals were denied access to the media, election officials failed to record the names of early voters, and no texts of the proposed constitution were made available to voters until several days after people began voting. As a result of these irregularities, the head of the Central Election Commission (CEC) announced prior to the event that he would not be able to certify the results of the referendum. President Lukashenko promptly fired him, although the Constitution in force at the time gave authority to appoint and dismiss the CEC chairman exclusively to the Parliament. Members of the security forces then forcibly removed him from his office. Shortly thereafter, the Prime Minister resigned in protest of President Lukashenko's refusal to cancel the widely criticized referendum.

Most of the international community chose not to send election monitors to observe the referendum, because of the illegitimacy of the entire process. Human rights organizations including the Lawyers Committee for Human Rights, the Committee to Protect Journalists, and Human Rights Watch protested the conduct of the referendum.

The Constitutional Court had ruled that the issues posed in President Lukashenko's referendum could not be legally decided through a referendum, and that its results should be purely advisory, consistent with the Constitution. However, after winning the referendum—according to the Government's results—President Lukashenko began to implement it immediately. The new Constitution establishes a bicameral legislature. Its 110-member lower house was formed out of the membership of the existing Supreme Soviet; deputies volunteered or were bribed by promises of free housing and other benefits to serve in the new body. The 64-member upper house was created by a combination of presidential appointments and elections by the 7 oblast councils and the Minsk City Council. Many electoral districts were left unrepresented in the new legislature as a result of the transition.

There are no legal restrictions on women's participation in politics and government. However, with the exception of the judiciary, social barriers to women in politics are strong, and men hold virtually all leadership positions. Only 9 of the 199 members of the now defunct Supreme Soviet were women. Lukashenko has said that the new legislature should include 30 percent women. The President appointed a woman as chair of the National Bank, and there are two female ministers in the Government—the Ministers of Health and of Social Welfare.

Section 4. Governmental Attitude Regarding International and Nongovernmental Investigation of Alleged Violations of Human Rights

Human rights monitors reported that the Government presented some obstacles when they tried to investigate alleged human rights violations. Belarus' human rights record drew the attention of many international human rights organizations, and there are several local human rights groups active in the country. In general, however, human rights monitors noted government willingness to discuss human rights, and international organizations were not hindered in visiting Belarus. The Ministry of Justice attempted to force the Belarus League for Human Rights to change its charter during the course of reregistration. However, the League argued that this effort was illegal, secured high-level support for this position, and continues to operate under its original registration.

Section 5. Discrimination Based on Race, Sex, Religion, Disability, Language, or Social Status

The Constitution states that "all are equal before the law and have a right, without any discrimination, to equal protection of their rights and legitimate interests," but it does not specifically prohibit discrimination based on factors such as race, sex, or religion.

The Law on Citizenship, passed by the Parliament, grants citizenship to any person living permanently on the territory of Belarus as of October 19, 1991. Those who arrived in Belarus after that date and wish to become citizens are required to submit an application for citizenship, take an oath to support the Constitution, have a legal source of income, and have lived in the country for 7 years. Parliament passed a new Law on Immigration and Migration in 1995 that provides numerical limits on new citizens but failed to budget funds for its implementation.

Women.—Although statistics are not available, domestic violence against women is a significant problem. Knowledgeable sources indicate that police generally are not hesitant to enforce laws against violence and that the courts are not reluctant to impose sentences. The main problem, according to women's groups, is a general reluctance among women to report incidents of domestic violence.

The law requires equal wages for equal work, and in practice women are paid the same as men. However, they have significantly less opportunity for advancement to the upper ranks of management and government.

Children.—The Government is committed to children's welfare and health, particularly as related to the consequences of the nuclear accident at Chernobyl, and, with the help of foreign donors, gives them special attention. The Government provides education; children begin school at the age of 6 and are required to complete 9 years, although the Government makes 11 years of education available. Families with children receive government benefits. A World Bank study found that the majority of those living in poverty are families with multiple children or single mothers.

There does not appear to be a societal pattern of abuse of children.

People With Disabilities.—A law mandating accessibility to transport, residences, businesses, and offices for the disabled came into force in 1992. However, facilities, including transport and office buildings, often are not accessible to the disabled. The Government, facing a deteriorating economic situation, failed to budget sufficient funds to implement these laws. However, when the Government slashed subsidies for most sectors of society, most subsidies for the disabled remained in force.

Religious Minorities.—Societal anti-Semitism exists, but it is not usually manifested openly. Instances of anti-Semitism included the desecration of Jewish cemeteries and monuments in Gomel, Borisov, Minsk, and other cities. In addition state-owned newspapers have published anti-Semitic articles, and anti-Semitic incidents did not evoke a government reaction.

Section 6. Worker Rights

a. *The Right of Association.*—The Constitution upholds the right of workers, except state security and military personnel, to form and join independent unions on a voluntary basis and to carry out actions in defense of workers rights, including the right to strike. However, these rights are not generally recognized in practice. The Government suspended the activities of the Free Trade Union of Belarus (SPB) in conjunction with a 1995 Minsk metro strike. International labor organizations, including the International Confederation of Free Trade Unions, joined Belarusian independent trade unions in presenting a case to the International Labor Organization, alleging violations of the right to strike, arrests of trade union leaders, and restrictive legislation on freedom of association.

The independent trade union movement is still in its infancy, and the Government is hindering its activities. Although several independent trade unions exist, the Belarusian branch of the former Soviet Union's All-Union Central Council of Trade Unions—currently the Federation of Trade Unions of Belarus (FTUB)—is by far the largest trade union organization. This trade union of 5 million members is not considered independent since it often follows government orders. However, one of the member associations of the FTUB, the Association of Independent Industrial Trade Unions of Belarus (AIITUB), has begun to break away from the progovernment line of the FTUB and is speaking out in defense of its members' rights.

Workers are often automatically inducted into the FTUB, and their union dues are deducted from their wages. Independent labor leaders believe that the official trade unions' control over social functions usually performed by the State (such as pension funds) is an obstacle to the growth of true, independent trade unions.

The two major independent trade unions are the Free Trade Union of Belarus (SPB) and the Belarusian Independent Trade Union (BNP). The BNP and the SPB formed the Congress of Free Trade Unions of Belarus, which coordinates the activities of the two largest unions of more than 16,000 members and serves as a resource center for the free trade union movement.

Although the SPB was reregistered following the 1995 Minsk metro strike, a presidential decree "suspending the activities" of the SPB continues to prevent it from carrying out its functions. The Ministry of Justice circulated a letter to enterprises where the SPB has local unions instructing them that the SPB "does not have the right to act."

A strike planned for February 28 by the AIITUB to protest delays in paying workers' wages was forbidden by the President's administration and by the Minsk City Council, which claimed that "since workers' demands had been met," there was no reason to approve plans for the strike. Throughout the year, workers staged 1-day strikes to protest delays in receiving wages.

The SPB invited Polish Solidarity Chairman Marian Krzaklewski to Belarus to meet with workers at the Minsk automated lines plant, but Krzaklewski was denied access to the plant despite having a valid entry permit. Krzaklewski met with workers outside the territory of the plant on May 14. Shortly thereafter, he and two colleagues were detained, denied access to the Polish consul for several hours, and ejected from Belarus for "conducting an unauthorized mass meeting."

Unions may freely affiliate with international bodies.

b. *The Right to Organize and Bargain Collectively.*—Legislation dating from the Soviet era provides for the right to organize and bargain collectively. Since the economy is still largely in the hands of the State, workers usually seek redress at the political level. Workers and independent unions have recourse to the court system.

c. *Prohibition of Forced or Compulsory Labor.*—The 1994 Constitution prohibits forced labor, and it is not known to occur.

d. *Minimum Age for Employment of Children.*—Current labor law establishes 16 years of age as the statutory minimum age for employment of children. With the written consent of one parent (or legal guardian), a child of 14 years may conclude a labor contract. Reportedly, the Prosecutor General's office enforces this law effectively.

e. *Acceptable Conditions of Work.*—The President's administration sets a minimum wage, which was raised once in response to inflation. As of October 1, the monthly minimum wage was less than $10 (120,000 Belarusian rubles). The minimum wage does not provide a decent standard of living for a worker and family.

The Labor Code sets a limit of 40 hours of work per week and provides for at least one 24-hour rest period per week. Because of the difficult economic situation, an increasing number of workers find themselves working considerably less than 40 hours per week. Factories often require workers to take unpaid furloughs due to shortages of raw materials and energy, and lack of demand for factory output.

The law establishes minimum conditions for workplace safety and worker health; however, these standards are often ignored. Workers at many heavy machinery plants do not wear even minimal safety gear, such as gloves, hard hats, or welding glasses. A State Labor Inspectorate exists but does not have the authority to enforce compliance, and violations are often ignored. There is no provision in law allowing workers to remove themselves from dangerous work situations without risking their jobs.

BELGIUM

Belgium is a parliamentary democracy under a constitutional monarch who plays a mainly symbolic role. The Council of Ministers (Cabinet), led by the Prime Minister, holds office as long as it retains the confidence of the lower house of the bicameral Parliament. Constitutional reforms enacted in 1993 transformed Belgium from a unitary into a federal state with several levels of government, including national, regional (Flanders, Wallonia, and Brussels), and community (Flemish, Francophone, and German) levels.

The Government maintains effective control of all security forces. The Police Judiciaire and the Belgian gendarmerie share responsibility for internal security with municipal police.

Belgium is a highly industrialized state with a vigorous private sector and limited government participation in certain industries. The economy, buttressed by an extensive social welfare system, supports a high standard of living for most citizens.

The Government fully respected the human rights of its citizens, and the law and an independent judiciary allow for effective means of dealing with instances of individual abuse.

RESPECT FOR HUMAN RIGHTS

Section 1. Respect for the Integrity of the Person, Including Freedom From:

a. *Political and Other Extrajudicial Killing.*—There were no reports of political or other extrajudicial killings.

b. *Disappearance.*—There were no reports of politically motivated disappearances.

c. *Torture and Other Cruel, Inhuman, or Degrading Treatment or Punishment.*—The law prohibits such practices, and there were no reports that officials employed them.

Prison conditions vary. Newer prisons meet international standards. Older facilities meet or strive to meet minimum international standards despite their Spartan physical conditions and limited resources. The Government permits visits by human rights monitors. In September the prison system designed to hold 6,616 prisoners had 7,371 occupants. In late 1995, the Government adopted measures that allow alternative sentencing, such as time in substance abuse treatment centers or community service. Additionally, the Cabinet adopted separate measures that are intended to reduce the judicial backlog. Both sets of measures are designed to reduce prison overcrowding problems.

d. *Arbitrary Arrest, Detention, or Exile.*—The law prohibits arbitrary arrest, detention, or exile, and the Government observes this prohibition. Arrested persons must be brought before a judge within 24 hours. Pretrial confinement is subject to monthly review by a panel of judges, which may extend pretrial detention based on established criteria (e.g., whether, in the court's view, the arrested person would be likely to commit further crimes or attempt to flee the jurisdiction if released). Bail exists in principle under the law but is rarely granted, and pretrial confinement is thus fairly common. Belgium no longer sees a need to separate convicted criminals and pretrial detainees. Pretrial detainees receive different benefits from convicted criminals, such as more frequent family visitation rights. Approximately 40 percent of the total prison population consists of pretrial detainees. Arrested persons are allowed prompt access to a lawyer of their choosing or, if they cannot afford one, an attorney appointed by the State.

e. *Denial of Fair Public Trial.*—The Constitution provides for an independent judiciary, and the Government respects this provision in practice. The judiciary provides citizens with a fair and efficient judicial process, enforcing the law's provision for the right to a fair trial. The judicial system is organized according to the principles of specialization and territorial jurisdiction, with 5 territorial levels: canton (222), district (27), province (9), courts of appeal (5), and the whole Kingdom—the Cour de Cassation. The latter is the highest appeals court. When a preliminary judicial investigatory phase is completed, a suspect is formally charged if the evidence so warrants. Charges are clearly and formally stated, and there is a presumption of innocence. All defendants have the right to be present, to have counsel (at public expense if needed), to confront witnesses, to present evidence, and to appeal. Military tribunals try military personnel for common law as well as military crimes. All military tribunals consist of four officers and a civilian judge. At the appellate level the civilian judge presides. The accused has the right of appeal to a higher military court.

There were no reports of political prisoners.

f. *Arbitrary Interference With Privacy, Family, Home, or Correspondence.*—The law prohibits such practices, government authorities respect these prohibitions, and violations are subject to effective legal sanction.

Section 2. *Respect for Civil Liberties, Including:*

a. *Freedom of Speech and Press.*—The law provides for these freedoms, and the Government respects these rights in practice. An independent press, an effective judiciary, and a functioning democratic political system combine to ensure freedom of speech and of the press, including academic freedom.

The Government operates several radio and television networks but does not control program content. Programs are supervised by boards of directors which represent the main political, linguistic, and opinion groups. A government representative sits on each board but has no veto power. Private radio and television stations operate with government licenses. Almost all homes have access by cable to television from other Western European countries and elsewhere abroad. Satellite services are also available.

There are restrictions on the press regarding libel, slander, and the advocacy of racial or ethnic discrimination, hate or violence.

b. *Freedom of Peaceful Assembly and Association.*—The law provides for these rights, and the Government respects them in practice. Citizens are free to form organizations and establish ties to international bodies, but the Antiracism Law (see Section 5) prohibits membership in organizations that practice discrimination overtly and repeatedly.

c. *Freedom of Religion.*—The Government does not hinder the practice of any faith. The law accords "recognized" status to Roman Catholicism, Protestantism, Judaism, Anglicanism, Islam, and Greek and Russian Orthodoxy, and these receive subsidies drawn from general government revenues. Taxpayers who object to contributing to religious subsidies have no recourse. By law each recognized religion has the right to provide teachers at government expense for religious instruction in schools, but not all avail themselves of this right.

In response to mass suicides in Switzerland in 1994 and in France in 1995, the Government established a commission to create a policy to combat the alleged dangers that sects may represent to society, especially children. The commission's first task is to establish a working definition of "sect." No specific groups have been targeted, although "Temple Solaire," the group involved in the incidents in France and Switzerland, was mentioned in the initial parliamentary discussion.

d. *Freedom of Movement Within the Country, Foreign Travel, Emigration, and Repatriation.*—The law provides for these rights, and the Government respects them in practice.

The Government cooperates with the United Nations High Commissioner for Refugees and other humanitarian organizations in assisting refugees. The Government provides first asylum and provided it to 12,232 applicants in 1996, an increase of 7 percent over the 1995 number of applicants. A total of 1,588 applicants, mostly from previous years, were granted permanent status in 1996. All asylum seekers can plead their cases before immigration authorities. There were no reports of forced expulsion of those having a valid claim to refugee/asylee status. Prior to March 1995, the Government had a special procedure for refugees from the former Yugoslavia under which 5,000 to 6,000 persons received "displaced person" status, while their cases were further considered. Many of these individuals have since received permanent status.

As a result of a 1996 amendment to existing immigration law, asylum seekers arriving by air with no papers may be detained indefinitely in closed centers while awaiting consideration of their cases. Children in such centers do not attend school. At the discretion of the Minister of Interior, the Cabinet may exempt certain cities, which have already accepted large refugee populations, from giving legal residence to new refugees/asylees. Pursuant to the 1996 amendment to immigration law, asylum seekers awaiting consideration of their cases will no longer qualify for financial assistance but will be provided room and board at refugee centers.

Section 3. Respect for Political Rights: The Right of Citizens to Change Their Government

The law provides citizens with the right to change their government peacefully. Citizens age 18 and older exercise this right in practice through periodic, free, and fair elections held on the basis of universal and compulsory (under penalty of fine) suffrage. Direct popular elections for parliamentary seats (excluding some Senators elected by community councils and others elected by Senate members) are held at least every 4 years. Opposition parties operate freely.

The federal Government is responsible for such matters of state as security, justice, social security, and fiscal and monetary policy. The regional governments are charged with undertakings that directly affect the geographical region and the material well-being of its residents, such as commerce and trade, public works, and environmental policy. The linguistic community councils handle matters more directly affecting the mental and cultural well-being of the individual, such as education and administration of certain social welfare programs.

Women hold some high-level positions in the Government formed after the May 1995 general elections. Two of 15 federal ministers are women. In the federal Parliament, 18 of 150 House members and 18 of 71 Senators are women. The law requires that 33 percent of the candidates on the ballot in the next general election, to be held no later than 1999, be women.

The existence of communities speaking Dutch, French, and German engenders significant complexities for the State. Most major institutions, including political parties, are divided along linguistic lines. National decisions often take into account the specific needs of each regional and linguistic group.

Section 4. Governmental Attitude Regarding International and Nongovernmental Investigation of Alleged Violations of Human Rights

Numerous human rights groups operate without government restriction, investigating and publishing their findings on human rights cases. Government officials are very cooperative and responsive to their views.

Section 5. Discrimination Based on Race, Sex, Religion, Disability, Language, or Social Status

The law prohibits discrimination based on the listed factors, and the Government enforces it. With Dutch, French, and German as official languages, Belgium has a complex linguistic regime, including language requirements for various elected and appointed positions.

Women.—The Government actively promotes a comprehensive approach to the integration of women at all levels of decisionmaking. The Division of Equal Opportunity, a part of the Ministry of Labor, focuses specifically on issues affecting women, including violence against women, sexual harassment, and the participation of women in the political process. Based on the results of the 1995 assessment of the effectiveness of two hot lines established in recent years to assist victims of sexual harassment, and the nature and volume of the calls that continue to come in, the Ministry of Labor continues to operate the French and Flemish hot lines.

The law prohibits physical abuse of women, and the Government enforces this ban.

The law prohibits organizing prostitution or assisting immigration for purposes of prostitution.

Children.—Belgium has comprehensive child protection laws, which the Government seeks to enforce. The Francophone and Flemish communities have agencies dealing with children's needs. Government and private groups provide shelters for runaways and counseling for children who have been physically or sexually abused. The Government provides a compulsory education program up to the age of 18.

In 1995 the Government enacted laws designed to repress the occurrence of child pornography by increasing penalties for those who commit such crimes and for those in possession of such materials. The law permits the Government to prosecute Belgians who commit such crimes abroad. Another 1995 law stated that criminals convicted of sexual abuse of children cannot receive parole without first receiving specialized assistance and must continue counseling and treatment upon release from prison.

In August Belgian authorities uncovered a pedophile/child pornography and trafficking ring, the extent of which was still being investigated at year's end. Police found two missing girls and the bodies of four others. They made 11 arrests in the case, but none of the suspects had come to trial by year's end. In response to allegations of corruption and complicity within the law enforcement and judicial system, including allegations that at least one policeman colluded with those charged in the case, the Ministry of Justice initiated several internal investigations into the conduct of the investigation of child disappearances. Consistent with the strong government response to this case, parliamentary committees were examining the performance of the judicial community in this investigation and evaluating the need to reform the judiciary. The policeman in question has been charged only in connection with the vehicle trafficking ring run by the same group. The Government had not released any results of these investigations by year's end.

The Government adopted a series of measures designed to strengthen its ability to fight organized crime rings domestically and internationally; to make it more difficult for those convicted of sexual crimes to be released from prisons early; and to create programs to support the victims and their families. Foreign Minister Erik Derycke made similar proposals at the World Congress Against the Commercial Sexual Exploitation of Children, which was held in Stockholm in August.

Children have the right to a voice in court cases that affect them, such as divorce proceedings. The law states that a minor "capable of understanding" can request permission to be heard by a judge, or a judge can request an interview with a child. Child prostitution is of limited scope, but, in response to recommendations made in a 1994 government study, police have received instructions to be especially diligent in combating prostitution of those who appear to be under the age of 18.

There is no societal pattern of abuse directed against children.

People With Disabilities.—The laws provide protection from discrimination against disabled people in employment, education, and in the provision of other state services. The Government mandates that public buildings erected since 1970 be accessible to the disabled and offers subsidies to induce owners of other buildings to make necessary modifications. Many older buildings, however, are not accessible to the disabled.

The Government provides financial assistance for the disabled. It offers special aid for parents of disabled children and for disabled parents. Regional and community programs provide other assistance, such as job training. Disabled persons are eligible to receive services in any of the three regions (Flanders, Wallonia, or Brussels), not just from the region in which they reside.

National/Racial/Ethnic Minorities.—Belgium is a pluralistic society in which individual differences in general are respected and linguistic rights in particular are protected. Some 60 percent of citizens are native Dutch speakers; about 40 percent French speakers; and fewer than 1 percent German speakers.

An Antiracism Law penalizes incitement of discrimination, hate, or violence based on race, ethnicity, or nationality. It is illegal for providers of goods or services (including housing) to discriminate on the basis of any of these factors and for employers to consider these factors in their decisions to hire, train, or dismiss people.

The Center for Equal Opportunity and the Fight Against Racism, a parliamentary organization tasked with investigating complaints of discrimination based on race, handled 1,120 calls asking for information in the first 10 months of 1995. Some 644 of these calls were to make actual complaints, leading to court action in only 8 cases. Statistics for 1996 are not yet available.

Section 6. Worker Rights

a. *The Right of Association.*—Under the Constitution, workers have the right to associate freely. This includes freedom to organize and join unions of their own choosing. The Government does not hamper such activities, and workers in fact fully and freely exercise their right of association. About 60 percent of the work force are members of labor unions. This number includes employed and unemployed workers. Retired workers are considered to be in the work force. Unions are independent of the Government but have important links with major political parties. As the Government does not require unions to register, there are no prohibitions against antiunion actions before registration.

Unions have the right to strike, and strikes by civil servants and workers in "essential" services are tolerated. The teachers, railway workers, and airport workers held strikes without government intimidation. Despite government irritation over wildcat strikes by air traffic controllers, no strikers were prosecuted. There were a number of significant labor strikes and work stoppages in 1996. (Ministry of Labor data indicate 45 strikes in 1995 with no data available for 1996.) Even though many strikes begin as wildcat actions, strikers are not prosecuted for conducting illegal strikes.

The International Confederation of Free Trade Unions (ICFTU) in its "Annual Survey of Violations of Trade Union Rights 1996" noted a 1995 practice of using civil court rulings to end strikes. The ICFTU report stated that the rulings include a threat of fines against strikers. After noting that these rulings had been made without giving a hearing to the unions, the ICFTU report concluded that such rulings call into question the free exercise of the right to strike. The ICFTU report acknowledged government efforts to solve this problem but also cited an assessment of the Socialist Trade Union Confederation that "nothing had come of the Government's commitment." On the other hand, there was a sharp decrease in the number of this kind of court ruling starting in late 1995 and throughout 1996. This development is a result of labor/management talks in 1996, which brokered an informal agreement to minimize court rulings in exchange for less secondary boycott activity by the unions.

Unions are free to form or join federations or confederations and are free to affiliate with international labor bodies.

b. *The Right to Organize and Bargain Collectively.*—The right to organize and bargain collectively is recognized, protected, and exercised freely. Every other year the Belgian Employers Federation and unions negotiate a nationwide collective bargaining agreement, covering 2.4 million private sector workers, that establishes the framework for negotiations at plants and branches. Public sector workers also negotiate collective bargaining agreements. Collective bargaining agreements apply equally to union and nonunion members, and over 90 percent of workers are thus under collective bargaining agreements. As part of the Government's global economic reform plan, wage increases in both private and public sectors remain suspended, but this did not affect Belgium's wage indexation policy. This policy permits an across-the-board wage increase to keep workers' pay level with inflation.

The law prohibits discrimination against organizers and members of unions and protects against termination of contracts of members of workers' councils, members of health or safety committees, and shop stewards. Employers found guilty of antiunion discrimination are required to reinstate workers fired for union activities. Effective mechanisms such as the labor courts exist for adjudicating disputes between labor and management.

There are no export processing zones.

c. *Prohibition of Forced or Compulsory Labor.*—Forced or compulsory labor is illegal and does not occur. Domestic workers and all other workers have the same rights as nondomestic workers. The Government enforces laws against those who seek to employ undocumented foreign workers.

d. *Minimum Age for Employment of Children.*—The minimum age for employment of children is 15, but schooling is compulsory until the age of 18. Youth between the ages of 15 and 18 may participate in part-time work/study programs and may work full time during school vacations. The labor courts effectively monitor compliance with national laws and standards. There are no industries where any significant child labor exists.

e. *Acceptable Conditions of Work.*—In May the monthly national minimum wage rate for workers over 21 years of age was set at $1,432 (43,665 Belgian francs); 18-year-olds must be paid at least 82 percent of the minimum, 19-year-olds 88 percent, and 20-year-olds 94 percent. The minimum wage rate, coupled with Belgium's extensive social benefits, provides workers with a standard of living appropriate to a highly developed nation. Minimum wages in the private sector are set in biennial nationwide collective bargaining (see Section 6.b.), which leads to formal agreements signed in the National Labor Council and made mandatory by royal decree for the entire private sector. In the public sector, the minimum wage is determined in negotiations between the Government and the public service unions. The Ministry of Labor effectively enforces the law regarding minimum wages. By law the standard workweek cannot exceed 40 hours and must have at least one 24-hour rest period. Many collective bargaining agreements set standard workweeks of 36 to 39 hours. The law requires overtime pay for hours worked in excess of the standard. Work done from the 9th to the 11th hour per day or from the 40th to the 50th hour per week is considered allowable overtime. Longer workdays are permitted only if agreed upon in a collective bargaining agreement. These laws/regulations are enforced effectively by the Ministry of Labor and the labor courts.

Comprehensive provisions for worker safety are mandated by law. Collective bargaining agreements can supplement these laws. Workers have the right to remove themselves from situations that endanger their safety or health, without jeopardy to their continued employment, and the law protects workers who file complaints about such situations. The Labor Ministry implements health and safety legislation through a team of inspectors and determines whether workers qualify for disability and medical benefits. Health and safety committees are mandated by law in companies with more than 50 employees. Labor courts monitor effectively compliance with national health and safety laws and standards.

BOSNIA AND HERZEGOVINA

The 1995 General Framework Agreement for Peace in Bosnia and Herzegovina (the Dayton Accords), signed after 3 years of war, provided for the continuity of Bosnia-Herzegovina, originally one of the constituent Republics of Yugoslavia, as a single state, Bosnia and Herzegovina, with two constituent entities, the Federation of Bosnia and Herzegovina (the Federation) and the Republika Srpska (RS). The Federation, which incorporates the areas with a Bosniak (Muslim) and Croat majority, occupies 51% of the territory; the RS, populated mostly by Bosnian Serbs, occupies 49%. The Dayton Accords established a constitution for Bosnia and Herzegovina that includes a central government with a bicameral legislature, a three-member presidency comprised of a representative of each major ethnic group, a council of ministers, a constitutional court, and a central bank. Defense remains under the control of the respective entities.

In a significant step toward implementing the Dayton Accords, elections for central, entity-level, and, within the Federation, cantonal offices were held on September 14. Alija Izetbegovic, Momcilo Krajisnik, and Kresimir Zubak were elected to the presidency representing respectively Bosniaks, Serbs, and Croats. Izetbegovic, who received a plurality of the votes, was named Chair in accordance with the new Constitution. Although the preelection period was marked by widespread limitations on the ability of opposition parties to campaign effectively and significant restrictions on freedom of interentity movement, the balloting was orderly and calm. The large turnout demonstrated that citizens were committed to the voting process.

Before and after the elections, the main political parties continued to exercise significant political power at all levels. These were the Party of Democratic Action (SDA) in predominantly Bosniak areas, the Serb Democratic Party (SDS) in the RS, and the Croatian Democratic Union of Bosnia and Herzegovina (HDZ) in Croat areas.

One of the two entities that make up Bosnia and Herzegovina, the Federation of Bosnia and Herzegovina, was established in March 1994 and transformed the internal structure of the Bosnian territories under Bosniak and Croat control. It is a mixed system with a president and a parliament that must approve the president's choice of Prime Minister. Federation structures have been implemented only gradually. Major steps were the creation of provincial structures in the form of cantons, the unification of Sarajevo under Federation control, and September elections to a Federation Parliament. In these elections, the mainly Muslim SDA and Croat HDZ won 59% and 22% of the votes, respectively. Widespread abuses of citizens on an ethnic basis in the Sarajevo suburbs that occurred during and after the transfer of authority there in March and inconclusive efforts to integrate separate Bosniak and Croat administrations in the ethnically bifurcated city of Mostar highlighted the willingness of political leaders of both Bosniaks and Croats to manipulate ethnic factors for political gain.

In most respects Federation authority did not extend effectively outside the areas in which Bosniaks constituted a majority. The self-proclaimed "Croat Republic of Herceg-Bosna" was a rival claimant to Croat-held territory in Bosnia and Herzegovina until March 1994. Although its official dissolution was called for under a separate agreement reached in Dayton, security and administrative structures associated with Herceg-Bosna persisted and remained closely associated with the military structure of the Croat Defense Council (HVO) and the political party structure of the HDZ. This relationship included close military ties, and along with the fact that Bosnian Croats had dual citizenship with Croatia and were able to vote in Croatian elections, brought into question the degree of the HDZ's independence from Croatia.

The Republika Srpska of Bosnia and Herzegovina is the other entity. Its de facto capital is the town of Pale, near Sarajevo, although Banja Luka is the seat of the RS Parliament and other entity ministries. A president and two vice presidents are directly elected for 4-year terms. Until July 18 Radovan Karadizic acted as the president of Republika Srpska, despite his indictment for war crimes. The legislative branch, the National Assembly, is elected on the basis of proportional representation. Real control, however, was exercised by the dominant political party, the SDS. The party ensured conformity among local authorities in many areas and used its authority to ensure adherence to nationalistic positions. In the September elections the SDS won 66% of the vote. Then-acting RS President, Biljana Plavsic, was elected President for a full term.

The Constitution of Bosnia and Herzegovina (Annex 4 of the Dayton Accords) made the Federation and RS responsible for maintaining civilian law enforcement agencies operating in accordance with internationally recognized standards. Law enforcement bodies of both entities have on many occasions violated these standards, giving preferential treatment on the basis of political, ethnic, and religious criteria. Police personnel and in some instances special military police were involved, but with the end of active hostilities, local police structures assumed a much greater role in people's daily lives throughout Bosnia and Herzegovina. However, the existence of special or secret police in all three ethnic areas, a throwback to the Communist heritage, poses another problem. They are not in the normal police chain of command but are directly responsive to the senior leadership. The police in Bosniak-controlled areas of the Federation are locally recruited and organized. They have been guilty of widespread human rights abuses.

A Federation army was created by agreement of the Croat and Bosniak leaders in October, to be comprised of five corps and two independent divisions. Four corps and the two independent divisions are mostly Muslim and one corps is Croat. A joint command is expected to develop into a unified organization in 3 years.

For most of 1996, the Bosnian Army (ABiH) was the military arm of the majority Muslim portion of the Federation. During the war it developed from a citizen militia into an army. It is in principle, and to some extent in reality, a multiethnic fighting force, comprised predominantly of Bosnian Muslims, but also of Croats, Serbs, and Bosnians of mixed ethnicity. During the year the influence of non-Muslims among the military command diminished, primarily as a result of the growing influence and ethnic orientation of the ruling Party of Democratic Action. The Bosnian Army generally respected citizens' human rights, although it did commit some violations.

The one Croat corps of the newly formed Federation army operated separately as the Croat Defense Council and appeared to remain under the effective control of the Croatian army. Police remained monoethnic, and those in predominantly Croat areas were outside the control of Federation officials. They were generally responsive to the direction of higher officials and the HDZ party, although they appeared somewhat less disciplined than police in the RS. Police in Croat areas committed numerous human rights abuses.

The Bosnian Serb Army is the military arm of the RS. It was amalgamated in 1992 from Serb paramilitary bands, local rural militias, and elements of the Yugoslav National Army (JNA). Its commander, Ratko Mladic, was indicted for war crimes and replaced in November. There were no reports of human rights violations by Bosnian Serb Army (BSA) units during the year, but individual soldiers or persons dressed in BSA uniforms were reported to have committed human rights violations. Serb police forces consist of locally recruited municipal forces and a special force responsible to the Ministry of the Interior. Both forces respond to central direction. Both were responsible for widespread human rights abuses.

The NATO-led Implementation Force (SFOR/IFOR) continued its mission to implement the military aspects of the Dayton Accords and create a more secure environment to facilitate implementation of the nonmilitary aspects of the settlement, such as civilian reconstruction, the return of refugees and displace persons, elections, and freedom of movement of the civilian population.

In addition to the human suffering, the war had a destructive impact on the economy and infrastructure. Gross domestic product (GDP) is estimated to have contracted by three-quarters with income losses of up to 85 percent in the Bosniak majority areas. Croat-controlled territory fared relatively well, with GDP contraction estimated at around 15 percent. The economy in Serb-controlled areas appear to have performed somewhere between the two. Since the Dayton Accords, there are signs of increased trade in the Croat-majority areas and significant growth (from a very low base) in the Bosniak parts of the country. Reconstruction programs initiated by the international community have financed physical construction of infrastructure and provided loans to the manufacturing sector, which is expected to increase employment.

Economic assistance is expected to lay the groundwork for a revival of the economy. The actual distribution of assistance to particular entities or areas continues to be conditioned on the parties' compliance with their Dayton obligations, including the turnover of persons indicted for war crimes to the International Criminal Tribunal for the Former Yugoslavia.

Unemployment was a major problem. The military demobilization on all sides subsequent to the Dayton Accords, the large number of displaced persons, and the destruction of a significant part of housing, have further contributed to economic and social insecurity. There are an estimated 650,000 unemployed persons in the Federation. In addition 40 percent of the estimated 1.2 million refugees would need work should they return.

The year 1996 was a period of transition in which the international community sought, through implementation of the Dayton Accords, to promote political reconciliation after more than 3 years of war during which more than 250,000 people were killed and some 3 million were uprooted and dispersed. The most egregious abuses of the war period—murder, rape, and widespread disappearances and displacements—largely ended. However, to varying degrees the authorities in both RS and the Federation continued to commit abuses, and the human rights situation remained precarious nearly a year after the signing of the peace agreement.

Members of the security forces physically mistreated citizens and made widespread use of arbitrary arrest and detention. Prison conditions are poor. Judicial institutions throughout the country did not effectively try cases of human rights abuses; even in cases where fair judgment was reached, local official refused to implement court decisions. Authorities in all areas infringed on citizens' right to privacy and home, and as a rule the right of refugees and displaced persons to return to their homes was not respected. Restrictions on freedom of movement, destruction of homes, and the displacement of large numbers of people for reasons of ethnicity constituted a serious problem, with the most serious such abuses committed by the RS. Members of all security forces harassed and intimidated refugees. The authorities on the Bosniak side exerted control over the media; in the RS the authorities dominated the media. Both sides constrained academic freedom and freedom of assembly and association.

Abuses based on ethnicity constituted a major problem, and interethnic differences were further complicated by religious differences. The large numbers of refugees and displaced persons, themselves often embittered victims of ethnic conflict, combined with greatly reduced housing resulting from the war, posed serious problems for interethnic relations.

Abuse of such human rights as privacy, freedom of movement, security of the person, and ethnic nondiscrimination were so frequent as to be almost routine, especially in the Croat and Serb areas. In the Muslim areas the situation was somewhat better, but when important interests of the political and administrative elite were at stake, for example, in the efforts of non-SDA partisans to return to Bihac and neighboring areas, the transfer of authority of the Sarajevo suburbs from RS to Federation control, and efforts to unify Mostar, the actions of Bosniak police did not differ greatly from those of their ethnic counterparts. In many instances, police reinforced the insecurity of ethnic minorities by failing to assist them when they were victimized by popular animosities on the part of the majority.

Bosniak police were responsible for the harassment of other ethnic groups and the mistreatment of detainees and prisoners, although some improvement has been noted by the International Police Task Force (IPTF). The Army of Bosnia and Herzegovina was reportedly responsible for the widespread mistreatment of returnees from the Kupljenska refugee camp in Croatia.

The leaders of the dominant political parties failed to demonstrate a commitment to ethnic nondiscrimination. The leaders of the SDS, who effectively ruled the RS, single-mindedly pursued policies of ethnic exclusivity, including ethnic cleansing, against Muslims and Croats and intimidated ethnic Serbs who opposed such policies. Leaders of the HDZ continued, in such places as Mostar, to place the interests of Croats above the ethnic integration to which they committed themselves in the Dayton Accords. The most conspicuous examples of discrimination in this connection related to the return of refugees and displaced persons to their former places of residence and the security of individuals from repressive measures designed to induce them to move, which represented continuing, if less massive and brutal, manifestations of ethnic cleansing characteristic of the war period.

The international presence throughout the country helped deter additional human rights abuses.

Nationwide elections on September 14 marked a significant milestone in the creation of a state based on democracy and the rule of law. The preelection period was marked by the unwillingness of important leadership elements in all three of the dominant parties to tolerate political opposition even from members of their own communities.

Although the Bosniak side of the Federation has surrendered persons indicted by the International Criminal Tribunal for the Former Yugoslavia, authorities in the Croat-controlled parts of the Federation and the RS continued their failure to apprehend and deliver indicted persons to the Tribunal. The International Criminal Tribunal for the Former Yugoslavia handed down its first verdict in November, sentencing a Bosnian Serb soldier to 10 years' imprisonment for war crimes.

RESPECT FOR HUMAN RIGHTS

Section 1. Respect for the Integrity of the Person, Including Freedom From:

a. *Political and Other Extrajudicial Killing.*—There was only one report of political or other extrajudicial killing by police under the effective control of the Federation. International organizations reported that two Croat special police officers were identified as the perpetrators of the murder of a Bosniak driving between Zenica and Zepce. After intervention by international officials, the two suspects were brought before a court in Vitez, in the Croat controlled area, and convicted of their crime.

In the RS, human rights officials from the Organization for Security and Cooperation in Europe (OSCE) reported a case in Banja Luka in which a Bosniak died due to physical abuse while in police custody. Arrested for alleged possession of illegal weapons, he suffered massive internal injuries produced by a blunt instrument. Another Bosniak man was found beaten to death in Doboj. Police involvement is suspected, but noncooperation by RS authorities with the investigation made responsibility difficult to confirm.

Extensive killings and other brutal acts committed in earlier years remained unpunished. Although all parties bore some responsibility for some of the killings, the RS was responsible for the most massive, egregious, and well-organized killings targeted on members of an ethnic group. These include, since 1995, about 7,000 persons missing and presumed killed by the Bosnian Serb Army after the fall of Srebrenica, the worst incident of mass killing in Europe since World War II, and another 1,500–5,000 missing and presumed killed as a result of "ethnic cleansing" in Northern Bosnia. The International Criminal Tribunal for the Former Yugoslavia by year's end had indicted 75 individuals on charges of war crimes and genocide in connection with these and other occurrences. Only the Bosniak side of the Federation has been willing to surrender persons under indictment. At year's end only seven of the accused were in custody. The Tribunal handed down its first verdict in November, sentencing a Bosnian Serb soldier to 10 years' imprisonment for war crimes. Authorities in both the Croat-controlled parts of the Federation and the RS have failed to apprehend and surrender indicted persons to the Tribunal. Those indicted include former RS President and SDS Chairman, Radovan Karadzic, and former Bosnian Serb Army Commander Ratko Mladic. Karadzic retained his positions in the RS long after the indictment was handed down, before being removed from office in July.

b. *Disappearance.*—There were no reports of politically motivated disappearances.

Despite delays there was some progress in solving earlier disappearances. With the cooperation of the RS, international and Bosniak experts began to exhume the bodies buried around Srebrenica. Several sites have been excavated and hundreds of bodies found, but many more persons are still missing from Srebrenica and Zepa.

In addition to those believed killed in Srebrenica and Zepa, the International Committee of the Red Cross reported in December that a total of 17,689 family members from the war years had requested assistance in tracing missing persons; 999 individuals have been found. Several hundred people expelled from Banja Luka, Prijedor, Bosanski Novi, and Bosanska Dubica may also have been killed. Local Bosnian officials in Bugojno have yet to provide satisfactory information on the whereabouts of 26 prominent Croats who disappeared when the Bosnian Army took the town in late 1993. Nor was there any resolution of the longstanding case involving the disappearance of approximately 180 Bosniak men from Hadzici in June 1992.

In September the International Commission on Missing persons in Former Yugoslavia was formed under the Chairmanship of former U.S. Secretary of State Cyrus Vance. Comprised of distinguished international public servants, the Commission is working to get the Bosnian parties, Serbia and Montenegro, and Croatia to provide a full and timely accounting of the missing.

c. *Torture and Other Cruel, Inhuman, or Degrading Treatment or Punishment.*—The Constitution provides for the right to freedom from torture and cruel or inhuman treatment or punishment. No reliable reports emerged that any of those in authority in Bosnia and Herzegovina employed torture as an instrument of state. However, in all areas of the country authorities, police, and prison officials were responsible for numerous instances of physical mistreatment.

For example, the IPTF reported in November that a Bosniak man and his family were forcibly expelled from their house in Dubica in the RS by local police. The man was arrested, beaten, and detained without charge for 3 days.

According to the IPTF, a Bosniak man was beaten in a restaurant in Teslic by two RS policemen in November after being asked for his identification papers. The man was arrested without being charged and released a week later.

The Human Rights Coordination Center of the Office of the High Representative for Implementation of the Peace Agreement on Bosnia and Herzegovina (OHR) reported the complaint of a Serb woman in the town of Hadzici (Federation) who said that local police refused to investigate an incident in November in which a group of men in uniform entered her house, beat her husband at gunpoint, and tried to forcibly evict them.

In December the United Nations High Commissioner for Refugees (UNHCR) in Mostar reported that an old Bosniak woman living in the Croat sector of the divided town was evicted from her residence. The woman reportedly died during the expulsion from heart problems.

Also in December a group of six Bosniak policemen severely beat and robbed a Croat driving through the Bosniak sector of Mostar. The victim was taken to the Bosniak police headquarters where he was beaten again. The victim suffered a fractured jaw and several broken teeth. There have been no arrests or reprimands.

Conditions in Federation prisons are poor and well below minimum international standards. There are accounts of beatings and mistreatment by officials in government detention centers. Conditions in RS prisons also remained poor.

d. *Arbitrary Arrest, Detention, or Exile.*—Arbitrary arrest and detention continue to be widely practiced in both the Federation and the RS. In some cases people are released after 2 or 3 days, although international organizations have reported several cases that remained unresolved for months. The victims are frequently members of ethnic minorities in their areas. Local officials are in many instances able to act in an entirely arbitrary manner with absolute impunity.

According to the OHR, three persons were arrested in February in Kiseljak, a predominantly Croat town and transferred into HVO custody in Mostar. They were kept in detention without being charged, and there was no evidence that judicial proceedings were under way. It appears that the detaining authority hoped to exchange them for Croats who were serving criminal sentences elsewhere in Federation territory. They were eventually released in September; however, others remain in detention.

Of major concern were prisoners held before the Dayton Accords came into effect who have not been registered and are unknown to monitors. OHR reports that in a particularly egregious and well-known case, a Croat priest from Prijedor, Tomislav Matanovic, and his parents have been detained in the RS since September 1995. RS authorities acknowledged that the priest is being held in private detention and have pledged that he will be released.

There were no reports that forced exile was practiced as a juridical device. However, authorities in all areas of the country and at all levels undertook to drive out individuals, especially members of minority groups, as a means of consolidating ethnic and political control. Moreover, police often failed to provide protection to individuals being mistreated by elements of the population or nongovernmental organizations, with the same end in mind. In the Federation, during the transfer of authority of the suburbs of Sarajevo, local authorities did little to prevent the exodus of non-Bosniaks, and there was no determination to forestall or stop acts by Bosniak displaced persons intended to drive them out. Similar practices were apparent in some parts of majority Croat areas within the Federation.

In the RS there were continuing expulsions, notably in Teslic and Urbanja. In the RS a joint fact-finding mission conducted by the OHR, the OSCE, and the U.N. Center for Human Rights uncovered evidence of significant numbers of expulsions of non-Serbs from the greater Teslic region. Bosnian Serbs intimidated or expelled dozens of families, mostly Bosniaks, during May and June. The principal perpetrators appeared to be displaced persons and Serb thugs from nearby villages.

e. *Denial of Fair Public Trial.*—The Constitution provides for an independent judiciary, extends the judiciary's independence to the investigative division of the criminal justice system, and establishes a judicial police force that reports directly to the courts. However, these provisions have not yet been implemented, and the executive appears to exercise authority over the judiciary. Yugoslav and wartime practices in which the executive and the leading political parties exerted considerable influence over the judicial system persisted in all areas. Party affiliation and political connections appeared to weigh heavily on the appointment process, and the ruling parties attempted to stack the courts with party loyalists.

The existing judicial hierarchy in the Federation is based on municipal courts, which have original jurisdiction in most civil and criminal cases, and cantonal courts, which have appellate jurisdiction over the canton's municipalities, as well as three federal courts (Constitutional, Supreme, and Human Rights). The Constitution provides for the appointment of judges until the age of 70 and for internal administration of the judicial branch. The Constitution also provides for open and public trials, and the accused has the right to legal counsel.

The Bosnian Serbs reportedly use a modified form of the old Yugoslav Republic of Bosnia's criminal code.

Human rights ombudsmen reported that judicial institutions in both entities, whose work was controlled by the ruling parties, were neither capable nor willing to try cases of human rights abuse referred to them, and that even when the courts rendered a fair judgment, local officials refused to implement their decision.

There have been no credible reports that the Bosnian Government holds political prisoners.

f. *Arbitrary Interference With Privacy, Family, Home, or Correspondence.*—The Constitution of Bosnia and Herzegovina provides for the right to "private and family life, home, and correspondence." These rights were generally better observed in the Federation than the RS, but neither entity brought property law into conformity with international norms, and implementation of the laws that did exist was often guided by considerations of ethnic or political advantage.

In the Federation, the authorities sporadically used their power over possession of property, including housing, in a manner that effectively dispossessed ethnic minorities (see Section 5). RS authorities tried to obstruct the reintegration of Sarajevo by forcing Serbs to leave the area and dismantling or destroying housing, industrial facilities, essential utilities, and other infrastructure. OSCE monitors reported that evictions of Muslims continued in Prijedor and Doboj, and in the latter town a Serb woman from the local Red Cross was reportedly interrogated and beaten by local police when she tried to help a Muslim woman who was being evicted. Bosnian Serbs who left the Sarajevo suburbs, in some cases because of intimidation by RS police and SDS party activists, were forced to resettle in Brcko, Pale, Sokolac, Srebrenica, Visegrad, Zvornik, and other areas previously purged of non-Serbs. Intimidation was also used to prevent Bosniak and Bosnian Croat refugees from returning to their homes in RS territory, as well as to influence the arbitration decision on the future of Brcko. Approximately 10,000 Serbs of an original population of 70,000 remained in the Sarajevo suburbs transferred to Federation control.

Local authorities responsible to the RS continued to expel Bosniaks. Several families that were expelled from the village of Vrbanja near Banja Luka in June and returned had to be evacuated for their physical safety by the United Nations. Following the evacuation, only 40 Muslims remained in this village, once inhabited by 4,500. However, RS authorities were not alone in seeking the ethnic purity of this region as the HVO evacuated ethnic Croats from RS territory to Croat-controlled territory (see Section 1.g.).

g. *Use of Excessive Force and Violations of Humanitarian Law in Internal Conflicts.*—The performance of Federation military and police forces did not indicate a policy of reliance upon force to achieve ethnic or other goals in the Bosnia-wide setting. However, excessive force was used with sufficient frequency in localized situations to suggest that such behavior was tolerated. In the region around Bihac, the Bosnian Army V Corps and the Bosniak police frequently harassed and intimidated refugees returning from Kuplensko Refugee Camp in Croatia. Representatives of the IFOR reported 56 such cases in January, and some refugees fled back to Croatia. The OHR indicates that such occurrences were considered a "rite of passage" by victims and authorities alike. It was unclear whether they represented an organized campaign against the returnees. In the transition to Federation rule of the Sarajevo suburbs, Federation police were reliably accused of mistreating ethnic Serbs or not intervening when others did so (See Section 5).

The Catholic Press Agency reported the protest of Catholic Bishop Komarica of Banja Luka over the forced repatriation by the HVO to "Herceg-Bosna" of 500 residents of his Diocese from the town of Majdan in the RS, despite their wish to remain in their ancestral homes. This village was designated by the Dayton Accords as part of RS. The Croats had lived in this village since before the war, experiencing no problems with their non-Croat neighbors.

Serb police often employed excessive force to prevent Bosniak former residents from returning to, or staying in, territory designated as RS territory by the Dayton Accords, to force ethnic Serbs living in other parts of Bosnia to move to RS territory, and to intimidate ethnic Serbs from registering as voters in territory other than that of the RS. Local Serb police apparently took no action against the perpetrators of severe harassment. The UNHCR described the expulsions as ethnic cleansing. Bosnian Serb police obstructed IPTF investigations through noncooperation and restrictions on movement by means of checkpoints.

Section 2. Respect for Civil Liberties, Including:

a. *Freedom of Speech and Press.*—The Constitution provides for freedom of speech and the press. This right was partially respected in the territory under effective control of the Bosniak Muslims; authorities in the RS and Croat-controlled areas of the Federation respected it to a considerably lesser extent, although some progress was made in establishing alternative print media in the RS.

The dominant political parties continued to exercise strong control over the most influential media outlets. However, in the Federation, a number of independent publications have consolidated their positions in terms of readership and influence, if not financial health. They include the leading daily Oslobodjenja and the weeklies Dani and Slobodna Bosna. In the Bosniak-controlled portions of the Federation there was a strong tendency to favor the positions of the governing SDA. Party influence was particularly notable in the State-run television outlets, the principal source of information in all areas. The OHR reported that on TV Bosnia and Herzegovina, announcers continued to use inflammatory generalizations to describe persons from the RS. In general the media of the RS and the Croat-controlled portions of the Federation were unremittingly biased in favor of the positions of their ruling parties.

Complying with commitments made in connection with the Dayton Accords, the authorities permitted other political parties limited access to television in advance of the September national elections. However the content of many broadcasts continued to reflect the views of nationalist hardliners.

In the Federation many private radio stations broadcast locally; a smaller number of private television stations served local markets in Sarajevo, Zenica, and Tuzla. In central Bosnia SDA officials appeared to be using their influence over government frequency allocation to restrict the further establishment of broadcast media outlets. After overcoming great resistance from Federation authorities, a Western-sponsored Independent Open Broadcast Network was established by broadcasting material through some of these independent television stations. The purpose was to create a strong independent television sector in all parts of Bosnia, drawing talent from among all ethnic communities. Despite a number of ongoing logistical and resource problems, its signal could be received in most major population centers.

The development of independent media was constrained by a number of structural factors including limited circulations, a lack of locally produced material with a wide appeal, poor advertizing revenues, and high operating costs. Few of the media were commercially viable; some survived through the sponsorship of private organizations, cultural societies, and political parties, others with help from Western aid organizations.

In Croat-controlled Federation territory, broadcast transmissions from neighboring Croatia, as well as local Croatian-nationalist broadcast entities, captured the majority of audiences, while few alternative or nonnationalist news sources were available. In the RS most media are a propaganda tool of the ruling SDS party. Srpska Radio-Televizija broadcasts from RS engage in negative ethnic stereotyping. The party uses its own information resources, an information ministry, and tight control of most media outlets to dominate most outlets. Nonetheless, some independent media were established. In Banja Luka an independent newspaper, Nezavisne Novine, began publication, as did a monthly and a weekly not under the control of the SDS. In some areas RS authorities have exerted considerable pressure against independent publications, forbidding local businesses to advertise in them, local presses to print them, and local kiosks to sell them.

Foreign journalists representing recognized media were generally free to report from all areas of the country, although local authorities occasionally reacted with force to prevent efforts to film incidents involving violence. The absence of telephone and fax links between the entities complicated journalists' work.

Academic freedom was constrained. In the Federation, Serbs and Croats complained that SDA party favorites were more likely to get promoted or obtain senior managerial positions. In Serb-controlled areas, the authorities' general lack of tolerance for dissent led to total control of the educational media. The curriculum in Serb-controlled areas has been revamped to teach solely Serb history, art, literature, etc.

b. *Freedom of Peaceful Assembly and Association.*—The Constitution provides for freedom of peaceful assembly and association. However, none of the parties fully respected these rights in practice. A wide range of social, cultural, and political organizations functioned without interference, but there were serious exceptions relating to efforts of certain opposition political parties to stage rallies and campaign in the September national elections (see section 3).

In the RS, control over security and police by the SDS imposed severe limitations on the right to assembly. There was a clear attitude of intolerance toward opposition parties. For example, the OHR reported the disruption in March of a Socialist Party of RS (SPRS) public meeting in Blatnica by a members of a local paramilitary group.

Although freedom of association is not directly limited, indirect pressure constrains the exercise of this right. While political membership is not forced, membership in the ruling SDA and HDZ parties in Federation territory was increasingly viewed as a way to obtain and keep housing and high-level jobs in the state-owned sector of the economy.

The OHR reported that in Croat-held areas, particularly West Mostar, opposition parties were reluctant to organize openly because of fear of retaliation by HDZ supporters.

Human rights groups in the RS pointed to a number of physical attacks on activists of the Alliance for Peace and Progress (SMP), a party opposing the ruling SDS. The atmosphere of intimidation was apparent in an incident in Kalesija, near Tuzla where, according to the OHR, 159 people were called in for informational interviews by the military police because they were accused of having heckled the Mayor of the municipality during a public appearance in April.

c. *Freedom of Religion.*—The Constitution provides for freedom of religion, including private and public worship, and in the Federation the authorities rarely interfered. In general, individuals in their ethnic majority areas, who constitute the great majority of the population, enjoyed unfettered freedom of religion. However, there were some incidents that resulted in damage to religious edifices. Some of these incidents resulted from actions by the authorities; others were due to societal religious violence (see Section 5).

In the RS, whose core ethnic group is traditionally Serb Orthodox, authorities demolished property at the site of the Ferhadija mosque in Banja Luka without consultation with religious leaders. Authorities repeatedly rejected efforts of Muslims to revisit religious sites and graveyards in their previous areas of residence, and international representatives had to negotiate on a case-by-case basis with the RS authorities for the few such visits that did take place. Muslim members of the RS Parliament, who were elected in October, were initially required to take an oath referring to the Christian Scriptures when they sought to take their seats in the opening session. They declined to do so and were barred from participation in parliamentary work until the legal commission of the assembly ruled that they were not required to take the oath. While now participating in parliamentary discussions, they remain isolated from the committees, where the substantive work is done.

d. *Freedom of Movement Within the Country, Foreign Travel, Emigration, and Repatriation.*—The Constitution provides for "the right to liberty of movement and residence." Within the Federation checkpoints between areas controlled by Bosniaks and those controlled by Croats have been largely dismantled. Travel across the Interentity Boundary Line (IEBL) separating the two entities within Bosnia, impossible during the war, has become possible in certain limited circumstances. Interentity bus connections were reestablished in certain areas and generally operated without interference. Thousands of people crossed the IEBL each day.

Nonetheless, the extent of travel between the entities remains far less than might normally be expected. Fears engendered by the 3-year conflict, reinforced by frequent police checks of vehicles, are in part responsible. There were also some examples of more forceful constraints: The road leading to the Federation town of Gorazde was under threat by Serb nationalists who threw stones at vehicles during most of the year. OSCE human rights reporting indicated that the road was attacked 13 times in less than a 2-day period in July and August. The persistence of roadblocks along the IEBL also frequently appeared designed to impede the freedom of individuals to travel to and from areas in which they were part of an ethnic minority.

There were credible reports that Bosnian Muslims restricted Croat freedom of movement in the Vares region. For much of the year both Croats and Muslims restricted freedom of movement between the divided communities in Mostar. Only continual prodding by representatives of the international community permitted some halting progress in permitting the return of refugees to the towns of Jajce, Bugojno, Stolac, and Travnik, as spelled out in the Dayton Displaced Persons Agreement.

A major aspect of freedom of movement in Bosnia and Herzegovina is the ability of refugees and displaced persons to return to their places of residence, a right established in the Dayton Accords. Some progress was made in this regard. By October between 220,000 and 240,000 individuals had returned, albeit primarily to areas in which they were part of the ethnic majority. This number must be evaluated, however, against an estimated total of 2.4 million refugees and displaced persons.

A number of policies and measures served to discourage the return of persons to their former homes. In both the Federation and the RS, property laws were manipulated both to prevent individuals who fled as a result of the war from returning, or to force others to flee. The parties have failed to implement adequate amnesty laws, which the OHR indicates is a substantial obstacle to freedom of movement and return of refugees and displaced persons.

In certain strategic or sensitive areas, such as Mostar, the suburbs of Sarajevo, and the Brcko region, population movement—including pressure for resettlement of some groups and restrictions on the movement away of others—strongly suggested policies adopted at the highest levels by the leadership of all three ethnic groups. In the Federation, with the possible exception of the specific areas described above, local authorities or popular sentiment more often appeared to be responsible for the violations, but Federation-level authorities often took little action to prevent or undo them. In general the pattern of violations in the RS suggested a systematic policy of attempting to achieve ethnic homogeneity.

The Federation Parliament adopted an amnesty law, described by the UNHCR as inadequate, on June 12. One of the intended effects of this law was to permit individuals who fled during the war and were subsequently charged with a variety of offenses to return. The UNHCR states that the law has not been fully respected, citing the arrests of returnees from the Kuplensko camp in Croatia on war crimes allegations and the reported initiation of criminal proceedings in Sarajevo courts against some 83 Bosnian Serb Army soldiers.

The RS Parliament adopted an amnesty law, flawed in certain respects, in July. Non-Serbs in the Banja Luka region were subjected to continuing pressure, including eviction or threats of eviction from their homes. Expulsions during the war greatly reduced the population of non-Serbs, who once numbered 250,000. They now number fewer than 4,000.

A few hundred Muslims have returned to areas of their former residence in Jusici, Mahala, and Dugi Dio on RS territory in the zone of separation between the entities. Press reports described RS efforts to prevent Muslims from returning to the town of Mahala: Serb Interior Ministry police beat 10 persons before NATO soldiers gained control of the situation. Efforts of Muslims to return to towns in the northern RS continued, however. Local Serbs who might be favorably disposed toward the returnees appeared to be afraid of the reaction of Serb authorities.

The Government grants asylum and refugee status in accordance with international standards. It cooperates with the UNHCR and other humanitarian organizations in assisting refugees. The issue of the provision of first asylum did not arise in 1996.

Section 3. Respect for Political Rights: The Right of Citizens to Change Their Government

The Dayton Accords commit the parties to "ensure that conditions exist for the organization of free and fair elections, in particular a politically neutral environment," and to the right to "vote in secret without fear or intimidation." Observance of these rights was first tested on the national, entity, and, in the case of the Federation, at the provincial level, in elections held on September 14. Alija Izetbegovic, Momcilo Krajisnik, and Kresimir Zubak were elected to the Presidency representing respectively Bosniaks, Serbs, and Croats. Izetbegovic, who received a plurality of the votes, was named Chair in accordance with the new Constitution. Voters throughout Bosnia and Herzegovina (and refugees abroad) also elected national and entity-level Assemblies.

Some human rights organizations charged that the elections were unfair because of the obstacles placed in the way of campaigns by political parties other than the three dominant nationalist parties, which have ruled in their respective ethnic areas. They also declared them undemocratic because of alleged fraud in the voting and counting of ballots. The Coordinator for International Monitoring concluded that the elections, "although characterized by imperfections, took place in such a way that they provide a first and cautious step toward the democratic functioning of the governing structures of Bosnia and Herzegovina." The Bosnian Provisional Election Commission "certified" them as valid. The three nationalist parties won large majorities in their respective areas. However, in both the Federation and the RS other parties garnered sufficient votes to win representation in Bosnia and Herzegovina's House of Representatives. The Dayton Accords specified that voters who had been forced to flee because of the war could return to the localities where they lived earlier in order to vote. The High Representative reported that there were no serious restrictions on freedom of movement in this connection, although fewer than expected chose to exercise this option.

In the Bosniak areas of the Federation, opponents of the governing SDA endured acts of hooliganism. Former Prime Minister Haris Silajdzic, running for President for the Party for Bosnia and Herzegovina (SBiH), was attacked prior to a campaign rally by local supporters of the dominant SDA. In July OSCE human rights monitors reported several other instances of personal intimidation and interruption of political meetings suffered by minority parties, to such an extent that it became effectively impossible for opposition parties to operate in some areas. There was a concerted campaign of harassment and intimidation of opposition party representatives and their supporters in Cazin and Velika Kladusa, including bombing and grenade attacks, assaults, and arbitrary arrests.

In Croat-controlled areas of the Federation few incidents were reported. Few opposition candidates and parties conducted large-scale activities during the campaign period, probably as a result of fear occasioned by earlier violence.

Although persons in the RS have a theoretical right to change their government, SDS control of the media and security apparatus precluded true citizen participation without intimidation. The SDS was intolerant of opposition political activity. In the period leading up to the polls, pressure on the opposition took various forms, both subtle and overt, including firing on party offices, disruptions of meetings, and harassment of party members.

The Dayton Accords also provided that local elections be held throughout Bosnia and Herzegovina if feasible. They were scheduled to take place at the same time as the national and provincial elections. However, logistical and political difficulties, including massive manipulation of Serb voter registration, resulted in their postponement.

Women are generally underrepresented in government and politics, although a few women occupy prominent positions. For example, a Serb woman, Biljana Plavsic, was appointed, and in September elected, to the Presidency of the RS. In the three legislatures, women are woefully underrepresented, particularly in RS and Bosnia and Herzegovina.

Section 4. Governmental Attitude Regarding International and Nongovernmental Investigation of Alleged Violations of Human Rights

In general, the authorities permitted outside investigations of alleged human rights violations. International and local NGO's involved in human rights appear to operate fairly freely. The OHR reports that human rights monitors, both those associated with government and NGO's, were able to travel without restriction in all areas of the country, although there were some threats directed at the Federation Ombudsmen. The International Police Task Force was given widespread access to detention facilities and prisoners in the RS as well as in the Federation. However, monitors experienced difficulties, especially in the RS, in obtaining relevant laws and procedural rules as well as documents pertaining to individual cases.

While monitors enjoyed relative freedom to investigate human rights abuses, they were less successful in persuading the authorities in all regions to respond to their decisions or interventions, often meeting with delays or outright refusal. In the Federation, for example, Ombudsmen tried without success to seek equitable resolution to hundreds of property cases. In other cases, interventions by international monitors to win the release of persons arbitrarily detained were met with frank acknowledgment of the unfounded nature of the detention, and offers to exchange the detainee for others who were allegedly wrongfully detained by another side (see Section 1.d.). The Federation Ombudsmen accused local Federation authorities of refusing to cooperate with them.

There are few reports of threats or harassment of international monitors, with the notable exception of the Mostar area. In one case, the OHR reports that in April an Italian European Union officer was shot in the neck by an off duty Croat policeman who reportedly demanded that the officer turn over two Bosniak policemen riding in his car.

Cooperation with the International Criminal Tribunal for the Former Yugoslavia (ICTY) in the Hague is a key factor in the implementation of the Dayton Accords, the establishment of respect for human rights, and the elimination of impunity for those responsible. While the Bosniak side of the Federation became the first party to surrender persons under indictment of their own dominant ethnicity to the Hague (two Bosniaks were transferred to the Tribunal after a decision of the Supreme Court in June), the RS continued its policy of defiance of the Tribunal and the Dayton Accords by allowing persons indicted for war crimes to remain in high political and military office for part of 1996. Karadzic was removed from political office in July and Mladic from the military command in November.

On November 29, the ICTY handed down its first verdict, sentencing a former soldier of the Bosnian Serb Army to 10 years' imprisonment for his role in the massacre of Muslim civilians in 1995 near Srebrenica. The soldier is appealing the verdict.

The parties have cooperated on several joint exhumations through a process facilitated by international organizations.

Section 5. Discrimination Based on Race, Sex, Religion, Disability, Language, or Social Status

In the Dayton Accords the parties agreed to reject discrimination on such grounds as sex, race, color, language, religion, political or other opinion, national or social origin, or association with a national minority. There were nevertheless many cases of discrimination.

Women.—Physical abuse of women has greatly diminished as a result of the end of the war, when rape was one of the most frequently used tools of ethnic cleansing by the Bosnian Serbs.

Although accurate statistics are not available, there appears to be little legal or social discrimination against women. Women hold some of the most responsible positions in society, including judges, doctors, and professors. A woman is President of the RS. A Bosnian woman heads Bosniak radio and television. Women are entitled to 12 months' maternity leave and required to work no more than 4 hours per day until a child is 3 years old. A woman with underage children may not be forced to do shift work.

Children.—The U.N. Convention on the Rights of the Child is incorporated by reference in the Dayton Accords and has the effect of law in both entities. The end of the fighting has brought a major improvement in the human rights of children. During the war nearly 17,000 children were killed, 35,000 wounded, and over 1,800 permanently disabled.

The domination by ethnic majorities adversely affects children of minorities, who must attend schools in which the educational content is skewed toward the values, history, and religious traditions of the local majority. Children also suffer from the extreme paucity of social services, especially the lack of adequate care for mentally retarded children.

There is no discrimination or societal pattern of abuse against children. Nonetheless, they have suffered and continue to suffer disproportionately from the societal stress being experienced in Bosnia. United Nations experts estimated that one-half of the children in Bosnia and Herzegovina—some 700,000—are refugees or displaced persons.

A U.N. official overseeing human rights in Bosnia reported two situations in which children were apparently singled out for abuse. In an ethnically motivated incident, a bus carrying Bosniak children was pelted by a stone-throwing mob near Banja Luka and received no assistance from local authorities. In the Velika Kladusa-Cazin area, the teenage children of returning Bosniaks who had not supported the SDA were assaulted because of their parents' alleged political beliefs. The perpetrators were identified to the local police, arrested, and speedily released.

People With Disabilities.—By law the Federation Government is required to assist people with disabilities in finding employment and protecting them against discrimination. In the current situation there are few jobs available, and approximately 12,000 newly disabled victims of the war are entering the job market. The Government had limited resources to address the special needs of the disabled.

Religious Minorities.—In July a Roman Catholic church in the Muslim-controlled town of Bugojno was firebombed. It was reportedly the last Catholic church in the town. This act followed by a few days a fire that damaged a mosque in the Croat-controlled town of Prozor and may have been in retaliation for the burning of the mosque. In the latter case police apprehended a Croat man in connection with the vandalism.

National/Racial/Ethnic Minorities.—Ethnic differences—complicated by religious differences—were at the heart of the war in Bosnia and Herzegovina. After family ties, ethnic identity remains the most powerful social force in the country. Both the SDS and the HDZ leaders have conveyed a commitment to the concepts of a "Greater Serbia" and a "Greater Croatia," even after having agreed in the Dayton framework to abandon them. These parties, and to a lesser extent the primarily Bosniak SDA as well, have sought to manipulate the movement of people and the access to housing and social services they control to ensure that the ethnic groups with which they are associated consolidate their position in their respective geographic regions.

Although in certain areas like Sarajevo and Tuzla mixed communities coexist relatively peacefully, there continue to be an extremely high number of incidents of harassment and discrimination directed against minority populations throughout Bosnia and Herzegovina. In some cases, these reflect popular animosities exacerbated by years of ethnic conflict. In many cases there is evidence of tacit or direct involvement of the authorities. Most such instances are clearly designed to intimidate remaining ethnic minorities. There have been numerous, well-documented instances of overt discrimination or violence; incidents commonly cited include forced evictions, beatings, and arbitrary arrest/detention.

Property disputes often form the basis of incidents of ethnic discrimination. The flight of hundreds of thousands of refugees during the war left many dwellings and other properties empty. Local officials continued to apply laws concerning abandoned property arbitrarily either to manipulate the ethnic make-up of a particular area or to falsely declare apartments abandoned in order to evict minorities. The

OHR reported that in Busovaca, in the Federation, municipal authorities refused to recognize the occupancy of about 95 Croat families who had lived in military-owned apartments prior to the war, apartments subsequently allocated to other families. An RS law on deserted property permits the return of such property to the original owner only if any subsequent occupant willingly departs, an unlikely eventuality in light of the large number of displaced persons, mostly Serb, and the lack of adequate alternative dwellings.

The departure of the majority of Serb inhabitants in connection with the transfer of authority over Sarajevo in March exemplified the effects of ethnic intolerance at all levels of authority and among the populace. RS authorities, expressing dissatisfaction with the reorganization, threatened to pull all Serbs out of Sarajevo and sought to dismantle or destroy housing, industrial facilities, essential utilities, and other services. Reliable reports indicate that the RS authorities made plans in advance to resettle Serbs in large numbers in areas of the RS from which Bosniaks had been forced to flee earlier. There were numerous reports of intimidation and harassment of those who indicated a willingness to remain in the suburbs after the 20 March transfer. A common tactic, according to the OHR, involved late-night visits to homes of persons who did not appear to be making preparations to leave. In such cases these individuals were asked repeatedly when they planned to leave, and others were told that their apartments would be looted or burned if they did not leave. In part as a result of such pressure, about 60,000 of the 80,000 Serbs in the Sarajevo canton moved away; others trickled out in the months that followed.

However, the arrival of Federation police did not result in a significant improvement in the situation for most of the Serbs who remained. Evictions and harassment of ethnic Croats and Serbs continued. Minorities remaining in these areas have trouble gaining or retaining employment. Many of these acts appear have been perpetrated by incoming displaced Bosniaks from eastern Bosnia, although there were incidents involving the Federation police using violence against Serbs. According to a statement made in June by the Chairman of the Helsinki Committee for Human Rights in Bosnia-Herzegovina, "the remaining Serbs in Sarajevo are currently in an alarming position." He claimed that neither the local nor the international police were providing sufficient protection for the remaining Serb population, with the result that Muslims arriving from Podrinje, Srebrenica, Zvornik, Zepa, and Visegrad were throwing Serbs out of their homes.

Ethnic discrimination was also evident repeatedly in international efforts to integrate Mostar, which had been divided for 3 years between the Croat-controlled Western sector and a Muslim controlled Eastern sector. European Union authorities responsible for overseeing the reunification enforced a political structure, including three districts for Croats, three for Bosniaks, and one mixed. Elections for the local government of Mostar in June demonstrated the highly charged atmosphere between Bosniak- and Croat-controlled areas. When the mainly Muslim SDA gained a majority of one seat on the new city council, Bosnian Croats initially refused to participate in Council sessions. Mostar remained a city bitterly divided along ethnic lines, and movement between the two ethnic halves of the city was minimal. Incidents of ethnically based violence persisted.

According to Bosnian Federation Ombudsmen, human rights violations based on ethnic origin continued to be committed at all levels of government in the Federation. According to one report from the Ombudsmen, the essential problem is the continued existence of two ethnically pure police forces; as a result, members of an ethnic community who are part of a minority in a certain area suffer. There is reportedly little difference in this respect between the police in the areas under Bosniak control or in those held by the Croatian Defense Council. Two examples cited by the Ombudsmen were Croat-held West Mostar and Moslem-held Bugojno, where local police forces not only tolerated violence and discrimination but were directly involved in it.

In the RS abuse of ethnic minorities has been tantamount to official policy. Ethnic minorities have been subjected to harassment and on occasion expulsion. Serb local authorities, whose numbers appear to have been purged by hard-line SDS officials, have been directly involved in restricting freedom of movement, conducting discriminatory policies, and fomenting, through propaganda, violence against non-Serbs. The return of minority refugees to their former place of residence in Serb-controlled areas was often hampered by the deliberate destruction of their homes.

There are indications that some resettlement efforts in "strategic" areas of the RS, including by persons not originally residents of those areas, had tacit support from Bosniak authorities.

Section 6. Worker Rights
   a. *The Right of Association.*—The Federation Constitution provides for the right of workers to form and join labor unions. The largest union is the Confederation of Independent Trade Unions of Bosnia and Herzegovina, the heir of the old Yugoslav Communist Trade Union Confederation. Unions have the right to strike, but there were few strikes during the year because of the economic devastation and joblessness caused by the war throughout much of the Federation.
   A threat to strike by representatives of 19,000 Bosnian miners was dropped in October after the Federation Prime Minister promised to pay back wages for August.
   Unions may affiliate internationally.
   b. *The Right to Organize and Bargain Collectively.*—The practice of collective bargaining in labor-management negotiations was used only in a limited way in 1996. There are no export processing zones.
   c. *Prohibition of Forced or Compulsory Labor.*—There were no reports of forced labor in either entity.
   d. *Minimum Age for Employment of Children.*—The minimum age for employment of children in the Federation was 16 years. Children sometimes assisted their families with farm work and odd jobs.
   e. *Acceptable Conditions of Work.*—The minimum monthly wage is $60 (96 DM) and $46 (74 DM) per month for pensioners. In principle this wage level is guaranteed, but in reality it is meaningless as the economy is only beginning to recover from the war. Many workers still have claims outstanding for salaries earned during the war but are being paid in full for current work.
   Occupational safety and health regulations were generally ignored because of the demands and constraints imposed by the war.

BULGARIA

Bulgaria is a parliamentary republic ruled by a democratically elected government. President Zhelyu Zhelev, former chairman of the Union of Democratic Forces (UDF), was elected in 1992 to a 5-year term in the country's first direct presidential elections. Petar Stoyanov of the UDF won new presidential elections in the fall and will succeed Zhelev in January 1997. The Bulgarian Socialist Party (BSP), heir to the Communist Party, and two nominal coalition partners won an absolute majority in preterm elections in December 1994 and have ruled since then. The judiciary is independent but continued to struggle with structural and staffing problems.
   Most security services are the responsibility of the Ministry of the Interior, which controls the police, the Central Service for Combating Organized Crime, the National Security Service (civilian intelligence), internal security troops, border guards, and special forces. A number of persons known to be involved in repressive activities during the Communist regime returned to senior-level positions in the security services in 1995 and retained these positions in 1996. Some members of the police force committed serious human rights abuses.
   The post-Communist economy remains heavily dependent on money-losing state enterprises, although the private sector now accounts for about 45 percent of economic activity. Most people are employed in the industrial and service sectors; key industries include food processing, chemical and oil processing, metallurgy, and energy. Principal exports are agricultural products, cigarettes and tobacco, chemicals, and metal products. The transformation of the economy into a market-oriented system has been retarded by continued political and social resistance. Slow progress in privatization of the large Communist-era state enterprises has been a major reason for economic stagnation. The Government is now implementing a mass privatization program which, if successful, would partially address this problem. The service and consumer goods sectors in private hands continued to be the most vibrant. After a period of superficial economic stability and revived growth in 1995, a crisis in the financial system occurred in early 1996, accompanied by a sharp devaluation of the country's currency, high inflation, and a serious grain shortage. This implosion helped prod the Government toward economic restructuring and, late in the year, to speed up privatization. Reform measures include an austerity package with layoffs at state-owned enterprises, which is expected to increase unemployment substantially. The economic crisis has affected the employment of people from ethnic minorities disproportionately. The annual per capita gross domestic product of $1,205 provides a low standard of living.
   The Government generally respected the human rights of its citizens, but problems remained in some areas. Police used unwarranted lethal force against suspects

and minorities in some cases, and security forces beat suspects and inmates. Human rights observers charged that the security forces are not sufficiently accountable to Parliament or to society and that the resultant climate of impunity is a major obstacle to ending police abuses. Prison conditions are harsh, and pretrial detention is often prolonged. The judiciary is underpaid, understaffed, and has a heavy case backlog. Most citizens have little confidence in their legal system. Constitutional restrictions on political parties formed on ethnic, racial, or religious lines effectively limit participation for some groups. Societal mistreatment of ethnic minorities is a serious problem, and both the Government and private citizens continued to obstruct the activities of some non-Eastern Orthodox religious groups. Human rights groups report that the Government does not adequately assist homeless and other vulnerable children, notably Romani children, and that security forces harass, physically abuse, and arbitrarily arrest and detain Romani street children. Discrimination and violence against women and Roma remain serious problems.

RESPECT FOR HUMAN RIGHTS

Section 1. Respect for the Integrity of the Person, Including Freedom From:
  a. *Political and Other Extrajudicial Killing.*—Police officers used unwarranted lethal force against criminal suspects, as well as against members of minority groups whether or not suspected of any crime, resulting in two deaths.
  On January 29, a 17-year-old Rom, Anguel Zabchikov, died while in police custody in Razgrad, apparently as a result of a beating. The police told Zavchikov's family that he fell and fractured his skull while fleeing the police and died instantly. The police later reported that he died as a result of excessive alcohol in the bloodstream. In addition to the fractured skull, Zabchikov's family described numerous signs of severe beating and handcuff marks on both wrists. An investigation is in progress.
  On April 15, Ivan Benchev was found beaten to death in Sofia. Benchev had been arrested with a friend on April 14 for making a false bomb threat. After the police released him, he was attacked and abducted 50 meters from the police station. In July the Ministry of Interior dismissed three policemen for organizing Benchev's beating and kidnaping with former police colleagues now working at a private security firm. A military prosecutor is investigating the case.
  On October 2, former Prime Minister Andrei Lukanov was shot and killed outside his home; neither motive nor perpetrators have yet been identified. Some of his colleagues claimed that his assassination was linked to his plans to publicize corruption at the highest levels of the BSP; others saw the killing as a gangland-style murder related to his business dealings.
  In June three policemen were convicted of the 1995 murder of a male in police custody. Two of the officers were sentenced to 20 years and the third to 18 years in prison. One of the remaining three policemen was convicted of inflicting bodily harm and extorting a confession and was given a lesser sentence; the other two received suspended sentences.
  The investigation into the February 1995 suspicious death of a Rom in Gradets was closed after a coroner determined that the man died as a result of freezing to death rather than as a result of a beating. There was little progress in the investigation of the March 1995 killing of a 22-year-old Rom by a police sergeant in Nova Zagora. The investigation into the September 1994 case of a detainee who died 1 day after being taken into police custody in Pleven was suspended in March by the district prosecutor's office. In July, after a local human rights organization appealed the district prosecutor's decision, the chief prosecutor's office overturned the suspension and ordered the investigation to resume.
  Interior Ministry data on serious police violations over the 18 months ending March 31, 1995, show 18 deaths due to police negligence, 59 cases of physical injury, more than 60 charges of serious offenses, and 58 convictions of police officers on these and lesser charges during the period. The then-Minister of Interior acknowledged that police abuses occur and made a commitment to address the problem. For example, penalties were reportedly imposed on 272 employees during the month of May for unspecified offenses and breaches of discipline: 7 were dismissed and 11 reduced in rank. The police have generally refused to make investigative reports available to the public. The climate of impunity that still prevails is the single largest obstacle to ending abuses.
  b. *Disappearance.*—There were no reports of politically motivated disappearances.
  c. *Torture and Other Cruel, Inhuman, or Degrading Treatment or Punishment.*— The Constitution expressly prohibits torture and cruel, inhuman, or degrading treatment.
  Despite this prohibition, police beat criminal suspects and Roma during arrests. In January, according to a report by the Starna Zagora Regional Directorate for In-

ternal Affairs, three men dressed in police uniforms, presenting themselves as officers of the Sofia Directorate for Internal Affairs, abducted and beat 23-year-old Kamen Chausev, who was in preventive detention in Kazanluk. In February police reportedly beat Vasilev Dobrev, a passenger in the car of Georgi Goergiev, when Dobrev intervened to support Georgiev's refusal to pay a bribe demanded by the police. Investigations were initiated in both cases. In February, according to newspaper reports, Ahmed Mustatov of Bratovo was arrested and allegedly beaten by three officers. The local prosecutor is reviewing the findings of a preliminary police inquiry.

In March, according to Human Rights Watch, an off-duty police officer in Russe beat a Romani couple when they refused to pay a bribe. No charges were brought. Police reportedly beat six Roma in the village of Barkatch in April after catching them stealing corn from a nearby field. The next day police broke into a house in the village and, after accusing the occupants of hiding stolen corn, beat a man and his 15-year-old son. No police officers were charged or investigated. In May the police reportedly beat two men after arresting them at the funeral of three murdered policemen. The men were not charged with a crime and, after they were released, sought medical attention for their injuries. The beatings were widely reported in the press, but again no officers have been charged.

In March a military court in Pleven sentenced two policemen to 8-month suspended sentences and 3 years' probation for abusing their authority and causing bodily injuries to two Romani juveniles in April 1995. This was the first time that policemen were sentenced to jail (although the sentence was suspended) for abusing Roma.

A European human rights organization concluded in a September 1995 report that criminal suspects arrested by the police run a significant risk of being mistreated at the time of their apprehension or while in police custody and on occasion may be subject to severe mistreatment or torture.

An Amnesty International (AI) report released in June described 7 deaths in custody under suspicious circumstances, 3 incidents in which 6 persons were shot without sufficient provocation, 17 cases of torture, and the mistreatment of dozens of victims spanning a period from 1993 to the date of the report's release. The report concluded that the recurring incidence of abuses revealed "a pattern of casual violence and illegal acts by police officers throughout the country." The Government in response looked into the cases raised by AI, reported on the results of inquiries into 16 of the cases, and expressed readiness to cooperate with AI. In October AI urged provision of additional information, noting that the information provided was "insufficient to assess whether these investigations have been prompt and impartial."

A Human Rights Watch report documenting police mistreatment of Romani street children stated that police harass and physically abuse the children. Children described being chased, kicked, and grabbed by police on the street.

Conditions in some prisons are harsh, including severe overcrowding, inadequate lavatory facilities, and insufficient heating and ventilation. Credible sources reported cases of brutality committed by prison guards against inmates; in some cases, prisoners who complained were placed in solitary confinement. The process by which prisoners may complain of substandard conditions or of mistreatment does not appear to function.

The Government cooperated fully with requests by independent observers to monitor prison conditions.

d. *Arbitrary Arrest, Detention, or Exile.*—The Constitution provides for access to legal counsel from the time of detention. Police normally obtain a warrant from a prosecutor prior to apprehending an individual; otherwise, in emergency circumstances judicial authorities must rule on the legality of a detention within 24 hours. Defendants have the right to visits by family members, to examine evidence, and to know the charges against them. Charges may not be made public without the permission of the chief prosecutor. Pretrial detention is limited to 2 months under normal circumstances, although this may be extended to 6 months by order of the Chief Prosecutor, who may also restart the process. In practice, persons are often detained for well over 6 months.

Nearly 4,000 of approximately 10,000 prison inmates are in pretrial detention. In the event of a conviction, time spent in pretrial detention is credited toward the sentence. The Constitution provides for bail, and some detainees have been released under this provision, although bail is not widely used.

A Human Rights Watch report found that "police often arbitrarily detain street children, hold them in custody, question them, and then release them after registering the children with the Children's Pedagogic Office or referring them to a local Commission, the body which is authorized under the Juvenile Delinquency Act to recommend confinement of a child in a Labor Education School."

The Government does not use forced exile.

e. *Denial of Fair Public Trial.*—Under the Constitution the judiciary is granted independent and coequal status with the legislature and executive branch. However, most observers agreed that the judiciary continued to struggle with problems such as low salaries, understaffing, and a heavy backlog of cases. Partly as a legacy of communism and partly because of the court system's structural and personnel problems, most citizens have little confidence in their judicial system. Human rights groups complain that local prosecutors and magistrates sometimes fail to pursue vigorously crimes committed against minorities. Few organized crime figures have been prosecuted.

The court system consists of regional courts, the Constitutional Court, and, until the end of 1996, an interim Supreme Court. The Government had not yet carried out several of the reforms provided for in a 1994 judicial reform bill, including the establishment of separate supreme courts of cassation (civil and criminal appeal) and administration. The failure to establish these courts led to a political confrontation between the Supreme Judicial Council and the ruling Bulgarian Socialist Party. In June the Supreme Judicial Council elected presidents for the two courts. The BSP-controlled Parliament retaliated by passing legislation prohibiting the Supreme Judicial Council from electing presidents, vice presidents, and judges of the two courts until Parliament passes legislation establishing them. In October the Constitutional Court declared this prohibition unconstitutional, and the supreme courts of cassation and administration were constituted in November.

The Constitutional Court is empowered to rescind legislation it considers unconstitutional, settle disputes over the conduct of general elections, and resolve conflicts over the division of powers between the various branches of government. Military courts handle cases involving military personnel and some cases involving national security matters. The Constitutional Court does not have specific jurisdiction in matters of military justice.

Judges are appointed by the 25-member Supreme Judicial Council and, after serving for 3 years, may not be replaced except under limited, specified circumstances. The 12 justices on the Constitutional Court are chosen for 9-year terms as follows: a third are elected by the National Assembly, a third appointed by the President, and a third elected by judicial authorities.

The Constitution stipulates that all courts shall conduct hearings in public unless the proceedings involve state security or national secrets. There were no reported complaints about limited access to courtroom proceedings. Defendants have the right to know the charges against them and are given ample time to prepare a defense. The right of appeal is guaranteed and widely used. Defendants in criminal proceedings have the right to confront witnesses and to have an attorney, provided by the state if necessary, in serious cases.

A Human Rights Watch report likened the Labor Education Schools to which problem children can be sent to penal institutions. However, since the schools are not considered prisons under the law, the procedures by which children are confined in these schools are not subject to minimal due process. Children sometimes appear despite the requirement that parents must attend hearings; the right to an attorney at the hearing is expressly prohibited by law. Decisions on these cases are not subject to judicial review and children typically stay in the Labor Education Schools for 3 years or until they reach majority age, whichever occurs first. At year's end the Parliament enacted legislation providing for court review of sentencing to such schools, setting a limit of a 3-year stay, and addressing other problems in these institutions (see Section 5, Children).

A number of criminal cases against former leaders for alleged abuses during the Communist period were carried forward. Former dictator Todor Zhivkov, who was serving a 7-year sentence under house arrest for abuse of power involving personal expense accounts and state privileges, was acquitted in February by the Supreme Court. The Court ruled that Zhivkov has immunity from prosecution for the criminal charges in this case. Zhivkov remains under house arrest for his indictment on other charges stemming from his involvement in the coercive campaign to rename and assimilate ethnic Turks in the mid-1980's, channeling funds to arm third-world countries, and establishing a fund to assist leftist workers' organizations worldwide.

In April the Prosecutor General's office suspended the investigation of the case in which 43 former high-level Communists were indicted in 1994 for having given grant aid during the 1980's to then-friendly governments in the developing world such as Cuba, Angola, and Libya. The Prosecutor General's office also suspended the investigation of a case begun in 1993 involving a charge of embezzlement for giving grant aid to Communist parties in other countries (the "Moscow case"). According to the prosecutor's office, the cases were suspended because many of the accused have immunity as deputies for the BSP. Some human rights observers criticized these and previous indictments, asserting that the activities in question were political and economic in nature, not criminal.

One of the primary figures in these cases, former Prime Minister and one-time senior Communist official Andrei Lukanov, brought a complaint against these proceedings to the European Commission of Human Rights. In March the Commission ruled that the detention of Lukanov from July to December 1992 was unlawful. The European Court of Human Rights is now considering the case, although Lukanov was shot and killed in Sofia on October 2.

There was no progress in a case begun in 1993 relating to the forced assimilation and expulsion of ethnic Turks in 1984–85 and 1989, nor in a trial relating to the notorious death camps set up by the Communists after they came to power in 1944.

There were no reports of political prisoners.

f. *Arbitrary Interference With Privacy, Family, Home, or Correspondence.*—The Constitution provides for the inviolability of the home and the right to choose one's place of work and residence and protects the freedom and confidentiality of correspondence. Human rights observers expressed concern that illegal wiretaps may still persist but provided no tangible evidence. In November the opposition Union of Democratic Forces charged that its headquarters had been wiretapped by the Interior Ministry during the fall presidential elections. The Ministry denied the charge but ordered an inquiry; the military prosecutor's office began investigating the charges.

Section 2. Respect for Civil Liberties, Including:

a. *Freedom of Speech and Press.*—The Constitution provides for freedom of speech and the press, and the Government generally respects this right in practice. However, in September Parliament passed, over President Zhelev's veto, legislation that was publicly criticized by Council of Europe experts and Bulgarian journalists for the inhibitions it would impose on freedom of the broadcast media. Critics of the media law were concerned, for example, that the makeup of the National Council for Radio and Television would subject the media to political influence by the party in power. Asked by 74 opposition Members of Parliament to rule on the law, the Constitutional Court in November declared this and numerous other provisions unconstitutional. Until a revised bill is enacted, the broadcast media are left in a legislative void.

The variety of newspapers published by political parties and other organizations represents the full spectrum of political opinion, although journalists frequently color their reports to conform with the views of the political parties or economic groups that own their respective newspapers.

In June the chief editor of the tabloid newspaper Noshten Trud was convicted of libeling the Prosecutor General in a June 1995 article. The editor was given a 3-month suspended sentence and 3 years' probation. Two journalists, correspondents for the national dailies Trud and 24 Hours in Smolyan, were arrested in February and charged with "libel against a government official" for writing unflattering reports about a local prosecutor. After spending a night in jail, the journalists were released by order of a local court. However, the official investigation against the two remains open. Some human rights observers charged that prosecutors, especially those in smaller towns, use their authority to issue arrest warrants to intimidate reporters who criticize their work.

Pending the new media legislation, national television and radio broadcasting both remained under parliamentary supervision. Some media observers expressed concern that such parliamentary supervision fosters censorship and a lack of balance in the state-controlled media. For example, on new year's eve 1995, the director of national television canceled the broadcast of a comedy program claiming that the show was disrespectful of political institutions. In June an agreement to give live coverage of the "no to fear" concert and rally held in downtown Sofia was abruptly canceled the day before, allegedly on the orders of a high-ranking government official.

There are two state-owned national television channels that broadcast in Bulgarian. There is also a national channel that broadcasts Russian programming, and another that carries a mixture of Cable News Network International and French language programming. Bulgarian national television has been planning Turkish-language programming for at least 3 years, but broadcasts have not yet begun. There is no private national broadcaster, but a number of privately owned regional stations operate. After initial government approval in the fall of 1994 of an application to create a privately owned national broadcast television station, further progress has floundered, with no action taken by the current Government.

Foreign government radio programs such as the British Broadcasting Corporation and the Voice of America (VOA) had good access to commercial radio frequencies.

However, a request by Radio Free Europe (RFE) to broadcast Voice of America programs on what was unused time on its frequency has not been granted and remains in limbo many months after the formal request was submitted. Television and radio news programs on the state-owned media present opposition views, but opposition members claim that their activities and views are given less air time and exposure than the those of the ruling party. There are no formal restrictions on programming. Both television and radio provide a variety of news and public interest programming, including talk and public opinion shows.

More than 30 independent radio stations are licensed. Some private stations complained that their licenses unduly restricted the strength of their transmissions in comparison with state-owned stations. Radio transmitter facilities are owned by the Government.

Private book publishing remained vigorous.

The Government respects academic freedom.

b. *Freedom of Peaceful Assembly and Association.*—The right to peaceful assembly is provided for by the Constitution, and the Government generally respected this right in practice. The authorities require permits for rallies and assemblies held outdoors, but most legally registered organizations were routinely granted permission to assemble. However, Jehovah's Witnesses reported difficulties obtaining permits for outdoor assemblies, and they and Word of Life also had difficulty renting assembly halls. In most cases, these religious groups had been denied registration by the Council of Ministers (see Section 2.c.). In September, at the behest of some Plovdiv residents, municipal officials issued and carried out an order to close a Pentacostal-Charismatic Church that was an outgrowth of the Bible Faith Center Immanuel founded in 1990 by Pastor Ivan Nestorov. On two separate occasions, members of the Word of Life were coerced by police into signing a declaration that they would not receive in their homes gatherings of church members.

Vigorous political rallies and demonstrations were a common occurrence and took place without government interference.

The Government has undertaken to respect the rights of individuals and groups freely to establish their own political parties or other political organizations. However, there are constitutional and statutory restrictions that limit the right of association and meaningful participation in the political process. For example, the Constitution forbids the formation of political parties along religious, ethnic, or racial lines, and prohibits "citizens' associations" from engaging in political activity. Nonetheless, the mainly ethnic Turkish Movement for Rights and Freedoms (MRF) is represented in Parliament. The other major political parties generally accept the MRF's right to participate in the political process. In December, however, a group of parliamentarians within the Socialist-led coalition filed a challenge to the MRF's constitutionality, based on MRF programs and goals that allegedly threatened Bulgaria's territorial integrity and national unity (see below). The Constitutional Court rejected their petition as inadmissible.

The Constitution also prohibits organizations that threaten the country's territorial integrity or unity, or that incite racial, ethnic, or religious hatred. The Government has refused since 1990 to register a self-proclaimed Macedonian rights group, Umo-Ilinden, on the grounds that it is separatist. In February and May, police broke up attempts by the group to hold public meetings. On May 14, the group was denied registration as an educational organization in the city of Blagoevgrad.

c. *Freedom of Religion.*—Although the Constitution provides for freedom of religion, the Government restricts this right in practice for some non-Orthodox religious groups, and discrimination against them increased. The ability of a number of religious groups to operate freely continued to come under attack, both as a result of government action and because of public intolerance. The government requirement that groups whose activities have a religious element register with the Council of Ministers remained an obstacle to the activity of some religious groups, such as Jehovah's Witnesses and Word of Life, which have been denied registration. Despite several applications, no new religious denominations were registered in 1996. The Government provides financial support for the Eastern Orthodox Church and other denominations it considers to be "traditional."

Dozens of articles in a broad range of newspapers depicted lurid and inaccurate pictures of the activities of non-Orthodox religious groups, attributing suicides of teenagers and the breakup of families to their activities.

The Government refused most requests for visas and residence permits for foreign missionaries, and some of them came under physical attack in the street and in their homes. Members of the Mormon church reported continued acts of harassment and assault, including some perpetrated by the police themselves. The police response was indifferent despite the expressed concern of the Government about such cases. Missionaries of Jehovah's Witnesses also reported an incident of beating by the police.

In December 1995, a Jehovah's Witness mother living in a Asenovgrad was denied custody of her son solely because of her religious beliefs. The woman has appealed to the Supreme Court.

In late 1995, Jehovah's Witnesses brought a complaint to the European Commission of Human Rights about the Government's refusal to register the organization. In January the Commission ruled that Jehovah's Witnesses appeal was admissible before the Commission, but it has not yet issued a decision on the merits of the case.

On several occasions the police shut down religious meetings of unregistered groups. In June the police broke up a Jehovah's Witness meeting at a public dance hall in Asenovgrad and confiscated religious material. In August the police raided a private hall in Sofia and closed down a meeting of Word of Life. The press was on hand and gave wide coverage to both of the police raids. These incidents give credence to charges by human rights activists that the police are monitoring the activities of certain unregistered groups.

The Constitution designates Eastern Orthodox Christianity as the "traditional" religion. Along with the Orthodox Church, a number of major religious bodies, including the Muslim and Jewish communities, receive government financial support. There was no evidence that the Government discriminated against members of any religious group in making restitution to previous owners properties that were nationalized during the Communist regime. For most registered religious groups there were no restrictions on attendance at religious services or on private religious instruction. A school for imams, a Muslim cultural center, university theological faculties, and religious primary schools operated freely. Bibles and other religious materials in the Bulgarian language were freely imported and printed, and Muslim, Catholic, and Jewish publications were published on a regular basis. Nevertheless, there were reports that police confiscated religious books and cassettes during searches of Word of Life members.

During compulsory military service most Muslims are placed into construction units where they often perform commercial or maintenance work rather than serve in normal military units. The mainly ethnic-Turkish Movement for Rights and Freedoms (MRF) protested this practice (see Section 5).

A significant proportion of Muslims considered the Government's continued recognition of the 1994 statutes on the Muslim faith and of Nedim Gendjev as Chief Mufti and head of the Supreme Theological Council to be government interference in the affairs of the community. The Government continued to refuse to recognize the election of a rival Chief Mufti, Fikri Salli, who was elected at an alternative Islamic conference in March 1995. In 1995 Fikri appealed the Government's action unsuccessfully to the Supreme Court.

The Government's Directorate of Religious Affairs hired Boncho Asenov, a former security official during the Communist regime. Reliable sources report that Asenov participated in repressive activities against the ethnic Turkish minority and religious groups before 1989.

By order of the Minister of Education, a private religious elementary school located in Lovetch was closed on August 6. The "School of Tomorrow" was run by the registered evangelical denomination, "Shalom" (this group is distinct from the Jewish community organization of the same name). According to Shalom, the school was part of a network of similar schools, founded by an American citizen and associated with several Protestant churches, in 108 countries.

At the Department of Theology of Sofia University all students are required to present a certificate of baptism from the Orthodox Church, and married couples must present a marriage certificate from the same in order to enroll in the Department's classes; in July two non-Orthodox applicants were denied admission to the Department when they were unable to present such certificates. The applicants have appealed to the local courts.

The schism that opened in the Orthodox Church in 1992 deepened, and the Government refused to recognize an alternative Patriarch elected by supporters in July. The Supreme Court ruled that the decision was unlawful, but the alternate Patriarch remained unregistered.

d. *Freedom of Movement Within the Country, Foreign Travel, Emigration, and Repatriation.*—The Constitution provides for freedom of movement within the country and the right to leave it, and these rights are not limited in practice, with the exception of limited border zones that are off limits both to foreigners and citizens not resident therein. Every citizen has the right to return to Bulgaria, may not be forcibly expatriated, and may not be deprived of citizenship acquired by birth. A number of former political emigrants were granted passports and returned to visit or live.

As provided under law, a prosecutor restricted foreign travel by several activists of Umo-Ilinden (see Section 2.b.) due to an investigation into their activities. The activists complained that the investigation was inactive and that the travel restrictions were being used punitively. A human rights organization took up the case and successfully appealed the travel restrictions to a higher ranking prosecutor. Observers criticized the lack of time limits on such inactive or "suspended" investigations.

Bulgaria has provisions for granting asylum or refugee status in accordance with the standards of the relevant U.N. acts in this field, and the Government provides first asylum. However, domestic and international human rights organizations expressed concern over the Government's handling of asylum claims and reported that there may be cases in which bona fide refugees are forced to return to countries where they fear persecution. The Bureau for Territorial Asylum and Refugees asserts that it gives a fair hearing to all persons seeking asylum or refugee status but admits that there may be cases which do not come to its attention before the applicant is returned to the country from which he entered Bulgaria. The Ministry of Interior reports that 2,600 people were denied entry at borders over the past few years; it is not known how many of these requested asylum.

The Bureau reports that 1,506 people have applied for asylum or refugee status in the past 3 years; 203 applicants were approved and 28 denied. Domestic and international human rights organizations complained that the asylum process is slow, and many of those who have been granted refugee status have yet to receive the necessary documents enabling them to move about freely and work. The Bureau is still seeking to establish registration and reception centers blocked in 1994 by skinheads and local citizens groups and has identified some new sites for the centers.

Section 3. Respect for Political Rights: The Right of Citizens to Change Their Government

Citizens have the right to change their government and head of state through the election of the President and of the members of the National Assembly, although the constitutional prohibition of parties formed on ethnic, racial, or religious lines has the effect of circumscribing access to the political process for some groups (see Section 2.b.). Suffrage is universal at the age of 18. The most recent parliamentary elections took place in December 1994. President Zhelev was elected in 1992 in the first direct presidential elections. Peter Stoyanov of the UDF, who was selected as a candidate in a primary election among opposition parties in June and then won presidential elections in the fall of 1996, will succeed Zhelev in January 1997.

There are no restrictions in law on the participation of women in government. A number of women hold elective and appointive office at high levels, including a cabinet-level post and several key positions in Parliament. Women hold about 13 percent of the seats in the current Parliament.

Section 4. Governmental Attitude Regarding International and Nongovernmental Investigations of Alleged Violations of Human Rights

Local and international human rights groups operate freely, investigating and publishing their findings on human rights cases. Local human rights groups reported some improvement in their dealings with government officials. The Human Rights Project stated that the police regularly answered the group's inquiries and have responded positively to a proposal for human rights training of police officers in several cities with large Roma populations. However, government officials, especially local officials, are otherwise often reluctant to provide information or active cooperation.

Section 5. Discrimination Based on Race, Sex, Religion, Disability, Language, or Social Status

The Constitution provides for individual rights, equality, and protection against discrimination, but in practice discrimination still exists, particularly against Roma and women.

There have been reports of inadequate police response to incidents of violence against gays, but few victims of such assaults are willing to press charges.

Women.—Domestic abuse is reportedly a serious and common problem, but there are no figures, official or otherwise, on its occurrence. Currently, the law exempts from state prosecution certain types of assault if committed by a family member, and the Government does not assist in prosecuting crimes of domestic assault unless the woman has been killed or permanently injured. The courts prosecute rape, although it remains an underreported crime because some stigma still attaches to the victim. The maximum sentence for rape is 8 years; convicted offenders often receive a lesser sentence or early parole. Police data released in August show that over the past 2 years 131 women were killed, 1,243 between the age of 17 and 30 were raped, 451 were crippled for life, and 236 sustained serious injuries as a result of violence. Marital rape is a crime but is rarely prosecuted. Courts and prosecutors tend to view domestic abuse as a family rather than criminal problem, and in most cases victims of domestic violence take refuge with family or friends rather than approach the authorities. No government agencies provide shelter or counseling for such persons, although there is a private initiative to address the problem.

Many of the approximately 30 women's organizations are closely associated with political parties or have primarily professional agendas. Of those that exist mainly to defend women's interests, the two largest are the Women's Democratic Union in Bulgaria, heir to the group which existed under the Communist dictatorship, and the Bulgarian Women's Association, which disappeared under communism but has now reemerged and has chapters in a number of cities.

The Constitution forbids privileges or restrictions of rights on the basis of sex. However, women face discrimination both in terms of recruitment and the likelihood of layoffs. Official figures show the rate of unemployment for women to be higher than that for men. Women are much more likely than men to be employed in low-wage jobs requiring little education, although statistics show that women are equally likely to attend university. Women, in the main, continue to have primary responsibility for child rearing and housekeeping even if they are employed outside the home. There are liberal provisions for paid maternity leave. However, in some cases these may actually work against employers' willingness to hire and retain female employees, especially in the private sector.

Children.—The Government is generally committed to protecting children's welfare but, with limited resources, falls short in several areas. It maintains, for example, a sizable network of orphanages throughout the country. However, many of the orphanages are in disrepair and lack proper facilities. Government efforts in education and health have been constrained by serious budgetary limitations and by outmoded social care structures. The Constitution provides that school attendance is mandatory until the age of 16. Groups that exist to defend the rights of children charge that an increasing number of children are at serious risk as social insurance payments fall further behind inflation and are often disbursed as much as 6 months late.

Credible sources report that there is no provision for due process of law for Romani and other juveniles when they are detained in labor education schools run by the Ministry of Education. Living conditions at these reform schools are poor, offering little medical, educational, or social opportunities. Generally, staff members at these institutions lack the proper qualifications and training to adequately care for the children. Degrading and severe punishment, such as the shaving of a child's head, reduction in diet, severe beatings, and long periods of solitary confinement, are common at the schools. The Ministry of Education (MOE) acknowledges problems at the schools, attributing the cause to a lack of funding. At the end of the year, Parliament enacted legislation providing for court review of sentencing to such schools and addressing other problems in the reform school system.

The vast majority of children are free from societal abuse, although some Romani children are frequent targets of skinhead groups; the homeless or abandoned were particularly vulnerable. Some Romani minors were forced into prostitution by family or community members. There was little police effort to address these problems. The new legislation calls for the establishment of shelters for homeless children.

People With Disabilities.—Disabled persons receive a range of financial assistance, including free public transportation, reduced prices on modified automobiles, and free equipment such as wheelchairs. However, as in other areas, budgetary constraints mean that such payments have fallen behind. Disabled individuals have access to university training and to housing and employment, although no special programs are in place to allow them to live up to their full employment potential. To date little effort has been made at the national level to change building or street layouts to help blind or otherwise physically disabled persons. The city of Varna allocated money for the installation of approximately 150 wheelchair ramps (curb cuts) in the city center.

At the end of 1995, Parliament passed legislation requiring the relevant ministry and local governments to provide a suitable living and architectural environment for the disabled within 3 years. However, there is a moratorium on the law taking effect until the Ministry of Construction has completed issuing new construction standards that more fully take into account the needs of the disabled. Policies of the Communist regime which separated mentally and physically disabled persons, including very young children, from the rest of society have persisted.

National/Racial/Ethnic Minorities.—Ethnic Turks comprise about 10 percent of the population. Although estimates of the Romani population vary widely, several experts put it at about 6 percent. (Bulgarian Muslims or "Pomaks" are a distinct group of Slavic descent, comprising 2 to 3 percent of the population, whose ancestors converted from Orthodox Christianity to Islam. Most are Muslim, although a number have become atheists or converted to Christianity.) These are the country's two largest minorities. There are no restrictions on the speaking of Turkish in public or the use of non-Slavic names.

Voluntary Turkish-language classes in public schools, funded by the Government, continued in areas with significant Turkish-speaking populations, although some observers complained that the Government was discouraging the optional language classes in areas with large concentrations of Bulgarian Muslims. According to the Ministry of Education (MOE), there are 844 Turkish language teachers for 64,000 children who study Turkish as their mother tongue. The MOE has reached an agreement with the Turkish Government to send teachers to study at Turkish universities; 30 such teachers participated in a training course over the summer. Some ethnic Turkish leaders, mainly in the MRF, demanded that Turkish-language schooling be made compulsory in ethnic Turkish areas, but the Government resisted this.

In the 1992 census approximately 3.4 percent of the population identified itself as Romani. The real figure is probably about twice that high, since many persons of Romani descent tend to identify themselves to the authorities as ethnic Turks or Bulgarians. Romani groups continued to be divided among themselves, although several groups had some success presenting Romani issues to the Government. As individuals and as an ethnic group, Roma faced high levels of discrimination.

Attacks by private citizens on Romani communities continued to occur. In April seven teenagers beat and stabbed to death Anguel Ivanov, a Roma, in the city of Shumen. While there were no witnesses to the attack, the victim was able to identify his attackers before dying. An investigation is in progress. In June a group of young men attacked and beat three Roma in the town of Samokov. Two of the victims suffered numerous injuries and were knocked unconscious. Local Roma told a human rights organization that skinhead attacks were common in the town, and the police did nothing to stop them. In January at the central rail station in Sofia, a group of skinheads attacked several homeless Roma children sleeping at the station. One of the victims was stabbed three times. Several witnesses reported that the police arrested some of the attackers, but later released them. Roma children living at the station allege that they are frequently attacked by skinheads and occasionally by police officers. No charges have been filed in the 1994 and 1995 cases of attacks by private citizens on two Romani communities. Authorities often fail to aggressively investigate cases of assault or other crimes against Roma, although there was some improvement in their responsiveness to inquiries of human rights organizations (see Section 4).

Roma encounter difficulties applying for social benefits, and rural Roma are discouraged from claiming land to which they are entitled under the law disbanding agricultural collectives. Many Roma and other observers made credible allegations that the quality of education offered to Romani children is inferior to that afforded most other students.

The Government admitted that it has been largely unsuccessful in attracting and keeping many Romani children in school, but it stated that improved education for these children is a government priority. The MOE, together with UNESCO, started seven pilot schools designed specifically for Romani children. The schools have had good results, but because of financial constraints the MOE is unable to expand the program. The MOE continued its program to introduce Romani-language schoolbooks into schools with Romani populations and issued follow-on textbooks for the program. The program has had mixed success, partly due to a lack of qualified teachers.

Workplace discrimination against minorities continued to be a problem, especially for Roma. Employers justify such discrimination on the basis that most Roma have relatively low training and education. Supervisory jobs are generally given to ethnic Bulgarian employees, with ethnic Turks, Bulgarian Muslims, and Roma among the first to be laid off. The National Employment Office is responsible for two programs designed to improve education, training, and labor market participation: an ongoing literacy and training program in ethnically mixed regions; and, with foreign assistance, a "from social assistance to employment" program aimed at reducing the number of persons receiving social assistance, many of whom are Turkish or Roma.

During compulsory military service most Roma (and Muslims—see Section 2.c.) are shunted into units where they often perform commercial, military construction, or maintenance work rather than serve in normal military units. The MRF protested this practice, as did human rights groups and labor observers who cited it as a violation of International Labor Organization (ILO) accords. There are only a few ethnic Turkish and Romani officers in the military.

Thousands of Bulgarians, mainly in the southwest, identify themselves as Macedonians, most for historical and geographic reasons. Members of the two organizations that purport to defend their interests, Umo-Ilinden and Tmo-Ilinden, are believed to number in the hundreds (see Section 2.b.).

Section 6. Worker Rights

a. *The Right of Association.*—The 1991 Constitution provides for the right of all workers to form or join trade unions of their own choice, and this right was apparently freely exercised. Estimates of the unionized share of the work force range from 30 to 50 percent. This share is shrinking as large firms lay off workers, and most new positions appear in small, nonunionized businesses.

There are two large trade union confederations, the Confederation of Independent Trade Unions of Bulgaria (CITUB), and Podkrepa. CITUB, the successor to the trade union controlled by the former Communist regime, operates as an independent entity. Podkrepa, an independent confederation created in 1989, was one of the earliest opposition forces but is no longer a member of the Union of Democratic Forces, the main opposition party. In 1995 a third trade union confederation, the Community of Free Union Organizations in Bulgaria (CFOUB), was admitted to the National Tripartite Coordination Council (NTCC), which includes employers and the Government (see Section 6.b.).

The 1992 Labor Code recognizes the right to strike when other means of conflict resolution have been exhausted, but "political strikes" are forbidden. Workers in essential services are prohibited from striking; in September the Constitutional Court ruled that this prohibition is constitutional. There was no evidence that the Government interfered with the right to strike, and several work stoppages took place. The Labor Code's prohibitions against antiunion discrimination include a 6-month period of protection against dismissal as a form of retribution. While these provisions appear to be within international norms, there is no mechanism other than the courts for resolving complaints, and the burden of proof in such a case rests entirely on the employee.

In 1993 the ILO requested further information on lustration proceedings, measures directed at compensating ethnic Turks for abuses under the previous regime, efforts taken to improve the economic situation of minorities, and measures to promote equality between men and women in workplace opportunity. At year's end, the ILO was still reviewing the information provided to it by the Government.

There are no restrictions on affiliation or contact with international labor organizations, and unions actively exercise this right.

b. *The Right to Organize and Bargain Collectively.*—The Labor Code institutes collective bargaining, which was practiced nationally and on a local level. The legal prohibition against striking for key public sector employees weakens their bargaining position; however, these groups were able to influence negotiations by staging protests and engaging in other pressure activities without going on strike. Both CITUB and Podkrepa complained that while the legal structure for collective bargaining was adequate, many employers failed to bargain in good faith or to adhere to concluded agreements. Labor observers viewed the Government's enforcement of labor contracts as inadequate.

Only the three labor members of the National Tripartite Cooperation Council are authorized to bargain collectively. This restriction led to complaints by smaller unions, which may in individual work places have more members than the NTCC members. Smaller unions also protested their exclusion from the NTCC. Podkrepa and CITUB walked out of the NTCC several times, charging that the Government was failing to negotiate in good faith. The Government acknowledges that the Council's record was inconsistent.

There were no instances in which an employer was found guilty of antiunion discrimination and required to reinstate workers fired for union activities. International labor organizations criticized the "national representation" requirement for participation in the NTCC as a violation of the right to organize.

The same obligation of collective bargaining and adherence to labor standards prevails in the export processing zones, and unions may organize workers in these areas.

c. *Prohibition of Forced or Compulsory Labor.*—The Constitution prohibits forced or compulsory labor. Many observers argued that the practice of shunting minority and conscientious-objector military draftees into work units that often carry out commercial construction and maintenance projects is a form of compulsory labor (Section 5).

d. *Minimum Age for Employment of Children.*—The Labor Code sets the minimum age for employment at 16 years of age; the minimum age for dangerous work is set at 18 years old. Employers and the Ministry of Labor and Social Welfare (MLSW) are responsible for enforcing these provisions. Child labor laws are enforced well in the formal sector. Underage employment in the informal and agricultural sectors is increasing as collective farms are broken up and the private sector continues to grow. In addition, children work on family-owned tobacco farms.

e. *Acceptable Conditions of Work.*—The national monthly minimum wage was approximately $24 (5,500 leva) effective October 1. The minimum wage is not enough to provide a wage earner and family with a decent standard of living. The Constitution stipulates the right to social security and welfare aid assistance for the temporarily unemployed, although in practice such assistance is often either late or not disbursed.

The Labor Code provides for a standard workweek of 40 hours with at least one 24-hour rest period per week. The MLSW is responsible for enforcing both the minimum wage and the standard workweek. Enforcement has been generally effective in the state sector (although there are reports that state-run enterprises fall into arrears on salary payments to their employees if the firms incur losses) but is weaker in the emerging private sector.

A national labor safety program exists, with standards established by the Labor Code. The Constitution states that employees are entitled to healthy and nonhazardous working conditions. The MLSW is responsible for enforcing these provisions. Under the Labor Code, employees have the right to remove themselves from work situations that present a serious or immediate danger to life or health without jeopardizing their continued employment. In practice, refusal to work in situations with relatively high accident rates or associated chronic health problems would result in loss of employment for many workers. Conditions in many cases are worsening owing to budget stringencies and a growing private sector that labor inspectors do not yet supervise effectively.

CANADA

Canada is a constitutional monarchy with a federal parliamentary form of government and an independent judiciary. Citizens periodically choose their representatives in free and fair multiparty elections.

Elected civilian officials control the federal, provincial, and municipal police forces. The armed forces have no role in domestic law enforcement except in national emergencies. Laws requiring the security forces to respect human rights are strictly observed, and violators are punished by the courts.

Canada has a highly developed, market-based economic system. Laws extensively protect the well-being of workers and provide for workers' freedom of association.

The Government generally respected the human rights of its citizens. However, there were occasional complaints in some areas, primarily regarding discrimination against aboriginals, the disabled, and women. The Constitution and laws provide avenues for legal redress of such complaints. The Government and private organizations seek to ensure that human rights are respected in practice at all levels of society and take steps to convict and punish human rights abusers. The Government has taken serious and active steps to address violence against women.

RESPECT FOR HUMAN RIGHTS

Section 1. Respect for the Integrity of the Person, Including Freedom From:

a. *Political and Other Extrajudicial Killing.*—There were no reports of political or other extrajudicial killings.

An investigation was continuing at year's end into the 1995 police killing of an aboriginal activist at Ipperwash, Ontario (see Section 5).

A civilian inquiry is continuing into the activities of a now disbanded Canadian military regiment during its 1993 peacekeeping mission in Somalia. The inquiry is reviewing the entire mission, with its current focus on allegations of a coverup of regiment activities, including the 1993 killing of a Somali teenager in its custody.

b. *Disappearance.*—There were no reports of politically motivated disappearances.

c. *Torture and Other Cruel, Inhuman, or Degrading Treatment or Punishment.*—The law prohibits such practices, and the Government observes the prohibition in practice.

Prison conditions generally meet minimum international standards, and the Government permits visits by human rights monitors. As a result of an inquiry into a

1994 incident at the women's prison in Kingston, Ontario, the Federal Government announced steps it will take to protect the privacy of female prisoners and the appointment of a deputy commissioner for corrections of women. The correctional service also changed its policy to ensure that no men will participate in strip searches of female inmates.

Inmates of Toronto's Don jail complained of inhuman conditions resulting from overcrowding and inadequate health facilities. A report identified the following problems: inadequate fire prevention controls; health hazards (including the risk of contracting tuberculosis and HIV) resulting from overcrowding; insufficient exercise and recreation facilities; and a lack of contact visits. Conditions were described as so depressing that some inmates purportedly pled guilty in order to be sent to other facilities and thus avoid awaiting trial in the jail.

d. *Arbitrary Arrest, Detention, or Exile.*—The law prohibits arbitrary arrest, detention, or exile, and the Government observes this prohibition. Lawyers for a Tamil refugee detained for over a year in a Toronto jail claimed that international standards of fair trial and detention were contravened. The refugee is being held under the Immigration Act, which allows for the detention of an individual the Minister of Justice certifies is a possible member of a terrorist organization.

e. *Denial of Fair Public Trial.*—The law provides for an independent judiciary, and the Government respects this provision in practice. The judiciary provides citizens with a fair and efficient judicial process and vigorously enforces the right to a fair trial.

The court system is divided into federal and provincial courts, which handle both civil and criminal matters. The highest federal court is the Supreme Court, which exercises general appellate jurisdiction and advises on constitutional matters. The judicial system is based on English common law at the federal level as well as in most provinces; in the province of Quebec, it is based on the Napoleonic Code. Throughout Canada judges are appointed. In criminal trials, the law provides for a presumption of innocence and the right to a public trial, to counsel (free for indigents), and to appeal.

In October the Quebec provincial Government announced a wide-ranging public inquiry into the Quebec police force. The inquiry's mandate is to examine allegations of evidence tampering, witness intimidation, and bungled investigations. It was announced after the judge who headed an internal investigation of the Quebec force resigned, terming inadequate a closed-door inquiry into a drug case that had been thrown out of court after allegations that police officers fabricated and tampered with evidence.

There were no reports of political prisoners.

f. *Arbitrary Interference With Privacy, Family, Home, or Correspondence.*—The law prohibits such practices, government authorities generally respect these prohibitions, and violations are subject to effective legal sanction.

Section 2. *Respect for Civil Liberties, Including:*

a. *Freedom of Speech and Press.*—The law provides for freedom of speech and of the press, and the Government respects these rights in practice. An independent press, an effective judiciary, and a functioning democratic political system combine to ensure freedom of speech and of the press, including academic freedom.

Journalists are occasionally banned from reporting some specific details of court cases until a trial is concluded, and these restrictions, adopted to ensure the defendant's right to a fair trial, enjoy wide popular support. Some restrictions on the media are imposed by provincial-level film censorship, broadcasters' voluntary codes curbing graphic violence, and laws against hate literature and pornography. The Canadian Human Rights Act prohibits repeated communications by telephone that expose a person or group to hatred or contempt. Human rights groups are exploring the possibility of extending this prohibition to the Internet.

b. *Freedom of Peaceful Assembly and Association.*—The Constitution provides for these rights, and the Government respects them in practice.

c. *Freedom of Religion.*—The Constitution provides for freedom of religion, and the Government respects this right in practice.

d. *Freedom of Movement Within the Country, Foreign Travel, Emigration, and Repatriation.*—The law provides for these rights, and the Government respects them in practice.

The Government cooperates with the United Nations High Commissioner for Refugees and other humanitarian organizations in assisting refugees and extends first asylum. Canada is a resettlement country, and in 1995 the Government granted refugee status and accepted for resettlement 9,611 persons (56 percent of all applicants for this status). From January to September 1996, the Government granted refugee status to 7,409 applicants (47 percent of applicants). There were no reports of forced expulsion of those having a valid claim to refugee status.

Section 3. Respect for Political Rights: The Right of Citizens to Change Their Government

The Constitution provides citizens with the right to change their government peacefully, and citizens exercise this right in practice through periodic, free, and fair elections held on the basis of universal suffrage.

The Quebec superior court allowed a suit to proceed that would prevent the Quebec government from holding another referendum on the sovereignty issue. The suit maintained that such an act would violate the Canadian Constitution and the filer's rights as a Canadian citizen. The suit was opposed by the Quebec government on grounds that the sovereignty question was a purely political one that could be decided only by the people of Quebec and their National Assembly. In September the federal Minister of Justice referred to the Supreme Court the question of whether Quebec can unilaterally separate from Canada.

Section 4. Governmental Attitude Regarding International and Nongovernmental Investigation of Alleged Violations of Human Rights

A wide variety of human rights groups operate without government restriction, investigating and publishing their findings on human rights cases. Government officials are very cooperative and responsive to their views.

Section 5. Discrimination Based on Race, Sex, Religion, Disability, Language, or Social Status

The Charter of Rights and Freedoms provides for equal benefits and protection of the law regardless of race, national or ethnic origin, color, religion, sex, age, sexual orientation, or mental or physical disability. These rights are generally respected in practice, but there are occasional charges of discrimination within this multicultural society.

Affirmative action (employment equity) legislation is a topic of some national and provincial debate. Federal employment equity legislation was passed by Parliament in December 1995, but the Ministry of Labor is still consulting on the regulations required by the act, and it has not yet entered into force. The legislation is designed to strengthen employment equity provisions for employees under federal jurisdiction.

The Ontario Human Rights Commission was criticized for its enormous backlog of cases, three-quarters of which are employment based, and for the procedures used to reduce the backlog. The criticism included charges that cases were dismissed after commission-caused delays, that basic rules of evidence were not followed by commission staff, and that the investigative process was neither open nor accountable. The Commission was hampered by a 6 percent cut in its budget by the provincial government, despite the ruling Conservative Party's promise to increase the Commission's funding.

The Constitution protects the linguistic and cultural rights of minorities. Despite Canada's federal policy of bilingualism, English speakers in Quebec and French speakers in other parts of Canada must generally live and work in the language of the majority.

In Quebec language laws restrict access to English-language publicly-funded schools through grade 11 to children whose parents were educated in English in Canada and to short-term residents. The law stipulates that French is the working language of most businesses and must be predominant in bilingual commercial signage.

In the summer, English-speaking activists successfully pressed several chain stores in Montreal to display more English signs. Some of these activists called for an end to all restrictions on the language of commercial signs and on access to English-language public schools. French-speaking activists called on the provincial government to do more to promote the use of French, e.g., by reinstituting a pre-1993 law limiting commercial signs to French only, or by extending language laws relating to schooling to grades 12 and 13. In the fall, the Quebec government considered legislation that would reconstitute a French-language inspection office abolished in 1993.

Provinces outside Quebec often lack adequate French-language schooling, which is of concern to local Francophones, although French-language schools are reported to be thriving in all three prairie provinces.

Women.—The law prohibits violence against women, including spousal abuse. The health and economic costs of violence against women have been calculated at $3.15 billion (Can $ 4.2 billion) annually. Nevertheless, according to Statistics Canada, 3 in 10 women currently or previously married or living in a common-law relationship have experienced at least one incident of physical or sexual violence.

In November the federal agency Status of Women Canada reported on Canadian initiatives to address violence against women, and in 1995–96, Status of Women Canada provided approximately $1.9 million (Can $ 2.5 million) to women's groups to address the root causes of violence. A 5-year federal initiative on family violence begun in 1991 provided over $102 million (Can $ 136 million) for the funding of nearly 3,000 projects and the establishment of emergency shelters and longer-term housing for battered women.

In June the federal/provincial-territorial ministers responsible for the status of women released a resource guide of provincial and territorial initiatives aimed at empowering women, youth, and children.

The Criminal Code prohibits criminal harassment (stalking) and makes it punishable by imprisonment for up to 5 years. In 1995 police departments reported 4,260 charges of criminal harassment. In April the Minister of Justice proposed amendments to the Code that would strengthen the criminal harassment provisions. The proposals would require that a person convicted of stalking while under a restraining order should have that fact treated as an aggravating factor in sentencing. Also, a person who commits murder while stalking and intends to make the victim fear for her safety or that of others could be found guilty of first degree murder without proof that the murder itself was planned and deliberate.

Women are well represented in the labor force, including business and the professions. The law prohibits sexual harassment, and the Government enforces this provision.

Women enjoy marriage and property rights equal to those of men. Over 85 percent of single parent households are headed by women. Child support reforms that will take effect in 1996 and 1997 include: Amendments to the income tax act to eliminate child support from the custodial parent's taxable income and the tax deduction available to payers of child support; amendments to the divorce act to establish fairer and more consistent child support payments; new measures to strengthen enforcement; and an enhanced income supplement for lower-income families.

Children.—The Government demonstrates its strong commitment to children's rights and welfare through its well-funded systems of public education and medical care. Federal and provincial regulations protect children from abuse, overwork, and discrimination and duly penalize perpetrators of such offenses. There is no societal pattern of abuse of children.

People With Disabilities.—There is no discrimination against disabled persons in employment, education, or in the provision of other state services. The law mandates access to buildings for people with disabilities, and for the most part the Government enforces these provisions. However, human rights groups report that a significant percentage of their complaints come from those with disabilities. Disabled persons are underrepresented in the work force; for example, they make up 2.6 percent of the federally regulated private sector work force, but those capable of working total 6.5 percent of the population.

The national strategy for the integration of persons with disabilities concluded its 5-year mandate in March. In 1995 the parliamentary Committee on Human Rights and the Status of Disabled Persons concluded that the strategy's programs had not had as much impact as they should have, in part because federal spending on employment programs and services for the disabled declined by $9 million (Can $ 12 million) since 1991.

Indigenous People.—Canada's treatment of its aboriginal people continued to be one of the most important human rights issues facing the country. Disputes over land claims, self-government, treaty rights, taxation, duty-free imports, fishing and hunting rights, and alleged harassment by police continued to be sources of tension on reserves. Aboriginal people remained underrepresented in the work force, overrepresented on welfare rolls, and more susceptible to suicide and poverty than other population groups.

After 5 years of work, the Royal Commission on Aboriginal Peoples released its final report in November. The 3,537 page report proposes a 20-year strategy for rebuilding First Nations through restoring aboriginal communities and restructuring their relationship with the Government. The report's recommendations include the passage of parliamentary acts to address broken treaty promises, the establishment of an aboriginal legislative body that would function alongside the House of Commons and Senate, and the creation of an independent tribunal to monitor land claims.

Although aboriginal leaders welcomed the report's recommendations, the Minister for Indian Affairs said that he believes current government policies are achieving change and that it is doubtful that Canada can afford the high cost that would be necessary to implement all the recommendations. The federal and provincial governments are examining the report and are expected to provide an official response in 1997.

Concern continued over the problem of teen suicides on the Big Cove Reserve in New Brunswick. Between 1992 and 1994, 10 youths on the reserve committed suicide, and observers predicted that deeply rooted social problems and inadequate housing would lead to more self-inflicted deaths. On the positive side, more youths sought counseling for their problems.

The Minister for Indian Affairs announced an increase of $105 million (Can $ 140 million) in funding for on-reserve housing over the next 5 years. In July the Government announced that it will spend $74 million (Can $ 98.5 million) in 1996–97 for water and sewage repairs on reserves. Department of Indian Affairs statistics show that 95 percent of houses on reserves have running water and 90 percent have sewage facilities.

Treaty rights for aboriginals are recognized in the Canadian Constitution, and the Federal Government is currently engaged in four sets of discussions with First Nations on various treaty issues. The Federal Government is also currently involved in self-government negotiations with 350 First Nations.

An investigation was ongoing at year's end into the 1995 police killing of an aboriginal activist at Ipperwash, Ontario. Family members of the slain man filed a $5.25 million ($ Can 7 million) wrongful death suit against the Ontario Premier, two cabinet ministers, the provincial government, and the Ontario Provincial Police, but said that they will drop the suit if a full public inquiry is held. The Premier maintains that a public inquiry cannot be held during an ongoing investigation. Indians still control Ipperwash provincial park, which they claim is on a sacred burial ground. A federal negotiator was appointed in January and has held monthly negotiating meetings with all concerned parties.

In March the Nisga'a tribal council signed an historic agreement in principle with the Federal and British Columbia Governments encompassing the disposition of forestry, fishing, environmental, and water claims. The agreement also includes procedures for taxation, governance, revenue sharing, and establishment of a justice system. Negotiation of the final treaty is under way but final agreement is pending public hearings by a provincial legislative select committee. First Nation representatives believe that public support in the province for a political settlement of aboriginal claims has subsided significantly from its high water mark in the early 1990's.

Quebec's Indians continue to regard the separatist provincial government with deep misgivings. The Pontiac tribe voted to demand that their territories remain part of Canada even if Quebec declares itself independent. A group of the Ottawa with lands in Quebec are petitioning their local municipality and the Federal Government for the same kind of guarantee.

Friction was generated when Quebec police arrested the Mohawk organizers of a "charity casino" set up to fund scholarships for Mohawk children, on the grounds that the organizers did not have a provincial permit to operate a gambling establishment. When Mohawk police refused to intervene, provincial police (without entering the reservation) arrested six suspects and took them into custody outside the reservation.

The last of several court cases involving a dispute over native fishing rights in New Brunswick concluded in August. Seventeen members of the Eel Ground band who fish the northwest Miramichi River were sentenced on a variety of fishing violations and assault charges. The 17 had staged a protest in June 1995 over the terms of a fishing agreement with the Federal Government, contending that the agreement's prohibition of nets on the river violated their right to fish using traditional methods.

A Micmac native in Nova Scotia was convicted in June of illegally netting eels and selling them. Micmac and Maliseet natives contended that 18th century treaties with the British guaranteed them the right to fish and hunt commercially without licenses; the Government argued that aboriginals may fish and hunt only for sustenance and ceremonial purposes.

Religious Minorities.—In March the B'nai Brith League for Human Rights reported that anti-Semitic harassment was up by 12.1 percent over 1995. Anti-Semitic vandalism dropped slightly for the second consecutive year, but harassment increased. Total incidents in 1995 numbered 331, up from 290 last year. B'nai Brith attributed the rise in part to the spread of hate propaganda on the Internet.

In April Jewish groups in Montreal expressed concern that Quebec government measures to promote compliance with Quebec language laws requiring French labelling on goods threatened Jews' access to imported "kosher for Passover" foods. In August the Quebec government formally exempted "kosher for Passover" products from Quebec's French labelling regulations under an agreement reached between the Canadian Jewish Congress and the Quebec French language office.

National/Racial/Ethnic Minorities.—The narrow defeat of the 1995 Quebec sovereignty referendum left unresolved the concerns of French-speaking Quebeckers about their minority status in Canada, while sharpening the concerns of English-speaking Quebeckers about their minority status in Quebec.

There have been visible efforts in Quebec by Parti Quebecois (PQ) leadership to lower tensions since the referendum and refocus attention on the economy. The PQ leader has repeatedly stated that there is a role for the English-speaking community in a sovereign Quebec and has made several overtures to the Anglophone business community. An English-language publication in Quebec City, however, recently described the Anglophone community there as "depressed" and "in decline."

There was increased tension in Nova Scotia's black community following the conviction of six young black men in February for their involvement in the beating of three white students in 1995. The black youths received sentences of 7 to 10 years. The black community believed that the sentences were racially biased and excessive. One of the youths has been granted a new trial after successfully arguing that his defense attorney did not have prior access to statements made by a key witness.

A report of the Commission on Systematic Racism in the Ontario criminal justice system showed that blacks and other racial minorities are more likely to be charged and imprisoned than whites in Ontario. Commission members stated that the systematic racism they found is based largely on discretionary decisions made by law enforcement personnel and attorneys. The Commission recommended training and education to alleviate the situation; minority community leaders said that they hope for an improved dialogue between police and community members.

Section 6. Worker Rights

a. *The Right of Association.*—Except for members of the armed forces, workers in both the public and private sectors have the right to associate freely. The Labor Code protects these rights for all employees under federal jurisdiction, while provincial legislation protects all other organized workers.

Trade unions are independent of the Government. They are free to affiliate with international organizations. Of the civilian labor force, 29.2 percent is unionized.

All workers have the right to strike, except those in the public sector providing essential services.

During the first 6 months of 1996, there were 91 work stoppages, 7 of which were illegal, and 33 unresolved labor disputes. The remainder were settled through direct bargaining or mediation.

The law prohibits employer retribution against strikers and union leaders, and the Government enforces this provision.

b. *The Right to Organize and Bargain Collectively.*—Workers in both the public (except for some police) and the private sectors have the right to organize and bargain collectively. While the law protects collective bargaining, for some public sector workers providing essential services there are limitations, which vary from province to province.

The law prohibits antiunion discrimination and requires employers to reinstate workers fired for union activities. There are effective mechanisms for resolving complaints and obtaining redress.

All labor unions have full access to mediation, arbitration, and the judicial system.

There are no export processing zones.

c. *Prohibition of Forced or Compulsory Labor.*—Forced labor is illegal, and there were no known violations.

d. *Minimum Age for Employment of Children.*—Child labor legislation varies from province to province. The Federal Government does not employ youths under 17 years of age while school is in session. Most provinces prohibit those under age 15 or 16 from working without parental consent, at night, or in any hazardous employment. These prohibitions are effectively enforced through inspections conducted by the federal and provincial Labor Ministries. The statutory minimum school-leaving age in all provinces is 16.

e. *Acceptable Conditions of Work.*—Although it was common practice among most federal jurisdiction employers (who employed less than 10 percent of the work force) to use the higher provincial/territorial minimum wage rates, in 1996 the Federal Government passed legislation to align the federal rate heretofore with the provincial/territorial rates. Ontario, Alberta, and the Northwest Territories have a minimum wage for youths and students lower than their respective standard minimums. A family whose only employed member earns the minimum wage would be considered below the poverty line.

Standard work hours vary from province to province, but in all the limit is 40 or 48 a week, with at least 24 hours of rest.

Federal law provides safety and health standards for employees under federal jurisdiction, while provincial and territorial legislation provides for all other employees. Federal and provincial labor departments monitor and enforce these standards. Federal, provincial, and territorial laws protect the right of workers with "reasonable cause" to refuse dangerous work.

CROATIA

The Republic of Croatia is a constitutional parliamentary democracy with a powerful presidency. President Franjo Tudjman, elected in 1992 for a 5-year term, serves as head of state and commander of the armed forces. He chairs the influential National Defense and Security Council and appoints the Prime Minister who leads the Government. President Tudjman's party, the Croatian Democratic Union (HDZ), holds the majority of seats in both houses of Parliament and has ruled since independence in 1991. Government influence weakens the nominally independent judiciary. The enormous constitutional powers of the presidency, the overwhelming dominance of one political party, and the continuing concentration of power within the central Government tend to stifle the expression of diverse views.

The Ministry of Interior oversees the police, and the Ministry of Defense oversees the armed forces. Civilian police have no authority over military police or over uniformed military personnel. The national police have primary responsibility for internal security but, in times of disorder, the Government may call on the army to provide security. Both the police and army are responsible for external security. While civilian authorities generally maintain effective control of the professional security forces, members of the police and armed forces committed human rights abuses.

The economy is slowly changing to a market-based free enterprise system. Agriculture is mostly in private hands. Family-owned small enterprises are multiplying, but industry is still largely state-owned. Although the Government maintained a strict austerity budget, inflation began to creep upward, which eroded a standard of living already much diminished due to the civil conflict.

The Government's human rights record remained poor. It continued to commit or allow serious abuses, in particular with regard to the treatment of ethnic Serbs from the reclaimed areas (former sectors north, south, and west), most of whom fled to Serbia-Montenegro or Bosnia and Herzegovina. Military and police forces were responsible for forced evictions and also allowed Croatian refugees to evict ethnic Serbs. Ethnic Serbs were largely denied the right to return to their homes in the reclaimed areas, and the Government was slow in reestablishing adequate civil authority in these regions. Police were unwilling or unable to take effective action against criminal activity directed against ethnic Serbs. Murders, looting, and threats continued, although in lesser numbers than last year, and the Government did not make sufficient efforts to seek out, investigate, and punish those responsible for such abuses. Many cases of abuse from 1995, the victims of which were almost exclusively ethnic Serbs, also remain unresolved. Key provisions of the Law on National Minorities remained suspended during the year, and the Government sought to legalize and institutionalize the population changes resulting from its armed offensives of 1995, rather than engage in confidence-building measures that would welcome back Serb refugees. The Government infringed on press freedom and used the courts and administrative bodies to restrain or shut down newspapers, radio stations, and television programs that criticized it. The Government amended the Criminal Code, making it a crime to insult high government officials in the press. Government intimidation induced self-censorship by journalists. The judicial system is subject to executive influence and denies citizens fair trials. The Government partially limited the right of citizens to freely change their government. It used manipulation of laws, intimidation, harassment, control of the media, and economic pressure to control the political process. It occasionally harassed local human rights monitors. Societal discrimination against ethnic Serbs and other ethnic minorities and discrimination and domestic violence against women are problems.

Croatia normalized relations with neighboring Serbia-Montenegro on August 23, which paved the way for passage in September of a comprehensive general amnesty for ethnic Serbs who fought on the side of the Serb Republic of Krajina ("RSK") against Croatia during the previous 4 years. However, the Government allowed only several thousand of the approximately 180,000 Serbs who fled the Croatian military action in 1995 to return in 1996. Although precise figures vary, the office of the United Nations High Commissioner for Refugees (UNHCR) estimates that approximately 50,000 to 60,000 Croatian Serb displaced persons fled to the last remaining Serb enclave in Eastern Slavonia.

With the cessation of hostilities and signing of the Basic Agreement between the Government and the Eastern Slavonia Serbs, the United Nations established the U.N. Transitional Administration for Eastern Slavonia (UNTAES) on January 15 to supervise the peaceful reintegration of Eastern Slavonia into Croatia. A U.N.-appointed transitional administrator had complete authority over affairs of the territory, which was effectively outside of Croatian government control through the year. The region was demilitarized by mid-summer, and elections for local officials are expected to be held sometime in the first half of 1997. UNTAES established the Transitional Police Force (TPF), in which Serb and Croat police jointly patrolled the region. By year's end, however, only a small number of Croats were integrated into the force. Although this force was supervised by a U.N. civilian police contingent, there were at times questions about the TPF's equal treatment of ethnic minorities.

As a signatory of the Dayton Accords, Croatia is obliged to cooperate fully with the International Criminal Tribunal for the Former Yugoslavia by turning over to the Tribunal persons on its territory who were indicted for war crimes. Croatia's cooperation with the Tribunal was uneven. It arranged for the surrender of Gen. Tihomir Blaskic, but it has not yet turned over another indictee in Croatian custody, Zlatko Aleksovski, and reports persisted that other persons indicted by the Tribunal were living or travelling in Croatia.

RESPECT FOR HUMAN RIGHTS

Section 1. Respect for the Integrity of the Person, Including Freedom From:

a. *Political and Other Extrajudicial Killing.*—There were no reports of political or other extrajudicial killings. There were, however, several reports of ethnically motivated killings by unknown persons in the parts of Croatia reclaimed by the Government's "Operation Storm" in August 1995. The vast majority of those killed were ethnic Serbs. The murders, although far fewer in number than in 1995, continue a pattern begun in the fall of that year of ethnically motivated killings carried out to intimidate Serbs who stayed behind after Croatia reclaimed these areas and discourage those Serbs who fled from returning. The authorities have made only a few arrests in these cases and attempts to seek out, investigate, and punish those responsible for such murders have been inadequate.

For example, an elderly Serb couple was murdered on February 29 in Plitvice, in former Serb-controlled territory, and their house destroyed by arson. In August retired Serb General Milorad Miscevic was killed when a bomb exploded in the courtyard of his house near Gospic, also part of former Serb-occupied territory. The Croatian Helsinki Committee called the event "a murderous and terrorist" act. In September a married couple of mixed nationality, one Serb and one Croat, was murdered in Bukovica, and their house destroyed by arson. There have been no arrests to date in any of these cases.

Six individuals charged with the August 1995 murders of 16 elderly Serbs in Varivode and Gasici (both near Knin) in the wake of Operation Storm were acquitted in July. A seventh man, Ivica Petric, was sentenced to 6 years in prison for murdering a Serb civilian at Zrmanja village, while an eighth man, Nikola Rasic, was sentenced to 18 months in jail for armed robbery and attempted murder of a Serb woman in Ocestovo near Knin. Despite provision of information by U.N. personnel on the Grubori murders in 1995, police still have made no progress on solving the crime.

b. *Disappearance.*—There were no reports of politically motivated disappearances. As of mid-November, government figures showed 2,534 citizens still missing in cases unresolved from the 1991–92 war and the 1995 military actions. The Government estimates that about 1,250 of those people are from Vukovar, while about 500 are thought by the Government to be buried in the formerly Serb-held areas of Croatia known as the Krajina (former sectors north and south). Steady, albeit slow, progress was made throughout the year in removing names from the list of those missing as a result of identification of corpses exhumed in the Krajina region and Eastern and Western Slavonia.

Exhumations from the mass grave at Ovcara, completed by the International Criminal Tribunal for the Former Yugoslavia (ICTY) under the protection of UNTAES, unearthed the remains of 200 people who had been missing since they were taken from Vukovar hospital by rebel Serbs in November 1991. Exhumations were conducted in some 20 villages around Petrinja, and in Pridraga, Islam Grcki, Smilcic, and Novigrad. In the village of Skabrnja in southern Croatia, 27 bodies were recovered from a mass grave where 60 civilians and 20 Croatian combatants were killed in the summer of 1991.

Some progress was also made in efforts to exchange information on missing persons between Serbia-Montenegro and Croatia. On April 17 the two Governments signed a protocol on cooperation between their respective commissions on missing persons. All prisoners held by either party or in an area under their influence were to be immediately released, and all information exchanged. However, cooperation between the commissions was often stymied for political reasons. As part of the normalization of relations agreement signed by Serbia-Montenegro and Croatia on August 23, both sides agreed to resolve without delay the issue of missing persons. The International Commission on Missing Persons (ICMP) was established with the goal of raising the level of discussion between Serbia-Montenegro, Bosnia and Herzegovina, and Croatia and bringing political pressure to bear on all parties in order to increase cooperation in resolving cases of persons who were missing or had disappeared. After being registered by the Red Cross as a prisoner of war in 1992, Croatian pilot Vladimir Sumanovac disappeared in December 1993. He was "found" and released in May.

c. *Torture and other Cruel, Inhuman, or Degrading Treatment or Punishment.—* The Constitution prohibits torture or cruel or degrading punishment, and there were no reports that officials employed such practices.

Prison conditions meet minimum international standards, and the Government permits visits by human rights monitors. Jails are crowded, but not to excess, and family visits and access to counsel are generally available. Rebel Serb detainees interviewed by international monitors reported good treatment, although some asserted that they were treated less favorably than common criminals. Prisons and detainees in Eastern Slavonia were monitored under the auspices of UNTAES.

d. *Arbitrary Arrest, Detention, or Exile.—*The Constitution contains provisions to protect the legal rights of all accused persons, but the Government does not always respect these rights in practice. Two new amnesty laws offered a framework under which some progress was made in resolving cases of arbitrary arrest and detention dating back as far as 1991. The first amnesty law, passed in May, covered only the specific geographic area of Eastern Slavonia and had numerous exceptions. Despite these weaknesses, however, 282 persons were amnestied under this legislation. The second country-wide general amnesty adopted in September incorporated many UNTAES recommendations. Under this amnesty, persons charged, arrested, or convicted in connection with the armed rebellion on the territory of Croatia were to have their cases reviewed. Those in custody determined eligible for amnesty were to be freed, while those who had been charged or convicted in absentia were to have all criminal proceedings against them canceled. Only war crimes (as determined by international convention) and common crimes not connected with the armed rebellion were exempted. By October 95 persons had been released from detention facilities across the country under this second amnesty, according to government figures. Of this number, 26 were charged again for war crimes ("crimes against civilian populations"). By year's end, lawyers involved with the cases claimed that, in at least some instances, no new evidence had been provided and that the Serbs had essentially been charged with reworded versions of the same crimes for which they had been amnestied; in effect double jeopardy in their view and a contradiction of the spirit, if not the letter, of the amnesty law. Among the persons amnestied were 15 Serbs arrested in 1995 on charges of espionage, including the prominent Croatian Serb judge, Radovan Jovic.

Police normally seek arrest warrants by presenting evidence of probable cause to an investigative magistrate. Police may carry out arrests without a warrant if they believe suspects might flee, destroy evidence, or commit other crimes. Such cases are not uncommon. The police then have 24 hours in which to justify their decision before the local investigative magistrate.

After arrest, the law states that persons must be given access to an attorney of their choice within 24 hours; if they have no attorney, and are charged with a crime for which the sentence is over 10 years' imprisonment, the investigative magistrate will appoint counsel from a list of public defenders. If the potential sentence is under 10 years, detainees can request court-appointed counsel if they so choose. The court will appoint counsel after charges are levied for the trial. The investigative judge must, within 48 hours of the arrest, decide whether sufficient cause exists to hold a person in custody pending further investigation. The judge must justify the decision in writing, including the length of detention ordered, which may not be longer than 1 month without review. The review by the county court may extend the period another 2 months if necessary. The usual period of investigative detention varies from a few days to a few weeks, but the Supreme Court may grant the State an additional 3 months for a total of not more than 6 months of pretrial detention in exceptional cases. These decisions may be appealed, either immediately or later in the detention period. Once the investigation is complete, detainees are usually released on their own recognizance pending trial, unless the crime is a major offense, the accused are considered a public danger, or the court believes that they may flee.

However, those persons held under investigative detention are often denied the right to have an attorney present whenever they wish during the investigative stage and during an appeal of investigative detention. In practice detainees are almost always bound over for investigation unless it is clear that no case exists against them. There are provisions for posting bail after charges are brought, but the practice is not common. Police will sometimes retain the passports of those released pending trial to prevent them from leaving the country.

With the cessation of hostilities and the establishment of UNTAES, the situation in Eastern Slavonia improved. UNTAES established the Transitional Police Force (TPF) in July, with joint Croatian-Serb patrols and international supervision of police activity.

The Red Cross estimated that approximately 120-130 ethnic Serbs were still in detention for acts related to the conflicts in 1995.

The Constitution prohibits the exile of Croatian citizens. However, Croatian Serbs who fled during the last 5 years have found themselves effectively exiled from Croatia. The Government's inability to create secure conditions in the formerly occupied regions and its slow pace in issuing identity papers to Serbs in Eastern Slavonia and abroad have combined to leave almost 180,000 ethnic Serb former citizens of Croatia effectively without citizenship. In December, however, substantial progress was made in talks between the U.N. Transitional Administration and the Government to establish a framework for expedited issuance of Croatian documents in preparation for the March elections.

Some 30,000 non-Croats (mostly Serbs) have applied to return from Serbia-Montenegro, but to date only approximately 1,000 to 1,500 have, in fact, been able to do so. Ethnic Muslims and Serbs who are currently living in Croatia have also been denied citizenship or residency permits, regardless of their previous residence, and are subject to exclusion and even deportation from Croatia (see Section 5).

e. *Denial of Fair Public Trial.*—Government influence weakens the nominally independent judiciary.

The judicial system consists of municipal and district courts, a Constitutional Court, a Supreme Court, an Administrative Court, and a State Judicial Council. A parallel commercial court system handles all commercial and contractual disputes. The State Judicial Council (with a president and 14 members from all parts of the legal community) appoints judges and public prosecutors. The upper house of Parliament nominates persons for membership on the State Judicial Council, and the lower house elects members to 8-year terms. The 11 judges of the Constitutional Court are elected to 8-year terms in the same manner.

The Provisional Court for Human Rights called for under the 1992 Constitutional Law on Minorities was never created. The Government cited a possible clash of jurisdiction between this court and the European Court of Human Rights because of Croatia's accession in November to the Council of Europe. In November the Parliament abolished the military court system which had functioned throughout the war. However, these military courts are to continue to function until all cases under way are resolved.

Although the Constitution provides for the right to a fair trial and a variety of due process rights in both civilian and military courts, in practice the prosecuting attorney has leeway in deciding whether to bring a case against an individual. Further, in cases considered "political", both the indictment and the conduct of trials are sometimes subject to outside influence. For example, in May charges were brought against the editor and one journalist of the satirical weekly, Feral Tribune, for articles that allegedly impugned the honor and dignity of the President (see Section 2.a.). The public prosecutor initiated charges on his own authority (with the consent of the President) and, when the journalists were acquitted, appealed the acquittal.

Nor is the judicial process free of ethnic bias. Numerous cases throughout the year dealing with residency and property claims were arbitrarily decided against ethnic Serbs and Muslims, often with little or no explanation for the decision. For example, in one extended ethnic Muslim family (resident in Croatia for 19 years) which applied for Croatian citizenship, the father and two of his siblings had their requests granted; a third sibling was granted permanent residency; while the two adult children were both denied legal status and face deportation (see Section 5). Following the general amnesty in September, there were repeated credible allegations that the Government rearrested several amnestied Serbs and charged them with war crimes, despite the lack of new evidence (see Section 1.d.).

The judicial system in Eastern Slavonia was put under the control of the U.N. Transitional Administrator in the summer. Although the local Serb entity continued to function with the same personnel and systems as previously, UNTAES asserted the right to review all cases and rescind or revise judgments as necessary.

There were no reports that the Government held political prisoners. At least one Croat was still being held as a political prisoner by Serb authorities in Eastern Slavonia.

f. *Arbitrary Interference With Privacy, Family, Home, or Correspondence.*—The Constitution declares the home inviolable. Only a court may issue a search warrant, stating the justification for the search of a home or other premises. Police may enter a home without a warrant or the owner's consent only if necessary to enforce an arrest warrant, apprehend a suspect, or prevent serious danger to life or important property. In practice the authorities generally complied with these norms although there were some notable exceptions. For example, in October an ethnic Serb Member of Parliament alleged that police searched his apartment and interrogated his wife without any warrant or stated cause.

The incidence of looting in the former sectors, while lower than last year, remained substantial. International organizations such as the European Community Monitoring Mission (ECMM) noted at least several incidents per week of looting, robbery, and intimidation, particularly in the Krajina. Indigenous nongovernmental organizations (NGO's) claimed that the treatment of the small Serb populations in the Krajina region actually deteriorated with the normalization of relations between Croatia and Serbia-Montenegro in September. With the notable exception of Pakrac (former sector west), police in the formerly Serb-held areas were often ineffective in either responding to incidents or in resolving cases where the victim was an ethnic Serb. According to a report issued by the Government in June, numerous judicial proceedings have been initiated to prosecute crimes committed against the indigenous Serb population after the military actions in 1995. However, the U.N. Special Rapporteur for Human Rights pointed out that, of those cases opened, a large number were for charges such as embezzlement and endangering traffic safety. In addition, a significant number of the cases were undertaken against Serbs for rebellion or war crimes.

Military and civil police continued to carry out forced evictions, involving numerous families of all nationalities. Croatian refugees, with at least the appearance of official countenance, forcibly entered the homes of ethnic Serbs and other minorities who had lived for years in family apartments, but who were themselves not listed as the official tenant. Although such evictions were often declared illegal in court, the authorities forbade the police to remove the intruders on the basis of a law requiring that a new home be found for a displaced or refugee family before it can be removed from any form of housing, whether legally occupied or not.

Forced evictions of ethnic Serbs, Croats, and others from former Yugoslav National Army (JNA) apartments continued throughout the year. The Ministry of Defense arbitrarily revoked the tenancy rights of individuals who had lived in apartments for decades, and soldiers frequently took residences by force of arms, either evicting current tenants or forcing them to share quarters. They justified their actions on the basis of property laws that remove tenancy rights as a result of any 6-month absence or if the tenant was ruled to "have acted against the interests of the Republic of Croatia." The courts increasingly used this legislation to deny tenancy rights to former JNA members, whether they had actually participated in activities against Croatia or not. Membership in the JNA at any time was deemed sufficient to brand them as "enemies of the state." Often court action was initiated to terminate tenancy rights when the tenant sought to purchase the residence under the rules for privatization adopted in 1995. In a positive development, the Constitutional Court in November abolished Articles 70 and 94 of the Law on Housing Relations, removing the right of administrative housing councils to evict tenants and reserving that right exclusively for the courts.

The Constitution provides for the secrecy and safety of personal data, but it was unclear if such provisions were observed in practice.

Section 2. Respect for Civil Liberties, Including:

a. *Freedom of Speech and Press.*—The Constitution provides for freedom of thought and expression, specifically including freedom of the press and other media of communication, speech and public expression, and free establishment of institutions of public communication. In practice, government influence on the media through state ownership of most print and broadcast outlets limits these freedoms. Government intimidation through the courts and other means also induces self-censorship. Journalists were increasingly reluctant to criticize the Government in public forums for fear of harassment, job loss, intimidation, criminal prosecution, or being branded as disloyal. A campaign of harassment of the independent media continued throughout the year.

After much delay, Parliament passed in October a comprehensive Law on Public Information to regulate the media. This law was adopted with input from both local and international organizations and had the general support of all parties. A controversial article requiring publishers to purchase mandatory insurance in case of libel suits (the expense of which would have effectively shut down many small publications) was removed after pressure from the Council of Europe.

More problematic were the amendments to the Penal Code adopted by the Parliament in March authorizing criminal prosecution of journalists who insult the honor or dignity of the President, Supreme Court judges, or parliamentary figures and also of those who publish "state secrets." The law was used to suppress systematically several independent publications, including the satirical weekly Feral Tribune, the independent daily Novi List, and the weekly Nacional. While Feral Tribune was eventually acquitted in September of slandering the President, the state prosecutor appealed the acquittal. In addition, charges under yet another statute, brought by the ruling HDZ party are still pending against Nacional and Novi List, both charged with damaging the honor and reputation of the HDZ party.

In addition to legal action against unfriendly media coverage, the Government frequently used administrative means to control the media. Radio 101, the best known and one of last remaining independent radio stations, lost its broadcast license after a costly legal battle with administrative authorities in which the State Broadcasting Council reallocated its frequency to those more favorably inclined towards the Government. After extensive public criticism, including two mass demonstrations in Zagreb in which tens of thousands of persons took part, the new owners of the frequency declined to accept it, and the Council announced that it would reconsider the issue. Radio 101 remained on the air with a temporary license pending final resolution of the issue. Another radio station, Radio North-Northwest in Varazdin lost its frequency in September. This station was similar in style to Radio 101, but lacked the outside attention the latter received. In April the newspaper Novi List was ordered to pay a $2.5 million fine for allegedly using printing equipment imported tax and duty free for the sole use of the Italian-language press. The fine was suspended in May by the Ministry of Finance, although technically it is still outstanding against the paper. Also in April, the financial police raided the offices of the independent weekly Panorama, charging the newspaper with violations of "ecological standards." The newspaper was shut down for a month and reopened in May only after substantial international criticism. The popular television news program "Slikom na Sliku" (frame by frame) was taken off state-run television station HTV without explanation in July, soon after its coverage of the Feral Tribune trial.

Government influence over the distribution network for print media, coupled with stiff value added taxes levied at several points during the production process also has an impact on press freedom. Certain independent newspapers and magazines claim that they must pay out more than 50 percent of their gross revenues for taxes and distribution costs alone. While the high circulation of some popular independent journals such as Globus has given them enough financial independence to survive despite these high taxes and high costs, other journals would likely shut down without support from international organizations like the Soros Foundation.

Foreign papers and journals were available throughout Croatia, including Serbian periodicals which subscribers continued to receive by mail.

Both public and private radio and television broadcasting coexist, although the Government controls all national broadcasting. Opposition figures and human rights activists uniformly charge that state-owned media outlets have a strong progovernment bias. Regulations governing access to the state-owned broadcast media restrict the ability of opposition parties to criticize government policies (see Section 3). Croatian state radio-television (HRT), broadcasts on three national television channels and three national radio channels. Technically under the supervision of the Parliament, HRT is in practice run by the ruling HDZ party, and its head has a seat on the National Security Council. HRT has its headquarters in Zagreb and also has radio and television studios in the country's major provincial cities. Its regional television studios broadcast ½ hour of local news daily; its regional radio stations offer more extensive local programming. Private local television stations operate in most major Croatian cities, and private local radio stations exist throughout the country, in cities large and small. However, these local outlets largely lack their own news and public affairs programs; most repeat HRT's news, while some also rebroadcast the Voice of America and the British Broadcasting Corporation.

In the U.N.-administered region of Eastern Slavonia, the local Serb authorities control a radio and television station in the town of Beli Manastir and a radio station in the city of Vukovar. There is no private broadcasting or local press in this region. UNTAES broadcasts a daily program over the Vukovar radio station. In this area (as elsewhere in Eastern Croatia) people receive radio and television broadcasts from neighboring Serbia; Serbian publications also circulate freely in the region.

While academic freedom is generally respected, some ethnic Serb professors and intellectuals have reported increasing pressure within academia to conform with the norms and opinions of the ruling HDZ party.

b. *Freedom of Peaceful Assembly and Association.*—The Constitution provides that all citizens have the right to peaceful assembly and association for the protection of their interests or the promotion of social, economic, political, national, cultural, and other objectives, and the Government respects these provisions in practice.

There were demonstrations during the year in several major cities, often related to the desire of internally displaced persons to return to their homes or to labor disputes (see Section 6.a.). In November two peaceful mass rallies were held in support of the best known and one of the last remaining independent radio station when the State Broadcasting Council awarded its frequency to a competitor (see Section 2.a.). In the area under UNTAES control, there were a number of demonstrations. Demonstrators in Baranja and also in Vukovar expressed their interest in autonomy and other grievances.

c. *Freedom of Religion.*—The Constitution provides for freedom of conscience and religion and free public profession of religious convictions, and the Government respects these rights in practice. There is no state religion. All religious communities are free to conduct public services and to open and run social and charitable institutions. Roman Catholicism, Eastern Orthodox Christianity, and Islam are the major faiths in Croatia, and there is also a small, though active, Jewish community. The majority of Croats are Roman Catholic, and the Government provides optional Catholic religious training in schools.

There are no formal restrictions on religious groups. The main mosque is in Zagreb, where it serves not only as a religious center but also as a social aid office for the large Bosnian Muslim refugee population. Croatian Protestants from a number of denominations, as well as foreign clergy, actively practice and proselytize, as do representatives of eastern-based religions. Some foreign religious organizations seeking to provide social services reported bureaucratic obstacles to their establishment, but it was unclear if this had any connection with their religious character.

A health care center in the main mosque in Zagreb was closed by Ministry of Health officials in September. The official reason given was that all health-related activity should be conducted only under the auspices of the Ministry, although other private clinics continued to operate.

Most Catholic churches in the formerly Serb-held areas were destroyed. In Eastern Slavonia, only one active Croatian Catholic priest remains.

The Government discriminates against Muslims in the issuance of citizenship documents. The Interior Ministry frequently uses Article 26 of the Law on Citizenship to deny citizenship papers to persons otherwise qualified to be citizens (see Section 5).

d. *Freedom of Movement Within the Country, Foreign Travel, Emigration, and Repatriation.*—The Constitution generally provides for these rights, with certain restrictions. All persons legally in the country must register their residence with the local authorities. Under exceptional circumstances, the Government may legally restrict the right to enter or leave the country if necessary to protect the "legal order, health, rights or freedoms of others."

The Government cooperates with the office of the U.N. High Commissioner for Refugees (UNHCR) and other humanitarian organizations in assisting refugees. Despite the absence of domestic implementing legislation, relevant U.N. acts in the refugee field have in practice been observed. The UNHCR estimates that the Government was providing first asylum to approximately 170,000 people from various parts of the former Yugoslavia as of August, and the Government stated that it was financially supporting another 150,000 internally displaced persons. The Government has resettled some of the refugees, almost exclusively ethnic Croats, but has stated that Bosnian Croat refugees from "safe," Federation-held portions of Bosnia as well as Bosnian Muslim refugees (some 43,000) must return home and has removed their refugee status.

The Government continued to relocate refugees from coastal tourist facilities to inland areas in an effort to rehabilitate those facilities for the slowly reviving tourist trade. The Kupljensko refugee camp was officially closed in August, its inhabitants either repatriated to Bosnia, transferred to other sites in Croatia, or resettled in third countries. There was one significant incident of forced return of refugees to Bosnia and Herzegovina in February, when 46 Bosnian Muslim refugees were forcibly repatriated to the Bihac area after the Government arrested them on charges of black market activities in the Kupljensko camp.

Serbs who fled the military operations in 1995 found their right to travel freely, particularly to the former sectors, difficult and at times impossible to exercise. Incidents of intimidation and beatings by local Croats of ethnic Serbs who attempted to visit their former homes were common and frequently went uninvestigated and unpunished. The Government actively encouraged the resettlement of Bosnian Croat refugees in the Krajina, further complicating any eventual return by the former Serb residents. Although reports vary, by some estimates as many as 55,000 Croats had been housed there by November. In Eastern Slavonia, all access was strictly controlled by UNTAES, with neither Serbs nor Croats moving freely across the boundaries of the sector without U.N. approval or escort.

The process of Serb return progressed only slowly during the year. While the Government was publicly committed to the return of all persons to their homes, regardless of ethnicity, in practice it did not fulfill this commitment. Between 20,000 and 30,000 Serbs filed applications to return, based almost exclusively on the principle of family reunification, and over 12,000 of these requests had been granted by August. The UNHCR estimated that 61 percent of those applications approved were for persons over the age of 60. The United Nations Special Rapporteur for Human Rights estimated that as many as 3,000 Serbs had actually returned to Croatia, and that the majority of these had joined family members who were living outside of the former occupied areas. There were no group returns of Serbs to Croatia (see Section 3). On November 1, UNTAES opened the five villages south of the Bosut river in the U.N.-administered area to unlimited Croatian return. This affected up to 10,000 former residents of the region.

Section 3. Respect for Political Rights: The Right of Citizens to Change Their Government

The Government partially limited the right of citizens to change their government. Croatia is a multiparty democracy in which all citizens 18 years of age and older have the right to vote by secret ballot. The President, elected for 5 years, exercises substantial power, authority, and influence but is constitutionally limited to two terms. Parliament comprises the House of Representatives and the House of Counties (Zupanije). The Croatian Democratic Union holds a majority in both houses and President Franjo Tudjman was reelected in 1992. The Cabinet is a one-party (HDZ) body. According to law, presidential elections must be held in mid-summer 1997, and elections for all local governing bodies as well as the House of Counties must be held no later than the spring of 1997.

Presidential powers include approving the mayor of Zagreb, who is elected by the city assembly. Opposition parties won control of the Zagreb city assembly in fall 1995 local elections. President Tudjman had refused to confirm four mayoral candidates by year's end, and the opposition parties in late 1996 began a boycott of the city assembly in protest. In November opposition Members of Parliament staged a 30-day walkout from Parliament to protest the HDZ decision not to debate the Zagreb situation in Parliament. Neither the boycott nor the walkout proved successful, and in December the opposition city assembly members submitted their resignations. However, further splits among the opposition parties led to the increased likelihood that new elections could be held in order to resolve the issue.

The "Zagreb City Council crisis," as it came to be known, was a visible example of the ruling party's manipulation of politics. In addition to liberal interpretation and implementation of laws to suit the Government's agenda, the ruling party used intimidation and harassment, as well as control of the media and government, to control the political process. Economic pressure was one of the most effective tools, and government agencies selectively issued or denied permits for businesses based on political affiliation. In at least a dozen towns and cities where the ruling party was not in power, it allegedly managed to coopt the local leader into joining the HDZ.

The HDZ used its control of Parliament to push through legislative changes that favored it. In addition to changes in the election law made in 1995, in July additional amendments were passed, which included changing the ratio of proportionally to directly elected seats from 2/3:1/3 to 3/4:1/4. (The last local elections were held with a 50:50 ratio; 1995 changes to the law put the ratio at 2/3:1/3.) The July amendments allow a party to put someone's name on its list as its "bearer" even if that person was not a candidate on the list. Also in July, the Parliament began discussions on redistricting which, if legislation is passed, could inhibit minority parties from achieving a 5 percent threshold. Changes to the electoral law were often done in "emergency parliamentary sessions" and pushed through hastily, with little debate.

Rules for access to state-owned electronic media restricted the ability of opposition parties to criticize government policies and activities and limited their ability to fully engage the Government in an open political dialog (see Section 2.a.).

The Government maintained rigid policies throughout the year that disenfranchised the Croatian Serb population. A nationwide census scheduled for April was not held. Consequently, Articles 21 and 22 (and all other relevant articles) of the 1992 Constitutional Law on Human Rights and Freedoms, rescinded in 1995, remained suspended throughout the year. These laws had established self-governing special status districts in areas where minorities made up more than 50 percent of the population, namely, municipalities in the Knin and Glina regions. This repeal of the special districts law combined with the unwillingness of the Government to facilitate the return of Serb refugees contributed to charges that the Government sought to legalize and institutionalize the population changes resulting from the 1995 military actions in order to create a homogenous country with no significant minorities.

In preparation for elections in sector east as called for under the Basic Agreement between the Government and the Eastern Slavonia Serbs, by year's end the Government increased the pace of residency document (domovnica) issuance for Serbs, thereby enabling them to participate in the political process. Elections were agreed upon for March 16, 1997, and, in a major positive development, the Government in December dropped its long-held opposition to voting rights in Eastern Slavonia for Serb citizens from other parts of Croatia who had fled to Eastern Slavonia after the fall of the Krajina. While some modalities remained to be worked out, one of the major impediments to peaceful reintegration was thus removed.

Although there are no legal restrictions on participation by women or minorities in the political process, they are represented in only small numbers in Parliament, the executive branch, and courts. In the 206-member Parliament, 13 women hold seats; 1 is the President of the House of Counties. Election law requires representation for minorities in Parliament, with proportional representation for any minority that makes up more than 8 percent of the population. Currently no minority meets that criteria. Representation for Croatia's Serb minority is based, however, on government estimates of the number of Serbs who fled Croatia between 1991–95 and the assumption that they will not return. There were no Muslim representatives in Parliament despite that fact that the Muslim minority was the next largest after Serbs.

Section 4. Governmental Attitude Regarding International and Nongovernmental Investigation of Alleged Violations of Human Rights

Human rights groups in the capital, Zagreb, and throughout the country worked to prevent human rights abuses and brought their concerns to the attention of local and national authorities as well as to that of domestic and international media. Most of these groups focused on legal advocacy programs and social services support for the remaining people in the former Serb-held areas. A coalition of groups called the Antiwar Campaign, formed in 1991, expanded its outlook and became a nationwide network of NGO's, dealing with issues as diverse as peace education and women's and minority rights, as well as lobbying Parliament for effective and fair legislation. Throughout the year, indigenous human rights groups were highly critical of the Government's human rights record.

International organizations worked freely throughout Croatia. These organizations usually reported an adequate level of cooperation with government authorities in Zagreb although, at times, government follow-through in the field was less than adequate. UNTAES reported that government cooperation was generally good, with demilitarization of Eastern Slavonia completed in June and establishment of the transitional police force with some joint Croat/Serb patrols in the summer. However, UNTAES complained that, at times, agreements made in Zagreb with ranking officials were openly ignored by local officials. For example, orders to the Osijek police to allow passage of documented Serbs across the sector boundary were countermanded by the local chief of police. The issuance of identity papers to Serbs desiring Croatian citizenship was slow and often marred by incomplete cooperation by the various ministries involved (see Section 5). There were also isolated incidents of threats and assaults against U.N. personnel in Eastern Slavonia.

The Government, after substantial delay, signed a memorandum of understanding that established a resident presence of the Organization for Cooperation and Security in Europe (OSCE). The agreement limited OSCE offices outside Zagreb to two (Knin and Vukovar) and the overall staff to 14 (8 in Zagreb, 3 in each field office), which did not allow for extensive operations throughout the country. OSCE officials reported instances of lack of cooperation by local government officials, especially in the Knin area, where it took local representatives almost 2 months to secure an initial appointment with the mayor. The ECMM and the United Nations Special Rapporteur for Human Rights moved freely throughout the country, reporting on human rights problems.

Domestic human rights groups reported that their activity was largely ignored by the Government. Unless a case received international attention through the media or an international organization, the Government took little or no action to address the problem cited. Increasingly, local NGO's and their staff were the target of government harassment, such as "informal" interviews at the Ministry of Interior or apartment searches. In the last quarter of the year a tougher, less tolerant attitude toward foreign NGO's became evident, in particular toward the Soros Foundation whose activities included promotion of a free press. In December the Open Society (the local Soros affiliate) was charged with tax evasion, and three of its representatives were indicted for falsifying documents in relation to that charge. The Government's charges, coming soon after several hardline speeches by the President, were widely viewed as politically motivated.

The NGO's also found themselves the targets of violence. The office of the NGO Homo in Lika was attacked three times during the year. First the office was set on fire; then two staff members were beaten and a vehicle damaged, allegedly by a Bosnian Croat refugee living in the area who opposed the organization's work promoting the rights of Serbs in the area; a second fire at the office was reported in November. In December a staff member of the human rights NGO "Otvorene Oci" (Open Eyes) was beaten in her apartment in Split. All of these incidents were still under investigation, but no suspects were in custody. In yet another incident, a small explosive device was thrown into the yard of the summer home of the President of the Croatian Helsinki Committee, a vocal advocate for human rights who was often critical of government policies.

The Government pledged its cooperation with the International Criminal Tribunal for the Former Yugoslavia (ICTY) in the Hague and passed legislation to facilitate that cooperation in April. However, the President of the Tribunal noted in October that the level of cooperation had been more verbal than actual and was cause to question the Government's commitment to work with that body. By year's end, the Government had arrested only two of seven indicted Croats, only one of whom had been turned over to the Tribunal. In several instances during the year, indicted war criminals were allegedly spotted on Croatian territory, but the Government apparently took little or no serious action to arrest them. The Government in July disbanded its war crimes commission, the main avenue for the flow of information to the Tribunal in the Hague, putting in its place a government panel which had yet to take effective shape by year's end, leading to increased dissatisfaction with the Government's performance. The Government repudiated its earlier pledge not to arrest war criminals absent prior review of the charges by the ICTY (the so-called rules of the road).

Section 5. Discrimination Based on Race, Sex, Religion, Disability, Language, or Social Status

The Constitution specifies that all citizens shall enjoy all rights and freedoms, regardless of race, color, sex, language, religion, political or other opinion, national or social origin, property, birth, education, social status, or other attributes. It adds that members of all national groups and minorities shall have equal rights. With the exceptions noted below, these rights are observed in practice. The Constitution provides for special "wartime measures" but states that restrictions shall be appropriate to the nature of the danger and may not result in the inequality of citizenship with respect to race, color, sex, language, religion, or national or social origin. Under these measures, these rights have been observed in practice.

Women.—Although the Government does not collect statistics on the issue, informed observers state that violence against women, including spousal abuse, is common and that the number of incidents has increased in the last few years. One NGO estimates that abuse or harassment affect as many as 30 percent of women. Alcohol abuse is commonly cited as a contributing factor. Centers for the psychological and medical care of abused women are open in several cities, and hot lines have been established in Zagreb (24-hour), Pula, and Osijek. A number of local institutions and voluntary agencies offer social, medical, and other assistance to abused women and to those traumatized by war experiences. Family crisis associations are also active.

The law does not discriminate by gender. In practice, however, women generally hold lower paying positions in the work force. According to government figures, 75 percent of elementary teachers and 33 percent of high school teachers are women. The majority of nurses and clerical workers are female as well. While there is no one national organization devoted solely to the protection of women's rights, many small, independent groups were active in the capital and larger cities. These groups together established a national Coordination Council of Women's Organizations. A nationwide organization established during the Communist era, "Hrvatska Zena" (Croatian Woman), also sought to remake itself into a more genuine advocacy group.

Children.—The Government is strongly committed to the welfare of children. Maternity leave was increased to 3 years under the new Labor Code that went into effect on January 1. Schools provide free meals for children, day care facilities are available in most communities even for infants, and medical care for children is free. Education is compulsory up to 14 years of age.

There is no societal pattern of abuse or discrimination against children.

People With Disabilities.—No specific legislation mandates access to buildings or government services for people with disabilities; access to such facilities is often difficult. While people with disabilities face no open discriminatory measures, job opportunities generally are limited. Special education is also limited and poorly funded.

Religious Minorities.—The Muslim community suffered from discrimination, and Croatian Muslims and Bosnian refugees continue to report widespread discrimination in many areas such as citizenship (see Section 2.c.) and employment rights. Religion as a reflection of ethnicity was frequently used to identify non-Croats and as another way of singling them out for discriminatory practices.

The close identification of religion with ethnicity previously caused religious institutions to be targets of violence. The Serbian Orthodox Church in downtown Zagreb nevertheless remained open, and several other Orthodox churches and monasteries operate freely. Despite being guarded by security forces, two Orthodox churches were bombed by unknown persons: one near Zadar on August 23 and another in Dubrovnik on September 5. There were no casualties. On December 24, UNTAES reported that the Catholic church in the town of Ilok (sector east) was attacked by a Serbian mob during its Christmas services, which were attended by a group of ethnic Croats from Croatia proper.

National/Racial/Ethnic Minorities.—Constitutionally, Croatian Serbs and other minority groups enjoy the same protection as other self-identified ethnic and religious groups. Schools with a significant number of minority students often have their own special curriculum in addition to standard ones, designed to teach history, geography, art, and music to students in their native language. In practice, however, a pattern of ever-present and often open discrimination continues against ethnic Serbs in such areas as the administration of justice, employment, housing, and the free exercise of cultural rights. A plan for the development of a school curriculum for Serbs remains incomplete due to the Government's requirement that all students in Eastern Slavonia be tested in Croatian to receive credit for course work completed under the Serb curriculum. Istrian Italians complained that access to Italian-language schools was limited by a government requirement that parents designate the ethnicity of their children at birth. Serbs continue to be particularly vulnerable to attack because of government reluctance to protect their rights rigorously. Although the rate declined from previous years, attacks against property owned by Serbs continued, particularly in the areas formerly under Serb control. Serbs continued to leave Croatia, and many who had fled did not return as a result of the combination of economic discrimination and physical threats and the lack of interest shown by the Government in restoring confidence among Serbs remaining in the formerly occupied areas.

The makeup of the police force, which consists almost exclusively of ethnic Croats—some with little or no previous experience or training in police work—contributed to the problem. Police responsiveness to complaints filed by Serb residents of the former sectors was mixed; in sectors north and west, adequate at best, and in sector south, uniformly poor. The U.N. Special Rapporteur on Human Rights reported that "the principal responsibility for the continued insecurity lies with the local police, who are either unable or unwilling to take effective action against the ongoing wave of criminal activity against Croatian Serbs." The ECMM, the International Federation of the Red Cross and Red Crescent Societies, and the ICRC all confirm that police action to stop the threats, theft, and violence is inadequate, particularly in former sector south, where a "climate of fear" still prevails. On the other hand, the situation is reported to have improved markedly in the town of Pakrac, in former sector west, largely due to the efforts of the local chief of police.

Serbs and other minorities also suffered from economic discrimination. While the difficult economic situation continued to cause high unemployment for all sectors of society, the rate of Serb unemployment is much higher than that of any other ethnic group, and a disproportionate number of layoffs and firings involve ethnic Serbs. In the Krajina (former sectors north and south), for example, one NGO estimated that unemployment for Serbs was as high as 80 percent and that the few jobs that existed went to Croats rather than Serbs. There are numerous documented cases of the inability of ethnic Serbs to obtain reconstruction assistance and loans to rebuild homes damaged in the war. In a positive development, 60 ethnic Serbs were rehired by the government-owned oil refinery INA in Djelotovci, Eastern Slavonia.

The Law on Citizenship distinguishes between those with a claim to Croatian ethnicity and those without. The "Croatian people" are eligible to become citizens of Croatia even if they were not citizens of the former Socialist Republic of Croatia, as long as they submit a written statement that they consider themselves Croatian citizens. Others must satisfy more stringent requirements through naturalization in order to obtain citizenship, even if they were previously lawful residents of Croatia as citizens of the former Yugoslavia. While an application for citizenship is pending, the applicant is considered an alien and is denied rights such as social allowances, including medical care, pensions, free education, and employment in the civil service. The Government's practice of discriminating against ethnic and religious minorities, particularly Serbs and Muslims, in the issuance of citizenship papers, drew harsh criticism. Human rights organizations reported numerous documented cases in which the Interior Ministry denied citizenship papers to long-term residents of Croatia (that is, resident in Croatia long before the country declared its independence). For example, residents of several ethnic Muslim villages near Slunj (a total of some 500 people) were unable to obtain Croatian citizenship, and in some cases entire villages were rendered stateless. Human rights groups complain that the Interior Ministry frequently based its denials on Article 26 of the Law on Citizenship, which permits it to deny citizenship papers to persons otherwise qualified to be citizens of Croatia for reasons of national interest. The law does not require the reasons to be explained, and human rights organizations reported that the police continued to refuse citizenship applications without full explanation.

The situation for Serbs in sector east and for those outside the country desiring to return to their homes in Croatia was particularly difficult. At the urging of UNTAES, the Government established document centers in several cities in Eastern Slavonia to facilitate provision of identity papers to Serbs who claimed Croatian citizenship. Due to government requirements for lengthy background checks and document verification, however, these centers initially issued identity documents only slowly. UNTAES and international pressure helped to speed up the process, and, by year's end, approximately 20,000 (or 10 percent of the population of the sector) had been issued their domovnica with a further credible promise from the Government that the remaining backlog of persons desiring Croatian citizenship would be processed in time to vote in local elections scheduled for March 16, 1997.

While, overall, Roma continued to face societal discrimination and official inaction when complaints were filed, some progress was made in education and cultural awareness. In its June report to the Council of Europe, the Government noted the publication of several studies on the subject of Romani education, and the Ministry of Education established a summer school for Romani children.

Other minority groups—Slovaks, Czechs, Italians, and Hungarians—did not report significant discrimination to the same extent as the Serb community. As power became increasingly centralized in Zagreb, the Istrian region (with a large Italian minority who had traditionally enjoyed a significant amount of autonomy) became increasingly disaffected. Agreements were signed with Hungary and Italy for the mutual protection of minority populations. The return of ethnic Hungarians to Croatia was much less controversial than that of Serbs and proceeded unhindered, if somewhat slowly.

Section 6. Worker Rights

a. *The Right of Association.*—All workers are entitled to form or join unions of their own choosing without prior authorization. There is an active labor movement with three major and three minor national labor federations and independent associations of both blue- and white-collar members. More than 80 percent of workers are members of unions of one sort or another. In general, unions are independent of the Government and political parties. The law prohibits retaliation against strikers participating in legal strikes. Workers may only strike at the end of a contract or in specific circumstances mentioned in the contract. Most importantly, they cannot strike for nonpayment of wages, currently a serious problem. The only recourse in the event of nonpayment is to go to court, a process that may take several years. If a strike is found to be illegal, any participant can be dismissed, and the union held liable for damages.

When negotiating a new contract, workers are required to go through mediation before they can strike. Labor and management choose the mediator together. If they cannot agree, the Labor Law which went into effect on January 1 calls for a tripartite commission of labor, business, and government representatives to appoint one. Arbitration is never mandatory, but can be used if both sides agree. Only after submitting to mediation and formally filing a statement that negotiations are at an impasse is a strike legal.

The right to strike is provided for in the Constitution with the above-mentioned limitations and with additional limits on the members of the armed forces, police, government administration, and public services. Even though salaries are very low relative to the cost of living, and wage increases have been minimal, there is little strike activity. The stringent requirements for calling a strike, the high rate of unemployment, and the Government's insistence on adhering to its austerity program of October 1993 all discourage strikes. However, despite these deterrents, there were several labor disputes, including some successful strikes and protests, of varying severity, during the year as the quest for a living wage clashed with government austerity measures.

Transportation workers, seeking a 100 percent wage increase, went on strike in February. Despite a demonstration of support by approximately 6,000 members of one of the largest trade unions in the capital, a general strike did not materialize. After 7 days, workers settled for a 19.75 percent increase. However, railway workers again went on strike for 2 weeks late in the year. When this strike was deemed illegal by the courts, the workers duly reported back to work, only to announce their intention to strike again when the proper procedures had been observed. This second strike lasted only several days before a compromise wage package was agreed upon.

A general strike planned for November 11 over labor-government negotiations on tax policy was called off when the talks began to make progress. In October shipbuilding workers struck in Karlovac over low wages and high unemployment.

Unions may freely affiliate internationally.

b. *The Right to Organize and Bargain Collectively.*—Collective bargaining is protected by law and practiced freely. The new Labor Code governs collective bargaining contracts, protection for striking workers, and legal limitations on the ability of employers to conduct "lockouts" during labor disputes. The process of "transforming" previously "socially owned" enterprises continues, albeit slowly, as the first step towards their eventual privatization. The current transition to private enterprise and a free market economy has put unions under pressure at the same time that they are trying to establish themselves as genuine trade unions. General unemployment is the most significant hurdle. Unions and foreign observers claim that unemployment was 22 percent throughout the year, and would be much higher except it did not include workers on "waiting lists"—employees at government-owned firms on partial pay but not working. International organizations working in the Krajina (former sectors north and south) estimated unemployment in these areas was 80 percent.

The Labor Code deals directly with antiunion discrimination issues. It allows unions to challenge firings in court and eliminated provisions under which illness had been a valid reason for employers to fire workers. However, the Government often employs coercion against employees, including government employees, involved in labor disputes and strikes to force them back to work. But no instances of severe coercion, such as physical attacks or destruction of workers' property, were reported.

There are no export processing zones.

c. *Prohibition of Forced or Compulsory Labor.*—Forced or compulsory labor is constitutionally forbidden, and there were no documented instances of it. The Ministry of Labor and Social Welfare is the agency charged with enforcing the ban on coerced or forced labor.

d. *Minimum Age for Employment of Children.*—The minimum age for youth employment is 15 years old, and it is enforced by the Ministry of Labor and Social Welfare. Under the Constitution, children may not be employed before reaching the legally determined age, nor may they be forced or allowed to do work that is harmful to their health or morality. Workers under the age of 18 are entitled to special protection at work and are prohibited from heavy manual labor. Education is mandatory to the age of 14.

e. *Acceptable Conditions of Work.*—There are national minimum wage standards. As of October, the minimum gross monthly wage was approximately $150 (800 kuna), which does not provide a decent standard of living for a worker and family. Government policy toward its employees is a major factor in setting wage standards. There is a large public sector, and the Government manages, through the privatization fund, employees of companies waiting to be privatized.

In January the Government announced a zero percent wage increase policy for all state employees as part of its austerity program. The policy was enforced only sporadically, however, and the Government signed a contract granting public sector employees a 5 percent raise effective July 1. (Public service wages are very low, and therefore public service unions have been very aggressive.) The Government then failed to pay the increase, claiming that the contract was not binding. Both sides initially agreed to mediation, but in the end rejected the compromise decision. The matter was finally resolved in November, when another less remunerative agreement was reached after collective bargaining.

National regulations provide for a 42-hour workweek with a ½-hour daily break, a 24-hour rest period during the week, and a minimum of 18 days of paid vacation annually. Workers receive time-and-a-half pay for any hours worked over 42.

Health and safety standards are set by the Government and are enforced by the Ministry of Health. In practice, industries are not diligent in meeting standards for worker protection—a visit to any construction site reveals workers without hard hats and equipment with safety devices removed. Workers can in theory remove themselves from hazardous conditions of work. A worker would have redress to the courts in a situation where he felt that he had been wrongfully dismissed for doing so.

CYPRUS

Cyprus has been divided since the Turkish military intervention of 1974, following a coup d'etat directed from Greece. Since 1974 the southern part of the country has been under the control of the Government of the Republic of Cyprus. The northern part is ruled by a Turkish Cypriot administration. In 1983 that administration proclaimed itself the "Turkish Republic of Northern Cyprus" ("TRNC"), which is recognized only by Turkey. The two parts are separated by a buffer zone patrolled by the United Nations Force in Cyprus (UNFICYP). A substantial number of Turkish troops remains on the island. In both the government-controlled areas and in the Turkish Cypriot community there is a generally strong regard for democratic principles. Glafcos Clerides was elected President of the Republic of Cyprus in 1993; in April 1995, Turkish Cypriots reelected Rauf Denktash as their leader.

Police in the government-controlled areas and in the Turkish Cypriot community are responsible for law enforcement. Police forces operating in the government-controlled areas are under civilian control, while Turkish Cypriot police forces are directed by military authorities. In general the police forces of both sides respect the rule of law, but instances of police abuse of power continued.

Both Cypriot economies operate on the basis of free market principles, although in each community there are significant administrative controls. The government-controlled part of the island has a robust, service-oriented economy, with a declining manufacturing base and a small agricultural sector. Tourism and trade generate 22 percent of gross domestic product and employ 26 percent of the labor force. In 1995 per capita income was approximately $12,500, inflation was 2.6 percent, and unemployment was 2.6 percent. Growth in 1995 was 5 percent. The Turkish Cypriot economy, which relies heavily on subsidies from Turkey, is burdened by an overly large public sector. It, too, is basically service-oriented but has a relatively smaller tourism base and a larger agricultural sector. In 1995 per capita income in the north was approximately $3,300, and inflation was 72 percent (down from 212 percent in 1994). The economy in the north grew 2.7 percent in 1995.

The Republic of Cyprus and the Turkish Cypriot authorities generally respect human rights norms and practices. However, deadly intercommunal violence flared in 1996. In August Turkish Cypriot police killed two Greek Cypriot demonstrators. In September unknown assailants shot and killed a Turkish Cypriot soldier. In October Turkish Cypriot security forces, who again used unwarranted deadly force, shot and killed a Greek Cypriot civilian.

In July a prominent Turkish Cypriot journalist was murdered in what was apparently a politically motivated killing. Police brutality continued to be a problem; discrimination and violence against women also remained problems. Although the Turkish Cypriot authorities again took some positive steps to improve the conditions of Greek Cypriots and Maronites living in the territory under their control, the treatment of these groups still falls short of Turkish Cypriot obligations under the Vienna III agreement of 1975. The Turkish Cypriot authorities continued to impose significant restrictions on meetings between members of the two communities outside of the United Nations-controlled buffer zone. Although they had earlier permitted most meetings inside the buffer zone, in October Turkish Cypriot authorities began denying permission for virtually all meetings. They said that they were acting in response to an effort by a Greek Cypriot parliamentarian to discourage tourists from entering the north. Greek Cypriot women are still denied the right to pass citizenship to their children if they are married to foreign spouses.

RESPECT FOR HUMAN RIGHTS

Section 1. Respect for the Integrity of the Person, Including Freedom From:

a. *Political and Other Extrajudicial Killing.*—A prominent, leftist Turkish Cypriot journalist, Kutlu Adali, was murdered outside of his home in Nicosia on July 6 (see Section 2.a.). Police reportedly prevented Adali's family from entering their apartment for nearly a day following his murder, saying that they were searching for evidence. Turkish Cypriot authorities have not, however, so far conducted a credible investigation into Adali's murder.

In August Turkish Cypriot civilian police shot and killed one Greek Cypriot demonstrator and participated in the beating death of another Greek Cypriot protester. During demonstrations on August 11, Greek Cypriot demonstrators throwing rocks entered the buffer zone after Greek Cypriot civil authorities allowed them unimpeded access. Turkish Cypriot authorities also allowed a group of Turkish Cypriot civilians into the buffer zone and may have even facilitated their entry through a restricted military area. One Greek Cypriot demonstrator was caught by a group of Turkish Cypriots, including three uniformed policemen, and clubbed to death. On August 14, following the funeral of the first victim, Greek Cypriot demonstrators again entered the buffer zone after government authorities once more failed to block their entry. A Greek Cypriot civilian was killed by shots fired by members of the Turkish Cypriot police force, who used lethal force disproportionate to any threat posed by the demonstrators. The Government of Cyprus stated that it will press for legal action against the killers and issued arrest warrants for those it believes are responsible for the murders.

In September unknown assailants shot and killed a Turkish Cypriot soldier manning an observation post.

In October Turkish Cypriot forces, again using unnecessary deadly force, killed a Greek Cypriot civilian who crossed the cease-fire line into the area controlled by the Turkish Cypriots.

b. *Disappearance.*—There were no reports of politically motivated disappearances.

c. *Torture and Other Cruel, Inhuman, or Degrading Treatment or Punishment.*—Both the Constitution of the Republic of Cyprus and the basic law governing the Turkish Cypriot community specifically prohibit torture. The law in both communities provides for freedom from cruel, inhuman, or degrading treatment or punishment. Respect is generally accorded to these prohibitions throughout the island.

In January the Government fired five Limassol police officers, including the chief of police and a senior officer, in connection with revelations that came to light last year that they had used torture to force confessions from suspects. The Government had originally planned to fire 12 officers but dropped its cases against 7 of them claiming a lack of evidence.

Also in January, the Government stated that some Greek Cypriot police were involved in murder, narcotics, gambling, and prostitution. The accusations were made in connection with the resignation of the assistant chief of police, Costas Papacostas. The Government has taken no further action on these allegations, however.

The Republic's ombudsman issued a report confirming that police used torture against a suspected Turkish Cypriot drug smuggler, Erkan Egmez. Egmez was arrested in October 1995 and tortured while in police custody. No official action has been taken against any of the police involved.

In July the European Commission of Human Rights decided that the rights of Lefteris Andronicou and Elsi Constantinou had been violated by the Cyprus Government during a botched hostage rescue attempt in 1993. Both persons died in the attempt, which took place in the village of Chlorakas. The European Commission of Human Rights referred the case to the European Court of Human Rights. The Government announced that it would comply with the verdict of the court.

Parliament again failed to pass a proposed bill addressing police brutality; the bill was reintroduced in the fall.

While there were no public allegations of police brutality in the Turkish Cypriot community, there are credible reports of pervasive police abuse of power and harsh treatment of detainees.

Prison conditions are generally adequate in both communities. In August eight inmates were injured during a prison brawl in Larnaca between Greek Cypriot and Iraqi inmates. A Council of Europe delegation visited Greek Cypriot jails in May but, in accordance with the Council's policies, no report was made public.

d. *Arbitrary Arrest, Detention, or Exile.*—Throughout Cyprus laws providing for freedom from arbitrary arrest and detention are respected by the police. Judicially issued arrest warrants are required. No one may be detained for more than 1 day without referral of the case to the courts for extension of the period of detention. Most periods of investigative detention do not exceed 8 to 10 days before formal charges are filed. Attorneys generally have access to detainees, and bail is permitted.

Some abuses of power occur at the hands of the Turkish Cypriot police, generally at the time of arrest. Suspects often are not permitted to have their lawyers present when testimony is being taken, a right guaranteed under the Turkish Cypriot Basic Law. Suspects demanding the presence of a lawyer are routinely threatened with stiffer charges or even physically intimidated. A high percentage of convictions in the Turkish Cypriot community are obtained with confessions made during initial police interrogation under these conditions. There are also credible reports that police routinely abuse their right to hold persons up to 24 hours before having to go before a judge. Police officers use this tactic against persons believed to have behaved in a manner deemed insulting to the officer. The suspects are them released within 24 hours without charges having been filed.

Exile is specifically prohibited by the Constitution and by the basic law governing the Turkish Cypriot community.

e. *Denial of Fair Public Trial.*—The judiciary is legally independent of executive or military influence in both communities. Cyprus inherited many elements of its legal system from the United Kingdom legal tradition, including the presumption of innocence, the right to due process, and the right of appeal. Throughout Cyprus a fair public trial is provided for in law and accorded in practice. Defendants have the right to be present at their trials, to be represented by counsel (at government expense for those who cannot afford one), to confront witnesses, and to present evidence in their own defense. There are no special courts to try security or political offenses. On the Turkish Cypriot side, civilians deemed to have violated military zones are subject to trial in a military court. These courts consist of one military and two civilian judges and a civilian prosecutor. Members of the Turkish Cypriot bar have complained that civilian judges tend to defer to their military colleagues in such hearings.

There were no reports of political prisoners.

f. *Arbitrary Interference With Privacy, Family, Home, or Correspondence.*—Both the Cyprus Constitution and the basic law governing the Turkish Cypriot community include provisions protecting the individual against arbitrary interference by the authorities. A judicial warrant is required for a police official to enter a private residence. Turkish Cypriot police reportedly prevented the family of a murdered Turkish Cypriot journalist, Kutlu Adali, from entering his home for nearly a day, claiming that they were searching for evidence (see Section 1.a.).

Section 2. Respect for Civil Liberties, Including:

a. *Freedom of Speech and Press.*—Freedom of speech and the press are provided for by law and are freely practiced throughout the island. The proliferation of party and independent newspapers and periodicals in both communities enables ideas and arguments to circulate freely. Opposition papers frequently criticize the authorities. Several private television and radio stations in the Greek Cypriot community compete effectively with the government-controlled stations. Turkish Cypriot authorities retain a monopoly over local radio and television, but a new, private radio station is operating in addition to two smaller, university-run stations. International broadcasts are available without interference throughout the island, including telecasts from Turkey and Greece.

In July journalist Kutlu Adali was killed (see Section 1.a.). Adali had written articles critical of Turkey's role in the north and particularly of the role of the Turkish military and of policies that allowed large numbers of Turkish workers into the north. Following Adali's murder, some Turkish Cypriot journalists have complained about surveillance and intimidation. Turkish Cypriot authorities have not responded adequately to such allegations.

Academic freedom is accorded wide respect throughout the island.

b. *Freedom of Peaceful Assembly and Association.*—The freedom to associate, organize, and hold meetings is protected by law and respected in practice.

c. *Freedom of Religion.*—Freedom of religion is respected in Cyprus. Although missionaries have the legal right to proselytize in both communities, missionary activities are closely monitored by the Greek Cypriot Orthodox Church and by both Greek Cypriot and Turkish Cypriot authorities. Turkish Cypriots residing in the southern part of the island and non-Muslims in the north are allowed to practice their religion. Restrictions on the right of Greek Cypriots resident in the north to visit Apostolos Andreas monastery have been eased. These Greek Cypriots may now visit the monastery every Sunday and on religious holidays. An application to replace a retiring priest is still pending.

d. *Freedom of Movement Within the Country, Foreign Travel, Emigration, and Repatriation.*—Turkish Cypriots and Greek Cypriots enjoy freedom of movement within their respective areas. For most of the year, the Turkish Cypriot authorities generally approved applications for bicommunal meetings in the U.N.-controlled buffer zone. In October, however, they began to deny all applications for such meetings, citing the activities of a Greek Cypriot Member of Parliament. The Parliamentarian attempted to discourage tourists from crossing the buffer zone into the north. His associates struck at least one tourist and pounded on the cars of diplomats and others as they attempted to cross the zone. Turkish Cypriots who apply for permission to visit the south are required to justify their applications with formal invitations to events arranged by individuals or organizations resident in the Greek Cypriot community. Many of these applications are denied, often without an official reason, although the basis for most denials is clearly political and related to the state of intercommunal relations.

Turkish Cypriot authorities usually grant the applications of Greek Cypriot residents in the north to visit the government-controlled area. The limit on visits to the south is 15 days per month. The applicants must return within the designated period or risk losing their right to return and their property, although this rule is rarely enforced in practice. Turkish Cypriot authorities also permit close family relatives of Greek Cypriots resident in the north to visit twice per month (it was once per month until July) and allow one overnight stay per month. As in the past, Turkish Cypriot authorities permit school holiday visits by children under the ages of 16 (male) and 18 (female) residing in the government-controlled area. Turkish Cypriot authorities apply generally similar but slightly looser restrictions to visits by Maronite residents of the north to the government-controlled area and visits by Maronites living in the south to Maronite villages in the north.

Previously, persons of Greek Cypriot or Armenian origin, or even persons having Greek or Armenian names, faced considerable difficulties entering the north. In 1995 the Turkish Cypriot authorities instituted a new policy under which third country nationals of Greek Cypriot origin would be permitted to visit the Turkish Cypriot-controlled areas. However, implementation of the procedures remains inconsistent, and several persons entitled to cross under the new guidelines were denied permission without apparent cause.

The Turkish Cypriot authorities since 1995 no longer require Greek Cypriots resident in the north to obtain police permits for travel to Famagusta or Nicosia. However, members of the Maronite community living in the north continued to need permits even to visit neighboring villages and are generally denied permission to visit areas in the north other than Morphou and Nicosia.

Republic of Cyprus authorities permit only day travel by tourists to the northern part of the island. They have declared that it is illegal to enter Cyprus except at authorized entry points in the south, effectively barring entry into the government-controlled area by foreigners who have entered Cyprus from the north. Following the March 1994 murder of the director of a Greek Cypriot association supporting Kurds in Turkey, the authorities placed significantly tighter controls on the movement of Turkish Cypriots to the areas under their control. Institutions and individuals sponsoring visits of Turkish Cypriots to the government-controlled areas must notify the police in advance and provide them with an exact itinerary.

The European Court of Human Rights ruled in an 11 to 6 vote in December that Turkey had committed a continuing violation of the rights of a Greek Cypriot woman by preventing her from going to her property located in north Cyprus. The ruling reaffirmed the validity of property deeds issued prior to 1974. The Court also found in this case that "It was obvious from the large number of troops engaged in active duties in northern Cyprus that the Turkish Army exercised effective overall control there. In the circumstances of the case, this entailed Turkey's responsibility for the policies and actions of the 'TRNC.'" Under the Council of Europe, each side has 6 months to make submissions regarding compensation.

In a similar development, the European Commission of Human Rights ruled that a complaint by the Government of Cyprus against Turkey was admissible. The case alleged that Turkey was responsible for the detention of persons missing since the 1974 conflict and for depriving Greek Cypriots from the northern part of Cyprus of the use of their lands. The Commission's procedural ruling made no judgment on the merits of the case.

The authorities respect the right to travel abroad and to emigrate. Turkish Cypriots have difficulty traveling to most countries because travel documents issued by the "Turkish Republic of Northern Cyprus" are recognized only by Turkey. Most Turkish Cypriots resort to utilizing Turkish travel documents instead.

Despite the absence of legislation, the Government of Cyprus regularly grants de facto first asylum. Cases are referred to the local office of the U.N. High Commissioner for Refugees for evaluation. There were approximately 60 such cases in 1996. If applicants are found to meet the criteria for refugee status, they are permitted to remain and are given temporary work permits. Applicants are not, however, generally granted permanent resettlement rights on the grounds that the Government already has enough responsibilities in caring for those displaced after the 1974 Turkish intervention. But they are permitted to remain until resettlement in a third country can be arranged. There were no reports of forced return of persons to a country where they fear persecution.

Section 3. Respect for Political Rights: The Right of Citizens to Change Their Government

Multiparty political systems exist throughout Cyprus. Under the Republic's Constitution, political parties compete for popular support actively and without restriction. Suffrage is universal, and elections are held by secret ballot. Elections for the office of president are held every 5 years and for members of the House of Representatives every 5 years or less. The small Maronite, Armenian, and Latin communities elect nonvoting representatives from their respective communities, in addition to voting in elections for voting members. However, under the terms of the 1960 Constitution, Turkish Cypriots may only vote for the position of the Vice President and for Turkish Cypriot Members of Parliament. As a result, Turkish Cypriots living in the government-controlled area may not vote.

The Turkish Cypriots elect a leader and a representative body every 5 years or less. In April 1995, Turkish Cypriot voters elected Rauf Denktash in elections deemed by observers to be free and fair. Greek Cypriots and Maronites living in the north are barred by law from participating in Turkish Cypriot elections. They are eligible to vote in Greek Cypriot elections but must travel to the south to exercise that right. They may also choose their own village officials, but those elected are not recognized by the Government of Cyprus.

In both communities, women face no legal obstacles to participating in the political process. While clearly underrepresented in government, they hold some cabinet-level and other senior positions.

Section 4. Governmental Attitude Regarding International and Nongovernmental Investigation of Alleged Violations of Human Rights

There are organizations in both parts of the island that consider themselves human rights groups, but they are generally concerned with alleged violations of the rights of their community's members by the other community. Groups with a broad human rights mission include organizations promoting awareness of domestic violence and others concerned with alleged police brutality.

There are no restrictions preventing the formation of human rights groups. Representatives of international human rights organizations have access throughout the island.

The United Nations, through the autonomous tripartite (United Nations, Greek Cypriot, Turkish Cypriot) committee on missing persons in Cyprus (CMP), is engaged in resolving the missing persons dilemma that remained from the intercommunal violence beginning in 1963–64 and the 1974 Turkish military intervention. The U.N. Secretary General has made continued support for the CMP contingent on evidence of a new spirit of cooperation between the Cypriot sides. In March Turkish Cypriot leader Denktash told an interviewer that some of the Greek Cypriots listed as missing since 1974 were killed by Turkish Cypriot irregulars after having been captured by the Turkish army. In August Amnesty International alleged that the rules governing the CMP were inconsistent with relevant U.N. instruments, particularly the U.N. Declaration on the Protection of all Persons from Enforced Disappearance and recommend that the CMP be replaced by a U.N. commission of inquiry. In response the U.N. clarified publicly that the CMP was not an organ of the United Nations, and the Government of Cyprus stated that there was no plan to replace the CMP. Also during the year, a U.S. team continued efforts to ascertain the fate of five American citizens of Greek Cypriot origin who disappeared in the 1974 conflict.

Section 5. Discrimination Based on Race, Sex, Religion, Disability, Language, or Social Status

Legislation in both communities provides for protection against discrimination based on sex, religion, or national, racial, or ethnic origin. While such laws are generally respected by each community, significant problems remain with the treatment of the Greek Cypriots and Maronites living in the north and, to a lesser extent, with the treatment of Turkish Cypriots living in the government-controlled area.

Women.—There are reports of spousal abuse in the Greek Cypriot community, and the problem is believed to be significant. A 1994 law aimed at making spousal abuse easier to report and prosecute has had little effect because key provisions remain unfunded and unimplemented. Many suspected cases of domestic violence do not reach the courts, largely because of family pressure and the wife's economic dependence on her husband. An organization formed to address the domestic abuse problem reports an increasing number of calls over its hot line, although definitive statistics on the number of incidents are not available. Very few cases tried in the courts result in convictions. There is little public discussion of domestic violence in the Turkish Cypriot community, although a report issued by the Women's Research Center described such violence as common. A women's shelter opened in 1994. Domestic violence cases are rare in the Turkish Cypriot legal system as they are often considered a "family matter."

Throughout Cyprus women generally have the same legal status as men. However, under Turkish Cypriot law, the man is legally considered to be the head of the family and can decide on the family's place of residence and insist that his wife take his name. Turkish Cypriot women are not permitted to marry non-Moslem men. While legal provisions in both communities requiring equal pay for men and women performing the same job are effectively enforced at the white collar level, Turkish Cypriot women employed in the agricultural and textile sectors routinely are paid less than their male counterparts.

In the Greek Cypriot community, women face discrimination that denies them the ability to pass on citizenship to their children if they marry foreign spouses. Under existing law, only a Greek Cypriot male may transmit citizenship to his children automatically or obtain expeditious naturalization for his foreign spouse.

In the Turkish Cypriot community, women face discrimination in divorce proceedings with regard to property acquired during the marriage. Divorced women also face a pervasive problem of inadequate awards of child support or nonpayment of child support. Legal remedies are difficult to obtain or enforce.

Republic of Cyprus law forbids forced prostitution. However, there continue to be allegations that women, generally East Asian or Eastern European night club performers, are forced into prostitution in the Greek Cypriot community. To date there have been few arrests since the women, fearing retaliation by their employers, generally do not press charges. However, at least one trial was in progress by year's end. In the Turkish Cypriot community, there are an estimated 300 to 350 women—mostly from Eastern Europe—working as prostitutes. These women often must surrender their passports to the club owners and are sometimes prohibited even from making private phone calls.

Reports on the mistreatment of maids are frequent in the Greek Cypriot press. These reports usually involve allegations that maids, often from East or South Asia, have been forced to work under inhuman circumstances. While these women generally receive fair treatment when their cases come before the courts, many women do not file charges, fearing retribution from their employers.

Children.—Both the Government and the Turkish Cypriot authorities demonstrate a strong commitment to children's welfare. There is no pattern of societal abuse of children nor any difference in the health care and educational opportunities available to boys and girls.

People With Disabilities.—In the Greek Cypriot community, disabled persons applying for a public sector position are entitled to preference if they are deemed able to perform the required duties and their qualifications equal those of other applicants. In the Turkish Cypriot community, regulations require businesses to employ 1 disabled person for every 25 positions they fill, although enforcement is ineffective. Disabled persons do not appear to be discriminated against in education and the provision of state services. Legislation also mandates that new public buildings and tourist facilities provide access for the disabled. The Turkish Cypriot community has not yet enacted legislation to provide for such access.

In August the University of Cyprus announced acceptance of its first legally blind student.

National/Racial/Ethnic Minorities.—Both the Government of Cyprus and the Turkish Cypriot administration have constitutional or legal bars against discrimination. The basic agreement covering treatment of Greek Cypriots and Maronites living in the north and Turkish Cypriots living in the south remains the Vienna III agreement signed in 1975. This document provides for voluntary transfer of populations, free and unhindered access by UNFICYP to Greek Cypriots and Maronites living in the north and Turkish Cypriots living in the south, and facilities for education, medical care, and religious worship. UNFICYP access to Greek Cypriots and Maronites living in the north remains limited. There are no Greek-language educational facilities for Greek Cypriot or Maronite children in the north beyond elementary education, forcing parents in many instances to choose between keeping their children with them or sending them to the south for further education (in which case they may no longer return permanently to the north). Despite recent improvements, Greek Cypriots and Maronites living in the north are unable to move about freely (see Section 2.d.) or to change their housing at will. Maronites living in the north also face a pervasive system of petty restrictions on their right of movement and generally lack public services available in most other Turkish Cypriot areas.

In February the rapporteur of the Council of Europe's Parliamentary Assembly visited Greek Cypriots living in the north. The rapporteur, the late Lord Finsberg, stated that he was "shocked" by the conditions he found among these Greek Cypriots. In May a Dutch member of the same organization also demanded substantial improvements in the living conditions of Greek Cypriots and Maronites living in the north. Some Turkish Cypriots living in the government-controlled area face difficulties in obtaining identification cards and other government documents, especially if they were born after 1974. Turkish Cypriots also appear to be subjected to harassment and surveillance by the Greek Cypriot police. A number of Turkish Cypriots who work in the government-controlled area but do not live there, along with their employers, received anonymous threats following the killing of two Greek Cypriots in August (see Section 1.a.). As a result, many of these Turkish Cypriots did not report to work and were dismissed. The Cyprus Government, which stated that it could not guarantee the safety of the Turkish Cypriot workers, undertook to provide unemployment benefits to those living in the mixed Greek Cypriot-Turkish Cypriot village of Pyla, located in the U.N.-patrolled buffer zone.

Section 6. Worker Rights

a. *The Right of Association.*—All workers, except for members of the police and military forces, have the legal right to form and join trade unions of their own choosing without prior authorization. In the government-controlled area, police officers also have the right to join associations that have the right to bargain collectively, although not to strike. More than 82 percent of the Greek Cypriot work force belong to independent trade unions. Approximately 50 to 60 percent of Turkish Cypriot private sector workers and all public sector workers belong to labor unions.

In the Turkish Cypriot community, union officials have alleged that various firms have been successful in establishing "company" organizations and then applying pressure on workers to join these unions. Officials of independent labor unions have also accused the Turkish Cypriot authorities of creating rival public sector unions to weaken the independent unions. The International Labor Organization (ILO) has not yet acted on these complaints. There are no complaints outstanding against the Government of Cyprus.

In both communities, trade unions freely and regularly take stands on public policy issues affecting workers and maintain their independence from the authorities. Two of the major trade unions, one in each community, are closely affiliated with political parties. Both of the remaining major unions are independent.

All workers have the right to strike, and several strikes, usually of short duration, occurred. In the northern part of the island, however, a court ruling from 1978 gives employers an unrestricted right to hire replacement workers in the event of a strike, thereby limiting the effectiveness of the right to strike. Authorities of both the Greek Cypriot and Turkish Cypriot communities have the power to curtail strikes in what they deem to be "essential services," although this right is rarely used.

Unions in both parts of Cyprus are able to affiliate with international trade union organizations.

b. *The Right to Organize and Bargain Collectively.*—Trade unions and confederations by law are free to organize and bargain collectively throughout Cyprus. This right is observed in practice in the government-controlled areas, and most wages and benefits are set by freely negotiated collective agreements. However, Greek Cypriot collective bargaining agreements are not enforceable under the law. In the rare instances when such agreements are believed to have been infringed, the Ministry of Labor is called in to investigate the claim. If the Ministry is unable to resolve the dispute, the union may call a strike to support its demands. In practice, however, such alleged violations are extremely rare; there were no reported instances in 1996.

In the Turkish Cypriot community, where inflation exceeded 70 percent over the year, wage levels are reviewed twice a year for the private sector and six times a year for public sector workers, and a corresponding cost-of-living raise is established. A special commission composed of five representatives each from organized labor, employers, and the authorities conducts the review. Union leaders contend that private sector employers are able to discourage union activity because enforcement of labor and occupational safety regulations is sporadic and penalties for antiunion practices are minimal. As in the Greek Cypriot community, parties to a dispute may request mediation by the authorities.

Small export processing zones exist in Larnaca Port and Famagusta, but the laws governing working conditions and actual practice are the same as those outside the zones.

c. *Prohibition of Forced or Compulsory Labor.*—Forced or compulsory labor is prohibited by law, and this prohibition is generally observed.

d. *Minimum Age for Employment of Children.*—In both the Greek Cypriot and Turkish Cypriot communities, the minimum age for employment of children in an "industrial undertaking" is 16 years of age. Turkish Cypriots may be employed in apprentice positions at the age of 15. There are labor inspectors in both communities. However, in family-run shops it is common to see younger children working, and according to press reports in August, children as young as 11 or 12 years of age were working in factories during their school holidays in the Turkish Cypriot community.

e. *Acceptable Conditions of Work.*—The legislated minimum wage in the Greek Cypriot community, which is reviewed every year, is approximately $484 (225 Cyprus pounds) per month for shop assistants, practical nurses, clerks, hairdressers, and nursery assistants. This amount is insufficient to provide an adequate living for a worker and family. All other occupations are covered under collective bargaining agreements between trade unions and employers within the same economic sector, and the wages set in these agreements are significantly higher than the legislated minimum wage. The legislated minimum wage in the Turkish Cypriot area, while subject to frequent review because of high inflation, is approximately $150 (14.8 million Turkish lira) per month as of mid-1996. This amount is not adequate to support a worker and family. Unskilled workers typically earn about $267 (26.4 million Turkish lira) per month, which is barely adequate to support a family.

A significant percentage of the labor force in the north consists of illegal workers, mostly from Turkey. According to some estimates, illegal workers constitute as much as 25 percent of the total work force there. There are frequent allegations that such workers are subject to mistreatment, including nonpayment of wages and threats of deportation.

In the Greek Cypriot community, the standard workweek is an average of 39 hours in the private sector. In the public sector, it is 37½ hours during the winter and 35 hours in the summer. In 1992, however, Greek Cypriot unions won concessions that reduce the workweek for most blue collar workers by one-half hour per year until 1997 when a 38-hour workweek will be in place for most sectors of the economy. In the Turkish Cypriot community, the standard workweek is 38 hours in winter and 36 hours in summer. Labor inspectors effectively enforce these laws.

Greek Cypriot labor union leaders have complained that occupational and safety standards lack important safeguards. Factories are typically licensed by municipalities rather than the Government, resulting in an uneven application of environmental and work safeguards. A proposed bill to harmonize health and safety standards with those of the European Union failed to win approval in 1995. It continues to receive widespread support and is expected to pass eventually.

Occupational safety and health regulations are administered at best sporadically in the Turkish Cypriot area. In both areas, factory inspectors process complaints and inspect businesses in order to ensure that occupational safety laws are observed. Turkish Cypriot workers who file complaints do not receive satisfactory legal protection and may face dismissal.

THE CZECH REPUBLIC

The Czech Republic is a parliamentary democracy. Prime Minister Vaclav Klaus and his Civic Democratic Party lead the current minority coalition Government, formed after the June parliamentary elections. The country has essentially completed the reform of political and economic structures initiated after the 1989 "velvet revolution." President Vaclav Havel is an internationally recognized advocate of human rights and social justice. The judiciary is independent.

The Ministry of the Interior oversees the police. The civilian internal security service, known as the Security and Information Service (BIS), is independent of Ministry control, but reports to Parliament and the Prime Minister's office. Police and BIS authorities generally observe constitutional and legal protection of individual rights in carrying out their responsibilities. However, there were occasional reports of abuses by some members of the police.

The market-based economy continued to show solid growth, with over two-thirds of the gross domestic product (GDP) produced by the private sector. Most macroeconomic indicators (balanced budget, low inflation and unemployment) were favorable. Significant trade and current account deficits persisted, which were financed by strong capital inflows. The work force was employed primarily in industry, retail trade, and construction. Leading exports were intermediate manufactured products and machinery and transport equipment, primarily to European Union countries. GDP per capita reached approximately $5,100.

The Government generally respected the human rights of its citizens. However, popular prejudice and skinhead violence against Roma remain problems. Other problems include the 1992 Citizenship Law; the law on lustration (screening), which forbids certain pre-1989 Communist officials and secret police collaborators from holding certain positions; and the laws criminalizing defamation of the State and presidency. There is increasing public awareness about violence against women.

RESPECT FOR HUMAN RIGHTS

Section 1. Respect for the Integrity of the Person, Including Freedom From:

a. *Political and Other Extrajudicial Killing.*—There were no reports of political or other extrajudicial killings.

In 1995 Frantisek Kahanek, the confessed rapist and murderer of a 10-year-old child, was found dead in his jail cell while awaiting trial. In December three of the four wardens charged with assault and abuse of public office in connection with the death were acquitted by the district court in Pilsen. The remaining warden was given a 6-month sentence with 1 year of probation.

In July the Prague-West district court sentenced a police officer to 8 months in prison for using excessive force during a roadside traffic check and banned him from the police force for 5 years. The officer caused the death of a German tourist during a traffic check in Pribram in October 1994.

b. *Disappearance.*—There were no reports of politically motivated disappearances.

c. *Torture and Other Cruel, Inhuman, or Degrading Treatment or Punishment.*—Torture is prohibited by the Constitution, and there were no reports of such practices.

In May some 60 armed police officers used truncheons to beat dozens of people attending a rock concert in a Prague club. Several attendees were injured as a result. Following the completion in November of an investigation by the Inspectorate of the Interior Ministry, the leader of the police action was charged with abuse of public office.

In August an officer was charged with abuse of public office in connection with a police action in 1995, when the Brno police allegedly used excessive force in breaking up a late-night party outside a theater.

The police underwent significant restructuring and have brought many new officers onto the force. Police approval ratings remained rather low in public opinion polls, but that may be partially explained by increased public anxiety over crime. There have been reports of police shakedowns and anecdotal stories of physical abuse and malfeasance, often directed at foreigners and Roma.

Prison conditions meet minimum international standards, and the Government permits visits by human rights monitors. There is overcrowding in some prisons. According to the prison authority, as of September the prison system was at 112 percent of capacity, and 7 of the country's 32 prisons were 25 percent or more over capacity.

d. *Arbitrary Arrest, Detention, or Exile.*—The law prohibits arbitrary arrest, detention, or exile, and the Government observes this prohibition. Authorities may hold persons without charge for 24 hours, during which time they have the right to counsel. A person charged with a crime has the right to appear before a judge for arraignment, when the judge determines whether custody is necessary pending trial.

Pretrial custody may last as long as 4 years, with periodic judicial review, for criminal charges. The law does not allow bail for certain serious crimes. If the court does not approve continued detention at any of the legally mandated review dates, the suspect must be released. A suspect may petition the appropriate investigating authorities at any time for release from custody.

Since 1989 the average length of pretrial detention has increased from 89 days to 216 in 1996, although that figure is down slightly from 1995. According to the prison service, nearly 39 percent of prisoners are currently awaiting trial or sentencing, down from 42 percent in 1995. The lack of experienced judges and investigators, combined with a still-evolving legal environment, led to a backlog of court cases. Attorney and family visits are permitted. The authorities follow these guidelines in practice.

e. *Denial of Fair Public Trial.*—The Constitution provides for an independent judiciary, and it is impartial and independent in practice. Judges are not fired or transferred for political reasons.

The court system consists of district, regional, and high courts. The Supreme Court is the highest court of appeal. In addition, a Constitutional Court rules separately on the constitutionality of legislation. The shortage of qualified judges is being gradually overcome by the hiring of new personnel. Public opinion polls indicate that over half of the population nevertheless remains somewhat skeptical of the courts' effectiveness as an instrument of justice.

The law stipulates that persons charged with criminal offenses are entitled to fair and open public trials. They have the right to be informed of their legal rights and of the charges against them, to consult with counsel, and to present a defense. The State provides lawyers for indigent defendants in criminal and some civil cases through the bar association. According to the International Helsinki Committee, many eligible parties fail to complete the demanding process of applying for such representation. Defendants enjoy a presumption of innocence and have the right to refuse to testify against themselves. They may appeal any judgments against them. The authorities observe these rights in practice.

The 1991 lustration law bars many former Communist Party officials, members of the people's militia, and suspected secret police collaborators from holding a wide range of elective and appointive offices, including appointive positions in state-owned companies, academia, and the media, for a period of 5 years; some other employers have also required applicants to produce proof of noncollaboration.

Late in 1992 the Czechoslovak Federal Constitutional Court eliminated the largest category of offenders from the law (those listed as collaborators but who in fact may only have been intelligence targets). According to the Interior Ministry, of approximately 300,000 requests for lustration received by late 1996, roughly 3 percent revealed that the applicants were suspected of some form of collaboration. Those positively identified may appeal to an Interior Ministry "Independent Commission" created to review such cases. They may also file a civil suit against the Interior Ministry for a charge similar to slander. From the beginning of lustration in 1993 until mid-October 1996, 581 such suits had been filed. According to the Ministry, of the 472 court cases that had been decided by then, about half were "fully successful," and another quarter were "partially successful." In January former member of the Czechoslovak Federal Assembly and longtime dissident publisher in London Jan Kavan, who had been accused of collaboration with the Czechoslovak secret police, was completely exonerated by the court. Many of those unjustly accused of collaboration feel that they have suffered diminished career prospects and damaged personal reputations.

The screening process has been criticized because it is based on the records of the Communist secret police, records many suspect were incomplete or unreliable. The law has also been criticized as a violation of human rights principles prohibiting discrimination in employment and condemning collective guilt. International criticism of the screening law was muted in 1996, as most organizations that had criticized lustration in the past, such as the Organization for Security and Cooperation in Europe and the Council of Europe (COE), rarely if ever received complaints from aggrieved parties. In 1995 Parliament voted to extend the law to the year 2000, overriding a veto by President Havel.

Although a 1993 law defining the pre-1989 Communist regime as criminal and lifting the statute of limitations for crimes committed by the Communist Party of Czechoslovakia during its 40-year rule remained on the books, it was rarely invoked. The anti-Communist law was upheld by the Constitutional Court in December 1993.

Several charges filed by the Office for the Documentation and Investigation of the Crimes of Communism (UDV) were dismissed by the state prosecutor's office for procedural errors or lack of evidence. In September President Havel ordered that charges against former Communist Defense Minister Milan Vaclavik be dropped, citing the advanced age and poor health of the accused. The UDV had charged Vaclavik with illegally supplying the people's militia with arms.

In October an individual who had been fired from the theological faculty at Prague's Charles University charged that secret police collaborators were still employed at his former workplace. The head of the UDV confirmed this information, but the office did not involve itself in the matter further, as no laws applied to the case.

There were no reports of political prisoners.

f. *Arbitrary Interference With Privacy, Family, Home, or Correspondence.*—Electronic surveillance, the tapping of telephones, and interception of mail require a court order. The Government complied with this requirement.

In November the head of BIS resigned amid charges that his agency placed a leading politician under surveillance in 1992, reportedly due to the politician's ties with a banker under investigation. A government investigator found that BIS had tampered with evidence in the case, but no evidence emerged of any political motivation for the surveillance.

Section 2. Respect for Civil Liberties, Including:

a. *Freedom of Speech and Press.*—The law provides for freedom of speech and the press, and the Government respects this right in practice. Individuals can and do speak out on political issues and freely criticize the Government and public figures. However, "defamation" of the Republic and the President are punishable by prison terms of up to 2 years under the Penal Code. In practice the courts gave suspended sentences in the handful of such cases to date. In 1994 the Constitutional Court struck out language that also criminalized defamation of the "Parliament, Government, or Constitutional Court." Nevertheless, these laws continued to be criticized by both domestic and international human rights observers as limiting freedom of expression.

In March President Havel pardoned Pavel Karhanek, who had been given a 9-month suspended sentence in 1995 under the law on defamation of the President for putting up posters in a local government office calling the President a former alcoholic, a swindler, and a Communist collaborator. According to the Office of the President, Havel routinely pardons those convicted under the law when they request it or when his office learns of such cases. In May the district court in Kromeriz pronounced a 4-month suspended sentence on Zdenek Spalovsky under the same law for publishing statements in local and emigre newspapers in 1994 that Havel was a traitor and a false prophet.

In October the Constitutional Court struck down a 1995 proclamation by the Znojmo town hall that placed limitations on the use of foreign languages in shop signs.

A wide variety of newspapers, magazines, and journals publish without government interference. The capital, Prague, is home to at least a dozen daily newspapers with national distribution, as well as a variety of entertainment and special interest newspapers and magazines. These publications are owned by a variety of Czech and foreign investors. Some newspapers are still associated with the interests of a political party; others are independent.

The electronic media are independent. There are 4 television stations, 2 public and 2 private, and more than 60 private radio stations in addition to Czech Public Radio. The leading television channel, Nova, is privately owned, partially by foreign investors. In addition, many viewers have access to foreign broadcasts via satellite and cable.

A parliamentary commission has broad oversight and power to approve or reject candidates for the Television and Radio Council. The Council has limited regulatory responsibility for policymaking and answers to the parliamentary media committee. The Council can issue and revoke radio and television licenses and monitors programming.

By year's end, Parliament had not yet voted on two long-delayed media laws: one for print and one for broadcast media. New laws are needed because the print law on the books dates from 1966 and the current broadcast law, dating from 1991, did not envision private media. The print media law has gone through several drafts in the process of working its way through various parliamentary committees. Czech journalists criticize the draft law for not affirming the right of a journalist to protect sources and for not requiring government officials to supply information to the media.

The law provides for academic freedom but also forbids activities by established political parties at universities.

b. *Freedom of Peaceful Assembly and Association.*—The law provides for the right of persons to assemble peacefully. Permits for some public demonstrations are required by law but are rarely refused. However, the law forbids political party activity at universities (see Section 2.a.). Police generally do not interfere with spontaneous, peaceful demonstrations for which organizers lack a permit.

In April the Constitutional Court struck down a proclamation by the central district of the city of Brno that placed restrictions on the use of Freedom Square for promotional, cultural, or political events. The proclamation had been adopted in 1993 after a rock musician was stabbed in the stomach by a man who was apparently irritated by noise from the musician's concert on the Square.

Since late 1995, the Constitutional Court has also overturned five "anti-Communist" decrees from various towns. In April the court overturned proclamations by the town councils of Brno and Nova Paka that banned the promotion of parties and movements spreading ethnic, racial, political, or class hatred. In June the same Court overturned two proclamations that banned Communist, Nazi, and Fascist propaganda in the towns of Pardubice and Jicin. The Court has also overturned a similar measure from Usti Nad Labem.

The right of persons to associate freely and to form political parties and movements is provided for by law, and the Government respected this right in practice. Either the Government or the President may submit a proposal to the Supreme Court calling for a political party to be disbanded, but there have been no such cases since 1989. Organizations, associations, foundations, and political parties are required to register with local officials or at the Interior Ministry, but there is no evidence that this registration is either coercive or arbitrarily withheld. The Communist Party, although fragmented, is represented in the Parliament and in local government.

c. *Freedom of Religion.*—The law provides for religious freedom, and the Government respects this right in practice. The State provides support to all religions that are registered with the Ministry of Culture. There are currently 21 registered churches. A church must have at least 10,000 adult members to register. Smaller religious groups, such as the Muslim minority, lack an alternative legal mechanism that would enable them to own community property.

One Christian political party, the Christian Democratic Union-Czechoslovak People's Party, is a member of the governing coalition. A smaller Christian party, the Christian Democratic Party, merged with the Civic Democratic Party, the largest party in the coalition Government, early in the year.

d. *Freedom of Movement Within the Country, Foreign Travel, Emigration, and Repatriation.*—There are no restrictions on domestic or foreign travel, emigration, and repatriation. Passports are readily available to all wishing to travel abroad. Czechs who emigrated during the period of Communist rule frequently return to visit, or even to settle, and are able to regain Czech citizenship if they wish, although to do so they must relinquish claim to any foreign citizenship. Citizenship is not revoked for political reasons. Nonetheless, the United Nations High Commissioner for Refugees (UNHCR) has expressed concern to the Government that its 1992 Citizenship Law has created a problem of statelessness that may lead to irregular movements (see Section 5).

The Government provides first asylum and cooperates with the UNHCR and other humanitarian organizations in assisting refugees. Most migrants used the Czech Republic as a transit route toward the West; however, the country is becoming the final destination for increasing numbers. According to the Interior Ministry, acceptance rates for asylum applications have decreased from over 35 percent in 1991 to just over 4 percent in 1996. This trend reflects the rationalization of border controls; a more restrictive attitude toward accepting economic migrants; and perhaps also the belief that certain foreigners have contributed to higher crime rates since 1989. There are 4 reception centers for asylum seekers, 6 humanitarian centers for Bosnians under temporary protection, and 10 integration centers for recognized refugees. In April the Parliament abolished a provision in the law on refugees allowing refugee status to be granted only for 5 years, thus bringing domestic law into harmony with the State's international commitments in the 1951 Convention Relating to the Status of Refugees and its 1967 Protocol. As a result of the April amendment, refugees may now apply for citizenship after 5 years. Nongovernmental organizations (NGO's) work closely with the Interior Ministry to ease the refugees' transition into society. In practice, however, many potential refugees choose to apply for permanent settlement elsewhere.

According to the Interior Ministry, as of October there were officially 334 Bosnians under temporary protection in humanitarian centers and approximately 470 in other living arrangements. Nearly 1,000 have obtained either long-term or permanent residency, and an unknown number remain in the country illegally. Participation by recognized refugees in the September elections in Bosnia was facilitated by the Organization for Security and Cooperation in Europe and the Embassy of Bosnia-Herzegovina in Vienna. Voluntary repatriation of Bosnian refugees began in July; by October, 277 had returned to Sarajevo on three flights specially chartered by the Government and were given a resettlement stipend.

The Government devoted increased attention to illegal migration into the country and took steps with its neighbors to control the movement of people across its borders. The Government has signed readmission agreements with all of the country's neighbors, and with Hungary, Romania, and Canada. In 1996 the UNHCR observed that these agreements "do not specifically take into account the special situation of asylum seekers" nor "ensure access to refugee status determination procedure," while noting that in practice the Government allows all interested parties to apply for such protections.

Section 3. Respect for Political Rights: The Right of Citizens to Change Their Government

The Constitution provides citizens with the right to change their government by democratic means, and citizens exercise this right in practice. Citizens over the age of 18 are eligible to vote by secret ballot in republic-wide and local elections. Opposition groups, including political parties, function openly and participate without hindrance in the political process. Prior to the June parliamentary elections, a number of small political parties protested the introduction of an election-deposit requirement, charging that they were unable to afford the sums demanded and were thus effectively excluded from participating in the democratic process. Prior to the November Senate elections, the district and central election committees were criticized for forcing several candidates from various parties to withdraw from the race for sometimes minor irregularities in their registration papers. There was no evidence of partisanship in such decisions. The Supreme Court in the overwhelming majority of cases ruled in favor of the candidates. International observers have noted that former Czechoslovaks who elected representatives to the Czech National Assembly in 1992 and whose current citizenship status is unclear continue to lack voting rights (see Section 5).

The ruling three-party center-right minority Government was formed in July following the Czech Republic's first national elections. There are also a number of left-of-center opposition parties and one party of the radical right. The Constitution mandates elections to Parliament at least every 4 years, based on proportional representation in eight large electoral districts. There is a 5-percent threshold for parties to enter Parliament. The first elections to the Senate were held in November. With its establishment, the Czech Republic's parliamentary system came into compliance with the country's Constitution. The President, who is elected by Parliament, serves a 5-year term. The President has limited constitutional powers but may use a suspense veto to return legislation to Parliament, which can then override that veto by a simple majority.

There are no restrictions, in law or in practice, on women's participation in politics. Nevertheless, relatively few women hold high public office. The state attorney and the mayors of Brno and a number of smaller towns are women; the 200-member Parliament includes 29 female deputies, including 1 deputy speaker. Nine women are senators in the newly elected 81-member Senate; one of the four vice chairmen is a woman.

Representatives from all minority groups sit on the government-sponsored Council for Nationalities. Slovaks, of whom there are an estimated 300,000, are almost all "Czechoslovaks" who elected to live in the Czech Republic after the split. Many serve in high positions in the civil service. For the most part, these Slovaks define their interests in the context of Czech politics, not along ethnic lines; there is no Slovak party in the Parliament.

Many of the estimated 200,000 to 250,000 Roma have not been fully integrated into society, and the party that represented their interests immediately following the demise of communism, the Romani Civic Initiative, is in disarray. The political culture generally defines Roma as outsiders. The Roma themselves have not united behind a program or set of ideals that would enable them to advance their interests in the democratic structures of the country (see Section 5). Since mid-1995, however, various Romani groups have joined forces to protest interethnic violence against them. Even if all Romani citizens of voting age were to unite behind a single party, they would not garner the required 5 percent of votes cast to be represented in the lower house, and no seats are reserved in either house for ethnic minorities. There are currently no Romani deputies in the Parliament.

Section 4. Governmental Attitude Regarding International and Nongovernmental Investigation of Alleged Violations of Human Rights

Human rights groups operate without government restriction, and government officials are generally cooperative and somewhat responsive to their views. The presidency of former dissident and human rights monitor Vaclav Havel serves as an important symbol for these groups. While the Government has demonstrated a willingness to examine and redress individual cases of human rights abuse, it has been less flexible when considering larger systemic changes. There is a government-sponsored Council for Nationalities, which advises the Cabinet on minority affairs. In this body, Slovaks and Roma have three representatives each; Poles and Germans, two each; and Hungarians and Ukrainians, one each. In Parliament there is a petition committee for human rights and nationalities, which includes a subcommittee for nationalities. The Senate has also formed a committee for human rights and nationalities.

Section 5. Discrimination Based on Race, Sex, Religion, Disability, Language, or Social Status

The law provides for the equality of citizens and prohibits discrimination. Health care, education, retirement, and other social services generally are provided without regard to race, sex, religion, disability, social status, or sexual orientation. In practice Roma face discrimination in such areas as education, housing, and job opportunity.

Women.—The true extent of violence against women is unknown, and public debate about it is rare, despite the efforts of a handful of women's groups to bring this issue to the attention of the public. The press devoted increased coverage to the issues of violence against women and trafficking in women. Official statistics fail to track violence against women effectively. Since 1989 official police statistics have recorded 700 to 900 rape cases per year, and approximately 80 percent of the cases are solved. Studies by the Sexology Institute found that 12 percent of women over the age of 15 had experienced some form of sexual assault in their lifetime and that only 3 percent of rape victims report the crime. Gender studies experts say that women are ashamed to speak about rape and that the police are not equipped, either by attitude or training to help. According to legal experts, there is an unspoken understanding in the court system that spousal abuse should be prosecuted as a crime only if a doctor determines that the victim's condition warrants medical treatment for 7 days or more. There are state-supported shelters that accept women in most major cities and towns. According to NGO's, the situation has improved in recent years, but there are still not enough spaces to meet demand.

In a 1995 study by the Sociology Institute, 43 percent of women reported experiencing some form of sexual harassment in the workplace during their career. A study by the Defense Ministry in 1996 found that nearly half of female soldiers experienced harassment on duty. In a landmark case, a major bank forced a local branch manager to resign in August after he made repeated, unwelcome advances toward female employees. The bank had declined to act following the first incident, and in the resulting national discussion, press commentators generally dismissed the concerns of women's groups over the extent of sexual harassment in the workplace.

Women are equal under the law and in principle receive the same pay for the same job. However, according to a survey of employers by the Ministry of Labor, women's median wages lagged behind those of men by roughly 25 percent in 1996 (a private survey produced comparable results), although the gap is narrowing. According to a 1995 study, women are concentrated in professions in which the median salary is low: medicine, teaching, and white-collar clerical jobs. At the same time, women have made deep inroads into the private sector since 1989, and the number in agricultural work has fallen by 50 percent over the last decade. Women have steadily represented roughly half of the labor force over the same period. They enjoy equal property, inheritance, and other rights with men.

Prostitution is legal, although a November 1995 amendment to the law on communities provides that it may be regulated by local authorities. Under the Penal Code, trafficking in prostitutes is punishable by a prison term of up to 8 years (up to 12 years if the victim is under the age of 15). According to the police unit responsible for fighting organized crime, the Czech Republic is largely a transit country for traffickers in women. A credible NGO that tracks this issue has concluded that the country is increasingly becoming a destination for many prostitutes from farther east. In February the police broke up a ring of traffickers in Kladno. Several hundred women and girls annually are smuggled into Western Europe and North America through the Czech Republic and forced to work as prostitutes. According to the same NGO, the trade in women is growing.

Children.—The Government is committed to children's welfare through programs for health care, compulsory education, and basic nutrition. Some Romani children do not receive these benefits for a variety of reasons, and the Government's largely bureaucratic and administrative approach has not adequately addressed the disadvantages faced by Roma in many municipalities. Some segments of the Romani community prefer to limit as much as possible their contacts with the majority society.

Child abuse and trafficking in children received increased attention in the press in 1996. A children's crisis center was founded in 1995 and is 70 percent state supported. According to its director, around 1 percent of children are neglected, mistreated, or sexually abused, but only about one-tenth of all cases are registered by the police. The increase in the number of reported cases of child abuse appears to be the result of an increased awareness of the problem. According to a special envoy of the U.N. Human Rights Commission who visited in 1996, there is no evidence of a societal pattern of child abuse.

Girls and boys enjoy equal access to health care and education at all levels. The Government ceased tabulating educational or other statistics on the basis of ethnicity following the breakup of the Czechoslovak federation in 1993; yet 1991 figures show that over 20 percent of the self-identified Romani population in the Czech lands had not completed elementary school and that over 95 percent had not completed high school. Since a large majority of Roma do not identify themselves as such for census-takers, however, such statistics provide only an approximate picture of reality. In 1993 the Government instituted a number of year-long programs (so-called "zero grades") to prepare disadvantaged youth for their first year in school, mostly in areas with high concentrations of Roma. Participation in the "zero grades" is voluntary. Some Romani parents do not send their children to school regularly for a variety of reasons, including the expense of books, supplies, and activities; subtle or overt discrimination; and sometimes, because of the parents' ambivalent attitudes toward education.

According to the Ministry of Education, Romani children make up 60 percent or more of pupils placed in "special schools" for those who suffer from mental or social disabilities, although Roma are estimated to comprise only 2 to 3 percent of the population. Language and cultural barriers frequently impede the integration of Romani children into mainstream schools. Moreover, some Romani parents appear to prefer that their children attend such schools, where they can be among others of the same ethnicity, regardless of their mental abilities.

During the year, some public discussion took place about lowering the age of criminal responsibility. The leader of a far-right political party represented in the Parliament called for lowering the criminal age of responsibility for Romani children to zero (see below). There was no change in the relevant legislation by year's end.

People With Disabilities.—At the beginning of the year, the Government introduced a new set of eligibility guidelines for disability benefits in an effort to rationalize the system. According to an NGO representing the disabled, under the new system as many as 30 percent of former recipients receive either fewer benefits or none. Businesses in which 60 percent or more of the employees are disabled qualify for special tax breaks, and 41 such companies are members of the union of Czech and Moravian producer cooperatives.

The disabled suffer disproportionately from unemployment, and the physically disabled have unequal access to education, especially in rural areas. This is less the result of government policy than of a lack of barrier-free access to public schools. Most buildings and public transportation are inaccessible to those in wheelchairs. However, a regulation of the Economic Ministry from 1994 requires architects to ensure adequate access for the disabled in new building projects, and this regulation is applied in practice. Numerous NGO's are actively working to diminish the disadvantages faced by the disabled. The integration of the disabled into society has not been the subject of significant policy or public debate. There is one disabled member of Parliament.

Religious Minorities.—The Jewish community numbers a few thousand. There were only isolated incidents of vandalism against Jewish property. In June a Prague synagogue that had repeatedly been the target of vandalism was defaced with swastikas and anti-Semitic graffiti. In February the Federation of Jewish Communities protested the publication of a new edition of "The Protocols of the Elders of Zion," a notorious anti-Semitic text, despite the inclusion in the new edition of a scholarly essay showing the work to be a fabrication. The police confirmed the existence of over 20 underground magazines with small circulations propagating fascism, racism, and anti-Semitism.

Religious groups with 10,000 or more adult members may register with the Ministry of Culture. Only registered religions are eligible for state subsidies. Smaller groups lack a legal mechanism by which they may own community property (see Section 2.c.). The Jewish community constitutes an exception, since it was recognized by the State before 1989.

In March the town council of Teplice voted 26 to 2 to deny a permit for the construction of a mosque on the grounds that the building could become a center for Islamic terrorism. In the same month, the city of Brno gave permission for a mosque to be built, but with the stipulation that the building not have a minaret. The small Muslim minority is otherwise free to assemble and worship in the manner of its choice. Its members can and do issue publications without interference. There is also a small Muslim cemetery in Trebic.

On the anniversary of Kristallnacht, a series of Nazi-inspired mob attacks on German Jews and their property in November 1938, an international crowd of about 700 people gathered in Kozolupy near Pilsen to attend a concert by skinhead bands. Police detained nine participants who made the "Heil Hitler" salute, an offense punishable under Czech law, and charged the owner of the venue with supporting and propogating a movement that aims to suppress citizens' rights and freedoms, a criminal offense. Police refrained from further intervention at the time of the concert, but an investigation is continuing.

National/Racial/Ethnic Minorities.—After ethnic Slovaks, the most significant minority in the Czech Republic by far is the Romani population, officially estimated to number approximately 200,000. Roma live throughout the country but are concentrated in the industrial towns of northern Bohemia, where more than 40 years ago many eastern Slovak Roma settled or were forced to settle in the homes of Sudeten Germans transferred to the West. They suffer disproportionately from poverty, interethnic violence, illiteracy, and disease. Efforts by foundations and individuals in the education and health fields to improve their living conditions, especially the conditions of Romani children, have had only minimal impact. There is a Czech-language program for Roma on state television and another on state radio. There are various publications for Roma, of which all but one are state supported. There is also an academic journal of Romani studies with several Roma on the editorial board. Romani leaders have had limited success thus far in organizing their local communities, which are often riven by conflicting loyalties and where many are pessimistic about improving relations with the majority.

Roma suffer from serious popular prejudice, as is repeatedly affirmed by public opinion polls. In 1996 a survey found that 22 percent of respondents would "give more room to the skinheads" as a means of resolving the problem of coexistence with the Roma; 35 percent were in favor of "concentrating and isolating" the Roma; and 45 percent would support "moving the Roma out of the Czech Republic if possible." However, a majority of respondents also supported the right of Roma to file complaints with international bodies, reserving seats for Romani representatives on municipal councils, the "zero grade" program, and efforts to bring more Roma onto the police force.

The International Helsinki Federation and Human Rights Watch criticized the Government in 1996 for not curbing skinhead violence against Roma. Racially motivated violence against Roma, usually by skinheads, has risen sharply in recent years. Statistics through October recorded a sixfold increase in the number of reported incidents over 1994. Local authorities have been unable (or, according to some observers, unwilling) to curb this violence. In the last 5 years, over 200 people have been charged with racial violence; to date, just under 100 have been convicted. In mid-1995 Parliament passed legislation to stiffen the penalties for certain categories of racially motivated crime, and the state attorney instructed prosecutors to act more vigorously in such cases. Nonetheless, many judges and police officers remain extremely reluctant to ascribe a racial motive to anti-Roma violence, even when skinheads are involved.

In February the district court in Breclav sentenced one skinhead to a 6-year prison term for the October 1995 attack on the Roma Josef and Jarmila Polak, which caused each to suffer a concussion and Josef Polak to lose an eye. The court gave the remaining three assailants in the Polak case suspended sentences because of their apparent repentance and because they had not reached the age of criminal responsibility at the time of the attack.

Skinheads organized several large gatherings in November, and police were sometimes effective in containing them. In late November, some 100 skinheads from several countries in the region gathered in Breclav to protest the verdict in the Polak case. The same night, police and local authorities in the southern Moravian municipality of Lanzhot successfully dispersed an estimated 200 skinheads who were attending a concert and who had begun to shout Fascist slogans. Police closely watched and escorted some of over 100 skinheads gathered in Senov in northern Moravia when they walked through an area of nearby Havoriv where many Roma live.

In May the high court in Olomouc overturned a lower court's ruling and attributed a racial motive to the 1995 skinhead attack on Rom Tibor Berki who died from his injuries. One of the assailants had been sentenced to 12 years in prison for murder and a second to 18 months; in the 1995 trial, the court did not find the attack to be racially motivated. Under the new ruling in 1996, the sentences were extended by 1 year and 2 months, respectively.

The investigation continues into the case of three Romani girls who were severely beaten by nine skinheads in 1995.

Witnesses are often afraid to testify in such cases for fear of reprisals. For example, in September and again in December the district court in Pisek again postponed court proceedings in the case of the death of Tibor Danihel, an 18-year-old Rom who drowned after a gang of skinheads forced him into the Otava river in Pisek in 1993, due to witnesses' unwillingness to testify. In a separate case in Uherske Hradiste, two Romani witnesses called upon to give testimony in January had to be summoned by the police; one witness told the court that he feared for his life if he testified.

The prosecution of racially motivated attacks is often slowed by the general backlog of court cases (see Section 1.d.). In other cases, suspects accused of brutal attacks were released by the courts pending trial. A Brno court released an 18-year-old female skinhead who attacked a Romani man with an infant in his arms in May, pending a hearing; she then assaulted another woman in September. An Olomouc court released a youth who had attacked a foreign student at the local university (see below). Overcrowding in some prisons (see Section 1.c.) may contribute to some judges' unwillingness to place youths, even violent offenders, in custody.

Central government officials remain engaged in problems affecting the Romani community. Romani representatives met separately with the Ministers of Labor and Education to discuss their concerns. The latter meeting was the first ever attended by spokespersons for the particularly isolated Vlach Roma. In July the leader of a far-right party delivered a speech on the floor of the Parliament in which he said that Romani children should be criminally responsible from birth; all other parties' deputies left the chamber in a protest against this statement. In November the mandate and immunity committee of the Chamber of Deputies fined the offender 1 month's salary. In 1996 the number of those charged with racially motivated crimes continued to rise, and the Attorney General directed state prosecutors to seek stiffer sentences for them.

Roma face discrimination in employment, housing, schools, and the rest of everyday life. NGO's estimate that unemployment among Roma is as high as 70 percent in some areas. Some restaurants, pubs, and other venues throughout the country routinely refused service to Roma and posted signs prohibiting their entry. In March a small political party forced a Breclav businessman to resign as its candidate for the parliamentary elections after he put up a sign in his hotel refusing service to Roma. In other cases, local authorities intervened to have offensive signs removed. In June the town of Kladno barred entry to the municipal swimming pool by Roma after an outbreak of hepatitis infected most of the local Romani community. Municipal health authorities stated that the measure would not be especially effective in containing the outbreak. The mayor subsequently proposed a conference that would include Roma participants to discuss interethnic relations; this initiative has been received with skepticism by local Roma.

In August, in the first prominent antidiscrimination case, the Rokycany district court found pub owner Ivo Blahout not guilty of discriminating against Romani patrons despite videotaped evidence and the incriminating testimony of two policemen. The pub owner argued both that all the tables in his establishment had been reserved on the day of the incident and that he had a right to take reasonable measures to protect his property from notoriously unruly customers. The district state attorney has appealed the ruling.

While local Romani leaders tended to focus on racially motivated violence and other problems, international and domestic legal and human rights organizations continued to criticize the discriminatory impact of the 1992 citizenship law. That law, created at the time of the Czech-Slovak split, allowed Czechoslovaks living in the Czech Republic until the end of December 1993, later extended to June 1994, to opt for Czech citizenship under conditions more favorable than those faced by non-Czechoslovaks in the normal naturalization process. Unlike its Slovak counterpart, which awarded Slovak citizenship to all former Czechoslovak citizens living within its borders regardless of their previous nationality (after 1970, Czechoslovaks were required to choose whether they were "Czechs" or "Slovaks," a choice with virtually no significance at the time), the Czech law posed conditions: "Slovak" applicants were required to prove they had a clean criminal record over the previous 5 years and were resident in the Czceh Republic for 2 years. Romani leaders protested that these provisions were designed to discriminate against Roma, most of whom are of Slovak origin.

Current "Slovak" applicants for Czech citizenship are required to meet the same conditions as all other foreigners except the Czech language requirement, and they may request a waiver of the clean criminal record requirement (below). The practical result of the citizenship law is that an unknown number of former Czechoslovaks of "Slovak" nationality resident in the Czech Republic at the time of the split—nearly all of them Roma—have found themselves without Czech citizenship. Some failed to meet the law's requirements; others never applied, either out of negligence or ignorance of the consequences. The Interior Ministry has never given an official estimate of the number of unresolved citizenship cases, but it has indicated that several thousand applications are currently pending. The Citizenship Project, an NGO which actively helps former Czechoslovaks through the citizenship application process, states that many more have not applied and that only the Government is in a position to gauge the scope of the problem.

In February the UNHCR released a report on the Czech and Slovak citizenship laws and the problem of statelessness; in April the Council of Europe (COE) issued a report on the same laws and their implementation. The UNHCR report noted that the placing of conditions such as the clean criminal record requirement on the right of former Czechoslovaks to opt for Czech citizenship "is not justified" and "does not follow the accepted pattern established under general international legal principles." The UNHCR also observed that the Czech Republic had drawn harsh criticism for thus disqualifying from citizenship even long-term and lifelong residents of the Czech lands (i.e., those with "a genuine and effective link" with the territory as described in international law). The COE report found that "conformity with European legal standards might be doubtful" with regard to the clean criminal record requirement, noting that this particular requirement could have untoward consequences in cases of state succession such as the Czech-Slovak split. Both reports expressed concern at the number of cases of "de facto statelessness" among Roma. In July Human Rights Watch also issued a report on the effects of the citizenship law on Roma. The law was further discussed in the COE's Committee of Ministers in June and in the Organization for Cooperation and Security in Europe Permanent Council in July and August.

In April Parliament amended the citizenship law to enable the Interior Ministry to waive the clean criminal record requirement, on an individual basis, for "Slovaks" who had been resident in the Czech lands since before the 1993 split. The waiver application can be included with the citizenship application. In July the Interior Ministry agreed to send letters to all those whose citizenship applications were currently pending in which applicants' right to request a waiver was explained. According to the Government, all who have applied for waivers have been granted them. However, relatively few former Czechoslovaks have taken advantage of this opportunity: as of November, the Interior Ministry had granted about 250 waivers.

Some problems with the application of the law have been addressed. For example, in addition to the Interior Ministry's ability to waive the requirement for a clean criminal record on an individual basis, Czech citizenship is now granted upon release from Slovak citizenship (thus diminishing the potential for de jure statelessness), and some fees have been reduced. However, other problems persist. The requirement for a clean criminal record is interpreted inconsistently and applied even to petty crimes. "Slovak" applicants who have never set foot in Slovakia must still obtain an official release from Slovak citizenship. This requirement is also applied to school-age children. Rules for certain social subsidies, which only citizens or residents may collect, require that all family members be eligible; the labor office in Usti Nad Labem suggested to one woman that she divorce her nonresident husband so that she and her children could receive benefits. Only legal guardians may apply for citizenship for a minor; thus, directors of children's institutions must first secure legal guardianship from the courts before applying for citizenship for their wards.

At year's end, police continued their investigation into the case of a Karvina district office official who accepted improper payments in 1994, primarily from Roma, to expedite citizenship applications. NGO's suggest that many applicants were unaware that this was an irregular practice. Karvina officials subsequently revoked hundreds of citizenship papers signed by that official, and the applicants were told that they had to begin anew the lengthy and expensive process of application for citizenship. The official and her immediate superior no longer work at the district office, yet many of those whose citizenship was revoked face severe economic hardship until their cases are resolved. Without citizenship or residency they do not have the right to work, to health insurance, or to any of the social benefits enjoyed by nearly all citizens and residents.

Fears that the situation would lead to mass deportations of Roma have thus far proven exaggerated. Yet several hundred individuals have been deported to Slovakia since the breakup of the federation, generally following an arrest and often without regard to long-term family ties in the Czech Republic. According to the police, 144 persons were deported to Slovakia during the first 6 months of 1996. Police who come across formerly Czechoslovak individuals without proper citizenship or residency papers have been known to expel them to Slovakia, an action which is within their authority. In addition, courts have issued "prohibitions of stay" to over 1,000 persons of Slovak nationality, of whom an unknown number are Roma.

Several skinhead attacks were directed against nonwhite foreigners, some of them foreign students at Palacky University in Olomouc. In January a Pakistani student was hospitalized with a concussion and other injuries after being attacked by local youth in Olomouc's main train station. Three skinheads were charged; however, despite the recommendation of the police and the local state attorney, the court released them pending trial. The Olomouc chief of police stepped up patrols and stated his intention to take stricter measures to combat extremism. Also in January, the Prague 3 district court sentenced 4 youths to prison terms and ordered them to pay damages to an Ethiopian man they had attacked; the victim suffered a concussion and open fractures of the lower arm and nose. The same court sentenced two other youths to conditional prison terms for attacking an Armenian man who managed to escape from them without injury. In August four skinheads in Prague mistook a Japanese scientist attending a conference for a Vietnamese, beat him, and broke his nose; the victim was hospitalized for 8 days. One of the assailants was detained and charged with assault. In September a biology professor from Benin was verbally assaulted in a tram in Brno and kicked in the face by a masked youth wearing spiked boots; the investigator has charged one suspect with racial defamation.

Section 6. Worker Rights

a. *The Right of Association.*—The law provides workers with the right to form and join unions of their own choice without prior authorization, and the Government respects this right. The work force was 45 to 50 percent unionized in 1996.

Most workers are members of unions affiliated with the Czech-Moravian Chamber of Trade Unions (CMKOS). CMKOS is a democratically oriented, republic-wide umbrella organization for branch unions. It is not affiliated with any political party and carefully maintains its independence.

Workers have the right to strike, except for those whose role in public order or public safety is deemed crucial. The law requires that labor disputes be subject first to mediation and that strikes take place only after mediation efforts fail. There were no major strikes in 1996.

Unions are free to form or join federations and confederations and affiliate with and participate in international bodies. This freedom was fully exercised.

b. *The Right to Organize and Bargain Collectively.*—The law provides for collective bargaining, which is generally carried out by unions and employers on a company basis. Scope for collective bargaining is more limited in the government sector, where wages are regulated by law.

There are 11 free trade zones. Their workers have and practice the same right to organize and bargain collectively as other workers in the country.

c. *Prohibition of Forced or Compulsory Labor.*—The law prohibits forced or compulsory labor, and it is not practiced.

d. *Minimum Age for Employment of Children.*—The Labor Code stipulates a minimum working age of 15 years, although children who have completed courses at special schools (schools for the severely disabled) may work at the age of 14.

e. *Acceptable Conditions of Work.*—The Government sets minimum wage standards. The current minimum wage is approximately $95 (2,500 crowns) per month. The minimum wage provides a sparse standard of living for an individual worker, although when combined with allowances available to families with children, provides an adequate standard of living for a worker and a family. Retraining efforts, carried out by district labor offices, seek to provide labor mobility for those at the lower end of the wage scale. Because of a very tight job market in most of the country, the enforcement of minimum wage standards was not an issue.

The law mandates a standard workweek of 42½ hours. It also requires paid rest of at least 30 minutes during the standard 8- to 8½-hour workday, as well as annual leave of 3 to 4 weeks. Overtime ordered by the employer may not exceed 150 hours per year or 8 hours per week as a standard practice. Overtime above this limit may be permitted by the local employment office. The Labor Ministry enforces standards for working hours, rest periods, and annual leave.

Government, unions, and employers have agreed to promote worker safety and health, but conditions in some sectors of heavy industry are problematical, especially those awaiting privatization. Industrial accident rates are not unusually high. The Office of Labor Safety is responsible for enforcement of health and safety standards. Workers have the right to refuse work endangering their life or health without risk of loss of employment.

DENMARK

Denmark is a constitutional monarchy with parliamentary democratic rule. Queen Margrethe II is Head of State. The Cabinet, accountable to the unicameral Parliament (Folketing), leads the Government. A minority three-party coalition took office in September 1994 following national elections, but dropped to only the Social

Democrats and Radical Liberals in December with the withdrawal of the Center Democrats from the coalition.

The national police have sole responsibility for internal security. The civilian authorities maintain effective control of the security forces.

Denmark has an advanced, market-based industrial economy. One-half of the work force is employed in the public sector. The key industries are food processing and metal working; the leading exports are a broad range of industrial goods. The economy provides residents with a high standard of living.

The Government fully respected the human rights of its citizens, and the law and judiciary provide effective means of dealing with instances of individual abuse.

RESPECT FOR HUMAN RIGHTS

Section 1. Respect for the Integrity of the Person, Including Freedom From:

a. *Political and Other Extrajudicial Killing.*—There were no reports of political or other extrajudicial killings.

b. *Disappearance.*—There were no reports of politically motivated disappearances.

c. *Torture and Other Cruel, Inhuman, or Degrading Treatment or Punishment.*—The law prohibits such practices, and there were no reports that officials employed them. The Government responded to a 1994 Amnesty International report by suspending police use of leg locks as a method of restraining detainees.

Prison conditions meet minimum international standards, and the Government permits visits by human rights monitors.

d. *Arbitrary Arrest, Detention, or Exile.*—The law prohibits arbitrary arrest, detention, or exile, and the Government observes this prohibition.

e. *Denial of Fair Public Trial.*—The law provides for an independent judiciary, and the Government respects this provision in practice. The judiciary provides citizens with a fair and efficient judicial process.

The judicial system consists of a series of local and regional courts, with the Supreme Court at the apex.

The law provides for the right to a fair trial, and an independent judiciary vigorously enforces this right.

There were no reports of political prisoners.

f. *Arbitrary Interference With Privacy, Family, Home, or Correspondence.*—The law prohibits such practices, government authorities generally respect these prohibitions, and violations are subject to effective legal sanction.

Section 2. Respect for Civil Liberties, Including:

a. *Freedom of Speech and Press.*—The law provides for freedom of the press, and the Government respects this right in practice. An independent press, an effective judiciary, and a democratic political system combine to ensure freedom of speech and of the press, including academic freedom.

b. *Freedom of Peaceful Assembly and Association.*—The law provides for these rights, and the Government respects them in practice.

c. *Freedom of Religion.*—The Constitution provides for religious freedom and the Government respects this right in practice. There is religious instruction in the schools in the state religion, the Evangelical Lutheran Church, but any student may without sanction be excused from religion classes with parental permission.

d. *Freedom of Movement Within the Country, Foreign Travel, Emigration, and Repatriation.*—The law provides for these rights, and the Government respects them in practice. The Government cooperates with the United Nations High Commissioner for Refugees and other humanitarian organizations in assisting refugees. The Government provides first asylum (and provided it to approximately 5,800 persons in 1996). There were no reports of forced expulsion of refugees to a country where they feared persecution or of those having a valid claim to refugee status.

Section 3. Respect for Political Rights: The Right of Citizens to Change Their Government

The law provides citizens with the right to change their government peacefully, and citizens exercise this right in practice through periodic, free, and fair elections held on the basis of universal suffrage.

The territories of Greenland (whose population is primarily Inuit) and the Faroe Islands (whose inhabitants have their own Norse language) have democratically elected home rule governments with powers encompassing all matters except foreign affairs, monetary affairs, and national security. Greenlanders and Faroese are Danish citizens, with the same rights as those in the rest of the Kingdom. Each territory elects two representatives to the Folketing.

In the current Government, 7 of 20 ministers are women.

Section 4. Governmental Attitude Regarding International and Nongovernmental Investigation of Alleged Violations of Human Rights

A number of human rights groups operate without government restriction, investigating and publishing their findings on human rights cases. Government officials are cooperative and responsive to their views.

Section 5. Discrimination Based on Race, Sex, Religion, Disability, Language, or Social Status

The Government's operations and extensive public services do not discriminate on the basis of any of these factors. The law prohibits discrimination on the basis of sex, and it is effectively enforced by the Government. Discrimination on the basis of race is at present covered by two laws, which prohibit racial slander and denial of access to public places on the basis of race. Human rights organizations such as the Antidiscrimination Center have criticized the Government for failing to expand legislation to other areas of potential discrimination. The rights of indigenous people are carefully protected.

Women.—An umbrella nongovernmental organization reports that in 1995, women's crisis shelters were contacted 11,516 times, and 2,060 women stayed at shelters. There were 795 sexual assaults including 270 rapes. The law requires equal pay for equal work, but some wage inequality still exists. The law prohibits job discrimination on the basis of sex and provides resources, such as access to the Equal Status Council, for those so affected. Women hold positions of authority throughout society, although they are underrepresented at the top of the business world. Women's rights groups are effective in lobbying the Government in their areas of concern, e.g., wage disparities and parental leave.

Children.—The Government demonstrates a strong commitment to children's rights and welfare through its well-funded systems of public education and medical care. Sections within the Ministries of Social Affairs, Justice, and Education oversee implementation of programs for children. There is no societal pattern of abuse against children.

People With Disabilities.—There is no discrimination against disabled persons in employment, education, or in the provision of other state services. Building regulations require special installations for the disabled in public buildings built or renovated after 1977, and in older buildings that come into public use. The Government enforces these provisions in practice.

Indigenous People.—The law protects the rights of the inhabitants of Greenland and the Faroe Islands. The Greenlandic legal system seeks to accommodate Inuit customs. Accordingly, it provides for the use of lay people as judges, and it sentences most prisoners to holding centers (rather than to prisons) where they are encouraged to work, hunt, or fish during the day. Education in Greenland is provided to the native population in both the Inuit and Danish languages.

National/Racial/Ethnic Minorities.—The inflow of ethnically and racially diverse refugees and immigrants has provoked a degree of tension between Danes and immigrants (mostly Iranians, Palestinians, and Sri Lankans until late 1992; refugees are now overwhelmingly former Yugoslavs and Somalis). Recent publicity on the involvement of foreigners in street-level drug dealing has increased these tensions to the point that Parliament is debating mandatory deportation for those convicted. Incidents of random, racially motivated violence do occur but are rare. The Government effectively investigates and deals with cases of racially motivated violence.

Section 6. Worker Rights

a. *The Right of Association.*—The law states that all workers, including military personnel and the police, may form or join unions of their choosing. Approximately 80 percent of wage earners belong to unions that are independent of the Government and political parties. The Social Democratic Party and the Danish Confederation of Trade Unions, at their respective conferences, severed their historic formal link. They no longer have representation on each other's governing boards but maintain close informal ties. Unions may affiliate freely with international organizations, and they do so actively. All unions except those representing civil servants or the military have the right to strike.

b. *The Right to Organize and Bargain Collectively.*—Workers and employers acknowledge each other's right to organize. Collective bargaining is protected by law and is widespread in practice. The law prohibits antiunion discrimination by employers against union members and organizers, and there are mechanisms to resolve disputes. Employers found guilty of antiunion discrimination are required to reinstate workers fired for union activities. In the private sector, salaries, benefits, and working conditions are agreed upon in biennial or triennial negotiations between the various employers' associations and their union counterparts. If the negotiations fail, a national conciliation board mediates, and its proposal is voted on by management and labor. If the proposal is turned down, the Government may force a legislated solution on the parties (usually based upon the mediators' proposal). The agreements, in turn, are used as guidelines throughout the public as well as the private sector. In the public sector, collective bargaining is conducted between the employees' unions and a government group, led by the Finance Ministry.

Labor relations in Greenland are conducted in the same manner as in Denmark. Greenlandic courts are the first recourse in disputes, but Danish mediation services or the Danish Labor Court may also be used.

There is no umbrella labor organization in the Faroes, but individual unions engage in periodic collective bargaining with employers. Disputes are settled by mediation.

There are no export processing zones.

c. *Prohibition of Forced or Compulsory Labor.*—Forced or compulsory labor is prohibited by law, which the Government effectively enforces.

d. *Minimum Age for Employment of Children.*—The minimum age for full-time employment is 15 years. The law prescribes specific limitations on the employment of those between 15 and 18 years of age, and it is enforced by the Danish Working Environment Service (DWES), an autonomous arm of the Ministry of Labor.

e. *Acceptable Conditions of Work.*—There is no legally mandated national minimum wage, but national labor agreements effectively set a wage floor. The lowest wage paid is currently about $13 (DKr 75) per hour, effective in September 1995, which is sufficient for a decent standard of living for a worker and family. The law provides for 5 weeks of paid vacation per year. A 37-hour workweek is the norm, established by contract, not by law. The law does, however, require at least 11 hours between the end of one work period and the start of the next.

The law also prescribes conditions of work, including safety and health; duties of employers, supervisors, and employees; work performance; rest periods and days off; and medical examinations. The DWES ensures compliance with labor legislation. Workers may remove themselves from hazardous situations or arms production without jeopardizing their employment rights, and there are legal protections for workers who file complaints about unsafe or unhealthy conditions.

Similar conditions of work are found in Greenland and the Faroes, except that their workweek is 40 hours. As in Denmark, this is established by contract, not by law.

ESTONIA

Estonia is a parliamentary democracy. With its statehood widely recognized as continuous for more than 70 years, Estonia regained its independence in 1991 after 50 years of Soviet occupation. The Constitution, adopted by referendum in 1992, established a 101-member unicameral legislature (State Assembly), a prime minister as Head of Government, and a president as Head of State. Free and fair indirect presidential elections took place in two rounds in August and September. A cabinet crisis was resolved in December.

The official conversion of the Soviet militia into the Estonian police preceded the reestablishment of the country's independence by about 6 months. Its conversion into a Western-type police force committed to procedures and safeguards appropriate to a democratic society is proceeding, with police leadership actively working to professionalize the force. The police, who are ethnically mixed, are subordinate to the Ministry of Internal Affairs. Corrections personnel are subordinate to the Ministry of Justice. The security service, called Security Police, is subordinate to the Interior Ministry but also reports to the Prime Minister. Police and corrections personnel continued to commit human rights abuses.

Estonia has a market economy. Reflecting the extent of its post-1992 reforms, Estonia signed a Europe Agreement with the European Union in 1995, which granted associate member status without a transition period. Services, especially financial and tourism, are growing in importance compared to historically more prominent light industry and food production. Privatization of small and medium firms is virtually complete, and privatization of large-scale enterprises is underway. The economy continues to grow steadily with gross domestic product (GDP) estimated to increase by about 3 percent in 1996. Although prices continue to rise, incomes are rising faster than the rate of inflation. Per capita GDP is about $2,400 per year. Two-thirds of Estonian exports (textiles, food products, wood and timber products) are now directed to Western markets. Unemployment remained fairly low overall (unofficially about 8 percent) but was significantly higher in rural areas.

The Government generally respected the human rights of its citizens and the large noncitizen community, but problems remained in some areas. The major human rights abuses continued to be mistreatment of prisoners and detainees, and the use of excessive force by the police. Prison conditions are poor. The deadline for noncitizens to file for permanent residency expired in 1996, after being extended twice. An undetermined number of noncitizens have still not filed for residency. Problems remain in processing the applications for permanent residency of some 19,000 Russian military retirees and family members. Processing of applications for alien passports continued. There were complaints about the low rate of issuance which, however, picked up late in the year. The Government continued to issue temporary travel documents and to accept former Soviet internal passports as identity documents.

RESPECT FOR HUMAN RIGHTS

Section 1. Respect for the Integrity of the Person Including Freedom From:

   a. *Political and Other Extrajudicial Killing.*—There were no reports of political or other extrajudicial killings.

   b. *Disappearance.*—There were no reports of politically motivated disappearances.

   c. *Torture and Other Cruel, Inhuman, or Degrading Treatment or Punishment.*—Such practices are prohibited by law. However, there continued to be credible reports that police used excessive force and verbal abuse during the arrest and questioning of suspects. Punishment cells ("kartsers") continued to be used, in contravention of international standards.

Two cases of hazing were prosecuted in the military; one perpetrator was punished; charges against another were dropped for lack of evidence. There were reports of more instances of recruit mistreatment.

Prison conditions remained poor. Overcrowding continued in the Tallinn Central Prison built in 1765. The Government continued measures to address poor prison conditions and to make prison staff more professional. The first group of professionally trained corrections officers graduated from the National Defense Academy in June. Following several widely reported prison escapes, the head of the Corrections Department resigned in August. By late September, 3 prisoners had been killed by other prisoners, in contrast to 1992 when there were 32 such killings. Opportunities to study or work in prison were limited.

The Government has drafted a multiyear plan to refurbish and restructure all the country's prisons and to close the Tallinn Central Prison, but it had not yet been implemented by year's end. Some suggestions to improve prison conditions made by Council of Europe (COE) representatives in 1993 have been implemented, but fulfillment of others is still hampered by lack of resources and high turnover among prison staff.

The Government permits human rights monitors to visit prisons.

   d. *Arbitrary Arrest, Detention, or Exile.*—The Constitution and laws forbid arbitrary arrest, detention, or exile, and the Government generally observes this prohibition. Under the Constitution, warrants issued by a court are required to make arrests. Detainees must be informed promptly of the grounds for the arrest and given immediate access to legal counsel. If a person cannot afford counsel, the State will provide one. A person may be held for 48 hours without formally being charged; further detention requires a court order. A person may be held in pretrial detention for 2 months; this may be extended up to a total of 12 months by court order. Police rarely violate these limits. At midyear 1,555 of the 4,406 persons held in prisons were awaiting trial.

   e. *Denial of Fair Public Trial.*—The Constitution establishes an independent judicial branch and the judiciary is independent in practice. It operates through a three-tier court system: rural and city courts; district courts; and the State Court (which functions as a supreme court). The district and state courts are also courts for "constitutional supervision." At the rural and city levels, court decisions are made by a majority vote with a judge and two lay members sitting in judgment. All judges and lay judges must be citizens. The President nominates and the State Assembly confirms the Chief Justice of the State Court. The Chief Justice nominates State Court judges who are subject to confirmation by the State Assembly. He also nominates the district, city, and rural court judges who are then appointed by the President. Judges are appointed for life.

The Constitution provides that court proceedings shall be public. Closed sessions may be held only for specific reasons, such as protection of state or business secrets, and in cases concerning minors. The Constitution further provides that defendants may present witnesses and evidence as well as confront and cross-examine prosecution witnesses. Defendants have access to prosecution evidence and enjoy a presumption of innocence.

Estonia continued to overhaul its criminal and civil procedural codes. An interim Criminal Code that went into effect in June 1992 basically revised the Soviet Criminal Code by eliminating, for example, political and economic crimes. The Code of Criminal Procedure was adopted in 1994. New codes in a variety of fields were being drafted at year's end. A multiyear plan is being compiled to replace present criminal codes with new penal codes.

There were no reports of political prisoners. In September former dissident Tiit Madisson was sentenced to 26 months in prison for attempting to organize an armed overthrow of the Government. The sentence is being appealed.

f. *Arbitrary Interference With Privacy, Family, Home, or Correspondence.*—The law requires a search warrant for search and seizure of property. During the investigative stage, warrants are issued by the prosecutor upon a showing of probable cause. Once a case has gone to court, warrants are issued by the court. The Constitution provides for secrecy of the mail, telegrams, telephones, and other means of communication. Police must obtain a court order to intercept a person's communications. Illegally obtained evidence is not admissible in court. In a widely reported case, the police in the summer of 1995 destroyed a field of alleged opium poppies without a warrant. A criminal case was filed against the owner of the field for growing opium poppies; the owner asserted that he was growing oil poppies. The case was settled out of court with the owner receiving compensation. At year's end, security police and parliamentary investigations were continuing into the 1995 case involving then-Interior Minister Savisaar who was implicated in making unauthorized recordings of conversations.

Section 2. Respect for Civil Liberties, Including:

a. *Freedom of Speech and Press.*—The Government generally respects constitutional provisions providing for freedom of speech and the press. The media routinely do probing and thorough investigative reporting. Foreign newspapers and magazines are widely available. Most newsprint, printing, and distribution facilities are now private companies. There are four major national Estonian language and two Russian language dailies.

State broadcast media, including one nationwide television (TV) channel, continue to receive large subsidies, and the State has assured that these subsidies will continue. There are several major independent television and radio stations. Several Russian language programs, mostly Estonian produced, are broadcast over state and private television channels. Russian state TV and Ostankino programs are widely available via cable.

Academic freedom is respected.

b. *Freedom of Peaceful Assembly and Association.*—The Constitution provides for the right to assemble freely, but noncitizens are prohibited from joining political parties, although they may form social groups. Permits for all public gatherings must be obtained 3 weeks prior to the date of the gathering. The authorities have wide discretion to prohibit such gatherings on public safety grounds but seldom exercise it. There were no reports of government interference in mass gatherings or political rallies.

c. *Freedom of Religion.*—The Constitution provides for freedom of religion, and the Government respects this right in practice.

The 1993 Law on Churches and Religious Organizations requires all religious organizations to have at least 12 members and to be registered with the Interior Ministry and the Board of Religion. Leaders of religious organizations must be citizens with at least 5 years' residence in Estonia.

The majority of Estonians are nominally Lutheran, but following deep-seated tradition there is wide tolerance of other denominations and religions. People of varying ethnic backgrounds profess Orthodoxy, including communities of Russian Old Believers who found refuge in Estonia in the 17th century. The Estonian Apostolic Orthodox Church (EAOC), independent since 1919, subordinate to Constantinople since 1923, and exiled under the Soviet occupation, reregistered under its 1935 statute in August 1993. Since then, a group of ethnic Estonian and Russian parishes preferring to remain under the authority of the Russian Orthodox Church structure imposed during the Soviet occupation has insisted that it should have claim to the EAOC name. This group has refused to register under any other name, although its refusal to register violates the law. During 1996 representatives of the Moscow and Constantinople Patriarchates formed a joint commission to resolve the question. The dispute, which centers on property issues, is the subject of ongoing discussions. The Government has taken a hands off approach to the issue but has assured parishes aligned with the Russian Orthodox Church that they may continue to worship unimpeded. Free worship has occurred in practice.

d. *Freedom of Movement Within the Country, Foreign Travel, Emigration, and Repatriation.*—The law permits free movement within the country, and it is honored in practice. It also provides for the right of foreign travel, emigration, and repatriation for citizens. There are no exit visas.

In July 1993, Parliament enacted a Law on Aliens that defines an alien as a person who is not a citizen of Estonia, i.e., a citizen of another country or a stateless person. The majority of noncitizens are ethnic Russians. The law provided a 1-year period during which noncitizens who came to Estonia prior to July 1, 1990, and were permanent residents of the former Estonian Soviet Socialist Republic, could apply for temporary residence permits. They could also apply for permanent residence at the same time. Following delays and confusion in implementation as well as criticism by international human rights observers, the application deadline was extended by a year, until July 12, 1995. By that date the vast majority of aliens—327,737 of the estimated 370,000—had filed applications. The Government extended the registration period until April 30, 1996. An indeterminate number of noncitizens—estimates range from 20,000 to 50,000—still have not registered.

There were complaints about the slow pace with which the Government was processing residence applications for some 19,000 Russian military pensioners. The process was complicated by the lack of Russian-provided passports in which to affix the permits. An estimated 35 percent of the first group of military pensioners missed the deadline to present their passports for residence permits. Technically, the Citizenship and Migration Board could move to have them deported. In fact, however, the Government is moving on a case-by-case basis to solve the outstanding issues. Late in the year, the Government decided to issue alien passports to those who could not or did not want to take out Russian citizenship.

No restrictions are placed on the right of noncitizens to foreign travel, emigration, or repatriation, although some noncitizens complain of delays in obtaining travel documents. The Government began issuing temporary travel documents valid for a single departure and reentry into the country to resident aliens in 1994. To accommodate entry visa requirements of other countries, the validity period of the document was extended in August 1994 from 6 months to 2 years. In late 1994, the Government began issuing alien passports. These are issued to resident aliens not in possession of any other valid travel document. Such aliens included: (1) persons who are designated as stateless; (2) foreign citizens who lack the opportunity to obtain travel documents of their country of origin or of another state; (3) persons who file for Estonian citizenship and pass the language examination if required; and (4) aliens who are permanently departing Estonia. The Government plans to expand the classes of noncitizens eligible for alien passports. It has already approved their issuance to noncitizens intending to study abroad and has agreed to issue them to former military personnel who cannot or do not want to take out Russian citizenship. By early December, the Government had received about 130,000 applications for alien passports; it had issued more than 65,000. Estonian officials admitted that the pace of issuance had been unsatisfactory initially, but picked up late in the year. The Citizenship and Migration Board planned to issue virtually all the documents by year's end.

The Government has deported a relatively small number of illegal aliens, usually those caught in criminal acts. By late September, 46 illegal aliens were held as internees, pending deportation or a court order granting them residence. After a large-scale escape from the internment prison, most internees were moved to a regular prison. In March 1995, the Government expelled Russian citizen and longtime resident of Estonia, Pyotr Rozhok, for repeated antistate activities. Rozhok was the representative of Vladimir Zhirinovsky's Russian Liberal Democratic Party in Estonia. He appealed the decision; after the case was adjourned in September, a hearing was held in October, and the court ruled that Rozhok's deportation had been procedurally flawed. The Citizenship and Migration Board did not appeal the decision, and Rozhok resides in Estonia.

The Government has no asylum law and does not accord refugee status or asylum. The representative of the United Nations High Commissioner for Refugees (UNHCR) in the Nordic and Baltic states continues to urge Estonia to develop and adopt legislation distinguishing between refugees, applicants for asylum, and illegal immigrants. In 1995 he distributed Estonian language copies of the UNHCR Handbook for Determining Refugee Status. Legislation that would bring Estonian law into conformance with the 1951 U.N. Protocol on the Status of Refugees and its 1967 Protocol has been presented to the Parliament. There were no reports of refugees being returned to areas where they would face persecution.

Section 3. Respect for Political Rights: The Right of Citizens to Change Their Government

Citizens have the right to change their Government. In March 1995, free and fair elections to the second post-Soviet Parliament were held. Among the deputies are six ethnic Russians. Indirect presidential elections were held in August and September. When the Parliament failed to muster the required two-thirds majority to elect the President, an Electoral Assembly consisting of parliament members and representatives of local governments convened and reelected the incumbent, Lennart Meri.

Local elections were held in late October. The Local Elections Law permits resident noncitizens to vote but not to run for office. About one-third of qualified noncitizens registered to vote in local elections, and the vast majority of these turned out to vote. The local elections were free and fair, although due to technical mishaps, some qualified voters were left off the rolls. In May the President rejected the draft of the local elections law that would have required language testing of those candidates who had not acquired an Estonian language education. Parliament agreed to drop this stipulation. All candidates must certify that they know Estonian sufficiently to be able to function in local government. Theoretically, elected council members can be removed from office for insufficient Estonian skills, but no such case has occurred. However, in late December the State Electoral Commission began hearings into a complaint filed by Sillamae town council members against the council chairman who, the complaint alleged, could not speak Estonian.

The Citizenship Law enacted in February 1992 readopted the 1938 Citizenship Law. According to that law, anyone born after 1940 to a citizen parent is a citizen by birth. The parent does not have to be an ethnic Estonian. The Government estimates that under this provision some 80,000 persons not ethnically Estonian have obtained citizenship. The law included requirements for naturalization, such as a 2-year residency requirement, to be followed by a 1-year waiting period, as well as knowledge of the Estonian language.

In January 1995, Parliament adopted a new Citizenship Law, revising the 1992 law and combining into one statute provisions regarding citizenship that were scattered among several pieces of legislation. This law became effective in April 1995. It extended the residency requirement for naturalization from 2 to 5 years and added a requirement for knowledge of the Constitution and the Citizenship Law. Persons who had taken up legal residence in Estonia prior to July 1, 1990, are exempt from the 5-year legal residence and 1-year waiting period requirements. The law allows the Government to waive the language requirement but not the civic knowledge requirement for applicants who have Estonian language elementary or higher education, or who have performed valuable service to Estonia.

According to the latest law, the following classes of persons are ineligible for naturalization: those filing on the basis of false data or documents; those not abiding by the constitutional system or not fulfilling the laws; those who have acted against the State and its security; those who have committed crimes and been punished with a sentence of more than 1 year or who have been repeatedly brought to justice for felonies; those who work or have worked in the intelligence or security services of a foreign state; or those who have served as career soldiers in the armed forces of a foreign state, including those discharged into the reserves or retired. (The latter includes spouses who have come to Estonia in connection with the service member's assignment to a posting, the reserves, or retirement.) A provision of the law allows for the granting of citizenship to a foreign military retiree who has been married to a native citizen for 5 years.

Between 1992 and late October, some 85,300 persons had received citizenship. Some observers attribute this growing but still relatively low number to indecision over whether to apply for Estonian citizenship or citizenship of another country, such as Russia. By August Russian Embassy data showed that more than 110,0000 persons had obtained Russian citizenship, however, the Embassy refused to supply the Government with a list. The Organization for Security and Cooperation in Europe (OSCE) Mission believes that the actual number of Russian citizens may be lower since the Embassy does not seem to keep records on those who die or depart Estonia.

The Citizenship Law was criticized by the Russian Foreign Ministry and by some in the local Russian community as discriminatory. Some Western observers also urged that there be some flexibility shown, especially regarding language requirements for the elderly. However, numerous international fact-finding organizations, including the Finnish Helsinki Committee and the Organization for Security and Cooperation in Europe (OSCE), confirm that the Citizenship Law conforms to international standards.

Bureaucratic delays and the Estonian language requirement are also cited as disincentives for securing citizenship. The Government has established language training centers, but there is a lack of qualified teachers, financial resources, and training materials. Some allege that the examination process, which 75 to 90 percent pass, is arbitrary.

There are no legal impediments to women's participation in government or politics. However, women are underrepresented in government and politics. There are 12 women among the 101 members of Parliament. One of the presidential candidates was also a woman. Two female ministers assumed office after the cabinet reshuffle at the end of the year. There are six ethnic Russian deputies in Parliament.

Section 4. Governmental Attitude Regarding International and Nongovernmental Investigation of Alleged Violations of Human Rights

The Government does not restrict the formation or functioning of human rights organizations. In response to allegations of poor treatment of ethnic minorities, the President established a Human Rights Institute, which first convened in 1992. The purpose of the Institute is to monitor human rights in Estonia and to provide information to the international community. It investigates reports of human rights violations, such as allegations of police abuse and inhuman treatment of detainees. In September the Institute established an information center in the heavily ethnic Russian town of Kohtla-Jarve. In addition because of tensions surrounding the adoption of the Elections Law and the Aliens Law in 1993, the President established a round table composed of representatives of Parliament, the Union of Estonian Nationalities, and the Russian speaking population's Representative Assembly. An analogous but independent round table meets in the county of East Virumaa. In addition with initial funding from the Danish government, a nongovernmental legal information center in Tallinn provides free legal assistance to individuals—citizen and noncitizen alike—seeking advice on human rights-related issues.

In the context of repeated Russian allegations of human rights violations among the noncitizen population, both the OSCE mission in Estonia and the OSCE High Commissioner on National Minorities have declared that they could not find a pattern of human rights violations or abuses in Estonia. Although the Government previously had expressed concern about what it termed biased reporting by the OSCE mission, government relations with the mission were cordial.

Section 5. Discrimination Based on Race, Sex, Religion, Disability, Language, or Social Status

The Constitution prohibits discrimination based on race, sex, religion, disability, language, social status or for any other reason. The Government reports that no court cases charging discrimination have been filed.

Women.—Violence against women, including spousal abuse, was the subject of increasing discussion and media coverage. According to women's groups and law enforcement officials, family violence is not pervasive. Rape and attempted rape occur relatively infrequently. In the first 11 months, there were 93 reported rapes and attempted rapes, compared with 97 for the same period in 1995. However, studies show that 40 percent of crime in Estonia goes unreported, including domestic violence. Even when the police are called, the abused spouse often declines to press charges.

Discussion of the role and situation of women has been extensive, especially in the wake of the Fourth World Conference on Women held in Beijing in 1995, as well as former Social Affairs Minister Siiri Oviir's run for the presidency. Women possess the same legal rights as men and are legally entitled to equal pay for equal work. Nevertheless, although women's average educational level was higher than men's, their average pay was lower, and the trend did not seem to be improving. There continue to be female- and male-dominated professions. Most women carry major household responsibilities in addition to comprising slightly more than one-half of the work force.

Children.—The Government's strong commitment to education is evidenced by the high priority it gives to building and refurbishing schools. The Government provides free medical care for children and subsidizes school meals. In 1992 the Government adopted a Law on Child Protection patterned after the U.N. Convention on the Rights of the Child.

There is no societal pattern of child abuse, but a 1995 research project conducted by the nongovernmental Estonian Union for Child Welfare on children and violence at home found that a significant proportion of children had experienced at least occasional violence at home, in schools, or in youth gangs. A 1996 poll reports that 3 percent of surveyed children had been sexually molested. Finnish press reports alleged large-scale child prostitution in Estonia; the Government called these reports exaggerated but admitted that underage prostitution occurs.

People With Disabilities.—While the Constitution contains provisions to protect disabled persons against discrimination, and both the State and some private organizations provide them with financial assistance, little has been done to enable disabled people to participate normally in public life. There is no public access law, but some effort to accommodate the disabled is evident in the inclusion of ramps at curbs on new urban sidewalk construction. Public transportation firms have acquired some vehicles that are accessible to the disabled, as have some taxi companies.

National/Racial/Ethnic Minorities.—The OSCE mission in Estonia, established in 1993, continued to promote stability, dialog, and understanding among communities in Estonia. In addition the President's Round Table, also established in 1993, which is composed of members of Parliament, representatives of the Union of Estonian Nationalities, and the Representative Assembly of the Russian Community, continued to work toward finding practical solutions to problems of noncitizens, as did the analogous but independent round table that met in the northeastern part of the country (see Section 4).

The Law on Cultural Autonomy for citizens belonging to minority groups was adopted by Parliament and went into effect in 1993. There is a tradition of protection for cultural autonomy going back to a 1925 law. Some noncitizens termed the law discriminatory, since it restricts cultural autonomy only to citizens. The Government replied that noncitizens can fully participate in ethnic organizations and that the law includes subsidies for cultural organizations.

Ethnic Russians total approximately 29 percent, and nonethnic Estonians as a whole some 37 percent, of the population of slightly less than 1.5 million. During the years of Estonia's forced annexation by the Soviet Union, large numbers of non-Estonians, predominantly ethnic Russians, were encouraged to migrate to Estonia to work as laborers and administrators. They and their descendants now make up approximately one-third of the total population; about 40 percent of them were born in Estonia. About 8 percent of the population of the pre-1940 Republic was ethnic Russian.

Some noncitizens, especially Russians, continued to allege job, salary, and housing discrimination because of Estonian language requirements. Russian government officials and parliamentarians echoed these charges in a variety of forums. The law makes no distinction on the basis of lack of citizenship concerning business or property ownership other than for land. A 1996 law on land ownership further liberalized land ownership by foreigners; such ownership is now restricted only in certain strategic areas. All legal residents of Estonia may participate equally in the privatization of state-owned housing.

Estonian language requirements for those employed in the civil service went into effect in 1993. The new Law on Public Service as originally passed required state employees to be proficient in Estonian by the end of 1995. In December 1995, Parliament amended the Law on Public Service to allow noncitizen local and national government employees without adequate Estonian to continue working until February 1, 1997. No noncitizens were to be hired after January 1, 1996. This amendment reflected the Government's awareness that in some sectors, the number of employees with inadequate Estonian remained high. Two railroad employees were dismissed for claiming adequate command of Estonian on the basis of fraudulent certificates. The employees filed suit: one was ordered reinstated and the other's case was pending at year's end.

The language office liberally grants extensions to persons who can explain their failure to meet their requisite competence level in 4 years. Estonian language training is available but, some claim, too costly. Some Russian representatives have asked for free language training. They also charge that the language requirement for citizenship is too difficult, and there has been talk of making the language requirement less rigorous. The examination fee for either language test—for employment or citizenship—is 15 percent of the monthly minimum wage, although it is waived for the unemployed.

Legislation and a government decision provide that in districts where more than one-half of the population speak a language other than Estonian, the inhabitants are entitled to receive official information in that language. Moreover, the local government may conduct business in that language. In practice city governments of predominantly Russian speaking communities conduct most internal business in Russian.

Section 6. Worker Rights

a. *The Right of Association.*—The Constitution provides for the right to form and join a union or employee association. The Central Organization of Estonian Trade Unions (EAKL) came into being as a wholly voluntary and purely Estonian organization in 1990 to replace the Estonian branch of the official Soviet labor confederation, the All-Union Central Council of Trade Unions (AUCCTU). The EAKL has 120,000 members. Another trade union, The Organization of Employee Unions (TALO), split from the EAKL in 1993 and has 50,000 members. About one-third of the country's labor force belongs to one of the two labor federations.

The right to strike is legal, and unions are independent of the Government and political parties. The Constitution and statutes prohibit retribution against strikers. There was a 1-day strike by employees of cultural institutions. Some worker demonstrations occurred to protest low salaries, poor working conditions, or public and private sector enterprise layoff plans.

Unions may join federations freely and affiliate internationally.

b. *The Right to Organize and Bargain Collectively.*—While Estonian workers now have the legally acquired right to bargain collectively, collective bargaining is still in its infancy. According to EAKL leaders, few collective bargaining agreements have been concluded between management and workers of a specific enterprise. The EAKL has, however, concluded framework agreements with producer associations, which provide the basis for specific labor agreements, including the setting of the minimum wage. The EAKL was also involved with developing Estonia's new Labor Code covering employment contracts, vacation, and occupational safety. The Labor Code prohibits antiunion discrimination, and employees have the right to go to court to enforce their rights. In 1993 laws covering collective bargaining, collective dispute resolution, and shop stewards were enacted.

There are no export processing zones.

c. *Prohibition of Forced or Compulsory Labor.*—The Constitution prohibits forced or compulsory labor. The Labor Inspections Office effectively enforces this prohibition.

d. *Minimum Age for Employment of Children.*—The statutory minimum for employment is 16 years of age. Minors 13 to 15 years of age may work with written permission of a parent or guardian and the local labor inspector, if working is not dangerous to the minor's health or considered immoral, does not interfere with studies, and if the type of work is included on a government-prepared list. Government authorities effectively enforce minimum age laws through inspections.

e. *Acceptable Conditions of Work.*—The Government, after consultations with the EAKL and the Central Producers Union, sets the minimum wage. The monthly minimum wage is $62 (680 Estonian crowns). The minimum wage is not sufficient to provide a worker and family with a decent standard of living. About 3 percent of the work force receive the minimum wage. The average monthly wage in the second quarter was about $250.

The standard workweek is 40 hours, and there is a mandatory 24-hour rest period. According to EAKL sources, legal occupational health and safety standards are satisfactory, but they are extremely difficult to achieve in practice. The National Labor Inspection Board is responsible for enforcement of these standards, but it has not been very effective to date. In addition the labor unions have occupational health and safety experts who assist workers into bringing employers in compliance with legal standards. Workers have the right to remove themselves from dangerous work situations without jeopardy to continued employment.

FINLAND

Finland is a constitutional republic with an elected head of state (president), parliament, and head of government (prime minister), and with an independent judiciary.

The security apparatus is effectively controlled by elected officials and supervised by the courts.

Finland has a mixed economy, primarily and extensively market based.

During 1996 there were no reported violations of fundamental human rights.

RESPECT FOR HUMAN RIGHTS

Section 1. Respect for the Integrity of the Person, Including Freedom From:

a. *Political and Other Extrajudicial Killing.*—There were no reports of political or other extrajudicial killings.

b. *Disappearance.*—There were no reports of politically motivated disappearances.

c. *Torture and Other Cruel, Inhuman, or Degrading Treatment or Punishment.*—The law prohibits such practices, and there were no reports that officials employed them.

d. *Arbitrary Arrest, Detention, or Exile.*—The law prohibits arbitrary arrest, detention, or exile, and the Government observes this prohibition.

e. *Denial of Fair Public Trial.*—The law provides for the right to fair public trial, and an independent judiciary vigorously enforces this right. The President appoints Supreme Court justices, who in turn appoint the lower court judges.

Local courts may conduct a trial behind closed doors in juvenile, matrimonial, and guardianship cases, or when publicity would offend morality or endanger the security of the State. In national security cases, the judge may withhold from the public any or all information pertaining to charges, verdicts, and sentences. The law provides for sanctions against violators of such restrictions.

There were no reports of political prisoners.

f. *Arbitrary Interference With Privacy, Family, Home, or Correspondence.*—The law prohibits such practices. Government authorities generally respect these prohibitions, and violations are subject to effective legal sanction.

Section 2. Respect for Civil Liberties, Including:

a. *Freedom of Speech and Press.*—The law provides for freedom of the press, and the Government respects this right in practice. An independent press, an effective judiciary, and a functioning democratic political system combine to ensure freedom of speech and of the press, including academic freedom.

b. *Freedom of Peaceful Assembly and Association.*—The law provides for these rights, and the Government respects them in practice.

c. *Freedom of Religion.*—The law provides for freedom of religion, and the Government respects this right in practice.

d. *Freedom of Movement Within the Country, Foreign Travel, Emigration, and Repatriation.*—The law provides for these rights, and the Government respects them in practice.

The Government cooperates with the United Nations High Commissioner for Refugees and other humanitarian organizations in assisting refugees. Approved refugees and asylum seekers are processed directly for residence. The issue of the provision of first asylum has never arisen. There were no reports of forced expulsion of those having a valid claim to refugee status.

Section 3. Respect for Political Rights: The Right of Citizens to Change Their Government

The Constitution provides citizens with the right to peacefully change their Government, and citizens exercise this right in practice through periodic, free and fair elections held on the basis of universal suffrage.

Women are fairly well represented in government. There are 67 in the 200-member Parliament, and 7 in the 18-member Cabinet. The Ministers of Foreign Affairs and Defense as well as the Associate Minister of Finance are women, as are the Speaker of Parliament and the President of the Bank of Finland. In 1995 Parliament passed quota legislation for all state committees, commissions, and appointed municipal bodies, requiring a minimum of 40 percent membership from each sex.

Section 4. Governmental Attitude Regarding International and Nongovernmental Investigation of Alleged Violations of Human Rights

A number of human rights groups operate without government restriction, investigating and publishing their findings on human rights cases. Government officials are very cooperative and responsive to their views.

Section 5. Discrimination Based on Race, Sex, Religion, Disability, Language, or Social Status

The law prohibits any discrimination based on race, sex, religion, disability, language, or social status, and the Government effectively enforces these provisions.

Assaults by local "skinheads" on a black American in November 1995 focused attention on racism and xenophobia in Finland. President Ahtisaari mentioned the danger of xenophobia and racism in his New Year's speech to the nation. A ministerial group was established to devise a government program against racism by year's end. Initial plans include improved human rights training for police and other officials and more antidiscrimination education. Antiracism public relations activities increased and include projects targeting elementary and secondary schools.

Women.—The law provides for stringent penalties for violence against women; this provision is vigorously enforced by the police and the courts. The Union of Shelter Homes as well as the municipalities maintain such homes for female, male, and child victims of violence in homes all over the country. The total number of shelter units is around 55. Studies show that the opening of a shelter home in an area brings cases of family violence out into the open. The concept of family violence in Finland includes negligence in care, psychological violence, and economic abuse. The annual number of calls to the police relating to domestic violence is no longer centrally compiled but is estimated at some 10,000 to 12,000. Shelter officials state that the figure is less than half of the number of actual incidents. Police statistics from January to June show an overall rise of 10 percent in the number of assaults (statistics not broken down by sex). There were 100 cases of rape reported to police during this period. Government experts note no evidence of a significant change in the incidence of rape in recent years but say that as many as half of all rapes may go unreported.

The government-established Council for Equality coordinates and sponsors legislation to meet the needs of women as workers, mothers, widows, or retirees.

In 1985 Parliament passed a comprehensive equal rights law which mandates equal treatment for women in the workplace, including equal pay for "comparable" jobs. In practice comparable worth has not been implemented because of the difficulty of establishing criteria, but the Government, employers, unions, and others continue to work on implementation plans. Women's average earnings are 80 percent of those of men, and women still tend to be segregated in lower paying occupations. While women have individually attained leadership positions in the private and public sectors, there are disproportionately fewer women in top management jobs. Industry and finance, the labor movement, and some government ministries remain male dominated. Women are permitted to serve in the military. The Government's Equality Ombudsman monitors compliance with regulations against sexual discrimination. Of the 100 complaints processed by the Ombudsman between January 1 and June 30, 29 cases were established as violations of the law.

Children.—The Government demonstrates its strong commitment to children's rights and welfare through its well-funded systems of public education and medical care. There is no pattern of societal abuse of children, and the national consensus supporting children's rights is enshrined in law.

People With Disabilities.—Although the law has required since the 1970's that new public buildings be accessible to people with physical disabilities, many older buildings remain inaccessible to them. There is no such law for public transportation, but each municipality subsidizes measures to improve accessibility to vehicles. Local governments maintain a free transport service that guarantees 18 free trips per month for a disabled person. The deaf and the mute are provided interpretation services ranging from 120 to 240 hours annually. The Government provides subsidized public housing to the severely disabled.

Indigenous People.—Sami (Lapps), who constitute less than one-tenth of 1 percent of the population, benefit from legal provisions protecting minority rights and customs. Sami language and culture are supported financially by the Government. The Sami receive subsidies to enable them to continue their traditional lifestyle, which revolves around reindeer herding. Sami have full political and civil rights and are able to participate in decisions affecting their economic and cultural interests.

Section 6. Worker Rights

a. *The Right of Association.*—The Constitution provides for the rights of trade unions to organize, to assemble peacefully, and to strike, and the Government respects these provisions. About 87 percent of the work force is organized. All unions are independent of the Government and political parties. The law grants public sector employees the right to strike, with some exceptions for provision of essential services. In the first quarter of 1996, there were 36 strikes, 35 of which were wildcat strikes.

Trade unions freely affiliate with international bodies.

b. *The Right to Organize and Bargain Collectively.*—The law provides for the right to organize and bargain collectively. Collective bargaining agreements are usually based on incomes policy agreements between employee and employer central organizations and the Government. The law protects workers against antiunion discrimination. Complaint resolution is governed by collective bargaining agreements as well as labor law, both of which are adequately enforced.

There are no export processing zones.

c. *Prohibition of Forced Compulsory Labor.*—The Constitution prohibits forced or compulsory labor, and this prohibition is honored in practice.

d. *Minimum Age for Employment of Children.*—Youths under 16 years of age cannot work more than 6 hours a day or at night, and education is compulsory for children from 7 to 16 years of age. The Labor Ministry enforces child labor regulations. There are virtually no complaints of exploitation of children in the work force.

e. *Acceptable Conditions of Work.*—There is no legislated minimum wage, but the law requires all employers—including nonunionized ones—to meet the minimum wages agreed to in collective bargaining agreements in the respective industrial sector. These minimum wages generally afford a decent standard of living for workers and their families.

The legal workweek consists of 5 days not exceeding 40 hours. Employees working in shifts or during the weekend are entitled to a 24-hour rest period during the week. The law is effectively enforced as a minimum, and many workers enjoy even stronger benefits through effectively enforced collective bargaining agreements.

The Government sets occupational health and safety standards, and the Labor Ministry effectively enforces them. Workers can refuse dangerous work situations, without risk of penalty.

FRANCE

France is a constitutional democracy with a directly elected President and National Assembly and an independent judiciary.

The law enforcement and internal security apparatus consists of a Gendarmerie, national police, and municipal police forces in major cities, all of which are under effective civilian control.

The highly developed, diversified, and primarily market-based economy provides residents with a high standard of living.

The Government fully respected the human rights of its citizens, and the law and judiciary provide effective means of dealing with individual instances of abuse. Racially motivated attacks by extremists doubled, from 207 in 1994 to 454 in 1995 (latest available data). The Government has taken important steps to combat violence against women and children. Women continue to face wage discrimination. A series of apparently politically motivated terrorist bombings killed over a dozen persons in Corsica.

RESPECT FOR HUMAN RIGHTS

Section 1. Respect for the Integrity of the Person, Including Freedom From:

a. *Political and Other Extrajudicial Killing.*—There were no reports of political or other extrajudicial killings by government officials.

Law enforcement officers have in the past used excessive force—particularly directed against immigrants—resulting in deaths, but there is no evidence of a pattern of such abuses. In February a Paris court found a police officer guilty of involuntary homicide in the 1993 death of Makome M'Bowole, a 17-year-old youth from Zaire shot during an interrogation at a Paris police station. Judges sentenced the officer to 8 years in prison, the longest sentence ever given to a police officer convicted of this crime. In May in a case involving the 1993 shooting death of 17-year-old Rachid Ardjouni, the Court of Appeal reduced the sentence imposed against a police officer found guilty of involuntary manslaughter. Amnesty International criticized the court's decision to expunge the conviction from the officer's criminal record, permitting him to continue to serve as a police officer carrying a firearm. Judicial and administrative inquiries have also been opened by the Government into the 1995 shooting death of 8-year-old Serbian refugee Todor Bogdanovic. Border police in the Bogdanovic case have been accused of using excessive force in attempting to halt a convoy of refugees who ran a border check point. The judicial inquiry into the December 1993 shooting and killing of 19-year-old Algerian Mourad Tchier by a police officer near Lyon continued at year's end. The U.N. Special Rapporteur on Extrajudicial, Summary or Arbitrary executions, in a 1996 report, cited the Tchier case in expressing his concern over what he characterized as the increasing use of excessive force by law enforcement officers. A judicial inquiry into the January 1994 death of an 18-year-old Algerian youth, Ibrahim Sy, shot by a gendarme near Rouen, continued at year's end.

Reza Mazoulman, an Iranian Deputy Education Minister under the Shah, was shot and killed in Paris in May. Two Iranian nationals are suspected in the shooting: One is being held in Germany awaiting extradition to France; the other is suspected of having fled to Iran.

In six cases, extreme rightwing youths attacked and killed members of minority ethnic groups (see Section 5).

In Corsica there were over a dozen killings and an average of one bombing a day, some of which were politically motivated.

On December 3, an apparently politically motivated terrorist bombing in the Paris Metro killed 2 people and injured 97. A third bombing victim died from his wounds a few days later.

b. *Disappearance.*—There were no reports of politically motivated disappearance.

c. *Torture and Other Cruel, Inhuman, or Degrading Treatment or Punishment.*— The law prohibits such practices and the authorities punish officials who employ them. However, there were credible reports that law enforcement officers used excessive force, particularly against immigrants. Isolated instances of police misconduct occurred, but there is no evidence of a pattern of such abuses.

Three Marseille police officers have been suspended and charged with illegal detention, premeditated assault, and theft in the 1995 beating of Algerian/French national Sid Ahmed Amiri. The officers have been released on bail pending trial. In January an officer of the intervention squad of the French anticriminal brigade was given a 4-month prison sentence (which was suspended) and fined for the 1994 assault and battery against Didier la Rouche. In 1995 an officer in the border police was sentenced in Nice to 24 months' imprisonment, with 16 months suspended, for the 1993 sexual assault of Moufida Ksouri, a French citizen of Tunisian origin. The Government has also opened an administrative inquiry into allegations that Tahitian trade union leader Hiro Tefaareve and 15 others were arrested and beaten in 1995 by members of the Gendarmerie Nationale following protests over the resumption of French nuclear testing in the Pacific.

Prison conditions generally exceed international standards, and the Government permits visits by human rights monitors. Most prisons provide opportunities for paid employment as well as recreational facilities. In a report released in January, the European Committee for the Prevention of Torture criticized overcrowding and unhygienic conditions in Paris' municipal jail cells. In its 1995 report, the French organization, "International Observer of Prisons (IOP)" noted an increasing number of deaths in detention attributable to neglectful surveillance and supervision. In one case, a prison guard was charged and held pending trial for not assisting an inmate who was being assaulted by four other prisoners. The report also criticized overcrowding in some prisons and a record number of 107 inmate suicides in 1995 (latest available data). IOP also observed that the promise of greater access to health care for prisoners offered by the passage of 1994 legislation has not been realized, because most prisons have delayed application of needed reforms.

d. *Arbitrary Arrest, Detention, or Exile.*—The law prohibits arbitrary arrest, detention, or exile, and the Government observes this prohibition.

In narcotics trafficking convictions, courts often assess a customs fine based on the estimated street value of the drugs, in addition to a jail sentence. At the end of their jail terms, prisoners who cannot pay the fine are detained for up to 2 years while customs officials attempt to reach the largest possible settlement. This practice has been criticized by the European Court of Justice.

A 1994 case continues against 6 of 26 resident non-French Muslims detained by police on suspicion of supporting Algerian terrorists. Twenty of the detainees had been deported after several weeks' detention.

There are no provisions for exile, and it does not occur.

e. *Denial of Fair Public Trial.*—The law provides for an independent judiciary, and the Government respects this provision in practice.

The judiciary provides citizens with a fair and efficient judicial process. There is a system of local courts, 35 regional courts of appeal, and the highest criminal court, the Court of Cassation, which considers appeals on procedural grounds only.

There were no reports of political prisoners.

f. *Arbitrary Interference With Privacy, Family, Home, or Correspondence.*—The law prohibits such practices, government authorities generally respect these prohibitions, and violations are subject to effective legal sanction.

Section 2. Respect for Civil Liberties, Including:

a. *Freedom of Speech and Press.*—The law provides for freedom of speech and the press, and the Government respects these rights in practice. An independent press, an effective judiciary, and a functioning democratic political system combine to ensure freedom of speech and of the press, including academic freedom.

In August the elected Mayor of Orange in southern France, a member of the far-right National Front (FN) political party, used his police powers to halt the distribution of anti-FN literature in Orange. The measures taken by the Mayor were promptly suspended by an administrative tribunal. A few weeks later, another mayor in the town of La Grande-Motte (also in southern France) again temporarily suspended the distribution of anti-FN literature just before the start of a 1-week FN convention. This action was also promptly suspended. There have been other reported incidents of similar efforts to suppress anti-FN speech.

In November a criminal court sentenced two singers to 3 to 6 months in prison and imposed a 6-month ban on their performing. The charges stemmed from a 1995 concert where the group "NTM" performed a song in which they advocated the murder of police officers. At year's end, neither singer had begun serving a jail sentence, since their cases were under appeal.

b. *Freedom of Peaceful Assembly and Association.*—The law provides for these rights, and the Government respects them in practice.

c. *Freedom of Religion.*—The law provides for separation of church and state, and the Government respects this right in practice.

The State subsidizes private schools, including those that are church-affiliated. Central or local governments also own and provide upkeep for other religious buildings constructed before 1905, the date of the law separating church and state. Cultural associations with religious affiliations may also qualify for government subsidies. Contrary to practice in the rest of France, the Jewish, Lutheran, Reformed, and Roman Catholic religions in three departments of Alsace and Lorraine enjoy special legal status. Adherents of these four religions may choose to have a portion of their income tax allocated to their church in a system administered by the central Government.

Debate continues over whether denying some Muslim girls the right to wear headscarves in public schools constitutes a violation of the right to practice their religion. In 1989 the highest administrative court ruled that the "ostentatious" wearing of these headscarves violated a law prohibiting proselytizing in schools. After much media attention—mainly unfavorable—to the wearing of such headscarves, in 1994 the Ministry of Education issued a directive that prohibits the wearing of "ostentatious political and religious symbols" in schools. The directive does not specify the "symbols" in question, leaving school administrators considerable authority to do so. The highest administrative court affirmed in 1995 that simply wearing a headscarf does not provide grounds for exclusion from school.

In 1995 the highest administrative court ruled that Jewish students could be excused from attending classes on Saturdays, the Jewish Sabbath. The court said that a 1991 law laying out the rights and responsibilities of students in public schools could not be used to prevent authorized absence from school for religious worship or the celebration of a religious holiday.

In November a former leader of the Scientologists in Lyon was convicted of involuntary homicide and fraud, sentenced to 18 months in prison, and fined about $100,000. The charges stemmed from a 1988 suicide of one of the church's members. The court found that the psychological pressure by the Scientologists caused the member's suicide, but specifically avoided ruling on the issue of whether Scientology is a religion. Other Scientologists were also convicted of fraud related to this incident, fined, and given suspended sentences. The convictions are being appealed.

d. *Freedom of Movement Within the Country, Foreign Travel, Emigration, and Repatriation.*—The law provides for these rights, and the Government respects them in practice.

France provides first asylum and provided it to approximately 17,200 persons in 1996. The Government cooperates with the United Nations High Commissioner for Refugees and other humanitarian organizations in assisting refugees. There were no reports of forced return of persons to a country where they feared persecution.

The pace of deportations of illegal aliens has increased, with reportedly double the number of charter flights returning illegal aliens to their homelands, compared with the previous year. In July and August, approximately 300 undocumented aliens occupied St. Bernard's Church in Paris, protesting against toughened immigration laws and asking to be allowed to remain in France. Ten staged a hunger strike. Ultimately, the Government forcibly entered the church and arrested the protestors, drawing praise and criticism from different sectors of political opinion. More than a dozen of the protestors were deported, but most were released within a few days of their arrest and remain at liberty while their individual cases are considered. There is no evidence that those deported had valid claims of refugee or legal status in France. In fact, at one point, the Government had reviewed the files of the St. Bernard protesters and authorized 48 of them to remain, primarily those with French citizen children.

Section 3. Respect for Political Rights: The Right of Citizens to Change Their Government

The Constitution provides citizens with the right to peacefully change their government, and citizens exercise this right in practice through periodic, free, and fair elections held on the basis of universal suffrage.

There are no legal restrictions on the participation of women in politics or government, but they remain significantly underrepresented in public offices, especially at the national level. Four of 32 cabinet members, 18 of 321 Senators, and 32 of 577 Deputies in the National Assembly are women. To increase women's participation, some parties have established quotas for them on electoral lists or in party management.

The citizens of the "collective territory" of Mayotte and the territories of French Polynesia, Wallis and Futuna, and New Caledonia determine their legal and political relationships to France by means of referendums, and they elect Deputies and Senators to the French Parliament.

Section 4. Governmental Attitude Regarding International and Nongovernmental Investigation of Alleged Violations of Human Rights

A wide variety of local and international human rights organizations operate freely, investigating and publishing their findings on human rights cases. Government officials are generally cooperative and responsive to their views. The National Consultative Commission on Human Rights (NCCHR)—which has nongovernmental as well as government members—also monitors complaints and advises the Government on policies and legislation. It is an independent body in the Office of the Prime Minister.

Section 5. Discrimination Based on Race, Sex, Religion, Disability, Language, or Social Status

Statutes ban discrimination based on race, religion, sex, ethnic background, or political opinion, and the Government effectively enforces them.

Women.—The penal code prohibits abuse as well as violence against women. Wife beating is a felony. The penalty for rape ranges from 5 to 20 years in prison, with no differentiation between spousal and other rape. There were 6,540 reported rapes or sexual assaults in 1995 (latest available data). Some 15,700 incidents of wife beating (including 98 which resulted in death) were reported to police in 1993 (latest available data). The Government offers shelter, counseling, and financial assistance, and operates a telephone hot line. The welcome centers for battered women added 500 staff members in 1995. About 60 private associations also help battered women.

While the law requires that women receive equal pay for equal work, this requirement is often not the reality. A 1994 study (latest available data) found a mean discrepancy between wages of women and men of 20 percent in the private sector and 18 percent in the public sector. The same study found that the unemployment rate for women averaged about 4 points higher than that for men. The law prohibits sex-based job discrimination and sexual harassment in the workplace. Thus far these laws have encountered difficulties in implementation. Women's rights groups criticize the scope of the law as narrow, and the fines and compensatory damages as often modest. For example, the law limits sexual harassment claims to circumstances where there is a supervisor-subordinate relationship, but fails to address harassment by colleagues or a hostile work environment.

Children.—The Government demonstrates a strong commitment to children's rights and welfare through well-funded systems of public education and medical care. The Ministry for Family Affairs oversees implementation of the government's programs for children. There are strict laws against child abuse, particularly when committed by a parent or guardian. In 1994 (latest available data) there were 15,000 reported cases of mistreatment (physical violence, sexual abuse, mental cruelty, or severe negligence) against children. Special sections of the national police and judiciary are charged with handling these cases. The Government provides counseling, financial aid, foster homes, and orphanages, depending on the extent of the problem. Various associations also help minors seek justice in cases of mistreatment by parents.

Some immigrants from countries where female genital mutilation (FGM) is customary subject their children to this practice, which is widely condemned by international health experts as damaging to both physical and psychological health. The authorities have prosecuted some cases involving FGM and have undertaken a campaign to inform immigrants that FGM is contrary to the law and will be prosecuted.

People With Disabilities.—There is no discrimination against disabled persons in employment, education, or in the provision of other state services. The Government announced several measures in 1995 to boost employment opportunities for the disabled. A 1991 law requires new public buildings to be accessible to the physically disabled, but most older buildings and public transportation are not accessible.

Religious Minorities.—The annual NCCHR report (see Section 4) released in March noted a 50 percent decrease in the number of threats or attacks against Jews, from 169 in 1994 to 78 in 1995 (latest available data). However, in July a former skinhead and neo-Nazi group member confessed to the 1990 desecration of a Jewish cemetery in the southeastern city of Carpentras. The Government is vigorously prosecuting those responsible, but the revelation of neo-Nazi involvement in this incident, in which 34 Jewish tombs were vandalized and freshly buried corpses unearthed and impaled, has further contributed to the perception that racist/anti-Semitic violence is a serious problem.

National/Racial/Ethnic Minorities.—Anti-immigrant sentiments sparked incidents including occasional attacks by skinheads on members of the large Arab/Muslim and black African communities. The annual NCCHR report noted that racist attacks and threats had doubled in 1 year, from 207 in 1994 to 454 in 1995 (latest available data). The number of deaths attributed by the NCCHR to racist anti-immigrant violence increased from two deaths in 1994 to six deaths in 1995 (latest available data). The racial attacks that resulted in deaths include the following cases. Three FN youths await trial in the 1995 killing in Marseille of Ibrahim Ali, a 17-year-old shot in the back when FN youths opened fire on a dozen Comoriens during a political rally. Three skinheads have been arrested and still await trial for the 1995 death of Brahim Bouraam, a young Moroccan bystander pushed off a quay during another FN political rally. Another skinhead was arrested for theft in May 1995 and confessed that one of his friends had killed a Tunisian in April 1995 in Le Havre, by throwing him into the harbor. In May 1995, an FN militant stabbed an Algerian to death after an altercation in Cherbourg. Another right-wing militant awaits trial for beating to death a North African immigrant in September 1995 in Bayonne.

The Government strongly condemns such actions and attacks, has strict antidefamation laws, and prosecutes perpetrators whenever possible. Government programs attempt to combat racism and anti-Semitism by promoting public awareness and bringing together local officials, police, and citizen groups. There are also antiracist educational programs in some public school systems.

Section 6. Worker Rights

a. *The Right of Association.*—The Constitution provides for freedom of association for all workers. Trade unions exercise significant economic and political influence, although only about 10 percent of the work force is unionized. Unions have legally mandated roles (as do employers) in the administration of social institutions, including social security (health care and most retirement systems), the unemployment insurance system, labor courts, and the economic and social council, a constitutionally mandated consultative body.

Unions are independent of the Government, and most are not aligned with any political party. Many of the leaders of the General Confederation of Labor and its unions, however, belong to the Communist Party. Unions can freely join federations and confederations, including international bodies.

Workers, including civil servants, are free to strike except when a strike threatens public safety. One-fourth of all salaried employees work for the Government: Strikes in the public sector tend to be fairly numerous and receive extensive media coverage. In May an estimated 7,000 workers demonstrated nationwide to demand a shorter workweek without a reduction in pay. In June an estimated 14,000 workers demonstrated nationwide to protest government-proposed cutbacks in public sector jobs and services. An estimated 150,000 workers joined a nationwide strike on October 17 to protest government austerity reforms expected to result in especially large cuts in education, defense, communications, and aviation. In October journalists also staged a day-long strike to protest a government proposal to repeal a tax exemption for journalists. A 12-day truckers' strike in late November to demand early retirement, a shorter workweek, and pay increases caused serious disruptions in highway and port traffic and in gasoline supplies nationwide.

The law prohibits retaliation against strikers and strike leaders, and the Government effectively enforces this provision.

b. *The Right to Organize and Bargain Collectively.*—Workers, including those in the three small export processing zones, have the right to organize and bargain collectively. The law strictly prohibits antiunion discrimination; employers found guilty of such activity are required to correct it, including the reinstatement of workers fired for union activities.

A 1982 law requires at least annual bargaining in the public and private sector on wages, hours, and working conditions at both plant and industry levels but does not require that negotiations result in a signed contract. In case of an impasse, government mediators may impose solutions that are binding unless formally rejected by either side within a week. If no new agreement can be reached, the contract from the previous year remains valid. Over 90 percent of the private sector work force is covered by collective bargaining agreements negotiated at national or local levels.

Trilateral consultations (unions, management, and government) also take place on such subjects as the minimum wage, temporary work, social security, and unemployment benefits. Labor tribunals, composed of worker and employer representatives, are available to resolve complaints.

The law requires businesses with more than 50 employees to establish a works council, through which workers are consulted on training, working conditions, profit-sharing, and similar issues. Works councils, which are open to both union and non-union employees, are elected every 2 years.

The Constitution's provisions for trade union rights extend to France's overseas departments and territories.

c. *Prohibition of Forced or Compulsory Labor.*—Forced or compulsory labor is prohibited by law, and the Government effectively enforces this provision. In its 1993 report, however, the International Labor Organization's Committee of Experts (COE) questioned the French practice of obliging prisoners to work for private enterprises at less than the national minimum wage. In 1995 the Government officially responded to the COE, pointing out that prisoners participate in a work program on a voluntary—not a mandatory—basis, that more prisoners request work than can be accommodated, and that the work is designed to prepare prisoners for reentry into the labor force.

d. *Minimum Age for Employment of Children.*—With a few exceptions for those enrolled in certain apprenticeship programs, children under the age of 16 may not be employed. Generally, work considered arduous or work between the hours of 10 p.m. and 5 a.m. may not be performed by minors under age 18. Laws prohibiting child employment are effectively enforced through periodic checks by labor inspectors, who have the authority to take employers to court for noncompliance with the law.

e. *Acceptable Conditions of Work.*—The administratively determined minimum wage, revised whenever the cost-of-living index rises 2 percentage points, is sufficient to provide a decent standard of living for a worker and family. The wage was changed to $7.23 (F 37.91) per hour as of July 1.

The legal workweek is 39 hours, with a minimum break of 24 hours per week. Overtime is restricted to 9 hours per week.

The Ministry of Labor has overall responsibility for policing occupational health and safety laws. Standards are high and effectively enforced. Workers have the right to remove themselves from dangerous work situations. The law requires each enterprise with 50 or more employees to establish an occupational health and safety committee. Over 75 percent of all enterprises, covering more than 75 percent of all employees, have fully functioning health and safety committees.

GEORGIA

Georgia declared independence from the Soviet Union in 1991. Multiparty parliamentary elections followed a short-lived military coup in 1992. In August 1995, Parliament adopted a Constitution that provides for an executive branch that reports to the President, a legislature, and an independent judiciary. In November 1995, Eduard Shevardnadze was elected President and a new Parliament was selected in elections described by international observers as generally consistent with democratic norms except in the region of Ajara. The President appoints ministers with the consent of the Parliament. The judiciary is subject to executive pressure.

Internal conflicts in Abkhazia and South Ossetia remain unresolved. These conflicts, together with problems created by roughly 250,000 internally displaced persons (IDP's), pose the greatest threat to national stability. In 1993 Abkhaz separatists forcibly took control of Abkhazia, and most ethnic Georgians, a large percentage of the population, fled the region. In 1994 Russian peacekeeping forces representing the Commonwealth of Independent States (CIS) deployed in the conflict area with the agreement of the Government and the Abkhaz separatists. Despite the presence of peacekeepers there has been little repatriation of ethnic Georgian IDP's apart from some spontaneous returns to the Gali region, where the security situation remains unstable. A Russian peacekeeping force has been in South Ossetia since June 1992. Repatriation to South Ossetia has also been slow. The Government has no effective control over either Abkhazia or South Ossetia. There were no large-scale armed hostilities in South Ossetia or Abkhazia in 1996, but Abkhaz and Georgian armed bands operated in the Gali region.

The Ministry of Interior (MVD) and Procuracy have primary responsibility for law enforcement, and the Ministry of State Security (MGB formerly KGB plays a significant role in internal security. In times of internal disorder, the Government may call on the army. Reformist, elected, civilian authorities maintain inadequate control of the security forces. The MVD and Procuracy especially committed serious human rights abuses.

The economy improved, led by gains in trade and services, agriculture, and transportation. The economy remains primarily agricultural. Foreign aid makes a large contribution to the economy. Per capita gross domestic product is estimated at over $500.

The Government continued efforts to improve its human rights record, but significant problems remain. These include police and security force abuse and beating of prisoners and detainees, forced confessions, inhumane prison conditions, deaths in custody, judicial corruption, denial of fair and expeditious trials, and arbitrary interference with privacy and home. Some press freedoms are constrained, the judiciary is subject to executive pressure, and discrimination against women is a problem. There is, however, a growing awareness on the part of the people of their individual rights. The number and variety of independent nongovernmental organizations (NGO's) is growing. The Parliament is more active and reformist than its predecessor. Independent newspapers show a greater willingness to criticize government policies.

RESPECT FOR HUMAN RIGHTS

Section 1. Respect for the Integrity of the Person Including Freedom From:

a. *Political and Other Extrajudicial Killing.*—In 1996, there was a sharp drop in the level of violence due to improved political and social stability. Perpetrators of atrocities and other political killings arising from the separatist conflict in the region of Abkhazia are not being investigated, prosecuted, or punished. President Shevardnadze proposed in 1995 that the United Nations create a body to investigate and punish those guilty of crimes against humanity in Abkhazia. The U.N. Observer Mission in Georgia (UNOMIG) and the Organization for Security and Cooperation in Europe (OSCE) mission in Georgia have sent teams into Abkhazia to investigate security incidents and human rights abuses.

The authorities reported that 13 people died while in pretrial detention, a decline from 40 last year. All deaths were officially attributed to medical causes, but physical abuse and torture of prisoners also played a role (see Section 1.c.).

Abkhaz separatist authorities continue to condone violence to discourage the repatriation of ethnic Georgian internally displaced persons to the Gali district. In spite of the cessation of large-scale hostilities in 1993 and the presence of peacekeepers, there has been little repatriation. About 10 percent of IDP's and refugees have returned. A series of politically motivated attacks occurred in Abkhazia directed at civilians by both Georgian and Abkhaz armed bands. The most serious occurred on January 5. Three young men wearing a mix of military and civilian clothing fatally shot eight members of an ethnic Georgian family in Shesheleti, Abkhazia. The U.N.'s report characterized the attack as "well-planned, not random, and carried out with ruthless efficiency." The identity of the perpetrators remains unknown.

b. *Disappearance.*—According to the State Committee on Human Rights and to Abkhaz separatist authorities, the fate of over 1,000 Georgians and Abkhaz who have disappeared since 1992 as a result of the Abkhaz conflict is still unknown. The OSCE reports that the Government has 10 Abkhaz in detention. The Abkhaz authorities reportedly hold about 24 ethnic Georgians (see Section 1.d.). Partisan groups active in Abkhazia periodically take hostages. There is some cooperation between the two sides on exchange of hostages.

c. *Torture and Other Cruel, Inhuman, or Degrading Treatment or Punishment.*—The Constitution forbids the use of torture, but serious abuses occur. Members of security forces continued, on a routine basis, to beat and abuse prisoners and detainees. According to Amnesty International and Human Rights Watch, there were instances of torture and mistreatment, including the use of electric shock. Government officials claim that a lack of proper training and supervision of investigators and guards often results in cases of abuse. Corruption and criminality also play a role. The most serious incidents of abuse occur in the investigative stage of pretrial detention when suspects are interrogated by police. A number of policemen have been arrested or disciplined for physical abuse, and five, including the former head of the MVD's narcotics unit, were put on trial.

Members of the Parliamentary Committee on Human Rights and Ethnic Relations have independently investigated claims of abuse. In particular the subcommittee on prisons has been very active.

Prison authorities admit that conditions are inhuman in many facilities. They blame inadequate cells, medicine, and food on a lack of resources. In the pretrial detention facility in Tbilisi for example, 2,050 inmates are housed in a prison designed for fewer than 1,000. Cells can contain as many as 36 inmates with so few beds that they must sleep in shifts. The lack of proper sanitation, medical care, and food poses a serious threat to the life and health of prisoners. Tuberculosis is a particular problem. Government plans announced in 1995 to build a new pretrial detention center remain unfulfilled. The poor condition of prisons is a contributing factor to the pretrial detention mortality rate. Thirteen people died in pretrial detention. Although officially attributed to medical causes, physical abuse and torture were also factors in these deaths.

Until March the International Committee of the Red Cross (ICRC) had only limited access to detainees and prisoners. From March to October, the ICRC found that its access improved, but it still had to make several applications and get senior-level approval for some visits.

On October 10, President Shevardnadze issued a decree instructing the Ministers of Security, Interior, and the Procuracy to allow ICRC access without obstacle to all detainees in all places of detention. The President issued his decree after months of unsuccessful negotiations between the ICRC and the ministries to ensure appropriate access. The President's instructions were carried out, and the ICRC had full access to detention facilities at year's end in accordance with its customary procedures, which include meetings with the detainees without the presence of third-party observers and the regular repetition of visits. This year the ICRC saw 243 prisoners in Georgian detention, as well as 60 in the custody of Abkhaz separatist authorities. Many of these detainees and prisoners were visited repeatedly. The OSCE mission and foreign diplomats had some access to detainees and prisoners.

International human rights monitors have faced obstacles in connection with prisoners arrested in 1995 for alleged involvement in the assassination attempt on President Shevardnadze. When eventually allowed to meet with some, though not all, of these individuals, government officials remained in the room. Despite earlier assurances of access, the Procuracy continued to prevent international monitors from meeting with several of these detainees. Following the attempted assassination of President Shevardnadze, the MVD arrested dozens of individuals. Many continue to be held and officials from the Office of the Prosecutor tried to prevent human rights monitors from meeting several of the detainees. At least one of those detained, former security service Captain Guram Papukashvili, was beaten severely. After several scheduled meetings with Papukashvili were canceled, officials allowed human rights monitors to meet him in March, but not alone. Papukashvili reported that since his arrest he had developed kidney problems and coughed up blood. In April he confirmed to his attorney that he had been beaten. These restrictions prevented independent verification of reports of torture and abuse, denial of medical care, and denial of prisoners' access to their attorneys. No appeal nor complaint was filed by Papukashvile's attorneys.

Human rights monitors were also denied permission to see Loti Kobalia, Badri Zarandia, and other members of the former Gamsakhurdia government on trial for high treason and other crimes, on the grounds that their cases were ongoing. Court officials allowed monitors and journalists to meet defendant Nugzar Molodinashvili, a onetime member of Gamsakhurdia's Supreme Council, after he declared a hunger strike that lasted more than 30 days.

Colonel Gia Korbesashvili, arrested and severely beaten as a suspect in the July 1995 attempted bombing of a bridge in Tbilisi, is still under investigation by the MVD. The case is in the Tbilisi city court, but the trial has not yet started. The Office of the Human Rights Defender created in 1995 is not yet functioning (see Section 1.d.).

d. *Arbitrary Arrest, Detention, or Exile.*—The Constitution provides for a 9-month period of maximum pretrial detention, mandated court approval of detention after 72 hours, and restrictions on the role of the prosecutor (see Section 1.e.). These safeguards are not yet in force and not observed. A new Criminal Code, which will bring into force the constitutionally mandated restrictions on the powers of the Procuracy and the police, is scheduled to be introduced in Parliament by the end of the first quarter of 1997 (see Section 1.e.). The Criminal Code of the former Georgian Soviet Socialist Republic continues to be used by a law enforcement and court system that has been slow to adapt to democratic norms. Under Soviet law, prosecutors issued warrants for arrests and searches without court approval. Persons could be legally detained for up to 72 hours without charge. After 72 hours, the prosecutor was required to approve the detention. However, this approval was often a formality as it was normally the prosecutor who initiated the arrest in the first place. The law allowed for a maximum of 18 months of detention before trial. In practice even these provisions are frequently violated. Virtually no means are available for accused individuals to present their cases to a judge prior to trial. This effectively means that pretrial detention is at the discretion of the prosecutor.

Persons detained on suspicion of involvement in the attempted assassination of President Shevardnadze in August 1995 have been held without trial for 15 months and no trial dates have been set. In a separate case, Giorgi Korbesashvili was arrested in July 1995, beaten several times, denied access to an attorney of his choosing for seven months, and not told of the charges against him. He continues to await trail on charges of plotting to blow up a bridge in Tbilisi (see Section 1.c.).

On August 7, police arrested Eldar Gogoladze, a colonel in the State Security Service, on suspicion of weapons possession. At the time of his arrest, Gogoladze had a permit to carry a weapon. Police searched Gogoladze's home 10 days after his arrest and found no weapons, but continued to press charges. Gogoladze was released from pretrial detention in November on grounds of insufficient evidence. However, the Procuracy has made no decision on dropping the charges.

Nikolay Ploshkin, held by the authorities for 3 years in pretrial detention, was released on May 2 after having been tried and found guilty on the charge of concealing a crime. He received a sentence of 2½ years and was released based on time already served.

There were no cases of forced exile.

e. *Denial of Fair Public Trial.*—The Constitution provides for an independent judiciary. Prior to adoption of the Constitution, the courts were often influenced by pressure from the executive branch. This pattern continues with judicial authorities frequently deferring to the executive branch, particularly at lower levels of the court system.

The court system is divided into three levels. At the lowest level are district courts, which hear both routine criminal and civil cases. City courts, the next level, serve as appellate courts for the district courts, reviewing cases and either confirming verdicts or returning the case to the lower court for retrial. City courts also try in the first instance major criminal cases. The Supreme Court, the highest level, acts as an appellate court. Parliament approved the creation of a Constitutional Court this year, which is now operating.

A new Criminal Code is due to be considered by Parliament by year's end. In its draft form, it is designed to reduce the pervasive powers of the Procuracy (see Section 1.d). A separate draft law to reorganize and reduce the power of the Procuracy was being debated in Parliament at year's end. Currently Soviet law continues to be used. Under Soviet law prosecutors are vested with powers greater than those of judges and defense attorneys. Prosecutors direct criminal investigations, supervise some judicial functions, and represent the State in trials. Trials are not conducted in an adversarial manner. Prosecutors continued to wield disproportionate influence over outcomes.

According to the Constitution, a detainee is presumed innocent and has the right to a public trial. A detainee has the right to demand immediate access to a lawyer and to refuse to make a statement in the absence of counsel. The detaining officer must inform the detainee of his or her rights and must notify the detainee's family of his or her location as soon as possible. These rights mark a significant departure from Soviet legal practice, but they are not observed.

The State must provide legal counsel if the defendant is unable to afford one. In fact the State provided virtually all attorneys as they remain by and large employees of the State. Attorneys are assigned to a case by the Office of Legal Assistance, a part of the state-controlled Bar Association, upon the recommendation of the Procurator's Office. Private attorneys are allowed in criminal and civil cases only with the express written approval of the Office of Legal Assistance.

Human rights observers report widespread judicial incompetence and corruption, including the payment of bribes to prosecutors and judges.

In the trials of Badri Zarandia, Loti Kobalia, and other members of the former Gamsakhurdia Government who fought against forces loyal to the Shevardnadze Government, the Government consistently violated due process during the investigation and trial. Torture, use of forced confessions, denial of legal counsel, and expulsion of defendants from the courtroom took place. On May 7, Zarandia and his codefendants Zviad Sherozia, Gabriel Bendeliani, Karlo Jichonaia, Gurgen Malania and Murman Gulua were expelled from court. On June 17, Zarandia was sentenced to death after being convicted of high treason, hooliganism, banditry, and other crimes. He was told of the sentence in his cell as he had not been permitted to return to the courtroom following his expulsion. On November 18, Kobalia was found guilty and also received the death sentence. In a separate case, Nugzar Molodinashvili, a former member of Gamsakhurdia's Supreme Council, was expelled from the courtroom on May 21 for "offending the Government" during his trial.

The two men condemned to death in the 1995 trial of the assassination attempt against parliamentary deputy Jaba Ioseliani filed appeals, which are still pending. The case was marked by procedural irregularities and acts of abuse, forced confessions, denial of legal counsel, and expulsion of defendants from the courtroom took place.

Former Member of Parliament and head of the Monarchist Party Temur Jhorjholiani was sentenced to 4-years imprisonment after being convicted of drug possession and assault on a police officer, despite having Parliamentary immunity at the time of his arrest in 1995. The judge disregarded the question of whether Jhorjholiani's immunity should have excluded the evidence that led to his conviction. Throughout the trial, the Court refused Jhorjholiani's requests for bail without explanation in violation of the Constitution's requirement that judges cite grounds for such decisions.

There are no known political prisoners. Political overtones, however, attended the cases of a number of individuals, including Gamsakhurdia supporters and MGB personnel, who were tried and sentenced on criminal grounds.

f. *Arbitrary Interference With Privacy, Family, Home, or Correspondence.*—Credible reports indicate that government security agencies monitor private telephone conversations without court order. Police and State tax authorities also enter homes and places of work without legal sanction. Police regularly stop and search vehicles without probable cause to extort bribes. The high level of unregulated police misconduct and corruption has undermined public confidence in government, especially law enforcement agencies.

Section 2. Respect for Civil Liberties, Including:

a. *Freedom of Speech and Press.*—The Constitution and the 1991 press law provide for freedom of the press, but the Government constrains some press freedoms. Security and law enforcement authorities attempted to intimidate the press through public comments and private meetings.

Numerous independent newspapers operate and the press increasingly serves as a check on government, frequently criticizing the performance of high-level officials. However, no independent newspapers have a national audience and most citizens get their news from television. The Government finances and controls two newspapers and a radio and television network, which have a national audience and reflect official viewpoints.

The State also exerts influence over the press in other ways. For example, it owns and operates the major printing facility. Earlier this year, the Government proposed to a number of independent newspapers that they centralize their operations and accept government assistance. They refused. Independent newspapers and television stations are harassed by state tax authorities.

Rustavi-2, a member station of the fledgling independent television network, TNG, for the second successive year encountered government attempts to shut it down. In spite of the legal decision in 1995 that confirmed Rustavi-2's right to broadcast television, the Ministry of Communications revoked the station's license in July and awarded its broadcast channel to a company with strong ties to government officials. Rustavi-2 had been broadcasting in Tbilisi only for a short time, but had demonstrated independence. Rustavi-2 appealed the revocation but lost in the district court. The subsequent appeal to the Supreme Court was successful. In November the Supreme Court overturned the lower court's decision. Other independent stations reported pressure by local governments to support them.

Academic freedom is widely respected.

b. *Freedom of Peaceful Assembly and Association.*—The Constitution provides for these rights, and the Government generally respects them in practice. The Government permits unannounced assembly in four locations in Tbilisi and requires 24-hour advance notice for assemblies in other areas. The Government generally grants permits for assembly and registration for associations without arbitrary restriction or discrimination. Government respect for freedom of assembly is, however, limited in some cases. On May 26 police, including elite "OMON" troops from the Ministry of the Interior, violently broke up a sanctioned assembly of 200 demonstrators, mostly supporters of former President Gamsakhurdia.

c. *Freedom of Religion.*—The Constitution provides for freedom of religion, and the Government respects this right in practice. Georgia has a tradition of religious tolerance. In two separate instances, however, foreign Christian missionaries were questioned by police for engaging in "anti-Christian activities." In one of those instances, Orthodox priests urged police to call in the missionaries for questioning. This action reflects a growing mistrust on the part of the Georgian Orthodox Church of the activities of missionaries of other denominations, especially evangelicals (see Section 5). The Georgian Orthodox Church stated publicly that foreign Christian missionaries should confine their activities to non-Christian areas.

d. *Freedom of Movement Within the Country, Foreign Travel, Emigration, and Repatriation.*—The 1993 law on migration provides for these rights, and the Government generally respects them in practice. Registration of an individual's place of residence is no longer required. In principle the Government respects the right of repatriation, although approximately 270,000 Meskhetian Turks (primarily Muslim), who were expelled to Central Asia by Stalin in the 1940's, still face public opposition to their return. The Government publicly supported the right of the Meskhetian Turks to return but did not develop a mechanism for repatriation, nor identify a community willing to accept returnees. The pilot effort to resettle 35–40 Meskhetian families proposed in 1995 did not take place. In 1996 the Government granted refugee status to 120 Meskhetian Turks who came to Georgia as students.

The 1994 quadripartite agreement (Russia, Georgia, Abkhazia, and the United Nations High Commissioner for Refugees) on repatriation in Abkhazia provided for the free, safe, and dignified return of displaced persons and refugees to their homes. The Abkhaz separatist regime prevented virtually all official repatriation before unilaterally abrogating the agreement in 1994. Over the past 2 years, some 30,000 to 35,000 of the estimated 250,000 IDP's from Abkhazia have returned spontaneously, most to the southern part of the Gali District where the Abkhaz militia operate only sporadically. Returnees continue to face security threats from Abkhaz separatist militia, and Abkhaz and Georgian armed bands (see Section 1.a.).

The 1992 ethnic conflict in South Ossetia also created tens of thousands of ethnic Georgian IDP's. South Ossetian separatists continue to defy OSCE and government attempts to repatriate people to their homes.

At present there is no effective law concerning the settlement of refugees or the granting of political asylum in Georgia. Parliament is considering a draft law. Georgia has so far not acceded to the 1951 Geneva Convention related to refugees. The Government has not provided first asylum, both because there are no legal provisions for it and because the matter has not yet been raised in practical terms.

Section 3. Respect for Political Rights: The Right of Citizens to Change Their Government

The Constitution and the 1995 Election Law provide citizens with the right peacefully to change their government. Citizens exercised this right in elections in October 1992 and November 1995. A democratically elected President and Parliament govern most of Georgia. The separatist regions of Abkhazia and South Ossetia are ruled by undemocratic leaders. In addition the region of Ajara is to a large extent self-governing, under conditions resembling a police state. Ajara's postindependence relationship to the rest of Georgia is still undetermined and in matters, such as elections, Ajara's authorities claim that regional laws take precedence over national laws. The Government does not challenge illegal, undemocratic activity by the Ajaran authorities, purportedly because Tbilisi seeks to avoid open separatism in this ethnic Georgian, historically Muslim region. Ajara held regional elections on September 22 and denied requests from international as well as Georgian organizations to monitor the elections. In the September election, the Ajaran authorities employed fraud and intimidation to ensure the victory of the local ruling party. In addition the most serious violations noted during the 1995 national elections occurred in Ajara.

The 223-member Parliament and President Eduard Shevardnadze were elected in multiparty elections in 1995. Despite some violations, international observers judged these elections to meet international standards, except in Ajara. There was no voting in the separatist regions of Abkhazia and South Ossetia. President Shevardnadze's party won a majority of the seats in Parliament. Only two other parties qualified for representation in Parliament, but opposition parties actively participated in preelection planning and election monitoring.

Women are poorly represented in Parliament. Only 16 women (7 percent) were elected to Parliament in 1995, and only 1 woman (6 percent) has been named to a ministerial post.

Section 4. Governmental Attitude Regarding International and Nongovernmental Investigation of Alleged Violations of Human Rights

The Government generally respects the right of domestic and international organizations to monitor human rights, but has limited the access of some organizations to prisoners (see Section 1.c.).

Domestic human rights monitoring is politicized. The Government claims that most local human rights groups are extensions of partisan political groups, while those groups criticized the State Committee on Human Rights, which has been disbanded, and the Parliamentary Committee on Human Rights, for favoring the Government. Pending since 1995, when filled, the constitutionally mandated Public Human Rights Defender will be selected and funded by Parliament, but accountable neither to the Parliament nor the executive. The extended delay in filling this position reflects continued disagreement between the President and Parliament over a mutually acceptable candidate.

Section 5. Discrimination Based on Race, Sex, Religion, Disability, Language, or Social Status

The Constitution recognizes the equality of all citizens without regard to race, language, sex, religion, skin color, political views, national, ethnic, or social affiliation, origin, social status, landownership, or place of residence. The Constitution provides for Georgian as the state language, but not all minorities in Georgia prefer to use Georgian. As a practical matter, the approximately 500,000 Armenians and 300,000 Azeris prefer to communicate in their own language. The Abkhaz, Ossetian, and Russian communities prefer to use Russian. Georgian and Russian are both used for interethnic communication.

Women.—Women's nongovernmental organizations (NGO's) report that family violence and rape are not common, although spousal abuse and sexual harassment occurs. Spousal abuse usually goes unreported, and police are reluctant to investigate complaints. Sexual harassment is increasingly reported as a problem in the workplace. The Government has no support services for abused women, although police reportedly investigate reports of rape.

Human rights monitors in Abkhazia continue to note reports of rape of non-Abkhaz women by young Abkhaz men, often in paramilitary dress, but these assaults reportedly declined in 1996.

Women's access to the labor market continues to be confined mostly to low-paying and low-skill positions frequently despite high professional and academic qualifications. Few women work in professional positions and women have suffered disproportionately when companies and organizations laid off workers. An NGO Association for the Employment of Women was established in 1995 by a group of concerned Georgian women for registering unemployed women, but has not been active.

Several organizations have been formed to promote women's rights, including Georgian Women's Choice and the Political Organization for the Defense of Women's Rights. The two organizations cooperate closely to promote an agenda concentrated on the "social and economic rights" of women.

Children.—Government services for children are extremely limited. The 1995 Health Reform Act withdrew the right of children over the age of 1 year to free medical care. While education is officially free, many parents are unable to afford books and school supplies, and most parents have to pay for their children's education.

The Georgian private voluntary organization (PVO), "Child and Environment," noted a dramatic rise in homeless children following the collapse of the Soviet Union. It estimates that there are approximately 1,000 street children in Tbilisi due to the inability of orphanages and the Ministry of Education to provide support. Child and Environment also reported a growing trend towards child involvement in criminal activity, narcotics, and prostitution despite the cultural tradition of protecting children.

People With Disabilities.—There is no legislative or otherwise mandated provision requiring accessibility for the disabled. The Law on Labor has a section that includes the provision of special discounts and favorable social policies for those with disabilities, especially disabled veterans.

Many of the state facilities for the disabled that operated in the Soviet period have been closed because of lack of government funding. Most disabled persons are supported by family members, or by international humanitarian donations.

Religious Minorities.—The Georgian Orthodox Church, wary of proselytism, has sought to hinder evangelical missionaries and the Salvation Army. In one instance, the Orthodox Church urged the police to question foreign Christian missionaries (see Section 2.c.). The Catholic Church also complains of continuing delays in the return of churches closed during the Soviet period and later given to the Georgian Orthodox Church. A prominent Armenian church in Tbilisi remains closed.

Organizations promoting the rights of Jews and Jewish emigration continue to report that the Government provides good cooperation and support. Jewish leaders in the country attribute isolated acts of anti-Semitism in previous years to general instability and disorder. The Government has been outspoken in denouncing anti-Semitism. A virulently anti-Semitic article that appeared in the independent newspaper Noi during the summer prompted a public rebuke from the President. The Prosecutor's Office filed charges against the editor for inciting interethnic hatred.

National/Racial/Ethnic Minorities.—The Government generally respects the rights of individuals of ethnic minorities in nonconflict areas, but limits self-government in the ethnic Armenian and Azeri enclaves. The Government provides funds for ethnic schools, and the teaching of non-Georgian languages is permitted. Violence in Abkhazia and South Ossetia reflects historic ethnic conflicts and the legacy of Soviet policy, designed to pit ethnic minorities against one another.

Section 6. Worker Rights

a. *The Right of Association.*—The Constitution provides for the right of citizens to form and join unions. The Soviet Labor Code, still in effect, specifies that these unions must be registered with the Ministry of Justice.

A union of trade unions (the Amalgamated Trade Unions of Georgia) has been established and comprises 25 sectoral unions. The union, jointly with the Ministry of Justice, has prepared a draft law on trade unions. The union sees the protection of social and economic rights of workers as the basic function of trade unions. Unions are remnants of the Soviet period when they were essentially administrative bodies concerned with property and finance rather than with workers' rights.

There are no legal prohibitions against affiliation and participation in international organizations. The right to form unions is protected under the Constitution.

b. *The Right to Organize and Bargain Collectively.*—The Constitution and the Soviet Labor Code allow workers to organize and bargain collectively, and this right is respected. The Labor Code also prohibits antiunion discrimination by employers against union members. Employers may be prosecuted for antiunion discrimination and be made to reinstate employees and pay back wages. The Ministry of Labor investigates complaints but is not staffed to conduct effective investigations.

There are no export processing zones.

c. *Prohibition of Forced or Compulsory Labor.*—The Labor Code prohibits forced or compulsory labor and provides for sanctions against violators; violations are rare. The Ministry of Labor enforces this law.

d. *Minimum Age for Employment of Children.*—According to current legislation, the minimum age for employment of children is 16 years; however, in exceptional cases, the minimum age can be 14 years. These laws are generally respected.

e. *Acceptable Conditions for Work.*—The nationally mandated minimum wage was abolished in 1995 and replaced by a wage scale that sets salaries for various grades in the public sector, the lowest of which is approximately $10 (13 lari) per month. There is no state-mandated minimum wage for private sector workers. A recent Government report concluded that $77 per month was required for the basic minimum needs of an individual. Pensions and salaries are usually insufficient to meet basic minimum needs.

The law provides for a 41-hour workweek, and for a 24-hour rest period. The government workweek is often shortened during the winter due to the continuing energy crisis. The Labor Code permits higher wages for hazardous work and permits a worker in such fields to refuse duties that could endanger life.

GERMANY

The Federal Republic of Germany is a constitutional parliamentary democracy with an independent judiciary; citizens periodically choose their representatives in free and fair multiparty elections. The head of the Federal Government, the Chancellor, is elected by the lower house of Parliament. The powers of the Chancellor and of the Parliament are set forth in the Basic Law (Constitution). The 16 states enjoy significant autonomy, especially as concerns law enforcement and the courts, education, the environment, and social assistance.

Law enforcement is primarily a responsibility of state governments, and the police are organized at the state level. The jurisdiction of the Federal Criminal Office is limited to international organized crime, especially narcotics trafficking, weapons smuggling, and currency counterfeiting. Police forces in general are well trained, disciplined, and mindful of citizens' rights, although there were occasional instances of police abuse.

Germany's highly advanced economy affords its residents a high standard of living. The economy has had difficulty pulling out of its 1993–94 recession, which followed a reunification boom in the early 1990's. The economy picked up in the second half of 1996, but unemployment remains high, as the structural rate of unemployment rose again with the most recent recession. In the East, where economic integration and growth continued particularly strongly, employment has increased more noticeably than in the West. Nonetheless, overall unemployment in eastern Germany remains significantly higher than in the country's western half as the region continues to grapple with adjustment to free market conditions. Unemployment in the East affects women disproportionately more than men.

The Government fully respects the human rights of its citizens, and the law and judiciary provide effective means of dealing with instances of individual abuse. However, there were continued allegations of police abuse of prisoners, especially foreigners. Although violence or harassment directed at foreigners continued to occur within society as a whole, the number of incidents declined markedly, as was the case in 1995. Rightwing violence against foreigners decreased by nearly 50 percent, with 154 cases reported in the first 6 months of 1996, compared with 313 in the same period of 1995. Rightwing extremist violence rose sharply after German unification but peaked in 1992 and has since been declining sharply. Still, there were a significant number of attacks on property or persons, and foreigners were disproportionately the victims.

Anti-Semitic incidents decreased in the first 6 months of 1996. Most involved graffiti or distribution of anti-Semitic materials. The overwhelming majority of the perpetrators of attacks on foreigners or anti-Semitic acts were frustrated, apolitical youths and a small core of neo-Nazis. All the major political parties and all the highest officials of the Federal Republic denounced violence against foreigners and anti-Semitic acts.

Women continue to face wage discrimination in the private sector. The Government is taking serious steps to address the problem of violence against women.

RESPECT FOR HUMAN RIGHTS

Section 1. Respect for the Integrity of the Person, Including Freedom From:

a. *Political and Other Extrajudicial Killing.*—There were no reports of political or other extrajudicial killings by government officials.

Some murders occurred among rival factions of Iranians, Kurds, Turks, and other foreign nationals. The federal and state authorities sought to find and prosecute the perpetrators of such crimes and pressed charges in several trials.

The trial of Red Army Faction member Birgit Hogefeld, which began in November 1994, ended on November 5. Hogefeld was sentenced to life imprisonment by the State Superior Court in Frankfurt. She was found guilty of participating in a 1993 bombing of a prison in Weiterstadt, Hessen; participating in a 1988 attack on Bundesbank President Hans Tietmeyer; and participating in the 1985 bomb attack at the U.S. Rhein-Main Air Base.

Lebanon extradited Yasser Mohammed Shraydi to Berlin in May in connection with his alleged participation in the April 1986 bombing of the Berlin discotheque "La Belle." The attack killed one Turkish and two U.S. citizens, and injured 230 persons. Prosecution is expected to begin in spring 1997. Three further suspects were arrested in October: Ali Chanaa, alias Alba; his former wife, Verena Helga Chanaa (a German national); and his wife's sister, Andrea Haeusler (also German). Also in October, warrants were issued for the arrest of three former Libyan diplomats and a former member of the Libyan Security Service who were stationed in East Berlin.

On September 10, six former East German generals were sentenced to prison for terms ranging from 3 years 3 months to 6½ years, for ordering the shooting of persons who fled across the Berlin Wall and the former border between East and West Germany. The six included former Deputy Defense Minister Klaus-Dieter Baumgarten, who was accused of direct complicity in 11 killings.

b. *Disappearance.*—There were no reports of politically motivated disappearances.

c. *Torture and Other Cruel, Inhuman, or Degrading Treatment or Punishment.*—Torture is not mentioned in the Basic Law, but it is forbidden by law.

There continue to be serious allegations of police brutality against foreigners, but fewer than in previous years. No action was taken against individual Hamburg policemen being investigated since 1995 for possible mistreatment of arrested foreigners as the witnesses were considered unreliable.

Prison conditions meet minimum international standards, and the Government permits visits by human rights monitors.

d. *Arbitrary Arrest, Detention, or Exile.*—The Basic Law prohibits arbitrary arrest, detention, or exile, and the Government observes this prohibition. To make an arrest, police must obtain a judicial warrant. By the day after arrest, police must bring the suspect before a judge and lodge a charge. The court must then either issue a warrant stating the grounds for detention or order the person's release.

There is no preventive detention. If there is evidence that the suspect might flee the country, police may detain the suspect for up to 24 hours pending a formal charge. The right of free access to legal counsel has been restricted only in the cases of terrorists suspected of having used contacts with lawyers to continue terrorist activity while in prison. Only judges may decide on the validity of any deprivation of liberty. Bail exists but is seldom employed; the usual practice is to release detainees unless there is clear danger of flight outside the country.

There is no use of forced exile.

e. *Denial of Fair Public Trial.*—The Basic Law provides for the right to a fair trial, and an independent judiciary vigorously enforces this right. The court system is highly developed and provides full legal protection and numerous possibilities for judicial review. Ordinary courts have jurisdiction in criminal and civil matters. There are four levels of such courts (local courts, regional courts, higher regional courts, and the Federal Court of Justice), with appeals possible from lower to higher levels. In addition there are four types of specialized courts: Administrative, labor, social, and fiscal courts. These courts are also established on different levels, with the possibility for appeal to the next higher level.

Separate from these five branches of jurisdiction is the Federal Constitutional Court, which is not only the country's supreme court but an organ of the Constitution with special functions defined in the Basic Law. Among other things, it reviews laws to ensure their compatibility with the Constitution and adjudicates disputes between constitutional organs on questions of competencies. It also has jurisdiction to hear and decide claims based on the infringement of a person's basic constitutional rights by a public authority. The judiciary provides citizens with a fair and efficient judicial process.

There were no reports of political prisoners.

f. *Arbitrary Interference With Privacy, Family, Home, or Correspondence.*—The Basic Law prohibits such practices, government authorities generally respect these prohibitions, and violations are subject to effective legal sanction.

Section 2. Respect for Civil Liberties, Including:

a. *Freedom of Speech and Press.*—The Basic Law provides for freedom of the press, and the Government respects this right in practice. There is no official censorship. An independent press, an effective judiciary, and a functioning democratic political system combine to ensure freedom of speech and the press, including academic freedom. Propaganda of Nazi and other proscribed organizations is illegal. Statements endorsing Nazism are also illegal. Several persons were indicted for making statements or distributing materials that were alleged to fall into these categories, including a U.S. citizen, Gary Lauck, who was sentenced August 22 to 4 years' imprisonment for instigating national hatred and dissemination of illegal propaganda materials.

In January the press reported that the authorities pressured a provider of Internet on-line service to block access to material—a neo-Nazi World Wide Web site—that the Government considers illegal under German law.

b. *Freedom of Peaceful Assembly and Association.*—The law provides for these rights, and the Government respects them in practice. The Basic Law permits banning political parties found to be "fundamentally antidemocratic." A 1950's ruling by the Federal Constitutional Court outlawed a neo-Nazi and a Communist party. State governments may outlaw only organizations that are active solely within their state. If a group's activities cross state lines, the Federal Government assumes jurisdiction.

Four far-right political groups, not organized as political parties, were banned in late 1992. The Kurdistan Workers' Party (PKK), along with 35 subsidiary organizations, was banned in 1993. Also in 1993 the Federal Government asked the Constitutional Court to ban the far-right Free German Workers' Party; the Court's decision was still pending at year's end. Several extremist parties were under observation by the Office for the Protection of the Constitution (BFV, the internal security service), although such monitoring may by law not interfere with the organizations' continued activities. The BFV reported that 46,100 people belonged to far-right organizations in 1994, a decline of 22 percent from the previous year.

c. *Freedom of Religion.*—The Basic Law specifically provides for religious freedom. The Government fully supports religious freedom. Most of the population belongs to the Catholic or Protestant churches. These denominations and the Jewish community hold a special legal status as corporate bodies under public law, giving them, for instance, the right to participate in a state-administered church tax system. State governments subsidize church-affiliated schools and provide religious instruction in schools and universities for those belonging to the Protestant, Catholic, or Jewish faith.

Groups of a religious character, which are not granted special legal status, do not benefit from the privileges granted by the State. A sharp debate surrounds the activities of the Church of Scientology, whose members allege both government-condoned and societal harassment, including expulsion from (or denial of permission to join) a political party and loss of employment. Business firms whose owners or executives are Scientologists may face boycotts and discrimination, sometimes with government approval. Scientologists continued to take such grievances to the courts. Legal rulings have been mixed.

During the year, the Church of Scientology came under increasing scrutiny by both federal and state officials, who claim that its activities do not fall within the legal definition of a religious organization. Several cabinet officials criticized the organization. In January Claudia Nolte, the Minister of Family Policy, described the Church as "one of the most aggressive groups in our society" and said she would oppose the organization "with all the means at my disposal." The Parliament created a special commission to investigate Scientology's activities and social impact. The press reported that the federal chancellery and state minister-presidents decided on December 19 to create an interministerial group to study Scientology.

Major political parties exclude Scientologists from membership, arguing that the Church is not a religion but a for-profit organization whose goals and principles are antidemocratic and thus inconsistent with those of the political parties. In late summer, the governing Christian Democratic Union (CDU) party approved a resolution saying that membership "in the Scientology organization is not compatible with employment in the public service," and urging that the Church be put under surveillance. The resolution also urged the banning of federal funding for cultural and artistic events featuring Scientologists. In December a state organization of the CDU confirmed the expulsion of three members for belonging to the Church.

Various artists have been affected because of their membership in the organization. Artists have been prevented from performing or displaying their works because of their membership in the Church. In the summer, the youth wing of the CDU in a number of German states urged a boycott of the film "Mission Impossible" because the leading actor in this film is a Scientologist. In Bavaria the Minister of Culture was criticized by the state parliament for allowing American musician Chick Corea, a Scientologist, to perform at a state-sponsored jazz festival.

Individual German states also took action against members of the organization. On November 1, the state of Bavaria began to screen applicants for state civil service positions for Scientology membership. Bavaria also said it would not fund arts-related activities in which Scientologists were to appear. It also decreed that private companies awarded state contracts in certain "sensitive" fields must sign a statement that they do not follow the tenets of Scientology.

The past year has also seen some positive developments. A former Minister of Justice editorialized that the Government should be more restrained in its dealings with Scientology. In an October report, the Ministry of Interior concluded that there was insufficient evidence to justify surveillance of Scientology by the Offices for the Protection of the Constitution (OPC). In response to the CDU's call for the organization to be placed under OPC observation, the report concluded that "no concrete facts exist currently to substantiate the suspicion of criminal acts." In closing the report reminded states requesting a ban on Scientology that "only economic considerations may be taken into account" when awarding public contracts.

d. *Freedom of Movement Within the Country, Foreign Travel, Emigration, and Repatriation.*—Citizens are free to move anywhere within the country, to travel abroad, to emigrate, and to repatriate, without restrictions that violate human rights.

For ethnic Germans entering the country, the Basic Law provides both for citizenship immediately upon application and for legal residence without restrictions. Persons not of German ethnicity may acquire citizenship (and with it the right of unrestricted residence) if they meet certain requirements, including legal residence for at least 10 years (5 if married to a German), renunciation of all other citizenships, and a basic command of the language. Long-term legal residents often opt not to apply; they receive the same social benefits as do citizens, and after 10 years of legal residency they are entitled to permanent residency. Representatives of the Turkish and Roma communities in Germany have criticized the citizenship policy as unjust and discriminatory and have opposed the policy against dual nationality.

The Basic Law and subsequent legislation provide for the right of foreign victims of political persecution to attain asylum and resettlement. In 1996 Germany received 116,367 applications for asylum and had a recognition rate of 12.4 percent for the 194,451 cases concluded. Since July 1993, when the criteria for granting asylum were tightened with an amendment to the asylum law, the overall trend in asylum applications has continued downward, decreasing by two-thirds from the 1992 all-time high of 438,191.

Under the tightened criteria, persons coming directly from any country that officials designate as a "safe country of origin" cannot normally claim political asylum but may request an administrative review of their applications while in Germany. Persons entering via a "safe third country"—any country in the European Union or adhering to the Geneva Convention—are also ineligible for asylum.

The legislated changes also limited legal recourse against denials of asylum applications. Critics argue that few countries can assuredly be designated as "safe third countries" and that the law unjustly fails to allow applicants to rebut such designations. While the law permits appeals against designations of "safe countries of origin," critics protest that the 48-hour period allotted for hearings is too brief.

However, in May the Constitutional Court upheld the constitutionality of the 1993 amendment.

Asylum seekers with applications under review enjoy virtually the full range of civil rights except the right to vote. While less than 5 percent of applicants have attained political asylum, denial does not automatically result in deportation. Most rejected applicants are allowed to remain in the country for humanitarian reasons, especially those from the former Yugoslavia.

Applicants who have been conclusively denied asylum are placed in detention pending deportation. Some police detention facilities, particularly in Berlin, are overcrowded or otherwise seriously substandard.

Repatriations of Vietnamese citizens living illegally in Germany have proceeded behind the schedule established in the protocols to the agreement signed with Vietnam in July 1995; 7,500 returns were foreseen for 1996, but the actual number of returns for the year only reached approximately 1,500.

Germany concluded two other repatriation agreements during the year. The first, signed on October 10 with Serbia-Montenegro, is intended to facilitate the return of the estimated 135,000 citizens of Serbia-Montenegro living without legal status in Germany. Of that number, it is estimated that two-thirds are ethnic Albanians from Kosovo. No returns within the context of this agreement occurred in 1996, but Germany has begun the application process to allow for returns in 1997. The second agreement, initialed with Bosnia on November 20, is intended to facilitate the repatriation of the estimated 320,000 Bosnian refugees. The Government provides first asylum and has granted "temporary protection" (first asylum) to these Bosnian refugees at an estimated cost of $2.8 billion annually for their support.

In response to the December 1995 Dayton Peace Agreement, Federal and state Interior Ministers decided in January to terminate the temporary protection regime and to begin a phased, compulsory if necessary, return of the Bosnian refugees residing in Germany. In the first phase (October 1996 to mid-1997), those refugees without accompanying minor children are to leave Germany; the Federal Interior Ministry estimates the number of people potentially included in the first phase to be 80,000. The second phase (mid-1997 onward) foresees the departure of all other Bosnian refugees. The starting date for "first phase" returns was originally July, but was postponed until October 1 when it became clear that conditions in Bosnia were not conducive to large-scale returns. Most states decided subsequently to delay returns until the spring of 1997. However, two states with large Bosnian refugee populations, Bavaria and Baden-Wuerttenberg, pursued returns beginning in October, deporting fewer than 60 Bosnians by year's end. Many, though not all, of the deportees were convicted of crimes in Germany, making priority candidates for deportation. The decision to proceed with compulsory returns led to disagreement with the Office of the United Nations High Commissioner for Refugees, which favored only voluntary returns during this period.

Section 3. Respect for Political Rights: The Right of Citizens to Change Their Government

The Basic Law provides citizens with the right to change their government peacefully, and citizens exercise this right in practice through periodic, free, and fair elections. The Government is elected on the basis of universal suffrage and secret balloting. Members of the Parliament's lower house, the Bundestag, are elected from a mixture of direct-constituency and party-list candidates. The upper house, the Bundesrat, is composed of delegations from state governments.

The law entitles women to participate fully in political life, and a growing number are prominent in the Government and the parties, but women are still underrepresented in those ranks. Slightly over 26 percent of the Federal Parliament is female, including its President. Women occupy 3 of 16 cabinet positions. One state minister-president is a woman. On the Federal Constitutional Court, 4 of the 16 judges are women, including the Chief Justice. All of the parties have undertaken to enlist more women. The Greens/Alliance 90 Party requires that women comprise half of the party's elected officials. The Social Democrats have a 40-percent quota for women on all party committees and governing bodies.

Section 4. Governmental Attitude Regarding International and Nongovernmental Investigation of Alleged Violations of Human Rights

A wide variety of human rights groups operate without government restriction, investigating and publishing their findings on human rights cases. Government officials are very cooperative and responsive to their views.

Section 5. Discrimination Based on Race, Sex, Religion, Disability, Language, or Social Status

The law prohibits denial of access to shelter, health care, or education on the basis of race, religion, disability, sex, ethnic background, political opinion, or citizenship. The Government enforces the law effectively.

Women.—While violence against women occurs and is almost certainly underreported, it is prohibited by laws that are effectively enforced. It is condemned in society, and legal and medical recourse is available. Police statistics on rape showed a slight increase to 6,175 cases in 1995 (latest available data) from 6,095 in 1994.

The Government has conducted campaigns in the schools and through church groups to bring public attention to the existence of such violence and has proposed steps to counter it. The Federal Government has supported numerous pilot projects throughout Germany. There are, for example, 330 "women's houses" in Germany, over 100 in the new states in the East, where victims of violence and their children can seek shelter, counseling, and legal and police protection. Germany supported the appointment of a special rapporteur on violence against women at the U.N. Human Rights Commission.

Trafficking in women and forced prostitution is also forbidden by law. The laws against trafficking in women were modified in 1992 to deal more effectively with problems stemming from the opening of Germany's eastern borders. In recent years, the Federal Ministry for Women and Youth commissioned a number of studies to gain information on violence against women, sexual harassment, and other matters, producing for example a special report on violence against women in 1995.

Children.—The Government is committed to protection of children's rights, and there is no societal pattern of abuse of human rights of children. Public education is provided and is mandatory through the age of 16. The Government recognizes that violence against children is a problem requiring its attention. Police figures indicate that there were 16,013 alleged cases of sexual abuse of children in 1995 (latest available figures), up slightly from 1994. Officials believe that the numbers of unreported cases may be much higher. The Child and Youth Protection Law stresses the need for preventive measures, and the Government has taken account of this in stepping up its counseling and other assistance.

The Criminal Code was amended in 1993 to further protect children against pornography and sexual abuse. For possession of child pornography, the maximum sentence is 1 year's imprisonment; the sentence for distribution is 5 years. The amendment made sexual abuse of children by German citizens abroad punishable even if the action is not illegal in the child's own country.

People With Disabilities.—There is no discrimination against the disabled in employment, education, or in the provision of other state services. The law mandates several special services for disabled persons, and the Government enforces these provisions in practice. The disabled are entitled to assistance to avert, eliminate, or alleviate the consequences of their disabilities and to secure employment commensurate with their abilities. The Government offers vocational training and grants for employers who hire the disabled. The severely disabled may be granted special benefits, such as tax breaks, free public transport, special parking facilities, and exemption from radio and television fees.

The Federal Government has established guidelines for attainment of "barrier-free" public buildings and for modifications of streets and pedestrian traffic walks to accommodate the disabled. While it is up to the individual states to incorporate these guidelines into building codes, all 16 states now have access facilities for the disabled.

Religious Minorities.—Anti-Semitic acts decreased, with 380 incidents reported in the first 6 months of 1996, compared with 634 incidents in the same period in 1995. There were only 17 cases involving the use of force. Over 90 percent of these anti-Semitic incidents involved graffiti, the distribution of anti-Semitic materials, or the display of symbols of banned organizations. The perpetrators of the 1995 firebombing of the Luebeck synagogue were deemed mentally ill and sent for treatment. There were no anti-Semitic bombings in 1996.

National/Racial/Ethnic Minorities.—Data from the Federal Office for the Protection of the Constitution show the number of violent offenses by rightwing extremists against foreigners decreased by nearly 50 percent in the first 6 months of 1996 compared with the same period in 1995. This continues a significant downtrend since

1992. According to police data, all violent acts against foreigners, regardless of the political leanings of the perpetrators, also declined by roughly 50 percent. As in previous years, most of these offenses were directed against foreign residents. Eight American exchange students of Asian descent were attacked and slightly injured by rightwingers in July 1995 in Merseburg. Charges have been brought in this case, but the trial had not convened by year's end.

Ethnic Turks continue to complain credibly about societal and job-related discrimination. Isolated firebombing incidents occurred again during the year targeting Turkish business establishments. The attacks were largely attributed to intra-Turkish disputes. There have been no arrests in connection with these firebombings. Turkish community leaders have sometimes complained of insufficient security efforts by German authorities in the face of these bombings.

In March Turkish Kurd supporters of the PKK held large demonstrations at German border crossing points. During one such demonstration in Elten near the Dutch border, two police personnel suffered severe head injuries.

Perpetrators of rightwing violence were predominantly young, male, and low in socioeconomic status, often committing such acts while inebriated. As in the past, most acts of violence against minority groups were committed spontaneously. There continued to be evidence in 1996 that neo-Nazi groups were making efforts to achieve greater coordination among themselves.

In addition to voicing condemnation of the violence, the Government has recommended tougher anticrime legislation and law enforcement measures, as well as measures aimed at the societal roots of extremist violence and other crime. Eastern state governments have also taken efforts to reinvigorate enforcement of laws against violence by extremists. For such projects, however, state governments have thus far allocated only limited funds in their tight budgets.

The police in the eastern states continued to become better versed in the federal legal system, better trained, and more experienced. They continued to move toward reaching the standards of effectiveness characteristic of police in the rest of Germany. The level of rightwing activity in the new states continued to decrease, and the police and state officials continued to show greater coordination in moving quickly and effectively to prevent illegal rightwing and neo-Nazi gatherings and demonstrations. The state of Saxony, for example, has a "Special Commission on Rightwing Extremism," which has been particularly active. Police at the local level in the new states are not always so active, however. After police in the Saxon town of Wurzen failed to move against local rightwing radicals, the Special Commission was forced to take independent action in May without informing the local police in advance. In the aftermath of the raid, nine Wurzen police officers were suspended. The case is still under investigation, but all the policemen involved have returned to regular duty.

Sinti and Romani leaders expressed satisfaction at the signing by the Government of the Council of Europe Convention on Minorities. Germany submitted an interpretation of the Convention in which Sinti and Roma were explicitly mentioned as ethnic minorities in Germany, providing them the recognition that they had long sought.

Section 6. Worker Rights

a. *The Right of Association.*—The right to associate freely, choose representatives, determine programs and policies to represent workers' interests, and publicize views is recognized and freely exercised. Some 35.5 percent of the total eligible labor force belong to unions. The German Trade Union Federation (DGB) represents 85 percent of organized workers.

The law provides for the right to strike, except for civil servants (including teachers) and personnel in sensitive positions, such as members of the armed forces. In the past, the International Labor Organization (ILO) has criticized the Government's definition of "essential services" as overly broad. The ILO was responding to complaints about sanctions imposed on teachers who struck in the state of Hesse in 1989 and, earlier, the replacement of striking postal workers by civil servants. In neither case did permanent job loss result. The ILO continues to seek clarifications from the Government on policies and laws governing labor rights of civil servants.

There were several large union-sponsored job actions protesting efforts to reduce fringe benefits. For example, on October 1, over 100,000 workers demonstrated to protest cuts in sick pay by major auto manufacturing companies.

The DGB participates in various international and European trade union organizations.

b. *The Right to Organize and Bargain Collectively.*—The Basic Law provides for the right to organize and bargain collectively, and this right is widely exercised. Due to a well-developed system of autonomous contract negotiations, mediation is uncommon. Basic wages and working conditions are negotiated at the industry level and then are adapted, through local collective bargaining, to particular enterprises.

However, some firms in eastern Germany have refused to join employer associations, or have withdrawn from them, and then bargained independently with workers. Likewise, some large firms in the West withdrew at least part of their work force from the jurisdiction of employer associations, complaining of rigidities in the industrywide, multicompany negotiating system. They have not, however, refused to bargain as individual enterprises. The law mandates a system of works councils and worker membership on supervisory boards, and thus workers participate in the management of the enterprises in which they work. The law thoroughly protects workers against antiunion discrimination.

There are no export processing zones.

c. *Prohibition of Forced or Compulsory Labor.*—The Basic Law prohibits forced or compulsory labor, and there were no known violations.

d. *Minimum Age for Employment of Children.*—Federal law generally prohibits employment of children under the age of 15, with a few exceptions: Those 13 or 14 years of age may do farm work for up to 3 hours per day or may deliver newspapers for up to 2 hours per day; those 3 to 14 years of age may take part in cultural performances, albeit under stringent curbs on the kinds of activity, number of hours, and time of day. The Federal Labor Ministry effectively enforces the law through its Factory Inspection Bureau.

e. *Acceptable Conditions of Work.*—There is no legislated or administratively determined minimum wage. Wages and salaries are set either by collective bargaining agreements between unions and employer federations or by individual contracts. Covering about 90 percent of all wage- and salary-earners, these agreements set minimum pay rates and are legally enforceable. These minimums provide an adequate standard of living for workers and their families. The number of hours of work per week is regulated by contracts that directly or indirectly affect 80 percent of the working population. The average workweek for industrial workers is 36 hours in western Germany and about 39 hours in the eastern states.

An extensive set of laws and regulations on occupational safety and health incorporates a growing body of European Union standards. These provide for the right to refuse to perform dangerous or unhealthy work without jeopardizing employment. A comprehensive system of worker insurance carriers enforces safety requirements in the workplace. This system now applies in the eastern states, where lax standards and conditions under the communist regime created serious problems. The Labor Ministry and its counterparts in the states effectively enforce occupational safety and health standards through a network of government organs, including the Federal Institute for Work Safety. At the local level, professional and trade associations—self-governing public corporations with delegates both from the employers and from the unions—oversee worker safety.

GREECE

Greece is a constitutional republic and multiparty parliamentary democracy with an independent judiciary in which citizens periodically choose their representatives in free and fair elections. In 1996 parliamentary elections, the Panhellenic Socialist Movement (PASOK) won a majority of the parliamentary seats, and its leader, Constantine Simitis, was returned to office as Prime Minister. The defeated New Democracy Party retained the role of the main opposition.

The national police and security services are responsible for internal security. Civilian authorities maintain effective control of all security forces, and police and security services are subject to a broad variety of legal and constitutional restraints. The Parliament, a vigorous free press, the judiciary, the European Parliament, and Greek and international human rights organizations monitor their activities. Some members of the police and security forces nevertheless committed human rights abuses.

Greece has a mixed economy in which the market system is overlaid by a large public sector that accounts for more than 40 percent of gross domestic product. Moderate growth, a high but declining inflation rate, a large but also declining budget deficit, and a 9.8 percent unemployment rate characterize the economy, which nevertheless provides residents with a relatively advanced standard of living. To promote further economic development, Greece relies heavily on the European Union for subsidies, grants, and loans, the latter two directed mainly toward major infrastructure projects.

The Government generally respected the human rights of most citizens, but problems remained in some areas. There continued to be credible reports that security force personnel sometimes abused suspects during arrests and interrogations and abused Albanian illegal aliens. Relations between Greece and Albania improved substantially, however, and an agreement was reached to regulate the flow of Albanian seasonal workers to Greece. The Government continued to use Article 19 of the Citizenship Code to revoke the citizenship of Greek citizens who are not ethnically Greek, and Article 20 of the same code was used to revoke the citizenship of Greek citizens abroad who have asserted a "Macedonian" ethnicity. On occasion the Government placed international and domestic human rights monitors under surveillance. Information about their private meetings and activities subsequently appeared in the press.

Responding to criticism, the Government continued to take corrective action to relieve severe overcrowding and harsh living conditions in some prisons and police holding centers. Problems remain, however, as evidenced by violent prison riots in March and June. There are some restrictions on freedom of religion; four persons were prosecuted for proselytizing, two persons were prosecuted for illegal operation of a "house of prayer," and a number of Jehovah's Witnesses were harassed by authorities. Discrimination against minorities continued to be a problem.

The Government formally recognizes only one minority, the Muslim minority referred to in the 1923 Treaty of Lausanne. It refuses to acknowledge formally the existence of any other ethnic groups under the term "minority" and denies members of the Slavophone community the right to identify themselves as a minority. As a result, some individuals who define themselves as members of a minority find it difficult to express freely their identity and to maintain their culture.

RESPECT FOR HUMAN RIGHTS

Section 1. Respect for the Integrity of the Person, Including Freedom From:

a. *Political and Other Extrajudicial Killing.*—There were no reports of political killings.

There were several reports of shootings at the Greek-Albanian border of illegal Albanian migrants being apprehended by Greek authorities. The Albanian Government protested four separate incidents to the Greek Government, including alleged shootings on the border in June and August and elsewhere in the country in January and April. At least two migrants were killed in these incidents. According to the Greek Government, each of the incidents was investigated, and criminal proceedings were initiated against the responsible officers. The Government emphasized that the incidents represented violations of an official policy against the use of force.

According to press reports, a man who died in police custody had suffered a heart attack after being beaten. An internal investigation concluded that he died of natural causes (see Section 1.c.).

b. *Disappearance.*—There were no reports of politically motivated disappearances.

c. *Torture and Other Cruel, Inhuman, or Degrading Treatment or Punishment.*— The Constitution specifically forbids torture, and a 1984 law makes the use of torture an offense punishable by a sentence of 3 years' to life imprisonment. However, this law has never been invoked, even though a 1993 report by the Council of Europe (COE) Committee for the Prevention of Torture and Inhuman or Degrading Treatment or Punishment (CPT) concluded that certain categories of persons detained or arrested by the police, particularly persons arrested for drug-related offenses or for crimes such as murder, rape, or robbery, run a significant risk of being mistreated and are occasionally subjected to severe mistreatment or torture.

The Government continued its own internal review of the CPT charges and as of September reported that of the 33 lawsuits filed against policemen in the period 1989–93 for abuse, torture, and mistreatment, 10 cases were still pending in court or under investigation. One case was closed when the police officer was found innocent.

Five police officers were under internal investigation following allegations that they severely beat a man arrested in January in Iraklion, Crete. Criminal charges filed by the individual were pending at year's end. Press reports claimed that a man found dead the same month in a police detention center in Vyron had died of a heart attack after being beaten. An internal investigation determined that he had died of natural causes and resulted in no disciplinary action; a related court case was also pending. In February a man arrested on robbery charges in Thessaloniki filed assault charges against several police officers. The charges and an internal investigation were pending. Some police also abused suspects during interrogations (see Section 1.d.).

In February a security team raided a Romani settlement near Athens in search of a murder suspect. Television coverage of the raid showed heavily armed team members dragging camp residents, including the elderly and juveniles, from their shacks, forcing them to lie face down in the dirt, and kicking them. Seventy persons were arrested, but the murder suspect was not found. A subsequent internal police investigation cleared the chief of police of wrongdoing, but it resulted in the dismissal of two other officers and the reprimand of a third officer for violations of police procedures and the use of excessive force.

Prison conditions remained poor. Despite several changes in the law to permit earlier parole of prisoners, substantial overcrowding continued to plague prisons throughout the country. Overcrowding contributed to unrest in six provincial prisons in March, and there were violent prison riots in March and June. While the capacity of Korydallos (the largest prison, located in Athens) is 480 inmates, some 960 were housed there in the first 10 months of the year. As of September 1, the Ministry of Justice reported that the number of prisoners was 5,178 (of whom approximately 2,000 were foreigners), while the total capacity of the prison system was 4,302.

The Government has instituted new training programs for wardens and new vocational training programs for inmates. The Ministry of Justice announced plans to begin construction of two major new prisons in 1997 in order to reduce overcrowding. Prison conditions for conscientious objectors continued to improve as a result of government actions to reduce overcrowding and to increase work opportunities in prisons, which reduced the time of imprisonment. A law passed in June granted voting rights to certain inmates.

In past years there were credible reports of rape by inmates (including rape of juveniles by other juveniles), physical abuse by prison guards, and violence perpetrated by inmates, including against foreign prisoners. There were no press reports of such incidents in 1996. In August, however, the Albanian Government protested mistreatment of inmates in the Patras and Iwannina prisons that was reportedly condoned by prison officials. Albanian consular officials were denied permission to visit either prison. Several inmate disturbances over conditions occurred.

A 1995 bilateral agreement between Greece and Albania provides for the transfer of Albanian inmates to Albanian prisons. Although there are approximately 1,000 Albanian prisoners in Greek jails, only 23 were repatriated under the agreement during the first 9 months of the year. The Government attributed low participation in the repatriation program to the unwillingness of Albanian prisoners to consent to repatriation.

The Government is inconsistent in granting permission for prison visits by nongovernmental organizations.

d. *Arbitrary Arrest, Detention, or Exile.*—The Constitution requires judicial warrants for all arrests, except during the actual commission of a crime, and the law prohibits arbitrary arrest orders. Police must, by law, bring a person arrested on the basis of a warrant or while committing a crime before an examining magistrate within 24 hours. The magistrate must issue a detention warrant or order the release of the detainee within 3 days, unless special circumstances require a 2-day extension of this time limit.

Defendants brought to court before the end of the day following the commission of a charged offense may be tried immediately, under a "speedy procedure." Although legal safeguards, including representation by counsel, apply in speedy procedure cases, the short period of time may inhibit the defendant's ability to present an adequate defense. Defendants may ask for a delay to provide time to prepare their defense, but the court is not obliged to grant it. The speedy procedure was used in less than 10 percent of misdemeanor cases. It does not apply to felonies.

The police sometimes violated these legal safeguards. CPT team members stated that the police, during investigation of serious crimes, occasionally interrogated suspects as "witnesses," allegedly because witnesses do not have the right to legal representation during police questioning. Statements made to the police in these circumstances may be used against these persons in court if they are later charged and brought to trial. Witnesses do not have the legal right to remain silent, although they are not required to testify against themselves. In such cases access to a lawyer can be effectively denied until after interrogation, which in some cases has resulted in torture or mistreatment and the subsequent signing of a statement. These circumstances were reportedly most likely to occur in cases of serious crimes, including drug offenses, in which the police did not have sufficient evidence to convict without a confession. The Government did not prosecute and punish any officials for such misconduct during the year.

The effective maximum duration of pretrial detention is 18 months for felonies and 9 months for misdemeanors. Defense lawyers complain that pretrial detention is overly long and overused by judges. A panel of judges may grant release pending trial, with or without bail. Pretrial detainees made up 32 percent of those incarcerated, according to government sources. A person convicted of a misdemeanor and sentenced to 2 years or less may, at the court's discretion, pay a fine in lieu of being imprisoned.

Exile is unconstitutional, and no cases have been reported since the restoration of democracy in 1974. However, Greek citizens not of ethnic Greek origin who travel outside the country may be deprived of their citizenship and refused readmittance to the country under Article 19 of the Citizenship Code. Article 20 of the Code permits the Government to strip citizenship from those who "commit acts contrary to the interests of Greece for the benefit of a foreign state." Article 19 was applied in 84 cases in 1996; the Government would not reveal the number of Article 20 cases it pursued in 1996 (see Section 2.d.).

e. *Denial of Fair Public Trial.*—The Constitution provides for the independence of the judiciary, but there have been charges that judges sometimes allow political criteria, including the desire to obtain promotion, to influence their judgments.

The judicial system includes three levels of courts, appointed judges, an examining magistrate system, and trial by judicial panels.

The Constitution provides for public trials, and trial court sessions are open to the public, unless the court decides that privacy is required to protect victims and witnesses, or the cases involve national security matters. According to defense attorneys, the latter provision has not been invoked since the restoration of democracy in 1974. The defendant enjoys the presumption of innocence, the standard of proof of guilt beyond a reasonable doubt, the right to present evidence and witnesses, the right of access to the prosecution's evidence, the right to cross-examine witnesses, and the right to counsel. Lawyers are provided to defendants who are not able to afford legal counsel only in felony cases. Both the prosecution and the defense have the right of appeal.

Although non-Greek speaking defendants have the right to a court-appointed interpreter, the low fees paid for such work often result in a poor quality of translation; foreign defendants complain that they do not understand their trials.

The legal system does not discriminate against women or minorities, with some exceptions: Article 19 of the Citizenship Code (see Section 2.d.) applies only to Greek citizens who are not ethnically Greek; Orthodox and non-Orthodox religions have different legal procedures for applying for a "house of prayer" permit (see Section 2.c.); nonethnic Greek citizens are legally prohibited from settling in a large "supervised zone" near the frontier (in practice this prohibition is not enforced); and a 1939 law prohibits the functioning of private schools in buildings owned by non-Orthodox religious foundations. (However, in practice this prohibition is not enforced.)

Although laws that limit freedom of expression remain in force (see Section 2.a.), no one has been imprisoned as a result of such charges in the last year. Those convicted in the past were allowed to convert their convictions into a fine of approximately $14 per day.

Amnesty International reported several derogations from international standards in group trials of students stemming from violent demonstrations in late 1995 at Athens Polytechnic University.

There were no reports of political prisoners.

f. *Arbitrary Interference With Privacy, Family, Home, or Correspondence.*—The Constitution prohibits the invasion of privacy and searches without warrants, and the law permits the monitoring of personal communications only under strict judicial controls. However, the number of persons and groups subjected to government surveillance in recent years raises questions about safeguards.

The security services continued to target human rights activists, non-Orthodox religious groups, and minority group representatives and to monitor foreign diplomats who met with such individuals. On several occasions, information about such private meetings, including official government documents, was published by the press. Human rights activists also reported the continuation of suspicious openings and diversions of mail, some of which was never delivered but was subsequently published in newspapers with apparent links to security services. As far as is known, the Government took no steps to stop such practices or to prosecute those involved.

Section 2. Respect for Civil Liberties, Including:

a. *Freedom of Speech and Press.*—Freedom of speech and the press is provided for in the Constitution, and the Government generally respected these rights in practice, but with some exceptions. Some legal restrictions on free speech remain in force; the Government continued to use such laws against individuals who raise politically sensitive topics such as the assertion of nonrecognized ethnic minority identification.

Articles of the Penal Code that are at times used to restrict free speech and the press include Article 141, which forbids exposing the friendly relations of the Greek state with foreign states to danger of disturbance; Article 191, which prohibits spreading false information and rumors liable to create concern and fear among citizens and cause disturbances in the country's international relations and inciting citizens to rivalry and division, leading to disturbance of the peace; and Article 192, which prohibits inciting citizens to acts of violence or to disturbing the peace through disharmony among them.

These laws were invoked in September when the public prosecutor of Florina ordered the Rainbow Party to remove a bilingual sign outside its office that used a Slavic place name for a Greek city, on the grounds that it "promoted divisiveness." The public prosecutor pressed charges against the Rainbow Party for the display of a similar sign in 1995. In addition, an official of the Rainbow Party was charged with a criminal offense under Article 191 for attempting to import two wall calendars in March that identified Greek cities by their Slavic names. No trial date had been set by year's end.

On matters other than those involving the question of ethnic minorities, Greece generally enjoys a tradition of outspoken public discourse and a vigorous free press. In 1993 the Government repealed a law that forbade "insulting authority" and it proscribed prosecution of otherwise actionable "offenses committed by or through the press."

Satirical and opposition newspapers do not hesitate to attack the highest state authorities. The Constitution allows for seizure (but not prior restraint), by order of the public prosecutor, of publications that insult the President, offend religious beliefs, contain obscene articles, advocate violent overthrow of the political system, or disclose military and defense information. Seizures have been rare, however, and none occurred in 1996.

Despite the official prohibition on prosecuting offenses committee by or through the press, Muslim journalist Abdul Dede was charged under Article 191 as well as under libel codes for an article he wrote in January concerning extremist groups in Thrace. His trial, originally scheduled for December, was postponed until 1997.

The Government is prosecutng Radio Icik, a Turkish-language station in Xanthi, for operating without a license in 1994 and 1995. No other radio stations have been prosecuted under these statutes despite the fact that many operate without licenses. The case is to be heard in February 1997.

In April a Turkish-language radio station in the Thracian village of Selero was damaged in a fire that the station owner claimed was caused by arson. He claimed that he had received warnings prior to the fire; he did not produce evidence, however, to refute the finding of the Government's investigation, which was that the cause was electrical.

The Constitution provides that the state exercise "immediate control" over radio and television. An independent, government-appointed body with the authority to enact rules governing private broadcasting established procedural regulations for radio several years ago. In 1993 it did so for television as well, issuing licenses to six private stations. Many other private television stations operated without licenses, however. State-run stations tended to emphasize the Government's views but also reported objectively on other parties' programs and positions. Private radio and television stations operated independently of any Government control over their reporting. Members of ethnic, religious, and linguistic minorities freely publish periodicals and other publications, often in their native language. In Thrace, Turkish-language television broadcasts are widely available.

An Athens court acquitted actor Vassilis Diamantopolous and professor George Roussis in May of charges of "praising a criminal act" in conjunction with their defense of rioting students on a television talk show. The public prosecutor appealed the decision, and the case was pending at year's end.

Academic freedom is respected.

b. *Freedom of Peaceful Assembly and Association.*—The Constitution provides for freedom of assembly. Police permits were routinely issued for public demonstrations, and there were no reports that the permit requirement was abused.

The Constitution provides for the right of association, which was generally respected, except in cases involving ethnic minorities. In 1994 the Supreme Court upheld the 1991 decision of lower courts to deny registration to the "Macedonian Cultural Center" in Florina, organized by Greeks who consider themselves of Slavic descent. The 1991 ruling held that "the true goal of the society * * * is to affirm the idea of the existence of a 'Macedonian' minority in Greece, which contradicts (Greece's) national interests and the law." The organizers have appealed the decision to the European Court of Human Rights, which declared the application admissible in June but had not delivered a judgment by year's end.

Government authorities legally recognize the existence of the Muslim minority but not any other minorities (see Section 5). The Government's position is contrary to the 1990 Copenhagen document of the then-Conference on Security and Cooperation in Europe (CSCE) to which the Government is a signatory, which asserts that "to belong to a national minority is a matter of a person's individual choice."

c. Freedom of Religion.—The Constitution establishes the Greek Orthodox Church, to which perhaps 95 to 97 percent of the population at least nominally adhere, as the prevailing religion, but it prohibits discrimination against adherents of other religions. The Greek Orthodox Church wields significant influence through its relationship with the Ministry of Education and Religion. Religious training is mandatory in public schools for Greek Orthodox pupils. Non-Orthodox students are exempt from this requirement. However, some teachers suspended Jehovah's Witnesses for not participating in school national day parades. The Constitution limits religious practice by prohibiting proselytizing; four Jehovah's Witnesses were prosecuted for proselytizing in 1996. More Jehovah's Witnesses were harassed by authorities who arrested and held them for several hours at police headquarters but subsequently released them without pressing charges. Several cases involving proselytism from previous years resulted in verdicts of acquittal in 1996; one such case was postponed until 1997. Several past convictions for proselytizing were pending before the European Court of Human Rights at year's end.

Traditionally, Jehovah's Witnesses ministers were not granted the exemption from military service accorded under the law to clergy of "known religions" and thus served prison sentences for refusing military service. Since 1990–91 the Council of State, the highest court dealing with civil and administrative matters whose opinions are binding on the Government, has ruled that Jehovah's Witnesses were a "known religion" and has ordered the release of ministers who had refused induction. However, the recruiting service of the armed forces regarded these rulings as applying only to individual appellants, rather than as binding precedents for subsequent Jehovah's Witnesses ministers who were called up. It thus continued to rely, in the first instance, on the opinion of the Ministry of Education and Religion, which in turn accepted the view of the Greek Orthodox Church that Jehovah's Witnesses are not a "known religion." As a consequence, for the past few years, ministers of Jehovah's Witnesses have been called up for military service and prosecuted for refusal to serve; only after conviction could they appeal to the Council of State.

To open and operate a non-Greek Orthodox house of worship requires approval by the Ministry of Education and Religion. The Ministry bases its decision on the advisory opinion of the local Orthodox bishop. In recent years, such permission has been granted to some groups only after long delays and withheld altogether from other denominations. Two Jehovah's Witnesses were charged in February with the illegal use of a house of prayer in Komotini.

In September the European Court of Human Rights ruled in favor of four Jehovah's Witnesses who had been found guilty by the Supreme Court in 1991 of illegally operating a house of prayer. The Court found that the house of prayer authorization procedure allowed the Government to limit the exercise of religious freedom by members of non-Orthodox religions and was therefore contrary to Article 9 of the European convention on human rights. The Government nevertheless denied after the verdict that any restrictions were imposed.

In May an appeals court considering the case of former Greek Orthodox priest Nikodomos Tsarknias overturned three of his previous convictions for "pretense of authority." Human rights monitors note that the language of the court's decision implied recognition of the Macedonian Orthodox Church.

Mosques operate freely in Western Thrace and in the islands of Rhodes and Kos, where most Greek citizens of the Muslim faith reside. However, in December 17 Muslims were arrested in Xanthi province for rebuilding a mosque without a proper permit. Their case had not been resolved by year's end.

In accordance with a 1990 presidential decree, the State appointed two muftis (Islamic judges and religious leaders) and one assistant mufti in Greece, all resident in Thrace, based on the recommendations of a committee of local Muslim scholars, religious authorities, and community leaders. The Government argued that it must appoint muftis because, in addition to their religious duties, they perform judicial functions in many civil and domestic matters under Muslim religious law, for which the State pays them.

The Muslim minority remains divided on the mufti selection issue. Some Muslims accept the authority of the two officially appointed muftis; other Muslims have chosen two other muftis to serve their communities. The Government prosecuted the two unofficial muftis again in 1996. Mehmet Amin Aga was sentenced in May to 12 months in jail, and again in July to 20 months in prison for usurping the authority of the mufti; he appealed both sentences and was not incarcerated. Ibrahim

Sherif was sentenced in October to 6 months in jail on identical charges. He elected to pay a fine instead of serving the jail sentence.

Some Muslims claimed that a 1980 law weakens the financial autonomy of the "wakfs," community associations which raise funds used for maintaining mosques and schools and for charitable works, by placing the Wakfs under the administration of appointed muftis and their representatives. Those who object to this system say that it violates the terms of the Treaty of Lausanne. A presidential decree issued in March put the Wakfs under the administration of a temporary committee as an interim measure toward resolving their outstanding problems.

Leaders of various non-Greek orthodox religious groups assert that their members face discrimination in reaching the senior ranks in government service. Furthermore, the historical record generally indicates that only those of the Greek Orthodox faith can become officers in the Greek military. To avoid this restriction some members of other faiths resort to declaring themselves Orthodox. Senior government officials, when questioned about such allegations of discrimination, deny that it exists and point out certain persons not of the Orthodox faith who have successful careers in the military. Although only two Muslim officers have been allowed to advance to the rank of reserve officer in the military, insufficient statistical evidence is available to support definitively either side.

A 1991 law mandates that citizens declare their religion on European Union (EU) identity cards that—if and when issued—could be used instead of passports to travel freely within the EU. Current national identity cards, which will be replaced when the new EU cards are issued, include reference to the holder's religion, although individuals have the option of leaving that section blank. The law mandating the declaration of religion on the EU cards has caused particular concern among the Catholic and Jewish religious communities in Greece and abroad and has drawn strong criticism from the European Parliament. Despite such criticism and concern, the Government declined to either change the law mandating the declaration of religion on the cards or to issue the new EU cards.

d. *Freedom of Movement Within the Country, Foreign Travel, Emigration, and Repatriation.*—The Constitution calls for freedom of movement within and outside the country and the right to return. However, Article 19 of the Citizenship Code distinguishes between citizens who are ethnic Greeks and those who are not. Most Article 19 cases involve Muslims from Western Thrace, since only the "Muslim minority" is recognized as having non-Greek ethnicity. Citizens who are not ethnic Greeks may be deprived of their citizenship if it is determined that they left Greece with no apparent intent to return. Determination of intent is made without input from the affected individual; in practice, this law is applied to members of the Muslim community considered to be "undesirable" by the security services. However, immigrants who are ethnic Greeks are normally recognized as citizens and accorded full rights, despite years or even generations of absence.

The Interior Ministry initiates proceedings under Article 19 on the basis of reports by local authorities or by Greek embassies or consulates abroad. Affected persons are not notified of Article 19 hearings and are not permitted to attend. Those who lose citizenship as a result of such hearings sometimes learn of this loss only when they seek to reenter Greece. According to the Ministry of the Interior, 84 persons lost Greek citizenship under Article 19 in 1996 (compared with 72 in 1995). Of this number, the Government claims that 35 voluntarily relinquished their citizenship (compared with 45 in 1995).

Persons who lose their citizenship under Article 19 have the right of "administrative appeal" to the Interior Ministry; they can also appeal to the Council of State and to the Council of Europe. Leaders of the Muslim community complained that the time and expense involved tended to discourage such appeals. In addition, some persons who lose their citizenship under Article 19 do not discover that fact until appeals deadlines have passed. Three persons who lost citizenship in 1994 have filed administrative appeals which are pending.

Another section of the Citizenship Code, Article 20, permits the Government to strip citizenship from those who "commit acts contrary to the interests of Greece for the benefit of a foreign state." While the law as written applies equally to all Greeks regardless of their ethnic background, to date it has been enforced only against citizens who identified themselves as members of the "Macedonian" minority. The Government would not reveal the number of Article 20 cases it pursued in 1996. Dual citizens who are stripped of Greek citizenship under Article 20 have been prevented from entering the country using the passport of their second nationality.

Greece maintains restricted military zones along its borders, including along the northern border with Bulgaria, an area where many Pomaks live. Until 1995 entry into the zone was controlled by authorities even for local inhabitants, causing residents to complain that their freedom of movement was restricted. The Government announced in 1995 that the sole remaining checkpoint into the village of Exinos within the zone would be removed and that restrictions for entry into the zone would be lifted. Although the regulations concerning the zone remain formally in place, in practice they are no longer enforced for Greek citizens. Several foreign groups were, however, turned away from the zone in 1996.

Ethnic Greek immigrants, including those who came from the former Soviet Union since 1986 and from the civil war in Georgia, normally qualify promptly for citizenship and special assistance from the Government. The returnees were settled initially in Western Thrace, where government programs encouraging them to remain have met with limited success. Most move to Athens, Thessaloniki, or other cities, where job prospects are better.

Greece frequently offers first asylum to a growing number of refugees from Turkey, Iraq, and Iran. The Government provides first asylum to an average of over 100 persons per month. However, it reserves the right to refuse first asylum to illegal immigrants who do not apply within 48 hours. If they do not, their applications can be denied at their "admissibility interviews" when and if they are apprehended regardless of the potential merit of claims of persecution.

Permanent resettlement is not normally available for refugees who are not ethnically Greek. Approximately 6,000 refugees were officially recognized between 1980 and 1995, including 400 Vietnamese refugees accepted since 1979 for permanent resettlement. Of the 858 individuals who submitted applications for refugee status in the first 9 months of 1996, 86 were approved. The remaining applications, many of which were submitted by ethnic Kurds from Turkey and Iraq, are under review by the Government in cooperation with the United Nations High Commissioner for Refugees.

The Government continues to apprehend and return to Albania illegal Albanian immigrants. Greece and Albania signed a treaty of friendship in March, followed in May by a seasonal employment agreement designed to regularize the flow of Albanian workers to Greece. The Parliament has not yet passed the implementing legislation necessary for the agreement to take effect.

Section 3. Respect for Political Rights: The Right of Citizens to Change Their Government

Greece is a multiparty democracy in which the Constitution provides for full political rights for all citizens and for the peaceful change of governments and of the Constitution. The Government headed by Prime Minister Constantine Simitis of the Panhellenic Socialist Movement (PASOK) won in free and fair elections in September. Parliament elects a President for a 5-year term. Voting is mandatory for those over the age of 18, but there are many conditions that allow one not to vote and penalties are not applied in practice. Members of the unicameral 300-seat Parliament are elected to maximum 4-year terms by secret ballot. Opposition parties function freely and have broad access to the media.

Although there are no legal restrictions on the participation of women or minorities in government or politics, they are underrepresented at the higher levels of political life. Women held 2 ministerial positions in the Government and only 1 of 29 subministerial positions. Of the 300 Members of Parliament, 17 were women. Women are also underrepresented in the leadership of the two largest parties. The head of the Communist Party is a woman.

While the Government generally respects citizens' political rights, there are sometimes charges that the Government limits the right of some individuals to speak publicly and associate freely on the basis of their self-proclaimed ethnic identity, thus impinging on the political rights of such persons. It also combined voting districts in Thrace, which had the consequence of making it difficult for Muslims to be elected to regional positions. However, candidates from the Muslim minority and members of the "Macedonian minority" ran in the national parliamentary elections. Three Muslim deputies were elected in Thrace, one each from PASOK, New Democracy, and the Coalition of the Left. Romani representatives report that local authorities sometimes deprive Roma of the right to vote by refusing to register them.

In April the Government transferred responsibility for oversight of all rights guaranteed to the Muslim minority under the Treaty of Lausanne, including education, zoning, administration of the "wakfs," and trade, from the governors to the Regional Development Director of Eastern Macedonia and Thrace. Because the governors are elected, but the Development Director is appointed by the central government, this reduced the ability of the minority to influence decisions that affect it through the democratic process. The Government stated that it made the change because Greece's treaty obligations could be administered more effectively by the central authorities.

Section 4. Governmental Attitude Regarding International and Nongovernmental Investigation of Alleged Violations of Human Rights

The Government allows domestic human rights organizations to operate, but cooperation with them varies. In principle it does not prohibit foreign diplomats from meeting with officials and other citizens, including critics of official policy. However, the security services on occasion monitor contacts of Greek human rights groups, including listening in on conversations held between those groups and human rights investigators and diplomats. The security services have also questioned monitors' interlocutors in the aftermath of meetings, reports of which have subsequently appeared in the press. Official government documents regarding the activities of human rights monitors have also been reproduced in the press. Monitors view this activity as a form of intimidation which deters others from meeting with investigators.

Section 5. Discrimination Based on Race, Sex, Religion, Disability, Language, or Social Status

The Constitution provides for equality before the law and the full protection of individual life, honor, and freedom irrespective of nationality, race, language, or religious or political belief. Government respect for these rights in practice is uneven.

Violence against homosexuals is not common. However, police occasionally harass gay bar owners and gay men, including detaining them at police stations overnight and sometimes physically mistreating them.

Women.—The incidence of violence against women reported to the authorities is low, but Athens' Equality Secretariat—which operates the only shelter for battered women—believes the actual incidence is "high." According to the Ministry of Public Order, 234 cases of rape were reported in 1995. No other statistics were available. The General Secretariat for Equality of the Sexes (GSES), an independent government agency, asserts that police tend to discourage women from pursuing domestic violence charges and instead undertake reconciliation efforts, although they are neither qualified for nor charged with this task. The GSES also claims that the courts are lenient when dealing with domestic violence cases.

As a result of pressure from women's groups, the Government established a center for battered women in Athens in 1988, and a residential facility for battered women and their children opened in 1993. These centers provide legal advice, psychological counseling, information on social services, and temporary residence for battered women and their children. Battered women can also go to state hospitals and regional health centers, although these facilities are often not adequately staffed to handle such cases properly.

According to the police, trafficking in women for prostitution, mostly from the former Soviet Union, Albania, Bulgaria, and Romania, has increased sharply in recent years. Of the 118 foreign women arrested in Attica province (which includes Athens) during the first 9 months of the year for prostitution without a license, 60 were from Albania, 19 were from Russia, and 25 were from elsewhere in the former Soviet Union. Police estimate that foreigners constitute 2,000 of the 5,000 prostitutes in Greece. Although information on this subject is fragmentary, January press reports indicated that Greek and Cypriot police were cooperating to break up a prostitution ring specializing in Russian women.

There are broad constitutional and legal protections for women, including equal pay for equal work. However, the GSES and the unions maintain that women receive lower salaries overall than men because they are hired for lower-level jobs. The National Statistical Service's most recent data (the fourth quarter of 1995) show that women's salaries in manufacturing were 71 percent of those of men in comparable positions; in retail sales, women's salaries were 83 percent of those of men in comparable positions. These same groups claim that women face a "glass ceiling" when they are considered for promotions in both the public and private sectors. A GSES report shows that although women make up 42 percent of permanent civil servants, only 10.6 percent hold directors' positions. Women represent 60 percent of the unemployed and 69 percent of those affected by long-term unemployment. Although there are still relatively few women in senior positions, in recent years women have entered traditionally male-dominated occupations such as the legal and medical professions in larger numbers.

Children.—The Government is committed to providing adequate basic health and education services for children. Education is compulsory through the ninth grade and free through university. However, some social groups, such as Roma and illegal immigrants, are underserved, according to child health specialists.

Welfare legislation enacted in 1992 prohibits the mistreatment of children and provides penalties for violators. The State provides preventive and treatment programs for abused children and for children deprived of their family environment; it also seeks to ensure that alternative family care or institutional placement is made available to them.

The Institute of Child Health, which receives referrals of children who have been abused, estimates that 4,000 children are abused each year. The Institute reports that its cases involve physical abuse (52.5 percent), neglect/malnutrition (37 percent), burns (7 percent), and sexual abuse (3.5 percent), the latter including sexual exploitation, incest, and rape. According to a report submitted by the Government at the 1996 Stockholm International Congress on the Sexual Exploitation of Children, 238 cases of sexual exploitation of children and young people up to the age of 18 were reported in 1995.

Children's rights advocacy groups claim that protection of high-risk children in state residential care centers is inadequate and of low quality. They cite lack of coordination between welfare services and the courts, inadequate funding of the welfare system, and poor staffing of residential care centers as systemic weaknesses in child abuse prevention and treatment efforts. Societal abuse of children in the form of prostitution, pornography, and child labor is rare.

In recent years, the number of street children who panhandle or peddle at city intersections on behalf of adult family members or for criminal gangs has grown. Many in the Athens area are ethnic Albanian. Police occasionally round up these children and take them to state or charitable institutions that care for wayward children. Parents can reclaim their children but risk deportation if they are illegal immigrants.

People With Disabilities.—Legislation mandates the hiring of disabled persons in public and private enterprises employing more than 50 persons. However, the law is reportedly poorly enforced, particularly in the private sector. The law states that disabled persons should number 3 percent of staff in private enterprises. In the civil service, 5 percent of administrative staff and 80 percent of telephone operator positions are reserved for disabled persons. Persons with disabilities have been appointed to important positions the civil service, including that of Secretary General of the Ministry of Welfare.

The Construction Code mandates physical access for disabled persons to private and public buildings, but this law too is poorly enforced. Ramps and special curbs for the disabled have been constructed on some Athens streets and at some public buildings, and sound signals have been installed at some city street crossings. Since 1993 the Government has been replacing old city buses with new ones with stairs specially designed for the disabled. Officials say that the new Athens subway lines under construction will provide full access for the disabled.

Religious Minorities.—Several religious denominations reported difficulties in dealing with the authorities on a variety of administrative matters. Privileges and legal prerogatives granted to the Greek Orthodox Church are not routinely extended to other recognized religions. Rather, the non-Greek Orthodox must make separate and lengthy applications to government authorities on such matters as arranging appointments to meet with Ministry of Education and Religion officials and gaining permission to move places of worship to larger quarters.

According to Jehovah's Witnesses, teachers no longer face difficulties gaining or keeping employment in public and private schools, except in rare instances in rural areas. Jehovah's Witnesses are now treated as a "known religion" for the purpose of employment by the Ministry of Education, which hires public school teachers.

Jehovah's Witness leaders have protested the existence of a derogatory passage in the high-school level textbook used nationwide in religious instruction classes. The segment criticizes minority religions as a threat to the nation.

Leaders of the Jewish community in Greece have lobbied the government for several years to delete anti-Semitic references from public school textbooks. The Ministry of Education and Religion agreed to delete all such references as new editions were published. The references have been deleted in the new editions that have since been released. The central board of Jewish communities in Greece expects the remaining references to be deleted in the coming years.

The Government gave approval for construction of a memorial for the 48,000 victims of the Holocaust in Thessaloniki. The city of Thessaloniki will open a Jewish folk and history museum, and a privately funded holocaust museum will open in early 1997.

National/Racial/Ethnic Minorities.—There are communities in Greece that identify themselves as Turks, Pomaks, Vlachs, Roma, Arvanites (ethnic Albanians), and "Macedonians" or "Slavomacedonians." Many are fully integrated into Greek society. The only minority the Government formally recognizes is the "Muslim minority" referred to in the 1923 Treaty of Lausanne. The Government insists on the use of that rubric to refer to several different ethnic communities. A substantial part of the Muslim minority is ethnically Turkish or consists of Turkish-speakers in Western

Thrace; the Government estimates their number at some 120,000 persons. In addition to people of Turkish origin, the Muslim minority includes Pomaks and Roma. Many Greek Muslims, including Pomaks, identify themselves as Turks and say that the Muslim minority as a whole has a Turkish cultural consciousness. The use of the word "tourkos" ("Turk") is prohibited in titles of organizations, though individuals may legally call themselves "tourkos." To most Greeks, the word "tourkos" connotes Turkish identity or loyalties, and many object to its use by citizens of Turkish origin. Use of a similar adjective, "tourkoyennis" (of Turkish descent, affiliation, or ethnicity) however, is allowed.

Northern Greece is home to an indeterminate number (estimates range widely, from under 10,000 to 50,000 or more) of citizens who are descended from Slavs or Slavophones. Some still speak a Slavic dialect, particularly in the Florina district. A small number of them consider themselves to be members of a distinct ethnic group which they identify as "Macedonian" (self-described "Macedonians" are hereafter referred to "Macedonian") and assert their right to minority status. The Government harasses and intimidates some of these people, including denying their right of association (see Section 2.b.), monitoring activists' meetings with human rights investigators (see Section 2.d.), and accusing activists publicly of being agents of a foreign government. As a result, some Greeks who consider themselves "Macedonian" do not declare themselves openly for fear of losing their jobs or other sanctions. The Government's sensitivity on this issue stems from its belief that people who claim to be members of a "Macedonian" minority may have separatist aspirations. Greece's dispute with the Former Yugoslav Republic of Macedonia over that country's name heightened this sensitivity.

Government officials and courts deny requests by individuals and groups to identify themselves using the ancient term "Macedonian," because some 2.2 million ethnic (and linguistically) Greek citizens in the northern Greek region of Macedonia already use the term to identify themselves. The Government does not define the Slavic dialect spoken by some thousands of northern Greeks as "Macedonian," and government officials deny that it is a separate language at all. The officials also note that Greece regulates the establishment of all commercial language academies and question whether advocates of "Macedonian" language schools meet the relevant requirements. They say that the Government would not interfere with the holding of informal language classes within the Slavophone community. When a political party hung a bilingual Greek and Slavic name sign outside its office, the public prosecutor in Florina ordered that it be removed (see Section 2.a.). Criminal charges were filed against an official of the same party under a law banning "inciting rivalry and division" when he attempted to import two wall calendars identifying Greek cities by their Slavic names (see Section 2.a.).

The Secretariat for Adult Education (a government agency) estimates the number of Roma at some 300,000. Almost half of the Romani population is permanently settled, mainly in the Athens area. The other half is mobile, working mainly as agricultural laborers, peddlers, and musicians throughout the country. Government policy is to encourage the integration of Roma. Poverty, illiteracy, and social prejudice continue to plague large parts of the Romani population. The Secretariat for Adult Education conducts education and training programs targeting the Romani population, including the use of mobile schools. The illiteracy rate among Roma is estimated at 80 percent. Some 1,200 Romani children attended the mobile school program during the last school year.

The usage of public health facilities by Roma is low because of the low rate of integration of Romani communities into Greek society and social security systems. Ninety percent of Roma are not insured by any of the government social security systems because they are self-employed or work in off-the-books jobs that do not make contributions to the social security system. The fact that health facilities are not located close to the Roma camps also contributes to their low rate of access.

In July the Government announced new projects, subsidized by EU social funds, to improve Romani living conditions. The projects include the establishment of organized camps, subsidies for the purchase of mobile homes, and the creation of mobile medical units. None of the projects was implemented by year's end.

The Treaty of Lausanne provides that the Muslim minority has the right to Turkish-language education, with a reciprocal entitlement for the Greek minority in Istanbul (now reduced to about 3,000). Western Thrace has both Koranic and secular Turkish-language schools. Government disputes with Turkey over teachers and textbooks caused these secular schools serious problems in obtaining faculty and teaching materials in sufficient number and quality. Under a 1952 educational protocol, Greece and Turkey may annually exchange 35 teachers on a reciprocal basis. The teachers serve in Istanbul and Western Thrace, respectively, but in recent years the Greek side limited the exchanges to 16 teachers per country due to the dwindling needs of the small and aging Greek population Turkey. In Greece over 9,000 Muslim children attended Turkish-language primary schools. Around 650 attended Turkish-language secondary schools, and approximately 1,000 attended Greek-language secondary schools. Many Muslims reportedly went to high school in Turkey due to the limited number of places in the Turkish-language secondary schools, which are assigned by lottery.

In 1995 the Government enacted several measures designed to improve the educational situation of Muslims in Thrace. A new education law provides incentives for Muslim and Christian educators to reside and teach in isolated villages. The new law also permits the Minister of Education to give special consideration to Muslims for admission to universities and technical institutes. Under this law, faculties of each university and technical institute nationwide created at least one position for Muslim students, a total of some 250 places. All Muslim students who applied were admitted to these institutes of higher learning, and about 70 attended.

The rate of employment of Muslims in the public sector and in state-owned industries and corporations is much lower than the Muslim percentage of the population. In Xanthi and Komotini, while Muslims hold seats on the prefectural and town councils, there are no Muslims among the regular employees of the prefecture. Muslims in Thrace claim that they are hired only for lower level, part-time work. The Government says lack of fluency in written and spoken Greek and the need for university degrees for high-level positions limit the number of Muslims eligible for government jobs. Muslims have not received any of the government subsidies offered to corporations establishing or expanding their business operations in Thrace. According to government sources, however, no Muslims applied for these subsidies.

Public offices in Thrace do their business in Greek; the courts provide interpreters as needed. In the Komotini district in Thrace, where many ethnic Turks live, the office of the district governor ("nomarch") has Turkish-language interpreters available.

Claims of discriminatory denial of Muslim applications for a license to operate businesses, own a tractor, or construct property have diminished greatly in recent years. One Muslim's application for membership in the Komotini chamber of commerce, which is necessary to obtain import licenses and other privileges, was refused because his business partner was Turkish. Basic public services provided to Muslim-populated neighborhoods and villages (electricity, telephones, paved roads) in many cases continue to lag far behind those provided in non-Muslim areas.

In August rightwing orthodox Christian extremists vandalized around 40 Muslim-owned businesses and institutions in Komotini, including the Muslim youth organization and the mosque that was the headquarters of the mufti. Four Muslims were hospitalized following the attacks. Police made five arrests in connection with the incident.

In 1995 the Defense Minister reported that members of the Muslim minority would for the first time be allowed to advance to the rank of reserve officers in the military. To date, two Muslims have done so. Members of the Muslim minority in the Dodecanese islands of Rhodes and Kos are much more integrated into local society.

Section 6. Worker Rights

a. *The Right of Association.*—The Constitution and subsequent legislation provide for the right of association. All workers, with the exception of the military, have the right to form or join unions. Police have the right to form unions but not to strike.

Approximately 30 percent of workers (nearly 1 million persons) were organized in unions. Unions receive most of their funding from a Ministry of Labor organization, the Workers' Hearth, which distributes mandatory contributions from employees and employers. Workers, employers, and the state are represented in equal numbers on the board of directors of the Workers' Hearth. Only the five most powerful public sector unions have dues-withholding provisions in their contracts, in addition to receiving Workers' Hearth subsidies.

Over 4,000 unions are grouped into regional and sectoral federations and two umbrella confederations, one for civil servants and one, the General Confederation of Greek workers (GSEE), for private sector employees. Unions are highly politicized, and there are party-affiliated factions within the labor confederations, but day-to-day operations are not controlled by political parties or the Government. There are no restrictions on who may serve as a union official. Legal restrictions on strikes include a mandatory period of notice, which is 4 days for public utilities and 24 hours for the private sector. Legislation mandates a skeleton staff during strikes affecting public services, such as electricity, transportation, communications, and banking. Public utility companies, state-owned banks, the postal service, Olympic

Airways, and the railroads are also required to maintain a skeleton staff during strikes.

The courts have the power to declare strikes illegal, although such decisions are seldom enforced. Unions complain, however, that this judicial power serves as a deterrent to some of their membership from participating in strikes. In 1996 the courts declared a majority of strikes illegal for reasons such as failure of the union to give adequate advance notice of the strike, or the addition of demands by the union during the course of the strike. No striking workers were prosecuted, however.

Unions are free to join international associations and maintain a variety of international affiliations.

b. *The Right to Organize and Bargain Collectively.*—Legislation provides for the right to organize and bargain collectively in the private sector and in public corporations. These rights are respected in practice. There are no restrictions on collective bargaining for private sector employees. The union of civil servants negotiates with the Office of the Minister to the Prime Minister.

In response to union complaints that most labor disputes ended in compulsory arbitration, legislative remedies were enacted providing for mediation procedures, with compulsory arbitration as a last resort. The legislation establishing a national mediation, reconciliation, and arbitration organization went into effect in 1992 and applies to the private sector and public corporations (the military and civil service excluded).

Antiunion discrimination is prohibited. The Labor Inspectorate or a court investigates complaints of discrimination against union members or organizers. Court rulings have mandated the reinstatement of improperly fired union organizers.

There are three free trade zones, operated according to EU regulations. The labor laws apply equally in these zones.

c. *Prohibition of Forced or Compulsory Labor.*—The Constitution prohibits forced or compulsory labor, and the Ministry of Justice enforces this prohibition. However, the Government may declare the "civil mobilization" of workers in the event of danger to national security, life, property, or the social and economic life of the country. The International Labor Organization (ILO) Committee of Experts has criticized this power as violating the standards of ILO Convention 29 on forced labor.

d. *Minimum Age for Employment of Children.*—The minimum age for employment in the industrial sector is 15 years, with higher limits for certain activities. The minimum age is 12 years in family businesses, theaters, and the cinema. These age limits are enforced by occasional Labor Inspectorate spot checks and are generally respected. However, families engaged in agriculture, food service, and merchandising often have younger family members assisting them, at least part time.

e. *Acceptable Conditions of Work.*—Collective bargaining between the GSEE and the Employers' Association determines a nationwide minimum wage. The Ministry of Labor routinely ratifies this minimum wage, which has the force of law and applies to all workers. The current minimum wage of $24 (Dr 5,746) daily and $533 (Dr 128,329) monthly, effective July 1, is sufficient for a decent standard of living for a worker and family. The maximum legal workweek is 40 hours in the private sector and 37½ hours in the public sector. The law provides for at least one 24-hour rest period per week, mandates paid vacation of 1 month per year, and sets limits on overtime.

Legislation provides for minimum standards of occupational health and safety. Although the GSEE characterized health and safety legislation as satisfactory, it charged that enforcement, the responsibility of the Labor Inspectorate, was inadequate. In its most recent review of this issue in 1992, the GSEE cited statistics indicating a high number of job-related accidents over the past two decades. Inadequate inspection, failure to enforce regulations, outdated industrial plant and equipment, and poor safety training of employees were cited as contributing to the accident rate. Workers do not have the legal right to remove themselves from situations they believe endanger their health. They do have the right, however, to lodge a confidential complaint with the Labor Inspectorate. Inspectors have the right to close down machinery or a process for a period of up to 5 days if they see safety or health hazards that they believe represent an imminent danger to the workers.

HUNGARY

Hungary is a parliamentary democracy with a freely elected legislative assembly. Prime Minister Gyula Horn, the leader of the Hungarian Socialist Party, heads a coalition government formed after the 1994 national elections. The Government respects the constitutional provisions for an independent judiciary.

The internal and external security services report directly to a minister without portfolio, and the police report to the Interior Minister. There continued to be credible reports of police abuses.

The Government has demonstrated through its macroeconomic policies and extensive privatization its commitment to the transition to a market economy. The private sector generates about 70 percent of gross domestic product. Services, trade, and government employ about 60 percent of the labor force, and industry nearly 30 percent. Major exports include manufactured goods (49 percent) and machinery and transport equipment (26 percent). An estimated 25 percent of the population live in poverty, with elderly pensioners, dependent housewives and children, and Roma most affected.

Although the Government generally respects human rights and civil liberties of its citizens, the authorities do not ensure due process in all cases. Prosecutors and judges impose—but rarely—what amounts to unlimited pretrial detention. Police on occasion enter private residences to check foreigners' identification without warrants. Although senior levels of the Interior Ministry and the National Police were more willing to address problems, police continued to use excessive force against suspects. Police harassed and abused both Roma and foreign nationals.

The print media enjoy a relatively high degree of independence. However, the Government still controls national television and most radio stations. The 1995 broadcast media law creates the conditions necessary to insulate the electronic media from state control or manipulation. The Government plans to privatize portions of the electronic media including one of the two state television channels in 1997. Opposition politicians criticized the Government's "monopolistic ownership" of the press and manipulation of distribution networks that limit opposition access to the media. Societal discrimination against Roma remains a serious problem. Anti-Semitic and racist attacks continued to decline. Spousal abuse of women is a serious problem, while discrimination against women is common in the workplace, as well as in most aspects of daily life.

RESPECT FOR HUMAN RIGHTS

Section 1. Respect for the Integrity of the Person, Including Freedom From:

a. *Political and Other Extrajudicial Killing.*—There were no reports of political or other extrajudicial killings.

After a suspect reportedly was beaten to death in Paszto in July 1995, one of the police officers involved was dismissed, three were suspended, and the police commander resigned. After 12 months of investigation, formal charges were brought in October. In November the trial was suspended until February 1997 to permit further investigation.

b. *Disappearance.*—There were no reports of politically motivated disappearances.

c. *Torture and Other Cruel, Inhuman or Other Degrading Treatment or Punishment.*—No known incidents of torture occurred. Police abuses continued, including harassment, use of excessive force, and beatings of suspects. Police also continued to harass and physically abuse Roma and foreign nationals.

In July the national chief of police announced a ban on the use of benzidin, a powerful chemical smeared on the skin of some suspects, because of its dubious benefit to criminal investigation. Benzidin is used to find traces of blood on human skin. In high doses, it can cause cancer. Hungarian human rights organizations allege that benzidin is used to coerce or force confessions from criminal suspects. Benzidin was used in several cases in Nograd county, resulting in itching, burning, and severe rashes on the suspects exposed to the chemical. In one case in April, Antal Fajd admitted his crime, but police treated him with benzidin as part of the ensuing criminal investigation. Police repeatedly denied Fajd medical treatment after the benzidin application resulted in rashes that festered on his arm. Romani suspects also were treated with benzidin in December 1995 with similarly strong reactions. In July Imre Furmann, director of the Legal Defense Bureau for National and Ethnic Minorities, reported that another person sought legal assistance after his genitals were smeared with benzidin.

The National Police have stiffened internal controls over the past several years. Of 41,000 police officers, 164 were accused of physical abuse in 1995, a three-fold increase over the previous year. The Hungarian Helsinki Committee reported in 1995 that police misconduct "* * * takes place every day, although the public is only informed by chance, only in conspicuous cases. Guilty police officers are very rarely condemned, and the majority of the officers suspected of such crimes remain on duty." In the first half the year 19 police officers were convicted for using excessive force.

Public sector salaries remain stagnant, and police are poorly paid. They frequently harass residents, charging questionable fines for erroneous traffic violations to earn petty cash. Police showed indifference towards foreigners who have been victims of street crime.

Although prisons are overcrowded, conditions meet minimum international standards, and the Government permits visits by human rights monitors. In a report covering the first half of the year for a local human rights organization, Dr. Agnes Kover identified 28 cases of physical abuse of detainees in prisons, although only 1 detainee brought charges against the police.

d. *Arbitrary Arrest, Detention, or Exile.*—Police must inform suspects upon arrest of the charges against them and may hold them for a maximum of 72 hours before filing charges. The law requires that all suspects be allowed access to counsel prior to questioning and throughout all subsequent proceedings. The authorities must provide counsel for juveniles, the indigent, and the mentally disabled. There are credible reports that police do not always allow access to counsel, particularly for minor crimes. There is no bail system; however, depending upon the nature of the crime, courts may release detainees upon their own recognizance.

Pretrial detention, based on a warrant issued by a judge, is initially limited to 1 year while criminal investigations are in progress; it may be extended indefinitely on the prosecutor's motion (provided the judge concurs). The lack of a bail system gives tremendous leeway to the judge. In addition, foreigners charged with crimes are considered likely to flee the country, which means that they are usually held until their trial. Roma allege that they are kept in pretrial detention longer and more frequently than non-Roma (see Section 1.e.). The law provides for compensation when the accused is released for lack of evidence, but the procedure is exercised rarely since victims must undertake a complicated legal procedure to pursue their claims.

The Penal Code does not provide for exile, and it is not employed.

e. *Denial of Fair Public Trial.*—The Constitution provides for an independent judiciary, and the Government respects this provision in practice. The judiciary provides citizens with a fair, although sometimes slow, process. Although counsel is appointed for indigent clients, public defenders are low paid and do not give indigent defendants priority; lawyers often meet such clients for the first time at trial.

Under the Constitution, the courts are responsible for the administration of justice, with the Supreme Court exercising control over the operations and judicature of all the courts. There are three levels of courts. Original jurisdiction in most matters rests with the local courts. Appeals of their rulings may be made to the county courts or to the Budapest municipal court, which have original jurisdiction in other matters. The highest level of appeal is the Supreme Court, whose decisions on nonconstitutional issues are binding. In the case of military trials, appeals also may be addressed to the Supreme Court.

The Constitutional Court is charged with reviewing the constitutionality of laws and statutes brought before it. Citizens may appeal directly to the Constitutional Court if they believe that their constitutional rights have been violated. Parliament elects the Court's members to 9-year terms, which may be renewed. In September the Parliament began debate on whether to increase the number of seats on the Constitutional Court, as well as providing life tenure for its members (the current retirement age is 70), thereby addressing concerns that vacancies on the bench could delay the Court's work. No judge or member of the Supreme or Constitutional Court may belong to a political party or engage in political activity. Although the Government has alleged that judges' political attitudes have affected decisions, these charges are undercut by unanimous decisions in controversial cases, with judges appointed by the government siding with those appointed by the opposition.

The law provides for the right to a fair trial, and the authorities respected this right in practice. In selected cases judges may agree to a closed trial to protect the accused or the crime victim, such as in some rape cases. There is no jury system; hence judges are the final arbiters.

Military trials follow civil law and may be closed if national security or moral grounds so justify. In all cases, sentencing must take place publicly. Defendants are entitled to counsel during all phases of criminal proceedings and are presumed innocent until proven guilty. Judicial proceedings are generally investigative rather than adversarial in nature.

Many human rights and Romani organizations claim that Roma receive less than equal treatment in the judicial process. Specifically, they allege that Roma are kept in pretrial detention more often and for longer periods of time than non-Roma. This allegation is credible in light of general discrimination against Roma; however, there is no statistical evidence because identifying the ethnicity of offenders is not allowed in police records.

In March the Parliament amended the Penal Code to crack down on hate crimes, spurred in part by the acquittal on technical grounds that month of neo-Nazi Albert Szabo on charges of disseminating anti-Semitic, fascistic materials.

There were no reports of political prisoners.

f. *Arbitrary Interference With Privacy, Family, Home or Correspondence.*—The law provides that the prosecutor's office may issue search warrants. Police must carry out house searches in the presence of two witnesses and must prepare a written inventory of items removed from the premises. Wiretapping, which may be done for national security reasons and for legitimate criminal investigations, requires a court's permission. These provisions appear to be observed in practice. However, police at times enter private residences without warrants to check foreigners' identification.

Section 2. Respect for Civil Liberties, Including:

a. *Freedom of Speech and Press.*—The Constitution provides for freedom of speech and the press, and the Government generally respects this right in practice. The last state-owned Budapest daily, Magyar Nemzet, was sold to a private owner in 1995. Four national political, 1 national economic, and 3 tabloid newspapers as well as 18 local dailies have been privatized. The print media enjoy considerable freedom; however, journalists and opposition politicians are concerned that the expression of different views in the press may be circumscribed by the small number of owners who control most of the print media.

Parliament passed a media law in December 1995 creating institutions designed to foster a free and independent electronic media. The law provides for the creation of national, commercial television and radio and insulates the remaining public service media from government control. There are no private national television stations, although the Government is negotiating the sale of two countrywide television channels and several government-owned radio stations. At present, there is one private national radio station and one national radio station in which the Government maintains a minority share. The Government recently announced plans to establish a third private television channel. However, at year's end state-owned Hungarian Radio and Hungarian Television continued to enjoy a near monopoly of nationwide broadcasting, and the Prime Minister controlled their budgets.

While some limited-range local television licenses were issued, partisan political wrangling and, less importantly, pressures from television and radio unions and employee associations continued to block the availability of national broadcast frequencies. (However, over half of the country's households have access to satellite television, cable, or both.)

Academic freedom is generally respected.

b. *Freedom of Peaceful Assembly and Association.*—There are essentially no restrictions on peaceful public gatherings. In general the Government does not require permits for assembly except when a public gathering is to take place near sensitive installations, such as military facilities, embassies, and key government buildings. Police may sometimes alter or revoke permits, but there is no evidence that they abuse this right.

Any 10 or more persons may form an association, provided that it does not commit criminal offenses or disturb the rights of others. Associations with charters and elected officers must register with the courts.

c. *Freedom of Religion.*—The Constitution provides for freedom of religion, and members of all faiths are allowed to practice their religion freely. There is no officially preferred religion, but only officially approved religions receive state subsidies. The Government distributed $113 million in state subsidies in 1995 among approximately three dozen religious groups for salaries, rehabilitation, education, and social work. Religious orders and schools have regained some property confiscated by the Communist regime.

In September the President officially reopened Budapest's Dohany Street synagogue. Two-thirds of the $800,000 reconstruction cost was financed by the Government with the rest funded by international donations. In October the Parliament passed the Jewish Restitution Decree; the Government has earmarked over $250 million for restitution. In December Parliament began debate on enabling legislation that will fund a new Jewish foundation. The foundation is expected to distribute funds to Hungarian Holocaust survivors and oversee property and restitution claims by heirs of Holocaust victims.

d. *Freedom of Movement Within the Country, Foreign Travel, Emigration, and Repatriation.*—There are no restrictions on the movement of citizens within or outside Hungary, including on the rights of emigration and repatriation. The Government may delay but not deny emigration for those who have significant court-assessed debts or who possess state secrets. It requires that foreigners from countries that do not have a visa waiver agreement with Hungary obtain exit visas each time they leave the country, although blanket permission is sometimes available.

The fighting in the former Yugoslavia resulted in a continued flow of refugees into Hungary. While approximately 5,000 refugees from the former Yugoslavia are registered in Hungary, the Government estimates that over 20,000 more are present in unregistered status. Most of the refugees are in private housing, with only 1,380 (as of September) housed in 3 refugee camps. In September the Government moved virtually all remaining refugees from their facility in Nagyatad to more modern facilities in Debrecen. Only a handful of refugees, mostly the mentally ill and those awaiting resettlement in third countries, remain in Nagyatad.

Hungary is a signatory to the 1951 United Nations Convention Relating to the Status of Refugees and to its 1967 Protocol, with a caveat that it will grant refugee status only to European nationals. The Government cooperates with the office of the U.N. High Commissioner for Refugees and other humanitarian organizations in assisting refugees. Hungary provided first asylum to refugees from the former Yugoslavia during the fighting in that neighboring country. Prospective refugees who seek only to transit to Western Europe are encouraged to return to their countries of departure.

Illegal aliens, mostly non-European, were housed at border guard facilities throughout Hungary. In 1996 6,927 illegal aliens were processed pending either deportation or qualification for resettlement in a third country. The determination is made by the local office of the United Nations High Commissioner for Refugees (UNHCR). While police seek the timely deportation of detainees who do not qualify for refugee status, a shortage of funds and the detainees' lack of proper documentation, such as passports, often result in lengthy stays. In September Amnesty International reported the forced repatriation of two Sudanese citizens who sought asylum. The two were returned to Syria, from where they had travelled to Budapest, and are expected to be repatriated to Sudan. The Government disputes the fact that this was a case of illegal forcible repatriation that placed the two at risk. In December a local nongovernmental organization (NGO) charged that 10 Iraqi citizens were held captive in handcuffs with their legs chained and their mouths taped before they were sent to Damascus without any assessment of the threat they faced if returned to Iraq. The Government denies the alleged mistreatment.

Section 3. Respect for Political Rights: The Right of Citizens to Change Their Government

Citizens age 18 and over have the right to change their government through national elections held at least every 4 years. The Parliament's members are elected through a complex voting procedure for individuals and party lists. In the 1994 national elections, Prime Minister Gyula Horn's Hungarian Socialist (formerly Communist) Party won an absolute majority and formed a coalition government with the Liberal Alliance of Free Democrats. Five parties, ranging from moderate to conservative, constitute an active opposition in Parliament.

There are no legal impediments to women's participation in government or the political process; 43 of 386 parliamentary deputies are women. There are few women in leadership positions in the Government or the political parties. Several minorities are represented in Parliament, including one Rom, one ethnic German, one ethnic Slovak, and one ethnic Croat.

Section 4. Governmental Attitude Regarding International and Nongovernmental Investigation of Alleged Violations of Human Rights

Numerous human rights organizations operate without government restriction or interference. Many NGO's report that the Government is generally responsive to their requests for information. However, individual police units are reportedly uncooperative at times, particularly in cases involving Roma. There is also a 20-member parliamentary Committee for Human, Minority, and Religious Rights.

Section 5. Discrimination Based on Race, Sex, Religion, Disability, Language, or Social Status

The Constitution provides for individual rights, equality, and protection against discrimination, but in practice discrimination still exists, particularly against Roma.

Women.—Spousal abuse is believed to be common, but the vast majority of such abuse is not reported, and victims who step forward often receive little help from authorities. While there are laws against rape, it is often unreported for cultural reasons. Police attitudes towards victims of sexual abuse are often reportedly unsympathetic, particularly if the victim was acquainted with her aggressor. Rape within marriage is not recognized in the Penal Code. According to the government statistics office, there were 406 reported rapes in 1995 and 2,862 reported cases of assaults on women; for the first 6 months of 1996, 189 rapes and 1,303 assaults were reported.

Legally, women have the same rights as men, including identical inheritance and property rights. While there is no overt discrimination against women, the number of women in middle or upper managerial positions in business and government is low. Women are heavily represented in the judiciary and in the medical and teaching professions. The law does not prohibit sexual harassment in the work place.

A 1995 report prepared under the auspices of the United Nations to evaluate compliance with the Convention on the Elimination of Discrimination Against Women termed sexual harassment in the workplace as "virtually epidemic." Women's groups report that a major problem is that women are not aware of their rights. The Government moved to address women's concerns by establishing an Office of Women's Issues in the Ministry of Labor.

Children.—The Government is committed to children's rights. Education is mandatory through 16 years of age, and employment is illegal below the age of 16. There is no societal pattern of child abuse. According to the government statistics office, there were 753 reported cases of violence against children in 1995, 100 of which took place within the family. For the first 6 months of 1996, 331 crimes against children were reported, of which 54 were within the home.

People With Disabilities.—The Government does not mandate accessibility to buildings or government services for people with disabilities. Services for the disabled are limited, and most buildings are not wheelchair accessible.

Religious Minorities.—There were few anti-Semitic incidents (almost all graffiti) and no reports of attacks by skinheads or neo-Nazi sympathizers against the Jewish community. However, in October two small bombs exploded in the Jewish quarter, one in the vicinity of the Dohany Street synagogue. In March tombstones in a Jewish cemetery in Budapest were vandalized with swastikas. In September a court fined the Debrecen soccer club $2,000 (300,000 forints) after unruly football fans chanted anti-Semitic slogans against a rival team from Budapest.

National/Racial/Ethnic Minorities.—The 1993 law on ethnic and minority rights establishes the concept of collective rights of minorities and states that minorities need special rights in order to preserve their ethnic identities. It explicitly permits organized forms of limited self-government in areas where ethnic groups constitute a majority and states that the establishment of self-governing bodies must be made possible in localities where an ethnic group constitutes less than a majority of the population. The law permits associations, movements, and political parties based upon an ethnic or national character and mandates unrestricted use of ethnic languages. Only those ethnic groups that have lived within the country's present borders for at least 100 years and whose members are citizens may obtain recognized status under this law.

On this basis, the law specifically grants minority status to 13 ethnic or national groups. Other groups may petition the Chairman of Parliament for inclusion if they comprise at least 1,000 citizens and have their own language and culture.

In 1994 the first elections were held for minority local self-government entities, which resulted in the formation of over 600 minority local bodies. The number grew in 1995 to 817 organizations, of which 477 are Roma groups. With funding from the central budget and logistical support from local governments, these bodies have as their primary responsibility influencing and overseeing local matters affecting the minorities. In 1995 these groups elected national minority self-government bodies, whose effectiveness has varied widely. The non-Romani minorities appear to be the most satisfied, while Romani leaders express frustration with the self-governments' lack of clear authority, responsibility, or resources. These entities' greatest value is that they provide a platform for minorities to address local and national government organizations; their greatest weakness is that the Government is compelled to listen, but not to act.

In 1995 Parliament appointed an Ombudsman—currently an ethnic German—specifically charged with defending minority rights. The office, however, does not include any Roma, the largest minority group.

Roma constitute at least 4 percent of the population; Germans, the second largest minority group, constitute about 2 percent. There are smaller communities of Slovaks, Croats, Romanians, Poles, Greeks, Serbs, Slovenes, Armenians, Ruthenians, and Bulgarians, which all are recognized as minorities.

Education is available to varying degrees in almost all minority languages. There are minority-language print media, and the state-run radio broadcasts 2-hour daily programs in the mother tongue of major nationalities, i.e., Slovak, Romanian, German, Croatian, and Serbian. State-run television carries a 30-minute program for the larger minority groups, complemented by 5-minute weekly news bulletins.

Conditions of life within the Romani community are significantly poorer than among the general population. Roma suffer from discrimination and racist attacks and are considerably less educated, with lower than average incomes and life expectancy. The Romani unemployment rate is estimated to be 70 percent, over six times the national average of 10.5 percent. With unemployment benefits exhausted and social services stretched thin, Roma often confront desperate situations. Roma constitute a majority of the prison population. The deplorable conditions within the Romani community were documented in July by the human rights NGO Helsinki Watch. The Helsinki Watch report states that Roma have suffered disproportionately in the post-Communist economic transition, particularly in terms of unemployment and the degradation of their urban communities into slums. Helsinki Watch reports that Roma continue to suffer widespread discrimination in education, housing, and access to public institutions, including restaurants and pubs. While commending government efforts to address minority issues, Helsinki Watch states that such efforts, for the Roma, have been largely ineffective to date.

The Government sponsors programs both to preserve Romani languages and cultural heritage and to assist social and economic assimilation. Nonetheless, widespread popular prejudice continues. Police commonly abuse Roma (see Section 1.c.).

The Martin Luther King Organization (MLKO), which documents assaults on nonwhites, recorded six such incidents in the first half of 1996, a higher rate of assaults than the total (seven) for 1995. MLKO sources commented that they believe many cases go unreported.

Section 6. Workers Rights

a. *The Right of Association.*—The 1992 Labor Code recognizes the right of unions to organize and bargain collectively and permits trade union pluralism. Workers have the right to associate freely, choose representatives, publish journals, and openly promote members' interests and views. With the exception of military personnel and the police, they also have the right to strike. Under a separate 1992 law, public servants may negotiate working conditions, but the final decision on increasing salaries rests with Parliament.

The largest labor union organization is the National Confederation of Hungarian Trade Unions, the successor to the former monolithic Communist union, with over 800,000 members. The Democratic League of Independent Unions and the Federation of Workers' Councils have approximately 250,000 and 150,000 members respectively.

There are no restrictions on trade union contacts with international organizations, and unions have developed a wide range of ties with European and international trade union bodies.

b. *The Right to Organize and Bargain Collectively.*—The Labor Code permits collective bargaining at the enterprise and industry level, although the practice is not widespread and is actively discouraged in the growing private sector. There is a willingness among labor organizations to cooperate with one another, and this is particularly evident in their relationship in forums such as the National Interest Reconciliation Council (ET), which provides a forum for tripartite consultation among representatives from management, employees, and the Government. The ET discusses issues such as wage hikes and the setting of the minimum wage, which is centrally negotiated within the ET in order to control inflation. Individual trade unions and management may negotiate higher levels at the plant level. The Ministry of Labor is responsible for drafting labor-related legislation, while special labor courts enforce labor laws. The decisions of these courts may be appealed to the civil court system. Employers are prohibited from discriminating against unions and their organizers. The Ministry of Labor enforces this provision.

There are no export processing zones.

c. *Prohibition of Forced or Compulsory Labor.*—The law prohibits forced or compulsory labor, and the Ministry of Labor enforces this prohibition.

d. *Minimum Age for Employment of Children.*—The National Labor Center enforces the minimum age of 16 years, with exceptions for apprentice programs, which may begin at the age of 15. There does not appear to be any significant abuse of this statute. Education is compulsory through 16 years of age. Roma are far more likely than non-Roma to stop attending school before 16 years of age.

e. *Acceptable Conditions at Work.*—The ET establishes the legal minimum wage, which is subsequently implemented by Ministry of Labor decree. The minimum wage, $95 (14,500 forints) per month, is insufficient to provide an adequate standard of living for a worker and family. Many workers supplement their primary employment with second jobs.

The Labor Code specifies various conditions of employment, including termination procedures, severance pay, maternity leave, trade union consultation rights in some management decisions, annual and sick leave entitlement, and labor conflict resolution procedures. Under the code, the official workday is set at 8 hours; it may vary, however, depending upon the nature of the industry. A 24-hour rest period is required during any 7-day period.

Labor courts and the Ministry of Labor enforce occupational safety standards set by the Government, but specific safety conditions are not generally up to internationally accepted standards. Enforcement of occupational safety standards is not always effective in part due to the limited resources the Ministry of Labor is able to commit to enforcement. In theory, workers have the right to remove themselves from dangerous work situations without jeopardy to continued employment.

ICELAND

Iceland is a constitutional republic and a multiparty parliamentary democracy. Its people participate in high percentages in regular, free, and fair elections which determine the distribution of power among political parties and leaders.

Elected officials control the police force, which scrupulously observes and enforces the laws that ensure protection of human rights.

Iceland has a mixed, open economy, in which citizens have the right to hold private property. It provides residents with a high standard of living. The leading export, marine products, accounts for almost 80 percent of export revenues.

The Government fully respects the human rights of its citizens, and the law and judiciary provide effective means of dealing with instances of individual abuse. There is some societal discrimination against women, which the Government has begun to address.

RESPECT FOR HUMAN RIGHTS

Section 1. Respect for the Integrity of the Person, Including Freedom From:

a. *Political and Other Extrajudicial Killing.*—There were no reports of political or other extrajudicial killings.

b. *Disappearance.*—There were no reports of politically motivated disappearances.

c. *Torture and Other Cruel, Inhuman, or Degrading Treatment or Punishment.*—Torture and other cruel, inhuman, or degrading treatment or punishment are prohibited by law and do not occur. Prison conditions are good, but most prisons are full, and many are antiquated. The Government has begun a construction program to alleviate these difficulties.

d. *Arbitrary Arrest, Detention, or Exile.*—The Constitution prohibits arbitrary arrest, detention, or exile, and the Government observes this prohibition.

e. *Denial of Fair Public Trial.*—The Constitution and law provide for an independent judiciary, and the Government respects this provision in practice. The Ministry of Justice administers the lower court system, while the Supreme Court guards its independence and fairness. Juries are not used, but multijudge panels are common, especially in the appeals process. All judges, at all levels, serve for life.

The judiciary provides citizens with a fair and efficient judicial process. Defendants are presumed innocent. They are guaranteed the right of access to legal counsel of their own choosing in time to prepare their defense. For defendants unable to pay attorneys' fees, the State assumes the cost. Defendants have the right to be present at their trial, to confront witnesses, and to participate otherwise in the proceedings. No groups are barred from testifying, and all testimony is treated alike. Trials are public and are conducted fairly, with no official intimidation. Defendants have the right to appeal.

There were no reports of political prisoners.

f. *Arbitrary Interference With Privacy, Family, Home, or Correspondence.*—The Constitution prohibits such practices, government authorities generally respect these prohibitions, and violations are subject to effective legal sanction.

Section 2. Respect for Civil Liberties, Including:

a. *Freedom of Speech and Press.*—The Constitution provides for freedom of speech and of the press, and the Government respects these rights in practice. An independent press, an effective judiciary, and a functioning democratic political system combine to ensure freedom of speech and of the press, including academic freedom.

b. *Freedom of Peaceful Assembly and Association.*—The Constitution provides for these rights, and the Government respects them in practice.

c. *Freedom of Religion.*—Although the official state religion is Lutheranism, the Constitution provides for freedom of religion, and the Government respects this right in practice.

d. *Freedom of Movement Within the Country, Foreign Travel, Emigration, and Repatriation.*—The Constitution provides for these rights, and the Government respects them in practice. The Government cooperates with the United Nations High Commissioner for Refugees (UNHCR) and other humanitarian organizations in assisting refugees. There were no reports of forced expulsion of those having a valid claim to refugee status. The issue of the provision of first asylum did not arise in 1996. The Government responded to the UNHCR's request that it take in refugees from the former Yugoslavia by accepting 31 in 1996. The Icelandic Red Cross and the town of Isafjordur, where the refugees were settled, made significant efforts to begin incorporating them into Icelandic society.

Section 3. *Respect for Political Rights: The Right of Citizens to Change Their Government*

The Constitution provides citizens with the right to change their government peacefully, and citizens exercise this right in practice through periodic, free, and fair elections held on the basis of universal suffrage. The most recent elections to the Althing (unicameral Parliament) were held in April 1995.

There are no legal or practical impediments to women's participation in government and politics. There is an active feminist political party, the Women's List, which won 3 of 63 seats in the 1995 parliamentary elections.

Section 4. *Governmental Attitude Regarding International and Nongovernmental Investigation of Alleged Violations of Human Rights*

A number of human rights groups operate without government restriction, investigating and publishing their findings on human rights cases. Government officials are generally cooperative and responsive to their views.

Section 5. *Discrimination Based on Race, Sex, Religion, Disability, Language, or Social Status*

The culture of the ethnically homogeneous population is strongly egalitarian and opposed to discrimination based on any of these factors. Government legislation and practice generally reflect this attitude.

Women.—Increased governmental awareness of violence against women, resulting from extensive media coverage, has led to stiffening of sentencing for sex offenders. The tougher sentencing derives from improved action by the courts in more strictly enforcing existing laws. A police program to train officers in correct interrogation procedures in rape and sexual abuse cases appears to be addressing prior concerns that police indifference and hostility to female victims did not assure victims of such abuses proper attention and consideration.

There is a public women's shelter that offers protection to approximately 350 women and 200 children per year; these figures are virtually unchanged since 1995. There is also a rape trauma center sponsored and operated by women's organizations; some 400 women and children seek assistance annually. Both facilities are funded by national and municipal governments, and private contributions. The Reykjavik City Hospital emergency ward has an all-female staff to care for rape victims. During the year the emergency ward reported 76 visits associated with incidents of rape or sexual abuse. Hospital officials estimate that only 55 percent of these victims press charges and only a handful of cases actually go to trial, attributing this to fear of publicity in such a small, tight-knit society.

The Women's List political movement and the female Mayor of Reykjavik have kept women's issues in the forefront of public debate. The 1996 Conservative Independence Party convention focused on increasing the political participation of women and on women's issues in general. While major political institutions and businesses remain male dominated, the Government is taking steps to enforce legislation requiring equal pay for equal work. The 20 percent gap in earnings between men and women in comparable jobs narrowed somewhat nationally but dropped significantly in Reykjavik to 10 to 15 percent.

Since 1991 complaints regarding the Equal Rights Law have been referred to a special committee under the Equal Rights Affairs Office of the Ministry of Social Affairs. However, the committee has only advisory powers, and its recommendations to employers do not have the force of law. Few complaints are made to the committee.

Children.—The Government demonstrates its strong commitment to children's rights through its well-funded systems of public education and medical care. The Government provides free prenatal and infant medical care, as well as heavily subsidized children's care. Compulsory education ends in the 10th grade. About 85 percent of students continue to upper secondary education, which is financed completely by the State. In 1994 the Government created the Office of the Children's Ombudsman in the Prime Ministry, with a mandate to protect children's rights, interests, and welfare by, among other things, exerting influence on legislation, government decisions, and public attitudes. The Parliament ratified the Hague Convention on Child Abduction which entered into force in December. This action is expected to facilitate the handling of international child custody cases.

There is no societal pattern of abuse directed against children.

People With Disabilities.—Disabled individuals are not subject to discrimination in employment, education, or provision of other state services. The Government has legislated accessibility to public buildings for the disabled.

Section 6. Worker Rights

a. *The Right of Association.*—Workers make extensive use of the right to establish organizations, draw up their own constitutions and rules, choose their own leaders and policies, and publicize their views. The resulting organizations are controlled neither by the Government nor any single political party. Unions take active part in Nordic, European, and international trade union bodies. With the exception of limited categories of workers in the public sector whose services are essential to public health or safety, unions have had and used the right to strike for many years. Some 76 percent of all eligible workers belong to unions.

b. *The Right to Organize and Bargain Collectively.*—There are no impediments to union membership in law or in practice. Virtually all unions exercise their right to bargain collectively. The central labor and management organizations periodically negotiate collective bargaining agreements that set nationwide standards and specific terms for workers' pay, workhours, and other conditions. The Government both plays a role in the negotiations, and sometimes undertakes commitments in order to bring the two sides together. Labor courts effectively adjudicate disputes over contracts and over the rights provided for in the 1938 Act on Trade Unions and Industrial Disputes, which prohibits antiunion discrimination.

By law, employers found guilty of antiunion discrimination are required to reinstate workers fired for union activities. In practice, the charges are difficult to prove.

In May the Parliament passed legislation updating the labor laws and bringing them into compliance with the European human rights convention.

There are no export processing or other special economic zones.

c. *Prohibition of Forced or Compulsory Labor.*—Forced or compulsory labor is prohibited by law and does not occur.

d. *Minimum Age for Employment of Children.*—The law requires children to attend school until the age of 16 years and prohibits employment of children under that age in factories, on ships, or in other places that are hazardous or require hard labor. This prohibition is observed in practice. Children 14 or 15 years old may be employed part-time or during school vacations in light, nonhazardous work. Their workhours must not exceed the ordinary workhours of adults in the same occupation. The Occupational Safety and Health Administration enforces child labor regulations.

e. *Acceptable Conditions of Work.*—Although there is no minimum wage law, union membership is so extensive and effective as to ensure that labor contracts afford even the lowest paid workers a sufficient income for a decent standard of living for themselves and their families.

Workers are protected by laws that effectively ensure their health and safety as well as provide for unemployment insurance, paid vacations, pensions, and reasonable working conditions and hours. The standard legal workweek is 40 hours. Work exceeding 8 hours in a workday must be compensated as overtime. Workers are entitled to 10 hours of rest within each 24-hour period and to a day off every week. Under defined special circumstances the 10-hour rest period can be reduced to 8, and the day off can be postponed by a week, in which case the worker has a right to 2 additional hours off in the following week.

Health and safety standards are set by the Althing and administered and enforced by the Ministry of Social Affairs through its Occupational Safety and Health Administration.

IRELAND

Ireland is a parliamentary democracy with a long tradition of orderly transfer of power. The Government is headed by a president and a prime minister, and there is a bicameral parliament. The judiciary is independent.

The national police are under the effective civilian control of the Minister of Justice and have sole responsibility for internal security. Ireland's principal internal security concern has been to prevent the spillover of terrorist violence from Northern Ireland. Despite the end of the Irish Republican Army's (IRA) cease-fire in February, the Government did not reinstate the state of emergency, which it lifted in 1995 when the cease-fire began.

Ireland has an open, market-based economy that is highly dependent on international trade. It is a large net recipient of funds from the European Union (EU) designed to raise per capita gross national product to the EU average. Despite strong economic growth over the past few years, unemployment remains high at 12.4 percent.

The Government generally respected the human rights of its citizens. Human rights problems arise primarily from: prison overcrowding and substandard facilities; instances of abuse by police and prison officials; the continuation of special arrest and detention authority and the nonjury court; discrimination and violence against women; abuse of children; occasional censorship of films, books, and periodicals; and a lack of explicit antidiscrimination legislation, especially in relation to persons with disabilities and "travelers" (an itinerant ethnic community).

RESPECT FOR HUMAN RIGHTS

Section 1. Respect for the Integrity of the Person, Including Freedom From:

a. *Political and Other Extrajudicial Killing.*—There were no reports of political or other extrajudicial killings.

b. *Disappearance.*—There were no reports of politically motivated disappearances.

c. *Torture or Other Cruel, Inhuman, or Degrading Treatment or Punishment.*—The law prohibits such practices, and security personnel generally did not employ them.

However, at least 66 cases were filed against the State by persons claiming damages for personal injuries resulting from alleged mistreatment while in police custody. While mistreatment by police officers is not widespread, in one case two persons accused of murdering a police officer alleged that they had been severely beaten by police while in custody. At their initial court appearance, the men showed physical injuries consistent with their allegations. No official public action was taken on their complaint.

Ireland has a low incarceration rate (73 inmates per 100,000 population), and the prison regime is generally liberal. However, the physical infrastructure of many prisons is barely adequate: facilities are plagued by chronic overcrowding, requiring doubling-up in many single-person cells. Almost all of the country's 12 prisons are very old buildings that were built originally for other uses; as a result, less than half the cells have toilets and running water. According to the May report of its oversight committee, a statutory body made up of ministerial appointees not connected to the prison service, drug abuse is widespread at Mountjoy prison, the country's largest. The report also cites overcrowding and describes medical services as "ad hoc and uncoordinated." The Government is in the process of upgrading prison facilities to improve sanitary conditions and to meet statutory health and safety standards.

Prisoners have filed 26 cases against the State for alleged mistreatment. The Government admitted that "in at least some prisons in Ireland * * * there are certain officers who have a propensity to ill-treat prisoners." There is no evidence that these officers have been reprimanded or removed. The Government has improved training of prison officials in order to reduce prisoner abuse.

The Government has continued to arrest and incarcerate at Portlaoise prison persons involved in paramilitary activity. Conditions for these inmates are the same, if not better, than those for the general prison population.

The Government has a 3-year prison construction plan to build 800 new cells and a new women's prison annex at Mountjoy prison. However, human rights observers are skeptical that the plan will lead to the end of the present chronic overcrowding given the Government's failure so far to expand prison capacity under the 5-year plan published in 1994. International human rights monitors are permitted to visit prisons without reservation.

d. *Arbitrary Arrest, Detention, or Exile.*—The Constitution stipulates that no person shall be deprived of personal liberty without due process under the law. A detainee has the right to petition the High Court, which is required to order release unless it can be shown that the person is being detained in accordance with the law. Under the 1984 Criminal Justice Act, the maximum period of detention for questioning in most cases is 12 hours, plus a possible extension of 8 hours overnight to allow a detainee to sleep.

Detention without charge is permitted for up to 48 hours, however, in cases covered by the 1939 Offenses Against the State Act. This act allows police to arrest and detain for questioning anyone suspected of committing a "scheduled offense," i.e., one involving firearms, explosives, or membership in an unlawful organization. Although the stated purpose of the act is to "prevent actions and conduct calculated to undermine public order and the authority of the state," it is not restricted to subversive offenses. Therefore, the police have broad arrest and detention powers in any case involving firearms.

The act also provides for the indefinite detention, or internment, without trial of any person who is engaged in activities that are "prejudicial to the preservation of public peace and order or to the security of the state." While this power has not been invoked since the late 1950's, the Government could do so by simply issuing a proclamation. There are no provisions for the 1939 Offenses Against the State Act to be renewed; it continues indefinitely.

The Criminal Justice (Drug Trafficking) Act of 1996 permits detention without charge for up to 7 days in cases involving drug trafficking. To hold a suspected drug trafficker for more than 48 hours, however, the police must seek a judge's approval.

The authorities do not impose exile.

e. *Denial of Fair Public Trial.*—The Constitution provides for an independent judiciary, and the Government respects this provision in practice. The judiciary provides citizens with a fair and efficient judicial process.

The judicial system includes 23 district courts, 8 circuit courts, the High Court, the Court of Criminal Appeal, and the Supreme Court. Judges are appointed by the President on the advice of the Government.

Most criminal cases are prosecuted by the Director of Public Prosecutions, a state official with semiautonomous status. Jury trial is the norm. The accused generally may choose his or her attorney. For indigent defendants, the state assumes the cost of counsel.

However, the Constitution explicitly allows "special courts" to be created when "ordinary courts are inadequate to secure the effective administration of justice and the preservation of public peace and order." In 1972, under the 1939 Offenses Against the State Act, the Government set up a nonjury "Special Criminal Court" (SCC) to try "scheduled offenses," i.e., ones involving firearms, explosives, or membership in an unlawful organization. Largely a reaction to the spillover of paramilitary violence from Northern Ireland, the SCC has been justified over the years as addressing the problem of jury intimidation in cases involving defendants with suspected paramilitary links.

Since the paramilitary cease-fire in 1994, far fewer cases have been handled by the SCC than during the "troubles." However, since the IRA resumed its campaign of violence, the Government may use the SCC more frequently in the future. It was used at least twice in 1996, and several additional cases are pending. In addition to the "scheduled offenses," the Director of Public Prosecutions can have any case tried by the SCC by simply certifying that the ordinary courts are "inadequate" to deal with it.

In lieu of a jury, the Special Criminal Court usually sits as a three-judge panel. Its verdicts are by majority vote. Rules of evidence are essentially the same as in regular courts, except that the sworn statement of a police chief superintendent identifying the accused as a member of an illegal organization is accepted as prima facie evidence. Sessions of the SCC are usually public, but the judge may exclude certain persons other than journalists. Appeals from the SCC are only allowed on points of law or against the sentence imposed.

There were no reports of political prisoners.

f. *Arbitrary Interference With Privacy, Family, Home, or Correspondence.*—The Supreme Court has affirmed that, although not specifically provided for in the Constitution, the inviolability of personal privacy, family, and home must be respected in law and practice. This is fully honored by the Government.

In 1996 the High Court upheld a referendum that removed the ban on divorce. The Government is expected to enact implementing legislation that allows courts to grant divorces under certain circumstances.

Section 2. Respect for Civil Liberties, Including:

a. *Freedom of Speech and Press.*—The Constitution provides individuals with the right to "express freely their convictions and opinions." Freedom of the press, however, is subject to the qualification that it not "undermine public order or morality or the authority of the state." Publication or utterance of "blasphemous, seditious, or indecent matter" is prohibited. While the press, in practice, operates freely, the 1961 Defamation Act (which puts the onus on newspapers and periodicals accused of libel to prove defamatory words are true) and the 1963 Official Secrets Act (which gives the State wide scope to prosecute unauthorized disclosures of sensitive government information) are believed to result in some self-censorship.

More than 80 libel actions against newspapers and other publications were pending before the courts; the National Newspapers Association of Ireland estimated that libel awards and related legal bills cost its members about $10 million (6 million Irish pounds) per year.

Broadcasting remains mostly state controlled, but under the 1988 Radio and Television Act, private sector broadcasting is growing. There are at least 22 independent radio stations, and negotiations are proceeding for an independent television station. The Broadcasting Complaints Commission oversees standards and investigates complaints about programming. The 1960 Broadcasting Act empowers the Government to prohibit the state-owned radio and television network from broadcasting any matter that is "likely to promote or incite to crime or which would tend to undermine the authority of the state." It was on this basis that the Government banned Sinn Fein (the legal political front of the IRA) from the airwaves from 1971 to 1994.

Films and videos must be screened and classified by the Office of the Film Censor before they can be shown or sold. Distributors must pay a fee between $1,100 and $1,300 (650 to 800 Irish pounds) per film, which is used to finance the censor's office. Under the 1923 Censorship of Films Act, the censor has the authority to cut or ban any film that is "indecent, obscene or blasphemous" or which tends to "inculcate principles contrary to public morality or subversive of public morality." There has been a diminishing use of this broad power in recent years: only two films were banned in 1996. Decisions of the censor can be appealed to a nine-member appeal board, but neither the censor nor the appeal board is required to hear arguments or evidence in public or to state reasons for its decisions.

Books and periodicals are also subject to censorship. The 1946 Censorship of Publications Act calls for a five-member board to examine publications referred to it by the customs service or a member of the general public. It can also examine books or periodicals on its own initiative. The board can prohibit the sale of any publication that it judges to be indecent or obscene. In 1996 the board banned at least 46 books and 43 periodicals, a sharp increase from 1995, when it banned 17 books and 3 periodicals.

Academic freedom is respected.

b. *Freedom of Peaceful Assembly and Association.*—The Constitution provides citizens with the right to "assemble peaceably and without arms" and to form associations and unions. However, it also allows the State to "prevent or control meetings" that are calculated to cause a breach of the peace or to be a danger or nuisance to the general public." Under the 1939 Offenses Against the State Act, it is unlawful to hold any public meeting on behalf of, or in support of, an illegal organization. Although the Government prosecutes and incarcerates persons for mere membership in a terrorist organization, it allows meetings and assemblies by some groups that are associated with illegal terrorist organizations.

c. *Freedom of Religion.*—The Constitution provides for freedom of religion, and the Government does not hamper the teaching or practice of any faith. Even though Ireland is overwhelmingly Roman Catholic, there is no state religion. However, almost all primary and secondary schools are denominational, managed and controlled by the Catholic Church. Religious instruction is an integral part of the curriculum, but there are provisions for parents to exempt their children from such instruction.

d. *Freedom of Movement Within the Country, Foreign Travel, Emigration, and Repatriation.*—There is complete freedom of movement within the country, as well as freedom to engage in foreign travel, emigration, and voluntary repatriation.

The Government approved a new refugee law in 1996, but it had not been implemented by year's end. Currently, there is no domestic law dealing with the status of refugees or procedures to be followed when a person applies for asylum. As a result, the legal rights and protections for asylum seekers and refugees are tenuous. The issue of provision of first asylum did not arise in 1996; nor were there reports of forced return of persons to a country where they feared persecution. Ireland implements its obligations under the 1951 Convention Relating to the Status of Refugees on an administrative basis. Specific administrative procedures for the determination of refugee status were drawn up in consultation with the U.N. High Commissioner for Refugees; in 1992 the Supreme Court ruled that these procedures were binding on the Minister of Justice. However, as the number of asylum seekers has increased (from only 31 in 1990 to 1,179 in 1996), these administrative procedures have proved inadequate. In particular, there have been complaints of long delays and a lack of transparency in decisions concerning refugee status. The Minister for Justice approved only 33 refugee petitions in 1996.

The new refugee law provides for a refugee commission, an appeals board, and provides criteria for evaluating refugee applications. These measures are designed to improve refugee processing and provide more openness.

Section 3. Respect for Political Rights: The Right of Citizens to Change Their Government

The Constitutional requirement that parliamentary elections be held at least every 7 years has always been met. Suffrage is universal for citizens over the age of 18, and balloting is secret. Several political parties have seats in the bicameral Parliament. Members of the Dail (House of Representatives)— the chamber that carries out the main legislative functions— are popularly elected; in the Seanad (Senate), some members are elected and some are appointed by various bodies. The President is popularly elected for a 7-year term and is limited to two terms. An appointed Council of State serves as an advisory body to the President.

Women are underrepresented in government and politics. Although a woman is president, only 23 of the 166 deputies in the Dail and 7 of the 60 senators are women. Of the 22 legislative committees, the only one chaired by a woman is the Joint Committee on Women's Rights. Two of the 15 government ministers are women, as are 3 of the 17 junior ministers. There are 3 women on the 20-member High Court; only 1 of the 8 Supreme Court judges is a woman. While women participate in all departments of government, they are underrepresented at senior levels. Women hold about 30 percent of public-sector jobs.

Section 4. Governmental Attitude Regarding International and Nongovernmental Investigation of Alleged Violations of Human Rights

The principal independent organization monitoring domestic human rights problems, the Irish Council for Civil Liberties, operates without hindrance from the Government. The Government is open to investigation of human rights abuses by international or other nongovernmental organizations.

Section 5. Discrimination Based on Race, Sex, Religion, Disability, Language, or Social Status

Except as regards employment, neither the Constitution nor the law prohibits discrimination on the basis of disability, race, sex, language, or social status. To address these and other shortcomings in Irish civil law, the Government in 1993 created the Department of Equality and Law Reform. The Department has drafted an equal status bill and an employment equality bill, but neither bill was passed by year's end. The Constitution, as amended, already forbids state promotion of one religion over another and discrimination on the grounds of religions profession, belief, or status.

Women.—There have been no systematic studies of violence against women, but indications are that it is significant. According to a 1995 survey by Women's Aid, a private organization, 7 percent of the women interviewed said that they had been abused by a partner or ex-partner in the past year, and 18 percent reported having been abused at some time. The Dublin Rape Crisis Center reports a 20 percent increase in the number of calls received in 1996. In 1995 it received more than 10,000 calls. The Center estimates that only 29 percent of rape victims report the crime to police and that only 8 percent of those go to trial. A 1990 act criminalized rape within marriage and provided for free legal advice to the victim. There are 12 women's refuges in the country, funded in part by the Government, with accommodation for about 50 families.

Another indication of the extent of violence against women is the number of applications for barring orders. In 1995 there were 4,448 applications for orders to bar the husband from the family home; the courts granted 1,891 barring orders. In 1996 the Government approved the Domestic Violence Act, which strengthens barring and protection orders and gives the police new powers to deal with these cases. A new working group on violence against women, chaired by a high-ranking government official, is scheduled to report in February 1997 on measures to deal further with the problem of violence against women.

Discrimination against women in the workplace is unlawful, but inequalities persist regarding pay and promotions in both the public and the private sectors. Working women are also hampered by the lack of adequate child-care facilities. The Maternity Protection Act was passed in 1994, providing a woman 14 weeks of maternity leave and the right to return to her job. The Anti-Discrimination (Pay) Act of 1974 and the Employment Equality Act of 1977 provide for protection and redress against discrimination based on gender and marital status. The Employment Equality Agency monitors their implementation. The number of cases brought to the agency has fallen in recent years, but progress in eliminating the differential in earnings has been modest. In 1996 the hourly industrial wage for women was 60 percent of that received by men, and weekly earnings of women averaged 68 percent of the weekly pay of men.

Children.—The Government is strongly committed to the welfare and rights of children, as demonstrated by its ongoing implementation of the 1991 Child Care Act. Education is compulsory for children 6 to 15 years of age. Among other things, the act places a statutory duty on government health boards to identify and help children who are not receiving adequate care and gives the police increased powers to remove a child from the family when there is an immediate and serious risk to health or welfare. The Minister of State (junior minister) for Health has special responsibility for children's policy, including implementation of the Child Care Act; by the end of 1996, only parts of the act remained to be implemented. The Status of Children Act of 1987 abolished the concept of illegitimacy and provided for equal rights for children in all legal proceedings.

Sexual abuse of children has been receiving increased media attention; the number of reported physical abuse cases is also rising. Surveys suggest that 12 to 15 percent of children experience physical, sexual, or emotional abuse or gross neglect. In 1996 there were several scandals involving allegations of sexual abuse of children by orphanage staff and members of the Roman Catholic clergy. In at least three cases, members of the clergy pled guilty to sexually abusing minors and were convicted. At least five more cases are pending.

People With Disabilities.—An estimated 15 percent of the adult population have a disability; 80 percent of those are unemployed. There is currently no legislation to protect persons with disabilities from discrimination in employment or in other matters or to improve their access to buildings or transportation. Few public or private buildings have facilities for people with disabilities. The Commission on the Status of People with Disabilities issued a comprehensive report of the conditions faced by persons with disabilities. The report, which makes 402 recommendations for legislative and policy changes, is regarded by government officials and advocates for persons with disabilities as a first step toward improving the rights of the latter.

National/Racial/Ethnic Minorities.—There are some 25,000 nomadic people within Ireland who regard themselves as a distinct ethnic group called "travelers," roughly analogous to the Roma of continental Europe. The "traveling" community has its own history, culture, and language. The travelers' emphasis on self-employment and the extended family distinguish them from the rest of Irish society. In 1991 a European Parliament committee reported that in Ireland, "the single most discriminated against ethnic group is the 'traveling people.'" That remained true in 1996.

Travelers are regularly denied access to premises, goods, facilities, and services; many restaurants and pubs, for example, have a policy of not serving them. Despite national school rules that provide that no child may be refused admission on account of social position, travelers frequently experience difficulties in enrolling their children in school. Sometimes they are segregated into all-traveler classes. Of an estimated 3,500 traveler families, more than 1,000 are residing on roadsides or on temporary sites without toilets, electricity, or washing facilities.

Indicative of public hostility towards travelers, a Waterford county councilman said at a council meeting in April that travelers should be "run out" of the country. He said that "they are not our people, they are not natives of this country." In 1996 there were fewer reported instances of violence against members of the traveling community than in the past.

The tense relations between the traveling community and the rest of Irish society led the Government in 1993 to establish a task force to study the problem and make recommendations. One of the main recommendations of the task force was that "the distinct culture and identity of the traveler community be recognized and taken into account," especially in the context of the proposed equal status legislation. The traveling community is specifically addressed in the 1989 Prohibition of Incitement to Hatred Act, but to date, there have been no prosecutions under that law.

Section 6. Worker Rights

a. *The Right of Association.*—The right to join a union is provided for by law, as is the right to refrain from joining. About 55 percent of workers in the private and public sectors are members of unions. Police and military personnel are prohibited from striking, but they may form associations to represent themselves in matters of pay, working conditions, and general welfare. The right to strike is freely exercised in both the public and private sectors. The Industrial Relations Act of 1990 prohibits retribution against strikers and union leaders; the Government effectively enforces this provision through the Department of Enterprise and Employment. In 1996 the number of strikes was significantly down from past years; however, the number of work days lost by strikes increased from 1995. The Irish Congress of Trade Unions (ICTU) represents 65 unions in the Republic of Ireland and Northern Ireland. Both the ICTU and the unions affiliated with it are independent of the Government and of the political parties. Unions may freely form or join federations or confederations and affiliate with international bodies.

b. *The Right to Organize and Bargain Collectively.*—Labor unions have full freedom to organize and to engage in collective bargaining. The Anti-Discrimination (Pay) Act of 1974 and the Employment Equality Act of 1977 make the Employment Equality Agency responsible for oversight of allegations of antiunion discrimination. If the Agency is unable to effect resolution, the dispute goes before the Labor Court, which consists of one representative each for the employer and the union, plus an independent chairperson. The Unfair Dismissals Act of 1977 provides various forms of relief in cases of employers found guilty of antiunion discrimination, including the reinstatement of workers fired for union activities.

Most terms and conditions of employment are determined through collective bargaining, in the context of a national economic pact negotiated every 3 years by the "social partners," i.e., representatives of unions, employers, farmers, and the Government. The social partners negotiated the current 3-year agreement, entitled "Partnership 2000," at the end of 1996. Formal ratification is expected early in 1997.

The Industrial Relations Act of 1990 established the Labor Relations Commission, which provides advice and conciliation services in industrial disputes. The Commission may refer unresolved disputes to the Labor Court, which may recommend terms of settlement and may set up joint employer-union committees to regulate conditions of employment and minimum wages in a specific trade or industry.

There is an export processing zone at Shannon airport that is subject to the same labor laws as the rest of the country.

c. *Prohibition of Forced Labor.*—Forced labor is prohibited by law and does not occur.

d. *Minimum Age for Employment of Children.*—By law children are required to attend school until the age of 15. The employment of children under the age of 15 is generally prohibited by the 1977 Protection of Young Persons (Employment) Act, but those 14 years of age are allowed to do light non-industrial work during school holidays with the written permission of their parents. They are limited to working 7 hours per day and 35 hours per week. For children 15 years old, the law limits work time to 8 hours per day and 40 hours per week. For those 16 or 17 years old, the limits are 9 hours per day and 45 hours per week. The Department of Enterprise and Employment effectively enforces these provisions.

The Government approved the Protection of Young Persons Act of 1996, which becomes effective in 1997. Under the new act, maximum work hours would be reduced slightly, and children the age of 14 or under would not be allowed to work in most circumstances.

e. *Acceptable Conditions of Work.*—There is no general minimum wage law, but there are several minimum rates of pay applicable to specific industrial sectors, mainly those with lower-than-average wages. Although the lowest of these minimum wages is not sufficient to provide a decent living for a family of four, low-income families are entitled to additional benefits such as subsidized housing and children's allowances.

The standard workweek is 39 hours. Working hours in the industrial sector are limited to 9 hours per day and 48 hours per week. Overtime is limited to 2 hours per day, 12 hours per week, and 240 hours in a year. The Department of Enterprise and Employment is responsible for enforcing four basic laws dealing with occupational safety that provide adequate and comprehensive coverage. No significant complaints arose from either labor or management regarding enforcement of these laws. Recent regulations provide that employees who find themselves in situations that present a "serious, imminent and unavoidable risk" may absent themselves without the employer being able to take disciplinary action.

ITALY

Italy is a longstanding, multiparty parliamentary democracy. Executive authority is vested in the Council of Ministers, headed by the President of the Council (the Prime Minister). The Head of State (the President of the Republic) nominates the Prime Minister after consulting with leaders of all political forces in Parliament. Parliament was elected in free and democratic elections in April. The judiciary is independent, but critics complain that some magistrates are politicized.

The armed forces are under the control of the Government and Parliament. There are four separate police forces under different ministerial or local authorities. Under exceptional circumstances, the Government may call on the army to provide security. The army supports the police in general guard duties in Sicily, a region with a high level of organized crime, thus freeing police resources for investigative and related activities. There were a number of credible reports that some members of the security forces committed abuses.

Italy has an advanced, industrialized market economy, and the standard of living is high. Small and midsized companies employ some 70 to 80 percent of the work force. Major products include machinery, textiles, apparel, transportation equipment, and food and agricultural products. The Government owns a substantial number of enterprises in finance, communications, industry, transportation, and services, but privatization is moving forward at a measured pace.

The Government generally respected the human rights of its citizens. The law and the judiciary generally provide effective means of dealing with instances of individual abuse. However, there were problems in some areas. There continued to be reports of police abuse of detainees, although abuse of inmates by prison guards declined. Prisons are overcrowded, and the pace of justice remains slow. Societal discrimination against women, abuse of children, and discrimination and sporadic violence against immigrants and other foreigners are problems. Parliament passed new comprehensive legislation to protect women against violence and sexual abuse. There were some reports of child labor in the underground economy.

RESPECT FOR HUMAN RIGHTS

Section 1. Respect for the Integrity of the Person, Including Freedom From:

a. *Political and Other Extrajudicial Killing.*—There were no reports of political or other extrajudicial killings.

Two Turin police officers were brought to trial on manslaughter charges in 1994 for beating a suspect to death after his arrest in December 1993. In January 1995, a court acquitted both officers, finding that one officer's use of physical force had been within the limits of the law. The suspect's family appealed in April 1995, but a hearing had not been scheduled by year's end.

The trial of four suspects charged with the March 1993 killing of an Iranian opposition leader took place in September. The court acquitted three of the suspects for insufficient evidence and the fourth was considered beyond the jurisdiction of the court by reason of diplomatic immunity.

b. *Disappearance.*—There were no reports of politically motivated disappearances.

c. *Torture and Other Cruel, Inhuman, or Degrading Treatment or Punishment.*—The law prohibits torture and cruel or degrading punishment. However, there have been some reports of abuse by police. Amnesty International (AI), the United Nations Human Rights Commission (UNHRC), the U.N. Committee Against Torture, and the Council of Europe's European Committee for the Prevention of Torture (ECPT) reported instances in which police abused detainees, commonly at the time of arrest or during the first 24 hours in custody, before detainees saw an attorney or a judicial authority. Examples of mistreatment include kicking, punching, beatings with batons, or deprivation of food. A high proportion of these cases involve non-European Union immigrants (mostly Africans), Roma, and persons held in connection with drug-related offenses. The U.N. Committee and the UNHRC expressed concern over a possible trend towards racism. Amnesty International (AI), the UNHRC and the U.N. Committee noted that, although authorities routinely investigate complaints of mistreatment in detention, some of the investigations lack thoroughness. The U.N. Committee and the UNHRC also questioned whether appropriate sanctions were imposed on those found guilty. Italy has ratified all of the principal international instruments prohibiting torture and cruel, inhuman, or degrading treatment or punishment, but the ECPT and the UNHRC recommended that the authorities take more effective steps to safeguard detainees and inmates from poor treatment. The ECPT's first visit to Italian prisons was in March 1992. Another visit took place in October 1995, but the report on that visit was not available by year's end.

Amnesty International reported several specific instances of mistreatment by law enforcement and prison officers. One involved the alleged beating and verbal abuse of the driver of a car by police officers acting as bodyguards for a judge in Sicily. Although the driver was released without charge, he had to be treated at a hospital for a perforated ear drum and bruises. He lodged a formal written complaint with the local judiciary in June 1995 and was given oral confirmation that October that judicial proceedings had been opened on his case. In another case, a Ghanaian citizen resident in Denmark was reportedly beaten by police officers at the Rome airport because they suspected him of travelling with illegal documentation. Although he was permitted to continue his journey the next day, he allegedly suffered hearing loss in one ear and facial disfigurement. The Ghanaian filed a written account of his experience with the Italian Embassy in Denmark. In addition AI reported that an Italian citizen of Nigerian origin was beaten by two police officers when she failed to produce identity documents upon their request. In May the prosecutor's office requested that the two officers involved be tried on charges of abuse of authority, threat, and causing injury. The prosecutor also asked that the woman be charged for resisting and insulting public officials, refusing to identify herself, and causing injury. Preliminary hearings have been scheduled.

Prison standards meet international levels. However, despite the creation of new prison space and a drop of almost 5 percent in the total jail population (due mainly to a law passed in 1995 changing the terms of preventive detention), the prison population exceeds maximum capacity of the nation's prisons by some 20 percent. In some cases, the number of inmates is two or three times greater than capacity. Overcrowding creates problems of poor sanitation and strains medical services, so much so that it was noted as a negative factor by the ECPT in its report on prison conditions after a visit in 1992 (published in Italy in 1995). AIDS is a major problem, although the law allows judges to release prisoners whose detention would prevent access to appropriate treatment or endanger the health of other inmates. According to data of the Association of Prison Doctors, about 5 percent of the total prison population is HIV positive. There were 43 suicides as of early December, compared with 50 during 1995.

The number of allegations of abuse of prisoners by guards is decreasing. In December 1994, the Naples judiciary committed to trial 71 prison officials of the Secondigliano prison, including the chief warden, on charges of mistreating some 300 inmates in early 1993. A court hearing for 65 of the defendants, all of them prison guards, began in March.

The Government permits independent monitoring of prison conditions by parliamentarians, local human rights groups, the media, and other organizations.

d. *Arbitrary Arrest, Detention, or Exile.*—In response to public concern over excessive use of preventive or investigative detention, Parliament passed a new law in 1995 clarifying that preventive detention can be imposed only as a last resort, or if there is clear and convincing evidence of a serious offense, such as crimes involving the Mafia, or those related to drugs, arms, or subversion. In these cases, a maximum of 2 years of preliminary investigation is permitted. Except in extraordinary situations, preventive custody is not permitted for pregnant women, single parents of children under 3 years of age, persons over 70 years of age, or those who are seriously ill. Despite these added protections, the practice of preventive detention reemerged as a concern when a former Senator accused of mafia-related crimes, who had fled Italy for 4 months but was returning to face the charges, committed suicide in August.

Detainees are allowed prompt and regular access to lawyers of their choosing (although occasional lapses in this general rule have been alleged) and to family members. If a detainee is indigent, the State provides a lawyer. The preliminary hearing judge's interrogation of an accused person must be conducted within 5 days, or the defendant must be released. Interrogation by a magistrate of a person in custody must be recorded on video or audio tape, or the statements cannot be utilized in any proceedings. The prosecutor is required to include in his request for preventive measures all evidence favorable to the accused. In addition the defense may present any favorable evidence directly to the court.

Preventive custody can be imposed only for crimes punishable by a maximum sentence of not less than 4 years.

There is no provision for bail, but judges may grant provisional liberty to suspects awaiting trial. As a safeguard against unjustified detention, panels of judges ("liberty tribunals") review cases of persons awaiting trial and decide whether continued detention is warranted. Despite these measures, as of mid-1996, 40 percent of inmates were in prison because they were awaiting either trial or the outcome of an appeal, rather than because they had been finally sentenced. The Constitution and law provide for restitution in cases of unjust detention.

Punishment by exile abroad is not practiced, and the law prohibits domestic exile.

e. *Denial of Fair Public Trial.*—The judiciary is formally autonomous, but the Constitution gives the Justice Minister the right to propose disciplinary action against magistrates. Friction between the magistrates and the Justice Ministry can develop when this right is exercised.

There are three levels of courts. The lower level has three separate tracks: Praetor Courts for offenses punishable by monetary fines or imprisonment for not more than 4 years; a Court of Assizes for crimes punishable by prison terms of more than 24 years; and a Tribunal Court for offenses falling between the jurisdiction of the first two. The Assizes Court of Appeals hears appeals from all three tracks. Decisions at this level can be further appealed to the highest level, the Court of Cassation, which is headquartered in Rome.

The law provides for trials to be fair and public, and the authorities observe these provisions. The law grants defendants the presumption of innocence. Trials are public, and defendants have access to an attorney sufficiently in advance to prepare a defense. Defendants can confront witnesses. All government-held evidence is normally made available to defendants and their attorneys. Defendants can appeal verdicts to the highest appellate court.

Cumbersome procedures slow the pace of justice. The average waiting period for trials is about 18 months. The Code of Criminal Procedure that took effect in 1989 sought to streamline the process, but it has not produced substantial improvement. The European Court of Human Rights ruled in favor of two Italian citizens who claimed that their rights had been violated by the length of the proceedings in their case. They were arrested on February 13, 1976, charged with murder, and after trials and appeals, the Court of Cassation gave a final ruling on February 28, 1992. The European Court ordered the Italian Government to pay $16,000 (24 million lire) to one of the accused and $10,000 (15 million lire) to the other, plus their court costs.

Since 1991 public prosecutors have conducted sweeping investigations into high level corruption. These inquiries continue and enjoy public support. However, there are critics who complain that some investigating magistrates are occasionally influenced by political or other interests in choosing targets of inquiry, or sometimes fail to show adequate respect for the rights of the suspects, by, for example, making excessive use of preventive detention (see Section 1.d.). In addition, since 1993 more than 200 magistrates have come under judicial investigation on charges of corruption, collusion, or mafia-related crimes. At least 15 were arrested and several others were committed to trial.

There were no reports of political prisoners.

f. *Arbitrary Interference With Privacy, Family, Home, or Correspondence.*—The law safeguards the privacy of the home, and the authorities respect this provision. Searches and electronic monitoring may be carried out only under judicial warrant and in carefully defined circumstances. Violations are subject to legal sanction.

Section 2. Respect for Civil Liberties, Including:

a. *Freedom of Speech and Press.*—The law provides for freedom of speech and the press, and the Government respects these rights in practice. An independent press, an effective judiciary, and a functioning democratic political system combine to ensure freedom of speech and of the press, including academic freedom.

b. *Freedom of Peaceful Assembly and Association.*—The Government does not restrict the right of peaceful assembly, including protests against government policies, except in cases where national security or public safety is at risk. Permits are not required for meetings, but organizers of public demonstrations must notify the police in advance. Professional and employer associations organize and operate freely. While allowing general freedom of association, the Constitution and law prohibit clandestine associations, those that pursue political aims through force, that incite racial, ethnic, or religious discrimination, or that advocate fascism.

c. *Freedom of Religion.*—The Constitution provides for freedom of religion and the Government respects this right. The Government subsidizes the Roman Catholic Church, the Adventist Church, and the Assemblies of God by allowing taxpayers to elect to designate a fixed percentage of their tax payment to one or another of these. In November 1993 the Buddhist community applied for the same funding, but the Government has not yet responded.

Roman Catholic religious instruction is offered in public schools as an optional subject. Those students who do not want to attend the "hour of religion" may take an alternative course.

d. *Freedom of Movement Within the Country, Foreign Travel, Emigration, and Repatriation.*—The Constitution and law provide for these rights, and the Government respects them in practice. Citizens who leave are guaranteed the right to return. The Constitution forbids deprivation of citizenship for political reasons.

The Government cooperates with the U.N. High Commissioner for Refugees and other humanitarian organizations in assisting refugees. It provides first asylum for refugees fleeing hostilities or natural disasters, for example. In these cases the refugees are granted temporary residence permits that must be renewed periodically and that carry no guarantee of future permanent residence. In 1996 the number of such refugees present in Italy, coming largely from the Balkans, declined to 49,630. The Government also provides political asylum, often for permanent residence, and 120 permits were granted in 1996 for political asylees. There were no reports of forced expulsion of any persons having valid claim to refugee status.

Section 3. Respect for Political Rights: The Right of Citizens to Change Their Government

All citizens over the age of 18 have the right to vote, by secret ballot, for the 630 members of the Chamber of Deputies. Those over 25 have the right to vote for 315 of the 325 members of the Senate, which also has 10 nonelected members, such as former Presidents of the Republic. Elections must be held every 5 years, or sooner if the President of the Republic so orders.

Parliament and a few representatives of regional bodies jointly elect the President of the Republic for a 7-year term. The Constitution states that the President need not be a member of Parliament, but must be over age 50. The President nominates the Prime Minister, who is the head of the executive and who in turn selects the cabinet members.

There are no restrictions in law on women's participation in government and politics. Fewer women than men, however, are office holders: in 1995 women held 3 of 23 cabinet positions. Women hold 25 of 325 Senate seats, and 63 of 630 seats in the Chamber of Deputies.

Section 4. Governmental Attitude Regarding International and Nongovernmental Investigation of Alleged Violations of Human Rights

A wide variety of human rights groups operate without government restriction, investigating and publishing their findings on human rights cases. Government officials are generally cooperative and responsive to their views.

Section 5. Discrimination Based on Race, Sex, Religion, Disability, Language, or Social Status

The law prohibits discrimination on the basis of race, sex (except with regard to hazardous work—see below), religion, ethnic background, or political opinion, and provides some protection against discrimination based on disability, language, or social status. However, societal discrimination persists to some degree.

Women.—Legislation to protect women from physical abuse, including from members of their family was updated and strengthened in February. The law regards spousal rape the same as any other rape.

Media reports of domestic violence are common, and Telefono Rosa, a prominent nongovernmental organization, reports that its hot line for assistance in cases of violence against family members received 1,621 calls in 1995 (latest available figures). The same organization reports that rape cases filed with the courts were 1,863 for 1995, compared with 1,689 for 1994 (latest available figures).

Law enforcement and court officials are not reluctant to bring perpetrators of violence against women to justice, but victims sometimes do not press charges due to fear, shame, or ignorance of the law. The new legislation passed in February makes prosecution of perpetrators of violence against women easier and shelters women who have been objects of attack from publicity. The Government provides a hot line through which abused women can obtain legal, medical, and other assistance. In May the city of Milan opened a clinic served by 40 doctors to provide free medical assistance to abused women and minors. Women's associations also maintain several shelters for battered women.

The media report cases of trafficking in women, often involving forced prostitution. The women (as well as their exploiters) are usually illegal immigrants and are therefore reluctant to contact the police. Nevertheless, the police have been able to make arrests on several occasions.

There are a number of government offices that work to ensure women's rights. The Prodi Government created a new cabinet-level position, the Office of Minister for Equal Opportunity, and named a woman to this position. In addition there is an Equal Opportunity Commission within the Office of the Prime Minister. Another such commission is in the Labor Ministry and focuses on discrimination and women's rights in the workplace. The Labor Ministry has a counselor who deals with these problems at the national level, and similar officials serve with regional and provincial governments. Many of these counselors, however, have limited resources for their work.

Some laws intended to protect women from hazardous work keep them out of jobs such as night shifts or underground work in mines, quarries, or tunnels. Maternity leave, introduced to benefit women, does add to the cost of employing them, with the result that employers sometimes find it advantageous to hire men instead.

Women generally receive lower salaries than men for comparable work. They are underrepresented in many fields, such as management or the professions (women, for example, account for only 25 percent of magistrates and only 10 percent of police officers). Women are often laid off more frequently than men.

While the law does not specifically prohibit sexual harassment, labor agreements covering broad sectors of the economy, in both the private and public sectors, do contain clauses that address the problem.

Women enjoy legal equality with men in marriage, property, and inheritance rights.

There are many groups actively and effectively involved in promoting women's rights. Most are close to labor unions or political parties.

Children.—The Government demonstrated a strong commitment to children's rights and welfare. It signed the European Convention on the Exercise of the Rights of Minors on January 25. It launched an extensive study of the living conditions of minors to serve as a data base for policies to improve their situation. The Ministry of Labor and Social Welfare and the Ministry of Public Administration brought employers' associations, national cooperative societies, and labor unions together to subscribe to a pact to battle exploitation of child labor by those organizations in their operations both in Italy and overseas. Signatories of the pact also agreed to contribute an hour's wage (for labor) or its equivalent for their staffs (for organizations) to United Nations Children's Fund (UNICEF) and International Labor Organization (ILO) programs aimed at improving the situation of children in less developed countries. Nevertheless, there were credible reports of instances of child labor in the underground economy.

Schooling is compulsory for children from age 7 to 14. The dropout rate for children in the compulsory schooling cycle is 0.75 percent for the nation as a whole, but 1.24 percent in the south. Boys and girls enjoy equal access and treatment with regard to education, health, and other government services.

Abuse of children is a societal problem. The National Statistical Office estimated that 600,000 children below the age of 15 suffered abuse of some kind within the last 2 years. A toll free number to help abused children under 14 years of age received an average of 5,000 calls daily nationwide. In the period from November 1994 to the end of May 1996, 3,580 of these calls required followup services. Social workers counsel abused children and are authorized to take action to protect them, including placing them in shelters.

People With Disabilities.—The law forbids discrimination against disabled persons in employment, education, or in the provision of state services. Legislation requires enterprises with more than 35 employees to draw on the disabled to staff 15 percent of their work force, directs that public buildings be made accessible to persons with disabilities, and spells out a number of specific rights for the disabled. Compliance with these requirements, however, is still only partial.

National/Racial/Ethnic Minorities.—Immigrants and other foreigners face societal discrimination. Some were even subjected to physical attack. The Romani people encounter difficulties finding places for their groups to stay. The city of Rome opened three camps for them so far and others are expected to be opened. The Romani population around Rome is between 5,000 and 6,500.

The Forum of Foreign Communities continues its work on behalf of immigrants and foreign residents. It has a hot line to report incidents of violence against foreigners. Other nongovernmental agencies, such as Caritas, provide a broad range of assistance to immigrants throughout the country.

Section 6. Worker Rights

a. *The Right of Association.*—The law provides for the right to establish trade unions, join unions, and carry out union activities in the workplace. Some 40 percent of the work force is organized. Trade unions are free of government controls and no longer have formal ties with political parties. The right to strike is embodied in the Constitution and is frequently exercised. A 1990 law restricts strikes affecting essential public services such as transport, sanitation, and health. Unions associate freely with international trade union organizations.

b. *The Right to Organize and Bargain Collectively.*—The Constitution provides for the right of workers to organize and bargain collectively, and these rights are respected in practice. By custom (though not by law), national collective bargaining agreements apply to all workers regardless of union affiliation.

The law prohibits discrimination by employers against union members and organizers. It requires employers who have more than 15 employees and who are found guilty of antiunion discrimination to reinstate the workers affected. In firms with less than 15 workers, an employer must state the grounds for firing a union employee in writing. If a judge deems these grounds spurious, he can order the employer to reinstate or compensate the worker.

There are no export processing zones.

c. *Prohibition on Forced or Compulsory Labor.*—The law prohibits forced or compulsory labor, and it does not occur.

d. *Minimum Age for Employment of Children.*—The law forbids employment of children under 15 years of age (with some limited exceptions). There are also specific restrictions on employment in hazardous or unhealthful occupations of males under age 18, and females under age 21. Enforcement of minimum age laws is effective only outside the extensive "underground" economy.

e. *Acceptable Conditions of Work.*—Minimum wages are not set by law but rather by collective bargaining agreements. These specify minimum standards to which individual employment contracts must conform. When an employer and a union fail to reach agreement, courts may step in to determine fair wages on the basis of practice in comparable activities or agreements.

The law provides a maximum workweek of 48 hours, with no more than 6 days per week and 8 hours per day, except that the latter can be exceeded in some specified kinds of jobs. Most collective agreements provide for a 36 to 38 hour workweek. Overtime may not exceed 2 hours a day or an average of 12 hours per week.

The law sets basic health and safety standards and guidelines for compensation for on-the-job injuries. European Union directives on health and safety have also been incorporated into the law; some provisions have already taken effect and others will be phased in during 1997. Labor inspectors are from local health units or from the Ministry of Labor. They are few, given the scope of their responsibilities. Courts impose fines and sometimes prison terms for violation of health and safety laws. Workers have the right to remove themselves from dangerous work situations without jeopardy to their continued employment.

KAZAKSTAN

The Constitution of Kazakstan concentrates power in the Presidency. President Nursultan Nazarbayev is the dominant political figure. The Constitution, adopted in 1995 in a referendum marred by irregularities, permits the President to legislate by decree and dominate the legislature and judiciary; it cannot be changed or amended without the President's consent. Presidential elections originally scheduled for 1996 did not take place, as President Nazarbayev's term in office was extended to 2000 in a separate 1995 referendum, also marred by irregularities. Under the new Constitution, Parliament's powers are more limited than before. However, members of Parliament have the right to introduce legislation and several bills were drafted for submission to the full Parliament. The judiciary remained under the control of the President and the executive branch. The lack of an independent judiciary made it difficult to root out corruption, which was pervasive throughout the Government.

The Ministry of Internal Affairs supervises the criminal police, who are poorly paid and widely believed to be corrupt. A new institution established in October 1995, the State Committee for Investigations (GSK), is a federal investigative and law enforcement agency. The Committee for National Security (KNB, successor to the KGB) continued efforts to legitimize its role by focusing on activities to combat terrorism, organized crime, and official corruption.

Kazakstan is rich in natural resources, chiefly petroleum and minerals, but its state-dominated economy continued to decline. Although the Government has been successful in stabilizing the local currency (tenge) and slowing inflation, structural reforms continue to lag. The agricultural sector, traditionally accounting for over one-third of national employment and production, has been slow to privatize. The Government successfully privatized most small- and medium-sized firms, and is working to privatize large-scale industrial complexes, particularly in the oil and gas sector.

The Government generally respected the human rights of its citizens. Citizens enjoy basic rights of freedom of religion, speech, and assembly. Nonetheless, democratic institutions are weak. The Government infringed on citizens' right to change their government. The legal structure, including the Constitution adopted in 1995, does not fully safeguard human rights. Members of the security forces often beat or otherwise abused detainees, and already harsh prison conditions continued to deteriorate. There were allegations of arbitrary arrest, and prolonged detention is a problem. The judiciary remains under the control of the President and the executive branch, and corruption is deeply rooted. The Government infringed on citizens' right to privacy. The Government generally tolerates independent media, although the media practiced self-censorship, and the Government maintained control of most printing facilities and supplies. Freedom of assembly was sometimes restricted, and freedom of association, while generally respected, was sometimes hindered by complicated registration requirements for organizations and political parties. The Government regulates the activities of foreign religious associations. The Government discriminated in favor of ethnic Kazaks. Domestic violence against women remained a problem. There was discrimination against women, the disabled, and ethnic minorities. The Government tried to limit the influence of independent trade unions, both directly and through its support for state-sponsored unions, and members of independent unions were harassed.

RESPECT FOR HUMAN RIGHTS

Section 1. Respect for the Integrity of the Person, Including Freedom From:

a. Political and Other Extrajudicial Killing.—There were no reports of political killings. There were credible reports that a few detainees died due to mistreatment during interrogation by the security forces (see Section 1.c.). Human rights organizations reported that there were several cases of detainees being killed while in custody during interrogations. In December the Chief of Criminal Investigations in the Moinkum Department of the State Committee for Investigations in Zhambyl was arrested on the charge that a detainee died due to mistreatment during interrogation while under his authority in December 1995. According to the press, the victim's death was due to serious bodily injuries and a lack of oxygen caused by the use of a gas mask to obtain a confession. The Prosecutor General's office confirmed that the investigation is continuing.

The Government reported that as of June, over 500 inmates imprisoned under harsh conditions with inadequate medical treatment had died of disease. Human rights monitors agreed, but estimated that 2500 prisoners had died by year's end.

b. Disappearance.—There were no reports of politically motivated disappearances.

c. Torture and Other Cruel, Inhuman, or Degrading Treatment or Punishment.— The Constitution states that "no one must be subject to torture, violence or other treatment and punishment that is cruel or humiliating to human dignity." However, there were credible reports that police beat or treated detainees abusively to obtain confessions. Human rights observers report that detainees are sometimes choked, handcuffed to radiators, or have plastic bags placed over their heads to force them to divulge information. Training standards for police are very low and individual law enforcement officials are often poorly supervised.

There are credible reports that a few detainees died as a result of mistreatment during interrogation. There is evidence that one detainee was killed during interrogation in December 1995 in Zhambyl province (see Section 1.a.).

In August security forces arrested and beat Nina Sidorova, the leader of an ethnic Russian political movement. The Prosecutor General's office admitted that Sidorova had been mistreated and ordered an internal investigation.

Army personnel subjected conscripts to brutal hazing, including beatings and verbal abuse.

Prison conditions were harsh and continued to deteriorate, due to diminishing resources. In June, while testifying before the Senate, the Minister of Interior noted that about $64.3 million (4.5 billion tenge) was needed to support the prison population, however, the Government allocated only about $37.1 million (1.9 billion tenge). In December the Ministry of Interior reported that, as of November 1, there were 72,305 prisoners in facilities designed for 60,000. Local human rights activists allege that there are 97,000 prisoners (including 20,000 in pretrial detention) in these facilities.

Overcrowding, combined with an inadequate prison diet and a lack of medical supplies and personnel, contributed to tuberculosis, hepatitis, and other diseases. In December the Government reported that more than 16,000 inmates suffered from tuberculosis with over 12,000 having the active form of the disease. The Kazakstan-American Human Rights Bureau estimated that 2,500 inmates had died of tuberculosis and other diseases as of June.

According to the Government, 2,531 inmates died. Tuberculosis was the cause of death in 56.7 percent of all cases; malnutrition accounted for 10.2 percent of deaths. The incidence of malnutrition doubled from 2,000 cases in 1995 to 4,000. According to the Government, budget cuts (penitentiaries received less than 50 percent of requested funds last year) have reduced the quality of food and the stocks of medicine. In virtually all prisons, medications are available for emergency care only; only 1 in 10 tuberculosis patients in prison receives medication.

Prison guards, who are poorly paid, steal food and medicines intended for prisoners. Violent crime among prisoners is routine.

To reduce prison overcrowding, President Nazarbayev announced in July an amnesty for 20,000 prisoners convicted of minor offenses. This number was later changed to 8,500 after concerns were expressed that the amnesty would lead to a resurgence in the crime rate, which had been falling. However, in December the

Ministry of Interior noted that more than 10,000 prisoners were able to take advantage of the amnesty offer. The first beneficiaries of the amnesty program were teenage offenders, war veterans, and the widows of war veterans. In August a similar amnesty law for the military came into force stipulating that all deserters who returned voluntarily to their army units before October 15 would not be tried by a military tribunal. Servicemen penalized for other offenses were also eligible for the amnesty. The press reported that about 3,000 soldiers were affected. No additional information about the amnesty was available from the Government.

Prisoners are allowed only one visit every 6 months, but additional visits may be granted in emergency situations. Juveniles are kept in separate facilities.

The Government worked with local human rights groups to improve prison conditions, but unlike the previous year did not permit monitoring of prison conditions by local media and human rights groups in 1996. However, in December, a visiting United Nations delegation was permitted to visit several penal institutions in Almaty.

d. *Arbitrary Arrest, Detention, or Exile.*—The Government continued the process of reforming the legal system throughout 1996. Much of the old Soviet legal system remained in force while new laws were being prepared to bring the legal system into accord with the Constitution. Local human rights organizations alleged that the Government used minor infractions of the law or manufactured charges to arrest and detain Government opponents arbitrarily, including leaders of ethnic Russian and Cossack organizations like Nina Sidorova, and opposition politicians like the leaders of the Azamat political movement who were arrested and fined for organizing an illegal demonstration in November in Almaty. In addition after a government-sanctioned opposition rally in December called for the resignation of the President and Prime Minister, one of the rally's organizers, Petr Svoik, was summoned by the State Committee for Investigations to discuss possible charges in connection with alleged wrongdoing during his tenure as the head of the State Antimonopoly Committee. In August, according to press reports, the Government responded to allegations that the arrests of two Cossacks in Kokshetau were politically motivated by asserting that the two were involved in a "terrorist plot".

The law sanctions pretrial detention. According to the Constitution, police may hold a detainee for 72 hours before bringing charges. After 72 hours, police may continue to hold the detainee for 10 days with the approval of a prosecutor. In practice, police routinely hold detainees, with the sanction of a prosecutor, for weeks or even months without bringing charges.

Defendants accused of serious crimes remain incarcerated until trial. Those accused of less serious crimes can be eligible for a "podpiska"—a system similar to bail. With the agreement of the Prosecutor General, the accused can be released from jail until trial if two persons make sworn written statements that the accused will not leave the locality. The law stipulates that the length of pretrial detention is 2 months, although the length of pretrial detention can be extended up to 1 year, with the approval of the Prosecutor General. The Prosecutor General stated that between 70 and 80 percent of those accused of a crime are considered to be eligible for bail; however, the Kazakstan-American Human Rights Bureau believes that the percentage of accused persons who actually obtain bail is small.

According to the Constitution, every person detained, arrested, or accused of committing a crime has the right to the assistance of a defense lawyer from the moment of detention, arrest, or accusation—a right generally respected in practice. However, human rights activists allege that members of the security forces have pressured prisoners to refuse the assistance of an attorney, sometimes resulting in a delay before the accused sees a lawyer. Detainees may also appeal the legality of detention or arrest to the prosecutor before trial; previously, detainees could appeal the legality of detention or arrest to the court. If the defendant cannot afford an attorney, the Constitution provides that the State must provide one free of charge. Human rights organizations allege that many prisoners are unaware of this provision of the law. Although some lawyers are reluctant to defend clients unpopular with the Government, there were no reports of government reprisals against attorneys. However, there were reports that several lawyers defending opposition figures were attacked and beaten by "unknown assailants."

The Government does not use forced exile.

e. *Denial of Fair Public Trial.*—Government interference and pressure compromised the court system's independence throughout 1996—a situation codified in the Constitution's establishment of a judiciary fully under the control of the President and the executive branch. At year's end, the Government was still in the process of restructuring the judicial system to bring it into line with provisions of the Constitution.

There are three levels in the court system: local; oblast (provincial); and the Supreme Court. According to the Constitution, the President proposes to the upper house of Parliament (the Senate) nominees for the Supreme Court (recommended by the "Highest Judicial Council", a body chaired by the President, which includes the chairperson of the Constitutional Council, the chairperson of the Supreme Court, the Procurator General, the Minister of Justice, senators, judges, and other persons appointed by the President). The President appoints oblast judges (nominated by the Highest Judicial Council) and local level judges from a list presented by the Ministry of Justice, based on recommendations from the "Qualification Collegium of Justice", an autonomous institution made up of deputies from the lower house of Parliament (the Majilis), judges, public prosecutors and others appointed by the President.

Judges are appointed for 10-year terms, although a new draft law on judges will reportedly give the President the power to appoint judges for life. The Constitution abolished the earlier Constitutional Court and established a Constitutional Council—three of its seven members, including the chairman, are directly appointed by the President. The Council rules on election and referendum challenges, interprets the Constitution, and determines the constitutionality of laws adopted by Parliament. Under the Constitution, citizens no longer have the right to appeal directly to a court that a government action is unconstitutional; this action is now the sole prerogative of the courts themselves.

Local courts try less serious crimes, such as petty theft and vandalism. Oblast courts handle more serious crimes, such as murder, grand theft, and organized criminal activities. The oblast courts may also handle cases in rural areas where no local courts are organized. Judgments of the local courts may be appealed to the oblast-level courts, while those of the oblast courts may be appealed to the Supreme Court. There is also a military court. Specialized and extraordinary courts can also be created—for example, economic, taxation, family, juvenile, and administrative courts—which have the status of oblast and local courts. The Constitution and existing law establish the necessary procedures for a fair trial. Trials are public, with the exception of instances in which an open hearing could result in secrets being divulged, or when the private life or personal family secrets of a citizen have to be protected.

According to the Constitution, defendants have the right to be present, the right to counsel (at public expense if needed), and the right to be heard in court and call witnesses for the defense. Defendants enjoy a presumption of innocence, are protected from self-incrimination, and have the right to appeal a decision to a higher court. Legal proceedings are to be conducted in the state language, Kazak, although Russian may also be used officially in the courts. Proceedings may also be held in the language of the majority of the population in a particular area.

The problem of corruption is evident at every stage and level of the judicial process. Judges are poorly paid; the Government has not made a vigorous effort to root out corruption in the judiciary. According to press reports, judicial positions can be purchased: A seat on the bench in a municipal district court, for example, reportedly costs $6,000. Anecdotal evidence stemming from individual cases suggests that judges solicit bribes from participants in trials and rule accordingly. In June the Chief Justice and another member of the Supreme Court were dismissed for taking bribes.

There were no reports of political prisoners. A few people were tried and convicted of violating laws on conducting rallies or demonstrations, or for slandering officials. None was incarcerated at year's end. According to local human rights monitors, journalist Boris Suprynuk, who was tried, sentenced, and imprisoned for "insulting" a public prosecutor in May 1995, was released from prison in the spring. He now lives and works in the Russian Federation.

f. *Arbitrary Interference With Privacy, Family, Home, or Correspondence.*—The Constitution provides that everyone has the right to "confidentiality of personal deposits and savings, correspondence, telephone conversations, postal, telegraph and other messages." Limitation of this right is allowed "only in the cases and according to the procedure directly established by law." However, the KNB and Ministry of Internal Affairs, with the concurrence of the General Prosecutor's office, can and do arbitrarily interfere with privacy, family, home, and correspondence. The law requires criminal police, who remain part of the internal security structure, to obtain a search warrant from a prosecutor before conducting a search, but they sometimes search without a warrant. The KNB has the right to monitor telephone calls and mail, but under the law it must inform the General Prosecutor's office within 24 hours of such activity.

Section 2. *Respect for Civil Liberties, Including:*
  a. *Freedom of Speech and Press.*—The Constitution and the 1991 Press Law provide for freedom of the press, and the Government generally tolerates independent media; however, the media practices self-censorship. The Government continued to own and control most printing and distribution facilities and to subsidize periodicals, including many which were supposedly independent. The potential for Government control, as well as reports of specific instances of Government officials making suggestions about what a journalist should and should not cover, resulted in widespread media self-censorship. The key subject considered to be "off limits" by journalists was personal criticism of the President and government officials.

  In April the Russian newspaper Komsomolskaya Pravda printed an article in which Russian writer Aleksandr Solzhenitsyn called for the reintegration of northern Kazakstan with Russia. The Prosecutor General's Office charged the newspaper with stirring up ethnic discord (a violation of Article 39 of the Constitution) and calling for the violation of Kazakstan's territorial integrity. The Prosecutor General demanded that the newspaper be suspended from publishing in Kazakstan for 6 months and its circulation throughout the country banned. Independent journalists quickly called on the Medeo district court of Almaty to reject the suit as contradictory to democratic ideals. The suit was dropped in July after the newspaper published a statement disassociating itself from Solzhenitsyn's remarks. Circulation of the newspaper was not affected.

  In July a journalist for the Kazak-language service of Radio Liberty was detained for several hours after he admitted to police that he was on his way to cover an "illegal demonstration" against Chinese nuclear testing. The journalist was not charged. He then sued the government for about $85,000 (6 million tenge) in "moral damages." In September the court awarded him about $140 (10,000 tenge).

  In the summer, a Russian citizen correspondent of the newspaper Izvestia, Vladimir Ardayev, was warned "unofficially" by the Ministry of Foreign Affairs that foreign correspondents should not interfere in internal Kazakstani affairs after he appeared on a local talk show. In September President Nazarbayev was angered by Ardayev's publication of a "confidential" letter from Uzbekistani President Karimov regarding integration within the Commonwealth of Independent States. Nazarbayev told the press that "Ardayev was already once driven out of Kazakstan, and if we drive him out again, he will never return." However, no official action was taken against Ardayev and he continued to live and work in Kazakstan.

  Despite these examples of official heavy-handedness, the press was generally permitted to criticize government decisions. Official corruption remained an acceptable topic for critical coverage. Many journalists have criticized the new bicameral Parliament as a "tame parliament in the President's pocket."

  Most political opposition groups freely issued their own publications. However, according to press reports, in December 1995, the editor of the Republican Party newspaper in Kokshetau oblast (province) was arrested and sent to a mental hospital after he criticized the akim (governor). In addition human rights activists reported that Yuri-Buravlyov, editor of the newspaper Era of Mercy, was detained by local authorities after publishing an article critical of the head of the north Kazakstan province administration. There are several independent newspapers that act as voices for the opposition, particularly Delovaya Nedelya (Business Week) and Novoye Pokoleniye (New Generation).

  There are many radio and television companies, both public and private, but the Government controls all broadcasting facilities. An association of independent broadcasters of Central Asia exists. However, Government officials and representatives of the state television corporation continued to call for a state-sponsored union of independent television stations.

  In October and November, several independent television and radio stations in Almaty had their broadcasting frequencies temporarily turned off, were told to prepare to vacate their technical offices in the state television tower, and were told that the frequencies they utilized would be sold to the highest bidder. The stations have independent news and political commentary as well as standard programming. With one exception, all of the independent electronic media continued to broadcast after brief interruptions. A government tender for the frequencies was announced in December. Bids will be accepted until January 14, 1997 and results will be announced on January 24, 1997. Bidders were required to pay $500 to bid. No minimum bid price was established. The "M" broadcasting company's television transmission from the television tower continued to be suspended because of allegations that its signal was interfering with another independent station; Radio M continued to broadcast on a radio cable network. Human rights activists and several media outlets claimed that these actions were part of a concerted government effort to harass and even eliminate independent media. The Government denied any intent to limit free speech and asserted that it was acting in its own fiscal interest.

In December the Government decided to suspend the broadcasting of the All-Russian Television and Radio Company (RTR) into Kazakstan. Although an independent station alleged that the decision was related to frequencies problems, the Government reported that RTR's broadcasting was suspended because of a $480 million debt to Kazakstan.

The law against insulting the President and other officials remained on the books and the Constitution provides for the protection of the dignity of the President. In August Nina Sidorova, the leader of an ethnic Russian political movement, was arrested and charged with insulting a prosecutor. In December Sidorova was sentenced to 2 years in prison after being found guilty of insulting officials of the court, insulting government officials, and assault and battery of court representatives. Sidorova's sentence was immediately suspended under a general amnesty declared earlier this year in conjunction with the fifth anniversary of independence.

Several laws control advertising in the mass media. One law restricts alcohol and tobacco advertising on television, as well as "pornography" and "violence" during prime viewing hours. Another law restricts the amount of advertising in newspapers to 20 percent of the total material in each issue. The Minister of Justice and the Minister of Press and Mass Media have interpreted this law as restricting paid articles, but not commercial advertisements.

The Government respects academic freedom.

b. *Freedom of Peaceful Assembly and Association.*—The Constitution provides for peaceful assembly and association, but there are significant restrictions. According to the law, organizations must apply to the local authorities for a permit to hold a demonstration or public meeting at least 10 days in advance, or the activity will be considered illegal. In some cases, local officials routinely issued necessary permits. However, human rights activists complained that complicated procedures and the 10-day notification period made it difficult to for all groups to organize public meetings and demonstrations. They argue that local authorities, especially those outside of the capital, turned down the majority of applications submitted. The press reported that there were numerous unsanctioned rallies of workers and pensioners protesting against difficult economic conditions and the nonpayment of wages and pensions. For the most part, no action was taken against these individuals. However, in November the leader of Azamat, a political opposition movement, and the leader of an independent trade union were arrested and fined for organizing an unsanctioned rally intended to protest the nonpayment of wages to workers. No government action was taken against the participants in the rally.

The Kazakstani Communist Party came under government scrutiny in March after it sponsored unsanctioned rallies and demonstrations in support of the Russian Duma's vote to nullify the 1991 accords that disbanded the former Soviet Union and founded the Commonwealth of Independent States. A number of local Communist Party chapters were fined and the national organization had difficulty renewing its registration. The General Prosecutor's office called for the suspension of the activities of the Communist Party until the Party brought its charter (which calls for the reconstitution of the Soviet Union) into compliance with existing law by recognizing the sovereignty of Kazakstan. The Communist Party was not banned; however, the ethnic Russian organization "LAD" of Ust-Kamenogorsk was suspended for its part in organizing the rallies. In November the Party agreed to revise its charter to acknowledge Kazakstani sovereignty. Its application for reregistration was submitted to the Ministry of Justice in December.

Organizations, movements and political parties that conduct public activities, hold public meetings, participate in conferences, or have bank accounts must register with the Government. Activity by nonregistered organizations is illegal. Registration on the local level requires a minimum of 10 members and on the national level, a minimum of 10 members in at least 11 of the 19 provinces (oblasts). In addition, a registration fee is required, which many groups consider to be a deterrent to registration.

The Constitution prohibits political parties established on a religious basis. The Government has refused to register ethnic-based political parties on the grounds that their activities could spark ethnic violence. The Constitution bans "public associations"—including political parties—whose "goals or actions are directed at a violent change of the constitutional system, violation of the integrity of the Republic, undermining of the security of the State (and), fanning of social, racial, national, religious, class and tribal enmity." Unregistered parties and movements, nonetheless, hold meetings and publish newspapers. All of the major religious and ethnic groups have independently functioning cultural centers.

To participate in elections, a political party must register with the Government. Under current law, a party must submit a list of at least 3,000 members from a minimum of 11 oblasts. The list must provide personal information about members, including date and place of birth, address, and place of employment. For many citizens, submitting such personal data to the Government is reminiscent of the former Soviet KGB's tactics and inhibits them from joining parties. The nationalist Alash Party and the Social Democratic Party have refused to register on the principle that they should not have to submit personal information about their members to the Government. Under the law, members of unregistered parties may run for elected office as individuals, but not as party members.

There are no public statistics available regarding the number of registered public parties; however, all parties asking to be registered have been successful. For the most part, political parties are very weak and, with the exception of the Communist Party and some of the ethnic-based political movements, have very little influence outside the capital. The majority of parliamentary deputies are independents; parties represented in the Parliament include several propresidential parties, the Communist Party, and the Socialist Party. Most opposition party members decided not to participate in the December 1995 elections and are, therefore, not represented in the Parliament.

The Constitution prohibits foreign political parties and foreign trade unions from operating in Kazakstan. In addition, the Constitution prohibits the financing of political parties and trade unions by foreign legal entities and citizens, foreign states, and international organizations. Some trade union associations have circumvented this prohibition by registering with the Government as "public organizations," in other words, nongovernmental organizations.

c. *Freedom of Religion.*—The Constitution provides for freedom of religion, and the various denominations worship without government interference. However, the Constitution also requires that the appointment by foreign religious centers of the heads of religious associations must be carried out "in coordination with the Government," as must the activities of foreign religious associations. In practice the Government does not interfere with the appointment of religious leaders. Foreign missionaries, unwelcome to some Orthodox and Muslim Kazakstanis, have complained of occasional harassment by low-level government officials. In June the government-controlled television station complained that more than 2,000 Kazakstanis had been converted to other religions and proposed stopping foreign missionaries who were preaching "Christianity and Krishna ideas on our own soil." However, no action has been taken against foreign missionaries working in the country.

The Islamic mufti and the Russian Orthodox archbishop have appeared together to promote religious and ethnic harmony.

d. *Freedom of Movement Within the Country, Foreign Travel, Emigration, and Repatriation.*—The Constitution provides for the right to emigrate and the right of repatriation; both are respected in practice. Kazakstanis have the right to change their citizenship, but are not permitted to hold dual citizenship.

According to the Constitution, everyone who is legally present on the territory of the Republic has the right to move freely on its territory and freely choose a place of residence except in cases stipulated by law. This provision formally abolishes the "propiska" system of residence permits, a holdover from the Soviet era. However, in the absence of a law for most of the year to bring legal practice into line with the Constitution, citizens were still required to have a propiska in order to prove legal residence and obtain city services. Obtaining a propiska for most of the country was generally routine. However, according to human rights activists, a bribery market in propiskas to live in Almaty continued to exist, because of Almaty's greater affluence. In August a new law replaced the propiska system with a system of registration for all citizens.

There were numerous reports of government efforts to restrict the movement of foreigners around the country. Internal visas were commonly required for foreigners traveling outside the capital.

An exit visa is required for both citizens and foreigners who wish to travel abroad, although refusals are rare. There have been reports of some officials demanding bribes for exit visas. The Government accords special treatment to ethnic Kazaks and their families who fled during Stalin's time and wish to return. Kazaks in this category are entitled to citizenship and many other privileges. Anyone else, including ethnic Kazaks who are not considered refugees from the Stalin era of political repression, such as the descendants of Kazaks who moved to Mongolia during the previous century, must apply for permission to return.

The Government cooperates with the United Nations High Commissioner for Refugees (UNHCR) and other humanitarian organizations in assisting refugees, especially with the resettlement of ethnic Kazaks from Afghanistan now living as refugees in Iran. In August President Nazarbayev estimated that about 200,000 ethnic Kazaks living abroad had returned over the past few years. In August representatives of the Association of Afghan Women Refugees appealed to the Government for financial assistance and protection, alleging that Afghan refugees had been assaulted. There were no reports of forced expulsion of refugees; however, there were complaints that the country had not yet adopted laws regularizing the status of refugees. The issue of the provision of first asylum has never arisen.

At the end of 1994, Kazakstan and Russia initialed agreements that established broad legal rights for the citizens of one country living on the territory of the other, and provided for expeditious naturalization for citizens of one country who moved to the other. These agreements were ratified by Parliament in January 1995 and by the Russian Duma in July.

Section 3. Respect for Political Rights: The Right of Citizens to Change Their Government

Although the Constitution provides for a democratic government, in practice the Government infringed on the right of citizens to change their government. The Constitution concentrates power in the presidency, granting the President considerable control over the legislature, judiciary, and local government. The Constitution cannot be modified or amended without the consent of the President. In 1995 President Nazarbayev extended his term of office to the year 2000 by referendum without a contested presidential election (which, according to the Constitution then in force, should have been held in 1996). A new, bicameral legislature took office in January (members were elected in December 1995). The lower house (the Majilis), consisting of 67 members, was elected directly. The upper house (the Senate), with 47 members, was elected indirectly, by members of oblast and city parliaments, 7 of its members are appointed by the President. The election law requires candidates for both houses to meet minimum age and education requirements, and to pay a nonrefundable registration fee of 50 times the minimum monthly wage (in December 1995 this fee was about $500 (30,000 tenge). The law does not require Majilis candidates to collect signatures in order to be placed on the ballot. Senate candidates are required to obtain signatures from 10 percent of the members of the local assemblies in their oblasts in order to be placed on the ballot. Some consider the election requirements, especially the registration fee, to be a barrier to participation.

The legislature cannot control the budget, initiate changes in the Constitution, or exercise oversight over the executive branch. Should Parliament fail to pass within 30 days an "urgent" bill brought by the President, the President may issue the bill by decree. While the President has broad powers to dissolve Parliament, Parliament can remove the President only for disability or high treason, and only with the consent of the Constitutional Council, which is largely controlled by the President.

Although the President maintained the right to legislate by decree, he respected the parliamentary procedures laid out in the Constitution. During its first session, Parliament passed a large number of bills and ratified several international agreements. However, the Parliament fell short in several areas. No parliamentarian exercised the right of legislative initiative (all legislation considered by the Parliament was introduced by the executive), parliamentary procedures were weak and constituent relations were nonexistent. Most parliamentary activities continued to be conducted behind closed doors. Sessions were neither open to the public nor televised. During the Parliament's second session beginning in September, individual deputies drafted and introduced several bills for consideration.

In June the Parliament twice rejected the Government's pension reform legislation, arguing that its constituents opposed the bill. The Government called for a vote of confidence. According to the Constitution, if the Government receives a vote of no confidence, the President can dissolve either the Government or the Parliament. In this case, the parliamentarians realized that, if forced to make a choice, the President would have chosen to dissolve the Parliament, not the Government. The Parliament gave the Government its vote of confidence and passed the bill.

The Constitution significantly constrains the independence of the judiciary. The Constitutional Court was abolished and replaced by a Constitutional Council. Three of its seven members, including its chairman, are directly appointed by the President. A two-thirds majority of the Council is required to overrule a Presidential veto of its decisions. All judges are appointed by the President.

According to the Constitution, the governors of oblasts (the "akims") are selected by the Prime Minister but serve at the discretion of the President, who may also annul their decisions.

Two national political opposition movements were established in 1996, both calling for the election of provincial governors and changes in the Government's economic reform policies. Azamat is a movement of intellectuals dedicated to constructive opposition. Republic is a popular front led by the Kazakstani Communist Party representing 20 political parties, public associations, and movements. The Government did not interfere with the development of either movement. However, the leaders of Azamat alleged that they were harassed by local officials while traveling through the countryside in the summer.

All adult citizens have the right to vote. Membership in political parties or trade unions is forbidden to members of the military, employees of national security and law enforcement organizations, and judges.

There are no legal restrictions on the participation of women and minorities in politics, but the persistence of traditional attitudes means that few women hold high office or play active parts in political life. There are no female federal ministers or provincial governors. Of 45 Senate members (2 seats were vacant in 1996), 3 are women; of 67 Majilis members, 9 are women.

Although minority ethnic groups are represented in the Government, Kazaks hold the majority of leadership positions. Of the 21 Government ministries, 8 are headed by non-Kazaks. Non-Kazaks are well-represented in the Majilis and the Senate.

Section 4. Governmental Attitude Regarding International and Nongovernmental Investigation of Alleged Violations of Human Rights

Helsinki Watch, the Kazakstan-American Human Rights Association, and Legal Development of Kazakstan are the most active of a small number of local human rights organizations. They cooperate on human rights and legal reform issues. Although these groups operated largely without government interference, they were subject to restrictions on assembly, and limited financial means hampered their ability to monitor and report human rights violations. Some human rights observers complained that the Government monitored their movements and telephone calls.

There is a presidential commission on human rights in the Government. In February the Prosecutor General's Office established a "Department for Supervising the Protection of Human and Civil Rights." In September the Prosecutor General's Office acknowledged that the jailed leader of an ethnic Russian political movement had been beaten and ordered an official investigation. However, the Government tended to deny or ignore charges of specific human rights abuses.

The Government permitted international and foreign nongovernmental organizations (NGO's) dealing with human rights issues to visit Kazakstan and meet with local human rights groups as well as government officials. The International Labor Organization, the International Federation of Red Cross and Red Crescent Societies, and the U.N. High Commissioner for Refugees have permanent offices in Kazakstan. However, the Constitution forbids "the financing of political parties and trade unions by foreign legal entities and citizens, foreign states and international organizations." Further, although the Civil Code allows the registration of NGO's, requirements for registration were burdensome and changed frequently. As a result, few NGO's were registered, leaving many without legal standing. Although some government officials made an effort to work with domestic and foreign NGO's, others continued to assert that foreign NGO's promote instability.

Section 5. Discrimination Based on Race, Sex, Religion, Disability, Language, or Social Status

The Constitution states "everyone is equal before law and court. No one may be subjected to any discrimination for reasons of origin, social position, occupation, property status, sex, race, nationality, language, attitude to religion, convictions, place of residence or any other circumstances." However, the Government does not effectively enforce this on a consistent basis. The Government has favored ethnic Kazaks in government employment and, according to many citizens, in the process of privatizing state enterprises.

Women.—According to human rights groups, there is considerable domestic violence against women. Police are often reluctant to intervene in cases of spousal abuse, considering it to be the family's business, unless they believe that the abuse is life threatening. The maximum sentence for wife beating is 3 years, but few cases are prosecuted. The Government has not specifically addressed the problem. Law enforcement authorities reported 1,905 cases of rape and adjusted 1995 figures to report 1,641 cases. The punishment for rape can range from 4 to 15 years. There is very little coverage of rape in the press, and it is generally believed that rapes often go unreported.

There is no legal discrimination against women, but women are severely underrepresented in higher positions in government and state enterprises and overrepresented in low-paying and some menial jobs. Women have unrestricted access to higher education.

Children.—The Government is committed in principle to children's rights, but, as in many other areas, budget stringencies and other priorities severely limit its effectiveness in dealing with children's issues. There is no established pattern of governmental or societal abuse against children. Rural children normally work during harvests (see Section 6.d.).

People With Disabilities.—Citizens with disabilities are entitled by law to assistance from the State. There is no legal discrimination against people with disabilities, but in practice, employers do not give them equal consideration. There are laws mandating the provision of accessibility to public buildings and commercial establishments for the disabled, but the Government does not enforce these laws. Disabled persons are a low priority for the Government.

National/Racial/Ethnic Minorities.—The population of about 17 million consists of approximately 44 percent Kazaks and 36 percent Russians, with many other ethnic groups represented.

The Government continued to discriminate in favor of ethnic Kazaks in government employment, where ethnic Kazaks predominate, as well as in education, housing, and other areas. However, the Government has continued to back away from its "Kazakification" campaign of the first year of independence. President Nazarbayev has publicly emphasized that all nationalities are welcome, but many non-Kazaks are anxious about what they perceive as expanding preferences for ethnic Kazaks. Many ethnic Kazaks, however, believe that such affirmative action is needed to reverse 200 years of discrimination.

Most of the population speaks Russian; only about half of ethnic Kazaks speak Kazak fluently. According to the Constitution, the Kazak language is the state language. The Constitution states that the Russian language is officially used on a basis equal with that of the Kazak language in organizations and bodies of local self-administration. This slight increase in the status of the Russian language (from its previous status as the Republic's "language of interethnic communication") did not satisfy some ethnic Russian Kazakstanis who had hoped that Russian would be designated as a second state language. The Government is encouraging more education of children in the Kazak language, but has done little to provide Kazak-language education for adults.

A new language law passed by the lower house of Parliament in November and forwarded to the Senate for consideration actively sought to further the use of the Kazak language. However, the draft bill does not appropriate any funding to improve Kazak language training. Its most controversial provision authorizes the Government to establish a list of government positions that could be held only by individuals fluent in Kazak. Ethnic Kazaks would have until 2001 to attain the necessary Kazak fluency; non-Kazaks would have until 2006.

Section 6. Worker Rights

a. *The Right of Association.*—The Constitution and the current Labor Code (since 1995 the Ministry of Labor has been in the process of drafting a new labor code, with input from labor representatives) provide for basic worker rights, including the right to organize and the right to strike. Kazakstan joined the International Labor Organization (ILO) in 1993.

Most workers remained members of state-sponsored trade unions established during the Soviet period, when membership was obligatory. At most enterprises, the state-sponsored unions continued to deduct 1 percent of each worker's wage as dues. In addition the Government withholds 30 percent of each worker's wage—85 percent of which is for the pension fund, 5 percent for social insurance, and 10 percent for health care. An additional 2 percent of each worker's wage is withheld for the unemployment fund. The state unions under the Communist system were, and for the most part still are, organs of the Government, and work with management to enforce labor discipline and to discourage workers from forming or joining independent unions.

The law gives workers the right to join or form unions of their own choosing and to stop the automatic dues deductions for the state unions. However, enterprises often continue to withhold dues for the state-sponsored union in spite of requests from individual workers to stop the deduction. The Independent Trade Union Center of Kazakstan claims membership of about 500,000 out of a total work force of about 5,600,000; however, the actual number of independent trade union members is estimated to be closer to 70,000. To obtain legal status, an independent union must apply for registration with the local judicial authority at the oblast level and with the Ministry of Justice. Registration is generally lengthy, difficult, and expensive. The decision to register a union appears to be arbitrary, with no published criteria. Judicial authorities and the Ministry of Justice have the authority to cancel a union's registration, however, there is no evidence that the Ministry of Justice has ever exercised this authority.

The law does not provide mechanisms to protect workers who join independent unions from threats or harassment by enterprise management or state-run unions. Members of independent unions have been dismissed, transferred to lower paying or lower status jobs, threatened, and intimidated. According to union leaders, state unions work closely with management to ensure that independent trade union members are the first fired in times of economic downturn.

A 1995 tripartite agreement between labor, management, and the Government, designed to help resolve labor issues and disputes, was moribund. However, in December a new tripartite agreement was signed by the Prime Minister, business representatives, the leaders of the state-sponsored trade unions, and the independent trade union center. According to press reports, the agreement is to support the Government's economic reform program. It is unclear whether this new agreement will be more successful that its predecessor.

Unions and individual workers exercised their right to strike in 1996, primarily in an effort to recover back wages owed to workers. Nonpayment of wages continued to be the priority issue for workers. Miners' strikes in the coal mining region of Karaganda continued throughout the year. According to legislation passed by the Parliament in June, workers may exercise the right to strike only if a labor dispute has not been resolved by means of existing conciliation procedures. In addition, the law requires that employers be notified that a strike will take place no less than 15 days before its commencement.

As a result of their inability to pay salaries, many enterprises continued to pay wages in script rather than in cash, a practice at odds with ILO Convention 95 on the protection of wages other than in the legal currency without the express consent of the workers. Enterprise directors claimed that the enterprises were not being paid in cash by their traditional trading partners in other parts of the former Soviet Union, which were also experiencing cash flow difficulties as a result of the general economic crisis. The script was often not accepted at stores or was accepted only at devalued levels.

By law, unions may freely join federations or confederations and affiliate with international bodies. Most independent trade unions belong to the Independent Trade Union Center (ITUC) headquartered in Almaty. The Independent Miners' Federation of Kazakstan, along with the State Miners' Union of Karaganda, are members of the Miners' International Federation. The unions belonging to the ITUC are not members of international federations but do maintain contacts with European and U.S. trade union federations. Independent unions were particularly concerned about a provision in the Constitution that forbids the financing of trade unions by foreign legal entities and citizens, foreign states, and international organizations. Since independence, independent trade unions have received financial assistance from a foreign trade union institute. However, most of this assistance terminated at the end of September when funding was reduced. Independent trade unions are now searching for new means of support. Some associations of trade unions were able to receive financing from foreign sources by registering as "public organizations" rather than labor unions.

b. *The Right to Organize and Bargain Collectively.*—There are significant limits on the right to organize and bargain collectively. Most large-scale enterprises remained state owned and were subject to the State's production orders. Although collective bargaining rights are not spelled out in the current law, in some instances unions successfully negotiated agreements with management. If a union's demands are not acceptable to management, it may present those demands to an arbitration commission composed of management, union officials, and independent technical experts. There is no legal protection against antiunion discrimination.

There are no export processing zones. Several free economic zones enjoy all the privileges of export processing zones, as well as other tax privileges and abatements, but labor conditions there appear to be no different than elsewhere in Kazakstan.

c. *Prohibition of Forced or Compulsory Labor.*—The Constitution prohibits forced labor except "at the sentence of the court or in the conditions of a state of emergency or martial law." However, in northern Kazakstan some persons were required to provide labor or the use of privately owned equipment with no, or very low, compensation to help gather the annual grain harvest.

d. *Minimum Age for Employment of Children.*—The minimum age for employment is 16 years. A child under age 16 may work only with the permission of the local administration and the trade union in the enterprise in which the child would work. Such permission is rarely granted.ABuse of child labor is generally not a problem, although child labor is routinely used in agricultural areas, especially during harvest season.

e. *Acceptable Conditions of Work.*—This year the Government stopped publishing an official minimum wage. However, the Government used a base minimum monthly wage of $7.35 (550 tenge) in the 1997 budget that was presented to the Parliament in November. The Government multiplies this base minimum wage by set coefficients to determine monthly payments for pensions, student stipends, and wages. Minimum wages vary by industrial sector and slowly increased throughout 1996. However, the minimum wage was far from sufficient to provide a decent living for a worker and family.

In June the Parliament ratified two ILO conventions: Number 14b regarding the protection of workers from professional risks caused by the pollution of the air, noise and vibrations in the workplace; and Number 155 regarding safety and hygiene of the labor and industrial environment.

The legal maximum workweek is 48 hours, although most enterprises maintained a 40-hour workweek, with at least a 24-hour rest period. The Constitution provides that labor agreements must stipulate the length of working time, vacation days, holidays, and paid annual leave for each worker.

Although the Constitution provides for the right to "safe and hygienic working conditions," working and safety conditions in the industrial sector are substandard. Safety consciousness is low. Workers in factories usually do not wear protective clothing, such as goggles and hard hats, and work in conditions of poor visibility and ventilation. Management largely ignores regulations concerning occupational health and safety, enforceable by the Ministry of Labor and the state-sponsored unions. Workers, including miners, have no legal right to remove themselves from dangerous work situations without jeopardy to continued employment.

KYRGYZ REPUBLIC

The Kyrgyz Republic became an independent state in 1991. Although the 1993 Constitution defines the form of government as a democratic republic with substantial civil rights for its citizens, the President, Askar Akayev, dominates the government. Akayev was reelected in December 1995 in an open, multicandidate presidential election, which was marred, however, by deregistration of three rival candidates immediately prior to the vote. Also in 1995, a new two-chamber Parliament was elected for a 5-year term. The Constitution was amended by referendum in February to strengthen substantially the presidency and define the role of Parliament. However, the referendum was marred by serious irregularities. In 1995 a Constitutional Court was sworn in, and a reform program was implemented to improve the quality of the judiciary in 1996. Parliament and the Constitutional Court are fairly weak in practice.

Law enforcement responsibilities are divided between the Ministry of Internal Affairs (MVD) for general crime, the Ministry of National Security (MNB) for state-level crime, and the procurator's office for both types of crime. Both the MVD and MNB deal with corruption and organized crime. These ministries inherited their personnel and infrastructure from their Soviet predecessors. Both appear to be under the full control of the Government and must conform their actions to the law. Kyrgyzstani borders are manned by Russian border troops under an agreement with the Russian Federation. The Government has little authority over these troops who sometimes enforce their own rules rather than Kyrgyzstani law.

The Kyrgyz Republic is a poor, mountainous country with a predominantly agricultural economy. Cotton, wool, and meat are the main agricultural products and exports. Other exports include gold, mercury, uranium, and hydroelectricity. The Government has carried out progressive market reforms. There was moderate growth in most sectors, and economic reform is now accepted by the general public. The level of hardship for pensioners, unemployed workers, and government workers with salary arrearages continues to be very high. Foreign assistance plays a significant role in the country's budget.

The Government generally respected the human rights of its citizens, but there were problems with freedom of speech and the press, due process for the accused, religious freedom, ethnic discrimination, and electoral procedures. Prison conditions remained poor. Two campaign workers and one journalist were arrested, tried, and convicted under criminal rather than civil statutes for libeling the President. Although receiving suspended sentences, they were held for months without bail before their trials. One was subsequently rearrested and convicted of additional criminal charges despite weak evidence. The Constitution was amended illegally in a referendum marred by irregularities. Local "elders'" courts used torture, and levied harsh sentences beyond their mandate, in one case ordering the death penalty. Although sanctioned by the Government, elders' courts are not part of the regular judicial structure and the Government has made efforts to curtail their activities. In general executive domination of the judiciary made assurances of due process problematic. The Government does not fully protect freedom of religion. Concerns about ethnic discrimination remain, but in general the situation of minorities has improved and emigration rates have fallen dramatically. Violence against women is a problem which the authorities often ignore.

RESPECT FOR HUMAN RIGHTS

Section 1. Respect for the Integrity of the Person, Including Freedom From:

a. *Political and Other Extrajudicial Killing.*—There were no reports of political or other extrajudicial killings by government officials. There was one report that an individual was killed by stoning after being sentenced to death by a local court of village elders (see Section 1.e.). These courts are supposed to handle petty disputes and are not authorized to try major crimes or impose punishment other than small fines. Apparently, the elders were not punished, but elders' courts are being monitored more closely.

b. *Disappearance.*—There were no reports of politically motivated disappearances.

c. *Torture and Other Cruel, Inhuman, or Degrading Treatment or Punishment.*—The Constitution prohibits such practices, and there were no reports that officials employed them. There were unconfirmed reports that police beat ethnic Chechens during their arrests (see Section 1.d.).

There have been allegations that local elders' courts in conjunction with unauthorized vigilantes have used torture to gain confessions in two villages (see Section 1.e.).

Prison conditions (including food shortages and lack of heat and other necessities) are poor but not so bad as to constitute cruelty. Those detained by the MNB rather than the MVD are kept in an MNB detention facility; after conviction they go to a regular prison.

d. *Arbitrary Arrest, Detention, or Exile.*—The judicial system continues to operate under Soviet laws and procedures. The procurator's office determines who may be detained, arrested, and prosecuted. The Interior Ministry, the MNB, and the General Procurator carry out investigations. Since 1990 persons arrested or charged with crimes have the right to defense counsel. The procurator's office responsible for the investigation often nominates the defense counsel, who is required to visit the accused within the first 3 days of incarceration. However, sometimes the accused first sees defense counsel only at the trial.

The Criminal Code permits the procurator to detain suspects for 72 hours before releasing them or accusing them of a crime. The procurator must issue an arrest warrant before a person can be detained. If a suspect is charged, the procurator must advise defense counsel immediately. The accused usually remains in detention while the procurator investigates and prepares the case for presentation in court. The procurator has discretion to keep the accused in pretrial detention for up to 1 year, but there are provisions for conditional release before trial. After 1 year, the procurator must release the accused or ask Parliament to extend the period of detention. Since independence, there have been no known instances in which Parliament extended a detention.

The procurator, not the judge, is in charge of criminal proceedings. Thus the courts are widely perceived as a rubber stamp for the procurator and not protectors of citizens' rights. In addition, very low judges' salaries have led to the apparently well-grounded view among the population that decisions can be bought easily. Numerous articles have appeared in the press about judges being charged and convicted for taking bribes.

Two days before the 1995 Presidential elections, the campaign chairman of opposition candidate Medetkan Sherimkulov and a campaign worker were arrested in Issyk Kul oblast while campaigning. They were charged with libeling the President by handing out leaflets saying that Akayev was ethnically Kazak. They and their colleagues denied that they had any leaflets. The men were detained without bail (which is usually available in cases of nonviolent crime) for 4 months and were allowed no visitors other than spouses and attorneys. In April they were convicted of libel and received 1-year suspended sentences. A third person was arrested on similar charges in Naryn in February and detained without bail until trial in July. He was convicted, given a suspended sentence of 1 year, and released. There were unconfirmed reports that police arbitrarily arrested and detained ethnic Chechens, some of whom were severely beaten during their arrests. The MVD noted that it had "cracked down on Chechen criminals" in 1996.

The Government does not employ forced exile.

e. *Denial of Fair Public Trial.*—The Constitution provides for an independent judiciary. However, the court system remains largely unreformed and the executive dominates the judiciary.

Cases originate in local courts, may move to appeals courts on a district or regional level, and finally to the Supreme Court. Separate courts of arbitration handle civil disputes, and traditional elders' courts handle low-level crime in rural areas.

The procurator brings the case to court and tries it before a judge and two people's assessors (pensioners or citizens chosen from labor collectives). The accused and defense counsel have access to all evidence gathered by the procurator. They attend all proceedings, which are generally public, and are allowed to question witnesses and present evidence. In fact nearly anyone in the court room may be allowed to question witnesses. Witnesses do not recapitulate their testimony in court; instead they affirm or deny their statements in the procurator's files. Defendants in criminal cases sometimes are treated in a demeaning manner by being kept in cages in the courtroom.

The court may render one of three decisions: Innocent, guilty, or indeterminate, i.e., the case is returned to the procurator for further investigation. In May the Constitutional Court ruled that only the defense has the right of appeal. Previously the prosecutor could appeal both acquittals and convictions so that defendants might be acquitted by the trial court but then convicted on appeal or have their sentences increased. The decision of a court to return a case to the procurator for further investigation may not be appealed, and the accused are returned to the procurator's custody where they may remain under detention.

Local elders' courts have committed a number of abuses. They are supposed to try petty crimes and decide local disputes but have tried major crimes and handed out harsher punishments than allowed in the form of high fines or detention. Torture is sometimes used to extract confessions (see Section 1.c.). In an extreme case, an elders' court sentenced a man to death by stoning for livestock rustling; the sentence was carried out (see Section 1.a.). Defendants in elders' courts may appeal to the local administrative court. Prosecutors' offices are monitoring these courts more closely but continue to report cases in which these courts exceeded their authority.

The Government has begun to reform the judicial system. Generally accepted international practices, including the presumption of innocence of the accused, have been introduced. A new system of court administration is being instituted, and sitting judges are being tested on their knowledge of the law and new civil codes. If they fail these tests, they are removed from office. In what may be an indication of growing judicial independence, in November the Constitutional Court ruled that the speaker of the legislative lower house had been unconstitutionally elected since mandated parliamentary procedure was not followed. The legislature accepted the Court's ruling and elected a new speaker.

The appointment of ethnic Kyrgyz to key positions in the judicial system has led to charges by non-Kyrgyz that the system is arbitrary and unfair, and that the courts treat Kyrgyz more leniently than members of other groups. Although systematic discrimination is not clearly evident, it is credible in some cases.

Economic crimes such as tax evasion, embezzlement, or theft of government property are common. Prosecution for these crimes, however, is relatively rare and sometimes appears to be directed at opponents of the Government.

On January 8, 1997, opposition activist Topchubek Turgunaliev was convicted of embezzlement, fraud, and abuse of position, stemming from his service as a university rector in 1994 (Turgunaliev also was convicted in April of defaming President Akayev and received a 1 year suspended sentence). He was arrested on December 17 after organizing a demonstration in Bishkek to protest high unemployment and nonpayment of pensions. The charges on which he was convicted had been brought previously, but rejected for lack of evidence. The timing of the case and the lack of new evidence suggested that the prosecution was politically motivated.

Many observers consider Topchubek Turgunaliev a political prisoner.

f. *Arbitrary Interference With Privacy, Family, Home, or Correspondence.*—The Constitution prohibits unlawful entry into a home against the wishes of the occupant and states that a person's private life, privacy of correspondence, and telephonic and telegraphic communications are protected. The law and procedures require the General Procurators's approval for wiretaps, searches of homes, interception of mail, and similar acts. A change in the law in 1995 weakened these protections by allowing the procurator to give approval for searches over the telephone; thus no written proof exists to verify that the search was approved. Furthermore, in certain cases law enforcement officers may first carry out a search and then get approval within 24 hours. If approval is not given, any evidence seized is inadmissible in court.

Personnel and organizations responsible for violations during the Soviet period have remained largely in place; however, no widespread nor systematic violations of the privacy of citizens were reported. There were some reports by citizens active in politics or human rights issues that the privacy of their communications was violated, but credible evidence is not available.

Section 2. Respect for Civil Liberties, Including:

a. *Freedom of Speech and Press.*—A 1992 law calls for freedom of the press and mass media but also provides guidelines proscribing publication of certain information. The law supports the right of journalists to obtain information, to publish without prior restraint, and to protect sources. However, it also contains provisions that the Government used to restrict press freedom. For example, the law prohibits publication of material that advocates war, violence, or intolerance toward ethnic or religious groups; desecration of national norms, ethics, and symbols like the national seal, anthem, or flag; publication of pornography; and propagation of "false information." The law also states that the press should not violate the privacy or dignity of individuals. It requires all media to register with the Ministry of Justice and to await the Ministry's approval before beginning to operate. The Ministry has ruled that foreign entities are not entitled to register. An amendment to the Constitution makes the dignity of presidents or former presidents inviolable.

There are fully independent newspapers and magazines, as well a few hours daily of independent television broadcasting and some independent radio stations. However, almost all electronic media and a significant portion of print media receive government subsidies, which permit the government to influence media coverage, especially on radio and television. Two print journalists are still barred from practicing their profession under a 1995 conviction for libel. No overt efforts to interfere with the press were observed in 1996, although at least one journalist complained of harassment by police and procurators for expressing independent views. The conviction of two campaign workers and one journalist for criminal defamation of the President during the election campaign emphasized the limits to freedom of speech. They were given 1-year suspended sentences in April and then released (see Section 1.d.).

Academic freedom is respected.

b. *Freedom of Peaceful Assembly and Association.*—Under the Constitution, citizens have the right to assemble and associate freely and do so without government interference.

Permits are required for public marches and gatherings but are routinely available. Some peaceful protests took place outside the President's office, mostly pensioners protesting late pension payments and market vendors protesting tax enforcement.

The 1991 Law on Public Organizations, which includes labor unions, political parties, and cultural associations, requires them to register with the Ministry of Justice. A bureaucratic mentality, carried over from the Soviet period, is at least partly responsible for the delay some organizations experience in registering. Ultimately all organizations have been able to register, with the exception of a Uighur organization with the stated goal of the creation of an independent Uighur state in northwest China.

c. *Freedom of Religion.*—The Constitution and the law provide for freedom of religion and the right of all citizens to choose and practice their own religion; however, the Government does not fully protect these rights. The Government does not support any religion and expressly forbids the teaching of religion (or atheism) in public schools.

In March the Government created a new State Commission on Religious Affairs, officially in order to promote religious tolerance, protect freedom of conscience, and oversee laws on religion. In its early months, the commission was not active and the Government appeared to resist calls by some Orthodox and Muslim leaders to limit the activities of "sects" and "nontraditional religions." By fall, however, the commission became more active. The President signed a decree requiring all religious organizations to register with the commission and announced that a new law on religion would be presented to Parliament. Under the new regulations, each congregation must register separately. As previously, if the group wishes to own property, it must also register with the Ministry of Justice as a legal entity.

Muslim leaders complain that the commission has begun to make decisions about religious events without consulting them. The main Baptist organization reported that a congregation of Baptists in Naryn oblast was denied registration both by the Ministry of Justice and by the Commission for Religious Affairs. The church filed lawsuits and appeals, but the courts upheld the denial of registration. The Baptists report that in October police broke into their services and threatened worshipers.

The Chairman of the Commission acknowledged that he was aware of the problems of the Naryn Baptists, and said that he had informed the authorities that they were to allow the Baptists to worship in peace, but was noncommittal on whether they would be allowed to register.

Religious leaders note with concern that the commission frequently uses the term "national security" in its statements. They also worry that references to "preserving interconfessional accord" could be used by traditional religious to prevent smaller churches from registering. Both Christians and Muslims have expressed concern about the State's apparent intention to take a more intrusive role in religion. Ethnic Kyrgyz Christian congregations appear to face special barriers, as do some Muslim congregations with foreign support.

d. *Freedom of Movement Within the Country, Foreign Travel, Emigration, and Repatriation.*—In general Government policy allows free travel within and outside the country. However, certain Soviet-era policies continue to complicate internal migration, resettlement, and travel abroad. Under the Soviet-era law still in force, citizens need official government permission (a "propiska") to work and settle in a particular area of the country. Home and apartment owners can legally sell their property only to buyers with such permission. This law is not enforced, however, and has become irrelevant as people move within the country, freely selling their homes and businesses.

There is no law on emigration. Administrative procedures permit movement of people; however, citizens who apply for passports must present a letter of invitation from the country they intend to visit or to which they intend to emigrate. They also need an exit visa. There were no reports, however, that citizens, after presenting such a letter, were denied a passport or an exit visa. A Soviet-era law prohibits emigration within 5 years of working with "state secrets." No one is believed to have been barred from emigration under this statute in 1996.

Emigrants were not prevented from returning to Kyrgyzstan, and there is reportedly a small but steady flow of returnees. The Government cooperates with the office of the United Nations High Commissioner for Refugees and other humanitarian organizations in assisting refugees. The issue of first asylum did not arise in 1996. There were no reports of forced return of persons where they feared persecution or expulsion of those having a valid claim to refugee status.

Section 3. Respect for Political Rights: The Right of Citizens to Change Their Government

Citizens have the constitutional right to change their government peacefully, but have limited ability to do so in practice.

The Constitution mandates presidential elections every 5 years. There is a two-term limit. The President was reelected to a second term in 1995 in a multicandidate election marred by irregularities. Parliamentary elections are also held every 5 years. In 1995 citizens elected a new Parliament in elections marred by irregularities. In February a referendum was held that amended the Constitution to redistribute power within the government. The referendum violated the Constitution in force at the time and the Law on Referendums. Voter apathy was high, and turnout low. The results were reminiscent of the Soviet era with a reported turnout of 98 percent and an approval margin of 95 percent. Ballot stuffing was rampant.

The amendments approved in the February referendum further strengthened the formal power of the President and his advisors who dominate the Government. The Parliament and the judiciary tend to be subordinate to the executive branch, but still show some independence. The overwhelming majority of local government officials are not elected but appointed by the President.

Women and most ethnic minorities are underrepresented in government and politics. Only 4 of 105 parliamentary deputies are women. There are four female ministers and the Constitutional Court chairman is a woman. A women's group has formed to recruit, advise, and campaign for women candidates in the next parliamentary elections. Russians and Uzbeks are underrepresented in government positions.

Section 4. Governmental Attitude Regarding International and Nongovernmental Investigation of Alleged Violations of Human Rights

A number of human rights groups operate without government restriction, investigating and publishing their findings on human rights cases. Government officials are generally responsive and sensitive to their views. However, in 1996 human rights groups and diplomats were denied access to the two opposition activists convicted of slandering the President (see Section 2.a.).

Section 5. Discrimination Based on Race, Sex, Religion, Disability, Language, or Social Status

The Constitution provides for the rights and freedom of individuals and prohibits discrimination, including on the basis of language. The Government expresses a strong commitment to protecting the rights of members of all ethnic, religious, and linguistic groups as well as those of women.

Women.—Research conducted in 1996 on violence against women showed a noticeable increase in such incidents since independence. Activists note that rape is becoming more common with authorities often ignoring such attacks. Official statistics show little change in the number of crimes against women, but medical records present a different story with increased hospital admissions of women who have been injured by a family member. Many of these incidents are alcohol related. Such crimes are treated by the normal criminal process if women press charges, but crime statistics indicate that most such crimes go unreported. There are no shelters for battered women. The Government has not devised a program to deal with this problem.

The law gives equal status to women, and they are well represented in the work force, in professions, and in institutions of higher learning. Women are prominent in law, accounting, and banking; and play an active role in the growing nongovernment sector.

Nonetheless, the deteriorating economic conditions have had a severe impact on women, who are more likely to lose their jobs. It is estimated that 70 percent of the unemployed are women. Women make up the majority of pensioners who are also in much worse condition than previously as inflation has eroded pensions, which are often paid late. Women's groups express general concern about the situation of rural women. With the end of communism, traditional attitudes toward women are reasserting themselves strongly in the countryside, where women are relegated to the role of wife and mother and educational opportunities are curtailed.

Women's groups are involved in drafting a family law that will include sections on the treatment of women and children within the family.

Children.—The Government continues to rely on former Soviet law in this sphere, but is finding it increasingly ineffective in dealing with adoption issues, custody disputes, and similar matters. A new family code is still in the drafting stage.

Human rights groups and the Kyrgyz Children's Fund monitor conditions of children. Human rights groups note that children who are arrested are usually denied lawyers. Police often do not notify parents of the arrest and neither parents nor lawyers are present during interrogation, despite laws to the contrary. Children are often intimidated into signing confessions and sometimes are placed in cells with adult criminals to frighten them. In practice children have restricted rights to travel abroad until 16. Before that age, they are not entitled to their own passport and usually may travel only when accompanying a parent on the parent's passport.

The Kyrgyz Children's Fund is concerned about the growing number of street children, many of whom have left home because of abusive or alcoholic parents. The organization has opened two shelters, one in Bishkek and one in Osh to provide food, clothing, and schooling to such children. The forced marriage of underage girls is becoming more common and the authorities often ignore this practice. Cultural traditions and social structures discourage victims from going to the authorities.

Children in rural areas commonly pick crops.

People With Disabilities.—There is no special law to protect disabled individuals, nor any law mandating accessibility. Former Soviet law continues to remain the basis for any resolution of complaints. Government officials are inattentive to the issue.

National/Racial/Ethnic Minorities.—Reported complaints of discrimination center on the treatment of citizens who are not ethnic Kyrgyz. In an estimated population of 4.5 million, some 59.7 percent are Kyrgyz, 16.2 percent Russians, 14.1 percent Uzbeks, and the rest Ukrainians, Tajiks, Kazaks, Tatars, Germans, and others. These groups, which make up over 40 percent of the population, are often called the Russian-speaking minority. Members of this minority allege discrimination in hiring, promotion, and housing. They complain that government officials at all levels favor ethnic Kyrgyz. The predominance of ethnic Kyrgyz in government lends weight to this claim.

Russian speakers (those who do not speak Kyrgyz) also allege that a ceiling exists in government employment that precludes their promotion beyond a certain level. The representation of ethnic Kyrgyz at high and intermediate levels of government is proportionally much greater than the percentage of ethnic Kyrgyz in the general population. This gives credence to perceptions that career opportunities are limited for those who are not ethnic Kyrgyz.

The Constitution designates Kyrgyz as the official language but provides for the preservation and equal and free development of Russian and other languages used in the country. In 1996 Russian was also declared an official language for some purposes. As a result of these reforms and difficult economic conditions in Russia, Russian emigration has significantly declined with some ethnic Russians returning.

Ethnic Chechens were reportedly subjected to arbitrary arrest and detention without charge or on false charges, but these reports could not be confirmed.

Section 6. Worker Rights

a. *The Right of Association.*—The 1992 Labor Law provides for the right of all workers to form and belong to trade unions, and there is no evidence that the Government tried to obstruct the formation of independent unions. Hearings were held on a draft labor law, but it has not been passed. The Federation of Trade Unions of the Kyrgyz Republic (The Federation), successor to the former official union, remains the only trade union umbrella organization in the country, although unions are not required to belong to it. The leadership is changing, and some properties are being sold off.

The Federation has been critical of government policies, especially privatization, and their impact on working class living standards. The Federation still regards itself as in a process of transition in which it is adjusting its relations with the Government, with other unions in the former Soviet Union, and with other foreign unions. A growing number of smaller unions are not affiliated with the umbrella organization.

While the right to strike is not codified, strikes are not prohibited. There were small strikes of short duration. There were no retaliatory actions against strikers, nor were there instances of human rights abuse directed at unions or individual workers.

The law permits unions to form and join federations and to affiliate with international trade union bodies. It calls for practices consistent with international standards. Since independent unions are still in their infancy, no meaningful affiliation with international trade union bodies has taken place.

b. *The Right to Organize and Bargain Collectively.*—The law recognizes the right of unions to negotiate for better wages and conditions. Although overall union structure and practice are slowly changing from that of the Soviet era, there is growing evidence of active union participation in state-owned and privatized enterprises. The Government sets the minimum wage, and then each employer sets its own wage levels.

The law protects union members from antiunion discrimination, and there were no recorded instances of discrimination against anyone because of union activities.

There are free economic zones that can be used as export processing zones. The minimum wage law does not apply to workers in the zones.

c. *Prohibition of Forced or Compulsory Labor.*—The law forbids forced or compulsory labor, and it is not known to occur.

d. *Minimum Age for Employment of Children.*—The minimum age for employment is 18 years. Students are allowed to work up to 6 hours per day in summer or in part-time jobs from the age of 16. The law prohibits the use of child labor (under age 16); the Ministry of Education monitors enforcement. However, families frequently call upon their children to work to help support the family.

e. *Acceptable Conditions of Work.*—The Government mandates a national minimum wage at a level theoretically sufficient to provide minimal subsistence. The minimum wage is about $6.00 (75 soms) per month. In practice even the higher median wage is considered insufficient to assure a decent standard of living for a worker and family. The Federation is responsible for enforcing all labor laws, including the law on minimum wages. Minimum wage regulations are largely observed. However, enforcement of labor laws is nonexistent in the growing underground economy. Market forces help wages in the unofficial sector to keep pace with official wage scales.

The standard workweek is 41 hours, usually within a 5-day week. For state-owned industries, there is a mandatory 24-hour rest period in the workweek.

Safety and health conditions in factories are poor. The deteriorating economy hindered enforcement of existing regulations and prevented investment to improve health and safety standards. A 1992 law established occupational health and safety standards, as well as enforcement procedures. Besides government inspection teams, trade unions are assigned active roles in assuring compliance with these measures, but the rapidly deteriorating economic situation in the country has made the compliance record of businesses spotty. Workers have the legal right to remove themselves from unsafe working conditions.

LATVIA

Latvia is a parliamentary democracy, having regained its independence in 1991 after forced annexation and more than 50 years of occupation by the Soviet Union. Elections for the 100-seat Parliament (Saeima) held in the fall of 1995 were free and fair, but the election law barred some citizens from competing due to prior activity in pro-Soviet organizations or lack of fluency in the state language. The Prime Minister, as chief executive, and the Cabinet are responsible for government operations. The President, as Head of State, is elected by the Parliament. The Saeima reelected President Guntis Ulmanis in a competitive election in June. The 1991 Constitutional Law, which supplements the 1922 Constitution, provides for basic rights and freedoms. The judiciary is independent but not well-trained, efficient, or free from corruption.

The security apparatus consists of: The national police and other services, such as the Special Immigration Police, subordinate to the Ministry of Interior; municipal police operating under local government control; the Counterintelligence Service and a protective service operating under the Ministry of Defense; and the National Guard, an element of the national armed forces, which also assists in police activities. Parliament approved the Government's proposal to transfer the Border Guard Force from the Ministry of Defense to the Ministry of Interior, effective January 1, 1997. Civilian authorities generally maintain effective control of the security forces and the Constitution Protection Bureau (SAB) is responsible for coordinating intelligence activities. However, Interior Ministry forces, municipal police, and intelligence personnel sometimes acted independently of central government authority. Some members of the security forces, including police and other Interior Ministry personnel, committed human rights abuses.

Traditionally dominated by agriculture and forestry products, with military and other industrial production introduced by the Soviets, the varied economy is increasingly oriented toward the service sector. As the transition from a centrally planned to a market-oriented economic system continues, private enterprise in trade and services is thriving. About 80 percent of agricultural land is farmed privately, and 60 percent of all land is now in private hands. In the industrial sector, progress toward privatization and revitalization is much slower. The currency remained stable and freely traded, unemployment was somewhat over 8 percent, and annual inflation was under 15 percent, down from 25 percent in 1995. Per capita gross domestic product (GDP) was slightly over $1,000. GDP began to rise slightly in 1996 as the economy recovered from the 1995 collapse of several commercial banks as well as from a severe governmental budget crisis.

The Government generally respected the human rights of its citizens and the large resident noncitizen community, although problems remained in certain areas. Members of the security forces, including the police and other Interior Ministry personnel, continued to use excessive force; police and prison officers beat detainees and inmates. The Government did not take adequate disciplinary action against those responsible. Prison conditions remained poor. The inefficient judiciary did not always ensure the fair administration of justice. The Citizenship and Immigration Department (CID) continued to act arbitrarily in some cases concerning the residence status of noncitizens, although independent observers noted improved performance and a reduction in the number of complaints. Over 100 asylum seekers continued to be detained without trial or final determination of their status until December, when Nordic countries accepted most of them for resettlement. Women are discriminated against in the workplace. Spousal abuse and trafficking in women, as well as child prostitution and abuse are significant problems.

Among key positive developments were the establishment of a Constitutional Court; establishment of a Presidential Consultative Council on Nationality Issues; naturalization of noncitizens under the 1994 Citizenship Law; and strengthening of an independent National Human Rights Office (NHRO). Proponents of a restrictive alternative citizenship law failed to gain enough signatures to force a referendum on their proposal. By year's end, in accordance with the 1995 Law on the Status of Former Soviet Citizens, the CID was preparing to begin issuing new travel documents verifying the rights of approximately 700,000 noncitizen residents to reside in, leave, and return to the country.

RESPECT FOR HUMAN RIGHTS

Section 1. Respect for the Integrity of the Person, Including Freedom From:

a. *Political and Other Extrajudicial Killing.*—There were no reports of political or other extrajudicial killings.

b. *Disappearance.*—There were no reports of politically motivated disappearances.

c. *Torture and Other Cruel, Inhuman, or Degrading Treatment or Punishment.*—The Constitution prohibits torture. However, there were credible reports that police and prison personnel beat prison inmates as well as asylum seekers and other detainees. Some law enforcement personnel were prosecuted and others were fired for abusing detainees. In November, for example, three former members of the Riga municipal police were convicted and given prison sentences ranging from 3 to 6 years for taking several persons hostage and extorting money from them in 1995. At least one guard was dismissed from the Interior Ministry for beating asylum seekers held at the Olaine Detention Center. Overall, however, oversight and punishment for improper behavior remained inadequate to deter abuses of authority by law enforcement personnel.

One of the legacies of the Soviet occupation is the regular practice of hazing military recruits. Despite high-level efforts to end harassment and abuse of soldiers, the practices continued. Early in 1996, several military officers were convicted of abusing recruits in 1995. Punishments ranged from suspended sentences to prison terms.

Prison conditions remained poor, despite new construction and foreign assistance, which has facilitated some improvements. Inadequate sanitation facilities, persistent shortages of blankets and medical care, and insufficient lighting and ventilation are common problems, as is the shortage of resources in general. The law continues to prohibit detainees awaiting trial from sending mail, but this prohibition is not universally enforced. The NHRO drew attention to the fact that many prison facilities fail to meet minimum international standards, that prison medical personnel are not sufficiently independent of the prison administration, and that prisoners' correspondence with government officials (except the prosecutor) is subject to censorship. The NHRO developed plans to work with the prison authorities to establish a human rights training program for prison personnel.

A detention center established at Olaine, outside Riga, provided substandard conditions for over 100 asylum seekers (including more than 40 children) who were held without trial until December, pending final determination of their status. Almost all were released and transported to Nordic countries, which had accepted them for resettlement as refugees.

The situation for some imprisoned children, who are not always separated from adults, remained poor. Children as young as 14 years of age were kept in unsanitary conditions, and suffer from disease and deprivation. Both boys and girls are subject to violence and possible sexual abuse.

d. *Arbitrary Arrest, Detention, or Exile.*—There were no known instances of arbitrary arrest. The responsibility for issuing arrest warrants was transferred from prosecutors to the courts in 1994. The law requires the prosecutor's office to make a formal decision whether to charge or release a detainee within 72 hours after arrest. Charges must be filed within 10 days of arrest. No detainee may be held for more than 18 months without the prosecutor presenting the case to the defendant and the court. Detainees have the right to have an attorney present at any time. These rights are subject to judicial review but only at the time of trial. There were credible reports that these rights are not always respected in practice, especially outside Riga.

There were no reports of forced exile, which is prohibited by law.

e. *Denial of Fair Public Trial.*—The Constitution provides for an independent judiciary, and the Government generally respects this provision in practice. However, the courts must rely on the Ministry of Justice for administrative support.

The Supreme Court does not have a clearly established right to rule on the constitutionality of legislation or its conformity with the country's international obligations. In June the Parliament amended the Constitution and adopted legislation to establish a Constitutional Court to fulfill these functions. The new seven-judge panel is authorized to hear cases at the request of state institutions (the President, Cabinet, prosecutor, Supreme Court, local governments, or one-third of Saeima members) but not of individuals. The Parliament approved six of the judges to sit on the court, which held its first organizational meeting and elected an acting chairman in December.

Although the criminal justice system was organized according to the former Soviet model, the Government is reforming the judicial system. In 1995 it completed the establishment of regional courts to hear appeals of lower court decisions. For more serious criminal cases, two lay assessors join the professional judge on the bench. There were no reports that the Government improperly influenced judges, but corruption is reportedly widespread. Most judges have inadequate judicial training, and the court system is too weak to enforce many of its decisions. There is a lack of information available on which to make informed decisions, especially outside Riga. Trials may be closed if state secrets might be revealed or to protect the interests of minors. All defendants have the right to hire an attorney, and the State will lend funds to destitute defendants for this purpose. Defendants have the right to read all charges, confront all witnesses, and may offer witnesses and evidence to support their case.

There were no reports of political prisoners. Former Latvian Communist Party First Secretary Alfreds Rubiks continued to serve an 8-year prison term for attempting to overthrow the independent Latvian State in 1991. While Rubiks' supporters describe him as a political prisoner, claiming that he acted in accordance with the prevailing Soviet legislation, there is no evidence that his conviction violated human rights standards.

f. *Arbitrary Interference With Privacy, Family, Home, or Correspondence.*—The law requires that law enforcement authorities have a judicial warrant in order to intercept citizens' mail, telephone calls, or other forms of communication. This protection is less comprehensive for the large noncitizen population.

Information came to light in 1996 about the unsanctioned taping that reportedly took place in late 1995 of an international telephone conversation between the President and a private citizen who subsequently became the Prime Minister. The prosecutor's office was conducting an investigation on the basis of a tape recording provided by a journalist, but there was no reliable information about those who may have been involved in this illegal activity.

Section 2. Respect for Civil Liberties, Including:

a. *Freedom of Speech and Press.*—The Constitutional Law provides for freedom of speech and the press, and the Government generally respects this right in practice. The 1991 Press Law prohibits censorship of the press or other mass media. Most newspapers and magazines are privately owned. New publications continued to appear, but economic difficulties forced others to close. Newspapers in both Latvian and Russian published a wide range of criticism and political viewpoints.

A large number of independent television and radio outlets broadcast in both Russian and Latvian, and the number of people receiving satellite television broadcasts continued to increase.

The Law on Radio and Television contains a number of restrictive provisions regulating the content and language of broadcasts. No more than 30 percent of private broadcasts may be in languages other than Latvian; in prime time, 40 percent of television broadcasts must be of Latvian and 80 percent of European origin. Moreover, foreign investment may not exceed 20 percent of the capital in electronic media organizations.

There are no restrictions on academic freedom.

b. *Freedom of Peaceful Assembly and Association.*—The authorities legally may not prohibit public gatherings. Organizers of demonstrations must provide advance notice to local authorities, who may change the time and place of public gatherings for such reasons as fear of public disorder. Numerous public meetings and political demonstrations took place without government interference. However, the Riga City Council regularly denied permission or sought to change the time and place of demonstrations by groups representing a portion of the noncitizen community.

The Constitution provides for the right to associate in public organizations. However, the Law on Registering Public Organizations was amended in late 1993 to bar registration of Communist, Nazi, or other organizations whose activities would contravene the Constitution. More than 35 political parties are officially registered. Noncitizens are prohibited from forming political organizations.

c. *Freedom of Religion.*—The Constitutional Law provides for freedom of religion, and the Government generally respects this right in practice. Although the Government does not require the registration of religious groups, the 1995 Law on Religious Organizations specifies that religious organizations can enjoy certain rights and privileges only if they register. Under this law the Justice Ministry has registered over 800 religious congregations, including Mormons, whose previous lack of official registration had created difficulties in obtaining visas and residence status. The only group denied registration was the Jehovah's Witnesses, whose appeal to the courts was still under review at year's end.

Foreign evangelists and missionaries are permitted to hold meetings and proselytize, but the law stipulates that only religious organizations in Latvia may invite them to carry out such activities. After the widely reported death of a Jehovah's Witness, whose religious beliefs affected her choice of medical treatment, the President sent a letter to Parliament asking lawmakers to specify the rights and responsibilities of unregistered religious organizations. He also suggested that the Saeima supplement the Criminal Code "with norms about inflicting physical or psychological damage on a person and about threatening a person's legal rights as a result of activities by a religious organization." The Saeima Human Rights and Legal Committees subsequently began considering a draft amendment to the Administrative

Code which would have prescribed fines for undefined "activities" by unregistered religious organizations. The NHRO and Ministry of Foreign Affairs pointed out that the provisions would violate international obligations in the field of religious freedom. The Saeima took no final action on this matter.

In July the Parliament adopted amendments to the Law on Religious Organizations, 1 of which reduced the number of persons necessary to seek registration of a religious group from a minimum of 25 citizens to 10 persons residing permanently in Latvia. Another amendment stipulated that religious education may be provided to students in public schools on a voluntary basis only by representatives of Evangelical Lutheran, Roman Catholic, Old Believer, Baptist, and Orthodox religious organizations. Students at state-supported national minority schools may also receive education in the religion "characteristic of the national minority." Other denominations may provide religious education, but may not do so in state-funded schools.

d. *Freedom of Movement Within the Country, Foreign Travel, Emigration, and Repatriation.*—There are no obstacles to freedom of movement within the country, foreign travel, or repatriation of citizens.

The 1995 Law on the Status of Former Soviet Citizens stipulates that registered permanent resident noncitizens enjoy the rights to establish and change residences, travel abroad, and return to the country. The law also provides for issuance of new noncitizen travel documents verifying these rights. After numerous delays, the CID announced that it would begin issuing the first of these documents in March 1997. Prior to the issuance of new noncitizen travel documents, and in apparent contradiction with this law, the CID continued to require noncitizens departing with former Soviet passports to obtain separate reentry guarantees. The CID also continued to issue temporary noncitizen identification documents, which are valid for 2 years and accepted as travel documents by most foreign countries.

Although the Government cooperates with the U.N. High Commissioner for Refugees (UNHCR), it is not a signatory to international conventions on refugees and does not have a law or established policy on political asylum, including first asylum or granting refugee status. Most of those seeking refugee status are persons from the Middle East and Central Asia entering by land from Russia or Belarus and hoping to reach Scandinavia. Latvia usually attempts to return such asylum seekers to the country from which they entered, but neighboring countries are generally willing to accept only their own citizens or legal residents.

One group of over 100 asylum seekers, originally detained in 1995, remained in detention without trial outside Riga until December. The authorities were unwilling to grant asylum to these persons, mainly of Iraqi origin, who were attempting to reach Sweden and other Western European countries. No other country was prepared to accept these individuals and no formal mechanism was in place to evaluate their claims or to convey any status other than that of illegal alien. In December, following extensive consultations with Latvia and the UNHCR, Nordic countries agreed to accept almost all the persons detained at Olaine. Nordic ministers emphasized that this was an extraordinary measure, noted that the Latvian Government had received a proposal for comprehensive refugee legislation, and "assumed" that Latvia would adopt and implement refugee legislation in accordance with the 1951 U.N. Convention Relating to the Status of Refugees.

There were credible reports that as many as several dozen asylum seekers were taken to border areas by Interior Ministry personnel and forcibly expelled or pressured to leave the country "voluntarily." This matter was under investigation by the Interior Ministry, the NHRO, and the Prosecutor's Office.

In August the Government established an interministerial working group to draft a comprehensive policy and legislation on refugee and asylum issues that would be consistent with the relevant international norms. In late November the working group submitted a draft law on refugee and asylum matters to the Cabinet, which was expected to review the proposal and transmit it to the Saeima in early 1997. Government officials characterized the draft law as the first important step in establishing a national framework on asylum and refugee issues. The working group also began to analyze the conditions under which Latvia could accede to the 1951 Convention and its 1967 Protocol. Officials continued to stress that their ability to deal with these problems would be greatly facilitated if neighboring countries would agree to readmit illegal migrants who entered Latvia from their territories. While Latvia was able to negotiate readmission agreements with its Baltic neighbors and some Nordic countries, it was particularly hampered by the lack of similar agreements with Russia and Belarus.

Section 3. Respect for Political Rights: The Right of Citizens to Change Their Government

Citizens have the right to change their government. There were free and fair elections for Parliament (the Saeima) in 1995, with the participation of numerous parties and factions representing a broad political spectrum. Candidates from 11 parties won Saeima seats, and 72 percent of eligible voters participated.

International observers deemed the parliamentary elections free and fair, although the elections law barred the candidacy of any citizen who remained active in the Communist Party or various other pro-Soviet organizations after January 13, 1991. There was also a Latvian language requirement for candidates. In 1996 several former candidates from the Socialist Party (including former Communist Party leader Alfreds Rubiks) were tried for making false statements about their past activities in connection with their 1995 candidacies. A few were convicted and given token fines; Rubiks was convicted but no penalty was added to the 8-year sentence he is serving for seeking to overthrow the Government in 1991.

In November the Saeima adopted a law with similar restrictions on the candidates for local elections scheduled to be held in March 1997. The Saeima reconsidered but did not alter these restrictions after widespread protests by the supporters of one official, the Mayor of Daugavpils, who was reportedly active in the Communist Party after January 13, 1991. The Saeima also rejected a proposal to allow noncitizen residents to vote in local elections.

In June the Parliament fulfilled its constitutional responsibility to elect an individual to serve a 3-year term as President. The Saeima chose freely among four candidates in a secret ballot that resulted in the reelection of the incumbent President. A parliamentary effort to restrict the pool of presidential candidates on the basis of language ability or past Communist activities was returned by the President for reconsideration and did not enter into force. The Saeima subsequently voted on all persons duly nominated, including Rubiks, who received 5 votes.

Following the restoration of independence in 1991, citizenship was immediately accorded only to those persons who were citizens of the independent Latvian Republic in 1940 and their direct descendants. Owing to the Russification policy pursued during the Soviet era, ethnic Latvians make up only about 54 percent of the total population and do not constitute a majority in seven of the eight largest cities. More than 70 percent of the registered residents are citizens, almost 400,000 of whom are not ethnic Latvian.

Under provisions of a 1994 law, various categories of noncitizens become eligible to apply for naturalization over a period extending from 1995 until early in the next century. Highest priority was given to spouses of Latvian citizens, citizens of other Baltic states, and persons born in Latvia. The law includes a Latvian language and residence requirement as well as restrictions on naturalization of several groups including former Soviet intelligence and military officers. The law requires applicants for citizenship to renounce previous non-Latvian citizenship, to have knowledge of the Constitution and Latvian history, and to take a loyalty oath.

International observers, including the resident Organization of Security and Cooperation in Europe (OSCE) mission, credit the Government with establishing a competent and professional naturalization board with offices throughout the country to implement the 1994 law. Early experience suggested that the board sought to apply the law fairly. About 1,000 persons were naturalized in 1995 and 3,000 in 1996. Of more than 33,000 persons ages 16 to 20 years who became eligible to apply for naturalization in 1996, only a few hundred expressed interest in doing so. The reasons for this relatively small number may include potential applicants' lack of confidence about their language ability, the restricted category of applicants eligible to seek naturalization in the first 2 years, certain benefits that flow from noncitizen status (such as travel without visas to Russia and exemption from compulsory military service), and a sense that the legal status of permanent resident noncitizens is relatively secure. Moreover, there were amendments to the citizenship law in 1995 that granted automatic citizenship (rather than requiring naturalization) to ethnic Latvians returning to the country as well as to persons successfully completing secondary education in Latvian language schools. These amendments allowed several thousand additional persons to register as citizens.

In early 1996 proponents of a much more restrictive alternative citizenship law exercised their right to conduct a signature campaign in favor of holding a referendum on this issue. The campaign fell about 5,000 signatures short of the number needed to force a referendum.

International experts, government officials, and domestic human rights monitors agreed that Latvia must continue to place high priority and devote sufficient resources to implementing the naturalization law in a fair, impartial manner. These same observers also agreed that the Government must provide greater opportunities for noncitizens to learn Latvian. In 1996 the Government worked with the United Nations Development Program (UNDP) to begin implementing a long-term nationwide Latvian language teaching program for adults and for children in non-Latvian schools.

The CID, which has administrative responsibility for registering noncitizens, has frequently failed to implement properly and fairly laws affecting noncitizens, most often by denying noncitizen residents' applications for permanent resident status. Negative CID decisions are subject to judicial review, and are frequently overruled. However, the CID was sometimes slow in complying with court rulings that overturned its negative decisions. The Minister of Interior personally criticized CID performance in these areas, which he cited as the reason to initiate changes in personnel and procedures. While problems remained, independent observers noted improvements in the quality of the CID's performance as well as a reduction in complaints about its work during the course of 1996.

There are no ethnic restrictions on political participation, and some nonethnic Latvians serve in various elected bodies. There was no mechanism for the many residents of Latvia who were not citizens to participate in the elections.

Women are underrepresented in government and politics. During the year less than 20 percent of parliamentarians and none of the full ministers in the Government were women. A woman was Speaker of the Parliament (the second ranking official after the President) for about 1 year before being replaced in late 1996.

Section 4. Governmental Attitude Regarding International and Nongovernmental Investigation of Alleged Violations of Human Rights

A growing number of nongovernmental organizations devoted to research and advocacy on human rights issues, including prison conditions and women's and children's rights, operate without government restriction. Several organizations deal with issues of concern to local noncitizens and other nonethnic Latvians, presenting them to the courts and the press.

The Government demonstrated a willingness to engage in dialog with nongovernmental organizations working on human rights issues. It welcomed visits by human rights organizations and received delegations from, among others, the OSCE, the Council of Europe (COE), and the United Nations. A resident OSCE mission continued to operate with a mandate to "address citizenship issues and other related matters."

The Government continued to implement its national program for the protection and promotion of human rights, which was adopted in 1995 upon the recommendations of key international organizations. In December the Saeima adopted a law strengthening the NHRO's status as an independent institution with a mandate to promote respect for human rights. Under an acting director, the NHRO continued to fulfill its mandate to provide information on human rights, inquire into individual complaints, and initiate its own investigations on alleged violations. Its permanent director will be appointed by the Government, confirmed by the Saeima for a 4-year term, and subject to dismissal only under limited circumstances. Initial financial difficulties for the NHRO were overcome when the Parliament allocated sufficient funds to facilitate a long-term agreement with the UNDP for training and other institutional support.

Section 5. Discrimination Based on Race, Sex, Religion, Disability, Language, or Social Status

According to the 1922 Constitution, all citizens are equal under the law. In December the Saeima decided to establish a working group to elaborate a second section of the Constitution that would strengthen the constitutional protection of basic human rights and freedoms. The 1991 Constitutional Law, which supplements the Constitution, states that "all persons in Latvia" are equal under the law regardless of race, sex, religion, language, social status, political preference, or other grounds and grants equal rights to work and wages to "persons of all nationalities." However, the Constitutional Law only grants to citizens the right to occupy state positions, establish political parties, and own land.

Women.—Sources indicate that domestic violence against women is fairly widespread and is often connected with alcohol abuse. There is anecdotal evidence suggesting that the entire legal system, including the courts, tends to downplay the seriousness of domestic violence. Observers suggest that police are sometimes reluctant to make arrests in such cases. The NHRO began to work with the Interior Ministry to assist victims of domestic abuse and train law enforcement personnel in dealing with this problem.

Both adult and child prostitution are widespread and often linked with organized crime. There is no legislation in force that specifically addresses these problems. In

May for reasons that remain unclear, the Parliament repealed the only such provisions contained in the Administrative Code.

Women possess the same legal rights as men. The Labor Code prohibits women from performing "hard jobs or jobs having unhealthy conditions," which are specified in a list agreed upon between the Cabinet and labor unions. Moreover, the code bans employment discrimination. In reality women frequently face hiring and pay discrimination, especially in the emerging private sector. It is not unusual to see employment advertising that specifically seeks men. Sexual harassment of women in the workplace is reportedly common. Women apparently have not brought any discrimination suits before the courts.

Women's advocacy groups are growing in size and number. They are involved in finding employment for women, lobbying for increased social benefits, assisting victims of domestic abuse, and opposing the hazing of military recruits.

Children.—Although it is government policy to ensure children's rights to basic health, welfare, and education, there is no general legislation outlining these rights, and the Government lacks the necessary resources to provide them fully. For example, despite the existence of mandatory education, published reports suggested that as many as 15,000 school-age children failed to attend school.

Evidence suggests that abandonment and child abuse, including sexual abuse, are relatively widespread, as is child prostitution. A few children's advocacy groups are active, particularly in lobbying for legislation to protect children's rights and for increased welfare payments for children. Law enforcement authorities have won court suits to remove children from abusive parents and secured convictions in child molestation cases.

Although legislation had long provided for the establishment of special institutions for rehabilitation and vocational training of juvenile offenders, the Government only opened the first such institution in 1996. This facility is designed to reduce the number of juveniles housed in regular prison facilities who have committed relatively minor offenses.

People With Disabilities.—There is no law banning discrimination against the disabled. The Government supports special schools for disabled persons. It does not enforce a 1993 law requiring buildings to be accessible to wheelchairs, and most buildings are not. However, Riga has undertaken an extensive wheelchair ramp program at intersections.

Religious Minorities.—There was no progress reported in apprehending the perpetrators of the 1995 bombing of a Riga synagogue.

National/Racial/Ethnic Minorities.—Of Latvia's more than 2.5 million registered residents, there are more than 765,000 ethnic Russians, 100,000 ethnic Belarusians, almost 70,000 ethnic Ukrainians, and more than 60,000 ethnic Poles. Nearly 400,000 persons belonging to national or ethnic minorities are citizens. Because the majority of persons belonging to national and ethnic minorities are not citizens, they have difficulty participating fully in civic life. Noncitizens who are temporary residents have particular difficulty, but the size of this group has greatly diminished since the adoption and implementation of the 1995 Law on the Status of Former Soviet Citizens who do not hold Latvian or any other citizenship.

This law reiterates guarantees of basic human rights and provides noncitizens who have been permanent residents continuously since July 1, 1992, with the rights to change residence, leave and return, and invite close relatives to join them for the purpose of family reunification. It also requires the registration of noncitizens regardless of their housing status, helping to resolve cases of persons previously unregistered because they lived in former Soviet military or dormitory housing. The law also provides for issuance of new travel documents reflecting these rights (see Section 2.d.).

Various laws prohibit employment of noncitizens in certain categories, some of which appear to be reasonable restrictions (e.g., only citizens can serve as Latvian diplomats) while others seem less justified (e.g., service as crew members on Latvian National Airlines). There are also a few distinctions in the manner of calculating eligibility for social benefits such as pensions, though there was progress in 1996 toward eliminating some of these differences. At the request of the parliamentary human rights committee, the NHRO undertook a major study of all differences between the status of citizens and noncitizens to determine whether they may be inconsistent with constitutional provisions or international obligations and to recommend revisions in legislation if necessary. The study, released in December, identified 10 differences between the rights of citizens and noncitizens that the NHRO considered to be inconsistent with obligations under the International Covenant on Civil and Political Rights. These included restrictions on noncitizen employment as firefighters, armed guards, private detectives, members of airline crews, and certified attorneys, as well as holding licenses as pharmacists. The NHRO found most other differences to be consistent with international standards and practices that allow a state to limit government employment, political participation, and some property rights to those persons who are citizens.

The language law requires employees of the State and of all "institutions, enterprises, and institutes" to know sufficient Latvian to carry out their profession. The law also requires such employees to be conversationally proficient in Latvian in order to be able to deal with the public. Despite the language law, there have been no reports of widespread dismissals, even in the city of Daugavpils, in which only 15 percent of the population is ethnically Latvian. Moreover, Russian is the prevailing language in state-owned industrial enterprises. Nevertheless, many nonethnic Latvians believe that they have been disfranchised and that the language law discriminates against them. In October the Cabinet issued regulations requiring Latvian language competence for a person to be registered and receive benefits as an unemployed person.

Some ethnic Russians have also complained of discrimination resulting from the property laws, which do not allow individual noncitizens to own land. Moreover, noncitizens were given fewer privatization certificates (which can be used to purchase shares of stock and to privatize apartments and land) than citizens. However, the law does allow land ownership by companies in which noncitizens own shares.

The Riga City Council adopted a decision in August requiring noncitizens privatizing their apartments to obtain an additional document from the CID regarding their eligibility to receive noncitizens' travel documents. The Minister for Environmental Protection and Regional Development used his authority to overturn this provision, arguing that it would have created an unjustified administrative requirement, and it did not enter into force.

The Government has agreed to continue using Russian as the language of instruction in public schools where the pupils are primarily Russian speakers. It also supports schools in eight other minority languages. Although all non-Latvian-speaking students in public schools are supposed to learn Latvian and to study a minimum number of subjects in Latvian, there are shortages of qualified teachers.

Most state-funded university education is in Latvian, and incoming students whose native language is not Latvian must pass a Latvian language entrance examination. However, there are several private institutions offering higher education in Russian. In midyear the Minister of Education declined to authorize establishment of a branch of the Moscow State University in Riga, but the issue may be revisited.

A lively debate continued over proposals in a draft education law that all secondary education in public schools be in Latvian by the year 2005. The Parliament was considering several hundred amendments to the education law, and it took no legally binding decision on the long term prospects of state-funded minority language education.

In July the President took the initiative to form an advisory council of nationalities residing in the country made up of persons nominated by the Latvian Association of National Cultural Societies and other prominent persons active in the field of interethnic relations. The council includes members representing a broad range of national minority groups, with a mandate "to discuss the most serious problems in order to promote their solution at the level of executive bodies or legislative initiative." Members of the council reportedly agreed that they would begin by working cooperatively to address questions relating to education, citizenship, and differences between the status of citizens and noncitizens. In December the advisory council began to consider concrete issues and to make recommendations regarding possible changes in regulations and legislation. For example, the council reportedly asked the Labor Department to reconsider the cabinet regulation adopted in October that requires persons to demonstrate Latvian language competence to qualify for unemployment benefits.

Section 6. Worker Rights

a. *The Right of Association.*—The Law on Trade Unions mandates that workers, except for the uniformed military, have the right to form and join labor unions of their own choosing. Union membership, which had been about 50 percent of the work force in 1993, continued to fall as workers left Soviet-era unions that include management or were laid off as Soviet-style factories failed. In general the trade union movement is undeveloped and still in transition from the socialist to the free market model.

The law does not limit the right to strike. Although many state-owned factories are on the verge of bankruptcy and seriously behind in wage payments, workers fear dismissal if they strike. While the law bans such dismissals, the Government has not effectively enforced these laws.

Unions are free to affiliate internationally and are developing contacts with European labor unions and international labor union organizations.

b. *The Right to Organize and Bargain Collectively.*—Labor unions have the right to bargain collectively and are largely free of government interference in their negotiations with employers. The law prohibits discrimination against union members and organizers. Some emerging private sector businesses, however, threaten to fire union members. These businesses usually provide better salaries and benefits than are available elsewhere. The Government's ability to protect the right to organize in the private sector is weak.

There are no export processing zones.

c. *Prohibition of Forced or Compulsory Labor.*—The law prohibits forced or compulsory labor, and it is not practiced. Inspectors from the Ministry of Welfare's Labor Department enforce this ban.

d. *Minimum Age for Employment of Children.*—The statutory minimum age for employment of children is 15 years, although those from 13 to 15 years of age may work in certain jobs after school hours. Children are required to attend school for 9 years. The law restricts employment of those under age 18, for instance, by banning night shift or overtime work. State authorities are lax in their enforcement of child labor and school attendance laws.

e. *Acceptable Conditions of Work.*—The Government raised the monthly minimum wage to about $70 (38 lats), far below the amount which trade union officials describe as the bare minimum for survival. Many factories are virtually bankrupt and have reduced work hours. The Labor Code provides for a mandatory 40-hour maximum workweek with at least one 24-hour rest period weekly, 4 weeks of annual vacation, and a program of assistance to working mothers with small children. The laws establish minimum occupational health and safety standards for the workplace, but these standards are frequently ignored. Workers have the legal right to remove themselves from hazardous work situations, but these standards are frequently ignored in practice.

LIECHTENSTEIN

The Principality of Liechtenstein is a constitutional monarchy and parliamentary democracy. The reigning Prince is the Head of State; all legislation enacted by the popularly elected Parliament (Landtag) must have his concurrence. The Landtag elects and the Prince appoints the members of the Government and of the functionally independent judiciary.

The Interior Ministry effectively oversees the regular and auxiliary police forces. There is no standing military force.

Despite its small size and limited natural resources, Liechtenstein has developed during recent decades from an agrarian society into a prosperous, highly industrialized, free-enterprise economy with a vital service sector. It participates in a customs union with Switzerland and uses the Swiss franc as its national currency. As a result of complex negotiations held with member states of the European economic area and Switzerland and a national referendum held in 1995, Liechtenstein is also a member of the European Economic Area. Citizens enjoy a very high standard of living. Unemployment was only 1.1 percent in 1996.

The Government fully respects the human rights of its citizens provided for in the Constitution, and the law and judiciary provide effective means of dealing with instances of individual abuse. Existing societal discrimination against women is being eliminated in accordance with government policy.

RESPECT FOR HUMAN RIGHTS

Section 1. Respect for the Integrity of the Person, Including Freedom From:

a. *Political and Other Extrajudicial Killing.*—There were no reports of political or other extrajudicial killings.

b. *Disappearance.*—There were no reports of politically motivated disappearances.

c. *Torture and Other Cruel, Inhuman, or Degrading Treatment or Punishment.*—The law prohibits torture and cruel punishment, and there were no reports of the use of such methods.

Prison conditions meet minimum international standards, and the Government permits visits by human rights monitors.

d. *Arbitrary Arrest, Detention, or Exile.*—The law provides for freedom from arbitrary arrest and detention, and the authorities honor these provisions. Within 24 hours of arrest, the police must bring suspects before an examining magistrate, who must either press formal charges or order release. The law grants suspects the right to legal counsel of their own choosing, at no cost if they are indigent. Release on personal recognizance or bail is granted unless the examining magistrate has reason to believe the suspects are a danger to society or will not appear for trial.

There is no provision for exile, and it does not occur.

e. *Denial of Fair Public Trial.*—The judiciary is independent of the executive and legislative branches. It has three tiers: lower court, high court, and Supreme Court. In addition, an Administrative Court hears appeals against government decisions. Also, the State Court protects the rights accorded by the Constitution, decides on conflicts of jurisdiction between the law courts and the administrative authorities, and acts as a disciplinary court for members of the Government.

The Constitution provides for public trials and judicial appeal, and the authorities respect these provisions.

The Constitution authorizes the Prince to alter criminal sentences or pardon offenders. However, if the offender is a member of the Government and is sentenced for a crime in connection with official duties, the Prince can take such action only if the Landtag requests it.

There were no reports of political prisoners.

f. *Arbitrary Interference With Privacy, Family, Home, or Correspondence.*—The Constitution provides for personal liberty and for inviolability of the home, of postal correspondence, and of telephone conversations. No violations were reported. Police need a judicial warrant to search private property.

Section 2. Respect for Civil Liberties, Including:

a. *Freedom of Speech and Press.*—An independent press, an effective judiciary, and a democratic political system combine to ensure freedom of speech and the press. Two daily newspapers are published, each representing the interests of one of the two major political parties, as is one weekly news magazine. There is a state-owned television station and a private radio station, but residents freely receive radio and television broadcasts from abroad. An information bulletin is also issued by the third party ("Freie Liste") represented in Parliament.

The Government respects academic freedom.

b. *Freedom of Peaceful Assembly and Association.*—The Constitution provides for freedom of assembly and association, and the authorities do not interfere with these rights in practice.

c. *Freedom of Religion.*—The Constitution provides for freedom of religion, and the Government does not hamper the teaching or practice of any faith. The finances of the Roman Catholic Church are integrated directly into the budgets of the national and local governments. Roman Catholic or Protestant religious education is compulsory in all schools, but the authorities routinely grant exemptions for children whose parents so request.

d. *Freedom of Movement Within the Country, Foreign Travel, Emigration, and Repatriation.*—Citizens have unrestricted freedom to travel in or outside the country, to emigrate, and to return.

The Government cooperates with the U.N. High Commissioner for Refugees and other humanitarian organizations in assisting refugees. The Government provides first asylum, but the country's lack of an airport or international train station means it receives few requests. Those entering to cross the Austrian border without permission are sent to Austrian authorities in accordance with a bilateral agreement. Those entering from a third country through Switzerland are dealt with on a case-by-case basis. A solution is sought which would avoid forcing people to return to a country where they would be subject to persecution on political, religious, or racial grounds.

There were 10 new asylum cases in 1996. The 18 Tibetans who entered in 1993 have not been granted asylum, but the Government has decided for the time being not to force them to return. Of the 295 refugees from the former Yugoslavia who were given permission to stay until April, 234 are still in country. Of this total, 39 will be allowed to stay until March 31, 1997, 148 will be allowed to stay until July 31, 1997, and 47 cases were still pending at year's end. Of the additional 40 refugees from the former Yugoslavia admitted in 1995, only 12 remain.

Section 3. Respect for Political Rights: The Right of Citizens to Change Their Government

The monarchy is hereditary in the male line. The 25-member unicameral legislature is elected every 4 years. Suffrage is universal for adults over age 20, and balloting is secret. A two-party coalition has formed the Government since 1938. Other parties operate freely; one nongovernmental party is currently in Parliament: the

Freie Liste. The Government regularly puts initiatives and referendums to popular vote.

Since women gained the right to vote in 1984, a growing number are active in politics. Two women are Members of Parliament, and two—one the Foreign Minister—are among the five members of the Cabinet. Women serve on the executive committees in the major parties.

Section 4. Governmental Attitude Regarding International and Nongovernmental Investigation of Alleged Violations of Human Rights

The sole local human rights organization, Justitia Et Pax, is an informal group of about 10 persons who monitor prison conditions and assist foreign workers with immigration matters.

No requests were received from any source for investigation of human rights violations.

Section 5. Discrimination Based on Race, Sex, Religion, Disability, Language, or Social Status

The law prohibits discrimination on the basis of race, language, or social status, and the authorities respect these provisions.

Women.—The law prohibits all forms of domestic violence, and the Government vigorously prosecutes those who violate the law. The local shelter provided refuge for 27 abused women in 1996, only 3 of whom were Liechtenstein citizens.

Societal discrimination still limits opportunities for women in fields traditionally dominated by men. In accordance with a 1992 constitutional amendment mandating equality for women, Parliament has amended a significant number of statutes to ensure equality of treatment, including the citizenship law, the employment law, the law on labor conditions, and the tax law.

Children.—The Government supports programs to protect the rights of children and matches contributions made to the four nongovernmental organizations monitoring children's rights. There is no societal pattern of abuse against children. The U.N. Convention on the Rights of the Child came into force in January. On October 30, the Parliament ratified the European Convention on Recognition and Enforcement of Decisions Concerning Custody of Children and on Restoration of Custody of Children. At the same time, it also ratified the European Convention on the Legal Status of Children Born out of Wedlock.

People With Disabilities.—Although the law does not expressly prohibit discrimination against people with disabilities, complaints of such discrimination may be pursued in the courts.

The Government has required that buildings and government services be made accessible for people with disabilities.

Section 6. Worker Rights

a. *The Right of Association.*—All workers, including foreigners, are free to associate, join unions of their choice, and select their own union representatives. The sole trade union represents 13 percent of the work force, but it looks after the interests of nonmembers as well. It is a member of the World Confederation of Labor but is represented on an ad hoc basis by a Swiss union.

Workers have the right to strike except in certain essential services. No strikes are known to have taken place in the last 26 years. The law does not provide specific protection for strikers. Employers may dismiss employees for refusal to work; such dismissals may be contested.

b. *The Right to Organize and Bargain Collectively.*—The law provides for the right of workers to organize and bargain collectively. However, collective bargaining agreements are generally adapted from ones negotiated by Swiss employers and unions.

There are no export processing zones.

c. *Prohibition of Forced or Compulsory Labor.*—The law prohibits forced or compulsory labor, and there were no reports of violations.

d. *Minimum Age for Employment of Children.*—The law generally prohibits employment of children under 16 years of age; however, exceptions may be made, under certain circumstances, for some employment of youths older than age 13 and for those leaving school after age 14.

e. *Acceptable Conditions of Work.*—There is no national minimum wage, but even the lowest actual wages afford a decent living for workers and their families. The law sets the maximum workweek at 45 hours for white-collar workers and employees of industrial firms and sales personnel, and 50 hours for all other workers. The actual workweek is usually 40 to 43 hours. With few exceptions, Sunday work is not allowed. Workers over age 20 receive at least 4 weeks of vacation; younger ones, at least 5 weeks.

The law sets occupational health and safety standards, and the Department for Worker Safety of the Office of the National Economy effectively enforces these provisions.

LITHUANIA

Lithuania is a parliamentary democracy, having regained its independence in 1990 after more than 50 years of forced annexation by the Soviet Union. The Constitution, adopted by referendum in 1992, established a 141-member unicameral legislature, the Seimas; a directly elected president, who functions as Head of State; and a government formed by a prime minister and other ministers, appointed by the President and approved by the Seimas. The Government exercises authority with the approval of the Seimas and the President. In fair elections in 1992, the Lithuanian Democratic Labor Party (LDDP)—the successor to the Communist Party of Lithuania, which in 1989 broke away from the Soviet Communist Party—won a majority of parliamentary seats and formed the Government. In 1993 voters elected Algirdas Brazauskas, then Chairman of the LDDP, as President. The Conservatives prevailed in the October and November parliamentary elections, followed by the Christian Democrats. The two parties formed a coalition government (the first in Lithuania's history) in December.

A unified national police force under the jurisdiction of the Interior Ministry is responsible for law enforcement. The State Security Department is responsible for internal security and reports to Parliament and the President. The police committed a number of human rights abuses.

Since independence Lithuania has made steady progress in developing a market economy. Over 40 percent of state property, including most housing and small businesses, has been privatized. Trade is diversifying, with a gradual shift to Western markets. The largest number of residents are employed in agriculture (24.8 percent), followed by industrial enterprises (19.8 percent, including electricity, gas, and water supply), followed by wholesale and retail trade (12.3 percent). About 35 percent of those employed work for state enterprises, while 65 percent are employed in private companies. The agricultural sector's high proportion of the work force reflects a lack of efficient consolidation of small private farms and represents a vocal protectionist current in economic policy debates. The banking system remains weak. The inflation rate for the first half of 1996 was 10.2 percent, compared with 16.7 percent for the same time period in 1995. Per capita gross domestic product in 1996 was estimated at $2,000 (8,000 litas) and unemployment in October was 6.4 percent. The balance of trade remains negative due to imports of gas and other energy products from Russia. Major exports include textile and knitwear products, timber and furniture, electronic goods, food, and chemical and petroleum products.

The Government generally respects the human rights of its citizens, but problems remain in some areas. Police on occasion beat detainees and abuse detention laws. Police corruption is on the rise, and prison conditions remain poor.

Some journalists allege that government officials apply pressure on them not to criticize governmental policies or acts. Jewish cemeteries are sporadically subjected to some vandalism and pilferage. Violence and discrimination against women and child abuse are serious problems. The Government took steps to assist people with disabilities.

RESPECT FOR HUMAN RIGHTS

Section 1. Respect for the Integrity of the Person, Including Freedom From:

a. *Political and Other Extrajudicial Killing.*—There were no reports of political or other extrajudicial killings.

b. *Disappearance.*—There were no reports of politically motivated disappearances. There is a problem, however, of women who have been forced—or willingly sold—into prostitution by mafia gangs (see Section 5). Their families, unaware of the situation, claim that they have disappeared or have been kidnaped.

c. *Torture and Other Cruel, Inhuman, or Degrading Treatment or Punishment.*—The Constitution specifically forbids torture, and there were no reports of its use. However, police sometimes beat or otherwise physically mistreated detainees. The local press reported that incidents of police brutality are becoming more common. In many instances, the victims reportedly are reluctant to bring charges against police officers for fear of reprisals. In past years the Ministry of the Interior has been unwilling to publicize statistics on reported cases of police brutality. However, this year the Ministry has compiled a detailed list of abuses: 371 officers were recalled from duty for negative activities in the first 9 months of 1996—231 for disciplinary problems, 72 for various traffic violations, 9 for abusing their occupational privileges, and 10 for brutality. The Interior Ministry states that district police inspectors are the most negligent in the force. The Minister requested the establishment of an internal affairs group that would be responsible for monitoring police abuses. However, the group has yet to be formed. The Commissar General states that during the year 337 officers were dismissed for wrongdoing, and 38 officers for criminal activity with the highest number of abuses occurring in the border police department. President Brazauskas has initiated an amendment to the Police Force Law, whereby the President would have the power to dismiss the Commissar General, and the police force would be separate from the Ministry of the Interior.

Human rights violations continue in the military despite renewed efforts by military to quash criminal bullying—a practice inherited from the former Soviet armed forces. Rolandas Slukinas, a 21-year-old married conscript deserted after 1 month in the army because of constant taunting and beatings. Moreover, the chief resident of one of the major hospitals in Vilnius stated that soldiers in the army are constantly being treated for injuries resulting from abuse. In the first 6 months of the year, that same hospital alone treated four soldiers for broken jawbones. The Lithuanian Human Rights Protection Association recommended that the Parliament take action on the problem and require the Ministry of Defense to prevent violations of human rights in the armed forces.

Prison conditions are poor. Due to limited resources, most are overcrowded and poorly maintained. Prisoners on death row or serving life sentences are required to wear special striped uniforms. Human rights monitors are permitted to visit prisons.

d. *Arbitrary Arrest, Detention, or Exile.*—Except in cases that come under provisions of the Preventive Detention Law (described below), police may detain a person for up to 72 hours based upon reliable evidence of criminal activity. Under a law passed in June, a judge must also approve the detention. At the end of that period, police must decide whether or not to make a formal arrest, and a magistrate must approve an arrest warrant. The authorities have a total of 10 days to present supporting evidence. Once a suspect is formally charged, prosecutors may keep the suspect under investigative arrest for up to 2 months before taking the suspect to court. In exceptional cases, investigative arrest may be extended by a further 6 to 9 months with the written approval of the Prosecutor General. The Constitution provides for the right to an attorney from the moment of detention.

In an effort to cope with the rise in violent organized crime, in 1993 Parliament passed the Preventive Detention Law pertaining to persons suspected of being violent criminals. The law, which was passed as a temporary measure, allowed police, but not the internal security and armed forces, to detain suspected violent criminals for up to 2 months rather than only for the standard 72-hour period. The effect of the law is to give prosecutors and investigators additional time to conduct an investigation and file formal criminal charges against the detainee. Those apprehended must be released after 2 months if an investigation does not lead to formal charges. Local police commissioners must obtain the Prosecutor General's approval of each arrest carried out under the provisions of this law. In the first 9 months of the year, 230 people were detained pursuant to this law compared with over 500 for all of 1995. Of these 230 detainees, only 66 were released after the specified 2 month time period.

The Parliament voted in December 1995 to extend this law for an additional year, maintaining provisions carried over from 1995 modifications, including checks on prosecutorial abuse. The law requires that a detainee: (1) must be informed within 3 hours following arrest about the length of the preventive detention being considered (not to exceed 2 months); and (2) must be brought before a court within 48 hours of arrest for a ruling on the legality of the detention. Furthermore, a detainee has the legal right to consult with an attorney during the period of detention. The law gives law enforcement officials wide latitude in making arrest decisions and may be open to abuse. Parliamentarians who voted against the extension stated that preventive detention was not in keeping with the Constitution and the European Convention on Basic Human Rights and Freedoms. The Prosecutor General, however, reported that although a drastic measure, it is effective. In several well-publicized cases, the law helped to convict and sentence dangerous criminals to lengthy prison terms. In many other instances, however, the suspects were freed without charge after expiration of the maximum detention period, leading some observers to believe that the police are abusing the length of the detention period provided by this law.

There is no provision for exile, nor is it practiced.

e. *Denial of Fair Public Trial.*—The Constitution provides for an independent judiciary, and the judiciary is independent in practice.

Efforts continued in 1996 to reform legal codes imposed during the Soviet era. Parliament passed new civil and criminal procedure codes as well as a Court Reform Law in 1995. The judicial system presently consists of a two-tier structure of district courts and a Supreme Court, which is an appellate court. There is also a Constitutional Court. Court decisions are arrived at independently. The Prosecutor General exercises an oversight responsibility through a network of district prosecutors who work with police investigators—employed by the Ministry of the Interior—in preparing the prosecution's evidence for the courts. The institution of lay assessors was abolished at the end of 1994.

Under the provisions of the Court Reform Law, two new kinds of courts are being created. Local district courts are being set up below the present district courts to handle cases at the municipal level, while a new appellate court level is hearing appeals arising from district court decisions, thereby reducing the case load of the overburdened Supreme Court. Moreover, a commercial court is in operation through the district courts.

An arbitration system is pending. In addition, as a result of accession to the Council of Europe, the Ministry of Justice has begun a thorough review of Lithuania's laws with a view towards bringing them into accord with the provisions of the European Convention on Human Rights.

The Constitution provides defendants with the right to counsel. In practice the right to legal counsel is abridged by the shortage of trained advocates who find it difficult to cope with the burgeoning numbers of criminal cases brought before the courts. Outside observers have recommended the establishment of a public defender system to regularize procedures for provision of legal assistance to indigent persons charged in criminal cases. By law defense advocates have access to government evidence and may present evidence and witnesses. The courts and law enforcement agencies generally honor routine, written requests for evidence.

Government rehabilitation of over 50,000 persons charged with anti-Soviet crimes during the Stalin era led to reports in 1991 that some people alleged to have been involved in crimes against humanity during the Nazi occupation had benefited from this rehabilitation. A special judicial procedure was established to examine each case in which an individual or organization raised an objection that a rehabilitated person may have committed a crime against humanity. In 1994 the Supreme Court overturned the rehabilitation of three persons whose cases were pending from 1993; there have been no such rulings by the Supreme Court since. Presently there is no legal procedure in Lithuania regulating the annulment of rehabilitation.

Formal charges have not been brought against Lithuanian-American Aleksandras Lileikis, an alleged war crime suspect. After being stripped of his U.S. citizenship in May for concealing his World War II activities, which allegedly included persecuting Jews when he headed the security police of the Vilnius district under Nazi control, the 89-year-old Lileikis returned to Vilnius. The Prosecutor General's office is passively investigating the case of Lileikis' activities in Nazi-occupied Lithuania but has not pressed charges against him. They have yet to complete their interrogation of Lileikis, ostensibly due to his poor health. Lileikis denies the charges.

There were no reports of political prisoners.

f. *Arbitrary Interference With Privacy, Family, Home, or Correspondence.*—The Constitution provides for the right to privacy. The authorities do not engage in indiscriminate or widespread monitoring of the correspondence or communications of citizens. With the written authorization of a prosecutor or judge, however, police and the security service may engage in surveillance and monitoring activities on grounds of national security. Except in cases of hot pursuit or the danger of disappearance of evidence, police must obtain a search warrant signed by a prosecutor before they may enter private premises.

It is widely assumed, however, that law enforcement agencies have increased the use of a range of surveillance methods to cope with the expansion of organized crime. There is some question as to the legal basis of this police surveillance, but there are no known legal challenges to such surveillance.

Section 2. *Respect for Civil Liberties, Including:*

a. *Freedom of Speech and Press.*—The Constitution provides for freedom of speech and of the press. The Government generally respects these rights in practice.

Prior restraint over either print or broadcast media and restrictions on disclosure are prohibited, unless the Government determines that national security is involved. Nevertheless, journalists working for the state-owned electronic media complained about pressure by superiors to avoid criticism of government policies in their television and radio reporting. The Parliament adopted its long-awaited media law in

July, after a draft public information law failed to pass in November 1995 because most independent news publications and many prominent journalists protested that it was too restrictive. The new media law introduced an element of self-regulation but postponed a difficult decision on television advertising. Under the new law, the media are to create a special ethics commission and ombudsman to check libel cases and other complaints. The final version of the law allows reporting on the private lives of officials as long as the information affects the welfare of the people.

The independent print media has flourished since independence, including a wide range of economic newspapers and specialty magazines. Officially there are over 2,000 newspapers and magazines registered, but only a fraction are still published.

Many investigative journalists covering organized crime were harassed by and received death threats from organized "crime families."

Five private radio stations, including one broadcasting in Polish, are on the air. Two private television stations also broadcast regular programming to wide audiences. Representatives of the private electronic media have complained for some time about unfair broadcasting rates that the Government sets, which allegedly favor the state radio and television stations.

There are no restrictions on academic freedom.

b. *Freedom of Peaceful Assembly and Association.*—There are no laws that prohibit public gatherings. Citizens must inform local government authorities of planned demonstrations. During the first 6 months of 1996, pensioners protested 12 times, demanding higher pensions and better health care.

The Constitution provides for, and the authorities respect, the right of citizens to associate freely. The Communist Party of Lithuania and other organizations associated with the Soviet regime continue to be banned. There are no special requirements to form an association or political party.

c. *Freedom of Religion.*—The Constitution provides for religious freedom, and the Government usually respects this provision in practice. The Law on Religious Communities and Associations was passed in October 1995. It grants religious communities, associations, and centers property rights to prayer houses, homes, and other buildings and permits construction necessary for their activities. Article 5 of this law mentions nine religious communities that have been declared "traditional" by the law and therefore are eligible for governmental assistance: Latin Rite Catholics, Greek Rite Catholics, Evangelical Lutherans, Evangelical Reformers, Orthodox, Old Believers, Jews, Sunni Muslims, and Karaites. There are no restrictions on the activities of other religious communities.

Relations between the Government and the officially registered Jewish community are good. However, the Hasidic Chabad Lubavich community is having difficulties registering as a traditional Jewish religion. The Ministry of Justice argues that the Chabad Lubavich is not a part of Lithuania's historical, spiritual, or social heritage and therefore cannot be registered as traditional (Article 5 of the Law on Religious Communities and Associations). The Ministry states that the Chabad Lubavich does not have a continuity of traditions and is a separate branch of Judaism than that followed by the traditional Lithuanian Jewish religious community. Furthermore, they state that the Hasidic movement only began in Lithuania in the 18th century and has been suspended twice. The Chabad Lubavich counter that the suspension of their activity during the war years and after was imposed by Nazi and Soviet occupiers. They also have protested the disassociation of the Hasidic movement from Judaism. The Chabad Lubavich continue to press for recognition as a traditional religion. They have been allowed to operate a kindergarten.

d. *Freedom of Movement Within the Country, Foreign Travel, Emigration, and Repatriation.*—Under the law, citizens and permanent residents are permitted free movement within the country and the right to return to the country. There are no restrictions on foreign travel. A growing number of refugees prompted the Government to begin plans for building a refugee detention center and other refugee facilities. Scandinavian countries are willing to assist this endeavor financially. The vast majority of refugees are fleeing economic, rather than political, conditions in their countries. However, in April a group of 40 Asian refugees briefly threatened to starve themselves if they were not granted political asylum. Officials placated them, ending the hunger strike, but stated that the refugees' request cannot be granted. There were about 500 refugees waiting to be deported at year's end. Lithuania is prepared to begin readmission agreement discussions with Russia and has concluded an agreement with Ukraine.

The refugee issue in Lithuania is closely linked to developments in Russia and other neighboring countries of the former Soviet Union, as it is mainly a transit country. Although a delimitation agreement has been signed between Lithuania and Belarus, the border has not yet been formally demarcated. Moreover, Lithuania has not signed readmission agreements with Belarus and Russia. During the year the

Government established a refugee registration center in the town of Pabrade. The reception center includes status determination procedures for those officially seeking asylum. There are approximately 400 economic refugees at the center.

Lithuania has not signed the 1951 Geneva Convention on the Status of Refugees or its 1967 Protocol. However, the Government adopted the Law on Refugee Status on July 4, which is expected to be ratified in 1997. It describes a refugee as foreigner who has reasonable grounds to fear persecution in his own country because of race, religion, national origin, social status, or political beliefs, cannot be efficiently defended in his own country, or has good reason to be afraid to request such defense. Moreover, Lithuania observes the principle that no person may be returned to a territory where he may be exposed to persecution. The Government cooperates with the Office of the United Nations High Commissioner for Refugees and other humanitarian organizations in assisting refugees. There were no reports of forced expulsion of those having a valid claim to refugee status.

The issue of first asylum did not arise in 1996.

Section 3. Respect for Political Rights: The Right of Citizens to Change Their Government

Lithuania is a parliamentary democracy. The election law provides for a secret ballot in parliamentary elections. Of 141 parliamentary seats, 71 are elected directly and 70 through proportional representation. According to a new election law adopted by the Seimas in June, only those parties that receive more than 5 percent of the total ballots (or 7 percent for coalitions) are allowed representation in the Parliament. National minority slates have been exempt from this rule in the past, but despite the new guidelines ethnic Lithuanians, Poles, Russians, and Jews were all elected to the new Parliament in the fall elections.

The Citizenship Law, adopted in 1991 and amended in October 1995, is inclusive with regard to the country's ethnic minorities. The law provides citizenship to persons who were born within the borders of the Republic; who were citizens of Lithuania prior to 1940 and their descendants; or who became citizens under previous legal authority. More than 90 percent of Lithuania's ethnic Russian, Polish, Belarusian, and Ukrainian inhabitants received citizenship.

Qualification for naturalization of persons not covered by the above-mentioned categories requires a 10-year residency, a permanent job or source of income, knowledge of the Constitution, renunciation of any other citizenship, and proficiency in Lithuanian.

While there are no legal restrictions on women's participation in politics or government, they are underrepresented in political leadership positions. There are now 24 female deputies in the 141-member Seimas up from 9 before the fall elections, and 2 female ministers (up from 1) will serve in the new Cabinet.

Section 4. Governmental Attitude Regarding International and Nongovernmental Investigation of Alleged Violations of Human Rights

Most government authorities cooperate with local nongovernmental organizations and actively encourage visits by international and nongovernmental human rights groups. A key exception is the Ministry of Interior, which has continually refused to release information on police brutality and statistics on corruption-related incidents. The Association for the Defense of Human Rights in Lithuania is an umbrella organization for several small human rights groups, all of which operate without government restriction. In 1994 the Government established the Department of International and Human Rights within the Ministry of Justice, which monitors law and legal practice to determine whether these are in accord with Lithuania's international obligations.

Section 5. Discrimination Based on Race, Sex, Religion, Disability, Language, or Social Status

The Constitution prohibits discrimination based on race, sex, religion, disability, or ethnic background. However, discrimination against women persists.

Women.—Abuse of women at home is reportedly common, especially in connection with alcohol abuse by husbands, but institutional mechanisms for coping with this problem are only now being formed. The Norwegian Ministry of Foreign Affairs and the women's organization Fokus have allotted 280,000 Norwegian krona ($111,947) for the establishment of a women's crisis center in Vilnius. At the shelter women will be able to receive professional counseling and support as well as medical aid. The religious organization Caritas opened a six-room shelter in Vilnius in September as well. According to one sociological survey, 20 percent of women reported experiencing an attempted rape, while another 33 percent reported having been beaten at least once in their lives. There was a 10 percent drop in rape occurrences in the first half of 1996. Official statistics on the incidence of abuse of women in the home are not filed separately from other categories of assault. The Ministry of Interior stated that 30 women were killed in the first half of 1996 due to arguments resulting from jealousy or domestic problems. This represents 34.5 percent of all murders during that time period. In addition, 43 women reportedly were severely beaten during the first half of 1996. Women's groups report some resistance among law enforcement officials to collecting and releasing such statistics. Persons convicted of rape generally receive sentences of from 3 to 5 years in prison.

There have been some women, mostly underage, who have been forced—or willingly sold—into prostitution by mafia gangs. Some agree to go out of naivete, others consciously, intending to become rich. Although some women go to the West of their own free will, many others are lured by deception: e.g., by advertisements in newspapers where seemingly innocent jobs are offered—work as "au pairs", bar dancers, or waitresses. Women are also tricked into prostitution through false marriage advertisements. According to 1995 statistics from the Ministry of the Interior, 80 Lithuanian women engaged in prostitution were deported from Israel (the number for 1996 was 30), 9 from Germany, 5 from the Netherlands, and 4 from Poland. Their families are often unaware of the situation and believe that they have disappeared or been kidnaped. An official from the Ministry of Foreign Affairs stated that about 99 percent of women who have been reported missing are actually willingly working as prostitutes in the West.

The Constitution provides for equal rights for men and women, and official policy specifies equal pay for equal work. Generally, men and women receive the same pay for comparable work, but women are significantly underrepresented in some professions and in the managerial sector as a whole. Significant inequalities in society based on gender continue, and there are still very conservative views about the role of women. The fact that women's enrollment now exceeds that of men in some university departments has prompted university administrators to introduce preferential entrance criteria for men to redress what is perceived as an abnormal state of affairs. Parliamentary deputies speaking about female deputies in public sometimes make unflattering comments based on gender stereotypes without eliciting any public reaction.

Children.—The Ministries of Social Protection and of the Interior share official responsibility for the protection of children's rights and welfare. Starting in 1994, the Children's Rights Service of the Ministry of Social Protection took on many of the functions formerly handled by the Interior Ministry and its subordinate police officers throughout the country, thereby focusing more attention on the social welfare needs of children. There are 56 branches of the Children's Rights Protection Council throughout Lithuania. This Council registers and cares for children in dysfunctional and abusive families, registering some 26,000 this year. Furthermore, a "village" for orphaned children has been built near Vilnius by the German organization SOS Kinderdorf for $10 million.

Child abuse is a problem. The press has been thorough in reporting increases in cruelty to children, including sexual abuse, intentional starvation, beatings, and murder. Authorities reported that seven children were killed as a result of severe beatings by parents in the first half of 1996. No department or organization collects information on child abuse, however. Moreover, there are no specific criminal codes for child pornography, sexual abuse, or sex tourism. There is only one rehabilitation center for children who have been sexually abused in the country.

Social welfare workers believe that child abuse in connection with alcohol abuse by parents is a serious problem. Moreover, the prevalence of authoritarian values in family upbringing has discouraged more active measures against child abuse.

People With Disabilities.—The Government designated 1996 the Year for Disabled Persons. More than 350,000 people with disabilities live in Lithuania—10,000 of them children. The Law on Integrating Disabled People, passed in 1991, provides for a broad category of rights and government benefits to which disabled people are legally entitled. The Parliament allotted $7.5 million (31 million litas—more than double the $3.25 million disbursed in 1994) for the betterment of facilities for the disabled, prosthetics, specially equipped vans, and other technology. An apartment building specially designed for people with various disabilities being built in Lithuania's second-largest city, Kaunas, should be completed in 1997. A center for deaf children is being created, as is a program for children with special orthopedic problems.

Religious Minorities.—A small Jewish community exists, largely in main cities. Jewish leaders called on officials to provide better police protection for Jewish cemeteries in Kaunas, Vilnius, and Klaipeda, which have been subject to some sporadic vandalism and pilferage.

National/Racial/Ethnic Minorities.—Minority ethnic groups—including Russians, Poles, Belarusians, and Ukrainians—comprise roughly 20 percent of the population.

A few hundred representatives of the Polish minority protested in June against a law depriving ethnic minorities of preference in elections (see Section 3). Poles also protested the redrawing of the boundaries of Vilnius to include a region heavily populated with ethnic Poles. They are angered by the rise in taxes that accompanies inclusion in the city of Vilnius.

Lithuania amended article 47 of its Constitution to allow foreigners to purchase land. The new law, which allows only citizens from European Union and NATO nations to own land, discriminates against citizens of other nations, notably those from the former Soviet Union.

Many public sector employees were required to attain a functional knowledge of Lithuanian within several years, although the authorities have been granting liberal extensions of the date by which this is to be achieved. During the first 8 months of 1996, language testing committees tested 4,025 people for whom Lithuanian is not a native language. Of those examined, 3,349 were certified as language qualified. To gain citizenship, 120 people were tested, 97 of whom passed. There is no documented evidence of job dismissals based on the language law. The authorities have indicated that the intent of the law is to apply moral incentives to learn Lithuanian as the official language of the State; they have asserted that no one would be dismissed solely because of an inability to meet the language requirement.

Section 6. Worker Rights

a. *The Right of Association.*—The Constitution and the 1991 Law on Trade Unions recognize the right of workers and employees to form and join trade unions. The Law on Trade Unions formally extends this right to employees of the police and the armed forces, although the Collective Agreements Law of 1991 does not allow collective bargaining by government employees involved in law enforcement and security related work. In 1990 the Lithuanian branch of the Soviet Union's All-Union Central Council of Trade Unions, including 23 of 25 trade unions, renamed itself the Confederation of Free Trade Unions (CFTU) and began asserting increased independence from its Soviet parent. In 1993 the CFTU joined eight other unions that also had been part of the All-Union Central Council to form the Lithuanian Trade Union Center (LTUC).

The Lithuanian Workers' Union (LWU) was formed in 1990 as an alternative to the CFTU. Unlike the CFTU/LTUC, the LWU was an early supporter of Lithuanian independence from the Soviet Union and actively sought Western free trade union contacts. The LWU claims a dues-paying membership of 50,000 workers organized in 35 regional groupings.

The Law on Trade Unions and the Constitution provide for the right to strike, although public officials providing essential services may not do so. Many workers threatened to strike because of low wages, but there were no major strikes in 1996. There are no restrictions on unions affiliating with international trade unions.

b. *The Right to Organize and Bargain Collectively.*—The Collective Agreements Law provides for collective bargaining and the right of unions to organize employees, although several provisions reportedly hinder the establishment of new union organizations. According to the law, unions, in order to be registered, must have at least 30 founding members in large enterprises or have a membership of one-fifth of all employees in small enterprises. Difficulties commonly arise in state enterprises in which employees are represented by more than one union. LWU officials charge that managers in some state enterprises discriminate against LWU organizers and have on occasion dismissed employees in retribution for their trade union activities. The LWU also charges that the judicial system is slow to respond to LWU grievances regarding dismissals from work. LWU representatives claim that state managers sometimes prefer the CFTU/LTUC over LWU unions as collective bargaining partners.

In general trade union spokesmen say that managers often determine wages without regard to trade union wishes, except in larger factories with well-organized trade unions. The Government issues periodic decrees that serve as guidelines for state enterprise management in setting wage scales. The LWU and the LTUC engage in direct collective bargaining over wages at the workplace level. Wage decisions are increasingly being made at the enterprise level, although government ministries still retain some control over this sphere in state-owned enterprises. The LWU reports that it supplements its bargaining efforts with active lobbying in government ministries that own enterprises. During the first 6 months of 1996 prices increased faster than the growth of wage increases, thereby reversing a process of real wage growth that had begun in 1993.

There are no export processing zones.

c. *Prohibition of Forced or Compulsory Labor.*—The Constitution prohibits forced labor, and this prohibition is observed in practice.

d. *Minimum Age for Employment of Children.*—The legal minimum age for employment of children without parental consent is 16 years. The legal minimum age with the written consent of parents is 14 years. Free trade union representatives assert that the mechanisms for monitoring minimum age legislation are rudimentary. Complaints about infringement of child labor regulations generally are referred to local prosecutors who investigate the charges and take legal action to stop violations. Available evidence suggests that child labor is rare.

e. *Acceptable Conditions of Work.*—The legal minimum wage was raised on September 1 from $30 (120 litas) to $75 (300 litas) per month. The minimum wage does not provide a decent standard of living for a worker and family. The average wage in the public sector is $166 (663 litas) per month. The Council of Ministers and the Ministry of Social Protection periodically set the minimum wage. Every 3 months these government bodies must submit their minimum wage proposals to the Parliament, which has the right to approve or revise the minimum wage level. Enforcement of the minimum wage is almost nonexistent, in part because the Government does not want to exacerbate the unemployment problem. (The unemployment rate during the second quarter of 1996 was 14.2 percent.) The 40-hour workweek is standard, with a provision for at least one 24-hour rest period. For a majority of the population, living standards remain low. The poorest households spend 68 percent of their income on food, compared to 45 percent in wealthier households.

The Constitution provides that workers have the right to safe and healthy working conditions. In 1993 a Labor Safety Law went into effect, setting the rights of workers confronted with hazardous conditions and providing legal protection for workers who file complaints about such conditions. The State Labor Inspection Service, which the law established, is charged with implementing the Labor Safety Law. Regional labor inspection offices, each of which employs only two or three officials, are severely understaffed. They closed 77 enterprises or departments of enterprises found to be in violation of safety regulations during the first 6 months of 1996. Unsafe conditions caused by worn, outdated industrial technologies are reportedly widespread, and 36 work-related deaths were recorded in the first 6 months of 1996.

LUXEMBOURG

Luxembourg is a constitutional monarchy with a democratic, parliamentary form of government. The role of the Grand Duke is mainly ceremonial and administrative. The Prime Minister is the leader of the dominant party in the popularly elected Parliament. The Council of State, whose members are appointed by the Grand Duke, serves as an advisory body to the Parliament. The judiciary is independent.

The Government effectively controls the security apparatus, which consists of police and gendarmerie.

Luxembourg has a prosperous market economy with active industrial and service sectors. The standard of living and level of social benefits are high.

The Constitution and laws provide for the full range of human rights, and the Government respects these rights in practice.

RESPECT FOR HUMAN RIGHTS

Section 1. Respect for the Integrity of the Person, Including Freedom From:

a. *Political and Other Extrajudicial Killing.*—There were no reports of political or other extrajudicial killings.

b. *Disappearance.*—There were no reports of politically motivated disappearances.

c. *Torture and Other Cruel, Inhuman, or Degrading Treatment or Punishment.*—The law prohibits such practices, and there were no reports that officials employed them.

Prison conditions meet minimum international standards. The Government permits prison visits by human rights monitors.

d. *Arbitrary Arrest, Detention, or Exile.*—The Constitution prohibits arbitrary arrest, detention, or exile, and the Government observes this prohibition.

The law stipulates that judicial warrants are required for arrests except in cases of hot pursuit. Within 24 hours of arrest the police must lodge charges and bring suspects before a judge. Suspects are not held incommunicado. They are given immediate access to an attorney, at government expense for indigents. The presiding judge may order release on bail.

Exile is never imposed.

e. *Denial of Fair Public Trial.*—The Constitution provides for an independent judiciary, and the Government respects this provision in practice. The judiciary provides citizens with a fair and efficient judicial process. The independent judiciary is headed by the Supreme Court, whose members are appointed by the Grand Duke. Defendants are presumed innocent. They have the right to public trial and are free to cross-examine witnesses and to present evidence. Either the defendant or the prosecutor can appeal a ruling; appeal results in a completely new judicial procedure, with the possibility that a sentence may be increased or decreased.

In response to a 1995 decision by the European Court of Human Rights, the Government passed legislation establishing an administrative court system. The European Court had held that Luxembourg's Council of State could no longer serve as both a legislative advisory body, approving all legislation enacted, and as an administrative court, reviewing citizen challenges to that legislation. The dual role of the Council of State was seen by the Court as a violation of the right to a fair trial. The new administrative courts were to begin functioning on January 1, 1997.

There were no reports of political prisoners.

f. *Arbitrary Interference With Privacy, Family, Home, or Correspondence.*—The Constitution prohibits such practices, government authorities generally respect these prohibitions, and violations are subject to effective legal sanction.

Section 2. *Respect for Civil Liberties, Including:*

a. *Freedom of Speech and Press.*—The law provides for freedom of speech and press, and the Government respects these rights in practice. Print media are privately owned. The privately owned national radio and television company has exclusive television broadcasting rights within the country. A permit system allows establishment of other private radio stations. Radio and television broadcasts from neighboring countries are freely available.

Academic freedom is fully respected.

b. *Freedom of Peaceful Assembly and Association.*—The law provides for these rights, and the Government respects them in practice.

c. *Freedom of Religion.*—The Constitution provides for freedom of religion, and the Government respects this right in practice. There is no state religion, but the State pays the salaries of Roman Catholic, Protestant, and Jewish clergy, and several local governments maintain sectarian religious facilities.

d. *Freedom of Movement Within the Country, Foreign Travel, Emigration, and Repatriation.*—The law provides for these rights, and the Government respects them in practice.

The Government cooperates with the United Nations High Commissioner for Refugees and other humanitarian organizations in assisting refugees. A new law establishes procedures for granting the right of asylum in conformity with procedures in other European Union countries. The Government provides first asylum and granted it to three persons in 1996. The Government also continued to allow about 1,800 persons from the former Yugoslavia to remain in protected status on humanitarian grounds. The Government does not expel those having a valid claim to refugee status; there were no reports during the year of the forced return of persons to countries where they feared persecution.

Section 3. *Respect for Political Rights: The Right of Citizens to Change Their Government*

Luxembourg is a multiparty democracy. Suffrage is universal for citizens ages 18 and above, and balloting is secret. National parliamentary elections are held every 5 years.

Women are active in political life. Of 60 Members of Parliament, 11 are women, as are 3 members of the Cabinet. The mayors of several major municipalities, including the capital, are women.

Section 4. *Governmental Attitude Regarding International and Nongovernmental Investigation of Alleged Violations of Human Rights*

Human rights groups operate without government restriction. Government officials are cooperative and responsive to their views.

Section 5. *Discrimination Based on Race, Sex, Religion, Disability, Language, or Social Status*

The law prohibits racial, sexual, or social discrimination, and the Government enforces these provisions. Blatant societal discrimination occurs only rarely.

Women.—Neither society nor the Government is tolerant of violence against women, and the Government prosecutes persons accused of such. The Government funds organizations providing shelter, counseling, and hot lines. The main shelter provides refuge to about 65 abused women per year, many with their children, and responds to between 40 and 45 telephone calls per day. About 150 to 200 cases of sexual abuse occur in an average year.

Women enjoy the same property rights as men. In the absence of a prenuptial agreement, property is divided equally upon dissolution of a marriage.

The law mandates equal pay for equal work. To date there have been no work-related discrimination suits. Women constitute 36.2 percent of the work force (1995 data). The Ministry for the Promotion of Women has a mandate to encourage a climate of equal treatment and opportunity in fact as well as in law. The Ministry has initiated a preschool education project on gender issues, a secondary school mentoring project for girls, and a study of the image of women in the media.

Children.—The Government demonstrates a strong commitment to children's rights and welfare through its well-funded systems of public education and medical care, which are available equally to girls and boys. Education law mandates school attendance from ages 4 to 16. Schooling is free through the secondary level, and the Government provides some financial assistance for postsecondary education.

There is no societal pattern of abuse directed against children. Child abuse does not appear to be widespread, and laws against child abuse are enforced. An organization for the prevention of child abuse estimates that there are about 300 new cases a year. Several organizations provide counseling and telephone hot line services to abused children and their families. The Government began a campaign in the schools to educate children about sexual abuse. A new shelter for girls who are victims of sexual abuse is scheduled to open in January 1997.

People With Disabilities.—There is no discrimination against disabled persons in employment, education, or in the provision of other state services. The law does not directly mandate accessibility for the disabled, but the Government pays subsidies to builders to construct "disabled-friendly" structures. Despite government incentives, only a modest proportion of buildings and public transportation have been modified to accommodate people with disabilities.

The Government helps disabled persons obtain employment and professional education. By law, businesses and enterprises with at least 25 employees must fill a quota for hiring disabled workers and must pay them prevailing wages. The quota is fixed according to the total number of employees, and employers who do not fulfill them are subject to sizable monthly fines. There have been no known complaints of noncompliance.

National/Racial/Ethnic Minorities.—Although foreigners constitute over 30 percent of the total population, antiforeigner incidents remain infrequent. The Government granted to citizens of European Union countries who reside in Luxembourg the right to vote and run in municipal elections. Minimum residency requirements are 6 years for voters and 12 years, including 6 months residence in the commune, for candidates to run for town councils. The Government also formed a commission to initiate projects against racism in conjunction with the European Year Against Racism.

Section 6. Worker Rights

a. *The Right of Association.*—All workers have the right to associate freely and choose their representatives. About 65 percent of the labor force is unionized. Membership is not mandatory. Unions operate free of governmental interference. The two largest labor federations are linked to, but organized independently of, major political parties. The law prohibits discrimination against strike leaders, and a labor tribunal deals with complaints.

The Constitution provides all workers with the right to strike except for government workers such as police, armed forces, and hospital personnel providing essential services. Legal strikes may occur only after a lengthy conciliation procedure between the parties; the Government's National Conciliation Office must certify that conciliation efforts have ended for a strike to be legal. There were no legal strikes during the year, and there have been no illegal strikes since 1979.

Unions maintain unrestricted contact with international bodies.

b. *The Right to Organize and Bargain Collectively.*—The law provides for and protects collective bargaining, which is conducted in periodic negotiations between centralized organizations of unions and employers. Enterprises having 15 or more employees must have worker representatives to conduct collective bargaining. Enterprises with over 150 employees must form joint works councils composed of equal numbers of management and employee representatives. In enterprises with more than 1,000 employees, one-third of the membership of the supervisory boards of directors must be employees' representatives.

The law provides for adjudication of employment-related complaints and authorizes labor tribunals to deal with them. A tribunal can impose a fine on an employer found guilty of antiunion discrimination, but it cannot require the employer to reinstate a worker fired for union activities.

There are no export processing zones.

c. *Prohibition of Forced or Compulsory Labor.*—The law prohibits forced or compulsory labor, and neither occurs.

d. *Minimum Age for Employment of Children.*—The law prohibits employment of children under age 15 and requires children to remain in school until age 16. Apprentices who are 15 or 16 years old must attend school in addition to their job training. Adolescent workers under age 18 have additional legal protection, including limits on overtime and the number of hours that can be worked continuously. The Ministries of Labor and Education effectively monitor the enforcement of child labor and education laws.

e. *Acceptable Conditions of Work.*—The law provides for minimum wage rates at levels that vary according to the worker's age and number of dependents. The minimum for a single worker over age 18 is approximately $8.29 (Lux F 253) per hour. Supporting a family is difficult on the minimum wage, but most employees earn more than the minimum.

National legislation mandates a workweek of 40 hours. Premium pay is required for overtime or unusual hours. Employment on Sunday is permitted in continuous-process industries (steel, glass, and chemicals), and for certain maintenance and security personnel; other industries have requested permission for Sunday work, which the Government has granted on a case-by-case basis. Work on Sunday, allowed for some retail employees, must be entirely voluntary and compensated at double the normal wage; and employees must be given compensatory time off on another day, equal to the number of hours worked on Sunday. The law requires rest breaks for shift workers and limits all workers to a maximum of 10 hours per day including overtime. All workers receive at least 5 weeks of paid vacation yearly, in addition to paid holidays.

The law mandates a safe working environment. An inspection system provides severe penalties for infractions. The Labor Inspectorate of the Ministry of Labor, and the Accident Insurance Agency of the Social Security Ministry, carry out their inspections effectively.

No laws or regulations specifically guarantee workers the right to remove themselves from dangerous work situations without jeopardy to continued employment, but every worker has the right to ask the Labor Inspectorate to make a determination, and the Inspectorate usually does so expeditiously.

THE FORMER YUGOSLAV REPUBLIC OF MACEDONIA

The Former Yugoslav Republic of Macedonia, which became independent following the breakup of Yugoslavia, is a parliamentary democracy. International monitors judged its second multiparty elections in 1994 to be generally free and fair despite numerous procedural irregularities. The judiciary is independent in practice.

The Ministry of Interior oversees a security apparatus that includes uniformed police, border police, and the state intelligence service. The Ministry is under the control of a civilian minister, and a parliamentary commission oversees operations. Some members of the police on occasion were responsible for instances of human rights abuses.

Historically, Macedonia was the least prosperous of the Yugoslav republics. Its economy was closely tied to the other republics, especially Serbia. Conflict in the region and sanctions imposed on Serbia and Montenegro, along with the problems of transition to a market economy, led to severe economic difficulties. A Greek trade embargo imposed in 1994, in a dispute over the country's name, flag, and constitution was lifted in October 1995 following the signing of an interim accord between the two countries. Trade sanctions against Serbia were suspended following conclusion of the Dayton Accords the next month. In the circumstances of these two border closures, gross domestic product had fallen an estimated 50 percent. Economic growth resumed during the year with a slight increase in industrial production, but recovery is expected to be slow. Official unemployment is about a third of the work force, and many people who are ostensibly employed are in fact furloughed. Even employed workers routinely receive their salaries several months late.

The Government generally respected the human rights of its citizens. However, there were credible reports of occasional police abuse of prisoners, and some unconfirmed charges of police harassment of political opponents of the Government. Violence and discrimination against women are problems.

Minorities, including ethnic Albanians, ethnic Turks, and ethnic Serbs, raised various allegations of human rights infringements and discrimination. Ethnic Macedonians hold a disproportionate number of positions in state institutions. Government promises to boost the number of minorities in these institutions have been implemented only slowly, except for the conscript ranks of the armed forces. Ethnic Albanians continue to demand increased Albanian-language education, greater representation in public sector jobs, and increased media access. Since a violent demonstration in 1995, an unofficial Albanian-language university in Tetovo has tacitly been allowed to operate but its rector and four other university activists were imprisoned in July in connection with the 1995 incident.

The Government has agreed in principle to many of the ethnic Albanian demands, but claims that resource constraints are slowing progress on implementing the agreements. A summer campaign by ethnic Albanian opposition parties demanding a change in the Constitution that would result in an ethnically based federalism, which was denounced by both the Government and its ethnic Albanian coalition partner, fueled underlying ethnic tensions. However, no major clashes took place during the year.

RESPECT FOR HUMAN RIGHTS

Section 1. Respect for the Integrity of the Person, Including Freedom From:

a. *Political and Other Extrajudicial Killing.*—There were no reports of political killings.

There were allegations that a Romani woman died in July as a result of being hit on the head with a police baton, but the Ministry of Interior announced that an autopsy determined she died of a heart attack.

The investigation continued at year's end into the 1995 car bomb attack on President Gligorov.

b. *Disappearance.*—There were no reports of politically motivated disappearances.

c. *Torture and Other Cruel, Inhuman, or Degrading Treatment or Punishment.*—The Constitution prohibits such treatment and punishment. However, police occasionally used excessive force during and following the arrest of criminal suspects.

Prison conditions are generally acceptable. Reports of abuse by prison authorities (who are separate from the police) are rare.

d. *Arbitrary Arrest, Detention, or Exile.*—The Constitution states that a person must be arraigned in court within 24 hours of arrest and sets the maximum duration of detention pending trial at 90 days. The accused is entitled to contact a lawyer at the time of arrest and to have a lawyer present during police and court proceedings. According to human rights monitors and criminal defense attorneys, police sometimes violate the 24-hour requirement and deny immediate access to an attorney. Although the law requires warrants for arrests, this provision is sometimes ignored, and the warrant issued only some time after the arrest. There is no systematic use of detention as a form of nonjudicial punishment. Incommunicado detention is not practiced. There were no confirmed reports of arbitrary arrest. Opposition political parties alleged police harassment of their members, but there were no clear, confirmed cases.

The Government does not use forced exile.

e. *Denial of Fair Public Trial.*—The Constitution provides that the courts are autonomous and independent, and the judiciary is independent in practice.

The court system is three tiered, comprising municipal courts, district courts, and a Supreme Court. A Constitutional Court deals with matters of constitutional interpretation. Few trials appear to be influenced by political considerations, although there is a widespread perception that bribery is common in the courts.

The Constitutional Court has a mandate to protect the human rights of citizens, but has not taken action in any case in this area. Parliament has yet to pass implementing legislation to establish a people's ombudsman to defend citizens' constitutional and legal rights.

Trials are presided over by government-appointed judges. The judges are assisted by two members of the community who serve essentially as consulting jurors, although the judge has the final word. Trials are open to relatives of the accused and the public with permission of the judge. The president of the court decides on the admission of journalists. Some trials—notably those of minors—are not open to the public.

Members of the Albanian community have charged that the Government holds two persons as political prisoners. They claim that the imprisonment of the Tetovo University rector and another activist is a violation of their human rights and that they are being punished for acts of speech that should be protected. The rector called on ethnic Albanians to resist police efforts to close the university 2 days before a violent incident in February 1995 and was convicted of inciting to riot on the basis of that statement. Another Albanian political leader was convicted of interfering with the duties of the police despite a lack of strong evidence that he was doing anything more than observing the incident. (The defendants' sentences were substantially reduced on appeal, and they returned to detention in July to serve out their terms.) Government officials say that they had to proceed against the defendants to prevent further violent incidents.

f. *Arbitrary Interference With Privacy, Family, Home, or Correspondence.*—The right to privacy of person, home, and correspondence is provided for in the Constitution. Although no instances of abuses were substantiated, officials of opposition parties charge that their telephones were tapped and their privacy violated by the state security service.

Section 2. Respect for Civil Liberties, Including:

a. *Freedom of Speech and Press.*—The Constitution forbids censorship and provides for freedom of speech, public access, public information, and freedom to establish private media outlets. The Government generally respects these provisions in practice.

Several daily newspapers are published in Skopje, as well as numerous weekly political and other publications. Newspapers in Albanian and a Turkish are distributed nationally and subsidized by the Government. Most newspapers and magazines published in the country are government owned and government oriented. Opposition parties allege that government control and manipulation of the media prevent them from getting their message across.

The state-owned media report opposition press conferences and statements, and in general do a reasonably creditable job of covering the major opposition parties. The overall balance of coverage, however, is in favor of the Government. The leading newspaper publisher is a government company that owns the only modern high-speed printing plant in the country, as well as most newspaper kiosks. Opposition groups complain that they are charged high prices for the services of the printing plant. Newspapers can be imported from Bulgaria, Serbia, Albania, and Greece only with the permission of the Ministry of Internal Affairs. Very few copies of Bulgarian newspapers are permitted into the country.

Academic freedom is respected in theory and practice. However, an attempt to open an Albanian-language university was declared illegal by the Government (see Section 5).

b. *Freedom of Peaceful Assembly and Association.*—The Constitution provides for these rights and the Government generally respects them in practice. Advance notification of large meetings is required, but the authorities do not appear to abuse that requirement, and opposition rallies occur regularly without major incident.

Political parties and organizations are required to register with the Interior Ministry in compliance with a comprehensive political party registration law. More than 40 political parties are registered, including ethnically based parties of Albanians, Turks, Serbs, and Roma. No cases of denial of registration were reported during the year.

c. *Freedom of Religion.*—The Constitution specifically provides for freedom of religion for the "Macedonian Orthodox Church and other religious communities and groups," and the Government generally does not interfere with the practice of religion.

While only the Macedonian Orthodox Church is mentioned by name in the Constitution, it does not enjoy official status. However, members of other religious communities credibly charge that the Government favors it, based on the ease with which it can obtain property and building permits for new construction. During 1995 the authorities destroyed at least two or three houses that did not have such permits and were being used as mosques.

The refusal of the Serbian Orthodox Church to recognize the independence of the Macedonian Orthodox Church has led to difficulties for ethnic Serbs who wish to worship in their own church. On a number of occasions the Government has refused Serbian Orthodox priests permission to enter the country and apparently plans to continue doing so until the Serbian Church recognizes the Macedonian Church.

Protestant groups have complained about incidents of harassment and vandalism to which police have failed to respond. They also complain that they cannot register their churches and obtain regular employment status for employees, and that on several occasions they have been prevented from holding religious meetings in venues outside churches.

d. *Freedom of Movement Within the Country, Foreign Travel, Emigration, and Repatriation.*—Citizens are permitted free movement within the country as well as the right to leave and return. These rights may be restricted for security, public health, and safety reasons, but are fully respected in practice.

The law on citizenship is highly restrictive, requiring, for example, 15 years of residence for citizenship. This has left some people who were living legally in the country at the time of independence without citizenship. The law particularly affects ethnic Albanians who had moved to the country from other parts of Yugoslavia before independence. As citizens of the predecessor state living legally in the territory of the country at the time of independence, they feel they have a right to citizenship. Some Albanian political leaders also charge that Ministry of Interior officials responsible for making citizenship determinations discriminate against Albanian applicants. The officials are said to make more demanding documentary requirements and to act on applications slowly. There were also plausible charges that officials were demanding bribes in return for a favorable decision. There is some truth to these charges, but citizenship problems also affected many ethnic Macedonians and others.

The Government cooperated with the office of the United Nations High Commissioner for Refugees and other humanitarian organizations in assisting refugees. It has provided protective status to several thousand refugees from Bosnia and Herzegovina but ceased admitting new claimants, except those with close family ties to the country, as of mid-1993. There were no reports of persons seeking first asylum in 1996. There were no reports of forced return of persons to a country where they feared persecution. The Government is concerned about the small flow of economic migrants from neighboring Albania. If caught, they are deported.

Section 3. Respect for Political Rights: The Right of Citizens to Change Their Government

Citizens elected a President by popular vote for the first time in 1994, and at the same time chose a new Parliament in the second multiparty elections in the country's postwar history, the first since independence. Opposition groups charged the Government with massive fraud and announced a boycott of the second round. International monitors, under the auspices of the Council of Europe and the then-Conference on Security and Cooperation in Europe, found the elections to be generally free and fair despite widespread irregularities attributed largely to careless organization. Local elections on November 17 were a further test of the relative strength of government versus opposition parties and of whether the Government has put in place internationally recognized electoral practices. Foreign monitors found the elections to be a considerable improvement over 1994 and concluded there was no need to mount a major monitoring for the second round on December 1. The governing party won a plurality of the vote.

The unicameral Parliament governs the country. The prime minister, as head of government, is selected by the party or coalition that can produce a majority in the Parliament. He and the other ministers may not be Members of Parliament. The Prime Minister is formally appointed by the President, who is head of state, chairman of the security council, and commander-in-chief of the armed forces.

Although no formal restrictions exist on the participation of women in politics and government, they are underrepresented in these areas. Only 1 of 20 ministers is a women, and only 4 of 120 Members of Parliament are women.

Minorities, including ethnic Albanians, ethnic Turks, ethnic Serbs, and Roma, have political parties to represent their interests. Minorities nevertheless complained that the political structures were biased against them. Some ethnic Albanians claimed that Albanian-majority districts had far more voters than ethnic Macedonian ones, thus violating the "one-person, one-vote" principle. There is some merit to this complaint, but the largest ethnic Albanian party was closely consulted by the Government during a redistricting of the country's municipalities in September, and obtained changes in the law that it sought. Some ethnic Albanians also complain that alleged discrimination against them in citizenship decisions effectively disenfranchises a large portion of their community (see Section 2.d.).

Ethnic minority Members of Parliament include 19 Albanians, 2 Roma, 1 Serb, and 1 Turk. Five Albanian ministers are in the cabinet, one of whom is both a deputy prime minister and minister of economy.

Section 4. Governmental Attitude Regarding International and Nongovernmental Investigation of Alleged Violations of Human Rights

Human rights groups and ethnic community representatives meet freely with foreign representatives without government interference. A forum for human rights exists and operates freely. The Government welcomes independent missions by foreign observers but objects to being included in the mandates of human rights observers for the former Yugoslavia.

Section 5. Discrimination Based on Race, Sex, Religion, Disability, Language, or Social Status

The Constitution provides for equal rights for all citizens regardless of race, sex, national or social origin, political or religious beliefs, property, or social status. However, societal discrimination against ethnic minorities and violence against women are problems.

Women.—Women's groups report that there is widespread familial violence against women. Cultural norms discourage the reporting of such violence; criminal charges on grounds of domestic violence are very rare. A crisis hot line received over 1,000 calls during 1996.

Women possess the same legal rights as men. Macedonian society, in both the Muslim and Christian communities, remains traditionally patriarchal, and advancement of women into nontraditional roles is limited. Some prominent professional women are now visible in society. Women's advocacy groups include the Union of Associations of Macedonian Women and the League of Albanian Women.

Children.—The country's strong commitment to the rights and welfare of children is limited by resource constraints. The Government provides compulsory education through the eighth grade. Both family budgets and the Government's ability to provide social relief in cases of need are under strain because of poor economic conditions.

There is no pattern of societal abuse against children.

National/Racial/Ethnic Minorities.—The population of 2.2 million is composed of a variety of national and ethnic groups, mainly Macedonians, Albanians, Turks, Roma, Serbs, and Vlakhs. All citizens are equal under the law. The Constitution provides for the protection of the ethnic, cultural, linguistic, and religious identity of minorities, including state support for education in minority languages through secondary school.

Ethnic tensions and prejudices are evident within the population. The Government is committed to a policy of peaceful integration of all ethnic groups into society but faces political resistance and the persistence of popular prejudices, especially in the lower levels of administration. Moreover, the economic crisis makes it difficult for the Government to find resources to fulfill minority aspirations, such as more education in minority languages. Despite underlying tensions, few incidents occurred during the year.

The main political opposition is more nationalistic than the governing coalition and objects even to some modest steps to meet the needs of minorities. Popular prejudices can affect the relationships that ethnic minorities have with the Government: For example, ethnic Macedonian parents in Kumanovo kept their children from attending school because the children's teacher, also an ethnic Macedonian, was married to an ethnic Turk, and thus considered of "doubtful religious confession." The parents were charged with the misdemeanor offense of not sending their children to school.

Representatives of the ethnic Albanian community, by far the largest minority group with 22.9 percent of the population, are the most vocal in charging discrimination. Expressing concern about government manipulation of the data, the Albanian community boycotted a 1990 census. An internationally monitored census held during the summer of 1994 to correct the situation was marred by some boycott threats. Experts from the Council of Europe monitored the conduct of the census and were generally satisfied that it was carried out fairly and accurately and that virtually the entire ethnic Albanian community took part. Turks make up about 4 percent of the population, Roma 2.3 percent, and Serbs 2 percent. About 8,500 citizens declared themselves Vlakhs.

Underrepresentation of ethnic Albanians in the military and police is a major grievance of the community. Even in areas dominated by ethnic Albanians, the police force remains overwhelmingly ethnic Macedonian. The Ministry of Interior says that the police force as a whole is only 4 percent ethnic Albanian. The Ministry is making efforts to recruit ethnic Albanian police cadets, but complains that it is very difficult to attract qualified candidates. Ethnic Albanian leaders allege that there is continued discrimination against those who do apply.

There has been more improvement in the proportion of ethnic Albanians recruited into the military. Military service is a universal male obligation, and it appears that most young men, whatever their ethnic origin, report for service. The proportion of ethnic Albanians in the ranks is now estimated at 25 percent. Fewer ethnic Albanians are in the officer corps, but some progress is being made in this area as well. Few ethnic Albanians serve as Defense Ministry civilian employees; however, the Deputy Minister is an ethnic Albanian.

Albanian-language education is a crucial issue for the ethnic Albanian community; it is seen as vital for preserving Albanian heritage and culture. Almost all ethnic Albanian children receive 8 years of education in Albanian-language schools. Less than 40 percent—a slight improvement over 1995—go on to high school, partly because of the lack of available classes and partly because the traditional nature of ethnic Albanian society means that many families in rural areas see no need to educate their children, especially girls, beyond the eighth grade.

The establishment of an unofficial Albanian-language university in Tetovo in 1995 led to a violent clash between demonstrators and police in which one ethnic Albanian died and about 30 people were injured. Since then the Government has tacitly allowed the University, which it still considers to be illegal, to function without giving it any official sanction.

Ethnic Turks, who make up about 4 percent of the population, have also complained of governmental, societal, and cultural discrimination. Their main complaints center on Turkish-language education and media. One continuing dispute has been over the desire of parents who consider themselves Turkish to educate their children in Turkish despite the fact that they do not speak Turkish at home. The Education Ministry refuses to provide Turkish-language education for them, noting that the Constitution provides for education in the mother tongue, not a foreign language. The parents have banded together to hire teachers of their own, but this kind of private education is not legally authorized.

Ethnic Serbs, who comprise about 2 percent of the population, also complained about discrimination, alleged censorship of the Serbian press, and their inability to worship freely in the Serbian Orthodox church.

Little tension is evident between the Roma and other citizens of the country. There has been some progress in providing supplementary Romani-language education, but no call has been made for a full curriculum. There is some Romani-language broadcasting.

There are also a number of Macedonian Muslims and Bosnian Muslims in the country.

The Government established a 13-member Council on Ethnic Relations with representatives of the country's main ethnic groups. The council has not, however, played an active role.

People With Disabilities.—Social programs to meet the needs of the disabled exist to the extent that government resources allow. Discrimination on the basis of disability is forbidden by law. No laws or regulations mandate accessibility for persons with disabilities.

Section 6. Worker Rights

a. *The Right of Association.*—The 1991 Constitution provides citizens with the right to form trade unions. There are restrictions in this area for the military, police, and the civil service.

The Council of Trade Unions of Macedonia is the successor organization to the old Communist labor confederation. It maintains the assets of the old unions and is the Government's main negotiating partner on labor issues. While its officers may tend to oppose strikes because of the legacy of the past, they appear to be genuinely independent of the Government and committed to the interests of the workers they represent. An Association of Independent and Autonomous Unions was formed in 1992, and independent unions have been allowed to organize without harassment by the Government or official unions.

The disastrous economic situation led to many brief strikes. These were undertaken mainly by employees of state-owned companies, many of which were shedding workers in the process of privatization and delaying their pay by up to several months. In most cases, the workers and unions understood the difficulties facing their companies and showed great restraint.

b. *The Right to Organize and Bargain Collectively.*—The Constitution implicitly recognizes employees' right to bargain collectively. Collective bargaining is still in its infancy. Legislation in this area has yet to be passed by Parliament.

There are no export processing zones.

c. *Prohibition of Forced or Compulsory Labor.*—Legal prohibitions against forced labor are observed in practice.

d. *Minimum Age of Employment for Children.*—The constitutional minimum age for employment of children is 15 years. Younger children, however, are often seen peddling cigarettes or other small items or working in family-owned shops or on family farms. Children may not legally work nights but are permitted to work 42-hour weeks. Education is compulsory through grade eight. The Ministries of Interior and Labor are responsible for enforcing laws regulating the employment of children.

e. *Acceptable Conditions of Work.*—The average monthly wage in September was about $220 (8,874 denars). The minimum wage is, by law, two-thirds of the average wage. The economic crisis meant that few workers could support a family on their wages alone and had to do additional work in the informal economy or draw on savings.

Yugoslavia had extensive laws concerning acceptable conditions of work, including an official 42-hour workweek with a minimum 24-hour rest period and generous vacation and sick leave benefits. The Former Yugoslav Republic of Macedonia adopted many of these provisions, including the workweek and rest period. The Constitution guarantees safe working conditions, temporary disability compensation, and leave benefits. Although there are laws and regulations on worker safety remaining from the Yugoslav era, credible reports suggest that they are not strictly enforced. The Ministry of Labor and Social Work is responsible for enforcing regulations pertaining to working conditions.

If workers have safety concerns, employers are supposed to address the dangerous situations. Should they fail to do so, employees may leave the dangerous situation without forfeiting their job.

MALTA

Malta is a constitutional republic and parliamentary democracy. The Head of State (President) appoints as the Head of Government (Prime Minister) the leader of the party that gains a plurality of seats in the quinquennial elections for the unicameral legislature.

The police are commanded by a civilian commissioner under the effective supervision of the Government.

The economy is a mixture of state-owned and private industry, with tourism and light manufacturing as the largest sectors, and it provides residents a moderate to high standard of living.

The Government is strongly committed to human rights. An independent judiciary upholds the Constitution's protections for individual rights and freedoms. Cultural and religious patterns reinforce the homogeneity of society. Societal discrimination against women persists, and domestic violence is a problem.

RESPECT FOR HUMAN RIGHTS

Section 1. Respect for the Integrity of the Person, Including Freedom From:

a. *Political and Other Extrajudicial Killing.*—There were no reports of political or other extrajudicial killings.

In October 1995, Fathi Shiqaqi, a leader of the Palestinian group, Islamic Jihad, was shot and killed in Sliema. There were no developments in the case.

b. *Disappearance.*—There were no reports of politically motivated disappearances.

c. *Torture and Other Cruel, Inhuman, or Degrading Treatment or Punishment.*—The Constitution prohibits inhuman or degrading punishment or treatment. There were no reports that officials employ them.

Prison conditions meet minimal international standards, and the Government permits visits by human rights monitors.

d. *Arbitrary Arrest, Detention, or Exile.*—The Constitution and law provide for freedom from arbitrary arrest, detention, or exile, and the Government observes this prohibition. The police may arrest a person for questioning on the basis of reasonable suspicion but within 48 hours must either release the suspect or lodge charges. Arrested persons have no right to legal counsel during this 48-hour period. Persons incarcerated pending trial are granted access to counsel. Bail is normally granted.

e. *Denial of Fair Public Trial.*—The judiciary is independent of the executive and legislative branches. The Chief Justice and nine judges are appointed by the President on the advice of the Prime Minister. There is a civil court, a commercial court, and a criminal court. In the latter, the presiding judge sits with a jury of nine . The Court of Appeal hears appeals from decisions of the civil and commercial courts. The Court of Criminal Appeal hears appeals from judgments of conviction by the criminal court. The highest court, the Constitutional Court, hears appeals in cases involving violations of human rights, interpretation of the Constitution, and invalidity of laws. It also has jurisdiction in cases concerning disputed parliamentary elections and electoral corrupt practices. There are also inferior courts presided over by a magistrate.

The Constitution requires a fair public trial before an impartial court. Defendants have the right to counsel of their choice, or (if they cannot pay the cost) to court-appointed counsel at public expense. Defendants enjoy a presumption of innocence. They may confront witnesses, present evidence, and have the right of appeal.

There were no reports of political prisoners.

f. *Arbitrary Interference With Privacy, Family, Home, or Correspondence.*—The Constitution protects privacy of the home and prohibits electronic surveillance. The

Government respects these provisions. Police officers with the rank of inspector and above may issue search warrants based on perceived reasonable grounds for suspicion of wrongdoing.

Section 2. Respect for Civil Liberties, Including:

a. *Freedom of Speech and Press.*—The Constitution provides for freedom of speech and the press, and the Government respects these rights in practice. However, the 1987 Foreign Interference Act bans foreign participation in local politics during the period leading up to elections. An independent press, an effective judiciary, and a functioning democratic political system combine to ensure freedom of speech and of the press, including academic freedom. One biweekly, three daily, and seven weekly newspapers freely express diverse views. Two government-owned television stations, an opposition party television station, a commercial cable network, and eight private radio stations also function freely.

b. *Freedom of Peaceful Assembly and Association.*—The Constitution provides for the right of peaceful assembly, and the Government respects this right in practice.

c. *Freedom of Religion.*—The Constitution provides for freedom of religion, and the Government respects this right in practice. The state-supported religion is Roman Catholicism. The Government grants subsidies only to Roman Catholic schools. Students in government schools may opt to decline instruction in Roman Catholicism.

d. *Freedom of Movement Within the Country, Foreign Travel, Emigration, and Repatriation.*—The Government does not arbitrarily restrict movement within the country, foreign travel, or emigration. A court order may prohibit the departure from the country of anyone who is the subject of a formal complaint alleging nonfulfillment of an obligation, such as nonpayment of a debt or nonsupport of an estranged spouse.

The Government cooperates with the Office of the United Nations High Commissioner for Refugees. It did not force the return of any refugees to a country where they feared persecution. Since 1992 the Government has granted temporary refugee status to over 1,000 persons, pending their relocation abroad, and on December 6, the first asylum refugee population amounted to 538 persons (275 cases involving 375 adults and 163 children). The largest refugee groups were: 279 Iraquis; 79 ex-Yugoslavs; 55 Sudanese; 40 Algerians; 39 Palestinians; and 11 Syrians. The Government, however, did not grant refugee status or accept anyone for resettlement. The Government expels or repatriates persons it deems to be economic refugees.

Section 3. Respect for Political Rights: The Right of Citizens to Change Their Government

Citizens exercise this right in multiparty, secret-ballot elections held every 5 years on the basis of universal suffrage for those 18 years of age or over. In the 1996 election, 97 percent of the electorate voted.

Women are underrepresented in government and politics.

Section 4. Governmental Attitude Regarding International and Nongovernmental Investigation of Alleged Violations of Human Rights

Various human rights organizations and persons interested in promoting and protecting human rights operate freely. The Government places no restrictions on investigations by international human rights groups.

Section 5. Discrimination Based on Race, Sex, Religion, Disability, Language, or Social Status

The Constitution and law prohibit discrimination based on sex. The Government respects this prohibition.

Women.—There is no widespread pattern of family violence against women, but continuing reports of such incidents have made plain that the problem exists. A special police unit and several voluntary organizations provide support to victims of domestic violence. For women who are threatened or physically abused, the Government also maintains an emergency fund and subsidizes a shelter.

Prostitution is a serious offense under Maltese law, and heavy penalties are reserved for organizers. Rape and violent indecent assault carry sentences of up to 10 years. The law treats spousal rape the same as any other rape. Divorce and abortion are not legal.

The Constitution provides that all citizens have access, on a nondiscriminatory basis, to housing, employment, and education. While women constitute a growing portion of the work force, they are underrepresented in management. Cultural and traditional employment patterns often direct them either into traditional "women's jobs" (such as sales clerk, secretary, bank teller, teacher, or nurse) or into more rewarding jobs in family owned businesses or select professions (i.e. academia or medicine). Therefore, women generally earn less than their male counterparts, and many leave employment upon marriage. The Government's Department of Equal Status of Women and women's rights groups actively address women's issues. Legislation enacted in 1993 granted women equality in matters of family law, and a 1991 constitutional amendment committed the Government to promoting equal rights for all persons regardless of sex. Redress in the courts for sexual discrimination is available.

Children.—The Government has expressed concern for children's rights and welfare but addresses those concerns within the context of family law. Although sensitive to children's rights, Parliament has failed to pass specific legislation to protect children's rights. The number of reported cases of child abuse has grown as public awareness has increased, but it is not clear whether the actual number of incidents has increased.

People With Disabilities.—The law protects the rights of the disabled. The 1969 Employment of Disabled Persons Act led to greater employment of disabled persons in government agencies. The 1992 Structures Act requires accessibility to public buildings for people with physical disabilities. Overall government and private sector efforts to advance the status of disabled persons have been uneven.

Section 6. Worker Rights

a. *The Right of Association.*—Workers have the right to associate freely and to strike, and the Government respects these rights in practice. Only noncivilian personnel of the armed forces and police are prohibited from striking. There are 24 registered trade unions, representing about 50 percent of the work force.

Although all unions are independent of political parties, the largest, the General Workers' Union, is generally regarded as having close informal ties with the Labor Party. There is no prohibition on unions affiliating internationally.

Under the Industrial Relations Act of 1976, the responsible minister may refer labor disputes either to the Industrial Tribunal (a government-appointed body consisting of representatives of government, employers, and employee groups) or to binding arbitration. The International Labor Organization Committee of Experts objects to a provision of the Act that permits compulsory arbitration to be held at the request of only one of the parties, but neither unions nor employers appear to object to this provision. In practice, a striking union can ignore an unfavorable decision of the Tribunal by continuing the strike on other grounds. No disputes were referred to the Tribunal in 1996.

b. *The Right to Organize and Bargain Collectively.*—Workers are free, in law and practice, to organize and bargain collectively. Unions and employers meet annually with government representatives to work out a comprehensive agreement regulating industrial relations and income policy.

Under the Industrial Relations Act, an employer may not take action against any employee for participation or membership in a trade union. Complaints may be pursued through a court of law, through a tripartite (union-employer-government) tribunal, or through the Commission Against Injustices (a government-appointed body composed of representatives of the Government and the opposition); but most disputes are resolved directly between the parties. Workers fired solely for union activities must be reinstated.

There are no export processing zones.

c. *Prohibition of Forced or Compulsory Labor.*—The Constitution bans forced labor, and it does not occur.

d. *Minimum Age for Employment of Children.*—The law prohibits employment of children younger than the age of 16. This is generally respected, but there is some employment of underage children during summer months, especially as domestics, restaurant kitchen help, or vendors. The Department of Labor enforces the law effectively but is lenient in cases of summer employment of underage youths in businesses run by their families.

e. *Acceptable Conditions of Work.*—The legal minimum wage, $115 (42.38 Malta liri) per week, provides a decent standard of living for a worker and family with the addition of government subsidies for housing, health care, and free education. Wage Councils, composed of representatives of government, business, and unions, regulate workhours; for most sectors the standard is 40 hours per week, but in some trades it is 43 or 45 hours per week.

Government regulations prescribe a daily rest period, which is normally 1 hour. The law mandates an annual paid vacation of 4 workweeks plus 4 workdays. The Department of Labor effectively enforces these requirements.

Enforcement of the 1994 Occupational Health and Safety (Promotion) Act is uneven, and industrial accidents remain frequent. Workers may remove themselves from unsafe working conditions without jeopardy to their continued employment.

MOLDOVA

Moldova gained its independence from the Soviet Union in 1991. In 1994 it adopted a Constitution that provides for a multiparty representative government with power divided among a president, cabinet, parliament, and judiciary. Parliamentary Speaker Petru Lucinschi, running as an independent, was elected President in a second-round runoff election, replacing the incumbent Mircea Snegur. International observers considered the elections to be free and fair. Prime Minister Andre Sangheli and the cabinet resigned immediately after the election, but agreed to remain as caretakers until President Lucinschi could appoint a new government after his January 15 inauguration.

Moldova remains divided, with mostly Slavic separatists controlling the Transnistrian region along the Ukrainian border. This separatist regime has entered negotiations with the national Government on the possibility of a special status for the region. Progress has been blocked, however, by the separatists' continuing demands for "statehood" and recognition of Moldova as a confederation of two equal states. The Organization for Security and Cooperation in Europe (OSCE), the Russian Federation, and Ukraine act as mediators. The two sides have generally observed the cease-fire of July 1992, which ended armed conflict between them, but other agreements to normalize relations have often not been honored. A Christian Turkic minority, the Gagauz, enjoys local autonomy in the southern part of the country.

The Ministry of Internal Affairs has responsibility for the police. The Ministry of National Security controls other security organs. The Constitution assigns to Parliament the authority to investigate the activities of these ministries to ensure that they comply with legislation in effect. There is also a protective service, which guards the President, the Prime Minister, and the Speaker of Parliament. Some members of the security forces committed human rights abuses.

Moldova continued to make progress in economic reform. A privatization program based on vouchers issued to all citizens is virtually complete. However, the economy is largely based on agriculture, and agricultural privatization continued to lag behind. In April the Constitutional Court declared unconstitutional a law slowing the conversion of land belonging to agricultural collectives into private property. In October the Constitutional Court declared unconstitutional a law forbidding private agricultural land sales until 2001 and limiting the period when farmers could withdraw from collectives to a few months a year. Some 50,000 private farmers are officially registered. Estimates of those persons seeking to register range from 100,000 to 150,000. Private land holdings represent only 4 percent of the total land available for agriculture. Per capita gross domestic product is about $430.

The Government generally respects the human rights of its citizens, however, there are problems in some areas. The police occasionally beat detainees and prisoners. Security forces monitor political figures, use unauthorized wiretaps, and at times conduct illegal searches. Prison conditions remain harsh. The judiciary is subject to the influence of the prosecutor's office. The Constitution potentially limits the activities of political parties and the press. Societal discrimination against women persists. Addressing a minority concern, the Constitution allows parents the right to choose the language of education for their children.

The Transnistrian authorities continue to be responsible for human rights abuses, including pressure on the media, questionable detentions, and discrimination against Romanian/Moldovan speakers. Detailed information about the human rights situation in the region is difficult to obtain.

RESPECT FOR HUMAN RIGHTS

Section 1. Respect for the Integrity of the Person, Including Freedom From:

a. *Political and Other Extrajudicial Killing.*—There were no verified reports of politically motivated killings either in Moldova or its separatist region. Information from Transnistria is, however, limited. In June the wife of a former Russian army special investigator being held without charge in Transnistria died under mysterious circumstances. The investigator was released in October, but continues to suffer from a medical condition that considerably worsened while he was being detained because of a lack of adequate treatment.

b. *Disappearance.*—A vice president of the independent television station, which at times has been pressured by the Government, was abducted by men wearing police uniforms in January and has not been seen since. The Ministry of Internal Affairs claims that its personnel were not involved and attributes the abduction to a private settling of criminal accounts.

c. *Torture and Other Cruel, Inhuman, or Degrading Treatment or Punishment.*—There were no allegations of torture by the authorities, but there were credible reports that police sometimes beat prisoners and suspects.

In late December 1995, the home of journalists Tamara Gorinci and her husband of the weekly Mesagerul was invaded by persons in police uniforms and the journalists were beaten. The weekly was running a series on corruption in the carabineri, a small, specialized police unit. There were other attacks on journalists from this publication, as well as others, in late 1995 and early 1996. Circumstances and identities of perpetrators are difficult to establish. The perpetrators in one case were arrested, reportedly nonpolicemen who were engaged in a robbery attempt, but no arrests were made in the other cases.

Conditions in most prisons remain harsh, with serious overcrowding. Spatial norms do not meet local legal requirements. Conditions are especially harsh in prisons used to hold people awaiting trial or sentencing; in September Council of Europe experts criticized the harsh conditions of the facilities for those in detention. These prisons especially suffer from overcrowding, bad ventilation, and a lack of recreational and rehabilitation facilities. Conditions for those serving sentences are only marginally better. The incidence of disease, especially tuberculosis, and malnutrition is high in all facilities. Abuse of prisoners by other prisoners or jailers themselves, ostensibly for disciplinary reasons, has been reduced by the dismissal or retirement of some of the worst offending guards. The Ministry of Justice took over authority for the prisons, replacing the Ministry of Interior.

Human rights monitors are permitted to visit prisons.

After questionable trials, four Moldovans are serving sentences in Transnistria for terrorism-related crimes (see Section 1.e.). The International Committee of the Red Cross (ICRC) was denied the possibility of visiting them despite numerous representations to the Tiraspol authorities.

d. *Arbitrary Arrest, Detention, or Exile.*—The former Soviet Code on Penal Procedure remains in force with some amendments. Prosecutors issue arrest warrants. Under the Constitution, a suspect may be detained without charge for 24 hours. The suspect is normally allowed family visits during this period. The 24-hour time limit was generally respected. If charged, a suspect may be released pending trial. There is no system of bail, but in some cases a friend or relative, in order to arrange release, may give a written undertaking that the accused will appear for trial.

Suspects accused of violent or serious crimes are generally not released before trial. The Constitution permits pretrial arrest for an initial period of 30 days, which may be extended to 6 months. In exceptional cases, Parliament may approve extension of pretrial detention on an individual basis of up to 12 months. The accused has the right under the Constitution to a hearing before a court regarding the legality of his arrest. According to figures provided by the Ministry of Justice in October, 1,746 persons were held in confinement awaiting trial.

According to the Constitution, a detained person must be informed immediately of the reason for his arrest, and must be made aware of the charges against him "as quickly as possible." The accused is provided with the right to a defense attorney throughout the entire process, and the attorney must be present when the charges are brought. Many lawyers point out that in practice, access to a lawyer is generally granted only after a person has been detained 24 hours. If the defendant cannot afford an attorney, the State requires the local bar association to provide one. Because the State is unable to pay standard legal fees, a lawyer who is less than competent or energetic is often chosen.

The Government does not use forced exile.

e. *Denial of Fair Public Trial.*—The Constitution provides for an independent judiciary. Although the prosecutor's office still has undue influence, the independence of the judiciary has increased since the dissolution of the Soviet Union. The Constitutional Court made several rulings that demonstrated its independence. In April the court overturned the Parliament's amendments to the land code that had in effect halted land reform by preventing peasants from individually withdrawing their land from collective farms. Also in April, the court ruled that President Snegur's attempted dismissal of Defense Minister Creanga was unconstitutional. In October the Court overturned a Central Electoral Commission decision to exclude a presidential candidate from competing in the November 17 election by questioning large numbers of the signatures on her electoral petitions. The respective parties complied with these decisions.

The Constitution provides that the President, on the nomination of an expert judicial body, the Superior Court of Magistrates, appoints judges for an initial period of 5 years. They may be reappointed for a subsequent 10 years, after which they serve until retirement age. This provision for judicial tenure is designed to increase judicial independence.

The judiciary consists of lower courts, an appellate court, a Supreme Court, and a Constitutional Court. The Constitutional Court provided for in the 1994 Constitution came into existence in February 1995. A July 1995 law on judicial reforms specified a system of appeals courts. There are district courts of the first instance and five regional tribunals. The Higher Appeals Court and the Supreme Court, which serves as a final court of appeal, are both in Chisinau. The Supreme Court supervises and reviews the activities of the lower courts.

By law defendants in criminal cases are presumed innocent. In practice prosecutors' recommendations still carry considerable weight and limit the defendant's actual presumption of innocence. Trials are generally open to the public. Defendants have the right to attend proceedings, confront witnesses, and present evidence. Defense attorneys are able to review the evidence against their clients when preparing their cases. The accused enjoys a right to appeal to a higher court. Because the Government has been unable to fund fully the new appeals courts mandated in 1995, most of the tribunals and the Higher Appeals Court are not functioning. Cases cannot be appealed directly to the Supreme Court, thereby creating a backlog of cases on appeal. Court decisions involving the restitution of salary or a position are not always implemented.

To date no pattern of discrimination has emerged in the judicial system. The new Constitution provides for the right of the accused to have an interpreter both at the trial and in reviewing the documents of the case. If the majority of participants agree, trials may take place in Russian or another acceptable language instead of Romanian/Moldovan.

There continue to be credible reports that local prosecutors occasionally bring unjustified charges against individuals in retribution for accusations of official corruption or for political reasons. Prosecutors occasionally use bureaucratic maneuvers to restrict lawyers' access to clients.

There were no reports of political prisoners.

In Transnistria four Moldovans, members of the "Ilascu Six," remain in prison following their conviction in 1993 for allegedly killing two separatist officials. International human rights groups raised serious questions about the fairness of the trial, and local organizations alleged that the Moldovans were prosecuted for political reasons, solely because of their membership in the Christian Democratic Popular Front, a Moldovan party that favors reunification with Romania. Family members have been allowed access. However, the Transnistrian "authorities" have refused to allow the ICRC access under standard ICRC terms and conditions, such as access to an entire detention facility and a private meeting. The most recent such attempt was in April.

f. *Arbitrary Interference With Privacy, Family, Home, or Correspondence.*—Both prosecutors and judges may issue search warrants. In some instances searches are conducted without warrants. Courts do not exclude evidence that was illegally obtained. There is no judicial review of search warrants.

The Constitution specifies that searches must be carried out "in accordance with the law," but does not specify the consequences if the law is not respected. It also forbids searches at night, except in the case of flagrant crime.

It is widely believed that security agencies continue to use electronic monitoring of residences and telephones without proper authorization. By law the prosecutor's office must authorize wiretaps and may do so only if a criminal investigation is under way. In practice the prosecutor's office lacks the ability to control the security organizations and police and to prevent them from using wiretaps illegally.

Section 2. Respect for Civil Liberties, Including:

a. *Freedom of Speech and Press.*—The Constitution and the law provide for freedom of speech and the press, although with some restrictions. The Government does not abridge freedom of speech and the print media express a wide variety of political views and commentary. National and city governments own a number of newspapers, but political parties and professional organizations, including trade unions, also publish newspapers.

There were several assaults on journalists engaged in investigations of alleged official corruption (see Section 1.c.). Circumstances and identities of perpetrators are difficult to establish. The perpetrators in one case were arrested; they were reportedly nonpolicemen engaged in a robbery attempt. However, no arrests have been made in the other cases. It is too early to tell if these attacks have had an inhibiting effect on the willingness of the press to investigate corruption.

Several independent radio stations broadcast in Moldova, including a religious one. An independent television station broadcasts in the Chisinau area. The independent media outlets maintain news staffs and conduct a number of public interest programs. The Government owns and operates a television channel that covers the whole country as well as several of the major radio stations. The city government of Balti operates its own television and radio stations.

Parliament removed language in the press law enforcing the prohibitions contained in the Constitution, which forbid "contesting or defaming the State and the people," and political parties that "militate" against the country's sovereignty, independence, and territorial integrity. However, these restrictions remain in the Constitution. They appear to be aimed at journalists publishing material in favor of reunification with Romania or questioning the legal right of the Republic of Moldova to exist.

The Government does not restrict foreign publications. However, Western European and American publications do not circulate widely since they are very expensive by local standards. Some Russian newspapers are available, but do not circulate widely due to their expense. Moldova receives television and radio broadcasts from Romania and Russia. Cable subscribers receive Cable News Network, the U.S. National Broadcasting Corporation, Super Channel, Euro-News, and a number of other news and entertainment networks.

Of the two major newspapers in Transnistria, one is controlled by the regional authorities and the other by the Tiraspol city government. The latter criticizes the regime from time to time. Other print media in Transnistria do not have large circulations and appear only on a weekly or monthly basis. Nonetheless, some of them also criticize local authorities. The one independent cable television station is under constant pressure from the authorities. It had to restrict its activity when it lost a libel suit brought by the local authorities this spring. Most Moldovan newspapers do not circulate in Transnistria. Circulation of all print media in Transnistria is greatly hampered by the local economic crisis, which is more severe than in the rest of Moldova.

The Government respects academic freedom.

b. *Freedom of Peaceful Assembly and Association.*—The law provides for the right to peaceful assembly. The local mayor's office generally issues permits for demonstrations; it may consult the national Government if the demonstration is likely to be extremely large.

The Constitution states that citizens are free to form parties and other social and political organizations. Private organizations, including political parties, are required to register, but applications are approved routinely. The Constitution declares unconstitutional parties that "militate against the sovereignty, independence, and territorial integrity of Moldova."

c. *Freedom of Religion.*—The Government generally permits free practice of religion. A 1992 law on religion codifies religious freedoms, although it contained restrictions that could inhibit the activities of some religious groups. The law provides for freedom of religious practice, including each person's right to profess his religion in any form. It also provides for alternative military service for conscientious objectors, protects the confidentiality of the confessional, allows denominations to establish associations and foundations, and states that the Government may not interfere in the religious activities of denominations. The law, however, requires that religious groups register with the Government in order to hire noncitizens. The law also prohibits proselytizing.

Some Protestant denominations are concerned that the prohibition on proselytizing could inhibit their activities, although many denominations hold revival meetings apparently without official interference. To date the authorities have taken no legal action against individuals for proselytizing. The Salvation Army, however, was unable to register as a religious denomination because it did not meet the requirement of having a Moldovan citizen as the organization's legal head.

Although Eastern Orthodoxy is not designated the official religion, it continues to be a strong religious force and exert significant influence. In 1992 a number of priests broke away from the Moldovan Orthodox Church, which is subordinate to the Moscow Patriarchate, in order to form the Bessarabian Orthodox Church. The Bessarabian Orthodox Church, which sees itself as the legal and canonical successor to the pre-World War II Romanian Orthodox Church in Bessarabia (the part of Moldova between the Dniester and Prut rivers), subordinated itself to the Bucharest patriarchate of the Romanian Orthodox Church. The Government has consistently refused to register the Bessarabian Church, citing unresolved property claims as the principal reason.

The Jewish community, although small, is very active. Jewish leaders reported that their relations with the Government and local authorities were good.

d. *Freedom of Movement Within the Country, Foreign Travel, Emigration, and Repatriation.*—The Government does not restrict travel within the country. Citizens generally are able to travel freely; however, there are some restrictions on emigration. Close relatives with a claim to support from the applicant must give their concurrence. The Government may also deny permission to emigrate if the applicant had access to state secrets. Such cases, however, are very rare, and none were reported in 1996.

Travel between Transnistria and the balance of the country is not prevented. There are regularly scheduled buses. However, the separatist "authorities" do stop and search both incoming and outgoing vehicles. They restrict the flow of information materials, preventing persons from bringing either Moldovan or Western publications into the separatist region.

Moldova is not a party to the 1951 United Nations Convention on the Status of Refugees or its 1967 Protocol. The issue of providing first asylum has never arisen. There were no reports of the forced return of persons to a country where they feared persecution.

Section 3. Respect for Political Rights: The Right of Citizens to Change Their Government

Citizens voted in the first multiparty parliamentary elections in 1994, and in the country's second presidential election in November. Parliamentary Speaker Lucinschi, running as an independent, won a second-round runoff election on December 1. International observers considered the elections to be free and fair. The peaceful transition of presidential power represents further progress in the transition to democracy.

The Transnistrian "authorities," however, refused to allow polling stations to be set up in the separatist region and restricted access of Transnistrian voters to stations in the rest of the country. Turnout from Transnistria in the election was less than 2 percent of those eligible to vote.

Preelection maneuvering caused a realignment of the various registered political parties in the country, plus a fragmentation of the leftist parties represented in Parliament, including both the former ruling party, the Democratic Agrarian Party, and its close ally, the Socialist/Unity Bloc. Incumbent President Snegur is moving to become leader of the rightist opposition, in preparation for parliamentary elections to be held by February 1998. Supporters of President-elect Lucinschi have also moved to establish their own party to compete in these elections. Leftist and agrarian groups are seeking to form coalitions.

The Constitution adopted in 1994 provides for the division of power between the popularly elected President, the Cabinet, the Parliament, and the judiciary. The President, as Head of State, in consultation with the Parliament, appoints the Cabinet and Prime Minister, who functions as the Head of Government. However, a minister can only be dismissed with the assent of the Prime Minister.

In March the President tried to dismiss the Defense Minister, an army general, by using his powers as Supreme Commander of the armed forces. In April the Constitutional Court ruled that the general's position as a government minister meant that he could not be fired without the assent of the Prime Minister. The President immediately accepted the Court's decision, thereby averting a constitutional crisis. Many observers thought that the incident showed a possible deficiency in the Constitution regarding the sharing of executive powers between the offices of the President and the Prime Minister.

Parliamentary elections must take place no later than every 4 years. Given the fragmentation of some of the parliamentary parties as well as the possible need to revise the Constitution, a number of parliamentarians called for parliamentary elections following the presidential elections. Early elections may be necessary if President-elect Lucinschi has difficulty forming a government.

The Constitution states that citizens are free to form parties and other social and political organizations. A controversial article states, however, that those organizations that "are engaged in fighting against political pluralism, the principles of the rule of law, the sovereignty and independence or territorial integrity of the republic of Moldova" are "unconstitutional." Opposition parties, some of which favor rapid or eventual reunification with neighboring Romania, have charged that this provision is intended to impede their political activities.

There are no restrictions in law or practice barring the participation of women or minorities in political life. However, women are generally underrepresented in leading positions of political parties. Women hold only 5 of 104 parliamentary seats. The Association of Moldovan Women, a social and political organization, competed in the 1994 elections, but was unable to gain parliamentary representation. Russian, Ukrainian, Bulgarian, and Gagauz minorities are represented in Parliament. Debate takes place in either the Romanian/Moldovan or Russian language, with translation provided.

Section 4. Governmental Attitude Regarding International and Nongovernmental Investigation of Alleged Violations of Human Rights

Several local human rights groups exist. The local Helsinki Watch organization maintains contacts with international human rights organizations, as does the Helsinki Citizens Assembly, whose president is the chairman of the Parliament's Human Rights Commission. Human rights groups operate without government interference.

The Government has welcomed and supported the work of the OSCE, which has had a mission in the country since 1993 to assist with finding a resolution for the separatist conflict. The OSCE participates in the Joint Control Commission—composed of Russian, Moldovan, Ukrainian, and Transnistrian members—which reviews violations of the cease-fire agreement. The mission now generally enjoys access to the "security zone" along the river dividing the separatist-controlled territory from the rest of Moldova.

Moldova has cooperated with the International Committee of the Red Cross (ICRC) in the past, permitting visits to prisoners from the 1992 conflict (since released).

Since 1993 Transnistrian separatist authorities have not allowed the ICRC access to the four members of the "Ilascu Six" still in prison (see Section 1.e.).

Section 5. Discrimination Based on Race, Sex, Religion, Disability, Language, or Social Status

The Constitution states that persons are equal before the law regardless of race, sex, disability, religion, or social origin. There are remedies for violations, such as orders for redress of grievances, but these are not always enforced.

Women.—Women abused by their husbands have the right to press charges; husbands convicted of such abuse may receive prison sentences (typically up to 6 months). Public awareness of the problem of violence in families is not very high and no special government programs exist to combat spousal abuse. According to knowledgeable sources, women do not generally appeal to police or the courts for protection against abusive spouses because they are embarrassed to do so. Police generally do not consider spousal abuse a serious crime. However, when cases do reach a court, they appear to be treated seriously. Women and legal authorities report that spousal abuse is not widespread. Through November the Ministry of Internal Affairs recorded 276 cases of rape or attempted rape. A newly formed women's crisis group believes that the number of rapes is greatly underreported.

The law provides that women shall be equal to men. However, according to statistics, women have been disproportionately affected by growing unemployment. By law women are paid the same as men for the same work. Although still victimized by societal discrimination, anecdotal evidence suggests that women are more employable than men (being seen as more flexible, better workers), and are working because of economic necessity. There are a significant number of female managers in the public sector; the president of Moldova's leading private sector bank is a woman.

Children.—There is extensive legislation designed to protect children, including extended paid maternity leave and government supplementary payments for families with many children. Ten years of basic education are compulsory, followed by either technical school or further study leading to higher education. The health system devotes extensive resources to child care. No special problems concerning child abuse came to light in 1996 nor is there a societal pattern of abuse of children, but child support programs suffered from inadequate funding along with other government programs.

People With Disabilities.—There is no legal discrimination against people with disabilities. However, there are no laws providing for accessibility of buildings, and there are few government resources devoted to training people with disabilities. The Government does provide tax advantages to charitable groups that assist the disabled.

Religious Minorities.—The Bessarabian Church has been harassed by unknown persons, including a grenade attack in September on the Metropolitan's (the presiding Bishop's) house, which caused no deaths or injuries and only small material damage.

National/Racial/Ethnic Minorities.—The population is about 4.3 million, of which 65 percent are ethnic Moldovans. Ukrainians (14 percent) and Russians (13 percent) are the two largest minorities. A Christian Turkic minority, the Gagauz, lives primarily in the southern regions of the country. They are largely Russian speaking and represent about 3.5 percent of the population.

The 1990 Citizenship Law offered an equal opportunity to all persons resident at the time of independence to adopt Moldovan citizenship. The OSCE's Office of

Democratic Institutions and Human Rights described the law as being very liberal. The law permits dual citizenship on the basis of a bilateral agreement, but no such agreements are in effect. In 1994 the Parliament voted to delay until 1997 implementation of the language testing called for in the Language Law of 1989 which was due to begin in 1994. The principle inherent in the Language Law is that, in dealing with any official or commercial entity, the citizen should be able to choose the language to use. Officials are therefore obligated to know Russian and Romanian/Moldovan "to the degree necessary to fulfill their professional obligations." Since many Russian speakers do not speak Romanian/Moldovan (while educated Moldovans speak both languages), they argued for a delay in the implementation of the law in order to permit more time to learn the language. Addressing a minority concern, the Constitution provides parents with the right to choose the language of instruction for their children.

In the separatist region, however, discrimination against Romanian/Moldovan speakers continued. Schools in the area are required to use the Cyrillic alphabet when teaching Romanian. Many teachers, parents, and students objected to the use of the Cyrillic script to teach Romanian. They believe that it disadvantages pupils in pursuing higher education opportunities in the rest of the Moldova or Romania. (Cyrillic script was used to write the Romanian language in Moldova until 1989, since "Moldovan," as it was then called, was officially decreed during the Soviet era to be a different language than Romanian, which is written in the Latin alphabet. The 1989 Language Law reinstituted the use of the Latin script.)

As a result of an agreement between the Government and the separatist authorities, 19 schools in the separatist region obtained permission in January 1995 to use the Latin alphabet, with salaries and textbooks to be supplied by the Moldovan Ministry of Education. Implementation was modest during the 1995-96 school year, largely due to bureaucratic obstacles imposed by authorities in the separatist region. Separatist authorities rescinded permission a few weeks after the 1996 school year opened in September, with the schools closed by local police and Cossacks. Teachers from these schools were taken from their homes in the evening and held for questioning for a number of hours before being released. Separatist authorities in early October detained several teachers for 6 days before releasing them. At least one teacher from such a school was fired. At year's end, the schools were open but teaching Romanian in Cyrillic script.

Section 6. Worker Rights

a. *The Right of Association.*—The 1990 Soviet Law on Trade Unions, which was enacted by Moldova's then-Supreme Soviet and is still in effect, provides for independent trade unions. Laws passed in 1989 and 1991, which give citizens the right to form all kinds of social organizations, also provide a legal basis for the formation of independent unions. The 1994 Constitution further declares that any employee may found a union or join a union that defends workers' interests. However, there have been no known attempts to establish alternate trade union structures independent of the successor to the previously existing official organizations that were part of the Soviet trade union system.

The successor organization is the General Federation of Trade Unions (GFTU). GFTU's continuing role in managing the state insurance system and its retention of previously existing official union headquarters and vacation facilities provide an inherent advantage over any potential organizers who might wish to form a union outside its structure. However, its industrial or branch unions are becoming more independent entities; they maintain that their membership in GFTU is voluntary and that they can withdraw if they wish. Virtually all employed adults are members of a union.

Government workers do not have the right to strike, nor do those in essential services such as health care and energy. Other unions may strike if two-thirds of the members vote for a strike in a secret ballot. There were several labor actions seeking payment of wage arrears, including a number of strikes by teachers in various parts of the country. High unemployment, both hidden and official, led to worker concern about job security.

Unions may affiliate and maintain contacts with international organizations. GFTU is currently negotiating membership in the International Confederation of Free Trade Unions, and hopes to accede in 1997.

b. *The Right to Organize and Bargain Collectively.*—The law, which is still based on former Soviet legislation, provides for collective bargaining rights. However, wages are set through a tripartite negotiation process involving government, management, and unions. On the national level, the three parties meet and negotiate national minimum wages for all categories of workers. Then, each branch union representing a particular industry negotiates with management and the government ministries responsible for that industry. They may set wages higher than the minimum set on the national level and often do, especially if the industry in question is more profitable than average. Finally, on the enterprise level, union and management representatives negotiate directly on wages. Again, they may set wages higher than had negotiators on the industry level.

There were no reports of actions taken against union members for union activities. The 1990 Soviet Law on Trade Unions provides that union leaders may not be fired from their jobs while in leadership positions or for a period after they leave those positions. This law has not been tested in Moldova.

There are no export processing zones.

c. *Prohibition of Forced or Compulsory Labor.*—The Constitution prohibits forced labor. No instances of it were reported.

d. *Minimum Age for Employment of Children.*—The minimum age for unrestricted employment is 18 years. Employment of those ages 16 to 18 is permitted under special conditions, including shorter workdays, no night shifts, and longer vacations. The Ministry of Labor and Social Protection is primarily responsible for enforcing these restrictions, and the Ministry of Health also has a role. Child labor is not used in industry, although children living on farms do sometimes assist in the agricultural sector.

e. *Acceptable Conditions of Work.*—There is a legal minimum monthly wage of $4 (18 Moldovan lei), but this is used primarily as a basis for calculating fines. The average monthly wage of approximately $41 (184 Moldovan lei) does not provide a decent standard of living for a worker and family. Lowest wages are in the agricultural sector, where they average approximately $23 (102 Moldovan lei a month). Due to severe budgetary constraints, the Government and enterprises often do not meet payrolls for employees. The Constitution sets the maximum workweek at 40 hours, and the Labor Code provides for at least 1 day off per week.

The State is required to set and check safety standards in the workplace. The unions within GFTU also have inspection personnel who have a right to stop work in the factory or fine the enterprise if safety standards are not met. Further, workers have the right to refuse to work but may continue to draw their salaries if working conditions represent a serious threat to their health. In practice, however, the depressed economic situation has led enterprises to economize on safety equipment and generally to show less concern for worker safety issues. Workers often do not know their rights in this area.

MONACO

Monaco is a constitutional monarchy in which the sovereign Prince plays a leading role in governing the country. The Prince appoints the four-member Government, headed by a Minister of State chosen by the Prince from a list of candidates proposed by France. The other three members are Counselors for the Interior (who is usually French), for Public Works and Social Affairs, and for Finance and the Economy. Each is responsible to the Prince. Legislative power is shared between the Prince and the popularly elected 18-member National Council. There are in addition three consultative bodies, whose members are appointed by the Prince: The 7-member Crown Council; the 12-member Council of State; and the 30-member Economic Council, which includes representatives of employers and trade unions.

In addition to the national police force, the "Carabiniers du Prince" carry out security functions. Both forces are controlled by government officials.

The principal economic activities are services and banking, light manufacturing, and tourism.

Individual human rights are provided for in the Constitution and respected in practice. The Constitution distinguishes between those rights that are guaranteed for all residents and those that apply only to the approximately 5,000 who hold Monegasque nationality. The latter enjoy free education, financial assistance in case of unemployment or illness, and the right to vote and hold elective office. Women traditionally have played a less active role than men in public life, but this is changing; women currently hold both elective and appointive offices.

RESPECT FOR HUMAN RIGHTS

Section 1. *Respect for the Integrity of the Person, Including Freedom From:*

a. *Political and Other Extrajudicial Killing.*—There were no reports of political or other extrajudicial killings.

b. *Disappearance.*—There were no reports of politically motivated disappearances.

c. *Torture and Other Cruel, Inhuman, or Degrading Treatment or Punishment.*—The Constitution prohibits such practices, and the authorities respect this prohibition. There were no reports of violations.

Prison conditions meet or exceed minimum international standards, and the Government permits visits by human rights monitors.

d. *Arbitrary Arrest, Detention, or Exile.*—The Constitution bars arbitrary arrest. Arrest warrants are required, except when the detainee is arrested while committing an offense. The police must bring the detainee before a judge within 24 hours to be informed of the charges and of the detainee's rights under the law. Most detainees are released without bail, but the investigating magistrate may order detention on grounds that the suspect might either flee or interfere with the investigation of the case. The magistrate may extend the initial 2-month detention for additional 2-month periods indefinitely. Detainees have the right to counsel, at public expense if necessary. The magistrate may permit family members to see the detainee.

The Government does not forcibly exile its own nationals. However, it does sometimes expel to France non-Monegasque nationals who are in violation of residency laws or who have committed minor offenses, such as disorderly conduct.

e. *Denial of Fair Public Trial.*—Under the 1962 Constitution, the Prince delegated his judicial powers to an independent judiciary. The law provides for fair, public trial, and the authorities respect these provisions. The defendant has the right to be present and the right to counsel, at public expense if necessary. As under French law, a three-judge tribunal considers the evidence collected by the investigating magistrate and hears the arguments made by the prosecuting and defense attorneys. The defendant enjoys a presumption of innocence and the right of appeal.

There were no reports of political prisoners.

f. *Arbitrary Interference With Privacy, Family, Home, or Correspondence.*—The Constitution provides for the individual's right of privacy in personal and family life, at home, and in correspondence, and the Government respects these rights in practice.

Section 2. Respect for Civil Liberties, Including:

a. *Freedom of Speech and Press.*—Freedom of expression is guaranteed. The Monegasque Penal Code, however, prohibits public denunciations of the ruling family. Several periodicals are published. Foreign newspapers and magazines circulate freely, including French journals that specifically cover news in the Principality. Foreign radio and television are received without restriction. Stations that broadcast from the Principality operate in accordance with French and Italian regulations.

Academic freedom is respected.

b. *Freedom of Peaceful Assembly and Association.*—The Constitution provides citizens with the rights of peaceful assembly and association. Outdoor meetings require police authorization, which is not withheld for political or arbitrary reasons. Formal associations must be registered and authorized by the Government.

c. *Freedom of Religion.*—Roman Catholicism is the state religion. The law provides for the free practice of all religions, and the Government respects this right in practice.

d. *Freedom of Movement Within the Country, Foreign Travel, Emigration, and Repatriation.*—Residents move freely within the country and across its open borders with France. Monegasque nationals enjoy the rights of emigration and repatriation. They can be deprived of their nationality only for specified acts, including naturalization in a foreign state. Only the Prince can grant or restore Monegasque nationality, but he is obliged by the Constitution to consult the Crown Council on each case before deciding.

The Government implements the 1951 United Nations Convention Relating to the Status of Refugees. In light of its bilateral arrangements with France, Monaco does not grant political asylum or refugee status unless the request also meets French criteria for such cases. The number of cases is very small. There were no reports of forced expulsion of those having a valid claim to refugee status.

Section 3. Respect for Political Rights: The Right of Citizens to Change Their Government

The 1962 Constitution cannot be suspended, but it can be revised by common agreement between the Prince and the National Council. The Prince plays an active role in government. He names the Minister of State (in effect, the Prime Minister) from a list of names proposed by the French Government. He names as well the three Counselors of Government (of whom the one responsible for the interior is usually a French national). Together the four constitute the Government. Each is responsible to the Prince.

Only the Prince may initiate legislation, although the 18-member National Council may send proposals for legislation to the Government. All legislation and the adoption of the budget require the Council's assent. Elections, which are held every 5 years, are based on universal adult suffrage and secret balloting. Two political parties are currently represented on the Council. There is one independent member.

The Constitution provides for three consultative bodies. The seven-member Crown Council (composed exclusively of Monegasque nationals) must be consulted by the Prince regarding certain questions of national importance. He may choose to consult it on other matters as well. The 12-member Council of State advises the Prince on proposed legislation and regulations. The 30-member Economic Council advises the Government on social, financial, and economic questions. One-third of its members come from the trade union movement, and one-third from the employers' federation.

Women are active in public service. The Mayor of Monaco and one member of the National Council are women.

Section 4. Governmental Attitude Regarding International and Nongovernmental Investigation of Alleged Violations of Human Rights

While the Government imposes no impediments to the establishment or operation of local groups devoted to monitoring human rights, there is none. There have been no requests from outside groups to investigate human rights conditions.

Section 5. Discrimination Based on Race, Sex, Religion, Disability, Language, or Social Status

The Constitution provides that all Monegasque nationals are equal before the law. It differentiates between rights that are accorded nationals (including preference in employment, free education, and assistance to the ill or unemployed) and those guaranteed to all residents (e.g., freedom of religion, inviolability of the home).

Women.—Reported instances of violence against women are rare. Marital violence is strictly prohibited, and any woman who is a victim of it may bring criminal charges against her husband. Women are fairly well represented in the professions, e.g., they constitute 6 of Monaco's 18 lawyers (including a former president of the bar), 5 of 42 physicians, and 8 of 26 dentists. Women are less well represented in the business world. The law governing transmission of citizenship provides for equality of treatment between men and women who are Monegasque by birth. However, women who acquire Monegasque nationality by naturalization cannot transmit it to their children, whereas naturalized male citizens can.

Children.—The Government is fully committed to the protection of children's rights and welfare and has well-funded public education and health care programs. There is no societal pattern of abuse of children.

People With Disabilities.—The Government has mandated that public buildings provide for access for the disabled, and this has been largely accomplished.

Section 6. Worker Rights

a. *The Right of Association.*—Workers are free to form unions, but fewer than 10 percent of workers are unionized, and relatively few of these reside in the Principality. Unions are independent of both the Government and the Monegasque political parties. The Monegasque Confederation of Unions is not affiliated with any larger labor organization but is free to join international bodies.

The Constitution provides for the right to strike in conformity with relevant legislation. Government workers, however, may not strike. The first strike in several years occurred in March when the Monegasque Confederation of Unions organized a 1-day work stoppage by bank, transportation, and factory employees.

b. *The Right to Organize and Bargain Collectively.*—The law provides for the free exercise of union activity. Agreements on working conditions are negotiated between organizations representing employers in a given sector of the economy and the respective union. Antiunion discrimination is prohibited. Union representatives can be fired only with the agreement of a commission that includes two members from the employers' association and two from the labor movement. Allegations that an employee has been fired for union activity may be brought before the Labor Court, which can order redress such as the payment of damages with interest.

There are no export processing zones.

c. *Prohibition of Forced or Compulsory Labor.*—Such practices are outlawed and do not occur.

d. *Minimum Age for Employment of Children.*—The minimum age for employment is 16 years. Special restrictions apply to the hiring, worktimes, and other conditions of workers 16 to 18 years old.

e. *Acceptable Conditions of Work.*—The legal minimum wage for full-time work is the French minimum wage plus 5 percent, i.e., currently $7.70 (Fr 39.60) per hour, which is adequate to provide a decent living for a worker and family. Most workers receive more than the minimum. The legal workweek is 39 hours. Health and safety standards are fixed by law and government decree. These standards are enforced by health and safety committees in the workplace and by the government Labor Inspector.

THE NETHERLANDS

The Netherlands is a constitutional monarchy with a parliamentary legislative system and an independent judiciary. Executive authority is exercised by the Prime Minister and Cabinet representing the governing political parties (traditionally a coalition of at least two major parties). The bicameral Parliament is elected through free and fair elections.

Regional police forces are primarily responsible for maintaining internal security. The police, the royal constabulary, and investigative organizations concerned with internal and external security are effectively subordinated to civilian authority.

The market-based economy is export oriented and features a mixture of industry, services, and agriculture. Key industries include chemicals, oil refining, natural gas, machinery, and electronics. The agricultural sector produces fruit, vegetables, flowers, meat, and dairy products. Living standards and the level of social benefits are high. At just over 6.3 percent, unemployment is a serious problem, and one which affects minorities relatively more than the general population.

The Government fully respects the rights of its citizens, and the law and judiciary provide effective means of dealing with instances of individual abuse. The Government is taking serious steps to address violence and discrimination against women. The Government has also taken steps to address societal discrimination against minorities.

Aruba and the Netherlands Antilles, which are two autonomous regions of the kingdom, also feature parliamentary systems and full constitutional protection of human rights. In practice, government respect for human rights on these islands generally is little different from that in the European Netherlands. The two Caribbean Governments have taken measures to address past reports of police brutality. The islands' prison conditions remain substandard.

RESPECT FOR HUMAN RIGHTS

Section 1. Respect for the Integrity of the Person, Including Freedom From:

a. *Political and Other Extrajudicial Killing.*—There were no reports of political or other extrajudicial killings.

b. *Disappearance.*—There were no reports of politically motivated disappearances.

c. *Torture and Other Cruel, Inhuman, or Degrading Treatment or Punishment.*— The Constitution prohibits such practices, and there were no reports that officials employed them.

A Dutch government-funded police professionalization program, as well as the establishment of a grievance committee, have contributed significantly to countering incidents of police brutality in both the Netherlands Antilles and Aruba. New incidents have not been reported, nor has there been any allegation of torture.

Prison conditions in the Netherlands meet minimum international standards, and the Government permits visits by human rights monitors.

Publication of two reports of the Committee for the Prevention of Torture of the Council of Europe encouraged the Governments of the Netherlands, the Netherlands Antilles, and Aruba to improve the "inhuman" conditions in Curacao's prison and in cell blocks at the police stations on the islands of St. Maarten, Bonaire, and Aruba. Complaints ranged from overcrowding and deplorable sanitary conditions to poor food and insufficient ventilation. The Dutch Government has offered substantial financial and logistic assistance. The authorities plan to ease overcrowding at Curacao's prison by the construction of a maximum security facility and a new wing for young delinquents, as well as through bilateral agreements with neighboring countries on the transfer of sentenced persons, since most prisoners are from these countries. The Governments of the Netherlands Antilles and Aruba allow access by nongovernmental organizations to prisons.

d. *Arbitrary Arrest, Detention, or Exile.*—The law prohibits arbitrary arrest, detention, or exile, and the Government observes this prohibition.

e. *Denial of Fair Public Trial.*—The Constitution provides for an independent judiciary, and the Government respects this provision in practice. The judiciary provides citizens with a fair and efficient judicial process. The law provides for the right to a fair trial, and the independent judiciary vigorously enforces this right.

There were no reports of political prisoners.

f. *Arbitrary Interference With Privacy, Family, Home, or Correspondence.*—The law prohibits such practices, government authorities generally respect these prohibitions, and violations are subject to effective legal sanction.

Section 2. Respect for Civil Liberties, Including:

a. *Freedom of Speech and Press.*—The law provides for freedom of speech and of the press, and the Government respects these rights in practice. An independent press, an effective judiciary, and a functioning democratic political system combine to ensure freedom of speech and of the press, including academic freedom.

b. *Freedom of Peaceful Assembly and Association.*—The law provides for these rights, and the Government respects them in practice.

c. *Freedom of Religion.*—The law provides for freedom of religion, and the Government respects this right in practice. State subsidies are provided to religious organizations that maintain educational facilities.

d. *Freedom of Movement Within the Country, Foreign Travel, Emigration, and Repatriation.*—The law provides for these rights, and the Government respects them in practice.

The Government cooperates with the United Nations High Commissioner for Refugees and other humanitarian organizations in assisting refugees. There were no reports of forced expulsion of those having a valid claim to refugee status. The Government does not provide first asylum as such, but most asylum seekers (87 percent in 1996), except those who obviously came from a "safe country of origin" or stayed for some time in a "safe third country," are permitted to apply for status. A sizable number (about 40 percent in 1996) of those whose applications are eventually denied are nonetheless permitted to stay temporarily on humanitarian grounds or as long as their country of origin is considered unsafe.

In 1996 Parliament passed a bill that aims to protect genuine refugees while shutting out economic refugees and illegal immigrants. The new bill will come into effect in early 1997. Since tighter criteria for granting asylum were introduced in January 1995, the number of new asylum applicants has decreased from 52,576 in 1994 to 29,258 in 1995 and to a projected 21,000 for all of 1996. The Government has adopted a remigration program for rejected asylum seekers from selected countries, including Somalia, Sri Lanka, and the former Yugoslavia, which aims to stimulate their voluntary repatriation through financial incentives.

The Government pursues an active policy against alien smuggling, the penalties for which were raised considerably.

Section 3. Respect for Political Rights: The Right of Citizens to Change Their Government

The Constitution provides citizens with the right to change their government peacefully, and citizens exercise this right in practice through periodic, free, and fair elections held on the basis of universal suffrage.

There are no restrictions in law or in practice on the participation of women and minorities in government and politics. The second chamber of Parliament includes 49 women among its 150 members. Four of 13 cabinet ministers and 80 of 633 mayors are women.

Although in the minority, women also hold positions in the parliaments and cabinets of the Netherlands Antilles and Aruba.

Section 4. Governmental Attitude Regarding International and Nongovernmental Investigation of Alleged Violations of Human Rights

Human rights groups operate without government restriction, investigating and publishing their findings. Government officials are very cooperative and responsive to their views.

Section 5. Discrimination Based on Race, Sex, Religion, Disability, Language, or Social Status

The law bans discrimination on the basis of any of these factors or on sexual orientation or political preference. The Government generally is effective in enforcing these provisions. Under a new Equal Treatment Act, complainants may take offenders to court under civil law.

Women.—The Government supports programs to reduce and prevent violence against women. Battered women find refuge in a network of 48 government-subsidized women's shelters offering the services of social workers and psychologists. In addition, battered women who leave their domestic partners become eligible for social benefits which include an adequate basic subsidy as well as an allowance for dependent children. Nongovernmental organizations also advise and assist women who have been victims of sexual assault. Since 1991 marital rape has been a crime and carries the same penalty as rape. Spousal abuse carries a one-third higher penalty than ordinary battery. However, since the judicial system does not compile statistics distinguishing spousal abuse from battery, it is difficult to estimate the extent of the problem. The most recent study, by the Ministry of Welfare, Health, and Culture in 1989, showed that over 20 percent of women in heterosexual relationships were victims of violence during their lifetimes. Slightly over half of these suffered repeated severe violence.

High-priority government measures to combat trafficking in women for prostitution include a more aggressive prosecution policy as well as closer international cooperation. A number of police forces have established special units to deal with the issue. The Dutch Foundation Against Trafficking in Women estimates that each year around 1,000 women are brought into the Netherlands for the purpose of prostitution, not only from Central and Eastern Europe, but also from the Far East and West Africa. Women who are forced to work illegally as prostitutes and who are apprehended have special exemptions in immigration law and receive counseling and legal assistance.

Women are increasingly entering the job market, but traditional cultural factors and inadequate child care facilities can discourage women—especially those with young children—from working. Although more than 40 percent of the Dutch work force is female, many women work only part time. Only 52 percent of women ages 15-64 have jobs, and only 42 percent of those work more than 35 hours a week. By contrast, 75 percent of men in this age group are employed, 88 percent of whom work 35 or more hours a week.

According to the Dutch Education Ministry, women have fully made up the arrears they had experienced in education. At present, girls form the majority in higher secondary education where they also score better, and in 1996, for the first time, as many women as men entered college and university.

Women are often underemployed and have less chance of promotion than their male colleagues. The unemployment rate of women reentering the labor market is high. A 1993 study of central government civil servants showed that, while 58 percent of those in the lowest salary grade were women, only 9 percent in the highest grade were women. These problems notwithstanding, women are making steady progress by moving into important professional and high-visibility jobs.

In 1988 the Government began instituting affirmative action programs for women. Collective labor agreements usually include one or more schemes to strengthen the position of women. Legislation mandates equal pay for equal work, prohibits dismissal because of marriage, pregnancy, or motherhood, and provides the basis for equality in other employment-related areas. A legislatively mandated Equal Treatment Commission actively pursues complaints of discrimination in these areas as well as allegations of pay differences.

The Dutch social welfare and national health systems provide considerable assistance to working women with families. Women are eligible for 16 weeks of maternity leave at full pay. The Parental Leave Law allows new mothers and fathers to work only 20 hours a week over a 6-month period. The Netherlands Antilles and Aruba allow 60 days of paid maternity leave at up to 80 percent of full salary.

Women have full legal and judicial rights and enter marriage with the option of choosing community property or separate regimes for their assets.

Women's groups dedicated to such issues as equal rights in social security, the legal position of women, sexual abuse, taxation, education, work, and prostitution operate freely. The law requires employers to take measures to protect workers against sexual harassment; research showed that one in three working women has experienced sexual harassment in the workplace. The Government runs an ongoing publicity campaign to increase awareness of the problem. As the biggest employer in the country, it has taken measures to counter harassment among civil servants, for example, in the police force.

Children.—The Government works to ensure the well-being of children through numerous well-funded health, education, and public information programs. The Council for the Protection of Children, operated through the Ministry of Justice, enforces child support orders, investigates cases of child abuse, and recommends remedies ranging from counseling to withdrawal of parental rights. In addition, the Government has set up a popular hot line for children and a network of pediatricians who track suspected cases of child abuse on a confidential basis. There is no societal pattern of abuse of children.

International sex tourism involving abuse of minor children is prosecutable under Dutch law. For the first time ever, a Dutchman was tried in the Netherlands in 1996 for abuse of minors in the Philippines. On October he was convicted and sentenced to 5 years' imprisonment for sexual abuse of minors, some as young as age 11. The maximum penalty for child pornography was raised from 3 months' to 4 years' imprisonment, 6 years in the event of financial gain, and the maximum fine was more than tripled. New legislation allows for provisional arrest, house searches, and criminal financial investigations. Moreover, the authorities will no longer have to prove that a person possesses child pornography for the purpose of distribution or public display. The possession of pictures of sexual behavior with minors alone will be sufficient cause for prosecution. The Government is considering raising the age limit under which sex with minors is automatically a criminal offense from 12 to 14 years. At present, the age of consent is 16. Prosecution of adults for sex with minors between the ages of 12 to 16 only occurs upon the filing of a complaint by an interested party.

People With Disabilities.—There is no discrimination against disabled persons in employment, education, or in the provision of other state services. Local governments are increasingly mandating access to public buildings for the disabled.

National/Racial/Ethnic Minorities.—Integration of racial and ethnic minorities into the social and cultural mainstream remains a difficult problem.

The Government pursues an active campaign aimed at increasing public awareness of racism and discrimination. The Constitution prohibits discrimination on the basis of race and nationality and allows those who claim that they have been discriminated against to take offenders to court under civil law. The rising trend in recent years in incidents of violence against ethnic minorities has been reversed. The Criminal Investigation Service reported in 1996 a significant decrease in racist incidents, particularly in those of a life-threatening nature. The decline in incidents was attributed to waning interest in racist extremism in politics and to a decrease in rightwing activists to a hardcore group of 50 to 60 in a total population of over 15 million.

Immigrant groups face some discrimination in housing and employment. These groups, concentrated in the larger cities, suffer from a high rate of unemployment. The Government has been working for several years with employers' groups and unions to reduce minority unemployment levels to the national average. As a result of these efforts, in recent years the rate of job creation among ethnic minorities has been higher than among the general population.

A 1994 law requiring employers with a work force of over 35 people to register their non-Dutch employees has run into implementation problems. Some employers find the law burdensome, and some minority employees object to being counted as "non-Dutch." Employers must submit confidential affirmative action plans, including recruitment targets and proposed means of reaching that target.

Section 6. Worker Rights

a. *The Right of Association.*—Membership in labor unions is open to all workers including military, police, and civil service employees. People are entitled to form or join unions of their own choosing without previous government authorization, and unions are free to affiliate with national trade union federations. This right is freely exercised.

Unions are entirely free of control by the Government and political parties. Union members may and do participate in political activities.

All workers have the right to strike, except for most civil servants who have other institutionalized means of protection and redress. The right to strike is exercised freely, but the number of strikes each year is very low: on average about 17 labor days per 1,000 workers are lost each year. There is no retribution against striking workers.

About 25 percent of the work force is unionized, but union-negotiated collective bargaining agreements are usually extended to cover about three-quarters of the work force. The white-collar unions' membership is the fastest growing.

The four union federations are active internationally, without restriction.

b. *The Right to Organize and Bargain Collectively.*—The right to organize and bargain collectively is recognized and well established. Discrimination against workers because of union membership is illegal and does not occur.

Collective bargaining agreements are negotiated in the framework of the "Social Partnership" developed between trade unions and private employers. Representatives of the main union federations, employers' organizations, and the Government meet each autumn to discuss labor issues, including wage levels and their relation to the state of the economy and to international competition. The discussions lead to a central accord with social as well as economic goals for the coming year. Under this umbrella agreement, unions and employers in various sectors negotiate sectoral agreements, which the Government usually extends to all companies in the respective sector.

Antiunion discrimination is prohibited. Union federations and employers' organizations are represented, along with independent experts, on the Social and Economic Council. The Council is the major advisory board to the Government on its policies and legislation regarding national and international social and economic matters.

There are no export processing zones.

c. *Prohibition of Forced or Compulsory Labor.*—Forced or compulsory labor is prohibited by the Constitution and does not occur.

d. *Minimum Age for Employment of Children.*—The minimum age for employment is 16 years, and for full-time work it is conditioned on completion of the mandatory 10 years of schooling. Those still in school at the age of 16 may not work more than 8 hours per week. People under the age of 18 are prohibited by law from working at night, overtime, or in areas dangerous to their physical or mental well-being. The laws are effectively enforced by the tripartite Labor Commission, which monitors hiring practices and conducts inspections.

e. *Acceptable Conditions of Work.*—The minimum wage for adults is established by law and can be adjusted every 6 months to changes in the cost-of-living index. Since 1982 few adjustments have been made, and the rise in the minimum wage has lagged well behind the rise in the index. The gross minimum wage is $1,350 (f. 2,204) per month. For workers earning the minimum wage, employers currently pay $3,750 a year (f. 6,000) in premiums for social security benefits, which includes medical insurance. Only 3 percent of workers earn the minimum wage because collective bargaining agreements, which are normally extended across a sector, usually fix a minimum wage well above the legislated minimum. The Government, unions, and employers have taken measures to increase the number of minimum wage jobs and to decrease employers' social payments in order to lower the cost of hiring new workers and to create more jobs, especially for the long-term unemployed.

There is a reduced minimum wage for young people under the age of 23—one of the demographic groups with the highest rate of unemployment—intended to provide incentives for their employment. This wage ranges from 34.5 percent of the adult minimum wage for workers 16 years of age to 85 percent for those 22 years of age. The legislated minimum wage and social benefits available to all minimum wage earners provide an adequate standard of living for workers and their families.

A 40-hour workweek is established by law, but collective bargaining agreements often set a shorter workweek. The rapid increase of telecommuting and high level of part-time work have lowered the estimated actual workweek to 35.8 hours. As a job creating measure, the Government now permits flexible hours. For some, this could mean more than an 8-hour day, within the weekly legal limits. However, collective bargaining negotiations are heading toward an eventual 36-hour week for full-time employees.

Working conditions, including comprehensive occupational safety and health standards set by law and regulations, are actively monitored by the tripartite Labor Commission. Enforcement is effective. Workers may refuse to continue working at a hazardous work site. The Ministry of Labor and Social Affairs also monitors standards through its labor inspectorate.

NORWAY

Norway is a parliamentary democracy and constitutional monarchy with King Harald V as the Head of State. It is governed by a prime minister, cabinet, and a 165-seat Storting (parliament) which is elected every 4 years and cannot be dissolved.

The national police have primary responsibility for internal security, but in times of crisis, such as internal disorder or natural catastrophe, the police may call on the military forces for assistance. In such circumstances, the military forces are always under police authority. The civilian authorities maintain effective control of the security forces.

Norway is an advanced industrial state with a mixed economy combining private and public ownership that provides a high standard of living for residents. The key industries are oil and gas, metals, engineering, shipbuilding, fishing, and manufacturing including of fish processing equipment. The leading exports are oil and gas, manufactured goods, fish, and metals. Between 60 and 70 percent of the labor force is in the service sector (including public service), and up to 15 percent is in the manufacturing sector.

The Government fully respects the rights of its citizens, and the law and judiciary provide effective means of dealing with instances of individual abuse.

RESPECT FOR HUMAN RIGHTS

Section 1. *Respect for the Integrity of the Person, Including Freedom From:*
   a. *Political and Other Extrajudicial Killing.*—There were no reports of political or other extrajudicial killings.
   b. *Disappearance.*—There were no reports of politically motivated disappearances.
   c. *Torture and Other Cruel, Inhuman, or Degrading Treatment or Punishment.*—The Constitution prohibits such practices, and there were no reports that officials employed them.
   Prison conditions meet minimum international standards, and the Government permits visits by human rights monitors.
   d. *Arbitrary Arrest, Detention, or Exile.*—The Constitution prohibits arbitrary arrest, detention, or exile, and the Government observes this prohibition.
   e. *Denial of Fair Public Trial.*—The law provides for the right to a fair trial, and an independent judiciary vigorously enforces this right.
   The court system consists of the Supreme Court, the Supreme Court Appellate Court (committee), superior courts, county courts for criminal cases, magistrate courts for civil cases, and claims courts. Special courts are the Impeachment Court (made up of Parliamentarians), the Labor Court, Trusteeship Courts, Fishery Courts, and something similar to land ownership severance courts. There are no religious, political, or security courts. All courts, which date back to laws passed in the eleventh century, meet internationally accepted standards for fair trials.
   There were no reports of political prisoners.
   f. *Arbitrary Interference With Privacy, Family, Home, or Correspondence.*—Both the Constitution and law prohibit such practices, government authorities generally respect these prohibitions, and violations are subject to effective legal sanction.

Section 2. *Respect for Civil Liberties, Including:*
   a. *Freedom of Speech and Press.*—The Constitution provides for freedom of the press, and the Government respects this right in practice. An independent press, an effective judiciary, and a functioning democratic political system, combine to ensure freedom of speech and of the press, including academic freedom.
   b. *Freedom of Peaceful Assembly and Association.*—The law provides for these rights, and the Government respects them in practice.
   c. *Freedom of Religion.*—The Constitution provides for freedom of religion, and the Government respects this right in practice.
   The state church is the Evangelical Lutheran Church of Norway, which is financially supported by the State, and to which 93 percent of the population nominally belong. There is a constitutional requirement that the King and one-half of the Cabinet belong to this church. The Workers' Protection and Working Environment Act permits prospective employers to ask job applicants in private or religious schools, or in day care centers, whether they respect Christian beliefs and principles.
   Other denominations operate freely. A religious community is required to register with the Government only if it desires state support, which is provided to all registered denominations on a proportional basis in accordance with membership. Although the state religion is taught in all public schools, children of other faiths are allowed to be absent from such classes upon parental request. Workers belonging to minority denominations are allowed leave for religious holidays.
   d. *Freedom of Movement Within the Country, Foreign Travel, Emigration, and Repatriation.*—The law provides for these rights, and the Government respects them in practice.
   The Government cooperates with the Office of the United Nations High Commissioner for Refugees and other humanitarian organizations in assisting refugees. The Government provides first asylum and provided it to 29 persons in 1995. (Statistics for 1996 are not available.) Overall, it provided residence permits on humanitarian grounds to asylum seekers in the first instance to 913 persons in 1995. There were no reports of forced expulsion of those having a valid claim to refugee status or to countries where they feared persecution.

Section 3. *Respect for Political Rights: The Right of Citizens to Change Their Government*
   The law provides citizens with the right to change their Government peacefully, and citizens exercise this right in practice through periodic, free, and fair elections held on the basis of universal suffrage.
   There are no restrictions, in law or practice, on the participation of women in government or in the political arena generally. Norway's female Prime Minister retired in October after 6 years in office. Her successor has appointed women to lead 8 of

the 18 ministries. Women constitute 65 of the 165 members of parliament (39.4 percent), chair 5 of 15 standing committees, lead 2 of the 6 main political parties.

In addition to participating freely in the national political process, Norwegian Sami (formerly known as Lapps) elected their own constituent assembly, the Sameting, in 1993 for the second time. Under the law establishing the 39-seat body, it is a consultative group which meets regularly to deal with "all matters which in (its) opinion are of special importance to the Sami people." In practice the Sameting has been most interested in protecting the group's language and cultural rights and in influencing decisions on resources and lands where Sami are a majority.

Section 4. Governmental Attitude Regarding International and Nongovernmental Investigation of Alleged Violations of Human Rights

A number of human rights groups operate without government restriction, investigating and publishing their findings on human rights cases. Government officials are very cooperative and responsive to their views.

Section 5. Discrimination Based on Race, Sex, Religion, Disability, Language, or Social Status

The Constitution prohibits discrimination based on race, sex, religion, disability, language, or social status, and the Government enforces this prohibition in practice.

Women.—In 1995 there were 16,314 contacts by women with crisis action centers and 2,380 overnight stays by women at shelters. Police authorities believe that increases in reported rapes and wife beatings in recent years have been largely due to greater willingness among women to report these crimes. The police vigorously investigate and prosecute such crimes. They have also instituted special programs to prevent rape and domestic violence and to counsel victims. Public and private organizations run several shelters which give battered wives an alternative to returning to a violent domestic situation.

The rights of women are protected under the Equal Rights Law of 1978 and other regulations. According to that law, "women and men engaged in the same activity shall have equal wages for work of equal value." An Equal Rights Council monitors enforcement of the 1978 law, and an Equal Rights Ombudsman processes complaints of sexual discrimination. There were 209 written complaints in 1995 and 399 by telephone. There had been 97 written complaints as of August. On average 55 percent of all complaints of sexual discrimination are filed by women, 19 percent by men, and 26 percent by organizations; in the latter cases, it is not clear whether the organizations represented men or women.

In 1995 the Parliament adopted a harassment amendment to the Working Environment Act, which states that "employees shall not be subjected to harassment or other unseemly behavior."

Children.—The Government demonstrates its strong commitment to children's rights and welfare through its well-funded systems of education and medical care. The Government provides education for children through the post-secondary level. There is no difference in the treatment of girls and boys in education or health care services. An independent Children's Ombudsman Office, within the Ministry of Children and Families, assures protection of children in law and practice. There is no societal pattern of abuse against children.

People With Disabilities.—There is no discrimination against disabled persons in employment, education, or in the provision of other state services. The law mandates access to buildings for people with disabilities, and the Government enforces these provisions in practice.

Indigenous People.—Apart from a tiny Finnish population in the northeast, the Sami constituted Norway's only significant minority group until the influx of immigrants during the 1970's. In recent years the Government has taken steps to protect Sami cultural rights by providing Sami language instruction at schools in their areas, radio and television programs broadcast or subtitled in Sami, and subsidies for newspapers and books oriented toward the Sami (see Section 3).

Section 6. Worker Rights

a. *The Right of Association.*—The law provides workers with the right to associate freely and to strike. Norway changed its wage negotiating process for 1996, shifting negotiations from the national to the local and company level. This change resulted in a substantially higher number of strikes. There were 10 nationwide strikes in 1996, and many smaller ones at regional, local, and company levels. Almost all have been settled through negotiations.

The Government has the right, with the approval of the Storting, to invoke compulsory arbitration under certain circumstances. The Government came under increasing criticism in 1995 for resorting to compulsory arbitration too quickly during strikes. In addition this procedure, which was also invoked several times in the

1980's, particularly in the oil industry, was criticized repeatedly by the Committee of Experts of the International Labor Organization, which argued that the situations were not a sufficient threat to public health and safety to justify invoking compulsory arbitration. The Supreme Court is reviewing a case that will allow it to rule on whether the Norwegian process in this regard violates the country's international commitments.

With membership totaling about 60 percent of the work force, unions play an important role in political and economic life and are consulted by the Government on important economic and social problems. Although the largest trade union federation is associated with the Labor Party, all unions and labor federations are free of party and government control. Unions are free to form federations and to affiliate internationally. They maintain strong ties with such international bodies as the International Confederation of Free Trade Unions.

b. *The Right to Organize and Bargain Collectively.*—All workers, including government employees and military personnel, exercise the right to organize and bargain collectively. Collective bargaining is widespread, with most wage earners covered by negotiated settlements, either directly or through understandings which extend the contract terms to workers outside of the main labor federation and the employers' bargaining group. Any complaint of antiunion discrimination would be dealt with by the Labor Court, but there have been none in recent years.

There are no export processing zones.

c. *Prohibition of Forced or Compulsory Labor.*—Compulsory labor is prohibited by law and does not exist. The Directorate of Labor Inspections ensures compliance. Domestics, children, or foreign workers are not required to remain in situations amounting to coerced or bonded labor.

d. *Minimum Age for Employment of Children.*—Children 13 to 18 years of age may be employed part-time in light work that will not adversely affect their health, development, or schooling. Minimum age rules are observed in practice and enforced by the Directorate of Labor Inspections. Education is compulsory for nine years. Children are normally in school up to the age of 16.

e. *Acceptable Conditions of Work.*—Normal working hours are mandated by law and limited to 37½ hours per week. The law also provides for 25 working days of paid leave per year (31 days for those over age 60). A 28-hour rest period is legally mandated on weekends and holidays. There is no specified minimum wage, but wages normally fall within a national scale negotiated by labor, employers, and the Government. Average income, not including extensive social benefits, is adequate to provide a worker and family a decent living.

Under the Workers' Protection and Working Environment Act of 1977, all employed persons are assured safe and physically acceptable working conditions. Specific standards are set by the Directorate of Labor Inspections in consultation with nongovernmental experts. According to the Act, working environment committees composed of management, workers, and health personnel must be established in all enterprises with 50 or more workers, and safety delegates must be elected in all organizations. Workers enjoy strong rights to remove themselves from situations which endanger their health. The Directorate of Labor Inspections ensures effective compliance with labor legislation and standards.

POLAND

Poland is a parliamentary democracy based on a multiparty political system and free and fair elections. The President shares power with the Prime Minister, the Council of Ministers, and the bicameral Parliament (Senate and Sejm). The coalition government, composed of the Democratic Left Alliance (SLD), a successor to the former Communist Party, and the Polish Peasant Party (PSL), a successor to the Peasant Party of the Communist era, has a nearly two-thirds majority in both houses of Parliament. Poland has held two presidential and two parliamentary elections in the 7 years since the end of communism. The next parliamentary elections are due by September 1997. The judiciary is independent.

The armed forces and the internal security apparatus are subject to governmental control. In January President Aleksander Kwasniewski signed a bill clarifying the chain of command within the Ministry of Defense and placing the Chief of the General Staff clearly under the authority of the civilian Minister. The law also transferred oversight of military intelligence from the General Staff to the Ministry of Defense. The commission established to implement the law eliminated the General Staff's parallel and autonomous structure, reformed the military justice system, and is instituting broad changes in the structure of the Ministry and the armed forces to enhance democratic oversight of the military.

Poland has made a successful transition to a free market economy. A burgeoning private sector and increasing exports to Western Europe produced a 7 percent rate of growth in 1995 and an estimated 6 percent in 1996. Both inflation (18.5 percent) and unemployment (13 percent) remained high. Since 1989, most small- and medium-sized state-owned enterprises have been privatized. Many of the largest enterprises (e.g., banks, the telephone company, mines, power plants, the national airline) await long-promised privatization. Generous social and retirement programs place an enormous strain on the budget and impede economic growth. Parliament, however, has moved slowly on addressing the politically sensitive subject of social programs reform.

The Government generally respected the rights of its citizens, but there were some problems. Freedom of speech and the press were subject to some limitations, particularly involving political influence over state-owned television. There were some incidents of intolerance toward minorities, but fewer than in 1995. Lack of public confidence as well as an inadequate budget plague the court system. Court decisions are frequently not implemented, particularly those of the administrative courts, and simple civil cases can take as long as 2 or 3 years. Many low-paid prosecutors and judges have left public service for more lucrative employment. The threat of organized crime has provoked legislative responses that could threaten the right to privacy. Women continue to experience serious discrimination in the labor market, are not full participants in political life, and are subject to various legal inequities as a consequence of paternalistic laws. Spousal abuse is a problem. The President and Government have worked constructively toward resolving issues of concern to the Jewish community. Although the rights to organize and bargain collectively were largely observed, there were employer violations of other worker rights provided by law, particularly in the growing private sector.

RESPECT FOR HUMAN RIGHTS

Section 1. Respect for the Integrity of the Person, Including Freedom From:

a. *Political and Other Extrajudicial Killing.*—There were no reports of political or other extrajudicial killings.

The trial of two militiamen accused in the 1983 beating death of Grzegorz Przemyk, a student, continues. The prosecutor's office expects a verdict in early 1997. The police are accused of covering up the death and blaming it on the ambulance drivers who took Przemyk to the hospital. The prosecution has been unable to establish the names of all militiamen involved in the incident, but charges have been filed against a third militiaman for obstructing the investigation by hiding documents.

On October 23, Parliament voted not to force General Wojciech Jaruzelski and other former Communist leaders to stand trial for the deaths and jailings of activists after the 1981 declaration of martial law. Approximately 25 Poles died in clashes between striking workers and riot police, and the Government jailed without trial more than 13,000 people during the 1½ years of martial law. Investigations continue in other cases relating to extrajudicial killings during the Communist period, including the shooting deaths of striking miners at the Wujek mine in 1981 and the December 1970 deaths of striking shipyard workers in several coastal cities.

b. *Disappearance.*—There were no reports of politically motivated disappearances.

c. *Torture and Other Cruel, Inhuman, or Degrading Treatment or Punishment.*—The Criminal Code prohibits torture, and there were no reported incidents of it.

In March a court in Warsaw sentenced Adam Humer to 9 years in prison for the torture of prisoners when he was a security service interrogator in the 1950s. In September the press reported that authorities had begun an investigation into the alleged beating of two men detained by police in Szczytno.

Prison conditions are generally adequate, according to reports by nongovernmental organizations (NGO's), although some facilities are old and in disrepair. Many prisons experience overcrowding. In a 1995 letter to the Prime Minister, the Ombudsman for Human Rights charged that the condition of many detention facilities and prisons was poor and recommended that several dozen be closed in whole or in part for renovation. The Ombudsman also recommended that actions be taken to reduce the prison population, including the decriminalization of certain offenses, such as failure to pay alimony. A 1996 report by the Helsinki Foundation for Human Rights stated that Polish prisons, mental hospitals, and other "isolating institutions" neither engage in nor tolerate violations of the rights of inmates. The Foundation did, however, observe isolated violations that were inconsistent with

Polish and international norms, specifically cases of beating in juvenile institutions run by the Ministry of Education.

The Government permits visits to civilian prisons by human rights monitors.

d. *Arbitrary Arrest, Detention, or Exile.*—The Constitution prohibits arbitrary arrest and detention, and the Government observes this prohibition. The law allows a 48 hour detention period before authorities are required to bring formal charges, during which detainees are normally denied access to a lawyer. Once a prosecutor presents the legal basis for a formal investigation, the law provides that the detainee be given access to a lawyer. Detainees may be held under "temporary" arrest for up to 3 months and may challenge the legality of an arrest through appeal to the district court. A court may extend this pretrial confinement period every 3 months until the trial date. Bail is available, and human rights organizations report that most detainees were released on bail pending trial. A new law went into effect in August that requires courts, rather than prosecutors, to issue arrest warrants. This law was adopted in order to comply with the European convention on human rights.

The Government does not employ forced exile.

e. *Denial of Fair Public Trial.*—The Constitution provides for an independent judiciary, and the Government respects this provision in practice. Poland has a three-tier court system consisting of regional and provincial courts and a Supreme Court, which is divided into five divisions: Military, civil, criminal, labor, and family. Judges are nominated by the National Judicial Council and appointed by the President. Judges are appointed for life and can be reassigned but not dismissed, except by a decision of the National Judicial Council. The Constitutional Tribunal rules on the constitutionality of legislation, but its decisions may be overruled by an absolute majority in the Sejm.

Although the pretrial waiting time in criminal courts can be several months, the courts generally provide fair and efficient trials, and there is no evidence of significant corruption. However, the court system continues to be plagued by an inadequate budget, which contributes to a lack of public confidence. Many effective judges and prosecutors have left public service for the more lucrative private sector. Court decisions are frequently not implemented, particularly those of administrative courts. Bailiffs normally guarantee the execution of civil verdicts such as damage payments and evictions. However, according to some observers, they are underpaid, subject to intimidation and bribery, and have a mixed record of implementing court decisions. Civil and administrative rulings against public institutions such as hospitals often cannot be complied with due to a lack of funds. Simple civil cases can take as long as 2 to 3 years before resolution. For example, the wait for official court recognition of land ownership deeds can inhibit the sale and development of property for several years. Furthermore, anecdotal evidence suggests that the judicial backlog and the costs of legal action deter some citizens from using the justice system at all, particularly in civil matters such as divorce. The long wait for routine court decisions in commercial matters is an incentive for bribery and corruption.

All defendants are presumed innocent until proven guilty. At the end of a trial the court renders its decision orally and then has 7 days to prepare a written decision. A defendant has the right to appeal within 14 days of the written decision. Appeals may be made on, among other grounds, the basis of new evidence or procedural irregularities.

Criminal cases are tried in regional and provincial courts by a panel consisting of a professional judge and two lay assessors. The seriousness of the offense determines which of these is the court of first instance. Once formal charges are filed, the defendant is allowed to study the charges and consult with an attorney, who is provided at public expense if necessary. Once the defendant is prepared, a trial date is set. Defendants are required to be present during trial and may present evidence and confront witnesses in their own defense. The right to testify is universal. A law allowing for the use of incognito witnesses, designed to assist in combating organized crime, threatens a defendant's ability to confront witnesses. In January and July, successive reforms were made in the legal system that allow citizens to make appeals to the high courts in both civil and criminal matters. Previously, provincial courts were the final court of appeal for individual citizens. The Ombudsman's office has raised concerns that government employees, particularly those in uniform, should have greater access to the courts in the event of disciplinary action.

Trials are normally public. The courts, however, reserve the right to close a trial to the public in some circumstances, such as divorce cases, trials in which state secrets may be disclosed, or cases whose content might offend "public morality." The courts rarely invoke this prerogative.

In December the Parliament accepted a committee report concluding that the intelligence services may have acted illegally in gathering evidence in the investigation of former Premier Oleksy. The report recommended that its findings be passed to the prosecutor's office, which would decide whether to investigate the intelligence officers involved in the case. Parliamentarians also began collecting signatures necessary to launch state tribunal proceedings against former Interior Minister Milczanowski for his role in the case.

There were no reports of political prisoners.

f. *Arbitrary Interference With Privacy, Family, Home, or Correspondence.*—The Constitution provides for the right to privacy of correspondence. There is no legislation that guarantees the general right to privacy. In response to the growing threat of organized crime and money laundering, Parliament has permitted the police and secret services to monitor private correspondence and to use wiretaps and electronic monitoring devices in cases involving a serious crime, narcotics, money laundering, or illegal arms sales. The Minister of Justice and the Minister of Interior, both political appointees, must authorize these investigative methods. In emergency cases, the police may initiate an investigation using wiretaps or opening private correspondence at the same time that they seek permission from the ministries.

Parliamentarians and human rights groups have expressed concern about the lack of control over this type of surveillance. There is no independent judicial review of these decisions, nor is there any control mechanism over how the information derived from these investigations is used. A growing number of agencies have access to wiretap information, and a recent law allows electronic surveillance to be used for the prevention of crime as well as for investigative purposes.

The Justice Minister reported that in the first half of 1996, his office agreed to the surveillance of 727 persons, and the Minister of the Interior has confirmed that covert security service (UOP) employees operate as post and telecommunications employees. The Ombudsman for Human Rights has condemned the lack of control over wiretapping and is trying to determine the extent to which the Ministry of the Interior is authorizing the tapping of telephones.

The law forbids arbitrary forced entry into homes. Search warrants issued by a prosecutor are required in order to enter private residences. In emergency cases, when a prosecutor is not immediately available, police may enter a residence with the approval of the local police commander. In the most urgent cases, in which there is not time to consult with the police commander, police may enter a private residence after showing their official identification. There were no reports that police abused search warrant procedures.

The Ombudsman for Human Rights is advocating reform of the rules governing how citizens are registered in their official places of residence. The law requires all adults to be officially registered at a given address and allows them access to public services established in that locality. However, the current law permits property owners to "unregister" tenants from rented residences, potentially cutting citizens off from public services if they cannot immediately find another landlord willing to let them register.

Section 2. Respect for Civil Liberties, Including:

a. *Freedom of Speech and Press.*—The Constitution provides for freedom of speech and the press, and the Government generally respects this right. However, there are some restrictions in law and practice.

The Penal Code states that acts that "publicly insult, ridicule, and deride the Polish nation, the Polish Republic, its political system, or its principal organs are punishable by between 6 months and 8 years of imprisonment." The code imposes a prison term of up to 10 years for a person who commits any of the prohibited acts in print or through the mass media. In October 1995 presidential candidate Leszek Bubel was charged with violating this law, and his case is currently before a judge. Bubel claimed on a radio program that when he served as Deputy Prosecutor General, a former head of the presidential chancellery protected a group of criminals. In August the Warsaw prosecutor refused to begin proceedings against Pawel Moczydlowski, former head of the prison system, for publicly slandering President Kwasniewski and the head of the Council of Ministers Office by suggesting their public complicity in an espionage case. The Gdansk prosecutor has announced an investigation into November remarks by talk show host Wojciech Cejrowski, who is alleged to have publicly insulted President Kwasniewski.

The Penal Code also provides for punishment of anyone who uses print or other mass media to "advocate discord" on national, ethnic, racial, or religious grounds. In July the Warsaw prosecutor's office brought charges against Mikolaj Siwicki, a Warsaw pensioner, for publication of a hate-mongering book, which, the prosecutor charged, "could seriously damage the interests of the Polish Republic in international affairs." The book allegedly condones crimes committed against Poles during the Second World War, makes historically dubious claims about Polish crimes against the Ukrainian nation, and calls for lands in southeastern Poland to be given to Ukraine. The case was ongoing at year's end.

The Penal Code also stipulates that offending religious sentiment through public speech is punishable by a fine or a 2-year prison term. In September the Gdansk prosecutor reopened his investigation of Father Henryk Jankowski for violation of this law for an allegedly anti-Semitic sermon he gave in 1995. However, the case was dropped in June for lack of evidence. Catholic organizations have challenged the legality of certain films and images published in the press on the basis of this provision. In October 1995, a provincial court charged presidential candidate Leszek Bubel with violating this article by publishing a pamphlet containing anti-Semitic humor. A verdict is not expected in this case until 1997. The print media are uncensored and independent, although they may be subject to prosecution under the Penal Code provisions described above.

The State Secrets Act allows for prosecution of private citizens who have published or otherwise betrayed state secrets. Human rights groups have criticized this law, since it restricts the right of free speech of private citizens who have not freely sworn to uphold state secrets. Jerzy Urban, editor in chief of the leftist weekly Nie, was found guilty of violating the State Secrets Act for his 1992 publication of the operational acts of the UOP concerning an agent. In June Urban was sentenced to 1 year in prison (suspended) and 2 years' probation, banned from working as a journalist for 1 year, and fined approximately $4,000 (10,000 zlotys). The Helsinki Committee criticized the decision, alleging that it was in conflict with the European convention on human rights. Urban has appealed the decision, and the prosecutor's office announced that it will ask for a harsher sentence when the case is reviewed.

The Supreme Court has ruled that a prosecutor or a judge, in the context of a criminal trial, may order a journalist to divulge the name of a source. The penalty for noncompliance is a fine of approximately $2,000 (5,000 zlotys) and 1 month in jail. There were no reported cases of this law being applied in 1996.

The National Broadcasting Council (NBC) has broad interpretive powers in monitoring and regulating programming on public television, allocating broadcasting frequencies and licenses, and apportioning subscription revenues. In order to encourage the NBC's apolitical character, the nine NBC members are legally obliged to suspend any membership in political parties or public associations. They are, however, chosen for their political allegiances and nominated by the Sejm, the Senate, and the President following political bargaining, raising serious questions about the independence of broadcasting oversight from political influence. The broadcasting law stipulates that programs should not promote activities that are illegal or against state policy, morality, or the common good. The law also requires that all broadcasts "respect the religious feelings of the audiences and in particular respect the Christian system of values." The law does not fully define the term "Christian values." The Constitutional Tribunal has confirmed the constitutionality of this provision. Since the NBC has the ultimate responsibility for supervising the content of programs, these restrictions could be used as a means of censorship if enforced. The penalty for violating this provision of the law is a fine of up to 50 percent of the annual fee for the transmission frequency, a suspension of the broadcaster's license, or difficulty in renewal when it expires.

Private broadcasters operate on frequencies selected by the Ministry of Communications and auctioned by the NBC. The first auction in 1994 gave Polsat Corporation and some smaller local and religious stations license to broadcast. Several private radio stations broadcast under the same licensing arrangement. A second auction in October 1996 selected two private firms to receive two large regional broadcasting licenses; by year's end they had not yet begun broadcasting.

The Government owns the two largest television channels and many local stations, as well as five national radio networks. PAP, the national wire service, is also government owned. Public television is the largest source of news and information. Although Polsat is the only nationwide private television station available to regular viewers, satellite television and private cable services (domestic and foreign) are widely available. Cable services carry the main public channels, Polsat, local and regional stations, and a variety of foreign stations. RTL, a Luxembourg-based firm, inaugurated a Polish-language cable channel in December that provides news and entertainment.

Recent actions by the government-appointed Television Managing Board raise concerns that public television is increasingly subject to partisan influence by the Government. In November the Independent Center for Monitoring Freedom of the Press criticized the "evident political actions which the State authorities take towards the media." Earlier in the summer Wieslaw Walendziak, President of the Public Television (TVP) Managing Board, resigned and was replaced by Ryszard Miazek of the PSL, a governing coalition party. Miazek made controversial statements when first chosen, criticizing aggressive journalism and calling for strict adherence to the management line. As President of TVP, he also controls TAI—the television news agency—and has appointed an SLD associate as programming chair. In August Tomasz Siemoniak was fired as director of the state-owned Channel One by the TVP managing board for his refusal to replace the production team of a political commentary program that often criticized the ruling coalition. Siemoniak's dismissal prompted several other editorial and production executives to resign in protest and generated public criticism from dissenting members of the board. TVP has also announced that it will not broadcast political commentary programs that are not produced in-house. Although TVP management has explained this decision on economic grounds, critics charge that it is another partisan attempt to clamp down on the editorial independence of public television.

The law on radio and television requires TVP to provide direct media access to the main state organs, including the presidency, "to make presentations or explanations of public policy." President Kwasniwski, however, has complained through his spokesman that his office does not receive adequate television coverage. In September the spokesman met directly with TVP head Miazek, who pledged to devote more attention to the activities of the President. Some observers and opposition politicians described the meeting as inappropriate pressure from the President on the programming decisions of public television. Despite these developments, evidence of overt political tampering in public broadcasting is scarce, and public and private television provide coverage of all ranges of political opinion. Political patronage in filling key positions, however, threatens the professional credibility of this major media institution.

There is no restriction on the establishment of private newspapers or distribution of journals; private newspapers and magazines flourish. Ruch, the national network of newspaper kiosks, remains in state hands, although the Government approved a privatization plan in December. However, there is no evidence that the Government has used this virtual monopoly on distribution to suppress any publications. Action has begun to privatize the operation. Books expressing a wide range of political and social viewpoints are widely available, as are foreign periodicals and other publications from abroad.

Academic freedom is generally respected.

b. *Freedom of Peaceful Assembly and Association.*—The law provides for these rights, and the Government generally respects them in practice. Permits are not necessary for public meetings but are required for public demonstrations; demonstration organizers must obtain these permits from local authorities if the demonstration might block a public road. For large demonstrations, organizers are also required to inform the local police of the time and place of their activities and their planned route. Every gathering must have a chairman who is required to open the demonstration, preside over it, and close it.

Private associations need governmental approval to organize and must register with their district court. The procedure essentially requires the organization to sign a declaration that it will abide by the law. In practice, however, the procedure itself is complicated and may be subject to the discretion of the judge in charge.

c. *Freedom of Religion.*—The Constitution, as amended, provides for freedom of conscience and belief, and the Government respects this right in practice. Citizens enjoy the freedom to practice any religion they choose. Religious groups may organize, select and train personnel, solicit and receive contributions, publish, and engage in consultations without government interference. There are no government restrictions on establishing and maintaining places of worship.

More than 95 percent of Poles are Roman Catholic, but Eastern Orthodox, Ukrainian Catholic, and much smaller Protestant, Jewish, and Muslim congregations meet freely. Although the Constitution provides for the separation of church and state, state-run radio broadcasts Catholic mass on Sundays. The Catholic Church is authorized to relicense radio and television stations to operate on frequencies assigned to the Church, the only body outside the NBC allowed to do so.

In January 1995 a "Soldier's Prayer Book," authored by General Kazimierz Tomaszewski, Chief of the Warsaw Military District, was published for the military. The book states that members of a special honor guard who do not take part in military mass are considered to be disobeying orders. While this publication does not constitute law, it bears the same weight. The Ombudsman is continuing his investigation into this matter.

Although the Sejm has ratified the human rights protocol providing parents with the right to bring up their children in compliance with their own religious and philosophical beliefs, religious education classes continue to be taught in the public schools at public expense. While children are supposed to have the choice between religious instruction and ethics, the Ombudsman's office states that in most schools ethics courses are not offered due to financial constraints. Although Catholic Church representatives teach the vast majority of religious classes in the schools, parents can request religious classes in any of the religions legally registered in Poland, including Protestant, Orthodox, and Jewish religious instruction. Such non-Catholic religious instruction exists in practice, and the instructors are paid by the Ministry of Education. The joint State-Episcopate Commission announced that beginning in September 1997, priests will receive salaries from the state budget for teaching religion in public schools. Church representatives are included on a commission that determines whether books qualify for school use.

A government-proposed resolution on ratification of the Concordat, a treaty regulating relations between the Government and the Vatican signed in 1993, remains under consideration in the Sejm. Critics of the Concordat have called for legislation requiring the Church to register all church marriages with civil authorities and forbidding the Church from denying burial to non-Catholics in cemeteries it controls.

d. *Freedom of Movement Within the Country, Foreign Travel, Emigration, and Repatriation.*—Although the Constitution does not address freedom of movement, the Government does not restrict internal or foreign travel. Citizens who leave Poland have no trouble returning. There are no restrictions on emigration. A July initiative by the Social Insurance Company's (ZUS) Chairwoman Anna Bankowska would require those who are delinquent on their ZUS payments to surrender their passports. This proposal could threaten a person's right to travel. Passport law entitles authorities to refuse passports to "persons failing to meet their legal obligations."

The Government generally cooperates with the United Nations High Commissioner for Refugees (UNHCR) and other humanitarian organizations in assisting refugees. There are no reports of forced repatriation of those having a valid claim to refugee status. Foreigners recognized as refugees under the 1951 U.N. Convention are granted full refugee status and permission to remain permanently. According to UNHCR figures, 3,200 persons applied for refugee status in 1996, more than double the number for 1995. Of that number, 120 people were granted refugee status and 380 applicants were denied. About 1,600 cases were discontinued due to the applicant's failure to appear for a hearing. The remaining cases are pending.

However, some observers have criticized how the Government deals with the ever-increasing numbers of asylum seekers, refugees, and illegal immigrants. Poland does not recognize the concept of first asylum or any other form of temporary protection.

Section 3. Respect for Political Rights: The Right of Citizens to Change Their Government

Citizens have the right and ability peacefully to change their government. This right is provided for in the Constitution and exists in practice. Poland is a multiparty democracy in which all citizens 18 years of age and older have the right to vote and to cast secret ballots.

Executive power is divided between the President and a government chosen by Parliament, which is composed of an upper house (the Senate) and a lower house (the Sejm). The Constitution provides for parliamentary elections at least every 4 years. The President, elected for 5 years, has the right to dissolve Parliament following a vote of no confidence or when Parliament fails to pass a budget within 3 months after the Government submits it. Parliament may impeach the President. The electoral law exempts ethnic minority parties from the requirement to win 5 percent of the vote nationwide in order to qualify for seats in individual districts.

The current interim Constitution consists of the "Small Constitution" of 1992, governing the structure of government, and several sections of the 1952 Communist-era Constitution, including a Bill of Rights. The latter includes so-called economic rights. The interim Constitution provides for an independent judiciary. The National Assembly's (joint Sejm and Senate) Constitutional Commission has completed its draft of a new constitution and plans to put it before a national referendum in early 1997.

Women are underrepresented in government and politics. Only 13 percent of parliamentarians are women. Of a total of 15 ministries, none is headed by a woman. None of the leaders of the parties represented in Parliament is a woman. One of the three Vice Marshals of the Sejm is a woman. Prime Minister Cimoszewicz chose a team of 40 advisers early in the year, which included only 2 women.

In November the Government dismissed the Gdansk region's independent prosecutor responsible for repossessing former Communist Party assets from that party's successor, the SDRP (of the current governing coalition). Opposition leaders have cited this as government interference in the political process on behalf of SDRP interests.

Section 4. Governmental Attitude Regarding International and Nongovernmental Investigation of Alleged Violations of Human Rights

A number of human rights groups operate without government restriction, investigating and publishing their findings on human rights cases. Government officials are generally cooperative and responsive to their views.

The Helsinki Committee, a major NGO, conducted human rights investigations without government interference. Members of the Committee report that the Government displays a generally positive and helpful attitude towards human rights investigations. Some local NGO's, however, sense that there is a hostile regulatory climate developing within the government bureaucracy.

The office of the Commissioner for Civil Rights Protection (The Ombudsman), established in 1987, is the Government's watchdog for human rights. The Ombudsman's office is an independent body with broad authority to investigate alleged violations of civil rights and liberties. The Ombudsman registers each reported case and files grievances, where appropriate, with the relevant government office. He has no legislative authority and is sworn to act apolitically.

The Senate Department of Correspondence and Intervention investigates a wide range of grievances and refers cases to senators who will be sympathetic to the grievance, regardless of their district or political affiliation. According to human rights NGO's, this office has been largely inactive and generally ineffective.

Section 5. Discrimination Based on Race, Sex, Religion, Disability, Language, or Social Status

The Constitution calls for equal rights "irrespective of sex, birth, education, profession, nationality, race, religion, social status, and origin." Other clauses provide equal rights to women and religious minorities. However, sufficient legislation does not yet exist to enforce these provisions fully.

Women.—Violence against women continued to be a problem, with occasional reports in the press of wife beating and spousal rape. According to a 1995 government report, 41 percent of women questioned said that they know someone personally who has been beaten by her husband. The report also stated that the Government does not have a program addressing violence towards women, nor has it provided an adequate research tool to determine the extent of the problem. Government and police statistics do not differentiate between male and female victims of violence. In addition, the Government has not supplied public information on the problem. Police do intervene in cases of domestic violence, and husbands can be convicted for beating their wives, but statistics provided by the Women's Rights Center suggest that a large majority of convictions result in suspended sentences. Punishment for domestic violence can range from probation to 10 years in prison, depending on the circumstances of the crime and the harm inflicted. The law has no provision for restraining orders to protect battered women against potential abuse. Women's advocacy groups have complained about the small number of state-supported shelters for battered women.

Trafficking in women is illegal. Two specific provisions in the Criminal Code address this problem. However, according to a government report, there is an increase in the incidence of such trafficking; most often, women are induced to work as prostitutes in Western Europe, often under false pretenses.

No official statistics are available about the extent of sexual harassment or discrimination in the workplace. According to some activists, few complaints about harassment or discrimination are registered because of the lack of specific provisions in the Labor Code that provide for redress. However, a 1996 survey published in a major national daily stated that 23 percent of all women believe that they face discrimination in the workplace. Another recent poll revealed that only 7 percent of women say that they have encountered sexual harassment in the workplace. Labor law was changed this year to grant men paternity leave in order to care for newborn children.

The Constitution provides for equal rights regardless of sex and grants women equal rights with men in all fields of public, political, economic, social, and cultural life, including equal pay for equal work. However, while the Constitution calls for equal treatment, it contains provisions that aim at protecting women rather than offering them true equality. In practice, women are frequently paid less for equivalent work, mainly hold lower level positions, are discharged more quickly, and are less likely to be promoted than men. A 1995 report issued by a committee of nongovernmental organizations stated that women on average earn 30 percent less than men for similar work.

Women are employed in a broad variety of professions and occupations, and a few women occupy high positions in government and in the private sector. However, legal barriers, such as clauses in social insurance law limiting child sick care benefits to women only and mandating earlier retirement for women, encourage discrimination in hiring.

The law does not address equality in hiring practices (there are no legal penalties for discriminatory hiring practices). Advertisements for jobs frequently indicate a gender preference. In May the Labor Code was modified to allow women access to a number of previously forbidden careers. However, women are still prevented from working underground or in jobs that require heavy lifting. The rise in unemployment and other social changes accompanying economic reforms and restructuring have affected women more than men: At the end of 1995, 14.4 percent of women were unemployed, compared with 13.7 percent of men.

The Ombudsman for Human Rights monitors the rights of women within the broader context human rights. Observers note that the broad scope of the office's mandate dilutes its ability to function as an effective advocate of women's issues. Within the Cabinet, the "Government Plenipotentiary for Women and the Family" is responsible for providing relevant information to the Government as it formulates policy. Incumbent Plenipotentiary Jolanata Banach has taken an activist approach, and her office is drafting the Government's "Action Plan for Women's Issues" to comply with the 1995 Beijing Declaration. Several women's rights NGO's. Among the most notable are the Polish Foundation for Women and Family Planning, and the Women's Rights Center. These groups are active advocates of gender equality and advance their goals through research, monitoring, and publication. There are also several church-sponsored women's advocacy organizations, but their cooperation with the above-mentioned NGO's is limited.

The 1962 citizenship law discriminates against women by not granting them the same right as men to transmit citizenship to their foreign-born spouses.

Children.—The Constitution extends some state protection to the family and children. Specifically, it states that children born in and out of wedlock shall be treated equally. It also charges the State with ensuring that alimony rights and obligations are implemented and tasks the Government with "devoting special attention to the education of youth." However, the realities of economic and social life make it difficult for the Government to implement these mandates.

The Government sponsors some health programs targeted specifically at children, including a vaccination program and periodic checkups conducted through the schools. In reality, however, budget shortfalls prevent complete implementation of these programs. The school system does not provide health education classes for children. Some NGO's have tried to fill this gap: the Batory Foundation has set up a program to provide health education for children by providing training and instructional materials to a group of teachers, but a spokesperson says the scope of the problem far outstrips this small program.

Education is compulsory until the age of 16, although the Government has proposed raising the age to 18. There are no procedures in schools to protect children from abuse by teachers; in fact, the teachers' work code guarantees legal immunity from prosecution for the use of corporal punishment in classrooms.

There is an increasing incidence of prostitution among 12- and 13-year-olds, and unemployment, alcoholism, and housing shortages have affected the quality of life of children. Moreover, there are no laws explicitly addressing violence against children or corporal punishment. Abuse is rarely reported, and convictions for child abuse are even rarer. Parents have the right to make all decisions concerning their children's medical treatment and education.

There is unequal treatment of young men and women in terms of the age of majority. Men and women reach majority at the age of 18 under the Civil Code. However, a young woman can reach majority at the age of 16 if she has entered into marriage with the consent of her parents and the guardianship court. In addition, men are not permitted to marry without parental consent until the age of 21, whereas women may do so at the age of 18. Lawmakers' rationale for this difference in treatment is the assumption that it is better that men entering compulsory military service not be encumbered with families.

People With Disabilities.—There are approximately 4.5 million disabled persons in Poland, and it is predicted that the number will reach 6 million by the year 2010. In 1995 the Central Bureau of Statistics reported that 17 percent of disabled persons who can work are unemployed. Disabled persons' groups claim that the percentage is much higher.

A number of laws protect the rights of people with disabilities. Implementation, however, falls short of rights set forth in the legislation. Public buildings and transportation are generally not accessible to people with disabilities; the law provides only that such buildings "should be accessible." The law created a state fund for the rehabilitation of the disabled that derives its assets from a tax on employers of over 50 persons, unless 6 percent of the employer's work force are disabled persons.

While the fund has adequate resources, its management has been fraught with difficulties, including frequent changes in leadership. According to newspaper reports, the fund has 4,000 applications pending. In addition, by law the fund cannot be used to assist disabled children, that is, persons under 16 years of age. In October the Polish Union of the Blind organized a protest in Opole to demand more accessibility to public buildings and the use of Braille in certain public documents and public welfare agencies.

Religious Minorities.—The law places the Protestant churches on the same legal footing as Catholic and Orthodox churches. Protestants have the same ability to claim restitution of property lost during the Communist era and have the same tax reduction granted to the Orthodox and Catholic churches. However, the law only covers church property seized by the People's Republic of Poland and does not address either the issue of private property or Jewish religious property taken during World War II.

The President and Government made efforts during the year to improve Polish-Jewish relations. In July the Prime Minister and the Mayor of Kielce apologized on behalf of the Polish nation for the 1946 pogrom in that city in which 42 Jews were murdered. The President and Prime Minister opposed the building of a supermarket near the Auschwitz concentration camp and successfully encouraged local authorities to find alternatives to the planned development. This cooperative approach was praised by Jewish organizations.

In July around 100 skinheads led by far-right politician Boleslaw Tejkowski marched on the Auschwitz-Birkenau camp. The provincial governor was criticized by national and local officials for his decision to allow the demonstration, which he said was based on the right to free speech. A similar, though smaller, demonstration in Krakow by Tejkowski in May failed to elicit support from curious onlookers.

In June 66 tombs at the Jewish cemetery in Warsaw were destroyed. The police presume that the perpetrators were hooligans without religious motivation, as no hate slurs were written on the site. However, members of the Jewish community believe that the attack was related to the anniversary of the Kielce pogrom. On July 6, a Jewish monument commemorating the Jews who lived at Kamien Pomorski before World War II was vandalized. The police said that it was an act of hooliganism and not a hate crime. A similar event occurred in November, when vandals defaced some graves in the Jewish cemetery in the town of Oswiecim, near the site of the Auschwitz concentration camp. Police have made no arrests in the case, but the city council made a public statement condemning the vandalism.

In September the Gdansk prosecutor reopened his investigation of Father Henryk Jankowski for an allegedly anti-Semitic sermon he gave in 1995 (see Section 2.a.).

National/Racial/Ethnic Minorities.—The law provides for the educational rights of ethnic minorities, including the right to be taught in their own language. Poland's bilateral treaties with Germany and Belarus contain provisions relating to the rights of those national minorities, and human rights groups have praised these provisions as "close to ideal." A program was initiated at the beginning of the 1996–97 school year to teach Lithuanian to pupils of Lithuanian descent in 12 schools in northeastern Poland. Some 4,000 students also will begin learning Belarusian in the Bialystok region this year.

In Przemysl a Greek Catholic cupola was torn down this spring, reportedly for safety reasons. This was done without the consent of the Ukrainian Greek Catholic minority in the city, and the event fueled ongoing tension between the Roman Catholic majority and the Ukrainian minority there.

The Romani community, numbering around 30,000, faced disproportionately high unemployment and was more negatively affected by the current economic changes and restructuring than were ethnic Poles, according to its leaders. The national Government does not overtly discriminate against Roma; however, some local officials sometimes do discriminate by not providing services in a timely manner or at all. Some schools have experimented with separate special classes for Romani children, stating that because of economic disadvantage, language barriers, and parental illiteracy, Romani children are behind their non-Romani counterparts when starting school. In July police raided and tore down a Romani camp in Warsaw and made over 100 arrests. Opposition politicians and Romani leaders protested against the alleged "strong-arm tactics" of the police in this action, although there was no evidence that the police violated any laws. After the raid, the authorities deported several Roma who were in Poland illegally. Human rights groups report that non-Polish Roma with valid visas were released immediately.

In March a court in the south rejected the appeal of six people convicted of throwing incendiary devices into a hostel occupied by participants in a Ukranian cultural festival in 1995. In December, 1995, the court had reduced the original sentence of 18 months in prison to a fine and 3 years' probation.

According to a 1995 study conducted by the Warsaw University Sociology Institute, 25 percent of visitors to Poland of African, Asian, or Arab descent experienced some type of aggression during their stay, and 60 percent experienced verbal abuse based on their skin color.

Section 6. Worker Rights

a. *The Right of Association.*—The law provides that all civilian workers, including military employees, police and frontier guards, have the right to establish and join trade unions of their own choosing. And unions have the right to join labor federations and confederations and to affiliate with international labor organizations. Independent labor leaders reported that these rights were largely observed in practice.

The law sets minimum size requirements for establishing a trade union: 10 persons may form a local union, and 30 may establish a national union. Unions, including interbranch national unions and national interbranch federations, must be registered with the courts. A court decision refusing registration may be appealed to an appeals court. In 1996 the number of registered national-level unions rose to 318 from 288. No precise data exists on work force unionization, but some estimates put membership at some 40 percent of state/public sector employees, with the figure at about 5 percent in the private sector. Newly established small- to medium-sized firms were as a rule nonunion, while union activity often carried over after state-owned enterprises were privatized.

The Independent Self-Governing Trade Union (NSZZ) Solidarity has a verified dues-paying membership that stabilized in 1996 at about 1.4 million. Small spinoffs from mainstream Solidarity include the rival factions "Solidarity '80," "August '80" and "Christian Trade Union Solidarity (Popieluszko)." There are no reliable estimates of their membership. The other principal national unions are those affiliated with the All-Poland Trade Union Alliance (OPZZ), the Communist-inspired confederation established in 1984 as the sole legal alternative to then-repressed NSZZ Solidarity, and its teachers' affiliate, ZNP. The OPZZ claims a membership of 4.5 million, but these figures are unverified and recent polls suggest that its regular dues-paying membership may be less than Solidarity's. The 1994 collective bargaining law did not require union membership figures to be verified or based on dues-paying members to be considered a "representative" negotiating partner. As a result, Solidarity has challenged the credentials of some unions (largely OPZZ affiliates) to negotiate with the Government on the grounds that membership figures are unproven.

In May President Kwasniewski signed a bill that could lead to partial resolution of the longstanding dispute over Solidarity assets seized during the martial law period and still administered by OPZZ. Solidarity called the law a step forward but stressed that it applied to only a fraction of disputed assets. The International Confederation of Free Trade Unions and European Trade Union Confederation continued to decline to cooperate with OPZZ, largely because of the outstanding assets issue.

Reports that the domestic branch of the UOP intelligence service had directed its officials to monitor strategically important enterprises caused a storm of controversy, particularly within organized labor. Labor leaders protested that the UOP order sanctioned infiltration of unions and penetration by technical means to obtain early information on strikes and the mood of the work force. The UOP later rescinded the order and clarified that any monitoring of the industrial climate would take place on the basis of open sources, not by recruiting agents from among the labor force or installing listening devices. Nevertheless, Solidarity President Marian Krzaklewski asserted in the fall that the UOP continued to monitor him, his family, and other Solidarity leaders.

Most trade unions operate independently of the Government, and some are particularly active in politics. More than two-thirds of the 169 governing Democratic Left Alliance (SLD) Deputies are, or have been, OPZZ members. Of these, the OPZZ formally sponsored 63 as "trade union deputies" during the 1993 elections, but many have since left the OPZZ. Solidarity and some OPZZ regional leaders charge that the OPZZ national leadership is not independent because the SLD enforces party discipline on important votes in the Sejm. Solidarity has a 13-member caucus in the Senate and in the summer brokered a coalition ("Solidarity electoral action"), a bloc of more than 35 center-right political groups to stand for the 1997 parliamentary elections. One Confederation of Independent Poland (KPN) Sejm Deputy chairs the KPN trade union wing, "Kontra."

Unions have the right to strike except in "essential services." According to the unions, the 1991 Act on Collective Dispute Resolution prescribes an overly lengthy process before a strike may be called. Employers considered the law too lenient as it allows only one-quarter of the work force to vote to call a strike. As a result, as many as 60 to 90 percent of strikes called in recent years have been technically "illegal" because one or both of the sides did not follow each step exactly as required by law. Labor courts act slowly on deciding the legality of strikes while sanctions against unions for calling illegal strikes, or against employers for provoking them, are minimal. Arbitration is not obligatory and depends on the will of disputing parties. Unions charge that laws prohibiting retribution against strikers are not consistently enforced and that fines imposed as punishment are so minimal that they are ineffective sanctions to illegal activity. Workers who strike in accordance with the law retain their right to social insurance but not pay. If a court rules a strike "illegal," however, workers may lose social benefits, and organizers are liable for damages and may face civil charges and fines.

The number of strikes called continued to fall sharply (to a dozen by mid-1996, from a high of several thousand in the early 1990's). A new Labor Code went into effect on June 1, representing a major overhaul of Communist-era labor regulations, but ambiguities in dispute resolution mechanisms remain.

Solidarity is affiliated with the ICFTU and the World Confederation of Labor (WCL).

b. *The Right to Organize and Bargain Collectively.*—The 1991 Law on Trade Unions created a favorable environment to conduct trade union activity.

Labor leaders, however, reported that the 1991 law has not prevented numerous cases of employer discrimination against workers seeking to organize or join unions, particularly in the growing private sector. The law also has not prevented employer harassment of union members for their union activity. Union leaders say the law also lacks provisions to ensure that a union has continued rights of representation when a state-owned enterprise undergoes privatization, commercialization, bankruptcy, or sale. This contributed to the very low unionization rate in the private sector.

The 1991 law provides for parties to take disputes over its implementation first to labor courts, then to the Prosecutor General, and, in the last resort, to the Supreme Court. In a typical year, Solidarity takes several thousand cases to labor courts, several hundred to the Prosecutor General, and dozens to the Supreme Court for resolution. In an overwhelming majority of these cases, the courts ordered employers to correct practices or reinstate dismissed workers. In other cases, the courts ordered unions to reimburse employers for activity found to be illegal. Penalties, however, are minimal and are not an effective deterrent.

The Government sought to make enterprise-level collective bargaining over wages and working conditions the central element of the new labor relations system. Labor and management at increasing numbers of enterprises have used the law to adapt their relationship to the demands of a market economy, but experience in modern labor relations is still minimal among unionists and employers reportedly often resist entering into negotiations. Thus, a substantial minority of enterprises continued to operate on the basis of agreements renewed from previous years.

Since its formation in early 1994, the Tripartite Commission (labor, employers, government), under the leadership of the Labor Minister, has become the primary forum that determines national-level wage and benefit increases in such politically sensitive areas as the so-called budget sector (health, education, and public employees), while rendering opinions on pension indexation, energy pricing, and other important aspects of social policy. The Commission serves as a very important "safety valve" by which the social partners air differences and discuss grievances before they erupt into social conflict. Most Commission members want it to become a permanent fixture on the national landscape, despite many initial doubts about its viability.

Many disputes arose because of the weakness of the employer side of the union/employer/government triangle. Key state sector employers still were unable to negotiate independently with organized labor without the extensive involvement of central government ministries to which they were subordinate, while the Government repeatedly stated its intention not to be drawn into labor disputes. This continued to complicate and politicize the Government's new labor relations paradigm.

There are no export processing zones.

c. *Prohibition of Forced or Compulsory Labor.*—Compulsory labor does not exist, except for prisoners convicted of criminal offenses, and is otherwise prohibited by law.

In April the Ukrainian Government protested to the Polish Embassy in Kiev about a case of alleged "forced labor," in which 19 Ukrainian and Belarusian women were reportedly required to work in restrictive and dangerous conditions in a Polish agricultural firm. Journalists investigated the case and reported that pay and working conditions at the farm, while lower than normal Polish standards, exceeded those in the countries of the workers' origin and therefore did not qualify as a "labor camp." Following the initial report, the case attracted no more attention.

d. *Minimum Age for Employment of Children.*—The law contains strict legal prescriptions about the conditions in which children may work. The Labor Code forbids the employment of persons under the age of 15. Those between the ages of 15 and 18 may be employed only if they have completed primary school and if the proposed employment constitutes vocational training and is not harmful to their health. The age floor rises to 18 if a particular job might pose a health danger.

Despite these prescriptions, the state Labor Inspectorate reported that increasing numbers of children now work and that employers often violate labor rules in employing them (underpayment, late payment, etc.). Inspectors found violations on stud farms, in restaurants, and, in some instances, in factories in the private sector.

e. *Acceptable Conditions of Work.*—The Ministry of Labor, the unions, and employers' organizations negotiate a revised national minimum wage every 3 months. The minimum monthly wage for employees in state-owned enterprises rose to roughly $140 (370 zlotys). While this was an increase over 1995, it was insufficient to provide a worker or family with a decent standard of living in view of rapidly rising prices. A large percentage of construction workers and seasonal agricultural laborers from the former Soviet Union earn less than the minimum. The large size of the informal economy, along with the insufficient numbers of state labor inspectors, make enforcement of the minimum wage very difficult. In late 1995, the State Labor Inspector concluded that as long as high unemployment persists, workers often agree to inferior working conditions in order to retain their jobs.

The standard legal workweek is 42 hours, which allows 6 or 7 hour days, including at least one 24-hour rest period. The law requires overtime payment for hours in excess of the standard workweek. The new Labor Code defines minimum conditions for the protection of workers' health and safety. Prescriptions are strict and extensive, and trade unions have the right to stop production or extract a worker from dangerous working conditions without jeopardy to continued employment. Enforcement, however, is a major problem because the State Labor Inspectorate is unable to monitor the state sector sufficiently, or the private sector, where a growing percentage of accidents take place. In addition, there is a lack of clarity concerning which government or legislative body has responsibility for enforcing the law.

Of the 112,205 work-related accidents reported in 1995, 621 involved deaths, slightly fewer than in 1994. This represents roughly 10 accidents per 1,000 workers, slightly more than in 1994. The Government reported in April that most accidents were in the public sector, while most serious accidents were in the private sector, where proportionally more deaths also occurred. Solidarity charges that the problem lies not in the law, which sets adequate standards, but in enforcement, as employer sanctions for illegal behavior are minimal. Standards for exposure to chemicals, dust, and noise are routinely exceeded.

PORTUGAL*

The Republic of Portugal is a constitutional democracy with a president, an independent judiciary, a prime minister, and a legislative assembly freely elected by secret ballot in multiparty elections.

Internal security is primarily the responsibility of the Ministries of Justice and Internal Administration. Security forces are controlled by, and responsive to, the Government.

Portugal has a market-based economy and is a member of the European Union. An increasing proportion of the population is employed in services, while employment in agriculture continues to decline and has been static or declining slightly in the industrial sector.

Citizens enjoy a broad range of civil and other human rights which the Government generally respects. Civil rights are outlined in the Constitution with specific reference to the Universal Declaration of Human Rights. The principal human rights problem is the occasional beating of detainees or prisoners by police or prison personnel. Credible although infrequent reports of this problem continued, as did reports of poor conditions in prisons. Also, violence against women, child labor, and discrimination against Roma are problems.

---

*A separate report on Macau, recognized by both China and Portugal as Chinese territory under Portuguese administration, follows this report.

RESPECT FOR HUMAN RIGHTS

Section 1. Respect for the Integrity of the Person, Including Freedom From:

a. *Political and other Extrajudicial Killing.*—There were no reports of political killings.

A criminal suspect was killed while in police custody in a widely publicized incident in May. A National Republican Guard officer confessed to the crime. A trial is pending.

b. *Disappearance.*—There were no reports of politically motivated disappearances.

c. *Torture and Other Cruel, Inhuman, or Degrading Treatment or Punishment.*—The Constitution forbids torture, inhuman or degrading treatment or punishment, and the use of evidence obtained under torture in criminal proceedings. An independent Ombudsman, chosen by the Legislative Assembly (parliament), investigates complaints of mistreatment by police and prison authorities. A recently appointed police inspector general has also begun examining cases of alleged mistreatment.

The Government and Amnesty International (AI) have continued their dialogue on allegations of police brutality. One case of mistreatment of two citizens by the National Republican Guard (GNR), which AI had been following since 1992, was finally resolved when the conviction and sentencing of several GNR soldiers to prison terms was upheld on appeal. The trial continued at year's end of six other GNR officers charged with assaulting another citizen in 1991. New credible complaints of police brutality continue to be lodged, including a widely publicized case in which a magistrate in the public prosecutor's office claimed to have been punched and kicked by GNR officers. AI continues to lament the delay in investigating such allegations.

The Council of Europe's Committee for the Prevention of Torture also continued its dialogue with the Government. In a November report, the Committee released the findings of its 1995 visit to prisons and police stations. The 1995 visit was a followup to a 1992 visit of the same facilities. The Committee's report cited improvements in prison conditions but criticized the continued high incidence of allegations of beatings of detainees at the time of arrest or while in police custody. The report further criticized the failure of police agencies to investigate allegations of mistreatment by their officers, or to adequately punish those found guilty of such offenses. It recommended that human rights training for the police receive increased emphasis, that allegations of mistreatment be fully investigated, and that persons alleging mistreatment be given a forensic medical examination for use in evidence. The Government announced plans in May to address problems of police mistreatment by sending veteran officers for training in human rights and proper police procedure. New recruits have been receiving such training for several years.

Prison conditions are poor. The Ombudsman submitted a critical report on prison conditions to the Government and parliament in June. He cited overcrowding, sanitation, medical care, security, and food quality as among the problem areas and recommended numerous corrective measures. Two new prisons opened during the year.

The Government permits prison visits by human rights monitors. Human rights organizations report no difficulties in gaining access to inmates at detention facilities.

d. *Arbitrary Arrest, Detention, or Exile.*—Under the law, an investigating judge determines whether an arrested person should be detained, released on bail, or released outright. Persons may not be held more than 48 hours without appearing before an investigating judge. Investigative detention is limited to a maximum of 6 months for each suspected crime. If a formal charge has not been filed within that period, the detainee must be released. In cases of serious crimes, for example murder or armed robbery, or of more than one suspect, investigative detention may be for up to 2 years and may be extended by a judge to 3 years in extraordinary circumstances. A suspect in investigative detention must be brought to trial within 18 months of being formally charged. If the suspect is not in detention, there is no specified period for going to trial. A detainee has access to lawyers; the State assumes the cost if necessary.

Exile is illegal and is not practiced.

e. *Denial of Fair Public Trial.*—The judiciary is independent and impartial. The court system, laid out in the Constitution, consists of a Constitutional Court, a Supreme Court of Justice, and judicial courts of first and second instance. There is also a supreme court of administration, which deals with administrative and tax disputes, and which is supported by lower administrative courts. An audit court is in the Ministry of Finance.

All trials are public except those which may offend the dignity of the victim, such as in cases of sexual abuse of children. The accused is presumed innocent. In trials for serious crimes, a panel of three judges presides. For lesser crimes, a single judge presides. At the request of the accused, a jury may be used in trials for major crimes; in practice, requests for jury trials are extremely rare.

The judicial system provides citizens with a fair legal process. It has been much criticized, however, for a large backlog of pending trials resulting from inefficient functioning of the courts.

There were no reports of political prisoners.

f. *Arbitrary Interference With Privacy, Family, Home, or Correspondence.*—The Constitution forbids such practices, and the Government respects these provisions in practice. Violations are subject to effective legal sanctions.

Section 2. Respect for Civil Liberties, Including:

a. *Freedom of Speech and Press.*—Freedom of speech and the press is provided for in the Constitution, and the Government respects these rights in practice. An independent press, an effective judiciary, and a functioning democratic political system combine to ensure freedom of speech and of the press, including academic freedom.

b. *Freedom of Peaceful Assembly and Association.*—The law provides for these rights, and the authorities generally respect these provisions.

c. *Freedom of Religion.*—The Constitution provides for freedom of religion, and the Government respects this right in practice.

d. *Freedom of Movement Within the Country, Foreign Travel, Emigration, and Repatriation.*—The Constitution and laws provide for these rights, and the Government respects them in practice.

The Government cooperates with the U.N. High Commissioner for Refugees and other humanitarian organizations in assisting refugees. Persons who qualify as refugees are entitled to residence permits. The issue of first asylum did not arise in 1996. There were no reports of forced expulsions of those having a valid claim to refugee status.

Section 3. Respect for Political Rights: The Right of Citizens to Change Their Government

Portugal is a multiparty, parliamentary democracy. The Constitution provides citizens with the right to change their government peacefully, and citizens exercise this right in practice through periodic, free, and fair elections on the basis of universal suffrage.

Women and minorities have full political rights. Women currently head 3 of 17 ministries: Health, employment, and environment. Women are represented in all major political parties but constitute only 13 percent of the deputies in the legislature, where 3 of the 15 committees are chaired by a woman. Race is rarely an issue in politics. Persons of minority origin have achieved prominence in politics.

Section 4. Governmental Attitude Regarding International and Nongovernmental Investigation of Alleged Violations of Human Rights

A number of local and international human rights groups operate freely, investigating and publishing their findings on human rights cases. Government officials are generally cooperative, although most groups complain of slow investigations or remedial actions.

Section 5. Discrimination Based on Race, Sex, Religion, Disability, Language, or Social Status

The Constitution forbids discrimination based on ancestry, sex, race, language, origin, religion, political or ideological convictions, education, economic situation, or social condition, and the Government enforces these prohibitions.

Women.—The deaths of three women in March drew attention to the reportedly common but largely hidden problem of domestic and other violence against women. Hundreds of battered women seek help each year from the Portuguese Association for the Support of Victims. The law provides for criminal penalties in cases of violence by a spouse. Traditional societal attitudes discourage many battered women from recourse to the judicial system. In 1996 a shelter for battered women opened in Oporto, and a Lisbon shelter is planned. The judicial system shows no apparent reluctance to prosecute suspects accused of abusing women.

The Civil Code provides for full legal equality for women. Sexual harassment, an issue gaining public attention, is covered in the Penal Code as a sex crime, but only if perpetrated by a superior and in the workplace. As in the case of violence, socially ingrained attitudes discourage many women from taking advantage of their legal protection.

The Commission on Equality in the Workplace and in Employment, made up of representatives of the Government, employers organizations, and labor unions, is empowered to examine complaints of sexual harassment but receives few. It does review numerous complaints of discrimination by employers against pregnant workers and new mothers, who are protected by law.

Women are increasingly represented in universities, business, science, and the professions. Traditional attitudes of male dominance persist but are changing gradually. The Commission for the Equality and Rights of Women, an official organization reporting to the newly-established High Commissioner for the Promotion of Equality and of the Family, is a leading and effective advocate of women's rights.

Children.—Nine years of education are compulsory. The Government is increasingly committed to improving children's welfare and has convened an interministerial commission reporting to the High Commissioner for the Promotion of Equality and of the Family to study whether the Government should implement a "global policy on children." The quasi-independent Institute for the Support of Children and the University of Minho's Institute for the Study of Children contribute to efforts to improve conditions for children. The primary role of the former is to promote the Government's child welfare policies by advising local authorities and employers as to the legal rights of minors. The mission of the newly-created Institute for the Study of Children is to research children's issues and to improve child care. There is no societal pattern of abuse of children, although child labor remains a problem (see Section 6.d.).

People With Disabilities.—There is no discrimination against disabled persons in employment, education, or the provision of other state services. Their access to public facilities is mandated by legislation, which is generally complied with. There is no such legislation covering private businesses or other facilities.

National/Racial/Ethnic Minorities.—The principal minority groups are immigrants, legal and illegal, from Portugal's former African colonies. There is also a resident Romani population. The Government devoted significant police resources to investigating the 1995 skinhead street attack on persons of African origin in which one victim died. The investigation led to the prosecution of at least 15 persons believed to have been involved in planning or carrying out the attack. Racism was a suspected motive in another case in which a person of African origin died; the accused was acquitted, but the prosecutor has appealed the verdict. A new law designed to combat race-related crimes permits antiracism associations as well as victims to lodge criminal complaints and to participate by retaining their own lawyers and calling witnesses. The Government appointed a High Commissioner for Immigration and Ethnic Minorities, and, in order to reduce exploitation of illegal workers, passed a law to regularize the status of many illegal immigrants, particularly those of Lusophone African or Brazilian origin. When one local government, reportedly pressured by popular suspicion of criminal activity by Roma, demolished allegedly illegal residential structures in an apparent attempt to evict a Romani family, the civil governor of the district was actively involved in efforts to resolve the issue and to assist the dislocated family to find shelter in a more tolerant community nearby. The incident focused press and public attention on the hostile local attitudes encountered by Romani communities in some areas.

Section 6. Worker Rights

a. *The Right of Association.*—Workers in both the private and public sectors have the right to associate freely and to establish committees in the workplace to defend their interests. The Constitution provides for the right to establish unions by profession or industry. Trade union associations have the right to participate in the preparation of labor legislation. Strikes are constitutionally permitted for any reason, including political causes; they are common and generally are resolved through direct negotiations. The authorities respect all provisions of the law on labor's rights.

Two principal labor federations exist. There are no restrictions on the formation of additional labor federations. Unions function without hindrance by the Government and are closely associated with political parties. There are no restrictions on the ability of unions to join federations or on federations affiliating with international labor bodies.

b. *The Right to Organize and Bargain Collectively.*—Unions are free to organize without interference by the Government or by employers. Collective bargaining is provided for in the Constitution and is practiced extensively in the public and private sectors.

Collective bargaining disputes rarely lead to prolonged strikes. Should a long strike occur in an essential sector such as health, energy, or transportation, the Government may order the workers back to work for a specific period. This did not occur in 1996. The Government has rarely invoked this power, in part because most strikes are limited to periods of 1 to 3 days. The law requires a "minimum level of service" to be provided during strikes in essential sectors, but this requirement has been infrequently applied. When it has, minimum levels of service have been established by agreement between the Government and the striking unions, although unions have complained, including to the International Labor Organization, that the minimum levels have been set too high. When collective bargaining fails, the Government may appoint a mediator, at the request of either management or labor.

The law prohibits antiunion discrimination, and the authorities enforce this prohibition in practice. Complaints are promptly examined by the General Directorate of Labor.

There are no export processing zones.

c. *Prohibition of Forced or Compulsory Labor.*—Forced labor is prohibited and does not occur.

d. *Minimum Age for Employment of Children.*—The minimum employment age is 15 years. It is to be raised to 16 years on January 1, 1997, to ensure that the Labor Code does not conflict with the decree mandating 9 years of compulsory education. The first students bound by the 9-year rule will complete 9 years of study in 1997.

The two main labor federations and observers from other European countries have charged that a number of "clandestine" companies in the textile, shoe, and construction industries exploit child labor. In September the Government created a new intergovernmental Commission to Combat Child Labor (CNCTI) tasked with eradicating child labor. New measures that the CNCTI is charged with implementing include stiffer fines for employers with children on the payroll, subsidies for vulnerable families with children, and curriculum changes to keep children in school. The CNCTI is tasked with presiding over an upgrade of the Government's General Labor Inspectorate, which is responsible for enforcing child labor laws. An increase is planned in the Inspectorate's funding, the number of inspectors, and inspections. The Inspectorate reports that thousands of children under age 15 are employed illegally but believes the number is declining. Government statistics derived from labor inspections suggest the incidence of child labor has been greatly reduced in recent years. Nevertheless, the Inspectorate acknowledges that the transfer of work involving children from factories and workshops into the home and other settings beyond the reach of inspectors complicates the task of accurately measuring and stopping child labor violations.

Union observers agree that the number of illegally employed children is falling, but they attribute this development to the general rise in unemployment. Unions continued to form local alliances with church groups, citizens groups, and local government bodies to address the multiple social and economic causes of child labor. While some improvements have been made, the Government does not allocate enough resources to address the problem fully.

e. *Acceptable Conditions of Work.*—Minimum wage legislation covers full-time workers, as well as rural workers and domestic employees age 18 or over. The monthly minimum wage of about $360 (Esc 54,600), which came into effect on January 1, is generally enforced. Along with widespread rent controls, basic food and utility subsidies, and phased implementation of a guaranteed minimum income, the minimum wage affords a basic standard of living for a worker and family.

A new law adopted in July provides for phased reduction of the normal maximum workweek from 44 hours to 40 hours by December 1997. The new law limits regular work hours to 8 hours per day, with a maximum of 2 hours paid overtime per day and 200 hours of overtime per year, and with a minimum interval of 12 hours between normal working days. The law also introduces job flexibility—employers may assign workers tasks beyond those specifically included in their job category. Another new law provides for the phased reduction of the normal maximum workweek for all public sector employees from 40 hours to 35 hours by 1999, beginning with a reduction to 39 hours in 1996. These working hour limits are respected in practice. Workers receive 22 days of paid annual leave per year, plus vacation and Christmas ("13th month") bonuses.

The Ministry of Employment and Social Security monitors compliance through its regional inspectors.

Employers are legally responsible for accidents at work and are required by law to carry accident insurance. An existing body of legislation regulates safety and health, but labor unions continue to argue for stiffer laws. The General Directorate of Hygiene and Labor Security develops safety standards, and the General Labor Inspectorate is responsible for enforcement, but the Inspectorate lacks sufficient funds and inspectors to combat the problem of work accidents effectively. A relatively large proportion of accidents is in the construction industry. Poor environmental controls in textile production also cause considerable concern. While the ability of workers to remove themselves from situations where these hazards exist is limited, it is difficult to fire workers for any reason. Workers injured on the job rarely initiate lawsuits.

MACAU

Macau, a 13 square mile enclave on the south China coast, is recognized by both China and Portugal as Chinese territory under Portuguese administration. The "Organic Statute" of 1976, which serves as the constitution, grants it considerable administrative, financial, and legislative autonomy. Both the Governor and the Legislative Assembly exercise legislative power. The Governor, appointed by the Portuguese President, holds extensive powers under the Organic Statute.

Under the 1987 Sino-Portuguese joint declaration, Macau will become a Special Administration Region (SAR) of China on December 20, 1999, and operate under the principle of "one country, two systems," to remain unchanged for 50 years. The future constitution, a joint Sino-Portuguese document called the "Basic Law," was promulgated on March 31, 1993.

Portuguese metropolitan law serves as the basis for the legal system, which features a judiciary and jury trials. The police force maintains public order and is under civilian control.

The market-based economy is fueled by legalized gambling, which generates approximately one-half of government revenue. A thriving tourist industry and the export of textiles and other light industrial products also contribute to economic growth. An international airport opened in December 1995 and is expected to promote economic growth. The economy provides a high standard of living for its citizens.

Although citizens derive a wide range of rights and freedoms from Macau's status as a Portuguese territory, they have limited ability to change their government. Voters directly elect only one-third of the legislators, and the territory's future path has been set by Lisbon and Beijing. Legislation, effective in November 1995 provided greater equality in the work force for women. Although China, through the Basic Law, agreed to continue the application of international covenants on civil and political rights and on economic, social, and cultural rights after 1999, human rights activists remain concerned that China made no obligation to submit regular reports in these areas. There are credible reports that media self-censorship continues on issues considered to be sensitive to China.

RESPECT FOR HUMAN RIGHTS

Section 1. Respect for the Integrity of the Person, Including Freedom From:

a. *Political and Other Extrajudicial Killing.*—There were no reports of political or other extrajudicial killings.

b. *Disappearance.*—There were no reports of politically motivated disappearances.

c. *Torture and Other Cruel, Inhuman, or Degrading Treatment or Punishment.*— Such abuses are prohibited by law, and the authorities respect this in practice. Prison conditions meet minimum international standards, and the Government permits visits by human rights monitors. Human rights groups have expressed concern that there has been no agreement to date within the Sino-Portuguese Joint Liaison Group on the application to Macau of the Covenant against Torture and Other Cruel, Inhuman or Degrading Treatment or Punishment, although both Portugal and China have ratified the covenant.

d. *Arbitrary Arrest, Detention, or Exile.*—Legal prohibitions against arbitrary arrest exist, and the authorities respect them in practice. The examining judge, who conducts a pretrial inquiry in criminal cases, has a wide range of powers to collect evidence, order or dismiss indictments, validate and maintain the detention of suspects, and determine whether to release accused persons. Police must present persons remanded in custody to an examining judge within 48 hours of detention. The accused's counsel may examine the evidence. If the judge is not convinced that the evidence is adequate, he may dismiss the accused.

A 1995 Macau Supreme Court ruling upholding a Portuguese Constitutional Court decision on the unconstitutionality of extraditing individuals to countries that practice the death penalty, clarified policy towards people alleged to have committed commercial or criminal violations in China. This ruling followed international criticism of the involuntary transfer to Chinese authorities of an Australian citizen of Chinese ancestry in 1994. The authorities investigated this matter and claimed to have found no evidence of police misconduct. Human rights activists assert that in numerous cases in the past, the police had "transferred" detainees to China, despite the absence of a Sino-Portuguese extradition treaty. The authorities have suggested that three persons affected by the 1995 court ruling could be tried in Macau for the crimes they allegedly committed in China, using evidence and witnesses furnished by China. Chinese officials on the Sino-Portuguese Joint Liaison Group, however, criticized the decision by the Macau Supreme Court, arguing that because Macau is considered to be a part of China, no formal extradition arrangements are necessary for the transfer of prisoners wanted by China.

Forced exile is not practiced.

e. *Denial of Fair Public Trial.*—Changes to the judicial system in 1993 designed to render the system autonomous from the Portuguese system—required to bring the system into line with the structure for the judicial system specified in the Sino-Portuguese Basic Law—raised some concerns among human rights observers and journalists. Prior to the reorganization, the judiciary had only subordinate (first instance) courts located in the territory. In the first stage of the reforms, new courts, most notably a Supreme Court of Justice, were established to allow appeals to be heard locally.

The Superior Court consists of six magistrates broken down into two panels, one of which hears only administrative, fiscal, and customs duties cases; the other oversees all other cases. An additional judge serves as President of the Court. Cases before the Supreme Court are heard initially by the relevant panel of three judges. In instances where a judgment has been rendered by such a panel and subsequently appealed, the case is then heard by all six judges, with the President voting only in case of a tie. This structure results in a situation where three of the individuals hearing an appeal have already rendered an opinion in the initial judgment, which critics charge calls into question the objectivity of the subsequent ruling. Until full autonomy of the Macau courts is achieved, however, some special appeal cases may still be either presented directly to courts in Portugal or sent to them through a local court.

Journalists and human rights activists have also voiced concerns that, as a result of the 1993 reforms, judges and public prosecutors are now appointed by the Governor based on proposals made by two administrative boards of the judiciary. The Supreme Council of Justice, recommends judges for appointment to the Macau Supreme Court as well as the local attorney general, and the Judiciary Council of Macau, which recommends judges for the common courts and delegates to the public prosecutor's office. In particular, critics charge that the strong ties members of the latter group have to the executive branch and to China raise questions about the independence of the judiciary, particularly as judges and public prosecutors rely on the Judiciary Council to win renewal of their 3-year assignments. The 3-year appointment of judges differs from the practice in Portugal, where appointments are generally for life.

The law provides for a fair trial, and this is generally observed. The Constitution provides for the right of access to law and the courts, and the authorities respect this right in practice.

There were no reports of political prisoners.

f. *Arbitrary Interference With Privacy, Family, Home, or Correspondence.*—Laws provide for the inviolability of the home and of communication, the right of ownership of private property and enterprises, and the freedom to marry and raise a family. The Government respects these rights in practice.

Section 2. Respect for Civil Liberties, Including:

a. *Freedom of Speech and Press.*—The law provides for these rights, and the Government respects them in practice. However, some journalists and human rights activists believe that the practice of media self-censorship is increasing as reversion approaches. Critics charge that the leading newspapers are pro-China publications that do not give equal coverage to liberal and pro-democracy voices. Chinese and Portuguese journalists and legislators have expressed concern over a draft law proposed by the Government in June to create a press council to monitor and advise the Government on press issues. Critics charge that the proposed makeup of the press council—a judge from Macau's Judiciary Council, three legislators from the Legislative Assembly, two persons appointed by the Governor, and three individuals chosen by the other members of the council—excludes press professionals, and the closed meetings of the council could lead to an erosion of press freedoms.

b. *Freedom of Peaceful Assembly and Association.*—The law provides for these rights, and the Government respects them in practice.

c. *Freedom of Religion.*—Portuguese law as extended to Macau provides for freedom of religion, and the Government respects this right in practice. Human rights groups have expressed concern, however, that the Legislative Assembly thus far has failed to entrench these rights in local law.

d. *Freedom of Movement Within the Country, Foreign Travel, Emigration, and Repatriation.*—The law provides for these rights, and the Government respects them in practice.

The Government has assisted in the resettlement of Vietnamese boat people. At year's end, there were only six Vietnamese refugees living in Macau. All other boat people have emigrated to host countries.

Section 3. Respect for Political Rights: The Right of Citizens to Change Their Government

Citizens have a limited ability to change their government. The 23-member Legislative Assembly is composed of 8 members elected in universal direct elections; 8 indirectly elected by local community interests; and 7 appointed by the Governor. The Consultative Council, an advisory group to the Governor composed of elected and appointed members, also provides some measure of popular representation. By tradition the Government also consults informally on a regular basis with local business and cultural leaders. Although the Legislative Assembly can enact laws on all matters except those reserved for bodies in Portugal or the Governor, in reality the Governor initiates the vast majority of legislation, either directly through "decree-laws" or in the form of "proposals of law" that require that he receive the permission of the Legislative Assembly prior to issuing legislation. While the Legislative Assembly has the legal power to refuse to ratify laws issued by the Governor, in practice this is seldom done.

Elections were held on September 22 for the Legislative Assembly. There was a large voter turnout with nearly 75,000 residents, 64 percent of the electorate, going to the polls. The elections were generally fair and open, although there were some charges of vote buying and other irregularities.

Although women traditionally have played a minor role in local political life, they increasingly are being found in senior positions throughout the administration. The Legislative Assembly currently has three female members including the President of the Assembly, which is the second most senior position. Other high-level positions in the ministries, including education and statistics, are filled by women.

Section 4. Governmental Attitude Regarding International and Nongovernmental Investigation of Alleged Violations of Human Rights

Human rights groups operate without government restriction, investigating and publishing findings on human rights cases.

Section 5. Discrimination Based on Race, Sex, Religion, Disability, Language, or Social Status

While the Constitution does not explicitly proscribe discrimination based on race, sex, religion, disability, language, or social status, it does incorporate the principle of nondiscrimination. Separate laws provide for many of these rights. Access to education, for example, is stipulated for all residents regardless of race, religious belief, or political or ideological convictions under the law which establishes the general framework for the educational system.

Women.—Violence against women is not common. For cases that are reported, the authorities enforce criminal statutes prohibiting domestic violence and prosecute violators. Police and doctors report abuses to the Social Welfare Department, which investigates them. If hospital treatment is required, a medical social worker counsels the victim and informs her about social welfare services. Until their complaints are resolved, battered women may be placed in public housing, but no facilities are reserved expressly for them.

Women are becoming more active and visible in business and government, and some enjoy considerable influence and responsibility in these areas. Equal opportunity legislation, enacted in 1995, applicable to all public and private organizations, mandates that women receive equal pay for equal work, states that discrimination based on sex or physical ability is not permitted, and establishes penalties for employers found to be in violation of these guidelines.

Children.—The Government has not promulgated any statutes specifically to protect the rights of children, relying on the general framework of civil and political rights legislation to protect all citizens. However, the Government seeks to protect the health and well-being of children, who represent a growing share of the population. The Social Welfare Institute is charged with implementing programs designed to provide services for children. A government-sponsored panel, set up to study the provision of social services to Chinese families, recommended in 1995 that greater effort be expended to address the need for additional educational and other services for children.

Child abuse and exploitation are not widespread problems.

People With Disabilities.—The extent to which physically disabled persons experience discrimination in employment, education, and the provision of state services is not known. The Government gives little attention to the subject, and there is little funding for special programs aimed at helping the physically and mentally disabled gain better access to employment, education, and public facilities. The Government has not mandated accessibility for the disabled, legislatively or otherwise.

National/Racial/Ethnic Minorities.—Although the governmental and legal systems place a premium on knowledge of the Portuguese language, which is spoken by less than 4 percent of the population, the Chinese language received official status in 1993, and the use of Chinese in the civil service is growing. By the end of May, local Chinese accounted for only one half of the 951 senior government posts and none of the top 30 positions.

There is considerable public pressure for the Government to speed up the process of making the civil service more representative of the population; however, the pace of adding native-born Chinese speakers to the senior civil service has been very slow.

Section 6. Worker Rights

a. *The Right of Association.*—The Portuguese Constitution recognizes the right and freedom of all workers to form and join trade unions and of private sector unions to strike, and these rights are extended to Macau. The Government neither impedes the formation of trade unions nor discriminates against union members. Human rights groups are concerned that no similar rights and protections have been incorporated into local law.

People's Republic of China interests heavily influence local trade union activities, including the selection of union leadership, and stress the importance of stability and minimum disruption of the work force. Nearly all of the private sector union members belong to a pro-China labor confederation. Many local observers claim that this organization is more interested in furthering the Chinese political agenda than in addressing trade union issues such as wages, benefits, and working conditions. A few private sector unions and two of the four public sector unions are outside Chinese control. Although the Portuguese Constitution provides workers with the right to strike, labor leaders complain that there is no effective protection from retribution should they exercise this right.

Unions may freely form federations and affiliate with international bodies. Three civil services unions are affiliated with the major non-Communist Portuguese union confederation.

b. *The Right to Organize and Bargain Collectively.*—Unions tend to resemble local traditional neighborhood associations, promoting social and cultural activities rather than issues relating to the workplace. Local customs, moreover, normally favor employment without the benefit of written labor contracts except in the case of labor from China. Unions traditionally have not attempted to engage in collective bargaining. Portuguese laws protecting collective bargaining apply, and the Government does not impede or discourage such activity. No rules apply to the setting of wages.

A significant amount of the total work force (approximately 16 percent) is composed of laborers from China and other countries who fill both blue- and white-collar positions. These workers often work for less than half the wages paid to a Macau citizen performing the same job, live in controlled dormitories, work 10 to 12 hours a day, and owe large sums of money to the labor-importing company for the purchase of their job. Labor interests claim that the high percentage of imported labor erodes the bargaining power of local residents to improve working conditions and increase wages.

The law prohibits antiunion discrimination, and there were no complaints of it. There are no export processing zones; Macau is a free port.

c. *Prohibition of Forced or Compulsory Labor.*—Compulsory labor is illegal and does not exist.

d. *Minimum Age for Employment of Children.*—The law forbids minors under the age of 16 to work, except in businesses operated by their families. The Labor Department enforces this law and refers offending employers to the judicial authorities for prosecution. The Labor Department claims that the incidence of child labor has declined radically since effective enforcement began in 1985. School attendance is not compulsory.

e. *Acceptable Conditions of Work.*—No minimum which exists for local or foreign workers. In the absence of any statutory minimum wage or publicly administered social security programs, some large companies have provided private welfare and security packages.

Labor legislation provides for a 48-hour workweek, an 8-hour workday, overtime, annual leave, medical and maternity care, and employee compensation insurance. Although the law provides a 24-hour rest period for every 7 days of work, worker representatives report that workers frequently agree to work overtime to compensate for low wages. The Department of Labor provides assistance and legal advice to workers on request, but government enforcement of labor laws is lax because of limited resources.

The Department of Labor enforces occupational safety and health. Failure to correct infractions leads to government prosecution. Although a recent law states that employers should provide safe working conditions, no guarantee exists to protect employees' right to continued employment if they refuse to work under dangerous conditions.

ROMANIA

Romania is a constitutional republic with a multiparty system and a directly elected president as chief of state. In the November election, opposition candidate Emil Constantinescu was elected President, and a new government headed by Victor Ciorbea was installed in December. The judicial system has been subject to executive branch influence, although it is increasingly independent.

The Ministry of Internal Affairs supervises the police. The national police have primary responsibility for security, but in times of national disorder the Government may call on the army and the border guard to assist the police. Sporadic reports of human rights abuse by the police continued.

Romania is a middle-income developing country in transition from socialism to a market economy. In 1995 the private sector accounted for about 45 percent of gross domestic product (GDP) and employed 49.1 percent of the work force, primarily in agriculture and services. Although privatization is well under way, government ownership remains dominant in industry, where about 86 percent of output is produced by state-owned enterprises. Major industries include steel and metal products, automobiles, shipbuilding, textiles and apparel, electrical machinery, and energy production. Following a severe contraction in 1989–92 (when GDP fell by nearly one-quarter), the economy has continued to grow, increasing 6.9 percent in 1995 and a forecast 3.5 percent in 1996. Projected GDP is about $37 billion in 1996 (or about $1,635 per capita). Exports have risen over 20 percent in the past 2 years, although they fell $400 million for the first 6 months of 1996 compared with the same period in 1995. Inflation, at 62 percent in 1994, was down to 27.8 percent in 1995 and is expected to be about 40 percent in 1996.

The Government generally respected the rights of its citizens. However, several serious problems remained. Although the police have become more cognizant of human rights, reports of their abuse of detainees continued, and the Government does not take effective action to punish abusers. Prison conditions remained poor. The judicial system has been subject to executive branch influence, although it is increasingly independent. There were reports of occasional infringements on citizens' right to privacy. New legislation is designed to ensure that the widespread dismissal of democratically elected mayors by government-appointed prefects that occurred in 1995 can no longer take place without due legal process. Discrimination and violence against Roma continued, and discrimination and violence against women remained serious problems. A growing number of impoverished and apparently homeless children continued to roam the streets of large cities.

RESPECT FOR HUMAN RIGHTS

Section 1. Respect for the Integrity of the Person, Including Freedom From:

a. *Political and Other Extrajudicial Killing.*—There were no reports of political killings.

In April Gabriel Carabulea died after 3 days in police custody during which he reportedly was severely beaten. After initially ruling that there were no grounds for an indictment of the police, the military prosecutor's office reopened its investigation at the urging of the Romanian Helsinki Committee and the deceased's relatives.

According to Human Rights Watch, Mircea-Muresul Mosor, a Rom from Comani, was shot and killed in May while in police custody in Valcele.

The case of Istvan Kiss, an ethnic Hungarian allegedly beaten to death by police in 1995, is still being investigated by a military prosecutor.

In several earlier cases of deaths in custody or deaths reportedly due to police brutality, investigations and trials are still dragging on, years later.

b. *Disappearance.*—There were no reports of politically motivated disappearances.

c. *Torture or Other Cruel, Inhuman, or Degrading Treatment or Punishment.*—The Constitution prohibits torture and inhuman or degrading punishment or treatment, and these prohibitions were generally respected in practice.

There were, nevertheless, reports that police continued to beat detainees, especially Roma. For example, Amnesty International reported that in July police officers in Targu-Mures mistreated three Romani minors, Gheorghe Notar Jr., Ioan Otvos, and Rupi Stoica, who were held for 5 days in a Center for the Protection of Minors on suspicion of theft of a watch. A representative of a local human rights organization observed bruises on the youths' arms and legs, which he said "appeared very similar, as if they resulted from beatings with the same object." Nonetheless, requests for medical treatment were rejected.

Judicial cases involving military personnel and the police (who fall under the jurisdiction of the military prosecutor) are tried in a military court system. Local and international human rights groups criticize this system, especially investigations conducted by the military prosecutor's office of police personnel accused of abuses. These critics claim that the investigations are unnecessarily lengthy and often purposefully inconclusive, that the military courts sometimes block proper investigation of police abuses, and that these mechanisms inhibit prosecution or discipline of police misconduct.

Prison conditions are poor, facilities are overcrowded and unhealthy, and medical assistance is meager. Several human rights organizations credibly reported that abuses occurred in prisons. Prisons continued to use the "cell boss" system in which some prisoners are designated to be in semiofficial charge of other prisoners. During four visits in 1996, members of the Romanian Helsinki Committee observed overcrowding and precarious hygienic conditions. The single penitentiary hospital also suffers from overcrowding and too few doctors. Prisoners who are pregnant generally are not transferred to the penitentiary hospital until the sixth month of pregnancy, and they suffer from an inadequate diet.

The Government permits prison visits by human rights monitors.

d. *Arbitrary Arrest, Detention, or Exile.*—The law forbids the detention of anyone for more than 24 hours without an arrest order from a prosecutor, who may order detention for up to 30 days. Detainees have the right to apply for bail and may ask for a hearing before a judge. Such a request must be granted within 24 hours. In the absence of a request, however, the authorities may hold a person for up to 65 days without a court order.

Police often do not inform citizens of their rights. The law requires the authorities to inform arrestees of the charges against them and of their right to an attorney at all stages of the legal process. Police must notify defendants of this right in a language they understand before obtaining a statement. However, the prosecutor's office may delay action on a request for a lawyer for up to 5 days from the date of arrest.

Under the law, minors detained by police and placed under guard in a Center for the Protection of Minors are not considered by judicial authorities to be "in detention or under arrest." Since the provisions of the Penal Code do not apply to minors in these centers until their cases have been referred to a prosecutor, police are permitted to question them without restrictions and may hold those suspected of criminal offenses in such centers for up to 30 days. This law appears to be in conflict with the Constitution, and both Amnesty International and local human rights groups have called on the Government to change it.

Exile was not used as a means of punishment.

e. *Denial of Fair Public Trial.*—Under the terms of a 1992 law, the judicial branch is independent of other government branches. However, 5 of the 15 members of the Superior Council of the Magistrature, which controls the selection, promotion, transfer, and sanctioning of judges, are prosecutors subordinate to a presidentially appointed Prosecutor General, and all Council members are nominated by Parliament. Certain labor unions have alleged that the courts side with the Government in ruling on the legality of strikes and other labor actions. The courts have ruled in favor of the workers in a labor action against a government entity only once. Although the judicial system was at times subject to executive branch influence, it demonstrated increasing independence.

The 1992 law reestablished a four-tier legal system, including appellate courts, which had ceased to exist under Communist rule. Defendants have final recourse to the Supreme Court or, for constitutional matters, to the Constitutional Court established in 1992.

The law provides for fair public trial, and defendants benefit from a presumption of innocence. The Criminal Code requires that an attorney be appointed for a defendant who cannot afford legal representation or is otherwise unable to select counsel. In practice, the local bar association provides attorneys to indigents and is compensated by the Ministry of Justice. Either a plaintiff or defendant may appeal. These provisions of the law are respected in practice. The law provides that confessions extracted as a result of police brutality may be withdrawn by the accused when brought before the court.

There were no reports of political prisoners.

f. *Arbitrary Interference With Privacy, Family, Home, or Correspondence.*—The Constitution provides for protection against the search of a residence without a warrant, but this protection is subordinate to "national security or public order." The 1992 National Security Law defines national security very broadly and lists as threats not only crimes such as terrorism, treason, espionage, assassination, and armed insurrection, but also totalitarian, racist, and anti-Semitic actions or attempts to change the existing national borders. Security officials may enter residences without proper authorization from a prosecutor if they deem a threat to national security "imminent."

The Constitution further states that the privacy of legal means of communication is inviolable; thus, the Romanian Intelligence Service (SRI) is legally prohibited from engaging in political acts (for example, monitoring the communications of a political party). However, the law allows security services to engage in such monitoring on national security grounds.

Similarly, although the law requires the SRI to obtain a warrant from a prosecutor to carry out intelligence activities involving "threats to national security," it may engage in a wide variety of operations, including "technical operations," to determine if a situation meets the legal definition of a threat to national security.

In 1996 there were occasional instances of interference with individual citizens' right to privacy. A number of citizens and diplomats from two foreign countries credibly reported opened mail or baggage, personal surveillance, and harassment. Protestant church groups also continued to allege that current or former government intelligence services' agents entered their members' homes and offices, opened their mail, and tapped their telephones.

Section 2. Respect for Civil Liberties, Including:

a. *Freedom of Speech and Press.*—Although the Constitution provides for freedom of expression and prohibits censorship, it limits the bounds of free expression by prohibiting "defamation of the country." An updated Penal Code passed by Parliament in September rectified many of the shortcomings of the former Communist-era code, although the new version was criticized in some quarters because it retains jail terms for those convicted of libel or slander.

Journalists Tana Ardeleanu and Sorin Rosca-Stanescu of Ziua, a then-pro-opposition daily, were convicted of seditious libel and sentenced to serve prison terms. The charges were filed in connection with an article that claimed former President Ion Iliescu was recruited by the Soviet KGB intelligence service when he was a student in Moscow. Free press advocates were concerned that the outcome may set a precedent, since the Ziua journalists were the first well-known reporters convicted for defamation of the authorities.

Radu Mazare and Constantin Cumpana, two journalists who published an article in the Constanta daily Telegraf about an illegal contract in the city council, were sentenced for libeling local elected authorities, one of whom, a member of an opposition party, brought a private criminal suit against the journalists. They lost their appeal and received 7-month sentences. Prior to leaving office, President Iliescu pardoned them. Lesser-known cases involving journalists and Penal Code provisions for libel were also active before the November elections.

The independent media continued to grow. Several hundred daily and weekly newspapers are published. Several private television stations broadcast nationwide, with the largest reaching approximately 46 percent of the country and 72 percent of the urban market. As of September, 53 private television stations and 110 radio stations were broadcasting. A sizable number of households are wired for cable, giving significant portions of the population access to both private and foreign broadcasts. However, Romanian State Television (RTV) and Radio Romania remained the only national broadcasters capable of reaching the bulk of the rural population.

The ability to broadcast nationwide by satellite allowed stations to make a significant impact on the June local elections; electoral campaigns were conducted in a diverse and competitive media market. The media's new role in nationwide election campaigns made them the target of some heated debates and public complaints regarding biased reporting from politicians on both sides.

The 1994 law that established a board of directors for RTV, appointed by Parliament, was still not fully implemented by year's end. In 1995 and 1996, Parliament, led by the opposition, refused to approve one of RTV's two candidates for the board, and new elections to choose another nominee failed to attract the necessary number of voters. The board cannot convene to choose a director for RTV until all 13 of its members have been confirmed by Parliament; at present the board lacks the 1 aforementioned RTV representative. The new Government, with Parliamentary approval, has appointed an interim director, who began his tenure by replacing a number of department heads and news directors. Prior to the November elections, studies indicated that state newscasts covered the President, the Government, and the ruling party significantly more than the opposition parties, leaving state broadcasters open to criticism.

Foreign news publications may be imported and distributed freely, but high costs limit their circulation.

Academic freedom is respected.

b. *Freedom of Peaceful Assembly and Association.*—The Constitution provides for freedom of assembly, and the Government generally respected that right in practice. The law on public assembly provides for the right for citizens to assemble peacefully while unarmed but states that meetings must not interfere with other economic or social activities and may not be held near locations such as hospitals, airports, or military installations. Organizers of demonstrations must inform local authorities and police before the events The authorities may forbid a public gathering by notifying the organizers in writing within 48 hours of receipt of the request. The law prohibits the organization of, or participation in, a counterdemonstration held at the same time as a scheduled public gathering.

The law forbids public gatherings to espouse Communist, racist, or Fascist ideologies or to commit actions contrary to public order or national security. It punishes unauthorized demonstrations or other violations by imprisonment and fines. Constitutional provisions and laws on free assembly were generally respected in 1996.

To reduce the number of small political parties, a new law approved by Parliament raised the number of members a party needs to obtain legal status from 251 to 10,000. Associations may still obtain legal status with proof of only 251 members.

c. *Freedom of Religion.*—The Constitution provides for religious freedom, and the Government does not generally impede the observance of religious belief. However, several Protestant denominations, including Jehovah's Witnesses, made credible allegations that low-level government officials harassed them and impeded their efforts at proselytizing and worship. In particular, foreign missionaries often experienced delays in obtaining long-term visas. An international conference of Jehovah's Witnesses, scheduled for June in Bucharest, was banned by the Government following public attacks by the Romanian Orthodox Church; a national conference later took place without incident in Cluj.

Under the provisions of a 1948 decree, the Government recognizes 15 religions whose clergy may receive state financial support. The State Secretariat for Religious Affairs has licensed 385 other faiths, organizations, and foundations as religious associations under two 1924 laws on juridical entities, entitling them to juridical status as well as to exemptions from income and customs taxes. But religious associations may not found churches and are not permitted to perform rites of baptism, marriage, or burial. The Romanian Orthodox Church, to which approximately 86 percent of the population nominally adheres, predominates. The official registration of faiths and organizations is extremely slow because of bureaucratic delays.

d. *Freedom of Movement Within the Country, Foreign Travel, Emigration, and Repatriation.*—The Government places no restrictions on travel within the country, except in the case of certain small areas used for military purposes. Citizens who wish to change their places of work or residence do not face any official barriers. The law stipulates that citizens have the right to travel abroad freely, to emigrate, and to return. In practice, citizens freely exercise these rights.

In 1991 Romania signed the 1951 U.N. Convention Relating to the Status of Refugees and its 1967 Protocol, and in March a Refugee Law was passed, providing implementing legislation. The new Law established a refugee office within the General Directorate of Border Police, Passports, Aliens, and Migration Issues to determine eligibility for refugee status. The Ministry of the Interior, in which the refugee office is found, was also assigned responsibility for providing accommodations for asylum seekers and refugees.

The Government cooperates with the U.N. High Commissioner for Refugees (UNHCR) and other humanitarian organizations in assisting refugees but does not provide any direct monetary or physical support for them. The issue of first asylum did not arise in 1996. There was one report of forced return of persons to a country where they feared persecution: In March a Syrian citizen was forced to return to Syria, where Amnesty International had reported that he was previously imprisoned for political reasons.

As of July 31, a total of 887 refugees and asylum seekers depended on the UNHCR for their subsistence, including food, accommodation, clothing, medical assistance, and language or vocational training.

Section 3. Respect for Political Rights: The Right of Citizens to Change Their Government

The Constitution provides citizens with the right to change their government through periodic and free elections held on the basis of universal suffrage.

Legislation passed in June prohibits government-appointed prefects from dismissing elected mayors and local council members for alleged abuses of authority prior to a binding legal ruling on the charges. (In recent years, government-appointed prefects had dismissed from office for various alleged abuses 133 freely elected mayors, 116 of whom were politically independent or from opposition parties.)

The general elections in November saw the first genuinely democratic transfer of power since 1928 and resulted in a victory for the two main allied opposition coalitions, the Romanian Democratic Convention (CDR) and the Union of Social Democrats (USD). Out of 343 seats in the Chamber of Deputies and 143 in the Senate, the two opposition coalitions together won 175 and 76, respectively. The two coalitions also have the support of the Hungarian Democratic Union of Romania (UDMR), which controls 25 seats in the Chamber and 11 in the Senate. The local elections in June also gave the former opposition greater representation in city halls and county councils. Both elections were generally free and fair.

There are no legal restrictions on the participation of women in government or politics, but societal attitudes constitute a significant impediment. Women hold only 5.9 percent of the seats in Parliament and no ministerial positions.

The Constitution and electoral legislation grant each recognized ethnic minority one representative in the Chamber of Deputies, provided that the minority's political organization obtains at least 5 percent of the average number of valid votes needed to elect a deputy outright (only some 1,784 votes in the 1996 elections). Organizations representing 15 minority groups elected deputies under this provision in 1996. The ethnic Hungarians, represented by the UDMR, obtained parliamentary representation through the normal electoral process. Roma are underrepresented in Parliament, due to a low turnout of Roma at the polls and internal divisions that worked against the consolidation of votes for one Romani candidate, organization, or party. They have not increased their parliamentary representation beyond the one seat provided them through the Constitution and electoral legislation.

Section 4. Governmental Attitude Regarding International and Nongovernmental Investigation of Alleged Violations of Human Rights

Domestic human rights monitoring groups include the Romanian Helsinki Committee (APADOR-CH), the independent Romanian Society for Human Rights (SIRDO), the League for the Defense of Human Rights (LADO), the Romanian Institute for Human Rights, and several issue-specific groups such as the Young Generation of Roma and the Center for Crisis Intervention and Study, also a Romani nongovernmental organization (NGO). Other groups, such as political parties and trade unions, continued to have sections monitoring the observance of human rights.

These groups, as well as international human rights organizations, functioned freely without government interference and visited prisoners and detainees. However, the authorities have not been cooperative with all human rights groups. The General Inspectorate of the police in the Ministry of Interior has refused to cooperate with the Romanian Helsinki Committee since January 1994, when RTV aired a prime-time 2-hour documentary prepared by the Committee.

Section 5. Discrimination Based on Race, Sex, Religion, Disability, Language, or Social Status

The Constitution forbids discrimination based on race, nationality, ethnic origin, language, religion, sex, opinion and political allegiance, wealth, or social background. In practice, however, the Government does not effectively enforce these provisions, and women, Roma, and other minorities are subject to various forms of extralegal discrimination.

Women.—Violence against women, particularly rape, continued to be a serious problem. Both human rights groups and women's rights groups credibly reported that domestic violence also is common. There are no support facilities for victims, and media coverage is virtually nonexistent. According to government statistics, 613 women were raped during the first 6 months of 1996. Prosecution of rape is difficult because it requires both a medical certificate and a witness. A rapist will not be punished if he marries the victim.

Both the Constitution and international conventions that Romania has signed grant women and men equal rights. In practice, however, the Government does not enforce these provisions, nor do the authorities focus attention or resources on women's issues.

Few recourses are available for women experiencing economic discrimination. The Government acknowledged in 1995 that despite existing laws women have experienced a higher rate of unemployment than men and have earned lower average wages since 1989, despite educational equality. Women occupy few influential positions in the private sector. In 1996, to address these concerns, the Government created a department in the Ministry of Labor and Social Protection (MOLSP) to advance women's concerns and family policies. The department organizes programs for women, proposes new laws, and monitors legislation for sexual bias. It also targets resources to train women for skilled professions, especially in rural areas, and to address problems of single mothers.

Children.—The Government administers health care and public education programs for children, despite scarce domestic resources. Most resources for children still flow mainly from international agencies and NGO's.

There was no perceptible societal pattern of abuse against children. Nevertheless, large numbers of impoverished and apparently homeless but not necessarily orphaned children roamed the streets of the larger cities—2,000 to 2,500 in Bucharest alone. The Government does not have statistics defining the scope of the problem, but some NGO's remain acutely concerned that deteriorating economic conditions contribute to increased juvenile delinquency and vandalism. NGO's working with children continued to cite special concern about the number of minors detained in jail and prison and were seeking alternative solutions, such as parole for juveniles. Because time served while awaiting trial counts as part of the prison sentence but does not count towards time to be served in a juvenile detention center, some minors actually requested prison sentences. The sexual exploitation of children, for example, child pornography and child prostitution, has attracted domestic press attention, and the police reported 676 cases of sexual abuse involving minors through the end of August. The law does not expressly outlaw pedophilia; instead pedophiles are charged with rape, corporal harm, and sexual corruption. Due to the minimal punishment given to pedophiles, police have little incentive to investigate cases of child prostitution or child pornography.

People With Disabilities.—Difficult economic conditions and serious budgetary constraints contributed to very difficult living conditions for those with physical or mental disabilities. Many disabled people cannot make use of government-provided transportation discounts because public transport does not have facilitated access. Accessibility for the disabled to buildings and public transportation is not mandated by law.

Religious Minorities.—After the signing of the Romanian-Hungarian bilateral treaty in September, the extreme wing of the nationalist press focused its attention on the Hungarian minority. However, the fringe press continued to publish anti-Semitic harangues, to the discomfiture of the small Jewish community (numbering less than 15,000). Former President Iliescu and most mainstream politicians have publicly condemned anti-Semitism, other types of racism, and xenophobia.

National/Racial/Ethnic Minorities.—The Government created a Consultative Council for National Minorities in 1993 to monitor specific problems of persons belonging to ethnic minorities, to establish contacts with minority groups, to submit proposals for draft legislation and administrative measures, to maintain permanent links with local authorities and the Government, and to investigate complaints. Many minorities and other observers have claimed that the Government seldom acted on the Council's recommendations. There was no action by year's end on a bill restoring nationalized, nonreligious communal property to minority communities, since the authorities had not yet received a catalog of the properties in question from these communities. The new Government has promoted the director of the Council to ministerial status: the new Minister for National Minorities is an ethnic Hungarian parliamentarian from the UDMR.

The 1.6 million ethnic Hungarians constitute the largest and most vocal minority, and the UDMR holds 36 seats in the Parliament. There was no violence in 1996 associated with ethnic Hungarian issues, despite the usual extremist rhetoric from the Party of Romanian National Unity (PUNR) and the signing of the Romanian-Hungarian Treaty, an act that was unpopular with the extremist political parties. The treaty ended 5 years of negotiations and included commitments on observance of the Helsinki Final Act and the status of Romania's ethnic Hungarians. Hungary dropped demands for ethnic autonomy for Romania's Hungarian minority, in exchange for provisions that provide for national minorities to be educated in their native language at all levels (according to local needs), to use the minority language with administrative and judicial authorities, to display road and street signs in the minority language in areas where the minority constitutes a substantial number of the local population (percentage undefined), and respect for the rights of national minorities in conformity with pertinent international documents.

A 1995 Law on Education deals with the right of the Hungarian ethnic minority to be educated in their own language. Although the law was deemed by the Organization for Security and Cooperations's High Commissioner for National Minorities to be in line with European and international standards, it rescinded the rights of Hungarians to take university entrance examinations in Hungarian for those subjects not taught in Hungarian. It also dictated that certain vocational schools use only Romanian, which some Hungarians charge would disadvantage ethnic Hungarians who work in these areas. However, implementation of the law has been postponed until 1997, and the Government has accepted OSCE review of the implementation process.

Roma continued to be subjected to discrimination, harassment, beatings, and violence. The cases of those responsible for the burning of 11 Romani homes in May 1994 and the beating of Roma and burning of 3 Romani houses in January 1995 are still being reviewed by the courts.

Section 6. Worker Rights

a. *The Right of Association.*—All workers except public employees have the right to associate freely, to engage in collective bargaining, and to form and join labor unions without previous authorization. Limitations on the right to strike apply only in industries that the Government considers critical to the public interest. No workers may be forced to join or withdraw from a union, and union officials who resign from elected positions and return to the regular work force are protected against employer retaliation. The majority of workers are members of about 18 nationwide trade union confederations and smaller independent trade unions.

Union members complain that unions must submit grievances to government-sponsored conciliation before initiating a strike and are frustrated with the courts' propensity to declare illegal the majority of strikes on which they have been asked to rule. Past studies have indicated that the labor legislation adopted in 1991 falls short of International Labor Organization standards in several areas, including free election of union representatives, binding arbitration, and financial liability of strike organizers. Although the 1991 legislation is supportive of collective bargaining as an institution, the contracts that result are not always enforceable in a consistent manner. Unions representing divergent sectors of the economy carried out strikes, or threatened to strike, throughout 1996. The Vacaroiu Government did not follow up on the 1995 ILO recommendation that the Government take steps to rescind all measures taken against suspended union leaders involved in a 1993 strike by railway locomotive engineers. The union leaders, who had initially defied a Supreme Court ruling to suspend the strike for 170 days, were fired by the national railway company when the strike ended.

The 1991 legislation stipulates that labor unions should be free from government or political party control, and the Government has honored this in practice. Unions are free to engage in political activity and have done so.

Labor unions may freely form or join federations and affiliate with international bodies. The National Confederation of Trade Unions-Fratia (CNSLR-Fratia) and the National Union Bloc (BNS) are affiliated with the International Confederation of Free Trade Unions and the European Trade Union Confederation. The Confederation of Democratic Trade Union of Romania (CSDR) is affiliated with the European Trade Union Confederation. Alfa cartel is affiliated with the World Labor Confederation. Representatives of foreign and international organizations freely visit and advise Romanian trade unionists.

b. *The Right to Organize and Bargain Collectively.*—Workers have the right to bargain collectively under the 1991 legislation, but collective bargaining efforts are complicated by continued state control over most industrial enterprises and the absence of independent management representatives. Basic wage scales for employees of state-owned enterprises are established through collective bargaining with the State (see Section 6.e.).

There are no export processing zones.

c. *Prohibition of Forced or Compulsory Labor.*—The Constitution prohibits forced or compulsory labor. The MOLSP effectively enforces this prohibition.

d. *Minimum Age for Employment of Children.*—The minimum age for employment is 16 years, but children as young as the ages of 14 or 15 may work with the consent of their parents or guardians, although only "according to their physical development, aptitude, and knowledge." Working children under the age of 16 have the right to continue their education, and the law obliges employers to assist in this regard. The MOLSP has the authority to impose fines and close sections of factories to ensure compliance with the law, which it enforces effectively.

e. *Acceptable Conditions of Work.*—Most wage rates are established through collective bargaining at the enterprise level. However, they are based on minimum wages for given economic sectors and categories of workers which the Government sets after negotiations with industry representatives and the labor confederations. Minimum wage rates are generally observed and enforced. In 1996 the minimum monthly wage of $28 did not keep pace with inflation and did not provide a decent standard of living for a worker and family. However, the Government still partly subsidizes basic necessities such as housing and medical care. The Labor Code provides for a standard workweek of 40 hours or 5 days, with overtime to be paid for weekend or holiday work or work in excess of 40 hours. It also includes a requirement for a 24-hour rest period in the workweek, although most workers receive 2 days off. Paid holidays range from 18 to 24 days annually, depending on the employee's length of service. The law requires employers to pay additional benefits and allowances to workers engaged in particularly dangerous or difficult occupations.

Some labor organizations press for healthier, safer working conditions on behalf of their members. The MOLSP has established safety standards for most industries and is responsible for enforcing them. However, it lacks sufficient trained personnel for inspection and enforcement, and employers generally ignore its recommendations. Although they have the right to refuse dangerous work assignments, workers seldom invoke it in practice, appearing to value increased pay over a safe and healthful work environment. Neither the Government nor industry, still mostly state owned, has the resources necessary to improve significantly health and safety conditions in the workplace.

RUSSIA

Russia continued its profound political, economic, and social transformation. Democratic institutions and practices are evolving but are not fully developed. The Constitution approved by voters in 1993 provides for a democratic government comprised of three branches with checks and balances. The executive branch consists of an elected president as its leader and a government headed by a prime minister. There is a bicameral legislature (Federal Assembly), consisting of the State Duma and the Federation Council, and a judicial branch. For the first time in Russia's history as an independent state, its head of state was chosen in a competitive election. It was judged largely free and fair. The judiciary showed signs of limited independence.

The Ministry of Internal Affairs (MVD), the Federal Security Service (FSB), the Procuracy, and the Federal Tax Police are responsible for law enforcement at all levels of government throughout the Russian Federation; the MVD also oversees most of the prison system. In addition to its core responsibilities of security, counterintelligence, and counterterrorism, the FSB has broad law enforcement functions, including fighting crime and corruption. The FSB operates with only limited oversight by the procuracy and the courts. The military participated in the conflict in Chechnya and is occasionally used for riot control. Some members of the security forces continued to commit human rights abuses.

For the past 5 years, Russia has been in the process of transition from a centrally planned to a market economy. Real gross domestic product had fallen 34 percent from the 1991 level by the end of 1995. The transformation has affected nearly every sector of the economy as labor resources shift from the former Soviet Union's emphasis on industrial output to a greater balance among production, trade, and services. Industrial output has shrunk from being over 75 percent of the country's economic activity in the 1980's to less than 40 percent in 1996. The energy and raw material sectors account for most of industrial output and constitute the majority of exports. Organized crime is active in many sectors of the economy. Per capita income is $3,400. A sharp reduction in inflation and stabilization of the exchange rate led incomes to grow significantly for the first time since the beginning of the transition. Income disparities have increased dramatically since the downfall of communism, and about 23 percent of the population live below the poverty line. By midyear official unemployment was 9 percent. Wage arrears were the cause of many strikes, including hunger strikes, and other forms of civil disturbance.

The Government's human rights record showed little progress in 1996. Domestic and foreign human rights groups continued to document serious violations of international humanitarian law and human rights in the Republic of Chechnya by both Russian military and Chechen separatist forces. Violations committed by Russian forces continued to occur on a much larger scale than those of the Chechen separatists. Russian forces engaged in the indiscriminate and disproportionate use of force, resulting in numerous civilian deaths. They also prevented civilians from evacuating from areas of imminent danger and humanitarian organizations from assisting civilians in need. These actions were in conflict with a number of Russia's international obligations, including those concerning the protection of civilian noncombatants. Security forces were also responsible for disappearances in Chechnya. Chechen forces executed some members of the federal forces and repeatedly seized civilian hostages. Both parties to the conflict at times used torture, mistreated prisoners of war, and executed some of them. Tens of thousands of civilians were killed and over 500,000 persons displaced since the conflict began in December 1994.

In August the two sides initiated a cease-fire and for the remainder of the year made steady progress toward a political settlement. Russian troops completed their withdrawal from Chechnya, leaving the separatist forces in effective control of the Chechen Republic. The two sides agreed to hold elections in early 1997 and to resolve Chechnya's status within 5 years.

Although the Government has made progress in recognizing the legitimacy of internationally recognized human rights, the institutionalization of procedures to safeguard these rights has lagged. Implementation of the constitutional provisions for due process, fair and timely trial, and humane punishment made little progress. In addition the judiciary was often subject to manipulation by political authorities and was plagued by large case backlogs and trial delays. Lengthy pretrial detention remained a serious problem.

In one high visibility case that was fraught with numerous violations of due process, Aleksandr Nikitin—a former navy captain who was researching the environmental dangers of nuclear waste from the Northern Fleet—was detained by the FSB for 6 months without charge on suspicion of espionage and revealing state secrets, crimes possibly punishable by death. He was subsequently charged formally and later released pending trial.

There were reports that law enforcement and correctional officials tortured and severely beat detainees and inmates. Prison conditions worsened and are extremely harsh. According to human rights groups, between 10,000 and 20,000 detainees and prison inmates died in penitentiary facilities, some from beatings, but most as a result of overcrowding, inferior sanitary conditions, disease, and lack of medical care.

In the military, the practice of "dedovshchina" (the violent hazing of new conscripts) continued. The Government and human rights groups offered sharply divergent estimates of the number of soldiers who died as a result of abuse or suicide.

Arbitrary arrest and detention remained problems. Police and other security forces in various parts of Russia continued their practice of targeting citizens from the Caucasus for arbitrary searches and detention on the pretext of maintaining public safety.

In the face of a variety of obstacles, the media continued to represent a wide range of opinion. The major print media organizations functioned relatively unhindered by the Government, although there was evidence that the broadcast media did not give equal time to candidates in the presidential election campaign. The media reported freely on the Chechen conflict despite government pressure and heavy-handed treatment of journalists by Russian troops in the war zone. Several journalists were killed during the war, some deliberately, others accidentally; other journalists were kidnaped. In addition journalists elsewhere in Russia covering controversial issues were subjected to pressure and physical violence, including death.

The effort to institutionalize official human rights bodies stalled. In January Sergei Kovalev resigned as chairman of the Presidential Human Rights Commission to protest President Yeltsin's human rights record. Parliament failed to pass a law establishing a human rights ombudsman, a position that is provided for in Russia's Constitution and is required of members of the Council of Europe, to which Russia was admitted in February. With a few important exceptions, however, nongovernmental organizations (NGO's) documented and reported on human rights abuses.

The Government continues to restrict freedom of movement. Violence against women and abuse of children remain problems, as do discrimination against women, and both religious and ethnic minorities.

RESPECT FOR HUMAN RIGHTS

Section 1. Respect for the Integrity of the Person, Including Freedom From:

a. *Political and Other Extrajudicial Killing.*—There were no confirmed political killings by agents of the Government. However, several journalists—including some covering the war in Chechnya—and government officials were murdered under suspicious circumstances. Some of these crimes have been attributed to organized crime or business disputes. In addition, 10,000 to 20,000 detainees and prison inmates died after beatings by security officials or due to harsh conditions (see Section 1.c.).

During the war in Chechnya, the Russian military continued its practice of using excessive force and targeting civilian populations, resulting in numerous casualties (see Section 1.g.).

Ten journalists have been killed by unknown assailants for their coverage of the war in Chechnya since December 1994—4 of them in 1996—according to the Committee to Protect Journalists. The body of Nadezhda Chaykova, a newspaper correspondent who had been missing for several months, was found in the Chechen village of Geikhi on April 11. Chaykova had been severely beaten, blindfolded, and shot in the back of the head. Chaykova was the author of articles on human rights violations in the Russian "filtration camps" in Chechnya. The body of Nina Yefimova, a correspondent for the newspaper Vozrozhdeniye, was found in Groznyy on May 9. She had been kidnaped and then shot repeatedly in the back of the head. According to news reports, Yefimova had received threats in connection with her articles.

Elsewhere in Russia, some journalists investigating crime and official corruption were also killed. Oleg Slabynko was killed in January, soon after producing a television program on government corruption. Photographer Feliks Solovev, who freelanced for the German newspaper Bild, was killed in Moscow on February 26. Viktor Mikhaylov, a journalist for Zabaykalskiy Rabochiy, was killed on May 12 in Chita while working on a series of articles on crime and the work of Russian law enforcement. At year's end, no one had been charged with these murders.

Several government officials were the targets of violent attacks, although the assailants' motives in many instances remained unclear. Prime Minister Viktor Chernomyrdin's personal physician, Dmitriy Nechayev, was shot and killed on April 26, perhaps for political reasons. Deputy Justice Minister Anatoliy Stepanov was killed by a blow to the head on May 23, reportedly after a dispute with an old friend. Viktor Mosalov, the Mayor of Zhukovskiy, a town outside of Moscow, was shot and killed on June 13. Galina Borodina, acting head of the Moscow Oblast Justice Administration, was shot and killed in her apartment building in Podolsk on June 25. Gamid Gamidov, Minister of Finance in the Republic of Dagestan, was killed on September 23 by a car bomb that exploded next to the Dagestani Ministry of Finance building.

There were several high-profile murders involving members of Russia's financial elite and other prominent figures. It is unclear whether any of these killings were politically motivated, and most appear to be linked to organized crime or business disputes. According to MVD figures cited in press reports in May and June, 560 of the 32,000 murders in 1995 were contract killings (twice as many as in 1994). The MVD reports that only 22 per cent of such cases are ever solved.

In November prominent American businessman Paul Tatum was murdered in Moscow. Although the authorities pledged to investigate the case vigorously, no suspects have been identified.

The administration of capital punishment continued to raise procedural and humanitarian concerns because of the secrecy with which such cases are treated.

In June a Moscow oblast court acquitted a suspect in the case of the murder of Aleksandr Men, a Russian Orthodox priest murdered in September 1990, ruling that the defendant was under duress and had given a false confession. Men's family had publicly stated that they believed that the evidence against the suspect was fabricated.

The high-profile murder case of Vladislav Listyev, a journalist and television executive killed in 1995, remained unsolved, as did the murder of Dmitriy Kholodov, a Moskovskiy Komsomolets journalist killed in 1994.

In December six ICRC workers were murdered and a seventh wounded in an ICRC compound, which was located in a region under the effective jurisdiction of the Chechen separatists. By year's end, no suspects had been identified, although there were widespread suspicions that the crime was committed by persons who sought to derail the peace process.

Three terrorist bombings, apparently politically motivated, occurred in Moscow during the summer. A bomb exploded in a Moscow subway on June 11, killing four people. A second bomb exploded on a Moscow bus on July 11; a third bomb exploded in Moscow on July 12. No one has been charged in these attacks.

b. *Disappearance.*—Both federal and Chechen separatist forces used hostage taking, including of civilians, as a tactic in the Chechen conflict (see Section 1.g.).

American relief expert Fred Cuny, who disappeared in Chechnya in April 1995, is believed to have been killed. His body still had not been located by year's end. No trace has been found of American photojournalist Andrew Shumack, who disappeared in July 1995 after reportedly entering Chechnya.

Police logged a number of reports about the disappearances of Russian citizens, particularly young men, elderly people, and children. Most were attributed to criminal foul play rather than to any political motivations. According to press reports, some of the young men reported as missing had been rounded up and conscripted for military service when they could not prove that they had performed their national service.

c. *Torture and Other Cruel, Inhuman, or Degrading Treatment or Punishment.*—The Constitution prohibits torture and other cruel, inhuman, or degrading treatment or punishment. However, prisoners' rights groups have documented numerous cases in which law enforcement and correctional officials tortured and beat detainees and prisoners. Russian forces and Chechen separatists used torture during the Chechen conflict (see Section 1.g.).

Law enforcement officials have admitted unofficially to the Moscow Center for Prison Reform (MCPR) that they use torture to coerce confessions from suspects, often by cutting off oxygen with a plastic bag or a gas mask. (The latter method is referred to as the "elephant" torture in which oxygen is slowly cut off until a suspect agrees to confess.) Guard brutality is rampant and notorious. In addition to raping and severely beating inmates, guards have been known to pour chlorine on cell block floors and cut off ventilation.

In a February report, the Presidential Human Rights Commission noted that existing legal norms and administrative instructions failed to provide specific, clear regulation of the application of physical force and that this allowed "the use of impermissible physical coercion directed against prisoners virtually without restraint."

The practice of "dedovshchina," the violent hazing of new recruits in the military, MVD, and border guards continued unabated. Dedovshchina includes various forms of physical and mental abuse, including the use of recruits as personal servants of more senior soldiers. Soldiers often do not report hazing to officers for fear of reprisals. In 1995 the Ministry of Defense (MOD) reported that 392 military personnel died from various noncombat related causes, one-third from suicide. The Mothers' Rights Foundation and the Soldiers' Mothers' Committee believe that many of those who committed suicide were driven to do so by violent hazing or in fact died from abuse. Although the Mothers' Rights Foundation has not compiled complete figures for 1996, the group estimated that thousands of soldiers died in 1996 as a result of criminal acts by fellow soldiers or officers, by committing suicide, or by not receiving sufficient medical attention. The Foundation stated that few of these cases were referred to the courts.

Senior MOD and MVD officials acknowledged that hazing is a problem but allege that it is difficult to eradicate given the quality of recruits, who are often youths raised on the streets who have spent time in prison. According to press reports, 5.2 percent of recruits have a criminal record. Military leaders claim to make every effort to punish both soldiers and officers who take part in or allow hazing. But there are credible reports that many officers continue to permit—and even encourage—dedovshchina, and that some officers hit recruits because they are "inattentive to their duties." In a number of units, hazing is at such high levels that officers have been ordered to sleep in the barracks until the situation improves. In August Itar-Tass reported that a preliminary investigation into the suicides of two sailors on a ship in the Arctic Sea attributed one of the deaths to brutal hazing from fellow sailors. Also in August, 30 MVD soldiers from Perm Oblast deserted, complaining of "unbearable," vicious hazing. They returned after a few days once a senior commander guaranteed their safety. Six soldiers suspected of hazing the recruits were sent to military prison and criminal cases were opened against them.

Despite the magnitude of the problem, the national military leadership apparently made no moves to implement training and education programs to combat dedovshchina systematically, nor was there any apparent progress in establishing a military police force.

The systematic abuse of psychiatry as a form of punishment has declined dramatically from Soviet-era practice, although human rights groups charge that psychiatric hospitals continue to conceal their archives and their practices. There were no reports of sane persons committed to psychiatric institutions.

Conditions in almost all pretrial detention centers and many penitentiary facilities worsened during the year and are extremely harsh and even life threatening. Yuriy Kalinin, head of the MVD's Main Directorate of Internal Affairs, stated in 1995 that "the conditions in our pretrial detention centers can be classified as torture under international standards. That is, the deprivation of sleep, air, and space."

According to the law "On the Detention of Those Suspected or Accused of Committing Crimes," which came into effect in July 1995, inmates must be provided with adequate space, food, and medical attention. Although most of its provisions were due to come in effect by the end of 1996, the authorities were not able to ensure compliance, primarily due to lack of funds and of a bail system. The law mandates provision of 2.5 square meters of space per detainee. However, detainees in SIZO's (investigative isolation wards) averaged only 1.6 square meters—only 0.9 square meters in urban areas. Under such conditions, prisoners sleep in shifts, and there is little, if any, room to move within the cell. At Kresty, St. Petersburg's largest SIZO, 5 to 15 prisoners are held in cells that were built 100 years ago to hold 1 prisoner. In most pretrial detention centers and prisons, there is no ventilation system. Cells are stiflingly hot in summer and dangerously cold in winter. Matches won't light in many SIZO cells during the summer because of a lack of oxygen.

Health, nutrition, and sanitation standards in penitentiary facilities declined due to a lack of funding. It is estimated that the MVD was able to provide only 15 to 20 percent of needed medications and medical care. Tuberculosis is perhaps the most serious health problem. The MCPR has asserted that rates of tuberculosis are 40 times higher in prison than in the free population, and death rates of those infected with tuberculosis in prison are 17 times higher than for those outside. Every month 2,000 former prisoners with active tuberculosis are released. Head lice, scabies, and various skin diseases are prevalent. It is estimated that MVD penitentiary facilities were able to provide only 60 to 70 percent of the daily food rations they envisioned providing. Prisoners and detainees typically rely on families to provide them with extra food.

Statistics are very closely held on the number of detainees and prisoners who were killed or died and on the number of law enforcement and prison personnel sanctioned for use of excessive force. According to Russian human rights groups, between 10,000 and 20,000 detainees and prison inmates died in penitentiary facilities throughout Russia, some due to beatings, but most as a result of overcrowding, inferior sanitary conditions, or lack of medical care. During 1996 the MCPR reported that according to official MVD statistics over 3,000 detainees died in IVS's (temporary holding isolators) and SIZO's and over 9,000 convicts died in prisons and penal colonies. The MCPR, however, reports that many detainees are transferred to hospitals just before dying so as to deflate the official mortality rate. Although hundreds of MVD officials have reportedly been dismissed for "unacceptable behavior" (usually corruption), there are no reports of any cases of law enforcement or correctional officers being punished for abusing detainees or convicts.

The penitentiary system is centrally administered from Moscow. The MVD, the Ministry of Health, the Ministry of Defense, and the Ministry of Education all maintain penitentiary facilities. The MVD oversees about 85 percent of the prison population, which the MCPR estimated to be about 1,150,000 at the beginning of 1996. There are five basic forms of detention in the MVD correctional system.

IVS's are detention centers in police stations where suspects are held upon arrest. Approximately 70,000 individuals spent time in IVS's in 1995. Under the Criminal Procedure Code, suspects can be detained in an IVS for up to 3 days; in practice, however, a presidential decree permits this period to be extended for up to 30 days. Conditions in IVS's vary considerably, but are as a rule harsh. In most cases, detainees are not fed and have no bedding, sleeping place, running water, or toilet.

SIZO's are prison-like detention centers where those awaiting completion of criminal investigation, trial, sentencing, or appeal are confined. At the end of 1996, there were about 170 SIZO's holding some 300,000 suspects. Convicts are on occasion imprisoned in SIZO's because there is no money to pay for them to be transported elsewhere. Conditions in SIZO's are extremely harsh. A suspect can be detained in a SIZO for 18 months or longer while the criminal investigation is conducted. In 1995 the average length of detention was 10 months (see Section 1.d.). Men and women are separated, but juveniles are routinely detained with adults charged with serious crimes because guards have found less abuse occurs than when juveniles are segregated from adults. Family access is not usually permitted.

ITK's (correctional labor colonies) are penal institutions, divided into minimum and maximum security, which handle the bulk of the convicts, a total of 722,000 in 743 facilities at the beginning of 1996. Conditions in ITK's are, as a rule, much better than those in SIZO's and prisons, with the exception of the 158 timber correctional colonies where hardened criminals serve and where beatings, torture, and rape are common. A number of colonies have their own factories where prisoners work.

"Prisons" are penitentiary institutions for those who repeatedly violate the relatively lax rules in effect in ITK's. At the beginning of 1996, there were 13 prisons with about 4,750 inmates. Conditions in many prisons are extremely harsh. Although they are not as crowded as SIZO's, guards severely discipline prisoners to break down resistance. Prisoners are humiliated, beaten, and starved.

VTK's (educational labor colonies for juveniles) are prisons for juveniles 14 to 20 years of age. At the beginning of 1996, there were 61 VTK's holding 20,900 juvenile offenders. Conditions in VTK's are significantly better than in ITK's, but juveniles in VTK'S and juvenile SIZO cells suffer greatly from beatings, torture, and rape.

In January President Yeltsin approved the MVD's project to reorganize criminal procedures and the penal system in order to bring Russia's penal system in line with international standards. The President's Commission for Prison Reform monitors prison conditions and has prepared recommendations and legislation for reform. None of these efforts have made demonstrable progress.

Inadequate supervision by guards and brutal conditions have resulted in gruesome crimes, including murder and cannibalism, by inmates. According to MVD statistics, in 1995 there were 102 murders and 230 incidents of serious bodily harm in MVD penitentiaries. Violence among inmates, including beatings and rape, are common, as are elaborate inmate-enforced caste systems in which informers, homosexuals, rape victims, child molesters, and others are determined to be "untouchable" and treated very harshly.

Moscow human rights groups make frequent visits to the prisons in the Moscow area, but they have neither the resources nor a national network to investigate conditions in all 89 regions.

d. *Arbitrary Arrest, Detention, or Exile*.—The Constitution provides that the arrest, taking into custody, and detention of persons suspected of crimes are permitted only by judicial decision. However, the Constitution's transitional provisions specify that these provisions will not go into effect until a new criminal procedure code is adopted, which is not expected until late 1997 at the earliest. The new Criminal Code that was passed in 1995 was scheduled to go into effect at the beginning of 1997.

In the absence of measures to implement the procedural safeguards contained in the Constitution, suspects were often subjected to uneven and arbitrary treatment by officials acting under the present Criminal Procedure Code and "temporary" presidential decrees. The current code gives procurators authority to issue an order of detention without a judge's authorization and, if police believe that the suspect has committed a crime or is a danger to others, he can be detained for up to 48 hours without a warrant. The Constitution and the Criminal Procedure Code provide that detainees are entitled to have a lawyer present from the time of detention, during questioning following detention, and throughout investigation up to and including formal charging. However, the President's 1994 decree on combating organized crime allows law enforcement authorities to detain persons suspected of ties to organized crime for up to 30 days without explanation of the reasons for detention and without access to a lawyer. Authorities employed this decree extensively during the year. President Yeltsin's July 10 decree on combating crime in Moscow goes even further, allowing officials to hold unregistered residents suspected of crimes for up to 30 days and in certain cases to expel them from Moscow. In addition suspects frequently fear exercising their rights to request judicial review of their detention and access to a lawyer out of fear of angering the investigating officer.

Valeriy Shchelukhin, who is currently being held in a pretrial detention center, contested the constitutionality of several provisions in the decree and on May 27 the Constitutional Court began reviewing the legality of the 1994 decree's provision that suspects can be held for 30 days without being charged.

The Criminal Procedure Code specifies that only 2 months should elapse between the date an investigation is initiated and the date the file is transferred to the procurator so that he can file formal charges against the suspect in court. However, investigations are seldom completed that quickly. Detainees are sometimes held longer than the maximum investigation period. Some suspects spend 18 months or longer in detention under harsh conditions (see Section 1.c.). The code provides that the regional procurator may extend the period of criminal investigation to 6 months in "complex" cases. If more time is required in "exceptional" cases, the Procurator General can personally extend the period up to 18 months. Extensions of the investigation period are often issued without explanation to the detainee. Until the investigation is completed, the suspect is under the jurisdiction of the procurator's office and the Ministry of Internal Affairs. There is no procedure for a suspect to plead guilty during the investigative period, although if a suspect informs the investigator that he is guilty, the period of the investigation is usually shorter than if he maintains his innocence.

The use of bail is extremely rare in Russia, even if suspects are not flight risks or have not been charged with violent crimes. This aggravates crowding in pretrial detention and, due to delays in bringing cases to trial, results in many suspects remaining in pretrial detention for longer than the maximum penalty they might face if convicted.

Delays also plague the trial stage. Although the Criminal Procedure Code requires court consideration to begin no more than 14 days after the judge issues the order designating where the trial will take place, the congested court system frequently produces long postponements. Some suspects actually serve the length of their sentence while awaiting trial.

Some human rights organizations believe that the authorities have taken advantage of the system's procedural weaknesses to arrest people on false pretexts for expressing views critical of the Government. The case of Aleksandr Nikitin, a retired Russian naval captain who was detained for much of the year, was fraught with serious violations of due process, suggesting that his detention was politically motivated. The FSB detained Nikitin in St. Petersburg in February on suspicion of espionage and revealing state secrets, a crime punishable by a jail sentence or even death. Nikitin had been working with a Norwegian environmental foundation, Bellona, to publish information on the dangers posed by the nuclear waste generated by the Northern Fleet, where Nikitin had served. Nikitin and Bellona have demonstrated that all of the information they published was from open sources.

The FSB detained Nikitin without charge for over 6 months before charging him with treason and forgery. The authorities unsuccessfully attempted to deny Nikitin the right to choose his own legal counsel. The Government's case hinged on Nikitin's alleged violation of a secret 1993 MOD decree that Nikitin did not have access to because he had retired in 1992. Prosecution under the decree was also contested on constitutional grounds: the Constitution specifies that "any normative legal enactments affecting human and civil rights, freedoms, and duties cannot be applied unless they have been officially published for universal information." Furthermore, neither Nikitin nor his lawyer was shown the findings of the expert panel on which the charges are based. Amnesty International concluded that Nikitin was being held for political reasons. In December the Federal Deputy Prosecutor ordered the FSB to release Nikitin on his own recognizance, because the FSB had no legal grounds for holding him in jail before his trial.

Human rights activists maintain that Yuriy Shadrin was detained because of his intention to speak to Moscow jurists about abuses involving the judiciary in Omsk. Shadrin was arrested on an automobile-related charge that does not require pretrial detention and held for over 1 month. He immediately embarked on a hunger strike and prominent activists brought his case to the attention of the Moscow authorities. He was released in December.

Charges against Sergey Belyayev, a lawyer and trade union activist in Yekaterinburg, who had been detained, were dropped in February (see Section 6.b.).

The Government does not use forced exile.

e. *Denial of Fair Public Trial.*—The Constitution provides for an independent judiciary; the development of an independent judiciary continued but slowed considerably. Judges remain subject to some influence from executive, military, and security forces, especially in high profile or political cases. The Government's inability to fully fund the operations of the justice system further undermined the independence of the judiciary, preventing it from acting as an effective counterweight to the other branches of government. In addition judges remain dependent on local authorities for allocation of a variety of benefits.

The court system is divided into three parts: the courts of general jurisdiction, with the Supreme Court at the apex; the arbitration (commercial) court system, headed by the High Court of Arbitration; and the Constitutional Court. The Constitutional Court is assuming a more active role in the judicial system after it was reestablished in early 1995 following its suspension for over 1 year. The Court has been asked to rule on a variety of cases involving the President's authority, the immunity of parliamentary deputies, parliamentary organization, the State's citizenship policy, and the constitutionality of oblast legislative actions. To date, however, the Court has had limited success in enforcing its decisions.

Disputes between business entities are tried in the system of courts of arbitration, which consists of lower level courts and the High Court of Arbitration. There are 82 courts of arbitration with over 2,000 judges. These courts hear over 360,000 cases per year. If a party to a civil suit is a private citizen, the dispute must be handled by a court of general jurisdiction.

Throughout Russia there are about 15,000 judges in approximately 2,500 courts of general jurisdiction at the district, regional, and federation level. Apart from the arbitration courts, there are no courts of special jurisdiction to handle cases such as domestic relations or probate. Within the regular court system, 90 percent of the civil and criminal cases are heard by trial courts of general jurisdiction called "rayon" courts. Only a limited category of cases involving the most serious crimes fall directly under the original jurisdiction of the next level of courts—the oblast (regional) court. Serious cases, such as those involving murder, can be tried by one of three methods: a judge and a panel of two "people's assessors;" a judge alone; or a jury. However, the latter is possible only in the nine regions where jury trials have been authorized. A decision of lower courts can be appealed through intermediate courts up to the Supreme Court. All higher courts have discretionary trial jurisdiction.

Procurators, like the courts, are organized at the district, regional, and federation levels. They are ultimately responsible to the Procurator General, who is nominated by the President and confirmed by the Federation Council. They supervise criminal investigations conducted by the MVD, except in serious crimes like murder where the procurator actually conducts the investigation. They then submit the results of their investigation to the judge or panel of judges. Procurators are quite influential in nonjury trials, which are inquisitorial, not adversarial.

The code provides for the court to appoint a lawyer if the suspect cannot afford one. The Society for the Guardianship of Penitentiary Institutions is often called upon by judges to provide legal assistance for suspects facing charges and trial without any representation. This Society operates primarily in Moscow, although it uses its connections throughout Russia to appeal to legal professionals to take on cases of the indigent. However, in many cases the indigent receive little legal assistance, because funds are lacking to pay for trial attorneys for them.

Because the right to a lawyer during pretrial questioning is often not exercised (see Section 1.d.), many defendants recant testimony given in pretrial questioning, stating that they were denied access to a lawyer or that they were coerced into giving false confessions or statements. Nevertheless, human rights monitors have documented cases in which convictions were obtained on the basis of original, illegal testimony which the defendant refuted in court, even in the absence of other proof of guilt.

In the 80 regions where adversarial jury trials have not yet been introduced, criminal procedures are heavily weighted in favor of the procurator. The judge or panel of judges conduct the trial by asking questions based on their prior review of the evidence. The constitutionally mandated presumption of innocence is often disregarded, and defendants are often expected to prove their innocence, rather than the procurators proving guilt. Judges, fearing that an outright acquittal will result in a procuratorial appeal, frequently send cases back to the procurator for "additional information." This greatly increases the defendant's time spent in the SIZO (see Section 1.c.).

Adversarial jury trials, at the option of the accused in cases where there is a risk of a death penalty, were introduced in 1993 in Stavropol kray and Saratov, Ryazan, Ivanovo, and Moscow oblasts and in 1994 in Ulyanovsk and Rostov oblasts and Altay and Krasnodar krays, covering 23 percent of Russia's population. The Department of Judicial Reform of the State Legal Administration of the President, which is charged with reintroducing jury trials to Russia, plans to expand jury trials to 12 new regions, including the cities of Moscow and St. Petersburg, the Republic of Karelia, and Chelyabinsk oblast. This expansion, which was proposed for 1996 but delayed due to lack of funds, would extend access to jury trials to approximately half of Russia's population.

In June the All-Russian Council of Judges adopted a resolution expressing lack of confidence in Justice Minister Valentin Kovalev because courts had received less than one-fifth the sums required to cover administrative costs and other expenses. Some courts stopped hearing cases. In October the support staff in 17 of 19 St. Petersburg courts went on strike because they had received no salary for over 2 months and only about one-quarter of their pay for the preceding 8 months. Justice officials also are at risk physically; two were killed in 1996 (see Section 1.a.), and court personnel are routinely threatened. Court security is minimal due to a lack of funds.

Journalist Valeriy Yerofeyev, editor of a Samara weekly called Vremya-Iks, was taken into police custody in September 1995 after writing a number of articles about city police officers accepting bribes from owners of "massage parlor" brothels. Yerofeyev started this series of articles in the spring of 1995 and was not deterred by 3 days of police detention in June 1995 during which he said that he was beaten by police and warned to stop writing. In July Yerofeyev was convicted of procuring the services of prostitutes following a closed trial by a court in Samara. He was sentenced to 10 months (exactly the amount of time he had spent in pretrial detention) and was released.

Viktor Orekhov, a former KGB officer who assisted dissidents under the Soviet regime, was released in March after serving 8 months of his reduced sentence of 1 year. Orekhov was arrested for illegally possessing a firearm shortly after he made unflattering remarks in an article about his former boss, now the FSB chief of intelligence for the Moscow region.

Semyon Livshits, a naval officer who was convicted after he had applied to emigrate to Israel, was freed from a Krasnoyarsk labor camp on July 2 and emigrated to Israel. Livshits had served 6 years of a sentence on criminal charges that many human rights activists regard as fabricated. The Government's handling of his case was marred by serious procedural flaws.

Chechen separatists have announced that they will institute the use of the Shari'a (the Islamic legal code) in areas that they control. Three men were executed for rape by a Shari'a court in September. Offenses such as trespassing and drunkenness are punished by canings.

There were no confirmed reports of political prisoners.

f. *Arbitrary Interference With Privacy, Family, Home, or Correspondence.*—The Constitution states that officials can enter a private residence only in cases prescribed by federal law or on the basis of a judicial decision. It permits the Government to monitor correspondence, telephone conversations, and other means of communication only with judicial permission. It prohibits the collection, storage, utilization, and dissemination of information about a person's private life without his consent. The implementing legislation necessary to bring these provisions into effect has not yet been passed. In 1995 legislation was passed that gave broad authority for the FSB to utilize domestic surveillance and to conduct searches of private residences, with only limited oversight by the courts and the procuracy. These measures remain in force. There were reports of electronic surveillance by government officials and others.

g. *Use of Excessive Force and Violations of Humanitarian Law in Internal Conflicts.*—In the conflict with the secessionist Republic of Chechnya, Russian forces continued to commit numerous, serious violations of human rights and international humanitarian law. Russian forces used indiscriminate and excessive force without regard for the presence of noncombatants, prevented civilians from evacuating areas of imminent danger, blocked humanitarian assistance from reaching civilians in need, mistreated detainees who may or may not have had any links with separatist forces, and tolerated incidents involving groups of federal soldiers engaging in murder, rape, assault, extortion, and theft. The Chechen separatists also committed human rights violations, though on a lesser scale. Both sides deployed antipersonnel landmines. A cease-fire agreed to in August resulted in a dramatic reduction in violence during the final 3 months of 1996. By year's end, all federal troops had departed Chechnya.

Estimates vary of the total number of casualties caused by the war. Interior Minister Kulikov claimed that fewer than 20,000 civilians were killed while then-Secretary of the National Security Council Aleksandr Lebed asserted that 80,000 to 100,000 had been killed and 240,000 had been injured. Chechen spokesmen claim that the true numbers are even higher. Human rights groups estimate that over 4,300 soldiers from the federal forces were killed. In addition international organizations estimate that up to 500,000 people have fled Chechnya during the war. Many ethnic Chechens have returned since the conflict ended, but a majority of ethnic Russians are likely to resettle elsewhere. Since many records were destroyed during the war and many of the refugees who departed Chechnya are undocumented, the true numbers of casualties and refugees may never be known.

In numerous well-documented incidents, federal troops used excessive force against the separatist forces and recklessly put civilians in harm's way. Federal use of helicopter gunships and artillery bombardments were cited as the most frequent causes of death among civilians. Breaking a cease-fire shortly after the presidential election, federal forces launched a "preemptive strike" on July 10 against Geikhi, a village in which Chechen forces said there were no rebel soldiers. The attack, which was preceded by aerial and artillery bombardments, killed at least 20 civilians. Similar attacks were mounted in July against the villages of Mairtup, Kurchaloy, and Artury. The brutality of these actions prompted the ICRC to call on all parties to respect international humanitarian law, "in particular to respect and protect civilians by refraining from launching indiscriminate attacks, spreading terror among the population or using it for military purposes." Attempts by federal forces in August to hold Groznyy were also characterized by indiscriminate use of air power and artillery, destroying several residential buildings and a hospital, according to credible sources.

In March federal forces shelled the village of Sernovodsk while refusing to allow civilians to leave the area, resulting in numerous deaths. Similarly, in an assault on Samashki, the federal forces gave inhabitants 2 hours' warning to evacuate before shelling commenced. Once the bombardment started, Chechen men were not permitted to leave. The relief organization Medicins Sans Frontiers (MSF) reported that civilians were often forced to pay federal forces for permission to escape areas under attack through "humanitarian corridors;" in some cases, however, civilians— including women—were fired upon while transiting these corridors. In Samashki the human rights group Memorial reported that small groups of federal forces forced civilians to walk ahead of military formations or sit on the outer hulls of armored vehicles, making them "human shields." According to Memorial, during the battle for Groznyy federal forces occupied a hospital and used patients as human shields.

Prior to attacks, Russian forces often would encircle a village and issue an ultimatum to surrender weapons, troops, and money or face attack. Often, however, even those villages that complied with those terms were subjected to Russian attack.

Domestic and international human rights groups have compiled a substantial number of credible accounts of torture and other cruel and inhuman or degrading punishment of Chechens by Russian military and internal security forces during the Chechen conflict. These abuses include beatings of combatants as well as of unarmed civilians suspected of involvement with, or support for, the secessionist Chechen rebels. Amnesty International reported that allegations of rape were made against Russian forces.

Federal forces continued to use "filtration centers" to detain suspected separatists and supporters. Detainees were frequently subjected to torture during interrogation in these centers. Memorial reports that Russian forces took hostages through the filtration center apparatus—including civilians—and used these hostages to exchange for federal prisoners held by the separatists.

Incidents were reported in the Russian press of undisciplined federal forces engaging in theft, looting, assault, rape, and murder—frequently while intoxicated. There are many documented cases of junior officers and ordinary soldiers participating in such incidents.

In violation of international humanitarian law, federal forces repeatedly denied aid organizations access to the victims of the conflict. The MSF reported that "during the systematic attacks on villages and civilians, aid agency vehicles, supplies and teams" were "blocked by the military at the roadblocks" and that during the siege of Sernovosk, "aid was only allowed through 25 days after the bombing ended." The ICRC reported a number of instances in which its representatives were denied access to detainees. Each side claimed that the other was still holding detainees at year's end.

Final responsibility for the conduct of the war in Chechnya by the federal side rests with the military leadership and, ultimately, with President Yeltsin as Commander-in-Chief. Russian military and civilian officials routinely characterized separatist forces as criminal groups or illegal armed formations. Remarks in the press in July attributed to an unidentified major general typify the attitude toward accountability projected by the federal forces: "since we are not waging war in Chechnya, we do not apply the law on criminal responsibility for crimes committed in war and combat." Human Rights Watch (HRW) reported that the Russian military procuracy was said to have convicted 27 servicemen for crimes against civilians, but that "it failed adequately to investigate, let alone prosecute, the most glaring combat-related violations of humanitarian law."

Separatist forces also violated international humanitarian law by taking and executing hostages and using prisoners as human shields. In January Chechen forces took about 100 civilians hostage in the city of Kizlyar and then transported them to Pervomayskoye (both in Dagestan). Following a stand-off of several days during which federal authorities claimed that hostages were executed, federal forces bombarded the settlement, resulting in extensive property damage and killing an unknown number of hostages and Chechen rebels. During the crisis, another group of rebels hijacked a passenger ship on the Black Sea with many Russians on board. The Turkish Government resolved the incident peacefully.

After the separatist takeover of Groznyy in August, Chechen forces also carried out summary executions of civilians deemed collaborators. Even after the cease-fire came into force, separatist forces detained, tortured, and killed members of the Moscow-backed administration of Doku Zavgayev. During the Pervomayskoye crisis, Chechen separatists tortured, burned alive, and left the remains of three hostages they had previously abducted from the Chechen Ministry of Internal Affairs. The separatist commanders, who were effectively functioning as a government by year's end, demonstrated no intent to punish violations committed by rebel forces.

As in 1995, journalists working in Chechnya were subjected to violence by both warring sides. Several were kidnaped and killed, while others were used in prisoner exchanges even though they are noncombatants (see Section 2.a.).

International relief workers in Chechnya were often targeted in kidnapings, most likely by local organized crime groups or segments of the rebel forces.

Efforts at producing a settlement, though ultimately successful, were uneven. In May during the final days of Yeltsin's reelection campaign, a cease-fire agreement was reached that lowered the intensity of the conflict for several weeks. Immediately after Yeltsin's victory, however, the federal forces unleashed an offensive that caused scores of civilian casualties, as they had in March. In subsequent weeks, Lebed took over the negotiations and in August he signed an agreement with Chechen commander Aslan Maskhadov that called for an end to hostilities, full exchange of prisoners, and joint administration by a coalition government. The agreement stated that Chechnya's political status would be decided within 5 years. Despite Yeltsin's dismissal of Lebed, the peace process continued during the fall and in November the two sides reached another agreement that called for the withdrawal of federal forces by the end of the year and the holding of elections in January 1997.

The Glasnost Fund established an "international intergovernmental tribunal on crimes against humanity and war crimes in Chechnya," which plans to conduct investigations and forward its findings to the Russian Procurator General, the Council of Europe, and the European Court of Human Rights. The tribunal's members include prominent human rights activists from throughout the world.

Section 2. Respect for Civil Liberties, Including:

a. *Freedom of Speech and Press.*—The Constitution provides for freedom of the press and mass information and the "right of each person to seek, pass on, produce, and disseminate information freely by any legal method." The Government generally respects these provisions; however, the law contains provisions regarding secrecy of information that federal, regional, and local authorities have on occasion chosen to interpret broadly in order to limit access to information and to prosecute journalists and media organizations publishing critical information. Despite this, the major print media organizations, most of which are independent of the Government and represent Russia's broad political spectrum, were able to work relatively unhindered. Independent and semi-independent television stations continued to develop, and the number of small private radio stations, mostly in the big cities, continued to increase. Nevertheless, reports of government pressure on the media continued, particularly when coverage dealt with the Chechen war, other security related issues, corruption, or criticism of the authorities. Furthermore, journalists were killed or beaten, and the Government was criticized for its apparent failure to investigate these cases.

During the presidential election campaign, all candidates had access to the mass media, including both free broadcast time granted by law and paid advertising. However, candidates complained about unequal access and biased reporting. According to the European Mass Media Institute, President Yeltsin received more than 52 percent of television news coverage broadcast time, while his main rival, Communist Party candidate, Gennadi Zyuganov, only got 18 percent. Each of the other presidential candidates received no more than 7 percent. Reports proliferated that senior media figures received generous "retainers" from the Yeltsin campaign to assure their loyalty and that even junior journalists received compensation for positive stories. Immediately after declaring his candidacy, President Yeltsin dismissed Oleg Poptsov, the head of Russian state television (ORT), an action that human rights organizations asserted was in response to critical coverage of the war in Chechnya, a key election issue.

Media organs openly appealed to their audiences to vote for a particular candidate, in most cases President Yeltsin, a fact that can be explained not simply by government pressure, but also by journalists' fear of a crackdown on the liberal media if Communist Party candidate Gennadi Zyuganov had won. Igor Golembiovskiy, Editor in Chief of the Moscow-based Izvestiya, said that he and his staff had agreed that a Yeltsin victory was "in their interests." In the print media, only a few pro-Communist, hardline opposition newspapers, such as Pravda and Sovetskaya Rossiya, gave positive coverage to Zyuganov. With some exceptions, journalists showed little interest in investigating important campaign issues that might have resulted in more balanced coverage.

The press actively covered the war in Chechnya, providing the Russian and international publics with a wide range of information about the conflict despite physical danger to journalists and government attempts to restrict access. This coverage (which was often extremely graphic) was a determining factor in crystalizing public opposition to the conflict.

Journalists were subjected to violence by both warring sides (see Section 1.g.). The Glasnost Defense Foundation (GDF) reported that combatants violated journalists' rights in Chechnya almost daily. Several journalists were killed (see Section 1.a); many were detained and beaten; and some were missing at year's end. Natalya Vasenina, editor-in-chief of a newspaper published in Chechnya called Nezavisimost, was kidnaped from her home in Groznyy on September 27 and forced into a car by two unidentified masked persons. A Chechen spokesman stated that regional and state security authorities were searching for her. Vitaliy Shevchenko and Andrey

Bazvluka, Ukrainian journalists working for Lita-M Television Company, were last seen on August 11 in Groznyy. Yelena Petrova, also of Lita-M, was kidnaped at the beginning of September and was believed held by Chechen forces in Achkoy-Martan. Journalists were also used in prisoner exchanges even though they are noncombatants. According to the Committee to Protect Journalists, on August 31 federal border guards detained Salman Betelgereyev and Bekhan Tepsayev, two Chechen journalists from the separatist television channel, at the airport in Makhachkala, Dagestan, upon their arrival from Turkey. Federal troops released Betelgereyev and Tepsayev on September 22 at the Khankala military base outside Groznyy in exchange for Russian MVD troops held by Chechen fighters.

Foreign and Russian journalists covering the conflict in Chechnya alleged that Russian forces fired upon and threatened them. On August 8, Russian army helicopters opened fire on two cars marked WTN (Worldwide Television News, a British company) and "press." On the same day in Groznyy, Russian troops shot at a Cable News Network car. Other reports of abuses by the Russian army included destruction of equipment, confiscation of exposed tape, and restriction of journalists' access to certain parts of Chechnya.

The Committee to Protect Journalists protested the "restrictive and aggressive manner in which Russian authorities" treated journalists in Dagestan during the Pervomayskoye events in January (see Section 1.g.). The newspaper Izvestiya complained that official attempts to manipulate information were "unprecedented," as journalists were denied free access to the released hostages. According to Russian press reports, the Russian military set up cordons 15 kilometers away from Pervomayskoye on January 16 and barred journalists from approaching the village. One reporter said that his car was fired on at a checkpoint by Russian soldiers; others were attacked by guard dogs at checkpoints. Two Russian journalists working for WTN had their equipment confiscated.

Human rights activists cited government pressure on the media in the cases of Yevgenia Albatz, an investigative journalist, and Valeria Novodvorskaya. Albatz was fired by the newspaper Izvestiya after she had completed a major article exposing alleged illegal activities by the FSB. Human rights activists charged that FSB pressure on the newspaper was responsible for her firing, noting that her editor had promised her article front page coverage only days before. Journalist and political activist Valeria Novodvorskaya was charged in 1995 with "promoting interethnic strife," apparently for her criticism of Russian citizens in Latvia and Estonia. During her trial the judge ordered an investigation of her organization "Democratic Choice." The Supreme Court subsequently overturned this order; however, her case is still pending. Human rights activists assert that the FSB is forcing the judiciary to prosecute Novodvorskaya.

Journalists publishing critical information about local governments and influential businesses, as well as investigative journalists writing about crime and other sensitive issues, were subjected to threats, beatings, and even murder (see Section 1.a.). Others were assaulted or harassed. In a report on violations of the rights of journalists, the Glasnost Defense Foundation found numerous instances of harassment, including financial pressure, physical assaults, and threats against journalists' families. Aleksandr Krutov, a correspondent for Moskovskiye Novosti who had just published an article entitled "The Chechen Syndrome in the Volga Region," was hit over the head with a metal pipe more than 10 times by two men in Saratov in February.

In the regions outside the major media markets of Moscow and St. Petersburg, local authorities continued to use city-owned media premises, printing facilities, government subsidies, and charges of libel to pressure the media. Vecherniy Neftekamsk, a newspaper in Bashkortostan, published a series of articles that accused Bashkortostan President Rakhimov's family of seizing control of the Bashkortostan oil industry and described corruption in the local government. As soon as the articles were published, the printing plants in Bashkortostan stopped printing the newspaper. In August the local prosecutor's office started libel proceedings against the newspaper's editor, Eduard Khusnutdinov, who also received phone threats.

In June the Tatarstan Parliament passed a law to prohibit insulting and humiliating the President of Tatarstan. According to the new law, journalists found guilty would be fined up to $5,900 (30 million rubles) and all copies of their publications confiscated. Tatarstan President Shaymiyev wrote in his letter to the Committee to Protect Journalists that Russian law prohibited insulting government officials, because doing so "encroaches upon the justice system and the established order of government."

In September the club of regional editors in chief announced that the head of the Komi Republic's Administration for Media and Law Enforcement issued written orders to all 23 heads of city and regional administrations in the Republic to begin judicial investigations against the newspaper, Krasnoye Znamya, because it had published an expose of alleged squandering of funds by senior Komi government officials. The President's Judicial Chamber on Information Disputes ruled in October that this action was unlawful and requested that the President of Komi take strong disciplinary action against his chief of staff who ordered this action. The Chamber, however, lacks the authority to enforce its decisions, and no disciplinary action was taken.

Meeting with a group of senior Moscow editors, President Yeltsin promised personally to examine each case of absorption of independent news organizations by other businesses to prevent media intimidation. Yeltsin also said that all cases of threats and violence against journalists should be reported directly to his office. The Committee to Protect Journalists, however, noted that it had received no response to its letters asking the President to investigate the cases of journalists who were killed, kidnaped, or harmed.

The Government's information policy remained restrictive by Western standards. Facts, documents, and statistical data are still frequently kept from the press. For example according to the GDF, in the Orel region all documents containing statistics on the region's economy are marked "not for the press." The secrecy of information, and the resistance of senior officials to releasing it, were typically cited as pretexts for refusing to provide information. The higher an organization's status, the more generally closed to the press it remained.

Institutions of higher learning enjoy academic freedom; however, extreme financial difficulties have slowed the revision of Communist-era curricula and textbooks. In larger cities, private high schools and universities have been formed without any government interference.

b. *Freedom of Peaceful Assembly and Association.*—The Constitution provides citizens with the right to assemble freely, and the Government respects this right in practice. Organizations must obtain permits in order to hold public meetings. The application process must begin between 5 and 10 days before the scheduled event. Citizens freely and actively protested government decisions and actions. Permits to demonstrate were readily granted to opponents and to supporters of the Government.

The Constitution provides for freedom of association and the Government respects this right in practice. Public organizations must register their bylaws and the names of their leaders with the Ministry of Justice. In 1995 a registration law was passed specifying that organizations had until 1999 to reregister. Despite this provision, the Jewish Agency, an organization operating around the world to promote Jewish cultural life and to facilitate emigration to Israel, was threatened in April by the Ministry of Justice with closure of its branch offices because its registration had expired. After protracted difficulties, the agency was reregistered as the Jewish Agency of Russia on September 13. The Agency's functions, including the facilitation of emigration to Israel, were unaffected by the reregistration difficulties.

In addition to submitting their bylaws and the names of their leaders, political parties must present 5,000 signatures and pay a fee to register. The Constitution and the law ban the participation in elections of those organizations that profess anticonstitutional themes or activities.

c. *Freedom of Religion.*—The Constitution provides for freedom of religion, and the Government respects this right in practice. The Constitution also provides for the equality of all religions before the law and the separation of church and state. In December 1990, the Soviet Government adopted a law on religious freedom designed to put all religions on an equal basis. It forbade government interference in religion and established simple registration procedures for religious groups.

The Government does not require that religious groups be registered. However, by being registered, religious groups are able to establish official places of worship. Religious groups have not reported problems obtaining registration, although some evangelical and other religious groups have not applied. Religious publishing is flourishing, and religious books from abroad are widely available. The Government does not designate religion on passports or national identity documents.

Despite official toleration for various religions, however, many public authorities make increasingly less effort to avoid the appearance that the Russian Orthodox Church (Moscow Patriarchate) and in some regions, the Muslim religion, have privileged positions, particularly in the return of church properties and in the allocation of public funds for restoration and construction of church properties.

The sharp increase in the activities of well-financed foreign missionaries has disturbed many sectors of Russian society, particularly nationalists and those in the Russian Orthodox Church, some of whom advocate limiting the activities of foreign religious groups. Some government officials have endorsed this idea. In June Lebed said that he viewed the activities of a number of religious groups as a "direct threat to Russia's security." Citing Aum Shinrikyo and the Mormons as examples, Lebed described foreign religious sects as "mold and scum" that "corrupt the people and ravage the State" and he argued that they should be banned. While Lebed later apologized for criticizing the Mormons, he reiterated his opposition to foreign sects in Russia.

About one-fourth of Russia's 89 regional governments have passed restrictive laws and decrees that violate the provisions of the 1990 Law on Religion by limiting or restricting the activities of religious groups or by requiring registration. Enforcement is uneven, but there are reports of local governments preventing religious groups from using venues, such as cinemas, suitable for large gatherings. As a result, denominations that do not have their own property are denied the opportunity to practice their faith in large groups or to hold prayer meetings. In 1996 the Constitutional Court refused to consider a challenge to the constitutionality of one such law on procedural grounds.

Although religious activity was generally not restricted, some religious groups encountered problems. In St. Petersburg in March, police raided a private apartment, disturbing a meeting of the Unification Church that was attended by six Russian students and one American. After searching the apartment without presenting a search warrant, the police took the American and three Russians to the police station for questioning and forced them to sign statements without the presence of legal counsel. There were reports that Jehovah's Witnesses were harassed in Tyumen. There was substantial negative Russian media coverage of so-called "totalitarian" or "nontraditional" groups, including such groups as Jehovah's Witnesses, the Unification Church, the Church of Scientology, the Church of Christ, Hari Krishna, and charismatic-fundamentalist Russian Christian groups.

Since 1993 governmental discrimination against people from the Caucasus and Central Asia, many of whom are Muslims, increased concurrently with new measures at both the federal and local levels to combat crime (see Section 2.d.). For example on October 2, a group of 40 OMON (MVD Special Forces) troops disrupted evening prayers at a mosque in central Moscow in order to check registration documents of the worshipers. Several Duma deputies demanded a thorough investigation of the incident and apologies from the appropriate authorities. The Government has not yet investigated the incident.

Although Jews and Muslims continue to encounter prejudice and societal discrimination, they have not been inhibited by the Government in the free practice of their religion. In some areas of the country, other religions, including Buddhism, various minority Christian faiths, and Shamanism are practiced in accord with local traditions.

For the most part, synagogues, churches, and mosques have been returned to communities to be used for religious services, but there have been problems. For example some Roman Catholic churches have not yet been returned, and the Moscow Anglican church did not regain full possession of its St. Andrew's Church. In addition some religious buildings have been "privatized," and local authorities often refuse to get involved in property disputes, which they contend are between private organizations. Even where state or municipal authorities still have undisputed control of properties, a number of religious communities continue to meet with significant obstacles when they request the return of religious buildings, or when they seek to acquire land and necessary building permits for new religious structures. Reports from Baptist ministers suggested that the Russian Orthodox Church influences the Government regarding land allocated for churches of minority sects.

d. *Freedom of Movement Within the Country, Foreign Travel, Emigration, and Repatriation.*—The Constitution provides citizens with the right to choose their place of residence freely. However, the Government continues to restrict this right through residential registration rules that closely resemble the Soviet-era "propiska" (pass) regulations. Although the rules, which came into effect at the beginning of 1996, were touted as a notification device rather than a control system, their implementation has produced many of the same results as the propiska system.

Citizens must register to live and work in a specific area within 7 days of moving there. Russian citizens changing residence in Russia as well as citizens of former Soviet republics who decide to move to Russia often face enormous difficulties or are simply not permitted to register in some cities, such as Krasnodar. The cost of registration is often prohibitive, far beyond the means of most migrants or refugees, who usually do not register. In October the fee in Moscow was set at 500 times the legal minimum wage, or about $7,500 (40 million rubles). In April the Constitutional Court struck down a Moscow city law that gives local officials the right to collect high fees for registration, but the Court did not outlaw charging fees or specify how much could legally be charged. The mayor's office protested the decision and has not lowered the fees. Those who are not registered cannot work legally, are not eligible for social or health services, may not send their children to school, and may not vote.

The Government and residents of Moscow and other big cities staunchly defend retaining registration as necessary in order to control crime, to keep crowded urban areas from attracting even more inhabitants, and to gain revenue. According to an MVD press release, during the first 6 months of 1996, one out of every four crimes in Moscow was committed by a non-Muscovite. The President's Human Rights Commission and many human rights groups have condemned the registration system as well as the requirement to register visits as infringements upon freedom of movement that create the possibility of arbitrary enforcement by corrupt local authorities.

Discriminatory document searches and expulsions increased in the summer and fall. In part in reaction to terrorist acts in Moscow, including a bomb that exploded in a Moscow subway on June 11 (killing four people), President Yeltsin issued a decree on July 10 "On Urgent Measures to Consolidate Law and Order and Intensify the Fight Against Crime in Moscow and Moscow Oblast." A second bomb exploded on a Moscow bus on July 11. On July 12, at the scene of the explosion of a third bomb, the mayor of Moscow Yuriy Luzhkov declared that "the entire [Chechen] diaspora must be evicted from Moscow!" (By contrast, earlier in the month, the mayor had publicly criticized police efforts to harass law-abiding Chechens, urging that they restrict their attention to those who violated the law.) After announcing that "we plan to clear Moscow of both homeless people and dangerous elements," Luzhkov signed a resolution in August ordering the deportation of all unregistered people living in Moscow back to the place where they were last registered to live. At the end of September, the press reported that 4,051 unregistered people had "voluntarily" departed from Moscow and that 812 were deported under armed guard.

Although citizens are generally free to travel within Russia, the Government also imposes registration requirements on domestic travel. All adults are issued internal passports, which they must carry while traveling and use to register with local authorities for visits of more than 3 days (in Moscow it is 24 hours). However, travelers not staying in hotels usually ignore this requirement.

The Constitution provides all citizens with the right to emigrate. The Government does not impose more than nominal emigration taxes, fees, or duties. On average it takes 3 to 5 months to process a passport application, although it can take much longer if documentation is needed from elsewhere in the former Soviet Union. Emigrants must have an exit stamp in their foreign passport in order to emigrate legally.

However, if a citizen had access to classified material, police and FSB clearances are necessary to receive an external passport. By law the Government can impose a moratorium of up to 5 years on foreign travel for citizens who have had access to such material, and there were hundreds of people awaiting external passports on these grounds. Persons denied external passports can appeal the decision to an interagency commission chaired by First Deputy Foreign Minister, Igor Ivanov. In 1996, the commission granted travel permission to 267 applicants and denied 27.

Potential emigrants must satisfy all financial obligations, including the obligation to support immediate family members who remain in Russia. Members of an emigrant's immediate family can prevent emigration by claiming that the emigrant is their sole source of support. "Immediate family" can include parents and children and can also include grandparents if the parents of the emigrant are deceased. Daughters, however, are relieved of their obligations to support parents when they marry. There were a number of cases of persons who were not permitted to emigrate because they could not get permission from close relatives, sometimes because of alimony or child support concerns, sometimes because a cash settlement was desired.

Emigrants who have permanently resettled abroad, including in Israel, Germany, or the United States have been able to visit or repatriate without hindrance.

Russia has been a party to the 1951 United Nations Convention Relating to the Status of Refugees and its 1967 Protocol since 1993. Although the Government provides first asylum, effective procedures to determine refugee status have not yet been formulated. The Government cooperates with the United Nations High Commissioner for Refugees (UNHCR). The Government is in the process of bringing its procedures up to UNHCR standards. Some progress has been made in developing appropriate mechanisms in St. Petersburg, where over 250 persons were interviewed in 1996. However, Moscow is still unable even to process applications. Human rights organizations claim that this is part of intentional efforts by the authorities to rid the city of foreign asylum seekers.

The UNHCR and Amnesty International are working with the Federal Migration Service and border officials to ensure that interviews of potential refugees are conducted in a timely fashion, that the UNHCR is allowed access to potential refugees in airport transit lounges, and that deportations of potential refugees are delayed until cases are adjudicated. The UNHCR has limited access to the transit areas of Moscow's airports. UNHCR officers were barred from entering the transit area of Sheremetyevo II airport in Moscow without prior notification. Denying UNHCR officials free access to the airport areas contradicts the agreement between the UNHCR and the Government. As a result, many would-be asylum seekers were deported without access to UNHCR. At the request of the Government, the UNHCR established three suboffices in the North Caucasus to handle the flow of people from Chechnya.

There are two groups of refugees recognized by the UNHCR in Russia. The first are citizens of the former Soviet Union, generally ethnic Russians, who wish to emigrate to Russia. For ethnic Russians who wish to emigrate to Russia, refugee status is usually granted in 5 to 6 months. April statistics indicate that there have been 137,000 refugees of this type since 1992. The other recognized group of refugees consists of persons from countries that were not part of the former Soviet Union. April statistics indicate that 67 persons have been granted refugee status from this group since 1992, including Afghans, Ethiopians, and Bosnian Muslims. Some refugees who sought refuge in Russia, such as Kurds, have left the country because cities would not issue them residence permits or because they were harassed by the police. Local legislation in Moscow, St. Petersburg, Rostov, and other major population centers prohibits the settlement of refugees within their cities, and Moscow refused to process any applications from asylum seekers. A large number of workers and students from Africa and Asia, who came to work or study in accordance with treaties between their countries and the former Soviet Union, remain in Russia. The Government has not deported them but encourages their return home.

The Russian Government does not recognize as refugees the Armenians evacuated in the wake of ethnic unrest in Baku, Azerbaijan, during the Soviet period. They are termed "internally displaced" and remain housed in the Moscow hotels where they were initially placed "temporarily." About half of them have emigrated. The remainder are unable to return to Azerbaijan, are not accepted by Armenia, and have no status or residency permits for Moscow. Without residency permits, the refugees cannot legally apply for work nor can they register their children for public schooling. They have rejected offers of relocation to other regions of Russia because they have no assurances of housing or employment. Their situation is becoming increasingly precarious as the formerly state-owned hotels in which they reside privatize and the new owners exert financial and other pressure on them to depart.

Several people in Russia accused of criminal acts, who are political opposition figures in other former Soviet countries, were extradited forcibly without due process.

Section 3. Respect for Political Rights: The Right of Citizens to Change Their Government

The Constitution provides citizens with the right to change their government, and citizens exercised this right in practice in presidential elections in July and in parliamentary elections in December 1995, both of which domestic and international observers declared to be generally free and fair.

The Federal Assembly comprises two chambers. The lower chamber, or the Duma, consists of 450 deputies, half elected in single mandate constituencies, half by party lists. In the December 1995 parliamentary elections, 43 political blocs appeared on the ballot. The upper chamber, the Federation Council, has 178 members—the 89 chief executives of regional administrations (many of whom had been appointed by the President) and the 89 chairpersons of regional legislatures. Under the terms of a 1995 law, all members of this chamber must be popularly elected by early 1997.

The Constitution provides the President and the Prime Minister with substantial powers, which they used in the absence of effective opposition from the Parliament and courts.

A democratic election for the President of the Russian Federation took place in July for the first time in the history of Russia as an independent state. President Yeltsin was reelected on July 3 with 54 percent of the vote in a generally free and fair election. The International Foundation for Electoral Systems (IFES) found that the technical election procedures have shown continuing improvement since 1993.

While concluding that the elections were generally free and fair, OSCE representatives expressed concern about biased election coverage in state-owned media and scattered irregularities in some areas, such as illegal proxy voting. The Central Electoral Commission (CEC) and the court system have ruled on charges of fraud against regional election officials, and the CEC reprimanded candidates for violating prohibitions on early campaigning.

Elections in 52 of Russia's 89 regions were scheduled to take place between September and January 1997. Results in two oblasts were appealed to the regional electoral commissions based on allegations of vote rigging. In Amur oblast, the incumbent governor appealed the results of the September election after it was announced that he had lost by fewer than 200 votes.

Women are underrepresented in government and politics. In the December 1995 elections, 46 female deputies were elected to the 450-member Duma, a decrease from the 58 female deputies in the previous Duma elected in 1993.

Section 4. Governmental Attitude Regarding International and Nongovernmental Investigation of Alleged Violations of Human Rights

Many domestic and international human rights groups operate freely. With the notable exception of Chechnya, most groups investigated and publicly commented on human rights issues, generally doing so without government interference or restrictions. Most are headquartered in Moscow and have branches throughout the country. Some of the more prominent human rights organizations are the Moscow Center for Prison Reform, the Society for the Guardianship of Penitentiary Institutions, the Glasnost Fund, Memorial, the Moscow Research Center for Human Rights, the Soldiers' Mothers' Committee, and the Mothers' Rights Foundation. Regional groups, which generally do not benefit from any international support or attention, reported that local authorities have obstructed their work and that law enforcement officers have begun criminal investigations based on fabricated charges against certain regional human rights groups' leaders.

In September the FSB prevented the Bellona Foundation, a Norwegian environmental group, from distributing its report on environmental hazards in the North Sea caused by Russian nuclear vessels, although Bellona had distributed the same report unhindered prior to the detention of Bellona employee Alexander Nikitin (see Section 1.d.). During Nikitin's detention, the Government restricted the movements of Bellona staff members who were visiting Russia in an attempt to assist Nikitin with his case.

The OSCE and the ICRC both reported that their access to areas of Chechnya was frequently curtailed by Russian forces. The Government strongly cautioned against, but did not specifically prohibit, travel by foreign diplomats and international organization staff to Chechnya. In the wake of the murder of six ICRC representatives and frequent kidnapings, all international organizations except the OSCE had withdrawn from Chechnya by year's end.

Russia's governmental human rights institutions were weakened during the year. The Human Rights Commission, created by presidential decree in 1993, which had the right to carry out independent investigation of human rights concerns, virtually ceased functioning after human rights activist Sergey Kovalev resigned as the head of the Commission in January in protest of the war in Chechnya. Four Commission members resigned in February, the day after releasing the Commission's Report on Human Rights in Russia in 1994–95. The Report declared that there had been a "visible retreat from democratic achievements" in many areas. The Report also noted that there was no official reaction to the Commission's 1993 Report.

In May President Yeltsin reaffirmed his commitment to the Commission and named new members, including law professor Vladimir Kartashkin as chairman. The reconstituted Commission is composed primarily of people from the Government whereas Kovalev's commission included independent human rights activists. The Commission plans to resume publishing a biannual report on human rights. Some human rights groups complained that the Commission's focus has changed from advocacy of human rights to defending the Government's policy.

In June President Yeltsin signed a decree entitled "On Certain Measures of State Support for the Human Rights Movement in the Russian Federation," which called for a high degree of coordination between federal structures and the human rights community. Specific measures laid out in the decree included the creation of three entities: an interregional human rights center to coordinate human rights activities; a human rights training center; and a center publishing human rights literature. Regional administrations were instructed to establish bodies analogous to the federal Human Rights Commission. The human rights group Memorial reported that no action has been taken on this decree.

By year's end, the Parliament had not approved a law establishing a human rights ombudsman. This position is provided for in the Constitution and is a condition for membership in the Council of Europe, which admitted Russia as a member in February.

In July President Yeltsin established by decree a Political Consultative Council (PCC) to assist in the creation of a legal framework for economic and political reforms with 12 standing chambers, including a human rights chamber, headed by

Duma Deputy Valeriy Borshchev, and a legal chamber, headed by Boris Zolotukhin, a former Duma deputy. The PCC meets monthly. The Human Rights Chamber includes representatives of the various Duma factions as well as 10 members of the human rights NGO community. The Chamber has held hearings on issues such as prison reform and has proposed legislation on a death penalty moratorium to comply with Russia's obligations to the Council of Europe.

Section 5. Discrimination Based on Race, Sex, Religion, Disability, Language, or Social Status

The Constitution prohibits discrimination based on race, sex, religion, language, social status, or other circumstances. However, both official and societal discrimination still exist.

Women.—Domestic violence remains a major problem, as victims rarely have recourse to protection from the authorities. Police are frequently reluctant or even unwilling to involve themselves in what they see as domestic disputes. Many women are deterred from reporting such crimes because of this and because the housing system makes it difficult either to find housing outside the family dwelling or to expel an abusive spouse, even after a final divorce action.

During the first 6 months of 1996, there were 46,000 rapes reported in Moscow, an increase over the first 6 months of 1995. The MVD estimated that 80 percent of violent crime occurred in the home. Hospitals and members of the medical profession provide assistance to women who have been assaulted. However, some doctors are reluctant to ascertain the details of a sexual assault, fearing that they will be required to spend long periods in court. Human Rights Watch criticized the Government for failing to provide guidelines for improving police response to violence or to call for the adoption of a domestic violence law.

There is credible evidence that women encounter considerable discrimination in employment. At a Duma-sponsored roundtable held on March 5, representatives of 53 women's associations appealed to the Duma to improve the legal status of women by creating a council to assess all draft legislation to ensure that it provided for equal opportunities for women and men. In their appeal to the Duma, the women's associations' representatives raised their concerns that women form a disproportionately high percentage (62 percent) of the officially registered unemployed, that women are discriminated against in hiring and firing, that the differences between the salaries of men and women have increased sharply, and that few women attain senior positions. In March the Public Opinion Fund released a poll that indicated that the higher the income bracket, the lower the proportion of women. Women made up 87 percent of the employed urban residents with a personal income of less than $21 (100,000 rubles) a month and only 32 percent of those earning more than $315 (1.5 million rubles) a month.

Human Rights Watch accused the Government of participating in discriminatory actions against women, contending that the Government seldom enforces employment laws concerning women. Employers prefer to hire men, thereby saving on maternity and child care costs, and avoiding the perceived unreliability that accompanies the hiring of women with small children. In July a change in the Labor Code went into effect prohibiting women between the ages of 15 and 49 from being hired for jobs that are considered to be harmful to their health, including working on the night shift. Many of these jobs pay more, allow early retirement, or both.

In an April survey of female trade unionists conducted by the Institute of Free Trade Unions, 20 percent of respondents reported that they were aware of female workers in their enterprises being more frequently assigned to the lowest paid work, and 28 percent said that women were more frequently laid off or placed on involuntary leave. In the same survey, 16 percent said that women were less likely to be promoted, that women with young children were the first to be dismissed, and that women were not paid the same wage for the same work (as their male coworkers). Almost 14 percent of respondents considered that their enterprises shortchanged female workers on benefits, including maternity leave, exemption from night shifts, and other benefits.

Children.—The Constitution assigns the Government some responsibility for safeguarding the rights of children. The State endeavors to provide, within its reduced means, for the welfare of children. A new family code regulating children's rights and marriage and divorce issues came into effect on March 1. Although the President stated in March that government policies to improve the situation of children were a top priority, the Government had not begun any significant programs in this area by year's end. Many Moscow charitable organizations have established productive relations with the city government to address the needs of disabled children, as well as other distressed groups.

The position of many children has deteriorated since the collapse of communism, because of falling living standards, an increase in the number of broken homes, and domestic violence. According to press reports, 40 percent of all children live below the poverty line. In November 1995, Duma Deputy Mariya Gaydash stated that 2 million children under 14 years of age suffer from physical or mental abuse with as many as 200,000 dying each year from injuries received at home, usually from parental abuse or neglect. About 50,000 children run away from home each year, Gaydash asserted, and 2,000 commit suicide. To combat the growing number of children being abducted, police organizations, like the Nizhny-Tagil Police Academy in Sverdlovsk oblast, are forming programs to protect children.

The most vulnerable group of children in society are orphans and the mentally disabled, who are often given up by their parents to state-run institutions. Human rights activists allege that children in state institutions are poorly provided for (often because funds are lacking) and in some cases are physically abused by staff.

People With Disabilities.—The Constitution does not directly address the issue of discrimination against disabled persons. Although laws exist that prohibit discrimination, the Government has not enforced them. The meager resources that the Government can devote to assisting disabled persons are provided to veterans of World War II and other military conflicts. Special institutions exist for children with various disabilities. The Government does not mandate special access to buildings for the disabled. The Society for the Defense of Invalids is working to broaden public awareness and understanding of issues concerning people with disabilities.

Indigenous People.—The State Committee for the Development of the North, based in Moscow, is charged with representing and advocating the interests of indigenous people. With only a small staff, its influence is limited. Local communities have organized in some areas to study and make recommendations regarding the preservation of the culture of indigenous people. People such as the Buryats in Siberia; the Tatar and Bashkiri in the Urals; the people of the north, including the Enver, Tafarli, and Chukchi; and others have worked actively to preserve and defend their cultures, as well as the economic resources of their regions. Most believe that they are treated equally with ethnic Russians within the Russian Federation.

Religious Minorities.—Muslims, who comprise approximately 10 percent of Russia's population, continue to encounter societal discrimination and antagonism.

There are between 600,000 and 700,000 Jews in Russia. Jews continue to encounter societal discrimination, and government authorities have been criticized for insufficient action to counter it. There were a number of anti-Semitic incidents reported in 1996, including the desecration of 60 gravestones in St. Petersburg's only Jewish cemetery; the disruption of a meeting in Orel by representatives of the paramilitary group Russian National Unity; the bombing of a Yaroslavl synagogue that damaged the library and offices; the robbery and spray painting of anti-Semitic graffiti in a Jewish center in Smolensk; vandalism of 40 gravestones in a Jewish cemetery in Kursk; and a bomb attack on Moscow's Marina Roshcha Chassidic Synagogue, which damaged masonry and shattered windows. With the exception of the Yaroslavl attack, no suspects have been identified in these crimes.

In addition anti-Semitic themes continued to figure prominently in hundreds of extremist publications, and some Russian politicians—including some who ran for president—made anti-Semitic remarks. Members of Russian National Unity, an anti-Semitic organization that uses a modified swastika as its symbol, patrolled two Moscow parks, reportedly at the request of local officials. A prominent foreign visitor was denied a visa to attend a conference in Russia on Jews in the former Soviet Union in July.

There were, however, a few important judicial developments in combating intolerant speech. In a notable decision, in March a Yaroslavl court sentenced Igor Pirozhok, leader of the neo-Nazi group Werewolf Legion, and another Werewolf Legion member to 5- and 9-year prison terms for murder and inciting ethnic hatred. Pirozhok had admitted to Izvestiya that his group commits terrorist acts against "Jews, Communists, and democrats." In February a St. Petersburg court found Yuriy Belyayev, head of the St. Petersburg branch of the National Republican Party of Russia, guilty of inciting ethnic hatred under the Criminal Code based on an interview he gave Izvestiya. However, although Belyayev was sentenced to 1 year in prison, he was immediately amnestied under President Yeltsin's 1995 general amnesty in connection with the 50th anniversary of World War II.

National/Racial/Ethnic Minorities.—Ethnic Roma from the Caucasus and Central Asia face widespread popular discrimination, which is often reflected in official attitudes and actions. Since 1993 discrimination against people from the Caucasus and Central Asia increased concurrently with new measures at both the federal and local levels to combat crime. Law enforcement authorities targeted people with dark complexions for harassment, arrest, and deportation from urban centers (see Section

2.d.). In May Amnesty International sent a letter to the Procurator General's office, the MVD, and law enforcement agencies in Moscow demanding that a series of cases be investigated in which Moscow police officers threatened and beat Chechen refugees. In August participants at a roundtable of organizations of the Helsinki Citizens' Assembly from the Caucasus expressed their concern over Russian authorities' intentional policy of open racial and national discrimination against Armenians, Georgians, and Azerbaijanis. They cited the arbitrary detention, beating, and humiliation of thousands of their compatriots in Moscow and the Moscow oblast as well as a campaign in the mass media against those originally from the Caucasus.

Section 6. Worker Rights

a. *The Right of Association.*—The law provides workers with the rights to join and to form trade unions, and roughly 65 percent of the work force are nominally organized. However, this number includes members of the successor organizations to the official Communist unions, which are themselves organized as the Federation of Independent Trade Unions of Russia (FNPR). The numerical dominance of the FNPR, its continued control over the extensive property and real estate of its predecessor, and its still-substantial role in the distribution of social benefits, function as practical constraints on the right to freedom of association. Moreover, almost all of the formerly official unions include management as part of the bargaining unit.

In practice the leaders of FNPR unions tend to remain dependent on enterprise managers or local political elites. The FNPR uses the leverage it has as the guardian of social benefits, including health care and recreation and vacation facilities, to dissuade workers from joining independent unions. Labor market analysts cite polls showing that the majority of workers either do not know that they belong to a union at all or belong solely because they believe that they would not be covered by social insurance or receive other benefits if they did not pay dues to their union.

On the national level, trade unions exist independently of the Government, political parties, and other political forces. The independent, or "free" labor unions supported a wide variety of political blocs in the December 1995 parliamentary elections. Political parties do not control or interfere in the function of any of the trade unions. At the national level, even the FNPR plays a very independent political role. On the regional and local levels, FNPR unions are often closely associated with lower-level political bosses.

Despite the thousands of strikes that took place in 1996, most strikes were technically illegal since the labor dispute at issue was not first reviewed by an arbitration court. (Frequently, however, local authorities do not bother to have the strikes declared illegal.) Unions have complained that arbitration court findings favor management. Transportation unions in particular have complained that, because transportation can be considered an essential service, their right to strike has been effectively negated.

There have also been incidents of reprisals for organizing and for strike activity. In October 1995, a district procurator initiated a criminal case against Sergey Belyayev, chairman of the Yekaterinburg Comradeship of Free Trade Unions. Belyayev was particularly active on behalf of the free trade unions and had initiated approximately 50 court cases on behalf of union members for wage arrears, failure to index payment of back wages, illegal layoffs, violations of collective bargaining agreements, and other matters. He was accused of hooliganism, a charge with a maximum prison sentence of 5 years, detained, and the local media launched a smear campaign against him. Union members protested the charges against Belyayev by picketing the prosecutor's office, and the charges were dropped on February 2.

In March in Lipetsk oblast, workers affiliated with the independent union federation SOTSPROF went on strike at a tractor factory over wages unpaid since December 1995. The oblast procurator began criminal proceedings against the strike's organizer, Igor Cherkasov. Investigators searched union premises and seized various documents relating to his union activities. In Krasnoyarsk kray, the management of an aviation company attempted to force three pilots active in the union to accept positions as repairmen, janitors, or drivers.

Unions may freely form federations and affiliate with international labor bodies.

b. *The Right to Organize and Bargain Collectively.*—While collective bargaining is protected under the law, its practice is limited by the frequent refusal of enterprise management to negotiate collective bargaining agreements with independent labor unions. This has been a particular problem for unions outside of the FNPR's organization. For example, the management of an electro-mechanical factory in Novosibirsk refused to recognize the independent federation SOTSPROF. In Tomsk oblast, the general director of a furniture factory refused to recognize an alternative union formed by his workers and ordered the mass dismissal of its members. Discrimination between the FNPR and alternative unions is not confined to enterprises. In Lipetsk oblast the SOTSPROF organized picketing in front of the oblast's administration building on July 1, in part to stem discrimination against union members, and in part to stop the administration from charging members of alternative unions more for vacation packages and other benefits than FNPR members.

Enterprises in special economic zones and export processing zones must comply with the Labor Code.

c. *Prohibition of Forced or Compulsory Labor.*—The Labor Code prohibits forced or compulsory labor, and there are no documented cases of violations. Soldiers are regularly sent to work on farms to gather food for their units. There are documented cases of soldiers being sent by their superior officers to perform work for private citizens or organizations. However, while such labor might violate military regulations, it is not clear that it violates International Labor Organization (ILO) conventions, which do not cover military personnel.

d. *Minimum Age for Employment of Children.*—The Labor Code prohibits regular employment for children under the age of 16, and also regulates the working conditions of children under the age of 18, including banning dangerous, nighttime, and overtime work. Children may, under certain specific conditions, work in apprenticeship or internship programs at the ages of 14 and 15. Although in some instances children sell consumer goods on street corners, accepted social prohibitions against employment of children and the availability of adult workers at low wage rates combine to prevent widespread abuse of child labor legislation. According to figures cited by a Duma committee, approximately 2 million 14- and 15-year-olds are neither in school nor officially at work. There are no reports of children being forced to work due to economic necessity, although children working after school in family businesses is not unknown.

e. *Acceptable Conditions of Work.*—The monthly minimum wage as of April was roughly $15 (75,900 rubles). While this figure does not constitute a living wage under prevailing conditions, most people receive several times the official minimum. At the same time, much of the population continues to reside in low-rent or subsidized housing and receive various social services from enterprises or municipalities. The official minimum wage is primarily a benchmark figure for calculating university stipends, old age pensions, civil service wages, and a host of other social benefits.

The Labor Code provides for a standard workweek of 40 hours, with at least one 24-hour rest period. The law requires premium pay for overtime work or work on holidays. Workers have complained of being forced to work well beyond the normal week, i.e., 10 to 12 hour days, of abrogations of negotiated labor agreements, and of forced transfers of workers.

Nonpayment of wages was the most widespread abuse of the Labor Code experienced by workers, and the primary reason for the more than 3,000 strikes that occurred during the first 6 months of 1996. Nonpayment of wages was a widespread and pervasive problem: A May poll indicated that 27 percent of all workers had not received their salary for the previous month and 26 percent received their salaries late. In the same poll, 34 percent of workers indicated that wage arrears were the cause of labor conflict in their enterprise. Wage arrears across industries range between 3 and 9 months. The Federation of Independent Trade Unions estimated that wage arrears totaled approximately $7.5 billion (40 trillion rubles) in September, while government statistics indicated that as of July 8, wage arrears had reached approximately $5.6 billion (29.8 trillion rubles).

Although roughly 4 percent of the workers owed back wages have sought relief through the court system, this has proved ineffective, as many enterprises are themselves owed substantial sums by their customers, and some cannot afford to pay wages. Others simply chose not to use their funds to pay workers. Although Labor Ministry inspectors have found, as in the case of a Kazan factory manufacturing gas fittings, that enterprises owing workers substantial wage arrears have accumulated capital funds overseas, and have pursued these cases, individual punishments have not been a sufficient deterrent to resolve the problem. There have been various laws and presidential decrees issued, but these have had little impact on the problem. In order to draw public and Government attention to their plight and to place political pressure on enterprises to resolve their wage arrears, workers have resorted to mass hunger strikes, demonstrations, picketing, blocking roads, and, occasionally, suicide.

The law establishes minimum conditions of workplace safety and worker health, but these standards are not effectively enforced. Workers wear little protective equipment in factories, enterprises store hazardous materials in open areas, and smoking is permitted near containers of flammable substances. The Labor Code does establish workers' right to remove themselves from hazardous or life-threatening work situations without endangering their continued employment.

Workers were at unacceptably high levels of risk of industrial accidents and death. According to statistics compiled for 1995 by the Federal Employment Service, 21 percent of workers in industry, 11 percent of workers in transport, and 9 percent of workers in construction labored under conditions not meeting occupational health norms. Particularly egregious conditions were found in the energy industry (80 percent violating norms), foundries/metallurgical enterprises (60 percent), and underground transport (50 percent). It is unlikely that occupational safety and health improved substantially in 1996 compared with 1995, as industrial accidents have consistently increased over the past 5 years.

SAN MARINO

San Marino is a democratic, multiparty republic. The popularly elected parliament (the Great and General Council—GGC) selects two of its members to serve as the Captains Regent (co-Heads of State). They preside over meetings of the GGC and of the Cabinet (Congress of State), which has 10 other members, also selected by the GGC. Assisting the Captains Regent are three Secretaries of State (Foreign Affairs, Internal Affairs, and Finance) and several additional secretaries. The Secretary of State for Foreign Affairs has come to assume many of the prerogatives of a prime minister.

Elected officials effectively control the centralized police organization (the Civil Police) and the two military corps (the Gendarmerie and the Guardie di Rocca).

The principal economic activities are tourism, farming, light manufacturing, and banking. In addition to revenue from taxes and customs, the Government derives much of its revenue from the sale of coins and postage stamps to collectors throughout the world and from an annual budget subsidy provided by the Italian Government under the terms of the Basic Treaty with Italy.

The Legal Code extensively provides for human rights, and the authorities respect its provisions. Although the parliament and the Government have demonstrated strong commitment to the protection of human rights, some laws discriminate against women, particularly with regard to the transmission of citizenship.

RESPECT FOR HUMAN RIGHTS

Section 1. Respect for the Integrity of the Person, Including Freedom From:

a. *Political and Other Extrajudicial Killing.*—There were no reports of political or other extrajudicial killings.

b. *Disappearance.*—There were no reports of politically motivated disappearances.

c. *Torture and Other Cruel, Inhuman, or Degrading Treatment or Punishment.*—The law prohibits such practices, and there were no reports that officials employed them.

Prison conditions meet minimum international standards, and the Government permits visits by human rights monitors.

d. *Arbitrary Arrest, Detention, or Exile.*—The law prohibits arbitrary arrests, detention, or exile, and the Government observes these prohibitions.

e. *Denial of Fair Public Trial.*—The law provides for an independent judiciary, and the Government respects this provision in practice. The judicial system delegates some of its authority to Italian magistrates, both in criminal and in civil cases. Cases of minor importance are handled by a local conciliation judge. Appeals go, in the first instance, to an Italian judge residing in Italy. The final court of review is San Marino's Council of Twelve, a group of judges chosen for 6-year terms (four replaced every 2 years) from among the members of the GGC.

The judiciary provides citizens with a fair and efficient process.

There were no reports of political prisoners.

f. *Arbitrary Interference With Privacy, Family, Home, or Correspondence.*—The law prohibits such practices. Government authorities respect these prohibitions, and violations are subject to effective legal sanction.

Section 2. Respect for Civil Liberties, Including:

a. *Freedom of Speech and Press.*—The law provides for freedom of speech and of the press, and the Government respects these rights in practice. An independent press, an effective judiciary, and a functioning democratic political system combine to insure freedom of speech and of the press, including academic freedom.

b. *Freedom of Peaceful Assembly and Association.*—The law provides for these rights, and the Government respects them in practice.

c. *Freedom of Religion.*—The law provides for freedom of religion, and the Government respects this right in practice.

d. *Freedom of Movement Within the Country, Foreign Travel, Emigration, and Repatriation.*—The law provides for these rights, and the Government respects them in practice.

The Government cooperates with the Office of the U.N. High Commissioner for Refugees and other humanitarian organizations. Although it does not formally offer asylum to refugees, it has given a few individuals de facto asylum by permitting them to reside and work in San Marino. Refugees and other foreigners are eligible to apply for citizenship only after 30 years of residence. The issue of the provision of first asylum did not arise in 1996; nor were there any reports of forced repatriation of refugees.

Section 3. Respect for Political Rights: The Right of Citizens to Change Their Government

The Constitution provides citizens with the right to peacefully change their government, and citizens exercise this right in practice through periodic, free, and fair elections held on the basis of universal suffrage.

There have been no impediments to women participating in government or politics since the passage of a 1973 law eliminating all restrictions. In 1974 the first female member was elected to the GGC. Since then, women have served on the Council as Secretary of State for Internal Affairs and as Captain Regent. All women's branches of the political parties have been integrated into the mainstream party organizations, and women hold important positions in the various parties.

Section 4. Governmental Attitude Regarding International and Nongovernmental Investigation of Alleged Violations of Human Rights

There are no domestic human rights organizations, although the Government imposes no impediments to the formation of such organizations. The Government has declared itself open to outsiders' investigations of alleged abuses. There have been no known requests of such a nature.

Section 5. Discrimination Based on Race, Sex, Religion, Disability, Language, or Social Status

The law prohibits discrimination based on race, religion, disability, language, or social status, and the authorities respect these provisions. The law also prohibits some forms of discrimination based on sex, but there remain vestiges of legal as well as societal discrimination against women.

Women.—The law provides for protection of women from violence, and occurrences of such violence, including spousal abuse, are unusual.

Several laws provide specifically for equality of women in the workplace and elsewhere. In practice there is no discrimination in pay or working conditions. All careers are open to women, including careers in the military and police as well as the highest public offices.

However, there is a law that discriminates against women in stipulating that a woman who marries a foreigner cannot transmit citizenship to her husband or children, but that a man who marries a foreigner can do so to both spouse and children.

Children.—The Government demonstrates its commitment to children's rights and welfare through its well-funded systems of public education and medical care. There is no difference in the treatment of girls and boys in educational or health care, nor is there any societal pattern of abuse directed against children.

People With Disabilities.—There is no discrimination against disabled persons in employment, education, or in the provision of other state services. A 1992 law established guidelines for easier access to public buildings, but implementation of its provisions has not yet reached all buildings.

Section 6. Worker Rights

a. *The Right of Association.*—By law, all workers (except the military, but including police) are free to form and join unions. A 1961 law sets the conditions for establishment of a union. The unions may freely form domestic federations or join international labor federations.

Union members constitute about half of the country's work force (which numbers about 10,000 San Marinese plus 2,000 Italians, from the country's total population of about 25,000).

Trade unions are independent of the Government and the political parties, but they have close informal ties with the parties, which exercise strong influence on them.

Workers in all nonmilitary occupations have the right to strike. No strikes have occurred in at least the last 6 years.

b. *The Right to Organize and Bargain Collectively.*—The law gives collective bargaining agreements the force of law and prohibits antiunion discrimination by employers. Effective mechanisms exist to resolve complaints. Negotiations are freely conducted, often in the presence of government officials (usually from the Labor and Industry Departments) by invitation from both the unions and the employers' association. For the last several years, all complaints have been resolved amicably by a "conciliatory committee" composed of judges and government officials.

There are no export processing zones.

c. *Prohibition of Forced or Compulsory Labor.*—The law prohibits forced or compulsory labor and is enforced.

d. *Minimum Age for Employment of Children.*—The minimum working age and compulsory education age is 16 years. The Ministry of Labor and Cooperation permits no exceptions. Most students continue in school until age 18.

e. *Acceptable Conditions of Work.*—Since January 1, 1995, the legal minimum wage has been approximately $1,200 (1.88 million lira) per month. This affords a decent living for a worker and family. Wages are generally higher than the minimum.

The law sets the workweek at 36 hours in public administration and 37½ hours in industry and private business, with 24 hours of rest per week for workers in either category.

The law sets safety and health standards, and the judicial system monitors them. Most workplaces implement the standards effectively, but there are some exceptions, notably in the construction industries.

SERBIA-MONTENEGRO

The United States and the international community do not recognize Serbia-Montenegro as the successor state to the former Yugoslavia. Serbia-Montenegro, a constitutional republic, is dominated by Slobodan Milosevic, who is serving his second term as President of Serbia. President Milosevic controls the country through the Socialist Party of Serbia (SPS) which, although it lacks majorities in both the federal and Serbian parliaments, controls governing coalitions and holds the key administrative positions. Serbia abolished the political autonomy of Kosovo and Vojvodina in 1990, and all significant decisionmaking since that time has been centralized under Milosevic in Belgrade. The Government's control of the judiciary was illustrated by its manipulation of the courts to annul opposition victories in the November local elections.

The Government precipitated a political crisis in November by orchestrating the annulment of election victories by the opposition coalition Zajedno in Belgrade and other major cities. The Government failed to act on the recommendations of former Spanish prime minister Felipe Gonzalez, who led a delegation from the Organization for Cooperation and Security in Europe (OSCE) to Belgrade in December, which confirmed the opposition victories and called for their recognition. Large demonstrations in Belgrade and other cities continued into January to protest the stolen elections and demand democratic reforms.

During 1996 the international community worked intensively with the Government of Serbia-Montenegro to secure implementation of the terms of the Dayton Peace Accord, a step-by-step process designed to end the war in Bosnia and secure the peace. While U.N. sanctions against the "Federal Republic of Yugoslavia" (FRY) were lifted in October, the FRY is still not permitted to participate in the United Nations (U.N.), the OSCE, or other international organizations.

As a key element of his hold on power, President Milosevic controls the police, a heavily armed force of over 100,000 that is responsible for internal security. The police committed extensive and systematic human rights abuses.

Despite suspension of U.N. sanctions against Serbia-Montenegro in December 1995, economic performance was anemic in 1996. Unemployment and underemployment remained high as the Government was unable and unwilling to introduce necessary restructuring measures. Industrial production, hampered by a lack of investment capital, averaged only 30 percent of capacity. By year's end, a typical family of four required 2.2 times the average wage to obtain sufficient food. Largely as a result of the central bank's tight monetary policy, hyperinflation was avoided.

The Government's human rights record continued to be poor. The police committed numerous, serious abuses including extrajudicial killings, torture, brutal beatings, and arbitrary arrests. Police repression continued to be directed against ethnic minorities, particularly the Albanians of Kosovo and the Muslims of Sandzak, and was also increasingly directed against any citizens who protested against the Government. The Government used its continued domination of the media and election law amendments to manipulate the electoral process, and in practice citizens cannot exercise their right to change their government. The Government used police and economic pressure against independent press and media. The judicial system is not independent of the Government and does not ensure fair trials. The authorities infringe on citizens' right to privacy and movement. Discrimination and violence against women remained serious problems, as did discrimination against Albanian, Muslim, and Romani minorities. The Government continues to harass international and local human rights groups, though to a lesser extent than in 1995. The Government limits unions not affiliated with the Government in their attempts to advance worker rights.

As a signatory of the Dayton Accords, Serbia-Montenegro is obliged to cooperate fully with the International Criminal Tribunal for the Former Yugoslavia by turning over to the Tribunal persons on its territory who were indicted for war crimes. The Government has so far been uncooperative. There are credible reports that some indictees live in Serbia and that others freely travel in and out of Serbia.

RESPECT FOR HUMAN RIGHTS

Section 1. Respect for the Integrity of the Person Including Freedom From:

a. *Political and Other Extrajudicial Killing.*—Political violence, including killings by police, resulted mostly from efforts by Serbian authorities to suppress and intimidate ethnic minority groups. According to the Council for the Defense of Human Rights and Freedoms (CDHRF), a monitoring organization based in Pristina, Kosovo, the authorities killed 14 ethnic Albanians during the year. One was shot by soldiers and the others died as a result of mistreatment or beatings while in police custody. In Belgrade a prodemocracy demonstrator was killed on December 24 after an altercation with government supporters.

According to a CDHRF report, in June Serbian police took Isuf Muse from his home in Gjurakoc, Kosovo, and tortured him. He was allowed to return home where he died of his injuries shortly afterward. The CDHRF photographed the remains in order to provide a record of the extent of the injuries.

In a particularly egregious incident, on December 9 police raided the home of Feriz Blakcori, a schoolteacher in Pristina, and demanded that he turn over a handgun, which police alleged that he owned. When he denied possessing a gun, police took him into custody and beat him. He subsequently died of his wounds. According to Blakcori's family members, who were contacted by police to pick up his remains from a local morgue, the police told his wife that if they provided approximately $21,000 (DM 35,000), they would spare her husband. She told the police that she did not have the means to pay.

Crimes against citizens of minority groups appear to have rarely been investigated, nor were police generally held accountable for their excesses. However, a court convicted and sentenced a Serbian policeman to 4½ years' imprisonment in April for the 1994 killing of a 6-year-old ethnic Albanian boy. However, there was no confirmation that the subject has actually served any prison time.

b. *Disappearance.*—There were no reports of politically motivated disappearances. There were no developments in the 1993 Strpci incident, in which 20 Muslim men disappeared (see Section 4).

c. *Torture and other Cruel, Inhuman, or Degrading Treatment or Punishment.*— Torture and other cruel forms of punishment—prohibited by law—continue to be a problem in the FRY, particularly in Kosovo directed against ethnic Albanians.

Police routinely beat people severely when holding them in detention. On December 7, a prodemocracy demonstrator in Belgrade was arrested and brutally beaten by police. Earlier in the day he had appeared at an opposition demonstration with a life-sized puppet of President Milosevic dressed in prison garb. The law permits the police to hold suspects for up to 72 hours before charging them. This period can be extended an additional 24 hours to establish a suspect's identity. The police have abused this provision by holding persons whose identity was not in question for 96 hours. It is during this period of "informative talks" that the worst police brutality takes place. These excesses are now primarily concentrated in Kosovo, and to a lesser extent in Sandzak, although prodemocracy demonstrators also face selective detention and abuse while in police custody.

Ethnic Albanians continue to suffer at the hands of security forces conducting searches for arms. Human rights observers report that the police, without following proper legal procedures, frequently extract "confessions" during interrogations that routinely include the beating of suspects' feet, hands, genital areas, and sometimes heads. The police use their fists, nightsticks, and occasionally electric shocks. Apparently confident that there would be no reprisals and, in an attempt to intimidate the wider community, police often beat persons in front of their families. According to various sources, ethnic Albanians are frequently too terrified to ask police to follow proper legal procedures—such as having the police provide written notification of "informative talks."

Police also used threats and violence against family members and have held them as hostages. According to Albanian and foreign observers, the worst abuses against ethnic Albanians took place outside urban centers in rural enclaves. In one July incident, several ethnic Albanian vendors in an open market near Pristina were beaten by Serbian financial police, who accused them of not having their vendor's licenses in order. According to the victims, the police stole all the merchandise from the vendors without even looking at their papers, and then left the scene.

Ethnic Albanian children also were not spared abuse. According to the CDHRF in Pristina, over 200 children faced mistreatment at the hands of the authorities between January and June alone. The Council reported an incident in Mitrovica on July 3 in which police broke into the home of Zymer Ahmeti to search for guns. When they could not find him they took his 16-year-old daughter into custody, releasing her only when they were assured that her father would appear the next day.

According to the CDHRF, some 3,657 ethnic Albanians were mistreated, many severely beaten, in the first 6 months of 1996. The Council suggests that the number may be higher owing to the threat of retaliation by police authorities. Other observers say that the situation improved in 1996.

Prison conditions meet minimum international standards. There were no reports of abuse of prisoners, once sentenced and serving time.

The Government permits prison visits by human rights monitors.

d. *Arbitrary Arrest, Detention, or Exile.*—Police use of arbitrary arrest and detention was concentrated primarily in Kosovo and Sandzak. Police often apply certain laws only against ethnic minorities, using force with relative impunity. Laws regarding conspiracy, threats to the integrity of the Government, and state secrets are so vague as to allow easy abuse by the State.

Federal and republic-level statutes permit police to detain suspects without a warrant and hold them incommunicado for up to 3 days—4 if required to establish a suspect's identity—without charging them or granting them access to an attorney. After this period, police must turn a suspect over to an investigative judge, who may order a 30-day extension and, under certain legal procedures, subsequent extensions of investigative detention up to 6 months. In Kosovo police often beat people without ever officially charging them and routinely hold suspects well beyond the 3-day statutory period. However, observers report the problem is not as pronounced in the rest of Serbia-Montenegro as in the past.

Defense lawyers and human rights workers complained of excessive delays in filing formal charges and opening investigations. The ability of the defense to challenge the legal basis of their clients' detention often was further hampered by difficulties in gaining access to detainees or acquiring copies of official indictments and decisions to remand defendants into custody. In some cases, judges prevented defense attorneys from reading the court file. The investigative judges often delegated responsibility to the police or state security service and rarely questioned their accounts of the investigation even when it was obvious that confessions were coerced.

The police carried out arrests and detentions for alleged crimes in an arbitrary fashion against members of ethnic minorities. In a country where the majority of ethnic Serbs are armed, police, according to some members of minorities, selectively enforced the laws regulating the possession and registration of firearms so as to harass and intimidate ethnic minorities, particularly Albanian Kosovars and Bosniak Muslims. The most frequent justification given for searches of homes and arrests was illegal possession of weapons. Observers allege that in Kosovo the police are known to use the pretext of searching for weapons when in fact they are also searching for hard currency. Local police authorities more easily approve registration of legal weapons for Kosovo Serbs and, according to observers, they frequently turn a blind eye to Serbs' possession of illegal weapons.

Exile is neither legally permitted nor routinely practiced. No specific instances of the imposition of exile as a form of judicial punishment are known to have occurred, although the practical effect of police repression in Kosovo and Sandzak is to cause many ethnic Albanians and Bosniak Muslims to go abroad to escape persecution.

e. *Denial of Fair Public Trial.*—The Constitution provides for an independent judiciary, but in practice the courts are largely controlled by the Government and rarely challenge the will of the state security apparatus. The authorities frequently deny fair public trial to non-Serbs and to persons they believe oppose the regime.

While judges are elected for life terms, they may be subjected to governmental pressure. For example, the opposition coalition Zajedno charged that the municipal court judge whose ruling overturned the opposition's majority in the Belgrade city assembly was convicted of a criminal offense that should result in his removal from the bench. Zajedno contends that the regime abused the situation to influence the ruling. The court system comprises local, district, and supreme courts at the republic level, as well as a federal Supreme Court to which republic supreme court decisions may be appealed. There is also a military court system. According to the Federal Constitution, the Federal Constitutional Court rules on the constitutionality of laws and regulations, relying on republic authorities to enforce its rulings. The Federal Criminal Code of the former Socialist Federal Republic of Yugoslavia still remains in force. Some confusion and room for abuse remain in the legal system because the 1990 Constitution of Serbia has not yet been brought into conformity with the 1992 Constitution of the Federal Republic of Yugoslavia.

Under federal law, defendants have the right to be present at their trial and to have an attorney, at public expense if needed. The courts must also provide interpreters. The presiding judge decides what will be read into the record of the proceedings. Both the defendant and the prosecutor may appeal the verdict. Although generally respected in form, defense lawyers in Kosovo and Sandzak have filed numerous complaints about flagrant breaches of standard procedure that they believed undermined their clients' rights. Even when individual judges have admitted that the lawyers are correct, courts have ignored or dismissed the complaints.

The Government continues to pursue cases brought previously against targeted minority groups, under article 116 of the Yugoslav Criminal Code, of jeopardizing the territorial integrity of the country and, under article 136, of conspiring or forming a group with intent to commit subversive activities—that is, undermining the "constitutional order." However, apparently no new cases were brought against ethnic Albanians in Kosovo in 1996. As a result, the estimated number of "political prisoners" in Kosovo declined from more than 250 to 200 overall. The Fund for Humanitarian Law found that proceedings on charges of subversion, all brought before 1996, have been initiated exclusively against Kosovar Albanians and Sandzak Muslims.

A high-profile case during the past year involved the leader of the Democratic Party, Zoran Djindjic. In September Djindjic lost a court case 6 weeks prior to the federal elections.

Djindjic was accused of "slandering" Serbian Prime Minister Marjanovic for Marjanovic's alleged role in a scam to line the pockets of political cronies from the profits on sales of wheat during sanctions. Djindjic was given a 4-month suspended sentence and told to refrain from criticizing government officials or face time in prison. In the course of the proceedings, the court rejected one defense motion to call the Prime Minister as a witness and another to appoint a court auditor to review the commodity reserve's book of accounts.

f. *Arbitrary Interference With Privacy, Family, Home, or Correspondence.*—Federal law gives republic Ministries of the Interior sole control over the decision to monitor potential criminal activities, a power routinely abused. Authorities monitor opposition and dissident activity, eavesdrop on conversations, read mail, and wiretap telephones. The federal post office registers all mail from abroad, ostensibly to protect mail carriers from charges of theft, even though this is illegal under provisions of all three constitutions: Federal, Serbian, and Montenegrin.

Although the law includes restrictions on searches, officials often ignored them. In Kosovo and Sandzak, police have systematically subjected ethnic Albanians and Bosniak Moslems to random searches of their homes, vehicles, shops, and offices, asserting they were searching for weapons. CDHRF records showed that the police carried out scores of home raids. For example, in November police entered the home of Samir and Sahit Seferi, neither of whom were home, threatened a family member, and took another brother to the police station where he was subjected to physical abuse, according to the CDHRF. In a similar incident, on November 14 police raided the home of Isuf Surkishi in Podujevo and demanded that he report to the police station for "informative talks." When he did not attend, police returned to his home, according to the CDHRF, physically "ill-treated" him in front of his family. In December police raided a home, took a schoolteacher into custody, and beat him so badly that he subsequently died of his wounds (see Section 1.a.).

The police also seize family members as hostages to compel the appearance of persons they wish to take into custody (see Section 1.c.).

The Government's law requiring universal military service is enforced only sporadically. It was not vigorously enforced in 1996, although during one campaign there were some 100 call-ups. Of approximately 100,000 draft evaders living abroad to avoid punishment, 40 percent were estimated to be ethnic Albanian. This number in part reflects the large number of conscription-age men in the FRY's Albanian community.

The climate appears to be moderating, no doubt as a result of the cessation of hostilities in Bosnia. Nevertheless, leaders of the Kosovar Albanian community have maintained that forced compliance of ethnic Albanians with universal military service was an attempt to induce young men to flee the country. According to an amnesty bill passed in June, young men for whom criminal prosecution for draft evasion had already started were granted amnesty. In a related development, under a 1996 agreement with Germany, ethnic Albanian refugees repatriated to the FRY will not be prosecuted for fleeing the draft.

Section 2. Respect for Civil Liberties, Including:

a. *Freedom of Speech and Press.*—Federal law provides for freedom speech and the press, but in practice the Government strongly influences most of the media. Prior to FRY federal elections in November, numerous complaints from democratic opposition leaders suggested that media manipulation by the Government was even worse than during previous elections. Serbian state-run radio and television (RTS), the prime source of news for the populace (especially outside Belgrade), has long been under the direct control of the regime and serves as its most powerful tool for manipulating public opinion.

The main emphasis of prime-time news programs in the past year was on the activities of the President, the ruling Socialist Party of Serbia (SPS), and JUL (United Yugoslav Left), whose leader, Mirjana Markovic, is President Milosevic's wife. The most striking example of media bias came in reaction to mass demonstrations that followed widespread government theft of elections won in November 17 voting by the opposition in several key municipalities, including Belgrade. The government-controlled media downplayed the size of crowds, sometimes ignoring demonstrations altogether—despite numbers of demonstrators in the tens of thousands. When state-run television did cover the demonstrations, it was in an effort to label protestors as "hooligans" and "traitors" determined to destroy Serbia. Meanwhile, the print media responded to prodemocracy demonstrations by stepping up a smear campaign against opposition leaders, frequently with personal, unsubstantiated stories of intrigue. One such story, for example, suggested that an opposition leader's political efforts were being funded by Albanian drug money.

The media's bias was also demonstrated in the coverage given a strike by workers at the Zastava munitions factory in Kragujevac in August and September. The coverage demonstrated the Government's use of progovernment media to obscure facts inimical to government objectives and to manipulate public opinion. Official media gave little or no coverage to the first weeks of the strike, despite the fact that thousands of workers and supporters were demonstrating every day in front of Kragujevac's municipal building. What limited coverage there was focused on government largesse in meeting some of the demands of the workers but avoided references to the size of the demonstrations. When the strike appeared to be waning, the progovernment press emphasized its demise. Later, when the strike flared up and temporarily drew support from workers at other factories, thus becoming an antigovernment rallying point, the official press lashed out with front page attacks—labeling the workers self-indulgent.

Economic pressure was the usual weapon of the regime against the free press. For example, state-owned enterprises were dissuaded from advertising in independent media. Although not the problem it was during the period of sanctions, the availability of newsprint continued to pose occasional problems, especially for the independent media. Also, while the state-controlled press got newsprint at subsidized prices, independent publications paid substantially higher market prices. According to a January announcement in the progovernment daily Politika, the cost of newsprint—even with subsidies—accounts for 71 percent of the expense of producing a daily paper. Nasa Borba, the most respected independent paper, continues to be prevented from using the distribution networks available to the progovernment press. This tactic has had the effect of reducing readership and raising distribution costs.

There were numerous cases of government harassment of the media. In April police temporarily prevented the publication of the Albanian-language Koha magazine. They interrogated the director of the printing company that publishes the magazine, informing the editor that Koha would not be allowed to resume publication unless future issues were screened by the authorities. After drawing public attention to the pressure, the company ignored the warning. No subsequent action has been taken by the Government. In May municipal authorities in the eastern Serbian town of Smederevo, following a similar tactic used previously elsewhere in Serbia, took control of the local radio station. The progovernment city council used transformation of property laws to change management at what had been one of the last independent stations in Serbia. Other stations faced similar pressures. In a related development, the Vranjske, an independent newspaper in southern Serbia faced financial ruin after pressure from the Government. Meanwhile, during key phases of the early stage of prodemocracy demonstrations, the Government blocked transmission of the independent radio stations B-92, in Belgrade, and Boom 93, in Pozarevac. Boom 93 remained off the air at year's end.

Academic freedom exists in a limited fashion. Many leading academicians are active members of the political opposition and human rights groups, and the adoption of antiregime positions would likely limit their advancement.

b. *Freedom of Peaceful Assembly and Association.*—The federal and republic-level constitutions provide for freedom of peaceful assembly and association. Numerous instances occurred in 1996 in which citizens exercised this right, including political rallies by opposition parties prior to the November elections. After the November elections, the opposition continued to organize political rallies; the Government, however, blocked marches after December 25.

The Government continued to treat political association by members of ethnic minorities as a threat. For example, in October the court in Kamenici sentenced Sevdi Tacija, the President of the local chapter of the Democratic League of Kosovo (LDK) and chairman of the local athletic society to 6 months' imprisonment for having in his possession 12 membership cards for the football club "Hogost." The court ruled that Tacija had committed a criminal offense because the organization he heads is not officially registered.

c. *Freedom of Religion.*—There is no state religion, but the Government gives preferential treatment, including access to state-run television for major religious events, to the Serbian Orthodox Church to which the majority of Serbs belong. On several occasions Muslims have been ordered to remove loudspeakers from some mosques in Kosovo and the Sandzak.

d. *Freedom of Movement Within the Country, Foreign Travel, Emigration, and Repatriation.*—The Constitution provides for freedom of movement, and the Government makes passports available to most citizens. However, many inhabitants of Serbia-Montenegro who were born in other parts of the former Yugoslavia, as well as large numbers of refugees, have not been able to establish their citizenship in the FRY, leaving them in a stateless limbo.

According to a report by the Humanitarian Law Center, authorities on several different occasions barred FRY citizens from reentering the country. On March 2, six ethnic Albanians holding valid passports were refused entry at Pristina airport. They were held in detention overnight and then transferred to Belgrade for 6 days before being returned to Pristina and sent back to Germany. One LDK official was detained at the airport on entering the FRY for over 4 hours and subjected to intensive interrogation related to his political activities.

In early 1996, the Government eliminated the need for an exit visa to visit Albania, greatly facilitating travel between the two countries. Prior to this development ethnic Albanians had traveled to Albania by way of Macedonia because of the great difficulty in obtaining exit visas. The Government occasionally continues to restrict the right of Albanian Kosovars to travel by holding up issuance or renewal of passports for an unusually long period of time and has reserved the option of prosecuting individuals charged previously with violating exit visa requirements.

FRY citizens reported difficulties at borders and occasional confiscation of their passports. Ethnic Albanians frequently complained of harassment at border crossings. There were numerous reports of border guards confiscating foreign currency or passports from travelers as well as occasional complaints of physical ill-treatment. The authorities have generally allowed political leaders, including Zajedno leaders and LDK head Ibrahim Rugova, to leave the country and return.

The Government has been very slow to issue passports to refugees. Albanian Kosovars also have problems with issuance and renewal of passports and are sometimes called in for interrogation by state security officers before passports are issued. In 1995 the Government passed a new citizenship law which, when it goes into effect in January 1997, is expected to affect adversely the rights of many inhabitants, including those born in other parts of the former Yugoslavia, refugees, and citizens who had migrated to other countries to work or seek asylum. Prior to the law's adoption, the U.N. human rights rapporteur noted that the new law would give the Ministry of Interior almost complete control over the granting of citizenship. The Government has served notice that it plans to limit severely the granting of citizenship to refugees from the conflicts in Bosnia and Croatia. The Government also plans to revise the eligibility status of a large number of people, chiefly refugees, who have been granted citizenship since 1992.

Observers in the Sandzak region also note that Muslim residents who were forced to flee to Bosnia from Sandzak in 1992 and 1993 may not be permitted to return to Serbia, particularly if they have obtained Bosnian passports in the interim.

Government policy toward refugee and asylum seekers continued to be uneven. Refugees are often treated as citizens of Serbia-Montenegro for labor and military purposes but are denied other rights such as employment and travel (see Section 1.f.). The Government has cooperated with the U.N. High Commissioner for Refugees to provide help for the more than 600,000 refugees in Serbia-Montenegro.

Section 3. Respect for Political Rights: The Right of Citizens to Change Their Government

The three constitutions—Federal, Serbian, and Montenegrin Republic—provide for this right, but in practice citizens are prevented from exercising it by the Government's monopoly on the mass media and manipulation of the electoral process. Federal and municipal elections were seriously flawed. At the federal level, in violation of constitutional statutes, the Government gerrymandered election districts to smooth the way for candidates in the ruling coalition. Media access was seriously restricted, to an extent worse than in 1992, according to opposition leaders.

At the municipal level, the opposition fared much better, gaining strong victories in key urban centers, including Belgrade. However, opposition victories in the November 17 voting were successively stolen by the government-controlled electoral commissions and courts—exposing vividly the Government's Potemkin village-style "democracy."

Leaders of opposition political parties complain that media access during the 1996 FRY elections was even more restricted than in 1992. Additionally, opposition politicians charge that changes in the election law, including redrawing of districts, implemented since the last election, were designed specifically to favor the ruling party.

Slobodan Milosevic dominates the political system. Although formally President of Serbia, one of the two constituent republics in the Federal Republic of Yugoslavia, Milosevic first consolidated his position by weakening the authority of the Federal Government through his control of the Serbian police, the army, and the state administration. He then placed his followers in key appointed positions, including the Federal Presidency and Federal Prime Ministership. Manipulating power within the federation based on the comparative size of the Serbian and Montenegrin populations and economies, Milosevic greatly circumscribes the Montenegrin Government's sphere for independent action and does not tolerate significant divergence from the ruling Socialist Party line. Nevertheless, the political crisis after the November elections did prompt a greater measure of Montenegrin criticism of the Serbian President's handling of events.

Although the domestic political opposition faces many obstacles, it coalesced into a united front for November's elections. Nevertheless, the Government's control over the media was a determining factor. Also, many citizens hesitate to join opposition parties unless they are economically self-sufficient because of SPS's and associated parties' control over many jobs. Although the SPS does not have an absolute majority in the Serbian Parliament, it coopted one of the smaller opposition parties and formed the previous government.

In Montenegro the ruling Democratic Party of Socialists (DPS) enjoys an absolute majority. In both Serbia and Montenegro, the ruling parties have effectively blocked legislation that would loosen their control over the state-run media.

There are no legal restrictions on women's participation in government and politics, and women are active in political organizations. However, women are greatly underrepresented in party and government positions, holding less than 10 percent of ministerial-level positions in the Serbian and federal governments. An exception is the controversial Mira Markovic, wife of Serbian President Milosevic. She is the leading force in the neo-Communist United Yugoslav Left Party, through which she exerts considerable influence on policymakers.

There are no legal restrictions on the role of minorities in government and politics, but ethnic Serbs and Montenegrins dominate the country's political leadership. Few members of other ethnic groups play any role at the top levels of government or the state-run economy. The same is true of women, although in both instances there are no legal restrictions preventing advancement. Ethnic Albanians have refused to take part in the electoral process, including federal and local elections in November and therefore have virtually no representation. Their refusal to participate in FRY federal elections has had the practical effect of increasing President Milosevic's and his supporters' political influence. Ultranationalist parties, which in the past were occasional Milosevic allies, have also taken advantage of the ethnic Albanian boycott to garner representation beyond their numbers.

Section 4. *Governmental Attitude Regarding International and Nongovernmental Investigation of Alleged Violations of Human Rights*

The Governments of Serbia and Montenegro formally maintain that they have no objection to international organizations conducting human rights investigations on their territories. However, they sporadically hindered such activities and regularly rejected the findings of human rights groups. In the most glaring example of the regime's uneven approach, Milosevic invited the OSCE to send a delegation to investigate the charges of election irregularities. However, prior to the arrival of the team, led by former Spanish Prime Minister Gonzalez, the President staged a mass demonstration of supporters in Belgrade condemning international interference in domestic affairs. As of year's end, he had refused to accept the OSCE team's findings.

A number of independent human rights organizations exist in Serbia-Montenegro, researching and gathering information on abuses, and publicizing such cases. The Belgrade-based Humanitarian Law Fund and Center for Antiwar Action researches human rights abuses throughout Serbia-Montenegro and, on occasion, elsewhere in the former Yugoslavia. The Belgrade-based Helsinki Committee publishes studies on human rights issues and cooperates with the Pristina-based Helsinki Committee in monitoring human rights abuses in Kosovo. In Kosovo the Council for the Defense of Human Rights and Freedoms collects and collates data on human rights abuses and publishes newsletters. In the Sandzak region, two similar committees monitor abuses against the local Muslim population and produce comprehensive reports. All of these organizations offer advice and help to victims of abuse.

Local human rights monitors (Serbs as well as members of ethnic minorities) and nongovernmental organizations (NGO's) worked under difficult circumstances. Sefko Alomerovic, chairman of the Helsinki Committee for Human Rights in Sandzak, was formally charged with libel by former FRY President Dobrica Cosic and his advisor Vladimir Matovic. His trial opened in October. Alomerovic had publicly accused Cosic and Matovic of direct complicity in the February 1993 Strpci incident, in which some 20 Muslim men were taken off the Belgrade-Bar train as it passed through Bosnian territory. The fate of these men remains a mystery, but Alomerovic believes that the Government, and Cosic specifically, were responsible for the kidnapings. While evidence directly linking Cosic to the kidnapings remains in doubt, the Government's reluctance to fully investigate the Strpci incident, as well as other disappearances, is clear.

Overall, however, most observers say the situation improved in 1996, with much less overt obstruction by the Government of human rights NGO's. For example, after revoking the license of the Soros Foundation in 1995, the Government later reversed its decision. It has also improved its record regarding issuing visas to visitors it believed would visit the ethnic minority areas of Serbia. After past problems obtaining a visa, the rapporteur for the U.N. Committee on Human Rights visited Serbia-Montenegro, including Pristina, on a regular basis. During 1996 the International Committee of the Red Cross was allowed to conduct ongoing prison visits in Kosovo. An NGO was also allowed to visit the mines at Trepca in Kosovo in order to investigate reports that forced labor from Bosnia was being used at the site. The Government also allowed the U.N. Committee on Human Rights and the International Criminal Tribunal for the Former Yugoslavia to open offices in Belgrade.

However, the authorities also refused numerous approaches by OSCE representatives to allow the reintroduction of the OSCE long-duration missions into Kosovo, Vojvodina, and Sandzak, maintaining that the FRY must first be "reinstated" in the OSCE. President Milosevic also refused to meet with the U.N. Special Rapporteur for Human Rights during her October visit, for as yet unspecified reasons.

Section 5. *Discrimination Based on Race, Sex, Religion, Disability, Language, or Social Status*

While federal and republic laws provide for equal rights for all citizens, regardless of ethnic group, religion, language, or social status and prohibit discrimination against women, in reality the legal system provides little protection to such groups.

Women.—The traditionally high level of domestic violence persisted. The few official agencies dedicated to coping with family violence have inadequate resources and are limited in their options by social pressure to keep families together at all costs. Few victims of spousal abuse ever file complaints with authorities. The Center for Autonomous Women's Rights offers a rape crisis and spousal abuse hot line, as well as sponsoring a number of self-help groups. The Center also offered help to refugee women, many of whom experienced extreme abuse or rape during the conflict in the former Yugoslavia.

Women do not enjoy status equal to men in the FRY, and relatively few women obtain upper level management positions in commerce. Traditional patriarchal ideas of gender roles, which hold that women should be subservient to the male members of their family, have long subjected women to discrimination. In some rural areas, particularly among minority communities, women are little more than serfs without the right to control property and children; in a few villages, brides are still bought and sold. Although underrepresented in party and government positions, women are active in political and human rights organizations. Women are entitled to equal pay for equal work and are granted maternity leave for 1 year, with an additional 6 months available. Women's rights groups continue to operate with little or no official acknowledgement.

Children.—The state attempts to meet the health and educational needs of children. The educational system is adequate, with 8 years of mandatory schooling.

The current division of Kosovo into parallel administrative systems has resulted in Serb and Albanian Kosovar elementary age children being taught in separate areas of divided schools, or attending classes in shifts. Older Albanian Kosovar children attend school in private homes. The quality of the education is thus uneven, and the tension and division of society in general has been replicated to the detriment of the children.

An agreement negotiated under the auspices of the Rome-based Sant-Egedio community and signed on September 1 by President Milosevic and Dr. Ibrahim Rugova, the leader of the LDK, seeks to resolve the division of the educational system and lend impetus to efforts to normalize the situation within Kosovo. No progress on implementation of the accord had been discerned by year's end, owing to intransigence on both sides.

Economic distress, owing primarily to the Government's abject mismanagement, has spilled over into the health care system, adversely affecting children. In Kosovo, the health situation for children remained particularly poor. Humanitarian aid officials blamed the high rate of infant and childhood mortality, as well as increasing epidemics of preventable diseases, primarily on poverty that led to malnutrition and poor hygiene, and to the deterioration of public sanitation. Ethnic minorities in some cases fear Serb state-run medical facilities, which results in a low rate of immunization and a reluctance to seek timely medical attention. Significant cooperation between Serbian medical authorities and ethnic Albanian-run clinics in Kosovo on a polio vaccination campaign represents a hopeful development. A similar drive took place in Sandzak for Muslim children, although there too local suspicions caused difficulty in implementing the vaccination program.

There is no governmental or societal pattern of abuse against children. Children are not conscripted into the army.

People With Disabilities.—Facilities for disabled people are inadequate, but the Government has made some effort to address the problem. The law prohibits discrimination against disabled persons in employment, education, or in the provision of other state services The law mandates access to new official buildings for people with disabilities, and the Government enforces these provisions in practice.

Religious Minorities.—Religion and ethnicity are so closely intertwined as to be inseparable. Serious discrimination and harassment of religious minorities continued, especially in the Kosovo and Sandzak regions. Violence against the Catholic minority in Vojvodina, largely made up of ethnic Hungarians and Croats, has also been reported.

National/Racial/Ethnic Minorities.—There were credible reports that Muslims and ethnic Albanians continued to be driven from their homes or fired from their jobs on the basis of religion or ethnicity. Other ethnic minorities, including ethnic Hungarians in Vojvodina, also allege discrimination.

The Romani population is generally tolerated, and there is no official discrimination. Roma have the right to vote, and there are two small Romani parties. However, prejudice against Roma is widespread, and local authorities often ignore or condone societal intimidation of the Roma community.

Section 6. Worker Rights

a. *The Right of Association.*—All workers (except military and police personnel) have the legal right to form or join unions. Unions are either official (government-affiliated) or independent organizations. There are 1.8 million members of the official unions and 85,000 members in the independent unions, but neither enjoys significant clout. Owing to the poor state of the economy, about 60 percent of union workers are on long-term mandatory leave from their firms pending increases in production.

The independent unions, while active in recruiting new members, have not yet reached the size needed to enable countrywide strikes that would force employers to provide concessions on workers' rights. The independent unions also claim that the Government has managed to prevent effective recruiting through a number of tactics including preventing the busing of workers to strikes, threatening the job security of members, and failing to grant visas to foreign visitors supporting independent unions. The largely splintered approach of the independent unions has left them with little to show in terms of increased wages or improved working conditions.

The ability of unions to affiliate internationally is not clear at present.

b. *The Right to Organize and Bargain Collectively.*—While this right is provided by under law, collective bargaining remains at a rudimentary level of development. Individual unions tend to be very narrow and pragmatic in their aims, unable to join with unions in other sectors to bargain for common purposes. The history of trade unionism in the country has centered not on bargaining for the collective needs of all workers, but rather for the specific needs of a given group of workers. Thus, coal workers, teachers, health workers, and electric power industry employees have been ineffective in finding common denominators (e.g., job security guarantees, minimum safety standards, universal workers' benefits, etc.) on which to negotiate. The overall result is a highly fragmented labor structure composed of workers who relate to the needs of their individual union but rarely to those of other workers. Additionally, job security fears—given the high rate of unemployment—have limited workers' militancy.

The Government is seeking to develop free trade zones.

c. *Prohibition of Forced or Compulsory Labor.*—Forced labor is prohibited by law and is not known to occur. Rumors surfaced that Bosnian Muslims were laboring in Kosovo's Trepca mines; an inspection of the mines and surrounding areas uncovered no evidence to substantiate the report.

d. *Minimum Age for Employment of Children.*—The minimum age for employment is 16 years, although in villages and farming communities it is not unusual to find younger children at work assisting their families. With an actual unemployment rate (registered unemployed plus redundant workers who show up at the workplace but perform only minimal work) in excess of 60 percent, real employment opportunities for children are nonexistent. Children can, however, be found in a variety of unofficial "retail" jobs, typically washing car windows or selling small items on the streets such as cigarettes.

e. *Acceptable Conditions of Work.*—Large government-owned enterprises, including all the major banks, industrial plants, and trading companies generally observe minimum wage standards. The current minimum wage is approximately $50 (240 Din) a month. This figure, however, is comparable to unemployment benefits and is paid to workers who have been placed in a "forced leave" status. The actual minimum wage would correspond to the lower level of the net average wage, approximately $120 (600 Din). It is not sufficient to meet basic needs, as the cost of food and utilities alone for a family of four is estimated at nearly $430. Private enterprises use the referenced wages as a general guide, but are often more flexible in paying higher wages. Reports of sweatshops operating in the country are rare. The official workweek, listed as 40 hours, had little meaning in an economy with massive underemployment and unemployment. Neither employers nor employees tended to give high priority to enforcement of established occupational safety and health regulations, focusing their efforts instead on economic survival.

In light of the competition for employment, and the fact that many industries are state-operated, workers are not free to leave hazardous work situations without risking loss of their jobs.

THE SLOVAK REPUBLIC

The Slovak Republic became an independent state in 1993, following the dissolution of the Czech and Slovak Federal Republic (CSFR). Its Constitution provides for a multiparty, multiethnic parliamentary democracy, including separation of powers and an independent judiciary. Slovakia chose to carry over the entire body of CSFR domestic legislation and international treaty obligations, which gradually are being renewed or updated.

The national police, which fall under the jurisdiction of the Ministry of Interior, are the primary law enforcement agency. In addition to domestic law enforcement, they also have responsibility for border security. The Slovak Information Service (SIS), an independent organization reporting directly to the Prime Minister, is responsible for all civilian security and intelligence activities. A six-member parliamentary commission, which includes no meaningful opposition participation, oversees the SIS. Civilian authorities maintain effective control of the security forces. Police have committed some human rights abuses.

Slovakia made significant but intermittent progress in moving from a command-based to a market-based economy, with almost 79 percent of gross domestic product (GDP) now generated by the private sector. However, the Government is reluctant to relinquish control over certain "strategic" sectors, e.g., transportation, telecommunications, and energy. GDP growth was strong at around 7 percent, inflation was under 7 percent, and the National Bank of Slovakia, in concert with the Government, continued a disciplined monetary and fiscal policy. The privatization process, while moving at a rapid rate, lacked transparency and largely excluded foreign investors. The economy is industrially based, with just 7 percent of GDP derived from agricultural production. Major exports are iron and steel, machinery and transport equipment, audio and video equipment, plastic materials, chemicals and fuels, paper, and paper products. GDP per capita is approximately $2,650, providing most of the population with an adequate standard of living. Unemployment was high, though declining, at 12.4 percent, with some areas of the country reaching levels as high as 28 percent. A disproportionate number of unemployed are Roma, who face exceptional difficulties in finding and holding jobs as a result of discrimination.

While the Government generally respected most of the human rights of its citizens, disturbing trends away from democratic principles continued. Human rights monitors reported police brutality against Roma, and there were credible allegations that the SIS conducted surveillance of senior political figures and their spouses. There were also credible allegations of politically motivated dismissals of public officials, intimidation of opponents of government policy, and interference with the electronic media. An atmosphere of intimidation restricted freedom of expression in certain areas. A new law infringed on academic freedom. The Government's failure to seriously investigate the issue of possible SIS involvement in the 1995 abduction and torture of the President's son undermines its commitment to the rule of law. Discrimination and violence against women are serious problems. Roma faced societal discrimination, and the police failed to provide adequate protection against continued attacks on Roma by skinheads.

RESPECT FOR HUMAN RIGHTS

Section 1. Respect for the Integrity of the Person, Including Freedom From:
a. *Political and Other Extrajudicial Killing.*—There were no confirmed reports of political or other extrajudicial killings by government officials.

However, press speculation is widespread that elements of the security services were involved in the death of Robert Remias. Remias was a friend and intermediary of Oskar Fegyveres (a former member of the SIS and a self-proclaimed witness to the kidnaping of the President's son in August 1995—see Section 1.c.). Remias died when his car exploded on April 29 in Bratislava.

A few hours after the incident, the Ministry of Interior released a statement saying that the blast had been caused by a defect in the propane/butane fuel burning system. The importer of the system claimed that there were no instances worldwide of such an accident. In September the authorities investigating the incident officially concluded that a bomb was the cause of the explosion. To date there are no suspects.

Other bombs that caused property damage but no deaths were placed in front of the homes of ethnic Hungarian Member of Parliament Bela Bugar in May and breakaway founding member of the ruling Movement for a Democratic Slovakia Frantisek Gaulieder in December. While the investigation into the Bugar bombing remained open at year's end, both Bugar and the police believe the attack was criminal and not political in nature. A police investigation into the Gaulieder bombing was in progress at year's end.

Skinhead violence against Roma led to three deaths (see Section 5).

b. *Disappearance.*—There were no reports of politically motivated disappearances.

c. *Torture and Other Cruel, Inhuman, or Degrading Treatment or Punishment.*—The Constitution prohibits such practices. However, certain events have raised questions about the observance of these prohibitions by government agents.

The 1995 case of the violent abduction of the President's son, Michael Kovac Jr., to Austria, during which he was tortured, remained unsolved. SIS personnel are alleged to be implicated. The SIS refused to permit its personnel to be questioned and has accused police investigators of wrongdoing. One lead police investigator resigned under pressure; another was removed from the case, as was their supervisor. The third investigator closed the case due to "insufficient evidence" and noted that the incident may have been staged to embarrass the Government. The Government's failure to seriously investigate the torture and kidnaping case undermines its commitment to the rule of law.

Human rights monitors reported cases of police brutality against Roma. In one case a Rom alleged he was beaten by police and forced to sign a confession that he had committed a murder. He was sentenced to 18 months' imprisonment but later released.

In May Dr. Vasilij Demidov was involved in an altercation at a department store in Martin. Police intervened, and he was arrested, taken to a police station, and allegedly beaten. The police denied the charges, saying that the man was drunk and hurt himself in his aggressive state. While doctors did not give official statements, one was quoted anonymously as saying that Demidov's injuries did not appear to be self-inflicted. In August police investigators dismissed charges against the policemen involved. At year's end, prosecutors were still considering charges against Demidov for interfering with the duties of a police officer and filing a false report.

Prison conditions meet minimum international standards, and the Government permits visits by human rights monitors.

d. *Arbitrary Arrest, Detention, or Exile.*—The Constitution prohibits arbitrary arrest and detention, and the Government observes this prohibition.

A person accused or suspected of a crime must be given a hearing within 24 hours and either set free or remanded to the court. During this time, the detainee has the right to an attorney. If remanded to a court, the accused is entitled to a hearing within 24 hours, at which the judge will set the accused free or issue a substantive written order placing the accused in custody. Investigative detention may last up to 2 months and may be extended. The total length of pretrial detention may not exceed 1 year, unless the Supreme Court extends it by determining that the person constitutes a serious danger to society. Pretrial detainees constituted roughly 25 percent of the total prison population, and the average pretrial detention period was 7.2 months. The law allows family visits and provides for a court-paid attorney if needed, although human rights monitors point out that this applies only to defendants whose alleged offenses are punishable by more than 5 years in prison. A system of bail exists. Noncitizens may be detained for up to 30 days for the purposes of identification.

The Constitution prohibits exile, and the Government observes this prohibition.

e. *Denial of Fair Public Trial.*—The Constitution provides for courts that are independent, impartial, and separate from the other branches of government. Some critics allege, however, that the dependence of judges upon the Ministry of Justice for logistical support, the granting of leave requests, and other services undermines their independent status. Also, the Ministry of Justice can remove presidents and vice presidents of the courts for any reason, although they remain judges; it has done so.

The court system consists of local and regional courts with the Supreme Court as the highest court of appeal except for constitutional questions. There is a separate Constitutional Court—with no ties to the Ministry of Justice—that considers constitutional issues. In addition, there is a separate military court system, the decisions of which may be appealed to the Supreme Court and the Constitutional Court. Under the Constitution, the President appoints and removes Constitutional Court judges based upon parliamentary nominations. Parliament elects other judges, based on recommendations from the Ministry of Justice, and can remove them for misconduct.

Persons charged with criminal offenses are entitled to fair and open public trials. They have the right to be informed of the charges against them and of their legal rights, to retain and consult with counsel sufficiently in advance to prepare a defense, and to confront witnesses. Defendants enjoy a presumption of innocence and have the right to refuse to testify against themselves. They may appeal any judgment against them.

The "lustration" law of the former CSFR, barring from high public office persons who previously collaborated with the Communist-era secret police, expired at year's end. It had not been enforced since independence in 1993.

With respect to the Roma minority, human rights monitors continued to charge that police appear reluctant to take the testimony of witnesses to skinhead attacks on Roma. Further, they reported that police used the device of countercharges to pressure Roma victims of police brutality to drop their complaints, that medical doctors and investigators cooperated with police by refusing to describe accurately the injuries involved, and that lawyers often were reluctant to represent Roma in such situations, for fear this would have a negative effect on their practice.

Several Roma complained to a human rights organization about the reluctance of police in Prievidza to deal with their reports of skinhead violence and threats. Police routinely refused to accept complaints and accused the Roma of abusing public officials. The human rights organization sent a complaint to police headquarters in Banska Bystrica. In this case, the police chief admitted the violation of police basic duties and promised to take disciplinary action against the officers involved. No known action had been taken by year's end.

There were no reports of political prisoners.

f. *Arbitrary Interference With Privacy, Family, Home, or Correspondence.*—The Criminal Code requires police to obtain a judicial search warrant in order to enter a home. The court may issue such a warrant only if there is a well-founded suspicion that important evidence or persons accused of criminal activity are present inside or if there is some other important reason. Police must present the warrant before conducting the house search or within 24 hours after the search.

The 1993 Police Law regulates wiretapping and mail surveillance for the purposes of criminal investigation, which may be conducted, on the order of a judge or prosecutor, only in cases of extraordinarily serious premeditated crimes or crimes involving international treaty obligations. However, in June a local radio station in Bratislava acquired and broadcast a tape of a conversation between then-Minister of Interior Hudek and chief of the SIS Ivan Lexa in which they appeared to be discussing the dismissal of the police investigator of the Kovac kidnaping case. A second tape, allegedly of a conversation between deputy Prime Minister Sergej Kozlik and Lubomir Dobrik (State Secretary of the Justice Ministry) discussing plans to shift control of the state insurance company into the hands of fellow members of the Movement for a Democratic Slovakia (HZDS) party was obtained, but not played due to its poor quality. It is not clear who made the tapes, but the independent media has alleged that SIS or police agents were involved in the former case while the latter may have been a more amateur, yet still illegal, undertaking. There were credible allegations that the SIS conducted routine surveillance of some senior political figures and their spouses. Radio Free Europe (RFE) representatives alleged that SIS agents tailed RFE deputy editor Luba Lesna.

In July 1995, police with a legal warrant searched the diocesean headquarters of Bishop Rudolf Balaz, Chairman of the Conference of Bishops. The search occurred soon after Balaz had led the Conference in a statement of support for President Michal Kovac, who has been the target of criticism by supporters of Prime Minister Vladimir Meciar. Police said Balaz was involved in the illegal sale of art works listed in the register of national treasures. Denying this, Balaz's office director stated that the Government was intent on discrediting Balaz and that police had searched areas clearly inconsistent with their alleged mission. The charges were dropped in March after a newspaper alleged SIS involvement in the case. A high church official said that the police had not returned either the art work or the money that had been seized.

There were no reports of mail tampering.

Section 2. Respect for Civil Liberties, Including:

a. *Freedom of Speech and Press.*—The Constitution provides for freedom of speech and of the press, and the Government generally respects this right in practice. However, both the law and an atmosphere of intimidation restrict freedom of expression in certain areas.

Although dependent on a state-owned distribution company, the print media are free and uncensored, and newspapers and magazines regularly publish a wide range of opinions and news articles. However, the politicization of state-owned broadcast media remains a significant problem. Private broadcast media are widespread but are threatened by huge cost increases imposed by the state-owned telecommunications company.

Many individuals reported an atmosphere of intimidation that made them reluctant to criticize the Government openly without fear of some form of reprisal. This led some to practice self-censorship. Among the events contributing to this view were: The mysterious death of former policeman Robert Remias (see Section 1.a.), who had assisted journalists investigating the 1995 kidnapping of the President's son; widespread reports of civil servants being dismissed for refusing to join the ruling political party; reports that the Government, acting through the Fund for National Property, required newly privatized companies to advertise exclusively in progovernment media; and public questioning by officials of the governing coalition of the patriotism of citizens and journalists who spoke critically of developments in the country.

In November a Banska Bystrica court ruled that an opposition daily was guilty of libel and sentenced it to pay $250,000 (7.5 million crowns) to the prime minister and each member of his cabinet for quoting a journalist who spoke at the funeral of Robert Remias (see Section 1.a.). The journalist was found not guilty because the paper used his quotation out of context. The newspaper filed an immediate appeal, which was pending at year's end.

The bitter dispute between the President and the Prime Minister generated multiple defamation suits. In May the President sued the Prime Minister for defamation. The President also sued Jan Smolec, a former editor of the newspaper

Slovenska Republika, for defamation in October. The newspaper SME was charged in October in a secret indictment with publishing secret documents from a government meeting. The editors of SME reported that they were told they could be punished if they revealed the existence of the indictment, which they nonetheless did.

An amendment to the Criminal Code, commonly referred to as "the Law on the Protection of the Republic" was passed in March despite domestic and international criticism that it is undemocratic. The amendment makes it a crime to facilitate the spread of false information damaging to the interests of the Slovak Republic. The amendment was returned by the President to Parliament in April. In December a revised law was passed and again returned by the President. The 1995 State Language Law also restricts freedom of expression by banning the use of foreign languages in the media. Broadcasting in minority languages continued, but several radio stations canceled English language programming in order to comply with the law.

Slovak radio and television are supervised by three boards appointed by majority vote of Parliament. The Slovak Television Council and the Slovak Radio Council establish broadcast policy for state-owned television and radio. The Slovak Radio and Television council issues broadcast licenses and administers advertising laws and some other regulations. The Radio and Television Council has made significant progress in fostering the spread of private broadcasting. It has issued 27 licenses for private radio broadcasting. A private company, Markiza Television, began broadcasting with a signal covering two-thirds of the country, and it quickly established a leading position in the ratings. In September Parliament passed a law to privatize the second channel of Slovak television (STV). Three private companies and one local government hold licenses and broadcast television regionally. The Radio and Television Council revoked the license of one regional broadcaster, TV Sever, because it changed programming abruptly. In December TV Sever won a court decision that restores its license. Cable television licenses are held by 73 municipalities and private companies.

The state-owned electronic media have continued to be highly politicized. Critics have charged that STV avoids controversial topics and provides limited space for opposition views or reporting the activities of the President. STV was censured by the Television and Radio Council for violating programming rules by abruptly interrupting its regular schedule to broadcast a program charging the President's son with fraud.

Slovak Radio's coverage of internal politics remains more objective. However, in April an editor at Slovak radio was fired after reporting erroneously that two intelligence service agents would testify in the kidnapping case involving the President's son. The error was in not noting that the two witnesses were former intelligence agents. The editor sued, and in December a court ruled that dismissal was too great a penalty for such an error. The dismissed editor charged that he was really fired for disseminating antigovernment commentaries.

In January the Radio and Television Council sharply criticized some programs of Radio Free Europe for being unbalanced, unobjective, and anti-Slovak. It nevertheless finally renewed Radio Free Europe's license for 18 months in November.

The Government continued to restrict the activities of minorities: It terminated the autonomous status of the ethnic Hungarian and Roma theaters (see Section 5).

The law provides for academic freedom, which is generally respected. However, the universities law adopted in September transferred final decisionmaking power regarding curriculum, the establishment of departments, faculty promotions, and the granting of degrees from individual universities to the Ministry of Education. Students and rectors characterized the law as an infringement on academic freedom.

b. *Freedom of Peaceful Assembly and Association.*—The Constitution provides for these rights, and the Government respects them in practice.

c. *Freedom of Religion.*—The Constitution provides for freedom of religious belief and faith, and the Government respects this provision in practice. Under existing law, only registered churches and religious organizations have the explicit right to conduct public worship services and other activities, although no specific religions or practices are banned or discouraged by the authorities. The State provides financial subsidies only to registered churches and religious organizations, of which there are 15.

d. *Freedom of Movement Within the Country, Foreign Travel, Emigration, and Repatriation.*—The Constitution provides for these rights, and the Government respects them in practice.

The Government cooperates with the U.N. High Commissioner for Refugees (UNHCR) and other humanitarian organizations in assisting refugees. The Government provides first asylum and provided it to 403 persons in 1996. Of these, 4 were granted citizenship, 128 were accepted as refugees, 62 claims were rejected, 193 persons terminated their cases, and the remainder are pending. In addition, under the auspices of the UNHCR, approximately 250 persons granted first asylum in previous years were repatriated to Bosnia-Herzegovina in 1996. There were no reports of forced expulsion of those having a valid claim to refugee status. However, some refugee claimants had difficulty in gaining access to initial processing.

Section 3. Respect for Political Rights: The Right of Citizens to Change Their Government

Citizens have the constitutional right to change their government through the periodic free election of their national representatives. Citizens over the age of 18 are eligible to vote, and voting is by secret ballot. The Constitution reserves certain powers to the President as Chief of State (elected by the Parliament), but executive power rests with the Government. Legislative power is vested in the National Council of the Slovak Republic (Parliament).

A number of actions served to consolidate the Government's power in a manner, which, taken as a whole, gave rise to continued concern over the future course of pluralism, separation of powers, and democratic development overall.

In December in a virtual party line vote, deputies ousted M.P. Frantisek Gauleider from Parliament against his will because he had earlier resigned his membership in the ruling party, the Movement for a Democratic Slovakia (HZDS). A bomb exploded at his residence 2 days later (see Section 1.a.). Gauleider's expulsion was referred to the Constitutional Court, where it was pending at year's end. The incident, along with the bombing which followed parliamentary action, undercuts the freedom to express opposing views without fear of reprisals.

Many academics criticized the new higher education law as an infringement on academic freedom (see Section 2.a.). In the absence of a civil service law, the Government continued to replace national and local government officials with its supporters, apparently based largely on political loyalty. In August Parliament passed a territorial administration law redistricting regional and local government. Details of the relationship between appointed heads of the newly created regions and counties and elected mayors are not yet clear, and further legislation is expected. Ethnic Hungarian and other opposition politicians accused the Government of gerrymandering and excessive patronage as the Government moved to appoint coalition party members to newly created positions associated with this law. Most politicians were unable to describe the role of the new regional entities except to say that they were dependent on central government funds and that their leaders were appointed, not elected like the local mayors. In its handling of the privatization of large state enterprises, the national property fund, nominally independent of the Government, appeared to favor primarily supporters of the ruling coalition.

Women are underrepresented in government. They hold 2 of 15 portfolios: Labor/Social Affairs and Education. One of three Deputy Prime Ministers is a woman. Women hold 22 seats in the 150-member Parliament.

The large ethnic Hungarian minority, whose coalition gained 17 seats in Parliament in the 1994 elections, is well represented in Parliament and in local government but not in the central government. Roma are not represented in Parliament and hold no senior government positions.

Section 4. Governmental Attitude Regarding International and Nongovernmental Investigation of Alleged Violations of Human Rights

A number of human rights groups operate without government restriction, investigating and publishing their findings on human rights cases. Nonetheless, nongovernmental organizations (NGO's) and foundations protested a government-sponsored law that required such organizations to have substantial financial resources in order to operate, a condition which would eliminate 95 percent of existing foundations. NGO's protested another provision of this law that required documentation of sources and origin of property donated to a foundation out of concern that this provision compels the public and perhaps unwelcome exposure of donors. In April, after no evidence of fraud was found, the General Prosecutor stopped the investigation of human rights foundations funded by international philanthropist George Soros. The investigation was started in 1995, at the behest of the head of the Slovak National Party (SNS), after Soros criticized the Government.

Section 5. Discrimination Based on Race, Sex, Religion, Disability, Language, or Social Status

The law prohibits discrimination and provides for the equality of all citizens. Health care, education, retirement benefits, and other social services are provided regardless of race, sex, religion, disability, language, or social status.

Women.—Violence, particularly sexual violence against women, remains a serious and underreported problem. Experts say that in 1993, the latest year studied, there were 47,000 acts of violence or intolerance against women (violence is defined as physical, sexual, emotional, and economic). Physical and sexual violence account for almost half of all reported cases. These experts conclude that most of the unreported cases, estimated to be as high as half of all cases, involve sexual violence. They note that although police (in 1993) reported a drop of 19 percent in officially reported cases of sexual violence, centers of psychological counseling registered a 60 percent increase in such cases. Police estimate that two-thirds of female rape victims fail to report the cases for personal reasons. Police deal with spousal abuse, child abuse, and other violence against women in the same way as other criminal offenses; specific sections in the Criminal Code deal with rape, sexual abuse, trade in women, and pandering.

As a result of amendments to the Criminal Code that took effect in 1994, prostitution is not an illegal act. However, the Code prohibits activities related to prostitution, such as renting apartments for conducting prostitution, spreading contagious diseases, or trafficking in women for the purpose of prostitution.

Women are equal under the law. They enjoy the same property, inheritance, and other legal rights as men. Women are well represented in the judicial and administrative professions but are underrepresented in other public service areas. Labor law prohibits women from engaging in certain types of work considered dangerous to their health.

Despite the lack of overt discrimination, women face large wage discrepancies in the workplace. Women receive 25 to 30 percent less pay than men for the same work. A February 1995 report prepared by the Ministry of Foreign Affairs stated that for the period 1988–93, "gross earnings of men are 71 percent higher than those of women." The report concluded that "since there is little difference in the level of education achieved by men and women, and since a significantly greater number of women are graduates of technical universities as well as universities, the discrepancy in wages is caused by factors other than educational achievement."

The Democratic Union of Women of Slovakia (DUZS) monitors observance of the rights of women and their families in light of internationally accepted documents and the Constitution, especially as they affect the social and family spheres. In August DUZS representatives stated that the number one problem facing women was insufficient resources to provide for everyday family needs. Other major problems included women's health and the health of their family members. The DUZS continued to promote creation of a parliamentary committee on women and the family, and passage of a law on the family. Regarding legislation, the DUZS was particularly interested in more day care and preschool programs. The DUZS also complained about growing discrimination against middle-aged and older women in employment.

After the 1995 U.N. Conference on Women in Beijing, the Government formed a Coordinating Committee for Women's Affairs. The Committee meets periodically to discuss the status of women's issues and any necessary followup from the Beijing Conference. The committee includes government officials as well as NGO participants. Some NGO representatives have chosen not to participate, characterizing the committee as ineffective.

Children.—The Government demonstrates its commitment to children's rights and welfare through its system of public education and medical care. The Ministry of Labor oversees implementation of the Government's programs for children. The Constitution, the law on education, the Labor Code, and the system of child welfare payments to families with children each provide in part for children's rights. Education is compulsory for 9 years, or until the age of 15.

While there is no evidence of a pattern of societal abuse of children, some problems remain. One NGO reported almost 400 cases of child beating and 500 cases of sexual abuse although the number of unreported cases could be much higher. In September police began an investigation into the legitimacy of an advertising agency that was sending children across the border into Austria for nude and seminude photo sessions. In cooperation with Interpol, police were also investigating a connection to the pedophile case in Belgium. Dutroux was in active contact with many families in the town of Topolcany and the police were investigating whether any girls there were subject to abuse.

People With Disabilities.—The Constitution and implementing legislation provide for health protection and special working conditions for mentally and physically disabled persons, including special protection in employment relations and special assistance in training. A 1994 decree provides incentives to employers who create a "sheltered" workplace (i.e., a certain percentage of jobs set aside for disabled). The law also prohibits discrimination against physically disabled individuals in employment, education, and the provision of other state services. Nevertheless, experts report discrimination in such areas as accessibility of premises and access to education (especially higher education). Although not specifically required by law, another 1994 government decree mandates the provision of accessibility with regard to new building construction. The decree provides for sanctions but lacks a control mechanism to enforce them. A spokeswoman for an NGO dealing with people with disabilities said that the Government made some limited progress on accessibility issues and in supplying prosthetics.

Religious Minorities.—Isolated instances of verbal harassment against Jews occurred during the year. Despite protests by the Federation of Jewish Communities, Slovak National Party members and the official Slovak cultural organization Matica Slovenska continued their efforts to revise the history of the pro-Nazi wartime Slovak state. These efforts included: Stopping publication of a new school history text, written by prominent historians, because it was not sufficiently positive in its treatment of then-president Tiso and his Nazi puppet state; television programs extolling the virtues of the Tiso Government; and statements by one SNS parliamentarian linking the deportation of Jews during the war to their excessive enrichment and their "paupering" of the Slovak people. However, the Prime Minister has publicly distanced himself from the glorification of the Tiso regime and has condemned fascism and anti-Semitism.

In December the Rabbi of Bratislava was attacked by three skinheads while on his way to inspect a large menorah in a public square. Bystanders chased the skinheads away, and the police were present during the subsequent candle-lighting ceremony, which proceeded without incident. One of the skinheads was identified and arrested.

National/Racial/Ethnic Minorities.—The Constitution provides minorities with the right to develop their own culture, receive information and education in their mother tongue, and participate in decisionmaking in matters affecting them. The Government continued to provide funding for cultural, educational, broadcasting, and publishing activities for the major ethnic minorities, but at greatly reduced levels. In April Parliament ratified a bilateral treaty with Hungary, which deals extensively with the treatment of ethnic minorities.

The politically active ethnic Hungarian minority, which is the most numerous, is concentrated primarily in southern Slovakia, with a population registered at 570,000 (150,000 of whom are thought to be Roma who speak Hungarian and choose to declare themselves as ethnic Hungarian). Most ethnic Hungarians and ethnic Slovaks living in mixed areas continued to coexist peacefully, but there were occasional outbreaks of anti-Hungarian feeling, mostly in areas where the two do not coexist.

Hungarian ethnic leaders complained about large cuts in government subsidies to Hungarian cultural organizations, as well as a number of government initiatives, which they said sought to reverse gains made in previous years. The Government took no action in 1996 on the proposed education law that would expand the use of Slovak in schools of the Hungarian minority, and in particular require that history and literature be taught in Slovak. In January then-Foreign Minister Juraj Shenk assured the High Commissioner for Minorities of the Organization for Security and Cooperation in Europe that the Government would pass a law codifying the use of minority languages. The Ministry of Culture did not draft a bill, but ethnic Hungarian Members of Parliament did. Parliament did not act on this proposal. A September law on state symbols restricts the playing of foreign anthems to events where official foreign representatives are present. Ethnic Hungarian leaders had yet to notice any impact of this law.

Roma constitute the second largest ethnic minority and suffer disproportionately from high levels of poverty and unemployment. Credible reports by human rights monitors indicated that Roma continued to suffer from discrimination in employment and housing, and administration of state services. Skinhead violence against Roma was a serious and growing problem, and monitors reported that police remain reluctant to take action. In April three serious incidents took place: A Roma house was set on fire killing Jozef Miklos and injuring three other Roma in the town of Hontianske Nemce. According to witnesses, the mayor was unwilling to call the police to intervene; a Roma man suffered burns when three men threw a bottle of flaming liquid into his house in Zalistie after having assaulted him and four other Roma; and in Topolcany a group of skinheads attacked mentally disabled Romani children from an orphanage attending a hockey game, yelling "we will kill all gypsies."

In August a Romani man, who was taunted on a bus, knifed and killed a skinhead in the town of Prievidza. In the aftermath, skinheads set fire to Romani houses and spray-painted anti-Semitic, anti-Roma, and pro-Nazi graffiti in town.

In December a father and son of Romani heritage were stabbed by a skinhead at the train station in Handlova. The father died while the son suffered serious wounds. The police found and arrested the perpetrator, who remained in custody at year's end charged with murder and attempted murder.

Human rights monitors reported cases of police brutality against Roma (see Section 1.c.). Both ethnic Hungarians and Roma protested the June decision of Culture Minister Ivan Hudec to end the autonomous status of the country's two ethnic Hungarian theaters and its only Roma theater. The theaters were placed under the direction of a state official appointed by the Minister. Government involvement in, and control of, cultural activities occurs throughout the country, however, and is not restricted to minority areas.

Persons of color also suffered from attacks or discrimination. In August a U.S. serviceman was called racially derogatory names and attacked by skinheads in Banska Bystrica before other citizens came to his rescue. Another person of color was verbally harassed at the airport due to the color of his skin.

Section 6. Worker Rights

a. *The Right of Association.*—The Constitution provides for the right to form and join unions, except in the armed forces. According to one reliable, independent estimate, approximately 50 percent of the work force is organized. Official sources stated that the figure is closer to 75 percent. Unions are independent of the government and political parties. There are no restrictions on the right to strike. Slovakia has been largely free of strikes since the 1989 revolution. However, in 1996 low-level labor unrest increased. In September state-employed doctors threatened to strike because of low wages. No strike took place, and negotiations continued. In October actors of the Slovak national theater protested the firing of the theater director through a public demonstration and a 1-day strike. All work actions were carried out peacefully with no government interference.

There were no reported instances of retribution against strikers or labor leaders, but the law and regulations do not explicitly prohibit such retribution. There were no reports of human rights abuses targeted against unions or workers.

Unions are free to form or join federations or confederations and to affiliate with and participate in international bodies.

b. *The Right to Organize and Bargain Collectively.*—The law provides for collective bargaining, which is freely practiced throughout the country. Employers and unions set wages in free negotiations. The Law on Citizens' Associations prohibits discrimination by employers against union members and organizers. Complaints may be resolved either in collective negotiations or in court. If found guilty of antiunion discrimination, employers are required to reinstate workers fired for union activities.

The Customs Act of 1996 regulates free customs zones and customs warehouses. Firms operating in such zones must comply with the Labor Code; to date there have been no reports of special involvement by the trade unions. No special legislation governs labor relations in free trade zones.

c. *Prohibition of Forced or Compulsory Labor.*—Both the Constitution and the Employment Act prohibit forced or compulsory labor. There were no reports of violations. The Ministry of Labor, Social Affairs, and Family, as well as district and local labor offices, have responsibility for enforcement.

d. *Minimum Age for Employment of Children.*—The law sets the minimum employment age at 15 years. Children must remain in school for 9 years, or until the age of 15. Workers under the age of 16 may not work more than 33 hours per week; may not be compensated on a piecework basis; may not work overtime or night shifts; and may not work underground or in specified conditions deemed dangerous to their health or safety. Special conditions and protections, though somewhat less stringent, apply to young workers up to the age of 18. The Ministry of Labor enforces this legislation. There were no reports of violations.

e. *Acceptable Conditions of Work.*—The minimum wage, effective April 1 is $88 (2,700 crowns) per month. Even when combined with special allowances paid to families with children, which were increased in September, it does not provide an adequate standard of living for a worker and family. The Ministry of Labor is responsible for enforcing the minimum wage. No violations were reported. The standard workweek mandated by the Labor Code is 42.5 hours, although collective bargaining agreements have achieved reductions in some cases (most often to 40 hours). For state enterprises the law requires overtime pay up to a maximum of 8 hours per week, and 150 hours per year, and provides 4 weeks of annual leave. Private enterprises can compensate their employees for more hours of overtime than stipulated by the law and sometimes provide 5 weeks of annual leave. There is no specifically mandated 24-hour rest period during the workweek. The trade unions, the Ministry of Labor, and local employment offices monitor observance of these laws, and the authorities effectively enforce them.

The Labor Code establishes health and safety standards that the office of labor safety effectively enforces. For hazardous employment, workers undergo medical screening under the supervision of a physician. They have the right to refuse to work in situations that endanger their health and safety and may file complaints against employers in such situations. Employees working under conditions endangering their health and safety for a certain period of time are entitled to paid "relaxation" leave in addition to their standard annual leave.

SLOVENIA

Slovenia is a parliamentary democracy and constitutional republic which declared its independence from the Socialist Federal Republic of Yugoslavia in 1991. Power is shared between a directly elected President, a Prime Minister, and a bicameral legislature. The third multiparty general elections since independence held in November represent a further consolidation of a vigorous, open, and democratic system. Constitutional provisions for an independent judiciary are respected by the Government in practice.

The police are under the effective civilian control of the Ministry of the Interior. By law, the armed forces do not exercise civil police functions.

The country has made steady progress toward developing a market economy. Privatization continues, and trade has been reoriented to the West. Manufacturing accounts for most employment; machinery and other manufactured products are the major exports. Unemployment remained a concern. Inflation continued to decline; real growth slowed to 3.5 percent in 1995 and was expected to decline to 3 percent in 1996. The currency is stable, fully convertible, and backed by substantial reserves. The economy provides citizens with a good standard of living.

The Government fully respected the human rights of its citizens, and the law and judiciary provide adequate means of dealing with individual instances of abuse. An Ombudsman deals with human rights problems, including citizenship cases. About 12 percent of the population is composed of minorities, most of whom are nationals of the former Yugoslavia. The Hungarian and Italian ethnic communities (under 1 percent) enjoy constitutionally provided representation in the National Assembly. Minorities are generally treated fairly in practice.

RESPECT FOR HUMAN RIGHTS

Section 1. Respect for the Integrity of the Person, Including Freedom From:

a. *Political and Other Extrajudicial Killing.*—There were no reports of political or other extrajudicial killings.

b. *Disappearance.*—There were no reports of politically motivated disappearances.

c. *Torture and Other Cruel, Inhuman or Degrading Treatment or Punishment.*—The Constitution prohibits torture and inhuman treatment as well as "humiliating punishment or treatment," and there were no reports of such treatment.

Prison conditions meet minimum international standards and were not the subject of complaint by any human rights organization.

d. *Arbitrary Arrest, Detention, or Exile.*—The Constitution prohibits arbitrary arrest, deprivation of liberty, and the use of exile. The detaining authority must advise the detainee in writing within 24 hours, in his own language, of the reasons for his arrest. The law also provides safeguards against self-incrimination.

The Constitution also spells out the rights of detainees and limits on the Government's power to hold them (3 months maximum, with right of appeal). These rights and limitations are fully respected in practice.

e. *Denial of Fair Public Trial.*—The Constitution provides for an independent judiciary, and the Government respects this provision in practice.

The judicial system comprises local and district courts, with the Supreme Court as the highest court. Judges, elected by the State Assembly (parliament) on the nomination of the Judicial Council, are constitutionally independent and serve indefinitely, subject to an age limit. The Judicial Council is composed of six sitting judges elected by their peers and five presidential nominees elected by the State Assembly. The nine-member Constitutional Court rules on the constitutionality of legislation.

The Constitution provides in great detail for the right to a fair trial, including provisions for: Equality before the law, presumption of innocence, due process, open court proceedings, guarantees of appeal, and a prohibition against double jeopardy.

These rights are respected in practice, although the judicial system is so burdened that justice is frequently a protracted process.
There were no reports of political prisoners.

f. *Arbitrary Interference With Privacy, Family, Home, or Correspondence.*—The Constitution provides protection for privacy, "personal data rights," and the inviolability of the home, mail, and other means of communication. These rights and protections are respected in practice.

Section 2. *Respect for Civil Liberties, Including:*

a. *Freedom of Speech and Press.*—The Constitution provides for freedom of thought, speech, public association, the press, and other forms of public communication and expression. Lingering self-censorship and some indirect political pressures continue to influence the media.

The press is now a vigorous institution emerging from its more restricted past. The media span the political spectrum. The major media do not represent a broad range of ethnic interests, although there is an Italian-language television channel as well as a newspaper available to the ethnic Italian minority who live on the Adriatic Coast. Hungarian radio programming is common in the northeast where there are about 10,000 ethnic Hungarians. Bosnian refugees and the Albanian community have newsletters in their own languages.

Six major daily and several weekly newspapers are published. The major print media are supported through private investment and advertising, although the national broadcaster, RTV Slovenia, enjoys government subsidies, as do cultural publications and book publishing. There are five television channels, two of them independent private stations. Numerous foreign broadcasts are available via satellite and cable. All major towns have radio stations and cable television. Numerous business and academic journals and publications are available. Foreign newspapers, magazines, and journals are widely available.

In theory and practice, the media enjoy full freedom in their journalistic pursuits. However, for over 40 years Slovenia was ruled by an authoritarian Communist political system, and reporting about domestic politics may be influenced to some degree by self-censorship and indirect political pressures.

In December a journalist from the Maribor daily, Vecer, came under direct pressure from the Government when the Defense Ministry accused him of revealing state secrets as a result of his reporting on ministry procurement practices. The Interior Ministry searched his home and confiscated documents. While these measures were undertaken with strict observance of the law, they may have a chilling effect on press coverage of sensitive government issues.

The election law requires the media to offer free space and time to political parties at election time. During the recent general election, television stations offered viewers a host of public-interest and debate programs featuring party figures and opinion-makers from the entire political spectrum.

The Constitution provides for autonomy and freedom for universities and other institutions of higher education. There are two universities, each with numerous affiliated research and study institutions. Academic freedom is respected, and centers of higher education are lively and intellectually stimulating.

b. *Freedom of Peaceful Assembly and Association.*—The Constitution provides for the rights of peaceful assembly, association, and participation in public meetings, and the Government respects these rights in practice. These rights can be restricted only in circumstances involving national security, public safety, or protection against infectious diseases, and then only by act of the National Assembly.

c. *Freedom of Religion.*—The Constitution explicitly provides for the unfettered profession of religious and other beliefs in private and in public, and the Government respects these rights in practice. No person can be compelled to admit his religious or other beliefs. There is no state religion. About 70 percent of the population adheres to the Roman Catholic faith, and 2.5 percent to the Orthodox. There are also Protestant congregations, especially in the eastern part of the country. Clergy, missionaries—some from abroad—churches, and religious groups operate without hindrance.

The appropriate role for religious instruction in the schools continues to be an issue of debate. The Constitution states that parents are entitled "to give their children a moral and religious upbringing.* * *" Before 1945 religion was much more prominent in the schools, but now only those schools supported by religious bodies teach religion.

d. *Freedom of Movement Within the Country, Foreign Travel, Emigration, and Repatriation.*—The Constitution provides that each person has the right to freedom of movement, to choice of place of residence, to leave the country freely, and to return. Limitations on these rights may be made only by statute and only where necessary in criminal cases, to control infectious disease, or in wartime. In practice, citizens travel widely and often.

The Constitution provides for a right of political asylum for foreigners and stateless persons "who are persecuted for their stand on human rights and fundamental freedoms." The Government cooperates with the office of the United Nations High Commissioner for Refugees and other humanitarian organization in assisting refugees. It also provides first asylum and extended it to approximately 2,500 refugees (primarily from Bosnia) in 1996. There were no reports of forced expulsion of those having a valid claim to refugee status. Since 1991 Slovenia has taken in refugees from the fighting in Croatia and especially Bosnia-Herzegovina, and has dealt with them humanely. There are some 16,000 in the country, about 10,500 of them registered.

Section 3. Respect for Political Rights: The Right of Citizens to Change Their Government

Citizens have the right to change their government, voting by secret ballot on the basis of universal suffrage. Of the 31 parties legally registered, 23 contested seats in the National Assembly in the November elections, which were conducted peacefully, without allegations of fraud. Slovenia has a mixed parliamentary and presidential system. The President proposes a candidate to the legislature for confirmation as Prime Minister, after consultations with the leaders of the political parties in the National Assembly.

The Constitution stipulates that the Italian and Hungarian ethnic communities are each entitled to at least one representative in the Assembly, regardless of their population.

There are no restrictions on the participation of women or minorities in politics. The Prime Minister's office has an active agency for monitoring and promoting participation by women in public life.

Section 4. Governmental Attitude Regarding International and Nongovernmental Investigation of Alleged Violations of Human Rights

Independent human rights monitoring groups promote respect for human rights and freedoms and freely investigate complaints about violations. The Government places no obstacles in the way of investigations by international or local human rights groups. The United Nations Human Rights Commission (UNHRC) in 1994 deleted Slovenia from the group of Yugoslav successor states monitored by the UNHRC for human rights abuses.

Section 5. Discrimination Based on Race, Sex, Religion, Disability, Language, or Social Status

The Constitution provides for equality before the law, and that is observed in practice. The population (excluding refugees) is approximately 2 million, of which 1,727,018 are Slovenes and the remainder persons of 23 other nationalities. There are 54,212 Croats, 47,911 Serbs, 26,842 Muslims, 8,503 Hungarians, and 3,064 Italians.

The Constitution provides special rights for the "autochthonous Italian and Hungarian ethnic communities", including the right to use their own national symbols, enjoy bilingual education, and other privileges. It also provides for special status and rights for the small Romani communities, which are observed in practice.

Women.—In general, the level of personal crime and violence is relatively low. The problem of spousal abuse and violence against women exists, and police are not reluctant to intervene in such cases. Crimes of abuse against women are dealt with in accordance with the Penal Code; there is no special legislation on crimes against women.

Equal rights for women are a matter of state policy. There is no official discrimination against women or minorities in housing, jobs, education, or other walks of life. Marriage, under the Constitution, is based on the equality of both spouses. The Constitution stipulates that the State shall protect the family, motherhood, and fatherhood.

In rural areas, women, even those employed outside the home, bear a disproportionate share of household work and family care because of a generally conservative social tradition. However, women are frequently encountered in business and in government executive departments.

Equal pay for equal work for men and women is the norm. Slovenia has gradually but steadily increased employment, although the unemployment rate is 13 percent. In such conditions, men and women both suffer from the loss of work. Both sexes have the same average period of unemployment. Women, however, still are found more often in lower paying jobs.

Children.—The Constitution stipulates that children "enjoy human rights and fundamental freedoms consistent with their age and level of maturity." Moreover, they are guaranteed special protection from exploitation and maltreatment.

The Government demonstrates its commitment to children's welfare through its system of public education and health care. There is no societal pattern of abuse against children.

People With Disabilities.—The disabled are not discriminated against, and the Government has taken steps to facilitate access to social and economic opportunities. In practice, modifications of public and private structures to ease access by the handicapped continue slowly but steadily.

Section 6. Worker Rights

a. *The Right of Association.*—The Constitution stipulates that trade unions, their operation, and their membership shall be free, and provides for the right to strike. Virtually all workers, except for the police and military, are eligible to form and join labor organizations. In 1993 the National Assembly for the first time passed legislation restricting strikes by some public sector employees. However, in the wake of government budget-cutting, some public sector professionals (judges, doctors, and educators) have become increasingly active on the labor front.

Labor has two main groupings, with constituent branches throughout the country. A third, much smaller, regional labor union operates on the Adriatic coast. Unions are formally and actually independent of Government and political parties, but individual union members hold positions in the legislature. The Constitution provides that the State shall be responsible for "the creation of opportunities for employment and for work."

There are no restrictions on joining or forming federations and affiliating with like-minded international union organizations.

b. *The Right to Organize and Bargain Collectively.*—The economy is in transition from the former Communist system, which included some private ownership of enterprises along with state-controlled and "socially-owned" enterprises. In the transition to a fully market-based economy, the collective bargaining process is undergoing change. Formerly, the old Yugoslav Government had a dominant role in setting the minimum wage and conditions of work. The Government still exercises this role, to an extent, although in the private sector wages and working conditions are agreed annually in a general collective agreement between the "social partners;" the labor unions and the Chamber of Economy. There are no reports of antiunion discrimination.

Export processing zones have been established in Koper, Maribor, and Nova Gorica. Worker rights are the same in these zones as in the rest of the country.

c. *Prohibition of Forced or Compulsory Labor.*—There is no forced labor.

d. *Minimum Age for Employment of Children.*—The minimum age for employment is 16 years. Children must remain in school until age 15. During the harvest or for other farm work, younger children do work. In general, urban employers respect the age limits.

e. *Acceptable Conditions of Work.*—The minimum wage is approximately $408 (Sit 55,061) per month, which provides a decent standard of living for a worker and family. The workweek is 40 hours. In general, businesses provide acceptable conditions of work for their employees. Occupational health and safety standards are set and enforced by special commissions controlled by the Ministries of Health and Labor. Workers have the right to remove themselves from unsafe conditions without jeopardizing their continued employment.

SPAIN

Spain is a democracy with a constitutional monarch. The Parliament consists of two chambers, the Congress of Deputies and the Senate. As a result of elections in March, Jose Maria Aznar of the Popular Party became Prime Minister. The Government respects the constitutional provisions for an independent judiciary in practice.

Spain has three levels of security forces. The National Police are responsible for nationwide investigations, security in urban areas, traffic control, and hostage rescue. The Civil Guard polices rural areas and controls borders and highways. Autonomous police forces have taken over many of the duties of the Civil Guard in Galicia, Catalonia, and the Basque Country. The security forces are under the effective control of the Government. The security forces also maintain anticorruption units. An adviser for human rights in the Ministry of Justice is charged with promoting humanitarian law and training senior law enforcement groups in human rights practices. An Ombudsman, called the "People's Defender" in the Constitution, serves as an independent advocate for citizen's rights. Some members of the security forces committed human rights abuses.

The economy is market based, with primary reliance on private initiative, although a number of public-sector enterprises remain in key areas. The economy grew by 2.3 percent in 1996. The nominal unemployment rate dropped from the 1994 high of 25 percent to 21.3 percent in July.

The Government generally respected the human rights of its citizens. However, there were problems in some areas, including police brutality, an inefficient judicial system, and investigations of past government wiretapping. Societal violence against women, discrimination against Roma, and incidents of racism and rightwing youth violence are also problems. The Government investigates allegations of human rights abuses by the security forces and punishes those found guilty of such abuses.

Continued allegations surfaced of involvement by the previous Gonzalez Administration in the "Antiterrorist Liberation Groups" (GAL), which were responsible for bombings, kidnapings, and extrajudicial killings during the mid 1980's. The Supreme Court was still investigating the GAL at year's end. There were accusations that the current Government, while clearly not involved in these incidents, was engaging in a deliberate coverup by declining to release classified documents that some allege contain evidence of the previous government's involvement in the GAL.

The principal source of human rights abuses continued to be the protracted campaign of terrorism waged by the Basque Fatherland and Freedom (ETA) separatist group, which committed killings, kidnapings, and other abuses.

RESPECT FOR HUMAN RIGHTS

Section 1. Respect for the Integrity of the Person, Including Freedom From:

a. *Political and other Extrajudicial Killing.*—There were no reports of political or other extrajudicial killings by government forces.

Courts continue to investigate the "dirty war" against terrorism, during which the GAL allegedly assassinated approximately 28 people in the mid-1980's. Hearings began in 1995, and high-ranking officials continue to testify. Several cases are expected to go to trial in early 1997.

In January the Supreme Court indicted former Interior Minister Jose Barrionuevo and former Secretary of State for Security Rafael Vera on charges of kidnaping, misuse of public funds, and association with an armed group in relation to the kidnaping of Segundo Marey in 1983 and the "dirty war" against ETA. They were indicted on additional charges in February. In November the Supreme Court decided not to summon to testify in this case former Prime Minister Felipe Gonzalez, former Vice President and Defense Minister Narcis Serra, or Basque socialist leader Jose Maria Benegas.

In April a witness testified that in 1983, highly decorated Civil Guard General Enrique Galindo and former Guipuzcoa civil Governor Julen Elgorriaga entered the Palace de la Cumbre where they presumably interrogated two kidnaped men, Jose Ignacio Lasa and Jose Antonio Zabala. The bodies of Lasa and Zabala, which showed signs of torture, were identified in 1995. Two Civil Guardsmen involved in the killings were imprisoned in May, the first persons to be sentenced in the GAL investigations. Galindo was held in preventive custody for 72 days for his role in this case. Elgorriaga remains in preventive detention.

In February the ex-head of operations of the National Intelligence Agency (CESID) provided new information about the 1983 assassination in the south of France of Roman Onaederra (also known as "Kattu") by Civil Guardsmen. In May Galindo and two generals were declared suspects in this case. Barrionuevo and Vera are expected to testify.

The case of the death of Mikel Zabaltza, a tram conductor who died while in police custody in 1985 after being taken from his home for alleged collaboration with terrorists, was reopened in November.

Also pending in the GAL investigations is the case of Frenchman Robert Caplanne, who was mistaken for an ETA member and murdered in 1985.

In September the Madrid daily El Mundo reported that CESID abducted a tramp and two drug addicts in July 1988 to test on them an anesthetic that CESID intended to use for the kidnaping of ETA leader Juan Antonio Urreticoechea (also known as "Josu Ternera"). El Mundo claimed that the injection of the anesthetic led to the death of one of the beggars and that CESID agents had to dispose of the body. The Defense Minister at the time and the current Defense Minister both denied the accusations; the investigation continued at year's end.

There continued to be frequent terrorist incidents. As of October, 49 attacks attributed to ETA had resulted in 5 deaths and 43 serious injuries. The Attorney General's report states that groups supporting ETA carried out 830 acts of sabotage, numerous disturbances, and attacks on persons, property, political parties, and security forces in 1995, a 300 percent increase from 1994. Actions by ETA and its affiliate groups caused millions of dollars worth of damage throughout Spain. In February then-Prime Minister Felipe Gonzalez said that terrorist violence reached levels in 1995 unheard of since 1985–87.

On February 6, Basque Socialist parliamentary candidate Fernando Mugica Herzog was shot and killed by four ETA youths in San Sebastian. On February 14, the former Vice Chairman of the Constitutional Court was assassinated by three shots to the back of the head in his office at Madrid University where he served as a professor. On March 4, a car bomb killed the former head of the Basque police intelligence service, 1 day before his scheduled testimony in the trial of 15 alleged ETA members. On May 12, a bomb killed an army sergeant and narrowly missed a busload of soldiers in Cordoba. On July 26, Basque businessman Isidro Usaiaga was shot five times as he was returning home from a party. Local officials say that he had refused to pay ETA's "revolutionary tax."

On June 23, ETA announced a 1-week unilateral cease-fire. The Government said that the short cease-fire could not be taken seriously when ETA continued to hold kidnaped prison official Jose Antonio Lara (see Section 1.b.). ETA ended the cease-fire on July 1, and followed its announcement with an attack on a Civil Guard outpost in Navarra and the resumption of its annual summer campaign against selected tourist areas in the south of Spain. The campaign moved to Catalonia with a July 20 explosion at the Reus airport that injured 35 people.

The Government took several steps to deal with the ETA problem. It increased its counterterrorism efforts, joined in the creation of a European police intelligence department, signing a Europe-wide extradition treaty, and sought tougher extradition rules from countries outside Europe where ETA terrorists reside. The Government offered the possibility of talks with ETA, provided that ETA renounced terrorism and made fundamental political commitments. It also sought tougher legislation to control street violence by separatists supporters.

French-Spanish cooperation led to the November arrest in Bordeaux of ETA's arms and explosives operative, Juan Maria Insausti Mugica (also known as "Karpov"); the November arrest in Bayona of ETA's chief of illegal commands, Juan Luis Agierre Lete (also known as "Patas" and "Isuntza"); and the July arrest in Pau of ETA's number three leader, Julian Achurra Egurola (also known as "Pototo"). In November France also carried out the extradition pending since 1994 of ETA leader Rosario Pikabea Ugalde (also known as "Errota"), charged in Spain with two murders. Two ETA members were also arrested in Brussels in January, and three more were detained in Venezuela in May.

In November the National High Court sentenced ETA member Henry Parot to 1,170 years' imprisonment for the bomb attack on the Civil Guard Directorate General.

b. *Disappearance.*—Since 1970 ETA has kidnaped 76 people; between then and year's end, it is estimated that ETA has obtained more than $33 million (4 billion pesetas) from the kidnapings.

ETA released Jose Maria Aldaya Etxeburua, a 54-year-old Basque industrialist, on April 14, after holding him hostage for 341 days. This was the longest kidnaping ever by ETA, during which time thousands of people participated in hundreds of demonstrations, urging Aldaya's release. The Ministry of the Interior estimates that ETA was able to acquire more than 100 million pesetas ($800,000) from various sources for the liberation of Aldaya.

Jose Ortega Lara, a worker at the prison of Logrono, was kidnaped on January 17. Unlike other ETA kidnapings, Ortega Lara's is widely viewed as an attempt by ETA to pressure the Government into ending the dispersion of more than 500 ETA prisoners in jails around Spain and concentrating them in prisons in the Basque country. As of December Ortega Lara was still a captive.

On November 28, ETA claimed responsibility for the November 12 kidnaping of Cosme Delclaux Zubriria, a 34-year-old Vizcaya lawyer whose family is heavily involved in Basque business and finance. Family members claim that they received a letter 2 years ago "advising" that they pay ETA's "revolutionary tax," which they said they did not do. Police also now believe a misspelling of the name "Delclaux" appeared on a list of ETA targets recovered in 1987 with the arrest of ETA member Santiago Arrospide Sarasola (also known as "Sani Potros"). At year's end, Delclaux was still a captive.

c. *Torture and other Cruel, Inhuman, or Degrading Treatment or Punishment.*—The law prohibits such acts. Spain is a signatory to the U.N. Convention Against Torture and in 1995 approved Protocol 1 of the Strasbourg European Convention for the Prevention of Torture and Inhumane or Degrading Treatment or Penalties.

Nonetheless, many detainees charged with terrorism assert that they have been abused during detention, and similar charges are sometimes made by other detainees. In March four policemen were charged with the rape and illegal detention of a Brazlian tourist.

While the situation of ETA prisoners appears to be improving, individuals, nongovernmental organizations(NGO's), and the media continue to accuse the Civil Guard of unprovoked brutality, particularly in the Basque region. According to the Spanish Association Against Torture (AAT), there were 267 accusations of torture in 1994 (latest figures available) involving 448 members of the security forces, of whom 128 were found guilty and sentenced, and 120 were found innocent. The remaining cases are still being processed.

The Madrid public prosecutor charged 14 Civil Guards of the Colmenar Viejo barracks near Madrid with torturing, injuring, annoying, and threatening 3 youths while they were detained in the barracks in October 1994. The three young men were arrested the day after a violent confrontation in a bar. The public prosecutor's report describes the injuries inflicted on the 3 detainees by the 14 Civil Guardsmen. The Civil Guard opened its own investigation into the case. The AAT filed a judicial complaint against 18 Civil Guardsmen in the case. The additional four are identified in the prosecutor's report as witnesses. The public prosecutor asked for penalties of between 4 months and 1 year in jail for the 14 it accused. The AAT asked for penalties of between 6 months and 6 years in jail for the 18 it accuses in the case.

In December 1995 the National High Court in Madrid sentenced 11 people accused of collaboration with ETA to 135 years' imprisonment. Some 50 persons had been arrested between January and May 1992, but the court ruled inadmissible a large number of the police declarations because nearly all of the detainees made detailed allegations (often supported by medical evidence) of torture. The allegations of torture were under judicial examination at year's end.

In March a judge suspended the trial of 10 Civil Guardsmen accused of the torture in 1980 of 6 detained ETA members in the jail of La Salve in Bilbao.

Prison conditions generally meet minimum international standards, and the Government permits visits by human rights monitors. In March the Government agreed to publish a medical report of a 1994 ad hoc visit by the European Committee for the Prevention of Torture, which recognized injuries compatible with eight 1994 detainees' allegations of mistreatment. The National High Court had originally rejected complaints of mistreatment.

d. *Arbitrary Arrest, Detention, or Exile.*—The Constitution prohibits arbitrary arrest, detention, and exile, and the authorities respect this provision. A suspect normally may not be held more than 72 hours without a hearing. The Penal Code permits holding a suspected terrorist an additional 2 days without a hearing or the possibility of incommunicado detention for such persons, provided that a request is granted by a judge. Many requests for extensions and incommunicado detention contain only minimal necessary details, which alarms Amnesty International. The U.N. Committee Against Torture, in its 1993 examination, raised the issue of the operation of "antiterrorist" legislation and expressed concern over incommunicado detention and the suspension of procedural rights, such as the initial denial of selection of free legal counsel.

The law on aliens permits detention of a person for up to 40 days prior to deportation but specifies that it must not take place in a prison-like setting.

In October two policemen were incarcerated for illegal detention of immigrants, extortion, drug trafficking, and robbery. Other policemen were also charged with illegal detention (see Section 1.c.).

e. *Denial of Fair Public Trial.*—The Constitution provides for an independent judiciary, and the judiciary is independent in practice.

The judicial structure consists of territorial, provincial, regional, and municipal courts with the Supreme Court at its apex. The Constitutional Court protects constitutional rights, but there is no clear distinction between its jurisdiction and that of the Supreme Court on some issues, nor is it clear which has ultimate authority. A National High Court handles cases involving crimes such as terrorism and drug trafficking. The European Court of Human Rights is the final arbiter in cases concerning human rights.

Over the past 2 years, Spain has almost completely overhauled its judicial system, in an effort to rectify the shortage of judges and the severe backlog of cases. A nine-person jury system was established in November 1995, and the first cases were tried in 1996. The entire Penal Code was revised and enacted in May. Changes included the restructuring of the criminal justice system, introduction of modern offenses and white-collar crimes, an increase in the penalties for fraud offenses, a rise in the legal age at which an individual may be tried for a criminal offense from 16 to 18 years of age, the establishment of other new offenses (including domestic violence and sexual harrasment), and authorizing judges to fine individuals with reference to their wealth. The new Code also allows judges more flexibility in sentencing. It eliminates the longstanding tradition of granting credits toward early release for time served for good behavior. The maximum penalty for any one offense under the new code is 25 years, and the maximum time a person can continuously serve is 30 years, regardless of the cumulative total of sentences. Judges can now deport foreigners sentenced to 6 years or less. The 1882 Criminal Procedural Law was not changed.

The Constitution provides for the right to a fair public trial, and the authorities respect this right in practice. Defendants have the right to be represented by an attorney (at state expense for the indigent). They are released on bail unless the court has some reason to believe they may flee or be a threat to public safety. The law calls for an expeditious judicial hearing following arrest. However, the Association of Victims of Terrorism and others have protested delays in the judicial process. By law, suspects may not be confined for more than 2 years before being brought to trial, unless a further delay is authorized by a judge, who may extend pretrial custody to 4 years.

In practice pretrial custody is usually less than 1 year; however, increasing criticism is heard in legal circles that some judges use "preventive custody" as a form of anticipatory sentencing. In cases of petty crime, suspects released on bail sometimes wait up to 5 years for trial. As of December, 25.8 percent of the prison population was in jail awaiting trial.

Following conviction, defendants may appeal to the next higher court. Human rights groups such as the Association Against Torture and members of the press complain that many persons convicted of offenses constituting violations of human rights have avoided judicial sentencing by prolonging the appeals process and that sentences for persons convicted of such offenses are unduly light. According to Amnesty International, custodial sentences of less than 1 year and 1 day are customarily not served by those convicted of such offenses.

There were no reports of political prisoners.

f. *Arbitrary Interference With Privacy, Family, Home, or Correspondence.*—The Constitution provides for the privacy of the home and correspondence. Under the Criminal Code, government authorities must obtain court approval before searching private property, wiretapping, or interfering with private correspondence. The present antiterrorist law gives discretionary authority to the Minister of Interior to act prior to obtaining court approval in "cases of emergency."

Investigation continues into allegations of wiretapping by the National Intelligence Agency (CESID) of private telephone conversations made by the King, various ministers, and other prominent figures between 1980 and 1991. The Minister of Defense, the Vice President, and CESID's chief resigned in 1995, after related government documents were leaked to the press. The judge closed the case on February 9; however, on May 14 the provincial court revoked that action and ordered the judge to continue investigating.

CESID has also been linked to the investigations of GAL crimes (see Section 1.a.). In February the judge in one GAL investigation "found" lists of CESID documents relating to GAL in the prison cell of the ex-director of CESID operations, which were subsequently leaked to the press. Based on the lists, the judge requested 18 official secret documents from the CESID in May, which allegedly contain information about GAL crimes. The Government declined to declassify these documents. The investigating judges criticized the Government for impeding the judicial process by not declassifying the documents and stated that they would work with parliamentary representatives, public officials, and other judges to obtain the information.

Section 2. Respect for Civil Liberties, Including:

a. *Freedom of Speech and Press.*—The Constitution provides for freedom of speech and the press, and the Government respects these provisions in practice. Opposition viewpoints, both from political parties and nonpartisan organizations, are freely aired and widely reflected in the media.

In July the dismissal of six top journalists from the state-run television network ignited controversy over whether the firings were politically motivated or driven by cost concerns (as the station management claimed). Several foreign newspapers took up the cause of the discharged journalists (all of whom had been appointed under the previous government), charging that their firings represented a threat to freedom of the press. Other foreign newspapers and the majority of the Spanish press declared that the personnel changes were "normal" in any media organization undergoing a change of top management.

Academic freedom is respected.

b. *Freedom of Peaceful Assembly and Association.*—The Constitution provides for these rights, and the Government respects them in practice.

c. *Freedom of Religion.*—The Constitution provides for freedom of religion, and the Government respects this right in practice. Roman Catholicism is the predominant religion, and its institutions receive official funding. Protestant and Jewish leaders refused the Government's offer of financial support.

The Government announced in June that it would make "religion" (or a similar class on "ethics") an obligatory class in public secondary educational institutions, reverting to a longstanding practice. The Spanish confederation of parents of students and some opposition political parties opposed the idea. Consequently, the Government agreed to search for a balance between the desire of the Catholic Church that religion be taught and parents' constitutional right to choose the kind of education they want for their children. A final decision had not been reached by year's end.

d. *Freedom of Movement Within the Country, Foreign Travel, Emigration, and Repatriation.*—Citizens are free to travel within and outside the country, to emigrate, and to repatriate. The Government respects these rights in practice.

The Government cooperates with the U.N. High Commissioner for Refugees (UNHCR) and other humanitarian organizations in assisting refugees. A recent asylum law (passed in 1994 and modified in February 1995) brought refugee and asylum cases together and gave full power to the Office of Asylum and Refugees (OAR) (a branch of the Ministry of the Interior) to adjudicate them but also mandates that cases can be referred to the UNHCR for appeal. Asylum requests can be made only at the point of entry, and applicants are detained until the case is resolved. Negative rulings must be made within 72 hours, but the asylum seeker has an additional 24 hours in which to make an appeal. No provisions are made for detainees to have access to translators or lawyers. Since 1994 the revised law has caused a major drop in the numbers of both requests for, and grants of, asylum. From January to June, only 110 of 1,638 applications for asylum were approved. An additional 98 humanitarian asylum applications were approved.

Spain is facing an unprecedented wave of illegal immigrants coming across the Strait of Gibraltar. More than 8,000 illegal immigrants had been caught as of October, the majority in Andalucia; authorities say that under "normal" circumstances they intercept no more than 30 percent of those who enter Spain through that zone. In response, the Government is resorting to a mix of tighter border controls, liberalized treatment for those who have already established themselves in Spanish society, and increased international coordination. In July the Government sedated and forcibly repatriated 103 sub-Saharan Africans, one of whom later died during a violent demonstration in Guinea-Bissau. The repatriation stirred protests from civil libertarians and opposition political parties, as well as hunger strikes and demonstrations by the affected persons in Africa and Spain. The man who was killed in Guinea-Bissau was one of several who had applied for asylum, but whose applications never reached the proper authorities because of faults in police procedure; such deportations violated Spanish law.

Section 3. Respect for Political Rights: The Right of Citizens to Change Their Government

Spain is a multiparty democracy with open elections in which all citizens 18 years of age and over have the right to vote by secret ballot for Parliament and for provincial and local bodies. At all levels of government, elections are held at least every 4 years. As a result of elections held in March, the People's Party (PP) received 38 percent of the votes. Jose Maria Aznar became Prime Minister, and 14 years of Socialist government came to a close. The Spanish Socialist Workers' Party (PSOE) followed closely with 37.5 percent of the votes. The next highest number of votes received were the United Left (IU) with 10.6 percent, the Catalan Union and Convergence Party (CIU) with 4.6 percent, and the Basque National Party with 1.3 percent.

Governmental power is shared between the central government and 17 regional "Autonomous Communities." Local nationalist parties give political expression to regional linguistic and cultural identities.

Women are increasing their participation in the political process. The number of female candidates increased in the 1996 national elections, but under the electoral system the percentage of votes won determines the number of candidates elected from the party list. Many women were placed in the lower half of the list, and as a consequence of the electoral system, the number of women elected has never reached 25 percent.

Women hold 19 percent of parliamentary seats. The 350-member Chamber of Deputies has 72 female representatives (22 percent of the total), and the 256-member Senate has 27 (10.4 percent of the total). There are 1,529 mayors (6.5 percent of the total), and 224 women in regional parliaments (19 percent of the total). Of all judges, 30 percent are women (a profession that was closed to women before 1977), but no women hold Supreme Court positions. The Ministers of Justice, Agriculture, Education and Culture, and Environment are women.

Section 4. Governmental Attitude Regarding International and Nongovernmental Investigation of Alleged Violations of Human Rights

A number of nongovernmental human rights groups, including the Human Rights Association of Spain in Madrid and the Human Rights Institute of Catalonia in Barcelona, operate freely without government interference. The Government cooperates readily with international organizations investigating allegations of human rights abuses (such as the European Commission of Human Rights) and international nongovernmental human rights groups, as well as with independent national groups.

Section 5. Discrimination Based on Race, Sex, Religion, Disability, Language, or Social Status

The Constitution provides for equal rights for all citizens and provides for an Ombudsman, called the "People's Defender", who actively investigates complaints of human rights abuses by the authorities. The Ombudsman operates independently from any party or government ministry, must be elected every 5 years by a three-fifths majority of Congress, and is immune from prosecution. He has complete access to government institutions and documents not classified secret for national security reasons. The office of the people's defender received 13,214 complaints in 1995 and an estimated 22,000 complaints in 1996. While the majority of the complaints pertained to education and social services, there were increases in complaints of racism and mistreatment by law enforcement agencies.

Women.—Sexual abuse, violence, and the harassment of women in the workplace continued to be areas of concern. The Women's Institute in the Ministry of Labor and Social Affairs reports that 47 women were killed by their male partners and that 1,863 rapes were reported in 1995. Police received 16,000 calls concerning abuse in 1995, 3,400 from Madrid. However, experts believe that only 10 percent of violent acts against women each year are reported to authorities. Some women's NGO's estimate that about 600,000 to 800,000 cases of abuse occur each year.

A 1989 law prohibits sexual harassment in the workplace, but very few cases have been brought to trial under this law.

Several levels of government provide assistance to battered women. A toll-free hot line advises women where to go for government shelter or other aid if mistreated. There are 54 official centers for mistreated women. The Government also runs educational programs seeking to change public attitudes that contribute to violence against women. The Women's Institute has charged that some judges are reluctant to get involved in cases of violence against women by members of their family. Similarly, in smaller towns some police officers have been reluctant to accept complaints from battered women. Recognizing the latter problem, the Ministry of the Interior initiated a program in 1985 that created special sections within the police department to deal with violence against women, staffed by trained female officers. In March the community of Madrid cut spending for women's organizations by 9 percent, paralyzing more than 1,000 women's programs until 1997.

In recent years, women have moved towards equality under the law, and there are larger numbers of women in the educational system and work force. According to the organization Active Population, women received 58 percent of university degrees in 1995. The Minister of Social Affairs in January claimed that women now constitute 43 percent of the work force. Women outnumber men in the legal, journalistic, and health care professions, but still play minor roles in many fields.

The law mandates equal pay for equal work. However, according to a report by the Economic and Social Council in April, women's salaries still remain 27 percent lower than those of their male counterparts. The Council claims that women are more apt to have temporary contracts and part-time employment than men. The National Association of Rural Women and Families (ANFAR) claimed in 1995 that 80 percent of rural women are not formally employed but instead aid their husbands in farming or fishing. ANFAR said that these women lack titles to family enterprises and do not receive the same social security benefits as the male head of household.

Children.—The Government demonstrates its commitment to children's welfare through well-funded and easily accessed programs of education and health care. The Constitution obligates both the State and parents to protect children, whether or not born in wedlock. The Ministries of Health and Social Affairs are responsible for the welfare of children and have created numerous programs to aid needy children. Numerous NGO's exist to further children's rights. For example, the school help program for the protection of children has a team of experts who work with educators to help them identify abused or abandoned children in the classroom.

The 1995 Law of the Child gives legal rights of testimony to minors in child abuse cases; it also obliges all citizens to act on cases of suspected child abuse and, for the first time, sets up rules regarding foreign adoptions. A 1987 signatory to the 1961 Hague Convention, Spain voted in 1995 to withdraw the reservations it held previously in regard to the protection of minors; the treaty's provisions now apply to all children in Spain, not just those who are Spanish citizens.

Under the new Penal Code, children under the age of 18 are not considered responsible for their actions and cannot be sent to prison. The seriousness of the violent acts in the Basque country by separatist youths, however, has led to accelerated negotiations between the central Government and the Basque government for the punishment of youthful offenders under age 18. Public debate centers on whether the age of responsibility should be set as low as 12 years. The Attorney General's report in September highlighted a 300 percent increase in youth vandalism in the Basque country since 1994.

A new penitentiary law passed this year lowered the age that a child can remain with an incarcerated mother from 6 to 3 years of age. It also provides a special unit for mothers with children, a kindergarten, psychological support, and ways for children to get out of prison regularly. Currently 169 children live in jails with their mothers under this law.

People With Disabilities.—The Constitution obliges the State to provide for the adequate treatment and care of people with disabilities, ensuring that they are not deprived of basic rights that apply to all citizens. Since 1982, a law on the integration of disabled citizens has been in effect, which aims to ensure fair access to public employment, prevent disability, and facilitate physical accessibility to public facilities and transportation. The national law serves as a guide for regional laws; however, levels of assistance and accessibility differ from region to region and have not improved in many areas.

The 1996 Penal Code continues to allow parents or legal representatives of a mentally disabled person to petition a judge to obtain permission for the sterilization of that person. In 1994 the Constitutional Court held that sterilization of the mentally infirm does not constitute a violation of the Constitution. In practice many courts have authorized such surgery. Religious groups continue to protest this ruling.

National/Racial/Ethnic Minorities.—Roma, who make up 3 percent of the population, continue to suffer discrimination in housing, schools, and jobs. Since 1991 the Madrid city government, in cooperation with the autonomous regional government, has been carrying out a program to relocate squatters (the great majority of whom are Roma) to housing projects in the region. A University of Navarra estimate indicates that 12,000 squatters live in camps at the margins of Madrid, although the Madrid public works councilor states that there has never been a reliable census of squatters. The daily El Pais reported in March that 16 prefabricated houses exist around Madrid for the "Chabolistas," with 140 more houses planned. The city government plans to relocate 449 of the 769 families of squatters in and around Madrid by 1998. Spain's largest Romani organization, Gypsy Presence, complains that the city has put up police checkpoints and fences that make Romani communities resemble prison camps. The group's complaint that such relocation areas lack basic services is supported by NGO's and the press. The city government denies any anti-Romani bias in its actions. In May, 31 illegal families destroyed their "houses" so that they would not be counted in the 1996 census and forced to relocate.

Six of the 17 autonomous communities use a language or dialect other than Castillian Spanish. The Constitution stipulates that citizens have "the duty to know" Castillian, which is the "official language of the state", but it adds that other languages can also be official under regional statutes and that the "different language variations of Spain are a cultural heritage which shall * * * be protected." Catalonia has passed a law whereby Catalan is taught in regional schools and used at official regional functions. Suits regarding specific applications of this law are pending in various courts. Both Galicia and Valencia have laws stating the duty to "promote" their regional languages in schools and at official functions.

In 1995 Congress modified the Penal Code to make it a crime to "incite, publicize, or otherwise promote the abuse or discrimination of people or groups because of race, ethnicity, nationality, ideology, or religious beliefs." No cases have been tried under the modified Penal Code.

Human rights groups and the media continued to give increasing attention to discrimination against the growing numbers of illegal immigrants from northern and sub-Saharan Africa (see Section 1.d.). According to the Youth Institute in the Ministry of Labor and Social Affairs, 91 percent of persons under the age of 29 would like to see immigration further restricted. Although only 1.3 percent of the population is foreign born and the Government reduced the number of work permits issued to foreigners by 10 percent in 1995, 60 percent of the respondents under 29 years old in a July Youth Institute survey said that they believed immigrants caused employment problems for them. The association of Moroccan immigrant laborers has offices in Madrid, Barcelona, and Seville to combat anti-Moroccan racism, and Madrid has a special administrative office to deal with immigrant complaints.

There may be a connection between opinions on immigration and the increasing number of race-related incidents being reported. Quasi-organized rightwing youth groups (called "skinheads" by the press) continued to commit violent acts throughout the year, terrorizing minorities, and in some instances, committing murder. National police estimate the total number of skinheads to be several thousand; however, they say that the skinheads are not organized to plan specific actions. SOS Racismo, an NGO, said that race-related violence increased in 1995, due in part to the reduction in police arrests and incarcerations of skinheads.

In May skinhead Oscar Hernandez Bernal was tried in Barcelona for racist comments and defense of the expulsion of African immigrants in a newspaper interview in 1993. Other incidents included an attack on a black immigrant by skinheads in Madrid which was stopped by the shouts of a 60-year-old woman, and the beating in Madrid of a Moroccan man by six skinheads who did not like the color of his skin.

Skinheads and ultra-right groups also attacked young radical-left supporters, Arabs, punks, homosexuals, and homeless persons. In April two skinheads received a 3-year sentence for publicly stating their opinion on television that killing transvestites did not constitute wrongdoing. In March five neo-Nazis were sentenced to a total of 12 years in jail for severely beating a youth for his leftist opinions. In September seven skinheads were detained for kidnaping, robbing, and beating a 22-year-old man in Barcelona. Perhaps the most widely publicized case was the murder of David Gonzalez in January, who was stabbed in the heart by Madrid skinheads. As a consequence, the President of the Madrid autonomous region, together with nine women and one man whose children had been brutally attacked (and in three cases, killed) by ultraright bands, launched an initiative in April to end the violence.

In May three of nine accused persons were sentenced to 7 total years in jail for the murder of a Polish citizen outside Madrid in 1990. The other six were declared innocent.

U.S. citizens regularly complain of discrimination and abuse by authorities and, more frequently, by ordinary citizens. Women and U.S. citizens of African and Latin American origin are those most frequently victimized.

Section 6. Worker Rights

a. *The Right of Association.*—All workers, except those in the military services, judges, magistrates, and prosecutors, are entitled to form or join unions of their own choosing. All that is required to organize a trade union is that more than two workers register with the Minister of Labor and Social Security. Spain has over 200 registered trade unions and 1 not legally registered (because the Constitutional Court ruled that it was ineligible, since it represents military personnel).

Under the Constitution, trade unions are free to choose their representatives, determine their policies, represent their members' interests, and strike. They are not restricted or harassed by the Government and are independent of political parties. A strike in nonessential services is legal if its sponsors give 5 days' notice. Any striking union must respect minimum service requirements negotiated with the respective employer. The right to strike has been interpreted by the Constitutional Court to include general strikes called to protest government policy. Strikes occur frequently, but most are brief. From January to April, there were 166,700 absent workers due to strikes, a 70 percent drop from the same period in 1995. In the first 3 months of 1996, the Labor Ministry reported that there were 277 strikes, in which 86,900 workers participated, compared with strikes by 190,900 workers for the same period last year.

The Government is reforming the labor and social security regime, particularly the pension system. On September 20, a preagreement on pension reform was signed between the Government and labor. Although trade unions have signed this agreement, they have not ruled out supporting the public employee confederations in protesting the government plan to save approximately $1.6 billion (200 billion pesetas) by freezing public employees' salaries through 1997. The trade unions have planned a number of actions in response to the salary freeze plan, including filing complaints with the International Labor Organization, lobbying Congress to protect employees' right to collective action, and holding demonstrations and strikes.

Unions are free to form or join federations and affiliate with international bodies and do so without hindrance.

b. *The Right to Organize and Bargain Collectively.*—A 1980 statute undergirds the right to organize and bargain collectively. Trade union and collective bargaining rights were extended in 1986 to all workers in the public sector, except military personnel. Public sector collective bargaining in 1990 was broadened to include salaries and employment levels, but the Government retained the right to set these if negotiations failed. Collective bargaining agreements are widespread in both the public and private sectors; in the latter they cover 60 percent of workers, notwithstanding that only about 15 percent of workers are actually union members.

The law prohibits discrimination by employers against trade union members and organizers. Discrimination cases have priority in the labor courts. Legislation in 1990 gave unions a role in controlling temporary work contracts to prevent abuse of these and of termination actions. Nonetheless, unions contend that employers discriminate in many cases by refusing to renew temporary contracts of workers engaging in union organizing. More than one-third of all employees are under temporary contracts, and the number is growing.

Labor regulations and practices in free trade zones and export processing zones are the same as in the rest of the country. Union membership in these zones is reportedly higher than the average throughout the country.

c. *Prohibition of Forced or Compulsory Labor.*—Forced or compulsory labor is outlawed and is not practiced. The legislation is effectively enforced.

d. *Minimum Age for Employment of Children.*—The statutory minimum age for the employment of children is 16 years. The Ministry of Labor and Social Security is primarily responsible for enforcement. The minimum age is effectively enforced in major industries and in the service sector. It is more difficult to control on small farms and in family-owned businesses. Legislation prohibiting child labor is effectively enforced in the special economic zones. The law also prohibits the employment of persons under the age of 18 at night, for overtime work, or in sectors considered hazardous.

e. *Acceptable Conditions of Work.*—The legal minimum wage for workers over 18 years of age is considered sufficient for a decent standard of living. The daily national minimum wage rate in 1996 was $18.03 (2,164 pesetas); for those 16 and 17 years of age it was $13.95 (1674 pesetas). These rates are revised every year in line with the consumer price index and are effectively enforced by the Ministry of Labor and Social Security. The law sets a 40-hour workweek with an unbroken rest period of 36 hours after each 40 hours worked. Workers enjoy 12 paid holidays a year and a month's paid vacation.

Government mechanisms exist for enforcing working conditions and occupational health and safety rules, but bureaucratic procedures are cumbersome and inefficient. Safety and health legislation is being revised to conform to European Union (EU) directives. The Law to Prevent Labor Risks was passed in 1995 by Parliament as the foundation for the completion of the rest of the EU directives. The National Institute of Safety and Health in the Ministry of Labor has technical responsibility for developing labor standards, but the Inspectorate of Labor has responsibility for enforcing the legislation through judicial action when infractions are found. Workers have legal protection for filing complaints about hazardous conditions.

SWEDEN

Sweden is a constitutional monarchy and a multiparty parliamentary democracy. The King is Chief of State. The Cabinet, headed by the Prime Minister, exercises executive authority. The judiciary is independent of the Government.

The Government effectively controls the police, all security organizations, and the armed forces.

Sweden has an advanced industrial economy, mainly market-based, and a high standard of living, with extensive social welfare services. More than 90 percent of businesses are privately owned.

Human rights are deeply respected and widely protected. Swedes are entirely free to express their political preferences, pursue individual interests, and seek legal resolution of disputes. The Parliament, police, or an ombudsman investigate thoroughly all allegations of human rights violations, including the occasional allegation of police misconduct. Sweden's ombudsmen, appointed by the Parliament but with full autonomy, have the power to investigate any private complaints of alleged abuses by authorities and to prescribe corrective action if required. Sweden has one of the world's most equal distributions of income, but wage levels for women still lag behind those for men. There are occasional incidents of violence against minorities. The Government, political parties, and youth organizations have active programs to promote tolerance and combat racism. The Government has established programs to deal with violence against women.

RESPECT FOR HUMAN RIGHTS

Section 1. Respect for the Integrity of the Person, Including Freedom From:

a. *Political and Other Extrajudicial Killing.*—There were no reports of political or other extrajudicial killings.

b. *Disappearance.*—There were no reports of politically motivated disappearances.

c. *Torture and Other Cruel, Inhuman, or Degrading Treatment or Punishment.*—The law prohibits these abuses, and the authorities respect such prohibitions. There are occasional reports of the use of excessive force by police in arrests, but thorough investigations have not produced evidence of a systematic problem. Typically, police officers found guilty of abuse have been suspended or otherwise disciplined. Such disciplinary actions numbered less than a dozen nationwide and usually involved officers-in-training found unfit for permanent duty.

Prison conditions meet minimum international standards, and the Government permits visits by human rights monitors.

d. *Arbitrary Arrest, Detention, or Exile.*—Arrests are public and by warrant. The police must lodge charges within 6 hours against persons detained for disturbing the public order or considered dangerous, and within 12 hours against those detained on other grounds. The law requires arraignment within 48 hours. The time between arrest and the first court hearing may be extended to 96 hours for detainees considered dangerous, likely to destroy evidence, or likely to flee, but this occurs very rarely. Other than such dangerous suspects, detainees are routinely released pending trial. Bail as such does not exist. If a person files for bankruptcy and refuses to cooperate with the official investigation, a court may order detention for up to 3 months, with judicial review every 2 weeks.

The Government does not impose exile.

Convicted foreign criminals who are not permanent residents often are deported at the conclusion of their prison terms, unless they risk execution or other severe punishment in their home country.

e. *Denial of Fair Public Trial.*—The Constitution forbids deprivation of liberty without a public trial by a court of law, and the Government respects this provision. The judiciary is free of governmental interference. The accused have the right to competent counsel, but the Government provides public defenders to indigents only in cases where the maximum penalty could be a prison sentence of 6 months or more. Convicted persons have the right of appeal in most instances.

There were no reports of political prisoners.

f. *Arbitrary Interference With Privacy, Family, Home, or Correspondence.*—The law limits home searches to investigations of crimes punishable by at least 2 years' imprisonment, such as murder, robbery, rape, arson, sabotage, counterfeiting, or treason. The authorities respect this provision. Normally, police must obtain court approval for a search or a wiretap. However, a senior police official may approve a search if time is a critical factor or the case involves a threat to life. A parliamentary committee each year reviews all monitoring of telephones, facsimile (fax), or computers.

Section 2. Respect for Civil Liberties, Including:

a. *Freedom of Speech and Press.*—The Constitution provides for freedom of speech and the press, and the Government respects these provisions in practice. Most newspapers and periodicals are privately owned. The Government subsidizes daily newspapers, regardless of political affiliation. Broadcasters operate under a state concession. Until a few years ago the State had a monopoly over ground-based broadcasting, but a variety of commercial television channels (one ground-based, and several via satellite or cable) and several commercial radio stations now exist.

The Government may censor publications containing national security information. A quasi-governmental body excises extremely graphic violence from films, television programs, and videos.

Criticism of child pornography was widespread, and the debate over its legality continued in 1996. Sweden hosted the United Nations (U.N.) Conference on the Sexual Exploitation of Children. The Queen has emerged as a strong and popular advocate of children's rights and opponent of child pornography.

Academic freedom is respected.

b. *Freedom of Peaceful Assembly and Association.*—The Constitution provides for freedom of peaceful assembly and association, and the Government respects these rights in practice. Police require a permit for public demonstrations. However, the authorities routinely grant such permits, with rare exceptions to prevent clashes between antagonistic groups.

c. *Freedom of Religion.*—The Constitution provides for freedom of religion, and the Government does not hamper the teaching or practice of any faith.

Sweden has maintained a state (Lutheran) church for several hundred years, supported by a general "Church Tax" (although the Government routinely grants any request by a taxpayer for exemption from that tax). After decades of discussion, however, in 1995 the Church of Sweden and the Government agreed to a formal separation. This reform will not become effective until the year 2000, and the Church will still receive some state support. Beginning in 1996 citizens are no longer automatically members of the state church at birth. Sweden is tolerant of the diverse religions practiced there, including the Mormon faith and Scientology.

d. *Freedom of Movement Within the Country, Foreign Travel, Emigration, and Repatriation.*—The law provides for free movement within, from, and returning to the country, and the Government respects these rights in practice. Foreigners with suspected links to terrorist organizations may be required to report regularly to police authorities, but may travel freely within Sweden. Courts must review the reporting requirement for each case at least once every 3 years.

The Government cooperates with the U.N. High Commissioner for Refugees (UNHCR) and other humanitarian organizations in assisting refugees. The Government provides first asylum. Sweden has adopted an increasingly restrictive asylum policy. The Government has sent some asylum seekers back to "safe" countries through which they arrived in Sweden. The number of asylum applications dropped to a 10-year low of 10,000 in 1995, and 2,715 in the first half of 1996. There is an ongoing debate over the plight of asylum seekers who have submitted applications that are considered "manifestly unfounded," those coming to Sweden through a "safe third country," and those whose applications remain under consideration for unduly long periods of time, in some cases as long as 9 years. There have also been complaints of exceedingly accelerated procedures and inadequate legal safeguards for some asylum seekers, e.g., asylum seekers who were deported within 72 hours of arrival and did not receive access to lawyers. A broad interpretation of what constitutes a "safe third country" permits the return of applicants to a third country without consideration of whether that country has an asylum policy under which the applicant might be admitted. Asylum seekers are occasionally detained upon arrival in Sweden and, when awaiting deportation after a negative decision on their claim, in cases where the authorities fear flight to avoid deportation. Detention facilities are clean, comfortable, and relatively unrestricted. On occasion, when no other facility is available, asylum seekers are detained in remand prisons.

Approximately 60,000 refugees from Bosnia and Herzegovina are living in Sweden. The Government provides funds for Bosnians to travel to their homeland in order to determine if they wish to be repatriated. The long-term status of those choosing not to return is uncertain. Sweden has accepted over 100,000 refugees from the former Yugoslavia.

Section 3. Respect for Political Rights: The Right of Citizens to Change Their Government

The Constitution provides ways and means for citizens to change the Government. Elections to the 349-member unicameral Parliament are held every 4 years. Suffrage is universal for citizens 18 years and older, with secret balloting. Noncitizen residents have the right to participate in local (city and county) elections.

Women participate actively in the political process and Government. They currently compose 41 percent of the Parliament and half of the Cabinet. The governing Social Democratic Party largely has held to its pledge to place women in half of all political appointments at all levels.

Section 4. Governmental Attitude Regarding International and Nongovernmental Investigation of Alleged Violations of Human Rights

Several private organizations actively monitor issues such as the impact of social legislation, anti-immigrant or racist activities, and the condition of the indigenous Sami population. The official ombudsmen also publicize abuses of state authority and have the right to initiate actions to rectify such abuses. Government agencies are in close contact with a variety of local and international groups working in Sweden and abroad to improve human rights observance.

Section 5. Discrimination Based on Race, Sex, Religion, Disability, Language, or Social Status

The Constitution provides for equal rights for all citizens, and the Government respects this provision.

Women.—Nearly 18,600 cases of assault against women took place in 1994 (the last year for which statistics are available), an increase of 600 over 1993. Most involved spousal abuse. In three-quarters of the assaults, the perpetrator was an acquaintance of the victim. Reported abuse against women occurs disproportionately in immigrant communities.

The law provides complainants protection from contact with their abusers, if so desired. In some cases the authorities help women obtain new identities and homes. Since 1994 the Government has provided electronic alarms or bodyguards for women in extreme danger of assault. Both national and local governments provide monetary support to volunteer groups that provide shelter and other assistance to abused women. The authorities strive to apprehend and prosecute abusers. Typically, the sentence for abuse is a prison term or psychiatric treatment.

The number of rapes rose sharply in 1993 (later figures are not available), from approximately 1,400 to over 2,100. In 1994 the number dropped somewhat to 1,800. Women's groups believe the increase in recent years is partly an effect of increased willingness to report rape (including spousal or "date" rape), but cannot rule out the possibility of a real increase resulting from worsened economic and social conditions. The law does not differentiate between spousal and nonspousal rape.

A study conducted by the U.N. Development Program (UNDP) in preparation for the U.N. Conference on Women gave Sweden the highest ranking on equality for women. The law requires employers to treat men and women alike in hiring, promotion, and pay, including equal pay for comparable work. The Equality Ombudsman, a public official, investigates complaints of gender discrimination in the labor market. Women may also pursue complaints through the courts. A third option, and by far the most common, involves settling allegations using the employee's labor union as mediator. Virtually all gains in the status of women have occurred through such negotiations, with relatively little resort to legislation or legal decisions.

Despite the available remedies, surveys show that women remain underrepresented in higher paying jobs, with salaries averaging only 72 percent of men's, a decrease from a high of 80 percent a decade ago. This decrease largely reflects recent substantial cuts in social sector jobs, where women comprise the vast majority of the work force. In addition, tight economic conditions in recent years have made unions less willing to pursue claims of pay discrimination. Women submit hundreds of complaints to the Equality Ombudsman each year, but almost all of these complaints are either resolved or dropped before the Ombudsman takes action.

As a result, women increasingly have begun to turn to the courts in cases of individual discrimination. Women initiated several test cases of the "equal pay for comparable work" clause in 1995, with at least one court decision in their favor in 1996. This court case is widely expected to be precedent setting.

The law prohibits sexual harassment. As with other forms of discrimination, women may take complaints to the Equality Ombudsman, the courts, or to their unions.

Children.—The Government allocates funds to private organizations concerned with children's rights and also supports a special ombudsman for children. The ombudsman has focused her work on ensuring adherence to the U.N. Convention on the Rights of the Child, which Sweden was among the first countries in the world to ratify.

Although child abuse appears relatively uncommon, the public and authorities remain concerned by consistent data indicating an increase over the past several years. The number of reported cases, for children under the age of 15, rose significantly in 1994, to 4,400 from 3,300 in 1993. Many children's rights advocates believe this change reflects a true increase (as opposed to increased incidence of reporting) due to the strains imposed on families by the difficult economic situation.

The law prohibits parents or other caretakers from abusing children mentally or physically in any way. Parents, teachers, and other adults are subject to prosecution if they physically punish a child, including slapping or spanking. Children have the right to report such abuses to the police. The authorities respect these laws, and the usual sentence is a fine combined with counseling and monitoring by social workers. If the situation warrants, however, authorities may remove children from the home and place them in foster care. However, foster parents virtually never receive permission to adopt long-term foster children, even in cases where the parents are seen as unfit or seek no contact with the child. Critics charge that this policy places the rights of biological parents over the needs of children for security in permanent family situations.

People With Disabilities.—The law prohibits discrimination against people with disabilities. The Government provides disabled persons with assistance aimed at allowing them to live as normal a life as possible, preferably outside an institutional setting. This includes educational aid, such as provision of personal tutors or assistants at all stages from day care to university studies, as well as assistance in the workplace, such as provision of a personal aide or improvement of the workplace's accessibility to wheelchairs. It also encompasses services such as home care or group living. Regulations for new buildings require full accessibility, but the Government has no such requirement for existing public buildings. As a result, many buildings remain inaccessible to disabled persons.

Indigenous People.—Sweden counts at least 17,000 Sami (Lapps) among its 8.6 million inhabitants (Sami organizations place that number somewhat higher, 25,000 to 30,000). In 1994 Sweden was the last of the Nordic countries to allow formation of a Sametinget, or Sami Parliament, as an advisory body to the Government. Under the current Government, Sami issues fall under the Ministry of Agriculture.

The Sami continue a protracted struggle for recognition as an indigenous people under a variety of international agreements, such as International Labor Organization (ILO) Convention 169. Historically, the Government has resisted granting the Sami such rights. For instance, Sami children had no right to education in their native language until provision of such education to immigrant children forced the Government to grant Sami at least equal treatment. As a result of such education, northern Sami dialects have enjoyed a recent renaissance. Sami dialects in the southern portions of traditional Sami lands, however, now may have too few native speakers to survive as living languages.

Late in 1994 the Government removed from the Sami the right to control hunting and fishing activities on Sami village lands, permitting instead totally unlimited hunting and fishing activity on all government property. Sami leaders continued to protest this change in 1996.

Although some Sami state that they face discrimination in housing and employment on an individual basis, particularly in the southern mountain regions, the Government does not condone such discrimination.

Religious Minorities.—Graffiti was painted on some synagogues in 1996. The Government supports activities by volunteer groups working against anti-Semitism.

National/Racial/Ethnic Minorities.—Scattered acts of violence or harassment against minorities continue, usually from "skinhead" groups with neo-Nazi ties. Although the Government does not compile national statistics on such acts, one newspaper counted over 100 violent incidents with racist overtones (most involving neo-Nazis) in a recent year. Most violent incidents involved assault on lone immigrants by teenage skinheads.

Most estimates place the number of active neo-Nazis at less than 2,000, and there appears to be little popular support for their activities or sentiments. Many Swedes doubt whether such youth actually embrace neo-Nazi ideology, and the Government supports activities by volunteer groups working against racism. The Government investigates and prosecutes race-related crimes, although in many clashes between Swedish and immigrant youth gangs, authorities judge both sides as at fault. In one 1996 case, an African man was murdered by a teenage Swede who was sentenced to 4 years' imprisonment despite his juvenile status. In a case involving a 17-year old sentenced to 100 days community service for wearing neo-Nazi badges, the Supreme Court ruled that it can be illegal to wear xenophobic symbols or racist paraphernalia.

Section 6. Worker Rights

a. *The Right of Association.*—The work force is 87 percent unionized. Career military personnel, police officers, and civilian government officials, as well as private sector workers in both manufacturing and service industries, are organized. Most business owners belong to counterpart employer organizations.

Unions and employer organizations operate independently of the Government and political parties (although the largest federation of unions has always been linked with the largest political party, the Social Democrats). The law protects the freedom of workers to associate and to strike, as well as for employers to organize and to conduct lockouts. Within limits protecting the public's immediate health and security, public employees also enjoy the right to strike. These laws are fully respected and are not challenged.

Unions have the right to affiliate with international bodies. They are affiliated with the International Confederation of Free Trade Unions and European Trade Union Confederation among others.

b. *The Right to Organize and Bargain Collectively.*—Labor and management, each represented by a national organization by sector (for example, retailers and engineering industries), negotiate framework agreements every 2 to 3 years. More detailed company-level agreements put such framework agreements into effect at the local level.

Framework agreements entered into force in 1996, with most valid until 1998. The few conflicts that took place included a January strike by public sector nurses for significantly higher wages and a 6-day strike by journalists.

The law provides both workers and employers with effective mechanisms for resolving complaints. The vast majority of complaints are resolved informally. If informal discussions fail, the issue goes to a labor court, whose ruling sets a precedent to be followed by employers and unions. Cases of an employer firing an employee for union activities are virtually unheard of; no cases occurred in 1996. Very few wildcat strikes took place in 1996, and only at a very small, local level and with quick resolution.

There are no export processing zones.

c. *Prohibition of Forced or Compulsory Labor.*—The law prohibits forced or compulsory labor, and the authorities effectively enforce this ban.

d. *Minimum Age of Employment of Children.*—Compulsory 9-year education ends at age 16, and the law permits full-time employment at that age under supervision of local authorities. Employees under age 18 may work only during daytime and under supervision. During summer and other vacation periods, children as young as 13 years may work part-time or in "light" work with parental permission. Union representatives, police, and public prosecutors effectively enforce this restriction.

e. *Acceptable Conditions of Work.*—There is no national minimum wage law. Wages are set by collective bargaining contracts, which nonunion establishments usually observe as well. Even the lowest paid workers can maintain a decent standard of living for themselves and their families through substantial benefits (such as housing or day care support) provided by social welfare entitlement programs. However, cutbacks in these programs have made it harder for some workers to make ends meet, particularly for low-paid single women with children.

The standard workweek is 40 hours or less. Both the law and collective bargaining agreements regulate overtime and rest periods. For workers not covered by a labor agreement, the law stipulates a limit for overtime at 200 hours a year, although exceptions may be granted for key employees with union approval; some collective bargaining agreements put the limit at 150 hours. The law requires a rest period after 5 hours of work but does not stipulate a minimum duration; in practice it is usually 30 minutes. The law also provides all employees with a minimum of 5 weeks of paid annual leave; labor contracts often provide more, particularly for higher ranking private sector employees and older public service workers.

Occupational health and safety rules are set by a government-appointed board and monitored by trained union stewards, safety ombudsmen, and, occasionally, government inspectors. These standards are very high, making workplaces both safe and healthy. Safety ombudsmen have the authority to stop unsafe activity immediately and to call in an inspector. An individual also has the right to halt work in dangerous situations in order to consult a supervisor or safety representative.

SWITZERLAND

Switzerland is a constitutional democracy with a federal structure and an independent judiciary. The bicameral Parliament elects the seven members of the Federal Council, the highest executive body, whose presidency rotates annually. Because of the nation's linguistic and religious diversity, the Swiss political system emphasizes local and national political consensus and grants considerable autonomy to individual cantons.

The Swiss armed forces are a civilian-controlled militia based on universal military service for able-bodied males. There is virtually no standing army apart from training cadres and a few essential headquarters staff functions. Police duties are primarily a responsibility of the individual cantons, which have their own distinct police forces kept under effective control. The National Police Authority has a coordination role and relies on the cantons for actual law enforcement.

Switzerland has a highly developed free enterprise industrial and service economy strongly dependent on international trade. The standard of living is very high.

The Government fully respects human rights, and there were no major human rights problems. However, there continue to be verbal abuse against foreigners by private citizens and complaints by NGO's of occasional police harassment against foreigners, particularly asylum seekers (see Section 2.d.). Some laws still tend to discriminate against women, although a new federal law came into force in July that is designed to promote gender equality in the labor market. The Government is taking serious steps to address violence against women.

RESPECT FOR HUMAN RIGHTS

Section 1. Respect for the Integrity of the Person, Including Freedom From:

a. *Political and Other Extrajudicial Killing.*—There were no reports of political or other extrajudicial killings.

b. *Disappearance.*—There were no reports of politically motivated disappearances.

c. *Torture and Other Cruel, Inhuman, or Degrading Treatment or Punishment.*—The Constitution proscribes such practices, and there were no reports of violations.

Prison conditions meet minimum international standards, although some nongovernmental organizations complain of prison overcrowding. The Government has taken measures to improve prison conditions and address overcrowding. The Government permits visits by human rights monitors.

d. *Arbitrary Arrest, Detention, or Exile.*—The legal prohibitions on arbitrary arrest, detention, or exile are fully respected at all levels of government. The cantons are responsible for handling most criminal matters, and their procedures vary somewhat from canton to canton. In general, a suspect may not be held longer than 48 hours without a warrant of arrest issued by an investigative magistrate. However, asylum seekers and foreigners without valid documents may be held for up to 96 hours without an arrest warrant. A suspect has the right to choose and contact an attorney as soon as the warrant is issued; the State provides free counsel for indigents in most situations. Investigations are generally prompt, even if in some cases investigative detention may exceed the length of sentence. Release on personal recognizance or bail is granted unless the magistrate believes the person is dangerous or will not appear for trial. Any lengthy detention is subject to review by higher judicial authorities.

There is no summary exile, nor is exile used as a means of political control. Non-Swiss convicted of crimes may receive sentences that include denial of reentry for a specific period following completion of a prison sentence.

e. *Denial of Fair Public Trial.*—The Constitution provides for an independent judiciary, and the Government respects this provision in practice. The judiciary provides citizens with a fair and efficient judicial process.

The Constitution provides for public trials in which the defendant's rights are fully respected, including the right to challenge and to present witnesses or evidence. All courts of first instance are local or cantonal courts. Minor cases are tried by a single judge, difficult cases by a panel of judges, and murder (or other serious cases) by a public jury. Trials are usually held expeditiously. Citizens have the right to appeal to a higher instance court, ultimately to the Federal Court.

There were no reports of political prisoners.

f. *Arbitrary Interference With Privacy, Family, Home, or Correspondence.*—Cantonal laws regulate police entry into private premises. These regulations differ widely from canton to canton, but all prohibit such practices without a warrant. All government authorities respect these provisions, and violations are subject to effective legal sanction.

Section 2. Respect for Civil Liberties, Including:

a. *Freedom of Speech and Press.*—The Constitution provides for freedom of speech and of the press, and the Government respects these rights in practice. An independent press, an effective judiciary, and a functioning democratic political system combine to ensure freedom of speech and of the press, including academic freedom. The authorities may legally restrict these freedoms for groups deemed to be a threat to the State, but no groups were restricted during the year. In addition, an article of the Penal Code criminalizes racist or anti-Semitic expression, whether in public speech or in printed material.

Most broadcast media are government-funded but possess editorial autonomy, and foreign broadcast media are freely available.

b. *Freedom of Peaceful Assembly and Association.*—The Constitution provides for these rights, and the Government respects them in practice.

c. *Freedom of Religion.*—The Constitution provides for complete freedom of religion, and the Government respects this right in practice. There is no single state church, but most cantons support one or several churches with public funds. In all cantons, an individual may choose not to contribute to church funding. In some cantons, however, private companies are unable to avoid payment of the church tax.

d. *Freedom of Movement Within the Country, Foreign Travel, Emigration, and Repatriation.*—Under the Constitution and the law, citizens are free to travel in or outside the country, to emigrate, and to repatriate.

Switzerland has traditionally been a haven for refugees, but public concern over the high number of asylum seekers generated pressure on the Government to tighten its policy.

Some human rights organizations have charged authorities with abuses in connection with the implementation of a law adopted in 1995 aimed at asylum seekers or illegal foreigners who are suspected of committing crimes or avoiding repatriation. In particular, these groups have alleged instances of abuse, including arbitrary detention as well as denial of access to established asylum procedures by police at the two main airports. They also charge that police have used the law to detain or harass refugees who are not suspected of having committed a crime. However, the allegations made by these groups have never been verified, and these groups now indicate that the situation has improved over the last year. Under the law, police actions are subject to judicial oversight and the federal court has overturned many cases in which it believed that there was not sufficient regard for the rights of asylum seekers or other foreigners.

The Government cooperates with the Office of the United Nations High Commissioner for Refugees (UNHCR) and other humanitarian organizations in assisting refugees. The Government provides first asylum and provided it to approximately 2,000 persons in 1996. Refugees whose applications are rejected are allowed to stay temporarily if their home country is experiencing war or insurrection.

Section 3. Respect for Political Rights: The Right of Citizens to Change Their Government

The Constitution provides citizens with the right to change their government peacefully (at all local, cantonal, and federal levels), and citizens exercise this right in practice through periodic, free, and fair elections held on the basis of universal suffrage. In addition, initiative and referendum procedures provide unusually intense popular involvement in the legislative process.

Participation by women in politics continues to expand. Women were disenfranchised until 1971 at the federal level, but since then their participation in politics has expanded progressively.

Women occupy 51 of the 246 seats in the Parliament, 1 of 7 seats in the Federal Council (Cabinet), and a record 19 in the cantonal government executive bodies. In 1995 and 1996, however, voters rejected two local initiatives designed to reserve a fixed percentage of elective seats for women. A vote on an initiative to mandate equal gender representation in all federal institutions will take place no later than 1999.

Section 4. Governmental Attitude Regarding International and Nongovernmental Investigation of Alleged Violations of Human Rights

All major international human rights groups are active and operate without government restriction.

Section 5. Discrimination Based on Race, Sex, Religion, Disability, Language, or Social Status

The Constitution and laws prohibit discrimination on the basis of race, sex, religion, language, or social status, and the Government effectively enforces these prohibitions.

Women.—While there are no data about violence against women, indications are that a problem exists and that many cases go unreported. The Federation of Women's Organizations and other groups have heightened public awareness on the problem of violence against women. The law prohibits wife beating and similar offenses, and spousal rape is explicitly considered a crime in the Penal Code. The Penal Code also criminalizes sexual exploitation and trafficking in women. The authorities effectively enforce these laws. Victims of violence can obtain help, counseling, and legal assistance from specialized offices sponsored by local and cantonal authorities.

Although the Constitution prohibits all types of discrimination, a few laws still tend to discriminate against women. However, as noted below, Parliament has passed significant legislation improving the treatment of women.

In July a new federal law on equal opportunity for women and men came into force. The law includes a general prohibition on gender-based discrimination and incorporates the principle of "equal wages for equal work." The new law also includes provisions aimed at eliminating sexual harassment and facilitating access to legal remedies for those who claim discrimination or harassment. At the aggregate level, men earn more than women, but it is not clear if this circumstance reflects overt discrimination or other factors. Individual cases of denial of equal pay for equal work would be subject to the new law. A revised labor law eliminated special restrictions on working hours for women (see Section 6.e.).

Children.—The Government demonstrates its strong commitment to children's rights and welfare through a well-funded public education system and medical care. The federal and cantonal governments, as well as organizations defending children's rights, have devoted considerable attention in recent years to child abuse, especially sexual abuse. For convicted perpetrators of the latter, the law provides imprisonment for up to 15 years. Officials have proposed changes in the law that would raise the statute of limitations in cases of child abuse from 5 to 10 years.

With respect to child abuse abroad, current law provides for prosecution only if the act is considered a crime in the country in which it took place. However, experts have proposed making such acts punishable in Switzerland regardless of where the crime took place.

People With Disabilities.—Switzerland has strong legal prohibitions against discrimination directed at disabled persons in employment, education, and the provision of other state services. Advocates for the disabled have called for new measures to ensure greater protection for the rights of the disabled, including easier access to buildings and public transportation. The Government has not mandated that building or transportation facilities be made accessible. A member of Parliament has proposed legislation to amend the Constitution to provide equality of opportunity for the disabled. The legislation has so far received broad support in Parliament, but it would be subject to a mandatory voter referendum.

In January 1995, a law came into force exempting disabled men from the tax imposed on those who have not fulfilled their military duty.

National/Racial/Ethnic Minorities.—According to nongovernmental organizations' statistics, which have not been verified, there were 41 reported attacks against foreigners in the first half of 1996, almost double the number reported for the same period in 1995. However, these figures include instances of verbal and written "attacks" which are much more common than physical assaults. Investigations of these attacks are conducted effectively and lead in most cases to the arrest of the persons responsible. Persons convicted of racist crimes are commonly sentenced to at least 1 year's imprisonment.

In accordance with the first antiracism law which was approved in September 1994 (and which criminalizes racist and anti-Semitic actions or public speech), the Government appointed in August 1995 a commission against racism. This group of experts is expected to focus on preventive measures and to serve as a mediator for conflicts between individuals.

Section 6. Worker Rights

a. *The Right of Association.*—All workers, including foreigners, have the freedom to associate freely, to join unions of their choice, and to select their own representatives. The Government does not hamper the exercise of these rights. About one-third of the work force is unionized.

The right to strike is legally recognized and freely exercised, but a unique labor peace under an informal agreement between unions and employers—in existence since the 1930's—has meant fewer than 10 strikes per year since 1975. There were no significant strikes in 1996.

Unions are independent of government and political parties, and laws prohibit retribution against strikers or their leaders. Unions can associate freely with international organizations.

b. *The Right to Organize and Bargain Collectively.*—By law, workers have the right to organize and bargain collectively, and the law protects them from acts of antiunion discrimination. The Government fully respects these provisions. Periodic negotiations between employer and worker organizations determine wages and settle other labor issues at the national and local levels. Nonunion firms generally adopt the terms and conditions fixed in the unions' collective bargaining.

There are no export processing zones.

c. *Prohibition of Forced or Compulsory Labor.*—Although there is no specific constitutional or statutory ban on forced or compulsory labor, it does not occur.

d. *Minimum Age for Employment of Children.*—The minimum age for employment of children is 15 years, and children are in school up to this age. Children over 13 years may be employed in light duties for not more than 9 hours a week during the school year and 15 hours otherwise. Employment of youths between the ages of 15 and 20 is strictly regulated; they cannot work at night, on Sundays, or under hazardous or dangerous conditions. The Federal Office for Industry, Trade, and Labor effectively enforces the law on working conditions.

e. *Acceptable Conditions of Work.*—There is no national minimum wage. The lowest wages fixed in collective bargaining are always adequate to provide a decent standard of living for workers and their families.

The Labor Act established a maximum 45-hour workweek for blue- and white-collar workers in industry, services, and retail trades, and a 50-hour workweek for all other workers. The law prescribes a rest period during the workweek. Overtime is limited by law to 120 hours annually.

The Labor Act and the Federal Code of Obligations contain extensive regulations to protect worker health and safety. There have been no reports of lapses in the enforcement of these regulations, but the degree to which enforcement is effective is unclear. The Government is currently overhauling the 1948 Labor Act, in part to strengthen provisions for workers' health and safety. Parliament passed a revised labor law, but it was defeated in a December referendum. A worker may opt out of a dangerous assignment without penalty.

TAJIKISTAN

Tajikistan remains in the hands of a largely authoritarian government, but has established some nominally democratic structures. The Government's narrow base of support renders it incapable of controlling the entire territory of the country. The Government of President Emomali Rahmonov, comprised largely of natives of the Kulob region, continued to dominate the State. Opposition to this control and frustration with declining public order led to large and sometimes violent demonstrations in several regions. The demonstrators sought improved security and the removal of officials (particularly those of Kulobi origin) and their replacement by local residents. In response to this popular pressure, the Government transferred substantial numbers of officials of Kulobi origin to other areas.

Tajikistan has not successfully achieved national reconciliation after its 1992 civil war. Under United Nations auspices, the Government and the armed, externally based opposition continued a series of inter-Tajik talks, including a round in Ashgabat in July. While a cease-fire agreement and an accord on exchange of prisoners were signed at that session, neither was immediately implemented, and repeated, continuing cease-fire violations were reported by the United Nations Mission of Observers to Tajikistan (UNMOT). Further talks were held in Tehran in October, and the President and opposition leader met in Afghanistan in December, signing a cease-fire agreement. A December 19-23 summit meeting in Moscow produced a framework document on national reconciliation whose details were to be completed in 1997. At the end of the year, the Government was intensively engaged in the U.N. peace process.

Internal security is the responsibility of the Ministries of Interior, Security, and Defense. The Russian Army's 201st Motorized Rifle Division, part of a Commonwealth of Independent States (CIS) peacekeeping force established in 1993, remained in the country. Some regions of the country remained effectively outside the Government's control. Government control in other areas was at the sufferance of local opposition commanders, or was limited to the daylight hours. Opposition forces, supported by at least some Afghan and Arab Islamic mercenaries, and local bandit units, used parts of the Gorno-Badakhshan Autonomous Oblast (GBAO) and Gharm Valley as a base for launching attacks. Some members of the security forces and government-aligned militias committed serious human rights abuses. The armed opposition also committed serious human rights abuses.

The economy continued to decline, and government revenue remains highly dependent on the government-owned cotton and aluminum industries. Most Soviet-era factories operate at a minimal level, if at all, while privatization has moved ahead only slowly. As much as one-third of the total population is unemployed or significantly underemployed, according to government estimates. However, inflation dropped sharply, and the exchange rate remained steady. Most wages and pensions are paid, although not all missed payments have been made. Current wages are extremely low and not enough to support adequate nutrition without supplemental income.

The Government's human rights record improved slightly, although serious problems remain. During fighting with the opposition, government artillery fire killed civilians. The Government limits citizens' right to change their government. Some members of the security forces and government-aligned forces were responsible for disappearances and forced conscription, and regularly tortured and abused detainees. The Government prosecuted few perpetrators of these abuses. The Minister of Interior continued efforts to remove from his Ministry some of the professionally unqualified and worst human rights abusers, but substantial problems remain. Prison conditions remain life threatening, and the Government continued to use arbitrary arrest and detention. There are often long delays before trials, and the judiciary is subject to political and paramilitary pressure. The authorities infringe on citizens' right to privacy.

The Government severely restricts freedom of speech and freedom of the press and essentially controls the electronic media. No genuine opposition media appeared during the year, although there are new semi-independent, largely nonpolitical media. The authorities strictly control freedom of assembly and association for political organizations. One new political party was allowed to register in 1996, bringing the total to seven; the three opposition parties and a branch of the fourth affiliated with the armed opposition remained suspended. The Government generally cooperated with the Organization on Security and Cooperation in Europe (OSCE) in Dushanbe, although it declined to act on OSCE proposals to establish a human rights ombudsman. The Government claimed it will establish its own ombudsman, but had not done so at year's end. Violence against women is a problem.

The external opposition also committed serious human rights abuses, including the killing of captured soldiers based on their ethnic (Uzbek) or geographic (Kulob) origin, as well as threats, extortion, and abuse of civilian populations.

RESPECT FOR HUMAN RIGHTS

Section 1. Respect for the Integrity of the Person, Including Freedom From:

a. *Political and Other Extrajudicial Killing.*—There were a significant number of extrajudicial killings. However, the unstable situation and the proliferation of armed groups make it difficult to assign responsibility in many individual cases. Some killings were probably committed by government forces, some by the opposition, and some by independent warlords. The Government has investigated some of the higher profile cases, but without positive results. The competence of those efforts as well as their independence are questionable.

Indiscriminate artillery fire by government forces killed an undetermined number of noncombatants (see Section 1.g.).

Several prominent figures were killed by unknown persons, including the mufti of Tajikistan and members of his family; a prominent member of Parliament; an ethnic Russian, Tajik citizen journalist (see Section 2.a.); and the rector of the medical institute. These cases remain unsolved.

Illustrative of such cases is the murder of Muhammad Osimi, a respected senior academic (see Section 2.a.). Osimi was prominent in promoting Tajik culture, but not politically active. No group claimed to have killed Osimi and there was no credible explanation for his death. The Government claimed that it partially solved the murder, as one of the alleged assailants in the case was killed by government units near Dushanbe. Due to the circumstances of the killing and the absence of publicly presented documentary evidence, however, the Government's assertion has not been widely accepted.

A number of local officials, businessmen, and professional figures were killed during the year for economic, ethnic, political, and other reasons. Few if any suspects have been identified. There have been arrests in some of the murders of businessmen, but there have been no arrests in any high-profile case, and none of those arrested has been brought to trial.

Since mid-August, an extended series of clashes between two groups seeking to control Tursunzade has resulted in at least 30 deaths; some of those killed were unarmed bystanders. These killings do not appear to be connected with the Government's conflict with the opposition, but reflect the lack of governmental control and the arrogation of local authority by regional strongmen.

Several Russian army officers, soldiers, and staff were killed during the year. One officer was shot in March; two were killed in August when a bomb exploded near their troop transport. The Russian border forces and the Government have generally blamed the opposition in these cases, but the armed opposition has denied the charges.

Poor prison conditions and lack of food and adequate medical treatment resulted in a significant number of deaths in custody (see Section 1.c.).

b. *Disappearance.*—A number disappearances were reported, most significantly the February disappearance of Zafar Rahmonov, opposition cochairman of the Joint Commission to observe the cease-fire. At year's end, there was still no information concerning his fate.

The Government has not been active in investigating claims of previous disappearances. There were no developments in the 1993 disappearances of judge Tagobek Shukurov or the surgeon and Democratic Party Dushanbe branch chairman Dr. Ayniddin Sodikov.

Many cases of young men thought to have disappeared actually involve forcible conscription (see Section 1.f.). Other missing young men may have defected to, or are being held prisoner by, the opposition.

c. *Torture and Other Cruel, Inhuman, or Degrading Treatment or Punishment.*—Security officials, particularly those in the Ministry of Interior, regularly beat detainees in custody. Security forces were responsible for widespread beatings, especially of prisoners and detainees to extort confessions. In April two Democratic Party activists were arrested for distributing leaflets and beaten, although no formal charges were filed against them. Police shot one demonstrator in Uro-Teppa in May (see Section 2.b.).

In previous years, there were reports of rape or threat of rape of women in prison or detention. There were no such reports this year; however, there is no reason to believe that circumstances have changed.

Prison conditions remain harsh and life threatening. Prisons are generally overcrowded, unsanitary, and disease-ridden, producing serious threats to many prisoners' health and a significant number of deaths from hunger and malnutrition. This reflects in part the self-funded status of most prisons, under which prisoners are supposed to grow much of their own food or make goods for sale. The general collapse of governmental programs and of the economy has caused the virtual disappearance of these programs. Conditions in most prisons improved somewhat in 1996, due primarily to the efforts of international relief groups and the International Committee of the Red Cross (ICRC). Some food production is resuming. Family members are allowed access to prisoners, in accordance with the law. Despite its standard modalities, the ICRC has not succeeded in gaining access to prisoners in pretrial detention (where most abuses occur) but has been able to establish a program to supply food for inmates in many institutions.

d. *Arbitrary Arrest, Detention, or Exile.*—The Criminal Code has not been significantly amended since independence, and it therefore retains many of the defects inherited from Soviet times. Revision of the Criminal Code is a high priority of the Majlisi Oli (parliament). The system allows for lengthy pretrial detention and provides few checks on the power of procurators and police to arrest persons. Public order, which broke down during the civil war, has yet to be fully restored, and the virtual immunity from prosecution of armed militia groups has further eroded the integrity of the legal system.

Police may legally detain persons without a warrant for a period of 72 hours, and the procurator's office may do so for a period of 10 days after which the accused must be officially charged. At that point, the Criminal Code permits pretrial detention for up to 15 months. The first 3 months of detention are at the discretion of the local procurator, the second 3 months must be approved at the regional level, and the Procurator General must sanction the remaining time in detention. The Criminal Code maintains that all investigations must be completed 1 month before the 15-month maximum in order to allow the defense time to examine government evidence. There is no requirement for judicial approval or for a preliminary judicial hearing on the charge or detention. In criminal cases, detainees may be released and restricted to their place of residence pending trial. Once a case is entered for trial, the law states that it must be brought before a judge within 28 days. However, it is common for cases to languish for many months before the trial begins.

The number of politically motivated arrests decreased compared with 1995. There are credible allegations of illegal government detention of members or relatives of members of opposition political parties for questioning. In most cases, the security officers do not obtain arrest warrants and do not bring charges. Those released sometimes claimed that they were mistreated and beaten during detention.

Opposition sources maintain that security forces detained dozens of persons unlawfully without charge. Since the law precludes visits to persons in pretrial detention, it is not possible to assess these allegations.

The Constitution states that no one can be exiled without a legal basis; no laws have been passed so far setting out any legal basis for exile. There were no reports of the use of forced exile.

e. *Denial of Fair Public Trial.*—The 1994 Constitution states that judges are independent and subordinate only to the Constitution and the law; it prohibits interference in their activities. However, judicial officials at all levels of the court system are heavily influenced by both the political leadership and, in many instances, armed paramilitary groups. Under the Constitution, the President has the right, with confirmation by the Parliament, to both appoint and dismiss judges and prosecutors. Judges at the local, regional, and republic level are, for the most part, poorly trained and lack understanding of an independent judiciary.

The court system, largely unmodified from the Soviet period, includes city, district, regional, and national levels, with a parallel military system. Higher courts serve as appellate courts for the lower ones. The Constitution establishes additional courts, including a Constitutional Court. This court has begun to function, has heard some cases, and issued decisions.

According to the law, all trials are public, except in cases involving national security or the protection of minors. The court will appoint an attorney for those who do not have one. Defendant may choose their own attorneys but may not necessarily choose among court-appointed defenders. In practice, arrested persons are often denied prompt, and in some cases any, access to an attorney.

The procurator's office is responsible for conducting all investigations of alleged criminal conduct. In theory, both defendant and counsel have the right to review all government evidence, to confront witnesses, and to present evidence and testimony. No groups are barred from testifying, and all testimony is theoretically given equal weight, regardless of ethnicity or gender of the witness. Ministry of Justice officials maintain that defendants benefit from the presumption of innocence, despite the unmodified Soviet legal statute, which presumes the guilt of all brought to trial. Thus, in practice, bringing charges tends to suggest guilt to most Tajiks.

Pressure continues to be exerted on the judicial system by local strongmen, their armed paramilitary groups, and vigilantes who operate outside of government control, sometimes leading to the dismissal of charges and dropping of cases. Bribery of prosecutors and judges is also considered to be widespread.

The Government holds political prisoners, although estimates of the number vary widely. The Government and the Tajik opposition exchanged multiple lists of prisoners of war (POW's) and political prisoners for exchange as a result of the fifth round of inter-Tajik talks in Ashgabat. The largest opposition list totaled 596 names of political prisoners believed by the opposition to be in government custody, while the largest government list totaled 463 soldiers believed by the Government to be held by the opposition. Both lists undoubtedly include names of many persons who were missing or dead, or, in the case of POW's held by the opposition, who defected. No prisoners were exchanged in 1996.

f. *Arbitrary Interference With Privacy, Family, Home, or Correspondence.*—The Constitution provides for the inviolability of the home and prohibits interference with correspondence, telephone conversations, and postal and communication rights, except "in cases prescribed by law." Police may not enter and search a private home without the approval of the procurator. In some cases, police may enter and search a home without permission, but they must then inform the procurator within 24 hours. Police are also permitted to enter and search homes without permission if they have compelling reason to believe a delay in obtaining a warrant would impair national security. There is no judicial review of police searches conducted without a warrant.

There are continuing credible reports of arbitrary illegal search and seizure by government forces.

Forced conscription occurred extensively as the armed forces sought to maintain sufficient strength to prosecute the war against the armed opposition in the face of both widespread reluctance to serve and draft evasion. There are numerous credible reports of young men being caught in public places and sent directly to the front line, or to very short-term training camps before being sent to battle zones. Checks on service liability are typically not made, so that persons with legal deferments were still forced into service. Some of these persons were killed in the line of duty, and there were reports of their bodies being dumped on their parents' doorsteps.

In some cases, particularly where the conscript is under age, parents have been able to obtain his release by appearing at the training camp or military base with appropriate documentation. The involvement of an OSCE representative may also have been central to obtaining these releases.

g. *Use of Excessive Force and Violations of Humanitarian Law in Internal Conflicts.*—Tajikistan signed a code of conduct at the OSCE conference in Budapest in 1994, obliging it to incorporate into domestic legislation the provisions of the code dealing with humanitarian standards in internal conflicts. This has not been done. The ICRC has sought access to all persons detained in connection with the conflict without success.

Despite continued political efforts under United Nations auspices to mediate a national reconciliation and the continued nominal existence of a cease-fire agreement, fighting increased in intensity and geographic extent over 1995 levels. Government artillery forces exercised little discipline, resulting in noncombatant deaths.

A May attack by the opposition on Tavildara led to many months of fighting in that central Tajikistan area, resulting in many deaths, much destruction of civilian property and public resources such as bridges and highways, the placement of landmines by both sides, and the internal displacement of several thousand persons. POW's are mistreated by both sides.

While precise figures are not available, several hundred troops died on both the government and opposition sides. Several times that number were injured, and many civilians were killed, wounded, or forced to flee.

On December 20, 23 persons in a U.N. convoy, including 7 U.N. military observers, were taken hostage by fighters loyal to a local commander, Rizvon Sadirov, who formerly supported the opposition, but recently was reported to have defected to the

Government. The hostage takers were not part of the government's military forces and were quickly persuaded to release the hostages unharmed.

Section 2. Respect for Civil Liberties, Including:

a. *Freedom of Speech and Press.*—Despite the Constitution and the 1991 law protecting freedom of speech and the press, the Government severely restricts freedom of expression in practice. Journalists, broadcasters, and individual citizens who disagree with government policies cannot speak freely or critically. The Government exercises control over the media both overtly through legislation and less obviously through such mechanisms as friendly advice to reporters on what news should not be covered. The Government also controlled the printing presses, the supply of newsprint, and broadcasting facilities, and subsidizes virtually all publications and productions. Editors fearful of reprisals exercise careful self-censorship.

Journalists of the newspaper Sadoi Mardum, published by the Parliament, were not permitted to publish an article critical of a parliamentary deputy. The journalists were able to publish the article in the executive branch newspaper, but were then threatened by the subject of their article. An independent television station in the northern city of Khojand, linked to a former provincial chairman, was closed by the regional government.

On March 28, Viktor Nikulin, an ethnic Russian native of Tajikistan who worked for a Moscow television station, was murdered in Dushanbe by unknown persons. No progress has been made in solving this death (see Section 1.a.).

There were some improvements regarding freedom of speech and the press. Several new, semi-independent publications appeared, although they are largely nonpolitical. Letters critical of the official version of the antigovernment demonstrations that took place in the northern city of Uro-Teppa in May were printed in Dushanbe in August. A semi-governmental Dushanbe television station that had been closed in September 1995, resumed limited broadcasting under a new name in September. A seminar to discuss the proposed new electronic media law was held in Dushanbe in August.

Academic expression is limited by fear of reprisals, the complete reliance of scientific institutes upon government funding, and by the need to find alternate employment to generate sufficient income, leaving little time for academic writing. Prominent Tajik academic Muhammad Osimi was killed during the year, but it appears unlikely that his death was connected to his academic work.

b. *Freedom of Peaceful Assembly and Association.*—The Constitution provides for freedom of peaceful assembly and association. In practice, however, the authorities exercise strict control over organizations and activities of a political nature. Although free assembly and association are permitted for nonpolitical associations, including trade unions, freedom of association is circumscribed by the requirement (in the law on nongovernmental associations) that all organizations must first register with the Ministry of Justice. This process is often slowed by the requirement to submit documents in both Russian and Tajik. The Ministry of Justice's verification of the text inevitably delays the granting of registration. Once registered an organization must apply for a permit from the local executive committee in order legally to organize any public assembly or demonstration.

In the spring there were demonstrations in the Khatlon region to protest rising bread prices and the nonpayment of salaries. In May large demonstrations took place in Khujand, sparked by the killing of a prominent local businessman and in protest of the presence of numerous government officials from the Kulobi region. Demands were made regarding military service by young men. After the demonstrations, some of the organizers were arrested. Similar demonstrations took place in several other northern cities. In Uro-Teppa in May police shot one demonstrator, leading to the burning of several buildings.

In August demonstrations in Hissor to protest the behavior of local militia led to the dismissal of the regional security chief, a Kulobi by origin.

There are six political parties officially registered with the Government. Three of the four political parties suspended in 1993—the Islamic Revival Party, the Rastokhez National Movement, and the Lali Badakhshan Movement for the Autonomy of the Pamirs—remained suspended. In March a seventh political party, Adolatkhoh (justice seeker), was registered. In addition a national front organization (Public Accord) established by the Government was registered in March.

In several cases, members of suspended political parties have been unable to find employment, apparently due to actions taken by the security services.

c. *Freedom of Religion.*—The Constitution provides for freedom of religion. Religion and State are separate, and neither the law nor the Government places restrictions on religious worship. However, according to the Law on Freedom of Faith, the Committee on Religious Affairs under the Council of Ministers registers religious communities and monitors the activities of the various religious establishments. While the official reason given is to ensure that they are acting in accordance with the law, the practical purpose is to ensure that they do not become overtly political.

d. *Freedom of Movement Within the Country, Foreign Travel, Emigration, and Repatriation.*—The Constitution provides for the right of citizens to choose their place of residence, to emigrate, and to return. In practice, the Government generally respects these rights, with some regulation.

The Government has stipulated that both citizens and foreigners are prohibited from traveling within a 25-kilometer zone along the country's borders with China and Afghanistan without permission from the Ministry of Foreign Affairs. In practice, however, international aid workers and diplomats travel freely in these regions without prior government authorization.

Residents of Dushanbe and those travelers wishing to remain longer than 3 days are supposed to register with central authorities, and regulations require registration at the local Ministry of Interior office upon arrival and departure from a city. However, these regulations are largely ignored in practice. There are no legal restrictions on changing residence or workplace. Citizens who wish to travel abroad must obtain an exit visa. There is no evidence that these are withheld for political reasons.

There is no law on emigration. Those wishing to migrate within the former Soviet Union notify the Ministry of Interior of their departure. Persons wishing to emigrate beyond the borders of the former Soviet Union must receive the approval of the relevant country's embassy in order to obtain their passport. Persons who settle abroad are required to inform the Tajikistan embassy or Tajikistan interests section of the nearest Russian embassy or consulate.

Persons who wish to return to Tajikistan after having emigrated may do so freely by submitting their applications to the Tajikistan embassy or Tajikistan interests section of the nearest Russian embassy or consulate. The Government adjudicates requests on a case-by-case basis. There is no indication that persons, other than those who fled Tajikistan for political reasons after the civil war, are not freely permitted to return. Persons currently active with the Tajik opposition whose travel documents have expired have at times had difficulty obtaining new documents permitting them to return.

Under the 1994 refugee law, a person granted refugee status is guaranteed the right to work and move freely throughout the country. The Central Department of Refugee Affairs under the Ministry of Labor has responsibility for the registration of refugees.

The Government cooperates with the Office of the United Nations High Commissioner for Refugees (UNHCR) and other humanitarian organizations in assisting refugees. There were no reports of forced expulsion of those having a valid claim to refugee status. There were no reports of forced return of persons to a country where they feared persecution. The Government, particularly the Ministry of Labor, worked closely with the UNHCR and the International Organization for Migration on behalf of refugees and internally displaced persons.

The Government provides first asylum, and has provided it to 1,060 refugees from Afghanistan since July 1995.

In July 1995, the Central Department of Refugee Affairs (CDR) under the Ministry of Labor took over from the UNHCR the registration of refugees, in accordance with the 1951 Convention on Refugees and Tajikistan's 1994 Law on Refugees. An unresolved problem stems from the unofficial government policy of denying official status to the Afghan spouses and children of returning Tajik refugees by denying them residence permits.

Tajik refugees continued to return from northern Afghanistan, as did internally displaced persons from Gorno Badakhshan, to the Dushanbe and Khatlon regions, albeit slowly. Approximately 20,000 to 22,000 refugees remain in Afghanistan. Opposition groups have reportedly blocked the return of these refugees through threats and harassment. The number of internally displaced persons increased sharply with the summer fighting in Tavildara, to approximately 14,000. While significant problems remain with illegal occupation of returnees' homes by those loyal to the victorious Popular Front militias, progress continues to be made in evicting the occupiers.

The UNHCR reported that the Government's responsiveness, including that of local authorities, was greater than in 1995 in investigating cases of illegal housing occupation and accusations of crimes against returnees, although not all cases were brought to successful conclusions.

Section 3. Respect for Political Rights: The Right of Citizens to Change Their Government

The Government limits the right of citizens to change their government peacefully and freely. The Government of President Rahmonov remains dominated by Kulobi regional political interests, although the prime ministers have been from the northern Khojand region. Three of the four opposition parties suspended in 1993 remain suspended. One new party was registered, joining six other legal parties. Many opposition party activists remained either jailed or in exile abroad, although one member of the opposition negotiating team resides in Tajikistan and the opposition members of the Joint Commission have spent extended periods in Tajikistan since early August.

The parliamentary (Majlisi Oli) elections conducted in 1995 were marked by numerous irregularities, such as voter intimidation and ballot-box stuffing, and did not result in a truly independent Parliament.

There are no formal barriers to women's participation in the electoral process, although since the removal of Soviet-era quotas the number of female deputies has declined. At year's end there were 16 female deputies in the Parliament, 1 woman serving as a deputy prime minister, 1 as a minister, and several as deputy ministers.

Section 4. Governmental Attitude Regarding International and Nongovernmental Investigation of Alleged Violations of Human Rights

The Government's record on dealing with international and nongovernmental investigation of alleged human rights abuses was mixed. Lingering fear of persecution by government or extragovernmental elements has discouraged efforts by citizens to form their own human rights organizations. The Government has not interfered, however, with citizens' and government officials' participation in international and local seminars sponsored by the Organization for Security and Cooperation in Europe, the International Commission of the Red Cross, United Nations agencies, NGO's, and foreign governments on such topics as the rule of law, an independent judiciary, and international humanitarian law. Discussion at such seminars, including those held in Tajikistan, has at times been critical of the Government.

The Government worked closely with the United Nations Mission of Observers in Tajikistan and the United Nations Secretary General's Special Representative in the course of the inter-Tajik talks.

The OSCE's mission continues to monitor human rights issues, including through three field offices, which receive generally good cooperation from local officials. While the Government at first agreed to establish a national human rights institution and ombudsman position with OSCE financial support, it later decided to establish such functions itself. Thus far no institution or ombudsman position has been established.

The ICRC intensified contacts with government entities concerned with prisoners, but still was not given access to prisoners in accordance with its standard modalities.

Section 5. Discrimination Based on Race, Sex, Religion, Disability, Language, or Social Status

The Constitution provides for the rights and freedoms of every person regardless of nationality, race, sex, language, religious beliefs, political persuasion, social status, knowledge, and property. It also explicitly states that men and women have the same rights. In practice, however, there is discrimination as a result of cultural traditions and the lingering hostilities from the 1992 civil war.

Women.—While no official data are available on the prevalence of spousal abuse, wife beating is a common problem. In both urban and rural areas, many cases of wife beating are unreported and many of those reported are not investigated. There is a widespread reluctance to discuss the issue or provide assistance to women in abusive situations. In addition abduction of brides is widely reported, and there are reliable reports of young women prevented from leaving the country due to threats against their families should they do so.

The Criminal Code prohibits rape, although it is widely believed that most rape cases are unreported. There are no rape crisis centers or special police units for handling these cases. The threat of rape is reliably reported as being used to coerce women. The situation is exacerbated by a general decline in public order, so that in many cities, including Dushanbe, women exercise particular care in their movement, especially at night.

Laws exist against keeping brothels, procuring, making or selling pornography, infecting another person with a venereal disease, and sexual exploitation of women.

According to the law, women have equal rights with men. Inheritance laws do not discriminate against women. In practice, however, inheritances may pass disproportionately to sons.

The participation of women in the work force and in institutes of higher learning is one of the positive legacies of the Soviet era. There is no formal discrimination against women in employment, education, or housing, and in urban areas women can be found throughout government, academic institutes, and enterprises. Divorce rates in urban areas are comparatively high, and women tend to carry the burden of child-rearing and household management whether married or divorced. In rural areas, women tend to marry younger, have larger families, and receive less education than women in cities. Due to the prevalence of large families, women in rural areas are also much less likely to work outside the home. Articles in the Criminal Code protect women's rights in marriage and family matters.

Children.—The extensive government social security network for child welfare continued to deteriorate. Women are provided 3 years of maternity leave and monthly subsidies for each child, which were increased at the time price controls on bread were lifted. Education is compulsory until age 16, but the law is not enforced. All health care is free. However, the Government's lack of financial resources left it unable to fulfill many of its obligations for the provision of subsidies and care for maternal and child health.

People With Disabilities.—The 1992 Law on Social Protection of Invalids stipulates the right of the disabled to employment and adequate medical care. In practice, however, the Government does not require employers to provide physical access for the disabled. Financial constraints and the absence of basic technology to assist the disabled result, in practice, in high unemployment and widespread discrimination. There is no law mandating accessibility for the disabled.

Religious Minorities.—The Baha'i community in Dushanbe suffered an arson attack in the spring. A newspaper that had published articles provided by the Baha'i community was pressured by the Government to stop publishing them, possibly at the instigation of the Iranian embassy.

National/Racial/Ethnic Minorities.—After the civil war, over 90,000 people of primarily Gharmi and Pamiri origin fled to Afghanistan to avoid reprisals by progovernment forces. Most of these persons returned to Tajikistan in 1994–95, and repatriation continued during 1996, with government encouragement. While making a good faith effort to assist with the repatriation of refugees, particularly those from Afghanistan, the Government did not fulfill many of its pledges, including the payment of reconstruction fees for returning refugee families. However, security for returning refugees improved, with the UNHCR reporting fewer cases of murder, rape, and harassment of returnees than in 1995. Similarly, local procurators took an active stance in investigating alleged crimes against returnees. However, some procurators and judges continued to be subjected to threats and intimidation for investigating or trying charges against militia members, often of Kulobi origin.

With the exception of the trilingual (Tajik/Uzbek/Russian) school structure, Uzbek has no official status in Tajikistan, although Uzbeks comprise nearly one-quarter of the population. The Government permits radio and television broadcasts in Russian and Uzbek, in addition to Tajik. In practice Russian is the language of inter-ethnic communication and widely used in government. Ethnic Russians and related Russian speakers, e.g., Ukrainians, now make up less than 2 percent of the population. While the Government has repeatedly expressed its desire for the ethnic Russian and Slavic population to remain in Tajikistan, economic conditions provide little incentive for them to do so, and some local Russians and other Slavs perceive an increase in negative social attitudes towards them. At the same time, a Slavic university opened in Dushanbe in September, with Russian as the language of instruction; President Rahmonov attended the opening ceremony. In 1996 President Rahmonov and Russian President Yeltsin signed an agreement on dual citizenship, which the Russian Duma ratified on December 4 to complete the process.

Members of the Government, particularly security forces, continued to discriminate against Afghan nationals by extorting bribes and not giving crime victims full police protection. Afghan spouses of returning Tajik refugees still suffer from the unofficial government policy of denying them official status (see Section 2.d.).

Section 6. Worker Rights

a. *The Right of Association.*—The Law on Social Organization and the Law on Trade Union Rights and Guarantees provide all citizens with the right of association, which includes the right to form and join unions without prior authorization, to organize territorially, and to form and join federations.

The Federation of Trade Unions, a holdover from the Communist era, remains the dominant labor organization, although it has since shed its subordination to the

Communist Party. The Federation consists of 20 professional trade unions and currently claims 1,500,000 members, virtually all nonagricultural workers. The separate Trade Union of Non-State Enterprises has registered unions in over 3,000 small and medium-sized enterprises, totaling about 50,000 employees, although many of these enterprises are not functioning due to the general economic depression. The same is true for many members of the Federation of Trade Unions. The Council of Ministers formally consults both labor federations during the drafting of social welfare and worker rights legislation.

The Law on Tariff Agreements and Social Partnerships mandates that arbitration take place before a union may legally call a strike. Depending on the scale of the labor disagreement, arbitration can take place at the company, sector, or governmental level. In the event that arbitration fails, unions have the right to strike, but both labor federations have publicly disavowed the utility of strikes in a period of deepening economic crisis and high unemployment and espoused compromise between management and workers.

While there were no official, union-sanctioned strikes, several wildcat strikes occurred. Workers at the aluminum smelter at Tursunzade struck in August to protest nonpayment of salaries, and similar demonstrations or brief strikes took place elsewhere during the year. None of these strikes had the sanction of the labor unions and were, hence, illegal. However, the Ministry of Labor recognized that nonpayment of salaries to workers was a violation of International Labor Organization regulations.

The law provides citizens with the right to affiliate with international organizations freely.

b. *The Right to Organize and Bargain Collectively.*—The right to organize and bargain collectively is codified in the Law on Trade Union Rights and Guarantees, the Law on Social Partnerships and Collective Contracts, and the Law on Labor Protection. Employees, members of the trade union, and management participate in collective bargaining at the company level. Negotiations involving an industry sector include officials from the relevant ministry and members of the union's steering committee for that particular sector. As the economic situation worsens, it is becoming increasingly difficult for enterprises to engage in effective collective bargaining.

The law prohibits antiunion discrimination or the use of sanctions to dissuade union membership, nor may a worker be fired solely for union activity. Any complaints of discrimination against a labor union or labor union activist are first considered by a local labor union committee and, if necessary, raised to the level of the Supreme Court and investigated by the Ministry of Justice. The law compels an employer found guilty of firing an employee based on union activity to reinstate the employee.

There are no export processing zones.

c. *Prohibition of Forced or Compulsory Labor.*—The Constitution prohibits forced labor, except in cases defined in law. No laws have been passed defining such cases since the adoption of the new Constitution. Neither the Law on Labor Protection nor the Law on Employment, both predating the 1994 Constitution, specifically prohibits forced or compulsory labor. The Soviet practice of compelling students to pick cotton was officially banned in 1989, although students in the Leninabad region continued to be sent to the fields to pick cotton. In previous years there have been reports of buses being stopped and passengers being sent to pick cotton for several hours before being allowed to proceed.

d. *Minimum Age for Employment of Children.*—According to labor laws, the minimum age for the employment of children is 16, the age at which children may also legally leave school. With the concurrence of the local trade union, employment may begin at the age of 15. By law workers under the age of 18 may work no more than 6 hours a day and 36 hours per week. However, children as young as 7 years of age participate in agricultural work, which is classified as family assistance. Trade unions are responsible for reporting any violations in the employment of minors. Cases not resolved between the union and the employer may be brought before the Procurator General, who may investigate and charge the manager of the enterprise with violations of the Labor Code.

e. *Acceptable Conditions of Work.*—The President, on the advice of the Ministry of Labor and in consultation with trade unions, sets the minimum monthly wage.

The nominal minimum wage of approximately $1.00 (288 Tajik rubles) falls far short of providing a minimal standard of living for a worker and family. The Government recognizes this problem and has retained certain subsidies for workers and their families at the minimum wage. Although the Government adopted a wage indexation law in 1993 and inflation has been high, the law has not been implemented.

The economy continued to decline, with a majority of industry standing idle by the end of the year. As factories and enterprises either remained closed or were shut down, workers were laid off or furloughed for extended periods. Some establishments, both governmental and private, compensated their employees in kind with food commodities or the output of the particular concern for which the employee worked. The employee could then sell or barter those products in local private markets. Citizens in rural areas intensified cultivation of food crops on their private or rented plots, while even urban residents started tending small vegetable gardens and raising livestock.

The legal workweek for adults (over age 18) is 40 hours. Overtime payment is mandated by law, with the first 2 hours of overtime to be paid at one and one-half times the normal rate and the rest of the overtime hours at double time.

The Government has established occupational health and safety standards, but these fall far below accepted international norms, and the Government does not enforce them in practice. The enforcement of work standards is the responsibility of the State Technical Supervision Committee under the Council of Ministers. While new statistics were not available, it is virtually certain, given the continuing economic decline, that 1993 statistics, which reported that over one-fifth of the population worked in substandard conditions, greatly underreport the number of persons working in substandard conditions. Workers can leave their jobs with 2 months' notice, but, given the bleak employment situation, few choose to do so. The Law on Labor Protection provides that workers can remove themselves from hazardous conditions without risking loss of employment.

TURKEY

Turkey is a constitutional republic with a multiparty parliament, the Grand National Assembly, which elects the President. Suleyman Demirel was elected President in 1993. December 1995 elections led to an unstable coalition government that fell in the spring, and in July Necmettin Erbakan, leader of the Refah party, became the first Islamist Prime Minister in the Republic's history. He heads a coalition government with the secular, center-right True Path Party (DYP), whose leader, Tansu Ciller, is Deputy Prime Minister and Foreign Minister. The Government respects the constitutional provisions for an independent judiciary.

For over a decade, Turkey has engaged in armed conflict with the terrorist Kurdistan Workers Party (PKK), whose goal is a separate state of Kurdistan in southeastern Turkey. A state of emergency, declared in 1984, continues in 9 southeastern provinces where the Government faces substantial terrorist violence from the PKK. (The state of emergency was lifted in Mardin province in November.) A regional governor for the state of emergency has authority over the ordinary governors in the 9 provinces, as well as 2 adjacent ones, for security matters. The state of emergency allows him to exercise certain quasi-martial law powers, including restrictions on the press and removal from the area of persons whose activities are deemed hostile to public order. The state of emergency decree was most recently renewed for 4 months in November.

The Turkish National Police (TNP) have primary responsibility for security in urban areas, while the Jandarma (gendarmerie) carry out this function in the countryside. The armed forces continued to combat the PKK in the state of emergency region, thereby taking on an internal security function. Although civilian and military authorities remain publicly committed to the establishment of a state of law and respect for human rights, some members of the security forces, particularly police "special teams," Jandarma, and TNP personnel, committed serious human rights abuses.

Turkey has a primarily market-based economy driven by an increasingly active private sector. The agricultural sector employs nearly one-half of the country's labor force but contributes only 15 percent of the gross national product (GNP) and total exports. The leading industrial sectors—textiles, iron, and steel—provide the leading exports. Impressive economic growth over the past 15 years has translated into an improved standard of living and the creation of a growing middle class. Per capita GNP is approximately $3,000. Such positive developments, however, have been accompanied by substantial macroeconomic imbalances. The Government had little success in implementing needed reforms to reduce the budget deficit and inflation. The introduction of populist economic measures pushed the budget deficit to nearly 10 percent of GNP, while inflation exceeded 80 percent. Persistently high inflation over the past decade has worsened income distribution. The conflict in the southeast and maintenance of a large national defense establishment continue to be a significant drain on the economy. As expected, implementation of the customs union with the European Union in January appears to have aggravated the trade deficit in the short term. Corruption has taken an economic toll and has sapped popular faith in the Government.

Serious human rights problems continued. The Government was unable to sustain improvements made in 1995 and, as a result, its record was uneven in 1996 and deteriorated in some respects. Human rights emerged as a priority public issue during the year. There was growing recognition in the Government, Parliament, the media, academia, big business, and the public at large that the country's human rights performance is inadequate and needs to be brought in line, not only with its international obligations and commitments, but also with popular aspirations and demands.

The situation in the southeast was of particular concern. The Government has long denied its Kurdish population, located largely in the southeast, basic cultural and linguistic rights. As part of its fight against the PKK, the Government forcibly displaced large numbers of noncombatants, tortured civilians, and abridged freedom of expression. The PKK has committed widespread abuses and regularly employed terrorism against the Government and civilians, mostly Kurds. In January a minibus carrying 11 people, including some supporters of a Kurdish political party, was ambushed in Sirnak province, and all were killed. The Government blamed the PKK, but an independent "Working Group for Peace" concluded that security forces were responsible.

Estimates of the total number of villagers forcibly evacuated from their homes since the conflict began vary widely: between 330,000 and 2 million. A credible estimate given by a former Member of Parliament from the region is around 560,000. Although the Government began a new resettlement program this year, its efforts to deal with and compensate the many internally displaced remained inadequate. As of October, 2,019 households with 15,314 people were resettled, according to government figures.

Human rights abuses were not limited to the southeast. Extrajudicial killings, including deaths in detention, from the excessive use of force, in safe house raids, and "mystery killings," continued to occur with disturbing frequency. Disappearances also continued. Torture remained widespread: Police and security forces often abused detainees and employed torture during periods of incommunicado detention and interrogation. Prolonged pretrial detention and lengthy trials continued to be problems.

In January journalist Metin Goktepe died from wounds he sustained while in police custody. Forty-eight police members were charged in his death; 14 of whom were dismissed from the force pending trial. In western Turkey, 10 police officers from the city of Manisa, including 2 superintendents, are being tried for torturing 14 people, mostly teenagers accused of ties to a leftist terrorist organization. In Istanbul, five police officers have been indicted for torturing Gulderen Baran and four others whom they suspected of being members of a terrorist organization. Prison conditions remained poor. At least 12 prisoners died during nationwide hunger strikes between March and July. At Diyarbakir prison, 10 prisoners were beaten to death by security forces called in to quell a disturbance in September; a parliamentary commission investigated and recommended that 68 police and security personnel be tried for their role in the violence. They were charged with manslaughter.

Limits on freedom of expression remained another serious problem. For example, at various times 135 journalists were detained, 11 of whom were formally arrested. Seven were reportedly attacked and one kidnaped. Academics, students, Members of Parliament, and intellectuals also had their freedom of expression limited. The Government continued to use the 1991 Anti-Terror Law, with its broad and ambiguous definition of terrorism, to detain both alleged terrorists and others on the charge that their acts, words, or ideas constituted dissemination of separatist propaganda. A book titled "The Euphrates Flows Sadly," published by a Kurdish former Member of Parliament (M.P.) from Erzurum, Abdulmelik Firat, was confiscated as separatist propaganda on orders of the Istanbul State Security Court prosecutor. Prosecutors also used Article 312 of the Criminal Code (incitement to racial or ethnic enmity) with increasing frequency. The translator and publisher of a Human Rights Watch report on the conflict in the southeast are being charged under Article 159 of the Code (defaming the military). Kurdish-language broadcasts remained illegal, despite the fact that Kurdish music broadcasts are growing. Despite these developments, private channel television programs and print media expanded the limits of debate on human rights and other issues of freedom of speech and the press. The number of licensed media rose substantially, the number of banned publications declined considerably, and the number of persons charged or convicted under the Anti-Terror Law fell significantly.

Four pro-Kurdish former M.P.'s who were convicted in 1994 on charges of separatism, and whose sentences were overturned on appeal in 1995, were retried and found guilty in April on similar charges. In September their sentences were upheld on appeal. Like the other M.P.'s from the Democracy Party (DEP) who were earlier convicted of separatism, they plan to appeal to the European Commission of Human Rights. The Ankara State Security Court pressed charges against three other former DEP Parliamentarians this year, also for promoting separatism.

In September and October, the Government prosecuted 43 members of the Pro-Kurdish People's Democracy Party (HADEP), including party chairman Murat Bozlak, based on an incident at the party's June 23 convention in Ankara, during which the Turkish flag was torn down and replaced by a PKK banner. The accused face minimum sentences ranging between 12 and 22½ years, and the party itself may be declared illegal (as were two of its predecessors). Of the 43 defendants, 16 remain in custody; by year's end, the trial had not yet concluded.

Officials of various government agencies continued to harass, intimidate, indict, and imprison human rights monitors, journalists, and lawyers for ideas that they expressed in public forums. In May Mustafa Cinkilic, a representative of the Adana branch of the Human Rights Foundation (HRF), and Dr. Tufan Kose, who operated a center for the treatment of victims of torture, were charged with operating an unlawful health center. Human rights monitors alleged that the prosecution of Cinkilic and Kose was a government attempt to harass the HRF. There were several hearings during the year, and the case is set to resume in February 1997. In May Seyfettin Kizilkan, president of the Diyarbakir Medical Chamber, was arrested on the grounds that he had PKK ties. He was sentenced in June to a 3-year prison term by the Diyarbakir State Security Court but remains free pending the outcome of his appeal.

Prosecutions of police or security officers for killings and torture increased somewhat. However, the climate of impunity reflected in the relatively small number of convictions probably remains the single largest obstacle to reducing these troubling human rights abuses. The lack of early access to an attorney by those detained is also a major factor in the use of torture by police and security forces.

The Government expanded human rights training for the police and military. The military improved the training of its officers and noncommissioned officers, which human rights nongovernmental organizations (NGO's) reported led to a reduction in human rights violations. Human rights education in primary schools is mandatory; it is an elective in high schools. The Refah/DYP coalition Government initially abolished the position of State Minister for Human Rights, but recreated it in November, appointing Lutfu Esengun to the position and providing him with more personnel and resources than his predecessors. Some discrimination against women persists. Spousal abuse and child labor remain serious problems.

PKK terrorists murdered noncombatants, targeting village officials, teachers, and other perceived representatives of the State and committed random murders in their effort to intimidate the populace. The PKK brutally murdered seven primary school teachers in predominantly Kurdish areas and often targeted civilians in an effort to prevent them from collaborating with security forces or to coerce them into assisting the insurgents. The PKK was also responsible for at least 23 disappearances.

RESPECT FOR HUMAN RIGHTS

Section 1. Respect for the Integrity of the Person, Including Freedom From:

a. *Political and Other Extrajudicial Killing.*—While accurate figures on the number of political and extrajudicial killings were unavailable, credible reports of such violations by government authorities continued. The Human Rights Foundation of Turkey, a respected nongovernmental organization, reported in its documentation center announcements a number of deaths under suspicious circumstances while in official custody, some as an apparent result of torture.

In January Metin Goktepe, a correspondent for Evrensel newspaper, died from wounds inflicted while in detention in Istanbul. Goktepe was detained by the police as he covered the funeral of a prisoner who died during a disturbance at Istanbul's Umraniye prison. Police initially denied that he had been detained, then later said that he died from a fall. Following large public demonstrations and a parliamentary outcry over the circumstances of his death, an investigation led to the arrest of 48 police officers, including 3 senior officers and a deputy commissioner. Some of these officers alleged that they were themselves tortured during interrogation. Fourteen of the accused were dismissed from the police force in October, and the case against all of the accused continued at year's end. The remaining police were suspended. (Some officers returned to work briefly, but due to public reaction they were again suspended.) In January a policeman shot and killed Cetin Karakoyun while the 14-

year-old was in custody in Magazalar. Authorities are obliged by law to investigate all deaths in custody. However, the number of serious prosecutions of security force members, while increasing, remained low.

The Human Rights Association (HRA) and other human rights (NGO's) recorded several mystery killings, in which the assailant's identity was unknown, many with the alleged complicity of security forces. Most of the reports pertain to the southeast where some of the victims were leaders or prominent members of the Kurdish community, local politicians, or members of the HADEP. The 1995 recommendations of a Parliamentary Committee, designed to purge "illegal formations" within the State which the Committee said committed some mystery killings, were not implemented.

In November a fatal car crash occurred involving: Abdallah Catli, a rightwing militant wanted by Interpol on charges of murdering seven Labor Party members in 1980; Huseyin Kocadag, former Istanbul deputy police chief; Gonca Uz, a former beauty queen; and Sedat Bucak (the only survivor), an ethnic Kurdish M.P. and clan leader with an important stake in the Government's village guard program. The incident resurrected serious concerns about corruption and the abuse of power in the security forces. It also led to the resignation of the Interior Minister, Mehmet Agar, who had been linked to the victims of the accident. A parliamentary committee was formed to investigate reputed links among politicians, police officials, and organized crime bosses.

There was an increase in the number of reports of deaths attributable to government authorities due to excessive use of force. According to Amnesty International, four prisoners died from beatings received in January in Umraniye prison. The Parliamentary Human Rights Commission concluded after an investigation that security forces killed 10 prisoners with truncheon blows to the back of the head while quelling a disturbance in Diyarbakir on September 24. A total of 37 people, including prison officers, were wounded (see Section 1.c.). The Commission recommended that 68 police and security personnel be tried for their role in the violence, and in January 1997 they were charged with manslaughter. Several NGO's have credibly reported that government forces used excessive force during some raids on alleged terrorist safe houses. Police killed three protestors during violent May Day demonstrations in Istanbul (see Section 2.b.).

Following an investigation, six of eight police officers originally accused have been charged in the case of Sinan Demirtas, who died in 1995 while in police custody. The 1995 death of journalist Safyettin Tepe in custody was ruled a suicide. In April the Bitlis prosecutor transferred the case to the provincial administrative board to determine if any further investigation into the conduct of police officers who had detained Tepe was warranted. The 1994 death in detention of Can Demirag was also ruled a suicide. Turkish authorities have in the past frequently claimed that deaths in custody were suicides. The case of police officer Abdullah Bozkurt, charged with the 1994 murder of Vedat Han Gulsenoglu, continues; Bozkurt has been reassigned from Istanbul to Van while his case is being prosecuted. The 1994 investigation into the murder of Diyarbakir tradesman Serif Avsar revealed that he was killed by six village guards, some of whom were his relatives. One defendant confessed that Avsar was killed as the result of a family vendetta. The case in absentia continues concerning the death in detention in 1993 of Vakkas Dost; policeman Nurettin Ozturk, the accused murderer, is still at large. The trial of the 11 police officers in the 1992 Basalak case continues.

The following cases remain unresolved: the 1992 case of Yucel Ozen, the 1994 murder of HEP party official Faik Candan, and the 1993 murder of journalist Ugur Mumcu.

A law under which terrorists who surrendered were eligible for lighter sentences was not renewed, but the Government continues to encourage their surrender. The courts also are more lenient with such terrorists. The Government asserts that it treats surrendered PKK members well and that only PKK coercion and propaganda—claiming that the Government kills all surrendered terrorists—has prevented an increase in the number surrendering.

The PKK continued to commit political and extrajudicial killings, primarily in rural southeast Anatolia. Political killings perpetrated by the PKK have in the past included those of state officials (Jandarma, local mayors, imams, and schoolteachers), state-paid paramilitary village guards and their family members, young villagers who refused to be recruited, and PKK guerrillas-turned-informants. According to government figures, for the first 10 months of 1996 the PKK killed 447 people in several operations, including at least 109 unarmed civilians, and wounded 900 other people. This total included 7 schoolteachers, bringing the total number of teachers killed by the PKK over the last 12 years to 153. The PKK also destroyed 70 primary and middle schools. This year the PKK began a new campaign of suicide bombings by women, who had usually been drugged or coerced in other ways.

Turkish Hizbullah, an Islamist Turkish terrorist group (not related to Lebanese Hizbullah), also targeted civilians in the southeast, committing at least eight gruesome murders and injuring several other people in Diyarbikar. Four trials continued against 89 Hizbullah members charged with a total of 113 murders. The Foreign Ministry states that a case has been opened against Hizbullah for the 1993 murder of DEP parliamentarian Mehmet Sincar; human rights groups consider the case a mystery killing.

b. *Disappearance.*—Accurate statistics on disappearances of those previously under dteention are hard to confirm; nonetheless, HRA figures indicate that such disappearances appear to have declined from a total of 221 in 1995 to 194 in 1996. Some persons disappeared after witnesses reported that security forces or law enforcement officials took them into custody. On September 16, at least five bodies were found on the outskirts of the village of Baharli, near Diyarbakir. Some of the victims had reportedly been in police custody earlier in September. The disappearances and deaths are under investigation; as yet no one has been formally charged.

For nearly a year, mothers who claim that their children have disappeared have gathered weekly in a square in Istanbul to ask for their return. In July police broke up one of these demonstrations, temporarily detaining at least 25 people and hitting others with truncheons, according to eyewitnesses. During the remainder of the year, the demonstrations took place unimpeded.

This year the Ministry of Interior created a missing persons bureau, which operates 24 hours a day. It has investigated disappearances reported by the HRA for 1995 and the first 5 months of 1996 and found that of 187 reported disappearances, 39 persons had since been found, 3 were fugitives from justice, 2 were killed by illegal groups, 82 who were allegedly in police custody had never been detained and were not being sought, 58 had been jailed for crimes, and 3 were active in terrorist groups.

The Government, human rights organizations, and the media report that the PKK routinely kidnaps young men or threatens their families as part of its recruiting effort. PKK terrorists continued their abductions of local villagers, teachers, journalists, and officials in the southeast. According to the Government, the PKK abducted 23 people through October, and killed at least 4 of them.

c. *Torture and Other Cruel, Inhuman, or Degrading Treatment or Punishment.*—Despite the Constitution's ban on torture, the Government's cooperation with unscheduled foreign inspection teams, and public pledges by successive governments to end torture, it continued to be widespread. The HRF's torture rehabilitation centers in Ankara, Izmir, Istanbul, and Adana reported that they accepted a total of 354 credible applications for treatment in the first 6 months of 1996. A total of 713 applications were received in 1995. Human rights attorneys and physicians who treat victims of torture say that most persons detained for or suspected of political crimes usually suffer some torture during periods of incommunicado detention in police stations and Jandarma headquarters before they are brought before a court. Government officials admit that torture occurs. Although they deny that torture is systematic, they explain its occurrence by stating that it is closely tied to the State's fight against terrorism. The Government's draft legislation before Parliament includes provisions for reducing lengthy prearraignment/pretrial detention periods cited by human rights monitors as providing occasions for torture; by year's end this legislation had not been passed into law.

Many cases of torture, however, occur in western Turkey, outside the zone of conflict. For example, 10 police officers, including 2 superintendents from Manisa (western Turkey) are being tried for allegedly torturing a group of 14 teenagers whom they suspected of belonging to a leftist terrorist organization. The December 1995 incident came to light through the intervention of a Manisa M.P. Widespread press coverage led to public outrage. The police officials' trial is set to resume in February 1997. Meanwhile the separate trials of the 15 alleged victims ended in January 1997. Five of the students were sentenced to 12½ years' imprisonment, one student was sentenced to 3 years, 9 months, and four students to 4½ years. The other five were acquitted. Lawyers have announced that they will appeal the convictions. The timing of the police and teenagers' trials precluded consideration that the teenagers' confessions may have been based on torture. Amnesty International published a report in November citing the Manisa case, and other alleged incidents of torture of children. In Istanbul, five police officers from the antiterror department were indicted in criminal court. The police are accused of torturing Gulderen Baran and four other detainees during an interrogation about their alleged membership in a terrorist organization.

Private attorneys reported neither better treatment of those charged under the Anti-Terror Law nor an overall decrease in the incidence of torture in 1996. In 1996 women again charged that sexual abuses occurred while under detention by security officials. In the 1995 case of Leman Celikaslan, who alleged that she was sexually abused by antiterror police, no evidence of rape was found, and the investigation was dropped, according to the HRF. In February she was found guilty of being a member of the PKK and sentenced to prison.

The 1992 Criminal Trials Procedure Law (CMUK) facilitates faster attorney access to those arrested for common crimes; however, the CMUK's provisions for immediate attorney access do not apply to those detained under the Anti-Terror Law or for other "security" crimes. The CMUK's allowable maximum prearraignment detention periods exceed Council of Europe maximums.

Human rights observers report that because the arresting officer is also responsible for interrogating the suspect, some officers may resort to torture to obtain a confession that would justify the arrest. Commonly employed methods of torture alleged by the HRF's torture treatment centers include: high-pressure cold water hoses, electric shocks, beating on the soles of the feet, beating of the genitalia, hanging by the arms, blindfolding, sleep deprivation, deprivation of clothing, systematic beatings, and vaginal and anal rape with truncheons and, in some instances, gun barrels. Other forms of torture were sexual abuse, submersion in cold water, use of truncheons, hanging sandbags on detainees' necks, forcing detainees to stand on one foot, releasing drops of water on their heads, and withholding food.

The Government maintains that medical examinations occur once during detention and a second time before either arraignment or release. However, former detainees assert that some medical examinations took place too long after the event to reveal any definitive findings of torture. According to a 1996 report by the Physicians for Human Rights (PHR) based on interviews with 39 torture survivors, a survey of 60 physicians who officially examine detainees, and a review of more than 150 official medical reports on detainees, law enforcement officers frequently coerce physicians, through the use of violence and intimidation, not to report evidence of torture. Members of security and police forces often stay in the examination room when physicians are examining detainees, resulting in intimidation of both the detainee and the physician. Physicians responded to the coercion by refraining from examining detainees, performing cursory examinations and not reporting findings, or reporting physical findings but not drawing reasonable medical inferences that torture occurred. Sixty percent of the physicians surveyed believed that "nearly everyone who is detained is tortured." The report also found that doctors and other health care professionals in the state of emergency region have been killed, tortured, imprisoned, internally exiled, and legally sanctioned in the course of their professional duties.

The Government attempted to deal with the problem doctors face in reporting evidence of torture by making improvements in medical examination procedures during the year. The Ministry of Health added some reporting requirements designed to increase accountability. A Ministry of Health circular from July requires "health station doctors" to examine detainees every 48 hours in areas where forensic doctors are not available. This requirement was adopted to promote independent and objective exams. While there is no information about the implementation and impact of this regulation, the Turkish Medical Doctors' Union noted that practices in 1996 were "more positive" than in the past. Ministry of Health efforts to disseminate information on forensic medicine were generally successful; however, according to the Medical Doctors' Union, not all the new monitoring practices were in place, especially in the southeast.

Credible sources in the human rights and legal communities estimate that judicial authorities investigate very few of the formal complaints involving torture and prosecute only a fraction of those. Security personnel accused of violating human rights are held to a different standard than other citizens. The Anti-Terror Law provides that officials accused of torture or other mistreatment may continue to work while under investigation and, if convicted, may only be suspended. Special provincial administrative boards rather than regular courts decide whether to prosecute such cases. Suspects' legal fees are paid by their employing agencies. Under the state of emergency, any lawsuit directed at government authorities must be approved by the state of emergency governor. Approval is rare. These constraints contribute to the paucity of convictions for torture.

Under the Administrative Adjudication Law, an administrative investigation into an alleged torture case is conducted to determine if there is enough evidence to bring a law enforcement officer to trial. Under the CMUK, prosecutors are empowered to initiate investigations of police and Jandarma officers suspected of torturing or mistreating suspects. In cases where township security directors or Jandarma commanders are accused of torture, the prosecutor must obtain permission to initiate an investigation from the Ministry of Justice, because these officials are deemed to have a status equal to that of judges.

In the first 9 months of 1996, seven complaints of torture or mistreatment were filed with the Parliamentary Human Rights Commission. This was a decrease from 1995 when 23 cases were filed during the same period. In each of the seven cases, the Commission wrote to the offices of the public prosecutor where the alleged incidents occurred. As prosecutors were not required to complete their investigations within strict deadlines, by year's end no further developments had occurred. There were no additional developments in the case of Baki Erdogan.

The Government accepted numerous unannounced visits by the Council of Europe's Committee for the Prevention of Torture (CPT) and is in regular dialog with the CPT. In December the CPT issued a very tough report about torture. The report acknowledged that progress had been made since 1992, but said that "although much of the legal framework necessary to combat torture is in place * * * in practice these measures are being ignored." The Government agreed that CPT reports on Turkey may be made public.

In December the European Court of Human Rights ruled against Turkey in the case of Zeki Aksoy. Specifically, the Court ruled that Aksoy had been tortured, detained for too long a time without being brought before a judge, and that he had not been provided with an effective remedy for his complaint of torture. The Court ordered Turkey to pay compensation, legal costs, and expenses. Aksoy did not live to hear the verdict, since he was murdered by unknown assailants in April 1994, reportedly after being threatened with death if he did not withdraw his petition before the Court.

The Turkish Medical Doctors Union states that women are no longer routinely subjected to virginity testing when they file complaints alleging sexual crimes.

Prison conditions remain poor. Prisons are overcrowded, and families often must supplement the poor quality food. Prisons are run on the ward system. Prisoners, often those of the same ideological bent, are incarcerated together and indoctrinate and punish their own. One of several examples of this practice was the death in August in Diyarbakir's central prison of PKK prisoner Emine Yavuz, who reportedly was strangled by other PKK militants for collaborating with the police. Torture in prisons decreased in the last few years, but security personnel continued to use excessive force in quieting disturbances. Four prisoners died of head injuries received in a January confrontation with security personnel, who also caused injury to 33 others. Ten prisoners were beaten to death in Diyarbikar in September by security forces called in to quell an uprising.

Hunger strikes in protest of prison conditions and poor treatment by guards occurred at many institutions throughout the year. In March prisoners at Diyarbakir prison, many convicted of terrorist-related crimes, began hunger strikes in protest of a government plan to transfer some prisoners to a new Western-style maximum security facility in Eskisehir, which would have broken up the ward system. According to Ministry of Health figures, by July an estimated 2,174 prisoners had gone on hunger strikes in 43 prisons in 38 cities. There were reports that some prisoners were forced by others to participate in the hunger strikes. Twelve prisoners who joined the hunger strikes eventually died. The strikes ended in August when an agreement rescinding the transfers was reached with the Justice Minister. As part of the accord, the Government agreed to the establishment of an independent "Prison Watch Committee," composed of prominent individuals such as novelist Yasar Kemal, to monitor negotiations and prison conditions.

Several monitoring groups, both domestic and international, carried out prison visits.

d. *Arbitrary Arrest, Detention, or Exile.*—To take a person into custody, a prosecutor must issue a detention order, except in limited circumstances such as when a person is caught committing a crime. The maximum detention period for those charged with common individual crimes is 24 hours. Those detained for common collective crimes may be held for 24 hours. The detention period may be extended for an additional 24 hours. Under the CMUK, detainees are entitled to immediate access to an attorney and may meet and confer with the attorney at any time. In practice, this access continued.

Persons detained for individual crimes that fall under the Anti-Terror Law must be brought before a judge within 48 hours, while those charged with crimes of a collective, political, or conspiratorial nature may be detained for up to 15 days in most of the country and up to 30 days in the 9 southeastern provinces under the state of emergency. Those detained and tried for the expression of views, generally for disseminating separatist propaganda, are charged promptly.

There is no guarantee of immediate access to an attorney under the law for persons whose cases fall under the jurisdiction of the State Security Courts; these include those charged with smuggling and with crimes under the Anti-Terror law. This lack of early access to an attorney is a major factor in the use of torture by police and security forces. The Government presented to Parliament draft legislation which, when passed, would grant more immediate access to an attorney, and return to the jurisdiction of the regular criminal courts some offenses now within the purview of the SSC system. By year's end, this legislation had not been passed into law.

The decision concerning access to counsel in such cases is left to the independent prosecutor, who often denies access on the grounds that it would prejudice an ongoing investigation. The Justice and Interior Ministries generally have not intervened in prosecutors' decisions or police actions denying access to counsel. Although the Constitution specifies the right of detainees to request speedy arraignment and trial, judges have ordered a significant number detained indefinitely, sometimes for years. Many cases involve persons accused of violent crimes, but it is not uncommon for those accused of nonviolent political crimes to be kept in custody until the conclusion of their trials.

By law, a detainee's next of kin must be notified "in the shortest time" after arrest, a requirement observed in practice. Once formally charged by the prosecutor, a detainee is arraigned by a judge and allowed to retain a lawyer. After arraignment, the judge may release the accused upon receipt of an appropriate guarantee, such as bail, or order him detained if the court determines that he is likely to flee the jurisdiction or destroy evidence.

There is no external exile. Turkey's internal exile law was repealed in 1987, but in 1990 the Government granted the southeast regional governor the authority to "remove from the region," for a period not to exceed the duration of the state of emergency (now in its twelfth year), citizens under his administration whose activities "give an impression that they are prone to disturb general security and public order." There were no known instances of the use of this broad authority during the year. Human rights monitors and residents of towns in the southeast report that officials continued to rely on "administrative transfers" to remove government employees thought liable to "create trouble."

e. *Denial of Fair Public Trial.*—The Constitution provides for an independent judiciary, and in practice the courts generally act independently of the executive. The Constitution requires that judges be independent of the executive in the discharge of their duties and provides for the security of tenure. The High Council of Judges and Prosecutors, which is appointed by the President and includes the Minister of Justice, selects judges and prosecutors for the higher courts and is responsible for oversight of those in the lower courts. The Constitution also prohibits state authorities from issuing orders or recommendations concerning the exercise of judicial power.

The judicial system is composed of general law courts, State Security Courts, and military courts. There is also a Constitutional Court. Most cases are prosecuted in the general law courts, which include the civil, administrative, and criminal courts. Appeals are heard either by the High Court of Appeals or the Council of State. Provincial administrative boards established under the Anti-Terror Law decide whether cases in which state officials are accused of misconduct should be heard in criminal court. Military courts, with their own appeals system, hear cases regarding infractions of military law by members of the armed forces, and cases in which civilians are alleged to have impugned the honor of the armed forces or undermined compliance with the draft.

The Constitutional Court examines the constitutionality of laws, decrees, and parliamentary procedural rules. However, it may not consider "decrees with the force of law" issued under a state of emergency, martial law, or in time of war.

State Security Courts (SSC) sit in eight cities. They are composed of panels of five members—two civilian judges, one military judge, and two prosecutors—and try defendants accused of crimes such as terrorism, drug smuggling, membership in illegal organizations, and espousing or disseminating ideas prohibited by law such as "damaging the indivisible unity of the state." There are 18 such SSC's. (In November changes in the relevant law abolished the SSC's in Erzincan, Konya, and Kayseri and established new ones in Ezurum, Van, and Adana. Cases have been redistributed among the new courts. The changes are meant to expedite existing cases by moving the courts closer to the cases.) SSC verdicts may be appealed only to a specialized department of the High Court of Appeals dealing with crimes against state security.

In 1996 SSC's predominantly handled cases under the Anti-Terror Law and Section 3.12 of the Criminal Code, which prohibits "incitement to racial enmity." The State claims that these courts were established to try efficiently those suspected of certain crimes. The heavy caseload often means that cases drag on for years. These courts may hold closed hearings and may admit testimony obtained during police interrogation in the absence of counsel. The trial of Diyarbakir lawyers charged with acting as couriers for the PKK continues at the Diyarbakir SSC, but the number of defendants has increased from 12 to over 20. There was no information available on the trial of nine Erzurum lawyers charged with similar crimes. None of the attorneys is being detained.

Defendants normally have the right to a public trial and, under the Constitution, can be proven guilty only in a court of law. By law the bar association must provide free counsel to indigents who make such a request to the court. Costs are borne by the association. There is no jury system; all cases are decided by a judge or a panel of judges. Trials may last for months or years, with one or two hearings scheduled each month.

Defense lawyers generally have access to the independent prosecutor's files after arraignment and prior to trial (a period of several weeks). In cases involving violations of the Anti-Terror Law and a few others, such as insulting the President or "defaming Turkish citizenship," defense attorneys may be denied access to files which the State asserts deal with national intelligence or security matters.

In law and in practice, the legal system does not discriminate against minorities. However, as legal proceedings are conducted solely in Turkish, and the quality of interpreters varies, some defendants whose mother tongue is not Turkish may be seriously disadvantaged. There are still some laws in effect that discriminate against women.

Turkey recognizes the jurisdiction of the European Court of Human Rights and the European Commission on Human Rights. Citizens may file applications alleging violations of the European Convention for the Protection of Human Rights and Fundamental Freedoms with the Commission. In September the European Court ruled against the Government in the case of Huseyin Adivar and six other Kurds, who claimed that the security forces had destroyed their homes in the village of Kelekci (see Section 1.f.). According to the Foreign Ministry, a total of 424 individual applications were made to the Commission as of August. Fifty cases were concluded, and 374 cases are still under review. The Commission has found 73 cases admissible to date. As of August, 6 new applications were made in 1996, compared to 71 new cases in all of 1995 and 96 in 1994. Bakir Caglar, a constitutional lawyer responsible for defending the Government's position before the European Court, resigned in the fall to protest the lack of progress on human rights.

There is no reliable estimate of the number of political prisoners. The Government claims that most alleged political prisoners are in fact security detainees, convicted of being members of, or assisting, the PKK or other terrorist organizations. The number of people charged, suspected, or convicted of offenses under the Anti-Terror Law was down significantly, probably because the late 1995 addition of an "intent" clause to the statute, as intended, made it more difficult to prosecute terrorist suspects. According to government statistics, during the first 10 months of 1996, 1,024 persons were in custody and an additional 1,943 were suspects not in custody related to offenses under the Anti-Terror Law. Eighty were convicted through October. Under the same law, 5,893 persons were arrested and charged with offenses in 1995, and 2,861 were convicted.

f. *Arbitrary Interference With Privacy, Family, Home, or Correspondence.*—The Constitution provides for the inviolability of a person's domicile and the privacy of correspondence and communication. Government officials may enter a private residence or intercept or monitor private correspondence only upon issuance of a judicial warrant. These provisions are generally respected in practice outside the state of emergency region.

A judge must decide whether to issue a search warrant for a residence. If delay may cause harm to the case, prosecutors and municipal officers authorized to carry out prosecutors' instructions may conduct a search. Searches of private premises may not be carried out at night, unless the delay will be damaging to the case or the search is expected to result in the capture of a prisoner at large. Other exceptions include persons under special observation by the Security Directorate General, places anyone can enter at night, places where criminals gather, places where materials obtained through the commission of crimes are kept, gambling establishments, and brothels.

In the 9 provinces under emergency rule, the regional state of emergency governor empowers security authorities to search without a warrant residences or the premises of political parties, businesses, associations, or other organizations. The Bar Association claims it is not constitutional for security authorities in these provinces to search, hold, or seize without warrant persons or documents. Roadblocks are common in the southeast; security officials regularly search vehicles and travelers. In August Parliament passed a law amending several laws affecting the security situation in the southeast. Key changes, which have been criticized by human rights activists, include authorizing security forces to shoot to kill when challenging a suspect, and granting all governors the power to declare a "state of emergency" and to call in security forces.

Security forces have forcibly evacuated villages in the southeast to prevent villagers from giving aid and comfort to the PKK (see Section 1.g.). The Government admits to village evacuations but claims that they occur as the consequence of pressures by and fear of the PKK and because security operations against the PKK in the region make continued occupancy unsafe. On September 16, the European Court of Human Rights ruled against the Government in the case of several Kurds who claimed that their human rights were violated when security forces destroyed their village. The Court ordered the Government to compensate the villagers (see Section 1.e.).

g. *Use of Excessive Force and Violations of Humanitarian Law in Internal Conflicts.*—Since 1984 the separatist PKK has waged a violent terrorist insurgency in southeast Turkey, directed against both security forces and civilians, almost all of them Kurds, whom the PKK accuses of cooperating with the State. The TNP, Jandarma, and armed forces, in turn, have waged an intense campaign to suppress terrorism, targeting active PKK units as well as persons they believe support or sympathize with the PKK. In the process, both government forces and PKK terrorists have committed human rights abuses against each other and noncombatants. In August Hurriyet newspaper reported that since 1984, 12,984 PKK, 4,133 security force members, and 4,922 civilians lost their lives in the fighting. The "Repentance Law," pursuant to which members of terrorist organizations who turn state's evidence could have their sentences decreased or annulled, was not renewed by Parliament beyond July 1995, but authorities claim that it is still being applied in some cases. According to press reports, 364 PKK terrorists were captured alive, and 271 turned themselves in during 1996. The Government asserts that it treats PKK members who surrender well and that it is only PKK propaganda—alleging that the surrendered members are killed—that has kept the number of individuals who surrender from rising.

Government security forces forcibly evacuated and destroyed some villages. According to the Foreign Ministry, as of October 1996, approximately 2,400 villages and hamlets (settlements of 3 or 4 houses) had been evacuated by the Government. The Government's stated purpose was to protect civilians or prevent PKK guerrillas from obtaining logistical support from the inhabitants. Some villagers alleged that security forces had evacuated them for refusing to participate in the paramilitary village guard system. The Government denied these allegations. The emergency region governor stated that villages were depopulated "for various reasons," including for security reasons; residents leaving of their own accord for security or economic reasons; and departures because of PKK pressure. The PKK burned some villages to seek revenge on paramilitary village guards.

The exact number of persons forcibly displaced from villages in the southeast since 1984 is unknown. Most estimates agree that 2,600 to 3,000 villages and hamlets have been depopulated. A few nongovernmental organizations have put the number of people forcibly displaced as high as 2 million. Official census figures for 1990—before large-scale forced evacuations began—indicate that the total population for the 10 southeastern provinces then under emergency rule was between 4 to 4.5 million people, half of them in rural areas. Since all rural areas in the southeast have not been depopulated, the estimate of 2 million evacuees is probably too high. On the low end, the then Interior Minister stated in July that the total number of evacuees was 330,000. Rapidly growing demands for social services in the cities indicate that migration from the countryside has been higher than this figure. Although the urbanization is also accounted for in part by voluntary migration for economic or educational reasons also related to the conflict, the figure given by a former M.P. from the region—560,000—appears to be the most credible estimate of those forcibly evacuated.

Whatever the actual number, government programs to deal with and compensate the forcibly evacuated villagers have been inadequate. The Foreign Ministry indicated that, as of October, 15,314 people or 2,019 households had returned to their villages in the southeast. The Ministry also noted that some of the displaced chose to resettle in urban areas and are receiving assistance there. The Government began a new "emergency support program" during the year to expedite resettlement in the southeast. The program is funded from the public budget and in September was allocated $2 million. The funds are used for rebuilding homes and roads, as well as for animal husbandry and beekeeping programs. Human rights activists dispute these figures, and officials overseeing these programs express dismay at the inadequacy of their funding.

There are credible allegations that serious security force abuses during the course of operations against the PKK continue. The Government organizes, arms, and pays for a civil defense force in the region known as the village guards. Participation in this paramilitary militia by local villagers is theoretically voluntary, but villagers are sometimes caught between the two sides. If the villagers agree to serve, the PKK may target them and their village. If the villagers refuse to participate, government security forces may retaliate against them and their village. The village guards have a reputation for being the least trained and disciplined of the Government's security forces and have been accused repeatedly of corruption, common crimes, and human rights abuses. In addition to the village guards, the Jandarma and police "special teams" are viewed as those most responsible for abuses.

A minibus containing 11 people, including 4 village guards, was ambushed on Sirnak's Guclukonak Highway on January 15. Its occupants were all killed and burned in the vehicle. Military officials claimed that it was a PKK attack, as many of those killed were supporters of the HADEP party. HADEP Vice Chairman Osman Ozcelik sought a parliamentary investigation of the incident, claiming that the victims had earlier been in the custody of security forces. The Diyarbakir HRA branch also said that the victims had previously been under police detention. An independent investigation concluded that the official explanation was inconsistent and laid the blame for the incident on security forces.

According to the Physicians for Human Rights 1996 report on torture, Law 169 of the Penal Code and Article 7 of the Anti-Terror Law, which prohibit assistance to illegal organizations or armed groups, have been used extensively to prosecute health professionals for providing care to individuals suspected of being members of terrorist organizations. Dr. Ilken Diken, convicted and imprisoned for failing to report that he had treated terrorists in 1994 and 1995, was released in 1996.

Government state of emergency decree 430, codified in 1990 and most recently renewed for 4 months in November, imposes stringent security measures in nine provinces in the southeast. The state of emergency was lifted in the province of Mardin on November 28. The regional governor for the state of emergency may censor news, ban strikes or lockouts, and impose internal exile (see Section 1.d.). The decree also provides for doubling the sentences of those convicted of cooperating with separatists. Informants and convicted persons who cooperate with the state are eligible for rewards and reduced sentences. Only limited judicial review of the state of emergency governor's administrative decisions is permitted.

As a result of an initiative by a coalition party M.P., seven soldiers being held by the PKK were released in November and December to a delegation that included their relatives and human rights activists. A prosecutor dropped charges that the members of the delegation were collaborating with the PKK during an earlier, unsuccessful effort to obtain the soldiers' release.

Although schools have remained open in most urban centers, in the southeast, rapid migration has led to severe overcrowding of schools and chronic teacher shortages. The PKK policy of murdering teachers exacerbated the situation (see Section 1.a.). Government officials claim that a significant effort is being made both to reopen schools and to build new schools in regions faced with acute overcrowding. For the 1995–96 school year, according to the Foreign Ministry, of 6,244 primary schools in the southeast, 3,455 are open, and 3,820 secondary schools are open.

In 1996 Turkish ground forces with air support conducted several preemptive operations into northern Iraq. These incursions, carried out by units of 1,000 to 2,000 men, were designed to destroy PKK infrastructure and to disrupt PKK supply lines. The most recent operation commenced December 31 and lasted 6 days (see Iraq report).

Section 2. Respect for Civil Liberties, Including:

a. *Freedom of Speech and Press.*—The Constitution provides for freedom of speech and the press; however, the Government continued to limit these freedoms. The Criminal Code provides penalties for those who "insult the President, the Parliament, and the army." Numerous other provisions in various laws restrict freedom of expression to one degree or another; those most frequently employed include Article 8 of the Anti-Terror Law and Article 312 of the Criminal Code that forbids "incitement to racial or ethnic emnity." Judges generally examine evidence rigorously and dismiss many charges brought under these laws.

In 1995 the Anti-Terror Law was amended by adding a retroactive intent clause to the article that prohibits dissemination of separatist propaganda. According to the Foreign Ministry, that change led to the judicial review of thousands of cases, resulting in the release of 143 prisoners in 1995 and an additional 126 prisoners by mid-November. Sentences were reduced over this period for another 1,408 prisoners.

Domestic and foreign periodicals providing a broad spectrum of views and opinions are widely available. Government censorship of foreign periodicals is very rare.

While the overall readership of the local press is not large for a country of 60 million, the newspaper business is intensely competitive and the product often sensationalist.

The electronic media reach nearly every adult, and their influence is correspondingly great. Radio and television have experienced explosive growth in the 5 years since privately owned broadcasting has been allowed: as of October, over 229 local, 15 regional, and 15 national television stations were registered, and 1,058 local, 108 regional, and 36 national radio stations were registered. Another 260 television stations and 1,202 radio stations have applied for broadcast licenses. Other television and radio stations broadcast without an official license. In 1994 Parliament passed regulatory legislation making it illegal for broadcasters to threaten the country's unity or national security and limiting the private broadcast of television programs in languages other than Turkish. The increasing availability of satellite dishes and cable television allows access to foreign broadcasts, including several Turkish-language private channels. Internet use is growing and faces no government restrictions.

Despite the restrictions noted, the media frequently criticizes government leaders and policies. Turkish media coverage of the situation in the southeast tended to be unreliable, underreporting it in some instances and sensationalizing it in others. Government Decree 430 requires self-censorship of all news reporting from or about the southeast and, upon the request of the regional governor, gives the Interior Ministry the authority to ban distribution of any news viewed as misrepresenting events in the region. In the event that such a government warning is not obeyed, the Decree provides for a 10-day suspension of operations for a first offense and 30 days for subsequent offenses.

The Press Law permits prosecutors to seek a court order for the confiscation of a newspaper or magazine and requires that each publication's "responsible editors" bear legal responsibility for the publication's content. Many editors have faced repeated criminal proceedings. Ismail Besikci served 10 years in prison between 1971 and 1987 for his publications on the Kurdish situation in Turkey. He now has been in prison since November 1993 on a variety of new charges based upon his ongoing articles on Kurdish issues. In August he was remanded to Istanbul's Metris prison to serve out his latest sentence. SSC prosecutors ordered the confiscation of numerous issues of leftist, Kurdish nationalist, and pro-PKK periodicals, although most continue to publish. The pro-PKK newspaper Ozgur Ulke and its successor Yeni Politika were both closed by court order in 1995. A successor, Demokrasi, which began publishing in December 1995, is available.

According to the Turkish Journalists' Association, during the year 109 issues of newspapers and magazines and 8 books' press runs were confiscated on court order. These numbers are down significantly from 1995 when 1,443 publications (56 books, 784 journals, 602 newspapers, and 1 bulletin) were similarly confiscated. Forty newspapers and magazines were shut down for some period during the year, including the leftist daily Evrensel, which was ordered closed four times early in the year for publishing issues that the Government claimed "incited hatred" or "promoted racism."

Individual journalists are subject to harassment and police violence. At various times 135 journalists were detained. The Committee to Protect Journalists (CPJ) has documented 14 arbitrary detentions. Eleven journalists were formally arrested. The CPJ reports 19 instances where journalists were physically assaulted by police while practicing their profession. One journalist was reportedly kidnaped during the year.

Sanar Yurdatapan, a well-known musician and spokesman for freedom of expression, was arrested on October 17 and charged with "aiding members of an armed organization" (the PKK) when he participated in a discussion on the PKK-associated MED-TV and signed a statement condemning a reported assassination attempt against the PKK leader, despite the fact that Yurdatapan has also publicly denounced the aims and methods of the PKK. He was released on November 11 when the Ankara SSC claimed that it did not have jurisdiction to prosecute him. His case is now pending review in Istanbul.

In 1995 the Istanbul SSC charged prominent Turkish novelist Yasar Kemal in connection with the article, "Black Sky Over Turkey," which he published in a German news magazine, and later reprinted in Turkey in a book entitled "Freedom of Expression." In it, Kemal accused the Turkish Government of waging a "campaign of lies" in its comprehensive censorship of reporting on the Kurdish question. Kemal was charged both under Article 8 of the Anti-Terror Law and under Article 312 of the Criminal Code for "inciting to racial or ethnic enmity." The court acquitted Kemal in December 1995, finding that he had no intent to promote separatism or racial enmity, but he was tried again and convicted in March on virtually the same charge. He was fined and given a 20-month suspended sentence, which he appealed; his appeal was denied in October. The 99 writers originally being tried for their involvement with the same book have been joined by many others. Currently, 1,000 individuals are involved. The case against them continued at year's end as testimony is being collected.

In May author Turgut Inal was acquitted of charges under Article 159/3 of the Criminal Code for "insulting the laws of the Turkish Republic" in his article "We Protect Human Rights with an Imperfect Constitution and Laws." The entire board of directors of the HRF, which published Inal's article in a book entitled "A Present to Emil Galip Sandalci," also was acquitted (see Section 4).

In August a Kurdish former M.P. from Erzurum, Abdulmelik Firat, was brought to trial for calling the Turkish Parliament the "most useless and characterless institution (in Turkey)" during an interview. On September 29, Firat was acquitted of the charges. A book that Firat wrote, however, was confiscated as separatist propaganda in September on orders of the Istanbul SSC prosecutor. HRA deputy secretary general Erol Anar, who wrote a book entitled "History of Human Rights," was charged in August by SSC prosecutors with disseminating separatist propaganda. At the request of the defense, the trial was moved from Ankara to Istanbul and was set to resume in February 1997.

In October Ertugrul Kurkcu and Ayse Nur Zarakolu, respectively the translator and publisher of a November 1995 report by the Human Rights Watch arms project, "Weapons Transfers and Violations of the Laws of War in Turkey," were charged under Article 159 of the Turkish Penal Code for "defaming the state's security and military forces." In December the prosecution decided to focus its case on only one section of the translated report, an unconfirmed comment attributed by HRW to an unnamed U.S. official describing police special counterinsurgency forces as "thugs." The trial is set to resume in February 1997.

Seven pro-Kurdish former DEP M.P.'s and one independent M.P., convicted in 1994 on charges ranging from disseminating separatist propaganda to supporting or being a member of an armed band or gang, appealed their sentences in 1995. The 15-year sentences of four of the defendants for being members of a terrorist group were upheld; they are appealing their case to the European Commission on Human Rights. The court overturned the sentences of the other four in 1995, but they were retried and found guilty in April on the reformed Article 8 charges. In September the Court upheld these sentences on appeal. These four defendants also plan to appeal to the European Commission of Human Rights; the Government pledged to abide by its decision.

In December the Ankara SSC prosecutor charged Mehmet Sever, Mahmut Uyanik, and Muzaffer Demir, former DEP M.P.'s, with assisting the PKK. The charges stem from a 1991 incident during which the accused publicly termed the parliamentary swearing-in oath as "racist, chauvinistic, antidemocratic, and a violation of human rights." Additionally, during the swearing-in ceremony the three defendants wore handkerchiefs in colors associated with the PKK. This new trial is apparently unrelated to the earlier DEP trials. The three defendants left the DEP party prior to its being banned in 1994 and remained in Parliament as independents until their terms expired in 1995. Until that time, they had parliamentary immunity and could not be tried for alleged offenses. The delay of a year between the end of the defendants' terms in Parliament and the bringing of charges is not considered unusually long, given the sensitive nature of the case. If convicted, they could face prison terms ranging from 4 to 7½ years.

The Government prosecuted 41 members of the pro-Kurdish People's Democracy Party (HADEP), including party chairman Murat Bozlak, based on an incident at the party's June 23 convention in Ankara, in which the Turkish flag was torn down and replaced by a PKK banner. The accused face minimum sentences ranging between 12 and 22½ years, and the party itself may be declared illegal (as were two of its predecessors). Of the 43 defendants, 16 remain in custody. Hearings were held in September, October, November, and December, and the trial is set to resume on an undetermined date. The chief judge has denied a defense motion for acquittal and refused requests for the release of the defendants. Following the party's convention, three party members were murdered by unknown assailants, and party offices were bombed.

In 1995 independent M.P. Hasan Mezarci was charged with insulting modern Turkey's founder, Kemal Ataturk, but the criminal court dropped the charges. Following this decision, Mezarci again was brought to court in January on similar charges, had his parliamentary immunity lifted, and was sentenced to 18 months in prison. In August the new verdict was upheld by the appeals court. Mezarci left the country and a warrant was issued for his arrest. He returned on December 26 and was arrested. Press reports indicate that he is being held at Istanbul's Metris prison.

Although the 5-month sentences of well-known journalist Mehmet Ali Birand and two other journalists for "harming the image of the military" were overturned in 1995 by the military court of appeals, they were retried in early 1996 on the same charges. The military court of appeals again overturned the sentences in June. According to current law, Birand may be retried one more time on the same charges.

Kurdish-language cassettes and publications on Kurdish subjects continued to be widely available, although suppression continued. The Kurdish-language weekly, Welate Me, continued to be available. Some potential customers are afraid to purchase Kurdish-language materials because possession of such items may be interpreted as evidence of PKK sympathies. Kurdish-language broadcasts are still illegal. Can-TV, a private station based in the southeast, broadcasts Kurdish-language music from a list of songs approved by security officials. In August police raided Can-TV offices during a live Turkish-language broadcast of a panel discussion on "Peace and the Kurdish Issue." The detainees were released within 2 days of the raid, and no charges were filed. Pro-PKK Med TV, based in Belgium and England, broadcasts via Intelsat and can be received by satellite dish in the southeast.

In February there was a large conference in Istanbul entitled "The Kurdish Problem and a Democratic Solution," which was attended by academics, human rights monitors, politicians, and labor leaders. The conference highlighted the growing visibility of these issues and the increasing discussion of the Kurdish issue in a democratic context. University professor Dogu Ergil continued throughout the year to publish articles and papers on the Kurdish issue without government interference.

Until 1995 the Constitution and the law governing political parties proscribed student and faculty associations and labor union involvement in political activities. Constitutional amendments passed by Parliament in 1995 provided for participation in political activities by students age 18 years or older and professors. No implementing legislation has been passed. Nonetheless, some students have been politically active.

Academic freedom is respected.

b. *Freedom of Peaceful Assembly and Association.*—The Constitution provides for freedom of assembly, but authorities may deny permission if they believe the gathering is likely to disrupt public order. Prior notification of gatherings is required, and the authorities may restrict meetings to designated sites.

Police committed serious abuses during crowd control situations. A May Day demonstration in Istanbul, attended by as many as 10,000 people, including hundreds of members of illegal leftist and Kurdish organizations, turned violent and resulted in some looting, destruction of stores, and armed clashes with the police. Police handled the demonstration very poorly and shot three demonstrators to death, in reaction to the serious beating of a police officer by rioting demonstrators. At the end of the rioting, 89 people were wounded (including 52 police officers) and 354 were arrested. Although complaints of excessive use of force were made against the police, none was prosecuted.

On November 6, university students took to the streets to protest the Higher Education Council's control over student life and academic curricula. Protests in Istanbul, Ankara, and Balikesir turned violent, and according to eyewitnesses and the media, police used excessive force to disperse the crowds. In Istanbul 545 students reportedly were detained, and 7 students and 3 police were wounded. In Ankara approximately 100 students were detained and 7 wounded. Nearly all students were released within 48 hours.

The Constitution provides for freedom of association, but associations and foundations must submit their charters for government approval, a lengthy and cumbersome process.

c. *Freedom of Religion.*—The Constitution establishes Turkey as a secular state and provides for freedom of belief, freedom of worship, and private dissemination of religious ideas. The Government generally observed these provisions in practice. About 99 percent of the population is Muslim. Under the law, religious services may take place only in designated places of worship.

Although Turkey is a secular state, religious instruction in state schools is compulsory for Muslims. Upon written verification of their non-Muslim background, Lausanne Treaty minorities (Greek, Armenian, and Jewish) are exempted by law from Muslim religious instruction, although students who wish to attend may do so with parental consent. Syriac Christians are not officially exempt because they are not an official Lausanne Treaty minority. However, according to a church official, because the community is mentioned in the Treaty, its members have not been forced to follow any specific curriculum.

Turkey's Alawi Muslim minority (an offshoot of Shi'ite Islam) is estimated to number at least 12 million. There are, however, no government-salaried Alawi religious leaders, in contrast to Sunni religious leaders, and no Religious Affairs Directorate funds go to the Alawi community. Some Alawis allege discrimination in the form of failure to include any Alawi doctrines or beliefs in religious instruction classes. Alawis are disgruntled by what they regard as the Sunni bias in the Religious Affairs Directorate and the Directorate's tendency to view the Alawis as a cultural group rather than religious group.

Many prosecutors regard proselytizing and religious activism on the part of either Islamic extremists or evangelical Christians with suspicion, especially when they deem such activities to have political overtones. Since there is no law explicitly prohibiting proselytizing, police sometimes arrest Islamic extremists and evangelical Christians for disturbing the peace. Courts usually dismiss such charges. If the prosyletizers are foreigners, they may be deported, but generally they are able to reenter the country easily.

Twice this year the armed forces dismissed groups of soldiers for prohibited religious and political activities. Some of these soldiers have indicated that they will bring their cases to the European Court of Human Rights.

Most religious minorities are concentrated in Istanbul. The number of Christians in the south has been declining as the younger Syriac generation leaves for Europe and North America. Minority religions not recognized under the Lausanne Treaty may not acquire additional property for churches. The Catholic Church in Ankara, for example, is confined to diplomatic property. The State must approve the operation of churches, monasteries, synagogues, schools, and charitable religious foundations, such as hospitals and orphanages.

The Government formed in July has sought a more cooperative relationship with religious minorities, particularly in Istanbul, according to prominent members of these communities. The state ministry responsible for the religious minority communities gave the Armenian Patriarchate permission to rebuild a church in Anatolia and informed the Patriarchate that requests to restore some other properties would be approved immediately. These requests have all been approved without delay.

The authorities monitor the activities of Eastern Orthodox churches and their affiliated operations. The Ecumenical Patriarchate in Istanbul has consistently expressed interest in reopening the seminary on the island of Halki in the Sea of Marmara. The seminary has been closed since the 1970's when the state nationalized most private institutions of higher learning.

Bureaucratic procedures relating to historic preservation impede repairs to some religious facilities. Under the law, religious buildings that become "extinct" (because of prolonged absence of clergy or lay persons to staff local religious councils or for lack of adherents) revert to government possession. Some non-Muslim minorities, particularly the Greek Orthodox and, to a lesser extent, the shrinking Armenian Orthodox and Jewish communities, are faced with the danger of losing some of their houses of worship.

d. *Freedom of Movement Within the Country, Foreign Travel, Emigration, and Repatriation.*—Citizens generally enjoy freedom of movement domestically and the freedom to travel abroad. The Constitution provides that a citizen's freedom to leave may be restricted only in the case of a national emergency, civic obligations (military service, for example), or criminal investigation or prosecution. The overseas travel $100 departure tax was repealed in March, spurring a boom in foreign travel.

Travel in the southeast often is restricted for security reasons. Roadblocks, set up by both security forces and the PKK, can seriously impede travel in the region. The PKK, in an effort to draw attention to its cause, kidnaped foreign tourists and other travelers in the region for short periods.

When Turkey ratified the 1951 United Nations Convention Relating to the Status of Refugees, it exercised the option of accepting the convention's obligations only with respect to refugees from Europe. It has not subsequently lifted the geographic limitation of its treaty obligation. As a result, the Government does not recognize non-European asylum seekers as refugees and requires that they register with the authorities within 5 days of entering the country. The Government screens these applicants, determines those that it considers bona fide, and then refers them to the U.N. High Commissioner for Refugees (UNHCR). It provides only very limited first asylum opportunities designed to allow non-European applicants time to process for onward resettlement. A negative decision usually leads to immediate expulsion. The UNHCR representative and foreign diplomats in Ankara continued to protest the turning back of Iranian and Iraqi asylum seekers, many of whom claimed religious persecution in their home countries. Since Turkey implemented new asylum regulations in 1994, more than 150 Iranians and Iraqi UNHCR-recognized asylum seekers were forcibly returned to their countries.

The Government declined numerous offers from the UNHCR to assist in establishing reception centers for undocumented asylum seekers in key border areas. The offer included funding and training for officers conducting interviews.

At the end of the year, Turkey facilitated the humanitarian evacuation from northern Iraq and immediate transit to the United States of some 6,700 employees and Iraqi political oppositionists who faced potential persecution.

Due to the cessation of fighting in the former Yugoslavia, the number of Bosnian refugees in Turkey decreased significantly. At year's end, it was estimated that fewer than 5,000 refugees remained, down from a peak of 15,000 to 20,000 in the early 1990's. As "guests" there is no restriction on the period that they are allowed to remain. They are not allowed to work or attend school; however, many do.

Section 3. Respect for Political Rights: The Right of Citizens to Change Their Government

The Constitution provides citizens with the right to change their government peacefully, and citizens exercise this right in practice. Turkey has a multiparty parliamentary system, in which national elections are held at least every 5 years on the basis of mandatory universal suffrage for all citizens 18 years of age and over. As of October, there were at least 30 political parties, 7 of which were represented in Parliament. The Grand National Assembly (Parliament) elects the President as head of state every 7 years or when the incumbent becomes incapacitated or dies.

The Government neither coerces nor forbids membership in any political organization, although the Constitutional Court may close down political parties for unconstitutional activities. In March the Court closed down the tiny pro-Kurdish Democracy and Transformation Party (DDP) on these grounds.

There are no restrictions in law against women or minorities voting or participating in politics. The Constitution calls for equal political rights for men and women. There were 13 women in the 550-seat Parliament. In addition to Deputy Prime Minister Ciller, there were three other female ministers. Some political parties now recruit female delegates for their party conferences and electoral lists. Women's committees are active within political party organizations.

Section 4. Governmental Attitude Regarding International and Nongovernmental Investigation of Alleged Violations of Human Rights

The nongovernmental Human Rights Association has branches in 50 provincial capitals. The HRA claims a membership of about 17,000. HRA branches in the southeast, closed at different times in 1994 and 1995 by the authorities, were reopened; nonetheless, periodic harassment continued. In March Adana's then acting provincial governor shut down the local HRA for a period of 15 days on the grounds that it possessed "illegal publications." As of October, HRA branches in the southeast were operating in Diyarbakir, Adiyaman, Malatya, Mardin, and Sanliurfa. HRA branches in Batman and Hakkari remain closed by the authorities.

In 1990 HRA established the Human Rights Foundation, which operates torture rehabilitation centers in Ankara, Izmir, Istanbul, and Adana and serves as a clearinghouse for human rights information. Other domestic nongovernmental organizations include the Istanbul-based Helsinki Citizens Assembly, the Ankara-based Turkish Democracy Foundation, human rights centers at a number of universities, and the Islamist-oriented Mazlum Der, the Association of Human Rights and Solidarity for Oppressed Peoples.

Government agents have harassed human rights monitors as well as lawyers and doctors involved in documenting human rights violations. According to a 1996 report by the Lawyers' Committee for Human Rights, "there is a close connection between the Turkish Government's hostility toward those who expose human rights violations, and its attacks on the integrity of the legal profession, and the persistence of severe human rights problems." Some human rights monitors have been aggressively prosecuted. Turgut Inal and members of the board of directors of the HRF were acquitted of criminal charges brought against them in 1995 for the publication of a book entitled "A Gift to Emil Galip Sandalci" (see Section 2.a.).

In May Mustafa Cinkilic, the Adana HRF representative, and Dr. Tufan Kose, who operated one of the HRF centers for the treatment of victims of torture, were charged with operating an unlawful health center. The case is scheduled to resume in February 1997. Similar charges had been leveled against the operators of the other HRF torture treatment centers. Charges in Izmir and Ankara were dropped; in Istanbul, the criminal court found that insufficient evidence had been presented to warrant the charges, and the defendant was acquitted.

In May Dr. Seyfettin Kizilkan, director of Diyarbakir's state insurance hospital and president of the southeast region's chamber of doctors was arrested after police allegedly found bomb materials and PKK documents in his home. In June the

Diyarbakir SSC sentenced him to a 3-year, 9-month prison term. His family and local activists allege that the police planted the evidence. Kizilkan is free pending an appeal. In May the Diyarbakir SSC acquitted the HRA representative in Hakkari, Abdulkerim Demirer, who was on trial for being a member of a terrorist organization.

In December the Ankara SSC acquitted HRA head Akin Birdal, Mardin HRA branch head Cemil Aydoagn, and Ihsan Aslan, Vice President of the Islamist human rights group Mazlum Der, of charges that they had collaborated with the terrorist PKK. The three men, together with Refah party M.P. Fethullah Erbas, had sought the release of seven Turkish soldiers being held captive by the PKK. (Erbas had parliamentary immunity and so was not charged.) The soldiers were eventually released.

Since 1991 Parliament has convened a Human Rights Commission. The Commission is authorized to oversee compliance with the human rights provisions of domestic law and international agreements to which Turkey is a signatory, investigate alleged abuses, and prepare reports. Previously underfunded and lacking the power to subpoena witnesses or documents, the Commission this year has asserted itself. It was instrumental in pressing for criminal charges against 68 security personnel for excessive use of force in the killing of 10 prison inmates in Diyarbakir.

Representatives of diplomatic missions who wish to monitor human rights are free to speak with private citizens. However, security police usually place such visitors in the southeast and the east under visible surveillance, intimidating those they meet.

Section 5. Discrimination Based on Race, Sex, Religion, Disability, Language, or Social Status

The Constitution proclaims Turkey to be a secular state, regards all citizens as equal, and prohibits discrimination on ethnic, religious, or racial grounds. Discrimination nevertheless remains a problem in several areas. The Government officially recognizes only those religious minorities mentioned in the Treaty of Lausanne (1923), which guarantees the rights of Eastern Orthodox, Armenian Apostolic, and Jewish adherents.

Women.—Spousal abuse is serious and widespread. However, it is still considered an extremely private matter, involving societal notions of family honor. Few women go to the police, who in any case are reluctant to intervene in domestic disputes and frequently advise women to return to their husbands. Turks of either sex may file civil or criminal charges but rarely do so. Laws and ingrained societal notions make it difficult to prosecute sexual assault or rape cases. Penalties may legally be reduced if a woman was not a virgin prior to a rape, or if a judge deems the woman to have acted provocatively.

During the year, a series of high-profile "honor murders"—the killing of women who are suspected of being unchaste—in rural areas or among recent immigrants to cities, has focused attention on some of the inequalities in the legal code as it applies to women. In one case, 16-year-old Sevda Gok was murdered by her family because she allegedly dishonored them by behaving too independently and consorting with boys. Often family members refuse to press charges and task minor family members with the actual killings. In this case, Gok's 14-year-old cousin did so and was sentenced to only 2 years in jail for the crime. The two men who held Sevda Gok down were never identified.

According to the Prime Ministry's Family Research Institute, beating is one of the most frequent forms of violence against women in the home. New figures were not available for 1996, but in the past the Institute has noted complaints of beatings, threats, economic pressure, and sexual violence.

There are several shelters for battered women, and at least two consultation centers—Istanbul's Purple Roof Foundation and Ankara's Altindag center city shelter. New NGO's have been formed to address women's issues, including honor murders.

The Civil Code, which prohibits granting gender-based privileges or rights, retains some discriminatory provisions concerning marital rights and obligations. Because the husband is the legal head of household, the wife automatically acquires the husband's surname with marriage; the husband is authorized to choose the domicile and represents the conjugal unit. As parents, husband and wife exercise joint child rearing rights, but when they disagree, the husband's view often prevails. Women's groups have lobbied to change this provision. A single woman who gives birth to a child out-of-wedlock is not considered automatically to be the legal guardian of her child. A court decision may be required. Divorce law requires that the divorcing spouses divide their property according to property registered in each spouse's name. Because in most cases property is registered in the husband's name, this can create difficulties for women who wish to divorce. Under inheritance laws, a widow generally receives one-fourth of the estate, her children the rest. There are reliable reports that under the current Government, female judges have been shifted from courtroom to administrative jobs.

The literacy rate for women has been revised upward to approximately 79 percent. Particularly in urban areas, women continue to improve their position, including in the professions, business, and the civil service, although they continue to face discrimination to varying degrees. Numerous women have become lawyers, doctors, and engineers since the 1960's. Women make up between 43 and 50 percent of the work force. They generally receive equal pay for equal work in the professions, business, and civil service jobs, although a large percentage of women employed in agriculture and in the trade, restaurant, and hotel sectors work as unpaid family help. Women may take the examination required to become a subgovernor. Several have been appointed subgovernors; one governor is a woman.

Independent women's groups and women's rights associations exist and are growing, but the concept of lobbying for women's rights is still in its infancy.

Children.—The Government is committed to furthering children's welfare and works to expand opportunities in education and health, including further reduction of the infant mortality rate. The State Minister for Women's and Family Issues oversees implementation of the Government's programs for children. Education for children is mandatory and government-provided through fifth grade, or the age of 10. Traditional family values in rural areas place a greater emphasis on advanced education for sons than for daughters. Far fewer girls than boys continue their education after primary school.

Children have suffered greatly from the cycle of violence in the southeast. The migration—forced or voluntary—of many families, terrorism against teachers, and school closings in the southeast have uprooted children to cities that are hard pressed to find the resources to extend basic, mandatory services such as schooling. Many cities in the southeast are operating schools on double shifts, with as many as 100 students per classroom (see Section 1.g.). The Government is establishing regional boarding schools to help combat this problem, but these are insufficient. In practice, in rural Anatolia and the southeast, the literacy rate for girls is very low, and many do not complete primary school. The literacy rate for boys, most of whom complete primary school, is higher. Some continue on to middle and high school, for which they generally must travel or live away from home.

Instances of child beating and abuse are more frequently reported than in previous years, according to women's groups. The increase may be attributable to greater public awareness of the problem.

People With Disabilities.—Legislation dealing with the disabled is piecemeal, and there is little legislation regarding accessibility for the disabled. Certain categories of employers are required to hire disabled persons as 2 percent of their employee pool, although there is no penalty for failure to comply.

Religious Minorities.—Extremist groups target minority communities from time to time. According to press reports, during an anti-Israel demonstration in October, Refah party officials in Ankara declared Jews to be the enemies of Muslims. Refah party journals also frequently publish anti-Semitic diatribes.

During the last few years, there have been instances of graffiti, stones tossed over the walls, and press attacks on the Ecumenical Patriarchate and the Patriarch. On September 30, a hand grenade was thrown over the wall of the Ecumenical Patriarchate compound in Istanbul causing minor damage. On December 17, a small pipe bomb exploded at St. Anthony's Catholic Church in Istanbul. The police responded promptly in both cases and are investigating the incidents. The Armenian Patriarchate also reported incidents of harassment against Armenian churches in Istanbul, and church officials complain of growing encroachment by certain Muslim extremist groups on lands belonging to the Armenian community, especially on the Princes' Islands in the Sea of Marmara. The police have responded with intensified security measures.

All religious minority groups fear the possibility of rising Islamic extremism.

National/Racial/Ethnic Minorities.—The Constitution does not recognize the Kurds as a national, racial, or ethnic minority. There are no legal barriers to ethnic Kurds' participation in political and economic affairs, but Kurds who publicly or politically assert their Kurdish ethnic identity risk harassment or prosecution. Some M.P.'s and senior officials and many professionals are ethnic Kurds. Kurds who are long-term residents in industrialized cities in western Turkey have been for the most part assimilated into the political, economic, and social life of the nation, and there has been much intermarriage over many generations. Kurds who are currently migrating westward (including those displaced by the conflict in the southeast) bring with them their culture and village identity, but often little education and few skills; many simply are not well prepared for urban life.

The 1991 repeal of the law prohibiting publications or communications in Kurdish legalized private spoken and printed communications in Kurdish. Under the law on political parties, however, all discussion that takes place at political meetings must be in Turkish. Kurdish may be used only in "nonpolitical communication." Materials dealing with Kurdish history, culture, and ethnic identity continue to be subject to confiscation and prosecution under the "indivisible unity of the state" provisions of the Anti-Terror Law (see Section 2.a.).

The Ministry of Education tightly controls the curriculum in foreign-language schools. Many Greek-origin students report difficulty in continuing their education in Turkey and go to Greece, often never to return.

The Romani population is extremely small, and there were no reported incidents of public or government harassment directed against them.

Section 6. Worker Rights

a. *The Right of Association.*—Workers have the right to associate freely and form representative unions, except police and military personnel. Constitutional amendments in 1995 gave civil servants, including schoolteachers, the right to form legally recognized unions; however, implementing legislation has not yet been enacted. (Even prior to passage, civil servants' unions existed and worked for legal recognition, collective bargaining, and the right to strike through demonstrations and 1-day work stoppages.) Parliament added language to Article 53 of the Constitution stipulating that civil servants' unions could bring cases to court on behalf of members, carry out collective talks with the Government to secure their objectives, and sign an understanding with the Government if agreement is reached. The amendment language did not mention strikes.

The Constitution stipulates that no one shall be compelled to become or remain a member of, or withdraw from, a labor union. The law states that unions and confederations may be founded without prior authorization based on a petition to the governor of the province of the prospective union's headquarters. Although unions are independent of the Government and political parties, they must have government permission to hold meetings or rallies and must allow police to attend conventions and record the proceedings. The Constitution requires candidates for union office to have worked 10 years in the industry represented by the union. Slightly over 12 percent of the total civilian labor force (15 years old and above) is unionized. There are three confederations of labor unions: the Turkish Confederation of Workers Unions (Turk-Is), the Confederation of Turkish Real Trade Unions (Hak-Is), and the Confederation of Revolutionary Workers Unions (DISK). Unions and their officers have a statutory right to express views on issues directly affecting members' economic and social interests.

Prosecutors may ask labor courts to order a trade union or confederation to suspend its activities or to go into liquidation for serious infractions, based on alleged violation of specific legal norms. The Government, however, may not summarily dissolve a union.

The right to strike, while provided for in the Constitution, is partially restricted. For example, workers engaged in the protection of life and property and those in the mining and petroleum industries, sanitation services, national defense, and education do not have the right to strike.

Collective bargaining is required before a strike. The law specifies the steps a union must take before it may strike or before an employer may engage in a lockout. Nonbinding mediation is the last of those steps. A party that fails to comply with these steps forfeits its rights. The employer may respond to a strike with a lockout but is prohibited from hiring strikebreakers or using administrative personnel to perform jobs normally done by strikers. Article 42 of Law 2822, governing collective bargaining, strikes, and lockouts, prohibits the employer from terminating workers who encourage or participate in a legal strike. Unions are forbidden to engage in secondary (solidarity), political or general strikes, or in slowdowns. In sectors in which strikes are prohibited, disputes are resolved through binding arbitration.

The Government has the statutory power under Law 2822 to suspend strikes for 60 days for reasons of national security or public health and safety. Unions may petition the Council of State to lift such a suspension. If this appeal fails, and the parties and mediators still fail to resolve the dispute, it is subject to compulsory arbitration at the end of the 60-day period. The International Labor Organization's (ILO) Committee of Experts and the Committee on the Application of Standards regard the Government's application of the law as too broad and have called on the Government to limit the application of the law and recourse to compulsory arbitration to essential services in the strict sense of the term. The Government asserts that the law does not contradict the committees' principles.

During the first 7 months of 1996, there were 31 strikes involving 1,160 workers, which resulted in approximately 114,010 lost work days. During the same period there were 2 lockouts involving 660 workers, resulting in 69,564 lost work days. No strikes or strike decisions were suspended by the first or second coalition governments since their formation following the December 24, 1995, general elections.

In some instances labor union members have been the subject of government limits on freedom of speech and assembly (see sections 2.a. and 2.b.). Implementing legislation for certain provisions of constitutional amendments, to permit the legal unionization of the civil service, has not yet been enacted. However, some civil service organizations continued to demonstrate for the right to strike and for higher salary. In response to these protests, the Ankara public prosecutor's office initiated two separate court cases against Turk-Is in 1995, charging that August 8 and September 20 demonstrations held by Turk-Is in Ankara to protest the deadlock in collective bargaining negotiations were illegal. In the first case, the public prosecutor demanded prison terms for the Turk-Is officials of a minimum of 6 months in accordance with Article 72 of Law 2822. In the second case, the prosecutor's office accused Turk-Is management of violating the associations law when it announced its support for opposition parties before the 1995 general elections. The trials began in the Ankara court of first instance on June 21. The Turk-Is president stated in his defense that he and other officials actually calmed down the workers during the demonstrations. Judicial officials postponed the trials to a later date to hear the testimony of other Turk-Is officials who were not present at the first trial.

With government approval, unions may and do form or join confederations and international labor bodies, as long as these organizations are not hostile to Turkey or to freedom of religion or belief. The International Confederation of Free Trade Unions (ICFTU) approved DISK as an affiliate in 1992. Hak-Is applied for ICFTU affiliation in 1993; however, its application has been held up by the international labor federation due to opposition expressed by Turk-Is, a longstanding member of the ICFTU. The application is still pending.

b. *The Right to Organize and Bargain Collectively.*—All industrial workers have the right to organize and bargain collectively, and most industrial activity and some public sector agricultural activities are organized. The law requires that, in order to become a bargaining agent, a union must represent not only 50 percent plus one of the employees at a given work site, but also 10 percent of all the workers in that particular industry. This 10 percent barrier has the effect of favoring established unions, particularly those affiliated with Turk-Is, the confederation that represents nearly 80 percent of organized labor.

The ILO has called on Turkey to rescind this 10 percent rule. Both Turk-Is and the Turkish employers' organization favor retention of the rule, however. The Government informed the ILO Committee on the Application of Standards that the Ministry of Labor and Social Security proposed to remove the 10 percent numerical restriction and that it had communicated its proposal to the social partners. The ILO took note of the Government's statement that it continued to study removal of this requirement despite objections from employer and worker organizations.

The law on trade unions stipulates that an employer may not dismiss a labor union representative without rightful cause. The union member may appeal such a dismissal to the courts, and if the ruling is in the union member's favor, the employer must reinstate him and pay all back benefits and salary. These laws are generally applied in practice.

In November thousands of teachers staged a protest march in Ankara to demand better treatment and salaries, better working conditions, and "cessation of exile to remote areas of the country of teachers who engage in union activities." Minister of Education Mehmet Saglam said that the Ministry of Labor had begun reviewing the government prohibition of teachers' gaining union rights and pledged to examine the cases of teachers who had been punished for union activity.

c. *Prohibition of Forced or Compulsory Labor.*—The Constitution and statutes prohibit compulsory labor. The laws are enforced.

d. *Minimum Age for Employment of Children.*—The Constitution and labor laws forbid employment of children younger than age 15, with the exception that those 13 and 14 years of age may engage in light part-time work if enrolled in school or vocational training. The Constitution also prohibits children from engaging in physically demanding jobs such as underground mining and from working at night. The Ministry of Labor effectively enforces these laws only in the organized industrial sector.

In practice many children work because families need the supplementary income. An informal system provides work for young boys at low wages, for example, in auto repair shops. Girls are rarely seen working in public, but many are kept out of school to work in handicrafts, especially in rural areas. The bulk of child labor occurs in rural areas and is often associated with traditional family economic activity such as farming or animal husbandry. It is common for entire families to work together to bring in the crop during the harvest.

The Government has recognized the problem of child labor and has been working with the ILO to define its dimensions and to determine solutions. The Ministry of Labor, the Ankara municipality, the Turk-Is labor confederation, and the Turkish Employers Association are among the institutions participating in the ILO's International Program on the Elimination of Child Labor (IPEC), a project to solve the problems of working children. The Ministry of Labor and the ILO have jointly produced a study showing that almost one-half (44 percent) of the children working in Turkey are below the age of 15, are paid less than the minimum wage, and have no insurance.

According to a study conducted by the Turk-Is child workers bureau released in September, for every 100 workers, 32 were between the ages of 6 and 19. Children employed at work sites and homes constitute 5 percent of the total working population and were mostly employed in the metal, shoe, woodworking, and agricultural sectors. The young workers employed on a monthly or daily wage payment basis worked over 40 hours a week, and those employed at home and not receiving a wage payment worked less than 40 hours per week. The study said that 56 percent of these workers were uninsured. It added that the total number of working young people between the ages of 12 and 19 was 3.5 million, and 45 percent of them were under the age of 16.

e. *Acceptable Conditions of Work.*—The Labor Ministry is legally obliged to set minimum wages at least every 2 years through a minimum wage board, a tripartite government-industry-union body. In recent years, it has done so annually. In August the nominal minimum wage was increased by approximately 101 percent over the year before. The monthly gross minimum wage rates, which became effective on September 1, are approximately $200 (tl 17,010,000) for workers older than 16 years of age and about $170 (tl 14,400,000) for workers under the age of 16.

It would be difficult for a single worker, and impossible for a family, to live on the minimum wage without support from other sources. Most workers earn considerably more. Workers covered by the labor law, who constitute about one-third of the total labor force, also receive a hot meal or a daily food allowance and other fringe benefits which, according to the Turkish Employers' Association, make basic wages alone account for only about 37 percent of total remuneration.

Labor law sets a 45-hour workweek, although most unions have bargained for fewer hours. The law prescribes a weekly rest day and limits the number of overtime hours to 3 a day for up to 90 days in a year. The Labor Inspectorate of the Ministry of Labor effectively enforces wage and hour provision in the unionized industrial, service, and government sectors, which cover about 12 percent of workers.

Occupational health and safety regulations are mandated by law, but the Government has not carried out an effective inspection and enforcement program. Law 1475 sets out procedures under which workers may remove themselves from hazardous conditions without risking loss of employment. The law also allows for the shutdown of an operation if a five-man committee, which includes safety inspectors, employee, and employer representatives, determines that the operation endangers workers' lives. In practice, financial constraints, limited safety awareness, carelessness, and fatalistic attitudes result in scant attention to occupational safety and health by workers and employers alike.

TURKMENISTAN

Turkmenistan, a one-party state dominated by its President and his closest advisers, made little progress in moving from a Soviet-era authoritarian style of government to a democratic system. Saparmurad Niyazov, head of the Turkmen Communist Party since 1985 and President of Turkmenistan since its independence in October 1990, may legally remain in office until 2002. The Democratic Party, the renamed Communist Party, retained a monopoly on power; the Government registered no parties in 1996 and continued to repress all opposition political activities. Emphasizing stability and gradual reform, official nation-building efforts focused on fostering Turkmen nationalism and glorification of President Niyazov. In practice, the President controls the judicial system, and the 50-member unicameral Parliament (Majlis) has no genuinely independent authority. The Government opened the Institute for Democratization and Human Rights in October, giving it a mandate to conduct research in support of the democratization of Turkmen government and society and to monitor the protection of human rights.

The Committee on National Security (KNB) has the responsibilities formerly held by the Soviet Committee for State Security (KGB), namely, to ensure that the regime remains in power through tight control of society and discouragement of dissent. The Ministry of Internal Affairs directs the criminal police, which works closely with the KNB on matters of national security. Both operate with relative impunity and have been responsible for abusing the rights of individuals as well as enforcing the Government's policy of repressing political opposition.

Turkmenistan is largely desert with cattle and sheep raising, intensive agriculture in irrigated oases, and huge oil and gas reserves. Its economy remains dependent on central planning mechanisms and State control, although the Government has taken a number of potentially significant steps to make the transition to a market economy. Agriculture, particularly cotton cultivation, accounts for nearly half of total employment. Gas, oil, gas derivatives, and cotton account for almost all of the country's export revenues. Seeking increased outlets for its gas exports (and, thereby, greater economic independence), the Government is considering construction of new gas export pipelines to or through a number of countries, including neighboring Iran and Afghanistan.

The Government continued to commit human rights abuses, notably by severely restricting political and civil liberties. Citizens do not have the ability to change their government peacefully. The Government placed dissident Durdymurad Khodzha-Mukhammed in a psychiatric hospital in Geok-Depe and imprisoned dissident Ata Aymamedov after he called for the President's removal from office. Senior government officials failed to respond to inquiries regarding these two cases. Security forces continued to beat suspects and prisoners, and prison conditions remained poor and unsafe. Arbitrary arrest, detention, unfair trials, and interference with citizens privacy remained problems. The Government completely controls the media, censoring all newspapers and rarely permitting independent criticism of government policy or officials. The Government generally gave favored treatment to ethnic Turkmen over minorities and to men over women. Women experience societal discrimination, and domestic violence against women is a problem.

RESPECT FOR HUMAN RIGHTS

Section 1. Respect for the Integrity of the Person, Including Freedom From:

a. *Political and Other Extrajudicial Killing.*—There were no reports of political or other extrajudicial killings.

b. *Disappearance.*—There were no reports of politically motivated disappearances.

c. *Torture and Other Cruel, Inhuman, or Degrading Treatment or Punishment.*—The 1992 Constitution makes torture or other cruel, inhuman, or degrading treatment illegal. Nevertheless, there were credible and widespread reports that security officials frequently beat criminal suspects and prisoners and often used force to obtain confessions.

International human rights organizations reported that on February 22, the authorities placed dissident Durdymurad Khodzha-Mukhammed in a psychiatric hospital in Geok-Depe where he remains against his will. Others who have protested government policies or economic conditions also are held in psychiatric hospitals.

Prisons are unsanitary, overcrowded, and unsafe. Food is poor, and facilities for prisoner rehabilitation and recreation are extremely limited. In the past, some prisoners have died due to overcrowding and lack of adequate protection from the severe summer heat. The Government does not permit independent monitoring of prison conditions.

d. *Arbitrary Arrest, Detention, or Exile.*—The Constitution states that citizens "have the right to freedom of belief and the free expression thereof and also to obtain information unless it is a State, official, or commercial secret." In practice, those expressing views critical of or different from those of the Government have been arrested on false charges of committing common crimes, such as Ata Aymamedov (see Section 1.e.), or the two journalists, Mukhammed Muradliev and Yowshan Anagurhan, for "hooliganism" in connection with a 1995 peaceful demonstration.

The precise number of political detainees held at year's end was unknown. Pretrial detainees are held 6 to 8 months on the average. One recent detainee was held for 61 days and released on October 1 after the presidential amnesty announced in conjunction with the fifth anniversary of independence.

Forced exile was not known to have occurred in 1996. However, almost all prominent political opponents of the present Government have chosen to move to either Moscow, Stockholm, or Prague for reasons of personal safety.

e. *Denial of Fair Public Trial.*—The Constitution provides for judicial independence. However, in practice, the judiciary is not independent; the President's power to select and dismiss judges subordinates the judiciary to the Presidency. The court system has not been reformed since Soviet days. It consists of a Supreme Court, 6 provincial courts (including 1 for the city of Ashgabat only), and, at the lowest level, 61 district and city courts. A Supreme Economic Court hears cases involving civil disputes between state-owned enterprises and ministries. There are also military courts, which handle crimes involving military discipline, criminal cases concerning military personnel, and crimes by civilians against military personnel.

The President appoints all judges for a term of 5 years without legislative review, except for the Chairman (Chief Justice) of the Supreme Court, and he has the sole authority to remove them from the bench before the completion of their terms.

The law provides for the rights of due process for defendants, including a public trial, the right to a defense attorney, access to accusatory material, and the right to call witnesses to testify on behalf of the accused. In practice, these rights are often denied by authorities, and there are no independent lawyers, with the exception of a few retired legal officials, available to represent defendants. When a person cannot afford the services of a lawyer, the court appoints one. A person may represent himself in court.

Decisions of the lower courts may be appealed to higher courts, and in the case of the death penalty the defendant may petition the President for clemency. In practice, adherence to due process is not uniform, particularly in the lower courts in rural areas. Even when due process rights are observed, the authority of the prosecutor vis-a-vis the defense attorney is so great that it is very difficult for the defendant to receive a fair trial.

In January the Government convicted 27 persons for involvement in a peaceful demonstration in July 1995; 20 were immediately amnestied. In February authorities arrested one more person, Charymurat Amandurdyev, on charges relating to the demonstration.

At the end of the year, the Government held at least 12 political prisoners, including 1 dissident committed to a psychiatric hospital for nonmedical reasons. According to Human Rights Watch, at least two other dissidents were also held in psychiatric hospitals. Of the 11 convicted prisoners, 8 were involved in the July 1995 demonstration. Two others were convicted in secret before the Supreme Court in 1995 for an alleged conspiracy to assassinate the President. Dissident Ata Aymamedov was sentenced in February to 4½ years' imprisonment for "hooliganism" after he criticized the President in a private conversation. He reportedly claimed that the only way to improve the country's situation would be to remove the President from office. The authorities tried and imprisoned him on the day of his arrest.

f. *Arbitrary Interference With Privacy, Family, Home, or Correspondence.*—The Constitution provides for the right of protection from arbitrary interference by the State in a citizen's personal life. However, there are no legal means to regulate the conduct of surveillance by the state security apparatus, which regularly monitors the activities of opponents and critics of the Government. Security officials use physical surveillance, telephone tapping, electronic eavesdropping, and the recruitment of informers. Critics of the Government, and many other people, report credibly that their mail is intercepted before delivery.

In the past, the authorities have dismissed children from school and removed adults from their jobs because of the political activities of relatives. Since his trial, the Government has reportedly persecuted Ata Aymamedov's entire family in this way.

Section 2. Respect for Civil Liberties, Including:

a. *Freedom of Speech and Press.*—The Constitution provides for the right to hold personal convictions and to express them freely. In practice, however, the Government severely restricts freedom of speech and does not permit freedom of the press. Continued criticism of the Government can lead to personal hardship, including loss of opportunities for advancement and employment.

The Government completely controls radio and television. Its budget funds almost all print media. The Government censors newspapers; the Committee for the Protection of State Secrets must approve prepublication galleys. There is at least one monthly newspaper that purports to be independent, but it is still censored. Russian language newspapers from abroad are generally available only to organizations by subscription; individuals are rarely able to subscribe. Individual issues are available in at least one Ashgabat hotel, but are sometimes confiscated from passengers arriving at international airports.

After publishing a series of articles critical of the Government in the Russian newspaper Pravda, Turkmen journalist Marat Durdyev was fired from three state jobs: at the state-owned newspaper; an archeological site, and a state school; and he was harassed by the KNB and other government organs.

The Government prohibits the media from reporting the views of opposition political leaders and critics, and it rarely allows even the mildest form of criticism in print. The Government press has condemned the foreign media, including Radio Liberty, for broadcasting or publishing opposing views, and the Government has subjected those quoted in critical foreign press items to threats and harassment. It revoked the accreditation of the Radio Liberty correspondent because of broadcasts by an opposition politician in exile, although it has not prevented him from continuing to file reports for broadcast.

The Government also restricts academic freedom. It does not tolerate criticism of government policy or the President in academic circles, and it discourages research into areas it considers politically sensitive. The government-controlled Union of Writers has in the past expelled members who have criticized government policy; libraries have removed their works. Intellectuals have reported that the security organs have instructed them to praise the President in their art and have warned them not to participate in receptions hosted by foreign diplomatic missions.

b. *Freedom of Peaceful Assembly and Association.*—The Constitution allows for peaceful assembly and association, but the Government restricts these rights. It does not permit peaceful demonstrations organized by alleged critics and in 1995 dispersed the first peaceful protest rally in years, convicting over 20 persons for their participation. Permits are required for public meetings and demonstrations, but there were reports of spontaneous demonstrations over bread prices during the year.

A few unregistered organizations without political agendas are permitted. Unregistered organizations with a political agenda are not allowed to hold demonstrations or meetings outside, but can hold small private meetings. No political groups critical of government policy have been able to meet the requirements for registration. The Government uses laws on the registration of political parties to prevent the emergence of potential opposition groups. At present the only registered party is the Democratic Party of Turkmenistan.

Social and cultural organizations without political aims are allowed to function, but often have difficulty registering. Theoretically, citizens have the freedom to associate with whomever they please. However, the authorities have fired or threatened to fire supporters of opposition movements from their jobs for political activities, removed them from professional societies, and even threatened them with the loss of their homes. In addition, some Turkmen with links to foreigners are subject to official intimidation.

c. *Freedom of Religion.*—The Constitution provides for freedom of religion and does not establish a State religion. The State generally respects religious freedom. Citizens are overwhelmingly Muslim, but Islam does not play a dominant role in society, in part due to the 70 years of Soviet rule.

A modest revival of Islam has occurred since independence. The Government has incorporated some aspects of Muslim tradition into its efforts to define a Turkmen identity, and it gives some financial and other support to the Council on Religious Affairs, which plays an intermediary role between the government bureaucracy and religious organizations.

Religious congregations are required to register with the Government, but there were no reports that the Government has denied registration to any religious groups.

There is no law specifically addressing religious proselytizing. The Government, however, must grant permission for any mass meetings or demonstrations for this purpose. The Government does not restrict the travel of clergy or members of religious groups to Turkmenistan. Islamic religious literature is distributed through the mosques. Orthodox churches offer a variety of Christian religious literature.

d. *Freedom of Movement Within the Country, Foreign Travel, Emigration, and Repatriation.*—The Government does not generally restrict movement within the country, although travel to southern border zones is tightly controlled. Citizens still carry internal passports. These are used primarily as a form of identification rather than as a means of controlling movement. Residence permits are not required, although place of residence is registered and noted in passports.

The Government uses its power to issue passports and exit visas as a general means of restricting international travel. Most nonofficial travelers find the process of obtaining passports and exit visas to be difficult. Many allege that officials solicit bribes in exchange for permission to travel abroad.

While most citizens are permitted to emigrate without undue restriction, some government opponents have been denied the opportunity to emigrate. In 1996 ethnic

Russians and other non-Turkmen residents, including Jewish residents, have been permitted to emigrate.

The government-funded Council of World Turkmen provides assistance to ethnic Turkmen abroad who wish to return to Turkmenistan and apply for citizenship. The Government, however, discourages immigration by ethnic Turkmen living in Iran, Iraq, Turkey, and other countries. Immigration of non-Turkmen from other areas of the former Soviet Union is discouraged by the unofficial policy of favoring employment of ethnic Turkmen.

The Government has not formulated a policy regarding refugees, asylees, or first asylum. The country does not provide first asylum, and the issue of its provision has never arisen. The Government has never granted refugee or asylee status to persons or accepted them for resettlement.

The Government cooperates with the Office of the United Nations High Commissioner for Refugees (UNHCR) and other humanitarian organizations in assisting refugees. There are no provisions for granting asylum or refugee status in accordance with the 1951 United Nations Convention and its 1967 Protocol Relating to the Status of Refugees. Although the Government is not a signatory to the Convention, President Niyazov has publicly stated that Turkmenistan will accede to all international conventions, including those governing human rights and refugees. There are no domestic structures in place for government adherence to the Convention. The UNHCR is assisting the Government in creating such structures as a first step towards signing the Convention. UNHCR officials estimate that the country is at least 2 years away from signing the Convention.

There were no reports of forced expulsion of those having a valid claim to refugee status. There has not been a pattern of abuse of refugees with the exception of low-level harassment.

Section 3. Respect for Political Rights: The Right of Citizens to Change Their Government

Citizens have no real ability to effect peaceful change in the Government and have little influence on government policy or decisionmaking. The 1992 Constitution declares Turkmenistan to be a secular democracy in the form of a presidential republic. It calls for the separation of powers between the various branches but vests a disproportionate share of power in the Presidency, particularly at the expense of the judiciary. In practice, President Niyazov's power is absolute, and the country remains a one-party state. Despite the appearance of decisionmaking by consensus, most decisions are made at the President's level.

In the 1992 presidential election, the sole candidate was Saparmurad Niyazov, the incumbent and nominee of the Democratic Party of Turkmenistan (formerly the Communist Party). The Government announced the election barely a month before voting day, giving opposition groups insufficient time to organize and qualify to submit a candidate. A 1994 national referendum extended the President's term to 2002, obviating the need for the scheduled presidential election in 1997. According to the official results, 99.9 percent of those voting cast their ballots to extend his term. The policy of the Democratic Party, according to its leadership, is to implement the policy of the President.

In the 1994 elections for a reconstituted Mejlis (Parliament) no opposition participation was permitted. The Government claimed that 99.8 percent of all eligible voters participated. The Mejlis routinely supports presidential decrees and, as yet, has no genuinely independent authority, although it has taken several measures to become a more professional body. The next parliamentary elections are scheduled for 1999.

There are no legal restrictions on the participation of women or minorities in the political process. Minorities are represented in the Government although preference is given to ethnic Turkmen. However, women are underrepresented in the upper levels of government. Women currently serve as the Deputy Chairman of the Parliament and as the Permanent Representative to the United Nations. However, there are no women serving in the influential positions of ministers or provincial governors.

Section 4. Governmental Attitude Regarding International and Nongovernmental Investigation of Alleged Violations of Human Rights

There are no local human rights monitoring groups, and government restrictions on freedom of speech, press, and association would preclude any effort to investigate and criticize publicly the Government's human rights policies. Several independent journalists report on these issues in the Russian press in Russia and have contact with international human rights organizations. On numerous occasions in the past, the Government has warned its critics against speaking with visiting journalists or other foreigners wishing to discuss human rights issues.

The National Institute for Democracy and Human Rights under the President opened in October. Its mandate is to support the democratization of the government and society and monitor the protection of human rights. Beginning in December, Institute personnel led an investigative tour of prisons and of regional and local government offices, reporting to the President on substandard prison conditions and abuses by regional and local authorities. The degree of the Institute's independence and the full scope of its prospective activities, remained unclear at year's end.

Section 5. Discrimination Based on Race, Sex, Religion, Disability, Language, or Social Status

Article 17 of the Constitution provides for equal rights and freedoms for all, regardless of one's nationality, origin, language, and religion. Article 18 specifies equal rights before the law for both men and women. There is no legal basis for discrimination against women or religious or ethnic minorities. Cultural traditions and the Government's policy of promoting Turkmen nationalism, however, limit the employment and educational opportunities of women and nonethnic Turkmen.

Women.—Anecdotal reports indicate that domestic violence against women is common, but no statistics are available. The subject is not discussed in Turkmen society. There are no court cases available and no media references to domestic violence in the media.

Despite constitutional provisions, women are underrepresented in the upper levels of state-owned economic enterprises and are concentrated in health care, education, and service industries. Women are restricted from working in some dangerous and environmentally unsafe jobs. Under the law, women enjoy the same inheritance and marriage rights as men. In traditional Turkmen society, however, the woman's primary role is as homemaker and mother, and family pressures often limit opportunities for women to enter outside careers and advance their education. Religious authorities, when proffering advice to practicing Muslims on matters concerning inheritance and property rights, often favor men over women.

There is only one officially registered women's group, headed by the Deputy Chairperson of the Mejlis and dedicated in honor of the President's mother. At least one other group to support battered women operates in Ashgabat. The Women's Council of Turkmenistan, a carryover from the Soviet system, was disbanded following the election of Parliament in December 1994, and the only professional businesswomen's organization is no longer active. The Government has no program specifically aimed at rectifying the disadvantaged position of women in society, as it does not believe that women suffer discrimination.

Children.—Turkmenistan's social umbrella covers the welfare needs of children. The Government provides 9 to 10 years of education for the nation's children. Generally, there is little difference in the education provided to girls and boys. The Government has not taken effective steps to address the environmental and health problems that have resulted in a high rate of infant and maternal mortality.

During the annual cotton harvest, some schools in agricultural areas are closed and children as young as 10 work in the cotton fields. Other than this, there is no societal pattern of abuse against children.

People With Disabilities.—Government subsidies and pensions are provided for those with disabilities, although the pensions are inadequate to maintain a decent standard of living. Those capable of working are generally provided with jobs under still-valid preindependence policies that virtually guarantee employment to all. According to existing legislation, facilities for the access of the disabled must be included in new construction projects. Compliance is spotty, however, and most older buildings are not so equipped.

National/Racial/Ethnic Minorities.—The Constitution provides for equal rights and freedoms for all citizens. Turkmen comprise approximately 77 percent of the population of about 4.5 million; Russians, 7 percent; and Uzbeks, 9 percent. There are smaller numbers of Kazaks, Armenians, Azerbaijanis, and many other ethnic groups. Since independence, Turkmenistan has not experienced ethnic turmoil.

As part of its nation-building efforts, the Government has attempted to foster Turkmen national pride, in part through its language policy. The Constitution designates Turkmen the official language, and it is a mandatory subject in school, although not necessarily the language of instruction.

The Constitution also provides for the rights of speakers of other languages to use them. Russian remains in common usage in government and commerce. The Government insists that discrimination against Russian speakers will not be tolerated. However, efforts to reverse past policies that favored Russians work to the benefit of Turkmen at the expense of the other ethnic groups, not solely ethnic Russians.

Non-Turkmen fear that the designation of Turkmen as the official language will put their children at a disadvantage educationally and economically. They complain that some avenues for promotion and job advancement are no longer open to them. Only a handful of non-Turkmen occupy high-echelon jobs in the ministries, and government employees from minority ethnic groups are sometimes assigned lesser positions than their experience and qualifications would merit.

Section 6. Worker Rights

a. *The Right of Association.*—Turkmenistan has inherited the Soviet system of government-associated trade unions. There are no legal guarantees entitling workers to form or join unions. The Colleagues Union is the only legal central trade union permitted, and it claims a membership of some 1.6 million; its unions are divided along both sectoral and regional lines. Unions may not form or join other federations.

While no law specifically prohibits the establishment of independent unions, there are no such unions, and no attempts were made to register an independent trade union in 1996. The State controls key social benefits such as sick leave, health care, maternal and childcare benefits, and funeral expenses. Deductions from payrolls to cover these benefits are transferred directly to the Government.

The law neither prohibits nor permits strikes and does not address the issue of retaliation against strikers. Strikes are extremely rare and no strikes were known to have occurred in 1996.

There is no information on union affiliation with international unions. Turkmenistan joined the International Labor Organization in late 1993.

b. *The Right to Organize and Bargain Collectively.*—The law does not protect the right to collective bargaining. In practice, in the state-dominated economy, the close association of both the trade union and the state-owned enterprise with the Government seriously limits workers' ability to bargain, and workers often go months without pay or receive their paychecks late.

The Ministry of Economics and Finance prepares general guidelines for wages and sets wages in health care, culture, and some other areas. In other sectors, it allows for some leeway at the enterprise level, taking into account local factors. The Government determines specific wage and benefit packages for each factory or enterprise.

The law does not prohibit antiunion discrimination by employers against union members and organizers, and there are no mechanisms for resolving such complaints.

There are no export processing zones.

c. *Prohibition of Forced or Compulsory Labor.*—The Constitution prohibits forced labor. No incidents of compulsory labor were reported.

d. *Minimum Age for Employment of Children.*—The minimum age for employment of children is 16 years; in a few heavy industries it is 18 years. The law prohibits children 16 through 18 years of age from working more than 6 hours per day (the normal workday is 8 hours).

A 15-year-old child may work 4 to 6 hours per day, but only with the permission of the trade union and parents. This permission rarely is granted. Violations of child labor laws occur in rural areas during the cotton harvesting season, when teenagers work in the fields and children less than 10 years of age sometimes help with the harvest.

e. *Acceptable Conditions of Work.*—There is no minimum wage in Turkmenistan. As of October 1, the average monthly wage in the state sector was approximately $16 (80,000 manats) per month. While the Government subsidizes the prices of many necessities and provides others free of charge, this wage falls short of the amount required to meet the needs of an average family. Most households are multigenerational, with several members receiving salaries, stipends, or pensions. Even so, many people lack the resources to maintain an adequate diet, and meat is a luxury for most of them.

The standard legal workweek is 40 hours with 2 days off. Citizens are commonly expected to work on Saturday in violation of the 40-hour workweek law. Individuals who work fewer hours during the week or are in certain high-level positions may also work on Saturdays.

Turkmenistan inherited from the Soviet era an economic system with substandard working conditions—one in which production took precedence over the health and safety of workers.

Industrial workers often labor in an unsafe environment and are not provided proper protective equipment. Some agricultural workers are subjected to environmental health hazards. The Government recognizes that these problems exist and has taken some steps to deal with them but has not set comprehensive standards for occupational health and safety. Workers do not always have the right to remove themselves from work situations that endanger health or safety without jeopardy to their continued employment.

UKRAINE

Under the new Constitution adopted in June, the President, elected for a 5-year term, and a one-chamber Parliament (the Rada), elected for a 4-year term, share responsibility for governance. (Transitional provisions continue the current President's and Parliament's terms until October 1999, and March 1998, respectively.) President Leonid Kuchma was elected in 1994. The President appoints the Cabinet and controls government operations. Under the new Constitution, the judiciary is funded independently, instead of through the Ministry of Justice. However, the court system remains subject to political interference.

The Security Service of Ukraine (SBU), the Ministry of Internal Affairs, and the Ministry of Defense all have equal status and report to the President through the Cabinet. The heads of these three institutions sit in the Cabinet of Ministers. The armed forces have largely remained outside politics. Although the SBU has not interfered in the political process, it can affect it through criminal investigations against politicians and influential businessmen. The SBU, police, and prosecutor's office have drawn public criticism for their failure to take adequate action to curb institutional corruption and abuse in the Government. Members of the security forces committed human rights abuses.

Ukraine is making a difficult transition from central planning to a market-based economy. According to official statistics, about half of the work force is formally employed in manufacturing, with the balance divided between services and agriculture, although in reality many industrial enterprises have reduced or stopped production. Exports are diversified and include metals, chemicals, sugar, and semi-finished goods. Annual per capita gross domestic product is approximately $800. President Kuchma's economic reform program has achieved partial macroeconomic stabilization and curtailed inflation, allowing the Government to introduce the new currency, the hryvna, in September. The private sector has grown significantly and now represents a substantial portion of the economy, although that growth which is in the unofficial shadow economy is not fully reflected in official government statistics. Nevertheless, the country remains in a serious economic crisis. Industrial output continues to decline, and shrinking revenue has left millions of employees unpaid for several months.

Overall, Ukraine continued to make significant progress toward building a law-based civil society. Reports of human rights violations remained at the same low level as last year. Problems remain in the unreformed legal and prison systems. Police and prison officials regularly beat detainees and prisoners, and the Government rarely punishes officials who commit such abuses. Prison conditions remain poor, and lengthy pretrial detention under poor conditions is a problem. The judiciary is overburdened and lacks sufficient funding and staff. Long delays in trials are a problem. While progress has been made toward ensuring the independence of the judiciary, political interference continues to affect the judicial process. There are occasional government attempts to control the press, and significant limits on freedom of association and on nonnative religious organizations. Significant societal anti-Semitism, violence against women, as well as discrimination against women, and both ethnic and religious minorities, persists.

The new Constitution provides safeguards for human rights and strengthens the courts by establishing the principle of judicial review. It establishes a Constitutional Court with the power to determine the constitutionality of acts and decisions by all branches of government. The new Constitution also provides for a human rights ombudsman, to be appointed by Parliament, who is to be responsible for assisting citizens in defending their rights. The efficacy of the new Constitution, however, depends on enabling legislation, most of which had not been passed by year's end.

RESPECT FOR HUMAN RIGHTS

Section 1. Respect for the Integrity of the Person, Including Freedom From:

a. *Political and Other Extrajudicial Killing.*—There were no known political killings by government agents, but in some instances the line between politically motivated killing and criminal activities was difficult to distinguish. The Government's inability to stem economic decline and check the growth of violent, organized criminal activity had major repercussions. Politicians continued to be the victims—

whether through killing or kidnaping—of organized criminal groups, aided in a few cases, either actively or passively, by corrupt officials. In July the Prime Minister narrowly escaped an alleged assassination attempt in Kiev when a bomb reportedly exploded near his car. No suspects have so far been identified. In November a Rada Deputy and business magnate was killed at Donetsk Airport by unknown persons. It was the first known killing of a deputy since independence. The number of contract killings of members of the business community, often managers of state-owned enterprises, remained high. Three senior officials of an important steel plant, Azov-Stal, were killed in a suspicious car crash. The heads of two major natural gas importing companies, one in Kiev and one in Donetsk, were murdered in March and April during a period of fundamental changes in the Government's gas supply policy. Politicians were also targeted because of their influence over state-owned enterprises.

The undermining of governmental authority was particularly serious in Crimea. The central Government in Kiev lacks institutional control over the peninsula, and the Crimean authorities are widely alleged to be compromised by ties to organized criminal elements. Early this year the central Government replaced the Crimean prosecutor and the leadership of the local police for their inability to curb violent crime, including their failure to solve any of the 35 alleged contract murders committed in 1995. The new Crimean police leadership claims to have solved 13 of 21 contract murders on the peninsula to date this year and to have detained some local criminal leaders. Officials of the Party of Economic Renaissance of the Crimea were the targets of a spate of shootings and bombings in April. A Simferopol municipal council deputy was wounded by automatic gunfire in his car in January, and another was killed in his apartment in September. The Mayor of Sevastopol was the victim of a bombing in October.

b. *Disappearance.*—In August the Speaker of the Crimean Legislature claimed that he had been kidnaped and beaten by unidentified assailants. The January 1994 disappearance of Myhailo Boichyshyn, a prominent leader of the Popular Movement of Ukraine (RUKH), remains unsolved.

c. *Torture and Other Cruel, Inhuman, or Degrading Treatment or Punishment.*— The Constitution prohibits torture; however, police and prison officials regularly beat detainees and prisoners. There is no effective mechanism for registering complaints about mistreatment or for obtaining redress, although the human rights ombudsman required by the new Constitution may provide such a mechanism. With the single exception of a police officer jailed for torturing detainees, the Government made no known efforts during the year to end the practice or to punish officials who committed such abuses.

A member of Parliament from Kiev, Myroslav Gorbatiuk (who was placed in an intensive care unit after a brutal assault), and a former parliamentarian from Zaporizhzhia, Victor Slesarenko (whose car was blown up), claimed that violent attacks against them were linked to their investigations into high-level corruption in the Government. The Government has not yet announced the results of its investigations of these allegations.

There were no reported cases of political abuse of psychiatry. However, human rights groups claim that there are isolated cases of abuse of psychiatric diagnosis for economic reasons, relating to property, inheritance, or divorce-related disputes. The disputes often entail the corruption of psychiatric experts and court officials. The Ukrainian Psychiatric Association submitted to the Rada a new draft law on psychiatry designed to curb such abuses. The government-owned media have begun reporting instances of psychiatric abuse.

Conditions in pretrial detention facilities routinely fail to meet basic human rights standards. Inmates are sometimes held in "investigative isolation" for extended periods and subjected to intimidation and mistreatment by jail guards. Overcrowding is common in blocks for prisoners who have been charged with a crime and are awaiting trial or are in investigative detention.

Prison conditions are poor. Despite government efforts to maintain minimum international standards in the prisons for convicted prisoners, the worsening economic crisis has led to a further deterioration of these facilities. Overcrowding, poor sanitation, and inadequate medical care are all problems in the prisons.

The Government generally permits visits by human rights monitors, although human rights groups have complained of being refused access to some prisons.

d. *Arbitrary Arrest, Detention, or Exile.*—The law provides that authorities may detain a person suspected of a crime for 3 days without a warrant. The new Constitution provides that only the courts may issue arrest warrants, but under its "transitional provisions" the prosecutor's office retains the authority to issue arrest and search warrants for 5 more years. An arrest order must be issued if the period of detention exceeds 3 days. The maximum period of detention after charges have been filed is 18 months, but the law does not limit the aggregate time of detention before and during the trial. The law permits citizens to contest an arrest in court or appeal to the prosecutor.

By law a trial must begin no later than 3 weeks after the defendant is indicted. This requirement is frequently not met by the overburdened court system, where months may pass before a defendant is finally brought to trial.

The law stipulates that a defense attorney be provided without charge to the indigent from the moment of detention or the filing of charges, whichever comes first. However, it has been credibly alleged that individuals held under preventive detention frequently have been denied timely access to counsel. In addition there are insufficient numbers of defense attorneys to protect suspects from unlawful, lengthy imprisonment under extremely poor conditions. Although the concept of providing attorneys from the state system remains in principle, public attorneys often refuse to defend indigents for the low government fee. Once a suspect is taken into detention, the prisoner may talk to a lawyer only in the presence of a prison official or an investigator. To protect the defendant, each investigative file must contain a document signed by the defendant attesting that his right to have a defender was explained as were the charges against him. An appeals court may dismiss a conviction or order a new trial if this document is missing. As defendants became aware of their rights, they increasingly insisted on observance of these procedures. However, many still were not aware and hence did not make use of these safeguards.

Exile as a punishment no longer exists in the law, and the Government observes this prohibition.

e. *Denial of Fair Public Trial.*—The new Constitution provides for the establishment of an independent judiciary; however, the judiciary remains subject to political interference.

The existing court system is divided into courts of general jurisdiction and arbitration, or commercial, courts. The courts of general jurisdiction are divided into criminal and civil sections. The courts are organized on three levels: rayon (district) courts (also known as peoples' courts), oblast (regional) courts, and the Supreme Court. There are 742 district and city courts, 27 regional courts, 26 military courts, and an interregional court. All may act as a court of first instance depending on the nature and seriousness of the crime. A case heard in the first instance by the Supreme Court, therefore, may not be appealed or overruled. Military courts only handle cases involving military personnel. Cases are decided by judges who sit singly (in principle with two public assessors), or in groups of three for more serious cases. As it has become increasingly difficult to find unpaid public assessors willing to attend a trial, most cases are tried by a single judge. There are no clear rules to determine which court first hears a case.

Under the new Constitution, justice is to be administered by the Constitutional Court and general jurisdiction courts with the Supreme Court at their head. The judicial system is also to include local and appeals courts, as well as special courts to be established by future legislation, headed by their respective highest courts. Pending formation of the new judicial system, the old system remains in place, including the present Supreme and Supreme Arbitration Court, for a maximum period of 5 years.

The Parliament, the President, and the Congress of Judges each appoint 6 of the 18 members for 9-year terms to the Constitutional Court. The Court Chairman is elected for a 3-year term by the 18 justices from among their own ranks. On October 18, 16 of the 18 justices were sworn in. The new Constitution strengthens the courts by establishing the principle of judicial review. The Constitutional Court is to be the ultimate interpreter of legislation and the Constitution. It will determine the constitutionality of legislation, of Presidential edicts, of Cabinet acts, and of acts of the Crimean Autonomy.

Prosecutors, like the courts, are also organized into offices at the rayon, oblast, and republic levels. They are ultimately responsible to the Prosecutor General, who is appointed by the President and confirmed by the Parliament for a 5-year term. Regional and district prosecutors are appointed by the Prosecutor General. Prosecutors and defense attorneys by law have equal status before the courts. In practice, however, prosecutors still are very influential because court proceedings are not conducted in an adversarial manner and the procuracy, in its pretrial investigative function, often acts in effect as a grand jury. The prosecutor directs all investigations of the Ministry of Internal Affairs and SBU, or he may use the investigative resources of his office. The new Constitution considerably curtails the prosecutor's authority, limiting it to prosecution, representing the public interest in court, oversight of investigations, and implementation of court decisions. However, the new Constitution allows the prosecutor's office to continue to conduct investigations and oversee general observance of the law.

Judges are appointed by the President for an initial 5-year term, after which they are subject to parliamentary approval for lifetime tenure. Judges are selected for nomination or dismissed by the Supreme Judicial Council, which is also authorized to discipline judges—including judges of the Supreme Court and supreme special courts—and prosecutors for violations of the law. The Supreme Judicial Council consists of 20 members nominated by the 3 branches of government and by professional associations from the law and procuracy sectors. It also includes the Chairman of the Supreme Court, the Minister of Justice, and the Prosecutor General of Ukraine.

Many serving judges and prosecutors were appointed during the Soviet era, when political influence pervaded the criminal justice system. Human rights lawyers claim that the judiciary is not free from government influence, particularly at the regional and local levels. Judges, prosecutors, and other court officials appear to remain closely attuned to local government interests. Organized crime elements are also widely alleged to influence court decisions. According to the Justice Ministry, in 1995 38 judges were disciplined, 8 dismissed, and several prosecuted on criminal charges, mostly for bribery. No higher court judge has been disciplined to date. Although statistics are not available, the Justice Ministry reports that some judges have been prosecuted and disciplined this year. Criminal elements routinely use intimidation to induce victims and witnesses to withdraw or change their testimony. Human rights groups contend that judicial processes are sometimes affected by the biases of expert advisers, who answer to government investigative and prosecutorial bodies.

The judiciary is inefficient and lacks sufficient staff and funds. Although the workload per judge is now only half that of the 1980's, the judiciary continues to draw criticism for its slowness and inefficiency. By October the judiciary had received only 36 percent of the funds earmarked for it in the budget; barely enough to pay the judges and staff the courts. According to the Justice Ministry, some 37 percent of the courts are inadequately housed. The authority of the judicial system is also undermined by a poor record of compliance with court decisions in civil and economic cases.

The new Constitution includes procedural provisions to ensure a fair trial, including the right of a suspect or witness to refuse to testify against himself or his relatives. However, pending passage of legislation implementing the Constitution, a largely Soviet-era criminal justice system remains in place. While the defendant is presumed innocent, conviction rates have not changed since the Soviet era. Nearly 99 per cent of completed cases result in convictions. Judges frequently send cases unlikely to end in convictions back to the prosecutor's office for "additional investigation." Such cases may then be dropped or closed, occasionally without informing the court or the defendant. It is commonly believed that suspects frequently bribe court officials to drop charges before cases go to trial. Consequently, conviction rates are a somewhat misleading statistic. According to the Justice Ministry, in the first half of the year 35.2 per cent of convicted defendants tried on criminal charges were sent to jail. The rest received suspended sentences. Complicated cases can take years to go to trial. In the interim, defendants wait in pretrial detention. Bail does not exist.

Present and former members of the Parliament, members of local councils, and judges enjoy immunity from criminal prosecution unless the Parliament or the respective council gives its consent to criminal proceedings. Consent is rarely given in practice.

There were no reports of political prisoners. A human rights group in Zaporizhzhia claims that its leader, currently serving a 1-year term in jail for insulting a judge, was framed for exposing corruption in the local courts. It alleges that he was denied a proper defense. A group of parliamentarians who appealed to the Prosecutor General's Office demanding a retrial has not yet received an answer.

f. *Arbitrary Interference With Privacy, Family, Home, or Correspondence.*—Although the new Constitution requires that courts issue search warrants, its provisions have not yet been implemented. Prosecutors are issuing search warrants during the transition period. The SBU, for reasons of national security, may conduct intrusive surveillance and searches without a warrant. Human rights groups report receiving no complaints of invasion of privacy by the SBU. The Prosecutor General's Office oversees the SBU, but the extent to which it utilizes that authority to monitor SBU activities and to curb excesses by security officials is unknown. The new Constitution provides citizens with the right to examine any dossier the SBU has on them and to sue for physical or emotional damages incurred by an investigation.

The remnants of Soviet control mechanisms survive in many guises. Militia personnel have the right to stop vehicles arbitrarily and need no probable cause to initiate extensive document checks and inspection of all parts of the vehicle. Citizens who have committed no violation, or only a minor one, often prefer to pay a bribe to avoid a time-consuming inspection.

Section 2. Respect for Civil Liberties, Including:

a. *Freedom of Speech and Press.*—The Constitution and a 1991 law provide for freedom of speech and the press; however, the Government occasionally attempts to control the press. Criticism of the Government is tolerated; however, some journalists practice self-censorship, and the Government largely controls the broadcast media.

The print media, both independent and government-supported, demonstrate a tendency towards self-censorship on matters sensitive to the Government. The executive branch, through the Ministry of Press and Information, subsidizes the operations of some large-scale publications. The Ministry has warned some periodicals against fomenting ethnic tensions and conducting antistate propaganda and has applied to the prosecutor's office to open investigations into those newspapers. However, no newspapers are known to have been prosecuted as a result. Private newspapers have also been established and are free to function on a purely commercial basis. However, they practice self-censorship and are subject to various pressures such as control of access to affordable state-subsidized newsprint; dependence on political patrons who may facilitate financial support from the State Press Support Fund; close scrutiny from government officials, especially at the local level; and politically motivated visits by tax inspectors. Foreign-owned newspapers are permitted.

The broadcast media remain largely under state ownership. They are managed by the State Committee on Television and Radio ("Derzhteleradio"), whose head, according to the new Constitution, is appointed by the President and confirmed by Parliament. The President and the Parliament each appoint half of the members of the regulatory board for broadcasting, the National Council for Television and Radio Broadcasting. Under current legislation, private and foreign companies are entitled to establish and operate their own transmission facilities, provided that they obtain a license from the National Council. News programs that cover domestic political developments, notably "Vikna" ("Windows") and "Pislamova" ("Epilogue"), have fended off attempts by Derzhteleradio to preview and revise the content of their programs. Derzhteleradio denied the independent news program "Vikna" its time slot. However, with widespread popular and official support, Vikna fought its way back on the air. Derzhteleradio suspended without warning the broadcast contract of "Pislamova," an investigative news show, which was unable to broadcast on a state channel for 8 months. During that time Pislamova was broadcast on a less widely received private channel. It returned to the state channel on September 6. In Kharkiv a television correspondent was fired and his editor reprimanded for criticizing the presidential draft of the Constitution. The Government disavowed any connection with the incident. Most local observers believe that it was the doing of an independent, overzealous local bureaucrat.

In 1994 President Kuchma abolished the State Committee for the Protection of State Secrets that had enjoyed broadly defined powers over all media. The Committee was absorbed into the Ministry of Press and Information, where it is now the Main Directorate for the Protection of State Secrets. According to journalists, this Department has not interfered with the practice of their craft. In 1996 the State Committee for State Secrets and Technical Protection of Information was reestablished. State secrets are prohibited from publication. An editor of the newspaper "Opositsiya" ("Opposition"), Ivan Makar, was sentenced by a metropolitan court to a suspended prison term of 2 years for libeling the President and his staff. The newspaper was closed by order of a Kiev court for publishing caricatures of the President and his staff. Its equipment was confiscated. In June more than 70 prominent journalists issued an appeal protesting increasing political and commercial pressure on the media.

Reporting on organized crime and corruption in the Government, including misconduct by high-ranking cabinet and administration officials, is becoming increasingly bold. Journalists contend that they have been subject to threats, including the threat of arrest, and violent assaults for aggressively reporting on crime and official corruption. The journalistic community links the suspicious death of an investigative reporter in Cherkasy to the corrupt elements he was investigating.

While the major universities are state owned, they now ostensibly operate under full autonomy. Academic freedom within universities, however, is an underdeveloped and poorly understood concept. University administrators are traditionally conservative establishment figures and possess the power to silence professors with whom they disagree by denying them the possibility to publish or more directly by withholding pay or housing benefits. This atmosphere tends to limit the spirit of free inquiry. Human rights groups report the restoration of special censorship offices in scientific and research institutes, including those not conducting classified research. Restrictions by the Communications Ministry on the mailing of scientific documents have also caused concern. Several private and religiously affiliated universities have been founded (or reestablished) since independence; all operate without any reported interference or harassment by the State.

b. *Freedom of Peaceful Assembly and Association.*—The law provides for the right of assembly, and the Government generally respects this right in practice. The Law on Public Assembly of 1989 stipulates that organizations must apply for permission to the respective local administration 10 days before a planned event or demonstration. The new Constitution requires that demonstrators merely inform the authorities of a planned demonstration in advance. Under the 1989 law, participants in demonstrations are prohibited from inciting violence or ethnic conflict and from calling for the violent overthrow of the constitutional order. Demonstrators may not interfere with traffic, obstruct the work of government bodies or enterprises, or otherwise hinder public order. Unlicensed demonstrations are common and have occurred without police interference. There were isolated cases of criminal prosecution of demonstrators for unauthorized demonstrations in Kharkiv and Dnipropetrovsk. In the most high profile case, a leader of the small People's Party in Dnipropetrovsk, Leopold Taburiansky, spent several months in jail pending trial on charges of repeatedly demonstrating without a permit on behalf of duped clients of pyramid schemes.

The Constitution, law, and government regulations impose significant limits on freedom of association, and the Government uses onerous registration requirements to circumscribe this right. The Constitution prohibits the establishment of parties and organizations that advocate the elimination of Ukrainian independence or the violent overthrow of the Government and of the constitutional order; that jeopardize Ukraine's sovereignty or territorial integrity; that undermine its security; that foment ethnic, racial or religious hatred; that violate individual rights and liberties; or that jeopardize public health. The Constitution also forbids political parties to form paramilitary branches. The Government enacted a regulation imposing limitations on the establishment of regional political parties through restrictive registration requirements. Informed international observers noted that the requirement to have representatives in at least half the oblasts of the country as a prerequisite for registration as a political party negatively affects primarily Russian and Tatar organizations in Crimea.

The 1992 Law on Public Organizations prohibits the State from financing political parties and other public organizations. According to the law, political parties may not receive funds from abroad or maintain accounts in foreign banks. It bars political parties from having administrative or organizational structures abroad. The law prohibits police authorities, members of the SBU, and armed forces personnel from joining political parties. The Constitution also prohibits establishment of political party organizations in the executive and judicial branches, military units, state-owned enterprises, educational, and other public institutions. Many members of such bodies nonetheless publicly associate themselves with specific parties.

By law the Ministry of Justice has the authority to warn or fine a political party for illegal activities or to temporarily suspend its activities for up to 3 months, provided that the prosecutor's office determined that the party violated the Law on Public Organizations. The Ministry used this authority to issue a warning to the Communist Party for collecting signatures calling for a referendum in support of socialism and reintegration of the former Soviet Republics.

Freedom of association is circumscribed by an onerous registration requirement that lends itself to abuse and bureaucratic manipulation. Groups must be registered with the Government to pursue almost any purpose, whether commercial, political, or philanthropic. The Ministries of Justice, Economy, and Foreign Economic Relations as well as the Committees on Religion and Broadcasting among others all have registration functions, which they have used at one time or another to prevent citizens from exercising their right of free association.

Not being registered has several important disadvantages. For example unregistered groups are prohibited from having bank accounts, acquiring property, or entering into contracts. Furthermore, the registration law gives the Government an unlimited right to inspect the activities of all registered groups. According to this law a registered group must: 1) keep the Government apprised of all its activities, including notification of any meetings; 2) make its meetings open to all persons at all times, regardless of whether or not they are members; and 3) upon request, present its registration documents to any government official, including the prosecutor's office, and be ready to prove that it is in compliance with the purposes of the group as set out in its registration documents. A change in the group's purposes necessitates reregistration. A registered group may not duplicate any function or service that the Government is supposed to provide. For example human rights lawyers who wish to represent prisoners are prohibited from establishing an association to do so because the Government is supposed to provide lawyers for the accused.

The Ministry of Justice revoked the registration of one of two rival Social Democratic Parties of Ukraine after a party split. One party leader, a former Justice Minister, is accused of using manipulation and fraud to register the parallel party. The Ministry alleges that the rosters of the party he sought to register were falsified.

c. *Freedom of Religion.*—The new Constitution and the 1991 Law on Freedom of Conscience and Religion provide for separation of church and state and permit religious organizations to establish places of worship and to train clergy. The Government respects these rights in practice. However, the law restricts the activities of nonnative religious organizations. There is no official state religion. Religious organizations are required to register with local authorities and with the Government's Committee for Religious Affairs, a process that generally takes about 1 month.

The Government initiated an attempt to mediate the ongoing dispute among competing churches claiming to be "the Ukrainian Orthodox Church." The Government proposed establishing a committee, the National Council of Churches, for interconfessional consultations to be headed by a deputy Prime Minister, which would hold an interreligious forum in 1997. This initiative is now under discussion by the churches. The Government moved to reduce church utility fees and rental payments, to exempt churches from the land tax, and to expedite the return of religious buildings to their former owners. However, implementation of a 1992 decree on restitution of religious community property seized during the Soviet era remains stalled. Jewish congregations in 33 towns and cities have negotiated successfully with local authorities for worship space. A Kiev arbitration court in September decided in favor of transferring title of the former Kiev Central Synagogue, which in Soviet times was used as a puppet theater, to a Chabad Hasidic congregation. While the theater directorship plans to appeal, the decision sets an important precedent for the judiciary's role in religious property restitution. The Government expanded already significant efforts to ensure that pilgrims of the Bratslav Hasidic sect were able to visit the tomb of their founding rabbi in the city of Uman on the occasion of the Jewish New Year. A breakthrough agreement was signed between representatives of the sect, a local Jewish community organization, and the local government to build a religious center and museum at the site.

A 1993 amendment to the 1991 law restricts the activities of nonnative religious organizations. It requires that members of the clergy, preachers, teachers, and other foreign citizen representatives of foreign organizations preach, administer religious ordinances, or practice other canonical activities "only in those religious organizations which invited them to Ukraine and with official approval of the governmental body that registered the statutes and the articles of the pertinent religious organization."

In addition local officials have occasionally impeded the activities of foreign religious workers. All regional administrations have departments responsible for registration of various denominations and religious groups, and for supervision of compliance with the Law on the Freedom of Conscience and Religion. Neither the State Committee on Religious Affairs, nor its regional departments have the authority to deregister religious groups; they can be deregistered only by court decision.

On February 12 a Kiev court sentenced three leaders of the "White Brotherhood" religious cult to jail terms ranging from 4 to 7 years (on charges of staging mass disorder and resisting authorities) for their involvement in the 1993 seizure of St. Sophia's Cathedral in Kiev, which resulted in a violent clash with police. A leader of the cult was granted early release under a mass amnesty, but the Supreme Court moved to prevent her release pending further consideration, apparently alarmed by her claims to be a living goddess.

d. *Freedom of Movement Within the Country, Foreign Travel, Emigration, and Repatriation.*—Freedom of movement within the country is not restricted by law. However, regulations impose a nationwide requirement to register at the workplace and place of residence in order to be eligible for social benefits, thereby complicating freedom of movement by limiting access to certain social benefits to the place where one is registered. People who move to other regions for work in the private sector, for instance, may not be eligible for registration and therefore may be denied formal access to free medical care and other services guaranteed by the State.

While Ukraine continues to assure the right of return for all those it considers citizens, in practice this assurance does not include the right of return for all Ukrainian "nationals." The ambiguity of the citizenship law regarding the acquisition of Ukrainian citizenship allows authorities to deny repatriation to nationals it considers undesirable. Persons born in Ukraine and living in Ukraine at the time of independence are considered citizens. Dual citizenship is not recognized.

Citizens who wish to travel abroad are able to do so freely, although exit visas are still required for most Ukrainian citizens. The Government may deny passports to individuals with access to state secrets, but a denial can be appealed. In two instances, exit visas for the purpose of emigration were denied on grounds that the requesting individuals had had access to state secrets. However, both subsequently left Ukraine on tourist visas.

The Government has not supported a foreign-funded program to facilitate the travel of some emigrants who qualify for resettlement as refugees. Some 260,000 Tatars have returned from exile to Crimea, mainly from Central Asia. The Crimean Tatar leadership has complained that their community has not received adequate assistance in resettling and that an onerous process of acquiring citizenship has excluded many of them from participating in elections and from the right to take part in privatization of land and state assets. The Crimean election law provides Crimean Tatars with a quota of seats in the Crimean legislature.

Ukraine is not a party to the 1951 United Nations Convention on the Status of Refugees or its 1967 Protocol. Its treatment of refugees is governed by the 1993 Law on Refugees, which entitles refugees to all the benefits accorded to citizens. According to international observers, the Government demonstrated a positive attitude toward those claiming refugee status. A total of 823 Afghans were given refugee status during 1996, and a commitment has been made to award refugee status to all Afghans who arrived in Ukraine before 1995. In cooperation with the U.N. High Commissioner for Refugees (UNHCR), the Government is in the process of establishing refugee receiving centers in Vinnitsa and Luhansk. Instances of police harassment of certain categories of refugees appear to have diminished during the year. The Government has not established a policy on first asylum.

Section 3. Respect for Political Rights: The Right of Citizens to Change Their Government

Citizens exercised this right in 1994, when they elected a new President, Leonid Kuchma, who replaced incumbent, Leonid Kravchuk, and elected a new Parliament representing a wide range of parties and ideologies. Because the current election law requires a minimum of a 50 percent voter turnout for elections to be valid, over 30 seats of the 450 seat legislature remain unfilled. The Parliament decided to hold no more by-elections for a year in the 24 constituencies where voter turnout has failed to reach the minimum threshold on two or more occasions. During several parliamentary by-elections, human rights groups received complaints of irregularities, especially in rural constituencies. The Central Election Commission invalidated the results in only one case, a by-election in Lviv. The winner, Olga Kolinko, Deputy Prosecutor General and an anticorruption campaigner, alleged that the decision was politically motivated and appealed to the Supreme Court. The Supreme Court was still hearing the case at year's end. According to the new Constitution, the Central Election Commission, not the Parliament, will decide the ultimate validity of future election results.

Women are active in political life but hold a disproportionately small percentage of offices. Women hold 16 of the 450 seats in Parliament. Only four women hold cabinet-rank posts. The 18-member Constitutional Court has 2 female members. The provincial governors are all men. There are more women in local and oblast governments than at higher levels of government.

Section 4. Governmental Attitude Regarding International Investigation of Alleged Violations of Human Rights

The Government allowed local and international human rights groups to operate freely, although some groups have been denied formal government registration, making it harder for them to obtain accreditation to official events and more difficult to register bank accounts and other financial aspects of their organizations. The Union of Councils for Soviet Jewry and Amnesty International have active offices in Kiev. The Government also welcomed visits by foreign human rights organizations.

Section 5. Discrimination Based on Race, Sex, Religion, Disability, Language, or Social Status

The new Constitution prohibits discrimination on the basis of race, sex, and other grounds; however, due in part to the absence of an effective judicial system, the Government has not been able effectively to enforce many of these provisions. Societal anti-Semitism exists, and the Government has not prosecuted anti-Semitic acts under the law forbidding the sowing of interethnic hatred. It also has not prosecuted those responsible for sexual harassment or discrimination. Human rights experts also note that the authorities' frequent harassment of dark-skinned young men is based on stereotypes that people from the Caucasus are involved in criminal activity.

Women.—While comprehensive information measuring the extent of violence against women is not readily available, survey results suggest that the problem is pervasive. The number of reported rapes and attempted rapes has increased by 80 percent over recent years. Surveys indicate that most women who have been subjected to physical abuse or rape never report it to the police. A 1995 poll of 600 women conducted by a women's organization in Kharkiv indicated that 10 to 15 percent had been raped and over 25 percent subjected to physical abuse over the course of their lifetimes. Hot lines, shelters, and other practical support for victims of domestic violence do not exist.

Separate statistics on prosecutions for wife beating or on average sentences are not available. Government representatives have acknowledged that when violence occurs the authorities often exert pressure on women to drop charges against their husbands in order to preserve the family. The low official incidence of reported crimes against women is mirrored by the lack of media attention to the subject. Many women's groups place a high priority on the issue but find it a difficult problem to combat.

Sexual trafficking in women to Western Europe, Turkey, and the Middle East is reputedly common. The problem has not been addressed by the Government. The authorities do not prosecute men for engaging women in the explosively growing sector of sexually exploitative work.

Labor law provides for equal rights for men and women, including equal pay for equal work, a principle that is generally observed. A controversial provision in the new Constitution bars women from hard labor and hazardous industries. Many women's advocates fear that it may be used to bar women from the best paying blue-collar jobs. Women are much more likely to be laid off than men. Government statistics report that over 70 percent of all registered unemployed are women, and it is estimated that women represent up to 90 percent of all newly unemployed persons.

Few women attain top managerial positions in government or in state and private industry. According to government statistics, 69.2 percent of Ukraine's 213,000 state administration jobs are held by women, including 45.2 per cent of the managerial positions. However, of the highest "first" and "second" category offices, only 5.6 percent in central or local governments are filled by women. (These numbers do not include the "power ministries"—the Ministries of Defense, Internal Affairs, Foreign Affairs, and the SBU.) Educational opportunities for women have generally been equal to those enjoyed by men, and they remain so. By law pregnant women and mothers with small children enjoy paid maternity leave until their children reach the age of 3, a privilege women value but one which is used as a justification to exclude women from responsible or career track jobs.

Children.—The Government is publicly committed to the defense of children's rights. Because of the deepening economic crisis, however, it has struggled to implement its agenda. The Government provides public education for children, which is compulsory to the age of 15 years. In principle there is free health care for children with special benefits for children affected by the Chornobil nuclear accident.

There is no societal pattern of abuse of children. Public concern over the fate of children adopted by foreigners triggered an amendment to the adoption law providing for thorough court examination of each case and followup monitoring of the children's well-being.

People With Disabilities.—The law prohibits discrimination against the disabled, but, especially with the economic crisis, the Government has been unable to support programs targeted at increasing opportunities for the disabled. The law mandates access to buildings for the disabled, but it is poorly enforced.

Religious Minorities.—Jews, the second largest religious minority in the country, have expanded opportunities to pursue their religious and cultural activities, but anti-Semitic incidents continue to occur. The Government has protected the rights of the Jewish community and speaks out against anti-Semitism. There are freely operating Jewish cultural centers and educational institutions, including several colleges. However, some ultranationalist Ukrainian groups, like UNA-UNSO and DSU ("National Independence of Ukraine"), circulate anti-Semitic tracts. Anti-Semitic articles continue to appear in a few local newspapers, especially in western Ukraine and Kiev. The Lviv newspaper "For a Free Ukraine" and the Kiev-based "Evening Kiev" regularly publish anti-Semitic diatribes, but have not been prosecuted under the law forbidding the sowing of interethnic hatred. The National Conference on Soviet Jewry and Union of Councils reported that anti-Semitic incidents continued in some regions. Union of Councils monitors have reported that death threats were made against Jews in Kharkiv.

Some Jewish cemeteries have been vandalized. On the eve of Hitler's birthday, the grave of a famous rabbi from Berdichev was desecrated. The problem of post-1940 demolition of or construction on Jewish cemeteries, both by Nazi occupiers and by the Soviet government, manifested itself during the year. In many instances Ukrainian officials inherited cases of Jewish cemetery land having been appropriated for other uses in the intervening years, as Soviet law permitted reuse of cemetery land 25 years after the final burial in the cemetery. The most problematic case, that of the historic Jewish cemetery in Lviv, saw its last burial in the 19th century, total ruin by Nazi forces in 1942, and construction of a market on the land by Soviet authorities in 1947–1964. Similarly, in Berdichev private garages had been constructed atop burial grounds; and in Mliniv a hotel and parking lot encroach on a cemetery site. Local government officials have responded with varying degrees of concern and immediacy. The Government quickly addressed the issue at the presidential level, issuing an order that all construction or privatization on the land of Jewish cemeteries be immediately frozen. Negotiations began late in the year to reach an ultimate resolution of the problem.

National/Racial/Ethnic Minorities.—With some important exceptions, there are only isolated cases of ethnic discrimination in Ukraine. The new Constitution provides for "the free development, use and protection of the Russian language and other minority languages in Ukraine." This compromise builds on a 1991 Law on National Minorities, which played an instrumental role in preventing ethnic strife by allowing individual citizens to use their respective national languages in conducting personal business and by allowing minority groups to establish their own schools. Russian speakers, who predominate in eastern Ukraine, complained about the increased use of Ukrainian in schools and in the media. They claim that their children are disadvantaged when taking academic entrance examinations, since all applicants are required to take a Ukrainian language test.

With the exception of two regions, there is no evidence of serious ethnic tension. In some parts of western Ukraine, small Russian, Jewish, and other minority groups credibly accuse some local Ukrainian ultranationalists of fostering ethnic hatred and printing anti-Semitic tracts. They also charge that local authorities have not taken action against those who foment ethnic hatred. In Crimea, Ukrainian and Tatar minorities credibly complain of discrimination by the Russian majority and demand that the Ukrainian and Tatar languages be given equal treatment to Russian. The Ukrainian community in Crimea has criticized the national Government for tolerating radical anti-Ukrainian and Russian chauvinistic groups on the peninsula. An investigation into the 1995 riots after the killing of two Tatar market vendors, which left four Tatars dead, ended inconclusively. While the Crimean Government, pleading insufficient funds, did not assent to requests from the Tatar community for assistance in reestablishing its cultural heritage through Tatar language publications and educational institutions, the central Government is working with the UNHCR, the Organization for Security and Cooperation in Europe, and the International Organization for Migration on support for the Tatar community.

Section 6. Worker Rights

a. *The Right of Association.*—The new Constitution provides for the right to join trade unions to defend "professional, social and economic interests." Under the new Constitution, all trade unions have equal status, and no government permission is required to establish a trade union. The 1992 Law on Citizens' Organizations (which includes trade unions) stipulates noninterference by public authorities in the activities of these organizations, which have the right to establish and join federations on a voluntary basis. In principle all workers and civil servants (including members of the armed forces) are free to form unions. In practice the Government discourages certain categories of workers (e.g., nuclear power plant employees) from doing so.

The successor to the Soviet trade unions, known as the Federation of Trade Unions (FPU), has begun to work independently of the Government and has been vocal in opposing draft legislation that would restrict the right to strike. The FPU urged Parliament to adopt a new trade union law to replace old Soviet-era legislation. It has defended strike organizers from the Donbass coal mines who were charged with provoking civil disorder during strikes in July. As during the Soviet era, most FPU affiliates work closely with management. Enterprise managers are free to join the FPU. The FPU has no official or legal relationship with any political party.

Independent unions now provide an alternative to the official unions in most sectors of the economy. Some, such as the Independent Miners' Union of Ukraine (NPGU), and unions representing pilots, civil air traffic controllers, locomotive engineers, and aviation ground crews have formed an umbrella organization, the National Federation of Trade Unions of Ukraine.

The new Constitution provides for the right to strike "to defend one's economic and social interests." The Constitution says that strikes must not jeopardize national security, public health, or the rights and liberties of others. The Law on Labor Conflict Resolution does not extend this right to members of the armed forces, civil and security services, and employees of "continuing process plants" (e.g. metallurgical factories). The law prohibits strikes that "may infringe on the basic needs of the population" (e.g., rail and air transportation). Strikes based on political demands are also illegal. The Government has relied on the prosecutors and courts to deal with strikes it considers illegal.

Following a protracted miners' protest over unpaid wages, several leaders were detained pending trial on criminal charges of disrupting public order by blocking roads and railways during the Donbass strike in July. The headquarters of the "Workers' Strike Committee," a loose labor organization in the coal sector in Donetsk, was searched and forcibly closed. On August 20 the oblast arbitration court ordered it disbanded. The leader of the strike committee, Mikhail Krylov, was arrested and later released on parole. The strike committee leaders have since defied the banning order. The NPGU leaders in the coal mining town of Krasnodon were found guilty of promoting public disorder and released with suspended sentences. In April a leader of the Independent Miners' Trade Union (NPG) of the Donbass coal mining region, Nykolay Volynko, was assaulted by unidentified assailants. The NPG of Donbass blamed opponents of the union for the assault.

There are no official restrictions on the right of unions to affiliate with international trade union bodies: The NPGU is a member of the International Miners' Union.

b. *The Right to Organize and Bargain Collectively.*—The law on enterprises states that joint worker-management commissions should resolve issues concerning wages, working conditions, and the rights and duties of management at the enterprise level. Overlapping spheres of responsibility frequently impede the collective bargaining process. The Government, in agreement with trade unions, establishes wages in each industrial sector and invites all unions to participate in the negotiations.

The manner in which the collective bargaining law is applied prejudices the bargaining process against the independent unions and favors the official unions (affiliates of the FPU). Most workers are never informed that they are not obligated to join the official union. Renouncing membership in the official union and joining an independent union can be bureaucratically onerous and is typically discouraged by management. The collective bargaining law prohibits antiunion discrimination. Under the law disputes are supposed to be resolved by the courts. There have been cases in which such disputes have not been settled in a fair and equitable manner.

There are no export processing zones.

c. *Prohibition of Forced or Compulsory Labor.*—The Constitution prohibits compulsory labor, and it is not known to exist.

d. *Minimum Age for Employment of Children.*—The minimum employment age is 17 years. In certain nonhazardous industries, however, enterprises may negotiate with the Government to hire employees between 14 and 17 years of age, with the consent of one parent. The new Constitution provides for general secondary education. School attendance is compulsory to the age of 15, a regulation vigorously enforced by the Ministry of Education.

e. *Acceptable Conditions of Work.*—During the year the Government raised the minimum monthly wage and pension in stages from $0.30 to $8.80 (15 hryvnas), which does not provide a decent standard of living for a worker and family. The official poverty line is now about $40 (68.1 Hryvnas) per month. It is estimated that some 50 per cent of the population officially lives below that line, although the practice of underreporting sources of income is widespread. Inflation was reduced significantly to an annual rate of around 47 per cent (down from 182 per cent in 1995) and is declining further.

The Labor Code provides for a maximum 40-hour workweek, a 24-hour day of rest per week, and at least 15 days of paid vacation per year. Stagnation in some industries (e.g., defense) significantly reduced the workweek for some categories of workers.

The Constitution and other laws contain occupational safety and health standards, but these are frequently ignored in practice. Lax safety standards caused many serious mine accidents, resulting in 243 deaths over the first 8 months of the year. This compares with 358 deaths for all of 1995, representing a considerable increase in the ratio of fatalities per ton of coal extracted in light of decreasing coal output. In theory workers have a legal right to remove themselves from dangerous work situations without jeopardizing continued employment. In reality, however, independent trade unionists report that asserting this right would result in retaliation or perhaps dismissal by management.

UNITED KINGDOM

The United Kingdom of Great Britain and Northern Ireland (UK) is a longstanding, constitutional monarchy with a democratic, parliamentary government. A lower legislative chamber (the House of Commons), the center of parliamentary power, is elected in periodic multiparty elections. An upper chamber (the House of Lords), with the power to revise and delay implementation of laws, is made up of hereditary and life peers and senior clergy of the established Church of England. There is an independent judiciary, but Parliament may overrule its decisions.

Throughout the United Kingdom, police forces are responsive to, and under the effective control of, civilian officials. The Security Service Act of 1996, giving the intelligence agency MI–5 jurisdiction to act in support of other law enforcement agencies in the prevention and detection of serious domestic crime, received royal assent in July. In some areas of Northern Ireland, because of continued terrorist violence, army units operated to reinforce the Royal Ulster Constabulary (RUC). Although the security forces generally respect human rights and the rule of law, some members of the police have committed human rights abuses.

The United Kingdom has a highly developed and diversified market-based economy that provides most residents with a high standard of living. Certain geographic areas, particularly older industrial areas including Northern Ireland, suffer from higher than average unemployment. In addition, unemployment tends to be higher among some demographic groups, such as youth and racial minorities. The Government provides comprehensive social welfare services, including a national health system, housing and family benefits, and heavily subsidized higher education.

The Government respected the human rights of its citizens, but there were problems in some areas. Police occasionally abused detainees. The controversial reversal by the RUC chief constable of his earlier decision allowed Protestant "Orangemen" to parade through a predominately Catholic nationalist area of Portadown on July 11, leading to serious and widespread public disturbances throughout Northern Ireland. Although the chief constable justified his decision as necessary to prevent loss of life, Irish nationalists argue that the RUC reacted more aggressively and vigorously to quell nationalist disturbances than toward loyalist lawbreakers.

In January the Government announced that it was setting up an independent inquiry into, and inviting public comment on, the future need for counterterrorism legislation in Northern Ireland. Such counterterrorism legislation was renewed and strengthened by Parliament following the resumption of Irish Republican Army (IRA) terrorist violence in February. At year's end there was an upsurge in terrorist violence in Northern Ireland.

The Government is taking steps to combat violence against women and societal discrimination against nonwhite minorities.

Police believe paramilitary groups in Northern Ireland were responsible for nine killings as of September. Both Republican and Loyalist paramilitary groups continued to engage in vigilante "punishment" attacks on alleged "antisocial elements" and to exile "informers" by force. There have also been instances of arson against (Protestant) Orange halls and Catholic churches.

RESPECT FOR HUMAN RIGHTS

Section 1. Respect for the Integrity of the Person, Including Freedom From:

a. *Political and Other Extrajudicial Killing.*—There were no reports of political killings by the Government, but several deaths of persons during civil unrest, in the course of apprehension, or while in custody raised questions about whether police and prison officers had used improper restraining techniques or excessive force against minority group members and criminal suspects. The Home Office banned the use of one restraining technique that was alleged to have been the cause of a prisoner fatality.

David Ewen, pursued by police after stealing an automobile in February, was cornered by police vehicles and verbally warned. When he did not get out of the car, a police officer opened fire on the side of the stolen vehicle, killing Ewen. The policeman was charged with murder, and his trial continued at year's end. A jury returned a verdict in December of unlawful killing in the case of Oluwashijibomi Lapite, who died in police custody in December 1994 after being placed in a suffocating choke hold. The cause of death was listed as asphyxiation. Following this incident, the police issued new guidelines banning the use of the choke hold. The independent Police Complaints Authority decided that no disciplinary action would be taken against any officer involved. In December an inquest jury returned a verdict of accidental death in the case of Wayne Douglas, a suspected burglar who died in police custody in 1995. Douglas' family will appeal the verdict to the High Court. A jury returned a verdict in November of "misadventure to which neglect contributed" in the case of Leon Patterson, who died in police custody in 1992 after being left naked and handcuffed on a jail cell floor. No police officers or jail personnel were punished in this case. In August an inquest reached a verdict of accidental death in the case of Brian Douglas, an Afro-Caribbean man who in 1995 died from hemorrhages and a fractured skull 5 days after his arrest. Earlier in the year the Crown Prosecution Service (CPS) said that it would not prosecute the officers involved due to "insufficient evidence."

A police tribunal dismissed a case of neglect of duty against a senior police officer who supervised the police squad involved in the death of illegal immigrant Joy Gardner. This brought an end to all disciplinary proceedings in the case of Gardner, who died of brain damage in 1993 after police officers gagged her with adhesive tape when she resisted arrest. The Home Office no longer permits mouth restraints to be used in the removal of people under Immigration Act powers.

During July disturbances in Londonderry, Northern Ireland, an armored personnel carrier ran over Dermot McShane, a convicted Republican terrorist who had taken refuge behind a board fence during street fighting. The army claimed that the death was accidental, and the RUC appointed a senior detective to investigate. A police inquiry is under way into the death of Dairmud O'Neil, who was killed in September when police stormed a London residence where IRA bomb-making and other terrorist-related materials were found. A decision is pending by the CPS about whether to bring charges in the case of Richard O'Brien, an Irishman whom a Coroners Court found had been unlawfully killed by police in 1994. The CPS had earlier decided there was insufficient evidence to prosecute, but the family's attorney petitioned the CPS to institute criminal proceedings against the officers involved. Human rights monitors complained about delays in the criminal process.

Killings by Republican and Loyalist groups continued. In January a group calling itself "Direct Action Against Drugs" (DAAD), but believed to have strong links to the IRA, killed one person. In September the group claimed responsibility for the shooting death of a 31-year-old man. As of September, while there were numerous arrests, no persons had been charged in the cases of the DAAD murders of 1995 or 1996.

The January killing of reputed Irish National Liberation Army (INLA) chief of staff Gino Gallagher sparked a feud between two INLA factions, which through September resulted in six other deaths, including that of a 9-year-old girl.

Two innocent bystanders were killed and several hundred persons injured by the IRA when it detonated a massive bomb in the Docklands area of London in February, ending the cease-fire it had declared in August 1994 (see Section 1.c.). James Bradwell, a British Army warrant officer, died on October 11 from injuries sustained in an October 7 IRA double-bomb attack on a barracks and, minutes later, on a hospital at the British Army headquarters in Northern Ireland. Bradwell was caught in both explosions, caused by around 500 pounds of homemade explosives.

In July Michael McGoldrick, a Catholic taxi driver, was found murdered in his car in County Armagh, Northern Ireland. No one claimed responsibility for his murder, but it had the hallmarks of a Loyalist assassination and probably was perpetrated by a renegade faction of the Ulster Volunteer Force (UVF). In December a policeman was wounded during an IRA attack at a children's hospital; the subsequent wounding of a Republican in a car bombing thought to be perpetrated by a Loyalist group prompted fears of a resurgence of sectarian violence in the province.

The 1989 killing of Patrick Finucane, counsel to many IRA suspects, remains an open case. Although it was alleged that Brian Nelson, a former Loyalist paramilitary and agent for British military intelligence, assisted in targeting Finucane, the Northern Ireland DPP determined that the evidence was insufficient and decided not to bring charges against him. In February Nelson was freed from prison.

Coroners do not have the power to compel people who are suspected of involvement in extrajudicial killing to give evidence at inquests, and the relatives of those who have died do not receive advance disclosure of information, statements, and other evidence. In the June inquest into the death of Patrick Shanaghan, murdered by Loyalist paramilitary groups in 1991, the coroner agreed to applications by the Shanaghan family's lawyer to admit evidence that police officers threatened Shanaghan's life while he was under arrest and said that they would leak his name to a paramilitary group. The chief constable rebuked the coroner for straying outside his authority and refused to uphold the ruling.

b. *Disappearance.*—There were no reports of disappearances attributed to the Government. At least 14 terrorist-perpetrated disappearances, dating back to 1972, remain outstanding without any significant investigative progress by the authorities. A seven-person RUC team works full time to solve the cases, but the victims, typically members of the security forces, suspected informers, or petty criminals have not been found.

c. *Torture and Other Cruel, Inhuman, or Degrading Treatment or Punishment.*—The law forbids torture and other cruel, inhuman, or degrading treatment. Confessions thus obtained are not admissible in court, and judges can exclude even voluntary confessions. Detainees who claim physical mistreatment have the right to an immediate medical examination. Such a claim must be examined by a trial judge. There were no reports that government officials used torture.

Several incidents of police brutality toward criminal suspects occurred, including toward ethnic minorities. In February Amer Rafiq, who is of Pakistani origin, lost an eye due to injuries sustained in a police van following his arrest in Manchester for alleged public disorder offenses. The London Metropolitan Police have had to pay damages in several instances. In March a Hong Kong native, who was thrown in the back of a police van, punched, kicked, and insulted by three constables, was awarded $374,000 (220,000 Pounds) in damages against the London Metropolitan Police by a jury. Scotland Yard refused to discipline the officers involved and appealed the verdict.

Corporal punishment is still on the statute books in several British Caribbean dependent territories. It is rarely used in practice, but in May a British Virgin Islands youth was subjected to flogging after failing to pay a $1,000 fine for illegal cultivation of marijuana.

The Independent Commission for Police Complaints (ICPC), established by the Government, supervises police investigations in Northern Ireland. Authorized to review all complaints, it automatically supervises cases involving death or serious injury. It accepts information provided by a complainant and by any other sources, as well as that discovered by the police. The ICPC can direct the chief constable to bring charges against police officers. The ICPC reported that in 1995 it had received 2,328 complaints of official abuse and that its investigations had led to informal disciplinary action in 99 cases, formal disciplinary charges in 22, and the lodging of criminal charges in 14 more. Local human rights groups complain that the ICPC's powers are inadequate because it cannot act autonomously; it can only review cases in which a state actor or a citizen has filed a complaint.

In 1993 the Northern Ireland Secretary named an independent assessor of military complaints to deal with procedures regarding complaints of abuses by the army; he, too, has no independent investigative powers. His third report, released in May, noted that the army had largely implemented the recommendations of the two earlier reports. There were only 19 complaints in 1995, down from 217 in 1994, as the cease-fires took hold. The assessor criticized delays in processing (nine cases took more than 8 weeks to resolve) and suggested that letters denying army culpability should, where reasonable, give the complainants the benefit of the doubt in order to improve community relations.

The United Nations Committee Against Torture and many human rights groups have raised concerns about mistreatment of detainees in Northern Ireland, where suspects arrested under emergency legislation are interrogated in special holding centers.

In 1992 the Government appointed a senior barrister as Independent Commissioner for Holding Centers in Northern Ireland, with authority to make irregular, unannounced visits to any holding center, observe interrogations, and interview detainees. In January he and his deputy noted that 11 complaints of physical assault during detention (in a detainee population of 449) were received in 1995. Their report welcomed the Government's decision in January (not yet implemented as of October) to introduce a system for silent video recording of interrogations of suspects (at which legal representatives are not allowed) but called for introduction of audio recording as well.

There have long been accusations that security forces in Northern Ireland harass citizens, particularly young people, in areas where support for terrorists is considered strong. The Government strongly denies that such behavior is widespread or officially tolerated.

Police continue to use plastic bullets in crowd control situations, a practice restricted to Northern Ireland. The number of plastic rounds fired this year surpasses all but one prior year. This practice has been widely criticized by human rights monitors and the U.N. Committee Against Torture. The European Parliament has called for a ban on their use. According to RUC rules, plastic bullets should be aimed at the lower half of the body; numerous head and upper body injuries nevertheless have resulted from their use.

Prison conditions meet minimum international standards, and the Government permits visits by human rights monitors. A 1995 security crackdown has resulted in harsher prison regimes, particularly for those inmates categorized as "high risk."

In January the Home Secretary announced that female prisoners admitted to the hospital to give birth would no longer have handcuffs or any other physical restraints applied to them at any time during their hospital stays; nor would restraints now be applied during prenatal checkups unless there was a particularly high risk of escape.

IRA bombings targeting buildings and economic activities in England have resulted in civilian casualties. Two bombs in February in London injured a total of 108 persons, 2 fatally; another in June in Manchester injured more than 200. In September a police raid resulted in the seizure of 10,000 pounds of explosive material, ammunition, firearms, and vehicle booby traps from several caches in London. Police officials said that the evidence pointed to a planned large-scale terrorist attack. Republican terrorists are also believed to be responsible for a double explosion within Thiepval Barracks, Lisburn (British Army headquarters in Northern Ireland) on October 7. One soldier died later of injuries, and 31 people, including an 8-year-old girl, were injured.

Joseph Kelly, Brian McHugh, James Murphy, and Michael Phillips were arrested in London on September 23 following discovery of bomb-making and other terrorist materials at a London residence. The four were charged with conspiracy to cause explosions under the Prevention of Terrorism Act. They are being held at Belmarsh Prison awaiting trial.

Both Loyalist and Republican terrorists in Northern Ireland have carried out increasingly frequent "punishment" attacks, typically involving beatings with iron pipes and spiked clubs. The RUC recorded 79 Loyalist and 175 Republican assaults of this nature in 1996. Young men ages 14 years and over were the most frequent victims. In 1995 there were 141 Republican assaults and 79 by Loyalists. The Loyalists often, but not exclusively, target members of their terrorist cells who have broken ranks, while the Republicans more frequently extend their vigilante activities to the broader Catholic community, punishing "antisocial" activities (such as drug-trafficking and car theft).

d. *Arbitrary Arrest, Detention, or Exile.*—British authorities can and often do make arrests or detain suspects without judicial warrants—especially in Northern Ireland, under laws applicable only there—when they believe that they have reasonable cause to suspect wrongdoing.

The Criminal Justice and Public Order Act of 1994 allows police officers to stop and search vehicles and pedestrians "where it appears expedient to do so in order to prevent acts of terrorism." The rules under the 1991 Northern Ireland Emergency Provisions Act permit an on-duty soldier or security officer to arrest and detain for up to 4 hours "a person who he has reasonable grounds to suspect is committing or has committed or is about to commit any offense." The Prevention of Terrorism Act (PTA) is the most reviewed piece of legislation in the United Kingdom. It expires every 2 years and, due to the changing security situation, is amended or altered to account for those changes.

Outside Northern Ireland, suspects arrested without warrants must be released within 24 hours (or 36 hours if a serious arrestable offense is involved) unless brought before a magistrate's court. The court may authorize extension of detention by 36 hours and on further application by another 24 hours. Defendants awaiting trial have a statutory right to be granted bail unless there is a risk that they would abscond, commit an offense, interfere with witnesses, or otherwise obstruct the course of justice, or unless they were on bail when the alleged offense was committed. The minority (about 3 percent) of defendants who are remanded in custody are protected by statutory custody time limits, which restrict the period for which they can be held while awaiting trial to a maximum of 182 days unless the court grants an extension. In 1995 (latest figures) the average period for which defendants awaiting Crown court trial were held in custody was 139 days.

The Prevention of Terrorism (Temporary Provisions) Act allows the police to arrest without a warrant anywhere in the UK persons they have reason to suspect of being involved in terrorism. The authorities may detain such persons (even those under the age of 18) up to 48 hours without legal representation or judicial review. Suspects may be interrogated during this time, and confessions obtained may be used in subsequent court proceedings. Under the 1989 PTA in England or Wales, detainees are granted the right to have lawyers present during interrogation, but this is not the case in Northern Ireland. Detention without charge may be extended up to a further 5 days on the authority of the Home Secretary or, in Northern Ireland, the Secretary of State for Northern Ireland. Extensive PTA detention powers were held in breach of a ruling by the European Court of Human Rights (ECHR) and have occasioned a derogation by the Government. For example, in February the ECHR ruled that the Home Secretary's power to decide whether or not to release young murderers violated article 5 of the European convention on human rights. The ruling calls for the Government to set up an independent judicial body to review the detention of juveniles who have committed murder.

Immigration legislation gives the power of administrative detention to immigration officers. There is no time limit for such detention and no right to have it reviewed by a court. In 1995 police detained a Punjab native with permanent residency in the UK, Raghbir Singh Johal, citing national security after the murder in London of a Punjabi newspaper editor. The Home Office has not permitted Singh to see any of the evidence on which it based its decision, has not told him what the allegations are against him, and will not afford him legal representation.

Refugee advocates complained about detention of about 750 asylum seekers, who are held in regular prisons and occasionally police cells, as well as in specially built detention centers. Unlike those accused of criminal offenses, the asylum seekers are given no written statement as to why they are detained, and their right to apply for bail is not automatic and requires a high level of surety. The Home Office states that detention is authorized only where there are good grounds to believe that a person will not comply with the terms of temporary admission and that the practice does not affect more than 1.5 percent of asylum seekers at any given time.

The Government does not practice exile (see Section 2.d. regarding exclusion orders), but terrorist organizations do. An organization that works with individuals and families under threat in Northern Ireland reported that up to the end of August it was aware of 238 cases of people who had been warned to leave the province, 63 of whom had actually done so. This compared with 215 cases for all of 1995.

e. *Denial of Fair Public Trial.*—The judiciary is independent and provides citizens with a generally fair and efficient judicial process.

The UK has several levels of courts. The vast majority of criminal cases are heard by magistrates' courts, which are managed by locally based committees. Their decisions may be appealed to the Crown Court, which also hears criminal cases requiring a jury trial, or to the High Court. From the Crown Court, convictions may be appealed to the Court of Appeal, which in turn may refer cases involving points of law to the House of Lords. The Appellate Committee of the House of Lords (which consists of senior judges and is functionally distinct from the legislative arm) is the final court of appeal. Once all of these appeals have been exhausted, defendants in England and Wales may appeal to the Home Secretary to refer a case back to the courts if fresh evidence has emerged that casts doubt on the conviction. (Appeals may be made to the Northern Ireland Office and the Scottish Office in those jurisdictions.)

The law provides for fair trial, and the authorities respect this. In August the Home Office appointed the head of a new Criminal Case Review Commission to direct and supervise investigations into possible miscarriages of justice. The Commission, called for by the 1995 Criminal Appeal Act, is supposed to refer cases in which routine appeals have been exhausted for further appeal on factual, legal, and sentencing grounds. Members of Parliament objected when it turned out that the appointee belonged to the Freemasons, a secretive fraternal organization that includes in its membership many police officers. By year's end the Commission was not yet operational. Thus, cases involving possible miscarriages of justice must be referred to the Home Office for review.

Under the Criminal Justice and Public Order Act of 1994, judges have the power to instruct juries that they may draw an inference of guilt from a defendant's refusal to answer questions during interrogation or trial, although no conviction can be based solely on such an inference. Human rights groups and the U.N. Human Rights Commission have sharply criticized this change in the law. A similar provision is in effect in Northern Ireland.

Indigent defendants have the right to free counsel of their choice, with some exceptions. In June the European Court of Human Rights faulted the Government for not extending the duty solicitor scheme to poll and council tax defaulters, some 900 of whom are jailed annually.

All criminal proceedings must be held in public except those in juvenile court and those involving public decency or security. In a trial under the Official Secrets Act, the judge may order the court closed, but the sentencing must be public. Convictions can be appealed to successively higher courts.

In Northern Ireland, special "emergency" restrictions affect due process. Under the Northern Ireland Emergency Provisions Act of 1991 (EPA), the Government can suspend the right to trial by jury for certain terrorist-related offenses. Such offenses are tried instead by a "Diplock Court" consisting of a judge presiding without a jury. If the decision is to convict, the judge must justify it in a document that becomes part of the court record, and an appellate court may overturn it on substantive as well as legal grounds. The Diplock Courts have been widely criticized. The EPA also permits the use of uncorroborated confessions, but they cannot be the sole basis for conviction.

The 1988 Criminal Evidence Order allows judges to draw an adverse inference when a suspect refuses to answer questions. In February the ECHR found in John Murray v. United Kingdom that the denial in Northern Ireland of access to counsel for the first 48 hours in a situation where the right of the defense might thus be irretrievably prejudiced was, whatever the justification, incompatible with article 6 of the European convention on human rights.

There were no reports of political prisoners.

f. *Arbitrary Interference With Privacy, Family, Home, or Correspondence.*—Warrants are normally required for a police search of private premises. However, under the 1991 EPA, on-duty members of the armed forces or policemen in Northern Ireland may enter and search "any premises for the purpose of arresting a person for an arrestable offense, but only if he or she has reasonable grounds for believing that the person being sought is on the premises."

Primarily due to fear of intercommunal violence, many Protestant and Catholic families in Northern Ireland moved away from mixed or border neighborhoods.

In Northern Ireland, paramilitary groups have attacked and threatened to attack the homes and families of police and politicians.

Section 2. Respect for Civil Liberties, Including:

a. *Freedom of Speech and Press.*—Strongly held common-law tradition, an independent press, and a democratic political system combine to secure freedom of speech and the press, including academic freedom. Viewpoints critical of the Government are well represented. The print media are dominated by a handful of national daily newspapers, all privately owned and independent (although often generally aligned with a political party). About half the electronic media are run by the British Broadcasting Corporation (BBC), which is funded by the Government but enjoys complete editorial independence. The remainder are run by corporations under renewable government license.

Human rights organizations and journalists criticized the 1981 Contempt of Court Act, which allows courts to order a journalist to disclose a source if this is deemed to be "in the interests of justice." In March the ECHR found that the Government had violated the right to free expression when it held journalist William Goodwin and his publishers in contempt of court for refusing to disclose the identity of a source who had given Goodwin confidential corporate information that, if published, might have caused financial harm to a company.

The doctrine of Public Interest Immunity (PII) allows government ministers to prevent certain information from being disclosed during litigation, on the grounds that its revelation would be contrary to the public interest. For those charged with disclosing official information, the 1990 Official Secrets Act denies any defense that the information is already in the public domain or that its publication is in the public interest.

b. *Freedom of Peaceful Assembly and Association.*—The law provides for the right of peaceful assembly, but the right is routinely limited where it would impose a cost on public convenience. The annual "Marching season" in Northern Ireland, a period of several weeks in the summer during which the 100,000 members of the Orange Order and similar Protestant organizations stage traditional parades to celebrate their history and cultural identity, posed special problems to the Government as it tried to respect this right in practice. Similar organizations in the nationalist community also march during the summer, although the smaller scale of those parades has presented law enforcement authorities with fewer difficulties.

After initially prohibiting it, police permitted Orangemen to march along Garvaghy road in Portadown in July, despite local nationalist residents' objections. The RUC chief constable said that he reversed his decision because the potential for loss of life was very high as the likelihood increased, during a 5-day standoff, that more than 50,000 Orangemen would try to breach police lines. Many observers on both sides of the community perceived the Government's reversal in the face of unlawful Unionist protests as a victory of might over the rule of law, and the incident damaged the RUC's reputation as an impartial police force.

In July the Secretary of State for Northern Ireland appointed an independent commission headed by the Vice Chancellor of Oxford University to examine the parades issue and make recommendations for the future. The Government also announced that a review of the RUC's handling of public order situations would be undertaken by the Inspector of Constabulary, an independent inspectorate covering every police force in the United Kingdom, including the use of plastic bullets and would include the issue of police protection in the face of determined assaults.

Under the PTA, the Secretary of State for Northern Ireland may proscribe any organization that "appears to him to be concerned in, or in promoting or encouraging terrorism occurring in the United Kingdom and connected with the affairs of Northern Ireland." Membership in proscribed Loyalist and Republican paramilitary groups is punishable by up to 10 years' imprisonment. Supporting these paramilitary groups is also illegal and an imprisonable offense, as is wearing clothing that arouses "reasonable suspicion" that the wearer belongs to or supports proscribed organizations. Human rights monitors, while acknowledging the deterrent effects of proscription powers, argue for the repeal of this law because it violates the fundamental right of freedom of association and the individual's right to hold opinions and beliefs.

c. *Freedom of Religion.*—Government policy and general practice ensure freedom of religion. There are two legally recognized official churches of the state: the (Anglican) Church of England and the (Presbyterian) Church of Scotland. Wales has not had an established church since 1920. Freedom of worship has been legally guaranteed to members of all faiths and denominations since the mid-19th century. Blasphemy of the Christian religion is outlawed. The blasphemy law, however, is rarely enforced. In Northern Ireland, the Constitution Act of 1973 prohibits public authorities from discriminating on the basis of religious or political belief.

d. *Freedom of Movement Within the Country, Foreign Travel, Emigration, and Repatriation.*—Citizens enjoy freedom of movement within the country and in foreign travel, emigration, and repatriation. However, the Home Secretary may exclude from Great Britain anyone believed linked with terrorism in Northern Ireland, except anyone born in Great Britain or resident there for 3 years; and the Secretary of State for Northern Ireland can likewise exclude persons not native to or resident in that province. Currently 31 persons (down from 36 in 1995) are subject to exclusion orders. Several Members of Parliament, human rights groups, and the media have objected to exclusion orders. The Secretary of State need not reveal the grounds for exclusion, and the evidence is not tested in any court. There is no right of appeal to the courts, but appeal may be made informally to an independent advisor.

The Government cooperates with the U.N. High Commissioner for Refugees (UNHCR) and other humanitarian organizations in assisting refugees. First asylum is provided under a temporary protection program started in 1992. All evacuees are screened by the UNHCR. Approximately 3,700 people have been accepted under the program, which allows them 6 months' "leave to enter the country" on arrival. They can then apply for an automatic 3½-year extension of their stay and may apply for refugee status at any time. Such applications are considered in accordance with the criteria in the 1951 U.N. refugee convention. If recognized as refugees, they may remain indefinitely.

New measures beginning in February denied social welfare benefits to refugees who had not sought asylum as soon as they entered the country. The measures are intended to discourage false asylum claims. According to government reports, new asylum applications fell dramatically. After an Appeals Court ruled in July that the Government's plan to withdraw all benefits was illegal, the number of asylum applications nearly doubled, from 920 received in June, to 1,700 received in July. Immigration officials claim that this is proof that many claiming to be political refugees are actually economic migrants.

Saudi dissident Mohammed al-Masari entered the UK illegally and applied for asylum. His initial request was denied, due to the circumstances of his entry, but the courts prohibited immigration officials from deporting him to his home country because his safety there could not be guaranteed. The Government then considered sending Al-Masari to a third country, Dominica, but he was able to demonstrate that his safety could not be assured there either. Finally, Al-Masari was granted permission to remain for 4 years, with the option of applying for permanent residency at the end of that period.

Section 3. Respect for Political Rights: The Right of Citizens to Change Their Government

Citizens have the right to change their government and freely exercise that right. The Government is formed on the basis of a majority of seats in the House of Commons. Elections are held at intervals not to exceed 5 years.

Participation in the political process is open to all persons and parties. All citizens 18 years of age and older may vote. Northern Ireland has city and district councils, as in the rest of the UK, but with somewhat fewer powers. England and Wales also have county councils, while Northern Ireland does not. (Scotland's structure is different still.) Despite periodic attempts, there has been no devolved government in Northern Ireland since 1972 because of the situation there.

Parties committed to the establishment of some form of Scottish parliament received some 75 percent of the vote during the last general election (in 1992). The Scottish National Party, which holds four seats in Parliament, advocates independence for Scotland.

British dependent territories, other than Hong Kong, have small populations, under 60,000, and all are ruled by appointed governors or administrators assisted by executive councils (usually appointed) and legislative assemblies or councils (partly elected).

Women and minorities face no legal constraints on voting or holding office. Women members constitute about 10 percent of the membership of the lower legislative chamber and 5 percent of the upper one. Several members of minority ethnic groups serve in Parliament.

Section 4. Governmental Attitude Regarding International and Nongovernmental Investigation of Alleged Violations of Human Rights

A wide variety of human rights groups operate without government restriction, investigating and publishing their findings on human rights cases. Government officials are cooperative and responsive to their views. In 1973 the Government established a Standing Advisory Commission on Human Rights (SACHR) to monitor human rights in Northern Ireland but has not adopted many of its security-related recommendations.

A number of international, nongovernmental human rights organizations, including Amnesty International and Article 19, are based in the UK. The Government cooperates fully with international inquiries into alleged violations of human rights.

Section 5. Discrimination Based on Race, Sex, Religion, Disability, Language, or Social Status

The Race Relations Act of 1976 prohibits discrimination on the basis of race, color, nationality, or national or ethnic origin and outlaws incitement to racial hatred. No legislation exists to specifically outlaw racial discrimination in Northern Ireland. Discrimination on grounds of religious or political opinion is unlawful in Northern Ireland but not in Great Britain. Discrimination on the basis of religion is only illegal in Great Britain when its effect is to discriminate against a member of a minority ethnic group. The Government respects and enforces all extant antidiscrimination laws, which concentrate on employment and the supply of goods and services.

Women.—Statistical and other evidence indicates that most victims of societal violence are women. Domestic violence constitutes one-third of all reported crimes against women and accounts for almost 25 percent of all reported violent crimes. The Government believed that the problem of stalking was becoming so acute that it promised to introduce a new law that could result in stalkers being jailed for up to 5 years.

The law provides for injunctive relief, personal protection orders, and exclusion orders for women who are victims of violence. The Government provides shelters, counseling, and other assistance for victims of battery or rape, and it offers free legal aid to battered women who are economically reliant upon their abusers. The Government actively prosecutes perpetrators of domestic violence, and the law provides for their imprisonment. The courts have held that nonconsensual marital sex can constitute a criminal offense. A 1994 law abolished the warning that judges had previously been required to give juries to the effect that a victim's testimony alone should not be adequate for a rape conviction. The Criminal Justice and Public Order Act of 1994 made sexual (as well as other intentional) harassment a criminal offense.

The law provides for equal opportunity between the sexes, but women experience some discrimination in practice. Nevertheless, according to the Equal Opportunities Commission, there has been significant progress in equal opportunity for women at work since the Commission was set up following the passage of the Sex Discrimination Act. The Equal Opportunities Commission supports persons who bring discrimination cases before industrial tribunals and courts, and it produces guidelines on good practice for employers. Women in Britain earn approximately 20 percent less than their male counterparts in comparable positions. A government minister cochairs the Women's National Commission, a forum for women's organizations that presents women's views to the Government.

The 1975 Sex Discrimination Act as amended in 1986 prohibits indirect as well as direct discrimination in training, education, housing, and provision of goods and services, as well as in employment. Women have equal rights regarding property and divorce.

Children.—The Government demonstrates its strong commitment to children's rights and welfare through its well-funded systems of public education and medical care.

While there is no societal pattern of abuse directed against children, indications are, despite the lack of reliable data, that child abuse is nevertheless a problem. Various laws covering England and Wales stipulate that children have the right to apply for court orders, to give or withhold consent for medical treatment (for those capable of making an informed decision), to make complaints to the relevant local authority, to have their ethnic, linguistic, and religious background considered in decisions affecting them, to have reasonable contact with their family (usually applied in a circumstance where there has been abuse), and in general to be consulted regarding their desires.

In September a tribunal commenced examination of allegations of child abuse in public children's homes in Wales over the last 20 years. The hearings followed allegations of systematic physical and sexual abuse of hundreds of children by staff and were expected to last for 12 months.

People With Disabilities.—The Disability Discrimination Act passed in 1995 outlaws discrimination against disabled persons in provision of access to public facilities, by employers of more than 20 workers, service providers (apart from those providing education or running transport vehicles), and anyone selling or renting property. The 1993 Education Act imposes specific duties on local education authorities to make provision for the special educational needs of disabled children. Disabled rights groups continued to complain that the Government had declined to create an enforcement body for the Discrimination Act.

Rights Now, a consortium of over 50 independent organizations campaigning for laws to end discrimination on the grounds of disability, reported that employers were 6 times more likely to turn down a disabled person for a job interview than a nondisabled applicant with the same qualifications; that only 80,000 wheelchair-accessible houses were available, and that in the last general election 88 percent of polling stations were inaccessible to disabled people.

Access to buildings is improving but inadequate. Many buildings and train stations are so old that they do not have elevators. Since 1985 government regulations have required that all new buildings meet the access requirements of all persons with impaired mobility. In 1992 the Government put in place similar regulations for sensory-impaired persons. Government regulations mandate that by the year 2000 all taxis be accessible to wheelchairs.

Religious Minorities.—Despite government efforts, the unemployment rate for Catholic men in Northern Ireland remained twice that for Protestant men. The Fair Employment (Northern Ireland) Act of 1989, as amended, aims to end even unintentional or indirect discrimination in the workplace. A fair employment tribunal adjudicates complaints. All public-sector employers and all private firms with over 10 workers must report annually to the Fair Employment Commission on the religious composition of their work force and must review their employment practices at least once every 3 years. Noncompliance can bring criminal penalties and loss of government contracts. Victims of employment discrimination may sue for damages. While critics of the act have asserted that its targets and timetables are too imprecise, most leaders of the Catholic community have praised it as a positive step.

There have been improvements in fair housing, education, and provision of goods and services, although there is no legislation to prohibit discrimination on the basis of religion in Great Britain.

While active recruitment of Catholics by the Northern Ireland civil service has produced rough proportionality in overall numbers, the service has acknowledged that Catholics remain significantly underrepresented in its senior grades, and in 1993 it declared its intention to overcome this imbalance. Service-wide employment cutbacks have thus far hampered its efforts. Government efforts to increase recruitment of Catholics into the police force (currently 92 percent Protestant) and related security fields in the province have been hampered by IRA assassinations and death threats, as well as widespread antipathy in the Catholic community to the security forces. The number of Catholics joining the RUC increased somewhat during the August 1994 to February 1996 cease-fire period but has fallen since, despite continuing recruitment efforts.

National/Racial/Ethnic Minorities.—Although the law prohibits discrimination based on race (except in Northern Ireland), persons of African or south Asian origin face occasional acts of societal violence and some discrimination. Incitement to racial hatred is a criminal offense punishable by a maximum of 2 years' imprisonment. The Government strictly enforces the laws and regulations in this area.

The U.N. Committee on the Elimination of Racial Discrimination noted with serious concern in March that among the victims of death in custody in the UK were a disproportionate number of members of minority groups; that police brutality appeared to affect members of minority groups disproportionately; and that allegations of police brutality and harassment were reportedly not vigorously investigated and perpetrators, once guilt was established, not appropriately punished.

A government-appointed but independent Commission for Racial Equality (CRE) provides guidelines on good practice, supports persons taking court action under the Race Relations Act of 1976, and may initiate its own court action. After investigating a complaint, the CRE may issue a notice requiring that the discrimination be stopped. The CRE monitors the response to such a notice for 5 years.

Following a 2-year examination of the army's household cavalry, the CRE in March found that there had been racial discrimination in recruitment and transfer and racial abuse and harassment in individual cases. The Ministry of Defense agreed to take steps, including monitoring of ethnic recruitment and prompt investigation of complaints, to redress these problems.

Section 6. Worker Rights

a. *The Right of Association.*—Workers have the right to form and join unions, and the Government fully respects this right in practice. Unions are free of government control. Like employers' associations, they must have their accounts certified by the Government. Senior union officers must be elected by secret ballot. The law mandates secret ballots before a strike call, prohibits unions from disciplining members who reject a legal strike call, and allows members to lodge complaints against their union with a government-appointed commissioner.

There is no specific statutory "right to strike." Voluntary cessation of work may be considered a breach of contract. A system of legal immunities from prosecution for unions engaged in lawful industrial action was narrowed by acts of Parliament in the 1980's. These acts exclude secondary strikes and actions judged to have political motives; unions encouraging such strikes are subject to fines and seizure of their assets. The legislation also restricts the ability of unions to act against subsidiaries of prime employers with which they are in dispute when the subsidiaries are not party to the dispute and are the employers of record.

In 1993 the Council of Europe (COE) determined that British labor law violated the European Social Charter by permitting an employer to dismiss all employees who take part in a strike and then, after 3 months, to rehire them selectively. The Council requested that the British Government notify them of the measures to be taken to remedy this defect, but the Government has not done so because it is no longer a party to the Charter.

Legislation in 1978 and 1990 made it illegal to deny employment on the grounds that the applicant is not a union member. The Trade Union Reform and Employment Rights Act of 1993 set new procedural requirements for union strikes, dues collection, and membership rules. It also made it possible for private citizens, when deprived of goods or services due to strike action, to seek damages and to obtain assistance in this effort from the Government. The Trade Unions Congress (TUC) in 1993 lodged complaints with the International Labor Organization (ILO) on various provisions of the 1993 Act (see Section 6.b.). In 1995 a court upheld a provision of the Employment Protection Act of 1978, as amended by the Employment Act of 1988, allowing employers to offer workers financial inducements to give up trade union representation. In 1996 the Committee of Experts of the ILO found this law in substantial violation of Convention 98 which guarantees the right to organize and bargain collectively and asked the UK to amend its legislation. The Government has not yet acted on this recommendation.

Unions participate freely in international organizations.

b. *The Right to Organize and Bargain Collectively.*—Although there is no legal obligation for employers to bargain with workers' representatives, and while labor-management contracts are not enforceable in the courts, collective bargaining is long standing and widespread, covering about 40 percent of the work force.

Workers who believe themselves victims of antiunion discrimination may seek redress through industrial tribunals. Remedies available include payment of indemnities and reinstatement.

Contrary to ILO Convention 98, it is lawful for employers or others to circulate blacklists of union members seeking employment. In 1993 the ILO concluded that the British Government was obliged to protect union members from such discrimination, but the Government has not responded to this.

There are no export processing zones in the UK.

c. *Prohibition of Forced or Compulsory Labor.*—Forced or compulsory labor is prohibited and is not practiced.

d. *Minimum Age for Employment of Children.*—School attendance until the age of 16 is compulsory. Children under the age of 16 are not permitted to work in an industrial enterprise except as part of an educational course.

e. *Acceptable Conditions of Work.*—There is no legislated minimum wage. The Trade Union Reform and Employment Rights Act of 1993 abolished the wage council system, which prior to September 1993 had established minimum hourly wages and overtime rates for adult workers in 26 low-wage industries. No legislation limits daily or weekly working hours.

The Health and Safety at Work Act of 1974 requires that the health and safety of employees not be placed at risk. A Health and Safety Commission effectively enforces regulations on these matters and may initiate criminal proceedings. Workers' representatives actively monitor the enforcement. Workers can remove themselves from hazardous conditions without risking loss of employment as provided in the European Union Framework Directive on Safety and Health.

In November the European Court determined that an EU directive limiting the workweek to 48 hours in most circumstances was applicable to the UK. The Government argued that EU directives dealing with the Social Chapter should not apply in the UK because of its "opt out" from this provision, but agreed to enforce the directive while undertaking to modify it via changes in the jurisdiction of the European Court.

HONG KONG

Hong Kong, a small, densely populated British dependency, is a free society with legally protected rights. Its constitutional arrangements are defined by the Letters Patent and Royal Instructions. Executive powers are vested in a British Crown-appointed Governor who holds extensive authority. The judiciary is an independent body adhering to English common law with certain variations. Fundamental rights ultimately rest on oversight by the British Parliament. In practice, however, Hong Kong largely controls its own internal affairs.

All 60 seats in the Hong Kong Legislative Council were open to direct or indirect balloting for the first time in September 1995, and the elections were widely considered to be fair and open.

The resulting Legislative Council has served as a forum for vigorous debate and planning for the period after July 1, 1997, when sovereignty over Hong Kong will revert from the United Kingdom to the People's Republic of China and it becomes the Hong Kong Special Administrative Region. However, China has stated its intention to dissolve the 1995 Legislative Council, district boards, and municipal councils in July 1997, noting that it did not agree to the electoral rules adopted by the Hong Kong Government in 1994 for election to these bodies.

On December 28, 1995, China appointed a Preparatory Committee, composed of 57 mainland Chinese and 93 Hong Kong residents, to establish the post-1997 Special Administrative Region Government. Democratic Party members of the Legislative Council responded on March 13, voting to condemn the Preparatory Committee's "unrepresentative composition," particularly the lack of democracy advocates. In March the Preparatory Committee announced that a provisional legislature will be formed before July 1, 1997, to "examine and approve" laws and other measures that take effect at midnight June 30, 1997. In early November, the Preparatory Committee members established the Selection Committee, composed of 400 Hong Kong residents. The Selection Committee in turn, chose the Chief Executive and provisional legislature in December. Thirty-three of the current Legislative Council members were selected to join the provisional legislature. However, none of those chosen were Democratic Party members, who opposed and therefore chose not to seek seats on the provisional legislature even though their party that had drawn the most popular support in the Legislative Council elections in 1995. There has been public concern that the selection of the provisional legislature was unnecessary, lacked transparency, was not based on open elections, and excluded groups or individuals critical of China.

A well-organized police force maintains public order and is under the firm control of civilian authorities. There were reports that some members of the police used excessive force.

Hong Kong is a major regional and international trade and financial center. It is the principal gateway for trade and investment with China. The territory's free market economy operates on the basis of minimal government interference and a thriving private sector. Per capita gross domestic product surpassed $23,200 in 1995 and continued to grow in 1996.

Human rights activists, journalists, and legislators continued to criticize the Government for opposing human rights initiatives such as the establishment of a human rights commission; laws against discrimination based on age, race, and sexual orientation; and freedom of information legislation. Human rights problems continued to include some instances of excessive use of force by the police, media self-censorship, limitations on citizens' ability to change their government, and violence and discrimination against women, and discrimination against the disabled.

The Government actively maintains a high degree of legal and judicial protection of fundamental rights and freedoms. The scrupulous protection of human rights, as pledged in Chinese commitments, is seen as a key element in the transition to Chinese sovereignty.

RESPECT FOR HUMAN RIGHTS

Section 1. Respect for the Integrity of the Person, Including Freedom From:

a. *Political and Other Extrajudicial Killing.*—There were no reports of political or other extrajudicial killings.

There were eight instances of death in police custody. The authorities determined that three were deaths by natural causes and four were suicides; the eighth remains under investigation.

b. *Disappearance.*—There were no reports of politically motivated disappearances.

c. *Torture and Other Cruel, Inhuman, or Degrading Treatment or Punishment.*—The law forbids torture and other extreme forms of abuse by the police and stipulates punishment for those who break the law. Disciplinary action can range from dismissal to warnings. Criminal proceedings may be undertaken independently of the disciplinary process of the police force. Allegations of excessive use of force are investigated by the Complaints Against Police Office, whose work is in turn monitored and reviewed by the Police Complaints Council, a body composed of members of the public appointed by the Governor. The Government, however, continued to resist public calls for the creation of an independent body to investigate allegations of abuse by police.

Although excessive use of force by police is not widespread, there are occasional complaints of force being used to coerce information or confessions during police interrogations. Human rights monitors in Hong Kong are concerned that this may be a growing problem and have documented victims' complaints of beatings during interrogation. In 1995 government officials reported 1,581 complaints against police, of which only 1 was substantiated by the Police Complaints Council. From January to June, there were 704 complaints, all for "assault by police officers," but none were substantiated. Human rights groups contrast the relatively large number of complaints with the very small number of cases substantiated by the Government to argue the need for revamping a system where the review process appears to favor the police.

Although conditions vary among facilities, prison conditions generally conform to international standards. The Government permits prison visits by human rights monitors.

d. *Arbitrary Arrest, Detention, or Exile.*—British legal protections and common law traditions govern the process of arrest and detention and ensure substantial and effective legal protections against arbitrary arrest or detention.

Exile is not practiced.

e. *Denial of Fair Public Trial.*—The judicial and legal systems are organized according to principles of British constitutional law and legal precedent and provide for an independent judiciary, which the Government respects in practice. According to the agreement signed by the United Kingdom and China in June 1995, Hong Kong's Court of Final Appeal will be established formally on July 1, 1997. Incoming officials of the post-1997 Hong Kong Special Administrative Region are to be responsible for setting up the Court and selecting judges. The agreement thus grants a principal role in the Court's establishment and membership to the Hong Kong Special Administrative Region Government. After reversion, the Court of Final Appeal is to have power of final judgment over Hong Kong law. The Special Administrative Region courts, however, are to have "no jurisdiction over acts of State such as defense and foreign affairs." The Basic Law also vests the Standing Committee of China's National People's Congress with the power to interpret the Basic Law in matters that are the "responsibility of the Central People's Government or concern the relationship between the Central authorities and the Special Administrative Region." If broadly applied and loosely interpreted, these exceptions to the Court of Final Appeal's power of final jurisdiction could be used to limit the independence of the judiciary after 1997.

The law provides for the right to a fair public trial, and this is respected in practice. Trial is by jury.
There were no reports of political prisoners.

f. *Arbitrary Interference With Privacy, Family, Home, or Correspondence.*—The law provides for the right of privacy, and the Government generally respects this right in practice. The Independent Commission Against Corruption is vested with powers that are normally exercised only by a judicial officer. Amendments to ordinances governing the Independent Commission Against Corruption have deprived it of the independent authority to issue arrest or search warrants (it must now go to the courts), but it still operates on the assumption that any excessive, unexplainable assets held by civil servants are ill-gotten until proven otherwise.

Section 2. *Respect for Civil Liberties, Including:*

a. *Freedom of Speech and Press.*—Hong Kong has a tradition of free speech and free press. Political debate is vigorous. Numerous views and opinions, including those independent or critical of the British, Hong Kong, and Chinese governments, are aired in the mass media, in public forums, and by political groups. International media organizations operate freely. Several ordinances permit restrictions on the press, but they are rarely imposed. The Hong Kong Journalists Association has continued to criticize the Government for not taking swift action to repeal these ordinances before 1997, warning that the post-1997 Government might be more prone to invoke them.

Residents of the territory continue to speak freely to the press, and there are no taboo subjects in the media. Although there are reports of self-censorship, it is difficult to verify specific instances in which self-censorship has killed a story. However, according to poll results published in February 1995 by Hong Kong University's Social Science Research Center, most journalists believe that self-censorship remains a problem. The pressures on journalists are subtle—there are no direct orders to refrain from writing—but a need for special care toward topics of particular sensitivity in China, such as leadership dynamics, corruption, or military activity is nonetheless perceived. Journalists in the Chinese-language press report a pervasive if tacit understanding that editors expect those reporting on China to be especially certain of their facts and careful in their wording. A few newspaper articles have reported self-censorship among Hong Kong publishers on such sensitive issues as Taiwan and Tibet. Another source of pressure comes from the belief of some publishers and editors that their advertising revenues would suffer if they were perceived to be too antagonistic to China in their editorial judgments.

Hong Kong press coverage of China continues to be extensive and is frequently critical. For example, there was strong criticism in the press of Chinese Foreign Minister Qian Qichen in October after he indicated that in post-July 1997 Hong Kong reporting of "rumors or lies," personal criticism of Chinese leaders in the press, and any demonstrations to commemorate the Tiananmen Square events of June 4, 1989, would not be allowed. Although overall there has been neither a sharp increase nor decrease of critical coverage over the past year, Hong Kong journalists based in or traveling to China face certain risks. China requires journalists to apply for permission to do any reporting in China. Those who bypass official channels—which many feel they must do to get the stories they want—run a risk of violating regulations. For example, according to a press report three Hong Kong journalists were detained and then deported by China after being accused of illegally entering a military zone in Fujian province to collect information during the Chinese military exercises near Taiwan in March. The New China (Xinhua) News Agency reported that they were detained because they did not follow rules and regulations for Hong Kong journalists working on the mainland. Hong Kong reporters continue, however, to enter China to cover sensitive stories related to Hong Kong, Taiwan, or China itself.

Commemorations of journalist Xi Yang's imprisonment in 1994 continue to take place, with a massive march on the offices of the New China News Agency (Xinhua) this year. A PRC national, Xi Yang was working for Hong Kong's Ming Pao Daily when taken into custody for reporting economic data China considered to be state secrets. His arrest was widely cited as having had a chilling effect on Hong Kong media.

Xinhua's treatment of one commentary from a university journalism program suggests an insensitivity to press freedom, reinforcing concerns in Hong Kong about the prospects on this score following reversion. In a recent issue of a journalism magazine published at the Chinese University, the "Editor's Note" column reported on the Chinese authorities' method of dealing with the press, gleaned from an interview with the Xinhua Deputy Director in Hong Kong. Xinhua, which had been shown an advance copy of the issue, tried without success to change the story. After the story was published, Xinhua contacted the student who conducted the interview and hinted that it would be "hard for the reporter to stay in the journalism field in the future if that attitude did not change."

Early in the year, the Hong Kong media were still reacting to a newspaper price war set off when the Oriental Daily News, the most popular daily in Hong Kong for the past 20 years, lowered its retail price in an attempt to woo readers away from Apple Daily, a tabloid-style daily newspaper that has captured a larger share of the market from other papers. The price war led to closure of four daily newspapers, a weekly entertainment periodical, and a newspaper supplement magazine. Another casualty was Eastern Express, the English-language daily published by the Oriental Group, which closed during the summer. Some commentators fear that the closings might lead to less diversity of opinion in the media but there has been no visible affect on the range of opinions expressed.

Media and general public access to government information is strictly controlled. The Government opposed freedom of information legislation proposed by Legislative Council members in 1995 and decided instead to develop an administrative code of practice on access to government information. Under the code, civil servants are required to provide information held by the Government, unless there are valid reasons not to do so. A pilot scheme to test the legal, practical, and resource implications arising from the code began in March 1995. By December 23, the code had been extended to the entire Government. The Government's efficiency unit reports a rejection rate of five percent for information requests from the public.

The Government respects academic freedom. There are a wide range of opinions represented in lively debate on Hong Kong campuses, and the issue of academic freedom has not generally caused much public comment. In June the Hong Kong University vice-chancellor ordered the removal of Tiananmen-era slogans criticizing China from university pavement. This order sparked strong student protests, and the slogans were repainted.

b. *Freedom of Peaceful Assembly and Association.*—Freedom of assembly is practiced without significant hindrance. Following a march by 3,000 people protesting the sentencing of Chinese dissident Wang Dan in November, police ordered protesters to remove banners from outside Xinhua News Agency headquarters. The police claimed that the banners were hazardous to motorists; demonstrators claimed that the order stemmed from pressure from People's Republic of China authorities.

Freedom of association is also practiced without significant hindrance, although the amended Societies Ordinance requires people to notify the Societies Officer of the formation of a society. The Societies Officer may recommend to the Secretary for Security prohibition of the operation or continued operation of a society if he reasonably believes that it may be prejudicial to the security of Hong Kong or to public safety or public order. The provision in the ordinance allowing the Government to refuse to register an organization "incompatible with peace, welfare, or good order," or affiliated with a political organization abroad was repealed in 1992. The Basic Law provides, however, that the Special Administrative Region "shall enact laws on its own" regarding subversion and overseas political affiliations of Hong Kong organizations. This could lead, after July 1, 1997, to reinstatement of certain restrictions on societies.

c. *Freedom of Religion.*—The Hong Kong Bill of Rights includes a provision prohibiting discrimination on the basis of religion. Government policy and general practice ensure freedom of religion.

d. *Freedom of Movement Within the Country, Foreign Travel, Emigration, and Repatriation.*—There is freedom of movement within Hong Kong, and travel documents are freely and easily obtained. The number of applicants for British Dependent Territories travel documents was more than five times the total for all of 1995. The last day of eligibility was in March.

Two Democratic Party members were denied entry to China in November, raising questions in Hong Kong about the existence of a "blacklist" of Hong Kong politicians. The two had planned to submit petitions in Beijing against the Selection Committee and the provisional legislature.

Hong Kong has never refused first asylum to Vietnamese boat people. Prior to June 1988, refugee status was automatically accorded them. Since then asylum seekers have been screened to determine their status and held in prison-like detention centers awaiting resettlement in other countries or repatriation to Vietnam. From October 1995 to September 1996, 5,660 persons were voluntarily repatriated to Vietnam through the auspices of the United Nations High Commissioner for Refugees. On May 12, 1992, the Hong Kong Government reached agreement with Vietnamese authorities on mandatory (involuntary) repatriation (the "Orderly Return Program") of those who were determined not to be refugees. There were 4,267 people repatriated under the Orderly Return Program from October 1995 to September

1996. Under the program, people are randomly chosen from the nonrefugee camp population and moved to a separate location several days before a flight's scheduled departure. Government security officers then escort, forcibly if necessary, all those being involuntarily returned on to the airplane and accompany the flight to Vietnam.

A total of 12,815 Vietnamese remained in the Hong Kong camps as of October 18, of whom 1,335 were screened-in as refugees but who, mostly for reasons of health or criminal acts, have not been resettled.

Hong Kong authorities continue to encounter physical resistance in the camps when attempting to remove those chosen for the Orderly Return Program flights. In May during a transfer of northern Vietnamese from the Whitehead Detention Center to the High Island Detention Center, a massive riot occurred in which many buildings and vehicles and records were burned by Vietnamese detainees. Hong Kong authorities used tear gas to restore order. All but 28 of the 119 Vietnamese who escaped from detention during the riot were found and returned to camp.

Voluntary Repatriation and the involuntary Orderly Return Program were regularly returning about 1,400 people a month during calendar year 1996. If continued, this rate of return is expected to leave the Hong Kong camps empty by the July 1, 1997, reversion to China. However, as of October 18, approximately 6,000 Vietnamese in camps had not been cleared for return by the Vietnamese Government.

The number of illegal Chinese immigrants has been estimated by knowledgeable observers to be at least 15,000. During 1996 the Government returned illegal Chinese immigrants to China at the rate of 68 per day. Only in those rare instances in which a person qualifies as a refugee under the terms of the international agreement on the status of refugees is permission to remain in Hong Kong granted. There are currently 289 ex-China Vietnamese illegal immigrants in Hong Kong. The repatriation of these people, who fled from China to Hong Kong, was stayed in 1996 pending the outcome of litigation in the Privy Council in London to free them from detention.

A well-known Chinese labor organizer and political dissident, Han Donfang, remains in Hong Kong. Chinese government authorities continued to refuse him entry into China as they have ever since his expulsion from China in August 1993.

Section 3. Respect for Political Rights: The Right of Citizens to Change Their Government

Hong Kong is a free society, with most individual freedoms and rights protected by law and custom. Although the Government has moved to democratize district and municipal boards and the Legislative Council, Hong Kong residents do not have the right to change the Government. The Governor is appointed by and serves at the pleasure of the Crown. He is advised on policy by the Executive Council, which he appoints.

The Legislative Council enacts and funds legislation and also debates policy and questions the administration. Although the Legislative Council's power to initiate legislation is limited (all bills with budgetary implications, for example, must be approved by the Government before introduction), it has become increasingly assertive. The Governor has ultimate control of the administration of Hong Kong but, by convention, rarely exercises his full powers. In practice, decisions are reached through consensus. Political parties and independent candidates are free to contest seats in free and fair elections. Representative government employing universal franchise exists at the local district board level.

All district and municipal board members were chosen by direct elections in 1994 and 1995, respectively. In 1995 the Government implemented legislation abolishing all appointed seats in the Legislative Council. In September 1995, 920,000 voters, by direct or indirect balloting, selected members to fill these seats in generally free and fair elections. Out of 60 seats, there were 20 geographic seats directly elected, 10 seats chosen by an election committee comprised of 283 locally elected officials, 9 seats selected by broad functional (occupational) constituencies, and 21 seats elected by more narrow functional groupings. Although the 1995 elections did not result in a fully representative, democratically elected government—a point on which they were criticized by the United Nations Human Rights Committee—they significantly increased voters' ability to influence government decisionmaking through a greater number of elected representatives.

China opposed the Hong Kong Government's election reforms. It stated that it does not recognize the validity of the 1995 legislative council elections, and that the present Legislative Council would have no mandate to serve past reversion and thus would "terminate" on June 30, 1997, along with elected district boards and municipal councils. China insisted that the crux of its disagreement was not the pace of democratization but Britain's failure to reach a mutually acceptable accord on the electoral changes before unilaterally announcing the reform package. Seventeen rounds of negotiations were held before the Hong Kong Government made its announcement. In March China's appointed Preparatory Committee announced that a provisional legislature would be formed to serve for not more than 1 year after reversion until the "first" Special Administrative Region legislature could be elected. According to the Preparatory Committee, a provisional legislature would "examine and approve" laws to take effect on July 1, 1997. One Preparatory Committee member who voted against the provisional legislature was initially declared by Beijing as disqualified to serve on the Selection Committee or the provisional legislature, but was later chosen for the provisional legislature.

The Preparatory Committee's Selection Committee panel held public consultations in April on forming a 400-member Selection Committee to choose the first Special Administrative Region chief executive and the provisional legislature. More than 1,000 people representing 362 organizations presented their views. Participation was controlled through selective invitations, but some dissenting views on the provisional legislature were voiced by the Hong Kong Bar Association and prodemocracy political figures. The Preparatory Committee received over 5,000 nominees for the Selection Committee.

There is public concern that the process of selecting a provisional legislature lacked transparency, was not based on a free and fair election, and excluded groups, political parties, and individuals critical of China. There is also concern that the provisional legislature may begin functioning before June 30, 1997, and thereby undermine the authority of the present Hong Kong Government. Finally, many representative groups see the process of selecting a provisional legislature as unnecessary and unjustified. On December 11, the Selection Committee chose Hong Kong's first postreversion Chief Executive, C. H. Tung. On December 21, it selected the 60-member provisional legislature. Those selected included 33 of the 34 current legislative councilors who sought inclusion. In addition, 10 persons who had been defeated in the 1995 legislative council elections were chosen. The 19 Democratic Party members in the current Legislative Council regarded the disbanding of that body as illegitimate and chose not to seek seats on the provisional legislature.

The Government is continuing efforts to place Hong Kong Chinese in senior government positions and has publicly committed to fill all "principal official" posts with local officers before 1997. At present 22 of 23 existing posts equivalent to future principal officer posts (Chief Secretary, Financial Secretary, 15 Branch Secretaries, Commissioner of the Independent Commission Against Corruption, Director of Audit, Commissioner of Police, Director of Immigration, and Commissioner of Customs and Excise) are filled by local officers. The remaining expatriate principal officer (Attorney General) is due to be replaced by a local officer before reversion to China. As of April, 70 percent of the Government's top directorate-level jobs and almost 85 percent of administrative and other senior management positions were filled by local staff.

Expatriates remain in key positions in the legal department and the judiciary; at the same time, 70 percent of the Crown counsel positions and 76 percent of police positions (police inspector and above) are currently filled by local officers.

The Government's efforts to add ethnic Chinese to the Government were opposed by a group of expatriate government workers who undertook legal action against the Government, claiming that they were being discriminated against under the provisions of the Hong Kong Bill of Rights. The Hong Kong High Court on October 31, 1995, ruled that most of the Government's arrangements to fill positions with local officers were lawful. The expatriates subsequently appealed the judgments and the Government cross-appealed on one judgment. At the substantive hearing of the appeal in November, the Court of Appeal ruled crucial parts of the localization policy unlawful. According to December 23 news reports, the Government decided not to appeal to the Privy Council given the slim chances of success but reiterated its determination to continue its localization policy.

In 1995 the Chinese authorities' public demands for personnel records of senior civil servants caused anxiety among some Hong Kong Government officials. Later that year, the Chinese authorities scaled back their demands and initiated a series of successful "informal" exchanges with Hong Kong civil servants, which continued throughout 1996.

In March a Chinese official told reporters that Hong Kong civil servants who opposed the idea of a provisional legislature would be barred from serving after reversion. Although Chinese authorities thereafter qualified this position, calling it only "personal opinions," civil service confidence was shaken. China has said no cadres would come to Hong Kong from Beijing to work in the civil service.

Women are playing a larger role in politics, with larger numbers running for public office in 1995 and 1996 than ever before. In 1996 women comprised 12 percent of the Legislative Council, 13 percent of the top government directorate-level posts, and 37 percent of government administrative officers.

Section 4. Government Attitude Regarding International and Nongovernmental Investigation of Alleged Violations of Human Rights

The international covenants on civil and political rights and on economic, social, and cultural rights currently apply to Hong Kong through the United Kingdom. China has agreed to extend these agreements to Hong Kong beyond 1997, but stated in October that it does not consider itself obligated to file reports to the United Nations on implementation of the agreements in Hong Kong because China is not a signatory. The Chinese Government's statement caused concern in Hong Kong, as well as in the United Nations Human Rights Committee, the Hong Kong section of the International Commission of Jurists, and among others in the international human rights community.

In October 1995, the China-appointed Preliminary Working Committee's legal subgroup issued a statement that called for striking key sections from Hong Kong's Bill of Rights Ordinance, including articles that require all past and future legislation to conform to the ordinance. The subgroup also recommended that six colonial-era public security ordinances relating to registration of societies, media licensing, broadcast authority, and police control of public meetings and processions, which were amended in 1991 to conform to the Bill of Rights Ordinance, be changed to restore the Government's original prerogatives under these laws. The Preliminary Working Committee's recommendation generated a strong negative public reaction in Hong Kong about the potential erosion of civil liberties and fundamental freedoms. By year's end, however, the Preparatory Committee had taken no action on any section of the Bill of Rights Ordinance.

Article 23 of China's Basic Law provides that the Hong Kong Special Administrative Region will enact laws to prohibit subversion, secession, treason, and sedition against the PRC Government. In late November, the Hong Kong Government introduced a draft amendment to the crime ordinance defining the implementation of these laws. China objected to this action because the Hong Kong Government did not secure its agreement, despite consultations, before presenting the legislation. Beijing also insists the Special Administrative Government, and not the current Hong Kong Government, should consider such laws. By the end of the year, it was unclear what, if any, action would be taken by the current Legislative Council on the draft legislation.

The U.N. High Commissioner for Refugees and nongovernmental human rights organizations have full access to Hong Kong's camps for Vietnamese boat people.

Although the present Government has interposed no official barriers to the formation of local human rights groups, some human rights activists believe that provisions of the Societies Ordinance provide the legal means whereby a future government could do so.

Section 5. Discrimination Based on Race, Sex, Religion, Disability, Language, or Social Status

The Government opposed measures supported by some Legislative Council members in 1994-95 addressing problems of sex, race, and age discrimination, and introduced instead its own bills, both adopted in 1995, banning discrimination on the basis of sex and disability. With the establishment of an Equal Opportunities Commission in September, to oversee the implementation of sex and disability discrimination laws, all nonemployment related provisions of the sex discrimination law took effect. Employment related provisions cannot come into force until the Legislative Council approves a code of practice on employment that is currently being developed.

The Chinese language has equal status with English in many government operations except in judicial proceedings. To help remedy the situation in judicial proceedings, the Government has increased the number of officers in the Legal Aid Department proficient in Chinese from three (of nine) to seven and initiated a pilot scheme for simultaneous interpretation in some court proceedings. The Government extended the use of bilingual prosecution documents to magistracies and district and high courts in 1995 and 1996. Bilingual charge sheets have been introduced in all magistrates courts, and bilingual indictments are used in the district and high courts. According to the Basic Law English may be used as an official language by the executive authorities, legislature, and judiciary of the Hong Kong Special Administrative Region.

Women.—Violence and discrimination against women remain significant problems in society. The only legislation to protect the rights of battered women is the 1987 Domestic Violence Ordinance, which enables a woman to seek a 3-month injunction against her husband, and which may be extended to 6 months. Domestic violence may also be prosecuted as common assault under existing criminal statutes. The Government enforces these laws and prosecutes violators. It also funds programs to stem domestic violence such as family life education counseling, a hot line service operated by the Social Welfare Department and nongovernmental organizations, temporary housing, legal aid, and child protective services. In 1995 the Government expanded the number of family service centers from 53 to 65; in 1996 it opened a third shelter for battered women and their children. Many women, however, do not seek help when they have been victims of violence, and many cases of domestic violence have not been reported because of cultural factors and inadequate information about the availability of assistance and resources. To address this, the Government set up a Working Group on Battered Spouses in April 1995; issued multidisciplinary procedural guidelines on handling battered spouse cases in March; and initiated public education and mass media programs. Women's action groups continue to press for better legal and government protection for battered wives.

Women have faced significant discrimination in the areas of employment, salary, welfare, inheritance, and promotion (see Section 6.e.). Discrimination on the basis of age, particularly in hiring practices, is openly practiced and is not prohibited by law. According to government statistics for early 1996, unemployment in all age groups among female workers was lower than for male workers. Women have suffered discrimination in the area of inheritance in the New Territories portion of Hong Kong, but a 1994 ordinance removed the inhibition against women inheriting land in the New Territories. Women now have equal rights with men to inherit land in the New Territories, as is the case elsewhere in Hong Kong.

For the years 1991-95, the number of female secondary school student candidates who took university advanced-level examinations accounted for between 51 to 55 percent of the total, and the number of female candidates who matriculated at universities during those years accounted for between 52 to 56 percent of all candidates who matriculated.

Children.—The Government displays a firm commitment to children's rights and welfare through a well-funded systems of public education, medical care, and protective services. It supports child welfare programs including custody, protection, day care, foster care, shelters, small group homes, and assistance to families. Child abuse and exploitation have not been considered widespread. However, the Secretary for Health told the Legislative Council in March that the number of child abuse cases had almost doubled in 2 years; 116 cases of child sexual abuse had been handled by the Social Welfare Department and NGO's in 1995, compared to 77 in 1994 and 61 in 1993. In 1995 the police set up a Child Abuse Investigation Unit to improve treatment of child abuse victims, and the Legislative Council adopted amendments to the law making it easier for abused children to give evidence in court. Legal penalties for ill-treatment or neglect of minors were also substantially increased. In 1996 the Government set up a video interviewing suite in a residential building for recording statements in a child-friendly environment, and initiated multidisciplinary procedures for handling child sexual abuse cases.

People With Disabilities.—Organizations and persons representing the interests of the disabled claim that discrimination against the physically and mentally disabled exists in employment, education, and the provision of some state services. Access to public buildings and transportation remain significant problems for the physically disabled. Advocacy groups have urged the Government to do more to encourage greater public acceptance of the physically and mentally disabled. The Government has been responsive, undertaking programs to foster greater public awareness and acceptance in this area. In 1995 the Legislative Council passed the Antidiscrimination Law to protect the rights of the disabled. This law calls for changes to the building ordinance to improve building access for the disabled and sanctions for those who discriminate against the disabled. In 1995 and 1996, the Government took additional actions to assist the disabled, introducing an integrated work extension program in sheltered workshops, increasing expenditures for the mentally disabled, expanding vocational assessment and training services, and conducting public education programs on rehabilitation. There are 4,231 disabled persons employed as civil servants out of a total civil service work force of 180,313—just over 2 percent, and there are 8,476 disabled persons in school—just under 1 percent.

National/Racial/Ethnic Minorities.—Racial discrimination against Filipino women, 140,000 of whom work under contract in Hong Kong, has been the focus of news reports. Also, despite official reassurance that Philippine workers would be welcome after 1997, reports indicate that employers of large numbers of Filipinos—hotels and the airport authority—are beginning to employ Chinese from the mainland instead.

Section 6. Worker Rights
  a. *The Right of Association.*—The right of association and the right of workers to establish and join organizations of their own choosing are provided for by law. Trade unions must be registered under the Trade Unions Ordinance. The basic precondition for registration is a minimum of seven persons who serve in the same occupation. The Government does not discourage or impede the formation of unions. During 1995, 21 new trade unions (including one mixed union of employers and employees) were registered. By the end of 1995, there were 522 registered employees' unions with a declared membership of 591,181, which represents 21.11 percent of a total of 2.8 million salaried employees and wage earners. Most registered unions belong to one of three major trade union federations.
  Work stoppages and strikes are permitted. However, there are some restrictions on this right for civil servants. Even though employees have the freedom to strike and there is no legislative prohibition of strikes, in practice most workers must sign employment contracts that typically state that walking off the job is a breach of contract and can lead to summary dismissal. The Employment Ordinance permits firms to discharge or deduct wages from staff who are absent due to a labor dispute. In 1995 there were nine strikes involving 1,018 workdays.
  Labor unions may form federations and confederations, although such affiliation cannot be cross-industry in scope. The two leading labor federations, the Hong Kong Federation of Trade Unions and the Hong Kong Confederation of Trade Unions, were active participants in the territory's 1995 Legislative Council elections.
  As a dependent territory of the United Kingdom, Hong Kong is not a member in its own right of the International Labor Organization (ILO). The United Kingdom makes declarations on behalf of Hong Kong concerning the latter's obligations regarding the various international labor conventions. To date Hong Kong has amended labor legislation and taken administrative measures to apply 49 conventions. In the Basic Law, China committed to adhere to these conventions after reversion in 1997.
  Unions may affiliate with international bodies. Any affiliation with foreign labor unions requires the consent of the Government. No application for such affiliation has thus far been refused.
  b. *The Right to Organize and Bargain Collectively.*—The ILO Convention on the Right to Organize and Bargain Collectively has been applied to Hong Kong without modification since 1975. This convention does not obligate the Government to impose collective bargaining by statute. There are no laws that stipulate collective bargaining on a mandatory basis. Wage rates in a few trades like tailoring and carpentry are now determined collectively in accordance with established trade practices and customs rather than as a statutory mechanism.
  In practice, collective bargaining is not widely practiced. Unions generally are not powerful enough to force management to engage in collective bargaining. The Government does not encourage it, since the Government does not engage in collective bargaining with civil servants' unions but merely "consults" with them. Free conciliation services are afforded by the Labor Relations Division of the Department of Labor to employers and employees involved in disputes that may involve statutory benefits and protection in employment as well as arrears of wages, wages instead of notice, or severance pay. The Department of Labor assists employers and employees in a dispute to reach amicable settlement but does not have the authority to impose a solution. The Department of Labor is not required by law to allow unions to represent employees in these proceedings, although it takes a positive attitude towards the participation by trade unions in dispute negotiations. The Labor Tribunal Ordinance provides that an officer of a registered trade union, who is authorized in writing by a claimant or defendant to appear as his representative, has the right of audience in the Labor Tribunal.
  The law protects workers against antiunion discrimination. Employees who allege such discrimination have the right to have their cases heard by the Department of Labor's Labor Relations Division. Violation of the antiunion discrimination provisions under the Employment Ordinance is a criminal offense carrying a maximum fine of $2,564. However, employers are not required to reinstate or compensate an employee.
  The International Confederation of Free Trade Unions is highly critical of Hong Kong labor legislation's failure to protect the right to strike and its provisions allowing dismissals and disciplinary action against striking trade unionists. Individual labor claims are adjudicated by the Labor Tribunal, a part of the judicial branch, which is supposed to provide quick and inexpensive machinery for resolving certain types of disputes. The Tribunal complements the conciliation service of the Labor Relations Division. Union leaders complain, however, that the Tribunal takes too long—an average of 130 days—to hear workers' cases. Labor unions and legislators

are concerned about government plans to allow increases in imported labor, fearing downward pressure on wages. There are few protections for almost 152,000 Filipino, Thai, and Indonesian domestic workers who face deportation if dismissed by their employers and are thus vulnerable to abuse.

There are no export processing zones.

c. *Prohibition of Forced or Compulsory Labor.*—Existing labor legislation prohibits forced labor, and it is not practiced.

d. *Minimum Age for Employment of Children.*—The Employment of Children Regulations prohibit employment of children under the age of 15 in any industrial establishment. Children 13 and 14 years of age may be employed in certain nonindustrial establishments, subject to conditions aimed at ensuring a minimum of 9 years' education and protecting their safety, health, and welfare. The Government conducts inspections to safeguard against the employment of children. Few violations were found, and child labor is not a problem.

e. *Acceptable Conditions of Work.*—There is no minimum wage except for foreign domestic workers. In 1996 the minimum wage for such workers was $480 (HK$3,750) a month. Because the law also requires employers of domestic labor to provide foreign domestic workers with housing, worker's compensation insurance, travel allowances, and meals or a meal allowance in addition to the minimum wage, foreign domestics have a decent standard of living.

Aside from a small number of trades and industries where a uniform wage structure exists, wage levels are customarily fixed by individual agreement between employer and employee and are determined by supply and demand. Many employees receive a year-end bonus of a month's pay or more. Some employers provide workers with various kinds of allowances, free medical treatment, and free subsidized transport.

There are no legal restrictions on hours of work for men. The Women and Young Persons (Industry) Regulations under the Employment Ordinance control hours and conditions of work for women and for young people 15 to 17 years of age in the manufacturing sector. Work hours for young people are limited to 8 per day and 48 per week between 6 a.m. and 11 p.m. Women are permitted to work only between 7 a.m. and 7 p.m.; however, this provision is very loosely enforced for persons at age 16 or over. For women, overtime is restricted to 2 hours per day with a maximum of 200 days per year, and overtime is prohibited for all persons under the age of 18 in industrial establishments. The regulations also prohibit women and young persons from working underground or, with the exception of males 16 and 17 years of age, in dangerous trades. The Labor Inspectorate conducts workplace inspections to enforce compliance with these regulations. During 1995 there were 8,978 prosecutions for breaches of various ordinances and regulations. Fines totaling $6.2 million were imposed. From January to September, there were 6,106 prosecutions, and fines for this period totaled $4.4 million. The employment of underage workers is generally not a serious problem.

The Department of Labor's Factory Inspectorate Department sets basic occupational safety and health standards, provides education and publicity, and follows up with enforcement and inspection in accordance with the Factories and Industrial Undertakings Ordinance and subsidiary regulations. The Inspectorate pays particular attention to safety in high-risk areas of factories and construction sites, with routine visits to such sites. During 1995, 89,138 enforcement visits including 82,746 inspections and 6,392 accident investigations were conducted. Department of Labor officials acknowledged that accidents in construction and service sectors remain very high. Apart from routine inspection, the Inspectorate also expanded special inspections targeting high-risk areas. The inspection campaigns included machine safety, fire and chemical safety, and summer job safety. During these campaigns, 21,859 manufacturing and catering establishments and 1,196 construction sites were inspected, and 1,234 summonses were issued. Fines were varied, depending on the seriousness of the violation. The Government also conducted a review of industrial safety in Hong Kong in 1995 and is implementing a range of measures and proposals recommended in the review for improving safety standards. The continued need for stronger government enforcement and inspection efforts, however, was demonstrated when the collapse in June of a bridge construction platform caused six deaths, prompting legislators to introduce several new safety bills.

As part of a complementary effort, the Department of Labor's Occupational Health Division investigates claims of occupational diseases and injuries at work, conducts environmental testing in the workplace, and provides medical examinations to employees in occupations that involve handling of hazardous materials. The small number of inspectors—about 200—and the inability of workers to elect their own safety representatives weaken the enforcement of workplace safety and health standards. There is no specific legal provision allowing workers to remove themselves from dangerous work situations without jeopardy to continued employment.

UZBEKISTAN

Uzbekistan is a state with limited civil rights. It took several steps toward creating a less authoritarian society in 1996, the full effect of which is unclear. The Constitution provides for a presidential system with separation of powers between the executive, legislative, and judicial branches. In practice President Islam Karimov and the centralized executive branch that serves him remain the dominant forces in political life. The Oliy Majlis (Parliament) is dominated by the executive branch, and only parties that support the President are represented. Although the Constitution provides for an independent judicial authority, in practice the judicial branch is heavily influenced by the executive branch in civil and criminal cases.

The police are controlled by the Ministry of Interior (MVD). The police and related MVD forces are responsible for most normal internal police functions. The National Security Service (NSS)—the former KGB—deals with a broad range of national security questions, including corruption, organized crime, and narcotics. The army and border guards are responsible for external defense. They are not routinely used in internal disturbances and rarely are implicated in human rights abuses. The police and the NSS committee numerous, serious human rights abuses.

The Government continued to move toward market reform, especially through improvement in the legislative framework. However, in the last quarter of the year, it took financial steps which led the International Monetary Fund to suspend its loan program. The economy is based primarily on agriculture and agricultural processing; Uzbekistan is the world's fifth largest producer of cotton, the seventh largest producer of gold, and has substantial deposits of copper, strategic minerals, gas, and oil. The Government has proclaimed its commitment to a gradual transition to a free market economy. It has achieved substantial progress in reducing inflation and the budget deficit. However, progress on privatization of the large state-owned enterprises that account for the bulk of gross domestic product remained slow, and a host of formal and informal barriers continued to constrain the nascent private sector.

The Government's human rights record improved, but serious problems remain. Citizens cannot exercise their right to change their government peacefully. Chosen president in a 1991 election that most observers considered neither free nor fair, Karimov had his stay in office extended to 2000 by a 1995 Soviet-style referendum. Parliament subsequently voted to make the extension part of Karimov's first term, thus making him eligible to run again in 2000. To control the political arena, the Government continues to deny registration to independent political parties and other groups potentially critical of the Government, and it prevents unregistered opposition parties and movements from operating freely or publishing their views. The Government continues to ban unsanctioned public meetings and demonstrations. Police and NSS forces used torture, harassment, and illegal searches, and arbitrarily detained or arrested opposition activists on false charges. They committed these and other abuses against both dissidents and other citizens, although reported abuses against dissidents decreased sharply. Arbitrary arrest and detention is common; even foreigners are not exempt. Police often beat criminal suspects, and detention can be prolonged. Prison conditions are poor. Although the Government says that it investigates abuses, those responsible for documented abuses rarely appear to be punished. The Government severely limits freedom of speech and the press, and freedom of expression is constrained by an atmosphere of repression that makes it difficult to criticize the Government publicly. Although the Constitution expressly prohibits it, press censorship continues. The Government sharply restricts the importation of foreign print media. The Government reimplemented a long-dormant, politically motivated property confiscation order against opposition leader and former vice president, Shukrullo Mirsaidov, and harassed his family, apparently in retaliation for Mirsaidov's remarks at an OSCE-sponsored seminar on national human rights institutions. The Government has harassed and arrested independent Islamic leaders on questionable grounds, citing the threat of Islamic extremism. Despite a constitutional prohibition, there continues to be significant traditional societal discrimination and domestic violence against women.

The Government took several steps to improve its international human rights image. President Karimov has made speeches calling for human rights reform and more press freedoms. During the summer, the Government released approximately 15 prisoners alleged to be held for political reasons. It permitted Human Rights

Watch/Helsinki (HRW/H) to open an office in Tashkent and invited exiled opposition leaders and human rights activists to return without fear of reprisal. Outspoken human rights activist Abdoumanob Pulat, chairman of the Human Rights Society of Uzbekistan (HRSU), visited Uzbekistan without incident. At a human rights conference in September, several government critics voiced their complaints about human rights abuses before an international audience in Tashkent. The Government registered one indigenous human rights organization, but declined to act on the registration application of the HRSU which has been seeking to register since 1992. In April Radio Free Liberty opened an office in Tashkent.

RESPECT FOR HUMAN RIGHTS

Section 1. Respect for the Integrity of the Person, Including Freedom From:

a. *Political and Other Extrajudicial Killing.*—There were no reports of political or other extrajudicial killings.

The Government has never announced the results of its internal investigation into the 1995 death in police custody, almost certainly from a beating, of Bokhtiar Yakubov, a witness linked to an opposition activist.

b. *Disappearance.*—There were no reports of politically motivated disappearances.

No developments were reported in the 1995 disappearance of Abduvali Kori Mirzaev, the imam of an Andijon mosque who along with his assistant allegedly was detained at the Tashkent airport by NSS officers while en route to a conference in Moscow. Similarly, there were no new developments in the 1992 disappearance of Abdullah Utaev, leader of the Uzbekistan chapter of the outlawed Islamic Renaissance Party, who, most observers believe, also was detained by security forces. There is no official admission that either man was arrested or detained and no further information on their whereabouts. However, most independent observers believe that the three missing Islamic activists are either dead or in NSS custody.

c. *Torture and Other Cruel, Inhuman, or Degrading Treatment or Punishment.*—Although the law prohibits these practices, police routinely beat and otherwise mistreat detainees to obtain confessions. Both police and the NSS used beatings and harassment against citizens.

On September 25, the Supreme Court completed its review of an appeal by the "Namangan 11," a group of young men who, evidence strongly suggests, were falsely accused of belonging to a Namangan city gang that committed a murder and several robberies. The Court commuted the death sentence of one and reduced the sentences of the other defendants. Lawyers at the hearing presented evidence that the defendants' confessions were obtained by beatings.

Dmitri Fattakhov, a young man allegedly beaten nearly to the point of insanity by police to obtain his confession in a 1995 murder case, was permitted to go to Israel for medical treatment in early 1996.

Police detained the representative of an international human rights nongovernmental organization (NGO) overnight and subjected him to verbal abuse and humiliating treatment (see Section 1.d.). There were no reported developments, in the investigation of the 1995 kidnapings of former vice president Mirsaidov and his son.

Prison conditions are poor, and worse for male than for female prisoners. Due to limited resources, prison overcrowding is a problem. Reportedly there are severe shortages of food and medicines. Political prisoners are often not allowed visitors or any other direct form of contact with family and friends. The Government operates labor camps, but little is known about the conditions of incarceration. The Government does not routinely permit prison visits by human rights monitors although diplomats have occasionally obtained access in specific cases.

d. *Arbitrary Arrest, Detention, or Exile.*—Uzbekistan continues to use the Soviet legal system, and laws on detention have not changed since independence. According to the law, police may hold a person suspected of committing a crime for up to 3 days. At the end of this period, the suspect must be either officially charged or released. A procurator's order is required for arrests but not for detentions. A court case must be scheduled within 15 days of the arrest, and the defendant may be detained during this period. A defendant may not have access to counsel while in detention but only after formal arrest. Delays between detention and trials can be lengthy—one Islamic cleric detained in September 1994 did not go on trial until May 1995.

In practice police arbitrarily stop and detain individuals, whether dissidents or not, without warrant or just cause. In the past, opposition and religious figures have been charged with offenses such as drug possession, illegal possession of firearms, or disorderly conduct in an effort to stifle their criticism of government policy. There were no such reports in 1996.

In March police detained opposition-linked human rights activist Paula Braunerg and her son when they found newspapers from Russia in her house during a search, allegedly for smuggled gold. She was later released, and government officials admitted privately that the security forces had acted incorrectly in detaining her for possession of the newspapers.

On August 30, three police officers, possibly intoxicated, arrested the local HRW/H representative, a British citizen, as he returned from a dinner engagement with friends. At the district police station, two senior officials intimidated and verbally abused him, and accused him without basis of illegally possessing narcotics and firearms. He was forced to spend the night in a cold jail cell in his underwear. Police never brought charges. The Government claims that it carried out an internal investigation and does not admit being at fault, but it has issued a written apology.

The Government does not use forced exile.

e. *Denial of Fair Public Trial.*—Although the Constitution provides for an independent judicial authority, the judicial branch takes its direction from the executive branch.

There is a three-tier court system: the people's court on the district level, the regional courts, and the Supreme Court. District court decisions may be appealed to the next highest level within 10 days of the ruling. The new Criminal Code reduces the list of crimes punishable by death to murder, espionage, and treason, eliminating the economic crimes punishable by death in the former Soviet code. Officially and in recent practice, most court cases are open to the public but may be closed in exceptional cases, such as those involving state secrets, rape, or young defendants.

Under the Constitution, the President appoints all judges for 10-year terms. They may be removed for crimes or failure to fulfill their obligations. Power to remove judges for failure to fulfill their obligations rests with the President, except for Supreme Court judges, whose removal must also be confirmed by Parliament.

Uzbekistan still uses the Soviet judicial system, which features trial by a panel of three judges: one professional judge and two "people's assessors" who are chosen by the workers' collectives for a period of 2½ years. The judge presides and directs the proceedings. Defendants have the right to attend the proceedings, confront witnesses, and present evidence. The State will provide a lawyer without charge, but by law the accused has the right to hire an attorney. In some political cases, the defendants have not had access to lawyers.

Detainees deemed not to be violent may be released on their own recognizance pending trial. No money need be posted as bond, but in such cases the accused must usually sign a pledge not to leave the city.

In practice defense lawyers are unskilled at defending their clients. Courts often do not allow all defense witnesses to be heard, and written documents are given more weight than courtroom witnesses. In the case of the Namangan 11 (see Section 1.d.), the defendants' written confessions, allegedly gained by beatings and repudiated by the defendants in court, appeared to have been given more weight than the testimony of eyewitnesses.

Human Rights Watch/Helsinki and the HRSU have compiled lists of 20 to 30 individuals believed to be political prisoners. Many were associated with the Birlik or Erk parties, or were involved in independent Islamic activities. Many were convicted of nonpolitical offenses such as tax evasion, misappropriation of funds, or illegal possession of narcotics or firearms. However, many observers question the fairness of the trials and believe that incriminating contraband was planted by arresting officers. Six of the prisoners on the lists were paroled during the year, five of them under President Karimov's August amnesty. Three other prisoners were either released or had their sentences reduced before 1996. The Government denies holding political prisoners.

f. *Arbitrary Interference With Privacy, Family, Home, or Correspondence.*—By law search warrants issued by a procurator are required. There is no provision for a judicial review of warrants. No legal mechanism exists for authorizing telephone tapping or monitoring. Security agencies routinely monitor telephone calls and employ surveillance and wiretaps in the cases of persons involved in opposition political activities.

The Government does not allow general distribution of foreign newspapers (with the exception of two or three very conservative Russian ones) and other publications. However, limited numbers of foreign periodicals began to appear in Tashkent's two major hotels, and authorized groups can obtain foreign periodicals through subscription. The publication of the local editions of Izvestia and Pravda and the sale of their Moscow editions remained suspended throughout 1996. The authorities black out Russian news broadcasts when they are critical of the Government (see Section 2.a.).

Section 2. Respect for Civil Liberties, Including:

a. *Freedom of Speech and Press.*—Although the Constitution provides for "freedom of thought, speech, and convictions," the Government continues to severely limit these rights.

A 1991 law against "offending the honor and dignity of the President" limits the ability to criticize the President. Journalists and ordinary citizens remain afraid to express views critical of the President and the Government.

Information remains very tightly controlled. Although the Constitution prohibits censorship, it is widely practiced and the Government tolerates little, if any, criticism of its actions. Newspapers may not be printed without the censor's approval. Journalists and writers who want to ensure that their work is published practice self-censorship. Several speakers at the OSCE conference openly challenged the Government's assertion that there is no censorship.

Although the President made several speeches advocating more freedom of the press, Vatan, the newspaper of the progovernment Fatherland Progress Party, ceased publication temporarily after publishing an analytical piece about the President's August 29 speech to Parliament on human rights, reportedly under pressure from government officials displeased by the article.

The Uzbekistan Information Agency cooperates closely with the presidential staff to prepare and distribute all officially sanctioned news and information. Nearly all newspapers are government owned and controlled; the key papers are organs of government ministries. State enterprises control the printing presses.

The last opposition newspaper to be published was that of the Erk party. In 1993 it was banned and has not been published since.

Magazines and weeklies have to be registered, a procedure that includes providing information about the sources of funding, means of distribution, founders, and sponsors. A resolution by the Cabinet of Ministers bans private persons and journalist collectives from founding newspapers or magazines. Foreign correspondents based in Tashkent report that the security services have harassed and threatened their translators and other local employees. Limited numbers of foreign periodicals are available, but the Government does not allow the general distribution of foreign newspapers (see Section 1.f.).

Television broadcasting is state controlled. Although there are local stations in various regions, nationwide programming is on two state-run channels that fully support the Government and its policies. The Ostankino channel from Russia broadcasts during the evening. Its news broadcasts are blacked out when they are critical of the Government. A cable television joint venture between the state broadcasting company and an American company broadcasts the Hong Kong-based "Star TV" channels, including the British Broadcasting Corporation (BBC) and Cable News Network world news, to Tashkent and a few other locations.

However, there were instances in which the Government eased its restrictions. For example, at a human rights conference in Tashkent in September sponsored by the Organization for Security and Cooperation in Europe (OSCE), numerous dissidents, including the head of the HRSU, the son of the missing Andijon Imam, and the former vice president were allowed at the last minute to participate and express views critical (in some cases extremely so) of the Government. In the wake of the conference, the head of the HRSU and another dissident were interviewed on government radio. Government television also aired a program in which short clips of critical speeches were aired, followed by longer rebuttals from government supporters.

In May the Government allowed Radio Free Liberty to open a bureau in Tashkent, staffed by two local Uzbek stringers. Radio Liberty, the Voice of America, and BBC radio, along with the more expensive cable television channels noted above, are among the few sources of uncontrolled news.

In addition to state-controlled television, at least one major station in Samarkand considers itself independent. It claims not to receive any government subsidy and to exist wholly on income derived from advertisers. It currently has two channels and plans a third, devoted to business news. However, it is clearly sensitive to political concerns from the center and concentrates on nonpolitical news but claims not to be formally censored.

There are no private publishing houses, and government approval is required for all publications.

Virtually all academic institutions and academies are experiencing increased autonomy, but freedom of expression is still limited. Most institutions are in the process of revising curriculums, and Western textbooks are in great demand.

b. *Freedom of Peaceful Assembly and Association.*—The Constitution provides for the right of peaceful assembly, however, it also states that the authorities have the right to suspend or ban rallies, meetings, and demonstrations on security grounds.

The Government must sanction demonstrations and does not routinely grant this permission.

The Constitution provides for the right of freedom of association, but the Government limits the exercise of this right by refusing to register opposition political parties and movements opposed to the established order. The Constitution places broad limitations on the types of groups that may form and requires that all organizations be formally registered with the Government in accordance with procedures prescribed by law. In December the Parliament passed new legislation on political parties which increases the number of signatures required to register a political party from 3,000 to 5,000. A party must meet other requirements, such as providing an official address. The process for registering NGO's and other public associations is also difficult and time consuming, with many opportunities for official obstruction.

Since 1992, the Government has repeatedly frustrated the efforts of the Human Rights Society of Uzbekistan (HRSU), a local human rights group with close ties to exiled opposition figures, to register officially. Immediately prior to the OSCE Conference in September, however, it granted permission for the HRSU to hold a founding organizational meeting (kurultai), a prerequisite for receiving registration. The Society subsequently pursued the next step in the registration process by submitting its registration petition on October 3. On January 3, 1997, the Government declined to act on HRSU's application to register, asserting technical deficiencies in its paperwork (see Section 4.). The Government earlier granted registration to another human rights NGO, the Committee for Protection of Individual Rights, a group formed with the support of the Government.

In earlier years, the Government repeatedly denied the attempts of the Birlik movement and Erk party to register as parties. Most of these organizations' leaders have since gone into exile, and these organizations made no attempt to register in 1996, reportedly because their remaining adherents in the country are afraid of government reprisals. The Constitution and a 1991 amendment to the law on political parties bans those of a religious nature. This principle is cited for previous denials of registration to religious parties, including the Islamic Renaissance Party (IRP). Other opposition activists have announced the formation of the "Adolat-True Path" party but have never pursued formal registration, claiming that their members are also afraid of government reprisals.

Nonpolitical associations and social organizations usually did not encounter comparable difficulties in registering, although bureaucratic delays and official suspicion continued to plague the registration process for such groups. Some evangelical churches and some foreign humanitarian assistance groups found it difficult to obtain registration or reregistration.

c. *Freedom of Religion.*—The Constitution provides for freedom of religion and for the principle of separation of religion and state. However, despite allowing many groups to worship freely, for example, the Russian Orthodox and several other Christian denominations, the Government suppresses some religious groups that defy the authority of state-appointed religious authorities, particularly Islamic dissidents. In addition, despite the principle of separation of religion and state, the government-controlled Spiritual Directorate for Muslims funds some Islamic religious activities.

After the enforced atheism of the Soviet period, religious communities are experiencing a significant revival. Religious education is becoming more widespread, although it is not included in state schools. While Islam is the religion of the majority, ethnic minorities may also practice their religion in relative freedom.

However, tensions arise when churches attempt to convert across ethnic lines, especially when they attempt to convert members of generally Muslim ethnic groups to Christianity. Although distribution of religious literature is legal in Uzbekistan, missionary activity and proselytizing is not.

Fearing the destabilizing influence of extremist Islamic forces, the Government has sought to control the Islamic hierarchy, the content of imams' sermons, and the extent and substance of published Islamic materials. However, Islamic groups not affiliated with the Government form a "parallel Islam". The Government has detained a number of Fergana Valley Islamic clerics on various charges (see Section 1.d.). Bureaucratic restrictions have also inhibited the free operation of numerous religious schools. Dissident Islamic figures deny that they are extremists and claim that they are being persecuted for their unwillingness to "slavishly" praise the Government's actions.

Muslim leaders have been detained and harassed for acts of perceived insubordination and independence. In early 1996, the government-appointed mufti fired imam Abidkhon Nazarov, head of the Tukhtoboi mosque in Tashkent, and several other independent-minded Islamic clerics. These clerics were fired ostensibly for failing a government-designed "imam test," which included questions about political and economic policy outside the traditional sphere of a religious cleric. The Government also closed the Andijon Friday mosque where missing imam Abduvali Kori Mirzaev (see Section 1.b.) formerly preached. The Kokand Friday mosque remains closed since mid-1995.

There is no pattern of official discrimination against Jews. Synagogues function openly; Hebrew education (long banned under the Soviets), Jewish cultural events, and the publication of a community newspaper take place undisturbed. However, the perception of bleak economic prospects; occasional harassment by low-level officials, which some believe is anti-Semitic in origin (other say that such incidents occur in the context of harassment which any resident of Uzbekistan may face); and the belief that militant Islam might become a strong force are motivating many Jews to consider emigration.

d. *Freedom of Movement Within the Country, Foreign Travel, Emigration, and Repatriation.*—The Constitution provides for free movement within the country and across its borders, and the Government generally respected these right. The Government has largely completed the process of issuing new passports to citizens in place of the old Soviet ones. The new passports serve as both internal identity cards and, when noted, as external passports. In addition the Government has greatly simplified the process of obtaining exit visas, which are valid for a period of 2 years and no longer require invitations.

Most barriers to emigration were lifted before the Soviet breakup. Although in some instances emigrants are delayed by long waits for passports and exit visas, potential emigrants who can find a host country willing to accept them are able to leave the country. Since independence, a significant number of non-Uzbeks, including Russians, Jews, Ukrainians, and others have emigrated, although no figures are available. These people have left because of their perception that economic conditions are better elsewhere and, in some cases, due to concern that future economic and social prospects for non-Uzbeks will be limited. A sizable number of Russian emigrants, finding poor economic conditions and discrimination in Russia, have returned to Uzbekistan.

The travel of local citizens within Uzbekistan is not controlled, unlike travel by foreigners, including journalists. Due to treaties between their countries and Uzbekistan, citizens of the United States, France, Germany, the United Kingdom, and the Republic of Korea receive visas valid for travel throughout Uzbekistan. Other foreign visitors must have each city they wish to visit noted on their visas. Tourists seeking to check into hotels without the appropriate internal visa often find themselves having to pay fines or bribes to local officials. In mid-1995, a presidential edict decreed that the ancient cities of Tashkent, Samarkand, Bukhara, and Khiva would henceforth be "open cities," for which a separate visa notation is not required for nationals of any country. However, it is not clear whether implementing regulations are yet in place.

The law on citizenship stipulates that citizens do not lose their citizenship if they reside overseas. However, since Uzbekistan does not provide for dual citizenship, those acquiring other citizenship lose Uzbekistani citizenship. If they return to Uzbekistan as foreign citizens, they are subject to foreign visa regulations. There is no evidence that anyone was denied permission to return.

There is no law concerning the rights of refugees and asylum seekers, and the Government does not recognize the right of first asylum. The Government considers asylum seekers from Tajikistan and Afghanistan to be economic migrants, and such individuals are subject to harassment and bribe attempts when seeking to regularize their status. They may be deported if their residency documents are not in order. The country hosts populations of ethnic Koreans, Mesketian Turks, and Crimean Tartars deported to Central Asia by Stalin during World War II. These groups enjoy the same rights as other citizens. Although they are free to return to their ancestral homelands, absorption problems in those countries have slowed that return. The UNHCR estimates there are 30,000 Tajik and 9,000 Afghan asylum seekers of which 2,000 have filed asylum requests with UNHCR; 960 had received mandate refugee status by year's end. There were no confirmed reports of forced repatriation of refugees.

Section 3. Respect for Political Rights: The Right of Citizens to Change Their Government

While the Constitution provides for this right, in reality citizens cannot exercise their right to change their government through peaceful and democratic means. The Government severely represses opposition groups and individuals and applies harsh limits on freedom of expression, although pressure on dissidents decreased in 1996. No true opposition groups participated in government or were allowed to function legally.

Uzbekistan is ruled by a highly centralized presidency, comprising the President, a small inner circle of advisers, and senior government officials. President Karimov, formerly the first secretary of the Communist party in Uzbekistan under Soviet rule, was elected in a limited multicandidate election in 1991. A 1995 Soviet-style referendum and subsequent parliamentary decision extended Karimov's term until the year 2000. President Karimov and the executive branch retain control through sweeping decree powers, primary authority for drafting legislation, and control of virtually all government appointments, most aspects of the economy, and the security forces.

Most government officials are members of the People's Democratic Party of Uzbekistan (PDP), formerly the Communist Party and still the country's largest party. However the Party as such does not appear to play a significant role in government, and the President resigned his chairmanship of the party in 1996.

The 1995 Parliamentary elections were limited to candidates and parties (the PDP and one other government-sponsored party) that support the President. Since then, several other government-sponsored parties have been created and entered Parliament through unchallenged by-elections and other arrangements. The Oliy Majlis is constitutionally the highest government body. In practice, despite assistance efforts by international donors to upgrade its ability to draft laws independently, its main purpose is to confirm laws and other decisions drafted by the executive branch rather than to initiate legislation.

Few people were willing to challenge the Government's grip on power or even risk criticizing it publicly. During a June visit to the United States, President Karimov invited opposition and human rights activists to return to Uzbekistan. In August Abdoumanov Pulat, head of the HRSU (see Section 4) and brother of exiled Birlik leader Abdurakhim Pulatov, returned temporarily from political asylum in the United States to reassume leadership of the HRSU after a 4½-year absence. Pulat moved freely about the country and was not harassed. Some of the many remaining opposition figures in exile have expressed tentative interest in returning, but others report that they do not trust President Karimov's offer and have no intention of returning.

The Government reimplemented a long-dormant, politically motivated property confiscation order against opposition leader and former vice president, Shukrullo Mirsaidov, and harassed his family, apparently in retaliation for Mirsaidov's remarks at an OSCE-sponsored seminar on national human rights institutions. Police placed the family under surveillance and questioned neighbors after Mirsaidov spoke at the conference. On November 28, the Government evicted the family from their apartments in Tashkent to enforce a long-standing but previously dormant property confiscation order against Mirsaidov. During the trial, the district representative withdrew the action on grounds of insufficient evidence, but the prosecutor and judge refused to halt the trial. On November 9, Hasan Mirsaidov, Shukrullo's son, was abducted by several unidentified men under circumstances suggestive of official involvement. He was handcuffed, beaten, and threatened with execution, only to be released after 12 hours. No ransom demand was made on the family. The culprits had not been identified by the police at year's end.

The Government does not officially forbid membership in any political organization. However, individuals whose names are linked with unregistered, opposition-linked organizations report that they are subject to telephonic and written harassment and discrimination in the workplace. Secular political dissidents report that harassment and surveillance have decreased significantly over the past year. Harassment and surveillance of Islamic dissidents continue.

Traditionally, women participate much less than men in government and politics. Only 13 of the 250 deputies in Parliament are female. In 1995 the President promoted the chairwoman of the governmental national women's committee to the position of Deputy Prime Minister. Her duties specifically include monitoring the rights and welfare of women.

Section 4. Governmental Attitude Regarding International and Nongovernmental Investigation of Alleged Violations of Human Rights

The Government generally disapproves of local nongovernmental organizations working on human rights, and restricts their operations. Local NGO's face many obstacles. Laws left over from the Soviet period present difficulties in registration and operation for NGO's and private business alike.

The Human Rights Society of Uzbekistan (HRSU), an opposition-linked group formed in 1992, has been the chief independent source on human rights abuses in Uzbekistan. In the past it was denied registration, and its activists were subject to prolonged harassment, including physical violence. Prior to the OSCE conference in September, however, the Government permitted the HRSU to take the first step in the registration process, the holding of a founding congress, or "kurultoi," in September. HRSU activists continued to suffer harassment, although less than in previous years. HRSU Chairman Pulat visited Uzbekistan for several months without incident. He participated openly in the OSCE human rights seminar and subsequently was interviewed by Uzbek radio. The HRSU publishes reports in Moscow and circulates materials in Uzbekistan, but has no formal right to publish materials locally. The Government declined to act on HRSU's registration petition, asserting technical difficulties in its paperwork.

A governmental human rights commission, headed by a parliamentary ombudsman, was founded in 1995. It responds to complaints from citizens but has insufficient trained staff to carry out in-depth investigations of human rights violations and does not vigorously pursue allegations against the police and security forces. The Government plans to upgrade its capabilities with United Nations assistance. After years of opposition and delay, the Government registered one human rights NGO in 1996, the Committee for Protection of Human Rights. It was formed with the support of the Government but has ties to opposition figures as well. It reportedly has had some success in investigating abuses and getting the Government to correct them, but it has been unable to publish its views because of censorship and lack of financial resources. Some sources affiliated with other groups have questioned its true degree of independence from the Government.

In the past, the Government sharply criticized international human rights groups and Western and Russian reporters for what it considered biased reporting on human rights in the country. The Government has continued to reject criticism from Moscow-based sources, but it has announced its willingness to hold an open dialog with international human rights NGO's. It permitted Human Rights Watch/Helsinki to open a Tashkent office in June. The opening followed two visits in 1995 by HRW/H monitors who met with both governmental and nongovernmental figures. A representative of Amnesty International also visited Uzbekistan in 1996.

From September 11 to 13, the Government and the Office for Democratic Institutions and Human Rights (ODIHR) of the OSCE cosponsored a seminar on national human rights institutions. At the seminar, representatives of indigenous and international NGO's, including secular and Islamic dissidents associated with those NGO's, gave presentations, several of which were extremely critical of government polices concerning the media, political parties, and religious freedom.

Section 5. Discrimination Based on Race, Sex, Religion, Disability, Language, or Social Status

Both the Constitution and the 1992 law on citizenship prohibit discrimination on the basis of sex, religion, language, or social status, however societal discrimination against women persists.

Women.—Spousal abuse is common, but local activists do not have statistics. Wife beating is considered a personal family affair rather than a criminal act, and thus such cases rarely come to court.

Although discrimination against women is prohibited by law, traditional cultural and religious practices severely limit their role in everyday society. For these reasons, women are severely underrepresented in high-level positions. In 1995 President Karimov issued an edict on measures to increase the role of women in society, particularly extending their participation in state and social administration and coordinating the activities of ministries and social organizations as they relate to women's issues. In this connection a new post, deputy Prime Minister, was established with responsibilities for the management of matters connected with furthering the role of women in society. The edict also created heads of women's affairs in the autonomous republic of Karakalpakstan, regions, cities, and districts. The Ministry of Finance was ordered to allocate the necessary funds to finance these new positions and working bodies.

Due to traditional roles, women, particularly in rural areas, usually marry before the age of 20, bear many children, and confine their activities within the family. In rural areas, women often find themselves limited to arduous labor in the cotton fields. However, women are not formally impeded from seeking a role in the workplace: the barriers to equality for women are cultural, not legal, and women who open businesses or seek careers are not legally hindered.

Children.—The Constitution provides for children's rights, stating that parents are obliged to support and care for their children until they are of age. In theory the State provides free universal primary education and health care. In practice shortages and budget difficulties mean that some services must be paid for privately. The State grants monetary allowances to families based on their number of children. There is no societal pattern of abuse of children. Uzbekistan has a very high birthrate; over one-half of the population is under the age of 15.

People With Disabilities.—One of the country's first laws, adopted only 2 months after independence in 1991, provided support for the disabled. This law was aimed at ensuring the disabled the same rights as other people. However, little effort is made to bring the disabled into the mainstream. The State cares for the mentally retarded in special homes. The Government has not mandated access for the disabled.

National/Racial/Ethnic Minorities.—Government statistics show that the population of approximately 23 million is about 71 percent Uzbeks, 8 percent Russians, 5 percent Tajiks, 4 percent Tatars, and 3 percent Kazaks, with many other ethnic groups represented.

The citizenship law, passed in 1992, does not impose language requirements for citizenship. Nonetheless, the language issue remains very sensitive. Uzbek has been declared the state language, and the Constitution requires that the President speak Uzbek. However, the language law provides for Russian as the "language of interethnic communication." Russian is widely spoken in the main cities, and Tajik is widely spoken in Samarkand and Bukhara. The language law, passed in 1989, originally required that Uzbek would be the sole method of official communication by 1997. Uzbekistan also plans to replace its Cyrillic alphabet with the Latin alphabet. However, realizing the difficulties for Uzbeks and minorities alike, the Government has delayed the full transition to both Uzbek and the Latin alphabet to 2005.

Section 6. Worker Rights

a. *The Right of Association.*—The 1992 law on unions specifically provides that all workers have the right voluntarily to form and join unions of their choice and that trade unions themselves may voluntarily associate territorially or sectorally. Membership in trade unions is optional. The law also declares all unions independent of the State's administrative and economic bodies (except where provided for by law), and states that trade unions should develop their own charters, structure, and executive bodies and organize their own work.

In practice, however, the overall structure of trade unions has not changed significantly since the Soviet era. Independence has eliminated subordination to the Soviet Union or Russia but has not altered the centralized trade union hierarchy, which remains dependent on the Government. No "alternative" central union structures exist. A few new professional associations and interest groups have been organized, such as a union of entrepreneurs, a union of renters, an association of private physicians and pharmacists, and one of lawyers. Their role, degree of independence from the Government, and strength are as yet uncertain. Some of these hope to play a significant role in licensing and otherwise regulating the economic activity of their members.

According to the law, the Council of the Federation of Trade Unions (CFTU) has a consultative voice in the preparation of all legislation affecting workers and is entitled to draft laws on labor and social issues. Trade unions are legally described as organizations that defend the right to work and protect jobs. They have lost their previous role in state planning and in the management of enterprises. The emphasis now is on the unions' responsibility for "social protection" and social justice—especially unemployment compensation, pensions, and worker retraining.

The trade union law does not mention strikes or cite a right to strike. However, the law does give the unions oversight over both individual and collective labor disputes, which are defined as those involving alleged violations of labor laws, worker rights, or collective agreements.

There were few reports of strikes. Both union and government officials assert that this reflects general support for the Government's policies and common interest in social stability. It probably also reflects the absence of truly representative trade unions as the standard of living fell, and growing unemployment raised social tensions. Worker collectives in rural areas conducted sit-ins and demonstrations for nonpayment of salaries. In most cases, the local government made arrangements for payment, and the groups dispersed peacefully.

The 1992 law on unions provides that unions may choose their own international affiliations.

b. *The Right to Organize and Bargain Collectively.*—Trade unions may conclude agreements with enterprises. Privatization is in its very early phases, so there is no experience yet with negotiations that could be described as adversarial between unions and private employers. With very few exceptions, the State is still the major employer, and the state-appointed union leaders do not view themselves as having conflicts of interest with the State.

The Ministry of Labor and the Ministry of Finance in consultation with the CFTU, set the wages for various categories of state employees. In the small private sector, management establishes wages or negotiates them with those who contract for employment.

The law forbids discrimination against union members and their officers, and no complaints were registered.

There are no export processing zones.

c. *Prohibition of Forced or Compulsory Labor.*—The Constitution specifically prohibits forced labor, except as legal punishment or as may be specified by law. Large-scale compulsory mobilization of youth and students (by closing schools) to help with the cotton harvest continues. Young people in rural areas are expected to participate "voluntarily" in harvesting activities of all kinds, and universities still shut down temporarily to send both students and faculty into the fields.

d. *Minimum Age for Employment of Children.*—The minimum working age is 16 years; 15-year-olds may work with permission but have a shorter workday. In rural areas, younger children and the elderly often turn out to help harvest cotton and other crops. The Labor Ministry has an inspection service responsible for enforcing compliance with these and other regulations governing employment conditions.

e. *Acceptable Conditions of Work.*—The Ministry of Labor, in consultation with the CFTU, sets the minimum wage. As of December 1, it was about $11.00 (600 som) per month. The minimum wage is not sufficient to provide a decent living for a worker and family. The workweek is set at 41 hours per week and includes a 24-hour rest period. Some factories have apparently reduced workhours in order to avoid layoffs. Overtime pay exists in theory but is not always paid.

The Labor Ministry establishes occupational health and safety standards in consultation with the unions. There is a health and safety inspectorate in the Ministry. Workers do leave jobs that are hazardous without apparent jeopardy to continued employment; but the local press occasionally published complaints about the failure of unions and government authorities to do enough to promote worker safety. Although written regulations may provide adequate safeguards, workers in hazardous jobs often lack protective clothing and equipment.

In theory workers may remove themselves from hazardous conditions without jeopardizing their continued employment. In practice high rates of underemployment make this step difficult.

NEAR EAST AND NORTH AFRICA

ALGERIA

After gaining independence in 1962, Algeria had a single-party state dominated by the country's military leadership and supported by the bureaucracy and the National Liberation Front (FLN). The FLN's rule ended in 1992 with the resignation of President Chadli Benjedid and the dissolution of the FLN-dominated Parliament.

President Liamine Zeroual, a former general, was elected in November 1995 to a 5-year term. Zeroual had previously served as president of a transition government established by the army in 1994. The President controls defense and foreign policy, appoints and dismisses the Prime Minister and cabinet ministers, and may dissolve the legislature. The presidential election was competitive. Three opposition candidates had some access to state-controlled television and radio and also received heavy coverage in the independent press. Zeroual received 61 percent of the votes according to government figures; losing candidates claimed that there were instances of fraud but did not contest Zeroual's victory. Algeria has not had an elected parliament since January 1992. In 1994 the military-backed Government appointed a National Transition Council as a surrogate parliament. The President pledged to hold new parliamentary elections in the first half of 1997.

Under the 1989 Constitution, there was to be a transition to a pluralist republic with a strong president. The democratization process was suspended in 1992 when the Army forced the President to resign, canceled the second round of parliamentary elections which the Islamic Salvation Front (FIS) was poised to win, and installed a ruling five-man High State Committee, which banned the FIS and jailed more of its leaders. The cancellation of the elections in 1992 escalated fighting between the security forces and armed Islamist groups seeking to overthrow the Government and impose an Islamic state.

In May the President began reviewing with legal opposition parties a memorandum containing his ideas on how to develop a political system. These included amending the Constitution to define acceptable political practices and to establish a second parliamentary chamber (a senate). The President also insisted the electoral and political party laws be changed. In September several important opposition political parties joined with the President to sign a national charter encompassing these ideas. In November the Government obtained approval of proposed changes to the Constitution, including provision of a second parliamentary chamber and greater presidential authority, in a flawed popular referendum.

The Government's security apparatus is composed of the army, air force, navy, the national gendarmerie, the national police, communal guards (a local police), and local self-defense forces. All of these elements are involved incounterinsurgency and counterterrorism operations. The security forces were responsible for numerous serious human rights abuses.

The economy is slowly developing from a centrally planned system to a more market-oriented system, in the wake of stabilization policies and structural reforms undertaken in 1994 and 1995. The pace of structural reform slowed in 1996. Uncompetitive and unprofitable state enteprises constituted the bulk of the industrial sector. The state-owned petroleum sector's output represented about a quarter of national income and about 95 percent of export earnings in 1996. Algeria is a middle-income country whose annual per capita income is about $1,700. Unemployment continued to rise in 1996, hitting young people especially hard. About 70 percent of persons under the age of 30 could not find adequate employment. Some made a living from petty smuggling or street peddling.

Although the Government's human rights performance improved somewhat, there were continued serious human rights abuses. The security forces carried out extrajudicial killings, were responsible for numerous cases of disappearance, routinely tortured or otherwise abused detainees, and arbitrarily arrested and held incommunicado many of those suspected of involvement with armed Islamist groups.

Although the Constitution provides for an independent judiciary, recent executive branch decrees have restricted some of the judiciary's authority. Poor prison conditions, lengthy trial delays, illegal searches, and infringements on citizens' privacy rights also remained problems. The Government heavily censored news about security incidents and the armed groups. The Government also continued to restrict freedoms of speech, press, assembly, and movement. During the November constitutional referendum, there were no independent observers at the polling stations during the vote or the ballot counting. Political parties opposing the constitutional amendments were denied access to the electronic media, and their activitists suffered occasional government harassment. The Family Code limited women's civil rights, while domestic violence against women remained a serious problem.

Armed groups and terrorists also committed numerous serious abuses, killing thousands of civilians. Armed Islamists have conducted a widespread insurgency since elections were canceled in January 1992. Although some areas of the country saw less conflict in 1996 that heretofore, acts of terrorism were still numerous. Islamist groups targeted government officials and families of security service members. They also assassinated political and religious figures, businessmen, teachers, journalists, state enterprise workers, farmers, and children. Armed Islamists targeted women specially; there were repeated instances of kidnaping and rape. Bombs left in cars, cafes, and markets killed and maimed people indiscriminately. By year's end, most commonly accepted casualty estimates were that 60,000 people had been killed during 5 years of turmoil.

RESPECT FOR HUMAN RIGHTS

Section 1. Respect for the Integrity of the Person, Including Freedom From:

a. *Political and Other Extrajudicial Killing.*—There were fewer credible reports that security forces killed persons suspected to be members or sympathizers of armed groups. According to an Algerian human rights organization, in August a group of self-defense force members killed 21 civilians outside of Boufarik. An Algerian human rights organization credibly reported that in September a communal guard killed the parents of a suspected terrorist in Draa Ben Khedda after the guard's father was murdered. There was also a credible report that security forces killed a dozen members of an armed group trying to surrender in a western Algerian province in June.

Human rights activists also stated that many persons arrested by police died in custody. For example, police took a young man from his Algiers home in January; his family learned that his body was at the Algiers morgue the following day. Neither the police nor other government authorities have explained how he died.

The Government maintains that the security forces resort to lethal force only in the context of armed clashes with terrorists. The Government also contends that as a matter of policy disciplinary action is taken against soldiers or policemen who are guilty of violating human rights, and this occurred in some cases. In September the Government put a group of self-defense force members on trial in Blida on charges of wrongly killing 5 persons in May. In December a Tipaza court found guilty two policemen for torturing a young man in Tipaza; the officers received suspended sentences. There were no other reports of action or serious sanctions taken against security force members for killings or other human rights abuses.

Armed groups targeted both security force members and civilians. Terrorists attacked civilians whom they regarded as instruments of the State or whose lifestyles they considered in conflict with Islamic values. Sometimes they killed in the course of armed robberies or to enforce local protection rackets. Some terrorist bombings seemed intended only to create social disorder by causing a high number of civilian casualties without any apparent concern for the particular target.

The terrorist Armed Islamic Group (GIA) claimed responsibility for dozens of murders, including the killing of seven French monks in June. Terrorist targets included current and former government officials, businessmen, teachers, doctors, and farmers. An official from the Hamas Movement, a legal Islamist party, was murdered at Ksar Al-Boukhari in January, while an official from the former Communist Party was killed in May. Three men murdered a French-language teacher in a classroom in front of her students in Blida in March. Also in March terrorists killed six textile plant workers near Tizi Ouzou because the workers' villages had organized local defense groups. Armed men shot and killed a popular singer in Constantine in September. There also were instances throughout the year of terrorists stopping buses and cars and murdering civilian passengers. In some cases the victims apparently were murdered merely because they were young men of draft age eligible for military service. In April an armed group assaulted the village of Larbaatache east of Algiers and reportedly killed 60 persons, including women and children. There were a series of massacres in Blida, Tipaza, and Boumerdes provinces during November and December.

Terrorist bombs also killed hundreds. In some cases, the terrorists targeted government buildings. In others they sought to retaliate against the families of members of the security services by exploding car bombs outside their homes. In January a bomb planted in a mosque in Baraki killed six persons. Another bomb killed the Bishop of Oran in August. The Algiers region suffered from a series of cafe bombings during the summer. Terrorists also left bombs at several street markets during the year; one such bomb in Boufarik killed 17 persons in September. Since 1993 at least 59 journalists have died in terrorist attacks; at least 9 were killed during the year. Three of the journalists killed in 1996 died in a February car bombing of the Main Press Building in Algiers, along with 12 other persons (see Section 2.a.). Terrorists also murdered a well-known Algerian news photographer, a reporter for the national television station, and a broadcaster for Algerian Radio. Many journalists had to change their addresses every few days to make themselves less accessible targets. Over 120 foreigners have been killed since 1993.

b. *Disappearance.*—The government-affiliated National Observatory of Human Rights (ONDH) received reports of about 50 cases of disappearance in 1996, down substantially from the 116 received in 1995. The ONDH did receive some responses to its inquiries about disappearance cases from 1996 and previous years. Some of these cases involved arrests by security forces, others involved persons kidnaped by armed groups, and still others involved persons who fled to join armed groups. These resolved cases represented only a small fraction of the total number of cases; the great majority remained unresolved. An independent Algerian human rights group said in December that it had 400 outstanding cases of persons arrested who have disappeared since 1992.

Independent human rights groups in Algeria had no specific total for 1996, but they also suggested that there were fewer cases of disappearance than in previous years. Armed men in uniforms took away an electrician named Mourad in Algiers in July in a vehicle clearly marked "security;" the family was unable to verify if or where he was being held. A man named Hakim was arrested in April by men in uniforms and taken away in the type of vehicle normally used by Defense Ministry elements, but his family could obtain no official confirmation of Hakim's detention. An electrician was arrested and taken from his home in Algiers by men in uniform in September, but his family could obtain no further information on his whereabouts. Families of 14 persons arrested by men in uniforms during a security force sweep of the district of Le Chevalier in March also could not obtain any news of their relatives. The Government asserted that terrorists disguised as security forces perpetrated numerous incidents.

Terrorist groups kidnaped hundreds of civilians, including family members of security service members. Sometimes the mutilated corpses of such victims were later found. In many other instances, however, the victims disappeared, and their families could obtain no information about their fate.

c. *Torture and Other Cruel, Inhuman, or Degrading Treatment or Punishment.*—Both the Constitution and legislation ban torture and other cruel, inhuman, or degrading treatment. However, according to human rights groups and lawyers, the police regularly resort to torture when interrogating persons suspected of involvement in or of having sympathies with armed Islamists. There were several credible reports of torture at the Algiers police facility called Chateau Neuf. Rachid Mesli, a defense lawyer for the FIS was detained in August; he had severe bruises on his face and arms when he appeared for his first Algiers court hearing. There also were credible reports that an Islamist party activist and his wife were arrested and tortured in Setif in March. Security forces reportedly tortured residents from the town of Belaoudi during interrogations in the midst of a sweep for armed groups in July.

There were repeated reports that police applied to prisoners a technique called "Le Chiffon," in which a cloth soaked in noxious fluid was put in the victim's mouth. There were also reports that the police applied electric shocks to sensitive body parts. Police beatings of detainees appeared to be common.

Many victims of torture hesitate to make public allegations due to fear of government retaliation. The Interior Ministry in 1992 said that it would punish those who violated the law and practiced torture, but it has never revealed whether any of those responsible for torture have been punished. In its 1996 report, the ONDH stated that there had been complaints of torture in the Government's campaign against terrorism. It also pointed to a connection between incommunicado detention and allegations of torture. The ONDH called on the Government to put an end to torture of detainees, noting that such practice hurt the credibility of the State.

Armed groups also committed abuses, including frequent beheadings and dismemberment of their victims. There were frequent reports of young women being abducted and repeatedly raped, often for weeks at a time. The terrorists sought to justify this sexual abuse by referring to it as "temporary marriage," but all other observers, including Islamic scholars, uniformly condemned the practice as rape.

Prison conditions are poor and prisons are very overcrowded. According to human rights activists, cells often contain several times the number of prisoners for which they originally were designed. Medical treatment for prisoners is also severely limited. The Government does not permit independent monitoring of prisons or detention centers by groups such as the International Committee of the Red Cross (ICRC) or Amnesty International (AI).

d. *Arbitrary Arrest, Detention, or Exile.*—The Constitution prohibits arbitrary arrest and detention. It stipulates that incommunicado detention in criminal cases prior to arraignment may not exceed 48 hours, after which the suspect must be charged or released. According to the Antiterrorist Law of 1992, the police may hold suspects in prearraignment detention for up to 12 days; they also must inform suspects of the charges against them.

However, the security forces routinely exceed the lawful detention limit in practice. The 1996 ONDH report noted that detainees frequently are held incommunicado much longer than allowed by law. In the spring, there were credible reports from three villages in Jijel province that Communal Guard forces arrested persons suspected of sympathies with armed groups and detained them at Guard barracks.

The most prominent case involving a prisoner held incommunicado was FIS vice-president Ali Benhadj; his family has heard nothing about him since mid-1995 despite repeated approaches to the Justice Ministry by Benhadj's lawyers.

The ONDH report and human rights activists also stated that court judges could not exercise effective control over the police to ensure that the law was applied consistently.

The Antiterrorist Law of 1992 suspended the requirement that the police obtain warrants in order to make an arrest. During the year, the police made a few broad nighttime sweeps of neighborhoods in the Algiers suburbs in search of suspected terrorists and often detained suspects without identifying themselves. In some cases, they purposely arrested close relatives of suspected terrorists in order to force those suspects to surrender. In June the police arrested a 69-year old woman named Daouia in Constantine in order to compel her son, wanted for involvement in an armed group, to surrender. As of late fall, the family was unable to determine where the woman was being held.

According to the ONDH, there are several hundred persons awaiting trial on security-related charges. Other human rights groups allege that the number is much higher. The 1996 ONDH report stated that 12,000 persons were serving prison sentences after being convicted of security-related offenses; an independent Algerian human rights monitoring group put the number at 40,000. In both estimates, however, many—if not most—of those being held were allegedly involved in acts of violence. There were cases, however, which clearly appeared political. For example, Abdelkader Hachani, a senior FIS official, has been imprisoned since January 1992 without trial. Similarly, lawyer Ali Zouita has been held since 1993 despite a court's acquitting him in 1993 of aiding a terrorist group; he has never been tried on other charges.

Persons accused of crimes sometimes did not receive expeditious trials. During the year, the Government arrested hundreds of state enterprise officials on charges of corruption. Only a few have received a trial. The rest remained in detention. Mid-level officials from an Annaba State Enterprise accused of corruption staged a hunger strike in August to protest their 6 months of detention without trial.

Under the state of emergency, the Minister of Interior is authorized to detain suspects in special camps administered by the army. The Government closed the last camp in November 1995, and announced that it had released the 641 prisoners there, although there were subsequent reports that some were rearrested later. The Government and other sources contended that some persons released from this prison had joined armed groups.

Exile is not a legal form of punishment and is not known to be practiced.

e. *Denial of Fair Public Trial.*—The Constitution provides for an independent judiciary. In practice, however, the Government does not always respect the independence of the judicial system.

The National Judges Syndicate publicly charged several times during the year that the executive branch was interfering in matters that properly belong to the judicial system. It cited a Justice Ministry order of March that denied judges the right to release provisionally those accused of corruption without approval from the Ministry. The Government did not retaliate openly against the National Syndicate after it made these charges. However, the authorities prevented the Syndicates's leadership from convening a syndicate meeting in Algiers in December and reportedly encouraged the emergence of new syndicate leadership.

The judiciary is composed of the civil courts, which try misdemeanors and felonies, and military courts, which have tried civilians for security and terrorism offenses. There also is a Constitutional Council which reviews the constitutionality of treaties, laws, and regulations. Although the Council is not part of the judiciary, it has the authority to nullify laws found unconstitutional.

The Government in 1995 abolished the Special Security Courts which human rights observers had contended did not provide defendants fair trials. Regular criminal courts now try those accused of security-related offenses, but there have been very few actual trials.

According to the Constitution, defendants are presumed innocent until proven guilty. They have the right to confront their accusers and may appeal the conviction. Trials are public, and defendants have the right to legal counsel. However, the authorities do not always respect all legal provisions regarding defendants' rights. Lawyers defending state enterprise managers accused of corruption in Annaba withdrew from the case after the Interior Ministry refused to share the evidence gathered against the managers as the law stipulates. Some lawyers would not accept cases of those accused of security-related offenses, due to fear of retribution from the security forces. Defense lawyers for members of the FIS have suffered harassment, death threats, and arrest (see Sections 1.c. and 1.d.).

There are no credible estimates of the number of political prisoners. An unknown number of persons who may be considered political prisoners were serving prison sentences or detained without charge because of their Islamist sympathies and membership in FIS (see Section 1.d.).

f. *Arbitrary Interference with Privacy, Family, Home, or Correspondence.*—The Constitution provides for the inviolability of the home, but the State of Emergency authorizes provincial governors to issue exceptional search warrants at any time. Security forces often entered residences without warrants. The security services also deployed an extensive network of secret informers against both terrorist targets and political opponents. The Government monitored telephones and sometimes disconnected service to political opponents (see Section 3). Security forces detained relatives of suspects to try to compel the suspects to surrender (see Section 1.d.).

There were credible reports that people had to leave their homes due to the Government's antiterrorist operations. In the spring, communal guards forced the evacuation of at least one small village in Jijel province in the midst of a security sweep. There were additional reports that Communal Guard forces blocked the supply of food and water to several villages in Jijel until they agreed to form self-defense forces. During the summer, gendarmerie forces compelled the residents of a village near Larbaa to abandon their homes when they refused to organize a self-defense force.

Armed Islamists routinely entered private homes either to kill or kidnap residents or to steal weapons, valuables, or food. In early 1996, armed groups kidnaped all of the daughters of several families in Jijel province. Armed Islamist groups consistently used threats of violence to extort money from businesses and families across Algeria.

Section 2. Respect for Civil Liberties, Including:

a. *Freedom of Speech and Press.*—The Constitution provides for the freedom of speech, but a 1990 law specifies that such speech must respect "individual dignity, the imperatives of foreign policy, and the national defense." The state of emergency decree gave the Government broad authority to restrict these freedoms and to take legal action against what it considered to be threats to the State or public order. In March 1994, the Government issued an interministerial decree that independent newspapers could print security information only from official government bulletins carried by the government press service APS.

In February the Interior Ministry reminded newspapers of the existing requirement that only APS bulletins about security incidents and the armed groups could be published. In September President Zeroual reiterated that the Government would restrict information about security incidents.

Compliance with the Government directive varied among independent newspapers, but they rarely reported information about security force losses. The Government seized some newspapers for reporting what it considered sensitive information. For example, in April an issue of Al-Watan was seized at the printers when it carried an unauthorized story about a massacre at Larbaatache. Similarly, the Interior Ministry blocked two issues of Al-Acil, printed in eastern Algeria, in June, for allegedly trying to publish information about security incidents.

The Government's definition of security information often extended beyond purely military matters to encompass broader political affairs. The Interior Ministry blocked publication of the weekly La Nation three times in February and March for articles which, it alleged, justified terrorism. However, one issue's articles were reprints of articles about human rights already printed in the French newspaper Le Monde Diplomatique. The Interior Ministry seized an issue of the weekly Al-Houriya in March when it tried to publish an article about the history of political assassination in Algeria. In May the Interior Ministry briefly jailed two journalists from the weekly political satire Al-Mesmar and then banned the paper permanently. In June the Interior Ministry brought charges of defamation against an Al-Watan journalist after she wrote about corruption at the Oran Customs Administration; the Oran court convicted her. The Government closed the independent daily La Tribune in July after the paper carried a cartoon that the Government alleged defamed the Algerian flag; an Algiers court decision in September suspended the newspaper for 6 months. The Government also revoked the credentials of the Spanish correspondent of the Madrid daily El Pais because of its dissatisfaction with his analysis of the security situation. In December the Government again seized an issue of Al-Houriya, although it never explained why. Al-Houriya's editor presumed the seizure stemmed from his effort to publish a story about a book published in France about Algeria's human rights situation.

The Interior Ministry cautioned newspapers to avoid printing interviews with officials from the banned FIS. In 1995 FIS officials who had been freed from detention in 1994 received direct orders from the Justice Ministry to make no further public statements. This ban remains in force.

Journalists at independent newspapers often avoided printing stories about the security situation and Islamist groups in order to avoid difficulties with the Government. The Government frequently sanctioned journalists who wrote offending articles by putting them under judicial control. This required them to check in regularly with the local police. It also prevented them from leaving the country. The ONDH stated in February that the Government should apply this measure less routinely.

The independent press remained free to criticize economic and social policy broadly, but the Interior Ministry and the courts often retaliated against newspapers that accused specific officials of policy failures or crimes. The editor in chief of Al-Watan was convicted and fined for defaming the Health Minister in March after the newspaper alleged that he did not control wasteful spending by the Ministry. The editor of El-Kilaa was jailed briefly in May after his newspaper pointed out that the governor of Tebessa did not attend a local province ceremony as expected. The Interior Ministry charged journalists from La Nation and its fellow weekly Ach-Chourouq with defamation after they wrote exposes about the internal maneuverings of the National Liberation Front in May. In general, journalists exercised self-censorship by not publishing specific criticism of specific officials.

President Zeroual in a September press conference said that the problems confronting the press resulted from market forces, not censorship. However, the Government maintained an effective monopoly of printing companies and newsprint imports and blocked a UNESCO grant to establish a private printing press.

The Government also tightened controls over vital newspaper advertising revenues, centralizing in April all state companies' advertising decisions in a single state agency called ANEP. (This advertising is crucial in an economy in which state companies' output and government services still represent approximately two-thirds of national income.) ANEP provided significant amounts of advertising to particular publications with an anti-Islamist editorial line and that did not undertake investigations of corruption. Other newspapers with different editorial policies received very little or no advertising, even though they had a larger national readership and sometimes even offered cheaper advertising prices. For example, the anti-Islamist newspapers L'Authentique and Le Matin received much more advertising than did L'Opinion or El Al-Alem As-Siyasi newspapers, even though the latter two newspapers had about the same circulation and cheaper advertising prices.

Radio and television remained under government control, with coverage biased in favor of the Government's policies. Opposition political parties occasionally were able to present their points of view, but these appearances represented only a small fraction of the total radio and television broadcast time. Satellite dish antennas are widespread, and millions of citizens have access to European and Middle Eastern broadcasting.

Armed groups continued to target journalists of both the government-controlled and independent media. The February bombing against the Main Press Building was the most visible incident, but at least 9 journalists were murdered during the year (see Section 1.a.).

Many artists, intellectuals, and university educators fled Algeria after widespread violence began in 1992 being especially fearful of Islamist terror. Few returned in 1996. As a result, there were few academic seminars and colloquia, although there appeared to be more in 1996 than in 1995. The Government did not interfere with nonpolitical seminars; it did sometimes with those that were more political in content. For example, it banned seminars that an Algerian youth group sought to hold to discuss human rights (see Section 2.b.).

b. *Freedom of Peaceful Assembly and Association.*—The Constitution provides for the rights of assembly and association, but the 1992 Emergency Law sharply curtails these freedoms. Citizens and organizations must obtain a permit from the appointed local governor before holding public meetings.

The Government had a mixed record of permiting public meetings during the year. The local Algiers authorities refused permission for a labor union in March to protest wage cuts in February. They also banned a sit-in by a nongovernmental organization called The Children of War Martyrs to protest social conditions. Another nongovernmental organization, The Rally for Youth Action, sought permission to hold seminars on human rights in June and on democracy in October, but both were denied. The Algiers authorities did permit a rally in front of the Main Press Building in support of freedom of the press in July, however. In addition the Socialist Forces Front obtained approval for a public rally in downtown Algiers in September. In December political parties and a coalition group called the "Call for Peace" sought permission to hold marches and meetings, but all requests were refused.

The authorities' record outside Algiers also was mixed. During the first half of the year, some legal Islamic parties could not obtain approval to hold public meetings in the provinces of Setif, Khenchala, and Tebessa. During the second half of the year, however, the local authorities granted permission to these same parties. The legal Islamist party An-Nahda could not obtain authorization for a rally in Algiers during the autumn. The Socialist Forces Front also sometimes could not obtain authorization for party rallies during the year. At various times throughout the year Interior Ministry officials sought to gather names of political party activists, and sometimes they summoned activists briefly to police stations to question them about their activities.

The Rally for Youth Action was able to hold human rights conferences in western Algeria and in the Kabylie region east of Algiers, but police later detained its activists in Oran and Bejaia temporarily.

The Interior Ministry licenses all nongovernmental associations, and regards all associations as illegal unless they have licenses. It may deny a license to, or dissolve, any group regarded as a threat to the existing political order. After the Government suspended the parliamentary election in 1992, it banned the FIS as a political party, and the social and charitable groups connected to it. Membership in the FIS is illegal.

According to a 1989 law, all citizens except judges, army, and security service personnel, and members of the Constitutional Council have the right to join political organizations. The Government was rewriting this law late in the year to bar some other government employees in positions of authority from joining political organizations. There were several political groups, including some centrist Islamist parties, such as Hamas and Al-Nahdah, which were able to conduct political activities, though not with complete freedom. Other associations include specialized groups such as human rights and women's rights groups, social welfare groups, and regionally-based cultural organizations.

c. *Freedom of Religion.*—The Constitution declares Islam to be the state religion but prohibits discrimination based on religious belief. The Government respects this right in practice. It permits the small Christian and Jewish populations to practice their faiths without interference.

The Government appoints preachers to mosques and gives general guidance on sermons. The Government monitors activities in mosques for possible security-related offenses.

Conversions from Islam to other religions are rare. Because of security worries and potential legal and social problems, Muslim converts practice their new faith clandestinely. The Family Code prohibits Muslim women from marrying non-Muslims, although this is not always enforced. The Code does not restrict Muslim men from marrying non-Muslim women.

In 1994 the GIA declared its intention to eliminate Jews, Christians, and polytheists from Algeria. The Christian community, composed mostly of foreigners, curtailed its activities. Some church workers left the country because of GIA threats. During 1996 the GIA kidnaped and killed seven Roman Catholic monks in central Algeria. The Catholic Bishop of Oran also was murdered at his home.

d. *Freedom of Movement Within the Country, Foreign Travel, Emigration, and Repatriation.*—The law provides for freedom of domestic and foreign travel and freedom to emigrate. The Government generally respects these provisions. It lifted the remaining nighttime curfew in 10 provinces in February. It has, however, placed some journalists under "judicial control" that does not allow them to leave the country (see Section 2.a.). In addition the Government does not allow foreign travel by senior officials from the banned FIS. The Government also does not permit young men who are eligible for the draft and have not yet completed their military service to leave the country if they do not have special authorization; this authorization can be granted to students and to those with special family circumstances. The Family Code does not permit women under 19 years of age and boys under the age of 18 to travel abroad without their husband's or father's permission.

Under the state of emergency, the Interior Minister and the provincial governors may deny residency in certain districts to persons regarded as threats to public order. The Government also restricts travel into four southern provinces where much of the hydrocarbons industry and many foreign workers are located in order to enhance security in those areas.

The police and the communal guards operate checkpoints throughout Algeria. They routinely stop vehicles to inspect identification papers and search for evidence of terrorist activity. They sometimes detain persons at these checkpoints.

The GIA in February warned young Algerians of draft age not to travel across the country on pain of death for collaboration with the Government. Armed groups establish temporary roadblocks in various regions, including the capital, to rob travelers of cash and vehicles or to kill them. According to credible reports, they sometimes massacred groups of civilian passengers at these roadblocks (see Section 1.a.).

The Constitution provides for the right of political asylum, and the Government occasionally grants asylum. The Government cooperates with the office of the United Nations High Commissioner for Refugees (UNHCR) and other humanitarian organizations in assisting refugees. It also provided first asylum. For example, it cooperates with the UNHCR on programs to help refugee Sahrawis, the former residents of the Western Sahara who left that territory after Morocco took control of it in the 1970's. The Government also has worked with international organizations helping the Tuaregs, a nomadic people of southern Algeria and neighboring countries. Some refugees came from Mali to escape fighting in the northern part of that country. There were no reports of forced expulsion of persons to a country where they feared persecution.

Section 3. Respect for Political Rights: The Right of Citizens to Change Their Government

President Zeroual was elected in a November 1995 presidential election, officially winning 61 percent of the votes cast; there is no elected legislature. The presidential campaign was generally freely contested. Three opposition candidates representing a spectrum of viewpoints had access to both the independent press and the government-controlled media, including radio and television. Their parties were permitted to hold rallies across the country, and they had authorization to send observers to polling stations. There was an independent election commission to supervise the election process, but the opposition parties complained that it did not carefully review complaints it received about the conduct of the election.

Legislative elections have been announced for the first half of 1997. The now-banned FIS and the Socialist Forces Front won a majority of votes cast in the first round of the last legislative election in December 1991. In 1992 the Army forced the President to resign, canceled the second round of parliamentary elections which the Islamic Salvation Front (FIS) was poised to win, and installed a ruling five-man High State Committee, which banned the FIS and jailed more of its leaders. In 1994 the military-backed High Council of State appointed delegates to a National Transition Council, which still acts as a surrogate legislature to ratify legislation proposed by the President. Some opposition parties have representatives on the Council, but their numbers do not reflect any proportional electoral base. Several opposition parties rejected the President's offer to join the Council.

The President called a popular referendum in November to amend the Constitution, and 79 percent of the voters approved the changes, according to the Government. There were no independent observers at the polling stations during the vote or the ballot counting. Political parties opposing the constitutional amendments suffered occasional harassment by local government officials and could not obtain access to the electronic media, which is government-controlled.

Under the new Constitution, the President has the authority to rule by decree in special circumstances. The President must subsequently submit to the Parliament for approval decrees issued while the Parliament was not in session. The Parliament will henceforth have a popularly elected lower chamber and a Senate, two-thirds of whose members will be elected by municipal councils. The President will appoint the remaining one-third of the Senate's members. Legislation must have the approval from three-quarters of both the upper and lower chambers' members to be made law. Laws must originate in the lower house.

The President also proposed changing the law regulating political parties. Under the proposed new law, parties will need official approval from the Interior Ministry. To obtain approval, they will also have to have 25 founders from across Algeria. Parties may not seek to utilize religion, Berberism, or Arabism for political purposes.

The existing political parties represent a wide spectrum of viewpoints and engage in activities ranging from holding rallies to printing newspapers. However, they sometimes encounter difficulties when dealing with local officials who hinder their organizational efforts (see Section 2.b.).

The Government monitored private telephone communications and sometimes disconnected telephone service to political opponents for extended periods (see Section 1.f.). Opposition parties have very limited access to state-controlled television and radio, but the independent press publicizes their views without difficulty (see Section 2.a.).

There is only one woman in the Cabinet, and there are few others in senior government positions. There are several women on the National Transition Council. About 25 percent of the judges are women, and this percentage has been growing in recent years. Only about 1 percent of the candidates in the 1991 legislative elections were women, and none of the four candidates in the 1995 presidential election was a woman. However, a woman heads a workers' party and a woman was the 1995 presidential campaign spokesperson for one of the candidates. The major political parties have women's divisions. The Government changed the electoral law in 1995 to ensure that women cast their own ballots, rather than to permit their husbands or fathers to vote for them, as frequently happened in previous elections. Women voted in large numbers in the 1995 presidential election.

The Government does not ban political participation by any ethnic minority group. The Berbers, an ethnic minority centered in the Kabylie region of Algeria, participate freely and actively in the political process. The Berber-populated region of Algeria has given birth to two political parties, the Socialist Forces Front and the Rally for Culture and Democracy. These two Berber-based parties will have to conform with changes in the new party law that stipulate that political parties have 25 founders from across Algeria.

Independent Berber associations tried in vain to obtain approval to hold conferences about the Berber language in Batna in July and in Ain Beinan in September. The local governor in the Berber city of Bejaia, however, allowed a major rally in September (see Section 2.b.). The Tuaregs, a people of Berber origin, do not play as important a role in politics, due in large part to their small numbers, estimated in the tens of thousands, and their nomadic existence.

Section 4. Governmental Attitude Regarding International and Nongovernmental Investigation of Alleged Violations of Human Rights

The most active independent human rights group is the Algerian League for the Defense of Human Rights (LADDH) which has members throughout Algeria. The LADDH president is a lawyer who speaks out publicly about the general human rights situation. In 1996 the LADDH brought some cases to the attention of the authorities without effect. The LADDH is not allowed access to the authorities or to prisons beyond the normal consultations allowed between a lawyer and client. Members of the LADDH have suffered harassment. Telephone service of their President, for example, was intermittently disrupted, and he and other LADDH activists received death threats from unidentified callers.

There are two other human rights groups in Algeria. The Algerian League for Human Rights (LADH), an independent organization based in Constantine, is less active. The LADH has members throughout Algeria who follow individual cases. It issued a report on the human rights situation in April. The other organization, the National Observatory for Human Rights (ONDH), is a government-affiliated body which was established by the Government in 1992. The ONDH is mandated to report human rights violations to the authorities. It prepares an annual report with recommendations to the Government. The 1996 report highlighted murders committed by terrorist groups but made no mention of killings by government forces. It did, however, recognize violations of the law regarding detention of prisoners. It also recommended that the Government reduce the frequency with which it places journalists under judicial control (see Section 2.a.).

There is an Amnesty International (AI) chapter in Algeria, but it does not work on cases in Algeria. An AI team of foreign human rights monitors came to Algeria during the year. The team moved around freely; however, it was not allowed to visit prisons. The Government has extended an invitation to the U.N. Human Rights Commission Special Rapporteur on Extrajudicial, Summary, or Arbitrary Executions.

Section 5. Discrimination Based on Race, Sex, Religion, Disability, Language, or Social Status

The Constitution prohibits discrimination based on birth, race, sex, belief, or any other personal or social condition. However, women continue to face legal and social discrimination.

Women.—Women's rights advocates assert that spousal violence is common, but there are no reliable studies regarding its extent. There are no laws to protect women from spousal rape or abuse. Battered women must obtain medical certification of the physical effects of the attack before they lodge a complaint with the police. According to women's rights advocates, fewer than half of the women attacked visit doctors for such certification. They also assert that the police and courts are lenient with men accused of beating their wives. Women's rights groups had great difficulty drawing attention to spousal abuse as an important social problem.

Some aspects of the law, and many traditional social practices, discriminate against women. The 1984 Family Code, based in large part on Islamic law or Shari'a, treats women as minors under the legal guardianship of a husband or male relative. A woman must obtain a father's approval to marry, for example. Divorce is difficult to obtain except in cases of abandonment or the husband's conviction of a serious crime. Husbands generally obtain the right to the family home in the case of divorce. Custody of the children normally goes to the mother, but she cannot enroll them in a particular school or take them out of the country without the father's authorization.

The Family Code also confirms the Islamic practice of allowing a man to marry four wives—a rare occurence. However, a wife may sue for divorce if her husband does not inform her of his intent to marry another wife prior to the marriage. Only males are able to confer citizenship on their children.

Women suffer from discrimination in inheritance laws; in accordance with Shari'a they are entitled to a smaller portion of an estate than male children or even a deceased husband's brothers. Women under 19 years of age cannot travel abroad without their husband's or father's permission (see Section 2.d.).

Social pressure against women pursuing higher education or a career is strong. Women comprise only 8 percent of the work force. Nonetheless, women may own businesses and enter into contracts; they pursue opportunities in government, medicine, law, education, the media, and even the armed forces. The 1990 Labor Law bans sexual discrimination in the workplace, but Labor Ministry inspectors do little to enforce this law.

During the year, Islamic extremists often specifically targeted women. For example, they killed wives of members of security forces and female French language teachers (see Section 1.a.). Armed Islamist groups reportedly kidnaped some young women in remote areas and kept them as sex slaves for group leaders (see Section 1.c.).

There are numerous small women's rights groups. Their main goals are to foster women's economic welfare and to amend aspects of the Family Law. No such amendments have yet been passed.

Children.—The Government is committed in principle to protecting children's human rights. It provides free education for children 6 to 15 years of age and free medical care for all citizens—albeit in often rudimentary facilities. The Ministry of Youth and Sports has programs for children, but these face serious funding problems. Legal experts maintain that the Penal and Family Codes do not offer children sufficient protection. Hospitals treat dozens of cases of child abuse every year, but many cases are unreported. Laws against child abuse have not led to notable prosecutions against offenders.

People With Disabilities.—The Government does not mandate accessibility to buildings or government services for people with disabilities. Public enterprises, downsizing the work force, generally ignore a law that requires that they reserve 1 percent of their jobs for people with disabilities. Social Security provides for payments for orthopedic equipment, and some nongovernmental organizations do receive limited government financial support. The Government also tries to finance specialized training, but this remains rudimentary.

National/Racial/Ethnic Minorities.—The Berbers are an ethnic minority, centered in the Kabylie region. Berber nationalists have sought to maintain their own cultural and linguistic identity while the Government's Arabization program continues. As part of the National Charter signed in September, the Government and several major political parties agreed that the Berber culture and language were one of the components of Algerian identity. The Charter did not meet the demands of some political groups that Berber be made an official language. In 1995 the Government established a commission to study how to promote teaching of the Berber language, and some elementary and high schools in the Kabylie region and Algiers started teaching it. However, school administrations decided to suspend these courses in September because they lacked qualified teachers and an approved curriculum. There are professorships in Berber language and culture at the University of Tizi Ouzou. The government-owned national television station began broadcasting a brief, nightly news program in Berber in May. Berbers hold influential positions in Government, the army, business, and journalism.

The Tuaregs, a people of Berber orgin, live a nomadic existence and are relatively few in number.

Section 6. Worker Rights

a. *The Right of Association.*—Workers have the right to establish trade unions of their choice. About two-thirds of the labor force belongs to unions. There is an umbrella labor confederation, the Union Generale Des Travailleurs Algeriens (UGTA), which dates from the era of a single political party and its affiliated entities. The UGTA encompasses national syndicates specialized by sector. There also are currently some autonomous unions, such as a Syndicate of Air Algerie Pilots, another for airport technicians, and another for teachers in the Kabylie.

Workers are required to obtain government approval to establish a union. The 1990 Law on Labor Unions requires the Labor Ministry to approve a union application within 30 days. Early in 1996 a second labor confederation, the Autonomous Syndicates Confederation (CSA), tried to organize the autonomous syndicates, but it did not gain wide support for this effort. It made its application to the Labor Ministry in September 1995 but had not received its approval by the end of 1996. It was allowed to function without official status.

The law prohibits unions from associating with political parties. The law also prohibits unions from receiving funds from foreign sources. The courts are empowered to dissolve unions that engage in illegal activities. The labor union organized by the banned FIS, the Syndicate Islamique Des Travailleurs (SIT), was dissolved in 1992 because it had no license.

Under the state of emergency, the Government is empowered to require workers in both the public and private sectors to stay at their jobs in the event of an unauthorized or illegal strike. According to the 1990 Law on Industrial Relations, workers may strike only after 14 days of mandatory conciliation, mediation, or arbitration. This law states that arbitration decisions are binding on both parties. If no agreement is reached in arbitration, the workers may legally strike after they vote by secret ballot to do so. A minimum of public services must be maintained during public sector service strikes.

The UGTA staged a 2-day general strike in February to protest the Government's decision to cut wages. This was the first nationwide general strike since 1991, but there were approximately 400 local strikes in 1994 and about 200 in 1995. The number of local strikes appeared to decrease further in 1996, but teachers in the Kabylie region staged a strike in April, textile workers staged a strike in March, and the pilots of Air Algerie held a series of strikes in August and September. University teachers staged a strike that lasted from October through the end of the year. With the exception of the pilots' and university teachers' strikes, most work stoppages ended quickly with mediation between company management and the unions. The Government did not invoke the state of emergency to block strikes. Some companies, such as Air Algerie, filed injunction appeals in court to prevent strikes. The courts upheld the companies' motions, and thereby denied the right to strike in these instances, in apparent contravention of the law.

Air Algerie in September fired several dozen pilots who went on strike in August. It claimed that it did so for financial reasons. Most of the pilots' syndicate organizers lost their jobs. Air Algerie later offered all strikers their jobs again, but only for 1-year contracts, providing much less security than their previous permanent positions.

Unions may form and join federations or confederations, affiliate with international labor bodies, and develop relations with foreign labor groups. The UGTA, for example, has contacts with French unions and the American Federation of Labor-Congress of Industrial Organizations.

b. *The Right to Organize and Bargain Collectively.*—The law provides for collective bargaining for all unions. The Government permits this right to be practiced.

The UGTA engaged in several rounds of negotiation with the Government over wage issues. It won concessions in February talks over the issue of salary deductions and it represented workers again in three-way discussions with the Government and business associations in September.

The law prohibits discrimination by employers against union members and organizers and provides mechanisms for resolving trade union complaints of antiunion practices by employers. It also permits unions to recruit members at the workplace.

c. *Prohibition of Forced or Compulsory Labor.*—Forced or compulsory labor is incompatible with the Constitution's provisions on individual rights. The Penal Code prohibits compulsory labor, and the Government effectively enforces the ban.

d. *Minimum Age for Employment of Children.*—The minimum age for employment is 16 years. Inspectors from the Ministry of Labor enforce the minimum employment age by making periodic or unannounced inspection visits to public-sector enterprises. They do not effectively enforce the law in the agricultural or private sectors. Economic necessity compels many children to resort to informal employment, such as street vending.

e. *Acceptable Conditions of Work.*—The law defines the overall framework for acceptable conditions of work but leaves specific agreements on wages, hours, and conditions of employment to the discretion of employers in consultation with employees. The Government fixes by decreee a guaranteed monthly minimum wage for all sectors. The minimum wage is $87 (4,500 dinars) per month. Ministry of Labor inspectors are responsible for ensuring compliance with the minimum wage regulations, although their enforcement is inconsistent.

Algeria has a 44 hour workweek and well developed occupation and health regulations codified in a 1991 decree. Government inspectors do not enforce these regulations effectively. There were no reports of workers being dismissed for removing themselves from hazardous working conditions.

BAHRAIN

Bahrain is a hereditary emirate with few democratic institutions and no political parties. The Al Khalifa extended family has ruled Bahrain since the late 18th century and dominates its society and government. The Constitution confirms the Amir as hereditary ruler. The current Amir, Shaykh Isa Bin Sulman Al Khalifa, governs Bahrain with the assistance of a younger brother as Prime Minister, the Amir's son as Crown Prince, and an appointed cabinet of ministers. In 1975 the Government suspended some provisions of Bahrain's 1973 Constitution, including those articles relating to the National Assembly, which the Government disbanded in the same year. There are few judicial checks on the actions of the Amir and his Government. Bahrainis belong to the Shi'a and Sunni sects of Islam, with the Shi'a comprising over two-thirds of the indigenous population. The Sunnis predominate because the ruling family is Sunni and is supported by the armed forces, the security service, and powerful Sunni and Shi'a merchant families. Bahrain experienced considerable political unrest throughout the year, including bomb and arson attacks on public and private property.

The Ministry of Interior is responsible for public security. It controls the Public Security Force (police) and the extensive Security Service, which are responsible for maintaining internal order. The Bahrain Defense Force (BDF) is responsible for defending against external threats; however, during the year it was called upon to deal with civil unrest. The security forces committed numerous serious human rights abuses.

Bahrain has a mixed economy, with government domination of many basic industries, including the important oil and aluminum industries. Possessing limited oil and natural gas reserves, Bahrain is intensifying efforts to diversify its economic base and has attracted companies doing business in banking, financial services, oilfield services, and light manufacturing. The Government has used its modest oil revenues to build an advanced transportation and telecommunications infrastructure. Bahrain has become a regional financial and business center. Tourism, particularly via the causeway linking Bahrain to Saudi Arabia, is also a significant source of income.

The Government's human rights record worsened in 1996. The main human rights problems continue to include the denial of the right of citizens to change their government; political and other extrajudicial killings; torture; deteriorating prison conditions; arbitrary arrest and incommunicado detention; involuntary exile; limitations on or the denial of the right to a fair public trial, especially in the Security Court; infringements on citizens' right to privacy; and restrictions on freedom of speech, press, assembly, association, and worker rights. Domestic violence against women and discrimination based on religion, ethnicity, and sex remain problems.

RESPECT FOR HUMAN RIGHTS

Section 1. Respect for Integrity of the Person, Including Freedom From:

a. *Political and Other Extrajudicial Killing.*—During the year, in an effort to control civil disturbances, measures taken by the police and security forces resulted in the deaths of five persons. In at least one case, the police may have beaten to death a young man in custody. Most of the deaths occurred when police used force on crowds of antigovernment demonstrators.

On January 5, during a peaceful demonstration in the Al-Qafool area of downtown Manama, security forces shot an unidentified 16-year-old male in the leg who was then fatally struck by a vehicle when he attempted to flee the scene. On May 3, Fadhel Abbas Marhoon of the village of Karzakkan was fatally shot by a patrolling BDF unit. On July 2, 17-year-old Ali Taher was shot and killed by security forces during a demonstration in Sitra. On July 23, 53-year-old Zahra Kadhem Ali reportedly suffered a fatal heart attack when security forces arrived at her home in Bani Jamrah to arrest her adolescent son. On August 15, 19-year-old Seyed Ali Amin from the village of Karbabad died in police custody, reportedly after being beaten and tortured during interrogation at the police station in the village of Khamis. To date the Government has not investigated or prosecuted any police or security force personnel for these incidents.

Seven expatriate laborers died on March 14 when antigovernment protesters barricaded them in a restaurant in the village of Sitra and set the building on fire. One expatriate was also killed under similar circumstances in a separate arson attack in September.

b. *Disappearance.*—There were no reports of politically motivated disappearances.

c. *Torture and Other Cruel, Inhuman, or Degrading Treatment or Punishment.*—Torture and other cruel, inhuman, or degrading treatment or punishment are prohibited by law. There are credible reports, however, that prisoners often are beaten, both on the soles of their feet and about the face and head, burned with cigarettes, forced to endure long periods without sleep, and in some cases are subjected to electric shock. At least one death probably occurred as a result of torture during detention (see Section 1.a.). The Government has difficulty in rebutting allegations of torture and of other cruel, inhuman, or degrading practices because it permits incommunicado detention and detention without trial. There were no known instances of authorities being punished for human rights abuses committed either this year or in any previous year.

Opposition and human rights groups allege that the security forces sometimes threaten female detainees with rape and inflict other sexual abuses and harassment on them while they are in custody. These allegations are difficult either to confirm or deny.

One death and one injury resulted from opposition bombing attacks on hotels and businesses in 1996. On June 30, a man was killed when an explosive device he was allegedly planting at a banking site detonated prematurely. On March 19, a female employee was severely injured when an explosive device detonated at a downtown hotel.

Prison conditions are reportedly deteriorating. There are credible reports that, because of overcrowding, the Government is now experiencing difficulties in providing prisoners with adequate sanitation, sleeping areas, food, water, and health care.

At the Government's invitation, the International Committee of the Red Cross (ICRC) sent a delegation to inspect the prisons in November. ICRC inspections are reportedly to continue into 1997.

d. *Arbitrary Arrest, Detention, or Exile.*—The 1974 Constitution stated that "no person shall be arrested, detained, imprisoned, searched or compelled to reside in a specified place * * * except in accordance with the provisions of the law and under the supervision of the judicial authorities." In practice, however, in matters regarding arrest, detention, or exile, the 1974 State Security Act takes precedence. Under the State Security Act, persons may be detained for up to 3 years without trial for engaging in activities or making statements regarded as a threat to the broadly defined concepts of national harmony and security, and the Government continued to arbitrarily arrest and detain citizens. In March the scope of the State Security Act of 1974 was expanded to include any case involving arson, explosions, or attacks on persons at their place of employment or because of the nature of their work. Detainees have the right to appeal such detentions after a period of 3 months and, if the appeal is denied, every 6 months thereafter from the date of the original detention.

Government security forces used the State Security Act regularly during 1996 to detain persons believed by the Government to be engaging in antiregime activities, as well as those attempting to exercise their right of free speech, association, or other rights deemed to be in opposition to the Government. Activities that can also lead to detention, questioning, warning, or arrest by the security forces include: membership in illegal organizations or those deemed subversive; painting antiregime slogans on walls; joining antigovernment demonstrations; possessing or circulating antiregime writings; preaching sermons considered by the Government to have an antiregime political tone; and harboring or associating with persons committing such acts.

In addition to overseeing the security service and police, the Ministry of Interior also controls the Office of the Public Prosecutor, whose officers initially determine whether sufficient evidence exists to continue to hold a prisoner in investigative detention. The Ministry is responsible for all aspects of prison administration. In the early stages of detention, prisoners and their attorneys have no recourse to any authority outside the Ministry of Interior. The authorities rarely permit visits to inmates who are incarcerated for security-related offenses and such prisoners may be held incommunicado for months, sometimes years. Prisoners detained for criminal offenses, however, generally may receive visits from family members, usually once a month.

The number of women detained for questioning or placed under arrest for antigovernment offenses increased during 1996. However, credible sources within the legal profession state that the authorities do not as a rule hold women in detention for long periods.

Security forces are estimated to have held over 3,000 people in detention in 1996, including some who were arrested, released, and then arrested again. At year's end, as many as 1,500 detainees still remained in detention.

Abdul Amir Al-Jamri, a prominent Shi'a cleric, longtime opposition activist, and one of the original 14 signers of the 1994 petition to the Amir calling for the restoration of the National Assembly, was arrested on January 21 and remains in detention. Al-Jamri is accused of committing a wide variety of security-related crimes, including treason. Several other Shi'a clerics associated with Al-Jamri, including Abdul Wahab Hussein, Hassan Mushaimaa, Hassan Sultan, Ali Bin Ahmed Al-Jedhafsi, and Haji Hassan Jarallah, were also arrested in January and remain in detention.

While the authorities reserve their right to use exile and the revocation of citizenship to punish individuals suspected of, or convicted of, antiregime activity, there were no reports of exile orders issued in 1996. In the past, the Government has revoked the citizenship of nationals who are considered security threats. The Government considers these individuals to have forfeited their nationality under the Citizenship Act of 1963 because they accepted foreign citizenship or passports, or engaged in antiregime activities abroad. Bahraini emigre groups and their local contacts have challenged this practice, arguing that the Government's revocation of citizenship without due process violates Bahrain's 1973 constitution. According to the emigre groups, as many as 500 Bahrainis continue to live in exile. This figure includes both those prohibited from returning to Bahrain and their family members who voluntarily live abroad with them.

During the year the Government released over 150 persons detained in connection with antigovernment activities.

e. *Denial of Fair Public Trial.*—The Constitution provides for an independent judiciary; however, the courts are subject to government pressure regarding sentencing and appeals.

The civil and criminal legal system consists of a complex mix of courts, based on diverse legal sources including Sunni and Shi'a Shari'a (Islamic law), tribal law, and other civil codes and regulations. The 1974 State Security Act created a separate, closed security court system which was given wider jurisdiction in cases of antigovernment activity and was expanded from one to three courtrooms.

The Bahrain Defense Force maintains a separate court system for military personnel accused of offenses under the Military Code of Justice. Military courts do not review cases involving civilian criminal or security offenses.

Defense attorneys are appointed by the Ministry of Justice and Islamic Affairs. Some attorneys and family members involved in politically sensitive criminal cases complained that the Government can and has interfered with court proceedings to influence the outcome or to prevent judgments from being carried out. There are periodic allegations of corruption in the judicial system.

In past cases, the Amir, the Prime Minister, and other senior government officials have all lost civil cases brought against them by private citizens. The courts ordered these judgments to be carried out. Members of the ruling Al Khalifa family are well represented in the judiciary and do not generally excuse themselves from cases involving the interests of the regime.

A person arrested may be tried in an ordinary criminal court or, if recommended by the prosecution, in the Security Court. Ordinary civil or criminal trials provide procedural guarantees for an open trial, the right to counsel (with legal aid available when necessary), and the right to appeal. Criminal court proceedings generally do not appear to discriminate against women, children, or minority groups. However, there is credible evidence that persons accused of antigovernment crimes and tried in the criminal courts were denied fair trials. The accused are not permitted to speak with an attorney until their appearance before the judge at the preliminary hearing. Trials in the criminal courts for antiregime activities were held in secret.

Security cases are tried in secret by the Supreme Court of Appeal, sitting as the Security Court. Family members are usually not permitted in the court until the final verdict is rendered. Procedures in the security courts do not provide for even the most basic safeguards. The Security Court is exempt from adhering to the procedural guarantees of the Penal Code. Defendants may be represented by counsel but seldom see their attorneys before the actual day of arraignment. Convictions may be based solely on confessions and police evidence or testimony that may be introduced in secret. There is no discovery. Defense lawyers complain that they are rarely given sufficient time to develop witnesses. There is no right to judicial review of the legality of arrests. There is no judicial appeal of a State Security Court verdict, but the defendant may request clemency from the Amir. Over 117 Security Court convictions were publicly acknowledged by the Government by year's end, compared with fewer than 50 the previous year.

The number of political prisoners is difficult to determine because the Government does not release data on security cases, such cases are not tried in open court, and visits to prisoners convicted of security offenses are severely restricted. The Government denies that there are any political prisoners, claiming that all inmates incarcerated for committing security offenses were properly convicted of subversive acts such as espionage, espousing or committing violence, or belonging to terrorist organizations.

In accordance with tradition, the Government releases and grants amnesty to some prisoners, including individuals imprisoned for political activities, on major holidays. The Government pardoned over 100 prisoners in May during the Eid Al-Adha holiday.

f. *Arbitrary Interference with Privacy, Family, Home, or Correspondence.*—Under the law, the Ministry of Interior is empowered to authorize entry into private premises without specific judicial intervention. Domestic and international telephone calls and correspondence are subject to monitoring. Police informer networks are extensive and sophisticated.

During the year, the Government infringed on citizens' right to privacy on a broad-scale, using illegal searches and arbitrary arrests as tactics to control political unrest. Security forces routinely raided villages at night, entered private homes without warrants, and took into custody residents who were suspected of either participating in or having information regarding antigovernment activities. While conducting these raids, security forces frequently confiscated, damaged, or destroyed personal property for which owners were not compensated by the Government. Security forces also regularly set up checkpoints at the entrances to villages, requiring vehicle searches and proof of identity from anyone seeking to enter or exit. In many villages, although there were no official curfews, security forces routinely arrested villagers who ventured outside their residences after sundown. On one occasion, at least two villages were locked down completely by security forces, with residents unable to enter or leave for several days. For a period of months in the early part of the year, the Government disabled all public telephones to prevent outside communications. The Government generally jams either in whole or in part foreign broadcasts that carry antigovernment programming or commentary. In May the authorities jammed a satellite transmission of the British Broadcasting Corporation (BBC) program Assignment because it contained a report on the political unrest that was critical of the Government. A government-controlled proxy prohibits user access to Internet sites considered to be antiregime or anti-Islamic (see Section 2.a.).

Section 2. Respect for Civil Liberties, Including:

a. *Freedom of Speech and Press.*—While the Constitution provides for the right "to express and propagate opinions," Bahrainis are not, in practice, free to express public opposition to the Government in speech or writing. Press criticism of ruling family personalities and of government policy regarding certain sensitive subjects—such as sectarian unrest and the dispute with Qatar over the Hawar Islands—are strictly prohibited. However, local press coverage and commentary on international issues is open, and discussion of local economic and commercial issues is also relatively unrestricted. Many individuals express critical opinions openly on domestic political and social issues in private settings but do not do so to leading government officials or in public forums.

The Information Ministry exercises sweeping control over all local media. Bahrain's newspapers are privately owned but routinely exercise self-censorship of stories on sensitive topics. In January the Government changed its policy of withholding information from the public regarding incidents of unrest and permitted more, albeit slanted, articles to be published in the local press. The Government does not condone unfavorable coverage of its domestic policies by the international media and has occasionally revoked the press credentials of offending journalists. Since the Ministry also sponsors foreign journalists' residence permits, this action can lead to deportation. There were no deportations of journalists during the year. Ahmed Al-Shamlan, a local columnist and attorney, was jailed in February for his antigovernment writings but was released in April when the charges against him were dropped. The Government generally afforded foreign journalists access to Bahrain and did not limit their contacts on the island, nor did they penalize reporters afterward for unfavorable stories.

The State owns and operates all radio and television stations. Radio and television broadcasts in Arabic and Farsi from neighboring countries and Egypt can be received without interference. International news services, however, including the Associated Press, United Press International, and Agence France Presse, frequently complain about press restrictions. The Cable News Network is available on a 24-hour basis by subscription and the BBC world news service is carried on a local channel 24 hours a day free-of-charge. However, the Government generally jams wholy or partially foreign broadcasts that carry antigovernment programming or commentary (see Section 1.f.).

Many senior government officials, ruling family members, and major hotels use satellite dishes to receive international broadcasts, as do well-to-do private citizens. The Ministry of Information closely controls access to satellite dishes, and the importation or installation of dishes without prior government approval is illegal.

The Internet system was introduced to Bahrain through the National Telephone Company (Batelco) in 1995. The number of users more than doubled during 1996. A government-controlled proxy prohibits user access to sites considered to be antiregime or anti-Islamic, but e-mail access to information is unimpeded, although it may be subject to monitoring.

Although there are no formal regulations limiting academic freedom, as a practical matter academics try to avoid contentious political issues. In 1996 the Government introduced a new university admissions policy that appears to favor Sunnis and others who pose no question of loyalty and security, rather than focusing only on professional experience and academic qualifications. This policy was accompanied by a major shakeup in the university's administration that removed many Shi'a from senior-level positions.

b. *Freedom of Peaceful Assembly and Association.*—Despite the Constitution's provision for the right of free assembly, the Government prohibits all public political demonstrations and meetings and controls religious gatherings that may take on political overtones. Unauthorized public gatherings of more than five persons are prohibited by law. The Government monitors gatherings that might take on a political tone and frequently disperses such meetings.

On a regular basis from January through July, the security forces used tear gas, rubber bullets, and, occasionally, live ammunition to disperse gatherings during which protesters called for the reestablishment of an elected parliament and the release of prisoners; objected to Al Khalifa rule; denounced police brutality; protested foreigners in the security forces and in the labor force; and demanded increased employment opportunities. After each of these incidents, suspected leaders and active participants were arrested.

The Government prohibits political parties and organizations. Some professional societies and social/sports clubs have traditionally served as forums for discreet political discussion, but they are restricted by law from engaging in political activity. Only the Bahraini Bar Association has been granted an exemption to the regulation requiring all associations to state in their constitutions that they will refrain from political activity. The Bar Association successfully argued that a lawyer's professional duties may require certain political actions, such as interpreting legislation or participating in a politically sensitive trial. Other organized discussions and meetings are still actively discouraged. Permits are required for most public gatherings, and permission is not routinely granted.

c. *Freedom of Religion.*—The population is overwhelmingly Muslim and Islam is the state religion. However, Christians and other non-Muslims, including Jews, Hindus, and Baha'is are free to practice their religion, maintain their own places of worship and may display the sumbols of their religion. Bibles and other Christian publications are displayed and sold openly in local bookshops, which also sell Islamic and other religious literature. Some small groups worship in their homes. Notables from virtually every religion and denomination visit Bahrain and frequently meet with government and civic leaders. Religious tracts of all Islamic sects, cassettes of sermons delivered by Muslim preachers from other countries, and publications of other religions are readily available.

Proselytizing by non-Muslims is discouraged, anti-Islamic writings prohibited, and conversions from Islam to other religions, while not illegal, are not well tolerated by society.

Both Sunni and Shi'a sects are subject to governmental control and monitoring. During the months of January and February, the Government closed mosques and ma'tams (Shi'a community centers) in certain locations to prevent religious leaders from delivering political speeches during their Friday prayers and sermons. There are also reports that security forces entered several religious facilities and removed communication equipment, such as computers, printers, and facsimile machines, that were alleged to be used to further political unrest. In March the Government established the High Council for Islamic Affairs which includes among its functions review and approval of all clerical appointments within both the Sunni and Shi'a communities and program oversight for all citizens studying religion abroad. The Council is still awaiting several key appointments and has yet to issue any directives. Public religious events, most notably the large annual commemorative marches by Shi'a, are permitted but are closely watched by the police. There are no restrictions on the number of citizens permitted to make pilgrimages to Shi'a shrines and holy sites in Iran, Iraq, and Syria. However, owing to conditions in Iraq, very few citizens make pilgrimages there. The Government monitors travel to Iran and scrutinizes carefully those who choose to pursue religious study there. Travel to Iran for pilgrimages, business trips, tourism, and family visits, however, is not forbidden.

d. *Freedom of Movement Within the Country, Foreign Travel, Emigration, and Repatriation.*—Citizens are free to move within the country and change their place of residence or work. Passports, however, may be denied on political grounds. Approximately 3 percent of the indigenous population, the "bidoon," or stateless persons, mostly Persian-origin Shi'a, do not have passports and cannot readily obtain them, although they may be issued travel documents as Bahraini residents (see Section 5). About 150 Sunni bidoon, mostly from the Arabian Peninsula, were granted citizenship in 1995, and about 15 Egyptian citizens resident in Bahrain also received citizenship.

Citizens living abroad who are suspected of political or criminal offenses may face arrest and trial upon return to Bahrain. Under the 1963 Citizenship Law, the Government may reject applications to obtain or renew passports for reasonable cause, but the applicant has the right to appeal such decisions before the High Civil Court. The Government has also issued temporary passports, good for one trip within a year, to individuals whose travel it wishes to control or whose claim to Bahraini nationality is questionable. Noncitizen residents, including Bidoon of Iranian origin, may also obtain Bahraini laissez passers, usually valid for 2 years and renewable at Bahraini embassies overseas. Laissez passer holders also require visas to reenter Bahrain.

Bahrain does not usually accept refugees due to its small size and limited resources.. In practice, however, refugees who arrive in Bahrain are not repatriated to countries from which they have fled. Many Iranian emigres who fled Iran after the Iranian revolution have been granted permission to remain in Bahrain, but they have not been granted citizenship. Although the Government cooperates with the U.N. High Commissioner for Refugees to the maximun extent possible, it has not formulated a formal policy regarding refugees, asylees, or first asylum.

Section 3. Respect for Political Rights: The Right of Citizens to Change Their Government.

Citizens do not have the right or ability peacefully to change their government or their political system, and political activity is strictly controlled by the Government. Since the dissolution of the National Assembly in 1975, there have been no formal democratic political institutions. The Government permits neither political parties nor opposition organizations. The Prime Minister makes all appointments to the Cabinet. All other government positions are filled by the relevant ministries. About one-third of the cabinet ministers are Shi'a Muslim, although they do not hold security-related offices. The ordinary citizen may attempt to influence government decisions through submission of personal written petitions and informal contact with senior officials, including appeals to the Amir, the Prime Minister, and other officials at their regularly scheduled public audiences, called majlises.

In 1992 the Amir establish by decree a Consultative Council (Majlis Al-Shura.) Its members are evenly divided between Sunni and Shi'a and are appointed by the Amir. They are selected to represent major constituent groups, including representatives from the business, labor, professional, and religious communities. There are no members of the ruling Al Khalifa family or religious extremists in the Majlis. In September two Amiri decrees amended the Council's structure and mandate to allow for an expanded membership—from 30 to 40—and increased powers, including debate on issues not submitted to it by the Cabinet. The Majlis may also summon cabinet ministers to answer questions, but its recommendations are not binding on the Government. The Majlis held its fourth session from October 1995 to June 1996 and began a new session on October 1. The chairman is a prominent Shi'a who formerly was Minister of Transport and Communications.

In 1996 the Majlis debated a number of contentious social and economic issues, including unemployment, labor policy, and education, drafting proposals on these and other subjects for government consideration. According to the Speaker of the Majlis, the Government responded positively to the majority of the Majlis's recommendations by incorporating them into legislation or by taking other appropriate actions.

There are no women in either the Consultative Council or at the ministerial levels of government. The majority of women who choose to work in government are in a support capacity and only a few have managed to attain senior positions within their respective ministries or agencies.

Section 4. Government Attitude Regarding International and Nongovernmental Investigations of Alleged Violations of Human Rights

There are no local human rights organizations. Because of the restrictions on freedom of association and expression, any independent, domestically based investigation or public criticism of the Government's human rights policies faces major obstacles. A number of groups based abroad claim to report on Bahraini human rights violations. These include the Damascus-based Committee for the Defense of Human Rights in Bahrain, the London-based Bahrain Freedom Movement and the Islamic Front for the Liberation of Bahrain, and the Copenhagen-based Bahrain Human Rights Organization, formerly the Committee for the Defense of Political Prisoners in Bahrain. These groups are composed of small numbers of emigres living in self-imposed exile and reportedly receive funding from sources hostile to the Government. They are viewed by many local observers as espousing a political, rather than a purely human rights, agenda.

The Government maintains that it is not opposed to visits in good faith by bona fide human rights organizations and has engaged in dialog with the International Committee of the Red Cross and Amnesty International (AI). In practice, however, international human rights organizations have found it difficult to conduct activities in Bahrain. In October the Government invited the ICRC to undertake inspections of Bahrain's prisons, reportedly on the grounds that the ICRC's findings would not be made public. The inspections have been under way since November and are expected to continue into early 1997.

Section 5. Discrimination Based on Race, Sex, Religion, Disability, Language, or Social Status

The Constitution states that "liberty, equality, security, tranquility, education, social solidarity, and equal opportunities for citizens shall be pillars of society assured by the State." It further states that every citizen shall have the right to medical care, welfare, education, property, capital, and work. In practice, however, these rights are unevenly protected, depending on the individual's social status, ethnicity, or sex.

Women.—Violence against women occurs, but incidents are usually kept within the family. In general there is little public attention to, or discussion of, violence against women. No Government policies explicitly address violence against women. Women's groups and health care professionals state that spouse abuse is common, particularly in poorer communities. There are very few known instances of Bahraini women seeking legal redress for violence. Anecdotal evidence suggests that the courts are not receptive to such cases.

Cases are not uncommon of foreign women working as domestic servants who have been beaten or sexually abused. Numerous cases have been reported to local embassies and the police. Most victims, however, are too intimidated to sue their employers. Those who do so appear to be received sympathetically in the courts.

Islamic law (Shari'a) governs the legal rights of women. Specific rights vary according to Shi'a or Sunni interpretations of Islamic law, as determined by the individual's faith, or by the court in which various contracts, including marriage, have been made.

While both Shi'a and Sunni women have the right to initiate a divorce, religious courts may refuse the request. Although local religious courts may grant a divorce to Shi'a women in routine cases, occasionally Shi'a women seeking divorce under unusual circumstances must travel outside of Bahrain to seek a higher ranking opinion than is available in Bahrain. Women of either sect may own and inherit property and may represent themselves in all public and legal matters. In the absence of a direct male heir, Shi'a women may inherit all property. In contrast, Sunni women—in the absence of a direct male heir—inherit only a portion; the balance is divided among brothers, uncles, and male cousins of the deceased.

In the event of divorce, the courts routinely grant Shi'a and Sunni women custody of daughters under the age of 9 and sons under age 7, although custody usually reverts to the father once the children reach those respective ages. In all circumstances except mental incapacitation, the father, regardless of custody, retains the right to make certain legal decisions for his children, such as guardianship of any property belonging to the child until the child reaches legal age. A non-Bahraini woman automatically loses custody of her children if she divorces their Bahraini father. Women may obtain passports and leave the country without the permission of the male head of the household. Bahraini women are free to work outside the home, to drive cars without escorts, and to wear the clothing of their choice (a large percentage wear Western dress outside the home), and have increasingly taken jobs previously reserved for men. Labor law does not discriminate against women; however, in practice, there is discrimination in the workplace, including inequality of wages and denial of opportunity for advancement. Women constitute over 20 percent of the work force. The Government has encouraged the hiring of women, enacted special laws to promote female entry into the work force, and is a leading employer of women. Labor law does not recognize the concept of equal pay for equal work, and women are generally paid less than men. Generally, women work outside the home during the years between secondary school or university and marriage. Women make up the majority of students at Bahrain's universities. There are women's organizations that seek to improve the status of women under both civil and Islamic law.

Some women have expressed the view that, despite their participation in the work force, women's rights are not significantly advancing and that much of the lack of progress is due to the influence of Islamic religious traditionalists. Other women, however, desire a return to more traditional religious values and support calls for a return to Islamic patterns of social behavior.

Children.—The Government has often stated its commitment to the protection of children's rights and welfare within the social and religious framework of this traditional society. It honors this commitment through enforcement of its civil and criminal laws and an extensive social welfare network. Public education for children below the age of 16 is free and compulsory. Limited medical services for infants and adolescents are provided free of charge.

The social status of children is shaped by tradition and religion to a greater extent than by civil law. Public discussion of child abuse is rare, and the preference of the authorities has always been to leave such matters within the purview of the family or religious groups. The authorities actively enforce the laws against prostitution, including child prostitution, procuring, and pimping. Violators are dealt with harshly and can be imprisoned, or if non-Bahraini, deported. In some cases, authorities reportedly will return children arrested for prostitution and other nonpolitical crimes to their families rather than prosecute them, especially for first offenses. Some legal experts have called on the Government to establish a separate juvenile court. Other Bahrainis, however, insist that the protection of children is a religious, not a secular, function and oppose greater government involvement. Independent and quasi-governmental organizations such as the Bahraini Society for the Protection of Children and the Mother and Child Welfare Society play an active part in protecting children by providing counseling, legal assistance, and advice, and, in some cases, shelter and financial support to distressed children and families.

Detentions and arrests of juveniles, some as young as 7 years old, increased in 1996 in connection with the political unrest. These children were generally released without charges within several days of their arrests. However, those juveniles charged with security offenses received the same treatment as adult prisoners, i.e., incommunicado detention and trial before a state security court.

People With Disabilities.—The law protects the rights of people with disabilities, and a variety of governmental, quasi-governmental, and religious institutions are mandated to support and protect disabled persons. The Regional (Arabian Gulf) Center for the Treatment of the Blind is headquartered in Bahrain and a similar Center for the Education of Deaf Children was established in 1994. Bahraini society tends to view people with disabilities as special cases in need of protection rather than as fully functioning members of society. Nonetheless, the Government is required by law to provide vocational training for disabled persons wishing to work and maintains a list of certified, trained disabled persons. The Labor Law of 1976 also requires that any employer of over 100 people must engage at least 2 percent of its employees from the Government's list of disabled workers. The Ministry of Labor and Social Affairs works actively to place people with disabilities in public sector jobs, such as in the public telephone exchanges. The Government's housing regulations require that access be provided to disabled persons. Most large public buildings are equipped with ramps and other aids that make them accessible to disabled persons.

Religious Minorities.—Although there are notable exceptions, the Sunni Muslim minority enjoys a favored status in Bahrain. Sunnis generally receive preference for employment in sensitive government positions and in the managerial ranks of the civil service. Shi'a citizens are not allowed to hold significant posts in the Bahrain defense and internal security forces. During 1996 employment opportunities for Shi'a citizens in the government sector became more restricted. In the private sector, Shi'a tend to be employed in lower paid, less skilled jobs.

Educational, social, and municipal services in most Shi'a neighborhoods, particularly in rural villages, are inferior to those found in Sunni urban communities. In an effort to remedy social discrimination, improve living conditions for the Shi'a, and encourage integration, the Government has built numerous subsidized housing complexes open to all citizens on the basis of financial need.

National/Racial/Ethnic Minorities.—A group of approximately 9,000 to 15,000 persons, mostly of Persian-origin and Shi'a, but including some Christians, are stateless. They are commonly known as bidoon and enjoy less than full citizenship under the Citizenship Act of 1963. Many of the bidoon are second- or third-generation residents whose ancestors emigrated from Iran. Although they no longer claim Iranian citizenship, they have not been granted Bahraini nationality. Without citizenship these individuals are officially unable to buy land, start a business, or obtain government loans, although in practice many do. The law does not address the citizenship rights of persons who were not registered with the authorities prior to 1959, creating a legal problem for such persons and their descendants and resulting in economic and other hardships. The Government maintains that many of those who claim to be bidoon are actually citizens of Iran or other gulf states who have voluntarily chosen not to renew their foreign passports. Bidoon and Bahrainis who speak Farsi, rather than Arabic, as their first language also face significant social and economic obstacles, including difficulty finding employment.

Section 6. Worker Rights

a. *The Right of Association.*—The partially suspended 1973 Constitution recognizes the right of workers to organize, but internationally affiliated trade unions do not exist. The Constitution states that "freedom to form associations and trade unions on national bases and for lawful objectives and by peaceful means shall be guaranteed in accordance with the conditions and in the manner prescribed by the law. No person shall be compelled to join or remain in any association or union."

In response to labor unrest in the mid-1950's, 1965, and 1974, the Government passed a series of labor regulations which, among other things, allow the formation of elected workers' committees in larger companies. Worker representation today is based on a system of Joint Labor-Management Committees (JLC's) established by ministerial decree. Between 1981 and 1984, 12 JLC's were established in the major state-owned industries. Four new JLC's were established in 1994 in the private sector, including one in a major hotel.

In 1995 elections were held for 2-year terms for representatives to the General Committee of Bahrain Workers (GCBW), which oversees the activities of the JLC's. Workers from all types of occupations were elected to the body in 1995, including Sunni and Shi'a Muslims, expatriates, and, for the first time, a woman. These elections, which were by secret ballot and appeared to be free, were carried out during the worst of the demonstrations. The Government is considering the further expansion of the JLC system into the tourism and banking sectors.

The JLC's are composed of equal numbers of appointed management representatives and worker representatives elected from and by company employees. Each committee is chaired alternately by the management and worker representative. The selection of worker representatives appears to be fair; under the law the Ministry of Interior may exclude worker candidates with criminal records or those deemed a threat to national security. The elected labor representatives of the JLC's select the 11 members of the GCBW, established in 1983 by law, which oversees and coordinates the work of the JLC's. The Committee also hears complaints from Bahraini and foreign workers and assists them in bringing their complaints to the attention of the Ministry of Labor or the courts. Although the Government and company management are not represented on the GCBW, the Ministry of Labor closely monitors the body's activities. It approves the GCBW's rules and the distribution of GCBW funds. The JLC-GCBW system represents nearly 70 percent of the island's indigenous industrial workers, although both government and labor representatives readily admit that nonindustrial workers and expatriates are clearly underrepresented in the system. The Ministry of Labor and Social Affairs has publicly urged the formation of JLC's in all public and private sector companies employing more than 200 workers. Although expatriate workers comprise 67 percent of the work force, expatriates are underrepresented in the GCBW. Expatriate workers can and do participate in JLC elections, and five expatriates currently serve on JLC's. None, however, currently sits on the board of the GCBW. It is a long-term goal of both the Government and the GCBW to replace expatriate workers with Bahrainis throughout all sectors of the economy and to create new jobs for Bahrainis seeking employment.

The Labor Law is silent on the right to strike, and there were no strikes in 1996. Actions perceived to be detrimental to the "existing relationship" between employers and employees or to the economic health of the State are forbidden by the 1974 Security Law. There are no recent examples of major strikes, but walkouts and other job actions have been known to occur without governmental intervention and with positive results for the workers.

The GCBW represents Bahraini workers at the International Labor Organization (ILO) and in the Arab Labor Organization, but does not belong to any international trade union organizations.

b. *The Right to Organize and Bargain Collectively.*—As in the case of strikes, the Labor Law neither grants nor denies workers the right to organize and bargain collectively outside the JLC system. While the JLC's are empowered to discuss labor disputes, organize workers' services, and discuss wages, working conditions, and productivity, the workers have no independent, recognized vehicle for representing their interests on these or other labor-related issues. JLC's hold discussions with management on some working conditions and limited aspects of wage issues. Minimum wage rates for public sector employees are established by Council of Minister decrees. Private businesses generally follow the Government's lead in establishing their wage rates.

There are two export processing zones. Labor law and practice are the same in these zones as in the rest of the country.

c. *Prohibition of Forced or Compulsory Labor.*—Forced or compulsory labor is prohibited by law. In practice, the labor laws apply for the most part only to citizens, and abuses occur, particularly those involving domestic workers and those working illegally. In some cases, workers arrive in Bahrain under the sponsorship of an employer and then switch jobs, while continuing to pay a fee to their original sponsor. The Government has announced its intention to abolish this illegal practice, which makes it difficult to monitor and control the employment conditions of domestic and other workers. However, no substantive action has yet been taken.

Amendments to the Labor Law passed in November 1993 stiffened the penalties for engaging in visa switching to include jail sentences of up to 6 months for the sponsor of every illegally sponsored worker. In such cases, the workers involved are likely to be deported as illegal immigrants after the case is concluded.

The sponsorship system leads to abuses. There are numerous reports that employers withhold salaries from their foreign workers for months, even years, at a time and may refuse to grant them the necessary permission to leave the country. The Government and the courts generally work to rectify those abuses brought to its attention, but fear of deportation or employer retaliation prevent many foreign workers from making complaints to the authorities.

Labor laws do not apply to domestic servants. There are credible reports that domestic servants, especially women, are sometimes forced to work 12- or 16-hour days, given little time off, and are subjected to verbal and physical abuse.

d. *Minimum Age for Employment of Children.*—The minimum age for employment is 14 years of age. Juveniles between the ages of 14 and 16 may not be employed in hazardous conditions or at night and may not work more than 6 hours per day or on a piecework basis. Child labor laws are effectively enforced by Ministry of Labor inspectors in the industrial sector; child labor outside that sector is less well monitored but is not believed to be significant outside family operated businesses.

e. *Acceptable Conditions of Work.*—Minimum wage scales, set by government decree, exist for public sector employees and generally afford a decent standard of living for workers and their families. The current minimum wage for the public sector is $236.60 (91 dinars) a month. Wages in the private sector are determined on a contract basis. For foreign workers, employers consider benefits such as annual trips home and housing and education bonuses part of the salary.

The Ministry of Labor enforces the labor laws, with periodic inspections and fines routinely imposed on violators. Provisions to the Labor Law passed in 1993 stiffened the fines and prison terms for certain violations. The press often performs an ombudsman function on labor problems, reporting job disputes and the results of labor cases brought before the courts. Once a complaint has been lodged by a worker, the Labor Ministry opens an investigation and often takes remedial action.

The Labor Law, enforced by the Ministry of Labor and Social Affairs, mandates acceptable conditions of work for all adult workers, including adequate standards regarding hours of work (maximum 48 hours per week) and occupational safety and health. The Fourth High Court (Labor) has jurisdiction over cases involving alleged violations of the Labor Law.

Complaints brought before the Ministry of Labor and Social Affairs that cannot be settled through arbitration must, by law, be referred to the court within 15 days. In practice, most employers prefer to settle such disputes through arbitration, particularly since the court and labor law are generally considered to favor the employee. Under the Labor Law workers have the right to remove themselves from dangerous work situations without jeopardy to their continued employment. In 1993 the Government strengthened the Labor Law by Amiri decree, announcing that significant fines and jail sentences would be imposed upon private sector employers who fail to pay legal wages. This law applies equally to employers of citizens and expatriates and is intended to reduce abuses against foreign workers who have sometimes been denied legal salaries. The law provides equal protection to Bahraini and foreign workers, but all foreign workers still require sponsorship by Bahrainis or Bahrain-based institutions and companies. Subject to sanctions for wrongful dismissal, sponsors are able to cancel the residence permit of any person under their sponsorship and thereby block them for 1 year from obtaining entry or residence visas from another sponsor.

Foreign workers, particularly those from developing countries, are often unwilling to report abuses for fear of losing residence rights and having to return to their native countries. Instances of foreign workers being denied full wages, days off, vacations, or other guaranteed conditions of employment without compensation are periodically reported in the local press, as well as the court rulings or Ministry of Labor and Social Affairs actions taken in response. Nonetheless, government attempts to address individual abuses in these and other cases are often hampered by the workers' unwillingness to make a formal complaint.

In addition, the Labor Law specifically favors citizens over foreign workers, followed by Arab expatriates over other foreign workers, in hiring and firing. Because employers include housing and other allowances in their salary scales, expatriate workers can legally be paid lower regular wages than their Bahraini counterparts, although they sometimes receive the same or a greater total compensation package because of home leave and holiday pay allowances. Western expatriates and Bahraini workers are paid comparable wages, with total compensation packages often significantly greater for the former. Women are entitled to 60 days of paid maternity leave, nursing periods during the day, and up to 1 year of unpaid maternity leave. However, women are generally paid less than men.

EGYPT

According to its Constitution, Egypt is a social democracy in which Islam is the state religion. However, the National Democratic Party (NDP), has governed since its establishment in 1978, has used its entrenched position to dominate national politics, and maintains a wide majority in the popularly elected People's Assembly and the partially elected Shura (Consultative) Council. The President, Hosni Mubarak, was reelected unopposed to a third 6-year term by the People's Assembly in 1993. The President appoints the Cabinet, which is responsible to him. The judiciary is independent.

There are several security services in the Ministry of Interior, two of which are primarily involved in combating terrorism: The State Security Investigations Sector (SSIS), which conducts investigations and interrogates detainees; and the Central Security Force (CSF), which enforces curfews and bans on public demonstrations, and conducts paramilitary operations against terrorists. The use of violence by security forces in the campaign against terrorists appeared more limited this year than in previous years. The security forces committed numerous serious human rights abuses.

Egypt continued to move from a command economy to a free market system. Manufacturing is still dominated by the public sector. The Government began accelerating its privatization program during the year. Agriculture remains the largest employer in the economy and is almost entirely in private hands. Transfers and remittances from approximately 2 million Egyptians working abroad are the largest source of foreign currency earnings. In 1995 tourism surpassed petroleum as the second largest hard currency earner and preliminary data for 1996 suggest a continued strong rebound of the tourism sector. In the past 5 years, the Government has enacted significant economic reforms, which have reduced the budget deficit, stabilized the exchange rate, reduced inflation and interest rates significantly, and built up substantial reserves. The success of the reform efforts has resulted in an increase in annual economic growth rates to 4.8 percent for fiscal year 1995–96 and 5.1 percent estimated for fiscal year 1996–97.

The Government continued to commit numerous serious abuses, although its human rights record improved somewhat over the past year. The Emergency Law, which has been in effect since 1981, continues to restrict many basic rights. The ruling NDP dominates the political scene to such an extent that citizens do not have a meaningful ability to change their government. The security forces and terrorist groups remained locked in a cycle of violence. In fighting the terrorists, the security forces continue to mistreat and torture prisoners, arbitrarily arrest and detain persons, hold detainees in prolonged pretrial detention, and occasionally engage in mass arrests. Aside from the antiterrorist campaign, local police abused common criminal suspects. However, security forces committed fewer abuses than in the previous year. The Government took disciplinary action against police officers accused of abusing detainees, but did not pursue most cases or seek adequate punishments. Prison conditions are poor.

The use of military courts to try civilians continues to infringe on a defendant's right to a fair trial before an independent judiciary. The Government again tried members of the Muslim Brotherhood in military courts on charges of illegal political activities, continuing to expand the jurisdiction of the military courts beyond terrorism-related offenses. The Government used the emergency law to infringe on citizens' privacy rights. Although citizens generally express themselves freely, the Government continues to place significant limitations on freedom of the press. Some of the harsher penalties of the 1995 press law were suspended; however, state prosecutors brought libel charges, some under the old law, against several journalists for criticizing corruption and abuse of authority among government officials and their families. The Government restricts freedom of assembly and association, and does not legally recognize local human rights groups, but which are allowed to operate openly. The Government places limits on the freedom of religion.

Women and Christians face discrimination based on tradition and some aspects of the law. Terrorist violence against Christians was a problem. Violence against women is a problem. Worker rights are not adequately protected. A new child labor law increases protections for children, but child labor remains widespread despite the government's efforts to eradicate it. Abuse by employers continues, and stricter government enforcement of the law is necessary. In a significant breakthrough, the Government issued a decree banning the practice of female genital mutilation (FGM), developed a program to address the problem, and increased efforts to educate the public as to its dangers.

Terrorists committed numerous serious abuses. Terrorist groups seeking to overthrow the Government and establish an Islamic state continued their attacks on police, Coptic Christians, and tourists. In April terrorists killed a group of 18 Greek tourists in Cairo; 13 Greeks and 2 Egyptians were wounded. Terrorists groups were responsible for the majority of the 132 civilian and police deaths, and committed bank and jewelry store robberies to get funds. They also attacked police, a train, and riverboats, mostly in upper (southern) Egypt.

RESPECT FOR HUMAN RIGHTS

Section 1. Respect for the Integrity of the Person, Including Freedom From:

a. *Political and Other Extrajudicial Killing.*—There were no reports of political killings by government officials; however, extrajudicial killings may have occured in certain antiterrorist operations.

There were no total figures for deaths in custody from government or human rights sources by year's end. Human rights groups were investigating eight deaths in police custody, six of which they believed were due to medical negligence, one to suicide, and one as a result of a beating or being tortured to death. They are also investigating 13 prison deaths related to medical negligence (see Section 1.c.).

In antiterrorist operations, the security forces killed 34 suspected terrorists; there were no reports of excessive use of lethal force. At least one civilian bystander was reported killed inadvertently by security forces. No suspects died while attempting to escape arrest. There were no reports of killings of relatives of suspected extremists in apparent vendettas.

The case against a policeman charged with torture and use of excessive force in the 1994 death of a detainee remained pending (see Section 1.c.).

In January state prosecutors ruled in the case of the 1994 death in custody of Amre Mohamed Safwat that there was no felony case. The prosecutors, however, ordered a reprimand for the head of the Ain Shams Cairo police station and the director of the hospital involved for violating the rules of admission to the hospital. An appeal by the family is currently under investigation by the Technical (Human Rights) Office of the Ministry of Justice. There were no new developments in the case of Mohammed Abdel Hamid Hassan, who reportedly died in police custody in 1994.

Terrorist groups were responsible for the majority of the deaths in civil unrest. They killed 132 persons, compared with 200 in 1995. This total included 48 police and security officers as well as 84 civilians. Terrorist attacks directed specifically against Coptic Christians continued, killing at least 22, including a group of 8 in Assiyut in February. They also attacked churches and other properties owned by Christians. In April four gunmen belonging to the extremist Islamic group Al-Gamma'a Al-Islamiyya attacked a group of Greek tourists at the entrance to the Europa Hotel near the pyramids. The terrorists killed 18 of the visitors, and wounded 13 other tourists and 2 Egyptians before escaping. Terrorists also attacked a passenger train in Minya in January and were involved in a number of bank and jewelry store robberies, mostly in upper Egypt. While the Europa Hotel attack brought the largest casualty count from a single incident in Egypt's modern history, the total number of deaths from extremist violence was sharply down in 1996 after increasing steadily during the previous 4 years.

b. *Disappearance.*—There were no reports of politically motivated disappearances.

Of the 11 individuals that local human rights groups claimed had disappeared in 1994 and the 1 cited in 1995, 8 have since been located in detention facilities, but 4 remain missing. The Government has not responded to queries from human rights monitors regarding the outstanding cases.

There were no concrete developments in the case of Mansur Kikhya, a former Libyan Foreign Minister and a prominent exiled dissident, who disappeared in Cairo in 1993.

c. *Torture and Other Cruel, Inhuman, or Degrading Treatment or Punishment.*— The Constitution prohibits the infliction of "physical or moral harm" upon persons who have been arrested or detained. However, abuse and torture of detainees by police, security personnel, and prison guards is common.

Under the Penal Code, torture of a defendant or orders to torture are felonies punishable by temporary hard labor or 3 to 10 years imprisonment. If the defendant dies, the crime is one of intentional murder punishable by a life sentence at hard labor. The crime of arrest without due cause through threat of death or physical torture is punishable by temporary hard labor. The use of cruelty against people by relying on one's position is punishable by imprisonment of no more than 1 year or a fine of no more that $65.00.

Despite these legal safeguards, there were numerous credible reports of mistreatment and torture by security forces, although fewer than in previous years. Reports of mistreatment and torture at police stations remain frequent.

In a June interview, the Minister of Interior stated that human rights was taught as a subject at the National Police Academy, and that police officers responsible for human rights infractions must be brought to trial and punished or administratively reprimanded in accordance with the law. While the Government has investigated torture complaints in criminal cases and punished some offending officers, the punishments are not in line with the seriousness of the offense. However, government officials have stated that administrative punishments can be severe enough to prevent further career advancement, and that some police officers have opted to face criminal charges instead. The Government has said that it will not disclose further details of individual cases of police abuse for fear of harming the morale of law enforcement officers involved in counterterrorist operations.

Reports of torture on the part of the SSIS dropped during the year. However, torture has reportedly taken place in police stations; SSIS offices, including its headquarters in Cairo; and at Central Security Force camps. Torture victims usually are taken to a SSIS office where they are handcuffed, blindfolded, and questioned about their associations, religious beliefs, and political views. Torture is used to extract information, coerce the victims to end their antigovernment activities, and deter others from such activities. While the law requires security authorities to keep written records of detained citizens, human rights groups report that such records often are not available, not found, or the police deny any knowledge of the detainee when they inquire about specific cases, effectively blocking the investigation of torture complaints.

Egyptian human rights groups and victims report a number of torture methods. Detainees are frequently stripped to their underwear; hung by their wrists with their feet touching the floor or forced to stand for prolonged periods; doused with hot and cold water; beaten; forced to stand outdoors in cold weather; and subjected to electric shocks. Some victims, including female detainees, report that they have been threatened with rape.

In late 1994, public prosecutors charged a policeman with torture, unlawful detention, illegal entry, and excessive use of force in the case of Fateh Al-Bab Abdel Moneim who died in police custody in 1994. At year's end, the case remained pending before the south Cairo Criminal Court.

In early 1995, the Public Prosecutor's office began an investigation into the case of Gamal El-Shazly, who allegedly had been tortured in December 1994, in a police station in Manshayit Nasser, a poor district of Cairo. The case remains under investigation.

Prison conditions remain poor. Despite the completion of five new prisons in 1995, human rights groups report that overcrowding and unhealthy conditions continue. The use of torture and other mistreatment, lack of medical care, the banning of visits, and substandard living conditions are reportedly common. Prisoners have claimed that their cells are poorly ventilated, their food is inadequate in quantity and nutritional value, and medical services are often unavailable. Health conditions in the High Security Prison ("The Scorpion") at Tora reportedly include widespread tuberculosis among the inmates. At the same prison, in June, 40 inmates were ordered to strip and were flogged, after 3 contraband items were found during an inspection of the prison. Human rights groups are investigating 13 prison deaths related to medical negligence.

Prisoners at two high security prisons, the New Valley Prison and Torah Prison, reported receiving physical and psychological abuse known as a "reception party" upon their arrival at prison. Under the supervision of a prison official and doctor, guards reportedly beat new arrivals for 30 minutes with fists and heavy plastic sticks. The inmates are then forced to crawl to their cells on their hands and knees.

The Ministry of Interior stated that the ban on prison visits by relatives and lawyers at a number of prisons, including Fayyom and the High Security Prison, has been lifted. Human rights groups report, however, that visits have been refused at several prisons. At others, restrictions have been placed on visits to political or extremist prisoners, limiting the number of visits allowed each prisoner, and the total number of visitors allowed in the prison at any one time. Human rights monitors are allowed to visit prisoners, but often face considerable bureaucratic obstacles before obtaining the proper paperwork.

d. *Arbitrary Arrest, Detention, or Exile.*—As part of the Government's antiterrorist campaign, security forces conducted mass arrests and detained hundreds of individuals without charge after specific terrorist incidents. Under the provisions of the Emergency Law, which has been in effect since 1981, the police may obtain an arrest warrant from the Ministry of Interior upon showing that an individual poses a danger to security and public order. This procedure nullifies the constitutional requirement of obtaining a warrant from a judge or prosecutor upon showing that an individual has likely committed a specific crime.

The Emergency Law allows authorities to detain an individual without charge. After 30 days, a detainee has the right to demand a court hearing to challenge the legality of the detention order, and may resubmit his motion for a hearing at 1-month intervals thereafter. There is no maximum limit to the length of detention if the judge continues to uphold the legality of the detention order, or if the detainee fails to exercise his right to a hearing.

In addition to the Emergency Law, the Penal Code also gives the State wide detention powers. Under the code, prosecutors must bring charges within 24 hours or release the suspect. However, they may detain a suspect for a maximum of 6 months, pending investigation. Arrests under the Penal Code occur openly and with warrants issued by a district prosecutor or judge. There is a system of bail. The Penal Code contains several provisions to combat extremist violence. These provisions broadly define terrorism to include the acts of "spreading panic" and "obstructing the work of authorities."

Human rights groups reported that hundreds, and according to one report, thousands, of people detained under the Emergency Law have been incarcerated for up to several years without charge. The courts have ordered the release of a number of these detainees, but prison officials have reportedly ignored the orders. Frequently, the Ministry of Interior reissues detention orders, sending detainees back to prison.

In March the Government lifted a 2-year dusk-to-dawn curfew on Mallawi and several surrounding villages in Minya province.

During the year, security forces and police arrested at least 120 members of the Muslim Brotherhood (an Islamist opposition organization) as well as 200 members of a new group, the Qutbiyoun, described as an offshoot of the Brotherhood. The charges ranged from inciting the masses against the Government, to distributing illegal leaflets and membership in an illegal organization. An undetermined number of Muslim Brothers were brought to trial during the year (see Section 1.e.).

Neither the Government nor human rights groups were able to provide firm figures for the total prison population. One human rights group cited a government figure of 12,000 registered and serving sentences, but provided a rough estimate of 32,000 for the total prison population, including those being held pending sentencing. However, in a June interview in the weekly magazine Al-Wasat, Interior Minister Hasan Al-Alfy asserted that the number of political detainees was considerably less than 10,000. The Minister also noted that 1,600 repentant convicted terrorists had been released during the previous few months.

The Government does not use forced exile.

e. *Denial of Fair Public Trial.*—The judiciary is independent. The Constitution provides for the independence and immunity of judges, and forbids interference by other authorities in the exercise of their judicial functions. The President appoints all judges upon recommendation of the Higher Judicial Council, a constitutional body composed of senior judges, and chaired by the President of the Court of Cassation. The Council regulates judicial promotions and transfers. In the last few years, the Government has added lectures on human rights and other social issues to its training courses for prosecutors and judges.

There are three levels of regular criminal courts: Primary courts; appeals courts; and the Court of Cassation, the final stage of criminal appeal. The judicial system is based on the Napoleonic tradition; hence there are no juries. Misdemeanors, that are punishable by imprisonment, are heard at the first level by one judge; at the second level by three judges. Felonies, that are punishable by imprisonment or execution, are heard in criminal court by three judges. Contestations of rulings are heard by the Court of Cassation. A lawyer will be appointed at the court's expense if the defendant does not have one. The appointment of lawyers is based on a roster chosen by the Bar Association; however, expenses are incurred by the State. Any denial of this right is cause for contestation of the ruling. However, detainees in certain high-security prisons alleged that they were denied access to counsel, or that such access was delayed until trial, thus denying counsel the time to prepare an adequate defense.

Defense lawyers generally agree that the regular judiciary respects the rights of the accused and exercises its independence. In the past, criminal court judges have dismissed cases where confessions were obtained by coercion. However, while the judiciary generally is credited with conducting fair trials, under the Emergency Law, cases involving terrorism and national security may be tried in military or state security courts, in which the accused do not receive all the constitutional protections of the judicial system. The majority of terrorist cases were again referred to Supreme State Security Emergency courts this year. High-profile cases involving Muslim Brotherhood members and a large number of terrorists went to military courts.

In the past, human rights groups and defense lawyers have claimed that the Government intimidated lawyers representing terrorist suspects by detaining and questioning them on the activities of their clients. There were no such reports during the year.

The use of military and state security tribunals under the Emergency Law has deprived hundreds of civilian defendants of their constitutional right to be tried by an ordinary judge. In 1992, with extremist violence on the rise, the Government began trying cases of persons accused of terrorism and membership in terrorist groups before military tribunals. In 1993 the Supreme Constitutional Court ruled that the President may invoke the Emergency Law to refer any crime to a military court.

From January to December, the Government referred approximately 66 civilian defendants to the military courts in five separate cases.

During the year security forces detained 13 members of the Muslim Brotherhood on suspicion of engaging in illegal political activities. The Government referred the

Muslim Brotherhood detainees to trial in a military court on charges of membership in an illegal organization, maintaining links to terrorists, and planning to overthrow the Government. In an August decision, the court acquitted five. The remainder were found guilty of the charges—seven were sentenced to from 7 months' to 3 years' imprisonment, and 1 to a suspended 1 year prison term (for health reasons).

In January 24 defendants accused of involvement in terrorist plots were brought to trial before a military court. The court acquitted six, sentenced six others to death, and sentenced the remainder to prison terms ranging from 3 to 15 years.

In November a higher military court in Assiyut handed down verdicts on 10 defendants accused of infiltrating Egypt and attempting to smuggle and sell weapons to terrorists. The court acquitted 3 defendants, sentenced 4 to life imprisonment at hard labor, and the remaining 3 to prison terms ranging from 10 to 15 years.

Two trials of 19 defendants from the Islamic Group opened in December at a supreme military court in Cairo. The first trial involved 3 defendants accused of attempting to assassinate the Military Prosecutor in 1993. In the second trial, 19 defendants, including the 3 defendants in the first trial as well as 16 others, are accused of killing a policeman, assaulting persons at two movie theaters in Helwan, and wounding 16 persons, including 8 tourists, during an attack on a tourist bus in Cairo in 1994.

In response to an appeal, the Supreme Court, as it did in 1993, found that the President may invoke the emergency law to refer any crime to a military court.

The Government defends the use of military courts as necessary in terrorism cases, maintaining that trials in the civilian courts are protracted, and that civilian judges and their families are vulnerable to terrorist threats. Some civilian judges have confirmed that they fear trying high-visibility terrorism cases because of possible reprisals. The Government claims that civilian defendants receive fair trials in the military courts and enjoy the same rights as defendants in civilian courts.

However, the military courts do not guarantee civilian defendants due process before an independent tribunal. While military judges are lawyers, they are also military officers appointed by the Minister of Defense and subject to military discipline. They are not as independent as civilian judges in applying the civilian Penal Code. There is no appellate process for verdicts by military courts; instead, verdicts are subject to review by other military judges and confirmed by the President, who in practice usually delegates the review function to a senior military officer. Defense attorneys have complained that they have not been given sufficient time to prepare defenses and that judges tend to rush cases with many defendants.

The state security courts share jurisdiction with military courts over crimes affecting national security. The President appoints judges to these courts from the civilian judiciary upon the recommendation of the Minister of Justice and, if he chooses to appoint military judges, the Minister of Defense. Sentences are subject to confirmation by the President but cannot be appealed. The President may alter or annul the decision of a state security court, including a decision to release a defendant. In 1996 state security courts tried at least 9 cases involving over 175 defendants charged with terrorist acts.

There are no reliable statistics on the number of political prisoners.

f. *Arbitrary Interference with Privacy, Family, Home, or Correspondence.*—Under the Constitution, homes, correspondence, telephone calls, and other means of communication "shall have their own sanctity, and their secrecy shall be guaranteed." Police must obtain warrants before undertaking searches and wiretaps. Courts have dismissed cases in which warrants were issued without sufficient cause. Police officials who conduct searches without proper warrants are subject to criminal penalties, although these are seldom imposed.

However, the Emergency Law has abridged the constitutional provisions regarding the right to privacy. The law empowers the Government to place wiretaps, intercept mail, and search persons or places without warrants. Security agencies frequently place political activists, suspected subversives, journalists, foreigners, and writers under surveillance, screen their correspondence (especially international mail), search them and their homes, and confiscate personal property.

Section 2. Respect for Civil Liberties, Including:

a. *Freedom of Speech and Press.*—The Constitution provides for freedom of speech and the press, however, the Government continues to place limitations on these rights. Citizens openly speak their views on a wide range of political and social issues, including vigorous criticism of the Government.

The Government owns stock in the three largest daily newspapers and the President appoints their editors in chief and chairmen of the board. However, although these papers generally follow the Government line, they frequently criticize government policies. The Government also enjoys a monopoly on the printing and distribution of newspapers including the opposition parties' papers. The Government has been known to use its monopolistic control of newsprint to limit output of opposition publications.

Opposition political parties publish their own papers but receive a subsidy from the Government and, in some cases, subsidies from foreign interests as well. Most are weeklies, with the exception of the centrist daily Al Wafd, the daily Al-Ahrar, and Al-Shaab, the semiweekly of the Islamist-oriented Socialist Labor Party. All have small circulations. Opposition newspapers frequently publish criticism of the Government, inspiring rejoinders from the government-owned press. They also give greater prominence to human rights abuses than the state-run newspapers. All party newspapers are required by law to reflect the platform of their party.

The Penal Code, Law 93 of 1995, the Press Authority Law, and the Publications Law govern press issues. The laws stipulate substantial fines for criticism of the President, members of the Government, and foreign heads of state. The Constitution restricts ownership of newspapers to public or private legal entities, corporate bodies, and political parties. However, there are numerous restrictions on legal entities that wish to estabish their own newspapers. Papers published outside Egypt can be distributed with government permission.

Libel laws provide protection against malicious rumor-mongering and unsubstantiated reporting. Jail terms may be imposed. Financial penalties increased substantially under Law 93 of 1995, although the judicial process remains long and costly, creating a bar to realistic legal recourse for those wrongly defamed. In recent years, opposition party newspapers have, within limits, published articles critical of the President and foreign heads of state without being charged or harassed. Most cases involving the press are brought by the Government, usually involving rumors or charges of corruption against members of the families of government officials. On several occasions in 1996, the Government detained and interrogated editors and journalists for publishing allegations of official misconduct and corruption.

In June 1995, an amendment to Law 93 was passed, stiffening penalties for and broadening the definition of criminal libel. Following a series of protests by the press syndicate, and a direct appeal to President Mubarak, he set aside this amendment in June. However, the Government continues to prosecute journalists under the law in effect at the time charges were filed. The process of determining whether the applicable sections of the law have been set aside is time-consuming and exprensive. Approximately 42 journalists are in various stages of prosecution under Law 93.

In July a court sentenced Magdy Ahmad Hussein, editor of the Islamic fundamentalist newspaper Al-Shaab, to a 1-year suspended sentence for libeling the son of Interior Minister Hassan Alfi. He was also ordered to pay a fine of 15,000 Egyptian pounds.

Various ministries are legally authorized to ban or confiscate books and other works of art, upon obtaining a court order. The Islamic Research Institute at Al-Azhar University has legal authority to censor, but not to confiscate, all publications dealing with the Koran and Islamic scriptural texts. In recent years the Institute has passed judgment on the suitability of nonreligious books and artistic productions.

In January 1995, an administrative court ruled that the sole authority to prohibit publication or distribution of books and other works of art resides with the Ministry of Culture. This decision voided a 1994 advisory opinion by a judiciary council that had expanded Al-Azhar's censorship authority to include visual and audio artistic works. The same year, President Mubarak stated that the Government would not allow confiscation of books from the market without a court order, a position supported by the then-Grand Mufti, who is now the Grand Sheik of Al-Azhar.

There were no court ordered confiscations during the year. However, two books were seized by police in June without a court order, after officials at Al-Azhar ruled that they should be banned for violating religious laws and norms. In August the police also seized five books on Shi'a Islam from Cairo bookstores, without a court order.

The Ministry of Interior regularly confiscates leaflets and other works by Muslim fundamentalists. It also has the authority to stop specific issues of foreign published newspapers from entering the country on the grounds of protecting public order. The Ministry of Defense may ban works about sensitive security issues.

The Council of Ministers may order the banning of works that it deems offensive to public morals, detrimental to religion, or likely to cause a breach of the peace.

Plays and films must pass Ministry of Culture censorship tests as scripts and as final productions. Many plays and films, highly critical of the Government and its policies, are not censored. The Ministry of Culture also censors foreign films for viewing in theaters, but it is more lenient when the same films are released in video cassette format. Government censors ensure that foreign films made in Egypt portray the country in a favorable light. Censors review scripts before filming, are present during filming, and have the right to review the film before it is sent out of Egypt.

Two films are currently in the courts. "The Emigrant" was banned this year after a long court case, but the decision is under appeal. A group of Islamic lawyers had brought the case in 1994, arguing that it violated Islamic tenets in its portrayal of the life of the Prophet Joseph. Despite the court case, the film has represented Egypt in several international festivals. The second case is against the film "Birds of Darkness," the plaintiffs charging that it is insulting to lawyers. The case is still pending.

The Ministry of Information owns and operates all domestic television productions. In the past, it has censored serious artistic works that criticized the Government or dealt with social problems from a nongovernmental perspective. The Ministry also censored nine articles of the English language weekly, The Middle East Times, during the year. Two of the articles had contained allegations of human rights violations. According to the editor, in October an issue of the newspaper al-Dustuur was confiscated because of previously published criticism of the Israeli Government.

Moderate Muslims and secularist writers continue to find themselves under attack by Islamic extremists.

In August the Court of Cassation, Egypt's highest court of appeal, supported a 1995 lower court ruling against Cairo University professor Nasr Abu Zeid. In 1993 Islamic fundamentalist lawyers had asked the courts to rule that Abu Zeid was an apostate because of his controversial interpretation of Koranic teachings. The petitioners argued that as an apostate, Abu Zeid should not be allowed to remain married to a Muslim woman in a Muslim country. After a lower court threw out this suit, an appellate court in June 1995 gave the plaintiffs standing to pursue their suit. Jurists and secular intellectuals criticized the court's decision as an infringement on the principle of privacy and freedom of expression.

The Government had joined Abu Zeid in his appeal, and the People's Assembly passed two laws during the year designed to derail other such lawsuits. The Hisba Law, ratified by the Assembly in late January, limits cases by third parties "on behalf of society." The Assembly also approved in May amendments to an article of the Law for Civil and Commercial Procedures requiring the direct personal involvement of the plaintiff prior to the filing of suits.

In its decision, the Court of Cassation, which rules on legal technicalities rather than the case itself, noted that the Hisba Law and Law 81 were issued after final arguments were made by the plaintiffs and the defense, and that the case and the lower court ruling were legally valid. Abu Zeid's defense team has filed for a reconsideration by the Court of Cassation, citing major mistakes in the decision against Abu Zeid, including the Court's ignoring of the Hisba Law and Law 81. In September a lower court judge stayed the execution of the decision against Abu Zeid pending the outcome of the reconsideration by the Court of Cassation. Meanwhile, Abu Zeid and his wife are residing together abroad. In December a Giza court of appeal upheld their stay.

In another Hisba case, a Cairo criminal court ruled against and fined two lawyers who brought a case against the actress Youssra and a magazine for printing an allegedly indecent picture of her on the cover.

The Government does not directly restrict academic freedom at universities. However, some university professors claim that the Government tightened its control over universities in 1994 when a law was passed authorizing university presidents to appoint the deans of the various faculties. Under the previous law, faculty deans were elected by their peers. The Government has justified the measure as a means to combat Islamist influence on campus.

b. *Freedom of Peaceful Assembly and Association.*—The Government continues to maintain substantial restrictions on freedom of assembly. Under a 1923 law, citizens must obtain approval from the Ministry of Interior before holding public meetings, rallies, and protest marches. Permits are generally granted for rallies held indoors or on university campuses.

The Government continues to maintain substantial restrictions on freedom of association. Under Law 32 of 1964, the Ministry of Social Affairs has extensive authority over associations and private foundations, including the right to license and dissolve them, confiscate their properties, appoint members to their boards, and intercede in other administrative matters. Licenses may be revoked if such organizations engage in political or religious activities. The law authorizes the Ministry to "merge two or more associations to achieve a similar function," a provision that may be used to merge an undesirable organization out of existence.

Since 1985 the Government has refused under Law 32 to license the Egyptian Organization for Human Rights (EOHR) and the Arab Organization for Human Rights (AOHR) on grounds that they are political organizations. Nevertheless, both continue to operate openly (see Section 4). Amnesty International, which had a petition pending for legal status for its local office, closed its local office this year for internal reasons.

Under 1993 legislation on professional syndicates, an association must elect its governing board by at least 50 percent of its general membership. Failing a quorum, a second election must be held in which at least 33 percent of the membership votes for the board. If such a quorum is impossible, the judiciary may appoint a caretaker board until new elections can be set. The law was adopted to prevent well-organized minorities, specifically Islamists, from capturing or retaining the leadership of professional syndicates. Members of these syndicates have reported that Islamists have used such irregular electoral techniques as physically blocking polling places, and limiting or changing the location of polling sites.

c. *Freedom of Religion.*—The Constitution provides for freedom of belief and the practice of religious rites. However, the Government places clear restrictions on this right. Most Egyptians are Muslim, but at least 10 per cent of the population, 5.7 million people, belong to the Coptic Orthodox Church, the largest Christian minority in the Middle East. There are other small Christian denominations, as well as a Jewish community numbering fewer than 50 individuals.

For the most part, members of the non-Muslim minority worship without harassment and maintain links with coreligionists abroad. Under the Constitution, however, Islam is the official state religion and primary source of legislation. Accordingly, religious practices that conflict with Islamic law are prohibited. While technically proselytizing is not a crime, Christians have been arrested on charges of ridiculing or insulting heavenly religions and/or inciting secular strife. At least one Christian was detained in 1996 on charges of ridiculing or insulting heavenly religions and/or inciting secular strife.

There are no restrictions on non-Muslims converting to Islam. However, Muslims face legal problems if they convert to another faith. Authorities have charged a few converts to Christianity under provisions of the Penal Code that prohibit the use of religion to "ignite strife, degrade any of the heavenly religions or harm national unity or social peace." In other cases, authorities have charged such persons with violating laws against falsifying documents, since Muslim converts to Christianity sometimes attempt to change their names and religious affiliation on their identification cards and other official documentation to reflect their conversion. These laws were upheld in a 1980 court decision. There were no confirmed reports of individuals detained during the year under these laws.

There were credible reports that state security officers in Cairo detained, interrogated, and, in at least two cases, physically abused several Christians and converts to Christianity, in an effort to obtain information about the identities and activities of other converts.

An 1856 Ottoman Decree still in force requires non-Muslims to obtain what is now a presidential decree to build or repair a place of worship. Coptic Christians maintain that they frequently have been unable to obtain such authorization, that such permits have been delayed, or that they have been blocked by the security forces from using the authorizations that have been issued. Other restrictions of the 1856 Decree were codified in 1934 into a list of 10 provisions that the police and other authorities should investigate prior to issuance of a presidential decree. A local human rights organization brought a legal case during the year requesting the abolition of the Ottoman Decree against Copts, including abolition of the 10 provisions. The case remains before the court.

As a result of these restrictions, some communities use private buildings and apartments for religious services. Between 1992 and 1995, the situation improved somewhat as the Government has increased the number of building permits issued to Christian communities to an average of more than 20 per year, compared to the average of 5 permits issued annually in the 1980's. During the year, the Government issued 10 permits for the construction of new churches and 8 for repairs and reconstruction. While Christian and Muslim reformers urge the abolition of the Ottoman Decree, Islamists who oppose the spread of Christianity in Egypt defend the building restrictions.

In 1994 the Alexandria government closed two buildings near the city that had been used by Coptic Evangelical Christians since 1990 for church activities. The Government claims that the church lacked a building permit. Lawyers for the church point out that the closures violated previous court rulings upholding the right to conduct religious services in private buildings without prior government approval. They also pointed out that the closed buildings were located in an area where unlicensed buildings are common. At year's end, the case remained with an administrative court in Alexandria.

The Government continued its efforts to extend legal controls to all mosques, which by law must be licensed. The Government appoints and pays the salaries of the imams officiating in mosques, and proposes themes for and monitors sermons. Of the country's approximately 70,000 mosques, slightly less than half remain unlicensed and operate outside the control of government authorities. In an effort to combat Islamic extremists, the Government announced that it intended to bring the remaining 30,000 unauthorized mosques under its control during the next 5 years.

d. *Freedom of Movement Within the Country, Foreign Travel, Emigration, and Repatriation.*—Citizens and foreigners are free to travel within Egypt except in certain military areas. The Government during the year removed the requirement for most foreigners to register within 7 days of their arrival in Egypt. Males who have not completed compulsory military service may not travel abroad or emigrate, although this restriction can be deferred or bypassed. Unmarried women must have permission from their fathers to obtain passports and travel; married women of any age require the same permission from their husbands. Citizens who leave the country have the right to return.

In recent years, the Government has denied permission to a small number of Christian converts from Islam to travel abroad. In October 1994, security officials arrested Ibrahim Sharaf Al Din, an Egyptian convert, at Cairo Airport as he attempted to enter Egypt from Kenya, where he had been granted asylum and resided with his family since the early 1980's. Sharaf Al Din was imprisoned for 8 months while prosecutors investigated the circumstances of his conversion. He was released without charge in June 1995. However, according to a local human rights group, in order to leave Egypt he is required to file a lawsuit in order to obtain a court order that indicates that he is not banned from leaving the country.

The Constitution forbids the deportation of citizens and aliens granted political asylum. Egypt grants first asylum for humanitarian reasons or in the event of internal turmoil in neighboring countries. Asylum seekers generally are screened by representatives of the United Nations High Commisioner for Refugees (UNHCR), whose recommendations regarding settlement are forwarded to the Ministries of Interior and Foreign Affairs for final determination. Refugees accepted by the Government are permitted to live and work, but cannot acquire Egyptian citizenship, with rare exceptions. During the year, the Government accepted over 6,000 refugees, including 3,000 Somalis and 1,400 Sudanese, for temporary resettlement.

Section 3. Respect for Political Rights: The Right of Citizens to Change Their Government

The ruling National Democratic Party (NDP) dominates the 454-seat People's Assembly, the Shura Council, local governments, the mass media, labor, the large public sector, and the licensing of new political parties, newspapers, and private organizations to such an extent that, as a practical matter, citizens do not have a meaningful ability to change their government.

In 1993 President Hosni Mubarak was elected unopposed to a third 6-year term by the People's Assembly. In October of that year, his reelection was approved by 96 percent of the voters in a national referendum. Under the Constitution, the electorate is not presented with a choice among competing presidential candidates. Two opposition parties urged the public to boycott the referendum, and two other parties urged the public to vote against the President. The other opposition parties endorsed the President's candidacy.

Over 100 losing candidates in the fall 1995 legislative elections filed complaints in the administrative courts, alleging ballot-rigging and other irregularities. The courts agreed with most of these claims, but while the courts have the authority to rule on whether irregularities took place, they may not remove an elected Member of the Assembly, a right that the Assembly claims solely for itself, under the concept of parliamentary sovereignty. To date the Assembly has not called for any new by-elections to cover these cases.

The Assembly debates government proposals, and members exercise their authority to call cabinet ministers to explain policy. The executive initiates almost all legislation. Nevertheless, the Assembly maintains the authority to challenge or restrain the executive in the areas of economic and social policy, but it may not modify the budget except with the Government's approval. The Assembly exercises limited influence in the areas of security and foreign policy, and there is little oversight of the Interior Ministry's use of Emergency Law powers. Many executive branch initiatives and policies are carried out by regulation through ministerial decree without legislative oversight. The military budget is prepared by the executive and not debated publicly. Roll-call votes in the Assembly are rare. Votes are generally reported in aggregate terms of yeas and nays, and thus constituents have no independent method of checking a member's voting record.

There are 15 recognized opposition parties. The law empowers the Government to bring felony charges against those who form a party without a license. New parties must be approved by the Parties Committee, a semi-official body including a substantial majority of members from the ruling NDP and some members from among the independents and opposition parties. Decisions of the Parties Committee may be appealed to the civil courts. The Parties Committee rejected the applications of at least four new parties this year; those applications and several from last year are before the courts for review.

According to the law, which prohibits political parties based on religion, the Muslim Brotherhood is an illegal political organization. Muslim Brothers are publicly known and openly speak their views, but have come under increasing pressure from the Government (see Sections 1.d. and 1.e.). Some have served in the Assembly as independents or as members of other recognized parties.

Women and minorities are underrepresented in government and politics. The Constitution reserves 10 Assembly seats for presidential appointees, which the President traditionally has used to assure representation for women and Coptic Christians. Five women and no Copts were elected in 1995; of the 10 presidential appointments, 6 were Copts and 4 were women. The ruling NDP nominated no Coptic candidates in the 1995 parliamentary election. Three women and two Coptic Christians are in the Cabinet.

Section 4. Governmental Attitude Regarding International and Nongovernmental Investigation of Alleged Violations of Human Rights

The Government refuses to license local human rights groups as private entities under Law 32 of 1964 (see section 2.b.). Since 1986 the Government has refused to license the Egyptian Organization for Human Rights (EOHR) on grounds that it is a political organization and duplicates the activities of an existing, although moribund, human rights group (see Section 2.b.). The EOHR has appealed the denial in the courts, and continues to conduct activities openly, pending a final judicial determination of its status.

The Arab Organization for Human Rights, EOHR's parent organization, has a long-standing request for registration as a foreign organization with the Ministry of Foreign Affairs. The issue remains pending.

A request by Amnesty International for legal status for its local chapter had been pending with the Ministry of Foreign Affairs for 6 years, until the office was closed for internal reasons. In the meantime it was allowed to conduct limited activities.

Despite their nonrecognition, the EOHR and other groups sometimes enjoy the cooperation of government officials. The Government allows EOHR field workers to visit prisons, to call on some government officials, and to receive funding from foreign human rights organizations. Representatives from EOHR met this year with Speaker of the Assembly Fathy Sorour. The Ministry of Foreign Affairs facilitated entry into the country for Africans in a training seminar held by EOHR, and the Supreme Constitutional Court cosponsored a seminar on human rights.

There were no reports during the year that the Government banned meetings of human rights groups, although the Government has on occasion made the holding of such meetings difficult.

Some human rights organizations have found requests for conference space turned down for "security reasons" or reservations later canceled for "maintenance reasons."

Other human rights organizations, such as the Center for Human Rights Legal Aid, are registered with the Government as corporations under commercial or civil law, thus avoiding the obstacles posed by law (see Section 2.b.) In 1995 the Ministry of Justice issued a nonbinding advisory ruling stating that such organizations properly should be considered nongovernmental organizations as defined by Law 32 and registered accordingly, or face punitive action. However, the Government did not close down any group during the year.

Section 5. Discrimination Based on Race, Sex, Religion, Disability, Language, or Social Status

The Constitution provides for equality of the sexes and equal treatment of non-Muslims, but aspects of the law and many traditional practices discriminate against women and Christians.

Women.—Family violence against women occurs and is reflected in press accounts of specific incidents. According to recent statistics, one out of every three women who have ever been married has been beaten at least once during marriage. Among those who have been beaten, less than half have ever sought help. In general neighbors and extended family members intervene to limit incidents of domestic violence. Abuse within the family is rarely discussed publicly, owing to the value attached to privacy in this traditional society. Several nongovernmental organizations have begun offering counseling, legal aid, and other services to women who are victims of domestic violence. "Honor killings" are not prevalent, but when they do occur, the punishment is generally lighter that in other cases of murder.

The law provides for equality of the sexes, but aspects of the law and many traditional practices discriminate against women. By law unmarried women under 21 must have permission from their fathers to obtain passports and travel; married women of any age require the same permission from their husbands (see Section 2.d.). Only males can confer citizenship. In rare cases, this means that children born to Egyptian mothers and stateless fathers are themselves stateless.

Laws affecting marriage and personal status generally correspond to an individual's religion, which is Islam for most Egyptians. A 1979 liberalization of the Family Status Law strengthening a Muslim woman's rights to divorce and child custody was repealed in 1985 after it was found unconstitutional for conflicting with Islamic law. A new marriage contract for Muslim women was proposed in 1995, to replace the current one drafted in 1931. It stipulates premarital negotiations on a wide variety of issues, including the woman's right to work, study and travel abroad, and divorce settlements. Government approval is still pending.

Under Islamic law, non-Muslim males must convert to Islam to marry Muslim women, but non-Muslim women need not convert to marry Muslim men. Muslim female heirs receive half the amount of a male heir's inheritance, while Christian widows of Muslims have no inheritance rights. A sole female heir receives half her parents' estate; the balance goes to designated male relatives. A sole male heir inherits all his parents' property. Male Muslim heirs face strong social pressure to provide for all family members who need assistance. However, this does not always occur.

Women have employment opportunities in government, medicine, law, academia, the arts, and, to a lesser degree, in business. According to government figures, women constitute 17 percent of private business owners, and occupy 25 percent of the managerial positions in the four major national banks. There are 123 women officers in the Egyptian diplomatic service, including 6 ambassadors and 7 consuls general. There are 3 women state counselors in the administrative court system. However, there are no women state prosecutors or judges in the civil court system. Although there is no legal basis to prohibit female judges, a woman under consideration for promotion to magistrate was denied the promotion on the basis of gender in 1993 and is suing the Government. Social pressure against women pursuing a career is strong, and some womens' advocates say that a resurgent Islamic fundamentalist trend limits further gains. Women's rights advocates also point to other discriminatory traditional or cultural attitudes and practices such as female genital mutilation (FGM) and the traditional male relative's role in enforcing chastity and appropriate sexual conduct.

There are a growing number of active women's rights groups working in diverse areas including reforming the Personal Status Code, educating women on their legal rights, combating FGM, and rewriting the marriage contract.

Children.—The Government remains committed to the protection of children's welfare within the limits of its budgetary resources. Many of the resources for children's welfare are provided by international donors, especially in the field of child immunization. Child labor is widespread, despite the Government's commitment to eradicate it (see Section 6.d.).

The Government provides public education, which is compulsory until the age of 15. In education the Government treats boys and girls equally at all levels of education, although only 74 percent of girls attend school. Literacy rates reflect this disparity: Female literacy is 34 percent, while male literacy is 63 percent.

The Government enacted a new Child Law in March. The law provides for more privileges, protection, and care for children in general. Six of the laws's 144 articles set advantageous rules for working children (see Section 6.d.). Other provisions include: Employers to set up or contract with a child care center if they employ more than 100 women; the right of rehabilitation for disabled children; defendants between the ages of 16 and 18 may not be sentenced to capital punishment, hard labor for life, or temporary hard labor; and defendants under the age of 15 may not be placed in preventive custody although the prosecution may order that they be lodged in an "observation house" and be summoned upon request.

In July following the death by hemorrhage of an 11-year-old girl, the Minister of Health and Population issued a decree calling for an end to the practice of FGM and prohibiting its performance by nonmedical and medical practioners. FGM is widely condemned by international health experts as damaging to both physical and psychological health. Statistics on the prevalence of FGM vary, but Government and private sources agree it is common. A recent study places the percentage of Egyptian women who have undergone FGM at 97 percent. The act is generally performed on girls between the ages of 7 and 10, probably with equal prevalence among Muslims and Coptic Christians. The Government broadcasts television programs condemning the practice, and a number of NGO's work actively to educate the public of the health hazards attached to the practice. A discussion of FGM and its dangers is being added to the curriculum at medical schools and in training courses given to traditional birth attendants. The new Sheik of Al-Azhar, the senior Muslim leader in the country, has stated that FGM is not required by Islamic tenets. However, despite strong government efforts to eradicate it, it is unlikely that the practice will disappear quickly due to traditional and family pressures.

People With Disabilities.—There are approximately 5.7 million disabled persons, of whom 1.5 million are severely disabled. The Government makes serious efforts to address their rights. It works closely with United Nations agencies and other international aid donors to design job-training programs for the disabled. The Government also seeks to increase the public's awareness of the capabilities of the disabled by using television programming, the print media, and educational material in public schools.

By law, all businesses must designate 5 percent of their jobs for the disabled, who are exempt from normal literacy requirements. Although there is no legislation mandating access to public accommodations and transportation, the disabled may ride government-owned mass transit buses without charge, are given priority in obtaining telephones, and receive reductions on customs duties for private vehicles.

Religious Minorities.—The Constitution provides that all citizens are equal before the law and prohibits discrimination based on religion. For the most part these constitutional protections are upheld by the Government. However, discrimination against Christians still exist.

The approximately 5.7 million Coptic Christians are the objects of occasional violent assaults by Muslim extremists. During the year, extremists were responsible for killing at least 22 Copts, most in the Minya and Assiuyut governorates in upper Egypt, where about 30 to 40 percent of the inhabitants are Christian. Acts of violence also were reported against churches and Copt-owned businesses; some carried out by extremists, but others committed by ordinary citizens. Rumors of church repairs or building without permits occasionally resulted in anti-Christian rioting by citizens. In one incident in the delta village of Kafr Demyan, local newspapers reported that the rioters were incited by Muslim preachers who utilized mosque loudspeakers to call for retaliation against the perceived violations.

Some Christians have complained that the Government is lax in protecting Coptic lives and property. Security forces arrest extremists who perpetrate violence against Copts, but some members of the Coptic community do not believe that the Government is vigorous in its efforts to prevent attacks and does little to correct nonviolent forms of discrimination, including its own.

There were reports of forced conversions of Coptic children to Islam, but even human rights groups find it extremely difficult to determine the actual degree of compulsion used, as most cases involve a Coptic girl converting to Islam to marry a Muslim boy. According to the Government, the girl in such cases must meet with her family, with her priest, and with the head of her church before she is allowed to convert. However, there are credible reports of government harassment of Christian families attempting to regain custody of their daughters, and of the failure of the authorities to uphold the law that states that a marriage of a girl under 16 is prohibited and between the ages of 16 and 21 is illegal without the approval and presence of her guardian.

Government discriminatory practices include: Suspected statistical underrepresentation of the size of the Christian population; anti-Christian discrimination in education; failure to admit Christians into schools of Arabic studies to become Arabic teachers since the curriculum involves study of the Koran; the production of some Islamic television programs with anti-Christian themes; job discrimination in the public sector—the police, the armed forces, and other government agencies; reported discrimination against Christians in staff appointments at universities; and their underrepresentation in government. There are no Coptic governors and no Copts in the upper ranks of the military, police, or diplomatic service.

Section 6. Worker Rights

a. *The Right of Association.*—Workers may join trade unions but are not required to do so. A union local, or workers' committee, may be formed if 50 employees express a desire to organize. Most union members, about 25 per cent of the labor force, are employed by state-owned enterprises. The law stipulates that "high administrative" officials in government and the public sector may not join unions.

There are 23 industrial unions, all required to belong to the Egyptian Trade Union Federation (ETUF), the sole legally recognized labor federation. The International Labor Organization's Committee of Experts repeatedly has emphasized that a law requiring all trade unions to belong to a single federation infringes on the freedom of association. The Government has shown no sign that it intends to accept the establishment of more than one federation. The ETUF leadership asserts that it actively promotes worker interests and that there is no need for another federation. ETUF officials have close relations with the NDP, and some are members of the People's Assembly or the Shura Council. They speak vigorously on behalf of worker concerns, but public confrontations between ETUF and the Government are rare. Disputes are more often resolved by consensus behind closed doors.

The labor laws do not adequately provide statutory authorization for the rights to strike and to engage in collective bargaining. Even though the right to strike is not guaranteed, strikes occur. The Government considers strikes a form of public disturbance and hence illegal.

Only a few strikes took place in either the public or private sector during the year, mainly over wage and dismissal questions. No violence was reported in any of the strikes.

Some unions within ETUF are affiliated with international trade union organizations. Others are in the process of becoming affiliated.

b. *The Right to Organize and Bargain Collectively.*—Under the law, unions may negotiate work contracts with public sector enterprises if the latter agree to such negotiations, but unions otherwise lack collective bargaining power in the state sector. Under current circumstances, collective bargaining does not exist in any meaningful sense because the Government sets wages, benefits, and job classifications by law. Larger firms in the private sector generally adhere to such government-mandated standards.

Labor law and practice are the same in the export processing zones (EPZ's) as in the rest of the country.

c. *Prohibition of Forced or Compulsory Labor.*—The criminal code authorizes sentences of hard labor for some crimes.

d. *Minimum Age for Employment of Children.*—Under the new Child Law (see Section 5), the minimum age for employment is 14 in non-agricultural work. Provincial governors, with the approval of the Minister of Agriculture, can authorize seasonal work for children between the ages of 12 to 14 years, provided that duties are not hazardous and do not interfere with schooling. Preemployment training for children under the age of 12 is prohibited. It is prohibited for children to work for more than 6 hours a day, including 1 or more breaks totaling at least 1 hour. Children are not to work overtime, during their weekly day off, between 8 pm and 7 am, or more than 4 hours continuously. Education is compulsory until the age of 15.

Ministry of Health figures for 1995 indicate that 2 million children between the ages of 6 and 15 are employed. A 1989 study estimated that perhaps 720,000 children work on farms. However, children also work as apprentices in repair and craft shops, in heavier industries such as brickmaking and textiles, and as workers in leather and carpet-making factories. While local trade unions report that the Ministry of Labor adequately enforces the labor laws in state-owned enterprises, enforcement in the private sector, especially in family-owned enterprises, is lax. Many of these children are abused and overworked by their employers and it is unlikely that the restrictions in the new Child Law will improve their condition without much stricter enforcement on the part of the Government.

e. *Acceptable Conditions of Work.*—For government and public sector employees, the minimum wage is approximately $25 (84 Egyptian pounds) a month for a 6-day, 42-hour workweek. Base pay is supplemented by a complex system of fringe benefits and bonuses that may double or triple a workers take-home pay. It is doubtful that the average family could survive on a worker's base pay at the minimum wage rate. The minimum wage is also legally binding on the private sector, and larger private companies generally observe it and pay bonuses as well. Smaller firms do not always pay the minimum wage or bonuses.

The Ministry of Labor sets worker health and safety standards, which also apply in the export processing zones, but enforcement and inspection are uneven. The law prohibits employers from maintaining hazardous working conditions, and provides legal recourse for employees who are asked to work in such conditions if they refuse.

IRAN*

The Islamic Republic of Iran was established in 1979 after a populist revolution toppled the monarchy. The Government is dominated by Shi'a Muslim clergy. Ayatollah Ali Khamenei is the Leader of the Islamic Revolution and functions as the Chief of State. He is also the Commander-in-Chief of the armed forces. President Ali Akbar Hashemi-Rafsanjani, first elected in a popular vote in 1989 and reelected in 1993, is constitutionally barred from a third term. The Constitution provides for a 270-seat unicameral Islamic Consultative Assembly, or Majles. The Government seeks to ensure that public policy is consistent with its view of political and socioreligious values, but some serious differences exist within the leadership. The authoritarian government maintains its power through widespread repression and intimidation. The judiciary is subject to government and religious influence.

Several agencies share responsibility for internal security, including the Ministry of Intelligence and Security, the Ministry of Interior, and the Revolutionary Guards, a military force established after the revolution and coequal with the regular military. Paramilitary volunteer forces known as Hezbollahis or Basijis conduct vigilante actions. Both regular and paramilitary security forces commit numerous and serious human rights abuses.

Iran has a mixed economy. The Government owns the petroleum and utilities industries and the banks. Oil exports are the primary source of foreign exchange. The economy has not yet recovered from the disruptions of the 1979 revolution and the destruction from the Iran-Iraq war. Iran's isolation from international financial markets has decreased slightly, but remains a problem. Economic performance is adversely affected by corruption and government mismanagement. Unemployment in 1996 was estimated at 30 percent, and inflation was about 50 percent.

The Government's human rights record remains poor; there was no evidence of significant human rights improvement during the year. Systematic abuses include extrajudicial killings and summary executions; disappearances; widespread use of torture and other degrading treatment; harsh prison conditions; arbitrary arrest and detention; lack of fair trials; infringement on citizens' privacy rights; and restriction of the freedoms of speech, press, assembly, association, religion, and movement. The Government represses political dissidents and the ruling clerics effectively control the electoral process, thereby denying citizens the right to change their government. Women face legal and social discrimination, and the Government discriminates against minorities and restricts important worker rights. Although a lively debate on political, economic, and social issues occurred during the parliamentary election campaign this year, freedom of expression remained firmly under government control and became more severely restricted in the wake of the parliamentary elections. The Government closed several newspapers, disqualified candidates, barred speakers, and intimidated opposition gatherings by encouraging Hezbollahi attacks.

However, the Government did allow the first visit in 5 years of the United Nations Human Rights Commission (UNHRC) Special Rapporteur on Human Rights in Iran. Canadian Maurice Copithorne, the newly appointed Special Rapporteur, visited Iran from February 10 to 16. The Special Rapporteur heard credible reports of abuses including: Inhuman or degrading treatment and punishment; arbitrary arrests, imprisonments, and executions; unfair judicial practices; and disregard for freedom of expression and religion. Human Rights Watch (HRW) and the UNHRC Special Rapporteur reported that the Government was generally cooperative during their visits, However, the Government continues to deny the universality of human rights and attempts to discredit critics. For example, in one Iranian press report, the chief of Evin prison described human rights inspectors as "sick" people who filed misleading and untruthful reports. The U.N. Special Rapporteur for Religious Freedom and the U.N. Special Rapporteur for the Freedom of Expression also traveled to Iran in 1996. In November the UNHRC continued the mandate of its Special Rapporteur.

RESPECT FOR HUMAN RIGHTS

Section 1. Respect for the Integrity of the Person, Including Freedom From:

a. *Political and Other Extrajudicial Killing.*—Most executions in political trials amount to summary executions because basic procedural safeguards are lacking. In his 1995 report, the U.N. Special Rapporteur on Extrajudicial, Summary, or Arbitrary Executions noted "the persistent allegations of violations of the right to life

---

*The United States does not have an embassy in Iran. This report draws heavily on non-U.S. Government sources.

in the Islamic Republic of Iran." Although the domestic press stopped reporting most executions as of 1992, executions appear to continue in substantial numbers. Amnesty International (AI) reported that at least 110 persons were executed in 1996, a substantial increase over the previous year's total of 50 executions. Inhuman punishments are used in some cases, including two cases of stoning (see Section 1.c.). Those executed included Mehrdad Kalany, who was executed on June 22 on charges that included "meeting and talking" with Reynaldo Galindo Pohl, the former U.N. Special Representative, and the delegation that accompanied him. Also on June 22, Ahmed Bakhtiari, a member of the Iranian People's Fedaian Organization (Minority), was executed on charges of participation in a terrorist group and terrorist operations, as well as other criminal charges. Rahman Radjabi Hamvand, a member of the Kurdish Democratic Party of Iran, was executed on July 28. The charges against him stemmed from a complaint by a private individual that was later withdrawn. AI reported that Hedayatollah Zendehdel and Abolghasem Majd-Abkahi were believed to have been hanged at the end of the year, after 7 years' detention without trial and conviction on mainly political charges.

Exiles and human rights monitors report that many of those executed for alleged criminal offenses, primarily narcotics charges, were actually political dissidents. In addition a November 1995 law criminalized dissent and applied the death penalty to offenses such as "attempts against the security of the State, outrage against high-ranking Iranian officials, and insults against the memory of Imam Khomeini, and against the Leader of the Islamic Republic."

The Government continued its repression of the Sunni minority, both inside and outside Iran. On January 28, a 50-year-old Sunni cleric, Molawi Ahamed Sayyad, imprisoned by the Government from 1990–95, disappeared at Bandar Abbas airport. His body was found in a suburb of the city on February 2. Allegedly, six members of the Revolutionary Guards arrested him at the airport; he is believed to have died in their custody. In early March, 46-year-old Molavi Abdul Malek, a Sunni cleric and Iranian Balouch leader, was reportedly killed by Iranian intelligence operatives in Karachi. Also reported killed in a related incident were Iranian Sunni Molavi Abdulmalek, the son of a prominent Iranian Sunni cleric, and Jamshid Zahi, another Iranian Sunni leader.

In December clashes erupted in Bakhtaran at a funeral after mourners accused the Government of killing Mohammad Rabil, a Sunni prayer leader. Officials said that Rabil died of a heart attack. It is unclear whether any persons were killed in the rioting.

The Government also continued to kill political opponents abroad. Opposition leaders Zahrah Rajabi and Abdul Ali Moradi were killed in Istanbul by agents of the Government on February 20. In Iraq eight members of the Kurdish Democratic Party of Iran were killed by elements of the Revolutionary Guards. The victims were: Ghafour Mehdizadeh; Ali Amini; and Saddig Abdulahi, who were killed on December 27, 1995 in Koya; Usman Ruyan and Abubaker Rahimi, who were killed on December 30, 1995 in Arbil; Rahman Schabannajad and Ali Abdulah, who were killed on January 2 in Suleimanya; and Cheder Mahmudi, who was killed in November 1995 in Suleimanya. In May a former official from the Shah's regime, Reza Masluman, was killed in Paris. The murder is believed to have been ordered by the Government.

Investigations of state-sponsored terrorism abroad continued in 1996. For example the trial of Kazem Darabi, an Iranian charged with murdering four Iranian Kurdish dissidents in Berlin in 1992 allegedly under instructions from the Iranian Government, continued in Germany. In November the German prosecutor stated that Iranian Head of State Ayatollah Khameini and President Rafsanjani were responsible for the murders. Iran responded by threatening the German embassy in Tehran, the German judiciary, and political and economic ties with Germany. In France a French prosecutor accused Iranian chief of intelligence Ali Fallahian of ordering a killing, and in Germany a warrant was issued for Fallahian's arrest.

The Government took no action to repudiate the religious ruling (fatwa), or its related bounty, calling for the death of Salman Rushdie and anyone associated with publishing his book, "The Satanic Verses" (see Section 2.a.).

b. *Disappearance.*—No reliable information is available on the number of disappearances. In the period immediately following arrest, many detainees are held incommunicado.

In early November, Faraj Sarkuhi, a magazine editor who had been critical of the Government, disappeared while traveling to Germany where his wife and children reside. His wife accused the Government of abducting him in Tehran. Sarkuhi reappeared in late December and held a press conference at the Tehran airport where he said that he had been in Germany but had not contacted his wife, with whom he was having problems. The German Government stated that he had not entered

Germany, and the press speculated that the Government had forced Sarkuhi to give a false account of his whereabouts.

c. *Torture and Other Cruel, Inhuman, or Degrading Treatment or Punishment.*—Credible reports indicate that security forces continue to torture detainees and prisoners. Common methods include suspension for long periods in contorted positions, burning with cigarettes, and, most frequently, severe and repeated beatings with cables or other instruments on the back and on the soles of the feet. A new law entered into force on July 10 that reinforces Islamic punishments such as flogging, stoning, amputations, and public executions. Two persons were stoned to death, while two others were executed after receiving lashes.

Prison conditions are harsh. Some prisoners are held in solitary confinement or denied adequate rations or medical care in order to force confessions. Female prisoners have reportedly been raped or otherwise tortured while in detention. In the past, prison guards have intimidated the family members of detainees and have sometimes tortured detainees in their presence. The UNHRC Special Rapporteur met privately with detainee Abbas Amir Entezam, a former deputy minister in the government of Prime Minister Mehdi Bazargan. Amir Entezam reported that the conditions in Evin prison improved after 1989, but that political prisoners were still housed with violent criminals and denied regular family visits. Some prisoners, who met with former U.N. Special Representative Galindo Pohl during his last visit in 1991, complained of reprisals. Amir Entezam claimed that he was beaten so extensively that he lost the hearing in his left ear.

The Government does not permit unrestricted to imprisoned dissidents by human rights monitors. The U.N. Special Rapporteur was not able to see all the dissidents he asked to see.

In September 1994, the International Committee of the Red Cross (ICRC) issued a report on "unresolved humanitarian issues" from the Iran-Iraq war. The ICRC noted that the Government failed to identify combatants killed in action and failed to exchange information on those killed or missing. The report criticized the Government for obstructing ICRC efforts to register and repatriate prisoners of war. Throughout 1996 the Governments of Iran and Iraq made little progress in resolving the issue of those missing in action.

d. *Arbitrary Arrest, Detention, or Exile.*—Although the Constitution prohibits arbitrary arrest and detention, there is reportedly no legal time limit on incommunicado detention, nor any judicial means to determine the legality of detention. Suspects may be held for questioning in jails or in local Revolutionary Guard offices.

The security forces often do not inform family members of a prisoner's welfare and location. Even if these circumstances are known, the prisoner still may be denied visits by family and legal counsel. In addition, families of executed prisoners do not always receive notification of the prisoner's death. Those that do receive such information may be forced to pay the Government to retrieve the body of their relative.

Although the Government claimed to have released Abbas Amir Entezam early in 1996, he is still detained. Initially arrested in 1979 on charges of espionage and condemned to life in prison, he is now held in a "security house."

Adherents of the Baha'i faith continue to face arbitrary arrest and detention. The Government appears to adhere to a practice of detaining a small number of Baha'is at any time.

The Government does not use forced exile, but many dissidents leave Iran because they feel threatened.

e. *Denial of Fair Public Trial.*—The traditional court system is not independent and is subject to government and religious influence.

Iran has two court systems: The traditional courts, which adjudicate civil and criminal offenses; and the Islamic Revolutionary Courts, established in 1979 to try political offenses, narcotics crimes, and "crimes against God."

Many aspects of the prerevolution judicial system survive in the civil and criminal courts. For example defendants have the right to a public trial, may choose their own lawyer, and have the right of appeal. Trials are adjudicated by panels of judges. There is no jury system. In the absence of postrevolution laws, the Government advises judges to base their decisions on Islamic law. These courts are not independent. The Revolutionary Courts may consider cases normally in the jurisdiction of the civil and criminal courts, and also may overturn their decisions. Assignment of cases to either system of courts appears haphazard. The Supreme Court has limited authority to review cases.

Trials in the Revolutionary Courts are not fair. Often, pretrial detention is prolonged and defendants lack access to attorneys. When legal help is available, attorneys are rarely given time to prepare an effective defense. Indictments are often for vague offenses such as "antirevolutionary behavior," "moral corruption," and "siding with global arrogance." Defendants do not have the right to confront their accusers or to appeal. Secret or summary trials of 5 minutes are common. Others are show trials intended to highlight a coerced public confession.

The Government often charges members of religious minorities with crimes rather than apostasy. Ayatollah Mohammad Yazdi, the head of the judiciary, stated in May that Baha'ism was an espionage organization rather than a religion. On February 18, the Iranian court confirmed death sentences for two Baha'is, Kayvan Khalajabadi and Bihnam Mithaqi. When they were sentenced in 1993, an Iranian member of the U.N. Human Rights Commission stated that they were sentenced to death not because they were Baha'is, but because they were spies (see Sections 2.c. and 5). In July a Muslim convert to Christianity was arrested on charges of espionage (see Section 2.c.).

In 1995 the Government began implementing a law authorizing judges to act as prosecutor and judge in the same case. The rights of defendants are further eroded by the fact that many judges retired after the revolution, and others were disbarred for ideological reasons. The Government has replaced them with judges who are regarded as politically acceptable to the regime. The law's effect was clear to the U.N. Special Rapporteur when he viewed a 45-minute session of a trial. He wrote in his report: "The judge was clearly not a neutral third party between the prosecution and the defense."

In June the Government requested technical assistance in training judges and administering prisons from the UNHCR, and from the U.N. Crime Prevention and Justice Branch.

No estimates are available on the number of political prisoners. However, the Government often arrests persons on questionable criminal charges, usually drug trafficking or espionage, when their actual "offenses" are political. In October 1994, the U.N. Special Rapporteur issued a report that noted that he had requested the Government to provide information on 78 reported political prisoners.

f. *Arbitrary Interference with Privacy, Family, Home, or Correspondence.*—The Constitution states that "reputation, life, property, (and) dwelling(s)" are protected from trespass except as "provided by law." However, security forces enter homes and offices, monitor telephone conversations, and open mail without court authorization.

Paramilitary volunteer forces, including the basijis and hizbollahis, and other security forces monitor the social activities of citizens. Such organizations may harass or arrest women whose clothing does not cover the hair and all of the body except the hands and face, or those who wear makeup. Enforcement varies with the political climate and the jurisdiction.

There were increasing reports of hizbollahi violence. Incidents included attacks on young people believed to be too foreign in their dress or activities. Reports indicate that the hizbollahi more frequently invaded private homes and intervened on the streets. They also disrupted memorial services for prominent literary figures. There are reports of several deaths resulting from these incidents. There have been other reports that hizbollahi or basiji question and abuse unmarried couples. Women have also been beaten if caught without proper clothing in public or in private houses when men are present.

In the past, prison guards have intimidated family members of detainees (see Section 1.c.). Iranian opposition figures living abroad have reported harassment of their relatives in Iran.

Section 2. Respect for Civil Liberties, Including:

a. *Freedom of Speech and Press.*—The Constitution provides for the freedom of the press, except when published ideas are "contrary to Islamic principles, or are detrimental to public rights." In practice the Government restricts freedom of speech and the press. The Government exerts strong control over most media, particularly publications. Some newspapers are associated with factions in the Government. They reflect different views and criticize the Government, but are prohibited from criticizing the concept of Islamic government or promoting the rights of ethnic minorities.

The U.N. Special Representative for Freedom of Opinion and Expression, Abid Hussain, visited Iran from January 6 to 10. He reported significant problems: The strong connection between adherence to the Government's version of Islam and the right to freedom of opinion and expression. He noted that the vagueness of criteria determining what forms of expression are allowable under Islamic law hampers free expression and also reported limits on women's right to free expression. He pointed out that the Government "generally fails to condemn strongly and unequivocally" both threats and the use of violence "by irregular groups of private persons against professionals in the field of information." He expressed concern that prominent members of the Government defend and encourage the hizbollahi in these attacks, and that no court cases have been brought against the hizbollahi.

The Government continued its heavy-handed censorship of the press. Iranian publisher and writer Abdolkarim Soroush again left Iran after continuing harassment by the Government and hizbollahi. In May a band of hizbollahi prevented Soroush from speaking at Amir Kabir University in Tehran.

Another influential writer, Abbas Maroufi, publisher of the now defunct magazine, Gardoun, was sentenced to 35 lashes and 6 months in prison for "publishing lies" after printing a survey stating that many Iranians are psychologically depressed. He was also convicted of "insulting the Leader of the Islamic Republic" for publishing an article comparing the Shah and Ayatollah Khamenei.

In January publisher Abolghassem Golbaf of the monthly magazine, Gouzarish, was sentenced to 3 months in prison for publishing a negative story on a state-owned fertilizer company. Under the press law, only the Ministry of Culture and Islamic Guidance may bring cases against a publisher or writer; however, the case against Golbaf was brought by the Minister of Agriculture.

The U.N. Special Rapporteur reported that several newspapers were closed by the authorities, and that the editor of Kinyan, a publication critical of government policies, was charged with publishing false information and "weakening the foundation of the Islamic Republic."

The Special Rapporteur also reported that the authorities broke up an informal gathering of writers protesting the intolerant atmosphere, threatening that if such meetings were held again, those involved would be detained.

The Government owns all broadcasting facilities, and their programming reflects its political and socio-religious ideology. In the fall, a new television program "Hovigat" (Identity) was launched. The program's apparent aim is to categorize targeted intellectuals as social misfits or foreign spies.

Government censorship extends to the film industry. Any cinema showing films not considered acceptable is vulnerable to hizbollahi attacks. In early June, a group of hizbollahi attacked the audience and employees of the Qods cinema because it played a movie in which a man appeared in women's clothing. Several persons were reported injured, including a pregnant woman.

The Ministry of Islamic Culture and Guidance is also charged with ensuring that books do not contain offensive material prior to publication. The Ministry inspects foreign printed materials prior to their release on the market. However, some books and pamphlets critical of the Government are published without reprisal.

The Government made no effort to repudiate the 1989 religious decree condemning to death British author Salman Rushdie for his book, "The Satanic Verses," which the Government considers blasphemous. Nor did the Government move to repudiate its promise of a cash award to any person who kills Rushdie or anyone associated with publishing his book. According to press reports, senior government officials declared that the Government would not take steps to enforce the decree. However, Ayatollah Yazdi, head of the Iranian judiciary, stated that the decree "applies to all Muslims and would eventually be carried out one day."

In the fall the authorities began rigorously enforcing the ban on satellite dishes. Many were seized and others were removed and hidden by their owners. The press speculated that the crackdown was related to the debut of a television program featuring popular Iranian performers that was broadcast by the Voice of America.

Academic censorship persists. In his interim report the UNHRC Special Representative noted the existence of a campaign to bring about the "Islamization of the universities," which seemed to be a movement to purge persons "who fight against the sanctities of the Islamic system." The deputy Dean of the law school at the University of Tehran, Dr. Javad Tabatabai, was dismissed after criticizing a 1994 law reorganizing the country's court system.

Government informers are said to be common on university campuses and monitor classroom material. Admission to universities is politicized; all applicants must pass "character tests" in which officials screen out applicants critical of the Government's ideology. To achieve tenure, professors must cooperate with government authorities over a period of years.

b. *Freedom of Peaceful Assembly and Association.*—The Constitution permits assemblies and marches "provided they do not violate the principles of Islam." In practice, the Government restricts freedom of assembly. Oppositionists tried to hold press conferences about the election on January 2 and again on January 31. The police broke up both meetings, first claiming they could not guarantee security for the event and then stating that the conference was sponsored by an illegal organization. The UNHCR Special Rapporteur also noted the tendency of government police and military forces not to intervene when unofficial groups attempted to break up opposition or cultural gatherings. The press reported significant antigovernment unrest in the western city of Kermanshah following the death of a Kurdish Sunni Muslim cleric in early December. Protests over the next week were violently suppressed by security forces, resulting in several deaths, many persons injured, and perhaps hundreds arrested.

The Constitution provides for the establishment of political parties, professional associations, and religious groups provided that they do not violate the principles of "freedom, sovereignty, and national unity," or question Islam or the Islamic Republic. In practice, most independent organizations are banned, co-opted by the Government, or moribund.

In 1995 the Ministry of Interior refused to grant a license to the Freedom Movement, a political group founded in 1961 and declared illegal in 1991. The Ministry decision effectively precluded the party from participating in the March Majles elections. No major opposition faction was represented in the elections. In the northwestern city of Bonab, demonstrations against the Government's handling of the elections were forcibly broken up, resulting in the deaths of a number of persons.

c. *Freedom of Religion.*—The Constitution declares that the "official religion of Iran is Islam and the sect followed is Ja'fari Shi'ism." It also states that "other Islamic denominations shall enjoy complete respect." However, the Government restricts freedom of religion. The Government is profoundly influenced by Shi'a Islam. The President and many top officials, including the Speaker of the Parliament and many parliamentary deputies, are Shi'a clergymen.

Approximately 90 percent of the population are Shi'a Muslims. Aside from slightly over 1 percent who are not Muslims, the rest of the population are Sunni Muslims, drawn largely from Kurdish, Arab, Turkoman, Baluchi, and other ethnic minorities.

The Constitution also recognizes Christianity, Judaism, and Zoroastrianism. Members of these religions elect representatives to reserved Parliamentary seats. They are free to practice their religion and instruct their children, but the Government interferes with the administration of their schools. Harassment by government officials is common (see Section 5).

Non-Muslims may not proselytize Muslims. Oppression of evangelical Christians increased in 1996. In early July, a Muslim convert, Shahram Sepehri-Fard, was arrested on charges of having "sensitive information." He has been denied visitors since shortly after his arrest, and his condition is unknown. In late September, another Muslim convert to evangelical Christianity, Pastor Mohammed Yussefi (also known as Ravanbaksh), was reportedly murdered by authorities. Yussefi had been imprisoned by the Government on several occasions prior to his death. Three members of the opposition movement Mojahadin-e-Khaleq (MEK), Farohnaz Anami, Betoul Vaferi Kalateh, and Maryam Shahbazpoor, are currently in prison for the 1994 murder of Reverend Tatavous Michaelian, an evangelical Protestant pastor. The three women claim that two other Christian pastors murdered in 1994, Reverend Mehdi Dibaj and Reverend Haik Hovsepian Mehr, were also killed by the MEK.

The Government regards the Baha'i community, the largest non-Muslim minority with 300,000 to 350,000 members, as a "misguided sect." It prohibits Baha'is from teaching and practicing their faith or maintaining links with coreligionists abroad. Recently, Baha'i youth have been denied admittance to the fourth year of high school. Universities continue to deny admittance to Baha'i students. In addition, Baha'i are regularly denied compensation for injury or criminal victimization. Government authorities claim that only Muslim plaintiffs are eligible for compensation.

In October 1993, the Majles approved legislation that prohibits government workers from membership in groups that deny the "divine religions." The Government uses such terminology to describe members of the Baha'i faith. The law also stipulates penalties for government workers who do not observe "Islamic principles and rules."

d. *Freedom of Movement Within the Country, Foreign Travel, Emigration, and Repatriation.*—Citizens may travel to any part of Iran, although there have been restrictions on travel to Kurdish areas during times of heavy fighting. People may change their place of residence without obtaining official permission. The Government requires exit permits for draft-age males and citizens who are politically suspect. Some Iranians, particularly those whose skills are in short supply and who were educated at government expense, must post bonds to obtain exit permits.

The Government permits Iranian Jews to travel abroad, but often denies them the multiple-exit permits normally issued to other citizens. The Government does not normally permit all members of a Jewish family to travel abroad at the same time.

The Government and the U.N. High Commissioner for Refugees (UNHCR) estimate that there are approximately 1.3 million Afghan refugees in Iran. Of this total, only about 21,800 are accommodated in refugee camps administered by the Government. The rest live seminomadic lives or reside in settlements. In 1996 about 10,000 refugees repatriated to Afghanistan. This was far fewer than the UNHCR had predicted would return and resulted from continued instability in Taliban-controlled areas of Afghanistan.

The UNHCR estimates that there are about 580,000 Iraqi Kurdish and Shi'a Muslim refugees in Iran who were displaced by the Gulf War. In September an additional 65,000 Iraqi Kurdish refugees fled to Iran following the eruption of fighting between two Kurdish factions in northern Iraq. Since the cessation of fighting in October, the majority of this most recent wave of refugees has returned to Iraq.

The Government generally cooperates with the UNHCR and other humanitarian organizations in assisting refugees. Iran is a signatory to the 1951 Convention Relating to the Status of Refugees and its 1967 U.N. Protocol. Although the Government generally provides first asylum (as demonstrated by the large number of Afghan and Iraqi refugees in Iran), there have been instances where pressure was applied to force refugees to return to their home countries. In late 1996, the Government hastened the return of many recently arrived Iraqi Kurdish refugees by depriving them of adequate food and other relief. The UNHCR protested this policy of forced repatriation to the Government.

Section 3. Respect for Political Rights: The Right of Citizens to Change Their Government

The right of citizens to change their government is severely compromised by the leadership of the Government, which effectively manipulates the electoral system to its advantage. Iran is ruled by a group of religious leaders and their lay associates who share a belief in the legitimacy of a theocratic state based on Ayatollah Khomeini's interpretation of Shi'a Islam. There is no separation of state and religion. The clerics dominate all branches of government. The Government represses any movement seeking to separate state and religion, or to alter the State's existing theocratic foundation. The selection of candidates for elections is effectively controlled by the ruling clerics.

The Constitution provides for a Council of Guardians composed of six Islamic clergymen and six lay members who review all laws for consistency with Islamic law and the Constitution. The Council also screens political candidates for ideological and religious suitability. It accepts only candidates who support a theocratic state, but clerics who disagree with government policies have also been disqualified.

Regularly scheduled elections are held for the President, members of Parliament (the Majles), and members of the Assembly of Experts, a body responsible for selecting the successor to the Leader of the Revolution. The Majles exercises a considerable amount of independence from the executive branch, but its decisions are reviewed by the Council of Guardians. Vigorous parliamentary debates take place on various issues, and in some cases the Majles has respected laws proposed by the executive branch. Most deputies are associated with powerful political and religious officials, but often vote independently and shift from one faction to another.

Majles elections in the spring were marred by government control and violence. Preelection debate was vigorous, but the Council of Guardians succeeded in controlling the elections by selectively approving candidates. Human Rights Watch (HRW) estimated that the Government disqualified about 44 percent of the 5,121 prospective candidates, including 32 sitting members of the Majles. The criteria for vetting candidates was vague; the Council did not have to give a reason for rejection; and there was no right of appeal. The U.N. Special Rapporteur noted a number of irregularities in the elections, in particular the nullification of election results in eight jurisdictions apparently on ideological grounds. Most of the candidates disqualified were pragmatists rather than conservative candidates.

Human Rights Watch received reports indicating that riot police opened fire on demonstrators protesting government interference in the northwestern city of Bonab during voting on March 8. On April 6, the Government annulled election results in Isfahan, Malayer, Najafabad, Naeen, Miandoab, Meimeh, Borkhar, and Khomeini Shahre. New elections for these constituencies were to be held after 5 months but they did not materialize. On April 19, runoff elections took place for 125 seats.

Women are underrepresented in government. They hold only 9 of 270 Majles seats, and there are no female cabinet members.

Section 4. Governmental Attitude Regarding International and Nongovernmental Investigation of Alleged Violations of Human Rights

In 1996 the Government continued to repress local human rights groups, but it was more cooperative with foreign groups. The U.N. Special Representatives on Human Rights in Iran, Freedom of Expression, and Religious Freedom visited Iran. In addition Human Rights Watch sent a representative. All reported reasonably good cooperation from the Government, but all found continuing serious abuses of human rights. The ICRC and the UNHCR both operate in Iran.

The Government established a human rights committee in the Majles and a human rights commission in the judiciary, but observers believe that they lack independence. Government officials regularly assert that Iran should be judged by Islamic, rather than Western, human rights principles, and reject the universality of human rights.

Section 5. Discrimination Based on Race, Sex, Religion, Disability, Language, or Social Status

In general the Government does not discriminate on the basis of race, disability, language, or social status. The Government does discriminate on the basis of religion and sex.

Women.—Although domestic violence is known to occur, little is known about its extent. Abuse in the family is considered a private matter and seldom discussed publicly. There are no official statistics on the subject.

Discrimination against women has increased since the revolution. In general women suffer discrimination in the legal code, particularly in family and property matters. It is difficult for many women, particularly those residing outside large cities, to obtain any legal redress. Under the legal system, a woman's testimony as a witness is worth only half that of a man's, making it difficult for a woman to prove a case against a male defendant. In addition the families of female victims of violent crime often have to pay the assailant's court costs to bring him to trial. Although women may be educated and employed in the professions, social constraints tend to inhibit their educational and economic opportunities. Illiteracy and the lack of university degrees also affect their standing. The enforcement of conservative Islamic dress codes has varied considerably since the death of Ayatollah Khomeini in 1989. Nonetheless, such dress codes persist and are enforced arbitrarily.

Under legislation passed in 1983, women have the right to divorce, and regulations promulgated in 1984 substantially broadened the grounds on which a woman may seek a divorce. However, a husband is not required to cite a reason for divorcing his wife. In 1986 the Majles passed a 12-article law on marriage and divorce that limited the privileges accorded to men by custom and traditional interpretations of Islamic law. The 1986 law also recognized divorced women's rights to a share of the property that couples acquire during their marriage and increased alimony rights.

In June the Government requested the U.N. High Commissioner for Human Rights to "render advisory services to the nongovernmental organization (NGO) network on women existing in the country," according to the U.N. Special Representative.

In 1995 the Government permitted women to attain the rank of judges. But the Government does not permit female judges to preside over legal hearings, so the practical effect of the change in the law remains unclear. Women's activities can be severely restricted by the hizbollahi as well.

Children.—Most children have access to education through the 12th grade, and to some form of health care. There is no known pattern of child abuse.

People With Disabilities.—There is no available information regarding whether the Government has legislated or otherwise mandated accessibility for the disabled. The Cable News Network (CNN) reported, however, in late October on the harsh conditions in an institution for retarded children who had been abandoned by their parents. The film showed children tied or chained to their beds, in filthy conditions, without appropriate care. It is not known to what extent this represents the typical treatment of the disabled Iran.

National/Racial/Ethnic Minorities.—The Kurds seek greater autonomy and continue to suffer from government discrimination.

Religious Minorities.—The Christian, Jewish, Zoroastrian, and Baha'i minorities suffer varying degrees of officially sanctioned discrimination, particularly in the areas of employment, education, and public accommodations (see Section 2.d.). Muslims who convert to Christianity also suffer discrimination.

University applicants are required to pass an examination in Islamic theology. Although public-school students receive instruction in Islam, this requirement limits the access of most religious minorities to higher education. Applicants for public-sector employment are similarly screened for their adherence to Islam.

Religious minorities suffer discrimination in the legal system, receiving lower awards in injury and death lawsuits, and incurring heavier punishments than Muslims. Sunni Muslims encounter religious discrimination at the local level.

In 1993 the U.N. Special Representative reported the existence of a government policy directive on the Baha'is. According to the directive, the Supreme Revolutionary Council reportedly instructed government agencies to block the progress and development of the Baha'i community; expel Baha'i students from universities; cut the

Baha'is' links with groups outside Iran; restrict the employment of Baha'is; and deny Baha'is "positions of influence," including those in education. The Government claims that the directive is a forgery. However, it appears to be an accurate reflection of current government practice.

The persecution of Baha'is persisted in 1996. The Government continued to return some property previously confiscated from individual Baha'is, although the amount returned is a fraction of the total seized. Property belonging to the Baha'i community as a whole, however, such as places of worship, remains confiscated. Other government restrictions have been eased, so that Baha'is may currently obtain food ration booklets and send their children to public schools. However, the prohibition against the admission of Baha'is to universities appears to be enforced. Thousands of Baha'is dismissed from government jobs in the early 1980's receive no unemployment benefits and have been required to repay the Government for salaries or pensions received from the first day of employment. Those unable to do so face prison sentences (see Sections 1.d. and 5).

Section 6. Worker Rights

a. *The Right of Association.*—Although the Labor Code grants workers the right to establish unions, there are no independent unions. A national organization known as the Worker's House, founded in 1982, is the sole authorized national labor organization. It serves primarily as a conduit for government control. The leadership of the Worker's House coordinates activities with Islamic labor councils, which are organized in many enterprises. These councils also function as instruments of government control, although they have frequently been able to block layoffs and dismissals. Moreover, a network of government-backed guilds issues vocational licenses, funds financial cooperatives, and helps workers find jobs.

The Government does not tolerate any strike deemed to be at odds with its economic and labor policies. In 1993 the Parliament passed a law that prohibits strikes by government workers. It also prohibits government workers from having contacts with foreigners and stipulates penalties for failure to observe Islamic dress codes and principles at work.

There are no known affiliations with international labor organizations.

b. *The Right to Organize and Bargain Collectively.*—Workers do not have the right to organize independently and negotiate collective bargaining agreements. No information is available on mechanisms used to set wages.

It is not known whether labor legislation and practice in the export processing zones differ from the law and practice in the rest of the country.

c. *Prohibition of Forced or Compulsory Labor.*—The Penal Code provides that the Government may require any person who does not have work to take suitable employment. This provision has been criticized frequently by the International Labor Organization (ILO) as contravening ILO Convention 29 on forced labor.

d. *Minimum Age for Employment of Children.*—The labor law prohibits employment of minors under 15 years of age and places special restrictions on the employment of minors under age 18. Education is compulsory until age 11. The law permits children to work in agriculture, domestic service, and some small businesses. By law women and minors may not be employed in hard labor or, in general, in night work. Information on the extent to which these regulations are enforced is not available.

e. *Acceptable Conditions of Work.*—The Labor Code empowers the Supreme Labor Council to establish annual minimum wage levels for each industrial sector and region. It is not known if the minimum wages are adjusted annually or enforced. The Labor Code stipulates that the minimum wage should be sufficient to meet the living expenses of a family and should take inflation into account. Many middle-class citizens must work two or even three jobs to support their families. It is unlikely that minimum wage laws alone can ensure a decent standard of living for a worker and family, given current economic conditions in Iran

Information on the share of the working population covered by minimum wage legislation is not available.

According to press reports, the Ministry of Labor in early December announced that employers had 1 month in which to fire foreign workers and replace them with Iranians. It is believed that approximately 1 million foreign workers, mostly Afghan refugees, would be affected. The Government apparently hoped to alleviate high unemployment by pressuring foreigners to leave.

The Labor Code establishes a 6-day workweek of 48 hours maximum, with 1 weekly rest day, normally Fridays, and at least 12 days of paid annual leave and several paid public holidays.

According to the Labor Code, a Supreme Safety Council, chaired by the Labor Minister or his representative, is responsible for promoting workplace safety and health. The Council has reportedly issued 28 safety directives, and oversees the activities of 3,000 safety committees established in enterprises employing more than 10 persons. It is not known how well the Ministry's inspectors enforce regulations. It is not known whether workers can remove themselves from hazardous situations without risking the loss of employment.

IRAQ*

Political power in Iraq is concentrated in a repressive one-party apparatus dominated by Saddam Hussein. The provisional Constitution of 1968 stipulates that the Arab Ba'ath Socialist Party (ABSP) governs Iraq through the Revolutionary Command Council (RCC), which exercises both executive and legislative authority. President Saddam Hussein, who is also Prime Minister, Chairman of the RCC, and Secretary General of the Regional Command of the ABSP, wields decisive power. Saddam Hussein and his colleagues continue to point to an October 1995, nondemocratic "referendum" on his presidency in which he received 99.96 per cent of the vote as legitimating the regime. However, his "referendum" included neither secret ballots nor opposing candidates, and many credible reports indicated that voters feared possible reprisal for a negative vote. The judiciary is not independent and is subject to presidential interference.

Ethnically and linguistically, the Iraqi population includes Arabs, Kurds, Turkomen, Yazidis, and Armenians. Historically, the religious mix is likewise varied: Shi'a and Sunni Muslims (both Arab and Kurdish), Christians (including Chaldeans and Assyrians), and Jews (most of whom have emigrated). Ethnic divisions have resulted in civil uprisings in recent years, especially in the north and the south. The Government has reacted against those who revolt with extreme repression.

The Government's security apparatus includes militias attached to the President, the Ba'ath Party, and the Interior Ministry. They play a central role in maintaining the environment of intimidation and fear on which government power rests. Security forces have committed widespread, serious, and systematic human rights abuses.

The Government controls most of the economy, which is largely based on oil production, and owns all major industries. Damaged by the Gulf War and subjected to United Nations sanctions as a result of Iraq's 1990 invasion of Kuwait, the economy continues to deteriorate. The sanctions ban all exports and allows imports only of food, medicine, and materials and supplies for essential civilian needs. The Government's failure to comply with U.N. Security Council resolutions has led to repeated extensions of the sanctions. In May, after a year of obstruction and delay, the Government reached agreement with the U.N. on a plan to implement U.N. Security Council Resolution (UNSCR) 986, which would allow a controlled sale of Iraqi oil to purchase food and other humanitarian goods to improve the deteriorating situation of the Iraqi people. Throughout the rest of 1996, however, the Government continued to engage in delaying tactics and other actions which the U.N. and other observers cited as delaying implementation. The Government's actions threatened the resolution's intended controls on oil sales and the conditions required to ensure fair and equitable distribution of relief. In mid-December, the U.N. announced that conditions were finally in place to allow implementation to begin, although it appeared likely that relief would not be delivered until early 1997.

The Government's abysmal record on human rights worsened in 1996. Human rights abuses remain extremely difficult to document because of the Government's efforts to conceal the facts, including its refusal to permit visits by human rights monitors or other observers and its continued restrictions designed to prevent dissent. Nevertheless, the Government's renewal of repression and threats in northern Iraq following its military attack on the city of Irbil on August 31 make it clear that serious human rights violations increased.

Summary executions of perceived political opponents reportedly increased, as did reports of disappearances. Both types of repression were particularly clear in the north during and after the August 31 attack on Irbil. Tens of thousands of political killings and disappearances remain unresolved from previous years. As socioeconomic conditions deteriorated, the regime punished persons accused of economic crimes, military desertion, and a variety of other charges with torture and cruel and inhuman penalties, including the extensive use of amputation. Prison conditions are

---

*The United States does not have diplomatic representation in Iraq. This report draws to a large extent on non-U.S. Government sources.

poor. The authorities routinely use arbitrary arrest and detention. The judiciary is not independent; the President can override any court decision. The Government continues to deny citizens the right to due process and privacy. Max van der Stoel, the Special Rapporteur for Iraq appointed by the U.N. Human Rights Commission (UNHRC), confirmed again that freedom of speech, the press, assembly, and association do not exist, except in some parts of the northern areas, beyond control of the Government. The Government severely limits freedom of religion and movement, discriminates against women, children, religious minorities, and ethnic groups. It also restricts worker rights.

Citizens do not have the right to change their government. The October "referendum" on Saddam's presidency was not free. It was dismissed by most international observers. As in years past, the Government forcibly transferred hundreds of government workers from one job to another, purportedly to prevent the development of potential opposition in any government institutions. After failed coup attempts and repressed protests between May and July, the Government arrested, removed from their jobs, or otherwise punishednumerous citizens for their alleged association with these incidents. The fate of many such persons remains unknown. After Saddam's daughters and his sons-in-law, Hussein Kamel and Saddam Kamel al-Majid, defected to Jordan in August 1995, the Government reportedly arrested scores of midlevel military and civilian officials for their association with the defectors. Evidence has emerged that the Government was behind the deaths of Saddam's sons-in-law, who returned to Iraq in February from Jordan after they received promises of amnesty. Shortly after entering Iraq, the two were separated from their families and were killed, allegedly in a gunfight with relatives. Other members of the al-Majid clan were also arrested or disappeared.

Iraqi military operations continued to target Shi'a Arabs living in the southern marshes. In central and southern Iraq, the regime continued to divert humanitarian supplies to its security forces, the military, and other supporters. For most of the year, the Government maintained an internal embargo against Iraq's northern governorates, blocking the shipment of food, medicine, and other goods from government-controlled territory to the Kurdish-controlled areas. The Government announced the lifting of the internal embargo on September 12, but anecdotal and other reports indicate that the regime still exercises tight control over the flow of goods and services into and out of northern areas.

The Government persisted in its flagrant interference with the international community's provision of humanitarian assistance, in contravention of the conditions of UNSC Resolution 688. It harassed and intimidated relief workers as well as U.N. security personnel throughout the country. The Government renewed a threat to arrest or kill relief workers, whether foreign or Iraqi, simply for association with a foreign relief organization. The Government initially objected to the distribution monitors required by the terms of Resolution 986, and it remains to be seen whether the Government will allow those monitors to carry out their work. In northern Iraq, fighting continued between the two main Iraqi Kurd groups, the Kurdistan Democratic Party (KDP) and the Patriotic Union of Kurdistan (PUK), in which both fighters and civilians were killed. KDP cooperation with the Government in the August 31 attack and PUK cooperation with Iran in August increased instability and, according to Iraqi and Iranian opposition reports, the ability of both governments to act against political opponents in the area. A cease-fire established on October 23 ended fighting for the rest of the year, albeit with a few sporadic clashes. At the end of the year, both groups were considering a mutual release of detainees as one of several confidence-building measures to strengthen the cease-fire and improve prospects for political reconciliation between the two groups. Terrorist actions in northern Iraq and Turkey by the Turkish terrorist organization, the Kurdistan Workers' Party (PKK), also resulted in the death of both fighters and civilians. Both Iraqi Kurdish groups and the PKK reportedly committed serious abuses, including killings, torture, arbitrary arrest and detention.

RESPECT FOR HUMAN RIGHTS

Section 1. Respect for the Integrity of the Person, Including Freedom From:

a. *Political and Other Extrajudicial Killing.*—The regime has a long record of executing perceived opponents. The U.N. Special Rapporteur, the international media, and other groups all reported an increased number of summary executions in 1996. In his November report to the U.N. Human Rights Commission, the Special Rapporteur stated that "the country is run through extrajudicial measures." In an April 10 report, Amnesty International noted that various decrees expanding the use of the death penalty in 1994 and 1995 have not been sufficiently clarified to ensure fair and just applicability, a problem compounded by the lack of an independent judiciary.

As in previous years, there were numerous credible reports that the regime executed persons allegedly involved in plotting against President Hussein, including high-ranking civilian, military, and tribal leaders, as well as members of his family and clan. The regime periodically eliminates large numbers of detainees; in May, according to unconfirmed reports, the regime executed as many as 100 detainees. In June some 400 officers of various ranks were executed, including some senior Republican Guard officers. Allegedly these executions were ordered directly by Saddam Hussein and supervised by his eldest son, Uday. Also in June, Uday reportedly ordered the killing of a former aide, Muhammad Al-Rawi, for trading stocks on the Baghdad stock market.

Hussein Kamel and Saddam Kamel, Saddam Hussein's sons-in-law, were executed by the Government in February, according to numerous credible sources, when they returned from Jordan after defecting in August 1995. Although the Government announced amnesties for both men, they and over 40 relatives, including women and children, were killed in what the official Iraqi press described as the spontaneous administration of tribal justice. The Special Rapporteur noted in his November report that "the killings occurred without any legal process and with total impunity." He also cited continued reports of the frequent use of the death penalty for such offenses as "insulting" the President or the Ba'ath Party, and the pervasive fear of death for any act or expression of dissent.

Government forces reportedly executed more Shi'a inhabitants of the southern marshes in 1996, but there remains no independent means to verify these reports (see Section 1.g.).

Indications persist that the Government has offered "bounties" to anyone who kills United Nations or other international relief workers in northern Iraq. A September 12 amnesty announcement specifically excluded anyone accused of espionage, a charge the Government has repeatedly made against foreign relief organizations working in northern Iraq.

As in previous years, the regime continued to deny totally the widespread killings of Kurds in northern Iraq during the "Anfal" Campaign of 1988 (see Sections 1.b. and 1.g.). The Special Rapporteur and Human Rights Watch have concluded that the Government's policies against the Kurds raise issues of crimes against humanity and violations of the 1948 Genocide Convention.

The most obvious extrajudicial killings occurred during and after the Iraqi army attacked northern Iraq in late August and early September. Numerous credible reports, including but not limited to eyewitness accounts collected by opposition organizations, confirm that 96 Iraqi army officers and soldiers who had previously deserted the army and fled to the north were captured in the town of Qushtapa, 22 kilometers south of Irbil, on August 31. Local residents were reportedly taken to the town center and forced to watch while soldiers executed these prisoners. As noted by the Special Rapporteur and media reports, a KDP spokesman acknowledged on September 11 that the Government was responsible for these executions. Numerous other individual executions and extrajudicial killings were reported over the next few months. For example, on October 16 the body of an Iraqi dissident, architectural engineer Qutaiba Ghazi Al-Samarra'i, was discovered in Dohuk. According to opposition reports, Al-Samarra'i was an opponent of Saddam Hussein's dictatorship and was eventually sought out and killed by government intelligence units.

There was no further information on the death of the prominent Shi'a oppositionist Taki Al-Khoei who, along with three others, was killed in 1994 in a suspicious automobile crash in southern Iraq. Strong circumstantial evidence points to the Government's involvement.

During the year, political killings and terrorist actions occurred in northern Iraq. Intra-Kurdish fighting from August through October between the PUK and the KDP resulted in the deaths of several fighters and civilians, and both groups complained of forced expulsions of one another's supporters from territory controlled by the other party. At the end of the year, both groups were working to confirm the whereabouts of one another's detainees and missing supporters and to end forced expulsion and other abuses as part of confidence-building measures to strengthen the October 23 cease-fire. Throughout 1996, elements of the PKK, a Turkish Kurd terrorist group, remained active in northern Iraq and reportedly killed local residents in an effort to control a territorial base. The PKK sometimes attacked civilians, foreign relief workers, and journalists.

b. *Disappearance.*—The Special Rapporteur stated in November that he continues to receive reports on widespread disappearances. The Government continued to ignore the more than 15,000 cases conveyed to it in 1994 and 1995 by the U.N. Working Group on Enforcement on Involuntary Disappearances, as well as other requests from the Governments of Kuwait and Saudi Arabia on the whereabouts of those missing from the 1990–91 occupation of Kuwait.

The United Nations has documented over 16,000 cases of persons who have disappeared According to the Special Rapporteur, most of these cases occurred during the Anfal campaign. He estimates that the total number of Kurds who disappeared during Anfal could reach the tens of thousands. HRW estimates the total at between 70,000 and 150,000, and Amnesty International (AI) at more than 100,000.

Disappearances in northern Iraq increased in 1996 as Iraqi and Iranian intelligence units grew more active. On September 11, a KDP spokesman confirmed various reports that Iraqi intelligence units arrested numerous individuals, including members of the oppositionist Iraqi National Congress (INC) and Turkomen and Islamist groups. According to the Special Rapporteur, the fate of these individuals remains unknown. Unconfirmed reports blamed Iran for the disappearances of several Iranian opposition figures who resided in the north.

The Special Rapporteur and several human rights groups continued to request that the Government provide information about the arrest in 1991 of the late Grand Ayatollah Abdul Qasim Al-Khoei and 108 of his associates. The Ayatollah died while under house arrest in Al-Najaf. Others arrested with him have not been accounted for, and the regime refuses to respond to queries regarding their status.

The Government failed to return or account for a large number of Kuwaiti citizens and other foreign nationals detained during the Iraqi occupation of Kuwait. Regime officials, including military leaders known to have been among the last to see the persons who disappeared during the occupation, have refused to respond to the hundreds of outstanding inquiries about the missing. The regime denies having any knowledge of them and claims that relevant records were lost in the aftermath of the Gulf War.

In addition to the tens of thousands of reported disappearances, human rights groups report that the Government continues to hold thousands of other Iraqis in incommunicado detention.

c. *Torture and Other Cruel, Inhuman, or Degrading Treatment or Punishment.*—The security services routinely torture detainees, even though the Constitution prohibits the practice. The Special Rapporteur and AI provided new, detailed accounts of the Government's systemic use of physical and psychological torture in recent years. They noted that government decrees and announcements that might reduce the use of torture had not been confirmed by demonstrable evidence. For example, the Special Rapporteur noted that an August 5 RCC decree suspending the use of amputation against army deserters did not apply to those convicted of various other crimes. The execution of 96 deserters in northern Iraq on August 31 (see Section 1.a) calls into question whether the Government intended any lesser punishments for army deserters.

According to former detainees, torture techniques include brandings, electric shocks administered to the genitals and other areas, beatings, burnings with hot irons, suspension from ceiling fans, dripping acid on the skin, rape, breaking of limbs, denial of food and water, and threats to rape or otherwise harm relatives. Tormentors kill many torture victims and mutilate their bodies before returning them to the victims' families.

Eyewitnesses reported that the Government carried out second amputations and brandings on repeat offenders and on those who sought corrective surgery for earlier disfigurements. In some of these cases, the regime executed the offenders as well as the doctors who either performed corrective surgery or refused to carry out amputations. The Special Rapporteur also reported the execution of a number of doctors who refused to tattoo army deserters on their foreheads as required by government decree. In his November report, the Special Rapporteur reconfirmed his previous analysis, that the amputations and brandings constituted "gross violations of human rights."

Several government officials cited Islamic law (Shari'a) as a rationale for amputating the right hands of convicted thieves, but none commented on the punishments imposed on repeat offenders or the Government's disregard for rights protected under Islamic law. One senior official claimed that brandings were instituted in order to avoid confusing criminals with war veterans who had lost limbs in battle.

The Special Rapporteur, human rights organizations, and opposition groups continue to receive numerous reports of women still suffering severe psychological trauma after they were raped while in custody. The security forces allegedly raped women captured during the Anfal Campaign and during the occupation of Kuwait. The Government has never acknowledged these reports of rape or conducted any investigation. Although the regime made a variety of pronouncements against rape and other violent crimes during the year, it took no action against regime activists who committed these abuses.

Prison conditions are poor. Certain prisons are notorious for routine mistreatment of prisoners. Al-Rashidiya Prison, on the Tigris River north of Taji, reportedly has torture chambers. The Al-Shamma'iya Prison, located in east Baghdad, holds the mentally ill and is reportedly the site of both torture and disappearances.

The Al-Radwaniyah Prison is a former prisoner-of-war facility near Baghdad and reportedly the site of torture as well as mass executions. This prison was the principal detention center for persons arrested following the civil uprisings of 1991. HRW and others have estimated that the Al-Radwaniyah Prison holds more than 5,000 detainees.

There were continued reports that Iraqi Kurdish groups tortured captured criminal suspects and political opponents. A wide variety of observers documented KDP abuses against the al-Sourchi tribe and others for alleged cooperation with the PUK and others. Some observers charged that the KDP was reportedly responsible for the death of a respected leader of the tribe, Hussein al-Sourchi, as well as for detaining tens of suspected KDP opponents and for property damage. The KDP claimed that Hussein al-Sourci's death was an accidental result of a preemptive strike against KDP opponents, and the KDP denied what it termed exaggerated reports of damage and of detainees. Numerous other reports of KDP and PUK abuses against perceived opponents also circulated during the year, especially in the aftermath of Iranian support for PUK military moves in August and of Saddam Hussein's August 31 attack on Irbil (see Section 1.g.). The PKK also reportedly tortured civilians captured in northern Iraq in the latter half of the year. The UNHCR and other observers noted that PKK influence at the Atrush refugee camp had grown to such a point that at year's end the UNHCR decided to close the camp, with its inhabitants offered the options of voluntary repatriation to Turkey or relocation elsewhere in northern Iraq.

d. *Arbitrary Arrest, Detention, or Exile.*—Although the Constitution and Legal Code explicitly prohibit arbitrary arrest and detention, the authorities routinely engage in these practices. In his November report, the Special Rapporteur stated that arbitrary arrests are still common throughout the country and often lead to detention for long periods of time without access to a lawyer or being charged. The military and security services, rather than the ordinary police, carry out most cases of arbitrary arrest and detention. Government officials have linked ending these practices to the lifting of the international embargo. They maintain that the arrests are a temporary preventive measure and do not constitute human rights violations.

It has also been reported that there is a widespread practice of holding family members and close associates responsible for the alleged actions of others. In the aftermath of several security incidents, security forces reportedly arrested hundreds of persons perceived as security threats, mainly on the basis of an individual's personal association or family connection with opponents of the regime. Many of those arrested were reportedly killed while in custody (see Section 1.a.). The Special Rapporteur also notes that "guilt by association" is facilitated by administrative requirements on relatives of deserters or other perceived opponents of the regime. Relatives who do not report deserters, for example, could lose their ration cards for purchasing government-controlled food supplies or be evicted from their residences.

According to international human rights groups, numerous foreigners arrested arbitrarily in previous years remain in detention.

According to the Special Rapporteur's report, Iraqi military and security authorities arbitrarily arrested hundreds of people during and after the Government's military operations against the northern city of Irbil in late August and early September. Among those arrested were several prominent local politicians, intellectuals, lawyers, journalists, and university lecturers. Reportedly 1,500 persons were arrested in Irbil alone, including women and children. In addition, 150 members of an opposition group and persons suspected of involvement with opposition groups were reportedly detained by government security personnel. Their fate remains unknown.

Opposition groups provide many detailed but unconfirmed reports of arbitrary arrest in other areas of the country. In April, for example, the regime reportedly launched a random arrest campaign in the Al-Basrah governorate. Troops reportedly raided a number of homes in the Al-Zubayr district and arrested about 30 citizens under the pretext that the detained persons had connections with Kuwaiti citizens who own farms near the Iraqi border. In the Abu Al-Khasib district, six citizens reportedly were arrested on the same charge.

The Government reportedly continued to target Shi'a Muslim clergy and their supporters for arbitrary arrest and other abuses. The Government also reportedly continued to forcibly move various Shi'a populations from the south to the north and other minority groups such as Assyrians and Turkomen from the north to government-controlled territory. There was no substantive evidence that the Government was implementing two "amnesty" decrees issued in 1995. AI stated on April 10 that it "remains concerned that Iraqi authorities may be attempting to bring deserters and government opponents out of hiding in order to penalize them." The Special Rapporteur reported in November that his similar analysis in 1995 remained accurate.

Although the figure is unknown, there are possibly thousands of political detainees.

The Government apparently does not practice forced exile.

e. *Denial of Fair Public Trial.*—The judiciary is not independent, and there is no check on the President's power to override any court decision. The Special Rapporteur and international human rights groups all observed during the year that the repressive nature of the political and legal systems precludes any concept of rule of law.

There are two parallel judicial systems: the regular courts, which try common criminal offenses; and special security courts, which generally try national security cases, but may also try criminal cases. There is a Court of Appeal. The Court of Cassation is the highest court.

Procedures in the regular courts theoretically provide for many protections. However, the regime often assigns to the security courts cases which, on their merits, would appear to fall under the jurisdiction of the regular courts. Trials in the regular courts are public, and defendants are entitled to counsel, at government expense in the case of indigents. Defense lawyers have the right to review the charges and evidence brought against their clients. There is no jury system; panels of three judges try cases. Defendants have the right to appeal to the Court of Appeal and then to the Court of Cassation. The Special Rapporteur noted in his November report that numerous laws lend themselves to continued oppression. He reported in detail on extrajudicial methods used by the Government in previous years to extract confessions or coerce cooperation with repressive actions by the Government's security forces.

The Government shields certain groups from prosecution for alleged crimes. A 1992 decree grants immunity from prosecution to members of the Ba'ath Party and the security forces who kill anyone while in pursuit of army deserters. Unconfirmed but widespread reports indicate that this decree was applied in 1996 to prevent trials or punishment of such government officials as Uday Saddam Hussein, the President's son. A 1990 decree grants immunity to men who kill their mothers, daughters, and other female family members who have committed "immoral deeds," e.g., adultery, fornication, etc.

Special security courts have jurisdiction in all cases involving espionage and treason, peaceful political dissent, smuggling, currency exchange violations, and drug trafficking. According to the Special Rapporteur and other sources, military officers or civil servants with no legal training head these tribunals, which hear cases in secret. Authorities often hold defendants incommunicado and do not permit contact with lawyers. The courts admit confessions extracted by torture, which often serve as the basis for conviction.

Many cases appear to end in summary execution, although defendants may appeal to the President for clemency. Saddam Hussein may grant clemency in any case that apparently suits his political goals.

There are no Shari'a, or Islamic law, courts as such. Regular courts are empowered to administer Islamic law in cases involving personal status, such as divorce and inheritance.

Because the Government rarely acknowledges arrests or imprisonments, it is difficult to estimate the number of political prisoners. Many of the tens of thousands of persons who have disappeared or been killed in recent years were originally held as political prisoners.

f. *Arbitrary Interference with Privacy, Family, Home, or Correspondence.*—The Government frequently disregards the constitutional right to privacy, particularly in cases allegedly involving national security. The law defines security offenses so broadly that authorities are virtually exempt from the legal requirement to obtain search warrants. In 1996 the authorities subjected citizens of various ethnic groups and tribal affiliations to searches without warrants (see Section 1.g.). The regime routinely ignores the constitutional provisions safeguarding the confidentiality of mail, telegraphic correspondence, and telephone conversations. The Government periodically jams news broadcasts, including those of opposition groups, from outside Iraq.

The security services and the Ba'ath Party maintain pervasive networks of informers to deter dissident activity and instill fear in the public. For example, the

Special Rapporteur reported in November that an operator was arrested and executed in 1993 for having warned a person not to use a bugged telephone line. The authorities also hold family members and close associates responsible for the alleged actions of others (see Section 1.d.).

g. *Use of Excessive Force and Violations of Humanitarian Law in Internal Conflicts.*—As in previous years, the armed forces conducted deliberate artillery attacks against Shi'a civilians in the southern marshes and against minority groups in northern Iraq. In 1992 the Gulf War allies imposed "no-fly zones" over both northern and southern Iraq. The no-fly zones continue to deter aerial attacks on the marsh dwellers in southern Iraq and residents of northern Iraq, but they do not prevent artillery attacks in either area, nor the military's large-scale burning operations in the south.

Credible reports confirm the ongoing destruction of the marshes. The army continued to construct canals, causeways, and earthen berms to divert water from the wetlands. Hundreds of square kilometers have been burned in military operations. Moreover, the regime's diversion of supplies in the south limited the population's access to food, medicine, drinking water, and transportation.

During 1996 the Government regularly reported on several water-diversion and other projects in the south, which continued the process of large-scale environmental destruction. The Government claims the drainage is part of a land reclamation plan to increase the acreage of arable land, spur agricultural production, and reduce salt pollution in the Tigris and Euphrates rivers. However, the evidence of large-scale human and ecological destruction appears to belie this claim.

The Government maintained an internal embargo against the three governorates in northern Iraq for most of the year. These governorates are populated primarily by Kurds, Assyrians, Turkoman, and other ethnic minorities. The embargo prevented the entry of food, medicine, and other humanitarian supplies to that area. Beginning in 1993, the embargo also included electrical power cut-offs in specific areas, causing the disruption of water and sanitation systems and interfering with the delivery of food and fuel. The United Nations and donor governments installed temporary generators to alleviate the crisis. The Government announced that the embargo was lifted in mid-September, but anecdotal and other reports indicate that some areas are still subject to more restrictive movements of goods and people than other parts of the country. The entire northern area remains subject to the threat of future cut-offs.

Operation Provide Comfort—a multinational coalition made up of the United States, United Kingdom, France, and Turkey—continued enforcement of a "no-fly zone" to inhibit government aerial activity to repress citizens in northern Iraq. However, government military forces continued intermittent, sometimes heavy shelling of northern villages by long-range artillery throughout the year, especially of areas controlled by the PUK. Iranian forces reportedly shelled military positions and civilian sites within KDP-controlled areas in August. The Government also continued to "Arabize" certain areas, such as the urban centers of Kirkuk and Mosul, through the forced movement of local residents from their homes and villages and their replacement by Arabs from outside the area (see Section 1.d.).

On August 31, government troops, tanks, artillery, and helicopters first shelled and then captured the city of Irbil in northern Iraq. Several other cities and villages in northern Iraq were shelled by artillery and then were entered by government troops. The Special Rapporteur stated in November that indiscriminate shelling by Iraqi forces of civilian settlements had been a recurrent practice well before these most recent clashes. He and numerous other observers confirmed that the Government's use of military forces against civilian targets is a clear violation of Security Council Resolution 688, which demands that the Government cease oppression of its civilian population.

According to the Special Rapporteur, there were at least 100 casualties following the drive by troops into Irbil, as well as many other casualties of a simultaneous push by the KDP. In addition, security forces reportedly executed several members of the INC, PUK, and other opposition groups in the streets following house-to-house searches.

It has also been reported that the troops that entered the villages upon the first attacks burned and destroyed houses after having looted valuable property. Major buildings, including hospitals, as well as water and sanitation systems, were reportedly looted, damaged, and in some cases destroyed. The armed conflict in Irbil also resulted in the cutting of electricity and water supplies by both Kurdish groups, which were restored fully a few weeks after a cease-fire was put in place on October 23.

The KDP was accused of several extrajudicial killings and indiscriminate attacks in September, including a confirmed attack on September 10 on a camp near the

Iranian border that held refugees from PUK-controlled areas. The KDP also detained PUK members and perceived supporters throughout this peroid, including PUK politburo member Fuad Massoum and 11 other PUK supporters who were released on September 25. The PUK was accused of similar indiscriminate attacks and detainees in August and October, which the KDP said were supported by Iranian forces. The vast majority of these reports could not be confirmed due to the absence of impartial observers and the general lack of security, but individual cases that were confirmed indicate that the abuses likely took place on both sides while fighting continued.

During this period, the KDP and PUK took steps to protect foreign workers engaged in humanitarian relief work. However, there were several reports that Kurdish relief workers were abused during the second half of the year.

The PKK committed numerous abuses against civilians in northern Iraq throughout the year. It also stepped up violence against UNHCR officials working in the Atrush refugee camp late in the year.

On several occasions in 1996, Turkish armed forces entered northern Iraq in pursuit of PKK terrorists and bases. Human rights organizations and political organizations charged that these operations resulted in some civilian deaths and destruction of residences. Turkish government authorities stressed that the operation sought to avoid civilian casualties.

Land mines in northern Iraq, mostly planted by the Government before 1991, continue to kill and maim civilians. Many of the mines were laid during the Iran-Iraq War, but the army failed to clear them before it abandoned the area. The mines appear to have been haphazardly planted in civilian areas. The Special Rapporteur has repeatedly reminded the Government of its obligations under the Land Mines Protocol to protect civilians from the effects of mines. Various nongovernmental organizations continue efforts to remove mines from the area and increase mine awareness among local residents.

Reports from victims and eyewitnesses show that the Iraqi regime engaged in war crimes—willful killing, torture, rape, pillage, hostage-taking, and associated acts—directly related to the Gulf War. Many governments continue to urge the U.N. Security Council to establish an international commission to study evidence of a broader range of war crimes, as well as crimes against humanity and possible genocide. HRW continues to work with various governments to bring a genocide case at the International Court of Justice against the Government for its conduct of the Anfal campaign against the Kurds in 1988. U.S. Government policy is to support these efforts to hold Saddam Hussein's regime accountable for its war crimes and crimes against humanity.

Section 2. Respect for Civil Liberties, Including:

a. *Freedom of Speech and Press.*—Freedom of speech and of the press do not exist, and political dissent is not tolerated in areas under the Government's control. The Special Rapporteur reports that "the possibility for citizens to freely express their opinions is seriously undermined if not totally meaningless."

The Government and the Ba'ath Party own all print and broadcast media and operate them as propaganda outlets. They generally do not report opposing points of view that are expressed either domestically or abroad. According to the Special Rapporteur, journalists are under regular pressure to join the Ba'ath party. The Special Rapporteur and other observers have described how journalists are under instruction to mention Saddam Hussein positively in any article, regardless of the subject. The same sources have detailed how journalists may fall under suspicion for not writing about Saddam Hussein every few months. Negative articles can carry extreme consequences: one journalist was reportedly executed extrajudicially for criticizing an article written by Saddam Hussein under a pseudonym, while another was sentenced to life imprisonment for telling a joke about the President.

The Special Rapporteur also reported that the Ministry of Culture and Information periodically holds meetings at which orientation and general guidelines for the press are provided. Furthermore, books can be published only with the authorization of the Ministry of Culture and Information. The President's son, Uday Hussein, also reportedly exercises control over journalists. He sometimes uses a newspaper under his personal control, Babel, to threaten members of a particular tribe or clan believed to be insufficiently supportive of the regime. In a more direct example of control, the Special Rapporteur reported that Uday Hussein and his cohorts pelted two elderly, well-respected journalists with tomatoes at a conference as punishment for not being sufficiently supportive of the regime. The Government also jams foreign news broadcasts (see Section 1.f.).

Several statutes and decrees suppress freedom of speech and the press. These include a 1986 decree stipulating the death penalty for anyone insulting the President or other high government officials; Section 214 of the Penal Code, which prohibits singing a song likely to cause civil strife; and the Press Act of 1968, which prohibits the writing of articles on 12 specific subjects, including those detrimental to the President.

Foreigners are also subject to restrictions on freedom of the press. The Government refused to admit a returning Danish member of the U.N. Guard Contingent in Iraq, which protects international humanitarian workers throughout the country, for carrying a foreign newspaper with unfavorable coverage of Saddam Hussein.

In northern Iraq, several newspapers have appeared over the past 5 years, as have opposition radio and television broadcasts. The absence of central authority permits some freedom of expression, although most journalists are influenced or controlled by various political organizations.

The Government has no respect for academic freedom, exercising strict control over academic publications. University staff is hired or fired depending on their support for the Government.

b. *Freedom of Peaceful Assembly and Association.*—Citizens may not peacefully assemble or organize for any political purpose other than to express support for the regime. The Government regularly orchestrates crowds to demonstrate support for the regime and its policies through financial incentives for those who participate and threats of violence against those who do not.

Unconfirmed reports continued to circulate of small demonstrations and even confrontations between farm workers and the security forces. The Special Rapporteur and other observers expressed doubts that the Government would allow such reports to be confirmed by monitors, whose mandate under Resolution 986 could cover such activities insofar as they are related to the distribution of relief.

The Government controls the establishment of political parties, regulates their internal affairs, and monitors their activities. Several parties are specifically outlawed, and membership in them is a capital offense. A 1974 law prescribes the death penalty for anyone "infiltrating" the Ba'ath Party.

c. *Freedom of Religion.*—The Government severely limits freedom of religion. The Provisional Constitution of 1968 states that "Islam is the religion of the State." The Ministry of Endowments and Religious Affairs monitors places of worship, appoints the clergy, and approves the publication of religious literature.

Although Shi'a Muslim Arabs, who compose between 60 and 65 percent of the population, are the largest religious group, Sunni Arabs (composing only about 12 to 15 percent of the population) have traditionally dominated economic and political life. Despite legal guarantees of sectarian equality, the regime has in recent years repressed the Shi'a clergy and followers of the Shi'a faith. Security forces have desecrated Shi'a mosques and holy sites, particularly in the aftermath of the 1991 civil uprisings.

The security forces reportedly were still encamped in the shrine to Imam Ali at Al-Najaf, one of Shi'a Islam's holiest sites, using it as an interrogation center. The former Shi'a theological school in Al-Najaf, which the Government closed following the 1991 uprising, continues to be used as a public market. Security forces continued to expel foreign Muslim clerics from Al-Najaf, under the pretext that the clerics' visas had expired.

The following government restrictions on religious rights remained in effect throughout 1996: a ban on the Muslim call to prayer in certain cities; a ban on the broadcast of Shi'a programs on government radio or television; a ban on the publication of Shi'a books, including prayer books; a ban on funeral processions; and the prohibition of certain processions and public meetings commemorating Shi'a holy days. Moreover, the Government also continued to insist that its own appointee replace the late Grand Ayatollah Abul Qasim Al-Khoei, formerly the highest ranking Iraqi Shi'a clergyman, who died in government custody in 1992 (see Section 1.b.). The Shi'a religious establishment refuses to accept the Government's choice. The Government also continued to harass and threaten members of the late Ayatollah Al-Khoei's family (see Section 1.a. and 1.b.).

The Special Rapporteur and others report that the Government has engaged in various abuses against the country's 350,000 Assyrian Christians. Most Assyrians traditionally live in the northern governorates, and the Government often has suspected them of "collaborating" with Kurds. Military forces destroyed numerous Assyrian churches during the Anfal Campaign and reportedly tortured and executed many Assyrians (see Section 4). According to HRW and Assyrian sources, the Government continues to harass and kill Assyrians throughout the country by forced relocations, terror, and artillery shelling.

d. *Freedom of Movement Within the Country, Foreign Travel, Emigration, and Repatriation.*—The Government controls the movement within the country of citizens and foreigners. Persons who enter sensitive border areas and numerous designated security zones are subject to arrest (see Section 1.d.). Police checkpoints are common on major roads and highways. High-ranking officials and other key supporters of the regime were exempt from these restrictions, but some reports indicate that the Government removed most of these exceptions and tightened internal and border travel controls at times of relative instability, such as reported internal disturbances in May and July.

The Government requires citizens to obtain expensive exit visas for foreign travel. Citizens may not make more than two trips abroad annually. Exit from the country requires possession of specific government authorization, and the Government reportedly prohibits some citizens from all international travel. Before traveling abroad, citizens are required to post collateral with the Government which is refundable only upon their return. There are restrictions on the amount of currency that may be taken out of the country. Women are not permitted to travel outside Iraq alone; male relatives must escort them.

The Government prohibits the granting of approval for foreign travel to journalists, authors, and all the employees of the Information Ministry. Security authorities interrogate all media employees, journalists, and writers who have traveled outside Iraq about the reasons for their travel and who they met during their trips. Some citizens without personal documents have turned themselves over to Jordanian border posts to avoid paying the departure tax levied on citizens who wish to travel abroad. Most citizens are unable to pay this tax. In addition, the Jordanian Government has asked the Iraqi regime to prevent Iraqi border guards from shooting at Iraqi soldiers who try to flee to Jordan. Iraqi border guards fire at fleeing soldiers even after they cross into Jordanian territory.

Students abroad who refuse to return to Iraq are required to reimburse any of their expenses that were paid by the Government. Each student wishing to travel abroad must provide a guarantor. The guarantor and the student's parents may be liable if the student fails to return.

Foreign spouses of citizens who have resided in Iraq for 5 years are required to apply for nationality. The requirement is 1 year of residence for the spouses of citizens employed in government offices. Many foreigners thus have been obliged to accept citizenship and are subject to official travel restrictions. The penalties for noncompliance include, but are not limited to, loss of the spouse's job, a substantial financial penalty, and repayment for any governmental educational expenses.

The Government prevents many citizens who also hold citizenship in another country—especially the children of Iraqi fathers and foreign-born mothers—from visiting the country of their other nationality.

The Government does not provide first asylum or respect the rights of refugees. In northern Iraq, the United Nations High Commissioner for Refugees (UNHCR) worked with the KDP and the PUK on the return of Iraqis who fled into Iran during the September clashes, and along with the Government of Turkey, on the disposition of the Atrush camp.

The Government continued to pursue its discriminatory resettlement policies, including demolition of villages and forced relocation of Kurds, Turkomen, Assyrians, and other minorities. Human rights monitors reported that the Government continues to force Kurdish and Turkomen residents of Mosul and Kirkuk to move to other areas in the north or the south.

Tens of thousands of refugees fled to Iran from northern Iraq after the Iraqi attack on Irbil and other attacks in early September. Hundreds of thousands of others temporarily fled their residences in these areas, although they did not leave Iraq itself. By December, most of these refugees and displaced persons had returned to their residences.

According to the Special Rapporteur, security forces continue to relocate Shi'a inhabitants of the southern marshes to major southern cities. Many have been transferred to detention centers and prisons in central Iraq, primarily in Baghdad, or even to northern cities like Kirkuk, as part of the Government's attempt to "Arabize" traditionally non-Arab areas.

According to the U.N. High Commissioner on Refugees (UNHCR), hundreds of thousands of Iraqi refugees remain abroad—mainly in Iran, Saudi Arabia, Kuwait, Syria, Turkey, Pakistan, and Jordan. Apart from those suspected of sympathizing with Iran, most fled after the Government's suppression of the civil uprising of 1991; others are Kurds who fled the Anfal Campaign of 1988.

Of the 1.5 million refugees who fled following the 1991 uprisings, the great majority, particularly Kurds, have repatriated themselves to northern Iraq, in areas where the allied coalition has prohibited overflights by Iraqi aircraft. Several hundred thousand Kurds remain unsettled in northern Iraq because political circumstances do not permit them to return to their former homes in government-controlled territory.

Both the KDP and the PUK fulfilled security guarantees and provided assistance in evacuating more than 6,000 relief workers and Iraqi oppositionists perceived to be affiliated with the United States.

Approximately 14,000 Turkish Kurds remain in the north who have fled civil strife in southeastern Turkey. The UNHCR is treating these displaced persons as refugees until it reaches an official determination on their status. In late 1996, the UNHCR and the Government of Turkey began implementing a plan to close the Atrush refugee camp and conduct voluntary repatriation of the refugees to Turkey.

Section 3. Respect for Political Rights: The Right of Citizens to Change Their Government

Citizens do not have the right to change their government. Although the Government has taken steps to provide an increased appearance of democracy, the political process is still controlled by the State. There are strict qualifications for candidates; candidates to the National Assembly, by law, must be over 25 years old and "believe in God, the principles of the July 17–30 revolution, and Socialism." In the 250-seat National Assembly 160 deputies reportedly belong to the Ba'ath Party and 60 are independent, Saddam Hussein appointed 30 deputies to represent the northern governorates. According to the Special Rapporteur, the Ba'ath Party allegedly instructed a number of its members to run as nominally "independent" candidates.

Full political participation at the national level is confined to members of the Arab Ba'ath Socialist Party, estimated at about 8 percent of the population. The political system is dominated by the Party, which governs through the Revolutionary Command Council, headed by President Saddam Hussein. However, the RCC exercises both executive and legislative authority. It overshadows the National Assembly, which is completely subordinate to it and the executive branch.

The President wields decisive power over all instruments of government. Almost all powerful officials are either members of his family or are family allies from his hometown of Tikrit.

Opposition political organizations are illegal and severely suppressed. Membership in certain political parties is punishable by death (see Section 2.b.). In 1991 the RCC adopted a law that theoretically authorized the creation of political parties other than the Ba'ath; in practice the law is used to prohibit parties that do not support Saddam Hussein and the current Government. New parties must be based in Baghdad and are prohibited from having any ethnic or religious character.

The Government does not recognize the various political groupings and parties that have been formed by Shi'a Muslims, as well as Kurdish, Assyrian, Turkomen, and other Iraqi communities. These political groups continued to attract support notwithstanding their illegal status.

Women and minorities are underrepresented in government and politics. The law provides for the election of women and minorities to the National Assembly, but they have only token representation.

In northern Iraq, all central government functions have been performed by local administrators, mainly Kurds, since the Government withdrew its military forces and civilian administrative personnel from the area after the 1991 uprising. A regional parliament and local government administrators were elected in 1992. These were the only free and open elections held in Iraq in recent decades, and those only for local officials and institutions. This parliament last met in May 1995. Discussions among Kurdish and other northern Iraqi political groups continue on the reconvening of parliament, but the tensions and maneuverings by both the PUK and KDP continue to prevent parliamentary activity.

Section 4. Governmental Attitude Regarding International and Nongovernmental Investigation of Alleged Violations of Human Rights

The Government does not permit the establishment of independent human rights organizations. It operates an official human rights group that routinely denies allegations of abuses. Citizens have established several human rights groups abroad and in northern areas not under government control.

As in 1995, the Government did not allow the U.N. Special Rapporteur to visit Iraq, nor did it respond to his requests for information on several cases. The Government continued to defy various calls from U.N. bodies to allow the Special Rapporteur to visit the southern marshes and other regions.

In 1996 the U.N. Human Rights Committee and the U.N. Subcommission on Prevention of Discrimination and Protection of Minorities adopted resolutions condemning the Government's human rights violations. For the fourth consecutive year, the UNHRC passed a resolution calling on the U.N. Secretary General to send human rights monitors to "help in the independent verification of reports on the human rights situation in Iraq." The U.N. Subcommission on Prevention of Discrimination and Protection of Minorities adopted a resolution reiterating the UNHRC request for the deployment of monitors. The Government has continued to defy these calls for the entry of monitors.

The Special Rapporteur nonetheless was able to gather more evidence, in part due to interviews with current and past government officials who shed new light on the systemic nature of human rights violations. The Special Rapporteur dispatched members of his staff to Jordan and other locations to interview victims of Iraqi human rights abuses. The Special Rapporteur repeatedly has asserted the need for further resources to carry out his mandate, while recalling that appropriate action on major issues like the Anfal Campaign are beyond the scope of his potential resources (see Section 1.g.).

The Government continues to fail to accept U.N. Security Council Resolution 688, which insists that the Government afford immediate, unrestricted access by humanitarian workers to all those in need of assistance in all parts of Iraq. Throughout 1995 the Government threatened, harassed, and assaulted employees of the U.N. and nongovernmental organizations working in Iraq (see Sections 1.g. and 2.a.).

Section 5. Discrimination Based on Race, Sex, Religion, Disability, Language, or Social Status

The Constitution and legal system provide for some rights for women, chldren, and minorities. However, in practice, the Government systematically abuses these rights.

Women.—Domestic violence against women occurs, but little is known about its extent. Such abuse is customarily addressed within the tightly knit family structure. There is no public discussion of the subject, and the Government issues no statistics. Spousal violence constitutes grounds for divorce and criminal charges, but suits brought on these charges are believed to be rare. Men who kill female family members for "immoral deeds" may receive immunity from prosecution under a 1990 law (see Section 1.c.).

The Special Rapporteur has noted that there is an unusually high percentage of women in the Kurdish areas, purportedly caused by the disappearances of tens of thousands of Kurdish men during the Anfal Campaign. The Special Rapporteur has reported that the widows, daughters, and mothers of the Anfal Campaign victims are economically dependent on their relatives or villages because they may not inherit the property or assets of their missing family members. Other reports suggest that economic destitution has forced many women into prostitution.

Evidence concerning the Anfal Campaign indicates that the Government killed many women and children, including infants, by firing squads and in chemical attacks. Government forces also raped many women during the Anfal campaign as well as during the occupation of Kuwait. Reports indicate that women are raped in custody, but the Government takes no action against the abusers (see Section 1.c.).

The Government claims that it is committed to equality for women, who make up about 20 percent of the work force. It has enacted laws to protect women from exploitation in the workplace and from sexual harassment; to permit women to join the regular army, Popular Army, and police forces; to require education for girls; and to equalize women's rights in divorce, land ownership, taxation, suffrage, and election to the National Assembly. It is difficult to determine to what extent these protections are afforded in practice. Reports indicate, however, that the application of these laws has declined as Iraq's political and economic crisis persists. Women are not allowed to travel outside Iraq alone (see Section 2.d.).

Children.—No information is available on whether the Government has enacted specific legislation to promote the welfare of children. However, the Special Rapporteur and several human rights groups have collected a substantial body of evidence pointing to the Government's continuing disregard for the rights and welfare of children.

The Government's failure to comply with relevant U.N. Security Council resolutions has led to a continuation of economic sanctions. As a result, general economic and health conditions have deteriorated dramatically. Children have been particularly susceptible to the decline in the standard of living. Increases in child mortality and disease rates have been reported.

There were continued accounts of aggressive government action against youths. In February security forces launched an arrest campaign against youths who frequented the Al-Tali'ah Youth Center in Baghdad, after the discovery of leaflets denouncing the ruling regime. In another report, three Jordanian youths, who were on their way to Baghdad aboard a truck laden with sugar, were killed by a gang led by an army midlevel officer. The gang reportedly killed the young men, hacked their bodies into pieces, and scattered them in the desert.

In late July, opposition sources reported that more than 300 children had died while undergoing compulsory training in Fedayeen camps. The Fedayeen system was widely reported by opposition and other sources as another systematic regime effort to extend and solidify its control through forced indoctrination of Iraqi youth.

People with Disabilities

No information is available on the Government's policy towards people with disabilities.

National/Racial/Ethnic Minorities.—Kurds, who make up approximately 20 percent of the population, historically have suffered political and economic discrimination, despite the token presence of a small number of Kurds in the national Government (see Sections 1.a., 1.b., and 1.g.).

Assyrians and Chaldeans are ethnic groups as well as separate Christian communities (see Section 2.c.). Assyrians speak a distinct language—Syriac. Public instruction in Syriac, which was to have been allowed under a 1972 decree, has never been implemented. Numerous reports indicated continued systematic discrimination against Assyrians throughout 1996, especially in terms of forced movements from northern areas and repression of political rights there.

Citizens considered to be of Iranian origin must carry special identification and are often precluded from desirable employment. Over the years, the Government has deported hundreds of thousands of citizens of Iranian origin (see Section 2.d.).

Religious Minorities.—Iraq's cultural, religious, and linguistic diversity are not reflected in the country's political and economic structure. Various segments of the Sunni Arab community, which itself constitutes a small minority of the population, have effectively controlled the Government since independence in 1932. Shi'a Arabs, the overwhelming majority of the population, have long been economically, politically, and socially disadvantaged. Like the Sunni Kurds and other ethnic and religious groups in the north, the Shi'a Arabs of the south have been targeted for particular discrimination and abuse, ostensibly because of their opposition to the Government.

Section 6. Worker Rights

a. *The Right of Association.*—Although Iraq is a party to the 1919 Constitution of the International Labor Organization (ILO), which provides for the freedom of association, trade unions independent of government control do not exist. The Trade Union Organization Law of 1987 established the Iraqi General Federation of Trade Unions, a government-dominated trade union structure, as the sole legal trade federation. The General Federation is linked to the Ba'ath Party, which uses it to promote party principles and policies among union members.

Workers in private and mixed enterprises—but not public employees or workers in state enterprises—have the right to join local union committees. The committees are affiliated with individual trade unions, which in turn belong to the General Federation.

The Labor Law of 1987 restricts the right to strike. No strike has been reported over the past two decades. According to the International Confederation of Free Trade Unions, the severe restrictions on the right to strike include penal sanctions.

The General Federation is also affiliated with the International Confederation of Arab Trade Unions and the formerly Soviet-controlled World Federation of Trade Unions.

b. *The Right to Organize and Bargain Collectively.*—The right to bargain collectively is not recognized. Salaries for public sector workers (the majority of the employed) are set by the Government. Wages in the much smaller private sector are set by employers or negotiated individually with workers.

The Labor Code does not protect workers from antiunion discrimination, a failure that has been criticized repeatedly by the ILO's Committee of Experts.

There are no export processing zones.

c. *Prohibition of Forced or Compulsory Labor.*—Compulsory labor is theoretically prohibited by law. However, the Penal Code mandates prison sentences, including compulsory labor, for civil servants and employees of state enterprises accused of breaches of labor "discipline," including resigning from a job. According to the ILO, foreign workers in Iraq have been prevented from terminating their employment to return to their native countries because of government-imposed penal sanctions on persons who do so.

d. *Minimum Age for Employment of Children.*—The employment of children under the age of 14 is prohibited except in small-scale family enterprises. Children reportedly are increasingly encouraged to work in order to support their families, given the country's harsh economic conditions. The law stipulates that employees between the ages of 14 and 18 work fewer hours per week than adults.

e. *Acceptable Conditions of Work.*—Theoretically, most workers in urban areas work a 6-day, 48-hour workweek. Hours for government employees are set by the head of each ministry. In practice, the rate of absenteeism has likely increased with the deterioration of socioeconomic conditions. There is contradictory information on whether laws and regulations mandate a minimum wage, but the Government makes no effort to protect this or other worker entitlements.

Working hours for agricultural workers vary according to individual employer-employee agreements.

Occupational safety programs are in effect in state-run enterprises. Inspectors theoretically inspect private establishments, but enforcement varies widely.

ISRAEL AND THE OCCUPIED TERRITORIES*

Israel is a parliamentary democracy with a multiparty system and free elections. There is no constitution; a series of "basic laws" provide for fundamental rights. The legislature, or Knesset, has the power to dissolve the Government and limit the authority of the executive branch. On May 29, Likud Party leader Benyamin Netanyahu was elected Prime Minister; he heads a center-right coalition government. The judiciary is independent.

Since its founding in 1948, Israel has been in a state of war with most of its Arab neighbors. It concluded a peace treaty with Egypt in 1979 and with Jordan in 1994. As a result of the 1967 War, Israel occupied the West Bank, the Gaza Strip, East Jerusalem, and the Golan Heights. The international community does not recognize Israel's sovereignty over any part of the occupied territories. Throughout its existence, Israel has experienced numerous terrorist attacks. It relies heavily on its military and security services and retains many security-related regulations from the period of the British Mandate.

An historic process of reconciliation between Israel and its neighbors began with the Madrid Conference in 1991 and continued with the September 1993 signing of the Israeli-Palestinian Declaration of Principles (DOP.) In September 1995, Prime Minister Yitzhak Rabin and Chairman Yasir Arafat of the Palestine Liberation Organization (PLO) signed the Interim Agreement on the West Bank and the Gaza Strip, which provided for the election and establishment of a Palestinian self-governing authority, transfer of civil authority, Israeli redeployment from major Palestinian population centers in the West Bank, security arrangements, and cooperation in a variety of areas. Palestinian elections were held in January. Negotiations on permanent status—which are to address the status of Jerusalem, Palestinian refugees, Israeli settlements in the West Bank and Gaza, final security arrangements, borders, and other issues of common interest—began on May 5 and were immediately adjourned.

Internal security is the responsibility of the General Security Service (GSS)—(Shin Bet, or Shabak), which is under the authority of the Prime Minister's office. The police are under the authority of the Minister of Interior Security. The Israel Defense Forces (IDF) are under the authority of a civilian Minister of Defense. The IDF includes a significant portion of the adult population on active duty or reserve status and plays a role in maintaining internal security. The Foreign Affairs and Defense Committee in the Knesset reviews the activities of the IDF and Shin Bet. Some members of the security forces committed human rights abuses.

Israel has an advanced industrial economy, and citizens enjoy a high standard of living, with a per capita income of almost $17,000. Unemployment among citizens was approximately 6.5 percent with nearly full employment in some areas. Along with rapid economic growth in recent years there has been a tendency toward increasing income inequality. The long-standing gap in levels of income between Jewish and non-Jewish citizens continues. Israel's growing reliance on foreign workers, principally from Asia and Eastern Europe who are generally employed in agriculture and the construction industry, and comprise about 10 percent of the labor force. Since the implementation of an economic stabilization plan in 1985, Israel has moved gradually to reduce state intervention in the economy. The new Netanyahu Government promised a renewed emphasis on market-oriented structural reforms, especially deregulation and rapid privatization of the economy, but had achieved little progress by year's end. Despite the continued dominant role of the Government in the economy, individuals generally are free to invest in private interests and own property.

---

*The human rights situation in the occupied territories is discussed in the annex appended to this report.

The Government generally respects human rights, and citizens enjoy a wide range of civil and other rights. Israel's main human rights problems have arisen from its policies and practices in the occupied territories. However, the redeployment of the IDF from most major Palestinian population areas in the West Bank in December 1995, and its previous withdrawal from Gaza and Jericho, have significantly reduced these problems. In September, however, Israel's opening of an archeological tunnel near the Temple Mount in Jerusalem and the subsequent calls by Palestinian leaders to protest this decision sparked confrontations between Israeli security forces and Palestinians expressing their frustrations over the slow pace of the peace process. These demonstrations escalated into several days of fighting between Israelis and Palestinians and left 16 Israelis and 58 Palestinians dead and many hundreds injured.

The authorities continue to hold and mistreat Palestinian security detainees, and detention and prison conditions, particularly for Palestinians, are poor. However, new legislation during the year set tighter limits on the length and grounds for pre-trial detention. New legislation also broadened children's rights and made the basis for comparing men's and women's compensation more equitable. Proposed legislation defining the basis for and limits of GSS activities, circulated to interested groups in 1995 for their comment, was widely criticized for because it authorized the Government to use force during interrogation and to issue secret guidelines defining the methods of interrogation. The legislation has not been formally submitted to the Knesset.

The Government responded to terrorist and security incidents by tightening existing restrictions on movement across borders with the West Bank and Gaza, and demolishing the homes of some suspected terrorists and their families in the occupied territories.

The Government took steps to address discrimination and violence against women. It pledged to eliminate the social and economic gap between Israel's Arab and Jewish citizens; however, the Arab minority still does not share fully in the rights granted to, and the obligations imposed on, Jewish citizens.

RESPECT FOR HUMAN RIGHTS

Section 1. Respect for the Integrity of the Person, Including Freedom From:

a. Political and Other Extrajudicial Killing.—There are no reports of political killings by government forces. During the year, however, at least two Palestinians died while in Israeli custody, two after apparently being tortured by other Palestinians (see Section 1.a. and Section 1.c. of the annex.)

Two extremist Islamic groups, the Islamic Resistance (Hamas) and the Palestine Islamic Jihad (PIJ), made a concerted effort during the year to undermine the authority of the Palestinian Authority and derail the Israeli-Palestinian peace process by killing Israeli civilians in a series of deadly suicide bombing attacks in Jerusalem, Tel Aviv, and Ashkelon (see Section 1.g.). On June 9, terrorists shot and killed an Israeli couple in a car 12 miles southwest of Jerusalem.

On October 3, a Tel Aviv court sentenced Yigal Amir, the killer of former Prime Minister Yitzhak Rabin, to an additional 5 years in prison. Amir is already serving a life term. The court also sentenced the killer's brother, Hagai Amir, to 12 years, and a third man, Dror Adani, to 7 years, for plotting Rabin's murder. The three men were also found guilty of planning attacks against Palestinians, and Hagai Amir was convicted of various weapons charges.

In September Israel's opening of a controversial tunnel near Muslim and Jewish holy sites in Jerusalem and calls by the Palestinian Authority (PA) for Palestinians to protest the move sparked several days of violent clashes between Israeli security forces and Palestinian security officers and civilians. Fifty-eight Palestinians (including 11 Palestinian security officers) and 16 IDF soldiers and border police officers died in the fighting, and some 1,500 persons were injured (see Section 1.g. of the annex).

b. Disappearance.—There were no reports of politically motivated disappearances.

c. Torture and Other Cruel, Inhuman, or Degrading Treatment or Punishment.— Although laws and administrative regulations prohibit the physical abuse of detainees, the head of Shin Bet is empowered to authorize security officers to use use "moderate physical and psychological pressure" in interrogating Palestinian detainees. In certain "ticking bomb" cases the GSS has "greater flexibility" to employ "special measures" when deemed necessary to obtain information to save lives. These measures have been applied against Palestinians suspected of involvement in planning terrorist acts, and include the practice of violent shaking (see Section 1.c. of the annex).

The practice of shaking was challenged repeatedly before the Israeli Supreme Court during the year by human rights groups and attorneys for individual detainees. In two cases in November, the Court upheld the right of the GSS to use "special measures" and "force" against Palestinian prisoners. However, in a number of cases, the Court ordered the GSS to show cause that this method of interrogation was necessary in order to obtain information directly related to citizens' safety. While in a number of cases the GSS succeeded in meeting the Court's standard, and shaking was authorized, the show-cause orders constitute some restriction on the use of the method.

In August the authorities detained Bashar Tarabieh, a part-time employee of the nongovernmental organization (NGO) Human Rights Watch, who had been visiting his family in the Golan Heights. For 8 days he was held without charge in a jail near Haifa, in a separate section for the detention and interrogation of security prisoners. Between repeated interrogation sessions he was frequently hooded and tied to a chair in a contorted position. He was held in a cell with poor sanitary conditions, and for much of his detention given food that was inedible. After international attention brought his case to light, he was released without charge.

Conditions vary in incarceration facilities in Israel and the occupied territories, which are administered by the Israeli Prison Service (IPS), the national police, or the Israel Defense Forces. IPS prisons usually meet minimum international standards. Generally, IPS inmates are not subject to physical abuse by guards, food is adequate, and prisoners receive basic necessities. Inmates receive mail, have television sets in their cells, and receive regular visits. Prisoners receive wages for prison work and benefits for good behavior. Many IPS prisons have drug treatment, educational, and recreational programs. The IPS has established an investigatory committee to look into charges of violence by guards against inmates.

Since the closure in 1995 of the main IDF detention camps in the occupied territories, all security detainees from the occupied territories who are held for more than a few days are transferred to facilities within Israel. Security detainees in 1996 were held in IDF camps in Israel, but also in IPS facilities and in special sections of police detention facilities. Prisoners incarcerated for security reasons are subject to a different regimen, even in IPS facilities. They are often denied certain privileges given to prisoners convicted on criminal charges. Security prisoners include some minors. Detention camps administered by the IDF are limited to male Palestinian security prisoners and are guarded by armed soldiers. The number of security prisoners, 4,900 at the beginning of 1996, varied between 3,800 and 4,200 during the year, and was approximately 3,800 at year's end.

Conditions at some national police detention facilities can fall below minimum international standards. Such facilities are intended to hold criminal detainees prior to trial, but often become de facto prisons. Those held include some security detainees and some persons who have been convicted and sentenced. Inmates in the national police detention facilities are often not accorded the same rights as prisoners in the IPS. Moreover, conditions are worse in the separate facilities for security detainees maintained both in police facilities and in IPS prisons.

In response to a series of reports by the Association for Civil Rights in Israel (ACRI) that were critical of the country's detention facilities, the Government in April presented a plan for widespread reform, including renovation of existing police and IPS facilities and construction of new ones. By year's end some improvements had been made in the country's major detention facilities. A new prison, built to modern standards for incarceration, was opened at Tsalmon. A detention facility in Beersheva that had been criticized for its very poor conditions was shut down. Some detainees from police facilities were moved to the IPS to relieve overcrowding. Funds were allocated to rebuild the Abu Kabir facility in the Tel Aviv area, and some minor renovations were made in Jerusalem's Russian Compound detention center, in which up to 50 Palestinian detainees had been crowded into 4-bed cells.

Thus far improvements have been limited in scope, and dilapidation and overcrowding (the latter aggravated by the closure of IDF detention facilities in the occupied territories) are still problems. New legislation enacted in May and scheduled to take effect in 1997 defines the minimum conditions for detainees. The minimum conditions for detainees include: The right to live in conditions that would not harm the health or dignity of the detainee; access to adequate health care; the right to a bed for each detainee; and access to exercise and fresh air on a daily basis.

Children's rights groups have expressed particular concern over the separate sections of holding facilities set aside for the detention of children. Overcrowding, poor physical conditions, lack of social workers, and denial of visits by parents are among the key problems. In addition to some Israeli minors held in criminal cases, there are juveniles among Palestinian detainees. Children's rights activists have recommended the construction of a separate detention facility for children.

Conditions in IDF detention camps have been criticized repeatedly over the years. In May the Ketziot Detention Camp in the Negev, regarded as having had the harshest conditions, was closed. Conditions at Meggido detention facility near Afula remain difficult, where 90 percent of detainees are housed in tents. Conditions in remaining facilities improved in some respects, with inmates given more time for exercise outside their cells. Nevertheless, recreational facilities remain minimal, and severe limitations remain on family visits to detainees. Visits were prevented for long periods during closures of the borders with Gaza and the West Bank, including a 4-month closure after the February-March bombings.

All incarceration facilities are monitored by various branches of the Government, by members of the Knesset, and by the International Committee of the Red Cross (ICRC) and other human rights groups. In somes instances, human rights groups and diplomatic officials encountered difficulties gaining access to specific detainees, usually Palestinians held for security offenses (see Section 1.d. of the annex).

d. *Arbitrary Arrest, Detention, or Exile.*—The law prohibits arbitrary arrest of citizens, and the Government observes this prohibition. Defendants are considered innocent until proven guilty, and have the right to writs of habeas corpus and other procedural safeguards. However, a 1979 law permits administrative detention without charge or trial. The Minister of Defense may issue a detention order for a maximum of a year. Within 48 hours of issuance, detainees must appear before a district judge who may confirm, shorten, or overturn the order. If the order is confirmed, an automatic review takes place after 3 months. Detainees have the right to be represented by counsel and appeal detention orders to the Supreme Court. At detention hearings, the Government may withhold evidence from defense lawyers on security grounds. It may also seek to renew administrative detention orders.

In felony cases, a district court judge may postpone for 48 hours the notification of arrest to the detainee's attorney. The postponement may be extended to 7 days by the Minister of Defense on national security grounds or by the Police Inspector General to conduct an investigation. Moreover, a judge may postpone notification for up to 15 days in national security cases.

New legislation enacted in May, which takes effect in 1997, defines more narrowly the grounds for pretrial detention, and reduces to 24 hours the length of time a person may be held without charge. Children's rights activists have recommended separate legislation to define when and how a child may be arrested and how long children may be detained.

Administrative orders issued by the IDF central command continued to restrict the movements of some members of the Jewish ultranationalist Kach and Kahane Chai organizations who live in the occupied territories. In October two Israeli settlers in Hebron were detained due to indications that they might incite violence as the Hebron negotiations were beginning.

Most of the protections afforded by law are not extended to Palestinian detainees, who fall under the jurisdiction of military law even if they are detained in Israel. With IDF redeployment on the West Bank, detention centers there were closed, and all Palestinian detainees held for longer than 1 or 2 days are incarcerated in Israel. The Government does, however, observe some humanitarian provisions of the Fourth Geneva Convention with regard to these detainees (see Section 1.d. of the annex).

The Government detains 140 non-Palestinian Arabs, who comprise a mixture of common prisoners, administrative detainees, and security detainees. It continues to deny the ICRC access to two Lebanese citizens, Sheikh Mustafa Dirani and Sheikh Obeid. The disposition of these two cases appears linked to government efforts to obtain information on Israeli military personnel believed to be prisoners of war or missing in Lebanon.

In 1995 the Government expelled a Jordanian citizen and a West Bank Palestinian into the security zone in southern Lebanon. While the Jordanian has since returned to Jordan, the Palestinian still is being given shelter by the United Nations Interim Force In Lebanon (UNIFIL). The ICRC has taken up his case with the Government.

The law prohibits forced exile of citizens, and it is not used.

e. *Denial of Fair Public Trial.*—The law provides for an independent judiciary, and the Government respects this provision in practice. The judiciary provides citizens with a fair and efficient judicial process.

The judicial system is composed of civil, military, religious, labor relations, and administrative courts, with the Supreme Court at the apex. The Supreme Court is an appellate court. Each of the cited courts, including the Supreme Court, have appellate courts or jurisdictions.

The law provides for the right to a hearing with representation by counsel, and authorities observe this right in practice. A planned regional and national system of public defenders operated by the Ministry of Justice was inaugurated in 1996 with the opening of a Tel Aviv office, although that office has suffered serious budget shortages and faces further cutbacks in 1997.

All nonsecurity trials are public except those in which the interests of the parties are deemed best served by privacy. Cases involving national security may be tried in either military or civil courts and may be partly or wholly closed to the public. The Attorney General determines the venue in such cases. The prosecution must justify closing the proceedings to the public. Adult defendants have the right to be represented by counsel even in closed proceedings but may be denied access to some evidence on security grounds. Convictions may not be based on any evidence denied to the defense. Nevertheless, in the 1995 case of Mohammed Salah, he was denied access to some evidence, but it is not clear that he was convicted on the basis of that evidence.

f. *Arbitrary Interference with Privacy, Family, Home, or Correspondence.*—Although privacy of the individual and the home are generally protected by law, authorities sometimes interfere with mail and monitor telephone conversations. In criminal cases, the law permits wiretapping under court order; in security cases, the order must be issued by the Ministry of Defense. Under emergency regulations, authorities may open and destroy mail on security grounds (see Section 1.f. of the Annex).

g. *Use of Excessive Force and Violations of Humanitarian Law in Internal Conflicts.*—In April in response to Katyusha rocket salvos launched by the terrorist organization Hizballah from southern Lebanon against towns and civilian areas in northern Israel, the Government responded with an aerial and artillery counterattack. The IDF attempted to confine its initial attacks to the Hizballah-controlled areas from which the rockets had come; however, many Hizballah launching sites were intermingled with, or located close to, Lebanese civilian areas. The fighting subsequently intensified to include attacks on Beirut and blockades of Lebanese ports. The conflict resulted in more than 150 civilian deaths and hundreds of wounded civilians on the Lebanese side, and dozens of wounded civilians in Israel.

The Israeli military operation—known as Grapes of Wrath—included a public call on Lebanese civilians in the south to move away from areas that Israel intended to attack. As a result, the operation created 200,000 to 300,000 or more temporary refugees. In northern Israel, Hizballah salvos caused 20,000 to 30,000 civilians to abandon their homes. Lebanese observers and some Israeli media commentators alleged that a central tactic of Grapes of Wrath was to put pressure on the Lebanese Government to restrain Hizballah by generating a large northward flow of Lebanese refugees toward Beirut. Israel clearly stated that it did not intend to injure civilians, but would not allow Hizballah to fire from within villages and conceal itself among the civilian population. Hizballah declared that its aim was to create a flow of Israeli refugees in retaliation.

On April 18, Hizballah fired mortar rounds at an Israeli military unit from a position very near the U.N. compound at Qana, and the IDF responded with artillery fire. A number of Israeli shells struck the compound, killing 102 civilians who had sought shelter there and wounding others. The Government expressed regret for these casualties, but insisted that the U.N. compound had not been shelled intentionally. A U.N. report concluded, however, that it was unlikely that the shelling was due to technical or procedural error.

Negotiations to end the fighting resulted in an April 26 understanding under which the two parties committed not to target civilians or to use civilian-populated areas or nonmilitary public installations as launching grounds for attacks. An international monitoring group was established to investigate complaints of violations of the understanding. This group, the Israel-Lebanon Monitoring Group (ILMG), continued to function throughout the remainder of the year, with the participation of the United States, France, Syria, Israel, and Lebanon.

Politically motivated intercommunal killings continued as extremists sought to disrupt the Israel-Palestinian peace process. On February 25, two Palestinian suicide bombers struck in Jerusalem and at a road junction near the southern coastal city of Ashkelon. The Jerusalem explosion killed 25 persons, including three U.S. citizens. In Ashkelon one person was killed and 36 injured. On March 3, another suicide bomber killed 19 persons, including Palestinian and Romanian workers, and wounded 7 in Jerusalem. The following day a fourth bomber killed 14 persons—including 6 children—and injured more than 100 others at an intersection in central Tel Aviv. On December 22, a court in Lod sentenced two Palestinians to consecutive life terms for driving suicide bombers to the scenes of the bombing attacks in Jerusalem and Ashkelon.

See also Section 1.g. of the annex.

Section 2. Respect for Civil Liberties, Including

　a. *Freedom of Speech and Press.*—The law provides for freedom of the press, and the Government generally respects this right in practice. The law authorizes the Government to censor any material reported from Israel or the occupied territories regarded as sensitive on national security grounds. A new censorship agreement signed on May 22 between the Government and media representatives continues the trend to broaden liberalization of Israel's censorship regime. The agreement provides that military censorship is to be applied only in cases involving national security issues that have a near certainty of harming Israel's defense interests, and now applies to all media organizations in Israel, including local and Arabic-language newspapers. All media organizations can appeal the censor's decision to the Supreme Court. Moreover, a new clause abolishes the right of the censor to shut down a newspaper for a censorship violation and eliminates the ability of the office of the censor to appeal a decision against it. News printed or broadcast abroad may be reported without censorship.

　Emergency regulations prohibit anyone from expressing support for illegal organizations. The Government occasionally prosecutes persons for speaking or writing on behalf of terrorist groups. No such cases were filed in 1996.

　Individuals, organizations, the press, and the electronic media freely debate public issues and criticize government officials and policies. A public debate on the legitimate exercise of the freedom of speech, sharpened by the November 1995 killing of Prime Minister Rabin, continued during the year. New concerns were raised by the actions of angry right-wing extremists who criticized the Supreme Court and issued threats against the life of Chief Justice Aharon Barak. There was also scattered praise from extremists for Rabin's killer. The head of the Zo Artsenu movement was tried for sedition and the case is still pending. For the most part, however, the Attorney General, while condemning hate speech, concluded that such speech could not be prosecuted.

　All newspapers are privately owned and managed. Newspaper licenses are valid only for Israel; separate licenses are required to distribute publications in the occupied territories.

　Directed by a government appointee, the quasi-independent Israel Broadcast Authority (IBA) controls television channel 1 and Kol Israel radio, both major sources of news and information. Six cable companies operate under franchises granted by government-councils. Privately owned channel2 television, the first commercial television channel, is operated by three franchise companies. Seven regional radio franchises were joined by another 6, bringing to 13 the number of private radio outlets. The Second Television and Radio Authority, a public body, supervises both channel 2 and the regional radio stations.

　The May elections focused public attention on a provision of the communications law that prohibits the visual image of candidates to be screened during the last 30 days of a campaign. A bill to change this law was debated in the Knesset, but deferred, even though cable news channels like Cable News Network (CNN) and the British Broadcasting Corporation (BBC) were not prohibited from broadcasting images of the candidates. Another part of the law that prohibits paid political advertising on television was also debated but was not changed.

　b. *Freedom of Peaceful Assembly and Association.*—The law provides for these rights, and the Government generally respects them in practice. After the Hebron massacre in 1994, the Cabinet invoked the 1948 Ordinance for the Prevention of Terror to ban the ultranationalist Kach and Kahane Chai organizations, a ban that remains in effect. The decision stipulates imprisonment for anyone belonging to, or expressing support for, either organization.

　Demonstrations by ultra-Orthodox Jews in July and August were organized to force the municipality of Jerusalem to close the city's Bar-Ilan Street, a main throughfare, to traffic on the Sabbath. The demonstrators committed acts of civil disobedience and violence. The police used excessive force in countering the demonstrators.

　c. *Freedom of Religion.*—The law provides for freedom of religion, and the Government respects this right. Approximately 81 percent of citizens are Jewish. Muslims, Christians, Druze, and members of other religions make up the remaining 19 percent. Each recognized religious community has legal authority over its members in matters of marriage and divorce. Secular courts have primacy over questions of inheritance, but parties, by mutual agreement, may bring cases to religious courts. Jewish and Christian families may ask for some family status matters, such as alimony and child custody in divorces, to be adjudicated in civil courts as an alternative to religious courts. New legislation passed during the year allows the rabbinical courts to sanction either party who is not willing to grant a divorce.

Many citizens object to the Orthodox Jewish religious authorities' exclusive control over marriage, divorce, and burial, whether persons are Jewish or not. These authorities do not recognize marriages or conversions to Judaism performed in Israel by Conservative or Reform rabbis. These issues have been a source of sharp division within society, particularly in recent years, as thousands of Jewish immigrants from the former Soviet Union have brought with them family members not recognized as Jewish by these Orthodox authorities. The divisions grew sharper during the year, as Jewish religious extremists, asserting the supremacy of religious law over democracy, threatened the life of the Chief Justice of the Supreme Court, and of local Reform rabbis.

A large number of Jews who wish to be married in secular or non-Orthodox religious ceremonies do so abroad. The Ministry of Interior recognizes such marriages. New Knesset legislation provided for the right to civil burials, and land for the first secular cemeteries was recently designated.

Missionaries are allowed to proselytize in Israel, although Mormons are specifically prohibited from doing so by mutual agreement between the Church of Jesus Christ of the Latter-Day Saints and the Government. A 1977 antiproselytizing law prohibits anyone from offering or receiving material benefits as an inducement to conversion, but the law has not been applied for several years.

A 1995 Supreme Court ruling allows small numbers of Jews under police escort to pray on the Temple Mount, which is the site of two Muslim holy places and also the location of the First and Second Jewish Temples.

d. *Freedom of Movement Within the Country, Foreign Travel, Emigration, and Repatriation.*—The law provides for these rights, and the Government respects them in practice for citizens, except with regard to military or security zones or in instances where citizens may be confined by administrative order to their neighborhoods or villages. During the year, rabbinical courts asserting jurisdiction over divorce cases refused at least two visiting U.S. citizens permission to depart the country until their cases were tried (see Section 5). The Government continued to limit the movements of some Jewish settlers living in the occupied territories who belonged to extremist Kach or Kahane Chai groups (see Section 2.d. of the Annex).

Citizens are free to travel abroad and to emigrate, provided they have no outstanding military obligations and are not restricted by administrative order. In 1996 the Government again permitted Muslim citizens over 30 years of age to perform the religious pilgrimage to Mecca, but it denied permission to Muslim citizens under 30 years of years of age on security grounds. The Government asserts that travel to Saudi Arabia, which is still in a state of war with Israel, is a privilege and not a right.

The Government welcomes Jewish immigrants, their families, and Jewish refugees, on whom it confers automatic citizenship and residence rights under the Law of Return. This law does not apply to non-Jews or to persons of Jewish descent who have converted to another faith. Other than the Law of Return, which applies only to Jews, and the family reunification statutes, which mainly apply to Arabs who fled Israel in 1948–49, Israel has no immigration law that provides for immigration to Israel, or for political asylum. The law does allow qualified individuals to live in Israel as permanent residents.

The issue of first asylum did not arise in 1996. The Government cooperates with the office of the United Nations High Commissioner for Refugees and other humanitarian organizations in assisting refugees.

Section 3. Respect for Political Rights: The Right of Citizens to Change Their Government

The law provides citizens with the right to change peacefully their government, and citizens exercise this right in practice through periodic, free, and fair elections held on the basis of universal suffrage for adult citizens. In May general elections were held for the 14th Knesset and, for the first time, the voters elected the Prime Minister by direct ballot.

Israel is a parliamentary democracy, with an active multiparty system representing a wide range of political views. Relatively small parties, including those whose primary support is among Israeli Arabs, regularly win seats in the Knesset. Elections are by secret ballot.

While there are no legal impediments to the participation of women and minorities in government, they are underrepresented. Women hold 9 of 120 Knesset seats, compared with 11 female members in the previous Knesset. There are 11 Arab and 1 Druze in the new Knesset, compared with 7 and 2 prior to the May election; most represent parties deriving their support largely or entirely from the Arab community. Of the Knesset's 12 committees, 2 (including the Committee on the Status of Women) are chaired by a woman and another is chaired by the Druze member of the legislature. There is one woman in the Cabinet, as compared with 2 in the previous government. There are no Arab or Druze ministers or deputy ministers in the new government. Three women, but no Arab or Druze citizens, serve on the 14-member Supreme Court.

Section 4. Governmental Attitude Regarding International and Nongovernmental Investigation of Alleged Violations of Human Rights

A wide variety of human rights groups operate without government restriction, investigating and publishing their findings on human rights cases. Government officials are generally cooperative and responsive to their views.

Section 5. Discrimination Based on Race, Sex, Religion, Disability, Language, or Social Status

The law prohibits discrimination on the basis of sex, marital status, or sexual orientation. The law also prohibits discrimination by both government and nongovernment entities on the basis of race, religion, political beliefs, and age. Local human rights groups are concerned that resources for implementing those laws, or mechanisms for their enforcement, are sometimes lacking.

Women.—There continued to be action, both in and out of government, to deal with the issue of violence against women in Jewish and Arab communities. The Government has allocated funds for a special campaign to combat such violence, and in June a parliamentary committee of inquiry issued a report recommending a number of measures to combat the problem at its source. Groups that focus on domestic violence include a committee established by the Ministry of Labor and Social Affairs that includes Jewish and Arab nongovernmental organizations (NGO's) as well as government representatives, and a coalition of human rights organizations. Approximately 16 women were killed by husbands or other male relatives during the year. According to the most recent estimates, some 200,000 women suffer from domestic violence each year, and some 7 percent of these are abused on a regular basis.

Arab human rights advocates also have formed a coalition to raise public awareness of so-called family honor killings, a term commonly used for the murder of a female by a male relative for alleged misconduct.

The Government supports seven shelters for battered women, including one exclusively for Arab women. There are plans for a total of 12 shelters, including 2 for Arab women, although women's rights advocates consider this number inadequate.

According to the 1991 Domestic Violence Law, a district or magistrate court may prohibit access by violent family members to their property. Women's groups cooperate with legal and social service institutions to provide women's rights education. While sentences handed down to men convicted of rape have increased in recent years, women's rights activists note that the penalties are not sufficiently harsh.

Civil rights groups also expressed concern about an increased incidence of physical attacks by Jewish religious extremists, particularly in Jerusalem, against women whom they consider to be immodestly dressed in public.

Women's advocacy groups report that women routinely receive lower wages for comparable work, are promoted less often, and have fewer career opportunities than their male counterparts. In March the Equal Pay Law, which required employers to pay male and female workers equal wages for equal work, was replaced by new legislation that redefines compensation to include important side benefits, and allows for class action suits. An amendment to the social security law allowed housewives some access to the nation's social security pension system.

Legislation in 1993, reinforced by a 1994 ruling of the High Court of Justice, or the Supreme Court in other circumstances, has increased the percentage of women on the boards of two-thirds of government-owned companies. Their numbers remain low overall, however. One study reported that in 1996 women made up more than 30 percent of the boards in only 39 of 118 government-owned companies.

The adjudication of personal status law in the areas of marriage and divorce is left to religious courts, where Jewish and Muslim women are subject to restrictive interpretations of their rights (see Section 2.c.). Legislation passed in 1995 broadens the civil sanctions made available to rabbinical courts in cases where a wife has ample grounds for divorce—such as abuse—but the husband has refused to agree. In some cases, however, rabbinical courts have failed to invoke these sanctions. In some cases where a wife has failed to agree, a husband has been allowed to remarry; this permission is not given to wives. Such imbalances have been used by husbands to extort concessions from their wives in return for agreeing to divorce.

In at least two cases during the year, the rabbinical court imposed civil sanctions on persons not citizens of Israel. This court asserted jurisdiction over Jewish U.S. citizens visiting Israel who had received civil divorces in the United States but whose former wives was seeking a religious divorce through the rabbinical court in

Israel. The U.S. citizens were denied permission to leave Israel until the courts heard the cases (see section 2.d.). In 1996 the court heard one of the cases and ruled in early 1997 that it had no jurisdiction in the matter because the U.S. citizen was not a resident or a citizen of Israel. However, the U.S. citizen was not permitted to leave the country when a second, related case was filed against him in the district rabbinical court.

Religious law can be even more restrictive for Muslims: some Islamic law courts have held that Muslim women may not request a divorce, but that women may be forced to consent if a divorce is granted to a man.

Jewish women are subject to the military draft but have been barred from combat positions. During the year the Israeli Air Force, acting on a landmark Supreme Court ruling handed down in 1995, for the first time admitted women to IDF pilot training, which would qualify them for combat aviation positions. Two classes with women members are in training. At the same time, a new petition before the Court charged the national police force with discrimination against women, in recruiting, assignments open to female officers, and promotions. The petition was still pending at year's end.

Children.—The Government is strongly committed to the rights and welfare of children, including in the areas of education and health care. However, resources are sometimes insufficient to put that commitment into practice, particularly in the case of low-income families. Education is compulsory to the age of 15, or until the child reaches the 10th grade, whichever comes first. Government ministries, children's rights groups, and members of the legislature often cooperate on children's rights issues.

Legislative landmarks in the area of children's rights during the year included the requirement that the psychiatric hospitalization of a child be reviewed by a court, as it must in the case of an adult; the extension to children of confidentiality in HIV testing; and the ruling that in any family status court case, such as divorce, the children affected or their legal representatives must be heard.

The Government has legislated against sexual, physical, and psychological abuse of children, and has mandated comprehensive reporting requirements. Although there has been a sharp increase in reported cases of child abuse in recent years, activists believe that this is largely due to increased awareness of the issue rather than a growing pattern of abuse. There are now four shelters in Israel for children at risk, and a fifth is scheduled to open. The Stockholm Conference raised public awareness of the issue of child prostitution. The Ministry of Justice formed a committee with police and NGO representatives that is attempting to assess the scope of the problem. Children's rights activists estimate that there may be several hundred prostitutes among the nation's children, and warn that the phenomenon is unlikely to be eradicated until the social problems that give rise to it—including child abuse and schools that give up too readily on dropouts—are addressed.

NGO's in the field of children's welfare concentrate their efforts on public education, on promoting the concept of children's rights as citizens, on improving legal representation for minors, and on combating the problems of poverty, which are most notable for the Bedouin children of the south. There has been concern over the children of Israel's growing population of foreign workers, many of them in the country illegally. Children of such families, believed to number in the thousands, exist in a legal and social limbo, without access to schools or adequate health services.

Privately funded children's rights information centers have been established in some communities, and the Government assists in funding additional centers in other cities.

People With Disabilities.—The Government provides a range of benefits, including income maintenance, housing subsidies, and transportation support for disabled persons, who comprise about 10 percent of the population. Existing antidiscrimination laws do not prohibit discrimination based on disability, and these citizens continue to encounter difficulties in areas such as employment and housing. A law requiring access for the disabled to public buildings is not widely enforced. There is no law providing for access to public transportation for people with disabilities. A new law extended disability assistance for deaf children from age 14 to maturity.

Religious Minorities.—In civic areas where religion is a determining criterion, such as the religious courts and centers of education, non-Jewish institutions routinely receive less state support than their Jewish counterparts. The status of a number of Christian organizations with representation in Israel has heretofore been defined by a collection of ad hoc arrangements with various government agencies. Several of these organizations are negotiating with the Government in an attempt to formalize their status. Attempts to establish meaningful negotiations are ongoing.

National/Racial/Ethnic Minorities.—The Government does not provide Israeli Arabs, who constitute 18 percent of the population, with the same quality of education, housing, employment, and social services as Jews. Government efforts to close the gaps between Israel's Jewish and Arab citizens have resulted in an estimated 160 percent increase in resources devoted to Arab communities between 1992 and 1996. Nevertheless, significant differences remain.

Relative to their numbers, Israeli Arabs are underrepresented in the student bodies and faculties of most universities and in higher-level professional and business ranks. A small number of Israeli Arabs have risen to responsible positions in the civil service, generally in the Arab departments of government ministries. A 1994 Civil Service Commission 3-year affirmative action program to expand that number has had only modest results. The Government has allocated only very limited resources to enforce landmark 1995 legislation prohibiting discrimination in employment.

In practice, Israeli Arabs are not allowed to work in companies with defense contracts or in security-related fields. The Israeli Druze and Circassian communities are subject to the military draft, although some have refused to serve. Some Bedouin and other Arab citizens who are not subject to the draft serve voluntarily. Those not subject to the draft have less access than other Israelis to those social and economic benefits for which military service is a prerequisite or an advantage, such as housing, new-household subsidies, and government or security-related industrial employment. Under a 1994 government policy decision, the social security child allowance for parents who have not served in the military is being increased over a 3-year period to equal the allowance of those who have served in the military.

The Government has yet to fulfill its commitment to resolve the legal status of unrecognized Arab villages. Eight villages have been recognized since 1994, but nearly a hundred more, of varying size and with a total population of nearly 70,000 people, remain in limbo. Such villages have none of the infrastructure, such as electricity, provided to recognized villages and towns. Private efforts have supplied some with water. In the Negev, a government program to provide housing for thousands of Bedouin in seven concentrated settlements has been criticized as likely to aggravate the severe poverty there and disrupt the indigenous culture.

Arab children make up about a quarter of Israel's public school population, but government resources for them are not equal to those for Jewish children. Many schools in Arab communities are dilapidated and overcrowded, lack special education services and counselors, have poor libraries, and have no sports facilities. Arab groups also note that the public school curriculum stresses Israel's Jewish culture and heritage.

Unresolved problems of many years' standing also include claims by Arab groups that land expropriation for public use has affected the Arab community disproportionately; that Arabs have been allowed too little input in planning decisions that affect their schools and municipalities; that mosques and cemeteries belonging to the Islamic Waqf have been unjustly expropriated for public use; and that successive governments have blocked the return of persons displaced in the early years of Israel's history to their homes. The Government has yet to agree with the pre-1948 residents of the northern villages of Bir Am and Ikrit, and their descendants, regarding their long-time demand to be allowed to rebuild their houses; in the meantime, permission has been given to Jewish settlements to increase their land holdings in the disputed areas.

Section 6. Worker Rights

a. *The Right of Association.*—Workers may join and establish labor organizations freely. Most unions belong to Histadrut (the General Federation of Labor in Israel), or to a much smaller rival federation, the Histadrut Haovdim Haleumit (National Federation of Labor.) These organizations are independent of the Government. Histadrut members democratically elect national and local officers, and officials of its affiliated women's organization Na'amat, from political party lists. Plant or enterprise committee members are elected individually.

During the year, the Histadrut administration continued its drastic reshaping of the labor federation, with further reductions in staff and services, as Histadrut shifted its concentration to those areas directly related to employment. In 1995 a new national health insurance law severed the link between Histadrut and Kupat Holim Clalit, the nation's largest health maintenance organization, in the process ending Histadrut's chief source of income. Membership in Histadrut dropped sharply once it was no longer necessary to join the federation in order to have access to its health plan. Histadrut is seeking to expand its membership in areas not presently organized, such as small businesses and factories, even where collective bargaining agreements do not exist. At the end of 1996, membership—which once reached 1.8 million people—had climbed back to about 700,000.

The right to strike is exercised regularly. Unions must provide 15 days' notice prior to a strike unless otherwise specified in the collective bargaining agreement. However, unauthorized strikes occur. Strike leaders—even those organizing illegal strikes—are protected by law. If essential public services are affected, the Government may appeal to labor courts for back-to-work orders while the parties continue negotiations. There were a number of strikes in both public and private sectors during the year by employees protesting the effects of privatization. Worker dismissals and the terms of severance arrangements were often the central issues of dispute.

Palestinians from the West Bank and Gaza Strip who work in Israel may not join Israeli trade unions or organize their own unions in Israel. Palestinian trade unions in the occupied territories are not permitted to conduct activities in Israel (see Section 6.a. of the annex). However, nonresident workers in the organized sector are entitled to the protection of Histadrut work contracts and grievance procedures. They may join, vote for, and be elected to shop-level workers' committees if their numbers in individual establishments exceed a minimum threshold. Palestinian participation in such committees is minimal.

Labor laws apply to Palestinians in East Jerusalem and to the Syrian Druze living on the Golan Heights.

Unions are free to affiliate with international organizations.

b. *The Right to Organize and Bargain Collectively.*—Israeli workers fully exercise their legal rights to organize and bargain collectively. While there is no law specifically prohibiting antiunion discrimination, the law against discrimination could be cited to contest discrimination based on union membership. No antiunion discrimination has been reported.

Nonresident workers may not organize their own unions or engage in collective bargaining, but they are entitled to be represented by the bargaining agent and protected by collective bargaining agreements. They do not pay union membership fees, but are required to pay a 1-percent agency fee which entitles them to union protection by Histadrut's collective bargaining agreements. The Ministry of Labor may extend collective bargaining agreements to nonunionized workplaces in the same industrial sector. The Ministry of Labor also oversees personal contracts in the nonorganized sectors of the economy.

There are no export processing zones.

c. *Prohibition of Forced or Compulsory Labor.*—The law prohibits forced or compulsory labor. Neither Israeli citizens nor nonresident Palestinians working in Israel are subject to this practice. Civil rights groups charge that unscrupulous employers often take advantage of illegal workers' lack of status (see Section 6.e.) to hold them in conditions amounting to involuntary servitude.

d. *Minimum Age for Employment of Children.*—Children who have attained the age of 15 years, and who are liable to compulsory education under the Compulsory Education Law, may not be employed unless they work as apprentices under the Apprenticeship Law. Notwithstanding these provisions, children who are 14 years old may be employed during official school holidays. Employment of those ages 16 to 18 years is restricted to ensure time for rest and education.

There are no reliable data on illegal child workers. They are concentrated among Israel's Arab population and its newest Jewish immigrants. Illegal employment is found primarily in urban, light-industrial areas. Children's rights groups have called for more vigorous enforcement of child labor laws, combined with a parallel effort to deal with the causes of illegal child labor.

e. *Acceptable Conditions of Work.*—Legislation in 1987 established a minimum wage at 45 percent of the average wage, calculated periodically and adjusted for cost of living increases. At year's end, the minimum wage stood at about $620 (roughly 2,000 new Israeli shekels) per month. The minimum wage is often supplemented by special allowances and is generally sufficient to provide workers and their families with an acceptable standard of living. Union officials have expressed concern over enforcement of minimum wage regulations, particularly with respect to employers of illegal non-resident workers who sometimes pay less than the minimum wage.

By law the maximum hours of work at regular pay are 47 hours a week, 8 hours per day, and 7 hours on the day before the weekly rest, which must be at least 36 consecutive hours and include the Sabbath. By national collective agreements, the private sector established a maximum 45-hour workweek in 1988. The public sector moved to a 5-day, 42½ hour workweek in 1989, while the military adopted it in 1993.

Employers must receive a government permit to hire nonresident workers from the occupied territories, certifying that no citizen is available for the job. All Palestinians from the occupied territories are employed on a daily basis and, unless they are employed on shiftwork, are not authorized to spend the night in Israel. Palestinians without valid work permits are subject to arrest.

Nonresident workers are paid through the Employment Service of the Ministry of Labor, which disburses wages and benefits collected from employers. The Ministry deducts a 1 percent union fee and the workers' required contributions to the National Insurance Institute (NII), the agency that administers the Israeli social security system, unemployment benefits, and other benefits. Despite these deductions, Palestinian workers are not eligible for all NII benefits. They continue to be insured for injuries occurring in Israel and the bankruptcy of a worker's employer. They do not have access to unemployment insurance, general disability payments, low-income supplements, or child allotments. By contrast Israeli settlers in the occupied territories who work in Israel have the same benefits as other Israeli workers. The International Labor Organization has long criticized this inequality in entitlements. The Government agreed to transfer the NII fees collected from Palestinian workers to the PA, which will assume responsibility for all the pensions and social benefits of Palestinians working in Israel. Implementation of this change is still underway.

Along with union representatives, the Labor Inspection Service enforces labor, health, and safety standards in the workplace, although resource constraints affect overall enforcement. Legislation protects the employment rights of safety delegates elected or appointed by the workers. In cooperation with management, these delegates are responsible for the safety and health of the workplace. Workers do not have the legal right to remove themselves from dangerous work situations without jeopardy to continued employment. However, collective bargaining agreements provide some workers with recourse through the work site labor committee. Any worker may challenge unsafe work practices through government oversight and legal agencies.

There was increased public debate over the role in the workplace and society of foreign workers, who are estimated to number 200,000 or more, perhaps half of them undocumented and illegally employed. The majority of such workers come from eastern Europe and southeast Asia, and most are employed in the construction and agricultural sectors. The law does not allow such workers citizenship or permanent residence in Israel. As a result, they and their families live in a legal and social limbo. Government deportations of such workers take place without benefit of due process.

THE OCCUPIED TERRITORIES

(INCLUDING AREAS SUBJECT TO THE JURISDICTION OF THE PALESTINIAN AUTHORITY)

Israel occupied the West Bank, Gaza Strip, Golan Heights, and East Jerusalem during the 1967 War. The West Bank and Gaza Strip are now administered to varying extents by Israel and the Palestinian Authority(PA). Pursuant to the May 1994 Gaza-Jericho Agreement, Israel transferred most responsibilities for civil government in the Gaza Strip and Jericho to the PA. The Agreement on Preparatory Transfer of Powers and Responsibilities of August 1994, and the Interim Agreement provided for the further transfer of civil authority to the Palestinians, including education, culture, health, tourism, taxation, social welfare, statistics, local government, insurance, commerce, industry, fuel, gas, agriculture, and labor. Israel continues to retain responsibility in the West Bank and Gaza Strip for external security, foreign relations, the overall security of Israelis, including public order in the Israeli settlements, and certain other matters. Negotiations on the final status of the occupied territories as well as of Jerusalem, borders, Israeli settlements, refugees, and other matters began in May but were immediately adjourned and did not resume by year's end. Israel and the Palestinian Authority agreed on January 15, 1997 to resume these talks within 60 days. According to the timetable set out in the DOP, the interim period is to conclude in May 1999.

In addition to most of the Gaza Strip and the Jericho area, which was turned over to the Palestinians in May 1994, Israel began redeploying its forces in the West Bank and turning over major towns and villages to the PA in late 1995. Pursuant to the Interim Agreement and the "Protocol Concerning Redeployment in Hebron," concluded on January 15, 1997, Israel redeployed its forces in Hebron. Israel continues to control some civil functions and is responsible for all security in portions of the occupied territories categorized as Zone C, which includes the Israeli settlements. The PA has jurisdiction over civil affairs and shares security responsibilities with Israel in areas known as Zone B, and the PA has control over civil affairs and security in Zone A. The PA also has jurisdiction over some civil affairs in Zone C. Accordingly, this report discusses the policies and practices of both the Israeli Government and the Palestinian Authority in the areas where they exercise jurisdiction and control.

Israel continues to exercise civil authority in some areas of the West Bank through the Israeli Ministry of Defense's Office of Coordination and Liaison, known by Hebrew acronym MATAK, which replaced the now defunct Civil Administration (CIVAD). The approximately 150,000 Israeli settlers living in the West Bank and Gaza Strip are subject to Israeli law and are better treated by Israeli forces than are Palestinians. The body of law governing Palestinians in the Israeli-controlled portions of the territories derives from Ottoman, British Mandate, Jordanian, and Egyptian law and Israeli military orders. In Palestinian-controlled areas, regulations promulgated by the PA are also in force. The United States considers Israel's authority in the occupied territories to be subject to the Hague Regulations of 1907 and the 1949 Geneva Convention relating to the protection of civilians in time of war. The Israeli Government considers the Hague Regulations applicable and states that it observes the Geneva Convention's humanitarian provisions.

In January the Palestinian Authority chose its first popularly elected government in democratic elections, which were generally well-conducted. An 88-member Legislative Council and Ra'ees (president or chairman) of the executive authority were elected. The PA also has an appointed cabinet of 20 ministers who oversee 19 ministries. PA Chairman Yasir Arafat continues to dominate the affairs of government and to make major decisions. Most senior government positions and positions of authority in the PA are held by individuals who are members of, or loyal to, Arafat's Fatah faction of the Palestine Liberation Organization (PLO). The elected 88-person Legislative Council meets frequently and discusses a range of issues significant to the Palestinian people and the development of an open, democratic society in the Gaza Strip and West Bank. Pursuant to a series of agreements between the PA and Israel, the PA now also has full or partial control over major Palestinian population centers in the Gaza Strip and West Bank.

Israeli security forces in Israeli-controlled parts of the West Bank and Gaza Strip consist of the Israel Defense Forces (IDF); the General Security Service (GSS or Shin Bet); the police; and the paramilitary border police. Israeli military courts try Palestinians accused of committing security crimes in Israeli-controlled areas. Members of the Israeli security forces committed human rights abuses.

The Palestinian Police Force (PPF) was established in May 1994 and includes the Palestinian National Security Force (PNSF); the Palestinian civil police; the Preventive Security Force (PSF); General Intelligence Service, or Mukhabarat; the civil defense force; and the Palestinian Presidential Security Force. Several other quasi-military security organizations, such as the coast guard and military intelligence, also exercise law enforcement powers. Palestinian police are responsible for security and law enforcement for Palestinians and other non-Israelis in PA-controlled areas of the West Bank and Gaza Strip. Israeli settlers in the occupied territories are not subject to Palestinian security force jurisdiction. Members of the PA security forces committed human rights abuses.

The economies of the West Bank and Gaza Strip are small, poorly developed, and highly dependent on Israel. The economic situation deteriorated significantly during the year as a result of closures of the territories imposed by Israel after security incidents, including several serious terrorist bombings. Both areas rely on agriculture, services, and to a lesser extent, light manufacturing. Many West Bank and Gaza workers are employed at day jobs in Israel and Jerusalem, making their employment vulnerable to disruption due to closures. The West Bank and Gaza economies were significantly damaged by a closure first imposed by Israel in 1993. In the wake of terrorist bombings in Israel in February and March and violent clashes between Israeli and Palestinian forces in September, Israel temporarily tightened the existing closure, sealing off the West Bank and Gaza Strip from Israel, prohibiting most travel between towns and villages within the West Bank (the "internal closure"), denying Palestinian workers access to jobs in Israel, and hampering the flow of goods and people between Israel and the occupied territories. The "internal closure" was lifted in each case after about 2 weeks. The general closures of Gaza and the West Bank followed a pattern of being eased but then reimposed in the wake of new security threats. Partly as a result of the closures, the per capita Gross National Product of Palestinians in the West Bank and Gaza Strip dropped by approximately 39 percent between 1992 and 1996 (from $2,425 to $1,480.) By year's end, however, the closure had eased in important ways.

There were some improvements in the human rights situation in the territories. However, both Israel and the PA were responsible for serious human rights abuses.

Two Islamic groups, the Islamic Resistance Movement (HAMAS) and the Palestine Islamic Jihad (PIJ), made a concerted effort this year to undermine the authority of the PA and restrict the Israeli-Palestinian peace process by killing Israeli civilians in a series of deadly suicide bombing attacks in Jerusalem, Tel Aviv, and Ashkelon. The most serious attacks occurred in late February and early March. On February 25, two Palestinian suicide bombers struck in Jerusalem and at a road junction near the southern coastal city of Ashkelon. The Jerusalem explosion killed 25 persons, including three U.S. citizens. In Ashkelon one person was killed and 36 injured. On March 3, another suicide bomber killed 19 persons, including Palestinian and Romanian workers, and wounded 7 in Jerusalem. The following day a fourth bomber killed 14 persons—including 6 children—and injured more than 100 others at an intersection in central Tel Aviv.

In the aftermath of those terrorist bombings, Israeli authorities arrested approximately 1,000 Palestinians suspected of affiliation with extremist Islamic and secular opposition groups. Israeli authorities in some cases mistreated prisoners to obtain information on further terrorist attacks. Following the bombings, Israeli authorities demolished the homes of eight Palestinians implicated in terrorist attacks, compared with one demolition in 1995. Israel also tightened its existing closure of the West Bank and Gaza Strip, sealing off the territories from Israel and imposing an "internal closure." There was one credible report that an Israeli undercover unit killed a Palestinian, compared with 10 such deaths in 1995. There were also credible reports that Israeli authorities continue to abuse and torture Palestinian detainees and prisoners. At least two Palestinians died in Israeli prisons, after possibly being tortured by other Palestinians in custody for cooperating with the Israelis. Prison conditions are poor.

In its intensive efforts to counter and prevent terrorism, the Palestinian Authority used excessive force on occasion in its searches of homes, and ordered two opposition newspapers closed. In the wake of terrorist bombings, PA authorities arrested approximately 1,000 Palestinians suspected of affiliation with extremist Islamic and secular opposition groups and held all but one without charge. There were credible reports that PA authorities mistreated prisoners to obtain information on further terrorist attacks. The PA also continued to harass, detain, and abuse journalists and political activists who criticized the PA. Although the PA claims to tolerate expression of a range of views, human rights watchers say that Palestinian commentators and critics practice self-censorship out of fear that they would be harassed or punished by the PA if they criticized it. The PA strongly discourages dissenting views. There were also credible reports that the PA continues to abuse and torture detainees. Four Palestinians died in PA custody, two after having been tortured, one shot and killed by a prison guard, and one apparently have committed suicide. Prison conditions are very poor.

In September Israel's opening of a controversial tunnel near Muslim and Jewish holy sites in Jerusalem and calls by the PA for mass demonstrations to protest the move sparked several days of violent clashes between Israeli security forces and Palestinian security officers and civilians. Fifty-eight Palestinians (including 11 Palestinian security officers) and 16 IDF soldiers and border police officers died in the fighting. Israeli and Palestinian security forces used excessive force during the clashes. During clashes in Ramallah and Rafah, Israeli forces shot at demonstrators from a helicopter gunship and from elevated sniper positions; Israeli forces also shot persons who were trying to evacuate wounded Palestinians. Palestinian security forces in Gaza prevented the timely evacuation of wounded Israeli journalists.

Terrorist attacks against Israelis continued after the series of deadly bombings in February and March. In April two gasoline firebombs were hurled at an Israeli commuter bus at Beit Omar, a village near Hebron, injuring 5 people. Two Palestinians with alleged Hamas sympathies shot and killed an Israeli with American citizenship and wounded another Israeli at a settlement at Beit El in May. In November Islamic militant Mohammud Assaf, who was reportedly preparing to launch a suicide attack against Israel, was killed in the West Bank town of Qabatya, when a bomb exploded prematurely in his hands. Palestinians believed to be affiliated with extremist Islamic and secular opposition groups killed two Israelis and wounded three in attacks in the West Bank.

Israeli settlers continued to harass and threaten Palestinians in the West Bank and Gaza Strip, and they killed three Palestinians in 1996, whereas settlers killed four Palestinians in 1995.

The number of Palestinians killed by other Palestinians for collaborating with Israel decreased again in 1996.

RESPECT FOR HUMAN RIGHTS

Section 1. Respect for the Integrity of the Person, Including Freedom From:

a. *Political and Other Extrajudicial Killing.*—There were credible reports that Israeli undercover units, disguised as Palestinians, operated in Palestinian areas during 1996. In June an alleged undercover unit shot and killed a 28-year old Palestinian man outside his home in the Ras al-Amud neighborhood of Jerusalem. In October three Palestinians were shot and wounded by a probable undercover unit in an incident outside of Bethlehem. In 1995 there were 10 deaths attributed to undercover units.

According to human rights organizations, undercover units have deliberately killed suspects under circumstances in which they might have been apprehended alive. Such operations normally have taken place at night when there are few eyewitnesses. Accounts of witnesses, when available, often differ from the IDF version.

Israeli authorities acknowledge that the undercover units conduct operations among Palestinians wanted for investigation, but claim that such units observe the same rules of engagement as other IDF units. They further claim that the IDF investigates all killings and allegations of misbehavior. However, human rights groups state that the investigations are not conducted efficiently and rarely lead to serious punishment. The IDF does not announce the findings of its investigations.

The IDF killed four Palestinians at military checkpoints and roadblocks at Israeli borders and inside the occupied territories in 1996. In these cases, the IDF said that the individuals were shot after they failed to obey soldiers' orders to halt.

In January armed Palestinians in a car fired on three Israeli soldiers a West Bank checkpoint near Jenin. The soldiers returned fire, killing three armed Palestinians. Palestinian witnesses largely agreed with the IDF's official account of the shooting.

In February following a suicide bus bombing in Jerusalem, Israeli security forces and civilians shot and killed a Palestinian-American after he drove a rented car into a crowded bus stop in Jerusalem, killing 1 Israeli and injuring 22 others. Israeli authorities investigated the incident and determined that the man, who had a history of mental problems, acted deliberately.

In November Israeli soldiers shot amd killed a Palestinian and wounded 11 others when a protest against expansion of a West Bank settlement near Ramallah turned violent. An Israeli army spokesperson said that the protesters hurled stones at the soldiers who at first tried to disperse the crowd with rubber bullets and gunshots into the air, but later shot into the crowd when they believed that their lives were in danger. Eyewitnesses dispute that Israeli soldiers lives were in danger. Also in November, Israeli soldiers shot and killed 18-year-old Iyad Mahmoud Badran, a passenger in a vehicle that the soldiers ordered to stop. The vehicle stopped, but when it moved into reverse, the soldiers fired.

A fine of less than $0.01 (one agora) fine was passed down by a military court in November on four soldiers who confessed to having killed a Palestinian in 1993.

In January Hamas operational leader Yahya Ayyash was killed in the Gaza Strip, when a remote-controlled booby-trapped cellular telephone blew up as he was using it. Ayyash was considered the mastermind of several suicide bombings that killed and wounded dozens of Israelis in 1994 and 1995.

At least two Palestinians died in an Israeli prison after being tortured, possibly by other Palestinians. 'Abdel-Rahman 'Omar Saleem Al-Kilani, an alleged Hamas member and suspected collaborator, died while in administrative detention in Israel's Megiddo military detention center on February 1. Human rights monitors and autopsy findings suggest that several Palestinian prisoners tortured him and that he died from the resulting shock. It is unclear why he was tortured. 'Adel 'Ayed Yousef Al-Shahateet, an administrative detainee, died at Megiddo military detention center in Israel on February 15 after being tortured. There are conflicting accounts as to whether Israeli prison officials or Palestinians tortured him.

The Palestinian Authority security forces, which lack equipment and training in crowd control, used excessive force to break up demonstrations in a number of instances. In September Palestinian police in Nablus shot and killed one Palestinian and injured two while trying to stop fans from rioting during a soccer match. Palestinian police in Nablus killed one Palestinian when trying to break up a demonstration in August. In March PA police injured six persons while breaking up a demonstration in Nablus.

In 1996 four Palestinians died in PA custody, two after being tortured, one after he apparently committed suicide. A fourth was shot and killed. The PA disciplined the officers involved in three of the four deaths.

In the first case, Mahmoud Jmaiel, a 26-year-old resident of Nablus, died while in the custody of the Palestinian coast guard in Nablus in July. An autopsy revealed that Jmaiel, who was brain dead for a day before dying, had been severely tortured. The autopsy and photographs of the body revealed burns from cigarettes and a hot iron device, deep bruises, a fractured skull, and extensive bleeding in the brain. Hundreds of demonstrators marched on police headquarters in Nablus and denounced the officers who tortured Jmaiel. The city was paralyzed by a general strike, the first time this protest tactic was used against the PA. Three coast guard officials found responsible for Jmaiel's death were tried and sentenced to 15 years' imprisonment by the Palestinian security court within days of the death. The Mandela Institute for Political Prisoners alleges that the three coast guard officers did not have adequate legal representation or time to prepare their case.

In a second case, there were reports that a Palestinian prisoner was killed in detention in Al-Bireh during interrogation on March 31. A PA military court in Jericho found two security officers, one a military intelligence officer and the other from the Preventive Security Service, guilty of "causing his death" and of "improper use of a weapon" in the incident.

In the third case, an elderly Palestinian man apparently hanged himself in PA custody in Ramallah after being arrested for beating to death a woman in a land dispute. The man's family initially accused the PA of torturing him. However, the PA maintained that the death had been a suicide; therefore, no disciplinary measures were taken.

In the final case, in December prison guard Assam Jalaiteh shot and killed a prisoner in Jericho. The prisoner, Rashid Fityani, was arrested in January 1995 with his brother-in-law, Salman Jalayta, on suspicion of killing a member of Hamas and cooperating with Israel. Jalayta died after 2 days in custody, apparently as a result of torture. No disciplinary action was taken against guards in that death. The prison guard who shot and killed Fityani, however, was convicted of using excessive force and sentenced to life imprisonment within days of the shooting.

Five members of the Palestinian security forces who allegedly killed suspected Palestinian collaborator Muhammad Al-Jundi in Gaza in 1995 have not yet been tried for the killing, according to the PA.

In September clashes between Israeli security forces and PA security forces and Palestinian civilians resulted in numerous deaths (see Section 1.g.).

Palestinians suspected of being members of organizations opposed to the peace process also killed six Israelis and wounded eight in attacks in the West Bank. On December 11, militants reportedly belonging to the Popular Front for the Liberation of Palestine ambushed a car with a family of seven Israelis at a crossroad outside the village of Surda. They killed a 12-year-old Israeli boy, Ephraim Tsur, and his mother, Etta Tsur, and wounded the five other persons in the vehicle. One week later, the PA State Security Court convicted three men for these killings. The Court sentenced two of the men—Abdel Nasser Qaisi and Ibrahim Qam—to life imprisonment at hard labor. The third, Ibrahim Mussad, was sentenced to 15 years' imprisonment for driving the getaway car. Two women were injured in a drive-by shooting near Bethlehem in August. A Palestinian with alleged Hamas sympathies stabbed and killed an Israeli soldier in Janin in January. Two Palestinians with alleged Hamas sympathies shot and killed an Israeli with American citizenship and wounded another Israeli at a settlement at Beit El in May. The Palestinian Authority arrested and is holding one of the killers, who has confessed to the killing at Beit El. Palestinian gunmen shot and killed two Israeli soldiers in January near the village of Halhoul, north of Hebron.

Israeli settlers continued to harass and attack Palestinians. In October a 10-year-old Palestinian boy died after being beaten by a settler near Bethlehem. The settler was indicted for manslaughter. In February a settler shot and wounded a Palestinian teenager. In August a settler from Jerusalem stabbed a Palestinian near Jerusalem. In December Ibrihim Abdullah Hamdan Abu Nasir was killed by a Israeli settler in Gaza in December; charges are pending.

Israel punished several settlers who attacked Arabs. One settler was sentenced to life in prison for killing a Palestinian in 1994. Rabbi Moshe Levinger served less than 5 months of a 7-month jail sentence for attacking Arabs in 1992. In February Israeli authorities arrested a Tapuah settler for allegedly shooting three Palestinians in 1995 and 1996.

Palestinian civilians killed an estimated 8 Palestinians during the year, for suspicion of collaboration with Israeli security services. In 1995, 14 Palestinians were killed for the same reason. Approximately six Palestinians suspected of collaboration with Israel were killed in the West Bank. Human rights organizations charge that at least two Palestinians suspected of collaboration were killed in jail by fellow Palestinian prisoners.

b. *Disappearance.*—There were no reports of politically motivated disappearances attributed to either Israeli or Palestinian security services.

c. *Torture and Other Cruel, Inhuman, or Degrading Treatment or Punishment.*—International, Israeli, and Palestinian human rights groups and diplomats continue to provide credible reports that Israeli security forces were responsible for widespread abuse, and in some cases torture, of Palestinian detainees. The Landau Judicial Commission in 1987 condemned torture but allowed for the use of "moderate physical and psychological pressure" to secure confessions and obtain information. There continued to be a high number of complaints of mistreatment and torture during interrogation, especially from those suspected of belonging to Islamic groups. Interrogation sessions are long and severe, and solitary confinement is used frequently for long periods. The GSS systematically uses interrogation methods which do not result in detectable traces of ill-treatment on the victims, or which leave marks that disappear after a short period of time.

Common interrogation practices reportedly include hooding; forced standing or squatting for long periods of time; prolonged exposure to extreme temperatures; tying or chaining the detainee in contorted and painful positions; blows and beatings with fists, sticks, and other instruments; confinement in small and often filthy spaces; sleep and food deprivation; and threats against the detainee's life or family. Israeli interrogators continued to subject prisoners to violent "shaking," which in at least one case has resulted in death. The apparent intent of these practices is to disorient and intimidate prisoners in order to obtain confessions or information. The International Committee of the Red Cross (ICRC) declared in 1992 that such practices violate the Geneva Convention. Human rights groups and attorneys challenged the practice of shaking before the Israeli High Court. In a number of cases, the Court ordered the GSS to show cause for use of this method to obtain information. In many of the cases, the Court authorized the GSS to use the shaking method.

Although the Israeli Penal Code prohibits the use of force or violence by a public official to obtain information, the GSS chief is permitted by law to allow interrogators to employ "special measures" that exceed the use of "moderate physical and psychological pressure" when it is deemed necessary to obtain information that could potentially save Israeli lives in certain "ticking bomb" cases. The GSS first permitted interrogators "greater flexibility" in applying the guidelines shortly after a bus bombing in Tel Aviv in October 1994 that killed 22 Israelis. The Government has not defined the meaning of "greater flexibility." At roughly quarterly intervals, the Government has approved the continued use of "special measures," arguing that they were vital because their use had prevented terrorist attacks. In November the Government granted another 3-month extension of the "special measures" provision. In November the Israeli High Court of Justice authorized the GSS to use "special measures" against a Palestinian prisoner, and "force" to extract information from another Palestinian prisoner. In both cases, the prisoners were alleged terrorists whom the Israelis believed had information concerning imminent terrorist attacks, making these "ticking bomb" cases.

Israeli authorities maintain that torture is not condoned, but acknowledge that abuses sometimes occur and are investigated. However, the Government does not generally make public the results of such investigations. Israel conducted 60 investigations into the 83 complaints received in 1996. In the investigations conducted, the Israeli Government concluded that the findings did not justify any steps being taken against the interrogators.

Most convictions in security cases before Israeli courts are based on confessions. A detainee may not have contact with a lawyer until after interrogation, a process that may last days or weeks. The Government does not allow ICRC representatives access to detainees until the 14th day of detention. Human rights groups point to this prolonged incommunicado detention as contributing to the likelihood of abuse. Detainees sometimes claim in court that their confessions are coerced but judges rarely exclude such confessions. Human rights groups also assert that Palestinian detainees frequently fail to make complaints either from fear of retribution or because they assume that their complaints will be ignored.

There were 83 formal complaints submitted by Palestinian detainees resident in the occupied territories against the GSS for mistreatment during interrogation. Complaints of abuse are forwarded to the Department for Police Investigations at the Ministry of Justice, which investigates complaints against the GSS. During the year, there were no known cases in which a confession was disqualified because of improper means of investigation or interrogation.

Israeli authorities also frequently treat Palestinians in an abusive manner at checkpoints. In November security officers were videotaped beating and humiliating a group of Palestinian workers. Following a public outcry in Israel when the videotape was shown on television, the two policemen involved were suspended. The Prime Minister condemned the incident, calling it "unpardonable." The chief of the Israeli border police confirmed that many such incidents occur. More than 300 formal complaints were filed against border policemen, and the Ministry of Justice confirmed that complaints of violence and harassment had increased this year. According to the Israeli government, 73 cases were closed because the petitioners did not cooperate with the investigation, 47 cases were closed for lack of evidence, and 26 were dismissed as unjustified. In 33 cases border guards were prosecuted; in 14 other cases they were referred for disciplinary action; and the rest remain under investigation.

Security officers who man checkpoints often act capriciously in honoring permits and travel passes held by Palestinians. Following the election of the Palestinian Legislative Council, PA council members from Gaza were subjected to long delays and searches at Israeli checkpoints in the West Bank, even though they were travelling on special passes issued by Israel. In September a leading Gazan businessman who had obtained Israeli approval to travel with foreign diplomats between Gaza and the West Bank was verbally abused and forced to walk almost a kilometer through the checkpoint to rejoin the diplomats. In October a blind Palestinian with American citizenship was detained at a checkpoint for 5 hours, verbally abused, and accused of "faking" her blindness. In March IDF soldiers in the northern West Bank arrested an elderly Palestinian man tending his animals, stripped him naked, and forced him to walk home.

According to credible reports, PA security forces abused, and sometimes tortured, Palestinian detainees. Such abuse generally takes place after arrest and during interrogation. The PA does not prohibit the use of force or torture against detainees. In 1995 the Gaza Civil Police commander issued to police officers in the West Bank and Gaza a circular forbidding torture during interrogation and directing the security forces to observe the rights of all detainees. The circular, however, does not have the force of law; Palestinian security officers have not been issued formal guidelines on the proper conduct of interrogations.

PA security officials reportedly abused prisoners by hooding, beating, tying in painful positions, sleep deprivation, threats, and burning detainees with cigarettes and hot instruments. A 1995 report by the Israeli human rights group B'tselem claimed that mistreatment of detainees and improper arrest and detention procedures by the Preventive Security Service (PSS) in Jericho reflects PA policy. The Palestinian Centre for Human Rights (PCHR) and other Palestinian human rights groups denied that there is evidence of systematic abuse, but cited numerous incidents of mistreatment, especially of detainees accused of collaboration with the Israelis, affiliation with certain political or extremist groups, or the commission of crimes, such as drug dealing, prostitution, or rape. On some occasions prisoners were denied prompt and adequate medical care after being abused.

In 1996 four Palestinians died in PA custody, two after being tortured, one after he apparently committed suicide, and one was shot and killed. In August Ayman Sabbah charged from his hospital bed that he had been tortured by PA security forces after being arrested during an anti-PA protest.

Israeli settlers harassed Palestinians. For example, settlers rampaged through Arab neighborhoods in the old city of Jerusalem in June, stoned Arab cars in Beit-El in February, and shot at Palestinians in Bethlehem in February.

Prison conditions in Israeli facilities are poor. Facilities are overcrowded, sanitation is poor, and medical care is inadequate. Palestinian inmates held strikes and protests in support of a number of causes and to protest prison conditions. Prisoners in Megiddo military detention center in Israel rioted in April over their treatment during investigations into the deaths of two Palestinians who were allegedly killed by other Palestinians. Palestinians in Israeli prisons also held several strikes to protest being held in administrative detention, lack of visits by family members or lawyers, Israel's refusal to release female Palestinian prisoners, and to protest abuse by prison authorities. Israel permits independent monitoring of prison conditions, although human rights groups and diplomats encountered difficulties gaining access to specific detainees.

Prison conditions in PA facilities are very poor. Facilities are overcrowded and dilapidated. Food and clothing for prisoners is inadequate and must be supplemented by donations from families and humanitarian groups. Palestinian inmates held strikes and protests in support of a number of causes and to protest prison conditions. Palestinians who were arrested by PA authorities after a wave of terrorist bombings in February and March went on strike in April and June to protest poor prison conditions, being held in solitary confinement, and being held in administrative detention. The PA has not allocated its Ministry of Justice funds to make improvements.

The PA permits independent monitoring of prison conditions, although human rights groups encountered difficulties arranging visits or gaining access to specific detainees. In September the PA signed an agreement with the International Committee of the Red Cross (ICRC) allowing the ICRC access to PA-run prisons. The ICRC had not had access to Palestinian detention facilities and prisons since 1995. In accordance with the agreement, the ICRC began prison visits in both the West Bank and Gaza in December.

d. *Arbitrary Arrest, Detention, or Exile.*—Any Israeli policeman or border guard may arrest without warrant a person who has committed, or is suspected of having committed, a criminal or security offense in the occupied territories, except for areas under exclusive PA control. Israeli soldiers may also detain Palestinians and hold them for questioning for the same reasons. Human rights groups say that the vast majority of arrests and detentions are for alleged security offenses. Persons arrested for common crimes are usually provided with a statement of charges and access to an attorney and may apply for bail. However, these procedures are sometimes delayed. Authorities issue special summonses for security offenses. Israeli Military Order 1369 stipulates a 7-year prison term for anyone who does not respond to a special summons delivered to a family member or posted in the MATAK office nearest his home address. Bail is rarely available to those arrested for security offenses. The courts treat persons over the age of 12 as adults.

Israeli authorities may hold persons in custody without a warrant for 96 hours; they must be released unless a warrant is issued. Prearraignment detention can last up to 11 days for Palestinians arrested in the occupied territories and up to 8 days for minors and those accused of less serious offenses. Authorities must obtain a court order for longer detentions—up to 6 months from the date of arrest. Detainees are entitled to be represented by counsel at their detention hearings, although the defense is routinely not allowed to hear the evidence against a suspect. Detainees must be released at the end of the court-ordered detention if they are not indicted. If there is an indictment, a judge may order indefinite detention until the end of the trial. Detainees have the right to appeal continued detention. A Palestinian administrative detainee who was arrested in 1992 for a security offense remains in detention in Israel, having had his detention orders extended eight times to enable the Government to prepare a case against him. A new administrative detention order was issued this fall against the Palestinian held since 1992.

Although a detainee generally has the right to consult with a lawyer as soon as possible, in security cases authorities may delay access to counsel for up to 15 days. Higher-ranking officials or judges may extend this period. Access to counsel is routinely denied while a suspect is being interrogated, which sometimes can last several weeks. Authorities must inform detainees of their right to an attorney and whether there are any orders prohibiting such contact. In April Israeli authorities agreed to let lawyers visit two Palestinians suspected of involvement in a bus bombing in Jerusalem after they had been in prison for nearly 1 month, according to press reports.

A number of factors hamper contacts between lawyers and their clients in Israeli prison and detention facilities. Human rights groups charge that authorities sometimes schedule appointments between attorneys and their detained clients, only to move the clients to another prison prior to the meeting. Authorities reportedly use such tactics to delay lawyer-client meetings for as long as 90 days. Israeli regulations permit detainees to be held in isolation during interrogation. The closure of the occupied territories, which was tightened after a series of terrorist bombings in Israel and Jerusalem in February and March, and again after Palestinian-Israeli clashes in September, also makes it difficult for lawyers to gain access to clients in prison inside Israel. According to the Mandela Institute, in February Israel began allowing only Palestinian lawyers with East Jerusalem identity cards and licenses issued by the Israeli Bar Association or by an official Israeli governmental body such as MATAK or the former Civil Administration to visit detainees in Israeli prisons.

Israeli authorities claim that they attempt to post notification of arrest within 48 hours. In February the Israeli High Court of Justice ordered the State to ensure that the families and attorneys of security prisoners are notified immediately that an arrest has occurred, the location of the prisoner, and whether the attorney may meet his client. Palestinian suspects are nonetheless often kept incommunicado for several days after their arrest.

Palestinians generally locate detainees through their own efforts. Palestinians can check with their local ICRC office to determine whether it has information on the whereabouts of a family member. A senior officer may delay for up to 12 days notification of arrest to immediate family members, attorneys, and diplomatic officials. A military commander may appeal to a judge to extend this period in security cases for an unlimited time.

Israeli district military commanders may order administrative detention (detention without trial) for up to 12 months without formal charges. Administrative detention orders may be extended. Many Palestinians administratively detained over the past 2 years have had their detention orders renewed repeatedly with no meaningful chance of appeal.

There were 270 Palestinians in administrative detention in Israel at year's end, compared with 220 at the end of 1995. Administrative detainees are usually held in the Megiddo prison. The Palestinian Society for the Protection of Human Rights and the Environment, and the Defence for Children International report that at least six children below the age of 16 are being held in administrative detention and have had their orders extended.

Evidence used at hearings for administrative detentions is secret and unavailable to the detainee or his attorney. Lawyers report that during hearings to appeal detention orders, the detainee and defense lawyer are required to leave the courtroom when secret evidence is presented. Israeli authorities maintain that they are unable to present evidence in open court because to do so would compromise the method of acquiring the evidence, which is often provided by informers whose lives would be jeopardized if their identities were known. Detainees may appeal detention orders, or the renewal of a detention order, before a military judge.

There were no deportations for security reasons in 1996.

At year's end, an estimated 3,800 Palestinian prisoners and detainees were incarcerated in Israeli prisons, military detention centers, and holding centers, a decrease from 4,900 incarcerated in 1995. The Israeli Government routinely transfers Palestinians arrested in Israeli-controlled areas of the occupied territories to facilities in Israel, especially Megiddo military detention center near Afula. In May Israel closed the Ketziot detention camp in the Negev desert and transferred its detainees to other prisons in Israel.

Families, human rights organizations, and lawyers have encountered barriers trying to gain access to Palestinian detainees and prisoners held in facilities in Israel as a result of closures of the West Bank and Gaza Strip. Family visits to Palestinian prisoners held in Israeli jails have sharply declined. Only immediate family members, including siblings under the age of 16, are allowed to visit relatives in facilities in Israel. Family members with security records are barred from visiting. Transferring of prisoners between facilities also makes it difficult for families, lawyers, and human rights organizations to locate and visit detainees. Due to travel restrictions, the ICRC suspended its family visits program to detainees in Israeli prisons several times during the year.

Israeli security forces conducted several mass arrests of Palestinians in response to acts or threats of violence against Israelis. Israel arrested approximately 1,000 Palestinians suspected of affiliation with Hamas, the Palestine Islamic Jihad, or the Popular Front for the Liberation of Palestine after a series of suicide bombings in February and March. Of these, approximately 100 were still being held in administrative detention at year's end.

The PA does not have a uniform law on administrative detention, and security officials do not always adhere to the existing Gazan and West Bank laws. Gazan law, which is not observed in the West Bank, stipulates that detainees held without charge be released within 48 hours. Gazan law allows the Attorney General to extend the detention period to a maximum of 90 days during investigations. Human rights organizations and the PA Ministry of Justice assert that PA security officials do not always adhere to this regulation. Five members of the Palestinian police force were detained in Gaza without charge for several months in an internal dispute. Prevailing West Bank law allows a suspect to be detained for 24 hours before being charged. The Attorney General can extend the detention period.

PA authorities generally permit prisoners to receive visits from family members, attorneys, and human rights monitors, except for prisoners held for security reasons. PA security officials are not always aware that lawyers have a right to see their clients. In principle, detainees may notify their families of their arrest, but this is not always permitted.

In 1996 the several PA security services had overlapping or unclear mandates. Although only the civil police are authorized to make arrests, other security services reportedly do so as well. The operating procedures and regulations for conduct of police in the various services are not well developed and have not yet been made available to the public.

There are many detention facilities in the West Bank and Gaza Strip administered by the overlapping PA security services, a situation that complicates the ability of families, lawyers, and even the Ministry of Justice, to track detainees' whereabouts. Security services including the Preventive Security, General Intelligence, military intelligence, and the coast guard have their own interrogation and detention facilities. In general, these services do not, or only sporadically, inform families of a relative's arrest. Most PA security officers remain ignorant of proper arrest, detention, and interrogation procedures as well as basic human rights standards. Approximately 450 Palestinian security officers from various security organizations in the West Bank were trained in basic human rights practices and principles in 1996 by Palestinian human rights groups.

PA security forces continued to arbitrarily arrest and detain journalists, political activists, and human rights advocates, who criticized the PA, such as Iyad Sarraj and Bassim Eid (see Sections 2.a. and 4).

Palestinian security forces in the Gaza Strip and West Bank arrested approximately 1,000 Palestinians in the wake of the suicide bombings in early 1996 and in response to pressure to crack down on terrorism. The majority of arrests were conducted without warrants, and approximately 150 individuals arrested in February and March remain in detention without being charged.

e. *Denial of Fair Public Trial.*—Palestinians accused by Israel of security offenses in Israeli-controlled areas of the occupied territories are tried in Israeli military courts. Security offenses are broadly defined and may include charges of political activity, such as membership in outlawed organizations. Charges are brought by military prosecutors. Serious charges are tried before three-judge panels; lesser offenses are tried before one judge. Defendants have the right to counsel and to appeal verdicts to the court of military appeals, which may accept appeals based on the law applied in the case, the sentence, or both. The right of appeal does not apply in all cases and sometimes requires court permission. The Israeli military courts rarely acquit Palestinians of security offenses, but sentences are sometimes reduced on appeal.

Trials are sometimes delayed for several reasons: Witnesses, including Israeli military or police officers, do not appear; the defendant is not brought to court; files are lost; or attorneys fail to appear, sometimes because they have not been informed of the trial date or because of travel restrictions on Palestinian lawyers. These delays add pressure on defendants to plead guilty to avoid serving a period of pretrial detention that could exceed the sentence. In cases involving minor offenses, an "expedited" trial may be held, in which a charge sheet is drawn up within 48 hours and a court hearing scheduled within days.

By law most Israeli military trials are public, although access is limited. Diplomatic officials are allowed to attend military court proceedings involving foreign citizens, but there have been delays in gaining admission. Most convictions in military courts are based on confessions.

Evidence which is not available to the defendant, his attorney, and occasionally the judges may be used in court to convict persons of security offenses. There is frequently no testimony provided by Palestinian witnesses because, Israeli authorities maintain, Palestinians refuse to cooperate with the authorities. Physical and psychological pressures and reduced sentences for those who confess make it more likely for security detainees to sign confessions. Confessions are usually spoken in Arabic, but translated into Hebrew for the record because, authorities maintain, many Israeli court personnel speak Arabic but few read it. Palestinian detainees seldom read Hebrew and therefore sign confessions that they cannot read.

Crowded facilities and poor arrangements for attorney-client consultations in prisons hinder legal defense efforts. Appointments to see clients are difficult to arrange, and prison authorities often fail to produce clients for scheduled appointments. The temporary tightening of the closure of the West Bank and Gaza Strip following terrorist bombings in February and March and violent Israeli-Palestinian clashes in the West Bank and Gaza Strip in September significantly decreased contact between lawyers and clients in jails in Israel.

Israeli settlers in the West Bank and Gaza Strip accused of security and ordinary criminal offenses are tried under Israeli law in the nearest Israeli district court. Civilian judges preside and the standards of due process and admissibility of evidence are governed by the laws of Israel, not military occupation decrees. Settlers convicted in Israeli courts of crimes against Palestinians regularly receive lighter punishment than Palestinians convicted in Israeli courts of similar crimes against either Israelis or other Palestinians.

The PA inherited a court system based on structures and legal codes predating the 1967 Israeli occupation. The Gaza legal code derives from British Mandate law, Egyptian law, and PA directives and laws. Pre-1967 Jordanian law applies in PA-controlled areas of the West Bank. Bodies of law in the Gaza Strip and West Bank have been substantially modified by Israeli military orders. According to the DOP and the Interim Agreement, Israeli military decrees issued during the occupation theoretically remain valid in both areas and are subject to review pursuant to a specific procedure. The PA is undertaking efforts to unify the Gaza and West Bank legal codes, but it has made little progress.

The PA court system in general is recovering from years of neglect. Judges and staff are underpaid and overworked and suffer from lack of skills and training; court procedures and record-keeping are archaic and chaotic; and the delivery of justice is often slow and uneven. Judges suffer from a lack of police protection. The ability of the courts to enforce decisions is extremely weak, and there is administrative confusion in the appeals process.

In June lawyers representing 10 Bir Zeit students arrested in March without a warrant by the PA for having suspected links to Hamas petitioned the PA to charge or release the students. In August the West Bank High Court of Justice in Ramallah demanded that the PA release the students for lack of cause. Senior PA officials, including Chairman Arafat and the Attorney General, ignored and failed to enforce the order in a timely fashion. According to a lawyer who represented the students, most of them were released more than a month after the order was handed down.

The PA Ministry of Justice appoints all civil judges for 10-year terms. The Attorney General, an appointed official, reports to the Minister of Justice and supervises judicial operations in both the Gaza Strip and West Bank.

In 1995 the PA established state security courts in Gaza and the West Bank to try cases involving security issues. Three military judges preside over each court, which applies civilian law. A senior police official heads the state security court in Jericho, and three judges preside over it. There is no right of appeal, but verdicts may be either ratified or repealed by the PA chairman, Yasir Arafat. According to the PA, during the year, the PA State Security Court handed down sentences to 12 defendants, ranging from a few years in prison to death. There are 10 Palestinians sentenced to death, but none of the sentences have been carried out. According to a press report, Chairman Arafat commuted the death penalties issued by PA courts.

Normal limits on the length of prearraignment detention do not appear to apply to suspects held by a PA security court. Defendants are brought to court without knowledge of the charges against them or sufficient time to prepare a defense. Defendants are represented by court-appointed lawyers. Court sessions often take place on short notice, sometimes even in the middle of the night, at times without lawyers present, all violations of a defendant's right to due process. In some instances, security courts try cases, issue verdicts, and impose sentences in a single session lasting several hours. Terrorists who murdered an Israeli settler and her young son were arrested, tried, and convicted shortly after the crime.

Local and international human rights groups have criticized the PA state security courts, arguing that they are subordinate to the power of the executive and that subordination undermines the independence of the judiciary and violates defendants' rights to a fair and open trial. The PA Ministry of Justice has no jurisdiction over the security courts, according to the PA Attorney General.

The Palestine Center for Human Rights reported that as of April, 83 persons suspected of collaborating with Israel were in PA detention. PA facilities held 150 political prisoners at year's end.

f. *Arbitrary Interference with Privacy, Family, Home, or Correspondence.*—Israeli military authorities in areas of the West Bank under their control may enter private Palestinian homes and institutions without a warrant on security grounds when authorized by an officer of the rank of lieutenant colonel. In conducting searches, the IDF has forced entry, and has sometimes beaten occupants and destroyed property. Israeli authorities say that forced entry may lawfully occur only when incident to an arrest and when entry is resisted. Authorities say that beatings and arbitrary destruction of property during searches are punishable violations of military regulations, and that compensation is due to victims in such cases. According to the Israeli Government, information on the claims against the Ministry of Defense for damages caused as a result of IDF actions has not yet been collected.

In September IDF soldiers forced their way into the West Bank apartment of a Palestinian-American family during clashes with Palestinian demonstrators. The IDF forced the family members out of their apartment, roughed them up, hitting and pushing them, and pointed guns at them. When the family was allowed back into the apartment 3 days later, they found that the soldiers had smashed windows, destroyed furniture and clothing, and fouled the apartment with excrement. The family was later compensated by the Government.

Israeli security forces may demolish or seal the home of a suspect, whether the owner or tenant, without trial. The decision to seal or demolish a house is made by several high-level Israeli officials, including the Coordinator of the MATAK (formerly Civil Administration) and the Defense Minister. Owners of houses ordered demolished have 48 hours to appeal to the area commander; a final appeal may be made to the Israeli High Court. A successful appeal generally results in the conversion of a demolition order to sealing. After a house is demolished, military authorities confiscate the land and prohibit the owner from rebuilding or removing the rubble.

Israeli authorities demolished eight homes for security reasons in 1996, compared with one in 1995. They also sealed one apartment, making it uninhabitable, compared with one partial sealing in 1995. The authorities carried out demolition orders issued in 1995 on the homes of 3 suicide bombers. In addition, authorities demolished the homes of five individuals implicated in suicide bombings, including one Palestinian involved in the 1995 bombing of a bus in Jerusalem who was tried and sentenced by the Palestinian Authority. Israeli authorities sealed the apartment of a suicide bomber after the High Court of Justice ruled that demolishing the apartment would harm other apartments in the building. Human rights groups report that Israeli security forces blew up five of eight houses that were demolished, in many cases damaging surrounding homes. Israel compensated the owners of the damaged homes in some cases.

Many human rights groups criticize the sealing or demolishing of homes because such acts target innocent families and children. The Israeli High Court has stated that the goal of such demolitions is to deter terrorists. An Israeli security official told the Israeli press that blowing up a home had a greater psychological effect than demolishing it using nonexplosive methods.

Owners may apply to regional military commanders for permits to rebuild or unseal their homes. Since 1994 the Israeli Government has allowed the opening or rebuilding of homes sealed or demolished as a result of security offenses committed by a family member after that person has been released from prison. Each former prisoner must apply for a permit to rebuild or unseal a home, which the Government may deny. In 1996 the Government allowed one home to be unsealed.

Israeli security services sometimes monitor the mail and telephone conversations of Palestinians, Israelis, and foreigners. The authorities sometimes interrupt telephone and electricity service to specific areas. In January electricity in villages near Janin was interrupted for several days after a Palestinian killed an Israeli soldier there.

In the Gaza Strip and PA-controlled areas of the West Bank, the PA requires the Attorney General to issue warrants for entry and searches of private property. These requirements are sometimes ignored in Palestinian police sweeps for security suspects. PA police have searched homes without the consent of their owners. In some cases, police have forcibly entered premises and destroyed property. In March Palestinian security forces searched the homes of journalist Rabi' Hussein Rabi and his brother and father without a warrant because they were believed to be affiliated with Hamas. Palestinian security in the Gaza Strip destroyed property during searches of private property and the Islamic University in Gaza in March.

g. *Use of Excessive Force and Violations of Humanitarian Law in Internal Conflicts.*—IDF regulations permit the use of live ammunition only when a soldier's life is in immediate danger, to halt fleeing suspects, to disperse a violent demonstration, or to fire on an "individual unlawfully carrying firearms." According to policy, soldiers should direct fire at the legs only and may fire at a fleeing suspect only if they believe that a serious felony has occurred and they have exhausted other means to apprehend the suspect. It is forbidden to open fire in the direction of children or women, even in cases of severe public disorder, unless there is an immediate and obvious danger to a soldier's life. However, Israeli soldiers and police sometimes used live ammunition in situations other than when their lives were in danger and sometimes shot suspects in the upper body and head.

On September 25, Yasir Arafat called for a general strike and marches to protest the opening of the Hasmonean Tunnel in Jerusalem. However, after the Palestinian reaction spiraled into spontaneous acts of violence and confrontations between Israeli security forces and Palestinians, intense gun battles erupted between Israeli and Palestinian security forces, causing Israeli and Palestinian casualties.

Both sides used excessive force. According to the PA Ministry of Health and human rights groups, 58 Palestinians were killed (including 11 security officers). Fifteen of those Palestinians killed were children under age 18, according to Defense for Children International. Sixteen Israeli soldiers died of wounds from live fire, according to the Israeli Government. The fatalities from this one incident exceeded the number of Israelis and Palestinians killed in violent confrontations in all of 1995.

Palestinian sources contend that Israeli forces in Ramallah and Rafah fired on demonstrators and Palestinian security personnel from helicopter gunships and from elevated sniper positions. Israel also used nonlethal means to disperse rioters, including batons and tear gas. Israeli security forces fired on and killed medical personnel and civilians while they were evacuating wounded. One Palestinian nurse was shot and killed in Gaza while evacuating wounded persons. Palestinian security forces prevented medical care from reaching a wounded Israeli journalist in the Gaza Strip.

In the face of violence, the PA promptly took steps to improve command and control of its forces. During the fighting, the head of the Palestinian security forces in the West Bank traveled with his Israeli central command counterparts to the scenes of the fighting to restore order and discipline. Before the fighting ended, the PA instituted a new procedure barring protests in proximity to Israeli checkpoints. This procedure greatly reduces the possibility of clashes between Israeli security forces and Palestinian protesters. Palestinian security forces reinforced existing instructions to their units forbidding the use of firearms without prior approval and have not hestitated to discipline those guilty of weapons infractions.

During and following the September disturbances, the PA provided protection for and assisted in the evacuation of Israeli security forces stranded at Joseph's Tomb in Nablus.

During the year, extremist Palestinians also killed 4 Israeli soldiers and civilians in the West Bank and PA areas and 58 people in terrorist bombings in Israel (see Section 1.g. of the Israel report).

Section 2. Respect for Civil Liberties, Including:

a. *Freedom of Speech and Press.*—The Israeli Government generally respects freedom of speech in the occupied territories, but prohibits public expressions of support for Islamic extremist groups, such as Hamas, and other groups avowedly dedicated to the destruction of Israel. Continuing a policy it began in 1994, the Israeli Government generally did not enforce its prohibition on the display of Palestinian political symbols, such as flags, national colors, and graffiti, acts which are punishable by fines or imprisonment. In May, however, the IDF raided an elementary school in Hebron and beat pupils for flying a Palestinian flag, according to press reports.

Overall, censorship of specific press pieces continued to be low. Israeli authorities continue to monitor the Arabic press for security-related issues. Military censors review Arabic publications in Jerusalem for material related to the public order and security of Israel and the territories. Reports by foreign journalists are also subject to review by Israeli military censors for security issues, and the satellite feed used by many foreign journalists is monitored.

Israel sometimes closes areas to journalists, usually in conjunction with a curfew or security incident. Israeli authorities have denied entry permits to Palestinian journalists travelling to their place of work in Jerusalem during closures of the territories.

The IDF requires a permit for publications imported into the occupied territories. Imported materials may be censored or banned for anti-Semitic or anti-Israeli content. Possession of banned materials is punishable by a fine and imprisonment. In 1996 Israel refused to allow publications into the Gaza Strip when it tightened its closure of the occupied territories after terrorist bombings in February and March.

Israel closed for 6 months at least six colleges, universities, and recreational and welfare institutions in Jerusalem and Israeli-controlled areas of the West Bank in March after a series of terrorist incidents. Israeli authorities claimed that the institutions served as centers of Hamas activity. In September Israel extended the closure orders on Hebron University, Hebron Technical Institute, and Islamic institutions. These closure orders were lifted in December in anticipation of IDF redeployment in Hebron.

Educational institutions in the West Bank and Jerusalem also closed for periods of time as a result of internal closures in the West Bank that Israel imposed after terrorist attacks in the spring and after clashes between Israeli security forces and PA security forces and Palestinians in September. These closures disrupted the operations of colleges, universities, and schools because significant numbers of students and staff could not travel to the schools from neighboring towns and villages. Following terrorist bombings in the spring, Israeli security forces arrested hundreds of Gazan students in the West Bank and returned them to Gaza. At years' end, Gazan students are still denied travel and residence permits to attend West Bank colleges and universities.

The PA has a generally poor record on freedom of expression and freedom of the press, although it professes to tolerate varying political views and criticism. PA chairman Arafat enacted a press law in 1995 prior to Palestinian elections that Palestinian journalists criticize for not adequately protecting press freedoms. In a report issued in September 1995, Reporters Without Frontiers, a Paris-based journalists' rights group, charged the PA with resorting to "pressure, harassment, arrests, and suspensions" to stifle the independence of the press. It labeled the PA Press Law as restrictive, because it prevents criticism of the police and permits the seizure of newspapers that do so. The Israeli human rights group B'tselem reported that Palestinian journalists now practice self-censorship to avoid antagonizing the

PA. Editors readily admit that they practice self-censorship to avoid being shut down by the PA.

PA officials imposed restrictions on the press in several instances, including closing some opposition newspapers. PA authorities do not permit criticism of Yasir Arafat or his policies or style of government. Twice in 1996, the PA arrested and detained human rights activist Iyad Sarraj for criticizing the PA and Yasir Arafat. On May 18, Palestinian policemen arrested Sarraj for investigation for "slander" based on comments Sarraj made to a Western journalist that were critical of arbitrary arrest and torture committed by PA authorities. Sarraj was released on May 26, and wrote a letter to Arafat reiterating his views. On June 9, police arrested Sarraj again. Sarraj alleged that he was beaten in custody. He was released from custody on June 26. In May the PA Preventive Security Force in Gaza pressured a journalist and his editor to reveal the source of a newspaper article on corruption in the Preventive Security Force. Also in May, PA Chairman Arafat fired a Voice of Palestine talk show host for allowing a caller to criticize the Palestinian security services. In Gaza PA authorities took a radio show off the air after the host complained that PA officials were driving luxury cars. In February and March, Palestinian authorities closed al-Watan and al-Istiqlal, the press organs of Hamas and the Palestinian Islamic Jihad. They have not been allowed to reopen by year's end. In September the PA shutdown the weekly independent Jenin allegedly because its editor criticized the policies of the Jenin municipality and the local trade organization. In August PA authorities prevented the distribution of books by one of Arafat's most vocal critics, Edward Said.

The PA has authority over all levels of education in the West Bank and Gaza Strip. There were no reports of PA interference with academic freedom.

b. *Freedom of Peaceful Assembly and Association.*—Israeli military orders ban public gatherings of 10 or more people without a permit, but authorities relaxed enforcement after the signing of the Declaration of Principles in September 1993. According to the Palestinian Society for the Protection of Human Rights and the Environment, Israeli authorities began to enforce this order more vigorously in response to Palestinian demonstrations held in 1996 over land issues in the West Bank.

Private organizations are required to register with the Israeli authorities, though some operate without licenses. The authorities permit Palestinian charitable, community, professional, and self-help organizations to operate unless their activities are viewed as overly political or opposed to the DOP.

PA officials maintain that they do not impose restrictions on freedom of assembly, although they do require permits for rallies, demonstrations, and many cultural events. These were rarely denied. In Gaza police approval is required for "political" meetings at several specific large meeting halls. Written permission is also required for buses to transport passengers to attend political meetings. In West Bank cities, the PA requires permits for outdoor rallies and demonstrations and prohibits calls for violence, a display of arms, and racist slogans. In December the PA issued permits to a number of rejectionist groups (Hamas, PFLP, DFLP) to celebrate their anniversaries on the condition they demonstrate peacefully and not advocate violence. At a Bir Zeit University rally Hamas supporters burned an Israeli bus in effigy, an act that suggested support for bus bombings. The PA reportedly approached Bir Zeit University officials to review security procedures for the rally.

There were periodic complaints during the year from Palestinian political parties, social, and professional groups, and other non-governmental organizations that the PA tried to limit their ability to act autonomously.

c. *Freedom of Religion.*—The Israeli Government respects freedom of religion and does not ban any group or sect on strictly religious grounds. It permits all faiths to operate schools and institutions. Religious publications are subject to the publications laws (see Section 2.a.). The IDF temporarily closed three mosques in the West Bank for security reasons for several months. In April the IDF closed a mosque in the West Bank town of Burqa for security reasons and in May closed mosques in Qabalan and A-Ram for 6 months after finding "inciteful material" in them, according to human rights monitors and press reports.

The PA does not restrict freedom of religion.

d. *Freedom of Movement Within the Occupied Territories, Foreign Travel, Emigration, and Repatriation.*—Israel requires that all West Bank and Gaza residents obtain identification cards to qualify for permits to enter Israel and Jerusalem. However, Israel sometimes denies applicants ID cards and permits with no explanation, and does not allow effective means of appeal. Palestinian residents of Jerusalem are sometimes prohibited from entering PA-controlled areas of the West Bank, and they require written permits from Israel to travel to the Gaza Strip. Residents of the Gaza Strip are rarely able to obtain permission to travel to the West Bank. Israel and the PA have yet to establish "safe passage" to facilitate travel between the West Bank and Gaza Strip, as set out in the Interim Agreement.

Israel continued to apply its policy begun in 1993 of closure of the West Bank and Gaza Strip in response to terror attacks. A closure was applied on February 25, following suicide bombings in Jerusalem and Ashkelon. During "normal" closure conditions that prevailed for most of 1996, any Palestinian holding a Gaza or West Bank identity card was required to obtain a permit to enter Israel or Jerusalem. Palestinian workers employed in Israel were prohibited from entering Israel to work for a significant portion of the year. Most Palestinians in the West Bank and Gaza Strip encountered difficulty obtaining permits to work, visit, study, obtain medical care, or attend religious services outside of the West Bank or Gaza. Israeli authorities do not permit Gazans to bring vehicles into Israel and rarely permit West Bank vehicles to enter Jerusalem or Israel.

As a security precaution, Israel also routinely tightens closures on the West Bank and Gaza during major Jewish or Muslim holy days, as well as during times of political sensitivity for Israel or the Palestinian authority, such as during the Israeli elections in May.

Twice in 1996—in the spring following terrorist bombings in Israel and Jerusalem, and after Palestinian-Israeli clashes in September—Israel imposed a total closure of the West Bank and Gaza as well as an "internal closure" on West Bank towns, isolating areas under PA control by preventing travel between them. The "internal closure" imposed in the spring, the first time such a closure was used, lasted for about 2 weeks, as did the second. Israeli government officials acknowledged that closures have limited effectiveness as a security measure; since at least 1994, all known perpetrators of terrorist attacks in Israel were not in possession of valid permits but were nonetheless able to enter Israel.

The tightening of these restrictions significantly hampered the flow of food, medicine, students, doctors, and patients into and out of the occupied territories, and seriously disrupted normal commerce. Human rights groups report that in February and March at least seven ill Palestinians, including three babies, died because they were unable to travel to hospitals in Jerusalem or Israel. Another Palestinian child died at an Israeli checkpoint while awaiting permission to enter Israel for medical treatment. Emergency cases were handled on an ad hoc basis throughout the September-October crisis. By year's end, more trucks and day laborers were permitted to enter and leave the territories.

Israel continues to impose periodic curfews in areas of the West Bank under its jurisdiction largely in response to security incidents, in anticipation of incidents, or as part of ongoing security operations. Israeli settlers are generally free to move about during curfews, while Palestinian residents are confined to their homes. Following clashes between Israeli security forces and Palestinian security forces and civilians in September, Hebron was put under a 20-hour per day curfew that lasted for 10 days. Palestinians periodically were allowed out of their homes for brief periods of time to buy food and other necessities.

The Government restricted travel for 21 Israeli settlers, prohibiting them from entering sensitive locations in the West Bank. The Yesha Council, an umbrella group of settler organizations, estimates that six Israelis were placed under administrative detention during the year.

The Israeli Government requires all Palestinians resident in areas under its control to obtain permits for foreign travel and has restricted the travel of some political activists. Bridge-crossing permits to Jordan may be obtained at post offices without a screening process. However, the fear of losing one's residency is an obstacle to travel. Palestinian males between the ages of 16 and 25 who cross into Jordan must remain outside the occupied territories for 9 months. Restriction on residence, tourist visas, reentry, and family reunification apply only to Palestinian residents of the occupied territories. Israeli authorities sometimes refuse to renew the laissez-passers of Palestinians from the occupied territories who live or work abroad, on the grounds that they have abandoned their residences.

The Israeli Government ordinarily does not permit Palestinians who obtain foreign citizenship to resume residence in Jerusalem; nor does it permit those who acquire legal residency abroad, or who remain outside Jerusalem for over 3 years, to resume their residency. Such persons are permitted to return only as tourists and are sometimes denied entry entirely. No such restrictions are applied to Israeli citizens.

Israel enforced these residency restrictions in Jerusalem with greater stringency in 1996, according to human rights groups and foreign diplomats. In 1996 approximately 2,000 Arab residents of Jerusalem had their residency permits revoked, or were told by Israeli officials they could not retain their resident status if they traveled out of the country or if they did not renounce citizenship or residency in another country. The Israeli Government has denied that greater enforcement of the Jerusalem residency requirements reflects a concerted policy to decrease the Arab population in Jerusalem. The Government explained in September that Palestinian residents of Jerusalem are not losing their residency status as a result of more rigorous enforcement of the Jerusalem residency requirements and that Israel had not changed its policies. The Government, however, has not yet responded to requests by foreign diplomats to explain why it revoked Jerusalem residency permits in several dozen individual cases, which apparently did not contradict Israeli policy.

Israeli authorities also place restrictions on family reunification. Most Palestinians who were abroad before or during the 1967 war or who have lost their residence permits for other reasons, are not permitted to reside permanently with their families in the occupied territories. Israeli security also singles out young (often unmarried) Palestinian males for harsher treatment than other Palestinians, citing them as more likely to be security risks. They generally are prohibited from working in Israel.

The MATAK usually denied permanent residency in the occupied territories to the foreign-born spouses and children of Palestinian residents, and to nonresident mothers. The Government usually issued temporary residency permits to persons in these categories.

The PA generally does not restrict the travel of Palestinians in Gaza and PA cities in the West Bank. During clashes with Israeli security in September, PA authorities placed Nablus under a temporary curfew. Passports and identification cards for the residents of PA areas are issued by the PA. PA authorities issued travel documents freely to male Palestinians, and the PA Ministry of Civil Affairs rescinded this past summer the law requiring women to show the written consent of a male family member before issuing them a travel document (see Section 5).

Section 3. Respect for Political Rights: The Right of Citizens to Change Their Government

Palestinian residents of the West Bank, Gaza Strip, and Jerusalem chose their first popularly-elected government on January 20. They elected an 88-member Palestinian Legislative Council and the head of the Executive Authority of the Council. Voter turnout was high, about 75 percent of the estimated 1 million registered voters. Yasir Arafat won almost 89 percent of the vote in a two-person race for chief executive of the Council. Some 700 candidates ran for Council seats. Council members were elected in multi-member electoral districts. As many as 35 of the elected members were independent candidates or critics of Arafat and his Fatah faction. The Council convened on March 7 and proceeded to elect their officers. International observers concluded that the election could be reasonably regarded as an accurate expression of the will of the voters, despite some irregularities.

Most Palestinians in Jerusalem do not recognize the jurisdiction of the Municipality of Jerusalem; less than 7 percent of Jerusalem's Palestinian population voted in 1993 municipal elections. No Palestinian resident of Jerusalem sits on the city council.

Women are underrepresented in government and politics. There are five women in the 88-member Council, and two women serve in ministerial-level positions.

Section 4. Governmental Attitude Regarding International and Nongovernmental Investigation of Alleged Violations of Human Rights

Many local groups—Israeli, Palestinian, and international—monitored the Israeli Government's human rights practices. The Israeli Government normally cooperates with human rights organizations; officials normally agree to meet with human rights monitors. The Israeli Government permits them to publish and hold press conferences.

However, some individual human rights workers have been subjected to interference. A fieldwork coordinator for the Palestinian human rights organization Al-Haq was arrested and detained without charge in February. A blind Palestinian-American human rights worker was detained at the Gaza border, interrogated, and prevented from presenting a human rights training session in Gaza.

Many local human rights groups—mostly Palestinian—as well as several international human rights organizations, monitored the PA's human rights practices. The PA generally cooperates with these organizations and PA officials normally meet with their representatives. Many of the Palestinian human rights organizations work behind the scenes with the PA to overcome alleged abuses in certain areas. They also publish criticism if they believe that the PA is not responding adequately to private entreaties.

The International Committee of the Red Cross (ICRC) operates in the PA areas under the terms of a memorandum of understanding signed in September between the ICRC and the PLO. The memorandum accords the ICRC access to all detainees held by the PA and allows regular inspections of prison conditions. Despite this memorandum, and an earlier one, the ICRC had not visited PA detention facilities since 1995. In September the PA signed an agreement with the ICRC allowing the ICRC access to PA-run prisons. The ICRC began prison visits in both the West Bank and Gaza in December in accordance with the agreement.

The PA police twice arrested and detained for several days the chairman of the Palestinian Independent Commission for Citizen's Rights, Iyad Sarraj, for criticizing the PA and its human rights practices (see Section 2.a.). In January Palestinian security forces arrested and held B'tselem field worker Bassam Eid for several hours without specifying why he was being held. In September 1995, the head of the Palestinian Preventive Security Force in Jericho had labeled Eid "an agent of the Israeli police."

Section 5. *Discrimination Based on Race, Sex, Religion, Disability, Language, or Social Status*

Under the complex mixture of laws and regulations that apply to the territories, Palestinians are disadvantaged under Israeli law and practices compared with the treatment received by Israeli settlers. This includes discrimination in residency, land and water use, and access to health and social services.

Women.—The problems of rape, domestic violence, and violence related to "family honor" have gained greater prominence, but public discussion is generally muted. Victims are often encouraged by relatives to remain quiet and are themselves punished or blamed for the "shame" that has been brought upon them and their families. Women's groups seek to educate women on these problems, but women's rights advocates claim that few resources are available to shelter the victims of violence. They also maintain that society has not been receptive to providing counseling or outreach services to victims of problems that they see as more widespread than is acknowledged. There are no reliable statistics available on family violence or other forms of violence against women.

Palestinian women in the Israeli-controlled areas of the occupied territories and in the Palestinian Authority areas endure various forms of social prejudice and repression within their own society. Because of early marriage, girls frequently do not finish the mandatory level of schooling. Cultural restrictions sometimes prevent them from attending colleges and universities. While there is an active women's movement in the West Bank and Gaza, attention has only recently shifted from nationalist aspirations to women's issues such as domestic violence, education, employment, and marriage and inheritance laws.

There are no laws providing for women's rights in the workplace. Some Palestinian women work outside the home. Women are underrepresented in most aspects of professional life. There are almost no women in decisionmaking positions in the legal, medical, educational, and scientific fields. However, a small group of women are prominent in politics, medicine, law, teaching, and in nongovernmental organizations.

Personal status law for Palestinians is based on religious law. For Muslim Palestinians, personal status law is derived from Shari'a (Islamic law). In the West Bank and Gaza, Shari'a law pertaining to women is part of the Jordanian Status Law of 1976, which includes inheritance and marriage laws. Under the law, women inherit less than male members of the family. The marriage law allows men to take more than one wife, but few do so. Women are permitted to make "stipulations" to protect them against divorce and questions of child custody. However, only 1 percent of women take advantage of this section of the law, leaving most women at a disadvantage when it comes to divorce or child custody. Following legal protests, the PA Ministry of Civil Affairs this year rescinded a law requiring women to obtain the written consent of a male family member before it would issue them a travel document.

Children.—While the PA provides for compulsory education, it does not provide specific health services for children. Current British Mandate, Jordanian, and military laws, from which West Bank and Gaza law is derived, offer protection to children under labor and penal codes. While there is no juvenile court system, judges specializing in children's cases generally sit for juvenile offenders. In cases where the child is the victim, judges have the discretion to remove the child from a situation deemed harmful. However, the system is not advanced in the protection afforded children.

There is no societal pattern of abuse of children, either among Israelis or Palestinians.

People With Disabilities.—There is no mandated accessibility to public facilities in the occupied territories under either Israeli or Palestinian authority. Approximately

130,000 Palestinians in the West Bank and Gaza are disabled. Some Palestinian institutions care for and train disabled persons; their efforts, however, are chronically underfunded. According to a report by the Palestinian human rights group Al-Haq, many Palestinians with disabilities are segregated and isolated from Palestinian society; they are discriminated against in most spheres, including education, employment, transportation, and access to public buildings and facilities.

Section 6. Worker Rights

a. *The Right of Association.*—Labor affairs in the West Bank came under Palestinian authority with the signing of the Interim Agreement in September 1995. Until a new law being drafted by PA authorities comes into effect, labor affairs in the West Bank are governed by Jordanian Law 21 of 1965, as amended by Israeli military orders, and in Gaza by PA decisions. The law permits workers to establish and join unions without government authorization. The earlier Israeli stipulation that all proposed West Bank unions apply for a permit is no longer enforced. No new unions were established in 1996. Israeli authorities have previously licensed about 35 of the estimated 185 union branches now in existence. There are almost 30 licensed trade unions in the West Bank and 6 in Gaza.

Palestinian workers in Jerusalem are governed by Israeli labor law. They are free to establish their own unions. Although the Government restricts Jerusalem unions from joining West Bank trade union federations, this restriction has not been enforced. Palestinian workers in Jerusalem may simultaneously belong to unions affiliated with a West Bank federation and the Israeli Histadrut labor federation.

West Bank unions are not affiliated with the Israeli Histadrut federation. Palestinian workers who are not resident in Israel or Jerusalem are not full members of Histadrut, but they are required to contribute 1 percent of their wages to Histadrut. Negotiations between Histadrut and West Bank union officials to return half of this fee to the Palestinian union federation were completed in 1995. Histradut did not return half of the fee.

Palestinians who work in Israel are required to contribute to the National Insurance Institute (NII), which provides unemployment insurance and other benefits. Palestinian workers are eligible for some, but not all, NII benefits. According to the Interim Agreement, Palestinians working in Israel will continue to be insured for injuries occurring in Israel, the bankruptcy of a worker's employer, and allowances for maternity leave. The Government of Israel agreed to transfer the NII fees collected from Palestinian workers to the PA, which will assume responsibility for the pensions and social benefits of Palestinians working in Israel. Implementation of this change is still underway.

The great majority of West Bank unions belong to the Palestinian General Federation of Trade Unions (PGFTU). The PGFTU acted as the informal coalition in the completion of the negotiations with Histadrut regarding workers' fees. The reorganization of unions under the PGFTU is intended to enable the West Bank unions and Gaza unions to better represent the union members' interests; the reorganization had not yet been finalized at year's end.

An estimated 86,000 workers are members of the GFTU, the largest union bloc. The PGFTU estimates actual organized membership, i.e., dues-paying members, at about 30 percent of all Palestinian workers, and is working to add more.

No unions were dissolved by administrative or legislative action this year. Palestinian unions seeking to strike must submit to arbitration by the PA Ministry of Labor. If the union disagrees with the final arbitration and strikes, a tribunal of senior judges appointed by the PA decides what, if any, disciplinary action is to be taken. There are no laws in the territories that specifically protect the rights of striking workers, and, in practice, such workers have little or no protection from employers' retribution.

The PGFTU has applied for membership in the International Confederation of Free Trade Unions (ICFTU).

b. *The Right to Organize and Bargain Collectively.*—A majority of workers in the occupied territories are self-employed or unpaid family helpers in agriculture or commerce. Only 35 percent of employment in the territories consists of wage jobs, most with the United Nations Relief and Works Agency (UNRWA), the PA, or in municipalities. Collective bargaining is protected. Labor disputes are adjudicated by committees of 3 to 5 members in businesses employing more than 20 workers.

Existing laws and regulations do not offer real protection against antiunion discrimination. One industrial zone is being developed in the Gaza Strip.

c. *Prohibition of Forced or Compulsory Labor.*—There is no forced or compulsory labor in the occupied territories.

d. *Minimum Age for Employment of Children.*—The minimum working age in the West Bank and Gaza is 14. This order is not effectively enforced, and underage workers are employed in agriculture and in some West Bank and Gaza factories. Work hours for young workers are not limited.

e. *Acceptable Conditions of Work.*—There is currently no minimum wage in the West Bank or Gaza area. In the West Bank, the normal workweek is 48 hours in most areas; in Gaza the workweek is 45 hours for day laborers and 40 hours for salaried employees. There is no effective enforcement of maximum workweek laws.

The Palestinian Authority Ministry of Labor is responsible for inspecting work places and enforcing safety standards in the West Bank and the Gaza Strip. The Ministry of Labor says that newer factories and work places meet international health and safety standards but that older ones fail to meet minimum standards.

JORDAN

The Hashemite Kingdom of Jordan is a constitutional monarchy ruled by King Hussein since 1952. The Constitution concentrates a high degree of executive and legislative authority in the King, who determines domestic and foreign policy. The Prime Minister and the Cabinet manage the daily affairs of government. The Parliament consists of a 40-member Senate appointed by the King and an 80-member Chamber of Deputies elected by the people. Since the elections of 1989 the Lower House has increasingly asserted itself in the areas of domestic and foreign policy. Reflecting this trend, the Cabinet appointed in February included 22 deputies from the lower house, the highest number ever. The judiciary is independent.

The General Intelligence Directorate (GID) and the Public Security Directorate (PSD) share responsibility for maintaining internal security and have broad authority to monitor the activities of persons believed to be security threats. The State Security Court and broad police powers remain in place as vestiges of martial law, which was in place from 1967 to 1991. The security forces continue to commit human rights abuses.

Jordan has a mixed economy with significant government participation in industry, transportation, and communications. The country has few natural resources and is financially dependent on foreign assistance and remittances from citizens working abroad. Because of the Government's policies during the 1990-91 Gulf crisis, some Arab Gulf state governments discontinued foreign assistance, expelled many Jordanian guest workers, and placed restrictions on imports of Jordanian goods. The domestic economy has been buffeted by high unemployment since the late 1980's. Traditional exports to Iraq dropped off sharply due to United Nations sanctions against that country and Jordanian initiatives to reduce the export of nonsanctioned goods under the bilateral trade protocol with Iraq. As part of a structural adjustment program mandated by the International Monetary Fund, the Government removed subsidies on bread and animal feed in August, resulting in a doubling of the price of bread and other price rises. The price increase was followed by riots in the south of the country. Some local commentators estimate that the standard of living for the average Jordanian has dropped by over half in the past 10 years. Per capita gross domestic product was estimated at $1,500 in 1996.

Since the revocation of martial law in 1991, there has been a steady improvement in the human rights situation. Nonetheless, problems remain, including: Arbitrary arrest; abuse and mistreatment of detainees; prolonged detention without charge; lack of due process; harassment of opposition political parties; restrictions on the freedoms of speech, press, assembly, and association; official discrimination against adherents of the Baha'i faith; and restrictions on women's rights. Opposition allegations of human rights abuses in 1996 peaked following August riots in southern Jordan. Human rights activists protested detentions, the arrest of journalists and opposition party members, and the harassment of political parties. Discrimination against the Bedouin, violence against women, and abuse of foreign servants are also problems. Citizens do not have the right to change their form of government, although in recent years the King has taken steps to increase participation in the political system, such as legalizing political parties. Parliamentary elections in 1993 and nationwide municipal elections in 1995 were largely free and fair although there were opposition accusations of government misconduct.

RESPECT FOR HUMAN RIGHTS

Section 1. Respect for the Integrity of the Person, Including Freedom From:

a. *Political and Other Extrajudicial Killing.*—There was one report of death in custody. Younis Mahmoud Abu Dawleh was arrested by officers of the PSD for his alleged involvement in the December 24 shooting of Hamzeh Nazzal, in what has been described in press reports as a dispute among former Democratic Front for the Liberation of Palestine members. He reportedly resisted arrest and police knocked him down a flights of stairs, sat on him, and beat him. He died of a heart attack on December 24 while enroute to the police station. His body reportedly showed signs of repeated blows to the genital area.

No progress was made in the Attorney General's review of the case of the death of Mahmud Khalifeh and wounding of his brother Bashir by security forces in June 1995. Opponents of the Government charge that security forces used excessive force against the two after the pair used firearms to resist arrest. The Khalifeh brothers were wanted for shooting at police patrol cars and sending faxes critical of the Government and the King to prominent citizens.

   b. *Disappearance.*—There were no reports of politically motivated disappearance.

   c. *Torture and Other Cruel, Inhuman, or Degrading Treatment or Punishment.*—Although the Legal Code provides prisoners with the right to humane treatment, security and other police forces abuse detainees physically during interrogation. Torture allegations are difficult to verify because security officials frequently deny detainees timely access to lawyers. The most frequently alleged methods of torture are sleep deprivation, beatings, and extended solitary confinement. Defendants in high-profile cases before the State Security Court claim to have undergone physical and psychological abuse while in detention. Government officials reject allegations of torture.

There were a number of allegations of torture in connection with those detained after the disturbances in the south. Human rights monitors charge that two doctors who were treating detainees for injuries sustained at the hands of government authorities were detained themselves. The doctors were reportedly taken into custody for sending detainees to the hospital to be treated for a bullet lodged in the spine in one case, and broken hands in another. Credible sources alleged that the doctors were then abused. In another case, opposition deputies charged the Government with detaining and torturing Essam Al-Najjar, a Hamas supporter, for two weeks. They alleged that Al-Najjar was beaten in the stomach, throat, and on the soles of his feet, was cursed by guards, and had excrement wiped in his face.

The Court of Cassation overturned the June 1995 death sentences of defendants in the so-called "Udwan Mills" case, ruling that the criminal court could not base its sentencing solely on the defendants' confessions, which defense lawyers claimed were extracted under duress. The convictions were based solely on confessions.

Local police detention facilities are spartan but generally clean. Prisons generally meet minimum international standards. Prisoners detained on national security grounds are often kept in separate prisons maintained by the GID.

The International Committee of the Red Cross (ICRC) is permitted unrestricted access to prisoners and prison facilities. In August members of Parliament's Public Freedoms Committee visited Suwaqa Prison to assess the condition of Layth Shubaylat and Ata Abu Rishtah (see Section 1.e.). Following the disturbances in the south, however, the Committee was not permitted to inspect prisons or assess the condition of detainees until October 15, 7 weeks after the first arrests. In September representatives of the Arab Organization for Human Rights (AOHR) were given permission by the court to visit the detainees but were not permitted by prison officials to tour the facility.

   d. *Arbitrary Arrest, Detention, or Exile.*—Under the Constitution citizens are subject to arrest, trial, and punishment for the defamation of heads of state, dissemination of "false or exaggerated information outside the country which attacks state dignity," or defamation of public officials.

The Criminal Code requires legal authorities to file formal charges within 10 days of arrest. The courts routinely grant requests from prosecutors for 15-day extensions as provided by law. This practice generally extends pretrial detention for lengthy periods of time. In cases involving state security, the authorities frequently hold defendants in lengthy pretrial detention, do not provide written charges, and do not allow defendants to meet with their lawyers until shortly before the trial. Security defendants usually meet with their attorneys 1 or 2 days prior to the trial.

Testimony in July in the case of the Bayat Al Imam defendants, charged with plotting to carry out extremist attacks and illegally possessing and manufacturing of explosives, revealed that they had been detained by security forces for 5 months without charge and without access to an attorney, before being transferred to a military prosecutor for questioning.

According to the Ministry of Information a total of 572 people were detained following August's disturbances in southern Jordan; 521 were released, without being charged. All those remaining in custody were released and charges against them dropped under a general amnesty in honor of the King's birthday on November 14.

The Government detains persons, including journalists, for varying amounts of time for what appear to be political reasons (see Sections 2.a. and 2.b.). During the year all such detainees were released within 3 months. Observers estimate that in previous years approximately 400 people were detained each year for national security reasons, of whom all but a few were released after questioning.

The Government does not use forced exile.

e. *Denial of a Fair Public Trial.*—The Constitution provides for an independent judiciary. Court rulings against the Government, including the Udwan Mills case (see Section 1.c.), indicate that the judiciary functions independently.

There are several types of courts. Most criminal cases are tried in the civilian courts, which include appeals courts, the Court of Cassation, and the Supreme Court. Cases involving sedition, armed insurrection, financial crimes, and drug trafficking are tried in the State Security Court, a remnant of the pre-1991 martial law period. Islamic, or Shari'a, courts, have jurisdiction over marriage and divorce among Muslims and inheritance cases involving both Muslims and non-Muslims (see Section 5). Under Shari'a law, a woman's testimony is only equal to half that of a man (see Section 5).

Most trials in the civilian courts are open. Defendants are entitled to legal counsel, may challenge witnesses, and have the right to appeal. Defendants facing the death penalty or life imprisonment must be represented by legal counsel. Public defenders are provided in such cases.

The State Security Court is comprised of panels of three judges, who may be either civilians or military officers. It frequently restricts public attendance at its trials. Defendants tried in the State Security Court are often held in pretrial detention without access to lawyers, although they are visited by representatives of the ICRC. In the State Security Court, judges have inquired into allegations that defendants were tortured and have permitted the testimony of physicians regarding these allegations. To date the Court has not invalidated confessions obtained under duress, but on review, the Court of Cassation has ruled that the State Security Court cannot issue a death sentence on the basis of such a confession alone (see Section 1.c.). Defendants in the State Security Court have the right of appeal to the Court of Cassation, which is authorized to review the testimony, evidence, and judgment. Appeals are automatic for cases involving the death penalty.

Defense attorneys have challenged the appointment of military judges to the State Security Court to try civilian cases as contrary to the concept of an independent judiciary. Military judges appear to receive adequate training in civil law and court procedure, and State Security Court decisions are reviewed by the Court of Cassation. At least partly in response to these charges, a panel of civilian judges was appointed to the court for the first time in December 1995 to try the case of Layth Shubaylat for slandering the King. The panel was dissolved in September and was replaced by military judges.

A number of the cases brought before the State Security Court in 1995 resulted in convictions. In the case of six members of the Islamic Revival Movement, three were sentenced to 7½ years at hard labor for possession of explosives. The other three defendants were acquitted due to a lack of evidence. In two separate cases involving free speech, Ata Abu Rishtah and Layth Shubaylat were convicted of slandering the King and sentenced to 3 years in prison, the maximum sentence for this crime. Both sentences were upheld by the Court of Cassation on appeal. On November 8, the King ordered the release from prison of Shabaylat after he had served 7 months of his sentence.

In the case of an attack on the office of the GID at Al Baqaa refugee camp in 1994, five men were found guilty of plotting to carry out an extremist attack and were sentenced to 15 years' imprisonment at hard labor. The five and another defendant were acquitted of charges of distributing pamphlets slandering the King. During the trial the defendants retracted their confessions, saying that they were extracted under duress.

In the case of two men accused of shooting a French diplomat in February 1995, the defendants were found innocent of attempted murder in criminal court, but were convicted of plotting to carry out extremist attacks and the manufacture and possession of illegal arms and explosives. The two men were sentenced to 10 years in prison at hard labor. Both men claimed that they were tortured while in custody.

In the "Bayat Al Imam" case, 4 of the 13 the defendants were found innocent, and 9 were convicted. Seven had been charged with plotting to carry out extremist attacks, illegal manufacture and possession of explosives with illicit intent, and slandering the King. The remaining six were accused with slandering the King. Of the seven charged with manufacturing explosives, two were found not guilty, four were convicted of the lesser charge of possession of explosives, and the seventh was found guilty of all charges. Three of the four were sentenced to 15 years at hard labor; the fourth was sentenced to 10 years at hard labor. The one defendant convicted on all charges was sentenced to death, but his sentence was commuted to life imprisonment at hard labor. Among those accused only of slander, one was found not guilty while the remaining five received sentences ranging from 2 to 3 years in prison. During the trial all the defendants claimed that they were forced to confess while in security detention for 5 months prior to being charged.

In 1996 the State Security Court began hearing the case of three men accused of planning attacks against Israeli tourists. The men are charged with plotting to carry out extremist attacks and possessing illegal explosives. The Court also heard the case of Mohammed Salameh Duwaik, an attorney arrested after neighbors accused him of making remarks that slandered the King and Government. Duwaik was cleared of the charges as a result of inconsistencies in witnesses' testimony. The press has carried details of the ongoing cases, including allegations of torture.

f. *Arbitrary Interference with Privacy, Family, Home, or Correspondence.*—The authorities generally respect the Constitutional prohibitions of such practices. Police must obtain a warrant from the Prosecutor General or a judge before conducting searches. However, in security cases, authorities sometimes—in violation of the law—obtain warrants retroactively or obtain preapproved warrants. Security officers reportedly monitor telephones, read correspondence, and engage in surveillance of persons who allegedly pose a threat to the Government. While these practices are not believed to be widespread, the law permits them if the Government obtains a court order.

Section 2. Respect for Civil Liberties, Including:

a. *Freedom of Speech and Press.*—The Constitution provides for freedom of speech and the press; however, the Government imposes some restrictions on these rights. Private citizens can be prosecuted for slandering the royal family or the Government and for inciting sedition. Citizens generally do not hesitate to criticize the Government openly but are more circumspect in regard to the King and the royal family. The Press and Publications Law of 1993 restricts media coverage of 10 subjects, most notably the military services, the royal family, and monetary policy. In addition, journalists engage in self-censorship when reporting on security issues and opposition to the Government to avoid government censorship or retaliation.

The Government exercises control over the print media through its ownership of 61 percent of the Jordan Press Foundation and 40 percent of the Jordan Press and Publications Company, which together publish the country's three main daily newspapers. The 1993 Law gives the Government until 1997 to reduce its shares in press establishments to a maximum of 30 percent. The Government also requires licenses for newspapers and periodicals, but the Press Law does not prescribe penalties for publishing without a license. The Government may revoke a license only if a company fails to publish for an extended period of time. The Government licensed eight new weekly newspapers in 1996. No licenses were revoked.

The Government also requires licenses for journalists, editors, and publishers. Journalists have long complained about the requirement that they must join the government-sponsored Jordan Press Association (JPA). However, the Government has not taken legal action against journalists who refuse to join the association. Foreign journalists and Jordanians working for foreign news agencies must register with the Ministry of Information. The Press Law offers limited protection for the confidentiality of a journalist's sources.

The Penal Code authorizes the State to take legal action against any person who incites violence, defames heads of state, disseminates "false or exaggerated information outside the country which attacks state dignity," or defames public officials. Ahmed Oueidi Abbadi, a former deputy, is charged with undermining national unity, inciting people to criminal acts, and fueling bigotry for writing a June editorial in which he called for Government confiscation of the property of Palestinians living in Jordan.

Persons accused of violating the Press and Publications Law are tried in a special court for press and copyright cases. During the year there were 13 cases involving violations of the Press and Publications Law. Journalists are also prosecuted for criminal and security violations in connection with their work. Most such cases result in acquittal or are dismissed before coming to trial. In 1995 only 2 of the 20 cases heard resulted in guilty verdicts. The Government uses detention and prosecution or the threat of prosecution of press and publications cases as a means to harass and intimidate outspoken journalists and encourage self-censorship. Fourteen journalists have been charged with security and press offenses related to the August disturbances in southern Jordan. Charges include "publishing material deemed offensive to the public," "carrying inaccurate or misleading reporting," slandering the King, and instigating public disorder or sedition. Salameh Na'mat, the Amman correspondent for Al Hayat, was acquitted in April of slander, inaccurate reporting, and "damaging national unity" under the Press and Publications Law. He was detained in October 1995 for 3 days in connection with the charges.

Two Lebanese journalists and the chief editor of an Egyptian opposition paper were denied entry by the Government into the country in December on the grounds that their writings were insulting and slanderous to the King and the Jordanian leadership.

Radio and television news is more restricted than the print media. Television news airs criticisms of the Government but rarely covers alleged human rights abuses. During the August disturbances foreign television crews were permitted to film the riots, but the crew from Jordan Television was denied access to Kerak, where the disturbances were taking place. All political parties have access to broadcast facilities, but the cost of air time is prohibitively high. Opposition parties have complained that Jordan Television reports only the Government's position on controversial matters. In August opposition parliamentarians boycotted Parliament over complaints that their views about the bread subsidy issue were not being aired. International television programs are widely available by satellite; Israeli and Syrian television can be received with an antenna.

Although the Government does not usually interfere with the importation of foreign newspapers and magazines, individual issues sometimes do not appear on the newstands, as was the case with a number of British publications immediately following the August disturbances. In October over 30 publications on display at Amman's International Book Fair were confiscated by officials from the Press and Publications Department because they had not been submitted to the Department in advance. The confiscated books covered political and social topics and included novels and poetry.

There were no cases of leftist or Islamist university professors being dismissed for advocating extremist political views. Intellectuals, however, believe that there are no safeguards to prevent such dismissals. University of Jordan sociology professor Ibrahim Abu Arkoub was detained in September without charge for 45 days, apparently for his connections with Hamas.

b. *Freedom of Peaceful Assembly and Association.*—Citizens must obtain permits for public gatherings. Since 1989 the Government has granted some permits for peaceful demonstrations. The Government denies permits for public protests and rallies that it determines pose a threat to security. Following riots and demonstrations in response to the August increase in bread prices, the Government denied opposition and Islamist organizers permission to hold a "hungry million march" to protest the price increase. The Government indirectly limits conferences, workshops, and seminars by requiring that the organizers obtain Government approval for any such gathering. The Government has not refused such permission in 1996.

The Government routinely licenses political parties. Twenty-six parties have been licensed since 1992. Membership in an unlicensed party is illegal. The High Court of Justice may dissolve a party if it violates the Constitution or the Political Parties Law. The Government has no discretion to deny a license to a party that submits a complete application, including names of the founders, financial information, and bylaws. There are over 50 political movements that are not licensed by the Government as full-fledged political parties.

In August the Government took action against opposition party members suspected of instigating unrest in the south. Members and officials of the Jordanian Arab Baath Socialist Party, the Jordan People's Democratic Party, and the Jordanian Communist Party from various parts of Jordan were detained and charged for involvement in the riots (see Section 1.d.).

c. *Freedom of Religion.*—According to the Constitution, Islam is the state religion. The Constitution prohibits discrimination based on religion and provides for "personal freedom." Sunni Muslims constitute over 90 percent of the population. Government control of Islamic institutions is managed by the Ministry of Religious Affairs and Trusts, which appoints imams and subsidizes activities sponsored by the mosques. The Political Parties Law prohibits houses of worship from being used for political party activity. This has been interpreted to prevent Islamist parliamentarians from preaching in mosques. However, enforcement of the law has not been consistent. Religious instruction is mandatory for all Muslim students in public schools.

The Government does not interfere with public worship by Jordan's Christian minority. The Government does not recognize the Baha'i faith as a religion but does not prohibit the practice of the faith.

The law prohibits non-Muslims from proselytizing. Muslims who convert to other faiths complain of social and government discrimination. The Government does not fully recognize the legality of such conversions. Under Shari'a law, converts from Islam are regarded as apostates and may be legally denied their property and other rights. In Jordan this principle is not applied. Converts from Islam do not fall under the jurisdiction of their new religion's laws in matters of personal status and are still considered Muslims under Shari'a law.

d. *Freedom of Movement Within the Country, Foreign Travel, Emigration, and Repatriation.*—The law provides for the right of citizens to travel freely abroad and within Jordan except in military areas. The law requires that Jordanian women and foreign women married to Jordanians obtain written permission from a male guardian to apply for a passport. A woman traveling abroad with children may also be asked for authorization from her spouse before being allowed to depart. Legal authorities enforce requests from fathers to prevent their children from departing the country, even when traveling with their mothers.

Many Palestinian residents are Jordanian citizens, with the rights of citizenship. Jordanians with full citizenship receive passports valid for 5 years. Until 1995 the Government issued passports valid for 2 years to Palestinians who arrived after 1967, as well as to Palestinians in areas under Israeli occupation who did not have other travel documentation. In 1995 the King announced that virtually all applicants would be eligible for 5-year passports. The Government stresses that these passports are for travel only; they do not denote nationality. Palestinians must obtain permits from the Ministry of the Interior for travel between Jordan and the Israeli-occupied territories. Such permission is routinely granted.

The Government cooperates with the office of the U.N. High Commissioner for Refugees (UNHCR) and other humanitarian organizations in assisting refugees. The Government provides first asylum. Since 1991 thousands of Iraqis have sought asylum in Jordan and been assisted by the UNHCR. There were no reports of forced return of persons to a country where they feared persecution. The Constitution prohibits the deportation of citizens.

Over 1.35 million Palestinian refugees are registered in Jordan with the United Nations Relief and Works Agency. The Agency counts another 800,000 Palestinians as either displaced persons from the 1967 war, arrivals following the 1967 war, or returnees from the Gulf.

Section 3. Respect for Political Rights: The Right of Citizens to Change Their Government

Executive and legislative powers are so concentrated in the hands of the King that citizens do not have any meaningful ability to change their system of Government. The King has sole discretionary authority to form and dismiss cabinets, appoint and remove prime ministers, dissolve Parliament, and establish the broad outlines of public policy. Appointments made by the King to high government posts do not require legislative approval. The executive power is vested in the King, who exercises his powers through his ministers in accordance with the provisions of the Constitution.

The Parliament is composed of a Senate appointed by the King and a Chamber of Deputies elected by the people. The Parliament is empowered to approve, reject, or amend legislation proposed by the Cabinet. In practice Members of Parliament ask the Government to submit specific legislation for consideration. The Parliament may amend such draft legislation. The King proposes and dismisses extraordinary sessions of Parliament and may postpone regular sessions up to 60 days. In August the King terminated the extraordinary session of Parliament in which the proposed hike in bread prices was to be discussed. The King must approve by decree all laws passed by Parliament. If the Government amends or enacts a law when Parliament is not in session, it must submit the law to Parliament for consideration during the next session.

Women have the right to vote, and women's groups encourage women to vote and become active in the political process. In the Amman area, over 43 percent of those who voted in the 1995 municipal elections were women. In 1996 there was one woman in the Cabinet, one in the Chamber of Deputies, and two in the Senate. Eleven women were elected to municipal posts in 1995, including one as mayor of Khirbet al Wahadneh, near Ajloun.

Of the 80 seats in the lower chamber, 9 are reserved for Christians, 6 for Bedouins, and 3 for the Circassian or Chechen ethnic minorities.

The Palestinian community, estimated to be slightly over one-half the total population, is not represented proportionately in the Government. Five of 31 ministers, 9 of 40 senators, and 13 of 80 lower house deputies are of Palestinian origin. The electoral system gives greater representation to south Jordan, which has few inhabitants of Palestinian origin.

Section 4. Governmental Attitude Regarding International and Nongovernmental Investigation of Alleged Violations of Human Rights

Local and international human rights groups investigate allegations of human rights abuses and have published and disseminated findings critical of government policy. However, the Press and Publications Law restricts the publication of information about the military and security services, which, in effect, prevents the publication by local groups of reports alleging torture and other abuses committed by the security services.

The ICRC is permitted to visit prisoners and assess the condition of security detainees, including those held by the GID. The AOHR and the Amman-based Peace Center for Humanitarian Studies are registered with the Government and have raised human rights cases with government officials. Both organizations have drawn public attention to alleged human rights abuses and have pressed the Government to explain the status of detainees and to charge or release them promptly. In February the AOHR released a report detailing human rights abuses in 1995. In October the AOHR released an "emergency report" about human rights abuses following the August disturbances. The Jordanian Human Rights Society (JHRS) received its license to operate on November 30 from the Ministry of Interior.

Section 5. Discrimination Based on Race, Sex, Religion, Disability, Language, or Social Status

Although Jordanian law does not distinguish between citizens on the basis of race, women and minorities are treated differently under the law and may face discrimination in employment, housing, and other categories.

Women.—Violence against women over the age of 15 is common. Reported incidents of crimes against women do not reflect the full extent of the problem. Medical experts acknowledge that spousal abuse occurs frequently. However, cultural norms constrain victims from seeking medical or legal help and frustrate an objective assessment of the extent of abuse.

Abused women have the right to file a complaint in court against their spouses for physical abuse, but in practice, familial and societal pressures discourage them from seeking legal remedies. Marital rape is legal. Nongovernmental organizations such as the Jordanian Women's Union, which has a hotline for victims of domestic violence, provide assistance in such matters. Wife beating is technically grounds for divorce, but the husband may seek to demonstrate that he has authority from the Koran to correct an irreligious or disobedient wife by striking her.

The Criminal Code allows for leniency for persons found guilty of committing a "crime of honor," the term commonly used for a violent assault against—or murder of—a female by a male relative for alleged sexual misconduct. Law enforcement treatment of men accused of "honor" crimes mirrors widespread social approval for such acts. As of September, the press reported 11 such cases in 1996. However, these figures likely understate the actual number of cases, as most crimes of honor are not reported by the press, and the actual number of such crimes is believed by a local expert to be four times as high. According to the law, a "crime of honor" defense may be invoked only by a defendant who "surprises his wife or any close female relative committing adultery," in which case there is no punishment. Although few defendants can meet the stringent requirements for a "crime of honor" defense, which requires that the defendant have witnessed the female victim engaging in sexual intercourse, convicted offenders rarely spend more than 2 years in prison. More commonly, such defenses rely on the male relative having acted in the heat of passion upon hearing of a female relative's sexual transgression, without any investigation on the part of the killer to determine the veracity of the allegation before committing an act of violence. Women may not invoke this defense for murdering a male relative under the same circumstances, nor may they use it for killing men who attempt to rape, sexually harass, or otherwise threaten their "honor." In contrast to "honor" crimes, the maximum penalty for first-degree murder is death; the maximum penalty for second degree murder is 15 years.

Women also experience legal discrimination in matters of pension and social security benefits, inheritance, divorce, and the value of testimony in court (see Section 1.e.). The Government provides men with more generous social security benefits than women. The Government continues pension payments of a deceased male civil servant to his heirs but discontinues payments of a deceased female civil servant.

Under Shari'a or Islamic law, female heirs receive half the amount of a male heir's inheritance, while the non-Muslim widows of Muslim spouses have no inheritance rights. A sole female heir receives half her parents' estate; the balance goes to designated male relatives. A sole male heir inherits all his parents' property. Male Muslim heirs have the duty to provide for all family members who need assistance. Shari'a law regards the testimony of two women to be equal to the testimony of one man. This technically applies only in religious courts but in the past has been imposed in civil courts as well, irrespective of religion. Men are able to obtain divorce more easily than women under Islamic law. Marriage and divorce matters for Christians are adjudicated by special courts for each denomination. The Government bans married women from applying for diplomatic posts. A woman was appointed as a judge for the first time in 1996.

The law requires a married woman to obtain her husband's permission to obtain a passport (see Section 2.d.). Married women do not have the legal right to confer citizenship on their children. However, they may obtain citizenship for their non-Jordanian husbands who may then confer citizenship on the children. Civil law grants women equal pay for equal work, but in practice this law is often ignored.

Social pressures discourage many women from pursuing careers. Nonetheless, women have employment opportunities in many professions, including engineering, medicine, education, and law. Women constitute approximately 14 percent of the work force. Women's groups stress that the problem of discrimination is not only one of law but also of women's lack of awareness of their rights or unwillingness to assert those rights. The United Nations Food and Agricultural Organization reported in 1995 that women who work in agriculture average 15-hour days and earn less than men. The Jordanian chapter of the Business and Professional Women's Club gives seminars on women's rights and assists women in establishing small businesses. Members of the royal family are working actively to improve the status of women.

Children.—The Government is committed to children's rights and welfare, especially in the areas of education and health. In October the Minister of Labor issued a memorandum to all ministry inspectors ordering them to fine every employer of children under 16 years of age. However, the Government's progress in these areas is constrained by limited financial resources. Education is compulsory to age 15. The children of Iraqi citizens living in Jordan without residence permits are not permitted to attend school.

The Government safeguards some children's rights, especially regarding child labor. Although the law prohibits children under the age of 16 from working, child peddlers work the streets of Amman. The Ministry of Social Development has a committee to address the problem and in most cases removes the children from the streets, returns them to their families or to juvenile centers, and may provide the families with a monthly stipend. However, the child usually returns to the streets soon afterward. The law prohibits corporal punishment in schools.

Although the problem is difficult to quantify, social workers believe that there is a significant incidence of child abuse in families. The law specifies punishment for specific abuses against children. Rape or sodomy of a child under 15 years of age carries the death penalty. In January the Court of Cassation upheld the death sentence of a man for repeatedly raping and threatening the life of a 10-year old girl. The incidence of crimes, especially sexual crimes, is significantly higher than reported in the press.

People With Disabilities.—High unemployment in the general population restricts job opportunities for the disabled. The Government passed legislation in 1993 requiring future public buildings to accommodate the needs of the disabled and the retrofitting of existing public buildings, but implementation has been slow. Since 1993 the Special Education Department of the Ministry of Social Development has enrolled approximately 10,000 mentally and physically disabled persons in public and private sector training courses. It has placed approximately 400 disabled persons in public and private sector jobs. A new law requires that 2 percent of the available jobs be reserved for the physically disabled. Private organizations and members of the royal family actively promote programs to protect and promote the interests of the disabled. Jordan participates in the Special Olympics with the active encouragement of the royal family.

Indigenous People.—The Bedouin, Jordan's nomadic people, carry Jordanian passports and are increasingly assimilated into society. However, the Bedouin face social, economic, and professional discrimination, although the Government reserves six seats for the Bedouin in the Chamber of Deputies. The military and police forces have special units primarily composed of Bedouin.

Religious Minorities.—The Government does not recognize the Baha'i faith as a religion. It does not record the religion on national identity cards issued to Baha'is, nor does it register property belonging to the community. Unlike Christian denominations, the Baha'i community does not have its own court to adjudicate personal status and family matters. Baha'i personal status matters are heard in Islamic law courts.

The Government does not officially recognize Jehovah's Witnesses, the United Pentecostal Church, the Church of Christ, and the Church of Jesus Christ of Latter-Day Saints, but it allows them to conduct their activities without interference.

Established religious groups, which include Muslims, Roman Catholics, Greek Orthodox, Baptists, Anglicans, Presbyterians, Syriacs, and Armenian Orthodox, require official government recognition in order to register property in the name of the church, but members may practice their religion without government recognition. In general Christians do not suffer discrimination. Christians hold cabinet and other government positions and are represented in the media and academia approximately in proportion to their presence in the general population, which is estimated at 6 percent. Christian and Baha'i children in public schools are not required to participate in Islamic religious instruction.

National/Racial/Ethnic Minorities.—The Government granted full citizenship to all Palestinians who fled to Jordan after the 1948 Arab-Israeli war and to a large number of refugees who arrived after the 1967 War. However, refugees who fled Gaza after 1967 are not entitled to citizenship and until 1995 were issued only 2-year passports. As of October 1995, most Palestinian refugees became eligible to receive 5-year passports, but the Government has stressed that these passports are for travel only and do not connote nationality (see Section 2.d.). Palestinians suffer disproportionate scrutiny in taxation and discrimination in the award of university scholarships and appointments to senior positions in the Government and the military.

Section 6. Worker Rights

a. *The Right of Association.*—Workers in the private sector and in some state-owned companies have the right to establish and join unions. Unions must be registered to be considered legal. The law prohibits union membership for noncitizens. Over 30 percent of the work force is organized into 17 unions. Although union membership in the General Federation of Jordanian Trade Unions (GFJTU), the sole trade federation, is not mandatory, all unions belong to it. The Government subsidizes and audits the GFJTU's salaries and activities. Union officials are elected by secret ballot to 4-year terms. Although the Government cosponsors and approves the timing of these elections, it does not interfere in the choice of candidates.

Labor laws mandate that workers must obtain permission from the Government in order to strike. Unions generally will not seek approval for a strike, but workers will use the threat of a strike or wildcat action as a negotiating tactic. Strikes are prohibited if a labor dispute is under mediation or arbitration. If a settlement is not reached through mediation, the Ministry of Labor may refer the dispute to an industrial tribunal by agreement of both parties. If only one party agrees, the Ministry of Labor refers the dispute to the Council of Ministers and then to Parliament. The tribunal is an independent arbitration panel of judges appointed by the Ministry of Labor. The decisions of the panel are legally binding. Labor law prohibits employers from dismissing a worker during a labor dispute. There was one reported strike in 1996.

The GFJTU belongs to the Arab Labor Organization, the International Confederation of Arab Trade Unions, and to the International Confederation of Free Trade Unions (ICFTU).

b. *The Right to Organize and Bargain Collectively.*—Unions have, and exercise, the right to bargain collectively. The Constitution prohibits antiunion discrimination, but the ICFTU claims that the Government does not adequately protect employees from antiunion discrimination and that the Government has dismissed public sector employees for political reasons. Workers may lodge complaints of antiunion discrimination with the Ministry of Labor, which is authorized to order the reinstatement of employees discharged for union activities. There were no complaints of antiunion discrimination lodged with the Ministry of Labor in 1996.

The national labor laws apply in the free trade zones in Aqaba and Zarqa. Private sector employees in these zones belong to one national union that covers both zones and have the right to bargain collectively.

c. *Prohibition of Forced or Compulsory Labor.*—The Constitution forbids compulsory labor, except in a state of emergency such as war or natural disaster. Compulsory labor is not practiced.

d. *Minimum Age for Employment of Children.*—Labor law forbids children under the age of 16 from working except as apprentices. At age 13 children may begin part time training for up to 6 hours a day with night work prohibited. Ministry of Labor inspectors attempt to enforce the law on child labor, but in practice enforcement often does not extend to some small family businesses that employ underage children. Education is compulsory to age 15. Families in remote areas frequently keep some school-age children at home to work. Child peddlers work on the streets of Amman (see Section 5).

e. *Acceptable Conditions of Work.*—There is no national minimum wage. The Government periodically adjusts a minimum wage schedule for various trades, based on recommendations of an advisory panel representing workers, employers, and the Government. The lowest minimum wage rate on the schedule is about $150 (80 dinars) per month, including allowances. Workers earning the lowest wage find it difficult to provide a decent living for their families. The Government estimates the poverty level at a monthly wage of about $93 (65 dinars) per month for a family of three.

The law prohibits most workers from working more than the customary 48 hours a week, and 54 hours for hotel, restaurant, and cinema employees. Workers may not work more than 16 hours in any continuous period or more that 60 hours' overtime per month. Employees are entitled to 1 day off each week.

The law does not apply to domestic servants, who do not have a legal forum to address their labor grievances and have no standing to sue in court for nonpayment of wages. Abuse of domestic servants, most of whom are foreign, is widespread. Imprisonment of maids and confiscation of travel documents by employers is common. Complaints of beatings, underfeeding, and rape are not generally reported to officials by victims, who fear losing their work permits and being sent back to their nation of origin should they file a complaint. Domestic servants are generally not given a day off.

The law specifies a number of health and safety requirements for workers, including the presence of bathrooms, drinking water, and first aid equipment at work sites. The Ministry of Labor makes an effort to enforce health and safety requirements but is hampered by the lack of qualified inspectors. The inspectors do not have the power to order firms to comply with health and safety standards. The law does not require employers to report industrial accidents or occupational diseases to the Ministry of Labor. Workers do not have a statutory right to remove themselves from hazardous conditions without risking the loss of their job.

KUWAIT

Amirs, or princes, from the Al-Sabah family have ruled Kuwait in consultation with prominent community figures for over 200 years. The Constitution, adopted in 1962 shortly after Kuwait's independence from British protectorate status, provides for an elected National Assembly and enumerates the powers of the Government and the rights of citizens. It also permits the Amir to suspend its articles during periods of martial law. The Amir twice suspended constitutional provisions from 1976 to 1981 and from 1986 to 1992 and ruled extraconstitutionally during these periods. Iraq occupied Kuwait from August 1990 until its forces were expelled in February 1991. The National Assembly resumed functioning after the 1992 elections, and elections were held again in October. New legislation in October granted the judiciary greater administrative and financial independence, but the Amir appoints all judges.

The Ministry of Interior supervises the security apparatus, including the Criminal Investigation Department (CID) and Kuwait State Security (KSS), two agencies that, in addition to the regular police, investigate internal security-related offenses. Some members of the security forces committed human rights abuses.

Richly endowed with oil, the country's estimated per capita gross national product is approximately $20,600. Costly reconstruction undertaken to recover from the destruction caused by the Iraqi occupation led the Government to incur a cumulative fiscal deficit of approximately $70 billion, which it covered by liquidating government-owned foreign assets and increasing the public debt. The Government is gradually reducing the deficit and plans to eliminate it by the year 2000. Despite its emphasis on an open market, the Government continues to dominate the local economy through direct expenditures and government-owned companies and equities. The Government has initiated a program of disposing of its holdings of stock in private companies.

The Government's human rights record improved, although problems remain in certain areas. Police abuse detainees during interogation, and guards beat a large number of prisoners after a January prison riot. Citizens cannot change their head of state. The Government bans formal political parties, and women do not have the right to vote. The Government restricts freedom of assembly and association, and places some limits on the freedom of religion. Journalists practice self-censorship. The Government prevents the return to Kuwait of stateless persons who have strong ties to the country. Deportation orders may be issued by administrative order, and hundreds of persons are being held in detention facilities pending deportation. Many have been held for a year or more. Discrimination and violence against women are problems. The Government restricts the rights of women, e.g., women do not have the right to vote. Domestic servants are not protected by labor law, and unskilled foreign workers suffer from lack of a minimum wage in the private sector and from failures to enforce labor law.

However, for the first time, sons of naturalized male citizens and citizens naturalized between 20 and 30 years ago were eligible to vote in the October National Assembly elections. Although the Government continues to be indifferent to the human rights problems of the more than 100,000 stateless people residing in Kuwait known as the "bidoon," the Government naturalized a small fraction of the bidoon, and made some efforts to address their status. The Amir commuted the sentences of four individuals who were convicted of security offenses in 1991 by the Martial Law Court. During the year the National Assembly passed laws granting the judiciary greater administrative and financial independence and providing for increased access and employment opportunites for the disabled.

RESPECT FOR HUMAN RIGHTS

Section 1. Respect for the Integrity of the Person, Including Freedom From:

a. *Political and Other Extrajudicial Killing.*—There were no reports of political or other extrajudicial killings.

There were no developments in the investigations into the extrajudicial killings that occurred during the chaotic period after Kuwait's liberation in 1991.

b. *Disappearance.*—There were no reports of politically motivated disappearances.

There have been no developments since 1994 in the cases of disappearance that occurred following Kuwait's liberation in 1991.

According to the International Committee of the Red Cross (ICRC), Iraqi authorities have not yet accounted for 602 Kuwaitis and residents of Kuwait, including 8 women, who were taken prisoner during Iraq's occupation of Kuwait. Iraq repatriated one woman in May. The Government of Iraq has refused to comply with U.N. Security Council Resolution 687, which stipulates the release of the detainees. Iraq denies that it holds Kuwaiti detainees.

c. *Torture and Other Cruel, Inhuman, or Degrading Treatment or Punishment.*— The Constitution prohibits torture, however, there continue to be credible reports that the police physically abuse detainees during interrogation. The police were more likely to inflict such abuse on non-Kuwaitis than on citizens. Reported abuse includes blindfoldings, verbal threats, slaps, and blows.

The Government says that it investigates all allegations of abuse and that it has punished at least some of the offenders. However, the Government does not make public the findings in its abuse investigations or what, if any, punishments are imposed. This omission creates a climate of impunity, which diminishes deterrence against torture and abuse. Prison guards beat a large number of prisoners following a prison riot in January. Although authorities apparently put an end to the abuse, it is not known if the guards involved in the beatings were disciplined.

Defendants have the right to present evidence in court that they have been mistreated during interrogation. However, the courts frequently dismiss abuse complaints because defendants are often unable to substantiate their complaints with physical evidence. Members of the security forces deliberately hide or misrepresent their identity, a practice that further complicates confirmation of abuse.

Prison conditions, including conditions for those held for security offenses, meet minimum international standards, in terms of food, access to basic health care, scheduled family visits, cleanliness, and opportunities for exercise and work. Continuing problems include overcrowding and the lack of specialized medical care. In addition, some minor children of female prisoners stay in the prison with their mothers. The Government is taking steps to improve prison conditions.

The National Assembly's Human Rights Committee continued to monitor prison conditions, and the Government allows the ICRC access to all detention facilities.

d. *Arbitrary Arrest, Detention, or Exile.*—The Constitution provides for freedom from arbitrary arrest and detention. There were no reports of arbitrary arrest during the year.

Police officers must obtain an arrest warrant from state prosecutors before making an arrest, although in misdemeanor cases the arresting officer may issue them. Security forces occasionally detain persons at checkpoints in Kuwait City (see Section 2.d).

Under the Penal Code, a suspect may not be held more than 4 days without charge. Security officers sometimes prevent families from visiting detainees during this confinement. After 4 days, prosecutors must either release the suspect or file charges. If charges are filed, prosecutors may remand a suspect to an additional 21 days in detention. Prosecutors may also obtain court orders for further detention pending trial.

Approximately 1,900 persons are serving sentences at the central prison of Kuwait. Although the number of persons in detention awaiting deportation reached almost 1,000 during the year, the Government granted temporary conditional releases to many detainees during the second half of the year, significantly lowering this figure. Many deportation orders are issued administratively, without benefit of a trial. The Government may expel noncitizens (including bidoon, i.e., stateless residents of Kuwait), even if they are native-born or long-term residents, if it considers them security risks. The Government may also expel foreigners if they are unable to obtain or renew work or residency permits. About 10 percent of the detainees awaiting deportation, especially Iraqis and bidoon, have been in detention for more than 1 year, some for up to 5 years. However, the Government does not deport such detainees to their country of origin against their will.

The law protects citizens from exile, and there were no reports of this practice.

e. *Denial of Fair Public Trial.*—The Constitution states that "judges shall not be subject to any authority;" however, until April the Ministry of Justice controlled the judiciary's administrative and financial matters. In April the National Assembly passed a law that regulates the Government's ability to appoint, transfer, discipline, or dismiss both Kuwaiti and non-Kuwaiti judges. The law also requires the Ministry of Justice to disclose the judiciary's appropriation recommendations to the National Assembly.

One court system tries both civil and criminal cases. The Court of Cassation is the highest level of judicial appeal. Sunni and Shi'a Muslims have recourse to courts of their respective denominations for family law cases; however, there is no Shi'a appellate court. Shi'a cases are referred to the Sunni court on appeal.

Defendants have the right to confront their accusers and appeal verdicts. The Amir has the constitutional power to pardon or commute all sentences. Defendants in felony cases are required by law to be represented in court by legal counsel, which the courts will provide in criminal cases. In misdemeanor cases, defendants have the right to waive the presence of legal counsel, but the court is not required to provide counsel to indigent defendants.

Both defendants and prosecutors may appeal court verdicts to the High Court of Appeal, which may rule on whether the law was properly applied, as well as on guilt or innocence of the defendant. Decisions of the High Court of Appeal may be presented to the Court of Cassation, which conducts a limited, formal review of cases to determine only whether the law was properly applied.

In the regular court system there are no groups, including women, who are barred from testifying or whose testimony is given lesser weight. However, the Islamic courts, which have jurisdiction over family law, apply Islamic law, which states that the testimony of two women equals that of one man.

There are no reported political prisoners. The Government continues to incarcerate persons convicted of collaboration with Iraq during the occupation. By law such collaboration is a felony. Most of the people convicted in the Martial Law Court in 1991, and the Special State Security Court, which was abolished in 1995, did not receive fair trials. In 1996 the Amir commuted the sentences of four individuals convicted by the Martial Law Court.

f. *Arbitrary Interference with Privacy, Family, Home, or Correspondence.*—The Constitution provides for individual privacy and sanctity of the home. The police must obtain a warrant to search both public and private property, unless they are in hot pursuit of a suspect fleeing the scene of a crime or if alcohol or narcotics are suspected on the premises. The warrant can be obtained from the state prosecutor or, in the case of private property, from a judge. The security forces occasionally monitor the activities of individuals and their communications.

By law males must obtain government approval to marry foreign-born women. Many citizens comply with this law by validating there foreign marriage certificate at a Kuwaiti embassy or consulate. Although the Government may advise against marriage to a foreign national, there are no known cases of the Government refusing permission to marry. The Government also advises women against marrying foreign nationals.

Section 2. Respect for Civil Liberties, Including:

a. *Freedom of Speech and Press.*—The Constitution states that "freedom of the press, printing, and publishing shall be guaranteed in accordance with the conditions and manner specified by law." With a few exceptions, citizens are free to criticize the Government at public meetings and in the media. However, journalists practice self-censorship. Several laws empower the Government to impose restrictions on freedom of speech and the press, but they are rarely invoked.

Newspapers are privately owned and free to publish on many social, economic, and political issues and frequently criticize government policies and officials, including the Crown Prince, who is also the Prime Minister.

The Government ended prepublication censorship in 1992, but journalists still censor themselves. The Press Law prohibits the publication of any direct criticism of the Amir, official government communications with other states, and material that serves to "attack religions" or "incite people to commit crimes, create hatred, or spread dissension among the populace." In 1995 the Government banned publication of one newspaper, Al Anba, for 5 days under a law that the media and opposition parliamentarians alleged was unconstitutional. The paper took the Government to court and has appealed an initial court ruling in favor of the Government. In 1996 six armed individuals threatened the employees of a newspaper that published a cartoon deemed offensive to Islam. No one was hurt in the attack, and the police arrested those involved.

In order to begin publication of a newspaper, the publisher must obtain an operating license from the Ministry of Information. Publishers may lose their license if their publications do not appear for 6 months. This 6-month rule prevents publishers from publishing sporadically—it is not used to suspend or shut down existing newspapers. Individuals must also obtain permission from the Ministry of Information before publishing any printed material, including brochures and wall posters.

The Government does not censor foreign journalists and permits them open access to the country.

The Government owns and controls the radio and television companies. The Middle East Broadcasting Company and Egyptian television transmit to Kuwait without censorship. The Government does not inhibit the purchase of satellite dishes. Citizens with such devices are free to watch a variety of programs, including those broadcast from Israel.

The Ministry of Information censors all books, films, videotapes, periodicals, and other imported publications deemed morally offensive. However, the Ministry has censored political topics as well. The General Organization of Printing and Publishing controls the printing, publishing, and distribution of informational materials in Kuwait.

There is no government censorship of university teaching, research, or publication. However, academics are subject to the same restraints as the media with regard to criticism of the Amir or Islam. In October Ahmed al-Baghdadi, a Kuwaiti University political science professor, received a death threat in response to a brief article he wrote for a university magazine. Both legislators and the Islamic movement were angered by a reference in the article to the Prophet that they viewed as critical of the Prophet. The Islamic magazine Al-Mojtama called for al-Baghdadi to be fired from the University. Al-Baghdadi has sued the magazine for libel. During the year, parliamentarians and university organizations publicly criticized several university professors for writings deemed critical of Islam and inconsistent with social mores. Some of the professors were subject to inquires by the university and the Ministry of Education, and some were referred to the Public Prosecution Department for investigation into possible criminal violations. None of the professors was suspended or charged with any criminal wrongdoing; however, investigations were still pending at year's end. Private citizens filed apostasy or blasphemy suits against two of the professors in Islamic (Personal Status) Court.

b. *Freedom of Peaceful Assembly and Association.*—Although the Constitution affirms the right to assembly, the Government restricts this right, as well as that of association, and bans political parties. Several informal blocs, acting much like parties, exist and were active during the October National Assembly elections. The Government has made no effort to constrain these groupings, which are organized on the basis of common ideological goals. Many may be categorized as opposition groups. Public gatherings, however, must receive prior government approval, as must private gatherings of more than five persons that result in the issuance of a public statement.

Political activity finds its outlet in informal, family-based, almost exclusively male, social gatherings known as diwaniyas. Practically every male adult, including the Amir, hosts and attends diwaniyas at which every possible topic is discussed. The diwaniya contributes to the development of political consensus and official decisionmaking.

All nongovernmental organizations (NGO's) must obtain a license from the Ministry of Social Affairs and Labor. The Government uses its power to license as a means of political control. The Ministry has licensed over 55 NGO's, including professional groups, a bar association, and scientific bodies. These groups receive Government subsidies for their operating expenses. They must obtain permission from the Ministry before attending international conferences. However, since 1985 the Ministry has issued only two licenses. The Ministry has disapproved other license requests on the grounds that previously established NGO's already provide services similar to those proposed by the petitioners.

By banning unregistered NGO's, the Government mainly sought to dissolve groups whose efforts were not coordinated with an official government committee working for the release of the missing persons presumed held in Iraq. The ban discourages these groups from fundraising and recruitment, and prevents them from holding public meetings and making their views known in the press. Nevertheless, the Government overlooks the activities of many unregistered NGO's, despite a 1993 decree ordering them to cease activities. No organization has challenged the 1993 decree in court.

c. *Freedom of Religion.*—Islam is the state religion. The Constitution states that Islamic law, Shari'a, is "a main source of legislation." The ruling family and many prominent Kuwaiti families belong to the denomination of Sunni Islam. However, 30 to 40 percent of the population belong to the Shi'a denomination. They are free to conduct their traditional forms of worship without government interference.

The Constitution states that "all people are equal in * * * public rights and duties before the law, without distinction as to * * * religion," and that "freedom of belief is absolute. The State protects the freedom to practice religion in accordance with established customs, provided that it does not conflict with public policy or morals." There are several legally recognized expatriate congregations and churches, including a Catholic diocese and several Protestant churches. Expatriates who are members of religions not sanctioned in the Koran, e.g., Hindus, Sikhs, and Buddhists, may not build places of worship but may worship privately in their homes. The Government prohibits missionaries to proselytize among Muslims; however, they may serve expatriate congregations. The Government prohibits Muslims from converting to other religions. The law prohibits religious education for religions other than Islam, although this law does not appear to be rigidly enforced. The Government does not permit the establishment of non-Islamic publishing companies or training institutions for clergy.

The law prohibits non-Muslims from becoming citizens. A non-Muslim male must convert to Islam when he marries a Muslim woman, if the wedding is to be legal in Kuwait. A non-Muslim female does not have to convert to Islam to marry a Muslim male, but it is to her advantage to do so, i.e., failure to do so may ultimately place custody of children in the hands of the Muslim father, should the couple later divorce.

In May a family law court applying Shari'a law convicted former Muslim Robert Hussein of apostasy for converting to Christianity in a case filed by a group of private Muslims citizens. The verdict ordered Hussein to pay all legal costs and affected certain personal rights, such as child custody and property inheritance, but did not carry a criminal penalty or affect his civil rights. The judge and some private citizens publicly quoted a Koranic reference to death being the punishment for apostasy. The Government later publicly affirmed Hussein's civil rights and stated that he would be protected. Hussein did not attend a scheduled appellate court session. Since that date, the court has not taken any action on his appeal.

d. *Freedom of Movement Within the Country, Foreign Travel, Emigration, and Repatriation.*—Citizens have the right to travel freely within the country and to change their workplace as desired. Unmarried women the age of 21 and over are free to obtain a passport and travel abroad at any time. However, married women who apply for passports must obtain their husband's signature on the application form. Once she has a passport, a married woman does not need her husband's permission to travel, but he may prevent her departure from the country by placing a 24-hour travel ban on her. He can do this by contacting the immigration authorities. After this 24-hour period, a court order is required if the husband still wishes to prevent his wife from leaving the country. All minor children must have their father's permission to travel outside of the country. Citizens are free to emigrate and to return.

A serious problem exists in the case of the bidoon, who are stateless persons, many of Iraqi or Iranian descent, who resided in Kuwait prior to the Iraqi invasion. The Government argues that many bidoon (the term means "without") are concealing their true citizenship in order to remain in Kuwait, become citizens, and enjoy the generous benefits provided to citizens. Some bidoon have had residency ties to Kuwait for generations. Others immigrated to Kuwait during the oil boom years. There are approximately 117,000 stateless persons in Kuwait, down from a prewar level of about 220,000. The Government does not wish the return of the bidoon who departed Kuwait during the Gulf War and frequently delays or denies issuing them entry visas. This policy imposes serious hardships and family separations.

The Government continued its postwar policy of reducing by deportation the number of nationals from those countries that supported Iraq during its invasion of Kuwait. The number of such residents is now only about 10 percent of its prewar total. The Government permits the ICRC to verify if a deportee objects to returning to his country of origin. The Government detains those deportees who have objections at the main deportation center. Many have been held for 1 year or more; some have been held for 5 years.

Security forces in Kuwait city occasionally set up checkpoints where they may detain individuals. The checkpoints are mainly for immigration purposes and are used to apprehend undocumented aliens.

There is no legislation governing refugees, asylees, or first asylum, and no clear or standard procedure for processing a person's claim to be a refugee. The Constitution prohibits the extradition of political refugees. The Ministry of Interior may issue residency permits to persons granted political asylum, although this is not a frequent occurrence. The Government states that it does not deport anyone who claims a fear of persecution in his home country, but it will often keep such persons in detention rather than grant them permission to live and work in Kuwait. The United Nations High Commissioner for Refugees (UNHCR) maintains an office in Kuwait and has access to refugees in detention.

Section 3. Respect for Political Rights: The Right of Citizens to Change Their Government

Citizens cannot change their head of state. Women and citizens naturalized less than 20 years ago may not vote. In addition members of the armed forces, police, and other uniformed personnel of the Ministry of Interior are prohibited from voting.

Under the Constitution, the Amir holds executive power and shares legislative power with the National Assembly. The Prime Minister presides over a 14-member cabinet. In accordance with the practice of the ruling family, the Prime Minister is always the Crown Prince. The Constitution empowers the Amir to suspend its provisions and to rule by decree. The Amir dissolved the National Assembly from 1976 to 1981, and in 1986 the Amir effectively dissolved the Assembly by suspending the constitutional provisions on the Assembly's election. The Assembly remained dissolved until 1992, when elections were held. Members serve 4-year terms, and National Assembly elections were held on in October. The elections were conducted freely and fairly among the minority of citizens who are permitted to vote; 229 candidates ran for the Assembly's 50 seats. Since the Government prohibits political parties, assembly candidates must nominate themselves. Nonetheless, informal political groupings are active in the Assembly. The Constitution empowers the National Assembly to overturn any Amiri decrees made during the dissolution, and the Assembly has done so in some cases.

Approximately 107,000 male citizens, almost the entire franchised population, registered to vote in the 1996 elections, and 80 percent of registered voters cast ballots. For the first time sons of naturalized citizens and Kuwaiti citizens naturalized 20 to 30 years ago were eligible to vote. Some women demonstrated at polling booths to demand that they be given voting rights before the next election.

Women are disenfranchised and have little opportunity to influence government. In the past, a majority of the members of the National Assembly have expressed opinions favoring women's right to vote; however, a draft law on this issue remained in committee for over a year, and was never put to a vote. No strong parliamentary support currently exists for this law, and the Government has made no effort to persuade the National Assembly to pass the legislation. Women's groups are divided on this issue.

Members of Kuwait's Shi'a minority are generally underrepresented in high government positions, although in recent years two Shi'a Muslims were appointed to the Cabinet and one was named to a high-ranking military post.

Section 4. Governmental Attitude Regarding International and Nongovernmental Investigation of Alleged Violations of Human Rights

The Government has prevented the establishment of local human rights groups by not approving their requests for licenses (see Section 2.b.). The Government permits international human rights organizations to visit Kuwait and to establish offices. Several organizations conduct field work and report excellent communication with and reasonable cooperation from the Government.

The National Assembly has a human rights committee, which takes testimony from individuals about abuses, investigates prison conditions, and has made nonbinding recommendations for redress.

Section 5. Discrimination Based on Race, Sex, Religion, Disability, Language, or Social Status

The Constitution prohibits discrimination based on race, national origin, language, or religion. However, laws and regulations discriminate against women, and non-Kuwaitis face widespread social, economic, and judicial discrimination.

Women.—According to some local experts, domestic abuse of women occurs in an estimated 15 percent of all marriages. Each of the country's 50 police stations receives approximately one to two complaints of spousal abuse each week. Women in such cases usually take refuge in the homes of relatives. The police and the courts generally seek to resolve family disputes informally and may ask the offending spouse to sign a statement affirming that he will end the abuse. The police refer serious cases to the Psychiatric Department at the Ministry of Health. The courts have found husbands guilty of spousal abuse. Although it is not common, there are reports of rape of female domestic servants by male employers.

A significant number of employers physically abuse expatriate women working as domestic servants, and sexual abuse is also a problem. The local press gives the problem considerable attention. Foreign-born servants have the right to sue their employers for abuse, but few do so owing to both fear of deportation and fear that the judicial system is biased against them. The Government has designated a police station to investigate complaints and provide some shelter for runaway maids. Both the police and the courts have taken action against employers when presented with evidence of serious abuse.

Runaway servants seek shelter at their country's embassy where they seek repatriation or a change in employers. On several occasions, the Philippine embassy has sheltered nearly 300 women at once. Although most of these women sought shelter due to contractual or financial problems with their employers, many also had suffered physical and sexual abuse.

Women experience legal and social discrimination. They are denied the right to vote (see Section 3); their testimony is not given equal weight to that of males in the Islamic courts (see Section 1.e.), and married women require their husband's permission to obtain a passport (see Section 2.d.). By law only males are able to confer citizenship, which means that children born to Kuwaiti mothers and stateless fathers are themselves stateless. Inheritance is governed by Islamic law, which differs according to sects. For example, Sunni female heirs receive half the male heirs' inheritance, while a sole Shi'a female heir may receive the whole of her parents' or brother's estate.

Women are traditionally restrained from choosing certain roles in society, and the law restricts women from working in "dangerous industries" and trades "harmful" to health. Educated women maintain that an Islamic fundamentalist trend limits career opportunities. Nonetheless, an estimated 28 percent of women of working age are employed. The law promises "remuneration equal to that of a man provided she does the same work." This promise is respected in practice. Women work as doctors, engineers, lawyers, and professors. A few have reached senior government positions in the Foreign Ministry, the Ministry of Education, and the state-owned Kuwaiti Petroleum Corporation. However, there are no female judges or prosecutors, and women may not run for election to the National Assembly.

In case of divorce, the Government makes family entitlement payments to the divorced husband, who is expected by law and custom to provide for his children even though custody of minor children is usually given to the mother. The law discriminates against women married to foreign men. These women are not entitled to government housing subsidies that are available to male citizens. The law also requires women to pay residence fees for their husbands and does not recognize marriage as the basis for granting residency to foreign-born husbands. Instead, the law grants residency only if the husband is employed. By contrast, men married to foreign-born women do not have to pay residency fees for their spouses, and their spouses' right to residency derives from marriage. A gender segregation bill passed the National Assembly in July, however the Amir has not signed it, and it was not in force by year's end.

Polygymy is legal. A husband is obliged to inform his first wife that he is taking a second wife. The husband is obligated to provide the first wife a separate household if that is her preference. It is the second wife's choice to get married. A first wife who objects to a second marriage can request a divorce, but the court's determination of divorce and child custody would be made on grounds other than the fact of the second marriage itself.

Children.—The Government is committed to the welfare of children. Children receive a free education. The Government provides free health care and a variety of other services to all children. There is no societal pattern of abuse of children.

Marriage of girls under the age of 17 is uncommon among the urban population but remains a practice of Bedouins in outlying areas.

People With Disabilities.—There is no institutionalized discrimination against physically disabled persons in housing, employment, education, and in the provision of state services. In addition to extensive government benefits for the disabled that cover transportation, housing, job training, and social welfare, the National Assembly passed a law mandating accessibility for the disabled to all facilities frequented by the public. The law also provides an affirmative action employment program for the disabled.

National/Racial/Ethnic Minorities.—The Government's failure to improve the plight of the 117,000 bidoon remains a significant human rights abuse. The bidoon have been the objects of hostile government policy since the late 1980's. Since then the Government has eliminated the bidoon from the census rolls, discontinued their access to government jobs and free education, and sought to deport many bidoon. In 1993 the Government decreed that bidoon males would no longer be allowed to enlist in the military service. Those presently in the armed forces are being gradually replaced. The Government does not routinely issue travel documents to bidoon, and if bidoon travel abroad, they risk being barred from returning to the country unless they receive advance permission from the immigration authorities. Marriages pose special hardships because the offspring of male bidoon inherit the father's undetermined legal status.

In 1996 the Government naturalized a small fraction of the bidoon, primarily bidoon who have served in the military and security forces, and children born to marriages between bidoon males and Kuwaiti women. As a step towards resolving the bidoon issue, the Government required all bidoon to register, and issued a card to each person that identifies whether the individual's family came to Kuwait before or after the 1965 census. The card does not accord the holder any legal status, nor is it an official identity document, but anyone who did not register is considered an illegal resident subject to deportation. The Government says that it will review the registrations; however, the Government has not announced the goal of the process, or its standards for review. The Government claims that it will issue a residency visa, and legal status, to any bidoon who can present a passport, regardless of the country of issuance. This has led some bidoon to acquire passports from countries with which they have no tie, but which have liberal "economic citizenship" programs. There are reports that the Government has denied residency visas to some bidoon who obtained passports, particularly Iraqis. In some cases the Government has unilaterally decided the "real" nationalities of bidoon without a hearing and without possibility of review.

Since the end of the Gulf War, government policy has been targeted against workers from those nations that supported Iraq, especially Jordanians and Yemenis, and also against Palestinians. The Government argues that during the Iraqi occupation many residents from these places sided with the Iraqi forces. The Government has delayed or denied the issuance of work and residency permits to persons in these groups and in many cases has hindered those workers that are permitted to reside in the country from sponsoring their families to join them.

Section 6. Worker Rights

a. *The Right of Association.*—Workers have the right, but are not required, to join unions. Nonetheless, the Government restricts the right of association by prohibiting all workers from freely establishing trade unions. The law stipulates that workers may establish only one union in any occupational trade and that the unions may establish only one federation. The International Labor Organization (ILO) has long criticized such restrictions.

Approximately 50,000 people are organized in 14 unions, 12 of which are affiliated with the Kuwait Trade Union Federation (KTUF), the sole, legal trade union federation. The Bank Worker's Union and the Kuwait Airways Workers Union are independent. The Government has shown no sign that it would accept the establishment of more than one legal trade union federation. The law stipulates that any new union must include at least 100 workers, of whom at least 15 are citizens. Both the ILO and the International Confederation of Free Trade Unions (ICFTU) have criticized this requirement because it discourages unions in sectors employing few citizens such as the construction industry and domestic sectors.

The Government's pervasive oversight powers further erode union independence. The Government subsidizes as much as 90 percent of most union budgets, may inspect the financial records of any union, and prohibits any union from engaging in political or religious activities, which the law does not clearly define. The law empowers the courts to dissolve any union for violating labor laws or for threatening "public order and morals." Such a court decision may be appealed. The Amir may also dissolve a union by decree. By law, the Ministry of Social Affairs and Labor is authorized to seize the assets of any dissolved union. The ILO has criticized this aspect of the law. Although no union has been dissolved, the law subordinates the legal existence of the unions to the power of the State.

Foreigners constitute most of the work force and about a third of its unionized work force. Yet the law discriminates against foreign workers by permitting them to join unions only after 5 years of residence and only as nonvoting members. Unlike union members who are citizens, foreign workers do not have the right to elect their leadership. The law requires that union officials be citizens. The ILO has criticized the 5-year residency requirement and the denial of voting rights for foreign workers. KTUF administers an Expatriate Labor Office which is authorized to investigate complaints of foreign laborers and provide them with free legal advice. Any foreign worker may submit a grievance to the Labor Office regardless of union status.

The law limits the right to strike. It requires that all labor disputes be referred to compulsory arbitration if labor and management cannot reach a solution (see Section 6.b.). The law does not have any provision guaranteeing strikers that they will be free from any legal or administrative action taken against them by the State.

Unions may affiliate with international bodies. The KTUF belongs to the International Confederation of Arab Trade Unions and the formerly Soviet-controlled World Federation of Trade Unions.

b. *The Right to Organize and Bargain Collectively.*—Workers have the right to organize and bargain collectively, subject to certain restrictions (see Section 6.a.). These rights have been incorporated in the Labor Law and have, according to all reports, been respected in practice.

The Labor Law provides for direct negotiations between employers and "laborers or their representatives" in the private sector. Most agreements are resolved in such negotiations; if not, either party may petition the Ministry of Social Affairs and Labor for mediation. If mediation fails, the dispute is referred to a labor arbitration board composed of officials from the High Court of Appeals, the Attorney General's office, and the Ministry of Social Affairs and Labor.

The Civil Service Law makes no provision for collective bargaining between government workers and their employer. Technically, wages and conditions of employment for civil service workers are established by the Government, but in practice, the Government sets the benefit scales after conducting informal meetings with officials from the civil service unions. Union officials resolve most issues at the working level and have regular access to other senior officials.

The Labor Law prohibits antiunion discrimination. Any worker who alleges antiunion discrimination has the right to appeal to the judiciary. There were no reports of discrimination against employees, based on their affiliation with a union. Employers found guilty of antiunion discrimination must reinstate workers fired for union activities.

There are no export processing zones.

c. *Prohibition of Forced or Compulsory Labor.*—The Constitution prohibits forced labor "except in cases specified by law for national emergency and with just remuneration."

Foreign workers may not change their employment without permission from their original sponsors unless they have been in the country for over 2 years. Domestic servants are particularly vulnerable to abuses from this practice because they are not protected by labor law. In many cases employers exercise some control over their servants by holding their passports, although the Government prohibits this practice and has acted to retrieve passports of maids involved in disputes.

Domestic servants who run away from their employers may be treated as criminals under the law. However, the authorities usually do not enforce this provision of the law. In some reported cases, employers illegally withheld wages from domestic servants to cover the costs involved in bringing them to Kuwait. The Government has done little, if anything, to protect domestics in such cases.

d. *Minimum Age for Employment of Children.*—The legal minimum age is 18 years for all forms of work, both full- and part-time. Employers must obtain permits from the Ministry of Social Affairs and Labor to employ juveniles between the ages of 14 and 18 in certain trades. Education is compulsory for children between the ages of 6 and 15. These laws are not fully observed in the nonindustrial sector, although no instances involving children have been alleged. Some small businessmen employ their children on a part-time basis, and there have been unconfirmed reports that some south Asian domestic servants are under the age of 18, but falsified their age in order to enter Kuwait.

Juveniles may work a maximum of 6 hours a day on the condition that they work no more than 4 consecutive hours followed by a 1-hour rest period.

e. *Acceptable Conditions of Work.*—The Ministry of Social Affairs and Labor is responsible for enforcing all labor laws. A two-tiered labor market ensures high wages for Kuwaiti employees while foreign workers, particularly unskilled laborers, receive substantially lower wages. There is no legal minimum wage in the private sector. In the public sector, the effective minimum wage is approximately $757 (226 dinars) per month for citizens and approximately $301 (90 dinars) per month for noncitizens. The public sector minimum wage provides an acceptable standard of living for a worker and family. Wages of unskilled workers in the private sector do not always permit a decent standard of living.

The Labor Law establishes general conditions of work for both the public and the private sectors, with the oil industry treated separately. The Civil Service Law also prescribes additional conditions for the public sector. The Labor Law limits the standard workweek to 48 hours with 1 full day of rest per week, provides for a minimum of 14 workdays of leave each year, and establishes a compensation schedule for industrial accidents. Domestic servants, who are specifically excluded from the Private Sector Labor Law, frequently work long hours, greatly in excess of 48 hours.

The ILO has urged the Government to guarantee the weekly 24-consecutive-hour rest period to temporary workers employed for a period of less than 6 months and workers in enterprises employing fewer than five persons. The law pertaining to the oil industry provides for a 40-hour workweek, 30 days of annual leave, and sick leave. Laws establishing work conditions are not always applied uniformly to foreign workers. Labor law also provides for employer-provided medical care and compensation to workers disabled by injury or disease due to job-related causes. The law also requires that employers provide periodic medical examinations to workers exposed to environmental hazards on the job (i.e., chemicals, asbestos, etc.). The Government has issued occupational health and safety standards; however, compliance and enforcement appear poor, especially with respect to unskilled foreign laborers. Employers often exploit workers' willingness to accept substandard conditions. Foreign workers, especially unskilled or semiskilled south Asian workers, frequently face contractual disputes, poor working conditions, and some physical abuse.

Workers have the right to remove themselves from dangerous work situations without jeopardy to their continued employment, and legal protections exist for workers who file complaints about such conditions. The latest available figures for occupational injuries show 1,472 such occurrences in 1994, primarily in the sectors of construction and building, manufacturing, hotels and restaurants, and transportation. To cut accident rates, the Government periodically inspects installations to raise awareness among workers and employers and ensure that they abide by the safety rules, control the pollution resulting from certain dangerous industries, train workers in specialized institutes to use new machines, and report violations.

LEBANON

Lebanon is a parliamentary republic in which the President is by tradition a Maronite Christian, the Prime Minister a Sunni Muslim, and the speaker of the Chamber of Deputies a Shi'a Muslim. The Parliament consists of 128 deputies, equally divided between Christian and Muslim representatives. The judiciary is generally independent, but is subject to political pressure.

Non-Lebanese military forces control much of Lebanon. These include about 30,000 Syrian troops; a contingent of Israeli army regulars; an Israeli-supported militia in southern Lebanon, and several armed Palestinian factions. All undermine the authority of the central Government and prevent the application of law in the patchwork of areas not under the Government's control. In 1991 the governments of Lebanon and Syria concluded a security agreement that provides a framework for cooperation between their armed forces. However, Syrian military intelligence units in Lebanon conduct their activities independently of the agreement.

In 1989 the Arab League brokered a peace settlement at Taif, Saudi Arabia, to end the civil war in Lebanon. According to the Taif Accord, Syrian troops were scheduled to be redeployed from their positions in Lebanon's coastal population areas to the Biqa' valley, with full withdrawal contingent upon fullfillment of other aspects of the Taif Accord and subsequent agreement by both the Lebanese and Syrian governments. Although the Syrian Government has refused to carry out this withdrawal from the coastal areas, it made some partial redeployments from Beirut and the Metn in the latter part of the year. One Syrian official cited the increased ability of Lebanese forces to fulfill security functions as a factor in the redeployment. However, strong Syrian influence over Lebanese politics and decisionmakers make Lebanese officials unwilling to press for a complete withdrawal. This relationship with Syria does not reflect the will of most Lebanese citizens.

Israel exerts control in and near its self-proclaimed "security zone" in south Lebanon through its surrogate, the South Lebanon Army (SLA), and the presence of about 1,000 Israeli regular troops. Also in south Lebanon, the Iranian-backed Shi'a Muslim militia, Hizballah, and allied Palestinian guerrillas continue to be locked in a cycle of attack and counterattack with Israeli forces and the SLA. Palestinian groups operate autonomously in refugee camps throughout the country. During the year, the Government continued to consolidate its authority in the parts of the country under its control, but made little effort to disarm Hizballah, Hizballah's allies, and the SLA, or to reassert state control over the Palestinian refugee camps.

The security forces comprise the Lebanese Armed Forces (LAF), which may arrest and detain suspects on national security grounds; the Internal Security Forces (ISF), which enforce laws, conduct searches and arrests, and refer cases to the judiciary; and the State Security Apparatus and the Surete General, both of which collect information on groups that may jeopardize state security. The Surete General is also responsible for the issuance of passports and residency permits and for the censorship of foreign periodicals and movies that treat national security issues. The security forces committed serious human rights abuses.

Before the 1975–90 hostilities, Lebanon was an important regional financial and commercial center. The war weakened its commercial leadership and inflicted massive damage on the economic infrastructure. In 1996 the economy continued to recover as the Government took steps to restore confidence and implement an ambitious reconstruction program.

Since the end of hostilities, the Government has made no substantial effort to improve human rights conditions, and serious problems remain in several areas. Members of the security forces used excessive force and tortured some detainees. Prison conditions remained poor. Government abuses also included the arbitrary arrest and detention of persons who opposed government policies. The Government infringed on citizens' privacy rights. The Government continued to restrict freedom of assembly and ban demonstrations. The Government also partially limited press freedom, particularly by passing a new media law to restrict radio and television broadcasting. The right of citizens to change their government has deteriorated in recent years. Although the August-September parliamentary elections represented a step forward, the electoral process was flawed by various shortcomings, as the elections were not prepared or carried out impartially. Discrimination against women and Palestinians, and violence against women are problems.

Although the overall level of armed conflict has declined in recent years, heavy fighting occurred in April, provoked by two lethal incidents in the south. Life and property, especially in the south, are still threatened by artillery and aerial attacks by the various contending forces. These forces continue to commit abuses, including killings, terrorist bombings and abductions.

The SLA maintains a separate and arbitrary system of justice in the zone, which is independent of Lebanese central authority. During the year, SLA officials reportedly arbitrarily arrested and detained persons, mistreated detainees, deported some alleged criminals to Israel to face legal charges, and expelled some local residents from their homes in the zone. Palestinian groups in refugee camps maintain a separate arbitrary system of justice for other Palestinians. Members of the various Palestinian groups that control the camps tortured and detained their Palestinian rivals.

RESPECT FOR HUMAN RIGHTS

Section 1. Respect for the Integrity of the Person, Including Freedom From:

a. *Political and Other Extrajudicial Killing.*—During the year, political killings declined as the Government further consolidated its authority over the country. Various factions and unknown persons committed extrajudicial killings. On August 9, unidentified assailants shot and killed Ibrahim 'Abdallah Bou-Hamdan, an official in the Shi'a Amal Movement in the Biqa' valley. One Iraqi national, Idriss Daoud Shayeh, was arrested as a suspect in the crime. On August 18, three members of the Druze Progressive Socialist Party (PSP) were accused of responsibility for the death of 'Akram Arbeed. They allegedly beat him while he was accompanying a candidate for parliamentary elections. The Government claimed that Arbeed died of a heart attack while being transported to the hospital for treatment. The three suspects were interrogated by the judiciary but released on bail. A trial is pending.

In February Lebanese army intelligence abducted Ahmad Al-Hallaq from inside the Israeli-defined security zone. Hallaq was convicted in absentia by a military court in June 1995 for the 1994 death of Hizballah figure Fua'd Mughniyah and two others in a car-bomb explosion. Tawfiq Nasser, who was also sentenced to death in the same case, surrendered to the Lebanese embassy in Argentina and was brought back to Lebanon for trial. In August the military court found Ahmad Al-Hallaq and Tawfiq Nasser guilty, and sentenced Hallaq to death and Nasser to 10 years' imprisonment at hard labor. Hallaq's death sentence was carried out on September 21, after President Hrawi refused his appeal for clemency.

In May the Criminal Court of Beirut found former Lebanese Forces commander Samir Ja'Ja' and codefendant Rafiq Saadah guilty of the 1990 of murder of former Kata'ib Party member Dr. 'Ilyas Al-Zayek. Ja'Ja' and Saadah were sentenced to death, but the sentence was subsequently commuted by the President to life at hard labor. The court also sentenced in absentia Ghassan Touma and Antonios Ilyas Ilyas (alias Tony Obayd) to death for the same murder but commuted their sentences to life imprisonment at hard labor. Neither is in custody.

On March 14, in a setback for government efforts to bring those responsible for terrorist acts during the war years to justice, the Court of Cassation found Bassem Al-Firkh and Nameq Kamal not guilty of murder for their roles in the 1976 assassination of U.S. Ambassador Francis Meloy, embassy officer Robert Waring, and their driver Muhamad Meghrabi. The two men were found guilty of the lesser crime of kidnaping, which the court ruled made them eligible for amnesty under the 1991 Amnesty Law.

There were no developments in the 1994 death of Tariq Hasaniyah, who was allegedly beaten to death by authorities at the Bayt Al-Din Prison, nor in the 1994 death of Fawzi Al-Rasi, who died while in the custody of the Ministry of Defense.

In 1994 security forces arrested four Iraqi diplomats assigned to Beirut and charged them with the murder of an Iraqi dissident. According to press reports the suspects have admitted their guilt, but as of year's end no trial had yet been held. One suspect died in custody in 1995, reportedly of natural causes.

b. *Disappearance.*—There were no reports of politically motivated disappearances.

The Government has taken no judicial action against groups known to be responsible for the kidnapings of thousands of people during the unrest between 1975 and 1990. In May 1995, Parliament approved a law that allows those who disappeared during the civil war to be officially declared dead. The law stipulates that interested parties may declare as dead any Lebanese or foreigner who has disappeared in Lebanon or abroad and for whose disappearance death was the most probable explanation. Petitioners may apply for a court certification 4 years after a declaration of disappearance and may not benefit from any properties inherited until 6 years after such a court certification. The law facilitates the resolution of inheritance claims and second marriages.

c. *Torture and Other Cruel, Inhuman, or Degrading Treatment or Punishment.*— There continued to be credible reports that Lebanese security forces used torture on some detainees. In January some members of Parliament accused the ISF of torturing detainees by beating them, especially during interrogation, and called on the Ministers of Justice and Interior to investigate. At least one prisoner reportedly suffered paralysis as a result of security force violence during interrogation. Authorities charged three policemen, but the case was still pending at year's end.

Abuses also occurred in areas outside the State's authority, especially in the Palestinian refugee camps. There were credible reports that members of the various Palestinian groups that control the camps detained and tortured their Palestinian rivals.

Prison conditions are poor and do not meet internationally recognized minimum standards. There are only 18 operating prisons with a total capacity of 2,000 inmates. However, prisons are overcrowded, and the total number of prisoners is nearly 5,000. According to a study prepared jointly by the Association for the Protection of Human Rights and the Ministry of Social Affairs, overcrowding is the main problem. Inmates also lack heat and adequate toilet and shower facilities. For example, the Zahle Prison for males consists of 4 rooms with a total of 194 prisoners. The same study also shows that of the 142 juveniles detained in prisons, only 9 were charged; the others are awaiting trial. The prison system is regulated by law. Although the Interior Minister requested $50 million at the end of 1995 to rehabilitate the prison system, the requested amount was subsequently turned down by the Government for lack of funds.

In addition to the regular prisons, the Surete Generale, which mans border posts, operates a detention facility. Hundreds of foreigners, mostly Egyptians and Sri Lankans, have been detained pending deportation. They are reportedly held in small, poorly ventilated cells.

The Government does not permit prison visits by human rights monitors.

The South Lebanon Army operates its own detention facility in Al-Khiyam Prison, and there are frequent allegations of mistreatment of detainees. The SLA permitted relatives to visit detainees since October 1995. Hizballah also detains SLA members and suspected agents at unknown locations. Hizballah reportedly mistreats them. Both groups occasionally release prisoners. Hizballah, for example, unilaterally released some prisoners in February and July. A German-brokered exchange of prisoners and prisoner remains involving Hizballah, Israel, and the SLA also took place in July.

Neither the SLA nor Hizballah permit prison visits by human rights monitors.

d. *Arbitrary Arrest, Detention, or Exile.*—The Government resorts to arbitrary arrests and detention. The law requires security forces to obtain warrants of arrest before making arrests. However, military prosecutors, who are responsible for cases including the military as well as those involving espionage, treason, weapons possession, and draft evasion, reportedly issue blank warrants of arrest to be completed after a suspect has reen arrested. Arresting officers must refer a suspect to a prosecutor within 24 hours of arrest, but frequently do not do so.

The law requires the authorities to release suspects after 48 hours of arrest if they do not bring formal charges against them. Some prosecutors flout this requirement and detain suspects for long periods in pretrial confinement without a court order. The law authorizes judges to remand suspects to incommunicado detention of 10 days with a possible extension of an additional 10 days. Bail is only available to those accused of petty crimes, not to those accused of felonies. Defendants have the right to legal counsel, but there is no public defender's office. The Bar Association has an office to assist those who cannot afford a lawyer.

Security forces continued the practice of arbitrary arrest, detaining mainly the opponents of the Government. In March security forces arrested five persons for distribution of antigovernment leaflets. The five, who were members of the Lebanese Popular Convention, were charged and later acquitted for lack of evidence.

In April the Lebanese army arrested members of the dissolved Lebanese Forces militia and some 'Awnist groups, who had gathered in the Maronite Patriarchate in Bkirki to protest government policies and practices on the occasion of the visit of French President Jacques Chirac. Most of those arrested were released a few hours later, after President Chirac had left the area.

On July 13, the Lebanese army arrested 88 supporters of the former commander of the Lebanese Forces, Samir Ja'Ja', in the village of Bsharre, in north Lebanon. Ja'Ja's supporters had been shooting into the air to celebrate Ja'Ja's acquittal on charges of bombing a church in February 1994. Several persons were reportedly beaten by LAF, including the priest of the village. The military court sentenced 65 of the 88 to from 5 to 20 days' imprisonment and acquitted the others.

After the December 18 rifle attack on a Syrian bus, security forces detained and interrogated scores of citizens, predominately Christians. These detentions and searches of homes reportedly took place without warrants, and detainees were not given access to lawyers. Although most were released after brief periods, some, including a prominent human rights activist and a journalist, were held for 10 days or more without charge. The journalist was subsequently charged with distributing leaflets that disturb Lebanon's relations with friendly nations and having friendly contacts with Israeli agents, and released on bail. The law allows for detention without charge for 24 hours and an additional 24 hours with court permission.

Human rights groups credibly allege that detained persons are sometimes transferred to Syrian custody and imprisoned in Syria. The number of such persons cannot be accurately determined, but on November 24, Prime Minister Hariri stated that 210 Lebanese were in Syrian custody.

The authorities often detain for short periods and without charges political opponents of the Syrian and Lebanese governments.

Local militias and non-Lebanese forces continued to conduct arbitrary arrests in areas outside central government control. The SLA detains an estimated 100 to 200 Lebanese citizens and an undetermined number of Palestinians at Al-Khiyam prison in south Lebanon. During the year, the SLA continued to allow the families of detainees to visit their relatives in the prison. It also released 82 detainees, most of whom were Lebanese citizens.

In July the SLA abducted the son of a parliamentarian from his home in Jazzine, in response to the abduction by Hizballah of an SLA member. The parliamentarian's son was released shortly thereafter. The SLA member is still believed to be held. In January press reports indicated that 3 Swedes were arrested by Hizballah forces in the southern suburbs of Beirut while they were taking photographs of a mosque. Hizballah denied the report.

Syrian forces reportedly detained persons.

Israel is known to hold several Lebanese citizens, including Shaykh Abd Al-Karim Obaid and Mustafa Dirani, figures associated with the Islamic Resistance (IR).

Palestinian refugees are subject to arrest, detention, and harassment by the state security forces, Syrian forces, the various militias, and rival Palestinians.

In the recent past, the Government resorted to exile as a means of punishment. In 1991 it pardoned former army commander General Michel 'Awn and two of his aides on the condition that they depart the country and remain in exile for 5 years. 'Awn was accused of usurping power. The 5-year period ended on August 29, but 'Awn still remains in France.

e. *Denial of Fair Public Trial.*—The judiciary is generally impartial and independent. However, influential politicians and Syrian intelligence officers sometimes intervene to protect their supporters from prosecution.

The judicial system is composed of the regular civilian courts, the military court, which tries cases involving military personnel and military-related issues, the Judicial Council, which tries national security offenses, and the religious tribunals of the various denominations, which adjudicate disputes including marriage, inheritance, and personal status.

The Judicial Council is a permanent tribunal of five senior judges that adjudicates threats to national security. On the recommendation of the Minister of Justice, the Cabinet decides whether to try a case before this tribunal.

The Ministry of Justice appoints judges according to a formula based on the confessional, i.e., the religious affiliation of the prospective judge. The shortage of judges has impeded efforts to adjudicate cases backlogged during the years of internal conflicts. Trial delays are also caused by the Government's inability to conduct investigations in areas outside its control. Defendants have the right to examine evidence against them. The testimony of a woman is equal to that of a man.

In May the Judicial Council started to try 17 persons charged with the August 31, 1995 killing of Shaykh Nizar Al-Halabi, a Sunni cleric who headed an Islamist socio-political organization. The 17 publicly admitted their guilt. The trial is ongoing. The leader of the 17, Ahmad Abd Al-Karim Al-Sa'di (alias Abu Muhjin) is still hiding in the 'Ayn Al-Hilweh Palestinian refugee camp near Sidon. Several arrest warrants were issued, but the authorities have not apprehended him, declining to enter the refugee camp because to do so might provoke unnecessary bloodshed.

In July the Judicial Council issued its verdict in the 1994 Al-Zuq church bombing. The tribunal acquitted Samir Ja'Ja' of charges of bombing the church but sentenced him to 10 years' imprisonment for creating illegal military cells. Ja'Ja' is still on trial for the 1991 assassination attempt against then-Minister of Defense Michel Al-Murr.

The SLA maintains a separate and arbitrary system of justice. Palestinian groups in refugee camps operate an autonomous and arbitrary system of justice. Hizballah applies Islamic law in areas under its control.

There were no reports of political prisoners.

f. *Arbitrary Interference with Privacy, Family, Home, or Correspondence.*—While the authorities generally show little interest in controlling the personal lives of citizens, they readily interfere with the privacy of persons regarded as foes of the Government. Laws require that prosecutors obtain warrants before entering houses, except when the army is in hot pursuit of an armed attacker.

The Government uses informer networks and monitors telephones to gather information on its adversaries. In May the Salvation Bloc, headed by former Prime Minister Salim Al-Huss, issued a communique asking the Government to stop telephone tapping. There were numerous reports that members of government security forces visited the homes of politicians in the Metn region on the eve of elections for purposes of intimidation.

Militias and non-Lebanese forces operating outside areas of central government authority have frequently violated rights of privacy. Various factions also use informer networks and monitor telephones to obtain information on their adversaries.

g. *Use of Excessive Force and Violations of Humanitarian Law in Internal Conflicts.*—An undetermined member of civilians continue to be killed in south Lebanon, as Lebanese and Palestinian militias on the one hand, and Israeli forces and SLA on the other, engage in a cycle of violence. The former organizations attacked SLA and Israeli troops deployed in Lebanon, and also launched rocket attacks against northern Israel. Israeli forces conducted repeated air strikes and artillery barrages on populated areas and on guerrilla and terrorist targets inside Lebanon.

There were numerous incidents in the cycle of attack and reprisals. For example, in April after Israeli aircraft raided several villages in both the western and central sectors of Lebanon and two Lebanese civilians were killed in two other incidents, Hizballah began firing Katyusha rockets at settlements in northern Israel. Israel conducted a large-scale military operation dubbed "Grapes of Wrath," in response to Hizballah's refusal to cease launching these rockets.

During the 16-day operation, hundreds of thousands of civilians in southern Lebanon fled their homes and sought refuge in safer parts of the country. About 164 Lebanese, primarily civilian noncombatants, were killed. Israeli planes hit two Beirut civilian power stations. During the operation, Katyusha attacks against northern Israel intensified.

On April 18, Hizballah fired mortar rounds at an Israeli military unit from a position very near the U.N. compound at Qana, and the Isreal Defense Forces (IDF) responded with artillery fire. A number of Israeli shells struck the compound, killing 102 civilians who had sought shelter there and wounding others. The government of Israel expressed regret for these casualities, but insisted that the U.N. compound had not been targeted intentionally. A U.N. report concluded, however, that it was unlikely the shelling was due to technical or procedural error.

Negotiations to end the fighting resulted in an April 26 understanding under which the two parties committed not to target civilians nor to use civilian-populated areas or nonmilitary public installations as launching grounds for attacks. An international monitoring group was established to monitor application of the undertanding and to (deal with) (hear) (review) complaints of violations of the understanding. This group, the Israel-Lebanon Monitoring Group (ILMG), continued to function throughout the remainder of the year, with the participation of the United States, France, Syria, Israel, and Lebanon.

In February the Israeli Navy detained three fishermen off the coast of Tyre in south Lebanon. On June 13, the IDF seized journalist Ali Daya, the Agence France Press (AFP) correspondent in the security zone. An Israel army spokesman said that Daya was arrested on suspicion of collaboration with Hizballah. Daya was released on July 18.

In August the Israeli air force raided Ba'labakk and damaged the building of The Voice of the Oppressed, the radio voice of Hizballah.

On September 21, the SLA expelled a family of 12 from the village of Mayss-Al-Jabal (Bint Jubayl province), allegedly due to the desertion from the SLA of one member of the family. The Israeli forces and the SLA reportedly expelled 18 additional persons from the security zone during the year, including 7 members of the Abdallah family and 8 members of Ali Khalil Nasrallah's extended family from Hula village, a husband and wife from the village of Markaba, and one individual from Tair Harfa.

Section 2. Respect for Civil Liberties, Including:

a. *Freedom of Speech and Press.*—The Constitution provides for freedom of the press, but the Government partially limits this right in practice. Freedom of the press declined significantly during the year as the Government prosecuted newspapers, passed a new media law to restrict radio and television broadcasting, and intimidated journalists and broadcasters into practicing self-censorship. The Government also imposes direct censorship on satellite broadcasts originating in Lebanon.

Lebanon has a long history of freedom of opinion, speech, and the press. Although there were repeated attempts to restrict these freedoms during the year, daily criticism of government policies and leaders continues. Dozens of newspapers and magazines are published throughout Lebanon, financed by various Lebanese and foreign groups. While the press is normally independent, press content often reflects the opinions of these financial backers.

The Government uses several tools at its disposal to control the freedom of expression. The Surete Generale is authorized to approve all foreign magazines and non-periodical works including plays, books, and films before they are distributed in the market. The law prohibits attacks on the dignity of the head of state or foreign leaders. The Government may prosecute offending journalists and publications in the Publications Court, a special court empowered to try such matters.

Moreover, the 1991 security agreement between Lebanon and Syria contains a provision that effectively prohibits the publication of any information deemed harmful to the security of either state. Under the risk of prosecution, Lebanese journalists censor themselves on matters related to Syria.

During the year, the Government severely attacked press freedoms by filing charges against several newspapers. In one 10-day period, three dailies (Ad-Diyar, Al-Liwa' and Nida' Al-Watan), and two weeklies (Al-Kifah Al-Arabi and Al-Massira) where charged with defaming the President and the Prime Minister, and for publishing materials deemed provocative to one religious sect. The daily Ad-Diyar alone was indicted five times and both the owner and editor-in-chief faced sentences of between 2 months' and 2 years' imprisonment and fines of $30,000 to $60,000 if found guilty.

In September the Government provoked widespread protest when it moved suddenly to implement its controversial Media Law. The stated purpose of the law is to impose order on the largely unregulated airwaves and to reduce religious and political tensions by forcing the country's many small, sectarian oriented stations to combine into a much smaller number of pluralist stations.

Most citizens, however, view the implementation of the law as political in nature. It would reduce 52 television stations to 4 stations, and approximately 100 radio stations to 11, only 3 of which would be permitted to broadcast news programs. All four television stations approved so far are owned by, or closely associated with, important government figures. Some of the approved stations are not yet operational, while a number of popular stations associated with opposition to the Government have been refused licenses, ostensibly for failing to comply with the law. As of year's end, the Government had not enforced the November 30 closure of unlicensed stations. It had stated that it would continue to consider new applications. Hizballah's radio and television stations were allowed to continue to broadcast without a license, including news related to "resistance" activities.

In May the Surete Generale confiscated all issues of the book entitled "Remove Peter's Mask from the Face of Christ," by the Saudi Arabian author Ahmad Zaki. The book was determined by the Surete Generale to defame Christianity.

In November the Interior Ministry's Public Security Department reportedly twice censored the scenes from the foreign movie "Independence Day" to remove scenes with Jewish characters, and Hizballah later demanded a complete ban on the film because one of its heros is a Jew. In September a public prosecutor charged a singer, Marcel Khalife, with demeaning religious rituals. The same prosecutor also charged Andre Yussef Haddad with demeaning religious rituals in his book "The Entrance to Arab Unity." However, on September 21, facing rising criticism from various factions, the Prime Minister asked the Justice Minister to drop the charges brought against Khalife. The charges against Haddad were dropped by an investigating judge on January 8, 1997.

Lebanon has a strong tradition of academic freedom and a flourishing private educational system born of inadequate public schools and a preference for sectarian affiliation. Students exercise the right to form campus associations and the Government usually does not interfere with student groups.

b. *Freedom of Peaceful Assembly and Association.*—Although the Constitution provides for freedom of assembly, the Government restricts this right. Any group wishing to organize a rally must obtain the prior approval of the Interior Ministry, which does not render decisions uniformly. The Government banned all rallies again in 1996 but made an exception during the parliamentary elections. Various political factions, such as oppositionist Amal, Hizballah, 'Awnists, and supporters of the Prime Minister held rallies without obtaining government permission.

In February the General Confederation of Labor (CGTL) submitted a request to hold demonstrations on February 29. The Government refused to grant permission, and called on the LAF to control the situation. The LAF was accorded a 90-day grant of exceptional powers necessary to maintain public order. Under this authority it imposed a nationwide curfew on February 29, which lasted 16 hours. The LAF also imposed a temporary ban on the public display of weapons by those licensed to carry arms. Several persons were arrested for violating the curfew, including three journalists. The three were accused of photographing a military installation but were released after 24 hours. The others, about 30 persons, were sentenced to 5 to 10 days in jail.

On April 4, the Government prevented the CGTL from staging a sit-in in front of Parliament during the visit of French President Jacques Chirac. The Lebanese army encircled CGTL headquarters and prevented CGTL leaders from leaving their offices, keeping them under provisional arrest for about 6 hours.

The Constitution provides for freedom of association. The Government generally respects this right; however, there were exceptions during the year. In general, the Government does not interfere with the establishment of private organizations. The law requires that persons forming organizations notify the Interior Ministry, which in turn issues permits for the formation of associations. The Interior Ministry refused to grant a permit to the Lebanese Association for the Democratization of Elections, declaring it nonexistent.

The Ministry of Interior also scrutinizes requests to establish political movements or parties, and to some extent monitors their activities. The Army Intelligence Service monitors the movement and activities of members of opposition groups.

Neither Israel nor Syria allows groups openly hostile to them to operate in areas under their control.

c. *Freedom of Religion.*—The Constitution provides for freedom of religion, and the Government respects this right in practice.

d. *Freedom of Movement Within the Country, Foreign Travel, Emigration, and Repatriation.*—The Constitution provides for these rights, and the Government generally respects them in practice. However, there are some limitations. Travel to Israel is prohibited by law, but many do so through Israeli-occupied territory in southern Lebanon. All male citizens between 18 and 21 years of age are subject to compulsory military service and are required to register at a recruitment office and obtain a travel authorization document before leaving the country. Husbands may block foreign travel by their wives and minor children.

Lebanese Armed Forces and Syrian troops maintain checkpoints in areas under their control. In south Lebanon, the Lebanese army, the Israeli army, and the SLA all maintain tight restrictions on the movement of people and goods into and out of Israel's self-declared security zone.

There are no legal restrictions on the right of all citizens to return. Many emigres, however, are reluctant to return for a variety of political, economic, and social reasons. After years of internal conflict, the recent increased legitimacy of government authority has removed barriers that previously hindered domestic travel. The Government has encouraged the return to their homes of over 600,000 persons displaced during the civil war. Although some people have begun to reclaim their homes abandoned or damaged during the war, the vast majority of displaced persons have not attempted to reclaim and rehabilitate their property. The resettlement process is slowed by tight budgetary constraints, shattered infrastructure, the lack of schools and economic opportunities, and the fear that physical security is still incomplete in some parts of the country.

Most non-Lebanese refugees are Palestinians. The United Nations Relief and Works Agency (UNRWA) reported that the number of Palestinian refugees in Lebanon registered with UNRWA was 352,668 as of June 30. The Government estimates the number of Palestinian refugees at 361,000, but this figure includes only the families of refugees who arrived in 1948.

The Government issues laissez-passers (travel documents) to Palestinian refugees to enable them to travel and work abroad. However, after the government of Libya announced in September 1995 its intention to expel Palestinians working in that country, the Lebanese Government moved to prohibit the return of Palestinians living abroad unless they obtain an entry visa. The Government maintained that the visa requirement is necessary to ensure the validity of Lebanese laissez-passers, as a large number of those documents were forged during the years of strife. The effect has been to discourage foreign travel by Palestinians resident in Lebanon.

The Government seeks to prevent the entry of asylum seekers and undocumented refugees. There have been no known asylum requests since 1975. There are legal provisions for granting asylum or refugee status in accordance with the 1951 Convention relating to the Staus of Refugees and its 1967 Protocol. The Government cooperates with the office of the United Nations High Commissioner for Refugees (UNHCR) and the United Nations Relief and Works Agency.

Section 3. Respect for Political Rights: The Right of Citizens to Change Their Government

The Constitution states that citizens have the right to change their government in periodic free and fair elections. However, while the August-September parliamentary elections represented a small step forward, the electoral process was flawed by significant shortcomings, as the elections were not prepared or carried out impartially.

According to the Constitution, elections for the Parliament must be held every 4 years. The Parliament, in turn, elects the President every 6 years. The President and Parliament nominate the Prime Minister, who with the President chooses the Cabinet. According to the unwritten "National Pact of 1943," the president is a Maronite Christian, the Prime Minister a Sunni Muslim, and the speaker of Parliament a Shi'a Muslim. Until 1990, seats in Parliament were divided on a 6 to 5 ratio of Christians to Muslims. Positions in the Government were allocated on a similar basis between Christians and Muslims. Under the National Reconciliation Agreement reached in Taif, Saudi Arabia in 1989, members of Parliament agreed to alter the National Pact to create a 50–50 balance between Christian and Muslim members of Parliament. The Taif Accord also increased the number of seats in Parliament and transferred some powers from the President to the Prime Minister and Cabinet.

In August and September, Lebanon held its second parliamentary elections since 1972. On balance they constituted a small step forward for the restoration of democracy in Lebanon, with significantly higher voter turnout than the last election in 1992. (The turnout reached about 45 percent; the historical average is near 50 percent.) Nonetheless, the elections were flawed by a variety of shortcomings. A call by Christian oppositionists to boycott the polling led to a result that did not entirely reflect the will of the entire populace. Moreover, the elections were not prepared and carried out in a manner that ensured broad national confidence in their fairness. For example, many citizens complained that the Electoral Law was tailored to favor some political groups over others by enhancing their electoral influence since the districting was not uniformly applied. There were also credible reports of Syrian government involvement in the formation of candidate lists and alliances, as well as numerous reports of irregularities in the process of voting and counting of ballots, including the failure to provide adequate privacy for voting at some polling places, restrictions on observers, the use of forged identification papers, buying of votes, stuffing of "misplaced" ballot boxes, and, according to some reports, the existence of officially sealed envelopes with the competing lists inside. The electoral rolls were themselves in many instances considered unreliable, among other reasons, because of the destruction of records. It is not clear how such acts may have influenced the outcome of individual races.

Government officials have acknowledged some electoral shortcomings and pledged to correct them in future elections. Moreover, unlike in the 1992 elections, losing candidates can challenge results through the Constitutional Council. Several candidates have submitted such challenges, and the Council has 2 months in which to issue its irrevocable decisions. There were no decisions by year's end.

The right of citizens to change their government also was undermined by a decision taken by Parliament in May 1995 to extend the term in office of the country's municipal officials to December 31, 1996. Municipal elections have not been held since 1963. Many serving officials are elderly or have been appointed by the central government. The Government has not announced any firm plans for new elections.

Women have the right to vote and there are no legal barriers to their participation in politics. No women hold Cabinet positions. Three women were elected to Parliament in 1996.

Palestinian refugees have no political rights. An estimated 17 Palestinian factions operate in Lebanon, generally organized around prominent individuals. Most Palestinians live in refugee camps controlled by one or more factions. The leaders of the refugees are not elected, nor are there any democratically organized institutions in the camps.

Section 4. Governmental Attitude Regarding International and Nongovernmental Investigation of Alleged Violations of Human Rights

Several human rights groups operate freely without overt government restriction, including the Lebanese Association for Human Rights, the Foundation for Human and Humanitarian Rights-Lebanon, and the National Association for the Rights of the Disabled. Some of these groups have sought to publicize the detention in Syria of hundreds of Lebanese citizens. The Government has made no public comment on the issue. The number of such persons cannot be accurately determined, but on November 24, President Hrawi stated that 210 Lebanese were in Syrian custody. Some human rights groups have reported harassment and intimidation by government, Syrian, and militia forces.

In April the Government granted an entry visa to a delegation from Amnesty International (AI), to allow its members to investigate the Qana incident (see Section 1.g.).

Section 5. Discrimination Based on Race, Sex, Religion, Disability, Language, or Social Status

The Constitution calls for "social justice and equality of duties and rights among all citizens without prejudice or favoritism." In practice, aspects of the law and traditional mores discriminate against women. Religious discrimination is built into the electoral system. Discrimination based on the other listed factors is illegal.

Women.—The press reports cases of rape with increasing frequency; what is reported is thought to be only a fraction of the actual level of this abuse. There are no authoritative statistics on the extent of spousal abuse. Most experts agree that the problem affects a significant portion of the adult female population. In general battered or abused women do not talk about their suffering for fear of bringing shame upon their families or accusations of misbehavior upon themselves. Doctors and social workers believe that most abused women do not seek medical help. The Government has no separate program to provide medical assistance to battered women. It does provide legal assistance to victims of crimes who cannot afford it, regardless of the gender of the victim. The Lebanese Association for Combating Violence Against Women, founded in 1994, has been active in lobbying to improve the socio-economic condition of women and to reduce violence against women.

The legal system is discriminatory in its handling of "crimes of honor." According to the Penal Code, the killer of a spouse may receive a reduced sentence if that partner demonstrates that the crime was in response to an illegitimate sexual relationship conducted by the victim. Since 1991, however, the Government has begun to increase sentences on violent crimes in general and to seek punishment for males who commit "crimes of honor."

Women have employment opportunities in government, medicine, law, academia, the arts, and, to a lesser degree, in business. However, social pressure against women pursuing careers is strong in some parts of society. Males sometimes exercise considerable control over female relatives, restricting their activities outside the home or their contact with friends and relatives. Women may own property but often cede effective control of it to male relatives for cultural reasons. In 1994 the Parliament removed a legal stipulation that a woman must obtain her husband's approval to open a business or engage in a trade. Husbands may block foreign travel by their wives (see Section 2.d.).

Only males may confer citizenship on their spouses and children. This means that children born to Lebanese mothers and foreign fathers may not become citizens. In late 1995, the Parliament approved a law allowing Lebanese widows to confer citizenship on their minor children.

Religious groups have their own family and personal status laws administered by religious courts. Each group differs in its treatment of marriage, family property rights, and inheritance. Many of these laws discriminate against women. For example, Sunni inheritance law gives a son twice the share of a daughter. Although Muslim men may divorce easily, Muslim women may do so only with the concurrence of their husbands.

Children.—The plight of children is a growing concern, but the Government has not allocated funds to protect them. Education is not compulsory, and many children take jobs at a young age to help support their families. In lower income families, boys generally get more education, while girls usually remain at home to do housework.

An undetermined number of children are neglected, abused, exploited, and even sold to adoption agents. There are hundreds of abandoned children in the streets nationwide, some of whom survive by begging, others by working at low wages. According to a U.N. Children's Fund (UNICEF) study, 60 percent of working children are below 13 years of age and 75 percent of them earn wages below two-thirds of the minimum wage. Juvenile delinquency is on the rise; many delinquents wait in ordinary prisons for trial and remain there after sentencing. Although their number is very small, there is no adequate place to hold delinquent girls, and they are currently held in the women's prison in Ba'abda. Limited financial resources have hindered efforts to build adequate facilities to rehabilitate delinquents. However, the Higher Relief Committee allotted some funds to the Association for the Protection of Juveniles to lease a two-story building in Ba'asir in order to accommodate 50 juvenile delinquents.

There are neither child welfare programs nor government institutions to oversee the implementation of children's programs. The Committee for Children's Rights, formed 3 years ago by prominent politicians and private citizens, has been lobbying for legislation to improve the condition of children. The Parliament passed a law to cease use of the word "illegitimate" on the identity cards of children born out of wedlock. The Ministry of Health requires the establishment of health records for every child up to 18 years.

People With Disabilities.—Over 100,000 people sustained disabilities during the civil war. Care of the disabled is generally a function performed by families. Most efforts to secure education, independence, health, and shelter for the disabled are made by some 100 private organizations for the disabled. In general, these organizations are poorly funded.

Lebanon's heavily damaged cities make no accommodation for the disabled. Building codes have no requirements for ease of access. The private "Solidere" project for the reconstruction of downtown Beirut has imposed requirements for disabled access. This project is widely considered a model for future construction efforts around the country.

Religious Minorities.—Discrimination based on religion is built into the system of government. The amended Constitution of 1990 embraces the principle of abolishing religious affiliation as a criterion for filling all government positions, but few practical steps have been taken to accomplish this. One notable exception is the Lebanese Armed Forces, which through universal conscription and an emphasis on professionalism, has significantly reduced the role of confessionalism (religious sectarianism) in that organization.

National/Racial/Ethnic Minorities.—According to the United Nations, an estimated 350,000 Palestinian refugees live in Lebanon, though estimates by other organizations are considerably higher. Most Palestinian refugees live in overpopulated camps that have suffered repeated heavy damage as a result of fighting. The Government has instructed relief workers to suspend reconstruction work in the camps, and refugees fear that in the future the Government will reduce the size of the camps or eliminate them completely.

The Government officially ended its practice of denying work permits to Palestinians in 1991; however, in practice, very few Palestinians receive work permits. Palestinians still encounter job discrimination, and most are funneled into unskilled occupations. They and other aliens may own land of a limited size but only after obtaining the approval of five different district offices. The law applies to all aliens, but for political, cultural, and economic reasons it is applied in a manner disadvantageous to Palestinians and, to a lesser extent, Kurds. The Government does not provide health services to Palestinian refugees, who must rely on UNRWA and UNRWA-contacted private hospitals.

In recent years, Palestinian incomes have declined as the Palestinian Liberation Organization closed many of its offices in Lebanon, which formerly employed as much as 50 percent of the Palestinian work force. Palestinian children have reportedly been forced to leave school at an early age because U.N. relief workers do not have sufficient funds for education programs. The U.N. estimates that 18 percent of street children are Palestinian. Drug addiction and crime reportedly are increasing in the camps, as is prostitution.

Section 6. Worker Rights

a. *The Right of Association.*—All workers, except government employees, may establish and join unions and have a legal right to strike. Worker representatives must be chosen from those employed within the bargaining unit. About 900,000 persons form the active labor force, 42 percent of whom are members of 160 labor unions and associations. Twenty-two of the unions, with about 200,000 workers, are represented in the General Confederation of Labour.

In general the Government does not control or restrict unions, although union leaders allege that the Government has tried to intervene in elections for union officials.

Palestinian refugees may organize their own unions, but restrictions on their right to work make this right more theoretical than real. Few Palestinians participate actively in trade unions.

Unions are free to affiliate with international federations and confederations, and they maintain a variety of such affiliations.

b. *The Right to Organize and Bargain Collectively.*—The right of workers to organize and to bargain exists in law and practice. Most worker groups engage in some form of collective bargaining with their employers. Stronger federations obtain significant gains for their members, and on occasion have assisted nonunionized workers. There is no government mechanism to promote voluntary labor-management negotiations, and workers have no protection against antiunion discrimination. The Government's ban on demonstrations arguably diminishes unions' bargaining power.

There are no export processing zones.

c. *Prohibition of Forced or Compulsory Labor.*—Forced labor is not prohibited by law. Children, foreign domestic servants, or other foreign workers are sometimes forced to remain in situations amounting to coerced or bonded labor.

d. *Minimum Age for Employment of Children.*—The 1946 Labor Code stipulates that workers between the ages of 8 and 16 may not work more than 7 hours per day, with 1 hour for rest provided after 4 hours. They are also prohibited from working between the hours of 7 p.m. and 6 a.m. There is a general prohibition against "jobs out of proportion with a worker's age." The Code also prohibits certain types of mechanical work for children of ages 8 to 13, and other types for those of ages 13 to 16. The Labor Ministry is tasked with enforcing these requirements, but the civil war left it with few resources and a demoralized and sometimes corrupt staff. The Ministry does not rigorously apply the law.

e. *Acceptable Conditions of Work.*—The Government sets a legal minimum wage, which was raised in April to about $200 (300,000 Lebanese pounds) per month. The law is not enforced effectively in the private sector. In theory the courts could be called upon to enforce it, but in practice they are not. The minimum wage is insufficient to provide a decent standard of living for a worker and family. Trade unions actively try to ensure the payment of minimum wages in both the public sector and the large-scale private sector, such as education and transport.

The Labor Law prescribes a standard 6-day workweek of 48 hours, with a 24-hour rest period per week. In practice workers in the industrial sector work an average of 35 hours per week, and workers in other sectors work an average of 30 hours per week. The law includes specific occupational health and safety regulations. Labor regulations call on employers to take adequate precautions for employee safety. Enforcement, the responsibility of the Labor Ministry, is uneven. Labor organizers report that workers do not have the right to remove themselves from hazardous conditions without jeopardizing their continued employment.

LIBYA*

The Great Socialist People's Libyan Arab Jamahiriya is a dictatorship ruled by Colonel Mu'ammar Al-Qadhafi (the "Brother Leader and Guide of the Revolution") who is aided by extragovernmental Revolutionary Committees and a Comrades Organization. Libya's governing principles are expressed in Qadhafi's "Green Book." Borrowing from Islamic and pan-Arab ideas, Qadhafi has created a political system that purports to establish a "third way" superior to capitalism and Communism. He uses extrajudicial killings and intimidation to control the opposition abroad and summary judicial proceedings to suppress it at home. The Government exercises tight control over ethnic minorities, such as Berbers, and continues to repress banned Islamic groups.

Colonel Qadhafi publicly called for violence against opponents of his regime after violent clashes between Islamic activists and security forces in Benghazi in September 1995. Outbreaks of violence continued between government forces and Muslim militants. Two serious prison mutinies occurred in the past year, causing more bloodshed and prompting the Government to conduct intense military operations against suspected oppositionists.

Libya maintains an extensive security apparatus, consisting of several elite military units, including Qadhafi's personal bodyguards; local Revolutionary Committees; and People's Committees; as well as the newly formed "Purification" Committees. The result is a multilayered, pervasive surveillance system that monitors and controls the activities of individuals. The various security forces committed numerous serious human rights abuses.

The Government dominates the economy through complete control of the country's oil resources, the principal source of foreign exchange. It uses part of the oil income for development, but much income has been lost to waste, corruption, and attempts to develop weapons of mass destruction.

The human rights situation is poor. Citizens do not have the right to change their government. Security forces arbitrarily arrest, detain, and torture prisoners during interrogations or for punishment. The Government restricts the freedoms of speech, press, assembly, association, and religion. The Government also restricts basic worker rights. Citizens do not have the right to a fair public trial, to be represented by legal counsel, to be secure in their homes or persons, or to own private property. Prison conditions are poor, and many political detainees are held for years without charge. Although there were no reports of mass expulsions of foreign workers and residents in 1996, the regime threatened to expel thousands of Palestinian residents in May. Traditional attitudes and practices continue to discriminate against women, and the Government discriminates against minorities. Female genital mutilation is still practiced in remote tribal areas.

Libya continues to be subject to economic and diplomatic sanctions imposed by the U.N. Security Council in connection with the bombings of Pan Am flight 103 over Scotland in 1988 and the bombing of UTA flight 772 over Chad in 1989. The Government took only limited steps to address the U.N. Security Council resolutions concerning the bombing of Pan Am flight 103 and UTA flight 722.

RESPECT FOR HUMAN RIGHTS

Section 1. Respect for the Integrity of the Person, Including Freedom From:

a. *Political and Other Extrajudicial Killing.*—Violent clashes between the security forces and militant Islamist opposition groups increased during the year. The clashes were predominantly concentrated in the eastern region of Libya and by some estimates, resulted in 600 deaths and 800 wounded during the year.

In response to numerous attacks against the regime and a prison mutiny in Benghazi, the Government tightened security measures, made hundreds of arrests, and conducted an intense military campaign in the areas where insurrection oc-

---

*The United States has no official presence in Libya. Information on the human rights situation is therefore limited.

curred. Government forces killed a number of people, but there were no definitive estimates of the total killed in these government attacks. On July 12, the Government officially stated that the actions were military exercises and operations against drug traffickers.

The Government officially admitted that 8 people died and 39 were injured as a result of a July 9 riot that broke out in Tripoli after Qadhafi family bodyguards fired upon spectators at a soccer game who were shouting anti-Qadhafi slogans (see Section 2.b.). There were reports of up to 50 deaths, caused by the gunfire and the resulting crowd stampede.

Security forces killed an undetermined number of persons while suppressing a prison mutiny that broke out on July 5 (see Section 1.c.).

Qadhafi uses extrajudicial killing and intimidation to control the opposition abroad, and summary judicial proceedings to suppress domestic dissent. There have been reports of Libyan security forces hunting down and eliminating dissidents living abroad.

A large number of offenses, including political offenses and "economic crimes," are punishable by death. A 1972 law mandates the death penalty for any person associated with a group opposed to the principles of the revolution. Despite his longstanding stated intention, Qadhafi has not acted to abolish the death penalty for this offense. On July 15, a new law went into effect that applies the death penalty to those who speculate in foreign currency, food, clothes, or housing during a state of war or blockade and for crimes related to drugs and alcohol.

Islamic factions reportedly made one failed coup attempt, two failed assassination attempts on Qadhafi, and mounted three major attacks on Libyan security forces.

The first major attack came on June 22, when 8 Libyan policemen were shot and killed by members of the Libyan Islamic Group at a training center near the city of Dirnah. On July 19, Muslim militants killed 26 members of an army convoy, and in mid-August 13 soldiers and one of Qadhafi's bodyguards were killed in attacks in the areas of Tripoli and Benghazi. An estimated 400 Islamic fundamentalists escaped from the Al-Kawafiyah prison near Benghazi on March 24 and fled to the mountain region of Dirnah, where they clashed with security forces for several days.

Libya continues to be subject to economic and diplomatic sanctions imposed by the U.N. Security Council in connection with the bombings of Pan Am flight 103 over Scotland in 1988 which killed 259 people on board and 11 people on the ground and the bombing of UTA flight 772 over Chad in 1989 which killed 171 people. These sanctions require that Libya fulfill the following conditions: ensure the appearance in a U.S. or Scottish court of those charged in the Pam Am 103 case; cooperate with U.S., British, and French investigations into the Pan Am and UTA bombings; compensate the victims of Pan Am 103; and renounce terrorism and support for terrorism.

The Government took limited steps to address the U.N. Security Council resolutions concerning the bombing of Pan Am flight 103 and UTA flight 722. On March 23, Qadhafi wrote a letter to French President Chirac pledging cooperation in resolving the UTA bombing short of extraditing the suspects (which is against Libyan law) or compromising Libya's sovereignty. France's chief antiterrorism magistrate, Jean-Louis Brugiuere, visited Libya in an effort to investigate the incident and was expected to issue international arrest warrants for two suspects, bringing to six the number that he said he would prosecute. He indicated that the suspects would be tried without being present in court. Press reports identified the suspects as Libyan intelligence officials Abdesslam Issa Shibari, Abdesslam Hamouda, and Abadallah Senousi (brother-in-law of Qadhafi); Libyan diplomat Abdullah Elazragh; and intelligence operatives Ibrahim Naeli and Musbah Arbas.

b. *Disappearance.*—There were no reports of politically motivated disappearances. The 1993 disappearance from Cairo of Libyan dissident Mansour Kikhia remained unresolved.

c. *Torture and Other Cruel, Inhuman, or Degrading Treatment or Punishment.*—Although Libya is a party to the U.N. Convention against Torture and Other Cruel, Inhuman, or Degrading Treatment or Punishment, security personnel reportedly torture prisoners during interrogations or for punishment. Government agents periodically detain and reportedly torture foreign workers, particularly those from sub-Saharan Africa. Torture reports are difficult to corroborate because many prisoners are held incommunicado.

Methods of torture reportedly include: chaining to a wall for hours; clubbing; electric shock; the application of corkscrews in the back; lemon juice in open wounds; breaking fingers and allowing the joints to heal without medical care; suffocation by plastic bags; deprivation of food and water; and beatings on the soles of the feet. The law calls for fines against any official using excessive force, but there are no known cases of prosecution for torture or abuse.

There is insufficient information to make a determination on overall prison conditions, but a mutiny on July 5 at the Abu Salim prison was caused by inmates protesting poor conditions. The prisoners went on a hunger strike and captured guards to protest the lack of medical care, overcrowding, and inadequate hygiene and diet provided at the facility. Security units were dispatched to suppress the uprising, and hundreds of people were left dead after the week-long incident, as many as 100 of them killed by security forces.

The Government does not permit prison visits by human rights monitors.

d. *Arbitrary Arrest, Detention, or Exile.*—By law the Government may hold detainees incommunicado for unlimited periods. It holds many political detainees incommunicado in unofficial detention centers controlled by members of the Revolutionary Committees. Thousands of political detainees, many associated with banned Islamic groups, are reported to be held in prisons throughout Libya. Many have been held for years without charge. Thousands of other detainees may have been held for periods too brief (3 to 4 months) to permit confirmation by outside observers.

Security forces intensified the campaign to arrest suspected members and sympathizers of banned Islamic groups and to monitor activities at mosques following numerous violent clashes. Some practicing Muslims have shaved their beards to avoid harassment from security services. Qadhafi has publicly denounced Libyan "mujaheddin" (generally, conservative Islamic activists who fought with the Afghan resistance movement against Soviet forces) as threats to the regime.

The Purge Law of 1994 was established to fight financial corruption, black marketeering, drug trafficking, and atheism. Since the enforcement of the Purge Law began in June by the "Purification" Committees, scores of businessmen, traders, and shop owners have been arbitrarily arrested and dozens of shops and firms have been closed on charges of corruption, dealing in foreign goods, and funding Islamic fundamentalist groups. As part of the campaign to implement the Purge Law, the wealth of the middle class and affluent have been targeted as well (see Section 1.f.).

The Government does not impose exile as a form of punishment; to the contrary, Qadhafi seeks to pressure Libyans working or studying abroad to return home. The Government arbitrarily expels noncitizens (see Section 6.e.).

e. *Denial of Fair Public Trial.*—The judiciary is not independent of the Government. There are four levels of courts: summary courts, which try petty offenses; the courts of first instance, which try more serious crimes; the courts of appeal; and the Supreme Court, which is the final appellate level. The private practice of law is illegal; all lawyers must be members of the Secretariat of Justice.

Special revolutionary courts were established in 1980 to try political offenses. Such trials are often held in secret or even in the absence of the accused. In other cases, the security forces have the power to pass sentences without trial, especially in cases involving political opposition. In the past, Qadhafi has incited local cadres to take extrajudicial action against suspected opponents.

According to Amnesty International, approximately 22 persons were convicted and imprisoned for political offenses during 1995.

f. *Arbitrary Interference with Privacy, Family, Home, or Correspondence.*—The Government does not respect the right to privacy. Security agencies often disregard the legal requirement to obtain warrants before entering a private home. They also routinely monitor telephone calls.

The security agencies and the Revolutionary Committees oversee an extensive informant network. Libyan exiles report that family ties to suspected regime opponents may result in government harassment and detention. The Government may seize and destroy property belonging to "enemies of the people" or to those who "cooperate" with foreign powers. In the past, citizens have reported that Qadhafi has warned members of the extended family of any regime opponent that they risk the death penalty.

The Purge Law of 1994 provides for the confiscation of private assets above a nominal amount, describing wealth in excess of such an undetermined nominal amount as the fruits of exploitation or corruption. In May Qadhafi ordered the formation of hundreds of "Purge" or "Purification" Committees composed of young military officers and students. The Committees, backed by thousands of Revolutionary Committees, implement the Purge Law. The "Purification" Committees began to enforce the Law in June and reportedly seized some "excessive" amounts of private wealth from the middle and affluent classes in Libya. The confiscated property was taken from the rich to be given to the poor, in an effort to appease the populace and to strengthen Qadhafi's power and control over the country.

Section 2. Respect for Civil Liberties, Including:

  a. *Freedom of Speech and Press.*—The authorities tolerate some difference of opinion in People's Committee meetings and at the General People's Congress, but in general severely limit freedom of speech. This is especially true with regard to criticism of Qadhafi or his regime. Infrequent criticism of political leaders and policies in the state-controlled media is interpreted as a government attempt to test public opinion, or weaken a government figure who may be a potential challenger to Qadhafi.

  The regime restricts freedom of speech in several ways: By prohibiting all political activities not officially approved; by enacting laws so vague that many forms of speech or expression may be interpreted as illegal; and by operating a pervasive system of informants that creates an atmosphere of mistrust at all levels of society.

  The State owns and controls the media. There is a state-run daily newspaper, Al-Shams, with a circulation of 40,000. Local Revolutionary Committees publish several smaller newspapers. The official news agency, JANA, is the designated conduit for official views. The regime does not permit the publication of opinions contrary to government policy. Such foreign publications as Newsweek, Time, the International Herald Tribune, Express, and Jeune Afrique are available, but authorities routinely censor them and may prohibit their entry onto the market.

  b. *Freedom of Peaceful Assembly and Association.*—Public assembly is permitted only with regime approval and in support of the regime's positions.

  Despite these restrictions, members of the Warfalla tribe staged several informal protests in 1995 to protest the regime's decision to carry out the death penalty against tribe members involved in the 1993 coup attempt. The Government responded by arresting hundreds of tribe members and expelling others from the military and security forces. The death sentences had not been carried out by year's end.

  A rare display of public discontent and resentment towards the Government occurred when a riot broke out during a soccer match in Tripoli on July 9. The unrest began when a contentious goal was scored by the team that Qadhafi's sons supported and the referee called the play in their team's favor. The spectators reportedly started chanting anti-Qadhafi slogans after the referee made the call and Qadhafi's sons and their bodyguards opened fire in the air, then on the crowd. The spectators panicked and stampeded out of the stadium and into the streets, where they stoned cars and chanted more anti-Qadhafi slogans. The Government officially admitted that 8 people died and 39 were injured as a result of the soccer riots, but there were reports of up to 50 deaths, caused by the gunfire and the stampede of the crowd.

  The Government limits the right of association; it grants such a right only to institutions affiliated with the regime. According to a 1972 law, political activity found by the authorities to be treasonous is punishable by death. An offense may include any activity that is "opposed * * * to the principles of the Revolution."

  c. *Freedom of Religion.*—Libya is overwhelmingly Muslim. In an apparent effort to eliminate all alternative power bases, the regime has banned the once powerful Sanusiyya Islamic sect. In its place, Qadhafi established the Islamic Call Society (ICS), which is the outlet for state-approved religion as well as a tool for exporting the Libyan revolution. In 1992 the Government announced that the ICS would be disbanded; however, its director still conducts activities, suggesting that the organization remains operational. Islamic groups at variance with the state-approved teaching of Islam are banned.

  Members of some minority religions are allowed to conduct services. Services in Christian churches are attended by the foreign community. A resident Catholic bishop, aided by a small number of priests, operates two churches.

  d. *Freedom of Movement Within the Country, Foreign Travel, Emigration, and Repatriation.*—The Government imposed blockades on many cities in eastern Libya in reaction to the Islamic rebel attacks on military and police forces and the prison mutiny in Benghazi. The Government usually does not restrict the internal movement of Libyan citizens, except in the security areas. It requires exit permits for travel abroad and limits access to hard currency. A woman must have her husband's permission to travel abroad. Authorities routinely seize the passports of foreigners married to Libyan citizens upon their entry into Libya.

  The right of return exists. In fact, the regime often calls on students, many of whom receive a government subsidy, and others working abroad to return to Libya on little or no notice. Students studying abroad are interrogated upon their return. Some citizens, including exiled opposition figures, refuse to return. There have been reports of Libyan security forces hunting down and eliminating dissidents living abroad (see Section 1.a.).

In September 1995, the Government expelled approximately 1,000 Palestinian residents to signal its displeasure with the signing of the Interim Agreement between Israel and the Palestine Liberation Organization. The Palestinians were forced to live in makeshift camps along the Egyptian border. The Government allowed the Palestinians living in the border camps to return to Libya, but over 200 Palestinians elected to remain, hoping to travel to the West Bank and Gaza or resettle in Egypt. The Governments of Libya, Egypt, and Israel refused to accept the Palestinian refugees, leaving them stranded in the deteriorating and squalid conditions of the temporary border encampments.

The Government threatened to expel thousands of Palestinian residents and workers in May and distributed questionnaires to identify and locate Palestinian residents. However, it did not act on the threat or undertake the mass expulsions of foreigners (see Section 6.e.).

The Government is not a signatory to the 1951 United Nations Convention relating to the Status of Refugees or the 1967 Protocol and, therefore, does not grant asylum, first asylum, or refugee status to foreigners in Libya. The U.N. High Commissioner for Refugees (UNHCR) reported that by April 1996 there were over 3,000 refugees of concern to the UNHCR in Libya, including some 2,000 Somalis, 750 Eritreans, 325 Sudanese, and 300 Ethiopians. The Government officially contacted the UNHCR Liaison Officer in Tripoli in 1995 in an effort to facilitate the repatriation of Arab and African refugees to their country of origin. The UNHCR assisted in the repatriation of 168 Eritreans and 129 Ethiopians in the first 4 months of 1996.

Section 3. Respect for Political Rights: The Right of Citizens to Change Their Government

Citizens do not have the right to change their government. Major government decisions are controlled by Qadhafi, his close associates, and committees acting in his name. Political parties are banned. Qadhafi appoints military officers and official functionaries down to junior levels. Corruption and favoritism, partially based on tribal origin, are major problems, adversely affecting government efficiency.

In theory political participation is guaranteed by the grassroots People's Committees, which send representatives annually to the national General People's Congress (GPC). In practice the GPC is a rubber stamp that approves all recommendations made by Qadhafi.

Qadhafi established the Revolutionary Committees in 1977. These bodies are composed mostly of Libyan youths who are charged with guarding against political deviation. Some Committees have engaged in show trials of regime opponents; in other cases, they have been implicated with killing opponents abroad. The Committees approve all candidates in elections for the GPC.

There is no reliable information on the representation of women and minorities in the Government.

Section 4. Governmental Attitude Regarding International and Nongovernmental Investigation of Alleged Violations of Human Rights

The regime prohibits the establishment of independent human rights organizations. It created the Libyan Arab Human Rights Committee in 1989, but the Committee has not published any known reports.

The regime does not respond substantively to appeals from Amnesty International (AI) on behalf of detainees. In 1994 the regime described AI as a tool of Western interests and dismissed its work as neocolonialist. AI representatives last visited Libya in 1988.

Section 5. Discrimination Based on Race, Sex, Religion, Disability, Language, or Social Status

Women.—There is little information on the extent of violence against women. In general the intervention of neighbors and extended family members tends to limit the prevalence and scope of such violence. Abuse within the family is rarely discussed publicly, due to the value attached to privacy in this traditional society. Libyans have been implicated in the purchasing of Sudanese slaves (see Section 6.c.).

Women were granted equal status under law by the Constitutional Proclamation in 1969. Despite this legal provision of equality, many traditional attitudes and practices continue to discriminate against women. A woman must have her husband's permission to travel abroad (see Section 2.d.).

Most observers agree that, with the advent of oil wealth in the 1970's, women have made notable social progress. Oil wealth, urbanization, development plans, education programs, and even the impetus behind Qadhafi's revolutionary Government have contributed to the creation of new employment opportunities for women. In recent years, a growing sense of individualism in some segments of society, especially among the educated young, has been noted. For example many educated young couples prefer to set up their own households, rather than move in with their parents, and view polygyny with scorn. Since the 1970's, the level of educational differences between men and women has continued to narrow.

In general the emancipation of women is a generational phenomenon: Urban women under the age of 35 tend to have more "modern" attitudes toward life and have discarded the traditional veil; at the same time, older urban women tend to be more reluctant to give up the veil or the traditional attitudes towards family and employment. Moreover, a significant proportion of rural women still do not attend school and tend to instill in their children such traditional beliefs as women's subservient role in society.

Employment gains by women also tend to be inhibited by lingering traditional restrictions that discourage women from playing an active role in the workplace and by the resurgence of Islamic fundamentalist values. Some observers have noted that even educated women tend to lack self-confidence and social awareness and seek only a limited degree of occupational and social participation with men.

The ambiguous position of women is illustrated by Qadhafi's own attitudes and utterances. His development plans have made an effort to include women in the modern work force, yet he has criticized women's emancipation in the West, including their employment gains.

Children.—The Government has subsidized education (which is compulsory to the age of 15) and medical care, improving the welfare of children in the past 25 years. However, declining revenues and general economic mismanagement have led to cutbacks, particularly in medical services. Some tribes located in remote areas still practice female genital mutilation (FGM) on young girls, a procedure that is widely condemned by international health experts as damaging to both physical and psychological health.

People With Disabilities.—No information is available on the Government's efforts to assist people with disabilities.

National/Racial/Ethnic Minorities.—Arabic-speaking Muslims of mixed Arab and Berber ancestry comprise 97 percent of the population. The principal non-Arab minorities are Berbers and Africans. There are frequent allegations of discrimination based on tribal status, particularly against Berbers in the interior and Tuaregs in the south. Qadhafi manipulates tribes to maintain his grip on power by rewarding some tribes with money and government positions and repressing and jailing members of the other tribes. Qadhafi also attempts to keep the tribes fractured by pitting one tribe against another.

Section 6. Worker Rights

a. *The Right of Association.*—Independent trade unions and professional associations are prohibited, and workers do not have the right to join unions of their own choosing. The regime regards such structures as unacceptable "intermediaries between the revolution and the working forces." They may join the sole official trade union organization, the National Trade Unions' Federation, which was created in 1972 and administered by the People's Committee system. The Government prohibits foreign workers from joining unions.

The law does not guarantee the right to strike. There have been no reports of strikes for years. In a 1992 speech, Qadhafi affirmed that workers have the right to strike but added that strikes do not occur because the workers control their enterprises.

The official trade union organization plays an active role in the International Confederation of Arab Trade Unions and the Organization of African Trade Union Unity. It exploits international trade union contacts to engage in propaganda efforts on behalf of the regime. The Arab Maghreb Trade Union Federation suspended the membership of Libya's trade union organization in 1993. The suspension followed reports that Qadhafi had replaced all union leaders, in some cases with loyal followers without union experience.

b. *The Right to Organize and Bargain Collectively.*—Collective bargaining does not exist in any meaningful sense because the labor law requires that the Government must approve all agreements.

c. *Prohibition of Forced or Compulsory Labor.*—In its 1995 report, the International Labor Organization's (ILO) Committee of Experts stated that "persons expressing certain political views or views ideologically opposed to the established political, social, or economic system may be punished with penalties of imprisonment * * * involving * * * an obligation to perform labor." The situation in 1996 remained largely the same. The 1995 ILO report also noted that public employees may be sentenced to compulsory labor "* * * as a punishment for breaches of labor discipline or for participation in strikes, even in services whose interruption would not endanger the life, personal safety, or health of the whole or part of the population."

The Government informed the ILO that legislation was enacted to abolish these provisions and submitted a report to the ILO, but the ILO did not comment on it this year.

There have been credible reports that the Government has arbitrarily forced some foreign workers into involuntary military service or has coerced them into performing subversive activities against their own countries. Libyans have been implicated in the purchasing of Sudanese slaves, who are largely southern Sudanese women and children who were captured by Sudanese government troops in the war against the southern rebellion.

d. *Minimum Age for Employment of Children.*—The minimum age for employment of children is 18 years.

e. *Acceptable Conditions of Work.*—The labor force is about 1.2 million workers (including 161,000 foreign workers) in a population of 5.2 million. Wages, particularly in the public sector, are frequently in arrears. A public wage freeze imposed in 1981 remains in effect and has seriously eroded real income. The average wage appears inadequate to provide a worker and family with a decent standard of living. The average wage is about $900 per month (300 dinars) at the official exchange rate, but is only worth $100 at the unofficial exchange rate.

The legal maximum workweek is 48 hours. The labor law defines the rights and duties of workers, including matters of compensation, pension rights, minimum rest periods, and working hours. Labor inspectors are assigned to inspect places of work for compliance with occupational health and safety standards. Certain industries, such as the petroleum sector, try to maintain standards set by foreign companies.

The labor law does not accord equality of treatment to foreign workers. Foreign workers may reside in Libya only for the duration of their work contracts and may not send more than half of their earnings to their families in their home countries. They are subject to arbitrary pressures, such as changes in work rules and contracts and have little option but to accept such changes or to depart the country. Foreign workers who are not under contract enjoy no protection.

The Government uses the threat of expulsion of their foreign workers as leverage against countries whose foreign policies run counter to Libya's. The Government expelled approximately 1,000 Palestinian residents in late 1995 to signal its displeasure with the agreement between Israel and the Palestine Liberation Organization, and in May the regime threatened to expel thousands of Palestinian workers for political and economic reasons (see Section 2.d.).

The regime had expelled thousands of foreign workers from Chad, Sudan, and Egypt by the end of 1995, claiming that they were in Libya illegally. Government fears of worker ties to Islamic extremist groups and the need to conserve foreign exchange may have motivated the wave of expulsions.

MOROCCO

The Constitution of Morocco provides for a monarchy with a parliament and an independent judiciary. Ultimate authority, however, rests with the King, who may at his discretion terminate the tenure of any minister, dissolve the Parliament, and rule by decree. The present Parliament was created in 1993 through a two-stage process: 222 deputies were elected by direct universal suffrage, and an additional 111 were selected by labor syndicates, professional organizations, and local authorities. The Cabinet continues to be composed largely of technocrats. Parliamentary elections are expected in 1997, following the September 13, 1996 referendum on the creation of a second legislative chamber. The referendum was approved by 99 percent of the vote. The Government reported that 82 percent of the electorate voted, although most observers believe this figure is exaggerated.

The security apparatus includes several overlapping police and paramilitary organizations. The border police, the national security police, and the judicial police are departments of the Ministry of Interior, while the Royal Gendarmerie reports directly to the Palace. The security forces continued to commit human rights abuses.

Morocco has a mixed economy based largely on agriculture, fishing, light industry, phosphate mining, tourism, and remittances from citizens working abroad. Illegal cannabis production is also a significant economic activity. While a series of debilitating droughts has challenged generally strong economic growth in recent years, good rainfall during the year was expected to contribute to an economic upswing.

The Government's human rights record remained largely the same as the preceding year. Security forces occasionally abuse and torture detainees and prison conditions remain harsh. The Government's anti-contraband (assainissement) campaign resulted in numerous violations of citizen's human rights. Allegations of arbitrary arrest and physical abuse increased in the wake of this campaign, and the Government failed to investigate thoroughly allegations of abuse by security forces. The then-Minister for Human Rights resigned, citing excesses committed by security forces during this campaign. The King then appointed the Minister of Justice as Minister of Human Rights, although the Ministry of Justice is considered by some to be one of the primary obstacles to improved human rights.

Citizens do not have the right to change their government. The judiciary is subject to corruption and Interior Ministry influence. The authorities at times ignore due process rights and infringe on citizens' privacy rights. The Government restricts freedom of speech and the press in certain areas, and limits the freedoms of assembly, association, religion, and movement. While the Government generally tolerates peaceful protests and sit-ins, it does not tolerate marches and demonstrations. On three occasions during the year, including on the eve of a 1-day general strike in June and during a female textile workers demonstration in March, several protesters were seriously beaten, and scores were arrested. Discrimination and domestic violence against women are common. Child labor is a problem, and the Government has not acted to end the plight of young girls who work in exploitive domestic servitude. Unions are subject to government interference.

A large number of the allegations of governmental human rights abuse involve the Ministry of Interior. The Ministry is responsible for: The direction of most security forces; the conduct of elections, including cooperation with the United Nations in a referendum on the Western Sahara; the appointment and training of many local officials; the allocation of local and regional budgets; the oversight of university campuses; and the licensing of associations and political parties. Less formally, the Ministry exerts substantial pressure on the judicial system.

RESPECT FOR HUMAN RIGHTS

Section 1. Respect for the Integrity of the Person, Including Freedom From:

a. *Political and Other Extrajudicial Killing.*—Although no deaths of persons in police custody could be conclusively attributed to security force brutality, there were several instances of death under suspicious circumstances that remain unresolved. In January Yahya Salhi was found dead in the Oujda gendarmerie detention center. Salhi had been arrested 2 days earlier for theft. Officials allege that Salhi committed suicide.

In February Babeha Lahssen died while in custody at the gendarmerie center in Khemisset. According to human rights activists, Lahssen was arrested following a fight with a tribal chief. Several days after the arrest, Lahssen's family was informed that he had committed suicide. The Lahssen family's request for an autopsy was reportedly denied by the Court of First Instance.

In May 16-year-old Abdelhamid M'rabet died while in police custody in Tangier. Press reports state that M'rabet was arrested during a fight with a local police officer's son. In the course of the arrest, M'rabet was reportedly severely beaten about the head. He died shortly after arriving at the police station. Tangier officials detained the arresting officer and launched an investigation. The outcome of the investigation has not been made public.

Hussein El Mernissi was arrested on July 11 and died the next day at Asfi police station, purportedly taking his own life. The Moroccan Organization for Human Rights (OMDH) has filed a court action regarding this case, demanding that a second autopsy be performed.

In May Jalal Mohamed died in prison. Human rights activists attribute his death to official negligence (see Section 1.c.).

Human rights organizations continue to complain that security forces too often act with impunity; deaths in custody and other instances of potential abuse are not thoroughly investigated. None of the cases outstanding from 1995 have been publicly resolved. These include the deaths in custody of Hamza Daghdagh and Mustapha Benderweesh. However, in October a court acquitted two police officers accused of the 1993 torture death of Mustapha Hamzaoui and earlier cases. Since October local media reported four other cases of persons who died while in police custody: Mohamed Fedaoui; Omar Bouhdoun; Said Hammouch; and Rachid Rami.

Detainees claimed that several prisoners died during the year due to harsh prison conditions and inadequate medical care (see 1.c.).

b. *Disappearance.*—There were no new cases of disappearance during the year. This contrasts with 1995 when there were reports of over 20. However, the practice of the forced disappearance of individuals who opposed the Government and its policies dates back several decades. Many of those who disappeared were members of the military who were implicated in attempts to overthrow the Government in 1971 and 1972. Others were Sahrawis or Moroccans who challenged the Government's claim to the Western Sahara or other government policies. Many of those who disappeared were held in secret detention camps. To this day, hundreds of Saharan and Moroccan families do not have any information about their missing relatives, many of whom have been missing over 20 years.

The Government continues to deny that it has any knowledge of the whereabouts of those still missing. In recent years it has quietly released several hundred persons who had disappeared, including about 300 in June 1991, but no explanation for their incarceration has ever been provided. Local human rights monitors have concluded that many others died while at the notorious Tazmamart Prison, which has since been closed. The Government has acknowledged 34 of these deaths and has provided death certificates to the families of all but 1 of the 34 who died.

OMDH and other human rights organizations continued to pursue the issue of unresolved disappearances. OMDH reports that its efforts to meet with the Minister of Justice and Human Rights to discuss this issue have been unsuccessful.

There were no developments in the disappearance of Abdullah Sherrouq, a student, who was reportedly detained by security services on June 22, 1981. After 15 years, his family has still been unable to learn anything of his whereabouts or his fate, despite appeals by Amnesty International.

A group representing Tazmamart prison survivors and the families of persons who disappeared continues to call for an accounting of unresolved cases, compensation to families of those who disappeared, proper burial of victims' remains, and prosecution of responsible officials. The Government has not responded to their demands.

The Government continued to pay a small monthly stipend to the 28 former prisoners who survived 18 to 20 years in solitary confinement at Tazmamaart prison—without health care or sanitary facilities. The 28 are former military men who had been arrested in connection with the failed coup attempts in 1971 and 1972. After their release, the Government prohibited them from speaking out publicly about their detention. In exchange, the Government gave the 28 assurances that it would help them find jobs and reintegrate them into society.

c. *Torture and Other Cruel, Inhuman, or Degrading Treatment or Punishment.*—Morocco ratified the U.N. Convention against Torture in 1993. The Government claims that the use of torture has been discontinued, but newspapers and other sources indicate that security forces still abuse and torture detainees. The fact that detainees are not allowed to have contact with family or lawyers during the first 48 hours of incarceration (see Section 1.d.) increases the likelihood of torture and abuse.

According to local human rights advocates, one of the problems in documenting torture and abuse is that autopsies are not routine. They are only carried out at the request of the state prosecutor and at the order of a judge. The lack of autopsies indicates that follow-up investigations into deaths in custody are inadequate.

In June OMDH issued a report charging that torture is still prevalent. OMDH officials attribute the phenomenon to officials' attempts to elicit information from detainees in the anticontraband and antinarcotics campaigns. In addition, the report charges that allegations of abuse are frequently not investigated, and that officials often act with impunity.

In January the press and human rights organizations reported eyewitness accounts that those arrested during the Government's anticontraband campaign were subjected to physical abuse and torture during interrogation. There were also reports of due process violations and irregularities in the course of their trials (see Section 1.e.). Government officials have denied that any abuses occurred.

In April defendants arrested during a government antinarcotics crackdown charged that they had been subjected to abuse while in police custody. They also alleged that their signed confessions had been obtained through police pressure and coercion.

Although prison conditions remain harsh, they have reportedly improved in recent years, due in part to reforms undertaken at the suggestion of the Royal Consultative Council of Human Rights. Nonetheless, credible reports indicate that harsh treatment and conditions continue, with state security prisoners more likely to be victimized. On October 24, detainees at Kenitra central prison sent an open letter countering the Government's assertions that the prisons are being reformed and detailing the poor conditions at Kenitra. The prisoners, mostly political and Islamist detainees, alleged that the prison lacks the most basic needs, including ventilation and medical care. The letter states that seven prisoners died this year and alleged medical neglect. Causes of death ranged from cancer and tuberculosis to injuries sustained through physical assault. In May Jalaal Mohamed, a prisoner at El-Jadida Civil Prison, died while unloading a supply truck. Mohamed reportedly suffered from heart and other health problems. Human rights activists charge that his death was due to the negligence of prison officials.

The Government does not generally permit prison visits by human rights monitors. Notable exceptions occurred in February and March 1995, when human rights monitors, along with several journalists and an investigating commission, visited prisons in Tangiers, Mohammedia, El-Jadida, Casablanca, and Khenifra following a prison riot in Khenifra.

d. *Arbitrary Arrest, Detention, or Exile.*—Legal provisions for due process have been revised extensively in recent years, although reports indicate that the authorties sometimes ignored them (see Section 1.c.). Although police usually make arrests in public, they do not always identify themselves and do not always obtain warrants. Incommunicado (garde-a-vue) detention is limited to 48 hours, with one 24-hour extension allowed at the prosecutor's discretion. In state security cases, the garde-a-vue period is 96 hours; this may also be extended by the prosecutor. It is during this initial period, when defendants are denied access to counsel, that the accused is interrogated and abuse is most likely to occur. Some members of the security forces, long accustomed to indefinite precharge access to detainees, continue to resist the new rules.

Lawyers are not always informed of the date of arrest, and thus are unable to monitor compliance with the garde-a-vue detention limits. While the law provides for a limited system of bail, it is rarely used. Defendants are, however, sometimes released on their own recognizance. The law does not provide for habeas corpus or its equivalent. Under a separate code of military justice, military authorities may detain members of the military without warrants or public trial.

Although the accused are generally brought to trial within2 months, prosecutors may order up to five 2-month extensions of pretrial detention. Thus, an accused person can be kept in pretrial detention for up to 1 year.

There are no known instances of enforced exile, although a number of dissidents live abroad in self-imposed exile. Their number has been steadily diminishing, however, as many returned to Morocco following a broad-based amnesty decree issued by the Government in 1994.

In May Mamoun Balghiti Alaoui returned to Morocco after30 years of exile in Syria. Alaoui was a dissident in the 1960's who was forced to flee the country. He was later tried and sentenced to death in absentia. He was included in the global royal pardon issued by the King in 1994.

Many human rights groups consider Abraham Serfaty to be a Moroccan exile. A member of the (now defunct) Communist Party and a supporter of Saharan independence, Serfaty was released in 1991 after 17 years in prison. Upon his release, the Government declared that Serfaty was a Brazilian rather than a Moroccan citizen because his father was a naturalized Moroccan citizen originally from Brazil. Based on this Serfaty was expelled from Morocco. This decision has been widely criticized by human rights groups. In July Serfaty's wife was stopped at the Casablanca airport and prohibited from entering the country.

e. *Denial of Fair Public Trial.*—The Constitution provides for an independent judiciary, but all courts are subject to extrajudicial pressures, including bribery and government influence.

There are three levels in the court system, courts of first instance, the appeals Court, and the Supreme Court. While in theory there is a single court system under the Ministry of Justice, two other courts also operate: the Special Court of Justice that handles cases of civil servants implicated in corruption and the Military Tribunal for cases involving military personnel and on certain occasions matters pertaining to state security, although state security also falls within the jurisdiction of regular court system.

Although there is a single court system for most nonmilitary matters, family issues such as marriage, divorce, child support and custody, and inheritance are adjudicated by judges trained in Islamic law, or Shari'a. Judges considering criminal cases or cases in non-family areas of civil law are generally trained in the French legal tradition. All judges trained in recent years are graduates of the National Institute for Judicial Studies, where they undergo 2 years of study heavily focused on human rights and the rule of law. It is not necessary to be a lawyer to become a judge and the majority of judges are not lawyers.

In general detainees are arraigned before a court of first instance. If the infraction is minor and not contested, the judge may order the defendant released or impose a light sentence. If an investigation is required, the judge may release defendants on their own recognizance. Cases are often adjudicated on the basis of confessions, some of which are obtained under duress, according to reliable sources.

All courts are subject to extrajudicial pressures. Salaries for both judges and their staffs are extremely modest; as a result, petty bribery has become a routine cost of court business. In many courts, especially in minor criminal cases, defendants or their families pay bribes to court officers and judges to secure a favorable disposition.

A more subtle corruption derives from the judiciary's relationship with the Ministry of Interior. Judges work closely with the Ministry's network of local officials, or caids, who serve as members of the judicial police and often assume personal responsibility for the questioning of criminal detainees. They also frequently prepare the written summary of an arrest and subsequent interrogation. The summary is admissible in court and may be the only evidence introduced at trial, effectively rendering it an instruction passed from the caid's office to the court. Credible sources report that judges who hope for higher salaries and career advancement follow the caid's guidance closely.

The law does not distinguish political and security cases from common criminal cases. In serious state security cases, communications between the Ministry of Interior and the court are more direct. At the Government's discretion, such cases may be brought before a specially constituted military tribunal, which is subservient to other branches of the Government, notably the military and the Ministry of Interior.

Aside from external pressures, the court system is also subject to resource constraints. Consequently, criminal defendants charged with less serious offenses often receive only cursory hearings, with judges relying on police reports to render decisions. Although the Government provides an attorney at public expense for serious crimes (i.e., when the offense carries a maximum sentence of over 5 years), appointed attorneys often provide inadequate representation.

In January the OMDH charged that defendants arrested in the anticontraband crackdown were denied access to attorneys during interrogation and that defendants were not allowed to submit evidence (some of which investigators had earlier requested they present) to counter charges against them (see Section 1.c.). Later, the attorneys for nine of the defendants walked out of court in protest after charging that they had not been given enough time to study the case against their clients. One of the more extreme examples involved the trial of David and Simon Chetrit, father and son importers, who were pronounced guilty at 3:30 AM after the defense team had spent more than 17 hours in the courtroom without a rest or food break, and were repeatedly denied an opportunity to present a defense. The Chetrits were each sentenced to 5 years' imprisonment and received one of the largest fines of any of those convicted during the campaign on charges of importing contraband and bribing customs officials. Among those criticizing the way in which the anticontraband campaign was conducted was Human Rights Minister Mohamed Ziane. Ziane's outspoken disapproval of the campaign led to his resignation from the Ministry in January, and the human rights portfolio was assumed by the Minister of Justice. However, some observers consider the Ministry of Justice to be a major obstacle to an improved human rights record. Although their missions are not completely incompatible, combining the Ministry of Justice and the Ministry of Human Rights portfolios does not advance the stated objective of the Government and the King to protect and promote human rights.

The Moroccan Organization of Human Rights (OMDH) estimates that there are some 60 political prisoners, of which 50 are Islamists and the remainder are leftists. Among the 50 alleged Islamists are 16 members of the "Group of 26." Three of this group were convicted of arms smuggling in 1986, but the others were apparently arrested for Islamist activities. International human rights groups estimate of the number of persons in prison for advocating independence for the Western Sahara vary from none to 700.

f. *Arbitrary Interference with Privacy, Family, Home, or Correspondence.*—The Constitution states that the home is inviolable and that no search or investigation may take place without a search warrant. The law stipulates that a search warrant may be issued by a prosecutor on good cause. Nonetheless, during the Government's recent anticontraband campaign several businesses and places of residence were entered without the requisite search warrant.

Government security services monitor certain persons and organizations, both foreign and Moroccan and government informers monitor activities on university campuses.

Section 2. Respect for Civil Liberties, Including:

a. *Freedom of Speech and Press.*—Although the Constitution provides for freedom of expression, the Government seriously restricts press freedom in certain areas.

The Government owns the official press agency, Maghreb Arab Press, and the Arabic daily Al-Anbaa. A 1958 decree grants the Government the authority to register and license domestic newspapers and journals. Authorities can use the licensing process to prevent the publication of materials that they believe cross the threshold of tolerable dissent. Offending publications may be declared a danger to state security, seized, and the publisher's license suspended and equipment destroyed. The Ministry of Interior can control foreign publications by collecting "banned" publications after they have been distributed. In general, however, the Government does not employ extreme measures since the media regularly engage in self-censorship to avoid the Government's attention and possible sanctions.

The Press Code empowers the Minister of Interior to confiscate publications that are judged offensive by the Government. Under the Code the Prime Minister may order the indefinite suspension of a publication. On November 19, the Government formally banned the Arabic-language weekly Al-Usbu Al-Sahfi Wa'l Siyassi, and declared all distribution of this weekly illegal. The police notice banning the paper offered no justification, but credible sources confirm that the Minister of Interior and the Prime Minister were both angered by a series of articles on the "business activities" of the Moroccan elite, including their sons. The publisher was warned several weeks earlier to "lay off people who work closely with the King." The Moroccan Press Syndicate and a Moroccan human rights organization are filing a court case in an effort to rescind the Government's decision.

The Press Code empowers the Government to censor newspapers directly by ordering them not to report on specific items or events. In most instances, government control of the media generally is exercised through directives and "guidance" from the Ministry of the Interior. Nonetheless, the Government generally tolerates satirical and often stinging editorials in the opposition parties' dailies. However, both law and tradition prohibit criticism on three topics: the monarchy, Morocco's claim to the Western Sahara, and the sanctity of Islam.

There were some notable instances of censorship during the year. The Government continues its November 1995 ban on Jeune Afrique, which had published an article describing the King's health and its impact on the political scene. Since October Jeune Afrique has been distributed, but has—perhaps not coincidentally—recently refrained from publishing any negative stories about the royal family.

In January the OADP daily, Anoual, was seized twice by local authorities in Casablanca. No reason was given for the seizure. Also in January, the weekly magazine Maroc Hebdo was sued for defamation at the request of the Prime Minister. Maroc-Hebdo had reprinted selections from a report by the European Observatoire Geopolitique Des Drogues implicating high-level Moroccan officials in drug trafficking.

In February comedian Ahmed Snoussi (also known as Bziz) was prohibited from performing in Casablanca. Bziz, Morocco's best-known political satirist, has been banned from television appearances for the past 5 years. In April the government-owned television station dismissed its editor-in-chief after she participated in a seminar on the role of journalism in the democratic process and the protection of human rights. The dismissal was severely criticized by press and human rights groups.

The Government owns the only television station whose broadcasts can be received nationwide without decoder or satellite dish antennas. The Government purchased a majority share in 2M, the country's sole private station, which can be received in most urban areas with the rental of an inexpensive decoder. The ostensible reason for the Government's action was to save 2M from bankruptcy; the Government now owns 68 percent of 2M stock and the Minister of Information by virtue of hsi position has become the chairman of the board. Dish antennas are available on the market and permit free access to a variety of foreign broadcasts. Residents of the north can receive Spanish broadcasts with standard antennas. The Government does not impede the reception of foreign broadcasts.

The universities enjoy relative academic freedom in most areas.

b. *Freedom of Peaceful Assembly and Association.*—Although the Constitution provides for freedom of assembly and association, the law also permits the Government to suppress even peaceful demonstrations and mass gatherings. Most conferences and demonstrations require the prior authorization of the Ministry of Interior, ostensibly for security reasons.

In January members of the Association of Unemployed University Graduates, an unofficial organization not sanctioned by the Government, began a sit-in in front of the Ministry of Education to protest high unemployment and government inaction. There was little official reaction until March, when security forces dispersed the group, allegedly injuring14 persons.

The unemployed graduates resumed their sit-in in May. For several weeks, police barricaded the building where the youths were assembled, preventing them from leaving as a group to demonstrate in the streets. Occasionally the police and the unemployed graduates clashed, most notably on May 24 when the protesters tried to march out of the building that they were occupying. Police blocked their exit and injured some60 demonstrators. On June 4, on the eve of a nationwide general strike, police beat and injured numerous demonstrators, including humorist Bziz, who had gone to the sit-in to express his support for the unemployed graduates. The sit-in continued until late June, when the graduates voluntarily returned to their homes.

The right to form organizations is limited. Under a 1958 decree, persons wishing to create an organization must obtain the approval of the Ministry of Interior before holding meetings. In practice the Ministry uses this requirement to prevent persons suspected of advocating causes opposed by the Government from forming legal organizations. Islamist and leftist groups have the greatest difficulty in obtaining official approval, although there are over 20 active Islamist groups. The Government has prohibited membership in two, Justice and Charity and Jama'a Islamia, due to their perceived antimonarchy rhetoric. Political parties must also be approved by the Ministry of Interior, which uses this power to control participation in the political process.

On January 9, a group of university professors, lawyers, and journalists formed an association, called Transparency Maroc, dedicated to fighting corruption at all levels. This organization is also not sanctioned by the Government. Transparency is operating, but always in concert with other organizations that are recognized by the Government.

  c. *Freedom of Religion.*—Although the Constitution provides for freedom of worship, only Islam, Christianity, and Judaism are tolerated in practice.

Islam is the official religion. Ninety-nine percent of Moroccans are Sunni Muslims, and the King bears the title Commander of the Faithful. The Jewish community of approximately 6,000 is allowed to practice its faith, as is the somewhat larger foreign Christian community. The Baha'i community of 150 to 200 people has been forbidden to meet or hold communal activities since 1983.

Islamic law and tradition calls for strict punishment of any Muslim who converts to another faith. Any attempt to induce a Muslim to convert is similarly illegal. Foreign missionaries either limit their proselytizing to non-Muslims or conduct their work quietly.

The Ministry of Islamic Affairs monitors Friday mosque sermons and the Koranic schools to ensure the teaching of approved doctrine. The authorities sometimes suppress the activities of Islamists, but generally tolerate activities limited to the propagation of Islam, education, and charity. Security forces commonly close mosques to the public shortly after Friday services to prevent use of the premises for unauthorized political activity.

  d. *Freedom of Movement Within the Country, Foreign Travel, Emigration, and Repatriation.*—Although the Constitution provides for freedom of movement, in practice security forces set up checkpoints throughout the country and stop traffic at will. In some regions the checkpoints have been maintained in the same places for years, creating what some characterize as internal frontiers. Reports persist that police use these checkpoints to demand monetary payments. In the Moroccan-administered portion of the Western Sahara, movement is restricted in areas regarded as militarily sensitive.

The Ministry of Interior restricts freedom to travel outside Morocco in certain circumstances. OMDH, a human rights group, has compiled a list of individuals who have reportedly been denied passports. In addition, all civil servants must obtain written permission from their ministries to leave the country.

In June Maria Oufkir, who had spent 14 years under house arrest, was able to leave Morocco and emigrate to France. Oufkir is the daughter of Mohamed Oufkir, a general and Interior Minister during the 1960's who was implicated in the 1971 coup attempt against King Hassan. Oufkir died under mysterious circumstances in 1972. His family spent the following 14 years under house arrest. Although they were nominally released in 1986, the Oufkir family remained barred from traveling outside Morocco until Maria Oufkir's move to France. While her flight has been described as an escape, sources report that the Oufkirs were issued passports shortly before her departure, and it is acknowledged that she departed with at least the tacit consent of the Government.

Moroccans may not renounce their citizenship, but the King retains the power—rarely used—to revoke it. Tens of thousands of Moroccans hold more than one citizenship and travel on passports from two or more countries. While in Morocco, they are regarded as Moroccan citizens. As a result, the Government has sometimes refused to recognize the right of foreign embassies to act on behalf of dual nationals or even to be informed of their arrest and imprisonment. Dual nationals sometimes complain of harassment by immigration inspectors.

The Government welcomes voluntary repatriation of Jews who have emigrated. Moroccan Jewish emigres, including those with Israeli citizenship, freely visit Morocco. The Government also encourages the return of Sahrawis who have departed Morocco due to the conflict in the Western Sahara—provided they recognize the Government's claim to the region. The Government does not permit Saharan nationalists who have been released from prison to live in the disputed territory. The Government cooperates with the U.N. High Commissioner for Refugees (UNHCR) and other humanitarian organizations in assisting refugees. There were no reports of forced expulsion of anyone having a valid claim to refugee status. While Morocco has from time to time provided political asylum to individuals, the issue of first asylum has never arisen.

Section 3. Respect for Political Rights: The Right of Citizens to Change Their Government

Constitutional provisions notwithstanding, in practice citizens do not have the right to change their national government by democratic means. The King, as Head of State, appoints the Prime Minister, who is the titular head of government. The Parliament has the theoretical authority to effect change in the system of government, but has never exercised it. Moreover, the Constitution may not be changed without the King's approval. The Ministry of Interior appoints the provincial governors and local caids. Municipal councils are elected.

Constitutional changes in 1992 authorized the Prime Minister to nominate all government ministers, but the King has the power to replace any minister at will. Any significant surrender of power from the Crown to the Prime Minister's office was further diluted when the King transferred to the Secretaries General, who serve at the King's pleasure, many of the powers previously vested in the ministers.

Morocco has a unicameral legislature, two-thirds directly elected, and another third indirectly selected by various labor and professional organizations. Eleven parties have members in Parliament. The opposition parties have consistently urged that all members of Parliament be directly elected by the people. Instead, the King proposed creating a bicameral legislature, whereby all members of the lower chamber would be directly elected by the people and all members of the second chamber indirectly selected. On September 13, a referendum was held in which voters approved a constitutional amendment creating this bicameral parliament. The referendum was approved by 99 percent of the vote. The Government reported that 82 percent of the electorate voted, although most observers believe this figure is exaggerated. There were no restrictions on the electorate and there were no serious accusations of fraud. Allegations of fraud during the 1993 elections are still pending before the Supreme Court.

Women are underrepresented in government and politics. There are no female ministers, and there are only two women among the 333 members of Parliament.

Section 4. Governmental Attitude Regarding International and Nongovernmental Investigation of Alleged Violations of Human Rights

There are three officially recognized nongovernmental human rights groups: The Moroccan Human Rights Organization, the Moroccan League for the Defense of Human Rights (LMDH), and the Moroccan Human Rights Association (AMDH). A fourth group, the Committee for the Defense of Human Rights (CDDH), was formed in 1992 by former AMDH members.

The Royal Consultative Council on Human Rights (CCDH), an advisory body to the King, exists in sometimes uneasy coordination with the Ministry of Human Rights, which was established by Parliament. While their common mission provoked an adversarial relationship in the past, a clearer division of roles has emerged, with the CCDH issuing advice on matters such as prison reform, and the Ministry of Human Rights exercising a principally executive role.

Amnesty International (AI) has local chapters in Rabat, Casablanca, and Marrakech. These chapters participate in AI international letter campaigns outside Morocco.

Section 5. Discrimination Based on Race, Sex, Religion, Disability, Language, or Social Status

Although the Constitution states that all citizens are equal, non-Muslims and women face discrimination in the law and traditional practice.

Women.—The law and social practice concerning violence against women reflects the importance society places on the honor of the family. The Criminal Code includes severe punishment for men convicted of rape or violating a woman or a girl. The defendants in such cases bear the burden of proving their innocence. However, sexual assaults often go unreported because of the stigma attached to the loss of virginity. A rapist may be offered the opportunity to marry his victim in order to preserve the honor of the victim's family. The law is more lenient toward men with respect to crimes committed against their wives; for example, a light sentence or reprimand may be accorded a man who has murdered his wife after catching her in the act of adultery.

Spousal violence is common. Although a battered wife has the right to complain to the police, as a practical matter she would do so only if prepared to bring criminal charges.

Women suffer various forms of legal and cultural discrimination. The civil law status of women is governed by the Moudouwana, or Code of Personal Status, which is based on Islamic law. Although the Moudouwana was reformed in 1993, women's groups still complain of unequal treatment, particularly under the laws governing marriage and divorce.

In order to marry, a woman is generally required to obtain the permission of her "tuteur," or legal guardian, usually her father. Except in unusual circumstances, only if her father is deceased may she act as her own "tuteur."

It is far easier for a man to divorce his wife than for a women to divorce her husband. Rather than asking for a divorce, a man may simply repudiate his wife. Under the 1993 reforms to the Moudouwana, a woman's presence in court is required in order for her husband to divorce her, although women's groups report that this law is frequently ignored. The divorce can be finalized even over the woman's objections, although in such cases the court grants her unspecified allowance rights.

A woman seeking a divorce has several alternatives. She may offer her husband money to agree to a divorce (known as a Khol'a divorce). The husband must agree to the divorce and is allowed to specify the amount that he will be paid—without limit. According to women's groups, many men pressure their wives to pursue this kind of divorce. A woman may also file for a judicial divorce if her husband chooses to take a second wife, if she has been abandoned by her husband, or if she is a victim of physical abuse. However, divorce procedures in these cases are lengthy and complicated. For example, while physical abuse is a legal ground for divorce, the court will only grant it if the woman can provide two witnesses to the abuse. Even medical certificates are not sufficient. If the court finds against the woman, she is returned to her husband's home. Consequently, few women report abuse to the authorities.

Under the Criminal Code, women are generally accorded the same treatment as men, but this is not the case for family and estate law, which is based on the Malikite school of Islamic law. Under this law, women inherit only half as much as male heirs. Moreover, even where the law guarantees equal status, cultural norms often prevent a woman from exercising those rights. When a women inherits property, for example, male relatives may pressure her to relinquish her interest.

While many well-educated women pursue careers in law, medicine, education, and government service, few make it to the top echelons of their professions. Women comprise approximately 35 percent of the work force, with the majority in the industrial, service, and teaching sectors. The illiteracy rate for women is 78 percent, compared with 51 percent for men. Women in rural areas suffer most from inequality. Rural women perform most hard physical labor, and the literacy rate in the countryside is significantly lower for women than for men. Girls are much less likely to be sent to school than are boys. Women who do earn secondary school diplomas, however, have equal access to university education.

Children.—The Government has taken little action to end child labor (see Section 6.d.). Young girls in particular are exploited as domestic servants. Some orphanages are knowing accomplices to the practice of adoptive servitude, in which families adopt young girls who perform the duties of domestic servants in their new homes. Credible reports of physical abuse are widespread. The practice is often rationalized as a better alternative to keeping the girls in orphanages. This practice is socially accepted, attracts little criticism and is unregulated by the Government.

Another problem facing orphans of both sexes is lack of civil status. Normally, men are registered at local government offices; their wives and unmarried children are included in this registration, which confers civil status. Civil status is necessary to obtain a birth certificate, passport, or marriage license. If a father does not register his child, the child is without civil status and the benefits of citizenship. It is possible for an individual to self-register, but the process is long and cumbersome.

People With Disabilities.—A high incidence of disabling disease, especially polio, has produced a large population of disabled persons. While the Ministry of Social Affairs contends that the Government endeavors to integrate the disabled into society, in practice this is left largely to private charities. However, even charitable special education programs are priced beyond the reach of most families. Typically, disabled persons survive by begging. The Government continued a pilot training program for the blind sponsored in part by a member of the royal family. There are no laws mandating physical changes to buildings to facilitate access by the disabled.

National/Racial/Ethnic Minorities.—The Constitution affirms, and the Government respects, the legal equality of all citizens. The official language is Arabic. Both French and Arabic are used in the news media and educational institution. Science and technical courses are taught in French, thereby eliminating the large, monolingual Arabic-speaking population from these programs. Educational reforms in the past decade have stressed the use of Arabic in secondary schools. Failure to similarly transform the university system has effectively disqualified many students from higher education in lucrative fields. This is especialy true among the poor, for whom French training is not always affordable.

Some 60 percent of the population claim Berber heritage. Berber cultural groups contend that Berber traditions and the three remaining Berber languages are rapidly being lost. Their repeated requests to the King to permit the teaching of Berber languages in the schools led to a royal decree authorizing the necessary curriculum changes, although no changes have yet occurred.

In June a number of Berber associations issued a communique petitioning the Government to recognize their language, Amzaghi, as an official language and to acknowledge the Amzaghi culture as a part of Moroccan society. The Government thus far has made no response to the petition.

Section 6. Worker Rights

a. *The Right of Association.*—Although workers are free to establish and join trade unions, the unions themselves are not completely free from government interference. Perhaps half a million of Morocco's 9 million workers are unionized in 17 trade union federations. Three federations dominate the labor scene: the Union Marocain de Travail (UMT), the Confederation Democratique de Travail (CDT), and the Union Generale des Travailleurs Marocains (UGTM). The UMT has no political affiliation, but the CDT is affiliated with the Socialist Union of Popular Forces, and the UGTM to the Istiqlal Party.

In practice the Ministry of Interior is believed to have informants within the unions who monitor union activities and the election of officers. Sometimes union officers are subject to government pressure. Union leadership does not always uphold the rights of members to select their own leaders. There has been no case of the rank and file voting out its current leadership and replacing it with another.

Workers have the right to strike and do so. Work stoppages are normally intended to advertise grievances and last 48 to 72 hours or less. Secondary school teachers and university professors held several strikes throughout the year and there were a number of limited duration strikes in the phosphate, banking, and health care sectors, and at the port of Casablanca.

On June 5, the CDT and UGTM labor federations joined forces to stage a 24-hour general strike throughout Morocco to protest perceived government indifference to the economic and social situation of the workers. The strike was relatively quiet and violence-free except in a neighborhood of the northern city of Tangier, where there was sporadic violence involving teenagers and young adults, rather than union activists. The UMT did not participate in the strike and, overall, an estimated 50 to 60 percent of shops and factories nationwide closed in compliance with the call to strike.

UMT unionists at a yeast production company in Casablanca began a strike in February, when management fired a union representative. The strike continues as the plant owner received permission to import yeast to make up for shortages in the market.

Unions belong to regional labor organizations and maintain ties with international trade secretariats.

b. *The Right to Organize and Bargain Collectively.*—The right to organize and bargain collectively is implied in the constitutional provisions on the right to strike and the right to join organizations. Trade union federations compete among themselves to organize workers. Any group of eight workers may organize a union and a worker may change union affiliation easily. A work site may contain several independent locals or locals affiliated with more than one labor federation.

In general the Government ensures the observance of labor laws in larger companies and in the public sector. In the informal economy, and in the textile and handicrafts industries, both the Government and management routinely ignore labor laws and regulations. As a practical matter, unions have no judicial recourse to oblige the Government to enforce labor laws and regulations.

The laws governing collective bargaining are inadequate. Collective bargaining has been a long-standing tradition in some parts of the economy such as the industrial sector, especially heavy industry, but the practice has not spread to other sectors such as the service and informal sectors. The wages and conditions of employment of unionized workers are generally set in discussions between employer and worker representatives. However, wages for the vast majority of workers are unilaterally set by employers.

Employers wishing to dismiss workers are required by law to notify the provincial governor through the labor inspector's office. In cases where employers plan to replace dismissed workers, a government labor inspector provides replacements and mediates the cases of workers who protest their dismissal. Any worker dismissed for committing a serious infraction of work rules is entitled by law to a court hearing.

There is no law specifically prohibiting antiunion discrimination. Employers commonly dismiss workers for union activities regarded as threatening to employer interests. The courts have the authority to reinstate such workers, but are unable to ensure that employers pay damages and back pay.

Ministry of Labor inspectors serve as investigators and conciliators in labor disputes, but they are few in number and do not have the resources to investigate all cases. Unions have increasingly resorted to litigation to resolve labor disputes.

The labor law applies equally to the small Tangier export zone. The proportion of unionized workers in the export zone is about the same as in the rest of the economy.

c. *Prohibition of Forced or Compulsory Labor.*—Forced or compulsory labor is prohibited by the International Labor Organization's (ILO) Convention 29, which was adopted by royal decree. When authorities become aware of instances of forced labor, courts enforce the decree. However, in practice, the Government lacks the resources to inspect all places of work to ensure that forced labor is not being used.

d. *Minimum Age for Employment of Children.*—Abuse of the child labor laws is common. The law prohibits the employment or apprenticeship of any child under 12 years of age. Education is compulsory for children between the ages of 7 and 13 years. Special regulations cover the employment of children between the ages of 12 and 16 years. In practice, children are often apprenticed before age 12, particularly in the handicraft industry. The use of minors is common in the rug-making industry and also exists to some extent in the textile and leather goods industries. Children are also employed informally as domestics and usually receive little or no wages. Safety and health conditions as well as wages in enterprises employing children are often substandard.

Ministry of Labor inspectors are responsible for enforcing child labor regulations, which are generally well observed in the industrialized, unionized sector of the economy. However, the inspectors are not authorized to monitor the conditions of domestic servants.

e. *Acceptable Conditions of Work.*—The June 5 general strike led to negotiations among the Government, the manufacturers' association, and the labor confederations over increasing the minimum wage and improving health benefits, social benefits, and housing. In August all three parties agreed to a 10 percent increase in the minimum wage retroactive to July 1, raising it to approximately $193 (1,661 dirhams) per month in the industrialized sector and to approximately $9.41 (80.96 dirhams) per day for agricultural workers. Neither provides a decent standard of living for a worker and family—even with government subsidies for food, diesel fuel, and public transportation. In many cases, several family members combine their income to support the family. Most workers in the industrial sector earn more than the minimum wage. They are generally paid between 13 and 16 months salary, including bonuses, each year.

The minimum wage is not enforced effectively in the informal and handicraft sectors, and even the Government pays less than the minimum wage to workers at the lowest civil service grades. To increase employment opportunities for recent graduates, the Government allows firms to hire them for a limited period at less than the minimum wage.

The law provides for a 48-hour maximum workweek with no more than 10 hours in any single day, premium pay for overtime, paid public and annual holidays, and minimum conditions for health and safety, including a prohibition on night work for women and minors. As with other regulations and laws, these are not universally observed in the informal sector.

Occupational health and safety standards are rudimentary, except for a prohibition on the employment of women in certain dangerous occupations. Labor inspectors endeavor to monitor working conditions and accidents, but lack sufficient resources. While workers, in principle, have the right to remove themselves from work situations that endanger health and safety without jeopardizing their continued employment, there were no reports of any instances in which a worker attempted to exercise this right.

WESTERN SAHARA

The sovereignty of the Western Sahara remains the subject of a dispute between the Government of Morocco and the Polisario Front, an organization seeking independence for the region. The Moroccan Government sent troops and settlers into the northern two-thirds of the Western Sahara after Spain withdrew from the area in 1975 and extended its administration over the southern province of Oued Ed Dahab after Mauritania renounced its claim in 1979. The Moroccan Government has undertaken a sizable economic development program in the Western Sahara as part of its long-term efforts to strengthen Moroccan claims to the territory.

Since 1973 the Polisario Front has challenged the claims of Spain, Mauritania, and Morocco to the territory. Moroccan and Polisario forces fought intermittently from 1975 to the 1991 ceasefire and deployment to the area of a United Nations peacekeeping contingent, known by its French initials, MINURSO.

In 1975 the International Court of Justice issued an advisory opinion on the status of the Western Sahara. The Court held that while the region's tribes had historical ties to Morocco, the ties were insufficient to warrant recognition of Moroccan sovereignty. According to the court, the people of the Western Sahara, called Sahrawis, are entitled to self-determination. Most Sahrawis live in the area controlled by Morocco, but there is a sizable refugee population near the Western Saharan border, in Algeria, and, to a lesser extent, in Mauritania. The bulk of the Sahrawi population lives within the area delineated by a Moroccan-constructed berm, which encloses most of the territory.

Efforts by the Organization of African Unity (OAU) to resolve the sovereignty question collapsed in 1984 when the OAU recognized the Saharan Arab Democratic Republic, the civilian arm of the Polisario Front. Morocco withdrew from the OAU in protest.

In 1988 Morocco and the Polisario Front accepted the United Nations' plan for a referendum that would allow the Sahrawis to decide between integration with Morocco or independence for the territory. The referendum was scheduled for January 1992, but was postponed because the parties were unable to agree on a common list of eligible voters—despite the previous acceptance by both parties of an updated version of the Spanish census of 1974 as the base for voter eligibility. A complicated formula for determining voter eligibility was ultimately devised, and in August 1994, MINURSO personnel began to hold identification sessions for voter applicants.

The voter identification process ground to a halt in December 1995 and, after several fruitless efforts to coax the two parties to cooperate, the United Nations Security Council formally suspended the identification process in May. The United Nations and friendly governments have continued to urge the two parties to seek a political solution to the conflict, but efforts thus far have yielded no results.

Since 1977 the Saharan provinces of Laayoune, Smara, and Boujdour have participated in local elections organized and controlled by the Moroccan Government. The southern province of Oued Ed Dahab has participated in Moroccan-controlled elections since 1983. Sahrawis whose political views are aligned with Rabat fill all 10 seats allotted to the Western Sahara in the Moroccan Parliament.

The civilian population living in the Western Sahara under Moroccan administration is subject to Moroccan law. U.N. observers and foreign human rights groups report that Sahrawis have difficulty obtaining Moroccan passports, that the Government monitors the political views of Sahrawis more closely than those of Moroccan citizens, and that the police and paramilitary authorities react especially harshly against those suspected of supporting independence and the Polisario Front. Access to the territory is limited by the Moroccan Government and international human rights organizations, and impartial journalists have sometimes experienced difficulty in securing admission.

After years of denying that Sahrawis were imprisoned in Morocco for Polisario-related military or political activity, the Government released 300 such prisoners in 1991. Entire families and Sahrawis who had disappeared in the mid-1970's were among those released. The Government has failed to conduct a public inquiry or to explain how and why those released were held for up to 16 years in incommunicado detention without charge or trial.

There are a number of other Sahrawis, including Kelthoum el-Ouanat, who remain imprisoned for peaceful protests urging Saharan independence. El-Ouanat is currently serving a 20-year term after being arrested in October 1992 following a demonstration in Smara. Prior to her trial she was held in secret detention for up to 10 months during which time she reportedly was beaten, tortured, and sexually abused.

In May 1995, 8 Sahrawi youths were arrested for demonstrating for Sahrawi independence; in June 1995, they were given 20-year sentences. The sentences were later commuted to 1 year by the King, and the 8 Sahrawis were released in July, 14 months after having been taken into custody. They report that they continue to be closely monitored by the Moroccan police.

There are credible reports that 10 Sahrawis were arrested, beaten, and kept in seclusion in May following demonstrations in several cities of the Western Sahara in support of Sahrawi independence. Reportedly these 10 demonstrators have been sentenced to terms of imprisonment ranging from 18 months to 7 years.

The Polisario Front claims that the Government continues to hold several hundred Sahrawis as political prisoners and approximately 300 prisoners of war (POW's). The Government formally denies that any Sahrawi noncombatants remain in detention. On October 31, Morocco released 66 Sahrawi combatants who were flown to the Tindouf area of Algeria under International Committee of the Red Cross (ICRC) auspices. They were accompanied by foreign diplomats. The Government also claims that 30,000 Sahrawi refugees are detained against their will by the Polisario in camps around Tindouf, Algeria. The Polisario denies this charge. There are credible reports that the number of refugees far exceeds 30,000, but their desire to return to their homeland is unclear.

The ICRC also reports that the Polisario now holds approximately 1,900 Moroccan POWs. A group of 185 POW's was repatriated to Morocco in a humanitarian airlift conducted under ICRC auspices in November 1995.

Both the Moroccan Government and the Polisario Front refuse to repatriate the remaining POW's, claiming that the U.N. settlement plan calls for the release of POW's only after the identification process is complete. This rationale only delays progress on this issue, given the indefinite suspension of the U.N. identification process in May.

Freedom of movement within the Western Sahara is limited in militarily sensitive areas. Elsewhere, security forces subject travelers to arbitrary questioning and detention.

There is little organized labor activity in the Western Sahara. The same labor laws that apply in Morocco are applied in the Moroccan-controlled areas of the Western Sahara. Moroccan unions are present in the Moroccan-controlled Western Sahara but are moribund. The 15 percent of the territory outside Moroccan control does not have any major population centers or economic activity beyond nomadic herding. The Polisario-sponsored labor union, the Sario Federation of Labor, is not active in the Western Sahara.

There were no strikes, other job actions, or collective bargaining agreements during the year, but on August 3 a group of approximately 1,000 young Sahrawis demonstrated in Rabat, urging the Government to create job opportunities for them. On August 8, this group attempted to block a major roadway, and reportedly several demonstrators and police officers were injured in the ensuing scuffle. On August 10, after receiving assurances of high-level attention, the demonstrators returned to the Western Sahara. A ministerial delegation from Rabat subsequently traveled to the Western Sahara to discuss the concerns of the demonstrators. Most union members are employees of the Government or state-owned organizations. They are paid 85 percent more than their counterparts outside the Western Sahara. Workers in the Western Sahara are exempt from income and value-added taxes and receive subsidies on such commodities as flour, oil, sugar, fuel, and utilities.

Moroccan law prohibits forced labor, which does not appear to exist in the Western Sahara.

Regulations on the minimum age of employment are the same as in Morocco. Child labor appears to be less common than in Morocco, primarily because of the absence of industries most likely to employ children, such as rug knotting and garment making. A government work program for adults, the Promotion Nationale, provides families with enough income that children need not be hired out as domestic servants. Children in the few remaining nomadic groups presumably work as shepherds along with other group members.

The minimum wage and maximum hours of work are the same as in Morocco. In practice, however, workers in some fish processing plants may work as much as 12 hours per day, 6 days per week, well beyond the 10-hour day, 48-hour week maximum stipulated in Moroccan law. Occupational health and safety standards are the same as those enforced in Morocco. They are rudimentary, except for a prohibition on the employment of women in dangerous occupations.

OMAN

The Sultanate of Oman is a monarchy which has been ruled by the Al Bu Sa'id family since the middle of the 18th century. It has no political parties or directly elected representative institutions. The current Sultan, Qaboos Bin Sa'id Al Sa'id, acceded to the throne in 1970. Although the Sultan retains firm control over all important policy issues, he has brought tribal leaders—even those who took up arms against his family's rule—as well as other notables into the Government. In accordance with tradition and cultural norms, much decisionmaking is by consensus among these leaders. In 1991 the Sultan established the 59-seat Consultative Council, or Majlis Ash-Shura, which replaced an older advisory body. The Government selects Council members from lists of nominees proposed by each of the 59 wilayats (regions). After the first national census in 1993, the Sultan expanded the membership of the new Council to 80 seats. The Council has no formal legislative powers but may question government ministers, even during unrehearsed televised hearings, and recommend changes to new laws on economic and social policy, sometimes leading to amendments to proposed decrees. On November 6, the Sultan promulgated by decree the country's first written "basic law," which provides for citizens' basic rights in writing for the first time. It also provides for a bicameral body known as the Majlis Oman (Council of Oman), which is to include a new Council of State (Majlis Al-Dawla), and the current Consultative Council.

The internal and external security apparatus falls under the authority of the Ministry of Palace Office which coordinates all intelligence and security policies. The Internal Security Service investigates all matters related to internal security. The Royal Oman Police, whose head also has cabinet status, performs regular police duties, provides security at airports, serves as the country's immigration agency, and maintains a small coast guard. There are credible reports that security forces occasionally abused detainees.

Since 1970 Oman has used its modest oil revenue to make impressive economic progress and improve public access to health care, education, and social services. Oman has a mixed economy with significant government participation in industry, transportation, and communications. The Government seeks to diversify the economy and stimulate private investment.

The Government continues to restrict or deny important human rights. Human rights abuses include arbitrary arrest, mistreatment of detainees, prolonged detention without charge, and the denial of due process. The Government restricts freedom of expression and association and does not ensure full rights for workers and women. As a practical matter, the people do not have the right to change their government.

The new basic law provides for many basic human rights, e.g., an independent judiciary, freedom of association, speech, and press. The basic law permits the Government 2 years to adopt the necessary implementing decrees.

RESPECT FOR HUMAN RIGHTS

Section 1. Respect for the Integrity of the Person, Including Freedom From:

a. *Political and Other Extrajudicial Killing.*—There were no reports of political or other extrajudicial killings.

b. *Disappearance.*—There were no reports of politically motivated disappearances.

c. *Torture and Other Cruel, Inhuman, or Degrading Treatment or Punishment.*—Security forces abuse some detainees, particularly during interrogation. The abuse does not appear to be systematic and often varies depending upon the social status of the victim and the official involved. Techniques range from sleep deprivation to harsher measures such as hanging a bound victim from a steel bar in such a way that the wrists must support the full weight of the body. Security officials sometimes beat detainees but are often careful to conceal evidence of abuse by employing such tactics as restricting blows to less visible areas of the body. Detainees are sometimes left in isolation with promises of release or improved treatment as a further means to elicit confessions or information. Although judges have the right to order investigations of allegations of mistreatment, there is no recent evidence that any officer has been punished for abusing detainees. The new basic law, yet to be implemented, specifically prohibits "physical or moral torture" and that all confessions obtained by such methods will be considered null and void.

The Government does not permit independent monitoring of prisons. Nevertheless, prison conditions appear to meet minimum international standards. Access to some prisoners is severely restricted.

d. *Arbitrary Arrest, Detention, or Exile.*—The police may obtain warrants prior to making arrests but are not required by law to do so. The authorities must obtain court orders to hold suspects in pretrial detention. Within 24 hours of arrest, the police are required to file charges or ask a magistrate judge to order continued detention. In practice, however, the police do not always follow these procedures. Judges may order detentions for 14 days to allow investigation and may grant extensions if necessary. There is a system of bail. The announced new basic law provides for certain legal and procedural rights for detainees.

Police handling of arrests and detentions constitutes incommunicado detention in some instances. The police do not routinely notify a detainee's family or, in the case of a foreign worker, the worker's sponsor of the detention. Sometimes notification is made only just prior to the detainee's release. The authorities post a list of persons scheduled for trial near the magistrate court building in Muscat. The police do not always permit attorneys and family members to visit detainees. Judges occasionally intercede to ensure that security officials allow such visits.

The Government does not practice exile as a form of punishment. The new basic law prohibits exile.

e. *Denial of Fair Public Trial.*—The various courts are subordinate to the Sultan and subject to his influence. The Sultan appoints all judges, acts as a court of final appeal, and intercedes in cases of particular interest, especially in national security cases. However, there have been no reported instances in which the Sultan has overturned a decision of the magistrate courts or the Authority for Settlement of Commercial Disputes (ASCD). The announced new basic law affirms the independence of the judiciary The judiciary comprises the magistrate courts, which adjudicate misdemeanors and criminal matters; the Islamic, or Shari'a, courts, which adjudicate personal status cases such as divorce and inheritance; the ASCD; the Labor Welfare Board; and the Rent Dispute Committee, which hears tenant-landlord disputes. A State Security Court tries cases involving national security and criminal cases which the Government decides require expeditious or especially sensitive handling. Magistrate court judges have presided over trials in the State Security Court.

The Criminal Code does not specify the rights of the accused. There are no written rules of evidence, or codified procedures for entering cases into the criminal system, or any legal provision for a public trial. Criminal procedures have developed by tradition and precedents in the magistrate courts. In criminal cases, the police provide defendants with the written charges against them; defendants are presumed innocent and have the right to present evidence and confront witnesses. The prosecution and the defense question witnesses through the judge, who is usually the only person to question witnesses in court.

There are no jury trials. A single judge tries misdemeanors; a panel of three judges tries felonies and security offenses. Magistrate court judges must be citizens. Public prosecutors are senior police officers. They may bring additional charges after defense attorneys have inspected the charge sheet or during trial.

A detainee may hire an attorney but has no explicit right to be represented by counsel. The Government does not pay for the legal representation of indigents. Judges often pronounce the verdict and sentence within 1 day after the completion of a trial. Defendants may appeal jail sentences longer than 3 months and fines over the equivalent of $1,300 to a three-judge panel. Defendants accused of national security offenses and serious felonies do not have the right of appeal. Death sentences, which are rare, cannot be carried out without the Sultan's approval.

In June the Omani press announced that the Government had convicted 69 males in the State Security Court of crimes involving rape, kidnaping, torture, theft, and fraud. An undisclosed number of persons were acquitted, and some of those convicted were minors. Since the cases were tried in the State Security Court, the convicts may appeal only to the Sultan. Their sentences ranged from 6 months to 25 years. Defendants tried by the Security Court are not permitted to have legal representation present. The timing and the location of the Court's proceedings are not publicly disclosed. The Court does not follow legal procedures as strictly as the magistrate courts, although prominent civilian jurists form the panel. The Sultan has exercised his powers of leniency including in political cases.

There are no reports of political prisoners.

f. *Arbitrary Interference with Privacy, Family, Home, or Correspondence.*—The police are not required by law to obtain search warrants. There is a widespread belief that the Government eavesdrops on both oral and written communications, and Omanis are guarded in both areas. Citizens must obtain permission from the Ministry of Interior to marry foreigners, except to nationals from the Gulf Cooperation Council (GCC) countries. Such permission is not automatically granted. Delays or denial of permission have resulted in secret marriages within Oman. Marriages in foreign countries can lead to denial of entry into Oman of the foreign spouse and prevent a legitimate child from claiming citizenship rights.

Section 2. Respect for Civil Liberties, Including:
   a. *Freedom of Speech and Press.*—The law prohibits criticism of the Sultan in any form or medium. The authorities tolerate criticism of government officials and agencies, but such criticism rarely receives media coverage. The announced new basic law provides for freedom of opinion expressed in words, writing, or all other media within the limits of the law.
   The 1984 Press and Publication Law authorizes the Government to censor all domestic and imported publications. Ministry of Information censors may act against any material regarded as politically, culturally, or sexually offensive. However, journalists and writers generally censor themselves to avoid government harassment. Editorials reflect the Government's views, although the authorities tolerate some criticism on foreign affairs issues. The Government discourages in-depth reporting on controversial domestic issues and seeks to influence privately owned dailies and periodicals by subsidizing their operating costs.
   The Government prohibits the entry onto the market of foreign newspapers and magazines containing reports or statements deemed critical of Oman. Customs officials sometimes confiscate video cassette tapes and erase offensive material. The tapes may or may not be returned to their owners. Government censorship decisions are periodically changed without apparent reason. At least two books for sale locally for a number of years were banned in 1996, one when it was released in Arabic translation. The lifting of the boycott against Israel has eliminated prohibitions on publications from or about Israel that meet other censorship standards. There is a general perception that the confiscation of books and tapes at the border from private individuals and restrictions on popular novels has somewhat eased. However, it has reportedly become more difficult to obtain permission to distribute books that censors decide have factual errors about Oman (including outdated maps) in the local market.
   The Government controls the local radio and television companies. They do not air any politically controversial material. The Government does not allow the establishment of privately owned radio and television companies. However, the availability of satellite dishes has made foreign broadcast information accessible to the public.
   The appropriate government authority, such as Sultan Qaboos University, the police, or the relevant ministry must approve public cultural events, including plays, concerts, lectures, and seminars. Most organizations avoid controversial issues due to fear that the authorities may cancel their events. Academic freedom is restricted, particularly regarding controversial matters, including politics. Professors may be dismissed for going beyond acceptable boundaries.
   b. *Freedom of Peaceful Assembly and Association.*—The law does not guarantee freedom of assembly. All public gatherings require government sponsorship. The authorities do not always enforce this requirement, and gatherings sometimes take place without formal government approval. Regulations implemented in 1994 restricting most types of public gatherings remain in effect. The new basic law provides for limited freedom of assembly.
   Current law states that the Ministry of Social Affairs and Labor must approve the establishment of all associations and their bylaws. Despite this ruling, some groups are allowed to function without formal registration. The Government uses the power to license associations as a means to control the political environment. It does not license groups regarded as a threat to the predominant social or political views of the Sultanate. Formal registration of associations for expatriates is limited to a maximum of one association for any nationality. The new basic law's provisions—not yet in effect—regulate the formation of associations.
   c. *Freedom of Religion.*—Islam is the state religion, which is affirmed by the new basic law. The new basic law provides that Islamic law (Shari'a) is the basis for legislation and preserves the freedom to practice religious rites, in accordance with tradition, provided that does not breach public order. Discrimination against individuals on the basis of religion or sect is prohibited. Implementing decrees for the new basic law have not yet been established.
   Most Omanis are Ibadhi or Sunni Muslims, but there is also a minority of Shi'a Muslims. Non-Muslims are free to worship at churches and temples built on land donated by the Sultan. There are many Christian denominations which utilize two plots of donated land on which two Catholic and two Protestant churches have been built. Hindu temples also exist on government provided land. Other land has been made available to Catholic and Protestant missions in Sohar and Salalah.
   The Government prohibits non-Muslims from proselytizing Muslims. It also prohibits non-Muslim groups from publishing religious material, although material printed abroad may be brought into the country. Members of all religions and sects are free to maintain links with coreligionists abroad and undertake foreign travel

for religious purposes. Due to government restrictions on public gatherings, there has been a substantial curtailment of non-Muslim religious celebrations in recent years.

The police monitor mosque sermons to ensure that the preachers do not discuss political topics and stay within the state-approved orthodoxy of Islam. The Government expects all imams to preach sermons within the parameters of standardized texts distributed monthly by the Ministry of Justice, Awqaf, and Islamic Affairs.

d. *Freedom of Movement Within the Country, Foreign Travel, Emigration, and Repatriation.*—The Government does not restrict travel by citizens within the country except to military areas. Foreigners, other than diplomats, must obtain a government pass to cross border points. While a man may travel abroad freely, a woman must have authorization from her husband, father, or nearest male relative to obtain a passport.

Until the promulgation of the basic law, the Government did not have a policy on refugees, or a tradition of harboring stateless or undocumented aliens. The new basic law prohibits the extradition of political refugees. The issue of the provision of first asylum did not arise in 1996. Oman offered temporary refuge to several thousand Yemenis in 1994 displaced by a civil war. They returned to Yemen following the war's end. Tight control over the entry of foreigners into the country has effectively screened out would-be refugees.

Section 3. Respect for Political Rights: The Right of Citizens to Change Their Government

Oman is an autocracy in which the Sultan retains the ultimate authority on all important foreign and domestic issues. The country has no formal democratic political institutions, and its citizens do not have the ability peacefully to change their leaders or the political system.

The Sultan promulgated Oman's first defacto written constitution, known as the basic law, in November. Although it has immediate force of law, laws and regulations to implement its provisions are to be phased in over a 2-year period. The law does not provide for political parties or direct elections. Citizens have indirect access to senior officials through the traditional practice of petitioning their patrons, usually the local governor, or wali, for redress of grievances. Successful redress depends on the effectiveness of the patron's access to appropriate decisionmakers. The Sultan appoints the governors. The Sultan makes an annual 3-week tour of the country, accompanied by his ministers. The tour allows the Sultan to listen directly to his subjects' problems.

In 1991 Sultan Qaboos established a Consultative Council, or Majlis Ash-Shura. In 1994 he expanded the number of council seats to 80 from the original 59, a move which allocated 2 members for districts with a higher population. The Government selected the council members from several nominees elected in caucuses of prominent persons in each district. Caucus participants are also subject to government approval. In some cases, nominees with the most votes did not win appointment to the Council. The Council has no formal legislative powers, which remain concentrated in the Sultan's hands. However, it serves as a conduit of information between the people and the government ministries. No serving government official is eligible to be a Council member. The Council may question government ministers in public or in private, review all draft laws on social and economic policy, and recommend legislative changes to the Sultan, who makes the final decision. The new basic law provides for a Majlis Oman (Council of Oman), which is to consist of the Majlis Ash-Shura (Consultative Council), and a new body, the Majlis Al-Dawla (Council of State). The Sultan announced that the members of the new Council are to be directly appointed, that the franchise in the 1997 Majlis Ash-Shura elections would be expanded, and that female candidates would be permitted in all districts for the first time.

The Sultan has publicly advocated a greater role for women in both the public and private sectors. In 1994 the Government selected two women to serve on the Consultative Council.

Section 4. Governmental Attitude Regarding International and Nongovernmental Investigation of Alleged Violations of Human Rights

The Government prohibits the establishment of human rights groups. The existing restrictions on the freedom of speech and association do not permit any activity or speech critical of the Government. There were no known requests by international human rights organizations to visit Oman.

Section 5. Discrimination Based on Race, Sex, Religion, Disability, Language, or Social Status

The announced new basic law prohibits discrimination on the basis of sex, ethnic origin, race, religion, language, sect, place of residence, and social class. However, decrees to implement its provisions have not been promulgated. Institutional and cultural discrimination based on gender, race, religion, social status, and disability exists.

Women.—There is no evidence of a pattern of spousal abuse although observers say that allegations of such abuse in the Shari'a Courts are not uncommon. Definitive information is scant and difficult to collect. Doctors do not have a legal responsibility to report either spouse or child abuse cases to the courts. Battered women may file a complaint with the police but more often seek family intervention to protect them from violent domestic situations. Likewise, families seek to intervene to keep such problems out of public view. There have been reports that employers or male coworkers have sexually harassed foreign females employed in such positions as domestic servants and hospital nurses. Foreign women employed as domestic servants and garment workers have complained that their employers have withheld their salaries and that government officials have been unresponsive to their grievances. Individuals known to be abusing domestics are not always brought to account for their actions. A few foreign women have had to ask their government's embassy for shelter to escape abuse.

Most women live within the confines of their homes. They continue to face many forms of discrimination. Illiteracy among older women hampers their ability to own property, participate in the modern sector of the economy, or even inform themselves of their own rights. Government officials frequently deny women land grants or housing loans and prefer to conduct business with a woman's husband or other male relative.

Some aspects of Islamic tradition also discriminate against women. Islamic law favors male heirs in adjudicating inheritance claims. Many women are reluctant to take an inheritance dispute to court for fear of alienating the family.

However, since 1970 conditions for women have improved dramatically in several areas. Whereas in 1970 no schools existed for girls, the most recent figures available from the Ministry of Education report an enrollment rate of 86.7 percent for all girls eligible for elementary school. In the 1995–96 school year, female students constituted 50 percent of the total number of students attending public schools. Women constitute roughly half of the 4,500 students at Sultan Qaboos University. In November, 453 women and 282 men received bachelors degrees as members of the seventh graduating class while 8 women and 2 men received masters degrees. The University has a quota system with the apparent goal of increasing the number of men studying certain specialities. Reportedly, women are being limited to 50 percent of the seats in the medical department and are not permitted to take degrees in engineering and archeology. The quotas will allow women to constitute a majority in some other departments.

Women have also made gains in the work force. Some educated women have attained positions of authority in government, business, and the media. Approximately 20 percent of all civil servants are women. In both the public and private sectors, women are entitled to maternity leave and equal pay for equal work. The bureaucracy, the country's largest employer of women, observes such regulations, as do many private sector employers. Still, many educated women face job discrimination because prospective employers fear they might resign to marry or raise families. Several women employees in the Government have complained that they have been denied promotion in favor of less capable men. Government grants for study abroad are limited almost exclusively to males.

Children.—The Government has made the health, education, and general welfare of children a budgetary priority. The infant mortality rate continues to decline, and comprehensive immunization rates have risen. There is no pattern of familial or other child abuse. A few communities in the interior and in the Dhofar region still practice female genital mutilation (FMG). FMG is widely condemned by international health experts as damaging to both physical and psychological heath. Experts believe that the number of such cases is small and declining annually. Oman ratified the U.N. Convention on the Rights of the Child in 1996 with reservations relating to freedom of children to choose a religion and government spending limits.

People With Disabilities.—The Government has mandated parking spaces and some ramps for wheelchair access in private and government office buildings and shopping centers. Compliance is voluntary. Students in wheelchairs have easy access to Sultan Qaboos University. The Government has established several rehabilitation centers for disabled children. Disabled persons, including the blind, work in government offices. Free government medical assistance to all citizens includes physical therapy and prosthetics support for the disabled.

Religious Minorities.—Some members of the Shi'a Muslim minority claim they face discrimination in employment and educational opportunities. Some members of this same community, however, occupy prominent positions in both the private and public sectors.

National/Racial/Ethnic Minorities.—Citizens of east African origin complain that they frequently face job discrimination in both the public and private sectors. Some public institutions reportedly favor hiring members of one or another regional, tribal, or religious group. However, no group is banned from employment.

Members of the Shihuh tribe in the strategic province of Musandam have charged that security authorities have harassed and detained tribe members who complain about alleged inattention or mistreatment by the central Government.

Section 6. Worker Rights

a. *The Right of Association.*—The Government has not yet promulgated a new labor law first drafted by the Ministry of Social Affairs and Labor in 1994. The Consultative Council later recommended some changes, and at year's end the Government continued to review these additional changes to the proposed law. Government officials have said that the new labor code will be consistent with international labor standards. The current law stipulates that "it is absolutely forbidden to provoke a strike for any reason."

Labor unrest is rare. Although strikes are technically illegal, workers sometimes stage job actions. In general these disputes are settled without police intervention. In 1994 the Government joined the International Labor Organization.

b. *The Right to Organize and Bargain Collectively.*—The current law does not provide for the right to collective bargaining. It requires, however, that employers of more than 50 workers form a joint labor-management committee as a communication forum between the two groups. The implementation of this provision is uneven, and the effectiveness of these committees is questionable. In general the committees discuss such questions as living conditions at company-provided housing. They are not authorized to discuss wages, hours, or conditions of employment. Such issues are specified in the work contracts signed individually by workers and employers and must be consistent with the guidelines of the Ministry of Social Affairs and Labor.

The current law defines conditions of employment for some Omanis and foreign workers. It covers domestic servants and construction workers but not temporary workers or those with work contracts that expire within 3 months. Foreign workers constitute at least 50 percent of the work force and as much as 80 percent of the modern-sector work force.

Work rules must be approved by the Ministry of Social Affairs and Labor and posted conspicuously in the workplace by employers of 10 or more workers. Similarly, any employer with 50 or more workers must establish a grievance procedure. Regardless of the size of the company, any employee, including foreign workers, may file a grievance with the Labor Welfare Board. Sometimes worker representatives file collective grievances, but most grievances are filed by individual workers. Lower paid workers use the procedure regularly. Plaintiffs and defendants in such cases may be represented by legal counsel.

There are no export processing zones.

c. *Prohibition of Forced or Compulsory Labor.*—The law prohibits compulsory labor but investigative and enforcement mechanisms are lacking. Foreign workers sometimes find themselves in situations amounting to forced labor. In such cases, employers withhold letters of release, a document releasing the worker from his employment contract, which allow him to switch jobs. Without the letter, a foreign worker must continue to work for his current employer or become technically unemployed—which is sufficient grounds for deportation. Many foreign workers are not aware of their right to take such disputes before the Labor Welfare Board. Others are reluctant to file complaints for fear of retribution from unscrupulous employers. In most cases, the Board releases the grievant from service and awards compensation for time worked under compulsion. Employers face no other penalty than to reimburse the worker's back wages.

d. *Minimum Age for Employment of Children.*—The law prohibits children under the age of 13 from working. The Ministry of Social Affairs and Labor enforces this prohibition. In practice, however, the enforcement often does not extend to some small family businesses which employ underage children, particularly in the agricultural and fisheries sectors. Children between 13 and 16 years of age may be employed but must obtain the Ministry's permission to work overtime, at night, on weekends or holidays, or perform strenuous labor.

e. *Acceptable Conditions of Work.*—The Ministry of Social Affairs and Labor issues minimum wage guidelines for various categories of workers. The minimum wage for nonprofessional workers is about $156 (60 rials) per month. Minimum wage guidelines do not cover domestic servants, farmers, government employees, or workers in small businesses. Many foreigners work in fields exempt from the minimum wage statute. The Government is lax in enforcing minimum wage guidelines for foreign workers employed in menial jobs. However, foreign workers with high skills are frequently paid more than their Omani counterparts.

The minimum wage is sufficient to provide a decent standard of living for a worker and family. The compensation for foreign manual laborers and clerks is sufficient to cover living expenses and to permit savings to be sent home.

The private sector workweek is 40 to 45 hours and includes a rest period from Thursday afternoon through Friday. Government officials have a 35-hour workweek. While the law does not designate the number of days in a workweek, it requires at least one 24-hour rest period per week and mandates overtime pay for hours in excess of 48 per week. Government regulations on hours of employment are not always enforced. Employees who have worked extra hours without compensation may file a complaint before the Labor Welfare Board, but the Board's rulings are not binding.

Every worker has the right to 15 days of annual leave during the first 3 years of employment and 30 days per year thereafter. Employers provide many foreign nationals, including maids, with annual or biannual round-trip tickets to their countries of origin.

All employers are required by law to provide first aid facilities. Work sites with over 100 employees must have a nurse. Employees covered under the labor law may recover compensation for injury or illness sustained on the job through employer-provided medical insurance. The health and safety standard codes are enforced by inspectors from the Department of Health and Safety of the Directorate of Labor. As required by law, they make on-site inspections.

The law states that employers must not place their employees in situations involving dangerous work. However, the law does not specifically grant a worker the right to remove himself from dangerous work without jeopardy to his continued employment.

QATAR

Qatar, an Arab state on the Persian Gulf, is a monarchy without democratically elected institutions or political parties. It is governed by the ruling Al-Thani family through its head, the Amir. In June 1995, the ruling family, in consultation with other leading Qatari families, replaced Sheikh Khalifa bin Hamad Al Thani with his son, Sheikh Hamad bin Khalifa Al Thani. This transition of authority did not represent a change in the basic governing order. While the change of rulers was accepted in public statements by most members of the ruling family and without notable objections from the general public, there remains a reservoir of support for the former Amir. However, in October the former Amir concluded an agreement to return several billion dollars from his private accounts to the state treasury. This agreement is apparently tacit recognition of the legitimacy of his son's regime. The former Amir and his retinue were implicated in a foiled coup attempt in February.

The amended Provisional Constitution, promulgated in April 1972, institutionalizes the customs and mores of the country's conservative Islamic heritage. These include respect for the sanctity of private property, freedom from arbitrary arrest and imprisonment, and punishment of transgressions against Islamic law. The Amir holds absolute power, the exercise of which is influenced by consultation with leading citizens, rule by consensus, and the right of any citizen to appeal personally to the Amir. The Amir considers the opinions of leading citizens, whose influence is institutionalized in the Advisory Council, an appointed body that assists the Amir in formulating policy.

Qatar has efficient police and security services. The civilian security force, controlled by the Interior Ministry, comprises two sections: The police and the General Administration of Public Security; and the Investigatory Police (Mubahathat) which is responsible for sedition and espionage cases. The armed forces have under their jurisdiction the Intelligence Service (Mukhabarat), which is responsible for combating terrorism and monitoring political dissidence.

The State owns most basic industries and services, but the retail and construction industries are in private hands. Oil is the principal natural resource, but the country's extensive natural gas resources will play an increasingly important role. The rapid development of the 1970's and 1980's created an economy in which expatriate workers, mostly South Asian and Arab, outnumber Qataris by a ratio of 4 or 5 to 1. The Government tries to reduce this ratio by offering many government jobs only to citizens.

There was no significant change in the human rights situation. Human rights remain restricted, particularly the denial of the right of citizens to change their government, arbitrary detentions in security cases, restrictions on worker rights, and the freedoms of speech, press, assembly, and association. Women's rights are closely restricted, and non-Qatari workers face systematic discrimination.

RESPECT FOR HUMAN RIGHTS

Section 1. Respect for the Integrity of the Person, Including Freedom From:

a. *Political and Extrajudicial Killing.*—There were no reports of political or other extrajudicial killings.

b. *Disappearance.*—There were no reports of politically motivated disappearances.

c. *Torture and Other Cruel, Inhuman, or Degrading Treatment or Punishment.*—There have been no reported instances of torture for several years. The Government administers most corporal punishment prescribed by Islamic law but does not allow amputation.

Prison conditions generally meet minimum international standards. The Government does not permit domestic human rights groups to exist, and no international human rights organization has asked to visit the country or its prisons.

d. *Arbitrary Arrest, Detention, or Exile.*—The authorities generally charge suspects within 48 hours. In most cases involving foreigners, the police promptly notify the appropriate consular representative. Suspects detained in security cases are generally not afforded access to counsel and may be detained indefinitely while under investigation. There are no known recent cases of incommunicado detention.

Involuntary exile has occurred but is rare. There were no reported cases this year.

e. *Denial of Fair Public Trial.*—The judiciary is nominally independent, but most judges are foreign nationals who hold residence permits granted by the civil authorities and thus hold their positions at the Government's pleasure.

The judiciary is buried under the bureaucratic layers of two ministries. Civil (or Adlea) courts are subordinate to the Ministry of Justice, and religious (or Shari'a) courts fall under the Ministry of Endowments and Islamic Affairs. The prosecutors fall under the Ministry of Interior.

There are three types of courts: the civil courts, which have jurisdiction in civil and commercial matters; the Shari'a Court, which has jurisdiction in family and criminal cases; and the rarely convened state security courts. There are no permanent state security courts. Security cases, which are rare, are tried by ad hoc military courts. Although state security cases may be conducted in secret, there have been no cases before these courts since the new Amir assumed power. Defendants tried by all courts have the right to appeal. Occasionally in the Shari'a Court, the same judge will hear the original case and the appeal.

The legal system is biased in favor of Qataris and the Government. A Muslim litigant may request the Shari'a Court to assume jurisdiction in commercial or civil cases. Non-Muslims are not allowed to bring suits as plaintiffs in the Shari'a Court. This practice prevents non-Muslim residents from obtaining full legal recourse. Trials in the civil courts are public, but in the Shari'a Court only the disputing parties, their relatives, associates, and witnesses are allowed in the courtroom. Lawyers do not play a formal role except to prepare litigants for their cases. Although non-Arabic speakers are provided with interpreters, foreigners are disadvantaged, especially in cases involving the performance of contracts.

Defendants appear before a judge for a preliminary hearing within 7 days of their arrest. Judges may extend pretrial detention a week at a time to allow the authorities to conduct investigations. Defendants in the civil courts have the right to be represented by defense attorneys but are not always permitted to be represented by counsel in the Shari'a court.

Shari'a trials are usually brief. Shari'a family law trials are often held without counsel. After both parties have stated their cases and examined witnesses, judges are likely to deliver a verdict after a short deliberation. Criminal cases are normally tried within 2 to 3 months after suspects are detained. There is no provision for bail in criminal cases. However, foreigners charged with minor crimes may be released to a Qatari sponsor. They are prohibited from departing the country until the case is resolved.

There were no reports of political prisoners.

f. *Arbitrary Interference with Privacy, Family, Home, or Correspondence.*

Traditional attitudes of respect for the sanctity of the home provide a great deal of protection against arbitrary intrusions for most citizens and residents. A warrant must be obtained before police may search a residence or business, except in cases involving national security or emergencies. However, warrants are issued by police officials rather than by judicial authorities. There were no reports of unauthorized searches of homes during the year. The police and security forces are believed to monitor the communications of suspected criminals, those considered to be security risks, and selected foreigners.

With prior permission, which is usually granted, Qataris may marry foreigners of any nationality and apply for residence permits for their spouses.

Section 2. Respect for Civil Liberties, Including:

a. *Freedom of Speech and Press.*—The freedom of speech and press is significantly restricted. However, censorship of the local print media was formally lifted in 1995. Since then, the press has been essentially free of government interference. On at least two occasions, however, local newspapers were closed temporarily when their contents ran afoul of government sensitivities: El Watan when it prematurely published the concluding document of the 1995 GCC Summit, and El Sharq for printing a poem considered offensive to Saudi Arabia. The censorship function continues, however, for movies, videos, radio and television programming (including cable), and the foreign press. Although they increasingly test the limits, journalists continue to practice self-censorship. Social and political pressures for self-censorship will determine whether the new policy will usher in a period of increased public information and debate. Although the Ministry of Information was dissolved in October 1996, the ultimate effect of the suspension of formal press censorship is mitigated by the existence of a separate and unaffected censorship organ within the Ministry of Endowments and Islamic Affairs. This office is charged with the protection of public morality and religious values. As a result, cable television programming is still delayed for censorship, and offensive photos and stories continue to be blacked out of some foreign publications.

Customs officials routinely screen imported video cassettes, audio tapes, books, and periodicals for politically objectionable or pornographic content. Foreign cable television service was introduced in 1993, but censors review broadcasts for objectionable material.

There is no legal provision for academic freedom. Most instructors at the University of Qatar exercise self-censorship.

b. *Freedom of Peaceful Assembly and Association.*—These rights are severely limited. The Government does not allow political parties, political demonstrations, or membership in international professional organizations critical of the Government or any other Arab government. Private social, sports, trade, professional, and cultural societies must be registered with the Government. Security forces monitor the activities of such groups.

c. *Freedom of Religion.*—The state religion is Islam, as interpreted by the puritanical Wahabbi branch of the Sunni tradition. Non-Muslims are prohibited from public worship and may not proselytize. The Government tolerates private gatherings of non-Muslims but closely monitors them for political content. Non-Muslim parents may raise their children in their own faiths. The Government allows Shi'a Muslims to practice their faith. However, the latter have tacitly agreed to refrain from such public rituals as self-flagellation.

Conversion from Islam to another religion is a capital offense, although no one is known to have been executed for it.

d. *Freedom of Movement Within the Country, Foreign Travel, Emigration, and Repatriation.*—There are no restrictions on internal travel, except around sensitive military and oil installations. Generally, women do not require permission from male guardians to travel. However, men may prevent female relatives from leaving the country by placing their names with immigration officers at ports of departure. Technically, women employed by the Government must obtain official permission to travel abroad when requesting leave, but it is not known to what extent this regulation is enforced. Citizens critical of the Government face restrictions on their right to travel abroad.

All citizens have the right to return. Foreigners are subject to immigration restrictions designed to control the size of the local labor pool. Foreign workers must have a sponsor, usually their employer, to enter or depart the country. Foreign women married to Qataris are granted residence permits and may apply for citizenship. However, they are expected to relinquish their foreign citizenship.

The Government has not formulated a formal policy regarding refugees, asylees, or first asylum. Those attempting to enter illegally, including persons seeking to defect from nearby countries, are refused entry. Asylum seekers who can obtain local sponsorship or employment are allowed to enter and may remain as long as they are employed.

Section 3. Respect for Political Rights: The Right of Citizens to Change Their Government

Citizens do not have the right to change their government or the political system peacefully. Qatar has no formal democratic institutions. There have been reports that some of the 19 signers of a December 1991 petition calling for greater political freedom and constitutional reform continued to be subject to travel restrictions. The political institutions blend the characteristics of a traditional Bedouin tribal state and a modern bureaucracy. There are no political parties, elections, or organized opposition groups.

The Amir exercises most executive and legislative powers, including appointment of cabinet members. However, his rule is tempered by local custom. Interlocking family networks, together with the right of citizens to submit appeals or petitions to the Amir, provide informal avenues for the redress of many grievances. The custom of rule by consensus leads to extensive consultations among the Amir, leading merchant families, religious leaders, and other notables on important matters.

Under the amended Provisional Constitution, the Amir must be chosen from and by the adult males of the Al Thani family.

Section 4. Governmental Attitude Regarding International and Nongovernmental Investigation of Alleged Violations of Human Rights

The Government does not permit local human rights organizations to exist. No international human rights organizations are known to have asked to investigate conditions in Qatar.

Section 5. Discrimination Based on Race, Religion, Sex, Disability, Language, or Social Status

Institutional, cultural, and legal discrimination based on gender, race, religion, social status, and disability exists.

Women.—Violence against women and spousal abuse occur but are not believed to be widespread. However, some foreign domestics, especially those from South Asia and the Philippines, have been severely mistreated by employers. In keeping with Islamic law, all forms of physical abuse are illegal. The maximum penalty for rape is death. The police actively investigate reports of violence against women. In the last few years, the Government has demonstrated an increased willingness to arrest and punish offenders, whether citizens or foreigners. Offenders who are citizens usually receive lighter punishments than foreigners. Abused domestic workers usually do not press charges for fear of losing their jobs.

The activities of women are closely restricted both by law and tradition. For example, a woman is prohibited from applying for a driver's license unless she has permission from a male guardian. This restriction does not apply to non-Qatari women. The Government adheres to Shari'a law in matters of inheritance and child custody. While Muslim wives have the right to inherit from their husbands, non-Muslim wives do not, unless a special legacy is arranged. In cases of divorce, wives rarely obtain custody of children and never if the wife is not a Muslim. Women may attend court proceedings but are generally represented by a male relative. There has been a steady increase in the number and severity of complaints of spousal abuse by foreign wives of Qatari and foreign national men.

Women are largely relegated to the roles of mother and homemaker, but some women are now finding jobs in education, medicine, and the news media. However, the number of professional women is too small to determine whether they are receiving equal pay for equal work. Increasingly, women are receiving government scholarships to pursue degrees at universities overseas. The Amir has entrusted his second wife, who is the mother of the Heir Apparent, with the high-profile task of establishing a university in Doha. In November the Government appointed its first female undersecretary, in the Ministry of Education. Although women are legally able to travel abroad alone (see Section 2.d.), tradition and social pressures cause most to travel with male escorts. There have also been complaints that Qatari husbands retrieved their foreign spouses' passports and, without prior approval, turned them in for Qatari documents. The husbands then inform these wives that they had lost their previous nationality. In other cases, foreign citizen wives report being forbidden by husbands or in-laws to visit or contact foreign embassies.

There is no independent women's rights organization, nor would the Government permit the establishment of one.

Children.—The Government demonstrates its commitment to children's rights through a well-funded, free public education system (elementary through university) and a complete medical protection program for Qatari children. However, children of most foreigners are denied free education and have only limited medical coverage. There is no societal pattern of abuse of children.

People With Disabilities.—The Government has not enacted legislation or otherwise mandated provision of accessibility for the handicapped, who also face social discrimination. The Government maintains a hospital and schools that provide free services to the mentally and physically handicapped.

Religious Minorities.—Non-Muslims experience discrimination in employment, particularly in sensitive areas such as security and education. Non-Muslims also encounter official prohibitions in the public practice of their religions (see Section 2.c.).

National/Racial/Ethnic Minorities.—The Government discriminates against some citizens of non-Qatari origin. In the private sector, many Qataris of Iranian extraction occupy positions of the highest importance. However, in government they are rarely found in senior decisionmaking positions.

Section 6. Worker Rights

a. *The Right of Association.*—The right of association is strictly limited, and all workers, including foreigners, are prohibited from forming labor unions. Despite this, almost all workers have the right to strike after their case has been presented to the Labor Conciliation Board and ruled upon. Employers may close a place of work or dismiss employees once the Conciliation Board has heard the case. The right to strike does not exist for government employees, domestic workers, or members of the employer's family. No worker in a public utility or health or security service may strike if such a strike would harm the public or lead to property damage. Strikes are rare, and there were none in 1995.

The labor law provides for the establishment of joint consultative committees composed of representatives of the employer and workers. The committees do not discuss wages but may consider issues including work organization and productivity, conditions of employment, training of workers, and safety measures and their implementation.

Since July 1995, Qatar has been suspended from the U.S. Overseas Private Investment Corporation (OPIC) insurance programs because of the Government's lack of compliance with internationally recognized worker rights standards.

b. *The Right to Organize and Bargain Collectively.*—Workers are prohibited from engaging in collective bargaining. Generally, wages are set unilaterally by employers without government involvement. Local courts handle disputes between workers and employers.

There are no export processing zones.

c. *Prohibition of Forced or Compulsory Labor.*—The law prohibits forced or compulsory labor. Three-quarters of the work force are migrant workers, who are frequently dependent on a single employer for residency rights. This leaves them vulnerable to abuse. For instance, employers must give consent before exit permits are issued to any foreigner seeking to leave the country. Some employers temporarily withhold this consent to force foreign employees to work for longer periods than they wish.

d. *Minimum Age for Employment of Children.*—Minors between the ages of 15 and 18 may be employed with the approval of their parents or guardians. However, younger non-Qatari children sometimes work in small, family-owned businesses. Education is compulsory through the age of 15. While the laws governing the minimum age for employment of children are not strictly enforced, child labor, either Qatari or foreign, is rare. Very young children, usually of African or South Asian background, have been employed as riders in camel racing. Little information is available on wages and working conditions for these children.

Minors may not work more than 6 hours a day or more than 36 hours a week. Employers must provide the Ministry of Labor with the names and occupations of their minor employees. The Ministry may prohibit the employment of minors in jobs which are judged as dangerous to the health, safety, or morals of minors. Employers must also obtain permission from the Ministry of Education to hire a minor.

e. *Acceptable Conditions of Work.*—There is no minimum wage, although a 1962 law gives the Amir authority to set one. The 48-hour workweek with a 24-hour rest period is prescribed by law, although most government offices follow a schedule of 36 hours a week. Employees who work more than 48 hours a week, or 36 hours a week during the Muslim month of Ramadan, are entitled to overtime. This law is adhered to in government offices and major private sector companies. It is not observed in the case of domestic and personal employees. Domestic servants frequently work 7 days a week, more than 12 hours a day, with few or no holidays, and have no effective way to redress grievances against their employers.

Qatar has enacted regulations concerning worker safety and health, but enforcement, which is the responsibility of the Ministry of Energy and Industry, is lax. The Department of Public Safety oversees safety training and conditions, and the state-run petroleum company has its own set of safety standards and procedures. The Labor Law of 1964, as amended in 1984, lists partial and permanent disabilities for which compensation may be awarded, some connected with handling chemicals and petroleum products or construction injuries. The law does not specifically set rates of payment and compensation.

Foreign workers must be sponsored by a citizen or legally recognized organization to obtain an entry visa and must have their sponsor's permission to depart the country. Any worker may seek legal relief from onerous work conditions, but domestic workers generally accept their situations in order to avoid repatriation.

SAUDI ARABIA

Saudi Arabia is a monarchy without elected representative institutions or political parties. It is ruled by King Fahd Bin Abd Al-Aziz Al Saud, a son of King Abd Al-Aziz Al Saud, who unified the country in the early 20th century. The King and the Crown Prince are chosen from among the male descendants of King Abd Al-Aziz. There is no written constitution. The concept of the separation of religion and state is not accepted by either society or the Government. The Government maintains adherence to the precepts of a rigorously conservative form of Islam.

The Government does not permit the establishment of political parties and suppresses opposition views. In 1992 King Fahd appointed a Consultative Council, the Majlis Ash-Shura, and similar provincial assemblies. The Council began holding sessions in 1994. The judiciary is generally independent but is subject to influence by the executive branch and members of the royal family.

Police and border forces under the Ministry of Interior are responsible for internal security. The Mutawwa'in, or religious police, compose the Committee to Prevent Vice and Promote Virtue, a semiautonomous agency that encourages adherence to Islamic values by monitoring public behavior. Members of the security forces committed human rights abuses.

The oil industry has fueled the transformation of Saudi Arabia from a pastoral, agricultural, and commercial society to a rapidly urbanizing one characterized by large-scale infrastructure projects, an extensive social welfare system, and a labor market comprised largely of foreign workers. Oil revenues account for 37 percent of the gross domestic product (GDP) and 72 percent of government income. Agriculture accounts for only about 8 percent of GDP. Government spending, including spending on the national airline, power, water, telephone, education, and health services, accounts for 36 percent of GDP. About 37 percent of the economy is in private hands, and the Government is promoting further privatization of the economy. The Government has also undertaken an aggressive campaign to increase the number of Saudi nationals represented in the private and public work forces. This has included restrictions on some categories of foreign workers, for example, limiting certain occupations to Saudis only, increasing fees for some work visas, and setting minimum wages for some job categories designed to increase the cost to employers of non-Saudi labor.

The Government commits and tolerates serious human rights abuses. There is no mechanism for citizens to change their government, and citizens do not have this right. Since the death of King Abd Al-Aziz, the King and Crown Prince have been chosen from among his sons, who themselves have had preponderant influence in the choice. A 1992 royal decree reserves for the King exclusive power to name the Crown Prince. The Government bases its legitimacy on governance according to Islamic law. Security forces continued to abuse detainees and to arbitrarily arrest and detain persons. Ministry of Interior officers abused prisoners and facilitated incommunicado detention in contradiction of the law, but with the acquiescence of the Government. Prolonged detention is a problem. The legal system is subect to executive and royal family influence. The Government prohibits or restricts freedom of speech, the press, assembly, association, and religion. Reports of harassment by the Mutawwa'in decreased in 1995 and 1996, though Mutawwa'in intimidation, abuse, and detention of citizens and foreigners of both sexes continued. Other problems include discrimination and violence against women, suppression of ethnic and religious minorities, and strict limitations on the rights of workers. The Government disagrees with internationally accepted definitions of human rights and views its interpretation of Islamic law as its sole source of guidance for human rights.

RESPECT FOR HUMAN RIGHTS

Section 1. Respect for the Integrity of the Person, Including Freedom From:

a. *Political and Other Extrajudicial Killing.*—There was one allegation of political or other extrajudicial killings by government officials. In early December, Haytham Al-Bahir, a Shi'a student, reportedly died of complications arising from detention and torture, which aggravated a preexisting medical condition.

On June 25, unknown persons exploded a truck bomb outside a U.S. military housing complex at Al-Khobar. The bomb killed 19 U.S. personnel and wounded hundreds of persons. Authorities arrested dozens of people, and the investigation was continuing at year's end.

On April 22, the authorities announced the arrest of four persons for the November 1995 car bombing of a U.S.-run military training center for Saudi military that killed 7 persons and wounded 60. All four were tried and found guilty in accordance with Saudi judicial procedures, which include several levels of appellate review, and mandatory review by the King prior to their execution on May 31.

b. *Disappearance.*—There were no reports of politically motivated disappearances.

c. *Torture and Other Cruel, Inhuman, or Degrading Treatment or Punishment.*—There were credible reports that the authorities continued to abuse detainees, including citizens and foreigners. Ministry of Interior officers are responsible for most incidents of abuse, which can include beatings and the deprivation of sleep during weeks of interrogation resulting in severe weight loss for the detainee. There were unverified reports of worse abuses. Efforts to confirm or discount reports of worse abuses, including torture, are hindered by the Government's refusal to grant members of diplomatic missions access to the Ministry of Interior detention facilities or allow members of international human rights groups into the country. The Government's past failure to denounce human rights abusers has contributed to the public perception that abuses can be committed with impunity.

Although reports of harassment by the Mutawwa'in decreased, Mutawwa'in intimidation, abuse, and detention of citizens and foreigners of both sexes continued (see Sections 1.d. and 1.e.).

The Government rigorously observes criminal punishments according to its interpretation of Islamic law, including amputation, flogging, and execution by beheading or stoning. No executions were performed during the 5-month period from October 17, 1995, to March 14. Executions resumed March 15, and by year's end the authorities had beheaded 40 men and 1 woman for murder, 14 men for rape, 6 men and 2 women for drug offenses, 5 men for armed robbery, and 1 man for witchcraft. In a reversal of previous years, those executed in 1996 were predominantly Saudi (39 men and 1 woman). There were no executions by stoning in 1996.

In accordance with Shari'a, the authorities punish repeated thievery by amputation of the right hand. However, amputation has not been imposed since June 1995. For less serious crimes, such as drunkenness or publicly flouting Islamic precepts, flogging with a cane is frequently the punishment.

Conditions in standard jails and prisons vary throughout the Kingdom. Prisons, particularly in the eastern province, are of generally high quality, with air-conditioned cells, good nutrition, regular exercise, and careful patrolling by prison guards. Some detainees in police station jails, however, have complained of overcrowding and unsanitary conditions. Family members are allowed access.

Boards of Investigation and Public Prosecution, organized on a regional basis, were established by King Fahd in 1993. The members of these boards have the right to inspect prisons, review prisoners' files, and hear their complaints. The Government, however, does not permit visits to jails or prisons by human rights monitors. Some diplomats have been granted regular access to incarcerated foreign citizens.

No impartial observers are allowed access to specialized Ministry of Interior prisons, such as Al-Hair Prison south of Riyadh, where the Government detains persons accused of political subversion.

Representatives of the United Nations High Commissioner for Refugees (UNHCR) are present at the Rafha refugee camp housing former Iraqi prisoners of war (POW's) and civilians who fled Iraq following the Gulf War. According to UNHCR officials, there is no systematic abuse of refugees by camp guards. When occasional instances of abuse surface, the authorities are generally responsive and willing to reprimand offending guards. The camp itself is comparatively comfortable and well run.

d. *Arbitrary Arrest, Detention, or Exile.*

The law prohibits arbitrary arrest. Despite the law, however, officers make arrests and detain persons without following explicit legal guidelines. There are few procedures to safeguard against abuse. However, there was a case in 1995 in which a

Saudi citizen successfully sued the Government for wrongful imprisonment and was awarded compensation.

Authorities usually detain suspects for no longer than 3 days before charging them, in accordance with a regulation issued by the Ministry of Interior in 1983, although serious exceptions have been reported. The regulation also has provisions for bail for less serious crimes. Also, detainees are sometimes released on the recognizance of a patron or sponsoring employer without the payment of bail. If not released, the accused are detained an average of 1 to 2 months before going to trial.

There is no established procedure providing detainees the right to inform their family of their arrest. If asked, the authorities usually confirm the arrest of foreigners to their country's diplomats. In general, however, foreign diplomats learn about such arrests through informal channels. The authorities may take as long as several months to provide official notification of the arrest of foreigners, if at all. In capital cases, foreigners have in the past been tried and executed without notification of their arrest ever having been given to their government's representatives.

The Mutawwa'in enforce a strict public code of proper dress and behavior. However, reports of harassment, intimidation, and detention of those deemed to be violating the code declined in 1995 and 1996. The Mutawwa'in have the authority to detain people for no more than 24 hours for violation of behavior standards. However, they sometimes exceeded this limit before delivering detainees to the regular police (see Section 1.f.). Current procedures require a police officer to accompany the Mutawwa'in before the latter make an arrest, although this requirement is sometimes ignored.

Detainees arrested by the General Directorate of Investigation (GDI), which is the Ministry of Interior's security service, are commonly held incommunicado in special prisons during the initial phase of an investigation, which may last weeks or months. The GDI allows the detainees only limited contact with their families or lawyers.

The authorities detain without charge people who publicly criticize the Government, or they charge them with attempting to destabilize the Government (see Sections 2.a. and 3). The authorities continued to detain Salman Al-Awdah and Safar Al-Hawali, Muslim clerics who were arrested in September 1994 for publicly criticizing the Government. Their detention that year sparked protest demonstrations resulting in the arrest of 157 persons for antigovernment activities. At the end of 1994, 27 of these persons remained in detention pending investigation; the Government has not announced the release of any of those detainees in the succeeding 2 years. The thousands of prisoners and detainees released under the annual Ramadan amnesty included no political dissidents. The total number of political detainees is impossible to determine.

The Government does not use forced exile. However, Mohammed al-Masari and Osama Bin Ladin, two critics of the Government who live outside of the country, have had their citizenship revoked.

e. *Denial of Fair Public Trial.*—The independence of the judiciary is prescribed by law and is usually respected in practice. However, judges occasionally accede to the influence of the executive branch, particularly members of the royal family and their associates. Moreover, judicial, financial, and administrative control of the courts rests with the Ministry of Justice.

The legal system is based on Shari'a, or Islamic law. Regular Shari'a courts exercise jurisdiction over common criminal cases and civil suits regarding marriage, divorce, child custody, and inheritance. These courts base judgments largely on the Koran and on the Sunna, another Islamic text. Cases involving relatively small penalties are tried in summary courts; more serious crimes are adjudicated in general courts. Appeals from both courts are heard by the appeals courts in Mecca and Riyadh.

Other civil proceedings, including those involving claims against the Government and enforcement of foreign judgments, are held before specialized administrative tribunals, such as the Commission for the Settlement of Labor Disputes and the Board of Grievances.

The military justice system has jurisdiction over uniformed personnel and civil servants charged with violations of military regulations. Court-martial decisions are reviewed by the Minister of Defense and Aviation and by the King.

The Government permits Shi'a Muslims to use their own legal tradition to adjudicate noncriminal cases within their community.

There is a Supreme Judicial Council, which is not a court and may not reverse decisions made by an appeals court. However, the Council may refer decisions back to the lower courts for reconsideration. Its members are appointed by the King, as are most senior jurists, called muftis. Only the Council may discipline or remove a judge.

There is also the Council of Senior Religious Scholars, which is an autonomous body of 15 senior religious jurists, including the Minister of Justice. It establishes the legal principles to guide lower court judges in deciding individual cases.

Defendants usually appear without an attorney before a judge, who determines guilt or innocence in accordance with Shari'a standards. Defense lawyers may offer their clients advice before trial or may attend the trial as interpreters for those unfamiliar with Arabic. The courts do not provide foreign defendants with translators. Public defenders are not provided. There is no licensing procedure for lawyers. Individuals may choose any person to represent them by a power of attorney filed with the court and Ministry of Justice. Most trials are closed. A woman's testimony does not carry the same weight as that of a man. In a Shari'a court, the testimony of one man equals that of two women.

In the absence of two witnesses, or four witnesses in the case of adultery, confessions before a judge are almost always required for criminal conviction—a situation that repeatedly has led prosecuting authorities to coerce confessions from suspects by threats and abuse.

Sentencing is not uniform. Foreign residents often receive harsher penalties than citizens. Under Shari'a, as interpreted and applied in Saudi Arabia, crimes against Muslims receive harsher penalties than those against non-Muslims. In the case of wrongful death, the amount of indemnity or "blood money" awarded to relatives varies with the nationality, religion, and sex of the victim. A sentence may be changed at any stage of review, except for punishments stipulated by the Koran.

Provincial governors have the authority to exercise leniency and reduce a judge's sentence. In some instances, governors have reportedly threatened and even detained judges over disagreements on their decisions. In general, members of the royal family, and other powerful families, are not subject to the same rule of law as ordinary citizens. For example, judges do not have the power to issue a warrant summoning any member of the royal family.

The King and his advisors review cases involving capital punishment to ensure that the court applied the proper legal and Islamic principles. The King has the authority to commute death sentences and grant pardons except for capital crimes committed against individuals. In such cases, he may request the victim's next of kin to pardon the murderer—usually in return for compensation from the family or the King.

There is insufficient information to determine the number of political prisoners because the Government does not provide information on such persons or respond to inquiries about them. Moreover, the Government conducts closed trials for persons who may be political prisoners and in other cases has detained persons incommunicado for long periods while under investigation. At year's end, at least nine persons were serving prison terms for their connections to the rigidly fundamentalist Committee for the Defense of Legitimate Rights (CDLR), an opposition group based in London (see Section 3), and their alleged involvement in a 1994 assault on an Interior Ministry official.

f. *Arbitrary Interference with Privacy, Family, Home, or Correspondence.*—The sanctity of family life and the inviolability of the home are among the most fundamental of Islamic precepts. Royal decrees announced in 1992 include provisions calling for the Government to defend the home from unlawful incursions.

The police must generally demonstrate reasonable cause and obtain permission from the provincial governor before searching a private home, but warrants are not required.

Customs officials routinely open mail for contraband including material deemed pornographic as well as non-Muslim religious material. They regularly confiscate materials deemed offensive. The authorities also open mail and use informants and wiretaps in internal security matters.

The Government enforces most social and Islamic religious norms, which are matters of law (see Section 5). Women may not marry non-Saudis without Government permission; men must obtain approval from the Ministry of Interior to marry women from countries outside the six states of the Gulf Cooperation Council. Although women are prohibited from marrying non-Muslims, men have the right to marry Christians and Jews, in accordance with Islamic law.

Both citizens and foreigners were targets of harassment by members of the Mutawwa'in and by religious vigilantes acting independently of the Mutawwa'in, though on a lesser scale than in 1995. The Government enjoins the Mutawwa'in to follow established procedures and to offer instruction in a polite manner; following especially egregious altercations, the authorities have exerted tighter control over the Mutawwa'in (see Section 1.d.). The Government, however, has not condemned the actions of religious vigilantes but has sought to curtail their activities.

Mutawwa'in enforcement of strict standards of social behavior included the closure of commercial establishments during the daily prayer observances, insistence upon modest dress in public, and harassment of patrons of videotape rental shops. They remonstrate with Saudi and foreign women for failure to observe strict dress codes and for being in the company of males who are not their close relatives. They also harassed and arrested non-Muslims attempting to conduct religious services (see Section 2.c.).

Section 2. Respect for Civil Liberties, Including:

a. *Freedom of Speech and Press.*—The Government severely limits freedom of speech and the press. The authorities do not countenance criticism of Islam, the ruling family, or the Government. Persons whose criticisms align them with an organized political opposition are subject to arrest and detention until they confess their crime or sign a statement promising not to resume such criticisms, which is tantamount to a confession.

The print media are privately owned but publicly subsidized. A 1982 media policy statement and a 1965 national security law prohibit the dissemination of criticism of the Government. The media policy statement urges journalists to uphold Islam, oppose atheism, promote Arab interests, and preserve the cultural heritage of Saudi Arabia. The Ministry of Information appoints, and may remove, the editors in chief. It also provides guidelines to newspapers on controversial issues. The Government owns the Saudi Press Agency (SPA), which expresses official Government views.

Newspapers typically publish news on sensitive subjects, such as crime or terrorism, only after it has been released by the SPA or when it has been authorized by a senior government official. Two Saudi-owned, London-based dailies, Ash-Sharq Al-Awsat and Al-Hayat, are widely distributed and read in Saudi Arabia. The authorities continue to censor stories about Saudi Arabia in the foreign press. Censors may remove or blacken the offending articles, glue pages together, or prevent certain issues of foreign publications from entering the market. However, the Ministry of Information continued to relax its blackout policy regarding politically sensitive news concerning Saudi Arabia reported in international media, although press restrictions on reporting of domestic news remain very stringent. The terrorist bombing of a U.S. military facility in Al Khobar on June 25 was promptly reported by the government media.

The Government's policy in this regard appears to be motivated in part by pragmatic considerations: Saudi access to outside sources of information, especially Cable News Network and other satellite television channels, is widespread.

The Government tightly restricts the entry of foreign journalists into the Kingdom but admitted a markedly increased number into the country in 1996.

The Government owns and operates the television and radio companies. Government censors remove any reference to politics, religions other than Islam, pork or pigs, alcohol, or any sexual innuendo from foreign programs and songs. Reflecting competition from outside satellite television networks, Saudi television has introduced some program changes, including "Face to Face," a weekly live talk show in which ministers and other senior officials interact with a moderator and answer phone and facsimile questions from citizens.

There are as many as 300,000 satellite receiving dishes in the Kingdom that provide citizens with foreign broadcasts. The legal status of these devices is ambiguous. The Government ordered a halt to their import in 1992, at the request of religious leaders who objected to foreign programming available on satellite channels. In March 1994, the Government banned the sale, installation, and maintenance of dishes and supporting devices, but the number of dishes continues to increase and residents may legally subscribe to satellite decoding services that require a dish.

The Government censors all forms of public artistic expression. The authorities prohibit cinemas and public musical or theatrical performances, except those that are strictly folkloric.

Academic freedom is restricted. The authorities prohibit the study of evolution, Freud, Marx, Western music, and Western philosophy. Some professors believe that government and conservative religious informers monitor their classroom comments.

b. *Freedom of Peaceful Assembly and Association.*—The Government strictly limits these freedoms. It prohibits public demonstrations as a means of political expression and the establishment of political parties or any type of opposition group (see Section 3). By its power to license associations, the Government ensures that groups conform to public policy.

Public meetings are segregated by sex. Unless meetings are sponsored by diplomatic missions or approved by the appropriate governor, foreign residents seeking to hold unsegregated meetings risk arrest and deportation. The authorities monitor any large gathering of people, especially of women.

c. *Freedom of Religion.*—Freedom of religion does not exist. Islam is the official religion, and all citizens must be Muslims. The Government prohibits the practice of other religions. There are isolated reports of harassment and arrest of foreign workers conducting clandestine worship services, particularly around non-Muslim religious holidays. One Christian worship service was broken up by police and Mutawwa'in, and the man who hosted the service was punished by lashing.

Conversion by a Muslim to another religion is considered apostasy. Public apostasy is a crime under Shari'a law and punishable by death.

Islamic practice is generally limited to that of the Wahhabi sect's interpretation of the Hanbali School of the Sunni branch of Islam. Practices contrary to this interpretation, such as visits to the graves of renowned Muslims, are discouraged.

The Ministry of Islamic Affairs directly supervises and is a major source of funds for the construction and maintenance of almost all mosques in the country. The Ministry pays the salaries of all imams and others who work in the mosques. A governmental committee is responsible for defining the qualifications of imams. The religious police, or the Mutawwa'in, receive their funding from the Government and the general president of the Mutawwa'in holds the rank of minister.

The Shi'a Muslim minority (roughly 500,000 of over 13 million citizens) lives mostly in the eastern province. They are the objects of officially sanctioned social and economic discrimination (see Section 5). Prior to 1990, the Government prohibited Shi'ite public processions during the Islamic month of Muharram and restricted other processions and congregations to designated areas in the major Shi'ite cities. Since 1990, the authorities have permitted marches on the Shi'a holiday of Ashura, provided the marchers do not display banners or engage in self-flagellation. In May Ashura commemorations in the eastern province passed without incident.

The Government seldom permits private construction of Shi'ite mosques. The Shi'a have declined government offers to build state-supported mosques because Shi'ite motifs would be prohibited in them.

The Government does not permit public or private non-Muslim religious activities. Persons wearing religious symbols of any kind in public risk confrontation with the Mutawwa'in. The general prohibition against religious symbols applies also to Muslims. A Muslim wearing a Koranic necklace in public would be admonished. Non-Muslim worshippers risk arrest, lashing, and deportation for engaging in any religious activity that attracts official attention.

d. *Freedom of Movement Within the Country, Foreign Travel, Emigration, and Repatriation.*—The Government restricts the travel of Saudi women, who must obtain written permission from their closest male relative before the authorities will allow them to board public transportation between different parts of the country or travel abroad (see Section 5). Males may travel anywhere within the country or abroad.

Foreigners are typically allowed to reside or work in Saudi Arabia only under the sponsorship of a Saudi national or business. The Government requires foreign residents to carry identification cards. It does not permit foreigners to travel outside the city of their employment or change their workplace without their sponsor's permission. Foreign residents who travel within the country are often asked by the authorities to show that they possess letters of permission from their employer or sponsor.

Sponsors generally retain possession of the workers' passports. Foreign workers must obtain permission from their sponsors to travel abroad. If sponsors are involved in a commercial or labor dispute with foreign employees, they may ask the authorities to prohibit the employees from departing the country until the dispute is resolved. Some sponsors use this as a pressure tactic to resolve disputes in their favor, or to have foreign employees deported.

The Government seizes the passports of all potential suspects and witnesses in criminal cases and suspends the issuance of exit visas to them, until the case is tried. As a result, some foreign nationals are forced to remain in the country for lengthy periods against their will. The authorities sometimes confiscate the passports of suspected oppositionists and their families. Some husbands of women who participated in a 1991 motorcade through the streets of Riyadh in protest of government restrictions on female driving reported that, 5 years later, they still have not had their passports returned. The Government prevents Shi'a Muslims believed to have pro-Iranian sympathies from traveling abroad.

Citizens may emigrate, but the law prohibits dual citizenship. Apart from marriage to a Saudi national, there are no provisions for long-term foreign residents to acquire citizenship. However, foreigners are granted citizenship in rare cases, generally through the advocacy of an influential patron.

The 1992 Basic Law provides that "the State will grant political asylum if the public interest mitigates" in favor of it. The language does not specify clear rules for adjudicating asylum cases. In general, the authorities regard refugees and displaced persons like other foreign workers: They must have sponsors for employment or risk expulsion. Of the 35,000 Iraqi civilians and former prisoners of war allowed refuge in Saudi Arabia at the end of the Gulf War, none has been granted permanent asylum by the Saudis; however, the Government has underwritten the entire cost of providing safe haven to the Iraqi refugees, and continues to provide excellent logistical and administrative support to the United Nations High Commissioner for Refugees (UNHCR) and other resettlement agencies.

At year's end, approximately 25,000 of the original 35,000 Iraqi refugees had been resettled in third countries or voluntarily repatriated to Iraq. Most of the remaining 10,000 refugees are restricted to the Rafha refugee camp. The UNHCR has monitored over 2,800 persons voluntarily returning to Iraq from Rafha since December 1991 and found no evidence of forcible repatriation.

The Government has temporarily allowed some foreigners to remain in Saudi Arabia in cases where their safety would be jeopardized if they were deported to their home countries.

Section 3. Respect for Political Rights: The Right of Citizens to Change Their Government

Citizens do not have the right to change their government. There are no formal democratic institutions, and only a few citizens have a voice in the choice of leaders or in changing the political system. The King rules on civil and religious matters within certain limitations established by religious law, tradition, and the need to maintain consensus among the ruling family and religious leaders.

The King is also the Prime Minister, and the Crown Prince serves as Deputy Prime Minister. The King appoints all other ministers, who in turn appoint subordinate officials with cabinet concurrence.

In 1993 the King appointed 60 members to a Consultative Council, or Majlis Ash-Shura. This strictly advisory body began to hold sessions in 1994, but the Council has maintained a low profile and is not regarded as a significant political force by the citizenry or those in power.

The Council of Senior Islamic Scholars is another advisory body to the King and the Cabinet. It issues decisions based on Shari'a in its review of the Government's public policies. The Government views the Council as an important source of religious legitimacy, and takes the Council's opinions into account when promulgating legislation.

Communication between citizens and the Government is usually expressed through client-patron relationships and by affinity groups such as tribes, families, and professional hierarchies. In theory, any male citizen or foreign national may express an opinion or air a grievance at a majlis—an open-door meeting held by the King, a prince, or an important national or local official. However, as governmental functions have become more complex, time-consuming, and centralized, public access to senior officials has become more restricted. Since the assassination of King Faisal in 1975, Saudi kings have reduced the frequency of their personal contacts with the public. Ministers and district governors more readily grant audiences at a majlis.

Typical topics raised in a majlis are complaints about bureaucratic delay or insensitivity, requests for personal redress or assistance, and criticism of particular acts of government affecting family welfare. Broader "political" concerns—social, economic, or foreign policy—are rarely raised. Complaints about royal abuses of power would not be entertained. In general journalists, academics, and businessmen feel that avenues of domestic criticism and feedback to the regime are closed.

An opposition group, the Committee for the Defense of Legitimate Rights, which advocates a rigidly fundamentalist Islamic viewpoint, was established in 1993 by six citizens. The Government acted quickly to repress the CDLR following its formation. In 1994 CDLR spokesman Mohammed Al-Masari secretly fled to the United Kingdom, where he sought political asylum and established an overseas branch of the CDLR. Al-Masari continued to criticize the Government, using computers and facsimile transmissions to send newsletters back to Saudi Arabia. In March internal divisions within the CDLR spawned the rival Islamic Reform Movement (IRM), headed by Sa'ad Al-Faqih. Al-Masari has expressed the group's "understanding" of two fatal terrorist bombings of American military facilities and sympathy for the perpetrators. The IRM also implicitly condoned the two terrorist attacks in Saudi Arabia, arguing that they were a natural outgrowth of a political system that does not tolerate peaceful dissent.

In April the Saudi Ambassador in the United Kingdom stated publicly that his Government would withdraw from large contracts for British weapons unless the United Kingdom expelled Al-Masari. The British Government denied Al-Masari's initial request for asylum, due to the circumstances of his illegal entry, but eventually Al-Masari was granted permission to remain in the United Kingdom for 4 years, with the option of applying for permanent residency at the end of that period. There is no evidence of Saudi Government retribution against the British Government for this decision.

Women play no formal role in government and politics, and are actively discouraged from doing so. Participation by women in a Majlis is restricted, although some women seek redress through female members of the royal family. Only 1 of the 60 members of the Majlis Ash-Shura is a Shi'a.

Section 4. Governmental Attitude Regarding International and Nongovernmental Investigation of Alleged Violations of Human Rights

There are no publicly active human rights groups, and the Government has made it clear that none critical of government policies would be permitted.

The Government does not permit visits by international human rights groups or independent monitors, nor has it signed major international human rights treaties and conventions. The Government disagrees with internationally accepted definitions of human rights and views its interpretation of Islamic law as the only necessary guide to protect human rights. Citations of Saudi human rights abuses by international monitors or foreign governments are routinely ignored or condemned by the Government as assaults on Islam.

Section 5. Discrimination Based on Race, Sex, Religion, Disability, Language, or Social Status

Systematic discrimination based on sex and religion are built into the law. The law forbids discrimination based on race, but not nationality. The Government and private organizations cooperate in providing services for the disabled. The Shi'a religious minority suffers social, legal, and religious discrimination.

Women.—The Government does not keep statistics on spousal or other forms of violence against women. Hospital workers report that many women are admitted for treatment of injuries that apparently result from spousal violence. Some foreign women have suffered physical abuse from their Saudi husbands, who can prevent their wives from obtaining exit visas.

Foreign embassies receive many reports that employers abuse foreign women working as domestic servants. Embassies of countries with large domestic servant populations maintain safehouses to which citizens may flee to escape work situations that include forced confinement, withholding of food, beating and other physical abuse, and rape. Often the abuse is at the hands of female Saudis. In general, the Government considers such cases family matters and does not intervene unless charges of abuse are brought to its attention. It is almost impossible for foreign women to obtain redress in the courts due to the courts' strict evidentiary rules and the women's own fears of reprisals. Few employers have been punished for such abuses. There are no private support groups or religious associations to assist such women.

By religious law and social custom, women have the right to own property and are entitled to financial support from their husbands or male relatives. However, women have few political and social rights and are not treated as equal members of society. There are no active women's rights groups. Women, including foreigners, may not legally drive motor vehicles and are restricted in their use of public facilities when men are present. Women must enter city buses by separate rear entrances and sit in specially designated sections. Women risk arrest by the Mutawwa'in for riding in a vehicle driven by a male who is not an employee or a close male relative. Women are not admitted to a hospital for medical treatment without the consent of their male relative. By law and custom, women may not undertake domestic and foreign travel alone (see Section 2.d.).

In public women are expected to wear the abaya, a black garment covering the entire body. A woman's head and face should also be covered. The Mutawwa'in generally expect women from Arab countries, Asia, and Africa to comply more fully with Saudi customs of dress than they do Western women; nonetheless, in recent years they have instructed Western women to wear the abaya and cover their hair.

Some government officials and ministries still bar accredited female diplomats in Saudi Arabia from official meetings and diplomatic functions.

Women are also subject to discrimination in Islamic law, which stipulates that daughters receive half the inheritance awarded to their brothers. In a Shari'a court, the testimony of one man equals that of two women (see Section 1.e.). Although Islamic law permits polygyny, it is becoming less common. Islamic law enjoins a man to treat each wife equally. In practice such equality is left to the discretion of the husband. Some women participated in al-Mesyar (or "short daytime visit") marriages, where the women relinquish their legal rights to financial support and nighttime cohabitation. Additionally, the husband is not required to inform his other wives of the marriage, and the children have no inheritance rights. The Government places greater restrictions on women than on men regarding marriage to non-Saudis and non-Muslims (see Section 2.d.).

Women must demonstrate legally specified grounds for divorce, but men may divorce without giving cause. If divorced or widowed, a woman normally may keep her children until they attain a specified age: 7 years for boys, 9 years for girls. Children over these ages are awarded to the divorced husband or the deceased husband's family. Divorced women who are foreigners are often prevented by their former husbands from visiting their children after divorce.

Women have access to free, but segregated, education through the university level. They constitute 55 percent of all university graduates but are excluded from studying such subjects as engineering, journalism, and architecture. Men are able to study overseas; women may do so only if accompanied by a spouse or an immediate male relative.

Women make up only 5 percent of the work force. Whereas salary and other benefits are the main concerns for men seeking employment, for women the primary goal is merely establishing some toehold in the private or public sector. Most employment opportunities for women are in education and health care, with lesser opportunity in business, philanthropy, banking, retail sales, and the media. Women wishing to enter nontraditional fields are subject to discrimination. Women may not accept jobs in rural areas if they are required to live apart from their families. All workplaces where women are present are segregated by sex. Contact with male supervisors or clients is allowed by telephone or facsimile machine. In 1995 the Ministry of Commerce announced that women would no longer be issued business licenses for work in fields that might require them to supervise foreign workers, interact with male clients, or deal on a regular basis with government officials.

Children.—The Government provides all children with free education and medical care. Children are not subject to the strict social segregation faced by women, though they are segregated by sex in schools starting at age 7. In more general social situations, boys are segregated at age 12, and girls at the onset of puberty. It is difficult to gauge the prevalence of child abuse, since the Government keeps no statistics on such cases and is disinclined to infringe on family privacy. Societal abuse of children does not appear to be a major problem.

People With Disabilities.—The provision of government social services has increasingly brought the disabled into the public domain. The media carry features lauding the public accomplishments of disabled persons and sharply criticizing parents who neglect disabled children. The Government and private charitable organizations cooperate in education, employment, and other services for the disabled. The law provides hiring quotas for the disabled. While there is no legislation for public accessibility, newer commercial buildings often include such access.

Religious Minorities.—Shi'a citizens are discriminated against in government and employment, especially in national security jobs. Several years ago the Government subjected Shi'a to employment restrictions in the oil industry and has not relaxed them. The Sunni majority discriminates socially against the Shi'a minority.

Shi'a face restrictions on access to several services, despite efforts by the Government to improve the social service infrastructure in predominantly Shi'a areas of the country. Since the Iranian revolution, some Shi'a suspected of subversion have been subjected periodically to surveillance and limitations on travel abroad.

National/Racial/Ethnic Minorities.—Although racial discrimination is illegal, there is substantial societal prejudice based on ethnic or national origin. Foreign workers from Africa and Asia are subject to various forms of formal and informal discrimination and have the most difficulty in obtaining justice for their grievances.

Section 6. Worker Rights

a. *The Right of Association.*—Government decrees prohibit the establishment of labor unions and any strike activity.

In 1995 Saudi Arabia was suspended from the U.S. Overseas Private Investment Corporation insurance programs because of the Government's lack of compliance with internationally recognized worker rights standards.

b. *The Right to Organize and Bargain Collectively.*—Collective bargaining is forbidden. Foreign workers comprise about half of the work force. There is no minimum wage; wages are set by employers and vary according to the type of work performed and the nationality of the worker.

There are no export processing zones.

c. *Prohibition of Forced or Compulsory Labor.*—Forced labor is prohibited by a 1952 royal decree that abolished slavery. Ratification of the International Labor Organization (ILO) Conventions 29 and 105, which prohibit forced labor, gives them the force of law. However, employers have significant control over the movements of foreign employees, giving rise to situations that might involve forced labor, especially in remote areas where workers are unable to leave their place of work.

Sometimes sponsors prevent foreign workers from obtaining exit visas to pressure them to sign a new work contract or to drop claims against their employers for unpaid salary (see Section 2.d.). In another pressure tactic, sponsors may refuse to provide foreign workers with a "letter of no objection" that would allow them to be employed by another sponsor.

The labor laws do not protect domestic servants. There were credible reports that female domestic servants were sometimes forced to work 12 to 16 hours a day, 7 days a week. There were numerous confirmed reports of runaway maids (see Section 5). The authorities often returned runaway maids to their employers against the maids' wishes.

There have been many reports of workers whose employers have refused to pay several months, or even years, of accumulated salary or other promised benefits. Nondomestic workers with such grievances have the right to complain before the labor courts, but few do so because of fear of deportation. The labor system abets the exploitation of foreign workers because enforcement of work contracts is difficult and generally favors Saudi employers. Labor cases can take many months to reach a final appellate ruling, during which time the employer can prevent the foreign laborer from leaving the country; alternatively, an employer can delay a case until a worker's funds are exhausted and the worker is forced to return to his home country.

d. *Minimum Age for Employment of Children.*—The minimum age for employment is 13 years of age, which may be waived by the Ministry of Labor with the consent of the juvenile's guardian. There is no minimum age for workers employed in family oriented businesses or in other situations that are construed as extensions of the household, e.g., farmers, herdsmen, and domestic servants.

Children under the age of 18 and women may not be employed in hazardous or harmful industries, such as mining or industries employing power-operated machinery. While there is no formal government entity charged with enforcing the minimum age for employment of children, the Ministry of Justice has jurisdiction and has acted as plaintiff in the few cases that have arisen against alleged violators. In general, however, children play a minimal role in the work force.

e. *Acceptable Conditions of Work.*—There is no legal minimum wage. Labor regulations establish a 48-hour workweek at regular pay and allow employers to require up to 12 additional hours of overtime at time-and-a-half pay. Labor law provides for a 24-hour rest period, normally Fridays, although the employer may grant it on another day.

Many foreign nationals who have been recruited abroad have complained that after arrival in Saudi Arabia they were presented with work contracts specifying lower wages and fewer benefits than originally promised. Other foreign workers have reportedly signed contracts in their home countries and were later pressured to sign less favorable contracts upon arrival. Some employees report that at the end of their contract service, their employers refuse to grant permission to allow them to return home.

The ILO has stated that the Government has not formulated legislation implementing the ILO Convention on Equal Pay and that regulations that segregate work places by sex, and limit vocational programs for women, violate ILO Convention 111.

Labor regulations require employers to protect most workers from job-related hazards and disease. Foreign nationals report frequent failures to enforce health and safety standards. Workers in family operated businesses, farmers, herdsmen, and domestic servants are not covered by these regulations. Workers would risk their employment if they were to remove themselves from hazardous work conditions.

SYRIA

Despite the existence of some institutions of democratic government, Syria's political system places virtually absolute authority in the hands of the President, Hafiz Al-Asad. Key decisions regarding foreign policy, national security, internal politics, and the economy are made by President Asad with counsel from his ministers, high ranking members of the ruling Ba'th Party, and a relatively small circle of security advisers. Although the Parliament is elected every 4 years, the Ba'th Party is guaranteed a majority. The Parliament does not initiate laws, but only passes judgment on and sometimes modifies those proposed by the executive branch. The judiciary is constitutionally independent, but this is not the case in the exceptional (state of emergency) security courts, which are subject to political influence. The regular courts display independence, although political connections and bribery can influence verdicts. In general, all three branches of Government are guided by the views of the leadership of the Ba'th Party, whose primacy in state institutions is mandated by the Constitution.

The powerful role of the security services in government, which extends beyond strictly security matters, stems in part from the state of emergency that has been in place almost continuously since 1963. The Government justifies martial law because of the state of war with Israel and past threats from terrorist groups. Syrian Military Intelligence and Air Force Intelligence are military agencies, while General Security, State Security, and Political Security come under the purview of the Ministry of Interior. The branches of the security services operate independently of each other and outside the legal system. Their members often ignore the rights of suspects and detainees and commit serious human rights violations.

The economy is based on commerce, agriculture, and oil production. It consists of a generally inefficient public sector, a private sector, and a mixed public/private sector. A complex bureaucracy and endemic corruption hamper economic growth. The Government has sought to promote the private sector through incentives and deregulation. Real economic growth is about 3.6 percent, although real per capita growth is less than 1 percent. Annual per capita gross domestic product is about $900, and inflation about 15 percent per year. Wage increases in the public sector have not kept pace with cost of living increases, and the gap between rich and poor has widened.

The human rights situation remained poor, and the Government continues to restrict or deny fundamental rights. Serious abuses include the widespread use of torture in detention; generally poor prison conditions; arbitrary arrest and prolonged detention without trial; fundamentally unfair trials in the security courts; an inefficient judiciary that suffers from corruption and, at times, political influence; infringement on citizens' privacy rights; limits on the freedom of movement; and, despite a slight loosening of censorship restrictions, the denial of the freedoms of speech, press, assembly, and association. Because the Ba'th Party's domination of the political system is guaranteed by the Constitution, citizens do not have the right to change the government. The Government uses its vast powers so effectively that there is no organized political opposition and there have been very few antiregime manifestations. There is some societal discrimination and violence against women and discrimination against the Kurdish minority. The Government suppresses worker rights. Reportedly about 100 political activists were arrested in March. In May up to 800 members of the ethnic Turkoman minority were arrested, and perhaps 100 remain in detention without charge. As many as 3,000 political prisoners were released in late 1995, but there were no additional releases in 1996.

RESPECT FOR HUMAN RIGHTS

Section 1. Respect for the Integrity of the Person, Including Freedom From:

a. *Political and Other Extrajudicial Killing.*—There were no reports of political killings and no confirmed reports of deaths in detention, although such deaths have occurred in previous years. There was an unconfirmed report of the death in detention of a Syrian schoolteacher, who allegedly was arrested for belonging to an Islamist group. The victim's body allegedly showed signs of torture, while security authorities reported that the detainee died in prison of a heart attack. Previous deaths in detention have not been investigated by the Government, and the number and identities of prisoners who died in prisons since the 1980's remains unknown. On December 31, a bomb exploded on a private transport bus in central Damascus, killing at least 11 persons and wounding 47 others. The perpetrators and motivations for this bomb attack were unknown at year's end.

b. *Disappearance.*—There were no confirmed reports of politically motivated disappearances. Despite inquiries by international human rights organizations and foreign governments, the Government offered little new information on the welfare and whereabouts of persons who have been held incommunicado for years or about whom no more is known other than the approximate date of their detention (see Section 1.d.).

c. *Torture and Other Cruel, Inhuman, or Degrading Treatment or Punishment.*— Despite the existence of constitutional provisions and several Penal Code penalties for abusers, there was credible evidence that security forces continue to use torture. Former prisoners and detainees have reported that torture methods include electrical shocks; pulling out fingernails; the forced insertion of objects into the rectum; beatings, sometimes, while the victim is suspended from the ceiling; hyperextension of the spine; and the use of a chair that bends backwards to asphyxiate the victim or fracture the spine. Although torture may occur in prisons, torture is most likely while detainees are being held at one of the many detention centers run by the various security services throughout the country, and particularly while the authorities are trying to extract a confession or information about an alleged crime or alleged accomplices.

The Government continues to deny the use of torture, and claims that it would prosecute anyone believed guilty of using excessive force or physical abuse. There was no news of any prosecutions of security officials during the year, although past victims of torture have identified the officials who beat them, up to the level of brigadier general. In allegations of excessive force or physical abuse made in court, the plaintiff is required to initiate his own suit against the alleged abuser in civil proceedings.

Prison conditions vary and generally are poor and do not meet minimum international health and sanitation standards. Facilities for political or national security prisoners are generally worse than those that house common criminals. The prison at Tadmur in Palmyra, where many political and national security prisoners have been kept, is widely considered to have the worst conditions. At some prisons, authorities allow visitation rights, but in other cases security officials demand bribes from family members wishing to visit incarcerated relatives. Overcrowding and substandard or insufficient food exist at several prisons. Some former detainees have reported that the Goverment prohibits reading materials, even the Koran, for political prisoners.

The Government does not permit independent monitoring of prison or detention center conditions.

In instances in which foreign nationals are arrested, the authorities sometimes delay or deny prison visits by foreign diplomats. The authorities consider Syrian nationals who hold dual nationality only as Syrians, and thus do not necessarily recognize or grant requests by foreign diplomats to visit or otherwise assist such persons. Even in some of those cases where the Government granted foreign diplomats access to dual nationals, the diplomats had to wait for over a month to gain access. The Government did not grant access in all cases.

d. *Arbitrary Arrest, Detention, or Exile.*—The Emergency Law, which authorizes the Government to conduct preventive arrests, overrides the Penal Code provisions against arbitrary arrest and detention, including the need to obtain warrants. Officials contend that the Emergency Law is applied only in narrowly defined cases. Nonetheless, in cases involving political or national security offenses, arrests are generally carried out in secret, and suspects may be detained incommunicado for prolonged periods without charge or trial and are denied the right to a judicial determination for the pretrial detention. Some of these practices are prohibited by the state of emergency, but the authorities are not held to these strictures.

The Government apparently has continued to detain the relatives of detainees or of fugitives in order to obtain confessions or the fugitive's surrender (see Section 1.f.).

Defendants in civil and criminal trials have the right to bail hearings and the possible release from detention on their own recognizance. There is no bail option for those accused of national security offenses. Unlike defendants in regular criminal and civil cases, security detainees do not have access to lawyers prior to or during questioning.

Detainees have no legal redress for false arrest. Security forces often do not provide detainees' families with information on their welfare or location while in detention. Consequently, many people who have disappeared in past years are believed to be in long-term detention without charge, or possibly to have died in such detention. The number of those who disappeared in this way probably has declined over the past few years, although this may be due to the Government's success in deterring political activity rather than a loosening of criteria for detention. The Government brought to trial many detainees who have been held incommunicado for years. However, those trials have been unfair (see Section 1.e.).

Pretrial detention may be lengthy even in cases not involving political or national security offenses. The criminal justice system is backlogged; many criminal suspects are held in pretrial detention for months, and may have their trials extended for additional months. Lengthy pretrial detentions and drawn-out court proceedings are caused by a shortage of available courts and the absence of legal provisions for a speedy trial or plea bargaining. According to local lawyers, the new civilian courts announced in 1995 have not come into existence, and the criminal justice system remains backlogged.

There were two reports of large-scale politically motivated arrests. There were local reports that the Government arrested up to 100 political activists in Dayr Al-Zur in March. No further information has become available on the whereabouts of these alleged political detainees. In May the Government detained without charge up to 800 members of the Turkoman minority, including community leaders, in connection with a series of small explosions in 4 cities. Most of the Turkomans were reportedly released in July, but as many as 100 still remain in detention.

The last significant releases of political detainees were in late November and December 1995 (see Section 1.e.). While most of the doctors, lawyers, and engineers arrested in a mass crackdown in 1980 have been released, some apparently remain in prolonged detention without charge. Many Palestinian, Jordanian, and Lebanese citizens had been detained without charge by Syrian security services in both Lebanon and Syria, without any public accounting by the Government.

The number of remaining political detainees is likely in the hundreds or more. The number of political detainees is difficult to estimate since the Government does not verify publicly the number of detentions without charge, the release of detainees, or whether detainees are subsequently sentenced to prison (see Section 1.e.).

The Government has exiled citizens in the past, although the practice is prohibited by the Constitution. There were no known instances of forced exile in 1996.

e. *Denial of Fair Public Trial.*—The Constitution provides for an independent judiciary, but the two exceptional courts dealing with alleged security cases are not independent of executive branch control. The regular court system displays independence, although political connections and bribery sometimes influence verdicts.

The judicial system is composed of the civil and criminal courts; the religious courts, which adjudicate matters of personal status such as divorce and inheritance; military courts; and the security courts. The Supreme Constitutional Court is empowered to rule only on the constitutionality of laws and decrees. It does not hear appeals.

Civil and criminal courts are organized under the Ministry of Justice. Defendants before these courts are entitled to the legal representation of their choice; the courts appoint lawyers for indigents; defendants are presumed innocent, are allowed to present evidence, and allowed to confront their accusers; and trials are public, except for those involving juveniles or sex offenses. Defendants may appeal their verdicts to a provincial appeals court and, ultimately to the Court of Cassation, which is the highest court of appeal. However, such appeals are hampered because the courts do not provide verbatim transcripts of cases—only summaries prepared by the presiding judges. There are no juries.

Military courts have the authority to try civilian as well as military personnel. The venue for a civilian defendant is decided by a military prosecutor. There were continuing reports that the Government operates military field courts, in locations outside of established courtrooms. Such courts reportedly observe fewer of the formal procedures of regular military courts.

The two security courts are the Supreme State Security Court (SSSC), which tries political and national security cases, and the Economic Security Court (ESC), which tries cases involving financial crimes. Both courts operate under the state of emergency, not ordinary law, and do not observe constitutional provisions safeguarding defendants' rights.

Charges against defendants in the SSSC are often vague. Many defendants appear to be tried for exercising normal political rights, such as free speech. For example, the Emergency Law authorizes the prosecution of anyone "opposing the goals of the revolution" or "shaking the confidence of the masses in the aims of the revolution," or trying to "change the economic or social structure of the State." Nonetheless, the Government contends that the SSSC tries only persons who have sought to use violence against the State.

Under SSSC procedures, defendants are not present during the preliminary, or investigative, phase of the trial, when evidence is presented by the prosecutor. Trials are usually closed to the public. Lawyers are not guaranteed access to their clients before the trial and are excluded from the court during their client's initial interrogation by the prosecutor. Lawyers submit written defense pleas, rather than oral presentations. The State's case is often based on confessions, but defendants have not been allowed to argue in court that the confessions were coerced. There is no known instance in which the court ordered a medical examination for a defendant who claimed that he was tortured. The SSSC has reportedly aquitted some defendants, but the Government does not provide any statistics on the conviction rate. Defendants do not have the right to appeal verdicts, but sentences are reviewed by the Minister of Interior, who may ratify, nullify, or alter sentences. The President may also intervene in the review process.

Many—perhaps hundreds—of cases passed through the SSSC in 1996. Most involved charges relating to membership in various banned political groups, including the Communist Party, the Party for Communist Action, and the pro-Iraqi wing of the Ba'th Party. In the recent past, sentences have ranged up to 15 years.

The Economic Security Court (ESC) tries persons for alleged violations of foreign-exchange laws and other economic crimes. Prosecution of economic crimes is not applied uniformly, as some government officials or business people with close connections to the Government have likely violated Syria's strict economic laws without prosecution. Like the SSSC, the ESC does not guarantee defendants due process. Defendants may not have adequate access to lawyers to prepare their defenses, and the State's case is usually based on confessions. Verdicts are likely influenced by high-ranking government officials. Those convicted of the most serious economic crimes do not have the right of appeal, but those convicted of lesser crimes may appeal to the Court of Cassation.

The last significant releases of political prisoners and detainees were in late November and December 1995. Originally the Government claimed to have released some 1,650 political prisoners in November, but local estimates now place the number released between 2,200 and 3,000. Many of those released apparently were members of the Muslim Brotherhood who had not been involved in acts of violence. The release also may have included some persons from banned Communist parties, pro-Iraqi Ba'athists, and Nasserites. Some former prisoners reported having to sign admissions of guilt or loyalty oaths as a condition of their release. Other prisoners released in November 1995 apparently were in poor health as a result of their incarceration; they had been incarcerated without charge or have been detained in prison beyond the expiration of their original prison sentences, sometimes for years.

A Presidential amnesty issued in December 1995 provided for the release of some 6,000 to 7,000 prisoners who had comitted common crimes. Among those released under this amnesty were 500 to 700 persons convicted by the extraconstitutional Economic Security Court. Consistent with past practice, the Government did not announce the number of prisoners released, nor has it responded to requests from international human rights groups and foreign governments for their names. In 1995 the Government also released four former Ba'th party officials imprisoned since 1970. The Government has released virtually all of those arrested at the time President Asad took power in 1970. At least three persons arrested during that period remain in prison, even though the sentences of two of them expired in 1985. The third apparently was never tried.

The Government denies that it holds political prisoners, arguing that, although the aims of some prisoners may be political, their activities, including subversion, were criminal. However, the Emergency Law and the Penal Code are so vague, and the Government's power so broad, that many persons were convicted and are in prison for the mere expression of political opposition to the Government. The current population of political prisoners may range from several hundred to over 2,000.

f. *Arbitrary Interference with Privacy, Family, Home, or Correspondence.*—Although laws provide for freedom from arbitrary interference, the Emergency Law authorizes the security services to enter homes and conduct searches with warrants if security matters—very broadly defined—are involved. The security services selectively monitor telephone conversations and facsimile transmissions and interfere with the mail. The Government opens mail destined for both citizens and foreign residents. It also prevents the delivery of human rights materials.

The Government apparently has continued its practice of threatening or detaining the relatives of detainees or of fugitives in order to obtain confessions or the fugitive's surrender.

The incidence of security checkpoints has diminished. There are fewer police checkpoints on roads and in cities and towns than in previous years. Generally, the security services set up checkpoints to search for smuggled goods, weapons, narcotics, and subversive literature. The searches take place without warrants. The Government and the Ba'th Party have monitored and tried to restrict some citizens' visits to foreign embassies and cultural centers.

Section 2. Respect for Civil Liberties, Including:

a. *Freedom of Speech and Press.*—The Constitution provides citizens with the right to express their opinions freely in speech and in writing, but the Government restricts these rights significantly. The Government strictly controls dissemination of information and permits no written criticism of the President, the President's family, the Ba'th Party, the military, or the legitimacy of the regime. The Emergency Law allows the Government broad discretion in determining illegal expression. It prohibits the publishing of "false information," which opposes "the goals of the revolution" (see Section 1.e.). In the past, the Government has imprisoned journalists for failing to observe press restrictions. There is no information on whether these journalists are still imprisoned, nor were there any known arrests of journalists during the year. There were, however, reports that the state security services threatened local journalists for articles printed outside Syria.

The Ministry of Information and the Ministry of Culture and National Guidance censor the domestic and foreign press. They usually prevent publication or distribution of any material deemed threatening or embarrassing to the Government. Censorship is usually stricter for materials in Arabic. Commonly censored subjects include: the Government's human rights record; Islamic fundamentalism; allegations of official involvement in drug trafficking; aspects of the Government's role in Lebanon; graphic descriptions of sex; material unfavorable to the Arab cause in the Middle East conflict; and material that is offensive to any of Syria's religious groups, or is partial to sectarianism. In addition, most journalists and writers in Syria practice self-censorship, in order to avoid provoking a negative government reaction.

The Ministry of Culture and National Guidance censors fiction and nonfiction works, including films. It also determines which films may not be shown at the cultural centers operated by foreign embassies.

There continued to be a modest relaxation of censorship during the year. The media demonstrated somewhat wider latitude in reporting on regional developments, including the Middle East peace process. The media covered some peace process events factually, but other events were reported selectively to buttress official views. The Government newspapers continued to publish reports on government malfeasance and low-level corruption. Stories on high-level government corruption were printed in non-Syrian Arabic newspapers available for purchase in Syria, but these cases were portrayed as positive examples of the Government's anticorruption campaign.

The Government or the Ba'th Party owns and operates the radio and television companies and the newspaper publishing houses. There are no privately owned newspapers. The Ministry of Information scripts the radio and television news programs to ensure that they follow the government line. The Government does not interfere with broadcasts from Israel. In late 1994, the Government announced that it would confiscate satellite receiving dishes and replace them with a government-controlled cable distribution system. However, no dishes were confiscated. It appears that the Government has informally sanctioned private ownership of satellite dishes, which continue to proliferate.

The Government restricts academic freedom. Public school teachers are not permitted to express ideas contrary to government policy, although authorities allow somewhat greater freedom of expression at the university level.

b. *Freedom of Peaceful Assembly and Association.*—Freedom of assembly does not exist. Citizens may not hold meetings unless they obtain permission from the Ministry of Interior. Most public demonstrations are organized by the Government or Ba'th Party. The Government applies the restrictions on public assembly in the Palestinian refugee camps, where controlled demonstrations have been allowed.

The Government restricts freedom of association. Private associations must be registered with the Government in order to be considered legal. Some groups have not been able to register presumably because the Government viewed them as political, even though the groups considered themselves strictly cultural or professional. Unregistered groups may not hold meetings, and the authorities do not allow the establishment of independent political parties. The Government usually grants registration to groups not engaged in political or other activities deemed sensitive.

In 1980 the Government dissolved, then reconstituted under its control, the executive boards of professional associations after some members staged a national strike and advocated an end to the state of emergency. The associations have not been independent since that time and are generally led by members of the Ba'th Party, although independents are allowed on their executive boards.

c. *Freedom of Religion.*—The Constitution provides for freedom of religion, and the Government generally respects this right in practice. The only advantage given to a particular religion by the Constitution is that which requires the President to be a Muslim. All religions and sects must register with the Government, which monitors fundraising and requires permits for all meetings by religious groups, except for worship. Although no law prohibits non-Muslims from proselytizing Muslims, the Government discourages such activity. The few remaining Jews are generally barred from government employment and do not have military service obligations. They are the only minority group whose passports and identity cards note their religion. There is mandatory religious instruction in schools, with government-approved teachers and curriculum. The religion courses are divided into separate classes for Muslim and Christian students, respectively. Syrian Jews have a separate primary school for Jews only, which includes religious instruction (see Section 5).

d. *Freedom of Movement Within the Country, Foreign Travel, Emigration, and Repatriation.*—The Government restricts travel near the Golan Heights and occasionally near Iraq. Travel to Israel is illegal. Citizens require government permission to travel abroad. Some have been denied such permission on political grounds, although government officials deny that the practice occurs. The authorities may prosecute any person found attempting to emigrate or travel abroad without official permission, or who is suspected of having visited Israel. On the other hand, there is no evidence that the Government persecuted upon their return those who applied for, but were denied, asylum abroad.

Women over the age of 18 have the legal right to travel without the permission of male relatives. In practice, either the husband or the wife may file a request with the Ministry of Interior to prohibit the spouse's departure from Syria. A father may request that the Ministry prohibit travel abroad by unmarried daughters, even if they are over 18 years of age.

The United Nations Relief and Works Agency (UNRWA) reported that as of June 1996 there were 347,391 registered Palestinian refugees in Syria. Palestinian refugees sometimes encounter difficulties in obtaining travel documents and reentering Syria after traveling abroad. The Government restricts entry by Palestinians who are not resident in Syria. The Government does not allow the Palestinian residents of Gaza to visit Syria.

The Government cooperates on a case-by-case basis with the office of the United Nations High Commissioner for Refugees (UNHCR) and other humanitarian organizations in assisting refugees. The Government provides first asylum; approximately 1,735 persons sought asylum through the UNHCR in 1996. Although the Government denied any forced repatriation of those who may have had a valid claim to refugee status, it apparently forcibly repatriated some Iraqi refugees, as well as some Sudanese, Iranian, Somali, and Libyan asylum seekers. At year's end there were an estimated 37,000 non-Palestinian refugees in Syria, of which approximately 3,500 were receiving assistance from the UNHCR, including 2,000 refugees of Iraqi origin at the El Hol camp and other locations.

Section 3. Respect for Political Rights: The Right of Citizens to Change Their Government

Although citizens ostensibly vote for the President and members of Parliament, they do not have the right to change their government. The President has run for election unopposed since taking power in 1970, and political opposition to his rule is not tolerated. The President and his senior aides, particularly those in the military and security services, ultimately make all basic decisions on political and economic life with no element of public accountability.

Moreover, the Constitution mandates that the Ba'th party is the ruling party in Syria and is guaranteed a majority in all government and popular associations, such as workers' and women's groups. Six smaller political parties are also permitted and, along with the Ba'th party, make up the National Progressive Front (NPF), a grouping of parties which represents the sole framework of legal political participation for citizens. While created ostensibly to give the appearance of a multiparty system, the NPF is dominated by the Ba'th party and does not change the essentially one-party character of the political system. The non-Ba'th party members of the NPF exist as political parties largely in name only and hew closely to Ba'th party and government policies.

The Ba'th party dominates the Parliament, or "People's Council." Although parliamentarians may criticize policies and modify draft laws, the executive branch retains ultimate control over the legislative process. Since 1990 the Government has allowed independent non-NPF candidates to run for a limited number of seats in the 250-member People's Council. The current number of independent deputies is 80, guaranteeing a permanent absolute majority for the Ba'th party-dominated NPF.

Persons who have been convicted by the State Security Court may be deprived of their political rights after they are released from prison. These restrictions include a prohibition against engaging in any political activity, the denial of a passport, and a bar on accepting a government job and some other forms of employment. The duration of such restrictions may last from 10 years to the remainder of the ex-prisoner's life. The Government contends that this practice is mandated by the Penal Code and has been law since 1949.

Women and minorities, with the exception of the Jewish population and the stateless Syrian Kurds, participate in the political system without restriction. There are 2 female cabinet ministers and 24 female members of Parliament.

Section 4. Governmental Attitude Regarding International and Nongovernmental Investigation of Alleged Violations of Human Rights

The Government does not allow the existence of local human rights groups. One or two human rights groups once operated legally but were banned by the Government.

In March 1995, the Government took the unprecedented step of allowing the international human rights group, Human Rights Watch (HRW), to conduct a 48-day fact-finding mission to Syria, with a follow-up visit in July 1995. The HRW delegation met with several government ministers and was allowed to travel around the country, meet with lawyers and families of detainees and prisoners, and attend Supreme State Security Court trials, where its members talked to defendants, lawyers, and the judges in ongoing trials.

The Government did not grant the group's request to visit prisons and detention centers holding political and national-security detainees, although it said the group could visit civilian prisons. When the group returned for a follow-up visit in July, it was told the SSSC was not in session, although the Court may indeed have been conducting proceedings. HRW produced a report sharply critical of the procedures of the SSSC and the absence of legal outlets for political opposition. The Government contended that the criticisms contained in the HRW report were unwarranted and inaccurate but later indicated its desire to continue a dialog with the group. Since the 1995 HRW visit, no international human rights groups have conducted fact-finding missions to Syria.

As a matter of policy, the Government denies to international groups, including the United Nations Human Rights Commission, that it commits human rights abuses. It does not permit representatives of the International Committee of the Red Cross (ICRC) to visit prisons. The Government says that it now responds in writing to all inquiries from nongovernmental organizations (NGO's) regarding human rights issues, including those regarding individual detainees and prisoners, through an interagency governmental committee established expressly for that purpose. Human Rights Watch reported in April that the Government has not responded to its request to account publicly for the possibly thousands of citizens who were executed at Tadmur Prison in the 1980's. In 1996 the Government had little new information to offer human rights organizations and foreign embassies on specific political prisoner inquiries. The usual government response is that information is lacking and that the prisoner in question has violated national security laws.

Section 5. *Discrimination Based on Race, Sex, Religion, Disability, Language, or Social Status*

The Constitution provides for equal rights and equal opportunity for all citizens. In practice, membership in the Ba'th Party or close familial relations with a prominent party member or government official can be important for prospering. Party or government connections can pave the way for entrance into better elementary and secondary schools, access to lucrative employment, and greater power within the Government, the military, and the security services. Certain prominent positions, such as that of provincial governor, are reserved solely for Ba'th Party members. Apart from some discrimination against Kurds, there are no apparent patterns of systematic government discrimination based on race, sex, religion, disability, language or social status.

Women.—Violence against women is known to occur. However, there are no reliable statistics for domestic violence or sexual assault in Syria. This is because the vast majority of cases go unreported, and victims generally are reluctant to seek assistance from nonfamily members. There are no laws against spousal rape. One preliminary academic study suggested that domestic violence is the largest single reason for divorces, and that such abuse is more prevalent among the less-educated. It appears to occur more in rural than in urban areas. Battered women have the legal right to seek redress in court, but few do so because of the social stigma attached to such action. The Syrian Women's Federation offers services to battered wives to remedy individual family problems. The Syrian Family Planning Association also seeks to deal with this problem. Some private groups, including the Family Planning Association, have organized seminars on violence against women, which were reported by the government press. There are no specifically designated shelters or safe-havens for battered women seeking to flee their husbands. There was a university seminar on violence against women in 1996.

The Government has sought to overcome traditional discriminatory attitudes toward women, and encourages women's education. However, the Parliament has not yet changed retirement and social security laws that discriminate against women.

Shari'a or Islamic law on divorce discriminates against women. For example, husbands may claim adultery as grounds for divorce, but wives face more difficulty in presenting the same argument. In addition, if a woman requests a divorce from her husband, she is not entitled to child support, even if she keeps the children.

Inheritance for Muslims is based on Shari'a. Accordingly, women are granted a smaller share of inheritance than male heirs. On the other hand, male heirs are mandated by Shari'a to provide financial support to the female relatives who inherit less; for example, a brother who inherits an unmarried sister's share from their parent's inheritance is obligated to provide for the sister's well-being. If there is a problem, she has the right to sue, but such cases are not common.

Shari'a law applies to Muslims only. Christians are subject to their church canon law on marriage and divorce, making divorces difficult to obtain in most cases. Christians are subject to civil laws on inheritance.

Polygyny is legal and practiced by a minority of Muslim men. Under Shari'a, a husband has the right to take up to four wives without asking the consent of his other wife/wives. The first wife and later wives have the right to seek a divorce if the husband takes an additional wife; however, in doing so, the wife loses the right to alimony or child support.

A father may request that the Government prohibit travel abroad by his married daughter (see Section 2.d.).

Women are not impeded from owning or managing land or other real property. Women constitute 6 percent of judges, 10 percent of lawyers, 57 percent of teachers below university level, and 20 percent of university professors.

Children.—There is no legal discrimination between boys and girls in school or in health care. Education is compulsory for all children, male or female, between the ages of 6 and 12. According to the Syrian Women's Union, about 46 percent of the total number of students through the secondary level are female.

Nevertheless, societal pressure for early marriage and childbearing interfere with girls' educational progress, particularly in rural areas, where dropout rates for female students remain high.

As for career aspirations, these are as much a function of social class as societal pressure. Some girls may aspire to marry, have children early, and be supported by a husband; other women are able to pursue education and career aspirations in addition to marrying and having children.

The law stresses the need to protect children, and the Government has organized seminars on the subject of child welfare. Although there are cases of child abuse, there is no societal pattern of abuse against children. The law provides for severe penalties for those found guilty of the most serious abuses against children.

People With Disabilities.—The law prohibits discrimination against the disabled and seeks to integrate them into the public sector work force. However, implementation is lax. Regulations reserving 2 percent of government and public sector jobs for the disabled are not rigorously implemented. The disabled do not have recourse to the courts regarding discrimination. There are no laws mandating access to public buildings for the disabled.

Religious Minorities.—Although there is a significant amount of religious tolerance, religion or ethnic affiliation can be a contributing factor in determining career opportunities. For example, members of the President's Alawi sect hold a predominant position in the security services and military, which is out of proportion to their percentage of the population. Nevertheless, government policy officially disavows sectarianism.

There is little evidence of societal discrimination or violence against religious minorities, including Jews. Government-run schools offer separate religious instruction for Christians and Muslims. Jews have a separate primary school which offers religious instruction on Judaism, in addition to traditional subjects. Although Arabic is the official language in public schools, the Government allows the teaching of Armenian, Hebrew, and Chaldean in some schools on the basis that these are "liturgical languages." Technically, all schools are government-run and nonsectarian, although some schools are run in practice by Christian and Jewish minorities.

National/Racial/Ethnic Minorities.—Although the Government contends that there is no discrimination against the Kurdish population, it has placed limits on the use and teaching of the Kurdish language, Kurdish cultural expression, and, at times, the celebration of Kurdish festivals. Some members of the Kurdish community have been tried by the Supreme State Security Court for expressing support for greater Kurdish autonomy or independence. Although the Asad Government stopped the practice of stripping Syrian Kurds of their Syrian nationality (some 120,000 lost their nationality under this program in the 1960's), it never restored this nationality. As a result, they and those who had their nationality taken away and their children have been unable to obtain Syrian nationality and passports, or even identification cards and birth certificates. Without Syrian nationality, these stateless Kurds are unable to own land, cannot be employed by the Government, and have no right to vote. They encounter difficulties in enrolling their children in school. Stateless Kurdish men may not legally marry Syrian citizens.

Section 6. Worker Rights

a. *The Right of Association.*—Although the Constitution provides for this right, workers are not free to establish unions independently of the Government's bureaucratic structure. All unions must belong to the General Federation of Trade Unions (GFTU) which is dominated by the Ba'th Party and is actually a part of the State's bureaucratic structure. The GFTU is an information channel between political decisionmakers and workers. The GFTU transmits instructions downward to the unions and workers but also conveys information to decisionmakers about worker conditions and needs. The GFTU provides the Government with opinions on legislation, organizes workers, and formulates rules for various member unions. The GFTU president is a senior member of the Ba'th Party. He and his deputy may attend cabinet meetings on economic affairs. The GFTU controls nearly all aspects of union activity.

The law does not prohibit strikes, except in the agricultural sector; nevertheless, workers are inhibited from striking because of previous government crackdowns on strikers. In 1980 the security forces arrested many union and professional association officials who planned a national strike. Some of those remain in detention or have been tried by the State Security Court (see Section 2.b.).

The GFTU is affiliated with the International Confederation of Arab Trade Unions.

In 1992 Syria's eligibility for tariff preferences under the U.S. Generalized System of Preferences was suspended because the Government failed to take steps to afford internationally recognized worker rights to Syrian workers.

b. *The Right to Organize and Bargain Collectively.*—This right does not exist in any meaningful sense. Government representatives are part of the bargaining process in the public sector. In state-owned companies, union representatives negotiate hours, wages, and conditions of employment with representatives of the employers and supervising ministry. Workers serve on the boards of directors of public enterprises.

The law provides for collective bargaining in the private sector, but any such agreement between labor and management must be ratified by the Minister of Labor and Social Affairs, who effectively has the power of veto. The Committee of Experts of the International Labor Organization (ILO) has long noted the Government's resistance to abolish the Minister's power over collective contracts.

Unions have the right to litigate disputes over work contracts and other workers' interests with employers and may ask for binding arbitration. In practice, labor officials and management settle most disputes without resort to legal remedies or arbitration. Management has the right to request arbitration, but this is seldom exercised. Arbitration usually occurs when a worker initiates a dispute over wages or severance pay.

Since the unions are absorbed into the Government's bureaucratic structure, they are protected by law from antiunion discrimination. There were no reports of antiunion discrimination.

There are no unions in the seven free trade zones. Firms in the zones are exempt from the laws and regulations governing hiring and firing, although they must observe some provisions on health, safety, hours, and sick and annual leave.

c. *Prohibition of Forced or Compulsory Labor.*—There is no law prohibiting forced or compulsory labor. There were no reports of forced or compulsory labor involving children or foreign or domestic workers. Forced labor has been imposed as a punishment for some convicts.

d. *Minimum Age for Employment of Children.*—The minimum age for employment is 14 in the public sector and 12 in the private sector. In all cases, parental permission is required for children under the age of 16. The law prohibits children from working at night. However, all these laws apply only to children working for a salary. Thus, those working in family businesses and who are not technically paid a salary—a common phenomenon—do not fall under the law. The Government claims that the expansion of the private sector has led to more young children working. The Ministry of Labor and Social Affairs is responsible for enforcing child labor laws but does not have enough inspectors to ensure compliance with the laws.

e. *Acceptable Conditions of Work.*—The Minister of Labor and Social Affairs is responsible for enforcing minimum wage levels in the public and private sectors. The minimum wage, which the Government had raised in 1994 (accompanying a cut in subsidies on basic food items), remained unchanged in 1996 at $50 (550 Syrian pounds) per month in the public sector and $44 (484 Syrian pounds) per month in the private sector. A committee of labor, management, and government representatives submits recommended changes in the minimum wage to the Minister. The minimum wage does not provide an adequate standard of living for a worker and family. As a result, many workers take additional jobs or are supported by their extended families.

The statutory workweek is 6 days of 6 hours each, but in some cases a 9-hour workday is permitted. The laws mandate one 24-hour rest day per week. Rules and regulations severely limit the ability of an employer to dismiss employees without cause. Even if a person is absent from work without notice for a long period, the employer must follow a lengthy procedure of trying to find the person and notify him, including through newspaper notices, before he is able to take any action against the employee. Dismissed employees have the right to appeal before a committee of representatives from the union, management, the Ministry of Labor and Social Affairs, and the appropriate municipality. Such committees usually find in favor of the employee. The law does not protect temporary workers who are not subject to regulations on minimum wages. Small private firms and businesses employ such workers to avoid the costs associated with hiring permanent employees.

The law mandates safety in all sectors, and managers are expected to implement them fully. In practice, there is little enforcement without worker complaints, which occur infrequently despite government efforts to post notices on safety rights and regulations. Large companies, such as oil field contractors, also employ safety engineers.

The ILO has noted that a provision in the Labor Code allowing employers to keep workers at the workplace for as many as 11 hours a day might lead to abuse. However, there have been no reports of such abuses. Officials from the Ministries of Health and Labor inspect work sites for compliance with health and safety standards. Such inspections appear to be haphazard, apart from those conducted in hotels and other facilities that cater to foreigners. Rural enforcement of labor laws is also more lax than that in urban areas, where inspectors are concentrated. Workers may lodge complaints about health and safety conditions with special committees established to adjudicate such cases. Workers have the right to remove themselves from hazardous conditions without risking loss of employment.

TUNISIA

Tunisia is a republic dominated by a single political party. President Zine el-Abidine Ben Ali and his Constitutional Democratic Rally (RCD) continue to control the government, including the legislature and the judiciary, and to deny opposition groups the opportunity to play a significant role. The President appoints the Prime Minister, Cabinet, and 23 governors. Four opposition parties hold 19 of the 163 seats in Parliament.

The police share responsibility for internal security with a paramilitary national guard. The police operate in the capital and a few other cities. In outlying areas, their policing duties are shared with, or ceded to, the national guard. Both forces are under the control of the Minister of Interior and the President. The security forces continued to be responsible for serious human rights abuses.

Tunisia has made substantial progress towards establishing a market economy based on agriculture, petroleum, textiles, manufactured exports, and tourism. The year 1996 marked the end of a 3-year drought and a consequent improvement in the rate of growth, estimated at 6 percent. The per capita gross national product for 1995 was approximately $1,900. Sixty percent of Tunisians are in the middle class and enjoy a high standard of living. Remittances from workers abroad also are an important source of revenue.

The Government's human rights performance did not improve, and it continued to commit some serious abuses. The ability of citizens to change their government has yet to be demonstrated. Members of the security forces reportedly tortured and beat prisoners and detainees. Security forces also monitor the activities of government critics and at times harass them, their relatives, and their associates. Prison conditions reportedly ranged from spartan to poor, and prolonged pretrial detention is a problem. The judiciary is subject to executive influence, and due process rights in trials of a political nature are not always observed. The Government generally did not respond effectively to allegations of human rights abuses, often not divulging the results of investigations. It demonstrated a pattern of intolerance of public criticism, and continued to stifle freedoms of speech, press, and association. Because of government pressure, newspapers did not carry press releases of the leading human rights group. The Government continued to use control of advertising revenue as a means to discourage newspapers and magazines from publishing material that it deemed undesirable. The Government frequently seized editions of foreign newspapers containing articles it considered objectionable, and it restricted ownership of satellite dishes and access to the Internet. The Government also restricted the freedom of movement of government critics.

The convictions of two opposition party leaders and that of a human rights lawyer were regarded by human rights observers as government attempts to suppress political dissent. In response to international criticism, the Government granted parole to all three in December and released them from prison. Membership both in the Islamist movement known as An-Nahda and the Tunisian Communist Workers Party is prohibited, and the Government sentenced several persons to prison for their association with these groups. The President made an unprecedented visit to prisons and authorized the National High Commissioner for Human Rights to make unannounced prison inspections.

As part of its efforts to advance the rights of women and children, the Government passed a body of legislation pertaining to community property, family allowances, child support, and survivors benefits. Nonetheless, legal and societal discrimination against women continues to exist.

RESPECT FOR HUMAN RIGHTS

Section 1. Respect for the Integrity of the Person, Including Freedom From:

a. *Political and Other Extrajudicial Killing.*—There were no reports of political or other extrajudicial killings.

Investigations of the deaths in detention of Abderraouf Laaribi and Abdelwahed Abdelzi, who died in 1991, are no longer being pursued.

b. *Disappearance.*—There were no reports of politically motivated disappearances.

c. *Torture and Other Cruel, Inhuman, or Degrading Treatment or Punishment.*—The Penal Code prohibits the use of torture, and other cruel, inhuman, or degrading treatment or punishment. Nonetheless, security services allegedly employed various means of torture to coerce confessions from detainees. Five students arrested in August for membership in an illegal organization claimed to have been tortured during their 6-day detention. The forms of torture allegedly used included electric shock, submersion of the head in water, beatings with hands, sticks, and police batons, and food and sleep deprivation. Jalel Ayachi, a former detainee, filed a complaint against the Government for his loss of hearing in one ear, the alleged result of a police beating. Police and prison authorities also reportedly mistreat prisoners by beating them. There were reports that Radhia Aouididi was tortured following her November 8 arrest.

A German citizen reported being severely beaten while serving his prison sentence, losing several teeth as a result, after complaining about prison food and making critical remarks. The authorities are investigating his complaints.

Human rights advocates maintain that charges of torture and mistreatment are difficult to substantiate, since government authorities often deny medical examinations until evidence of abuse has disappeared. The Government maintained that it investigates all complaints of torture and mistreatment filed with the prosecutor's office and noted that alleged victims sometimes publicly accused authorities of acts of abuse without taking the steps required to initiate an investigation. Absent a formal complaint, the Government may open an administrative investigation but is unlikely to make the results public. According to defense attorneys and human rights advocates, prison conditions ranged from spartan to poor. Overcrowding is common, with as many as 30 to 50 prisoners sharing a common cell, often sharing beds. Human rights advocates report that prisoners receive inadequate medical care and are unable to obtain either medical evaluations to determine special needs or treatment for injuries or illness. Healthy prisoners are sometimes confined with ill inmates. There were credible reports that conditions and prisons rules are more stringent for political prisoners than for the general prison population and that the authorities limit the quantity and variety of food that families can bring to supplement prison fare. One credible report alleged the existence of special cell blocks and prisons for political prisoners. Political prisoners may be held in solitary confinement for months on end. Convicted opposition Movement of Democratic Socialists (MDS) party president Mohamed Moaada was held in solitary confinement since his 1995 arrest until his release in December.

The Government does not permit international organizations or independent human rights organizations to inspect or monitor prison conditions. In August the President visited certain prisons and subsequently authorized the National High Commissioner for Human Rights to make unannounced prison inspections. The High Commissioner made his first such inpections on October 12 and announced to the press that prisoners in the two facilities he had visited lived relatively well and received adequate medical care.

d. *Arbitrary Arrest, Detention, or Exile.*—The law authorizes the police to make arrests without warrants in the cases of suspected felons or crimes in progress. The Government may hold a suspect incommunicado for 10 days following arrest. Detainees have the right to be informed of the grounds for arrest before questioning and may request a medical examination. They do not have a right to legal representation during prearraignment detention. Attorneys, human rights monitors, and former detainees maintain that the authorities illegally extend the 10-day limit by falsifying the date of arrest. There are reports that authorities held Radhia Aouididi, arrested on November 8, incommunicado for a period exceeding the 10-day legal limit.

Detainees have a right to be represented by counsel during arraignment. The Government provides legal representation for indigents. At arraignment, the examining magistrate may decide to release the accused or to remand him to pretrial detention. Since 1993 the law has allowed for release of accused persons on bail or on the personal surety of a third party. This provision is little-known and rarely invoked. During the year the Government publicized its support of release-on-bail as a means of reducing or eliminating prison stays. In cases involving crimes for which the sentence may exceed 5 years, or which involve national security, pretrial detention may last an initial period of 6 months and may be extended by court order for 2 additional 4-month periods. During this period, the court conducts an investigation, hears arguments, and accepts evidence and motions of both parties.

A case proceeds from investigation to the Criminal Court of Appeals, which sets a trial date. There is no legal limit to the length of time the court may hold a case over for trial; nor is there a legal imperative to a speedy hearing. Complaints of prolonged detention awaiting trial were common, and President Ben Ali publicly encouraged judges to make better use of release on bail and suspended sentences.

There is no reliable estimate of the number of political detainees.

The law prohibits exile, and the Government observes the prohibition.

e. *Denial of Fair Public Trial.*—The judiciary is part of the Ministry of Justice and therefore not independent of the executive branch, which appoints, assigns, grants tenure to, and transfers judges. In addition, the President is head of the Supreme Council of Judges. This situation renders judges susceptible to pressure in politically sensitive cases.

The court system comprises the regular civil and criminal courts, including the courts of first instance, the courts of appeal, and the Court of Cassation, the nation's highest court, as well as the military tribunals within the Defense Ministry. Trials in the regular courts of first instance and appeals are open to the public.

The Code of Procedure is patterned after the French legal system. By law, the accused has the right to be present at trial, represented by counsel, question witnesses, and appeal verdicts. However, in practice, judges do not always observe these rights. For example, defense attorneys representing Mohamed Moaada, an opposition leader convicted of treason (see Section 2.a.), were unable to question the prosecution's principal witness, who had been released from prison and allowed to return to Libya prior to Moaada's trial. The law permits trial in absentia of fugitives from the law. Both the accused and the prosecutor may appeal decisions of the lower courts. The Court of Cassation, which considers arguments on points of law, as opposed to the facts of a case, is the final arbiter. Trials in the courts of first instance and in the courts of appeals are open to the public.

The presiding judge or panel of judges dominates a trial, and defense attorneys have little opportunity to participate substantively. Defense lawyers contend that the courts often fail to grant them adequate notice of trial dates or allow them time to prepare their cases. Some also reported that judges have begun to restrict access to evidence and court records, requiring in some cases, for example, that all attorneys of record examine the court file on one appointed day, in judges chambers, and prohibiting copying of material documents. They also complained that the judges sometimes refused to allow them to call witnesses on their clients' behalf or to question key government witnesses.

In July the Government convicted opposition MDS Party Deputy Khemais Chammari of divulging information from the grand jury investigation of Mohamed Moaada. Chammari's attorneys denounced the trial, protesting that they had received inadequate notice of the review before the Court of Cassation and inadequate access to court records, including the final judgment of the Criminal Court of Appeals, and that the Court illegally restricted attorney-client visits. In the last week before the hearing, the Court provided the defense attorneys access to the records and to their client but refused a continuance of the case and upheld the conviction. At the end of December, both Chammari and Moaada were granted parole and released from prison.

In January Nejib Hosni, a lawyer who had defended clients accused of political offenses, was convicted and sentenced to 8 years in prison for forging the name of a terminally-ill client on a land transaction. Defense attorneys asserted that the judge's wide discretionary authority allowed him to ignore critical eyewitness and expert testimony, thus denying Hosni a fair trial. In October Hosni was acquitted of the charges of passing arms to Islamists and, in December, released from prison on parole. At the same time, the Government paroled and released Mohamed Hedi Sassi, convicted of having distributed tracts of the illegal Tunisian Communist Workers Party.

Military tribunals try cases involving military personnel and civilians accused of national security crimes. The tribunal consists of a civilian judge from the Supreme Court and four military judges. Defendants may appeal the tribunal's verdicts to the Supreme Court.

There is no reliable information on the number of political prisoners. However, Human Rights Watch and Amnesty International report that there may be hundreds of political prisoners, convicted and imprisoned for membership in the Islamist group An-Nahda and the Communist Workers Party, for disseminating information of these banned organizations, and for aiding relatives of convicted members.

f. *Arbitrary Interference with Privacy, Family, Home, or Correspondence.*—The Constitution provides for the inviolability of the person and the home and for the privacy of correspondence, "except in exceptional cases defined by law." The law requires that the police have warrants to conduct searches, but police sometimes ignore the requirement if authorities consider that state security is at stake or that a crime is in progress. Authorities can invoke state security interests to justify telephone surveillance. There were also reports of Government interception of facsimile and computer-transmitted communications. The law does not explicitly authorize these activities, although the Government stated that the Code of Criminal Procedure implicitly gives investigating magistrates such authority. The security services monitor the activities of political critics, and sometimes harass, follow, question, and otherwise intimidate their relatives and associates. Many political activists experience frequent and sometimes extended interruptions of residential and business telephone and facsimile services. The security services question citizens seen talking with foreign visitors or residents, such as visiting international human rights monitors. One organization reported government interference with the delivery of its mail. Police presence is heavy throughout the country. The Government prohibits the receipt of some foreign publications (see Section 2.a.). Traffic officers routinely stop motorists to examine their personal identification and vehicular documents.

Section 2. Respect for Civil Liberties, Including:

a. *Freedom of Speech and Press.*—The Constitution provides for freedom of thought, expression, and the press. In practice, however, the Government limits exercise of these freedoms. The President convoked newspaper editors in August and affirmed the right of freedom of the press, "as long as it is properly used."

In February Mohamed Moaada, then president of the opposition MDS party, was convicted of treason for allegedly selling information relating to national security to a Libyan citizen. He was sentenced to serve 11 years in prison. The arrest (for an act that had allegedly transpired a year before) took place the day after Moaada had written a letter to President Ben Ali complaining of the lack of political freedoms.

In May Khemais Chammari, an MDS colleague of Moaada and member of the Chamber of Deputies, was arrested following a 7-month investigation for having divulged information about the grand jury investigating Moaada. Chammari's arrest took place the day after the Director of the Arab Institute for Human Rights had been detained at the airport, allegedly in possession of documents written by Chammari. Observers believed that the Government proceeded with the prosecution because of Chammari's outspoken criticism of the Government. Convicted and sentenced to 5 years' imprisonment, Chammari was released on parole at the end of the year.

Indications of continuing press restrictions were evident throughout the year. The confiscation of two journalists' passports prevented them from attending a regional seminar on promoting an independent Arab press. The Government also refused to renew the passport of Salah Bechir, a Tunisian journalist residing in France. The law permits such denials in cases where "the good reputation of Tunisia" might be tarnished. The Government also exerts control over the media by issuing or withholding credentials to journalists. It continued to deny accreditation to a journalist dismissed from the government news agency, Tunis Afrique Presse (TAP), in 1994 for publishing an interview with an opposition politician in a foreign publication.

Authorities used the placement of government advertising, a significant source of revenue for newspapers and magazines, as a means of controlling the press. There were reports that the Government withheld advertising orders in publications that published articles that the Government deemed offensive. As a result of such pressure, the Tunisian Human Rights League (LTDH) was unable to find a publisher for its annual report, and newspapers did not print its press releases. On one ocassion, however, local television did report an LTDH press release praising the Government. The Government monitored the activities and speech of human rights activists traveling abroad and interrogated individuals upon their return to Tunisia.

The Press Code contains broad provisions prohibiting subversion and defamation, neither of which is clearly defined. The Government prevents distribution of editions of foreign newspapers and magazines that contain articles critical of Tunisia—editions of Le Monde and Al Hayat, for example, were blocked 8 to 10 times a month—and has reportedly advised universities against subscribing to Le Monde. The authorities prosecuted citizens during the year on charges of distributing tracts—during the elections of 1994 and, later, in 1995—critical of the Government and, in particular, the absence of democratic freedoms and pluralism. While clandestine organizations publish several underground newspapers, their contributors risked trial for dissemination of false information. The Government provides official texts on major domestic and international events and has reprimanded publishers and editors for failing to publish these statements. These factors induce a high degree of self-censorship in the media.

In July the World Association of Newspapers (WAN) suspended the Tunisian Newspaper Association for failing to fight against press repression and noted "numerous instances * * * of jailing and harassment of journalists, the banning of foreign publications and broadcasts, and the withdrawal of passports from Tunisian journalists."

Before marketing publications, printers and publishers are required by law to deposit copies with the Chief Prosecutor (Procureur), the Ministry of Interior, the Secretary of State for Information, and the Ministry of Culture. Similarly, distributors must deposit copies of publications printed abroad with the Chief Prosecutor and various ministries prior to distributing them. While publishers need not wait for an authorization, they must obtain a receipt of deposit before distribution. On occasion such receipts are reportedly withheld, sometimes indefinitely. Without a receipt, publications may not be legally distributed. The Press Code stipulates fines and confiscations for failure to comply with these provisions. The Government canceled at the last minute a conference dealing with human rights issues, to have been co-sponsored by several activist organizations, allegedly because of the objectionable content of some of the conference materials submitted for government review (see Section 4).

In July 1995, the National Assembly passed legislation regulating the purchase and installation of satellite receiving dishes. While the Government continued to accept applications for permits to own a satellite dish, it issued few, if any, licenses. The black market reportedly supplies most of the stock of dishes.

The Government owns and operates the Tunisian Radio and Television Establishment (ERTT). ERTT's coverage of government news is taken directly from the official news agency, TAP. There are several regional radio stations and one local television channel. Bilateral agreements with France and Italy permit Tunisians to receive the French channel France 2 and the Italian Rai Uno.

Like journalists, university professors often practice a form of self-censorship, avoiding classroom criticism of the Government or statements supportive of the Islamist An-Nahda movement. The presence of police on campuses also discourages dissent.

b. *Freedom of Peaceful Assembly and Association.*—The Constitution provides for freedom of assembly. Groups wishing to hold a public meeting, rally, or march must obtain a permit from the Ministry of Interior. The authorities routinely approve such permits, except in cases involving proscribed organizations.

In April the Tunisian Association of Democratic Women sponsored a national conference celebrating the international observance of Women's Day (April 8.) It was the first time in 2 years that the group was able to hold a meeting in a public place. The Human Rights League (LTDH) celebrated its 19th anniversary also in a public gathering place.

The Government restricts freedom of association. The law bars membership in political parties organized by religion, race, or region. On these grounds, the Government prosecutes members in the Islamist movement An-Nahda. It also bans organizations that threaten disruption of the public order and prosecutes members of the Communist Workers Party. In May the Government withdrew authorization for a conference that was to be jointly held by several nongovernmental organizations including the Human Rights League, allegedly because of conference handouts that the Government found objectionable. In November it canceled a League educational program on the law concerning arrest and detention.

On the basis of a procedural error and without ruling on the merits of the case, a court annulled a 1992 Ministry of Interior ruling that the LTDH was in violation of rules governing associations because it refused to open its membership to all applicants. The LTDH sought to control the process of enrolling new members as a means of ensuring its independence.

c. *Freedom of Religion.*—Islam is the state religion, but the Government permits the practice of other religions. The Government controls mosques and pays the salaries of the prayer leaders. The 1988 Law on Mosques provides that only personnel appointed by the Government may lead activities in the mosques.

The Government regards the Baha'i faith as a heretical sect of Islam and permits its adherents to practice their faith only in private. With 1,300 adherents, the Jewish community is the country's largest indigenous religious minority. The Government assures the Jewish community freedom of worship and pays the salary of the Grand Rabbi. The Christian community, estimated at about 2,000, is composed mainly of foreigners. It freely holds church services and operates a small number of schools.

The Government views proselytizing as an act against "public order." Authorities ask foreigners suspected of proselytizing to depart the country and do not permit them to return. There were no reported cases of official action against persons suspected of proselytizing.

In a gesture toward tolerance and ecumenism, Tunisia hosted a visit in April by the Pope.

d. *Freedom of Movement Within the Country, Foreign Travel, Emigration, and Repatriation.*—The Constitution provides for these rights. People are free to change their place of residence or work at will. In practice, the Government restricts the freedom of movement and foreign travel of those critical of the administration.

Human rights monitors complained that the Government arbitrarily withholds passports from citizens. The Government again confiscated the passport of Moncef Marzouki, an opposition politician who unsuccessfully sought to run for the Presidency in 1994. The Government had restored his travel documents in 1995 following a previous confiscation in 1994. A member of the LTDH was prevented from traveling abroad as part of a human rights delegation. The director of a human rights research institute on his way to a conference overseas was arrested and detained for 4 days for allegedly having on his person objectionable documents (see Section 2.a.). The Government confiscated the passport of Hamma Hammami, former editor of the Communist Workers Party newspaper, when he attempted to attend an international symposium on torture.

Political activists reported that their movements were closely monitored and that they were sometimes harassed by security services personnel. Moncef Ben Salem, a former university professor who served a 3-year prison term for defaming the Government, said that he was prevented from leaving the limits of the southern city of Sfax where he resides.

The Government has signed the 1951 Convention Relating to the Status of Refugees, and the 1967 Protocol, and cooperates with the office of the United Nations High Commissioner of Refugees (UNHCR) in assisting refugees. The Government acknowledged UNHCR determination of refugee status which was accorded to approximately 150 persons during the year. Approximately 150 cases (300 to 400 individuals) await determination by the UNHCR. There is no pattern of abuse of refugees in Tunisia. Although a few refugees were deported during the year, none was forced to return to countries where they feared persecution.

Section 3. *Respect for Political Rights: The Right of Citizens to Change Their Government*

The Constitution provides that the citizenry shall elect the President and members of the legislature for 5-year terms. However, the ability of citizens to change their government through democratic means has yet to be demonstrated. The ruling RCD party and its direct predecessor parties have controlled the political arena since Tunisia gained independence in 1956. The party dominates the Cabinet, the Chamber of Deputies, and regional and local governments. The President appoints the Cabinet and the 23 governors. The Government and the party are closely integrated: The President of the republic is also the President of the party, and the party's Secretary General holds the rank of Minister of State.

The 163-seat Chamber of Deputies does not function as an effective counterweight to the executive branch. The Electoral Code provides for a winner-take-all formula for 144 of its seats. The ruling party won all seats in the 1994 parliamentary elections. Nineteen additional seats were reserved for unsuccessful candidates and were divided among four opposition parties after the 1994 elections. Election is by secret ballot. All legal parties are free to present candidates. Candidates for president, however, must receive the endorsement of 30 sitting deputies to launch a campaign. In 1995 the ruling party won 4,084 of 4,090 seats in countrywide municipal elections. In December the Government held special elections to fill two seats, one of which had been vacated by convicted MDS deputy Khemais Chammari. After the RCD declined to enter a candidate for Chammari's seat in order to ensure that the opposition retained the seat, the candidate of the opposition Unity Party won the election. The RCD retained control of the second seat. National presidential and legislative elections are next scheduled for 1999.

The most vocal and active of the opposition parties, the Movement of Democratic Socialists, suffered a split in its ranks following the convictions and imprisonment of party president Moaada and party vice-president Chammari. The Government denied reports that it financed the faction that favored cooperation with the Government and that it manipulated the press to portray this group as legitimate. Newspapers rarely carried stories about or press releases of the other faction. Because of MDS financial difficulties, it was unable to pay its rent and was evicted from its headquarters.

Women participate in politics. Eleven of the 163 members of the Chamber of Deputies are women. In addition one women is the junior Minister for Women's and Children's Affairs in the Prime Minister's office. Nevertheless, women's presence in public office is disproportionately low, and they hold few senior government posts.

Section 4. Governmental Attitude Regarding International and Nongovernmental Investigation of Alleged Violations of Human Rights

There are human rights offices in certain ministries, and a governmental body, the Higher Committee for Human Rights and Basic Freedoms, that address and sometimes resolve human rights complaints. The Committee's last publicly distributed report covered the 1993–1994 period.

The Tunisian Human Rights League is the most active independent advocacy organization, with branches in many parts of the country. The organization receives and researches complaints, and protests individual and systemic abuses. The Government places significant obstacles in the way of its effective operation, however. League members and other human rights activists report government harassment, interrogation, property loss or damage, unauthorized home entry, and denial of passports. The LTDH continues to be unable to find local newspapers willing to publish communiques issued by the League that are critical of the Government.

The Arab Institute for Human Rights, headquartered in Tunis, was founded in 1989 by the LTDH, the Arab Organization for Human Rights, and the Union of Arab Lawyers. It is an information, rather than advocacy, organization.

Amnesty International (AI) continued to maintain a Tunisian chapter. Its Tunis office, however, suffered repeated loss of telephone and facsimile service. In August a Tunisian staff member from AI's London headquarters was arrested when entering the country for a family vacation. Authorities allegedly detained him incommunicado for a week and interrogated him. The Government continued to deny entry to a London-based AI researcher responsible for Tunisian affairs, claiming that she has an anti-Tunisia bias. It did permit the International President of AI to visit on an occasion coinciding with the visit of the U.N. High Commissioner for Human Rights.

In June AI released its annual report for 1995, containing a section critical of Tunisia. Also in June, the Ministry of Foreign Affairs' Human Rights Section published a booklet entitled "Reflections on Human Rights in Tunisia" in which it dismissed most criticisms of its human rights record by suggesting that the authors were members of organizations infiltrated by religious and political extremists.

The Government denied entry to the head of the International Federation for Human Rights. The Government allowed a few foreign human rights researchers entry. One reported being followed regularly. Another's computer data disks, notes, and documents were stolen from his hotel room. A third was interrogated at the airport for 2 hours upon arrival. Resident foreign human rights monitors found it increasingly difficult to arrange meetings with some government human rights officers. When the Government did grant meetings, officials often delayed, sometimes indefinitely, responding to questions about human rights. The Government canceled at the last minute a conference dealing with human rights issues, to have been cosponsored by several activist organizations, allegedly because of the objectionable content of some of the conference materials submitted for government review.

In May the European Union (EU) passed a resolution criticizing Tunisia's human rights policies and practices. In concluding its Euro-Mediterranean Trade Agreement with Tunisia, the EU also linked respect for human rights and democratic principles to economic cooperation. The Government agreed to allow periodic monitoring of the human rights situation and to engage in ongoing discussions on human rights with its European partners.

Section 5. Discrimination Based on Race, Sex, Religion, Disability, Language, or Social Status

The Constitution provides that all citizens shall have equal rights and responsibilities and be equal under the law. The Government generally observes this practice. Legal or social discrimination is not prevalent.

Women.—Violence against women occurs, but there are no reliable statistics to measure its extent. The Tunisian Association of Democratic Women operates the country's only counseling center for women who are victims of domestic violence. The center, located in Tunis, assists approximately 20 women per month. Instances of rape or assault by someone unknown to the victim are rare. Battered women first seek help from family members. Police intervention is often ineffective because police officers and the courts tend to regard domestic violence as a problem to be handled by the family. Nonetheless, there are stiff penalties for spouse abuse, double that for normal battery. Both the fine and imprisonment for battery or violence committed by a spouse or family member are double those for the same crimes committed by an individual not related to the victim.

Women enjoy substantial rights, and the Government has made serious efforts to advance women's rights. However, women still face legal and societal discrimination in certain social and economic areas and in employment. Most property acquired during marriage, including property acquired solely, is held in the name of the husband. Inheritance laws, based on Shari'a (Islamic) law and tradition, discriminate against women.

Overseeing programs concerning women's issues is the Junior Ministry for Women and the Family. It maintains effective links with women's professional associations and with the government-supported Women's Union and Women's Research Center.

Passage in April of a body of legislation on women's rights appeared to represent significant progress. The legislation authorized joint application for loans and encouraged discussion prior to marriage of the possibility of joint ownership of property acquired during the marriage and inclusion in the marriage contract of relevant language. While the new laws are technically in effect, since passage there has been little public attention paid to the legislation and no public discussion. Some women's advocates believe that more traditional segments of society urged the Government not to publicize and promote the new laws. There were also new provisions regarding family allowance, alimony, child support, and survivors' benefits that especially benefit households headed by women.

Women in increasing numbers are entering the work force, employed particularly in the textile industry, manufacturing, health, and agricultural sectors. According to government statistics for 1995, women constituted 22 percent of the work force. Excluding the agricultural sector, they accounted for 44 percent. There are an estimated 1,500 businesses headed by women. Women represent 25 percent of the civil service, employed primarily in the fields of health, education, and social affairs at the middle or lower levels. Approximately 43 percent of the university students enrolled in the 1995–96 academic year were women. On the other hand, while the rate of illiteracy has dropped markedly in both rural and urban areas, the rate of female illiteracy in all categories is at least double that of men. Among 10- to 14-year olds, 5.5 percent of urban girls are illiterate, compared with 2.2 percent of urban boys; and 27 percent of rural girls, compared with less than 7 percent of rural boys.

Several active nongovernmental organizations (NGO's) focus, in whole or in part, on women's advocacy, or research women's issues, and a cadre of attorneys represent women in domestic cases. Media attention focuses on women's economic and academic accomplishments and usually omits reference to culturally sensitive issues.

Children.—The Government demonstrates a strong commitment to public education, which is compulsory until the age of 16. Primary school enrollment for the 1996–97 scholastic year was roughly the same as the preceding year; secondary school enrollment showed an 8 percent increase over last year. The Government offers a maternal and child health program, providing prenatal and postnatal services. It also sponsors an immunization program targeting preschool-aged children.

In 1995 the Government promulgated laws to constitute a code for the protection of children. The code proscribes child abuse, abandonment, and sexual or economic exploitation. Penalties for convictions for abandonment and assault on minors are severe. There is a Ministry for Children and Youths and a presidential delegate to safeguard the rights and welfare of children.

People With Disabilities.—The law prohibits discrimination based on disability and mandates that at least 1 percent of the public and private sector jobs be reserved for the disabled.

All public buildings constructed since 1991 must be accessible to physically disabled persons. Many cities, including the capital, have begun to install wheelchair access ramps on city sidewalks. There is a general trend toward making public transportation more accessible to disabled persons. The Government issues special cards to the disabled for benefits such as unrestricted parking, priority medical services, preferential seating on public transportation, and consumer discounts.

Indigenous People.—The small Berber minority constitutes less than 2 percent of the population. Some older Berbers have retained their native language, but the younger generation has been assimilated into Tunisian culture through schooling and marriage. Berbers are free to participate in politics and to express themselves culturally.

Section 6. Worker Rights

a. *The Right of Association.*—The Constitution and the Labor Code stipulate the right of workers to form unions. The Tunisian General Federation of Labor (UGTT) is the country's only labor federation and claims about 15 percent of the work force as members, including civil servants and employees of state-owned enterprises. There is no legal prohibition against the establishment of other labor federations. A union may be dissolved only by court order.

The UGTT and its member unions are legally independent of the Government and the ruling party but operate under regulations that restrict their freedom of action. The UGTT's membership includes persons associated with all political tendencies, although Islamists have been removed from union offices. The current UGTT leadership follows a policy of cooperation with the Government and its economic reform program. There are credible reports that the UGTT receives substantial government subsidies to supplement modest union dues and funding from the National Social Security Account.

Unions, including those representing civil servants, have the right to strike, provided they give 10 days' advance notice and the UGTT approves of the strike. These restrictions, however, are rarely observed in practice. In recent years, the majority of strikes have been illegal because the UGTT had not approved them in advance. The Government does not prosecute workers involved in illegal strike activity. The law prohibits retribution against strikers, but some employers punish strikers, who are then forced to pursue costly and time-consuming legal remedies to protect their rights.

Labor disputes are settled through conciliation panels in which labor and management are equally represented. Tripartite regional arbitration commissions settle industrial disputes when conciliation fails.

Unions are free to associate with international bodies.

b. *The Right to Organize and Bargain Collectively.*—The right to organize and bargain collectively is protected by law and observed in practice. Wages and working conditions are set by triennial negotiations between the UGTT member unions and employers.

Forty-seven collective bargaining agreements set standards for industries in the private sector and cover 80 percent of the total private sector work force. The Government's role in these negotiations is minimal, consisting mainly of lending its good offices if talks appear to be stalled. However, the Government must approve, but may not modify, the agreements.

The UGTT also negotiates wages and work conditions of civil servants and employees of state-owned enterprises.

The law prohibits antiunion discrimination by employers. The UGTT, however, is concerned about antiunion activity among private sector employers, especially the firing of union activists and the use of temporary workers to avoid unionization. In certain industries, such as textiles and construction, temporary workers account for a large majority of the work force. The Labor Code protects temporary workers, but enforcement is more difficult than in the case of permanent workers. A committee, chaired by an officer from the Labor Inspectorate of the Office of the Inspector General of the Ministry of Social Affairs, includes a labor representative and an employers' association representative; it approves all worker dismissals.

c. *Prohibition of Forced or Compulsory Labor.*—Tunisia abolished compulsory labor in 1989. The practice of sentencing convicts to "rehabilitation through work," which had been of concern to the International Labor Organization's (ILO) Committee of Experts as a possible violation of ILO Convention 29 on forced labor, ended in 1995.

d. *Minimum Age for Employment of Children.*—An August revision of the Labor Code raised the minimum age for employment in manufacturing from 15 to 16 years. The minimum age for light work in agriculture and some other nonindustrial sectors is 13 years. The Government requires children to attend school until the age of 16. Workers between the ages of 14 and 18 must have 12 hours of rest a day, which include the hours between 10 pm and 6 am. Children between the ages of 14 and 16 may work no more than 2 hours a day. The time that they spend in school and work may not exceed 7 hours per day. Inspectors of the Ministry of Social Affairs examine the records of employees to verify that employers comply with the minimum age law. Nonetheless, young children often perform agricultural work in rural areas and work as vendors in urban areas.

The UGTT has expressed concern that child labor continues to exist disguised as apprenticeship, particularly in the handicraft industry, and in the cases of young girls whose families place them as household domestics in order to collect their wages.

e. *Acceptable Conditions of Work.*—The Labor Code provides for a range of administratively determined minimum wages, which are set by a commission of representatives from the Ministries of Social Affairs, Planning, Finance, and National Economy in consultation with the UGTT and the employers' association. The President approves the commission's recommendations. When supplemented by transportation and family allowances, the minimum wage covers only essential costs for a worker and family. The minimum wage schedule was adjusted twice during the year, in May and September. The industrial minimum wage is $168.59 (161.696 dinars) per month for a 48-hour workweek and $147.71 (141.664 dinars) per month for a 40-hour workweek. The agricultural minimum wage is $5.17 (4.960 dinars) per day.

The Labor Code sets a standard 48-hour workweek for most sectors and requires one 24-hour rest period. The standard workweek is 40 hours in the energy, transportation, petrochemical, and metallurgy industries.

Regional labor inspectors are responsible for enforcing standards. They inspect most firms about once every 2 years. However, the Government often encounters difficulty in enforcing the minimum wage law, particularly in nonunionized sectors of the economy. Moreover, more than 240,000 workers are employed in the informal sector, which falls outside the purview of labor legislation.

The Ministry of Social Affairs has responsibility for enforcing health and safety standards in the workplace. There are special government regulations covering such hazardous occupations as mining, petroleum engineering, and construction. Working conditions and standards tend to be better in firms that are export-oriented than in those producing exclusively for the domestic market. Workers are free to remove themselves from dangerous situations without jeopardizing their employment, and they may take legal action against employers who retaliate against them for exercising this right.

UNITED ARAB EMIRATES

The United Arab Emirates (UAE) is a federation of seven Emirates established in 1971. None has any democratically elected institutions or political parties. Each emirate retains control over its own oil and mineral wealth and some aspects of defense and internal security, although the Federal Government asserts primacy in most matters of law and government. Traditional rule in the emirates has generally been patriarchal, with political allegiance defined in terms of loyalty to the tribal leaders.

Political leaders in the emirates are not elected, but citizens may express their concerns directly to their leaders via traditional mechanisms, such as the open majlis, or council. In accordance with the 1971 Provisional Constitution, the seven emirate rulers constitute a Federal Supreme Council, the highest legislative and executive body. The Council selects a President and Vice President from its membership; the President in turn appoints the Prime Minister and Cabinet. The Constitution provides that the Council meets annually, although individual leaders meet frequently in more traditional settings. The Cabinet manages the Federation on a day-to-day basis.

Each emirate maintains its own police force, but only the Federal Government and the Emirate of Dubai have independent internal security organizations.

The UAE has a free market economy based on oil and gas production, trade, and light manufacturing. The Government owns the majority share of the petroleum production enterprise in the largest emirate, Abu Dhabi. The Emirate of Dubai is likewise an oil exporter, as well as a growing financial and commercial center in the Gulf. The remaining five emirates have negligible petroleum or other resources and therefore depend in varying degrees on federal government subsidies, particularly for basic services such as health care, electricity, water, and education. The economy provides citizens with a high per capita income, but it is heavily dependent on foreign workers, who comprise at least 80 percent of the general population.

The Government continued to restrict human rights in a number of areas; e.g., denial of the right of citizens to change their government, the right to a speedy trial, and limitations on the freedoms of speech, press, assembly, association, and worker rights. Women continue to make progress in education and in the work force, but some types of discrimination persist. The press continued to avoid direct criticism of the Government and exercised self-censorship.

RESPECT FOR HUMAN RIGHTS

Section 1. Respect for the Integrity of the Person, Including Freedom From:

   a. *Political and Other Extrajudicial Killing.*—There were no reports of political or other extrajudicial killings.

   b. *Disappearance.*—There were no reports of politically motivated disappearances.

   c. *Torture and Other Cruel, Inhuman, or Degrading Treatment or Punishment.*—There were no reports of torture. The Provisional Constitution prohibits torture or degrading treatment. There are consistent but unconfirmed reports from foreign prisoners of beatings and coerced confessions by police during the initial detention. The Government has conducted internal investigations of these reports. These inquiries found the reports to be groundless. Shari'a courts frequently impose flogging (except in Dubai) on Muslims found guilty of adultery, prostitution, and drug and alcohol abuse. In practice, flogging is administered in accordance with Shari'a so as to prevent major or permanent injuries. The individual administering the lashing traditionally holds a Koran under the arm and swings the whip using the forearm only. According to press accounts, punishments for adultery and prostitution have ranged from 80 to 200 lashes. Individuals convicted of drunkenness have been sentenced to 80 lashes.

The Federal Supreme Court ruled in 1993 that convictions in the Shari'a courts do not necessarily require the imposition of Shari'a penalties on non-Muslims, but sentences have been carried out in a few cases.

No amputations were known to have been carried out.

In central prisons holding long-term inmates, cells may hold 8 to 10 prisoners. They are provided with food, medical care, and adequate sanitation facilities but sleep on blankets on concrete floors. The central prisons are not air-conditioned during the intense heat and humidity of the summer. Prisoners normally may receive visitors up to three times each week and may also make occasional telephone calls.

   d. *Arbitrary Arrest, Detention, or Exile.*—The Provisional Constitution prohibits arrest, search, detention, or imprisonment except in accordance with the law. The laws of each emirate prohibit arrest or search without probable cause.

Under the Criminal Procedures Code, the police must report arrests within 48 hours to the Attorney General, who must determine within the next 24 hours whether to charge, release, or order further detention pending an investigation. The Attorney General may order detainees held for up to 21 days without charge. After that time, the authorities must obtain a court order for further detention without charge.

Although the code does not specify a right to a speedy trial, authorities bring detainees to trial in reasonable time. Trials may last a substantial period of time, depending on the seriousness of the charges, number of witnesses, and availability of judges. For example, one drug trafficking case involving two U.S. citizens has been in the trial phase for over 1 year. There is no formal system of bail, but the authorities may temporarily release detainees who deposit money or an important document such as a passport. The law permits incommunicado detention, but there is no evidence that it is practiced. Defendants in cases involving loss of life, including involuntary manslaughter, may be denied release in accordance with the local custom of protecting the defendant from the victim's aggrieved family. Bail is usually permitted, however, after payment of "diya', i.e., financial compensation paid for death or injury cases.

The Provisional Constitution prohibits exile, which is not practiced.

   e. *Denial of Fair Public Trial.*—The Provisional Constitution provides for the independence of the judiciary. There is a dual system of Shari'a (Islamic) and civil (secular) courts. The civil courts are generally part of the federal system and are answerable to the Federal Supreme Court, located in Abu Dhabi, which has the power of judicial review as well as original jurisdiction in disputes between emirates or between the Federal Government and individual emirates. Courts and other parts of the judicial system in the Emirate of Dubai tend to maintain independence from the federal system.

The Shari'a courts are administered by each emirate but are also answerable to the Federal Supreme Court. In 1994 the President decreed that the Shari'a courts, and not the civil courts, would have the authority to try almost all types of criminal cases. The decree did not affect the emirates of Dubai, Umm Al-Qaiwain, and Ras Al-Khaimah which have lower courts independent of the federal system.

Legal counsel may represent defendants in both court systems. Under the new Criminal Procedures Code, the accused has a right to counsel in all cases involving a capital crime or possible life imprisonment. Only the Emirate of Dubai has a public defender's office. If the defendant is indigent, the Government will provide counsel. In Dubai, however, the Government provides indigents counsel only in felony cases. The Supreme Court ruled in 1993 that a defendant in an appeals case has a "fundamental right" to select his attorney and that this right supersedes a judge's power to appoint an attorney for the defendant.

Defendants are presumed innocent until proven guilty. There are no jury trials. A single judge normally renders the verdict in each case, whether in Shari'a or civil courts; three judges sit for Dubai felony cases. All trials are public, except national security cases and those deemed by the judge likely to harm public morality. Most judges are foreign nationals, primarily from other Arab countries; however, the Ministry of Justice has trained some UAE citizens as judges and prosecutors.

Each court system has an appeal process. Death sentences may be appealed to the ruler of the emirate in which the offense was committed or to the President of the Federation. Non-Muslims tried for criminal offenses in Shari'a courts may receive civil penalties at the discretion of the judge. Shari'a penalties imposed on non-Muslims may be overturned or modified by a higher court.

The Office of the President in Abu Dhabi Emirate (also known as the Diwan), following the traditional prerogatives of a local ruler, maintains the practice of reviewing many types of criminal and civil offenses (such as alcohol use, drug-related cases, firearm use, cases involving personal injury, and cases affecting tribal harmony) before cases are released to the prosecutor's office. The Diwan also reviews sentences passed by judges and reserves the right to return cases to the courts on appeal. The Diwan's involvement leads to long delays prior to and following the judicial process, causing prisoners to remain in prison after they have completed their sentence. In a recent case, a prisoner served twice her sentence of 2 months and was only released after foreign embassy intervention. Although there are reports of intervention by other emirates' rulers in specific cases of personal interest, it does not appear to be done routinely.

The military has its own court system based on Western military judicial practice. Military tribunals try only military personnel. There is no separate national security court system. In Dubai convicted criminals are eligible for executive pardon, often based on humanitarian grounds, once they have served at least half of their sentence.

There were no reports of political prisoners.

f. *Arbitrary Interference with Privacy, Family, Home, or Correspondence.*—The Provisional Constitution prohibits entry into homes without the owner's permission, except in accordance with the law. Although the police may enter homes without a warrant and without demonstrating probable cause, an officer's actions in searching premises are subject to review, and he is subject to disciplinary action if he acts irresponsibly. Officials other than a police officer must have a court order to enter a private home. Local custom and practice place a high value on privacy, and entry into private homes without the owner's permission is rare. There is no known surveillance of private correspondence.

Section 2. Respect for Civil Liberties, Including:

a. *Freedom of Speech and Press.*—Although the Provisional Constitution provides for freedom of speech, most people, especially foreign nationals, refrain from criticizing the Government in public. All published material is subject to Federal Law 15 of 1988, which stipulates that all publications, whether books or periodicals, should be licensed by the Ministry of Education. It also governs content and contains a list of proscribed subjects. Mindful of these provisions, journalists censor themselves when reporting on government policy, the ruling families, national security, religion, and relations with neighboring states.

Many of the local English and Arabic language newspapers are privately owned but receive government subsidies. Foreign publications are routinely subjected to censorship before distribution.

All television and radio stations are government owned and conform to government reporting guidelines. Satellite receiving dishes are widespread and provide access to international broadcasts without apparent censorship. Censors at the Ministry of Information and Culture review imported newspapers, periodicals, books, films, and videos and ban any material considered pornographic, violent, derogatory to Islam, favorable to Israel, unduly critical of friendly countries, or critical of the Government or the ruling families.

The unwritten but generally recognized ban on criticism of the Government also restricts academic freedom, although in recent years academics have been more open in their criticism.

b. *Freedom of Peaceful Assembly and Association.*—These freedoms are tightly restricted. Organized public gatherings require a government permit. Each emirate determines its own practice on public gatherings. Some emirates are relatively tolerant of seminars and conferences on sensitive subjects.

Citizens normally confine their political discussions to the numerous gatherings or majlis, held in private homes. There are no restrictions on such gatherings. However, private associations must follow the Government's censorship guidelines if they publish any material. Unauthorized political organizations are prohibited.

c. *Freedom of Religion.*—Islam is the official religion of all the emirates. Citizens are predominantly Sunni Muslims, but Shi'a Muslims are also free to worship and maintain mosques. In 1993 the Emirate of Dubai placed private mosques under the control of its Department of Islamic Affairs and Endowments. This move gave the Government control over the appointment of preachers and the conduct of their work. Throughout the emirates, most mosques are government funded or subsidized, and the Ministry of Awqaf and Religious Affairs ensures that clergy do not deviate from approved topics in their sermons.

Non-Muslims are free to practice their religion but may not proselytize publicly or distribute religious literature. Major cities have Christian churches and Hindu and Sikh temples, some built on land donated by the ruling families. Other religious communities (mostly expatriates residing in Dubai and Abu Dhabi) include Ismailis, Parsis, and Iranian Baha'is. The Government permits foreign clergy to minister to expatriate congregations. Non-Muslim religious groups are permitted to engage in private charitable activities and to send their children to private schools.

d. *Freedom of Movement Within the Country, Foreign Travel, Emigration, and Repatriation.*—There are no limitations on freedom of movement or relocation within the country, except for security areas such as defense and oil installations.

Unrestricted foreign travel and emigration are permitted to male citizens except those involved in financial disputes under adjudication. A husband may bar his wife and children from leaving the country. All citizens have the right to return. There is a small population of stateless residents, many of whom have lived in the UAE for more than one generation. They are Bedouins or the descendants of Bedouins who are unable to prove that they are of UAE origin.

Citizens are not restricted in seeking or changing employment. However, foreign nationals in specific occupations, primarily professional, may not change employers without first leaving the country for 6 months. This law is not often enforced. Foreign nationals involved in disputes with UAE citizen employers can be blacklisted by the employer with UAE immigration authorities, effectively preventing their return.

The Government has not formulated a formal policy regarding refugees, asylees, or first asylum. It may detain persons seeking refugee status, particularly non-Arabs, while they await resettlement in a third country. There is no formal procedure for naturalization, although foreign women receive citizenship by marriage to a UAE citizen, and anyone may receive a passport by presidential fiat.

Section 3. Respect for Political Rights: The Right of Citizens to Change Their Government

There are no democratically elected institutions, and citizens do not have the right to change their government or to form political parties. Although there are consultative councils at the federal and emirate levels, most executive and legislative power is in the hands of the Federal Supreme Council. The seven emirate rulers, their extended families, and those persons and families to whom they are allied by historical ties, marriage, or common interest wield most political power in their own emirates. Decisions at the federal level are generally made by consensus of the sheikhs of the seven emirates and leading families.

A federal consultative body, called the Federal National Council (FNC), consists of advisers appointed by the rulers of each emirate. The FNC has no legislative authority but may question ministers and make policy recommendations to the Cabinet. Its sessions are usually open to the public.

The choice of a new emirate ruler falls to the ruling family in consultation with other prominent tribal figures. By tradition, rulers and ruling families are presumed to have the right to rule, but their incumbency ultimately depends on the quality of their leadership and their responsiveness to their subjects' needs. Emirate rulers are accessible, in varying degrees, to citizens who have a problem or a request.

Tradition rather than law has limited the political role of women. Women are free to hold government positions, but there are few women in senior positions. Although the small Shi'a minority has enjoyed commercial success, few Shi'a Muslims have top positions in the Federal Government.

Section 4. Governmental Attitude Regarding International and Nongovernmental Investigation of Alleged Violations of Human Rights

There are no independent human rights groups. Government restrictions on freedom of the press and public association make it difficult for such groups to investigate and publicly criticize the Government's human rights restrictions. A human rights section exists within Dubai Emirate's police force to monitor allegations of human rights abuses.

A few informal public discussions of human rights have taken place in recent years, such as a seminar in December 1992 and an international symposium in late 1993. These events, along with some press coverage of selected local human rights problems, have led to a small increase in public awareness of human rights.

Section 5. Discrimination Based on Race, Sex, Religion, Disability, Language, or Social Status

The Provisional Constitution provides for equality before the law with regard to race, nationality, religious beliefs, or social status. However, there is institutional and cultural discrimination based on sex, nationality, and religion.

Women.—There are reported cases of spousal abuse. When reported, the local police authorities may take action to protect women from abuse. The laws protect women from verbal abuse or harassment from men, and violators are subject to criminal action. There continue to be credible reports of abuse of female domestic servants by some UAE and foreign employers (see Section 6.e.).

Most women play a subordinate role in this family centered society because of early marriages and traditional attitudes about women's activities. Husbands may bar their wives and children from leaving the country (see Section 2.d.), and a married woman may not accept employment without her husband's written consent. Islamic law is applied in cases of divorce. Mothers receive custody of their children under 7 years of age. Older children live with their fathers unless judicial authorities decide otherwise. Courts usually grant custody to the father regardless of the child's age in divorce cases. A woman who remarries forfeits her right to the custody of children from a previous marriage. Islamic law permits polygyny.

Women are restricted from holding majority shares in most businesses. A woman's property is not commingled with that of her husband. Women who work outside the home do not receive equal benefits, such as housing, and may face discrimination in promotion. In June 1995, the UAE Cabinet provisionally extended paid maternity leave for citizen women in the private sector to 3 months at full pay from 45 days, and up to 1 year's leave at half pay and a second year's leave at quarter pay.

Opportunities for women have grown in government service, education, private business, and health services. According to UAE government figures, 19.4 percent of the country's work force in 1995 was female. The Federal Government has publicly encouraged women to join the work force, guaranteeing public sector employment for all who apply. Cultural barriers and the lack of economic necessity have limited female participation. A symposium promoting the rights of women in the labor force was held in October. Participants called for increasing rights granted to women including the elimination of the requirement that a husband give approval before his wife can work.

Women continue to make rapid progress in education. They constitute over 75 percent of the student body at the National University in Al-Ain, largely because women, unlike men, rarely study abroad.

Women are officially encouraged to continue their education, and government-sponsored women's centers provide adult education and technical training courses. The Federal Armed Forces accept female volunteers, who may enroll in a special training course started after the Gulf War. The Dubai Police College recruits women, many of whom are deployed at airports, immigration offices, and women's prisons. As of mid-1995, about 85 women had graduated from the college.

The law prohibits cohabitation by unmarried couples. The Government may imprison and deport noncitizen women if they bear children out of wedlock. In the event that the courts sentence women to prison for such an offense, local authorities will hold the newborn children in a special facility until the mother's release and deportation. Children may remain in this facility longer in the event of a custody dispute.

Children.—The Government is committed to the welfare of children. Children who are citizens receive free health care, free education, guaranteed housing, and other perquisites of citizenship. A family may also be eligible to receive aid from the Ministry of Labor and Social Welfare for sons and daughters who are under the age of 18 or unmarried or disabled. There is no pattern of societal child abuse.

People With Disabilities.—There is no federal legislation requiring accessibility for the disabled. However, the Ministry of Labor and Social Affairs sponsors centers which provide facilities and services to the disabled. Services range from monthly social aid funds, special education, and transportation assistance to sending a team to the Special Olympics.

National/Racial/Ethnic Minorities.—Discrimination based on national origin, while not legally sanctioned, is prevalent (see Section 2.d.). Employment, immigration, and security policy, as well as cultural attitudes towards foreign workers, are conditioned by national origin.

Section 6. Worker Rights

a. *The Right of Association.*—There are no unions and no strikes. The law does not grant workers the right to organize unions or to strike. Foreign workers, who make up the bulk of the work force, risk deportation if they attempt to organize unions or to strike.

Since July 1995, the UAE has been suspended from the U.S. Overseas Private Investment Corporation insurance programs because of the Government's lack of compliance with internationally recognized worker rights standards.

b. *The Right to Organize and Bargain Collectively.*—The law does not grant workers the right to engage in collective bargaining, which is not practiced. Workers in the industrial and service sectors are normally employed under contracts that are subject to review by the Ministry of Labor and Social Affairs. The purpose of the review is to ensure that the pay will satisfy the employee's basic needs and secure a means of living. For the resolution of work-related disputes, workers must rely on conciliation committees organized by the Ministry of Labor and Social Affairs or on special labor courts.

Labor laws do not cover government employees, domestic servants, and agricultural workers. The latter two groups face considerable difficulty in obtaining assistance to resolve disputes with employers. While any worker may seek redress through the courts, this process puts a heavy financial burden on those in lower income brackets.

In Dubai's Jebel Ali Free Zone, the same labor laws apply as in the rest of the country.

c. *Prohibition of Forced or Compulsory Labor.*—Forced or compulsory labor is illegal and not practiced. However, some unscrupulous employment agents bring foreign workers to the UAE under conditions approaching indenture.

d. *Minimum Age for Employment of Children.*—Labor regulations prohibit employment of persons under the age of 15 and have special provisions for employing those 15 to 18 years of age. The Department of Labor enforces the regulations. Other regulations permit employers to engage only adult foreign workers. In 1993 the Government prohibited the employment of children under the age of 15 as camel jockeys and of jockeys who do not weigh more than 45 kilograms. The Camel Racing Association is responsible for enforcing these rules. However, children under the age of 15 working as camel jockeys have still been observed. Otherwise, child labor is not permitted.

e. *Acceptable Conditions of Work.*—There is no legislated or administrative minimum wage. Supply and demand determine compensation. However, according to the Ministry of Labor and Social Affairs, there is an unofficial, unwritten minimum wage rate which would afford a worker and family a minimal standard of living. As noted in Section 6.b., the Labor and Social Affairs Ministry reviews labor contracts and does not approve any contract that stipulates a clearly unacceptable wage.

The standard workday and workweek are 8 hours a day, 6 days per week, but these standards are not strictly enforced. Certain types of workers, notably domestic servants, may be obliged to work longer than the mandated standard hours. The law also provides for a minimum of 24 days per year of annual leave plus 10 national and religious holidays. In addition, manual workers are not required to do outdoor work when the temperature exceeds 45 degrees Celsius (112 degrees Fahrenheit).

Most foreign workers receive either employer-provided housing or housing allowances, medical care, and homeward passage from their employers. Most foreign workers do not earn the minimum salary of $1,090 per month (or $817 per month, if a housing allowance is provided in addition to the salary) required to obtain residency permits for their families. Employers have the option to petition for a 6-month ban from the work force against any foreign employee who leaves his job without fulfilling the terms of his contract.

The Ministry of Health, the Ministry of Labor and Social Affairs, municipalities, and civil defense units enforce health and safety standards. The Government requires every large industrial concern to employ a certified occupational safety officer. An injured worker is entitled to fair compensation. Health standards are not uniformly observed in the housing camps provided for foreign workers. Workers' jobs are not protected if they remove themselves from what they consider to be unsafe working conditions. However, the Ministry of Labor and Social Affairs may require employers to reinstate workers dismissed for not performing unsafe work. All workers have the right to lodge grievances with Ministry officials, who make an effort to investigate all complaints. However, the Ministry is understaffed and underbudgeted; complaints and compensation claims are backlogged.

Rulings on complaints may be appealed within the Ministry and ultimately to the courts. However, many workers choose not to protest for fear of reprisals or deportation. The press periodically carries reports of abuses suffered by domestic servants, particularly women, at the hands of some employers. Allegations have included excessive work hours, nonpayment of wages, and verbal and physical abuse.

Newspaper reports continue to highlight the difficult conditions of domestic workers. However, there have been no cases in 1996 as highly publicized as the 1995 Balabagan case. (Sarah Balabagan was the Filipina maid convicted of killing her employer, who she claimed had raped her.) The UAE Government quietly released Balabagan in July at the completion of her sentence.

YEMEN

The Republic of Yemen, comprising the former (northern) Yemen Arab Republic and (southern) People's Democratic Republic of Yemen, was proclaimed in 1990. Following a brief but bloody civil war in mid-1994, the country was reunified under the rule of the Sanaa-based government. Later in 1994, a new postwar governing coalition was formed, composed of the General People's Congress (GPC) and the Yemeni Grouping for Reform (Islaah). The Yemeni Socialist Party (YSP), formerly the main party of the south and a previous coalition partner, is now an opposition party.

Lieutenant General Ali Abdullah Salih is the President and leader of the GPC. He was elected by the legislature in 1994 to a 5-year term. However, the Constitution provides that henceforth the President will be elected by popular vote from at least two candidates selected by the legislature. The 301-seat House of Representatives was elected in 1993—the first multiparty Parliament elected by popular vote and universal suffrage. The next parliamentary elections are scheduled for April 1997. The Parliament is not yet an effective counterweight to executive authority; real political power rests with a few leaders, particularly the President. The judiciary, nominally independent, is severely hampered by corruption, executive branch interference, and frequent failure of the authorities to impose sentences.

The primary state security apparatus is the Political Security Organization (PSO) which reports directly to the President. It is independent of the Ministry of Interior and its leaders are all military officers. The Criminal Investigative Department (CID) of the police conducts most criminal investigations and makes most arrests. The Central Security Organization (CSO), a part of the Ministry of Interior, maintains a paramilitary force. Members of the security forces, particularly those in the PSO, committed human rights abuses.

Yemen is a poor country with an emerging market-based economy that is impeded by excessive government regulation and unchecked corruption. Its annual per capita gross national product is estimated at $340. Oil is the primary source of foreign exchange, but remittances from Yemenis working abroad (primarily in Saudi Arabia) are also important. Remittances were sharply reduced after Saudi Arabia and other Gulf states expelled up to 850,000 Yemeni workers during the Gulf War because of the Government's pro-Iraq position. The Gulf States also suspended most assistance programs, and much Western aid was reduced.

The human rights situation changed little in 1996. Problems include violence by security forces, which in one incident lead to a killing; arbitrary arrest and detention, especially of people still regarded as separatists; significant limitations on citizens' rights to change their government; infringements on the freedom of speech and the press; judicial corruption and inefficiency; and widespread discrimination based on sex, race, disability, and to a lesser extent, religion. The Government rarely punished human rights abusers. Government response to demonstrations in the southern city of Mukallah in June resulted in several deaths, at least one of which occurred while the victim was in custody. PSO officers have broad discretion over perceived national security issues, and, despite constitutional constraints, routinely detain citizens for questioning, sometimes mistreat detainees, monitor their activities, and search their homes. Prison conditions are poor. Female genital mutilation is practiced to an undetermined extent by some families; although publicly discouraged, it is not prohibited by the authorities.

RESPECT FOR HUMAN RIGHTS

Section 1. Respect for the Integrity of the Person, Including Freedom From:

a. *Political and Other Extrajudicial Killing.*—Police killed several persons during demonstrations on June 11 in the city of Mukallah. In addition, one young man active in the Yemen Socialist Party (YSP) died in custody following his arrest for participating in the demonstrations. His body was buried without being returned to his family. The Government has not assessed any blame nor punished any member of the security forces for this death.

There were no other reports of political or extrajudicial killings.

b. *Disappearance.*—Security forces continue to arrest and detain citizens for varying periods of time without charge or notification to concerned families. Many detainees, especially in southern governorates, are associated with the YSP and accused of being separatists. Most such disappearances are temporary, and detainees are released within months. A southern poet and singer whose recorded songs satirically criticized government leaders was detained in April without charge or notification to his family. He was released in August.

Hundreds of cases of disappearances dating since the 1970's, implicating the former governments of both north and south Yemen, remain unresolved.

Some tribes, seeking to bring their concerns to the attention of the Government, kidnap and hold hostages. Victims include foreign businessmen and tourists, as well as Yemenis. Foreign victims are rarely injured. The authorities have succeeded in obtaining the fairly quick release of foreign hostages.

c. *Torture and Other Cruel, Inhuman, or Degrading Treatment or Punishment.*—The Constitution, which asserts that Shari'a (Islamic law) "is the source of all legislation," is ambiguous on its prohibition of cruel or inhuman punishment. It states that the Government may not impose illegal punishments—a formulation that could be interpreted as permitting amputations according to Shari'a. There were, however, no reports of amputations.

Although there is no evidence of the systematic use of torture in detention facilities, arresting authorities are known to use force during interrogations, especially of those arrested for violent crimes. A young man arrested for participating in a political demonstration died in custody (see Section 1.a.). Authorities still use leg-irons and shackles, and flogging is occasionally inflicted as punishment for minor crimes. A woman detained in Mukallah in May complained to authorities that she was raped by a police officer while being interrogated. Upon making her complaint, she was arrested, and charged with prostitution. She was acquitted at her August trial while the officer accused of assaulting her was convicted of "abuse of authority" and sentenced to prison. The arrest caused riots, which resulted in several deaths.

Prison conditions do not meet internationally recognized minimum standards. Prisons are overcrowded, sanitary conditions poor, and food and health care inadequate. Inmates must depend on relatives for food and medicine. Prison authorities and guards often exact money from prisoners and even refuse to release prisoners until family members pay a bribe. Conditions are equally bad in women's prisons, where children are likely to be incarcerated along with their mothers. All prison guards are male.

The Government tightly controls access to detention facilities. Nonetheless, it permits most impartial observers to visit prisoners and detainees, including representatives of the International Committee of the Red Cross (ICRC). Nongovernmental organizations (NGO's) have distributed food, medical supplies, and clothing directly to prisoners.

d. *Arbitrary Arrest, Detention, or Exile.*—According to the law, detainees must be arraigned within 24 hours of arrest or released. The judge or prosecuting attorney must inform the accused of the basis for the arrest and decide whether detention is required. In no case may a detainee be held longer than 7 days without a court order. Despite these constitutional and other legal provisions, arbitrary arrest and prolonged detention without charge are common practices. Such practices often result, in effect, in the disappearance of such persons (see Section 1.b.).

Detainees have the right to inform their families of their arrests and may decline to answer questions without an attorney present. There are also provisions for bail. In practice many authorities respect these rights only if bribed.

The Government has failed to ensure that detainees and prisoners are incarcerated only in authorized detention facilities. The Ministry of Interior and the PSO reportedly operate extrajudicial detention facilities. Unauthorized, private prisons also exist in tribal areas, where the central Government exercises very little authority. People detained in these prisons are often held for strictly personal reasons and without trial or sentencing.

In cases where a criminal suspect is at large, security forces sometimes detain a relative while the suspect is being sought. The detention may continue while the concerned families negotiate compensation for the alleged wrongdoing.

Thousands of people have been imprisoned for years without documentation concerning charges against them, their trials, or sentences. While a few such cases have been redressed through the efforts of the Yemeni Human Rights Organization, the authorities have done nothing to investigate or resolve the problem. The authorities continue to detain politically active persons for limited periods of time.

At the end of the 1994 civil war, the President pardoned nearly all who fought against the central Government, including military personnel and most leaders of the unrecognized, secessionist Democratic Republic of Yemen (DRY).

The Government does not use forced exile. However, the Government denied the amnesty to only the 16 most senior leaders of the DRY, who fled abroad. Although they were technically not forced into exile, they are subject to arrest if they return. After more than a year of postponment, the Attorney General in November summoned the 15 to be tried.

e. *Denial of Fair Public Trial.*—The Constitution provides for an autonomous judiciary and independent judges, however, the judiciary is not fully independent. Judges are appointed by the executive branch of government, and some have been reassigned or removed from office following rulings against the Government. Many litigants maintain that a judge's social ties and susceptibility to bribery sometimes have greater influence on the verdict than the law or facts of the case. Others maintain that judges appointed since mid-1994 are poorly trained and that those closely associated with the Government often render decisions favorable to it. The judiciary is further hampered by the frequent reluctance of the authorities to implement sentences.

There are 2 types of courts: Islamic law or Shari'a courts, which try criminal cases and adjudicate civil disputes (such as divorce and inheritance cases), and commercial courts. There are no jury trials under Shari'a. Criminal cases are adjudicated by a judge who plays an active role in questioning witnesses and the accused. Defense attorneys are allowed to counsel their clients, address the court, and examine witnesses. Defendants, including those in commercial courts, have the right to appeal their sentences. Trials are public. However, both Shari'a and Commercial courts may conduct closed sessions "for reasons of public security or morals." foreign litigants in commercial disputes have complained of biased rulings.

Female judges who worked in the south prior to the civil war have been reappointed to positions. There are no female judges in the north.

There were no reports of political prisoners.

f. *Arbitrary Interference with Privacy, Family, Home, or Correspondence.*—Despite constitutional provisions against government interference with privacy, security forces routinely search homes and private offices, monitor telephones, read personal mail, and otherwise intrude into personal matters for alleged security reasons. Such activities are conducted without legally issued warrants or judicial supervision. Security forces regularly monitor telephone conversations and have interfered with the telephone service of government critics and opponents. Security forces sometimes detain relatives of suspects (see Section 1.d.).

Section 2. Respect for Civil Liberties, Including:

a. *Freedom of Speech and Press.*—The Constitution restricts the freedom of speech and press by allowing it only "within the limits of the law." Although many citizens are uninhibited in their private discussions of domestic and foreign policies, some are cautious, believing that they may be harassed for publicly expressed criticism of the Government.

The relative freedom of the press experienced prior to the 1994 civil war has not been fully reestablished. Although there were fewer official restrictions on newspapers in 1996 than in 1995, a level of government pressure on independent and political party journals continues that was not present before the civil war.

The Ministry of Information influences the media by its ownership of the television and radio companies, printing presses, and by subsidies to certain newspapers. The Government selects the items to be covered in news broadcasts and does not permit broadcast reporting critical of the Government. Even televised debates in the Parliament are edited to delete the most biting commentary on the Government.

Although newspapers are allowed to criticize the Government, journalists sometimes censor themselves, especially when writing on such sensitive issues as government policies toward the southern governorates, relations with Saudi Arabia and other foreign governments, or official corruption. The penalties for exceeding these self-imposed limits can be arrest for slander or libel, dismissal from employment, or extralegal harassment. In 1995 the Ministry of Information sought a court order to close the opposition newspaper Al-Shura. The case was decided in favor of the paper, which resumed publication in June.

The Government permitted the independent newspaper Al-Ayam, whose publication had been limited to Sanaa at the end of 1995 to resume publication in Aden. The paper was also allowed to import a printing press this year, the first privately-owned newspaper in Yemen to own its own press. Despite these positive developments, the paper came under pressure to comply with the standards of expression adhered to by government papers.

The independent English-language weekly, the Yemen Times, has frequently criticized the Government. The management has been periodically subjected to anonymous threats of violence, and government authorities have interfered with the paper's operations.

The newspaper Al-Tajammu was denied access to government presses for a period of 4 weeks after publishing a story criticizing government policies toward Hadramaut Governorate, where there had been increased civil disorder.

There were reports throughout the year of journalists—particularly in the south—being subjected to minor physical harassment and short periods of arbitrary incarceration. One such journalist, writing for the YSP paper Al-Thawry, was beaten by soldiers in the Parliament building in July.

Customs officials confiscate foreign publications regarded as pornographic or objectionable because of religious or political content. In June the Ministry of Information began routinely delaying the distribution of international Arabic-language dailies, such as Al-Hayat and Al-Sharq Al-Awsat, in an apparent effort to decrease their sales in Yemen. On a few occasions, the Ministry has banned the entry of international Arabic publications. In almost all cases, this was because they carried news about, or statements by, leaders of the 1994 secession attempt.

Academic freedom is restricted by the presence of security officials on university campuses and at most intellectual forums. Government informers monitor the activities of professors and students. The authorities review prospective university administrators and professors for their political acceptability before they are hired. In addition to Government activities, individuals identified with various Islamic political groups are also believed to gather information on the activities of professors and students.

b. *Freedom of Peaceful Assembly and Association.*—Although there are no constitutional restrictions on the right to peacefully assemble, government informers monitor meetings and assemblies.

Demonstrations in May and September in Mukallah protesting government actions deteriorated into violence which resulted in several shooting deaths of both demonstrators and security officers. At least one such demonstrator died in custody (see Section 1.a.).

The Constitution does provide for the right of association. Associations must obtain an operating license from the Ministry of Labor and Social Affairs, usually a routine matter.

c. *Freedom of Religion.*—Islam is the state religion, and there are restrictions on the practice of other religions. Virtually all citizens are Muslims, either of the Zaydi branch of Shi'a Islam or the Shafe'ei branch of Sunni Islam. There are also some Ismailis in the north. Private Islamic organizations may maintain ties to pan-Islamic organizations and operate schools, but the Government monitors their activities.

Most Christians are foreign residents, except for a few families of Indian origin in Aden. There are several churches and Hindu temples holding regular services in Aden, but no non-Muslim public places of worship in the former north Yemen. Church services are, however, regularly held without harassment in private homes or facilities such as schools.

Nearly all of Yemen's once sizable Jewish population have emigrated. There are some restrictions on those Jews who remain (see Section 5).

d. *Freedom of Movement Within the Country, Foreign Travel, Emigration, and Repatriation.*—The Government does not obstruct domestic travel, although the army and security forces maintain checkpoints on major roads. Likewise, the Government does not obstruct foreign travel or the right to emigrate and return. Women must obtain permission from a male relative before applying for a passport or departing the country, although enforcement of this restriction is irregular. The Constitution prohibits the extradition of a citizen to any country.

The Government cooperates with the office of United Nations High Commissioner for Refugees (UNHCR) and other humanitarian organizations in assisting refugees. The Government has provided de facto first asylum to approximately 30,000 in 1996. There are no reports of forced return of persons to a country where they feared persecution. The UNHCR is negotiating with the Government to improve the living conditions of the more than 50,000 Somali refugees in Yemen.

Section 3. Respect for Political Rights: The Right of Citizens to Change Their Government

Although the Government is accountable to the Parliament, there are significant limitations on the ability of the people to change their government. Although international observers judged the 1993 parliamentary elections as generally free and fair, to date the Parliament is not an effective counterweight to executive authority; it does little more than debate issues. Decisionmaking and real political power still rest in the hands of relatively few leaders, particularly the President.

The President has the authority to introduce legislation and promulgate laws by decree when Parliament is not in session. Decrees must be approved by Parliament 30 days after reconvening. In theory, if a decree is not approved, it does not become law; in practice, a decree remains in effect even if not approved. The President appoints the Prime Minister, who forms the Government. The Cabinet comprises 24 ministers; the majority of ministers come from the GPC and the remainder from Islaah.

In some governorates, tribal leaders retain considerable discretion in the interpretation and enforcement of the law. Central government authority in these areas is often weak.

There is a functioning multiparty system. All parties must be registered in accordance with the Political Parties Law of 1991, which stipulates that each party must have at least 75 founders and at least 2,500 members. In preparation for the 1997 parliamentary elections, 10 political parties have been registered under the law with 6 more applications pending at year's end.

The Constitution prohibits the establishment of parties that are contrary to Islam, oppose the goals of the Yemeni revolution, or violate Yemen's international commitments. The Government provides financial support to all parties represented in Parliament. The parties are permitted to publish their own newspapers.

Although women may vote and hold office, these rights are limited by cultural customs. Only 2 women have been elected to the 301-member Parliament, and few hold senior leadership positions in the Government or political parties.

Section 4. Governmental Attitude Regarding International and Nongovernmental Investigation of Alleged Violations of Human Rights

The Yemeni Human Rights Organization (YHRO) is the best known local nongovernmental human rights group. It is headquartered in Sanaa with branches in seven other cities. While the Government does not overtly restrict its activities, its senior staff are subject to petty harassment from the authorities and its work has subsequently decreased during the year. Another group, the Yemeni Organization for the Defense of Liberties and Human Rights, is based in Aden but has also been less active than in the past. There is a Human Rights Committee in Parliament, which has investigated some reports of human rights abuses. It suffers from lack of official and financial support and has no authority to do anything other than issue reports.

Amnesty International and Human Rights Watch observe Yemen closely. There is an International Committee of the Red Cross representative resident in Yemen. The Government has given these groups relatively broad access to government officials, records, refugee camps, and prisons.

Section 5. Discrimination Based on Race, Sex, Religion, Disability, Language, or Social Status

Prior to 1994, the Constitution stated that "no discrimination shall be practiced due to sex, color, racial origin, language, occupation, social status, or religious beliefs." However, as amended in 1994, the Constitution now states that "all citizens are equal in general rights and duties." There is widespread discrimination based on sex, race, disability, and to a lesser extent, religion.

Women.—Although spousal abuse occurs, it is undocumented and difficult to quantify. In Yemen's traditional society, an abused woman would be expected to take her complaints to a male relative (rather than the authorities) who would intercede on her behalf or provide her short-term sanctuary if required.

Women face significant restrictions imposed by law, social custom, and religion. Men are permitted to take as many as four wives, though few do so for economic reasons. The practice of dowry payments is widespread, despite efforts to limit the size of such payments. Husbands may divorce wives without justifying their action in court. Following a divorce, the family home and children (who are older than a certain age) are often awarded to the husband. Women also have the right to divorce, in accordance with the precepts of Shari'a. Women seeking to travel abroad must obtain permission to receive a passport and to travel from their husbands or fathers and are expected to be accompanied by male relatives.

Islamic law permits a Muslim man to marry a Christian or Jewish woman, but no Muslim woman may marry outside of Islam. Married women do not have the right to confer citizenship on their foreign-born spouses; they may, however, confer citizenship on children born in Yemen of foreign-born fathers.

An estimated 80 percent of women are illiterate, compared with approximately 35 percent of men. In general, women in the south are better educated and have had somewhat greater employment opportunities. Since the 1994 civil war, however, the number of working women in the south appears to have declined, in part due to the stagnant economy, but also because of increasing cultural pressure from the north. Nevertheless, female judges, magistrates, and prosecutors in southern governorates have been reappointed.

The Government has established a women's association to promote female education and civic responsibilities, and a nongovernmental organization has also been established for the same purpose.

Children.—While the Government has asserted its commitment to protecting children's rights, it lacks the resources necessary to ensure adequate health care, education, and welfare services for children.

Child marriage is common, especially in rural areas. Although the law requires that a girl be 15 years of age to marry, it is not enforced. Marriages of 13-year-old girls are not unusual. The Government has cooperated with foreign embassies in cases involving dual national girls brought back from overseas for forced marriages.

Female genital mutilation (FGM), which is widely condemned by international health experts as damaging to both physical and psychological health, is practiced by some Yemenis, particularly those of African origin living mainly in the coastal areas. It is not known to exist among the majority Zaydi and Shafi'i populations. There is no available information on its extent. While some government health workers actively and publically discourage the practice, the Government has not passed legislation outlawing it.

People With Disabilities.—There are distinct social prejudices against persons with mental and physical disabilities. The disabled often face discrimination in education and employment. The Government has not enacted legislation or otherwise mandated accessibility for the disabled nor provided special clinics or schools for them. Mentally ill patients, particularly those who commit crimes, are imprisoned and even shackled when there is no one to care for them. There is a charity project to construct separate detention facilities for mentally disabled prisoners.

Religious Minorities.—Apart from a small but undetermined number of Christians and Hindus in Aden, and a few Baha'is in the north, Jews are the only indigenous religious minority. Their numbers have diminished dramatically due to voluntary emigration. Jews are traditionally restricted to living in one section of a city or village and are often confined to a limited choice of employment, usually farming or handicrafts. Jews may, and do, own real property.

Christian clergy who minister to the foreign community are employed in teaching, social services, and health care. A hospital in Jibla operated by the Baptist Church has, in the past, experienced occasional threats and harassment from local Islamic extremists who feared that the hospital may be used to spread Christianity. Since an August 1995 incident of mob violence at the hospital, which was eventually controlled by the authorities, the hospital has not been threatened. Mother Theresa has active charity operations in three cities.

National/Racial/Ethnic Minorities.—Yemenis with a non-Yemeni parent, called "Muwalladin," may face discrimination in employment and in other areas. Persons seeking employment at Sanaa University or admission to the military academy must by law demonstrate that they have 2 Yemeni parents. Nonetheless, many senior government officials, including Members of Parliament and ministers, have only one Yemeni parent. In some cases, naturalization of the non-Yemeni parent is sufficient to overcome the "two-Yemeni parent" requirement.

A small group believed to be descendants of ancient Ethiopian occupiers of Yemen, who were later enslaved, are considered the lowest social class. Known as the "akhdam" (servants), they live in squalor and endure persistent social discrimination.

Section 6. Worker Rights

a. *The Right of Association.*—The Constitution provides that citizens have the right to form unions. A March 1995 law governs labor relations. It provides workers with the right to strike and equal labor rights for women, and it renews the freedom of workers to associate. The Labor Law does not stipulate a minimum membership for unions, nor does it limit them to a specific enterprise or firm. Thus, Yemenis may now associate by profession or trade.

The Yemeni Confederation of Labor Unions (YCLU) remains the sole national umbrella organization. The YCLU claims 350,000 members in 15 unions and denies any association with the Government, although it works closely with the Government to resolve labor disputes through negotiation. Observers suggest that the Government likely would not tolerate the establishment of an alternative labor federation unless it believed it to be in its best interests.

By law, civil servants and public sector workers, and some categories of farm workers, may not join unions. Only the General Assembly of the Yemeni Confederation of Labor Unions may dissolve unions.

Three strikes occured during the year; negotiated solutions resolved two of them. However, a strike by Hodeidah port workers against the private companies for which they work was declared illegal by the Government. The leaders were arrested and jailed, breaking the work action. The dispute eventually was resolved through negotiation and those imprisoned were released.

The International Labor Organization cited Yemen this year for not providing since 1994 required reports on the freedom of association, the application of ratified conventions, and the application of standards.

The Yemeni Confederation of Labor Unions is affiliated with the Confederation of Arab Trade Unions and the International Confederation of Free Trade Unions (ICFTU).

b. *The Right to Organize and Bargain Collectively.*—The new Labor Law provides workers with the right to organize and bargain collectively. All collective bargaining agreements must be deposited with and reviewed by the Ministry of Labor. Unions may negotiate wage settlements for their members and can resort to strikes or other actions to achieve their demands.

The law protects employees from antiunion discrimination. Employers do not have the right to dismiss an employee for union activities. Employees may appeal cases of antiunion discrimination to the Ministry of Labor. Employees may also take a case to the labor courts, which are often favorably disposed toward workers, especially if the employer is a foreign company.

There are no export processing zones.

c. *Prohibition of Forced or Compulsory Labor.*—The Constitution prohibits forced or compulsory labor. There were no reports of its practice.

d. *Minimum Age for Employment of Children.*—Because most Yemeni families feed themselves through subsistance agriculture, child labor is common. Even in urban areas, children may be observed working in stores, workshops, selling goods on the streets, and begging. The established minimum age for employment is 15 years of age in the private sector and 18 years of age in the public sector. By special permit, children the age of 12 to 15 may work. The Government rarely enforces these provisions, especially in rural and remote areas.

e. *Acceptable Conditions of Work.*—The Labor Law sets monthly and daily minimum wages, which are incredibly low (as little as $.80 per day (YR 100) and even these are not enforced. The minimum wage does not provide a worker and family with a decent standard of living. Inflation substantially eroded wages during the past few years, but it subsided in 1996.

The law specifies a 40-hour workweek with a maximum 8-hour workday, but many workshops and stores operate 10- to 12-hour shifts without penalty. The workweek for government employees is 35 hours, 6 hours per day, Saturday through Wednesday, and 5 hours on Thursday.

Workers have the right to remove themselves from dangerous work situations and can challenge dismissals in court. The law establishes workplace health and safety standards which the Ministry of Labor has the responsibility to enforce; however, the Ministry's budget does not provide sufficient resources to fulfill its obligations under the law. Some foreign-owned companies implement higher health, safety, and environmental standards than required in Yemen.

SOUTH ASIA

AFGHANISTAN*

Afghanistan in 1996 continued to experience civil war and political instability, although more of the country was free of fighting and violence than in past years. There was no central government. At year's end, the Pashtun-dominated ultra-conservative Islamic movement known as the Taliban had captured the capital of Kabul and expanded its control to over two-thirds of the country. General Abdul Rashid Dostam, an ethnic Uzbek, controlled several north-central provinces. After the loss of Kabul, former President Burhanuddin Rabbani and his military commander, Ahmed Shah Masood, controlled only three northeastern provinces. Rabbani and Dostam formed an alliance to check the growing power of the Taliban.

Taliban forces took Kabul on September 26–27 after Masood's forces retreated northward. The Taliban gained some ground north of Kabul, but were pushed back by the combined forces of Masood and Dostam. The year ended in a military stalemate. Despite intensive efforts, United Nations Special Envoy Norbert Holl did not secure a cease-fire agreement but made some progress towards getting the factions to begin political talks. The fighting forced thousands of Afghans to flee their homes in Kabul, areas north of Kabul, and in the northwestern and eastern parts of the country.

There is no constitution, rule of law, or independent judiciary. Former President Rabbani, relocated to Takhar in the north, claimed that he remained the head of the Government of Afghanistan. His delegation retained Afghanistan's U.N. seat after the U.N. General Assembly deferred a decision on Afghanistan's credentials. The Taliban, led by Mullah Mohammed Omar, formed a six-member ruling council in Kabul which ruled by edict. Ultimate authority for Taliban rule rested in the Taliban's inner Shura (Council), located in the southern city of Kandahar, and in Mullah Omar. In Taliban areas, order was established by disarming the local commanders and the populace and by instituting stiff punishments for crimes. Several provincial administrations maintained limited functions. Civil institutions were mostly nonexistent. General Dostam has established some administration in the 5–6 north-central provinces under his control, including customs collection at border points, but law and order in these areas is enforced by local commanders. The ethnic Tajik-majority areas of the northeast were controlled by Masood's commanders and his political organization.

Agriculture, including high levels of opium poppy cultivation, remained the mainstay of the economy. Afghanistan has become the second largest opium producer in the world. Lack of resources and the war have impeded reconstruction of irrigation systems, repair of market roads, and replanting of orchards in some areas. The presence of an estimated 10 million land mines has restricted areas for cultivation and slowed the return of refugees who are needed to rebuild the economy. The laying of new mine fields, primarily by pro-Rabbani forces but also by General Dostam's forces, exacerbated an already difficult situation. Trade was mainly in fruits, minerals, and gems, as well as goods smuggled to Pakistan. Formal economic activity remained minimal and was inhibited by recurrent fighting and roads blocked by local commanders. These blockages were removed in territory taken by the Taliban. Reconstruction was continuing in Herat, Kandahar, and Jalalabad, although efforts in the latter city were slowed by renewed hostilities in the fall. Reconstruction in some northern areas, including Balkh province, reportedly continues.

Serious human rights violations continued to occur and citizens were precluded from changing their government peacefully. Political killings, torture, rape, arbitrary detention, looting, abductions and kidnapings for ransom were committed by armed units, local commanders, and rogue individuals. Prison conditions were poor.

---

*The American Embassy in Kabul has been closed for security reasons since January, 1989. Information on the human rights situation is therefore limited.

Various factions infringed on citizens' privacy rights. Summary justice was common. The Taliban instituted Islamic courts and enforced their interpretation of appropriate Islamic punishments, such as public executions and amputations of one hand and one foot for theft. For minor infractions, Taliban militiamen often decided right or wrong and meted out punishments such as beatings on the spot. Both Taliban and anti-Taliban forces were responsible for the indiscriminate bombardment of civilian areas, particularly Kabul. Taliban forces rocketed and shelled Kabul when it was held by Rabbani, killing hundreds of civilians. After Kabul fell, Dostam and Masood's forces also bombed the city, but caused many fewer casualties. Civil war conditions and the unfettered actions of competing factions effectively limited the freedoms of speech, press, assembly, association, religion, and movement. There was widespread discrimination against women and girls, and the condition of women and girls in Kabul and Herat after the Taliban captured these cities was significantly worse than in 1995. The Taliban prohibited women from working outside the home except in the health care field. Girls were prohibited from attending school. However, the imposition of Taliban control in rural areas resulted in reduced incidents of rape, kidnaping, and forced marriage. Worker rights were not defined.

RESPECT FOR HUMAN RIGHTS

Section 1. Respect for the Integrity of the Person, Including Freedom From:

a. *Political and Other Extrajudicial Killing.*—A number of personal and politically-motivated killings reportedly took place during the chaos when the Taliban took Jalalabad in mid-September. For example, a group of commanders and members of the Nangarhar Council were ambushed and killed near the border town of Torkham. The attack was presumed to be retaliation for a Council-sanctioned killing of the assailant's brother several years earlier. When the Taliban captured Kabul in late September, one of their first acts was to invade the U.N. compound, seize former President Najibullah and his brother, and summarily execute them. Najibullah was head of the secret police during the Soviet occupation and President of Afghanistan from 1986–92. The corpses were hung in the street for 2 days following the executions. According to Amnesty International, at least 30 men were taken from Herat prison in July and executed by Taliban authorities. In October there were unconfirmed reports that 20 civilians were executed by Taliban forces north of Kabul as the Taliban forces withdrew under pressure from Masood's forces. There were also reports of atrocities against civilians by Dostam's forces.

Commander Rasul Pahlawan, a prominent northern leader, was killed in June, reportedly by one of his bodyguards who then was killed by the other bodyguards. Dostam, who many thought ordered the killing, denied involvement and established a commission of inquiry into the slaying. The assassin's family reportedly had had land and political disputes with Pahlawan. Since Pahlawan's slaying, intra-factional fighting within Dostam's political organization reportedly has resulted in some deaths.

In other areas, combatants sought to kill rival commanders and their sympathizers. The perpetrators of these killings and their motives were difficult to identify, as political motives are often entwined with family and tribal feuds, battles over the drug trade, and personal vendettas. In March fighting broke out in Baghlan near the town of Pul-i-Khumri after Ismaili forces reportedly ambushed and killed a Hezb-i-Islami commander loyal to Gulbuddin Hekmatyar and some of his men.

The Taliban used swift summary trials and implemented strict punishments according to Islamic law; the Taliban ordered public executions and death by stoning (see Sections 1.c. and 1.e.)

b. *Disappearance.*—Abductions, kidnapings, or hostage-taking for ransom or political reasons occurred in non-Taliban areas, but specific information was lacking. An unconfirmed report claimed that in July, political associates of Ahmed Shah Masood kidnaped six individuals in Takhar who were accused of being political opponents of Masood and held them for ransom. The strict security enforced by the Taliban in areas under their control has resulted in a decrease in such crimes.

There were unconfirmed reports of girls and young women being kidnaped by local commanders in the southeast, Jalalabad, Kabul, and other areas before these areas came under Taliban control. Some of the women were then forced to marry their kidnapers. Others simply remained missing. To avoid this situation, some families sent their daughters to Pakistan. There were also reports that women had been killed by their male relatives to prevent forced marriages (see Section 5).

Groups in Russia listed nearly 300 former Soviet soldiers who had served in Afghanistan as missing in action or prisoners of war. Most were thought to be dead or to have voluntarily assimilated into Afghan society. Some allegedly continued to be held against their will by their Afghan captors. A number of persons from

Ukraine, Belarus, and Kazakstan remain missing from the period of the Soviet occupation and are presumed dead. Their remains have not been found.

c. *Torture and Other Cruel, Inhuman, or Degrading Treatment or Punishment.*—Afghanistan is in a state of civil war and torture is used against opponents and prisoners of war (POW's), though specific information is generally lacking. Torture does not appear to be a routine practice in most areas. Some of Masood's commanders in the north reportedly used torture routinely to extract information from and break the will of prisoners and political opponents; some of the victims were said to have been tortured to death. Local authorities maintain prisons in territories under their control and established torture cells in some of them. The Taliban freed many prisoners as they took control of new areas, but also incarcerated new prisoners. The Taliban operate prisons in Kandahar, Herat, Kabul, and Jalalabad. There are also prisons in the north in Mazar-i-Sharif and Faizabad, Badakhshan province. According to Amnesty International (AI), some Taliban prisoners have been forced to labor in life-threatening conditions such as digging trenches in mined areas, though these reports are unconfirmed.

The Taliban ruled strictly in areas they controlled, establishing ad hoc and rudimentary judicial systems. Taliban courts imposed their interpretation of Islamic laws and punishments following swift summary trials. Murderers were subjected to public executions (see Section 1.a.) and thieves had a limb or two (one hand, one foot) severed. Adulterers were stoned to death. In July a couple was convicted of adultery by a Taliban court. The couple was reportedly stoned to death in a public place in Kandahar. In August a man was hanged from a crane for murder and left dangling for 20 minutes. The body was reportedly taken to the hospital before burial. However, the hospital staff discovered that the man was still alive. The Taliban reportedly pardoned the man who is now venerated.

Prison conditions are poor. Prisoners are given no food. Normally, this is the responsibility of prisoners' relatives who are allowed to visit to provide them with food once or twice a week. Those who have no relatives have to petition the local council or rely on other inmates. Prisoners live in collective cells. The U.N. Special Rapporteur for Human Rights in Afghanistan visited prisoners in Mazar-I-Sharif and Kandahar in July. Local authorities allowed the ICRC to visit detainees throughout the country.

d. *Arbitrary Arrest, Detention, or Exile.*—With the absence of formal legal and law enforcement institutions, justice was not administered according to formal legal codes. Judicial and police procedures varied from locality to locality. Little is known about the procedures for taking persons into custody and bringing them to justice. In both Taliban and non-Taliban areas, the practices varied depending on the locality, the local commanders, and other authorities. Some areas have more of a judicial structure than others. A seven-member Russian air crew, detained by the Taliban in Kandahar since August 1995, managed to escape in August. While performing maintenance on their downed aircraft at the airport, the crewmen overpowered their guards and took off in their plane to freedom.

Between January and June, the International Committee of the Red Cross (ICRC) visited over 2,000 detainees in 38 places of detention. Following the Taliban's capture of Kabul in September, the ICRC confirmed that all the detainees it had previously visited in the capital had been released. There were unconfirmed reports that the Taliban had freed prisoners in the southeast and the east as they captured these areas in August and September. In early October, the ICRC began visits to detainees newly-arrested by the Taliban in Kabul and Jalalabad.

In October AI claimed that the Taliban had detained up to 1,000 civilians during house to house searches in the initial days after the fall of Kabul. The families feared that the prisoners were sent to clear mine fields for the Taliban in the Panjshir valley. This report was not confirmed. AI reported other cases of individuals detained by the Taliban because of their ethnic origin, suspected sympathy with Taliban opponents, or opposition to Taliban religious decrees. Political detainees are probably held by all factions but no firm numbers are available. Perhaps as many as 1,000 soldiers are held by opposing groups as POW's. In November the ICRC reported that 600 former Rabbani/Masood soldiers were held by the Taliban. Masood reportedly holds several hundred Taliban soldiers as POWs.

The authorities are not known to use forced exile.

e. *Denial of Fair Public Trial.*—With no functioning nationwide judicial system, many municipal and provincial authorities relied on some form of Shari'a (Islamic) law and traditional tribal codes of justice.

Little is known about the administration of justice in the areas controlled by Dostam and Rabbani/Masood in the northern provinces. The administration and implementation of justice could vary from area to area and depend on the whims of local commanders or other authorities, who could summarily execute, torture, and mete out punishments without reference to any other authority. In Rabbani/Masood-controlled Badakhshan province, one commander used a scaffold outside his headquarters to hang several individuals convicted of serious crimes by local Islamic courts. In March three alleged criminals were hanged in public in Kabul, then under Rabbani's control.

The Taliban established Islamic courts in areas under their control to judge criminal cases and resolve disputes. These courts meted out punishments to dozens of prisoners, including execution and amputation. These courts are said to have heard cases in sessions that lasted only a few minutes. Reportedly one such court in Kandahar usually consisted of four judges who gathered in a room or courtyard. Both the witnesses and the accused were brought before the judges to recount testimony and plead their cases. Prisoners were often brought forward in shackles. The court reportedly dealt with all complaints, relying on Islamic law and punishments as well as traditional tribal customs (see Section 1.c.). In cases involving murder, convicted prisoners were generally ordered executed by relatives of the victim (see Section 1.a.), who could choose to accept other restitution. Decisions of the courts were reportedly final.

In January, according to press reports, a man was executed in Logar province for murdering a neighbor during a dispute. Local Taliban authorities arrested and tried the man, who was executed by a firing squad led by the victim's brother after the victim's family refused to forgive the man or accept money as compensation. Also in January, a man in Herat, also controlled by the Taliban, was executed by hanging at a local sports arena, reportedly for murder.

In February according to press reports, a Taliban court in Khost tried and convicted two men of murder in separate crimes. After rejecting any offer of money as compensation, the victims' male relatives carried out the sentence with a Kalashnikov rifle. The convicted men were blindfolded with hands and feet tied, placed one at a time in front of a large tree in a public area, and executed.

In July the Taliban allegedly executed without trial 30 to 50 pro-Rabbani troops or supporters captured by the Taliban in Herat and Ghor provinces. In the western province of Nimruz, three men were publicly hanged in August by the Taliban after having been found guilty of planting landmines. In November, according to press reports, two men were executed in Kandahar by order of an Islamic court for sexually assaulting and murdering a boy and a girl. In December, a man convicted of killing a woman and children by Rabbani's courts in Kabul and who escaped from prison in the confusion following the Taliban takeover, was recaptured by the Taliban. A Taliban Islamic court affirmed the earlier conviction and allowed the husband of the murdered woman to forgive the murderer or kill the murderer himself. He chose the latter and shot the murderer to death in Kabul stadium.

Shi'a Islamic legal norms are reportedly imposed in the Hazarajat in central Afghanistan. According to the October report of the U.N. Special Rapporteur for Human Rights in Afghanistan (see Section 4), the Shi'a Unity Party (Hezb-i-Wahdat) in Bamian province has established a Judicial Committee. The Committee has a prosecutor's office composed of three branches for political, military, and social offenders. There were also courts of the first and the final instance.

All factions probably hold political prisoners but no firm estimates of numbers are available.

f. *Arbitrary Interference with Privacy, Family, Home, or Correspondence.*—Intrafactional fighting often resulted in the homes and businesses of civilians being invaded and looted by the opposing forces—whether victor or loser. Armed gunmen acted with impunity given the absence of any legal protection from the law or a responsive police force. In Kabul and Jalalabad prior to the Taliban takeover, armed individuals reportedly forced their way into homes without fear of reprisal. It was unclear what authority controlled the actions of Taliban militiamen who patrolled the streets of cities and towns, and several incidents were reported of Taliban soldiers entering private homes without prior notification or informed consent in Kabul, Herat, Kandahar, and elsewhere. In Kabul the soldiers allegedly searched homes for evidence of cooperation with the former authorities. Individuals were beaten on the streets by the Taliban for what were deemed infractions of Taliban rules. However, following a written order in December by Mullah Omar to Taliban followers warning against beating citizens, the practice diminished.

According to the U.N. High Commissioner for Refugees (UNHCR), approximately 300 single men were registered in October who claimed to be fleeing forced conscription by the Taliban. There were unconfirmed reports that after the takeover of Kabul, the Taliban rounded up young men to be soldiers and Panshiri Tajiks were seized in Kabul and taken to undisclosed locations.

The Taliban and Dostam's political organizations infringed on women's freedom of expression by requiring strict Islamic garb in public (see Section 5).

g. *Use of Excessive Force and Violations of Humanitarian Law in Internal Conflicts.*—The Taliban killed approximately 325 civilians in Kabul in 1996 by indiscriminately firing rockets into the city. Approximately 675 civilians in Kabul were injured during the year because of the civil war. The Taliban reportedly conducted aerial bombing raids in October around Kalakan, approximately 12 miles north of Kabul, and caused the deaths of 16 to 20 civilians, including women and children. According to press reports, in October Taliban units destroyed 120 houses in the Tajik-dominated village of Sar Cheshma, five miles north of Kabul. From October to December, Dostam's and Masood's forces engaged in sporadic bombing and rocket attacks against Kabul. Several persons, including children, were killed and injured in separate attacks.

At the beginning of the year, the UNHCR reported that there were approximately 150,000 internally displaced persons (IDP's) in camps near Jalalabad and as many as 200,000 living independently in and around Jalalabad city. Between 25,000 and 27,000 IDP's were reported to be living in camps in the north in Pul-i-Khumri, Mazar-i-Sharif, Shibergan, and Hairatan. In November thousands of persons fled fighting in the northwest province of Badghiz. Twelve hundred of these IDP's passed through UNHCR camps in the Herat area, and 700 remained in camps as of late December Some 6,000 to 7,000 had headed north into Turkmenistan, but many of those had returned. The UNHCR said that 15,000 Afghans, mostly from Kabul, had crossed into Pakistan since October and that 600 to 700 were arriving daily. From October to December, UNHCR estimated that about 40,000 Afghans fled to Pakistan due to the intensified civil war.

The Afghan countryside remains plagued by an estimated 10 million land mines sown during and since the Soviet occupation. With funding from international donors, the United Nations has organized and trained mine detection and clearance teams, which operated throughout Afghanistan. Nevertheless, the mines are expected to pose a threat for years to come. The laying of new mine fields by Masood forces around Kabul and Sarobi, a strategic city southeast of Kabul, posed new dangers. U.N. agencies and other nongovernmental organizations (NGO's) have instituted a number of mine awareness campaigns and educational programs for women and children in various parts of the country, but many were curtailed as a result of Taliban restrictions on women and girls.

Section 2. Respect for Civil Liberties, Including:

a. *Freedom of Speech and Press.*—There are no laws effectively providing for freedom of speech and the press, and the Kabul authorities under Rabbani for the first 9 months of the year lacked the authority to protect these rights. Senior officials of various warring factions allegedly attempted to intimidate reporters and influence their reporting. The Afghan Islamic Press (AIP) is an unaffiliated reporting service. The few newspapers, all of which were published only sporadically, were largely affiliated with different factions. There was a pro-Rabbani radio and television service in Kabul until it came under Taliban control and was renamed the Voice of Shariat. The various regions had their own radio and television stations: Dostam had his own in the northern city of Mazar-I-Sharif and Hekmatyar had his own near Kabul until they were taken over by the Taliban. Herat's media came under Taliban control when they captured the city in September 1995.

International journalists in Kabul reported that they were routinely pressured by the Rabbani regime to slant their coverage. The Taliban by and large cooperated with the international press who arrived in Kabul in September and took few steps to curb their access. However, a female Western journalist was not allowed to attend the Taliban's first press conference in Kabul. In another incident, one commander discouraged Taliban officials from responding to questions posed by Western female journalists. One female correspondent reported that she and her camera crew were jostled by Taliban soldiers while filming in Kabul. There were several incidents in which photographers' film was seized after taking pictures of women. In October two Argentine journalists were reportedly detained for 24 hours and beaten by Taliban militia after they attempted to interview two Afghan women in Kabul. At times Western journalists were prevented from traveling to the front lines, although many succeeded in doing so on other occasions. Despite some incidents most journalists, including women, were able to do their jobs. In November the Taliban imposed a rule requring journalists to stay at the Intercontinental Hotel in Kabul (allegedly for security and economic reasons). Journalists also reported at year's end that the Taliban were attempting to control who could act as drivers and interpreters for journalists.

The Taliban imposed its interpretation of Islam on popular culture, banning music, movies, and television. Cinemas in Kabul had already been closed by authorities in June before the Taliban takeover.

The Taliban severely restricts academic freedom, particularly education for girls (see Section 5).

b. *Freedom of Peaceful Assembly and Association.*—Civil war, tenuous security, and likely opposition from local authorities seriously inhibited freedom of assembly and association. Nonetheless, Afghans demonstrated in several cities. There were credible reports of women demonstrating in Herat against Taliban strictures, of persons encouraged by the Taliban to demonstrate in Kabul and Kandahar against Iranian interference, and of demonstrations in Mazar-i-Sharif against the Taliban. In one demonstration in Herat, Taliban adherents reportedly beat the female demonstrators.

There were reports of Taliban harassment of international aid agencies and NGOs. In the fall, the Taliban detained Afghan staffers of UNHCR, broke into the office and home of one international staffer, and confiscated vehicles. Other NGO staffers, mostly Afghan, were also detained. Some female Afghan staffers were threatened with punishment if they went to work.

It is unknown whether laws exist governing the formation of associations. The Taliban reportedly issued an edict at year's end which outlawed all social organizations, but this was unconfirmed. Many Afghan NGOs have been formed. Some are based in neighboring countries, mostly Pakistan, with branches inside Afghanistan. Others are based in Afghan cities. The focus of their activities is primarily humanitarian assistance, rehabilitation, health, education, and agriculture.

c. *Freedom of Religion.*—Afghanistan's official name, the Islamic State of Afghanistan, reflects the country's adherence to Islam as the state religion. Some 85 percent of the population is Sunni Muslim, with Shi'a Muslims comprising most of the remainder. The Hazara ethnic group is Shi'a; Shi'as are among the most economically disadvantaged people in Afghanistan. The Shi'a minority want a national government to give them equal rights as citizens. There were unconfirmed reports that under Taliban rule, the Shi'a populations in Kabul and Herat were forced to pray in the open-handed Sunni style, rather than in their own closed-handed style. Miniature stones, representing the sacred black stone at the Kaaba in Mecca, were removed from Shi'a mosques. Shi'as were forced to pray at the same time as Sunnis, although traditionally their prayer schedules differ. However, at year's end it appeared the Taliban were not interfering in Shi'a prayer practices.

The Taliban sought to impose their strict form of Islamic observance in areas that they control. Men were hauled out of their vehicles and forced to attend services at mosques. Taliban members attempted to force men to pray five times a day at set times and to grow long beards. Ismaili women were not allowed to leave home to attend Ismaili religious services and Ismaili girls were not allowed to attend school. The Taliban also ordered women to dress in strict Islamic garb (see Section 5).

The small number of non-Muslim residents in Afghanistan may practice their faith, but may not proselytize. The country's small Hindu and Sikh population, which once numbered about 50,000, continued to shrink as its members emigrated or took refuge abroad. Some Taliban leaders claimed tolerance of religious minorities. There were unconfirmed reports that a number of Sikhs, who have long felt unwelcome by the various mujaheddin commanders, had returned to Jalalabad, Ghazni, and Kabul under the Taliban to reclaim their property and resume residence.

d. *Freedom of Movement Within the Country, Foreign Travel, Emigration, and Repatriation.*—Although in principle citizens have the right to travel freely both inside and outside the country, their ability to travel within the country was hampered by warfare, brigandage, millions of land mines, a road network in a state of disrepair, and limited domestic air service, complicated by factional threats to air traffic. Despite these obstacles many people continued to travel relatively freely with buses plying routes in most parts of the country. Security conditions have improved along roads in Taliban-controlled areas. However, due to intermittent fighting in various areas, international aid agencies often found that their ability to travel, work, and distribute assistance was hampered. International travel continued to be difficult as both Dostam and the Taliban threatened to shoot down any planes that overflew areas of the country that they controlled without their permission. In December, the Taliban forced down a U.N. plane carrying a Tajik opposition leader from Iran to Afghanistan. The Taliban said the U.N. had not informed them of the flight. After a diversion to Kandahar, the plane was allowed to proceed.

Commercial trade was impeded in certain non-Taliban areas as local commanders continued to demonstrate their control over the roads by demanding road tolls and sometimes closing roads. In January one road stoppage at Sarobi on the Kabul-Jalalabad road by a Hekmatyar commander prevented trucks carrying food supplies from reaching Kabul for about a week. Roads leading to Bamian province reportedly contained dozens of checkpoints controlled by local commanders, where travelers were sometimes subject to extortion.

According to the UNHCR, approximately 10,000 people reportedly fled Jalalabad following the Taliban takeover in mid-September, but most later returned. Villagers were forced to flee the fighting north and northeast of Kabul in several locations as factions contended for control village by village. A large number of Kabul inhabitants were also displaced by the Taliban takeover in late September, but there were no reliable estimates as to their number. In November fighting in Badghis province in the northwest caused thousands to flee their homes. More than 9,000 displaced persons were concentrated in 3 areas of northern Afghanistan by mid-November. The UNHCR said that 15,000 Afghans, mostly from Kabul, had crossed the border to Pakistan since the beginning of October. While, according to UNHCR statistics, the overall number of families returning to Kabul was greater than the number departing in 1996, the number of departing families rose sharply in September and continued at a high level throughout the remainder of the year. The rate of arrival in Pakistan in October was 600 to 700 a day. By year's end, the UNHCR and NGO's were assisting more than 1,600 newly arrived families (11,200 persons) in Nasir Bagh camp in Pakistan. Since October the Taliban have reportedly removed dozens of checkpoints on the Kabul-Jalalabad road; at year's end there were only six. They routinely checked passengers for weapons and "stolen state property."

Afghans continued to form one of the world's largest refugee populations. According to the UNHCR, about 2.4 million Afghans remain outside the country in 1996 as registered refugees. Of these, 1.3 million are in Iran, 864,000 are in Pakistan, and 28,000 are in Russia. Approximately 19,000 Afghans reside in parts of the former Soviet Union other than Russia. Pakistan claimed an additional 500,000 unregistered Afghan refugees in its territory. Over 3.8 million Afghan refugees have been repatriated since 1988, with over 1.5 million returning to Afghanistan in the peak year of 1992. According to the UNHCR, 127,500 Afghans repatriated in 1996, 120,000 from Pakistan and 7,500 from Iran. The repatriation from Iran was much lower than in previous years. This reflected in part the Iranian Government's decision not to encourage repatriation while the Taliban remained in control of western Afghanistan and to postpone use of a new repatriation route through Turkmenistan. It also reflected the judgment of many refugees that their prospects for earning a livelihood were better in Iran than in Afghanistan.

According to the UNHCR, approximately 18,800 refugees from Tajikistan remain in Afghanistan. About 1,000 Tajik refugees were repatriated to Tajikistan during 1996. Tajiks living in the UNHCR-run Saki camp near Mazar-i-Sharif have been able to repatriate relatively freely. Those in camps in the Kunduz area, which is controlled by Masood, Hekmatyar, and independent commanders and where the Tajik opposition actively opposes repatriation, have not had free access to information on repatriation. The UNHCR does not have access to these camps. The refugees have also faced considerable difficulty in repatriating when they have wished to do so. However, according to the UNHCR, the opposition's hold on the camps has decreased in recent months, and some repatriation has occurred.

Section 3. Respect for Political Rights: The Right of Citizens to Change Their Government

The continuing struggle for political power among the three major armed groups precluded citizens from changing their government or form of government peacefully and democratically. Most political changes came about through shifting military fortunes. No faction held elections or respected the right to change government democratically.

The faction controlling Kabul for the first 9 months of the year, headed by nominal President Rabbani, held power with the military backing of de facto Defense Minister Masood, until the Taliban takeover in late September. General Dostam was aligned with Hezb-I-Islami (Islamic Party) leader Gulbuddin Hekmatyar and with an opposition Shi'a party in an alliance called the Supreme Coordination Council of Afghanistan. The Taliban controlled all of southern and western Afghanistan to the Turkmenistan and Iranian borders. In June former Rabbani rival Gulbuddin Hekmatyar switched sides and joined the Rabbani government as Prime Minister. The move was intended to broaden the base of the Kabul regime to include Pashtuns. However, the step weakened the allegiance of Hekmatyar's commanders in the southeast and east and led to the crumbling of the formerly neutral Nangarhar Shura (Council) in the east. After the fall of Jalalabad, Sarobi, and then Kabul, Rabbani fled to Takhar in the north where he proclaimed that the Government had relocated. At year's end, Rabbani and Masood controlled two Tajik majority northeastern provinces, Badakhshan and Takhar, as well as pockets in Kunduz, Parwan, and Kapisa, including the Panjshir valley. Hekmatyar continued to command allegiance from several commanders located in Baghlan and Kunduz provinces. Dostam's National Islamic Movement controlled five to six north central provinces. After the fall of Kabul, Rabbani/Masood, Dostam, and the Khalili-led Shi'a Party formed an alliance, the Supreme Council for the Defense of Afghanistan, to combat the Taliban.

Although there are governors and local councils in the north, most power there is concentrated in the hands of Dostam and a few generals. Masood retains control in the northeastern ethnic Tajik-majority provinces through his commanders and political organization. The three eastern provinces—Nangarhar, Laghman, and Konar—were controlled by a neutral commander, but all fell to the Taliban in mid-September. The Taliban controlled more than two-thirds of the country by year's end, including Kabul. However, discontent with Taliban strictures and village values was strong in large non-Pashtun cities such as Herat and Kabul.

In September former King Zahir Shah declared from his residence in exile that he was prepared to return to Afghanistan and discuss with the relevant parties the formation of an interim government. Although many representatives of the factions visited the former King, he did not return to the country. The Taliban were ambivalent about a possible role for the former King, although some Taliban adherents supported his return. Some observers believed that some Afghans welcomed the Taliban to their areas because they thought that they were the former King's vanguard.

The United Nations and the international community continued their efforts to help Afghans reach a political settlement. In April and October, the U.N. Security Council held open discussions on Afghanistan. In October a Security Council resolution was adopted that called for an end to the fighting and the start of a political dialogue aimed at national reconciliation and a lasting political settlement. It also called upon the outside parties to stop supplying arms and ammunition to the warring factions and for all Afghan groups to respect human rights and permit the delivery of humanitarian assistance.

In the fall, attempts by U.N. Special Envoy Holl to broker a ceasefire among the parties failed. However, Holl succeeded in getting talks underway between two of the major groups, Dostam and the Taliban. In October the Organization of Islamic States (OIC) called for a peace conference of Afghans in Jeddah, but received no positive response. On November 18, the U.N. Secretary General convened a meeting of countries concerned with the Afghan situation to bolster international support for the U.N.'s mediation efforts and to engage the neighboring and regional states in a common approach to the conflict.

Section 4. Governmental Attitude Regarding International and Nongovernmental Investigation of Alleged Violations of Human Rights

There was no functioning central government in the country. The Rabbani regime cooperated with the U.N. Special Rapporteur for Human Rights in Afghanistan, Dr. Choong-hyun Paik, who traveled to Afghanistan in January and May 1995, visiting Kabul, Herat, Kandahar, Jalalabad, and Mazar-i-Sharif. In February his report to the U.N. Commission on Human Rights concluded that the lack of a central government posed extreme difficulties and complexities in redressing human rights violations. He concluded that it was necessary then to stress the importance of accountability at the level of regional administrations, which might assume responsibility for violations of human rights committed in their particular region. He noted that the collapse of an impartial judicial system prevented the administration of justice, which posed an insurmountable challenge to citizens' right to a fair trial and affected, in particular, detainees in prisons.

In April Dr. Paik's mandate as special rapporteur was renewed by the U.N. Commission on Human Rights. In July he traveled again to Afghanistan, as well as Pakistan and Iran. Also in July, the Kabul authorities under Rabbani permitted a 2-day visit to Kabul by three representatives of Amnesty International. They met with Rabbani and Dostam to discuss the human rights situation in the country. AI's requests to meet with Taliban representatives were denied.

In October the U.N. Special Rapporteur noted in his interim report that Afghanistan over the years had signed a number of international human rights conventions. However, the Taliban recognize only the validity of Islamic law. They do not accept the notion of secular law, nor binding international human rights norms. In early October, Jose Ayala Lasso, the U.N. High Commissioner for Human Rights, publicly invited the Taliban leadership to ensure respect for women's rights, such as the right of women to work and the right of girls to an education without discrimination.

The Afghan League of Human Rights operated both in Afghanistan and Pakistan; it produces an annual report. The Cooperation Center for Afghanistan (CCA) is an

Afghan NGO that operated in both Pakistan and Afghanistan. CCA maintains an office in Peshawar where it produces a monthly newsletter on the Afghan human rights situation. It also works inside Afghanistan to document human rights abuses. However, the civil war and lack of security made it difficult for human rights organizations to adequately monitor the situation inside the country. In October a 2-day workshop on human rights in Afghanistan was held in Peshawar, Pakistan.

Section 5. Discrimination Based on Race, Sex, Religion, Disability, Language, or Social Status

There are no constitutional provisions that prohibit discrimination based on race, sex, religion, disability, language, or social status. It is not known whether specific laws prohibit discrimination; local custom and practices generally prevail. Discrimination against women varies from area to area, depending on the local leadership's attitude towards work and education for women. Traditionally, the minority Shi'a faced discrimination from the majority Sunni population. There was more general acceptance of the disabled as the number of people maimed by land mines increased and the presence of the disabled became more prevalent.

Women.—As lawlessness and interfactional fighting continued in some areas, violence against women occurred frequently, including beatings, rapes, forced marriages, disappearances, kidnapings, and killings. Such incidents generally went unreported and most information was anecdotal. It was difficult to document rapes, in particular, given the social stigma that surrounded the problem.

Afghan tradition imposes limits on women's activities beyond the home, particularly in the Taliban-dominated Pashtun areas of the south. Under the Communist regime of the 1980's, a growing number of women, particularly in urban areas, worked outside the home in nontraditional roles. This trend was reversed when the Communists were ousted in 1992 and an Islamic government was installed. In 1996 the trend towards excluding women from public service continued, although some women retained employment as artisans, weavers, doctors, and nurses in some areas. In northern Afghanistan and pre-Taliban controlled Kabul, women were allowed to work and girls to attend school.

When the Taliban took Kabul in late September, they immediately issued pronouncements forbidding women to work, including female doctors and nurses in hospitals. This move affected as many as 40,000 women, including civil servants, teachers, bakers, and charwomen. Some working women appealed to the Taliban that they had no other means of livelihood to support several family members if they did not work. Taliban gender restrictions often interfered with the ability of UN relief agencies and NGO's to employ women and deliver assistance to women and girls. Many relief organizations had to scale back their activities, and at least one, Oxfam, suspended operations altogether in Taliban areas. However, most continued their principal programs. After gender restrictions threatened to disrupt the delivery of health services, the Taliban allowed some female medical staff, including doctors and nurses, to resume their jobs in Kabul and elsewhere, but generally only under strict guidelines. Female nurses were discouraged from working alongside male doctors. Male doctors could not attend to female patients. Actual practice, however, varied from place to place. The Taliban allowed female doctors and nurses to tend other females and even, in some instances, to attend to male patients. In one province, a male doctor who ran a clinic was allowed to see female patients but only with his wife present.

Female employment outside of the health sector was forbidden by the Taliban in Kabul, Herat, and elsewhere. The Taliban have completely stopped women from teaching in boys' schools, thereby preventing many boys from getting an education. In Kabul and elsewhere, women were prohibited from working outside the home. The Taliban promised to pay women salaries to remain at home but did not. In Herat resistance to the Taliban's edicts forbidding employment led to punishment, including beatings. The Taliban also limited women's access to education by stopping most women's educational programs in areas they took over, including the closure of a nursing school in Kandahar.

The Taliban decreed what women would wear in public. They were required to don an all-encompassing head-to-toe garb known as the chadori which has only a mesh screen for vision. In conservative areas, this was the normal garb for rural women. In Kabul women found in public not wearing the chadori were beaten by Taliban militiamen. In one incident, a woman covered by a chadori was reportedly harassed by a Taliban street patrol in Kabul for not properly covering her bare feet. A few reports indicated that some women in Herat are covering their heads with large scarves that leave the face uncovered and have not faced reprisals.

The appearance and movement of women in public has been discouraged, even with approved clothing. In the days after the Taliban takeover of Kabul, a Taliban patrol stopped two women and beat them with a broken-off car antenna, even though they were appropriately dressed. However, women were not prevented from leaving their homes altogether. They went to the market without accompanying male relatives in Kandahar, the most socially conservative of the larger cities, as well as in Herat and Kabul, though in smaller numbers than before the Taliban takeover. Women also visited open bazaars, but were sometimes discouraged from entering small shops. Instead, they had to conduct business with the shopkeepers from the street.

Most women in Dostam-controlled Mazir-i-Sharif now wear the chador, a marked change from last year. Dostam's political organization issued strict instructions that women on the streets should be modestly attired.

In October the U.N. Secretary General issued a statement criticizing the Taliban's directive on women and warned that international assistance to Afghanistan could be jeopardized if international human rights standards were not observed. The U.N. Security Council held an open discussion on October 16 at which many countries addressed the problem of human rights in Afghanistan, particularly the rights of women and girls.

Children.—Local administrative bodies and international assistance organizations undertook further children's welfare to the extent possible. Taliban restrictions on the movement of women and girls in areas that they controlled hampered the ability of U.N. agencies and NGO's to effectively implement education programs aimed at both boys and girls. UNICEF discontinued programs in Herat, Kandahar, and Kabul where girls were denied access to education. One NGO decided not to proceed with a planned program aimed at girls' education in Herat. The general disruption of health services countrywide due to the Soviet invasion and civil war put many young people at grave risk. UNICEF continued to operate some health-related programs in Taliban-controlled areas. Local authorities in all parts of Afghanistan have supported UNICEF/WHO mass vaccination campaigns. Education, also disrupted due to the Soviet invasion, 10 years of resistance, and civil war caused a generation of children to miss all of their schooling, reportedly raising illiteracy levels above 75 percent.

The Taliban have stopped most of the few opportunities for girls' education that were in place in areas they have taken over. Since capturing Kandahar in 1994, there has been no girls' education—either secular or religious—in the city. Since capturing Herat city in 1995, girls' schools have remained closed. Kabul had more girls' schools than any other city. According to a U.N. survey conducted in May, Kabul had 158 public schools accommodating 148,223 boys and 103,256 girls in grades K-12. Of 11,208 teachers, 7,793 were women. According to UNICEF, no women were teaching in and no girls were attending public schools in Kabul at year's end as a result of Taliban policies on female employment and education. The effect on boys' education was unknown; 3,415 male teachers presumably were still employed. UNICEF believed that girls may still be attending a few private schools, but no details were available. However, Taliban authorities reportedly permitted girls' education in some of the rural areas of Herat province. Limited girls' education continued in Taliban-controlled Ghazni, Khost, and Konar provinces in the south, at schools and in private homes. Even in areas where education is possible, facilities are inadequate and access is limited by custom and poverty. Simple education for boys, both secular and religious, continued in Taliban-controlled areas, including Kabul. However, these opportunities were diminished since female teachers were prohibited from teaching in boys' schools.

People With Disabilities.—Both the former Rabbani regime and the new Taliban authorities in Kabul took few measures to protect the rights of the mentally and physically disabled or to mandate accessibility for them. Victims of land mines were a major focus of international humanitarian relief organizations, which devoted resources to providing prostheses, medical treatment, and rehabilitation therapy to amputees. In Jalalabad an NGO provided bicycles to amputees for transportation as well as physical therapy, rehabilitation skills, and literacy training. There was more public acceptance of people with disabilities because of the prevalence of the maimed due to land mines. The U.N. Development Program (UNDP) conducted a million dollar project to strengthen comprehensive community-based rehabilitation services for disabled citizens. The ICRC and some NGO's were actively involved in programs for people with disabilities throughout the country.

Section 6. Worker Rights

a. *The Right of Association.*—Little is known about labor laws and practices, although only an insignificant fraction of the work force has ever labored in an industrial setting. There were no reports of labor rallies or strikes. Labor rights are not defined, in the context of the breakdown of governmental authority, and there is no effective central authority to enforce them. Many of Kabul's industrial workers are unemployed due to the destruction or abandonment of the city's minuscule manufacturing base. The only large employer in Kabul is the governmental structure of minimally functioning ministries.

b. *The Right to Organize and Bargain Collectively.*—Afghanistan lacks a tradition of genuine labor-management bargaining. There are no known labor courts or other mechanisms for resolving labor disputes.

c. *Prohibition of Forced or Compulsory Labor.*—No information is available on edicts regarding forced or compulsory labor. There were no confirmed reports of alleged forced-work road projects.

d. *Minimum Age for Employment of Children.*—There is no evidence that authorities in any part of the country enforce labor laws, if they exist, relating to the employment of children. Children from the ages of 6 to 14 often work to help support their families by herding animals in rural areas, and by collecting paper and firewood, shining shoes, begging, or collecting scrap metal among street debris in the cities. Some of these practices expose children to the danger of land mines.

e. *Acceptable Conditions of Work.*—There is no available information regarding a statutory minimum wage or the enforcement of safe labor practices. Many workers are apparently allotted time off regularly for prayers and observance of religious holidays.

BANGLADESH

Bangladesh is a parliamentary democracy headed by Prime Minister Sheikh Hasina Wajed, leader of the Awami League, which came to power in national elections in June. Major opposition parties include the previous ruling Bangladesh Nationalist Party (BNP), the Jatiyo Party and Jamaat-E-Islami. Elections under the BNP in February were boycotted by all other major parties (which demanded that the BNP hand over power to a neutral caretaker administration) and marred by rigging and violence. Faced with mounting antigovernment agitation, the Parliament in March passed a constitutional amendment requiring a caretaker regime for all future general parliamentary elections. The June elections, under a caretaker government headed by a retired Chief Justice, were deemed to be generally free and fair by domestic and international observers. Although the BNP blamed its losses on vote-rigging by the Awami League and partisan government employees, it nonetheless joined Parliament as the largest opposition party. The judiciary displays a high degree of independence.

The Home Affairs Ministry controls the police and paramilitary forces, which bear primary responsibility for maintaining internal security. The army and paramilitary forces are responsible for security in the Chittagong Hill Tracts (CHT), where a tribal group has waged a low-level insurgency since 1974. A cease-fire between government forces and insurgents generally held throughout the year; however, there were sporadic violations. Police officers committed a number of serious human rights abuses.

Bangladesh is a poor country. Annual per capita income is approximately $250; about 43 percent of the country's 123 million people exist on incomes insufficient to meet minimum daily needs. Eighty percent of the work force is involved in agriculture, which accounts for approximately one-third of the gross domestic product. There is a growing industrial sector, based largely on the manufacture of garments, textiles, industrial goods such as rerolled steel, cement, and jute. There is a small wealthy elite, and a middle class is emerging. Efforts to reform the economy have been hampered by political turmoil and the opposition of public sector enterprises, government bureaucrats, and other vested interests.

The Government continues to restrict or deny many fundamental rights. Police committed extrajudicial killings, and 17 detainees reportedly died in police custody. Police routinely use torture and other forms of abuse in interrogating suspects. The Government rarely convicts and punishes those responsible for torture or unlawful deaths. The Government continues to use national security laws to detain political opponents and other citizens without formal charge. A large case backlog slows the judicial process, and lengthy pretrial detention is a problem. The Government places some limitations on freedom of assembly. Women, minorities, the disabled, religious minorities, and indigenous people face societal discrimination. Violence against women and prostitution and trafficking of children remain serious problems. The Government continues to limit worker rights, and child labor is a problem.

RESPECT FOR HUMAN RIGHTS

Section 1. Respect for the Integrity of the Person, Including Freedom From:

a. *Political and Other Extrajudicial Killing.*—There were numerous extrajudicial killings during the year. In the western city of Bogra, from August 22 to 25, violence between police and students lead to the death of three students and a police officer. The violence began when, following the death of a student in a traffic accident, other students staged a violent demonstration and attacked buses. Police then fired on the demonstrators, killing two students, and the demonstrators in turn shot and killed a police officer. During a confrontation the next day at the police station, police shot and killed another student. The firings wound many other persons. The Government established a judicial investigation committee, which has yet to issue a report. While in this well-publicized case the Government compensated the families of those killed, and withdrew several police officers from the post, a general climate of police impunity from punishment remains a serious obstacle to ending police abuse and extrajudicial killings.

According to human rights monitors, 17 persons died while in custody in the first 9 months of 1996. According to the Government, six persons died in custody, but there was no evidence that any died from mistreatment. However, numerous press and human rights reports concerning police abuse and deaths of prisoners indicate that this claim is inaccurate and masks serious abuse. For example, in July police reportedly beat to death two men in their custody in Dhaka. In October police reportedly tortured to death an activist of the BNP youthwing, the Jatiybadi Jubo Dal, in Dhaka.

Violence, often resulting in killings, is a pervasive element in the political process. Demonstrators from all parties, and even within parties, often clash with police and with each other during rallies and demonstrations. The year was marked by widespread political violence leading to numerous deaths. In June journalist and Awami League member S. M. Alauddin was killed, possibly due to factional fighting within the party (see Section 2.a.). BNP activists used deadly force to disrupt opposition party gatherings. The Awami League, and other opposition parties, used armed violence and intimidation to enforce their boycott of the February national elections and to enforce numerous general strikes. They similarly disrupted BNP gatherings and government activities. The violence perpetrated by both sides resulted in more than 100 deaths, hundreds of injuries, extensive property damage, and large business losses across the country.

Violence among student political groups, allied with the major national parties, is endemic and reportedly resulted in at least 12 deaths, hundreds of injuries, and the closure of dozens of educational institutions. For example, in August struggles between rival student groups for control of dormitories resulted in approximately 100 injuries and the closure of Dhaka University for 20 days. In September a clash between student activists of rival parties in Cox's Bazar led to one shooting death, and a day-long hartal (general strike) stopping commerce and movement in that town.

In 1995 the Government charged former President Hossain Mohammed Ershad with ordering the 1981 murder of the alleged assassin of President Ziaur Rahman. Previously held in Dhaka central jail, Ershad is currently held in converted quarters (a "subjail") within the Parliament compound. He was moved there by the new Awami League government in July, when Parliament convened. He enjoys periods of 24-hour parole to attend Parliament sessions (he was elected as a Member of Parliament for the second time in June), although he cannot leave the Parliament premises. The murder case is not being actively pursued by the Government. Ershad was already serving a 20-year sentence for corruption (see Section 1.c.).

In August the Government arrested under the Special Powers Act (SPA) retired Lt. Colonel Farook Rahman, the self-confessed organizer of the 1975 assassination of Prime Minister Sheikh Mujibur Rahman. The Government initially told the press that Farook was suspected of illegal weapons possession and plotting to assassinate government officials; later, however, it officially accused him with the 1975 killings in Dhaka Central Jail of four Awami League leaders. Two alleged accomplices in the 1975 murders were arrested at the same time as Farook. Several diplomats were also recalled from abroad as suspected coconspirators (see Section 1.c.).

b. *Disappearance.*—There was one possible incident of politically motivated disappearance during the year. On June 12, Kalpana Chakma, Central Organizing Secretary of the Hill Womens' Federation, an organization of tribal people in the Chittagong Hill Tracts, disappeared from her house. Witnesses and human rights monitors allege that the army abducted her, but one human rights group reported that she was alive in India. The Government formed an investigative committee which has yet to issue any findings.

c. *Torture and Other Cruel, Inhuman, or Degrading Treatment or Punishment.*—Although the Constitution prohibits torture and cruel, inhuman, or degrading punishment, police routinely employ psychological and physical torture and other abuse during arrests and interrogations. Torture may consist of threats, beatings, and, occasionally, the use of electric shock. The Government rarely convicts or punishes those responsible for torture, and a climate of impunity allows such police abuses to continue.

Police brutality occurs regularly, and government inaction allows it to continue. In January police raided a dormitory at Dhaka University inhabited mainly by ethnic and religious minority students, ostensibly to search for illegal weapons. The dormitory was well-known as a stronghold of the Awami League Student Front Organization. Police reportedly used excessive force, and more than 200 students were injured. In June police attacked and injured at least 30 journalists who were covering the swearing-in of new members of Parliament.

Numerous press and human rights monitors' reports indicate that police abuse of detainees is a widespread problem and fequently results in death (see Section 1.a.). Lt. Col. Farook Rahman was arrested on August 13 under the SPA, and later accused in connection with the 1975 deaths in Dhaka Central Jail of four senior Awami League party officials. During his 32 days in police remand, the police refused to grant his family and lawyers access to him. According to unconfirmed press reports and sources close to his family, he was subjected to various forms of torture.

Rape in police custody is also a problem. In July a police officer in a village near Dinajpur reportedly raped a woman. In October four police officers raped a woman they had arrested near Chittagong. In this case, the four officers were suspended from their positions and arrested. The press reported seven instances of rape in police custody during the first 9 months of the year, but women's rights activists estimate that the real number was several times higher.

Most prisons are overcrowded and lack adequate facilities. The current prison population, nearly 45,000 in August, is more than double the official prison capacity. There are three classes of cells: A, B, and C. Common criminals and low-level political workers are generally held in C cells, which often have dirt floors, no furnishings, and poor quality food. The use of restraining devices on prisoners in these cells is common. Prisoners in the C cells reportedly suffer the worst abuses, including beatings or being forced to kneel for long periods. Conditions in B and A cells are markedly better; A cells are reserved for prominent prisoners.

A government-appointed committee of private citizens monitors prisons monthly but does not release its findings. In general, the Government does not permit prison visits by independent human rights monitors but does make occasional exceptions.

Former President Ershad is serving a 20-year sentence for corruption. He was also charged during 1995 with the 1981 murder of the alleged assassin of President Zia (see Section 1.a.). Ershad's treatment and condition came under scrutiny in late 1995 due to complaints from his family about inadequate medical care to treat his health problems (hepatitis), and poor living conditions. His health slowly improved, however, and the Government insisted that it was providing treatment equal to or better than that of any local hospital. In July the Government moved Ershad to a sub-jail within the Parliament compound.

d. *Arbitrary Arrest, Detention, or Exile.*—Both the BNP and Awami League Governments continued to use national security legislation, namely the Special Powers Act (SPA) of 1974, to detain citizens without formal charges or specific complaint being filed against them. Past governments have vowed to abolish the SPA, but so far there has been no action.

Under the SPA, the Government or a district magistrate may, to prevent the commission of an act likely "to prejudice the security of the country", order anyone detained for 30 days. The Government (or magistrate) must within 15 days inform the detainee of the grounds for detention, and the Government must within 30 days approve the grounds for detention or release the detainee. In practice, detainees are sometimes held for longer periods without the Government stating the grounds for the detention or formally approving it. Detainees may appeal their detention, and the Government may grant early release.

After 4 months, an advisory board composed of two persons who have been, or are qualified to be High Court judges, and one civil servant examines cases of detainees. If the Government adequately defends its detention order, the detainee remains imprisoned; if not, the detainee is released. Detainees are allowed to consult with lawyers while in detention, although usually not until a charge is filed. Detainees may receive visitors, and incommunicado detention is generally not practiced. However, the Government has held incommunicado some prominent prisoners, notably Lt. Col. Farook Rahman. In addition, it several times extended Farook's time in police remand (see Section 1.c.).

According to the Government, the authorities detained more than 3,600 persons under the SPA during the first 9 months of the year, approximately 1,400 during the BNP government (January to March) and 1,250 following the elections (July to September). As of September, the courts had ordered about 2,700 detainees released. Government figures indicate that almost 1,000 persons were in detention under the SPA at the end of September. Human rights monitors and political activists charge that both the BNP and Awami League governments have used the SPA as a tool to harass and intimidate political opponents. They claim that both governments arrested hundreds of opposition activitists under the SPA, most being later released when no charges could be brought. Actual numbers of party activists arrested were not verifiable.

In February the Government arrested five senior opposition party leaders under the SPA, including the Awami League mayor of Chittagong. All were released within 2 weeks.

The Government allowed another widely used statute, the Anti-Terrorism Act, to expire in 1994. However, 120 cases filed under this act were still pending on September 30, and 52 cases came to trial during the first 9 months of the year.

The Government does not use forced exile.

e. *Denial of Fair Public Trial.*—The judiciary displays a high degree of independence, as mandated by the Constitution, especially at the higher levels. The judiciary often rules against the Government in criminal, civil, and even politically controversial cases.

The court system has two levels, the lower courts and the Supreme Court. Both hear civil and criminal cases. The lower court consists of magistrates, who are part of the administrative branch of government, and session judges, who belong to the judicial branch. The Supreme Court is divided into two sections, the High Court and the Appellate Court. The High Court hears original cases and also reviews cases from the lower court. The Appellate Court has jurisdiction to hear appeals of judgments, decrees, orders, or sentences of the High Court. Rulings of the Appellate Court are binding on all other courts.

Trials are public. The law provides the accused with the right to be represented by counsel, to review accusatory material, to call witnesses, and to appeal verdicts. In practice, the largely rural, illiterate population does not always understand these rights, nor do the authorities always respect them. There is a system of bail, and bail is commonly granted for both violent and nonviolent crimes. However, if bail is not granted, the law does not specify a time limit on pretrial detention. State-funded defense attorneys are rarely provided, and there are few legal aid programs to offer financial assistance.

There is corruption within the legal process. Small sums must be paid to a number of court officials in order for a civil suit to be filed. While these may appear to be processing fees, they are more in the nature of bribes; they are not established by statute or regulation, are paid to officials personally, and there is no accountability for failure to discharge duties paid for. Defendants can sometimes pay to avoid being served with a notice or suit. Because of the difficulty accessing the courts and because litigation is time-consuming, alternate dispute resolution by traditional village leaders is popular in rural communities.

A major problem of the court system is the overwhelming backlog of cases. According to government testimony in Parliament, about 720,000 cases in July were pending in criminal and civil courts (almost a 50 percent increase from 1995), and more than 30,000 people, or 67 percent of the country's total prison population, were awaiting trial. Government sources show that the period between detention and trial averages 6 months, but press and human rights groups report many instances of pretrial detention lasting for several years. These conditions, and the corruption encountered in the judicial process, effectively prevent many people from obtaining a fair trial or justice.

The Government claims that it holds no political prisoners, but both the BNP and Awami League charge that their activists have been arrested under the SPA for political reasons (see Section 2.d.).

f. *Arbitrary Interference with Privacy, Family, Home, or Correspondence.*—The law requires authorities to obtain a judicial warrant before entering a home. However, according to human rights monitors, police rarely obtain warrants, and officers violating the procedure are not punished. In addition, the SPA permits searches without a warrant. The Government reportedly opens international mail and monitors telephone calls on occasion.

g. *Use of Excessive Force and Violations of Humanitarian Law in Internal Conflicts.*—The Shanti Bahini, a tribal group, has waged a low-level conflict in the Chittagong Hill Tracts (CHT) since the early 1970's to deter nontribal Bengali settlers who seek to exploit the Tracts' fertile and sparsely populated land. Government settlement programs increased the number of Bengali inhabitants in the CHT from 3 percent of the region's total population in 1947 to an estimated 48 percent in 1996. Although the Government prohibits further settlement of the area except for the purpose of starting a business, such as rubber planting, citizens from the flatlands continue to arrive.

All of the groups that participate in or are affected by the conflict—indigenous tribes, settlers, and security forces—have accused each other of human rights violations. It is difficult to verify facts in specific incidents because government travel restrictions, tight security, difficult terrain, and unsafe conditions created by the insurgency limit access to the area.

In September the most violent incident occurred in several years of conflict. Twenty-eight Bengali woodcutters were abducted by the Shanti Bahini and murdered, possibly the result of a dispute over payment of "tolls" (protection money extorted by the Shanti Bahini). A government-appointed committee is investigating the killings.

In other violence related to the Chittagong Hills conflict, several police officers, soldiers, rebels, and noncombatants were killed during the first 9 months of the year.

During the political turmoil of the first half of the year, there was little progress in the Government's talks with Shanti Bahini's political wing, the Jana Sanghati Samiti (JSS). However, the two sides agreed at short regular intervals to extend their cease-fire. Talks between the two groups resumed in late December, during which they extended the cease-fire until March 31, 1997.

The Government estimates that 45,000 Chakma tribal members fled the conflict in the CHT and sought shelter in refugee camps in India. Few of them returned to Bangladesh in 1996. The Shanti Bahini allegedly discouraged refugees from repatriating, and organizations based in the hills claim that returnees face persecution by the Government. Government officials claim that voluntary refugee returns, although small in number, increased slightly from the previous year and that the Government assisted returned refugees in their resettlement.

Section 2. Respect for Civil Liberties, Including:

a. *Freedom of Speech and Press.*—The Constitution provides for freedom of speech, expression, and the press, subject to "reasonable restrictions" in the interest of security, friendly relations with foreign states, public order, decency, and morality, or to prohibit defamation or incitement to an offense. With some exceptions the Government generally respects freedom of speech. On occasion the BNP government censored criticism of Islam.

Following the boycotted February elections, the press played a key role in persuading the BNP Government to turn over power to a caretaker government in April, setting the stage for the national elections in June, won by the Awami League. Demonstrations in front of the National Press Club in Dhaka and nationwide strikes were widely reported. Candidates from dozens of political parties campaigned freely prior to the June elections, and in several subsequent by-elections. Allegations by the BNP of Awami League voter fraud in September by-election balloting in two constituencies were reported openly in the press. The BNP regularly stages walk-outs of parliamentary sessions and threatens noncooperation with the Government, all of which is widely reported in the press.

There is one government-owned and one privately owned wire service that distribute news nationally. In September the Awami League reportedly issued verbal guidance to the government wire service to allow stories that are critical of the Government but not those that are "atrocious" or "unfairly overly critical."

Newspaper ownership and content are not subject to direct government restriction. The press, numbering hundreds of daily and weekly publications, is a forum for a wide range of views. Newsprint is allocated from government factories at subsidized prices. Papers that cannot obtain enough government newsprint to meet their needs must buy it on the open market at higher prices. On occasion government favoritism in allocating newsprint is alleged. An acute shortage of newsprint in early 1996 resulted in many newspapers reducing the number of their pages.

Some editors complain that the Government places advertising to reward supporters and punish critical newspapers, a practice that fosters self-censorship.

Foreign publications are subject to censorship. When enforced, this is most often for immodest or obscene photographs or perceived misrepresentation of Islam.

In August the Awami League Government allowed the circulation of the Indian-published Bengali language magazine Desh. It had been banned since 1994 for publishing an article containing comments perceived to cast doubt on the legitimacy of Bangladesh.

The Government owns and controls radio and television, which under both the BNP and Awami League have provided more extensive and favorable coverage to the ruling party than to the opposition. While several local business people have expressed interest in establishing private radio and television stations, there are no indications that this is likely to happen in the near future. However, the British Broadcasting Corporation (BBC) and the Cable News Network (CNN) international news and features are retransmitted live and uncensored for several hours each day. There are no restrictions on the installation of satellite dishes, which are widely owned both in Dhaka and throughout the country, including remote villages.

The Government's film censor board did not ban any films during the year; however, in past years the board banned several locally produced and foreign films, usually on the grounds that the films promoted immorality. The film censor board also considers issues of state security, law and order, religious sentiment, foreign relations, defamation of a person, and plagiarism in deciding whether to ban a film.

In June S.M. Alauddin, editor of the Khulna newsweekly Patradut, was killed in the town of Satkhira. Alauddin was a member of the ruling Awami League, which the week before had gained power. Five persons were arrested in connection with the murder, but speculation persists that others escaped and that the killing was the result of factional fighting within the party.

In June at least 30 journalists were injured at the Parliament building when baton-wielding police charged reporters and photographers covering the oathtaking of newly elected members of Parliament from the Jatiyo Party.

In September, following the by-election in which the opposition BNP lost seats, several BNP activists assaulted eight photographers covering a BNP rally in Dhaka near Bangla Motor Crossing. They also threatened to seek out journalists from a newspaper critical of the BNP. BNP officials condemned the attack while blaming it on Awami League infiltrators.

Feminist author Taslima Nasreen, whose writings and statements provoked death threats from some Islamic groups in 1993 and 1994, has remained abroad since her departure for Europe in 1994. The Government charged Nasreen in 1994 under a section of the Penal Code that stipulates punishment for anyone convicted of intentionally insulting religious beliefs, but it did not actively pursue its case against her during 1996. The Government has taken no action against those who issued death threats against Nasreen, even though such threats also violate the law.

Academic freedom is generally respected. Teachers and students at all levels are free to pursue academic assignments except on extremely sensitive religious and political topics.

b. *Freedom of Peaceful Assembly and Association.*—The Constitution provides for freedom of assembly, subject to restrictions in the interest of public order and public health. The Government sometimes prohibits rallies for security reasons.

Both the Government and opposition parties frequently interfere with each other's rallies and public meetings. Throughout the year partisans of the ruling and opposition parties used violence to disrupt political gatherings. In addition, both have used a statute that allows public assemblies to be prohibited—to prevent possible violence—if two or more parties have scheduled rallies for the same time and place. Political parties, after learning of planned opposing-party public gatherings, schedule other rallies for the same time and place, in hopes of forcing authorities to cancel both events.

The Constitution provides for the right of every citizen to form associations, subject to "reasonable restrictions" in the interest of morality or public order, and in general the Government respects this right. In practice, individuals are free to join private groups, but a local magistrate must approve public meetings.

c. *Freedom of Religion.*—The Constitution establishes Islam as the state religion but also stipulates the right to practice the religion of one's choice, and the Government respects this provision in practice. Approximately 88 percent of the 123 million population is Muslim. Some members of the Hindu, Christian, and Buddhist minorities continue to perceive and experience discrimination toward them from the majority community (see Section 5).

The law permits citizens to proselytize. However, strong social resistance to conversion from Islam means that many of the missionary efforts by non-Muslims are aimed at Hindus and tribal groups. The Government allows various religions to establish places of worship, train clergy, travel for religious purposes, and maintain links with coreligionists abroad. Foreign missionaries may work in Bangladesh, but their right to proselytize is not protected by the Constitution, and proselytization is frequently discouraged by the Government. Missionaries sometimes face problems in obtaining visas.

d. *Freedom of Movement Within the Country, Foreign Travel, Emigration, and Repatriation.*—Citizens are able to move freely within the country. Travel by foreigners is restricted in the CHT and some other border areas. Citizens are generally free to travel abroad and emigrate. The right of repatriation is generally observed.

Approximately 250,000 Rohingyas (Muslims from Burma's Arakan province) crossed into southeastern Bangladesh in late 1991 and early 1992, fleeing repression. Following voluntary repatriation efforts by the U.N. High Commissioner for Refugees (UNHCR), approximately 31,000 Rohingyas remain in the area of Cox's Bazar. The UNHCR estimates that the majority of the remaining refugees will repatriate in 1996; however, repatriation efforts were slowed by reports early in the year of violence and other abuse inside Burma against returning refugees and by the limited number of clearances issued by Burmese authorities.

During the first 5 months of 1996 another influx of Rohingyas arrived. Estimates of their numbers vary from 6,000 to 15,000, and most are thought to be living in villages and towns in the southeast. Many other Rohingyas, considered by both the BNP and Awami League governments to be economic migrants rather than refugees, were reportedly forced back into Burma by Bangladesh security forces. On April 20, 15 Rohingyas drowned near Teknaf when their boat capsized after Bangladeshi security forces ordered it back to Burma.

In August about 200 people, reported to be Bangladeshis working illegally in Pakistan, were forced back to Pakistan when they attempted to enter Bangladesh. The Government said that they carried false passports, denied their claim to citizenship, and excluded them from the country without judicial process. This occurred despite efforts by their local family members to persuade the Government that the returnees were citizens.

There are about 238,000 non-Bengali Muslims, known as Biharis, who have remained in Bangladesh since 1971 awaiting settlement in Pakistan.

Bangladesh is not a party to the 1951 United Nations Convention Relating to the Status of Refugees and its 1967 Protocol. The Government generally cooperates with the UNHCR and other humanitarian organizations in assisting refugees. The law does not provide for first asylum or resettlement of asylum seekers. However, the Government does in practice grant temporary asylum to individual asylum seekers whom the UNHCR has interviewed and recognized as refugees, on a case by case basis. At the request of the UNHCR, the Government has allowed about 200 asylum seekers, mostly from Somalia and Iran, to remain in Bangladesh for several years, until they can arrange their resettlement in a third country. In the case of the early 1996 Rohingya arrivals and attempted arrivals, the Government effectively denied first asylum by catagorizing them as illegal economic migrants, denying the UNHCR official access to those that did successfully enter Bangladesh, jailing at least 200 of them with common criminals, and turning back as many as possible at the border. Abuses such as the forced return and mistreatment of individual refugees already living in UNHCR camps have been reported, but these appear to be the exception rather than the rule. Nongovernmental organizations (NGO's) with access to the camps claimed that the new arrivals had fled various hardships and mistreatment, including forced labor.

Section 3. Respect for Political Rights: The Right of Citizens to Change Their Government

Bangladesh is a multiparty, parliamentary democracy in which elections by secret ballot are held on the basis of universal suffrage. Members of Parliament are elected at least every 5 years. The Parliament has 300 elected members, with 30 additional seats reserved for women, who are in turn elected by Parliament.

Bangladesh held national elections twice in 1996, in February and June. Since March 1994, when opposition parties accused the BNP of intimidation and vote-rigging in a parliamentary by-election, the Parliament had been attended only by BNP Members of Parliament. The combined opposition parties, led by the Awami League under Sheikh Hasina, first boycotted Parliament and later resigned their seats (146 in all), demanding that general elections be held under a neutral caretaker administration. Despite the boycott, resignations, and continuing agitation programs (rallies, demonstrations, transport blockades, and general strikes), the Parliament remained in session until the end of its 5-year term. The February elections, held under the BNP Government, were boycotted and actively resisted by all major opposition parties. Illegal actions by both opposition and ruling party activists marred the election. Opposition parties, led by the Awami League, engaged in widespread intimidation of voters, including attacks on polling places and theft of ballot boxes, in order to reduce turnout. The ruling BNP engaged in ballot-box stuffing to ensure the victory of its candidates. Many BNP candidates were elected unopposed in many constituencies, and the BNP ended up with all but two seats in Parliament.

In the face of increasing pressure from the combined opposition (a continuous general strike or "noncooperation movement" virtually shut down the country for 3 weeks in March), the Parliament drafted and passed a constitutional amendment mandating a neutral caretaker government for future interim periods after the dissolution of Parliament prior to general elections. The BNP then dissolved Parliament and, according to the terms of the amendment, handed over power to a caretaker administration headed by the President. All parties participated in the June elections; domestic and international observers deemed these to be generally free and fair, and high voter turnout set new records for the country. The Awami League won a majority of seats (more than 170, including reserved women's seats) and formed a government. The BNP charged the Awami League and government employees with conspiring to rig the vote, but it nevertheless joined Parliament and, with 113 seats, became the largest opposition party in the country's history.

In addition to the 30 parliamentary seats reserved for women (whose occupants are chosen by Parliament), women are free to contest any seat in Parliament. Seven women were elected in their own right in the June national elections. Seats are not specifically reserved for other minority groups, such as tribal peoples. However, tribal peoples have some parliamentary representation; eight members from minority groups won seats in the last elections.

Section 4. Governmental Attitude Regarding International and Nongovernmental Investigation of Alleged Violations of Human Rights

The Government generally permits human rights groups to conduct their activities. In 1996 such groups published reports, held press conferences, and issued appeals to the Government with regard to specific cases. The Government is sensitive to international opinion regarding human rights issues. It has been open to dialog with international organizations and foreign diplomatic missions regarding issues such as detention of opposition leaders and problems of trafficking in women and children.

The Government has put pressure on individual human rights advocates. Father Richard Timm, an American Catholic priest and human rights advocate who has worked in Bangladesh for over 40 years, has faced long delays in obtaining a new reentry visa. After his visa's expiration in May, he waited until August before receiving another, valid only until October. Other missionaries who advocate human rights have faced similar problems in the past.

The Government has since 1991 refused to register the Bangladesh section of Amnesty International. However, the Government recently registered the Bangladesh Human Rights Commission's Treatment Center for Trauma Victims. No major incidents of attacks on NGO workers or human rights activists were reported during the year. In past years representatives of local human rights groups have at times been physically attacked by religious extremists, who considered their activities unIslamic. The Government has failed to bring to justice those who engaged in such violence.

Section 5. Discrimination Based on Race, Sex, Religion, Disability, Language, or Social Status

The Constitution states that "all citizens are equal before the law and are entitled to equal protection by the law." In practice, the Government does not strongly enforce laws aimed at eliminating discrimination. In this context, women, children, minority groups, and the disabled often confront social and economic disadvantages.

Women.—Violence against women is difficult to quantify because of unreliable statistics, but wife beating appears to be widespread. A widespread and growing awareness of the problem is fostered by the Government, media, and by women's rights organizations.

Much of the violence against women is related to disputes over dowries. According to one human rights group, there were 73 dowry related killings during the first 9 months of the year. Human rights groups and press reports indicate that incidents of vigilantism against women—sometimes led by religious leaders—are common occurrences, particularly in rural areas. These include humiliating, painful punishments, such as whipping of women accused of moral offenses. For example, in January in Habiganj local religious leaders reportedly subjected a woman to 101 lashes for adultery, and in October in Maulvibazar district, a woman reportedly died after being beaten by village leaders for the same offense. Few perpetrators are prosecuted.

The Government has enacted laws specifically prohibiting certain forms of discrimination against women, including the Antidowry Prohibition Act of 1980, the Cruelty to Women Law of 1983, and the Women Repression Law of 1995. Enforcement of these laws is weak, however, especially in rural areas, and the Government seldom prosecutes vigorously those cases that are filed. However, in August the

Government accepted a suit against the State by a women's activist group in connection with the 1995 rape and murder of a 14-year-old girl by police officers.

Women remain in a subordinate position in society. The Government has not acted effectively to protect their basic freedoms. Approximately 30 percent of women are literate, compared to 35 to 40 percent of the general population. In recent years, female school enrollment has improved. Approximately 50 percent of primary and secondary school students are female. Women are often unaware of their rights, because of continued high illiteracy rates among adults and unequal educational opportunities. Strong social stigmas and lack of economic means to obtain legal assistance frequently keep women from seeking redress in the courts.

According to the 1961 Muslim Family Ordinance, female heirs receive less inheritance than male heirs, and wives are more restricted in divorce rights. Men are permitted to have up to four wives, although this right is rarely exercised. Laws provide some protection for women against arbitrary divorce and the taking of additional wives by husbands without the first wife's consent, but the protections generally apply only to registered marriages. Marriages in the countryside are often not registered because of ignorance of the law.

While employment opportunities have been stronger for women than for men in the past few years, this is to a large extent due to the growth of the garment industry, in which female workers are prevalent. Programs extending credit to large numbers of rural women have also contributed to greater economic power for them. However, women still occupy only a small fraction of other wage-earning jobs, and hold fewer than 5 percent of government jobs. The Government's policy to include more women in government jobs has had limited effect.

Children.—The Government undertakes programs in the areas of primary education, health, and nutrition. The Government made universal primary education mandatory in 1991 but stated that it could not fully implement the law because of a lack of resources. The Government has also initiated programs that offer incentives for female children between the ages of 12 and 16 to remain in school.

Reports from human rights monitors indicate that child abandonment, kidnaping, trafficking for labor bondage, and prostitution continue to be serious and widespread problems. UNICEF recently estimated that there were about 10,000 child prostitutes in Bangladesh. Other estimates have been as high as 29,000. The law does not allow anyone under 18 years of age to engage in prostitution and stipulates a maximum sentence of life imprisonment for persons found guilty of forcing a child into prostitution. However, procurers of minors are rarely prosecuted. Prostitution is legal for those over 18 with government certification. Human rights monitors report that police and local government officials often either ignore prostitution and trafficking, including that of children, or actually profit from it. Awareness of the issue is increasing, and it receives press coverage.

There is extensive trafficking in both women and children, primarily to the Middle East, India, Pakistan, and Southeast Asia, and also within Bangladesh. The trade, which mainly is for purposes of prostitution and labor servitude, is difficult to quantify. Press reports and evidence from human rights monitors indicate that it is widespread. The connivance of officials at various levels allows the trade to function. Enforcement of laws against it is hampered by poor records and easy access to forged identity documents. Most trafficked persons are lured by promises of good jobs or marriage. The BNP and Awami League governments have expressed concern about the problem and have worked with U.N. agencies and nongovernmental organizations to seek ways to combat it.

People With Disabilities.—The laws provide for equal treatment and freedom from discrimination for the disabled, but they face social and economic discrimination. The Government has not enacted specific legislation or otherwise mandated accessibility for the disabled.

Indigenous People.—Tribal peoples, especially in the Chittagong Hill Tracts, have a marginal ability to influence decisions concerning the use of their lands. Until 1985 the Government regularly parceled out land in the Chittagong Hill Tracts to Bengali settlers.

The Government has moved toward granting the tribal peoples more authority in the Chittagong Hill Tracts. In July 1991, tribal-dominated local government councils assumed control over primary education, health, family welfare, and the agricultural extension service, although the real extent of their autonomy is limited. The Government continues to withold from the councils authority in several governmental functions for which they were originally intended, including law and order as well as land use (see Section 1.g.).

Tribal peoples in other areas have reported similar problems of loss of land to Bengali Muslims through questionable legal practices and other means. The Garos, who live in the Madhapur Forest region in north central Bangladesh, have encountered problems in maintaining their cultural traditions and livelihoods in the face of reforestation projects. Human rights monitors in the region claim that the Garos are being harassed and intimidated into leaving their homes to make way for government-run, internationally financed economic development projects.

Religious Minorities.—Hindus, Christians, and Buddhists make up an estimated 10 percent of the population. Although the Government is secular, religion exerts a powerful influence on politics. The Government is sensitive to the Muslim consciousness of the majority of its citizens. However, the Jamaat-E-Islami, the country's largest Islamic political party, went from 18 seats in Parliament after the 1991 elections, to 3 in the June elections. The Awami League Government has not actively sought its political support.

Islamic extremists have occasionally violently attacked women, religious minorities, and development workers. The Government has sometimes failed to denounce, investigate, and prosecute perpetrators of these attacks.

Religious minorities are in practice disadvantaged in such areas as access to government jobs and political office. Selection boards in the government services are often without minority group representation.

Property ownership, particularly among Hindus, has been a contentious issue since independence in 1971, when many Hindus lost landholdings because of anti-Hindu discrimination in the application of the law. Prior to its June election victory, the Awami League promised to repeal the Vested Property Act, the law used to deprive Hindus of their property. However, The Government has so far taken no action. There have been cases of violence directed against religious minority communities that have also resulted in the loss of property. Such intercommunal violence has caused some members of religious minority groups to depart the country. While intercommunal violence occurred infrequently during the year, there were violent incidents in which Hindus were targeted in Chittagong during the June elections.

Section 6. Worker Rights

a. *The Right of Association.*—The Constitution provides for the right to join unions and—with government approval—the right to form a union. Approximately 1.6 million members of the country's total work force of about 45 to 50 million workers belong to unions. Only about 3 million workers are involved in the formal industrial sector. There is a large unreported informal sector, regarding which no reliable labor statistics exist.

For a union to obtain and maintain its registration, 30 percent employee participation in the workplace is required. Moreover, would-be unionists are technically forbidden to engage in many labor "activities" prior to registration. Labor activists have protested that this requirement severely restricts workers' freedom to organize.

With the exception of workers in the railway, postal, telegraph and telephone departments, government civil servants are forbidden to join unions. This ban also applies to security-related government employees such as the military and police. Civil servants forbidden to join unions, such as teachers and nurses, have formed associations that perform functions similar to labor unions, i.e., providing for members' welfare, offering legal services, and airing grievances. Collective bargaining, however, is prohibited. Some workers have formed unregistered unions, particularly university employees and workers in the construction and transport (both public and private) industries.

Ten to 15 percent of Bangladesh's approximately 4,200 labor unions are affiliated with 23 officially registered national trade union (NTU) centers (there are also several unregistered NTU's). There are no legal restrictions on political activities by labor unions, although the calling of nationwide general strikes or transportation blockades by unions is considered a criminal rather than a political act and thus forbidden. Some unions had complained that the BNP government used its Anti-Terrorism Law as a means to suppress both opposition political workers and union members rather than bona fide terrorists. In late 1994, however, the Anti-Terrorism Law lapsed, and the BNP government decided not to renew it. No arrests of labor leaders under the law have been made since 1993.

While unions are not part of the government structure, they are highly politicized. Virtually all the NTU centers are affiliated with political parties, including one with the ruling Awami League. Some unions are militant and engage in intimidation and vandalism. Illegal blockades of public transportation routes by strikers occurred frequently during the year. Pitched battles between members of rival labor unions occur regularly; hundreds were injured (and at least three combatants died) in 1996 in various large jute and textile mills, as well as in the inland water transport and overland transport sectors. Fighting often is over the control of rackets or extortion payoffs and typically involves knives, guns, and homemade bombs.

Workers are eligible for membership on their unions' executive staff, the size of which is set by law in proportion to the number of union members. Registration of a union may only be canceled by the Registrar of Trade Unions with the concurrence of the Labor Court, but no such actions were known to have been taken in 1996. Several cases were filed, invariably by employers claiming a union's membership had fallen below the requisite level, but, because of a backlog and other administrative problems, these cases have not come under review.

The right to strike is not specifically recognized in the law, but strikes are a common form of protest. The most prominent recent strikes have been by inland water transport employees, who claimed that they were not receiving the required minimum wage. Other major strikes have been by jute and textile workers, who sought increased wages and benefits along with guarantees against future privatization and job loss. Employees organized in professional associations or nonregistered unions also strike. In 1996 nurses, private elementary teachers, and members of the nonadministrative cadre of the civil service were among the striking groups. They sought better pay or benefits, a greater share of the public budget, inclusion in the public sector, or administrative reform. University teachers strike for short periods from time to time over the continuing problem of campus violence. General strikes are standard tools of political opposition groups and are used to pressure the Government to meet political demands. They caused significant economic and social disruption during the year. Wildcat strikes are illegal but occur frequently, with varying government responses. Wildcat strikes in the transportation sector are particularly common.

The Essential Services Ordinance permits the Government to bar strikes for 3 months in any sector that it declares essential. This ban, generally obeyed, has so far been applied to national airline pilots, water supply workers, shipping operations employees, and electricity supply workers. The bans tend to be renewed every 3 months. The Government is empowered to prohibit a strike or lockout at any time before or after the strike or lockout begins and to refer the dispute to the Labor Court. Mechanisms for conciliation, arbitration, and Labor Court dispute resolution were established under the Industrial Relations Ordinance of 1969. Workers have the right to strike in the event of a failure to settle. If a strike lasts 30 days or longer, the Government may prohibit the strike and refer the dispute to the Labor Court for adjudication. This has not happened since 1993.

There are provisions in the Industrial Relations Ordinance for the immunity of registered unions or union officers from civil liability. Enforcement of these provisions is uneven. In the case of illegal work actions, such as transportation blockades, police have arrested union members under either the Special Powers Act, the Antiterrorism Law (now no longer in effect), or regular criminal codes.

There are no restrictions on affiliation with international labor organizations, and unions and federations maintain a variety of such links. Trade unionists are required to obtain government clearance to travel to International Labor Organization (ILO) meetings, but no clearances were reported denied in 1996.

b. *The Right to Organize and Bargain Collectively.*—Collective bargaining is legal only for private sector workers, on condition that the workers are represented by unions legally registered as collective bargaining agents by the Registrar of Trade Unions. Collective bargaining occurs on occasion in large private enterprises such as pharmaceuticals or jute and textiles, but with unemployment in the 30 percent range, workers' concerns over job security often outweigh wage and other issues. Collective bargaining generally does not occur in small private enterprises.

Public sector workers' pay levels and other benefits are recommended by the National Pay and Wages Commission. The Commission's recommendations are binding and may not be disputed except on the issue of implementation.

Under the Industrial Relations Ordinance, there is considerable leeway for discrimination against union members and organizers by employers. For example, the ordinance allows arbitrary transfer of workers suspected of union activities or termination with payment of mandatory severance benefits (2 weeks' salary). Complaints that employers routinely engage in antiunion discrimination and harrassment, including physical attack, are particularly common in the garment industry. In practice, private sector employers, sometimes working in collaboration with local police, tend to discourage any union activity. The Registrar of Trade Unions rules on discrimination complaints. In a number of cases the Labor Court has ordered the reinstatement of workers fired for union activities. However, the Labor Court's overall effectiveness is hampered by a serious case backlog, and there have also been allegations that some of its deliberations have been corrupted by employers.

The law prohibits professional and industry-based unions in the two export processing zones (EPZ's). A small number of workers in the EPZ's have skirted prohibitions on forming unions by setting up associations. The BNP government stated in

1992 that labor law restrictions on freedom of association and formation of unions in the EPZ's would be lifted by 1997. So far neither the BNP nor the Awami League governments have taken action toward this end. In the burgeoning garment industry there have been numerous complaints of workers being harassed and fired in some factories for trying to organize unions. In addition to the prohibition on unions, no collective bargaining takes place in the EPZ's.

c. *Prohibition of Forced or Compulsory Labor.*—The Constitution prohibits forced or compulsory labor. The Factories Act and Shops and Establishment Act, both passed in 1965, set up inspection mechanisms to enforce laws against forced labor. These laws are not rigorously enforced, partly because resources for enforcement are few. While there is no large-scale bonded labor, there is forced labor to the extent that workers are often required to work later than stipulated by law, with no special compensation. This is a notable problem in the garment industry.

d. *Minimum Age for Employment of Children.*—The law prohibits labor by children. The Factories Act of 1965 bars children under the age of 14 from working in factories. This law also stipulates that young workers (children and adolescents) are only allowed to work a maximum 5-hour day and only between the hours of 7 a.m. and 7 p.m.

Enforcement of these rules is inadequate. According to a 1990 labor force survey by the Bureau of Statistics, the country has 5.7 million working children 10 to 14 years of age. The United Nations estimates that about one-third of the population under the age of 18 is engaged in some type of formal or informal employment. Children are commonly seen driving rickshaws, breaking bricks at construction sites, carrying fruit, vegetables, and dry goods for shoppers at markets, and working at tea stalls. They are found as peelers, packers, and beachcombers in the shrimp industry. Also, children work side by side with other family members in small-scale and subsistence agriculture. Children routinely perform domestic work. Cases of children being physically abused and occasionally killed by heads of households where they work are reported in the press. Under the law, every child must attend school through the fifth grade. However, the Government continues to maintain that it does not yet have the resources to implement this law effectively.

In anticipation of possible foreign legislation prohibiting the import of products made by child labor, thousands of underage workers employed in Bangladesh's ready-made garment industry were fired in 1993. Many were probably rehired later by other factories or in subcontracting operations, but the Bangladesh Garment Manufacturers and Exporters Association (BGMEA) pledged to make its member factories child labor-free. Protracted negotiations led to the July 1995 signing of a Memorandum of Understanding (MOU) between the BGMEA, UNICEF, and the ILO to eliminate child labor in the garment sector. The MOU establishes a cooperative program to identify underage workers (through surveys of the garment factories), remove them from their factories, and place them in new schools. It also provides that no children would be fired until education programs were ready to receive them. The children receive a monthly stipend while attending school to help replace their lost income. The ILO takes the lead on monitoring implementation of the MOU, and UNICEF on providing education. As of mid-November, 285 schools had opened, with 7,622 former child workers enrolled. The number of children working in nonexport, or nonfactory garment production is unknown. UNICEF estimates that as many as 200,000 children under the age of 14 are employed in some connection to the garment industry. The ILO calls that estimate exaggerated. Child labor in the industry has not ended, but the process of the elimination of child labor in this sector appears to be making progress.

e. *Acceptable Conditions of Work.*—There is no national minimum wage. Instead, the Wage Commission, which convenes every several years, sets wages and benefits industry by industry. In most cases, private sector employers ignore this wage structure. Organized jute and textile workers have called strikes in an attempt to win wage parity for their industry's private sector workers. The average monthly wage is sufficient to provide an individual with a minimal standard of living but is not sufficient to provide a decent standard of living for a worker and family.

The law sets a standard 48-hour workweek with 1 day off mandated. A 60-hour workweek, inclusive of a maximum 12 hours of overtime, is allowed. The law is poorly enforced in industries such as hosiery and ready-made garments.

The Factories Act of 1965 nominally sets occupational health and safety standards. The law is comprehensive but appears to be largely ignored by employers. Workers may resort to legal action for enforcement of the law's provisions, but few cases are actually prosecuted. Enforcement by the Labor Ministry's industrial inspectors is weak. Due to high unemployment and inadequate enforcement of the laws, workers demanding correction of dangerous working conditions or refusing to participate in perceived dangerous activities risk losing their jobs.

BHUTAN

Bhutan is a monarchy without a constitution or a bill of rights. The Wangchuk Dynasty of hereditary monarchs has ruled the country since 1907. King Jigme Singhye Wangchuk, on the throne since 1972, has continued efforts toward social and political modernization begun by his father. In recent years, there has been rapid progress in education, health, sanitation, and communications, and an increase in elected representatives and their role in decisionmaking. The judiciary is not independent of the King.

Three quarters of the population of 600,000 is composed of Buddhists with cultural traditions akin to those of Tibet. The remaining quarter of the population are mostly Hindus of Nepalese origin inhabiting the country's southern districts. The rapid growth of this ethnic Nepalese segment of the population led the Buddhist majority to fear for the survival of their culture. Government efforts to tighten citizenship requirements and control illegal immigration resulted in political protests and led to ethnic conflict and repression of ethnic Nepalese in southern districts during the late 1980's and early 1990's. Tens of thousands of ethnic Nepalese left Bhutan in 1991–92, many forcibly expelled. Approximately 91,000 ethnic Nepalese remain in refugee camps in Nepal and upwards of 15,000 reside outside the camps in the Indian states of Assam and West Bengal.

The Royal Bhutan Police, assisted by the Royal Bhutan Army, including those assigned to the Royal Body Guard, and a national militia, maintain internal security. Some members of these forces committed human rights abuses against ethnic Nepalese.

The economy is based on agriculture and forestry, which provide the main livelihood for 90 percent of the population and account for about half of the gross domestic product. Agriculture consists largely of subsistence farming and animal husbandry. Cardamon, citrus fruit, and spices are the leading agricultural exports. Cement and electricity are the other important exports. Strong trade and monetary links align the economy closely to that of India. Hydroelectric power production potential and tourism are key resources, although the Government limits foreign tourist arrivals by means of pricing policies. The gross national product per capita is estimated to be $470. Bhutan remains among the poorest and least developed countries in the world.

The Government significantly restricts the rights of the Kingdom's citizens. The King exercises strong and active, although indirect, influence over the Government. Citizens do not have the right to change their government. The Government discourages political parties, and none operates legally. Judges serve at the King's pleasure. There are no written criminal and civil procedure codes; judicial processes are based on traditional practices. Programs to build a body of written law and train lawyers are progressing. The Government restricts freedom of speech, the press, assembly, association, and worker rights. There are significant limitations on the right to a fair trial, freedom of religion, and citizens' privacy. Private television reception has been banned since 1989. The Government has failed to reach agreement with the Government of Nepal on procedures for screening and repatriation of ethnic Nepalese in refugee camps. The Government claims that it has prosecuted government personnel for unspecified abuses committed in the early 1990's; however, public indications are that it has done little to investigate and prosecute security force officials responsible for torture and other abuses committed against ethnic Nepalese residents.

RESPECT FOR HUMAN RIGHTS

Section 1. Respect for the Integrity of the Person, Including Freedom From:

a. *Political and Other Extrajudicial Killing.*—There were no reports of political or other extrajudicial killings.

b. *Disappearance.*—There were no reports of politically motivated disappearances.

c. *Torture and Other Cruel, Inhuman, or Degrading Treatment or Punishment.*—According to the Center for the Treatment of Victims of Torture, numerous ethnic Nepalese refugees attempting to return to Bhutan were captured by security forces, tortured, and sent back across the border.

Refugee groups credibly claim that persons detained as suspected dissidents in the early 1990s were tortured by security forces, who also committed acts of rape. During those years, the Government's ethnic policies and the crackdown on ethnic Nepalese political agitation created a climate of impunity in which the Government tacitly condoned the physical abuse of ethnic Nepalese. The Government denies these abuses but also claims it has investigated and prosecuted three government personnel for unspecified abuses of authority during that period. Details of these cases have not been made public and there is little indication that the Government has adequately investigated or punished any security force officials involved in the widespread abuses of 1989–92.

Prison conditions are reportedly adequate if austere. A prison visit program begun in 1993 by the International Committee of the Red Cross (ICRC) and opening of a new prison in Chemgang in 1994 contributed to substantial improvement in conditions of detention over the primitive conditions that existed until a few years ago.

d. *Arbitrary Arrest, Detention, or Exile.*—Under the Police Act of 1979, police may not arrest a person without a warrant and must produce an arrested person before a court within 24 hours of arrest, exclusive of travel time from place of arrest. Legal protections are incomplete, however, due to the lack of a fully elaborated criminal procedure code and deficiencies in police training and practice. Arbitrary arrest and detention remain a problem but are not routinely used as a form of harassment. There sometimes have been delays in informing family members of an arrest. Incommunicado detention of suspected militants was a serious problem in 1991 and 1992, but the initiation of ICRC prison visits and establishment of an ICRC mail service between detainees and family members has helped allay this problem. Of those detained in connection with political dissidence and violence in southern Bhutan in 1991–92, 1,685 were ultimately amnestied, 9 acquitted, and 46 released after serving their sentences, and 88 are serving prison sentences. As of October, charges were pending against two persons arrested for "anti-National activities" in southern Bhutan in 1996.

Although the Government does not formally use exile as a form of punishment, many accused political dissidents freed under government amnesties say that they were released on the condition that they depart the country. Many of them subsequently registered at refugee camps in Nepal.

e. *Denial of Fair Public Trial.*—There is no written constitution, and the judiciary is not independent of the King.

The judicial system consists of district courts and a High Court in Thimphu. Judges are appointed by the King on the recommendation of the Chief Justice and may be removed by him. Minor offenses and administrative matters are adjudicated by village headmen.

Criminal cases and a variety of civil matters are adjudicated under a legal code established in the 17th century and revised in 1965. For offenses against the State, state-appointed prosecutors file charges and prosecute cases. In other cases, the relevant organizations and departments of government file charges and conduct the prosecution. Defendants are supposed to be presented with written charges in languages that they understand and given time to prepare their own defense. This practice is not always followed, however, according to some political dissidents. In cases where defendants cannot write their own defense, courts assign judicial officers to assist defendants. A legal education program is gradually building a body of persons who have received formal training in the law abroad.

Defendants have the right to appeal to the High Court and may make a final appeal to the King, who traditionally delegates the decision to the Royal Advisory Council. Trials are supposed to be conducted in open hearings, however, political dissidents claim that this is not always the case in practice.

Questions of family law, such as marriage, divorce, and adoption, are resolved according to a citizen's religion: Buddhist tradition for the majority of the population and Hindu tradition, which predominates in areas inhabited by ethnic Nepalese, for the minority.

Some or all of the 88 prisoners serving sentences for offenses related to political dissidence or violence, primarily by ethnic Nepalese during 1991–92, may be political prisoners.

Tek-Nath Rizal, an ethnic Nepalese and internationally recognized political prisoner, remained in prison following his 1993 conviction under the National Security Act for writing and distributing political pamphlets and attending political meetings. Nevertheless, a United Nations Human Rights Commission working group on arbitrary detention that visited Bhutan in 1994 at the Government's invitation determined that Rizal had received a fair trial and declared his detention "not to be arbitrary."

f. *Arbitrary Interference with Privacy, Family, Home, or Correspondence.*—There are no laws providing for these rights. The Government requires all citizens, including minorities, to wear the traditional dress of the Drukpa majority when visiting Buddhist religious buildings, monasteries, government offices, and in schools and when attending official functions and public ceremonies. According to human rights groups police regularly conduct house to house searches for suspected dissidents without explanation or legal justification.

Section 2. Respect for Civil Liberties, Including:
   a. *Freedom of Speech and Press.*—The Government restricts freedom of speech and the press.
   The country's only regular publication is Kuensel, a weekly newspaper with a circulation of 10,000 published by an independent corporation that receives government subsidies. Kuensel, which publishes simultaneous editions in the English, Dzongkha, and Nepali languages, supports the Government but does occasionally report criticism of the King and government policies in the National Assembly. Indian and other foreign newspapers are available.
   The Government bans all private television reception in the country. Since 1989 all television antennas and satellite receiving dishes have been ordered dismantled.
   The Government radio station broadcasts each day in the four major languages (Dzongkha, Nepali, English, and Sharchop).
   English is the medium of instruction in schools and the national language, Dzongkha, is taught as second language. The teaching of Nepali as a second language was discontinued in 1990.
   b. *Freedom of Peaceful Assembly and Association.*—The Goverment restricts freedom of assembly and association. Citizens may engage in peaceful assembly and association only for purposes approved by the Government. Although the Government allows civic and business organizations, there are no legal political parties. The Government regards parties organized by ethnic Nepalese exiles—the Bhutan People's Party (BPP), the Bhutan National Democratic Party (BNDP), and the Druk National Congress (DNC)—as "terrorist and anti-national" organizations and has declared them illegal. These parties do not conduct activities inside the country. They seek the repatriation of refugees and democratic reform.
   c. *Freedom of Religion.*—Buddhism is the state religion. The Government subsidizes monasteries and shrines and provides aid to about a third of the kingdom's 12,000 monks. The monastic establishment enjoys statutory representation in the National Assembly and Royal Advisory Council and is an influential voice on public policy. Citizens of other faiths, mostly Hindus, enjoy freedom of worship but may not proselytize. Under the law, conversions are illegal.
   The King has declared major Hindu festivals to be national holidays, and the royal family participates in them. Foreign missionaries are not permitted to proselytize, but international Christian relief organizations and Jesuit priests are active in education and humanitarian activities.
   d. *Freedom of Movement Within the Country, Foreign Travel, Emigration, and Repatriation.*—Citizens traveling in border regions are required to show their citizenship identity cards at immigration check points, which in some cases are located at a considerable distance from what is in effect an open border with India. By treaty, citizens may reside and work in India.
   See Section 5 regarding the ethnic Nepalese refugee situation.

Section 3. Respect for Political Rights: The Right of Citizens to Change Their Government

   Citizens do not have the right to change their government. Bhutan is a monarchy with sovereign power vested in the King. There are, however, elected or partially elected assemblies at the local, district, and national levels, and the Government purports to encourage decentralization and citizen participation. Since 1969, the National Assembly has had the power to remove ministers, who are appointed by the King, but has never done so. Political authority resides ultimately in the King and decisionmaking involves only a small number of officials; however, major decisions are routinely made by officials subject to questioning by the National Assembly.
   Political parties do not legally exist, and their formation is discouraged by the Government as unnecessarily divisive. The Government prohibits parties established abroad by ethnic Nepalese (see Section 2.b.).
   The National Assembly established in 1953, has 150 members. Of these, 105 are elected by the people, 10 are selected by the Buddhist clergy, and the remaining 35 are appointed by the King to represent the Government. Elections to the National Assembly are contested, with candidates filing their own nominations. The Assembly enacts laws, approves senior government appointments, and advises the King on matters of national importance. Voting is by secret ballot, with a simple majority needed to pass a measure. The King may not formally veto legislation, but may return bills for further consideration. The Assembly occasionally rejects the King's recommendations or delays implementing them, but in general, the King has enough influence to persuade the Assembly to approve legislation that he considers essential or to withdraw proposals he opposes. The Assembly may question government officials and force them to resign by a two-thirds vote of no confidence.

Women are underrepresented in government and politics, although they have made small but visible gains. Three women hold seats in the National Assembly.

All major ethnic groups, including ethnic Nepalese, are represented in the National Assembly. There are 17 "southern Bhutanese" in the National Assembly.

Section 4. Governmental Attitude Regarding International and Nongovernmental Investigation of Alleged Violations of Human Rights

There are no legal human rights nongovernmental organizations (NGO's) in Bhutan. The Government regards human rights groups established by ethnic Nepalese exiles—the Human Rights Organization of Bhutan, the People's Forum for Human Rights in Bhutan, and the Association of Human Rights Activists—Bhutan—as political organizations and does not permit them to operate in Bhutan. Amnesty International visited Bhutan in 1992 to investigate and report on the alleged abuse of ethnic Nepalese. It has not been permitted to return in the years since.

ICRC representatives continue their periodic prison visits, and the Government has allowed them access to detention facilities, including those in southern districts inhabited by ethnic Nepalese. The chairman and members of the United Nations Human Rights Commission Working Group on Arbitrary Detention made a second visit to Bhutan in May as a follow-up to an October 1994 visit. In addition to meetings with government officials, members of the working group visited prisons and interviewed prisoners in Thimphu, Phuntsoling, and Samtse.

Section 5. Discrimination Based on Race, Sex, Religion, Disability, Language, or Social Status

Ongoing Government efforts to cultivate a national identity rooted in the language, religion, and culture of the Drukpa ethnic group constrain cultural expression by other ethnic groups. In the 1980's and early 1990's, concern over rapid population growth and political agitation by ethnic Nepalese resulted in policies and abusive practices that led to the departure of tens of thousands of members of this group, many forcibly expelled.

The Government claims that ethnic and gender discrimination in employment is not a problem. It claims that ethnic Nepalese fill 28 percent of Government jobs, which slightly exceeds their share of the current total population. Women are accorded respect in the traditions of most ethnic groups; however, persistence of traditional gender roles apparently accounts for the low proportion of women in Government employment. Exile groups claim that ethnic and gender discrimination is a problem.

Women.—There is no evidence of extensive rape or spousal abuse. Kuensel reported that charges of rape or attempted rape were brought in several cases. However, convictions and sentences were not reported.

There are credible reports by refugees and human rights groups that security forces raped large numbers of ethnic Nepalese women in southern Bhutan in 1991 and 1992. According to Amnesty International, some women were said to have died as a result. In one independent survey of 1,779 refugee families, 26 percent of the respondents cited rape, fear of rape, or threat of rape as a prime reason for their departure from Bhutan. The Government has denied these reports.

Rape was made a criminal offense in 1953, but that law had weak penalties and was poorly enforced. In 1993 the National Assembly adopted a revised rape act with clear definitions of criminal sexual assault and stronger penalties. In cases of rape involving minors, sentences range from 5 to 17 years. In extreme cases, a rapist may be imprisoned for life.

Women comprise 48 percent of the population and participate freely in the social and economic life of the country. Forty-three percent of enrollment in school is female, and women account for 16 percent of civil service employment. Inheritance law provides for equal inheritance among all sons and daughters, but traditional inheritance practices, which vary among ethnic groups, may be observed if the heirs choose to forego legal challenges. Dowry is not practiced, even among ethnic Nepalese Hindus. Inheritance practices favoring daughters among some groups are said to account for large numbers of women among owners of shops and businesses and an accompanying tendency of women to drop out of higher education to go into business. On the other hand, female school enrollment has been growing in response to government policies. Women are increasingly found among senior officials and private sector entrepreneurs, especially in the tourism industry. Women in unskilled jobs are generally paid slightly less than men.

Polygyny is sanctioned provided the first wife gives her permission. Marriages may be arranged by partners themselves as well as by their parents. Divorce is common. Recent legislation requires that all marriages must be registered and favors women in matters of alimony.

Children.—The Government has demonstrated its commitment to child welfare by its rapid expansion of primary schools, health-care facilities, and immunization programs. The mortality rates for both infants and children under 5-years have dropped dramatically since 1989, and primary school enrollment has increased at 9 percent a year since 1991, with enrollment of girls increasing at a yet higher rate. In 1995 the participation rate for boys and girls in primary schools was estimated at 72 percent, with the rate of completion of 7 years of schooling at 60 percent for girls and 59 percent for boys. Children enjoy a privileged position in society and benefit from international development programs focused on maternal and child welfare.

A study by UNICEF found that boys and girls receive equal treatment regarding nutrition and health care and that there is little difference in child mortality rates between the sexes. Government policies aimed at increasing enrollment of girls have increased the proportion of girls in primary schools from 39 percent in 1990 to 43 percent in 1995.

There is no societal pattern of abuse against children.

People With Disabilities.—There is no evidence of official discrimination toward people with disabilities but the Government has not passed legislation mandating accessibility for the disabled.

National/Racial/Ethnic Minorities.—Ethnic Nepalese have lived in southern Bhutan for centuries, and the early phases of economic development at the turn of the century brought a large influx of additional ethnic Nepalese. In the late 1980's, concern over the increase of population and political agitation among ethnic Nepalese prompted aggressive government efforts to assert a national culture, tighten control over southern regions, control illegal immigration, expel ethnic Nepalese, and promote national integration. Early efforts at national integration focused on assimilation, including financial incentives for intermarriage, education for some students in regions other than their own, and an increase in development funds in the south.

Beginning in 1989, more discriminatory measures were introduced, aimed at shaping a new national identity, known as Drukpa, based on the customs of the non-Nepalese Ngalong ethnic group predominant in central Bhutan. Measures included a requirement that national dress be worn for official occasions and as a school uniform, the teaching of Dzongkha as a second language in all schools, and an end to instruction in Nepali as a second language (English is the language of instruction in all schools). Also, beginning in 1988, the Government refused to renew the contracts of tens of thousands of Nepalese guest workers. Many of these workers had resided in Bhutan for years, in some cases with their families.

Citizenship became a highly contentious issue. Requirements for citizenship were first formalized in the Citizenship Law of 1958, which granted citizenship to all adults who owned land and had lived in Bhutan for at least 10 years. In 1985, however, a new citizenship law significantly tightened requirements for citizenship and resulted in the denaturalization of many ethnic Nepalese. While previously citizenship was conferred upon children whose father was a citizen under the 1958 law, the 1985 law raised this standard by requiring that both parents be citizens to confer citizenship on offspring. The law permits residents who lost citizenship under the 1985 law to apply for naturalization if they can prove residence during the previous 15 years. The Government declared as illegal immigrants all residents who could not meet the new requirements.

The 1985 Citizenship Act also stipulates the revocation of citizenship of any naturalized citizen who "has shown by act or speech to be disloyal in any manner whatsoever to the King, country, and people of Bhutan." The Home Ministry, in a circular notification in 1990, advised that "any Bhutanese nationals leaving the country to assist and help the anti-nationals shall no longer be considered as Bhutanese citizens * * * such people's family members living in the same household will also be held fully responsible and forfeit their citizenship." Human rights groups allege that these provisions were widely used to revoke the citizenship of ethnic Nepalese who were subsequently expelled or otherwise departed from Bhutan. Beginning in 1988, the Government expelled numbers of ethnic Nepalese through enforcement of the citizenship laws.

Outraged by what they saw as a campaign of repression, ethnic Nepalese mounted a series of demonstrations, sometimes violent, in September 1990. The protests were spearheaded by the newly-formed Bhutan People's Party (BPP) which demanded full citizenship rights for ethnic Nepalese, the reintroduction of Nepali as a medium of education in the south, and democratic reforms. Characterizing the BPP as a "terrorist" movement backed by Indian sympathizers, the authorities cracked down on its activities and ordered the closure of local Nepalese schools, clinics, and development programs after several were raided or bombed by dissidents. Many schools were reportedly turned into Army barracks. There were credible reports that many ethnic Nepalese activists were beaten and tortured while in custody, and that security forces committed acts of rape. There were also credible reports that militants, including BPP members, attacked and murdered census officers and other officials, and engaged in bombings. Local officials took advantage of the climate of repression to coerce ethnic Nepalese to sell their land below its fair value and emigrate.

Beginning in 1991, ethnic Nepalese began to leave southern Bhutan in large numbers and take refuge in Nepal. Many were forcibly expelled. According to Amnesty International, entire villages were sometimes evicted en masse in retaliation for an attack on a local government official. Many ethnic Nepalese were forced to sign "voluntary migration forms" wherein they agreed to leave Bhutan, after local officials threatened to fine or imprison them for failing to comply. By August 1991, according to NGO reports, 2,500 refugees were already camped illegally in Nepal, with a steady stream still coming from Bhutan. The UNHCR began providing food and shelter in September of that year, and by year's end, there were 6,000 refugees in Nepal. The number of registered refugees grew to approximately 62,000 by August 1992, and to approximately 80,000 by June 1993, when the UNHCR began individual screening of refugees. The flow slowedly considerably thereafter and is now less than a dozen persons a month. At the close of 1996, there were approximately 91,000 refugees registered in camps in Nepal, with much of the increase since 1993 the result of natural increase. An additional 15,000 refugees, according to UNHCR estimates, are living outside the camps in Nepal and India.

Ethnic Nepalese political groups in exile complain that the revision of Bhutan's citizenship laws in 1985 denaturalized tens of thousands of former residents of Bhutan. They also complain that the new laws have been selectively applied and make unfair demands for documentation on a largely illiterate people in a country that has only recently adopted basic administrative procedures. They claim that many ethnic Nepalese whose families have been in Bhutan for generations were expelled in the early 1990's because they were unable to document their claims to residence. The Government denies this and asserts that a three-member village committee—typically ethnic Nepalese in southern Bhutan—certifies in writing that a resident is a Bhutanese citizen in cases where documents cannot be produced.

The Government maintains that many of those who departed Bhutan in 1991–92 were Nepalese or Indian citizens who came to Bhutan after the enactment of the 1958 Citizenship law but were not detected until a census in 1988. The Government also claims that many persons registered in the camps as refugees may never have resided in Bhutan. A royal decree in 1991 made forcible expulsion of a citizen a criminal offense. In a January 1992 edict, the King noted reports that officials had been forcing Bhutanese nationals to leave the country but stressed that this was a serious and punishable violation of law. Nevertheless, only three officials were ever punished for abusing their authority during this period. According to the UNHCR, the overwhelming majority of refugees who have entered the camps since screening began in June 1993 have documentary proof of Bhutanese nationality. Random checks and surveys of camp residents—including both pre- and post-June 1993 arrivals—bear this out.

A Nepal-Bhutan ministerial committee met seven times in 1994–96 in efforts to resolve the Bhutanese refugee problem. These discussions have made little progress. At the end of the year, no date has been set for another round of talks. In March refugees began a series of "peace marches" from Nepal to Bhutan to assert their right to return to Bhutan. Marchers who crossed into Bhutan in August, November, and December were immediately detained and deported by Bhutanese police. In the December incident, police reportedly used force against the marchers.

Section 6. Worker Rights

a. *The Right of Association.*—Trade unionism is not permitted, and there are no labor unions. Workers do not have the right to strike, and the Government is not a member of the International Labor Organization.

b. *The Right to Organize and Bargain Collectively.*—There is no collective bargaining in industry, which accounts for about 25 percent of the gross domestic product, but it employs only a minute fraction of the total work force. The Government affects wages in the manufacturing sector through its control over wages in state-owned industries.

There are no export processing zones.

c. *Prohibition of Forced or Compulsory Labor.*—The Government abolished its system of compulsory labor taxes in December 1995. Laborers in rural development schemes previously paid through this system will now be paid regular wages. There is no evidence to suggest that domestics or children are subject to coerced or bonded labor.

d. *Minimum Age for Employment of Children.*—The law set the minimum age for employment at 18 years for citizens and 20 years for noncitizens. A UNICEF study suggested that children as young as 11 years are sometimes employed with road-building teams.

e. *Acceptable Conditions of Work.*—A circular effective February 1, 1994, established wage rates, rules and regulations for labor recruiting agencies, and regulations for payment of workmen's compensation. Wage rates are periodically revised, and range upward from a minimum of roughly $1.50 (50 ngultrums) per day for unskilled and skilled laborers, with various allowances paid in cash or kind in addition. This minimum wage does provide a decent standard of living for a worker and family in the local context. The workday is defined as 8 hours with a 1 hour lunch break. Work in excess of this must be paid at one and a half times normal rates. Workers paid on a monthly basis are entitled to 1 day's paid leave for 6 days of work and 15 days of leave annually. The largest salaried work force is the government service, which has an administered wage structure last revised in 1988 but supplemented by special allowances and increases since then, including a 25 percent increase on July 1. Only about 30 industrial plants employ more than 50 workers. Smaller industrial units include 69 plants of medium size, 197 small units, 692 "mini" units, and 651 cottage industry units. Bhutan's rugged geography and land laws that prohibit a farmer from selling his last five acres result in a predominantly self-employed agricultural work force. Existing labor regulations do not grant workers the right to remove themselves from work situations which endanger health and safety without jeopardizing their continued employment.

INDIA

India is a longstanding parliamentary democracy with a bicameral parliament. Prime Minister H. D. Deve Gowda, whose United Front (UF) party heads a 13-member parliamentary coalition, took office in June and heads the Government. President Shankar Dayal Sharma, who was elected by an electoral college made up of members of parliament and members of state assemblies, is Head of State and also has special emergency powers. The judiciary is independent.

Although the 25 state governments have primary responsibility for maintaining law and order, the central government provides guidance and support through use of paramilitary forces throughout the country. The Union Ministry for Home Affairs controls most of the paramilitary forces, the internal intelligence bureaus, and the nationwide police service; it provides training for senior police officers for the state-organized police forces. The armed forces are under civilian control. Security forces have committed significant human rights abuses, particularly in Jammu and Kashmir.

India has a mixed economy. The private sector is predominant in agriculture, most nonfinancial services, consumer goods manufacturing, and some heavy industry. Economic liberalization and structural reforms begun in 1991 continued largely unchanged despite a change of government. The economic problems are compounded by rapid population growth of 2 percent per year with a current total well above 900 million. Income distribution remained very unequal. Forty percent of the urban population and half the rural population live below the poverty level.

There continue to be significant human rights abuses, despite extensive constitutional and statutory safeguards. Many of these abuses are generated by intense social tensions, violent secessionist movements and the authorities' attempts to repress them, and deficient police methods and training. These problems are acute in Kashmir, where the judicial system has been disrupted by terrorist threats including the assassination of judges and witnesses, by judicial tolerance of the Government's heavy handed antimilitant tactics, and by the refusal of security forces to obey court orders. A decrease in abuses by security forces in Kashmir coincided with increased abuses by progovernment countermilitants.

Serious human rights abuses include: Extrajudicial executions and other political killings and excessive use of force by security forces; torture, rape, and deaths of suspects in police custody throughout the country; poor prison conditions; arbitrary arrest and incommunicado detention in Kashmir and the Northeast; continued detention throughout the country of thousands arrested under special security legislation; prolonged detention while under trial; widespread intercaste and communal violence; legal and societal discrimination as well as extensive violence, both societal and by police and other agents of government, against women; discrimination and violence against indigenous people and scheduled castes and tribes; child prostitution; and widespread exploitation of indentured, bonded, and child labor.

During 1996 India made further progress in resolving human rights problems. Following state elections in September and October, elected government was restored in Jammu and Kashmir for the first time in 6 years. Insurgency-related deaths were at the same level as last year, although the proportion of civilian deaths increased slightly apparently due to militant efforts to prevent elections and disrupt the newly elected government. State elections were also held in Uttar Pradesh, but results failed to resolve a political impasse and President's Rule was extended for an additional 6 months. In Punjab serious abuses of the early 1990's were acknowledged and condemned by the Supreme Court. Visits by international human rights groups, as well as continuing International Committee of the Red Cross (ICRC) prison visits in Kashmir, demonstrated increased transparency on human rights problems. The National Human Rights Commission (NHRC) continued to enlarge its useful role in addressing patterns of abuse, as well as specific abuses. The NHRC helped foster human rights education among the police and security forces, and advanced its program of human rights education in the schools.

Separatist militants were responsible for numerous, serious human rights abuses, including extrajudicial executions and other political killings, torture, and brutality. Separatist militants were also responsible for kidnaping and extortion in Kashmir and Northeast India.

RESPECT FOR HUMAN RIGHTS

Section 1. Respect for the Integrity of the Person, Including Freedom From:

a. *Political and Other Extrajudicial Killing* Political killings by government forces *(including deaths in custody and faked encounter killings), progovernment countermilitants, and insurgents continued at a high level in the state of Jammu and Kashmir and the seven northeastern states, where separatist insurgencies continued.*

Security forces committed an estimated 100–200 extrajudicial killings of suspected militants in Kashmir. Although well-documented evidence to corroborate cases and quantify trends is lacking, most observers believe the number of killings declined from previous years. However, the decline was at least partially offset by an increased number of killings by progovernment countermilitants. According to press reports and anecdotal accounts, those killed typically had been detained by security forces, and their bodies, bearing multiple bullet wounds and often marks of torture, were returned to relatives or were otherwise discovered the same day or a few days later. Security forces claim that these killings, when acknowledged at all, occur in armed encounters with militants. Members of the security forces are rarely held accountable for these killings.

Throughout the country, numerous accused criminals continue to be killed in encounters with police. Police personnel were wounded in a number of cases, however, and such incidents do not appear to reflect a pattern of extrajudicial execution. The most recent statistics, for 1995, show that 525 civilians and 159 police died in exchanges of gunfire involving police.

While extrajudicial killings continued in areas buffeted by separatist insurgencies, the press and judiciary continued to give attention to deaths in police custody and faked encounter killings elsewhere. According to NHRC statistics, 136 persons died in police custody in the year ending March 31. Many such persons were tortured (see Section 1.c.). The NHRC has focused on torture and deaths in custody. It has directed district magistrates to report all deaths in police and judicial custody and stated that failure to do so will be interpreted as an attempted coverup. Magistrates apppear to be complying with this directive. However, the NHRC has no authority directly to investigate abuses by the security forces, and security forces are therefore not required to—and do not—report custodial deaths in Kashmir or the Northeast. In February 24-year-old union leader Ram Gopal died in Faridabad while undergoing police interrogation on a theft charge. Charges related to the death were brought against a police inspector and the owner of a factory where the unionist was active. In July liquor dealer Debu Pramanik died after being detained and beaten by police in West Bengal, reportedly in revenge for selling liquor that sickened a policeman. In January the Supreme Court ordered prosecution of 27 Punjab policemen for abduction, illegal confinement, and murder of 4 suspected militants in a January 1994 incident described at the time as an encounter. Over 300 persons died in prison, many from natural causes, in some case aggravated by poor prison conditions (see Section 1.c.).

Killings and abductions of suspected militants and other persons by progovernment countermilitants emerged as a significant pattern in Kashmir. Countermilitants are former separatist militants who have surrendered to government forces but have retained their arms and paramilitary organization. Some observers number them at several thousand strong, but the precise figure is unknown.

They committed an estimated 100 to 200 political killings in Kashmir, although this figure is speculative. For example, on March 20 journalist Sheikh Ghulam Rasool was abducted from his home by countermilitants reportedly angered by a news report criticizing their activities; Rasool's body was found in the Jhelum river a month later. There are credible reports that government agencies fund, exchange intelligence with, and direct operations of countermilitants as part of the counterinsurgency effort. Countermilitants are known to screen passersby at roadblocks and guard extensive areas of the Kashmir Valley from attacks by militants. In sponsoring and condoning countermilitant activity, which takes place outside the legal system, the Government cannot avoid responsibility for abductions, murders, and other abuses by these irregulars.

In March countermilitants believed to be fronting for the Rashtriya Rifles paramilitary force abducted lawyer and human rights activist Jalil Andrabi from his car in Srinigar. (At least one eyewitness alleged that paramilitary soldiers participated directly in the abduction, but testimony on this point was inconsistent.) Andrabi was preparing to attend the U.N. Human Rights Commission in Geneva at the time of his abduction. His body, displaying marks of torture, was later discovered in the Jhelum river. Five countermilitants believed to be the abductors were found dead a month later. A court-directed investigation into Andrabi's abduction and murder was stymied when the Rashtriya Rifles did not respond to the court's request for assistance and denied investigators access to witnesses. However, the investigation continues and appears at year's end to be making progress. countermilitants also killed human rights monitor Parag Kumar Das in Assam in May.

As a result of terrorism aimed at preventing the holding of parliamentary and state assembly elections and, later, at disrupting and discrediting the newly elected state government, the proportion of civilian deaths in insurgency-related violence increased compared with 1995, although the total number of deaths was little changed. On October 23, two persons were killed by a car bomb outside the assembly members' hostel in Srinagar. In December 3 persons were killed and 40 injured, including a state assembly member, when a militant opened fire on and threw a grenade into a political meeting in Kulgam Towq. Newly elected chief minister Farooq Abdullah had been expected to visit Kulgam on the day of the attack and was the apparent target of two other grenade or bomb attacks in which several people were injured. Earlier in the year, terrorists were responsible for a number of mass killings of non-Muslims: In January 15 members of the Hindu community in the Doda district were abducted and later killed by terrorists; in May a group of 8 guest workers from Nepal were abducted near Srinagar and killed a few hours later; and in July another group of 10 non-Kashmiri laborers were shot and killed near Kupwara.

The total number of deaths in Kashmir was little changed compared with the total in 1995, although the proportion of civilian deaths increased. Reliable press reports indicate that 1,214 civilians, 94 security force personnel, and 1,271 militants died in insurgency-related violence in Kashmir in 1996. 1995 figures were 1,050 civilians, 202 security force personnel and 1,308 militants. The decrease in security forces deaths apparently reflects the increased role of countermilitants. Nongovernment organization (NGO) and other sources agree that civilian deaths attributed to security forces have decreased. Press reports indicate that the increase in civilian deaths is attributable to militant efforts to disrupt elections and the new government.

Prior to 1995, Andhra Pradesh police engaged in numerous encounter killings of Maoist Revolutionary Naxalites. Few such incidents were reported in 1995 and 1996, when the state unilaterally refrained from many enforcement actions. This restraint ended in August when, in response to continued Naxalite violence, the state reimposed a ban on the group. Although police did threaten to "liquidate" two human rights monitors (see Section 4), there were no reports that police had returned to previous patterns of abuse.

Killings by the Naxalites increased substantially after August. In November 13 policemen were killed in a Naxalite attack on a police station, and a deputy superintendent of police, his wife, and three others were killed by a Naxalite land mine. Also active in Bihar, Orissa, and West Bengal, Naxalites dispensed summary justice in "people's courts," which in some cases condemned to death suspected police informers, village headmen, and others as "class enemies" and "caste oppressors." In one such incident near Visakhapatnam, Andhra Pradesh in November, 13 Naxalites reportedly dragged a teacher from his home and cut his throat. In January in the Karimnagar district of Andhra Pradesh, five Naxalites and four civilians died in a shootout after police surrounded a people's court. In Bihar four policemen were killed in January in an attack on a police station in the Gaya district.

There were many allegations that military and paramilitary forces in the Northeast engage in arbitrary detention, abduction, torture, and extrajudicial execution of militants, as well as rape (see Sections 1.c. and 1.g.). According to human rights group, abuses in the Northeast are similar to those in Kashmir, though perhaps on a lesser scale. In Assam countermilitants have from time to time conducted abductions and killings, as exemplified in 1996 by the Parag Kumar Das killing (see below.) However, precise information on human rights violations in this relatively remote region is rare. Extensive, complex patterns of violence continued in the seven states of northeastern India. Numerous killings can be attributed to conflicts in each of the following categories:Between indigenous people, usually Buddhist or animist, and immigrant groups, usually Muslim or Hindu; between tribes of indigenous people; between security forces and militants of 1 or more of at least 17 insurgent groups; and among factions of insurgent groups.

Violence escalated in Assam following the death of the former chief minister in May and a change of government after elections in the same month. Between May and the end of August, more than 150 people were killed in the state. Bodo tribal militants and United Liberation Front of Assam (ULFA) insurgents killed 15 members of the security forces. Bodos also killed more than 50 members of the Santal minority and rendered roughly 200,000 homeless in a "cleansing" operation of Bodo-dominated areas.

In May ULFA claimed responsibility for killing the superintendant of police of the Tinsukhia district of Assam, together with his bodyguard and driver. Journalist Parag Kumar Das, known to be close to ULFA, was shot and killed a day later, allegedly by progovernment former ULFA gunmen.

In Nagaland in December, Naga militants killed 29 members of the rival Kuki tribal group and injured 29 others in an attack on a bus. In Tripura, also in December, tribal militants reportedly belonging to the National Liberation Front of Tripura killed 25 Bengali villagers and wounded 30. Tripura tribal militants also killed seven paramilitary personnel in an ambush in December.

b. *Disappearance* According to human rights groups, unacknowledged, incommunicado detention of suspected militants continued in Kashmir although the practice again decreased compared with previous years. The Government acknowledges that, as of December, it held 2,070 persons in connection with the insurgency in 5 detention centers in Jammu and Kashmir. Of these, 1,298 were held under the Public Safety Act and 772 under other laws, including the Terrorist and Disruptive Activities Act. Several thousand others are held in short-term confinement in transit and interrogation centers.

Human rights groups maintain that as many as 3,000 more are held by the military and paramilitary forces in long-term unacknowledged detention in interrogation centers and transit camps nominally intended for only short-term confinement.

The Government maintains that screening committees run by the state government provide information about detainees to their families. However, other sources indicate that families are able to confirm the detention of their relatives only by bribing prison guards. A program of prison visits by the ICRC, which began in October 1995, is designed in part to help assure communications between detainees and their families. All acknowledged detention centers in Kashmir and Kashmiri detainees elsewhere in the country have been visited. The ICRC is not authorized access to interrogation centers or transit centers.

In Punjab the pattern of disappearances prevalent in the early 1990's appears to be at an end. Hundreds of police and security officials have not been held accountable for serious human rights abuses committed during the counterinsurgency of 1984–94. However, steps have been taken against a few such violators. In January the Supreme Court ordered the Central Bureau of Investigation (CBI) to prosecute 27 Punjab policemen in connection with the alleged encounter killing of 4 suspected militants in Gurdaspur in January 1994. The Court stated that, on the basis of a CBI report, there appeared to be prima facie cases against some police in the abduction and illegal confinement and against all 27 for conspiracy to murder.

The Supreme Court, acting on a report of the CBI ordered by the Court, in July directed the Punjab state government to permit prosecution of a superintendant of police and eight other policemen for the September 5, 1995 abduction of human rights activist Jaswant Singh Khalra. The Court also ordered that compensation be paid to Khalra's wife.

Khalra had been investigating reports that police in the Tarn Taran district had secretly disposed of bodies of suspected militants believed to have been abducted and extrajudicially executed. In connection with its report on Khalra's abduction, the CBI reported that 984 unidentified bodies were cremated by Punjab police in the Tarn Taran district. Supreme Court justices, reportedly expressing horror and shock at this report, ordered that the CBI continue its investigation and that the state government turn over relevant information. Although the CBI report has not been made public, a magazine reported that CBI confirmed that 1,683 unclaimed bodies were cremated by police in the Tarn Taran district alone between 1984 and 1995. Of these, 698 were identified but not claimed by relatives. Of the 985 unidentified bodies: 407 were reportedly killed by border security forces while trying to cross into India from Pakistan, many of whom were probably militants; 291 were subsequently identified; 84 died by drowning, in road accidents or by suicide; and 70 reportedly died in clashes between militant factions. Implicitly 133 were unidentified militants killed in the interior of the district. Police reportedly filed "first information reports" (FIR) accounting for each of the bodies. These numbers testify to the extent of the bloodshed during those years and, given the pattern of police abuses prevalent during the period, credibly include many killed in extrajudicial executions.

There are credible reports that police throughout the country often do not file required arrest reports. As a result, there are hundreds of unsolved disappearances in which relatives claim an individual was taken into police custody and never heard from again. Police usually deny these claims, countering that there are no records of arrest.

Militants in Kashmir and the Northeast continued to use kidnapings to sow terror, seek the release of detained comrades, and extort funds. According to the Government, as of July 31 terrorists in Kashmir kidnaped 418 persons in 1996—compared with 548 for all of 1995—of which 222 were killed by their captors. The July 1995 kidnaping of American, British, German, and Norwegian nationals by terrorists remains unresolved. The Norwegian captive was beheaded in August 1995. A captured terrorist stated that the remaining hostages—one American, two Britons, and a German—were murdered by their captors in December 1995. There has been no reliable evidence that they are alive since the fall of 1995. In the northeast state of Tripura, militants kidnaped 22 persons during January alone, including a state legislator. According to the Government, Tripura militants kidnaped 366 persons during 1995, of whom 20 are known to have been killed and 35 are unaccounted for. In Assam Bodo militants kidnaped the son of a state minister in February and a few days later killed a businessman who had been kidnaped for ransom in January.

c. *Torture and Other Cruel, Inhuman, or Degrading Treatment or Punishment.—* The law prohibits torture, and confessions extracted by force are generally inadmissible in court. Nevertheless, there is credible evidence that torture is common throughout India and that the authorities often use torture during interrogations. In other instances, they torture detainees to extort money and sometimes as summary punishment. The NHRC has called on the Government to sign the 1984 International Convention Against Torture. The new United Front Government vowed that it would.

In 1995 the U.N. Special Rapporteur on Torture reported that torture was practiced routinely by the army, the Border Security Force, and the Central Reserve Police Force against the vast majority of persons arrested for political reasons in Jammu and Kashmir. According to the Rapporteur, official investigations into allegations of torture, including those that resulted in custodial deaths, were rare. This state of affairs did not change. Past practices have included beating, rape, burning with cigarettes and hot rods, suspension by the feet, crushing of limbs by heavy rollers, and electric shocks. Because many alleged torture victims die in custody, and others are afraid to speak out, there are few firsthand accounts, although the marks of torture have often been found on the bodies of deceased detainees.

The prevalence of torture by police in detention facilities throughout the country is borne out by the number of cases of deaths in police custody (see Section 1.a.). A post mortem examination of a young man who died in police custody in August reportedly found evidence of 51 external injuries, including burns and 30 injuries by a blunt object, and concluded that he had been tortured; police holding him claimed that the man died when he jumped from a jeep in an escape attempt.

According to the U.N. Special Rapporteur, torture victims or their relatives have reportedly had difficulty in filing compliants because police in Kashmir were issued instructions not to file a FIR without permission from higher authorities. In addition, Section 7 of the Armed Forces (Jammu and Kashmir) Special Powers Act provides that unless approval is obtained from the central government, "(n)o prosecution, suit, or other legal proceeding shall be instituted * * * against any person in respect of anything done or purported to be done in exercise of the powers of the Act." This provision reportedly allows the security forces to act with virtual impunity.

The rape of persons in custody is part of the broader pattern of custodial abuse. Limits placed on the arrest, search, and police custody of women appear effectively to limit the frequency of rape in custody, although it does occur on occasion. The NHRC received reports of only three cases of custodial rape during the 1995–96 fiscal year. The 24-hour reporting requirement applies to custodial rape as well as custodial death. However, the requirement does not apply to rape by policemen outside police stations. NGO's claim that rape by police, including custodial rape, is more common than NHRC figures indicate. Although evidence is lacking, a larger number appears credible, in light of other evidence of abusive behavior by police and the likelihood that many rapes go unreported due to a sense of shame. A pattern of custodial rape by paramilitary personnel allegedly exists in the Northeast (see Section 1.g.), but is not included in NHRC statistics because it involves military forces.

Although custodial abuse is deeply rooted in police practices, increased press reporting and parliamentary questions offer evidence of growing public awareness of the problem. The NHRC has identified torture and deaths in detention as one of its priority concerns. As a result of NHRC investigations during the fiscal year, 22 police personnel were prosecuted during the fiscal year and 79 were suspended, most in both cases due to involvement in custodial abuse. Charges against police prosecuted for custodial abuse include murder; in one case in Bihar, six policemen were convicted and sentenced to death (the decision is under appeal.)

Prison conditions are poor. Prisons are grossly overcrowded, often housing over three times their designed capacity. The largest class of prisoners typically sleeps on bare floors, has inadequate sanitary facilities, and receives inadequate food and medical care. Prisoners with privileged status or with the personal or family means can supplement what is normally provided. There are three classes of prison facilities. Prisoners are not classified by the nature of their crimes, but by their standing in society. Class "C" prisoners are those who cannot prove they are college graduates or income taxpayers. Their cells are overcrowded, often have dirt floors, no furnishings, and poor quality food. The use of handcuffs and fetters is common. Class "B" prisoners—college graduates and taxpayers—are held under markedly better conditions. Class "A" prisoners are prominent persons, as designated by the Government, and are accorded private rooms, visits, and adequate food, which may be supplemented by their families. Class "A" prisoners are usually held in government guest houses.

Overcrowding in jails is severe. According to a statement in Parliament in 1994 by the Minister of State for Home Affairs, New Delhi's Tihar Jail, considered one of the best-run in the country, housed 8,577 prisoners—in facilities designed to hold 2,487. According to the Minister, 7,505 detainees awaited the completion of their trials, while 672 others had been on trial for 3 years or longer. Press reports, statements in court cases, and statements by government officials indicate that conditions remained essentially unchanged in 1996.

Nevertheless, prison conditions are a subject of press reports and court cases and have received attention from human rights groups. Press accounts of prison conditions include reports of sexual abuse of prisoners, the use of prisoners by prison officials as domestic servants, the sale of food and milk for prisoners on the black market, the sale of female prisoners to brothels, and the marketing and export of prison-made goods. Women constitute 2 to 6 percent of the total prison population, according to the 1987 report of Justice Krishna Aiyer. Although Parliament passed a Children's Act in 1960 to safeguard young prisoners against abuse and exploitation and a Juvenile Justice Act in 1986 provides that boys under 16 and girls under 18 are not to be held in prison, most states have not implemented these acts. The Supreme Court has criticized the state governments for not providing reformatories and separate detention facilities for children.

With the exception of an agreement with the ICRC for visits to detention facilities in Kashmir, the Government does not allow NGO's to monitor prison conditions.

During the 1995–96 fiscal year, 441 cases of custodial death and three cases of custodial rape were reported to the NHRC, including 133 deaths and 3 rapes in police custody. (The 308 deaths in judicial custody, occurring in a prison population of 155,000, much of which is held for years, include a large proportion of deaths from natural causes, in some cases aggravated by poor conditions in prisons. Deaths in police custody, which typically occur within hours or days of initial apprehension, more clearly imply violent abuse. The NHRC has no authority to investigate abuses by security forces directly, and security forces in Kashmir and the Northeast are not required to report custodial deaths to the Commission.)

d. *Arbitrary Arrest, Detention, or Exile.*—The Government implemented during the early 1980's a variety of special security laws intended to help law enforcement authorities fight separatist insurgency. There were credible reports of widespread arbitrary arrest and detention under these laws.

Although one of these laws—the Terrorist and Disruptive Practices (Prevention) Act (TADA)—that had been subject to the most extensive abuse lapsed in May 1995,

3,785 persons previously arrested under the act continued to be held in a number of states at year's end, and a small number of arrests under TADA continued for crimes allegedly committed before the law lapsed. Criminal cases are proceeding against most of those still held under TADA, with more than 3,000 charged under other laws in addition to TADA. In February the Supreme Court eased bail guidelines for persons accused under TADA, taking into account the large backlog of cases in special TADA courts.

The Constitution requires that detainees have the right to be informed of the grounds for arrest, have the right to be represented by counsel, and, unless the person is held under a preventive detention law, the right to appear before a magistrate within 24 hours of arrest. At this initial appearance, the accused must either be remanded for further investigation or released. The Supreme Court has upheld these provisions. An accused person must be informed of his right to bail at the time of arrest and may, unless he is held on a nonbailable offense, apply for bail at any time. The police must file a charge sheet within 60 to 90 days of arrest; if they fail to do so, court approval of a bail application becomes mandatory.

The Constitution permits preventive detention laws in the event of threats to public order and national security. These laws provide for limits on the length of detention and for judicial review. Several laws of this type remain in effect.

The National Security Act (NSA) of 1980 permits detention of persons considered security risks; police anywhere in the country (except Kashmir) may detain suspects under NSA provisions. Under these provisions the authorities may detain a suspect without charge or trial as long as 1 year on loosely defined security grounds. The state government must confirm the detention order, which is reviewed by an advisory board of three high court judges within 7 weeks or arrest. NSA detainees are permitted visits by family members and lawyers and must be informed of the grounds for detention within 5 days (10 to 15 days in exceptional circumstances). At year's end, approximately 500 persons continue to be detained under the NSA.

The Jammu and Kashmir Public Safety Act (PSA) of 1978 covers corresponding procedures for that state. Over half of the detainees in Jamrau and Kashmir are held under the PSA.

The court system is overloaded. The result has been the detention of persons awaiting trial for periods longer than they would receive if convicted. Prisoners may be held months or even years before obtaining a trial date. According to a reply to a parliamentary question in July 1994, more than 111,000 criminal cases were pending in the Allahabad High Court, the most serious case backlog in the country, of which nearly 29,000 cases had been pending for 5 to 8 years. A statement to Parliament in July, indicated that criminal and civil cases pending before the country's high courts numbered nearly 2.9 million in 1995, roughly the same as in 1994 but an increase from 2.65 million in 1993.

The Government does not use forced exile.

e. *Denial of Fair Public Trial.*—India has an independent judiciary with strong constitutional safeguards. Under a Supreme Court ruling, the Chief Justice,in consultation with his colleagues, has a decisive voice in selecting judicial candidates. The President appoints the judges, and they can serve up to the age of 62 on the state high courts and to the age of 65 on the Supreme Court.

Courts of first resort exist at the subdistrict and district levels. More serious cases and appeals are heard in state-level High Courts and by the national-level Supreme Court, which also rules on constitutional questions. Subdistrict and district judicial magistrates are appointed by state governments. High Court judges are appointed on the recommendation of the federal Law Ministry, with the advice of the Supreme Court, the High Court Chief Justice, and the chief minister of the state usually from among district judges or lawyers practicing before the same courts. Supreme Court judges are similarly appointed from among High Court judges. The Chief Justice is selected on the basis of seniority.

When legal procedures function normally, they generally assure a fair trial, but the process can be drawn out and inaccessible to the poor. Defendants have the right to choose counsel from a bar that is fully independent of the Government. There are effective channels for appeal at most levels of the judicial system.

The Criminal Procedure Code provides for an open trial in most cases, but it allows exceptions in proceedings involving official secrets, trials in which statements prejudicial to the safety of the State might be made, or under provisions of special security legislation. Sentences must be announced in public.

Muslim personal status law governs many noncriminal matters involving Muslims—including family law, inheritance, and divorce. The Government does not interfere in the personal laws of the minority communities, with the result that laws that discriminate against women are upheld.

In Kashmir the judicial system barely functions due to threats by militants against judges, witnesses, and their family members, because of judicial tolerance of the Government's heavy handed antimilitant actions, and the frequent refusal by security forces to obey court orders. Courts there are not willing to hear cases involving terrorist crimes or fail to act expeditiously on habeas corpus cases, if they act at all. As a result, there have been no convictions of alleged terrorists in Kashmir since before 1994, even though some militants have been in detention for years.

There were no reports of political prisoners.

f. *Arbitrary Interference with Privacy, Family, Home, or Correspondence.*—The police must obtain warrants for searches and seizures. In a criminal investigation, the police may conduct searches without warrants to avoid undue delay, but they must justify the searches in writing to the nearest magistrate with jurisdiction over the offense. The authorities in Jammu and Kashmir, Punjab, and Assam have special powers to search and arrest without a warrant.

The Indian Telegraph Act authorizes the surveillance of communications, including monitoring telephone conversations and intercepting personal mail, in case of public emergency or "in the interest of the public safety or tranquility." These powers have been used by every state government.

g. *Use of Excessive Force and Violations of Humanitarian Law in Internal Conflicts.*—Both government forces and militants continue to commit serious violations of humanitarian law in the disputed state of Jammu and Kashmir. Between 350,000 and 400,000 Indian army and paramilitary forces are deployed in Jammu and Kashmir. The Muslim majority population in the Kashmir Valley is caught between the repressive tactics of the security forces and acts of wanton violence committed by the militants. Under the Jammu and Kashmir Disturbed Areas Act, and the Armed Forces (Jammu and Kashmir) Special Powers Act, both passed in July 1990, security forces personnel have extraordinary powers, including authority to shoot suspected lawbreakers and those disturbing the peace, and to destroy structures suspected of harboring militants or arms.

In March paramilitary and police forces clashed with militants who had attempted to occupy the Hazratbal shrine in Srinagar. Nine militants were killed in a gun battle while within the shrine compound. Later, after the militants voluntarily evacuated the shrine, 24 more were killed when security forces surrounded houses near the shrine in which the armed militants had taken shelter and opened fire with mortars, grenades, and firearms. Those surrounded were offered a chance to surrender, but only three women and two children left the houses before firing began. The houses were completely destroyed and the militants killed.

Civilian deaths caused by security forces diminished for the third consecutive year in Kashmir. The explanation appears to lie in press scrutiny and public outcry over abuses in previous years, increased training of military and paramilitary forces in humanitarian law, and greater sensitivity of commanders to rule of law issues. The improvement has taken the form of increased discipline and care in avoiding collateral civilian injuries and deaths (i.e., deaths in crossfire). The security forces have not abandoned the abduction and extrajudicial execution of suspected militants, much less embraced accountability for these abuses. However, the inclination of many commanders to distance their units from such practices has led to diminished participation in them and a transfer of some of this role to countermilitants.

In Manipur in August, the unusual willingness of a victim to speak up sparked a massive protest demonstration against a pattern of rape by security force personnel.

In an effort to sensitize paramilitary forces to human rights problems, the Director General of the Border Security Force and the NHRC sponsored a debate in February on the role of human rights among personnel of all seven paramilitary forces. In August the Chief of Army Staff issued revised human rights guidelines for military forces at a seminar on international humanitarian law sponsored by the Army Judge Advocate General, in cooperation with the ICRC and the Indian Red Cross.

Kashmiri militant groups were also guilty of serious human rights abuses. Terrorists attacked politicians in an effort to obstruct national parliamentary elections in May and June and state assembly elections in September. In addition to political killings and kidnapings (see Sections 1.a. and 1.b.), terrorists engaged in extortion and carried out acts of random terror that left hundreds of Kashmiris dead. Terrorist acts by Kashmiri groups have also taken place outside Jammu and Kashmir. A Kashmiri terrorist group detonated a bomb at a railway station in New Delhi in January, killing 6, and a car bomb in a crowded market in New Delhi in May, killing 25. Many of the terrorists are not Indian citizens.

Kashmiris continued to be caught in the crossfire between militants on one side and security forces and countermilitants on the other. Unlike past years, however, there were no large-scale or prolonged clashes resulting in extensive loss of civilian life or property.

In the Northeast, militant violence directed against civilians resulted in numerous deaths and drove thousands from their homes. In an upsurge of violence related to a change of elected government in the state, Bodo militants in Assam killed nearly 50 members of the Santal minority and forced some 200,000 persons to flee their homes (see Section 1.a.). In Tripura, as of February, repeated militant attacks over preceding months had forced more than 10,000 tribals opposed to extremism or aligned with the political opposition to flee their homes. A December 30 bomb blast on a passenger train in Assam, which left at least 34 dead, was believed to be the handiwork of Bodo militants.

Section 2. Respect for Civil Liberties, Including:

a. *Freedom of Speech and Press.*—The Constitution provides for these rights, and with some limitations they are exercised in practice. A vigorous press reflects a wide variety of public, social, and economic beliefs. Newspapers and magazines regularly publish investigative reports and allegations of government wrongdoing, and the press as a whole champions human rights and criticizes perceived government lapses. The Press Council of India is a statutory body of journalists, publishers, academics, and politicians with a chairman appointed by the Government. Designed to be a self-regulating mechanism for the press, it investigates complaints of irresponsible journalism and sets a code of conduct for publishers. This code includes not publishing articles or details that might incite caste or communal violence. The Council publicly criticizes newspapers or journalists it believes have broken the code of conduct, but its findings, while noted by the press community, carry no legal weight.

National television and radio, which are government monopolies, are frequently accused of manipulating the news to the benefit of the Government. However, international satellite television is widely distributed in middle class neighborhoods by cable and is gradually eroding the Government's monopoly on television.

Under the Official Secrets Act (OSA), the Government may restrict publication of sensitive stories, but the Government sometimes interprets this broadly to suppress criticism of its policies. The 1971 Newspapers Incitements to Offenses Act remains in effect in Jammu and Kashmir. Under the act, a district magistrate may prohibit the press from carrying material resulting in "incitement to murder" or "any act of violence." As punishment the act stipulates that the authorities may seize newspapers and printing presses. Despite these restrictions, newspapers in Srinagar regularly carry militant press releases attacking the Government and report in detail on alleged human rights abuses. The authorities allowed foreign journalists to travel freely in Kashmir, where they regularly spoke with militant leaders, and filed reports on government abuse.

A government censorship board reviews films before licensing them for distribution. The board deletes material deemed offensive to public morals or communal sentiment. Producers of video news magazines must also submit their products to the board, which occasionally censors stories that portray the Government in an unfavorable light. The board's ruling may be appealed and overturned. Kashmiri groups threatened journalists and editors and even imposed temporary bans on some publications. In July 19 journalists were detained by countermilitants, and 6 were threatened with death. All were released later the same day, following the intervention of paramilitary forces. On August 1, Ashraf Shaban, editor of the Urdu language Al Safa was abducted and held overnight.

Citizens enjoy complete academic freedom, and students and faculty espouse a wide range of views. In addition to 10 national universities and about 160 state universities, states are empowered to accredit locally run private institutions.

b. *Freedom of Peaceful Assembly and Association.*—The Constitution provides for the right of peaceful assembly and the right to form associations, and the Government generally respected these rights in practice.

The authorities sometimes require permits and notification prior to holding parades or demonstrations, but local governments ordinarily respect the right to protest peacefully. At times of civil tension, the authorities may ban public assemblies or impose a curfew under the Criminal Procedure Code. The authorities in Punjab frequently imposed such restrictions in previous years but limited their use since 1994; opposition Akali parties were permitted to hold public rallies and conduct membership drives.

Srinagar and other parts of Jammu and Kashmir were under curfew sporadically during much of the year.

c. *Freedom of Religion.*—The Constitution provide for freedom of religion, and the Government repects this right in practice. India is a secular state in which all faiths generally enjoy freedom of worship. Government policy does not favor any religious group. There is no national law to bar proselytizing by Indian Christians. Foreign missionaries can generally renew their visas but since the mid-1960's the Government has refused to admit new resident foreign missionaries. Those who arrive now do so as tourists and stay for short periods. As of January 1993, there were 1,923 registered foreign Christian missionaries. As in the past, state officials refused to issue permits for foreign Christian missionaries to enter some northeastern states. Tension between Hindus and Muslims continue to pose a challenge to the secular foundation of the State (see Section 5).

d. *Freedom of Movement Within the Country, Foreign Travel, Emigration, and Repatriation.*—Citizens enjoy freedom of movement within the country except in certain border areas where, for security reasons, special permits are required. Under the Passports Act of 1967, the Government may deny a passport to any applicant who "may or is likely to engage outside India in activities prejudicial to the sovereignty and integrity of India." The Government uses this provision to prohibit the foreign travel of some government critics, especially those advocating Sikh independence.

Citizens may emigrate without restriction.

Although India is not a signatory to the U.N. Convention and Protocol on Refugees, the Government follows its general principles. The Government cooperates with the office of the United Nations High Commissioner for Refugees (UNHCR) to a limited extent in connection with some categories of refugees, specifically those who fled Afghanistan. In earlier years the Government accepted a UNHCR role in overseeing the repatriation of refugees to Sri Lanka. The Government accepts the cooperation of other nongovernmental humanitarian organizations in assisting Tibetan and Sri Lankan refugees. The Government provided first asylum to approximately 6,000 additional refugees from renewed fighting in Sri Lanka in 1996. There were no reports of forced return of persons to a country where they feared persecution.

The Government recognizes certain groups, including Chakmas from Bangladesh, Tamils from Sri Lanka, and Tibetans, as refugees, providing them assistance in refugee camps or in resettlement areas. According to a government statement to Parliament in July, there were 98,000 Tibetans, 87,729 Sri Lankan Tamils, 66,234 Chakmas and Hajongs from Bangladesh, and 52 Burmese refugees. In the statement, the Government indicated that 18,932 Afghans, 255 Somalis, and 308 persons of other nationalities were living in India "under the mandate" of the UNHCR. Although the Government does not formally recognize persons in this latter category as refugees, it does not deport them. Instead, these people receive renewable residence permits or their status is ignored.

No further Chakma refugees were repatriated during 1996, pursuant to a 1993 agreement with the Government of Bangladesh. Human rights groups claimed that the Government reduced rations, medical care, and cash assistance to refugee camps holding Chakmas to encourage them to repatriate. In May the NHRC sent a team to investigate conditions in the camps. The team reported a shortage of water, meager rations, inadequate accommodations, inadequate medical care, inoperative wells, and evidence of malaria, water-borne diseases, and malnutrition among children. The NHRC subsequently directed concerned agencies to improve the administration of the camps.

The Supreme Court, in response to a case filed by the NHRC, intervened to protect another group of Chakmas who had come to India as refugees in the 1960's. The state government of Arunachal Pradesh, where these Chakmas had been settled, had threatened to remove them forcibly from the state in response to resentment expressed by the indigenous people.

According to the UNHCR, as of late November, there were 62,281 Tamil refugees from Sri Lanka living in 115 camps in India, including approximately 6,000 who fled the upsurge in fighting in Sri Lanka during 1996 and 338 suspected of militant activities, who are detained in special camps. An estimated 30–60,000 more Sri Lankan Tamils are not registered as refugees and are living outside the camps. NGO's report refugee complaints about deteriorated housing, poor sanitation, delayed dole payments, and inadequate medical care. Such complaints notwithstanding, minimum standards are being met. The state government, using central government resources, provides shelter and subsidized food for those in the camps. Enforcement of a Tamil Nadu government ban on NGO assistance to the camps has been relaxed and NGO's have visited the camps.

There are Chin ethnics among nonrecognized refugees in the northeastern states, particularly Mizoram. Their presence is generally tolerated. However, recent tensions between security forces and Chin National Force (CNF) insurgents operating in Burma have allegedly resulted in detention, interrogation, and expulsion of some persons associated with the CNF.

Section 3. Respect for Political Rights: The Right of Citizens to Change Their Government

Citizens exercise this right freely. India has a democratic, parliamentary system of government with representatives elected in multiparty elections under universal adult suffrage. A parliament sits for 5 years unless dissolved earlier for new elections, except under constitutionally defined emergency situations. State governments are elected at regular intervals except in states under President's Rule, i.e., rule by the central Government.

On the advice of the Prime Minister, the President may proclaim a state of emergency in any part of the national territory in the event of war, external aggression, or armed rebellion. Similarly, President's Rule may be declared in the event of a collapse of a state's constitutional machinery. The Supreme Court in May 1995 upheld the Government's authority to suspend fundamental rights during an emergency.

National elections for the popularly elected lower house of Parliament were held in several rounds from late April through June; more than half of the electorate of more than 600 million voted. The elections were generally free, fair, and peaceful. Repolling was undertaken in a number of polling places where the Election Commission suspected significant irregularities, and tightly enforced new restrictions on campaign expenditures, wall-painting, and the use of vehicles and loudspeakers were credited with enhancing the representative character of these elections.

State assembly elections were held in Jammu and Kashmir in September, resulting in an end of President's Rule and return to elected government for the first time in 6 years. Security forces in some places were seen to coerce members of the public to go to polling places, after militants called for a boycott of the elections. Some individuals said they welcomed this procedure as a pretext for evading militant retaliation against voters. Although state assembly elections were held in Uttar Pradesh in September and October, results failed to produce any clear majority in the assembly, and President's Rule was extended for an additional 6 months. This decision was subsequently approved by Parliament but was declared unconstitutional by the Allahabad High Court in mid-December on grounds that it exceeded the 1-year limit on President's Rule set by the Constitution and that all recourse to formation of an elected government had not been exhausted. An appeal of the High Court decision to the Supreme Court was pending at year's end, and President's Rule continued. In Gujarat President's Rule was declared and the assembly suspended in October, when the chief minister lost his majority. President's Rule was revoked and the assembly reconvened when a new government was formed a few weeks later.

There are no legal impediments to participation by women in the political process. A large proportion of women participate in voting throughout the country, and numerous women represent all major parties in the national and state legislatures. There are 57 women in the Parliament, including the deputy speaker of the upper house, but only one women in the Cabinet. Thirty percent of seats in elected village councils (panchayats) are reserved for women.

The Constitution reserves seats in Parliament and state legislatures for "scheduled tribes" and "scheduled castes" in proportion to their population (see Section 5). Indigenous people participate actively in national and local politics, but their impact depends on their numerical strength. In the northeastern states, indigenous people are a large proportion of the population and consequently exercise a dominant political influence in the political process. In Maharashtra and Gujarat, on the other hand, tribal peoples are a small minority and have been unsuccessful in blocking projects they oppose.

Section 4. Governmental Attitude Regarding International and Nongovernmental Investigation of Alleged Violations of Human Rights

Independent human rights organizations operate throughout the country investigating abuses and publishing their findings, which are often the basis for reports by international human rights groups. However, the police have targeted human rights monitors for arrest and harassment. In Tamil Nadu, the previous state government intimidated NGO's, including human rights groups, by enacting a law permitting the government to take over the management of any such group. Two persons involved in human rights activities, Jalil Andrabi in Kashmir and Parag Kumar Das in Assam, were killed by soldiers or progovernment counter militants, or both (see Section 1.a.). A court-directed investigation of the murder of Andrabi was in progress. On October 7 police in Warangal district, Andhra Pradesh, threatened Dr. Burra Ramulu and Amabati Srinivas, both members of the Andhra

Pradesh Civil Liberties Committee, after they called for judicial inquiries into alleged police abuses against suspected Maoist guerrillas. On October 9, the Andhra Pradesh High Court ordered the state to provide protection for the men.

The Government appointed a National Human Rights Commission in October 1993 with powers to investigate and recommend policy changes, punishment, and compensation in cases of police abuse.

In addition, the NHRC is directed to contribute to the establishment, growth, and functioning of nongovernmental human rights organizations. The Government appoints the members and finances the operations of the NHRC. Although the NHRC is seriously understaffed and prohibited by statute from directly investigating allegations of abuse involving army and paramilitary forces, the Commission has made effective use of indirect inquiries to address abuses by the armed forces.

During the 1995–96 fiscal year, the NHRC registered 9,751 complaints of human rights abuses, as well as 444 cases of custodial death or rape. A total of 1,277 cases remained pending from the preceding year. At the end of the fiscal year, 5,984 cases had been dismissed, 1,178 "disposed of with directions," 546 concluded, and 3,535 remained pending.

The NHRC organized or participated in several joint programs with NGO's and worked with human rights NGO's in its investigation of individual complaints. The NHRC has also worked to build a "culture of human rights" by actively encouraging the introduction of human rights syllabuses into universities and public schools. In March it launched a program to train instructors of teachers in human rights. Sixteen hundred instructors are receiving 6 months training on a continuing basis with a goal of giving human rights training to all of the country's 1 million teachers at the elementary and secondary levels. NHRC-supported programs are already underway at the university level. In February the NHRC cosponsored debates by personnel of Indian paramilitary forces on the role of human rights, in what is to be the first in an annual series; in December the Commission cosponsored an essay contest by police on "custodial crime" and "The role of police in human rights." It also sponsored human rights education programs for the police and a seminar in July on human rights and terrorism in which senior police officials and NGO representatives participated. State human rights commissions have been established in West Bengal, Himachal Pradesh, Assam and Madhya Pradesh. In addition, special courts to hear human rights cases have been established in Tamil Nadu, Uttar Pradesh, and Andhra Pradesh.

The NHRC was also involved in programs to eliminate child labor (see Section 6).

The prison visits program in Kashmir of the International Committee of the Red Cross (ICRC), initiated in October 1995, continued through the year. ICRC representatives also continued training police and border security force personnel in international humanitarian law. In August the ICRC and Indian Red Cross Society, together with the Army's Judge Advocate General, cosponsored a seminar on international humanitarian law.

Several international human rights organizations visited India during the year. An Amnesty International (AI) delegation made a month-long visit in July-August, the first AI visit since 1992. The team visited Delhi, Karnataka, and Rajasthan but was not permitted to visit Kashmir. After discussions with the AI team, (now retired) NHRC Chairman Ranganath Misra publicly urged that AI be permitted to visit the Kashmir valley. A Human Rights Watch researcher visited Kashmir in January. U.N. Human Rights Commission Special Rapporteur on Religious Intolerance Abdul Fateh Amor visited India, including Kashmir, as part of a three-member delegation in December.

An Asia-Pacific human rights NGO congress was held in New Delhi in December, attended by delegates from throughout the region.

Section 5. Discrimination Based on Race, Sex Religion, Disability, Language, or Social Status

The traditional caste system as well as differences of ethnicity, religion, and language deeply divide Indian society. Despite laws designed to prevent discrimination, there are other laws as well as social and cultural practices that have a profound discriminatory impact.

Women.—Domestic violence in the context of dowry disputes is a serious problem. In the typical dowry dispute, a groom's family will harass a woman they believe has not provided sufficient dowry. This harassment sometimes ends in the woman's death, which family members often try to portray as a suicide or kitchen accident. Although most "dowry deaths" involve lower and middle-class families, the phenomenon crosses both caste and religious lines.

In an answer to a parliamentary question in July, the Government reported that 5,817 dowry deaths occurred in 1993, 4,936 in 1994, and 4,811 in 1995. Under a

1986 amendment to the Penal Code, the court must presume the husband or the wife's in-laws are responsible for every unnatural death of a woman in the first 7 year of marriage—provided that harassment is proven. In such cases, police procedures require that an officer of deputy superintendent rank or above conduct the investigation and that a team of two or more doctors perform the post mortem procedures.

According to information presented to the Parliament by the Home Ministry in July, 6,735 cases of dowry death were before the courts in 1994. Of these, 461 resulted in conviction, 973 in acquittals, and 212 were compounded or withdrawn. This compares with 5,713 cases, 341 convictions, and 647 acquittals in 1993. Sentences included life imprisonment.

There is an elaborate system of laws to protect the rights of women, including the Equal Remuneration Act, the Prevention of Immoral Traffic Act, the Sati (widow burning) Prevention Act, and the Dowry Prohibition Act. However, the Government often is unable to enforce these laws, especially in rural areas where traditions are deeply rooted. Female bondage and forced prostitution are widespread in parts of society. Government statistics show that registered cases of violence against women—including molestation, rape, kidnaping, and wife murder (dowry deaths)— numbered 83,964 in 1993, 98,948 in 1994 and 100,846 in 1995. There were reports during the year of gang rapes as penalties for alleged adultery or as means of coercion or revenge in rural property disputes and feuds. Higher female mortality at all age levels, including female infanticide, accounts for a decline in the ratio of females to males to 927 per 1,000 in 1991, from 955 per 1,000 in 1981 and 972 per 1,000 at the turn of the century.

The personal status laws of the religious communities discriminate against women. Under the Indian Divorce Act of 1869, a Christian woman may demand divorce only in the case of spousal abuse and certain categories of adultery while for a man adultery alone is sufficient. Under Islamic law, a Muslim husband may divorce his wife spontaneously and unilaterally; there is no such provision for women. Islamic law also allows a man to have up to four wives but prohibits polyandry.

The Hindu Succession Act provides equal inheritance rights for Hindu women, but married daughters are seldom given a share in parental property. Islamic law recognizes a woman's right of inheritance but specifies that a daughter's share should be only one-half that of a son.

Under tribal land systems, notably in Bihar, tribal women do not have the right to own land. Other laws relating to the ownership of assets and land accord women little control over land use, retention, or sale.

There are thousands of grassroots organizations working for social justice and economic advancement of women, in addition to the National Commission for Women. The Government usually supports these efforts, despite strong resistance from traditionally privileged groups.

Children.—The Government formed in June made compulsory elementary education and an increase in expenditure on elementary education part of its program. The new Government also affirmed its support for the existing program for the elimination of child labor, which is aimed at progressively withdrawing children from the workplace and placing them in schools by 2000 through initiatives in education, rural development, women and child development, health, and labor programs. A Supreme Court decision in December raised penalties for employers of children in hazardous industries and establishing a welfare fund for formerly employed children. (See Section 6.d.).

There are an estimated 500,000 street children nationwide. Child prostitution in the cities is rampant, and there is a growing pattern of traffic in child prostitutes from Nepal. According to one estimate 5,000 to 7,000 children, mostly aged 10 to 18, are victims of this traffic annually.

The Child Marriage Restraint (Amendment) Act of 1976 prohibits child marriage, a traditional practice in northern India. The act raised the age of marriage for girls to 18 from 15, but the Government does not enforce it effectively. According to one report, 50 percent of the girls in Bihar, Rajasthan, Uttar Pradesh, and Madhya Pradesh are married at or before age 16.

The traditional preference for male children continues. Although a law passed in September 1994 prohibits the use of amniocentesis and sonogram tests for sex determination, they are widely misused for this purpose and termination of a disproportionate number of pregnancies with female fetuses occurs. Human rights groups estimate that at least 10,000 cases of female infanticide occur yearly, primarily in poor rural areas. In addition, parents often give priority in health care and nutrition to male infants. Women's rights groups point out that the burden of providing girls with an adequate dowry is one factor that makes daughters less desirable. Although abetting or taking dowry is theoretically illegal under the Dowry Prohibition Act of 1961, it is still widely practiced.

People with Disabilities.—The Ministry of Welfare has principal responsibility for programs for the disabled, and it delivers comprehensive rehabilitation services to the rural population through 16 district centers. A national rehabilitation plan commits the Government to putting a rehabilitation center in each of more than 400 districts, but services are still concentrated in urban areas. The Government reserves 3 percent of positions in official offices and state-owned enterprises for people with visual, hearing, or orthopedic disabilities. The Government provides special railway fares, education allowances, scholarships, customs exemptions, and rehabilitation training to assist people with disabilities. There is no legislation or otherwise mandated provision of accessibility for the disabled.

Indigenous People.—The Innerline Regulations enacted by the British in 1873 still provide the basis for safeguarding tribal rights in most of the border states of northeastern India. These regulations prohibit any person, including Indians from other states, from going beyond an inner boundary without a valid permit. No rubber, wax, ivory, or other forest products may be removed from the protected areas without prior authorization. No outsiders are allowed to own land in the tribal areas without approval from tribal authorities.

Despite constitutional safeguards, the rights of indigenous groups in eastern India are often ignored. There has been encroachment on tribal land in almost all the states of eastern India, including by illegal immigrants from Bangladesh and businesses that have removed forest and mineral products without authorization. Moreover, persons from other backgrounds often usurp places reserved for members of tribes and lower castes in national education institutions.

Such violations have given rise to numerous tribal movements demanding protection of land and property rights. The Jharkhand Movement in Rihar and Orissa, and the Bodo Movement in Assam, reflect deep economic and social grievances among indigenous people. In the Jharkhand area, tribal people complain that they have been relegated to unskilled mining jobs, have lost their forests to industrial construction, and have been displaced by development projects. The Government has considered the creation of an independent Jharkand state, but the affected state governments oppose the idea.

However, there is some local autonomy in the northeast. In Meghalaya tribal chiefs still wield influence in certain villages. The Nagaland government controls the rights to certain mineral resources, and autonomous district councils in Tripura, Assam, and Meghalaya control matters such as education, rural development, and forestry in cooperation with the state governors.

National/Racial/Ethnic Minorities.—The Constitution gives the President authority to specify historically disadvantaged castes and tribes which are entitled to affirmative action in employment and other benefits. These "scheduled" tribes and castes benefit from special development funds, government hiring quotas, and special training programs.

The Scheduled Castes and Scheduled Tribes (Prevention of Atrocities) Act of 1989 specifies new offenses against disadvantaged people and provides stiffer penalties for offenders. However, this act has had only a modest effect in curbing abuse. Government statistics indicate that 36,310 cases of abuse were committed against members of scheduled castes and tribes in 1995, compared with 38,927 in 1994. In a particularly gruesome incident on June 11, 20 low-caste villagers in the Bihar village Barki Kharwan, including pregnant women and children, were massacred by an upper caste private militia group. The Home Minister visited the village to investigate the incident personally, and 18 policemen were subsequently suspended for failing to intervene. A Government commission is charged with giving special attention to the problems of the scheduled castes and tribes and submits an annual report.

The practice of untouchability was in theory outlawed by the Constitution and the 1955 Civil Rights Act, but it remains an important aspect of life. Intercaste violence claims hundreds of lives each year.

Religious Minorities.—Controversy between Hindus and Muslims continues with regard to three sites where mosques were built centuries ago on sites where temples are believed to have previously stood. The potential for renewed Hindu-Muslim violence remains considerable. The NHRC undertook to continue investigation of 1992 Hindu-Muslim violence in Bombay after the Maharashtra state government in January ordered that a commission of inquiry be disbanded without completing its report. The commission was reinstated in May.

The Religious Institutions (Prevention of Misuse) Act makes it an offense to use any religious site for political purposes or to use temples for harboring persons accused or convicted of crime. While specifically designed to deal with Sikh places of worship in the Punjab, the law applies to all religious sites.

Fear of political violence drove most Hindus in the Kashmir Valley (Pandits) to seek refuge in camps in Jammu or with relatives in New Delhi or elsewhere. The Pandit community criticizes bleak conditions in the camps and fears that a negotiated solution giving greater autonomy to the Muslim majority might threaten its own survival in Kashmir as a culturally and historically distinctive group. The Pandits were permitted to vote in their districts of origin by absentee ballot in national and state elections during the year.

Section 6 Worker Rights

a. *The Right of Association.*—The Constitution provides for the right of association. Workers may establish and join unions of their own choosing without prior authorization. There are five major recognized national trade union centrals, each of which is associated with, but not necessarily controlled by, a political party.

Trade unions often exercise the right to strike, but public sector unions are required to give at least 16 days' notice prior to striking. Some states have laws requiring workers in certain nonpublic sector industries to give prior strike notice.

The Essential Services Maintenance Act allows the Government to ban strikes and requires conciliation or arbitration in specified essential industries. Legal mechanisms exist for challenging the assertion that a given dispute falls within the scope of this act. The Industrial Disputes Act prohibits retribution by employers against employees involved in legal strike actions. This prohibition is observed in practice.

Abuses against nationally organized unions or unionized workers are generally not a problem. However, unaffiliated unions of low caste or tribal workers are not always able to secure for themselve the protections and rights guaranteed by law. In February the death of a plant-level union leader in police custody, after he had been arrested on theft charges brought by his employer (see Section 1.a.), was an unusual instance of abuse. Charges related to the killing have been brought against both the police and the employer.

Unions are free to affiliate with international trade union organizations.

b. *The Right to Organize and Bargain Collectively.*—The right to bargain collectively has existed for decades. The Trade Union Act prohibits discrimination against union members and organizers, and employers may be penalized if they discriminate against employees engaged in union activities.

Collective bargaining is the normal means of setting wages and settling disputes in unionized plants in the organized industrial sector. Trade unions vigorously defend worker interests in this process. Although a system of specialized labor courts adjudicates labor disputes, there are long delays and a backlog of unresolved cases. When the parties are unable to agree on equitable wages, the Government may set up boards of union, management, and government representatives to determine them.

In practice legal protections of worker rights are effective only for the 28 million workers in the organized industrial sector, out of a total work force of more than 376 million. Outside the modern industrial sector, laws are difficult to enforce. Union membership is rare in this informal sector and collective bargaining does not exist.

There are seven export processing zones (EPZ's). Entry into the EPZ's is ordinarily limited to the employees. Such entry restrictions apply to union organizers. While workers in the EPZ's have the right to organize and bargain collectively, union activity is rare. In addition unions, content with their role in public sector enterprises, have not vigorously pursued efforts to organize private-sector employees anywhere in the years since EPZ's were established. Women constitute the bulk of the work force in the EPZ's.

c. *Prohibition of Forced or Compulsory Labor.*—The Constitution prohibits forced labor, and legislation passed in 1976 specifically bans the practice of bonded labor. A Supreme Court decision defined forced labor as work at less than the minimum wage, which is usually set by the state governments. Under this definition, which differs from that of the International Labor Organization (ILO), forced labor is widespread, especially in rural areas.

Bonded labor, the result of a private contractual relationship whereby a worker incurs or inherits debts to a contractor and then must work off the debt plus interest, is illegal but widespread. The Government estimates that between enactment of the Bonded Labor (Regulation and Abolition) Act in 1979 and March 31, 1993, approximately 251,424 bonded workers had been released from their obligations. Other sources maintain that those released are only one-tenth of the total number of bonded laborers. State governments are responsible for enforcing the act. Offenders may be sentenced to up to 3 years in prison but prosecutions are rare.

d. *Minimum Age for Employment of Children.*—The Constitution prohibits employment of children under 14 years of age in factories, mines, or other hazardous employment. It also encourages the state governments to provide free and compulsory education for all children up to the age of 14. A law passed in 1986 banned the employment of children under age 14 in hazardous occupations, such as glass making, fireworks, match factories, and carpet weaving and regulated their employment in others. The Factories Act and the Child Labor Registration Act limit the hours of workers below the age of 15 to 4.5 hours per day.

The Government estimates that there were 17.5 million child workers in 1985. The ILO estimates the number at 44 million, while NGO's claim that the figure is 55 million. Interpolation of census figures by the National Labor Institute indicates that of a total of 203 million children between the ages of 5 and 14, 116 million are in school, 12.6 million are in full time employment, and the status of 74 million is unknown. Most, if not all of the 87 million children not in school do housework, work on family farms, work alongside their parents as paid agricultural labor, work as domestic servants, or are otherwise employed.

The enforcement of child labor laws is the responsibility of the state governments. Enforcement is not effective, especially in the informal sector where most of the children are employed. The continuing prevalence of child labor may be attributed to social acceptance of the practice and the failure of the state governments to make primary school education compulsory.

The new national Government formed in June has continued a comprehensive plan to eliminate child labor from hazardous industries by the year 2000. This program, for which approximately $260 million has been budgeted, includes enhanced enforcement of child labor laws, income supplements for families, subsidized school lunches in areas where child labor is concentrated, and a public awareness campaign. Recognizing a need to ensure that primary education is made universal and compulsory by state governments, the new Government committed itself to making primary education a fundamental constitutional right, not merely a directive principle. It has also pledged to raise educational expenditures to 6 percent of the budget and to spend at least 50 percent of this amount on primary education. The NHRC, continuing its own child labor agenda, organized NGO programs to provide special schooling, rehabilitation, and family income supplements for children in the glass industry in Firozabad. The NHRC also intervened in individual cases. A December 10 Supreme Court decision imposed a penalty of about $570 (20,000 rupee) on persons employing children in hazardous industries and stipulated that parents or guardians of children receive an income supplement payment from a fund created with this money, on condition that the children removed from employment attend school.

e. *Acceptable Conditions of Work.*—The directive principles of the Constitution declare that "the State shall endeavor to secure * * * to all workers * * * a living wage, conditions of work ensuring a decent standard of life and full enjoyment of leisure and social and cultural opportunities." Laws set minimum wages, hours of work, and safety and health standards. Laws governing minimum wages and hours of work are generally observed in industries subject to the Factories Act but are largely unenforced elsewhere and do not ensure acceptable conditions of work for the nine-tenths of the work force not subject to the Factories Act. Enforcement of safety and health standards is lax.

Minimum wages vary according to the state and sector of industry. Such wages are considered adequate only for a minimal standard of living. Most workers employed in units subject to the Factories Act receive much more than the minimum wage, including mandated bonuses and other benefits. The state governments set a separate minimum wage for agricultural workers but do not enforce it well.

The Factories Act establishes an 8-hour workday, a 48-hour workweek, and various standards for working conditions. These standards are generally enforced and accepted in the modern industrial sector, but tend not to be observed in older and less economically robust industries. State governments are responsible for enforcement of the Factories Act. However, the large number of industries covered by a small cadre of factory inspectors and their limited training and susceptibility to bribery make for lax enforcement.

Although occupational safety and health measures vary widely, in general neither state nor central government resources for inspection and enforcement of standards are adequate. Safety conditions tend to be better in the EPZ's. The law does not provide workers with the right to remove themselves from work situations that endanger health and safety without jeopardizing their continued employment.

MALDIVES

The Republic of Maldives comprises 1,190 islands scattered across an area 500 miles long by 75 miles wide in the Indian Ocean. The population is about 245,000 persons. The Maldives has a parliamentary form of government with a very strong executive. The President appoints the Cabinet, members of the judiciary, and one-sixth of the Parliament. The President derives additional influence from his constitutional role as the protector of Islam. Political parties are officially discouraged, and candidates for the unicameral legislature, the Citizens' Majlis, run as individuals. The Majlis selects a single presidential nominee who is approved or rejected in a national referendum. The Majlis must approve all legislation and can enact legislation without presidential approval. Civil law is subordinate to Islamic law, but civil law is generally applied in criminal and civil cases. The judiciary is subject to executive influence.

The National Security Service (NSS) performs its duties under effective civilian control. The NSS includes the armed forces and police, and its members serve in both police and military capacities during their careers. The police division investigates crimes, collects intelligence, makes arrests, and enforces house arrest.

Fishing, small-scale agriculture, and tourism provide employment for over one-half the work force. Tourism accounts for over one-quarter of government revenues and roughly 40 per cent of foreign exchange receipts. Manufacturing accounts for 6 percent of Gross Domestic Product (GDP).

The Government restricts human rights in several areas. Although the political process is increasingly open, the Government still holds political prisoners. The Majlis assumed a more active political role and its members routinely differed with government policy on many issues. However, the President's power to appoint a significant portion of the Parliament still constrains citizens' ability to change their government. An easing of government restrictions and the Press Council's balanced handling of issues related to journalistic standards allowed a greater diversity of views in the media. Nevertheless, a journalist was convicted for comments in an article about the 1994 general elections. The Government limits freedom of assembly and association. There are significant restrictions on the freedom of religion, and women face a variety of legal and social disadvantages. Some of these restrictions are linked to the Government's observance of Shari'a (Islamic law) and other Islamic customs. The Government restricts worker rights.

RESPECT FOR HUMAN RIGHTS

Section 1. Respect for the Integrity of the Person, Including Freedom From:

a. *Political and Other Extrajudicial Killing.*—There were no reports of political or other extrajudicial killings.

b. *Disappearance.*—There were no reports of politically motivated disappearances.

c. *Torture and Other Cruel, Inhuman, or Degrading Treatment or Punishment.*—There were no reports of beatings or other mistreatment of persons in police custody. Convicted criminals may be flogged under judicial supervision when this punishment is prescribed by Islamic law. However, there were no reported floggings. Punishments are usually confined to fines, compensatory payment, house arrest, imprisonment, or banishment to a remote atoll. The Government generally permits those who are banished to receive visits by family members.

Prison conditions, including food and prisoner housing, are adequate. Prisoners are allowed to work in prison and given the opportunity for regular exercise and recreation. Spouses are allowed privacy during visits with incarcerated partners. The Government has permitted prison visits by foreign diplomats.

d. *Arbitrary Arrest, Detention, or Exile.*—The Constitution states that no person shall be apprehended, except on a verdict specified by Shari'a or civil law. Police initiate investigations based on suspicion of criminal activity or in response to written complaints from citizens, police officers, or government officials. They are not required to obtain warrants for arrests. Based on the results of police investigations, the Attorney General refers cases to the appropriate court. The authorities generally keep the details of a case confidential until they are confident that the charges will be upheld.

Depending on the charges, a suspect may remain free, detained in prison, or under house arrest for 15 days during investigations. The President may extend pretrial detention for an additional 30 days, but in most cases the suspect is released if not brought to trial within 15 days. Those who are released pending trial may not leave a specific atoll. The law, however, permits indefinite detention without charge for suspects accused of drug abuse, terrorism, or attempted overthrow of the

Government. There is no right to legal counsel during police interrogation. There is no provision for bail.

The Government may prohibit access to a telephone and nonfamily visits to those under house arrest. While there have been no reported cases of incommunicado detention in recent years, the law does not provide safeguards against this abuse.

The Government detained three individuals in April 1995 who remained under house arrest without charge until October 1995, when their detention was lifted. No charges were brought against them. The Government has offered no reasons for their detention. It is widely believed, however, that their detention was the result of political differences with the Government rather than due to any threat that the men—all of whom are elderly and well known figures—pose to national security.

There were no reports of external exile. However, the Government sometimes banishes citizens to remote atolls.

e. *Denial of Fair Public Trial.*—The Constitution does not provide for an independent judiciary. The judiciary is subject to executive influence. In addition to his authority to review High Court decisions, the President influences the judiciary through his power to appoint and dismiss judges, all of whom serve at this pleasure and are not subject to confirmation by the Majlis. The President has nevertheless removed only two judges since 1987. Both dismissals followed the recommendation of the Justice Ministry which found the judges' professional qualifications to be below standard. The President may also grant pardons and amnesties.

There are four summary courts, falling under the Ministry of Justice, on the capital island, Male'. These summary courts adjudicate specialized cases, such as debt, theft, or property claims. There is also a High Court on Male', which is independent of the Justice Ministry and which handles a wide range of cases, including politically sensitive ones, and acts as a court of appeal. Under a 1995 presidential decree, High Court rulings can be reviewed by a 5-member advisory council appointed by the President. The President also has authority to affirm judgments of the High Court, order a second hearing, or overturn the Court's decision. In addition to the Male' courts, there are 204 general courts on the islands.

There are no jury trials. Most trials are public and are conducted by judges and magistrates trained in Islamic, civil, and criminal law. Cases on outer islands are usually adjudicated by magistrates, but when more complex legal questions are involved, the Justice Ministry will send more experienced judges to handle the case.

During a trial, the accused may defend himself, call witnesses, and be assisted by a lawyer. Courts do not provide lawyers to indigent defendants. Judges question the concerned parties and attempt to establish the facts of a case.

Civil law is subordinate to Islamic law, or Shari'a. Shari'a is applied in situations not covered by civil law as well as in certain acts such as divorce and adultery. Courts adjudicating matrimonial and criminal cases generally do not allow legal counsel in court because, according to a local interpretation of Shari'a, all answers and submissions should come directly from the parties involved. However, the High Court allows legal counsel in all cases, including those in which the right to counsel was denied in the lower court. Under Islamic practice, the testimony of two women is required to equal that of one man in matters involving finance and inheritance. In other cases, the testimony of men and women are equal.

Ilyas Ibrahim, the President's chief rival for the 1993 presidential nomination, had been tried in his absence in 1994 and sentenced to 15 years' banishment on the charge of illegally attempting to become President and to 6 months banishment for violating his oath as minister. Ilyas returned from his self-imposed foreign exile in April and has been under house arrest since that time.

There was one known political prisoner, Ibrahim Shareef (see Section 2.a.).

f. *Arbitrary Interference with Privacy, Family, Home, or Correspondence.*—The Constitution prohibits security officials from opening or reading letters, telegrams, and wireless messages or monitoring telephone conversations, "except in accordance with the specific provisions of the law." The NSS may open the mail of private citizens and monitor telephone conversations if authorized in the course of a criminal investigation.

Although the Constitution requires the authorities to respect private premises and dwellings, there is no legal requirement for search or arrest warrants. The Attorney General or a commanding officer of the police must approve the search of private residences.

Section 2. Respect for Civil Liberties, Including:

a. *Freedom of Speech and Press.*—Law No. 4/68 of 1968 prohibits public statements that are contrary to Islam, threaten the public order, or are libelous. In April a journalist was sentenced under this law to 2 years' imprisonment for comments made about the 1994 general elections in an article published in the Philippines. On appeal the High Court reduced his sentence to 6 months.

The Penal Code prohibits inciting the people against the Government. However, a 1990 amendment to the Penal Code decriminalized "any true account of any act of commission or omission past or present by the Government in a lawfully registered newspaper or magazine, so as to reveal dissatisfaction or to effect its reform."

The Press Council established by the Government in 1994 is composed of government official and private media representatives, lawyers, and government officials. The Council met regularly and private journalists were satisfied with its objectivity and performance. Regulations that made publishers responsible for the content of the material they published remained in effect, but did not result in any legal actions against publishers. The Government agreed that private journalists, rather than the Government, should take responsibility for preparation of a journalistic code of ethics. Individual newspapers and journals established their own ethical guidelines in many cases. The Government has not amended regulations that make publishers responsible for the content of the material they publish, despite reports in 1994 that the regulations were under review and a change was likely.

There were no reports of government censorship of either the print or electronic media, nor were there closures of any publications or reports of intimidation of journalists. The only journalist, Ibrahim Shareef, convicted under Law 4/68 of 1968 had been originally arrested in 1994. No journalists were arrested in 1996. The Government discontinued its practice of providing reporting guidelines to the media in 1994.

Television news and public affairs programming routinely discussed topics of current concern and freely criticized government performance. Regular press conferences instituted with government ministers in 1995, continued. Journalist are more self-confident than in the past and self-censorship seems to have abated.

The Government owns and operates the only television and radio station. It does not interfere with foreign broadcasts or the sale of satellite receivers. Reports drawn from foreign newscasts are aired on the government television station. Cable News Network is shown, uncensored, daily on local television. In October a private company began providing Internet services. The Government enacted no regulations governing Internet access but does seek to block distribution of pornographic material via Internet.

Ninety-two newspapers and periodicals are registered with the Government. Aafathis, a morning daily, is published by the brother of the President's principal political rival, Ilyas Ibrahim, and is often critical of government policy. A new daily, Miadhu, began publishing in October and Haveeru is the evening daily. Both Miadhu's and Haveeru's publishers are progovernment.

There are no legal prohibitions on the import of foreign publications except those containing pornography or material otherwise deemed objectionable to Islamic values. No seizures of foreign publications were reported during the year. There are no reported restrictions on academic freedom, nor any governmental censorship or control over classroom materials. Some teachers are reportedly vocal in their criticism of the Government.

b. *Freedom of Peaceful Assembly and Association.*—The Constitution provides for the right to assembly, as long as the law or the Islamic code of behavior are upheld. The Home Ministry permits public political meetings during electoral campaigns but limits them to small gatherings on private premises.

The Government registers clubs and other private associations if they do not contravene Islamic or civil law. While not forbidden by law, political parties are officially discouraged by the President on the grounds that they are inappropriate to the homogeneous nature of society. However, many Majlis members were active and outspoken critics of the Government and have stimulated closer parliamentary examination of government policy.

c. *Freedom of Religion.*—Freedom of religion is significantly restricted. The Constitution designates Islam as the official religion and requires all citizens to be Muslims. The practice of any religion other than Islam is prohibited by law. However, foreign residents are allowed to practice their religion if they do so privately.

There are no places of worship for adherents of other religions. The Government prohibits the importation of icons and religious statues. It also prohibits non-Muslim clergy and missionaries from proselytizing and conducting public worship services. Conversion of a Muslim to another faith is a violation of Shari'a and may result in a loss of the convert's citizenship, although law enforcement authorities say this provision has never been applied.

d. *Freedom of Movement Within the Country, Foreign Travel, Emigration, and Repatriation.*—Citizens are free to travel at home and abroad, emigrate, and return.

Because of overcrowding, the Government discourages migration into the capital island of Male' or its surrounding atoll. The issue of the provision of first asylum did not arise in 1996. The Government has not formulated a policy regarding first asylum. There were no reports of forced expulsion of those having a valid claim to refugee status.

Section 3. Respect for Political Rights: The Right of Citizens to Change Their Government

Citizens' ability to change their government is constrained, as a strong executive exerts significant influence over both the legislature and the judiciary. The Majlis chooses a single presidential nominee who must be a Sunni Muslim male. The candidate is not permitted to campaign for the nomination and is confirmed or rejected by secret ballot in a nationwide referendum. In 1993 President Gayoom was reelected to a fourth 5-year term.

The elected members of the Majlis serve 5-year terms. All citizens over 21 years of age may vote. Of the body's 48 members, 40 are elected—2 from each of the 19 inhabited atolls and 2 from Male'—and the President appoints 8 members. Individuals or groups are free to approach members of the Majlis with grievances or opinions on proposed legislation, and any member may introduce legislation.

The Office of the President is the most powerful political institution. The Constitution gives Islamic law preeminence over civil law and designates the President as the protector of Islam. The President's authority to appoint one-sixth of the Majlis members, which is one-third of the total needed for nominating the President, provides the President with a power base and strong political leverage.

Relations between the Government and Majlis have been constructive. The Government may introduce legislation, but may not enact a bill into law without the Majlis' approval. However, the Majlis may enact legislation into law without presidential assent if the President fails to act on the proposal within 30 days or if a bill is repassed with a two-thirds majority. In recent years, the Majlis has become increasingly independent, challenging government policies and rejecting government proposed legislation.

In 1993 the Majlis introduced a question time in which members may question government ministers about public policy. Debate on the floor has since become increasingly sharp and more open. The last Majlis election was held in December 1995. According to South Asian Association for Regional Cooperation observers, the elections were generally free and fair. Irregularities were observed and repolling required in one of 29 constituencies. Over 200 candidates campaigned freely for 40 seats.

Women are not eligible to become president but may hold other government posts. For reasons of tradition and culture, few women seek or are selected for public office. Two women served in the Majlis and one in the Cabinet.

Section 4. Governmental Attitude Regarding International and Nongovernmental Investigation of Alleged Violations of Human Rights

There are no active local human rights groups. The Government has been responsive to at least one foreign government's interest in examining human rights issues. The Government also facilitated the visit of a team of South Asian Association for Regional Cooperation election observers in 1994.

Section 5. Discrimination Based on Race, Sex, Religion, Disability, Language, or Social Status

The Constitution declares all Maldivians equal before the law, but there is no specific provisions to prohibit discriminiation based on these factors. Women have traditionally been disadvantaged in Maldivian society, particularly in terms of education and the application of Islamic law to matters such as divorce, inheritance, and testimony in legal proceedings.

Women.—There are no firm data on the extent of violence against women because of the value attached to privacy in this conservative society. Police officials report that they receive few complaints of assaults against women. Maldivian women's rights advocates agree that wife beating and other forms of violence are not widespread. Rape and other violent crimes against women are rare.

Women traditionally have played a subordinate role in society, although they now participate in public life in growing numbers and gradually are participating at higher levels. Well-educated women maintain that cultural norms, not the law, inhibit women's education and career choices. In many instances, education for girls is curtailed after the seventh grade, largely because parents do not allow girls to leave their home island for one having a secondary school. Due largely to orthodox Islamic training, there is a strong strain of conservative sentiment—especially among small businessmen and residents of the outer islands—which opposes an active role for women outside the home.

Under Islamic practice, husbands may divorce their wives more easily than vice versa, absent any mutual agreement to divorce. Islamic law also governs inheritance, granting male heirs twice the share of female heirs. A woman's testimony is equal to only one-half of that of a man in matters involving finance and inheritance (see Section 1.e.). Women who work for wages receive pay equal to that of men in the same positions. About 10 per cent of uniformed NSS personnel are women.

Children.—The Government does not have a program of compulsory education. The Government is committed to protection of children's rights and welfare. Government policy provides for equal access to educational and health programs for both male and female children. Laws protecting children's rights apply with equal force to children of either sex.

Children's rights are incorporated into law, which specifically protects children from both physical and psychological abuse, including abuse at the hands of teachers or parents. The Ministry of Home Affairs has the authority to enforce this law, takes its responsibility seriously, and has received strong popular support for its efforts. There is no reported societal pattern of abuse directed against children.

People With Disabilities.—There is no law that specifically addresses the rights of the physically or mentally disabled. However, the Government has established programs and provided services for the disabled. There is no legislated or mandated accessibility for the disabled.

Section 6. Worker Rights

a. *The Right of Association.*—While the Government does not expressly prohibit unions, it recognizes neither the right to form them nor the right to strike. There were no reports of efforts to form unions during the year. The only strike involved a short-lived protest by some foreign workers upset over the deportation of one of their countrymen.

The work force consists of approximately 60,000 persons, about 20 percent of whom are employed in fishing. About 20,000 foreigners work in Maldives, many in tourist hotels, factories, or on construction projects. The great majority of workers are employed outside the wage sector. The Government estimates that the manufacturing sector employs about 15 percent of the labor force and tourism another 10 percent.

In 1995 the U.S. Government suspended Maldives' eligibility for tariff preferences under the U.S. Generalized System of Preferences because the Government failed to take steps to afford internationally recognized worker rights to Maldivian workers.

b. *The Right to Organize and Bargain Collectively.*—The law neither prohibits nor protects workers' rights to organize and bargain collectively. Wages in the private sector are set by contract between employers and employees and are usually based on the rates for similar work in the public sector. There are no laws specifically prohibiting antiunion discrimination by employers against union members or organizers. The Government has exerted pressure in the past to discourage seamen from joining foreign seamen's unions as a means to secure higher wages. There have been no reported complaints alleging such discrimination or claiming government interference with workers' attempts to join unions in the past 3 years.

There are no export processing zones.

c. *Prohibition of Forced or Compulsory Labor.*—Forced or compulsory labor is not prohibited by law. However, there were no reports that it is practiced.

d. *Minimum Age for Employment of Children.*—There is no compulsory education law. A 1992 law bars children under 14 years of age from "places of waged works and from work that is not suitable for that child's age, health, or physical ability or that might obstruct the education or adversely affect the mentality or behavior of the child." An earlier law prohibits government employment of children under the age of 16. There are no reports of children being employed in the small industrial sector, although children work in family fishing, agricultural, and commercial activities. The hours of work of young workers are not specifically limited by statute.

e. *Acceptable Conditions of Work.*—In 1994 the Government promulgated its first set of regulations for employer-employee relations. The regulations specify the terms that must be incorporated into employment contracts and address such issues as training, work hours, safety, remuneration, leave, fines, termination, etc. There is no national minimum wage for the private sector, although the Government has established wage floors for certain kinds of work. Given the severe shortage of labor, employers must offer competitive pay and conditions to attract skilled workers.

There are no statutory provisions for hours of work, but the regulations require that a work contact specify the normal work and overtime hours on a weekly or monthly basis. In the public sector, a 7-hour day and a 5-day workweek have been established through administrative circulars from the President's office. Overtime pay in the public sector was instituted in 1990. Employees are authorized 20 days of annual leave, 30 days of medical leave, maternity leave of 45 days, and special annual leave of 10 days for extraordinary circumstances. There are no laws governing health and safety conditions; however, there are regulatory requirements that employers provide a safe working environment and ensure the observance of safety measures. It is unclear, however, whether workers can remove themselves from unsafe working conditions without risking the loss of their jobs.

NEPAL

Nepal is a constitutional monarchy with a parliamentary form of government and an independent judiciary. In 1990 the King, formerly an absolute monarch, legalized political parties after which an interim government promulgated a new constitution. The King retains important residual powers, but has dissociated himself from direct day-to-day government activities. The democratically elected Parliament consists of the House of Representatives (lower house) and the National Council (upper house). Since 1990 Nepal has held three national elections, two for the Parliament and one for local officials. International observers considered these elections to be generally free and fair. The Government changed in September 1995 and the transfer of power to the new coalition was peaceful and orderly. However, in February the leaders of the United People's Front launched a "People's War" in central Nepal, which has been waged through killings and bombings involving both soldiers and civilians.

The National Police Force maintains internal security, assisted as necessary by the Royal Nepalese Army. Police reaction to the insurgency led to allegations that unwarranted force was used against prisoners and noncombatants. The army is traditionally loyal to the King and avoids overt involvement in domestic politics. The police are subject to civilian control, but local officials have wide discretion in maintaining law and order. The police committed human rights abuses.

Nepal is an extremely poor country, with an annual per capita gross domestic product of approximately $200. Over 80 percent of its 20 million people support themselves through subsistence agriculture. Principal crops include rice, wheat, maize, jute, and potatoes. Tourism and the export of carpets and garments are the major sources of foreign exchange. Foreign aid accounts for more than half the development budget. The economy is mixed with 54 public sector firms. Eight former government firms have been privatized since 1992.

Since political reform began in 1990, Nepal has made progress in its transition to a more open society with greater respect for human rights. However, problems remain, and the Government fails to enforce all the Constitution's provisions. The police continue to abuse detainees, using torture as punishment or to extract confessions. The Government rarely investigates allegations of police brutality or takes action. There were also allegations that police killed unarmed civilians in the course of operations against the insurgents, and while in custody. The authorities use arbitrary arrest and detention, and prison conditions remain poor. Judicial susceptibility to political pressure and corruption, long delays before trial, and lengthy pretrial detention remain problems. The Government continues to impose some restrictions on freedom of religion and expression. Lower castes and women suffer widespread discrimination. Trafficking in women and girls, violence against women, forced labor, and child labor also remain serious problems.

In July Parliament unanimously enacted a bill to establish a permanent human rights commission with the authority to investigate human rights abuses.

The insurgents committed numerous human rights abuses, including killings, bombings, and mutilations.

RESPECT FOR HUMAN RIGHTS

Section 1. Respect for the Integrity of the Person, Including Freedom From:
   a. *Political and Other Extrajudicial Killing.*—On a number of occasions, the Government is alleged to have used unwarranted lethal force against persons suspected of involvement in the "People's War" in central Nepal. Some human rights groups have reported several instances of police killings in the districts affected by the unrest. Some of these incidents occurred during armed combat, but several allegedly involved unarmed civilians. An investigation team of prominent human rights groups reported that Tilak Ram Budha, the elected village development committee chairman of Kot Gaon in Rolpa district and political representative of the United

People's Front (UPF), was shot by the police on April 12, reportedly while in custody after arrest. The team also reported that iman Singh Rokka of Uwa village in Rolpa died while being transferred to a jail under police custody. In this case, a medical doctor reportedly stated that the cause of death was chronic jaundice. The general perception, given the the brutality of insurgent attacks against civilians, is that the police have shown restraint.

The insurgents were responsible for numerous human rights abuses. Launched in February by UPF leaders Baburam Bhattarai and Pushpa Kamal Dahal, the "People's War" is a self-declared Maoist insurgency. Guerrillas, usually armed with homemade guns, explosives, knives, and sticks, attacked landowners, government officials, and government facilities in a number of districts. The Government responded to the insurgency by sending more than 1,500 police to the affected districts. Fifty-five persons died in the subsequent violence, most of them killed by the insurgents.

b. *Disappearance.*—There were no reports of politically motivated disappearances. Two student activists that the police took into custody in 1993 and 1994 remain missing. The Supreme Court has investigated these disappearances, but the police maintain that they are not holding the students.

c. *Torture and Other Cruel, Inhuman, or Degrading Treatment or Punishment.*— The Constitution and criminal law prohibit torture; however, the police often use beatings and torture to punish suspects or to extract confessions. The Government has failed to conduct thorough and independent investigations of reports of police brutality and has refused to take significant disciplinary action against officers involved. Police are often unwilling to investigate and discipline fellow officers, and people are afraid to bring cases against police for fear of reprisals. The Constitution provides for compensation for victims of torture, and a bill providing for such compensation was passed by Parliament in September. The Government has begun human rights education for the police force.

Human rights groups have reported instances of torture in areas affected by the "People's War." On March 7, Jhakku Prasad Subedi, the elected UPF chairman of the Rolpa District Development Committee, was reportedly so severely beaten while in police custody that he was unable to walk for 25 days. Dozens of other male detainees reported torture inflicted on them by police. Women in these areas have reported instances of rape and sexual abuse by the police.

Human rights groups have also documented Maoist violence in these areas, including the severing of arms and limbs. The Maoists have specifically targeted opposition political leaders, local elites, and suspected informers. On February 25, four persons shouting Maoist slogans seriously assaulted Communist Party of Nepal-United Marxist Leninist (UML) worker Bhim Bahadur Bhandari. On February 27, Maoist activists cut off the left hand and right hand fingers of Narajit Basnet, the brother of the Nepali Congress Party (NCP) president of his village development committee.

Prison conditions are poor. Overcrowding is common in prisons and authorities sometimes handcuff or fetter detainees. Women are normally incarcerated separately from men, but in similar conditions. The Government has not implemented a provision in the 1992 Children's Act calling for the establishment of a juvenile home and juvenile court. Consequently, children are sometimes incarcerated with adults—either as criminals or with an incarcerated parent. The Department of Prisons says that 75 noncriminal dependent children remain in prison, but the number of child prisoners charged or convicted of a crime is unknown.

There has been some improvement in prison conditions. The authorities are more likely to transfer sick prisoners to hospitals than they were in the past. Due to the inadequacy of medical facilities in the country, the authorities sometimes place the mentally ill in jails under inhumane conditions. The Government permits local human rights groups to visit prisons.

d. *Arbitrary Arrest, Detention, or Exile.*—The Constitution stipulates that the authorities must arraign or release a suspect within 24 hours of arrest, but the police often violate this provision. Under the Public Offenses Act of 1970, the police must obtain warrants for an arrest unless a person is caught in the act of committing a crime. For many offenses, the case must be filed in court within 7 days of arrest. If the court upholds the detention, the law authorizes the police to hold the suspect for 25 days to complete their investigation, with a possible extension of 7 days. However, the police often hold prisoners longer. The Supreme Court has on occasion ordered the release of detainees held longer than 24 hours without a court appearance.

Detainees do not have the legal right to receive visits by family members and they are permitted access to lawyers only after the authorities file charges. In practice the police grant access to prisoners on a basis that varies from prison to prison. Persons have a right to legal representation and a court appointed lawyer, but government lawyers or access to private attorneys is provided only on request. Consequently, those unaware of their rights may not have legal representation. There is a system of bail, but bonds are usually too expensive for most citizens. According to the Department of Prisons, over half of the 6,000 people imprisoned are awaiting trial. Due to court backlogs, a slow appeals process, and poor access to legal representation, it is common for persons to be held for periods longer than their sentences after conviction.

Under the Public Security Act, the authorities may detain persons who allegedly threaten domestic security and tranquility, amicable relations with other states, and relations between citizens of different classes or religions. Persons whom the Government detains under the Act are considered to be in preventive detention and are not brought to trial.

The 1991 amendments to the Public Security Act allow the authorities to extend periods of detention after submitting written notices to the Home Ministry. The police must notify the district court of the detention within 24 hours, and it may order an additional 6 months of detention before authorities file official charges.

Other laws, including the Public Offenses Act, permit arbitrary detention. This Act and its many amendments cover such crimes as disturbing the peace, vandalism, rioting, and fighting. Under this Act, the Government detained hundreds of civil servants during a 55-day antigovernment strike in 1991. Human rights monitors express concern that the Act vests too much discretionary power in the Chief District Officer (CDO), the highest ranking civil servant in each of the country's 75 districts. The Act authorizes the CDO to order detentions, to issue search warrants, and to specify fines and other punishments for misdemeanors without judicial review.

Under the Public Offenses Act hundreds of people were arrested on March 18 for staging a peaceful protest of the human rights situation organized by Amnesty International (AI) in Kathmandu in China. Although most were released the same day, several AI officers and 14 Tibetans were held in jail for up to 7 days, some without charge.

Human rights groups allege that the police have used arbitrary arrest and detention during the "People's War" to intimidate communities considered sympathetic to the Maoists. In one example, Jun Maya Rokaya, a UPF representative in the Uwa Village Development Committee, was reportedly arrested without a warrant on March 14 and kept in police custody for 2 months before being presented before a court.

The Constitution prohibits exile; it is not practiced.

e. *Denial of Fair Public Trial.*—The Constitution provides for an independent judiciary and the Supreme Court has demonstrated independence. However, lower level courts remain vulnerable to political pressure. In addition, bribery of lower level judges and court staff is endemic.

The Supreme Court has ruled that important provisions in the 1992 Labor Act and in the 1991 Nepal Citizenship Act are unconstitutional. In 1995 the Court also decided that the dissolution of the Parliament at the request of a former Prime Minister was unconstitutional, and ordered the body restored.

Appellate and district courts have become increasingly independent, although they sometimes bend to political pressure. In Rolpa, one of the districts most affected by the "People's War," human rights groups have accused the district courts of acting in complicity with CDO's in violating detainees' rights. These groups allege that arrest without a warrant, prolonged detention without trial, and police torture occur in these areas.

The judicial system consists of three levels: district courts, appellate courts, and the Supreme Court. The King appoints judges on the recommendation of the Judicial Council, a constitutional body chaired by the Chief Justice. The Council is also responsible for the assignment of judges, disciplinary action, and other administrative matters. Judges decide cases; there is no jury system.

Delays in the administration of justice are a severe problem. The Supreme Court has a backlog of approximately 11,000 cases, which it expects will take 5 years to clear. A case appealed to the Supreme Court may take more than 10 years to conclude.

The Constitution provides for the right to counsel, equal protection under the law, protection from double jeopardy, protection from retroactive application of the law, and for public trials, except in some security and customs cases. All lower court decisions, including acquittals, are subject to appeal. The Supreme Court is the court of last appeal, but the King may grant pardons. The King can also suspend, commute, or remit any sentence. On the recommendation of the Government, the King often pardons up to 12 prisoners—if they have served 75 percent of their sentence and shown good behavior—on national holidays.

Military courts adjudicate cases concerning military personnel, who are immune from prosecution in civilian courts. In 1992 the Supreme Court ruled that military courts may no longer try civilians for crimes involving the military services.

The authorities may prosecute terrorism or treason cases under the Treason Act. Specially constituted tribunals hear these trials in closed sessions. No such trials took place during the past 2 years.

There were no reports of political prisoners.

f. *Arbitrary Interference with Privacy, Family, Home, or Correspondence.*—The Government generally respected the privacy of the home and family. Search warrants are required before search and seizure except in cases involving suspected security and narcotics violations. As amended, the Police Act of 1955 empowers the police to issue warrants for search and seizure in criminal cases upon receipt of information about criminal activities. Within 24 hours of their issuance, warrants in misdemeanor cases must be approved by the CDO. Court judges must approve them in felony cases.

Section 2. *Respect for Civil Liberties, Including:*

a. *Freedom of Speech and Press.*—The Constitution specifies that all citizens shall have freedom of thought and expression and that the Government may not censor any news item or other reading material. Nevertheless, the Constitution prohibits speech and writing that would threaten the sovereignty and integrity of the Kingdom; disturb the harmonious relations among people of different castes or communities; promote sedition, defamation, contempt of court, or crime; or contradict decent public behavior or morality.

The Press and Publications Act provides for the licensing of publications and the granting of credentials to journalists. The Act includes penalties for violating these requirements. The Act also prohibits publication of material that, among other things, promotes disrespect toward the King or royal family; that undermines security, peace, order, the dignity of the King, and the integrity or sovereignty of the Kingdom; that creates animosity among people of different castes and religions; or that adversely affects the good conduct or morality of the public. The regulation also provides a basis for banning foreign publications. However, foreign publications are now widely available.

There are hundreds of independent vernacular and English newspapers representing various political points of view, most have a small circulation and limited impact. The Government owns the daily Nepali Language newspaper with the largest circulation. Editors and writers at the Government newspaper practice self-censorship and generally reflect government policy. Ruling political parties have influenced the editorial policy of the government newspaper to their advantage. However, despite the sensitivity of the Government to the "People's War," the press has not faced overt pressure to report on it in a particular way. Views of human rights groups, the statements of the police, and the press releases of UPF leader Bhattarai have all been reported in the local press.

The Government owns and controls the major radio and television stations. Radio reaches the greatest number of people and has the largest influence. Programming currently reflects a broader range of interests and political viewpoints than prior to the political transformation in 1990, but still closely follows the government line. The Government does not restrict access to foreign radio broadcasts or to the purchase of television satellite dishes that can access international news from the British Broadcasting Corporation (BBC) and the Cable News Network (CNN). A small but growing number of Nepalis have access to foreign news.

The Broadcast Act of 1993 allows private parties to broadcast television and FM radio, but implementation by the Government has been slow. Private broadcasters sometimes waited years for the Government to assign them a bandwidth and issue the operating license. There are two private television stations (cable and microwave), which have been operating for over a year in the Kathmandu valley. They provide mainly entertainment programming and do no local research or reporting.

There has been much debate about liberalizing the media and privatizing government-owned media. This debate has put pressure, so far successfully resisted, on successive governments to open the air waves and divest government-controlled printing operations.

The Government limits academic freedom to the same extent as the media. No overt efforts to enforce these limitations were reported this year.

b. *Freedom of Peaceful Assembly and Association.*—Although the Constitution provides for freedom of assembly, this right may be restricted by law on vague grounds such as undermining the sovereignty and integrity of the State or disturbing law and order. Persons protesting Chinese human rights policy were arrested and detained in March before and during peaceful protests (see Section 1.d.).

c. *Freedom of Religion.*—The Constitution describes Nepal as a Hindu Kingdom, although it does not establish Hinduism as the state religion. The majority of citizens are Hindu. The Constitution permits the practice of all religions and prohibits discrimination on the basis of caste except for traditional religious practices at Hindu temples.

Although the Government has generally not interfered with the practice of other religions, conversion is prohibited and punishable with fines or imprisonment, the police occasionally harass members of minority religions. Some groups are concerned that the ban on proselytizing limits the expression of non-Hindu religious belief. Foreigners convicted of proselytizing can be expelled from the country.

Eleven Christians were arrested in September 1994 for proselytizing. They were convicted by the Ilam district court and sentenced to 2 years' imprisonment in August 1995. The case received considerable international attention. The 11 were held in prison until they were pardoned by the King and released unconditionally in November 1995.

d. *Freedom of Movement Within the Country, Foreign Travel, Emigration, and Repatriation.*—The Constitution provides for freedom of movement and residence, and the Government generally does not restrict travel abroad. However, the Government restricts travel to some areas near the Chinese border for foreign tourists and for foreign residents, such as Tibetans residing in Nepal. The Government allows citizens abroad to return, and is not known to revoke citizenship for political reasons.

The Government has no official refugee policy and is party to neither the 1951 U.N. Convention relating to the Status of Refugees nor the 1967 Protocol. However, it does provide asylum for refugees and has cooperated with the office of the United Nations High Commissioner for Refugees (UNHCR), and with other humanitarian organizations, in assisting refugees from Bhutan and Tibet (China). The UNHCR has maintained an office in Kathmandu since 1989. Since 1959 the Government has accepted approximately 20,000 Tibetan refugees, many of whom still reside in the country. Since 1991 it has also provided asylum to more than 90,000 Bhutanese refugees, the great majority of whom are now living in UNHCR-administered camps in eastern Nepal.

In the mid-1960's, the Government suspended issuance of identification cards to Tibetans. Undocumented Tibetan residents face difficulties in obtaining basic citizens' rights and are unable to travel abroad or access such services as banking. The UNHCR donates blank resident identification cards to the Government for Tibetans. In early 1995, the Government reversed this policy and resumed issuance of identification cards to Tibetans. By mid-July issuance of identification cards to virtually all 7,300 Tibetan residents outside the Kathmandu valley was completed. However, approximately 4000 Tibetan refugees within the Kathmandu valley still remain without identification cards.

China and the Government of Nepal tightened control of movement across their border in 1986, but both sides have enforced these restrictions haphazardly. Police and customs officials occasionally harass Tibetan asylum seekers who cross the border from China. Border police often extort money from Tibetans in exchange for passage. With the change from a Communist Party government to a coalition government headed by the Nepal Congress Party, the former practice of forcibly returning asylum seekers to China has stopped, and there were no reports of forced expulsion of Tibetan asylum seekers in 1996.

There are approximately 91,000 ethnic Nepali refugees from Bhutan in UNHCR-administered camps in southeastern Nepal. An additional 15,000 to 20,000 refugees reside outside the camps in either Nepal or India. The total represents approximately one-sixth of Bhutan's estimated pre-1991 population.

The UNHCR monitors the condition of the Bhutanese refugees and provides for their basic needs. The Government accepts the refugee presence as temporary, on humanitarian grounds, but offers little more than a place to stay. The Government officially restricts refugee freedom of movement and work, but does not strictly enforce its policies. Living conditions in the camps have improved dramatically since 1992. Adequate clean water is available and health, sanitation, and nutrition standards are acceptable. Violence has sometimes broken out between camp residents and the surrounding local population. The UNHCR and other donors and relief organizations have defused tensions through a refugee affected areas assistance plan aimed at improving conditions in communities adjacent to the camps.

In 1993 the Governments of Nepal and Bhutan formed a joint committee to resolve the refugee problem and to determine different categories of refugees in preparation for future repatriation. Seven rounds of bilateral talks have been held, but with little concrete progress. The Government expressed concern during the latest round of talks in April that many refugees would become stateless if Bhutan refuses to take them back. The lack of progress in bilateral negotiations has led to increased frustration in the camps, and to a recent campaign of "peace marches" by refugees seeking to return to Bhutan.

Section 3. Respect for Political Rights: The Right of Citizens to Change Their Government

Citizens, through their elected representatives, have the right to amend the Constitution with the exception of certain basic principles that they may not change— sovereignty vested in the people, the multiparty system, fundamental rights, and the constitutional monarchy.

Parliamentary elections are scheduled at least every 5 years. Midterm elections may be called if the ruling party loses its majority, loses a vote of no confidence, or calls for elections. The Constitution grants suffrage to all citizens of age 18 and over.

A three-party coalition, which now has a majority in Parliament, passed a no-confidence motion against the previous minority government in September 1995. That coalition formed a new government later that same month.

The House of Representatives, or lower house, may send legislation directly to the King by majority vote. The National Council, or upper house, may amend or reject lower house legislation, but the lower house can overrule its objections. The upper house may also introduce legislation and send it to the lower house for consideration.

The King exercises certain powers with the advice and consent of the Council of Ministers. These include exclusive authority to enact, amend, and repeal laws relating to succession to the throne. The King's income and property are tax-exempt and inviolable, and no question may be raised in any court about any act performed by the King. The Constitution also permits the King to exercise emergency powers in the event of war, external aggression, armed revolt, or extreme economic depression. In such an emergency, the King may suspend without judicial review many basic freedoms, including the freedoms of expression and assembly, freedom from censorship, and freedom from preventive detention. However, he may not suspend habeas corpus or the right to form associations. The King's declaration of a state of emergency must be approved by a two-thirds majority of the lower house of the Parliament. If the lower house is not in session, the upper house exercises this power. A state of emergency may be maintained for up to 3 months without legislative approval and up to 6 months, renewable only once for an additional 6 months, if the legislature grants approval.

The Constitution bars the registration and participation in elections of any political party that is based on "religion, community, caste, tribe, or region," or that does not operate openly and democratically.

There are no specific laws that restrict women, indigenous peoples, or minorities from participating in the Government or in political parties. Conservative traditions limit the roles of women and of some castes and tribes in the political process. The Constitution requires that women constitute 5 percent of each party's candidates for the House of Representatives. Seven of the 205 members of the lower house of the current Parliament are women. In the upper house, 4 of the 60 members are women.

Section 4. Governmental Attitude Regarding International and Nongovernmental Investigation of Alleged Violations of Human Rights

There are a dozen nongovernmental (NGO) human rights organizations. These include the Human Rights Organization of Nepal (HURON), the Informal Sector Services Center (INSEC), the International Institute for Human Rights, Environment, and Development (INHURED), and the Forum for the Protection of Human Rights (FOPHUR). The Nepal Law Society also monitors human rights abuses and a number of NGO's focus on specific areas such as torture, child labor, women's rights, or ethnic minorities. Groups are free to publish reports on human rights abuses. The Government has also allowed groups to visit prisons and prisoners. The Government rarely arrests or detains those reporting on human rights problems. However, one worker for FOPHUR was reportedly arrested on February 18 without warrant or charge and held incommunicado for 6 days before release.

Section 5. Discrimination Based on Race, Sex, Religion, Disability, Language, or Social Status

The Constitution specifies that the State shall not discriminate against citizens on grounds of religion, race, sex, caste, or ideology. However, there is still a caste system. Discrimination against lower castes and women remains common, especially in rural areas.

Women.—There is no law against domestic violence, which is widespread. In one study, 50 percent of the respondents said that they know someone who was the victim of domestic violence. Little public attention is given to violence against women in the home; the Government makes no special effort to combat it. Rape and incest are also problems, particularly in rural areas. There is a law against rape of nonprostitute women which imposes sentences of from 3 to 5 years. In the case of rape of prostitutes, sentences range from a fine of 500 rupees ($9.00) to 1 year's imprisonment.

The dowry tradition is strong, with greater prevalence in the Terai region. Killing of brides because of defaults on dowry payments is rare, but does occur. More common is the physical abuse of wives by the husband and the husband's family to obtain additional dowry or to force the woman to leave to enable the son to remarry.

Trafficking in women and girls remains a deeply ingrained social problem in several of the country's poorest areas. Estimates of the number of girls and women working as prostitutes in India range between 40,000 and 100,000. The best available data suggest that approximately 5,000 to 7,000 girls between the ages of 10 and 18 are lured or abducted into prostitution each year. Prostitution is also a problem in the Kathmandu valley. A children's human rights group in Nepal states that 20 percent of prostitutes are younger than 16 years old. In many cases, parents or relatives sell women and young girls into sexual slavery. Among the Badini and Devaki of western Nepal, religious prostitution remains a problem.

There is legislation to protect women from coercive trafficking, but it is not well enforced. The fear of the spread of AIDS by returning prostitutes has discouraged the Government from promoting the rehabilitation of prostitutes. Government efforts focus more on preventing voluntary prostitution. The Ministry of Labor and Social Welfare sponsors job and skill training programs in several poor districts known for sending prostitutes to India. Several NGO's have similar programs.

Although the Constitution provides protections for women, including equal pay for equal work, the Government has not taken significant action to implement its provisions. Women face discrimination, particularly in rural areas, where religious and cultural tradition, lack of education, and ignorance of the law remain severe impediments to their exercise of basic rights such as the right to vote or to hold property in their own names.

Women have benefited from changes in marriage and inheritance laws. In 1994 the Supreme Court struck down provisions of the Citizenship Law that discriminated against foreign spouses of Nepalese women. However, many other discriminatory laws still remain. According to legal experts, there are more than 20 laws that discriminate against women. For example, the law grants women the right to divorce, but on narrower grounds than those applicable to men. The law on property rights also favors men in its provisions for inheritance, land tenancy, and the division of family property. In August 1995, the Supreme Court also ordered the Council of Ministers to enact legislation within 1 year giving women property rights in regard to inheritance and land tenancy equal of those of men. As of year's end, however, such legislation had not been introduced in Parliament.

According to the 1991 census, the female literacy rate is 26 percent, compared with 57 percent for men. Human rights groups report that girls attend secondary schools at a rate half that of boys. There are now many NGO's focused on integrating women into society and the economy. These NGO's work in the areas of literacy, small business, skills transfer, and against trafficking in women and girls.

There are a growing number of women's advocacy groups and nearly all political parties have their own women's group. Members of Parliament have begun working for the passage of tougher laws for crimes of sexual assault, but have had little success so far.

Children.—The Government provides free primary education for children of ages 6 to 12, but many families cannot afford school supplies or clothing. Schools charge fees for further education. Free health care is provided through government clinics, but they are poorly equipped and too few in number to meet the demand. Community-based health programs assist in the prevention of childhood diseases and provide primary health care services. Due to poor or nonexistent sanitation in rural areas many children are at risk from severe and fatal illnesses.

The Child Act of 1992 provides legal protection for children in the workplace and in criminal proceedings. Although it calls for the establishment of child welfare committees and orphanages, the Government has established few such facilities. The Labor Act of 1992 prohibits employment of minors under 14 years of age, but employers, particularly in the informal sector or agriculture, widely ignore the law.

Children under the age of 16 work in all sectors of the economy. Children's rights groups estimate that up to half of all children work. As recently as early 1994, the carpet industry employed large numbers of children, an estimated 23,000, nearly one-third of all workers in that industry. Due to negative publicity in consumer nations, children now account for approximately 5 percent of the carpet industry's employees, about 6,000 workers (see Section 6.d.). A consortium of carpet manufacturers is moving to establish a certification system for carpets made without child labor. The Ministry of Labor is increasing its efforts to monitor the use of child labor.

Prostitution and trafficking in young girls remain serious problems (see above).

Approximately 75 innocent children under the age of 12 are incarcerated with their parents because the Government has not established juvenile homes (see Section 1.c.).

People With Disabilities.—The disabled face widespread discrimination. Families often are stigmatized by and ashamed of disabled family members, who may be hidden away or neglected. Economic integration is further hampered by the general view that the disabled are unproductive. The mentally retarded are associated with the mentally ill. Sometimes, mentally ill and retarded persons are placed in prisons due to the lack of facilities or support.

The Government has long been involved in providing for the disabled, but the level of government assistance has not met the needs of the disabled. The 1982 Disabled Persons Protection and Welfare Act and additional 1994 rules mandate accessibility to buildings, transportation, employment, education, and other state services. However, despite government funding for special education programs, the Government does not implement or enforce laws regarding the disabled. A number of NGO's working with the disabled receive significant funding from the Government, but persons who are physically or mentally disabled rely almost exclusively on family members to assist them.

National/Racial/Ethnic Minorities.—Nepal has over 75 ethnic groups speaking 50 languages. The Constitution provides that each community "shall have the right to preserve and promote its language, script, and culture." It further specifies that each community has the right to operate schools up to the primary level in its mother tongue.

Discrimination against lower castes is especially common in the rural areas of western Nepal. Although the Government has outlawed the public shunning of "untouchables," an exception was retained for traditional practices at Hindu religious sites. Economic, social, and educational advancement tend to be a function of historical patterns, geographic location, and caste. Better education and higher levels of prosperity, especially in the Kathmandu valley, are slowly reducing caste distinctions and increasing opportunities for lower socioeconomic groups. Better educated urban-oriented castes (Brahmin, Chhetri, and certain elements of the Newar community traditionally dominant in the Kathmandu valley) continue to dominate politics, senior administrative and military positions, and to control a disproportionate share of natural resources in their territories.

In remote areas, school lessons and national radio broadcasts are often in the local language. However, in areas with nearby municipalities, education at the primary, secondary, and university levels is conducted almost exclusively in Nepali. Human rights groups report that the languages of the small Kusunda, Dura, and Meche communities are nearly extinct and that non-Hindu peoples are losing their culture.

Section 6. Worker Rights

a. *The Right of Association.*—The Constitution provides for the freedom to establish and join unions and associations. It permits restriction of unions only in cases of subversion, sedition, or similar conditions. Despite the political transformation in 1990, trade unions are still developing their administrative structures to organize workers, bargain collectively, and conduct worker education programs. The prior UML government "automatically" registered its own affiliated unions but interfered in the registration of unions associated with the Nepali Congress Party's labor organization.

Union participation in the formal sector is significant, but it accounts for only a small portion of the labor force. In 1992 Parliament passed the Labor Act and the Trade Union Act, and formulated enabling regulations. However, the Government has not yet fully implemented the laws. The Trade Union Act defines procedures for establishing trade unions, associations, and federations. It also protects unions and officials from lawsuits arising from actions taken in the discharge of union duties, including collective bargaining.

The law permits strikes, except by employees in essential services such as water supply, electricity, and telecommunications. The law empowers the Government to halt a strike or suspend a union's activities if the union disturbs the peace or if it adversely affects the nation's economic interests. Under the Labor Act, 60 percent of a union's membership must vote in favor of a strike in a secret ballot for the strike to be legal.

The Trade Union Act prohibits employers from discriminating against trade union members or organizers. There have been few reports of discrimination against union members.

The Government does not restrict unions from joining international labor bodies. Several trade federations and union organizations maintain a variety of international affiliations.

b. *The Right to Organize and Bargain Collectively.*—The Labor Act provides for collective bargaining, although the organizational structures to implement the Act's provisions have not been established. Collective bargaining agreements cover an estimated 20 percent of wage earners in the organized sector. However, labor remains widely unable to use collective bargaining effectively due to inexperience and employer reluctance to bargain.

There are no export processing zones.

c. *Prohibition of Forced or Compulsory Labor.*—The Constitution prohibits slavery, serfdom, forced labor, or traffic in human beings in any form. The Department of Labor enforces laws against forced labor in the small formal sector, but remains unable to enforce the law outside that sector.

Large numbers of women are still forced to work against their will as prostitutes (see Section 5). Bonded labor is a continuing problem, especially in agricultural work. Bonded laborers are usually members of lower castes. Over 25,000 ethnic Tharu families are estimated to be under the "Kamaiya" or bonded labor system in the southern Terai region. The Government has not yet enacted legislation or taken other significant steps to address the problem.

d. *Minimum Age for Employment of Children.*—The Constitution stipulates that children shall not be employed in factories, mines, or similar hazardous work. The law also establishes a minimum age for employment of minors at 16 years in industry and 14 years in agriculture. The Constitution limits children between the ages of 14 and 16 years to a 36-hour work week. Despite the law, child workers are found in many sectors of the economy (see section 5).

Up to half of all children work, mostly in agriculture. A consortium of carpet factory owners are moving to establish a certification system for carpets made without child labor (see Section 5). Partially as a result of this initiative, and of consumer pressure, children now reportedly constitute only 5 percent of the workforce in the export-oriented carpet industry. Few or no children work in the garment industry.

The Ministry of Labor's enforcement record is improving. In the urban formal sector, it has had some success in enforcing laws relating to tenure, minimum wage, and holidays. Government inspectors are also increasing their monitoring of the use of child labor in carpet factories.

e. *Acceptable Conditions of Work.*—The Labor Act sets a minimum wage of $23 (1,150 rupees) per month for unskilled workers in factories and in the organized labor sector. This wage is sufficient only for the most minimal standard of living. Wages in the unorganized service sector and in agriculture are often as much as 50 percent lower.

The Labor Act calls for a 48-hour work week, with 1 day off per week, and limits overtime to 20 hours per week. Health and safety standards and other benefits such as a provident fund and maternity benefits are also established in the act. Implementation of the new Labor Act has been slow, as the Government has not created the necessary regulatory or administrative structures to enforce its provisions. Workers do not have the right to remove themselves from dangerous work situations. Although the law authorizes labor officers to order employers to rectify unsafe conditions, enforcement of safety standards remains minimal.

PAKISTAN

Pakistan is an Islamic republic in which power is shared between the Prime Minister, as the leader of the National Assembly, and the President. The Chief of Army Staff also wields considerable influence on many major policy decisions and is the third member of the unofficial "troika" that governs the nation. During the first 10 months of 1996, Prime Minister Benazir Bhutto dominated political policymaking, with President Farooq Leghari playing a complementary role. Chief of Army Staff General Jehangir Karamat consulted closely with the Government but avoided open involvement in governing. The Constitution provides for an independent judiciary; however, it is subject to executive branch influence.

On November 5, 1996, President Leghari, invoking Section 58 (2)b of the Constitution, dismissed Prime Minister Bhutto and her Cabinet, and dissolved the National Assembly. Over the subsequent 2 weeks the provincial assemblies were also dissolved. President Leghari and caretaker Prime Minister Meraj Khalid have stated that new national elections would be held on February 3, 1997. Bhutto has challenged her dismissal and the dissolution of the National Assembly in the Supreme Court.

Responsibility for internal security rests primarily with the police, although paramilitary forces, such as the Rangers and Frontier Constabulary are responsible for maintaining law and order in Karachi and frontier areas. Provincial governments control the police and paramilitary forces when they are assisting in law and order operations. Members of the security forces committed numerous human rights abuses.

Pakistan is a poor country, with great extremes in the distribution of wealth and social stratification. Its per capita annual income is $495, and its rate of illiteracy is extremely high and is increasing, especially among women. The economy includes both state-run and private industries, and financial institutions. The Constitution provides for the right of private businesses to operate freely in most sectors of the economy. The Government continues to pursue economic reforms, emphasizing the privatization of government-owned financial institutions, industrial units, and utilities. Cotton, textiles and apparel, rice, and leather products are the principal exports.

Although the Government has publicly pledged to address human rights problems, particularly those involving women, child labor, and minority religions, the overall human rights situation remains poor. Security forces committed extrajudicial killings, used arbitrary arrest and detention, tortured or abused prisoners and detainees, and raped women. The police, investigative and intelligence agencies, and politically motivated court cases were used to harass and arrest political opponents of the Government. Prison conditions are poor. The judiciary has been subject to influence through constitutionally permitted transfers of judges and appointment of temporary judges to the High and Supreme Courts. A Supreme Court ruling in March, however, has limited the Government's power over judicial appointments and transfers. There was no serious government effort to reform the police or judicial systems or to prosecute those responsible for abuse. Police continued to conduct illegal searches and infringe on citizens' privacy, for example through mail censorship. Case backlogs led to long delays in trials, and lengthy pretrial detention is a problem. The Government imposes limits on the freedom of assembly, religion, and movement.

Political groups including the Mohajir Quami Movement (MQM) and their opponents were responsible for a large number of killings in Karachi. Religious zealots continued to discriminate against and persecute religious minorities, basing their activities in part on legislation that discriminates against non-Muslims. Government-imposed procedural changes have made the registration of blasphemy charges more difficult. Religious and ethnic-based rivalries resulted in numerous murders and civil disturbances. Traditional social and legal constraints kept women in a subordinate position in society. They continued to be subjected to abuse, rape, and other forms of degradation by their spouses and members of society at large. The Government and employers continued to restrict worker rights significantly. The use of child and bonded labor remained widespread, in spite of legislation to restrict these practices and the signing of a memorandum of understanding on child labor with the International Labor Organization (ILO). Little was done to improve basic conditions for children. Female children actually fell further behind their male counterparts in such measures as levels of health care and education.

RESPECT FOR HUMAN RIGHTS

Section 1. Respect for the Integrity of the Person, Including Freedom From:

a. *Political and Other Extrajudicial Killing.*—The number of extrajudicial killings committed by security forces, often in the form of deaths in police custody or staged encounters in which the police shoot and kill the suspects, increased. Prior to the removal of the Bhutto government, police killings of suspected criminals and others had become so common that no government officials gave due attention to the practice. There are allegations that rival political groups and mafias use police to kill each other's activists in such fake encounters. There are also widespread reports that suspected criminals are murdered by the police to prevent criminals from implicating police in crimes during court proceedings. Police officials agree in private that due to the lack of concrete evidence, to corruption in the judiciary, and sometimes to political pressure, courts often fail to punish criminals involved in serious crimes.

The police view these killings as appropriate in light of the lack of action by the judiciary against criminals.

President Leghari charged in his dissolution order against Prime Minister Bhutto's government that thousands of persons in Karachi and other parts of Pakistan, who were killed in police encounters and under police custody, had been deprived of their right to life in violation of Article 9 of the Constitution. Most such killings occurred in Sindh province in clashes between the Government and factions of the Mohajir Quami Movement (MQM).

The MQM was formed in 1984 as a response to a set of real and perceived political grievances of the part of the Mohajirs, the Urdu-speaking Muslims who migrated from India to Pakistan following partition in 1947. The MQM, in part because of its successful organizational structure and its willingnes to use violence and intimidation to further its ends, grew to become a dominant political party in urban Sindh, sweeping to power in November 1987 local elections in Karachi and Hyderabad. Relations between the MQM and the national Government have been contentious and often violent. Repeated government crackdowns against the party and its activists have failed to diminish, and may have increased, support for the party among the Mohajirs. Negotiations between the MQM and the Government have failed to make progress toward a political settlement in Karachi.

In Karachi the Government regularly used excessive force, including torture and alleged encounter killings, against MQM activists. Press reports put the total number of political killings at around 500, a sharp decrease from last year. Most of the MQM activists killed in encounters with police were not criminal suspects, and a sampling of cases shows that the official version of the encounters was often contradicted by other evidence.

In January MQM activist Faheem Bhoora died in police custody. The police claimed that Bhoora had taken them to a building under construction to recover arms that he had hidden there. According to the police, Bhoora then tried to escape by leaping from the second story, falling to his death. According to press reports, Bhoora's injuries—skull crushed from behind, broken ribs, and internal injuries—could not have occurred in the fall.

In March Rangers shot and killed Naeem Sherri and Amjad Beg, claiming that the two had opened fire on them. Sherri had been accused of numerous crimes, including murder. The Government claimed that the two were killed in a shootout inside Beg's house. Other witnesses reported that Sherri was trying to hide behind a stand when he was shot numerous times at close range. Beg was reportedly taken alive, moved outside, and then shot and killed in the street.

In June MQM activist Nadeem Sarwar was killed in an encounter with the police. The MQM claimed that he was killed after being arrested. Also in June two MQM workers were killed in an encounter. The police claimed that the two were driving an unregistered vehicle and opened fire on police when asked to stop. Other witnesses reported that the men were brought to the area in a police van.

In September police shot and killed Murtaza Bhutto, the brother of the Prime Minister, and seven of his supporters near his residence in Karachi. The police claimed that they intended only to arrest some of Bhutto's armed bodyguards. After the incident, there was confusion and delay over the registration by police of first information reports (FIR's) for the case, and one of the policemen allegedly injured in the encounter later died under circumstances that many view as suspicious. On December 18, prosecutors charged Asif Ali Zardari, the husband of former Prime Minister Bhutto, with the murder of her brother. A former intelligence chief was also charged with the killing, and several policemen were arrested but not charged. At year's end, a tribunal in Karachi was continuing its investigation into the case, and Asif Zardari remained in custody.

During 1996 the Lahore High Court (LHC) ordered an inquiry into several cases of such alleged fake encounters, but no police official was convicted. In a few cases of extrajudicial killings, in which allegedly innocent people were targeted, some police officials were suspended and arrested, but their cases are still under trial.

In a similar case in January, Lahore police shot and killed a man named Tanveer. Police arrested Tanveer for his alleged involvement in multiple murders and armed robberies. During the interrogation police sent him to a hospital in police custody, but he escaped. In a subsequent encounter, the police shot him when he allegedly opened fire on them. The press declared the incident a staged encounter. The Human Rights Commission of Pakistan (HRCP) reports that during the interrogation police had tortured Tanveer so harshly that he had to be sent to a hospital. Upon doctors' refusal to treat him and fearing that he might die from his injuries, the police shot him. Lahore police also killed other persons in questionable encounters and in custody.

In July Bahawalnagar district police killed a schoolteacher and wounded his brother in a police encounter. According to the police, the teacher, Ashraf, was wanted for robbery. When police attempted to arrest him, Ashraf and his brothers fired on the police party, and in an exchange of fire Ashraf was killed and his brother was wounded. However, according to friendly relatives, Ashraf had a long-running property dispute with hostile relatives who paid police to kill him, allowing them to take his property. Following Ashraf's death, the friendly relatives, colleagues, and neighbors demonstrated in front of the police station and the residence of the police officer in charge. The police opened fire on the demonstrators, killing 4 persons and injuring 10. The Punjab Chief Minister ordered that a murder case be registered against the Deputy Superintendent of Police and the police station house officer.

In March an employee of the Criminal Investigation Agency and several colleagues reportedly killed a Christian laborer to avenge a purported insult. Following the Christian community's protest, a case was registered against the police, but no action had been taken against them by year's end.

In April in a clash with Pakistan Muslim League-Nawaz (PML-N) activists, police killed PML-N Lahore Additional Secretary General Javed Ashraf and wounded two other persons. Police arrested 10 PML-N activists and registered a case against them on charges of attacking the police, burning a police kiosk, and damaging public property. Police claimed that Ashraf and his associates then tried to break into a nearby bank and that the bank guard fired on them. The PML-N leaders, however, claimed that the police had fired on the procession without provocation and that they had deliberately targeted Javed Ashraf on the instructions of the Government. PML-N leaders charged that the Government killed Ashraf in order to warn PML-N activists that they could meet the same fate if they took part in the opposition's campaign against the Government.

At times police used excessive force against demonstrators. In June police killed three antigovernment marchers in a clash with protestors (see Section 2.b.). Also in June, police killed 4 Jamaat-i-Islami (JI) demonstrators in Rawalpindi and wounded about 100 (see Section 2.b.).

In October army major Arshad Jamil was hanged for the murder of nine members of a family during an anticriminal operation in Sindh in 1992.

In November the Lahore District Magistrate ordered his subordinates to follow up and resolve all allegations of killings in police custody. At year's end, over a dozen were reportedly completed. However, neither the results of the investigations nor any charges were publicly announced. Also in November in Karachi, the caretaker Sindh provincial Government initiated a wholesale housecleaning of the local police department, which had been accused of extrajudicial killings.

b. *Disappearance.*—There were no known politically motivated disappearances.

c. *Torture and Other Cruel, Inhuman, or Degrading Treatment or Punishment.*— Torture and other cruel, inhuman, or degrading treatment by police remained common practice. Police routinely use force to elicit confessions.

Common torture methods include: Beating, burning with cigarettes, whipping the soles of the feet, sexual assault, prolonged isolation, electric shock, denial of food or sleep, hanging upside down, forced spreading of the legs, and public humiliation. Some magistrates and doctors help coverup the abuse by issuing investigation and medical reports stating that the victims died of natural causes.

The overall failure of successive governments to prosecute and punish abusers is the single greatest obstacle to ending or even reducing the incidence of abuse. The authorities sometimes transferred, suspended, or arrested offending officers, but seldom prosecuted or punished them. Investigating officers generally shield their colleagues.

A presidential ordinance, promulgated in April 1995, which permits confessions or statements against third persons obtained during police interrogations in parts of the country declared to be "terrorist-affected areas" to be used in court, remains on the books. The law is currently not applied, because no part of the country has been declared a terrorist-affected area.

According to press reports, torture is common at Hyderabad Central Prison. In July three newspapers published photographs of prisoners inside the prison who were blindfolded and being held in cross-bar fetters. Prisoners who were awaiting trial claimed that they were kept in chains, fetters, and handcuffs, unable to move or sleep. The immediate reaction of the prison officials to the story was to file a lawsuit against the reporter. The reporter's case was taken up by the HRCP, and the reporter was granted bail. At year's end hearings in the case had not taken place. The superintendent of Hyderabad prison has been suspended. In September the news magazine Herald published similar pictures and stories from prisoners.

Police and prison officials frequently use the threat of abuse to extort money from prisoners and their families. Police accept money for registration of cases on false charges and may torture innocent citizens. For example, in July a 75-year old man, Muhammad Ali, was physically tortured and brutalized by a Gujranwala police sub-inspector. People pay police to humiliate their opponents and to avenge their personal grievances.

In July the Inspector General of Police Punjab (IGP) stated that political interference was the major factor affecting the performance of the police. He added that successive governments recruited police officers in violation of merit considerations and the department's regulations. In some instances, recruits had criminal records.

The Government's decision to appoint police officials at the direction of parliamentarians has greatly damaged police effectiveness. In response to political pressure, police officials sometimes follow orders of legislators to harass political opponents. In return the legislators shield illegal activities by police.

Addressing a seminar in the spring, President Leghari alleged that police stations are sold—meaning that police officials pay bribes to the politicians and senior officials in the department in order to get posted to police stations of their choice. They then recoup their investments by extorting money from the citizenry.

The womens' police stations staffed by female personnel in Karachi, Lahore, Faisalabad, and Rawalpindi remained understaffed. Despite court orders and regulations requiring that female suspects only be interrogated by female police officers, they continued to be detained overnight at regular police stations and abused by male officers. According to HRCP's monthly report of incidents for January, a young woman was raped in a police station in front of her mother by police attempting to find the whereabouts of her son, and a wife was sexually and physically abused in front of her husband to force him to confess to a criminal charge. A female prisoner confined under the Hadood Ordinances was raped by the jail warden that same month. HRCP officials claim that the number of such incidents is increasing. According to human rights advocate Hina Jilani, the majority of women in jails were subjected to torture and sexual abuse by the jail staff. She claimed that 85 percent of women were tortured and 62 percent raped by prison officials in 1996. There is no independent confirmation of these claims. In 1995 the High Court ruled that no woman should be kept in any police station overnight without a male person from her family. According to human rights advocates, these High Court orders were rarely enforced in 1996.

The Hadood Ordinances, promulgated by the central Government in 1979, were an attempt to make the Penal Code more Islamic. These ordinances provide for harsh punishments for violations of Islamic law, or Shari'a, including death by stoning for unlawful sexual relations and amputation for some other crimes. In practice the standard of evidence for imposing these punishments is exceptionally high and to date they have not been carried out. Nonetheless, these laws have been applied to Muslims and non-Muslims alike and weigh most heavily on women (see Section 5).

Prison conditions are poor. Overcrowding is a problem. For example, according to the then provincial Law Minister, in August there were 41,605 prisoners in Punjab prisons which have space for only 17,271. There are three classes (A, B, and C) of prison facilities. Class "C" cells generally hold common criminals and those in pretrial detention. Such cells often have dirt floors, no furnishings, and poor food. The use of handcuffs and fetters is common. Prisoners in these cells reportedly suffer the most abuse, such as beatings and being forced to kneel for long periods. Conditions in "B" and "A" cells are markedly better. The authorities reserve the latter for prominent persons. Especially prominent individuals, including some political figures, are sometimes held under house arrest and permitted to receive visitors.

The Government permits prison visits by human rights monitors.

There were reports that wealthy landlords or political parties operated private jails. Many such jails are believed to exist in tribal and feudal areas. Some of the prisoners have reportedly been held in them for many years.

d. *Arbitrary Arrest, Detention, or Exile.*—The law regulates arrest and detention procedures; however, the authorities do not always comply with its provisions. The law permits a Deputy Commissioner (DC) of a local district to order detention without charge for 30 days of persons suspected of threatening public order and safety. The DC may renew detention in 30-day periods, for a total of 90 days. For other criminal offenses, the police may hold a suspect for 24 hours without charge. If the police can provide material proof that detention is necessary for an investigation, a court may extend detention for a total of 15 days.

In practice, however, the authorities do not fully observe the limits on detention. Police are not required to notify anyone when an arrest is made and often hold detainees without charge until they are challenged by a court. The police sometimes detain individuals arbitrarily without charge, or on false charges, in order to extort payment for their release. Some women continue to be arbitrarily detained and sexually abused (see Section 1.c.). Police also detain relatives of wanted criminals in order to compel suspects to surrender (see Section 1.f.). The law stipulates that detainees must be brought to trial within 30 days of their arrest. However, in many cases trials do not start until about 6 months after the filing of charges.

The authorities generally permit family members and lawyers to visit inmates. However, in some cases, authorities refuse such visits. In the case of politicians and party workers charged with various offenses, the Government incarcerated some of them outside their home districts, thereby discouraging visits by family members, supporters, and attorneys.

The Federally Administered Tribal Areas (FATA) have a separate legal system, the Frontier Crimes Regulation, which recognizes the doctrine of collective responsibility. Authorities are empowered to detain the fellow members of a fugitive's tribe, or to blockade the fugitive's village, pending his surrender or punishment by his own tribe in accordance with the local tradition. The Government exercised such authority in 1996. In one instance, in August the Government used this authority in the Khyber Agency following the kidnaping and murder of an income tax official.

Police may arrest individuals on the basis of a First Information Report (FIR) filed by a complainant. The police have been known to file FIR's without supporting evidence. FIR's are thus frequently used to harass or intimidate individuals. Charges against an individual may also be based on a "blind" FIR, which lists the perpetrators as "person or persons unknown." If the case is not solved, the FIR is placed in the inactive file. When needed, a FIR is reactivated and taken to a magistrate by the police, who then name a suspect and ask that the suspect be remanded for 14 days while they investigate further. After 14 days, the case is dropped for lack of evidence, but another FIR is then activated and brought against the accused. In this manner, rolling charges can be used to hold a suspect in continuous custody.

If the police can provide material proof that detention (physical remand or police custody for the purpose of interrogation) is necessary for an investigation, a court may extend detention for a total of 15 days. Such proof, however, may be little more than unsubstantiated assertions by the police. The Government sometimes uses mass arrests to quell civil unrest. For example, in June the Northwest Frontier provincial (NWFP) government arrested several leaders of the All Pakistan Clerk's Association in an effort to quell their almost year-long antigovernment protest.

The Government selectively used criminal charges and arrests to harass political opponents who were perceived as potential threats. In July police arrested four opposition leaders on different charges. Two of them, including General Secretary of the Metropolitan Muslim League Pervez Rashid, were arrested on charges of involvement in bomb explosions. They were later released on bail by the Lahore High Court when it became clear that there was no credible evidence to support police claims. Opposition leaders alleged that the Government had implicated these activists in false cases in order to discourage opposition activists from participating in antigovernment campaigns.

Political activists are sometimes arrested on trumped up criminal charges. It is possible that hundreds of people are incarcerated under these circumstances, though the exact number is unknown. MQM claims that 5,000 of its workers are held in prison on trumped up charges for what were, in reality, political activities. However, this number is impossible to confirm.

e. *Denial of Fair Public Trial.*—The Constitution provides for an independent judiciary, however, in practice, the judiciary is not independent. Through the President's power to transfer High Court justices and appoint temporary and ad hoc justices, the executive branch has been able to influence the Supreme Court, the provincial high courts, and the lower levels of the judicial system.

The judicial system involves several different court systems with overlapping and sometimes competing jurisdictions. There are civil and criminal systems with special courts for high-profile cases, as well as the federal Shari'a appeals courts for certain Hadood offenses. The appeals process in the civil system is: Civil court, district court, high court, and the Supreme Court. In the criminal system, the progression is magistrate, sessions court, high court, and the Supreme Court.

It had become standard practice to appoint judges to the high courts and Supreme Court on a temporary basis for a period of 1 year and later confirm or terminate their appointments after an evaluation of their performance. Legal experts say that temporary judges, eager to be confirmed following their probationary period, tend to favor the Government. The permanent judges of the high courts who can serve until retirement—age 62—are also vulnerable to the executive in that they could be transferred to the Federal Shari'a Court (FSC), which is deemed by many to signal the end of their career. Judges in the Special Courts for Suppression of Terrorist Activities and banking tribunals are appointed directly by the Government and are hired on renewable contracts. Their appointments can be terminated any time without going through the Supreme Judicial Council, which is applicable to the judges of the high courts and Supreme Court. However, executive branch power regarding some judicial appointments was restricted early in the year.

On March 20, a full bench of the Supreme Court of Pakistan (SC) issued orders curtailing the powers of the executive to appoint and transfer judges of the high courts. The SC made the consent of the chief justices of the high courts and Supreme Court mandatory in the appointment and transfer of any high court judge. It also ruled that it is not desirable to send a SC judge as acting Chief Justice (CJ) to a high court and that no ad hoc judge can be appointed to the SC when permanent vacancies exist. The full bench directed the executive to fill permanent vacancies of judges to the high courts and appoint permanent chief justices in high courts within 30 days of the issuance of the orders. Chief Justice of Pakistan Sajjad Ali Shah directed chief justices of all provincial high courts to process the cases of the judges affected by the Supreme Court's verdict within 30 days. The SC verdict was widely welcomed by the legal community, as well as by opposition political parties. Former Prime Minister Bhutto, on the floor of the house, criticized the judicial verdict, saying that the Chief Justice had issued the verdict in anger and accused him of amending the Constitution by exceeding his jurisdiction.

Despite its strong opposition to the ruling, the Government replaced ad hoc or acting chief justices of the high courts in Punjab, Sindh, and NWFP with those recommended by the Chief Justice of Pakistan. The new Chief Justices of Lahore and NWFP high courts recommended termination of 14 judges (11 from the Lahore High Court) who had been appointed in violation of the Constitution as interpreted by the SC in its March verdict. The Chief Justice of the LHC stopped referring cases to the affected judges. All affected judges have subsequently resigned. The LHC, entitled to have 50 judges, is now functioning with only 29 judges, which is causing delays in the judicial process. In September President Leghari approved 29 judges appointed by the PPP Government to the Sindh, Lahore, and Peshawar high courts and denotified (removed) 11. The 11 denotified were among the 17 justices not recommended by the Chief Justice following the March 20 ruling on appointments. The other six had already resigned after having their judicial work taken away. The effects of the SC ruling appeared quickly. In April a division bench of the LHC granted bail to Punjab opposition leader Shahbaz Sharif, whose appeals for bail hearings had been repeatedly delayed since his arrest in November 1995.

The civil judicial system provides for an open trial, cross-examination by an attorney, and appeal of sentences. Attorneys are appointed for indigents only in capital cases. There are no jury trials. Owing to the limited number of judges, the heavy backlog of cases, and lengthy court procedures, cases routinely take years, although defendants are required to make frequent court appearances. Under both the Hadood and standard criminal codes, there are bailable and nonbailable offenses. According to the Criminal Procedures Code, the accused in bailable offenses must be granted bail and the accused in nonbailable offenses should be granted bail if accused of a crime that carries a sentence of less than 10 years.

The Federal Shari'a Court and the Shari'a Bench of the Supreme Court serve as appeals courts for certain convictions in criminal court under the Hadood Ordinances. The Federal Shari'a Court also may overturn any legislation judged to be inconsistent with the tenets of Islam. However, these cases may be appealed to the Shari'a Bench of the Supreme Court.

The judicial process continued to be impeded by bureaucratic infighting, inactivity, and the overlapping jurisdictions of the different court systems. Scores of positions in the lower magistracy remained unfilled. Persons in jail awaiting trial are sometimes held for periods longer than the sentence they would receive if convicted. An HRCP team recently interviewed a prisoner in Dadu prison, Sindh, who had been in the jail for the last 9 years and had never been produced before a court. Arrested in a theft case, the prisoner's trial continued being adjourned due to the inability of the police to produce records. If convicted, he would have been sentenced to not more than 3 years' imprisonment.

The Government may refer cases involving terrorism, bombings, sabotage, highway robberies, banditry, kidnaping, or similar offenses to special terrorism courts established by the Suppression of Terrorist Activities Act of 1975. Many legal experts believe the special courts do not provide a fair trial. They maintain that the short time for investigations and trial procedures have effectively repudiated the presumption of innocence. They also cite the encroachment by federal authorities on the provincial governments' constitutional authority to administer justice and the inherent unfairness of parallel courts to which cases may be assigned arbitrarily. Moreover, the special courts may deny bail if the judges decide that the accused may have reasonably committed an offense. These courts had hundreds of cases pending in 1996. The court in Hyderabad alone had 380 cases pending at the beginning of the year.

Government officials and some attorneys maintain that despite their deficiencies, the special courts are necessary because of the judicial backlog. They also maintain that the rules of evidence apply in the courts, defendants have the right to counsel, and the judges must meet the same standards as those appointed to a high court. Defendants also have the right to appeal, but only one appeal is allowed.

The Penal Code incorporates the doctrines of Qisas (roughly, an eye for an eye) and Diyat (blood money), with the result that compensation is sometimes paid to the family of a victim in place of punishment of the wrongdoer. Consequently, wealthy or influential persons sometimes escape punishment for such crimes as murder and assault. The right to seek pardon or commutation is not available to defendants under the ordinance. The Hadood and Qisas and Diyat ordinances apply to both ordinary criminal courts and Shari'a courts. According to Christian activists, if a Muslim murders a non-Muslim, he can compensate for the crime by paying the victim's family diyat; however, if a non-Muslim murders a Muslim, he does not have the option of paying diyat and must serve a jail sentence or face the death penalty for his crime. However, there were no reported cases of this during the year. Appeals of certain Hadood convictions involving penalties in excess of 2 years' imprisonment are referred exclusively to the Shari'a courts and are heard jointly by Islamic scholars and high court judges using ordinary criminal procedures. Cases referred to the Shari'a Bench of the Supreme Court are heard jointly by Islamic scholars and Supreme Court judges using ordinary criminal procedures. Judges and attorneys must be Muslim and be familiar with Islamic law. Within these limits, defendants in a Shari'a court are entitled to the lawyer of their choice. There is a system of bail.

The Hadood Ordinances criminalize nonmarital rape, extramarital sex (including adultery and fornication), and various gambling, alcohol, and property offenses. Offenses are distinguished according to punishment, with some offenses liable to Hadd (Koranic punishment) and others to Tazir (non-Koranic punishment) (see Section 1.c.). Although both types of cases are tried in ordinary criminal courts, special rules of evidence apply in Hadd cases. A non-Muslim, for example, may not testify against a Muslim but may testify against another non-Muslim. Likewise, the testimony of a woman is not admissible in cases involving harsher punishments (lashing, amputation, and stoning), and a woman's testimony regarding financial matters is not admissible unless corroborated by another woman.

There continued to be charges that magistrates and police, under pressure to achieve high conviction rates, persuade detainees to plead guilty without informing them of the consequences. Politically powerful persons also attempt to influence magistrates' decisions and have used various forms of pressure on magistrates, including the threat to transfer them to other assignments.

Administration of justice in the FATA is normally the responsibility of tribal elders and maliks, or leaders. They may conduct hearings according to Islamic law and tribal custom. In such proceedings, the accused have no right to legal representation, bail, or appeal. The usual penalties consist of fines, even for murder. However, the Government's political agents, who are federal civil servants assigned to local governments, oversee such proceedings and may impose prison terms of up to 14 years. In remote areas outside the jurisdiction of federal political agents, tribal councils occasionally levy harsher, unsanctioned punishments, including flogging or death by shooting or stoning. Paramilitary forces under the direction of the political agents frequently perform punitive actions during enforcement operations. For example in raids on criminal activities, the authorities have been known to damage surrounding homes as extrajudicial punishment of residents for having tolerated nearby criminal activity.

In July a full bench of the LHC declared the constitution of banking tribunals and Special Courts for Suppression of Terrorist Activities to be unconstitutional. The full bench observed that appointment of judges to these courts are made by the Federal Government in its sole discretion, in some cases of persons who were officeholders of the ruling party and in other cases of persons who may not be qualified to be appointed as a judge of the high court or a district judge. The LHC's decision was welcomed by the public, the legal community, and opposition political parties. The opposition had been alleging that the Government victimized it by referring opposition leaders' cases to the special tribunals and courts, which were headed by the PPP-affiliated judges. However, in response to a government appeal, the SC stayed action on the LHC's decision.

One example of the alleged victimization of opposition leaders through the special tribunals and courts is an August judgment of the banking tribunal, Lahore, which ordered the Ittefaq group (owned by opposition leader Nawaz Sharif's family) to immediately return 409 million rupees (approximately $10,200,000) worth of loans to banks. The judgment was issued by the banking tribunal despite the fact that the defendants had moved an application in the LHC for transfer of the case to the LHC and that the LHC had stayed proceedings at the banking tribunal.

f. *Arbitrary Interference with Privacy, Family, Home, or Correspondence.*—By law the police must obtain a warrant to search a house but do not need a warrant to search a person. However, the police often enter homes without a warrant and have been known to steal valuables during searches. In the absence of a warrant, a policeman is subject to charges of criminal trespass. However, policemen are seldom punished for illegal entry. Paramilitary forces sometimes damage homes as extrajudicial punishment of residents for having tolerated nearby criminal activity (see Section 1.c.).

The Government maintains several domestic intelligence services that monitor politicians, political activists, suspected terrorists, and suspected foreign intelligence agents. Credible reports indicate that the authorities commonly resort to wiretapping and occasionally intercept and open mail. In his order dismissing former Prime Minister Bhutto, President Leghari accused the Government of massive illegal wiretapping, including the telephone conversations of judges, political party leaders, and military and civilian officials. On December 15, the caretaker government announced that effective immediately all foreign and domestic mail was to be subject to censorship by the Special Branch and the Intelligence Bureau.

Police arrest and detain relatives of wanted criminals in an attempt to compel suspects to surrender. In some cases, the authorities have detained whole families to force a relative who was the subject of an arrest warrant to surrender.

The Frontier Crimes Regulation, the separate legal system in the FATA, permits collective responsibility, and empowers the authorities to detain innocent members of the suspect's tribe, or blockade an entire village (see Section 1.d.).

Section 2. Respect for Civil Liberties, Including:

a. *Freedom of Speech and Press.*—The Constitution provides for freedom of speech and the press, and citizens are generally free to discuss public issues. There were increased efforts by the Government and private groups to restrict press freedom, but those efforts had little practical effect on press reporting. The Constitution stipulates the death penalty for anyone who damages the Constitution by any act, including the publication of statements against the spirit of the Constitution. The Constitution prohibits the ridicule of Islam, the armed forces, or the judiciary. Moreover, the Penal Code mandates the death sentence for anyone convicted of blaspheming the Prophet Mohammed (see Section 2.c.). Journalists censor themselves on such subjects. The competitive nature of Pakistani politics helps to ensure press freedom since the media serve as a forum for political parties to compete with one another.

The state-owned dailies Pakistan Times and Mashriq were sold to the private sector in 1996. The Ministry of Information controls one of the two main wire services, the other is privately owned. The wire services are circumspect in their coverage of the news and generally follow the Government line. A Print, Press, and Publications Ordinance requires the registration of printing presses and newspapers and allows the Government to confiscate newspapers or magazines deemed objectionable. Foreign books must pass government censors before being reprinted, although the importation of books is freely allowed. Government censors occasionally ban publications, usually for objectionable religious content, but for other reasons as well.

Privately owned newspapers freely discuss public policy and criticize the Government. They report remarks made by opposition politicians, and their editorials reflect a wide spectrum of views. The Government continued to influence editorial policy of privately owned newspapers by its power to allocate duty free newsprint and its placement of government advertising, an important source of newspaper revenue.

The Government owns and operates most radio stations. Private radio stations operate in Islamabad, Rawalpindi, Lahore, and Karachi, but they are not allowed to report news independent of that supplied by the government-run Associated Press of Pakistan (APP.) The Government also operates all but one semiprivate television station. It strictly controls their news broadcasts. However, the semiprivate Shalimar Television Network (STN) provides programs including Cable News Network (CNN) and British Broadcasting Corporation (BBC) programs, with considerable independence from government oversight. The Government censors segments of CNN and BBC programs considered socially offensive but rarely if ever censors the news content. The Ministry of Information monitors the advertisements on STN, editing or removing those deemed objectionable. Satellite dishes are readily available on the local market, and many Pakistanis use them to watch uncensored foreign broadcasts. Government-owned electronic media continued to convey the views of the party in power.

Literary and creative works remain generally free of censorship. Obscene literature, a category broadly defined by the Government is subject to seizure. Dramas and documentaries on previously taboo subjects, including corruption, social privilege, narcotics, violence against women, and female inequality, are frequently broadcast on television.

In July a senior subeditor of the newspaper Dawn was abducted at night from outside his residence in Karachi. He later said publicly that he had been interrogated by personnel of a government security agency regarding the whereabouts of an alleged fugitive. He was released the next day.

Zafaryab Ahmad, a free-lance Lahore-based journalist was arrested in 1995 and charged with sedition after he reported on child labor. He was accused of working with Indian intelligence to damage Pakistan's carpet industry exports through false reporting. At year's end, he was out on bail and his case still pending in the courts.

The Law of Defamation often makes it difficult for the press to report events of great public importance. Similarly, the Law of Contempt bars public debate on matters of public importance under litigation on the grounds that it would influence the process of adjudication. A March judgment by the LHC in a defamation case met with widespread approval from journalists. The court observed that to prove defamation the complainant must demonstrate malice or personal ill will on the part of the press. The court also observed that since public men are public property, discussion or criticism of their public conduct is in the public interest.

According to the HRCP, different law enforcement agencies and the Ministry of Information employed extralegal methods under various pretexts. These included: Harassment, attempts to influence photographers and reporters, interference in the distribution of publications, and delays and discrimination in the issuance of security passes to report on events of great public interest.

The press and electronic media continued facing nonstate pressure as well. Different political parties, ethnic, sectarian, and religious groups, and militant student bodies tried to influence the policies of the media through demonstrations and physical threats. The Government rarely if ever takes legal action in response to the activities of these groups.

In May activists of Jamaat-i-Islami (JI) attacked the Film Censor Board's office in Lahore, ransacked the office, and injured the staff. They demanded that the staff ban an Urdu feature film that they deemed obscene. The producer had to obtain a court order to continue showing the film publicly. In July activists of a Shi'a organization, Tehrik-I-Jafria Pakistan (TJP) demonstrated in front of an Urdu daily's office. JI and other religious groups' activists also demonstrated against Pakistan Television (PTV) for telecasting obscene programs and, on several occasions, threatened PTV officials.

The Government and universities generally respect academic freedom. However, the atmosphere of violence and intolerance fostered by student organizations, typically tied to political parties, continued to threaten academic freedom. On some campuses, well-armed groups of students, primarily from radical religious organizations, clash with and intimidate other students, instructors, and administrators on matters of language, syllabus, examination policies, doctrine, and dress. These groups facilitate cheating on examinations, interfere in the hiring of staff at the campuses, control new admissions, and sometimes control the funds of their institutions. At Punjab University, the largest university in the province, Islami Jamiat-e-Tulaba (IJT-student wing of the JI) frequently imposes its self-styled code of conduct for teachers and other students.

Human rights groups remain concerned about the implementation of a 1992 Supreme Court ruling that prohibits student political organizations on campuses. While they acknowledge that the ruling led to a reduction in campus violence, they question the legality of school officials expelling students for membership in a political organization.

b. *Freedom of Peaceful Assembly and Association.*—The Constitution provides for freedom "to assemble peacefully and without arms subject to any reasonable restrictions imposed by law in the interest of public order." Although the Government generally permits peaceful assembly, it occasionally interferes with large political rallies, which are held by all political parties.

The Constitution provides for freedom of association subject to restriction by government ordinance and law. There are no banned groups or parties. District magistrates occasionally exercised their power under the Criminal Procedures Code to ban meetings of more than four people when demonstrations seemed likely to result in violence. This provision was invoked frequently in May during the Islamic month of Muharram, when tensions between Sunni and Shi'a Muslims traditionally peak.

The Government usually did not interfere with large political rallies. However, police killed three Jamaat-i-Islami protesters during a clash with antigovernment marchers in June. Opposition leader Nawaz Sharif and other opposition politicians traveled largely unhindered across the country throughout the year, holding large rallies critical of the Government. However, the authorities sometimes prevented leaders of politico-religious parties from traveling to certain areas if they believed that the presence of such leaders would increase sectarian tensions or cause public violence.

In June police used batons and tear-gas and fired on JI demonstrators in Rawalpindi, killing 4 and injuring about 100. The demonstrators were trying to force their way through a maze of barbed wire to stage a sit-in in front of the Prime Minister's Secretariat against the "harsh tax-laden budget."

c. *Freedom of Religion.*—Pakistan is an Islamic republic in which 96 percent of the people are Muslim. The Constitution requires that laws be consistent with Islam. The Government permits Muslims to convert to other faiths but prohibits proselytizing among Muslims. "Islamiyyat" (Islamic studies) is compulsory for all Muslim students in state-run schools. Students of other faiths are not required to study Islam but are not provided with parallel studies in their own religion. In practice, however, many non-Muslim students are compelled by teachers to complete the Islamiyyat studies.

Minority religious groups fear that the Shari'a Law and its goal of Islamizing the Government and society may further restrict the freedom to practice their religions. Discriminatory religious legislation has encouraged an atmosphere of religious intolerance, which has led to acts of violence directed at Ahmadis, Christians, Hindus, and Zikris.

A 1974 constitutional amendment declared Ahmadis to be a non-Muslim minority because they do not accept Mohammed as the last prophet of Islam. However, Ahmadis regard themselves as Muslims and observe many Islamic practices. In 1984 the Government inserted Section 298(c) into the Penal Code (PC), which prohibited an Ahmadi from calling himself a Muslim and banned Ahmadis from using Islamic terminology. The punishment is up to 3 years' imprisonment and a fine. Since that time, the Government has used this provision to harass Ahmadis.

In 1986 the Government inserted Section 295(c) into the Penal Code, which stipulates the death penalty for blaspheming the Prophet Mohammad. This has been used by litigants to threaten and intimidate Ahmadis, Christians, and even Muslims in the past. According to the HRCP, the Government's unofficial changes to the procedures for filing formal blasphemy charges, made in 1995, have been followed by a significant drop in the number of blasphemy charges. According to the HRCP, one FIR was registered against a Christian, Ayub Masih, under section 295(c) in 1996. No such charge was brought against a Muslim this year. However, three cases were filed under this section against Ahmadis. Under the new procedures, magistrates are now required to investigate allegations of blasphemy to see whether they are credible before filing formal charges.

In October in one well-publicized case, 14 (some say 19) Christian families fled the Punjab village Number 35 Eb Arfiwala following the arrest of one of their community for alleged blasphemy. The families allegedly feared attack by Muslim neighbors angered over the alleged incident. By December the families had not returned to their homes in the village.

Ahmadis continue to suffer from a variety of problems, including violation of their places of worship, barring them from burial in Muslim graveyards, denial of freedom of faith, speech and assembly, restrictions on their press, a social boycott, and alleged official support of extremist elements who act against the Ahmadi community. Several Ahmadi mosques remained closed. In 1996 dozens of Ahmadis were charged with preaching their faith, which is illegal under the law. According to the Amir of the Islamabad Ahmadi community, there are approximately 140 Ahmadis charged with representing themselves as Muslims, most of whom are presently out on bail. Scores of Ahmadis were injured in attacks by religious extremists.

The police at times refuse to prevent harassment and violence against Ahmadis or to prosecute those who commit such acts. In January a group of Khatm-e-Nabuwwat Youth Force (Finality of Prophethood Youth Force) accompanied by police attacked the house of an Ahmadi in Abbottabad, NWFP, where Ahmadis were offering their Friday prayer. (Use of the house was necessary because activists of this militant organization had earlier demolished the Ahmadi mosque.) The mob dragged the Ahmadis out of the building and beat them in the presence of the police. The police refused to register a case against the attackers. An Urdu daily added to the tension by reporting that Ahmadis had attacked the Khatm-e-Nabuwwat Vice President, which resulted in threats to Ahmadis living across the district. Under pressure by the mullahs, the district administration sealed the Ahmadi house that had been used as a place of worship, and charged seven Ahmadis under Section 298(c) of the PC.

In April an Ahmadi, Abdul Khaliq, was arrested in Faisalabad under Section 188 of the PC for tearing an anti-Ahmadi poster printed and displayed by local mullahs. He was later released on bail by the court. The outraged mullahs exploited the situation by holding public meetings. The authorities arrested 22 Ahmadis and 12 mullahs who were later released. The mullahs, however, succeeded in getting an elderly Ahmadi, Mohammad Iqbal, arrested under section 298(c).

In March two Ahmadi women were attacked in Karachi for reportedly using a piece of cloth with Koranic inscriptions. Both were seriously injured. Under pressure from the militant Sunni organization, Sunni Tehrik, police registered a case against the women under section 295(a) and 295(c) of the PPC. The sessions court released the women on bail, finding that the piece of cloth had no script on it.

In December demonstrations broke out in Karachi against the appointment of an Ahmadi to the caretaker Sindh government.

According to a press report, in January there were 658 cases under blasphemy and anti-Ahmadi laws pending in different courts across the country. Reportedly, 2,467 individuals either are on bail or in jail under blasphemy charges, awaiting a decision on their cases.

When such religious cases are brought to court, extremists often pack the courtroom and make public threats about the consequences of an acquittal. As a result, judges and magistrates, seeking to avoid a confrontation with the extremists, often continue trials indefinitely, and the accused is burdened with further legal costs and repeated court appearances. Lahore High Court Justice Arif Iqbal Hussain Bhatti, one of the two judges who in 1995 ruled to acquit accused Christian blasphemers Salamat and Rehmat Masih has received several death threats.

In May the Peshawar High Court acquitted on appeal two Shi'a Afghans condemned to death in January 1995 for blasphemy. The Afghans had been convicted of violating Penal Code Section 295(c) prohibiting the use of representations of the Prophet Mohammad after they allegedly attempted to have 10,000 copies made of a "photo print" of the Prophet. The High Court concluded that the prosecution had failed to substantiate the blasphemy charges.

In September, 20 persons were killed in an attack by gunmen on a Sunni mosque in the Punjab city of Multan.

d. *Freedom of Movement Within the Country, Foreign Travel, Emigration, and Repatriation.*—Most citizens enjoy freedom of movement within the country and to travel abroad, but the Government occasionally prohibits the movement of persons within Pakistan through "externment orders" when it believes that their presence will lead to a threat to public order. Travel to Israel is legally prohibited. Government employees must obtain "no objection certificates" before traveling abroad. Students are also required to have these certificates from their institutions, however, this requirement is rarely enforced. Citizens have and regularly exercise the right to emigrate. Exit control lists (ECL), however, are used to prevent the departure of wanted criminals. The Government increasingly included businessmen, journalists, and political figures on the exit control list as a form of political harassment. No judicial action is required to add a name to the exit control list, and there is no judicial recourse or formal appeal mechanism if one's name is added. However, in some cases courts have directed the Government to lift restrictions on some ECL-listed politicians' travel abroad.

The Government cooperates with the Office of the United Nations High Commissioner for Refugees (UNHCR) and other humanitarian organizations in assisting refugees. First asylum has been provided to refugees from Afghanistan since 1979, when several million Afghans fleeing Soviet occupation fled across the border into Pakistan. There are currently over 865,000 Afghan refugees in Pakistan who have been granted first asylum. Between September and December, approximately 40,000 Afghans returned to Pakistan fleeing a resumption of fighting in Kabul. Initially the Government closed the border but soon after reopened it, allowing the refugees to enter Pakistan unhindered.

The Government has not legally granted permanent resettlement to Afghan refugees but allows them to live and work in Pakistan. Many are self-supporting and live outside of refugee camps.

According to the UNHCR, there were no reports of forced return of persons to a country where they feared persecution. Also according to the UNHCR, approximately 1.3 to 1.4 million registered and unregistered Afghan refugees remained in Pakistan at year's end. A total of 105,000 Afghan refugees were repatriated in the first 8 months of 1996. Since 1988 over 2.5 million Afghans have been repatriated from Pakistan.

Afghan refugees in Pakistan have limited access to legal protection and depend on the ability of the UNHCR and leaders of their groups to resolve disputes among themselves and with Pakistani society. Police also frequently prevent Afghan nationals from entering the cities. Most able-bodied male refugees have found at least intermittent employment but are not covered by labor laws. Women and girls obtained increasingly better education and health care as NGO's provided increased services.

The repatriation of Biharis continued to be a contentious issue. The Biharis are Urdu-speaking people from the Indian State of Bihar who went to East Pakistan—now Bangladesh—at the time of partition in 1947. Since 1971 when Bangladesh became independent, approximately 250,000 Biharis have been in refugee camps in Bangladesh. The repatriation of these people is tied to Pakistan's various ethnic problems. While the Mohajir community—descendants of Muslims who emigrated to present-day Pakistan from India during partition—supports repatriation, the Sindhi community opposes the move. In 1993 the Government flew 342 Biharis to Pakistan and placed them in temporary housing in central Punjab. No further repatriation occurred in 1996.

Section 3. Respect for Political Rights: The Right of Citizens to Change Their Government

Citizens have the right and the ability to change their government peacefully. With certain exceptions, citizens 21 years of age and over have the right to vote. However, several million bonded laborers and nomads may not vote because the National Election Commission has ruled that they do not "ordinarily reside in an electoral area, nor do they own or possess a dwelling or immovable property in that area." Political parties have been allowed to operate freely since the full lifting of martial law in 1988. Unregistered political parties are permitted to participate in elections. Members of the national and provincial assemblies are directly elected.

The Constitution requires that the President and Prime Minister be Muslims. In February the federal Cabinet approved the Electoral Reforms Bill that, among other changes, abolished the requirement that a voter's identity card be presented during polling. The opposition parties called the electoral reforms a government ploy to rig elections, and the opposition party PML-N stressed that it would not take part in the elections under the new electoral reforms.

In July the Muslim Conference boycotted the elections of the constituent assembly of Azad Jammu and Kashmir for the Kashmiris living in Punjab. The Muslim Conference alleged that with the abolition of the identity card requirement, the PPP massively rigged the polls. They also alleged that the Government brought non-Kashmiris to the polling stations to cast bogus votes. These allegations appear to be valid.

Under the present system, minorities vote for reserved at-large seats, not for non-minority candidates who represent actual constituencies. Because of this, local parliamentary representatives have little incentive to promote their minority constituents' interests. The Electoral Reforms Bill would give religious minorities the right to vote for at-large candidates as well as local candidates (the so-called "double vote") but different Muslim religious groups and the main opposition party—the PML-N—rejected the bill, alleging that it ignored the feelings of the Muslim majority. To date the bill has not been adopted by the Parliament. The Government claimed that the double vote right had been introduced in order to give minorities the leverage to influence their local members of the Parliament. The Government did not have the two-thirds majority necessary to pass the measure in the National Assembly.

In May the SC stayed further action on the new electoral rolls which were recently revised by the Election Commission of Pakistan. In their petition, opposition PML-N leaders alleged that the PPP Government had harassed election commission officials to enroll bogus voters and delete PML-N voters. A final decision in the case has not yet been made.

In June the Supreme Court restored the Punjab local government bodies that were dissolved in 1993 by the caretaker government based on charges of corruption. However, these local bodies were suspended a day later when the Punjab Assembly repealed the 1979 Local Government Ordinance under which the local bodies operated. The opposition alleged that the Government repealed the ordinance because the restored local bodies were dominated by PML-N members.

The more than 2 million Pashtun people living in the FATA do not vote for their National Assembly representatives and have no representation in the assembly of the Northwest Frontier province. In keeping with local traditions, FATA's National Assembly members are elected by tribal leaders, or maliks, who are appointed in the governor's name by the central Government's political agents. Many people living in this area have expressed dissatisfaction at having no vote. However, the majority of Pashtun people live outside the FATA and, while retaining their tribal identity, are fully integrated into politics and society. On December 15, the caretaker Government announced that all eligible voters in the tribal areas would be registered for the general elections. By year's end, over 370,000 persons, including almost 75,000 women, had registered to vote. However, rejecting the enrollment of female voters in the tribal areas, a grand jirga (council) of the Afridi tribe of the Khyber Agency unanimously decided on December 31 to impose a penalty of 1 million rupees and demolish the home of any woman who registers with the voters list.

Because of a longstanding territorial dispute with India, the political status of the northern areas—Hunza, Gilgit, and Baltistan—is not resolved. As a result, more than 1 million inhabitants of the northern areas are not covered under any constitution and have no representation in the federal legislature. The area is administered by an appointed civil servant. While there is an elected Northern Areas Council, this body serves in an advisory capacity to the Federal Government and has no authority to change laws or raise and spend revenue.

Although women participate in government, they are underrepresented in political life at all levels. Only 4 women—including the then-Prime Minister—held seats in the 217-member National Assembly that was dissolved in November. While women participate in large numbers in elections, some women are dissuaded from voting in elections by family, religious, and social customs in rural areas.

Section 4. Governmental Attitude Regarding International and Nongovernmental Investigation of Alleged Violations of Human Rights

There are several domestic human rights organizations, and new human rights and legal aid groups continue to form. These groups are generally free to operate without government restriction. The Government has provided protection to human rights lawyers defending accused blasphemers following threats and attacks on the lawyers by religious activists.

International human rights organizations have been permitted to visit Pakistan and travel freely. The Government has not always been responsive to foreign NGO's, however. The Government's Human Rights Cell established branch offices in Karachi, Lahore, and Peshawar. The Cell brought attention to the problem of spousal abuse by arranging visits by the then-Prime Minister to hospitalized abuse victims and began a television and radio campaign to educate the public on human rights issues.

The Government established a new Ministry of Human Rights in November 1995. The caretaker Government has merged the Ministry of Human Rights into the Ministry of Law, Justice, Human Rights, and Parliamentary Affairs. The former ministry did not accomplish much of note prior to and following the merger.

Section 5. Discrimination Based on Race, Sex, Religion, Disability, Language, or Social Status

The Constitution provides for equality before the law for all citizens and broadly prohibits discrimination based on race, religion, caste, residence, or place of birth. In practice, however, there is significant discrimination based on these factors.

Women.—Domestic violence is a widespread and serious problem. The Ministry of Women's Development estimates that 80 percent of women are victims of domestic violence. The press continued to draw attention to murders of married women by relatives over dowry or other family related disputes. Most of the victims are burned to death, allegedly in kitchen stove accidents. The police rarely visit the scene of the crime or conduct investigations to determine how the woman was burned. Increased media coverage of cases of wife burnings, spousal abuse, spousal murder, and rape cases has helped to raise awareness about violence against women

While abusive spouses may be charged for assault, cases are rarely filed. Police usually return battered wives to their abusive husbands. Women are reluctant to file charges because of societal mores that stigmatize divorce and make women economically and psychologically dependent on their husbands and male relatives. Relatives are also reluctant to report cases of abuse in order to protect the reputation of the family.

Rape is a widespread problem. However, it is estimated that less than one-third of all rapes are reported to the police. According to a police official, in a majority of rape cases the victims are pressured to drop rape charges because of the threat of Hadood adultery charges being brought against them. All consensual extramarital sexual relations are considered violations of the Hadood Ordinances. However, according to an HRCP lawyer, the Government has brought fewer charges against women under the Hadood Ordinances than in the past, and the courts have shown greater leniency toward women in their sentences and in the granting of bail. Nevertheless, according to a July HRCP report, 90 per cent of the reported rape victims are in prisons because of their failure to present credible witnesses, in strict terms, as required under the Hadood Ordinances. In Hadood cases, a woman or non-Muslim witness is not accepted. This means that if a man rapes a woman in the presence of several women, he cannot be convicted under the Hadood Ordinances because female witnesses will not be accepted. Similarly, if a Muslim man rapes a Christian woman in the presence of several Christian men and women, he cannot be convicted under Hadood Ordinances because non-Muslim witnesses are not accepted.

Marital rape is not a crime. The 1979 Hadood Ordinances abolished punishment for raping one's wife. It is a common practice in Pakistan, that "nikah" (marriage registration) is performed whereas "rukh sati" (consummation of marriage) takes place some years later. The "nikah" (non-consummated) marriage is also regarded as a formal marital relationship. In one such case, a 13-year-old girl, whose nikah had been performed but rukhsati had not taken place, decided to divorce her husband. The husband kidnaped the girl, raped her, and then released her. The police refused to register a rape case arguing that they were a married couple.

In 1996 there were scores of incidents involving violence against women. For example, in one period of 33 days (May 11 to June 13) 212 cases of violence against women were reported in the newspapers. Sixty-one women were killed by husbands, in-laws, relatives, or criminals. Forty-six women were burned, most of them seriously. Relatives often claimed that they were preparing food when their clothes accidentally caught fire. Of the 46 women who were burned, 9 were burned to death by their husbands and in-laws for domestic reasons. Most human rights monitors believe that the "stove deaths" are in fact murders based upon a suspicion of illicit sexual relationship or on dowry demands.

During this same period from May to June, 67 women were reported kidnaped, and most of them are still missing. Twenty-eight women, including some young girls, were reported to have been gang-raped, and several subsequently died from shock or torture. There were several press reports of in-laws burning daughters-in-law with boiling water or oil, acid, or fire. In some incidents, parents killed daughters to prevent love marriages. In one incident, a man disfigured a woman by throwing acid on her face because she had refused to marry him. A woman was badly beaten by her husband because she insisted on working. In few of these types of cases do the police or courts become involved, and it is rare for the perpetrator of domestic rape or murder to be convicted. There were several reports in 1996 of parents arranging marriages for their daughters with elderly men for financial gain. Reports of feudal landlords raping peasant women in the rural areas continued to appear in the press in 1996.

There are an increasing number of reports of women killed or mutilated by male relatives who suspect them of adultery. Few such cases are investigated seriously. Scores of men and women from Baluchistan and rural areas of Sindh and Punjab provinces are killed annually for alleged illicit sexual relations. While the tradition of such killing applies equally to offending men and women, women are more likely to be killed than men.

There are significant barriers to the advancement of women, beginning at birth. In general female children are less valued and cared for than male children. According to a United Nations study, girls receive less nourishment, health care, and education than boys. According to the Government, only 23.5 percent of females over 10 years of age are literate, compared with 48.9 percent of males; the level of literacy among females is declining. Discrimination against women is particularly acute in rural areas.

Human rights monitors and women's groups believe that the Shari'a Law has had a harmful effect on the rights of women and minorities, reinforcing popular attitudes and perceptions, and contributing to an atmosphere in which discriminatory treatment of women and non-Muslims is more readily accepted.

Both civil and religious laws protect women's rights in cases of divorce, but, as in the case of inheritance laws, many women are unaware of them, and often the laws are not observed. In inheritance cases women generally do not receive—or are pressed to surrender—their due share of the inheritance. In rural areas, the practice of a woman "marrying the Koran" is still widely accepted if the family cannot arrange a suitable marriage or wants to keep the family wealth intact. A woman "married to the Koran" is forbidden to have any contact with males over 14 years of age, including her immediate family members. The Government's Council of Islamic Ideology (CII) condemned the practice as un-Islamic, but the CII ruling is not legally binding. Press reports indicate that the practice of buying and selling brides still takes place in parts of NWFP and the Punjab. In September a Lahore High Court judge ruled that a woman's marriage without the consent of her parents or guardian is invalid. The judge further ruled that children born of such an invalid marriage are to be considered illegitimate, and that widows and divorcees also are forbidden to marry without the consent of their parents or guardians.

In 1992 the Supreme Court observed that under Islamic law, a husband is not required to give written notice of a divorce to a local union council. The husband's statement, with or without witnesses, is the defining legal step. The woman, lacking written proof of divorce, remains legally and socially vulnerable. Human rights organizations expressed concern that a woman could be charged with adultery if her former spouse were to deny having divorced her. However, the Court's opinion was never implemented.

There are also limits on the admissibility and value of women's testimony in court (see Section 1.e.).

Women's organizations operate primarily in urban centers. Many concentrate on educating women about existing legal rights. Other groups concentrate on providing legal aid to poor women in prison who may not be able to afford an attorney.

According to an independent observer, the Government through 1996 had trained and deployed over 40,000 female rural health workers. The Government plans to train another 10,000 in 1997 with the goal of having a total of 100,000 by 1998. The Government also produced television documentaries on women in development. Although a small number of women study and teach in universities, postgraduate employment opportunities remain largely limited to teaching, medical services, and the law. Nevertheless, an increasing number of women are entering the commercial and public sectors. In the urban areas of the Punjab, more and more parents send their daughters to schools.

Children.—There is no federal law on compulsory education, and neither the federal or provincial governments provide sufficient resources to assure universal education. Government provision of health care is somewhat better—especially with the program deploying rural health workers—but health care services in most areas remain seriously inadequate. Many children begin working at a very early age. At the age of 5 or 6, female children are often responsible for younger siblings. Children are sometimes kidnaped to be used as forced labor, for ransom, or to seek revenge against an enemy (see Sections 6.c. and 6.d.). Child prostitution involving boys and girls is widely known to exist but is rarely discussed. The Government does little to deter it.

Legal rights for children are theoretically protected by numerous laws that incorporate elements of the U.N. Convention on the Rights of the Child. However, the Government frequently fails to enforce these laws. Federal law allows, but does not require, offenders under the age of 14 to be placed in reform schools; however, no such facilities exist. There is only one jail in each province for convicted prisoners under the age of 21. A 1995 HRCP report estimated that there were more than a thousand children in various jails nationwide. Although Punjab and Sindh provinces have laws mandating special judicial procedures for child offenders, in practice, children and adults are essentially treated equally. Very young children accompany their convicted mothers to jail.

Incidents of kidnaping, rape, and murder of minor teenage children are on the rise. In January two girls in Faisalabad, both 4th grade students, were kidnaped and killed. The culprit was immediately arrested and sentenced to death by a special court. In such incidents against children, the courts appear to be far more active than in cases of domestic violence.

According to press reports, there are several madrassahs (religious schools) in southern Punjab where children are illegally confined and kept in unhealthy conditions. In March Multan district police raided such a madrassah where 22 children, 8 to 14 years of age, were kept chained by the superintendent of the madrassah. According to the assistant commissioner, the children were chained round the clock, and some of them had been chained for over 1 year. Following the police raid, there was no reported judicial action taken against officials of the madrassah.

People With Disabilities.—There are no laws requiring equal accessibility to public buildings for disabled persons. The Human Rights Cell has requested all city administrations to incorporate facilities for the disabled—including wheelchair access ramps and elevators—in local building codes.

Religious Minorities.—Government authorities afford religious minorities less legal protection than is afforded to Muslim citizens. Members of religious minorities are subject to violence and harassment, and police at times refuse to prevent such actions or to charge those who commit them. Ahmadis are often targets of violence, often instigated by local religious leaders

A Sunni Muslim shopkeeper stabbed and seriously wounded an Ahmadi teacher in Khushab. According to Ahmadi sources, the attack was instigated by the anti-

Ahmadi speech of a local mullah. A case could not be registered against the culprit because the hospital refused to issue a report of attempted murder.

In May about 300 religious extremists demolished an Ahmadi place of worship in Dulmial. When the district administration barred them from occupying the mosque, furious mullahs forced Ahmadi shopkeepers to evacuate properties owned by non-Ahmadis, boycotted businesses owned by Ahmadis, forced parents to withdraw their children from a school owned by an Ahmadi, and filed false cases against several Ahmadis.

Human rights activist and lawyer Asma Jehangir, who represents minorities in cases involving religious persecution, remained the target of religious extremists' criticism. She is accused by extremists of being "an infidel" and "a foreign agent." Following an attack on her family last year, widely assumed to have been carried out by religious extremists, Jehangir now is accompanied by an armed guard.

In April the district Sessions Court of Lahore acquitted three persons accused of murdering an alleged Christian blasphemer, Manzoor Masih. Masih was killed allegedly by religious extremists in April 1994. The court refused to accept written evidence of two eyewitnesses, Salamat and Rehmat Masih (accused along with the deceased in the 1995 blasphemy case) who fled to Germany following their acquittal.

Due largely to the efforts of the Milli Yakjehti Council (MYC-Alliance of Religious/Sectarian Groups to Develop Tolerance and Harmony) and strict measures taken by the Punjab government, in 1996 there were no bombings or attacks on Shi'a or Sunni places of worship. However, tension between the Sunni extremist organization Sipah-i-Sahaba Pakistan (SSP), and the Shi'a organizations Tehrik-i-Jafria Pakistan (TJP) and Sipah-i-Muhammad Pakistan (SMP) erupted in mid-year with a rash of sectarian-motivated killings. Those murdered included the Commissioner of Sargodha division, an excise and taxation officer, a renowned poet, and the spokesman of the extremist Shi'a organization SMP. Government officials have publicly blamed the SSP and the SMP for these murders.

According to a press report, from January 1 to August 19, 52 people were killed and 100 injured in 53 sectarian-motivated incidents across the country. In 2 weeks of August alone, 25 people were killed. On August 14, 11 people were killed when an Independence Day rally in Karachi, organized by the Sunni militant organization SSP, was attacked by unknown gunmen. Also in August, armed persons fired on a Shi'a religious gathering in Vehari district, killing 14 persons.

Religious minority groups also experience considerable discrimination in employment and education; the laws facilitate discrimination in employment based on religion. In Pakistan's early years, minorities were able to rise to the senior ranks of the military and civil service. Today, many are unable to rise above mid level ranks. Because of the lack of educational opportunities for some religious minority groups, discrimination in employment is believed to be increasingly prevalent. There are also restrictions on testimony in court by non-Muslims (see Section 1.e.).

Christians in particular have difficulty finding jobs other than those of menial labor. Many Christians continue to express the fear of forced marriages between Muslim males and Christian women, although the practice is relatively rare. Christians are among the least educated citizens. According to one Christian rights advocate, only 8 percent of Christian males and 6 percent of Christian females are literate.

Ahmadis suffer from harassment (see Section 2.c.) and discrimination and have limited chances for advancement into management levels in government service. Even the rumor that someone may be an Ahmadi or have Ahmadi relatives can stifle opportunities for employment or promotion. Young Ahmadis and their parents complain of increasing difficulty in gaining admittance to good colleges, forcing many children to go abroad for higher education.

Section 6. Worker Rights

a. *The Right of Association.*—The Industrial Relations Ordinance of 1969 (IRO) enunciates the right of industrial workers to form trade unions but is subject to major restrictions in some employment areas. The Essential Services Maintenance Act of 1952 (ESA) covers sectors associated with "the administration of the State," i.e., government services and state enterprises, such as oil and gas production, electricity generation and transmission, the state-owned airline, and ports. Workers in these sectors are allowed to form unions. However, the ESA sharply restricts normal union activities, usually prohibiting, for example, the right to strike in affected organizations. In response to international criticism, the Government took steps in 1995 to limit application of the ESA. In addition in 1996 the Cabinet decided to withdraw the exemption of the export promotion zones (EPZ's) from the IRO's provisions granting the right to workers to form trade unions.

Union members make up only about 10 percent of the industrial labor force and 3 percent of the total estimated work force. Contract labor continues to flourish, undercutting the power of the unions and exploiting workers willing to work on temporary contracts. These workers receive fewer benefits and have no job security. There is no provision in the law granting the right of association to agricultural workers.

Legally required conciliation proceedings and cooling-off periods constrain the right to strike, as does the Government's authority to ban any strike that may cause "serious hardship to the community" or prejudice to the national interest. The Government may also ban a strike that has continued for 30 days.

Strikes are rare. When they occur, they are usually illegal and short. The Government regards as illegal any strike conducted by workers who are not members of a legally registered union. Police do not hesitate to crack down on worker demonstrations. The law prohibits employers from seeking retribution against leaders of a legal strike and stipulates criminal penalties for offenders. The courts may imprison employers for violating this prohibition, but they are more likely to fine them. The law does not protect leaders of illegal strikes.

Unions may belong to federations, and there are seven major federations in Pakistan. The Government permits trade unions all across the political spectrum. While many unions remain aloof from party politics, the most powerful are those associated with political parties. After the PPP came to power in 1988, it successfully organized trade unions under the banner of the People's Labor Bureau (PLB). The PLB's main competitors are the Jamaat-i-Islami's National Labor Federation and the MQM-backed labor unions.

The International Labor Organization (ILO) has stated that current law and practice violate the Government's commitments under ILO Convention 87. The ILO has urged the Government to lift prohibitions against union activity in respect to teachers, radio, television, railway, forestry, hospital, and other government employees, as well as to rescind the existing ban on strikes. The ILO also expressed concern about the practice of artificial promotions that exclude workers from the purview of the Industrial Relations Ordinance and stated that nonapplication of labor laws in proposed new "special industrial zones" would be a violation of Convention 111. In response to a Government request, the ILO has provided technical assistance to help bring the country's labor laws into conformity with the world body's conventions. In 1994 a government task force on labor prepared a report recommending improvements on worker rights problems, which were the basis for the development of a new labor policy by the Government. As of year's end, the Government had not yet approved the new labor policy

Federations are free to affiliate with international federations and confederations.

b. *The Right to Organize and Bargain Collectively.*—The right of industrial workers to organize and freely elect representatives to act as collective bargaining agents is established in law. The IRO prohibits antiunion discrimination by employers. If found guilty of antiunion discrimination, employers are required to reinstate workers fired for union activities.

In general legally constituted unions have the right to bargain collectively. However, the many restrictions on forming unions (see Section 6.a.) preclude collective bargaining by large sections of the labor force, e.g., agricultural workers, who are not guaranteed the right to strike, bargain collectively, or make demands on employers.

The ESA also restricts collective bargaining. For each industry subject to the ESA, the Government must make a finding, renewable every 6 months, on the limits of union activity. In cases in which the Government prohibits collective bargaining, special wage boards decide wage levels.

These boards are established at the provincial level and are comprised of representatives from industry, labor, and the provincial Labor Ministry, which provides the chairman. The chairman may name additional industry and labor representatives to the board. Despite the presence of the labor representatives, unions are generally dissatisfied with the boards' findings. Disputes are adjudicated before the National Industrial Relations Commission. A worker's right to quit may also be curtailed under the ESA. Dismissed workers have no recourse to the labor courts.

c. *Prohibition of Forced or Compulsory Labor.*—The Constitution and the law prohibit forced labor. However, critics argue that the ESA's limitation on some worker rights constitutes a form of compulsory labor. The Government informed the ILO's Committee on the Application of Standards in 1990 that amendments were under consideration to rectify the problem. However, the Government has taken no further action.

Illegal bonded labor is widespread. Bonded labor is common in the brick, glass, and fishing industries and is found among agricultural and construction workers in rural areas. Conservative estimates put the figure of bonded workers at several million.

According to press reports, in the remote areas of rural Sindh, reports of bonded agricultural labor and debt slavery have a long history. Landlords have kept entire families in private prisons and families have been sold by one landlord to another. Press and other sources report that raids by government officials and human rights activists this year liberated a few of the bonded laborers.

In January a raid led by government human rights officials freed about 30 bonded laborers from three different private jails run by local landlords. According to government officials, the freed laborers were taken to safe places with relatives, but other prisoners in the same jails had been raped or killed, and the landlords fled.

In April, 140 bonded laborers were freed from two different landlords in rural Sindh in a raid conducted by the police and the HRCP. A few of the laborers had been held in bondage for as long as 25 years. The police allegedly acted only after urging by the HRCP, which had gathered videotaped evidence of the abuses.

The Bonded Labor System (Abolition) Act adopted in 1992, outlawed bonded labor, canceled all existing bonded debts, and forbade lawsuits for the recovery of existing debts. However, the provincial governments, which are responsible for enforcing the law, have failed to establish enforcement mechanisms. Hence, the law is largely ineffective. Lacking employment alternatives, many workers have voluntarily returned to bonded labor.

Children are sometimes kidnaped to be used as forced labor.

d. *Minimum Age for Employment of Children.*—Child labor is common and results from a combination of severe poverty, employer greed, and inadequate enforcement of laws intended to control it. The current estimate of working children is between 8 and 10 million. In response to international criticism, however, the Government has begun to push provincial authorities to enforce child labor laws. In the first 6 months of 1996, according to the Labor Minister, 7,003 raids on businesses suspected of violating child labor laws had been made, resulting in 2,538 prosecutions and 395 convictions. Fines have ranged from $10 to $117. There have been no reported jail terms. Private sector exporters and nongovernmental organizations, supported by the Government, are creating an independent child labor welfare organization to oversee implementation of a child labor free certification system as well as education and welfare programs for working children. The Government is offering financial support and nationally known human rights activists have agreed to sit on the proposed board.

While much child labor is in the traditional framework of family farming or small business, the employment of children in large industries and, according to labor activists, in state-sponsored training programs, is also widespread. Child labor is widely employed in the carpet industry, much of which is family run. Children have also been employed in other export industries, such as textiles, leather tanning, surgical instruments, and sporting goods, though the extent is unclear. Children are sometimes kidnaped to be used as forced labor (see Section 6.c.). The Government is establishing a pilot program of 24 rehabilitation centers for former child laborers in cooperation with the ILO's International Program for the Elimination of Child Labor (IPEC). Twelve of these centers are currently operating. About 1,400 children are involved with the centers. UNICEF is working with the National Commission for Child Welfare and Development and the Labor Ministry to establish a child labor community awareness media program. Soccer ball manufacturers are working with major foreign sporting goods companies to eliminate child labor from their products. One firm in Sialkot has formed a partnership with a foreign company to make child-labor-free soccer balls at village centers. Another Sialkot firm is building a plant in collaboration with a foreign partner with a program of schooling for workers' families.

e. *Acceptable Conditions of Work.*—Labor regulations are governed by federal statutes applicable throughout the country. The minimum wage is approximately $47 (1,650 rupees) per month. Although this wage provides a meager subsistence living for a small family, the minimum wage affects only a small part of the work force, and most families are large.

The law, applicable nationally, provides for a maximum workweek of 54 hours, rest periods during the workday, and paid annual holidays. These regulations do not apply to agricultural workers, workers in factories with fewer than 10 employees, and to the small contract groups, which are subdivisions within factories of 10 or fewer workers. Many workers are unaware of the regulations protecting their rights because of their lack of education.

The provinces have been ineffective in enforcing labor regulations, because of limited resources, corruption, and inadequate regulatory structures. In general, health and safety standards are poor. Although organized labor presses for improvements, the Government has done little and weakly enforces existing legal protection. Workers cannot remove themselves from dangerous work conditions without risking loss of employment.

SRI LANKA

Sri Lanka is a longstanding democratic republic with an active multiparty system. Constitutional power is shared between the popularly elected President and the 225-member Parliament. President Chandrika Kumaratunga leads the People's Alliance (PA), a coalition of parties, which holds a single seat majority in parliament. Both the Parliament and the President were elected in free and fair elections in 1994. The Government respects constitutional provisions for an independent judiciary.

The conflict between the Government and the Liberation Tigers of Tamil Eelam (LTTE), an insurgent organization fighting for a separate state for the country's Tamil minority, continued beyond its 13th year and intensified. A 6-month government military offensive captured the LTTE heartland of the Jaffna Peninsula in April, adding tens of thousands to the ranks of displaced persons. The LTTE inflicted a major military defeat on government forces at Mullaitivu army base in the north, killing upwards of 1,500 troops.

The Government controls all security forces. The 50,000-member police force is responsible for internal security in most areas of the country. The 80,000 member army, and the small navy and air force, conduct the war against the LTTE insurgents. The police paramilitary Special Task Force (STF) also battles the LTTE. The 5,000 strong Home Guards, an armed force drawn from local communities, provides security for Muslim and Sinhalese village communities in or near the war zone. The Government also arms and directs various Tamil militias opposed to the LTTE, though at times these groups act independently of government authority. During the year, some members of the security forces committed serious human rights abuses.

Sri Lanka is a low-income country with a market economy that is based on the export of textiles, garments, tea, rubber, coconuts, and gems, and on earnings from tourism. The gross domestic product per capita is about $700. The economy grew in excess of 5 percent per year during 1990–1995. However, a severe drought coupled with the ongoing civil war, slowed economic growth to less than 4 percent during 1996. During the year, the Government made significant steps toward economic reform, including trimming subsidies, privatizing government enterprises, and promoting foreign investment and trade.

The Government generally remained committed to the human rights of its citizens. However, the intensification of the war with the LTTE was accompanied by a deterioration in the human rights record of the security forces in some areas. In February the security forces were responsible for the extrajudicial killings of at least 50 Tamils, including the murder of 24 civilians in the eastern village of Kumarapuram by army troops. At least 300 individuals are believed to have disappeared from security force custody on the Jaffna Peninsula, while 50 more disappeared elsewhere on the island. Torture remained a serious problem, and prison conditions remained poor. There were an increase in detentions and short-term mass arrests, often accompanied by failure to comply with some of the protective provisions of the Emergency Regulations (ER). Impunity for those responsible for human rights abuses remained a problem. Progress was made in some unresolved, high-profile cases of extrajudicial killing and disappearance. In others, however, the investigations or judicial processes were inactive, giving the appearance of impunity for those responsible for human rights violations. At year's end concern was mounting over the failure of both the Government and the LTTE to take prisoners of war on the battlefield. From April to October, the Government censored all domestic news reports relating to military or police matters. Discrimination and violence against women, child prostitution, and child labor continued to be problems.

In positive developments, the Government took steps to control the abuses. Legislation was passed establishing a permanent human rights commission, although the commission was not yet operational at year's end. Prosecutions of security force personnel alleged to have engaged in human rights abuse continued, including that of 8 soldiers charged in the Kumarapuram massacre. There was no attempt, as in the past, to use the ER to cover up security force misdeeds. Sixteen police and army personnel were arrested for the rape and murder of two young women in Jaffna. Through its rulings, the judiciary continued to uphold individual civil rights. Government security forces took effective measures to limit civilian casualties during the military offensive against the LTTE in Jaffna. The Government also provided relief to those displaced by the conflict even though many were still under the control of the LTTE. Three regional commissions established to investigate disappearances continued their investigations. The Government ratified the Optional Protocol to the International Covenant on Civil and Political Rights.

The LTTE made terrorist attacks against civilians, although there were no reported attacks in the second half of the year. The LTTE regularly committed extrajudicial killings (including civilian massacres and assassinations), and was also responsible for disappearances, arbitrary arrests, detentions, and torture. The LTTE terrorist bombing of the Central Bank in Colombo in January killed 90 civilians. Seventy commuters in Colombo died in a train bombing in July. LTTE guerrillas routinely used excessive force in the war. In the attack on Mullaitivu, which killed 1,500 government troops, the LTTE claims to have taken no prisoners. Though largely dislodged from the Jaffna Peninsula by government forces, the LTTE continued to control large sections of the north and east of the country through authoritarian military rule, denying the people under its authority the right to change their government, routinely violating their civil liberties, and severely discriminating against ethnic and religious minorities. The use of rape by the LTTE as a weapon of terror, first noted in 1995, did not reoccur.

RESPECT FOR HUMAN RIGHTS

Section 1. Respect for the Integrity of the Person, Including Freedom From:

a. *Political and Other Extrajudicial Killing.*—Police (mostly STF officers) and army personnel committed extrajudicial killings in both Jaffna and the Eastern Province. Most of these were associated with operations against the LTTE insurgents or interrogation of suspected rebels. In excess of 50 individuals were killed, although the exact number was impossible to ascertain due to a long period of censorship of news relating to military or police operations, and lack of access to the north and east where the civil war was being waged. In February army troops murdered 24 Tamil villagers, including 2 children under 12 years of age, in the eastern village of Kumarapuram. Eight soldiers were arrested and the Attorney General's office recommended to the High Court that they be indicted on 101 counts of murder and attempted murder. They had not yet come to trial at year's end.

In some cases these extrajudicial killings were reprisals against civilians for LTTE attacks in which members of the security forces were killed or injured. Several such reprisals occurred during operations by the STF. In many cases, the security forces claimed that the victims were members of the LTTE. However, human rights monitors have determined that these victims were civilians. With the exception of the Kumarapuram incident, the perpetrators of these killings had not been arrested by the Government at year's end. There were also a number of suspicious deaths attributed to the security forces, mostly involving detainees acting as government informants who died during operational missions against the LTTE.

In October 1995, 22 members of the STF were arrested and detained under the ER on suspicion of murdering 23 Tamil youths whose bodies were found floating in Bolgoda Lake and other bodies of water near Colombo. The suspects were released on bail and resumed their police functions in February. In July the charred body of a Tamil textile merchant who had been detained under the ER was found at Giribawa in North Central Province. Six police officers, including the officer in charge of the police countersubversive unit in Vavuniya, were arrested and detained under the ER. In both cases, the police investigation was submitted to the Attorney General's department, which had not yet made any recommendations to the High Court by year's end. In the case of the Bolgoda Lake killings, problems with the Government's evidence have reportedly contributed to the delay.

A presidential commission was established to investigate torture and murder in the late 1980's at a government-run detention center at Batalanda Housing Estate near Colombo. In August five police officers were arrested for alleged complicity. The investigation was continuing at year's end.

In November, 16 police and army personnel were arrested for the rape and murder of Krishanthi Kumaraswamy, the murder of her family member, and the rape and murder of Rajini Velayuthapillai in Jaffna. The 11 accused in the Kumaraswamy case were brought before the magistrate's court in Colombo and charged with rape and murder.

The PA Government came to power in 1994 promising to bring to justice the perpetrators of extrajudicial killings from previous years. In 1994 it began prosecutions of suspects in several extrajudicial murders allegedly perpetrated by members of the security forces. The trial of 21 soldiers, accused of massacring 35 Tamil civilians in 1992 in the village of Mailanthani in Batticaloa district, was transferred to the Colombo High Court. The Attorney General recommended to the Court that the suspects be indicted on 40 counts of murder. The trial of 4 police officers indicted in

1994 for the 1990 murders of 12 civilians in Wavulkelle was still ongoing at year's end.

There were no developments in the government investigations into the mass graves at Sooriyakanda, which contain an estimated 300 bodies, or the grave at Ankumbura, which is thought to contain the bodies of 36 people killed by the police in 1989. In addition, there were no developments in the Nikaweratiya army camp incident in which 20 youths were allegedly killed by soldiers in 1989.

In April the ER, which had previously been in force only in areas of the north and east directly affected by the insurgency and in Colombo, was reimposed nationwide. There was no evidence that the Government was using them, as in previous years, to conceal extrajudicial killings or disappearances. However, crucial safeguards built into the ER were being routinely ignored by the security forces—especially those provisions requiring receipts to be issued for arrests and ordering the security forces to notify the Human Rights Task Force (HRTF) of any arrest within 24 hours. The HRTF is a quasi-independent government body established by an ER to register detainees held under the ER and the Prevention of Terrorism Act (PTA), and monitor their welfare. Although security force personnel can be fined or jailed for failure to comply with the ER, none was known to have been punished during the year.

In the east and in Vavuniya in the north, the military wing of the People's Liberation Organization of Tamil Eelam (PLOTE), the Mohan Group, and the Rasheek Group—progovernment Tamil militant organizations—were responsible for the killing of a number of people. Though armed and nominally under the control of the security forces, these groups frequently acted independently of government authority. It was imposible to determine the number of victims because of the secrecy with which these groups operated. However, those killed included both LTTE operatives and civilians who failed to comply with extortion demands.

Violence between supporters of the major political parties worsened during the year. Politically motivated attacks resulted in a number of deaths, including eight people in the coastal town of Negombo in September.

There were no developments in the October 1994 suicide bombing that killed the United National Party's presidential candidate, Gamini Dissanayake, and 58 other people, although it is generally believed to be the work of the LTTE.

The LTTE continued to commit extrajudicial killings. In January a midmorning bomb blast at the Central Bank in the heart of Colombo killed more than 90 civilians. In July, 70 commuters in Colombo died in a train bombing. In the same month, an attempted assassination attempt against the Minister of Housing by a suicide bomber in Jaffna left 25 dead, including an army brigadier. Numerous assassinations of political opponents in the east were perpetrated by "pistol gangs", who successfully carried out their attacks using motorcycles and revolvers. Massacres of civilians continued. In June, 14 Sinhalese villagers were killed in Puttalam district. In September, 11 Sinhalese travelers were murdered in an ambush on a bus in Ampara district. The LTTE continued to execute suspected government informants. In the past, the LTTE has killed university professors, members of nonviolent Tamil opposition parties, and human rights monitors.

b. *Disappearance.*—Disappearance at the hands of the security forces increased alarmingly, especially in the east and north, though some occurred in Colombo. Most of these were associated with the arrest of suspected LTTE insurgents. In excess of 300 individuals are believed to have disappeared on the Jaffna Peninsula in the second half of the year, and more than 50 elsewhere in the country throughout the year. As with extrajudicial killings, the exact number was impossible to ascertain due to censorship of news about security force operations, and lack of access to the north and east.

There were 34 confirmed cases of disappearance in 1995, and 10 cases in 1994, the lowest number on record in at least a decade. Those who disappeared in 1996 and in previous years are presumed dead. The disappearances involved persons last known to be in police or army custody. The Commander of the Army and the Inspector General of Police have both issued directives condemning disappearances and stating that perpetrators would be called to account. In November, the Ministry of Defense established a Board of Investigation to look into disappearances in the north and east and review security forces procedures. However at year's end, the Government had not identified or charged those responsible for disappearances during the year.

The Government continued investigations into past disappearances. The three regional commissions set up in November 1994 to inquire into disappearances occurring after January 1, 1988, worked throughout the year. Through August the commissions received 61,300 complaints. Most of these cases date from 1988–90, when a terrorist insurrection organized by the Janata Vimukti Peramuna (JVP) threatened to plunge the country into chaos until it was put down by a brutal counterinsurgency campaign. Of these, they were able to review 38,000 individual cases, leaving 23,000 outstanding. Charged with producing final reports for President Kumaratunga, including recommendations for legal action, the commissions were believed to have accumulated sufficient information to prosecute as many as 200 members of the security forces for human rights violations. No final reports were produced, as the mandates of the commissions were extended into 1997. The November 1995 final report of the Presidential Commission of Inquiry into the Involuntary Removal of Persons was made available to the three regional commissions. The Commission was formed in 1991 to investigate disappearances after that date.

The trial of 11 suspects, including an army brigadier general, in the disappearance of 32 school boys from the southern town of Embilipitiya in 1989 and 1990 continued at year's end. However, there were no developments in the Vantharamulle case, in which army troops allegedly abducted 158 Tamils from a refugee camp in Batticaloa district in 1990. Observers maintain that there is credible evidence identifying the alleged perpetrators. There were also no developments in the case of 31 youths who allegedly disappeared following their arrests in Divulapitiya in 1989.

The Government continued to give the International Committee of the Red Cross (ICRC) unhindered access to detention centers, police stations, and army camps. This played an important role in enabling the ICRC to monitor the human rights practices of the security forces, as did the work of the HRTF. However, at year's end the HRTF had not yet established operations on the Jaffna Peninsula, in part because government approval had been delayed until October.

Progovernment Tamil militants in the east and north, acting independently of government authority, were also responsible for disappearances. As in the case of extrajudicial killings, it was impossible to determine the exact number of victims because of the secrecy with which these groups operated. The Government has taken no clear public steps to condemn the militants' actions or to stop them.

The LTTE was responsible for an undetermined number of civilian disappearances in the northeastern part of the island. Most of the 400 to 600 police officers captured by the LTTE in 1990 are believed to be dead, as are over 200 security force personnel captured at a battle in Pooneryn in 1993. Although the LTTE denies taking any prisoners following the Mullaitivu battle in July, it is suspected of holding some. The vice chancellor of Eastern University, who was kidnaped by the LTTE in November 1995, was released in January.

c. *Torture and Other Cruel, Inhuman, or Degrading Treatment or Punishment.—* In 1994 the Government acceded to the Convention Against Torture and Other Cruel, Inhuman, or Degrading Treatment or Punishment. Parliament also enacted legislation to implement the Torture Convention by making torture a punishable offense. However, the Government has not yet developed effective regulations under the new legislation to prosecute and punish military and police personnel responsible for torture, although it has ceased paying fines incurred by security force personnel guilty of the offense.

Members of the security forces continued to torture and mistreat detainees and other prisoners, both male and female, particularly during interrogation. Although the number of torture reports was somewhat lower than in previous years in the Colombo area, the situation in Eastern Province did not improve. Torture also emerged as a problem in the newly recaptured Jaffna Peninsula. In November a Supreme Court judge stated publicly that torture continued unabated in police stations in spite of a number of judicial pronouncements against its use. Progovernment Tamil militants in the east and north, directly responsible to the security forces, also engaged in torture. Most torture victims were Tamils suspected of being LTTE insurgents or collaborators.

Methods of torture included electric shock, beatings (especially on the soles of the feet), suspension by the wrists or feet in contorted positions, burning, near drownings, placing of insecticide, chili powder, or gasoline-soaked bags over the head, and forced positions. Detainees have reported broken bones and other serious injuries as a result of their mistreatment. There were no reports of rape in detention.

Under fundamental rights provisions in the Constitution, torture victims may file civil suit for compensation in the Supreme Court. The Court granted awards ranging from $200 to $2,000. Most cases, however, take 2 years or more to move through the courts. Moreover, because the new antitorture law imposes a heavy minimum punishment of 7 years' imprisonment, the Court is scrutinizing fundamental rights cases more carefully than in the past, since findings would weigh heavily in criminal prosecutions of torturers. During the year, no one was convicted of torture under the antitorture law.

The LTTE reportedly used torture on a routine basis. However, because of the secretive nature of the LTTE, no first-hand information was available.

Prison conditions are generally poor and do not meet minimum international standards because of overcrowding and lack of sanitary facilities. An increase in the number of detentions associated with the war with the LTTE caused a significant deterioration in already poor standards in short-term detention centers. However, the Government permitted representatives from the ICRC to visit more than 400 places of detention.

Conditions are also believed to be poor in prisons operated by the LTTE.

d. *Arbitrary Arrest, Detention, or Exile.*—Under ordinary law, authorities must inform an arrested person of the reason for arrest and bring that person before a magistrate within 24 hours. In practice, persons detained under ordinary law generally appear before a magistrate within a few days of arrest. The magistrate may authorize bail or order continued pretrial detention for up to 3 months or longer. Under the ER and the PTA, security forces may detain suspects for extended periods of time without court approval. The ER, in force throughout the nation, allow pretrial detention for a maximum of four consecutive 3-month periods. A magistrate must order further detention. Detainees may challenge their detention and sue the Government for violating their civil rights in the Supreme Court.

In spite of government announcements that it would close all secret detention centers, there were continued reports that the security forces held people in such a manner, especially on the Jaffna Peninsula. Tamil militant groups, ostensibly under the direct control of the security forces, were known to be operating illegal—and unmonitored—detention centers in the east and in Vavuniya.

Detention of Tamils continued to increase as a result of the continuing hostilities with the LTTE. At year's end the Government held as many as 1,500 detainees under the ER, up from 380 at the end of 1994 and 940 at the end of 1995. Many of these detainees were arrested during operations against the LTTE. Between June and September, 460 suspected members of the LTTE were detained on the Jaffna Peninsula. The Government continued to detain up to 300 individuals under the PTA, which permits detention without charge for up to 18 months. A hunger strike in June by Tamils detained without charge under the PTA highlighted the fact that some had been so incarcerated for up to 4 years.

Arrests and detentions by the police increasingly took place in violation of the legal safeguards built into the ER, particularly regarding requirements that receipts be issued and that the HRTF be notified of any arrest within 24 hours. Due to censorship and lack of access, it was unclear what happened to detainees on the Jaffna Peninsula.

Security forces continued to conduct mass arrests of young Tamils, both male and female, especially following the LTTE assassination attempt in Jaffna against the Minister of Housing, and the LTTE attack on Mullaitivu in July. Major sweeps and arrests occurred in Colombo, the east, and increasingly, on the Jaffna Peninsula. Although exact numbers of arrests were impossible to determine, they clearly numbered in the thousands. Upwards of 1,000 Tamils at a time were picked up during police actions. Most were released after identity checks lasting several hours to several days. The Government justified the arrests on security grounds, but many Tamils claimed that the arrests were a form of harassment. In addition, those arrested, most of whom were innocent of any wrongdoing, were detained in prisons together with hardened criminals.

The HRTF continued to investigate the legality of detention in cases referred to it by the Supreme Court and private citizens. Although the HRTF is legally constituted under the ER to exercise oversight over arrests and detentions by the security forces and to undertake visits to prisons, members of the security forces routinely breached the regulations and failed to cooperate with the HRTF. Moreover, following the capture of Jaffna in April, the HRTF was not given permission by the Ministry of Defense to set up operations on the peninsula until October, in spite of provisions in the ER legally requiring the security forces to assist the statutory body. At year's end the HRTF had not yet opened an office on the Jaffna Peninsula.

There were unconfirmed reports that the LTTE was detaining more than 2,000 civilians in the northern part of the island. The LTTE did not permit the ICRC or any other humanitarian organization to visit its detainees—aside from 22 security force personnel, 17 Sinhalese fishermen, and 8 crew members of a civilian ferry hijacked in 1995.

The Government does not practice exile. There are no legal provisions allowing or prohibiting its use.

e. *Denial of Fair Public Trial.*—The Constitution provides for an independent judiciary, and the Government respects these provisions in practice.

The President appoints judges to the Supreme Court, the courts of appeal, and the high courts. A judicial service commission, comprised of the Chief Justice and two Supreme Court judges, appoints, transfers, and dismisses lower court judges. Judges serve until mandatory retirement age, which is 65 for the Supreme Court and 62 for judges on other courts.

In criminal cases, defendants are tried in public by juries. They are informed of the charges and evidence against them, may be represented by the counsel of their choice, and have the right to appeal. The Government provides counsel for indigent persons tried on criminal charges in the high courts and the court of appeal but not in other cases; private legal aid organizations assist some defendants. There are no jury trials in cases brought under the PTA. Confessions, which are inadmissible in criminal proceedings, are allowed in PTA cases. Most convictions under the PTA rely heavily on them. Defendants bear the burden of proof to demonstrate that their confessions were obtained by coercion. Defendants in PTA cases have the right to appeal.

The Government claims that all persons held under the ER and the PTA are suspected members of the LTTE and therefore legitimate security threats. There is insufficient information to determine whether these detainees or members of the now legal Sinhalese Janatha Vimukhti Peramuna (JVP), similarly detained in past years, were political prisoners. Between 200 and 300 of those previously detained—mostly JVP members—have been convicted under criminal law and remain incarcerated. In many cases, human rights monitors question the legitimacy of the criminal charges brought against these people.

The LTTE has its own court system, composed of young judges with little or no legal training. The courts reportedly impose severe punishments. However, the courts operate without codified or defined legal authority, and essentially operate as agents of the LTTE rather than as an independent judiciary.

The LTTE also holds a number of political prisoners. The number is impossible to determine because of the secretive nature of the organization.

f. *Arbitrary Interference with Privacy, Family, Home, or Correspondence.*—The Government generally respects the constitutional protections of individual privacy and the sanctity of the family and home. The police obtain proper warrants for arrests and searches conducted under ordinary law. However, the security forces are not required to obtain warrants for searches conducted under the PTA. The Secretary of Defense is responsible for providing oversight for such searches. There is no judicial review or other means of redress for alleged illegal searches under the PTA.

The Government is believed to monitor telephone conversations and correspondence on a selective basis. The security forces routinely open mail destined for the LTTE-controlled areas and seize contraband.

The LTTE routinely invades the privacy of citizens. It maintains an effective network of informants. In 1990 the LTTE evicted thousands of Muslim residents from their homes in the north. They currently live in refugee camps.

g. *Use of Excessive Force and Violations of Humanitarian Law in Internal Conflicts.*—Hostilities between the Government and the LTTE continued throughout the year. However, the security forces generally exercised much greater restraint in the use of excessive force than they had previously. From October 1995 through April 1996, the Government conducted coordinated military attacks on LTTE-held territory in the Jaffna Peninsula, resulting in the capture of Jaffna City in December 1995 and the remainder of the peninsula by April. Government forces also captured the town of Kilinochchi in September. Altogether, the fierce fighting in the north resulted in many casualties on both sides and upwards of 480,000 displaced persons.

The Government, however, took measures to limit the number of civilian casualties in the war. Notices were dropped warning civilians to congregate in schools, churches, and temples to minimize risk. In addition, during the Jaffna offensive, shelling in advance of troops attacking through populated areas was kept to a minimum in order to spare civilians, though Kilinochchi was shelled to a much greater extent in the July advance. Civilian casualties were also reduced due to the relatively slow and methodical manner in which government security forces pushed forward, which enabled civilians to flee well in advance of troop movements. The Government, assisted by international relief organizations, continued to channel emergency food and limited medical supplies to the civilians displaced in the fighting, including those living in areas controlled by the LTTE. The security forces also continued to carry out human rights instruction as part of their training courses (see Section 4).

Nonetheless, a massacre of villagers by army troops occurred at Kumarapuram in the east (see Section 1.a.). In an incident in December 1995, members of the STF in Batticaloa district in the east commandeered a civilian bus to move quickly to defend an STF camp at Pudukudiirippu that was under attack by the LTTE. They forced the civilians to remain on board, resulting in several civilian deaths when the bus came under LTTE fire. There has been no investigation into this incident.

The Government held only three LTTE cadres as prisoners of war (POW's). All were captured in previous years. In the past the number of POW's was limited by the guerrilla tactics of the LTTE, the LTTE practice to make every effort to remove wounded cadres from the battlefield before they fell prisoner, and the proclivity of LTTE cadres to choose suicide over capture. However, at year's end concern was mounting over the army's failure to report new POW's in spite of large offensives that resulted in heavy battlefield casualties for the LTTE, although there were no specific reports that POW's had been killed. Some observers were worried that a take-no-prisoners policy was in effect. The LTTE admits that it kills security force personnel rather than take them prisoner. It admits to holding only 22 security force prisoners. The LTTE is believed to have killed most of the police officers and security force personnel it has captured in recent years.

The LTTE used excessive force in the war, killing an undetermined number of civilians. It was accused of using church and temple compounds (where civilians are instructed by the Government to congregate in the event of hostilities) as shields for the storage of munitions. In the July attack on the army base at Mullaitivu, the LTTE killed upwards of 1,500 government troops, reportedly killing even those troops who attempted to surrender. During the government offensive on the Jaffna Peninsula, LTTE cadre forced some civilians to abandon their homes and retreat with them, allegedly as human shields, in the face of advancing government troops. The LTTE also reportedly recruited children into its military forces. The bodies of dead LTTE insurgents recovered by the Government following a major battle at Weli Oya in July 1995 were found to be as young as 14 years of age. Reports that the LTTE was conscripting children were impossible to verify.

Section 2. Respect for Civil Liberties, Including:

a. *Freedom of Speech and Press.*—Although the Constitution provides for freedom of speech and expression, restrictions are permitted on national security grounds.

The Government controls the country's largest newspaper chain, two major television stations, and the Sri Lanka Broadcasting Corporation. However, there are also a variety of independent newspapers, journals, radio, and television stations. Independent journalists reported that from the death of United National Party (UNP) President Premadasa in 1993 until September 1995 their freedom to report openly and critically about the Government had improved markedly. They had been able to provide an unimpeded range of views and openly criticize the Government and political parties. However, from September to December 1995, and from April until October, the Government abridged press freedom. Under the ER, it subjected all news relating to the conduct of the war by the armed forces and the police to government censorship. Journalists believe that the Government's implementation of the censorship regulations was arbitrary and overly broad.

A number of other government actions during the year were also of concern to the media. The Government failed to reform the Press Law and privatize government-owned media as promised during the election campaign. Two defamation of character suits stemming from news stories filed by President Kumaratunga in 1995 against leading editors were still pending. They were viewed by journalists as frivolous, intended only to harass and intimidate the media. Journalists were also concerned about the fierce nature of political attacks on the local press by leading politicians. In August the President charged newspapers with publishing deliberate lies and threatened those that published false reports on the war effort with closure.

In an incident that called the Government's commitment to press freedom into question, four Danish journalists were detained under the ER in November. The journalists came to Sri Lanka to cover the story of a teenage Tamil girl deported from Denmark. According to the Government, their detention was necessary because of their close association with the girl, who allegedly had ties to the LTTE. The Government also claimed that they failed to register with the Department of Information and lied on their airport disembarkation cards about the purpose of their visit to Sri Lanka. After a brief detention, the four were deported. A local journalist was also arrested in connection with the incident and was scheduled to appear in court in January 1997. On December 31, in another incident, the police arrested Ishini Perera, news director of an independent television and radio company, charging her under the Prevention of Terrorism Act (PTA) with broadcasting erroneous news. Most journalists regarded the use of the PTA in this matter as heavy handed harassment.

The Parliamentary Powers and Privileges Act stipulates an unlimited fine or up to 2 years' imprisonment for anyone who criticizes a Member of Parliament (M.P.).

Although the Government has not invoked the law since 1992, journalists and civil libertarians complain that the act is an unjustified infringement on freedom of the press.

The Government generally respects academic freedom. During 1996 the ER were not used, as in the past, to control students.

The LTTE does not tolerate freedom of expression. It tightly restricts the print and broadcast media in areas under its control and has often killed those who oppose it. The LTTE also does not respect academic freedom and has repressed and killed intellectuals who criticize it, such as Thiagarajah Selvanithy, a Jaffna poet and women's rights activist killed in 1991 for her views. In November 1995, the LTTE kidnaped a university vice chancellor; he was released in January. It has severely repressed the University Teachers for Human Rights, which was formerly based on the Jaffna Peninsula; most former members of this group have been killed.

b. *Freedom of Peaceful Assembly and Association.*—The law provides for these rights, and the Government respects them in practice. Although the PTA may restrict such freedoms, the Government did not use the Act for that purpose in 1996. The Government generally granted permits for demonstrations, though it banned May Day processions. In spite of this ban, the police allowed a political party supporting the Government to march on May Day, while they broke up an attempted procession by an opposition group.

c. *Freedom of Religion.*—The Constitution establishes Buddhism as the official national religion, but it also provides for the right of members of other faiths to practice their religions freely. The Government respects this right in practice. Foreign clergy may work in Sri Lanka, but for more than 30 years the Government has prohibited the entry of new foreign Jesuit clergy. It permits those already in the country to remain.

Evangelical Christians, who constitute less than 1 percent of the population, have expressed concern that their efforts at proselytization are often met with hostility and harassment by the local Buddhist clergy and others opposed to their work (see Section 5). They sometimes complain that the Government tacitly condones such harassment. However, there is no evidence to support this.

d. *Freedom of Movement Within the Country, Foreign Travel, Emigration, and Repatriation.*—The Constitution grants every citizen "freedom of movement and of choosing his residence" and "freedom to return to Sri Lanka." the Government generally respects the right to domestic and foreign travel. However, the war with the LTTE prompted the Government to impose more stringent checks on travelers from the north and the east and on movement in Colombo, particularly after dark. These security measures had the effect of restricting the movement of Tamils, especially young males.

Prior to the government military offensive on the Jaffna Peninsula in 1995 and 1996, an estimated 600,000 citizens had been displaced by the insurgency. Most live in camps financed by the Government and nongovernmental organizations (NGO's). The Jaffna offensive, in addition to the military advance on Kilinochchi in the Vanni region in July, resulted in the displacement of 480,000 people in LTTE-controlled areas of the Vanni. Some lived with friends or relatives, or in "welfare centers" in schools, religious institutions, and other public buildings. Many others lived in makeshift shelters or camped out under trees. The Government continued to supply them with food, medicine, and other essential supplies.

Prior to 1996, the LTTE severely restricted the movement of Tamils under its control, often levying a large "exit tax" on persons wishing to travel to areas under government control and requiring travelers to leave all their property in escrow. In addition, it would usually grant permission to only one family member to travel at a time. However, following the Government capture of Jaffna, the LTTE began to allow people to move more freely into government-controlled areas. About 16,000 people are estimated to have moved out of LTTE-controlled regions into Vavuniya during the last 3 months of the year. About 6,000 persons moved on to the government-controlled Jaffna Peninsula or returned to the LTTE-controlled Vanni. The remaining 10,000 displaced persons were effectively detained under substandard conditions in camps in Vavuniya pending security clearances which had not been granted at year's end.

In response to the military action in the north, upwards of 6,000 refugees are believe to have fled LTTE-controlled areas to Tamil Nadu in southern India as of October 1. An estimated 69,000 Tamil refugees were already estimated to live in camps there. Another 100,000 refugees are believed to have been integrated into Tamil society in southern India.

The Government cooperates with the U.N. High Commissioner for Refugees (UNHCR) and other humanitarian organizations in assisting refugees. The issue of the provision of first asylum did not arise in 1996. The Government does not permit the entry of refugees into the country, nor does it aid those who manage to enter to seek permanent residence elsewhere. There were, however, no instances of forcible repatriation.

Section 3. Respect for Political Rights: The Right of Citizens to Change Their Government

Citizens have the constitutional right to change their Government through periodic multiparty elections based on universal adult suffrage. This right was last exercised during parliamentary elections in August 1994, when the People's Alliance party ended the 17-year rule of the United National Party, and during the presidential election in November 1994, when PA presidential candidate Chandrika Kumaratunga won 62 percent of the vote. International election monitors judged the elections to be free and fair.

Local elections for municipal, urban, and village councils, which should have been held by June under existing legislation, were postponed by the President under the ER, at least temporarily denying the people the right to change their local government bodies. The Government cited an adverse security environment. The opposition charged that the Government initiated the delay to gain political advantage. The elections were rescheduled for 1997.

In January the Government attempted to dissolve two legally elected provincial councils controlled by the opposition UNP, citing mismanagement and malfeasance. The opposition claimed that the move was politically motivated and that it denied the electorate due process. In March the Court of Appeal overturned the dissolution, stating that the Government had not acted in accordance with the law.

In November the Government announced and set in motion mechanisms to hold elections for local government bodies on the Jaffna Peninsula in early 1997.

The Commissioner of Elections recognizes 26 parties; 9 hold seats in the 225-member Parliament. The two most influential parties, the PA and the UNP, generally draw their support from the majority Sinhalese community. Historically, these two parties have alternated in power. There are 27 Tamil and 21 Muslim M.P.'s.

Although there are no legal impediments to the participation of women in politics or government, the social mores in some communities limit women's activities outside the home. In August 1994, voters elected a female prime minister for the third time in Sri Lanka's history. In November 1994, for the first time, a woman was elected president. Eleven women hold seats in the Parliament. In addition to the Prime Minister and the Minister of Transport, Environment, and Women's Affairs, four deputy ministers are women.

The LTTE refuses to allow elections in areas under its control.

Section 4. Governmental Attitude Regarding International and Nongovernmental Investigation of Alleged Violations of Human Rights

In July Parliament passed the Human Rights Commission Act, which created a permanent human rights commission. The five-member body is empowered to monitor government human rights practices, to ensure compliance with constitutional fundamental rights provisions, and to investigate complaints of human rights abuse. The legislation also provides safeguards for people detained under the PTA and ER, and gives the commission the power to monitor the welfare of detainees. Although the legislation was passed, the commission had not yet been established by year's end.

The Cabinet ratified the Optional Protocol to the International Covenant on Civil and Political Rights in September. The Protocol provides for the right of individual petition and permits individuals to submit complaints about governmental violations of Sri Lankan obligations under the Covenant, i.e., any citizen of Sri Lanka has the right to petition individually to the United Nations Human Rights Committee in the event that he or she has been the victim of human rights violations as set out in the Covenant, and has not received justice. As a party to the Optional Protocol, Sri Lanka is obliged to recognize the competence of the Committee to receive and adjudicate such petitions.

There are several local human rights groups, including the Movement for Interracial Justice and Equality (MIRJE), the University Teachers for Human Rights, the Civil Rights Movement (CRM), and the Law and Society Trust (LST), which monitor civil and political liberties. There are no adverse government regulations governing the activities of local and foreign NGO's.

The Government continued to allow the ICRC unrestricted access to detention facilities. The ICRC provided human rights training materials and training to the security forces. The UNHCR, ICRC, and a variety of international NGO's assisted in the delivery of food, medical, and other essential supplies to the northern war zone.

However, following the capture of the Jaffna Peninsula in April, the army seriously restricted the movement of supplies by international organizations and NGO's to LTTE-controlled areas. Restricted supplies include materials the LTTE might use in its war effort, such as surgical supplies and antibiotics, building and shelter materials, well-drilling and water purification equipment, diesel fuel and gasoline. There have also been serious delays in approving the movement of many other medical supplies into LTTE-controlled areas.

Section 5. Discrimination Based on Race, Sex, Religion, Disability, Language, or Social Status

The Constitution guarantees equal rights under the law for all people in Sri Lanka. The Government generally respects these rights. The Supreme Court regularly upholds court rulings in cases in which individuals file suit over the abridgement of their fundamental civil rights.

Women.—Sexual assault, rape, and spousal abuse (often associated with alcohol) represent serious and pervasive forms of societal violence against women. However, new amendments to the Penal Code were introduced in 1995 that specifically addressed sexual abuse and exploitation. Rape laws were modified to create a more equitable burden of proof and to make punishments more stringent. Marital rape is now considered an offense in cases of spouses living under judicial separation, and new laws govern sexual harassment in the workplace and sexual molestation. While the new Penal Code may ease some of the problems faced by victims of sexual assault, many women's organizations believe that greater sensitization of police and judicial officials are also required. Laws against procuring and trafficking were strengthened in 1995, facilitating the prosecution of brothel owners. Police statistics indicated that there were 31,241 crimes against women during the period from January to June, compared with 24,766 crimes during the same period in 1995.

The Constitution provides for equal employment opportunities in the public sector, but women have no legal protection against discrimination in the private sector, where they are sometimes paid less than men for equal work and often face difficulty in rising to supervisory positions. Women constitute approximately one-half of the formal work force.

Women have equal rights under national civil and criminal law. However, issues related to family law, including divorce, child custody, and inheritance, are adjudicated by the customary law of each ethnic or religious group. In 1995 the Government raised the minimum age of marriage for women from 12 to 18 years, except in the case of Muslims, who continue to follow their customary marriage practices. The application of different legal practices based on membership in a religious or ethnic group often results in discrimination against women.

During massacres of civilians in the east in October 1995, the LTTE raped a number of the victims. This marked the first time in the ethnic conflict that the LTTE deliberately used rape as a weapon of terror. However, such abuses was not reported in 1996.

Children.—The Government is committed to protecting the welfare and rights of children but is constrained by lack of resources.

The Government demonstrates a strong commitment to children's rights and welfare through its widespread systems of public education and medical care. Education is compulsory to the age of 12 and free through university. Health care, including immunization programs, is also free.

There is a significant problem of child prostitution in certain coastal resort areas. The Government estimates that there are more than 2,000 active child prostitutes in the country, but private groups claim that the number is much higher. Many of these prostitutes are boys who sell themselves to foreign tourists. The Penal Code was amended to strengthen punishments for trafficking of persons. In 1995 the Ministry of Media, Tourism, and Aviation created a task force specifically to study the problem of sex tourism and related offenses, but no new legislation has resulted.

During the first half of 1996, police recorded a total of 3,687 crimes (of all types) against children, an increase from 1,997 crimes in the first half of 1995. NGO's attribute the problem of exploitation of children to the lack of law enforcement rather than inadequate legislation.

Upwards of 20,600 children are known to be fully employed. Additional thousands of children are believed to be working in domestic service. There have been reports that rural children working as domestic servants in urban households—often given into service by poverty stricken parents—have been abused by their employers. Some of these children have reportedly been starved, beaten, sexually abused, and forced into prostitution. The Government does not have sufficient resources to protect these children from such exploitation (see Section 6.d.).

People With Disabilities.—The law does not mandate accessibility to buildings or government services for people with disabilities. The World Health Organization estimates that 7 percent of the population is disabled. Most disabled people who are unable to work are cared for by their families. The Department of Social Services runs eight vocational training schools for the physically and mentally disabled and sponsors a program of job training and job placement for graduates. The Government provides some financial support to NGO's assisting the disabled, subsidizes prosthetic devices and other medical aids for the disabled, makes some purchases from disabled suppliers, and has registered 74 schools and training institutions for the disabled run by NGO's. In December an act of Parliament was passed forbidding discrimination against any person on the grounds of his or her disability.

Indigenous People.—The indigenous people of Sri Lanka, known as Veddas, number less than a thousand. They prefer to maintain their isolated traditional way of life and are protected by the Constitution. There are no legal restrictions on their participation in the political or economic life of the nation. However, some Veddas complain that they are being forced off their traditional land and not allowed to live according to their own culture and traditions. For the first time in 1996, Veddas were allowed by the Government to participate in the U.N. Working Group on Indigenous People in Geneva, where they were able to air their grievances.

Religious Minorities.—Discrimination based on religious differences is much less common than discrimination based on ethnic group or caste. In general, the members of the various faiths tend to be tolerant of each other's religious beliefs. However, evangelical Christians have, on occasion, been harassed by Buddhist monks for their attempts to convert Buddhists to Christianity (see Section 2.c.).

In the northern part of the island, LTTE insurgents expelled some 46,000 Muslim inhabitants from their homes in 1990—virtually the entire Muslim population. The LTTE has expropriated Muslim homes, lands, and businesses and threatened Muslim families with death if they attempt to return.

National/Racial/Ethnic Minorities.—There are approximately 1 million Tamils of comparatively recent Indian origin living in Sri Lanka. About 85,000 of these people do not qualify for either Indian or Sri Lankan citizenship and face discrimination, especially in the allocation of government funds for education. Without national identity cards, they are vulnerable to arrest by the security forces. However, the Government has stated that none of these people will be forced to depart the country.

Tamils maintain that they have long been the victims of systematic discrimination in university education, government employment, and in other matters controlled by the Government. However, in recent years there has been little clear evidence of overt discrimination in university enrollment or government employment, although some groups continue to assert that it exists.

In January the Government established a parliamentary select committee to consider a "devolution" package originally proposed in August 1995, which is designed to devolve wide-ranging powers to local governments, thereby providing ethnic minorities greater autonomy in governing their local affairs. The devolution proposals were still being debated at year's end.

Section 6. Worker Rights

a. *The Right of Association.*—The Government respects the constitutional right of workers to establish labor unions. Any seven workers may form a union, adopt a charter, elect leaders, and publicize their views. About 75 percent cf the plantation work force is unionized. Approximately 50 to 60 percent of the nonagricultural work force (about 25 to 30 percent of the total work force) is also unionized. Most workers in large private firms are represented by unions, but those in small-scale agriculture and small businesses usually do not belong to unions.

Most large unions are affiliated with political parties and together play a prominent role in the political process. More than 30 labor unions have political affiliations, but there are also a small number of unaffiliated unions.

The Department of Labor registered 96 new unions and canceled the registration of 12 others. The Department of Labor is authorized by law to cancel the registration of any union that does not submit an annual report. That requirement is the only legal grounds for cancellation of registration.

All workers, other than civil servants and workers in "essential" services, have the right to strike. By law, workers may also lodge complaints with the Commissioner of Labor, a labor tribunal, or the Supreme Court to protect their rights. Before September 1994, the Government controlled strikes by declaring some industries to be essential under the ER. Subsequently, this practice largely ceased. However, the President retains the power to designate any industry as an essential service. The International Labor Organization (ILO) has pointed out to the Government that essential services should be limited to services where an interruption would endanger the life, personal safety, or health of the population.

Civil servants may collectively submit labor grievances to the Public Service Commission but have no legal grounds to strike. Nonetheless, government workers in the transportation, telecommunication, and ports sectors have staged brief strikes and other work actions in past years. In May government power sector workers walked out. The President declared the government-run power sector to be an essential service and ordered the workers back to work to end a 3-day nationwide power outage. During 1996 there were 187 strikes.

The law prohibits retribution against strikers in nonessential sectors. Employers may dismiss workers only for insubordination. Incompetence or low productivity are not grounds for dismissal.

Unions are free to affiliate with international bodies and many of them have done so.

In September 1995 the Ministry of Labor and Vocational Training released a "workers' charter" designed to provide a basis for legislation to strengthen worker rights. The proposed charter consolidates existing labor legislation and reaffirms the rights of workers to organize and bargain collectively. It also proposes new amendments to the Labor Law that would guarantee the right of workers to join unions, ensure that employers recognize and bargain with unions, establish a national wages commission to review minimum wages in all industries, ensure that all workers are covered under relevant labor laws, and establish a social security scheme. It is opposed by business leaders, largely because of the provisions that compel management to recognize all unions, collect union dues, and pay above-market wages. The charter had not become law by year's end.

b. *The Right to Organize and Bargain Collectively.*—The law provides for the right to collective bargaining, and it is widely practiced. Large firms may have employees in as many as 60 different unions. In enterprises that do not have unions, including those in the Export Processing Zones (EPZ's), work councils—composed of employees, employers, and often a public sector representative—are often the forums for labor/management negotiation. However, the councils are not mandatory outside the EPZ's and do not have the power to negotiate binding contracts.

The law currently does not require management to recognize or bargain with unions, and in some cases, employers have declined to recognize the unions in their factories. However, the law prohibits antiunion discrimination. Employers found guilty of such discrimination are required to reinstate workers fired for union activities but have the right to transfer them to different locations.

There are 95,464 workers employed in the EPZ's. Under the law, workers in the EPZ's have the same rights to join unions as other workers. However, few if any unions have been formed, in part because employers in the EPZ's offer higher wages and better working conditions. In the past, there have been allegations that the Government's Board of Investment (BOI), which manages the EPZ's, has discouraged union activity. Work councils in the EPZ's are chaired by the BOI and consist of equal delegations from labor and management.

In most instances, wage boards establish minimum wages and conditions of employment, except in the EPZ's, where wages and work conditions are set by the BOI.

c. *Prohibition of Forced or Compulsory Labor.*—Forced or compulsory labor is prohibited by law and is almost nonexistent. However, according to some reports, a few rural children are employed in debt bondage as domestic servants in urban households. The Government does not have sufficient resources to protect these children from such exploitation.

The LTTE continues to conscript high-school age children for work as cooks, messengers, and clerks, and in some cases, building fortifications. Children as young as 10 are said to be recruited and placed for 2 to 4 years in special schools that provide them with a mixture of LTTE ideology and formal education.

d. *Minimum Age for Employment of Children.*—The minimum age for employment is 15 years of age. However, the law permits the employment of younger children by their parents or guardians in limited agricultural work. It also permits employment in any school or institution for training purposes.

Persons under the age of 16 may not be employed in any public enterprise in which life or limb is endangered. Children are not employed in the EPZ's, the plantations, the garment industry, or any other export industry. About 85 percent of children below the age of 16 attend school. The law provides that the employment of such persons is permitted for not more than 1 hour on any day before school.

Despite legislation, some child labor still exists. A 1995 labor department survey found that 20,600 children between the ages of 10 and 14 were fully employed. This included 13,700 males and 6,900 females. Additional thousands of children were believed to be employed in domestic service, though this situation was undocumented.

A significant portion of employed children work outside their families. In addition to domestic service, regular employment of children occurs mainly in the informal sector and in family enterprises such as family farms, crafts, small trade establishments, eating houses, and repair shops. Children are also involved in the manufacture of coconut fiber products, fishing, wrapping tobacco, street trading, domestic service, and farming. Government inspections have been unable to eliminate these forms of child labor (see Section 5.).

e. *Acceptable Conditions of Work.*—The Department of Labor effectively enforces the minimum wage law. While there is no universal national minimum wage, some 38 wage boards set minimum wages and working conditions by sector and industry. According to the Statistics Department of the Labor Ministry, current minimum wage rates average $36 (2,000 rupees) per month in industry, commerce, and the service sector; and $1.40 (75 rupees) per day in agriculture. The minimum wage in the garment industry is $36 (2,000 rupees) per month. These minimum wages are insufficient to support a worker and the standard family of five, but the vast majority of families have more than one breadwinner.

Most permanent full-time workers are covered by laws that prohibit them from working regularly more than 45 hours per week (a 5½ day workweek). Such workers also receive 14 days of annual leave, 14 to 21 days of medical leave, and some 20 local holidays each year. Maternity leave is available for permanent and casual female workers. Employers must contribute 12 percent of a worker's wage to an employee's provident fund and 3 percent to an employee's trust fund. Employers who fail to comply may be fined.

Several laws protect the safety and health of industrial workers. However, the Department of Labor's small staff of inspectors is inadequate to enforce compliance with the laws. Workers have the statutory right to remove themselves from situations that endanger their health, but many workers are unaware of, or indifferent to, health risks, and fear that they will lose their jobs if they remove themselves.

APPENDIX

Appendix A.—Notes on Preparation of the Reports

We base the annual Country Reports on Human Rights Practices on information available from all sources, including American and foreign government officials, victims of human rights abuse, academic and congressional studies, and reports from the press, international organizations, and nongovernmental organizations (NGO's) concerned with human rights. We find particularly helpful, and make reference in most reports to, the role of NGO's, ranging from groups in a single country to those that concern themselves with human rights worldwide. While much of the information we use is already public, information on particular abuses frequently cannot be attributed, for obvious reasons, to specific sources.

By law, we must submit the reports to Congress by January 31. To comply, we provide guidance to United States diplomatic missions in July for submission of draft reports in September and October, which we update by year's end as necessary. Other offices in the Department of State provide contributions and the Bureau of Democracy, Human Rights, and Labor prepares a final draft. Because of the preparation time required, it is possible that yearend developments may not be fully reflected. We make every effort to include reference to major events or significant changes in trends.

We have attempted to make these country reports as comprehensive as space will allow, while taking care to make them objective and as uniform as possible in both scope and quality of coverage. We have given particular attention to attaining a high standard of consistency despite the multiplicity of sources and the obvious problems related to varying degrees of access to information, structural differences in political and social systems, and trends in world opinion regarding human rights practices in specific countries.

It is often difficult to evaluate the credibility of reports of human rights abuses. With the exception of some terrorist organizations, most opposition groups and certainly most governments deny that they commit human rights abuses and often go to great lengths to conceal any evidence of such acts. There are often few eyewitnesses to specific abuses, and they frequently are intimidated or otherwise prevented from reporting what they know. On the other hand, individuals and groups opposed to a particular government sometimes have powerful incentives to exaggerate or fabricate abuses, and some governments similarly distort or exaggerate abuses attributed to opposition groups. We have made every effort to identify those groups (e.g., government forces, terrorists, etc.) that are believed, based on all the evidence available, to have committed human rights abuses. Where credible evidence is lacking, we have tried to indicate why. Many governments that profess to oppose human rights abuses in fact secretly order or tacitly condone them or simply lack the will or the ability to control those responsible for them. Consequently, in judging a government's policy, it is important to look beyond statements of policy or intent in order to examine what in fact a government has done to prevent human rights abuses, including the extent to which it investigates, tries, and appropriately punishes those who commit such abuses. We continue to make every effort to do that in these reports.

To increase uniformity, the introductory section of each report contains a brief setting, indicating how the country is governed and providing the context for examining the country's human rights performance. A description of the political framework and the role of security and law enforcement agencies with respect to human rights is followed by a brief characterization of the economy. The setting concludes with an overview of human rights developments in the year under review, mentioning specific areas (e.g., torture, freedom of speech and press, discrimination) in which abuses and problems occurred.

We have continued the effort from previous years to expand reporting on human rights practices affecting women, children, and indigenous people. We discuss in the appropriate section of the report any abuses that are targeted specifically against women (e.g., rape or other violence perpetrated by governmental or organized opposition forces, or discriminatory laws or regulations). In Section 5, we continue to discuss socioeconomic discrimination; societal violence against women, children, or minority group members; and the efforts, if any, of governments to combat these problems.

With regard to governmental policies on the welfare of children, readers may wish to consult "The State of the World's Children 1997," published by the United Nations Children's Fund, which provides a wide range of data on health, education, nutrition, and rates of infant mortality and mortality under 5 years of age in some 145 countries, as well as information on the degree of progress that these countries are making in reducing the key mortality rate for those under age 5.

The following notes on specific categories of the report are not meant to be comprehensive descriptions of each category but to provide definitions of key terms used in the reports and to explain the organization of material within the format:

Political and Other Extrajudicial Killing.—Includes killings in which there is evidence of government instigation without due process of law or of political motivation by government or by opposition groups; also covers extrajudicial killings (e.g., deliberate, illegal, and excessive use of lethal force by the police, security forces, or other agents of the State whether against criminal suspects, detainees, prisoners, or others); excludes combat deaths and killings by common criminals, if the likelihood of political motivation can be ruled out (see also Section 1.g.). Although mentioned briefly here, deaths in detention due to official negligence are covered in detail in Section 1.c.

Disappearance.—Covers unresolved cases in which political motivation appears likely and in which the victims have not been found or perpetrators have not been identified; cases eventually classed as political killings are covered in the above category, those eventually identified as arrest or detention are covered under "Arbitrary Arrest, Detention, or Exile."

Torture and Other Cruel, Inhuman, or Degrading Treatment or Punishment.—Torture is here defined as an extremely severe form of cruel, inhuman, or degrading treatment or punishment, committed by or at the instigation of government forces or opposition groups, with specific intent to cause extremely severe pain or suffering, whether mental or physical. Discussion concentrates on actual practices, not on whether they fit any precise definition, and includes use of physical and other force that may fall short of torture but which is cruel, inhuman, or degrading. This section also covers prison conditions, including whether conditions meet minimum international standards, and deaths in custody due to negligence by government officials.

Arbitrary Arrest, Detention, or Exile.—Covers cases in which detainees, including political detainees, are held in official custody without charges or, if charged, are denied a public preliminary judicial hearing within a reasonable period. Also discusses whether, and under what circumstances, governments exile citizens.

Denial of Fair Public Trial.—Briefly describes the court system and evaluates whether there is an independent judiciary and whether trials are both fair and public (failure to hold any trial is noted in the category above); includes discussion of "political prisoners" (political detainees are covered above), defined as those imprisoned for essentially political beliefs or nonviolent acts of dissent or expression, regardless of the actual charge.

Arbitrary Interference With Privacy, Family, Home, or Correspondence.—Discusses the "passive" right of the individual to noninterference by the State; includes the right to receive foreign publications, for example, while the right to publish is discussed under "Freedom of Speech and Press"; includes the right to be free from coercive population control measures, including coerced abortion and involuntary sterilization, but does not include cultural or traditional practices, such as female genital mutilation, which are addressed in Section 5.

Use of Excessive Force and Violations of Humanitarian Law in Internal Conflicts.—An optional subsection for use in describing abuses that occur in countries experiencing significant internal armed conflict. Includes indiscriminate, nonselective killings arising from excessive use of force, e.g., by police in putting down demonstrations, or by the shelling of villages (deliberate, targeted killing would be discussed in Section 1.a.). Also includes abuses against civilian noncombatants. For reports in which use of this section would be inappropriate, i.e., in which there is no significant internal conflict, lethal use of excessive force by security forces (which is herein defined as a form of extrajudicial killing) is discussed in Section 1.a.; nonlethal excessive force in Section 1.c.

Freedom of Speech and Press.—Evaluates whether these freedoms exist and describes any direct or indirect restrictions. Includes discussion of academic freedom.

Freedom of Peaceful Assembly and Association.—Evaluates the ability of individuals and groups (including political parties) to exercise these freedoms. Includes the ability of trade associations, professional bodies, and similar groups to maintain relations or affiliate with recognized international bodies in their fields. The right of labor to associate and to organize and bargain collectively is discussed under Section 6, Worker Rights (see Appendix B).

Freedom of Religion.—Discusses whether the constitution or laws provide for the right of citizens of whatever religious belief to worship free of government interference and whether the government respects that right. Includes the freedom to publish religious documents in foreign languages; addresses the treatment of foreign clergy and whether religious belief affects membership in a ruling party or a career in government.

Freedom of Movement Within the Country, Foreign Travel, Emigration, and Repatriation.—Includes discussion of forced resettlement; "refugees" may refer to persons displaced by civil strife or natural disaster as well as persons who are "refugees" within the meaning of the Refugee Act of 1980, i.e., persons with a "well-founded fear of persecution" in their country of origin or, if stateless, in their country of habitual residence, on account of race, religion, nationality, membership in a particular social group, or political opinion.

Respect for Political Rights: The Right of Citizens to Change Their Government.—Discusses the extent to which citizens have freedom of political choice and have the legal right and ability in practice to change the laws and officials that govern them; assesses whether elections are free and fair.

Governmental Attitude Regarding International and Nongovernmental Investigation of Alleged Violations of Human Rights.—Discusses whether the government permits the free functioning of local human rights groups (including the right to investigate and publish their findings on alleged human rights abuses) and whether they are subject to reprisal by government or other forces. Also discusses whether the government grants access to and cooperates with outside entities (including foreign human rights organizations, international organizations, and foreign governments) interested in human rights developments in the country.

Discrimination Based on Race, Sex, Religion, Disability, Language, or Social Status.—Every report contains a subheading on Women, Children, and People With Disabilities. As appropriate, some reports also include subheadings on Indigenous People, Religious Minorities, and National/Racial/Ethnic Minorities. Discrimination against groups not fitting one of the above subheadings is discussed in the introductory paragraphs of Section 5. In this section we address discrimination and abuses not discussed elsewhere in the report, focusing on laws, regulations, or state practices that are inconsistent with equal access to housing, employment, education, health care, or other governmental benefits by members of specific groups. (Abuses by government or opposition forces, such as killing, torture and other violence, or restriction of voting rights or free speech targeted against specific groups would be discussed under the appropriate preceding sections.) Societal violence against women, e.g., "dowry deaths," wife beating, rape, trafficking in women, and government tolerance of such abuse, is discussed in this section under the subheading on women. We also discuss under this subheading the extent to which the law provides for, and the government enforces, equality of economic opportunity for women. Similarly, we discuss violence or other abuse against children under that subheading. Because female genital mutilation is most often performed on children, we discuss it under that subheading.

Worker Rights.—See Appendix B.

Appendix B.—Reporting on Worker Rights

The Generalized System of Preferences Renewal Act of 1984 requires reporting on worker rights in GSP beneficiary countries. It states that internationally recognized worker rights include "(A) the right of association; (B) the right to organize and bargain collectively; (C) a prohibition on the use of any form of forced or compulsory labor; (D) a minimum age for the employment of children; and (E) acceptable conditions of work with respect to minimum wages, hours of work, and occupational safety and health." All five aspects of worker rights are discussed in each report in a final section under the heading "Worker Rights." The discussion of worker rights considers not only laws and regulations but also their practical implementation, taking into account the following additional guidelines:

A. "The right of association" has been defined by the International Labor Organization (ILO) to include the right of workers and employers to establish and join organizations of their own choosing without previous authorization; to draw up their own constitutions and rules, elect their representatives, and formulate their programs; to join in confederations and affiliate with international organizations; and to be protected against dissolution or suspension by administrative authority.

The right of association includes the right of workers to strike. While strikes may be restricted in essential services (i.e., those services the interruption of which would endanger the life, personal safety, or health of a significant portion of the population) and in the public sector, these restrictions must be offset by adequate guarantees to safeguard the interests of the workers concerned (e.g., machinery for mediation and arbitration; due process; and the right to judicial review of all legal actions). Reporting on restrictions affecting the ability of workers to strike generally includes information on any procedures that may exist for safeguarding workers' interests.

B. "The right to organize and bargain collectively" includes the right of workers to be represented in negotiating the prevention and settlement of disputes with employers; the right to protection against interference; and the right to protection against acts of antiunion discrimination. Governments should promote machinery for voluntary negotiations between employers and workers and their organizations. Reporting on the right to organize and bargain collectively includes descriptions of the extent to which collective bargaining takes place and the extent to which unions, both in law and practice, are effectively protected against antiunion discrimination.

C. "Forced or compulsory labor" is defined as work or service exacted from any person under the menace of penalty and for which the person has not volunteered. "Work or service" does not apply in instances in which obligations are imposed to undergo education or training. "Menace of penalty" includes loss of rights or privileges as well as penal sanctions. The ILO has exempted the following from its definition of forced labor: compulsory military service, normal civic obligations, certain forms of prison labor, emergencies, and minor communal services. Forced labor should not be used as a means of (1) mobilizing and using labor for purposes of economic development; (2) racial, social, national, or religious discrimination; (3) political coercion or education, or as a punishment for holding or expressing political views or views ideologically opposed to the established political, social, or economic system; (4) labor discipline; or (5) as a punishment for having participated in strikes. Constitutional provisions concerning the obligation of citizens to work do not violate this right so long as they do not take the form of legal obligations enforced by sanctions and are consistent with the principle of "freely chosen employment."

D. "Minimum age for employment of children" concerns the effective abolition of child labor by raising the minimum age for employment to a level consistent with the fullest physical and mental development of young people. In addition, young people should not be employed in hazardous conditions or at night.

E. "Acceptable conditions of work" refers to the establishment and maintenance of machinery, adapted to national conditions, that provides for minimum working standards, i.e., wages that provide a decent living for workers and their families; working hours that do not exceed 48 hours per week, with a full 24-hour rest day; a specified annual paid holiday; and minimum conditions for the protection of the safety and health of workers. Differences in levels of economic development are taken into account in the formulation of internationally recognized labor standards. For example, many ILO standards concerning working conditions permit flexibility in their scope and coverage. They may also permit countries a wide choice in their implementation, including progressive implementation, by enabling countries to accept a standard in part or subject to specified exceptions. Countries are expected to take steps over time to achieve the higher levels specified in such standards. It should be understood, however, that this flexibility applies only to internationally recognized standards concerning working conditions. No flexibility is permitted concerning the acceptance of the basic principles contained in human rights standards, i.e., freedom of association, the right to organize and bargain collectively, the prohibition of forced labor, and the absence of discrimination.

Appendix C.—International Human Rights Conventions
[See footnote references at end of table]

Country	A	B	C	D	E	F	G	H	I	J	K	L	M	N	O	P	Q	R	S	T	U	V	W
Afghanistan	P			P		P	P	P		P	P	P	P	P	P						S	P	P
Albania*	P	P	P	P	P	P	P	P	P	P	P		P	P	P	P		P	P	P	P	P	P
Algeria	P	P	P	P	P	P	P	P			P	P	P	P	P	P		P	P	P	P	P	P
Andora					P	P		P														P	
Angola		P			P	P	P			P		P		P	P	P		P		P			P
Antigua & Barbuda	P	P	P	P	P	P	P			P	P	P	P		P	P		P	P	P	P	P	P
Argentina		P	P	P	P	P	P	P		P	P	P	P	P	P	P	P	P	P	P	P	P	P
Armenia				P									P	P	P	P		P	P	P	P	P	P
Australia	P	P	P	P	P	P	P			P	P	P	P	P	P	P		P	P	P	P	P	P
Austria	P	P	P	P	P	P	P		P	P	P	P	P	P	P	P		P	P	P	P	P	P
Azerbaijan		P	P	P	P									P	P	P		P			P		P
Bahamas	P	P		P	P	P	P			P	P	P	P		P			P	P	P			P
Bahrain	P	P		P		P	P				P		P					P	P	P			P
Bangladesh	P	P	P		P	P	P	P			P	P	P					P	P	P	P		P
Barbados	P	P	P	P	P	P	P			P	P	P	P	P	P		P	P	P	P	P		P
Belarus	P	P	P	P	P	P	P	P		P	P		P	P	P			P	P	P	P	P	P
Belgium	P	P	P	P	P	P	P	P	P	P	P	P	P	P	P	P		P	P	P	P	S	P
Belize	1	P	P		P	P	P				1	P	P	1	1	P		P	P	P	P	P	P
Benin	2	P	P		P	P						P	S	P	P	P		P	P	P	P	P	P
Bhutan*													S								P		P
Bolivia	P		P	S	P	P	P			P	P	P	P	P	P	P	P	P	P	P	S		P
Bosnia & Herz.	P	P	P	P	P			P		P	P		P	P	P	P		P	P	P	P	P	P
Botswana	1				P	P					1		P		P			P	P				P
Brazil	P	P		P	P	P	P			P	P	P	P	P	P	P		P	P	P	P	P	P
Brunei*	1				P	P				1	1							P	P				P
Bulgaria	2	P	P	P	P	P	P	P	P	P	P		P	P	P	P		P	P	P			P
Burkina Faso		P	P	P	P	P	P	P					P		P			P	P	P			P
Burma	P	P	P			P	P	S	S											P			P
Burundi		P	P		P	P				P		P	P	P	P			P	P		P	P	P
Cambodia		P		P	P	P					P		P	P	P	P					P	P	P
Cameroon	P	P	P		P	P	P	P			P	P	P	P	P	P		P	P	P	P	P	P
Canada	P		P	P		P	P			P	P	P	P	P	P	P		P	P	P	P	P	P
Cape Verde		P			P	P	P				P		P	P	P	P		P	P	P	P	P	P
Cen. African Rep.	2	P	P		P	P	P			P	P	P	P	P	P	P		P	P	P	P	P	P
Chad		P	P		P	P	P					P	P	P	P	P				P	P	P	P
Chile	P	P		P		P	P			P	P		P	P	P	P	P	P	P	P	P	P	P
China			P		P	P				P	P		P			P		P	P	P	P	P	P
China (Taiwan only)*	P			P						P	P		P	S	S			P	P	P	P	P	P
Colombia		P	P	P	P	P	P			P		P	P	P	P	P	P	P	P	P	P		P
Comoros		P	P		P	P	P					P						P	P	P			P
Congo	2	P	P			P	P	P		P	P		P	P	P	P		P	P	P			P
Costa Rica		P	P	P	P	P	P			P		P	P	P	P	P	P	P	P	P	P	P	P
Cote D'Ivoire	2	P	P	P	P	P	P			P	P	P	P	P	P	P		P	P	P	P	P	P
Croatia	P	P	P	P	P	P	P	P	P	P	P		P	P	P	P		P	P	P	P	P	P
Cuba	P	P		P	P	P	P	P		P	P	P	P		P		P	P		P			P
Cyprus	P	P	P	P	P	P	P	P	P	P	P	P	P	P	P	P		P	P	P	P	P	P
Czech Republic	2	P	P	P	P	P	P	P	P	P	P		P	P	P	P		P	P	P	P	P	P
Denmark	P	P	P	P	P	P	P	S	P	P	P	P	P	P	P	P		P	P	P	P	P	P
Djibouti		P	P		P	P	P	P			P	P						P	P	P			P
Dominica	P	P	P		P	P	P			1	P		P	P	P			P	P	P			P
Dom Republic		P	P	S	P	P	P			P	P	P	P	P	P	P	P	P	P	P	S		P
Ecuador	P	P	P	P	P	P	P	P		P	P	P	P	P	P	P	P	P	P	P	P	P	P
Egypt	P	P	P	P	P	P	P	P			P	P	P	P	P	P		P	P	P	P	P	P
El Salvador				P		P	P			S	S	P	P	P	P	P	P	P	P	P			P
Equatorial Guinea					P	P							P	P	P		P	P	P				P
Eritrea																					P		P
Estonia	2			P				P			P		P	P				P	P	P	P		P
Ethiopia	P		P	P	P	P	P			P	P		P	P	P	P		P	P	P	P	P	P
Fiji	P	P		P	P	P	P				P	P	P		P						P		P
Finland	P	P	P	P	P	P	P	P	P	P	P	P	P	P	P	P		P	P	P	P	P	P

Appendix C.—International Human Rights Conventions—Continued

[See footnote references at end of table]

Country	A	B	C	D	E	F	G	H	I	J	K	L	M	N	O	P	Q	R	S	T	U	V	W
France	P	P	P	P	P	P	P	P	P	P	P	P	P	P	P	P		P	P	P	P	P	P
Gabon		P	P	P	P	P	P			P		P	P	P	P	P			P	P	P	S	S
Gambia*	1			P		P	P				1		P	P	P	P			P	P	P	S	P
Georgia				P		P	P							P	P				P	P	P	P	P
Germany	P	P	P	P	P	P	P		P	P	P	P	P	P	P	P		P	P	P	P	P	P
Ghana	2	P	P	P	P	P	P			P	P	P	P		P			P	P	P	P	P	P
Greece	P	P	P	P	P	P	P		P	P	P	P		P	P	P		P	P	P	P	P	P
Grenada	1	P		1	P	P	P			1	1	P	S	P	P		P			P			P
Guatemala	P	P	P	P	P	P				P	P	P	P	P	P	P	P	P	P	P	P	P	P
Guinea	P	P	P		P	P	P	P		P	P	P	P	P	P	P			P	P	P	P	P
Guinea-Bissau		P			P	P	P					P			P	P			P	P	P		P
Guyana	1	P	P		P	P	P				1	P	P	P	P				P	P	P	P	P
Haiti	2	P	P	P	P	P	P	P		P	P	P	P	P		P	P			P			P
Holy See*					P	P	P						P			P			P	P			P
Honduras				P	P	P	P	P				P		S	P	P	P	P	P	P	P		P
Hungary	P	P	P	P	P	P	P	P	P	P	P		P	P	P	P			P	P	P	P	P
Iceland		P	P	P	P	P	P		P	P	P	P	P	P	P				P	P	P	S	P
India	P	P		P		P	P	P		P	P		P	P	P					P			P
Indonesia		P			P	P	P			P										P	P	S	S
Iran	S	P		P		P	P	S			P	P	P	P	P	P			S	S			S
Iraq	P	P		P	P	P	P			P	P	P	P	P	P			P		P			P
Ireland	P	P	P	P	P	P	P		P	P	P	S	P	P	P	P		P	S	S	P	S	P
Israel	P	P	P	P	P	P	P	P		P	P	P	P	P	P	P		P	P		P	P	P
Italy	P	P	P	P	P	P	P	P	P	P	P	P	P	P	P	P		P	P	P	P	P	P
Jamaica	P	P	P	P	P	P	P			P	P	P	P	P	P	P	P		P	P			P
Japan		P	P		P	P	P	P		P			P	P	P	P				P			P
Jordan	P	P		P	P	P	P	P		P	P	P	P	P	P				P	P	P	P	P
Kazakhstan					P	P													P	P			P
Kenya		P			P	P	P					P		P	P	P		P		P			P
Kiribati*	1				P	P				1	1			1	1	1							P
Korea, Dem. Peo.*				P		P	P						P	P	P				P				P
Korea, Rep. of				P		P	P	P		P			P	P	P	P			P	P	P	P	P
Kuwait	P	P	P	P	P	P	P				P	P	P	P	P				P	P	P		P
Kyrgyzstan		P	P		P	P	P							P	P	P		P	P	P	P		P
Laos		P		P		P	P	P		P	P		P						P	P	P		P
Latvia	2		P	P	P	P	P	P	S	P	P	P	P	P	P				P	P	P	P	P
Lebanon		P			P	P	P			P			P	P	P					P			P
Lesotho	P	P	P	P	P	P	P			P	P	P	P	P	S	P			P	P			P
Liberia	P	P		P	P	P	P	S		S	S	P	P	S	S	P		P	P	P			P
Libya	P	P		P	P	P	P	P		P	P	P	P	P	P			P	P	P	P	P	P
Liechtenstein*				P		P	P		P							P			P		P	P	P
Lithuania				P					P					P	P				P	P	P		P
Luxembourg		P	P	P	P	P	P	P	P	P	P	P	P	P	P	P		P	P	P	P	P	P
Macedonia	2			P		P	P		S	P	P	P	P	P	P				P	P	P		P
Madagascar	P	P			P	P	P			P	P	P	P	P		P			P	P	P		P
Malawi	P		S		P	P	P	P			P	P							P	P	P		P
Malaysia		P		P	P	P	P				P	P								P			P
Maldives*				P	P	P	P						P						P	P	P		P
Mali	P	P	P		P	P	P	P		P	P	P	P	P	P			P	P	P	P		P
Malta	P	P	P		P	P				P	P	P	P	P	P			P	P	P	P	P	P
Marshall Isl.*																							P
Mauritania	P	P	P			P	P	P		P	P		P			P		P	P	P			P
Mauritius	P	P		P	P	P	P	P		P	P	P	P	P	P				P	P	P	P	P
Mexico	P	P	P	P		P	P	P		P	P	P	P	P	P		P		P	P	P	P	P
Micronesia*																				P			P
Moldova				P		P			S	P		P	P	P					P	P	P	P	P
Monaco*	P			P	P	P				P											P		P
Mongolia	P		P	P	P	P	P			P	P	P	P	P	P				P	P	P		P
Morocco	P	P		P	P	P	P	P		P	P	P	P	P	P	P			S	S	P	P	P
Mozambique				P		P	P							P		P			P				P

Appendix C.—International Human Rights Conventions—Continued

[See footnote references at end of table]

Country	A	B	C	D	E	F	G	H	I	J	K	L	M	N	O	P	Q	R	S	T	U	V	W
Namibia				P		P	P						P	P					P	P	P	P	P
Nauru*																							P
Nepal				P		P	P			P	P		P	P	P					P	P	P	P
Netherlands	P	P	P	P	P	P	P		P	P	P	P	P	P	P	P		P	P	P	P	P	P
New Zealand	P	P		P		P	P			P	P	P	P	P	P				P	P	P	P	P
Nicaragua	P	P	P	P	P	P	P			P	P	P	P	P	P		P	P	S	S	P	S	P
Niger	P	P			P	P	P	P		P	P	P	P	P	P			P	P	P	P		P
Nigeria	P	P	P		P	P	P			P	P	P	P	P	P				P	P	P	S	P
Niue																							P
Norway	P	P	P	P	P	P	P	P	P	P	P	P	P	P	P			P	P	P	P	P	P
Oman*						P	P												P	P			
Pakistan	P	P	P	P	P	P	P	P		P	P	P	P						S	S	P		P
Palau						P	P												P	P			P
Panama		P	P	P	P	P	P						P	P	P	P	P		P	P	P	P	P
Papua New Guinea	P	P		P	P	P	P			P			P	P						P			P
Paraguay			P	S	P	P	P			P		P		P	P	P	P		P	P	P	P	P
Peru		P	P	P	P	P	P			P	S	P	P	P	P	P	P		P	P	P	P	P
Philippines	P	P	P	P	P	P	P	P		P	P	P	P	P	P				S	P	P	P	P
Poland	2	P	P	P	P	P	P	P	P	P	P	P	P	P	P			P	P	P	P	P	P
Portugal	2	P	P		P	P	P	P	P		P	P	P	P	P	P			P	P	P	P	P
Qatar						P	P						P						P				
Romania	P	P	P	P	P	P	P	P	P	P	P		P	P	P	P		P	S	S	P	P	P
Russia	P	P	P	P	P	P	P	P	S	P	P	P	P	P	P	P		P	P	P	P	P	P
Rwanda			P	P	P	P	P					P	P	P	P	P		P	P	P	P		P
San Marino		P		P	P	P	P		P		P			P	P				P	P	P		P
Sao Tome & Prin.			P		P	P	P							S	S	P			P		P	S	P
Saudi Arabia	P	P		P		P	P				P	P							P				P
Senegal	2	P	P	P	P	P	P	P		P	P	P	P	P	P	P			P	P	P	P	P
Seychelles	2	P	P	P		P	P	P		1	P	P	P	P	P				P	P	P	P	P
Sierra Leone	P	P	P		P	P	P			P	P	P	P		P				P	P	P	S	P
Singapore		P		P		P	P	P			P	P							P	P			P
Slovak Republic	2	P	P	P	P	P	P	P	P	P	P		P	P	P			P	P	P	P	P	P
Slovenia		P	P	P	P	P	P	P	P	P	P		P	P	P	P		P	P	P	P	P	P
Solomon Isl.	P	P			P					P	P		1		1	P			P	P	S		P
Somalia		P			P	P						P	P	P	P						P		P
South Africa*	P				P	P	P			S			S	S	S	P			P	P	P	S	P
Spain	P	P	P	P	P	P	P	P	P	P	P	P	P	P	P			P	P	P	P	P	P
Sri Lanka	P	P		P	P	P	P	P			P		P	P	P					P	P	P	P
St. Kitts/Nevis*	1					P	P			1	1								P	P	P		P
St. Lucia	P	P	P	1	P	P	P			1	P	P	P	1		1			P	P	P		P
St. Vincent*	P		P		P	P				1	P		P	P	P				P	P	P		P
Sudan	P	P			P	P	P				P		P	P	P	P			P	P		S	P
Suriname	2	P	P		P	P	P			1	P		P	P	P	P	P		P	P			P
Swaziland	1	P	P		P		P			P	1	P	P		P				P	P			P
Sweden	P	P	P	P	P	P	P		P	P	P	P	P	P	P	P		P	P	P	P	P	S
Switzerland	P	P	P		P	P	P	P		P	P	P	P	P	P			P	P	P	S	P	S
Syria	P	P		P	P	P	P	P			P		P	P	P			P					P
Tajikistan*		P	P		P	P	P						P			P		P	P	P	P	P	P
Tanzania	P	P		P	P	P	P			P	P	P	P	P	P				P	P	P		P
Thailand		P			P	P					P		P		P						P		P
Togo	2	P	P	P	P	P	P	P			P		P	P	P	P		P	P	P	P	P	P
Tonga*	1			P		P	P	P			1	1	P										P
Trinidad & Tobago	P	P	P	P	P	P	P			P	P	P	P	P	P				P		P		P
Tunisia	P	P	P	P	P	P	P			P	P	P	P	P	P			P	P	P	P	P	P
Turkey	P	S	P	P	P	P	P		P	P	P	P	S		P				P	P	P		P
Turkmenistan						P	P						P			P			P	P			P
Tuvalu*	1					P	P			1	1												P
Uganda	P	P		P	P	P	P			P	P	P	P	P	P				P	P	P	P	P
Ukraine	P	P	P	P	P	P	P	P	S	P	P	P	P	P	P			P	P	P	P	P	P
United Arab Em		P			P	P							P						P	P			

Appendix C.—International Human Rights Conventions—Continued

[See footnote references at end of table]

Country	A	B	C	D	E	F	G	H	I	J	K	L	M	N	O	P	Q	R	S	T	U	V	W
United Kingdom	P	P	P	P	P	P	P		P	P	P	P	P	P	P	P			S	S	P	P	P
United States	P			P		P	P			P	P	P	P	S	P	S	S		S	S	S	P	S
Uruguay			P	P	P	P	P		S		P	P	P	P	P	P	P	P	P	P	P	P	P
Uzbekistan						P	P						P		P				P		P	P	
Vanuatu*						P	P				1								P	P	P		P
Venezuela		P	P	P	P	P	P	P		P		P	P	P	P	P	P	P			P	P	P
Vietnam*		P		P	P	P	P						P	P	P				P		P		P
Western Samoa*						P	P									P			P	P	P		P
Yemen	P	P	P	P	P	P	P	P		P		P	P	P	P	P			P	P	P	P	P
Zaire		P		P	P	P	P			P	P		P	P	P	P			P		P	P	P
Zambia	P	P			P	P			P	P	P	P	P	P			P	P	P	P			P
Zimbabwe	1		P		P	P				P			P	P	P	P			P	P	P		P

P=Party   S=Signatory   *=non-ILO member.
1 Based on general declaration concerning treaty obligations prior to independence.
2 Party to 1926 Convention only.

INTERNATIONAL HUMAN RIGHTS CONVENTIONS

A) Convention to Suppress the Slave Trade and Slavery of September 25,1926, as amended by the Protocol of December 7, 1953.

B) Convention Concerning Forced Labor of June 28, 1930 (ILO Convention 29).

C) Convention Concerning Freedom of Association and Protection of the Right to Organize of July 9, 1948 (ILO Convention 87).

D) Convention on the Prevention and Punishment of the Crime of Genocide of December 9, 1948.

E) Convention Concerning the Application of the Principles of the Right to Organize and Bargan Collectively of July 1, 1949 (ILO Convention 98).

F) Geneva Convention Relative to the Treatment of Prisoners of War of August 12, 1949.

G) Geneva Convention Relative to the Protection of Civilian Persons in Time of War of August 12, 1949.

H) Convention for the Suppression of the Traffic in Persons and of the Exploitation of the Prostitution of Others of March 21, 1950.

I) European Convention for the Protection of Human Rights and Fundamental Freedoms of November 4, 1950.

J) Convention on the Political Rights of Women of March 31, 1953.

K) Supplementary Convention on the Abolition of Slavery, the Slave Trade, and Institutions and Practices Similar to Slavery of September 7, 1956.

L) Convention Concerning the Abolition of Forced Labor of June 25, 1957 (ILO Convention 105).

M) International Convention on the Elimination of All Forms of Racial Discrimination of December 21, 1965.

N) International Covenant on Civil and Political Rights of December 16, 1966.

O) International Covenant on Economic, Social and Cultural Rights of December 16, 1966.

P) Protocol Relating to the Status Of Refugees of January 31, 1967.

Q) American Convention on Human Rights of November 22, 1969.

R) Convention Concerning Minimum Age for Admission to Employment of June 26, 1973 (ILO Convention 138).

S) Protocol Additional to the Geneva Conventions of August 12, 1949, and Relating to the Protection of Victims of International Armed Conflicts (Protocol I), of June 8, 1977.

T) Protocol Additional to the Geneva Conventions of August 12, 1949, and Relating to the Protection of Victims of Non-International Armed Conflicts (Protocol II), of June 8, 1977.

U) Convention on the Elimination of All Forms of Discrimination Against Women of December 18, 1979.

V) Convention Against Torture and Other Cruel, Inhuman or Degrading Treatment or Punishment of December 10, 1984.

W) Convention on the Rights of the Child of November 20, 1989.

Appendix D.—Explanation of Statistical Table

A table listing the amounts of U.S. bilateral assistance for Fiscal Year 1995 is provided in Appendix E. Fiscal Year 1996 data was not available at the time this publication went to print.

Key Abbreviations

DA—	Development assistance provided under the Functional Development Assistance Program and the Development Fund for Africa.
ESF—	Assistance provided under the Economic Support Fund.
FMF—	Foreign Military Finance Programs, loan and grant assistance programs.
IMET—	International Military Education and Training Program.
NARCS—	Assistance provided under the International Narcotics Control Program of the Department of State.
Peace Corps—	Assistance provided by the Peace Corps.
PL 480—	Assistance provided under Titles II and III of the Food for Peace legislation.
Other Econ—	Primarily includes Special Assistance Initiative funding for Eastern Europe and Multilateral Assistance Initiative funding for the Philippines.
SAI/NIS—	Special Assistance Initiatives/New Independent States.

Appendix E.—FY 1995 U.S. Economic and Military Assistance—Actual Obligations

(Data for FY 1996 U.S. Economic and Military Assistance was not available at the time this publication went to print)

[Dollars in thousands]

	DA	ESF	SA/NIS	PL 480 Title II	PL 480 Title III	NARCS	Peace Corps	Other ECON	FMF loans	FMF grants	IMET	Total
AFRICA												
Angola	14,821			44,750								44,750
Benin	2,648			2,491			1,516				161	18,989
Botswana	16			2,279			2,583				440	7,950
Burkina Faso				14,802			748					15,566
Burundi	4,996										44	5,040
Cameroon							3,039					3,039
Cape Verde	800			4,869			1,003				75	6,747
CAR	2,267						1,570				186	4,023
Chad	1,970			1,406			1,264				62	4,702
Comoros				975			449					1,424
Congo	700						771				150	1,621
Cote D'Ivoire				189			1,186				120	1,495
Djibouti				1,719							125	1,844
Eq. Guinea				161								161
Eritrea	3,820			5,653			854				200	10,527
Ethiopia	24,264			53,840	40,000		962				248	119,314
Gabon							2,733					2,733
Gambia	1,556			2,061			1,363					4,980
Ghana	27,900	780		7,361			2,250				222	38,513
Guinea	16,423			32			2,016				155	18,626
Guinea Bissau	4,150			859			1,159				75	6,243
Kenya	14,650			7,748			3,044				283	25,725
Lesotho	3,948			3,324			2,246				32	9,450
Liberia				51,643								51,643
Madagascar	25,250			3,080			945					29,275
Malawi	33,338			20,150			1,667				125	55,280
Mali	27,779						3,128				163	31,070
Mauritania				1,270			1,284					2,554
Mauritius				64								64
Mozambique	26,768			24,458	13,000		1,805				138	64,364
Namibia	6,800						2,458				126	8,731
Niger	11,950			272			2,458				189	14,869
Nigeria	2,377						429					2,806
Rwanda	5,748	3,900		157,040							50	166,738
Sao Tome	300						794				29	1,123
Senegal	17,540			1,454			3,230				598	22,822

Seychelles							10	373
Sierra Leone	450						52	8,714
Somalia	5,018			8,212				14,778
South Africa	99,979			9,760			297	100,276
Sudan				30,067			57	13,378
Swaziland	10,464			1,746			81	29,459
Tanzania	27,662							3,956
Togo				2,117		1,111	138	55,935
Uganda	44,250			10,439		1,716	92	28,813
Zambia	19,789			7,800		1,839	232	19,212
Zimbabwe	17,650					1,109		
						1,132		
						1,330		
CENTRAL AND SOUTH AMERICA								
Argentina							109	713
Bahamas	2,599				700	969	13	3,622
Belize	16,874	16,350		20,095	1,892		54	69,808
Bolivia					1,000		368	1,100
Brazil						1,793	100	1,913
Chile		850			16,000		120	27,438
Colombia	2,585			1,124		1,927	588	5,704
Costa Rica	8,361	869		3,755	500	1,971	68	15,169
Dominican Rep.	8,062			221		2,480	213	11,556
Ecuador	23,681	38,991		15,393	2,100	643	293	77,626
El Salvador	15,412	4,150	13,907	743		2,593	404	39,648
Guatemala	1,651			34,090		325		5,816
Guyana	56,539			7,578			97	186,718
Haiti	14,265	83,054				2,195	35	29,363
Honduras	9,814				600	1,925	325	12,513
Jamaica				4,275			174	4,675
Mexico	17,706	4,985		4,944	4,800	1,343	400	33,778
Nicaragua	2,893	4,964		64		1,276	425	9,558
Panama				58,576		3,147	134	3,345
Paraguay	17,780	37,300			15,000		325	128,981
Peru						413	28	441
Suriname						1,430	143	1,573
Uruguay					500		250	750
Venezuela								
EAST ASIA AND THE PACIFIC								
Burma	100							100
Cambodia	15,993	19,500		6,622		624	273	42,388
China						1,606		624
Fiji								1,606
Indonesia	55,040			3,776				58,816
Kiribati						472		472
Korea, Rep. of							10	10
Laos					2,200			2,200

1507

Appendix E.—FY 1995 U.S. Economic and Military Assistance—Actual Obligations—Continued

(Data for FY 1996 U.S. Economic and Military Assistance was not available at the time this publication went to print)

[Dollars in thousands]

	DA	ESF	SA/NIS	PL 480 Title II	PL 480 Title III	NARCS	Peace Corps	Other ECON	FMF loans	FMF grants	IMET	Total
Malaysia											504	504
Micronesia							2,193					2,193
Mongolia		3,500					915				98	12,332
Papua N Guinea	7,819						1,535				125	1,660
Philippines	35,941			14,132			1,605				1,193	52,871
Singapore											20	20
Solomon Is.							1,226				101	1,327
Thailand							3,077				999	5,876
Tonga						1,800	959					1,009
Vanuatu											50	50
Western Samoa											48	48
EUROPE												
Albania			29,956				1,205				226	31,387
Armenia			51,523				1,003					52,526
Azerbaijan			9,848									9,848
Baltics							2,399					2,399
Belarus			2,263								94	2,357
Bosnia-Herzegovina			12,640									12,640
Bulgaria			37,388				1,137				400	38,925
Croatia			12,345								105	12,450
Czech Republic			18,037				1,497				500	20,034
Estonia			2,368								108	3,254
Georgia			39,273							706	82	39,355
Greece											48	48
Hungary	19,600	19,600	23,727				2,285				796	26,808
Ireland												39,200
Kazakhstan			38,443				1,748				97	40,288
Kyrgystan			23,297				943				60	24,300
Latvia			6,326							706	197	7,229
Lithuania	485		11,767							706	196	13,154
Malta											58	58
Moldova			10,518				864				106	11,488
Poland			81,576				3,158			1,000	747	86,481
Portugal											500	500
Romania			39,599				1,296				460	41,355
Russia			282,307				2,724		(229,635)		413	285,444

1508

Slovak Rep.	......	......	27,597	......	......	......	253	29,118
Slovenia	......	......	3,417	......	......	......	150	3,567
Spain	......	......	......	......	......	......	52	52
The FYRO Macedonia	......	......	13,512	......	......	......	125	13,637
Tajikistan	......	......	8,401	......	......	......	......	8,401
Turkey	......	165,709	......	400	......	(328,959)	1,102	167,211
Turkmenistan	......	......	4,382	57,964	......	......	118	63,425
Ukraine	......	......	151,499	......	2,280	......	707	154,486
Uzbekistan	......	......	10,561	......	954	......	95	11,610
NEAR EAST								
Algeria	......	......	......	......	......	......	74	74
Bahrain	......	......	......	......	......	......	75	75
Egypt	......	974,077	......	......	......	......	1,000	2,275,077
Israel	......	1,200,000	......	......	......	......	......	3,000,000
Jordan	5,000	7,200	......	......	......	......	1,003	20,503
Lebanon	8,082	5,226	......	......	......	7,300	394	13,702
Morocco	12,862	......	......	......	2,173	......	724	15,759
Oman	......	......	......	......	......	......	131	131
Tunisia	......	......	......	......	1,181	......	800	1,981
West Bank/Gaza	824	79,439	......	......	604	......	......	80,867
Yemen	6,994	......	......	......	1,084	......	......	8,078
SOUTH ASIA								
Afghanistan	......	......	......	12,390	......	......	......	12,390
Bangladesh	21,099	......	......	31,521	......	......	209	92,829
India	56,861	......	......	104,810	......	......	208	161,879
Maldives	......	......	......	......	......	......	50	50
Nepal	14,280	......	......	510	2,160	......	96	17,046
Pakistan	7,480	......	......	7,141	2,500	......	......	17,121
Sri Lanka	11,366	......	......	1,141	608	......	96	13,211

Appendix F.—52d UNHRC Voting Record

The following resolutions were adopted without a vote (by consensus) at the 52nd session of the UN Commission on Human Rights:

1996/1	Situation of human rights in Burundi
1996/6	Question of Western Sahara
1996/7	Middle East peace process
1996/8	Implementation of the Programme of Action for the Third Decade to Combat Racism and Racial Discrimination
1996/10	Human rights and extreme poverty
1996/11	Question of the realization in all countries of the economic, social and cultural rights contained in the Universal Declaration of Human Rights and in the International Covenant on Economic, Social and Cultural Rights, and study of special problems which the developing countries face in their efforts to achieve these rights
1996/13	Human rights and the environment
1996/15	The right to development
1996/16	Status of the International Covenants on Human Rights
1996/17	Violence against women migrant workers
1996/18	International Convention on the Protection of the Rights of All Migrant Workers and Members of Their Families
1996/19	Tolerance and pluralism as indivisible elements in the promotion and protection of human rights
1996/20	Rights of persons belonging to national or ethnic, religious and linguistic minorities
1996/21	Measures to combat contemporary forms of racism, racial discrimination, xenophobia and related intolerance
1996/22	Effective implementation on international instruments on human rights, including reporting obligations under international instruments on human rights
1996/23	Implementation of the Declaration on the Elimination of All Forms of Intolerance and of Discrimination Based on Religion or Belief
1996/24	Traffic in women and girls
1996/25	Work of the Sub-Commission on Prevention of Discrimination and Protection of Minorities
1996/26	Minimum humanitarian standards
1996/27	Human rights of persons with disabilities
1996/28	Question of arbitrary detention
1996/29	Staff members of the United Nations and of the specialized agencies in detention
1996/30	Question of enforced disappearances
1996/31	Human rights and forensic science
1996/32	Human rights in the administration of justice, in particular of children and juveniles in detention
1996/33	Torture and other cruel, inhuman or degrading treatment or punishment
1996/34	Independence and impartiality of the judiciary, jurors and assessors and the independence of lawyers
1996/35	The rights to restitution, compensation and rehabilitation for victims of grave violations of human rights and fundamental freedoms
1996/36	Question of human rights and states of emergencies
1996/37	Question of a draft optional protocol to the Convention Against Torture and Other Cruel Inhuman or Degrading Treatment or Punishment
1996/38	Working Group of the Commission on Human Rights to elaborate a draft declaration in accordance with paragraph 5 of General Assembly resolution 49/214 of 23 December 1994
1996/39	International Decade of the World's Indigenous People
1996/40	Report of the Working Group on Indigenous Populations of the Sub-Commission on Prevention of Discrimination and Protection of Minorities

1996/41	A permanent forum for indigenous people in the United Nations system
1996/42	Preparations for the fiftieth anniversary of the Universal Declaration on Human Rights
1996/43	The protection of human rights in the context of human immunodeficiency virus (HIV) and acquired immune deficiency syndrome (AIDS)
1996/44	United Nations Decade for Human Rights Education
1996/45	The Olympic Ideal
1996/46	Human rights and thematic procedures
1996/47	Human rights and terrorism
1996/48	Question of integrating the human rights of women throughout the United Nations system
1996/49	The elimination of violence against women
1996/50	National institutions for the promotion and protection of human rights
1996/51	Human rights and mass exoduses
1996/52	Internally displaced persons
1996/53	Right to freedom of opinion and expression
1996/54	Situation of human rights in Cambodia
1996/55	Advisory services, technical cooperation and the Voluntary Fund for Technical Cooperation in the Field of Human Rights
1996/56	Assistance to states in strengthening the rule of law
1996/57	Assistance to Somalia in the field of human rights
1996/58	Situation of human rights in Haiti
1996/59	Assistance to Guatemala in the field of human rights
1996/60	Question on fundamental trade union and workers' rights
1996/61	Contemporary forms of slavery
1996/62	Hostage-taking
1996/63	Protection of the heritage of indigenous people
1996/64	Regional arrangements for the promotion and protection of human rights in the Asian and Pacific region
1996/66	Situation of human rights in Equatorial Guinea
1996/67	Situation of human rights in Togo
1996/70	Cooperation with representatives of United Nations human rights bodies
1996/71	Situation of human rights in the Republic of Bosnia and Herzegovina, the state of Bosnia and Herzegovina, the Republic of Croatia and the Federal Republic of Yugoslavia (Serbia and Montenegro)
1996/73	Situation of human rights in the Sudan
1996/74	Extrajudicial, summary or arbitrary executions
1996/75	Situation of human rights in Afghanistan
1996/76	Situation of human rights in Rwanda
1996/77	Situation of human rights in Zaire
1996/78	Comprehensive implementation and follow-up to the Vienna Declaration and Programme of Action
1996/79	Situation of human rights in Nigeria
1996/80	Situation of human rights in Myanmar
1996/81	Question of a draft declaration on the right and responsibility of individuals, groups and organs of society to promote and protect universally recognized human rights and fundamental freedoms
1996/82	Strengthening of the Office of the United Nations High Commissioner for Human Rights/Centre for Human Rights
1996/83	Evaluation of the human rights programme of the United Nations system, in accordance with the Vienna Declaration and Programme of Action
1996/85	Rights of the child

The following resolutions were adopted by vote at the 52nd session of the UN Commission on Human Rights (letter designations refer to vote chart):

A	1996/2	Human rights in the occupied Syrian Golan (adopted 22–1–29)
B	1996/3	Question of the violation of human rights in the occupied Arab territories, including Palestine (adopted 27–2–23)
C	1996/4	Israeli settlements in the occupied Arab territories (adopted 49–1–3)[1]
D	1996/5	Situation in occupied Palestine (adopted 28–1–23)
E	1996/9	Human rights and unilateral coercive measures (adopted 32–14–7)[2]
F	1996/12	Effects on the full enjoyment of human rights of the economic adjustment policies arising from foreign debt and, in particular, on the implementation of the Declaration on the Right to Development (adopted 34–16–1)
G	1996/14	Adverse effects of the illicit movement and dumping of toxic and dangerous products and wastes on the enjoyment of human rights (adopted 32–16–3)
H	1996/65	Composition of the staff of the Centre for Human Rights (adopted 33–16–4)
I	1996/68	Human rights situation in southern Lebanon and West Bekaa (adopted 50–1–2)
J	1996/69	Human rights in Cuba (adopted 20–5–28)
K	1996/72	Situation of human rights in Iraq (adopted 30–0–21)
L	1996/84	Situation of human rights in the Islamic Republic of Iran (adopted 24–7–20)

The following procedural votes were also taken at the 52nd session of the UN Commission on Human Rights (letter designations refer to vote chart):

M Vote on Chinese motion to take no action on the draft resolution on the situation of human rights in China. (No-action motion adopted by vote of 27–20–6.)

N Paragraph vote requested by Russian Federation on the seventh preambular paragraph and operative paragraphs 1, 25, 26, and 27 of the resolution (1996/71) on the situation of human rights in the Republic of Bosnia and Herzegovina, the state of Bosnia and Herzegovina, the Republic of Croatia, and the Federal Republic of Yugoslavia (Serbia and Montenegro). (Paragraphs were retained by a vote of 38–0–12.)

Commission member	A	B	C[1]	D	E[2]	F	G	H	I	J	K	L	M	N
Algeria	Y	Y		Y	Y	Y	Y	Y	A	A	Y	Y	Y
Angola	A	A	A	Y	Y	Y	Y	Y	A	A	A	Y	A
Australia	A	A	A	N	N	N	N	Y	Y	Y	Y	N	Y
Austria	A	A	A	N	N	N	N	Y	Y	Y	N	Y	Y
Bangladesh	Y	Y	Y	Y	Y	Y	Y	Y	A	A	Y	Y	Y
Belarus	A	A	A	A	N	N	N	Y	A	Y	A	Y	A
Benin	A	A	A	Y	Y	Y	Y	Y	A	A	A	Y	Y
Bhutan	Y	Y	Y	Y	Y	Y	Y	Y	A	A	A	Y	Y
Brazil	A	Y	Y	Y	Y	Y	Y	Y	A	Y	Y	N	Y
Bulgaria	A	A	A	N	N	N	N	Y	Y	Y	Y	N	Y
Cameroon	A	A	A	Y	Y	Y	A	A	A	A	A	Y	A
Canada	A	A	A	N	N	N	N	Y	Y	Y	Y	N	Y
Chile	Y	Y	Y	Y	Y	Y	Y	Y	Y	Y	Y	N	Y
China	Y	Y	Y	Y	Y	Y	Y	Y	N	A	N	Y	A
Colombia	Y	Y	Y	Y	Y	Y	Y	Y	A	A	Y	A	Y
Cote d'Ivoire	A	A	Y	A	Y	Y	Y	A	A	A	A	Y	Y
Cuba	Y	Y	Y	Y	Y	Y	Y	Y	N	A	N	Y	—
Denmark	A	A	A	N	N	N	N	Y	Y	Y	Y	N	Y
Dominican Rep.	A	A	A	A	—	—	A	Y	Y	Y	Y	N	Y
Ecuador	A	A	A	Y	Y	Y	Y	Y	Y	Y	Y	N	Y
Egypt	Y	Y	Y	Y	Y	Y	Y	Y	A	A	Y	Y	Y
El Salvador	A	A	A	A	Y	Y	A	Y	Y	Y	—	N	Y
Ethiopia	Y	Y	Y	Y	Y	Y	Y	Y	A	A	A	Y	A
France	A	A	A	N	N	N	N	Y	Y	Y	Y	N	Y
Gabon	A	Y		Y	Y	Y	Y	Y	Y	Y	Y	Y	Y
Germany	A	A	A	N	N	N	N	Y	Y	Y	Y	N	Y

Commission member	A	B	C[1]	D	E[2]	F	G	H	I	J	K	L	M	N
Guinea	A	Y		Y	Y	Y	Y	Y	Y	A	—	A	Y	A
Hungary	A	A		A	N	N	N	N	Y	A	Y	Y	N	Y
India	Y	Y		Y	Y	Y	Y	Y	Y	N	A	N	Y	A
Indonesia	Y	Y		Y	Y	Y	Y	Y	Y	N	A	N	Y	Y
Italy	A	A		A	N	N	Y	N	Y	Y	Y	Y	N	Y
Japan	A	A		A	N	N	N	N	Y	Y	Y	Y	N	Y
Madagascar	A	A		A	Y/A	Y	Y	Y	Y	Y	—	—	Y	—
Malawi	—	—		—	—	—	—	A	Y	A	Y	A	N	Y
Malaysia	Y	Y		Y	Y	Y	A	Y	Y	A	A	N	Y	Y
Mali	A	Y		Y	Y	Y	Y	Y	Y	A	A	A	Y	—
Mauritania	Y	Y		Y	Y	Y	Y	Y	Y	A	A	A	Y	Y
Mexico	Y	Y		Y	Y	Y	Y	Y	Y	A	Y	Y	A	A
Nepal	Y	Y		Y	Y	Y	Y	Y	Y	A	A	A	Y	A
Netherlands	A	A		A	N	N	N	N	Y	Y	Y	Y	N	Y
Nicaragua	A	A		A	Y	Y	Y	Y	Y	Y	Y	Y	N	Y
Pakistan	Y	Y		Y	Y	Y	Y	Y	Y	A	A	N	Y	Y
Peru	A	Y		Y	Y	Y	Y	Y	Y	A	Y	Y	Y	Y
Philippines	Y	Y		Y	Y	Y	A	Y	Y	A	A	A	A	Y
Rep. of Korea	Y	Y		Y	N	A	A	A	Y	Y	Y	A	A	Y
Russia	A	N		A	A	N	N	N	Y	A	Y	Y	A	A
Sri Lanka	Y	Y		Y	Y	Y	Y	Y	Y	A	A	A	Y	A
Uganda	Y	Y		Y	Y	Y	Y	Y	Y	A	A	A	Y	Y
Ukraine	A	A		A	A	N	N	N	Y	A	Y	A	Y	Y
United Kingdom	A	A		A	N	N	N	N	Y	Y	Y	Y	N	Y
United States	N	N		N	N	N	N	N	N	Y	Y	Y	N	Y
Venezuela	Y	Y		Y	Y	Y	Y	Y	Y	A	Y	Y	A	Y
Zimbabwe	Y	Y		Y	Y	Y	Y	Y	Y	N	A	A	Y	A

[1] Resolution was adopted by show—of—hands (49–1–3) rather than role call vote.
[2] Madagascar vote was recorded by UN both as Yes and Abstention.

Y=Yes.   N=No.   A=Abstain.   —=Absent.

ISBN 0-16-054190-5

90000